CONTEMPORARY
ARTISTS

OTHER ART TITLES FROM ST. JAMES PRESS

Contemporary Architects

Contemporary Artists

Contemporary Designers

Contemporary Fashion

Contemporary Hispanic Artists

Contemporary Masterworks

Contemporary Photographers

Contemporary Women Artists

International Dictionary of Architects and Architecture

International Dictionary of Art and Artists

St. James Guide to Black Artists

St. James Guide to Hispanic Artists

St. James Guide to Native North American Artists

C O N T E M P O R A R Y

ARTISTS

FIFTH EDITION

VOLUME 2: L-Z

Editor:
Sara Pendergast and Tom Pendergast

Advisers:
Jean-Christophe Ammann, Robert Atkins,
Szymon Bojko, Jorge Glusberg,
Carin Kuoni, Hans Ulrich Obrist,
Frank Popper, Robert Rindler,
Jose Lebrero Stals, Atsuo Yasuda

ST. JAMES PRESS

Detroit • New York • San Diego • San Francisco
Boston • New Haven, Conn. • Waterville, Maine
London • Munich

Sara Pendergast and Tom Pendergast, *Editors*

Christa Brelin, Joann Cerrito, Stephen Cusack, Kris Hart, Margaret Mazurkiewicz, Carol A. Schwartz, Michael J. Tyrkus, *Contributing Editors*

Peter M. Gareffa, *Managing Editor, St. James Press*

Mary Beth Trimper, *Manager, Composition and Electronic Prepress*
Evi Seoud, *Assistant Manager, Composition Purchasing and Electronic Prepress*
Dorothy Maki, *Manufacturing Manager*
Rhonda Williams, *Buyer*

Barb Yarrow, *Manager, Imaging and Multimedia*
Dean Dauphinais, *Senior Editor, Imaging and Multimedia*
Kelly A. Quin, *Editor, Imaging and Multimedia*

Maria Franklin, *Manager, Permissions*
Kim Davis, *Permissions Associate*

Library of Congress Catalog Cataloging-in-Publication Data
Contemporary artists / editors, Sara Pendergast and Tom Pendergast; advisers, Jean-Christopher Ammann . . . [et al.].—5th ed.
p. cm. — (Contemporary arts series)
Includes bibliographical references and index.
Contents: v. 1. A-K — v. 2. L-Z.
ISBN 1-55862-407-4 (alk. paper)
1. Artists—Biography. 2. Art, Modern—20th century. I. Pendergast, Sara. II. Pendergast, Tom. III. Series.

N6490 .C6567 2001
709'.2'2—dc21
[B]

2001048443

British Library Cataloguing-in-Publication Data
A catalogue record for this book is available from the British Library

ISBN 1-55862-407-4 (set)
ISBN 1-55862-488-0 (volume 1)
ISBN 1-55862-489-9 (volume 2)

Printed in the United States of America

St. James Press is an imprint of Gale Group
Gale Group and Design is a trademark used herein under license
10 9 8 7 6 5 4 3 2 1

CONTENTS

EDITOR'S NOTE

Contemporary Artists provides comprehensive profiles of nearly 850 of the most significant artists working in the contemporary era. The vast majority of these artists have done their most significant work in the years after 1960.

Artists were nominated for inclusion by an advisory board of international art scholars and curators. The artists selected for inclusion have exhibited in major galleries or museums and have attracted significant critical attention. All areas of the fine arts are represented, including painting, graphics, sculpture, mixed media, and performance; this edition, like the one before it, also contains a number of artists active in the fields of computer and Internet art. *Contemporary Artists* includes some deceased artists, but in order to provide coverage of a greater number of living artists we have removed any artist who has died before 1990 (with several exceptions). Several of these artists are among the best known artists of this century; however, the editors feel certain that researchers will be able to gather adequate information on these artists from previous editions of this work and from other published sources.

Each artist entry includes biographical data, a selected list of both individual and group exhibitions, a list of public collections that include work by the artist, and primary and secondary bibliographies. Many entries also include mention of permanent public installations, performances, or other categories of artistic production. Many artists have contributed a statement about their work or about art in general, as well as a photograph of a representative work. Finally, critical essays have been contributed by specialists in the field.

In order to provide accurate and up-to-date profiles, the editors have made every attempt to gather information directly from the artists themselves. In many cases, however, the information has been provided by galleries or gathered through research in secondary sources.

Acknowledgments

This work could not have been completed without the efforts of hundreds of people, from artists and gallery owners who provided us with up-to-date information, to writers who contributed their specialized knowledge, to the researchers and copyeditors who tried their best to be sure that the information provided was recent and accurate, to those at the publisher who will turn all this information into the book you hold today.

We wish to extend a special thanks to the following people: Christa Brelin, our contact at the St. James Press, for her consistent support and professionalism throughout the project; Michael Najjar, for his dogged research; Amy Moeller, Joyce Youmans, and Marcia Welsh, for taming the chaos of artist CVs into the entries you see in this book; and translators Stanley Anderson, Joerg Fiegler, Claudia Hoffmann, and Dan Newland. Finally, we would like to thank our advisers, whose thorough knowledge of contemporary art helped bring to this collection a wide variety of fascinating artists.

ADVISERS

Jean-Christophe Ammann
Museum für Moderne Kunst, Frankfurt am Main

Robert Atkins
Editor, AIDS-Art Forum, and Media Arts Editor, The Media Channel, New York

Szymon Bojko
Art Critic, Warsaw

Jorge Glusberg
Museo Nacional de Bellas Artes, Buenos Aires

Carin Kuoni
Independent Curators International, New York

Hans Ulrich Obrist
Musee d'Art Moderne de la Ville, Paris

Frank Popper
University of Paris VIII

Robert Rindler
School of Art, Cooper Union, New York

Jose Lebrero Stals
Museu d'Art Contemporani de Barcelona (MACBA)

Atsuo Yasuda
Hara Museum of Contemporary Art, Tokyo

CONTRIBUTORS

Daniel Abadie
Dietrich Albrecht (Albrecht D.)
Lawrence Alloway
Jean-Christophe Ammann
Sharon Matt Atkins

Marius Babias
Bradley Bailey
Carrie Baker
D. C. Barrett
Peter Barton
Konstantin Bazarov
Andreas Bee
László Beke
Jane Bell
Maurice Berger
Florent Bex
Eugen Blume
Willard Bohn
Szymon Bojko
Achille Bonito Oliva
Jean-Luc Bordeaux
David Bourdon
Betty Ann Brown
David Brown
Glen R. Brown
Maria Elena Buszek
Carly Butler

James D. Campbell
Massimo Carboni
Valerie Cassel
Gary Catalano
Barbara Cavaliere
Martin Clark
Robin Clark
Ronny Cohen
Michael Compton
Lynne Cooke
Barbara Cortright
Fenella Crichton

Aline Dallier-Popper
Natalie de Ligt
Janneke de Vries
Giorgio Di Genova
Deirdre Donohue
Gillo Dorfles
Merridawn Duckler
Mari Dumett
Beth Duncan

Mary Ellis
Muriel Emanuel
Thomas Epstein
Britta Erickson

Zdenek Felix
Michael Alistair Findlay
Uwe Fleckner
Marnie Fleming
Michael Florescu
Andrew Forge
Claude Fournet
Marietta Franke
Alison Fraser
B. H. Friedman
Kenneth Friedman

Edda Gazzerro
Sabine Gebhardt
Marcin Giżycki
Ron Glowen
Jorge Glusberg
Janet Goleas
Petra Gördüren
Klaus Görner
Olle Granath
Andy Grundberg

Jaimey Hamilton
James Harithas
Herbert R. Hartel, Jr.
Dean Higgins
Vanessa Hirsch
Roman Hollenstein
Ihor Holubizky
Klaus Honnef
Rosemarie Martha Huhn

Aaron Jacobs
Demetra James
Heather Belnap Jensen
Jill Johnston
Dorothy Joiner

Paul J. Karlstrom
Fiona Kearney
Victoria Keller
Jane Kelly
Alicja Kepinska
Joshua Kind
Elaine A. King
April Kingsley
Tammy A. Kinsey
Mason Klein
Daniel Kletke
Helena Kontova
Richard Kostelanetz
Mario Kramer
Rachel E. Kuhn
Udo Kultermann

Roberto G. Lambarelli
Sharon Lancer
Elise LaRose
Lavinia Learmont
Dominique Liquois
Marco Livingstone
Peter Lunenfeld

Alfred Mac Adam
Alastair Mackintosh
Audrey Mandelbaum
Elizabeth Mangini
Andrée Maréchal-Workman
Henry Martin
Carine Maurice
Marguerite K. Mayhall
Cecile N. McCann
Paul McGillick
Arthur McIntyre
Marco Meneguzzo
Thomas Messer
Günter Metken
Tamon Miki
Yusuke Minami
Christine Miner Minderović
Alan Moore
Joan Murray
Italo Mussa

Yusuke Nakahara
Fumio Nanjo
Roald Nasgaard
Percy North
Anna Novakov

Joan Oleck
Harold Osborne

Demetrio Paparoni
Loredana Parmesani
Keith Patrick
Ralph Pomeroy
Frank Popper

Cay Sophie Rabinowitz
Hans Rudolf Reust
John Roberts
John Robinson
Marlee Robinson
Ken Rogers

Richard Salkeld
Britt Salvesen
Merle Schipper
Eva Schmidt
Werner Schulze-Reimpell

Barry Schwabsky
Dieter Schwarz
Peter Selz
Michael Shepherd
Tazmi Shinoda
Dagmar Sinz
Jennifer A. Smith
Katherine Smith
Lucy Soutter
Charles Spencer
Heinz Spielmann
José Lebrero Stals
Ryszard Stanislawski
Shepherd Steiner
Mary Stofflet
Anne Swartz
Mark Swartz
Marie Luise Syring

Agnieszka Taborska
Daniel Thomas
Miang Tiampo
Yoshiaki Tono
Alan Trachtenberg

Dorothy Valakos
H. J. A. M. van Haaren
Radu Varia
Luca Venturi
Giorgio Verzotti
Alicia Volk
Monika von Zitzewitz
A. F. Wagemans
Sarah Wagner
Sarah Webb
Kathleen Wentrack
G. S. Whittet
Karen Wilkin
Sheldon Williams
Adina Wingate
Paula Wisotzki
Mara Witzling
Lisa Wolford
Aida-Yuen Wong

Joyce Youmans
Tara Reddy Young

Jennifer S. Zarro
Annalisa Zox-Weaver

C O N T E M P O R A R Y

ARTISTS

LIST OF ENTRANTS

Magdalena Abakanowicz
Marina Abramovic
Vito Acconci
Valerio (Romani) Adami
Dennis Adams
Nicholas Africano
Yaacov Agam
Vincenzo Agnetti
Doug Aitken
Pierre Alechinsky
Rene Pierre Allain
Terry Allen
Laurie Anderson
Carl Andre
Giovanni Anselmo
Horst Antes
Eleanor Antin
Stephen Antonakos
Richard (Joseph) Anuszkiewicz
Siegfried Anzinger
Karel Appel
Shusaku Arakawa
Nobuyoshi Araki
Siah Armajani
Arman
Kenneth Armitage
John M(ichael) Armleder
Robert Arneson
Eduardo Arroyo
Richard (Ernst) Artschwager
Roy Ascott
Michael Asher
David Askevold
Nora Aslan
Conrad Atkinson
Bernard Aubertin
Frank Auerbach
Ay-O
Alice Aycock
(Anthony) Aziz and
(Sammy) Cucher

Silvia Bächli
Francis Bacon
Enrico Baj
John Baldessari
Miroslaw Balka
Stephan Balkenhol
Balthus
Walter Darby Bannard
Clive Barker
Matthew Barney
Stéphan Barron
Robert Barry
Jennifer (Losch) Bartlett
Gianfranco Baruchello
Georg Baselitz
Leonard Baskin
Carlo Battaglia
Herbert Bayer
Thomas Bayrle
Jack Beal
Romare (Howard) Bearden
Bernhard and Hilla Becher
Bill Beckley
Jacques Bedel
Krzysztof M(aria) Bednarski
Vanessa Beecroft
Larry Bell
Claude Bellegarde
Maurice Benayoun
Lynda Benglis
Billy Al Bengston
Lucie Beppler
Jake Berthot
Jean-Pierre Bertrand
Joseph Beuys
Mike Bidlo
Sanford Biggers
Max Bill
Dara Birnbaum
James Bishop
Peter (Thomas) Blake
Peter Blume
Mel Bochner
Alighiero E. Boetti
Marinus Boezem
Christian Boltanski
Peter Booth
Jacobo Borges
Jon(athan) Borofsky
Derek Boshier
Fernando Botero
Martha Boto
Louise Bourgeois
Arthur (Merrick
Bloomfield) Boyd
Mark Boyle
Monika Brandmeier
Erich (or Arik) Brauer
Claudio Bravo
George Brecht
Robert C. Breer
K. P. Brehmer
Stuart Brisley
Stanley Brouwn
Larry Brown
Tania Bruguera
Günter Brus
Stephen Buckley
Chris Burden
Daniel Buren
Victor Burgin
Alberto Burri
Nancy Burson
Pol Bury
Michael Buthe

Paul Cadmus
John Cage
Miriam Cahn
Cai Guo-Qiang
Sophie Calle
Pier Paolo Calzolari
Peter Campus
Louis Cane
Rafael (Gomez) Canogar
Janet Cardiff
Anthony (Alfred) Caro
Ian Carr-Harris
Leonora Carrington
Pietro Cascella
Enrico Castellani
Luciano Castelli
Maurizio Cattelan
Patrick Caulfield
Alik Cavaliere
Vija Celmins
Mario Ceroli
(Baldaccini) Cesar
Lynn (Russell) Chadwick
John (Angus) Chamberlain
Alan Charlton
Grégory Chatonsky
Sandro Chia
Judy Chicago
Eduardo Chillida
Marek Chlanda
Christo and Jeanne-Claude
Chryssa
Roman Cieslewicz
Jürgen Claus
Francesco Clemente
Chuck Close
Susanna Coffey
Bernard Cohen
James Coleman
Robert Colescott
James Collins
Gianni Colombo
Alex Colville
Bruce Conner
Pietro Consagra
William Nelson (CPLY) Copley
Corneille
Claudio Costa
Robert Cottingham
Tony Cragg

Alan J. Shields
Mieko (Chieko) Shiomi
Katharina Sieverding
Charles Simonds
Lorna Simpson
Andreas Slominski
Alexis Smith
Kiki Smith
Richard Smith
Kenneth Snelson
Michael (James Aleck) Snow
K.R.H. Sonderborg
Alan Sonfist
Keith Sonnier
Peter Sorge
Jesus Rafael Soto
Pierre Soulages
Giuseppe Spagnulo
Nancy Spero
Daniel Spoerri
Klaus Staeck
Theodoros Stamos
Peter Stämpfli
Robert Stanley
Henryk Stazewski
Jeffrey Steele
Saul Steinberg
Frank Stella
Ian Stephenson
Jana Sterbak
Harold Stevenson
John Stezaker
Beat Streuli
Thomas Struth
Michelle Stuart
Kishio Suga
Kumi Sugai
George Sugarman
Hiroshi Sugimoto
Philip Sutton
Jan Švankmajer

Emilio Tadini
Shinkichi Tajiri
Takis
Pierre Tal-Coat
Rufino Tamayo
Antoni Tàpies
Ernest Tatafiore
Carroll (formerly Moppett) Taylor-Lindoe
Hervé Telémaque
Paul Thek
Wayne Thiebaud
Imants Tillers
Sidney Tillim
Joe Tilson
David Tindle
Jean Tinguely
Rirkrit Tiravanija
Gérard Titus-Carmel
Henryk Tomaszewski
Niele Toroni
Patrick Tosani
Endre Tōt
Claude Tousignant
David Tremlett
Rosemarie Trockel
David Troostwyk
Antonio A. Trotta
Anne Truitt
Costas Tsoclis
Albert Tucker
William Tucker
Giulio Turcato
William Turnbull
James (Archie) Turrell
Richard Tuttle
Cy Twombly

Günther Uecker
Timm Ulrichs
Ken Unsworth
Janos Urban
Nicolas (Garcia) Uriburu

DeWain Valentine
Jiri Valoch
Woody van Amen
J(acob) C(ornelis) J(ohan) Vanderheyden
Ger(ard Pieter) van Elk
Rob van Koningsbruggen
Inez Van Lamsweerde and Vinoodh Matadin
Jan van Munster
Gian Berto Vanni
Gregorio Vardanega
Victor Vasarely
Ben Vautier
Emilio Vedova
Vladimir Velickovic
Bernar Venet
Victoria Vesna
Claude Viallat
Marie-Helene Vieira da Silva
Dario Villalba
Jacques (Mahé) de la Villeglé
Bill Viola
Carel (Nicolaas) Visser
Eva von Platen
Ursula von Rydingsvard
Jan Voss
Wolf Vostell
Peter Voulkos

Robert (Schrope) Wade
John Walker
Brian Wall
Jeff Wall
Franz Erhard Walther
Andy Warhol
Robert Marshall Watts
Gillian Wearing
William Wegman
Lawrence Weiner
Roger Welch
Günter Weseler
Tom Wesselmann
Co Westerik
Colette Whiten
Rachel Whiteread
Robert Whitman
Joyce Wieland
William T. Wiley
Stephen Willats
John Willenbecher
Fred Wilson
Robert M. (Byrd Hoffman) Wilson
Gerd Winner
Rolf Winnewisser
Jacqueline Winsor
Krzysztof Wodiczko
David Wojnarowicz
Derrick Woodham
Bill Woodrow
Paul Wunderlich
Andrew (Newell) Wyeth

Xu Bing

Nil Yalter
Masaaki Yamada
Katsuhiro Yamaguchi
Yukinori Yanagi
Kenji Yoshida
Fumio Yoshimura
Peter (Ford) Young
Jack Youngerman

Gianfranco Zappettini
Rémy Zaugg
Gilberto Zorio
Zush

L

LAING, Gerald (Ogilvie)

Nationality: British. **Born:** Newcastle-upon-Tyne, 11 February 1936. **Education:** Berkhamsted School, Hertfordshire, 1945–53; Royal Military Academy, Sandhurst, Camberley, Surrey, 1953–55 (Commissioned Fifth Fusiliers, 1955–60); St. Martin's School of Art, London, 1960–64. **Career:** Painter since 1962, and sculptor since 1965, in New York, 1964–69, in Ross-shire, Scotland, since 1969: concentrated on Pop paintings, 1962–65, abstract wall-pieces and three-dimensional sculptures, 1965–69; rebuilt Kinkell Castle, Ross and Cromarty, Scotland, 1969–70; created sculpture in the landscape, 1969–73 and figurative sculpture since 1973: established a tapestry workshop, Conon Bridge, Ross-shire, 1970–74. Artist-in-residence, Aspen Institute for Humanistic Studies, Colorado, 1965; visiting professor, University of New Mexico, Albuquerque, 1976–77; professor of sculpture, Columbia University, New York, 1986–87. Art committee member, Scottish Arts Council, Edinburgh, 1978–80; commissioner, Royal Commission for Fine Art for Scotland, Edinburgh, 1987–98. **Awards:** Civic Trust Award, 1970. **Addresses:** Kinkell Castle, Dingwall, Ross-shire IV7 8AT, Scotland; 139 East 66th Street, New York, New York 10021, U.S.A. **Web site:** www.geraldlaing.com.

Individual Exhibitions:

1963 Laing Art Gallery, Newcastle upon Tyne
1964 Institute of Contemporary Arts, London
Richard Feigen Gallery, New York
Feigen Palmer Gallery, Los Angeles
1965 Richard Feigen Gallery, New York
Richard Feigen Gallery, Chicago
1966 Kornblee Gallery, New York (with Peter Phillips)
Richard Feigen Gallery, Chicago
1967 Richard Feigen Gallery, New York
Galerie M. E. Thelen, Essen
Pennsylvania State University, College Park
1969 Richard Feigen Gallery, New York
Galerie M. E. Thelen, Essen
1970 Richard Feigen Gallery, Chicago
Richard Demarco Gallery, Edinburgh
1971 Multiples Gallery, New York
Cincinnati Center for Contemporary Art, Ohio
Aspen Institute for Humanistic Studies, Colorado
Scottish National Gallery of Modern Art, Edinburgh
1973 Arthur Tooth and Sons, London
University of New Mexico, Albuquerque
1974 Arthur Tooth and Sons, London
1975 Aberdeen Art Gallery, Scotland
1977 Max Hutchinson Gallery, New York
1978 Gladstone Court, Edinburgh
1979 Max Hutchinson Gallery, Houston
Max Hutchinson Gallery, New York
1980 Scottish Gallery, Edinburgh
1981 Gallery Camino Real, Boca Raton, Florida
1982 Bacardi Gallery, Miami Florida
1983 Herbert Art Gallery, Coventry, Warwickshire (retrospective)
Joanne Lyon Gallery, Aspen, Colorado
1987 Albert Totah Gallery, London
1989 Scottish Gallery, London
1993 Independent Gallery, London
Harris Gallery, Houston, Texas
Fruit Market Gallery, Edinburgh (retrospective)
1994 Inverness Museum, Scotland
1996 Whitford Fine Art, London
1999 Fine Art Society Plc, London
2000 Fine Art Society Plc, London

Selected Group Exhibitions:

1963 *Young Contemporaries,* RBA Galleries, London
1964 *Contemporary British Painting and Sculpture,* Albright-Knox Art Gallery, Buffalo, New York
1966 *New Forms and Shapes of Colour,* Stedelijk Museum, Amsterdam
Primary Structures, Jewish Museum, New York
1967 *Bienal,* Sao Paulo
1968 *Annual Sculpture Exhibition,* Whitney Museum, New York
Prospect '68, Dusseldorf
1969 *Contemporary American Painting and Sculpture,* Krannert Art Museum, University of Illinois, Champaign-Urbana
1978 *Cubist Syntax in the '70s,* Ingber Gallery, New York
1993 *The Sixties Art Scene In London,* Barbican Art Gallery, London
1996 Berardo Collection, Lisbon
1998 *From the Bomb to the Beatles,* Imperial War Museum, London
2001 *PopArt, U.S/U.K. Connections 1956–66,* Menil Museum, Houston

Collections:

Victoria and Albert Museum, London; Museum of Modern Art, New York; Whitney Museum, New York; Minneapolis Museum of Art; Tate Gallery, London; Scottish National Gallery of Modern Art, Edinburgh; Nagaoka Museum, Japan; Cornell University, Ithaca, New York; National Portrait Gallery, London; Scottish National Gallery of Modern Art, Edinburgh; Scottish National Portrait Gallery, Edinburgh; Glasgow Art Gallery; Glasgow Royal Infirmary; Scottish Arts Council; Inverness Museum; Smithsonian Institute, Washington, D.C.; Indianapolis Museum; Government of Sierra Leone.

Publications:

By LAING: Book—*Kinkell: The Reconstruction of a Scottish Castle,* London 1974. **Articles—**''Notes Toward a Definition of U.S. Automobile Painting as a Significant Branch of Mobile Heraldry'' with Reyner Banham in *Art in America* (New York), September 1966; ''How We Turned a Ruined Castle into a Home'' in *The Observer* (London), November 1974.

Gerald Laing: *An American Girl,* 1977. ©Gerald Laing, courtesy of Fine Art Society PLC.

On LAING: Books—*Pop Art and After* by Mario Amaya, New York 1966; *Pop Art* by Lucy Lippard, New York 1966, London 1967; *Gerald Laing Retrospective,* exhibition catalog, Edinburgh 1971; *Art Now* by Edward Lucie Smith, New York 1977; *Produktionsasthetische Probleme Zeitgenossischer Schottischer Bildhauerei* by Babette Peters, Frankfurt and New York 1984; *Open Air Sculpture in Britain* by W. J. Strachan, London 1984; *The Sixties Art Scene in London* by David Mellor, London 1990; *Pop Art: A Continuing History* by Marco Livingstone, London 1990. **Articles—**''Hybrid: A Time of Life'' by G. R. Swenson in *Art and Artists* (London), June 1966, ''Gerald Laing'' in *Catalyst* (London), January 1971.

*

Mine was the first generation of young artists of whom some were lionized immediately after leaving art school. This was a matter of luck, timing and social climate; it had nothing particularly to do with extraordinary talent or skill. Art seemed suddenly to be both profitable and sexy; and therefore it gradually ceased to be an area of interest for a comparatively small proportion of the population. It suited the zeitgeist of the 1960s and was no longer ignored or treated with disdain.

Just as we were the first to receive early adulation and reward, so we were the last to go to art school with no such expectations. Our predecessors never experienced such pumping; a photograph of John Bratby and Derrick Greaves at an opening of the Zwemmer Gallery in the 1950s shows them in corduroys and tweed jackets with leather elbow patches, clutching half pints of beer. This is in marked contrast to an opening of, say, the Saatchi Gallery nowadays, with its black-clad throng of hopeful acolytes resembling nothing so much as the three-eyed toys in *Toy Story,* hoping against hope that they will be chosen by the Claw which hovers above them—hoping that they can do what has never been done, win what has never been won; meanwhile life goes on all around them. (Apologies to Bob Dylan.)

What each generation forgets—and it is human nature so to do—is that only a tiny proportion will be chosen; and like as not these select few will have careers like a boxer perhaps glorious but necessarily brief.

My unsuspecting generation suffered this fate. We were not ready for the event. We had the rest of our lives to live, years of work ahead, but we were expected to be fully formed before we were properly out of the womb.

The current state of affairs is very confusing. It seems to be a matter of hysteria. I have sat on art committees myself and watched the group as a whole, endorse work which no individual member of the group would support. I am, albeit reluctantly, forced to conclude that the same number of truly art-literate people exist as in the 1950s and earlier, before commercial techniques were brought so blatantly to the promotion of art. I am certain that a good patron is more rare than a good artist.

Ambition of the type which feeds on contemporary notions of fame is not relevant to the making of art. An artist must have skills; his standards of expertise must at least be comparable with that of a doctor or an engineer or any other professional. And because of the special nature of the creative act, he has to be his own chief critic; he cannot expect significant moral and critical endorsement from anyone, nor can he rely upon their opinion. By choosing to be an artist, he or she has chosen to stand alone.

Whether or not the groups of young artists, including my own, who have been subjected to early promotion have been ready and able to sustain and exploit such advantages throughout the length of an entire career, is debatable. The typical pattern is one of short-lived high-pitched success followed by comparative oblivion. Whether or not this is the case depends ultimately on the staying power of the work in its own right once the props of publicity and promotion have been, inevitably, removed.

Certainly I was not prepared to remain permanently in the mould into which I first was cast, that of Pop artist. I was a core member of the group of British Pop artists, yet I produced work of this type for only 3 years (1962–65). In 1965 I began making works which were abstract and cut out of metal, but which referred to the formal elements in my earlier ''Skydiver'' series of paintings. Several of these were included in the first and defining exhibition of Minimal Art (*Primary Structures,* Jewish Museum, New York, 1967)—though I did not completely accept the theories of the hard-core Minimalists such as Judd and Flavin. In 1965 I made a multiple which I called ''Print'' in order to propose that such an art object did not necessarily have to be a work on paper. I believe this to have been the first of this type of work which was later to become a popular manifestation. In 1965–66 Peter Phillips and I produced ''Hybrid'' which is regarded as the precursor of ''Process Art'' by people who are interested in such things.

Later, after moving from New York to the North of Scotland in 1969, I produced properly volumetric sculpture intended to be placed in a landscape—by ''landscape'' I meant any real open environment, either urban or rural. This was a contrast to my last New York works, which were highly finished and intended to occupy a pure white space which was otherwise empty and sterile.

I made each change in my work because it seemed at the time the logical, relevant, indeed essential course to take. At the same time a common thread runs through all of it; there are no sudden seismic shifts. The main themes are twofold: formal concerns of line and volume, and literary ones of context and meaning. The relevant proportions of these two ingredients create the major differences between one work and another.

After spending time with writers and engineers and others whose creativity I admired, but who could not, with the best of will, get as much from my work as I could from theirs, had to face the fact that my system of communication was at fault. I realised that if I was not to be marginalised then I must make fundamental changes. An epiphany occurred when one dawn in 1973, after a long party, I found myself standing contemplating the Royal Artillery Memorial at Hyde Park Comer in London. I realised then that no abstract art could contain a fraction of the love, passion, pain, pride, sorrow, beauty and acceptance that this great work of art effortlessly projects. It is intricate and grand, of its time and timeless, so abstract and formal, so realistic and human, sprung from the great tradition and yet new-born.

At last I understood that the process of creation, the aesthetics of form and composition which give this monument its strength and staying power are the artist's essential tools. They are the means by which these qualities are achieved to make concrete and convincing the content of the work, they are not an end in themselves, but their quality governs the quality of the work. They are the artist's business, or rather it is the artist's business to master them; but they need not necessarily even be apparent. It is the re-stating by each generation of the same truths and perceptions which must be the main purpose of an artist's endeavour, so that in each generation they are once more accepted, and the fact that this has been done repeatedly is understood and becomes a source of comfort and a means of orientation, a lifebelt in the chaos.

Carefully and slowly I returned to the human figure, discarding fabrication as a process and instead modeling in clay. By this simple move I increased to infinity the vocabulary of form available to me. The earliest figures I made are quite subjective. They still utilise the geometry which was the main part of my abstract sculpture; the difference is that because they have the human figure as their subject, they have gesture and emotion as well. Some people think that the changes in my work show me to be travelling backwards from abstraction to an objective figuration. The implication is that abstract art is ''advanced'' and figurative art ''old hat.'' I cannot subscribe to this linear view of art history in any case, but in fact at the time I knew that I was making the most radical move that I could possibly make, simply by following my conscience. This was confirmed for me by the fact that immediately my work was deemed by my peers to be completely unacceptable. No dealer would look at it—it was figurative, it was cast in bronze, for goodness' sake! It just wasn't groovy.

My income took a complete nosedive, my career was in ruins, and for four years I couldn't sell a thing. My debts shot up, I was in despair. I took the family back to America, where the smell of panic and failure which I seemed to be emitting made people run for cover. They don't like losers in America—they think that they are infectious. I spent a frightening period in a beach house in Amagansett in the off season, at that time a deserted and icy cold windswept resort, subsisting on the charity of friends. Eventually I was evicted, together with my wife and children. A year's Visiting Professorship at the University of New Mexico enabled me to survive (just); then, with a very small amount of cash in hand I returned to Scotland, determined to cast as much bronze sculpture as I could before I was forced to sell up and leave. It was a very difficult part of my life, one in which everything seemed to be disintegrating; but I had brought it on myself I had blasphemed against the canon, and as my daughter said at the time, I had become apostate. I looked up ''apostate'' in the dictionary so as to be sure that it meant what I thought it did; at the top of the next page my eyes fell upon the word ''artless.''

—Gerald Laing

* * *

The career of Gerald Laing illustrates very neatly one of the central problems of the present-day art system. The interested observer, who reads the views of the critics and catches up with one of those instant guides to contemporary art that appear every two or three years, will have the impression that art follows a logical course through history. Abstract Expressionism leads to Pop. Pop to Op. Op to Minimalism. Minimalism to Conceptualism and so on, and he might justifiably be under the impression that artists themselves follow the same course.

Art movements are created by critics, but artists are not. They pursue their own paths, waiting for the climatic moment when the searchlight of fashion sweeps across them and they ''make it.'' The problem is that the searchlight does not stop, and in time it moves on, leaving with expectations of a response that is no longer forthcoming. It may be that their best work is to come, but the ride of ''art history'' has swept past them and leaves them flapping on the beach, largely forgotten and without the supporting environment they have grown used to. More galling still, they find they are associated with work that they have long since surpassed.

Laing has been particularly affected by this process. His work became fashionable almost as soon as he left art college, and for five years he was associated with the Pop boom and sold widely. The irony is that this early and successful work, although stylish, has none of the depth and presence of the later sculpture which is hardy known at all.

Laing left St. Martin's School of Art in 1964 and with impeccable strategic instinct headed straight for New York, where the Pop boom was just beginning, and, thanks to the Beatles, anybody young and British was very much in demand. After a short period working with Robert Indiana, he landed a contract with Feigen and immediately began to sell.

The early work was mainly in the form of paintings and prints using the iconography of a confident and booming society: pin-up girls, dragster cars, free-fall parachutists, speed, flash, hard colour and bright style, the polished aluminum of a technological age coupled with a hint of Art Deco nostalgia—a winning combination for the mid-60s. And with the style went the life: custom painted cars, drinks at Max's Kansas City, smooth girls and sex on the studio floor. Move over Barnett Newman, 'cos we're going to rock n' roll right through the doors of the Metropolitan itself.

But an artist is not an ad-man. He has to follow his own vision or perish. Laing's work slowly crept down the wall onto the floor, the images faded and the works became abstract sculpture; and then there was Altamont and Kent State and Charlie Manson and Pop went pop! leaving nothing but a stain on the floor.

Most of the Pop artists took refuge in binding contracts with the hard men of 57nd Street, but Laing fled to Scotland, found a derelict castle, which he rebuilt, and then turned back to sculpture. What now emerged was very different: solid and massive, rusting steel, straight edged, hieratic presences that he grouped in the wild landscape around the castle, monuments to an older and more lasting reality than he found in New York. But the tide of art had by now moved into the arid desert of conceptualism and no one was interested in straightforward sculpture. Even his massive work for Strathclyde University in the heart of Glasgow passed virtually unnoticed, although, quite apart from being the largest single work of art in Britain including Stonehenge, it is an impressive and moving piece.

Since 1974, Laing has been experimenting with smaller works, usually based upon the human body and showing the influence of Matisse and other important sculptors of the early 20th century.

Whether Laing will surface again, in terms of fashionable success, will depend upon the justice of the art market. His current work is much superior to the Pop work, and one can only hope that soon dealers and public will recognize that fact.

—Alastair Mackintosh

LAKNER, László

Nationality: German. **Born:** Budapest, 15 April 1936; emigrated to West Germany, 1974; naturalized, 1980. **Education:** Attended Kepzo and Imparmuveszeti Gymnasium, Budapest, 1950–54; Fine Arts Academy, Budapest, 1954–60. **Family:** Married 1965 (divorced 1973): 1 son, Antal. **Career:** Independent artist since 1960; has lived and worked in Berlin and Essen since 1974. Produced first photo-document paintings, first book objects and book paintings, 1970. Artist-in-residence, Museum Folkwang, Essen, 1972. Professor, Folkwang-Hochschule, Essen. **Awards:** Museum Folkwang grant, 1968, 1972; D.A.A.D. Scholarship, Berlin, 1974; Roselius Foundation Prize, Bremen, 1976; German Critics Prize, 1976; P.S. 1 Scholarship, New York, 1980. **Agents:** Galerie Folker Skulima, Fasanenstrasse 68, 1 Berlin 15; Galerie Denise René-Hans Mayer, Dusseldorf; Galerie Georg Nothelfer, Berlin; and Galerie Isy Brachot, Brussels. **Address:** Home, Wilmersdorferstrasse 69, 1 Berlin 12, Germany; Office, University of Essen Faculty 4, Universitatsstrasse 12, 4300, Essen 1, Germany.

Individual Exhibitions:

1969 Institute of Cultural Relations Galerie, Budapest
1974 *Found Documents,* Neue Galerie, Aachen, Germany
Overbeck-Gesellschaft, Lübeck
Bilder, Bücher, Filme, Zettel, Neue Berliner Kunstverein
1975 Galerie Folker Skulima, Berlin
1976 Galerie Isy Brachot, Brussels
Kasseler Kunstverein, Kassel, Germany

1977 Galerie Denise René-Hans Mayer, Dusseldorf
Galerie Folker Skulima, Berlin
1978 Galerie Art in Progress, Munich
Book Works, Galerie ABF, Hamburg
1979 *Malerie 1974–1979,* Westfälischer Kunstverein, Münster
1980 *Small Sizes,* Galerie Zellermayer-Lorenzen, Berlin
1981 *Small Sizes,* Galerie Jaspers, Munich
1982 Galerie Heimeshoff, Essen
1983 Bertha Urdang Gallery, New York
Galerie Inge Baecker, Cologne (with Emmett Williams)
1984 Galerie Abras, Brussels
1985 Galerie 7, Freiburg
Galerie Nothelfer, Berlin
1987 Galerie Heimeshoff, Essen
1991 *László Lakner: Papierarbeiten, Objekte & 3 Skulpturen, 1976–1990,* Daadgalerie, Berlin (catalog)
2001 *Aura,* G.A.M.E.S. of Art Gallery, Mönchengladbach

Selected Group Exhibitions:

1968 *Modern Ungärische Kunst,* Museum Folkwang, Essen
1972 *Biennale,* Venice
1975 *8 from Berlin* at the *Edinburgh Festival,* (travelled to the Kunstmuseum, Bonn, and the Neuer Berliner Kunstverein)
1977 *Documenta,* Kassel, Germany
1979 *Biennale,* Sydney
1980 *Festa di Lettra,* Galleria Polygrapha, Barcelona
1981 *100 Jahre Kolner Dom,* Cologne
1983 *Neue Malerei in Deutschland,* Nationalgalerie, Berlin
1985 *Rollbilder,* Kunstverein, Kassel, Germany
1987 *Six Artists from Berlin,* Hara Museum, Tokyo
1999 *I Love Pop: International Pop Artists,* Chiostro del Bramante, Rome

Collections:

Museum Folkwang, Essen; Museum Ludwig, Aachen; Paula Modersohn-Becker Foundation, Bremen; University of Freiburg; Nationalgalerie, Berlin; Dahlem Museum, Berlin; Berlinische Galerie; National Gallery, Budapest; Museum of Modern Art, Lodz, Poland; Museum Boymans van Boeningen, Rotterdam.

Publications:

By LAKNER: Books—*Bildersprache: Celan-Motive bei László Lakner und Anselm Kiefer,* with Theo Buck and Anselm Kiefer, Aachen 1993. **Films**—*Toys,* 1968; *Spielzeug,* 1968; *Intervention,* with Geza Schnoller, 1969; *Ode,* 1973; *Video Program,* 1975; *Ode,* 1980; *Countenance,* 1981.

On LAKNER: Books—*László Lakner,* exhibition catalog by György Kemèny, Budapest 1969; *Found Documents,* exhibition catalog by Dr. Wolfgang Becker, Aachen 1974; *László Lakner: Bilder, Bücher, Filme, Zettel,* exhibition catalog with texts by Heinz Ohff and Karl Ruhrberg, Berlin 1974; *László Lakner,* exhibition catalog with text by Heiner Stachelhaus, Dusseldorf 1977; *László Lakner: Malerie 1974–1979,* exhibition catalog with text by Thomas Deecke, Münster 1979; *László Lakner: Herliche Grusse aus Babel,* exhibition catalog with text by Walter Grasskamp, Essen 1982; *László Lakner,* exhibition catalog with texts by Manfred de la Motte and Roland Wiegenstein, West Berlin 1985. **Articles**—article by Alain Jouffroy in *Opus International* (Paris), no. 1, 1971; article by Alain Jouffroy in *Opus International* (Paris), no. 5, 1972; article by Karl Ruhrberg in *Magazine Kunst* (Mainz), no. 1, 1976; ''Magyar Avantgárd: Izmusok Nélkül (II)'' by Éva Körner in *Új Müvészet,* vol. 5, no. 5, May 1994; ''Utolsó Pár, Elöre Fuss!'' by Edit András in *Új Müvészet,* vol. 5, no. 7–8, July-August 1994; ''Max Ernst Nyomdokain: A Magyar Szürnaturalizmus'' by Judit Szabadi in *Új Müvészet,* vol. 7, no. 5, May 1996.

LANCELEY, Colin

Nationality: Australian. **Born:** Dunedin, New Zealand, 1938; moved to Sydney, 1939. **Education:** Apprenticed as a photo engraver in Sydney; attended art classes at North Sydney Technical College, 1954; East Sydney Technical College, graduated 1960. **Family:** Married to Kay Morphett. **Career:** Independent artist. Founding member, Imitation Realist group, with Michael Brown and Ross Crothall, 1961–62; lived and worked primarily in England, 1964–80; returned to Sydney, 1981. Lecturer: Bath Academy of Art; Gloucestershire College of Art and Design; Chelsea School of Art, London; City Art Institute, Sydney, 1983–86. Lives and works in Sydney. **Awards:** Europe Prize for Painting, Belgium, 1980; Order of Australia, 1990. **Member:** Council of the National Gallery of Australia; Chairman of the Advisory Board of the National Art School, Sydney. **Agent:** Michael Carr Art Dealer, Level 3, 31 Bligh Street, Sydney NSW 2000, Australia. **Address:** 2 Esther Lane, Surry Hills, NSW 2010, Australia.

Individual Exhibitions:

1962 Rudy Komon Gallery, Sydney
1966 Marlborough Gallery, London
1967 Galerie Feigel, Galerie Alice Pauli, Lausanne
1968 Marlborough-Gerson Gallery, New York
1970 Boynthon Gallery, Sydney
1972 Galerie Pryzmat, Krakow
1976 Realities Gallery, Melbourne
Tate Gallery, London
1984 Macquarie Galleries, Sydney
1986 Allan Frumkin Gallery, New York
1987 Art Gallery of New South Wales, Sydney
1993 Sherman Galleries—Goodhope, Sydney
1994 Frumkin Adams Galleries, New York
1995 Sherman Galleries—Goodhope, Sydney
Sherman Galleries—Hargrave, Sydney
Patrick Heron and Colin Lanceley: Recent Works on Paper, Sherman Galleries—Goodhope, Sydney
1997 Za Mola Foundation, Japan
1999 Michael Carr Art Dealer, Sydney
2000 Solander Gallery, Canberra
Two Modern Masters, Michael Carr Art Dealer, Sydney
Drawings from Hill End, Bathurst Regional Gallery

Colin Lanceley: *Nature Morte,* 2000. Photo by Chris Shain. ©2001 Artists Rights Society (ARS), NY/VISCOPY, Sydney.

Selected Group Exhibitions:

1962 *Imitation Realists,* Museum of Modern Art, Melbourne
1968 *British Kunst Heute,* Kunstverein, Hamburg
1980 *Europa Prijs 1980,* Musee de Verviers, Belgium
1981 *Biennale der Europaischen Grafik,* Baden Baden, Germany
1982 *Carnegie International,* Carnegie Museum of Art, Pittsburgh
1986 *Biennale,* Sydney
1988 *The Great Australian Art Exhibition,* Rex Irwin, Sydney
1990 *Australian Contemporary Art Fair,* Melbourne
1992 *Australian Masters,* Solander Gallery, Canberra
200 Years of Australian Painting, National Museum of Western Art, Tokyo
1993 *Summer Exhibition,* Frumkin Adams Gallery, New York
1995 *Windows on Australia 1,* Australian Embassy, Tokyo
1997 *The AMCOR Works on Paper Awards,* Melbourne
1999 *Important International and Australian Paintings, Sculpture and Works on Paper,* Michael Carr Art Dealer, Sydney
2000 *Summer Exhibition,* Michael Carr Art Dealer, Sydney
2001 *Australian Collection Focus,* The Art Gallery of New South Wales, Sydney

Collections:

Museum of Modern Art, New York; Guggenheim Museum, New York; National Gallery, Washington, D.C.; Los Angeles County Museum; Tate Gallery, London; Baltimore Museum; National Gallery of Australia, Canberra; Stedelijk Museum, Amsterdam; Museum Narodowe, Cracow; Victoria and Albert Museum, London.

Publications:

On LANCELEY: Books—*Colin Lanceley* by Robert Hughes and William Wright, Sydney 1987. **Films—***Colin Lanceley: The Poetry of Place* produced by Australian Broadcasting Company, 1988.

*

Since my early collages of the 1960s, I have been exploring the ambiguous space in front of the picture plane as an arena in which to create a pictorial language. My works are constructed with carved and painted wood and canvas, and are, in effect, painted reliefs characterised by an emphasis on visual poetry.

—Colin Lanceley

* * *

An artist's career creates its own context. That is probably why good artists, as they mature, seem to be able to say more with less.

The single piece resonates with the collective meaning of its tribe of predecessors. Just as the expressive power of language is an inheritance passed on enriched from generation to generation, so each successive work by an artist adds to the communicative resources available to all the works to follow.

Of course, if you are one of those artists who change their styles like the rest of us change their underwear, you are going to have a problem getting it all to make sense.

But there is nothing fickle about Colin Lanceley. Even his most recent work highlights a continuity which goes back to the early 1960s, when he first became known as a member of the Annandale Imitation Realists.

This small group of East Sydney Tech art students whose whimsical, satirical, and sometimes provocative experiments—somewhat surreal, partly Pop and often deliberately arbitrary—signalled, like a lantern in the night, that there was an alternative to the ill-digested and turgid abstract expressionism then dominant in Sidney art.

They were, in Robert Hughes's words, "our first totally urban art guerilla group," not in any explicitly political sense, but in the way their work combined the exploratory and the satirical to expose the shabby assumptions affecting the local art scene.

Lanceley shortly disappeared to Europe with the aid of a Helena Rubinstein scholarship. The Imitation Realists had broken up and moved on. They had proved their point by already becoming part of a desperately needed mythology of postwar Australian art.

During the next 14 years abroad, Lanceley established a successful career based in London. It was a period when he could work close to the sources which fed his work, basically the early French modernists.

It was also a period when he enlarged and refined the vocabulary already laid out in the collages of the imitation realist phase. Back in the provinces, of course, where each new naughty boy of the art world is a sign of hope, Lanceley was still the *enfant terrible* of Annandale and it was partly to lay this fallacy to rest that he returned to Australia in 1981.

"An artist's greatness," said Matisse, "is measured by the number of new signs he introduces to the language."

The language metaphor is one to which Lanceley often resorts—dangerous in these semiotic times. But he is anything but a theory-driven artist. On the contrary, Lanceley stands outside most of the rules of the game.

Or, at least, so it seems. He has consistently worked away at what he calls "the dialogue between painted and three-dimensional forms." From collage, he moved to shaping his own sculptural elements which inhabit the shallow space in front of the painting's surface.

For some time, he had problems creating a unity between the three-dimensional elements and the painted surface, and it was only in the late 1970s that he was able to achieve that integrity. The illusory unity of the sculpture and the painted surface was essential if the painting were to work the modernist magic that Lanceley was aiming for—namely, getting the viewer to participate in resolving the apparent mismatch between what is and what seems to be, between the illusion of objects in space and the fact of the painting's artificial construction.

Lanceley's unique contribution to this traditional device in Western art has been to reverse the process. Instead of a two-dimensional surface appearing to be three-dimensional (and hence an illusion of reality), he often has a three-dimensional surface present itself as a two-dimensional plane. So, the question becomes: What is real?

That is the challenge thrown out by these quirky, richly colourful and endlessly inventive paintings. They are almost conundrums, provoking the viewer into solutions—except that the solutions can only ever be provisional. Anyway, the paintings are not contrived in the way a detective mystery is contrived. They have the spirit of that kind of mystery, but none of the mechanics.

Sculptural elements or not, Lanceley is a painter and, true to the tradition of Western painting (a context which Lanceley insists is vital to the integrity of contemporary painting—hence his alliance to the much-maligned modernists), he is intrigued by the issue of illusion in painting and tension between the illusory effects of colour, tone, and line and the concrete fact of the painting itself.

His painting has consistently been constructed with three-dimensional elements intruding into the space in front of the picture. These may be inert pieces of wood against a background of painted landscapes, but they set up a drama in which the viewer becomes a participant, trying to make sense of the relationships between these contradictory elements.

This is his theatre, as he calls it—a kind of theatre he sees mirrored in other art forms. The collage techniques of Bela Bartok's music or, more often, the poetry of T. S. Eliot, have been a constant source for him, where the tatty and familiar objects of the everyday world accrete meanings.

But in the drama of the dialogue between the illusory landscape of the painting and the concrete fact of the sculptural bits and pieces (including the frame) which cling to it, the objects themselves become both familiar and unfamiliar.

Sinewy, tubular appendages, ovoid drop-ins and domestic discards all hint at something we know but can't put our fingers on.

Like the painters he most admires—Matisse, Picasso, Braque, Miro—Lanceley has never been a pure abstractionist. He likes, he says, "to keep a finger on the pulse of human experience."

Hence, when he talks about forging a language with which to address his contemporaries, he is aiming at a common language, jointly constructed by a painter and a spectator. Nothing esoteric, but growing out of a shared experience.

What is always overlooked in the recent haste to trash-can the modernists is their central idea—namely, the way we make sense of our lives through art is a result of a dialogue between the collective inheritance (the Tradition) and our individual offerings.

Art, then, is both an exploration into an unknown territory and an attempt to recover a sense of belonging. Perhaps Eliot best sums up what Lanceley's art is all about:

We shall not cease from exploration
And the end of all our exploring
Will be to arrive where we started
And know the place for the first time.

—Paul McGillick

(This article was first published in the *Sydney Morning Herald,* 28 August 1993.)

LANE, Lois

Nationality: American. **Born:** Philadelphia, Pennsylvania, 6 January 1948. **Education:** Studied at Yale Summer School of Music and Art, New Haven, Connecticut, 1968; Philadelphia College of Art, B.F.A. 1969; Yale University, New Haven, Connecticut, M.F.A. 1971. **Career:** Painter. **Awards:** Creative Artists Public Service Program Grant, New York State Council on the Arts, 1977; Fellowship in painting, National Endowment for the Arts, 1978. **Agent:** Willard Gallery, New York. **Address:** c/o Willard Gallery, 29 East 72nd Street, New York, New York 10028, U.S.A; and 12 E. 12th St., New York, New York, 10003–4428.

Individual Exhibitions:

1977 Willard Gallery, New York
1979 Willard Gallery, New York
1980 *New York by Lois Lane,* Willard Gallery, New York
Greenberg Gallery, St. Louis
1981 Akron Art Museum, Ohio
1983 Willard Gallery, New York
1987 John Berggruen Gallery, San Francisco
1988 Barbara Mathes Gallery
1992 Barbara Toll Fine Arts, New York

Selected Group Exhibitions:

1978 *Ronald Greenberg Collection,* Brooks Memorial Art Gallery, Memphis, Tennessee
1979 *New Image Painting,* Whitney Museum, New York
Biennial, Whitney Museum, New York
10 Artists/Artists Space, Neuberger Museum, Purchase, New York
American Painting: The 80s, Grey Art Gallery, New York University
1980 *Printed Art: A View of Two Decades,* Museum of Modern Art, New York
American Prints 1960–1980, Bronfman Centre, Montreal
1995 *Point of View,* Avanti Galleries, New York

Publications:

On LANE: Articles—review by Lois E. Nesbitt in *Art News,* vol. 87, September 1988; review by Lisa Liebmann in *Artforum International,* vol. 30, March 1992; "Prints & Photographs Published" in *Print Collector's Newsletter,* vol. 25, September/October 1994; "Working Proof: Reviews of Prints, Photographs, and Multiples" in *On Paper,* vol. 1, July/August 1997.

* * *

Since her inclusion in the well-publicized exhibition at the Whitney Museum of American Art, *New Image Painting,* Lois Lane's career has been surveyed in the critical literature. The phrase used in the title of that exhibition, the first "new trend" show in several years, has become a part of the critical discourse in the past few years: "new image" refers to artists who make little distinction between abstraction and figuration. Lane herself has said "I was never that interested in painting per se, I was much more interested in image making. . . . "

Characteristic of Lane's approach to the canvas have been large scale (5 by 8 feet is not uncommon) surfaces covered with a single color, or a contrast of matte and shiny variant of a color, and an extremely sparse array of figurative matter set against that ground. Reminiscent of Ron Gorchov's dual placement of similar marks against a large color field, for instance, were the paintings which Lane produced about 1977–78, where two bud-like forms and other clearly figurative shapes were placed at each side of the rectangle of the canvas.

In works from the early 1980s she used collaged pictures from magazines in a single line across the monochromatic rear ground. It may be the overall modesty and humbled quality of their depiction whether drawn or collaged—despite their overall heroic size—that leads to an effect describable as enigmatic pathos. Lane's partisans insist on the intense and visionary significance of these images; and her commitment to an eclectic abstraction has remained unabated. More recently, there is a pleasure in the process and brushwork of her surfaces, while the domestic allusion—silhouetted forms of gowns, children, houses, et al.—remain as heretofore to set up the surreal expressiveness in her untitled paintings.

—Joshua Kind

LANG, Nikolaus

Nationality: German. **Born:** Oberammergau, 12 February 1941. **Education:** Studied at the Volksschule, Oberammergau, 1948–53, and the Gymnasium, Ettal, Garmish, 1953–56; studied woodcarving, under Julius Himpel, at the Staatliche Schnitzschule, Oberammergau, 1956–60, and art at the Akademie der Bildenden Künste, Munich, 1960–66, and the Camberwell School of Arts and Crafts, London, 1967–69. **Family:** Married Celia Hewitt in 1974; . **Career:** Independent artist, Bayersoien, since 1969: associated with Rainer Wittenborn and "Gruppe Spur" artists, Munich, 1960–63; with artists Gilbert and George, Richard Hamilton, and Mark Boyle, London, 1966–68, Camberwell School of Arts and Crafts, London; artist-in-residence, South Australian College of Art, Adelaide, Australia, 1987; professor, Akademie der bildenden Künste, Munich, 2000. **Awards:** D.A.A.D. Stipendium, Berlin, for travel to London, 1966–67, for travel to Japan, 1971–72; Staatlicher Bayerischer Forderungspreis, 1975; Villa Romana Prize, Florence, 1976; Glockengasse 4711 Art Prize, 1980; first prize, Environment of the Free University Competition, Berlin, 1982; Prinz Albrecht Palast Prize, Berlin, 1983; Defet Prize, Kunstlerbund Deutschlands, 1986; Gabriele Munther-Johannes Eichner Stiffung Award, 1986; Kunstfonds Award, Bonn, 1986; Artist in Residence Award, South Australia College of Art, Adelaide, 1987; Award from Friedrich-Baur-Stiftung, Bayerische Akademie der Schönen Künste, 1997. **Address:** Grundbauernhof, 82435 Bayersoien, Germany.

Individual Exhibitions:

1968 Hagen Residence, London
1969 Kleine Galerie, Frankfurt
1970 Galerie Leonhardt, Munich
1971 Wimbledon Common, London
Galerie de Gestlo, Hamburg (with Rainer Wittenborn)
Galleri Ostergen AB, Malmo, Sweden
1972 Maltzahn Gallery, London
1973 Galerie de Gestlo, Hamburg
Japanische Landschaften, Städtische Galerie im Lenbachhaus, Munich
1974 *Nikolaus Lang's Museum,* Neue Galerie, Aachen, Germany
1975 Kunst Forum, Rottweil, Germany
Kestner-Gesellschaft, Hannover
1976 Wurttembergischer Kunstverein, Stuttgart
1978 Westfalischer Kunstverein, Münster
Galerie Defet, Nuremberg, Germany
1980 Städtische Galerie, Nordhorn, Germany
1982 Goethe Institut, Paris
1984 Kunstlerhaus Bethanien, Berlin
1985 Galerie Defet, Nuremberg, Germany
1987 College Gallery, South Australian College of Art, Adelaide
1988 Art Gallery of South Australia, Adelaide
1989 Australian Centre for Contemporary Art, Melbourne
1991 Kunstraum München, Munich
Städtische Galerie im Lenbachhaus, Munich
Kunsthalle Bremen
Stadtgalerie, Saarbrücken
1992 Daedalus, Vienna
Institut für Auslandsbeziehungern, Stuttgart
Kunstverein Ruhr, Essen
Kunstraum, Wuppertal
1993 *Nunga und Goonya,* The Douglas Hyde Gallery, Dublin
1995 *Druckstock 1, 1980,* Sprengel Museum, Hannover
1998 *Points of View,* Neuer Berliner Kunstverein, Berlin
2000 *Kunst auf der zugspitze,* Staatliches Museum für Kunst und Design, Nürnberg
Roadkill, Agentur für Zeitgenössische Kunst, Christoph Grau, Hamburg

Selected Group Exhibitions:

1969 *Kunstmesse,* Kunstverein, Munich
1973 *8th Biennale de Paris,* Musée d'Art Moderne, Paris
1977 *Documenta 6* (and *Documenta 8,* 1987) Kassel, Germany
1979 *Sydney Biennale,* New South Wales, Australia
1981 *Myth and Ritual,* Zurich (travelled to Hamburg)
1983 *Aktuell 83,* Städtische Galerie im Lenbachhaus, Munich
1985 *Kunst in der Bundesrepublik 1984–85,* Nationalgalerie, Berlin
1990 *Animalia: Stellvertreter,* Haus am Waldsee, Berlin
1993 *Différentes Natures,* Paris
1994 *Localities of Desire,* Museum of Contemporary Art, Sydney
1995 *Bildhauer in Deutschland,* Kunstverein Augsburg
Bildhauerzeichnungen, Mitglieder der Akademie, Bayerische Akademie der Schönen Künste, Munich
1996 *Maurer, Kalk und Sand oder der Maler Franz Anton Maulbertsch,* daedalus, Vienna
1997 *Memoria e Progetto,* Abbazia di San Martino delle Scale, Palermo
Der Mann im Eis, Tiroler Landesmuseum Ferdinandeum, Innsbruck
Alpenblick, Kunsthalle Wien, Vienna
Deep Storage, Kulturforum Berlin, Berlin
1998 *Der Vogel Selbsterkenntnis,* Tiroler Volkskunstmuseum, Innsbruck
1999 *The Painted Coast: Views of the Fleurieu Peninsula South of Adelaide,* Art Gallery of South Australia, Adelaide
Vom Skarabäus zum new beetle, Kunstverein Bad Salzdetfurth
Das xx. jahrhundert: ein jahrhundert kunst in deutschland, Altes Museum, Neue Nationalgalerie, Hamburger Bahnhof, Berlin
Das Gedächtnis öffnet seine Tore, Kunst der Gegenwart im Lenbachhaus, Munich

Nikolaus Lang, *The Other Life of a Stag,* 1977. ©Nikolaus Lang.

2000 *Kulturräume: Skulptur seit 1970,* Wilhelm Lehmbruck Museum, Duisburg

Collections:

Stedelijk Museum, Amsterdam; Tate Gallery, London; Nationalgalerie, Berlin; Stadtische Galerie im Lenbachhaus, Munich; Australian National Gallery, Canberra; South Australia Art Gallery, Adelaide.

Publications:

On LANG: Books—*Nikolaus Lang: Japanische Landschaften,* exhibition catalog with text by Armin Zweite, Munich 1973; *Nikolaus Lang's Museum,* exhibition catalog with text by Wolfgang Becker, Aachen, Germany 1974; *Spurensicherung: Archaeologie und Erinnerung,* exhibition catalog with texts by Günter Metken and Uwe M. Schneede, Hamburg 1974; *5 from Germany,* exhibition catalog with text by Robert Kudielka, London 1974; *Nikolaus Lang,* exhibition catalog with texts by Carl-Albrecht Haenlein and Günter Metken, Hannover 1975; *Vergangenheit-Gegenwart-Zukunft,* exhibition catalog with an introduction by Tilman Osterwald, Stuttgart 1982; *Nikolaus Lang: Australian Imaginary Figurations 1986—1988,* exhibition catalog, Adelaide, Australia 1988; *Performance Ritual Process* by Elisabeth Jappe, Munich and New York, 1993; *Points of View*, exhibition catalog by Alexander Tolnay and Eugen Blume, Kunstverein 1998. **Films—***Nikolaus Lang,* television film by Dieter Wieland, 1970; *Nikolaus Lang und Ulrich Ruckriem,* television film by Jurgen Hohemeyer, 1975; *Nikolaus Lang—Spectral Sands* by Christopher Faull, 1987; *Nikolaus Lang* by Armin Kratzert, 1991; *German Artist Uncovers Australia* by Margaret Hazelgrove, South Australian Film Corporation, 1995; *Nikolaus Lang* by H. Ammer, 2000. **Articles—** ''Nikolaus Lang: The Prehistoric Voyage Through the Torres Straits, 1984–1986'' by Armin Zweite in *Zurück zur Natur, aber wie?,* exhibition catalog, Karlsruhe 1986; ''From the Earth: Nikolaus Lang talks with Rosemary Brooks'' by Rosemary Brooks in *Artlink,* March/April 1987; ''Nikolaus Lang's Recent Work'' by Rosemary Brooks in *Artlink,* June/August 1988; ''Out of Anxiety into Gridlock'' by Robert Hughes in *Time* (Special Issue), 25 June 1990; ''The Art

Diviners'' by Arnd Schneider in *Anthropology Today,* April 1993; ''Nikolaus Lang at the Neuer Berliner Kunstverein'' by Ulf Erdmann Ziegler in *Art in America,* March 1999.

* * *

Nikolaus Lang collects traces and remains. He preserves a situation which is both an objective detection and subjective finding, as well as a discovery of oneself. The investigation of the terrain imparts information about himself. Should one thus describe his activity as field research or a search for personal traces? Both apply, in my opinion, for ethnology too—at least according to Levi-Strauss' interpretation—involves a searching for oneself in others. A description of alien communities is of significance only in relation to our own; who could disregard himself in exploring remote circumstances?

Ethnology is concerned with groups whose relics can still be traced in our epoch. Nikolaus Lang found himself in a similar situation when he attempted to place the Gotte brothers and sisters. They were the children of a Swiss immigrant who purchased an isolated farmstead near Bayersoien, Germany. Four of the seven children were rejected by the old-established village community, so they built themselves cottages on the remote farm lands; they remained single and without progeny. One of the Gotte offspring emigrated to America.

These outsiders have since died. At the same time, the village community has begun to disintegrate due to the exodus from the land, tourism and mechanization. The distinct social division between the centre and the periphery, which determined the marginal, bachelor existence of the Gotte children as small farmers, cobblers and odd-job men, has become blurred and will probably soon be indistinguishable. This event provides the insight into the social structure of rural areas. Obvious are the problems of a brief happening and its far-reaching consequences, which is today the concern of historical researchers. Therefore over and above old customs and folklore, this case must be seen from many more perspectives; comparison with other phenomena of social rejection and non-integration could be illuminating.

Naturally, Nikolaus Lang is not concerned with comparative studies; although he proceeds in accordance with modern concepts in that he tackles a current problem and not a documented case, evaluates all the vestiges, even the most trivial, and not only documents or fashioned, possibly aesthetic objects. For example, he has collated villagers' statements about the Gotte family, searched their houses and, insofar as these have fallen into decay, the immediate vicinity. The discovered objects, which are partly clothing, household effects, religious items and tools, and partly paper, almanacs and farming catalogs, are displayed in the upper tray of a grain chest; its remaining two sections contain plants, fruit, snail shells, excrement of martens and the bones of deer found close to the houses, a mummified female hare, a roebuck skeleton and fossil impressions discovered further afield. This leads to pages from the land register, geological maps, climatic charts and descriptions replete with photographs. However, in contrast to scientists, the artist consciously fails to exhaust all his sources; he selects a small section, limits himself to the tangible.

For here, in the middle of this apparently objective preservation of remains, we encounter the personal quintessence of his work.

Nikolaus Lang, who grew up near Oberammergau, was once a frequent visitor to the meadows where he met Ludwig Gotte. Now he has reacquainted himself with terrain across which he once roamed so cursorily. It is a kind of magical taking-possession ceremony when he defines the sources and other places, sets up walls of leaves and interwoven objects, breaks coal and stones, when he collects, gathers, patches up Joseph's house or paces off the field to check his cartographical data. ''Ethnology'' now probes into itself. ''Objective'' research becomes an inward-looking quest. By exploring the terrain he maps out his own dimensions, latent clues are activated, a link is forged between earlier recollections and present-day topographical reality, a continuity emerges from intervals of time and becomes immersed in the period of experience. Lang spent over one year working on the project which incorporates part of himself and his time. The search for apparently predetermined phenomena becomes essentially an exploration of oneself, the search for a standpoint in our rapidly changing society.

Similar to his French colleagues, Lang is fascinated by natural history museums and herbariums, which emphasize both the creative and display aspects of collecting. This explains the painstaking arrangement and lettering of the trays, and the precise documentation. Combined with this is the feeling acquired in Japan for the sensuality of objects and the linguistic-semantic declarative force of their arrangement. Lang's trays thus contain hieroglyphics. They speak to the eyes and store time. One instant is preserved and codified. Their meaning is twofold, being related to the Gotte clan and those who investigate its traces. Finally, the brothers and sisters only sparked off a personal delimitation of a position—an impulse which appears to be transferable.

—Günter Metken

LATHAM, John

Nationality: British. **Born:** Zambesi River, Rhodesia, 23 February 1921. **Education:** Winchester College, Hampton; studied at Chelsea School of Art, London, 1946–1950. **Military Service:** Served in the Royal Navy, 1940–46. **Family:** Barbara Steveni in 1951; children: Noa, John Paul and Xenia. **Career:** Lives and works in London. Founder-member, Institute for the Study of Mental Images, London, 1954; executed first spray paintings, 1954; first book sculptures, 1958; first happenings and films, 1959; inaugurated Skoob Tower ceremonies, London, 1964; founder-member, Artists Placement Group, London, 1966; part-time lecturer, St. Martin's School of Art, London, 1966–67. **Address:** 5 Boscombe Road, London W12 9HS, England.

Individual Exhibitions:

1948 Kingly Gallery, London
1955 Obelisk Gallery, London
1957 Obelisk Gallery, London
1960 Institute of Contemporary Arts, London
Galerie Schmela, Dusseldorf
1962 Galerie International d'Art Moderne, Paris
1963 Bear Lane Gallery, Oxford
Kasmin Gallery, London
Alan Gallery, New York
1965 Bangor City Art Gallery, Wales
1970 Lisson Gallery, London
1974 Art Net, London
1975 Städtische Kunsthalle, Dusseldorf
1976 Tate Gallery, London

1978 Riverside Studios, London
1982 Riverside Studios, London
1983 Van Abbemuseum, Eindhoven, Netherlands
1986 Christ Church Picture Gallery, Oxford
1987 Lisson Gallery, London
1988 Josh Baer Gallery, New York
1989 Lisson Gallery, London
1991 *Art After Physics,* Staatsgalerie, Stuttgart (catalog)
1992 *Art After Physics,* Museum of Modern Art, Oxford, England (catalog)
1993 Lisson Gallery, London
1995 *New Displays 1995,* Tate Gallery, London
1996 The Mattress Factory, Pittsburgh

Selected Group Exhibitions:

1959 *Group Exhibition,* Galleria dell'Ariete, Milan
1961 *Art of Assemblage,* Museum of Modern Art, New York (travelled to the Museum for Contemporary Arts, Dallas, and the Museum of Art, San Francisco)
1964 *Painting and Sculpture of a Decade 1954–64,* Tate Gallery, London
1967 *The 1950s,* Museum of Modern Art, New York
1970 *Information,* Museum of Modern Art, New York
1971 *APG's Art and Economics,* Hayward Gallery, London
1975 *Structures and Codes,* Royal College of Art, London
1977 *APG's Incidental Personal Approach to Government,* at *Documenta 6,* Kassel, Germany
1985 *Next Tomorrow,* Kettle's Yard Gallery, Cambridge
1986 *From a Broad Time Base,* Time Based Arts, Amsterdam
1988 *Starlit Waters: British Sculpture—An International Art 1968–1988,* Tate Gallery Liverpool, England (catalog)
1989 *British Sculpture 1960–88,* Museum voor Hedendaagse Kunst, Antwerp, Belgium (catalog)
1992 *From Matisse to Today,* Musee Matisse, Le Cateau-Cambresis, France (also Musee des Beaux-Arts, Cambrai, France) (catalog)
1996 *Life/Live: The Artistic Scene in the United Kingdom in 1996—New Adventures,* Musee d'Art Moderne de la Ville de Paris, France (catalog)
1997 *Material Culture: The Object in British Art of the 1980s and 90s,* Hayward Gallery, London
2000 *A Shot in the Head,* Lisson Gallery, London (with Lindsay Seers and John Murphy)
Live in Your Head: Concept and Experiment in Britain, 1965–75, Whitechapel Art Gallery, London

Collections:

Tate Gallery, London; Ulster Museum, Belfast; Städtische Kunsthalle, Dusseldorf; Museum of Art, Caracas; Museum of Modern Art, New York; Newark Museum, New Jersey; Gallery of Modern Art, Washington, D.C., University of Lethbridge Art Gallery, Alberta, Canada.

Publications:

By LATHAM: Books—*Least Event, One Second Drawings, Blind Work, 24 Second Paintings,* London 1970. **Articles—**statement in *Alloway's Gazette* (London); ''Time Base and Determination in Events'' in *John Latham,* exhibition catalog, Dusseldorf 1975; statement in *Arte Inglesse Oggi,* exhibition catalog, Milan 1976; interview, with Richard Dunares in *Studio International* (London), August 1982; ''The 20C Trajectory: A Black Hole at the Core?'' with Ian MacDonald Munro in *AND: Journal of Art and Education,* no. 17, 1988; ''Time vs Space'' with Karl Birjukov in *AND: Journal of Art and Education,* no. 22, 1990; ''John Latham and Ian Macdonald Munro'' with Ian Macdonald Munro in *WhiteWalls,* no. 25, Spring 1990; ''A New Interpretation of History'' in *AND: Journal of Art and Art Education,* no. 27, 1992; interview with Hans Ulrich Obrist in *Neue Bildende Kunst,* no. 6, December 1995–January 1996.

On LATHAM: Books—*John Latham,* exhibition catalog by Lawrence Alloway, London 1960; *Art of Assemblage,* exhibition catalog by William C. Seitz, New York 1961; *John Latham,* exhibition catalog by Terry Measham, London 1976; *John Latham,* exhibition catalog with text by Richard Hamilton, London 1987; *John Latham* by John Albert Walker, Middlesex 1995. **Articles—**''In the Beginning Was the Word'' by Eddie Wolfram in *Art and Artists* (London), August 1966; ''10 Years of Conceptual Enquiring'' by John A. Walker in *Studio International* (London), September 1976; article by Waldemar Janusz in *New Scientist* (London), February 1982; ''The Last Avant-gardist: John Latham's Holistic Vision'' by John A. Walker in *Performance,* no. 65–66, Spring 1992; ''From Black Holes to Boardrooms: John Latham, Barbara Stevini, and the Order of Undivided Wholeness'' by Michael Corris in *Art and Text,* no. 49, September 1994; ''Consumed by Fire'' by John A. Walker in *Art Monthly,* no. 185, April 1995.

* * *

Though it has taken many forms, John Latham's work always poses a deliberate and radical challenge, since he wants to use art as a polemical means of changing the world and the conceptual basis we use to think and talk about it. Behind his versatility of style is a consistently evolving philosophy, though one which he seems capable of expressing only in clumsy and obscure language, since he is certainly no master of the written word. Nevertheless he quotes approvingly James Joyce's well known saying ''I go to forge . . . the conscience of my race,'' and this is obviously Latham's own aim. ''The human being's root source of alienation is to be found in the concept whereby he relates to the rest of the 'material world,''' he declares. And he wants to heal the ever-widening split between intellect and emotions by giving much more emphasis to the intuitive and the non-rational.

Latham proposes that traditional thought based on the tangible, visible material world, on extendedness in space, with objects as the basic unit, should be replaced instead by a description based on extendedness in time, which would make events the basic unit. Latham is therefore a performance artist, his exhibited works being not independent aesthetic objects for their own sake but only the residue of events—events which pose questions and challenge assumptions. But their significance may change even for the artist himself, since his respect for intuitive processes means his acknowledgement that earlier works may express ideas which he hadn't consciously recognized at the time but which have surfaced later.

His obsession with finding ''a language which shall copy Nature'' began as early as 1954, when the paint-spray technique he was then using made droplets of paint pass through the air and settle on a surface. He was witnessing what appeared to be a statement of pure process, which seemed to him to offer the possibility of a language analogous to natural laws. But he really sprang into prominence with his Skoob art—''Books'' spelt backwards. This could mean painting on books, cutting books up, building great towers of them or burning them and sticking them on canvas to form highly emotive ''matter'' paintings. The desire to shock, the violation of a cultural taboo, was clearly a factor, as well as the stated desire to question books as ''tools of the Mental Furniture Industry,'' to attack the tyranny of received opinion by mutilating these guided tours of intellectual knowledge. In the 1950s these Skoob towers were fashionably neo-Dada, paralleling Rauchenberg's assemblages. But none of Latham's events, not even the scandal-provoking book and magazine burnings outside the British Museum in 1966 as part of the Destruction in Art Symposium, can compare in theatrical effect with the huge Nazi book bonfire outside the Reichstag in Berlin stagemanaged by Dr. Goebbels, the greatest neo-Dadaist of them all. Latham's attitude to books, however, shows a characteristic ambivalence, since although he has poked fun at pretentious titles he is usually concerned with books as objects rather than with their actual content. The one exception is his chewing up page by page and fermenting a library copy belonging to the St. Martin's School of Art of a book which had been treated in the art world with ridiculous awe and reverence, Clement Greenberg's *Art and Culture,* the remains of which are decorously exhibited in the Museum of Modern Art in New York.

Body art and life-style art of the kind now most closely identified with Gilbert and George, the use of the artist's own person demonstratively, was also pioneered by John Latham as another means of shocking the public out of its normal complacency. Certainly one of the most effective of his attempts to relate his work directly to the everyday was his 1971 exhibition recreating the experience of a car crash in which he was nearly killed. The documentation included the wrecked car itself, and a series of X-ray photographs showing his slow recovery in hospital. Here for once Latham's work was not overloaded with verbiage, but allowed to speak directly, creating a moving record of maiming and restoration to health, with the car as a potent symbol of destruction and death, as opposed to the Futurists' enthusiastic use of it as a symbol of progress.

Latham has become increasingly concerned with the artist's social responsibility, with the function and use of art in society. He likes to describe himself not as an artist but an Incidental Person, who can operate on the fringes of society, diagnosing its faults and bringing his specially developed intuition to bear on every conceivable aspect of it. This is the rationale behind the APG or Artist's Placement Group which Latham developed in 1966 with his wife Barbara as a means of placing artists within large industrial firms, hopefully for each other's mutual benefit, and allowing the artist to bring his insight and fresh perception to bear in raising questions. In the mid-1970s Latham himself worked in this manner on environmental projects for the City of Glasgow, both on the urban renewal of a city which is running down and on trying to solve the problem of the colossal slag-heaps in the countryside resulting from coal-mining. His proposed solutions included turning these man-made mountains into tourist attractions by building huge Skoob monuments on top of them, and altering attitudes to them by photographing some of them from angles which make them look like ancient fertility goddesses.

Other Latham projects range from paintings on roller blinds which change continuously through time as the blind is rolled, or one-second drawings, to ''Spaceship Earth'' type of photographs of the earth from outer space. He is generally recognized as a valuable thorn in the flesh, pinpointing the tragic waste of human and earth's potential, raising all sorts of questions from trivial to fundamental, but sometimes weakening his own impact by surrounding his activities with too much of the incomprehensible verbiage of which he seems over-fond, while himself criticizing it.

—Konstantin Bazarov

LAW, Bob

Nationality: British. **Born:** Brentford, Middlesex, 22 January 1934. **Education:** Apprentice architectural designer: geometry, trigonometry, perspective drawing and planning at night school, 1949; also studied ornithology and zoology. **Military Service:** Served in the British Army, in North Africa, 1952–54. **Family:** married Gina Cann in 1965; children: Vanessa and Daniel. **Career:** Independent painter, since 1957: first ''field'' drawings and paintings, 1959, series of black paintings, 1964, white paintings, 1969, and sculpture, from 1980; lived in St. Ives, Cornwall, 1957–60, in Richmond, Surrey, 1960, 1964–69, in Froxfield, Hampshire, 1960–61, 1962–64, in Aix-en-Provence, France, 1961–62, in Twickenham, Surrey, since 1969. Has also worked as a carpenter, 1952, 1955–57, and furniture maker, 1962–64. Visiting lecturer, Exeter School of Art, Devon, 1964–71. **Awards:** French Government Scholarship, University of Aix, 1961; Purchase Award, 1967, and Major Award, 1978, Arts Council of Great Britain; Greater London Arts Association Award, 1981. **Address:** 17 Second Cross Road, Twickenham, Middlesex TW2 5QY, England.

Individual Exhibitions:

1962 Graboswki Gallery, London
1963 Christchurch College, Oxford
1967 Grabowski Gallery, London
1970 Galerie Konrad Fischer, Dusseldorf
Onnasch Galerie, Berlin
1971 Lisson Gallery, London
1974 Museum of Modern Art, Oxford
1975 Lisson Gallery, London
1977 Galerie Rolf Preisig, Basel
Lisson Gallery, London
1978 Whitechapel Art Gallery, London
1979 Galerie Gillespie/De Laage, Paris
1980 Whitfield Street Lisson, London
1982 Lisson Gallery, London
Gunnersbury Park, London
1987 Karsten Schubert Gallery, London
1988 Karsten Schubert Gallery, London
Black Watercolours, Karsten Schubert Ltd, London
1989 *Bob Law, Drawings 1959–1966,* Karsten Schubert Ltd, London
Clinton Tweedie, Lenox St. Gallery, Melbourne
1990 Paul Kasmin Gallery, New York
1992 The Platform Gallery, Folkestone
1996 Marlene Eleini Gallery
1999 Newlyn Art Gallery, Cornwall and Kettle's Yard, Cambridge

Selected Group Exhibitions:

1960 *Two Young British Painters,* ICA, London
1977 *British Artists of the 60s,* Tate Gallery, London
1980 *British Art 1940–1980,* Hayward Gallery, London
1982 *British Contemporary Art Exhibition,* Tokyo Metropolitan Museum (travelled to Tochigi Prefectoral Museum of Fine Arts; National Museum of Modern Art, Osaka; Fukuoka Art Museum; Hokkaido Museum of Modern Art, Sapporo)
1985 *The British Show,* Art Gallery of Western Australia, Perth (travelled to Art Gallery of New South Wales, Sydney; Queensland Art Gallery, Brisbane; National Gallery of Victoria, Melbourne; National Art Gallery, Wellington)
1986 *Falls the Shadow,* Hayward Gallery, London
1987 *British Art in the 20th Century,* Royal Academy of Arts, London
1988 *Le Couleur Seule, L'Experience du Monochrome,* Musée Saint Pierre d'Art Contemporain, Lyon, France
1991 *The LeWitt Collection,* Wadsworth Atheneum, Hartford, Connecticut
1996 *From Figure to Object, a Century of Sculptors' Drawings,* Frith Street Gallery and Karsten Schubert Gallery
1999 *As Dark as Light,* Tate Gallery, St. Ives
Small Sculptures and Early Drawings by Bob Law, Richard Salmon Gallery, London
Jerwood Painting Prize 1999, exhibition of the Seven Shortlisted Artists, Jerwood Space Gallery, London
2000 *Live In Your Head: Concept and Experiment in Britain, 1965–75,* Whitechapel Art Gallery, London, and Museu do Chiado, Lisbon
2001 Whitechapel Centenary, Whitechapel Art Gallery, London

Collections:

Tate Gallery, London; Arts Council of Great Britain; Victoria and Albert Museum, London; Southampton Art Gallery; Worcester College, Oxford; New College, Oxford; Contemporary Art Society, London; The British Council, London; City Museum and Art Gallery, Peterborough; Stedelijk Museum, Amsterdam; The Panza Collection, Milan; Museum of Modern Art, New York; City Art Gallery, Johannesburg; Guggenheim Museum New York; The Sol LeWitt Collection, Connecticut; The Gallery of New South Wales, Sydney; The British Museum, London.

Publications:

By LAW: Book—*16 Drawings,* London 1971. **Articles—**statements in *Bob Law,* exhibition catalog, London 1962; *7 aus London,* exhibition catalog, Berne 1973; *Arte Inglese Oggi,* exhibition catalog, Milan 1976; *A Chronology of Works and Writings,* catalog to Bob Law paintings and drawings, 1959–1978, London 1978; *Contemporary British Artists,* London 1979; *ROSC 84,* exhibition catalog, Dublin 1984.

On LAW: Books—*10 Black Paintings 1965–70,* exhibition catalog with text by Richard Cork, Oxford 1974; *Bob Law: Paintings and Drawings 1959–78,* exhibition catalog, London 1978; *Art in the Seventies* by Edward Lucie-Smith, London 1980; *St. Ives 1939–64* by David Brown, London 1985; *British Art since 1900* by Frances Spalding, London 1986; *The Landscape of Experience* by Jeremy Hooker, London 1987; *British Art in the Twentieth Century* by Susan Compton, London and Munich 1987; *Painting and Poetry, The Landscape of Experience* by Jeremy Hooker, 1987; *English Contemporary Art 1910–90, 80 Years of Collecting by the Contemporary Arts Society* by Daniel Wheeler, 1990; *Art Since Mid Century (1945-Present)* by Daniel Wheeler, 1991; exhibition catalog with text by Peter Keene, Galerie Luc Queyrel, Paris 1991; Jerwood Painting Prize Catalogue by Judith Bumpus, 1999. **Articles—**''Bob Law at Marlene Eleine Gallery'' by Andrew Wilson, *Art Monthly,* no. 198, July-August, 1996; ''Drawings, Sculpture, Paintings—Bob Law'' by S. Hobson, *Inside Cornwall,* February-March, 1999; ''Bob Law, Kettle's Yard, Cambridge'' by Margaret Garlake, *Art Monthly,* no. 226, May 1999; ''Bob Law'' by John Russell Taylor, *The Guardian,* 1999; ''Artist in Focus: Bob Law'' by Felicity Lunn, *Royal Academy Magazine,* no. 63, summer 1999. **Films—***Tree* and *Under Pressure* by Polywylde, 1971; *Film Show,* Situation Gallery, London, 1971, digital movie by Polywylde, 2000.

*

Above all, be happy in your work.

—Bob Law

* * *

At first encounter one of Bob Law's ''black'' paintings appears just that—an uncompromising black square, pure geometry—but to an attentive and perceptive eye there is a gradual awareness of almost imperceptible nuances of rich, dense colour within the immaculate surface of a carefully crafted work.

The scale of his ''black'' paintings is, typically, 66'' x 69'', that of ''a man with his arms out-stretched, large enough to be peripheral when viewed.'' They may appear modest in comparison with the size of the New York School of Abstract Expressionists whose paintings dominated the art scene in the late 1950s and 1960s when Law first commenced his own series. His work developed parallel to theirs but in a gentler, less expansive, more introverted and perhaps more English way.

He has used acrylic paint and has always paid meticulous attention to the edge conditions. There is a confining edge all the way round the colour field so that ''the paintings don't go off edges . . . (and) start relating to the architecture outside the complete object.''

A surface, which would when complete be violet/black/blue/black, is built up with a minimum of nine or ten coats, each having to be floated on with perfect evenness. In his obsessional search for the unflawed surface, Law rejects the canvas even after days of work if any irregularities or marks develop. Such is the delicacy of the final surface that it is extremely vulnerable to careless handling. His works are also practically unreproducable, as they photograph as simply black squares. To know his work, one has to know the real thing. The real thing, the almost-black, vibrant surfaces are essentially contemplative objects. The viewer cannot judge them by the sequential standards of tradition Western art. The response has to be totally subjective.

The artist has said that his works need time. He says that they may then start ''to eat you up, grow on you. If you openly go to them and you are a receptive type of person for this sort of work, they may swallow you up and take you inside. If you don't like them, it's too bad: I don't care. They're just things.''

—Mary Ellis

LE BROCQUY, Louis

Nationality: Irish. **Born:** Dublin, 10 November 1916. **Education:** Irish primary schools; studied chemistry at Trinity College, Dublin, 1936–37; self-taught in art. **Family:** Married Jean Stoney in 1938 (divorced, 1948); one daughter; married the painter Anne Madden Simpson, in 1958; children: Alexis and Pierre. **Career:** Independent painter, since 1938; worked in the family oil refining business, 1935–38; travelled in Europe, 1938–40, then returned to Dublin; organizer, with others, *Irish Exhibition of Living Art,* 1943; worked on Irish tinker paintings and theatre designs, stained glass and murals; settled in London, 1946; produced first tapestries, 1948; lived in France and Switzerland, 1958–60, and settled near Nice, 1960; destroyed many of his works, 1963; has worked on series of human head images, since 1964. Visiting lecturer in paintings and mural design, Central School of Arts and Crafts, London, 1947–54; visiting tutor, Royal College of Art, London, 1955–58; director, Kilkenny Design Workshop, 1965–77. **Member:** Irish Council of Design, 1963–65; Society of Designers in Ireland, 1974–75; board member, Irish Museum of Modern Art, 1989—. **Awards:** Premio Prealpina, *Biennale,* Venice, 1956; D.Litt.: University of Dublin, 1962; fellow, Society of Industrial Artist, 1960; Chevalier, Légion d'Honneur, 1974; honorary member, Royal Hibernian Academy, Dublin, 1983; LL.D.: National University, 1988; named Officier des Arts et des Lettres, Paris, 1996; Glen Dimplex Prize for ''sustained contribution to the visual arts in Ireland,'' 1998. **Agents:** Gimpel Fils, London, England; Taylor Galleries, 6 Dawson Street, Dublin 2, Ireland. **Address:** c/o Gimpel Fils, 30 Davies Street, London W1, England.

Selected Individual Exhibitions:

1956 Biennale, Venice
1966 Municipal Gallery of Modern Art, Dublin
1967 Ulster Museum, Belfast
1973 Fondation Maeght, St. Paul-de-Vence, France
1976 Musée d'Art Modern de la Ville, Paris
1981 New York State Museum, New York
1982 Palais des Beaux-Arts, Charleroi, Belgium
1988 Festival Centre, Adelaide
National Gallery of Victoria, Melbourne
Museum of Contemporary Art, Brisbane
1989 Musée Picasso, Antibes
1991 Museum of Modern Art, Kamakora
Itami Museum of Art, Osaka
City Museum of Contemporary Art, Hiroshima
1992 Taylor Galleries, Dublin
Gillian Jason Gallery, London
1993 Taylor Galleries, Dublin
Bell Gallery, Belfast
1994 Taylor Galleries, Dublin
Galerie Bernard Bouche, Paris
1995 Taylor Galleries, Dublin
Grant Fine Art, Newcastle
1996 Retrospective, Irish Museum of Modern Art, Dublin
Bibliothèque Municipal, Tours, France
Espace Paul Ricard, Paris
1998 Taylor Galleries, Dublin
Municipal Gallery of ARt, Lubliana, Slovenia
1999 Taylor Galleries, Dublin
2000 *Studies Towards an Image of Federico Garcia Lorca,* Museum of Contemporary Art, Oaxaca, Mexico
Taylor Galleries, Dublin
2001 Gimpel Fils, London

Selected Group Exhibitions:

1980 *ROSC,* Dublin
1987 *Painting since World War II,* Guggenheim Museum, New York
1988 *Olympiad of Art,* Seoul
1989 *L'Europe des Grands Maitres, 1870–1970,* Musée Jacquemart Andre, Paris
1990 *Seoul Art Festival,* Seoul
Collection du Musée Picasso, Antibes
1991 *Premiers Chef d'Oeuvres des Grands Maitres Européens,* M.E.O. Museums of Art, Ibaraki, Tokyo
1992 *11 en Francia, Artistas de la Communidad Europa,* I.C.F., Saragossa Madrid, Valencia
Le Portrait dans l'Art Contemporain, Musée de l'Art Moderne, Nice
1993 *Collection de la Fondation Maeghte,* St. Paul-de-Vence
1995 *Irish Art, 1770–1995,* Crawford Municipal Gallery of Modern Art, Cork (toured)
1997 *A Century of Irish Painting,* Hugh Lane Municipal Gallery of Modern Art, Dublin
1998 *When Time Began to Rant and Rage,* Walker Art Gallery, Liverpool; Berkeley Art Museum; Grey Art Gallery, New York; Barbican Art Gallery, London
1999 *Collection de la Fondation Van Gogh,* Mikata Gallery of Art, Tokyo
2000 *Reunion,* Rugby Art Gallery and Museum, Ireland

Selected Collections:

Albright-Knox, Buffalo; Detroit Institute of Arts, Michigan; Irish Museum of Modern Art, Dublin; Municipal Gallery, Dublin; Guggenheim Museum, New York; Hirshhorn Museum, Washington, D.C.; Ho Am Museum, Seoul; Itami Museum, Osaka; Kunsthaus, Zurich; Tate Gallery, London; Ulster Museum, Belfast; Museum of Modern Art, Paris.

Publications:

By LE BROCQUY: Illustrated books—*The Táin,* translated by Thomas Kinsella, 1969; *The Playboy of the Western World* by J. M. Synge, 1970; *Dubliners* by James Joyce, 1986; *Stirrings Still* by Samuel Beckett, 1988.

On LE BROCQUY: Books—*From Sickert to 1948* by John Russell, London 1948; *Art since 1945* by Herbert Read, London 1959; *A Letter to a Young Painter* by Herbert Read, London 1962; *A Concise History of Irish Art* by Bruce Arnold, London 1969; *Modern Master* by Brahamer and Garner, Malmo, Sweden 1980; *Louis Le Brocquy* by

Dorothy Walker, Dublin 1981; *Louis Le Brocquy and the Celtic Head Image,* exhibition catalog by Proinsias MacCana and Anne Crookshank, Albany, New York 1981; *Le Brocquy; Images 1975–87,* exhibition catalog, Dublin 1987; *Images, Single and Multiple,* exhibition catalog, Hiroshima 1991; *Seeing His Way* by Anne Madden Le Brocquy, Dublin 1994; *Louis le Brocquy, Procession* by George Morgan, Kinsale 1994; *Louis le Brocquy, The Head Image* by George Morgan, Kinsale 1996. **Articles—**''Headmaster'' by Tom Rosenthal in *New Statesman,* 21 May 2001.

* * *

Among the few extant early paintings by Louis Le Brocquy is one called *The Picnic* (1940), which, though very different from his later pictures, is a key to his future development as an artist. It has certain defects of draughtsmanship (the articulation of the limbs and their relationship with the ground, etc.) which were the sort of thing to be seized on by his critics and may have been an excuse for his work being rejected by the Royal Hibernian Academy in 1942 and again in 1943. It would have been the equivalent of refusing to print Joyce on the grounds that his spelling was bad and he made the occasional grammatical mistake. After all, Le Brocquy was self-taught and did not take up painting seriously until 1938. What is interesting and prophetic about this picture is the sadness and isolation of the figures. Each one is absorbed in his or her own thoughts. There is no communication, no human warmth, at least not on the surface. Isolation is a theme to which Le Brocquy constantly returns.

His next phase, however, was more fiery. The pictures of this period have been described as the *Traveller* series because of the predominance of tinkers, men and women who are euphemistically known in Ireland as ''travelling people.'' In fact they are a hard, ruthless, mean and vindictive lot. It is thus Le Brocquy portrays them, in a Cubist idiom, similar to that of Colquhoun and Keith Vaughan, admirably suited to his purpose. This, to my mind, was a splendid period of his work. Herbert Read had the good judgment to reproduce one of the masterpieces, *Man Creating a Bird* (1948), in his *Contemporary British Art* (1951).

There followed an equally fruitful period, known as the *Grey Series.* Though faintly Cubist, these pictures were more suave and smooth, with subtle modulations of tone, whites, blacks, and, of course, grey. In this period there is a return, with greater emphasis, to the theme of isolation. Not only are humans—father, mother and child—isolated and cut off from one another, but they are cut off even from their domestic pets. At this time, Le Brocquy captured, as no one else has, the loneliness, isolation and bewilderment of being a child (*Child in a Yard, Boy behind a Door,* 1954). All this was summed up in his prize-winning work, *A Family,* which, not surprisingly, horrified the pious folk of Ireland, who have different views of family life; but, for all that, it is a superb work, which earned the somewhat fulsome remark: ''the most ambitious attempt to trace and categorize the development of painting and sculpture from Cézanne and Robin to our time.''

There followed a period in which Le Brocquy's paintings became increasingly exiguous. The series has been called *Presences,* but, insofar as the human figure progressively disappears into the semblance of a ghost or an X-ray photograph of a human form, they might more properly be described as absences. I do not say this in any derogatory sense. It is not my favourite Le Brocquy period, but is was a period in which his texture (*impasto*) became richer as detail became thinner and vaguer. It had a purity, simplicity, pared down quality which one associates with the plays of Beckett at that time and subsequently. And it paved the way for his latest phase devoted to heads.

Some of the heads are of famous literary personages—W. B. Yeats, Joyce, Beckett, Lorca. Others are what he calls ''ancestral heads,'' or heads of Irish heros or victims or martyrs. The impasted technique is used, but the brushlines have become more fluent and the whole effect is more painterly—and the psychological effect more horrendous. The *Presences* were isolated in that they were either views from the back or transparent views. The heads bring back the human presence, but only just. Even the faces of the living have a remote, deathlike look, as if seen behind frosted glass or through a mist. The mist of memory, perhaps; for these heads, though recognizable, are not strictly portraits; they are reconstructed. Some are sinister in the extreme: a mouth open in agony, a hidden face behind what seen to be blood-stained hands pressed against glass. It is Bacon country; not surprisingly: the two are friends, and there is a series of Bacon heads.

Le Brocquy's versatility as an artist is remarkable. Besides painting, he has been engaged in stage and costume design, textile design, book illustration, stained glass, mosaics and tapestry. What is most remarkable is his ability to adapt faithfully to each medium (a quality he shares with Beckett). His illustrations for Thomas Kinsella's translation of *The Táin* are masterly in capturing the spirit of the poem, though the style is quite different from that of his paintings. Again, in a series of designs for the Tabard tapestry, unfettered by excessive naturalism, is capable.

—D. C. Barrett

LE GAC, Jean

Nationality: French. **Born:** Tamaris, Alès, 6 May 1936. **Education:** Section preparatoire, Professorat de Dessin, Paris, 1954–58. **Family:** Married Jacqueline Denoyel in 1958; children: Renaud, Agnes and Martine. **Career:** Painter, Paris, 1958–68; has worked with phototexts, Paris, since 1969. Has taught in various art schools in Paris, since 1958. **Agent:** Galerie Daniel Templon, 30 rue Beaubourg, 75003 Paris. **Address:** 67 Avenue Gambetta, 75020 Paris, France.

Selected Individual Exhibitions:

1970 Galerie Daniel Templon, Paris
1971 Galerie Rive Droite, Paris
1972 Galerie Daniel Templon, Paris
Galleria Daniel Templon, Milan
Kunstmuseum, Lucerne
1973 Museum of Modern Art, Oxford
Galerie t'Venster, Rotterdam
Galerie Daniel Templon, Paris
Galleria Daniel Templon, Milan
1974 John Gibson Gallery, New York
Galleria Nuovi Strumenti, Brescia, Italy
Israel Museum, Jerusalem
Galerie Daniel Templon, Paris
Galerie Loeb, Bern
Galleria Daniel Templon, Milan
Galerie Ricke, Cologne

Jean Le Gac: *La salle des voyages,* 2000. Photo by Marc Domage. ©Jean Le Gac.

1975 Galleria Cannaviello, Rome
Galerie Daniel Templon, Paris
Galleri St. Petri, Lund, Sweden
Galleri Daner, Copenhagen
Galerie Art in Progress, Munich
Galleria Daniel Templon, Milan
1976 John Gibson Gallery, New York
Galerie Daniel Templon, Paris
1977 Kunstverein, Hamburg
John Gibson Gallery, New York
Galerie Ricke, Cologne
Städtische Galerie im Lenbachhaus, Munich
Neue Galerie, Aachen, Germany
Galleria d'Arte Spagnoli, Milan
1978 Centre Georges Pompidou, Paris
Cannaviello Studio d'Arte, Milan
1979 Galerie Daniel Templon, Paris
John Gibson Gallery, New York
Galerie Ricke, Cologne
Kunstverein, Krefeld, Germany
1980 Le Coin du Miroir, Dijon, France
1981 Galerie Daniel Templon, Paris
1982 Galerie France Morin, Montreal
Galerie Catherine Isser, St. Paul-de-Vence, France
Hal Bromm Gallery, New York
1983 Galerie Daniel Templon, Paris
Galerie Le Chanjour, Nice, France
Musée La Roche sur Yon, France
1984 Studio Marconi, Milan
Galerie Athanor, Marseille, France
Galerie Catherine Issert, St. Paul-de-Vence, France
Musée d'Art Moderne de la Ville, Paris
1985 Andata/Ritorno, Geneva
Galerie Daniel Templon, Paris
Chapelle des Carmelites, Toulouse, France
1986 Galerie Catherine Issert, St. Paul-de-Vence, France

1987 Galerie Daniel Templon, Paris
Elisabeth Franck Gallery, Knokke-le-Zoute, Belgium
Chapelle du Mejean, Arles, France
1988 Galerie Reckermann, Cologne
Institut Francais, Cologne
Galerie Daniel Templon, Paris
Galerie Arte Unido, Barcelona
Galerie Catherine Issert, St. Paul-de-Vence
Galerie Isy Brachot, Bruxelles
1994 Galerie Sandmann et Haak, Hannover, Germany
Galerie Camille Von Scholtz, Brussels
Galerie Catherine Issert, St. Paul-de-Vence, France
Sala Parpallo, Paulau dela Scala, Valencia, Spain
Galerie Pascual Lucas, Valencia, Spain
1995 Galerie Alesandro Sales, Barcelona
Galleria Francese Piazza Navona, Rome
Galerie Knapp, Lausanne, Switzerland
1996 Musée Archéologique, Milan
1997 Galerie Fortlaan 17, Gand, Belgium

Selected Group Exhibitions:

1969 *Biennale de Paris,* Musée d'art Moderne, Paris
1972 *Pour Memoires,* Enterpots Laine, Bordeaux (toured France)
1977 *Europe in the 1970s,* Art Institute of Chicago, Illinois (travelled to San Francisco Museum of Modern Art, California; Fort Worth Art Museum, Texas; Contemporary Art Center, Cincinnati)
1981 *Westkunst,* Messehallen, Cologne
1984 *International Survey of Recent Painting and Sculpture,* Museum of Modern Art, New York
1987 *L'Epoque, la mode, la morale, la passion,* Musée d'Art Moderne de la Ville, Paris
1989 *L'Art en France, un siecle d'invention,* Pushkin Museum, Moscow (travelled to the Hermitage, Leningrad)
1992 *Manifeste,* Musée Moderne de la Ville, Paris
1993 *Ateliers de France,* Ludwig Museum, Koblenz, Germany
1995 *Album,* Musée Boysmans-Van Beuningen, Rotterdam
L'Effet Cinéma, Quand l'Image Raconte, Musée d'Art Contemporain de Montréal, Canada
1996 *Les Sept Pêchés Capitaux—La Paresse,* Galerie du Musée, Centre Georges Pompidou, Paris
1997 *Made in France,* Musée National d'Art Moderne, Centre Georges Pompidou, Paris
1999 *The Promise of Photography,* Centre National de la Photographie, Paris
2000 *Epiphanies,* Cathédrale d'Evry, Mission de l'An 2000

Collections:

Centre Georges Pompidou, Paris; Bibliothèque Nationale, Paris; Musée d'Art Moderne de la Ville, Paris; Fond National d'Art Contemporain, Paris; Musée d'Art et d'Industrie, St. Etienne, France; Neue Galerie, Aachen, Germany; Museum Boymans-van Beuningen, Rotterdam; Museum of Modern Art, New York; Palais de L'Elysée, Paris; Staatsgalerie, Stuttgart, Germany.

Publications:

By LE GAC: Books—*Les Cahiers 1968–1971,* Lucerne 1972; *Jean Le Gac/Florent Max,* Paris 1972; *Le Recit,* Hamburg 1972; *Le Decor,* Paris 1972; *The Painter,* Rotterdam 1973; *The Imitation of Jean le Gac,* Oxford 1973; *Les Anecdotes,* Jerusalem 1974; *Le Fantome des Beaux-Arts,* Brussels and Hamburg 1975; *Le Professeur de dessin,* Brussels and Paris 1976; *Der Maler,* with an introduction by Günter Metken, Brussels and Hamburg 1977; *Le Peintre-exposition romancée,* with an introduction by Günter Metken, Paris 1978; *Le Peintre de Tamaris près d'Alès,* Liege, Belgium 1980; *Introduction aux oeuvres d'un artiste dans mon genre,* Arles 1987; *Le peintre Intercalaire,* Paris 1990; *A l'aveuglette,* Brussels 1994. **Article**—''Le ruines emotionnelles de Jean Le Gac,'' interview by Emmanuel Pernoud in *Nouvelles de l'Estampe* (Paris), no. 128, 1993; **Films**—*Signal,* 1970; *Jean Le Gac, artiste peintre,* with Michel Pamart, 1973; *La Fausse Ruine et el Peintre,* with Michel Pamart, 1979; *L'Hydravion et le Peintre,* with Renaud Le Gac, 1980; *La sieste pittoresque* with Renaud Le Gac, 1985; *L'absent et l'inconnu* with Brigitte Cornaud and Philippe Gauthier, 1987; *Rythme de Robert Delaunay avec Jean Le Gac* with Pierre Coulibeuf, 1991; *Jean Le Gac* with Sylvie Boulloud and Philippe Brach, 1994; *Jean Le Gac, IN MEMORIAM* with Michel Nuridsany, 1999.

On LE GAC: Books—*Art en France, une nouvelle generation* by Jean Clair, Paris 1972; *Jean Le Gac* by Catherine Francblin, Paris 1984; *Jean le Gac, un peintre de reve,* exhibition catalog with text by Catherine Francblin, Michel Nuridsany and Bernard Marcade, Paris 1984; *Jean Le Gac* exhibition catalog with text by Martin Le Gac, Knokke-le-Zoute 1987; *Das echo und sein Maler,* exhibition catalog with text by G. Metken, 1988; *Le peintre bléssé,* text by Dèmosthénes Davvetas and Bernard Marcade, Paris, 1988; *Soleil immatériel, chemin dans l'art contemporain* by Démosthenes Devvetas, Paris, 1989; *Au dessous des deux verriéres de la gare de Colmar* exhibition catalog by Lextes de Francois Barré and Gilbert Lascault, Paris 1991; *Jean Le Gac par Le Gac, Jean* monograph with text by Ann Hindry, Brussels 1992; *Le peintre qui s'éloigne* text by Francois Chaval, St. Denis-de-la-Réunion, 1993; *Jean Le Gac,* exhibition catalog with text by Démosthènes Davvetas, Ann Hindry, Bernard Marcade, Valencia 1994; *Jean Le Gace* by Anne Dagbert, Paris 1998; *Un Peintre,* exhibition catalog by Evelyne Artuad, Nathalie Roux, and Michel Nuridsany, Clermont-Ferrand, France 2000. **Articles**—''Les Activités Myterieuses de Jean Le Gac'' by Bernard Borgeaud in *Chroniques de l'Art Vivant* (Paris), June 1971; ''Adventure Stories'' by Effie Stephano in *Art and Artist* (London), May 1973; ''Jean Le Gac et le Singulier Plural'' by Claire Stouling in *Art Press* (Paris), May 1974; ''The Enigmatic Images of Jean Le Gac'' by Kate Linker in *Arts Magazine* (New York), March 1977; ''Jean Le Gac commentateur de Jean Le Gac'' by Catherine Francblin in *Art Press* (Paris), March 1978; ''Trouvez l'Artiste'' by Anne Dagbert in *Art Press* (Paris), no. 59, 1982; ''On the Trial of Jean Le Gac'' by Kate Linker in *Artforum* (New York), summer 1986; ''La caméra-work de Jean Le Gac'' by Catherine Francblin in *Beaux-Arts Magazine,* July/August 1987; ''La peinture pour seul horizon'' by Philippe Arbaizar in *Artstudio* (Paris), no. 5, 1987; ''Jean Le Gac, histoires de peintre'' by Philippe Piguet in *Le quotidien de Paris,* 11 January 1990; ''Auto-portraits de dos'' by Marc Lebot in *Artstudio* (Paris) no. 20, June 1991; ''La memoire pour unique bagage'' by Daniele Gillemon in *Le Soir,* 2 February 1994; ''Jean Le Gac'' by Jean François Debailleux in *Libération,* 5 May 1995; ''El Pintor Detective'' by Luisa Borras in *Vanguardia,* 16 June

1995; ''Le Gac Peintre au Conditionnel'' by Michel Nuridsany in *Figaro,* 26 August 1997; ''Le Gac Célèbre les Femmes, la Photo, Matisse et la Mode'' by Philippe Dagen in *Monde,* 13/14 December 1998; ''Jean Le Gac, Faux Adieux'' by H. F. Debailleux in *Libération,* 18 December 1998; ''La Modernité Dynamité de Jean Le Gac'' by Roland Doclos in *Montagne,* April 2000.

*

In 1980 I would have nothing to add to that which I told you for your first edition: I was, quite simply, rather tired of the painter's role. The emotive strength I gained from his lightning appearance in my stories with photos had diminished by force of repetition. I had to make a major effort to invent new approaches. I lost all hope that the painter might again be able to appear in my eyes as ''an early messenger of the meaning of the World'' (Marcel Lecomte).

Fortunately in 1981 I discovered some pastels given to my daughter, a whole box which without me would have continued to wait impatiently in a drawer, and some poor quality cardboard which reminded me of my youthful years of poverty. I immediately reopened my books from childhood and, without respite, began to copy the illustration which in the past has awakened me to Art. Since then I feel like a Far Eastern calligrapher or a monk illuminator of the Middle Ages, that is to say a painter whose ''greatest pleasure is to recopy masterpieces indefinitely'' until he reaches effusion by the simple means of spellbinding repetition.

From 1986 to 1987 I pursued my attempt at copying childhood images on large painted canvas connected with old movie-projectors. Ideally I see my wide wall-decorations adorning a rich idle painter's home who has broken with Art History and the common species ''contemporary artist.''

—Jean Le Gac

* * *

Although Jean Le Gac has been active as an artist since the 1960s, it was not until 1973 that he became known internationally—the year that a name was given to the genre, ''Narrative Art.'' What had been a formal tendency, paradoxically notable for the catholicity of its practitioners, became a ''school,'' visible and coherent. Le Gac shares with his colleagues—Bill Beckley, David Askevold, Peter Hutchinson, and others—the concern with ''story,'' mythic, frequently humorous, inverted parable, often without a point but replete with and dependent upon penetrating content. Like them, he binds text and photographic visual image indissolubly, neither assuming more significance that the other. Yet the oeuvre as a whole presents a deeper sense of intimate mystery than others in the same mode; he eschews the theatricality of Mac Adams, the deliberate twists of Beckley, and the expository tone of Hutchinson.

Le Gac, in fact, is a latter-day *intimiste.* Delving deep into his gentle and modest imagination, he ''constructs'' characters, unassuming and non-heroic, and places them in the French landscape, or static, comfortably unpretentious domestic interiors. They operate on a level of nostalgia or wistful fantasy, one which is sometimes explicitly autobiographical but which just as often is an inevitable function of the characters themselves, who seem to play out real or imaginary incidents almost separately from the artist who has created them. The consciousness at work here is hardly that of a naif, however, and concerns itself with a re-ordering and rendering of its own ''flow,'' very much aware of both formal ad mental parallels. In one of Le Gac's first major narrative series, *The Anecdotes* (1974), the artist's humorous modesty is inescapable, but a sharp an sophisticated edge comes to the surface in his introductory text: ''An artist can become famous overnight. Therefore, it is no doubt wise to anticipate such an event by practicing at answering for your works in the presence of an interviewer.'' This piece echoes the sly—but genuine—humility that underlies Le Gac's frequent references to his own profession, that of the artist, which emerge in such series as *The Painter* (1973), *The Drawing Master,* and *The Phantom of the Beaux-Arts.* Formally, this spirit is made palpable by the linear, active drawings presented in some of the photographic panels—executed, interestingly enough, not by Le Gac but by his wife, Jacqueline.

In his seminal essay on Narrative Art, originally printed in *Artforum* and later used as the catalog essay for the first exhibition of his genre, James Collins likened Le Gac's work to that of Robbe-Grillet and Eric Rohmer, invoking, in particular, the film *Claire's Knee.* There is a certain inevitability to this comparison: Le Gac's work unravels themes, suggests at motivations, and meanders through an apparently unconnected series of incidents. Just as Rohmer's hero fixes his attention upon Claire's knee as erotic object—and subject—Le Gac displaces the banal and raises it to the level of significant myth. In the series of ten black-and-white and color panels called *The Painter,* Le Gac surfaces this sensibility to great effect: he begins by likening the obsession with his principal character, the French painter himself, with his attempt to stop smoking, leads us through the painter's daughter's marriage to a local tradesman, and ends with a parenthetical comment on the resurrection of a certain hairstyle. What appears to be significant is mentioned, then tucked away; what appears to be insignificant at first takes on the aspect of the drama.

This is characteristic of all of Le Gac's work to date, and it is what enables it to operate on such a level of effectiveness (as well as the fact that the texts themselves are so brilliantly written and so superbly linked to the visual sing): the elegiac quality of revery and imagination, a mingling of multiple layers of past, present, future, an on-going search for what Baudelaire termed Correspondences.

—Jane Bell

LENICA, Jan

Nationality: Polish. **Born:** Poznan, 4 January 1928. **Education:** Studied piano in Poznan, 1933–40, and architecture in Warsaw, 1947–52, Dip. Arch. 1952. **Career:** Independent artist, known for posters, Warsaw, 1950–63, and in Paris, since 1963; also cartoon filmmaker, since 1957, and theatre decor designer, since 1972. Teaching assistant to Henryk Tomaszewski, Art Academy, Warsaw, 1954; professor, Kunstakademie Gesamthochschule, Kassel, West Germany, 1979; professor, Hochschule der Künste, Berlin, since 1986. **Awards:** Toulouse-Lautrec Prize, Paris, 1961; first prize, *International Poster Biennale,* Warsaw, 1966; Bundes-film Preis, West Germany, 1969; Preis der Stadt Essen, West Germany, 1980;

Painting by Jan Lenica. ©2001 Artists Rights Society (ARS), NY/VG Bild-Kunst, Bonn.

Jules Cheret Prize, France, 1985; Alfred Jurzykowski Award, New York 1987; Graphics Award, Childrens Book Fair, Bologna, 1987, **Address:** Passauer Str. 34, 10789 Berlin, Germany.

Individual Exhibitions:

1948 Young Artists Club, Warsaw
1963 Stuck-Villa, Munich
1973 National Museum Poznan, Poland (retrospective)
1980 Centre Georges Pompidou, Paris
1988 Tampereen Nykytaiteen Museo, Finland
1990 Haus am Lützowplatz, Berlin
Polish Museum of America, Chicago
1991 Museum für Kunst und Gewerbe, Hamburg
2000 Center of Contemporary Art, Warsaw

Selected Group Exhibitions:

1971 *Vier Polnische Plakatkunstler,* Deutsche Plakat-Museum, Essen
1980 *Triennale '80: Die Besten Plakate der Jahre 1977 bis 1980,* Deutsche Plakat-Museum, Essen
1991 *Jestesmy,* Warsaw.
1993 *100th Anniversary of Polish Poster Art,* Krakow
1994 *Poster Biennal,* Warsaw and Brno

Collections:

Deutsches Plakat-Museum, Essen; Centre Georges Pompidou, Paris; Narodni Museum, Warsaw; Muzeum Narodowe, Poznan, Poland; Israel Museum Jerusalem; Museum of Modern Art, New York; Bibliothéque Nationale, Paris; Museum für Kunst und Gewerbe, Hamburg; Library of Congress, Washington, D.C.

Publications:

By LENICA: Books—*The Train,* Munich 1969, London 1970; *The Magic Bird,* with text by Max Bolliger, London 1987; *Jan Lenica: Noir et Blanc,* Paris 1988. **Film**—*Adam 2,* 1969.

On LENICA: Books—*Vier Polnische Plakatkunstler,* exhibition catalog with text by H. Schardt, Essen 1971; *Graphic Designers in Europe,* volume I, edited by Henri Hillebrand, London 1971; *Art without Boundaries 1950–1970,* edited by Gerald Woods, Philip Thompson and John Williams, London 1972; *Polish Poster Art Today* by Szymon Bojko, Warsaw 1972; *Triennale '80: Die Besten Plakate der Jahre 1977 bis 1980,* exhibition catalog with text by Frieder Mellinghof, Essen 1980; *Jan Lenica,* edited by Frolich and Kaufmann, West Berlin 1981. **Articles**—''Le plus important c'est l'o-reille'' in *Opus International,* April 1969; ''Adam 2: A New Cartoon Film by Jan Lenica'' by A. Brustellin in *Graphis* (Zurich), no. 145, 1969/70; ''Poland's Poster Genius'' by Frank Fox in *The World and I* (USA), May 1990; ''Jan Lenica'' by Shoji Katagishi in *Cration* (Tokyo), 1993.

*

I have always liked moving on the outskirts of Art, on the borderline of various spheres, penetrating regions situated far from the main routes and others, less noble so to say. I used to find amusing an action against the rules which were considered in force in various fields, a combination of elements seemingly remote from, if not strange to, each other, the blurring of boundaries separating adjacent domains, grafting of nobler qualities onto ''lower'' species; in short—a quiet subversion. I have always been attracted to forms, sort of commonplace, held in disregard by those who work in more refined areas. These remarks may seem surprising today, at the time of the general integration of various arts, of the emancipation of such fields as graphic art, photography and many others. But I remember the time when painters despised graphic art, and when there was something contemptuous about the word ''graphic artist.'' Where are those days? Art galleries are open to graphic art, and posters have been accepted into museums. Where is the boundary today between painting and graphic art? And who cares about the ''purity of the species'' these days? In the 1950s I was accused of using in my posters non-graphic art techniques, which apparently disagreed with the printing technique; I was blamed for the introduction into my posters of subjects which originated straight from painting, such as portraits. Today there is no technique which has not been adapted by poster art which has disposed of the cramping cloak of graphic design and freed itself from an embarrassing isolation, has forgotten its service role so far as to make the mere definition of poster art impossible. Posters have returned to their sources: they are against multiplied pictures done on a ''set subject.''

The situation in films is somewhat different. I must admit that I have chosen a beastly uncomfortable position for myself. An action against the accepted rules brings about painful consequences. The ruling principles of supply and demand are ruthless in that they repudiate everything which does not find its place in the market. In the past I thought that the animated film could become an instrument of fantastic possibilities when dealt with by an artist. Film appeared to me as the most contemporary raw material, of unparalleled means of expression, as a vast and fruitful area of activity. I was not aware then of the enormous difficulties accumulating before those who do not want to bow to the commercial system of the cinema. The margin of creative freedom and experiment which existed until recently in the short film has virtually disappeared. No one needs it, there is no place for it in the picture houses, and festivals of short films are deserted, filled with the melancholy of past glamour. Apart from socialist countries, these is a *raison d'etre* for it only in the United States where the distribution and audience are assured by universities and film lending libraries. The development of film pursues a traditional line as a performance. Film as an object and manifestation of art in time and movement has not found either its sponsor or its recipient and collector. I see a chance for it in the development of modern techniques of reproduction, in the video cassettes and picture disks now appearing on the market. They may change the situation radically and result in a distribution of films which is now the privilege of works of literature and music.

—Jan Lenica

* * *

During an interview, Jan Lenica gave the following reply in answer to the question, ''Who are you?'': ''I move on the fringes of fine art, film and literature, no dictionary has a name for this kind of occupation.'' But as art dictionaries are all in favor of subdivision into disciplines and media, any mention of Lenica must refer to him as a graphic artist, producer of posters, collages and drawings, and creator of animated films.

Apart from these characteristic traits—great self-irony, skepticism, and anger as a philosophical attitude—the intellectual and political climate of the period in which he grew up had a great influence on Lenica. Born into an artistic family, he inherited a traditional, political leaning towards the left, together with a certain sympathy for Communism, from his father who was a known, nonconformist painter. Hence, it is easy to understand why the social changes in Poland, and revolutionary art like that of Mayakowski, Grosz and Brecht, were so close to the artist's heart. He was fascinated by the Russian avant-garde of the 1920s—political theatre, agit-prop, revolutionary posters. Soon, however, like all of his generation, Lenica was to know the bitterness of disillusion. Their simplified view of life began to crack, revealing non-existent foundations. A period of moral and artistic reflection followed—a period of rational, lucid thinking, a farewell to the myths of youth. Criticism came to the fore, together with new values and motivation. Lenica began to search in art for that which exists universally, guides man's fate, explains his obsessions, fears—that which threatens him, his hopes and illusions. Lenica's mature work enters into a literary-artistic sphere, joining a surrealistic vision of the word with a perversely absurd interpretation of human life. Romantic fantasy and a rationalistic, merciless hunting down of mystification and appearances are equally to be found in this kind of work. The movement made a name for itself in 20th century world culture through the works of famous writers like Witkiewicz, Gombiowicz, Mrozek, not to mention Ionesco, who was the scriptwriter for Lenica's film *Monseiur Tête* in 1959.

Lenica's romanticism and literary roots—they are the sources of his symbols and metaphoric images. They also originate in lay-culture. Polish folklore in particular. In spite of his having lived abroad since the middle of the 1960s, Lenica's imagination is still full of the naive and fantastic images of his compatriots. Images of people drawn into an urban, industrial way of life, viewing that Moloch of technology, the city, and in fact all innovations, from a distance, with an air of distrust. Bypassing stylization, Lenica skillfully draws on the experience of primitive art. He values coarse, unyielding materials and makes great use of a technique similar to folk cut-outs, fairground woodcuts and bazaar bric-a-brac in his workshop.

Over the years (Lenica's first poster appeared in 1953), he has not kept to any one cultural tradition. He likes mixing various methods and conventions in order to achieve his own style. The large monograph/catalog printed in the German Federal Republic in 1981 contains all his work hitherto—posters and animated films; it also proposes subdivisions into periods for poster art; periode du realisme; recherches formelles; and signature trouvée.

Lenica's animated films share all the stylistic and ideological attributes of his graphics. One might call them an extreme, condensed form of graphics enriched by flexible narration and the length of time that the film runs. In *Adam 2,* Lenica's only feature film—which has subtitles as in a silent film instead of dialogue or commentary—the artist has gathered a kind of catalog of visual ideas: autocollage, photocollage, assemblage, cut-outs, old engravings tastefully embedded in the crude contours of a drawing, pictures from 19th century prospectuses, and catalogs that recall Max Ernst's fantastic world.

''Film is a dream,'' says Lenica. Indeed, one watches his films as one would experience a dream—fantasies but of this world. In his surrealistic-successional-grotesque cinema, whose sole author he is, Lenica leaves the moving pictures to speak of the greatness and the smallness of modern man.

—Szymon Bojko

LENK, Thomas

Nationality: German. **Born:** Kaspar Thomas Lenk, Berlin, 15 June 1933. **Education:** One term at the Kunstakademie, Stuttgart. **Family:** Married Maria Bendig in 1959; daughters: Mira and Ilona. **Career:** Sculptor, based in Stuttgart, since 1954; has worked on architectural sculpture projects, throughout Germany, since 1968. Guest professor, Heluwan University, Cairo, 1978; Ehrenmitgliedschaft der Art Gallery of Ontario, 1988; Ernennung zum Professor, 1989. **Awards:** Carnegie International Purchase Award, Pittsburgh, 1967; Third Prize, Socha piestanskych Parkov, Bratislava, 1969; First Prize, *Norwegian Graphics Biennale,* Frederikstad, 1974; Ehrengast der Villa Massimo, Rome, 1995. **Agents:** Galerie Krohn, Hintere, Au 1, 79410 Bandenweiler; Galerie Schlichtenmaier, Schloß Dätzingen,

Thomas Lenk: *ADGA—Triangel II,* 1993–94. ©2001 Artists Rights Society (ARS), NY/VG Bild-Kunst, Bonn.

71117 Grafenau; Galerie Neher, Moltkeplatz 61, 45138 Essen. **Address:** D-74542 Schloß Tierberg, Germany.

Individual Exhibitions:

1958 Galerie Boukes, Wiesbaden
1962 Galerie Mueller, Stuttgart
1963 Galerie Parmass, Wuppertal
1964 Studio F, Ulm
1965 Galerie Mueller, Stuttgart
1966 Galerie Handschin, Basel
Galerie Bischofberger, Zurich
Galerie Riche, Kassel, Germany
Galerie Thomas, Munich
1967 Fischbach Gallery, New York
Rowan Gallery, London
Galleria del Naviglio, Milan
1968 Westfälischer Kunstverein, Münster

Hessisches Landesmuseum, Darmstadt
Städtische Galerie, Stuttgart
1969 Galerie Renée Ziegler, Zurich
1970 Galerie Mueller, Stuttgart
Studio F, Ulm
1971 Kunstmuseum, Bochum, Germany
Museum Folkwang, Essen
Kunstmuseum, Dusseldorf
Galerie St. Johann, Saarbrucken
1973 Galerie Richard Foncke, Ghent
Museum Folkwang, Essen
1974 Württembergischer Kunstverein, Stuttgart
Kunsthalle, Dusseldorf (with Ad Dekkers and Philip King)
1976 Kölnischer Kunstverein, Cologne (with Karl Pfahler and Hans Uhlmann)
1977 Staatsgalerie, Stuttgart
1978 Fikrum wa Fann Gallery, Alexandria, Egypt
1980 Städtische Kunsthalle, Dusseldorf (travelled to Kunsthalle, Tübingen, and the Westfälischer Kunstverein, Münster)
1983 Galerie Holbein, Lindau, Germany
Kunsthalle, Nuremberg
Galerie von Aberron, Munich
1984 Kunstverein, Heilbronn
Galerie Cuenca, Ulm
1985 Kunsthalle, Mannheim
Erholungshaus Bayer AG, Leverkusen
Neue Galerie de Stadt Linz, Austria
Galerie Holbein, Lindau
1986 Staatsgalerie, Stuttgart
Kunstverein, Heilbronn
1987 Manuspresse, Stuttgart
1991 Galerie Spielvogel, Munich
1993 Stiftung für Konkrete Kunst, Reutlingen
Hällisch-Fränkisches Museum, Schwäbisch-Hall
Galerie Schlichtenmaier, Cologne
1995 Brandenburgische Kunstsammlungen, Cottgus
Anhaltische Gemäldegalerie, Dessau
Museum Für Konkrete Kunst, Ingolstadt
1998 Stadt Galerie, Waiblingen
Badisches Landesmuseum, Karlsruhe
2000 Goetheinstitut Budapest und Ungarisches Kulturinstitut Stuttgart

Selected Group Exhibitions:

1964 *Sculpture Allemande du Vingitième Siècle,* Musée Rodin, Paris
1967 *Sculpture from 20 Nations,* Guggenheim Museum, New York
1969 *1st Biennale Nurnberg, Kunsthalle,* Nuremberg
1971 *International Biennale of Prints,* Museum of Modern Art, Tokyo
1973 *12th Biennale Middelheim,* Antwerp
1975 *20th Century German Graphics,* The New School Art Center, New York (travelled to the Staatsgaleri, Stuttgart)
1979 *13th Graphics Biennale,* Ljubljana, Yugoslavia
1981 *Avantgarden retrospektiv,* Westfälischer Kunstverein, Münster
1985 *Kunst in der Bundesrepublik 1945–85,* Nationalgalerie, Berlin
1987 *Mathematik in der Kunst,* Wilhelm-Hack-Museum, Ludwigshafen
1990 *Bis jetzt. . . ,* Herrenhäser Gärten, Hannover
1991 *Position Konkret,* Neuer Sächsischer Kunstverein, Dresden
1997 *Magie der Zahl,* Staatsgalerie Stuttgart
Fort! Da!, Villa Merkel, Esslingen
1998 *Schwarz—Rot—Gold,* Badisches Landesmuseum, Karlsruhe
Stiftung—ganz konkret, Stiftung Wandel, Reutlingen
2000 *Farbe Farbe Farbe,* Galerie Neher, Essen

Collections:

Museum Folkwang, Essen; Kunstmuseum, Dusseldorf; Kunsthalle, Mannheim; Staatsgalerie, Stuttgart; Tate Gallery, London; Muzeum Narodowe, Warsaw; Museum of Contemporary Art, Nagaoka, Japan; Soto Museum, Ciudad Bolivar, Venezuela; Museum of Modern Art, New York; Carnegie Institute, Pittsburgh.

Publications:

By LENK: Books—*Nachbilder zu Mahler,* with Theodor W. Adorno, Stuttgart 1962; *Auseinandersetzen,* with Helmut Heissenbüttel, Stuttgart 1970; *Der Tod der Jugovic-Mutter,* with Johannes Wiedenheim, Stuttgart 1971; *Aufenthaltsraum,* with Franz Mon, Duisburg 1972; *Die Quatratur des Triptichons,* Stuttgart 1972; *Reminiszenzen,* Karlsruhe 1978; *Texte,* Stuttgart 1978; *Lob Der Geometrie,* Karlsruhe 1980; *Grossvogel,* with Kuno Ulshofer, Schwabisch-Hall 1983. **Film**—*Schichten,* with Walter Ruedel and Helmut Heissenbüttel, Essen 1973.

On LENK: Books—*Lenk,* exhibition catalog with text by Samuel Reppenko, Stuttgart 1962; *Junge Deutsche Bildhauer* by Udo Kultermann, Mainz 1964; *Plastik der Gegenwart* by Ulrich Gertz, Berlin 1964; *Kaspar Thomas Lenk,* exhibition folder, Kassel 1966; *Neue Dimensionen der Plastik* by Udo Kultermann, Tübingen 1967; *Positionen* by Rolf-Gunter Dienst, Cologne 1968; *Plastik der Gegenwart* by Heinz Fuchs, Baden-Baden 1970; *Deutsche Kunst: Eine Neue Generation* by Rolf-Günter Dienst, Cologne 1970, *Bis Heute* by Karin Thomas, Cologne 1971; *Deutsche Kunst der 60er Jahre* by Jürgen Morschel, Munich 1972; *Thomas Lenk* by Dieter Honisch, Stuttgart 1976: *Bildende Kunst der BRD und Westberlins* by Hermann Raum, Leipzig 1977; *Werkverzeichnis der Serigrafien* by Dieter Honisch and Rolf Krauss, Karlsruhe 1979; *Thomas Lenk: Serie ADGA,* exhibition catalog with texts by Gotz Adriani, Jürgen Harten and Heiner Stachelhaus, Dusseldorf 1980; *Thomas Lenk: Werkverzeichnis der Seriegrafien,* with text by Helmut Heissenbuttel, Dieter Honisch, Franz Mon and others, Karlsruhe 1985; *Thomas Lenk: Skulpturen und Zeichnungen,* with text by Helmut Heissenbuttel and Dieter Honisch, Berlin 1985; *Eulenspiegels Zunge,* Eigenverlag, 1988; *Cometa,* Galerie Waiblingen, 1998. **Films**—*Deutsche Bildhauer der Gegenwart* by Gerd Winkler, 1965; *Inn-Skulptur von Thomas Lenk* by Walter Rudel, 1969; *Thomas Lenk* by Frantiszek Kuduk, 1974.

*

In 1964 (via a casual game with beer tops) I made the significant discovery of "layerings," and took a step towards serial, technological construction. The creation of vertical or horizontal layers with geometric base elements (square, circle, triangle or parallelogram) was no more than a stereotyped accumulation of volumes in graduated planes. I increased the unreality of such constructions by the use of luminous colours, which tend to destroy rather than strengthen the effect of a sculpture. I had soon amassed a whole collection of designs, models and sculptures which tested out the various possibilities of ''layering''—for which initially only my wife and few friends (how could it be otherwise?) had any understanding or regard. Following exhibitions in Stuttgart, Zurich, Milan, London and New York, and conversations with friends, colleagues and critics, I realized that my work had at last been accepted. Elsewhere too, people were thinking and working along similar lines.

—Thomas Lenk

* * *

Kaspar Thomas Lenk—or Thomas Lenk, as he currently prefers to be known—is an articulate engagierter Kunstler. He is fiercely and basically political, even if his politics have a personal flavour not usually identified with that area of thought and behavior. He believes that the true artist has an established place and pattern of production in society from which he should not deviate. He subscribes to many of the aims and objects of Malevich's *Suprematist Manifesto* of 1924 but thinks that they should be expanded and made more precise. He is particularly opposed to the sort of art that reflects in outrage-pictures, activist political demos, and taking to the streets, and he is equally against any respect for ''fool's license'' art (the cultural upgrading of the work of phantasists, eccentrics, naives, schizophrenics and any others who might be eligible for representation in Dubuffet's Art Brut museum).

Because Lenk goes to some lengths to give clear and direct associated definition to his opinions and cultural philosophy, all these attitudes are relevant to the way in which the work of this sculptor has developed. He not only holds his views with fanatical intensity; he also confirms the standpoints he has taken by translating them into practical visual form.

Like Malevich, he believes that art should be for the people—and hopefully, for the State as well—but unlike his Russian predecessor, he also maintains that art (in his case his sculpture and its related graphics) should be essentially *businesslike* and devised to be incorporated into business itself. In this sense Lenk's sculpture is intended to become part of the *business architecture* and its ambience.

Although he realizes the isolated character a work of art can express (in an art gallery, in a museum, even in a private collection), Lenk has tried to extirpate this element by making his sculpture ally itself to the space factor (and the non-space factor) instead of invading the same space and, in so doing, interfering with it. Thus in theory, although not visually recognizable, there is a strong affinity between his intentions and those of the Polish Jan Berdyszak. Both are seeking to ensure that their work, while it is a visible additive, is physically absorbed into the site expected for it.

Lenk would say that he is not an abstractionist but a concrete artist. His gradual approach to this position has taken him from the personalized surrealism of his early days through a number of later stages all of which have led up to the style by which he is recognized today, a style that is still being expanded and variegated: ''Heaps'' (1957–61), ''Stones'' (1961), ''Additions'' (1961–64) and so on into the complex twists and turns in his work which he has introduced over the past two decades.

Those familiar with his sculpture are most likely to think of him as the creator of distorted columns composed of wood slates, aluminum (and sometimes plastics), each horizontal sliver matching its fellows, either quadri-rectangular or with rounded corners, or even circular—these are painstakingly built up, layer upon layer, and given a brilliant colour, often pillarbox red. Much variation on this central method of working has been carried out, and in some cases more than one colour has been employed. In recent years, besides the basic sprawl of the undulating columns, Lenk has investigated the opportunities of angling his sculptural forms to sprout from walls and, taking this experiment to still further extremes, he has actually constructed ''independent rooms'' through whose apertures, walls, windows and doors his inventions are able to spill out and make their ''escape.''

His claim to being a viable contributor to the contemporary art scene must surely rest upon his pragmatic ingenuity at adaptation, his ability to weld concrete art onto the mundane fabric of a technological age so that it ceases to be merely decorative or just evidence of high culture, but is actually an injected feature of the epoch it embellishes and encourages.

—Sheldon Williams

LE PARC, Julio (Alcides)

Nationality: Argentinian. **Born:** Mendoza, 23 September 1928. **Education:** Studied at the School of Fine Arts, Buenos Aires, under Lucio Fontana, 1942–54. **Family:** Married Martha Garcia in 1959; children: Juan, Pablo and Yamil. **Career:** Has lived and worked in France since 1958. Co-founder, Groupe de Recherches d'Art Viseul (GRAV), Paris, 1960–68; professor, arts plastiques et sciences de l'art, Université Paris I Pantheon/Sorbonne, 1972–73. **Awards:** Gold Medal, with GRAV, *Biennale di San Marino,* 1963; Premier Prix Travail d'Equipe, with GRAV, *Biennale de Paris,* 1963; Special Di Tella Prize, Buenos Aires, 1964; International Grand Prix for painting, *Biennale,* Venice, 1966. Chevalier, Ordre des Arts et Lettres, France. **Agent:** Galerie Denise René, 124 rue la Boetie, 75008 Paris. **Addresses:** 29 rue Couste, 94230 Cachan, France; and 41 rue des Rabats, 92160 Antony, France.

Individual Exhibitions:

1966 Howard Wise Gallery, New York
Galerie Denise René (Rive Drote and Rive Gauche), Paris
Op Art Galerie, Esslingen, Germany
1967 Halfmannshof, Gelsenkirchen, Germany
Galerie Francoise Mayer, Brussels
Howard Wise Gallery, New York
Galerie Saint-Laurent, Saint-Laurent-du-Pont, France
Istituto di Tella, Buenos Aires
Istituto General Electric, Montevideo
Museo de Bellas Artes, Caracas
1968 Moderna Museet, Stockholm
Galerie Buchholz, Munich
Museu de Arte Moderna, Rio de Janeiro
Museo de Bellas Artes, Mexico City
Galleria del Naviglio, Milan
1969 Henie-Onstad Art Center, Oslo
Galleria de Foscherari, Bologna

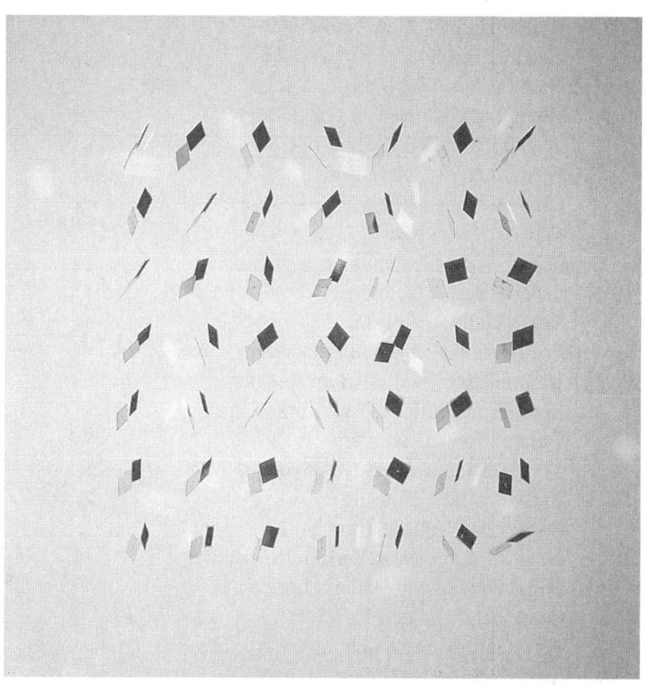

Julio Le Parc: *Continual Mobile, Continual Light.* ©2001 Artists Rights Society (ARS), NY/ADAGP, Paris.

Konsthallen, Gothenburg, Sweden
Galleria del Cavillino, Venice
1970 Galerie Denise René, Paris
Casa de las Americas, Havana
Ulmer Museum, Ulm, Germany
1972 Galerie Antanona, Caracas
Galerie Denise René, Paris
Galerie Francoise Mayer, Brussels
Städtische Kunsthalle, Dusseldorf (retrospective)
Haus am Waldsee, Berlin-Zehlendorf
Galerie Denise René-Hans Mayer, Dusseldorf
1973 Galleria La Polena, Genoa
Denise René Gallery, New York
1974 Galerie Denise René, Paris
1975 Museo de Arte Moderno, Mexico City
Galleria Lorenzelli, Bergamo, Italy
1976 Galeria Studium, Valladolid, Spain
Galeria Rayuela, Madrid
Modulations, Galerie Denise René, Paris
Le Parc en la Coruna, Galeria Mestre Mateo, La Coruna, Spain Museo de Arte Moderno, Bogotá
1977 *Festivals de Royan* at the *Quadriennale,* Rome
Galeria Torques, Santiago de Compostela, Spain
1981 *Retrospective,* Museo de Bellas Artes, Caracas
2000 *Retrospective,* Museo Nacional de Bellas Artes, Spain

Selected Group Exhibitions:

1965 *The Responsive Eye,* Museum of Modern Art, New York
Lumiere, Mouvement et Optique, Palais des Beaux-Arts, Brussels
1966 *Biennale,* Venice
1967 *Bienal,* Sao Paulo
1968 *Kinetische Kunst,* Haus am Waldsee, Berlin-Zehlendorf
1970 *Kinetics,* Hayward Gallery, London
1971 *Multiples: The First Decade,* Philadelphia Museum of Art
1973 *Electric Art,* Kunsthalle, Hamburg
1976 *Creadores Latinamericanos Contemporaneos 1950–1976,* Museo de Arte Moderno, Mexico City
1977 *L'Art et L'Automobile,* Centre Georges Pompidou, Paris
2000 *Force Fields: Phases of the Kinetic,* Hayward Gallery, London

Publications:

By LE PARC: Articles—"Propositions sur le Mouvement," with GRAV, in *Bewogen-Beweging,* exhibition catalog, Stockholm 1961; text, with GRAV, in *Le Parc: XXXIII Biennale de Venise 1966,* Paris 1966; text with GRAV in *Lumière et mouvement,* exhibition catalog, Paris 1967; text with GRAV in *GRAV,* exhibition catalog, Krefeld, Germany 1968; "L'Art Valeur Bourgeoise au Travail Révolutionnaire" and interview, with Frederic Chaleuil, in *Politique d'aujourd'hui* (Paris), no. 9, 1971; interview, with B. Breecken, in *Vendredi hebdo,* January 1971; "Je me déclare Incapable de prendre une décision pour accepter ou refuser l'invitation de M. Lassaigne" in *Les Lettres francaises* (Paris), April 1972; text with GRAV in *Le Parc,* exhibition catalog, Dusseldorf 1972.

On LE PARC: Books—*L'Art actuel en France* by Anne Tronche and Hervé Gloaguen, Paris 1973. **Articles—**"Julio Le Parc: Recherches 1959–1971" by P. Kress in *Kunstwerk* (Baden-Baden), March 1972; "Dusseldorf: Julio Le Parc" by A. Pohribny in *NAC* (Milan), April 1972; "52 interventi sulla Proposta di Comportamento di Enzo Mari" by Lea Vergine in *NAC* (Milan), August 1971; "Szene Rhein-Ruhr" by B. Kerber in *Art International* (Lugano, Switzerland), April 1972: "Julio Le Parc: The Laws of Chance" in *Studio International* (London), January 1973; "Arte Programmata: a cura di Lea Vergine" in *NAC* (Milan), March 1973; "The Game-as-art Form: Historic Roots and Recent Trends" by Michael J. Thomas in *Leonardo,* vol. 21, no. 4, 1988.

* * *

From being an artist interested in kinetics and light, Julio Le Parc has gradually moved to environments and play, and become more and more politicized into what he calls a "cultural guerrilla." Coming to Paris from Argentina on a scholarship in 1958, he joined with Vasarely's son Yvaral and other like-minded artists the following year to found the Groupe de Recherche d'Art Visuel (GRAV), one of the many kinetic groups formed in Europe during the late 1950s and early 1960s. It was a deliberate reaction against the fashion for informal tachism, and was influenced by the ideas of Vasarely, with his belief in impersonality and the anonymity of the artist; these artists set up a communal studio and constructed some works under the group name alone.

At first the group's aim was scientific or pseudo-scientific research into visual problems, but gradually, as Le Parc became more and more dominant, it was led towards the other main tendency of kinetic art, the "game aesthetic" of building environments for play and spectator participation. The group built complex environmental *Labyrinths* through which the public had to crawl while playing visual games of many kinds, manipulating mirrors, or balls which run through labyrinths. Le Parc aims at *instability,* a situation in which any permanent form of a work becomes impossible to discern. His works are designed to disorient the spectator, and he uses all sorts of devices like distorting glasses and spring-loaded shoes to achieve this disorientation.

Play and entertainment are basic even to his more serious mobiles and kinetic-light murals, which use simple suspended metallic elements to produce a constantly shifting play of light and shade. Other games demonstrate velocity, vibration or the way ping-pong balls are shot radially from a fast-spinning pivot to the sides of the box. The increasingly polemical and political nature of his work was shown when for a retrospective in Dusseldorf in 1972 he arranged a participative environment of large punch-me dolls, with faces painted to represent the pillars of established society: typically for him not only policemen, politicians, priests and journalists, but also the artist.

Le Parc has remarked that kineticism ''runs the risk of becoming a new academicism,'' and he has increasingly become one of those artists who are seeking a new orientation for art as the direct manipulation of the environment. His own statements make clear the relationship of his political views to this earlier belief in artistic instability and disorientation: ''One must become a kind of cultural guerrilla against the present state of things and point out all the contradictions. One must create new situations in which people may rediscover their capacity to bring about changes; fight any tendency towards stability, permanence, lastingness; fight anything that heightens the state of dependence, apathy, passivity which is linked to habits, established criteria and myths.''

—Konstantin Bazarov

LE VA, Barry

Nationality: American. **Born:** Long Beach, California in 1941. **Education:** Studied at California State University, Long Beach, 1960–63; Los Angeles College of Art and Design, 1963; Otis Art Institute, Los Angeles, 1963–67, BFA 1964, MFA 1967. **Career:** Independent artist, since 1967; now lives and works in New York. Instructor, Minneapolis College of Art and Design, 1969–70, and Princeton University, New Jersey, 1973–74, and Yale University, 1976. **Awards:** Young Talent Grant, Los Angeles County Museum of Art, 1968; Guggenheim Fellowship for Sculpture, 1974; National Endowment for the Arts Fellowship, 1976. **Agent:** Nolan/Eckman Gallery, 560 Broadway, New York, New York 10012, U.S.A.

Individual Exhibitions:

1969 Walker Art Center, Minneapolis
Institute of Fine Art, Minneapolis
University of Wisconsin at River Falls
Wisconsin State University at Menomenie
Ohio State University, Columbus
1970 Galerie Ricke, Cologne
La Jolla Museum of Art, California
1971 Nigel Greenwood Gallery, London
University of Utrecht, Netherlands
1972 Galerie Projection, Cologne
Galerie Ricke, Cologne
1973 Bykert Downtown Gallery, New York
Rudolf Zwirner and Rolf Ricke, Cologne
1974 Bykert Gallery, New York
Hartford Art School, Connecticut
Galleria Toselli, Milan
1975 Weinberg Gallery, San Francisco
Weinberg Gallery, New York
Bykert Gallery, New York
Claire Copley Gallery, Los Angeles
Espace 5, Montreal
Musée d'Art Contemporain, Montreal
1976 Galerie Ricke, Cologne
Texas Gallery, Houston
Weinberg Gallery, San Francisco
Claire Copley Gallery, Los Angeles
Sonnabend Gallery, New York
Galerie Sonnabend, Paris
1977 Wright State University, Dayton, Ohio
1978 Texas Gallery, Houston
Sonnabend Gallery, New York
1979 New Museum, New York (retrospective)
1980 Nigel Greenwood Gallery, London
1981 Sonnabend Gallery, New York
New Gallery of Contemporary Art, Cleveland, Ohio
1982 Yarlow-Salzman Gallery, Toronto
1983 Sonnabend Gallery, New York
1985 Texas Gallery, Houston
1986 Daniel Weinberg Gallery, Los Angeles
Sonnabend Gallery, New York
1988 Rijksmuseum Kroller-Muller, Otterlo, The Netherlands
Sonnabend Gallery, New York
Barry Le Va 1966–88, Carnegie-Mellon University Art Gallery, Pittsburgh, Pennsylvania; Newport Harbor Art Museum, California; High Museum of Art, Atlanta, Georgia; Neuberger Museum, State University of New York, Purchase, New York
1989 *Barry Le Va: Woodblock Prints and Related Drawings,* David Nolan Gallery, New York
Barry Le Va Sculpture, Daniel Weinberg Gallery, Los Angeles, CA
Barry Le Va: Glass, Bullets, Cleavers, 1968–1970, Staadtisches Museum Abteiberg, Mönchengladbach, Germany
Sculpture, Texas Gallery, Houston, TX
1990 *Barry Le Va: The Texas Variations,* David Nolan Gallery, New York
1991 Sonnabend Gallery, New York
1992 Galerie Fred Jahn, Münich
1993 *Barry Le Va: Collage and Drawing 1988–1993*, Nolan/Eckman Gallery, New York
Galerie Georges-Philippe Vallois, Paris
1994 *Barry Le Va: Zeichnungen 1965–1993*, Staatlichen Graphischen Sammlung, Munich
Staadtischen Museum Leverkusen, Schloß Morsbroich
1995 *Barry Le Va: Pages from a Sketchbook—Japanese Lacquerware*, Nolan/Eckman Gallery, New York
Sonnabend Gallery, New York
1996 Galerie Zell-am-See, Austria
Bunker Drawings, Galerie Fred Jahn, München
Sculpture and Drawings, Galerie Georges-Philippe and Natalie Vallois, Paris, France
1997 *Diagrams of Thought*, Nolan/Eckman Gallery

Danese Gallery, New York
1998 Sonnabend Gallery, New York
Staatliche-Kunstsammlungen, Dresden
Zeichnungen, Keramische Werkstatt Margaretenhöhe, Essen, Germany

Selected Group Exhibitions:

1967 *Newcomers 1967,* Lytton Center of Visual Arts, Los Angeles
1969 *Anti-Illusion Procedures and Materials,* Whitney Museum, New York
1970 *Art in the Mind,* Allen Art Museum, Oberlin College, Ohio
1972 *Documenta 5,* Museum Fridericianum, Kassel, Germany (and *Documenta 7,* 1982)
1975 *Bochner/Le Va/Rockburne/Tuttle,* Contemporary Arts Center, Cincinnati, Ohio
1976 *200 Years of American Sculpture,* Whitney Museum, New York
1978 *Contemporary Drawing; New York,* University of Santa Barbara, California
1979 *Drawings about Drawing Today,* University of North Carolina, Chapel Hill
1984 *Minding Measure: Measuring Mind,* Islip Art Museum, East Islip, New York
1986 *Art from Two Continents,* Helander Gallery, Palm Beach, Florida
1987 *1967: At the Crossroads,* Institute of Contemporary Art, University of Pennsylvania, Philadelphia
Drawings from the Eighties, Carnegie Mellon University Art Gallery, Pittsburgh, Pennsylvania
1988 *Sonnabend Collection,* Sonnabend Gallery, New York (toured galleries throughout the world)
Three Decades: The Oliver-Hoffman Collection, The Museum of Contemporary Art, Chicago
Recent American Prints, Galerie Fred Jahn, Munich, Germany
1989 *A Decade of American Drawing: 1980–1989,* Daniel Weinberg Gallery, Los Angeles
New Works by Gallery Artists, Sonnabend Gallery, New York
1990 *The New Sculpture 1965–1975: Between Geometry and Gesture,* The Whitney Museum of American Art, New York; The Museum of Contemporary Art, Los Angeles, California
Conceptual Art, Conceptual Forms, Galerie 1900–2000, Paris, France; Galerie Faust, Geneva, Switzerland
1991 *New Editions,* Nigel Greenwood Inc., London, England
Mel Bochner, Carroll Dunham, Barry Le Va, Terry Winters, Galerie Faust, Geneva, Switzerland
Immaterial/Objects: Works from the Permanent Collection of the Whitney Museum of American Art, Whitney Museum of American Art, New York
A View from the Sixties: Selections from the Leo Castelli Collection and the Michael and Ileana Sonnabend Collection, Guild Hall, East Hampton, New York
1992 *American Art: 1930–1970,* Lingotto, Turin, Italy
The New Museum Auction: 15th Anniversary Benefit Auction, New York
1993 *European and American Drawings 1961–1969,* Nolan/Eckman Gallery, New York
1995 *1995 Biennial Exhibition,* Whitney Museum of American Art, New York
Drawings from a Private Collection, Nolan/Eckman Gallery, New York
1997 *Drawings,* Nolan/Eckman Gallery, New York
1998 *Bill Jensen, Barry Le Va, Pat Steir,* Danese Gallery, New York
Summer Group Show, Nolan/Eckman Gallery, New York
1999 *Barry Le Va, Kirsten Ortwed, Lawrence Weiner,* Malmö Konsthall, Sweden
Drawings from the Sixties: Mel Bochner, Barry Le Va, Keith Sonnier, Richard Tuttle, Curt Marcus Gallery, New York

Collections:

Los Angeles County Museum of Art.

Publications:

By LE VA: Articles—"Clocked Clown Outward" in *Studio International* (London), November 1971; "Discussions with Barry Le Va" in *Avalanche* (New York), Fall 1971.

On LE VA: Books—*Barry Le Va: 1966–1988,* Pittsburgh, Carnegie Mellon University Press, 1988; *Barry Le Va,* exhibition catalog, Otterlo, Holland, 1988; *Barry Le Va: Dreaded Intrusions- Institutional Templates,* notes by Le Va, and interview with Fred Jahn, Munich, 1992; *Barry Le Va: Zeichnungen, München Diary-African Sketchbook,* exhibition catalog, Munich, 1993. **Articles—**"Barry Le Va: Distributional Sculpture" by Jane Livingston in *Artforum* (New York), November 1968; "Barry Le Va and the Nondescript Description" by Larry Rosing in *Artnews* (New York), September 1969; "Notes on Piece by Barry Le Va" in *Studio International* (London), November 1971; review in *Artforum* (New York), June 1973; review in *Artforum* (New York), May 1975; "Barry Le Va's Sculpture: Ellipsis and Ellipse" by Klaus Kertess in *Artforum,* vol. 21, no. 5, January 1983; "Barry Le Va" by Saul Ostrow in *Bomb,* Summer 1997.

* * *

Beginning with his early scatter pieces of 1967–68, Barry Le Va's main intention has been to reject the "object aesthetic" and art tied to a "single glance" by creating works which are composed of widely dispersed arrangements of abstract elements. Usually termed a Postminimalist, Le Va rejects Minimalist rigorous geometrics, using open forms and eccentric materials and emphasizing process in compositional methods which apply expressionistic painterly ideas to sculptural forms. In Le Va's conceptually based works, visual structures are expressive of thinking processes, communicating ideas about the tension between seeming randomness and more coherent ordering principles. His scattered arrangements explore the perimeters of defined spaces as experienced by the viewer/participant who, through choice, moves through the environmental layout preordained by the artist to discover and perceive the underlying content.

During 1966 and 1967, while Le Va was still in art school in Los Angeles, he began to develop what soon came to be known as "distributional pieces" using scraps lying around his studio, which were meant to be elements in the pictures with cutout collage/ elements he was making at that time. Separately from New York-based artists such as Robert Morris and Richard Serra, Le Va was experimenting to find new possibilities based on ideas inherent in expressionist painting of the 1950s and in minimal structures of the 1960s. His methodology and syntax in place, Le Va proceeded to locate variations on his consistently held ideas through the 1970s.

Among Le Va's chosen materials have been felt, dust, flour, cement powder, paper toweling and wood. Determining his choices by the specific site in which his elements are to be dispersed, Le Va sets his limits, establishing the number, size and shape of his components. Because of the enlarged scale and summary dispersal of the elements, the plan underlying the piece is not first visually apparent. To apprehend and decode the underlying schema, the viewer must move through the space, locating and perceiving elements such as direction, overlap and separation, filling in the gaps and recreating the situation set up by the artist in his or her own way. Memory becomes an important issue in the real time, physical experiencing of the participant of what at first seemed to be bunches of isolated forms. By the very nature of the scattered materials, permutations occur in the works' configurations, adding to the tension which already involved chance as well as choice. The physical experience of the ephemeral plan is suggestive of psychological states involving accumulation, continuities, discontinuities, expansion, dispersal, blockage. To my mind, Le Va's work is a kind of conceptualized methodology. As is true with much work of this kind, Le Va has tended to the repetitive, and the result has been a lapsing into aestheticized dryness and esoterica which doesn't seem to hold much possibility by this time.

—Barbara Cavaliere

LEVERETT, David

Nationality: British. **Born:** Nottingham, 12 January 1938. **Education:** Studied at Nottingham College of Art, 1957–61, at Royal Academy Schools, London, 1961–64. **Family:** Married Sonia Loretta Wilhelmina Holme in 1961; sons: Jason and Simeon. **Career:** Worked as builder-designer, London, 1954–57; scenic design assistant, Nottingham Repertory Theatre, 1956–57. Independent painter, since 1965: lives and works in London. Lecturer, Croydon College of Art, Surrey, 1965; director of studies, East Ham Technical College, London, 1966–69; visiting lecturer, Ravensbourne College of Art, Kent, 1969; visiting artist, Royal Academy Schools and Royal College of Art, London, and visiting lecturer, Hornsey College of Art, London, 1971–73; visiting lecturer, Slade School of Fine Art, London, since 1971; visiting artist, Norwich College of Art, Norfolk, 1972–74; visiting lecturer, Cooper Union, New York, 1974; and Dublin College of Art, 1980–82. **Awards:** Arts Council Grant, 1974; Sargant Fellowship, British School at Rome, 1990–91. **Agent:** Jill George Gallery, 38 Lexington St., London W1, England. **Address:** 132 Leighton Road, London, NW5, England.

Individual Exhibitions:

1965 Redfern Gallery, London
1968 Redfern Gallery, London
1970 Alecto Gallery, London
Editions Alecto, New York
Redfern Gallery, London
1971 Studio La Città, Verona (with Patrick Heron)
1972 Redfern Gallery, London
Bear Lane Gallery, Oxford
Galleria del Cavellino, Venice
Galerie Britta Heberie, Frankfurt
Alecto International, London
Studio La Città, Verona
1973 Ikon Gallery, Birmingham
1974 Studio La Città, Verona
Institute of Contemporary Arts, London
Galleria Godel, Rome (with Bernard Cohen and Robyn Denny)
Galleria La Chicciola, Padua
1975 Studio la Città, Verona
Galleria G7, Bologna
Gallery Demos, Athens
Galerie Folker Skulima, Berlin
1976 Galleria Vinciana, Milan
Galleria del Cavallino, Milan
1977 Oliver Dowling Gallery, Dublin
Galerie Skulima, Berlin
1978 House Gallery, London
Osieki Plein-air, Poland
Galleria del Cavellino, Venice
1979 Riverside Studios, London
Jordon Gallery, London
1980 Studio Gallery, Palace of Culture, Warsaw
Gallery Dom Sztuki, Krakow, Poland
1981 University of Reading, Berkshire
Zen Gallery, Porto, Portugal
1983 Gallery III, Lisbon
1984 Bildornan Gallery, Umea, Sweden
1985 Curwen Gallery, London
1986 Jersey Arts Centre, St. Helier
1987 Redfern Gallery, London
1990 Redfern Gallery, London
Thumb Gallery, London
1992 Jill George Gallery, London

Selected Group Exhibitions:

1965 *Young Contemporaries,* FBA Galleries, London
1968 *British Painting and Sculpture,* Whitechapel Art Gallery, London
1977 *British Painting 1952–1977,* Royal Academy of Arts, London
1979 *Bienal,* Sao Paulo
1983 *New Directions in British Art,* Puck Building, New York
1985 *One of a Kind,* St. Andrews University, Fife, Scotland (traveled to Edinburgh and Nottingham)
1987 *National Print Competition,* Royal Festival Hall, London
1988 *Mediterranean Biennale of Graphic Art,* Greece
1991 *Cabinet Paintings,* Gillian Jason Gallery, London (travelled to Hove Museum and Art Gallery and Glynn Vivian Art Gallery and Museum, 1992)
Special Presentation, Merrill Chase Gallery, Chicago

Collections:

Tate Gallery, London; Victoria and Albert Museum, London; Glasgow City Art Gallery; Museum de Arte Moderna, Sao Paulo; Museum of Modern Art, Zagreb; Museum of Contemporary Art, Athens; Art Gallery of New South Wales, Sydney; Umea Arts Council, Sweden; State Collection, Palace of Culture, Warsaw, Poland; Whitworth Art Gallery, Manchester.

Publications:

By LEVERETT: Books—*The Citadel: The Paintings of David Leverett from 1988 to 1994,* London 1994; *A Dance Through the Labyrinth of Sand: Paintings and Poems by David Leverett,* London 1997. **Articles**—''Artists Notebook'' in *Art and Artists* (London), June 1969; statement in *Leverett,* exhibition catalog, Verona 1974; statement in *Cratyus,* Sao Paulo, 1974; ''Fragments from the Laminates of Continuous Time'' in *Words and Images,* Verona 1976; ''Views from a Citadel'' in *David Leverett,* exhibition catalog, London 1985; ''Sacred Gardens'' in *David Leverett,* exhibition catalog, St. Helier 1986.

On LEVERETT: Books—*Play Orbit,* edited by Jasia Reichardt, London 1969; *Riflessioni sulla Pittura,* exhibition catalog, Acireale, Italy 1973; *Empirica 1975, Verona, 1975; Colours in Painting: A European Situation,* exhibition catalog, Rome 1976: **Article**—''A Discussion of Multiples'' by Paul Overy, in *Studio International* (London), September 1970.

*

The use of landscape as a metaphor is an important theme in my work. I use it as a means of exploring two important preoccupations that depend on the landscape for interpretation. The first takes the form of an inquiry into the way I perceive time and express it. The attempt to project a sensation of extended time that implies references to past, present and future is crucial to the inquiry. These various indicators of time invest the work with a sense of duration, with age, with perpetuity. References that reflect a sense of continuity that is carried in the formations of the land and the behavior of the seasons. The action of the weather, the motion of light are daily forces that confirm the histories of the Earth. In their effect they are the dynamics of change and turbulence that contrast against the durability of the rocks.

My second preoccupation is more difficult to describe because, ultimately, it is concerned with identity. It is the need to find and determine my position within the wider reaches of time. What I seek to do is to release this need by creating a primary sense of place through the work. The qualities of time that exist in the land allow this release to occur. The locations I choose on which to base my work are very important. They must contain features I can use to convey the sense of primary belonging to the earth. My views and perspective of the land are not just specific to its topographical characteristics. The spirit of place exists in the pervading wholeness of nature. The way we recognize it through a particular location only heightens its effect and draws our attention to it. The earth is our fundamental point of recognition to the vastness to which we belong. These considerations of time and space require forms of pictorial engagement that go much deeper than the surface landscape. They involve questions about the fragile state of one's identity as measured against time. Particular landscapes become for me a means of expressing the union which exists between the individual and nature. I believe the Earth is a sacred garden and that we are a part of it. We will interpret its mysteries with signs, symbols and images that affirm this union. Because of our primary link with the Earth, because we cannot be separated from it, we are its guardians too. Consequently, ignorance and abuse of this fact influences and damages the sacred gardens as much as it injures us.

—David Leverett

* * *

David Leverett's work can be described as concerned with narrative, in the sense of being less related to single, final images, than with communicating the process of creative thought and action. His work has gradually assumed a kind of manual serialization, so that each step is allowed its own clarity, no matter how complex the total structure. In fact, he describes his laminated, resin paintings as ''diaries of an event in time, the residue of remembrance of an event, as well as the activity whereby one records the event.''

His development has been demonstrated in a series of paintings and prints which intimately interrelate much of the experience derived from printmaking later being translated into paint. They begin with solid patterns in flat colours, positive and unconcerned with formative processes. A grid system then appeared, which seemed to undermine this positiveness, concerned with the structure beneath the solidity. The titles of these prints, referring to seasons, to shift and change, express the artist's growing concern with time and light, with the result that floating, rather than anchored form, and an image of a changeable world of sensations, began to emerge.

These prints required precise planning and control, but it was the overlaying of colour areas in the printing process which led to the first sprayed paintings. Here, even more than in the printing, Leverett became obsessed with the need to retain the narrative of creation, as a personal record and as a means of communication. Thus his pictures are not fixed points in time, but vortexes of creative time, inviting us into the intimacy of their structures. In recent years he has increasingly experimented with acrylics, first as the surfaces on which he projected spray techniques, and more recently laminated resins holding transparent sheets of drawn and painted paper. What emerges are living X-rays in which the artist describes time and experience.

—Charles Spencer

LEVINE, Les

Nationality: American. **Born:** Dublin, Ireland, 6 October 1935; emigrated to United States, 1964; naturalized, 1981. **Education:** Central School of Arts and Crafts, London, 1953–55. **Family:** Married Catherine Kanai in 1973. **Career:** Independent artist, since 1959. Feature writer, *Aspen Times,* Colorado, 1967–68; founder-director, Levine's Restaurant, 1969; founder, Museum of Mott Art Inc., New York, 1970. Artist-in-residence, Design Conference, Aspen, Colorado, 1967, 1969; associate professor of art, New York University, 1972–73; artist-in-residence, Nova Scotia College of Art and Design, Halifax, 1973; Distinguished Professor of Video Art, William Paterson

Les Levine, *Win the Race,* 1992, and *Sex Won't Save You,* 1993. Photo by Les Levine. Both ©2001 Les Levine/Artists Rights Society (ARS), NY.

College, Wayne, New Jersey, 1975; artist-in-residence, University of Illinois, Circle Campus, Chicago, 1975. **Awards:** *Canadian Sculpture Biennale* Prize, Paris 1969; Architectural League Grant, New York, 1972; Sculpture Fellowship, National Endowment for the Arts, 1974, 1980; Creative Artists Service Program Award for Video, New York, 1979; Gustave Klimt Prize for best billboard campaign, Austria, 1994. **Address:** 20 East 20th Street, New York, New York 10003. U.S.A.

Individual Exhibitions:

1964 Hart House, University of Toronto
Blue Barn Gallery, Ottawa
David Mirvish Gallery, Toronto
1965 Isaacs Gallery, New York
Book of Graphics, Toronto
1966 Blue Barn Gallery, Ottawa
Fischbach Gallery, New York
Art Gallery of Ontario, Toronto
Lofthouse Gallery, Ottawa
University of Western Ontario, London
1967 Walker Art Center, Minneapolis
Musem of Modern Art, New York
Isaacs Gallery, New York
Fischbach Gallery, New York
Architectural League, New York
1968 Glendon Campus Art Gallery, York University, Toronto
Fischbach Gallery New York
Gibson Gallery, New York
New York State Council on the Arts
1969 Molly Barnes Gallery, Los Angeles
Jack Burnham to Wed Judith Benjamin, Levine's Restaurant, New York
New York Stock Market
Museum of Contemporary Art, Chicago
University of Michigan, Ann Arbor
Rowan Gallery, London
Phyllis Kind Gallery, Chicago
Loeb Student Center, New York (and at West 4th Street, New York; New York City Department of Parks Show)
Fischbach Gallery, New York
1970 Galerie de Gestlo, Bremen, Germany
Isaacs Gallery, New York (twice)
Fischbach Gallery, New York
1971 Protetch-Rivkin Gallery, Washington, D.C.
Galerie M. E. Thelen, Cologne
Galerie de Gestlo, Hamburg
1972 Finch College Museum of Art, New York

Fischbach Gallery (Downtown), New York
Harold Rivkin Gallery, Washington, D.C.
Galerie M. E. Thelen, Cologne
1973 Galerie de Gestlo, Hamburg
Michael C. Rockefeller Art Center Gallery, State University of New York at Fredonia
Isaacs Gallery, New York
Seton Hall University, South Orange, New Jersey
Anna Leonowens Gallery, Nova Scotia College of Art and Design, Halifax
1974 Galerie de Gestlo, Hamburg
Vancouver Art Gallery
University of California at San Diego
Galerie Gerald Piltzer, Paris
Video Distribution Inc., New York
Galleria Schema, Florence
Stefanotty Gallery, New York
1975 A Space, Toronto
Adler Castillo, Caracas, Venezuela
Anthology Film Archives, New York
Miami-Dade Junior College, Florida
1976 Galerie Gilles Gheerbrant, Montreal
M. L. d'Arc Gallery, New York
Lions Gallery of the Senses, Wadsworth Atheneum, Hartford
California State University at Los Angeles
Art Gallery of New South Wales, Sydney
National Gallery of Victoria, Melbourne
Paterson Ewing Gallery, University of Melbourne
Jam Factory, Adelaide, South Australia
1977 Everson Museum, Syracuse, New York
Albright-Knox Gallery Buffalo, New York
Galerie de Gestlo, Hamburg
Isaacs Gallery, Toronto
Vehicule Art, Montreal
Galerie Arnesen, Copenhagen
AIR/ZBS Foundation, Fort Edward, New York
M. L. d'Arc Gallery, New York
1978 International Cultureel Centrum, Antwerp
Rotterddamse Kunststichting, Rotterdam
Station Gallery, Whitby, Ontario
Laurentian University, Sudbury, Ontario
Mary J. L. Black Library, Thunder Bay, Ontario
1979 Parry Sound Public Library, Canada
Paysages du Grand Nord, Canadian Cultural Centre, Paris
Northern Illinois University, DeKalb
Ronald Feldman Gallery, New York
Galerie Jollenbeck, Cologne
Philadelphia Museum of Art
Video-As-Art, Myers Fine Arts Gallery, State University of New York at Plattsburgh
Alberta College of Art, Calgary
1980 Marian Goodman Gallery, New York (twice)
Isaacs Gallery, Toronto
Enzo Cannaviello Gallery, Milan
Ronald Feldman Gallery, New York
Studio d'Arte Cannaviello, Milan
1981 Ronald Feldman Gallery, New York
Galerie Jollenbeck, Cologne
1982 Lower Manhattan Cultural Council, in New York subways
Galleria del Cavallino, Venice
Elizabeth Galasso Fine Arts, Ossining, New York
1983 N.A.M.E. Gallery, Chicago
Isaacs Gallery, Toronto
Ronald Feldman Gallery, New York
80 Langton, San Francisco
Honolulu Academy of Art, Hawaii
Real Artways, Hartford, Connecticut
Midtown Y Gallery, New York
1984 Lelia Ivy Gallery, Los Angeles
Elizabeth Galsso Fine Arts, Ossining, New York
Los Angeles Institute of Contemporary Art
Ted Greenwald Gallery, New York
1985 Millennium, New York
A Space, Toronto
Mo David, New York
Spectacolor Lightboard, Times Square, New York
Institute of Contemporary Arts, London
Orchard Gallery, Londonderry, Northern Ireland
1986 Carpenter & Hochman, New York
Trinity College, Dublin
Ted Greenwald Gallery, New York
Akademie der Kunst, Copenhagen
1988 Mai 36 Galerie, Lucerne, Switzerland
1989 International Center of Photography, New York
ArtFrankfurt, Frankfurt
New York City subway project
1990 Mai 36 Galerie, Lucerne, Switzerland
Central Museum, Utrecht, Holland
Brigitte March Galerie, Stuttgart
1991 Beck Forum, Munich
Wasserman Galerie, Munich
Brigitte March Galerie, Stuttgart
1992 New York City Billboard Campaign
MUKHA, Antwerp, Belgium
1993 Mai 36 Galerie, Zurich
Stadtraum Remise, Vienna
Galerie In Situ, Aalst, Belgium
1994 Lutz Teutloff Modern Art, Cologne
1995 Stadt Langenhagen, Hannover
1996 Alternative Museum, New York
Temporary Contemporary at the Baltic Flour Mills, Gateshead, England
1997 Galerie der Stadt, Stuttgart
1999 Velan, Carignano, Turin, Italy
2000 Brigitte March Galerie, Stuttgart
Asbaek Galerie, Copenhagen

Selected Group Exhibitions:

1988 *Committed to Print,* Museum of Modern Art, New York
Computers and Art, IBM Gallery of Science and Art, New York
1989 *Kolnischer Kunstverein,* Cologne
Image World, Whitney Museum of American Art, New York
1990 *Word as Image,* Milwaukee Art Museum
Art & Pub, Centre Georges Pompidou, Paris
Foundation van Gogh, Amsterdam
1993 *The Language of Art,* Kunsthalle, Vienna

1994 *Public Interventions,* Institute of Contemporary Art, Boston
1995 *International Sculptors Symposium,* Bursa, Turkey
1999 Massachusetts Museum of Contemporary Art
Art Gallery of Windsor, Canada
2000 Stadtische Galerie, Karlsruhe, Germany

Collections:

Museum of Modern Art, New York; Whitney Museum, New York; Philadelphia Museum of Art; National Gallery of Australia, Canberra; New Orleans Museum of Art, Louisiana; Institute of Contemporary Art, Boston; Corcoran Gallery of Art, Washington, D.C.; Honolulu Academy of Art, Hawaii; Art Gallery of Ontario, Toronto; Stadtische Museum im Lenbachhaus, Munich; Metropolitan Museum of Art, New York; Stadtsgalerie, Stuttgart; National Gallery of Canada, Ottawa.

Publications:

By LEVINE: Books—*Poem Disposable,* co-author, New York 1969; *Museum of Mott Art Catalog of Services,* New York 1970; *House,* Hilversum, Netherlands 1971, 1976; *After Art,* New York 1974; *Camera Art,* exhibition catalog, Wayne, New Jersey 1974; *Bear News,* New York 1976; *Using the Camera as a Club/Not Necessarily a Great One,* New York 1976; *Five OHHH Disposable Sculptures,* Ontario 1977; *On Subjectivity,* portfolio, Cambridge, Massachusetts 1978; *Media: The Bio-Tech Rehearsal for Leaving the Body,* Calgary, Alberta 1979; *Hand Printed Etchings,* exhibition catalog, New York 1980; *Les Levine: Large Format Polaroid Photographs,* exhibition catalog, New York 1985; *Blame God: Billboard Projects,* exhibition catalog, London 1986. **Television films—***The Last Sculpture Show,* META-TV, Arlington, Virginia 1972; ''Les Levine Festival'' on *Televisionaries, Channel J Cable-TV,* New York 1975. **Videotapes—**(all New York) *Bum,* 1965; *Critic,* 1965; *The Nude Model,* 1966; *Slipcover,* 1966; *White Noise,* 1967; *Destruction in Art,* 1967; *Clothing and the Law,* 1967; *Architecture,* 1967; *The London Scene,* 1968; *Photon Strangeness,* 1968; *Electric Shock,* 1968; *The Big Eye,* 1968; *Iris,* 1968; *Contact,* 1969 *Columbia,* 1969; *Blank,* 1969; *Fashion Show Poetry Event,* 1969; *Paint,* 1969; *Topesthesia,* 1970; *John and Mimi's Book of Love,* 1970; *Mott Art Hearings,* 1970; *Body Control Systems,* 1970; *A.I.R. Software Show,* 1970; *Train,* 1971; *Stand-Up Cop,* 1971; *Mrs. Hunt,* 1972; *The Last Sculpture Show,* 1972; *The Troubles: An Artist's Document of Ulster,* 1972; *Outside the Republican Convention,* 1972; *Chain of Command,* 1972; *Supervision,* 1973; *The Last Book of Life,* 1973; *Topesthesia III,* 1973; *Gilbert and George,* 1973; *Christmas Card,* 1973; *Ritual,* 1973; *Language—Emotion + Syntax = Message,* 1973; *Space Walk,* 1974; *The Story of Three Children,* 1974; *Spaghetti,* 1974; *Les Levin's Firenze,* 1974; *Visiting Artist,* 1974; *Brainwash,* 1974; *If I Graduate,* 1974; *Artistic,* 1974; *Les Levine's Greatest Hits,* 1974; *A Portrait of Anna,* 1974; *A Portrait of Les,* 1974; *Watergate Au Revoir,* 1974; *I Am an Artist,* 1975; *We Are Still Alive,* 1975; *An Interview with Bob Mulholland,* 1975; *Magic Carpet,* 1975; *Landscape I,* 1975; *Fortune Cookie,* 1975; *Cheap Thrill,* 1975; *One Gun,* 1975; *What Can the Federal Government Do for You?,* 1975; *Federal Fashions,* 1975; *Landscape II,* 1975; *Video Lecture,* 1975; *Starry Night,* 1975; *Mr. Abstract,* 1975; *The Last Art Student Has Been Eaten,* 1975; *I'm Lost,* 1976; *The Selling of a Video Artist,* 1976; *I Am Not Blind,* 1976; *Les Levine's Cornflakes,* 1977; *2 Yous,* 1980; *Einstein: A Nuclear Comedy,* 1983; *Performance 70's,* 1971–83; *Anxiety, Religion and Art,* 1985; *Close Frenzies,* 1986; *The Les Levine Video Catalog: Works from 1961–1989,* 1990; *The Media Tent,* 1994; *See Your Mind,* 1995; *Looking Out Seeing In,* 1997; *Group Shows Twist the Truth & Statements on the Sublime,* 2000; *Accused,* 2000.

On LEVINE: Books—*Beyond Modern Sculpture* by Jack Burham, London 1968; *Minimal Art: A Critical Anthology,* edited Gregory Battcock, New York 1968; *Recorded Activities,* exhibition catalog, Philadelphia 1970; *The Structure of Art* by Jack Burnham, New York 1971; *Icons and Images of the 60s* by Nicolas and Elena Calas, New York 1971; *Great Western Salt Works* by Jack Burnham, New York 1974; *The Great American Chewing Gum Book* by Robert Hendrickson Radnor, Pennsylvania 1976; *Art Actuel/Skira Annuel 1977,* Geneva 1977; *New Artists Video: A Critical Anthology,* edited by Gregory Battcock, New York 1978; *ZBS Foundation,* exhibition catalog, Fort Edward, New York 1978; *The Great American Foot,* exhibition catalog with an introduction by Paul J. Smith, New York 1978; *Images of Self,* exhibition catalog with an essay by Irving Sandler, Westfield, Massachusetts 1979; *Biennale de l'Association Belge des Critiques d'Art,* exhibition catalog, Antwerp and Charleroi 1979; *Journées Interdisciplinaries sur l'Art Corporel et Performances,* exhibition catalog with text by Pontus Hulten, Paris 1979; *Les Levine,* exhibition catalog, Antwerp 1979; *Les Levine: Paysages du Grand Nord,* exhibition catalog with text by Mela Constantinidi, Paris 1979; *Video-As-Art by Les Levine,* exhibition catalog with an introduction by Judith K. Van Wagner, Plattsburg, New York 1979; *Time and Space Concepts in Art* by Marilyn Belford and Jerry Herman, New York 1980; *Museums by Artists,* edited by A. A. Bronson and Peggy Gale, Toronto 1983; *Kunst und Video,* by Bettina Gruber and Maria Vedder, Cologne 1983; *The Art of Performance,* edited by Gregory Battcok and Robert Nickas, New York 1984; *Street Art* by Allan Schwartzman, New York 1985; *Digital Visions* by Cynthia Goodman, New York 1987; *Postmodern Currents* by Margot Lovejoy, Ann Arbor, Michigan 1989; *The Artist Project* by Peter Bellamy, New York 1991; *True Colors—The Real Life of the Art World* by Anthony Haden-Guest, New York 1996; *Plastic—The Making of a Synthetic Century* by Stephen Fenichell, New York 1996; *Les Levine, Media Sculptor—Art Can See,* exhibition catalog, Stuttgart 1997; *The Promise of Photography,* edited by Luminita Sabau, Munich 1998; *The Artists' Museum,* Lodz, Poland 2000.

*

When an artist is asked why he does what he does, he is dumbfounded because he thinks he's already answered the question by doing what he does. He sees the question as a penalty and tries to imagine what rule he has broken so he can prove himself innocent.

For many years I've concerned myself with the systems of art as they relate to society in general, that is to say, the questions of the society. I have been forced to ask myself, are the social and political problems of society a valid medium for art? The answer is, ''Yes, of course.'' If art is to mean anything to society, it is the duty of the artist to employ his sensibilities in interpreting existing social systems.

I have on numerous occasions described myself as a media sculptor, a nomenclature which has puzzled the art world at large. Their difficulty in understanding seems to be the juncture between the word ''sculpture'' which is physical and the word ''media'' which is non-physical and ephemeral. The feeling amongst them seems to be that a non-physical medium, such a communications media, has no physical substance, shape or form, and so therefore, to use the word ''sculpture'' which implies a shaping and forming technique would seem ridiculous.

However, in my case the media are my materials. I am interested in using my media to effect change and understanding of our environment; I want to consider media as a natural resource and to mold media the way others would mold matter. As with television the subject is the medium, i.e., if one has a politician on television, what we're really dealing with is the medium of politics. So in a sense, the subject of my work has to be considered the real medium. When I do a piece on Northern Ireland or games or the federal government no matter what technical medium I may be using, the real medium for the work is Northern Ireland, game rooms or the federal government. So I feel that communications media, particularly electronic media, have indeed a shape and form (though non-physical). My work deals with that shape and form and, therefore, I call myself a media sculptor. If media changes man, i.e., the television generation, then man must change media.

From where I stand, media is one of the few mysteries, both visual and audible, left for the 20th-century artist to decipher. By now, most formal problems connected with art production are a matter of academic knowledge. As a matter of fact, there is so much knowledge about color, form, shape, composition, relationships, esthetics, et al available that one has to assume that a lack of knowledge on the part of any individual amounts to not really wanting to know. It is also clear that making processes have revealed all of their secrets through industry. No one is going to learn much about the making process by making art anymore. We know so much about art that it can now make itself.

Of course, some artists would say. ''I only make art for myself. I don't care about the rest of society. I'm doing my own thing.'' A basic premise of my work is, ''You can't do it for yourself.'' Why should anybody look at the wonderful experience you've produced for yourself? No, the artist's job is to show society the shape of what it's got and how it works.

Media is obviously the most viable for showing society anything as it is the most direct sub-carrier of language and culture. Simply, it is connected to more people than any other medium. It replaces talking. It replaces direct seeing, direct feeling, traveling. It moves the image through space instead of you having to move your body through space to see the image. It is more believable, less processed than any other medium. Being non-physical, television reaches the mind more directly than any physical medium. It affected knowledge and perception that understand and refer to realities in the environment that make us behave the way we do. It also does a lot more that one can't cover here, but it is clear to me that electronic media still holds many mysteries.

One other thing I like to think art does and that is to constantly reprocess our understanding of what we think we already understand. For me, good art is like a growing up process in which one is constantly forced to reassess the problem and reevaluate the conditions of existence. A situation in which one is never quite sure of one's ground totally—in which nothing can be taken for granted completely—in which there is always something else to be understood about the situation.

In other words, I am for an art that develops new knowledge and understanding, without that new knowledge and understanding becoming an excuse or barrier for further understanding. The process of artmaking can never become complacent. The artist is like a hunter who must be on his toes at all times, with eyes and ears fully open to respond to the anxious signals the world sends out.

—Les Levine

* * *

Since the mid-1960s, Les Levine, who has termed himself a ''media sculptor,'' has produced more than 200 videotapes and plethora of works in a variety of media including plastic, ''disposable'' sculptures, electronic environments, photographs, prints, and installations which combine all of these and other elements as well. Levine believes that art for and of the present must use the new electronic media and materials because of their pervasive and mystical powers as carriers of information, communicating directly, mind-to-mind, a specific and precise kind of knowledge about the moment. His work is based on a persistent analysis of the ideas which operate in the current communications systems and in art alike. His intention is to apprehend and maneuver them into ideas which, by redefining the meaning and functions of media and art, can send out signals to show people who and what we are and make us more conscious of our anxieties and our choices for survival.

Works such as ''Photon: Strangeness 4'' (1967), ''Iris'' (1968) and ''Contact'' (1969) use electronic equipment to provide us with a new perception of how we take in, digest and receive information fed to us by the cybernetic wonders of our post-industrial, ''software society.'' ''Iris'' is a cybernetic eye which ''sees'' through three TV cameras located at the center of her bronze plastic facade. The cameras scan the viewer at close-up, medium and long range and show you your many sides, simultaneously, six at a time, live and moving in the multiple possibilities that you provide by placing them into her pre-coded system. It is a home entertainment video ''humanoid'' that portrays directly how television changes who we are.

It is in the field of video art that Levine has made his most pertinent contribution. Beginning as soon as the porta-pak became available to the individual, Levine made his 1965 videotape ''Bum.'' From the start to the present, he has always opted to use the strategies and methods of television to attain the most direct message-making power. Levine's videotapes use the best high-tech means available, are edited for timing and incorporate special effects only as they are intrinsic to communication of the subject matter at hand. His video installations are visually colorful and complexly interwoven so as to simulate the ways we experience life in our rapidly paced electronic age.

Because Levine is a first-generation video artist, he has made many works which examine the nature and techniques intrinsic to the video medium. Works such as ''Brainwash'' (1972), ''Video Lecture'' (1975), ''Landscape I and II'' (1971, 1975) and ''The Selling of the Video Artist'' (1976) both show and tell us the information we need to perceive more clearly the structural and psychological tactics which television uses to make us receive and believe. Some videotapes are about the role of the artist in the present, using the artist's direct presence in them as a model to portray what he feels and thinks as he is going through an experience. In ''I Am an Artist'' (1975) a video camera pursues Levine down the street, persistently asking him question while the ''celebrity'' artist becomes increasingly annoyed and turns away with an above-it-all, ''ivory tower'' attitude. In ''Artistic'' (1974), Levine, writhing in a chair as if in a state of autism, rambles about the vulnerability of the artist who offers himself as model without heroics. Sarcasm, with and/or poignancy are employed as needed to convey the message of the artist's role as communicator.

When Levine is commentating on the state of the art, as in ''The Last Sculpture Show'' (1971), ''Mr. Abstract'' (1975) or ''Cornflakes'' (1976), a biting humor takes precedence, poking fun to convey the follies of formalist abstraction. It's the same in the art world as in the rest of the world, Levine transmits in works such as ''Game Room: A Tribute to the Great American Loser'' (1976) and ''Deep Gossip'' (1979), the conniving for psychological and sociological control.

Among Levine's most powerful and challenging video works are those which directly confront issues in the world, using interview and/or documentary formats to convey the ideas that what we've seen is different both from television and from formalized art alike. These include ''The Troubles: An Artist's Document of Ulster'' (1972), an intermix of moving and still images with captions and text about the conflicts and torments of Northern Ireland, and ''We Are Still Alive'' (1975), a moving document of the Inuits, an Eskimo tribe who depend on artmaking for their survival. Confronting and interacting with his subjects/participants in their own environments, Levine uses the specific power of the video medium to artistically interpret our sociological and political systems.

In his 1978 video installation, ''Diamond Mind,'' Levine proclaimed the necessity for always ''moving on, continuing'' if we are to survive in our age of global, instant information-giving via media, and he also implied his continuous intention not to become repetitive in his own work. Living up to this commitment. Levine tooke his video camera to Hawaii to create a video work titled ''Visions from the God World'' (1981) which is a kaleidoscopic view of that location where East meets West in setting of mesmeric pleasure. Levine also made a series of ads, large photographed and drawn images juxtaposed with captions which are meant to offer new ways to perceive the basic ideas underlying ordinary everyday experiences. One of these, ''We Are Not Afraid,'' appeared in the spring of 1982 in the advertising spaces on New York City subway cars, disguising its identity to advertise an open-ended message concerning our anxieties. As in all Levine's works, the major concern is to harness the powerful methods and tactics of commercial media and make them the sources for artistic power.

—Barbara Caveliere

LEVINE, Marilyn (Anne)

Nationality: Canadian. **Born:** Marilyn Hayes in Medicine Hat, Alberta, 22 December 1933. **Education:** University of Alberta, Edmonton, 1953–59, B.Sc. 1957, M.Sc. 1959; University of California, Berkeley, 1969–71, M.A. 1970, M.F.A. 1971. **Family:** Married Sidney Levine in 1959. **Career:** Ceramicist: now lives and works in the San Francisco area. Worked as a chemist on the geological survey of Canada, Ottawa, 1959–61; instructor in chemistry, Campion College, University of Saskatchewan, Saskatoon, 1962–64; instructor in Ceramics, University of Regina, Saskatchewan, 1971–73; assistant professor of art, University of Utah, Salt Lake City, 1973–76; visiting lecturer, University of California, Berkeley, 1975–80, and California State University, Hayward, 1981. **Awards:** Gold Medal, *Concorso Internazionale della Ceramica d'Arte,* Faenza, Italy, 1969; Sculpture/Ceramics Prize, Louise and Adolf Schwenck Memorial, Montreal, 1969; Canada Council Arts Grant, 1969, 1973; International Academy of Ceramics Medal, Calgary, 1973; Research Fellowship, University of Utah, 1975; National Endowment for the Arts Grant, 1976, 1980. **Agents:** O.K. Harris Gallery, 383 West Broadway, New York, New York 10012; Rena Bransten Gallery, 77 Geary, San Francisco, California 94108. **Address:** 950 61st Street, Oakland, California 94608, U.S.A.; info@marilynlevine.com. **Web site:** http://users.lmi.net/ml/index.html.

Individual Exhibitions:

1966 The Craftsman, Regina, Saskatchewan
1967 Dunlop Art Gallery, Regina, Saskatchewan
University of Calgary, Alberta
1968 Dunlop Art Gallery, Regina, Saskatchewan
1969 Dunlop Art Gallery, Regina, Saskatchewan
Moose Jaw Art Museum, Saskatchewan
University of Lethbridge, Alberta
1970 Canadian Guild of Potters, Toronto
1971 Northwest Handicraft House, North Vancouver
University of California Art Museum, Berkeley
Hansen Fuller Gallery, San Francisco
University of Calgary, Alberta
1973 Bernard Danenberg Galleries, New York
1974 Norman McKenzie Art Gallery, Regina, Saskatchewan (retrospective)
O. K. Harris Gallery, New York
Morgan Gallery, Kansas City
1976 O. K. Harris Gallery, New York
1979 O. K. Harris Gallery, New York
1980 Fuller Goldeen Gallery, San Francisco
1981 O. K. Harris Gallery, New York
Institute of Contemporary Art, Boston (retrospective)
Galerie Alain Blondel, Paris
1983 Fuller Goldeen Gallery, San Francisco
Asher Faure Gallery, Los Angeles
1984 O. K. Harris Gallery, New York
1985 Elaine Horwitch Gallery, Santa Fe, New Mexico
O. K. Harris Gallery, New York
1986 Lubbock Fine Art Gallery, Texas
1990 Rena Bransten Gallery, San Francisco
1991 O. K. Harris Gallery, New York
1996 Huntington Museum of Art, Huntington, West Virginia
1998 *Marilyn Levine: A Retrospective,* Mackenzie Art Gallery, Regina, Saskatchewan, Canada (catalog)

Selected Group Exhibitions:

1970 *Survey 70: Realisms,* Museum of Fine Arts, Montreal
1972 *Painting and Sculpture Today,* Indianapolis Museum of Art
1973 *Ceramic Objects,* Art Gallery of Ontario, Toronto (travelled to the New York Cultural Center)
1974 *Hyperrealisme,* Galerie Isy Brachot, Brussels
New/Photo Realism: Painting and Sculpture of the 1970s, Wadsworth Atheneum, Hartford, Connecticut
1981 *Illusion and Reality,* Australian National Gallery, Canberra
1985 *International Ceramics Exhibition,* Taipei Fine Arts Museum
1986 *California Sculpture 1959–80,* San Francisco Museum of Modern Art
1987 *Ceramics from the Smits Collection,* Los Angeles County Museum of Art

The Eloquent Object, Philbrook Museum of Art, Tulsa, Oklahoma (travelled 1987–89)
1989 *Craft Today USA,* Musee des Arts Decoratifs, Paris (toured Europe; catalog)
1994 *Revolution in Clay: The Marer Collection of Contemporary Ceramics,* Scripps College, Claremont, California (toured; catalog)
1995 *A Bay Area Connection: Works from the Anderson Collection, 1954–1984,* Triton Museum of Art, Santa Clara, California (catalog)

Collections:

Museum of Contemporary Art, Chicago; Claridge Collection, Montreal; Los Angeles County Museum of Art; Crocker Art Museum, Sacramento, California; Limoges Museum, France; Everson Museum, Syracuse; San Francisco Museum of Modern Art; Israel Museum, Jerusalem; Oakland Museum, California; Australian National Gallery, Canberra; University Art Museum, Berkeley; Nelson-Atkins Museum of Art, Kansas City; Museum of Modern Art, Kyoto; Everson Museum of Art, Syracuse; Philbrook Museum of Art, Tulsa.

Publications:

By LEVINE: Article—''The Photo Realists: 12 Interviews,'' with Nancy Foote, in *Art in America* (New York), November/December 1972.

On LEVINE: Articles—''Ceramics 74: The Clay's the Thing'' by Christopher Lowell in *Tactile* (Toronto), July/August 1974; ''The Ceramics of Marilyn Levine'' by Susan Peterson in *Crafts Horizons* (New York), February 1977; ''American West Coast Artist Marilyn Levine'' by Hiroshi Matsubara in *Contemporary Sculpture* (Tokyo), June 1978; ''Marilyn Levine: A Decade of Ceramic Sculpture'' exhibition catalog by Stephen Prokoff, Boston, 1981; ''Marilyn Levine'' by Elaine Levin in *Ceramics Monthly,* vol. 33, no. 3, March 1985; ''Marilyn Levine: A Retrospective'' in *Espace,* no. 47, Spring 1999; ''Virtual Reality'' by Edward Lucie-Smith in *Ceramic Review,* no. 179, September/October 1999.

*

I am involved with both a sense of confrontation and a story in my work.

The confrontation results from the translation of a normally supple, changing material (leather, canvas, etc.) into an enduring, unyielding, rigid material (fired clay), giving it a stillness removed from the time-flux of everything around it. The conflict between visual and tactile clues disturbs one's sense of reality, with the result that one's relationship to the object can no longer be the same.

The story lies in the cracks, sags, tears, scuffs, and stains. These non-conscious marks left on the object through its use are the trace of man acting and reacting in his environment.

—Marilyn Levine

* * *

Marilyn Levine arrived in California in 1969 and found herself in one of the most active ceramics environments in American art history. Peter Voulkos, John Mason, Jerry Rothman, Stephen De Staebler, Ron Nagle, and Jim Melchert had all established themselves as part of the force which propelled clay into the art world. Sculpture and ceramics began to merge as artists created large scale organic forms, some reaffirming and some denying the importance of vessels in ceramic art. Levine, who was influenced at first by California funk and later began to make bags and shoes from clay, chose an unusual direction for the time. Instead of concentrating on formalist issues in clay, as did many of her colleagues whose ceramics were influenced by the abstract expressionists, she chose everyday subjects akin to pop art or even an earlier *trompe l'oeil* sensibility, and constructed life, or slightly larger than life, sized objects.

Levine has added a multi-layered chapter to the history of ceramic art; her subjects, borrowed from pop and funk, seem avant-grade for her medium, yet in reality they are vessels, the oldest of clay forms. At the same time they possess the timeless quality that Levine consciously seeks in her art. They subtly embody the oldest of all clay arguments: is it art or craft? decorative or useful? Levine's shoes, bags, and brief cases are objects and vessels simultaneously, a dual identity which adds as much to the appreciation of her art as the carefully constructed age marks on the leatherlike clay add to the ''history'' of the object.

—Mary Stofflet

LeWITT, Sol

Nationality: American. **Born:** Hartford, Connecticut, 1928. **Education:** Syracuse University, New York, 1945–49, B.F.A. 1949. **Career:** Lives and works in New York. Instructor, Museum of Modern Art School, New York, 1964–67, Cooper Union, New York, 1967–68, School of Visual Arts, New York, 1969–70, and New York University, 1970. **Agent:** Office, c/o Susanna Singer, 50 Riverside Drive, New York, New York, 10024–6555.

Individual Exhibitions:

1965 Daniel Gallery, New York
1966 Dwan Gallery, New York
1967 Dwan Gallery, Los Angeles
1968 Dwan Gallery, New York
Galerie Bischofberg, Zurich
Galerie Heiner Friedrich, Munich
Konrad Fischer Galerie, Dusseldorf
Ace Gallery, Los Angeles
1969 Konrad Fischer Galerie, Dusseldorf
Galerie L'Attico, Rome
Galerie Ernst, Hannover
Museum Haus Lange, Krefeld, Germany
1970 Wisconsin State University at River Falls
Dwan Gallery, New York
Art and Project, Amsterdam
Galerie Yvon Lambert, Paris
Galleria Sperone, Turin
Gemeemtemuseum, The Hague
Museum of Art, La Jolla, California
1971 Dwan Gallery, New York
Art and Project, Amsterdam

Pasadena Art Museum, California
Guggenheim Museum, New York
John Weber Gallery, New York
Lisson Gallery, London
Museum of Modern Art, New York
Galerie Stampa, Basel
Galerie Konrad Fischer, Dusseldorf

1972 Kunsthalle, Bern
Galerie Ernst, Hannover
Walker Art Center, Minneapolis
Massachusetts Institute of Technology, Cambridge
California Institute of the Arts, Valencia

1973 Galerie Yvon Lambert, Paris
John Weber Gallery, New York
Lisson Gallery, London
Museum of Modern Art, Oxford
Galleria Toselli, Milan

1974 Galerie Yvon Lambert, Paris
John Weber Gallery, New York
Palais des Beaux-Arts, Brussels
San Francisco Museum of Art (retrospective, toured the United States)
Galleria Sperone, Turin
Stedelijk Museum, Amsterdam

1975 Max Protetch Gallery, Washington, D.C.
Konrad Fischer Galerie, Dusseldorf
Galleria Gian Enzo Sperone, Turin
Galleria Scipione, Macerata, Italy
Israel Museum, Jerusalem
Art and Project, Amsterdam
Galerie Annemarie Verna, Zurich
Kunsthalle, Basel

1976 Visual Arts Museum, New York
Hammarskjold Plaza Sculpture Garden, New York
Kunstverein, Cologne

1977 Konrad Fischer Galerie, Dusseldorf
Lisson Gallery, London
John Weber Gallery, New York
National Gallery of Victoria, Melbourne
Art Gallery of New South Wales, Sydney
Galleria Genoa, Italy

1978 John Weber Gallery, New York
Brooklyn Museum, New York
Museum of Modern Art, New York (retrospective; toured the United States)

1979 Lisson Gallery, London
Konrad Fischer Galerie, Dusseldorf
Young-Hoffman Gallery, Chicago
Galerie Yvon Lambert, Paris

1980 John Weber Gallery, New York

1981 *Wall Drawings 1968–81,* Wadsworth Atheneum, Hartford, Connecticut
Paula Cooper Gallery, New York
Weinberg Gallery, San Francisco
RAW Gallery, Hartford, Connecticut
Wadsworth Atheneum, Hartford, Connecticut
Graphics I and II, Boston
Paul Cooper Gallery, New York

1982 John Weber Gallery, New York
Galleria Banco, Milan

1983 Lisson Gallery, London

1984 Stedelijk Museum, Amsterdam
Van Abbemuseum, Eindhoven, Netherlands
Wadsworth Atheneum, Hartford, Connecticut

1986 Tate Gallery, London

1987 Musée d'Art Moderne de la Ville, Paris
Cleveland Museum of Art, Ohio

1988 Galerie Schiessel, Munich
Pick Up the Book, Turn the Page and Enter the System: Books by Sol LeWitt, Minnesota Center for Book Arts, Minneapolis (catalog)
Sol LeWitt: Walldrawings, Kestner-Gesellschaft, Hannover (catalog)

1989 *Sol LeWitt,* Gibbes Art Gallery, Charleston, South Carolina (catalog)
Sol LeWitt: Wall Drawings 1984–1988, Kunsthalle Bern, Switzerland (catalog)

1991 *Magdalena Jetelova, Sol LeWitt, Allan McCollum, Pat Steir,* Galerie Franck und Schulte, Berlin (catalog)

1992 *Sol LeWitt: Drawings 1958–1992,* Gemeentemuseum, The Hague (catalog)

1993 *Sol LeWitt: Twenty-five Years of Wall Drawings, 1968-1993,* Addison Gallery of American Art, Amherst (catalog)
Sol LeWitt: Structures 1962–1993, Museum of Modern Art, Oxford (catalog)

1994 *Sol LeWitt's System in Book Form,* Neues Museum Weserburg, Bremen, Germany (catalog)

1995 Ace Gallery, New York

1996 *Of Sun and Stars: Sol LeWitt Wall Drawings,* 23rd Sao Paulo Biennale, Brazil (catalog)
Sol LeWitt: Prints 1970–1995, Museum of Modern Art, New York (catalog)

1997 Ace Gallery, New York

1998 Museum of Contemporary Art, Sydney, Australia
Pace Wildenstein Gallery, New York

2000 *Sol LeWitt: A Retrospective,* San Francisco Museum of Modern Art (traveled to Museum of Contemporary Art, Chicago; Whitney Museum of American Art, New York) (catalog)

2001 *Sol LeWitt: Incomplete Open Cubes,* Wadsworth Atheneum, Hartford

Selected Group Exhibitions:

1965 *Box Show,* Byron Gallery, New York

1968 *Documenta 4,* Museum Fridericianum, Kassel, Germany (and *Documenta 5,* 1972)

1971 *Guggenheim International,* Guggenheim Museum, New York

1974 *Kunst uber Kunst,* Kunstverein, Cologne

1978 *Book Art,* Cleveland Museum of Art

1979 *The Reductive Object,* Institute of Contemporary Art, Boston

1980 *Biennale,* Venice

1984 *Olympian Gestures,* Los Angeles County Museum of Art

1985 *Art Minimal I,* CAPC/Musee d'Art Contemporain, Bordeaux, France

1988 *Contemporary American Art,* Sara Hilden Art Museum, Tampere, Finland (traveled to Oslo)

1989 *The Presence of Absence: New Installations,* Gallery 400, University of Illinois at Chicago (catalog)
Essential Painting, Nelson-Atkins Museum of Art, Kansas City, Missouri (catalog)
Minimalism, Tate Gallery Liverpool, England (catalog)
1990 *American Masters of the '60s: Early and Late Works,* Tony Shafrazi Gallery, New York (catalog)
Collection, CAPC Musee d'Art Contemporain, Bordeaux, France (catalog)
Object and Content: Meaning in Minimal Art, Australian National Gallery, Canberra (catalog)
1991 *Immaterial Objects,* Whitney Museum of American Art, New York (catalog)
Sculptors' Drawings in the Wilhelm-Lehmbruck-Museum Duisburg, Germany (catalog)
1993 *11th Cleveland International Drawing Biennale,* Cleveland Gallery, Middlesbrough, England (also Middlesbrough Art Gallery, England) (catalog)
1994 *American Art 1962–92: In French Provincial Public Collections,* Musee de Toulon, France (catalog)
Contemporary Art from the Collection of the Federation of Migros Co-operatives, Museo Cantonale d'Arte, Lugano, Switzerland (catalog)
Even If It's Night-Time, CAPC Musee d'Art Contemporain, Bordeaux, France (catalog)
1995 *Revolution: Art of the Sixties from Warhol to Beuys,* Hara Museum of Contemporary Art, Tokyo (catalog)
American Drawings and Graphic Works: From Sol LeWitt to Bruce Nauman, Kunsthaus, Zurich (catalog)
The Marzena Collection: Arte Povera, Minimal Art, Concept Art, Land Art, Museum Moderner Kunst, Vienna (catalog)
1996 *Dutch Bath: Etchings—On the Technological Renaissance,* Kunsthaus Hamburg (catalog)
Minimal Art, Kolda Mitxelena Kulturunea, San Sabastian, Spain (catalog)
1997 Skoto Gallery, New York (with El Anatsui)
Multiple Identity, Kunstmuseum Bonn (catalog)
1998 *The Edge of Awareness,* World Heath Organization Headquarters, Geneva (catalog) (traveled to New York, Sao Paulo, New Delhi, Milan)
Waves Breaking the Shore...Ad Dekkers in His Time, Stedelijk Museum, Amsterdam (catalog)
1999 *Lyons Biennale,* Partage d'Exotismes, France
Minimal Maximal: Minimal Art and Its Influence on the International Art of the 1990s, Neues Museum Weserburg, Bremen, Germany (catalog)

Collections:

Museum of Modern Art, New York; Guggenheim Museum, New York; Albright-Knox Art Gallery, Buffalo, New York; Detroit Institute of Arts; Los Angeles County Museum of Art; Art Gallery of Ontario, Toronto; Tate Gallery, London; Centre National d'Art Contemporain, Paris; Stedelijk Museum, Amsterdam; Australian National Gallery, Canberra; Gemeentemuseum, The Hague; Kunsthalle, Berne; Rijksmuseum Kroller-Muller, the Netherlands; Wadsworth Atheneum, Hartford; Museum of Contemporary Art, Chicago; Art Institute of Chicago; Centre Georges Pompidou, Paris; Whitney Museum of American Art, New York; Mercury Art Collection, Celebrity Cruise Lines.

Public Installations:

High Museum of Art, Atlanta; National Airport Terminal, Washington, D.C.; Chapel of Madonna delle Grazie, Brunate, Italy (restoration with David Tremlett).

Publications:

By LeWITT: Books—*Arcs, Circles and Grids,* Berne 1972; *Sol LeWitt: Wall Drawings 1984–1992,* edited by Susanna Singer, Berne 1992. **Articles—**''Ziggurats'' in *Arts Magazine* (New York), November 1966; ''American Sculpture'' in special issue of *Artforum* (New York), summer 1967; ''Drawings Series 1968'' in *Studio International* (London), April 1969; ''I Am Still Alive: On Kawara'' in *Studio International* (London), July/August 1970; ''Sentences Are Conceptual Art'' in *Flash Art* (Milan), July 1971; ''Page Drawings'' in *Arts Magazine* (New York), February 1972; ''Sol LeWitt'' in *Flash Art* (Milan), June 1973; ''Paragraphs on Conceptual Art'' and ''Sentences on Conceptual Art'' in *Uber Kunst,* Cologne 1974; interview with Andrew Wilson in *Art Monthly,* no. 164, March 1993; interview with Claude Gintz in *Art Press,* no. 195, October 1994; interview with Gary Garrels in *New Art Examiner* (Chicago), December/January 2000/2001.

On LeWITT: Books—*Minimal Art: A Critical Anthology,* edited by Gregory Battcock, New York 1968; *Conceptual Art* by Ursula Meyer, New York 1972; *Incomplete Open Cubes,* exhibition catalog, New York 1974; *Sol LeWitt,* exhibition catalog, Amsterdam 1974; *Sol LeWitt 1968–84,* exhibition catalog, Amsterdam 1984; *Sol LeWitt,* exhibition catalog with text by Jeremy Lewison, London 1986; *Sol LeWitt: Openings Series,* Edinburgh 1994. **Articles—**''Abstract Art Refuses: Notes on LeWitt and Reinhardt'' by David Batchelor in *Artscribe International,* no. 79, January-February 1990; ''Dimensions of Drawing: The Prints of Sol LeWitt'' by John T. Paoletti in *On Paper,* vol. 1, no. 1, September-October 1996; ''Sol LeWitt: Puzzles & Prints'' by Sylvia Solochek Walters in *Contemporary Impressions,* vol. 5, no. 2, Fall 1997; ''Sum and the Parts'' by Yve-Alain Bois in *Artforum,* vol. 38, no. 6, February 2000; ''A Beauty Really Bare'' by Robert Hughes in *Time,* vol. 157, no. 5, 5 February 2001.

* * *

Since the 1960s, the artist Sol LeWitt has been elaborating and extending the notion of the Modernist grid in his sculptures, works on paper, and site-specific wall drawings. Usually associated with the Minimalist movement, LeWitt in fact coined the term ''conceptual art'' to reflect his abiding interest in the significance of the artist's thought process, rather than the physical appearance of the work of art, as the basis for meaning. Systematic and intellectual though it is, LeWitt's process has expanded over time to allow for arbitrary and unplanned creative decisions. Early in his career he stated, ''there are many side effects that the artist cannot imagine. These may be used as ideas for new works. . . . The concept of a work of art may involve the matter of the piece or the process in which it is made.''

LeWitt's early sculptures investigated the sculptural possibilities of the cube and its manipulation as a modular unit. Austere works such as *Open Modular Cube,* 1966, with its latticed grids made of painted white aluminum, were realized by an abstract process of mathematical calculation, devoid of emotion or traces of the artist's hand. As homogeneous, serial forms, LeWitt's cubes encapsulated space as space—they existed as the result of the artist's rationally applied system, but were ontologically pure nonetheless. His modular units thus invoked Platonic notions of harmony and order and the utopian ideals of the Bauhaus, de Stijl and Constructivism, even as they suggested the impersonality and uniformity of the grid as inherent in much modern architecture and city planning. *All Variations of Incomplete Open Cubes,* from 1974, makes the artist's mental process even more explicit, consisting as it does of all the possible variants of a fragmentary open cube, here presented as 122 small wood sculptures and 131 framed photos with drawings.

LeWitt's drawings of the same period also treated variations of simple geometric forms, such as line broken into its essential directions—vertical, horizontal, and diagonal, and the manipulation of the modular unit. Over time, LeWitt's drawings, an especially rich and exploratory aspect of his oeuvre, have become less purely reductive and more sensual and improvisatory. A series of gouache drawings from the early 1980s starts with modular geometric forms executed in primary colors and black; soon the artist has introduced irregular forms and jewel-like tonal variations achieved by overlapping the primaries in countless variations. More recent drawings consist of wavy lines of rich hues in overlapping spontaneous gestures.

With his first wall drawings of 1968 and 1969, LeWitt had invented a format that was to prove his most enduring and significant up to the present day. As impermanent and site-specific, the wall-drawings call attention to the procedures that determine them. They heighten our experience of not just specific architectural spaces, but the larger arena in which art is received, positing the art-making process directly in the museum or gallery. LeWitt's white cube becomes the white walls of the art institution itself, which frames the work with its implicit neutrality and authority. The wall drawings are generally executed by assistants who follow a set of written instructions from the artist. Concept and procedure are thus simultaneously emphasized and depersonalized, with a certain element of indeterminacy built in, since some aspects of the instructions are left open-ended, to be interpreted by the draftspersons executing them.

The artist's early wall drawings consisted of delicate, ruled lines of graphite applied directly on the wall, which nonetheless revealed slight irregularities in their making and in the walls' surface. Of these Kenneth Baker has written, "The impersonal shimmer of their visual effect seemed to be the radiance of their economy and elegance as art ideas. . . . To LeWitt, the wall drawings made sense because they were systematic yet unpredictable." (*Minimalism,* Abbeville Press, 1988). Over time, LeWitt's wall drawings have gradually become more complex. An example from 1975, *All Combinations of Arcs from Corners and Sides; Straight, Not-Straight, and Broken Lines,* uses simple white chalk on black walls, but the patterns and relationships between the drawn elements yield a visual result that appears both confoundingly random and pleasingly graceful and airy, like the hermetic chalkboard formula for some profound and fundamental law of physics.

The increasingly exuberant wall drawings from the 1980s to the present have relied on sophisticated color to enhance their spatial and psychological effects. Often executed in translucent inks which are overlaid to create subtly modulated, saturated tones, LeWitt's creates richly varied plays on his recurrent geometries—symphonies of striped bands that recall Color-Field paintings, grandly illusionistic isometrics, glowing lozenges that seem to shift back and forth in space, or punchy interlocking patterns that recall Johns, Op, and Pop. Subversive and sublime, calculated and random, vibrantly sensual and rooted in the objective here-and-now, the expressive range of these recent wall drawings testifies to the seemingly endless inventiveness and intellectual rigor with which Lewitt fashions complex variations from a simplicity of means.

—Dorothy Valakos

LEXIER, Micah

Nationality: Canadian. **Born:** Winnipeg, 13 November 1960. **Education:** University of Manitoba, B.A., 1982; Nova Scotia College of Art and Design, M.A., 1984. **Career:** Lived in Winnipeg; moved to Halifax, 1982; moved to Toronto, 1986; full-time artist since 1988. **Awards:** Numerous awards from the Canada Council, Ontario Arts Council, and the Toronto Arts Council. **Agent:** Jack Shainman Gallery, 513 West 20th Street, New York, New York 10011, U.S.A.; Robert Birch Gallery, 451 King Street East, Toronto, Ontario M5A 1J9; Trépanier Baer Gallery, Suite 105, 999 8th Street S.W., Calgary, Alberta T2R 1J5; Gitte Weise Galery, 56 Sutherland Street Paddington, Sydney, Australia 2021. **Address:** 464 W23rd Street Apt. 5F, New York, New York 10011, U.S.A.

Individual Exhibitions:

1987 Forest City Gallery, London
Centre for Art Tapes, Halifax
YYZ Artists Outlet, Toronto
1988 Definitely Superior Gallery, Thunder Bay
Eye Level Gallery, Halifax
New Gallery, Calgary
Plug-In Inc., Winnipeg
1989 Mercer Union, Toronto
Latitude 53, Edmonton
1990 Southern Alberta Art Gallery, Lethbridge
Hart House, Toronto
Galerie Brenda Wallace, Montreal
Niagara Artists' Centre, St. Catherines
Open Studio Gallery, Toronto
AKA, Saskatoon
1991 Jack Shainman Gallery, New York
Surrey Art Gallery, British Columbia
Main Access, Artspace, Winnipeg
1992 Stride Gallery, Calgary
Temiskaming Art Gallery, Haileybury
Galerie Brenda Wallace, Montreal
Andy Fabo and Micah Lexier, Canada House, London
Andy Fabo and Micah Lexier, Chapter, Cardiff
Andy Fabo and Micah Lexier, John Hansard Gallery, University of Southampton
1993 *Perspectives '93,* Art Gallery of Ontario, Toronto
Jack Shainman Gallery, New York
Oakville Galleries, Oakville, Ontario
Kamloops Art Gallery, Kamloops
Confederation Centre Art Gallery and Museum, Charlottetown, Prince Edward Island

Open Space, Victoria, British Columbia
Open Studio Gallery, Toronto
1994 Fay Gold Gallery, Atlanta
Winnipeg Art Gallery, Winnipeg
McIntosh Gallery, University of Western Ontario, London
Art Gallery of Peterborough, Ontario
Artspace, Peterborough, Ontario
Library and Gallery, Cambridge, Ontario
Tom Thomson Memorial Art Gallery, Owen Sound, Ontario
1996 Jach Shainman Gallery, New York
St. Mary's University Art Gallery, Halifax, Nova Scotia
1997 Trépanier Baer Gallery, Calgary, Alberta
Toronto Photographer's Workshop, Toronto
1998 Musée d'Art Contemporain de Montréal, Québec
Dunlop Art Gallery, Regina, Saskatchewan
Charles H. Scott Gallery, Emily Carr Institure of Art and Design, Vancouver, B.C.
McDonald Stewart Art Centre, Guelph, Ontario
Robert Birch Gallery, Toronto
Open Studio Gallery, Toronto
1999 Jack Shainman Gallery, New York
Gitte Weise Gallery, Sydney, Australia
Whyte Museum of the Canadian Rockies, Banff, Alberta
Trépanier Baer Gallery, Calgary, Alberta
2000 Hallwalls, Buffalo, New York
1 Space Gallery, University of Illinois at Champaign-Urbana, Chicago, Illinois
Agnes Etherington Art Centre, Queen's University, Kingston, Ontario
Robert Birch Gallery, Toronto
2001 Gitte Weise Gallery, Sydney, Australia

Selected Group Exhibitions:

1983 *Appropriation/Expropriation,* Mount Saint Vincent University Art Gallery, Halifax
1986 *Halifax-Auckland Exchange Show,* Artwork, Auckland
1987 *Young Contemporaries '87,* London Regional Art Gallery, London
1988 *As Told To: Structures for Conversation,* Walter Phillips Gallery, Banff Centre, Banff
1990 *Visions 90,* Centre International d'Art Contemporain de Montreal
11th British International Print Biennale, Bradford
1991 *Parallel Allegories,* Museum of Holography, New York
1992 *Artedomani—Punti di vista 1992,* Spoleto
1994 *Alliances: The Family,* Canadian Museum of Contemporary Photography, Ottawa, Ontario
1995 *Das Américas II,* Museu de Arte de Sao Paulo, Brazil
1996 *Containers 96: Art Across Oceans,* Copenhagen
1997 *Musé Imaginaire,* Museum of Installation, London
1998 *Speed,* Whitechapel Art Gallery, London
1999 *The Time of Our Lives,* New Museum of Contemporary Art, New York
2000 *Proposals from Halifax. . . (Library and Archives Exhibition No. 7),* National Gallery of Canada, Ottawa, Ontario
2001 *Travels in Time,* 200 Gertrude Gallery, Melbourne, Australia

Collections:

Art Gallery of Hamilton, Hamilton, Ontario; Confederation Centre Art Gallery and Museum, Charlottetown, Prince Edward Island; Gallery/Stratford, Stratford, Ontario; Jewish Museum, New York; Kamloops Art Gallery, Kamloops, British Columbia; Oakville Galleries, Oakville, Ontario; Surrey Art Gallery, Surrey, British Columbia; Vancouver Art Gallery, Vancouver, British Columbia; Winnipeg Art Gallery, Winnipeg, Manitoba; The British Museum, London; Macdonald Stewart Art Centre, Guelph, Ontario; Museum of Contemporary Art, Sydney, Australia.

Permanent Public Installations:

Hamilton Public Library, Hamilton, Ontario; Tom Thomson Memorial Art Gallery, Owen Sound, Ontario; Metropolitan Toronto Metro Hall, Toronto; Scurfield Hall, University of Calgary, Alberta; Vivian and David Campbell Sculpture Terrace, Art Gallery of Ontario, Toronto; Whitby Psychiatric Hospital, Whitby; National Trade Centre, Toronto; Air Canada Centre, Toronto; Agnes Etherington Art Centre, Queen's University, Kingston, Ontario; Toronto Transit Commission, Shepard/Leslie Subway Station.

Publications:

By LEXIER: Articles—''Dual Bi-Cycle Dual'' in *Midcontinental,* no. 2, 1982; ''Micah from Bab Sarah'' in *Impulse,* Spring 1990; ''Making'' in *Impulse,* Spring 1991; ''Love Letters'' in *Public,* Fall 1994; ''An Artist and Books'' in ''The Book; Twenty-Five Anniversary, Part One'' in *Descant 90,* vol. 23, no. 3, Fall 1995; ''A Minute of My Time'' in *Gallery Largeness,* issue 2, October 1996; ''if, then'' in *Atopia Journal,* issue 0.66, February 2000.

On LEXIER: Books—*Micah Lexier at Southern Alberta Art Gallery,* exhibition catalog with text by Renee Baert and Don Goodes, Lethbridge, Alberta 1991; *Micah Lexier: Name and Family Name,* exhibition catalog with text by Reesa Greenberg, Calgary, Albert 1992; *Andy Fabo and Micah Lexier,* exhibition catalog with text by Emmauel Cooper and Carolyn Bell Farrell, London, 1993; *Perspective '93: Micah Lexier and Lani Maestro,* exhibition catalog with text by Michele Theriault, Toronto, 1993; *Micah Lexier: Book Sculptures,* exhibition catalog text by Marnie Fleming and Nancy Tousley, Oakville, Ontario 1993; *Micah Lexier: A Portrait of David,* interview of the artist by Jon Tupper, Winnipeg, Manitoba, 1994; *Micah Lexier: A Project for Surrey and Other Site-Specific Works,* exhibition catalog with text by Liane Davison and Helga Pakasaar, Surrey, British Columbia, 1994; *Micah Lexier: Cross Reference— Dictionary Illustration Works 1981–1993,* exhibition catalog with text by Robin Metcalfe. **Articles—**''Installation Traces Coming of Age'' in *Calgary Herald,* 16 June 1988; ''Voyaging through the Rites of Passage'' in *Metropolis,* 30 November 1989; ''Micah Lexier/Mercer Union'' in *C Magazine,* spring 1990; ''Micah Lexier: A Growing Presence in Toronto'' in *The Globe & Mail Art Gallery Showcase,* Spring 1991; ''Micah Lexier Retrospective Taps Universal Themes'' in *Now Magazine,* 9 September 1993; ''Flip Sides of the New Narcissism'' in *The Globe & Mail* (Toronto), 18 September 1993; ''Report from Toronto'' in *Art in America,* November 1994; ''Micah Lexier: Cross Reference..,'' in *Arts Atlantic 50,* Fall 1994; ''Portrait of a Man'' in *Calgary Herald,* 13 August 1994; ''What's in a Name?'' by Tanya Stephan in *List,* issue 264, 6–19 October 1995;

''Micah Lexier: Together by Circumstance'' by Gil McElory in *Arts Atlantic 56,* Fall/Winter 1996; ''Lexier Scores with Monumental Hall of Names'' by Deirdre Hanna in *Now Magazine,* 10–16 April 1997; ''A Minute of My Time: Micah Lexier'' by Kyo Maclear in *Toronto Life,* September 1998; ''Micah Lexier: Life Expectancy'' by Ihor Holubizky in *Art/Text,* no. 62, August/October 1998; ''The Time of Our Lives'' by Jennifer Dalton in *Review Magazine,* 15 September 1999; ''Aging Artistically'' by Hilarie M. Sheets in *Newsday,* 23 July 1999; ''Time Warp and Vinyl'' by Gerald Mead in *Artvoice,* 19–25 October, 2000; ''Don't Fence Them In'' by Fred Camper in *Chicago Reader,* 17 May 2000.

* * *

Micah Lexier has a remarkable ability to inscribe complex meanings on to what is common, everyday and familiar. For almost a decade his work has been drawing from the personal—history, feelings, memories and images. To these he brings a refined sense of attention to place and materials, so that the subjectivity in his work does not remain personal but is transferred to objects which can then be carriers of collective moments.

Lexier's work—in the form of fabricated and found objects, sound recordings, texts, graphic design and photographs—is not easily characterized. Yet he has noted: ''Many of the issues and ideas that I work with (masculinity, relationships, education, memory, language) are ones that affect me personally.'' Taking on these issues, Lexier produces work that gives the impression his subjects are episodes from a personal history, not that far removed from our own. Many of his pieces return us to a sense of wonderment—a condition we often associate with childhood; those moments when we are first surprised and delighted by the world around us. Out of that wondering (both his and ours) comes the desire to know. His many works relating to childhood filter past episodes through an adult lens, suggesting both the continuing need to re-examine and unravel these experiences, and the ways in which they have an abiding influence on one's life. Lexier illuminates the conditions of childhood, the often difficult experience of coming of age, and draws attention to the constructs which shape personal identity.

Starting with the 1987 exhibition, *Mr. Caldwell* (titled after his grade six teacher), the artist explored issues of paternal authority, rites of passage and the anxiety of relationships of unequal power. Like many contemporary artists who deal with concerns of authorship and originality, Lexier openly borrows from existing forms found in everyday experience. His method is one which looks at an object as a sign capable of expressing and reflecting issues of social identification.

His practice is also highly conscious of systems of display, as evidenced in *Touch Down*, 1988, a three-image rotating electric sign. The first image is a found photograph of a group of male athletes on all fours, one on top of the other, forming a pyramid. It holds for a few seconds and then rotates downward to reveal the second image of the same group of athletes in a state of collapse. The third rotation displays the words ''touch down'' and then returns to the first image. By the recontextualization of both photograph and display sign to form a new object, the viewer is caught in an oscillating closed-circuit of construction and de-construction. The title, *Touch Down,* serves to introduce another ongoing theme in Lexier's production: the notion of touch. The title's implied reference is to the predominantly male sport of football and the ''legitimate'' touch which comes with contact sport. However, these images are not from football, but gymnastics, where a careful, stacked unit of balance is displaced by much closer contact through a collapse. Exploring codes of touching from the vantage point of a gay male, he probes the social constructs, or even hidden conditions, of gender and sexuality.

In *Touch to Change (Micah from Baba Sarah),* 1988, the act of touching is again a prominent theme, only here it is about affectionate familial touch. The phrase ''Micah from Baba Sarah'' was written on a gift note Lexier's grandmother had given him. He enlarged her handwriting in laser cut steel and then connected each of the words to a light socket which reacts to the viewer's touch. The measured effect of the viewer's touch determines the level of the light's intensity. Physical contact, in this case, is integral to the work, for in touching the metal one is invited in a very public way to interact, share an intimate experience, and reflect on personal relationships. Again, a very simple transaction is made complex, for while the text is a mundane phrase used in the giving of a gift, it can also be read as a homage and a valued recognition of his matriarchal lineage in that he, Micah, is descended from Baba Sarah.

There is a generosity in Lexier's use of the familiar, but there is also an unsettling quality. His visual clues have been dislocated from the site of memory, and have been selected and reframed to reside in an alternative exterior reality, thereby testing or creating new meanings. By giving his images a new context he makes possible re-interpretations in order to engage an audience in the process and outcome of his explorations. He creates, in fact, an interface in the reading of the work that moves between the social and the subjective, the past and the present.

These issues also inform the recent *Book Sculptures,* 1993, which actually consist of quantities of books stacked on top of each other, symbolic of knowledge built up in many layers, thus a synecdoche for all learning and linguistic structure. On the spine of each of these books is a portion of a photographic portrait, so that one stack of books sitting on the floor adds up to create one life-size image of a human figure. The images are pairings of parents with children, siblings and lovers. They are not so much portraits of specific people as they are of relationships between people. Exploring themes of family, relationships, knowledge and measurement, Lexier places the viewer in a situation where the systems of substantiation fall under intensive review. His measured methods give themes back to us, so that through wonderment and questioning we can come to learn again.

—Marnie Fleming

LIBERMAN, Alexander

Nationality: American. **Born:** Kiev, Russia, September 1912; emigrated to the United States, 1941; naturalized, 1946. **Family:** Married Tatiana Yacovleff Du Plessix, 1942 (died 1991): 1 stepdaughter: Francine Du Plessix Gray; Married Melinda Pechangco, 1992. **Education:** Studied at the Académie André Lhote, Paris, 1929–31; studied architecture, under Auguste Perret, at the Ecole des Beaux-Arts, Paris, 1930–32. **Career:** Independent painter since 1936, and sculptor since 1959. Art editor, *Vu* magazine, Paris 1933–37; staff member, 1941–43, and art director 1943, *Vogue* magazine, New York; art director, 1944, and editorial director, since 1962, Condé Nast Publications United States and Europe, New York. **Awards:** D.F.A., Rhode Island School of Design, Providence, 1980; Decorated Chevalier Legion of Honor, France; Recipient, Henry Johnson Fisher Award, 1994, 1995. **Agent:** c/o André Emmerich Gallery, 41 East

57th Street, New York, New York, 10022. **Died:** Of heart ailment in Miami Beach, Florida, 19 November 1999.

Individual Exhibitions:

1959 Museum of Modern Art, New York
1960 Betty Parsons Gallery, New York
1962 Betty Parsons Gallery, New York
1963 Betty Parsons Gallery, New York
1964 Betty Parsons Gallery, New York
Robert Fraser Gallery, London
Bennington College, Vermont
1965 Galleria dell'Ariete, Milan
Galerie Denise René, Paris
Galleria d'Art, Naples
1966 Jewish Museum, New York
Betty Parsons Gallery, New York
1967 André Emmerich Gallery, New York (2 shows)
Betty Parsons Gallery, New York
1968 André Emmerich Gallery, New York
1969 Betty Parsons Gallery, New York
André Emmerich Gallery, New York
1970 *Painting and Sculpture 1950–1970,* Corcoran Gallery, Washington, D.C. (retrospective)
Museum of Fine Arts, Houston (retrospective)
1971 Hammarskjold Plaza, New York
1972 Honolulu Academy of Art (retrospective)
1973 André Emmerich Gallery, New York
1974 André Emmerich Gallery, New York (2 shows)
Jane C. Lee Gallery, Houston
1977 Van Straaten Gallery, Chicago
Storm King Art Center, Mountainville, New York (retrospective)
1978 Vernissage, Rome
1979 Greenberg Gallery, St. Louis
Landau/Alexander Gallery, Los Angeles
The Arts Gallery, Baltimore
André Emmerich Gallery, New York
1980 André Emmerich Gallery, New York
1981 Hokin Gallery, Bay Harbor Island, Florida
André Emmerich Gallery, New York
1983 André Emmerich Gallery, New York
1985 Fort Worth Art Museum, Texas
Aldrich Museum of Contemporary Art, Ridgefield, Connecticut
1988 *Alexander Liberman: New Paintings,* Andre Emmerich Gallery, New York (catalog)
1991 André Emmerich Gallery, New York
1993 *The Circle Paintings 1949–1961,* Gagosian Gallery, New York (catalog)

Selected Group Exhibitions:

1954 *Younger American Painters,* Guggenheim Museum, New York
1965 *The Responsive Eye,* Museum of Modern Art, New York
1966 *New Shapes of Color,* Stedelijk Museum, Amsterdam
1968 *Art of the Real: 1948–1968,* Museum of Modern Art, New York
1972 *Contemporary Sculpture,* Phillips Collection, Washington, D.C.
Annual Exhibition of Contemporary American Painting, Whitney Museum, New York
1975 *Color as Language,* Museum of Modern Art, New York (and world tour)
1977 *Drawings for Outdoor Sculpture: 1946–1977,* John Weber Gallery, New York
1979 *Black and White Are Colors: Paintings of the 1950s-1970s,* Pomona College, Claremont, California (traveled to Scripps College, Claremont, California)
1981 *The Fine Art of Business,* De Cordova Museum, Lincoln, Massachusetts
1990 *The Great Decade: The 1960s,* Andre Emmerich Gallery, New York (catalog)
1996 Hamilton Gallery, London (with Ellen von Unwerth)

Collections:

Guggenheim Museum, New York; Metropolitan Museum of Art, New York; Museum of Modern Art, New York; Whitney Museum, New York; Storm King Art Center, Mountainville, New York; Corcoran Gallery of Art, Washington, D.C.; Smithsonian Institution, Washington, D.C.; Art Institute of Chicago; Museum of Fine Arts, Houston; Tate Gallery, London; Condé Nast Publications, New York; Yale University, New Haven; Virginia Museum of Fine Arts, Richmond; Bibliothèque Nationale, Paris.

Publications:

By LIBERMAN: Books—*The Art and Technique of Color Photography,* New York 1951; *The Artist in his Studio,* New York 1960; *Steichen the Photographer,* exhibition catalog, with others, New York 1961; *Greece, Gods, and Art,* with Iris C. Love, New York 1968; *Then: Photographs 1925–1995,* with Charles Churchward, New York 1996. **Articles—**"Farewell to Hard Edge: Interview with Alexander Liberman," with Lawrence Alloway, in *Alexander Liberman: Paintings,* exhibition catalog, Bennington, Vermont 1964; introduction to *Vogue Book of Fashion Photography 1919–1979* by Polly Devlin, New York 1979; interview with Jean-Jacques Lafaye in *Connaissance des Arts,* no. 455, January 1990; interview with Susan Morris in *Eye,* vol. 3, no. 10, 1993; interview with Suzanne Ramljak in *Sculpture* (Washington, D.C.), vol. 13, no. 2, March-April 1994. **Film—***La femme francaise,* Paris 1936; *Alexander Liberman: A Lifetime Burning* with Julius Potocsny, 1982.

On LIBERMAN: Books—*American Abstract Painters,* exhibition catalog with an introduction by Lawrence Alloway, London 1961; *Alexander Liberman,* exhibition catalog with introduction by Lawrence Alloway, New York 1962; *Alexander Liberman,* exhibition catalog, Bennington, Vermont 1964; *Hard Edge,* exhibition catalog, Paris 1964; *Alexander Liberman,* exhibition catalog, London 1964; *Pattern Art,* exhibition catalog, with an introduction by Lawrence Alloway, New York 1966; *Alexander Liberman,* exhibition catalog with text by Sam Hunter, New York 1966; *Minimal Art: A Critical Anthology,* edited by Gregory Battcock, New York 1968; *Alexander Liberman: Painting and Sculpture 1950–1970,* exhibition catalog with an introduction by James Pilgrim, Washington, D.C. 1970; *Alexander Liberman,* exhibition catalog, New York 1971; *Alexander*

Liberman, exhibition catalog, New York 1973; *Alexander Liberman: The Circle Paintings 1950–1964,* exhibition catalog with text by Thomas Hess, New York 1974; *Alexander Liberman,* exhibition catalog, New York 1979; *Black and White Are Colors: Paintings of the 1950s-1970s,* exhibition catalog with an essay by David S. Rubin, Claremont, California 1979; *The Place of Art in the World of Architecture* by Donald E. Thalacker, with a preface by Sam Hunter, New York 1980; *Handbook: The Guggenheim Collection 1900–1980* by Vivian Edicott Barnett, New York 1980, *Sculpture at Storm King,* with text by H. Peter Stern and David Collens, New York 1980; *Alexander Liberman* by Barbara Rose, New York 1982; *Alex: The Life of Alexander Liberman* by Dodie Kazanjian and Calvin Tomkins, New York 1993. **Articles—**''High Society: Portraits by Alexander Liberman'' by Trevor Gett in *British Journal of Photography,* no. 7071, 10 April 1996; ''Alexander Liberman: On Overcoming Aesthetics'' by Voronique Vienne in *Graphis,* no. 315, May-June 1998; Obituary in *Art in America* (New York), 1 February 2000.

* * *

Since his arrival in the United States as a refugee from the war in Europe during the 1940s, Alexander Liberman has balanced the dual careers of designer for Condé Nast Publications and fine artist of paintings, sculpture, and photographs. Born in Kiev, Russia, Liberman left his homeland with his parents during his adolescence, settling in Paris where he studied painting with Andre Lhote and architecture with August Perret at the Ecole des Beaux-Arts. He also received a baccalaureate degree in philosophy and mathematics from the Sorbonne. Liberman's design career began in 1933 when he was hired by *Vu* magazine. During the four years that he worked for *Vu* he rose quickly from art director to magazine editor. His innovative layouts reflected the avant-garde tendencies of contemporary European art, but his personal artistic talents were subordinated to his design interests until he returned to painting in 1945 in the United States. His initial gestural abstraction was quickly followed in the 1950s by hard-edge paintings of two-dimensional geometric shapes that prefigure the minimal aesthetic of the 1960s. It is, however, in the construction of monumental abstract geometric metal sculptures that Liberman is best known to the art world.

In 1959 Liberman learned arc welding which led to his first welded metal sculpture. The following year he held his first one-man exhibition at Betty Parson's Gallery featuring both his painting and sculpture. His first large sculpture, *Fire,* was commissioned for the exhibition *The Responsive Eye* that was held at the Museum of Modern Art in 1965. Renowned American architect Philip Johnson commissioned Liberman's first large scale public sculpture in 1964 for the New York World's Fair. He titled the hanging aluminum construction, featuring a painted disk framed with curving bands of metal, *Prometheus,* indicating his interest in classical mythological subjects. Here the geometric shapes symbolize ancient and persistent human concerns translated into the abstract imagery characteristic of twentieth-century thinking. As Barbara Rose has pointed out, Liberman is preoccupied ''with the symbolic content of abstract work.''

Since the early 1960s Liberman worked in increasingly larger scale to fulfill his desire to create art that is epic and monumental. He has so frequently painted his constructions in a vivid scarlet hue that it has become a trademark of his sculpture. His giant metal constructions of abstract shapes complement large urban architectures as well as the more pastoral settings of sculpture parks, where a number of his works are installed. They demonstrate the artist's use of industrial methods and materials as an expression of a particularly twentieth-century artistic consciousness that relates in scale and technique to contemporary architecture.

Given his first camera when he was eight years old, Liberman used photography as ''a way of taking notes.'' He was also involved in the artistic side of photography, which is attested to by his 1960 exhibition of photographs at the Museum of Modern Art titled *The Artist in his Studio.* In 1963 Liberman printed his first lithograph and since that time he explored graphic art as another extension of his talent. In 1968 Liberman published his book *Greece, Gods and Art.* Although he began working as the art director for *Vogue* magazine in 1943, Liberman became editorial director of all Condé Nast publications, a position that would hardly have seemed to leave him time to produce art, yet he managed to maintain a high level of artistic production.

—Percy North

LICHTENSTEIN, Roy

Nationality: American. **Born:** New York City, 27 October 1923. **Family:** Married Isabel Wilson, 1949 (divorced): children: David, Mitchell; Married Dorothy Herzka, 1968. **Education:** Attended Ohio State University, Columbus, 1940–43, 1946–49, B.F.A. 1946, M.F.A. 1949; also studied at the Art Students League, New York, under Reginald Marsh. **Military Service:** Served in the United States Army, 1943–46. **Career:** Painter and sculptor; lives in New York City and Southampton, New York. Taught at Ohio State University, Columbus, 1946–51, New York State College of Education, Oswego, 1957–60, and Douglas College, Rutgers University, New Brunswick, New Jersey, 1960–63. **Awards:** Skowhegan Award for Graphics, 1977. D.F.A., California Institute of the Arts, 1977; D.F.A., Ohio State University, 1988; D.F.A., Bard College, 1989. **Agent:** Leo Castelli, 420 Broadway, New York, New York 10012. **Address:** Post Office Box 1369, Southampton, New York 11968, U.S.A. **Died:** In New York, 29 September 1997.

Individual Exhibitions:

1951 Carlebach Gallery, New York
1952 John Heller Gallery, New York
1953 John Heller Gallery, New York
1954 John Heller Gallery, New York
1957 John Heller Gallery, New York
1962 Leo Gallery, Los Angeles
Galerie Sonnabend, Paris
1964 Leo Gallery, Los Angeles
Galleria Il Punto, Turin
Leo Castelli Gallery, New York
1965 Galerie Sonnabend, Paris
Leo Castelli Gallery, New York
1966 Cleveland Museum of Art
1967 Pasadena Art Museum, California (retrospective)
Walker Art Center, Minneapolis
Leo Castelli Gallery, New York

Contemporary Art Center, Cincinnati, Ohio
1968 Stedelijk Museum, Amsterdam
Tate Gallery, London (retrospective)
Kunsthalle, Bern
Kestner-Gesellschaft, Hannover
Irving Blum Gallery, Los Angeles
1969 Irving Blum Gallery, Los Angeles
Guggenheim Museum, New York (retrospective)
Castelli Graphics, New York
1970 Galerie Sonnabend, Paris
University of Puerto Rico, Mayaguez
Nelson Gallery of Art, Kansas City
Museum of Contemporary Art, Chicago
Seattle Art Museum
Columbus Gallery of Fine Arts, Ohio
University of California at Irvine
1971 Leo Castelli Gallery, New York
Irving Blum Gallery, Los Angeles
1972 Leo Castelli Gallery, New York
Contemporary Art Museum, Houston
1973 Leo Castelli Gallery, New York
Greenberg Gallery, St. Louis
Galerie Beyeler, Basel
1974 Galerie Mikro, Berlin
Margo Leavin Gallery, Los Angeles
Current Editions, Seattle
Mayor Gallery, London
Leo Castelli Gallery, New York
1975 Centre National d'Art Contemporain, Paris
Leo Castelli Gallery, New York
Ace Gallery, Los Angeles
Albert White Gallery, Toronto
1976 Mayor Gallery, London
Galerie de Gestlo, Hamburg
School of Visual Arts, New York
1977 Leo Castelli Gallery, New York
Mayor Gallery, London
California State University at Long Beach
Städtische Kunsthalle, Mannheim
Blum Helman Gallery, New York
1978 Leo Castelli Gallery, New York
Aced Gallery, Los Angeles
Institute of Contemporary Art, Boston
Washington Gallery, Indianapolis
1979 Leo Castelli Gallery, New York
University of Miami
State University of New York at Stony Brook
1981 Leo Castelli Gallery, New York
Whitney Museum Downtown, New York
Whitney Museum, New York
Fort Worth Art Museum, Texas
Seattle Art Museum
Blum Helman Gallery, New York
1988 *Lichtenstein's Picassos 1962–1964,* Gagosian Gallery, New York (catalog)
1989 *Roy Lichtenstein: Brushstroke Figures 1987–1989,* Waddington Graphics, London (catalog)
1990 *Lichtenstein: Prints,* Palazzo delle Albere, Trento (traveled to Villa Croce, Genoa) (catalog)
1991 *Roy Lichtenstein: Collages, Brushstroke Landscapes, Reflections on Comics, Interiors,* Galerie Daniel Templon, Paris (catalog)
1992 *Roy Lichtenstein: Water Lilies,* Mayor Gallery, London (catalog)
1993 *The Prints of Roy Lichtenstein,* Guggenheim Museum, New York (traveled to Los Angeles County Museum of Art; Montreal Museum of Fine Arts)
1995 *Roy Lichtenstein: Collages 1994,* Galerie Lawrence Rubin, Zurich (catalog)
Wexner Center for the Arts, Columbus, Ohio
1996 *Landscapes in the Chinese Style,* Leo Castelli Gallery, New York
1997 Leo Castelli Gallery, New York
Roy Lichtenstein: New Paintings, Galerie Lawrence Rubin, Zurich (catalog)
1998 Fondation Beyeler, Riehen, Switzerland (catalog)
1999 Corcoran Gallery of Art, Washington, D.C.

Selected Group Exhibitions:

1962 *New Paintings of Common Objects,* Pasadena Art Museum, California
1964 *Americansk Pop Konst,* Moderna Museet, Stockholm
1969 *New York Painting and Sculpture 1940–70,* Metropolitan Museum of Art, New York
1971 *Art and Technology,* Los Angeles County Museum of Art
1974 *Idea and Image in Recent Art,* Art Institute of Chicago
1976 *Drawing Now,* Museum of Modern Art, New York
1978 *About the Strange Nature of Money,* Kunsthalle, Dusseldorf
1979 *American Portraits of the 60s and 70s,* Aspen Center for the Visual Art, Colorado
1984 *Olympian Gestures,* Los Angeles County Museum of Art
1985 *Painterly Visions 1940–84,* Guggenheim Museum, New York
1988 *Red, Yellow, Blue: Primary Colours in 20th Century Art,* Kunstmuseum, Switzerland (traveled to Kassel) (catalog)
Made in the Sixties, Whitney Museum of American Art, New York (catalog)
American Print Renaissance 1958–1988, Whitney Museum of American Art, Fairfield County, Stamford (catalog)
1989 *Selections from the Beatrice and Philip Gersh Collection,* Museum of Contemporary Art, Los Angeles (catalog)
Art in Place: Fifteen Years of Acquisitions, Whitney Museum of American Art, New York (catalog)
1990 *American Masters of the '60s: Early and Late Works,* Tony Shafrazi Gallery, New York (catalog)
Early/Later, Whitney Museum of Modern Art, New York (catalog)
1991 *Pop Muses: Images of Women by Roy Lichtenstein and Andy Warhol,* Isetan Museum of Art, Tokyo (traveled to Chiba and Osaka) (catalog)
Roy Lichtenstein, Frank Stella, Galerie Beyeler, Basel (catalog)
Seven Master Printmakers: Innovations in the Eighties, Museum of Modern Art, New York (catalog)
1993 *Magic Blue: From Monet to Lichtenstein,* Galerie Beyeler, Basel (catalog)

Directions in Modernism: The Beyeler Collection, Nationalgalerie, Staatliche Museen Preussischer Kulturbesitz, Berlin (catalog)
American Art in the 20th Century: Painting and Sculpture, 1913–1993, Martin-Gropius-Bau, Berlin (traveling exhibition) (catalog)
1994 Museum of Fine Arts, Montreal (with Tamara de Lempicka)
Art After Art, Nassau County Museum of Art, Roslyn Harbor, New York (catalog)
Gemini G.E.L.: Recent Prints and Sculptures, National Gallery of Art, Washington, D.C. (catalog)
1996 *Picasso: A Contemporary Dialogue,* Galerie Thaddaeus Ropac, Paris (catalog)
1997 *Contemporary Prints,* Yvonne Andrews Gallery, London (catalog)
Venice Biennial, Italy
1998 *Glancing at the Century,* Museum of Modern Art, Basil & Elise Goulandris Foundation, Andros, Greece (catalog)
1999 *The Rutgers Group: Garden State Avant-Garde,* Newark Museum, New Jersey
44th Kunst-Messe, Munich

Collections:

Whitney Museum, New York; Museum of Modern Art, New York; Guggenheim Museum, New York; Detroit Institute of Art; Art Institute of Chicago; Tate Gallery, London; Stedelijk Museum, Amsterdam; Wallraf-Richartz Museum, Cologne; Norton Simon Museum of Art, Pasadena, California.

Publications:

By LICHTENSTEIN: Books—*The Artist Observed: 28 Interviews with Contemporary Artists* with John Gruen, Chicago 1991; *Some Kind of Reality: Roy Lichtenstein Interviewed by David Sylvester in 1966 and 1997,* exhibition catalog, London 1997; *Roy Lichtenstein: New Paintings,* exhibition catalog, with David Sylvester, Zurich 1997. **Articles—**''An Interview with Roy Lichteinstein,'' with John Coplands, in *Artforum* (New York), October 1963; ''What Is Pop Art?'' with Gene Swenson, in *Artnews* (New York), November 1963; ''Oldenberg, Lichtenstein, Warhol: A Discussion,'' with Bruce Glaser, in *Artforum* (New York), February 1966; ''Metamorphoses: L'Ecole de New York,'' with Jean Antoine, in *Quadram* (Paris), March 1966; ''Interview with Roy Lichtenstein,'' with David Pascal, In *Giff Wiff* (Paris), May 1966; ''Conversation with Roy Lichtenstein,'' with Alan Solomon, in *Fantazaria* (Rome), July/August 1966; ''Interview de Roy Lichtenstein,'' with Colette Roberts, in *Aujourd'hui* (Paris), December 1966; ''Sensibility of the 60s'' with Barbara Rose and Irving Sandler, in *Art in America* (New York), January/February 1967; ''Talking with Roy Lichtenstein,'' in *Artforum* (New York), May 1967; ''Le Classicisme du Hot Dog,'' with Raphael Sorin, in *La Quinzaine Litteraire* (Paris), January 1968; interview with Paul Taylor in *Flash Art,* no. 148, October 1989; ''Roy Lichtenstein: 'How Could You Be Much Luckier Than I Am?''' in *Artnews,* vol. 90, no. 5, May 1991; interview with Ann Hindry in *Artstudio,* no. 20, Spring 1991; interview with Robert Enright in *Border Crossings,* vol. 13, no. 3, Summer 1994; interview with Stephen Goode in *Insight on the News,* vol. 10, no. 48, 28 November 1994; interview with David Bowie in *Interview,* vol. 28, no. 1, January 1998.

On LICHTENSTEIN: Books—*Pop Art and After* by Mario Amaya, New York 1965; *Happenings, Fluxus and Pop Art* by Jurgen Becker and Wolf Vostell, Hamburg 1965; *Pop Art One* by Dorothy Herzka, New York 1965; *The New Art,* edited by Gregory Battock, New York 1966; *Lichtenstein,* edited by Alberto Boatto and Giordano Falzoni, Rome 1966; *Pop Art* by Lucy Lippard, New York 1966; *Pop Art: Object and Image* by Christopher Finch, New York 1968; *Pop Art Redefined* by John Russell and Suzi Gablik, London 1969; *Roy Lichtenstein: Drawings and Prints* by Diane Waldman, New York 1969; *Roy Lichtenstein,* edited by John Coplans, New York 1972; *Roy Lichtenstein 1970–1980* by Jack Cowart, London 1987. **Articles—**''The Work of Roy Lichtenstein in the Age of Walter Benjamin's and Jean Baudrillard's Popularity'' by Carter Ratcliff in *Art in America* (New York), vol. 77, no. 2, February 1989; ''The Unbearable Lightness of Roy Lichtenstein'' by David Joel Shapiro in *Artstudio,* no. 20, Spring 1991; ''Roy Lichtenstein: Past, Present, Future'' by Robert Rosenblum in *Artstudio,* no. 20, Spring 1991; ''Roy Lichtenstein: Precious Stepping-Stones'' by Henry Geldzahler in *Graphis,* vol. 48, no. 279, May-June 1992; ''Borrowed Spots'' by Cecile Whiting in *American Art,* vol. 6, no. 2, Spring 1992; ''Wham! Blam! Pow! Roy Lichtenstein!'' by Diane Waldman in *ARTnews,* vol. 92, no. 9, November 1993; ''Reflections on Lichtenstein'' by Mark Henshaw in *Artonview,* no. 5, Autumn 1996; Obituary in *Art in America* (New York), December 1997; ''Frederic Tuten on Roy Lichtenstein: Beauty Secrets'' by Frederic Tuten in *Artforum,* vol. 36, no. 5, January 1998.

* * *

Roy Lichtenstein's work in the 1950s was concerned with the pioneer passages of American history, such as the opening of the West: he painted canvases recalling the cowboys and Indians in their figurative Remington style. From 1957 he went through a phase of Abstract Expressionism that by 1961 had broken into the imagery he has now made his own. Those pictures were crudely based on advertising illustration, comic-strip characters, everyday objects and the adaptation of works by artists of the past. A prerequisite of the treatment was an overt reliance on the line. The painting was not a direct blow-up of a newspaper detail, but the method of composing the motive including the lettered caption was simplified in bold two-dimensional terms linked to printing processes.

It goes without saying that the content of the picture had only incidental relevance to its treatment, the enlargement emphasizing its abstract qualities of design and rhythm. Painting *per se* was useful for its contrasting ability to bowlderize commercial images while concentrating on their banality. This calculated pastiche emphasized its throw-away life, and also depersonalized the artist's autographic quality.

In his brushstroke paintings of 1965/66 Lichtenstein seemed to send up the subjective concern for the working of the pigment that characterized Abstract Expressionism. Like the paintings, his sculptures are completely removed from the conventions of the art so that ''Standing Explosion'' of 1966 is a cut-out in enameled metal of a blown-up line drawing, suggesting an explosion such as might appear in a strip cartoon. Likewise, the so-called ''Modern Sculptures'' are no more in effect than copies of Art Deco interior design in the apartments of the 1930s. His ''Modern paintings'' series of 1966/67 are based less upon the paintings themselves than on the proliferation of colour plates in art magazines and books.

The difficulty in placing Lichtenstein is not upon his self-contained identity as a painter but in the true personality of his work. By the act of pastiche he seeks to abdicate the right to be considered on his own terms. In their way, Lichtenstein's paintings and especially his sculptures enter the No Man's Land of Oldenburg, where the art is camouflaged to the point that imitation takes on an import and significance of its own. Like Picasso's "Maninas" after Velasquez, Lichtenstein's strip romances and vinyl seascapes are ready-made subjects after their contemplative reproductions.

—G. S. Whittet

LIEBSCHER, Martin

Nationality: German. **Born:** 2 October 1964. **Education:** Attended Slade School of Fine Arts, London, 1993; studied with Martin Kippenberger and Thomas Bayrle at Städelschule, Stadtliche Hochschule für bild. Künste, Frankfurt, 1990–95; Städelschule, Frankfurt, M.F.A. 1996. **Awards:** Frankfurter Künstlerhilfe, 1996; Hans Purrmann Price, 1996; MAK Grant, Mackey Appartment House, Los Angeles, 1997; world record for "The longest group photograph in the world," Guiness Book of Records, 1998; 1. Kunstpreis der "Frankfurter Welle," 1999; Kunstpreis der Volksbank, 1999; Staatspreis, Rheinland Pfalz, 1999. **Agent:** Voges + Deisen, Frankfurt/Main, Germany; Cato Jans, Hamburg, Germany; Kari Kenetti, Helsinki, Finland. **Address:** Marchlewskistr. 107, D-10243 Berlin, Germany. **Web site:** www.m-liebscher.de.

Individual Exhibitions:

1994 *Liebscher-Lehanka besucht London,* City Racing, London (catalog)
1995 *16 Works,* Airport, Frankfurt
1996 *Loose Lips Sink Ships,* Voges + Deisen Gallery, Frankfurt
Familientreffen, Friedensallee 12, Hamburg (catalog)
X-ing, Stefan Stux Gallery, New York
1997 *Liebscherhaus*, Kunstverein Speyer (catalog)
GROOV V, Michael Kapinos-Dogenhausprojekte, Berlin
1998 *Leebshers Bed & Breakfast,* Mackey Apt. House, Los Angeles
Autobahnkreuzungen, Schindler House-MAK Center, Los Angeles
If you lived here, you'd be home by now, Voges + Deisen Gallery, Frankfurt (catalog)
1999 *Liebscher-eine Künstlerfamilie aus der Pfalz,* Pfalzgalerie Kaiserslautern
Geschwindigkeitsübertretung, Cato Jans Gallery, Hamburg (catalog)
Volles Haus, Heart Gallery/Fotomeile, Mannheim
TKO, Berlin
2000 *Bensiiniä,* Kari Kenetti, Helsinki
visurbia, Kunstverein Ludwigshafen
drivebyshooting, Voges + Deisen, Frankfurt
2001 *380,* Cato Jans, Hamburg

Selected Group Exhibitions:

1991 *Virtuosen ihrer Zeit,* Gallery Grässlin, Frankfurt (catalog)
Give Me a Hand, Before I Call You Back, Gallery Bleich-Rossi, Graz, Österreich (catalog)
1992 *Ss. Ss. R.*, Gallery Grässlin, Frankfurt
1993 *The Lure of the Object,* Goethe Institute, London (catalog)
European Photography Awards, Bad Homburg
Chambre 763, Carlton Palace Hotel, Paris (with Liebscher-Lehanka) (catalog)
1994 *By the Way,* Leipziger Strasse, Frankfurt (catalog)
1995 *444&222 TOO (Karaoke),* South London Gallery, London
Kulturprämie, BASF Feierabendhaus, Ludwigshafen/Lindenaumuseum, Altenburg (catalog)
1996 *The Luminous Image,* The Alternative Museum, New York (CD-Rom)
1997 *Stadt,* Schloß Plön, Germany
Huge Garage Sale, MAK Center Los Angeles
Why don't we do it in the road?, Cato Jans, Hamburg
1998 *Pfalz-Price of Photography,* Pfalzgalerie, Kaiserslautern
Revue, Art Lab, Gallery Hilger, Vienna
1999 *Emy Roeder Price,* Kunstverein Ludwigshafen (catalog)
Save the day!, Museum of Modern Art, Frankfurt (catalog)
Fotobücher von Künstlern, Fototriennale/Künstlerhaus, Hamburg
Unidentified Fotografic Objects, Noorderlicht/Halte Kropswolte, Netherlands (catalog)
2000 *XL Photography,* Neue Deutsche Börse, Frankfurt (catalog)
one of these days, Kunstverein Mannheim (catalog)
A good cast is worth repeating, Voges + Deisen, Frankfurt
Youth Welcomes the III Millenium, Central House of Artists, Moscow (catalog)
Desert and Transit, Kunsthalle, Kiel/Museum der bildenden Künste, Leipzig (catalog)
Some Parts of This World, Helsinki Photography Festival (catalog)
2001 *True Fictions,* Schloß Arolsen

Collections:

Deutsche Flugsicherung, Langen/Leipzig; Deutsche Bank, Frankfurt/London; Commerzbank, Frankfurt; Museum für Moderne Kunst, Frankfurt; Vereins und Westbank, Hamburg; Olympus Optical, Hamburg; City of Tampere, Finland; West LB, London.

Publications:

On LIEBSCHER: Books—*Kulturprämie,* BASF Ludwigshafen 1995; *WRMM,* Heidelberg 1995; *Liebschers gute Fotobücher,* 5 volumes, Berlin, Frankfurt 1996–2001; *Liebschers Kunstkalender* by Martin Pesch, Frankfurt 1997; *C&L,* Frankfurt 1997; *Inside Out* by Andreas Bee, Kunstverein Speyer 1997; *Save the day!* MMK Frankfurt 1999; *1.LIGA!,* Pfalzgalerie Kaiserslautern 1999; *1. Kunstpreis der Frankfurter Welle* by Jean-Christophe Ammann, Frankfurt 1999; *Martin Liebschers Familienbilder* by Raimar Stange, Dölling und Gallitz, Hamburg 1999; *Desert & Transit,* exhibition catalog, Museum für zeitg. Kunst, Leipzig 2000; *XL Photography,* hatje/cantz, 2000;

Martin Liebscher: *Tokio Crosswalk,* 1999. ©2001 Artists Rights Society (ARS), NY/VG Bild-Kunst, Bonn.

Heimweh by Tim Staffel, Berlin 2000; *Visurbia,* Wunderhorn, Heidelberg 2000. **Articles**—*Kunstforum,* no. 136, 1997; ''Das längste Gruppenfoto mit einer Person'' in *Guiness Buch der Rekorde,* Berlin 1998; *Artist,* no. 39, July 1999; *Frankfurter Rundschau,* 17 June 1998; *FAZ,* 21 July 1998; *Mannheimer Morgen,* 7 September 2000; *Kunstzeitung,* January 2001.

* * *

One's gaze goes from left to right, from right to left, up and down, through light and dark zones, through swirling fore- and backgrounds, at times more quickly, at times more slowly, progressing like a car on an optical roller coaster that careens through time and space. It is nearly impossible to distinguish a clear, singular goal in Martin Liebscher's panoramas. Well hidden is the one solid point to which all lines connect and from which the image can be conventionally deciphered. Rarely recognizable is the established orientation of a horizon that is capable of holding the wandering glance in balance. The world appears to tumble completely out of control. Images such as these agitate the nerves like the sound of scratching on a chalkboard. Yet they also rouse and stimulate the lethargic mind into intensity.

It is obvious from the start: Liebscher's images are about speed, about acceleration and deceleration. Even in the first encounter, one realizes the different velocities in the photographs, achieved by the exaggeration and constriction of time. Those wanting to zero-in on the image will be hindered abruptly, only to momentarily be drawn into another dizzying whirl. Take for example the photograph from a helicopter in New York (''Helicopter NYC 1997''), which tells—in all its facets—of movement. We see through the action of the rotating blades, and we understand that the camera itself, during the exposure, is in motion, and that the film too was spooled by the open lens. We register in the photograph a variety of effects: the condensation stripe-like wiping of the object, suggesting its speed; changes in exposure comparable to the diminishing and swelling of music; and not lastly the extreme horizontal rhythm of the vertical elements. All of this has a meaning, it has a goal: the presentation of movement in a space.

Similarly compressed are the pans from moving automobiles. Again interior and exterior space is being melted, but sometimes with unlike movements on the most unrelated levels, flowing into one another. Thus Liebscher creates pictures that remind one of the condition of zero gravity, of a perspective in which above and below exist simply as conventions. If we could, for a short moment, become a feather blown by the wind across the interior of a church, we would perceive an image similar to the one which, in another photograph, melted into an image of time and space. The majority of his photographs are not meant to show clarity but—through blurs and underand overexposure—to create a singular atmosphere. The effect is comparable to a characteristic smell, intense and informative, such that the time and location of the photograph can approximately be determined. It is also like the swelling of a spring in a river, in which the clear water mixes with the muddying flow and yet remains evident.

Liebscher's images speak about the multifaceted phenomena of a mobile existence. They are not selectively repeatable, because in them, chance plays a role and the conventional distribution of an object's cognitive properties fundamentally calls stationary subjects into question. The boundary between the contradictory sides dissolves; their positions change their purpose, so that motion appears in what was stationary, and vice-versa. While a painter must move his entire body, a draftsman must at least use his hand to create an image, such movements become superfluous, even undesirable with the invention of photography. It became necessary—at least during the crucial moment of exposure—to hold the camera and oneself still. Blurred photographs were rarely accepted. Yet Liebscher moves not only the camera held to his moving body, but the film as well. The light-sensitive stripe of celluloid is spooled past the open lens in a more or less even motion. Thereby the movement of body and camera, in coordination with the movement of the film, is accelerated only to the extent that the resulting images can still be read as individual pieces and not just as a possibly atmospheric, but illegible glimmer.

Liebscher's pictures illustrate in a poetic way life as a race, as a process, to which the viewer can not quietly and noncommittally stand opposed; rather life is a process that engages. Here time is presented as something which actually does not exist, but is rather a condition in which there is no stopping or standing still. But even a fleeting comprehension of the world leaves behind traces, and Liebscher captures some of the duality between stasis and speed in his images. Thus the photographs depict motion without moving themselves; they illustrate the comprehension of time. The tension of ''before-now-later'' is never completely resolved, thus giving no sense of direction. The viewer forms his own opinions and impressions on the Before, Now, and Later. Perhaps he understands motion as a changing continuous game and not as a flight from a ''punktzeit''—a time point—or the push towards a goal.

—Andreas Bee

LIGON, Glenn

Nationality: American. **Education:** Rhode Island School of Design, Providence, 1980; Wesleyan University, Middletown Connecticut,

1978–82, B.A. 1982; Whitney Museum Independent Study Program, 1985. **Career:** Administrative assistant, Boys' Harbor, New York, 1982–83; proofreader, Skadder Arps, New York, 1983–91. **Awards:** National Endowment for the Arts internship, 1982; P.S. 1 National Studio Program, The Clocktower, New York, 1989–90; National Endowment for the Arts Fellowship (drawing), 1989; Dewar's Young Artist Recognition Award, 1990; Art Matters, Inc., Fellowship, 1990; National Endowment for the Arts Fellowship (painting), 1991; Rockefeller Foundation, Bellagio Study Center, Italy, 1994; Joan Mitchell Award, 1996; ArtPace International Artist-in-Residence Program, San Antonio, Texas, 1997–98. **Agent:** Max Protetch, 560 Broadway, New York, New York 10012, U.S.A. **Address:** 168 Prospect Place, Brooklyn, New York 11238, U.S.A.

Selected Individual Exhibitions:

1982 Davison Art Center, Wesleyan University, Middletown, Connecticut
1990 BACA Downtown, Brooklyn, New York
P.S. 1 Museum, Long Island City, New York
1991 Project Room, Jack Tilton Gallery, New York
1992 Whitney Museum of American Art at Philip Morris, New York (traveling)
1993 Max Protetch Gallery, New York
1994 Ruth Bloom Gallery, Santa Monica, California
1995 Des Moines Art Center, Iowa
MIT List Visual Arts Center, Cambridge, Massachusetts
Max Protetch Gallery, New York
1996 San Francisco Museum of Modern Art, California
Brooklyn Museum, New York
1998 *Nothing Under the Sun,* Max Protetch Gallery, New York (catalog)
Unbecoming, Institute of Contemporary Art, Philadelphia (catalog)
2000 *Coloring: New Work by Glenn Ligon,* Walker Art Center, Minneapolis, Minnesota

Selected Group Exhibitions:

1991 Grey Art Gallery, New York (traveling)
Black Male: Representations of Masculinity in Contemporary American Art, Whitney Museum of American Art, New York (catalog)
1995 Fabric Workshop, Philadelphia and Beaver College, Glenside, Pennsylvania
Twenty-Five Americans Paintings in the 90s, Milwaukee Art Museum, Wisconsin
1996 Frankfurt Kunstverein, Germany
Maison des Arts et de la Culture, Paris-Creteil
Fogg Art Museum, Cambridge, Massachusetts
Art Gallery of New South Wales, Sydney, Australia
Museum of Modern Art, New York
Steirischer Herbst 96, Graz, Austria
1997 *Community of Creativity: A Century of MacDowell Colony Artists,* National Academy Museum, New York (catalog)
No Man, Max Protetch Gallery, New York (catalog)
1998 *Histories (Re)membered,* PaineWebber Art Gallery, New York (catalog)
1999 *The Ecstatic,* Trans Hudson Gallery, New York (catalog)
The American Century: Art & Culture 1900–2000; Part II, 1950–2000, Whitney Museum of American Art, New York (catalog)

Collections:

Baltimore Museum of Art, Maryland; Boston Museum of Fine Art; Eli Broad Family Foundation, Santa Monica, California; Fisher Landau Center, New York; Carnegie Museum of Art, Pittsburgh; Des Moines Museum, Iowa; Detroit Institute of Arts; High Museum, Atlanta, Georgia; Hirshhorn Museum and Sculpture Garden, Washington, D.C.; List Art Gallery, MIT, Boston; Museum of Modern Art, New York; Norton Family Foundation, Santa Monica, California; Philadelphia Museum of Art; San Francisco Museum of Modern Art; Walker Art Center, Minneapolis, Minnesota; Whitney Museum of American Art, New York.

Publications:

By LIGON: Articles—''Artist Page'' in *Documents,* Summer 1994; ''Narratives,'' in *Yale Journal of Criticism,* Summer 1994; ''Memorial,'' in *New York Times Magazine,* 9 April 1995; ''A Feast of Scraps'' in *The Masculine Masquerade: Masculinity and Representation*, edited by Andrew Perchuk and Helaine Posner, Cambridge, Massachusetts 1995.

On LIGON: Books—*The Pressure of Voices,* exhibition catalog, New Jersey, State Museum at Trenton and Michael Brenson, 1992; *Glenn Ligon/Matrix 120,* exhibition catalog, Connecticut, Wadsworth Atheneum and Andrea Miller-Keller, 1992. **Articles—**''The Art of Questioning Identity'' by Christine Temin in *The Boston Globe,* 4 August 1991; ''Review'' by Yoshi Suznobu in *The New Yorker,* 31 July 1995; ''Lack of Location Is My Location'' by Roberta Smith in *New York Times,* 16 June 1991; ''Review'' by Lois Nesbitt in *Artforum,* Summer 1991; ''Skin Pigmentation as a Determinant of Attitudes'' by Helen Harrison in *New York Times,* 1 December 1991; ''Glenn Ligon at Max Protetch Gallery'' by Ken Johnson in *Art in America,* November 1992; ''Prints and Photographs Published'' in *The Print Collector's Newsletter,* vol. 24, March/April 1993; ''Fast Forward'' by Robin Cembalest, Marchy Haus, and Raphael Rubinstein in *Art News,* vol. 92, November 1993; ''Prints and Photographs Published'' in *The Print Collector's Newsletter,* vol. 24, January/February 1994; ''Possible Identities'' by Elizabeth Converse in *Artweek,* vol. 25, May 19 1994; ''Body Politic'' by Sarah Kent in *Time Out, London,* 24 May 1995; ''Glenn Ligon'' by Glenn C. Tomlinson in *Bulletin* (Philadelphia Museum of Art), vol. 90, Winter 1995; ''Prints and Photographs Published'' in *The Print Collector's Newsletter,* vol. 27, March/April 1996; ''To Disembark: The Slave Narrative Tradition'' by Kimberly Rae Conner in *African American Review,* vol. 30, no. 1, May 1996; ''Glenn Ligon at Max Protech'' by Anastasia Aukeman in *Art in America,* February 1996; ''Glenn Ligon: The Limits of Visibility'' by Richard Meyer in *Art Text,* no. 58, August/October 1997; ''Neo-archival and Textual Modes of Production: An Interview with Glenn Ligon'' by Lauri Firstenberg in *Art Journal,* vol. 60, no. 1, Spring 2001.

* * *

Glenn Ligon was born in 1960 and grew up in the South Bronx. He attended Rhode Island School of Design and Wesleyan University before moving to New York City in the early 1980s where he participated in the Whitney Museum Independent Study Program. Ligon began his career as an abstract painter and his early work is minimalist in style. The majority of Ligon's mature works focus on issues of race, identity, and sexuality. Appropriated materials, such as texts by African American writers, childhood coloring books, or photographs by other well-known artists, have played an important role in Ligon's work. Generally, his work explores and interrogates the complexities that arise when one tries to describe or define cultural, racial, or sexual identity.

Ligon's best known works are his text paintings from the early 1990s such as ''Untitled (I Feel Most Colored When I am Thrown Against a Sharp White Background)'' (1990–91). These text paintings utilize the language of famous African American authors such as Zora Neale Hurston, James Baldwin, and Ralph Ellison. The paintings are made by stenciling black letters onto white canvas. The letters form repeating phrases or sentences excerpted from the writings of these authors. Ligon uses the same stencil repeatedly from the top of the work to the bottom of the canvas. This technique produces legible words at the top of the canvas and smudged and blurry words towards the bottom. Ultimately, the works demonstrate the inefficacy of language to convey the African American lived experience and identity. Ligon has noted that the text also highlights the idea of obsessively reading or repeating a phrase and still not being heard or understood.

Much of Ligon's work from the mid-1990s explores the history of slavery and the contemporary implications of this history. In 1993 Ligon produced *Narratives*, a series of etchings containing autobiographical facts about himself written and printed in the style of frontispieces from nineteenth-century slave narratives. Ligon's amalgam of historical format and contemporary production creates a dialogue between the past and the present. In these works, Ligon also references the narrative tradition in African American culture. Slave narratives were typically written by white abolitionists because it was illegal for slaves to learn to read and write. However, many slaves did become literate and write their own stories, an act that was ultimately rebellious and empowering. Ligon references this history in his *Narratives* series, and appropriates historical documents that still have resonance in contemporary society. In another series of lithographs from 1993, titled *Runaways*, Ligon had friends write biographical and descriptive details about him—medium height, very short hair cut, medium complexion—which were used as the text in copies of nineteenth-century runaway slave advertisements. In these works, Ligon identifies with and is identified by slavery's painful past. These lithograph series allow Ligon to explore issues of contemporary African American identity in light of the history of slavery in America.

Ligon utilizes these nineteenth-century formats to illuminate histories of hate, pain, struggle, and identity formation. In one example from the *Narrative* series the artist reveals his homosexual history and identity. In this example, the frontispiece reads: ''The Narrative of the Life and Uncommon Sufferings of Glenn Ligon, a colored man, who at a tender age discovered his affection for the bodies of other men, and has endured scorn and tribulations ever since.'' The appropriation of the historical format allows Ligon to use the past as a springboard for identity explorations and autobiographical art making. Ligon himself suggests that a person's identity can be understood only in relation to a larger social picture.

Text, race, homoeroticism, and sexuality first merged in Ligon's work in 1993 when he exhibited his ''Notes on the Margins of the Black Book'' at the Whitney Biennial. Framing quotations from scholars and critics under images from Robert Mapplethorpe's famous *Black Book*, Ligon drew attention to the theoretical controversies surrounding Mapplethorpe's work. Through the added texts by writers such as James Baldwin, Kobena Mercer, and Franz Fanon, Ligon created a work where all issues of the *Black Book*—desire, racism, erotica—are enlightened and questioned. Ligon's installation cast light on the stereotypical images of nude black men by Mapplethorpe and questioned the significance of these images to the African American community and to the art community in general.

''Notes on the Margin of the Black Book'' is considered by many to be Ligon's first openly gay and homoerotic work of art. In the mid to late 1990s Ligon began exploring themes of sexual identity in his installations and projects. In 1996 Ligon exhibited an installation at the Max Protech Gallery which explored themes of gay sexuality within the realm of the home. In this exhibition, Ligon exhibited a twin bed with the mattress drawn back to reveal gay porn magazines. The installation suggests that in the realm of the home sexuality, especially gay sexuality, is something to be hidden. ''A Feast of Scraps'' is another project which Ligon worked on in the 1990s that explores sexuality in relation to the artist's family life and childhood. This work takes the form of a family photo album and displays the typical celebratory snapshots that every family shares—graduations, births, etc. But ''A Feast of Scraps'' also incorporates pornographic images of black men that Ligon culled from a porn shop. The combination of family photos and nude photos suggest that Ligon is perhaps rewriting the family history of denial and shame by including the objects of his desire in the safety and warmth of his family.

Ligon's most recent works are silk-screened images of 1970s black-themed coloring books. Using appropriated images from the era of the civil rights movement, the recreated coloring books explore an era when racial consciousness and the black power movement were burgeoning. As in much of Ligon's work, here he is addressing and interrogating racial and identity formation in America through the reappropriation of visual and pop culture.

—Jennifer S. Zarro

LIJN, Liliane

Nationality: American. **Born:** Liliane Segall in New York City, 22 December 1939; adopted name ''Lijn,'' 1961. **Education:** Solebury School, New Hope, Pennsylvania, 1950–54; Liceo Cantonale di Lugano, Switzerland, 1955–57; studied archaeology at the Sorbonne, Paris, 1958–59; studied art history, Ecole de Louvre, Paris, 1959–60; mainly self-taught in art, 1958–64. **Family:** Married the artist Takis in 1961 (divorced, 1967); children: Athanasios, Thanos. **Career:** Independent artist, in Paris 1960–61, 1963–64, in New York, 1961–62, and in London, since 1967; produced first light and kinetic sculptures, 1961; worked on house-building project, with Takis, in Athens, 1964–66. **Awards:** Arts Council Award, 1976; Alecto Award, *Bradford Print Binennale,* 1976; Arts Council Publishing Award, 1981; Arts Council Holography Bursary, 1982; London Film Production Award, 1996. **Address:** 99 Camden Mews, London NW1 9BU, England.

Liliane Lijn: *My Body My Self,* 1996. ©Liliane Lijn. Photo by Stephen Weiss.

Individual Exhibitions:

1963 La Librairie Anglaise, Paris
1967 Indica Gallery, London
1970 Hanover Gallery, London
1972 Galerie Germain, Paris
1973 Jordan Gallery, London
1974 Great Georges Project, Liverpool
1976 Serpentine Gallery, London
1977 Alecto Gallery, London
Durham Light Infantry Museum
Mappin Gallery, Sheffield
Walker Art Gallery, Liverpool (toured the U.K.)
1979 Central Art Gallery, Wolverhampton
1980 Eagle Walk Gallery, Milton Keynes
Roundhouse Gallery, London
1982 Aberdeen Art Gallery, Scotland
1983 Paton Gallery, London
1985 Galerie Peter Ludwig, Cologne
1987 Fischer Fine Art, London
1993 National Arts Library, Victoria & Albert Museum, London
1996 *Liliane Lijn: Her Mother's Voice,* The Eagle Gallery, London
1997 *Koanscones,* Galerie Lara Vincy, Paris

Selected Group Exhibitions:

1967 *Lumière et Mouvement,* Musée d'Art Moderne, Paris
1970 *Kinetic Art,* Hayward Gallery, London
1981 *British Sculpture in the 20th Century,* Whitechapel Art Gallery, London
1983 *Electra,* Musée d'Art Moderne, Paris
1985 *Livres d'Artistes,* Centre Georges Pompidou, Paris
1986 *Technologia e Informatica,* at the *Biennale,* Venice
1988 *Licht und Tranparenz,* Museum Bellerive, Zurich
1989 Artec '89, Nagoya, Japan
1991 *Les Artistes et la Lumière,* Le Manège, Reims, France
1992 *Estampes et Livres d'Artistes du XXe Siècle,* Bibliothèque Nationale, Paris
1993 *The Sixties Art Scene in London,* Barbican Art Gallery, London
1994 *Art Unlimited,* South Bank Centre Touring Exhibition, Glasgow
1995 *Modern British Sculpture,* Tate Gallery, Liverpool
British Abstract Art: Sculpture, Angela Flowers Gallery, London
Livres d'Artiste, Galerie Lara Vincy, Paris
Artists Books, Asbaek Gallery, Copenhagen
1996 *Chimeriques Polymeres,* Musée d'Art Modern de la Ville de Nice, Nice

Collections:

Tate Gallery, London; Arts Council of Great Britain, London; Victoria and Albert Museum, London; Musée de la Ville, Paris; Museum of Modern Art, New York; Aberdeen Art Gallery; Arts Council of Great Britain; Bibliothèque Nationale, Paris; Centre Nationale d'Art Contemporain, Paris; Museum of Fine Arts, Bern; Museum of New South Wales, Sydney.

Publications:

By LIJN: Books—*Crossing Map,* New York 1975, London 1983; *6 Throws of the Oracular Keys,* Paris 1982; *Her Mother's Voice,* published privately, 1996. **Articles—**''The Takis Dialogues 2'' and ''1964 Electron Notes'' in *Signals* (London), October 1964; ''Poem Machines'' in *Rohbo* (Paris), no. 4, 1968; ''The Inside of a Work Is to Find Out'' in *Art and Artist* (London), January 1971; ''Inside and Out'' and ''Notes on Anti-Gravity Koans'' in *Flash Art* (Milan), February 1971; ''All People Are Artists'' in *Ink* (London), September 1971; ''Reflection,'' ''3 Poems'' and ''Time Zone'' in *Grosseteste Review* (Bicester), vol. 4, no. 2, 1971; ''What Is Art?'' in *Ostrich* (Whitley Bay), September 1973; ''A Code of Form'' in *Upstart* (New York), Spring 1978; ''Hexagram'' in *Harpers and Queens* (London), December 1980; ''Receiving Change'' in *Resurgence* (London), May/June 1981; ''Artists on the 70s'' in *Studio International* (London), 1981; ''If'' in *New Departures* (London), no. 14, 1982; ''Fans—An Unrealised Project, from Unrealised Projects'' in *Arte Factum,* vol, 8, no. 8, April/May 1987; ''Imagine the Goddess!'' in *Leonardo* (Oxford), no. 2, 1987; ''Light Matters'' in *Women's Art Magazine,* no. 62, January/February 1995. **Films—***What Is the Sound of*

One Hand Clapping?, 1973; *The Power Game,* with Alastair Mackintosh, 1974.

On LIJN: Books—*La Lune en Rodage* by Karl Lazlo, Basel 1964; *Kinetic Art* by Frank Popper, Paris 1967; *Kinetic Art* by Guy Brett, London 1967; *Movements in Art since 1945* by Edward Lucie Smith, London 1969; *Open Air Sculpture in Britain* by W.J. Strachan, London 1984; *British Art Since 1900* by Frances Spalding, London 1986; *Liliane Lijn: Imagine the Goddess,* exhibition catalog with text by Jasia Reichardt, London 1987; *Sculpture Since 1945* by Edward Lucie-Smith, London, 1987; *University of Warwick Collection* by Katherine Eustace and Victoria Pomery, Warwick, 1991; *Architects Choice: Art and Architecture in Great Britain Since 1945* by Eugene Rosenberg, London, 1992; *Art in the Electronic Age* by Frank Popper, London 1993; *Art Unlimited, Multiples of the 1960s and the 1990s,* Tokyo, 1994. **Articles—**''Art as Research: The Experiments of Liliane Lijn'' by Cyril Barrett in *Studio International* (London), June 1967; ''Liliane Lijn in Discussion with Vera Lindsay'' in *Studio International* (London), May 1969; ''Functionalism of Art'' by Alastair Mackintosh in *Art and Artists* (London), March 1973; ''Beyond Light'' by John Spurling in *New Statesman* (London), 24 December 1976; ''Patterns of Light and Shadow'' by Marina Vaizey in *The Sunday Times* (London), 2 January 1977; ''Let There be Light'' by Michael Shepherd in *The Sunday Telegraph* (London), 9 January 1977; ''Liliane Lijn'' by Cyril Barrett in *Art Monthly* (London), February 1977; ''Feminist Themes'' by Richard Rush in *The Listener* (London), 28 September 1978; ''Liliane Lijn'' by Michael Shepherd in *Arts Review* (London), 19 December 1980; ''Liliane Lijn at the Roundhouse'' by Tam Giles in *Artscribe* (London), no. 27, 1981; ''Interference in Plain Air'' by Deanna Peterbridge in *Architectural Review* (London), April 1982; ''Die Grosse Verfurhrung'' by Friedmann Malsch in *Kunstforum International* (Mainz), October 1986; ''Artists Books: On the Map'' by Cathy Courtney in *Art Monthly* (London), July-August 1993; ''Energie'' in *Art,* no. 10, October 1993; ''Dragon's Dance'' by Henry Lydiate in *Art Monthly,* no. 186, May 1995; ''Family Matters'' by Cathy Courtney in *Art Monthly,* no. 197, June 1996.

*

I am particularly interested in the different ways time embeds itself in our bodies and in the earth. By time I mean changes. I have in the past worked with time in geometrical, formal and kinetic works. In the 1990s I explored Time through the medium of Memory. I asked myself if memories could be stored in the body and if so what would they tell and how would that appear. I wanted to make the unconscious visible, to see its eerie light. I began with cast bronze fragments taken off my body, which I later assembled contrasting the figurative bronze body casts with stacked mica and argon or neon. The mica symbolised the earth for me, the ''gleb'' we all emerge from and to which we will eventually return. The argon or neon which runs like a river of light through the centre of the body to the head refers both to the unconscious and the *kundalini* or *chi* energy.

I wanted to look at my *self* from as many points of view as possible. I knew little about my family history and I thought of writing an autobiography. (Autobiography = life/time.) I interviewed my mother beginning with her memories of her grandparents and her parents, then her childhood during the turbulent period of the Russian Revolution and her experience of Nazi Germany where she had lived before immigrating to the United States. From these interviews I created an artist's book, *Her Mother's Voice,* in which I looked for myself through her. I found the material I had collected in the form of sound tapes, vido and hundreds of archival photographs so interesting and rich that I decided to look at the same subject through the medium of video. From that came a film and five narrative sculptures. In the latter I use small fragments of my body such as an elbow or a shoulder and with them create landscapes through which memory speaks in the form of very brief and miniature video images. I am fascinated by the connections between on the one hand memory and dreams, and on the other the body and the earth. I am interested in change and the way we perceive it framed in a linear unidirectional time. Could there be a different way of perceiving change, another kind of time?

—Liliane Lijn

* * *

Liliane Lijn is an artist who is fascinated by science, philosophy (particularly oriental philosophy) and words, that is, what one can do with words. She is not so much concerned with science itself or ''art for a scientific age,'' as much the beauties and mysteries which science reveals and the possibilities for exploring these beauties which modern technology can offer the artist. And overriding all this is her oriental philosophical approach to the phenomena which science investigates.

Her approach to her work is intuitive, pragmatic and aesthetic. It has nothing to do with scientific research into optics, motion or related topics. This impression may have been given by the fact that, after a period of painting surrealist pictures (a not insignificant factor in her future development), she burst on the artistic scene as an optical-kinetic artist; and, like it or not, so, in part, she has remained, though by no means exclusively.

Among her early works in this field was a series of rotating perspex discs containing globules of water which acted as lenses and changed in size as the temperature and movement and the pressure of transparent spheres crossing the surface of the disc affected them. The moving spheres in turn reflected and magnified the globules or watery lenses, which, because of their liquidity, were alive and vibrant. A wonderful combination of rhythmic movement, light and vitality.

Light, pure white or refracted (coloured), as it traverses a prism, has been a persistent interest of hers since that time. So has the prism as a solid, crystalline object. The prisms, arranged in groups, bear a curious relationship to one another, like the monumental stones in a megalithic complex. Added to this, they produced spectral colours as one moves around them.

Another preoccupation of Lijn's is with cones. She has to put them to all manner of artistic uses. At first they were used as a kind of kinetic concrete poetry. Letters were written on rotating cones. These could be formed into words. But, unlike static poetry, the spectator did not know (or could not remember) what letters were coming next: it was a new form of concrete poetry.

Subsequent uses to which the cones have been put include (a) their articulation, so that parts can swivel, and, in so doing, set up various kinds of relationships with other cones; (b) the insertion of tubes of neon light into the cones, which spiral upwards and downwards as the cones rotate; (c) dissected, transparent cones, made of wire mesh or metal sections. The latter two uses of the cone have been developed to form monumental works, such as the ''White Koan,'' which now stands outside the Arts Centre of the University of Warwick, and ''Split Spiral Spin'' in the Birchwood Science Park, Warrington New Town. Both are objects of interest in their own right, that is, as static objects of contemplation; but they are interesting also for their kinetic effects, the liquid flow of light or the sounds of the wind in the mesh and the changing moiré patterns as one walks around the object.

Another device which Lijn has used to good effect is the rotating cylinder, unevenly coiled with wire (as on a resistance coil), which produces subtle ripples of light as it rotates. These come in various sizes and in combinations, usually groups of two or three. They may also be combines, to stunning effect, with ''lenses,'' as in the ''denslens'' series, where a cylinder is embedded in a plexiglass hemisphere which refracts spectral colours as the cylinder rotates. These cylinders lend themselves to expansion, as in the 23 rotating columns forming a curved circle of 20 feet (6.1 m) in diameter in Milton Keynes; it can look magnificent at night.

In her more recent work Lijn has returned to the confrontation of objects and has begun to produce what she calls ''totemic'' objects. These ''totems'' usually consist of a lens, mounted on a metal stem and supported by two metal flanges. Sometimes they stand on their own, sometimes they confront ''waveguides'' (a large group of rotating cylinders). They are called ''figures of light.'' This might, uncharitably, as described as ''science mysticism.'' So too might her ''kori''—stone embedded with prisms and placed in a natural environment. But, if one has a puzzled interest in what she is now doing, the quality of the works (from a, perhaps, irrelevant aesthetic point of view) is as high as ever.

—D. C. Barrett

LIN, Maya

Nationality: American. **Born:** Maya Ying Lin in Athens, Ohio, 10 October 1959. **Education:** Yale College, Major in Architecture, B.A., cum laude 1981, Yale University, School of Architecture, M.Arch. 1986. **Career:** Architect and artist best known for her design of the Vietnam Veterans Memorial; worked at Maya Lin Studio, New York, from 1986. Visiting Artist, Yale University School of Art, Sculpture Department, 1992; Artist in Residence, Wexner Center for the Arts, 1993; Pilchuck Residency, Pilchuck, Washington, 1994; Avenalli Professorship, University of California at Berkeley, Townsend Center for the Humanities, 1995; William A. Bernoudy Resident in Architecture, American Academy in Rome, Rome, Italy, 1998. Visiting lecturer at Rochester Arts and Lectures Series, Rochester, New York; Smithsonian Institution, Washington, D.C.; City Arts and Lectures, San Francisco, California; Portland Arts and Lectures, Portland, Oregon; University Bookstore, Seattle, Washington; Walker Art Center, Minneapolis, Minnesota; Cooper Union School of Art, New York; Ball State University, Muncie, Indiana; Denver Art Museum, Denver, Colorado; Duke University, Durham, North Carolina; Philadelphia Museum of Art, Philadelphia, Pennsylvania; Whitney Museum, New York; University of Washington, School of Art; American Institute of Architects National Convention, ''Women in Architecture''; Metropolitan Museum of Art, New York; Harvard University, Boston; Qinghua University, School of Architecture, Beijing; San Francisco Museum of Modern Art. **Awards:** American Institute of Architects Honor Award, 1984; NEA Visual Artists Fellowship, Sculpture, 1988; Presidential Design Award, 1988; New York Women's Agenda, Star Award, 1994; American Academy of Arts and Letters Award in Architecture, 1996; LVMH, Science pour L'Art Award, 1996; The Industrial Designers Excellence Awards, Industrial Designers Society of America, for the Knoll series,1999; Frank Annunzio Award Winner for the Arts, Christopher Columbus Foundation, 2000; Honorary Doctorate of Fine Arts: Yale University, Williams College, Smith College. **Address:** Maya Lin Studio, New York.

Selected Individual Exhibitions:

1993 *Public/Private,* Wexner Center for the Arts, Columbus, Ohio
1997 *Designing Industrial Ecology,* Bronx Community Paper Company, Municipal Art Society, New York,
1998 *Maya Lin,* American Academy, Rome
Maya Lin: Topologies, Southeastern Center for Contemporary Art, Winston-Salem, North Carolina (traveled)
1999 *Maya Lin: Recent Work,* Gagosian Gallery, Los Angeles
2000 *Between Art and Architecture,* Arthur A. Houghton Jr. Gallery, Cooper Union School of Art, New York

Selected Group Exhibitions:

1984 *American Women Artists-The Younger Generation,* Sidney Janis Gallery, New York
1985 *Sites and Solutions: Recent Public Art,* Freedman Gallery, Albright College
1987 *Avante-Garde in the Eighties,* Los Angeles County Museum of Art, California
1988 *60's to 80's Sculpture Parallels,* Sidney Janis Gallery, New York
1991 *Social Sculpture,* Vrej Baghoomian Gallery, New York
Working with Wax, Tibor di Nagy Gallery, New York
1992 *Culture Bites,* Connecticut College, New London, Connecticut
Ornament, John Post Lee Gallery, New York
1993 *Presence,* Ramnarine Gallery, Long Island City, New York
1994 *Critical Mass,* Yale University, New Haven, Connecticut
1996 *Extended Minimalism,* Max Protetch Gallery, New York
1997 *The Private Eye in Public Art,* New York
Stung by Splendor, Cooper Union, New York
1999 *Capturing Time: The New York Times Capsule,* American Museum of Natural History
Tomorrow Land, Alan Koppel Gallery, Chicago, Illinois
Designing the Future: Three Directions for the New Millennium, Philadelphia Museum of Art, Philadelphia, Pennsylvania
Urban Mythologies: The Bronx Represented Since the 1960's, Bronx Museum of the Arts, New York
Powder, Aspen Art Museum, Colorado
Group Show, Gagosian Gallery, New York
2000 *Women Designers in the USA, 1900–2000: Diversity and Difference,* Bard Graduate Center, New York

Maya Lin's Vietnam Veterans Memorial in Washington, D.C.

Silver and Gold, Baldwin Gallery, Aspen, Colorado (traveled)

Illusions of Eden: Visions of the American Heartland, Columbus Museum of Art, Ohio (traveled United States and abroad)

Nature: Contemporary Art and the Natural World, Marywood University, Scranton, Pennsylvania

Public Installations:

Vietnam Veterans Memorial, Washington, D.C., 1981; *Civil Rights Memorial,* Southern Poverty Law Center, Montgomery, Alabama, 1989; *Topo,* (with Henry Arnold, Landscape Architect), Charlotte Coliseum, Charlotte, North Carolina, 1991; *The Womens' Table,* Yale University, New Haven, Connecticut, 1993; *Groundswell,* Wexner Center for the Arts, Columbus, Ohio, 1993; *Eclipsed Time,* Long Island Railroad, Pennsylvania Station, New York, 1994; *The Wave Field,* FXB Aerospace Building, University of Michigan, Ann Arbor, Michigan, 1995; *Sounding Stones,* GSA/Federal Courthouse, New York, 1996; *100 North,* Rockefeller Foundation, New York, 1997; *A Shift in the Stream,* Principal Financial Headquarters, Des Moines, Iowa, 1997; *Reading a Garden,* (collaboration with Tan Lin), Cleveland Public Library, Cleveland, Ohio, 1998; *Time Table,* Stanford University, Palo Alto, California, 2000.

Publications:

By LIN: Books—*Maya Lin Boundaries,* New York 2000.

On LIN: Books—*Earthworks and Beyond* by John Beardsley, New York 1988; *Contemporary Public Sculpture* by Harriet Senie, Oxford University Press, 1992; *Civil Architecture: The New Urban Infrastructure* by Richard Dattner, New York 1994. **Articles—**''A Tale of Two Memorials'' by Elizabeth Hess in *Art in America,* April 1983; ''Vietnam Memorial'' edited by Alice Hall in *National Geographic,* May 1985; ''First She Looks Inward'' by Jonathan Coleman in *Time,* November 6, 1989; ''Like A Mighty Stream'' by John Beardsley in *Landscape Architecture,* vol. 80, no. 1, January 1990; ''The Symmetry of Maya Lin'' by Jill Kirschenbaum in *MS,* September 1990; ''Assemblage, Bricollage and the I- Meg Cranston, Melissa Kretchmer and Maya Lin'' by Saul Ostrow in *BOMB,* Spring 1991; ''Monument Maker'' by Peter Tauber in *New York Times Magazine,* February 24, 1991; ''On Nationality: 13 Artists'' by Lillian Wei in *Art in America,* September 1991; ''Civil Rights Memorial'' by William Zinsser in *Smithsonian,* September 1991; ''Culture Bites, Slices of Modern Life'' by William Zimmer in *New York Times,* Connecticut Ed. February 22, 1992; ''Cross Cultural Journey'' by Donald Albecht in *Architecture, Architecture for the Arts,* July 1993; ''Profile: Maya Lin After the Wall'' by Mark Alden Branch in

Progressive Architecture, August 1994; ''Maya Lin, *Groundswell,* Wexner Center for the Arts, Columbus, Ohio'' by Kate Hensley in *Sculpture,* January-February 1994; ''Maya Lin: Art and the Discreet Architect'' by Carol Vogel in *International Herald Tribune,* May 11, 1994; ''Maya Lin: Space and Place'' by Judith Stein in *Art in America,* December 1994; ''Les Paysages de Maya Lin'' by Philip E. Jodidio in *Connaissance des Arts,* September 1995; ''Beyond the Wall: Maya Lin's New Projects Share the Simple Elegance of Her Vietnam Memorial'' by Benjamin Forgey in *Washington Post,* October 22, 1995; ''She Got Where She Is Because She Is an Artist'' by Michael S. Bell in *Artweek,* August 1995; ''The Other Side of Maya Lin'' by Charles Gandee in *Vogue,* April 1995; ''Maya Lin's Power of the Serene'' by Paul Goldberger in *New York Times,* October 29, 1995; ''Making Waves at Michigan'' by Leslie Findlen in *ID,* May-June 1996; ''Maya Lin Finds Inspiration in the Architecture of Nature'' by Victoria Rowen in *Architectural Record,* September 1998; ''Distillations of Landscape'' by Eleanor Heartney in *Art in America,* September 1998; ''Maya Lin: Grey Art Gallery'' by Katie Clifford in *ArtNews,* November 1998; ''Maya Lin: Southeastern Center for Contemporary Art'' by Linda Johnson Dougherty in *Sculpture,* May-June 1998; ''Architect Maya Lin Creates Her First Line of Furniture For Knoll,'' in *Architectural Record,* June 1998; ''Maya Lin Finds Inspiration in the Architecture of Nature'' by Victoria C. Rowan in *Architectural Record,* September 1998; ''Greening a South Bronx Brownfield'' by Herbert Muschamp in *New York Times,* January 23, 1998; ''Maya Lin: Southeastern Center for Contemporary Art'' by Chuck Twardy *New Art Examiner,* September 1998; ''Grand Illusions'' by Pilar Viladas in *New York Times Magazine,* February 21, 1999; ''Record Interiors 1999'' by Sarah Amelar in *Architectural Record,* September 1999; ''More Than A Memorialist in The Guardian,'' by Hugh Aldersey-Williams in *Space* (London), April 22, 1999; ''Architecture's Quiet Soul'' by Fred Bernstein in *Blueprint,* May 1999; ''Maya Lin Reconsidered'' by Eleanor M. Hight in *Design Book Review,* Fall 1999; ''The A. 100: 100 Most Influential Asian Americans of the Decade,'' in *A. Magazine,* October-November 1999; ''Apartment in New York'' in *Detail Magazine,* March 2000; ''Somewhere Between Art and Architecture'' by Christopher Hawthorne in *Metropolis,* October 2000; ''Kuhler Kunstgriff'' by Claudia Steinberg in *Architektur & Wohnen,* February-March 2000; ''Making Waves'' by Cay Sophie Rabinowitz in *Art Papers Magazine,* March-April 2000; ''Rock, Paper, Vision Artist Maya Lin Goes Beyond Her Powerful Vietnam Memorial'' by Robert Campbell in *Boston Globe,* November 30, 2000. **Film**—*Maya Lin: A Strong Clear Vision,* Frieda Mock (director), American Film Foundation Production (Academy Award Winner, Best Documentary), 1995.

* * *

Maya Lin achieved notoriety at age twenty-one, when her design was selected for the Vietnam Memorial in Washington D.C. in 1981. Since then Lin has produced three kinds of work: architecture, public monuments, and smaller sculptures shown in galleries (what she calls ''studio art''). She never got her architect's license. She admits to not knowing how to draw on a computer and is not interesting in doing so. ''Architects call me a sculptor, and sculptors call me an architect. I don't think either wants to claim me,'' she told a sold-out audience at the Metropolitan Museum of Art in 1990.

All of her work maintains a sense of human scale and intimacy and establishes a connection between the viewer and the art object. Lin filters the massive and popular into the private and individual with her work. Her employment of pure indigenous materials, including rock, wood, and water; her respect for the natural environment and her keen observation mark her as an architectural humanist. In her recent book Lin says, ''Sculpture to me is like poetry, and architecture is like prose.''

A minimalist par excellence, her artwork follows a program of pared-down forms that make reference to landscape. She has an interest in stratigraphic layers of earth and topography and oceanography, which provide inspiration for her large and small works alike. Ancient burial mounds in Southeastern Ohio, where Lin grew up, informed her ''Wave Field'' (1995). ''Wave Field'' a work at the University of Michigan in Ann Arbor, is one Lin feels is among her finest. It is an earthwork based on a repetitive wave that suggests the dynamics of flight. Soil and sand make the swells and sod the crests of the waves. (It was commissioned for the university's Aerospace Engineering Building.) ''10 Degrees North'' (1997), which Lin designed for the Rockefeller Foundation in New York, contains a stone map of the earth with water percolating up through it.

When the Wexner Center for the Arts in Columbus, Ohio, awarded her a visual arts residency in 1993 to create a permanent, site-specific work in the building, exhibitions director Sarah J. Rogers decided to organize the first comprehensive survey of Lin's creative output. The retrospective show, *Maya Lin: Public/Private,* covered ten years of Lin's work. It consisted of photographs, drawings, and scale models of her public monuments and commissions, a selection of her studio sculpture, and ''Groundswell,'' the permanent installation that she created for the Center. ''Groundswell'' is forty tons of recycled auto glass from Ford Motor Co. carefully poured into mounds in the three outdoor spaces at the Center.

Topologies, an exhibition of her work at the Southeastern Center for Contemporary Art (SECCA) in Winston-Salem, North Carolina, comprises seven major artworks, including sculptures, installations, and works on paper. In it, the monumental ''Untitled (Topographic Landscape)'' possesses movement expressed in particle-board waves. ''Avalanche'' was a 21-foot tall mountain of glass shards poured into a gallery corner. ''Flatlands,'' a series of 10 monoprints from 1997, created by inking pieces of broken glass, is minimal and pure in form, like fragments of water, rock, or ice—captured on paper.

''Phases of the Moon'' (1998) is eight luminescent orbs of beeswax formed in subtle variations in size, thickness, and angle. Mounted on the wall, the orbs cast crescent shadows. ''Crater Series'' (1997) is eleven small rectangular slabs of wax, each pierced with an eroded irregular-shaped hole, on a steel shelf. ''Rock Field'' (1997) is forty-three blown glass ''rocks'' scattered randomly on the floor, like an imaginary beach or moonscape. Her clock-sculpture ''Eclipsed Time'' (1994) commissioned by New York's Metropolitan Transportation Authority was based on a lunar eclipse, and made up of a moving disk and frame without traditional hands. In Penn Station's Long Island Railroad Station ticketing area, Lin hopes it will become a fulcrum in the station that sees over 250,000 visitors a day.

Lin has created a line of furniture to honor Knoll's design philosophy and tradition on the occasion of its 60th anniversary. ''The Maya Lin Collection: The Earth is Not Flat'' was inspired by her travels to New Zealand and the South Pacific. In muted earth tones and sturdy shapes, the collection recalls the Knoll legacy of purist form and clean materials.

Freida Lee Mock's documentary, *Maya Lin: A Strong Clear Vision,* won the Academy Award for Best Documentary in 1995. It provided much needed closure to the artist over the controversy surrounding her earliest monument designs and inspired her to document her work with supporting texts. She spent three years creating *Boundaries,* which she calls a visual-verbal sketchbook, half written and half images. In her essay ''Shaping the Earth'' she pays tribute to her father's pervasive influence, as a working potter and artist of Chinese origin and zen aesthetic.

Although her greatest reputation is as a monument maker, she hopes to do only one more memorial: one to the vanished species of the earth.

—Deirdre Donohue

LINS, Pam

Nationality: American. **Born:** Chicago, Illinois, 1959. **Education:** University of Minnesota, B.A.; Hunter College, CUNY, M.F.A., 1993. **Family:** Married Jeff Davis in 1995 (divorced 1998). **Career:** Adjunct assistant professor, Fashion Institute of Technology, New York, 1994 to present; sculpture instructor, Caldwell College, 1998; visiting artist, Princeton University, 1998; faculty, fine arts, Cooper Union School of Art, 1999. **Awards:** Macdowell Colony Residency, 1990; Pollack/Krasner Grant, 1992; Yaddo Artist Residency, 1993. **Agent:** Ten in One Gallery, 426 West 26th Street, New York, New York. **Address:** 285 North 6th Street, Brooklyn, New York 11211.

Selected Individual Exhibitions:

1997 Ten in One Gallery, New York
1999 *Hot Snow,* Ten in One Gallery, New York
2001 Ten in One Gallery, Chicago, Illinois

Selected Group Exhibitions:

1993 *Projects,* Sculpture Center, New York
1994 *Karen Bowie/Pam Lins,* ad hoc Gallery, Toronto, Canada
1995 *Ooooze,* Black and Heron Gallery, New York
1997 *Working in Brooklyn,* Brooklyn Museum of Art, New York
1999 *Answer Yes, No, or I Don't Know,* Andrew Kreps Gallery, New York
Hang Time, White Columns, New York
New Museum Benefit, New Museum of Contemporary Art, New York
2000 *New York Projects,* Delfina Arts, London
Achieving Failure, Cincinatti Art Museum, Ohio

Publications:

On LINS: Articles—''The Suggestive Object'' by Roberta Smith in *New York Times,* 1991; ''The Kitsch Connection'' by Fred Camper in *Chicago Reader,* 24 January 1997; ''Hey, You Never Know'' by Sarah Schmerler in *Time Out New York,* 23 April 1998; ''Hang Time'' by Bill Arning in *Time Out,* 29 July, 1999; ''Cheer for the Brit Art Scene'' by Allison Roberts in *Evening Standard,* July 2000; ''Delphina Projects'' by Laura Moffet in *Art Monthly,* September 2000.

*

I have always felt that I work more like a fiction writer than a visual artist—I guess. In art—it is what I don't know that I am interested in. That I don't know what I will make next. In looking at art, it is the work that is difficult, and a struggle to comprehend, that takes me in.

—Pam Lins

LIPPOLD, Richard

Nationality: American. **Born:** Milwaukee, Wisconsin, 3 May 1915. **Education:** School of the Art Institute of Chicago, 1933–37; University of Chicago, 1933–37, B.F.A. in industrial design 1937; also studied music and dance in Chicago during the 1930s. **Family:** Married Louise Greuel in 1940; children: Lisa, Tiana, and Ero. **Career:** Industrial Designer, Cherry-Burrell Corporation, Chicago, New York, Cedar Rapids, Iowa, and Baltimore, 1937–41; also worked in a freelance design partnership, Milwaukee, 1937–41; began to work in wire sculpture and wrote music, 1942; moved to New York, 1944; lives in Locust Valley, New York, since 1955. Instructor, University of Michigan, Ann Arbor, 1941–44, and Goddard College, Plainfield, Vermont, 1945–47; head of the art department, Trenton Junior College, New Jersey, 1947–52; part-time teacher, Queens College, New York, 1947–48; artist-in-residence, Black Mountain College, Beria, North Carolina, 1948; professor of art, Hunter College, New York, 1952–65. **Awards:** Third Prize, Sculpture Competition, Tate Gallery, London, 1952; Creative Arts Award, Brandeis University, Waltham, Massachusetts, 1958; Honor Award, American Institute of Architects, Chicago, 1959; Silver Medal, Architectural League of New York, 1960; Merit Award, Municipal Art Society, New York, 1963; Fine Arts Medal, American Institute of Architects, Chicago, 1970. D.F.A.: Ripon College, Wisconsin, 1968. Member, National Institute of Arts and Letters, 1963. **Address:** Post Office Box 248, Locust Valley, New York 11560. U.S.A.

Individual Exhibitions:

1947 Willard Gallery, New York
Detroit Institute of Arts (with Peter Blume and David Smith)
1948 Willard Gallery, New York
1950 Willard Gallery, New York
1952 Willard Gallery, New York
1953 Willard Gallery, New York
Layton Art Gallery, Milwaukee
1958 Brandeis University, Waltham, Massachusetts

Richard Lippold. Library of Congress.

1960 Corcoran Gallery, Washington, D.C.
1962 Willard Gallery, New York
1968 Willard Gallery, New York
1973 Willard Gallery, New York
1988 Biennale, Venice
1990 Haggerty Museum, Milwaukee (catalog)
1999 Nassau County Museum of Art, New York
Whitney Museum of Art, New York

Selected Group Exhibitions:

1946 *Origins of Modern Sculpture,* Detroit Institute of Arts
1947 *Whitney Annual,* Whitney Museum, New York
1954 *Salute to France,* Musée d'Art Moderne, Paris
15 Americans, Museum of Modern Art, New York
1964 *New Members,* National Institute of Arts and Letters, New York
1979 *200 Years of American Sculpture,* Whitney Museum, New York
1980 *Photographs by Artists,* Los Angeles County Museum of Art
1981 *Contemporary Art Since 1939,* Kunsthalle, Cologne
1985 *Flying Tigers: Painting and Sculpture in New York,* Rhode Island School of Design, Providence (traveled to Worcester, Massachusetts)
1988 *43rd Biennale,* Venice

Collections:

Museum of Modern Art, New York; Metropolitan Museum of Art, New York; Whitney Museum, New York; Wadsworth Atheneum, Hartford, Connecticut; Virginia Museum of Fine Arts, Richmond; Detroit Institute of Arts; Milwaukee Art Center; Des Moines Art Center, Iowa; Addison Gallery of American Art, Andover; Detroit Art Institute; Brooks Gallery, Memphis; Mobile Art Museum, Alabama; Musee de Vin, Pavillac; Munson-Williams-Proctor Institute, Utica.

Permanent Public Installations:

Inland Steel Building, Chicago; Lincoln Center, New York; Pan-Am Building, New York; St. Mary's Cathedral, San Francisco; Duomo, Viterbo, Italy; House of God Shinto Shrine, Kyoto Japan; Deutsche World Bank Headquarters, Frankfurt; Darina Mandarin Hotel, Singapore.

Publications:

On LIPPOLD: Books—*Contemporary American Sculptures,* by C. Ludwig Brumme, New York 1948; *Sculpture of the 20th Century* by Andrew Carnduff Ritchie, New York 1952; *Masters of Modern Art* by Alfred H. Barr, New York 1959; *The Sculpture of This Century* by Michael Seuphor, New York 1960; *Art and Life in America* by Oliver Lemkin, New York 1960; *Between the Fairs: 25 Years of American Art 1939–1964* by John I. H. Baur, New York 1964; *Direct Metal Sculpture* by Dona Z. Moilach, New York 1966; *Constructivism: Origins and Evolution* by George Rickey, New York 1967; *American Art since 1900: A Critical History* by Barbara Rose, New York 1967; *Form and Space: Sculpture in the 20th Century* by Eduard Trier, New York 1968. **Articles**—''Richard Lippold's Wired Universe of Gold and Silver'' by Andrea Oppenheimer Dean, vol. 13, February 1983; ''The Ascendancy of Abstraction for Public Art: The Monument to the Unknown Political Prisoner Competition'' by Joan Marter in *Art Journal,* vol. 53, no. 4, Winter 1994.

*

Born into a place and an age in which space and time are our principal companions, I find it inevitable to love them more than the solid materials with which my ancestors were involved. We of this moment have learned to hurl ourselves through space, time, and energy with speeds and sensations beyond even the dreams of our forefathers. Yet for all the excitements of these experiences, the means of sensory perception, of intellectual contemplation, and of emotional response are unchanged; they continue to be responsible for all the tensions of human behavoir, both within the individual and in his contact with all other beings; human, natural and artificial.

What a pleasure to be secure in the heart of all mankind and at once to be free in this security for exploration into aspects of earthly and cosmic realities which have been hidden to our knowledge until

Richard Lippold with one of his wire sculptures. ©Corbis.

this instant! Courage to explore is not involved; it is simply a question of ''doing what comes naturally'' when one is free to find the form for his work in the challenge of new technologies and concepts—from suspension bridges to nuclear fission and space probes—from ancient yearnings for communication with the unknown. Wherein else lies the creative impulse?

—Richard Lippold

* * *

Richard Lippold may not be a pioneer, but he is definitely one of the most successful light experimentalists in the United States, where interest in light sculpture increased suddenly during the 1960s as it took many different forms. Since the late 1940s Lippold has produced a series of impressive and memorable architectural/sculptural structures which are intricately composed of polished gold wires and plaques. His metallic creations have acquired over the years a philosophical-symbolic-religious bent which makes them even more relevant to our pragmatic society.

Although modernist in conception and style, Lippold's works often bring to mind the illusionistic virtuosity of the great Baroque decorators of the seventeenth century in Italy, for example his ''Baldacchino'' over the alter of St. Mary's Cathedral in San Francisco (1965–67). The great majority of his works shine with iridescent luminescence.

—Jean-Luc Bordeaux

LOBDELL, Frank

Nationality: American. **Born:** Kansas City, Missouri, 1921. **Education:** St. Paul School of Fine Arts, Minnesota, 1938–39; California School of Fine Arts, San Francisco, 1947–50; and Academie de la Grande Chaumiere, Paris, 1950–51. **Military Service:** Served as a lieutenant in the United States Army, 1942–46. **Career:** Painter: lived and worked in St. Paul and Minneapolis, 1940–42, and in Sausalito, California, 1945–48; established studio in the Mission District of San Francisco, 1948. Instructor, 1957–65, and chairman of the graduate program, 1963, California School of Fine Arts, San Francisco. Artist-in-residence, 1965, and from 1966 member of the faculty, Stanford University, California. **Awards:** Artists Council Prize, 1948, and Purchase Prize, 1950, *Annual Drawing and Painting Exhibition,* San Francisco Museum of Art; San Francisco Bank Prize, Annual Oil,

Tempera and Sculpture Exhibition, San Francisco Museum of Art, 1950; Adaline Kent Annual Award for a Californian Artist, 1960; Nealie Sullivan Award, San Francisco Museum of Art, 1960; Tamarind Fellowship, 1966; Medal for Distinguished Achievement in Painting, American Academy and Institute of Arts and Letters, 1988; Academy Purchase Award, American Academy and Institute of Arts and Letters, 1992 and 1994. **Agents:** Campbell-Thiebaud Gallery, 645 Chestnut Street, San Francisco, California 94133, U.S.A. **Address:** 2769 Octavia Street, Apt. 3, San Francisco, California 94123, U.S.A.

Individual Exhibitions:

1958 Martha Jackson Gallery, New York
1960 De Young Memorial Museum, San Francisco
Martha Jackson Gallery, New York
1961 Pasadena Art Museum, California
Drawings by Richard Diebenkorn and Frank Lobdell, Pasadena Art Museum, California
1962 Ferus Gallery, Los Angeles
1963 Martha Jackson Gallery, New York
Pasadena Art Museum, California (retrospective)
Drawings by Elmer Bischoff, Richard Diebenkorn and Frank Lobdell, Palace of the Legion of Honor, San Francisco
1964 Galerie D. Benador, Geneva
1965 Galerie Anderson-Mayer, Paris
1966 Pasadena Art Museum, California
1967 Maryhurst College, Oregon
1969 San Francisco Museum of Modern Art
1970 St. Mary's College, Moraga, California
1972 Martha Jackson Gallery, New York
1978 Smith-Anderson Gallery, Palo Alto, California
1981 Reed College Art Gallery, Portland, Oregon
1983 San Francisco Museum of Modern Art
1990 Campbell-Thiebaud Gallery, San Francisco, California
1991 Smith Andersen Gallery, Palo Alto, California
1992 M. H. deYoung Memorial Museum, San Francisco, California
Campbell-Theibaud Gallery, San Francisco, California
1993 *Works, 1947–1992,* Stanford University Art Museum, California
1995 Campbell-Thiebaud Gallery, San Francisco, California
1996 Davidson Gallery, Seattle, Washington
1998 *Master Artist V,* Hearst Art Gallery, Saint Mary's College of California, Moraga, California

Selected Group Exhibitions:

1955 *Bienal,* Sao Paulo
1956 *California Artists,* Santa Barbara Museum of Art, California
1962 *The Artist's Environment: West Coast,* University of California at Los Angeles (traveled to the Oakland Art Museum, California, and the Amon Carter Museum, Fort Worth, Texas)
50 California Artists, Whitney Museum, New York
1969 *Kompas 4,* Van Abbemuseum, Eindhoven, Netherlands
1972 *Painting Annual,* Whitney Museum, New York
1980 *Bay Area Art: Then and Now,* Suzanne Brown Gallery, Scottsdale, Arizona
1987 *American Painting: Abstract Expressionism and After,* San Francisco Museum of Modern Art
1991 *Abstraction Redefined,* Olga Dollar Gallery, San Francisco, California
1992 IPA Gallery, Boston, Massachusetts
Recent Acquisitions in Context, M. H. deYoung Memorial Museum, San Francisco, California
1994 *Purchase Exhibition,* American Academy and Institute of Arts and Letters, New York
1995 Mulligan-Shanoski Gallery, San Francisco, California
1996 SFMOMA Rental Gallery, San Francisco
1997 Emmie Smock Gallery, San Francisco
Portland Art Museum International Print Exhibition, Portland, Oregon

Collections:

Los Angeles County Museum of Art; Norton Simon Museum of Art, Pasadena, California; Stanford University, Berkeley, California.

Publications:

On LOBDELL: Books—*Frank Lobdell, Paintings and Graphics from 1948–1965,* exhibition catalog with essay by Walter Hopps, Stanford, California 1966; *Frank Lobdell,* exhibition catalog with essays by Thomas Albright and Peter Boswell, San Francisco 1983; *Frank Lobdell, Works 1947–1992,* exhibition catalog with essay by Caroline A. Jones, Stanford, California 1993; *Frank Lobdell, Master Artist V,* exhibition catalog with essay by Marcia Tanner, Moraga, California 1998.

* * *

A large, writhing biomorphic figure, evocative at once of a human being, enveloped by volcanic blacks in thick impastos, retreats toward the edge of the canvas, arms raised, with head thrown back and mouth open in a howl of anguish, pain, and despair. Such is the tenor of Frank Lobdell's early works which, as a statement of his existential vision, create figures with enormous legs and feet, engendering a feeling of earth-boundedness, of the futility of any attempt at physical flight from pain. His work can be seen as a powerful religious experience which, as in Dante's psychic journey through the *Divine Comedy,* charts the gradual evolution of the artist's own existential philosophy. Because of the fundamental unity between art and psyche in Lobdell's work, artistic maturation and personal growth go hand in hand, each contributing to the other's development. The tragic sense of elemental conflict which gives way to a lyrical and exalted liberation in his recent work illustrates Lobdell's personal transition.

Images of personal torment and spiritual pain stemming from unknown sources emerge during the brooding period of 1953–54. The paintings frequently incorporate a smaller form alternately represented as a circle, or winged or armspread figure, usually shown in conjunction with a horizontal crescent shape. Lobdell then creates a larger figure which nearly always grasps for or surrounds the smaller form. Central to this period is the theme of the anguish caused by the discrepancy between human aspiration, symbolized by the circle or armspread figure, and human limitation, represented by the larger figure. Yet the cruciform, the armspread figure, the circle, and the crescent are all archetypal symbols, forms with associations deeply rooted in the human unconscious. Lobdell's early paintings seem to point towards an individual striving for spiritual fulfillment.

In the late 1950s Lobdell begins to augment the torment of this large ''pursuer'' figure. His piece *April 1959* depicts a figure whose main features—head, arms, and hands—are emphasized with greater detail, yet they are assembled with no reference to the body as a whole. It is, in fact, no longer a figure at all, but an agglomeration of parts—howling mouths and rigid arms culminating in clenched fists all tied together in one inchoate mass, reflecting the pursuer's anguish, frustration, and impotence.

The body/spirit duality soon evolves into the juxtaposition of a single figure in the early 1960s. The succession of figurally derived symbols of torment found in *April 1959* becomes increasingly attenuated, forming a serpentine meander which twists through the paintings with an elusive ''spirit-figure'' always at its head. As this form becomes less identifiable as a figure, a new figure emerges outside this chain with arms upraised and mouth howling. Essentially, the ''pursuer'' is a bystander witnessing the turmoil of his own internal struggle represented by the interaction between the ideal ''spirit-figure'' and the tormented forms of the serpentine trail. The paintings no longer express the juxtaposition of body and spirit, but of the self and the psychic forces which besiege it.

Lobdell's work toward the late 1960s and early 1970s incorporates nearly all the formal motifs he had developed until this time. Yet this period is distinguished by several traits which follow his subsequent career. The heavily outlined shapes that seemed to have tortuously struggled for so long for liberation from the protoplasmic environment to which they were bound, at last begin to free themselves. Lobdell achieves this by integrating symbolic and figurative forms. Inspired by Picasso's 1925 painting entitled *The Dance,* Lobdell composes a ''Dance'' series of 1970–71 which appears to be purely figurative. Yet his favorite forms and motifs embed themselves deep within the series. In *Dance V,* for example, the legs of the central figure cross to form a ''spirit-figure,'' and the mouth and edge of the arm of the right figure, painted in white, combine to form a circle-and-crescent. Because of the incorporation of symbols stemming from the unconscious into these figures, the figures themselves are not only physical entities but psychic ones as well, with body and spirit integrated into a single form.

His piece *Fall 1971* revolves in two figures overlapping in a bewildering welter of lines, with the human figure even more distorted and difficult to identify. This trend to eliminate the central figure gradually continued through the late 1970s and into the 1980s. By 1977 all figural references are abstracted beyond recognition. The central images are dominated by crescents, spheres, and spirals. Lobdell also abandons his favorite motif, the cross or ''spirit-figure.'' The paintings no longer represent the quest or yearning after the spirit. They are themselves expressions of this spirit.

From the beginning Lobdell has chosen to express himself through symbols. His career has been determined by a continuous effort to develop a visual vocabulary at once personal yet capable of achieving ever greater resonance and universality. His paintings appeal directly to the unconscious, and their power and life rests in their indefinability, their mutability, and their enigmatic persistence.

—Carrie Barker

LONG, Richard (J.)

Nationality: British. **Born:** Bristol, 2 June 1945. **Family:** Married Denise Johnston, 1969: two children. **Education:** Studied at West of England College of Art, Bristol, 1962–65; St. Martin's School of Art, London, 1966–68. **Career:** Produced first landscape artworks in England, 1967; and in Europe, North and South America, Mexico, Africa, Nepal, Australia and Japan, since 1969. **Awards:** Recipient, Turner Prize, 1989; Decorated Chevalier Order Arts & Lettres, 1990. **Agents:** Anthony d'Offay Gallery, 21 Dering Street, London, W1R 9AA; Gallery Sperone Westwater Fischer, New York. **Address:** Bristol, England.

Individual Exhibitions:

1968 Galerie Konrad Fischer, Dusseldorf
1969 John Gibson Gallery, New York
Galerie Konrad Fischer, Dusseldorf
Museum Haus Lange, Krefeld, West Germany
Galerie Yvon Lambert, Paris
Galleria Lambert, Milan
1970 Dwan Gallery, New York
Städtische Museum, Mönchengladbach, West Germany
Galerie Konrad Fischer, Dusseldorf
1971 Galleria Gian Enzo Sperone, Turin
Museum of Modern Art, Oxford
Art and Project, Amsterdam
1972 Whitechapel Art Gallery, London
Museum of Modern Art, New York
Galerie Yvon Lambert, Paris
1973 Stedelijk Museum, Amsterdam
Wide White Space, Antwerp
Galerie Konrad Fischer, Dusseldorf
Lisson Gallery, London
1974 John Weber Gallery, New York
Scottish National Gallery of Modern Art, Edinburgh
Lisson Gallery, London
1975 Galerie Konrad Fischer, Dusseldorf
Wide White Space, Antwerp
Galerie Yvon Lambert, Paris
Art and Project, Amsterdam
Galerie Rolf Preisig, Basel
Plymouth School of Art, Devon
1976 Galleria Gian Enzo Sperone, Rome
Galerie Konrad Fischer, Dusseldorf
Wide White Space, Antwerp
Lisson Gallery, London
Biennale, British Pavilion, Venice
Art Agency, Tokyo
Arnolfini Gallery, Bristol
Sperone-Westwater-Fischer, New York
1977 Whitechapel Art Gallery, London
Art and Project, Amsterdam
Gallery Akumulatory, Poznah, Poland
Galerie Rolf Preisig, Basel
Lisson Gallery, London
Kunsthalle, Bern
National Gallery of Victoria, Melbourne
Art Gallery of New South Wales, Sydney

1978 Art and Project, Amsterdam
Galerie Yvon Lambert, Paris
Galerie Konrad Fischer, Dusseldorf
Lisson Gallery, London
Park Square Gallery, Leeds, Yorkshire
Gallery Sperone-Westwater-Fischer, New York
Austellungsraum Ulrich Ruckriem, Hamburg
1979 Tate Gallery (with Naum Gabo and Paul Nash), Zurich
Anthony d'Offay Gallery, London
Galerie Rolf Preisig, Basel
Orchard Gallery, Londonderry, Northern Ireland
Photographic Gallery, Southampton University
Stediljk van Abbemuseum, Eindhoven, Netherlands
Lisson Gallery, London
Art Agency, Tokyo
Museum of Modern Art, Oxford
Tate Gallery, London (with Paul Nash and Tom Phillips)
1980 Karen and Jean Bernier, Athens
Art and Project, Amsterdam
Fogg Art Museum, Harvard University, Cambridge, Massachusetts
Sperone-Westwater-Fischer, New York
Anthony d'Offay Gallery, London
Galerie Konrad Fischer, Dusseldorf
1981 Anthony d'Offay, London (with Robert Bevan)
Sperone-Westwater-Fischer, New York
Graeme Murray Gallery, Edinburgh
Galerie Konrad Fischer, Dusseldorf
Anthony d'Offay, London
David Bellman Gallery, Toronto
Centre d'Arts Plastiques Contemporains, Bordeaux
1982 Art and Project, Amsterdam
Galerie Yvon Lambert, Paris
Flow Ace Gallery, Los Angeles
Sperone-Westwater-Fischer, New York
National Gallery of Canada, Ottawa
1983 David Bellman Gallery, Toronto
Arnolfini Gallery, Bristol
Anthony d'Offay Gallery, London
Antonio Tucci Russo, Turin
Art Agency, Tokyo
Century Cultural Center, Tokyo
Galerie Konrad Fischer, Dusseldorf
1984 Coracle Press, London
Galleria Lucio Amelio, Naples
Galerie Crousel-Hussenot, Paris
Jean Bernier Gallery, Athens
Sperone Westwater, New York
Dallas Museum of Art, Texas
Butler Gallery, Kilkenny Castle, Ireland
Orchard Gallery, Londonderry, Northern Ireland
Anthony d'Offay Gallery, London
Galerie Konrad Fischer, Dusseldorf
1985 Galerie Buchmann, Basel
Anthony d'Offay Gallery, London
Abbot Hall, Kendal, Westmoreland
Konsthall, Malmo, Sweden
Padiglione d'Arte Contemporanea, Milan
1986 Palacio de Cristal, Madrid
Galerie Croussel-Hussenot, Paris
Guggenheim Museum, New York
Sperone Westwater, New York
Anthony d'Offay Gallery, London
Porin Taidemuseo, Finland
Antonio Tucci Russo, Turin
1987 Musée Rath, Geneva
Coracle Atlantic Foundation, Liverpool, Merseyside
Donald Young Gallery, Chicago
Cairn Gallery, Nailsworth, Gloucestershire
Centre National d'Art Contemporain de Grenoble Magasin, Grenoble
Jean Bernier Gallery, Athens
1988 Galerie Konrad Fischer, Dusseldorf
Neue Galerie—Sammlung Ludwig, Aachen
Anthony d'Offay Gallery, Athens
1989 Kunstverein St. Gallen, Switzerland
Jean Bernier Gallery, Athens
Tucci Russo Gallery, Turin
Bristol Old Vic Theatre
Sperone Westwater, New York
Bristol Old Vic Theatre
Pietro Sparta Gallery, Chagny, France
La Jolla Museum of Contemporary Art, California
Henry Moore Sculpture Trust Studio, Dean Clough, Halifax, Yorkshire
1990 Arnolfini Gallery, Bristol
Anthony d'Offay Gallery, London
Angles Gallery, Los Angeles
Gallery Tschudi, Glarus, Switzerland
Galerie Konrad Fischer, Dusseldorf
Tate Gallery, London
Magasin 3 Konsthall, Stockholm
Chateau de Rochechouart, France
1991 Tate Gallery, Liverpool
St. Delsches Kunstinstitute und Stadtische Gallery, Frankfurt
Hayward Gallery, London
Galleria Tucci Russo, Turin
Sperone Westwater, New York
Scottish National Gallery of Modern Art, Edinburgh
Galerie Tschudi, Glarus
1992 Jean Bernier Gallery, Athens
Angles Gallery, Los Angeles
Mead Gallery, University of Warwick
Fundacio Espai Poblenou, Barcelona
Galerie Konrad Fischer, Dusseldorf
1993 65 Thompson Street, New York
Musée d'Art Moderne de la Ville, Paris
Inkong Gallery, Seoul
Anthony d'Offay Gallery, London
Kunstverein Bremerhaven
Center for Contemporary Art, Santa Fe, New Mexico
Newen Museum Weserburg, Bremen
Sperone Westwater, New York
1994 Kunstsdammlung, Dusseldorf
New York Public Library
Center for Contemporary Arts of Santa Fe
Palazzo delle Esposizioni, Rome
Richard Long: No Where, Pier Arts Center, Pier Arts Centre, Stromness, Scotland (catalog)

Sperone Westwater, New York
1995 *Richard Long: Here and There,* Modern Art Museum of Fort Worth, Texas (catalog)
1996 *Richard Long: Circles—Cycles—Mud—Stones,* Contemporary Art Museum, Houston (catalog)
1997 *Richard Long: Wind Circle Memory Sticks,* Wilhelm-Lehmbruck-Museum, Duisburg (catalog)
A Road from the Past to the Future: Work by Richard Long from the Haldane Collection, Crawford Arts Centre, St. Andrews, Scotland (catalog)
2000 Griffin Contemporary Gallery, Venice, California

Selected Group Exhibitions:

1972 *Documenta 5,* Kassel, Germany
1977 *Europe in the Seventies,* Art Institute of Chicago (travelled to Hirshhorn Museum and Sculpture Garden, Washington, D.C.; San Francisco Museum of Modern Art; Contemporary Arts Center, Cincinnati)
1979 *Un Certain Art Anglais,* Musee d'Art Moderne de la Ville, Paris
1980 *Biennale,* Venice
1982 *Documenta 7,* Kassel
1984 *Primitivism in 20th Century Art: An Affinity of the Tribal and the Modern,* Museum of Modern Art, New York
The Turner Prize Exhibition, Tate Gallery, London
1989 *Magiciennes de la Terre,* Grand Halle de la Villette, Paris
1994 *Biennale,* Sao Paulo
1995 *Our 100th Anniversary of Paintings of People—Pictoral Worlds,* Museum Ludwig, Cologne (catalog)
Sculpture, Anthony d'Offay, London (catalog)
1996 *A Century of English Sculpture,* Galerie Nationale du Jeu de Paume, Paris (catalog)
Public Works, Stedelijk Van Abbemuseum, Eindhoven, Netherlands (catalog)
In the Limelight, Kunsthaus Zurich (catalog)
1997 *Treasure Island,* Centro de Arte Moderna Jose de Azeredo Perdigao, Lisbon (catalog)
The Hirshhorn Collects: Recent Acquisitions, Hirshhorn Museum and Sculpture Garden, Washington, D.C. (catalog)
1998 *Arktis-Antarktis,* Kunst-und Ausstellungshalle der Bundesrepublik Deutschland, Bonn
Waves Breaking on the Shore...Ad Dekkers in His Time, Stedelijk Museum, Amsterdam (catalog)
Conceptual Photography from the 60s and 70s, David Zwirner Gallery, New York
1999 *Histoire d'Are,* Versailles
Inner Eye, Chrysler Museum, Norfolk (traveling exhibition)
Circa 1968, Serralves Museum of Contemporary Art, Oporto, Portugal
2000 *Diary on Show,* Cornerhouse, Manchester, England (traveled to Firstsite, Colchester, England)

Collections:

Tate Gallery, London; Stedelijk Museum, Amsterdam; Wallraf-Richartz Museum, Cologne; Louisiana Museum, Humlebaek, Denmark; Museum des 20 Jahrdunderts, Vienna; Musée d'Art Moderne de la Ville, Paris; Art Gallery of Victoria, Adelaide, Melbourne; Art Gallery of Ontario, Toronto; Museum of Modern Art, New York; Art Institute of Chicago; Musee d'Art Moderne Grand-Duc Jean, Luxembourg.

Public Installations:

Sculpture Park, Goodwood, England.

Publications:

By LONG: Books—*Richard Long: Skulptures,* Mönchengladbach, West Germany 1970; *From along a Riverbank,* Amsterdam 1971; *2 Sheepdogs Cross in and out of the Passing Shadows, the Clouds Drift over the Hill with a Storm,* London 1971; *South America,* Dusseldorf 1975; *From around a Lake,* Amsterdam 1973; *John Barleycorn,* Amsterdam 1973; *Inca Rock Campfire Ash,* Edinburgh 1974; *The North Woods,* London 1977; *100 Stones,* Berne 1977; *A Straight 100 Mile Walk in Australia,* Sydney 1977; *River and Stones,* Penzance, Cornwall 1978; *River Avon Book,* London 1979; *Richard Long,* Eindhoven, Netherlands 1979; *Aggie Weston's No. 16,* London 1979; *A Walk Past Standing Stones,* London 1980; *Five, Six, Pick up Sticks,* London 1980; *12 Works 1979–1981,* London 1981; *Mexico 1979,* Eindhoven 1982; *Selected Works/Oeuvres Choisies 1979–1982,* Ottawa 1982; *Touchstones,* Bristol 1983; *Countless Stones,* Eindhoven 1983; *Fango Pietre Legni,* Turin 1983; *Planes of Vision,* Aachen 1983; *Sixteen Works,* London 1984; *Mud Hand Prints,* London 1984; *River Avon Mud Works,* Londonderry 1984; *Postcards 1968–1982,* Bordeaux 1984; *Muddy Water Falls,* Noordwijk 1985; *Il Luogo Buomo,* Milan 1985; *Richard Long in Conversation,* Bristol and Noordwijk 1985; *Piedras,* Madrid 1986; *Lines of Time,* Amsterdam 1986; *Stone Water Miles,* Geneva 1987; *Richard Long: A Walk Across England,* London 1997; *Richard Long: Mirage,* with Georgia Lobacheff, Mario Codognato and Alison Sleeman, London 1998. **Articles**—interview with Colin Kirkpatrick in *Transcript,* vol. 2, no. 2, November 1996.

On LONG: Books—*Land Art:Long/Flanagan/Oppenheim/Smithson/Boezem/Dibbets/De Maria,* Berlin 1969; *Arte Povera* by Germano Celant, Turin 1970; *Richard Long ; Land Art in Museum Haus Lange,* Krefeld, Germany 1970; *The New Art,* exhibition catalog by Anne Seymour, London 1972; *Some Notes on the Work of Richard Long* by Michael Compton, London 1976; *Richard Long* by Rudi Fuchs, New York and London 1986; *No Where,* Orkney, 1994. **Articles**—"Some Recent Sculpture in Britain" by Charles Harrison in *Studio International* (London), January 1969; "Richard Long" by Willoughby Sharp in *Avalance* (New York), no. 1, 1970; "Richard Long" by Jasia Reichardt in *Architectural Design* (London), March 1972; "Memories of Passing: A Note on Richard Long" by Rudi H. Fuchs in *Studio International* (London), April 1974; "Long Walks" by N. Foote in *Artforum* (New York), Summer 1980; "Richard Long at Anthony d'Offay" by Michael Craig-Martin in *The Burlington Magazine* (London), November 1980; "In the Nature of Things" by John Haldane in *Modern Painters* (London), vol. 10, no. 2, Summer 1997; "Stone in the Soul: On Not Meeting Richard Long" by Bill Drummond in *Modern Painters* (London), vol. 11, no. 2, Summer 1998; "Richard Long" by John Haldane in *Tate: The Art Magazine,* no. 15, Summer 1998. **Film**—*Stones and Flies: Richard Long in the Sahara,* 1988.

*

My art is about working in the wide world, wherever. It has the themes of materials, ideas, movement (walking), and time. The beauty of objects, thoughts, places and actions. I hope to make images and ideas which resonate in the imagination, that mark the earth and the mind. My work is about my senses, my scale, my instinct. I use the world as I find it, by design and by chance.

—Richard Long

* * *

Richard Long works lightly on the earth with great economy of means. His art is concerned with ideas about time, movement and places, with making marks on the earth, by walking or by re-arranging things that are found in a place, such as stones, sticks, pieces of brushwood or seaweed. He uses them to re-create simple basic shapes common to all humankind for many millennia: straight lines, circles, spirals, zig-zags, crosses and squares. These works may be as transient as walking a ten-mile straight line across a moor in England or splashing water onto rocks in Bolivia, or as long-lasting as a line of rocks placed together high in the wilderness of the Himalayas. Such anchors have a resonance partly because of their economy of image and partly because of the congruity between material, place and uninsistent calmness.

Long is a classical artist, imposing a configuration on the landscape. He shows his work in galleries in several ways. There are photographs of the marks and the places where they have been made. Others are presented in the form of maps, drawings or words sharing the routes and shapes of the walks.

There are also sculptures made from stone, slate, pieces of wood, or pine needles arranged in simple shapes on the floor, in form and medium to suit the ambiance. Recently Long has made circles of river mud on the walls of galleries.

—David Brown

LONGO, Robert

Nationality: American. **Born:** Brooklyn, New York, 7 January 1953. **Education:** State University College of New York, Buffalo, B.F.A. 1975. **Career:** Sculptor, painter, filmmaker. **Address:** c/o Metro Pictures, 519 W. 24th Street, New York, New York 10011, U.S.A.

Selected Individual Exhibitions:

1985 Brooklyn Museum, New York
1989 Los Angeles, California
1993 Galeria Joan Prats, Barcelona
Espace Lyonnais D'Art Contemporain, Lyon (exhibition of films and videos)
1994 Metro Pictures, New York
Galerie Gana-Beaubourg, Paris
1995 Galerie Lupke, Frankfurt

Selected Group Exhibitions:

1976 *Convergence and Disperal,* SEM Festival, Albright-Knox Art Gallery, Buffalo, New York
1977 *In Western New York,* Albright-Knox Art Gallery, Buffalo, New York
1981 *Figures: Forms and Expressions,* Albright-Knox Art Gallery, Buffalo, New York
Empire: A Performance Trilogy, Corcoran Gallery Art, Washington
1982 *Focus on the Figure: Twenty Years,* Whitney Museum of American Art, New York
New Figuration in America, Milwaukee Art Center
1983 *Biennial,* Whitney Museum of American Art, New York
An International Survey of Recent Painting and Sculpture, Museum of Modern Art, New York
1984 *The Human Condition: Biennial III,* Museum of Modern Art, San Francisco
Currents, Institute of Contemporary Art, Boston
The Heroic Figure, Contemporary Arts Museum, Houston (traveled)
1986 *The American Exhibition,* Art Insitute of Chicago, Illinois
Monumental Drawing: Works by 22 Contemporary Americans, Brooklyn Museum, New York
1987 *Avante-Garde in the Eighties,* Los Angeles County Museum of Art, California
1989 *Image World: Art and Media Culture,* Whitney Museum of American Art, New York
1990 *Affinities and Intuitions,* Art Institute of Chicago, Illlinois
1991 *Power,* Indianapolis Museum of Art, Indiana
1992 *Allegories of Modernism: Contemporary Drawing,* Museum of Modern Art, New York
1994 *New York Unplugged,* Gallery Cothem, Zeedijk
1995 *It's Only Rock and Roll,* Contemporary Arts Center, Cincinnati, Ohio
Passions Privee, Musee d'Art Moderne, Paris
1996 *New York Unplugged II,* Cotthem, Belgium

Collections:

Museum of Modern Art, New York; Solomon R. Guggenheim Museum, New York; Whitney Museum of American Art, New York; Walker Art Center, Minneapolis; Tate Gallery, London; Art Institute of Chicago, Illinois; Wadsworth Atheneum, Hartford, Connecticut.

Publications:

By LONGO: Articles— ''The Dynamics of Power: An Interview with Robert Longo'' by Maurice Berger in *Arts Magazine,* vol. 59, January 1985.

On LONGO: Books—*Robert Longo* by Carter Ratcliff, New York 1985; *Robert Longo* by Howard N. Fox, New York 1989. **Articles—** ''Double Takes—Illustration and Allegory: Brooke Alexander Gallery, New York'' by Joan Simon in *Art in America,* vol. 68, October 1980; ''Performance—Art for All?'' by RoseLee Goldberg in *Art Journal,* vol. 40, no. 1/2, Fall-Winter 1980; ''Lois Lane and Robert Longo: Interpretation of Image'' by Jeanne Siegel in *Arts Magazine,* vol. 55, November 1980; ''Robert Longo's Men in the Cities: Quotes and Commentary'' by Barry Blinderman in *Arts Magazine,* vol. 55, March 1981; ''Metro Pictures Gallery, New York'' by C. Owens in *Art in America,* vol. 69, March 1981; ''Artists the Critics Are Watching: New York'' by Kay Schwartz and Ellen Larson in *Art News,* vol. 80, May 1981; ''Heute: Westkunst'' by R. Armstrong in

Artforum, vol. 20, September 1981; ''From Performance to Painting'' by Helena Kontova in *Flash Art* (International Edition), no. 106, February-March 1982; ''Return of the Emotive'' by John M. Moore in *Connaissance des Arts,* no. 26, March 1982; ''New Reliefs'' by Jeanne Siegel in *Arts Magazine,* vol. 56, April 1982; ''Contemporary American Art'' by Carter Ratcliff in *Flash Art* (International Edition), vol. 16, Summer 1982; ''Defenestrations: Robert Longo and Ross Bleckner'' by Robert Pincus-Witten in *Arts Magazine,* vol. 57, November 1982; ''Will Success Spoil Bob and Jim, Louise and Larry (Motherwell, Dine, Nevelson, Rivers, etc)'' by Paul Gardner in *Art News,* vol. 81, November 1982; ''New Editions'' by Ronny H. Cohen, Sarah Cecil, Cynthia Nadelman, and Melinda Wortz; in *Art News,* vol. 82, April 1983; ''Art of Spectacle'' by H. Foster in *Art in America,* vol. 71, April 1983; ''Robert Longo: Static Violence'' by T. Milazzo and R. Collins in *Flash Art* (International Edition), no. 112, May 1983; ''Robert Longo: The City of Sheer Image'' by Carter Ratcliff in *The Print Collector's Newsletter,* vol. 14, July-August 1983; ''Heritage Renewed: Representational Drawing Today'' by Phyllis Plous in *American Artist,* vol. 47, July 1983; ''Leo Castelli Gallery and Metro Pictures, New York'' by R. Brooks in *Artforum,* vol. 21, Summer 1983; ''Making It Neo (Young Generation Has Taken Center Stage)'' by Lisbet Nilson in *Art News,* vol. 82, September 1983; ''New Graphic Sensibility Transcends Media'' by Ronny H. Cohen in *The Print Collector's Newsletter,* vol. 14, November-December 1983; ''Entries: Propaedeutica'' by Robert Pincus-Witten in *Arts Magazine,* vol. 58, March 1984; ''Prints and Photographs Published'' in *The Print Collector's Newsletter,* vol. 15, July-August 1984; ''Jumbo Prints: Artists Who Paint Big Want to Print Big'' by Ronny H. Cohen in *Art News,* vol. 83, October 1984; ''Prints and Photographs Published'' in *The Print Collector's Newsletter,* vol. 16, March-April 1985; ''Longo: Making Art for Brave Eyes'' by Paul Gardner in *Art News,* vol. 84, May 1985; ''What Is Postmodern about Painting: The Scandinavia Lectures'' by Steven-Henry Madoff in *Arts Magazine,* vol. 60, October 1985; ''The Brooklyn Museum, New York'' by John Howell in *Artforum International,* vol. 24, October 1985; ''When is a Painting Finished?'' by Paul Gardner in *Art News,* vol. 84, November 1985; ''Prints and Photographs Published'' in *The Print Collector's Newsletter,* vol. 16, January-February 1986; ''Alchemy and the Rediscovery of the Human Figure in Recent Art'' by Paul Groot in *Flash Art* (International Edition), no. 126, February-March 1986; ''Donald Young Gallery, Chicago'' by Deven K. Golden in *New Art Examiner,* vol. 14, December 1986; ''Metro Pictures, New York'' by Eleanor Heartney in *Art News,* vol. 86, January 1987; ''Killing Angels'' by Richard Huntington in *High Performance,* vol. 10, no. 4, 1987; ''Auf der Suche nach Verbindlichkeiten: zur Documenta 8'' by Thomas Wagner in *Das Kunstwerk,* vol. 40, September 1987; ''Object Ghost and Love Collectors'' by Robert Longo in *Artforum International,* vol. 26, March 1988; ''Metro Pictures, New York'' by David Rimanelli in *Artforum International,* vol. 27, January 1989; ''Figure Painting in an Ambivalent Decade'' by Thomas West in *Art International,* no. 9, Winter 1989; ''Bravo Longo'' by Marchlaine Glicksman in *Film Comment,* vol. 25, March-April 1989; ''Film-Video: Mondo Longo'' by Christopher Lewis in *Art in America,* vol. 77, March 1989; ''Metro Pictures, New York'' by Holland Cotter in *Art in America,* vol. 77, March 1989; ''Hope for Corporate Redemption'' by Andrea Liss in *Artweek,* vol. 20, 16 November 1989; County Museum of Art'' by Michael Petry in *Arts Review* (London, England) vol. 41, 1 December 1989; ''Los Angeles ''Longo's Logos'' by Carter Ratcliff in *Artforum International,* vol. 28, January 1990; ''Art and Argument'' by Jeanne Siegel in *Women Artists News,* vol. 16–17, 1991–1992; ''Metro Pictures, New York'' by Eleanor Heartney in *Art News,* vol. 90, January 1991; ''Ma Lasciatemi D'Ivertire'' by Nanda-van-den Berg in *Kunst and Museumjournaal,* vol. 3, no. 1, 1991; ''Robert Longo: Quest for God and Country'' by G. Roger Denson in *Flash Art* (International Edition), no. 160, October 1991; ''Making Art, Making Artists'' by Wade Saunders in *Art in America,* vol. 81, January 1993; ''Installazione: When Heaven And Hell Change Places, Dusseldorf'' by Heinz-Norbert Jocks in *Domus,* no. 747, March 1993; ''Prints and Photographs Published'' in *The Print Collector's Newsletter,* vol. 24, January-February 1994; ''Metro Pictures, New York'' by Eleanor Heartney in *Art in America,* vol. 82, March 1994; ''Robert Longo'' by Heinz-Norbert Jocks in *Kunstforum International,* no. 129, January-April 1995; ''Cyber Johnny'' by Manohla Dargis in *Sight and Sound,* no. 5, July 1995; ''Artist's Dream Machines: The Films of Longo, Salle and Clark'' by Dike Blair in *Flash Art,* (International Edition), no. 187, March-April 1996; ''Foiled Again'' by Ihor Holubizky in *Art and Design,* vol. 11, May-June 1996; ''Artists Making Movies'' by Christina Lanzl in *Art New England,* vol. 18, April-May 1997; ''Robert Longo: Metro Pictures'' by Grady T. Turner in *Flash Art,* (International Edition), no. 199, March-April 1998; ''American Psychos: The End of Art Cinema in the 1990s'' by Laurence A. Rickels in *Art Text,* no. 67, November 1999-January 2000.

* * *

Robert Longo came into the art scene in the 1970s bringing with him a turbulent twist on the traditional media of painting, drawing, and sculpture. His works often include all three, plus appropriated images from films. His bravado technique and dramatic poses force one to respond to the images and materials he presents.

One of Longo's most well known works is the *Men in the Cities Series* (1979–82). The figures twist and turn as if caught in a moment of torture. It is hard to calmly watch these writhing figures exhibit the brutality and intensity of life. They seem to be in need of some type of help or comfort. Using active yet elegantly rendered figures with hard materials provides a harsh juxtaposition. *Corporate Walls: Walls of Influence* (1982) depicts a corporate battle between business men and women similar to Greek and Roman battles. Longo uses figures to entrance and frighten.

By the end of the 1980s and into the 1990s, Longo stepped away from using the figure to demonstrate emotion. He pared down the elements from his figurative work and captured them in one forceful motion especially in his sculpture, *The Fire Next Time (for G.B.)* 1988.

Longo has continued using film as a thread throughout his work. In *Empire (The Performance Trilogy)* (1981), he throws the world of dance and war together as in many of his other works of the early 1980s. He begins pulling these screen captures out of the film and onto canvas or into sculpture. His figures are often crawling out of their surface surrounding. He made fuller length films with *Arena Brains* in 1987 and *Johnny Mnemonic* in 1996. Also in 1996, Longo produced a large scale drawing effort of 366 uniformly sized pieces documenting the year, *Metro Pictures.* These drawings provide individual documentation of private life and popular events as daily time capsules.

In all of Longo's work there is a sense of a documentation of life. The message is sometimes more obscured, but always reflects the turbulence of the sacred and the profane.

—Rachel E. Kuhn

LÓPEZ ARMENTIA, Gustavo

Nationality: Argentine. **Born:** Buenos Aires, 9 February 1949. **Education:** Self-educated. **Awards:** Young Artist Award, Argentine Association of Art Critics, 1985; First Prize, First Biennial Exhibition of Latin American Art, Miami, 1986; Gold Medal, Latin American Biennial Exhibition of Works on Paper, Argentine Association of Art Critics, 1986; First Prize, Alto Palermo Prize, CAYC, 1990; First Prize for Painting, Hoechst Award, 1991; Artist of the Year-1991, Argentine Association of Art Critics, 1992; 1st *Spirit of Greece* Painting Biennial, Second Prize, 1992; Gold Medal, CAYC *New Center* Competition, Argentine Association of Art Critics, 1992; Honorable Mention, Prodaltec Prize, Digital Art, Borges Cultural Center, Buenos Aires, 1997. **Agent:** The Reece Galleries 24 West 57th Street, New York, New York 10019, U.S.A.; Principium Gallery, Esmeralda 1357, Buenos Aires, Argentina.

Selected Individual Exhibitions:

1984/86/88 Vermeer Gallery, Buenos Aires
CAYC, Buenos Aires
1989 Paulo Figueiredo, Sao Paulo, Brazil
1995 National Museum of Fine Arts, Buenos Aires
1996–2000 Reece Galleries, Inc., New York
1999–2000 *ArteBA,* Altera Gallery, Buenos Aires

Selected Group Exhibitions

1983 *The Younger Generation,* CAYC, Buenos Aires
62nd National Exhibition of Fine Arts, Buenos Aires
Realism, Three Styles, American Museum, Madrid
Maison de L'Amerique Latin, Paris, Amsterdam and Moscow
Ideas and Images in Argentina Today, Museum of Modern Art of Mexico, Caracas and Sao Paulo
1st International Biennial Exhibition, Cuenca, Ecuador
19th International Biennial Exhibition, Sao Paulo, Brazil
8th Biennial Exhibition, Valparaiso, Chile
Beau Lezard Gallery, Paris
Museum of Modern Art, Rio de Janeiro, Brazil
1989 *Ideas and Images of Argentina,* The Bronx Museum of Art, New York
9th Valparaiso International Biennial, Chile
1990 *Artists from Buenos Aires,* Museum of Modern Art, Mexico; La Tertulia Museum, Cali, Colombia; Sao Paulo Museum of Art, Brazil
1995 Cairo Biennial, Egypt
Milan Triennial, Italy
1996 *Container '96—Art Across Oceans,* Copenhagen
70–80–90, National Museum of Fine Arts, Buenos Aires
1997 47th Venice Biennial, Italy
Art Beyond Borders, TIMOTCA/UNESCO, New York
Graph Actual/12, Engraving Shows, National Museum of Fine Arts, Buenos Aires
1999 *Latin America, Vanguards at the Turn of the Millennium,* Culturgest Gallery, Lisbon, Portugal
2nd Latin American Biennial, Lima, Peru
2nd Mercosur Biennial, Porto Alegre, Brazil

Collections:

National Museum of Fine Arts, Buenos Aires; Rosa Galisteo de Rodríguez Museum, Santa Fe, Argentina; Carafa Museum, Córdoba, Argentina; Museum of Modern Art, Sao Paulo, Brazil; Museum of Modern Art, Rio de Janeiro, Brazil; Museum of Modern Art, Skopje, Yugoslavia; Andean Institute of Popular Arts, Quito, Ecuador; *Casa de las Americas* (House of the Americas), Havana, Cuba; Domecq Institute, Mexico; Museum of Art, Sao Paulo, Brazil; Museum of Contemporary Art, Buenos Aires; Rosa Galisteo de Rodríguez Museum, Santa Fe, Argentina.

Publications:

On LOPEZ ARMENTIA: Exhibition Catalogues—*Gustavo López Armentia* by Jorge Glusberg, Buenos Aires, 1992; *De Borges a María Kodama,* Buenos Aires, 1995; *70–80–90 in the National Museum of Fine Arts,* Buenos Aires, 1996; *Eckell, García, López Armentia en la XLVII Bienal Internacional de Venecia,* Buenos Aires, 1997; *Art Beyond Borders,* Los Angeles, 1997; *Gustavo López Armentia, Paintings and Sculptures,* Buenos Aires, 1997; *Gustavo López Armentia, New Works and Installations,* Buenos Aires, 1998; *Das Vanguardas ao Fin do Milenio,* Lisboa, 1999; *Masterpieces of the National Museum of Fine Arts,* Buenos Aires, 1999; *Gustavo López Armentia, New Works,* Buenos Aires, 1999; *Siglo XX Argentino Arte y Cultura,* Buenos Aires, 2000; *Gustavo López Armentia,* Valencia, Spain, 2000.

* * *

Gustavo López Armentia has received the influence of Expressionism in a broad sense—as a questioning and controversial movement. His brushstrokes are often vehement, rapidly executed and one of his most noteworthy characteristics is the frequent independence of signs in relation to motif. His paintings always maintain the characteristics and effects of the Expressionist School.

The linking of the abstract and the figurative is an expressly recognized intention of this painter. *Figuration/Abstraction,* not as polar peers, but as a synthesis. His figurative legibility is disseminated (in human characters, objects and actions in the work as such, unrelated among themselves, not even occupying the same place) while his figurative trait is only suggested and ambiguous, because the pictorial mass has no real boundaries.

In the mid-1980s, he introduced the use of a ''reflected perspective.'' He began working with the palette knife and denser impastos and did it with great sensuality, seeking to make his scenes more dynamic. The passage is structured via almost chaotic lines in which different elements have one and the same value. Also clear is another trait of his paintings: namely, *accumulation,* an aspect that appears contradictory in light of the dispersion we have been describing up to now. But in the end, it is not, since he accumulates his proposals, marking the scope and degrees of what he disperses.

Just as he makes use of the syringe, so too he uses the airbrush (an element that is linked to the concept of dispersion) and this technique permits him to introduce certain peculiar traits to his forms. His oil-painting, *Paisaje urbano I* (Urban Landscape I), is a landscape assembled from fragments of spots where the artist has lived or walked (another means of accumulation).

In a first stage, López Armentia swiftly—and unhesitatingly, we might add—introduces a series of elements that, in an incipient but clear-cut way, indicate the guidelines and language, the sense of which gradually unfolds and deepens.

In a second stage, the figurative tends to become diluted and two resources appear that characterize the depth of his language. On the one hand, there is dispersion, which projects images over the entire surface of the painting and cancels out any possibility of finding a central point, a common universe, with different systems. On the other, there is the ever more frequent appearance of an irregular and aqueous scheme that often plays within two dimensions, on top of and underneath the figures and objects. In qualifying this scheme as aqueous, we do so because of the similarity of the pattern with drops of water as they slide over the surface of a windowpane.

At the end of the 1980s, López Armentia enriched his images, adopting a climate where all naiveté, placidness, and playfulness disappeared. Here he would start to question reality more deeply, introducing a sometimes more somber palette, applying paint more abundantly, but tempering the flow and movement of objects, opening the way to resources that lend dynamics to matter.

His profiles and shadows of profiles mark, as if with luminous signs, an incorporeal world generated by the material. The painter's repertory is convoked, attracted, and fragmented from a viewpoint that dominates the key aspects of praxis. Here parade the metaphors of technological power and enlightenment, where cars fly and planes turn into mechanical birds (*Aeroparque*—Airport); matter launched with no intention of form and where, moreover, water, bridge, and ship emerge, almost like phantoms, signs assembled as if on a map (*Puerto Azul*—Blue Port). Childish images (ships or trains) are also dramatic, and the characters portrayed no longer slip by or float but are inserted into a dense impasto as if they were melting beneath the sun (*Una estación cualquiera*—Any Station). His painting becomes "textualized" to an ever-greater extent and the metaphors are covered with a matter that is the main protagonist, as the situations multiply with interlaced meanings.

Some of the paintings from the 1990s go deeper into the concepts we have just been explaining. In *Rincones cotidianos* (Everyday Corners), López Armentia presents a street along which advances a train, whose lights cast two yellowish lines on the viewer. The train cars are transparent. A few people are waiting to board the train that others have just got off. This soliloquy between interior and exterior is also developed in the houses on the right-hand side of the work, seen like a floor plan, even though their inhabitants are seen in cross section (sitting, walking, standing, taking a shower). In the left-hand section, only dark façades appear, as if they were the background set for a decorated theater, held up by ropes and whipped by the wind. The train splits the urban scene in two, separating intimacies from things hidden.

López Armentia seeks a concert of the ephemeral with the enduring, the circumstantial with the invariable, in that minimal measure of the present that is the everyday. By the everyday he refers to that of Latin America in general and Argentina in particular. His cities, his trains, his houses, and his people are Latin Americans, and they are, as is the painting itself, both rough and subtle.

The painter's last works of the 1990s have to do with the world of information in which we live today. There are other forms of time generated by the computer, the TV, and satellites. The immediate past can return in seconds with the mere rewinding of the videotape. The near future can be part of our today by simply rolling the tape forward and seeing the latest news flash or film. The present has become, then, a mere transit point.

López Armentia mixes the human being's times and creations. But he does this also mixing the materials with which he creates his works. The combination of materials with which he organizes the plaster—in the last few years he has discovered the use of plaster instead of canvas—permits him to come up with proposals that are personal and novel and works that are no less singular. As a matter of reference, we call them paintings or sculptures, but they are, in any case, objects of greater or lesser volume, which, when developed in this new support material (an amalgam of plaster and resin) have permitted him to invent a new and significant rhetoric.

—Jorge Glusberg

LOPEZ GARCIA, Antonio

Nationality: Spanish. **Born:** Tomelloso, Ciudad Real, 1936. **Education:** Escuela de Bellas Artes de San Fernando, Madrid, 1950–55. **Family:** Married the painter Maria Moreno. **Career:** Independent painter, Madrid, since 1955. **Awards:** Spanish Ministry of Education grant, to Italy 1955; Kunstpreis der Stadt Darmstadt, 1975; Prince of Asturias Prize, Madrid, 1985. **Address:** Plaza de la Infancia 5, Madrid, Spain.

Individual Exhibitions:

1957 Ateneo, Madrid
1961 Galeria Biosca, Madrid
1968 Stampfli Gallery, New York
1970 Galerie Buccholz, Munich
1971 Galerie Claude Bernard, Paris
1972 Galleria Galatea, Turin
1993 Centro de Arte Reina Sofía, Madrid (catalog)

Selected Group Exhibitions:

1955 *Hernandez/Lopez/Lopez Garcia/Munoz,* Sala de la Direcion de Bellas Artes, Madrid
1968 *Spanische Kunst der Gegenwert,* Neue Galerie, Bochum, Germany
1970 *Magische Realismus in Spanien Heute,* Frankfurter Kunstkabinett H. Bekker von Rath, Frankfurt
1973 *Contemporary Spanish Realists,* Marlborough Fine Art, London
1974 *Ars '74,* Kunstmuseum Athenseum, Helsinki
1975 *Realismus + Realitat,* Kunsthalle, Darmstadt
1976 *5 Spanische Realisten,* Kunsthalle, Baden-Baden, Germany
1977 *Documenta 6,* Kassel, Germany
1978 *Internationaler Realismus heute,* Kunstverein and Kunsthaus, Hamburg
1980 *Spanische Realisten,* Kunstverein, Braunschweig, Germany
1988 *Works on Paper by Contemporary Artists,* Marlborough Fine Arts, London
1995 Venice Biennale
1996 *City Scapes: A Survey of Urban Landscape,* Marlborough Gallery, New York

Publications:

On LOPEZ GARCIA: Books—*Magischer Realismus in Spanien heute,* exhibition catalog with text by Ernst Wuthenow, Frankfurt 1970; *Antonio Lopez Garcia,* exhibition catalog with text by Santiago Amon, Paris 1971; *Contemporary Spanish Realists,* exhibition catalog with text by Santiago Amon, London 1973; *5 Spanische Realisten,* exhibition catalog with text by Ernse Wuthenow, Baden-Baden, Germany 1976; *Spanische Realisten: Maria Moreno/Antonio Lopez Garcia/Isabel Quintanilla/Francisco Lopez,* exhibition catalog with text by Jurgen Schilling, Braunschweig, Germany 1980; *Works on Paper by Contemporary Artists,* exhibition catalog, London 1988; *Antonio Lopez Garcia: Drawings, Paintings, Sculptures* by Michael Brenson, F. Calvo Serraller, and Edward J. Sullivan, New YOrk 1990; **Articles—**''Connoisseurs of Classicism'' by Mark Stevens in *The New Republic,* vol. 194, 9 June 1986; ''Victor Erice et Antonio Lopez'' by Laurence Giavarini in *Cahiers du Cinema,* no. 457, June 1992; ''Clash of the Titans: Antoni Tàpies and Antonio Lopez Face Off Over the Merits of Realism'' by George Stolz in *Art News,* vol. 92, September 1993; ''Antonio Lopez, Painter of Madrid'' by Max Kozloff in *Art in America* (New York), vol. 81, October 1993; ''The Spirit of the Quince Tree'' by Laurel Berger in *Art News,* vol. 92, November 1993; ''Dead or Alive: Molds, Modeling and Mimesis in Representational Sculpture'' by Robert Taplin in *Sculpture* (Washington, D.C.), vol. 13, May/June 1994; ''Interior Gardens: Victor Erice's Dream of Light and the Bodegón Tradition'' by Linda C. Ehrlich in *Cinema Journal,* vol. 34, Winter 1995. **Films—***El Sol del Membrillo* by Victor Erice, 1993.

Sarah Lucas: *Bunny Gets Snookered No. 7,* 1997. ©Tate Gallery, London/ Art Resource, NY; courtesy of Tate Gallery.

LUCAS, Sarah

Nationality: British. **Born:** London, 1952. **Education:** Working Men's College, London, 1982–83; London College of Printmaking, 1983–84; Goldsmith's College, London, 1984–87. **Agent:** Barbara Gladstone Gallery, 515 West 24th Street, New York, New York 10011, U.S.A.

Selected Individual Exhibitions:

1993 *The Shop* (with Tracey Emin), 103 Bethnal Green Road, London
From Army to Armani (with Tracey Emin), Galerie Analix, Geneva
Penis Nailed to a Board, City Racing, London
The Whole Joke, Kingly Street, London
1994 *Got a Salmon On (Prawn),* Anthony d'Offay Gallery, London
Where's My Moss, White Cube, London
1995 *Supersensible,* Barbara Gladstone Gallery, New York
1996 *Sarah Lucas,* Museum Boymans-van Beuningen, Rotterdam (catalog)
Sarah Lucas, Portikus, Frankfurt
Is Suicide Genetic?, Contemporary Fine Arts, Berlin
2000 *The Fag Show,* Sadie Coles HQ, London
Sarah Lucas, Tecla Sala, Barcelona, Spain (catalog)
Beautiness, Contemporary Fine Arts, Berlin
Odd-bod Photography (with Angus Fairhurst), Sadie Coles HQ, London, and Kölnischer Kunstverein, Köln
The Old In Out, Barbara Gladstone Gallery, New York
The Law, St Johns Lofts, London
Bunny Gets Snookered, Sadie Coles HQ, London
Car Park, Ludwig Museum, Köln
Self Portraits 1990–98, Tomio Koyama Gallery, Tokyo

Selected Group Exhibitions:

1986 Showroom, London
1988 *Freeze,* PLA Building, London
1990 *East Country Yard Show,* Surrey Docks, London (catalog)
1992 Karsten Schubert Gallery, London
Stein Gladstone and Barbara Gladstone Gallery, New York
1993 *Sarah Lucas and Steven Pippin,* Project Room, Museum of Modern Art, New York (catalog)
Young British Artists II, Saatchi Collection, London (catalog)
1994 *Watt,* Witte de With and Kunsthal, Rotterdam (catalog)
Football Karaoke, Portikus, Frankfurt (catalog)
Not Self Portrait, Karsten Schubert Gallery, London
1995 *Minky Manky,* South London Gallery (catalog)
Corpus Delicti: London in the 1990s, Kunstforeningen, Copenhagen (catalog)
ARS 95, Museum of Contemporary Art, Helsinki (catalog)
Brilliant! New Art From London, Walker Art Center, Minneapolis, and Museum of Fine Arts, Houston (catalog)

1996 *Co-Operators,* Southampton City Art Gallery and Huddersfield Art Gallery (catalog)
Live/Life, ARC Musee d'Art Moderne de la Ville de Paris, and Belem Museum, Lisbon (catalog)
Full House, Wolfsburg Kunstmuseum, (CD-rom catalog)
Masculin/Feminine, Musee National d'Art Moderne, Centre Georges Pompidou, Paris (catalog)
1997 *Material Culture,* Hayward Gallery, London (catalog)
Assuming Positions, Institute of Contemporary Art, London (catalog)
Strange Days, Claudia Gian Ferrari Arte Contemporanea, Milan (catalog)
Sensation: Young British Artists in the Saatchi Collection, Royal Academy of Art, London (catalog)
1998 *Artists from the UK, Part Two,* Sammlung Goetz, Munich (catalog)
Real Life: New British Art, Tochigi Prefectural Museum of Fine Arts, Japan (toured Japan; catalog)
Contemporary British Art, National Museum of Contemporary Art, Korea (catalog)
No Sex Please We're British, Shiseido Gallery, Tokyo
New Art From Britain, Innsbruck Kunstraum, Austria (catalog)
2000 *Quotidiana: The Continuity of the Everyday,* Castello di Rivoli, Turin (catalog)
Human Being and Gender: 2000 Kwangju Biennale, Kwangju, Korea (catalog)
The British Art Show 5, Hayward Touring Exhibitions, Scottish National Gallery of Modern Art, Royal Botanic Gardens, Edinburgh (catalog)
New British Art 2000, Tate British, Millbank, London (catalog)
Sensation: Young British Artists in the Saatchi Collection, Brooklyn Museum, Brooklyn, New York
2001 *City Racing,* Institute of Contemporary Art, London

Publications:

On LUCAS: Books—*Shark Infested Waters: The Saatchi Collection of British Art in the 90s* by Sarah Kent, London 1994; *Blimey! From Bohemia to Britpop: The London Artworld from Francis Bacon to Damien Hirst,* Cambridge 1997; *Moving Targets: A User's Guide to British Art Now,* London 1998; *Ant Noises at The Saatchi Gallery* by Gemma De Cruz, London 2000. **Articles—**''Can an Old Kebab Be the Cutting-Edge of British Art? Does the London Art Scene Mean Anything in the North? A Few Questions We Ought to Ask'' by Michael Bracewell in *New Statesman,* 15 August 1997; ''The Royal Academy Is Casting Its Mantle Upon Saatchi's Brit Kids. . .'' by Will Self in *New Statesman,* 19 September 1997; ''The Freeze Generation and Beyond'' by Alexandra Anderson-Spivy in *Art Journal,* 22 September 1998; ''Remains of the Day'' by Robert Storr in *Art in America,* 1 April 1999.

* * *

Sarah Lucas' work is about sex: it is crude, vulgar, confrontational and funny. *Bitch* (1994–95) consists of a scruffy second-hand table ''wearing,'' at one end, a white T-shirt containing a pair of melon breasts and displaying, at the other end, vacuum-packed smoked fish genitalia. It is a vivid and powerfully offensive image of a woman as sex object, kneeling on all fours, submissively inviting abuse. It is, also, a witty reference to Allen Jones' notorious *Table* (1969) in which a realistic figure of a woman, scantily clad in fetishistic garb, kneels on all fours with a glass table-top screwed to her back.

The female nude has been a persistent theme in the history of art and popular culture and a troubling issue in gender politics. Allen Jones' *Table*, in particular, provoked a heated debate about the role of language and image in relation to the perpetuation of a sexist ideology which constructs women as passive, submissive sexual objects and men as active and dominant. The male gaze, it can be argued, has dominated the production of images of women, not only by men and for men, but by women and for women, too.

Precisely where Lucas stands in relation to these issues is not clear, for she resists articulating a political position. Her achievement lies in finding a fresh and funny, visual vocabulary that allows her to reposess a subject that has been so tainted with sexism and misogyny. Rather than constructing a critique of sexism she simply exposes it in all its ''innocence'' and revels in its earthiness: the viewer is put in an ambivalent position, unsure whether this is ideological critique or ironic celebration. Lucas takes crude but inventive colloquialisms, such as the insultingly reductive description of a woman as ''two fried eggs and a kipper,'' improves them, and gives them literal form: *Two Fried Eggs and a Kebab* (1991) is a reclining nude which, like *Bitch*, consists of a second-hand table but with a pair of fried eggs for breasts and a sliced-meat filled pita bread for a vagina; a photograph of the table with eggs and kebab stands at the top of the table to represent the figure's face, a witty reference to Magritte's *Rape* (1934) in which breasts and genitals form a face. *Au Naturel* (1994) brings male and female together: on a worn and stained mattress, one end bent up against the wall, the female (a pair of melons and a tin bucket) lies beside the male (a cucumber and a pair of oranges).

In these representations of women and men, Lucas roughs up the visual language of sexual iconography in a way that allows an escape from the repressive conventions which still dominate the production of images. This strategy had an appropriate setting when, in 2000, Lucas was invited to install work in the Freud Museum in London, the house in which Freud lived from 1938 until his death in 1939. Into this elegant interior of polished, antique furniture and oriental rugs, with its atmosphere of learning and culture, Lucas' *Pleasure Principle* (2000) was an unruly eruption from the unconscious: on the dining table stands a ''female'' wooden chair, dressed in knickers and globe-light filled brassiere, being penetrated by a glowing flourescent tube penis emanating from the ''male'' chair dressed in vest and underpants, on the floor.

Lucas herself features in many works: an androgynous figure in jacket, T-shirt, jeans, and boots unsmilingly stares down the viewer in *Divine* (1991); a black and white photograph of her dominates a collage of pinups culled from tabloid newspapers in *Great Dates* (1991). With dead-pan expression, she is eating a banana: it is unclear whether this symbolises a sexual service or the threat of castration. Perhaps the most compelling self portrait is constructed from the fragments which comprise: a life-size wax middle finger, tiny on its oversized plinth, it appears both vulnerable and phallic, and an obscene gesture to the world (*Receptacle of Lurid Things*, 1991); a pair of wax armpits, with hair (*Figleaf in the Ointment*, 1991); and a pair of steel toed boots with razor blades (*1–123–123–12–12*, 1991). Together with a later work, a painted wax cast of her chin and mouth, teeth exposed in grimace, with cigarette jammed into the corner of the mouth (*Where does it all end?*, 1994) these intimate fragments add up to a portrait of the artist as ''other,'' demonstrating a defiant refusal to be typecast, to be pigeonholed by gender, to be sanitised by convention.

Lucas is a sharp observer of the world around her in all its ugliness, shabbiness, and humour. She is not in the least precious about her work and uses materials that come easily to hand: tabloid newspapers, beercans, old furniture, foodstuffs, cigarettes. She is alive to their expressive possibilities, recognising the richness of new meanings and perceptions which can be achieved simply through deft adjustments.

—Richard Salkeld

LUCASSEN, Reinier

Nationality: Dutch. **Born:** Amsterdam, 16 April 1939. **Education:** Rijksnormaalschool voor Tekenlaren and Rijkascasemie voor Beeldende Kunsten, Amsterdam, 1957–60. **Career:** Independent artist, Amsterdam, since 1960; worked on environmental paintings, with Etienne Elias, Raoul de Keyser and Roger Raveel, Beervelde Castle, Ghent, 1966; collaborated on paintings with Ger Van Elk, 1972. Founder member, with Jan Dibbets and Ger Van Elk, International Institute for the Reeducation of Artists, Amsterdam, 1967. Artist-instructor, Ateliers '63, Haarlem, since 1968. **Awards:** Cassandra Foundation Award, 1970; David Roell Prize, Amsterdam, 1976. **Agents:** Galerie Espace, Keizersgracht 548, 1017 Amsterdam; and Galerie Nouvelles Images, Westeinde 22, The Hague. **Address:** Valeriusstraat 116, 1075 GD Amsterdam, Netherlands.

Individual Exhibitions:

1963 Galerie 845, Amsterdam
1964 Galerie Espace, Amsterdam
1965 Stedelijk Museum, Amsterdam
1966 Galerie Espace, Amsterdam
Markt 17, Enschede, Netherlands
Groninger Museum, Groningen, Netherlands
Galerie Kaleidoskoop, Ghent
1967 Galerie Espace, Amsterdam
1968 Galerie Espace, Amsterdam
1969 Rotterdamse Kunstkring, Rotterdam
Dordrechts Museum, Dordrecht, Netherlands
Galerie Espace, Amsterdam
1970 Tentoonstellingsdienst Den Bosch, Netherlands
Galerie Espace, Amsterdam
1972 Stedelijk Museum de Lakenhal, Leiden
Galerie Grafiek 50, Wakken, Belgium
Tentoostellingsdienst Den Bosch, Netherlands
1973 *Lucassen 63–73,* Frans Halsmuseum, Haarlem (toured the Netherlands)
Galerie Grafiek 50, Wakken, Belgium
1974 Galerie Espace, Amsterdam
Galerie Grafiek 50, Wakken, Belgium
1975 *Lucassen en de grote stijl,* Lens Fine Art, Antwerp
1976 Van Abbemusuem, Eindhoven, Netherlands
1977 *Lucassen 1977,* Galerie Espace, Amsterdam
1978 Lens Fine Art, Antwerp
1979 Stedelijk Museum, Amsterdam
Galerie Espace, Amsterdam

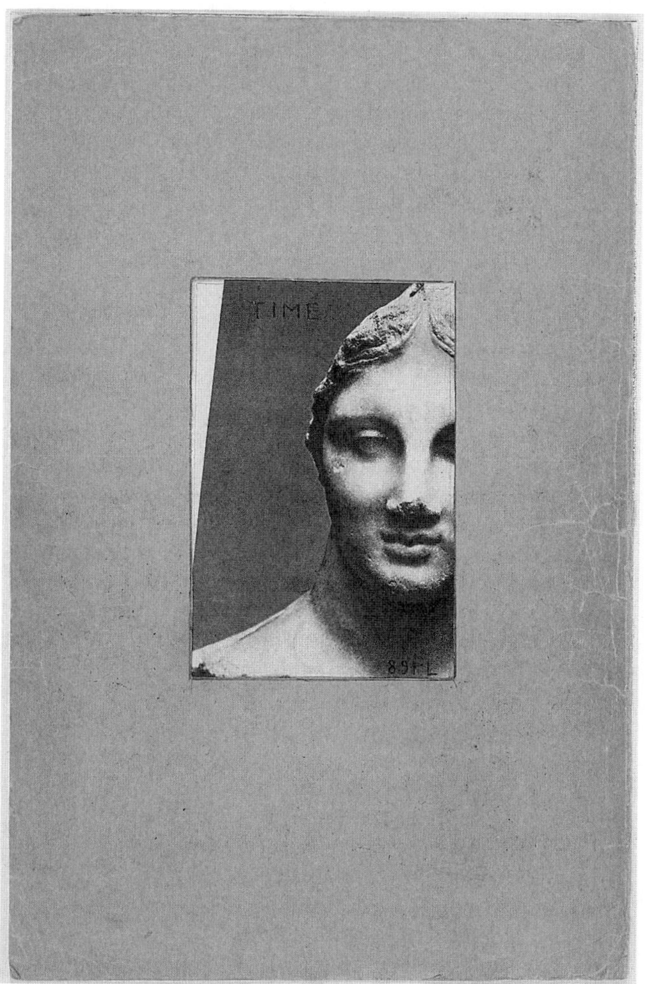

Reinier Lucassen: *Steentijd komt,* 1989. Photo by Henni van Beek. ©Reinier Lucassen.

1980 Gemeentemuseum, Aarnhem
1981 Galerie Espace display, *Fiac 81,* Paris
Galerie Espace, Amsterdam
Kunsthandel Lambert Tegenbosch, Heusden, Netherlands
1982 Lens Fine Art, Antwerp
1983 Galerie Espace, Amsterdam
Museum Fodor, Amsterdam
1984 Galerie Espace, Amsterdam
1985 Lens Fine Art, Antwerp
1986 Dutch Pavilion at the *Biennale*, Venice
Galerie Espace, Amsterdam
Museum Boymans-van Beuningen, Rotterdam
1987 Dutch Pavilion at the *Biennale,* Venice
1989 Galerie Espace, Amsterdam
1990 Galerie van Esch, Eindhoven
1992 Galerie Espace, Amsterdam
1993–96 Galerie Nouvelles Images, The Hague
1997 Galerie Nouvelles Images/KunstRAI, Amsterdam
1998 Galerie Wansink, Roermond
1999 Cobra Museum voor Moderne Kunst, Amstelveen
Galerie Espace/KunstRAI, Amsterdam
Galerie Nouvelles Images, The Hague

Selected Group Exhibitions:

1965 *Premio Lissone*, Italy
1967 *Junge Kunst aus Holland,* Kunsthalle, Bern
1969 *Profile 4,* Städtische Kunstgalerie, Bochum, West Germany
1971 *Stedelijk 60–70,* Ateneum, Helsinki (travelled to the Palais des Beaux-Arts, Brussels)
1973 *Fortunately There is Still Some Grass,* Camden Arts Centre, London
1976 *Reflektie en Realiteit,* Palais des Beaux-Arts, Brussels (toured Europe and Brazil)
1980 *Belgie-Nederland,* Palais des Beaux-Arts, Brussels (traveled to Museum Boymans-van Beuningen, Rotterdam)
1983 *Modern Dutch Painting,* National Gallery, Athens (traveled to Amsterdam and Nuremberg)
1985 *Aspecten von Nederlandse tekenkunst 1945–85,* Museum de Lakenhal, Leiden, Netherlands (traveled to Oberlin, Ohio)
1987 *Out of Holland,* Musée d'Art Contemporian, Montreal
1988 *Een Keuze uit de collectie van de Amro bank,* Stedelijk Museum, Amsterdam (catalog)
1989 *Gemeentelijke Kunstaankopen 1989,* Museum Fodor, Amsterdam (catalog)
1991 *De uitnodiging tot de reis/L'Invitation au Voyage; hedendaagse kunst uit Nederland,* Rijksdienst Beeldende Kunst, The Hague (catalog)
1993 *Grossbild: overeenkomsten en verschillen tussen hedendaagse Westerse en niet Westerse kunst,* Galerie van Esch, Eindhoven (catalog)
1994 *L'Orizonte, da Chagall a Picasso, da Pollock a Cragg,* Catello di Rivoli, Rivoli (catalog)
1995 *Genummerd + gesigneerd 1,* Museum van Bommel van Dam, Venlo (catalog)
1996 *20 jaar verzamelen, Bouwfonds Kunstcollectie,* Museum Boymans van Beuningen, Rotterdam (catalog)
1997 *Flemish and Dutch Painting from Van Gogh, Ensor, Magritte, Mondrian to Contemporary Artists,* Palazzo Grassi, Venice (catalog)
1998 *Rondom Picabia/Around Picabia,* Museum Boymans van Beuningen, Rotterdam

Collections:

Stedelijk Museum, Amsterdam; Van Abbemuseum, Eindhoven; Museum Boymans-van Beuningen, Rotterdam; Gemeentemuseum, The Hague; Stedelijk Museum de Lakenhal, Leiden; Frans Halsmuseum, Haarlem; Groninger Museum, Groningen; Museum voor Hedendaages Kunst, Utrecht; Museum voor Schone Kunsten, Ghent; Galleria degli Uffizi, Florence.

Publications:

By LUCASSEN: Articles—''Hommage san het einde van de schilderkunst'' in *Lucassen,* exhibition catalog, Amsterdam 1969; ''Dagboekfragmenten'' in *Reinier Lucassen,* exhibition catalog, Haaerlem 1973; ''Dagboekfragmenten 2'' in *Reiner Lucassen,* exhibition catalog, Utrecht 1973; ''Een appelte schillen'' in *NRC-Handelsblad* (Amsterdam), 23 November 1974; ''De mythe Sandberg is interessanter dan de werkelijheid'' in *Die Tijd* (Amsterdam), 7 November 1975; ''Dagboek getekend Lucassen'' in *De Revisor* (Amsterdam), 3 July 1975; ''De kunstenaar heeft alleen verantwoording tegenover zichzelf'' in *Keesings Reflector* (Amsterdam), 5 January 1976; ''Dagboekfragment 11 Juli 1972'' in *Reflectie en Realiteit,* exhibition catalog, Brussels 1976; ''Charchoune, meester van de schijnbare eevoud'' in *Tableau II* (Amsterdam), March/April 1980; ''De kunst en het geld'' in *De Revisor* (Amsterdam), June 1980; ''Nieuwe Figuratie; een opvatting, geen stijl, Pop-Art: Een incident'' in *Raster* (Amsterdam), no. 19, 1981; ''De architect'' in *De Gids* (Amsterdam), no. 10, 1983; ''Vraagen aan Lucassen'' in *Jong Holland* (Amsterdam), no. 2, 1986.

On LUCASSEN: Books—*Lucassen* by Roland Jooris, Hans Sizoo and Marchel Vos, Ghent 1969; *Lucassen,* exhibition catalog with text by Hans Sizoo, Leiden 1972; *Lucassen en Ger Van Elk. . . zogezed* by Roland Patteeus, Tielt, Netherlands 1973; *Lucassen 63–73,* exhibition catalog with text by Hans Sizoo, Haarlem 1973; *Lucassen de grote stijl,* exhibition catalog with text by Hans Sizoo, Antwerp 1975; *Lucassen,* exhibition catalog edited by Rudi H. Fuchs, Eindhoven, Netherlands 1976; *Lucassen 1977,* exhibition catalog with text by Hans Sizoo, Amsterdam 1977; *Dutch Painting* by Rudi H. Fuchs, London 1978; *Lucassen,* exhibition catalog with text by Hans Sizoo, Amsterdam 1979; *Lucassen: schilderijen, tekeningen, assemblages 1960–86,* with essays by Anna Tilroe, Hans Sizoo and Nicole Lasseel, Amsterdam 1986; *Biennale di Venezia: Lucassen,* exhibition catalog with texts by Gijs van Tuyl and Karel Schampers, Amsterdam and The Hague 1986; *Lucassen,* with texts by Elly Stegeman, Ed Wingen, Tijs Goldschmidt, Ansuya Blom, and Lucassen, Eindhoven 1999.

*

The essence of my work is determined by the fact that I do not care about notions, conceptions and forms such as figurative, non-figurative, rational, emotional, etc. I use (i.e., interpret) incompatible elements of style that should reject each other, in such a way the they assume a logical and organic form in the context of my work. When seen from the traditional notions of my style, my art has no style; I have turned the problem of style into a senseless problem.

Both in form and meaning this is a new aspect, possibly the only essentially new one in art since the great revolutions of the years 1900 to 1930.

—Reinier Lucassen

LUM, Ken

Nationality: Canadian. **Born:** Vancouver, British Columbia, Canada, 26 September, 1956. **Education:** Simon Fraser University, B.G.S. 1980; New York University, 1981–82; University of British Columbia, M.F.A. 1985. **Career:** First outdoor performances and installations, 1978. Naturalist and illustrator, Burnaby Parks Board, 1978; pestologist, Ministry of the Environment and Ministry of Agriculture, British Columbia, 1978–79; artist and graphic designer, Vancouver Public Library, 1980; director and curator, OR Gallery, Vancouver, 1984. Instructor, University of Ottawa, 1988–89, and Simon Fraser University, 1989; professor, University of British Columbia, 1989 to present. Guest professor, Akademie der Bilden Kunsten, Munich, Germany, 1992, and Ecole des Beaux-Arts, Paris,

1994. Has lectured at universities and gatherings throughout the world. Lives and works in Vancouver. **Agent:** Andrea Rosen Gallery, 130 Prince Street, New York, New York, 10012, U.S.A.

Individual Exhibitions:

1978 Ian Wallace Studio, Vancouver
1979 Ian Wallace Studio, Vancouver
1982 Artists Space, New York
Simon Fraser University Downtown Studio Gallery, Vancouver
1983 OR Gallery, Vancouver
1984 Simon Fraser University Downtown Studio Gallery, Vancouver
Coburg Gallery, Vancouver
1985 Plug-In Gallery, Winnipeg
Coburg Gallery, Vancouver
XYZ Gallery, Toronto
1986 Ydessa Gallery, Toronto
Convertible Showroom Gallery, Vancouver
Nature Morte Gallery, New York
1987 Galerie Daniel Buchholz, Cologne
Robbin Lockett Gallery, Chicago
1988 Cold City Gallery, Toronto
Galerie Ralph Wernicke, Stuttgart
Musée d'Art Contemporain, Montreal
Galerie Nelson, Lyon, France
Nature Morte Gallery, New York
1989 Galerie Johnen & Schöttle, Cologne
Galerie Daniel Buchholz, Cologne
Galleria Massimo de Carlo, Milan
1990 Galerie Meert Rihoux, Brussels
Galleri Nordanstad-Skarstedt, Stockholm
Andrea Rosen Gallery, New York
Winnipeg Art Gallery (travelled to Vancouver and Rotterdam)
1991 Galerie Rüdiger Schöttle, Paris
Galerie Daniel Buchholz, Cologne
Fine Arts Gallery, University of British Columbia, Vancouver
Galerie Rüdiger Schöttle, Munich
Kunstmuseum, Lucerne
1992 Andrea Rosen Gallery, New York
Galleria Massimo de Carlo, Milan
1993 Galerie Daniel Buchholz, Cologne
Galerie Johnen & Schöttle, Cologne
Stadtische Galerie im Lenbachhaus, Munich (travelled to Graz, Saarbrucken, and Karlsruhe)
1994 Andrea Rosen Gallery, New York
Catriona Jeffries Gallery, Vancouver
Oakville Galleries, Oakville, Ontario
1995 Galerie Drantmann, Brussels
San Francisco Art Institute
Galerie Nelson, Paris
DRAC, Lorraine, France
L'Aquarium, Valenciennes, France
1996 Stills Gallery, Edinburgh
1997 FRAC de Haute-Normandie
Galerie Art & Public, Geneva
Andrea Rosen Gallery, New York
1998 XXIV Sao Paulo Bienal, Sao Paulo
The Agency Contemporary Art, London
1999 Plug-In Gallery, Winnipeg, Canada
Walter Phillips Gallery, Banff Centre, Alberta, Canada
2000 L.A. Galeria, Frankfurt
The Gate Foundation, Amsterdam

Selected Group Exhibitions:

1985 *The Public Art Show,* Nexus Center for Contemporary Art, Atlanta (travelled throughout the South)
1987 *Material Fictions,* 49th Parallel Centre for Contemporary Canadian Art, New York (travelled to Binghampton, New York)
Nightfire, De Appel Foundation, Amsterdam
1988 *New York Now,* Esbo Museum of Art, Helsinki (travelled throughout Sweden)
1989 *Prospect 89,* Kunstverein and Schirn Kunsthalle, Frankfurt
1990 *(Not So) Simple Pleasures,* MIT List Visual Arts Center, Boston
Art et Publicité, Centre Georges Pompidou, Paris
1991 *Carnegie International,* Carnegie Museum of Art, Pittsburgh
1992 *Sidney Biennnale,* Sydney
1993 *Die Sprach der Kunst,* Kunsthalle, Vienna (travelled to the Kunstverein, Frankfurt)
1996 *Fact or Fiction? Four Canadian Artists,* Museum of Contemporary Art, Sydney
1997 *In Visible Light: Photography and Classification in Art, Science, and the Everyday,* Museum of Modern Art, Oxford, England (toured)
Cities on the Move, Vienna Secession, Vienna (traveled to CAPC Musie d'Art Contemporain de Bordeaux)
2000 *Contemporary Photography II: Anti-Memory,* Yokohama Museum of Art, Japan

Publications:

By LUM: Articles—"Thomas Lawson and Ken Lum: A Conversatoin between Two Artists," in *Flash Art,* April/May 1984; interview with Jerome Sans in *Flash Art,* May/June 1988.

On LUM: Exhibition catalogs—*Ken Lum,* with text by Manon Blanchette, Montreal 1988; *Ken Lum,* with text by Linda S. Boersma and Jeff Wall, Winnipeg, 1990; *Ken Lum,* with text by Marnie Fleming, Oakville, 1994. **Articles—**"Image and After Image" by Ian Wallace in *Vanguard,* December/January 1987; "Ken Lum" by Jutta Koether in *Artscribe,* March/April 1988; "Focus: Ken Lum" by Earl Miller in *Canadian Art,* fall 1989; "The Art World: Empty Frames" by Adam Gopnik in *The New Yorker,* 25 November 1991; "The Discomfort Zone" by Scott Watson in *Canadian Art,* spring 1992; "Global Art: Ken Lum" by Liam Gillick in *Flash Art,* January/February 1994; "Ken Lum" by Scott Watson in *Art + Text,* January 1995.

* * *

Ken Lum's work has always called into question the function of art, as well as the clichés that fill life in general, whether it be in his furniture sculptures, logo portraits or language paintings. Hailing from what has now become known as the Vancouver Photo-Conceptualist school, Lum is interested in the people who inhabit the streets of Vancouver (although it could be any major city), and no encounter, however brief, is too slight to escape his notice, nor too banal to become the source of one of his pieces. One could say that he speaks to us from a suffocating nearness, for the world he depicts is that of everyday life and the fullness of human experience.

The important series of diptychs have their roots in a ''logo series'' which was begun in 1984. In this work Lum combined portraits made by a commercial photographer with a number of corporate-looking logotypes. Life-size representations of ordinary people were juxtaposed brusquely beside shiny plexiglas logos of their name. The convergence of the portrait and logo established an intense polarity which created a dialogue that pointed to the increasingly vague distinction between art and commerce as well as to the social structure in which art is sanctioned as art.

This series was followed by a more dramatic-narrative series of 1989–90 in which the text contained not only the sitter's name, but also some aspects of the characters or circumstances of the figures portrayed. For example, a work from 1990 depicted a couple posed beside a massive tree trunk, dressed in outdoor wear, paired with the words ''A Woodcutter and his Wife.'' The title was spelled out in little logs of faux-wood against an acid-green monochrome surface. This work offered a number of possibilities: was it an advertisement promoting a product? the title of a film? or did it represent a logging promotion? Far from explaining the image, Lum's text merely added to the ambiguity and confusion. The state of tension between picture and words directed the viewer through a variety of associations. The same can be said of other works which also offered immediately recognizable clichés, such as a heavy-metal rock group posed theatrically in a suburban rec-room, or a seedy customer-service rep offering a handshake over his dishevelled desk. Each photo was accompanied by a genial or winsome text (*We Are Sacred Blade,* and *Ask for Larry Meyers*) laid out in an appropriate graphic style which had a correlation to the subjects. The meaning of picture and text came together as a whole, and metaphors from advertising clichés became ironic and critical commentaries.

In a new series of diptychs begun in 1993, Lum presents situations of concentrated emotion. On one side is a photograph of an everyday scenario, and on the other, texts that augment the slice-of-life scenes. In these works Lum depicts a moment of eruption or outburst, paired with the subject's subsequent feelings of anxiety, guilt, or remorse in the texts. The texts read like much repeated mantras or ''word-bites''; the most under-valued bits of speech. As spectators we are both witness to the scene, and privy to the state of mind of the subject.

The situations depicted in the photos are wholly contrived ''real-life moments,'' staged with actors. One example presents a photograph of a distressed young woman in jeans, standing in a phone booth and talking on the phone. The text reads: ''You don't love me. You've never loved me. When have you ever loved me? When have you ever given a shit about me?!'' By repeating parts of the text, Lum further integrates language into image.

The diptychs also come close to cinema, with their photographic subjects' interior thoughts revealed to us, like lines of script. Through their thoughts or their ''dialogue'' we enter their minds, or an emotionally charged ''inner'' life. Both photo and text serve to create an underlying tension: the seemingly objective representation of an emotionally charged scene with an inwardly psychological landscape. It must be said that while objectivity is the premise, subjectivity is the tacit organizer in Lum's exploration between the world and words. The words in the text are sufficiently large and aggressive to encroach upon our mental space and force an identification, or translation, of personal recollections. The time we spend in reading also more actively engages us as participants. No matter what kind of situation Lum chooses to depict, whether it be a spontaneous outburst, a moment of conscious action, a crisis, or a quiet recollection, it references decisive events in our day-to-day lives. It is in the banal and humdrum moments that Lum creates new assertions for a heightened awareness of reality.

This anecdotal take on contemporary life can also be seen in his sculptural work, comprised of modular sofas and chrome lamps. These items figured in some of his *Untitled* furniture installations from the early 1980s. Lum would arrange the rented furniture into the gestalts of Minimalist sculpture all the while making a point of talking about how modernism had curbed the ability to provide intimacy and hospitality: ''I am interested in making privateness a public issue.'' The exhibition space consequently became a public space in which pieces of furniture, normally private objects, were transposed into art objects. The furniture, like the recent diptychs, was an extension of that private world. Always walking a tightrope between art and non-art, Lum has consistently questioned the relationship between high modernism and everyday living.

—Marnie Fleming

LUNDQUIST, Evert

Nationality: Swedish. **Born:** Stockholm, 17 July 1904. **Education:** Educated in Stockholm, until 1920; studied at Carl Willhelmson's School of Painting, Stockholm, 1924; Académie Julian, Paris, 1924–25; Royal College of Fine Arts, Stockholm, 1925–31. **Military Service:** Served in the Swedish Army, 1927. **Family:** Married Ebba Reutercrona; sons: Hybner and Emanuel. **Career:** Independent painter, Stockholm, 1931–91, retired 1991. Professor of Painting, Royal College of Fine Arts, Stockholm, 1960–70. **Awards:** Swedish Association of Graphic Arts grant, 1959; Painting Prize, *Bienal,* Sao Paulo, 1961; Prince Eugene Medal, 1962; Artist Laureat, Stockholm, 1964; Tessin Medal, 1980. **Address:** 17893 Drottningholm, Stockholm, Sweden.

Individual Exhibitions:

1934 Konstnarshuset, Stockholm
1938 Konstnarshuset, Stockholm
1941 Konstnarshuset, Stockholm
1944 Royal Academy of Fine Arts, Stockholm (retrospective)
1945 Konstnarshuset, Stockholm
1949 Samlaren, Stockholm
1953 Museum of Art, Eskildstuna, Sweden
Konstnarshuset, Stockholm
1957 Royal Academy of Fine Arts, Stockholm
Konsthalle, Gothenberg, Sweden
1960 Galerie Rive Gauche, Paris
Beaux-Arts Gallery, London
1961 Little Studio Gallery, New York
Renaissance Society, Chicago

Evert Lundquist: *Woman with Apple.* Photo by Torbjorn Grundstrom. ©Evert Lundquist.

1962 Gummeson Gallery, Stockholm
Galleria del Cavallino, Venice
Galerie Zodiaque, Brussels
Beaux-Arts Gallery, London
1964 Swedish Pavilion, at the *Biennale*, Venice
1970 Royal Academy of Fine Arts, Stockholm
Museum of Art, Gavle, Sweden
1971 *Malningar, Etsningar 1963–1971,* Lunda Konsthall, Lund, Sweden
Museum of Art, Kalmar, Sweden
1974 Moderna Museet, Stockholm
1977 Royal Academy of Fine Arts, Stockholm
1979 *Peintures à l'Huile 1936–1979,* Centre Culturel Suedois, Paris
Konsthall, Gothenburg, Sweden
1980 Centre Culturel Suedois, Paris
Thielska Galleriet, Stockholm
1982 Clocktower Gallery, New York
1985 Kunstnernes Hus, Oslo
Thielska Galleriet, Stockholm
1989 Thielska Galleriet, Stockholm
1993 Studio Museum of Evert Lundquist, Stockholm (permanent)
1996 Royal Academy of Fine Arts, Stockholm

Selected Group Exhibitions:

1952 *Carnegie international,* Carnegie Institute, Pittsburgh (and 1959)
1960 *Triennale,* Milan
1961 *Bienal,* Sao Paulo
1962 *Biennale,* Venice (and 1982)
1963 *Dunn International,* Fredericton, New Brunswick, Canada
1964 *Guggenheim International,* Guggenheim Museum, New York
1992 Barbican Centre, London
1993 Museum of Modern Art, Stockholm

Collections:

Moderna Museet, Stockholm; National Museum, Stockholm; Goteborgs Konsthall, Gothenberg, Sweden; Centre Georges Pompidou, Paris; Bibliothèque Nationale, Paris; Museum of Modern Art, New York; Tate Gallery, London; Museu de Arte Moderna, Sao Paulo; National Gallery of Victoria, Melbourne; Musee d'Uffizi, Florence; Nasjonalgalleriet, Oslo.

Publications:

By LUNDQUIST: Books—*From a Painters Life,* Stockholm 1984, second enlarged edition, Stockholm 1996.

On LUNDQUIST: Books—*Evert Lundquist,* exhibition catalog, Stockholm 1957; *Evert Lundquist: Malningar, Etsningar 1963–1971,* exhibition catalog with text by Oscar Reutersvard, Lund, Sweden 1971; *Evert Lundquist,* exhibition catalog with text by Philip von Schantz and Ulf Linde, Stockholm 1974; *Evert Lundquist,* exhibition catalog with text by Ulf Linde, Stockholm 1975; *Evert Lundquist: Peintures à l'huile 1936–1979,* exhibition catalog with text by Ulf Linde, Paris 1979; *Lundquist,* exhibition catalog with text by Erik Blomberg, Oslo 1985; *E.L.: A Frustrated Classicism,* exhibition catalog by Jane Alison and Carol Brown, New York 1992; *Catalog for the Studio Museum of Evert Lundquist* by Ulf Linde *et al,* Stockholm 1992.

*

My personal and artistic taste and my temperament have always tended—in spite of many deviations and aberrations—to a predilection for classical art (from that day in 1922 when at the age of 19 I bought in London some photographic reproductions of the Elgin Marbles in the British Museum). This has now become ever more clearly my domain, and on this balanced, sound and largely universal art I exclusively feed; I feel at home in it, and its spirit I try to express in my work, in my own and my age's formal language. This is the way of the grand tradition, the way that endures in all ages and countries where the basic grounds of the Western spirit are still respected and revered. Particularly in this ravaged and—in its artistic life—so fragmented age, I believe this so-called "reactionary" attitude of mine to be valuable as a counterweight to all that is fleeting, chaotic, primitive, artificial, and unfinished.

An artist can relate to his own work only to the extent to which he has mastered the language of others, the extent to which he is in a tradition. In certain respects, he may find himself incapable of adopting the tradition. He may feel a more or less compelling need to alter it, but the work he then creates cannot be understood by anyone, not even himself, other than in relation to the tradition that was to be changed. His deviations, and thus also his will, can be read off in this way.

What characterizes the art that rises above mere incidentals is its great and timeless nature. And this does not come about from new attitudes, fresh initiatives, etc., but is the result of a lifelong, devoted adherence to and retrenchment of a limited position. It is in his restriction, says Goethe, that the master revels himself. It is not in absolute freedom, faithlessness and a desire for renewal that the strength of artistic creativity is expressed, but in an obstinate, devoted limitation to a single field, in which one voluntarily renounces so-called freedom. There are examples in our own time. Take someone like Mondrian, or Brancusi.

—Evert Lundquist

* * *

Probably the most distinguished modern Swedish painter, and the best known outside his native country, Evert Lundquist had, for a while, a particular rapport with British art as a result of his meeting the painter Cliff Holden who lives in Sweden. Holden was a pupil of the important painter David Bomberg, who has decisively influenced an important area of post-war British art, including Auerbach and Kossoff, who paint in deep, heavy impasto, intimate, emotional or passionate views of their domestic circle or immediate physical surroundings. This group of artists exhibited regularly at the now defunct Beaux-Arts Gallery in London, and it was through Holden that Lundquist was introduced to this gallery and to the British art scene.

Lundquist was first influenced by a brand of realistic-impressionism, infused with a special sense of dynamic emotionalism, gradually thickening the impasto of the paint to almost relief proportions, in heightened colors. He developed more and more powerful and expressive pictorial forms. His subjects have always been landscape, still-life and figures in space, but whilst these remain the inspirational starting point, they became more and more abstracted, the outline of the forms merging into the heavy impasto, and at the same time he adopted an almost monochromatic palette, selectively and dramatically broken by well chosen reds, browns, and blue-greys.

There is something moving and heroic in Lundquist's work, a combination of anxiety, and understanding of the frailty of human flesh and human spirit, with an idealistic determination to battle through, to face life and the world with that mixture of sensitivity, pride and defiance, which, perhaps, reflects his nation's experience as a small, vulnerable community, surrounded by a sea and potential enemies.

Lundquist has exerted a considerable influence in his native country, as a result of his own achievements and stature, the dignified stance of an artist of communicable seriousness, and a teacher at the Stockholm College of Art. In the 1940s he was one of the founders of the Saltsjo Duvnas group of figurative painters, and although he soon outstripped most of his colleagues, developing a style combining stronger emotional and abstract elements than the artists of the group, he has retained his leading national position.

—Charles Spencer

LUPAS, Ana

Nationality: Rumanian. **Born:** Cluj, 30 August 1940. **Education:** Studied at the Fine Arts Lyceum in Cluj and Bucharest, 1952–56; graduated from Academy of Fine Arts, Cluj, 1962. **Career:** Sculptor, performance and environmental artist, and writer, Cluj-Napoca. Professor, Fine Arts Academy, Cluj, 1967–79; exhibition organizer for groups of artists working in Studio 35, 1983–88. **Awards:** Prize of the Rumanian Union of Artists, 1969; gold medal, *International Art Triennale,* Stuttgart, 1969; silver medal, *International Art Triennale,* Milan, 1973; Grand Prize (ex aequo), *International Drawings Biennale,* Lisbon, 1979; silver medal, *International Triennale,* Lodz, 1981; The One and Only Prize, *International Vehtaprijs Biennale,* Vichte, Belgium, 1982; The Great Prize of the Rumanian Union of Artists, 1982; Silver Prize, *International Drawing Biennale,* Seoul, South Korea, 1984; Acquisition Prize, *Art-Expo,* Budapest, 1991. **Address:** Academia de Arta, Str. G-ral Budisteanu 19, Sect. 1, Cod. 70 744, Bucharest, Rumania.

Individual Exhibitions:

1966 *Solemn Process,* Margau, Rumania
1967 Leud, Rumania
1968 *Process of Determination* (performance), Marginea, Rumania
1970 *Wet Installation,* Margau, Rumania
1972 Galeria Apollo, Bucharest
National Theatre, Cluj, Rumania
1973 Galeria Wspolczesna, Warsaw
Salon BWA, Wroclaw, Poland
1974 Agence des Expositions Artistiques, Lublin, Poland
Kudontaa-Văv-A Tese-Tisser, Amos Andersonin Arts Museum, Helsinki
1975 Sveagalleriet, Stockholm
1976 Abbaye de Ronceray, Angers, France
The Reality and Its Ways of Expression, Museum of Rumanian Contemporary Art, Galati, Rumania
1978 Pulchri Studio, Den Haag, Holland
1982 *Meeting with . . . Ana Lupas,* Musée Cantonal des Beaux-Arts, Lausanne, Switzerland
1983 Gallery Obalna, Piran, Slovenia
1985 Vlahuta Street, Cluj, Rumania
1989 *Borrowed Clothes,* Cluj, Sibiu, Oradea, Cluj, Romania
1991 Art Expo, Szállás Street 4, Budapest, Hungary
Memorial of Cloth, University Square, Bucharest

Selected Group Exhibitions:

1973 *The 8th Biennale from Paris International Manifestation of Young Artists,* Musée d'Art Moderne, Paris
1974 *Premi Internacional Dibuix Joan Miró,* Colegio d'Arquitectos, Barcelona
1977 *03 23 03: The First International Meetings on Contemporary Art,* Bureau de Poste Désaffecté, Montreal, Quebec
1979 *The Third Biennale of Sydney,* Art Gallery of New South Wales, Sydney
1982 *International Vehtaprijs Biennale,* Oude Kerk, Vichte, Belgium
1984 *First Seoul International Drawing Triennale,* Art Center, Seoul, South Korea
1985 *18th Biennale of São Paulo,* Brazil
1990 *Visual Works and Witnesses,* Les Salons de l'Hotel de Lassay, Paris
1992 *International Exhibition,* Berlin-Mitte, Germany

1994 *Europe, Europe: The Century of the Avant-Garde in Central and Eastern Europe,* Kunst-und Ausstellungshalle der Bundesrepublik Deutschland, Bonn, Germany

1999 *Global Conceptualism: Points of Origin, 1950s-1980s,* Queens Museum of Art, New York (travelled to Walker Art Center, Minneapolis; Miami Art Museum, Florida)

Collections:

Savaria Múzeum, Syombathely, Hungary; Seoul International Fine Arts Center, South Korea; Centralne Muzeum Wlókiennictwa, Lodz, Poland; Museum of Rumanian Contemporary Art, Galati, Rumania; Amos Andersonin Konstmuseum, Helsinki; University Babes-Bolyai, Cluj, Rumania; Fundaçao Calouste Gulbenkian, Lisbon; Museum of History, Iassy, Rumania; National Art Museum, Bucharest; Hungarian National Gallery, Budapest.

Publications:

On LUPAS: Books—*Pueblos, hombres y formas en arte el tapis* by Gratia Cutulli, Buenos Aires 1976; *Textile* by Keiko Fujioka and Mikiko Sakima, Tokyo 1980; *Rumanian Modern and Contemporary Art* by Vasile Florea, Bucharest 1982; *Die Kluge genossin* by Renate Windich, Freiburg 1984. **Articles—**''Die kleine Triennale'' by Anneliese Lehmann in *Heimtex* (Stuttgart), September 1969; ''A Plastic Profile: Ana Lupas'' by Negotia Laptoiu in *Tribuna* (Cluj, Rumania), February 1971; ''Ana Lupas'' by Georges Boudaille in *Les Lettres Francaises* (Paris), July 1971; ''Ana Lupas'' by Neaga Graur in *Contemporanul* (Bucharest), September 1972; ''Ana Lupas'' by Ion Frunzetti in *Romania Literara* (Bucharest), March 1972; ''Ana Lupas/Warsaw'' by Zbigniew Macarevicz in *Projekt* (Warsaw), no. 4, 1973; ''Le deuxième souffle de la Biennale de Paris'' by Daniel Abadie in *L'Oeil* (Paris), October 1973; ''Texkstiile on Viesti'' in *Omamarka* (Helsinki), no. 1, 1974; ''Lodzban, a Triennalen'' by Frank Ianos, in *Elet Es Irodalom* (Budapest), November 1975; ''Rencontre avec Ana Lupas,'' by Francois Jaunin, in *Tribune du Matin* (Lausanne), January 1982; ''Contemporary Glass Art in Romania'' by Alexandru Vlad in *Neues Glas*, no. 2, 1993; ''Conceptualism: An Expanded View'' by Marcia E. Vetrocq in *Art in America* (New York), vol. 87, no. 7, July 1999; ''Global Conceptualism'' by Tony Godfrey in *Burlington Magazine* (London), vol. 141, no. 1157, August 1999. **Films—**Interview with Marina Bartsch Rüdiger in *Berlin-Mitte, Kunst Besetzt Raume,* Berlin 1992; interview with Sebastian Muenchmeyer in *Titel Geschichte Ost Kunst Westwärst,* Cologne 1994.

*

The Meaning of my Work—Social Therapeutics

Our society—which in its course of wider removals, removals which revolutionized and revolutionize its structure, gives new dimensions to the universe of its material and spiritual values and generates changes in our mind and behaviour—henceforth needs people who integrate themselves creatively, and not in a conformist manner, in the life of society; I think that the problems which art sets, and which arise regarding its genesis, creative means, manifold consequences, finality and significance, exceed its own realm; and these problems oblige art to contribute, to shape and to give new dimensions to the social existential universe, a universe indispensable to the individual who is to be formed and educated in order to express himself as a distinct personality, as a centre of initiative and creation.

My Task: Building-Site Worker, Hero of Thought

The Artist should sink down his roots to the common source, to the general background. An identification with the essential facts of culture and work.

—Ana Lupas

* * *

Ana Lupas is a Rumanian artist living in Cluj (Kolozsvár, Klausenburg), a town inhabited also by Hungarians. Her grandmother being Hungarian, she speaks this language fluently. Her grandfather was called the lawyer of the Jews. It was necessary to mention these biographical details in advance in order to emphasize the fact that, to my knowledge, her name has never been mentioned in connection with the internationally well-known, unfortunate Hungarian-Rumanian conflict. And yet, a first glance at her work is enough to make it apparent that they could not have been born anywhere outside of this far-away corner of Europe. As András Bán once remarked, ''There are very few artists in Eastern Europe who consciously take up the position of being Eastern European. . . . one of these is Ana Lupas.''

In this sense, to be an Eastern European does not imply any kind of narrow-mindedness or nationalism; rather, it means that the artists react to their environment, instead of turning to abstract theoretical or pure formal questions, and that they are especially sensitive to their natural environment, to objects and materials taken directly from nature or from their immediate social surrounding. Ana Lupas belongs to the first generation of artists on the international art scene who discovered the possibilities inherent in land art and who succeeded in the always honourable but often shaky endeavour: the integration of folklore traditions into contemporary avant-garde art. For example, she organized a land-art action in the course of which she persuaded an entire village to spread wet sheets on a nearby hillside according to her instructions (Margau, 1970). On another occasion, the village people created decorative three-dimensional objects out of the ears of wheat, which could be interpreted as avant-garde harvest relictums and country minimal art-space marks, ''vegetable sculpture'' (Marginea, 1964). These examples were taken from the early, heroic period of land art, but the reconstruction of the sheet-environment at the *Europa, Europa* exhibit (Bonn, 1994) proved that this artistic attitude is interesting once again. This time, instead of water, paint was dripping from the drying sheets into dishes placed on the floor, or to describe it more accurately, the result of the drying and dripping process solidified at a certain moment—it turned into sculpture. This transformation refers at the same time to the process when the one-time happenings and actions gradually transformed into performance, the environments and objects became installations, and they were converted into elements of—to quote some exhibition titles—''Ressource Kunst'' and ''Art into Nature.''

Ana Lupas feels comfortable in working with different materials and in various media, chiefly painting, textile, and ceramics, but in a rather individual way. In the beginning, the young art students had ''to be allowed'' to express themselves in other ways than by the use of pencil and paintbrush. She plaited a five-meter-long abstract braid for a college exhibition at the end of the 1950s. (Incidentally, a local official of the communist party interpreted it as a cross and filed a complaint.) This was her first installation. And if we are looking for examples of Lupas's ''intermediality,'' it is easy to realize that the solidified paint dripping appears simultaneously in the context of both painting and textile. (It should be born in mind that Ana Lupas was a top international artist in experimental textile art in the 1970s.) Then the solidified textiles logically connected to ceramic reliefs and sculpture. (I am referring to her famous ''shirt relief'' series and her coloured ceramic ''eyeballs'' measuring almost one metre in diametre.)

Recently, together with the artist, we attempted to compile a list of the different materials she has used thus far. Textile, thread, wax, fibre, iron, wire, wood, dirt, wheat (and other plants), plaster, water, skin (animal and human), bone, blood—practically anything. It could be more helpful to mention a few works instead of this list. *Ecce homo,* 1969: plaster statue of a fellow artist wrapped in a bloody bandage. *Preliminary to Resurrection,* 1986: plucked bird carcass, grotesquely alluding to the disharmony between body and soul, but at the same time also arousing strange anthropomorphic and gastronomic associations. A whole crowd of bird carcasses were included in an installation at Berlin (1992)—as if grilled chickens were waiting to migrate to the south. Naturally man himself is also granted a place in the ''Resurrection'' series in the form of ''faces'' turned upside down. (Upside down, since they have not resurrected yet.)

With regard to Ana Lupas's most recent works, it is hard to decide whether they are sculptures, objects or installations, or even some other—so far unnamed—category. This question in not necessarily an academic one, since even the artist herself cannot give a name to her latest works of art. She has a storage place in Cluj, where she seems to have created some order; it appears as if a strange space was created as a result of the process of tidying up, and as if the storage place was being transformed into a kind of studio. I have seen photographs of this place, but I would be reluctant to name the forms and materials I recognized (architectural details, catafalque, trough, black cell, cage?), because this half storage, half studio in transition, half way to aesthetic and half way beyond aesthetics. It was almost like seeing it all in a dream. As if it had also been a dream when Ana Lupas burned grey adobe in her self-made smoking oven at the Budapest Art Expo in 1991 in a grey, dusty factory yard. *The Raft of Medusa* of 1977 still had some symbolic context, although in that case, too, the materials left in pitiful shapelessness played a dominant role: nylon foil, broken table, pieces of mirror on the wooden plate. It is in this respect—the almost tragic emphasis on the dejection of materials and objects—that I seem to be able to detect some resemblances between Ana Lupas's works and those made by Tadeusz Kantor, the deceased Polish artist and theatre producer. In the late 1990s, Ana Lupas, too, established a theatre, although not for the broader public. She shapes her own space, although it is still far from certain whether she herself wants to live in it: she arranges objects in this space, although she will perhaps run away from them. She has not yet decided where she would stay in the near future; nevertheless, she is preparing the objects for survival, and herself for the Resurrection.

—László Beke

LÜPERTZ, Markus

Nationality: German. **Born:** Liberec, Bohemia (now Czech Republic), 5 April 1941. **Education:** Educated in Rheydt, Rheinland, 1948–55; studied art under Laurens Goosens, Werkkunstschule, Krefeld, 1956–61; also studied at the Kunstakademie, Dusseldorf, 1960–61. **Career:** Independent artist, in Krefeld, 1961, in West Berlin from 1962, and in Dusseldorf from 1986: first Dithyrambic paintings, 1962; first stage decors, 1982. Founder, Galerie Grossgroschen 35, West Berlin, 1964. Guest instructor, 1974, and professor from 1976, Städtliche Akademie der bildenden Kunst, Karlsruhe; guest professor, summer academy, Salzburg, 1983; professor, Städtliche Kunstakdemie, Dusseldorf, since 1986. Designer of stage designs for opera *Werther,* 1983, and church windows for the gothic choir in the cathedrals in Nevers, 1989–90. **Awards:** Villa Romana Prize, Florence, 1970; Deutscher Kritikerverband Prize, West Berlin, 1971. Agent: Galerie Michael Werner, Cologne. **Address:** c/o Galerie Michael Werner, Gertrudenstrasse 24–28, 5000 Cologne 1, Germany.

Individual Exhibitions:

1964 Galerie Grossgörschen 35, West Berlin
1966 Galerie Grossgörschen 35, West Berlin
Galerie Potsdamer, West Berlin
1968 Galerie Rudolf Springer, West Berlin
Galerie Michael Werner, West Berlin
Galerie Hake, Cologne
1969 Galerie Gerda Bassenger, West Berlin
Galerie Benjamin Katz, West Berlin
Galerie Hake, Cologne
1972 Galerie der Spiegel, Cologne
1973 Städtliche Kunsthalle, Baden-Baden, West Germany
Galerie im Goethe-Institut/Provisorium, Amsterdam
1974 Galerie Michael Werner, Cologne
1975 Galerie Rudolf Zwirner, Cologne
Galerie Michael Werner, Cologne
Galerie Hans Neuendorf, Hamburg
1976 Galerie Michael Werner, Cologne
Galerie Rudolf Zwirner, Cologne
Galerie Serial, Amsterdam
1977 Kunsthalle, Hamburg
Kunsthalle, Bern
Van Abbemuseum, Eindhoven, Netherlands
Galerie Hans Neuendorf, Hamburg
Galerie Michael Werner, Cologne
1978 Galerie Heiner Freidrich, Munich
Galerie Michael Werner, Cologne
Galerie Helen van der Mejj, Amsterdam
Galerie Gillespie-Laage, Paris
1979 Whitechapel Art Gallery, London
Barry Barker Gallery, London
Josef-Haubrich Kunsthalle, Cologne
1980 Galerie Michael Werner, Cologne
Galerie Helen van der Meij, Amsterdam
Galerie Rudolf Springer, West Berlin
Galerie Heiner Friedrich, Munich
Galerie Dr. Stober, West Berlin
1981 Galerie Rijs, Oslo
Whitechapel Art Gallery, London
Galerie Michael Werner, Cologne
Galerie Rudolf Springer, West Berlin
Marian Goodman Gallery, New York
Waddington Galleries, London
Galerie Fred Jahn, Munich
Kunstverein, Freiburg, West Germany

Galerie Dr. Stober, West Berlin
1982 Galerie Rudolf Springer, West Berlin
Galerie Onnasch, West Berlin
Galerie Michael Werner, Cologne
Galerie Gillespie-Laage-Salomon, Paris
Galerie Fred Jahn, Munich
Marian Goodman Gallery, New York
1983 Van Abbemuseum, Eindhoven, Netherlands
Musée d'Art Moderne, Strasbourg, France
Galerie Thaddäeus Ropac, Salzburg, Austria
Galerie Michael Werner, Cologne
Waddington Galleries, London
Galerie Maeght, Zurich
DAAD-Galerie, West Berlin
Galerie im Kornerpark, Neukolln-West Berlin
Kestner-Gesellschaft, Hannover
Galerie Winter, Vienna
Marian Goodman Gallery, New York
Galerie Rudolf Springer, West Berlin
1984 Waddington Galleries, London
Galerie Gillespie-Laage-Salomon, Paris
Galerie Michael Werner, Cologne
Galerie Maeght-Lelong, Zurich
Galerie Fred Jahn, Munich
Galerie Winter, Vienna
Wiener Sezession, Vienna
Galerie Thaddeus Ropac, Salzburg, Austria
Mary Boone/Michael Werner Gallery, New York
Galerie Ascan Crone, Hamburg
Maximilianverlag Sabine Knust, Munich
1985 Galerie Ulysses, Vienna
Galerie Michael Werner, Cologne (twice)
Galerie Herbert Meyer-Ellinger, Frankfurt
Galerie Fred Jahn, Munich
Galerie Beaumont, Luxembourg
1986 Städtische Galerie im Lenbachhaus, Munich
Kunstlerhaus, Salzburg, Austria
Galerie Thaddäus Ropac, Salzburg, Austria
Galerie Sabine Knust, Munich
Galerie Gillespie-Laage-Salomon, Paris
Galerie Maeght Lelong, Paris
Galerie Reinhard Onnasch, West Berlin
Galerie Folker Skulima, West Berlin
Neuer Berliner Kunstverein, West Berlin
Galerie Rudolf Springer, West Berlin
Galerie Michael Werner, Cologne
Galerie Maeght Lelong, Zurich
Waddington Galleries, London
Mary Boone/Michael Werner Gallery, New York
1987 Museum Boymans-van Beuningen, Rotterdam
Galerie Michael Werner, Cologne
Kunstverein, Braunschweig, West Germany
Galerie Beaumont, Luxembourg
1988 Cleto Polcina Artemoderna, Rome
Galerie Lelong, Zurich
Kunsthalle zu Kiel und Schleswig-Holsteinischer Kunstverein, Kiel
Galerie Kaj Forsblom, Helsinki
Rena Bransten Gallery, New York
1989 Galerie Lelong, Paris
Obalne Galerije Piran, Ljubljana
Kunstverein Arnsberg, Arnsberg
Haus am Waldsee, Berlin
Abbaye Saint-Andre, Centre d'Art Contemporain, Meymac Correze
Maximilianverlag, Sabine Knust, Munich
Galleria In Arco, Turin
Galerie Michael Werner, Cologne
Galerie Beaumont, Luxembourg
1990 Galerie Sfeir-Semler, Kiel
Galleria Gian Ferrari, Milan
Mary Boone Gallery, New York
Galerie Lelong, Zurich
Venice Design Art Gallery
Galerie Tegenosch, Heusden, Netherlands
Galerie Michael Werner, Cologne
Galerie Volker Diehl, Berlin
Galerie Philippe Guimont, Brussels
Cleto Polcina, Artemoderna, Rome
1991 Centro de Arte Reina Sofia, Madrid
Michael Werner, New York
Galerie Michael Werner, Cologne
Städtische Galerie im Prinz-Max-Palais, Karlsruhe
1994 Galerie Chobot, Vienna
Manner ohne Frauen—Parsifal, Michael Werner Gallery, Cologne (also Michael Werner Gallery, New York)
Museum Moderner Kunst Stiftung Ludwig Wien, Ausstellung im Palais Liechtenstein, Wein (catalog)
1995 *L'Homme Sans Femmes,* Galerie Montenay, Paris
Skulpturen in Bronze, Städtische Kunsthalle Mannheim (traveled to Städtische Kunstsammlungen Augsburg) (catalog)
Museum für Moderne Kunst, Bozen (catalog)
1996 Künstsammlung Nordrhein-Westfalen, Dusseldorf, Germany (retrospective) (catalog)
Michael Werner Gallery, Cologne
1997 Michael Werner Gallery, New York (catalog)
Arbeiten auf Papier, 1964–1983, Museum in der Alten Post, Mülheim an der Ruhr (catalog)
Kunsthalle der Hypo-Kulturstiftung, Munich (catalog)
Stedelijk Museum, Amsterdam (catalog)
1998 Michael Werner Gallery, New York
Michael Werner Gallery, Cologne (catalog)
Sculpture, Lowe Gallery, Atlanta (catalog)
Kulturstiftung Dessau-Wörlitz, Wörlitz (catalog)
2000 Galerie Werner, Koln
Gemälde aus den Jahren 1994 bis 1999, Galerie Schultz, Berlin (catalog)
18 Bilder, 3 Skulpturen, Michael Werner Gallery, New York (catalog)

Selected Group Exhibitions:

1969 *Eskalation: 14 mal 14,* Kunsthalle, Baden-Baden, West Germany
1972 *The Berlin Scene,* Gallery House, London (travelled to Hamburg)
1974 *Erste Biennale der Kunst,* West Berlin
1980 *Apres le classicisme,* Musée d'Art et d'Industries, St. Etienne, France

1982 *Documenta 7,* Museum Fridericianum, Kassel, West Germany
1984 *Expressions: New Art from Germany,* Museum of Contemporary Art, Chicago
1986 *Raumbilder in Bronze,* Kunsthalle, Bielefeld, West Germany
1987 *Berlinart 1961–87,* Museum of Modern Art, New York (travelled to San Francisco)
1993 *Paintings, Sculpture and Drawings,* Kunstmuseum, Bonn
1994 Galerie Michael Haas, Berlin (catalog)
1995 *Skulpturen in Bronze,* Städtische Kunsthalle Mannheim (travelled to Augsburg and Bremen)
The Muse?, Galerie Thaddaeus Ropac (traveled to Salzburg Festival 1995) (catalog)
1996 Locks Gallery, Philadelphia (catalog)
Ölbilder, Aquarelle, Graphik, Galerie Vömel, Düsseldorf (catalog)
1997 *New Paintings,* Michael Werner Gallery, New York (catalog)
1998 Kunstsammlung Nordhein-Westfalen, Düsseldorf

Collections:

Nationalgalerie, Berlin; Berlinische Galerie, Berlin; Staatsgalerie Moderner Kunst, Munich; Städtische Museum im Lenbachhaus, Munich; Städtische Museum, Monchengladbach; Museum Ludwig, Cologne; Kunsthalle, Hamburg; Van Abbemuseum, Eindhoven; Museum Boymans-van Beuningen, Rotterdam; Australian National Gallery, Canberra.

Public Installations:

Deutsche Telekom AG Headquarters, Bonn; Haus Pietzsch, Berlin; Galerie Wache, Düsseldorf.

Publications:

By LUPERTZ: Books—*9 Gedichte, Zeichnungen,* West Berlin 1975; *Markus—Vogue,* Munich 1984; *Tagebuch New York 1984,* Berne and West Berlin 1984; *Bleiben Sie sitzen Heinrich Heine,* Vienna 1984; *Poems and Lithographs,* New York 1991; *Markus Lüpertz,* Bonn 1993; *Markus Lüpertz,* with Giovanni Carandente, Milan 1994.

On LUPERTZ: Books—*Markus Lüpertz; Kunst, die im Wege staht, Dithyrambisches Manifest,* exhibition catalog, West Berlin 1966; *Markus Lupertz: Fasanenstr. 13,* exhibition catalog with text by Christos Joachimides, West Berlin 1968; *Markus Lüpertz: Bilder, Gouachen und Zeichnungen 1967–1973,* exhibtion catalog with texts by Klaus Gallwitz and George Tabori, Baden-Baden 1973; *Markus Lüpertz: Dithyrambische und Stil Malerie,* exhibition catalog with texts by Johannes Gachnang and Theo Kneubuhler, Berne 1977; *Markus Lüpertz: Still Painting 1977–79,* exhibition catalog with text by Siegfried Gohr, London 1969; *Markus Lüpertz: Bilder 1970–83,* exhibition catalog with texts by Carl Haenlein Reiner Speck and others, Hannover 1983; *Markus Lüpertz: Skulpturen 1981–86,* exhibition catalog with texts by Lucie Schauer, Siegfried Gohr and others, West Berlin 1986; *Markus Lüpertz: Arbeiten auf Papier, Bilder und Skulpturen,* exhibition catalog with texts by Wilhelm Bojescul, Andreas Franzke and Remo Guidieri, Braunschweig 1987; *Ink, Paper, Metal, Wood: Painters and Sculptors at Crown Point Press,* San Francisco 1996. **Articles—**''Germany: Markus Lüpertz: The Doubling Dandy'' by Ferdinand Protzman in *Art News,* vol. 92, October 1993; ''Markus Lüpertz: Portrait by Armin Linke'' by Silvio R. Baviera in *Du,* no. 1, January 1994.

* * *

In the second half of the 1970s, Markus Lüpertz's painting was already showing its dramatic dimension, particularly in the assemblage of form and space—as in *Interior III* (1974) and *Lupolis: Dithyrambic* (1975). The surface is thick with matter, and the forms seem ''imprisoned'' in the very act of appearing or disappearing. A material abstraction where the surface appears in a spatial instability, almost surreal.

A forerunner of the German transvantgarde together with Baselitz, Immendorff, Penck and Kirkeby, Lüpertz emerged as the most symbolic of all. His abstraction in the first place and his figuration in the second come from the dark depth of the unconscious, unleashing a kind of visionary ambiguity. In Lupertz's work, matter is constantly convulsed by striking, vivid colours and sharp, cutting marks. His symbolic expressionism, though, is also crosscut by ancestral energies forming a peculiar ''stylistic eclecticism'' (Archille Bonito Oliva). The strangest forms are condensed, as in *Big Spoon* (1982), in which a diagonally placed spoon prevails upon the whole surface of the picture.

The language of painting, in order to be vital, has to deviate to measure itself against contradictory statements, as in Penck's primitive signs, in Immendorff's matter, in Baselitz's figurations, where the gestural action breaks into the surface in a narrative guise, conquering spatiality. Lüpertz seeks in art an edifying collision: he captures an oneiric vision, always stylistically different. Through this difference he mobilizes his gestural force, conquering the surface while his penetrating gaze leaves nothing untouched. The surface is the locus in which manifestations of the picture become the urgency of artistic language.

In this Lüpertz is categorical; only matter in the very act of its making guarantees the mobility of the gesture, as much as of the artist's vision. The dramatic mobility which he deeply engraves into the surface strengthens the emotion.

Paraphrasing Gertrude Stein, one could say that in Lüpertz's painting everything is destroyed and nothing really continues. For this reason it has a dramatic splendour of its own. The gesture, in its competitive and contingent urgency, takes hold of everything, making reality appear as kaleidoscopic, impossible to grasp, and so losing any referential human measure.

Therefore, in Lüpertz's works—especially those of the 1980s—the inside and the outside are amalgamated (as in *Brooklyn*), a whole in which the visual plane is impenetrable. In works where monumental figuration prevails, this impenetrability is complete; the mark appears as if fragmenting the figure, almost always totally unrecognizable.

Lüpertz is a painter of events. In his work everything must have a pictorial significance which can be found in the space of life. His expressionism is humane. It is humane inasmuch as it loves painting as it appears to the painter's own gaze which enters inside the surface, modifying things and images. An essential solitude prompts the artist to stand outside himself, to make contact with everyday, unforeseen events. Through his engagement with the exterior world, Lupertz violates the unknown, uncovers reality, abbreviates endless visual distances, to favour a kind of strategic osmosis. This advantage of penetration and gesture, which arrests the abstract/figurative instant, is apparent in Lüpertz's most recent work.

—Italo Mussa

LÜTHI, Urs

Nationality: Swiss. **Born:** Lucerne, 10 September 1947. **Education:** Kunstgewerbeschule, Zurich, 1963–64. **Family:** Married Elke Kilga in 1974. **Career:** Independent painter, 1965–69, performance and photographic artist, 1969–80, painter since 1980: lives in Zurich and Munich. **Agents:** Galerie Kaufman, Quellenstrasse 27, Zurich; Galerie Stadler, 51 Rue de Seine, 75006 Paris; Galerie Ernesto, Neusserstrasse 27, Cologne. **Addresses:** c/o Kaufmann, Kanzleistrass 105, 8004 Zurich, Switzerland; Wendl-Dietrichstrasse 17, 8000 Munich 19, Germany.

Individual Exhibitions:

1966 Galerie Beat Mader, Bern
Galerie Palette, Zurich
1969 Galerie Junge Generation, Hamburg
Kabinett für Aktuelle Kunst, Bremerhaven, West Germany
Kunstverein, Bremen, West Germany
Galerie Palette, Zurich
1970 Galerie Toni Gerber, Bern
1972 Galleria Diagramma, Milan
Galeria Palette, Zurich
Galleria La Bertesca, Genoa
1973 Galerie Krinzinger, Innsbruck
Galerie Nachst St. Stephan, Vienna
Galleria Diagramma, Milan
Galleria Conz, Venice
1974 Studio Morra, Naples
Galerie Stadler, Paris
Galerie Stahli, Lucerne
Studio Marconi, Milan
Galleria Schema, Florence
1975 Galerie Stahli, Zurich
Galleria Diagramma, Milan
Studio Morra, Naples
Galerie De Appel, Amsterdam
Galerie Stadler, Paris
Galerie Stadler, at *Art '75,* Basel
Galerie Palette, Zurich
Modern Art Agency, Naples
Neue Galerie am Landesmuseum Joanneum, Graz, Austria
Musëe d'Art et d'Histoire, Geneva
1976 Kunsthalle, Basel
Nishima Gallery, Tokyo
Galerie Gaetan, Geneva
Galerie Stahli, Zurich
Galerie Isy Brachot, Brussels
1977 Galerie Stadler, Paris
Galerie Krinzinger, Innsbruck
1978 Studio d'Arte Cannaviello, Milan
Museum Folkwang, Essen
Galerie Zellermayer, West Berlin
Galerie Stadler, Paris
1979 Galerie Stahli, Zurich
Galerie Isy Brachot, Brussels
Kunstmuseum, Aarau, Switzerland
Studio d'Arte Cannaviello, Milan
Galerie AK, Frankfurt
Galerie Gugu Ernesto, Cologne
1980 Galerie Krebs, Berne
Neue Galerie am Landesmuseum Joanneum, Graz, Austria
1981 *Bilder 1977–1980,* Kunstmuseum, Bern
1982 Studio d'Arte Cannaviello, Milan
Galerie Stahli, Zurich
Galerie Gugu Ernesto, Cologne
Galerie Nachst St. Stephen, Vienna
Galerie Krinzinger, Innsbruck
Kunstverein, St. Gallen, Switzerland
Galerie Buchmann, St. Gallen, Switzerland
Kunstverein, Frankfurt
Galerie AK, Frankfurt
Studio d'Arte Cannaviello, Milan
Galerie Gugu Ernesto, Cologne
Kunstmuseum, Olten, Switzerland
1983 Galerie Anton Meier, Geneva
Kulturhaus Palazzo, Liestal, Switzerland
Wolfgang Gurlitt Museum, Linz, Austria
Wilhelm-Hack-Museum, Ludwigshafen, West Germany
Studio d'Arte Cannaviello, Milan
Galerie Gugu Ernesto, Cologne
1984 Galerie Stahli, Zurich
Abbaye de Fontevraud, Loire, France
Maison des Arts de Genas, France
1985 Maison de la Culture, St. Etienne, France
Galerie Stadler, Paris
Galerie Klein, Bonn
Galerie Gugu Ernesto, Cologne
1986 Kunstmuseum, Winterthur, Switzerland
Galerie Hubert Winter, Vienna
1987 Galerie Stadler, Paris
Galerie Gugu Ernesto, Cologne
Kunstverein Munich
Galerie Elisabeth Kaufman, Zurich
Gesellschaft für Atktuelle Kunst, Bremen, West Germany
1990 *Urs Lüthi, 1990,* Helmhaus, Zurich (catalog)
1991 Musée d'Art et d'Histoire, Geneva
Kunsthaus Glarus, Switzerland (catalog)
Urs Lüthi: l'Oeuvre Multiplié: 1970–1991, Musée d'Art et d'Histoire, Cabinet des Estampes, Geneva (catalog)
1993 Kunstverein, Bonn (retrospective) (traveled to Bremen, Klagenfurt and Wiesbaden) (catalog)
1994 Galleria Civica di Modena, Bologna
1996 *Urs Lüthi,* Pilkington-Olsoff Fine Arts, New York
2000 *Urs Lüthi: Run For Your Life; Placebos & Surrogates,* Lenbachhaus Kunstbau, Munich (also SI/NY Swiss Institute, New York) (catalog)

Selected Group Exhibitions:

1966 *Zurcher Kunstler,* Helmhaus, Zurich
1970 *Visualisierte Denkprozesse,* Kunstmuseum, Lucerne, Switzerland
1971 *Swiss Avantgarde,* Cultural Center, New York
1974 *Transformer,* Kunstmuseum, Lucerne, Switzerland
1976 *Identite, Identification,* Centre d'Art Plastique Contemporain, Bordeaux
1977 *Documenta 6,* Museum Fridericianum, Kassel, West Germany
1979 *Biennale of Sydney,* New South Wales, Australia
1981 *Autoportraits,* Centre George Pompidou, Paris
1983 *Kunst mit Fotografie,* Nationalgalerie, West Berlin
1984 *Ecritures dans la peinture,* Centre National des Arts Plastiques, Nice, France
1993 *Gegendruck,* Graphische Sammlung der Eidgenössischen Technischen Hochschule, Zurich (traveled to Bonn and Innsbruck) (catalog)
1994 *Hors Limites,* Centre Georges Pompidou, Paris
1996 *Barbara Hamann, Urs Lüthi, Norbert Radermacher, Rob Scholte, Alf Schuler, Dorothee von Windheim,* KünstlerProfessorinnen, Kassel (catalog)
1998 *29th Annual Recontres Internationales de la Photographie,* Arles, France
2001 *Autoritratto,* The Cavellini Gallery, Brescia, Italy

Collections:

Kunsthaus, Zurich; Kunstmuseum, Winterhur; Kunstmuseum, Lucerne.

Publications:

By LÜTHI: Books—*Just Another Story About Leaving,* Paris 1974; *The Personal Dissolves So Easily In The Typical,* exhibition catalog, Innsbruck 1977; *Urs Lüthi: Run for Your Life: Placebos & Surrogates,* with Helmut Friedel and Anne Maier, Ostfildern 2000. **Article—** ''Image as Emotion'' interview with Effie Stephano, in *Art and Artists* (London), August 1974.

On LÜTHI: Books—*Realismus* by Peter Sager, Cologne 1972; *Body Language* by Peter Gorsen, Graz 1973; *Transformer; Aspekte der Travestie,* exhibition catalog with texts by Jean-Christophe Ammann and Peter Gorsen, Lucerne 1974; *Il Corpo Come Linguaggio* by Lea Vergine, Milan 1974; *Bodyworks,* exhibition catalog by Ira Licht, Chicago 1975; *Some Day When My Longing Is Gone, I'm Gonna Take A Smile For a Walk In The Sun,* exhibition catalog with texts by Wilfried Skreiner and Jean-Christophe Ammann, Graz 1975; *Urs Lüthi,* exhibition catalog with texts by Jean-Christophe Ammann, Wilfried Skreiner, Maria Netter and Carlo Huber, Basel 1976; *Urs Lüthi,* exhibition catalog with text by Zdenek Felix, Essen 1978; *Urs Lüthi: Bilder 1977–1980,* exhibition catalog by Wilfried Skreiner, Rolf Winnewisser, Martin Disler and others, Graz 1980; *Ecritures dans la peinture,* exhibition catalog by Francois Pluchart, Nice 1984; *Urs Lüthi: Sehn-Sucht,* exhibition catalog with texts by Rudolf Koella and Annelie Pohlen, Winterthur 1986; *Urs Lüthi: Die Editionen 1970–1994* by Rainer Michael Mason, Geneva 1994; *Urs Lüthi* by Caryn Faure Walker, Cardiff 1994. **Articles—**''Urs Lüthi: Portrait by Armin Linke'' by Bruno Steiger in *Du,* no. 1, January 1994; ''Once Upon a Place and Time'' by Susan Butler in *Creative Camera,* no. 330, October/November 1994.

* * *

The theme of the self-portrait runs like a red ribbon through the work of the Swiss artist Urs Lüthi. The self-portrait in all its colorful variations accompanies him along the road to an unknown inner world, but also serves him as the expression of artistic egocentricity. This artistic self-centerdness finally betrays his affinity with Picabia, whose spirit gently hovers over Lüthi's most recent pictures with their shifting chameleon-like quality.

An exhibition of his insignia and photo-portraits at the Museum of Art in Lucerne in 1970 first brought Lüthi before a wider audience. As a relentless self-portraitist he was already fascinated at that time by the myth of individual personality. To render in visual terms every facet of personal reality subsequently became his central creative aim. In order to emphasise their many-sidedness, he staged his photographic self-portraits in a varied sequence of inner landscapes which evoked changing moods and psychic aspects. And in the double pictures a tension between self-portrait and environment was effectively created.

Although he gained international recognition through Jean-Christophe Ammann's *Transformer* exhibition in Lucerne in 1974, Lüthi was not content merely to produce transformer works. He was more concerned in his relentless photo-series, to investigate the conceptual isolation of modern man and the contradictions inherent in individual personality; he even went so far as to set out in picture form his own physical death. At the beginning of the eighties he switched from photography to painting in the hope of capturing and projecting new aspects of his self-portrait. In these latest works he was aiming less at illustrating external features than at transposing onto canvas intangible factors such as feelings, desires and fears.

Urs Lüthi risked—successfully, it seems—the difficult switch to a second career: that of painting. In order to satisfy his obsession with his own mirror image, he began in 1984 a large, complex series whose allure lies in its mannered style, its fresh wit and irony—qualities generally seldom seen in Swiss artists. In these he tries repeatedly to fathom his own ''I,'' demonstrating in the process his prolific creativity. His large exhibition at the Museum of Art in Winterthur in 1986 alone showed fifty new paintings in ten series, including large-format diptychs and triptychs. Each series revolved round a theme of self-portraiture from *Vague Memories* through *Dreams* and *Adventures* to *Pure Delivery.*

Lüthi transposes his multiple meanings and contradictions onto the canvas in a dry, only barely painterly manner. This brittle and in a certain sense analytical art links his paintings with his erstwhile photo-series. He manages to preserve his artistic anonymity and non-commitment by constantly changing his techniques and introducing references to recent art history. Out of a variety of influences—Cubism, Contructivism, Surrealism, Automatism and Abstract Expressionism—he contructs a personal, frequently strange and alienating amalgam. His *Self-Portraits from the Intense Feelings Series,* in which Eros triumphs, are reminiscent of Picabia, David Salle and Donald Baechler equally, *Vague Memories* are reminiscent of Gerhard Richter, and *Heads* of Sigmar Polke. A hint of Léger and Mondrian breathes through *Mistaken Dreams,* and Picabia's Constructivism of the late forties is mirrored in *Dream Pairs.*

The many-layeredness of Lüthi's paintings also recalls Picabia. Abstract blocks of colour are superimposed with several constructive layers; figurative representations are built up with abstract symbols; images are distanced and called into question by counter-images. Thus, out of an undefined area of colours the torso of a naked woman emerges, over which the outlines of a pin-up model and, painted with a thick brush, a sexually aroused matchstick man appear. Aesthetics are suggested, then immediately negated, trivialised with kitsch and the mundaneness of the day-to-day.

Lüthi's puzzle pictures are like a bottomless pit in which the eye can find no area to fix upon. The complex superimposition of ideas and planes, of drawing and painting, construction and free-form runs through the whole of this latest work. From such perspectives the most disparate works are reconciled, and an area of sea, which at first sight produces a confusing effect, becomes intelligible. In this sea-landscape the various planes of colour, overtopped by a network of clouds and white foam, serve the ends of a pseudonaturalism which at botton is as abstract as any bare constructive painting. The single work has something banal about it; only in the context of the series as a whole does it gain its deeper meaning. And so, ultimately, Lüthi's self-portraits are the portrait in outline of the aspirations of our time.

—Roman Hollenstein

M

MACK, Heinz

Nationality: German. **Born:** Lollar, 8 March 1931. **Education:** Studied art at the Staatliche Kunstakademie, Dusseldorf, 1950–53, and philosophy at University of Cologne, 1953–56, M.A. 1956. **Family:** Married Ute Tietze in 1985; daughters: Maria-Valeria, Simone, Bettina. **Career:** Independent artist in Dusseldorf, beginning 1950, in New York, 1964–66, in Mönchengladbach, 1964—, and in Ibiza, Spain, 1989—; founder, with Otto Piene, of ''ZERO'' movement, Dusseldorf, 1958; first light pillar, 1958. Editor, *MacKazin,* Dusseldorf, 1957–67, and, with Otto Piene, *ZERO,* Dusseldorf, 1958–61. **Awards:** City Art Prize, Krefeld, 1958; Premio Marzotto, 1963; Painting Prize, Biennale de Paris, 1965; Adolf-Grimme Preis, 1970. **Agent:** Galerie Am Lindenplatz, Schaan, Fürstentum Liechtenstein, Landstr. 1–3, 9494 Schaan; Galerie Schoeller, Poststr. 2, 40213 Dusseldorf, Germany. **Address:** Ueddingerstr. 232, Huppertzhof, 41066 Mönchengladbach, Germany.

Individual Exhibitions:

1957 Galerie Alfred Schmela, Dusseldorf
1958 Galerie Alfred Schmela, Dusseldorf
1959 Galerie Iris Clert, Paris
Galerie Behr, Stuttgart
Galerie Dr. Griescebach, Heidelberg
1960 Galleria Azimut, Milan
New Vision Centre, London
Galerie Alfred Schmela, Dusseldorf
Galerie Diogenes, West Berlin
Studio F, Ulm, West Germany
1961 Galerie Nota, Munich
Galerie Ad Libitum, Antwerp
Galerie Dato, Frankfurt
Galerie Stephan, Vienna
1963 Galleria Cadario, Milan
Galerie Ad Libitum, Antwerp
1964 Galerie D, Frankfurt
Galleria La Polena, Genoa
Galleria Il Bilico, Rome
Museum Haus Lange, Krefeld, West Germany
1965 Galleria L'Elefante, Venice
Galerie Alfred Schmela, Dusseldorf
McRoberts and Tunnard Gallery, London
Kestner-Gesellschaft, Hannover
1966 Howard Wise Gallery, New York
1967 Op-Art Galerie, Esslingen, West Germany
Galerie Rotloff, Karlsruhe
Galerie Denise René, Paris
1968 Galleria dell'Ariete, Milan
Galerie Handschin, Basel
Gallerie Notizie, Turin
Galerie Heseler, Munich
Kunstlerhaus Halfmannshof, Gelsenkirchen, West Germany
1969 Galerie Ursula Lichter, Frankfurt
Galerie Reckermann, Cologne
1971 Museum Folkwang, Essen
Zacheta Museum, Warsaw
Galerie Krinzinger, Bergenz, Austria
Galerie Langer, Braunschweig, West Germany
Galerie Reckermann, Cologne
Galerie Jesse, Bielefeld, West Germany
Kunstverein, Mannheim
Galerie Dröscher, Hamburg
Galerie Müller, Stuttgart
Galerie Ursula Lichter, Frankfurt
1972 Galerie Denise René/Hans Mayer, Dusseldorf
Modern Art Galerie, West Berlin
Galerie Argelander, Bonn
Akademie der Künste, West Berlin
Städtische Kunsthalle, Dusseldorf
1973 Musée d'Art Moderne de la Ville, Paris
Galerie Denise René, Paris
Denise René Gallery, New York
Galerie Lohri, Schiefbahn, West Germany
Stedelijk Van Abbemuseum, Eindhoven, Netherlands
Galerie Stoll, Cologne
1974 Bottcherstrasse, Bremen, West Germany
Städtische Museum, Mönchengladbach, West Germany
Städtische Museum, Dusseldorf
Gallerie E, Balzano, Italy
Galleria della Trinita, Rome
Galerie Reckermann, Cologne
Junior-Galerie, Hannover (toured Germany, Netherlands, Denmark and Switzerland)
1975 *Arbeiten aus den Jahren 1955–1975,* Galerie Denise René/Hans Mayer, Dusseldorf
Städtische Museum, Mulheim/Ruhr, West Germany
Markisches Museum, Witten, West Germany
Nordiyllands Kunstmuseum, Aalborg, Denmark
Galerie Keller, Starnberg, West Germany
Städtische Museum, Ravensburg, West Germany
Städtische Palais, Linz, Austria
1976 Galerie Christa Bocker, Moens, Belgium
Galleria E, at *Arte Fiera,* Bologna
Kunstverein, Oldenburg, West Germany
Galerie Denise René/Hans Mayer, Dusseldorf (with Gunther Uecker)
1977 Junior-Galerie, Goslar, West Germany
Junior-Galerie, Dusseldorf
Galerie Brockstedt, Hamburg
Galerie St. Johann, Saarbrucken
Westdeutscher Landesbank, Münster, West Germany
Kunsthalle, Hamburg
Stadtmuseum, Munich
Städtisches Kunsthalle, Dusseldorf
Galerie Photo-Selection, Dusseldorf
Galerie Schoeller, Dusseldorf
Galerie Klaus Lincke, Dusseldorf
Kunstkabinett Dr. Griesebach-Grewenig, Heidelberg
Kunsthalle, Darmstadt

1978 Junior-Galerie, Hannover
Nikon Galerie, Zurich
Galerie Bossin, West Berlin
Kunstverein, Detmold, West Germany
Städtische Museum, Mönchengladbach, West Gemany
Rizzoli Gallery, New York
Amstutz Fine Art, Zurich
Unac Gallery, Tokyo
1979 Schlosspark, Stuttgart
1980 Kleine Grafik-Galerie, Bremen, West Germany
Galerie A, Munich
1981 Galerie Lauter, Mannheim, West Germany
Galerie Loehrl, Mönchengladbach, West Germany
Galerie Reckermann, Cologne
Galerie Holtmann, Cologne
1982 Galerie Dibbert, West Berlin
Galerie Holtmann, Hannover
1983 Galerie der Deutschen Bank, Bielefeld, West Germany
Galerie der Deutschen Bank, Dusseldorf
Galerie der Deutschen Bank, Freiburg, West Germany
Galerie der Deutschen Bank, Hamburg
Galerie der Deutschen Bank, Cologne
Galerie Loehrl, Mönchengladbach, West Germany
Galerie der Deutschen Bank, Wiesbaden, West Germany
1984 Skulpturenpark, Dusseldorf
Galerie Heseler, Munich
Deutsche Bank, Tokyo
1985 Galerie Denise René/Hans Mayer, Dusseldorf
Galerie Lauter, Mannheim, West Germany
Galerie Wack, Kaiserslautern, West Germany
Verein Deutscher Ingenieure, Dusseldorf
Galerie Babel, Heilbronn, West Germany
1986 Galerie Bossin, West Berlin
Galerie Hoffmeister West, Ludenscheid, West Germany
Galerie Schoeller, Dusseldorf
Kunsthaus Schaller, Stuttgart
Galerie Wahlandt, Stuttgart
Galerie Loehrl, Mönchengladbach, West Germany
1987 Galerie Holtmann, Cologne
1988 Arteba-Galerie, Zurich
Galerie St. Johann, Saarbrücken
Europäische Galerie für Bildende Kunst, Trier
Galerie Ursula Erhardt, Nürnberg
Stadthaus, Papenburg
Galerie Hete Hünermann, Dusseldorf
Galerie Hans Mayer, Dusseldorf
Kunsthaus Schaller, Stuttgart
Galerie von Braunbehrens, Munich
1989 Galerie Neher, Essen
Galerie Döbele im Hindenburgbau, Stuttgart
1990 Reuchlinhaus, Pforzheim
Galerie von Braunbehrens, Munich
Kunsthaus Schaller, Stuttgart
Galerie Herrenhof-Mussbach, Neustadt
1991 Kulturring Sundern, Sundern
Galerie Am Lindenplatz, Schaan
Galerie Franz Swetec, Griesheim
Galerie Loehrl, Mönchengladbach
ZERO-Mack: The Forest of Light 1960–69, Städtische Museum Abteiberg, Mönchengladbach
BIS-Zentrum, Mönchengladbach
1992 *Mack: Sculptures and Paintings,* Galerie Lauter, Mannheim
Galerie Lauter, Mannheim (catalog)
Stadtsparkasse, Mönchengladbach
1993 Kunsthaus Schaller, Stuttgart
Galerie Loehrl, Mönchengladbach
Galerie Schoeller, Dusseldorf
Jüdisches Museum der Stadt Wien, Vienna
1994 Stadtmuseum, Dusseldorf
Brandenburger Kunstsammlungen, Cottbus
Lindenau-Museum, Altenburg
Neuer Sächsischer Kunstverein, Dresden
Galerie am Fischmarkt, Erfurt
1995 *Heinz Mack: Mediterranean Time—Paintings and Sculptures 1994–95,* Galerie Neher, Essen, Germany
1996 *Mack: Light in View,* Galerie Landesgirokasse, Stuttgart

Selected Group Exhibitions:

1959 *Documenta,* Kassel, West Germany
1962 *NUL=ZERO,* Stedelijk Museum, Amsterdam
1964 *Painting and Sculpture of a Decade,* Tate Gallery, London
1965 *The Responsive Eye,* Museum of Modern Art, New York
1968 *Biennale,* Venice (and 1970)
1974 *From Picasso to Lichtenstein,* Tate Gallery, London
1985 *Kunst in der Bundesrepublik 1945–85,* Nationalgalerie, West Berlin
1991 *Sammlung Lenz-Schönberg,* Tiroler Landesmuseum (and 1992)
1992 *L'Art en mouvement,* Fondation Maeght, Saint Paul, France
1993 *Art from Postwar Europe, 1945–1968: New Realities,* Tate Gallery, Liverpool
1996 *Art After '45: A Selection,* Galerie Neher, Essen, Germany
1998 *The Eye's Pop: Op Art from the Albright-Knox Art Gallery,* Anderson Gallery, Buffalo

Collections:

Städtische Kunstsammlungen, Bonn; Städtische Kunstmuseum, Bonn and Dusseldorf; Kunstbesitz DaimlerBenz, Stuttgart; Wallraf-Richartz Museum, Cologne; Museum des 20. Jahrhunderts, Vienna; Musée Royal des Beaux-Arts, Brussels; Museum of Modern Art, New York; Guggenheim Museum, New York; Bradley Sculpture Garden, Milwaukee; Hirshhorn Museum and Sculpture Garden, Washington, D.C.

Publications:

By MACK: Books—*Mackazin,* Frankfurt 1960; *ZERO,* 3 vols., Cologne 1973; *Strukturen,* Dusseldorf 1975; *Skulpturen im Raum der Natur,* Cologne 1991; *Das Lied der Lieder,* Vienna 1993. **Films—** *Tele-Mack,* 1969; *Lichtkunst,* 1990.

On MACK: Books—*Mack: Monographie* by Margit Staber, Cologne 1968; *Kunst in der Wüste* by Max Bense, Stuttgart 1969; *Werkkatalog* by Eberhard Roters and Wieland Schmied, Academie der Künste, Berlin 1971; *Imaginationen,* Berlin 1973; *Mack,* exhibition catalog with texts by Jacques Lassaigne, Wieland Schmied, Margit Staber, and others, Paris 1973; *Sculptors Safari,* New York 1976; *Mack: Skulpturen* by Dieter Honisch, Dusseldorf 1986; *Sculptures,* New York 1989; *Sehverwandtschaften,* Stuttgart 1989; *Skulptur im Licht,* Stadt Pforzheim 1990; *Drei von Hundert* by Anette Kuhn, Stuttgart 1990; *Neue Gemalte Bilder,* exhibition catalog, Mönchengladbach 1991; *Die Grosse Stele,* Stuttgart 1991; *ZERO-Mack,* exhibition catalog, Mönchengladbach 1991; *Mack: Outdoor Sculptures,* edited by Ute Mack, Cologne 1992; *Mack: Sculpture and Paintings,* exhibition catalog, Mannheim 1992; *Mack . . . in . . . ,* Dusseldorf, Vienna, New York, and Moscow 1992; *Neue Arbeiten: Skulptur und Malerei, 1992–93,* Dusseldorf 1993; *Lichtkunst,* Cologne 1994; *Heinz Mack: Mediterranean Time—Paintings and Sculptures 1994–95,* exhibition catalog, Essen 1995; *Mack: Light in View,* exhibition catalog, with text by Cantz Verlag, Ostfildern 1996. **Articles**—''Metaphors in Glass: The Role of Glass in Contemporary Art'' by Christina Schroeter in *Neues Glas,* no. 1, 1996.

*

The discovery, taking place almost by accident, that art comes about unexpectedly, irritates our naive consciousness and makes it critical. Theoretical reflection is only a trap for the artist if it is speculative, that is to say if not preceded and again followed by the sensation of the picture that has come about. I have never hesitated to reflect on my own activity as an artist.

The shaping of forms in the existing sense can no longer be discussed. The conquering of colorfulness by color itself corresponds to the abandonment of composition in favor of a simple structure zone—in other words the simple juxtaposition of all picture elements. The artist must be aware of the function of the individual picture elements in order to attain unity in his work; attractive details are superseded by completely unattractive structure elements, meaningful only if they have a relationship to the picture or represent such a relationship. By this means, a structural element obtains its individuality, its unmistakable meaning; in itself, such an element is meaningless.

The physical-objective picture space must be rejected, even when it has abstract form. In the same way, the atmospheric picture space is naturalism.

An unexpected opportunity to make the aesthetic movement visible arose when I accidentally trod on a thin metal sheet lying on a sisal carpet. As I picked up the sheet the light was able to vibrate. Since the carpet was a mechanical product, the impression it left was also mechanical and decorative. The movement of the reflected light was entirely monotonous and boring. My metal reliefs, which I would prefer to call ''light reliefs,'' are formed solely by finger pressure and need light in place of color to come alive. If given a mirror polish, even slight relief effect will suffice to disturb the peace of the light and cause it to vibrate. If these picture compositions are found attractive, then this is purely the expression of the beauty of light.

Luckily nature has not yet allowed the complete inventory of our world to be distributed evenly over the available space on the globe. Under the same sky we can still find nature reservations—unusual spaces of large size, which create the impression that atom bomb explosions would dwindle and be lost inside them.

I admit that such spaces fill my imagination; I admire the casual manner in which they spread out so untiringly. The deep, open space, not willing to stop even at the horizon, is the free sphere for my gaze, which hurries without purpose or direction over near and far, weightless, until it returns to me. The experience of the vastness remains in me then.

In such spaces the clarity of light and the fullness of calm can spread themselves permanently. Light gives the space its purpose, its atmosphere, its transparency. Light removes weight from space. Calm gives space its weight. Through calm the space becomes audible; in such spaces we feel that our senses are finely tuned.

I desire to seek out ungraspable natural spaces in order to realize in them the second, comprehensible space, that of art. I call this artificial space the art of reservation. In this reservation, intended one day to be total, art shall find a new freedom. The Sahara project is intended to bring about freedom.

The problem of integration between architecture and pictorial art has been discussed a thousand times but will not be shaken until patrons, architects, and artists face up to the common task of producing an architecture entirely without purpose. Such architecture would require the same conditions as the fantastic classical architecture throughout the world still reveals: an irrational desire for beauty, expressed by all humanity, conveyed by the patron, realized by the builder, and completed by the artists.

The most pleasant surprise for my eyes was the recognition that space and light are indeed more powerful than my artificial works but that my relatively small constructions can reduce the endless expanse of space in themselves and can articulate and intensify the all-embracing luminosity of light.

My art is not an abstraction of nature and does not seek victory over nature. Nature is not my enemy. The museums are against me even though they buy my works. This has strengthened one of my convictions: my artistic expectations are best fulfilled by those works with a manifestation which causes the observer to forget the old guilty question as to whether what he sees is art or not. I am content with the unreality of fascination.

—Heinz Mack

* * *

Heinz Mack was one of the leading members of Group ZERO, along with Otto Piene and Gunther Uecker. Like them, he has been above all concerned with the use of light and movement in art and with such new materials as glass and aluminum. Group ZERO, which Mack cofounded in 1958, was one of the many groups and associations of kinetic artists formed during the late 1950s and early 1960s, all dedicated to using new means and new technologies in art. But in contrast to the scientifically purist approach of the French Group de Recherche d'Art Visuel, ZERO was at the romantic end of the spectrum in adopting an intuitive relationship with technology and an individualist, rather than a collectivist, approach.

The ZERO artists believed in light as *the* expansive medium, carrying energy from the artist to the spectator; they also believed that the artist should help to change the environment on a large scale, which led them to the demonstrations and performances that Piene and Mack held in Dusseldorf, including the 1960 show in which dozens of white balloons were set adrift in the night sky and their paths followed up into the heavens by searchlights.

''Movement is the true form of a work,'' Mack has said. One form of such movement was the recurrent wave of his Cardiogram paintings. He found his conception of painting realized in Mondrian's late Boogie-Woogie paintings, which he saw as a profusion of little repetitive forms unified by the ''allover form'' of the whole work. Increasingly, however, Mack's work became involved in light play, and he has recounted how the fruitful accident of stepping on a thin piece of metal foil and thus imprinting it with the pattern of a mass-produced fibre mat led him to create the pieces that he called ''light reliefs.'' These depend on distorted reflectivity as light passes over the creased, rippled, and slotted surfaces of aluminum sheet, producing sparkling, ever-changing landscapes of reflection.

Mack has also experimented with vibrating columns of light, and since 1958 he has been constantly developing the theme of rotating reliefs and light dynamos—metal plates driven by an electromotor so that they rotate behind a rippling plane of corrugated glass, causing light to be reflected from it in changing patterns. The patterns are based on the *moiré* principle used by many purely ''Optical'' artists—the slow disturbance of the light rays reflected back at the viewer generating an optical illusion that gives a disturbing psychological effect of unbalance.

But like Piene, Mack has also been turning to environmental art, dreaming of realizing works such as his ''Sahara Relief'' and ''Light Pyramid'' in some vast open space such as the Sahara Desert, where there is an abundance of calm, space, and light to extend the ''limitless stretch'' of art.

—Konstantin Bazarov

MALER, Leopoldo (Mario)

Nationality: Argentinian. **Born:** Buenos Aires, 2 April 1937. **Education:** Studied social sciences at the New School for Social Research, New York, 1957–58; studied law at the University of Buenos Aires, 1958–60, University College, London, 1961–62, and the International Academy of Comparative Law, Helsinki, 1962. **Family:** Married Silvia Oclander in 1967 (divorced, 1970); married Joyce Pieck in 1974. **Career:** Practiced as a lawyer in Buenos Aires, 1960–61, 1965–67; producer, External Services, British Broadcasting Corporation, London, 1961–64, 1968–74; also assistant editor, *Talia* magazine, and announcer for Radio Municipal de Buenos Aires, 1965–67; art critic and current affairs writer for *El Dia* newspaper, Buenos Aires, 1967–72; lived in Paris, 1973; created daily three-hour one-man program on Radio Belgrano, Buenos Aires, 1974–75; lived in London, 1975–77, and worked for the BBC and taught at Hornsey College of Art, London and Leeds Polytechnic, Yorkshire; moved to New York, and commenced work with lasers and synthesizers, 1977. **Awards:** Special Prize, *Leipzig Film Festival,* 1964; Di Tella Institute Grant, Buenos Aires, 1965; Camden Arts Centre Grant, London, 1971–72; Grand Prize, *Biennal,* Sao Paulo, 1977; Guggenheim Foundation Fellowship, 1977–78; Premios Konex, 1982. **Address:** 414 East 75th Street, New York, New York 10021, U.S.A.

Individual Exhibitions:

1964 *Men in Silence,* National Film Theatre, London
1966 *Caperucita Rota,* Instituto Torcuato di Tella, Buenos Aires
1967 *Exhibition of an Opening,* Galeria Rubbers, Buenos Aires
1968 *Listen Here Now,* Art Laboratory, Drury Lane, London
1969 *Outrage,* Roundhouse, London
X-IT, The Place, London
1970 *X-IT2,* The Place, London
1971 *Silence,* Camden Arts Centre, London
Crane Ballet, Kentish Town Playground, London
1972 *Q,* Camden Arts Centre, London
Carmen et Cyclum, Great Georges Project, Liverpool
1975 *Mortal Issues,* Whitechapel Art Gallery, London
1976 Galeria Pecanins, Barcelona
1981 Gallery Watari, Tokyo

Selected Group Exhibitions:

1974 *Art System in Latin America,* International Cultureel Centrum, Antwerp (toured Europe)
1975 *Open Encounter on Video,* Espace Cardin, Paris (toured Europe)
1977 *Last Supper,* Fondation Miró, Barcelona
Bienal, Sao Paulo
21 Argentinos, Museo de Artes y Ciencias, Universidad Autonoma de Mexico, Mexico City
1978 *Grupo de los 13,* Museo de Arte Moderno, Rio de Janeiro
Hayward Annual, London
1979 *3 Easy Pieces,* Centre Georges Pompidou, Paris
Bienal, Sao Paulo
1980 *Biennale,* Venice
1998 *Out of Actions: Aktionismus, Body Art, and Performance, 1949–1979,* Museum of Contemporary Art, Los Angeles (traveled to Vienna, Barcelona, and Tokyo; catalog)

Publications:

By MALER: Article—''Silence'' in *Art and Artists* (London), June 1971.

On MALER: Book—*Q,* exhibition catalog with an introduction by Jasia Reichardt, London 1972. **Articles—**''Visual Arts: June 1970-June 1971'' by Charles Spencer in *Design in Greece* (Athens), no. 3, 1972; ''Outside the Galleries'' by Michael Shepherd in the *Sunday Telegraph* (London), November 1972; ''Leopoldo Maler's Special Effects'' by Guy Brett in *The Times* (London), November 1972; ''Leopoldo Maler'' by Georgina Oliver in *Arts Review* (London), November 1972; ''Wring Out the Old'' by Caroline Tisdall in *The Guardian* (London), December 1974; ''Leopoldo Maler, o injusticado de CAYC'' by Leonor Amarante in *O Estado de Sao Paulo,* 26 November 1978; ''Karuptures: A Symposium on Monumental Sculpture in Lamentin (Guadeloupe)'' by Valere Bertrand in *Cimaise,* no. 230, vol. 41, June-August 1994; ''Puerto Rico's Sculpture Park'' by Manuel Alvarez Lezama in *Art Nexus,* no. 32, May/July 1999.

*

Excess as a source of creativity: On experiencing ''excess'' one begins to explore limits of our knowledge. Excess demolishes ignorance and brings man closer to his inner nature . . . that of the unanswerable questions. Contemplation is a creative action. Any creative action implies an expansion. Expansion involves excess.

Choreographies: I became interested in choreographies as a medium for the development of ceremonies. It deals with the kinaesthetical perfection and precision that other media lack for this purpose. It deals with action, and therefore one could plot a series of movements for either human beings, machines or any other object.

On working with a machine which has been designed to perform a specific series of industrial tasks, and including it in a creative event, we may experience NOT its liberation—as that would be irrelevant and unreal—but OUR own, from the standards of knowledge imposed by a productivitarian culture. To be able to play and to enjoy ourselves with a huge crane or lorry should—as an attitude—be as valid as any other social conquests. It involves the destruction of respect and fear for any utilitarian programming, and may help to convert the factories one day for other purposes, such as playgrounds. The day industrial plants may become useless and enjoyable will mark the real birth of a humane technology (the same as when TV shall find its very raison d'etre).

Film (that strange medium recorded in the past and able to create the illusion of the present): Same as in the case of the industrial machines I tried to liberate the film from its square screen and the multiplicity of objects and subjects inhabiting each single sequence.

In order to reach this purpose, I tried to recreate a magic environment, and ''staged'' films in art galleries and museums. They are frequently presented in the form of mixed media ''tableaux'' (e.g., ''Siglence,'' ''Q'' etc.). They are films of people—in full scale—projected into screens built in the same shape as the image, so there takes place a coincidence between it and the reflecting surface. You walk into a large dark room. There are several people looking at you, moving slowly and dreamlike. These people are in fact films watching YOU.

On another level these films are linked with the presence of a real object: a car, a preserved carcass, etc. So in this instance films act as a memory for the objects; a memory that visually manifests itself as an hallucinatory image. Memory acts here as an alternative possibility; what the film IS might or might not have happened.

Meanwhile, the spectator experiences two dimensions of time within the same spatial context.

SPACE is an all-important element of these exhibitions or ''situations.'' The objects involved in these experiences, as sculptures in themselves, are perishable to some degree. But it is the emotional signalling of the space involved that most interests me, as I found that memory does not travel through the paths of time, but rather zigzags around spaces of our previous experiences.

In some ways I could describe my work in this field as that of ''staging films.'' It may be explained more conceptually as a creative process which destroys that of the editing. It is a dismantling of images gathered in a single shot. I want the spectator to walk through the individual images of the film in order to experience them spatially. Why? I feel that one could—helped with the crutches of hallucination—start walking through the experiencing of large dark spaces which might finally give us the measure of our own beings. It is not by chance that religions put so much emphasis on the architectonics and grandeur of their prayer palaces.

Other of my past works, such as ''Carmen et Cyclum''—a spectacular ritual produced in a deconsecrated Church in Liverpool—was intended to rescue the ''original''—that is, the reawakening of the origins.

A ritualized act with choruses and 15 butchers trussing lamb carcasses hanging from a mechanized circular chain, aided by a conveyor belt which carried the meat pieces into the cooking area.

How many people have seen in their life a living lamb, a real animal whose meat they are going to chew and eat for the rest of their life? It is not unlikely that if a child were asked, what is a rump steak, he may well describe it as a ''white polyurethane tray with a red solid substance on it'' as presented in its alienated form with the compliments of the local supermarket! One of the most striking views I ever had was on a visit to the largest meat-packing factory in Argentina, where cattle walks in alive and well, just to be ready for export, tinned down the conveyor belt some 80 yards from its entering point. Miracles of consumers' excesses!

Human figure: Few images awaken so much our feelings, anxieties or fears as the human presence. Only a body lying in a street can—even for a split second—slow down noises, speed and alienation, and make us consider our nature. It is the mortal presence which puts us back in touch with ouselves in time of deep alienation.

The human figure—sometimes in films, others as real people performing some action or sitting still; or life size inflatable bodies, etc.—is a recurring image in my work. Unlike other artists it is not the aesthetical proposition that is the content of my aim, but the secret ceremonial that the slow movement of a body may recall for us when contemplating it.

Fire: Fire is extinguishable and therefore mortal. My most recent works include fire as a formal part of an object. Right, it is quite ephemeral, like life, and unlike stone, cast iron, or even papyrus.

The only possible permanence of these works is in the mind of some spectator, and past pieces could only be found in the intangible collection of man's own hallucinations.

—Leopoldo Maler

* * *

I would like to go through the world organizing feasts for weddings and births, ceremonies for leave-takings and welcomes. In a word, doing all that which, when there is celebration in common with other human beings, takes away from the word ''artist'' the meaning of a man isolated within society.

In a certain way, Leopoldo Maler accomplishes these desires. Although he has not yet gone all round the world, he travels every day. As an artist, many of his works are in fact feasts and ceremonies, that is, celebrations in dance, theatre, cinema, video; and all of these manifestations have to do with life and death, with the welcomes and leave-takings of the human being.

Maler prefers to call his works ''situations,'' because—he maintains—his interest is not directed to the creation of an object or the examination of the substance but to the elaboration of a ''climate'' by means of images. It is that he believes in the inventive power of contemplation as a form of participating—the best form possible. His images thus exercise the functions of catalysts, without necessarily supporting a narrative content. They are symbols of a personal ritual, and Maler develops them with the minutiae of a person writing a book.

His situations, for these reasons, are in most cases ephemeral. However, Maler's message resides in this very transience. ''Perhaps all work should be ephemeral,'' he has declared, ''so that it will not constitute a burden for its creator, so that the creator may be reborn from the ashes of each experience.'' Nevertheless, there is more; man is by nature ephemeral, since none of his gestures, his motions, are ever repeated in the same way. Maler wishes precisely to redeem these gestures and movements as an uneven, secret and mysterious cipher of human happenings.

—Jorge Glusberg

MANESSIER, Alfred

Nationality: French. **Born:** Saint-Ouen, 5 December 1911. **Education:** Studied architecture at the Ecole des Beaux-Arts, Amiens, 1926–29; studied at the Ecole des Beaux-Art, Paris, 1929–33. **Military Service:** Served as a technical draughtsman, Ministry of War, Paris, 1939. **Family:** Married Therese Simonnet in 1938; children: Jean-Baptiste and Christine. **Career:** Painter and graphic artist, Paris. **Awards:** Painting Prize, *Bienal,* Sao Paulo, 1953; First Prize, *Exhibition of Sacred Art,* Vienna, 1954; Grand Prix, *Carnegie International,* Pittsburgh, 1955; International Painting Prize, Valencia 1955; International Institute of Liturgical Art Prize, *Biennale,* Venice 1958, 1962; First Prize, *Print Biennale,* Grenchen, 1958; Painting Prize, *Biennale,* Venice 1962. **Agent:** Galerie de France, 52 rue de la Verrerie, 75004 Paris, France. **Died:** In Orleans, France, in an automobile accident, 1 August 1993.

Individual Exhibitions:

1949 Galerie Billiet Caputo, Paris
Galerie Jeanne Bucher, Paris
1951 Galerie Apollo, Brussels
1952 Galerie de France, Paris
1953 Galleria Lattea, Turin
Pierre Matisse Gallery, New York
1955 Galleri Blanche, Stockholm
Institut Francais, Copenhagen
Palais des Beaux-Arts, Brussels
Stedelijk Van Abbemuseum, Eindhoven, Netherlands
1956 Galerie de France, Paris
1958 Kestner-Gesellschaft, Hannover
Galerie de France, Paris
1959 Kunsthaus, Zurich
Dienst voor Schone Kunsten, The Hague
Museum Folkwang, Essen
Haute Provence 1958–1959, Galerie de France, Paris
1961 Musée D'Amiens, France
1962 Galerie Tony Spinazzola, Aix-en-Provence, France
1964 Phillips Collection, Washington, D.C.
University of Notre Dame, South Bend, Indiana
Forum, Stadtpark, Graz, Austria
1965 Maison de la Culture, Caen, France
Kunstnernes Hus, Oslo
Konsthall, Lund, Sweden
1966 Galerie de France, Paris
Galerie Wünsche, Bonn
Galerie Emmy Widman, Bremen, West Germany
1967 Galerie Wünsche, Bonn
1968 Maison de la Culture, Amiens, France
Maison de la Culture, Thonon-les-Bains, France
Musée Fabre, Montpellier, France
Maison de la Culture, Bourges, France
Centre Culturel, Toulouse, France
1969 Musée de Metz, France
Musée d'Art et d'Histoire, Luxembourg
Städtische Museum, Trier, West Germany
1970 Kunsthalle, Bremen, West Germany
Mittelheim Museum, Koblenz, West Germany
Musée de Dijon, France
Oeuvres de 1935 à 1969, L'Abbaye de Ballelay, France
Maison des Arts et Loisirs, Sochaux, France
Galerie de France, Paris
1971 Galerie d'Art, Esche-sur-Alzette, Luxembourg
1972 Société des Arts, Mulhouse, France
University of Notre Dame, Indiana
Musée d'Art Moderne de la Ville, Paris
Marais 19, Paris
Musée de Metz, France
1973 Fundncao Calouste Gulbenkian, Lisbon
Museu Soares des Reis, Porto, Portugal
1974 Musée Fabre, Montpellier, France
Musée d'Art et d'Histoire, Neuchatel, Switzerland
Librairie Feret, Bordeaux
Neue Galerie am Wolfgang Gurlitt Museum, Linz, Austria
Provincial Museum, Graz, Austria
Provincial Museum, Kragenfurt, Austria
Galerie de France, Paris
Museum des 20. Jahrhunderts, Vienna
1975 Galleria Editalia, Rome
Galerie de France, Paris
Galerie Lafond, Chateauroux, France
1976 Musée Dynamique, Dakar, Senegal
Galerie le Castrum-Rousillon, Gordes-Rousillon, France
Galerie Candela, Cannes
Hotel de Ville, Tours, France
Galerie Municipale, Esch-sur-Alzette, Luxembourg
1977 Centre des Arts et Lettres, Saint-Nazaire, France (toured France)
Hotel de Ville, Bayonne, France
1978 Galerie de France, Paris
Palais de l'Europe, Le Touquet, France
Centre Culture Saint-Jacques, Lisieux, France
1979 *Manessier: Retrospective,* Palais des Beaux-Arts, Charleroi, Belgium
1981 *Schilderijen, Grafiek,* Gemeentemuseum, The Hague
Musée de Poste, Paris
1983 Galerie de France, Paris
Galerie Patrice Trigano, Paris
1984 Galerie du Vieux, Chene, Geneva
Mjallby Konstgard, Hamstad, Sweden
1986 Centre Noiroit, Arras, France
Musée Thomas Dobrée, Nantes
1988 *Manessier: La Passion 1948–1988,* ELAC, Lyon (travelled to Besançon and Chateau de Vianden, France; Halmstad, Sweden; and Dublin)
Prieuré de Graville, Le Havre
1989 *Manessier, le regard, la couleur, la pierre,* Institut Franco-Japonais, Tokyo (retrospective; toured the Mediterranean, Caribbean, and South America)
1990 Musée Boucher de Perthes, Abbeville
Chateau de la Roche-Jagu, Ploëzal-Pontrieux
1992 Grand Palais, Paris
Cellier de Loëns, Chartres
Galerie Gravure Actuelle, Paris

1993 *Alfred Manessier: Retrospective of His Stained Glass Work, 1948 to 1993,* Centre International de Vitrail, Chartres, France
Académie de France, Villa Médicis, Rome
Abbatiale-Musée, Payerne
Galerie de l'Institut des Arts Visuel, Orleans
Musée Suisse du Vitrail, Romont
Museum of Fine Arts, Budapest
Eglise du Chateau, Felletin
Musée des Beaux Arts, Arras
Tour des Archives de l'Abbaye, Ambronay
Galerie de France, Paris
1994 Musée des Beaux Arts, Angers
Musée Jean Lurçat et de la Tapisserie Contemporaine, Angers
Abbaye du Ronceray, Angers

Selected Group Exhibitions:

1953 *Biennale,* Sao Paulo
1958 *Biennale,* Venice
1969 *French Painting since 1900,* Royal Academy of Art, London
1981 *Paris-Paris, 1937–57,* Centre Georges Pompidou, Paris
1984 *Sur invitation,* Musee des Arts Decoratifs, Paris
1985 *Depuis Matisse, la couleur,* Musée des Beaux Arts, Nantes (traveled to Edinburgh, Humlebaek, and Brussels)
1988 *Les Anées 50,* Centre Georges Pompidou, Paris
1991 *Art of the Forties,* Museum of Modern Art, New York
1992 *30 Ans de Creation en Perspective,* Musée National d'Art Moderne, Paris
1993 *Manifeste: Une Histoire Parallele,* Musée National d'Art Moderne, Paris
1997 *Embroidered Chasubles of the 19th and 20th Centuries,* Musee de la Dentelle, Caudry, France (travelled to Musee Matisse, Le Cateau-Cambresis, France)
1999 *L'Ecole de Paris? 1945–1964,* Musee National d'Histoire et d'Art, Luxembourg

Collections:

Centre Georges Pompidou, Paris; Neue Nationalgalerie, West Berlin; Museum Folkwang, Essen; Stedelijk Van Abbemuseum, Eindhoven, Netherlands; Sonia Henie-Nils Onstad Kunstsenter, Oslo; Moderna Museet, Stockholm; Kunsthaus, Zurich; Museu de Arte Moderno, Sao Paulo; Museum of Modern Art, New York; Carnegie Institute, Pittsburgh; Musée National d'Art Moderne, Paris.

Publications:

On MANESSIER: Books—*Manessier,* exhibition catalog, with text by Edy de Wilde, Paris 1956; *Alfred Manessier,* exhibition catalog, with text by Werner Schmalenbach, Hannover 1958; *Manessier: Haute Provence 1958–1959,* exhibition catalog, Paris 1959; *Alfred Manessier,* exhibition catalog with texts by Fredrik Matheson and Ole Henrik Moe, Oslo 1965; *Alfred Manessier,* exhibition catalog with text by Jacques Lassaigne, Paris 1966; *Alfred Manessier: Oeuvres de 1935 à 1969,* exhibition catalog with text by Bernard Dorival, Bellelay, France 1970; *Manessier,* exhibition catalog with an introduction by Michel Georges Bernard, and an interview by Leonie de la Grandville, Paris 1970; *Manessier* by J. P. Hoden, Bath and New York 1972; *Manessier,* exhibition catalog with text by Gaston Diehl, Lisbon 1973; *Manessier 1970–1974,* exhibition catalog with text by Camille Bourniquet, and an interview by Pierre Encrere, Paris, 1974; *Alfred Manessier: Retrospective,* exhibition catalog with text by Robert Rousseau, Charleroi, Belgium 1979; *Manessier: Schilderijen, Grafiek,* exhibition catalog with an introdution by John Sillevis, The Hague 1981; *Alfred Manessier 83,* exhibition catalog with intoduction by Pierre Encreue, Paris 1983; *Manessier: La Passion,* exhibition catalog with preface and interview by Pierre Encrevé, Lyon 1988; *Manessier,* Geneva 1992; *Alfred Manessier,* Angers 1994. **Articles—** review in *Stained Glass* (Kansas City), vol. 88, Spring 1993; ''Acquisitions 1992–94 at the Musee National d'Art Moderne, Centre Georges Pompidou, Paris'' in *Burlington Magazine* (London), vol. 137, no. 1105, April 1995. **Films—***Peintres d'aujourd hui: Alfred Manessier* by Jacques Simonnet and Camille Bourniquet, 1963; *Alfred Manessier* by Robert Essens, 1969; *Manessier* by Yvan Butler, 1971; *Manessier* by Pascal Bony, 1983.

* * *

Alfred Manessier came to maturity after the 1939–1945 war, following a period of spiritual retreat in a monastery. His beginnings date back to his study of architecture in Amiens until 1929 before he entered the Academy of Montparnasse to follow a figurative style of painting under Bissière and became friendly with Le Moal.

From 1934 to 1935, Manessier was painting Cubist pictures after meeting Picasso and Braque, then from 1935 to 1937 he experimented with pure abstraction. His isolation in Normandy during the war forced a fresh consideration of his aims. After some attempts at refinement, he decided that the transmission of light from within the canvas itself was the major effect to be aimed for. Medieval stained glass, and the clarity and purity of their colours, were echoed in his compositions, where frameworks of thickened line conveyed the suggestion of the leading of window openings. Signs and symbols highly schematised became the rigging on which he flew the pennants of high-keyed colour. The linear structure often performed a two-fold purpose as in ''Crown of Thorns'' (1951), where the religious connotation is strikingly evident in a symbolism that is comparable to the use of emblems by Klee.

Klee, in fact, has the most obvious affinity in the animation of the picture plane, where Manessier's free employment of semaphors gives a two-dimensional elasticity. Light is in constant movement through and beyond the surface, controlled by the density and warmth of the pure hues in jewel-like juxtaposition. Manessier's spiritual involvement contributed to his designs for stained glass windows, many of them for modern churches, and also to tapestries and lithographs.

Within his own highly inflected and rhythmic notation of a picture, Manessier has evolved his individual system of attack, lending each work its autographic identity inevitably expressive of its theme. There is something of the mystic semantics of Oriental calligraphy in a Manessier canvas, allied frequently to the abstract economy of a Chinese water-colour landscape. This esoteric content is revealed in the evocative disposition of signs, nonallusive to natural phenomena, but carrying in the arabesques a flatly painted choregraphy of silent import.

—G.S. Whittet

MANGOLD, Robert (Peter)

Nationality: American. **Born:** North Tonawanda, New York, 12 October 1937. **Education:** Cleveland Art Institute, 1956–59; Yale University, New Haven, Connecticut, 1960–63, B.F.A. 1961, M.F.A. 1963. **Family:** Married the artist Sylvia Plimack (Sylvia Mangold, *q.v.*) in 1961; sons: James A. and Andrew P. **Career:** Instructor, School of Visual Arts, New York, since 1963. Instructor, Hunter College, New York, 1964–65; Skowhegan Summer Art School, Maine, 1968; Yale-Norfolk Summer Art School, New Haven, Connecticut, 1969; and Cornell University Summer Art School, Ithaca, New York, 1970. **Awards:** Summer Art Fellowship, Yale University, 1959; National Council for the Arts Award, 1966; Guggenheim Memorial Grant, 1969. **Address:** c/o Karen McCready Fine Art, 425 W. 13th Street, 5th Fl., New York, New York 10014, U.S.A.

Individual Exhibitions:

1964 Thibaut Gallery, New York
1965 Fischbach Gallery, New York
1967 Fischbach Gallery, New York
1969 Fischbach Gallery, New York
1970 Fischbach Gallery, New York
1971 Fischbach Gallery, New York
Guggenheim Museum, New York
1973 Max Protetch Gallery, Washington, D.C.
Daniel Weinberg Gallery, San Francisco
Galerie Yvon Lambert, Paris
Fischbach Gallery, New York
Galleria Toselli, Milan
Lisson Gallery, London
Galerie Annemarie Verna, Zurich
Galleria Mari-Lena Bonomo, Bari, Italy
1974 Museum of Contemporary Art, La Jolla, California
John Weber Gallery, New York
Galerie Konrad Fischer, Dusseldorf
Daniel Weinberg Gallery, San Francisco
1975 Cusack Gallery, Houston
Ace Gallery, Los Angeles
Lisson Gallery, London
Galerie Yvon Lambert, Paris
Galerie Swart, Amsterdam
Galleria D'Allessandro Ferranti, Rome
Galerie Konrad Fischer, Dusseldorf
John Weber Gallery, New York
1977 *Four Large Works,* Museum Hans Lange, Krefeld, West Germany

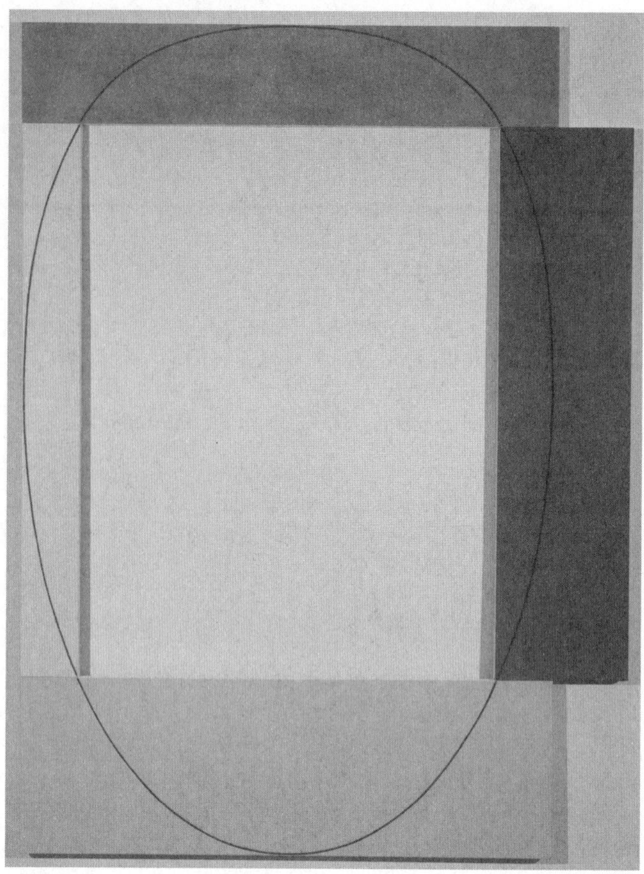

Shaped color field painting by Robert Mangold, 1965–95. ©Robert Mangold/ Artists Rights Society (ARS), NY.

Portland Center for the Visual Arts, Oregon
Kunsthalle, Basel
John Weber Gallery, New York
Young-Hoffman Gallery, Chicago
1978 Galerie Annemarie Verna, Zurich
Jean and Karen Bernier, Athens
Yarlow-Salzman Gallery, Toronto
Studio La Città, Verona
Galerie Schellmann und Kluser, Munich
Protech-McIntosh Gallery, Washington, D.C.
1979 John Weber Gallery, New York
Galerie Konrad Fischer, Dusseldorf
1980 Young-Hoffman Gallery, Chicago
John Weber Gallery, New York
Texas Gallery, Houston
Gremälde, Kunsthalle, Bielefeld, West Germany
Richard Hines Gallery, Seattle
1981 Galerie Annemarie Verna, Zurich
Lisson Gallery, London
Hoshour Gallery, Albuquerque, New Mexico
Carol Taylor Gallery, Dallas
1982 Sidney Janis Gallery, New York
Stedelijk Museum, Amsterdam
1983 Daniel Weinberg Gallery, Los Angeles
1984 Paula Cooper Gallery, New York

1985 Akron Art Museum, Ohio
La Jolla Museum of Contemporary Art, California
University of California, Berkeley
1986 Neuberger Museum, Purchase, New York
1995 *Curve Plane/Figure Paintings,* PaceWildenstein (Soho), New York
1997 PaceWildenstein (Soho), New York, and PaceWildenstein, Los Angeles (catalogs)

Selected Group Exhibitions:

1966 *Systemic Painting,* Guggenheim Museum, New York
1972 *Documenta 5,* Museum Fridericianum, Kassel, West Germany (and *Documenta 6,* 1977)
1975 *Painting, Drawing and Sculpture of the 60s and 70s from the Dorothy and Herbert Vogel Collection,* University of Pennsyvania, Philadelphia (travelled to the Contemporary Arts Center, Cincinnati)
1976 *Drawing Now,* Museum of Modern Art, New York
1977 *Less Is More,* Sidney Janis Gallery, New York
1978 *American Painting of the 70s,* Albright-Knox Art Gallery, Buffalo, New York
1979 *Whitney Biennial,* Whitney Museum, New York
1980 *The Geometric Tradition in American Painting 1920–1980,* Rosa Esman Gallery, New York
1984 *American Art Since 1970,* La Jolla Museum of Contemporary Art, California (travelled to Mexico City; Raleigh, North Carolina; Lincoln, Nebraska; Miami, Florida)
1985 *Art Minimal,* CAPC/Musée d'Art Contemporain, Bordeaux, France
1995 *Color and Structure,* Galerie Lelong, New York
1996 *Drawings by American and European Artists,* Margarete Roeder Gallery, New York
Limited Edition Artists Books since 1990, Brook Alexander, New York
1997 *Systematic* and *Great Graphics,* Karen McCready Fine Arts, New York

Collections:

Albright-Knox Art Gallery, Buffalo, New York; HHK Foundation of Contemporary Art, Milwaukee; Museum of Fine Arts, Houston; La Jolla Institute of Contemporary Art, California; Crex Collection, Zurich; Kunstmuseum, Basel; Städtische Museum, Mönchengladbach, West Germany; Museum Hans, Krefeld, West Germany; Van Abbemuseum, Eindhoven, Netherlands; Museum Boymans-van Beuningen, Rotterdam.

Publications:

By MANGOLD: Book—*6 Arcs,* New York 1978. **Articles—**''Work Comments 1965–1966'' in *Systematic Painting,* exhibition catalog, New York 1966; ''Robert Mangold: An Interview,'' with R. Krauss, in *Artforum* (New York), March 1974; ''Interview with Robert Mangold,'' with Robin White in *View* (Oakland, California), 1978.

On MANGOLD: Books—*Minimal Art: A Critical Anthology,* edited by Gregory Battcock, New York 1968; *Robert Mangold,* exhibition catalog with an essay by Dianne Waldman, New York 1971; *Robert Mangold,* exhibition catalog with an essay by Naomi Spector, La Jolla, California 1974; *Today/Tomorrow,* exhibition catalog with an introduction by Paul E. Thompson, Miami 1976; *Robert Mangold: Four Large Works,* exhibition catalog, West Germany 1977; *Robert Mangold: Gemälde,* exhibition catalog, Bielefeld, West Germany 1980; *Robert Mangold,* exhibition catalog with text by Alexander van Gravenstein, Amsterdam 1982; *Robert Mangold,* exhibition catalog with essays by Mark Stevens and J. Michael Danoff, Akron, Ohio 1985; *Between Image and Object: The Prints of Robert Mangold,* Andover, Massachusetts 2000. **Articles—**''Robert Mangold: Nuanced Deviance'' by Robert Berlind in *Art in America,* May 1985; ''Robert Mangold: 'A Maker of Images—Nothing More and Nothing Less''' by John Gruen in *ARTnews,* Summer 1987; ''The State of the Art World: The Nineties Begin'' by Arthur C. Danto in *The Nation,* 9 July 1990; ''Robert Mangold'' by Saul Ostrow and Shirley Kaneda in *Arts Magazine,* October 1990; ''What Artists Like About the Art They Like When They Don't Know Why'' by Paul Gardner in *ARTnews,* October 1991; ''Robert Mangold: Searching for 'Something in Between''' by Gus Gregg in *ARTnews,* September 1996; ''Robert MAngold at PaceWildenstein'' by Stephen Westfall in *Art in America,* September 1997.

* * *

Robert Mangold's career might be taken as a successful attempt to amalgamate some personal warmth and at times even dignified caprice within larger Minimalist commitment to anonymity, literalism, and precise measure. Only his earliest works, in the mid-1960s, were three-dimensional forms, and resembled grayed and abstracted building wall parts. But at that time, the artist made a self-conscious decision not to follow a sculpture course; nonetheless, the general character of his painted art has appeared ''architectural'' in both the geometric clarity of his form-shapes and his continuing fascination with works composed of sections abutted together and comprising a single concept.

In the later 1960s, with Barnett Newman still an important influence, Mangold worked with oil sprayed on masonite surfaces such as the ''Areas,'' 1966. More recently, he has used acrylic on canvas for works which became distinguished by large and clearly non-free-hand linear forms atop usually mellifluosly colored and monotonal grounds. These works have so developed during the course of the 1970s that at times the careful adjustment of the external shape edge to the internal patterns leads to the sensation that the normal neutrality of the outer edge of his works has become the real focus of the visual drama—or at least equally vital in establishing the significance of a single work. Where there appears to be error, as for instance ''8 Circle Drawings,'' 1973, as if miscalculations of the regularized forms were unseen by the artist who then permitted such works to be exhibited, there is both the character of wit and as well Mangold's absorption with an uncompleted form—continually avoiding stasis by its suggestion of movemet outside the boundaries of a particular work. He brings the old parlor game of visual illusion to bear upon images which have no apparent implication of such meaning at first glance.

Works of the later 1970s continued with internal linear marking but with a new emphasis on geometry, and went on to become shaped canvas as X and Plus, with clear allusion to De Stijl and Constructivism in a new kind of ease with European art traditions. As well, such visual play can be felt as a returning interest in compositional devices, and leaving off of the negation of Minimalism. But then his work may have always conveyed more interest in internal relationships rather than developing a sense of objectness.

For the past decade, he has used a brush (rather than a roller, as earlier) to make his surfaces more available and turned to a lyric ensemble of color—chocolate brown, sky blue, et al. With the mid-1980s, the paintings became marked with this-wordly suggestions—in fascinating counterpoint to the evolution of his wife's imagery (Sylvia Plimack Mangold) which has become more abstracted and diffused. In this time, in such a series as the *Frame Paintings* and the *Irregular Areas,* earlier motifs occur: the abutting of canvases, the play with curvilinear patterns within the geometry, and the emphasis on edge.

Although Mangold has said that he is much more interested in preparation of his ideas than in the actual concretization of them in pictures, he is clearly an intuitive artist and does not work through formula or system.

In the last decade Mangold continued to work in his accostomed series, moving with high confidence into very large scale and more complex configurations but without losing his essential direct immediacy and somehow, his concommitant charm. The early 1990s saw the completion of the 18 works of the ''Attic'' series. Influenced by the Metropolitan Museum of Art's collection of early classic Greek Red and Black figure pottery—which ironically Mangold had already known well years before as a museum guard—the artist evolved a series of irregular rhomboid and trapezoidal edged paintings. These featured the artist's usual flat fields of here muted, yet softly radiant color and surface reminscent of the vases; and as well Mangold's omnipresent linear play—here a double loop often akin to the infinity sign—seemed an echo of the incisive clarity of the ancient drawing style.

This group was followed by the ''Plane/Figures'' of 1992–94. In an irregular trapezoidal format, divided in half and each filled with intense coloration these works were reminscent of the landscape color outside the artist's rural studio. It was as if Mangold had here reflected his wife, Sylvia Mangold's, career-long and intense gaze at this same landscape, but of course in his own warmly austere abstract idiom.

Several writers have spoken of the humanoid sense of Mangold's inscribed linear images which, according to Westfall, ''sometimes feel like sentimental symbols for the figure.'' And such surmise becomes then less so in the light of Mangold's own assertion that he enjoys the sense—if it aids access to his work—that the viewer may project human form and nuance into his usual ovoid linear patterns.

The ''Curved Plane/Figures'' of the mid-1990s, with their semi-circular and strict half-circle upper borders, revived, in reversal, the lower-edge curve of Mangold's early body of work in 1968, the ''Curved Areas.'' And although the ''Curved Plane'' group offers overlapped ellipses and hue value changes within a single work, it seems a fond return to early maturity in the formal regularity of quarter circle edges and perpendicular color bands. In the ''Zones'' grouping of the later 1990s, a great complexity appears as if Mangold would assert an interplay, for the first time, between flatness and spatiality. In these very large scale and thus quasi-architectural works reaching beyond 16 feet in length, the arc-like upper border encompasses three panels; the older irregularity of both panel and inscribed ovoids as well reappears. But new to his work, Mangold has made the central panel a neutral color, most often black—it is the ''Zone''—and so then appearing like a void into or through which move the linear oval forms of the side panels. There may well be a sense of mystery beyond geometry that is intended. In a recent print series ''Fragments'' (1998), Mangold extended a chance view of a fractured lithographic stone into perhaps a vital part of his further formal evolution in painting as well: he has used the entire stone surface for printing so as to include the irregular edges and internal blemishes as part of the image. It is as if Mangold might now want his visual idiom to include chance as a given rather than as heretofore, chance as a self-made event.

—Joshua Kind

MANZÙ, Giacomo

Nationality: Italian. **Born:** Giacomo Manzoni in Bergamo, 22 December 1908. **Education:** Apprenticed to a wood carver and gilder and later to a plasterer, Bergamo, 1919; attended evening classes at the Fantoni School, Bergamo, 1921; studied briefly at the Accademia di Belle Arti, Verona, 1928; mainly self-taught in art. **Military Service:** Served in the Italian Army, in Verona, 1927. **Family:** Married Antonia Oreni in 1934 (separated, 1952); children: Carlo and Mileta (both died in 1937) and Pio; married Inge Schabel in 1958; children: Giulia and Mileto. **Career:** Sculptor and painter since 1928; lived in Milan, 1930–33, then returned to Bergamo; worked on decorations for the chapel of the Catholic University, Milan, 1930; decorated main hall, Ardiano House, Selvino, near Bergamo, 1933; produced many drawings and paintings during the 1930s, also worked in chased copper; first bronzes, 1934; moved to Clusone, near Bergamo, 1942; settled in Milan, 1945; moved to Rome, 1958; worked on decorations of chapel in house of Don Giuseppe de Lucca, Rome, 1961, moved to the Vatican, 1963; settled in Campo del Fico, Ardea, near Rome, 1964; first theatre designs, for *Oedipus Rex* by Stravinsky, Rome, 1964; founded Raccolta Amici di Manzù, Ardea, 1969, which was donated to the Italian State, 1981. Professor of sculpture, Brera Accademia di Belle Arti, Milan, 1941–54; lecturer, Albertina Accademia, Turin, 1941–42; lecturer, Kokoschka's International Summer School 1954–60. **Awards:** Gold Medal, *Triennale,* Milan 1937; Grand Prize, *Quadriennale,* Rome, 1942; Italian Sculpture Prize, *Biennale,* Venice, 1948; International Lenin Prize, 1966, Via Condotti Award, Rome, 1981; Italian Gold Medal of Merit, Rome, 1981; Le Muse Medal, Academy of the Muse, Florence, 1981. Honorary doctorate, Royal College of Art, London, 1971. Corresponding member, 1947, and Academician, 1954, Accademia di San Luca, Rome. **Member:** Académie Royal de Belgique, 1954; American Academy of Arts and Letters, 1964; Academia Nacional de Bellas Artes, Buenos Aires, 1964; Académie des Beaux-Arts, Paris, 1969; Academy of Arts of the U.S.S.R., 1969; American Academy of Arts and Sciences, 1978; European Academy of Sciences, Arts and Letters, Paris, 1981; Honorary Academician: Royal Academy of Arts, London, 1970. **Died:** In Ardea, Italy, 17 January 1991.

Individual Exhibitions:

1933 Galleria del Milione, Milan
1934 Galleria delle Tre Arti, Milan
1937 Galleria Cometa, Rome
1938 Galleria Genova, Genoa (with Renato Birolli)
1941 Galleria Barbaroux, Milan
1942 Centro d'Azione per le Arti, Turin
1944 Galleria Galatea, Turin
1945 Galleria Galatea, Turin
1947 Palazzo Reale, Milan

Giacomo Manzù: *Deposition,* 1933. ©Scala/Art Resource, NY, courtesy of a private collection, Milan, Italy.

Giacomo Manzù: *Woman.* ©Scala/Art Resource, courtesy of Collezione d'Arte Religiosa Moderna, Vatican Museums, Vatican State.

Galleria La Palma, Rome
1949 Instituto de Arte Moderno, Buenos Aires
1953 Hanover Gallery, London
1954 Galerie Welz, Salzburg (with Oskar Kokoschka)
1955 Galerie Welz, Salzburg (toured Europe)
1956 Hanover Gallery, London
Kunsthaus, Winterthur, Switzerland (with Giorgio Morandi)
1957 World House Gallery, New York
Palazzo Strozzi, Florence
1958 Opera Barilacqua di Musa, Venice
American Federation of Arts, New York (with Giorgio Morandi) Galerie Welz, Salzburg
1959 Haus der Kunst, Munich (toured Europe, 1959–60)
1960 World House Gallery, New York
La Nuova Pesa Galleria, Rome (with Renato Guttuso)
1962 Galerie Welz, Salzburg
Palazzo della Pinacoteca Carrara, Bergamo
1964 Galleria Galatea, Turin
Sala Napoleone, Venice
1965 Hanover Gallery, London
Paul Rosenberg Gallery, New York
1966 Gallery Cube, Tokyo
Academy of Art, Moscow (travelled to the Academy of Arts, Leningrad)
1967 Galleria Galatea, Turin
1968 Paul Rosenberg Gallery, New York
Galleria Ciranna, Milan
Museum Boymans-van Beuningen, Rotterdam
1969 Galerie des Beaux-Arts, Bordeaux
Hanover Gallery, London
Lumley Cazalet Gallery, London
Academie der Künste, East Berlin
Museum of Modern Art, New York
Pushkin Museum, Moscow (travelled to the Hermitage Museum, Leningrad, and the Academy of Fine Arts, Kiev)
Museo Nazionale, Reggio Calabria, Italy
1970 Galleria Odyssia, New York (with Giorgio Morandi and Ennio Morlotti)
Teatro San Carlos, Naples
1971 Galleria Luigi Bellini, Florence
Raccolta Amici di Manzù, Ardea, Rome
1972 Städtsgalerie Modernen Kunst, Munich
1973 National Museum of Modern Art, Tokyo
Carolino Augusteum Museum and Galerie Welz, Salzburg
Galleria Toninelli, Rome
Galerie G, Berlin
Pinacoteca Brera, Milan (travelled to the Galleria Civica d'Arte Moderna, Turin, and the Galleria Ghelfi, Verona)
Belvedere Palace, Prague
Palazzo Comunale, Pienza, Italy
Galleria Idea, Florence
1974 Galerie am Hohen Markt, Krems-an-der-Donau, Austria
Teatro Accademico del Bibbiena, Mantua, Italy

National Gallery, Budapest
1975 Palazzo Diamanti, Ferrara, Italy
Italo-Latin American Institute, Rome
1976 Universe Gallery, Tokyo
Mariani Galleria, Ravenna, Italy
Kunstmuseum, Münster
Raccolta Amici di Manzù, Ardea, Rome
1977 Palazzo della Ragione, Bergamo
Carrara Academy, Bergamo
San Bartolomeo, Bergamo
Studio d'Arte A2, Rome
1978 Art Museum, Phoenix, Arizona (travelled to the Fine Art Museum, San Diego, California)
Raccolta Amici di Manzù, Ardea, Rome
1979 Accademia delle Arti e del Disegno, Florence
Galerie Nichide, Paris
Universe Gallery, Tokyo
Galleria Ellequadro, Genoa
Gallery Tasende, La Jolla, California
1980 Galleria della Bezuga, Florence
Centro Dantesco, Ravenna
Pushkin Museum, Moscow
Galleria Bergamini, Milan (travelled to the Galleria Forni, Bologna)
100 Works 1938–1980, Art Gallery of Hamilton, Ontario (toured Canada, 1980–82)
1981 Galleria Ca'd'Oro, Rome
1986 Kunstnerforbundet, Oslo
Bergen Billedgalleri, Norway
Galleria l'Isola, Rome
1987 Carlsburg Glyptotek, Copenhagen
1988 Museum of Modern Art, Oxford
1991 *Manzù e il sacro,* Venice (catalog)
2000 *Manzù: Opere da e per Michelangelo da Caravaggio,* Bergamo (catalog)

Selected Group Exhibitions:

1932 *Group Exhibition,* Galleria del Milione, Milan
1936 *Biennale,* Venice
1937 *International Exhibition,* Musée National d'Art Moderne, Paris
1939 *Italian Art, Ancient and Modern,* San Francisco Museum of Art
1951 *Bienal,* Sao Paulo
1955 *Biennale,* Open-Air Sculpture Garden, Antwerp
1958 *Pittsburgh International,* Carnegie Institute, Pittsburgh
1966 *Italian Sculptors,* Tate Gallery, London
1972 *Masters of Modern Italian Art,* Museum of Modern Art, Kyoto, Japan

Collections:

Raccola Amici di Manzù, Ardea; Galleria Nazionale d'Arte Moderna, Rome; Tate Gallery, London; Middelheim Park, Antwerp; Wallraf-Richartz Museum, Cologne; Kunstnernes Hus, Oslo; National Museum of Modern Art, Tokyo; Manzù Room, Open-Air Museum, Hakone, Japan; Museum of Modern Art, New York; Guggenheim Museum, New York.

Publications:

By MANZÙ: Book—*Moscow,* 1972. **Illustrated books—***Il falso e vero verde* by Salvatore Quasimodo, 1954; *Works and Days* by Hesiod, Rome 1966; *The New Testament,* Paris 1966; *King Oedipus* by Sophocles, New York 1966; *The Odyssey* by Homer, translated by Salvatore Quasimodo, Rome 1977. **Articles—**''Dove va l'arte italiana? in *Domus* (Milan), February 1937; ''La disciplina dell'Arte'' in *Pinifarina* (Turin), no. 5, 1964; ''Paris Giacomo Manzu'' in *Domenica del Corriere* (Milan), March 1970; ''Il disegno e sempre una speranza'' in *Didattica del Designo* (Brescia, Italy), March 1970.

On MANZÙ: Books—*Manzù* by Giovanni Schweiller, Milan 1932; *Human and Religious Values in the Great Pietà of Giacomo Manzù for a Papal Monument* by Bruno Calzaferri, Milan 1943; *Giacomo Manzù; Sculptor* by Carlo Ludovico Ragghianti, Milan 1957; *Manzù* by John Rewald, London 1967; *Catalog of the Graphic Work of Manzù 1929–1968* by Alfonso Ciranna, Milan 1968; *An Artist and the Pope* by Curtis Bill Pepper, New York 1968; *Manzù* by Mario de Micheli, Milan 1971 (includes bibliography); *Manzù and the Stage* by Blida Heynold von Graefe, Ardea, Italy 1972; *Manzù and the Theme of Peace* by Glauco Pellegrini, Florence 1976; *Giacomo Manzù,* exhibition catalog by M. Homma, J. P. Hodin and H. Kon, Tokyo 1973; *Manzù: 100 Works 1938–1980,* exhibition catalog, Hamilton, Ontario 1980. **Film—***Giacomo Manzù* by Glauco Pellegrini, 1959.

* * *

''You have produced more than my portrait. You have told the story of my pontificate in bronze,'' said Pope John XXIII, the peasant's son from ''Sotto il Monte'' in the province of Bergamo, to Giacomo Manzù, the eleventh of a Bergamo shoemaker's twelve children. So the sculptor had again succeeded in what for him according to his own words is the most important element in sculpture: ''The form should embrace what people have in them.''

Manzù's sculptures, drawings and bas relief are always much more than an artist's perfect forms governed by the technique of his handicraft. The word handicraft in this instance is not accidental. Manzù is self-taught; he had been apprenticed as an 11 year old first to a wood carver, then to a plasterer. Only when he was 20 years of age, overwhelmed by his reaction to Impressionism in Paris, did he decide to become an artist. He was influenced by the Etruscans and the Roman and Gothic stonemasons of Lombardy but also by the great Medardo Rosso, much too little known outside Italy, who like Manzù modelled with light. But the impressionist Medardo almost dissolved his forms in the light, while the realist Manzù surrounds his with light, stresses their materiality as if with an inner light.

Manzù has always remained an outsider whose strengths grew with solitude. In 1954 he gave up the professorship at the Milan Brera Academy which he had held since 1941 so as to be able to work in peace.

Sensitivity and perceptive awareness dictate his work whose thematic breadth gives at first glance the impression of a contradiction. For it extends from the biblical themes of his bronze doors at St. Peter's in Rome, the cathedrals of Rotterdam and Salzburg to the almost ironically stylised Cardinals, from the sculptures and drawings for which his wife Inge and his children were models, to the erotic in the series of the lovers and of strip-tease.

Delicacy in him will never be feeble. The control of technique will never become routine. The handsome realism of his sculptures knows nothing of the smoothness of the neo-classic. His drawings are so little academic, like his bas reliefs which retain the sensitive freshness of his drawings. Only in the political caricatures of this ardent anti-fascist and anti-militarist does his soft line harden, is his otherwise lively sense of humour replaced by anger.

Manzù is the first Italian artist for whom a museum was established in his lifetime. The ''Amici di Manzù'' (Friends of Manzù) was inaugurated at the beginning of the 1970s near to his workshop in the ''Fig-garden'' of Ardea near Rome. Grown solitary and continuing to work untiringly, the artist bequeathed the museum to the state in 1981. For he knew, in all grumbling modesty, that his works no longer belong to him but to the people.

—Monika von Zitzewitz

MARCA-RELLI, Conrad

Nationality: American. **Born:** Boston, Massachusetts, 5 June 1913; moved to New York City in 1926. **Education:** Cooper Union, New York, 1930. **Military Service:** Served as a private first class in the United States Army, 1941–45. **Family:** Married Anita Gibson in 1951. **Career:** Painter, lived and worked in New York from 1930: influenced by associations with De Kooning, Pollock, Franz Kline and John Graham; Easel and Mural Painter, Federal Art Project, New York, 1935–38; lived in Rome and Paris, 1948–49; organizing member, 8th Street Club of painters and intellectuals, New York, 1949–50; lived in Easthampton, Long Island, New York, 1969–83, and in Sarasota, Florida, since 1983; also maintained a home in Ibiza, Spain. Guest critic, Yale University, New Haven, Connecticut, 1954–55, 1959–60; guest professor, University of California, Berkeley, 1958; artist-in-residence, New College, Sarasota, Florida, 1966; lived in Parma, Italy, 1996–2000. **Awards:** Logan Medal, Art Institute of Chicago, 1954; Ford Foundation Grant, 1959; Purchase Prize, Detroit Institute of Arts, 1960; Kohnstamm Prize, Art Institute of Chicago, 1963. **Member:** American Academy of Arts and Letters. **Died:** In Parma, Italy, 29 August 2000.

Individual Exhibitions:

1947 Niveau Gallery, New York
1949 Niveau Gallery, New York
Galleria Il Cortile, Rome
1951 New Gallery, New York
1953 Stable Gallery, New York
1955 Stable Gallery, New York
1956 Stable Gallery, New York
Frank Perls Gallery, Hollywood, California
1957 Galleria La Tartaruga, Rome
Galleria del Naviglio, Rome
1958 Stable Gallery, New York
1959 Kootz Gallery, New York
1960 Kootz Gallery, New York
Playhouse Gallery, Sharon, Connecticut
1961 Kootz Gallery, New York
Bolles Gallery, San Francisco
Joan Peterson Gallery, Boston
Istituto de Arte Contemporaneo, Lima, Peru
Galerie Schmela, Dusseldorf
1962 Kootz Gallery, New York
Galerie de France, Paris
1963 Galerie Charles Lienhard, Zurich
Kootz Gallery, New York
Tokyo Gallery
1964 Kootz Gallery, New York
1965 Galeria Bonino, Buenos Aires
1967 James David Gallery, Coral Gables, Florida
Markler Gallery, Philadelphia
Whitney Museum, New York (retrospective)
Rose Art Museum, Brandeis University, Waltham, Massachusetts
1968 University of Alabama, Tuscaloosa
Dorazio/Marca-Relli/Pasmore, Arts and Crafts Center, Pittsburgh
Alpha Gallery, Boston
Albright-Knox Members Gallery, Buffalo, New York
1969 Reed College, Portland, Oregon
Seattle Art Museum
1970 Marlborough Gallery, New York
University of Maryland Art Gallery, College Park
Norton Gallery, West Palm Beach, Florida
Gallery Van der Voort, Ibiza, Spain
1971 Museum of Fine Arts, Fort Lauderdale, Florida
Lowe Art Museum, University of Miami
Galerie Schmela, Dusseldorf
1972 Gallery Van der Voort, Ibiza, Spain
Galeria Inguanzo, Madrid
1973 Galeria Inguanzo, Madrid
1974 Marlborough Galerie, Zurich
1975 Marlborough Goddard Gallery, Toronto
Markler Gallery, Philadelphia
1981 Aronson Gallery, Atlanta
Hokin Gallery, Chicago
1985 Marisa del Re Gallery, New York
1990 Galleria d'Arte Niccoli, Parma (catalog)
Marca-Relli: Four Decades of Collage, January 11-February 8, 1990, Riva Yares Gallery, Scottsdale (catalog)
1992 Marisa del Re Gallery, New York
1998 *Exposition: Tribute to Conrad Marca-Relli,* Collezione Peggy Guggenheim, Venice (catalog)

Selected Group Exhibitions:

1959 *Documenta,* Kassel, West Germany
1960 *Segunda Bienal Interamericana de Mexico,* Mexico City
1961 *The Art of Assemblage,* Museum of Modern Art, New York
1966 *Art of the United States,* Whitney Museum, New York
1968 *American Painting: The 50s,* American Federation of Arts Gallery, New York (toured the United States)
1969 *American Drawings of the 60s,* New School Art Center, New York
1970 *Bienal de Arte Coltejer,* Medellin, Colombia
American Painting 1970, Virginia Museum, Richmond
Biennale, Venice
1976 *Newly Elected Members,* American Academy of Arts and Letters, New York
2000 *A Theatre of Art III,* Riva Yares Gallery, Santa Fe

Collections:

Museum of Modern Art, New York; Metropolitan Museum of Art, New York; Guggenheim Museum, New York; Pennsylvania Academy of Fine Arts, Philadelphia; Detroit Institute of Arts; Art Institute of Chicago; High Museum of Art, Atlanta; Cleveland Museum of Art; Los Angeles County Museum of Art; San Francisco Museum of Modern Art; The Caldwell Gallery, Manlius, New York; Telfair Museum of Art, Savannah; Columbia Museum of Art, South Carolina; Albright-Knox Art Gallery, Buffalo; Brandeis University, Waltham; Carnegie Institute, Pittsburgh; Fogg Art Museum, Harvard University, Boston; Guggenheim Museum, New York; Wadsworth Atheneum, Hartford; Whitney Museum of American Art, New York; Walker Art Center, Minneapolis.

Publications:

By MARCA-RELLI: Books—*Conrad Marca-Relli: Works 1945–1996,* with Klaus Wolbert, Darmstadt 2000. **Article--**''Collage Transformed: Interview with Marca-Relli,'' with Bernard Chaet, in *Arts Magazine* (New York), June 1959.

On MARCA-RELLI: Books--*Marca-Relli,* exhibition catalog with a preface by William Rubin, New York, 1959; *Collage: Personalities, Concepts, Techniques* by Harriet Janis and Rudi Blesh, Philadelphia 1962; *Marca-Relli* by H. H. Arnason, New York 1963; *Marca-Relli,* exhibition catalog by William C. Agee, New York 1967; *Marca-Relli* by Gerard Miracle and Harold Rosenberg, Barcelona 1975; *Marca Relli: New Works,* exhibition catalog with essay by David L. Shirey, New York 1985. **Article—**Obituary in *Art in America* (New York), 1 December 2000.

* * *

Within the gambit of the New York School of Abstract Expressionism Conrad Marca-Relli evolved a highly personal style of his own. After working with broken shapes, jagged lines and smeared colour in a manner analogous to that introduced by Jackson Pollock and Willem de Kooning, he matured in the early 1950s a technique of collage painting in which cut-out shapes of painted canvas were attached to a canvas ground in expressive patterns with a thick black glue which emphasized their outlines. A characteristic example of his work in this style, which combined taut vigour with a certain gracefulness, is ''The Battle'' (1956), which combines oilcloth, toned canvas pieces, enamel and oil paint on a canvas ground. In *American Art of the 20th Century,* Sam Hunter says of this work: ''Using cut-out canvas shapes attached to a canvas base with a black glue line that both demarcated and blurred their separate identities, Marca-Relli developed new and dramatic modes of juxtaposition and structure in an original collage idiom. Qualities of the elementary were mixed with refinement, and, in an early figurative mode, metaphysical allusion poetically transformed the brute physical fact of his canvas fragments.'' His work in this manner has been likened to the painting of de Kooning at the end of the 1940s.

In the 1960s Marca-Relli experimented with three-dimensional constructions using white plastic or sheets of aluminum. These had a precision and purity of facture which approximated to the geometrical abstraction of certain of the Minimal school of artists, although they retained something of the spontaneity of his earlier work and usually avoided giving the impression of machine-like inevitability. He also experimented with a new type relief painting which approximated more closely to the objective and impersonal manner of Post-Painterly Abstraction. During the 1960s, indeed, his work contained features both of Expressionist and of Constructivist abstraction. If he failed to attain the highest peaks in either mode, his work had inventiveness, mastery and assured individuality in both.

—Harold Osborne

MARCLAY, Christian

Nationality: American. **Born:** San Rafael, California, 1955. **Education:** Massachusetts College of Art.

Selected Individual Exhibitions:

1987 The Clocktower, P.S. 1 Museum, New York
1990 *Directions: Christian Marclay,* Hirshhorn Museum and Sculpture Garden, Washington, D.C. (brochure)
1991 Interim Art, London
Residue Politics, Beaver College Art Gallery, Glenside, Pennsylvania (catalog)
1992 *The Wind Section,* Galerie Jennifer Flay, Paris
1993 Margo Leavin Gallery, Los Angeles, California
1994 Daadgalerie, Berlin (traveled to Fri-Art Centre d'Art Contemporain Kunsthalle, Fribourg, Germany) (catalog)
1995 *Accompagnement Musical,* Musée d'Art et d'Histoire, Geneva, Switzerland
Arranged and Conducted, Kunsthaus, Zurich (catalog)
1997 *Pictures at an Exhibition,* Whitney Museum of American Art at Philip Morris, New York (brochure)
1999 Paula Cooper Gallery, New York

Selected Group Exhibitions:

1982 The Kitchen, New York
1985 The Kitchen, New York
1988 *Group Material: Politics and Election,* DIA Art Foundation, New York
1989 *Strange Attractors: Signs of Chaos,* New Museum of Contemporary Art, New York
1990 *Status of Sculpture,* Espace Lyonnais d'Art Contemporain, Lyon, France (traveled to ICA, London; Lion's Palais; Stiftung Starke, Berlin)
1991 *Biennial Exhibition,* Whitney Museum of American Art, New York (catalog)
Post Human, FAE Musée d'Art Contemporain, Pully/Lausanne, Switzerland (toured) (catalog)
1993 *At the Edge of Chaos,* Louisiana Museum, Humlebaek, Denmark
1994 *Outside the Frame: Performance and the Object,* Cleveland Center for the Arts, Ohio (catalog)
Solo Impression Inc., College of Wooster Art Museum (catalog)
1996 *Art and Film Since 1945: Hall of Mirrors,* Museum of Contemporary Art, Los Angeles, California (catalog)

1997 *Rrose is a Rrose is a Rrose: Gender Performance in Photography,* Guggenheim Museum, New York (catalog)
1998 *White Noise,* Kunsthalle, Bern, Switzerland
1999 *Releasing Senses,* Tokyo Opera City Art Gallery, Japan
2000 *Le Temps, Vitel,* Centre Georges Pompidou, Paris

Publications:

By MARCLAY: Articles—''Interview with Christian Marclay'' by Vincent Katz in *Print Collector's Newsletter,* March-April 1991; ''An Interview with Christina Marclay'' by Jonathan Seliger in *Journal of Contemporary Art,* Spring 1992; ''Christian Marclay Interview'' by Sabine Vogel in *Kunstforum,* September 1996; ''Christian Marclay: SCRRATCHH. . .'' article/interview by Yves Botz and Michel Henritzi in *Supersonic Jazz,* no. 4, 1997; ''Christian Marclay Interview'' by Jason Gross in *Perfect Sound Forever,* March 1998.

On MARCLAY: Books—*The Kitchen Turns Twenty: A Retrospective Anthology,* edited by Lee Morrissey, New York 1992; *New Art,* New York 1997; *Performance: Live Art Since 1960* by Laurie Anderson and Roselee Goldberg, New York 1998. **Articles—**''Notes on a Sculpture'' by Jerry Saltz in *Arts Magazine,* December 1989; ''Christian Marclay'' by Michael Archer in *Art Monthly,* April 1991; ''Verbranne CD's sind Geruchslos'' by Diedrich Dietersichsen in *Kunst Bulletin,* June 1995; ''Spin Doctor'' by David Krasnow in *Artforum,* November 1998; ''Christian Marclay at the Whitney Museum at Philip Morris'' by Michael Amy in *Art in America,* March 1998; ''Indexically Concrète: The Aesthetic Politics of Christian Marclay's Gramophonia'' by Thomas Y. Levin in *Parkett,* no. 56, 1999.

* * *

Christian Marclay was a college art student when he began experimenting with the use of record albums as musical instruments in 1979. Inspired by artists working with performance such as Vito Acconci and Joseph Beuys as well as the energy found in the punk rock movement, Marclay formed a duo with guitarist Kurt Henry. They called themselves ''The Bachelor, Even,'' in tribute to Marcel Duchamp, and began working with varieties of sound-making almost immediately. Marclay found encouragement in the punk notion that one did not need to really be able to play an instrument to play one. He began creating rhythmic, drum-like sounds by causing vinyl records to skip on turntables. In 1980, Marclay organized the Eventworks festival ''to explore the relation and influence of rock music on the art world.'' This ''happening'' brought together film makers, musicians, and artists in a fascinating exchange of ideas. Marclay's work continues to delve into the connections between popular entertainment and high art.

Marclay is very interested in recycling materials to make art, and he often uses records and equipment in the garbage or in thrift stores. His methods of performance are varied and show a great love for experimentation and chance occurrences. Marclay works with standard scratching of records, dragging the turntable's needle across the grooves in random patterns. He has also had success in playing recordings on damaged turntables. Marclay's most intriguing experiments have grown out of his physical destruction of records. He cuts them into pie-slice shapes and reassembles them with glue to create new works. These assemblages create auditory sculptures from the juxtaposition of widely varied musical styles and tones. Marclay finds audience response to this is very interesting. ''Once different unrelated records are combined, they sometimes have the power to trigger the memory of a tune. I don't consciously make music to trigger memory but it happens naturally. Music has such powers in triggering memory, collective memory and private memory. What I *consciously* try to do is to use the widest variety of music. These records often have different sets of references for different people, because most memories are personal and subjective. Whatever happens in their mind is something that I can't control, I can't control what they think about what I'm doing. It's like silent audience participation.''

Marclay's experiments with sound and performance quickly became popular in the New York art world. In 1982, he performed at The Kitchen for the first time, where he did a solo piece with six turntables and participated in an ensemble of fifteen using records as acoustic sound objects. *His Master's Voice: The Art of the Record Player* was curated by Tim Carr and featured such artists as Marclay, Roger Thrilling, Stuart Sherman, Danceteria DJ Bill Bahlman, DJ Whiz Kid, and others. Each was working in a realm outside the standard scene in which disc jockeys spin records at dance clubs. The potential here is obvious.

In 1985, The Kitchen presented Marclay's *Ghost (I Don't Live Today),* an homage to guitar legend Jimi Hendrix. In the piece, Marclay used his Phonoguitar creation, a turntable console strapped around his neck like a guitar. His first solo exhibition came in 1987 at the Clocktower Gallery. Marclay created an installation in which the floor of a room was filled with records. Visitors were invited to walk on them, leaving footprints, scuff marks and other signs of human trampling. The records were later packaged and sold. Marclay is interested in the sound of decay inherent in the aging process of recordings. ''I realized that when I listened to a record, there were all these unwanted sounds, clicks and pops, because of the deterioration of the record, the surface noise, scratches. Instead of rejecting these residual sounds, I've tried to use them, bringing them to the foreground to make people aware that they're listening to a record and not live music.''

Marclay's sculptural installations expanded to include such works as *Möbius Loop* (1994), a construction made of audiocassette tapes connected by nylon ties. His 1991 *Body Mix* piece featured eleven album covers stitched together with thread. Marclay continues to work in both audio experimentation and sculpture. His recordings are numerous and show a growing interest in collaboration with such artists as John Zorn and Otomo Yoshihide. He has had solo exhibitions at the Whitney Museum of American Art in New York, the Kunsthaus in Zurich, the Hirshhorn Museum in Washington, D.C., and at galleries throughout Switzerland. The exhibition catalog for the *Residue Politics* exhibition in 1991 spoke of Marclay as ''memorializing the relics of popular culture as [he] examines their underlying sexual and economic ideologies.''

—Tammy A. Kinsey

MARDEN, Brice

Nationality: American. **Born:** Bronxville, New York, 15 October 1938. **Education:** Boston University School of Fine and Applied Arts, Massachusetts, 1952–61, B.F.A. 1961, and Yale University

School of Art and Architecture, New Haven, Connecticut, 1961–63, M.F.A. 1963. **Family:** Married Pauline Baez in 1960 (now divorced); son: Nicholas Brice; married Helen Harrington in 1969; daughters: Maya Mirabelle Zahara and Melia Io Bricia. **Career:** Painter: lives and works in New York. Instructor, School of Visual Arts, New York, 1969–73. Member, Board of Governors, Skowhegan School of Painting and Sculpture, Maine, 1972. **Awards:** Third Prize, American Exhibition, Art Institute of Chicago, 1976. **Agent:** Pace Gallery, 32 East 57th Street, New York, New York 10022. **Address:** Office, 170 Varick Street, New York, New York 10013–1221.

Individual Exhibitions:

1966 Bykert Gallery, New York
Galerie Yvon Lambert, Paris
1968 Bykert Gallery, New York
1969 Bykert Gallery, New York
1970 Bykert Gallery, New York
Galleria Francoise Lambert, Milan
1971 Galerie Konrad Fischer, Dusseldorf
Galleria Gian Enzo Sperone, Turin
1972 Bykert Gallery, New York
Locksley Shea Gallery, Minneapolis
1973 Galerie Konrad Fischer, Dusseldorf
Galerie Yvon Lambert Paris
Galleria Francoise Lambert, Milan
1974 Contemporary Art Museum, Houston
Webster College, St. Louis
Bykert Gallery, New York
Locksley Shea Gallery, Minneapolis
1975 Forth Worth Museum of Art, Texas
Minneapolis Institute of Arts
Knoedler Contemporary Prints Gallery, New York
Galerie Konrad Fischer, Dusseldorf
Galleria Alessandro/Ferranti, Rome
Guggenheim Museum, New York
Hester Royen Gallery, London
Brice Marden/David Novros/Mark Rothko, Rice University, Houston
1976 Sperone-Westwater-Fischer Gallery, New York
1977 Galleria Sperone, Turin
Brown University, Providence, Rhode Island
Jean and Karen Bernier, Athens
Max Protetch Gallery, Washington D.C.
1978 Pace Gallery, New York
1979 Kunstraum, Munich
1980 Pace Gallery, New York
Institut für Moderne Kunst, Nuremberg
1982 Pace Gallery, New York
1984 Pace Gallery, New York
1987 Galleria Stampa, Basel
1988 Anthony d'Offay Gallery, London
1990 *American Masters of the '60s: Early and Late Works,* Tony Shafrazi Gallery, New York (catalog)
1991 *Cold Mountain,* Dia Center for the Arts, New York (catalog)
Brice Marden: Boston—A 'Connections' Project, Museum of Fine Arts, Boston (catalog)
Brice Marden: The Grove Group, Gagosian Gallery, New York (catalog)
1992 *Brice Marden: Prints 1961–1991,* Tate Gallery, London (also Musee d'Art Moderne de la Ville de Paris; Baltimore Museum of Art) (catalog)
1993 *Brice Marden,* Museum fur Gegenwartskunst, Basel (catalog)
Brice Marden: Paintings 1985–1993, Kunsthalle, Bern (also, Wiener Secession, Vienna) (catalog)
1995 *Brice Marden: Drawings,* Pace Wildenstein Gallery, New York (catalog)
1996 Matthew Marks Gallery, New York
1997 *Brice Marden: Work Books 1964–1995,* Staatliche Graphische Sammlung, Neue Pinakothek, Munich (traveled to Winterthur, Columbus, Cambridge, Dusseldorf, Munich) (catalog)
1999 *Brice Marden: Work of the 1990s,* Dallas Museum of Art (traveled to Hirshhorn Museum and Sculpture Garden, Washington, D.C.; Miami Art Museum; Carnegie Museum of Art) (catalog)
Brice Marden: Drawings, The Whitney Museum of American Art, New York
Brice Marden: Classic Paintings, C&M Arts, New York (catalog)
2000 Serpentine Gallery, London

Selected Group Exhibitions:

1969 *Concept,* Vassar College Art Gallery, Poughkeepsie, New York
1970 *Modular Painting,* Albright-Knox Art Gallery, Buffalo, New York
1972 *Painting: New Options,* Walker Art Center, Minneapolis
Documenta 5, Kassel, West Germary
1973 *Whitney Biennial,* Whitney Museum, New York
Options and Alternatives: Some Directions in Recent Art, Yale University Art Gallery, New Haven, Connecticut
1974 *Some Recent American Art,* Museum of Modern Art, New York
8 Contemporary Artists, Museum of Modern Art, New York
1976 *3 Decades of American Art,* Seibu Museum, Tokyo
1988 *Contemporary American Art,* Sara Hilden Art Museum, Tampere, Finland (travelled to Oslo)
1989 *Essential Paintings,* Nelson-Atkins Museum of Art, Kansas City (catalog)
Abstraction, Geometry, Painting, Albright-Knox Art Gallery, Buffalo (traveling exhibition) (catalog)
Yves Klein, Brice Marden, Sigmar Polke, Hirschl and Adler Modern, New York (catalog)
1990 *Brice Marden, Samuel Buri, Ernst Messerli: Projects for the Basle Cathedral,* Kunsthalle Palazzo, Liestal, Switzerland (catalog)
Object and Content: Meaning in Minimal Art, Australian National Gallery, Canberra (catalog)
American Drawings in the 1980s, Graphische Sammlung Albertina, Vienna (catalog)
1991 *Selection: Works from the Collection,* Musee d'Art Contemporain, Lausanne (catalog)
1992 *Allegories of Modernism: Contemporary Drawing,* Museum of Modern Art, New York (catalog)

1994 *Traces of Berne Kunsthalle: Exhibitions in Collections of Contemporary Art,* Kunsthalle, Bern (catalog)
1995 *Diary of a Human Hand,* Centre Saidye Bronfman, Montreal (also Center for Curatorial Studies, Bard College, New York) (catalog)
A Perspective on Contemporary Art: Painting—Singular Object, National Museum of Modern Art, Tokyo (also National Museum of Modern Art, Kyoto) (catalog)
Abstraction: Pure and Impure, Museum of Modern Art, New York (catalog)
1997 *47th Venice Biennale,* Italy
On the Edge, Museum of Modern Art, New York (catalog)
Deep Storage—Arsenals of Memory, Haus der Kunst, Munich (also Neue Nationalgalerie, Berlin; Kuntmuseum Dusseldorf; Henry Art Gallery, Seattle) (catalog)

Collections:

Museum of Modern Art, New York; Whitney Museum of American Art, New York: Walker Art Center, Minneapolis; Fort Worth Museum of Art, Texas; San Francisco Museum of Modern Art; Stedelijk Museum, Amsterdam.

Publications:

By MARDEN: Book—*Suicide Notes,* Lausanne 1974; *Brice Marden: Cold Mountain Studies,* with Bastian Heiner, Munich 1991; *Brice Marden,* with David Rimanelli, New York 1995; *Brice Marden: Work of the 1990s: Paintings, Drawings, and Prints,* with Charles Wylie, Dallas 1999; *Brice Marden Drawings: The Whitney Museum of American Art Collection,* with Janie C. Lee, New York 1999. **Articles—**''New in New York: Line Work'' in *Art Magazine* (New York), May 1957; ''Points of View: A Taped Conversation with 4 Painters'' in *Arts Magazine* (New York), December/January 1971; ''Three Deliberate Greys for Jasper Johns'' in *Art Now: New York,* March 1971; statement in *Arts Magazine* (New York), Summer 1972; ''The Quality Problem'' in *Artforum* (New York), October 1972; statement in *Eight Contemporary Artists,* exhibition catalog, New York 1974; ''Conversations with Brice Marden,'' with Robinson de Ak Moore, in *Art Rite* (New York), Spring 1975; interview with Saul Ostrow in *Bomb,* no. 22, Winter 1988; interview with William Furlong in *Art Monthly,* no. 117, June 1988; interview with Robert Mahoney in *Flash Art,* no. 155, November-December 1990; ''Curiously Determined Objects: An Interview with Brice Marden'' by Vincent Katz in *On Paper,* vol. 2, no. 3, January-February 1998.

On MARDEN: Books—*Minimal Art: A Critical Anthology,* edited by Gregory Battcock, New York 1968; *Contemporary American Art,* exhibition catalog with foreword by Peter Schjeldahl, Tampere 1988. **Articles—**''New York: Brice Marden, Bykert Gallery'' by J. Masheck in *Artforum* (New York), January 1971; ''Ryman, Marden, Manzoni: Theory, Sensibility, Mediation'' by Robert Pincus-Witten in *Artforum* (New York), June 1972; ''Brice Marden's Paintings'' by Roberta Smith in *Art Magazine* (New York), May/June 1973; ''Brice Marden's Paintings'' by Jeremy Gilbert-Rolf in *Artforum* (New York), October 1974; ''Brice Marden's Paintings'' by Jeremy Gilbert-Rolfe in *Artforum* (New York), January 1975; ''Brice Marden, David Novros, Mark Rothko: The Urge to Communicate Through Non-Imagistic Painting'' by Janet Kutner in *Arts Magazine* (New York), September 1975; ''Abstract Painting, Specific Spaces: Novros and Marden in Houston'' by Carter Ratcliff in *Art in America* (New York), September/October 1975; ''Vehicles for Rare Color'' by William Zimmer in the *Soho Weekly News* (New York), May 1978; ''Brice Marden'' by Jane Bell in *Artnews* (New York), November 1978; review by Elizabeth Franklin in *Art in America* (New York), January 1981; ''Brice Marden'' by John Yau in *Flash Art,* no. 142, October 1988; ''Marden's Web'' by Stephen Westfall in *Art in America* (New York), vol. 80, no. 3, March 1992; ''The Prints of Brice Marden'' by Pat Gilmour in *Print Collector's Newsletter,* vol. 23, no. 2, May-June 1992; ''Brice Marden'' by Christophe Marchand-Kiss in *Beaux Arts Magazine,* no. 103, July-August 1992; '''An Offhand Sublime''' by Gail Gregg in *ARTnews,* vol. 99, no. 3, March 2000.

* * *

Brice Marden began to develop his reductivist abstract painting during the early to mid 1960s. From the beginning his technical proficiency and adeptness with color have been pronounced, and his studied comprehension of art historical precedents is evident, stimulated, no doubt, by his training at Yale University.

By the time Marden left Yale in 1963, he had already begun to use two to four rectangular areas as the basic structure for his paintings. In 1965, he started to mix beeswax with oil to achieve a more physical, dense quality in his monochrome fields. From his first one-man exhibition in 1966 until the early 1980s, Marden's work showed a continuous and persistent development of variations based on the limited format he had arrived at at that time. Marden sought to achieve a balance by interrelating and distributing color surface and shape. His was a slow process of refinement, a seeking out of a subtler, more distilled expression of the possibilities inherent in a set of purposeful limitations. After spending 1964 to 1967–68 concentrating on one-panel, one-color works, Marden worked for several years on the development of paintings which use various color combinations on two or three panels, joining single-colored panels in either vertical or horizontal formats.

Marden's color was highly individualistic and idiosyncratic. He achieved tones which are impossible to characterize through words which name colors, and it was his considerable ability as an intuitive inventor of color which helped give Marden's work an evocative, emotive quality which suggests content beyond the purely formal level. Although he was often characterized as a Minimalist, Marden did not fit in comfortably with minimalism's stress on the literal objecthood of the artwork. In Marden's pictures, abstract form as well as color were infused with a mysterious quality more associative with the mythic undertones of Barnett Newman than with the reductivism of Donald Judd. To see Marden's early work in a clearer historical context is to understand him as a second generation Abstract Expressionist of the color-field variety.

Also more in line with predecessors such as Newman and Mondrian was Marden's continual use of geometrical proportions which clearly showed an involvement with the proportions of dynamic symmetry. It has been written that Marden always preferred to measure his surfaces. Beginning with his early work, a number of Marden's panels approximated the ''golden section'' rectangle and its related proportions. A 1966 ''Study,'' for example, measuring 30 x 48 inches, is in the proportion 1.6 (golden section is 1.618), and in

Marden's large three-panel painting, ''Thira,'' (1979–80), each panel measures 1.6. The classical, intellectual nature of Marden's work found another level in his use of these proportions, which placed him in line with a long tradition of art ranging from the Parthenon to Renaissance painting and architecture to any number of abstract painters of the twentieth century. In addition, these shapes have long been thought to convey a sense of balance, stability, continuity and universality, qualities which are primary in Marden's paintings.

Working within this narrow range of elements, Marden located a variety of possibilities, so that underlying the seeming simplicity and non-referentiality of his works was a strong sense of place and of specific color-light conditions, the distillation of a refined classical grandeur. The finely honed use of color relationships and panel divisions in ''Thira'' make the suggestion of classical temple architecture visually alive and capable of sustained contemplation. Here Marden's color-saturated, burnished encaustic surfaces seem to encapsulate light, creating a sense of a translucent volume that is furthered by his use of extra heavy stretcher bars to physically project the surface of the painting forward, like a light-filled sculptural relief.

Throughout the 1970s, concurrent with his elegant monochromatic canvases, Marden produced great numbers of drawings and etchings which reveal aspects of his artistic practice and concerns that were soon to come to the fore. In particular, he executed numerous drawings using long branches of the ailanthus tree or long-handled brushes, dipped in ink or gouache to create woven clusters of twisting, gestural lines. The irregular, loose quality of these drawings, which clearly relinquished precision and control in their facture, stood in sharp contrast to the architectonic structuring and subtly articulated surfaces of Marden's paintings. Beginning in the early 1980s, Marden began to introduce this linear structuring in his canvases, culminating in the *Cold Mountain* series of 1988–92.

Inspired by the work of the Tang Dynasty poet Han Shan, or ''Cold Mountain,'' the series alludes to processes of change and transformation, to the ephemeral and to the essentially unknowable. The eggshell surfaces of these large canvases are inscribed with webs of calligraphic lines painted in subdued tones of black, red, or blue on pale underlying fields. Tracks and traces of previous linear markings are scrubbed out but not entirely obliterated, ''buried like bones in silt or veiled like winter tree branches in fog'' (Stephen Westfall, *Art in America,* March 1992), to reveal constant shifts in direction as they move from background to foreground, coalescing or colliding with other skeins of color. Thus activated, the negative spaces between the lineaments and pentimenti become quietly charged with an atmospheric, Zen-like emptiness. The stripped-down materiality of the paintings reads like a physical residue of their making, simultaneously invoking absence and presence.

In recent paintings, such as *Aphrodite,* 1992–93, or *Muses,* 1991–93, Marden returns to the art of Greece and the West as a source of inspiration. Here line becomes less calligraphic and more organic, undulating and then dissolving into the depth of the pictorial space to suggest the curves of figures turning and gesturing in motion.

With their sense of inscribed light, space, and volume, their subdued tonalities, their relative containment in relationship to the edge of the canvas, and their sense of controlled spontaneity, of accident, and of improvisation, the meandering brushstrokes of Brice Marden's paintings extend the lexicon of Abstract Expressionism, endowing its heroic individualism and transcendental aspirations with pictorial lyricism and contemplative mystery. Marden's personal variant of modernist abstraction lies at the end of the line, but his talent and persistence have allowed him to create a body of work that supports the continued viability and integrity of formalist abstraction in the postmodern era.

—Essay by Barbara Cavaliere; updated by Dorothy Valakos

MARIONI, Tom

Nationality: American. **Born:** Cincinnati, Ohio, 21 May 1937. **Education:** Cincinnati Art Academy, 1955–59. **Career:** Sculptor and percussionist, since 1959. Founder, Museum of Conceptual Art (MOCA), San Francisco, 1970. Editor and designer, *Vision* (art journal), Oakland, California, 1975–82; artist-in-residence, Djerassi Foundation, Woodside, California, 1981, Pilchuck Glass School, Stanwood, Washington, 1990, and The Fabric Workshop, Philadelphia, 1992; consultant for public art, Central Embarcadero Project, City of San Francisco, 1992; founder, The Art Orchestra, San Francisco. **Awards:** Artist Fellowship, National Endowment for the Arts, 1976, 1979, 1984; Guggenheim Fellowship, 1981; Asian Cultural Council Award, 1986; Flintridge Foundation Award for Sculpture, 1998 **Address:** 657 Howard St., San Francisco, California 94105, U.S.A.

Individual Exhibitions:

1963 Bradley Memorial Museum of Art, Columbus, Georgia
1968 Richmond Art Center, California
1970 *The Act of Drinking Beer with Friends Is the Highest Form of Art,* Oakland Art Museum, California
1972 Richard Demarco Gallery, Edinburgh
DeSaisset Museum, University of Santa Clara, California
Reese Palley Gallery, San Francisco
1975 Galeria Foksal, Warsaw
1977 M. H. de Young Museum of Art, San Francisco
Paule Anglim Gallery, San Francisco
1978 Los Angeles Institute of Contemporary Art
1979 *Museum of Conceptual Art,* San Francisco Museum of Modern Art (sculpture installation with free beer)
Modern Art Gallery, Vienna
Cochise Fine Arts Center, Bisbee, Arizona
1980 Felix Handschin Gallery, Basel
University of California Art Museum, Berkeley
1981 Site Inc., San Francisco
1984 Gallery Paule Anglim, San Francisco
A La Limite, Dijon, France
1985 Eaton/Shoen Gallery, San Francisco
1986 New Langton Arts, San Francisco
Kuhlenschmidt/Simon Gallery, Los Angeles
1987 Museo Italo Americano, San Francisco
Margarete Roeder Gallery, New York
1990 Capp Street Project, San Francisco
1993 Gallery Paule Anglim, San Francisco
1994 Margarete Roeder Gallery, New York
1995 *Conceptual Works 1969–1973,* Refusalon, San Francisco
1996 *Elegant Solutions,* Gallery Paule Anglim, San Francisco
1998 Gallery Paule Anglim, San Francisco
Margarete Roeder Gallery, New York
1999 *beer with friends etc,* Y-1 Gallery, Stockholm, Sweden

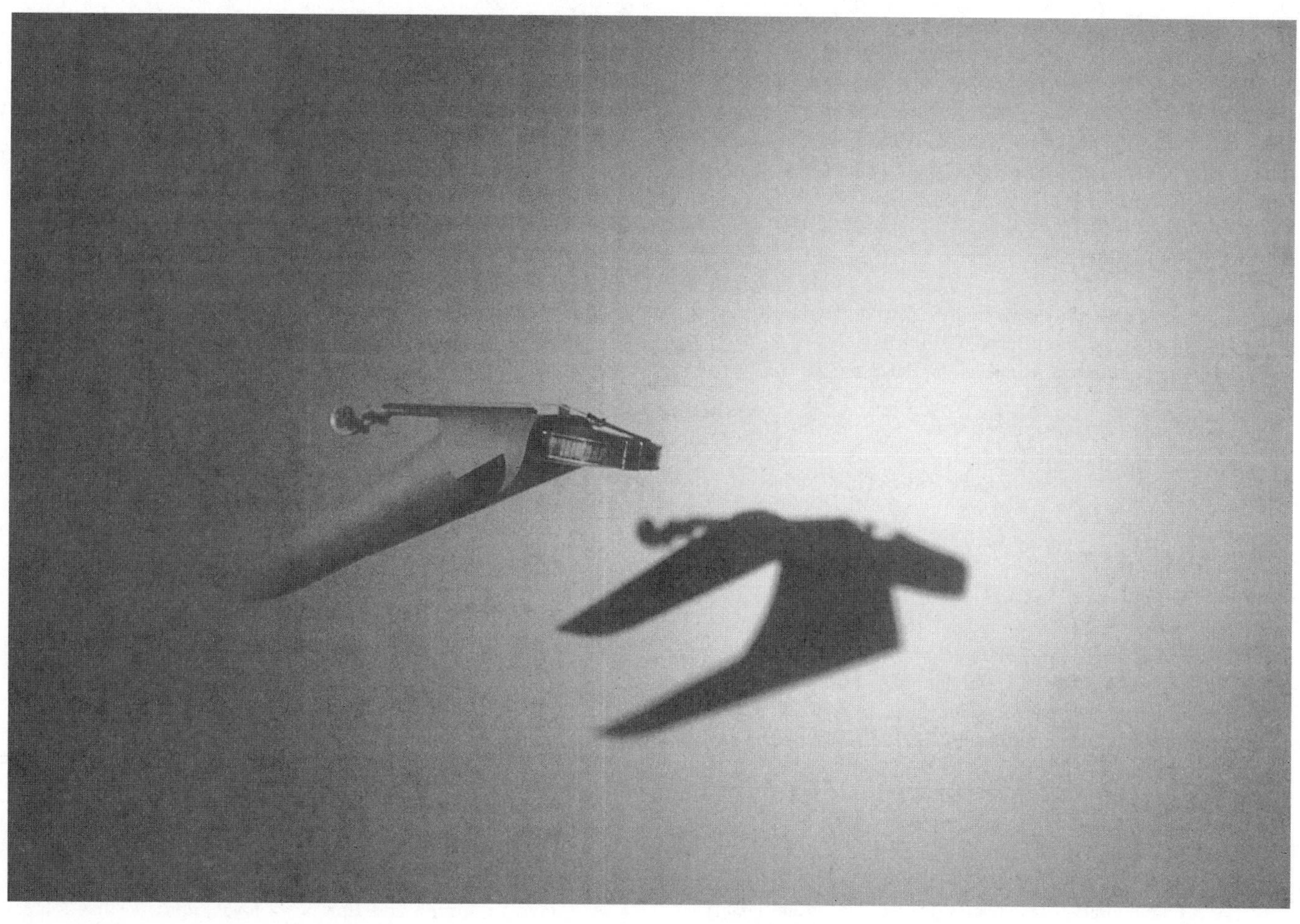

Tom Marioni: *Violin Bird,* 1972. ©Tom Marioni.

Trees and Birds 1969–1999, Mills College Art Museum, Oakland, California
Cincinnati Art Academy, Cincinnati, Ohio
2000 Margarete Roeder Gallery, New York
Gallery Paule Anglim, San Francisco

Sculpture Performances:

Worked in night club, sketching nude model, San Francisco, 1966; ''One Second Sculpture,'' San Francisco, 1969; ''Chain Reaction,'' DeSaisset Museum, University of Santa Clara, California, 1971; ''Identity Transfer,'' with Allan Fish, Berkeley Gallery, California, 1971; ''The Creation of a Situation and Environment While Becoming Increasingly More Intoxicated,'' Reese Palley Gallery, San Francisco, 1971; ''Sunday Scottish Landscape,'' Richard Demarco Gallery, Edinburgh, 1972; ''The Creation: A 7-Day Performance,'' Reese Palley Gallery, San Francisco, 1972; ''Christmas Poem,'' San Francisco, 1972; ''A Talk,'' Project Inc., Boston, 1973; concert at St. Mary's Cathedral, *Edinburgh Festival,* 1973; concert at the Institute of Contemporary Arts, London, 1973, ''Sculpture in 3/4 Time,'' San Francisco Museum of Art, 1973; ''Concert/Lecture/Demonstration,'' University of California Art Museum, Berkeley, 1973; ''The Sun's Reception,'' Marin County, California, 1974; ''A Sculpture in 2/3 Time,'' Student Cultural Center, Belgrade, 1974; ''One-Minute Demonstration,'' Gallery of Contemporary Art, Zagreb, 1974; ''Drum Lecture,'' 63 Bluxome Street, San Francisco, 1974; ''Lecture/Reception/Action,'' Indianapolis Museum of Art, 1974; ''Duologue,'' with Terry Fox, Los Angeles, 1975; ''Morning Action,'' Salon of the Museum of Modern Art, Belgrade, 1975; ''East-West,'' with Peter Stembergh, Prague, 1975; ''Thinking Out Loud,'' Galerie Foksal, Warsaw, 1975; ''Bird in Space: A Psychic Sculpture,'' and/or Gallery, Seattle, 1976; ''Yellow Is the Color of the Intellect,'' Portland Center for the Visual Arts, Oregon, 1977; ''The Sound of Flight,'' M. H. de Young Museum of Art, San Francisco, 1977; ''Now We'll Have a Party,'' at the *First International Performance Festival,* Vienna, 1978; ''Freibier'' at the *Vienna Performance Biennial,* 1979; ''A Social Action,'' Dany Keller Galerie, Munich, 1979; ''Praying with Chinese Firecracker,'' Krinzinger Gallery, Innsbruck, 1979; '''Liberating Light and Sound,'' Pellegrino Gallery, Bologna, 1979; ''Talking-Drumming,'' Los Angeles Institute of Contemporary Art, 1979; ''A Theatrical Action to Define Non-Theatrical Principles,'' Santa Barbara Museum of Art, California, 1979; ''Studio,'' Kunst Museum, Berne, 1980; ''Studio,'' Kunsthalle, Basel, 1980; ''Bending Light,'' Berner Gallery, Berne, 1980; ''Atelier,'' Centre Georges Pompidou, Paris, 1980; ''Studio,'' University of California Art Museum, Berkeley, 1980; ''Spirit in the Dark,'' Crown Point Press, Oakland, California, 1980; ''Drawing,'' Teahouse of the Saito Family, Kamakura, Japan, 1981; Museum of Contemporary Art, Chicago, 1981; Museum Folkwang, Essen, 1982; Kunstverein, Cologne, 1982; Ohara Shrine, Kyoto, Japan 1982; American Center, Kyoto, Japan,

1986; *Studio,* WDR Radio, Acoustic Festival, Cologne, Germany, 1996; The Art Orchestra, California Palace of the Legion of Honor, San Francisco, 1997; *Studio Berkeley 1980,* University of California, Berkeley Art Museum, 1998; *A Social Action 1978,* Austrian Museum of Applied Arts, Vienna, Austria, 1998; *Studio* and *Beer Drinking Sonata,* Chester Springs Center for Visual Art, Pennsylvania, 2000.

Selected Group Exhibitions:

1972 *The San Francisco Performance,* Newport Harbor Art Museum, Newport Beach, California
1979 *Art as Photography,* Kunstverein, Salzburg, Austria
1980 *For Eyes and Ears,* Akademie der Kunst, Berlin
1981 *California Performance Now and Then,* Museum of Contemporary Art, Chicago
Italians and American Italians, Crown Point Gallery, Oakland, California
1982 *100 Years of California Sculpture,* Oakland Museum, California
1983 *In Other Words,* Franklin Furnace, New York
1984 *The Sound Art Show,* Sculpture Center, New York
1985 *From Sound to Image,* Staatsgalerie, Stuttgart
1993 *Rolywholyover A Circus,* Museum of Contemporary Art, Los Angeles (traveled to Guggenheum Soho, New York, and to museums in Houston, Texas, Philadelphia, and Tokyo)
1995 *1965–1975 Reconsidering the Object of Art,* Museum of Contemporary Art, Los Angeles
1998 *Out of Actions: Between Performance and the Object, 1949–1979,* Museum of Contemporary Art at the Geffen Contemporary, Los Angeles (toured Europe and Japan)
1999 *Die Kunst Der Linie,* Landesmuseum, Linz, Austria

Collections:

Oakland Museum, California; Santa Barbara Museum of Art, California; Museum of Art, Lodz, Poland; Newport Harbor Art Museum, Newport Beach, California; Museum of Modern Art, New York; San Francisco Museum of Modern Art; Städtische Kunsthalle, Mannheim, Germany; Museo Italo Americano, San Francisco.

Publications:

By MARIONI: Book—*Vision 1, 2, 3, 4, 5,* Oakland, California; *Writings About Art, 1969–1999*, San Francisco 1999.

On MARIONI: Books—*Il Corpo Come Linguaggio* by Lea Vergine, Milan 1974; *The Painted Word* by Tom Wolfe, New York and London 1975; *Music, Sound, Language, Theater: John Cage, Tom Marioni, Robert Barry, Joan Jonas* by Kathan Brown, New York 1980; *Italians and American Italians,* exhibition catalog with essay by Kathan Brown, Oakland, California 1981; *Art in the San Francisco Bay Area 1945–1980* by Thomas Albright, Berkeley, California 1985; *Reconsidering the Object of Art 1965–1975,* exhibition catalog, with text by Ann Goldstein, Los Angeles 1995; *Tom Marioni: Sculpture and Installations 1969–97*, San Francisco 1997; Out of Actions, Between Performance and the Object, 1949–1970, exhibition catalog, with text by Paul Schimmel, Los Angeles 1998. **Articles**—''Tom Marioni,'' interview, in *Studio International,* (London), June 1972; ''Activity as Sculpture,'' interview, in *Art and Artists* (London), August 1973; ''Tom Marioni at Margarete Roeder Gallery'' by Ken Johnson in *Art in America,* February 1989; ''Stonehenge Chiaroscuro'' by Mark Levy in *Art International,* Spring 1989; ''Significant Engagement'' by Terri Cohn in *Art Week,* 7 June 1990; ''Tom Marioni'' by Marcia Tanner in *ARTnews,* April 1993; ''Artists Working with Words'' by Terri Cohn in *Artweek,* June 1997; ''Sacred Geometry'' by Terri Cohn in *Sculpture Magazine,* March 1998; ''Light as Medium'' by Terri Cohn in *Artweek,* October 1998; ''Works'' in *Site of Sound: Of Architecture and the Ear,* edited by Brandon LaBelle and Steven Roden, Los Angeles 1999; ''Tom Marioni at Margarete Roeder'' by Sarah Valdez in *Art in America,* July 2000.

*

I see the world as a sculptor. I make tableau sculpture, installations, action/performances, video tapes, drawings and prints. I organize exhibitions and social events (the act of drinking beer with friends is the highest form of Art—1970). I make sound in my performance actions. I also use light reflection and shadow in my actions and installations. I use found objects in my work and put them together to create new associations.

Many of my tableaux and installation sculptures are about a place, a city or a country, and usually they include objects from the music world and art world together, making a marriage of art and music.

The titles of my works usually are common expressions: *Thinking Out Loud* (1975), *The Power of Suggestion* (1979), *Room for Interpretation* (1987), *Birds of a Feather* (1986), and *Word of Mouth* (1980).

I love California and Europe; I love Leonardo and Marcel Duchamp; I love wine, women and song.

—Tom Marioni

* * *

On Friday the 13th of August, 1982, Tom Marioni created a café. The piece was called ''A Social Action'', and it contained elements which have characterized Marioni's work since 1970, when he performed ''The Act of Drinking Beer with Friends Is the Highest Form of Art'' at the Oakland Museum. The performance space was set as a still-life, a roomscape which contained a table and chair, a bottle of beer, a refrigerator, and a record player. Area spotlights gave each element the heightened emphasis of individual installations, but the presence of Marioni the activator tied the elements and the space into a cohesive setting. The piece, which took place in North Beach, San Francisco, successfully duplicated the ambience of a North Beach café as it might exist in the mind of one who had never visited such a place, or, in other words, in an ideal state—no crowds, no noise, etc. This North Beach café of the mind had jazz on the record player and the kind of stillness in which one imagines the creation of great works. Marioni, dressed in jeans and red shoes, began to create the café by writing CAFE with red and green chalk on a dull black wall. He worked very hard, using enormous concentration, right down to the final crossbar on the E. Occasionally he stopped to photograph the work in progress. As he built up the chalk strokes, the letters became more three dimensional, more smudged, and more sculptural in effect. Powdered chalk dust dripped down the wall.

Marioni's gestures were rhythmic, if not hypnotic. By the time the audience was approaching the same trance that governed the artist's activity, Marioni returned to the table in the center of the room, smiled, and spoke his only words: ''Now we can have a party.'' He opened the door to the refrigerator, and everyone participated in the highest form of art.

Marioni, who has said that for him the act is the art and the documentation is just a record of the activity, treads such a thin line between life and art that even after a decade of intense performance activity in California, there are those who doubt the validity of his work. Perhaps it is the highest compliment that in a time when everything is accepted as art, Marioni still provokes the question: But is it art?

In 1986, two galleries in San Francisco simultaneously mounted exhibitions focusing on Marioni's work. One, at New Langton Arts, included *The Back Wall of MOCA 1970–1986,* an installation homage to the Museum of Conceptual Art that Marioni founded and directed in San Francisco. The other, at Eaton/Shoen Gallery, was a miniretrospective of work done since 1972 and included recent pieces on national identities, *The Italians, Part I,* and *The Germans, Part I.* Although Marioni protests that ''I intend to hang onto the part—that's why I like San Francisco so much,'' he continues to expand the nations (in 1986 he added *The Japanese, Part I* to the series) and to record the ideas of art in stimulating and enlightening reifications.

—Mary Stofflet

Tom Marioni has been one of the most creative and daring Conceptualist and Performance artists in San Francisco since the late 1960s. He continues to create conceptual images and installations and performances that often straddle the boundary between the ephemeral and the tangible, between the purely cerebral and the fundamentally visual. Although many of his works are made as sculptures, drawings, and prints, they continue to originate in what seem like highly unlikely and unorthodox sources, but sources which have been of great importance to the avant-garde that emerged in the late 1960s and early 1970s, in the era of the dematerialization of the art object. Marioni became famous, if not notorious, for three-dimensional, visual works that often lacked the permanence and materiality of traditional art, and which originated in his interest in his body movements, his theatrical and even bombastic behavior, eccentric and even bizarre social activities in which he participated, and the undeniably intangible phenomena of sound and time. His work intrigues in that it is richly imbued with his sharp wit, sardonic humor, and willingness to undermine social mores. He is at his best when his work is sparse, uninhibited, and genuine; as a Conceptualist, less is truly more for him.

Marioni became prominent around 1970 with numerous performances that challenged the limits of decency, morality and social inhibitions in amusing, clever and yet shocking ways. *One Second Sculpture* consisted of tossing a tightly wound tape measure in the air and allowing it to unravel. In *Piss Piece*, Marioni stood over a galvanized tub and urinated after an afternoon of drinking beer. In his notorious *The Act of Drinking Beer with Friends Is the Highest Form of Art*, the artist created what he described as ''social sculpture:'' performances involving numerous people engaged in ordinary social events. In this event, the artist and his friends sat in a bar and drank beer all afternoon. When they were done, Marioni declared the work complete. Marioni continued his interest in socialization and beer when in 1997 he coordinated *Beer Drinking Sonata*, a performance that involved thirteen people drinking bottles of beer accompanied by music Marioni conducted and which was performed by a full orchestra. Marioni established the Museum of Conceptual Art in San Francisco in 1970 and remained its director until it closed in 1984. It was one of the first of what would become known as ''alternative spaces'' for the creation and exhibition of all kinds of art. Some of Marioni's early performances were conducted in the disguise of a fictitious alter ego, Allan Fish.

Some of Marioni's works are more tangible and permanent. In *Drawing a Line as Far as I Can Reach*, the first of many drawings and prints done since the early 1970s that are part of the ongoing series called *Trees*, the artist sits on the floor and draws or paints lines in various configurations on large sheets of paper and other materials as far up, down, or around himself as he can reach. He has created images based on the shadows of figures and objects, including his own shadow. In the 1990s, with works such as *Flying with Friends* of 1999, he created drawings with colored pencils by running and jumping in front of paper mounted on a wall and making marks on it as he passed. He has also created many photogravure prints which document his physical presence as artist, a maker of things and images, or simply as a person leaving traces of his existence wherever he goes and whatever he does. In such works he essentially continued his Zen-inspired interest in the spiritual and intellectual activity of the artist at work. Such works combine the existential chance of Jackson Pollock with the self-abandon of the Performance Art which Marioni pioneered thirty years ago.

Some of Marioni's works have been room-sized installations consisting of many ordinary, found objects placed together to construct various possible meanings. A number of them deal with social activities, including drinking beer. *Astronomy Piece (Galileo's Finger)* of 1989 was a room-size installation featuring an enlarged photograph of Stonehenge with a speaker's podium, a police officer's billy club, a glass lens, and other objects in front of a focused spotlight. *The Golden Room* of 2000 features beer bottles of different, supposedly symbolic shapes. Over the years he has created many prints in association with the San Francisco-based Crown Point Press that visually document his conceptual and performance activities. In the early 2000s, Marioni has also experimented with creating images for online viewing, thereby probing the creative and expressive possibilities of the latest in computer and information technology.

—Herbert R. Hartel, Jr.

MARKER, Chris

Nationality: French. **Born:** Christian François Bouche-Villeneuve in Ulan Bator (Mongolia), Belleville (a quarter of Paris), or Neuilly-sur-Seine in Paris, 29 July 1921. **Education:** Studied philosophy. **Military:** Left school to fight for the French Resistence during German occupation of France in World War II; left France to join the United States Air Force as a paratrooper for the remainder of the war. **Career:** Staff writer, *Esprit* (a Marxist-oriented, neo-Catholic journal), after the war; contributor, *Cahiers du cinéma*; traveled the world as a journalist and photographer; founder and editor of *Édition du Seuil's Petite Planète* series; began making films, 1952; part of the Left Bank group that included Alain Resnais, Jean Cayrol, and Henri Colpi; called the only ''essayist'' of French cinema.

Selected Films as Director

1952 *Olympia 52* (and screenwriter, co-cinematographer)
1953 *Les Statues meurent aussi*
1956 *Dimanche à Pekin* (and screenwriter, cinematographer)
1958 *Lettre de Sibérie*
1960 *Description d'un combat* (and screenwriter)
Les Astronautes (co-director, screenwriter)
1961 *Cuba Si!* (and screenwriter, cinematographer)
1964 *La Jetée* (completed 1962) (and screenwriter)
1965 *Le Mystère Koumiko* (and screenwriter)
1966 *Si j'avais quatre dromadaires* (and screenwriter)
1968 *La Sixième Face du Pentagone* (collaboration with Francois Reichenbach) (and screenwriter)
1969 *A bientôt j'espère* (and screenwriter)
1970 *La Bataille des dix millions* (and screenwriter)
Les Mots ont un sens (and screenwriter)
1973 *Le Train en marche* (and screenwriter)
1977 *Le Fond de l'air est rouge* (in 2 parts) (and screenwriter)
1984 *2084* (and screenwriter)
1985 *A.K.* (and screenwriter)
1986 *Hommage à Simone Sihnoret* (and screenwriter)
1989 *L'Heritage de la Chouette* (for TV, 13-part series) (and screenwriter, producer)
1993 *Le Dernier Bolchevik* (and screenwriter)
1997 *Level Five* (and cinematographer)

Group Exhibitions:

Publications:

By MARKER: Books—*Le Coeur net,* Paris 1949, translated as *The Forthright Spirit* by Robert Kee and Terence Kilmartin, 1951; *La Jetée: Ciné-roman*, New York 1992; *Silent Movie: La Petite Illustration Cinématographique*, Columbus Ohio 1995; *Immemory* (CD ROM), Paris 1998.

On MARKER: Books—*French Cinema Since 1946* by R. Armes, 1970; *Un cinéma réel* edited by R. Bellour, 1963; *Le cinéma et la vérité* by R. Bellour, 1963; *The Oxford Companion to Film,* 1976; *The Theory and Practice of the Ciné-Roman,* W.F. Van Wert, 1978; *Cinema: A Critical Dictionary* edited by R. Roud, 1980; *Le Documentaire français,* 1987. **Articles**—''Four Recent French Documentaries'' by N. Burch in *Film Quarterly,* vol. 13, no. 1, Fall 1959; ''Left Bank'' by Richard Roud in *Sight and Sound,* vol. 32, no. 1, Winter 1962/1963; ''Chris Marker and the Mutants'' by Gilles Jacob in *Sight and Sound,* vol. 35, no. 4, Autumn 1966; ''SLON'' by Richard Roud in *Sight and Sound,* vol. 42, no. 2, Spring 1973; ''Left Bank Revisited'' by Richard Roud in *Sight and Sound,* vol. 46, no. 3, Summer 1977; ''William Klein'' in *Graphis,* vol. 33, no. 194, 1977/1978; ''Chris Marker: The SLON Films (Societe pour le lancement des oeuvres nouvelle)'' by William F. Van-Wert in *Film Quarterly,* vol. 32, no. 3, Spring 1979; ''Time and Stasis in La Jetee'' by Bruce F. Kawin in *Film Quarterly,* vol. 36, no. 1, Fall 1982; ''Marker Changes Trains'' by Terrence Rafferty in *Sight and Sound,* vol. 53, Autumn 1984; ''Japant-Garde Japanorama'' by J. Hoberman in *Artforum International,* vol. 24, October 1985; ''Label hellene de Chris Marker'' by Francois Niney in *Cahiers du Cinema,* no. 422, July/August 1989; ''Insane Memory'' by Chris Petit in *Sight and Sound,* no. 4, July 1994; ''The Movement of Shadows: Video as Electronic Writing'' by John Conomos in *Art and Design,* vol. 10, November/December 1995; ''Chris Marker'' by Molly Nesbit in *Artforum International,* vol. 34, April 1996; ''Rouge Vertige'' by Laurent Roth in *Cahiers du Cinema,* no. 502, May 1996; ''Chris Marker's Reality Bytes'' by Jan-Christopher Horak in *Aperture,* no. 145, Fall 1996; ''Chris Marker: Truth, First Person Singular'' in *Art Press,* no. 224, May 1997; ''Trois Videos et un CD-Rom Autour de Chris Marker'' by Thierry Jousse in *Cahiers du Cinema,* no. 515, July/August 1997; '''. . . And Then Turn Away?' An Essay on James Coleman'' by Rosalind E. Krauss in *October* (Cambridge, Mass.), no. 81, Summer 1997; ''Chris Marker'' by Natascha Carron in *Flash Art* (International Edition), no. 196, October 1997; ''L'ordre et le desordre des memoires: Andre Bazin, Chris Marker, Alain Resnais et L'Espece humaine'' by Jean-Luc Alpigiano in *Cahiers du Cinema* nouvelle vague, special issue 1998; ''Chris Marker, dans le regard du chat'' by Stephane Bouquet in *Cahiers du Cinema,* no. 522, March 1998; ''Chris Marker: Beaconsfield'' by Ian Hunt in *Art Monthly,* no. 228, July/August 1999; ''Photography as Cinema: La Jetee and the Redemptive Powers of the Image'' by G. Uriel Orlow in *Creative Camera,* no. 359, August/September 1999.

* * *

Iconoclast, enigma, and shadow-artist Chris Marker has been known among film intelligentsia for almost half a century. There is something pleasingly ironic about this octogenarian now leap-frogging over the cyber-punks to provoke and stretch the definition of art, albeit with a veteran's witness to what has moved art off of canvas and beyond the textual in the past century.

In recent years Marker has surfaced as a post-film and video modernist. With his embrace of digital media and sometime disavowal of his earlier documentaries and essays, he continues to plunge forward into the unknown. A reclusive anti-celebrity, Marker was utilizing computers as early as 1984, when he submitted to a Q&A via computer terminal that was subsequently published in *Monthly Film Bulletin.*

Marker's tools—serious philosophical and political writing with evocative and provocative still photography—are blended with cinematography and music to produce works wistfully personal, yet decidedly in the avant-garde. His themes have been explorations of alienation, globalism, and Marxism as well as personal explorations of unreliable identity, memory, and time.

Marker was born Christian François Bouche-Villeneuve, and is supposed to have adopted his surname from the Magic Marker, but of the Oxford English Dictionary's definitions, ''one who notes or observes'' seems suitable enough. The artist was a student of philosophy before World War II transformed him into a paratrooper. After the war, he pursued a variety of travels and literary pursuits culminating in filmic essays of Siberia, China, Japan, and Israel. These endeavors were manifested in a variety of formats, and combinations of media.

His fascination with multi-media seems to have grown from his interest in Soviet Agit-Prop, with its montages, cartoons, interventions, and appropriation. Furthermore, an anti-auteurist film collective he helped form, dubbed SLON [Société pour le Lancement des Oeuvres Nouvelles and the Russian word for elephant], is reminiscent of those in Soviet Russia. His SLON collaborators: Agnes Varda, Jean-Luc Godard, Alain Resnais, Joris Ivens, among them, joined together to make *Loin du Viet-Nam* (*Far from Viet-Nam*) and reconvened during the tumultuous period around May 1968.

Marker's interest in cinematic and artistic precedents inspired works such as *The Last Bolshevik*, which is a meditation on the Soviet director Alexander Medvedkin (1900–1989), who had traveled through Russia in a famous train outfitted as a film lab and editing facility, capturing reverential images of workers in collectives and screening them for their subjects. The video is in the form of letters from the filmmaker, much as Marker's more autobiographical *San Soleil* takes the form of ''letters'' from one ''Sandor Krasna'' who has much in common with Marker. These letters, along with meditative visual essays, are techniques favored by Marker, who shares with his colleague Alain Renais the ambition to move beyond traditional narrative in his moving pictures.

Filmmakers and artists have attracted his attention, resulting in film and video portraits of numerous kindred creators such as Andrei Tarkovsky, Christo, and Kurosawa. An affinity between Marker and Kurosawa is summed up in the late director's words in the 1985 documentary about the filming of *Ran* called *A.K.*, ''To create is to remember.''

The more Marker has moved away from film convention and toward a new concept of multi-media and abstraction, the less enchanted film critics seem and the more welcoming the embrace of the fine art community. Through digital means he has discovered in multi-media the definitive added collage element that is supplied by interactivity: the unknown.

In recent years, Marker has had fertile associations with two art institutions who have commissioned and exhibited his experiments in video and beyond, the Musée national d'art moderne du Centre Georges Pompidou in Paris and the Wexner Center for the Arts at Ohio State University.

Silent Movie is a concise artwork that nevertheless indicates that Marker has thoroughly digested the whole century of cinema into his oeuvre. It was commissioned to commemorate the centenary of the motion picture, and subsequently included in the exhibition *Hall of Mirrors: Art and Film Since 1945*. The installation is five monitors stacked in a vertical tower with randomly shuffled scenes and cuts of music, chiefly drawing on Marker's personal visceral experience of cinema. The work also includes film posters created digitally by Marker, in a pastiche of classic cinema epics.

The best known work of Marker's oeuvre remains the 1962 ''photoroman'' *La Jétée*, a 29-minute film composed entirely of still images except for one blinking eye. Its setting in the post-apocalyptic future shown in rich black and white images with inter-titles, as well as its romantic theme, make it his most approachable work, perhaps, but its realization and themes are extraordinarily complex.

Level Five, the last full-length film, melds cyber-concept and video documentary, as the female protagonist endeavors to create a computer game of the notorious Battle of Okinawa. Among the facets of the film are scenes from a John Huston 1945 documentary *Let There Be Light* and an interview with the filmmaker Nagisa Oshima, who remembers the events.

His 1998 CD-ROM, produced for the Musée national d'art moderne du Centre Georges Pompidou, titled *Immemory One*, is a collage and fluttering image essay for realizing his philosophical considerations on art and the mind. The CD-ROM cleaves music and rapidly changing repetitive images to many-layered texts. Some of the reliable Chris Marker repertory appears: the Japanese good-luck cat with the tag ''En savoir plus?'' is joined by Proust, Hitchcock, and still images with philosophical and political briefs between them.

The artist's career, appropriately, has been documented on the web beginning in 1995 by Australian academic Adrian Miles. The website includes the credits of his films, an exhaustive bibliography, texts, images, and is an affectionate digital profile that is in excess of 150 pages.

Chris Marker has said that he will make no film or video in the new century, yet has already accepted a commission from ATOM films to create filmic work in a digital format for the web.

—Deirdre Donohue

MARTIN, Agnes

Nationality: American. **Born:** Maklin, Saskatchewan, Canada, 22 March 1912; immigrated to the United States, 1931: naturalized, 1950. **Education:** Attended primary and secondary schools, Vancouver, British Columbia; Western Washington College of Education, Bellingham, 1935–38; Teacher's College, Columbia University, New York, 1941–42, B.S. 1942, and 1951–52, M.A. 1952; University of New Mexico, Albuquerque, 1946–47. **Career:** Teacher at public schools in Washington, Delaware, and New Mexico, 1937–46 and 1948–50; painting instructor, University of New Mexico, Albuquerque, 1947–48, and East Oregon College, La Grande, 1952–53. Independent painter since 1957: joined Ruins Gallery group with Louis Reiback, Bea Mandelbaum, and Clay Spohn, Taos, New Mexico, 1956; associated with Ellsworth Kelly, Robert Indiana, Jack Youngerman, and James Rosenquist, New York, 1957–67. Abandoned painting and concentrated on writing, 1967–73; resumed painting in the early 1970s. **Agent:** PaceWildenstein, 32 East 57th Street, New York, New York 10022. **Address:** c/o PaceWildenstein, 32 East 57th Street, New York, New York 10022.

Individual Exhibitions:

1958 Betty Parsons Gallery, New York
1959 Betty Parsons Gallery, New York
1961 Betty Parsons Gallery, New York
1962 Robert Elkon Gallery, New York
1963 Robert Elkon Gallery, New York
1965 Robert Elkon Gallery, New York
Nicholas Wilder Gallery, Los Angeles
1966 Robert Elkon Gallery, New York
1967 Nicholas Wilder Gallery, Los Angeles
1970 Robert Elkon Gallery, New York
Nicholas Wilder Gallery, Los Angeles
1971 Visual Arts Gallery, School of Visual Arts, New York
1972 Robert Elkon Gallery, New York
1973 Institute of Contemporary Arts, University of Pennsylvania, Philadelphia (retrospective; travelled to the Pasadena Museum, California)
Kunstraum, Munich (travelled to Kunsthalle, Tübingen, West Germany; Kaiser Wilhelm Museum, Krefeld, West Germany)
1974 Scottish National Gallery of Modern Art, Edinburgh
Museum of Modern Art, New York
1975 Pace Gallery, New York
1976 Robert Elkon Gallery, New York
Pace Gallery, New York

Agnes Martin: *Untitled Number 1* 1981. The Museum of Modern Art, New York; gift of the American Art Foundation. Photo ©Museum of Modern Art, 1999.

1977 Arts Council of Great Britain, London (travelled to Hayward Gallery, London; Stedelijk Museum, Amsterdam)
Pace Gallery, New York
1978 Mayor Gallery, London
Galerie Rudolf Zwirner, Cologne
Pace Gallery, New York
Harcus-Krakow Gallery, Boston
1979 Margo Leavin Gallery, Los Angeles
Museum of Fine Arts, Santa Fe, New Mexico
Pace Gallery, New York
1980 Richard Gray Gallery, Chicago
Pace Gallery, New York (toured the United States and travelled to Glenbow Museum, Calgary, Alberta; Mendel Art Gallery, Saskatoon, Saskatchewan)
1981 Pace Gallery, New York
1982 Centre Saidye Bronfman, Montreal
Pace Gallery, New York
1984 Pace Gallery, New York
Mayor Gallery, London
1985 Pace Gallery, New York
Margo Leavin Gallery, Los Angeles
1986 Waddington Galleries, London
Annemarie Verna Galerie, Zurich
Pace Gallery, New York
1987 Galerie Yvon Lambert, Paris
1988 Barbara Krakow Gallery, Boston
1989 Pace Gallery, New York
Akira Ikeda Gallery, Tokyo
Cleveland Museum of Art
1990 Waddington Galleries, London
Pace Gallery, New York
1991 Mary Boone Gallery, New York
Westfälisches Landesmuseum für Kunst und Kulturgeschichte, Münster, Germany
Stedelijk Museum, Amsterdam (retrospective; travelled to Germany and France)
Pace Gallery, New York
1992 Kunstmuseum Winterthur, Winterthur, Switzerland
Hochschule für angewandte Kunst, Vienna
Galerie Yvon Lambert, Paris
Whitney Museum of American Art, New York (retrospective; toured the United States and travelled to Madrid)
1993 Wildenstein Gallery, Tokyo
Serpentine Gallery, London
1994 Galerie Michael Werner, Cologne
Santa Fe Museum of Fine Arts
Stockholm Konsthall, Magasin 3, Stockholm

Selected Group Exhibitions:

1976 *Aspects of Post-War Painting in America,* Guggenheim Museum, New York
Biennale, Venice
Drawing Now, Museum of Modern Art, New York (toured Europe)
1977 *Whitney Biennial,* Whitney Museum, New York
1978 *4 Contemporary Painters,* Cleveland Museum of Art
American Painting of the 1970s, Albright-Knox Gallery, Buffalo, New York (toured the United States)
1979 *The Reductive Object: A Survey of the Minimalist Aesthetic in the 1960s,* Institute of Contemporary Art, Boston
American Exhibition, Art Institute of Chicago
1980 *20 Americans,* San Francisco Museum of Modern Art
1987 *American Painting: Abstract Expressionism and After,* San Francisco Museum of Modern Art
1989–90 *Abstraction-Geometry-Painting: Selected Geometric Abstract Painting in America since 1945,* Albright-Knox Gallery, Buffalo (travelled to Miami; Milwaukee; and New Haven, Connecticut)
1992–93 *The Geometric Tradition in American Art: 1930–1990,* Whitney Museum of American Art, New York
1993 *American Art in the Twentieth Century: Painting and Sculpture, 1913–1993,* Martin-Gropius-Bau, Berlin and Royal Academy of Arts, London
Singular Dimensions in Painting, Guggenheim Museum, New York

Collections:

Museum of Modern Art, New York; Whitney Museum, New York; Guggenheim Museum, New York; Hirshhorn Museum, Washington, D.C.; Art Institute of Chicago; Art Gallery of Ontario, Toronto; Tate Gallery, London; Stedelijk Museum, Amsterdam; Australian National Gallery, Canberra.

Publications:

By MARTIN: Books—*On a Clear Day,* portfolio, 1971; *Writings/Schriften,* edited by Dieter Schwarz, Kunstmuseum Winterthur/Edition Cantz 1992. **Articles—**''Reflections'' in *Artforum* (New

York), April 1973; interview with Irving Sandler in *Art Monthly,* September 1993.

On MARTIN: Books—*Systematic Painting,* exhibition catalog, New York 1966; *Agnes Martin,* dissertation, by Frank Kolbert, Yale University, New Haven, Connecticut 1970; *Agnes Martin,* exhibition catalog with text by Lawrence Alloway and others, Philadelphia 1973; *Agnes Martin,* exhibition catalog with text by Herman Kern and others, Munich 1973; *Agnes Martin: Paintings and Drawings, 1974–1990,* exhibition catalog edited by Marja Bloem, Stedelijk Museum, Amsterdam 1991; *Agnes Martin,* exhibition catalog with text by Barbara Haskell and others, Whitney Museum of American Art, New York 1992. **Articles**—''Agnes Martin: An Appreciation'' by Kasha Linville in *Artforum* (New York), June 1971; ''Agnes Martin'' by Lawrence Alloway in *Artforum* (New York), April 1973; ''Early Work'' by Lizzie Borden in *Artforum* (New York), April 1973; ''Agnes Martin and the Artificial Infinite'' by Carter Ratcliff in *ARTnews* (New York), May 1973; ''Agnes Martin: The American Woman in Art'' by Barbara Rose in *Vogue* (New York), June 1973; ''Giving Art History the Slip'' by Stephanie Barron in *Art in America* (New York), March/April 1974; ''A Visit with Agnes Martin'' by Anne Hillerman in *The New Mexican,* 26 July 1974; ''An Art That's Almost a Prayer'' by Hilton Kramer in the *New York Times,* May 1976; ''Agnes Martin: 'Everything, Everything Is about Feeling . . . Feeling and Recognition''' by John Gruen in *ARTnews* (New York), September 1976; ''Whispers from Nature'' by Adrienne Rosenthal in *Artweek* (Oakland, California), 28 April 1979; ''Grey Geese Descending: The Art of Agnes Martin'' by Thomas McEvilley in *Artforum* (New York), summer 1987; ''Thin Gray Line'' by Mark Stevens in *Vanity Fair,* March 1989; ''Nature's Mystical Poetry, Written in Paint'' by Michael Kimmelman in the *New York Times,* 15 November 1992; ''Life Lines'' by Benita Eisler in the *New Yorker,* 25 January 1993; ''Agnes Martin: All the Way to Heaven'' by Holland Cotter in *Art in America* (New York), April 1993.

*

Artwork is a representation of our devotion to life. Everyone is devoted to life with an intensity far beyond our comprehension. The slightest hint of devotion to life in artwork is received by all with gratitude.

In all the arts a performance without devotion is dead, and our conditioning in life is toward the absolutely dead, because prideful, performance. Our whole inclination is to race forward. This racing is not an ordinary race to win over others. That is the prideful interpretation. It is an irresistible urge to win through to life. It is devotion to life. The simplest devotion in the Pyramids and the most profound and complicated exultations of Beethoven are understood by all.

The enormous pitfall is devotion to oneself instead of to life. All works that are self-devoted are absolutely ineffective. Even though they are often purchased by prideful people, they are soon recognized as dead.

Devotion to life is a feeling. Artwork is made with this feeling, and response to artwork is exactly the same feeling. This feeling of devotion literally carries us through life, past all distractions and pitfalls to a perfect awareness of life, to measureless happiness and perfection.

With no experience of real happiness, no conscious experience of devotion to life, one cannot be an artist. One must be lifted up, out of oneself, unconscious of self, as in the contemplation of beauty.

Life is consciousness of life itself. Our feelings of devotion are the measure of this consciousness. They are the measure of our lives and the measure of the effectiveness of our work.

The response to artwork is unchanging, even in thousands of years, proving that it is of life.

—Agnes Martin

* * *

Delicate, powdery tonalities share the space with a thin linear all-over grid, transmitting a sense of vast spatial continuity both rigorously defined and subtly intangible. Agnes Martin reached her mature form and substance in 1961, and since then she has continued to find multiple variations based on her chosen schema.

Martin is not a painter who came by her mature visualization either rapidly or easily. Although she achieved prominence in the 1960s, she had been working through her process of distillation since the 1940s, honing down each element through many levels and combinations. In the late 1940s Martin was making rather traditional still lifes and portraits, and by the early 1950s she had developed from these into an area of biomorphic abstraction related with the work of William Baziotes and Adolph Gottlieb. The linear quality of Arshile Gorky and Miró enters into her works of around 1955, combining with a painterly atmosphere, translucent and palely toned, already suggestive of her mature pictures. Martin's felt relationship with the landscape and particularly with the light quality of the American Southwest was by this time already in evidence, and this connection persisted later in her career, throughout the years she lived in New York City.

Martin left New Mexico for New York in 1957. During the next few years her work became more geometric and unitary in form. Image and ground were coalescing in compositions that employed concentric rectangles and/or circles in symmetry. In ''Lamp'' (1959), a patterning of circles line up across an atmospheric surface, signalling Martin's imminent return to her characteristic grid format. Until around 1964, the grid was centered and framed within the canvas surface; on finely textured brown canvases, roughly drawn marks appear in repetitive patterns, showing a directness and handmade quality. By 1964 the grid extends to the canvas edge, and Martin's system is complete.

Although Martin is often compared with the ''Hard-Edge'' abstractionists who gained popularity in the 1960s, her work is closer in feeling with first generation abstract expressionism, particularly with Ad Reinhardt's move into systematic, distilled form. Martin's visual development shows her working through elements similar to this group of painters of her own generation, with whom she shares a commitment to exalted subject matter transmitted through the painterly abstract language. The difference between Martin and the abstract expressionists lies in her less outwardly heroic and intellectual nature. Her works are more directly based on the intuitive and informed by a fragile quality that is both stately and unobtrusive.

In 1967 Martin stopped painting and left New York to return to the Southwest. She resumed working in the early 1970s, her new pictures emitting a continued austerity and delicacy and moving more intently into the realm of self-identification with the space and light of her landscape environment. Finding the most nuanced of textual and tonal variations, Martin's body of paintings is a distinctive statement of authority and reserve, fusing elements of stability and change with an economy and touch achieved over many years of concentration and practice. Any given group of Martin's paintings seems to subtly commemorate changing seasons and prevailing moods. One series contains only spare whites, blacks, and occasional grays, while another consists of multicolored bands of pink, orange, blue, and beige, overlaid with white to achieve the sheer tonality and airiness of a watercolor. Yet another evinces a more brooding, somber tone, with dense chromatic grays, vigorously applied surfaces, and heavier compositional sequences. Recently, Martin has begun to use only the horizontal component of her grid. Within these refined permutations, and in her systematic blending of the fragile, graphite grid with light-filled washes of pale color, Martin has used rigorous ordering to make visual the mysterious interior reality of timeless, shadowy vibrations.

—Essay by Barbara Cavaliere; updated by Dorothy Valakos

MARTIN, Ron

Nationality: Canadian. **Born:** London, Ontario, 28 April 1943. **Education:** Studied commercial art at Beal Secondary School, London, Ontario, 1960–64. **Career:** Contributing editor, *20 Cents,* London, Ontario, 1967–70. Independent painter. **Awards:** Best Oil Award, *Western Fair,* London, Ontario, 1966; Canada Council Centennial Purchase Award, Ottawa, 1967; Canada Council Arts Bursaries, Ottawa, 1968 through 1973; Visual Arts Grant, Ontario Arts Council, Toronto, 1973 through 1976. **Agent:** Christopher Cutts Gallery, 21 Morrow Avenue, Toronto, Ontario, Canada M6R 2H9.

Individual Exhibitions:

1965 Pollock Gallery, Toronto
1966 Pollock Gallery, Toronto
1967 Talbot College, University of Western Ontario, London
20/20 Gallery, London, Ontario
1969 20/20 Gallery, London, Ontario
York University, Toronto
1971 Carmen Lamanna Gallery, Toronto
1972 Carmen Lamanna Gallery, Toronto
1973 Carmen Lamanna Gallery, Toronto
1974 London Public Library and Art Museum, Ontario
Carmen Lamanna Gallery, Toronto
Forest City Gallery, London, Ontario
1975 Forest City Gallery, London, Ontario
Carmen Lamanna Gallery, Toronto
1976 Forest City Gallery, London, Ontario
Carmen Lamanna Gallery, Toronto
World Paintings, Art Gallery of Ontario, Toronto
Southern Alberta Art Gallery, Lethbridge, Alberta
1977 Carmen Lamanna Gallery, Toronto
1978 Galerie Michael Werner, Cologne
Galerie Marielle Mailhot, Montreal
Carmen Lamanna Gallery, Toronto
1979 Carmen Lamanna Gallery, Toronto
1980 Forest City Gallery, London, Ontario
Carmen Lamanna Gallery, Toronto
1982 Carmen Lamanna Gallery, Toronto
1983 Carmen Lamanna Gallery, Toronto
1984 Carmen Lamanna Gallery, Toronto
1985 49th Parallel Gallery, New York
Carmen Lamanna Gallery, Toronto
1986 Carmen Lamanna Gallery, Toronto
1989 Art Gallery of Ontario, Toronto
Ron Martin, 1971–1981, Art Gallery of Ontario, Toronto (also Vancouver Art Gallery; National Gallery of Canada, Ottawa; Musee d'Art Contemporain de Montreal) (catalog)
1991 Waddington & Gorce Inc., Montreal
Ron Martin: Geometric Paintings 1981–1985, Norman Mackenzie Art Gallery, Regina (catalog)
1992 Christopher Cutts Gallery, Toronto
1993 Christopher Cutts Gallery, Toronto
Retrospective, Moore Gallery, Hamilton
1995 Christopher Cutts Gallery, Toronto
Voice Box, Off-Whites, Ron Martin Bottled and Jammed 1993, Chinati Foundation, Marfa, Texas
Faith, 1990–1991, Kitchener-Waterloo Art Gallery, Ontario (catalog)
1996 Christopher Cutts Gallery, Toronto
Black-White-Grey Paintings 1987–88, Kitchener-Waterloo Art Gallery (traveled to London Regional Art and Historical Museum)
1997 *To Foil Oils,* Christopher Cutts Gallery, Toronto
London Regional Art and Historical Museum, Ontario

Selected Group Exhibitions:

1964 *Young Contemporaries,* London Public Library and Art Museum, Ontario
1967 *Centennial Exhibition,* National Gallery of Canada, Ottawa (toured Canada)
1968 *7th Biennale of Canadian Painting,* National Gallery of Canada, Ottawa
1971 *Contemporary Canadians,* Albright-Knox Gallery, Buffalo, New York
1973 *Boucherville, Montreal, Toronto, London,* National Gallery of Canada, Ottawa
1975 *Carmen Lamanna Gallery at the Owens Art Gallery,* Mount Allison University, Sackville, New Brunswick
1978 *Biennale,* Venice
1980 *10 Canadian Artists in the 1970s,* Art Gallery of Ontario, Toronto (international travelling exhibition)
1981 *20th Century Canadian Painting,* National Gallery of Canada, Ottawa (travelled to Japan)
1984 *Toronto Painting 84,* Art Gallery of Ontario, Toronto
1987 *Present Time Contemporary Abstraction,* National Gallery of Canada, Ottawa
1991 *Spectrum Time-Frame 6,* Extension Gallery, Toronto
The Empirical Presence: Caruso, Delaville, Gaucher, Martin, Poldaas, Saxe, Optica, Montreal
1992 Christopher Cutts Gallery, Toronto
1995 *Milieu Of The Order of Presentation,* S.L. Simpson Gallery, Toronto
1997 *Ten Years of Collecting,* MacKenzie Art Gallery, Regina, Ontario
Moore Gallery, Toronto
2001 *Pleasures of Sight and States of Being: Radical Abstract Painting,* Appleton Museum of Art, Ocala, Florida

Collections:

Art Gallery of Vancouver; Canadian Broadcasting Corporation, Vancouver; London Public Library and Art Museum, Ontario; McIntosh Art Gallery, University of Western Ontario, London; Art Bank, Canada Council, Ottawa; National Gallery of Canada, Ottawa; Art Gallery of Ontario, Toronto; Rothman's Art Gallery, Stratford, Ontario; Department of External Affairs, Cultural Affairs Division, Ottawa; Agnes Etherington Art Centre, Queens University, Kingston, Ontario; National Gallery of Canada, Ottawa; Albright-Knox Gallery, Buffalo; Art Gallery of Hamilton; Kitchner-Waterloo Art Gallery, Ontario; Montreal Museum of Fine Arts; Musee du Quebec; Vancouver Art Gallery; Christopher Cutts Gallery, Toronto.

Publications:

By MARTIN: Books—*Two Essays on Art and Knowledge,* with Walter Klepac and Brydon E. Smith, Toronto 1993. **Articles—** contributions to *20 Cents* (London, Ontario), 1967–70; ''Ron Martin Interview,'' with David Bolduc, in *For Proof Only,* Toronto 1974; ''Ron Martin Interview,'' with Anne Garwood, in *Ron Martin,* exhibition catalog, London, Ontario 1974; ''Ron Martin Interview,'' with Joan Murray, in *Ron Martin,* exhibition catalog, London, Ontario 1974; ''A Justification for Abstraction 1988'' in *Ron Martin 1971–1981,* Toronto, Art Gallery of Ontario 1989; ''Design, Form and Method 1998,'' typed, self-distributed artist's statement, 1998. **Audio recording—***Invisible Roots,* with London Experimental Jazz Quartet, 1974.

On MARTIN: Books—*Diversity—Canada East,* exhibition catalog by N. E. Dillow, Edmonton, Alberta 1972; *Ron Martin: World Paintings,* exhibition catalog by Roald Nasgaard, Toronto 1976; *10 Canadian Artists in the 1970s* by Roald Nasgaard, Toronto 1980; *Pleasures of Sight and States of Being: Radical Abstract Painting Since 1990* by Roald Nasgaard, Tallahassee, Florida State University Museum of Fine Arts 2001. **Articles—**''Ron Martin's New Paintings'' by David Rabinowitch in *Artscanada* (Torotno), August 1969; ''Ron Martin at the 20/20 Gallery'' by R. Woodman in *Artscanada* (Toronto), October/November 1970; ''In the Galleries, Toronto'' by G.M. Dault in *Artscanada* (Toronto), April/May 1971; ''Here is One Hand: One Pilgrim's Progress'' by Jerry McGrath in *Vanguard,* vol. 18, no. 3, Summer 1989; ''Object Relations: On Ron Martin's Recent Colour Paintings'' by James D. Campbell in *C Magazine,* no. 27, September 1990; ''Our Vincent'' by Richard Rhodes in *Canadian Art,* vol. 15, no. 4, Winter 1998.

* * *

The essential nature of Ron Martin's paintings is that our perception of them requires from us a self-conscious act of subjective attention, their meaning residing as much in the patterns of our response as in their attributes as objects: in the meeting of matter and psyche. As Martin once described it, in a now much quoted 1971 statement from *Artscanada*: ''I'd like to feel I could make a painting that is primarily about the experience of the experiencer.'' In so far as Martin's paintings need to be looked at as physical and phenomenal facts placed in the world of experience, they partake of the concerns that in the United States would be described as the ''art of the real'' or as ''minimalist.'' But if indeed the paintings are generated via carefully determined depersonalizing procedures—Martin has always profoundly taken into account the material base and the physical elements of painting: the character of the paint used, its quantity, his means of application and distribution, and the particularity of his interaction with the material used—they as often emerge as exuberantly gestural and chromatically dramatic events that reflect the passionate nature of the artist that produced them. As a whole Martin's body of work, which now covers over thirty-five years of undiminished creative activity, is uniquely inflected and not easily subsumed within broader critical categories. Broader international recognition, I believe, is long overdue.

Working in London, Ontario, in a lively artistic milieu that included such figures as Greg Curnoe, Murray Favro, David Rabinowich, and Royden Rabinowich, Martin came in to his own in 1967 with the *Conclusions and Transfer* series in which each work consisted of two identical hard-edged color paintings, the first the original, the second its copy, an exploration of the conceptual and phenomenal relation between the two. His second series, the *World Paintings* (1970–71)—constructed as a grid of one-inch squares each containing three strokes in N-configurations, set upright or sideways, each stroke a single color chosen from a palette of eight—interrogated the temporal nature of our apprehension of literal reality. During the 1970s he made one-color paintings, red, blue, green, yellow, white, until 1974 after which they were all been black. Most are characterized by broad sweeping traces, first of the brush, later of the fingers and the hand, moving the paint across the surface of the canvas to cover it. Towards the end of the decade they became less gestural, flatter, and more anonymously made.

In 1980, in *10 Canadian Artists in the 1970s,* I described a body of one-color paintings as follows. ''Despite the marks of making in Martin's paintings, it would be a mistake to assume that he is engaged in some expressionist enterprise, because of our usual association of gestural painting with the intention of directly rendering personal emotions. The paintings are unambiguously the product of real physical and deeply felt human action. But once they have left the painter's studio, the works insist on being curiously autonomous. They are made of paint, as paintings are, but the paint has retained its own identity. It displays its mass. It has depth and extension. It glistens when light hits it; it even retains the look of its previous viscosity which yielded under, resisted and sometimes overruled the artist's hand or the tools he used to spread it. Nor do the paintings represent anything. They are not models of something, and they have no parts physically or visually separable. They simply exist as indivisible wholes which must be dealt with directly in terms of their measurable physical properties.''

''Yet the paintings continue to fascinate because each is like nothing that we have seen before, or that we can quite understand. Though the paint retains its literal integrity, it is not methodically applied, in the manner of Robert Ryman, for instance. It seems to be fixed where it is, in one painting as a consequence of a heroic gesture of displacement, in another due to an act like that of stilling a turbulent sea. Thus read, the paintings become records of struggle against adversity, and of success, or relative success because the paint too has had its way, and are therewith in Martin's words, ''a symbol, an analogy of the reality you and I exist in.''

Writing in 1988 for the catalog for an exhibition at the Art Gallery of Ontario, Martin defined the concern of his work as follows: ''My art is . . . based in the idea that matter and the psyche are equivalent and in essence draw on an abstracted symbolism within us implicit in the projective issues manifest in painting.'' By then the one-color paintings had ceded to an exploration of the fact of color, color planes organized in grid formations, the paint smoothly and evenly applied, the eye scanning and measuring the effect of constant against shifting hues and values. By the late 1980s the grid pattern, black and white or multicolored, dissolved into thick, turbulent flowing paint matter, and by the early 1990, a new order of severity emerged in, among others, a series of black sand and acrylic surfaces articulated by regular horizontal striations as if made by a comb. Perhaps by implication the comb is Duchamp's ready-made *Comb*, because Martin has always been intensely engaged in the theoretical issues of painting, not only in his writing, but in an ongoing group of Duchampian object installations (*Dedication to Jackson Pollock*, 1974; *Bottle of Paint, Tube of Paint, Box of Paint*, 1988; etc.), as well as in several text works culminating most recently in *Pages*, 1998–99, whose premise it is that ''if we can project our soul onto material, we can project our soul onto viewers, [the latter] a medium of insight and knowledge through their comprehension of the medium of the painted text as image.''

—Roald Nasgaard

MASON, John

Nationality: American. **Born:** Madrid, Nebraska, 30 March 1927; moved to Nevada, 1937, and to Los Angeles, 1949. **Education:** Otis Art Institute, Los Angeles, 1949–52; Chouinard Art Institute, Los Angeles, 1953–54. **Career:** Sculptor: has lived and worked in Los Angeles since 1954. Associate professor of art, 1967–73, and professor and chairman of studio art, 1973–74, University of California at Irvine. Since 1974, professor of art, Hunter College, New York. **Awards:** Ford Foundation Award, Art Institute of Chicago, 1964; University of California Creative Arts Institute Award, 1969–70. **Agents:** Fuller Goldeen Gallery, 228 Grant Avenue, San Francisco, California 94108; Max Hutchinson Gallery, 138 Greene Street, New York, New York 10012. **Address:** Department of Studio Art, Hunter College, 695 Park Avenue, New York, New York 10021, U.S.A.

Individual Exhibitions:

1956 Gump's Gallery, San Francisco
1958 Ferus Gallery, Los Angeles
1959 Ferus Gallery, Los Angeles
1960 Pasadena Art Museum, California
1961 Ferus Gallery, Los Angeles
1962 Ferus Gallery, Los Angeles
1966 *Scuplture,* Los Angeles County Museum of Art (retrospective)
1974 *Ceramic Sculpture,* Pasadena Museum of Modern Art, California
1976 Hansen Fuller Gallery, San Francisco
1981 *Drawings, Sculpture and Proposals,* Max Hutchinson Gallery, New York
1990 Garth Clark Gallery, New York
1998 Perimeter Gallery, Chicago

Selected Group Exhibitions:

1964 *Annual American Exhibition,* Art Institute of Chicago
Annual Exhibition of Contemporary American Sculpture, Whitney Museum, New York
1967 *American Sculpture of the 60s,* Los Angeles County Museum of Art
1969 *West Coast 1945–1969,* Pasadena Art Museum, California
Kompas 4, Van Abbemuseum, Eindhoven, Netherlands
1971 *Contemporary Ceramic Art Canada, U.S.A., Mexico,* National Museum of Modern Art, Kyoto, Japan
1974 *Public Sculpture/Urban Environment,* Oakland Museum, California
1976 *200 Year of American Sculpture,* Whitney Museum, New York
1977 *Foundations in Clay,* Los Angeles Institute of Contemporary Art
1986 *California Sculpture 1959–80,* San Francisco Museum of Modern Art
1996 *Large Drawings and Objects,* Arkansas Arts Center, Little Rock
Abstract Expressionist Ceramics, Garth Clark Gallery, New York (catalog)
1998 *John Mason, Ken Price, Peter Voulkos at Frank Lloyd,* Frank Lloyd, Los Angeles
Gold, Association Gallery, London

Publications:

On MASON: Articles—''Beads, Body, and Soul: Art and Light in the Yorùbá Universe'' with Henry John Drewal in *African Arts,* vol. 31, Winter 1998.

On MASON: Books—*John Mason: Sculpture,* exhibition catalog with text by John Coplans, Los Angeles 1966; *John Mason: Ceramic Sculpture,* exhibition catalog with text by Barbara Haskell and an introduction by R. G. Barnes, Pasadena, California 1974; *John Mason: Installations from the Hudson River Series,* New York 1978. **Articles—**''John Mason'' by Mac McCloud in *Ceramics Monthly,* vol. 36, January 1988; review by Matthew Kangas in *American Ceramics,* vol. 8, no. 4, 1990; ''John Mason's Conceptual Journey'' by Ben Marks in *American Craft,* vol. 50, December/January 1990–1991; ''John Mason'' by Suzanne Muchnic in *Art News,* vol. 96, April 1997; ''Golden Years'' in *British Journal of Photography,* vol. 145, no. 7192, 16 September 1998; review by Fred Camper in *American Ceramics,* vol. 13, no. 2, 1998; review by Carmine Iannaccone in *Art Issues,* no. 55, November/December 1998; ''Boston's Nineteenth-Century Ship Carvers'' by Jane L. Port in *The Magazine Antiques,* vol. 158, no. 5, November 2000; ''John Mason's Initiation'' by Patricia Scott in *Hand Papermaking,* vol. 15, no. 2, Winter 2000.

* * *

In the mid-1950s, John Mason, along with a talented group of Southern California artists, undertook a radical reorientation of the ceramic medium. Interested in exploring the physical properties of clay and its expressive potential, Mason embarked on a direct attack on traditional techique and craftsmanship. In participation with Peter

Voulkos, Mason at first explored the expressionist possibilities inherent in the making of pottery. Playing on the innate qualities of clay (i.e., a malleable substance that requires quick and instantaneous working), the artist's gestural handling later evolved into a direct sculptural extrapolation of Abstract Expressionist painting. (Japanese pottery with its acceptance of asymmetry and imperfection was also an important influence.) Like Abstract Expressionism in general, these early sculptures, in their anthropomorphic or totemic bearing, never entirely relinquished figurative associations. At the verge of becoming primitive icons, they were suspended somewhere between pure expression and signification.

In its attention to the action of the hand and the processes that result in the transmutation of a volatile natural substance into a stable, culturally encoded object, Mason's work goes beyond expressionist assertion. After his Abstract Expressionist phase, the artist experimented with massive monolithic forms, creating primordial shapes reminiscent of crosses, double crosses, and spearheads. The increased size and homogeneity of these works combined with the general fragility of clay resulted in a number of complex technical problems. Standing between instability and permanence, Mason's primitive articulations, existing at the threshold of culture, echoed the concerns of his earlier expressionist work.

As Mason's work became increasingly smooth and monolithic throughout the 1960s, technical problems (such as cracking and breakage due to uneven shrinkage of the clay in the firing) became more severe. The artist's interest in a larger and more uniform format provoked an intense rethinking of the earlier concern with expressive handwork. After experimenting for several years with new materials, Mason settled on firebrick, a choice predicated on his increasing alienation from ceramic processes. Because the kiln is constructed from them, firebricks vestigially retain the mythology of the ceramic medium; within the furnace the clay undergoes a transition from nature to culture. Playing on firebrick's rich tonal and color variations, the artist created structures that were both systematic and sensuous. His early explorations were self-contained and more traditionally sculptural, such as his "Arch" (1976), a firebrick arch supported by the tension and pressure of its own weight. Since 1972, Mason has been working on floor pieces, deploying simple plinths of firebrick over large areas of gallery space. Under these special conditions, his elegant and beautiful structures assume a commanding territorial imperative in the reorientation of the spectator's sense of scale and place. Outside the domain of sculptural convention, works like "Hudson River Series" (1978) blast the logic of the self-contained monument, suggesting instead the conditions of landscape or architecture. Thus, in the traversal from the modernist sensibility of paradox, mysticism, and expression to the minimal, expansive, and temporal concerns of postmodernism, John Mason became one of the few artists to bridge, if not entirely reconcile, the often dissonant concerns of the two epochs.

—Maurice Berger

MASSON, André (Aimé René)

Nationality: French. **Born:** Balagny, Oise, 4 January 1896; moved with his family to Brussels, 1904, settled in Paris, 1912. **Education:** Studied at the Ecole Nationale Supérieure des Beaux-Arts, Paris, under Paul Baudouin, 1912. **Military Service:** French Army, 1914–19; wounded and hospitalized for many months. **Family:** Twice married. **Career:** Painter: worked as a ceramic decorator, deliveryman for a glass factory, proofreader, etc., in Paris, in the 1920s; associated with the Surrealists, 1924–29; first book illustrations, 1925; first sculptures, 1928; co-founder, *Minotaure* review, Paris, 1930; moved to Grasse, Southern France, 1932; first theatre designs, for Ballet Russe de Monte Carlo, 1933; worked as an illustrator for *Acephale,* edited by Georges Bataille, 1933; lived in Tossa de Mar, Catalonia, Spain, 1934–36, and Lyons-la-Foret, France, 1937; produced theatre designs for Jean-Louis Barrault, Leonide Massine and Jean-Paul Sartre, from 1937; lived in Freluc, Auvergne, France, 1940–41; lived in Connecticut, 1941–45; organized the conference Origins of Surrealism at the Baltimore Museum of Art, 1941, and Mount Holyoke College, Massachusetts, 1943; associated with the exiled Surrealists, organizing conferences, lectures and exhibitions, New York, 1941–45; lived in Poitiers, France, and Aix-en-Provence, 1946–47; first lithographs, 1948; travelled extensively in Europe, particularly in Italy, from 1950; worked on designs for the ceiling of the Odéon theater, Paris, 1965; first tapestry designs, 1967; with Max Ernst and Dorothea Tanning, organized concerts with Karlheinz Stockhausen, 1970; participated in the film *Arts et l'Emphemere* by Pierre Schneider, 1971, and a televison film on Matisse, with Hans Hartung and Georges Mathieu, 1973. **Member:** Council of National Museums, 1962. **Awards:** Grand Prix National des Arts, 1954. **Died:** Paris, 28 October 1987.

Individual Exhibitions:

1923 Galerie Simon, Paris
1929 Galerie Simon, Paris
1935 Pierre Matisse Gallery, New York
1936 Wildenstein and Company, London
Galerie Simon, Paris
1941 Baltimore Museum of Art
1942 Buchholz Gallery and Willard Gallery, New York
Arts Club of Chicago
1943 Buchholz Gallery, New York (with Paul Klee)
1944 Buchholz Gallery, New York
Paul Rosenberg Gallery, New York
1945 Buchholz Gallery, New York
Galerie Louise Leiris, Paris
1946 Palais des Beaux-Arts, Brussels
1947 Arts Council Gallery, London
Buchholz Gallery, New York
Gallery Louise Leiris, Paris
1948 Gallery Louise Leiris, Paris
1949 Landesamt für Museen, Fribourg, Switzerland
Buchholz Gallery, New York
1950 Kunsthalle, Basel (with Alberto Giacometti)
Galerie Louise Leiris, Paris
1952 Galerie Louise Leiris, Paris
1953 Paul Rosenberg Gallery, New York
Curt Valentin Gallery, New York
1954 Kunstverein, Dusseldorf (toured West Germany)
Galerie Louise Leiris, Paris
1955 Kestner-Gesellschaft, Hannover
Leicester Galleries, London

André Masson in Paris, 1987. ©2001 Artists Rights Society (ARS), NY/ADAGP, Paris.

1956 Galerie Lucien Blanc, Paris
1957 Galerie Louise Leiris, Paris
Galerie der Spiegel, Cologne
Galerie R Hoffman, Hamburg
1958 Albertina Akademie, Vienna
Saidenberg Gallery, New York
Biennale, Venice
Marlborough Fine Art, London
Edgardo Acosta Gallery, Beverly Hills, California (travelled to the Pasadena Art Museum and the Santa Barbara Museum of Art)
Kunstkabinett Klihm, Munich
Galerie Furstenberg, Paris
Meijishobo, Tokyo
1959 Galleria Bussola, Turin
1960 Galerie Louise Leiris, Paris
Galleria Il Segno, Rome
Galerie Renée Ziegler, Zurich
Svensk-Franska Konstgalleriet, Stockholm
1961 Saidenberg Gallery, New York
Richard Feigen Gallery, Chicago
1962 Galerie Louise Leiris, Paris
Marlborough Fine Art, London
1963 Galerie Gerald Cramer, Geneva
Galerie du Perron, Geneva
1964 Stedelijk Museum, Amsterdam
Akademie der Künste, Berlin
1965 Musée National d'Art Moderne, Paris
Galerie Michael Hertz, Bremen, West Germany
Tel Aviv Museum
Galerie Gerald Cramer, Geneva
Galerie Francoise Ledoux, Paris
1966 Galerie les Contards, Lacoste, Vaucluse, France
Saidenberg Gallery, New York
Galerie Renée Ziegler, Zurich
Galerie Wünsche, Bonn
1967 Musée des Beaux-Arts, Lyon
La Nuova Loggia, Bologna
Galerie Vincent Kramer, Prague
1968 Musée Cantini, Marseilles
Galerie Louise Leiris, Paris
Galerie Lucie Weil, Paris
Musée St. Ethienne du Rouvray, France
1969 Galleria Il Fauno, Turin
Galerie Sagot-le-Garrée, Paris
Casino Comunal, Knokke-le-Zoute, Belgium
Palazzo dei Diamanti, Ferrara, Italy
Galleria del Milione, Milan
1970 La Nuova Loggia, Bologna
Galleria Schwarz, Milan
Galleria La Bussola, Turin
Galerie Louise Leiris, Paris

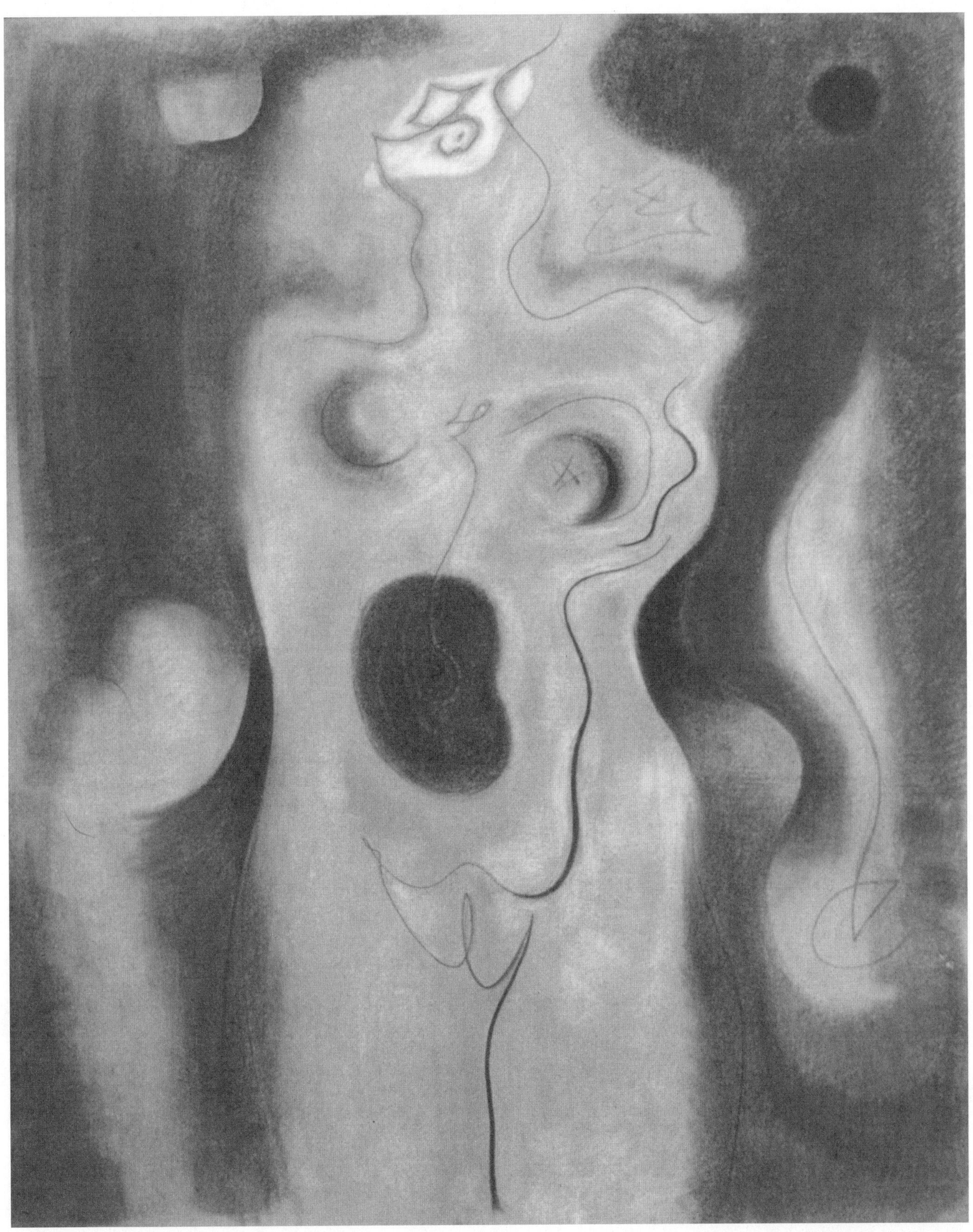

André Masson: *Nu a la Flamme*. ©2001 Artists Rights Society (ARS), NY/ADAGP, Paris.

Museum am Ostwall, Dortmund (travelled to the Klingenmuseum, Solingen, West Germany, and the Pfalzgalerie, Kaiserslauten, West Germany)
1971 Centre d'Art, Beirut
Basil Jacobs Fine Art, London
Salle des Fètes, Bobigny, France
Galerie Andelt, Wiesbaden
Galerie Gerald Cramer, Geneva (with Max Ernst)
Galerie de l'Editeur, Paris
Maison de la Culture, Amiens, France
1972 Maison des Arts et Loisirs, Montbeliard, France
Galerie de Seine, Paris
Waddington Galleries, London
Galerie Michael Hertz, Bremen, West Germany
Lerner-Heller Gallery and Blue Moon Gallery, New York
Salon de la Quinzaine d'Art en Quency, Montauban, France
Galerie Verrière, Paris
Galerie Ariane, Gotbenburg, Sweden
1973 Galleria Zanini, Rome
Galleria Schwarz, Milan
Galleria San Sebastianello, Rome
Galerie Louise Leiris, Paris
Centre d'Art 2, Beirut
Mayor Gallery, London
Galerie Jacques Davidson, Tours, France
Galerie du Lion, Paris
Musée de l'Art et d'Histoire, Fribourg, Switzerland (travelled to the Galerie Gerald Cramer, Geneva)
Lerner-Heller Gallery and Blue Moon Gallery, New York
1974 Galerie Benador, Geneva
Opere 1925–1973, Il Collezionista d'Arte Contemporanea, Rome
Galerie Claude Tchou, Paris
1975 Galerie de Seine, Paris
Lerner-Heller Gallery and Blue Moon Gallery, New York
Musée Grand-Palais de Malte, Aix-en-Provence
1976 Musée d'Art Moderne de la Ville, Paris
Museum of Modern Art, New York
Lerner-Heller Gallery and Blue Moon Gallery, New York
1977 Grand Palais, Paris
1978 Galerie Patrick Cramer, Geneva
1981 Orsanmichele, Florence
Marisa del Re Gallery, New York
1983 Galerie Louise Leiris, Paris
1985 Fondation Royaumont, Belgium
1986 Artcurial, Paris
Galerie Louise Leiris, Paris
1987 Marisa Del Re Gallery, New York
Galerie Jade, Colmar, France
1988 Edward Totah Gallery, London
1989 Villa Medici, Rome
1990 Listasafn Islands, Reykjavik
1992 Chateau des Rohan, Strasbourg
1993 Grand Jardin, Paris
1995 Museo Archeologico, Aosta
Mayor Gallery, London
1996 Zabriskie Gallery, New York
1998 Ludwig Museum, Deutschherrenhaus, Koblenz

Selected Group Exhibitions:

1925 *Peintures Surrealistes,* Galerie Pierre, Paris
1936 *International Surrealist Exhibition,* Burlington Galleries, London
1937 *Fantastic Art, Dada, Surrealism,* Museum of Modern Art, New York
1942 *First Papers of Surrealism,* Reed Mansion, New York
1952 *Surrealistische Malerei in Europa,* Saarbrucken Museum, West Germany
1966 *Art Francais Contemporain,* Palais des Beaux-Arts, Brussels
1968 *Dada, Surrealism and Their Heritage,* Museum of Modern Art, New York (travelled to the Los Angeles County Museum of Art and the Art Institute of Chicago)
1973 *Futurism: A Modern Focus,* Guggenheim Museum, New York
1975 *Surrealism,* National Museum of Modern Art, Tokyo
1977 *Neue Wirklichkeit: Surrealismus und Neue Sachlichkeit,* Orangerie, Schloss Charlottenburg, Berlin
1988 *Impressionist and Modern Masters,* Galerie Daniel Malingue, Paris
1993 *Masson & Bataille,* Musee des Beaux-Arts d'Orleans, Orleans
1995 *Le transparence dans l'art du Xxe siecle,* Musee des Beaux-Arts Andre Malraux, Le Havre
1997 *Annees 30 en Europe: le Temps Menacant,* Musee d'Art Moderne de la Ville de Paris, Paris
La luxure, Centre Georges Pompidou, Paris
1998 *The Surrealist Object,* IVAM Centre Julio Gonzalez, Valencia

Collections:

Centre Georges Pompidou, Paris; Musée d'Art Moderne de la Ville, Paris; Wallraf-Richartz Museum, Cologne; Folkwang Museum, Essen; Nationalgalerie, Berlin; Tate Gallery, London; Museum of Modern Art, New York; Hirshhorn Museum, Washington D.C.; National Gallery of Victoria, Melbourne.

Publications:

By MASSON: Books—*Mythology of Being,* New York 1942; *Anatomy of My Universe,* New York 1943; *Nocturnal Notebook,* New York 1944; *Bestiaire,* New York 1946; *Mythologies,* Paris 1946; *Carnet de croquis,* Paris 1950; *Le Plaisir de peindre,* Nice 1950; *Voyage à Venise,* Paris 1952 *Metamorphose de l'artiste,* Geneva 1956; *La memoire du monde,* Geneva 1974. **Books illustrated**—*Soleils bas* by Georges Limbour, Paris 1924; *L'Anus solaire* by Georges Bataille, Paris 1931; *Terre sur terre* by Tristan Tzara, Paris 1946; *Le Dit du vieux marin, Christobel et Koubla Khan* by Samuel Taylor Coleridge, Paris 1948; *Un saison en enfer* by Rimbaud, 1960; *Oeuvres completes: Essais philosophiques* by Albert Camus, Paris 1962; *L'Idiot* by Dostoievsky, Paris 1966. **Articles**—''Lettre à André Breton'' in *La Révolution Surrealiste* (Paris), October 1925; ''Tyrannie du Temps'' in *La Révolution Surrealiste* (Paris), March 1926; ''André Masson beantwortet einige Fragen'' in *Das Kunstblatt* (Berlin), August 1931; ''Du Haut de Montseratt'' in *Minotaure* (Paris), June 1936; ''Enquete'' in *Les Cahiers d'Art* (Paris), vol. 14, nos. 1–4,

1939; ''Mythologie de la Nature'' in *Les Cahiers d'Art* (Paris), vol. 14, no. 56, 1939; ''Peindre est une Gageure'' in *Les Cahiers du Sud* (Marseilles), March 1941, reprinted as ''Painting Is a Wager'' in *Horizon* (London), March 1943; ''The Bed of Plato'' in *View* (New York), October/November 1941; ''Life and Liberty'' in *Art in Australia* (Sydney), March/May 1942; ''Re-Minotaure'' in *View* (New York), May 1942; ''L'Homme Emblématique'' in *VVV* (New York), June 1942; ''Mallarmé, Portraitist of Baudelaire and Poe'' in *View* (New York), October 1942; ''Page from a Notebook'' in *View* (New York, vol. 3, no. 1, 1943; ''Antille'' in *Hemispheres* (New York), Autumn/Winter 1943/44; ''Une Crise de l'imaginaire'' in *Fontaine* (Algiers), no. 35, 1944, reprinted in Masson's book *Le Plaisir de peindre,* Nice 1950, and as ''A Crisis of the Imaginary'' in *Horizon* (London), July 1945, and in *Magazine of Art* (New York), January 1946; ''Unité et variété de la peinture française'' in *Renaissance* (New York), vol. II-III, 1944–45; ''Peinture tragique'' in *Les Temps Modernes* (Paris), January 1946; ''Eloge de Paul Klee'' in *Fontaine* (Paris), June 1946, reprinted in Mason's book *Le Plaisir de peindre,* and as ''Homage to Paul Klee'' in *Partisan Review* (New York), January/February 1947; ''Le Peintre et el temps'' in *Les Temps Modernes* (Paris), July 1946; ''Un grand siècle pictural'' in *Critique* (Paris), November 1946; ''Notes'' in *Les Cahiers du Sud* (Marseilles), vol. XXIII, no. 279, 1946; ''Le Roi fou à la couronne de flammes'' in *Les Cahiers du Sud* (Marseilles), vol. XXXIII, no. 275, 1946; statement in *11 Europeans in America* by James Johnson Sweeney, New York 1946; ''Commentaries'' in *Saisons* (Paris), Winter 1946/47; ''L'Artiste et son portrait: Corot reconte par luimeme et par ses amis'' in *Critique* (Paris), March 1947; ''Note sur l'imagination sadique'' in *Les Cahiers du Sud* (Marseilles), vol. XXXIV, no. 285, 1947; ''La Balance faussée'' in *Les Temps Modernes* (Paris), February 1949; ''Color and the Lithographer'' in *The Tiger's Eye* (New York), June 1949; ''Divagations sur l'espace'' in *Les Temps Modernes* (Paris), June 1949; ''Mouvement et Metamorphose'' in *Les Temps Modernes* (Paris), October 1949; ''L'Atelier de Calder'' in *Les Cahiers d'Art* (Paris), vol. XXIV, no. 2, 1949; ''Peinture et Rhétorique'' in *Les Cahiers du Sud* (Marseilles), vol. XXXVI, no. 295, 1949; ''La Création artistique est-elle affectée par les evénements contemporains'' in *Transition 49* (Paris), no. 5, 1949; ''Courbet: Le réaliste fabuleux'' in *Critique* (Paris), January 1951; ''Instant Notes for a New Style'' in *Artnews* (New York), October 1951; ''Vue d'ensemble: Fenise retrouvé'' in *Critique* (Paris), November 1951; ''Proposition'' in *Le Point* (Souillac, France), April 1952; ''Monet: Le fondateur'' in *Verve* (Paris), nos. 27–28, 1952; ''Notes sur la peintures'' in *Les Cahiers du Sud* (Marseilles), vol. XXXIX, no. 314, 1952; ''Le Surrealisme et après: Un entretien au magnétophone avec André Masson'' in *L'Oeil* (Paris), May 1955; ''L'Effusioniste'' in *La Nouvelle Revue Francaise* (Paris), July 1955; ''Une Peinture de l'Essentiel'' in *Quadrum* (Brussels), May 1956; ''Le Peintre es ses fantasmes'' in *Les Etudes Philosophiques* (Paris), October/December 1956; ''Redon: Mystique with a Method'' in *Artnews* (New York), January 1957; ''L'Art commence ou le réalisme finit,'' interview, with Alain Jouffroy, in *Arts Magazine* (New York), February 1958; ''La Brume dans la Vallée de l'Arc'' in *L'Arc* (Aix-en-Provence), Spring 1958; ''Dialogues avec André Masson'' in *Entretiens avec Georges Charbonnier,* Paris 1958; ''Entretien avec André Masson'' in *Le monologue du peintre* (Paris), vol. 1, 1959; preface to *Paris/New York: Arts Yearbook 3,* New York 1959; ''Le Jardin des dèlices'' in *Critique* (Paris), May 1959; ''Nicolas Poussin en 1960'' in *La Nouvelle Revue Francaise* (Paris), June 1960; ''Le Peintre et la Culture'' in *Art de France* (Paris), vol. 4 1964; ''Some Notes on the Unusual Georges Bataille'' in *Art and Literature* (Lausanne, Switzerland), Autumn/Winter 1964; ''Mon plafond à l'Odéon'' in *Connaissance des Arts* (Paris), January 1966; ''The Artist Speaks: André Masson'' in *Erotic Art: A Survey of Erotic Fact and Fancy in the Fine Arts* by Phyllis and Eberhard Kronhausen, New York 1968; letter in ''Letters from 31 Artists'' by Ethel Moore in *Albright-Knox Art Gallery Notes* (Buffalo, New York), Spring 1970; ''André Masson, graveur et illustrateur: Histoire d'une de mes folies'' in *XXe Siècle* (Paris), June 1972; ''Comment j'ai illustre des livres'' in *Bulletin du Bibliophile* (Paris), part 2, 1972; ''Conversation avec Matisse: La decoration Barnes'' in *Critique* (Paris), May 1974; ''A propos de Claude Monet'' in *Paintings by Monet,* exhibition catalog, Chicago 1975; ''Interview with André Masson,'' with D. Rosenthal, in *Arts Magazine* (New York), November 1980.

On MASSON: Books—*André Masson* by Jean-Louis Barrault, Georges Bataille, André Breton and others, Rouen 1940; *André Masson and His Universe* by Michael Leiris and Georges Limbour, Geneva 1947; *André Masson* by Hubert Juin, Paris 1963; *Masson* by Otto Hahn, Paris, New York and London 1965; *Mythologie d'André Masson* by Jean-Paul Clébert, Geneva 1971; *André Masson* by L. M. Sapphire, New York 1973; *André Masson: Opere 1925–1973,* exhibition catalog, by Michel Leiris, Paul Eluard, André Breton and others, Rome 1974; *André Masson et les puissances du signe* by René Passeron, Paris 1975; *André Masson,* exhibition catalog by William Rubin and Carolyn Lanchner, New York 1976; *André Masson,* exhibition catalog by William Rubin, Carolyn Launchner and Michel Leiris, Paris 1977; *André Masson,* exhibition catalog with text by Bernard Noel, Royaumont 1985; *André Masson,* exhibition catalog with text by Claude Duthuit, Paris 1986; *André Masson: du signe a'lecriture,* exhibition catalog, Strasbourg 1992; *André Masson,* exhibition catalog, Paris 1993; *André Masson,* by Dawn Ades, New York 1994; *André Masson,* exhibition catalog, with text by Dawn Ades, London 1995; *André Masson: Nature's Delirious Wisdom,* exhibition catalog, with text by Georges Duby, Aosta 1995; *André Masson in America (1941–1945),* exhibition catalog, New York 1996; *The Surrealist Object,* exhibition catalog with text by Maria Casanova, Valencia 1997; *Premiere fur einen Rebellen,* exhibition catalog, Koblenz 1998. **Articles—**''Andre Masson's Earth-Mothers in their Cultural Context'' by Robert Belton in RACAR, vol. 15, no. 1, 1988; ''Masson Before Surrealism'' by David Sylvester in *Modern Painters* (London), vol. 9, no. 3, Autumn 1996. **Films—***André Masson et les quatre elements* by Jean Gremillon, 1959; *A la source de la femme Aimé* by Nelly Kaplan, 1966; *Perspectives surrealistes: Les Metamorphoses,* ORTF-TV Film, 1971; *Le Monde Imaginaire d'André Masson,* with the sculptor Hansjorg Gesiger, TV Film, 1973.

* * *

Do fishes come at each other with knives? Does one praying mantis stand flexing his knees while another prepares to duel with him to the death in an arena whose ringside is crowded with an insect audience come to see battle done *mis-a-morte?* These have been the subjects of drawings and paintings by André Masson, carried out with figurative expertise that suggests spontaneous verve.

Such pictures seem remote in time and style from the artist's early juggling with a kind of classicist cubism, faceted works that looked only one remove from Greco-Roman culture, and which even shared with antiquity a palette of subdued hues and light-relief chiaroscuro, whereas the scenes of piscean and insect mortal combat were coloured in mid-day brilliance, only a shade more reserved than the lightning flashes of scarlet and yellow which set alight the "handwriting" pictures of the late 1930s. In that period, immediately before the Second World War, Masson painted like one possessed. There was, for instance, a lithograph carried in one of the earlier copies of *Verve* where some stellar object in richest red was poised in a sky of intensest blue and in a way so vivid that it made the eyes blink and, should they be closed a moment after, remained imprinted on the retina.

There have been many inventive pictures made by Masson since those days of 40 years ago. A wonderful and magical interior from a late stage of his development was bought not long ago for the Sztuka Museum in Lodz by Richard Stanislawsky. And there was an astonishing exhibition in Paris of Masson's oriental style and how this related to jewelry. But, nevertheless, probably his finest moments came before the War and one must be thankful that he was never idle for long.

At its best, Masson's line, and especially the painted line, is something never matched in the history of art, either before his time or since.

—Sheldon Williams

MATHIEU, Georges

Nationality: French. **Born**: Boulogne-sur-Mer, 27 January 1921. **Education:** Lycée Mariette, Boulogne, 1932; Lycée Hoche, Versailles, 1933–35; Lycée Corneille, Rouen 1936; studied law and English; mainly self-taught in painting. **Career:** Painter, in Douai, Cambrai and Biarritz, 1942–47, in Paris, since 1947: first abstract works, 1944; developed lyrical abstraction/tachist work, from 1947. Instructor in English, Lycée de Douai, 1943; instructor for the United States Army, Cambrai 1944; instructor in French, American University, Biarritz, 1945–46; head of public relations, United States Lines shipping company, Paris 1947; director/editor, *Paris Review* (for United States Lines), Paris, 1953–63. **Member:** Académie des Beaux-Arts, Paris, since 1975. **Agents:** Galerie Protée, 38 Rue de Seine, Paris, France; Galerie Semiha Huber, 16 Talstrasse, Zurich, Switzerland; Galerie Sapone, 25 Boulevard Victor Hugo, Nice, France. **Address:** c/o Academie des Beaux-Arts, 23 Quai de Conti 75006 Paris, France.

Individual Exhibitions:

1950 Galerie Drouin, Paris
1952 Studio Paul Facchetti, Paris
Stable Gallery, New York
1953 Galerie Marcel Evrard, Lille, France
1954 Kootz Gallery, New York
Galerie Rive Droite, Paris
Arts Club of Chicago
1955 Iolas Gallery, New York
Kootz Gallery, New York
1956 Galerie Rive Droite, Paris
Institute of Contemporary Arts, London
Galerie Pierre, Paris
Kootz Gallery, New York (2 shows)
1957 Palais des Beaux-Arts, Brussels

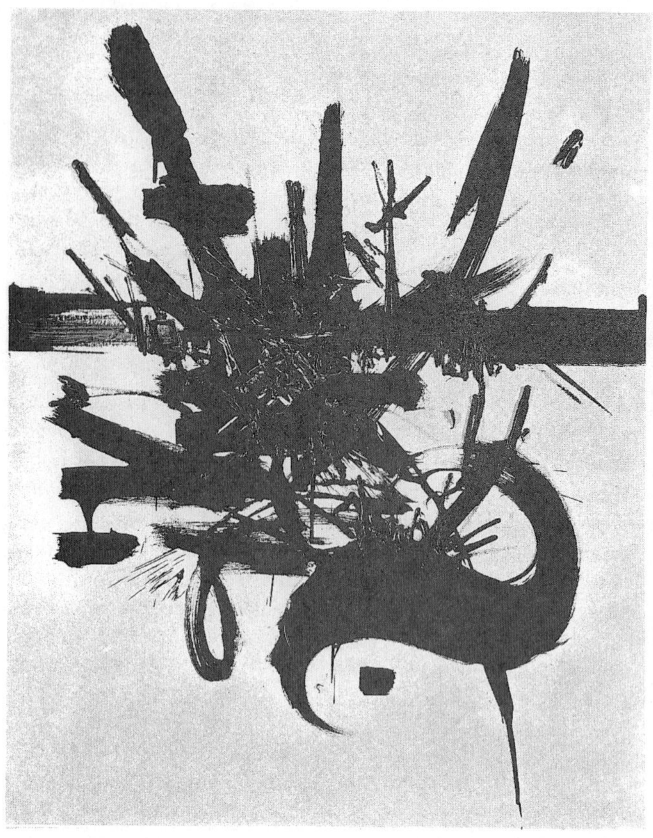

Georges Mathieu: *Zoroastre,* 1970. ©Georges Mathieu.

Galerie Kleber, Paris
Galleria dell'Naviglio, Milan
Galerie Helios Art, Brussels
Lyrical Abstraction in New Paintings by Mathieu, Kootz Gallery, New York
Galleria Selecta, Rome
1958 Galerie Schmela, Dusseldorf
Galerie d'Art Latin, Stockholm
Galerie Grange, Lyons
Galerie Chichio Haller, Zurich
Galerie d'Art Moderne, Basel
Galleria Castelnuovo, Ascoma, Switzerland
Kunstmuseum, Basel
Galerie Internationale d'Art Contemporain, Paris
Musée des Beaux-Arts, Liège, Belgium
Galerie Rive Droite, Paris
Hallwylska Museum, Stockholm
1959 Kunstverein, Cologne
Iolas Gallery, New York (retrospective)
Museum Haus Lange, Krefeld, West Germany
Musée des Beaux-Arts, Neuchatel, Switzerland
Musée de l'Athenée, Geneva
Atelier Riehentor, Basel
Galleria San Babila, Milan
Galerie St. Stephan, Vienna
Kootz Gallery, New York
Galerie Jacques Dubourg, Paris
Galerie Internationale d'Art Contemporain, Paris

Museu de Arte Moderno, Rio de Janeiro
Galeria Bonino, Buenos Aires
1960 Museu de Arte Moderno, Sao Paulo
Museo del Ateneo, Madrid
New London Gallery
Kootz Gallery, New York
Galerie Internationale d'Art Contemporain, Paris
Galleria del Cavallino, Venice
1961 Palais de la Presidence, Beirut
Galerie Schmela, Dusseldorf
Galerie Rive Droite, Paris
Galleria dell'Naviglio, Milan
Galerie Jacques Dubourg, Paris
1962 Galerie Hilt, Basel
18 Peintures, Bezalel National Museum, Jerusalem
Neue Galerie im Kunstlerhaus, Munich
Galleria Bussola, Turin
Galleria dell'Ariete, Milan
Galleria la Loggia, Bologna
Tel-Aviv Museum
1963 Dominion Galley, Montreal
Musée d'Art Moderne de la Ville, Paris
Galerie Internationale d'Art Contemporain, Paris
Palais des Beuax-Arts, Brussels
1964 Gimpel Fils, London
1965 Galerie Charpentier, Paris
Galerie Schmela, Dusseldorf
Mostra dell'Opera Recenta di Georges Mathieu, Galleria Il Milione, Milan
1967 Musée d'Art Moderne, Paris
Gemalde-Gouachen-Aquarelle-Collagen, Kunstverein, Cologne
1968 Gimpel & Hanover Galerie, Zurich
Gimpel Fils, London
1969 Manufacture Nationale des Gobelins, Paris
Arts Council Gallery, Belfast
Galerie Rive Droite, Paris
Musée des Beaux-Arts, Rennes, France
Opere Recenti di Georges Mathieu, Galleria Il Milione, Milan
1971 Galerie Veranneman, Brussels
Musée Monetaire, Paris
1972 Gimpel Fils, London
Galerie Stadler, Paris
1973 Berlin Oper, West Berlin
1974 *Oeuvres Anciennes 1948–1960,* Galerie Beaubourg, Paris
1976 Musée des Beaux-Arts, Antibes, France
1977 Casino Communal, Ostend, Belgium (retrospective)
Chateau de Simiane, France
1978 Musée des Beaux-Arts, Aix-en-Provence, France (retrospective)
Quelques Oeuvres Peintes de 1963 à 1978, Grand Palais, Paris
1979 Wildenstein Gallery, New York
Dominion Gallery, Montreal
1980 *Bilder, Gouachen, Aquarelle und Zeichnungen von Georges Mathieu aus den Jahren 1944–1979,* Gallerie Lauter, Mannheim
Galerie Arts Contemporaine, at *Art 80,* Basel
Musee de la Poste, Paris
1981 Galerie Protée, at *FIAC 81,* Grand Palais, Paris
1982 Hotel Meridien, Tunis
Galerie Jade, Colmar, France
1983 Regency Intercontinental Hotel, Bahrain
Chateau de Vascoeuil, France
Galerie Pro Arte, Morges, Switzerland
1984 Hotel Meridien, Singapore
Theatre Municipal, Brive, France
1985 Galerie Alain Moyon-Avenard, Nantes, France
Wally Findlay Galleries, New York
Galerie Rue Calvin, Geneva
Palais des Papes, Avignon, France (retrospective)
1986 Findlay Gallery, Palm Beach, Florida
Galerie du Luxembourg, Luxembourg
Galerie Protée, Paris
1987 Findlay Gallery, New York
Galerie Semiha Huber, Zurich
Galerie Sapone, Nice, France
Galerie de Bellecour, Lyon, France
Galleria Tedia, Milan
Galerie Protée, Toulouse, France
Palazzo di Caserta, Italy
1988 Fondation de Maddaloni, Caserta, Italy
Galleria Narciso, Turin, Italy
Galerie R. Mischkind, Lille, France
Studio d'Arte Crescenzo, Rome
Centre Arti Visive Beniamino, San Remo, Italy
Galerie Protée, Paris
Villa degli Angeli, Fiesole, Italy
Galleria della Scudo, Verona, Italy
Galerie Guy Pieters, Ghent, Belgium
1989 Centre Culturale Santandrea, Savona, Italy
Galerie Protée, Paris
Maison de la Culture, Metz, France
Galerie de Bellecour, Lyon
Art Valley, Forte di Marmi, Italy
1990 Galleri Ostermalm, Stockholm
Galleri Scandinavia, Göteborg, Sweden
Galleria Elleni, Bergamo, Italy
Abbaye des Cordeliers, Châteauroux, France
Galerie Semiha Huber, Zurich
1991 Conseil Général, Martinique
Galerie Arte 92, Milan
Musée Léon Dierx, Réunion
Hôtel de la Province Sud, Nouméa, New Caledonia
1992 Galerie Dominion, Montreal
Château-Musée de Boulogne-sur-Mer

Selected Group Exhibitions:

1947 *L'Imaginaire,* Galerie du Luxembourg, Paris
1948 *HWPSMTB,* Galerie Colette Allendy, Paris
1951 *Vehemences Confrontees,* Galerie Nina Dausset, Paris
1953 *Young European Painters,* Guggenheim Museum, New York
1957 *4 Paris Artists,* Otto Seligman Gallery, Seattle
1968 *Painting in France 1900–1967,* National Gallery of Art, Washington, D.C. (toured the U.S.A.)
1977 *Paris-New York,* Centre Georges Pompidou, Paris
1981 *Westkunst,* Messehallen, Cologne

1983 *Les Années 60,* Musée de St. Etienne, France
1986 *Biennale,* Venice

Collections:

Centre Georges Pompidou, Paris; Museum des 20. Jahrhunderts, Vienna; Kaiser-Wilhelm Museum, Krefeld, Germany; Kunstmuseum, Cologne; Kunsthaus, Basel; National Museum of Modern Art, Tokyo; Museum of Modern Art, New York; Guggenheim Museum, New York; Art Institute of Chicago; Art Gallery of Ontario, Toronto; Musées Royaux de Belgique, Brussels; Musée National d'Art Moderne, Paris; Fonds National d'Art Contemporain, Paris; Tel Aviv Museum, Israel; Galleria d'Arte Moderne, Rome; Albright-Knox Art Gallery, Buffalo, New York; Hirshhorn Museum, Smithsonian Institution, Washington D.C.

Publications:

By MATHIEU: Books—*Anagogie de la non-figuration,* Paris 1949; *De l'abstrait au possible,* with introduction by Blaise Distel, Zurich 1959; *Au-dela du Tachisme,* Paris 1963; *Le privilege d'etre,* Paris 1967; *De la revolte à la renaissance,* Paris 1973; *La response de l'abstraction lyrique,* Paris 1975; *L'abstraction prophetique,* Paris 1984; *Le Massacre de la Sensibilité,* Paris 1996; *Desormais Seul au Face de Dieu,* Paris 1998.

On MATHIEU: Books—*Georges Mathieu,* exhibition catalog with text by Michel Tapie, Paris 1952; *Georges A. Mathieu,* exhibition catalog with texts by Stephane Lupasco, Mark Tobey and Michel Tapie, Paris 1954; *Mathieu,* exhibition catalog with texts by Herbert Read and Toni del Renzio, London 1956; *Mathieu,* exhibition catalog with text by Toni del Renzio, Rome 1957; *Mathieu,* exhibition catalog with text by Julien Alvard, London 1960; *Georges Mathieu: 18 Peintures,* exhibition catalog with text by John Ashbery, Jerusalem 1962; *Mathieu,* exhibition catalog with text by Julien Alvard and Pierre Restany, Munich 1962; *Mathieu,* exhibition catalog with texts by René Heron de Villefosse and Marie-Claude Dane, Paris 1963; *Mostra dell'opere recente di Georges Mathieu,* exhibition catalog with text by Giulio Carlo Argan, Milan 1965; *Mathieu,* exhibition catalog with texts by Raymond Nacenta, Georges Schehade and Francois Mathey, Paris 1965; *Mathieu: Gemalde-Gouachen-Aquarelle-Collagen,* exhibition catalog with text by Werner Haftmann, Cologne 1967; *Mathieu,* exhibition catalog with text by François Bergot, Rennes 1969; *L'Art de notre temps: Georges Mathieu* by Francois Mathey, Paris and Milan 1969; *Opere recente di Georges Mathieu,* exhibition catalog, Milan 1969; *Mathieu* exhibition catalog with text by Pierre Dehaye, Paris 1971; *La peinture, le geste, l'action: l'existentialisme en peinture* by Margit Rowell, Paris 1972; *Mathieu* by Dominique Quignon-Fleuret, Paris 1973; *Mathieu: Oeuvres Anciennes 1948–1960,* exhibition catalog with texts by Patrice Trigano and Dominique Quignon-Fleuret, Paris 1974; *Georges Mathieu et la poetica del signo* by Maria Rosaria Mioni, Padua 1977; *Bilder, Gouachen, Aquarelle und Zeichnungen von Georges Mathieu aus den Jahren 1944–1979,* exhibition catalog with text by Rolf Lauter, Mannheim 1980; *Georges Mathieu: Retrospective,* exhibition catalog, Avignon 1985; *Mathieu,* introduction by Renato Barilli, Nice 1987; *Georges Mathieu* by Gillo Dorfles, Milan 1991; *Mathieu* by Patrick Grainville and Gerard Xuriguera, Paris 1992.

*

The only true creation is one which invents its means on the spot, calling everything into question. Who has lived those sublime, those tremendously heroic, moments when the artist, seeing the signs he recognises as his own appearing under his brush, butchers them like Cronos his children? Cronos whom the Romans foolishly identified with Saturn though he is the finest incarnation of Uranus! Oh! What a prodigy is this birth of new forms, this transition from Chaos to Cosmos, but what pain too in this birth unlike any other!

In that fundamental solitude, where security depends on speed and which has nothing to do with the work ''to measure'' of those who relied on something real, or on an existing architecture, the painter, first spectator of the imaginary reality which he creates before living it, is as an actor—hero by the same right as those rare military geniuses who have taken charge of events, creating challenges only to take them up, and traps only to defuse them. During the improvised execution of his works, the lyrical abstract artist initiates a strategy and a set of tactics similar enough to those of the great captains who, not content merely to win battles, left on them their own personal and original stamp, producing miracles rather than precedents. The artist ceases then to be the skillful executant of a vision composed by him in advance; he leads the action on his own account, an action in which the stake is not a victory over the enemy, but over himself.

That's where the drama lies. Every second it is his duty to usher in not only forms, but techniques of whose efficacy and extent he knows nothing, blinding himself to the havoc he is causing, never able to go back, condemned to proceed in the dark until, after a thousand approaches, he gets a glimpse of the clearing from whence he will see the paths that lead to the light. What exhilaration in the gesture which suddenly transcends the whole past of art, the whole of our own past!

From the soaked and folded towel dashed against the surface of *Hommage á Hideyoshi* on the roof of Osaka, to the white gashes of Stockholm, to the blood bath of Rio, to the luxuriant golden garlands of the *Election of Charles the Fifth,* born of the trajectory of the liquid pigment projected through space, landing on the canvas and flattening out there according to the laws of an unknown ballistics where speed, force, weight, fluidity and colour—the brush then ceasing to be in contact with the surface to be painted—all play their part, we witness as it were liberating expansion of the artistic means, which would be as nothing if not accompanied at each step by a fresh sense of vertigo.

One has to have experienced the anguish which paralyses the arm at the very moment of the ''uncontrolled explosion'' of which I spoke thirty years ago, if one is to understand the ill-timed intervention of reason and ''aesthetics'' in this fight to the death which finds its resolution only in victory, not over three centuries of Cartesian orthopedics, but over thirty years of pictorial awareness! Oh! If others could only know!

In this world where there is no help and no recourse, and where the most desperate cries fall on deaf ears, we must still reject sort of buoy or life raft . . . and nor are we allowed to swim according to the established laws of swimming.

We must cross to the other side by walking on the water.

(2000)The truth is that all of the above information reveals *nothing* of the work of art itself. It is just what is given on the internet, i.e., information and communication which has nothing to do with culture.

—Georges Mathieu

* * *

Georges Mathieu began painting in 1942, and in 1944 after reading a book on the novelist Joseph Conrad by Edward Crankshaw he adopted a nonfigurative style. The year of decision was 1947, and then he moved to Paris and organised the first exhibition of Abstraction Lyrique. For him this was a protest against the retrogressive direction in art relating back to the classical tradition resurrected by the painters of the Renaissance. At first he was influenced by abstract surrealism as seen in the work of Wols. Later he went through a period when Pollock and de Kooning had their effect.

It was about 1948 when he developed his own individual style of painting that had its foundation in the gesture and a flow of spontaneous continuity of image across the canvas. Speed and improvisation have often been the foundation of some of his most succesful paintings. He has painted a picture in front of an invited audience in a theatre within a few hours, a form of action painting that required confidence, energy and a total command of resources. Stage design, tapestries and mosaics as well as plans for the architecture of a new factory have issued almost ceaselessly from Mathieu's fertile imagination.

While much of his production is directed towards publicity, there is nevertheless a sound footing of competence in Mathieu's art that precludes its dismissal as facile. He has written much about art and philosophy. His admired masters of the past include El Greco, Goya, Rembrandt, van Gogh, and Le Brun. The choice of the last is not surprising, for Mathieu sees the role of the artist as a controller of the environment to the extent that he is architect, industrial designer, landscape gardener and consultant on all environmental problems as they demand visual consideration.

Mathieu sees contemporary painters as failing in their responsibility to the future because of a constant preoccupation with the art of the past. He endorses Pater's dictum that paintings should aspire to the condition of music. He believes that painting should exist in the same fashion as an autonomous art.

—G. S. Whittet

Yutaka Matsuzawa: *Warning,* a recitalive performance at an esoteric temple in Nagano, 2000.

MATSUZAWA, Yutaka

Nationality: Japanese. **Born:** Shimosuwa, 2 February 1922. **Education:** Studied architecture at Waseda University, Tokyo, 1941–46; contemporary poetry at Wisconsin State College, Superior, 1955–56; religious philosophy at Columbia University, New York, 1956–57. **Family:** Married Misuzu Kamishima in 1948; child: Kumiko; married Haruo Takizawa; child: Yoko; married Yoji Nakamura. **Career:** Worked as an architect, Azusa Architectural Office, Japan, 1946–48; now an independent artist pursuing spiritual and metaphysical explorations through both traditional and conceptual art-making, since 1952; lecturer, Bigakko Art School, Tokyo, 1971–81. **Awards:** Fulbright Fellowship, 1955; Japan Society Fellowship, 1956; Painting Prize, *Bienal,* Sao Paulo, 1977. **Member:** Accademia Tiberina, Rome, 1978. **Address:** 5370 Shimosuwa-machi, Nagano-ken 393–0057, Japan.

Individual Exhibitions:

1963 Aoki Gallery, Tokyo
1964 Naika Gallery, Tokyo
1965 Naika Gallery, Tokyo
1966 Modern Art Center of Japan, Tokyo
1967 Azuma Gallery, Tokyo
1970 Aoki Gallery, Tokyo
1971 Art & Project, Amsterdam
1974 Galeria Akumulatory 2, Poznán, Poland
1977 CAYC, Buenos Aires
1979 Ginza Kaiga Kan, Tokyo
1980 Podio del Mond Per L'Arte, Middelburg, Netherlands
1982 Galeria Media, Neuchâtel, Switzerland
Okazaki Tamako Gallery, Tokyo
1983 Okazaki Tamako Gallery, Tokyo
1984 Galerie Christian Cheneau, Paris
Okazaki Tamako Gallery, Tokyo
1985 Galerie Brigitte March, Stuttgart
Okazaki Tamako Gallery, Tokyo
1986 Art Com, San Francisco
Okazaki Tamako Gallery, Tokyo
1988 Okazaki Tamako Gallery, Tokyo
Wewerka Gallery, Berlin
Kunstverein Wolfsburg, Germany
1990 Okazaki Tamako Gallery, Tokyo
Galerie Brigitte March, Stuttgart
1992 Okazaki Tamako Gallery, Tokyo

1994 Okazaki Tamako Gallery, Tokyo
Yamaguchi Prefectural Museum, Japan
1995 Satani Gallery, Tokyo
Museum Haus Kasuya, Yokosuka
1996 Isahai Museum, Maebashi
1997 Saito Memorial Kawaguchi Contemporary Art Museum, Kawaguchi
1998 Komagane Modern Art Museum, Komagane
1999 Ohkashorin, Nagano
2000 Ohkashorin, Nagano

Selected Group Exhibitions:

1953 *Yomiuri Independent Exhibition,* Metropolitan Art Gallery, Tokyo (and each subsequent year through 1963)
Contemporary Japanese Art, Guggenheim Museum, New York
1971 *Sonsbeek '71,* Netherlands
1976 *Biennale,* Venice
1977 *Bienal,* Sao Paulo
1981 *The 2nd International Drawing Triennale,* Wroclaw, Poland
1983 *New Trends in Japanese Art of the 1960s,* Metropolitan Gallery of Art, Tokyo
1985 *Reconstructions: Avant-Grade Art in Japan 1945–65,* Museum of Modern Art, Oxford
1987 *Nihon no Matsuri,* San Francisco Museum of Modern Art
1994 *Avanguardi Giapponesi Degli Anni 70,* Bologna Contemporary Art Museum
1995 *Japanese Culture: The Fifty Postwar Years 1945–1995,* Meguro War Museum, Hiroshima Contemporary Art Museum, Hyogo Prefectural Modern Art Museum, Fukuoka Prefectural Museum, International Sculpture Symposium, and Uluda University Bursa
1996 *Japanese Art 1964,* Tokyo Metropolitan Contemporary Art Museum
1997–2000 Sakushima Art Festival, Ishikicho
1999 *Global Conceptualism: Points of Origin 1950s-1980s,* Queens Museum of Art, New York City
Artist Book Exhibition, Kofu
2000 *Õno Kazuo and Matsuzawa Yutaka,* Nagano
2001 *Century City: Art and Culture in the Twentieth Century Metropolis,* Tate Museum of Modern Art, London

Collections:

Yamaguchi Prefectural Museum, Japan.

Publications:

By MATSUZAWA: Books—*Psi Black Box,* Tokyo 1982; *9 Mandalas,* Neuchâtel, Switzerland 1982. **Articles—**''From Cybernetics to Mandala'' in *Geijutsushincho* (Tokyo), no. 8, 1960; ''Matter Vanishing'' in *Gendaibijutsu* (Tokyo), no. 6, 1965; ''Wander around Tantra'' in *Mizue* (Tokyo), no. 19, 1969; ''About Sonsbeek '71'' in *Bijutsu-techo* (Tokyo), no. 11, 1971; text in *Art and Strategy* by Walter Aue, Cologne 1972; ''On Lawrence Weiner and Other Artists'' in *Mizue* (Tokyo), no. 5, 1975; ''Making Public Fine Art Works on the Radio'' in *Gengo Seikatsu* (Tokyo), no. 2, 1981; ''Biography Autographical'' in *Kikan* (Tokyo), no. 13, 1982; ''Foss-Maguna Chinbotsu'' in *kaki no Ha,* Tokyo 1983; *Quantum Art Manifesto,* Tokyo 1992; ''Toward Yutaka Matsuzawa's Final Hypothesis,'' 1995.

On MATSUZAWA: Books—*Deai wo Motomete* by U-Fan Lee, Tokyo 1971: *Art Now II* by Ichiro Haryu, Tokyo 1972; *Mirukoto no Shinwa* by Yusuke Nakahara, Tokyo 1972; *On Matsuzawa* by U-Fan Lee, Tokyo 1974; *P.S. Tokyo* edited by Shuji Takashima, Yoshiaki Tono and Tusuke Nakahara, Tokyo 1974; *Apocalypse in Contemporary Art* by Tsuyuhiko Hinatsu, Tokyo 1986; *The Deviation History of Contemporary Art* by Shigeo Chiha, 1986; *Yukata Matsuzawa: Memento Mori,* exhibition catalog, Tokyo 1994; *The Complete Words of Nagano Prefecture Art,* 1997; *Japanese Contemporary Art* by Hiroshi Okabuyashi, 1998; *Ku no rinsho: An Introduction to Yutaka Matsuzawa,* 1998; *Japanese Art,* Sekikasho, China, 2000. **Articles—**''Outside of Psi's Chamber'' by Yoshie Yoshida in *Sansai* (Tokyo), no. 10, 1963; ''On Matsuzawa'' by Shuzo Takiguchi in *Tohaka ni Kaku,* Tokyo 1966; ''A Self-Portrait of the Messiah—Yutaka Matsuzawa'' by Ikuya Kato in *Bijutsu-techo* (Tokyo), no. 6, 1969; ''Yutaka Matsuzawa: A Commune Penetrating the Dark'' by Yoshie Yoshida in *Bijutsu-techo* (Tokyo), no. 11, 1972; ''On Yutaka Matsuzawa'' by Arata Tani in *Bijutsu-techo* (Tokyo), no. 2, 1974; ''On Yutaka Matsuzawa'' by Arata in *Bijutsu-techo* (Tokyo), no. 2, 1974; ''On Yutaka Matsuzawa'' by Yusuke Nakahara in *Mizue* (Tokyo), no. 5, 1975; special number of *Kikan* (Shiosuwa, Japan), no. 3, 1982; ''Matsuzawa Yutaka no Uchu'' in *Suwa Genso Sha* (Suwa), 1985.

*

In 1995, in ''Temporary Emptiness, True Emptiness,'' the latest work of quantum art and my final hypothesis, I wrote, ''A student of a student of a student of mine predicted the time of nirvana, saying that 1995 would be the turning point. I rejected this completely. I believe and feel that 1991 marked a change in the basic flow of the earth which contains a much more meaningful truth. Why? I am using quantum art as a way of solving this problem. Therefore:

Oh! Emptiness which is conditioned and the true emptiness.
Emptiness. What is it? How is it brought about?
Asking that, we try to solve a *koan* together.
Bit by bit in painful effort. No answer comes.
All things together beyond the end of all time.
When we attain a clear view of the emptiness.
There will be eight hundred more of these emptinesses.
And then beyond them another 108 of those emptinesses.
Which are to be found around time and space.

Look at this in your mind. A solution to the ultimate riddles has been attempted since ancient times by philosophy, religion, and science. Now quantum art is radically trying to do the same thing. It moves ahead in the midst of the universe, of being, and of human beings, all of which are to vanish, and with a method still unknown, attempts to see God. It is coming into view, coming into view.

Yutaka Matsuzawa's final hypothesis is
Based on the principle that
Everything has a Janus-like nature.
At once particle and wave.
At once matter and spirit.
Together God and the Devil.
Together man and, oh, woman.

Together being and, ah, nothing.

—Yutaka Matsuzawa

* * *

Yutaka Matsuzawa was born in 1922, and graduated from the Department of Architecture of Waseda University in 1946. He spent 1955 to 1957 in America, but discarded his study of architecture in favour of the philosophy of religion, which he studied at Columbia University. It has been Matsuzawa's accomplishment that since then he has combined his perception and knowledge gained from the study of the philosophy of religion with his artistic work, becoming in the process a true original in contemporary Japanese art.

Matsuzawa first produced a series of works called "psi," and since performing a ceremony "All Being Disappear," in 1966, he has concentrated on painting. What identifies Matsuzawa is his underlying, intense eschatological feeling in which all that is visible must become invisible. With such thought in mind, he persisted in dispensing information in the form of a succession of postcards. Typical titles of those postcards were "A Blank Sheet Picture for All Living and Non-Living Entities," and "The Picture Which Is Not Seen and Which Cannot be Seen," and "Picture Showing a Spirit in the Mist."

Matsuzawa's thinking thus is not aesthetic as much as it is cosmic. He takes the invisible as being real, not the visible. In the 1970 Tokyo *Biennal,* Matsuzawa gave to a gallery room in the museum the name "My Death," where he put on a performance and had this to say: "I exhibited my own death and the future. It was infinite existences in every mind of the contemplators, and it exists only in time. It is my death and your death, also his painting and her painting; it is involved in the Nirvana which does not increase nor decrease nor come nor go."

This Nirvana which neither increases nor decreases, neither comes nor goes, is Matsuzawa's Utopia.

Since the ceremony, "All Being Disappear," all of Matsuzawa's activities, in taking aims at this Utopia, are religious manifestations. Depending on one's viewpoint, it may be possible to classify this work as conceptual art. To identify accurately Matsuzawa's work, it must be called meta-art. That is because what Matsuzawa is aiming at is a plane at which distinctions cannot be made between concept and perception. In this, a critique of contemporary culture also emerges.

—Yusuka Nakahara

MATTA, Roberto (Sebastian Antonio Echaurren)

Nationality: Chilean. **Born:** Chiloe, 11 November 1911. **Education:** College of the Sacred Heart, Santiago, until 1928; studied architecture, Catholic University, Santiago, 1929–31. Dip. Arch. 1931; mainly self-taught in painting, from 1937. **Family:** Married Ann Matta (divorced); married Patricia Matta (divorced 1949); married Italian actress Angiola Fernanda (divorced 1954), married Malitte Pope; children: Batan, Gordon, Paino, Federica, Remuntcho, Iago and Alisee. **Career:** Worked as an interior decorator, Santiago, 1928; as merchant seaman, Compagnie Transatlantique ship, to Europe, 1933; as achitectural assistant, Le Corbusier studio, Paris, 1934–36. Independent painter, Paris, 1938–39, in New York, 1939–48, Rome, 1950–54, and in Paris, since 1955. Visiting instructor, Minneapolis School of Art, 1966. **Member:** With Federico Garcia Lorca, André Breton, Salvador Dali, Marcel Duchamp, Surrealist Group Paris, 1937–48, and from 1959, founder, Etrusculudens, Etruscan crafts artisan group, 1972. President, Cultural Congress, Havana, 1968. **Awards:** Premio Marzotto, Rome, 1962. **Address:** 145 Boulevard Saint-Germain, 75006 Paris, France.

Individual Exhibitions:

1940 Julien Levy Gallery, New York (with Pavel Tchelitchew)
1942 Pierre Matisse Gallery, New York (and regularly until 1948)
1945 Sidney Janis Gallery, New York
1947 Galerie René Drouin, Paris
Hugo Gallery, New York
1948 William Copley Gallery, Beverly Hills, California
1950 Galleria del'Obelisco, Rome
Galleria Schneider, Rome
Galleria del Cavallino, Venice
Galleri del Naviglio, Milan
1951 Institute of Contemporary Arts, London
1952 Allan Frumkin Gallery, New York
1953 Sala Napoleonica, Venice
Alexander Iolas Gallery, New York
1954 Museo de Arte Moderno, Lima, Peru
Museo de Arte Moderno, Santiago, Chile
Galleria del Cavallino, Venice
1955 Galerie du Dragon, Paris
Galleri Colibu, Malmo, Sweden
Pan American Union, Washington, D.C.
Alexander Iolas Gallery, New York
1956 *Matta: Terres Nouvelles,* Galerie du Dragon, Paris
1957 Museum of Modern Art, New York
Ruth Moskin Gallery, New York
1958 Galleria Galatea, Turin
1959 Foundation Mendoza, Caracas
Moderna Museet, Stockholm
Galerie Daniel Cordier, Frankfurt
Galerie Daniel Cordier, Paris
1960 Galleria del Naviglio, Milan
1961 Gimpel Fils Gallery, London
Cordier and Warren Gallery, New York
1962 Galleria L'Attico, Rome
Galerie Le Point Cardinal, Paris
Gimpel Fils Gallery, London
1963 Allan Frumkin Gallery, New York
Alexander Iolas Gallery, New York
Galleria Schwarz, Milan
Museo Civico, Bologna
Galerie Edwin Engelberts, Geneva
Casa de la Americas, Havana
Auslander Gallery, New York
University of Chicago
Frank Perls Gallery, Los Angeles
Kunsthalle, Dusseldorf
Robert Fraser Gallery, London
Museum des 20. Jahrhunderts, Vienna
Galerie Le Point Cardinal, Paris
1964 Palais des Beaux-Arts, Brussels

Stedelijk Museum, Amsterdam
Städtische Kunsthalle, Mannheim, West Germany
Galerie Michael Hertz, Bremen, West Germany
Casa de la Americas, Havana
Galerie Van de Loo, Munich
Gimpel und Hanover Galerie, Zurich
1965 Kunstmuseum, Lucerne
Galeria del Techo, Caracas
Gimpel Fils Gallery, London
1966 Institute of Contemporary Arts, Lima, Peru
Galerie Alexander Iolas, Paris
1967 Walker Art Center, Minneapolis
Palais de Mutualité, Paris
Gelleria Senior, Rome
Galleria S. Luca, Rome
Casa de las Americas, Havana
Musée d'Art et d'Histoire, Saint-Denis, France
1968 Alexander Iolas Gallery, New York
Musée d'Art Moderne de la Ville, Paris (with Alfredo Lam and Alicia Penalba)
Galleria La Medusa, Rome
1970 Nationalgalerie, Berlin
Maison de la Culture, Ameins (with Claude Parent)
Centre Culturel Municipal, Villeparisis, France
Galerie Michael Hertz, Bremen, West Germany
1973 Galleria Il Fauno, Turin
Palazzo di Diamanti, Ferrara, Italy (toured Italy)
Alexander Iolas Gallery, New York
Museo Civico, Bologna
Pinacoteca Comunale, Ravenna, Italy
Centro Storico, Livorno, Italy
1974 Belle Ciao, Terni, Italy
Kestner-Gesellschaft, Hannover (toured Germany)
Office Culturel, St. Etienne du Rouvray, France
Galeria Aele, Madrid
Museo de Arte Moderno, Mexico City
Museo de Arte Moderno, Bogota
Museo de Bellas Artes, Caracas
1975 Andre Crispo Gallery, New York
Alexander Iolas Gallery, New York
L'homme descend du signe: Mattapastelli, Galleria dell'Orca, Rome
Palazzo della Loggia, Brescia, Italy
Kettles Yard Gallery, Cambridge
Hotel de Ville, Venissieux, France
1976 Casa de las Americas, Havana
1977 Palazzo degli Alessandri, Viterbo, Italy
Coigitum, Hayward Gallery, London
1978 Kettles Yard Gallery, Cambridge
Galerie du Dragon, Paris
1979 Stamperia della Beauga, Florence
Centre Culturel Municipal, Villeparisis, France
Universita di Urbino, Italy
1980 Palazzo degli Alessandri, Viterbo, Italy
Galerie Kinge, Paris
Paintings and Drawings 1971–79, Tasende Gallery, La Jolla, California (travelled to Blanden Memorial Art Gallery, Fort Dodge, Iowa)
1982 *Roberto Matta: Architecte du Temps,* Theatre d'Ivry, Ivry-sur-Seine, France
Riverside Studios, Hammersmith, London
1983 Palacio de Cristal, Madrid
1984 City Museum and Art Gallery, Plymouth, Devon (travelled to Oxford, Swansea, Sheffield, Bolton, and Newcastle-upon-Tyne)
1988 *Matta: Drawings 1937–88,* Museum Bochum, Germany (catalog)
Matta, Louisiana Museum, Humlebaek (catalog)
Italy Matta: Matta in Italy, Palazzo Venezia, Rome (catalog)
Matta: The Early Years, Maxwell Davidson Gallery, New York (catalog)
1990 *Matta: Drawings 1937–1946,* Acquavella Contemporary Art, New York (catalog)
1991 *Matta,* Kunsthalle der Hypo-Kulturstiftung, Munich (also Kunsthaus, Vienna) (catalog)
Matta Exhibition: One Verse 11–11-11, Museo Nacional de Bellas Artes, Santiago (also Museo de Bellas Artes, Caracas) (catalog)
Matta, Galeria Arte Actual, Santiago (catalog)
1993 *Matta: Engravings,* Galeria Arte Actual, Santiago (catalog)
Matta: Works from Chicago Collections, Arts Club of Chicago (catalog)
1997 *Roberto Matta: Paintings and Drawings 1937–1959,* Galeria Lopez Quiroga, Mexico City (catalog)
Matta: Paintings & Drawings, André Emmerich Gallery, New York (catalog)
Matta: Re-generation, Boca Raton Museum of Art, Florida (catalog)
Maxwell Davidson Gallery, New York
1998 *Matta: Surrealism and Beyond,* Haggerty Museum of Art, Chicago
1999 *Matta,* Museo Nacional Centro de Arte Reina Sofia, Madrid (catalog)
Almirante Art Gallery, Madrid
Borges Cultural Center, Buenos Aires, Argentina (retrospective)
2000 *Matta: Opere Dal 1957 al 1993,* Galleria Patrizia Poggi, Ravenna (catalog)
Matta: El Ano de los Tres 000, Fundación Telefónica, Santiago (catalog)

Selected Group Exhibitions:

1937 *Surrealisme,* Galerie Wildenstein, Paris
1938 *Exposition Internationale du Surrealisme,* Galerie des Beaux-Arts, Paris
1942 *Artists in Exile,* Pierre Matisse Gallery, New York
1946 *5 Big Paintings,* Museum of Modern Art, New York
1955 *Bienal,* Sao Paulo
1958 *World's Fair,* Brussels
1959 *Documenta 2,* Museum Fridericianum, Kassel, West Germany
1968 *Dada, Surrealism and their Heritage,* Museum of Modern Art, New York
1974 *Biennale,* Venice
1981 *A New Spirit in Painting,* Royal Academy of Art, London
1989 *Aspects of Modern Art in France,* Galerie Daniel Malingue, Paris (catalog)

1992 *Crosscurrents of Modernism: Four Latin American Pioneers—Diego Rivera, Joaquin Torres-Garcia, Wilfredo Lam, Matta,* Hirshhorn Museum and Sculpture Garden, Washington, D.C. (catalog)
1995 *Transparency in the Art of the 20th Century,* Musee des Beaux-Arts Andre Malraux, Le Havre, France (catalog)
1997 *Latin American Masterpieces,* Robert Miller Gallery, New York (catalog)
1998 *Art Miami 98,* Miami Beach, Florida
1999 *Vivre Paris,* Espace Electra, Paris
La Utopía Latinoamericana, Fundación Pan Klub, Buenos Aires (catalog)

Collections:

Musée National d'Art Moderne, Paris; Nationalgalerie, Berlin; Stedelijk Museum, Amsterdam; Baltimore Museum of Art; City Art Museum, St. Louis, Missouri; Lawrence Art Museum, Williamstown, Massachusetts; Walker Art Center, Minneapolis; Museum of Contemporary Art, University of Chile, Santiago.

Publications:

By MATTA: Books—*Duchamp's Glass,* with Katherine S. Drier, New York 1944; *Come detta dentrovo signifiando,* Lausanne 1962; *Dialogo con Tarquinia,* Tarquinia 1975; *Matta: Un Día Lovestein, Una Piedra de Amor,* Buenos Aires 1999. **Articles—**interview with Celia Sredni de Birbragher in *Art Nexus,* no. 27, January-March 1998.

On MATTA: Books—*Matta: Terres nouvelles,* exhibition catalog with text by E. Glissant, Paris 1956; *Matta,* exhibition catalog with text by L. Hoctin, New York 1957; *Matta,* exhibition catalog with text by I. Gustafson, Stockholm 1959; *Histoire de la peinture surrealiste* by Marcel Jean, Paris 1959; *Matta,* exhibition catalog with text by Werner Hofmann, Vienna 1963; *Un revolution du régard* by Alain Jouffroy, Paris 1964; *Matta; Le Multiplicateur de progrès* by José Pierre, Paris 1967; *Catalog raisonne de l'oeuvre gravée de Matta,* compiled by Ursula Schmitt, Silkeborg 1969; *Developpements sur l'infrarealisme de Matta* by Jean Schuster, Paris 1970; *Matta,* exhibition catalog with an introduction by Ursula Schmitt, Berlin 1970; *Matta* exhibition catalog with text by Wieland Schmied, Hannover 1974; *L'homme descend du signe: Mattapastelli,* exhibition catalog with text by Giuliano Briganti, Rome 1975; *Matta: Catalog raisonné de l'oeuvre gravée 1943–1974,* compiled by Roland Sabatier, Stockholm and Paris 1975; *Matta: Opere dal 1939 al 1975* by Luisa Laureati, Rome 1976; *Matta: Coigitum,* exhibition catalog with interview by Peter de Francia, text by André Breton, London 1977; *Matta: Index dell'opere grafica dal 1969 al 1980,* edited by Germana Farrari, Viterbo, Italy 1980; *Roberto Matta; Paintings and Drawings 1971–1979,* exhibition catalog with texts by Peter Selz, J. M. Tasende and André Breton, La Jolla, California 1980; *Roberto Matta: Architecte du Temps,* exhibition catalog by Thierry Sigg and Jean-Pierre Faye, Ivry, France 1982; *Matta: The Logic of Hallucination,* exhibition catalog with text by Paul Overy, London 1984; *Latin American Art of the Twentieth Century* by Edward Lucie-Smith, London 1993. **Articles—**''The Mobile Matter of Roberto Sebastian Matta'' by Alvaro Medina in *Art Nexus,* no. 17, July/September 1995.

* * *

In 1938, when the Surrealist movement seemed to be breaking up, new life was breathed into it by two new painters, the Chilean-born Roberto Matta and the Cuban Wilfredo Lam. And in contrast to the realistic or veristic surrealist imagery of Dali or Magritte, the surrealist aim of automatism, of painting out the inner impulses and tapping inner srpings of energy in a spontaneous, improvisatory way, found a remarkable fulfilment in Matta's early paintings. He called them ''inscapes'' or ''psychological morphologies'' because he was trying in them to project visual metaphors for his inner feelings, impulses and passions. The results are violent, agitated explosions of luminous colour suggesting some cosmic creation or collapse—deep luminious space in whose shifting clouds float vaguely biomorphic or geological shapes, with everything in violent motion. Matta is above all the creator of imaginary worlds which manage to suggest the profound depths of the psyche simultaneously with the vastness of the universe.

When Matta fled to America during the 1939–45 war, along with other surrealists including Ernst, Tanguy, Breton and Masson, this sort of psychic automatism, came like a revelation to American artists, and was one of the basic influences on the growth of abstract expressionism. Matta had a particularly profound influence on the work of Arshile Gorky, which shares a similar sort of lyricism, and on Robert Motherwell, who painted with Matta in Mexico in 1941.

Towards the end of the war, however, Matta's own style was undergoing a profound change: ''My main preoccupation . . . was looking into myself. Suddenly I realized that while trying to do this I was *being with* a horrible crisis in society. My vision of myself was becoming blind for not being made one with people around me, and I sought to create a new morphology of others within my own field of consciousness.'' And so under the influence of the early machinist pictures of his friend Duchamp, man-like creatures with mechanical features began to appear in his works, in nightmare architectural settings, often amidst aggressive machinery and the crackling of high voltage electricity. Some of his bizarre anthropomorphs are like monstrous insects, lustful and erotic as they lunge aggressively at their female prey.

His mechanical monsters are painted on giant canvases, forming a wide-screen theatre in which his bizarre personages undergo transformation and struggle, tortured and torturing, reflecting the cruelty and destruction of war. Radical political aspirations were always an essential feature of surrealism, and some of Matta's more recent works have been more overtly political. But he is most successful when he poetically suggests rather than more specifically depicts ''man's struggle against oppression and exposes the cruel constant of daily life,'' and the best of his later works reflect his own struggle to interpret the specific terrors and obsessions of contemporary humanity and to evolve a pictorial mythology for our technological age.

—Konstantin Bazarov

MAU, Bruce

Nationality: Canadian. **Born:** Sudbury, Ontario, 25 October 1959. **Education:** Attended the Department of Communications and Design, Ontario College of Art, Toronto, 1978–80. **Career:** Designer, Fifty Fingers Inc., Toronto, 1980–82; designer, Pentagram Design, London, 1982–83; principal, Public Good Design and Communications Inc., Toronto, 1983–85; principal, Bruce Mau Design Inc., Toronto, from 1985; creative director, *I.D.* magazine, New York, 1991–93; editor, Swerve Editions, Toronto and New York, from 1991. Visiting instructor, Technical University of Nova Scotia, Faculty of Architecture, 1986, 1988; visiting critic, University of Toronto, 1988; Artist in Residence, Department of Fine Arts, California Institute of the Arts, 1989; visiting scholar, Getty Center for the History of Art and The Humanities, 1992; visiting Cullinan professor, Rice University, School of Architecture, 1996. **Awards:** Alcuin Citation for excellence in book design, Canada, 1989, 1991; IOAAG Design Award, 1991; Annual 100 Show, American Center for Design, 1992, 1994; AIGA award, 1993; Publication Design Award, American Association of Museums, 1993; TDC 40, Type Directors Club Exhibition, 1993; Book Builders West Award, 1994; Cassie Award, Art Gallery of Ontario, 1995; Best of Category in graphics, *I.D.* magazine, 1996. **Address:** Bruce Mau Design Inc., 197 Spadina Avenue, Suite 501, Toronto, Ontario M5T 2C8, Canada. **Web site:** www.brucemaudesign.com.

Exhibitions:

1992 *Canada Designs for Business,* Tokyo
1994 *Regeneration:A Series of Exhibitions,* sponsored by Ellis/ Don Construction Ltd., Toronto
S.M.L.XL. in Progress: Rem Koolhaas and Bruce Mau, Southern California Institute of Architecture, Los Angeles
1995 *From Toronto, l'actualité du design graphique,* Villeurbanne, France
Pop in Orbit, Design Exchange, Toronto
2000 *The Art of the Book: An Exhibit of Work by Johanna Drucker and Bruce Mau,* New Library Building, University at Albany, State University of New York
Canada at Work, Rest & Play, Design Exchange, Toronto
''STRESS'' (interactive video), Weiner Festwochen, Vienna

Publications:

By MAU: Books—With Rem Koolhaas, *S.M.L.XL.: Office for Metropolitan Architecture, Rem Koolhaas, and Bruce Mau,* New York 1995; With Rem Koolhaas, *Living: Rem Koolhaas and Bruce Mau,* New York 1997; *Life Style,* New York 2000; with others, *Remembering the Body*, Hatje 2000. **Articles—**''Beyond Typography'' in *The Lectures,* Rotterdam, 1992; *Insite* (Toronto), January 1996; ''Where Are We Going?: An Incomplete Manifesto for Growth'' in *Domus,* no. 822, January 2000.

On MAU: Books—*The Graphic Edge* by Rick Poyner, London, 1994. **Articles—**''Zone Maps Life in the Big City'' by Adele Freedman in *Globe and Mail* (Toronto), 31 May 1986; ''La ville, zone érogène'' by Pascaline Cuvelier in *Liberation,* 20 September 1986; ''The Magazine Rack'' by May Castleberry in *Afterimage,* March 1988; ''Publisher Aims at the Intellect'' by H. J. Kirchoff in *Globe and Mail* (Toronto), 13 April 1988; ''On the Borderline'' by Annetta Hanna in *I.D.* (New York), May/June 1988; ''Producer as Author'' by Rick Poynor in *Blueprint* (London), December 1989; ''International Bruce Mau'' by Freedman in *Canadian Art* (Toronto), Summer 1990; ''The Mau Zone'' by Howard Rombough in *Creative Review* (London), February 1992; ''Notes on the Tendencies Exhibited through Free Time'' by Burton Hamfelt and Mark Wasiuta in *Span* (Toronto), Spring 1992; ''A Font of Innovation Down to the Letter'' by Freedman in *Globe and Mail* (Toronto), 5 June 1992; ''Chairman Mau'' by John Barber in *Globe and Mail* (Toronto), 18 June 1992; ''Museum Quality'' by Barber in *Globe and Mail* (Toronto), 3 September 1992; ''Bruce Mau'' by Will Novosedlik in *Studio Magazine* (Rexdale), September/October 1992; ''Canadian Accent'' by Claudia Neri in *Linea Graphica* (Milan), March 1993; ''Toronto Graphic Designers Export Decidedly Different Styles'' in *Financial Post* (Toronto), 10 September 1993; ''The Producer as Author'' by Novosedlik in *Eye* (London), Winter 1994; ''Grafisch ontwerper Bruce Mau'' by Corine Koole in *Eigenhuis & Interieur,* April 1994; ''Maximal Mau'' by Elizabeth Crinion in *Azure,* May/June 1994; ''The Tall Order of Sizing Up a Very Large Book'' by Freedman in *Globe and Mail* (Toronto), 5 November 1994; ''A Fascination for an Unstable Quality: Bruce Mau More than just a Designer'' by Renny Ramakers in *Items* (Amsterdam), December 1994; ''Plump Fiction'' by John Shnier in *Canadian Architect* (Toronto), November 1995; ''Buildings Born of Dreams and Demons'' by Herbert Muschamp in *New York Times,* 7 January 1996; ''Koolhaas in 2-D'' by Brendan Gill in *New Yorker,* 12 February 1996; ''Hot Type'' in *The Chronicle of Higher Education,* 16 February 1996; ''Rem Koolhaas Sizes Up the Future'' by Muschamp in *New York Times,* 3 March 1996; ''Going beyond Attention and Distraction'' by Pamela Young in *Globe and Mail* (Toronto), 16 May 1996; ''The Designer as Author'' by Michael Rock in *Eye* (London), Spring 1996; ''Bruce Mau: Book Maker'' by Ken Coupland in *Graphis,* March-April 1998; ''The Generic City'' by Maarten Hajer in *Theory, Culture & Society,* vol. 16, no. 4, August 1999; ''We Produce Things No One Else Does'' by Robert Sheppard in *Maclean's,* 18 December 2000.

* * *

Bruce Mau is arguably Canada's premier graphic designer. Beginning in the early 1980s Mau eschewed the ''end of graphics'' rant that was heard and seen in such publications as *Raygun* and *Beach Culture*—both designed by David Carson—with a contemporary take on early 20th Century Swiss minimalism. With the initial publications of the cultural ''magazine'' *Zone 1/2* and the subsequent publications of its parent company Urzone, Mau began to gain international acclaim, which was furthered by the invitation to redesign the magazine *International Design* (*I.D.*). While David Carson's busy layouts and ''distressed'' type are quite overt in their relation to a formal postmodernism, Mau's subtler play on the pioneering work of German-born typographer Jan Tschichold and U.S. graphic artist Quentin Fiore places his work in a more linguistic model of deconstruction.

The aesthetic spirits of both Tschichold and Fiore are crucial to an understanding of Mau as a graphic designer. Tschichold (1902–1974) began his career as a champion of a high Modern graphic design, which relied on the asymmetry and juxtaposition of radically spatial layouts as a means to communicate the content of the text. Later, however, he turned towards a more classical model of composition as seen in the series of paperback books that he oversaw for Penguin (1947–49). Mau used both of these approaches in his work for Urzone, in which the typographical layouts he devised for the books were a literal hybridization of the two sides of Tschichold's character. The influence of Quentin Fiore, the designer and collaborator of a number of books with the Canadian media theorist Marshall McLuhan, most notably *The Medium is the Massage*, can be perceived in Mau's belief in collaboration as essential to practice and his inclination to manipulate images. In *The Medium Is the Massage*, Fiore employed images from disparate sources, rotating them and allowing them to bleed off the page in such a way as to focus the reader's attention on the theories of McLuhan. Similarly, Bruce Mau slips what he terms a ''cinematic'' layer of images behind the cover text, thereby creating a dynamic relationship between image and word.

Mau's stature as an intellectual was elevated when he was asked to be a contributor to the Netherlands Design Institute conference ''Play.'' It was here that Mau delivered his most ambiguous work, the aptly titled ''Incomplete Manifesto for Growth.'' The piece was then reproduced in its entirety in the April 1999 issue of *I.D.* magazine. Essentially 43 points towards an effective cultural practice, Mau implores us to learn, live, love, work hard, borrow, not be cool, make and repeat mistakes, and ultimately, as the title of the conference implies, be playful. It is easy, it appears, if you just do not take life so seriously. Within this seeming frivolity lies a social critique akin to that found in Guy Debord's book *The Society of the Spectacle*, which Mau redesigned for Zone with the author's blessing. In Mau's commitment to exposing, while to a certain degree embracing, our hyper-mediated world, can feigned innocence be read as a provocative strategy?

After the ''Incomplete Manifesto for Growth'' appeared, Mau became more involved in cross-disciplinary projects. These included a contest-winning proposal, ''Tree City'' (1999), for a decommissioned army base north of Toronto with Rem Koolhaas' firm O.M.A., and an interactive video, STRESS, which was produced for the Weiner Festwochen in 2000. These projects somehow do not replicate the quality of Mau's work with the printed book. Indeed, Mau's difficulty in transitioning to the installation format can be seen in an earlier exhibition he designed and curated at the Design Exchange in Toronto. Entitled *Pop in Orbit* (1995), the exhibition comprised an unfocused collection of remnants from the Pop era in North America. Visitors encountered such things as television and stereo equipment, architectural drawings and clips from the television show ''The Prisoner.'' While an effort was made to historically contextualize the objects on display, the show was ultimately limited by its reliance on the entertainment value of kitsch and a lack of critical analysis.

The publication in 2000 of the ideological monograph *Life Style* culminates what has been a steady and deliberate fifteen-year effort by Bruce Mau and his collaborators. It is a book that is even slightly larger than the one that he produced in 1995 with Rem Koolhaas, *S.M.L.XL.* It seems as though *Life Style* was meant to re-establish the general notoriety that followed the Koolhaas publication since its introduction, while refracting some of the limelight dominated by Koolhaas back to its co-author. It can be argued that the importance of *S.M.L.XL.* was that, in collaboration with Koolhaas, Mau reinvented the monograph as a pluro-graph. As Mau has ambiguously stated, it is a book that is authored but without an author. By incorporating statistics, Koolhaas' architectural writings, and O.M.A.'s work in production and work produced, the book constantly slips between being an advertisement, a critique, and an indoctrination into O.M.A.'s world. *Life Style* shares this methodology, as Mau attempted to theoretically frame his own work by dispersing the studio's projects amid his own cultural musings.

At its best, the strength of Mau's graphic design lies in its active engagement of the viewer. The critical integration of design and content prompts viewers to reconsider the role of design and the ways it informs the production of meaning—in Mau's books but also within society at large. Mau's clients, including such institutions as the Guggenheim Museum and the Getty Center, and his artist, architect, and author collaborators benefit from the clarity and conviction that he brings to their work.

—Mari Dumett

MAURI, Fabio

Nationality: Italian. **Born:** Rome, 1 April 1926. **Education:** University of Milan, 1945–47; Faculty of Modern Literature, University of Rome, 1948–50. **Family:** Married Adriana Asti in 1955 (separated, 1958). **Career:** Independent artist, since 1956. Instructor of painting and drawing, Boys Town of Italy, Civitavecchia, 1947–53; lecturer in aesthetics, Academy of Art, L'Aquila, since 1979. Has written for the theatre, since 1958; general manager, Editrice Valentino Bompiani, and editor, *Almanacco Letterario Bompiani and Sipario,* Rome, 1959–71; editor, *Quindici,* Rome, 1967–68; and *La Città di Riga, nos. 1 and 2,* Macerata, Italy, 1976; president, Messaggerie Italiane books and periodicals, Rome, since 1982. **Agent:** Studio Casoli, Corso Monforte, 23–20121 Milan, Italy. **Address:** Via Santa Maria dell'Anima, 39–00186 Rome, Italy.

Individual Exhibitions:

1954 Galleria del Cavallino, Venice
1955 Galleria Apollinaire, Milan
Galleria L'Aureliana, Rome
1956 Galleria San Babila, Milan
Galleria Apollinaire, Milan
1960 Galleria San Marco, Rome
1963 Galleria La Salita, Rome
1965 Galleria Arco d'Alibert, Rome
1967 Galleria La Salita, Rome
1968 Galleria de Nieubourg, Milan
1969 Studio d'Arte Toninelli, Rome
1970 Palazzo Ricci, Montepulciano, Italy
1971 Stabilmenti Safa Palatino, Rome (performance)
Galleria Barozzi, Venice (travelled to Galleria Acme, Brescia, Galleria La Steccata, Parma, and Galleria La Salita, Rome).
1972 Studio Barozzi, Milan
Centro Multipli, Rome
Galleria Seconda Scala, Rome
1974 Pilotta, Parma, Italy
1975 *Intellettuale,* Museo Civico, Bologna (with Piero Paolo Pasolini)
1976 *Senza,* Galleria Toselli, Milan
1977 *Brunelleschi e noi,* Chiostri di Santa Maria Novella, Florence
1978 *News from Europe,* A Space, Toronto
1979 *What is Fascism,* Performing Garage, New York
1980 *Muro d'Europa/La Barca,* De Appel, Amsterdam
1981 *Umanesimo/Disumanesimo nell'Arte Contemporanea,* Florence
1982 *1909–1930 Gran Serata Futurista,* Assessorato ala Cultura, Rome
Galleria Il Falconiere, Ancona

1983 Facolta di Magistero, L'Aquila (performance)
Assessorato alla Cultura, Florence (performance)
1984 Assessorato alla Cultura, L'Aquila (performance)
University of Rome (performance)
University of L'Aquila (performance)
Palazzo Trinci, Foligno (performance)
1985 Civica Scuola Piccolo Teatro, Milan (performance)
Galleria Mara Coccia, Rome
Teatro Universitario, L'Aquila (performance)
Mercati Traianei, Rome
1986 Palazzo Grassi, Venice
Palazzo San Domenico, L'Aquila
1987 Studio Marconi, Milan (performance)
1989 Centro Multimediale Quarto di S. Giusta, L'Aquila (performance)
1990 Galleria d'Ascanio, Rome
Galleria Carini, Florence
1992 Studio Casoli, Milan (performances)
Galleria L'Eroica, Milan (performance)
1993 Galleria Elleni, Bergamo, Italy
1994 Galleria Nazionale d'Arte Moderna e Contemporanea, Rome (performances)
1995 Studio Bocchi, Rome
1997 Kunsthalle, Klagenfurt, Germany (performance)
Studio Casoli, Milan (performance)
1998 La Tartaruga, Castelluccio di Pienza, Siena, Italy (performance)
Galleria Nazionale d'Arte Moderna, Rome
1999 Fundaciò La Caixa, Barcelona (performance)
Edicola Notte, Rome

Selected Group Exhibitions:

1954 *11th Triennale,* Milan
1960 *Collettiva Internazionale,* Galleria La Tartaruga, Rome
1973 *Art around 70,* Philadelphia Museum of Art
1976 *032303,* National Gallery of Canada, Ottawa
1978 *I Numeri Malefici,* at the *Biennale,* Venice
1980 *Camere Incantate: Espansione dell'Immagine,* Palazzo Reale, Milan
1982 *Generazioni a Confronto,* University of Rome
1983 *Il Pop Art e l'Italia,* Castello Visconti, Milan
1985 *Arte Italiana degli anni '60,* Galleria Civica d'Arte Moderna, Turin
1987 *Sogno Italiano,* Castello di Genazzano, Italy
1988 *La Couleur Seule, l'Expérience du Monochrome,* Musée St. Pierre, Lyon, France
1990 *Roma Anni '60,* Palazzo delle Esposizioni, Rome
1991 *Bildlicht,* Moderner Kunst Museum, Vienna
1993 *Arte Poetica,* Weisman Museum, Los Angeles, California
1994 *Four Italian Masters of Contemporary Art,* Smith's Gallery, London
1995 *After Auschwitz,* Royal Festival Hall, London (travelled to Edinborough, Sunderland, Potsdam)
1996 *Cina ASIA Nuova,* Opera Paese, Rome
1997 *Città Natura,* Palazzo delle Esposizioni, Rome
1998 *Arkipelag TV,* Nordic Museum, Stockholm
1999 *Minimalia,* P.S. 1 Contemporary Art Center, New York
2000 *Novecento: Arte e Storia in Italia,* Scuderie Papali del Quirinale e Mercati di Traiano, Rome

Collections:

Galleria Nazionale d'Arte Moderna, Rome; Museo d'Arte Moderna, Turin, Museo d'Arte Moderna, Bologna; Instituto d'Arte Contemporanea, Parma; Museo d'Arte Moderna, Livorno; Museo d'Arte Moderna, Republic of San Marino; Galleria Comunale d'Arte Moderna, Rome; The Jewish Museum, New York; Museo Sperimentale d'Arte Contemporanea, L'Aquila, Italy.

Publications:

By MAURI: Books—*Giro a vuoto cabaret,* Milan 1959; *Crack,* Milan 1960; *Artecronache,* with Plinio de Martiis and Cesare Vivaldi, Rome 1961; *Giovanna di lo,* in *Potentissima Signora,* Milan 1965; *Der Politische Ventilator,* Rome 1970; *Osuramento,* exhibition catalog, Rome 1975; *Manipolazione di cultura,* Macerata, Italy 1976; *Dramophon,* Rome 1980; *Narcissus in the Cold,* Toronto 1982; *Blu Cobalto,* Rome 1985; *Storia di un manifesto mancato,* Milan 1987; *Idee per la Cultura,* Milan 1989; *Per Diana!,* exhibition catalog, Rome 1990; *Il Monocromo Vuoto,* exhibition catalog, Perugia 1993. **Articles—**''21 modi per non pubblicare un libro'' in *Tempo Presente* (Rome), September/October 1966; ''Riflessioni in Apnea sulla critica'' in *Techne,* Florence 1968; ''Azione teoria e illustrazione'' in *La Città di Riga,* (Macerata, Italy), no. 1. 1976; ''Intervista'' in *Parachute* (Toronto), no. 14, 1978; ''Appunti per un Elogio Assiomatico della Critica'' in *Flash Art* (Milan), 1979; ''Conferenza non fatta'' in *Il viandante e la sua ombra,* edited by V. Artioli and F. Bartoli, Bologna 1981; ''Nel 1970 gli anni 50 avevano 10 anni'' in *Flash Art* (Milan), no. 112, 1983; ''Dio e la scena'' in *L'immagine: Arte, scienza, teoria,* Milan 1987; ''Ricostruzione della Memoria a Percezione Spenta'' in *Nuova Civiltà delle Macchine,* Torino 1989; ''Piazza del Popolo: 1950–1960,'' interview with Gabriella De Marco in *Quaderni d'Arte e Letteratura,* no. 5–6, March 1989; ''Interno—Spazio Contro Tempo'' in *Tridente V,* exhibition catalog, Rome 1990; ''Un Appartamento'' in *Via Tasso: Un Appartamento,* Rome 1993; ''Fabio Mauri: Linguaggio o Verità,'' interview with Vittoria Coen in *Titolo,* vol. IV, no. 14, 1993/94; ''I Suoi Studenti a Bergamo,'' interview with Anna Maria Maggi in *Qui Bergamo,* no. 16, November 1993. **Plays—** *L'isola,* 1964; *Lezione di inglese,* 1970; *Che Cosa è il Fascismo,* 1971; *Gran Serata Futurista (1909–1930),* 1980; *Che Cosa è la Filosofia: Heidegger e la Questione Tedesca, Concerto da Tavolo,* 1989.

On MAURI: Books—*Teatro delle mostre* by Maurizio Calvesi, Lerici, Italy, 1968; *Panorama di pitture internazionale* by Udo Kultermann, Milan 1969; *Fabio Mauri 1959–1969* by Cesare Vivaldi, Rome 1969; *Amore mia* by Achille Bonita Oliva, Florence 1970; *Il corpo come linguaggio* by Lea Vergine, Milan 1974; *Nuove prospettive della critica* by Gillo Dorfles, Milan 1976; *Brunelleschi e noi,* exhibition catalog by Achille Bonita Oliva, Florence 1977; *Umanesimo/ Disumanesimo nell'arte contemporanea,* exhibition catalog by Lara Vinca Masini, Florence 1980; *Fantasmi italiani* by Alberto Arbasino, Rome 1980; *Fabio Mauri,* exhibition catalog, Vancouver 1982; *Il Pop Art e l'Italia* by Bossaglia and Zatti, Pavia 1983; *Lo spettacolo dell'arte* by Lara Vinca Masini, Rome 1984; *Arte italiana 1960–1985* by C. Christov Bakargiev, Milan 1987; *Roma Anni '60,* exhibition catalog by Maurizio Calvesi, Rome 1990; *Arte Pericolosa* by Francesca Alfano Miglietti, Milan 1991; *Opere e Azioni 1954–1994* by Carolyn Christov Bakargiev, Augusta Monferini, Lea Vergine, Marcella Cossu, Ferdinando Taviani and Umberto Silva, Milan 1994; *L'Arte in*

Trincea by Lea Vergine, 1996; *Hall of Mirrors: Art and Film Since 1945* by Kerry Brougher, Los Angeles, California 1996; *Das Böse und das Schöne* by Arnulf Rohsmann, Klagenfurt 1997; *La Meva Cosina Marcella i la Guerra Civil* by Martì Peran, Angelo Trimarco and Sergio Givone, Barcelona 1999; *L'Arte di Fabio Mauri* by Floriano de Santi, Rome 2000; *Nell'inferno una Utopia* by Domenico Scudero, Rome 2000; *Arte e Storia in Italia,* exhibition catalog by Maurizio Calvesi and Paul Ginsborg, Rome 2000. **Articles—**''Fabio Mauri, la Pintura Llamada Postmoderna es un Retroceso'' by Mariana Diaz in *La Nueva Espagna,* 22 March 1988; ''Cinquanta Ben Portati'' by Lorenza Trucchi in *Il Giornale,* 12 March 1989; ''Quattro Passi Romani tra l'Artista e lo Spazio'' by Carolyn Christov-Bakargiev in *Il Sole 24 Ore,* 21 April 1990; ''Fabio Mauri'' by Carolyn Christov-Bakargiev in *Flash Art,* no. 156, 1990; ''Fabio Mauri Evoca il Martirio Nelle Celle de Via Tasso a Roma'' by Sandra Giannattasio in *L'Avanti,* 1 April 1993; ''Fabio Mauri, la Memoria Come Guerriglia'' by Francesca Alfano Migletti in *D'Ars,* no. 138, 1993; ''Fuori Uso'' by Adriana Martino in *Il Segno,* no. 128, December 1993.

*

At this point, what I am interested in is expression, not art. Or rather, to avoid the limitations of paradox, poetry as illumination, born from an uninterrupted process of expression and moving towards knowledge of the objective expression of the world of appearances. This involves a complex theory which describes, in a logical, intuitive manner, the complex creative system of at least one individual: myself. It is obviously impossible to elucidate this theory in two lines. One can only indicate a couple of relatively simply derivatives:

1. No distinction between ''genres,'' or perhaps, the reduction of all of them (music, painting, theatre, etc.) to single, exclusive ''genre'' of the mind which *had* to express itself to avoid obliteration at the hands of the ''active'' expression of the tangible world.

2. Knowledge, along with all forms of mental expression, should be considered an act of legitimate defense, as simple and natural as eating food; the only way of survival against the armies of error which are constantly nourished by the unqualifiable objectivity of the world.

No particular sign of culture is able to lie out of a general historical text, and no general historical text or interpretation of the world lies out of the more general enigma of the universe.

The interrogatives of the world are hitting us from various sides. I answer to the world from as many points. I am pretending to be many people.

I can detect exactly what is ''no thing.''

The ''screen'' is not a single (one) monochrome. There are two.

So similar to the monochrome, better to say identical, the screen is the second form or catetgory in the ground.

In a strict sense it does not coat the world with his body. Neither is it a substance, the same substance to which it reduces the world.

His aim, slightest or immeasurable, is to contain the world while veiling it. It is the continuity of the slightest diaphragm between inside and outside. The screen discretely awaits the images almost neglecting to suggest them. It is not particularly enigmatic, if ever, it is hidden.

But it's waiting is extremely skilled.

It is aware of containing substances.

It is not stating any thing.

But holds tightly its inside meaning.

The screen is a paintng hidden in a real object.

It is a complex statement shown as if it were simple and easy.

No man of culture can be so primitive as to love only things of high quality.

The idea is not a flash of lightning as in the ancient mythology, neither a bulb which lights as in the cartoon strips. It is a complex system of the significatum.

Language, when we talk about art is full of proposals.

It lends objectivity to thinking and to any outward appearance.

It enucleates the sense, more than science does, possibly more than philosophy.

It holds up in a very similar way God, man, feelings and thoughts, the general and particular appraisal judgement on the enigma of the Universe.

I would't know why one should have thoughts if one does not necessarily reach the truth.

When we are in art's surroundings, art does not lose its right to an effective existence.

—Fabio Mauri

* * *

During the 1950s, Fabio Mauri held a series of exhibitions in Milan, where he took part in, among other events, the Milan Triennale of 1954 and, in the following year, the Milan Biennale. In 1956 he returned to his native city of Rome. Toward the end of the 1950s, he produced a series of neo-Dada works, a tendency then imposing itself on the Italian art scene.

Since then, Mauri's painting has a characteristic of its own, stemming from a combination of developed 'action painting' and new ways of expression linked to the mass media. *Autoritratto Cancellato* is dated 1959–60: inside a drawer a number of tentative brushstrokes are superimposed on a portrait. Atop the whole, a box of pasta is set. In that period, Mauri also produced the series *The End;* one example from the series is *Helzapopping,* where in an enclosure are made a number of marks, and the words, 'The End' appear.

Within this kind of poetic Mauri developed a theme that was to remain constant throughout his work. In time he would employ all possible expressive means. Cesari Vivaldi has written: ''In his early work *The End* represents a cinema screen, whereas later the screen will stand for the cinema itself.'' This applies to the artist's works up to the end of the 1960s, a period ending with *Cinema a luce solida.*

Mauri's interest in cinema is constantly declared in a more or less explicit way. In a later work of 1968 in which plexiglass is used, cinema is idealized and 'frozen' within the magic of a projection hall. A stand symbolizes the projector, and a pyramid connected to the side and base of the stand and fixed to the wall symbolizes the light beam from the projector. Mauri became so interested in cinema that he has never abandoned themes connected to projection, the film, etc.

Following important works such as *Che cosa e il Fascismo* (1971), *Ideology and Nature* (1973) and *Oscuramento* (1975), he produced *Senza,* a series of installations in which films are projected onto animated or still objects. In them, he was seeking a relationship between thought (concretized as film) and the real world. The result was a continuously changing event, revealing new aspects of filmic language contaminated by the outside world.

Between the period of *Solid Light Cinema* at the end of the 1960s and this new chapter in his production, a number of changes took place. Dominant among them is Mauri's increasing awareness of how impossible it was to crystallize the core of European culture with the aim of affirming the validity of the work of art. The realization of this impossibility produced a reflection upon art and culture in an attempt to understand where such limitations originate. Mauri writes: "At the time I intuited that Europe contained invisible operating elements. The model of a consumer society in which Europe was caught was incapable of accounting for this. I decided to exhibit a series of ready-mades produced by recent history: Mussolini's megaphone which I had found, uniforms, military badges, and so on." So was born *What Is Facism,* a work that concludes one epoch and opens another, where ideology takes on a fundamental role to reflect on this.

A theatrical element underlines *A Fest in Honour of General Ernest Von Hussel Passing through Rome,* a complex sequence of performances simulating past reality, but a reality which nevertheless still has the power to influence people's current behaviour. It is such relationships between past and present, between fiction and reality that interest Mauri, and in such a light it is possible to see a common trend in his latest works, from *Ebrea* of 1971 to *Wall of Europe* of 1979. The latter work is an installation: a boat is divided into two equal halves along a longitudinal axis. The fundamental sense of the work is revealed in the author's own words: "The *Wall of Europe* alludes to the Berlin Wall, a scar that cuts across Europe, separating and splitting every thought and action."

—Roberto Lambarelli

McCOY, Ann

Nationality: American. **Born:** Boulder, Colorado, 8 July 1946. **Education:** Studied philosophy, theology and the classics at the University of Colorado, Boulder, 1966–69, B.F.A. 1969; studied sculpture and drawing at the University of California at Los Angeles, 1969–72, M.A. 1972. **Career:** Painter and printmaker, Los Angeles, 1972–77, in New York since 1977; art instructor, School of Visual Arts, New York, since 1977; Columbia University, New York, since 1985; Barnard College, New York, 1980–2000. **Awards:** New Talent Award, Los Angeles County Musuem of Art, 1972; Norman Wait Harris Award, Art Institute of Chicago, 1974; American Association of University Women Award, 1976; D.A.A.D. Kunstlerprogramm Fellowship, West Berlin, 1977; National Endowment for the Arts Award, 1978; Prix de Rome, 1989; National Endowment for the Arts grant, 1989; The Alice Baber Award, 1990; The Pollock Krasner Award, 1993; The Adolph and Esther Gottlieb Foundation, 1996; The Pollock Krasner Award, 1998. **Address:** 5–31 50th Avenue, Long Island City, New York, New York 11101. **Web site:** http://www.annmccoy.com.

Individual Exhibitions:

1970 Esther Bear Gallery, Santa Barbara, California
1974 Parrish Art Museum, Southampton, New York
Fourcade Droll Inc., New York
Nancy Hoffman Gallery, New York
1975 Institute of Contemporary Art, Boston
Harcus-Krakow-Rosen-Sonnabend Gallery, Boston
Betty Gold Fine Modern Prints, Los Angeles
1976 Margo Leavin Gallery, Los Angeles
1977 Wallraf-Richartz Museum, Cologne
1978 Brooke Alexander Inc., New York
Chandler Coventry Gallery, Paddington, Australia
1979 Arts Club of Chicago
Roy Boyd Gallery, Chicago
Margo Leavin Gallery, Los Angeles
Thomas Segal Gallery, Boston
Brooke Alexander Inc., New York (travelled to the Portland Center for the Visual Arts, Oregon)
1981 Augen Galleries, Portland, Oregon
Brooke Alexander Inc., New York
1988 A.C.A. Contemporary, New York (catalog)
1989 *Revelations: The Transformative Impulse in Recent Art,* Aspen Art Museum, Colorado (catalog)
1990 *Ann McCoy: New Roman Works, Rome 1989–90,* Arnold Herstand Gallery, New York (catalog)
1991 The Contemporary Museum, Honolulu, Hawaii
1993 The Jack Wright Gallery, Palm Beach, Florida
1994 The Alex Gallery, New York
The University of Colorado Art Gallery, Boulder
1998 *The Death of the King,* Central Fine Arts, New York

Selected Group Exhibitions:

1972 *15 Young Artists,* Pasadena Art Museum, California
1973 *New American Landscapes,* Vassar College, Poughkeepsie, New York
1974 *Drawings: Works by Contemporary Artists,* University of Miami
1975 *Both Kinds: Contemporary Art from Los Angeles,* University of California, Berkeley
1976 *America 1976,* Corcoran Gallery, Washington, D.C. (travelled to the Wadsworth Atheneum, Hartford, Connecticut, and the Fogg Art Museum, Cambridge, Massachusetts)
1978 *31st Annual Exhibition,* Brooklyn Museum, New York
1980 *Painting and Sculpture Today,* Indianapolis Museum of Art (travelled to the Contemporary Art Center, Cincinnati, Ohio)
1981 *Los Angeles Prints 1883–1980,* Los Angeles County Museum of Art
1985 *Memento Mori,* Moore College of Art, Philadelphia
1986 *Myths and Symbols,* Bruno Facchetti Gallery, New York
1988 *Selections from the Charles Craig Collection,* Santa Barbara Museum of Art, California
1989 *Awards in the Visual Arts,* High Museum of Art, Atlanta
The Boat Show: Fantastic Vessels, Fictional Voyages, Smithsonian Institution, National Museum of American Art, Renwick Gallery, Washington, D.C.
Animals in Art, Hudson River Museum, Yonkers, New York
1991 *Women and Surreal Narrative,* California State University, Fullerton
The Alice Baber Art Fund, Inc., Helander Gallery, New York
1992 *Bronze,* Gallery Camino Real, Boca Raton, Florida
1993 *Sanctuaries: Recovering the Holy in Contemporary Art,* Museum of Contemporary Religious Art, St. Louis University, Missouri
Beasties, Springfield Art Museum, Missouri
1995 *Critters II,* Des Moines Art Center, Iowa
New Acquisitions, New Orleans Museum of Art, Louisiana

Inspired by Nature, Neuberger Museum of Art, Purchase, New York

1996 *Views from a Golden Hill,* The Equitable Gallery, New York

Divine Flesh, Artopia Gallery, New York

1997 *A Natural Selection,* Z. Gallery, New York

Obsessed by Magic, A.C.A. Gallery, New York

Collections:

Allen Memorial Art Museum, Oberlin, Ohio; Art Institute of Chicago; Dallas Art Museum; Denver Art Museum; Des Moines Art Center; Hirshorn Museum of Art, Chattanooga; Honolulu Academy of Art, Hawaii, Indianapolis Museum of Art, Indiana; Los Angeles County Museum of Art; The Museum of Modern Art, New York; Museum of Fine Arts, Houston; The Metropolitan Museum of Art, New York; The National Gallery of Australia, Canberra; New Orleans Museum of Art, Louisiana; Newport Harbor Art Museum, Newport Beach; Whitney Museum of American Art, New York; San Francisco Museum of Modern Art.

Publications:

By McCOY: Articles—''The Demon and the Night Sea'' in *Art International* (Zurich), nos. 3–4, 1980; ''Mythologies of the Feminine: Conversation with Ann McCoy'' with Claudia Gould in *Arts Magazine,* vol. 63, no. 6, February 1989.

On McCOY: Articles—''The Rise and Decline of Younger Los Angeles Art'' by Peter Plagens in *Artforum* (New York), May 1972; ''The Strangeness of Reality'' by Melinda Terbell in *Artnews* (New York), November 1973; ''Artists in Love with Their Art'' by Peter Schjeldahl in the *New York Times,* 3 November 1974; ''The Silent World of Ann McCoy'' by Jean Luc Bordeaux in *Art International* (Lugano, Switzerland), January 1977; ''Drawings from the Natural World'' by Dorothy Burkhardt in *Artweek* (Oakland, California), 4 November 1978; ''Looking for Ann McCoy'' by John Loring in *Arts Magazine* (New York), December 1978; ''Ann McCoy'' by Jeff Perrone in *Artforum* (New York), December 1980; ''Ann McCoy at Brook Alexander'' by Carter Ratcliff in *Art in America* (New York), Februrary 1980; ''Ann McCoy at Central Fine Arts'' by Jonathan Goodman in *Art in America* (New York), vol. 86, no. 10, October 1998.

*

The works are concerned primarily with a kind of visual experience. At times in nature, I have felt like an instrument of perception, an optical lens viewing the scene before me in a non-judgemental, precognitive, mindless state. The visual experience becomes so intense that what James referred to as the whirring-buzzing confusion of the mind stills, the lobe of the brain which is concerned with logic, discourse, reason, seems to be non-existent. It is a visual experience that is solely dependent upon the optical mind. I feel this is the visual experience that Stan Brakhage refers to in *Metaphors on Vision:* ''Yet I suggest that there is a pursuit of knowledge foreign to language and founded upon visual communication demanding a development of the optical mind and dependent upon perception in the original and deepest sense of the word.''

I wanted the works to be concerned with a kind of visual communication that was not dependent upon literal discourse, problematical thought, discursive symbolism . . . the intellect and its restrictive manifestations. I perceive nature in a particular way. All of the paintings of landscapes I have seen seemed removed moved from this kind of perception. I wanted to draw the world as I perceived it.

The works are drawings. Four years ago I was working with transparency, luminosity and landscape; I was making sculptures that looked like Chinese jade mountains. I began to realize that I was more interested in the working drawings than in the sculptures. It was around that time I also saw the first Sol Le Witt wall drawing. I liked the notion of drawing on such a large scale, drawing as an ultimate concern. I have always preferred drawings to paintings . . . liked old master's notebooks better than their paintings. My first drawings were very much like silver-point drawings. My first drawing of Highland Mary Falls was all done with black and silver graphite . . . and had the same shimmering quality. The shimmering delicate quality of pencil seemed to capture the visual experience I had in nature.

Color became a concern about two years ago. I like the prismatic color sense one finds in Church and Bierstadt. I also like the kind of color one finds in film . . . color projected . . . has a transparent quality only found occasionally in watercolor paintings. The color in the drawings is determined by mood, weather and is generally the ''natural'' color of what is being drawn. I was interested in the work of Church for another reason . . . also in the work of Pollock. I like the general lack of emphasis on a particular area of the canvas. . . . I don't mean to confuse this with the notion of field painting generally. If one were to cut the canvas up into grid squares, one square would be no more important than another. When I am viewing a scene in nature, my visual field seems to defy the singling out of a particular object. I wanted to make the works, so that they, like nature, could not be perceived quickly. I have always liked the notion of complexity . . . gradual revelation . . . of several layers of perception of something being difficult to perceive or comprehend. This idea goes very much against much of the work of the sixties. . . . I often wonder if a viewer who is used to looking at Stellas can have to spend several hours looking at one of my drawings.

The ''cosmic landscape painters'' felt that nature was man's salvation, a transcendental substitute for organized religion. They painted the world in a pre-Adamic state: a world without the hedgerow or structure of European thought. In the drawings I am indeed concerned with a kind of Garden of Eden world . . . but not a world viewed through the eyes of a noble savage or primitive man. I am concerned with an outer landscape . . . altered by consciousness . . . seen through the eyes of an inner part of one's being. I do not want the drawings to be thought of as the extension of an historical tradition . . . as a celebration of a kind of Yankee idealism. For me they are like shadow pictures of an inner world that bears a striking resemblance to an outer world. In many ways they are as mysterious to me as they are to the viewer. When I finish one, I am always totally surprised that I have drawn a place that I have not seen, that I have drawn it at all.

I work from photographs . . . often as many as fifty different photographs of different locations. *The Andes* was inspired by photographs of the Andes, and also by photographs of Yosemite. The underwater drawings are drawn from photographs usually of a particular place . . . like photographs of the Great Barrier Reef. I have often not seen the place I am drawing, but try to study a similar place to observe the lighting conditions. I drew *The Andes* after studying the light falling on the peaks where I ski. I drew the underwater works after diving in California, Mexico and Hawaii. The basic inspiration always comes from actually being out in nature. My studio is within a half hour of mountains, octopi, buffalos, starfish and swans . . . a situation that one could not duplicate in New York.

The works grow spontaneously, I never know what the work will look like in advance. I use photographs, some actual objects like sea shells and lantern slides to help create the weather effects. I sometimes do geological research and also study oceanography. I have always liked scientific textbooks with diagrams. The drawings in the margins of the works are often notes or associations, that may or may not relate to the place in reality, but to places in my dreams. I like to combine scientific observation and detail with a dreamlike or unconscious element. The most recent works—*Le Pays Des Reves, Palou*—were aided by researching the ocean life in Australia, and also Palou, at the Sea Library.

Enough said; I hope that people will look at the works for themselves, and pay very little attention to anything that I have said about them. They are made to be seen without verbiage . . . are made for a part of the psyche that has nothing to do with the intellect.

—Ann McCoy

* * *

Influenced by Larry Bell, DeWain Valetine and Peter Alexander, Ann McCoy started her career by making cast resin sculptures of icebergs. Feeling there was a lack of support for her sculptures, she destroyed a great number of them and went on to experiment with drawing on a large scale. Water, however, continued to be (and still is) the main theme of her works, which are generally executed in colored pencil with acrylic ground on paper mounted on canvas.

The artistic world of Ann McCoy is located below the surface of the sea, which she explores and photographs herself. Since the early 1970s her drawings have been increasingly inhabited by sea ferns, sells, corals and fishes. Before her move from Venice, California, to Berlin in January 1977 when she was awarded the coveted Berliner Kunstlerprogram grant, her works were essentially luminous and calm. When she came back to the United States in 1978, to New York, where she now lives, her ocean drawings became more and more tormented and darker.

McCoy called the drawings which she exhibited in 1979 ''The Night.'' She wrote that these works ''have their origin in the unconscious. . . . Many of the images from these realms are primordial, preancestral.'' The presence of threatening sea creatures such as voracious eels, octopus and serpents reflects the artist's current deep state of introversion. She wrote that the monsters she researched in oceangraphic photo archives have been turned in her drawings into metaphors for the shadowy figures she has been encountering within herself. This journey into the sea of the unconscious takes her deeper and deeper, a dive which may partly explain the increasing darkness of the subaquatic element.

Unintimidated by any past or current fashions,McCoy offers the viewer a strong sensibility which is nourished by a great amount of reading ranging from St. Augustine, Thomas Aquinas, Irish poetry, St. John Perse and the Bible to art historical studies on, for example, 19th century American landscape painters. As the creator of a new form of visionary landscape (which also includes astronomical imagery), she has enjoyed great critical acclaim.

—Jean-Luc Bordeaux

McCRACKEN, John

Nationality: American. **Born:** Berkeley, California, 9 December 1934. **Education:** Studied under Gordon Onslow-Ford and Tony De Lap, California College of Arts and Crafts, Oakland, 1957–65, B.F.A. 1962. **Family:** Married Gail Barringer, 1991; children: David Gordon, Patrick Daniel. **Military Service:** Served in the United States Navy, 1953–57. **Career:** Instructor, University of California at Irvine, 1965–66; assistant professor, University of California at Los Angeles, 1966–68; assistant professor, School of Visual Arts, New York, 1968–69; assistant professor, Hunter College, New York, 1971–72; lecturer, University of Nevada, Reno, 1972–73; lecturer, University of Nevada, Las Vegas, 1973–75; lecturer, College of Creative Studies, University of California at Santa Barbara, 1975–85. Lives and works in Santa Fe, New Mexico. **Awards:** National Endowment for the Arts Grant, 1968. **Agents:** Sonnabend Gallery, New York; L.A. Louver Gallery, Los Angeles; Galerie Konrad Fischer, Dusseldorf; Lisson Gallery, London; Galerie Nordenhake, Stockholm; Galerie Froment & Putnam, Paris; Galerie Xavier Hufkens, Brussels; Art & Public, Geneva. **Address:** 1001 E. First St. #7, Los Angeles, California 90012, U.S.A.

Individual Exhibitions:

1965 Nicholas Wilder Gallery, Los Angeles
1966 Robert Elkon Gallery, New York
1967 Nicholas Wilder Gallery, Los Angeles
Robert Elkon Gallery, New York
1968 Robert Elkon Gallery, New York
Nicholas Wilder Gallery, Los Angles
1969 Ileana Sonnabend Gallery, Paris
Sculpture 1965–1969, Art Gallery of Ontario, Toronto
1970 Sonnabend Gallery, New York
Ace Gallery, Vancouver
1972 Robert Elkon Gallery, New York
1973 Robert Elkon Gallery, New York
1974 Seder-Creigh Gallery, Coronado, California
1978 Meghan Williams Gallery, Los Angeles
1979 Dobrick Gallery, Chicago
1980 Meghan Williams Gallery, Los Angeles
1982 Schaffner Gallery, Santa Barbara, California
1985 Flow Ace Gallery, Los Angeles
1986 P.S. 1, Long Island City, New York
1987 Newport Harbor Art Museum and Univerity of California, Irvine
Contemporary Arts Museum, Houston
1988 HoffmanBorman Gallery, Santa Monica
1989 Galerie Konrad Fischer, Dusseldorf
1990 Lisson Gallery, London
Galerie Nordenhake, Stockholm
Fred Hoffman Gallery, Santa Monica
1991 Galerie Froment & Putman, Paris
1992 Sonnabend Gallery, New York
1993 L.A. Louver Gallery, Los Angeles
Galerie Xavier Hufkens, Brussels
1994 L.A. Louver Gallery, Los Angeles
Galerie Art & Public, Geneva
1995 L.A. Louver Gallery, Los Angeles
Kunsthalle Basel, Switzerland (catalog)

Hochschule für Angewandte Kunst, Vienna (catalog)
Galerie Tanit, Munich
1996 Galerie Froment & Putnam, Paris
1997 L.A. Louver Gallery, Los Angeles
David Zwirner Gallery, New York
Lisson Gallery, London
1998 Studio La Citta, Verona
A Arte Studio Invernizzi, Milan
Galerie Art & Public, Geneva
1999 Galerie Hauser & Wirth, Zurich
James Kelly Contemporary, Santa Fe
2000 L.A. Louver Gallery, Los Angeles
Galerie Almine Rech, Paris
Zwirner & Wirth, New York
2001 Lisson Gallery, London
L.A. Louver Gallery, Los Angeles

Selected Group Exhibitions:

1967 *Biennale,* Paris (travelled to Pasadena Art Museum, California)
Guggenheim International Exhibition, New York
1969 *Art of the Real,* Museum of Modern Art, New York (travelled to Paris and London)
1970 *American Exhibition,* Art Institute of Chicago
1975 *University of California at Irvine 1965–75,* La Jolla Museum of Contemporary Art, California
1986 *Biennale,* Venice
1988 *La Couleur Seule,* Musée St. Pierre d'Art Contemporain, Lyon
1989 *Geometric Abstraction and Minimalism in America,* Guggenheim Museum, New York
1991 *Carnegie International,* Carnegie Museum of Art, Pittsburgh
1994 Inaugural exhibition, Musée d'Art Moderne et Contemporain, Geneva
Basic Black & White, Herbert Palmer Gallery, Los Angeles
1995 *Shape: Forming the L.A. Look,* California State University, Fullerton
From Behind The Orange Curtain, Muckenthaler Cultural Center, Fullerton, California
Object and Image, Newport Harbor Art Museum
Vue du Collectionneur, L'Espace de l'Art Concret, Mouans-Sartoux, France
1996 *Chimeriques Polymères,* Musée d'Art Moderne et d'Art Contemporain, Nice, France (catalog)
Black and White, Gallery Seomi, Seoul, Korea
Squares or Lines, Galerie Art & Public, Geneva, Switzerland
Painting Outside Painting: 44th Biennial Exhibition of American Painting, The Corcoran Gallery of Art, Washington, D.C. (catalog)
1997 *Sunshine & Noir: Art in L.A. 1960–1997,* The Louisiana Museum of Modern Art, Humblebaek, Denmark (also Castello di Rivoli; Hayward Gallery, London, Haus der Kunst, Munich; UCLA at the Armand Hammer Museum of Art, Los Angeles) (catalog)
Continuity and Contradiction, Miami Art Museum, Miami
1998 *Pop/Abstraction,* Museum of American Art of the Pennsylvania Academy of the Fine Arts, Philadelphia
Elevator, Steffany Martz Gallery, New York
Five Years, 1993–1998, David Zwirner Gallery, New York
1999 *The American Century: Art and Culture 1900–2000 (Part 2),* Whitney Museum of American Art, New York
Tang, Turner & Runyon Gallery, Dallas
2000 *Painting Zero Degree,* Cranbrook Museum of Art, Bloomfield Hills, Michigan (also Fred Jones Jr. Art Museum, University of Oklahoma, Norman)

Collections:

Art Gallery of Ontario, Toronto; Art Institute of Chicago; Arte Contemporaneo, A.C., Mexico City; French National Art Collection; Honolulu Academy of Art; La Jolla Museum of Contemporary Art; Los Angeles County Museum of Art; Milwaukee Art Center; Musée d'Art Contemporain de Montreal; Musée d'Art Moderne et Contemporain, Geneva; Museum of Contemporary Art, Los Angeles; The Museum of Modern Art, New York; Newport Harbor Art Museum, Newport Beach, California; Norton Simon Museum of Art, Pasadena; Oakland Museum, Oakland, California; Palais des Beaux Arts, Brussels; Rijksmuseum Kröller-Müller, Otterlo, Holland; San Diego Museum of Art; San Francisco Museum of Art; Santa Barbara Museum; The Solmon R. Guggenheim Museum, New York; University Art Museum, University of California, Berkeley; University Art Museum, University of California, Santa Barbara; Whitney Museum of American Art, New York.

Publications:

By McCRACKEN: Articles—''John McCracken: Remote Viewing/Psychic Traveling'' in *Frieze,* June-July 1997; ''Between Two Worlds,'' interview with Frances Colpitt in *Art in America* (New York), April 1998.

On McCRACKEN: Books—*5 Los Angeles Sculptors at Irvine,* exhibition catalog by John Coplans, Irvine, California 1966; *Primary Structures,* exhibition catalog by Kynaston McShine, New York 1966; *American Sculpture of the 60s* exhibition catalog by Maurice Tuchman, Los Angeles 1967; *A New Aesthetic,* exhibition catalog by Barbara Rose, Washington, D.C. 1967; *Guggenheim International Exhibition '67,* catalog by Thomas Messer and Edward Fry, New York, 1967; *Minimal Art: A Critical Anthology,* edited by Gregory Battcock, New York 1968; *Options,* exhibition catalog by Lawrence Alloway, Milwaukee 1968; *Art of the Real,* exhibition catalog by E. C. Goosen, New York 1968; *Los Angeles 6,* exhibition catalog by John Coplans, Vancouver 1968; *Whitney Annual,* exhibition catalog, New York 1968; *John McCracken: Sculpture 1965–1969,* exhibition catalog by Dennis Young and James Monte, Toronto 1969; *Late Modern: The Visual Arts Since 1945* by Edward Lucie-Smith, New York 1969; *James McCracken,* exhibition catalog, Paris, 1969; *American Art of the 20th Century* by Sam Hunter, New York 1972; *University of California at Irvine 1965–75,* exhibition catalog by Melinda Wortz, La Jolla California 1975; *Art Now* by Edward Lucie-Smith, Secaucus, New Jersey, 1989; *Minimal Art: The Critical Perspective* by Frances Colpitt, Ann Arbor, Michigan, 1990. **Articles—** ''Rejective Art'' by Lucy Lippard in *Art International* (Lugano,

Switzerland), October 1966; ''American Sculpture of the 60s'' by Kurt Von Meier in *Art International* (Lugano, Switzerland), summer 1967; ''Sculpture of the 60s'' by Edward Fry in *Art in America* (New York), September/October 1967; ''Art Bloom'' by John Coplans in *Vogue* (New York), 1 November 1967; ''Los Angeles 1971'' by Elizabeth Baker in *Artnews* (New York), September 1971; ''Diversity in Unity: Recent Geometicizing Styles in America'' by Lucy Lippard in *Art since Mid-Century, Vol. 1: Abstract Art Since 1945,* Greenwich, Connecticut 1971; ''Centering'' by Emily Wasserman in *Arts Magazine* (New York), November 1972; ''John McCracken'' by Colin Gardner in *Artforum,* November 1990; ''John McCracken: Visionary Realization'' by Peter Clothier in *Artspace,* January/February 1991; ''John McCracken: Paintings of Sculptures'' by Adachiara Zevi in *L'Architecttura,* vol. 471, no. 1, January 1995; ''John McCracken'' by Martin Herbert in *Time Out* (London), 12 February 1997; ''McCracken Sculptures as Objective as Objects Get'' by Ellen Berkovitch in *Journal North,* 5 August 1999.

*

My sculptures have always tended to emphasize, it seems to me, a general outward simplicity, and, so far as my abilities, and patience with the aspects of craft have gone, with a noticeable degree of material beauty. The making of ''dumb but interesting things,'' or ''just beautiful things,'' is more or less how I've thought of my attempts. Or to put it another way, I'd say that a consistent characteristic of my approach to art-making is that of trying to draw or put together, in the midst of earth-life experience, clear focusings, or centerings, in the form of concretized, archetypal-tending representations, or images, or objects that, I speculate, might function as ''anchor points'' in the sea of human consciousness, much as can a piece of wood, or stone, that one finds oddly or for some reason interesting and therefore keeps around somewhere in one's space.

Beyond a certain point, I feel I can, in relation to my own work, speak only as a viewer, with no more authority as to what's actually what than any other viewer. Therefore, I try to make as few claims as possible about it so as to avoid either preventing someone from seeing something they might have seen had I not suggested I knew what was there for everyone's perceptions, or, too, to avoid sounding too pompous. This is one round-about way of saying that I wish my things to be not only engaging, but as open as possible in terms of how they are seen and felt and interpreted.

But I do nevertheless have some definite ideas, even things I might be insistent about—one being that an issue very central to my work is that of human (or psychic) self-realizing, self-transforming, self-imaging, self-illuminating. Not merely, that is, the so-called 'ego'-self, but the self that begins with something like ego-awareness and expands from there to fill all the space (and time) one might come to imagine. I tend to view the things I make, and also all art objects—and, as a matter of fact, all objectifications of all kinds—as concentration or meditation devices. I try to make things which are, one the one hand, capable of drawing and sustaining one's interest, and on the other, of such a nature as to leave one free to enjoy whatever experiencing or dreaming or 'tripping'—or integrating—one might be inwardly inclined to do through them. I like the idea, for instance, of a person looking with such peculiar intensity of something that he then finds himself seeing ''through'' it, ''beyond'' it. To further distill this thought, or to risk an over-idealization, it seems in my view to be a matter of perceptually touching the infinite, the total universe ''picture,'' through a finite device or three-dimensional object-point; it's the attempt at seeing and feeling something of the sphere that contains all time and all space through a particularly attuned chunk of the regular material stuff we live in and walk around in and make waves through.

—John McCracken

* * *

In the mid 1960s, John McCracken began making monochromatic columns and planks of wood and fiberglass covered with bright reflective color. His series of planks which lean against the wall were, at the time of their development, a perceptive and inventive accomplishment, combining as they did a geometrical minimal rigor with flashy color and casual informality. They were also a nifty fusion of painting and sculpture, blending elements from the two- and three-dimensional with a stylistic emphasis very prominent in vanguard circles of that period.

McCracken's stated intentions are the desire to create unitary forms which are integrated dynamically with their environmental space. In all his works, the whole form is simply and directly perceptible, arriving at completion in relationship with the wall and floor. The element of interconnectedness (certainly neither a new nor a radical idea) is further aided by McCracken's scale, one just larger than humansize which is big enough to impress but not huge enough to encompass, and by the reflective quality of the light bouncing off laquer-like, glossy surfaces. By 1969, McCracken had begun using more neutral hues and more regular spacing in his installations, while continuing within the same general formal methodologies he had already come to prefer rather exclusively. His uses of chalky whites and matte grays attempt, it seems, to achieve a more integral energetic continuity between sculpture and surrounding environment. The regular ordering of congruent forms also serves as suggestive of ritualizing references, but these associations, as well as McCracken's intuited proportions, remain in the static realm, more dormant and classicizing than dynamic or mystical.

It is those leaning planks which use bright, hip colors such as lipstick red or plum, for instance, that attain the greatest degree of independence and character in McCracken's unitary oeuvre. His is a sort of success quotient which might be characterized by his choices of chic, L.A.-flavored titles which he finds in fashion magazines. Although McCracken chooses not to acknowledge illusionistic relationship with seen objects such as diving board or surfboards, it is such Pop-like connections which enliven his more openly seductive and flamboyant works with a personality that is capable of setting them apart from the more earnestly serious minimalisms of so many of his contemporaries.

Where McCracken went downhill was in his moves deeper and deeper into minimal aesthetics, taken too seriously and stripped of humor and of meaning outside the purely formalistic. He has continued to produce variation upon variation of his earlier works, pursuing them long past the time and context of their original potential, getting himself caught in a situation of endless repetition all too common among late-blooming modernists whose variations on a single theme become more dry and obvious through years of overuse. McCracken has acknowledged a major debt to Barnett Newman in his similar search for the basic elemental form. In McCracken's case, as in too many others, emulation of Abstract Expressionism's less-is-more vocabulary and syntax tends to miss the point that each generation must find its own possibilities and instead leads the artist into a small corner of what was previously an open arena for big ideas.

—Barbara Cavaliere

McGARRELL, James

Nationality: American. **Born:** Indianapolis, Indiana, 22 February 1930. **Education:** Indiana University, Bloomington, 1948–53; Skowhegan School of Painting and Sculpture, Maine, summer 1953; University of California at Los Angeles, 1953–55, M.A. 1955; Academy of Fine Arts, Stuttgart, 1956. **Family:** Married Ann Harris in 1955; children: Andrew and Flora. **Career:** Painter. Worked as short order cook, bus boy, factory assembly-line worker, and door-to-door salesman, 1941–53. Independent artist, since 1955: travelled in Italy and Spain, 1955–56; resided in Paris, 1964–65, and in Grimaud, France, 1970–71. Artist-in-Residence, Reed College, Portland, Oregon, 1956–59; Professor of fine arts and director of graduate painting studies, Indiana University, Bloomington, 1959–80; Professor of fine arts, Washington University, St. Louis, since 1980; Professor Emeritus, Washington University, St. Louis, 1993; Artist-in-Residence, Dartmouth College, 1993; Artist-in-Residence, Roswell Foundation, New Mexico, 1999. **Awards:** Fulbright Fellowship, 1955–56; Tamarind Lithographic Workshop Grant, Los Angeles, 1962; Citation and Grant, National Institute of Art and Letters, 1963; Guggenheim Fellowship, 1964; National Endowment for the Arts Grant, 1966, 1985; Jimmy Ernst Award in Art, American Academy of Arts and Letters, 1995. **Member:** Académie des Beaux Arts de l'Institut de France, 1970. **Agent:** Allan Frumkin Gallery Inc., 41 East 57th Street, New York, New York 10022. **Address:** PO Box 39, Newbury, VT 05051–0039.

Individual Exhibitions:

1955 Frank Perls Gallery, Beverly Hills, California
1957 Frank Perls Gallery, Beverly Hills, California
1958 Frank Perls Gallery, Beverly Hills, California
1959 Portland Art Museum, Oregon
1960 Indiana University, Bloomington
1961 Allan Frumkin Gallery, Chicago
Allan Frumkin Gallery, New York
1962 Allan Frumkin Gallery, Chicago
Salt Lake City Art Center, Utah
Frank Perls Gallery, Beverly Hills, California
1963 Indiana University, Bloomington
Portland Art Museum, Oregon
1964 Allan Frumkin Gallery, New York
Berkshire Museum, Pittsfield Massachusetts
Florida State University, Tallahassee
Frank Perls Gallery, Beverly Hills, California
1965 *The Graphic Works of James McGarrell,* Allan Frumkin Gallery, Chicago
Galleria Galatea, Turin
1966 Allan Frumkin Gallery, New York
1967 Tragos Gallery, Boston
Galerie Claude Bernard, Paris
Galleria Galatea, Turin
Il Fante di Spade, Rome
1969 Allan Frumklin Gallery, New York
1970 Galerie Claude Bernard, Paris
Galleria dei Lanzi, Milan
1971 Allan Frumkin Gallery, New York
Allan Frumkin Gallery, Chicago
Quincy Art Center, Illinois (toured the United States)
Galleria Il Fante di Spade, Rome
1972 Museum of Fine Art, Salt Lake City, Utah
Galleria dei Lanzi, Milan
1973 Allan Frumkin Gallery, New York
1974 Galerie Claude Bernard, Paris
Galleria Il Fante di Spada, Rome
1976 Galleria Il Fante di Spada, Rome
1977 Allan Frumkin Gallery, New York
Clark-Benton Gallery, Santa Fe, New Mexico
1980 Allan Frumkin Gallery, New York
1981 Allan Frumkin Gallery, New York
Eason Gallery, Santa Fe, New Mexico
New Mexico Museum of Art, Albuquerque
1984 Allan Frumkin Gallery, New York
1985 Southern Methodist University, Dallas
St. Louis Art Museum, Missouri
Signet Arts Gallery, St. Louis, Missouri
1986 Allan Frumkin Gallery, New York
1987 Signet Arts Gallery, St. Louis, Missouri
Charles Moore Gallery, Philadelphia
Jane Haslam Gallery, Washington, D.C.
Wichita State University, Kansas
1989 Galerie Simonne Stern, New Orleans
The More Gallery, Philadelphia
Scottish Gallery, London
Flowers East, London
1990 *Art of James McGarrell,* Museum of Art, University of Arizona, Tucson
Struve Gallery, Chicago
1991 *Bruce McLean: Minimal Moves,* Galerie Gmyrek, Düsseldorf
William Jackson Gallery, London
Glasgow Print Studio, Scotland
1993 Frumkin/Adams Gallery, New York
1994 Galerie Fortlaan 17, Gent, Belgium
1997 George Adams Gallery, New York
1998 Art Museum, University of Arizona, Tucson
The Art Gallery, University of New Hamshire, Durham
2000 *Table Top Joys: New Still-life Paintings,* George Adams Gallery, New York

Selected Group Exhibitions:

1956 *Whitney Annual,* Whitney Museum, New York (and 1958, 1960, 1963, 1967, 1969)
1959 New Images of Man, Museum of Modern Art, New York
1964 *Documenta,* Kassel, West Germany
1970 *The American Scene 1900–1970,* Indiana University Art Museum, Bloomington
1972 *Narrative Painting,* Kansas City Art Institute
1974 *American Prints 1913–63,* Museum of Modern Art, New York
1978 *Art about Art,* Whitney Museum, New York

1984 *Nueva Pintura Narrativa,* Museo Rufino Tamayo, Mexico City
1987 *Night Light, Night Life,* Sherry French Gallery, New York
1988 *Starlit Waters: British Sculpture—An International Art 1968–1988,* exhibition catalog, Tate Gallery Liverpool
1989 *British Sculpture 1960–1988,* exhibition catalog, Museum voor Hedendaagse Kunst, Antwerp, Belgium
1992 *Work and Turn: Artists' Bookworks from the United Kingdom,* National Gallery of Iceland, Reykjavik
1993 *Contemporary British Artists' Books,* Hardware Gallery, London
1995 *Sculpture,* Anthony d'Offay, London

Collections:

Museum of Modern Art, New York; Whitney Museum, New York; Brooklyn Museum, New York; Pennsylvania Academy of Fine Arts, Philadelphia; Baltimore Museum of Fine Art; National Gallery of Art, Washington, D.C.; Hirshhorn Museum and Sculpture Garden, Washington, D.C.; Art Institute of Chicago; Kansas City Art Museum; Centre Georges Pompidou, Paris; Santa Barbara Museum of Art; San Francisco Art Museum; Hamburg Museum of Art; Rose Art Museum, Brandeis University.

Publications:

By McGARRELL: Articles—''On Being a Provincial Artist'' in *New Art Examiner* (Chicago), June 1986; ''Flip Sides of Vision'' with Jonathan Williams in *Modern Painters* (London), vol. 11, no. 1, Spring 1998.

On McGARRELL: Books—*The Graphic Works of James McGarrell,* exhibition catalog, Chicago 1965; *James McGarrell,* exhibition catalog by Luigi Carluccio, Turin 1965; *James McGarrell,* exhibition catalog by Giovanni Testori, Paris, 1967; *The Quincy Inventions,* exhibition catalog with text by Mark Strant, New York 1971; *James McGarrell,* exhibition catalog, Paris 1974; *Starlit Waters: British Sculpture—An International Art 1968–1988,* exhibition catalog, Liverpool 1988; *Bruce McLean* by Mel Gooding, Oxford 1989; *Bruce McLean: Minimal Moves,* exhibition catalog, Düsseldorf 1991. **Articles—**''James McGarrell'' by Max Kozloff in *Art International* (Lugano, Switzerland), April 1964; ''The Essence of Reality'' by Paul Moses in the *Chicago Daily News,* 20 March 1965; ''Art: Symbolism of the Quincy Inventions'' by John Canaday in the *New York Times,* 15 May 1971; ''James McGarrell'' by Glenn O'Brien in *Artforum* (New York), May 1984; ''James McGarrell's Universe: Realism, Magic, Abstraction, and the Enigmatic Narrative'' by Tom Bolt in *Arts Magazine* (New York), vol. 60, April 1986; ''A Whirl of Ideas Spread on Canvas'' by Victoria Donothoe in the *Philadelphia Enquirer,* 17 January 1987; ''Bruce McLean'' by John Berry in *Ceramic Review,* no. 124, July/August 1990; review by Guy Burn in *Arts Review* (London), vol. 43, 12 July 1991; review by Tom Gross in *New Art Examiner,* vol. 19, June/Summer 1992; review by Reagan Upshaw in *Art in America* (New York), vol. 81, July 1993; review by Edith Doove in *Artefactum,* vol. 11, Autumn 1994; ''Bruce McLean: Profile of the Artist'' by David Lee in *Art Review* (London), vol. 47, November 1995; ''The Art Square, Barnsley, England'' in *Architectural Design* (London), vol. 67, July/August 1997; ''Social Space'' by Mel Gooding in *Architects' Journal,* vol. 212, no. 3, 20 July 2000; ''James McGarrell at George Adams'' by Lance Esplund in *Art in America* (New York), vol. 88, no. 5, May 2000.

*

I have always thought of painting as an artificial, synthetic construct which must, none-the-less, look organic, as inevitable as if it had grown, like a tree, according to natural processes.

In contradistinction with the great number of works being done in the past 25 years in the ''less is more'' tradition, my own seek to be inclusive. I like to get a lot going on, to paint over my head, to paint objects and visual complexes that are too difficult for me to understand entirely, or handle but which, when finally left on the canvas, have a sense of rightness of, again, inevitability.

Although I constantly study them, I have not, for several years, painted from direct visual sources or photographs.

—James McGarrell

* * *

Much of McGarrell's surreal-expressionist imagery appears the attempt to convey the poignance (if not the pathos as well) of the most specific, personal, and temporal of human moments, but transformed by the intrusive fantasy of the artificial and timeless realm of literary, historical, and intellectual inventions. And so the characteristic look of his work has been that of a complex amalgam of human figures—at times in spatially distorted environments—involved in interchange with other figures; the surroundings are often filled with emblematic-appearing accessories, and so an overall cast of the inexplicable is created.

The Expressionist aspect of his work, parallel to that of other mid-western American painters such as Robert Barnes, Seymour Rosofsky, and June Leaf, lies in his often loose and slurried paint-handling and aura of the foreboding. McGarrell has himself stated that in the mid-1960s ''salvation for me was to be found in the thickening of the plot rather than with simplification.'' But likewise that his multi-referential pictures ''do not stand for anything else, but represent themselves.'' If so, then McGarrell's dense visual and symbolic ambiguities are clearly his intention; and with his frequent reference, both hidden and overt, to the great works and eras of the European figurative tradition, his evolution may appear the technical exercises of an artist imbued with the pervasive Mannerism so often cited as characteristic of the postmodern period. McGarrell's largest work, exhibited in 1981, ''Travestimento,'' 8 by 20 feet, is both a summation of the previous two decades of work, and as well as a new assertion of confidence in his approach.

With the decade of the 1980s, the artist has only increased the verve of his images, letting go any painterly qualities still remaining from the earlier work to perfect a more precise illusionism. Even with his continuing use of a large format, McGarrell has often presented multi-panel arrangements, with a predella and small vertical flanking pictures to produce a resemblance to the archaic polyptych; his narratives have remained as densely non-specific as heretofore, and so there surrounding images allow him more complex enigmatic weaves of space and sentiment. Another aspect of his mastery—perhaps like the sudden explosion of verbal nonsense in the midst of Dickens' narration—is his ''micro-abstraction,'' little free-floating bits of non-representation which become an inexplicable part of the material density of the large fictions depicted. The whole is then well-labelled "Illusionist Abstraction."

—Joshua Kind

McLEAN, Bruce

Nationality: British. **Born:** Glasgow, 6 November, 1944. **Education:** Glasgow School of Art, 1961–63; St. Martin's School of Art, London, 1963–66. **Career:** Gave numerous performances, recorded by photographs, before forming the first Pose Band, Nice Style, with Paul Richards and Ron Carr, 1971; lecturer, Maidstone College of Art, Kent, 1971; senior lecturer, Slade School of Fine Art, London, 1985–95; visiting lecturer, Rijksacademie, Amsterdam, 1990–96, Real Academie de Bellas Arts, Madrid, 1991, and Städelschule, Staatliche Hochschule für Bildende Kunste, Frankfurt, 1992; external examiner, Royal College of Art, Lond, 1993–1996, and University of Reading, 1994–96; Professor of Fine Art, Slade School of Fine Art, London, 1996. **Awards:** Pratt Sculpture Bequest, 1965; Sainsbury Sculpture Award, 1966; Arts Council Award, 1975; Arts Council Bursary, 1978; DAAD Fellowship, West Berlin, 1981; Mercedes Benz Prize, 1985; John Morres 1st Painting Prize, 1985; Royal Television Society Design Award for Production Design (non-drama), 1994. **Agent:** Anthony d'Offay Gallery, 9 Dering Street, New Bond Street, London W1. **Address:** 34 Cleveland Road, London SW 13, England.

Individual Exhibitions:

1965 St. Martin's School of Art, London (performance)
1969 Konrad Fischer Galerie, Dusseldorf
Royal College of Art, London (performance)
1970 Nova Scotia College of Art, Halifax
1971 Situation Gallery, London
Galerie Yvon Lambert, Paris
1972 Galleria Francoise Lambert, Milan
Tate Gallery, London (one day only)
Sonja Henie Foundation, Oslo (with Nice Style)
1973 Tooth's Gallery, London (with Nice Style)
Hanover Grand Hotel, London (with Nice Style)
Royal College of Art, London (with Nice Style)
1974 Architectural Association, London (with Nice Style)
Garage Gallery, London (with Nice Style)
1975 Robert Self Gallery, London (with Nice Style)
Museum of Modern Art, Oxford
Robert Self Gallery, Newcastle upon Tyne
1976 Battersea Art Centre, London (performance with William Furlong)
1977 Battersea Art Centre, London (performance with Sylvia Ziranek)
Robert Self Gallery, London
1978 The Kitchen, New York (with Rosey McLean)
1979 Southampton University Gallery, Hampshire (performance with Rosey McLean, Sylvia, Ziranek, and Peter Lacoux)
Halle für Internationale Neue Kunst, Zurich
Barry Barker Gallery, London
Hayward Gallery, London (performance with Rosey McLean)
Riverside Studios, London (performance with Paul Richards)
1980 Third Eye Centre, Glasgow (travelled to Fruit Market Gallery, Edinburgh and Arnolfini Gallery, Bristol)
Basement Group, Newcastle upon Tyne (performance)
Mikery Theatre, Amsterdam (performance with Paul Richards)
1981 Musée d'Art et d'Industrie, St.-Étienne, France
Anthony d'Offay Gallery, London
Art Project, Amsterdam
Kunsthalle, Basel (travelled to the Whitechapel Art Gallery, London, and the Stedelijk van Abbemuseum, Eindhoven, Netherlands)
1982 Anthony d'Offay Gallery, London (with Gilbert and George and Richard Long)
Galerie Chantal Crousel, Paris
Galerie Greta Insam, Vienna
Kanransha Gallery, Tokyo
Mary Boone Gallery, New York
Modern Art Gallery, Vienna
Van Abbemuseum, Eindhoven, Netherlands
1983 Kanransha Gallery, Tokyo
Galerie Kiki Maier-Hahn, Dusseldorf
DAAD-Galerie, West Berlin
Galerie Dany Keller, Munich
Whitechapel Art Gallery, London
Institute of Contemporary Arts, London
1984 Galerie Fahnemann, West Berlin
Badischer Kunstverein, Karlsruhe, West Germany
Galerie Dany Keller, Munich
Art Palace, New York
Kanransha Gallery, Tokyo
Bernard Jacobson Gallery, New York
1985 Anthony d'Offay Gallery, New York
Bernard Jacobson Gallery, London
Galerie Gmyrek, Dusseldorf
Tate Gallery, London
1986 Bernard Jacobson Gallery, London
Anthony d'Offay Gallery, London
Scottish Gallery, Edinburgh
1987 Anthony d'Offay Gallery, London
Galerie Fahnemann, West Berlin
Hillman Holland Gallery, Atlanta, Georgia
1988 Galerie Gmyrek, Düsseldorf
Kanransha Gallery, Tokyo
1989 Scottish Gallery, London
1990 Glasgow Print Studio, Glasgow
Henry Moore Sculpture Studio, Dean Clough, Halifax
1991 Miriam Shield Fine Art, Toronto
Berkely Square Gallery, London
1992 Scottish Gallery, Edinburgh
1993 Kunstmuseum Soro, Soro
1994 Galerie Fortlaan 17, Ghent
1995–96 *Urban-Turban,* Cornerhouse, Manchester (traveled to Norwich Gallery, Norwich, and Ormeau Baths, Belfast)
1997 Galerie se, Bergen

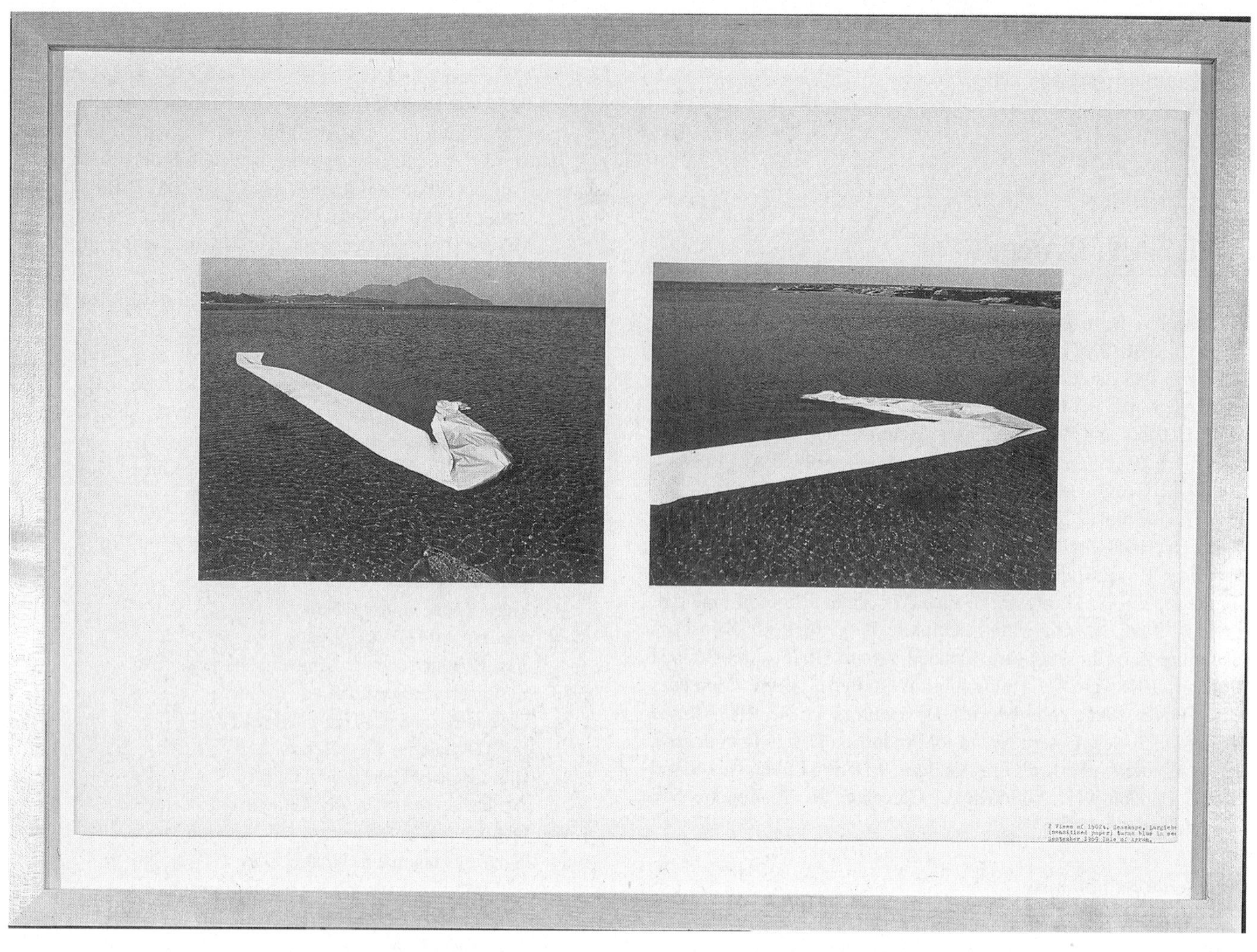

Bruce McLean: *150ft. Seaskape, Largiebeg,* 1969. ©Tate Gallery, London/Art Resource, NY; courtesy of Tate Gallery.

Selected Group Exhibitions:

1965 *5 Young Artists,* Contemporary Arts, London
1966 *Painting and Sculpture Today,* Grabowski Gallery, London
1970 *Information,* Museum of Modern Art, New York
1979 *Un Certain Art Anglais,* Musée d'Art Moderne de la Ville, Paris
1980 *Biennale,* Venice
1981 *A New Spirit in Painting,* Royal Academy, London
1982 *Vergangenheit/Gegenwart/Zukunft,* Württembergischer Kunstverein, Stuttgart
1983 *Thought and Action,* Laforet Museum, Tokyo
1985 *7000 Oaks,* Kunsthalle, Tubingen, West Germany
1987 *British Art in the 20th Century,* Royal Academy of Arts, London
1989 *Scottish Art since 1900,* Scottish National Gallery of Modern ARt, Edinburgh
1993 *The Sixties: The Art Scene in London,* Barbican Art Gallery, London
1993–94 *The Raw and the Cooked,* Barbican Art Gallery, London (traveled to Museum of Modern Art, Oxford)
1995 *Power to Change,* BBC, Wales
2000 *Live in Your Head,* Whitechapel Art Gallery, London

Collections:

Arts Council of Great Britain, London; British Council, London; Contemporary Arts Society, London; Tate Gallery, London; Victoria and Albert Museum, London; Glasgow Museums and Art Galleries, Scotland; University of Southampton, Hampshire; Van Abbemuseum, Eindhoven, Netherlands; National Museum of Modern Art, Osaka, Japan; Tochigi Prefectural Museum of Fine Art, Japan.

Publications:

By McLEAN: Books—*King for a Day,* exhibition catalog, London 1972; *Dream Works,* London 1985; *Ladder,* London, 1987; *Home Manoeuvres,* London, 1987. **Articles—**''Not Even Crimble'' in *Studio International* (London), October 1970; ''Nice Style at the Hanover Grand'' in *Audio Arts* (London), no. 2, 1973; ''Nice Style at Garage'' in *Audio Arts* (London), supplement 1973; ''Sorry: A Minimal Musical Parts'' in *Audio Arts* (London), supplement 1977; ''9 Works for Tape/Slide Sequence and a National Anthem'' in *Audio Arts* (London), 1977; ''I Want To Be a Seagull'' in *Salon Arts Magazine* (Dusseldorf), 1978; ''Ways of Viewing Mackerels and Mandolins'' in *Aspects* (Newcastle), no. 4, 1978; ''Titles: Teacups'' in *Salon Arts Magazine* (Dusseldorf), 1979; ''The Masterwork:

Award Winning Fish Knife'' in *Audio Arts* (London), supplement 1979; ''Tape/Slide Piece'' in *Audio Arts* (London), supplement 1979; interview with Nena Dimitrijevic in *Bruce McLean,* exhibition catolog, London 1981; ''Bruce McLean: Drawings'' in *Aspects* (Newcastle), no. 16, 1981; ''Late Evening, Sunday,'' interview with Mel Gooding in *Versus,* no. 5, 1995. **Films—***6 Waiter Waiter Works,* 1970; *In the Shadow of Your Smile, Bob,* 1970; *The Elusive Sculptor: Richard Long,* 1970; *Wheedle, Deedle Work,* 1970; *A Million Smiles for One of Your Miles, Walter,* 1971; *Crease, Crisis* (with Nice Style), 1973; *The Masterwork,* 1979.

On McLEAN: Books—*Performance 1909–1979* by Roselee Goldberg, London 1979; *Bruce McLean,* exhibition catalog by Sarah Kent and David Brown, Glasgow 1980; *Bruce McLean,* exhibition catalog by Nena Dimitrijevic, London 1981; *Bruce McLean,* exhibition catalog with text by Mario Amaya, New York 1984; *Bruce McLean,* exhibition catalog by Jean-Christophe Ammann, Basel and Florence 1984; *Bruce McLean: Simple Manners or Physical Violence,* exhibition catalog with text by Norman Rosenthal, Dusseldorf 1985; *Bruce McLean,* exhibition catalog by Mary Rose Beaumont, Edinburgh 1986; *McLean,* edited by Jeremy Hunt, London 1992.

* * *

McLean studied at the Glasgow School of Art from 1961 to 1963 and then went to St. Martin's School of Art in London to study sculpture from 1963 to 1966. McLean went to St. Martin's at the time when Anthony Caro's teaching predominated in the sculpture department. The sculptural debates at this time revolved round subjects such as whether sculpture should sit on the ground or on plinths and the placement of abstract elements of metal and wood and colour arrangements. McLean and another student eventually, in 1965, responded to this with the placement of life-sized silhouettes of human figures, one on the roof and one in the street with the sculptors waving in the direction of Charing Cross Station; this was entitled *Mary Waving Goodbye to the Trains.* This heralded McLean's sardonic style of art using a mixture of props and people in highly staged performances.

Since 1965 McLean's work has involved making sculpture using found materials, photography, performance and, most recently, paintings strongly influenced by his work with performance. He is probably best known for his 'pose works,' some of the earliest of which were produced in collaboration with Gilbert and George. To take an example, *Pose Work for Plinths* (1972), in a series of photographs, shows McLean posing in various awkward positions suggesting the stances of Henry Moore sculptures, on plinths of different heights. *Nice Style: The World's First Pose Band,* was founded by McLean in 1971 with students from Maidstone College of Art, where he was teaching. They produced pose performances in a multi-media from, (with their roots in Dada and Futurism), and were highly complicated performances devoted to achieving the perfect pose for a given context. For example, there were consumerism themes such as *Freeze: An Opera Based on the Life-Style and Values of a Midwest American Vacuum Cleaner Company* and *Semi-Domestic Poses* of 1973.

McLean developed various performances with an emphasis on irreverence and wit throughout the 1970s, climaxing in 1979 with the most ambitious, *The Masterwork: Award Winning Fishknife,* an elaborate criticism of the consumer society and particularly the professions of architects and designers.

McLean has produced his performances around the world, and with the late 1970s these were becoming more often static installations. With the 1970s his *Nice Style* drawings were closely linked to performance, but by 1977 his gouaches show thematic links only with performanc—brightly coloured, simple, flat forms are acrobats against schematic drawings denoting space.

With the 1980s his paintings have become the dominant work of his output, (though there is still the occasional performances). His past interests are still evident in the organization of his picture surfaces. Backgrounds are divided up as he might have devised a score for a performance, and, in a painting of 1980, *Rock to Rock, Cheek to Cheek,* the dancing figures on the right of the picture are caught in a bright yellow triangle like a spotlight beam. Wording appears in the picture surface, yet the whole painting is dominated by an expressionistic brush style.

In the late 1980s he has been turning his attention to monumental some sculpture. Yet as Richard Cork has written in the 1987 catalog, *British Art in the 20th Century,* ''McLean's sly, anti-heroic attitude is still in the sculpture, and his debunking sense of humour is never very far away.''

—Victoria Keller

McWILLIAM, F(rederick) E(dward)

Nationality: Irish. **Born:** Banbridge, 30 April 1909. **Education:** Slade School of Art, London (Robert Ross Scholarship), 1928–31. **Family:** Married Elizabeth Marion Crowther in 1932; daughters: Sarah and Bridget. **Military Service:** Royal Air Force, Great Britain and the Far East, 1940–45. **Career:** Sculptor: worked in Paris, 1931–32; has since then lived and worked in London: member, British Surrealist Group, 1938; member, Royal Academy, London, 1959 (resigned, 1962). **Awards:** Prix de Concours, Unknown Political Prisoner Competition, London, 1953; Prize, *John Moore's Exhibition,* Liverpool, 1961; Oireachtas Prize, Trinity College, Dublin, 1961. Fellow, University College, London, 1962; D. Litt.: Queens University, Belfast, 1964. C.B.E. (Commander, Order of the British Empire), 1966. **Died:** 1992.

Individual Exhibitions:

1939 London Gallery
1949 *Recent Sculpture,* Hanover Gallery, London
1952 Hanover Gallery, London
1953 Hanover Gallery, London
1956 Hanover Gallery, London
1958 Royal West of England Academy, Bristol
1960 Queens University, Belfast
1961 Waddington Galleries, London
1963 Waddington Galleries, London
1st American Exhibition, Felix Landau Gallery, Los Angeles
1966 Waddington Galleries, London
1968 Waddington Galleries, London
1969 Travers Gallery, London
1973 *Scuplture 1972–73: Women of Belfast,* Waddington Galleries, London

Women of Belfast: New Bronzes by F.E. McWilliam 1972–73, McClelland Galleries International, Belfast
Dawson Gallery, Dublin
1975 Waddington Galleries, London
1976 Waddington Galleries, London
1977 Bell Gallery, Belfast
1979 Waddington Galleries, London
1980 Taylor Gallery, Dublin
1981 Ulster Museum, Belfast (retrospective; travelled to the Douglas Hyde Gallery, Dublin, and the Orchard Gallery, Londonderry)
1982 Warwick Arts Trust, London (retrospective)
1984 Waddington Galleries, London
Gordon Gallery, Londonderry
1987 Gordon Gallery, Londonderry
1989 *F.E. McWilliam: Sculpture 1932–1989,* Tate Gallery, London
1992 The Mayor Gallery, London
1995 *F.E. McWilliam (1909–1992),* Solomon Gallery, Dublin

Selected Group Exhibitions:

1939 *British Surrealist and Abstract Exhibition,* Northampton Art Gallery, England
1940 *Surrealism,* Zwemmer Gallery, London
1953 *2nd Biennale,* Biennale, Middleheim Park, Antwerp
1961 *Carnegie International,* Pittsburgh
1964 *Painting and Sculpture of a Decade 1954–1964,* Tate Gallery, London
1972 *Decade 40,* Whitechapel Art Gallery, London
1978 *Dada and Surrealism Revisited,* Hayward Gallery, London
1980 *The Delighted Eye,* Earlham Street Gallery, London
1982 *Surrealism in England,* Galerie 1900/2000, Paris
1984 *English Contrasts 1950–60,* Artcurial, Paris (travelled to Serpentine Gallery, London)
1986 *Sculpture in Britain Between the Wars,* Fine Art Society, London
1990 *Contemporary Artists from Ireland,* Austin/Desmond Fine Art, London
British Modernism: Henry Moore and His Circle of Hampstead in the Thirties, City Art Gallery, Leeds, England

Collections:

Tate Gallery, London; Museum of Modern Art, New York; National Portrait Gallery; City Art Gallery, Leeds; Belfast Museum and Art Gallery; Middelheim Park, Antwerp; Art Institute of Chicago; National Gallery of South Australia, Adelaide.

Publications:

By McWILLIAM: Articles—article in *Architectural Design* (London), September 1958; interview with William Gaunt, in *The Times* (London), 17 March 1960; ''Harriet Cooke Talks to the Sculptor F.E. McWilliam'' in the *Irish Times* (Dublin), October 1963; interview with Mel Gooding, in *Art Review* (London), 6 November 1981; ''The Irish Sculptor, F.E. McWilliam in Conversation with James Burr'' in *Apollo* (London), no. 130, July 1989.

On McWILLIAM: Books—*British Sculpture* by Eric Newton, London 1947; *F. E. McWilliam: Recent Sculpture,* exhibition catalog with text by Merlyn Evans, London 1949; *F. E. McWilliam: First American Exhibition,* exhibition catalog, Los Angeles 1963; *F. E. McWilliam: Sculpture 1972–73: Women of Belfast,* exhibition catalog, London 1973; *Women of Belfast: New Bronzes by F. E. McWilliam 1972–73,* exhibition catalog, with an introduction by Roland Penrose, Belfast 1973; *Towards Sculpture* by W.J. Strachan, London 1974; *F. E. McWilliam,* exhibition catalog and book by Judy Marle and T.P. Flanagan, Belfast 1981; *F.E. McWilliam: Sculpture 1932–1989,* exhibition catalog, London 1989; *Contemporary Artists from Ireland,* exhibition catalog, London 1990; *F.E. McWilliam (1909–1992),* exhibition catalog, Dublin 1995. **Articles**—''The Sculpture of F. E. McWilliam'' by Bryan Robertson in *Nimbus* (London), no. 2, 1954; ''The Sculpture of F. E. McWilliam'' by Albert Garnett in *Studio International* (London), November 1954; ''F. E. McWilliam, ARA'' by J. Wood Palmer in *Motif* (London), September 1959; ''F. E. McWilliam, Waddington II'' by J. Sexton in *Arts Review* (London), January 1971; ''Art out of Torment'' by Bruce Arnold in the *Irish Independent* (Dublin), October 1973; review by John Russell in *The Sunday Times* (London), November 1973; review by James Burr in *Apollo* (London), no. 129, May 1989; ''Unconformist Wit: F.E. McWilliam, Sculptor'' by Paddy Kitchen in *Country Life,* vol. 183, no. 20, 18 May 1989; review by David Cohen in *The Burlington Magazine,* vol. 131, August 1989; ''F.E. McWilliam: Inventor of Styles'' by Janet Barber in *Journal of Arts and Crafts,* vol. 2, no. 3, September 1989; review by Mary Rose Beaumont in *Arts Review* (London), vol. 44, March 1992; ''F.E. McWilliam'' by Brian McAvera in *Sculpture* (Washington, D.C.), vol. 16, February 1997.

*

I have rather lost my interest in abstract art, and looking back now it seems as though the ''New Generation'' movement was the last flowering before it got inbred and academic. I don't think it had much influence on my own work: my commitment was to sculpture of another kind. I worked within as well as against the older tradition. I have never seen any reason why representation should eliminate the formal design element which is the potent factor in abstract art. Perhaps what's needed now is another close look at the incredible diversity in Nature, bearing in mind John Fowle's words about creating ''a world as real as but other than the world that is.''

I've always welcomed commissions, even when the site or subject involved me in activity quite different from my current interests. But then, unlike the British Council, I have never set any store by consistency; life is too short for restrictive practices. Indeed, even if (as has often happened) the commission proves abortive, I enjoy having imposed upon me the *raison d'etre* for a new obsession. Nothing masochistic about that sort of provocation. Sometimes it has meant one off, finish; but more often it has led to variations on the theme. My dream remains to achieve a synthesis of classical and romantic, the romantic side providing the irrational element, as art that is public and private at the same time.

—F. E. McWilliam

* * *

Not many artists go up so many avenues. Most of them, after their student days and their first experiences of comparative freedom, find a style of their own, improve upon it, modify it, perhaps even change it to a point approaching non-recognition, but never actually desert their chosen path. This is a general rule, of course; it is not always the case. The example of Picasso flashes before the eye, and even he was far from unique in this context.

F. E. McWilliam has made many changes, some of them radical. In the late 1940s he was exploring a kind of surrealism. A reassembly of the ''immaculate corpse.'' Heads and limbs could be exact in academic terms, but the trunk would be missing. By 1950 he had moved on. This time he was associated with giant profiles, very 3-dimensional but sporting outsize nose and eyes. The figuration was utterly recognizable but distorted. And so on to a rough non-figuration in metal—for example, his ''Witch of Agnesi'' (1959) which might have claimed relationship with early Paolozzi or Peter King.

The tortuous route—for a sculptor—is set out here because it helps to explain how many things in sculpture the name McWilliam can mean. In 1956 he even made a striking full-lengh (6 ft.) portrait of Elisabeth Frink, a follow-up of the hieratic figures he had been making (one of which graces a cathedral in Wales).

By the early 1960s it seemed as if McWilliam had finally found the furrow he intended to plough. He gradually foreswore the semi non-figurative pieces he had been welding in metal and became absorbed in figures whose pyramid shoulders, knees and feet came together in physical contortions that at times grew close to abstraction. These were the ''crankshaft'' figures. A book was published by Tiranti which concentrated upon this phase of his work.

But then came more swift changes, including an astonishing re-jigging of the figures encrusted with miniature tiles of gold and blue mosaic. Then—all sorts of non-figurative shapes, rounded and tactile, the absolute opposite of the rough and gritty crankshaft works. Were polished bronzes such as ''May Day'' (1965) to be the terminal point in McWilliam's complex development? Indeed, no.

His ''Women of Belfast'' (1972–73) brought back figuration. Not the crankshaft type this time, although elbows and knees were once again dramatically angular. ''Women of Belfast'' had a terrible social significance. They gave the impression that they had been physically and mentally crumpled just as if these pathetic pliable females had been caught and crushed in a giant fist.

McWilliam has his admirers, but can they always be the same admirers? Did Picasso have fans who genuinely applauded his every change of tempo?

—Sheldon Williams

MEGERT, Christian

Sculpture by Christian Megert, 1985. Photo by Mathias Möller. ©2001 Artists Rights Society (ARS), NY/ProLitteris, Zürich.

Nationality: Swiss. **Born:** Bern, 6 January 1936. **Education:** Studied art at the Kunstgewerbeschule, Bern 1952–56. **Family:** Married Lydia Christoffel in 1964 (divorced, 1972); son: Boris; married Franzkiska Vogt in 1976. **Career:** Independent artist in Bern, 1955–58 and 1960–73; in Paris, 1958–60; in Düsseldorf, since 1973. Produced monochrome black and white paintings, 1955–59; light-reflector works, 1959–63; mirror objects, since 1961; light-kinetic works, since 1963; stone sculptures, since 1975; professor, Kunstakademie, Düsseldorf, since 1976. **Member:** Founding member of Nouvelle Ecole Européenne (NEE; artists' group), Lausanne, 1960; associated with ZERO group, Copenhagen and Düsseldorf, 1960–63; cofounder and art director, Galerie Aktuell (artists' collective), Bern, 1964–69; cantonal art commission member, Bern, 1970–73, and exhibitions commission member, Kunsthalle, Bern, 1974. **Awards:** Swiss State art scholarships, 1962–64. **Agent:** Hubertus Schöller, Poststrasse 3, D-40213, Düsseldorf, Germany; Edith Wahlandt, Hölderlinstrasse 55, D-70193 Stuttgart, Germany. **Address:** Drakestrasse 7, D-40545 Düsseldorf, Germany.

Individual Exhibitions:

1959	Club des 4 Vents, Paris
1960	Galleri Koepcke, Copenhagen (with Dieter Roth)
1961	Galerie Punt 31, Dordrecht, Netherlands
	Galerie St. Luc, Barcelona
	Galleri Koepcke, Copenhagen
1962	Galerie A, Arnhem, Netherlands
	Galerie Orez, The Hague
1963	Galerie D, Frankfurt
	Galerie Knoll, Basel
	Galerie Kasper, Lausanne
	Rijksuniversiteit, Leiden
1964	Schweizerische Landesausstellung, Lausanne
1965	Galerie Aktuell, Bern
	Halfmannshof, Gelsenkirchen, West Germany
1966	Galerie Loehr, Frankfurt
	Galerie Toni Gerber, Bern
1967	Op Art Galerie, Esslingen, West Germany
	Galleria Vismara, Milan
1968	Galerie Swart, Amsterdam
	Galerie Toni Gerber, Bern
	Galerie Reckermann, Cologne
1969	Galerie Bischofberger, Zurich
	Galerie Latzer, Kreuslingen, Switzerland
1970	Galerie Ernst, Hannover
	Galerie Lichter, Frankfurt

1971 Galerie Reckermann, Cologne
Galerie Bernhard, Solothurn, Switzerland
Galerie Thomas Keller, Starnberg, West Germany
1972 Stadtische Galerie, Bern
Forum Kunst, Rottweil, West Germany
Galerie Ernst, Hannover
1973 Galerie Media, Neuenberg
Galerie Reckermann, Cologne
1974 Studio Casate, Milan
Galerie Edith Wahlandt, Schwabisch Gmund, West Germany
1975 Lucy Milton Gallery, London
Kunsthalle, Heilbronn, West Germany
Galerie St. Johann, Saarbrucken
Galerie 68, Rapperswil, West Germany
Galerie Ubu, Karlsruhe
1977 Galerie G. Herzog, Buren and der Aare, Switzerland
1978 Galerie Edith Wahlandt, Schwabisch Gmund, West Germany
1979 *Werke 1956–1978, Bilder, Objekte, Zeichnungen,* Kunstverein, Düsseldorf
Galerie Reckermann, Cologne
1980 Galerie Edith Wahlandt, Schwabisch Gmund, West Germany
1981 Galerie Schöller, Düsseldorf
Rosenthall Werk, Seib, West Germany
Rosenthall Werk, Amberg, West Germany
1982 Galerie Edith Wahlandt, Schwabisch Gmund, West Germany
Galerie Buhler, Biel, Switzerland
1985 Galerie Schöller, Düsseldorf
1986 Galerie Edith Wahlandt, Stuttgart
Bonefantenmuseum, Maastricht
Jan van Eick Akademie, Maastricht
1987 Museum für Moderne Kunst, Cuxhafen
1988 Galerie Schöller, Düsseldorf
Galerie Edith Wahlandt, Stuttgart
1989 Galerie Hermanns, Munich
Galerie von Gunten, Thun
1991 *Kunsträume,* Galerie Krebs, Bern
1992 Galerie Krebs, Bern
Galerie Schöller, Düsseldorf
1995 Sala 1, Rome, Italy
1996 Galerie Edith Wahlandt, Stuttgart
Galerie Schöller, Düsseldorf
1997 Städtische Museum Gelsenkirchen, Germany
Kunstmuseum, Bern, Switzerland
Galerie Krebs, Bern, Switzerland
2000 Galerie Lilo Marti, St. Paul de Vence, France

Selected Group Exhibitions:

1958 *Salon des Realites Nouvelles,* Paris
1961 *ZERO Group,* Institute of Contemporary Art, Philadelphia
1971 *The Swiss Avantgarde,* New York Cultural Center
1976 *Rationle Konzepte,* Galerie Pa Szepan, Gelsenkirchen, West Germany
1977 *Museum of Drawers,* Kunsthalle, Düsseldorf (travelled to the Israel Museum, Jerusalem)
1978 *Konkrete Kunst aus der Scheweiz,* Kunstmuseum Badhuis, Gorinchem, Netherlands (travelled to Stedelijk Museum, Apeldoorn)
1979 *Lichtsculptures,* Informationszentrum, Eindhoven, Netherlands
1980 *ZERO International,* Koninklijke Museum, Antwerp
1981 *Real und Irreal,* Galerie Schöller, Düsseldorf
1982 *Spiegel,* Kunstverein, Hannover (travelled to Haus am Waldsee, West Berlin, and the Wilhelm Lehmbruck Museum, Duisburg, West Germany)
1985 *ZERO,* Städtische Museum, Ulm
1989 *Goepfert, Holwek, Megert,* Galerie Edith Wahlandt, Stuttgart
1992 *Sammlung Lenz,* Geleria Zacheta, Warschau, Poland
Paradigmi della Frammentazione nell'Art Svizzera, Villa Corce, Genova, Italy
1997 *Zero in Paris 1960: Und Heute,* Musée d'art moderne et contemporain, Nizza, France
Regel und Abweichung: Schweiz Konstruktiv 1960–1997, Stiftung für Konkrete und Konstruktive Kunst, Zürich
1998 *Regel und Abweichung: 40 Jahre Konstruktive Kunst in der Schweiz,* Frankfurter Kunstverein, Germany
1999–2000 *Geometrie als Gestalt, Strukturen der modernen Kunst,* Sammlung DaimlerChrysler, Nationalgalerie, Berlin (traveled to Stiftung für Konstruktive und Konkrete Kunst, Zürich)

Collections:

Kunstmuseum, Bern; Progressive Museum, Basel; Städtische Sammlung, Bern; Landesmuseum, Hannover; Neues Landesmuseum, Münster; Städtische Kunsthalle, Recklinghausen, Germany; Museum der Stadt, Düsseldorf; Museum der Stadt, Mönchengladbach, Germany; Stadt Gorinchem, Netherlands; Albany Museum, New York; Staatliche Galerie Stuttgart, Germany; Museum Gelsenkrichen, Germany; Kunstmuseum Bern, Switzerland; DaimlerChrysler Collection, Stuttgart.

Publications:

By MEGERT: Books—*Ein neuer Raum,* Copenhagen 1961; *Glas und Spiegel Buch,* Bern 1962, 1974; *Wenn Sie einen Spiegel gegen Spiegel halten,* Cologne 1964; *Christian Megert,* Bern 1965; *Tam Tek,* Basel 1969; *Portfolio,* Starnberg, West Germany 1970; *Retro Megert,* Hinwil 1970; *Portfolio,* Zofingen 1974; *Der Raum und das Selbst,* with G. J. Lischka, Bern 1975.

On MEGERT: Books—*Kunst unserer Zeit* by Will Grohmann, Cologne 1966; *Der Doppelte Masstab* by John Anthony Thwaites, Frankfurt 1966; *Licht Kunst Licht,* exhibition catalog with text by Frank Popper, Eindhoven, Netherlands 1966; *Christian Megert,* exhibition catalog with text by Harald Szeemann, Esslingen, West Germany 1967; *Constructivism: Origin and Evolution* by George Rickey, New York 1967; *Neue Dimensionen der Plastik* by Udo Kultermann, Tübingen 1967; *Origins and Development of Kinetic Art* by Frank Popper, London 1968; *Kunst ist Revolution* by Louis Peter, Cologne 1969; *Op Art* by Cyril Barrett, London 1970; *ZERO Raum,* exhibition catalog with text by Gerhard Storck, Düsseldorf 1974; *Christian Megert; Werke 1956–1978; Bilder, Objekte, Zeichnungen,* exhibition catalog with texts by Karl-Heinz Hering,

Eugen Gomringer, Claus Bremer, and Harald Szeemann, Düsseldorf 1979; *Eine europäische Avantgarde,* exhibition catalog, Salzburg 1985; *Bern 66–87,* exhibition catalog, Bern 1987; *ZERO,* exhibition catalog, Düsseldorf 1988; *Skulptur 88,* exhibition catalog, Düsseldorf 1988; *Konkret Schweiz heute,* exhibition catalog, Münster and Berlin 1988, Neubrandenburg 1989; *Sammlung Lenz,* exhibition catalog, Warsaw 1992; *Tre Prospettive,* exhibition catalog, Rome 1995; *Christian Megert* by Anette Kuhn, Bern 1997; *ZERO und Paris 1960: Und heute* by Renate Damsch-Wiehager, Stuttgart 1998; *Von Dada bis Beuys—30 Jahre Kunstverein für die Theinlande und Westfalen mit Karl-Heinz Hering* by Marie-Luise Otten, Ratingen 1998; *Lexikon der Schweizer Kunst,* Zürich 1998; *Geometrie als Gestalt, Strukturen der modernen Kunst, von Albers bis Paik,* Berlin 1999; *ZERO aus Deutschland 1957–1966: Und heute,* 1999.

*

I will build a new space—a space without beginning and without end, in which everything lives and is called to live—which is at the same time quiet and loud, dynamic and static. It shall be high, as high as I want it and low if I want it low. It shall be constructable everywhere, on the smallest spot or big like a town, a country, or even a thought.

It shall be a space which is merry, full of vitality, full of color and movement, at the same time calmly calling for reflection without asking for anything, colorless and cold, which may change with the speed of thought after my desires, as I want it to be.

All the problems of space in the past and in the future will be found in my space, the solved ones and the unsolved ones, visible for everybody who is willing to see. It will contain only things existing in reality; everything unreal and unoriginal will no more be found in my space.

As it is real and surrealist and constructive and informal and colored and colorless, concrete and abstract, naive and intellectual, and synchronized, it will also need no art, because it is art itself—and the inhabitants of this space become the greatest artists of our time, and everybody may become an inhabitant of this space. Try to find a space without beginning and end and limit; if you hold a mirror against a mirror you will find a space without end or limits, a space with unlimited possibilities—a new metaphysical space.

—Christian Megert

MEIRELES, Cildo

Nationality: Brazilian. **Born:** Rio De Janeiro, 1948. **Agent:** Galerie Lelong, 20 West 57th Street, New York, New York 10019.

Selected Individual Exhibitions:

1967 Museu De Art Moderna Bahia, Salvador
1975 *Eureka/Blindhotland,* Museu de Arte Moderna, Rio de Janeiro
1981 Galeria Luisa Strina, São Paulo
1986 *Cinza (Gray),* Galeria Luisa Strina, São Paulo
1990 *Projects,* The Museum of Modern Art, New York
1992 *Metros I,* Galeria Luisa Strina, São Paulo
1996 Retrospective, Museu de Arte Do Porto, Portugal
1997 *Cildo Meireles,* Galerie Lelong, New York (catalog)
1998 *Camelô,* Galeria Luisa Strina, São Paulo
1999 Retrospective, New Museum of Contemporary Art, New York, in conjunction with Museums of Modern Art, Sao Paulo and Rio de Janeiro (catalog)
Ku Kka Ka Kka, Galerie Lelong, New York (catalog)
2000 Galeria Luisa Strina, São Paulo

Selected Group Exhibitions:

1970 *Information,* Museum of Modern Art, New York
1976 *International Actuality,* Venice Biennale
1981 *The Sermon of the Mountain,* Fiat Lux Museum of Modern Art, Medellin, Colombia
1987 *Non-Magic World,* Museum of Contemporary Art, São Paulo
1990 *The Rhetorical Image,* The New Museum of Contemporary Art, New York
1992 *America, Bride of the Sun,* Musee Real de Beaux Arts, Antwerp, Belgium
1995 *Temporarily Possessed: The Semi-Permanent Collection,* New Museum of Contemporary Art, New York (catalog)
1997 *You Are Here,* Royal College of Art, London
Re-Aligning Visions: Alternative Currents in South American Drawing, El Museo del Barrio, New York (catalog)
1998 *The Garden of the Forking Paths,* Kunstforeningen, Copenhagen
XXIV Biennal of São Paulo
1999 The Queens Museum of Art, New York
2000 *Worthless,* Moderna Galerija Ljubljana, Slovenia

Publications:

By MEIRELES: Articles—''Through the Labyrinth: An Interview with Cildo Meireles'' by John Alan Farmer in *Art Journal,* Fall 2000.

On MEIRELES: Books—*Cildo Meireles,* exhibition catalog, with text by Dan Cameron, Paulo Herkenhoff, and Jorge Luis Borges, New York 1999; *Cildo Meireles,* Helsinki 1999. **Articles—**''Cildo Meireles, Tunga'' by Michael Tarantino in *Artforum,* January 1990; ''Cries from the Wilderness'' by Lawrence Weschler in *ARTnews,* Summer 1990; ''Art from Brazil in New York'' by Barry Schwabsky in *Artforum,* Summer 1995; ''Raw Meal'' by Carlos Basualdo in *Artforum,* April 1996; ''Maxima Moralia'' by Carlos Basualdo in *Artforum,* February 1997; ''Memory of the Senses'' by Charles Merewether in *Grand Street,* Spring 1998; ''Cildo Meireles'' by David Joselit in *Artforum,* February 2000; ''Seeing Red'' by Steven Henry Madoff in *Time International,* 6 March 2000; ''Unspoken Stories'' by Edward Leffingwell in *Art in America,* July 2000.

* * *

Born in 1948, Cildo Meireles is one of Brazil's most significant living artists of the postwar period. A pioneer of installation art since the 1960s, Meireles is best known for his dramatic and politically charged walk-in environments which often incorporate sound, smell, and touch alongside visual experience, requiring the viewer's full perceptual involvement. For several decades Meireles' work has been included in the most significant international surveys, from the landmark *Information* exhibition at The Museum of Modern Art, New York, in 1970, to the XXIV Biennal of São Paulo in 1998, and most recently in a major retrospective at the New Museum of Contemporary Art in New York in association with the Museums of Modern Art in Rio de Janeiro and São Paulo.

Beginning with his first museum exhibition in 1967, Meireles played a key role in the transition in Brazilian art between the preceding generation of Neoconcretists—Lygia Clark, Hélio Oiticica, and Lygia Pape—and his own generation, informed by conceptual art, installation, and anti-form. The Neoconcretists favored creating participatory artworks and their principal achievement was a collective re-imagining of spatial perception—art not as pure symbolism, but art proposed as a new reality. In the early 1960s, Meireles favored the medium of drawing as a way to work out abstract concepts; however, he only produced drawings of things he wanted to construct. As a way to invest imagined ideas with the tensions of the world in his work ''Espaços Virtuais: Cantos'' (''Virtual Spaces: Corners,'' 1967–68), Meireles transferred his drawn investigations of space into three-dimensional sculptural environments resembling corners of rooms.

''During the late 1960s,'' writes curator Dan Cameron, ''the imposition of a ruthless military dictatorship in Brazil along with the proliferation in Latin America of radical political theory prompted Meireles to create works that conflated current events and the mechanics of perception.'' His *Inserções em Circuitos Ideologicos* (*Insertions into Ideological Circuits*, 1970) consisted of various projects where Meireles produced formulas that could potentially have a political effect. His *Insertions* were exhibited at The Museum of Modern Art in 1970 as part of an international exhibition of conceptual art. Meireles combined interest in the concept of circuits and systems study with international issues specific to Brazil. By imprinting the text ''Yankees go home'' onto Coca Cola bottles and then putting them back into circulation in his *Coca-Cola Project*, Meireles used the Coca Cola bottle as a symbol of ''the painful political, social, and economic reality of Brazil'' which he felt was ''a consequence of the American system of politics and culture and its expansionist, interventionist, hegemonic, centralizing ideology.'' Citing the influence of Duchamp's ready-mades, Meireles aimed to expand thinking about art in terms which were not limited to the visual. In a repressive political atmosphere of censorship and the restriction of legal rights, Meireles considered the public as potential agents of action and his art as a mechanism of provocation.

Meireles grew to feel that much of the conceptual art in the 1970s ended up as dry verbal discourse and maintained that the element of seduction should always be present in his work. Undertaken in response to the murder of a journalist by the police, Meireles created the temporary installation, *Desvio para o Vermelho* (*Red Shift*, 1967–84). This three-roomed environment transports the spectator from a tranquil monochrome domestic interior into a crime scene. The spectator enters a white-walled living room in which every object—the carpet, furniture, fish tank, books, plants, and paintings—is the color red. The connotations of red, specifically of blood and terror, become more prominent in the second part of the work. When turning into an underlit corridor, the spectator encounters a tiny bottle spilling out a vast red flood, far larger than could have been contained and which eventually covers the entire floor. Upon the third physical shift, the spectator traverses a darkened room. Across the space, an off-angle washbin has been dramatically illuminated, and with closer inspection a gushing red liquid pumps from the spigot into the sink. Meireles creates an experience in which the powerful tactile and visual impressions push the metaphorical meanings of the work into emotional and psychological spaces.

In *Volatil* (*Volatile*, 1980–94), the spectator enters a j-shaped room filled to mid-calf with several tons of light gray powdered talc. As the bare-footed participant slowly rounds the corner of the room, the smell of gas and a hissing sound are encountered. One single candle is visible. Meireles creates a strange mixture of feelings; he intends the combination of tranquility and apprehension to heighten the senses. A similar mechanism is employed in *Através* (*Through*, 1983–89), which Meireles first presented at the Kanaal Art Foundation in Belgium in 1989. The title of the piece serves as an impossible challenge, for the participant is confronted with a prohibitive labyrinth of barriers of all descriptions, including fishing nets, venetian blinds, prison bars, barbed wire, museum rope barriers, and eight tons of broken reinforced glass on the floor. The broken glass, while dangerous, shimmers seductively and the barriers are constructed in an elegant box-like grid; however, only at the risk of personal injury could a person pass through this work.

Meireles' work functions through condensation; it is dense, simple, direct, and open without being overly analytical. In *Cruzeiro do Sul* (*The Southern Cross*, 1969–70), a piece in which two minuscule adjacent blocks of wood sacred to the indigenous people of Brazil are installed in the vast space of an empty museum, Meireles brings forth ''a region that does not exist on the official maps.'' His work bears more resemblance to poetry than official discourse, its meaning becomes active in the peripheral regions of our consciousness.

—Sarah Wagner

MELOTTI, Fausto

Nationality: Italian. **Born:** Roverto, Trento, 8 June 1901. **Education:** Studied mathematics and physics, University of Pisa, 1918; electrical engineering, Milan Politecnico, 1924; sculpture, under Adolfor Widt, Brera Accademia di Belle Arti, Milan, 1929. **Career:** Sculptor: lives and works in Milan; close friendship with Lucio Fontana from 1928; founder, with Fontana, Antonasio Soldati and others, Gruppo del Milione, Milan, 1934–35; co-founder, *Quadrante;* lived in Rome, writing poetry, 1941–43; after many of his works were destroyed by a bombing raid on Milan in 1943, he retired into obscurity for many years; worked on ceramics after the war and returned to sculpture in the 1960s. Lecturer, Scuola Artigana di Cantu, 1932. **Awards:** Premio Internazionale, La Sarraz, Switzerland, 1937; Grande Medaglio d'Oro ad Artifice Italiano, Comune di Milano, 1958; Gold Medal, Prague, 1959; Gold Medal, Munich, 1964; Rembrandt Prize, Hamburg, 1974; Premio Diano Marina, 1975; Premio Biancamano, 1977; Premio Feltrinelli dell'Accademia dei Lincei, 1978. **Address:** Corso Magenta 66–20123 Milan, Italy.

Individual Exhibitions:

1935 Galleria del Milione, Milan
1956 Galleria Annunciata, Milan
1967 Galleria Toninelli, Milan
Galleria Notizie, Turin
Palazzo del Comune, Reggio Emilia, Italy

1968 Galleria II Segno, Rome
Palazzo dei Diamanti, Ferrara, Italy
Galleria Notizie, Turin
1969 Galleria dell'Ariete, Milan
1971 Galleria Martano, Turin
Galleria Galatea, Turin
Museum am Ostwall, Dortmund, West Germany
Galleria dell'Ariete, Milan
1972 Galleria Civica d'Arte Moderna, Turin
Galleria Galatea, Turin
1973 Galleria Il Segno, Rome
Galerie Marlborough, Zurich (travelled to Marlborough Galleria d'Arte, Rome and Marlborough Fine Art, London)
1974 Galleria St. Luca Bologna, Italy
Galleria Il Sole, Bolzano, Italy
Galleria Morone, Milan
Galleria Atena, Meda, Italy
1975 Galerie Schmela, Dusseldorf
Galleria La Piramide, Florence
Centro Rizzoli, Milan
Galleria dell'Oca, Rome
Galleria Beniamino, San Remo, Italy
Galleria La Parisina, Turin
Galleria Martini e Ronchetti, Genoa
1976 Galleria Rotta, Genoa
Palazzo della Pilotta, Parma
Galleria Editalia, Rome
Galleria 3A, Turin
1977 Castello del Buonconsiglio, Trento, Italy
Galleria Il Gabbiano, La Spezia, Italy
Graphica Club, Milan
1978 Galleria Duchamp, Cagliari, Italy
Galleria Morone 6, Milan
Galleria Niccoli, Parma
1979 Galeria A 2, Rome
Galleria Il Nome, Vigevano, Italy
Galleria Pero, Milan
Palazzo Reale, Milan
1980 Westend Galerie, Frankfurt
Galerie Wintersberger, Cologne
L'Uomo e l'Arte, Biella, Italy
Villa Cicogna, Bologna San Lazzaro, Italy
1981 Musée des Beaux-Arts, La Chaux de Fonds, Switzerland (travelled to the Galerie Lopez, Zurich)
Il Mercante di Stampe, Milan
Forte di Belvedere, Florence
1982 Galleria Il Millennio, Rome
Galleria Martano, Turin
1983 Galleria Nazionale d'Arte Moderna, Rome
Galleria Pancheri, Rovereto, Italy
1985 Gallerie dell'Accademia, Venice
Westend Galerie, Frankfurt
1987 Padiglione d'Arte Contemporanea, Milan
1990 *Fausto Melotti,* Museo Cantonale d'Arte, Lugano, Switzerland
Fausto Melotti, Palazzo Fortuni, Milan
1994 *Fausto Melotti: Anti-sculpture,* Paolo Baldacci Gallery, New York
Melotti, IVAM Centre Julio Gonzalez, Valencia, Spain
1997 *Fausto Melotti: Teatrini 1931–1985,* Galleria dello Scudo, Verona
2000 Lawrence Rubin, New York

Selected Group Exhibitions:

1930 *Triennal,* Milan
1935 *Gruppo del Milione,* Galleria del Milione, Milan
1943 *Quadriennale,* Rome
Biennale, Venice (and 1966)
1963 *Aspetti dell'Arte contemporanea,* Castello Cinquecentesco, L'Aquila, Italy
1969 *Aspetti del Primo Astratismo Italiano,* Galleria Civica d'Arte Moderna, Monza, Italy
1971 *Konkrete Kunst,* Westfälischer Kunstverein, Münster, West Germany
1973 *Sculpture Italienne contemporanée,* Musée Royal d'Art et d'Histoire, Brussels
1977 *Gli Ultimi 15 Anni d'Arte in Italia,* Galleria Civica d'Arte Moderna, Turin
1980 *Anni Creativi al Milione, 1932–1939,* Palazzo Novellucci, Prato, Italy
1990 *Sculpture in Milan 1945–1990,* Stadtische Kunsthalle, Mannheim, Germany; Kunsthalle, Darmstadt, Germany
1991 *The World of Carlo Belli: Italy in the 1930s—Artistic Culture,* Museo d'Arte Moderna e Contemporanea di Trento e Rovereto, Trento, Italy
1997 *Annees 30 en Europe: Le Temps Menacant,* Musee d'Art Moderne de la Ville de Paris, Paris

Publications:

By MELOTTI: Books—*Il triste minotauro,* Milan 1944; *Progetting di Melotti,* with Carlo Belli, Turin 1970; *Linée,* 1974; *Linée: Secondo quaderno,* 1978. **Articles—**''Idee sull'insegnamento artistico'' in *Bolletino della Galleria del Milione* (Milan), June 1934; ''L'arte e stato d'animo angelico geometrico'' in *Bollentino della Galleria del Milione* (Milan), May 1935; ''Sculture astratte del 35 e 65'' in *Domus* (Milan), July 1962; ''Cesar: Sculture e disegni'' in *Domus* (Milan), September 1962; ''Un gioco che, quando nesce, e poesia'' in *Sculture Astratte,* Milan 1962; ''Incertezza'' in *Domus,* (Milan), March 1963; ''Testimonianza'' in *Homage to Gino Ghiringhelli,* exhibition catalog by Zeno Birolli, Milan 1964, reprinted in *Domus* (Milan), May 1965; ''Bacon'' in *Domus* (Milan), May 1966; ''Un gioco che, quando riesce, e poesia'' in *Sculture Astratte,* (Milan) 1967; letter in *Experienze dell'astrattismo italiano,* exhibition catalog, Turin 1968; ''Foglietti'' in *Lo spazio inquieto,* edited by P. Fossati, Turin 1971; ''L'arte e fenomeno dello spirito'' in *Fausto Melotti,* exhibition catalog, Milan 1971; ''The Consolation of Poetry'' in *Arte Milano* (Milan), May 1972; ''Fausto Melotti'' in *Flash Art* (Milan), May/July 1972.

On MELOTTI: Books—*Melotti,* exhibition catalog by Carlo Belli, Rome 1968; *Melotti: Sculture, disegnie pitture 1933–1968* by Carlo Belli, Reggio Emilia, Italy 1968; *Fausto Melotti,* exhibition catalog by Renato Barilli, Turin 1971; *Progetti di Melotti, 1932–36,* by Maurizio Fagioli, Turin 1971; *Fausto Melotti,* exhibition catalog by Zeno Birolli and Aldo Passoni, Turin 1972; *Melotti* by A. M. Hammacher, Milan 1975; *Fausto Melotti* by Maurizio Calvesi, Parma 1976; *Fausto Melotti,* exhibition catalog by Carlo Belli, Rome 1976;

Melotti: Fedele al fantasma by Gabriella Drudi, Rome and Milan 1979; *Fausto Melotti,* exhibition catalog by Carlo Pirovano and Erich Steingraber, Milan 1979; *Melotti,* exhibition catalog by A. M. Hammacher and Vanni Bramanti, Florence 1981; *Melotti; Ottantotto Disegni* by Carlo Pirovano, Florence 1981; *Fausto Melotti,* exhibition catalog with texts by Mercedes Barberi and Giovanni Carandente, Milan 1987; *Fausto Melotti,* exhibition catalog, with text by Germano Celant, Milan 1990; *Fausto Melotti,* exhibition catalog, Lugano 1990; *Melotti,* exhibition catalog with introduction by J.F. Yvars, Valencia 1994; *Fausto Melotti: Anti-sculpture,* exhibition catalog, New York 1994; *Fausto Melotti: Teatrini 1931–1985,* exhibition catalog, Verona 1996; *Fausto Melotti: Segno, Musica e poesia* by Alberto Fiz, Milan, 2000. **Articles—**''The Enchanted Lyricist'' by Jole de Sanna in *Artforum* (New York), May 1990; ''Who Are the Most Underrated and Overrated Artists?'' by Paul Gardner in *ARTnews,* vol. 93, no. 2, February 1994; ''Fausto Melotti at Paolo Baldacci'' by Raphael Rubinstein in *Art in America* (New York), vol. 83, no. 3, March 1995.

* * *

In front of one of Fausto Melotti's ''Anti-Sculptures'' one thinks of music by Mozart or of a Paul Klee who, instead of canvas, discovered thread, scraps of metal and shreds of material. For they are created out of poor material and out of the most expensive substances by an imagination which restricts itself to essentials in form and so returns to the happiness and significance of the world of childhood. Weightless, delicate metal creations which like musical notations make things heard visually perceptible. Fables made from thread with a coloured spot of material, very cheerful and very serious stories mostly full of irony. His terracottas called ''Teatrini,'' reminders of Etruscan house urns, conjure up metaphysical ideas behind a magical reality, as do the rare pictures and graphic works which survived the bombardment of Milan in 1943.

In 1974 in Hamburg, when the then-73-year-old Fausto Melotti was honored with the Rembrandt prize, the donor A. Toepfer asked why this poet and musician was not greatly renowned among the sculptors of his native land. The answer was that he had indeed been well known for 40 years but that at his first exhibition in 1935 at the Milan Galleria del Millione, Carlo Carra had commented: ''It is intelligent, but it is not sculpture.''

Melotti was, like all his contemporaries, influenced by the Bauhaus and Constructivism, then silenced by fascism because such influences did not fit into any of the conventional rhetorical schemes. He remained silent far into the postwar era and devoted himself, frequently distinguished by the *Triennale,* to ceramics, which he did not like. ''Because there is always a little cheating in it and one never knows what the result will be. For the management above controls the fire.''

On his 70th birthday Gillo Dorfles toasted him as the ''youngest and most mature sculptor of Italy''; Maurizio Calvesi called him ''the most consistent interpreter of the independence of the avant-garde, which also means independence from the gravity and rhetoric of sculpture.'' Franco Russoli, the now deceased director of Milan's Brera, wrote in 1975: ''this fundamental poetic independence is the great moral and aesthetic quality which makes Melotti's art into one of the most supreme and genuine testimonies of the European cultural tradition.'' But Melotti is his own quietest and best interpreter. In 1935 he noted in his diary: ''Art is an angelic geometric spiritual condition. It makes use of the intellect, not the senses.'' Another time he spoke of ''the game which, when it succeeds, becomes poetry.''

In his long life Fausto Melotti's game has often been successful.

—Monika von Zitzewitz

MELZL, Stephan

Nationality: Swiss. **Born:** Basel, Switzerland, 1959. **Education:** School of Arts and Crafts, Basel, 1980; Academy of Visual Arts, Städelschule, Frankfurt/Main, 1981–86. **Career:** Teacher of nude drawing, Academy of Visual Arts, Städelschule, Frankfurt/Main, 1986—. **Awards:** Hessische Kulturstiftung Grant, 1994; Franfurter Künstlerhilfe Grant, 1995; Künstlerhaus Schloß Balmoral Grant, Bad Ems, 1996; Hessische Kultur GmbH Grant, 1997. **Agent:** Galerie Martina Detterer, Hanauer Landstrasse 20–22, 60314 Frankfurt/Main, Germany. **Address:** Schwanthalerstrasse 42, 60596 Frankfurt/Main, Germany.

Selected Individual Exhibitions:

1990 Forum Sparkasse, Frankfurt
1993 Galerie Martina Detterer, Frankfurt
1995 Galérie Gilles Peyroulet, Paris (with Max Mohr)
1996 Albrecht Dürer Gesellschaft/Der Nürnberger Kunstverein, Germany
1997 Galerie Martina Detterer, Frankfurt/Main
1999 Galerie Martina Detterer, Frankfurt/Main
2000 Galerie Lindig in Paludetto, Nürnberg, Germany
2001 Galerie Thomas Rehbein, Cologne, Germany

Selected Group Exhibitions:

1987–88 *Forum Junger Kunst,* Kunsthalle Baden-Baden (travelled to Württembergischer Kunstverein, Stuttgart)
1992 *Foregrounds and Distances,* Galleria dei Serpenti, Rome
1993–94 Galerie Jousse Seguin, Paris
1994 Kunsthalle Palazzo, Liestal, Switzerland (catalog)
Szenenwechsel VI, Museum für Moderne Kunst, Frankfurt
1995 *Hortus Conclusus,* Museum für Moderne Kunst, Frankfurt
1996 *Pittura,* Castello di Rivara, Italy (catalog)
Views from Abroad, Museum für Moderne Kunst, Frankfurt (travelled to Whitney Museum, New York) (catalog)
1997 *Augenzeugen,* Kunstmuseum Düsseldorf im Ehrenhof, Germany
1998 *DACH,* Galerie Krinzinger im Bengerpark, Bregenz, Vienna (catalog)
1999 *No.site.specific,* Mellow Birds, London

Collections:

Museum für Moderne Kunst, Frankfurt/Main; Städelsches Kunstinstitut, Frankfurt/Main; Kunstmuseum Basel, Switzerland; Kanton Basel, Switzerland.

Publications:

On MELZL: Books—*Stephan Melzl,* museum catalog with text by Jean-Christophe Ammann and Rudolf Schmitz, Frankfurt 1996;

Painting by Stephan Melzl, 2000. ©Stephan Melzl.

Stepahn Melzl, catalog with text by Klaus Görner, Bad Ems, Germany 1997.

MEREDITH, John

Nationality: Canadian. **Born:** Fergus, Ontario, 24 July 1933. **Education:** Brampton High School, Ontario; studied under J. W. G. Macdonald, Ontario College of Art, Toronto, 1950–53. **Family:** Married Kyoko Hyaski in 1975. **Career:** Independent painter, Toronto, since 1953. **Died:** Of pneumonia, Toronto, Canada, 9 September 2000.

Individual Exhibitions:

1958 Gallery of Contemporary Art, Toronto
1959 Gallery of Contemporary Art, Toronto
1961 Isaacs Gallery, Toronto
1963 Isaacs Gallery, Toronto
1965 Isaacs Gallery, Toronto
Blue Fern Gallery, Ottawa
1967 Isaacs Gallery, Toronto
Wieland/Meredith, National Gallery of Canada, Ottawa
1973 Isaacs Gallery, Toronto
1974 *John Meredith: 15 Years,* Art Gallery of Ontario, Toronto (toured Canada)
1977 Isaacs Gallery, Toronto
1980 *John Meredith: Drawings, 1957–1980,* Art Gallery of Greater Victoria
Isaacs Gallery, Toronto
1981 Isaacs Gallery, Toronto
1983 Isaacs Gallery, Toronto
1986 Region of Peel Art Gallery, Brampton, Ontario
1987 Isaacs Gallery, Toronto

Selected Group Exhibitions:

1965 *Biennal de Paris*
1967 Painting in Canada, Canadian Government Pavilion, at *Expo '67,* Montreal
International Black and White Exhibition, Lugano, Switzerland
1968 *Canada: Art d'Aujourd'hui,* Musee National d'Art Moderne, Paris
9 Canadians, Institute of Contemporary Art, Boston
1970 *8 Artists from Canada,* Tel Aviv Museum
1972 *Toronto Painting 1953–1965,* National Gallery of Canada, Ottawa
1976 *Abstractions,* Province of Ontario Exhibition, at the *Olympic Games,* Montreal
1978 *Modern Painting in Canada,* Edmonton Art Gallery
1981 *Linear Variables,* Winnipeg Art Gallery, Manitoba
1988 *Contemporary Canadian Works on Paper,* Concordia Art Gallery, Montreal (catalog)

Collections:

Art Gallery of Greater Victoria; Art Gallery of Ontario, Toronto; Department of External Affairs, Ottawa; Museum of Fine Arts, Montreal; National Gallery of Canada, Ottawa; Toronto Dominion Bank; Vancouver Art Gallery; Winnipeg Art Gallery; Museum of Modern Art, New York; Philadelphia Museum of Art.

Publications:

On MEREDITH: Books—*Contemporary Canadian Painting* by William Withrow, Toronto 1972; *A Concise History of Canadian Painting* by Denis Reid, Toronto 1973; *John Meredith: 15 years,* exhibition catalog by Marnie Fleming, Toronto 1974. **Articles—** ''John Meredith: Painter'' by Barry Lord in *Artscanada* (Toronto), April 1969; ''The John Meredith Poems Untitled'' by Barry Callaghan in *Exile* (Downsview, Ontario), June 1973; ''William Ronald and John Meredith'' by Robert Fulford in *National Post* (Don Mills, Ontario), 19 September 2000.

* * *

For the last decade John Meredith has been one of the important, ''big attack'' painters on the Canadian scene. His ''landscapes of the mind'' have always been distinguished in the Toronto school by their use of line and deft handling of colour. Meredith was a ''painter's painter.'' Younger members of the Toronto scene speak of him as the one they admire.

Painting for Meredith was a way of encompassing what he called ''the great mystery.'' In his early work, he explored flattened vertical bands of central images within a linear framework, sometimes with a semifigurative reference, in a shallow spatial depth. In 1964, he began to smudge the still wet lines in the paintings for a more lyrical, electrifying effect. At the same time his colour became higher in key.

Since 1966 (as in the Art Gallery of Ontario's ''Seeker''), Meredith had been trying to transfer the spontaneous quality of his sketches to his canvases. Now in his work the sketch is more than ever a starting point. He took liberties with it, transforming its vivacious qualities into a vigorous, broadly handled whole. These paintings, done very directly, recall fresh and exuberant watercolours. Big areas of cheerful, bustling colour predominate. But Meredith's idiosyncratic calligraphy, with its touch of Oriental influence, still shows up in works like ''Black and White Painting, May 1979.''

Meredith's later work turned a sharp corner. He painted the female nude standing, reclining, or floating using his smudged black line and glowing colour effect.

—Joan Murray

MERKIN, Richard (Marshall)

Nationality: American. **Born:** Brooklyn, New York, 9 October 1938. **Education:** Attended New York City public schools, 1943–53; Erasmus Hall High School, Brooklyn, 1953–56; Syracuse University, New York, 1956–60, B.F.A. 1960. **Family:** Married in 1960 (divorced, 1963). **Career:** Worked as a department store stockperson, in a bindery, as a clothing salesperson, and as a chauffeur, 1953–60; Michigan State University, East Lansing, graduate assistant, 1960–61; Rhode Island School of Design, Providence, teaching fellow, 1961–63, assistant professor of painting, 1963–70, and adjunct professor, since 1970. Visiting artist-in-residence, Syracuse University, New York, 1972; contributing editor, *Vanity Fair,* since 1986. **Awards:** Purchase Prize, *Printmaker's Show,* Washington, D.C., 1962; Louis Comfort Tiffany Foundation Fellowship, 1962–63; Richard and Hinda Rosenthal Foundation Award, National Institute of Arts and Letters, 1975. **Agent:** Helander Gallery, Palm Beach, Florida. **Address:** 500 West End Avenue, Apartment 12D, New York, New York 10024, U.S.A.

Individual Exhibitions:

1965 Obelisk Gallery, Boston
1967 Byron Gallery, New York
1968 Obelisk Gallery, Boston (with James Melchert)
1969 Hayden Art Gallery, Massachusetts Institute of Technology, Cambridge
Obelisk Gallery, Boston
1971 Obelisk Gallery, Boston
Galleria dell'Ariete, Milan
1972 Woods-Gerry Gallery, Rhode Island School of Design, Providence (with Seaver Leslie)
1973 Terry Dintenfass Gallery, New York
1974 Terry Dintenfass Gallery, New York
1975 Harcus, Krakow, Rosen, Sonnabend Gallery, Boston
1976 Anhalt Barnes Gallery, Los Angeles
Kingpitcher Gallery, Pittsburgh
1977 Newport Art Association, Newport, Rhode Island
1978 Terry Dintenfass Gallery, New York
Johnson Museum, Middlebury College, Vermont
1979 Gallery Camino Real, Boca Raton, Florida
1980 Chrysler Museum, Norfolk, Virginia
Terry Dintenfass Gallery, New York
Central Falls Gallery, New York
1981 Gallery Camino Real, Boca Raton, Florida
Eric Makler Gallery, Philadelphia
Terry Dintenfass Gallery, New York
1982 Marilyn Butler Gallery, Scottsdale, Arizona
Karen Lennox Gallery, Chicago
Reynolds Minor Gallery, Richmond, Virginia
Lily Iselin Gallery, Providence, Rhode Island
1983 Central Falls Gallery, New York
Eric Makler Gallery, Philadelphia
1984 Terry Dintenfass Gallery, New York
Susan Montezinos Gallery, Philadelphia
Galleria Giulia, Rome
1985 Joe and Emily Lowe Art Gallery, Syracuse University, New York
1986 Terry Dintenfass Gallery, New York
Gallery Camino Real, Boca Raton, Florida
1987 Central Falls Gallery, New York
Helander Gallery, Palm Beach
Foster-White Gallery, Seattle
1988 JRS Fine Art, Providence, Rhode Island
1989 Helander Gallery, Palm Beach
1990 Helander Gallery, Palm Beach
Jon Oulman Gallery, Minneapolis
1992 Helander Gallery, Palm Beach
Bentley-Tomlinson Gallery, Scottsdale, Arizona

Selected Group Exhibitions:

1964 *Paintings on Paper,* DeCordova Museum, Lincoln, Massachusetts
1965 *New England Contemporary Artists,* Northeastern University, Boston
Art '65—Lesser Known and Unknown Painters and Sculptors, New York World's Fair, Flushing
1969 *Annual Exhibition,* Whitney Museum, New York
1970 *American Painting, 1970,* Virginia Museum, Richmond
1974 *20th Annual Drawing and Small Sculpture Show,* Ball State University Art Gallery, Muncie, Indiana
Summer Exhibition, Royal Academy of Art, London
1976 *Painting and Sculpture Today,* Indianapolis Museum of Art, Indiana
1979 *Alumni Artists Exhibition,* Syracuse University, New York
1983 *Fiac '83,* Paris
1987 *The Grand Game of Baseball,* Museum of the Borough of Brooklyn, New York
Modern American Realism, National Museum of American Art, Washington, D.C.
1990 *New Work/New York,* Helander Gallery, Palm Beach (travelled to New York)

1991 *Tenth Anniversary Show,* Helander Gallery, Palm Beach

Collections:

American Federation of Arts, New York; Museum of Modern Art, New York; Whitney Museum of American Art, New York; Smithsonian Institution, Washington, D.C.; Pennsylvania Academy of the Arts, Philadelphia; Minnesota Museum of Art, Minneapolis; Rose Art Museum, Brandeis University, Waltham, Massachusetts; Museum of Art, Rhode Island School of Design, Providence; Massachusetts Institute of Technology, Cambridge; Fisk University Art Gallery, Nashville, Tennessee; Miami-Dade Junior College, Florida; Michigan State University, Lansing; First National City Bank, Chicago; Hallmark Collection, Kansas City, Missouri.

Permanent Public Installations:

Blackstone School, Boston, 1975–76.

Publications:

By MERKIN: Books—*On Art and Perfume; or, Did Mondrian Use Masking Tape?,* catalog, Cambridge, Massachusetts 1969; *Velvet Eden,* photo collection, New York 1979.

On MERKIN: Books—*The Grand Game of Baseball,* exhibition book, Brooklyn, New York 1987; *Diamonds Are Forever,* exhibition book, Albany, New York 1987; *This Face You Got: The Art of the Illustrator* by Jim McMullan, Boston 1994.

*

John Gregory Dunne, the novelist, once said, ''I think you write to find out what you think.'' At the risk of not sounding particularly original, and perhaps a bit glib, I think that it is fair to say that I paint, I make pictures, to see what I saw.

—Richard Merkin

* * *

You can almost see him strutting the boulevard, bedecked and bejewelled as to fit the scenery. He pauses briefly to straighten his tie, smooth his hair, glance side to side with a casual indifference about the city. But the ambition in his inner eye is alarmingly steadfast; the smallest details of the scenery imbued with a life of their own call to him: a Turkish cigarette, a glove, a capped-toe shoe, a walking stick (and no artist has ever had a more exquisite eye for cigarettes, gloves, shoes, and walking sticks), not to mention tennis collars and boutonnieres. Such details become a discreet element of design.

Richard Merkin is one of the few outstanding colorists and designers who exploits the energy and the dazzle of the boulevard, the city, the high-life, and the low-life in his work. Rising out of the sixties, he employed his wholly maverick qualities to a technique polished by Rabelaisian and Gautierian mannerisms. The blocks of color in his brilliant pastels remain flat and yet are built up with a depth and chromatic density that defies every conventional notion of the medium. To create this effect, his pastels are custom-made with an extraordinary proportion of pigment.

Merkin takes great splendor in lushness. His paintings radiate with a warmth and opulence that is not easily found in modern art. Splashed with macaw greens, flamingo pinks, scuba blues, and mimosa magentas, his is a palette bursting with a tropical *joie de vivre.* During a period in which modern art needs to be solved like riddles or deciphered like puzzles, Merkin remains loud, direct, disinterested in nostalgia or in a readily translatable language of symbols. In this respect he is a colorist in the tradition of French modernism—excluding anything but the barest formal statement. With such wit and simplicity, he hardly has the right to be called an artist when the ideal of the modern art world is both solemn and non-rational.

In ''Cafe Megalomania'' Merkin again emerges as the ''boulevardier,'' tipping his hat, as he loves to do, to the wits and antics of kings of yesterday, in this case to satiric German artists George Grosz and Edouard Thöny. His spirit is with Henry Lamb, or perhaps Andy Warhol—artists who repeat the images of daily life, images that appear on the streets and on the breakfast table in newspapers. Repetition both celebrates and devalues. How large a gap do we habitually make between the image offered by a work of art and the real-life thing to which it refers? Such a question is at the center of Merkin's work.

—Carrie Barker

MERZ, Mario

Nationality: Italian. **Born:** Milan in 1925. **Family:** Married to the artist Marisa Merz. **Career:** Independent artist, now living in Turin. **Agents:** Galleria Christian Stein, Piazza San Carlo 206, 10121 Turin; and Sperone Westwater, 142 Greene Street, New York, New York 10012, U.S.A. **Address:** Corso Tassoni 56, 10122 Turin, Italy.

Individual Exhibitions:

1953 Galleria Bussola, Turin
1956 Galleria del Milione, Milan
1962 Galleria Notizie, Turin
1967 Gian Enzo Sperone, Turin
1968 Gian Enzo Sperone, Turin
1969 Gian Enzo Sperone, Turin
Galleria l'Attico, Rome
Galerie Sonnabend, Paris
1970 Galerie Konrad Fischer, Dusseldorf
Sonnabend Gallery, New York
Galleria Francois Lambert, Milan
1971 Gian Enzo Sperone, Turin
Sonnabend Gallery, New York
John Weber Gallery, New York
1972 Walker Art Center, Minneapolis
Jack Wendler Gallery, London
1974 Haus am Lutzowplatz, Berlin
Cassino Ova, Tortona, Italy
Galleria Area, Florence
1975 Kunsthalle, Basel
1976 Galleria Mario Pieroni, Pescara, Italy
Villa Pignatelli, Naples

Gian Enzo Sperone, Rome
Gian Enzo Sperone, Turin
Galleria Tucci Russo, Turin
Galerie Annemarie Verna, Zurich
Galerie Konrad Fischer, Dusseldorf
1977 Galleria Salvatore Ala, Milan
Galerie Annemarie Verna, Zurich
1978 Galerie Jean and Karen Bernier, Athens
Galleria Lucio Amelio, Naples
Galleria dell'Oca, Rome
Galleria Tucci Russo, Turin
1979 Museum Folkwang, Essen
Sperone Westwater Fischer, New York
Institute of Modern Art, Brisbane, Autralia
Galerie Durand-Dessert, Paris
Galerie Annemarie Verna, Zurich
Galleria Franco Toselli, Milan
Galleria Giuliana de Crescenzo, Rome
1980 Whitechapel Art Gallery, London
Galleria Christian Stein, Turin
Stedelijk van Abbemuseum, Eindhoven, Netherlands
Galerie Albert Baronian, Brussels
Sperone Westwater Fischer, New York
Gian Enzo Sperone, Turin
Galleria Salvatore Alan, Milan
1981 Konrad Fischer, Dusseldorf
Musée d'Art Moderne de la Ville, Paris
Kunsthalle, Basel
Galerie Studio, Warsaw
Konrad Fischer, Zurich
Galleria Tucci Russo, Turin
Galleria Christian Stein, Turin
Joslyn Art Museum, Omaha, Nebraska
Galleria Franco Toselli, Florence
Galleria Lucio Amelio, Naples
1982 Sperone Westwater Fischer, New York
Ackland Art Museum, Chapel Hill, North Carolina
Galleria Mario Diacono, Rome
Galerie Munro, Hamburg
Galleria Marilena Bonomo, Bari, Italy
Galleria Salvatore Ala, Milan
Museum Folkwang, Essen, West Germany
Staatsgalerie, Stuttgart
Galleria d'Arte Moderna, Bologna, Italy
Kestner-Gesellschaft, Hannover
1983 Anthony d'Offay Gallery, London
Flow Ace Gallery, Venice, California
Israel Museum, Jerusalem
Galleria Pieroni, Rome
Neuberger Museum, Purchase, New York
Moderna Museet, Stockholm
Galerie Nachst St. Stephan, Vienna
Palazzo Congressi ed Esposizioni, Republic of San Marino
Galerie Buchmann, Basel
1984 Galerie Konrad Fischer, Dusseldorf
Albright-Knox Art Gallery, Buffalo, New York
Hallwalls, Buffalo, New York
Institute of Contemporary Art, Boston
Galerie Sparta, Chagny, France
Galeria Christian Stein, Turin
Musée Toulouse-Lautrec, Albi, France
Kunstverein, St. Gallen, Switzerland
Sperone Westwater, New York
1985 Galerie Nachst St. Stephan, Vienna
Galleria Christian Stein, Turin
Kunsthaus, Zurich
Galerie Durand-Dessert, Paris
Galerie Munro, Hamburg
Sperone Westwater/Leo Castelli Gallery, New York
Musée d'Art et d'Industrie, Geneva
Westfälischer Kunstverein, Munster, West Germany
Galerie Pietro Sparto/Pascale Petit, Chagny, France
1986 Galleria Antonio Tucci Russo, Turin
1987 CAPC/Musée d'Art Contemporain, Bordeaux, France
Galleria Toselli, Milan
Chapelle de la Salpetriere, Paris
Galerie Konrad Fischer, Dusseldorf
Kunstverein, Munich
Musée d'Art Contemporain, Montreal
1988 Anthony d'Offay Gallery, London
1994 Barbara Gladstone Gallery, New York
1996 Anthony d'Offay Gallery, London
1998 Galerie Konrad Fischer, Düsseldorf
1999 Christian Stein Gallery, Milan
Fundaçao Serralves, Portugal (catalog)
2000 Fondazione Antonio Ratti, Como, Italy

Selected Group Exhibitions:

1961 *International Art Exhibition,* Galleria Kaspers, Lausanne
1967 *Contemplazione,* Galleria Sperone/Galleria Stein, Turin
1969 *When Attitudes Become Form,* Kunsthalle, Bern (toured Europe)
1972 *Documenta 5,* Kassel, West Germany (and *Documenta 6, 1977; Documenta 7, 1982)*
1977 *Europe in the Seventies,* Art Institute of Chicago (travelled to Washington, D.C.; San Francisco; Fort Worth, Texas; Cincinnati, Ohio)
1979 *Third Biennale of Sydney,* Art Gallery of New South Wales, Sydney (travelled to Brisbane)
1981 *Identité Italienne: L'Art en Italie depuis 1959,* Centre Georges Pompidou, Paris
1983 *Arte a Torino 1946–53,* Accademia Albertina di Belle Arti, Turin
1985 *Transformation in Sculpture,* Guggenheim Museum, New York
1987 *Turin 1965–87: Arte Povera,* Musée d'Art et d'Histoire, Chambery, France (travelled to Lille)
1991 *Visionare Schweiz,* Kunsthalle, Zurich, and Stadtische Kunsthalle, Düsseldorf
Recent Acquisitions: 1989–1991, Hirshhorn Museum and Sculpture Garden, Washington, D.C.
1993 Venice Biennale, Italy
1994 *The Italian Metamorphosis, 1943–1968,* Guggenheim Museum, New York
1996 *Passion Privée,* Musée d'Art Moderne, Paris
1998 *100 Years of Sculpture: From the Pedestal to the Pixel,* Walker Art Center, Minneapolis

2001 *Zero to Infinity: Arte Povera 1962–1972,* Walker Art Center, Minneapolis

Collections:

Galleria d'Arte Moderna, Turin; Stedelijk Museum, Amsterdam; Kaiser Wilhelm Museum, Krefeld, Germany.

Publications:

By MERZ: Books—*Fibonacci 1202-Mario Merz, 1970,* edited by Germano Celant and Pierluigi Pero, Turin 1970; *Fibonacci 1202-Mario Merz 1972,* edited by Pierluigi Pero, Turin 1972; *It Is as Possible to Have a Space with Tables for 88 People as it Is Possible to Have a Space with Tables for No-One: Tables from Drawings of Mario Merz,* New York 1974; *Tavole con le zampe diventano tavoli: Cascina ova, tortona,* Milan 1974; *La frutta e qui. . . ,* edited by Lucio Amelio, Naples 1976. **Articles**—interview with Richard Koshalek, in *Art and Artists* (London), June 1972; interview, with M. Haerditerin, in *Mario Merz,* exhibition catalog, Berlin 1974; ''Limmaginazione vivente e in movimento continuo'' in *Mario Merz,* exhibition catalog, Berlin 1974; ''Annahern: Statistiche Zeichnungen an Dynamische. . .'' in *Projekt 74,* exhibition catalog, Cologne 1975; ''Texte 1970–1974'' in *Mario Merz,* exhibition catalog, Basel 1975; ''Una domenica lunghissima dura approssimativamente dal 1966 e ora siamo al 1976'' in *Citta di Riga I,* Rome 1977; ''La mancanza di iconografia e la nostra conquista o la nostra dammazione?'' in *Citta di Riga II,* Rome 1978; ''April 1980, May 1980'' in *Kunstforum International* (Mainz, West Germany), vol. 39, no. 3, 1980; ''Interview mit Mario Merz,'' with Jean-Christoph Ammann and Suzanne Page, in *Mario Merz,* exhibition catalog, Paris 1981; ''Project for Artforum'' in *Artforum* (New York), January 1985.

On MERZ: Books—*Arte Povera* by Germano Celant, Milan 1969; *Mario Merz,* exhibition catalog by Ruhrberg and Schmeid, Berlin 1974; *Mario Merz,* exhibition catalog, Essen 1979; *Mario Merz,* exhibition catalog, by Zdenek Felix, Essen 1982; *Mario Merz,* exhibition catalog with text by Carl Haenlin, Stockholm 1983; *Mario Merz,* exhibition catalog with texts by Germano Celant and others, San Marino 1983; *Arte Povera: The Knot* by Germano Celant, New York 1985; *Mario Merz,* Turin 1995; *Arte Povera* by Carolyn Christov-Bakargiev, London 1999; *Zero to Infinity: Arte Povera 1962–1972,* edited by Richard Flood and Frances Morris, Minneapolis 2001.

* * *

Mario Merz is an artist who works within and among contradictions, paradoxes, and dialectics. In his work one finds simultaneous expansion and contraction, natural and artificial materials, tradition and innovation. He began making his major work in the 1960s, a turbulent time in Italy as in the rest of the world. Becoming well-known as one of a group of Italian artists working and exhibiting together—loosely joined by critics under the name Arte Povera—Merz explored the spaces between contemporary life and historical patterns and precedents. Like most of these Italian artists, Merz shook off the weight of historical academicism—the traditions of and nostalgia for the Italy of antiquity and the Renaissance—replacing elegant and refined forms with primordial or pre-cultural gestures and modern technology and social politics.

We can see this technique working through the three major motifs in Merz's *oeuvre*: the igloo, the spiral, and the table, all of which are essential and enduring forms. The igloo corresponds to earlier nomadic times and basic systems. Often constructed of base materials such as lead, glass, or faggots of branches, these simple structures carry the energies of improvisation and invention. Sometimes the framework is combined with birds' nests and foodstuffs, and other times it is contrasted with neon lights. Interacting with his work always teaches one something fundamental about basic human needs, desires, and patterns.

Of central interest to Merz throughout his career has been the intuitive and acculturated working of systems, both ancient and contemporary. Finding the common structures and logics among orders which humans impose on and ''discover'' in the natural world can often teach us more about ourselves than about nature itself. In the early 13th century, the Italian mathematician Leonardo Fibonacci proposed a sequence of natural growth, based on his observations. This sequence, in which each number is the sum of the two preceding numbers, can be seen to correspond, like the spiral, to all patterns in nature: the number of seeds in fruit, petals on a flower, offspring of an animal, etc. Merz has used the fibonacci series in many of his works to allude to such intuitive systems of scientific observation, often contrasting their medieval origins with their continued relevance by ''writing'' them in neon sequences across gallery walls. The series is also compelling because of its implications towards the infinite. The sequence begins 1, 1, 2, 3, 5, 8, and theoretically continues on into infinity. The infinite alludes to the outer reaches of man's ability to control and interpret the world, the possibilities of both the future and the past, and the anticipation of new forms, materials, and beings.

Merz uses the system's endless refinements to build ideal structures that are synchronized with the natural needs of humankind, and which are infinitely modifiable within the system to absorb growth and reduction. In recent works, Merz combines many of these signature elements of his vocabulary to create a powerful tableau: an igloo with branches and schist gathered from his hometown, a spiral table covered in lead that begins/ends at a central table covered with bountiful fruits and vegetables, fragments of the fibonacci series floating overhead, a motorcycle signifying infinite acceleration that leaves a trail of fibonacci numbers accelerating in the opposite direction. In such complex works we find the expansion and contraction of the spiral, the juxtaposition of natural and artificial materials, and a suggestion of the universal human needs of home and shelter. The opposition of accelerating forces in the motorcycle and the neon fibonacci series questions the concept of progress in contemporary culture, the flux of abundance and famine, the interconnectedness of systems and natural forms and the critical balance of supply and demand in an increasingly global economy.

As the world marches into the ever more technological times of the 21st century, Mario Merz persists in seeking a symmetry between primordial forms and contemporary cultural structures. The Fibonacci series continues to inject a Dionysian progression of growth to oppose the Apollonian or hyper-rational systems of the cultural world. The expanding/contracting spirals and advancing/receding numbers challenge our sense of the continuity of time and space. In a 1999 exhibition at Fundçao Serralves, Portugal, Merz shakes the steady ground of classical architecture by inserting an igloo, a spiral table, basic animal forms, and a Fibonacci series into an archetypal modern house. The intervention of these primal forms and energies into a highly standardized architecture draws attention to the differences between the basic requirements for human shelter and the acculturated style and comforts of most dwellings.

—Elizabeth Mangini

MESSAGER, Annette

Nationality: French. **Born:** Berck, 30 November 1943. **Education:** Ecole Nationale Supérieure des Arts Décoratifs, Paris, 1962–66. **Career:** Independent artist, working with photography and painting. **Awards:** First Prize, *Kodak Photography International,* 1964. **Address:** Marian Goodman Gallery, 79, rue du Temple, 75003 Paris, France; 146 Boulevard Camelinat, 92240 Malakoff, France.

Individual Exhibitions:

1973 *Annette Messager Kunstlerin, Annette Messager Sammlerin,* Städtische Galerie im Lenbachhaus, Munich
Musée de Grenoble, France
Musée Rude, Dijon, France (with Boltanski and Le Gac)
Galerie Yellow Now, Liège, Belgium
1974 Galleria Diagramma, Milan
Galleri Daner, Copenhagen
Galleri St. Petri, Lund, Sweden
Musée d'Art Moderne de la Ville, Paris
1975 Galerie 't Venster, Rotterdam
Galerie Ecart, Geneva
Gallery of Contemporary Art, Zagreb
Gallery Space, Wiesbaden, West Germany
1976 Galleria Multimedia, Erbusco, Italy
Rheinisches Landesmuseum, Bonn
1977 Galerie Isy Brachot, Brussels
Galerie Seriaal, Amsterdam
1978 Holly Solomon Gallery, New York
Rheinisches Landesmuseum, Bonn
Galerie Voksal, Warsaw
1979 Galerie Gillespie-Laage, Paris
1980 Galerie Gillespie-Laage, Paris
St. Louis Art Museum
Galerie le Coin du Mur, Dijon, France
1981 University of California at Irvine
San Francisco Museum of Modern Art
P.S. 1, New York
Galerie Denise René-Hans Mayer, Dusseldorf
Artists' Space, New York
1982 Artists' Space, New York
1983 Galerie Gillespie-Laage-Salomon, Paris
Musée des Beaux-Arts, Calais, France
1984 ARC/Musée d'Art Moderne de la Ville, Paris
Galerie Grita Insam, Vienna
Elisabeth Kaufmann, Zurich
1985 Riverside Studios, Hammersmith
Galerie Gillespie-Laage-Salomon, Paris
1986 Galerie d'Art Contemporain, Nice
1987 Vancouver Art Gallery
Ministere de la Culture et de la Communication, Paris
Elisabeth Kaufmann, Zurich
1988 Galerie Laage-Salomon, Paris
Centre d'Art Contemporain, Dijon
Centre d'Art Contemporain de Castres
1989 *Annette Messager: Comédie-Tragédie de 1971–1989,* Musée de Peinture et de Sculpture, Grenoble
1990 Bonner Kunstverein, Bonn (travelled to Musée de la Roche sur Yon; and Kunstverein für die Rheinlande und Westfallen, Dusseldorf)
Contes d'été (with Christian Boltanski), Musée Départemental, Château de Rochechouart, Rochechouart
1991 *Faire des histoires/Making Up Stories,* Mercer Union, Toronto (travelled to Cold City Gallery, Toronto; Vancouver Art Gallery; and Contemporary Art Gallery, Vancouver)
1992 *Telling Tales,* Camden Arts Center, London (travelled to New York)
Salzburger Kunstverein-Kunstlerhaus, Salzburg
Monika Sprüth Galerie, Cologne
1993 Monika Sprüth Galerie, Cologne
Annette Messager—Faire Figures, FRAC Picardie, Amiens
Les Piques, Josh Baer Gallery, New York
1994 Elisabeth Kaufmann, Basel
1995 *Faire Parade* (retrospective) ARC/Musée d'Art Moderne de la Ville de Paris, Paris (travelled to The Museum of Modern Art, New York; Art Institute, Chicago; LACMA, Los Angeles) (catalog)
1997 *Dépendance/Indépendance,* Gagosian Gallery, New York
1999 *La procesion va por dentro,* Palacio de Velasquez—Museo Nacional Centro de Arte Reina Sofia, Madrid
2000 Monika Sprüth Gallery, Cologne
Marian Goodman Gallery, Paris

Selected Group Exhibitions:

1973 *Boltanski, Le Gac, Messager,* Biennale des Nuits de Bourgogne, Musée Rude, Dijon
1974 *Ils Collectionnent,* Musée des Arts Décoratifs, Paris
1975 *New Media,* Konsthall, Malmo Sweden
1976 *Les Boites,* Musée d'Art Moderne de la Ville, Paris (travelled to Maison de la Culture, Rennes, France)
1977 *Bookworks,* The Museum of Modern Art, New York
Documenta 6, Kassel
1978 *Biennale de Paris,* Musée d'Art Moderne de la Ville, Paris
1979 *Photography as Art,* Institute of Contemporary Arts, London
1980 *Works for Walls,* Cincinnati Art Center, Ohio
1981 *Szenen der Volkskunst,* Kunstverein, Stuttgart
1982 *Facons de Peindre,* Chalon-sur-Saône, France
1983 *New Art,* Tate Gallery, London
1984 *Biennale of Sydney,* Art Gallery of New South Wales, Sydney
1986 *Photography as Performance: Message through Object & Pictures,* The Photographers' Gallery, London
1987 *Les années 70, Les années mémoire,* Abbaye Saint-André, Centre d'Art Contemporain, Meymac
1989 *Histoire de Musée,* ARC/Musée d'Art Moderne de la Ville de Paris, Paris

1993 *Multiples Images: Photographs since 1965 from Collection,* MOMA, New York
1995 *Féminin/Masculin, le sexe de l'art,* Centre Georges Pompidou, Paris
Passions Privés, Musée d'Art Moderne de la Ville de Paris, Paris
1996 *Thinking Print,* Museum of Modern Art, New York
1997 *Unmapping the Earth,* The 2nd Kwangju Biennale, Korea
Deep Storage, Arsenal der Erinnerrung, Haus der Kunst, Münich; National Galerie, Berlin; Kunstmusem, Düsseldorf
1998 *Plaisir déplaisir,* CAPC, Musée d'Art Contemporain, Bordeaux
Mirror Images: Women, Surrealism, and Self-Representation, MIT List Visual Arts Center, Cambridge; Miami Art Museum
1999 *Private Eye, Crimes and Cases,* Haus am Waldsee, Berlin
2000 *Zeitwenden,* Kunstmuseum, Bonn
Ich ist etwas Anderes, Kunstsammlung, Düsseldorf
La Beauté, Palais des Papes, Avignon
Voilà, Musée d'Art Moderne de la Ville de Paris, Paris
L'Empire du Temps, mythes et créations, Musée du Louvre, Paris
Closer to One Another, Biennale de la Havane, La Havane
Partage d'exotisme, Biennale de Lyon, Lyon

Collections:

Centre Georges Pompidou, Paris; Musée d'Art Moderne de la Ville, Paris; Musée de Grenoble, France.

Publications:

By MESSAGER: Books—*Les Approches,* Hamburg 1973; *Mes cliches temoins,* Liège, Belgium 1974; *La Femme et. . . ,* Geneva 1975; *Mes jeux de main,* Zagreb 1975; *Le Bonheur illustre,* Bonn 1976; *Ma collection de proverbes,* Milan 1976; *Mes enluminures,* Dijon, 1988; *Mes Ouvrages,* Arles, 1989. **Articles**—''Dans l'intimite d'Annette Messager'' in *Chroniques de l'Art Vivant* (Paris), February 1974; ''Annette Messager,'' interview with Barbara Radice, in *Flash Art* (Milan), June 1974; ''Ma collection d'expressions et d'attitudes diverses'' in *Chorus* (Paris), no. 12, 1975; ''Annette Messager,'' interview with Aline Dallier, in *Les Cahiers du Griff* (Brussels), May 1976.

On MESSAGER: Books—*Annette Messager Kunstlerin, Annette Messager Sammlerin,* exhibition catalog with text by Armin Zweite, Munich 1973; *Annette Messager,* exhibition catalog with text by Gosse Oosterhof, Rotterdam 1975; *Modellbilder,* exhibition catalog with text by Klaus Honnef, Stuttgart 1976; *Identité/Identifications,* exhibition catalog with text by Jacques Clayssen, Bordeaux 1977; *Annette Messager,* exhibition catalog with text by Suzanne Pagé, Paris 1984; *Anonymity and Identity,* Richmond, Virginia 1993; *L'envers des choses,* Paris 1993; *D'approche* edited by Jean-Dominique Carré, Archives-Librairie, Paris 1995; *Nos témoignages* by Hans Ulrich Obrist, Stuttgart 1995; *Annette Messager, Penetrations: A Survey of Recent Sculptures and Installations* edited by Ealan Wingate, New York 1997. **Articles**—''Annette Messager: Los Angeles County Museum of Art'' by Amy Gerstler in *Artforum,* vol. 34, no. 2, October 1995; ''Life Stilled: From Norman Bates to Annette Messager, Taxidermy for a Reason'' by Lisa Wainwright in *New Art Examiner,* vol. 23, no. 9, May 1996; ''Annette Messager'' by Virginia Pitts Rembert in *Woman's Art Journal,* Fall 1996-Winter 1997; ''Annette Messager: Gagosian Gallery'' by Kristin M Jones in *Artforum,* vol. 35, no. 9, May 1997; ''Annette Messager'' by Tami Katz-Freiman in *Art Papers,* vol. 22, no. 2, March-April 1998; ''Body Malaise: Annette Messager's Anatomical Theater'' by Elisabeth Bronfen in *Parkett,* no. 59, 2000.

*

As time goes by I feel less like talking about my work.

''My work,'' words that evoke research and effort, when actually I would like so much to have a light, mobile and flexible activity (and also go back and see all of Hitchcock's films; yes, I would like to be the ''Hitchcock of painting"!).

I am an artist who would like to reconcile painting and photography—these two opposed media that hate each other, are jealous of one another or ignore each other. . . a rocky marriage. So, for this union, the two media must ''explode.'' Photography must come out of its usual form, out of its small format anecdotal aspect. It must meet painting in the most unexpected forms and places. They must separate again to rejoin each other later, more freely, somewhere in space.

Photography, it is said, is cold, temporal, always linked to the present or the past (never to the future). United with painting which is physical, timeless, what disturbing disorder!

I don't have too much respect for the history of art and culture. Perhaps the weight of culture is less strong for women and that is our luck today. Let's go!

We live in history: the street, stores, advertisements, television, newspapers and the movies are a large part of our culture. This culture is a mixture of diverse elements, a big ''do-it-yourself'' arrangement of strange reminiscences, a ''patchwork'' of juxtaposed events which constitutes our identity. This is why the notion of ''do-it-yourself'' interests me so: ''do-it-yourself'' media, ''do-it-yourself'' assemblies of different cultures. These are our myths and our legends today.

—Annette Messager

* * *

The work of the French artist Annette Messager transcends borderlines between existing media and at the same time the borderlines between art and the social and political reality of women. Feminist argumentation is manifested on a level of artistic articulation, and both the intimate-private and the social-political are required components in this process. In terms of the making of her art the artist speaks of the unification of photography and painting, but this does not remain on the formalistic level of existing media, it is a basic crossing of borderlines of traditional taboo: and cliches of social behaviours.

In her earliest exhibitions of 1973 Annette Messager was directed toward a combined confrontation of painting and photography, corresponding to the theme of ''Men-women and women-men.'' In these works photographs of couples are manipulated in regard to the domination within the individual couple so that as a result masculine women and feminine men are documented in their accepted roles within the union.

In sequential works of 1972 and 1973 these tendencies toward a transcendence of media limitations are continued: in *Mes jalousies* of 1973 the artist manipulated photos of people in regard to aging; lines in the faces reveal the aging process specifically demonstrating the absurdities of eternal youth illusions in the media industry. Messager here successfully demonstrates the discrepancies between false ideals and a more accurate perception of reality.

In the works to follow the concentration on role behaviour and a conscious decision-making process is evident and the thematics are extended into areas such as commercials, comic strips and other forms of popular imagery, all re-evaluated under the insights of a radically feminist argumentation.

Since 1975 these endeavors more and more concentrate on the body of the artist which becomes her major medium. In *La femme et la mort* Messager outlines the skeleton of her body directly on her skin, and in *La femme et le dessin,* using the same technique, she draws the anatomical details of her internal organs on her body. The process of the drawing becomes an additional part of the work, a work which in its essence is an analogy to the life process itself. In *La femme et l'operation* the same principle is applied to the drawing of her reproductive organs. Other works since the late 1970s are devoted to photographic series, such as *The Lover's Portraits* of 1977, *The Serials* of 1978 in which the behavioral cliches of man and woman in public and commercial media are the theme.

Works of this kind and those in the years to follow, such as *La femme-homme* of 1975, *Quel beau spectacle* of 1976, *Chimeres* of 1982/1983 and *Le piege Arachneen* of 1983 are pioneering for a new and authentic feminist art, which is not only a legitimate continuation of earlier tendencies in the art of women, but, in addition, exciting and often mysterious levels of reality are explored from an earlier unknown perspective. The fact that these endeavors manifest themselves in a newly created medium and in the programmatically crossing of existing borderlines between accepted media is significant for the necessity to challenge accepted cliches not only in art but also in life.

In a series of works around 1990, for example *Mes Voeux* (*My Wishes*) of 1988/1989, *My Little Sister* of 1988/1989, *Maman* of 1989/1990, *Histoire des robes* (*Story of Dresses*) of 1990, *Pesche* (*Sin*) of 1990, and *Les Piques* (*The Pikes*) of 1993 Annette Messager reveals in the continuing manipulation of various media (photography, collage, watercolor, and stuffed toys) unknown, hidden and often uncomfortable facts in the life of women, partly within the sadomasochistic tradition of artists like William Blake, Henry Fuseli, and Odilon Redon, while encompassing humour and the popular imagery of daily life sequences. In an interview Messager defined her art in the rejection of the ideological intent of conceptual and performance art: ''Conceptual art interests me in the same way Art Brut, astrology, or religious art might. The ideologies such arts convey do not interest me in any way. They are sources of forms. . . . I pinch their beautiful forms from them; selfishly, I hoard and steal them, and transform all these different worlds into my own thing, my own world.''

—Udo Kultermann

In 1995 the Los Angeles County Museum of Art and New York's Museum of Modern Art co-organized the first major American retrospective of Messager's work. The show toured the country and for many in the United States served as a long-overdue introduction to the artist's work. Having felt that ''doing a retrospective means opening up your heart,'' Messager's next work, 1997's *DépendanceIndépendance*, was a heart-shaped installation of dangling ropes and objects—ropes of yarn from unraveled sweaters, doll clothes, human limbs made of soft cloth—that were ''activated'' as the viewers walked through the installation as if though through the body of the artist herself. Her recent works present the artist returning to more macabre, but certainly no less playful themes. With typical candor, the artist attributed this tendency to her own approach to aging, asserting: ''As one approaches death, one would like to scoff at it, appropriate it for oneself!'' As viewers guiltily giggle at the silliness and pathos of newer works like *Ensemble* (1998) and *The Replicants* (1999–2000), in which the artist constructs pseudo-scientific ''specimens'' and hybrid creatures made of taxidermied animals and skinned stuffed toys, it is easy to follow Messager's lead in mocking mortality.

—Maria Elena Buszek

METZGER, Gustav

Nationality: Stateless. **Born:** Nürnberg, Germany, of Polish-Jewish parents, 10 April 1926; emigrated to Britain 1939. **Education:** Studied woodworking, O.R.T.-O.S.E. Technical School, Leeds, 1941–42; part-time drawing studies, Cambridge School of Art, 1945; full-time art studies, Sir John Cass Institute, under David Bomberg at Borough Polytechnique, Anglo-French Art Centre, all in London, and at Antwerp Academy, Belgium, and Oxford School of Art, 1946–50; evening classes, under David Bomberg, Borough Polytechnic, London, 1950–53. **Career:** Worked as furniture maker, carpenter, farmer and gardener, 1942–44; as junk-dealer, King's Lynn, Norfolk 1953–58. Independent artist, London, since 1958, and in Frankfurt since 1980: first stone carvings, 1944; paintings, 1945–57; auto-destruction works from 1959. Secretary, Destruction in Art symposium, London, 1966; editor, *PAGE,* bulletin of the Computer Arts Society, London, 1969–72; London organizer, International Coalition for the Liquidation of Art, Tate Gallery Demonstration, London 1970; vice-chairman, Artists Union, London, 1972; founder, with Cordula Frowein and Klaus Staeck, Kollektiv group and *Passiv-Explosiv* exhibition, Cologne, 1981. **Address:** c/o Cris Bittong, Oppeheimerlandstrasse 19,6000 Frankfurt 70, Germany.

Individual Exhibitions (including lecture/demonstrations):

1959 *Paintings* 14 Monmouth Street, London
Cardboards, 14 Monmouth Street, London
1960 *Paintings & Drawings 1945–60,* Temple Gallery, London
Demonstration: Auto-Destructive Art, Temple Gallery, London
Lecture/Demonstration, Heretics Society, Trinity College, Cambridge
1963 *Lecture/Demonstration,* Bartlett Society, School of Architecture, London University
1965 *Auto-Destructive Art,* Better Books, London (window display)
Lecture/Demonstration: Liquid Crystals, Society of Arts, Cambridge University
1966 *Liquid Crystals in Art,* Lamda Theatre Club, London
Lecture/Demonstration, Ravensbourne College of Art, Kent
1968 *Extremes Touch,* University College, Swansea, Wales

1971 *Lecture/Demonstration,* National Film Theatre, London
1972 *Unrealizable Disintergrative Architecture,* Architectural Association, London
Executive Profile, Institute of Contemporary Arts, London
1981 *Faschismus Deutschland: Darstellung Analyse,* University of Bern
1999 *Gustav Metzger,* Museum of Modern Art, Oxford, England (catalog)
Spacex Gallery, Exeter, England

Selected Group Exhibitions:

1953 *Borough Bottega,* Gallery, London
1969 *Event 1: Computer Arts Society,* College of Art, London
1970 *Tendencije 4,* Galeria Suvremene Umjetnosti, Zagreb
1971 *Art Spectrum,* Alexandra Palace, London
1972 *3 Life Situations,* Gallery House, London
1974 *Art into Society/Society into Art,* Institute of Contemporary Arts, London
1977 *Towards Another Picture,* Midland Group Gallery, Nottingham
1981 *Vor dem Abbruch,* Kunstmuseum, Bern
Passiv-Explosiv, Hahnentorburg, Cologne, West Germany
1996 *Life/live: The Artistic Scene in the United Kingdom in 1996—New Adventures,* Musee d'Art Moderne de la Ville de Paris
1999 *Sublime: The Darkness and the Light—Works from the Arts Council Collection,* John Hansard Gallery, Southampton, England (travelling exhibition)

Collections:

Archiv Hanns Söhm, Staatsgalerie, Stuttgart; Tate Gallery Archive, London.

Publications:

By METZGER: Books and pamphlets—*Auto-Destructive Art Manifesto 1,* London 1959; *Auto-Destructive Art, Manifesto 2,* London 1960; *Auto-Destructive Art, Machine Art, Auto-Creative Art,* London 1961; *3 Manisfestos,* London 1961; *Manifesto World,* London 1962; *Centre for Advanced Creative Studies,* with Marcello Salvadori, London 1963; *On Random Activity in Material/Transforming Works of Art,* London 1964; *Auto-Destructive Art,* London 1965; *DIAS Information,* 6 broadsheets, London 1967–78; *Passiv-Explosiv,* exhibition broadsheet, with Cordula Frowein and Klaus Staeck, Cologne 1981; *Gustav Metzger: ''Damaged Nature, Auto-destructive Art''* with Andrew Wilson and Clive Phillpot, London 1996. **Articles**—''3 Manifestos'' in *De-collage* (Cologne), no. 6, 1967; ''Machine Art, Auto-Creative Art, Auto-Destructive Art'' in *Ark* (London), no. 32, 1962; ''An Overwhelming Need for Shelter'' in *Peace News* (London), 2 September 1966; ''Automata in History,'' parts 1 and 2, in *Studio International* (London), March and October 1969; ''Zagreb Manifesto,'' with Jonathan Benthall and Gordon Hyde, in *Studio International* (London), June 1969; ''Kinetics'' in *Arts and Artists* (London), September 1970; ''Social Responsibility and the Computer Professional: The Rise of an Idea in America'' in *PAGE* (London), October 1970; ''A Critical Look at the Artist Placement Group'' in *Studio International* (London), January 1972; ''Art in Germany under National Socialism'' in *Studio International* (London), March/April 1976; ''Art Strike 1977–1980'' in *Yawn,* no. 38, March 1993; ''A Terrible Beauty: Interview'' by Andrew Wilson in *Art Monthly,* no. 222, December 1998/January 1999.

On METZGER: Books—*Mud Pie: The CND Story* by Herb Greer, London 1964; *4 Essays on Kinetic Art* by Stephen Bann, Reg Gadney, Frank Popper and Phil Steadman, London 1966; *Bomb Culture* by Jeff Nuttall, London 1968; *Origins and Development of Kinetic Art* by Frank Popper, London 1968; *Artworks and Packages* by Harold Rosenberg, London 1969; *The New Painting* by Udo Kultermann, London 1969; *Computers in Everyday Life* by Laura Tatham, London 1970; *Experimental Painting* by Stephen Dann, London 1970; *The Computer in Art* by Jasia Reichardt, London 1971; *Science and Technology in Art Today* by Jonathan Benthall, London 1972; *Environments and Happenings* by Adrian Henri, London 1974; *Art-Action and Participation* by Frank Popper, London 1975; *Art of the 60s* by Hugh Adams, London 1978; *Rubbish Theory: The Creation and Destruction of Value* by Michael Thompson, Oxford 1979; *The Assault on Culture* by Stewart Home, Aporia Press and Unpopular Books, 1988; *Gustav Metzger: Manifeste, Schriften, Konzepte,* edited and with introduction by Justin Hoffmann, Munich 1997; *Art and Outrage: Provocation, Controversy and the Visual Arts* by John A. Walker, London 1999. **Articles**—''Message from the Margin: Chronology of the Movements of Gustav Metzger'' by John Albert Walker in *Art Monthly,* no. 190, October 1995; ''Gustav Metzger,'' exhibition review, with text by Michael Archer in *Artforum* (New York), vol. 37, no. 6, February 1999; ''Yoko Ono, Gustav Metzger and Ilya Kabakov'' by David Jeffreys in *Burlington Magazine,* vol. 141, no. 1153, April 1999.

* * *

Gustav Metzger himself traces the auto-destructive art of which he is the founder back to roots in Dadaism, Russian revolutionary art, and the work of Moholy-Nagy. But his own practice of destruction in art is a reflection of his extreme political and social radicalism, of feelings of a world in crisis which have been with him ever since he arrived in Britain in 1939 as a refugee from the menace of Hitler, and which the atom bomb and environmental pollution have only served to strengthen. He is repelled by the threat of technology, arguing that it has built a ''self-destroying society,'' which demands an auto-destructive art in response. With other pioneers like Tinguely he was one of the first to theorize about and to practise destruction in art around 1960. And he has been one of the influences behind the emphasis on art as action and process, radically questioning consumer society, with the consequent withering away of the consumable art object which has been a marked feature of recent avant-garde activity.

Metzger was a painter until 1957, though he had long been dissatisfied with painting, having told his teacher Bomberg that he was looking for something ''extremely fast and intense. About ten years later I saw Pollock's drip paintings. They came nearest to that conception of paintings I had in 1946.'' Thinking this fast, intense vision couldn't be captured with paint on canvas, he tried painting and scraping on mild steel. In 1960 he at last found what he was looking for by painting with acid on sheets of nylon stretched in a frame. This has the opposite effect from building up paint on canvas, for the acid dissolves the nylon, so that the artist actually destroys the work in the process of creating it. Such auto-destructive art is material that is undergoing a transformation in time, so that Metzger converted the act of painting into a performance at which the audience participated. And he was also hoping to involve his audience in the "aesthetic revulsion" that he was thus trying to express for the self-destructive course of Western society.

The tension between an auto-creative art of change, growth and movement and auto-destructive decay as the natural forces run their course was even more dramatic when Metzger started demonstrating the colour changes of chemicals. Always eager to get closer to the transformation processes of nature, Metzger used liquid crystals between polaroid screens. By heating them and letting them cool, he was able to project a constantly changing imaging of translucent colour as the chemical broke down.

Yet Metzger is really interested less in such demonstrations than in what at first sight may seem a contradiction in terms, more "permanent" forms of auto-destructive art. In the lecture *Auto-Destructive Art* (1965) that he delivered to the Architectural Association he outlines several such monumental or sculptural projects. One for instance would be a construction of three slabs of mild steel, 18 feet high with a base about 24 feet by 18 feet which when exposed to the corrosion of an industrial atmosphere would decay over a period of about ten years. Much more complex and expensive is his idea for a sculpture of five walls, each about 30 feet high and 40 feet long, each wall composed of 10,000 uniform elements, square in one, rectangular or hexagonal in another. Each element is ejected under the control of a digital computer, so that again over a period of about 10 years the work would cease to exist.

Metzger is thus not averse to using technology in his own works. And he has indeed been an active and ardent supporter of the British Society for Social Responsibility in Science, dedicating himself to redirecting science and technology towards less destructive and militaristic ends. The final purpose of his auto-destructive art is to transform social attitudes through an aesthetic of revulsion. However, though like the performance artists who create happenings one of Metzger's aims has been to get away from the privileged situation of easel painting in galleries, his audiences have been small and elitist, and he has never been one of those artists eagerly courted by the press.

—Konstantin Bazarov

MILOW, Keith (Arnold)

Nationality: British. **Born:** London, 29 December 1945. **Education:** Baldock, Hertfordshire primary schools; studied at Camberwell School of Art, London, 1962–67; Royal College of Art, London, 1967–68. **Career:** Painter: now lives and works in New York; travelled to Morocco, 1965, Rome, 1966, and Amsterdam, Paris and Kassel, 1968; worked on experimental projects for the Royal Court Theatre, London 1968. Lecturer in printmaking, Ealing School of Art, London, 1968–70; artist-in-residence, University of Leeds, 1970–72; lecturer, Reading University, Berksire, 1971; lecturer, Royal College of Art, London, since 1974; visiting lecturer in painting, Canterbury School of Art, Kent and Chelsea School of Art, London, since 1975. **Awards:** Gregory Fellowship, University of Leeds, 1970; Harkness Fellowship, London, 1972; Calouste Gulbenkian Foundation Visual Arts Award, 1976; First Prize, *Tolly Cobbald Eastern Arts National Exhibition,* 1979. **Agent:** Nigel Greenwood **Address:** c/o Nigel Greenwood Inc., 4 New Burlington Street, London W1, England.

Individual Exhibitions:

1968 Axiom Gallery, London
1970 Nigel Greenwood Inc., London
1971 Arnolfini Gallery, Bristol
Institute of Contemporary Arts, London
1972 King's College, Cambridge
Leeds City Art Gallery
Utrechtkring, Utrecht
Nigel Greenwood Inc., London
1973 J. Duffy and Sons, New York
Nigel Greenwood Inc., London
1974 Nigel Greenwood Inc., London
1975 Hester van Royen Gallery, London
Arnolfini Gallery, Bristol
Galerie Jacomo Santiveri, Paris
Nigel Greenwood Inc., London
1976 Kettles Yard Gallery, Cambridge
Nigel Greenwood Inc., London
1977 Walker Art Gallery, Liverpool
1978 Nigel Greenwood Inc., London
Roundhouse Gallery, London
1979 Galerie Loyse Oppenheim, Nyon, Switzerland
Rowan Gallery, London
1981 Annina Nosei Gallery, New York
1982 Annina Nosei Gallery, New York
1986 Nigel Greenwood Inc., London
1988 Alexander Wood Gallery, New York
1989 John Davis Gallery, New York
1991 Nigel Greenwood Inc., London
Pence Gallery, Los Angeles
1995 *Keith Milow: Recent Work,* Nohra Haime Gallery, New York
1999 *Keith Milow: New Work,* Nohra Haime Gallery, New York
2000 Ron Judish Fine Arts Gallery, Denver, Colorado

Selected Group Exhibitions:

1967 *Young Contemporaries,* Tate Gallery, London
1970 *Works on Paper,* Museum of Modern Art, New York
1971 *Bienal,* Sao Paulo
1973 *From Henry Moore to Gilbert and George,* Hayward Gallery, London
1976 *Arte Inglese Oggi 1960–76,* Palazzo Reale, Milan
1978 *Britisk Samtidskunst,* Kunstnernes Hus, Oslo (travelled to Trondheim and Bergen, Norway)
1980 *British Art Now,* Guggenheim Museum, New York
1982 *Aspects of British Art Today,* Metropolitan Art Museum, Tokyo (toured Japan)
1984 *Chill Out,* Kenkeleba Gallery, New York
1985 *Smart Art,* Harvard University, Cambridge, Massachusetts
1995 *Important Works,* Nohra Haime Gallery, New York
1996 *The Power of Color,* Nohra Haime Gallery, New York

Collections:

Arts Council of Great Britain, London; Tate Gallery, London; Victoria and Albert Museum, London; Contemporary Arts Society, London; Art Gallery of Ontario, Toronto; Museum of Modern Art, New York; Oberlin College, Ohio.

Publications:

By MILOW: Articles—"Choice States," interview, with Anne Seymour, in *Studio International* (London), March 1972; statement in *Keith Milow: Drawings,* exhibition pamphlet, Liverpool 1977.

On MILOW: Books—*6 at the Hayward,* exhibition catalog by Michael Compton, London 1969; *Keith Milow,* exhibition catalog by J. Grosfed, Utrecht, 1972; *The New Art,* exhibition catalog by Anne Seymour, London 1972; *From Henry Moore to Gilbert and George,* exhibition catalog by Anne Seymour, London 1973; *Art as Thought Process,* exhibition catalog by Michael Compton, London 1974; *Keith Milow,* exhibition catalog by William Feaver, Cambridge 1976; *Keith Milow: Recent Work,* exhibition catalog, with text by Robert Rosenblum, New York 1995; *The Twentieth Century: Thames—by Keith Milow,* London 1998; *Keith Milow: New Work,* exhibition catalog, New York 1999. **Articles**—"Keith Milow" by Marina Vaizey in the *Financial Times* (London), August 1972; "Keith Milow" by William Feaver in *Art International* (Lugano), September 1972; "Keith Milow" by William Feaver in the *Financial Times* (London), November 1974; "Keith Milow" by Donald Kuspit in *Artforum* (New York), January 1983; review by Mary Rose Beaumont in *Arts Review* (London), vol. 43, 28 June 1991; "Keith Milow at Nohra Haime" by Ann Wilson Lloyd in *Art in America* (New York), November 1995; "Keith Milow" by Donald Kuspit in *Artforum International,* vol. 36, January 1998; "Keith Milow at Nohra Haime" by Lilly Wei in *Art in America* (New York), June 1998.

* * *

Keith Milow is a painter whose pictures are by no means confined to the two-dimensional surface of a canvas. Early works included printed images, usually of architecture, that were divided and rearranged or spaced out regularly across the surface. The breaking down and reconstruction of an image soon invaded the third dimension. Milow would take a drawing of work he revered, such as a Caro sculpture, and turn that drawing into a sculpture by partially slicing it into strips and folding each strip, imbued with resin, back so that its end would adhere to the previous strip. The overall silhouette was that of a hyperbole.

The strategy of taking an image, usually of a work of art but sometimes that of the real space around the work, and reconstructing or recycling it in one or more stages, has been a constant one in his art. It is related to that of several other British artists and may be considered a British tradition, including, for example, Michael Craig Martin and Stephen Buckley. Its doyen is Richard Hamilton. However, the character of Milow's work, as of himself, is very different from that of any of these other artists. It is exemplified in his most recent and persistent series.

For more than five years he has taken as his starting point that most central image of the western culture, the Latin across. The image remains always quite recognizable and is most often intact in outline. However, its surface is divided by orthogonal and diagonal shifts of plane. Surfaces are offset, staggered or rebated. This simple, powerful configuration has served as the basis of hundreds of variations not only of form but of surface. Milow employs wood, resin, paint, metal powders, plaster and cement. Very often the first impression, of great weight for example, may be subtly contradicted by the slightest indication that the object is hollow and somehow provisional. Through real, the object has the effect of being an illusion. The shadows cast by or on the piece are integrated with the arises that denote the changes of level and both appear pictorial.

Architecture is one of Milow's recurrent themes. It may appear in the form of synecdoche (the *beton brut* of one of his crosses recalling the chapel of Corbusier), of quotation (the photograph of Stirlings History Library in prints of the late '60s), or the real life relationship of the image in paintings to one's perception of them and of the space around them (the "Split Definitive" series of 1977).

—Michael Compton

MITCHELL, Joan

Nationality: American. **Born:** Chicago, Illinois, 12 February 1926. **Education:** Francis Parker School, Chicago, graduated 1942; Smith College, Northampton, Massachusetts, 1942–44; Art Institute of Chicago, 1944–49 (on travel fellowship in Europe, 1948–49), B.F.A. 1947, M.F.A. 1950; Columbia University, New York, 1950. **Career:** Independent painter, since 1950; established studio at St. Mark's Place, New York, 1950, and attended meetings at The Club, frequenting Cedar Tavern (with Willem de Kooning, Philip Guston, Franz Kline and others); travelled to Paris, 1955, and established studio, 1959, working in the circle of Jean-Paul Riopelle, Kimber Smith and Shirley Jaffe; Joan Mitchell Foundation established, Virginia Commonwealth University School of the Arts, 1993. **Awards:** Brandeis Creative Arts Award Medal, Waltham, Massachusetts, 1973. Honorary doctorate: Ohio Wesleyan University, Delaware, Ohio, 1971; Recipient, Creative Arts Citation, Brandeis University, 1973; Distinguished Artist Award, College Art Association, 1989; Painter of the Year citation, French Ministry of Culture, 1989. **Agent:** Xavier Fourcade Inc., New York. **Died:** Of lung cancer, 30 October 1992.

Individual Exhibitions:

1951 New Gallery, New York
1953 Stable Gallery, New York
1954 Stable Gallery, New York
1955 Stable Gallery, New York
1957 Stable Gallery, New York
1958 Stable Gallery, New York
1960 Galerie Neufville, Paris
Galleria dell'Ariete, Milan
1961 Stable Gallery, New York
B. C. Holland Gallery, Chicago
Dwan Gallery, Los Angeles
Southern Illinois University, Carbondale
1962 Massachusetts Institute of Technology, Cambridge
Galerie Jacques Dubourg, Paris
Galerie Lawrence, Paris
Galerie Klipstein und Kornfeld, Bern
1965 Stable Gallery, New York
1967 Galerie Jean Fournier, Paris
1968 Martha Jackson Gallery, New York
1969 Galerie Jean Founier, Paris
1971 Galerie Jean Fournier, Paris
Martha Jackson Gallery, New York

Joan Mitchell: *Afternoon,* 1969–70. ©Christie's Images/Corbis.

Joan Mitchell: *Sunflower III,* 1969. ©Smithsonian American Art Museum, Washington, DC/Art Resource, NY; courtesy of Smithsonian American Art Museum.

1972 *Fresh Air School: Sam Francis/Joan Mitchell/Walasse Ting,* Carnegie Institute, Pittsburg (toured the United States)
Martha Jackson Gallery, New York
Everson Museum, Syracuse, New York
1974 Whitney Museum, New York
Arts Club of Chicago
1976 Galerie Jean Fournier, Paris
Xavier Fourcade Inc., New York
1977 Xavier Fourcade Inc., New York
1978 Galerie Jean Fournier, Paris
Ruth Schaffner Gallery, Los Angeles
Webb and Parsons Galley, Bedford Village, New York
1979 Paula Anglim Gallery, San Francisco
1980 Galerie Jean Fournier, Paris
Xavier Fourcade Inc., New York
Richard Hines Gallery, Seattle
1981 Gloria Luria Gallery, Florida
Xavier Fourcade Inc., New York
Janie C. Lee Gallery, Houston
1982 Musée d'Art Moderne de la Ville, Paris
1983 Xavier Fourcade Inc., New York
1984 Galerie Jean Fournier, Paris
1985 Xavier Fourcade Inc., New York
1986 Xavier Fourcade Inc., New York
Keny and Johnson Gallery, Columbus, Ohio
1987 Galerie Jean Fournier, Paris
1988 Corcoran Gallery of Art, Washington, D.C. (travelled to San Francisco; Buffalo, New York; San Diego, California; Ithaca, New York, 1988–89)
Joan Mitchell: Selected Paintings Spanning Thirty Years, Manny Silverman Gallery, Los Angeles (catalog)
1989 *Joan Mitchell,* Robert Miller Gallery (catalog)
1994 *Joan Mitchell: ''My Black Paintings'' 1964,* Robert Miller Gallery, New York (catalog)
1997 *Joan Mitchell,* IVAM Centre Julio Gonzalez, Valencia (catalog)
1998 *Joan Mitchell: Paintings 1950 to 1955,* Robert Miller Gallery, New York (catalog)
1999–2000 *Joan Mitchell: The Nature of Abstraction* (retrospective), Walker Art Center, Minneapolis

2001 Whitney Museum of American Art, New York

Selected Group Exhibitions:

1959 *Documenta 2,* Kassel, West Germany
1961 *American Abstract Expressionists and Imagists,* Guggenheim Museum, New York
1962 *40 Artists Under 40,* Whitney Museum, New York (toured the United States)
1967 *Large American Paintings,* Jewish Museum, New York
1971 *Younger Abstract Expressionists of the 50s,* Museum of Modern Art, New York
1974 *5 American Painters: Recent Works,* Ruth Schaffner Gallery, Santa Barbara, California
1978 *American Painting of the 1970s,* Albright-Knox Art Gallery, Buffalo, New York
1980 *The Fifties: Painting in New York 1950–60,* Hirshhorn Museum, Washington, D.C.
1984 *Action the New Direction: Precision in New York 1955–60,* Newport Harbor Art Museum, Newport Beach, California (toured the United States)
1987 *Prints of Contemporary American Artists,* Mount Holyoke College, South Hadley, Massachusetts (travelled)
A Graphic Muse: Prints by Contemporary American Women, Mouth Holyoke College Art Museum, South Hadley, Massachusetts (catalog)
1999 *Selected Paintings 1975–77,* Lennon, Weinberg Gallery, New York

Collections:

Museum of Modern Art, New York; Guggenheim Museum, New York; Whitney Museum, New York; Rockefeller Institute, New York; Carnegie Institute, Pittsburgh; Corcoran Gallery, Washington, D.C.; Phillips Collection, Washington, D.C.; Walker Art Center, Minneapolis; Art Institute of Chicago; Musée d'Art Moderne, Paris; Albright-Knox Art Gallery, Buffalo; Fogg Art Museum, Massachusetts.

Publications:

By MITCHELL: Books—*Joan Mitchell 1992,* edited by John Cheim, New York 1992; *Joan Mitchell: Paintings 1956 to 1958,* New York 1996. **Articles—**"Reply to Irving H. Sandler" in *Artnews* (New York), September 1958; statement in *Nature in Abstraction,* exhibition catalog, New York 1958; "Statement" in *Artnews* (New York), May 1967.

On MITCHELL: Books—*40 Artists Under 40,* exhibition catalog, New York 1962; *Fresh Air School: Sam Francis/Joan Mitchell/Walasse Ting,* exhibition catalog, Pittsburgh 1972; *Joan Mitchell: My 5 Years in the Country,* with an introduction by James Harithas, Syracuse, New York 1972, introduction reprinted as "Weather Paint" in *Artnews* (New York), May 1972; *Joan Mitchell,* exhibition catalog, by Marcia Tucker, New York 1974; *5 American Painters: Recent Works,* exhibition catalog, Santa Barbara, California 1974; *Joan Mitchell: New Paintings,* exhibition catalog, New York 1976; *American Women Artists* by Charlotte Rubinstein, Avon 1982; *Joan Mitchell* by Judith E. Bernstock, New York 1988; *Originals: American Women Artists* by Eleanor Munro, New York 2000. **Articles—**"Mitchell Paints a Picture" by Irving Sandler in *Artnews* (New York), October 1957; "Joan Mitchell" by Irving H. Sandler in *School of New York: Some Younger Artists,* edited by B. H. Friedman, New York 1959; "An Expressionist in Paris" by John Ashbery in *Artnews* (New York), April 1965; "Joan Mitchell: To Obscurity and Back" by Peter Schjeldahl in the *New York Times,* April 1972; "Joan Mitchell's Envisionments" by Carter Ratcliff in *Art in America* (New York), July/August 1974; "Sensations of Landscape" by Thomas B. Hess in *New York Magazine,* 20 December 1976; "New York Letter: Joan Mitchell" by Carter Ratcliff in *Art International* (Lugano, Switzerland), January 1978; "On Winter's Traces" by John Ashbery in *New York Magazine,* 24 March 1980; "Joan Mitchell; Art and Life at Vetheuil" by Linda Nochlin in *House and Garden* (New York), November 1984; "Joan Mitchell" by John Russell in the *New York Times,* 25 April 1986; "In Living Chaos: Joan Mitchell" by Bill Berkson in *Artforum,* vol. 27, no. 1, September 1988; "Joan Mitchell: The Last Decade" by Klaus Kertess in *Art in America* (New York), vol. 80, no. 12, December 1992; "Joan Mitchell: Beyond Words" by Michael Gibson in *Cimaise,* vol. 39, no. 221, November-December 1992; "Joan Mitchell" by Philippe Piguet in *Oeil,* no. 464, September 1994; "Abstract Art's Gutsy Poet: Joan Mitchell" by Edward M. Gomez in *Art and Antiques,* vol. 19, no. 5, May 1996.

* * *

Joan Mitchell has been true all along to abstract expressionism. Historically she is one of the so-called second generation painters belonging to that movement. Originally from the American Midwest, she has spent the greater part of the career working in Paris. I mention this fact because I think it is important. Perfectly aware of and friendly with many of the painters of the New York scene, she has nevertheless been able to "keep her distance" from much of the merely fashionable and trendy that infects so many New York artists (not that Paris doesn't produce its own dangers!). By absenting herself from the hot center, so to speak, of abstract expressionism, she has been able to develop in a steady and consistent way—to follow her own nose. Much the same could be said of Sam Francis who also spent considerable time in France.

A case could even be made for the larger view one often experiences living amid an older culture—and the clearer vision sometimes experienced in looking on from afar. In any event, the paintings that have resulted from Mitchell's independence are wonderfully fresh and individual while clearly within the abstract expressionist idiom. There is definitely a kind of Joan Mitchell painting.

Much of the time it has to do with her response to nature—to streams, ponds, rocks, trees, hills, etc.—to places, to landscapes. There is even something of Cezanne's passion of blues and greens although little of his geometry. Mitchell's paintings are gutsy, lavish, exhilarating works full of grace notes. They are both lyric and robust and work splendidly at every scale.

Unlike many artists of her generation, Mitchell has not opted for successive art movements, for Pop or Op or Minimalism of New Realism. At the same time her steadfastness is not merely a form of stubbornness or the result of being locked-in. Rather it is expressive of the nature of her talent and indicative of the quality of her art—which it would appear is mined from a deep and inexhaustible vein.

—Ralph Pomeroy

When Mitchell moved from Paris to Vetheuil (about an hour train ride from Paris) in 1968, she became a city person transplanted to the country. (Interestingly, she lived in the same landscape as Claude Monet.) That proximity to the natural world may have kept her coming back to it for artistic inspiration, again and again; landscape and its rhythms remained an important ''subject'' of her art until her death from lung cancer in 1992. Her works are suffused with color and light, and she used the negative space of the unarticulated surface with great expressiveness.

During the 1970s Mitchell painted a series of triptychs, and for the remainder of her life she continued to create monumental, multi-paneled works that embodied the sensations of ''being in'' various landscapes. Her painting *Canada* (1972) effectively evokes the feeling of cold isolation; a later work, *Chord* (1987), is a visual evocation of the thunder of nature. Like many artists of the Abstract Expressionist era, Mitchell was very sensitive to the link between music and the visual arts; she often painted to musical accompaniment. Her artistic strength and vision remained strong, even in her later years. The etching *Little Weeds II* (1992, a triptych) is characterized by sinuous, calligraphic lines; *Ici* (1992), French for ''here,'' is a 9' x 13' diptych that asserts her presence with bold, color-laden gestures. Sunflowers in their various states of growth and decay also are a repeated theme in the last decade of her life, although they first appeared in her graphic art in the early 1970s.

Joan Mitchell: The Nature of Abstraction was a major retrospective of her work at the Walker Art Center in Minneapolis from November 1999 through May 2000. Despite its apparent spontaneity, Mitchell's working method was thoughtful and deliberate; she always developed her work from a concept. Despite the pitfalls of superlatives, perhaps one could say that she was the last true Abstract Expressionist, still exploring gesture, color, and paint in its purest terms into the 1990s.

—Mara Witzling

MIYAJIMA, Tatsuo

Nationality: Japanese. **Born:** Tokyo, 1957; lives in New York. **Education:** Graduated from Tokyo National University of Fine Arts and Music, 1984; completed postgraduate studies at Tokyo National University of Fine Arts and Music, 1986. **Agent:** Luhring Augustine, 531 West 24th St., New York, New York 10011, U.S.A.

Selected Individual Exhibitions:

1983 Gallery Paregon, Tokyo
1986 Maki Gallery, Tokyo
Akiyama Gallery, Tokyo
1987 Suntory Art-Box Gallery, Tokyo
Lunami Gallery, Tokyo
1988 Heineken Gallery, Tokyo
Gallery Vivita, Firenze, Italy
1989 Galeria Takagi, Nagoya
1990 *Hiroshima Installation,* Hiroshima City Museum of Contemporary Art, Hiroshima
Luhring Augustine Gallery, New York
Gallery Takagi, Tokyo
1991 Museum Het Kruithuis, The Netherlands
D.A.A.D., Berlin
Region, Nagoya City Art Museum, Nagoya
Projects by Artists Series, National Gallery of Canada, Ottawa
Galerie Max Hetzler, Cologne
Anthony D'Offay Gallery, London
1992 *133651.,* Iwaki City Art Museum, Japan
Gallery Takagi, Nagoya
1993 Kunsthalle Zurich, Zurich
1994 Gallery Takagi, Nagoya, Japan.
Galerie Buchmann, Basel, Switzerland
Nasubi Gallery, Tokyo
1995 Luhring Augustine, New York
Running Time, Queen's House, Greenwich
Gallery Takagi, Nagoya, Japan
Anthony d'Offay Gallery, London
1996 Fort Worth Art Museum, Fort Worth
Galerie Froment & Putman, Paris
Clear Zero, Foundation Cartier pour l'art contemporain, Paris
1997 *Big Time,* Hayward Gallery, London
San Francisco Museum of Modern Art
1998 *Running Time,* Johnson County Community College, Overland Park, Kansas
1999 La Biennale di Venezia, 48 Esposizione Internazionale d'Arte, Japan Pavillion, Venice
2000 *MEGA DEATH: shout! shout! count!,* Tokyo City Art Gallery, Tokyo
Dallas Museum of Art, Dallas, Texas
*Tatsuo Miyajima,,*Galeria Javier Lopez, Manuel Gonzalez Longoria, Madrid, Spain
Floating Time, Luhring Augustine, New York

Selected Group Exhibitions:

1982 *Video, Computer and Copy Art Show,* Seibu Department Store, Tokyo
1983 *Performance Week,* Kaneko Art Gallery, Tokyo
Bigs Once More, Plan-B, Tokyo
SCAN, Spring Competition, Video Gallery SCAN, Tokyo
1984 *Sound Object Exhibition,* Wave Gallery, Tokyo
1985 *The Hidden Animals in the City,* Osaka Prefectural Contemporary Art Center, Osaka
1988 *Hara Annual,* Hara Museum of Contemporary Art, Tokyo
Aperto '88, The Venice Biennale, Venice
Movement and Modern Art, The Museum of Modern Art, Saitama
1989 *East Meets West: Japanese and Italian Art Today,* Los Angeles Art Gallery at Silpakorn University, Thailand
Magician de la Terre, Centre Georges Pompidou, Paris
What is Contemporary Art?, Rooseum, Malmo, Sweden
Against Nature, San Francisco Museum of Modern Art, San Francisco (toured the United States)
Moving Images Now: The Fourth Contemporary Art Festival, Toyama Prefectural Museum of Modern Art, Toyama
1990 *The Game of Manners: Japanese Art in 1990,* Contemporary Art Gallery of Art Tower Mito, Mito
Japanische Kunst der 80 Jahre, Frankfurter Kunstverein, Frankfurt (toured Germany)
The Disappearance of Distance, Dutsches Postmuseum Frankfurt

Rhetoric Image, The New Museum of Contemporary Art, New York

1991 *Contemporary Arts: The Mind of Japan,* Museum of Fine Arts, Gifu

Zone of Love—Contemporary Art from Japan: Touring Australia and New Zealand, Tokyo Museum of Art, Tokyo, Art Gallery of Western Australia, Perth, Art Gallery of South Australia, Adelaide, Waikato Museum of Art and History

A Cabinet of Sign—Contemporary Art from Postmodern Art, Tate Gallery, Liverpool, White Chapel Art Gallery, London, Malmo Kunsthall, Malmo

1992 *Shiga Annual '92,* The Museum of Modern Art, Shoga, Japan

Occupied Territory: Installation at the Armory, Museum of Contemporary Art, Chicago

Performing Objects, Institute of Contemporary Art, Boston

1993 *Drawing the Line Against AIDS,* Guggenheim Museum SoHo, New York

Azure, Foundation Cartier pour l'art contemporain, Jouy-en Josas, France

Special Exhibition of Recycling Through Art, Taejon Expo, Korea

1994 *Of the Human Condition: Hope and Despair at the End of the Century,* Spiral Garden, Tokyo

Scream Against the Sky: Post-War Japanese Art, Guggenheim Museum SoHo, New York

Jetztzeit, Kunsthalle Wien, Austria

Exotic Excursions, Institute of International Visual Arts, London

1995 *Everything That's Interesting Is New,* Athens School of Fine Arts, Athens, Greece

Art Japan Today, Museum of Contemporary Art Tokyo, Japan

Japan Today, Louisiana Museum, Denmark

1996 *Tranquility,* Chiba City Museum of Art, Japan

Emits Light, Moves, Makes Noises-Non-Static Art in the 20th Century, The Museum of Modern Art, Wakayama, Japan

1997 *La Collection de la Fondation Cartier pour l'art contemporain,* Fondation Cartier pour l'art contemporain, Paris

1998 *New Science,* Edmonton Art Gallery, Canada

Luhring Augustine, New York

1999 *Infra-Slim Spaces: The Physical and Spiritual in the Art of Today,* Birmingham Museum of Art, Birmingham, Alabama

New Modernism for a New Millennium: Works by Contemporary Asian Artists from the Logan Collection, San Francisco Museum of Modern Art

2000 *Monism/Dualism,* SCAI The Bathhouse, Tokyo

Art in Technological Times, San Francisco Museum of Modern Art

Collections:

Hara Museum of Contemporary Art, Tokyo; Dannheisser Foundation, New York; Iwaki City Art Museum, Fukushima, Japan; Tate Gallery, London; Deste Foundation for Contemporary Art, Athens, Greece; National Gallery of Canada, Ottawa, Ontario; The Museum of Modern Art, Shiga, Shiga, Japan; Hiroshima City Museum of Contemporary Art, Hiroshima, Japan; Nagaya City Art Museum, Nagoya, Japan; Samsung Cultural Foundation, Seoul, Korea; Art Gallery of New South Wales, Sydney, Australia; National Museum of Modern Art Kyoto, Kyoto, Japan; Chiba City Museum of Art, Chiba, Japan; Fondation Cartier pour l'art contemporain, Paris, France; Tokyo Opera City, Tokyo, Japan; The Museum of Modern Art, Saitama, Saitama, Japan.

Public Installations:

Fortress of Human Rights, Geneva, Switzerland, 1996.

Publications:

On MIYAJIMA: Articles—''Gaining Face'' by Carol Lutfy in *ARTnews,* no. 89, March 1990; ''Tatsuo Miyajima: Dreaming of Numbers'' by Mary Haus in *ARTnews,* November 1991; ''Tatsuo Miyajima—Luhring Augustine'' by Neville Wakefield in *Artforum,* March 1995; ''Tatsuo Miyajima'' by Godfrey Worsdale in *Art Monthly,* March 1995; ''Tatsuo Miyajima'' by Carol Lutfy in *ARTnews,* April 1995; ''Tatsuo Miyajima—Luhring Augustine'' by Peter von Ziegesar in *Art in America,* May 1995; ''Tatsuo Miyajima: Carter Foundation and Froment & Putnam'' by Laurie Attias in *ARTnews,* Summer 1996; ''Tatsuo Miyajima—Luhring Augustine'' by Kirby Gookin in *Artforum,* March 2001; ''Tatsuo Miyajima—Luhring Augustine'' by Reena Jana in *ARTnews,* April 2001.

* * *

Best known for his environmental installations of digital gadgets, Japanese artist Tatsuo Miyajima's ''mathematical landscapes'' are meditations on time, space, and human existence. His art revolves around three key concepts: continuous change, communication, and perpetuity.

Miyajima's career began in the early 1980s, where his first work was as a performance artist. Walking the streets of Tokyo and screaming at the top of his lungs, the artist sought to critique the anonymity and rootlessness endemic in contemporary urban society. Frustrated by the fleeting nature of such gestures, Miyajima began exploring the idea of creating installations out of the detritus of Akihabara, the Tokyo electronics district. The light-emitting diodes (LEDs) that have come to characterize his work mesmerized viewers of the 1988 Venice Biannale, where his *Sea of Time,* an installation that consisted of dozens of digital watches with blinking red digits strewn about a darkened floor, each set to a different time, declared Miyajima an important presence in the contemporary art world. In the 1990s, Miyajima continued to explore the expressive possibilities of these gadgets with such works as *Lattice* (1990), a wall or ''field'' of hundreds of changing numbers, and *Spiral Time* (1992), two floor-to-ceiling columns adorned with spirals of digital counters. Perhaps his most engaging work of this period is *Running Time* (also referred to as *U-Car*) of 1994, an installation in which 30 or so battery-operated cars, topped by digital counters and placed in a pitch-dark gallery space, move about the viewers in a fascinating choreography of chance. Divided between green and red, ascending and descending number counts from 1 to 9 (Miyajima never uses zero, as it signifies both death and conformity), the courses and collisions of these cars suggest temporal and spatial subjectivity. Concepts such as

Heisenberg's uncertainty principle, as well as Buddhist notions of futility and transience clearly inform Miyajima's art.

Over the course of his career, Miyajima has demonstrated a desire to address controversial political issues in his art. His *Wine and Water* (1996) paired decanters, one holding wine and the other holding sea water from the South Pacific, where France had recently conducted nuclear tests, in such a manner as to question the relationships between nature and culture. In the mid-1990s, Miyajima also founded the Kaki Tree Project, a program dedicated to assuaging the pain caused by the Nagasaki bombing through the distribution of second-generation atomic bombing victim kaki trees to children throughout Japan. The artist characterizes this project as a performance-art piece in which he records the successful transplants on a digital counter that will eventually become part of an installation titled *Time Restorer*.

In recent years, Miyajima has explored a wider range of media and attempted to incorporate a more humanist dimension into his installations. For example, his *Counter Voice in Wine* (2000) is a video projection in which three figures count down from 9 to 1 in various languages and then plunge their faces into large bowls of wine, resurfacing to begin this process again. In this work, the existential topos of acting despite the absurdity of the situation is explored, and the mechanistic counting that is often associated with Miyajima's art is now humanized. In another work, *Floating Time* (2000), a darkened room is illuminated by four low, brightly lit platforms, where an array of numbers varying in size and color, counting backward and forward and bouncing from edge to edge, drift around the gallery space. The viewer stands within these squares of luminous color and watches the numbers flow across one's body while more pass on the floor and onto other viewers. It is in such environmental installations, where the viewer is lulled into contemplation of the intersections of time, space, and subjectivity, that Miyajima's work most effectively speaks of our postmodern age.

—Heather Belnap Jensen

MIYAMOTO, Ryuji

Nationality: Japanese. **Born:** Tokyo, Japan, 24 April 1947. **Education:** Tama Art University, Tokyo, B.A. in graphic design, 1973. **Career:** Assistant, Graphic design department, Tama Art University, 1974; Editorial staff, *Jutaku Kenchiku* (architectural magazine), 1975; Artist, since 1976. **Awards:** 14th Ihei Kimura Prize, 1989; Leone d'oro for the Best National Pavilion, 6th International Architecture Exhibition, Venice Biennale, 1996; 11th Shashin-no-kai Prize, 1999. **Address:** 3–21-35 Tokura Kokubunji-shi, Tokyo 185–0003 Japan.

Selected Individual Exhibitions:

1977 Shimizu Gallery, Tokyo
1986 Hillside Gallery, Tokyo
1988 INAX Gallery, Tokyo
1989 Minolta Photo Space, Tokyo
1990 Min Lowinsky Gallery, New York
1991 Silk Gallery, Seoul
1992 Petit Musee, Tokyo
1994 Yokohama Portside Gallery, Yokohama
1998 Zeit Poto Salon, Tokyo
Gilles Peyroulet and Cie, Paris
Form Zero, Santa Monica
Centre National de la Photographie, Paris
1999 Museum für Moderne Kunst, Frankfurt

Selected Group Exhibitions:

1985 *15 Contemporary Photographic Expressions,* Tama Art University Gallery, Tokyo
1986 *15 Contemporary Photographic Expressions,* Tama Art University Gallery, Tokyo
1987 *Icons in Contemporary Art,* Museum of Modern Art Saitama, Urawa
1989 *New Age Photography,* Ikebukuro Seibu Art Vivant, Tokyo
1990 *Fotofesta, The International Month of Photography,* George R. Brown Convention Center, Houston
Tokyo-Tokyo, Yurakucho Seibu Art Forum, Tokyo
1991 *Beyond Japan,* Barbican Art Gallery, London
Site Work, Photographers Gallery, London
1992 *My Home Sweet Home in Ruins; The Urban Environment and Art in Japan,* Setagaya Art Museum, Tokyo
1993 *About Big Cities,* New Society for Fine Art, Berlin
Yokohama Portside Gallery Exhibition: Ryuji Miyamoto and Toshio Shibata, Pacifico Yokohama, Yokohama
1994 *Liquid Crystal Future,* Fruit Market Gallery, Edinburgh
Kawasaki Monument, Kawasaki City Museum, Kawasaki
Fotofesta, The International Month of Photography, George R. Brown Convention Center, Houston
1995 *Tokyo City of Photos,* Tokyo Metropolitan Museum of Photography, Tokyo
Ginzabout, Ginza Art Space, Tokyo
1996 *Venice Biennale: 6th International Architecture Exhibition,* Tokyo
New Japanese Photography in 1990s The Resonance of Unconsciousness, Yokohama Civic Art Gallery, Yokohama
1997 *On Hong Kong,* The Photographer's Gallery, London
1998 *AIR Exhibition,* Gallery Yamaguchi, Tokyo
Invisible Cities, Hong Kong Arts Centre, Hong Kong
Donai yanen!, National Fine Arts School of Paris, Paris
AIR Exhibition, Tokyo Gallery, Tokyo
AIR Exhibition Annex, Gallery TE, Tokyo
1999 *Cities on the Move,* Hayward Gallery, London
Attack, Holland Festival, Amsterdam
Galleria Civica Modena, Modena
5th International Fototage Herten, Herten
La Mort, Gilles Peyroulet and Cie Gallery, Paris
2000 Tanlay Art Fare, Centre d'Art de Tanlay, Tanlay
City of Architecture of the City, Neues Museum, Berlin
Genealogy of Contemporary Photography, Nikon Salon, Tokyo

Collections:

Setagaya Art Museum; Tokyo Metropolitan Museum of Photography; Kawasaki City Museum; Japan Foundation; Asahi Shimbun

Publishing Company; Museum of Fine Arts Houston; Maison Europeene de la Photographie; Museum für Moderne Kunst, Frankfurt; Caisse des Depots et Consignations; Deutsches Center of Photography; Staatliche Museen zu Berlin Prussia Kulturbesitz.

Publications:

On MIYAMOTO: Books— *Kau Lung Shing Chai—Kowloon Walled City,* Tokyo 1988; *Architectural Apocalypse,* Tokyo 1988; *Daitokuji Temple,* Tokyo 1992; *Angkor,* Tokyo 1994; *KOBE 1995 After the Earthquake,* Tokyo 1995; *Kowloon Walled City,* Tokyo 1997; *Ryuji Miyamoto,* Germany 1999; *Museum Island,* Germany 2001.

*

There is a scene which keeps coming back to my memory like an underlying refrain. It is Toyama heights, an apartment in Shin-okubo in Shinjuku Ward. There were a number of military facilities in this area before the war, including a military hospital and school for children. When I saw it about 35 years ago, there were crumbling concrete structures here and there on a hill. It was a strange scene including a city apartment, an elementary school, and a church. My family is still there in a room created by remodeling a two-story wooden barracks. There is a tall chimney with no smoke coming out of it, a square pool with no water, a concrete base said to have been used for an antiaircraft gun, and a long concrete wall which is beginning to lean precariously. This kind of scene was common in Tokyo right after the war. I remember the sign on top of Isetan department store which could be seen from the window, a bright red neon sigh contrasting with the gray of the city. there was also a firing range which was taken over and used by the American army. It was in the shape of a large Quonset hut with one end open. the soldiers used real ammunition, and I can remember seeing the red-faced GIs shooting their rifles. I also saw an accident where a big military truck carrying tanks knocked down two or three shops on Meiji Street. I was amazed that the truck was hardly scratched even though the buildings were completely demolished. I also remember pushing my way through the crowd on the same street to see a black hose-drawn hearse in a funeral procession for a member of the Imperial family. These scenes only exist in my memory coming back from time to time. I might remember them differently if there were any photographs of the same scenes.

After the appearance of photography, people have had a tendency to think that things which were never photographed do not exist. Things which have been photographed definitely exit, but things which are not in photographs seem not to have existed at all. the difference between things which have and have not been photographed is absolute. the indefinite and vague things which fill the interval between what remains in a photograph and what does not gradually disappear. Existence and non-existence is clearly differentiated. Therefore, a photograph is a limited form which can only be spoken of in the past tense and the picture which appears now is a scene which existed a moment before. It is never simultaneous with the present. It is something which is absolutely gone and which we can do nothing about; it has the same meaning as death. It is the past holding on to the present. A photograph is a wordless memory, an abandoned structure built on layer upon layer of time stretching from the past to the present.

—Ryuji Miyamoto

* * *

MOLINARI, Guido

Nationality: Canadian. **Born:** Montreal, Quebec, 12 October 1933. **Education:** Ecole de Beaux-Arts, Montreal, 1948–51, studied under Marian Scott and Gordon Webber, Musée des Beaux-Arts, Montreal, 1951. **Career:** Painter; director, Galerie l'Actuelle, Montreal, 1955–57. Chairman, department of painting, Sir George William Univeristy, Montreal, since 1970. Jury member, *91st Annual Exhibition,* Royal Academy of Arts, Montreal, 1971. **Awards:** Laureat, Province of Quebec Artistic Competition, 1961; Jessie Dow Award, Musée des Beaux-Arts, Montreal, 1962; Buyer's Awards, *Biennial,* Winnipeg Art Gallery, 1962; Samuel and Ayala Zacks Purchase and Gift Award, Montreal, 1964; Grand Award, *Annual Spring Exhibition,* Musée des Beaux-Arts, Montreal, 1965; Guggenheim Fellowship for Creative Painting, New York, 1967. **Agent:** c/o Paul Kuhn Gallery, 722–11th Avenue S.W., Calgary, Alberta, Canada T2R 0E4. **Address:** 3290 Sainte Catherine Street East, Montreal, Quebec HIW 2C6, Canada.

Individual Exhibitions:

1954 Galerie l'Echourie, Montreal
1956 Galerie l'Actuelle, Montreal
1958 Galerie Artek, Montreal
1962 Galerie Nova et Vetera, College de St.-Laurent, Quebec
1963 Galerie Libre, Montreal
East Hampton Gallery, New York
1964 Jerrold Morris International Art Gallery, Toronto
Norman MacKenzie Art Gallery, University of Saskatchewan, Regina
Vancouver Art Gallery
Galerie du Siècle, Montreal
1965 East Hampton Gallery, New York
1966 Edmonton Art Gallery, Alberta
Galerie du Siècle, Montreal
1967 20/20 Gallery, London, Ontario
Galerie Nova et Vetera, College de St.-Laurent, Quebec
East Hampton Gallery, New York
1968 Galerie du Siècle, Montreal
Canada: Ulysse Comtois, Guido Molinari, at the *Biennale,* Venice
1971 Galerie Campo, Antwerp
1972 *Paintings,* Dalhousie University, Halifax, Nova Scotia
1976 National Gallery of Canada, Ottawa (retrospective; toured Canada)
1979 Musée d'Art Contemporain, Montreal
York University, Toronto
1988 49th Parallel Gallery, New York
1989 *Guido Molinari 1951–1961: The Black and White Paintings,* Vancouver Art Gallery, British Columbia

(traveled to Art Gallery of Windsor, Ontario; Art Gallery of Ontario, Toronto) (catalog)
1994 Stiftung für konkrete Kunst, Reutlingen
1995 *Guido Molinari: A Retrospective,* Musee d'Art Contemporain, Montreal (catalog)
1998 *Reconnaître Guido Molinari,* Musée de Grenoble, France (catalog)
Musée de Grenoble, France

Selected Group Exhibitions:

1955 *Espace 55,* Musée des Beaux-Arts, Montreal
1959 *Biennial Exhibition of Canadian Painting,* National Gallery of Canada, Ottawa
1961 *Guido Molinari and Claude Tousignant,* Musée des Beaux-Arts, Montreal
1965 *The Responsive Eye,* Museum of Modern Art, New York
1967 *9 Canadians,* Institute of Contemporary Art, Boston
1968 *Canada: Art d'Aujourd'hui,* Musée National Art Moderne, Paris
1970 *Grands Formats,* Musée d'Art Contemporain, Montreal
1977 *Contemporary Canadian Painters,* Canadian Department of External Affairs travelling exhibition (world tour)
1984 *Reflections: Contemporary Art Since 1964,* National Gallery of Canada, Ottawa
1989 *Montreal on Paper: Part One,* Saidye Bronfman Centre, Montreal (catalog)
1993 *Pictures for the Sky: Parallel Flight,* Museum of Fine Arts, Montreal (catalog)
1994 *The Festival de Peinture in Mascouche: Abstraction in Montreal 1950–70,* Hotel de Ville, Mascouche, Quebec (catalog)
Studios on Show 1994, Centre de Diffusion en Arts Visuels Cobalt, Montreal (catalog)
The Lavalin Collection of the Musee d'Art Contemporain in Montreal: The Sharing of a Vision, Musee d'Art Contemporain, Montreal (catalog)
1995 *The Glenn and Barbara McInnes Family Collection: A Selection from the Gift,* Carleton University Art Gallery, Ottawa (catalog)
1996 *The Eye of the Collector,* Musee d'Art Contemporain, Montreal (catalog)
1998 *Ecstasy,* Jack Shainman Gallery, New York
Kaleidoscope: An Exhibition by Quebec Members of the Royal Canadian Academy of Arts, Palais Montcalm, Hull, Quebec (also Academie Royal des Arts du Canada/Royal Canadian Academy of Arts, Toronto) (catalog)
Visions Géometriques, Musée de Grenoble, France
1999 *A Century of Canadian Drawing,* Dalhousie Art Gallery, Halifax, Nova Scotia (catalog)

Collections:

Musée des Beaux-Arts, Montreal; Sir George Williams University, Montreal; Art Gallery of Ontario, Toronto; Winnipeg Art Gallery, Manitoba; Norman Mackenzie Art Gallery, Regina; Vancouver Art Gallery; National Gallery of Canada, Ottawa; Museum of Modern Art, Guggenheim Museum, New York; Chrysler Museum, Provincetown, Massachusetts.

Publications:

By MOLINARI: Book—*Ecrits sur l'art, 1954–1975,* edited by Pierre Theberge, Ottawa 1976. **Articles—**''Sans Titre'' in *Le Petit Journal* (Montreal), September 1954, ''L'Espace tachiste ou situation de L'automatisme'' in *L'Autorite* (Montreal), April; 1955; ''L'Affaire du musée: G. Molinari demandé la demission de M. Steegman'' in *Le Devoir* (Montreal), August 1958; ''Le langage de l'art abstrait'' in *Art Abstrait,* exhibition catalog, Montreal 1959; ''Notes sur la peinture: Re-evaluation de Wassily Kandinsky'' in *Situations* (Montreal), March 1959; ''Le Salon et les peintres'' in *Situations* (Montreal), April 1959; ''Les Automatistes au Musée,'' ''Huit dessins de Claude Tousignant,'' and ''A Nui Cri'' in *Situations* (Montreal), September 1959; ''Reflexions sur l'automatisme et le plasticisme'' in *Situations* (Montreal), March/April 1961; statement in *Prize Winner Paintings: Books III* by Margaret Harold, Fort Lauderdale, Florida 1963; ''Sans Titre'' in *Guido Molinari,* exhibition catalog, Regina, Saskatchewan 1964, reprinted in *Molinari,* exhibition catalog, Montreal 1964; ''Sans Titre'' in *Canadian Art* (Toronto), January 1966; ''Sans Titre'' in *Statements: 18 Canadian Artists,* exhibition catalog, Regina 1967; ''La Perception des Structures'' in *La Presse* (Montreal), December 1967; ''L'Ecrivain a des Antennes'' in *Liberté* (Montreal), December 1967; ''Molinari'' interview, with Pierre Theberge, in *Artscanada* (Toronto), March 1969; ''L'Ecrivain a des Antennes'' in *Liberté* (Montreal), May/July 1969; ''Molinari: Pour un art de participation'' in *La Presse* (Montreal), January 1970; ''Sur: Le choix de peintre sur de grandes surfaces'' in *Grands Formats,* exhibition catalog, Montreal 1970; ''Molinari: Un Geste Social'' in *La Presse* (Montreal), April 1971; ''Sans Titre'' in *Paintings by Guido Molinari,* exhibiton catalog, Halifax, Nova Scotia 1972; ''Sans Titre'' in *Contemporary Canadian Painting* by William Withrow (Toronto), 1972; interview with Gary Michael Dault in *Canadian Art,* vol. 12, Summer 1995.

On MOLINARI: Books—*Guido Molinari,* exhibition catalog, Regina, Saskatchewan 1964; *Molinari,* exhibition catalog, Montreal 1964; *Statements: 18 Canadian Artists,* exhibition catalog, Regina, Saskatchewan 1967; *Paintings by Guido Molinari,* exhibition catalog, Halifax, Nova Scotia 1972; *Guido Molinari,* exhibition catalog with text by David Burnett, Montreal 1979; *Les Arts Visuels au Quebec Dans Les Annees Soixante: Tome II-l'Eclatement du Modernisme* by Francine Couture and others, Montreal 1997; *Pleasures of Sight and States of Being: Radical Abstract Painting Since 1990,* by Roald Nasgaard, Tallahassee, Florida State University Museum of Fine Arts 2001. **Articles—**''Du Molinarisme au Plasticisme avec Guido Molinari'' by Robert Millet in *Le Nouveau Journal* (Montreal), April 1962; ''Molinari, intuition rationalisée!'' by Paul Borduas in *Le Laurentien* (Montreal), October 1962; ''Une heure avec Guido Molinari'' by Robert l'Heureux in *Le Droit* (Ottawa), October 1964; ''Molinari on Molinari'' by Rea Montbizon in *The Gazette* (Montreal), October 1964; ''Molinari a quitte l'aureole pour une ancre d'une tonne'' by Robert Millet in *Le Magazine Maclean* (Montreal), February 1968; ''Molinari et le serie verticale'' by Yves Robillard in *La Presse* (Montreal), February 1968; ''Sans tire'' by Pierre Theberge in *Canada: Ulysse Comtois, Guido Molinari,* exhibition catalog, Venice 1968; ''An Artist Unites Man and Environment'' by Gail Dexter in *The Toronto Star,* March 1969; ''Molinari: The Medium Is Colour'' by Michael White in *The Gazette* (Montreal), October 1971; ''The Precociousness of Guido Molinari'' by Francois Gagnon in *Artscanada* (Torondo), December 1976; ''The Definitive

Eye'' in *Canadian Art,* vol. 5, no. 3, September 1988; ''Molinari: Tira le Noir, Visa le Prisme'' by Louise Beaudry in *Parcours,* vol. 1, no. 3, Summer 1995; ''Guido Molinari and the Destructive Element in Art'' by Roald Nasgaard in *Guido Molinari, une retrospective,* Musée d'art contemporain de Montréal, 1995.

* * *

Guido Molinari is perhaps the most pre-eminent personality among the several important artists, especially Claude Tousignant (b. 1932) and Yves Gaucher (1934–2000), to emerge in Montréal during the early 1960s, who rejected painterliness in favour of flat, geometric formats. Montréal, it must be remembered, was, after New York, one of the few cities on the international map to produce a genuinely original response to pre-war European traditions of abstract painting. During the early 1950s Molinari undertook some important automatist and tachist experiments, but by the mid 1950s he was entirely eschewing gesture in favour of a hard-edged impersonal application of color. The transformation of his painting was accompanied by his activity as a polemicist, his significant 1955 article, ''L'Espace tachiste ou Situation de l'automatisme'' attacking, while astutely analyzing, the basic premises and authority of Montreal Automatism.

Molinari's fully independent work emerged in the early 1960s after an intense period of engagement with Mondrian. From a broader perspective, however, Molinari must be defined as developing within the historical continuity of Malevich, Mondrian, Pollock, and Newman, working with the objectivity of Mondrian and the scale of Newman, but without the idealism of the former or the transcendental expressionism of the latter. As well Molinari has attached crucial importance to his study of the pre-structuralism of the American scientist and writer, Alfred Korzybski, who offered two interrelated propositions that would be crucial for his work; the principle of the non-identity of words and things, and the concept of non-Euclidian space.

The work that resulted, the Stripe Paintings, whose precepts would underlie all his future work, was simply composed of rows of equal vertical bands whose respective colours were arranged serially, the paint surface smooth, even and eventless, and closed to penetration by the eye, devoid of even a hint of that Matissian lyricism and illusion that still clung, during those same years, to the postpainterly abstraction of other stripe painters like Kenneth Noland and Gene Davis. Unlike postpainterly abstraction, nor were Molinari's Stripe Paintings in any sense meant to be instantaneously or holistically seen, as it were, but functioned as events over time caused by the visual interaction of the juxtaposed colours. Here Molinari's concern was not so much with the aesthetics of color, but its dynamics, color released to give full expression to its chromatic energies and interactions, never ceasing to perform before the eye, or indeed with respect to the body of the viewer, as he/she became caught up in the space that radiated outwards from the paintings. The paintings in effect become worlds in constant process, evoked and constructed by viewers willing to give over to them their perceptual and emotional commitments, structural enactments, through their ''synthesis of the energies of duration and chromatic energies,'' as the artist put it, of our relations to reality's state of perceptual transformation; or put more simply: they are visual equivalents of everyday personal experience.

The Stripe Paintings came to a close around 1969, when Molinari engaged himself with a series of alternative structures, from simple binary systems to more complicated checkerboard and triangular patterns, sometimes looking over his shoulder to re-engage earlier problems. At the risk of simplification it might be said that the work over the next five years or so re-explored, to paraphrase the artist, the space-generating potential of heterogeneous masses and their vectorial relationships, painting activity that would by the mid 1970s result in the Quantificateurs, a series to which he would devote himself until the end of the century. If the previous work, often brash and bright hued, seems to function on the larger public stage of the world, the latter quasi-monochromatic series points to an interior world of intimacy and contemplation. Seeing the Quantificateurs is slow, intense, and demanding, their chromatic values sometimes as close and subtle as to be on the edge of invisibility. But whether the first Dark Quantificateurs, or the Red and Blue ones (''my mystical period''), that followed, they construct a slow meditative space that reaches deep into the inner recesses of the body. By the end of the 1990s, the Quantificateur series had become Molinari's longest preoccupation. Then suddenly, as if it were once again time to return to sources, he began a new series entitled *Continuum*: ecstatic, in-your-eye, large scale, no-holds-barred, red yellow and blue revisitations of Mondrian's Boogie-Woogie paintings, the latter's heterotopian dispersals and destructions of form and colour having long been one of his touchstones. These have launched him, as I write, into new, yet unpredictable directions.

Molinari's work did not find much critical favour outside Canada in the 1960s, perhaps because they appeared to embrace something from the idealist tradition of geometric abstraction and thus seemed separate from other North American painting, suspiciously European and therefore regressive. Even more problematic, of course, was how these paintings presented themselves to the viewer. New York taste preferred holistic compositions in which ''at every moment the work itself is fully manifest,'' in the words of critic Michael Fried. Molinari's, as we have seen, tended to function like a never-ending event caused by the visual dynamics of the juxtaposed colours under the scrutiny of the eye. A painting whose variable appearances were only revealed as it was seen through time offered a very different experience from a painting, such as a Noland, that presumably was to be seen instantaneously. Perhaps Molinari also shared with Bridget Riley the consequences of having participated in MOMA's *Responsive Eye*, 1965, a fun-fair of an Op Art show that in retrospect was less a coherent summation of genuine artistic concerns than a superficial inventory of a variety of artistic paths that momentarily shared some technical strategies, but had no real common artistic programs. Both artists did indeed root their work in the physical and psychological processes of vision that defined Op Art, with the consequence that international opinion too often reduced their work to simple mechanistic concerns with optics. On their respective home turf, Britain and Canada, of course, neither was seen with such critical limitations, and each new body of work out of the studio was eagerly anticipated. And while Riley had her critical revenge in New York in 2000, Molinari has over the past decade attracted increased attention in Europe, with museum exhibitions at the Stiftung für konkrete Kunst (1994–95), Reutlingen and the Musée de Grenoble (1998).

—Roald Nasgaard

MONORY, Jacques

Nationality: French. **Born:** Paris, 25 June 1934. **Education:** Ecole Technique des Arts Appliques, Paris, 1951–55. Served in French

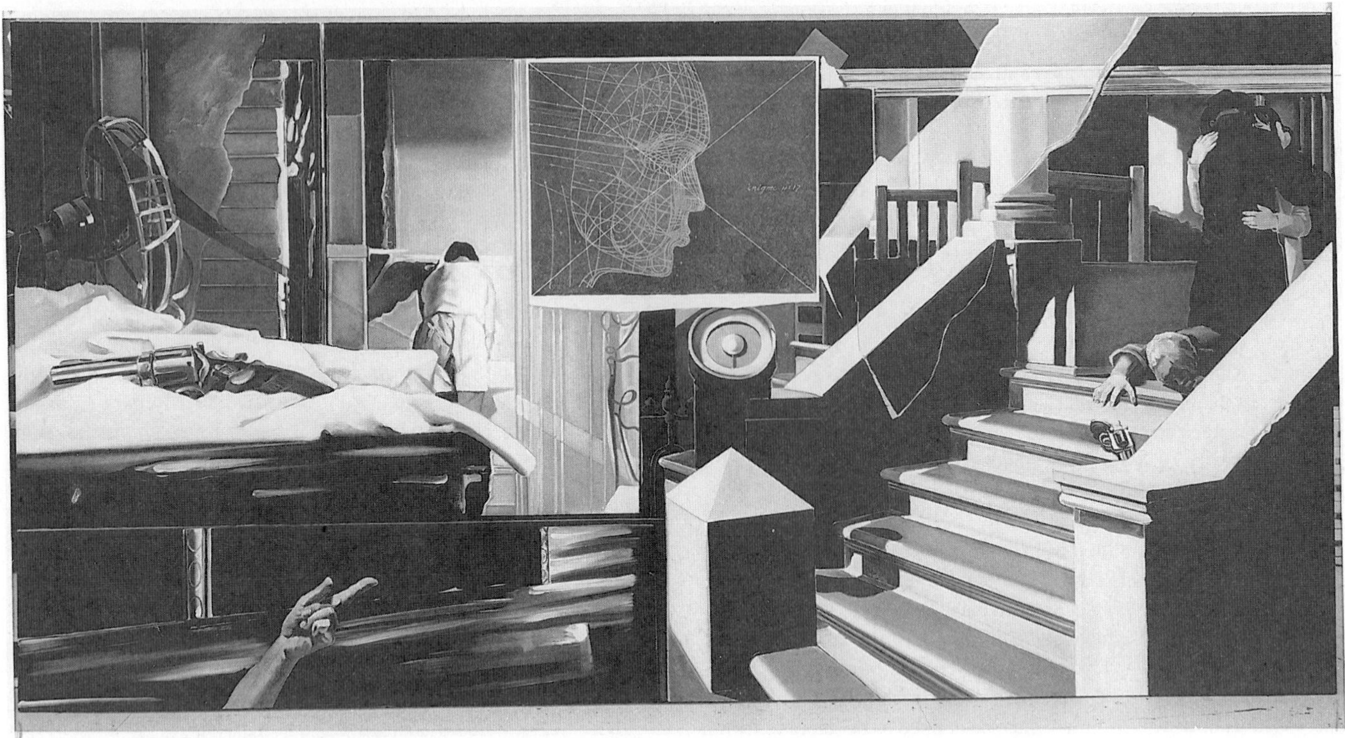

Jacques Monory: *Enigme No. 17,* 1996. ©Jacques Monory.

transport company, attached to the United States Army, 1955–56. **Family:** Married Sabine Monirys in 1960 (divorced, 1968); son: Antoine; married Paule Mominot, 1993. **Career:** Director, Editions Delpire publishing company, Paris, 1956–64; independent painter and graphic artist, Paris, since 1964; first paintings, 1952; first films, 1968. **Agent:** Galerie Lelong, 13 rue de Teheran, 75008 Paris. **Address:** 9 Villa Carnot, Cachan 94230, France. **Web site:** www.artnetart.com/monory.

Individual Exhibitions:

1955 Galerie Kleber, Paris
1959 Galerie La Hune, Paris
1965 Galerie Henriette Legendre, Paris
1966 Galleria Schwarz, Milan
1967 Galerie Blumenthal-Mommaton, Paris
Galleria Il Punto, Turin
1968 *Meurtes,* Galerie Blumenthal-Mommaton, Paris
1969 Galleria Forni, Bologna
Studio d'Arte Condotti 85, Rome
Galleria Il Punto, Turin
1971 Galerie Klang, Cologne
Velvet Jungle/N.Y., Musée d'Art Moderne de la Ville, Paris (travelled to the Palais des Beaux-Arts, Brussels)
1972 Stedelijk Museum, Amsterdam
Musée d'Art et d'Historie, Saint-Etienne, France
Neue Galerie, Aachen, West Germany
1973 Galleria Borgogna, Milan
1974 *Les Images Incurables,* Centre National d'Art Contemporain, Paris
1975 Louisiana Museum, Humlebaek, Denmark
Galerie Maeght, Zurich
Galerie Lanzenberg, Brussels (with Erro)
1976 *Operas Glaces,* Galerie Maeght, Paris
1977 Fondation Maeght, St. Paul-de-Vence, France
Images Incurables/Opera Glaces, Palais des Beaux-Arts, Charleroi, Belgium
Recits tremblants, Galerie de Larcos, Paris
Hommage à C. D. Friedrich, Kunsthalle, Hamburg
1978 *Technicolor,* Galerie Maeght, Paris
Galerie Maeght, Zurich
Figuration, Musée des Beaux-Arts, Grenoble (with Peter Klasen)
1979 Maison de la Culture, Rennes, France
1980 *Monory 3,* Galerie Maeght, Barcelona
Lunds Konsthall, Lund, Sweden
1981 *Ciels, Nebuleuses et Galaxies,* Galerie Maeght, Paris
Galerie Claude Riedel, Paris (with Jean Dupuy)
1982 Musée de la Chartreuse, Douai, France
Maison de la Culture, Nevers, France
Musée des Beaux-Arts, Pau, France
1983 *Dynamite,* Maison de la Culture, Grenoble, France
1984 *Toxique,* Musée d'Art Moderne de la Ville, Paris
Galerie Fuji TV, Tokyo
Encore une Fois Paraître à la Terasse, Galerie Pierre Hubert Geneva
Galerie Andate/Ritono, Geneva
1986 Musée des Sciences de La Villette, Paris
1987 Musée Gare D'Orsay, Paris
La Voleuse, Galerie Maeght Lelong, Paris
1988 *Le Peintre,* Centre de Development Culturel, Calais
1989 Galerie Lelong, Paris

Grand Formats en Bleu, Rose et Noir, Galerie La Defense, Paris
1990 *Come-back,* Galerie Zannettacci, Geneva
Alptraum, Galerie Loft, Paris
Sade-Révolution-Impossible, Centre Culturel, Aoste
1991 *Le Dernier Tableau,* Galerie Andata Ritorno, Geneva
Galerie Lelong, Paris
1992 *Monory,* Pavillion Français, Seville
1994 *Noir,* Galerie Lelong, Paris
1995 *Jardinage 3,* Champ-Clause F.60
1996 *Énigmes 1,* Centre Culturel, Galerie du Théâtre, Cherbourg, France
Énigmes 2, Galerie du Grand Café, Saint-Nazaire, France
1997 *Froid,* Municipal Art Museum, Reykjavik, Iceland
Énigmes 4, Nova Sin Gallery, Prague
Cinénigme, Villa Tamaris, La Seyne-sur-Mer, France
1998–99 *Épilogue,* Maison d'Art Contemporain, Chailloux-Fresnes, France
Monory, Musée de l'Abbaye de Sainte-Croix, Les Sables-D'Ollone (travelled to Musée des Beaux-Arts, Chartres; Musée des Beaux-Arts, Dôle)
1999 *La Nuit,* Galerie Zannettacci, Geneva
Ex-Crime, Musée des Beaux-Arts, Salle Chemellier, Angers, France
Documents, Palais des Congrès, Paris
Monory, Ecole de Beaux-Arts de Rouen, France
Monory, Galerie Gimpel, London
2000 *Tremblement,* FIAC, Paris

Selected Group Exhibitions:

1964 *Mythologies Quotidiennes,* Musée d'Art Moderne de la Ville, Paris
1968 *European Painters Today,* Musée des Arts Décoratifs, Paris (toured the United States)
1972 *Douze Ans d'Art Contemporain en France,* Grand Palais, Paris
1973 *Hyperrealistes Americains/Realistes Europeens,* Centre National d'Art Contemporain, Paris
1977 *Guillotine et Peinture,* Centre Georges Pompidou, Paris
1979 *De la Nature Etrange de l'Argent,* Kunsthalle, Dusseldorf (travelled to Eindhoven and Paris)
1982 *Alea,* Musee d'Art Moderne de la Ville, Paris
1986 *Espace* at the *Biennale,* Venice
1994 *Hors les Murs,* Musée de Clermont-Ferrand, France
1995 *Une Collection du 20th Siecle-Maeght,* Tokyo (toured Japan)
1997 *Face à l'Histoire,* Musée National d'Art Moderne, Centre Georges Pompidou, Paris
Pop Art, Centre Culturel de Bellem, Portugal
1998 *L'Art et le Crime,* Musée de Blois, France
1999 *Éclipse,* Centre Européen d'Action Artistique Contemporaine, Strasbourg, France
2000 *Times Suspend Your Flight,* Musées de Bergen (travelled to Musée de Reykjavik)

Collections:

Centre Georges Pompidou, Paris; Musée d'Art Moderne de la Ville, Paris; Musée Cantini, Marseilles; Musée d'Art Moderne, St. Etienne; Musée des Beaux-Arts, Genoble; Musée des Beaux-Arts, Pau, France; Stedelijk Museum, Amsterdam; Museum Boymans-van Beuningen, Rotterdam; Neue Galerie, Aachen, Germany; Louisiana Museum, Humlebaek, Denmark; Fonds National d'Art Contemporain, Paris; Museum of Modern Art, Fukuoka, Japan.

Publications:

By MONORY: Books—*Document bleu,* Paris 1970; *Deux* with Franck Venaille, Paris 1973; *USA 76, Bicentenaire Kit,* book/object, with Michel Butor, Paris 1975; *Hommage à C.D. Friedrich,* with Jean-Christophe Bailly, Paris 1977; *Recits tremblants,* with Jean-Francois Lyotard, Paris 1977; *Poétes charcutiers,* Paris 1978; *Diamondback,* Paris 1979; *Rien ne bouge assez vite au bord de la mort,* Paris 1984; *Quick,* Paris 1985; *Eldorado,* Paris 1991; *3'30'',* Paris 1993. **Books illustrated—***La mort sans phrase* by Charles Autrand, Paris 1968; *La baignoire verte* by Francoise Thieck, Paris 1974; *La Victoire à l'ombre des ailes* by Stanislas Rodanski, Paris 1975; *Eternité, zone tropicale* by Alain Jouffroy, Paris 1976. **Films—** *Ex,* 1968, *Brighton Belle,* 1974; *La voleuse,* 1986; *Le moindre geste peut faire signe,* 1989.

On MONORY—*Jaques Monory,* exhibition catalog with text by Gerald Gassiot-Talabot, Paris 1967; *Art et Contestation* by Gérald Gassiot-Talabot, Brussels 1968; *Depuis 45* by Gérald Gassiot-Talabot, Brussels 1970; *Monory* by Pierre Gaudibert and Alain Jouffroy, Paris 1972; *Jacques Monory,* exhibition catalog with text by Wolfgang Becker, Aachen, West Germany 1972; *Art en France, une nouvelle generation* by Jean Clair, Paris 1972; *L'Art Actuel en France* by Anne Tronche and Hervé Gloaguen, Paris 1973; *Monory: Les Images incurables,* exhibition catalog, with text by Alain Jouffroy, Paris 1974; *Jacques Monory: Operas glaces,* exhibition catalog with text by Gilbert Lascault, Paris 1976; *Figures de l'art contemporain* by M. LeBot, Paris 1977; *Guillotine et peinture* by Alain Jouffroy, Paris 1977; *Monory: Images incurables/Operas glaces,* exhibition catalog with text by Jean-Christophe Bailly, Charleroi, Belgium 1977; *Monory: Technicolor,* exhibition catalog with text by Alain Jouffroy, Zurich 1978; *Monory* by Jean Christophe Bailly, Paris 1979; *Monory 3,* exhibition catalog with texts by Jacques Adelin Brutaru and Marianne Nanne-Brahmmar, Lund, Sweden 1980; *Monory: Ciels, nebuleuses et galaxies,* exhibition catalog with text by Jean-Francois Lyotard, Paris 1981; *Monory: L'Assassinat de l'experience par la peinture* by Jean-Francoise Lyotard, Paris 1981; *Monory et la peinture-Avion* by H.F. Debailleux, Paris 1983; *Jacques Monory en Dandy* by H.F. Debailleux, Paris 1984; *Entretien presque imaginaire avec Jacques Monory* by Georges Charbonnier, Paris 1987; *Monory* by Pierre Tilman, Paris 1992; *Postmodern Romantics* by Sarah Wilson, London 1998; *Monory,* France 1998; *The Assasination of Experience by Painting* with preface by Sarah Wilson, London 1999.

*

My work has always been a catharsis for the anguish of death. Very directly in *Meutres* (*Murders*), always more or less slyly, a taste of *Catastrophe* throughout my extremely cinematographic subjects. Personal obsessions at play with collective obsessions, an impassioned pessimist, my painting, films, texts, make me a pertinent witness of our times.

Painting in its substance has only concerned me recently after my series *Ciels, Nebuleuses et Galaxies* (*Skies, nebulae and galaxies*), and the recent series *Fragile, Toxique, Le Peintre,* and *La Voleuse.* I work with it to question the pleasure of painting. Since 1991 I'm coming back to my favorite color painting, only made of blue and black. Thus my last series: *Noir Énigmes, Elements du Disastre, Nuit, A.N.G., Documents, Tremblement,* and now *La Vie Imaginaire de Jonq'erouas Cym.*

I am a romantic at a time when my expression can only appear as realistic dandyism, if possible with a little humour.

Since 1991 I'm coming back to my favorite color painting, only made of blue and black. Thus so my last series: noir, enigmes, elements du disastre, nuit, A.N.G., Documents, tremblement and mou la vie imaginaire de JONQ'EROUAS Lym.

—Jacques Monory

* * *

There can be little doubt, after one's first encounter with the 'pictures' of Jacques Monory, that this artist—who did not take seriously the creation of works of art from his own hand until 1952 when he was still a student at the Ecole Technique des Arts Appliques, was from the outset an accomplished performer, strange in his imagery but nonetheless amazingly adept.

A picture like *Meutre Novi* (at a time when he was making a series of 'meutres'), oil painted on canvas under plexiglass, declares a total bleakness. Three-quarters of this work shows—at an angle—a relentlessly undecorated tiled wall and, only at the bottom left-hand corner, a crouching half-figure of a man posed with his bald cranium bowed towards the picture-viewer, his hands clutched across his breast, the bent left arm caught by three out of four tracer bullets that have pierced the overall covering of plexiglass creating small starshapes at the point of impact. The dramatic perplexity of such a pictorialised situation attracts and repels simultaneously. Perhaps this is the predominant message of Monory's terrifying appeal.

What, after all, is so sinister about a sort of classic young homburgered American-style "Daddy" in corresponding shoes charging with outstretched hand into a characterless sitting-room to greet a kind of Hollywood girl-child type, neat white bow in hair, faultless knee-length white dress, her arms thrown wide in exaggerated welcome, careering towards him? All this against a tedious duplex background. The huge boring window behind has a large scribble over the lower edge of one of its immense panes, the stuffed easy chair is supremely uncluttered, making furniture and fittings seem like props on a stage for an acting company who could afford nothing better. Admittedly, to one side of the window there is a door ajar, and jackboots slouch beside another armchair which is casually slipping out of the front of the picture, clothes strewn with unconcerned abandon over one of its tightly upholstered arms and across a well-padded back. But where is the Drama? Although this work is 19 years younger than the *Meutre Novi* of 1967, it still conveys a sense of alarm—albeit without the bullet-holes showing.

Maybe it was his dalliance with films and filming in the late seventies that gave him this quixotic Cartier-Bresson flavour of the normal couched in abnormal terms (although actually he provides nothing like the photos of the great cameraman, except in his capacity to evoke the magnetism of a chance happening helping him to build up such a knack for portraying-unusual at its most usual—or vice-versa).

In fairness, not all the works of Monory are quite so worrying in their reticence. Sometimes the murder weapon and the one holding it are only too vivid in visual italics. The *usual* in a world steeped in violence? Happily, not for most of us. But then, if not in style, in intent Monory is a *realist.*

Not surprisingly, besides making his chilling picture inventions, he is also an author and essayist, and he has been able to turn his dauntless talent as an artist to illustrations for books written by others as well. He is a Jack-of-all-Trades, but Master of many, even enhancing a melange of these abilities to transform photography—very much his own photography, of course—into an art-form.

—Sheldon Williams

MOORE, Henry

Nationality: British. **Born:** Castleford, Yorkshire, 30 July 1898. **Education:** Castleford primary schools; studied at Teachers Training College, 1915–16, and at Leeds College of Art, 1919–21, and Royal College of Art, London, 1921–24. **Military Service:** Served as a lance-corporal in the 15th London Regiment, in France and England, 1916–19, and as an official war artist, London, 1940–45. **Family:** Married Irina Radetzky in 1929; daughter: Mary. **Career:** Sculptor: lived in London, 1921–40; produced first Mother and child sculptures, influenced by pre-Columbian art, 1922; lecturer in sculpture, Royal College of Art, 1924–32; founder, with Barbara Hepworth, Ben Nicholson and others, Unit One, London, 1931; founder of the department of sculpture, 1932, and lecturer in sculpture, 1932–39, Chelsea School of Art, London; settled in Much Hadham, Hertfordshire, 1940; also worked in Forte dei Marmi, Italy, from 1977; founded Henry Moore Foundation, Much Hadham, 1977. **Member:** Trustee, Tate Gallery, London, 1941–56; art panel, British Council, 1945; Royal Fine Art Commission, 1948–71; trustee, National Gallery, London, 1955–71; chairman, Auschwitz Memorial Commitee, 1958. **Awards:** International Prize for Sculpture, *Biennale,* Venice, 1948; Sculpture Prize, *Bienal,* Sao Paulo, 1953; Second Prize, *Carnegie International,* Pittsburgh, 1957; Stefan Lochner Medal, Cologne, 1957; Commemorative Award for the Arts, Yeshiva University, New York, 1968; Erasmus Prize, Netherlands, 1968; Gold Medal, Society of the Friends of Art, Cracow, Poland, 1969; Grand Cross of the Order of Merit, Federal German Republic, 1980 ; Order of the Aztec Eagle, Mexico, 1984. Honorary doctorate: University of London, 1953; Harvard University, Cambridge, Massachsetts, 1958; Oxford University, 1961; University of Sussex, Brighton, 1965; Yale University, New Haven, Connecticut, 1966; University of Toronto, 1968; University of Durham, 1970; and Columbia University, New York 1974; Honorary Fellow, Churchill College, Cambridge, 1965, Royal Institute of British Architects, 1971; member, Royal Scottish Academy of Painting, Sculpture and Architecture, 1974. Corresponding member, 1948, and associate, 1975, Académie Royal Flamande des Sciences, Lettres et Beaux-Arts de Belgique; foreign member, Swedish Royal Academy of Fine Arts, 1950, American Academy of Arts and Sciences, 1955; corresponding academician, Academia Nacional de Bellas Artes, Buenos Aires, 1959; member, Wiener Secession, Vienna, 1969; L'Institut of the Académie de Beaux-Arts, Paris, 1975; Academie Europêene des Sciences des Arts et des Lettres, 1981; Commandeur

Henry Moore: *Reclining Figure No. 5*, London, England, 1966. ©Archive Photos, Inc.

de L'Ordre des Arts de des Lettres, Paris, 1973; Cavaliere di Gran Croce dell'Ordine al Merito della Repubblica Italiana, 1972; Companion of Honour, 1955; Order of Merit, 1963. **Died:** Following declining health from arthritis and diabetes, in Much Hadham, Hertfordshire, 31 August 1986.

Individual Exhibitions:

1928 Warren Gallery, London
1931 Leicester Galleries, London
1933 Leicester Galleries, London
1935 Zwemmer Gallery, London
1936 Leicester Galleries, London
1939 Mayor Gallery, London
1941 Temple Newsam, Leeds Yorkshire
1943 Buchholz Gallery, New York
1945 Berkeley Galleries, London
1946 Leicester Galleries, London
Phillips Memorial Gallery, Washington, D.C.
Museum of Modern Art, New York
1947 Art Institute of Chicago (travelled to the San Francisco Museum of Art)
National Gallery of New South Wales, Sydney (toured Australia)
1948 Arts Council Gallery, Cambridge
Galleria d'Arte Moderna, Milan
Roland Browse and Delbanco, London
1949 Wakefield City Art Gallery, Yorkshire
Galerie de Arte Mexicano, Mexico City
1951 Tate Gallery, London
Leicester Galleries, London
Haus am Waldsee, Berlin
Bucholz Gallery, New York
Albertina, Vienna
1952 National Gallery of South Africa, Cape Town
Academian, Stockholm (toured Europe)
Neue Galerie der Stadt, Linz, Austria
Boymans-van Beuningen Museum, Rotterdam
Institute of Contemporary Arts, London
Comite voor Artisticke Werking, Antwerp

Henry Moore. Library of Congress.

Kestner Gesellschaft, Hannover (toured West Germany)
Galerie Welz, Salzburg (with Mario Marini and Fritz Wotruba)
1954 Leicester Galleries, London
Kunsthalle, Mannheim (toured West Germany)
Stadverwaltung, Göttingen, West Germany
Curt Valentin Gallery, New York
1955 Leicester Galleries, London
Kunsthalle, Basel
University of Colorado, Boulder (toured the United States)
Museum of Fine Arts, Montreal (toured Canada and New Zealand)
1958 Hatton Gallery, Newscastle upon Tyne
Marlborough Fine Art, London
Ashmolean Museum, Oxford
1959 Palacio Foz, Lisbon (toured Spain)
Metropolitan Art Gallery, Tokyo (toured Japan)
Middelheim Park, Antwerp
Marlborough Fine Art, London
Zachenta Gallery, Warsaw (toured Poland)
1960 Kunsthalle, Hamburg (toured West Germany)
1962 Arts Council Gallery, Cambridge
Marlborough Fine Art, London
1963 Marlborough Fine Art, London
Wakefield City Art Gallery, Yorkshire
Ferens Art Gallery, Hull, Yorkshire
La Jolla Art Center, California (toured California)
1964 Marlborough Fine Art, London
Palacio de Bellas Artes, Mexico City (toured South America)
1965 Marlborough Fine Art, London
Orleans Gallery, New Orleans
Marlborough Galleria d'Arte, Rome
University of Arizona Art Gallery, Tucson
Arkansas Art Center, Little Rock
Museum des 20 Jahrhunderts, Vienna (with Jean Dubuffet and Mark Tobey)
1966 Marlborough Fine Art, London
City Museum and Art Gallery, Folkstone, Kent (travelled to the Museum and Art Gallery, Plymouth,Devon)

Philadelphia College of Art
Israel Museum, Jerusalem
Sala Delles, Bucharest (toured Eastern Europe)
Cordova Museum, Lincoln, Nebreaska
Sheffield Art Gallery and Museum, Yorkshire
Trinity College, Dublin
Smithsonian Institution, Washington, D.C.
1967 Marlborough Fine Art, London
1968 Tate Gallery, London
Rijksmuseum Kröller-Müller, Otterlo, Netherlands (toured West Germany and the Netherlands)
1969 National Museum of Modern Art, Tokyo (toured Japan and travelled to Hong Kong)
York University
Norwich Castle Museum, Norfolk
1970 Marlborough Gerson Gallery, New York
Knoedler Gallery, New York
Galerie Beyeler, Basel
Galerie Cramer, Geneva (toured Europe and travelled to New York)
Marlborough Fine Art, London (with Pablo Picasso and Graham Sutherland)
1972 Forte di Belvedere, Florence
1973 Fischer Fine Art, London
1974 Los Angeles County Museum of Art
Wilhelm Lehmbruck Museum, Duisburg, West Germany (toured West Germany and Belgium)
1976 Zürcher Forum, Zurich
Imperial War Museum, London
Scottish National Gallery of Modern Art, Edinburgh (with Kenneth Martin)
Fischer Fine Art, London
Grafton Gallery, Bury St. Edmonds, Suffolk
Lillian Heidenberg Gallery, New York
1977 Orangerie des Tuilleries, Paris
Bibliothèque Nationale, Paris
Gracefield Arts Centre, Dumfries, Scotland
Art Gallery of Ontario, Toronto (toured Japan and travelled to London 1977–78)
1978 Cartwright Hall and Lister Park, Bradford, Yorkshire
Serpentine Gallery, London
Tate Gallery, London
Bayerischen Staatsgemaldesammlungen, Munich
Galeira Joan Prats, Barcelona
Festival Gallery, Aldeburgh, Suffolk
Gallery Kasahara, Osaka, Japan
Stiftung Landis und Gyr, Zug, Switzerland
Schossgut Wolfsberg, Ermstigen, Switzerland
Galeria Pieter Coray, Lugano, Switzerland
1979 Prince Henry's High School, Evesham, Worcestershire
Wildenstein Gallery, New York
Jersey Museum, Channel Islands
Bundeskanzleramt, Bonn (travelled to William Hack Museum, Ludwigshafen, West Germany)
Umetnosti Pavilijon, Slovenj Gradec, Yugoslavia (travelled to the Serbian Academy, Belgrade)
1980 Il Bisonte, Florence
Victoria and Albert Museum, London
Galerie Levy und Forderkreis, Hamburg
Campus West Library, Welwyn Garden City, Hertfordshire
Fishcer Fine Art, London
Galerie Patrick Cramer, Geneva
1981 125 Raskowsky, Sofia, Bulgaria
Retire Park, Madrid
Gulbenkian Foundation, Lisbon
Royal Museum, Folkestone
Galleria Bergamini, Milan
Wildenstein Gallery, London
Contemporary Sculpture Center, Tokyo
Gallery Welz, Salzburg
Alex Rosenberg Gallery, New York
1982 Joan Miró Foundation, Barcelona
Fine Arts Center, Colorado Springs
Galleria Comunale, Forte dei Marmi, Italy
Hoam Art Museum, Seoul, Korea
Durham Light Infantry Museum, County Durham
Fischer Fine Art, London
Linda Goodman Gallery, Sandton, South Africa
1983 Galerie Maeght, Paris
Alex Rosen Gallery, New York
1984 Marlborough Fine Art, London
Marlborough Graphics, London
Kunstmuseum, Herning, Denmark
Columbus Museum of Art, Ohio
1985 San Francisco Museum of Modern Art
Art Gallery of Ontario, Toronto
1986 Kent Fine Art, New York
Galerie Patrick Cramer, Geneva
Thomas Gibson Fine Art, London
1987 Marlborough Fine Art, London
Fischer Fine Art, London
Vallecchi Editore, Florence, Italy
Hofstra University, Hempstead, New York
1988 Art Gallery of Ontario, Toronto
Marlborough Fine Art, London
1990 Mead Gallery, Coventry
1991 Gosudarstvennyi Muzei Al.S. Pushkina, Moscow
1992 Art Gallery of New South Wales, Sydney
Waddington Galleries, London
Didier Imbert Fine Art, Paris
1995 Galeria BWA, Krakow
Waddington Galleries, London
Grosvenor Gallery, London
1998 Berkeley Square Gallery, London
Brighton Museum and Art Gallery, Brighton
Yorkshire Sculpture Park, West Bretton

Selected Group Exhibitions:

1936 *Fantastic Art, Dada and Surrealism,* Museum of Modern Art, New York
1948 *Biennale,* Venice
1962 *Art since 1950,* Ca'Pesaro, Venice
1967 *Guggenheim International,* New York
1968 *British Sculpture of the 50s,* Musée des Augustins, Toulouse
1973 *Henry Moore to Gilbert and George,* Palais des Beaux-Arts, Brussels

1982 *Gauguin to Moore: Primitivism in Modern Sculpture,* Art Gallery of Ontario, Toronto
1983 *Aspects of British Art,* Guggenheim Museum, New York
1988 *Sculpture: Inside Outside,* Walker Art Center, Minneapolis
1989 *Selections from the Beatrice and Philip Gersh Collection,* Museum of Contemporary Arts, Los Angeles
1990 *British Modernism,* City Art Gallery, Leeds
1991 *The Marlborough Gallery Re-opening Exhibition,* London
1992 *Modern Sculpture,* Marlborough Gallery, New York
1995 *Here & Now,* Serpentine Gallery, London
1945: the End of the War, Annely Juda Fine Art, London
1996 *A Century of English Sculpture,* Galerie Nationale du Jeu de Paume, Paris
A Century of Sculpture: the Nasher Collection, Fine Arts Museums, San Francisco
1997 *British Art: a Selection from Waddington Galleries,* Foire Internationale d'Art Contemporain, Paris
1998 *Art Treasures of England: the Regional Collections,* Royal Academy of Arts, London
The Thirties: Influences on Abstract Art in Britain, Annely Juda Fine Art, London

Collections:

Tate Gallery, London; Victoria and Albert Museum, London; Henry Moore Foundation, Much Hadham, Hertfordshire; Stedelijk Musaeum, Amsterdam; Israel Museum, Jerusalem; National Gallery of Victoria, Melbourne; Art Gallery of Ontario, Toronto; Hirshhorn Museum and Sculpture Garden, Washington, D.C.; Museum of Modern Art, New York; Experimental Museum, Mexico City.

Publications:

By MOORE: Books—*Henry Moore's Sheep Sketchbook,* London, New York and Paris 1980; *Henry Moore: Sculpture,* edited by David Mitchinson, Barcelona, London, New York and Stuttgart 1981. **Articles**—statement in *Architectural Association Journal* (London), May 1930; statement in *Unit One: The Modern Movement in English Architecture, Painting and Sculpture,* London 1934; ''Mesopotamian Art'' in *The Listener* (London), June 1953; ''The Sculptor Speaks'' in *The Listener* (London), August 1937; ''Primitive Art'' in *The Listener* (London), April 1941; ''The Living Image: Art and Life'' in *The Listener* (London), November 1941; ''Note on the Madonna and Child Statue'' in *Transformation* (London), no. 3, 1945; ''Message de la Sculpture'' in *XXe Siécle* (Paris), 1951; ''Interview with Ark Magazine'' in *Ark* (London), November 1952; ''The Sculptor in Modern Society'' in *Artnews* (New York), November 1952; ''Henry Moore Talking to David Sylvester'' in *The Listener* (London), August 1963; statements in *Henry Moore at the British Museum,* London 1981.

On MOORE: Books—*Henry Moore, Sculptor* by Herbert Read, London 1934; *Henry Moore: Sculpture and Drawings,* volume I and II by Herbert Read, volume III by Herbert Read and Alan Bowness, volumes IV and V by Alan Bowness, London and New York 1944–82; *Meaning and Symbolism in Three Modern Artists: Edvard Munch, Henry Moore, Paul Nash* by George Wingfield-Digby, London 1955; *The Archetypal World of Henry Moore* by Eric Neuman, New York 1959; *The Art of Henry Moore* by Will Grohmann, London 1960; *Henry Moore: A Study of His Life and Work* by Herbert Read, London 1965; *Henry Moore: Carvings 1923–1966* by Robert Melville, London 1967; *Henry Moore: Sculpture and Drawings 1921–1969* by Robert Melville, London, 1970; *Henry Moore in America* by Henry J. Seldis, London 1973; *Henry Moore: Catalog of Graphic Work,* 3 volumes, by Gerald and Patrick K. Cramer, Alistair Grant and David Mitchinson, Geneva 1973–80; *Henry Moore: Drawings* by Kenneth Clark, London and New York 1974; *Henry Moore: Sculpture and Environment* by David Finn, New York and London 1977; *With Henry Moore: The Artist at Work* by Gemma Levine, London and New York 1978; *Henry Moore: Sculptures in Landscape* by Geoffrey Shakerley and Stephen Spender, London, Oslo and New York 1978; *The Moore Collection in the Gallery of Ontario* by Alan G. Wilkinson, Toronto 1979; *Henry Moore: Portrait of an Artist* by John Read, London 1979; *Henry Moore: The Reclining Figure,* exhibition catalog with essays by Steven W. Rousen, Ann Garrould and others, Columbus, Ohio 1984; *Henry Moore's Photographs of his Sculpture,* exhibition catalog with essay by Van Deren Coke, San Francisco 1985; *Henry Moore: Drawings* by Ann Garrould, New York 1988;*The Life of Henry Moore* by Roger Berthoud, London 1986; *Henry Moore Remembered* by Alan G. Wilkinson, Toronto 1988; *Henry Moore: Mother and Child—Etchings and Small Sculpture,* by Julian Stallabrass, London 1990; *Henry Moore: the Human Dimension* by Henry Meyric Hughes, V.V. Znamenov and Irina Antonova, Halifax 1991; *Henry Moore, 1898–1986,* exhibition catalog, with essays by Susan Compton, Nick Waterlow, Alan Bowness and Edmund Capon, Sydney 1992; *Henry Moore, 1898–1986,* exhibition catalog, London 1992; *One Man's Henry Moore* by David Finn, Redding Ridge 1993; *Of the Human Form,* exhibition catalog, London 1995; *Henry Moore: Sculpture from the 40s and 50s,* exhibition catalog, London 1995; *Henry Moore 1898–1986: a Centenary Exhibition,* exhibition catalog, London 1998; *Art Treasures of England: the Regional Collections,* exhibition catalog, with text by Giles Waterfield, London 1998. **Articles**—''Henry Moore and the Pub'' by Robin Peck in *C Magazine,* no. 17, Spring 1988; ''Looking at Henry Moore'' by Glynn Williams in *Modern Painters* (London); ''Figurative Sculpture After Henry Moore'' by Anthony O'Hear in *Modern Painters* (London), vol. 4, no. 2, Summer 1991; ''Henry Moore as Medalist'' by Karen Coke in *Medal,* no. 21, Autumn 1992; ''Sculpture in the Tuileries'' by Karen Wilkin, in *New Criterion,* vol. 18, no. 1, September 1999. **Films**—*Henry Moore, Sculptor,* directed by John Read, 1951; *Henry Moore: London 1940–42,* directed by Nancy Thomas, 1963; *Henry Moore: Man of Form,* directed by Anthony Roland, 1965; *Henry Moore: At Home,* directed by John Read, 1973; *A Henry Moore for Moline,* directed by Arthur Wolf, 1975; *Henry Moore at 80,* directed by John Read, 1978.

* * *

Owing to his service in the First World War, Henry Moore was a late starter in art. On demobilization from the army in 1919, he went to Leeds School of Art. He stayed two years and went on to the Royal College of Art until 1925, when he visited Italy. He joined the staff of the Royal College and later transferred to the Chelsea School of Art until 1939.

The human figure has always been at the root of Moore's work and, as he has said, he found principles of form and rhythm from the study of natural objects. From his earliest productions there existed a formal difference between the carved and the modelled work. From

1922 his carvings in wood and stone follow an intense interest in extra-European sculptures: the Egyptian, the Sumerian, the African and chiefly the Mexican pre-Columbian epitomised in the Aztec Chacmool. The chunky solidity of the last contrasted with the more naturalistic flow of the few bronzes from the female life modes. After 1930 he was clearly coming to terms with the amalgam of form and feeling. An abstraction of shape in the figure carvings lends them an added warmth.

There followed a flirtation with forms owing something to the example of Picasso in their distorted imagery, and also to the surrealist juxtapositions of Giacometti. Hollowing out of the centred mass of his figures occured in the 1930s, when Moore was experimenting in various directions, some to be abandoned quickly, others continuing profitably, such as the opened-out interiors of a torso in clay, concrete and subsequently wood. Developing from the opening-out came the stringed and enclosed objects as seen through the aperture in the outer shell.

During the 1940s Moore returned to a more figurative idiom best known in his ''Madonna and Child'' for St. Matthew's Church, Northampton. This carving in stone has obvious debts to Massaccio and Michelangelo in its simple dignity and broad fullness of form that were to be stylised in the family groups and standing figures of the period. In parallel to his sculptures came the exciting activity between 1940 and 1942 as an official war artist, when he made his famous Shelter Drawings. Undeniably the most monumental to emerge from the hostilities, they have a strong similarity to the iconography of Mantegna.

Moore always worked in a continuous and varied investigation of glyptic possibilities, going back to ideas begun 20 or 30 years before, and making new works taking up from the previous ones as departure points. Relationships of man and woman, and mother and child, as well as the free-standing single figures, make the 1950s a productive and important phase of Moore's career. Bronzes predominate with occasional exceptions, like the grand ''Internal and External Forms,'' 1954, almost nine feet high, carved like a mammoth paepod pierced to reveal its figure sheltering symbolically within. ''King and Queen'' of a year earlier is separate yet unified by its stylised affinity. In an outdoor setting the bronze group has an imposing character when seen from a distance. In the 1960s Moore produced some of his most telling abstract works, developing the separation and locking-together motives that underlined the unified concepts of the whole. More than any other sculptor before him, though acknowledging the pioneering example of Brancusi, Moore revealed an extensive vocabulary of form symbols that he employed in the creation of significant total images.

Paraphrases of human anatomy found in rocks and pebbles, and even in the contours of mountain ranges, have been enlarged and enhanced by Moore in numinous artifacts that carry their intrinsic proportions of scale acceptable in any size from maquette to massive cast. While he may instil into an inert bronze some of the overpowering atmosphere of its theme, like ''Atom Piece'' (1964), or endow the warmth of the glowing red Soroya marble ''Three Rings'' of 19667 with a purified balance of mass and distanced voids, it is man in the universe that dominates Moore's prodigious and prolific output. He fulfils his contemporary role as explorer of continents never before examined, recycling inherited universal visual experiences in catalytic fusion of imagination and eminent tactile reality.

—G. S. Whittet

MORELLET, François

Nationality: French. **Born:** Cholet, 30 April 1926. **Education:** College Colbert, Cholet, 1932–36, 1940–41; Lycée Charlemagne, Paris, 1937–39, 1942–44; Ecole des Langues Orientales, Paris, 1945–47; received degree in Russian, 1947; mainly self-taught in art from 1947; influenced by meeting Almir Mavignier, 1950, and Max Bill, 1954. **Family:** Married Danielle Marchand in 1946; children: Frederic, Christophe and Florent. **Career:** General Manager, Morellet-Guerineau toy factory, Cholet, 1948–75. Artist, working with kinetic and optical experiments, Cholet, since 1950. Founder, with Sobrino, Le Parc, Stein, Yvaral and Rossi, Groupe de Recherche d'Art Visuel, Paris, 1960–68. **Awards:** First Prize (with G.R.A.V.), *4th Biennale di San Marino,* 1963; Ohara Museum Prize, *Tokyo Print Biennale,* 1974; First Prize, *Bienal,* Sao Paulo, 1975; Will Grohmann Prize, West Berlin, 1979; Silver Medal, *2nd Triennale of Drawing,* Wroclaw, 1981; Grand Prix National de la Sculpture, France, 1986; Superior Prize and 5th Henry Moore Grand Prize, Hakone, Japan, 1987. **Agents:** Galerie Liliane et Michel Durand-Dessert, 3 rue des Haudriettes, 75003 Paris, France; Galerie M, Haus Weitmar, 4630 Bochum, Germany. **Address:** 83 rue Porte-Baron, 49300 Cholet, France.

Individual Exhibitions:

1950 Galerie Creuze, Paris
1958 Galerie Colette Allendy, Paris
1960 Galerie Aujourd'hui, Palais des Beaux-Arts, Brussels
1961 Galerie Nota, Monaco
Galerie Studio F, Ulm, West Germany
1962 Studio G, Zagreb
1966 Galerie der Spiegel, Cologne
1967 Galerie Denise René Rive Droite, Paris
Galerie Denise René Rive Gauche, Paris
Indica Gallery, London
1969 Galerie Plus Kern, Ghent
Galerie Swart, Amsterdam
Halfmannshof, Gelsenkirchen, West Germany
1970 Galerie M. Bochum, West Germany
Galerie Denise René-Hans Mayer, Dusseldorf
Galerie Swart, Amsterdam
Galleri Artestudio, Macerata, Italy
1971 Galleria Cenobio-Visualita, Milan
Van Abbemuseum, Eindhoven, Netherlands
Centre National d'Art Contemporain, Paris
Galerie Denise René Rive Gauche, Paris
Kunstverein, Hamburg
Städtische Museum, Leverkusen, West Germany
Eat Art Galerie, Dusseldorf
Galerie M, Bochum, West Germany
Kunstverein, Frankfurt
Galerie Thomas Keller, Starnberg, West Germany
Galerie Lichter, Frankfurt
1972 White Gallery, Lutry, Switzerland
Palais des Beaux-Arts, Brussels
Galerie Plus Kern, Ghent
Kunstmuseum, Bochum, West Germany
Lucy Milton Gallery, London
Musee des Beaux-Arts, Grenoble, France

Kunstmuseum, Dusseldorf
Galerie Media, Neuchâtel, Switzerland
1973 Galerie Zodiak, Geneva
Musée des Beaux-Arts, Nantes, France
Galeria Arte Contacto, Caracas
Museum Sztuki, Lodz, Poland
Galerie Swart, Amsterdam
Galerie Le Disque Rouge, Brussels
Galerie Müller-Roth, Stuttgart
Centre Culturel, St. Pierre des Corps, France (toured France)
1974 Lucy Milton Gallery, London
Galerie Lydia Megert, Bern
Studio Plus Kern, Brussels
Galleria Cavallino, Venice
Galleria Trinita, Rome
Galleria Uxa, Novara, Italy
Galerie 58, Rapperswil, Switzerland
Studio Casati, Merate, Italy
Galerie Ernst, Hannover
Gallerie 2B, Bergamo, Italy
Musee Bargoin, Clermont Ferrand, France (toured France)
1975 Studio Marconi, Milan
Galleria Sincron, Brescia, Italy
Galleria Il Centro, Naples
Galleria E, Bolzano, Italy
Galerie M, Bochum, West Germany
Galerie M, The Hague
Galerie A, Parma
Galerie Swart, Amsterdam
Art Research Center, Kansas City
1976 Verfindustrie, Heerlen, Netherlands
Club 44, La Chaux de Fonds, Switzerland
Galerie Hermanns, Munich
Galerie 13, Angers, France
Galerie Müller-Roth, Stuttgart
Galerie F. L., Rome
Multipla de Arte, Sao Paulo
Galleria Beniamino, Sanremo, Italy
Lichtobjekte, Westfälischer Kunstverein, Münster, West Germany
Galleria Giuli, Lecco, Italy
Centro Serre Ratti, Como, Italy
1977 Nationalgalerie, West Berlin
Staatliche Kunsthalle, Baden-Baden, West Germany
Musée d'Art Moderne de la Ville, Paris
Kunsthalle, Kiel, West Germany
Galerie Swart, Amsterdam
Annely Juda Gallery, London
Galerie Nancy Gillespie-Elisabeth De Laage, Paris
Centro del Portello, Genova
Galerie Le Disque Rouge, Brussels
Studio Casati, Merate, Italy
Galerie Latzer, Kreuzlingen, Switzerland
Galerie Dritte, Zofingen, Switzerland
Atelier de Recherche Esthetique, Caen, France
1978 Commanderie van St. Jan, Nijmeegs Museum, Netherlands
Electric Gallery, Toronto
Galerie Gilles Gheerbrant, Montreal
Cloitre St. Trophime, Arles, France
Galeria Cadaques, Cadaques, Spain
Galerie Seestrasse, Rapperswil, Switzerland
Galerie Lydia Mergert, Bern
Galerie Nancy Gillespie-Elisabeth De Laage, Paris
Galerie Lachowsky, Brussels
Galerie Magazijn, Groningen, Netherlands
Studio Marconi, Milan
Galleria Piero Cavellini, Brescia, Italy
Galleria Uxa, Novara, Italy
1979 Galeria Eude, Barcelona
Galerie Swart, Amsterdam
Galerie Mörner, Stockholm
1980 Galerie Nordenhake, Malmo, Sweden
Galerie Le Coin du Miroir, Dijon, France
Galerie Genevieve et Serge Mathieu, Besancon, France
Galerie Hermanns, Munich
Galerie Müller-Roth, Stuttgart
Musée des Beaux-Arts, Toulon
Galleria La Bottega del Quátro, Bergamo, Italy
Galerie Fritz Buhler, Biel-Bienne, Switzerland
Galerie M, Bochum, West Germany
1981 Centre Jean Vilar, Angers, France
Helsingin Kaupungin Taidesmuseo, Helsinki
Galerie Gilles Gheerbrant, Montreal
East Gallery, London
Annely Juda Gallery, London
Galerie Durand-Dessert, Paris
1982 Galerie Lydia Megert, Bern
Musée Savoisien, Chambery, France
Kunstcentrum Badhuis, Gorinchem, Netherlands
Centre Culturel, Cherbourg, France
Musée des Beaux-Arts, Angers, France
1983 Galerie Convergences, Nantes, France
Musée Municipal, La Roche sur Yon, France
Tour Narbonnaise, Carcassonne, France
Galerie au Fond de la cour a droite, Chagny, France
Ecole d'Architecture Saint Luc, Ghent
Stadtmuseum Quadrant, Bottrop, West Germany
1984 Wilhelm-Hack-Museum, Ludwigshafen, West Germany
Galerie Nordenhake, Malmo, Sweden
Albright-Knox Art Gallery, Buffalo, New York (travelled to Montreal, New York and Miami)
1985 Galerie Durand-Dessert, Paris
Musée Saint Pierre, Lyon, France
Galerie M, Bochum, West Germany
Galerie Zographia, Bordeaux, France
Galerie Kunst + Architektur, Hamburg
Abbaye Royale de Fontevraud, France
1986 Centre Georges Pompidou, Paris (retrospective travelled to Amsterdam)
Galerie Plus-Kern, Brussels
Artothèque, Montpellier, France
Musée des Arts, Cholet, France
Galerie Steendrukkerij, Amsterdam
Galerie Oniris, Rennes, France
Musée Fabre, Montpellier, France
Galerie Blanche, Stockholm
Bruno Facchetti Gallery, New York
Oscarsson-Siegeltuch Gallery, New York

Galerie Emmerich/Margrit Bauman, Zurich
Centre d'Art Contemporain, Dijon, France
1987 Bruno Facchetti Gallery, New York
Rijksmuseum Kröller-Müller, Otterlo, Netherlands
Groninger Museum, Groningen, Netherlands
1988 Galerie Müller-Roth, Stuttgart
Ecole Régionale des Beaux-Arts Georges Pompidou, Dunkerque
Galerie Liliane et Michel Durand-Dessert, Paris
Ecole Supérieure d'Art Visuel, Genève
Maison du Livre, Villeurbanne
Château Génicart, Lormont
Galerie Dorothea van der Koelen, Mayence
Galleria Piero Cavellini, Milan
Galerie Municipale de l'Ancienne Poste, Calais
1989 Université Rennes 2, Rennes
La Crieé, Hall d'Art Contemporain, Rennes
Musée Denys Puech, Rodez
Regards sur l'oeuvre 1957–1989, Galerie im Taxispalais Innsbruck (travelled to Westfälisches Landesmuseum, Münster; Institut Français, Vienne; Galerie Municipale Prisma, Bolzano; Galerija suvremene Umjetnosti, Zagreb; Galerie Hermanns, Munich)
1990 *Collection Morellet du Musée des Arts de Cholet,* Musée San Telmo, San Sébastian (travelled to Galerie Artaffairs, Amsterdam; Sala Amarica-Vitoria; Palais des Beaux-Arts, Brussels; Palacio de Los Condes de Gabia, Granada)
François Morellet à l'Institut Francais, Institut Français, London
Néons: Tournus Art Contemporain, Réfectoire et Cellier des Moines, Tournus
Hommage aux Tilleuls et à Rodin par François Morellet, Musée Rodin, Paris
Musée des Beaux-Arts et de la Dentelle, Calais
Galerie Sollertis, Toulouse
Galerie Theo, Barcelona
1991 Saarland Museum, Saarbrücken
Dessins des années 40 et 50: Tableaux Blancs des Années 80, Musée des Beaux Arts, Grenoble (travelled to Stiftung für Konkrete Kunst, Reutlingen; Musée National d'Art Moderne, Centre Georges Pompidou, Paris)
1992 Forum des Landes Museums, Hanover
Van Reekum Museum, Apeldoorn (catalog)
1993 Galerie Durand-Dessert, Paris
Musée Denys Puech, Rodez
Galerie Art Attitude, Nancy
Galerie Hlavniho Města Prahy, Prague
1994 Maçka Sanat Galerisi, Istanbul
Installations, Städtische Kunstsammlungen Chemnitz, Stuttgart
1995 *Neonly,* Städtische Galerie im Lenbachhaus, Munich (catalog)
50 Werke aus 50 Jahren Künstlerischer Arbeit 1945-1995, Stadtmuseum Oldenburg (catalog)
1996 Neues Museum Weserburg Bremen, Bremen (catalog)
Espace de l'Art Concret, Mouans-Sartoux, France (catalog)
Galerie Dorothea van der Koelen, Mainz (catalog)
1997 *L'Armor Relais de l'Art Morellet,* Musée des Beaux- Arts, Rennes (catalog)
Musée des Beaux-Arts d'Angers (catalog)
1998 Nicholas Davies Gallery, New York
1999 *Gravure, 1980–1999,* Musée de la Cohue, Vannes (catalog)
Centre de Creation Contemporaine, Tours, France
2000 Musée Zadkine, Paris (catalog)
Galerie Friebe, Lüdenscheid

Selected Group Exhibitions:

1961 *Movement,* Moderna Museet, Stockholm (travelled to Stedelijk Museum, Amsterdam)
1965 *The Responsive Eye,* Museum of Modern Art, New York, (toured the United States)
1967 *Lumiére et Mouvement,* Musée d'Art Moderne, Paris
1975 *Bienal,* Sao Paulo
1977 *Documenta 6,* Kassel, West Germany
1980 *Printed Art since 1965,* Museum of Modern Art, New York
1983 *Concepts in Construction 1910–80,* Tyler Museum of Art, Texas (toured the United States and Canada)
1985 *Vom Zeichen: Aspekte der Ziechnung 1960–85,* Kunstverein, Frankfurt (travelled to Kassel and Vienna)
1988 *Biennale of Sydney,* Art Gallery of New South Wales (travelled to National Gallery of Victoria, Melbourne)
1992 *The Principle of Chance: Games, Methods and Systems in Twentieth Century Art,* Wilhelm-Hack Museum, Ludwigshafen
1994 *Collection 1991,* Musée d'Art Contemporain de Lyon, France (catalog)
Dadamaino, A. Arte Studio Invernizzi, Milan (catalog)
1995 *KA! Editions, 1990–1995,* Eagle Gallery, London (catalog)
1997 *Hommages a Vasarely,* Musee des Beaux-Arts, Charleroi, Belgium
Retrospective Soto, Jeu de Paume, Paris
1998 *Waves Breaking on the Shore. . . Ad Dekkers in His Time,* Stedelijk Museum, Amsterdam (catalog)
Centre d'Art Contemporain, Grenoble, Magasin (catalog)
2000 *Light Pieces,* Forum d'Art Contemporain, Casino Luxembourg (catalog)

Collections:

Centre Georges Pompidou, Paris; Hirshhorn Museum, Washington, D.C.; Tate Gallery, London; Stedelijk Museum, Amsterdam; Nationalgalerie, Berlin; Kunstmuseum, Dusseldorf; Kunsthaus, Zurich; Moderna Musset, Stockholm; Albright-Knox Gallery, Buffalo, New York; Musée des Beaux-Arts, Montreal; Städtische Museum Schloss Morsbroich, Leverkusen, Germany.

Public Installations: Debis Complex, Potsdamer Platz, Berlin.

Publications:

By MORELLET: Books—*Pour une peinture experimentale programmee,* with Groupe de Recherche d'Arte Visuel, Paris 1962;

Pour un art abstrait progressif, with F. Molnar, Zagreb 1963; *90 (degrees),* Cholet, France 1970; *François Morellet: Relâches et free-vol,* exhibition catalog, Paris 1993. **Articles**—"Für eine programmierte experimentelle Malerei" in *Francois Morellet,* exhibition catalog, Calogne 1966; "Mise en condition du spectateur" in *Lumière et Mouvement,* exhibition catalog, Paris 1967; "The Choice in Present-Day Art" in *Data,* edited by Anthony Hill, London, 1968; "Zur Situation des Kunstbetrachters" in *Fordererkreis des Wilhelm Lehmbruck Museums,* exhibition catalog, Duisburg, West Germany 1970; "Du spectatuer au spectatuer ou l'art de deballer son pique-nique" in *Morellet,* exhibition catalog, Eindhoven, Netherlands, 1971; "Auto-critique/Autokritika" in *10 Biennale de Gravure,* exhibition catalog, Ljubljana 1973; "1st History—2nd, The Moral" in *Morellet,* exhibition catalog, London 1974; "Fragen an Francois Morellet," with Gisland Nabakowski, in *Heute Kunst* (Dusseldorf), June/August 1975; "Die direkten Lichtquellen" in *Francois Morellet: Lichtobjekte,* exhibition catalog, Münster 1976; "Les Années 70" in *Skira Annuel,* Geneva 1980; "Pourquoi ai-je été incapable d'écrire un article dans Quad" in *Quad* (Paris), July 1980; "Apropos d'oeuvres éphemères et d'integrations architecturales" in *Mise en pieces, Mise en place, Mise au point,* exhibition catalog, Chalon-sur-Saône, France 1981; "La geometrie des contraintes" in *Media 81,* exhibition catalog, Neuchâtel, Switzerland 1981; "J'ai realise depuis 1968 de nombreuses oeuvres ephemeres" and "Nota" in *Murs,* exhibition catalog, Paris 1981; "Doctor de Stijl and Mister Bonset" in *Colloque International: Theo van Doesburg,* Dijon 1982; "Geometrees" in *Francois Morellet: Geometrie,* exhibition catalog, Fontevraud 1985; interview with Serge Lemoine in *CNAC Magazine* (Paris), January/February 1986; "Au secours la droite revient" in *Francois Morellet: Geometrie dans les spasmes,* exhibition catalog, Dijon 1987; interview with Marie-Francoise Le Saux in *Nouvelles de l'Estampe,* no. 163, March 1999.

On MORELLET: Books—*A la recherche d'une base: Peintures de Morellet,* by Francois Molnar, Nantes 1958; *Constructivism: Origins and Evolution* by George Rickey, New York 1967; *L'Art cinetique* by Frank Popper, Paris 1967; *Kinetic Art* by Guy Brett, London and New York 1968; *Optical Art* by René Parola, New York and London 1969; *Late Modern: The Visual Arts since 1945,* by Edward Lucie-Smith, London and New York 1969; *Op Art* by Cyril Barrett, London and New York, 1970; *History of Art,* H.W. Janson, New York 1971; *Human Information Processing* by P. H. Lindsay and D. A. Norman, New York and London 1972; *Francois Morellet: Les regles du jeu* by Michel Baudson, Brussels 1972; *L'Art actuel en France* by Anne Tronche and Hervé Gloaguen, Paris 1973; *Beyond Modern Sculpture* by Jack Burnham, New York 1973; *Geschichte der abstrakten Kunst 1900–1960* by Cor Blok, Cologne 1975; *Art: Action and Participation* by Frank Popper, London 1976; *Le Declin de l'object* by Frank Popper, Paris 1975; *Constructive Concepts,* by Willy Rotzler, Zurich 1977; *Concepts of Modern Art,* edited by Tony Richardson and Nikos Stangos, New York and London 1979; *Francois Morellet: Systems,* exhibition catalog with texts by Jan Van der Marck and Charlotta Kotik, New York 1984; *Francois Morellet: Retrospective,* exhibition catalog with texts by Dominique Bozo, Catherine Millet and others, Paris 1986; *François Morellet,* by Serge Lemoine, Zurich 1986; *Francois Morelett: Lichtinstallaties,* exhibition catalog with text by Frans Haks, Groningen 1987; *L'art contemporain en France* by Catherine Millet, Paris 1987; *Skulptur Projekte in Münster,* exhibition catalog, Cologne, Germany 1987; *Pluralisme depuis 1960: Histoire de l'art moderne* by Marco Livingstone, Paris 1988; *Les années 50,* exhibition catalog, Paris 1988; *Liberté et Egalité,* exhibition catalog, Saarbrücken, Germany 1991; *Künstler: Kritisches Lexikon der Gegenwartskunst,* Munich 1992. **Articles**—"Francois Morellet" by Gerard Denizeau in *L'Oeil* (Lausanne), no. 448, January-February 1993.

*

Part 1—History.

1926–1952 Nothing of interest. From 1952 onwards I have been making useless, therefore artistic, objects with the constant purpose of reducing to a minimum my arbitrary decisions. I have suppressed composition, removed all interest in the execution, and above all I have applied rigorously systems which are both simple and obvious. The only elements of "fantasy" are brought about by genuine chance or by the spectator's participation. All this has been done in an atmosphere of total apathy as regards the general public.

Recently, however, the specialists have discovered in my "work," according to their particular temperament, severity, mirth, nihilism, anguish, virtuosity, asceticism, etc. It has reminded them of planetary constellations, rain on puddles, "la petite madeleine" of Proust and so on.

Part 2—The Moral.

They are right in thinking all this, for the plastic arts must allow the spectator to find in them what he wants—that is to say what he brings to them himself. Works of art are like picnic areas or Spanish Inns, where one consumes what one takes there oneself.

Art is meant to say nothing (or everything). Specialists who respect each other experience each of them a different picnic, in opposition to one another and often contrary to the intention which the artist would himself have formulated. When, during their life-time, artists seem to agree with certain of their commentators, it is most cases because they have accepted, with astonishment and delight the significance given by these people to their work. Even more they have then sought to resemble the image, now given them.

The impossibility of conveying "messages" is evident, for example, in politics. How well I understand the distrust felt by dictators towards the artists of the avant-garde—even those of the same political turn of mind! (I cannot on the other hand conceive why those obsessed by politics choose, to express themselves, something so ambiguous and corrupt as art).

It is the great fraternity, the great conspiracy of the "great men" to make the "little men" believe that if Pasteur, Karl Marx, de Gaulle, Cezanne, had died at birth, no one would have been saved from rabies, capitalism, nazism, or impressionism. Of course, the cult of personality is natural. It was natural that we should worship Jesus Christ, Hitler or Elvis Presley. It is those who are worshipped who commit the fault in allowing themselves to be worshipped. They are the real reactionaries, those artist who, voluntarily or not, cultivate the arbitrary, allow one to believe in the existence of some secret justification, play the unknown despot, all the while considering themselves to be the revolutionary element in art. Since Duchamp, all the numerous revolutionary artists have been equally skillful in destroying the art of their predecessors as they have been in building up their own brilliant image.

All this will never change unless the geniuses cease being brilliant and concern themselves with becoming simply the awakeners, the masters of ceremony of the general public—that public which still does not realise that it is itself a genius (see Filliou).

Alternatively perhaps, the spectators might come to realise that, as in that tale by Hans Christian Andersen, ''The Emperor's New Clothes,'' it is they, they spectators, thanks to their brilliant imagination, who invest with splendour the Emperors and the artist. It would be a marvellous entertainment (but it would all the same be ironic that it should happen just as the picnickers begin to invest me with brilliance).

—François Morellet

Prominent in the activities of the Group de Recherche d'Art Visuel, of which he was a founding member, and a constant exhibitor with the Nouvelle Tendence, François Morellet combined aesthetic proclivities with a scientific interest in new and out-of-the-way avenues of perception. His activities in his field were extremely versatile. He sought new applications for graphic techniques, explored new effects of light, and made important uses of scientific investigations into the effects of cyclical rotation.

From the early 1950s he explored the possibilities of the statistical distribution of identical elements over a picture surface in order to create an impression of complete homogeneity vibrant with optical energy. At the same time he was working with the superimposition or partial superimposition of uniform grills in order to create unexpected or semihallucinatory effects in space. Particular attention was attracted by his *Sphére-trames,* which were cellular spheres built up of metal rods and tubes set at right angles to each other and sometimes measuring as much as six feet in diameter, and by his *Grillagés,* which were metal frames and meshes set one above the other with different axes. Many of them were hung as mobiles for the sake of their curious properties in regard to the reflection of light and for the optical illusions they effected. Later they were sometimes given an architectural context by being designed for a particular site. These were considered to mark the early stages in the passage from statis to kinetic Op art. In 1970 Morellet collaborated with the architect Claude Parent in designing a room with ''oblique space'' for the French Pavilion at the 35th Venice *Biennale.* And in 1970 and 1971 he applied his earlier techniques to a large-scale commission for the Plateau Beaubourg, Paris, designing decorations in blue and red on the blind walls of houses to give the impression of superimposed grills. Both these works were considered to be important landmarks of Op art.

From about 1963 Morellet also turned his attention to the creation of rhythmical effects by the use of a light source, working first with white light and later with white and red neon rods or tubes in order to produce rhythmic accents in space. In this, as also of course in his mobiles, stochasticism or the element of chance, played a significant part. Morellet was also among the foremost of those who advocated spectator participation. In his light structures the spectator was allowed to initiate and control the rhythmical processes by means of buttons and switches. Morellet's theory was that the artist provides the basic elements, but the work of art emerges only with the collaboration of the spectator—together with the play of chance. In a small publication of 1971 entitled *Du Spectateur au spectateur ou l'art de déballer son pique-nique* he wrote: ''For roughly 20 years I have obstinately continued to produce works which have been based on the guiding principle of reducing my arbitrary decisions to a minimum. To put limits on my 'artist's sensibility,' I among others have made use of simple and obvious systems, of pure chance, and of spectator participation.'' He concludes the spectator should ''cease to be the humble vassal of the great genius. Let him recover his dignity, his activity before those who should be no more than the leaders of the game.''

—Harold Osborne

MORIMURA, Yasumasa

Nationality: Japanese. **Born:** Osaka, Japan, 1951. **Awards:** Hugo Boss Prize nomination, New York, 1997. **Agent:** Luhring Augustine, 531 West 24th St., New York, New York 10011, U.S.A. **Web site:** http://www.morimura.gr.jp.

Selected Individual Exhibitions:

1983 Galerie Marronnier, Kyoto
1984 Hiramatsu Gallery, Osaka
1986 *Mon amour violet et autres,* Gallery Haku, Osaka
1988 ON Gallery, Osaka
Gallery NW House, Tokyo
1989 *Criticism and the Lover,* Mohly Gallery, Osaka
1990 *Daughter of Art History,* Sagacho Exhibit Space, Tokyo
Nicola Jacobs Gallery, London
1991 Thomas Segal Gallery, Boston
Luhring Augustine, New York
1992 *Options,* Museum of Contemporary Art, Chicago
The Carnegie Museum of Art, Pittsburgh, Pennsylvania
Homage to Spanish Still Life by Morimura and Fukuda (with Miran Fukuda), Nagoya City Art Museum, Nagoya
Shugo Satani Art Room, Tokyo
1993 Foundation Cartier pour l'art Contemporain, Jouy-en-Josas
1994 Ginza Art Space, Shiseido Corporate
Psychoborg, The Power Plant, Toronto, and Walter Philips Gallery, Branff, Alberta
Rembrandt Room, Hara Art Museum, Hara
1996 Yokohama Museum of Art, Yokohama
Luhring Augustine, New York
1997 *Yasumasa Morimura,* Actor/Actress, The Contemporary Arts Museum, Houston, and The McKinney Avenue Contemporary, Dallas
Thaddeus Ropac Gallery, Paris, France
1998 *Self-Portrait as Art History,* Museum of Contemporary Art, Tokyo; National Museum of Modern Art, Kyoto; Marugame Inokuma Museum of Contemporary Art, Kagawa
Galleria Severiarte, Arte Contemporanea, Bologna
1999 *Daughter of Art History,* Luhring Augustine, New York
Yasumasa Morimura: The Name with No Name, The Self with no Name, The Center of Academic Resources, Chulalongkorn University, Bangkok
2000 *Fundacion Telefonica: Yasumasa Morimura Historia Del Arte,* Madrid, Spain

Selected Group Exhibitions:

1984 *Can't You See We Are Not Reticent?*, Gallery Osaka
1985 *Smile with Radical Will,* Gallery 16, Kyoto

Yasumasa Morimura: *Doublonage (Portrait A),* 1988. ©Christie's Images/Corbis.

1986 *The 4th Kyoto Art and Craft Exhibition,* Kyoto Municipal Art Hall

1987 *Panache,* ON Gallery, Osaka

Yes Art Deluxe, Sagacho Exhibit Space, Tokyo, and Gallery Haku, Osaka

Photographic Aspect of Japanese Art Today, Tochigi Prefectural Museum of Fine Arts

1988 *ART NOW '88,* Hyogo Prefectural Museum of Modern Art, Kobe

La Biennale Di Venezia, Aperto '88,'' Venice, Italy

East Meets West: Japanese and Italian Art Today, ART/LA '88,'' Los Angeles Convention Center

1989 *Against Nature: Japanese Art in the Eighties,* San Francisco Museum of Modern Art, San Francisco (toured)

Art Exciting'89—Beyond the Present, The Museum of Modern Art, Saitama, and Queensland Art Gallery, Brisbane, Australia

Europalia '89 JAPAN—Japanese Contemporary Art 1989, Museum of Contemporary Art, Ghent, Belgium

1990 *Culture and Commentary: An Eighties Perspective,* Hirshhorn Museum and Sculpture Garden, Washington, D.C.

Japanese Contemporary Photography—Twelve Viewpoints, Tokyo Metropolitan Museum of Photography, Tokyo/ Pavillon des Arts, Paris

Japanische Kunst der 80 Jahre, toured Germany

Images in Transition, The National Museum of Modern Art, Kyoto, and The National Museum of Modern Art, Tokyo

1991 *Japanart,* Art Gallery of Western Australia, Perth; Art Gallery of Southern Australia, Adelaide

Zones of Love: Contemporary Art from Japan, Toyko Museum of Contemporary Art

A Cabinet of Signs: Contemporary Art from Post-Modern Japan, Tate Gallery Liverpool; Whitechapel Art Gallery, London; Malmo Konsthall, Sweden

1992 *Quotations,* Aldrich Museum of Contemporary Art, Ridgefield, Connecticut, and Dayton Art Institute, Museum of Contemporary Art, Ohio

Post-Human, Musee d'Art Contemporain Pully/Lausanne, Lausanne; Castello di Rivoli, Turin; Deste Foundation for Contemporary Art, Athens

Homage to Spanish Still Life by Yasumasa Morimura & Miran Fukuda, Nagoya City Art Museum

1993 *Building a Collection, Part I,* Museum of Fine Arts, Boston

Dress Codes, Institute of Contemporary Art, Boston, March-May

1994 *Of the Human Condition: Hope and Despair at the End of the Century,* Spiral Garden, Tokyo

Japanese Art After 1945: Scream Against the Sky, Guggenheim Museum SoHo, New York, and Yokohama Museum of Art, Yokohama

Inside Out: Contemporary Japanese Photography, The Light Factory, Charlotte, North Carolina, and Kemper Museum of Contemporary Art, Kansas City, Missouri

From Beyond the Pale, Irish Museum of Modern Art, Dublin

1995 *Cocido y Crudo,* Museo Nacional Centro de Arte Reina Sofia, Madrid

Japan Today, Museum of Modern Art Louisiana, Denmark (toured)

More than Real, Royal Palace, Casaerta, Italy

Duchamp's Leg, Walker Art Center, Minneapolis, and Center for the Fine Arts, Miami, Florida.

1996 *The Second Asia-Pacific Triennial of Conteporary Art,* Queensland Art Gallery

10th Biennale of Sydney, Sydney, Australia

1996 Melbourne International Festival of the Arts, Melbourne, Australia

Everything That's Interesting Is New, Athens School Of Fine Art, Athens, Greece

Hugo Boss Prize Exhibition, Guggenheim Downtown, New York.

1997 *Rrose is a Rrose is a Rrose,* Guggenheim Museum, New York

Japanishe Photografie der Gegenwart, Kunsthalle Wien, Vienna, Austria

About Face: Artists' Portraits in Photography, Harvard University Art Museum, Cambridge

1998 *Recycling Art History,* Pittsburgh Center for the Arts, Pittsburgh, Pennsylvania

Luhring Augustine, New York

A Portrait of Our Times: An Introduction to the Logan Collection, San Francisco Museum of Modern Art, San Francisco, California

1999 *Art at Work: Forty Years of the Chase Manhattan Collection,* Museum of Fine Arts, Houston, and the Contemporary Arts Museum

New Modernism for a new Millennium: Works by Contemporary Asian Artists from the Logan Collection, San Francisco Museum of Modern Art, San Francisco

Regarding Beauty: A View of the Late Twentieth Century, Hirshhorn Museum and Sculpture Garden, Haus der Kunst, Munich, Germany

Ghost in the Shell: Photography and the Human Soul, 1850–2000, Los Angeles County Museum of Art, Los Angeles

2000 *Contemporary Photography from Japan,* De Pont Foundation for Contemporary Art, Tilburg, The Netherlands

Beauty Now, Haus der Kunst, Munich, Germany

Photography Now, Contemporary Arts Center, New Orleans

Contemporary Photography from Japan, De Pont Foundation, Tilburg, Holland

2001 *A Contemporary Cabinet of Curiosities: Selections from the Vicki and Kent Logan Collection,* CCAC Institute, Oakland, California

Publications:

On MORIMURA: Books—*Yasumasa Morimura: 9 Visages*, exhibition catalog, Foundation Cartier pour l'art contemporain, 1993; *Yasumasa Morimura,* Yokohama 1996. **Articles**—''Yasumasa Morimura an NW House'' by Janet Koplos in *Art in America,* June 1989; ''Yasumasa Morimura'' by Azby Brown in *Artforum,* May 1990; ''Made in Japan'' by Kay Larson in *New York,* 1 October 1990; ''Who Is That Girl, Anyway?'' by Alexandra Anderson-Spivy in *Esquire,* February 1991; ''Yasumasa Morimura'' by Robert Mahoney in *Arts Magazine,* March 1992; ''The Great Impersonator'' by Peter Plagens in *Newsweek,* 6 April 1992; ''Yasumasa Morimura at the Museum of Contemporary Art'' by Susan Snodgrass in *Art in America,* May 1992; Yasumasa Morimura'' by Norman Bryson in *Artforum,* January 1994; ''Glamour Girls'' by Lynn Gumpert in *Art in America,* July 1996; ''Morimura Art Embodied'' in *The Daily Yomiuri*, 4 October 1996; ''But Is it Art?'' by Holly Brubach in *New York Times Magazine,* 17 November 1996; ''Elvis, Marilyn and Visions of Gods'' by John Christakos in *The Daily Yomiuri*, 18 November 1997; ''Women's Fashion: Wear Your Art on Your Sleeve'' by Andrew Lambirth in *The Independent* (London), 28 February 1998; ''The Many Faces of Morimura'' by Midori Kimura in *The Daily Yomiuri*, 26 May 1998; ''Yasumasa Morimura'' by Kay

Itoi in *ARTnews,* November 1998; ''Osaka Artist Finds the Hodgepodge of Street Life Inspiring'' by Yoko Kinoshita in *Mainichi Daily News*, 17 May 1999.

* * *

For the past decade, Morimura has been recognized throughout the world for his photographic self-portraits that mix painting and photography. One of Japan's most popular artists, he has won the praise of critics for dressing-up and re-creating works of art

Born in Osaka, Morimura achieved worldwide prominence in 1985 with a work titled ''The Self-Portrait'' in which he imitated a Van Gogh. Morimura made a detailed reproduction of Van Gogh's work in clay and oils and then placed a print of his own face over Van Gogh's. He continued his unique series of self-portraits using works by other great painters.

In 1989, Morimura began experimenting with a style in which he implanted his face in great paintings using computer graphics. In his show ''The Daughter of Art History'' (1990), Morimura attempted to expose the mystification of the other in modern Western masterpieces and, by ironically mimicking that process, to return the controlling gaze to the privileged viewer.

Reconstituting Manet's *Olympia,* Morimura's impersonations of both the white prostitute and the black servant reveal the similarity between sexual and colonial exploitation.

Brother's Slaughter (1991) transformed Goya's *Third of May* with Morimura appearing as the peasants about to be slaughtered, his Asian face, expressing despair and compassion, evoked the war in Vietnam, while the superfluous insertion of King Kong, Dracula and other monsters satirized the Japanese media implosion that strips reality of meaning by juxtaposing the real with the fictitious.

Portrait, Nine Faces (1990), features Morimura as the professor, students, and corpse in Rembrandt's *The Anatomy Lesson of Professor Nicholas Kulp*. The ubiquitousness of his face indicates his desire to fill space with his own image, beyond the critical purpose of dissolving the boundary between the East and the West, the subject and the object. In *Angels Descending the Stairs* (1991), Morimura presents himself as 34 angels after a Burne-Jones painting, and beautifully embodies the vertiginous pleasure of seeing oneself multiplied.

Morimura has held numerous solo exhibitions and he has participated in numerous international exhibitions such as the Venice Biennale, Sydney Biennale, and Asia-Pacific Triennial. *Self-Portrait as Art History,* the first comprehensive retrospective of Morimura's works, revealed the humor of his idiosyncratic self-portraits, cast as revisualizations of masterpieces of Western art.

Like his forebears, the great Ukiyo-e artists, Morimura's social criticism is lurking just below the surface of these humorous, splashy self-portrait tableaus. Although the images are mass-production worthy, these portraits explore the shaping of identity through visual media, and question proscriptions of nationality, gender, and class by performance and comic exposure.

Pretending to be someone else has been a popular artistic strategy since Durer painted himself as Christ in 1500. Acknowledging that the practice is already established, Morimura good-humoredly gives a nod to frequent comparisons to Cindy Sherman, Gerhard Richter, and Andy Warhol by incorporating their works into his latest exhibition. These all concern the relationship between reality and illusion in representation—a problem dating from the advent of photography.

Morimura has reminisced about how disguise once functioned for him as a ''combat suit,'' in which he was able to tap his still unexplored artistic talent by putting himself into someone else's body. Subverting this convention, Yasumasa Morimura works with both occidental and Japanese images with equal aplomb. His photographs seize on traditional Japanese classics in the same vein as his western favorites. His intrusive self-portrait digital transfers combined with zinc relief print and woodblock techniques are a narcissistic play in a half-serious attempt to usurp the roles and go under the skin of the Sharaku iconic prints of Kabuki stars.

Most recently he has produced a series of photographs of himself dressed as legendary Hollywood actresses. His Brigitte Bardot in a bath full of bubbles is well nigh perfect. His high-kicking Liza Minnelli is staggeringly convincing. His Jodie Foster, in *Taxi Driver*, is a bubble gum-chewing marvel of teenage lippiness. His Catherine Deneuve lying on a bed in her bra is exactly *Belle du Jour* with a difference. All are black and white like Hollywood studio stills, yet are not explorations of his sexuality but accusations directed at yours.

U.S. software mogul Peter Norton commissioned a Christmas keepsake paper fan from the artist, which seemed to be that famous photo of Marilyn Monroe taken in her early pin-up days. In ''Self-Portrait (Actress)/Red Marilyn'' (1996), we see the hands behind her head, eyes half closed, red lips open, then still brownish hair in waves around her naked shoulders. A closer look reveals the image to be not that of Marilyn, but of artist Morimura, wigged, rouged, and sporting false breasts.

When leading Japanese fashion artist Issey Miyake began to engage visual artists to contribute to the decoration of his ''Pleats Please'' line of clothes in 1996, Yasumasa Morimura was the first of the Guest Artist Series. Morimura's design has the nude woman of Jean-Auguste-Dominique Ingres' ''La Source'' (1856) photomontaged on to a male body—his own. Spliced horizontally in mirror juxtaposition, the result was printed on a high-necked pleated tunic and skirt or dress. In the press materials for the collection Morimura states, ''The celebrated painting by Ingres is the embodiment of classical beauty epitomized by the female body. I have combined this figure with my own, a male body, in the same painting. The image of the two bodies is then worn on yet another body. I find the contrast of bodies quite fascinating.''

—Deirdre Donohue

MORLEY, Malcolm

Nationality: British. **Born:** London, 1931. **Education:** Royal College of Art, London, 1954–57. **Career:** Independent painter, living in New York, since 1957. Worked as a waiter, Longchamps Restaurant, New York, 1964. Associated with Barnett Newman, New York, 1964–65. Instructor, Royal College of Art, London, 1956; Ohio State University, Columbus, 1965, 1966; School of Visual Arts, New York, 1967–69; State University of New York at Stony Brook, since 1972; lives and works in Long Island, New York. **Awards:** Turner Prize, Tate Gallery, London, 1984.

Individual Exhibitions:

1957 Kornblee Gallery, New York
1964 Kornblee Gallery, New York

1967 Kornblee Gallery, New York
1969 Kornblee Gallery, New York
1973 Galerie Gerald Piltzer, Paris
Stefanotty Gallery, New York
1974 Stefanotty Gallery, New York
1976 Clocktower Gallery, New York
1977 Galerie Jurka, Amsterdam
Galerie Jollenbeck, Cologne
1979 Nancy Hoffman Gallery, New York
Suzanne Hilberry Gallery, Detroit
1980 Wadsworth Atheneum, Hartford, Connecticut
1981 Xavier Fourcade, Inc., New York
1982 Akron Art Institute, Ohio
Xavier Fourcade Inc., New York
1983 Whitechapel Art Gallery, London (travelled to Basel)
Corcoran Gallery of Art, Washington, D.C.
1984 Museum of Contemporary Art, Chicago
Brooklyn Museum, New York
1985 Piccadilly Gallery, London
Fabian Carlsson Gallery, London
1987 Piccadilly Gallery, London
1990 *Malcolm Morley,* Anthony d'Offay Gallery, London (catalog)
1991 *Malcolm Morley: Watercolours,* Bonnefantenmuseum, Maastricht, Netherlands (catalog)
Pace Gallery, New York
1995 *Malcolm Morley 1965–1995,* Fundacion 'La Caixa,' Madrid (retrospective) (catalog)
Mary Boone Gallery, New York
Malcolm Morley Drawings, Michael Klein, New York (catalog)
1998 Baumgarten Galleries, Washington, D.C.
1999 Sperone Westwater Gallery, New York (catalog)

Selected Group Exhibitions:

1966 *The Photographic Image,* Guggenheim Museum, New York
1969 *Aspects of a New Realism,* Milwaukee Art Center (travelled to the Museum of Contemporary Arts, Houston, and Akron Art Institute, Ohio)
1972 *Contemporary American Painting,* Whitney Museum, New York
Sharp Focus Realism, Sidney Janis Gallery, New York
1973 *Photo-Realism,* Serpentine Gallery, London
1974 *Projekt 74,* Cologne
Dealers' Choice/Choice Dealers, New York Cultural Center
1977 *Painting in the Age of Photography,* Kunsthaus, Zurich
1981 *A New Spirit in Painting,* Royal Academy, London
1987 *The Long Perspective,* Thomas Agnew and Sons, London
1991 *New Acquisitions: The MCA Collects,* Museum of Contemporary Art, Chicago (catalog)
Bonnefanten Museum, Maastrich
Kunsthalle Basel, Switzerland
1992 Parish Art Museum, Southampton, New York
1994 *Painters' Images,* Museum Moderner Kunst, Vienna (catalog)
1995 *International and Norwegian Paintings from the Collection of the Astrup Fearnley Museum of Modern Arts Festival Exhibition,* Bergen Museum of Art, Norway (catalog)
1997 *Birth of the Cool: American Painting from Georgia O'Keeffe to Christopher Wool,* Deichtorhallen, Hamburg (traveled to Kunsthaus Zurich) (catalog)
1999 Liverpool Biennial, England

Collections:

Metropolitan Museum of Art, New York; Whitney Museum, New York; Fordham University, New York; Hirshhorn Museum, Washington, D.C.; Detroit Institute of Arts; Museum of Contemporary Art, Chicago; Louisiana Museum, Humlebaek, Denmark; Utrecht Museum, Netherlands; Neue Galerie der Stadt Aachen, Germany.

Publications:

By MORLEY: Books—*Malcolm Morley: Itineraries,* with Jean-Claude Lebensztejn, London 2001. **Articles**—interview with Nena Dimitrijevic in *Flash Art,* no. 142, October 1988; interview with Robert Storr in *Art Press,* no. 180, May 1993; interview with Richard Francis in *Bomb,* no. 55, Spring 1996; ''On Painting'' in *Parkett,* no. 52, May 1998.

On MORLEY: Books—*Pop Art Redefined* by John Russell and Suzi Gablik, New York 1969; *Pop Art* by Michael Compton, London 1970; *Icons and Images of the 60s* by Nicholas and Elena Calas, New York, 1971; *New Realism* by Udo Kultermann, New York 1972; *Super Realism: A Critical Anthology,* edited by Gregory Battcock, New York 1975; *Photorealism* by Louis K. Meisel, New York 1980; *Malcolm Morley,* exhibition catalog with texts by Michael Compton and Nicholas Serota, London 1983; *Malcolm Morley,* exhibition catalog with text by Arnold Glimcher, New York 1988. **Articles**—''New Names This Month'' by Jill Johnston in *Artnews* (New York), October 1964; ''Morley Paints a Picture'' by Lawrence Alloway in *Artnews* (New York), Summer 1968; ''The Reception of Figurative Art'' by Sidney Tillim in *Artforum* (New York), February 1969; ''New York: Super-Real Is Back in Town'' by Ralph Pomeroy in *Art and Artists* (New York), May 1969; ''Pop Reappraised'' by John Russell in *Art in America* (New York), July/August 1969; ''Real and the Artificial: Painting of the New Environment'' by William C. Seitz in *Art in America* (New York), November 1972; ''Malcolm Morley: Post Style Illusionism'' by Kim Levin in *Arts Magazine* (New York), February 1973; ''Malcolm Morley: Toward Erotic Painting'' by Valentine Tatransky in *Art International* (Lugano, Switzerland), October 1979; ''Malcolm Morley: Talking About Seeing'' by Klaus Kertess in *Artforum* (New York), Summer 1980; ''Malcolm X Morley'' by Catherine Grenier in *Art Press,* no. 180, May 1993; ''Malcolm Morley's Method'' by Jorn Houborg in *Hrymfaxe,* vol. 27, no. 2, June 1997; ''Malcolm Morley or Painting as Adventure'' by Enrique Juncosa in *Parkett,* no. 52, May 1998; ''Seasickness'' by Jean-Claude Lebensztejn in *Parkett,* no. 52, 1998.

* * *

As a result of the paintings he made from 1965 to 1970, Malcolm Morley became known as the first Photo-Realist. The title is a well-deserved one, and yet Morley is much more than this label implies.

Never satisfied to rest on previous accomplishments, he continued to develop a body of work during the 1970s which prove him to be one of the most astute painter's painters practicing at the present time.

Morley's abstract paintings from the early 1960s made use of the grid system. In a 1964 picture titled *High July* he introduced representational imagery arranged in a composition of striated pattern which reads from top to bottom as clouds, sky, sea and beach. Extracting and combining from these two elements, Morley began, in 1965, to use the grid to paint handmade enlargements of reproduced images which originated out of posters and photographs of contemporary scenes and events as well as from the paintings of masters such as Vermeer. During this period Morley stated that he had no interest in subject matters as such, and that he accepted it ''as a byproduct of surface.'' Painting square by square and often upside down, Morley questioned perceptions of literalness and reduplication. He was exploring the character of the confusions about meaning which occur through time and changing context. These paintings were a new kind of synthesis of painterly expression and content gleaned from the mass-produced sources through which we see most visual information from past and present, from art and life alike. From the start, there is a painterly quality which differs from the character of the photographic precursor. His use of devices such as the white border and the three-dimensional foldout form amplify these issues.

On his incredibly detailed painting titled *Racetrack* (1970), Morley superimposed a large red ''X'' in a gesture which destroyed, in effect, the literalness of the photo-real image and communicated the reality of paint as paint. *L.A. Yellow Pages* (1971, acrylic in wax) integrates into the work the rough tears Morley had made in his pocketbook source, not as collage but as painted surface. Paintings of the next few years become even rougher and denser in paint quality. *Rotterdam* (1974) is exemplary of this period; folds from the photographic source become painted elements in this picture which, in effect, negates Morley's earlier, more photo-real depiction of the same image in *SS Rotterdam in Rotterdam* (1966).

Among Morley's most effective pictures to date is *The Ultimate Anxiety* (1978). The model is a postcard showing part of painting by the 18th century Venetian scene painter Francesco Guardi. Morley transforms this reproduced image into a painterly rendition of color and light which, on close inspection, breaks up the scene into gestural strokes. Over the scene, Morley paints a colorful toy train which moves diagonally across the composition in a swipe of defiance towards the idea of meaning in literal depiction. *Christmas Tree (The Lonely Ranger in the Jungle of Desires)* (1979) mixes images of toys with those of parrot, snake and woman's legs, all of which cohabit in their jungle setting. It is a move further penetrating into Morley's continual concerns, dealing with what he had earlier called the ''pornographic'' element in the two-dimensional surface which controls ''because you can't penetrate it.''

Morley's recent pictures of animals in the landscape seem to come more directly from memories of seen experience, incorporating beside Morley's homage to Delacroix and Cezanne the hint that perhaps an unencumbered perception of things seen directly is in order at this time if we are to understand the nature of meaning as it really is, in paint and in life. In addition to Morley's investigations into the nature of his medium, the strength in his work lies in his ability to communicate the anxieties felt by the individual always on the edge of continuing or being destroyed, hovering, as it were, on the beach, ship or train, in the jungle or the city. He has accomplished much to convey the continued relevancy of the painter for the present by maintaining a fierce independence and persistence, refusing to be waylaid by trendiness or stylishness.

—Barbara Cavaliere

Boats and images of the ocean and the beach have ranked among Morley's major subjects in the 1990s. To create the ship paintings, Morley constructs a small paper model of each vessel. By using the model as a point of reference, Morley separates the viewer and the subject by yet another step, emphasizing that painting is a construction rather than a window on reality.

In addition to the nautical motifs, Morley's work has also included images of medieval knights, the game of chess, and, as a continuation of his long-standing interest in the experience of being a tourist, postcards from exotic locales. As always, Morley's work addresses issues of painting theory and our perception of the picture plane, as much as it does any particular subject. In recent years, he has moved away somewhat, although not entirely, from the traditional grid format. In this process, Morley paints one small area of the canvas at a time, often using watercolor sketches as preliminary works that determine the composition. This bit-by-bit painting technique has allowed Morley to concentrate on the paint itself, rather than being distracted, as it were, by subject matter.

—Tara Reddy Young

MORRIS, Robert

Nationality: American. **Born:** Kansas City, Missouri, 9 February 1931. **Education:** Studied engineering, University of Kansas City; art, Kansas City Art Institute, 1948–50; California School of Fine Arts, San Francisco, 1951; Reed College, Portland, Oregon, 1953–55; art history, Hunter College, New York, 1961–62, M.A. 1962. **Military Service:** Army Corps of Engineers, Arizona and Korea, 1951–52. **Career:** Worked in theatre improvisation, San Francisco, 1955–60; collaborated in performance works with Yvonne Rainer, New York 1963. Contributor, *Artforum,* New York, since 1966. Assistant professor, Hunter College, New York, since 1967. **Awards:** Prize, Walker of Art Center, Minneapolis, 1966; First Prize, International Institute, Torcuato di Tella, Buenos Aires, 1967; Guggenheim International Award, 1967; Guggenheim Fellowship, 1969; Sculpture Award, Society Four Arts, 1975; Skowhegan Medal for Progress and Environment, Maine, 1978. D.F.A.: Williams College, Williamstown, Massachusetts, 1986. **Agent:** Leo Castelli Gallery, 4 E. 77th Street, New York, New York 10021–1727. **Address:** Office, Department of Studio Art, Hunter College, 695 Park Avenue, New York, New York 10021–5024.

Individual Exhibitions:

1957 Dilexi Gallery, San Francisco
1958 Dilexi Gallery, San Francisco
1963 Green Gallery, New York
1964 Green Gallery, New York
Galerie Schmela, Dusseldorf
1965 Green Gallery, New York
1966 Dwan Gallery, Los Angeles

1967 Leo Castelli Gallery, New York
1968 Leo Castelli Gallery, New York
Galerie Ileana Sonnabend, Paris (2 shows)
Van Abbemuseum, Eindhoven, Netherlands
1969 Leo Castelli Gallery, New York
Galleria Enzo Sperone, Turin
Irving Blum Gallery, Los Angeles
Corcoran Gallery, Washington, D.C.
David Gallery, Houston
1970 Irving Blum Gallery, Los Angeles
Detroit Institute of Arts
Whitney Museum, New York
Stedelijk Museum, Amsterdam
Castelli Graphics, New York
1971 Tate Gallery, London
Galerie Ileana Sonnabend, Paris
1972 Leo Castelli Gallery, New York
David Gallery, Houston
1973 Galerie Ileana Sonnabend, Paris
Konrad Fischer Gallery, Dusseldorf
Max Protech Gallery, Washington, D.C.
Galleria Forma, Genoa
Lucio Amelio Modern Art Agency, Naples
Ace Gallery, Venice, California
1974 *Projects,* Institute of Contemporary Art, University of Pennsylvania, Philadelphia
Sonnabend-Castelli Gallery, New York
Galerie Art in Progress, Munich
Alessandra Castelli Gallery, Milan
Grand Rapids Project, Belknap Park, Grand Rapids, Michigan
1975 Galleria D'Allesandro-Ferranti, Rome
Carlson Gallery, University of Bridgeport, Connecticut
1976 Leo Castelli Gallery, New York
Sonnabend-Castelli Gallery, New York
1977 Louisiana Museum, Humlebaek, Denmark
Williams College, Williamstown, Massachusetts
James Corcoran Gallery, Los Angeles
Portland Center for the Visual Arts, Oregon
Stedelijk Museum, Amsterdam
Het Observatorium, Oostelijk Flevoland Netherlands
Galerie Art in Progress, Dusseldorf
Galerie Ileana Sonnabend, Paris
1978 Florence Wilcox Gallery, Swarthmore College, Pennsylvania
Beaver College, Glenside, Pennsylvania
Galleria Civica d'Arte Moderna, Comune di Ferrara, Italy
1979 Leo Castelli Gallery, New York
Ileana Sonnabend Gallery, New York
Wright State University, Dayton, Ohio
1980 Waddington Galleries, London
Richard Hines Gallery, Seattle
Art Institute of Chicago
Leo Castelli/142 Greene Street Gallery, New York
1981 Contemporary Arts Museum, Houston
1982 Williams College, Williamstown, Massachusetts (travelled to Boston, Seattle, Austin and Grand Rapids)
1983 Leo Castelli Gallery, New York
Sonnabend Gallery, New York
University of Illinois, Champaign
Galerie Daniel Templon, Paris
Rijkmuseum, Amsterdam
1984 Konsthall, Malmo, Sweden
Galerie Nordenhake, Malmo, Sweden
Contemporary Arts Museum, Houston
Padiglione d'Arte Contemporanea, Milan
Portland Center for the Visual Arts, Oregon
1985 Sonnabend Gallery, New York
Leo Castelli Gallery, New York
1986 Galerie Daniel Templon, Paris
Museum of Contemporary Art, Chicago
1989 *Robert Morris: The Felt Works,* Grey Art Gallery & Study Center, New York (catalog)
1990 *Robert Morris: Sculptures 1962–1984,* Lang and O'Hara, New York (catalog)
Inability to Endure or Deny the World: Representation and Text in the Work of Robert Morris, Corcoran Gallery of Art, Washington, D.C. (catalog)
1994 Solomon R. Guggenheim Museum, New York
Soho Museum, New York
1995 Centre Georges Pompidou, Paris (catalog)
1996 *Robert Morris: Recent Felt Pieces and Drawings,* Association L.A.C. Lieu d'Art Contemporain, Sigean, France (traveling exhibition) (catalog)
1997 Leo Castelli Gallery, New York
Henry Moore Institute, Leeds
2000 Musee d'Art Contemporain de Lyon, France

Selected Group Exhibitions:

1963 *Black, White and Grey,* Wadsworth Atheneum, Hartford, Connecticut
1966 *The Other Tradition,* Institute of Contemporary Art, Philadelphia
1970 *Information,* Museum of Modern Art, New York
1975 *Sculpture, American Directions 1945–1975,* National Collection of Fine Arts, Smithsonian Institution, Washington, D.C.
1978 *Art About Art,* Whitney Museum, New York (toured the United States)
1979 *The Reductive Object: A Survey of the Minimalist Aethetic in the 1960s,* Institute of Contemporary Art, Boston
1980 *Biennale,* Venice
1982 *Postminimalism,* Aldrich Museum, Ridgefield, Connecticut
1984 *Content: A Contemporary Focus 1974–84,* Hirshhorn Museum, Washington, D.C.
1987 *Avant-Garde in the Eighties,* Los Angeles County Musem of Art
1988 *Identity: Representations of the Self,* Whitney Museum of American Art, Downtown at Federal Reserve Plaza, New York (catalog)
Sculpture Since the Sixties, Whitney Museum of American Art, Equitable Center, New York (catalog)
Conceptual Art I, Centre d'Arts Plastiques Contemporains de Bordeaux, France (catalog)
1989 *Art in Place: Fifteen Years of Acquisitions,* Whitney Museum of American Art, New York (catalog)
Minimalism, Tate Gallery, Liverpool (catalog)
1990 *Object and Content: Meaning in Minimal Art,* Australian National Gallery, Canberra (catalog)

1991 *Selection: Works from the Collection,* Musee d'Art Contemporain, Lausanne (catalog)
1993 *Gravity & Grace,* Hayward Gallery, London (catalog)
1994 *The Body as Measure,* Davis Museum and Cultural Center, Wellesley, Massachusetts (catalog)
1995 *''Self Construction,''* Museum Moderner Kunst, Vienna (catalog)
Attitudes/Sculptures, CAPC Musee d'Art Contemporain, Bordeaux (catalog)
1996 *Minimal Art,* Kolda Mitxelena Kulturunea, San Sebastian, Spain (catalog)
1997 *The Lois Beurman Torf Print Collection for the University of Massachusetts,* Amherst (catalog)
1998 *Waves Breaking on the Shore...Ad Dekkers in His Time,* Stedelijk Museum, Amsterdam (catalog)
Minimal Maximal: Minimal Art and its Influence on the International Art of the 1990s, Neues Museum Weserburg, Bremen, Germany (catalog)

Collections:

Museum of Modern Art, New York; Whitney Museum, New York; Wadsworth Atheneum, Hartford, Connecticut; Allen Memorial Art Museum, Oberlin College, Ohio; Walker Art Center, Minneapolis; Dallas Museum of Fine Arts; National Gallery of Canada, Ottawa; Tate Gallery, London; Moderna Museet, Stockholm; National Gallery of Victoria, Melbourne.

Publications:

By MORRIS: Book—*Continuous Project Altered Daily,* 1969. **Articles—**''Notes on Sculpture, Part 1'' in *Artforum* (New York), February 1966; ''Notes on Sculpture, Part 2'' in *Artforum* (New York), October 1966; ''Notes on Sculpture, Part 3'' in *Artforum* (New York), June 1967; ''Anti-Forum'' in *Artforum* (New York) April 1968; statement in *Art Now: New York* (New York), June 1969; ''Some Notes on the Phenomenology of Making: The Search for the Motivated'' in *Artforum* (New York), April 1970; ''Pace and Process'' in *Avalanche* (New York), Fall 1970; ''A Method of Sorting Cows'' and ''A Dialogue,'' with David Sylvester, in *Robert Morris,* exhibition catalog, London 1971; ''The Art of Existence: 3 Extra-Visual Artists, Work in Process'' in *Artforum* (New York), January 1971; ''Interview mit Robert Morris,'' with Lil Picard, in *Kunstwerk* (Baden-Baden, West Germany), January 1972; ''Robert Morris Interviewed by A. B. Oliva'' in *Domus* (Milan), November 1972; ''Some Splashes in the Ebbtide'' in *Artforum* (New York), February 1973; ''Aligned with Nazca'' in *Artforum* (New York), October 1975; ''The Present Tense of Space'' in *Art in America* (New York), January/February 1978; ''Looking Back: An Interview,'' with J. Fineberg, in *Arts Magazine* (New York), September 1980; ''Robert Morris: A Conversation in 1985'' by Benjamin H.D. Buchloh in *October,* no. 70, Fall 1994; ''Golden Memories'' with W.J.T. Mitchell in *Artforum,* vol. 32, no. 8, April 1994; ''Yo Morris'' with Thomas Crow in *Artforum,* vol. 32, no. 10, Summer 1994; interview with Rosalind E. Krauss in *Art Press,* no. 193, July-August 1994; interview with Pepe Karmel in *Art in America* (New York), vol. 83, no. 6, June 1995; interview with Richard J. Williams in *Art Monthly,* no. 208, July-August 1997.

On MORRIS: Books—*Robert Morris,* exhibition catalog, Eindhoven, Netherlands, 1968; *Robert Morris,* exhibition catalog, Washington, D.C. 1969; *Robert Morris,* exhibition catalog by Marcia Tucker, New York 1970; *Robert Morris,* exhibition catalog by Michael Compton and David Sylvester, London 1971; *Robert Morris: Felt Pieces,* exhibition catalog by Walter Kambartel, Stuttgart 1971; *Robert Morris: Projects,* exhibition catalog with text by Edward Fry, Philadelphia 1974; *Line as Language: Six Artists Draw,* exhibition catalog by Rosalind Krause, Princeton, New Jersey 1974; *Robert Morris: Grand Rapids Project,* Grand Rapids, Michigan 1975; *Het Observatorium von Robert Morris in Oostelijk Flevoland,* exhibition catalog with text by E. de Wilde and others, Amsterdam 1977; *Structures for Behavior,* exhibition catalog by Roald Nasgaard, Toronto 1978. **Articles—**''Robert Morris: Une Esthetique de Transgression'' by A. Michelson in *Art Press* (Paris), July/ August 1973; ''Robert Morris: The Complication of Exhaustion'' by J. Gilbert-Rolfe in *Artforum* (New York), September 1974; ''Minimalism and Critical Response'' by P. Tuchman in *Artforum* (New York), May 1977, ''Authoritarian Abstraction'' by D. B. Kuspit in *Journal of Aesthetics and Art Criticism* (Cleveland), Fall 1977; ''Earthworks as Reclamation: Problems and Promises'' by R. Glowen in *Artweek* (Oakland, California), 25 August 1979; ''Monument-Sculpture-Earthwork'' by N. Foote in *Artforum* (New York), October 1979; ''Morris: Prisoner of Modernism'' by Carter Ratcliff in *Art in America* (New York), October 1979; ''Artist (Neo-Dandy) Stripped Bare by His Critic (Neo-Careerist) Almost'' by D. B. Kuspit in *Arts Magazine* (New York), May 1980; ''Space of the Self: Robert Morris in the Realm of the Carceral'' by S. F. Eisenman in *Arts Magazine* (New York), September 1980; ''Work for Landscape and Gallery'' by R. Glowen in *Artweek* (Oakland, California), 4 October 1980; ''Robert Morris: Death and the Picture Frames'' by Corinne Robbins in *Arts Magazine,* vol. 62, no. 9, May 1988; ''Robert Morris's Wake-up Call'' by Ken Johnson in *Art in America* (New York), vol. 78, no. 12, December 1990; ''The Work of Robert Morris 1961–71: A Criticism'' by Brian Hatton in *Issues in Architecture, Art and Design,* vol. 2, no. 2, Winter 1992–93; ''Robert Morris's Ambiguous Containers'' by Steven Peterson in *Athanor,* no. 11, 1992; ''Robert Morris: Building the Entropy Machine'' by Owen Drolet in *Flash Art,* vol. 27, no. 176, May-June 1994; ''Robert Morris'' by Eric de Chassey in *Beaux Arts Magazine,* no. 137, September 1995; ''Back Page: Robert Morris'' in *Arts Indiana,* vol. 18, no. 6, September 1996; ''Robert Morris and John Cage: Reconstructing a Dialogue'' by Branden Joseph in *October,* no. 81, Summer 1997; ''Robert Morris'' by Michael Compton and David Sylvester in *Tate: The Art Magazine,* no. 12, Summer 1997.

* * *

I seem to speak, it is not I, about me, it is not about me. —Samuel Beckett, *The Unnamable.*

In its ironic relationship to representation, Robert Morris' ''I-Box'' (1962) invokes Beckett's drained vision of the world, where ''I'' is simply a word, a verbal sign that is seeking to assume an ''eloquent silence'' while still clinging to the vestiges of life. The work, a small box with a door in the shape of the letter ''I,'' is not as much ''about'' an ''I'' as it is ''about'' the futility of representation itself. The door opened, the phonetic ''I'' yields to a silent one—a photograph of the artist naked and grinning. The polemic waged in ''I-Box,'' on the pre-eminence of one category of signs over the other, is ironic; the signs themselves, never able to be the represented object, are trapped on the surface, engaged in a self-directed and incestuous dialogue.

Like Beckett, Morris wished to divest the art object of the kind of *a priori* intellectual determination rooted in logical, rationalist thought. ''Disengagement with preconceived enduring forms and orders for things,'' Morris has said, ''is a positive assertion. It is part of the work's refusal to continue estheticizing form by dealing with it as a preconceived end.'' After his early, Duchamp-inspired work, Morris explored the possibilities of process and experience. Concentrating on temporal states, Morris produced pieces such as ''Metered Bulb'' (1963), in which a meter records a light bulb's expenditure of electricity, or ''Site'' (1963), a performance piece (with Carolee Schneeman) in which various tasks were acted-out around an updated tableau-vivant of Manet's ''Olympia.'' Later, sculptures composed of simple geometric forms (L-beams, cubes) or of interchangeable units constituted an immediate, self-referential presence that forced the spectator to confront his physical (and psychological) situation. Eventually, Morris employed freely formed materials such as thread and felt in order to defeat the resolute Gestalt of the earlier minimalist works (i.e., a cube is a shape the mind already knows). These ''anti-form'' pieces further asserted the work's independence from the sacred hegemony of art history.

Morris' divestment of the art object of predetermined psychological content is tempered by his understanding that ''experience'' is never entirely free of historical or psychological nuances. The philosopher Jacques Derrida has observed that while ''experience'' has always designated the relationship with a presence, it always corresponds to a certain type of factual or regional experience (historical, psychological, physiological, sociologial, etc.).'' Underlying many of Morris' projects is an almost ''archaeological'' awareness of concomitant art historical situations: in ''Observatory'' (1971), a monumental earthwork consisting of sloped circular walls, a seemingly self-referential situation is charged with allusions to Stonehenge and other neolithic buildings. ''Hearing'' (1972) juxtaposes an arrangement of heat-activated objects (a copper chair, a zinc table, and a lead bed) with a three-and-a-half hour recording of a hypothetical interrogation between a council, a witness, and an investigator, a self-reflexive drama of ideas on ''various questions about art history and about the relation of perception to language.'' In ''Box with the Sound of Its Own Making'' (1961), a nine-inch walnut cube containing a three-hour recording of the sounds of its being constructed, Morris literally interposes a temporal historical supplement into the viewer's experience. More recently in ''Preludes (for A.B.)'' (1980), crosses, skulls, and inscribed marble slabs are placed in darkened gallery as morbid commentaries on various cultural phenomena (eg. ''Roller Disco: Cenotaph for a Public Figure'' or ''Cenotaph for Cancer''). The representational statement implied in Morris' coffin-like ''I-Box'' is recast two decades later by his cenotaphs, cynical gravestones that mark the bankruptcy of much of the modernist utopian vision.

—Maurice Berger

MORTON, Margaret

Nationality: American. **Born:** Akron, Ohio, 16 October 1948. **Education:** Kent State University, B.F.A.; Yale University School of Art, M.F.A. **Career:** Professor, Cooper Union School of Art, 1980—. **Awards:** Individual Artist Grant, New York State Council on the Arts, 1992; Visual Artist Grant in Photography, National Endowment for the Arts, 1992; Graham Foundation Grant for Advanced Studies in the Fine Arts, 1994; The Catalog Project, New York Foundation for the Arts, 1995. **Agent:** Margaret Bodell, The Viewing Room, 114 West 17th Street, New York, New York 10011. **Address:** The Cooper Union School of Art, 30 Cooper Square, New York, New York 10003. **Web site:** http://www.fragiledwelling.org.

Selected Individual Exhibitions:

1990 55 Mercer Street Gallery, New York
1991 Photography Gallery, Cathedral Church of St. John the Divine, New York
Moore College of Art and Design, Philadelphia
Urban Center Gallery III, New York
1992 Institut für Gegenwartskunst, Vienna
1993 Lowinsky Gallery, New York (with Skeet McCaulay)
Mednick Gallery, Philadelphia
N.A.M.E. Gallery, Chicago
Louis Abrons Gallery, New York
1994 Urban Center Gallery, Municipal Art Society, New York
Glyndor Galleries, Wave Hill, New York
1995 Lowinsky Gallery, New York
National Building Museum, Washington, D.C.
1996 Kunstverein, Bremen, Germany
Boston Architectural Center
1997 Galerie M20, Hamburg
1999 Casa Italiana, New York
2000 Burden Gallery, Aperture Foundation, New York
Palazzo Te, Mantova, Italy
2001 Cleveland Center for Contemporary Art

Selected Group Exhibitions:

1990 *Bearing Witness: Five Documentary Photographers,* Lubalin Gallery, Cooper Union, New York
The First Amendment Exhibition, 308 Bedford Avenue Gallery, Brooklyn
1991 *Beyond Photography,* Laguna Gloria Art Museum, Austin, Texas; traveled to Texas A & M University Gallery, and Cullen Center, Houston
Giving Shelter, BAUhouse, Baltimore
1993 *In Transit,* New Museum of Contemporary Art, New York
The Architecture of Despair, Educational Alliance for the Arts, New York
Design and the Vernacular, Lubalin Gallery, Cooper Union, New York
1994 *Beyond the Label,* Joseloff Gallery, University of Hartford, Connecticut
House Sweet House, New Jersey Center for the Visual Arts, Summit
Building, Dwelling, Thinking, Lowinsky Gallery, New York
1995 *Designations of Home,* WKP Kennedy Arts Center, Ontario
Perifio: The Edges of the City, Milan Triennale
En Passant, Academy of Fine Art, Vienna (traveled to Kunstverein, Hamburg)

A Century Apart: Images of Struggle and Spirit, Jacob Riis & Five Contemporary Photographers, Museum of the City of New York; traveled to Nationalmuseet, Copenhagen
1996 *Fences,* National Building Museum, Washington, D.C.
1997 *Evidence: Photography and Site,* Wexner Center for the Arts, Columbus, Ohio; traveled to Cranbrook Art Museum, Bloomfield Hills, Michigan, and Power Plant Gallery, Toronto (catalog)
Thresholds: Limits of Perception, Eighth Floor Gallery, New York
Unmapping the Earth, Kwangju Biennale, Kwangju, Korea
Home, Bullet Space, New York
1998 *New York Photographs,* Houghton Gallery, Cooper Union School of Art, New York (catalog)
Domain, Islip Art Museum, Islip, New York
Politically Direct, McClean County Arts Museum, McClean, Illinois
1999 *Mumia 911,* Hugo Martinez Gallery, New York
In Sites, Margaret Bodell Gallery (at La Mama Galleria), New York
2000 *New York Now 2000,* Museum of the City of New York

Collections:

Library of Congress, Washington, D.C.; New York Public Library; Museum of the City of New York.

Publications:

By MORTON: Books—*Transitory Gardens, Uprooted Lives,* New Haven, Connecticut 1993; *The Tunnel,* New Haven, Connecticut 1995; *Fragile Dwelling,* New York 2000. **Articles—**''Anna's Garden'' with Diana Balmori in *Ms. Magazine,* November-December 1993; ''The Tunnel'' in *Grand Street,* 1994; photographs from ''The Tunnel'' in *Utne Reader,* September-October 1995; ''José Camacho's House'' in *Lingo 6,* September 1996; ''Fragile Dwelling,'' in *NY Arts,* February 1997; ''Mobile Homeless'' in *The Village Voice,* March 9, 1999.

On MORTON: Articles—''Ephemeral Spaces: Photographs of Homeless People's Shelters'' by Margaret Stevens in *Landscape Architecture,* September 1995; ''Fragile Dwelling: The Architecture of Despair'' by Elizabeth S. Padjen in *Art New England,* June-July 1996.

*

In 1989, when my ongoing photography project began, there were more homeless people in New York City than at any time since the Great Depression. That year alone, some twenty-five thousand homeless poor sought beds in city shelters each night. Converted armories, such as Fort Washington in Upper Manhattan and the Atlantic Avenue Armory in Brooklyn, slept as many as 1,200 men, billeted on floors once used for military drills. These crowded and dangerous conditions led thousands more to sleep outside: huddled in plastic bags or discarded refrigerator boxes, seeking protection in empty doorways, or finding warmth on top of steam grates.

As the situation worsened, a startling phenomenon occurred: homeless people began to improvise housing for themselves. Shantytowns soon became visible in Lower East Side vacant lots. These encampments, unseen on such a scale since the Hoovervilles of the 1930s, also appeared in public parks, under bridges and highway exit ramps, along the rivers, and beneath the streets in subway and railroad tunnels. Within these communities, people literally rebuilt their lives, constructing makeshift housing for themselves when no acceptable alternatives had been made available. The piles of trash along the streets of New York City, the refuse of those more fortunate, were scavenged, then carefully reconstructed into homes. As time passed, these cardboard boxes and plastic tarpaulins went far beyond the need for mere shelter and evolved into plywood shanties that were personalized and where possessions could be kept safe. Frequently, the men and women added details that evoked memories of an earlier home: a roof of the same pitch, a nameplate over an entrance, religious artifacts, seasonal decorations, a guardian figure, a garden.

In 1991, I began to audiotape oral histories of individual lives. These stories, which provided further insight into the daily existence of people struggling to establish a sense of community on the margins of society, became an integral part of my project.

As these homeless New Yorkers continued to be pushed out of their fragile, self-made dwellings by political pressures, police, and bulldozers, I also documented the cycle of demolition, relocation, and reconstruction that underscored the profound need among the homeless to create a sense of place, no matter how inevitable its demise. Since 1997, when the last encampment in Manhattan was demolished, the numbers of homeless poor have not diminished, but they have become less visible. Fearful of police, the dispossessed journey the streets alone, urban nomads forever on the move: riding subways throughout the night; sleeping on dark, silent streets; hiding in the shadows of construction sites; tucking themselves into decaying structures along the waterfront; disappearing before dawn.

—Margaret Morton

* * *

For ten years, Margaret Morton has journeyed with her camera into spaces of New York City little imagined, let alone frequented, by most of its residents. With a combination of determined curiosity and tactfulness, she has visited these occluded spaces and made them visible in remarkable pictures of human survival. One wonders how she achieved this feat, how she managed to break through the protective wall with which city dwellers remove themselves from unwanted scenes of wretchedness and disarray. Moreover, this achievement goes beyond the shattering of a wall or the rending of a veil. Morton shows us something beyond a culture of despair, something to wonder at, to admire, even to celebrate, in an act of courage parallel to the courage she perceives.

In 1989, Morton observed a settlement of improvised shacks and tents that had mushroomed near her home, a community of ''fragile dwellings'' pieced together out of every imaginable shred of material at hand for scavengers of the city's bourgeois debris. Here was a kind of vernacular architecture that instantly caught her photographic eye: living examples of bricolage shaped by the most urgent of human needs for shelter, warmth, community, the pleasure of making a place of one's own and calling it home. It's no surprise that the shelters erected without license in a public park were doomed to fall beneath police clubs and city bulldozers, doomed as a public nuisance. Witnessing those makeshift structures so pitilessly scooped into a dumpster marked the onset of her explorations of the underside of the city's multifarious life.

Drawn at first to the imaginative forms of the temporary housing erected throughout the city out of simple need, Morton found herself drawn to the people themselves, the city's most abused and allegedly helpless underclass. Recording their stories on tape, she came to define her project as something more than the making of photographs. She became an investigator, probing dark, often dangerous places for disclosures of hidden truths. But there is a great difference between Morton's investigations and those of Jacob Riis and other nineteenth-century charitable reformers, who viewed the inhabitants of slums with distaste and some disdain. Without a hint of condescension, Morton gives us images that tell stories of survival in the face of unimaginable odds. These stories tell of persistence and creativity: dwellings get put together, gardens designed and planted, laundry hung out to dry, breakfast and dinner laid out on whatever makes do as a table. It's a precarious existence of the sort impossible to comprehend without having witnessed it firsthand. And firsthand is clearly what these photographs are.

Morton's pictures invert the pathos and aversion usually attached to the word homeless. Not that they flinch from the facts of abject poverty. But the ''culture of poverty'' in the usual sense of the term is not quite the issue here. It's not simply the result of unemployment or hard luck we see, but something even more affecting: abandonment, reclusiveness, the outcast condition. Perhaps most striking about the photographs is the way they communicate the effects of recognition that the camera itself produces. We see people see themselves seen, acknowledged and respected. Morton invites her subjects to participate in her pictures of them, to arrange themselves and their surroundings as they want to be perceived. And she shows the places they create as environments nested within and pressing against the larger environment of the city, with all its emblems of indifference and abstract power. She allows her subjects the dignity of presenting themselves as artists in their own right, creators of a domestic architecture which, though it may emerge from despair, gives testimony to the possibility of joy and pride even in conditions of utmost deprivation. Look at the images and icons pinned on shabby walls, the touches of elegance in scale and shape. Fragility itself becomes a whole way of life, certainly not idealized, but taken for what it is: making the best of it with what's at hand. And she allows us to see and feel their world as if from the inside.

No small feat, this transposition of subject and viewer. And the montage effect of images and voices comprise a phenomenology of living art among the most marginalized of our population. It's with a shock of recognition that we see these people as pioneers of a sort, camping out on the frontier of bottom-rung urban existence. The bleakest of settings become, in Morton's pictures, sites of a kind of ''improvement'' that comments trenchantly on the shameless claim of real estate values, the ''market'' that has ruled these lost but undefeated souls out of bounds, beyond the pale of normal existence.

Fragile Dwelling crystallizes the paradox at the root of Morton's work: not only the coexistence of wealth and poverty in the world's richest metropolis, but the coexistence of despair and hope in the devices whereby the rejected contrive a life for themselves. We have the paradox of fragility itself: the dangers of hanging on by your fingernails, and the pride of creative survival. We see the hardship, the desperation, but also the will to live. Strangely uplifting and affirming, the pictures give a different look to the solidly planted structures towering with disdain above the ''fragile dwellings,'' the improvised and impermanent homeplaces of the ''homeless.'' The pictures compel us to confront not only their despair of homelessness, but our despair at having these encampments in our midst without comprehending what they mean to the assurances of ''normal'' life. What truths about our common life are we likely to recognize in Morton's pictures? How do they impinge on our ''normalcy''? Can we ever imagine ourselves occupying those spaces, dwelling in those structures, living such vulnerable lives?

Pictures and texts work so well together here that they seem one, emanating from and reflecting each other, urging the reader deeper into the imagination of an underground society brutally shoved to the margins of our awareness. *Fragile Dwelling* also brings home an unrelenting moral predicament. The predicament of the sympathetic viewer is made more severe by the fact that Margaret Morton's pictures neither stereotype nor sentimentalize, idealize or pity. Like their subjects, they take the world as it is. It's an old dilemma we face here: art or reform, beauty or anger, pleasure or discontent. Nightmares of an underground have haunted modern society since the onset of industrialism. *Fragile Dwelling* presents a familiar ordeal of modernity: shocking inequalities, exclusions, abjection. But no one looking at these pictures with any degree of empathy can fail to be moved by the thought that we have among us, while socially invisible for the most part, creative and worthy persons capable of fashioning a kind of beauty. In their tactfulness, the pictures do not judge; whatever judgments we derive from them become our own, and therefore our society's, responsibility.

—Alan Trachtenberg

MOSER, Wilfrid

Nationality: Swiss. **Born:** Zurich, 10 June 1914. **Education:** André Lhote studio and the Ecole Fernand Léger, Paris, 1945. **Family:** Married to Eva Puig; son: Gabriel. **Career:** Painter, Paris and Zurich, since 1946: tachiste paintings, 1950–59; collages and assemblage reliefs, 1959–69; three-dimensional objects and models, 1963–77; returned to figurative landscape painting, 1974. Central President, Swiss Painters, Sculptors and Architects' Society, Zurich, 1964–71; Federal Commission for Fine Arts, Zurich, 1964–72. **Awards:** Chevalier des Arts et Lettres, 1985; Grand Prize of the City of Zurich, 1989; Officier des Arts et Lettres, 1993. **Agents:** Galerie Jeanne Bucher, 53 rue de Seine, 75006 Paris; Galerie Louis Carre, 10 Avenue de Messine, 75008 Paris. **Died:** Zurich, 14 December 1997.

Individual Exhibitions:

1958 Galerie Jeanne Bucher, Paris
1961 Galerie Jeanne Bucher, Paris
1963 Galleri Haaken, Oslo
1964 Kunstmuseum, Lucerne
1965 Galerie Jeanne Bucher, Paris
1967 Galerie Alice Pauli, Lausanne
1970 Galerie Jeanne Bucher, Paris
Kunsthaus, Zurich
1971 Kunsthaus Chur, Switzerland
Galerie Scheidegger and Maurer, Zurich
1973 Kunstmuseum, Thun, Switzerland
1974 Kunsthverein, Bienne, Switzerland
Galerie 57, Bienne, Switzerland
Musée de Metz, France

1975 Galerie G4, Winterthur, Switzerland
Musée de Metz, France
1977 Galerie RB, Fribourg, Switzerland
1978 Galerie E. Schiedegger, Zurich
Galerie G4, Winterthur, Switzerland
Galerie Jeanne Bucher, Paris
1979 Museum Schaffhausen, Switzerland
1980 Swiss Pavilion, *Biennale,* Venice
Kunsthkeller, Bern
1981 Galerie Jeanne Bucher, Paris
Galerie Semiha Huber, Zurich
1982 Kunsthkeller, Bern
1983 Galerie G4, Winterthur, Switzerland
Galerie Jeanne Bucher, Paris
1988 Galerie Jeanne Bucher, Paris
1992 Galerie Jeanne Bucher, Paris
1993 Kunsthaus, Zurich (retrospective)
1998 *Wilfrid Moser: Le pont Alexandre III, oeuvres ultimes 1994–1997,* Galerie Jeanne-Bucher, Paris
1999 *Wilfrid Moser,* Graphische Sammlung der ETH, Zurich

Selected Group Exhibitions:

1951 *6 Young Paris Painter,* Gallerie Blanche, Stockholm
1957 *The Molzau Collection,* Kunsthaus, Zurich (travelled to Copenhagen and The Hague)
1958 *Carnegie International,* Carnegie Institute, Pittsburgh
1959 *Bienal,* Sao Paulo
1961 *Kompas-Paris: Carrefour de la peinture,* Van Abbemuseum, Eindhoven, Netherlands
1968 *Premio Marzotto,* Museo di Valdagno, Italy
1972 *31 Swiss Artists,* Grand Palais, Paris
1977 *Artistes Zurichois,* Musée Rath, Geneva
1978 *Beginn des Tachismus in der Schweiz,* Kunsthaus, Zurich
1982 *Salon de Mai,* Paris
1996 *6 x informel,* Le Musée de Pully, France
1999 *Informal Painting,* Galerie Carzaniga+Ueker, Basel

Collections:

Kunsthaus, Zurich; Kunstmuseum, Lucerne; Kunstmuseum, St. Gallen; Kunstmuseum, Thun, Switzerland; Museo d'Arte Contemporaneo, Locarno; Musée National d'Art Moderne, Paris; Musée de Peinture et Sculpture, Grenoble; Musée de Metz, France; Sonja Henie/Niels Onstad Foundation, Oslo; Museum of Contemporary Art, Chicago.

Publications:

On MOSER: Books—*Premier Bilan de l'art actuel* by R. Lebel, Paris 1953; *Propos sur la peinture actuelle* by R.V. Gindertael, Paris 1955; *Musée de poche: 16 Peintres de la jeune école de Paris* by H. Wescher and H. Juin, Paris 1956; *Dictionnaire de la peinture abstraite* by Michel Seuphor, Paris 1957; *Moser,* exhibition catalog with preface by Franz Meyer, Paris 1961; *Moser,* exhibition catalog with text by P. F. Althaus, Lucerne 1964; *Ecole de Paris* by Raymond Nacenta, Neuchâtel, Switzerland 1969; *Wilfrid Moser,* exhibition catalog with text by F. A. Baumann, Zurich 1970; *Moser,* exhibition catalog with text by P. F. Althaus, Chur, Switzerland 1971; *Swiss Made* by Paul Nizon, Zurich 1971; *Moser,* exhibition catalog with text by Fritz Billeter, Bienne, Switzerland 1974; *Actualité 77,* edited by Skira Verlag, Geneva 1977; *Moser* by F. A. Baumann, Zurich 1978; *Moser,* exhibition catalog with interview by Dominique Bozo, Paris 1978; *Moser,* exhibition catalog with text by M. Freivogel, Schaffhausen, Switzerland 1979; *Moser,* exhibition catalog with text by Daniel Abadie, Paris 1981; *Wilfrid Moser: Kitharou,* exhibition catalog with text by P. Killer, Zurich 1981. **Articles—**Obituary in *Le Monde,* 24 December 1997. **Films—***Moser,* television film, by W. Bolliger and P. F. Althaus, 1970; *Moser,* television film, by P. K. Wehrli, 1977; *Moser,* film by P. Münger and G. Maguaguagno, 1988.

*

The dramatizing of the third dimension, that is, space as a factor of expression, takes place on a flat surface, canvas, paper, etc; and this dramatization of space which strikes the onlooker, disturbs and attracts him, has been neglected since the Renaissance. Artists such as Grünewald, later Piranesi and some romanticists like the German Caspar David Friedrich or the French Theodore Géricault, had based their art on the dramatizing of space. Dürer had tamed space into perspective, brought a convention, formal rendering of the third dimension.

It is only after the destruction of the old visual habits through new forms of expression like cubism or contructivism, that the following generations were put in the situation of formulating anew the problem of the third dimension and reflecting fundamentally upon the possibilities of its realization.

—Wilfrid Moser

* * *

Painting without image, if not without subject, is the paradoxical proposition of the latest works of Wilfrid Moser. Not that distinctly portrayed elements of reality are not recognizable therein. (Some might even say: Moser paints stones or Moser paints trees.) It is however a question of nothing less than what we call certainty. Masses of fallen stones, confusion of stripped branches: in this world stricken with indescribable disaster is heard again the echo, from now on devoid of meaning, of the great romantic themes—the forest, solitude in the mountains, the dream of communion with natural forces. But our age is no longer one of innocence. It is of the world *after* to which Moser has for some years begun to call attention.

The obvious ''difference'' in his latest works has naturally led commentators to search for that which made the break in his work. The passage, in 1968, from painting to sculpture seems to be the indisputable turning point. Nothing, however, separates Moser's sculpture from his former painted work: both share the same confidence of expression. It is rather a matter of a different degree in the understanding of forms. It was in fact portraying sculptures among heaps of stones in works on paper, completed between 1973 and 1975, that Moser established a different relationship to the object and to his style.

Until then art for Moser had an absolute value. His urban images, just as much as his abstract works or his sculptures, affirm the reality of the world, the power of the painter to recognize and convey it. The works in volume—assemblages of planks or constructions—go so far as to deny the fiction of the image so as to register directly in the inventory of reality. Portraying them, as he did in the works on paper which mark his return to expression in paint, no doubt led him to perceive the accepted character of every image, its value directly in tune with that of the language which expresses it. Truth, touchstone of his experience, reveals itself, he discovers, not in the image but in the form. The warm confidence of his works, their generous aesthetic, is followed by an ethic of parsimony. Metaphor for a collapsed language, the stones of Moser are also the very materials for its reconstruction. From this point on, all his work will be a slow and careful experiment to name the unnameable.

Moser's works on paper are in a way the laboratory for his painting and also for his language. Preparatory to and in parallel with his paintings, they experiment with problems, give rise to solutions, prepare in their multiplicity the successful route. According to the material used—gouache or pastel—they seek more to define the image or to invent its plastic transcription. Everything reflects the major problem of Moser's painting: the creation of violent spatial tension, of a *dramatization of space.* Even more than in the paintings, one can follow in the juxtaposition of the works on paper the incessant search to render present and palpable a non figurative subject. Tension will often result from only minute modifications: a more accentuated curve emphasizing a plane, the different value of a color suddenly giving the necessary density to a block of stone. As in two versions of an identical drawing, like ''Caved-in-Wall,'' each shows a different truth by the sole play of color: one, an opalescent white, emphasizes the structure of the blocks until it is transformed into a coagulation of signs close to his former abstract paintings; the other, a constant ocher, tends to accentuate reliefs and cavities, to hollow out intervening space. In Moser's work it is no longer a question of a motive to paint, but of a motive of painting. In fact these works display a veritable ''rage of expression.''

It is true that the margin between their intention and the dangers of a dull naturalism is narrow. The damp squib of the ''new objectivity'' has clearly demonstrated what confusion could reign among figuration, postmodernism and academic reaction. Moser is not looking for a nostalgic return to tradition, a desire to paint according to the masters, but rather the establishment of another tradition where without hesitation he blazes the trail: the Master E. S., Altdorfer, Géricault, Caspar David Friedrich or the Picasso of ''Blue Train.'' As for all of these painters, Moser's realism is an anti-naturalism. Without doubt the various ''Undergrowths'' are the extreme example of this attitude. A constantly repeated subject, banished from modern art and left to commercial artists, it was impossible at the beginning to imagine a worse example. It is true that vegetal nature according to Moser is not more appealing than his ''Ends/Bits/Scraps of the World'' or his masses of fallen stones: dead trees, defoliated copses, inextricable confusion of branches—and it would be difficult to reproach him his choice of subject for its pleasing character. But it is in the very method of painting that the ''difference'' is first established.

Painting without a model, whether stones or trees, he cannot be said to ''imitate,'' and the veracity of his branches owes more by contrast to the abstract space on which they are inscribed than to realistic observation. For Moser does not site his derisory trophies of the forest, unless by a colored shore which takes the place of both light and space. What is important to him is to introduce in parallel to the concise drawing of the stones, curve and intertwinings, to play, in the face of overlapping and stacked arrangements, an involved and complex game, to work the empty space in the place of the full. In order to hem in more closely these creations of space Moser invents in this series a genuine negative writing: what he does show is less the branches than that which they define, less the bars of the cage than concretely its interior dimension.

Truth puts out one's eyes. Moser's painting hollows out the canvas. Nothing is apparently more in contradiction to the lesson of modern art than this evident will to open up space; nothing, in reality, is more customary. The ''Sainte-Victores'' of Cezanne do not suppress the display in depth of the planes but affirm, in opposition to reviving conventions, the pictorial equality of the foreground and the background, the primacy of the painting over the illusion of perspective. The landscapes of Le Cannet by Bonnard are surrounded by foliage, for that which encloses them in the foreground, sets the surface, renders the view of the subject more distant by the contrast of colors. The problem of space remains inherent in figuration, even if by modernist theories deny it, and one could envisage a history of thought which would be that of successive spatial transcriptions and their invention.

Affirmation of the picture plane and creation in its interior of genuine pockets of space is the very stuff of Wilfrid Moser's work. Temporary equilibrium, of opposing principles, each of his works, in its frenzied search, calls to mind the Frenhofer of ''Unknown Masterpiece.'' They intend to determine an imperceptible certainty.

—Daniel Abadie

MOSES, Ed

Nationality: American. **Born:** Long Beach, California, 9 April 1936. **Education:** University of California at Irvine, M.A., 1958. **Career:** Independent painter, in Venice, California, since 1958. Instructor, University of California at Irvine, 1968–71. Instructor, University of California at Los Angeles; visiting instructor, Skowhegan School of Painting and Sculpture, Maine, 1983. **Awards:** Tamarind Lithography Workshop Fellowship, 1968; National Endowment for the Arts Fellowship Grant, 1976; Guggenheim Fellowship, 1980; California Arts Council Commission, 1984; Honorary Ph.D., Otis Art Institute, Los Angeles, 1996. **Agent:** L.A. Louver Gallery, 55 North Venice Boulevard, Venice, California 90291. **Address:** 1233 Palms Boulevard, Venice, California 90291, U.S.A.

Individual Exhibitions:

1958 Ferus Gallery, Los Angeles
Dilexi Gallery, San Francisco
1959 Area Gallery, New York
Ferus Gallery, Los Angeles
Dilexi Gallery, San Francisco
1960 Dilexi Gallery, San Francisco
1961 Ferus Gallery, Los Angeles
1963 Ferus Gallery, Los Angeles
1969 Mizuno Gallery, Los Angeles
1970 Mizuno Gallery, Los Angeles
1971 Hansen-Fuller Gallery, San Francisco
Ronald Feldman Fine Arts, New York
1972 Nicholas Wilder Gallery, Los Angeles
Dayton's Gallery 12, Minneapolis
Felicity Samuel Gallery, London
1973 Ronald Feldman Fine Arts, New York
Art in Progress, Zurich
Dayton's Gallery 12, Minneapolis

1974 Art in Progress, Munich
André Emmerich Gallery, New York
1975 André Emmerich Gallery, New York
1976 University of California at Los Angeles
Los Angeles County Museum of Art
1979 Sidney Janis Gallery, New York
1980 Jacobson-Hochman Gallery, New York
James Corcoran Gallery, Los Angeles
1981 James Corcoran Gallery, Los Angeles
1982 Musee d'Art Moderne, Paris
Jacobson-Hochman Gallery, New York
1983 Dorothy Rosenthal Gallery, Chicago
1984 Larry Gagosian Gallery, Los Angeles
1985 L.A. Louver Gallery, Venice, California
1988 Ianetti-Lanzone Gallery, San Francisco
L.A. Louver Gallery, Venice, California
1989 *Ed Moses: Recent Paintings,* L.A. Louver Gallery, Venice, California
Ed Moses: Works on Paper, L.A. Louver Gallery, Venice, California
Gallery Georges Lavrov, Paris
Ed Moses, Louver Gallery, New York (catalog)
1990 *Ed Moses: Prints,* Santa Monica Heritage Museum
L.A. Louver Gallery, Venice, California
1991 Louver Gallery, New York
1992 *Ed Moses,* Zolla/Liberman Gallery, Inc., Chicago
Apparitions and What: Works on Paper, L.A. Louver Gallery, Venice, California
1993 *Structural Reoccurence & Cloud Cover: Paintings of the 80's & 90's,* Sharon Truax Fine Art, Venice, California
Apparition and What, Louver Gallery, New York
Ed Moses: Paintings and Drawings, Davis/McClain Gallery, Houston
1994 *Drawings,* Earl McGrath Gallery, Los Angeles
Recent Paintings, L.A. Louver Gallery, Venice, California
1995 *Paint,* L.A. Louver Gallery, Venice, California
1996 *A Retrospective of the Paintings and Drawings, 1951–1996,* Museum of Contemporary Art, Los Angeles (retrospective) (catalog)
At 70 from the 70's, Bobbie Greenfield Gallery, Santa Monica
Elpoep Ebolg, L.A. Louver Gallery, Venice, California
1997 *New Paintings and Works on Paper,* Barbara Davis Gallery, Houston
Up Against the Wall, L.A. Louver Gallery, Venice, California
1998 *Ec-topic: Drawings,* Bobbie Greenfield Gallery, Santa Monica
Peter Blake Gallery, Laguna Beach, California
1999 L.A. Louver Gallery, Venice, California
2001 *Moses @ Klein '01,* Klein Art Works, Chicago

Selected Group Exhibitions:

1962 *50 California Artists,* Whitney Museum, New York
1968 *Late 50s at the Ferus,* Los Angeles County Museum of Art
1969 *West Coast 1945–1969,* Pasadena Art Museum
1972 *Documenta,* Kassel, West Germany
1973 *70th American Exhibition,* Art Institute of Chicago
1974 *Art Now '74,* Kennedy Center, Washington, D.C.
1977 *20th National Print Exhibition,* Brooklyn Museum, New York
1988 *Visions of Inner Space,* Wight Art Gallery, University of California, Los Angeles (also National Gallery of Modern Art, New Delhi, India)
1990 *In Perfect Silence,* Art Center College of Design, Pasadena
Abstraction: John Altoon, Sam Francis, Craig Kauffman, Jon McLaughlin & Ed Moses, Nagoya City Art Museum (also Museum of Modern Art, Shiga; Hara Museum ARC, Japan)
1991 *Recent Acquisitions, Part II—1950–1991,* Achenbach Foundation, San Francisco
Moses, Richter, Scully, Louver Gallery, New York
Biennial Exhibition, The Whitney Museum of American Art, New York
1992 *American Drawings Since 1960,* Los Angeles County Museum of Art, Los Angeles
The Last Picture Show: An Evolution of Works by Los Angeles Artists, Bank of America, Gallery at the Plaza, Los Angeles
Choice Encounters, The Long Beach Museum of Art, California
1993 *Tony Berlant, John McCracken, Ed Moses,* Works Gallery, Costa Mesa
Art in Los Angeles: Eight Artists in the Sixties, Asher Faure, Los Angeles
Elegant, Irreverent & Obsessive: Drawing in Southern California, Main Art Gallery, California State University, Fullerton (catalog)
1994 *In Plain Sight: Abstract Painting in Los Angeles,* Blue Star Art Space, San Antonio, Texas
1995 *Object and Image,* Newport Harbor Art Museum, Newport Beach, California
Made in L.A.: The Prints of the Cirrus Editions, Los Angeles County Museum of Art (catalog)
California Collection, Hunsaker/Schlesinger, Santa Monica
Timeless Abstraction, Davis/McClain Gallery, Houston
1996 *Lobby Installation,* Whitney Museum of American Art, New York
Made in L.A.: The Prints of Cirrus Editions, Los Angeles County Museum of Art, Los Angeles
Washi: Collaborations in Spirit, Beckstrand Gallery, Palos Verdes Art Center
1997 *A Thought Intercepted,* California Museum of Art, Santa Rosa
California: State of the Art, Art of the State, Chac Mool Contemporary Fine Art, West Hollywood, California
1998 *Radical Past: Contemporary Art & Music in Pasadena, 1960–1974,* Norton Simon Museum of Art, Armory Center for the Arts, Pasadena
Sunshine & Noir, Art in L.A. 1960–1997, UCLA Hammer Museum, Los Angeles
LA Cool, Rocket Gallery, London (also Bruning & Zischke, Dusseldorf)
The Forty-fifth Biennial: The Corcoran Collects, 1907–1998, The Corcoran Gallery of Art, Washington, D.C.
The Edward R. Broda Collection, Orlando Museum of Art, Orlando, Florida

1999 *Contemporary Abstraction,* Klein Art Works, Chicago

Collections:

Albright-Knox Gallery, Buffalo; Akron Art Institute, Akron; Art Institute of Chicago; Cincinnati Museum of Art; Corcoran Gallery of Art, Washington, D.C.; Dartmouth College Gallery, Hanover; Denver Museum of Art; La Jolla Museum of Contemporary Art; Long Beach Museum of Art, California; Los Angeles County Museum of Art; Museum of Modern Art, New York; Museum of New Mexico, Santa Fe; National Museum of American Art, Smithsonian Institution, Washington, D.C.; Neuberger Museum, Purchase; Newport Harbor Art Museum, Newport Beach; Oakland Museum of Art; Palm Spring Desert Museum; Norton Simon Museum of Art, Pasadena; Philadelphia Museum of Art; San Francisco Museum of Modern Art; Seattle Art Museum; Walker Art Center, Minneapolis; Whitney Museum of American Art, New York.

Publications:

By MOSES: Books—*Ed Moses: A Retrospective of Paintings and Drawings, 1951–1996,* with John Yau, Berkeley, 1996. **Article—** interview, with Stephanie Barron, in *Moses,* exhibition catalog, Los Angeles 1976.

On MOSES: Articles—''Los Angeles: Ed Moses, Mizuno Gallery'' by Peter Plagens in *Artforum* (New York), September 1970; ''New York: Edward Moses, Ronald Feldman Fine Arts'' by Joseph Masheck in *Artforum* (New York), February 1972; ''Ed Moses: The Problem of Regionalism'' by Peter Plagens in *Artforum* (New York), March 1972; ''London Commentary'' by Bernard Denvir in *Studio International* (London), September 1972; *Documenta 5,* exhibition catalog, Kassel, West Germany 1972; ''Print as Surface'' by J. Loring in *Arts Magazine* (New York), September 1973; ''New York Letter'' by P. Derfner in *Art International* (Lugano, Switzerland), April 1974; ''Wholly Moses'' by Sean Mitchell in *Los Angeles Magazine,* vol. 40, no. 7, July 1995; ''Tracking Ed Moses'' by Frances Colpitt in *Art in America* (New York), December 1996.

* * *

Ed Moses—exhibiting originally as Edward Moses y Branco—did not receive the early acclaim enjoyed by his younger Ferus Gallery (1957–66) colleagues, Larry Bell, Billy Al Bengston, Robert Irwin and Craig Kauffman, although director Walter Hopp's singular eye undoubtedly saw the seeds of vanguard work in his New York-inspired Abstract Expressionism. He seemed to lag behind the others who abandoned that style soon after the turn of the decade to venture boldly and directly into ''finish fetish'' and the ''L.A. Look.'' Unlike their work Moses' *Rose* drawings and paintings of the early 1960s were not easily identified with rising national movements like Pop—despite their source in the design on cheap Mexican oilcloth—or with Minimalism. It wasn't until the late 1970s, when his flat, deceptively smooth, monochrome planes emerged that Minimalism was ascribed to the paintings which actually evolved from diagonal grids, densified by layering and smoothed by scraping and sanding. The *Roses* however, cut out, with the spaces in between filled with shimmering graphite hatchings, can now be seen by hindsight to forecast the later trend in pattern painting.

Moses, earlier a premedical student, drew schematized landscapes of the Venice boardwalk in 1952 revealing the propensity for structure that came to underlie even the gestural work that followed. The outer frame of *Rafe* (1958), reminiscent of Philip Guston, whose abstract style, as well as de Kooning's and Milton Resnick's, marked his work at the time, is reiterated inside the edge and echoed in the predominantly right-angled disposition of bright skeins of paint weaving over the center. In drawings of erotically suggestive organic forms much like those of Kauffman, whose work made a significant impact, and John Altoon, spontaneous marks exist in a structured framework.

Moses' constructive bent was given full rein outside the province of studio art—he worked as a technical draftsman from 1954 to 1956, then briefly served as a design engineer for solar aircraft. Later, he designed the Chapellet Winery at St. Helena, California (1969). Those skills came into play in the creation of an environment at the Mizuno Gallery (1970). By cutting a rectangle out of the roof, leaving the rafters to permit sunlight to fall on the floor in slanted stripes of light and dark, he elegantly introduced rough lumber and other raw materials into the realm of light and space art.

Prior to that, the *Roses* had given way to geometric abstraction, by no means rigidly drawn, but as loose and intuitively rendered grids, at first tending to horizontal lines recalling Agnes Martin, whom he came to know while maintaining a studio at Coenties Slip in New York City (1958–60).

While Moses' grids have also reflected the influence of Mondrian—even a Mondrianesque *Chrysanthemum* emerged in drawings (1961)—they became characteristally diagonal, sometimes like tartans but more often suggesting designs on Navajo blankets, a phenomenon the artist has intensively researched within a lifelong interest in fabric and pattern. *Loom* (1971) is a testimonial to this pursuit, a fiber and resin painting with loosely tied threads extending from the warp.

The use of resin as a support came about in the late 1960s, at first joined to unstretched canvas; his *Indian Blanket Series* (1970–71) awarded him critical acclaim. The loose-hanging ''soft'' paintings also cast him in the role of guru to many younger artists involved in creating ''meditative'' surfaces and sharing the interest in Tibetan Buddhism to which he was drawn in 1971.

That engagement is reflected in a 1981 series, the ''Raw Wood Paintings,'' which, at first glance, appear to be diametrically opposed to the monochromes which preceded them, but, unlike those, they expose, rather than conceal his process. Here, multipatterned constructions of rectangular boards incorporate different sizes of finished and unfinished woods, rough and finish carpentry procedures. Strident in color and varied in gesture, bearing strong references to primal and non-Western cultures, they ultimately suggest altarpieces the right-angled *Ohbo,* partly wood-finished and partly painted, embraces cornering walls, kimono-like an exterior shape.

Moses has since returned to canvas, tending to alternate between somewhat more structured diagonally ''woven'' grids, predominantly red, gold and black, and the more spontaneous, organic ''worm'' paintings, whose serpentine forms tend to neutral tones.

Both series are executed with oil and acrylic pigments which were poured together into a bucket and applied to canvases stretched horizontally on a wooden platform out of doors. Often incorporating a stenciled spider, the diagonal grids are executed with large brushes sweeping over the canvas alongside a board rotated to a 45-degree angle serving as a straight-edge, the diagonal format maintained even as successive layers of pigments, each cancelling out the one preceding, tend to undermine it.

All control is abolished in the organic paintings. There, intention and preconception give way entirely to the unconscious automatist mark. With a household mop rapidly swabbing the layers onto the soaked canvas, membranous strands collide and separate before the oil finally floats to the top and the acrylic bleeds into the support, their action forming lightning-like streaks and misty, atomized implosions, with the artist acting merely to ''distribute'' paint over the support. On occasion, that process overtakes rejected or incomplete gridded canvases so that throbbing and surging linear elements penetrate and overlay the existing organization, both demolishing it and becoming one with it.

Moses' drawings, which reveal the full extent of his researches, are, like his prints, no less valuable in their own right. They complete a body of work, which, he confesses, is frequently ''as much a surprise to me as it to anyone else.'' A dialogue between structure and spontaneity, and between medium and maker, his oeuvre records the progress of a career in which intuition, always open to provocation but never submitting to fashion, has been an unfailing guide.

—Merle Schipper

MOSSET, Olivier

Nationality: Swiss. **Born:** Bern, 11 May 1944. **Education:** Attended several Swiss schools until 1965; also worked with the artists Jean Tinguely, Daniel Spoerri and Arman, 1962–65. **Career:** Independent painter, in Paris, 1965–77, in New York, since 1977. Member, with Daniel Buren, Michel Parmentier and Niele Toroni, Groupe Gallery BMPT, Paris, 1966–68; lives and works in Tucson, Arizona. **Agents:** John Gibson Gallery, 205 East 78th Street, New York, New York, 10021; Tony Shafrazi Gallery, 328 East 11th Street, New York, New York 10003; Galerie Gilbert Brownstone, 17 rue Saint Gilles, 75003 Paris, **Address:** c/o Elizabeth Cherry Contemporary Art, 437 E. Grant Road, Tucson, Arizona 85705, U.S.A.

Individual Exhibitions:

1968 Galerie Jean Larcade, Paris
Galerie J. Paris (with Daniel Buren and Niele Toroni)
Galerie Rive Droite, Paris
1969 Galerie Jean Larcade, Paris
Galerie Rive Droite, Paris
1971 Galerie Mathias Fels, Paris
1974 Chez Ben Vautier, Nice
Galerie Daniel Templon, Paris
Galleria Daniel Templon, Milan
1976 Galerie l' Oeil 2000, Chateauroux, France
A.D.D.A., Marseilles
Galerie Ecart, Geneva
1977 Galerie Daniel Templon, Paris
Galerie Media, Neuchâtel, Switzerland
Laboratorio, Milan
1979 Tony Shafrazi Gallery, New York
1980 C. Space, New York
Galerie Claude Givaudan, Geneva
Galerie Marika Malacorda, Geneva
Galerie Gillespie-Laage, Paris
1981 Patrick Verelst Gallery, Antwerp
1982 Olsen Gallery, New York
1984 Galerie Susanna Kulli, St. Gallen, Switzerland
Galerie Marika Malacorda, Geneva
1985 Musée St. Croix, Poitiers, France
Centre d'Art Contemporain, Chateaurox, France
Musée des Beaux-Arts, La-Chaux-de-Fonds, Switzerland
1986 Tony Shafrazi Gallery, New York
Aargauer Kunsthaus, Aarau, Switzerland
Centre d'Art Contemporain, Geneva
Villa Arson, Nice, France
Galerie Gilbert Brownstone, Paris
1987 Galerie Daniel Buchholz, Cologne
Galerie Gilbert Brownstone, Paris
Musée St. Pierre d' Art Contemporain, Lyon, France
John Gibson Gallery, New York
1988 Galerie Susanna Kulli, St. Gallen, Switzerland
John Gibson Gallery, New York
Julian Pretto Gallery, New York
Gilbert Brownstone & Cie, Paris
1989 *Intuition,* John Gibson Gallery, New York (catalog)
Galerie Sollertis, Toulouse, France
Galerie Massimo de Carlo, Milan
Julian Pretto Gallery, New York
1990 John Gibson Gallery, New York
Galerie Jean-Francois Dumont, Bordeaux
Galerie Isy Brachot, Brussels
Galerie Frernando Alcolea, Barcelona
Galerie Pierre Huber, Geneva
Dart Gallery, Chicago
Galerie Tanit, Munich
Galerie Tanit, Cologne
Galerie Marika Malacorda, Genève
Gilbert Brownstone & Cie, Paris
1991 Galerie Jean-François Dumont, Bordeaux, France
Galerie Sollertis, Toulouse, France
Vrej Baghoomian Gallery, New York
Tony Shafrazi Gallery, New York
Galerie Anselm Dreher, Berlin
1992 Galerie Mark Müller, Zürich
Ecole Régionale d'Art, Dunkerque, France
Château de Grand Jardin, Joinville, France
Galerie Massimo de Carlo, Milan
1993 L'Usine, Dijon, France
CCC, Tours, France
Château de Fraissé, Fraissé-des-Corbières, France
Gilbert Brownstone & Cie, Paris
1994 Galerie Susanna Kulli, St. Gallen, Switzerland
Galerie John Gibson, New York
La Box, Ecole Nationale Supérieure d'Art de Bourges, France
1995 F.R.A.C. Auvergne, Clermont-Ferrand, France
Galerie de l'Ecole des Beaux-Arts, Quimper, France
Ecole Regionale des Beaux-Arts, Dunkerque
1996 Galerie Van Gelder, Amsterdam
Centre d'Art Neuchâtel, Switzerland
Galleria Massimo de Carlo, Milan
1997 Gilbert Brownstone & Cie, Paris

Galerie Guy Ledune, Brussels
1998 Terrain, San Francisco
Galerie Eric Linard, la Garde Adhemar, France
Galerie Martine & Thibault de la Chatre, Paris
1999 Salon, San Miguel de Allende, Mexico
Exit, Lausanne, Switzerland
Galerie Susanna Kulli, St. Gallen, Switzerland
Galerie Bruno Bischofberger, Zurich, Switzerland

Selected Group Exhibitions:

1967 *Salon de la Jeune Peinture,* Musée d'Art Moderne, Paris
1968 *Biennale di Lignano,* Italy
1974 *L' Art au Present,* Musée Gallieria, Paris
1976 *I Colori della Pittura,* Instituto Latino-Americano, Rome (travelled to the Galleria del Milione, Milan)
1978 *Fracture du Monochrome,* Musée d'Art Moderne de la Ville, Paris
1979 *Tendances de l'Art en France,* Musée d'Art Moderne de la Ville, Paris
1980 *22 Artistas Suicos,* Galeria Nacional de Arte Moderna, Lisbon
1981 *Painting about Painting,* William Paterson College, Wayne, New Jersey
1985 *On View,* New Museum of Contemporary Art, New York
1987 *Primary Structures,* Rhona Hoffman Gallery, Chicago
1988 *Abstract,* IGI, Javit Center, New York
Works, Concepts, Processes, Situations, Information, Galerie Hans Meyer, Düsseldorf, Germany
1989 *NY Kunst,* Louisiana Museum of Modern Art, Humlebaek, Denmark
Centre d'Art Contemporain, Genéve (catalog)
1993 *Live in Your Head,* Heiligenkreuzerhof, Vienna (catalog)
XLV Biennale di Venezia, Italy
1994 *Unbound: Possibilities in Painting,* Hayward Gallery, London (catalog)
1995 *Purple 8½,* Galerie Jousse Seguin, Paris
1996 *Spring Benefit,* The Sculpture Center, New York
Visual Reality, Petra Bungert Gallery, New York
1997 *Raindrops on Roses,* Sarah Cottier Gallery, Sydney, Australia
Magasin, Centre National d'Art Contemporain de Grenoble, France
1998 *Regle et Deviance,* Musee d'Art et d'Histoire, Neuchâtel, Switzerland
Forde's Needles, Galerie Forde, Geneva, Switzerland
1999 *Special Offer,* Kasseler Kunstverein, Kassel, Germany
Postmark: An Abstract Effect, Site Santa Fe, New Mexico
Olivier Mosset/Cady Noland, Migros Museum für Gegenwartskunst, Zurich
2000 *The Tao of Painting: Principles in Monochrome,* The McKinney Contemporary, Dallas, Texas
Texere, Skopia Art Contemporain, Geneva, Switzerland (catalog)

Collections:

Musée d'Art Moderne de la Ville, Paris; Centre Georges Pompidou, Paris; Kunstmuseum, Bern; Museum of Modern Art, New York.

Publications:

By MOSSET: Book—*Ecrits et Entretiens,* with John Armleder and Helmut Federle, Grenoble 1987. **Articles—**''Armleder and Mosset in Conversation'' in *Artscribe* (London), November/ December 1986; ''Oliver Mosset,'' interview with Robert Nickas in *Flash Art* (Milan), February/March 1987; interview with Jeanne Siegel in *Arts Magazine,* vol. 64, May 1990; interview with Hubert Besacier in *Artefactum,* vol. 10, no. 47, March-May 1993.

On MOSSET: Books—*Olivier Mosset: Catalog No. 1,* with text by Serge Bard, Paris 1967; *Mosset,* exhibition catalog with text by Jean-Paul Dolle, Paris 1969; *Art actuel en France* by Anne Tronche, Paris 1973; *I colori della pittura,* exhibition catalog with text by Italo Mussa, Rome 1976; *Fracture du monochrome,* exhibition catalog with text by Bernard Lamarche-Vadel, Paris 1978; *Tendances de l'art en France,* exhibition catalog with text by Marcelin Pleynet, Paris 1979; *Painting about Painting,* exhibition catalog with text by Nancy Einreinhofer, Wayne, New Jersey 1981; *Olivier Mosset,* exhibition catalog with text by Maurice Besset, Chateauroux 1985; *Oliver Mosset,* exhibition catalog with texts by Ulrich Loock and Adelina von Furstenberg, Geneva 1986. **Articles—**''BMPT'' by Gregoire Muller in *Robho* (Paris), Autumn 1967; ''Olivier Mosset'' by Otto Hahn in *L'Express* (Paris), November 1968; ''BMPT'' by Michel Claur in *VH 101* (Paris), Spring 1971; ''Le Groupe BMPT'' by Otto Hahn in *Art Press* (Paris), June/August 1974; ''Olivier Mosset'' by Otto Hahn in *+ -0* (Genval-Lac), September 1976; ''Olivier Mosset'' by Bernard Lamarche-Vadel in *Artistes* (Paris), June/July 1980; ''Getting on with Painting'' by Marcia Hafif in *Art in America* (New York), April 1981; ''Armleder, Mosset, Toroni'' by Dieter Schwarz in *Noema* (Zurich), Summer 1987. **Film—***Fun and Games for Everyone* by Serge Bard, 1968.

*

Even though nothing escapes the laws of history, the main problem remains a praxis, material and formal, that of applying color on the canvas, that of painting. Far from cutting the work off from reality, such practice should indeed give painting its full meaning: to make it be what it is, instead of being a reflexion upon reality which, though not preventing it from being, would, nevertheless, obfuscate its own reality.

I have difficulties speaking about my work; in fact, I have difficulties speaking about painting, and frankly, I am slightly disturbed by this conversation. Of course, we do talk about these things, and more or less in this way, but what bothers me is to be in a position to defend the conceptions we have of our work, because as I see it, such conceptions are not defendable. If I entertain a relationship of rightness to my work, it is a private relationship. It is up to others to say something.

—Olivier Mosset

* * *

Olivier Mosset's painting began in 1965 with a series of canvases carrying minimal images, such as a full stop mark or a letter ''A.'' From 1967 to 1968 Mosset belonged to the group BMPT (Buren, Mosset, Parmentier, Toroni) in which he pursued and radicalized his choice of a neutral and anonymous intervention in painting. Each artist chose and repeated his own ''distinctive'' mark. Buren's vertical stripes equalled Mosset's circle painted in the middle of the canvas.

The group produced a number of ''actions'' intended to present the work: a way of ''giving itself to the public'' in codified places. The group also transgressed a central artistic convention—the instance of recognizability, the ''personal mark'' that renders the work identifiable as produced by a particular artist.

The repetition of a visual element is also in contrast to the logic of chronological evolution within a body of work, and thus the needs of the market. But the constant repetition of a constant element itself became a ''stylistic cipher'' bringing the artist back to his own subjectivity, and once more the repetition itself had to be rejected.

Mosset's gesture in that period was still highly ideological, while his aim was directed at producing an analysis of the material reality of painting, from which both biography and ideology were to be banned. For this reason, in 1972 a move was made towards a series of paintings of ''constant dimensions,'' marked by vertical bands (seldom diagonal), firstly white and grey, later of different colours, at times tonally consistent, on other occasions dissonant. The passage from series to the next is dependent on purely accidental causes determined by practical considerations: running out of a supply of a particular kind of colour, the commission of a particular kind of picture, or simply the will to experiment with new pigments.

In this way Mosset's work is qualified by an investigation into colour, which is progressively reduced to a two-tone analysis—whereas later on he concentrates on tone alone in paintings where the vertical bands are delimited only by thin graphic lines (1977). Later on, this delineating element is also discarded, and the artist then engaged himself with a poetic of monochrome only, a kind of work that has absorbed him up to the present day.

Mosset is inspired by the work of Ad Reinhardt, though he does not posit the painting as an absolute, or the monochrome choice as an extreme statement at the core of a reflection which is purely metalinguistical as the American master does. Mosset deconstructs the system of painting, moving away from the absolute to the contingent.

The monochrome stands metonymically for the whole painting and represents the most appropriate vehicle for research into the signifiying potentialities of colour. In any case, the monochrome is considered by its nature as an event bearing a ''zero degree'' potential for expression. It is the very matter of painting of which Mosset analyses the mechanisms.

—Giorgio Verzotti

MOTHERWELL, Robert

Robert Motherwell, 1980. ©Dedalus Foundation, Inc./Licensed by VAGA, New York, NY.

Nationality: American. **Born:** Aberdeen, Washington, 24 January 1915. **Education:** Studied painting, California School of Fine Arts, San Francisco, 1932; studied philosophy, Stanford Institute, California, 1932–37, B.A. 1937; Harvard University Graduate School of Arts and Sciences, Cambridge, Massachusetts, 1937–38; studied, under Meyer Shapiro, Columbia University, New York, 1940; studied engraving, under Kurt Seligman, 1941, and under Stanley William Hayter, 1945. **Family:** Married Maria Emilia Ferreira y Moyers in 1941; daughters: Jeannie and Lise; married Helen Frankenthaler in 1958; married Renate Ponsold in 1972. Art instructor, University of Oregon, Eugene, 1939; Black Mountain College, Beria, North Carolina, 1945–51; co-founder, with William Baziotes, Barnett Newman and David Hare, Subject of the Artist School, New York, 1948 (closed, 1949); founder, School of Fine Arts, New York, 1949 (closed, 1950); painting instructor, 1951–58, and distinguished visiting professor, 1971–72, Hunter College, New York; instructor, graduate seminar, Oberlin College, Ohio, 1952; instructor, Colorado Springs Fine Arts Center, summer 1954; visiting critic, 1964–65, and advisor on art, 1972, graduate program of the arts, Columbia University, New York; co-chairman of seminar, with Anthony Caro and Alex Colville, University of Toronto, Ontario, 1970; instructor of seminars at Provincetown Art Workshop, Massachusetts, and at Calhoun College, Yale University, New Haven, Connecticut, 1971. Advisor, Bliss International Study Center, Museum of Modern Art, New York, 1968; education adviser, Guggenheim Foundation, New York, 1968–75; special adviser, National Council on the Arts, Washington, D.C., 1969; consultant, National Collection of Fine Arts, Smithsonian Institution, Washington, D.C., 1971. Editor, *Documents of Modern Art* series, from 1944; with John Cage, Pierre Chareau, and Harold Rosenberg, only issue of *Possibilities,* New York, 1947; general editor, *Documents of 20th Century Art,* New York and London, 1968; advisory editor, *American Scholar,* Washington, D.C., 1968–75. **Awards:** Guggenheim Award, 1964, and Fellowship, 1969; Belgian Arts Critics Prize, 1966; National Council on the Arts Grant, 1966; Fellowship in Perpetuity, Metropolitan Museum of Art, New

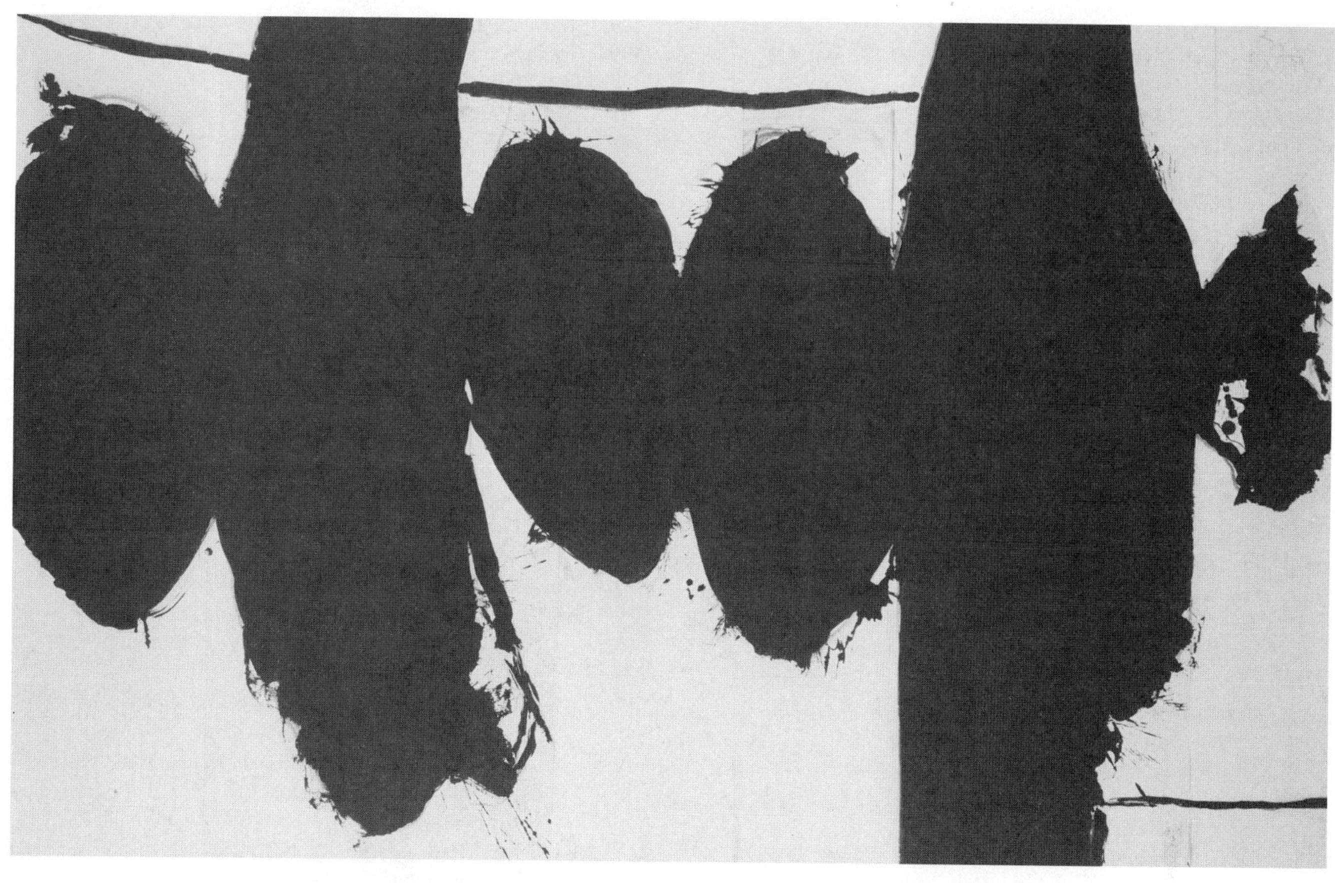

Robert Motherwell: *Elegy to the Spanish Republic No. 159,* 1979. ©Dedalus Foundation, Inc./Licensed by VAGA, New York, NY.

York, 1967; Benjamin Franklin Fellow, Royal Society of Arts, London 1968; Award for Distinction in Visual Arts, University of South Carolina, Columbia, 1974; Grande Medaille de Vermeil, Paris, 1977; Gold Medal, Pennsylvania Academy of Fine Arts, 1979; Medal of Merit, University of Salamanca, Spain, 1980; Skowhegan Award for Printmaking, Maine, 1981; Mayor's Award of Honor, New York, 1981; Gold Medal, National Arts Club, New York, 1983; Great Artists Award, New York University/Guggenheim Museum, 1985; MacDowell Colony Medal, 1985; Medalla d'Oro de Bellas Artes, Madrid, 1986; National Medal of Arts, 1990. D.F.A.: Bard College, Annandale-on-Hudson, New York, 1973; Maryland Institute, Baltimore, 1974; Southeastern Massachusetts University, North Dartmouth, 1974; University of Connecticut, 1979; Rhode Island School of Design, 1980; Otis Art Institute/New School for Social Research, 1985; Brown University, 1985; Hunter College, 1985. **Member:** National Institute of Arts and Letters, 1969; American Academy of Arts and Sciences, Cambridge, Massachusetts; Royal Society of Arts, London. **Agent:** Knoedler Gallery, 19 East 70th Street, New York, New York 10021. **Died:** Of stroke, Provincetown, Massachusetts, 16 July 1991.

Individual Exhibitions:

1939 Raymond Duncan Gallery, Paris
1944 Art of this Century Gallery, New York
1946 Kootz Gallery, New York
Museum of Art, San Francisco
1947 Kootz Gallery, New York
1949 Kootz Gallery, New York
1950 Kootz Gallery, New York
1952 Allen Memorial Art Museum, Oberlin College, Ohio
1953 Kootz Gallery, New York
1957 *Paintings and Collages,* Sidney Janis Gallery, New York
1959 *First Retrospective Exhibition,* Bennington College, Vermont
Sidney Janis Gallery, New York
1961 *Recent Paintings and Collages,* Sidney Janis Gallery, New York
Collages (1958–60), Galerie Berggruen, Paris
1962 Pasadena Art Museum, California
I Collages di Motherwell, Galleria Odyssia, Rome
Galerie Der Spiegel, Cologne
Sidney Janis Gallery, New York (retrospective)
1963 Smith College, Northampton, Massachusetts
Massachusetts Institute of Technology, Cambridge
1965 *Collages,* Phillips Collection, Washington, D.C. (retrospective)
Museum of Modern Art, New York
Galerie Schmela, Dusseldorf (with Conrad Marc-Relli)
1966 Contemporary Art Museum, Houston
Baltimore Museum of Art
Stedelijk Museum, Amsterdam
Whitechapel Art Gallery, London
Folkwang Museum, Essen

Palais des Beaux-Arts, Brussels
Museo Civico, Galleria d'Arte Moderna, Turin
Museum of Art, San Francisco
Indiana University Art Museum, Bloomington
University of California at Riverside
1968 Whitney Museum, New York
Museum of Art, Richmond, Virginia
Marlborough Galleria d'Arte, Rome
Museum of Modern Art, New York
1970 David Mirvish Gallery, Toronto
1971 *Bilder und Collagen 1967–70,* Galerie im Erker, St. Gall, Switzerland
Kunstverein, Freiburg, West Germany
1972 Walker Art Center, Minneapolis
Dayton's 12 Gallery, Minneapolis
Lawrence Rubin Gallery, New York
Metropolitan Museum of Art, New York
University of Iowa Art Museum, Iowa City
Frederick Gallery, Washington, D.C.
Gertrude Kasle Gallery, Detroit
The Collages of Robert Motherwell: A Retrospective Exhibition, Museum of Fine Arts, Houston
1973 Cleveland Museum of Art
Recent Works, Princeton Museum, New Jersey
Current Editions, Seattle
Wadsworth Atheneum, Hartford, Connecticut
John Berggruen Gallery, San Francisco
Museum of Fine Arts, Boston
David Mirvish Gallery, Toronto
1974 Knoedler Contemporary Art Gallery, New York
Brooke Alexander Inc., New York
1975 Waddington Gallery, London
Retrospective del Gran Pintor Norteamericano, Museo de Arte Moderno, Mexico City
1976 Knoedler Contemporary Art Gallery, New York
1977 Museum des 20. Jahrhunderts, Vienna (retrospective; travelled to Musee d'Art Moderne, Paris; Royal Scottish Academy, Edinburgh; and the Royal Academy of Arts, London)
1978 *David Smith/Robert Motherwell,* Museo de Arte Contemporaneo de Caracas, Venezuela
1979 *Robert Motherwell and Black,* William Benton Museum of Art, Storrs, Connecticut
William Ehrlich Gallery, New York
Janie C. Lee Gallery, Houston (retrospective)
Brooke Alexander Gallery, New York
1980 Centre Cultural de la Caix de Pensions, Barcelona (retrospective; travelled to Fundación Juan March, Madrid)
1981 American Federation of Arts, New York (retrospective)
1983 Albright-Knox Art Gallery, Buffalo, New York (retrospective; travelled to Los Angeles, San Francisco, Seattle, Washington, and New York, 1983–85)
Bavarian State Museum of Modern Art, Munich
1988 Associated American Artists, New York
1989 Bobbie Greenfield Fine Art, Los Angeles
Padiglione d'Arte Contemporanea, Milan
M. Knoedler Gallery, New York
1990 Artcurial, Paris
Associated American Artists, New York
1991 Museo Rufino Tamayo, Mexico City
1992 Modern Art Museum of Fort Worth, Fort Worth
Ars Multiplicata, Surry Hills
1996 Walker Art Center, Minneapolis
1997 Fundacio Antoni Tapies, Barcelona
Centro de Arte Reina Sofia, Madrid

Selected Group Exhibitions:

1958 *Biennale,* Venice
1959 *Documenta 2,* Kassel, West Germany
1964 *Dunn International,* Tate Gallery, London
1968 *Carnegie International,* Pittsburgh
1969 *New American Painting and Sculpture,* Museum of Modern Art, New York
1972 *Abstract Painting in the 70s,* Museum of Fine Arts, Boston
1974 *Prints from Gemini G.E.L.,* Walker Art Center, Minneapolis
1978 *American Art at Mid-Century: The Subjects of the Artist,* National Gallery of Art, Washington, D.C.
1985 *Painterly Visions 1940–84,* Guggenheim Museum, New York
1987 *American Painting: Abstract Expressionism and After,* San Francisco Museum of Modern Art
1988 *A Golden Age: the Artist Works with Paper,* Meredith Long Contemporary, Houston
Abstract Expressionist Drawings 1941–1955, Janie C. Lee Master Drawings, New York
1989 *Master Drawings 1859–1989,* Janie C. Lee Master Drawings, New York
The Artist's Book: the Most Beautiful Artists' Books from the Collection of the Herzog August Library in Wolfenbuttel, Kestner-Gesellschaft, Hanover
1990 *Abstract Expressionism: Other Dimensions,* Whitney Museum of American Art, New York
1992 *Abstract Expressionism: Works on Paper—Selections from the Metropolitan Museum of Art,* Metropolitan Museum of Art, New York
1993 *20th International Biennial of Graphic Art,* Moderna Galerija, Ljubljana
1995 *Abstract Expressionism: Works on Paper—Selections from the Metropolitan Museum of Art,* National Museum of Art, Tokyo
1999 *The New York School: Selections from the Collection,* Museum of Modern Art, New York

Collections:

Museum of Modern Art, New York; Metropolitan Museum of Art, New York; Whitney Museum, New York; Albright-Knox Art Gallery, Buffalo, New York; National Gallery of Art, Washington, D.C.; Smithsonian Institution, Washington, D.C.; Cleveland Museum of Art; Art Institute of Chicago; San Francisco Museum of Modern Art; Stedelijk Museum, Amsterdam; Phillips Academy, Addison Gallery of American Art, Andover, Massachusetts; Brooklyn Museum, New York; Dallas Museum of Fine Arts, Texas; Fogg Art Museum, Harvard University; The Hirshhorn Museum, Washington, D.C.; Los Angeles County Museum of Art, California; Museum of Art, Tel Aviv, Israel; Art Gallery of Toronto, Canada; Washington University,

St. Louis; University of Washington, Seattle; Yale University, New Haven.

Publications:

By MOTHERWELL: Books—*Plastic Art and Pure Plastic Art* by Piet Mondrian, editor, New York 1945; *Robert Motherwell: Collages 1943–1949,* with Marianne Moore, New York 1949; *The Dada Painters and Poets: An Anthology,* editor, New York 1951; *Modern Artists in American,* edited with Ad Reinhardt, New York 1951; *Robert Motherwell's "A la Pintura": The Genesis of a Book,* exhibition catalog with John McKendry and Diane Kelder, New York 1971. **Articles—**"Notes on Mondrian and Chirico" in *VVV* (New York), June 1942; "The Modern Painter's World" in *Dyn* (Coyoacán, Mexico), November 1944; "Painter's Objects" in *Partisan Review* (New York), Winter 1944; "Henry Moore" in *New Republic* (New York), 22 October 1945; "Beyond the Aesthetic" in *Design* (London), April 1946; statement in *14 Americans,* exhibition catalog, New York 1946; statement and editorial preface, with Harold Rosenberg, in *Possibilities: An Occasional Review* (New York), Winter 1947; preface to *Arp, On My Way: Poetry and Essays 1912–1947,* New York 1948; preface to *Beyond Painting and Other Writings by the Artist and His Friends* by Max Ernst, New York 1948; "The Ideas of Art: A Tour of the Sublime" in *Tiger's Eye* (New York), 15 December 1948; preliminary notice to *The Rise of Cubism* by Daniel-Henry Kahnweiler, New York 1949; preface to *Black or White: Paintings by European and American Artists,* exhibition catalog, New York 1950, reprinted in *Black and White,* exhibition catalog, New York 1963; preliminary notice to *Baudelaire to Surrealism,* New York 1950; preface to *The Fauvist Painters* by Georges Duthuit, New York 1950; preface to *David Smith,* exhibition catalog, New York 1950; "What Abstract Art Means to Me" in *Museum of Modern Art Bulletin* (New York), spring 1951; "The Public and the Modern Artist" in *Catholic Art Quarterly* (Boston), Easter 1951; "The Rise and Continuity of Abstract Art" in *Arts and Architecture* (Los Angeles), September 1951; preface to *The School of New York: 17 Modern American Painters on Painters,* exhibition catalog, Beverly Hills, California, reprinted in *The School of New York,* exhibition catalog, Santa Barbara, California 1951; "Artists Sessions at Studio 35 (1950)" in *Modern Artists in America* (New York), no. 1, 1951; preface to *Motherwell,* exhibition catalog, New York 1952; "The Painter and the Audience" in *Perspectives USA* (New York), Autumn 1954; "A Painting Must Make Human Contact" in *New Decade* (New York), 1955, reprinted in *Painters on Painting,* edited by Eric Protter, New York 1963; statement in *Bradley Walker Tomlin,* exhibition catalog, New York 1957; "The Significance of Miró" in *Artnews* (New York), May 1959; "Painting as Self-Discovery," recorded interview, with David Sylvester, for the BBC, October 1960; "In Support of the French Intellectuals," with others in *Partisan Review* (New York), January/February 1961; "What Should a Museum Be?" in *Art in America* (New York), vol. 49, no. 2, reprinted in *VI Bienal de Museo de Arte Moderna,* exhibition catalog, Sao Paulo 1961, and in *Robert Motherwell: A Retrospective Exhibition,* catalog, Pasadena, California 1962; statement, in *The Cubist Painters: Aesthetic Meditations* by Guillaume Apollinaire, New York 1962; "A Conversation at Lunch" in *An Exhibition of the Work of Robert Motherwell,* exhibition catalog, Northampton, Massachusetts 1963; statement, in "The Creative Use of the Unconscious by the Artists and the Psychotherapist" in *Annals of Psychotherapy: Journal of the American Academy of Psychotherapists,* vol. 5, no. 1, 1964; interview, with Bryan Robertson, in *Art: New York* (New York), 15 December 1964; "A Major American Sculptor: David Smith" in *Vogue* (New York), February 1965, reprinted in *People and Things in "Vogue,"* edited by Allene Talmey, Englewood Cliffs, New Jersey 1970; "A Letter from Robert Motherwell to Frank O'Hara" in *Robert Motherwell,* exhibition catalog, New York 1965; "The Motherwell Proposal" in *Seminar on Elementary and Secondary School Education in the Arts,* edited by Howard Comant, New York 1965; "An interview with Robert Motherwell," with Max Kozloff in *Artforum* (New York), September 1965; article in *Robert Motherwell,* exhibition catalog, by Luigi Mallé, Turin 1966; interview, with Sidney Simon, in *Art International* (Lugano, Switzerland), Summer 1967; statement in *Art Now: New York* (New York), May 1969; "Addenda to the Museum of Modern Art Lyric Suite Questionnaire: From Memory. . . with Possible Chronological Slips" in *Museum of Modern Art Newletter* (New York), Fall 1969; "David Smith: Erinnerungen" in *Robert Motherwell: Bilder und Collagen 1967–1970,* exhibition catalog, St. Gall, Switzerland 1970; "The Universal Language of Children's Art and Modernism" in *The American Scholar* (Washington D.C.), Winter 1970; "The Artist Speaks" in *Robert Motherwell at Saint Paul's School,* Concord, New Hampshire, 1970; preface to *Dialogues with Marcel Duchamp* by Pierre Cabanne, New York 1971; "Robert Motherwell," interview, with Irmelin Lebeer, in *Chroniques de l'Art Vivant* (Paris), July/August 1971; introduction to *The Journal of Eugene Delacroix,* New York 1972; "Robert Motherwell: Words and Images," interview with Heidi Golsman-Freyberger, in *The Print Collector's Newsletter* (New York), January/February 1974; reprinted in *Art Journal* (New York), Fall 1974; "A Talk with Robert Motherwell," interview with Vivian Raynor, in *Artnews* (New York), April 1974; "Interview with Robert Motherwell, June 14, 1974," with Richard Wagener, in *Robert Motherwell in California Collections,* exhibition catalog, Los Angeles 1974; "The Humanism of Abstraction" in *Tracks* (New York), November 1974; "A Conversation with Robert Motherwell, Painter," with Janet Baker-Carr, in *Hayward Magazine* (Cambridge, Massachusetts), October 1975; "Correspondence" in *Art Press* (Paris), January/February 1976; "An Artist's Odyssey" in *Art and Antiques,* February 1989.

On MOTHERWELL: Books—*Robert Motherwell,* exhibition catalog with a preface by James Johnson Sweeney, New York 1944; *Abstract-Expressionist Painting in America: An Interpretation Based on the Work and Thought of Six Key Figures,* dissertation by William C. Seitz, Princeton University, New Jersey 1955; *Robert Motherwell: Paintings and Collages,* exhibition catalog, New York 1957; *Motherwell: First Retrospective Exhibition,* exhibition catalog with text by Eugene C. Goosen, Bennington, Vermont 1959; *Recent Paintings and Collages,* exhibition catalog, New York 1961; *American Abstract Expressionists and Imagists,* exhibition catalog with text by H.H. Arnason, New York 1961; *Robert Motherwell Collages (1958–60),* exhibition catalog with text by Sam Hunter, Paris 1961; *VI Bienal de Museo de Arte Moderna,* exhibition catalog with text by Sam Hunter, Sao Paulo 1961; *I Collages di Motherwell,* exhibition catalog with text by Sam Hunter, Rome 1962; *Robert Motherwell: A Retrospective Exhibition,* exhibition catalog, with texts by T. W. Leavitt, Frank O'Hara and Sam Hunter, with a poem by Barbara Guest, New York 1962; *An Exhibition of the Work of Robert Motherwell,* exhibition catalog, Northampton, Massachusetts 1963; *Collages by Robert Motherwell,* exhibition catalog, with text by Sam

Hunter, Washington, D.C. 1965; *Robert Motherwell,* exhibition catalog with text by Frank O'Hara, Amsterdam 1966; *Robert Motherwell,* exhibition catalog by Luigi Mallé, Turin 1966; *Robert Motherwell: Bilder und Collagen 1967–70,* exhibition catalog, St. Gall, Switzerland 1970; *The Collages of Robert Motherwell: A Retrospective Exhibition,* exhibition catalog with an introduction by Philippe de Montebello, text by E. A. Carmean, Jr., Houston 1972; *Robert Motherwell: Recent Works,* exhibition catalog with an introduction by Sam Hunter, Princeton, New Jersey 1973; *Robert Motherwell: Selected Prints 1961–74,* exhibition catalog with a foreword by Arthur A. Cohen, New York 1974; *Robert Motherwell in California Collections,* exhibition catalog with texts by Emerson Woelffer, Gifford and Joanne Philipps, Los Angeles 1974; *Robert Motherwell: Retrospectivea del Gran Pintor Norteamericano,* exhibition catalog with text by Dore Ashton, Mexico City 1975; *Robert Motherwell* by H.H. Arnason, New York 1977; *Inside New York's Art World* by Barbara Diamonstein, New York 1979; *Robert Motherwell: Reconciliation Elegy,* paper, presented by E. A. Carmean, Jr., New York 1980; *Robert Motherwell and Black,* exhibition catalog, with text by Stephanie Terenzio, Storrs, Connecticut 1980; *Robert Motherwell: The Painter and the Printer* by Stephanie Terenzio, New York 1980; *Robert Motherwell* by Jack Flam and Dore Ashton, New York 1983; *Stephen's Iron Crown and Other Related Works* by E. A. Carmean, Fort Worth, Texas 1985; *Robert Motherwell: a Decade of Prints, 1979–1989,* exhibition catalog, Los Angeles 1989; *Prints of Robert Motherwell: a Retrospective,* exhibition catalog, New York 1990; *Robert Motherwell: the Open Door,* exhibition catalog, Fort Worth 1992; *Robert Motherwell: Reality and Abstraction,* exhibition catalog, text by Kathy Halbreich, Minneapolis 1996; *Robert Motherwell: What Art Holds* by Mary Ann Caws, New York 1996. **Articles—** ''Was There a Myth in the Making?—A Structuralist Approach to Robert Motherwell's Elegies to a Spanish Republic'' by Alice S. Brooker in *Athanor,* no. 7, 1988; ''Robert Motherwell's First Collages: 'All My Life I've Been Obsessed by Death''' by Robert S. Mattison in *Studies in Iconography* (Tempe), vol. 12, 1989; ''The World of Essences: the Prints of Robert Motherwell'' by Susan Tallman in *Arts Magazine* (New York), vol. 66, no. 3, November 1991; ''Selections from Robert Motherwell's 'Lyric Suite''' in *American Art* (Washington, D.C.), vol. 7, no. 1, Winter 1993.

* * *

Robert Motherwell is unique among the New York School Abstract Expressionists in his ability to change with the times yet remain relevant. Instead of developing a single ''trademark'' image, like Mark Rothko's soft rectangles or Jackson Pollock's dripped-line maze, Motherwell has allowed his image world to evolve naturally, feeding on itself while taking additional nourishment from the art ideas that are in the air around him. Finding himself surrounded by European artists-in-exile, particularly Surrealists, at the outset of his career, he took inspiration from Cubist collage, and Surrealist automatism and their trust in the unconscious, to produce some of the most ambitiously scaled and daring collages of the early 1940s. In addition, he produced some of the most perversely austere abstractions, such as ''Little Spanish Prison'' (1941), ever painted by an Abstract Expressionist. He also created a few marvelously crude, brutalized little paintings which have turned out to be a rich vein to mine in recent years as he explores the depths of atavism and the primitive impulse.

Toward the end of the 1940s, in paintings such as the Museum of Modern Art's ''Voyage,'' his collages were transformed into monumental canvases. In the ''Elegy to the Spanish Republic'' series the juxtaposition of repeated columnar verticals with organic ovoid masses, all painted in stark black and white, created a somber, processional mood that underlined the psychological profundity of his imagery. He continued to explore the structural potential of the early collages in the paintings of the 1950s and emphasized the calligraphic aspects of paint handling in paintings like ''Je t'aime,'' 1955. A series of small oils on panel, where raw, personnage-like forms seemed to emerge from the inchoate calligraphy like the matter in a void, led him to attempt monsterish images in a huge scale. ''Monster (for Charles Ives),'' 1959 and ''Spanish Painting with the Face of the Dog,'' 1958 are among the few survivors of this period; he destroyed most of the others—much to his regret, since they both harked back to some of his earliest, and perhaps most personal, images, and prefigured the primitivizing painting that enthralls him today.

He continued to work out of the ideas of the Elegy series during the 1960s, and he enlarged the scale of his collages as well as the scope of his printmaking and the freedom of his drawing. Even more daringly, he began to explore the possibilities of acrylic paint and huge expanses of pure color in the ''Open'' series. These monochromatic canvases were activated more often than not by only a single charcoal or painted line signifying a window. The spare geometry of ''Little Spanish Prison'' resurfaced in paintings as did the Matissean notion the ''more blue is bluer than less blue.'' But the 1960s were a cool period when emotionalism was a low priority in the visual arts, and Motherwell's life and career were at an especially smooth and untroubled passage. In the following decade severe illness, emotional upheavals, a change of physical surroundings, plus the repeated reassessments of his life's work and his aims that were demanded by numerous major monographs and retrospective exhibitions, all worked to upset the status quo for him, and he painted more unevenly, more energetically, more freely than he ever had. He took more and greater risks, but when he brought the painting off—as he did his ''Elegy to the Spanish Republic No. 100'' after 12 years of intermittent effort in 1975—he hit some of the highest points of his more than two score-long artistic life.

—April Kingsley

MUEHL, Otto

Nationality: Austrian. **Born:** Grodnau, Burgenland, 16 June 1925. **Education:** Studied German culture and history, University of Vienna, 1947–52, B.A., 1952; studied art at the Akademie der Bildenden Künste, Vienna, 1952–57. **Military Service:** German Army, 1943–45; lieutenant; Infantry Storm Decoration and Iron Cross, 1944. **Family:** Married Friedrike Neiss in 1965 (divorced, 1970); son: David. **Career:** Worked as teacher in a high school, Vienna, 1952; drawing therapist, Therapie Heim, Vienna, 1953; tutor in mathematics, Vienna, 1953–68. Independent artist, working with psychoanalytic actions, in Vienna, from 1960, and subsequently also in Gols, Burgenland; founder, with Gunter Brus, Direct Art Institute, Vienna, 1966; AA Kommune, Gols, 1970; and AAKK Actions Analytical Kommune children's group, Gols, 1974; editor-publisher, *AA Kommune News* quarterly, Gols, 1974; worked with phylogenetic and onthogenetic parabolas, Gols, from 1975. Adopted occasional pseudonyms Uni Ferkel, Franz Knoedl and AA OO, from 1970. **Awards:** Dirty Old Man Prize, *Wet Dream Festival,* Amsterdam, 1971. **Agent:** Karl Heinz Hein, Progressive Art Productions, Foehrenstrasse 11A, 8031 Groebenzell, Austria. **Addresses:** Praterstrasse 32/2/12, 1020 Vienna, Austria; AA Kommune, Friedrichshof, Gols, 7122 Burgenland, Austria.

Individual Exhibitions:

1961 Galerie Junge Generation, Vienna
1963 *Swamping the Venus,* Vienna
Mama & Papa, Vienna
Penis Action, Vienna
Breading an Ass, Vienna
Leda & the Swan, Vienna
Rumsti Bumsti, Vienna
Bimmel Bimmel, Vienna
Silver Ass, Vienna
1964 *2 Human Heads and a Cow Head,* Dusseldorf
Still-Life with Horses' Heads, Perinetgasse, Vienna
O Tannenbaum, Augartenstrasse, Vienna
1965 *Gymnastics Class in Food,* Perinetgasse, Vienna
1966 *Grimoid,* Perinetgasse, Vienna
1967 *Defense-Training,* Perinetgasse, Vienna
Psycho-Motoric Sound Action, Perinetgasse, Vienna
1969 *Christmas Action: Pig Slaughtered in Bed,* Braunschweig, West Germany
1970 *Investment Fund,* Vienna
Action, Bremen, West Germany
Action, Bern
1971 *Action with Goose,* at the *Wet Dream Festival,* Amsterdam
1973 *Last Art Action,* University of Ohio, Columbus
1992 *Arbeiten auf Papier aus den 60er Jahren,* Portikus, Frankfurt am Main (catalog)

Selected Group Exhibitions:

1962 *Blut Orgel Actions,* Perinet Keller, Vienna
1963 *Festival of Psycho-Physical Naturalism,* Vienna
1966 *Action Concert for Al Hansen,* Galerie St. Stephen, Vienna
1967 *Zock Festival,* Grunen Tor, Vienna
1968 *Revolution and Art,* University of Vienna
1970 *Happening und Fluxus,* Kunstverein, Cologne
1976 *Weiner Aktionistenszene um 1960,* Stichting De Appel, Amsterdam
1977 *The Spirit of Vienna,* René Block Gallery, New York
1978 *Paris-New York,* Centre Georges Pompidou, Paris
1984 *Arte Austriacca 1960–84,* Galleria d'Arte Moderna, Bologna, Italy
1998 *Out of Actions: Between Performance and Object, 1949–1979,* Museum of Contemporary Art, Los Angeles
1999 *Bad-Bad: That Is a Good Excuse,* Staatliche Kunsthalle Baden-Baden, Germany
30th Recontres Internationales de la Photographie, Arles, France
2000 *Posseder et Detruire,* Musee du Louvre, Paris
Works on Paper, Baron/Boisante Gallery, New York

Publications:

By MUEHL: Books—*Mama and Papa,* Frankfurt 1969; *Zock: Aspects of a Total Revolution 1966–71,* Vienna 1971; *History and Development of Human Consciousness,* Gols, Austria 1975; *Viennese Actionism 1960–71: The Shattered Mirror,* edited by Hubert Klocker, Klagenfurt 1989; *Brus, Muehl, Nitsch, Schwarzkogler: Writings of the Vienna Actionists,* with Malcolm Green, London 1999. **Films—***Amose,* 1968; *Sodonna,* 1969; *Scheiss Kerl,* 1970; *The Cherries in Papa's Garden,* 1974; *Sweet Movie,* Paris, 1974, Chicago 1999; *Selbstdarstellungs Aktions,* 1975. **Audio recording—***AA Selbstdarstellungs Musik,* Vienna 1975.

On MUEHL: Books—*Wein* by Peter Weibel, Frankfurt 1970; *Film as Subversive Art* by Amos Vogel 1974; *Paris-New York,* exhibition catalog edited by K. G. Pontus Hulten, Paris 1978. **Articles—**''Return to Reason: On Experimental Film in West Germany and Austria'' by B. Hein in *Studio International* (London), November/December 1975; ''L'Art Corporel'' by Francois Pluchart in *Artitudes* (St. Jeannet, France), January/March 1975; ''L'Art Corporel'' by Arthur McIntyre in *Art and Australia* (Sydney), July/September 1976; ''Einbruche unreflektier Wirklichkeit: Wiener Aktionismus in Amsterdam'' by G. F. Schwarshauer in *Kunstmagazin* (Mainz), vol. 17, no. 1, 1977; ''Wiener Aktionismus'' by J. Willink in *Museumjournaal* (Amsterdam), April 1979; ''Otto Mühl in Prison'' by Robert Fleck in *Flash Art (International Edition),* no. 160, October 1991; ''Seven-year Sentence for Otto Mühl'' by Christopher Phillips in *Art in America* (New York), vol. 80, January 1992; ''Otto Müehl: Dionysus in Jail'' by Michael Onfray in *Art Press,* no. 204, July-August 1994.

*

i am convinced that only people become artists who have been physically damaged through their upbringing in the small family. seen in this way, my actions as an artist were actually an attempt to resolve these damages. at first i tried it with painting, but i soon noticed that it wasn't making me healthier. painting was not a strong enough medicine for me; my fever remained. i noticed that beneath the mask of my good-citizen conformity, a very aggressive guy was hiding, a fact that i had previously kept secret even from myself. this was my sickness. the problem at this point was to find ways and means of fitting this aggressive guy into art. i succeeded. i discovered for this purpose the junk sculpture. i acted like a murderer against sheet metal, wood, against all possible useful objects of our civilization. i smashed everything. i smashed it into junk art. my tools were no longer the paintbrush, they were the pick-axe and hatchet. but even this wasn't enough for me, i invented the material action. this gave me the possibility of coming out with my aggressions much more directly and intensively. i worked with women and men, i showered and smeared them with food, i literally buried them in consumer products. this produced an extension, a social aspect came into the foreground.

i understood that it is the assignment of the artist to destroy art, that means coming closer to reality. the artist has the social responsibility to change himself and eventually society as well. only after many years did i realize that this is impossible through art, that the artist himself is nothing other than one of the socially accepted professional roles. because i didn't know this and knew no way other than art to get to reality, i intensified my actions to extremely aggressive undertakings, in the end it brought me fines and jail sentences but at the same time fame.

in spite of this, these actions had a happy result for me personally. they made it possible for me to destroy my still conservative existence, although i defended myself against the change, at that time i was still married, had a family, and lived by tutoring mathematics. one action at the university of vienna got me into jail for two months. a professor of early history ran distracted out of the lecture hall in which my action took place, broke down, crying and tearing his hair, in the arms of colleagues. he sobbed "this disgrace, this disgrace! it is unbearable! the honour of the university is ruined!" the minister of education called out during an assembly "i am ashamed to be austrian!" overnight i was styled into a scandal figure. i became known as the university pig. mothers did not dare send their children to me for tutoring. for the leftists who helped organize the action with me, i was a bourgeois pig who had destroyed their successful political work. i had scared away the working class.

in any case, suddenly i stood there alone. it dawned on me that there was nothing more to be done with art as i had practised it up to this point. i could not abolish the discrepancy between art and reality, i couldn't achieve an identity through art, i couldn't unify art with reality, i had failed in my attempt. aside from that i noticed that it wasn't my personal fault, that the gap between artist and social reality could not be resolved and had never been resolved by any artist in the world. for this reason i gave up the picture surface, the sculptures, and finally the art action as well. i changed to a new medium and had the idea of using, instead of paints or food, the direct social reality as modelling material. in 1970 i started to set up the experiment of living work, a continuous living experiment, developing and advancing with time. this environment has been growing and expanding without interruption. this living environment, i would like to speak of life as art, has now developed itself into art once again. it is art in art. whereby instead of the word art, the word reality can be interpolated. therefore reality in reality, art in reality, reality in art. reality art—art reality. real reality, real art, artificial reality. identity of art and reality. art unmasks itself here as a derivative of reality. reality without art is only half-reality. art without reality is no art.

—Otto Muehl

* * *

Otto Muehl calls his Material Action a kind of representational painting, a form of visual self-therapy using edible substances. To the audience, these actions often appear to be complete self-alienation, accidentally produced. In fact, they are planned to the last detail, and their effects are entirely calculated.

Many of Muehl's actions evoke associations of human birth. Beaten eggs, a slimy substance, tomato ketchup, flour, powder, paint and buttermilk are poured over the bodies of the women who take part; a balloon explodes. Such symbolism is easily explained. Associations of death, of violence, are called forth by the slaughtering of animals. Sexuality is directly expressed within the actions. Fundamental experiences which are not consciously noticed play an essential role in the actions. These are such everyday things as eating, drinking, urinating, shitting and vomiting.

Muehl's defencelessness vis-a-vis the press and his audiences is indicated by the criticism that he has got stuck in the phase of anal fixation. This seems quite mistaken, for as everyone knows from developmental psychology, too-early toilet training and an abrupt transition from the anal period causes children irreparable damage. Such criticisms of Muehl rebound on those who make them. For one cannot but make the presumption that such people have themselves been considerably affected by too-early toilet training.

Life within society is governed by countless norms which are only consciously perceived by very few individuals. Life begins with birth in the labour ward, and ends with fully automated cremation. If we consider our own sexuality, we notice the difficulties which are put in the way of expressing it fully according to our desires. Perhaps it was considerations such as these which led to Muehl's style of action. Muehl had very negative experiences with the Austrian authorities, experiences which directly incited them to continue and intensify his actions. Muehl has had nearly 70,000 schillings worth of fines and legal costs, and spent 77 days in prison.

By the end of the 1960s Muehl's actions were attended almost exclusively by voyeurs. Perhaps this was the reason for Muehl's withdrawal from the art scene. His experiences with actions form the basis of the work of the AKTIONSANALYTISCHEN ORGANISATION, a kind of community based on free love and communal possessions. Within the AAO a form of therapy has been developed, self representation in groups or individuality. The high point of the self-portrayal consists of recounting one's birth experiences. The goal of the self-portrayal is to eliminate the damage wreaked by the nuclear family. Muehl is the sovereign-master, the emperor of the AAO.

—Albrecht D.

MÜLLER, Robert

Nationality: Swiss. **Born:** Zurich, 17 June 1920. **Education:** Handelsschule, Zurich; studied art, under Charles-Otto Banninger and Germaine Richier, Zurich, 1939–45; under Germaine Richier, Paris, 1949; studied blacksmithing, Paris, 1952–53. **Career:** Sculptor and graphic artist, in Zurich, 1940–45; in Lonay, Lake Leman, 1945–47; in Genoa, 1947–49; in Paris, 1949–60; in Villiers-le-Bel, Val d'Oise, France, since 1960. Associated with war-time avant-garde artists, Galerie Gasser, Zurich, 1940–45; influenced by *Marino Marini* exhibition, Zurich, 1943; associated with painters Fieschi and Scanavino, cineaste Ribulsi, and sculptor Alfieri, in Genoa, 1947–49; with artists Geist, Rivers, Sugarman and Tajiri, in Paris, 1949; with Surrealist group, Paris, 1959. Produced first works in steel, Paris, 1951; wood engravings, Paris, 1958. **Awards:** Sculpture Prize, *Biennale,* Venice, 1956; Regina-Feigel Prize, *Bienal,* Sao Paulo, 1957; Jean Arp Prize, Biel, 1966, Kunstpreis, City of Zurich, 1971; Foundation for Graphic Arts Prize, Switzerland, 1981, **Agents:** Galerie Renée Ziegler, Zurich; and Galerie Ernst Scheidegger, Wettingerweis 2, 8032 Zurich. **Address:** 8 rue Jules Ferry, F-95400, Villiers le Bel, France.

Individual Exhibitions:

1954 Galerie Craven, Paris
1955 Galerie de France, Paris
1959 Kunsthalle, Basel (retrospective)
1960 Galerie d'Eendt, Amsterdam

1962 Albert Loeb Gallery, New York (with Jean Ipousteguy and Miguel Berrocal)
1963 Albert Loeb Gallery, New York
1964 Galerie Renée Ziegler, Zurich
Galerie de France, Paris
Plastiken, Stedelijk Museum, Amsterdam (retrospective; travelled to Kunsthalle, Bern; Kunsthalle, Dusseldorf; and the Museum des 20. Jahrhunderts, Vienna, 1964–65)
1967 Galerie de France, Paris
1968 *Tekeningen,* Stedelijk Museum, Amsterdam
Zeichnungen von Robert Müller, Jean Tinguely, Bernard Luginbuhl, Kunstmuseum, Basel
1971 Galerie de France, Paris
Werke 1967–71, Kunsthalle, Basel
Helmhaus, Zurich
Galerie Renée Ziegler, Zurich
1972 Galerie Renée Ziegler, Zurich
Plastik, Zeichnungen und Graphik, Galerie Bernard, Solothurn, Switzerland
1974 Galerie Scheidegger, Zurich
1977 Galerie Scheidegger, Zurich
1978 *Robert Müller/Bruno Müller: Skulpturen, Zeichnungen, Malerei, Graphik,* Kunsthaus, Aarau, Switzerland
1979 *Dessins 1937–1978,* Musée Rath, Geneva
1982 Galerie Scheidegger, Zurich
Galerie Renée Ziegler, Zurich
L'Oeuvre Grave, Musée d'Art et d'Histoire, Geneva
1983 Graphische Sammlung der ETH, Zurich
1985 Galerie Carzaniga & Ueker, Basel
1988 Galerie Carzaniga & Ueker, Basel
1990 Kunstmuseum, Solothurn, Switzerland
1991 Galerie Carzaniga & Ueker, Basel
1994 Galerie Carzaniga & Ueker, Basel
1996 Aargauer Kunsthaus, Aarau, Switzerland

Selected Group Exhibitions:

1946 *Nationale Kunstausstellung,* Geneva
1956 *Biennale,* Venice
1958 *World's Fair,* Brussels
1961 *Bewogen Bewegung,* Stedelijk Museum, Amsterdam (toured Denmark and Sweden)
1964 *Painting and Sculpture of a Decade 1954–1964,* Tate Gallery, London
1967 *Expo '67,* Montreal
1970 *Carnegie International,* Carnegie Institute, Pittsburgh
1973 *Contemporary French Sculpture,* National Art Gallery, Wellington, New Zealand (toured Australia and South America)
1975 *60 Ans d'Art Abstrait,* Maison de la Culture, Rheims
1981 *Zeichnungen von 13 Schweizer Bildhauern,* Tiroler Kunstpavillon, Innsbruck, Austria (travelled to the Modern Art Galerie, Vienna; and the Karntner Landesgalerie, Klagenfurt, Austria)
1984 *Neue Schweizer Graphik,* Kunsthaus Zug
1989 *Eisen 89—Perspektiven Schweizer Eisenplastik 1934–1989,* Dietikon *Künstlerwerkplatz Industrie,* Kunstmuseum Solothurn
1991 *Visionäre Schweiz,* Kunsthaus Zurich
1993 *Gegendruck Schweizer Künstlergraphik von Alberto Giacometti bis Urs Lüthi,* Galerie der Friedrich-Ebert-Stiftung, Bonn (toured)
1995 *Europäische Plastik des Informel,* Wilhelm Lehmbruck Museum, Duisburg

Collections:

Kunsthaus, Zurich; Kunstmuseum, Basel; Kunstmuseum, Winterthur, Switzerland; Kunstverein, Hannover; Stedelijk Museum, Amsterdam; Centre Georges Pompidou, Paris; Musée d'Art Moderne de la Ville, Paris; Museu de Arte Moderna, Sao Paulo; Museum of Modern Art, New York; Hirshhorn Museum and Sculpture Garden, Smithsonian Institution, Washington D.C.

Publications:

On MÜLLER: Books—*Sculpture Moderne en Suisse* by Marcel Joray, Neuchâtel, Switzerland 1955; *Robert Müller: Plastiken,* exhibition catalog with texts by Karl-Heinz Hering and Harald Szeeman, Dusseldorf 1965; *Robert Müller: Plastiken,* exhibition catalog with text by Werner Hofmann, Vienna 1965; *Robert Müller: Tekeningen,* exhibition catalog with foreword by Jan Martinet, Amsterdam 1968; *Zeichnungen von Robert Müller, Jean Tinguely, Bernhard Luginbuhl,* exhibition catalog with foreword by Dieter Koeplin, Basel 1968; *Robert Müller, Werke 1967–71,* exhibition catalog, with texts by Peter F. Althaus and Dorothea Christ, Basel 1971; *Robert Müller* by Gregoire Müller, Paris 1971; *Robert Müller* by Pierre Descargues, Brussels 1971; *Robert Müller: Plastik, Zeichnungen und Graphik,* exhibition catalog with a preface by Peter F. Althaus, Solothurn, Switzerland 1972; *Robert Müller, Bruno Müller: Skulpturen, Zeichnungen, Malerei, Graphik,* exhibition catalog with texts by Paul Nizon and Heiny Widmer, Aarau, Switzerland 1978; *Robert Müller: Dessins 1937–1978,* exhibition catalog with texts by Rainer Michael Mason and Paul Nizon, Geneva 1979; *Robert Müller: L'Oeuvre Grave,* exhibition catalog with text by Rainer Michael Mason, Geneva 1982; *Robert Müller: Et in Creta Ego,* exhibition catalog, Basel 1988; *Robert Müller: Skulpturen, Zeichnungen und Druckgraphik,* with text by Herausgegeben von Beat Wismer, Aarau 1996; *Robert Müller: L'Oeuvre Imprimé Des Débuts à 1996,* with texts by Richard Häsli and Dieter Koeplin, Geneva 1997; *Robert Müller: Estampes 1981–1996,* exhibition catalog, Geneva, 1996.

MUNARI, Bruno

Nationality: Italian. **Born:** Milan, 24 October 1907. **Career:** Sculptor, filmmaker and designer: lives and and works in Milan: associated with the Secondo Futurismo Group, Milan, 1927–33; executed first Fotogrammi works, after Man Ray and Moholy-Nagy, Milan, 1932; first Macchine Inutili, Milan 1933; co-signed. *Manifesto Tecnico dell'Aeroplastica Futurista,* 1934; worked on large abstract mosaic for *6th Triennale,* Milan, 1937; first kinetic works, 1945; ''Libri Illeggibili'' and children's books, 1949; published *Manifesto del Meccanismo,* 1949; co-founder, Movimento d'Arte Concreta, Milan, 1949; created animated wind mobile for Societá Motta, *Milan Fair,* 1950; worked with polarized light from 1953; with films from 1962; first Xerox works from 1965; visiting professor of design at Harvard University, 1970–71. **Awards:** Gold Medal of the Triennale, Milan;

Compasso d'Oro, Milan, 1954, 1955, 1979; *New York Times* Best Illustrated Chidren's Books of the Year awards, 1960 and 1969; New York Academy of Sciences award, 1974. **Agent:** Bruno Danese, Milan. **Died:** Of heart attack, in Quebec City, 29 September 1998.

Individual Exhibitions:

1933 Galerie Tre Arti, Milan
1934 Galleria Milano, Milan
1954 Museum of Modern Art, New York
1966 Museum of Modern Art, Tokyo
1967 Howard Wise Gallery, New York
1971 Galleria San Fedele, Milan
1973 Galerija Suvremene Umjetnosti, Zagreb
1979 University of Parma, Italy

Selected Group Exhibitions:

1927 *Secondo Futurismo,* Galleria Pesaro, Milan
1929 *Trentate Futuriste,* Galleria Pesaro, Milan
Peintres Futuristes Italiens, Galerie 23, Paris
1930 *Biennale,* Venice
1932 *Secondo Futurismo,* Galerie Renaissance, Paris
1933 *Triennale,* Milan
1951 *Arte Astratte e Concreta in Italia,* Galeria Nazionale d'Arte Moderna, Rome
1955 *Mouvement,* Galerie Denise Renée, Paris
1996 *The Italian Metamorphosis, 1943–1968,* The Solomon R. Guggenheim Museum, New York

Collections:

Galleria Nazionale d'Arte Moderna, Rome; Kunstmuseum, Krefeld, Germany; Museum of Modern Art, New York.

Publications:

By MUNARI: Books—*Design as Art,* Harmondsworth, Middlesex 1971; *Alfabetiere,* Turin 1972; *Cappucetto Verde,* Turin 1972; *Cappucetto Giallo,* Turin 1972. **Articles—**''Un Metodo di Progettizione'' in *Ottagono* (Milan), September 1970; ''Statements by Munari'' in *Studio International* (London), October 1970; ''L'Equilibrio degli Opposti'' in *Ottagono* (Milan), March 1971, ''Che cose'e un Abitacolo'' in *Domus* (Milan), March 1971; ''Libri per bambini: Intervista con Bruno Munari'' in *NAC* (Milan), June/July 1971; ''L'Autorita offi'' in *Ottagono* (Milan), September 1971; ''Strutturazione interna di spazii cubici'' in *Ottagono* (Milan), January 1972; ''L'Uomo a piu Dimensioni'' in *Ottagono* (Milan), March 1972; ''La machine antropomorfa'' in *Ottagono* (Milan), June 1972; ''Le Luci-spia'' in *Ottagono* (Milan), September 1972; ''Compasso d'oro a ignoti'' in *Ottagono* (Milan), December 1972; ''Moduli combinabili in strutture quadrale'' in *Ottagono* (Milan), June 1973; ''Bruno Munari Interview'' by I. Lebeer in *Chroniques de l'Art Vivant* (Paris), November 1974; ''Entrevista a Bruno Munari'' by Antonella Soldaini in *Kalias,* no. 10, vol. 5, 1993; ''The Essence of an Object'' in *Ottagono* (Milan), no. 118, vol. 31, March-May 1996. **Films—***Colori della Luce,* 1963; *Moiré* 1964.

On MUNARI: Books—*Munari 71,* exhibition catalog by Paolo Fossati and others, Milan 1971; *Munari,* exhibition catalog by Paolo Fossati, Zagreb 1973; *Bruno Munari,* exhibition catalog by Giulio Carlo Argan and Alessandro Mendini, Parma 1979; *L'arte anomala di Bruno Munari* by A. Tanchis, Bari, Italy 1981. **Articles—**''The Solomon R. Guggenheim Museum Exhibition, 'The Italian Metamorphosis, 1943–1968','' by Luisa Orto in *Issues in Architecture, Art and Design* (London), vol. 4, pt. 2, 1996; ''Munari: Making Air Visible'' by Stefano Casciani in *Abitare,* no. 360, March 1997; ''Munaria: Abitare Celebrates Bruno Munari's 90th Birthday'' by Beppe Finessi in *Abitare,* no. 366, October 1997; ''Top Ten'' by Rob Pruitt in *Artforum International,* vol. 38, no. 6, February 2000.

*

I search for a balance between the case and the rule. The case makes me discover some new aspects of life both inside and outside of myself. The rule helps me to construct the images with art. With these images I search to communicate, with exactness, the way I happen to do it and to let others also know.

—Bruno Munari

* * *

Sculptor, filmmaker and designer, Bruno Munari has been active in kinetic art, the art of luminism, machine art, the art of the multiple and Ludic art. In tribute to his great versatility he was called by Picasso ''the new Leonardo.''

After a brief association with the later school of Futurism—he contributed to the *Aeropittura* exhibition of 1931—he began making wire mobiles and kinetic sculpture in 1933. With these he anticipated and influenced Tinguely, whom he met in 1954. He called them ''machines inutiles,'' and the best known of them is his ''L'Ora X,'' a clock constructed during the 1940s in which the hands move mechanically round a clock face without numbers. After the war he made his mark at the important exhibition *Mouvement* staged by the Denise René Gallery, Paris, in 1955.

As a founding member of the Movimento per l'Arte Concreta in 1949, he began to investigate the problems of the fragmentation of light, displaying the aesthetic applications of fragmented light in his series of ''Projections'' and in ''Direct Applications of Polarized Light'' in 1957. He also made transparent and coloured collages from plastic materials.

Munari has made perhaps his most important impact in the field of Machine Art, which he pioneered and of which he has been the chief theoretician. He published *Manifesto de Meccanismo* in 1949 and a series of manifestos on this theme in 1952. He believed that industrial design has a social function to reawaken in the general public that sensibility for fine form which, in the words of Gillo Dorfles, ''otherwise threatens to be overwhelmed by the widespread contemporary pseudo-art disseminated by the machine.'' In opposition to the subjectivism inherent in our heritage of Romanticism, Munari held that there exists a genuinely objective code of good design which can be understood and appreciated by ordinary people in every part of the world. It is the duty of the artist to know and understand machines and by their designs to ensure that machine-made productions conform to these standards of good taste. In close conjunction with this he was a pioneer of the art of the ''Multiple''—called in Italy ''Arte Programmata''—that is, the machine-made article produced in many examples with no other function than to exist as a work of art for appreciation and contemplation. It has been his view that industrial design can do more than handicraft or fine art to educate the public to appreciation of genuine artistic values.

In pursuances of the foregoing ideas Munari also turned his attention to Ludic art and in collaboration with Giovanni Belgrado he produced a series of ''Visual Games'' and a ''Composable ABC'' designed to evoke and encourage a critical awareness of visual images in children. In the words of Frank Popper: ''The child is induced to discover the meaning and value of forms and colours, and to recognize their logical development in the interests of his own thought processes and critical judgment.''

There is something of the social apostle in all Munari's artistic activities and interests.

—Harold Osborne

MUNTADAS, Antonio

Nationality: Spanish. **Born:** Barcelona, Spain, 1942; moved to the United States in 1980. **Education:** University of Barcelona, Spain, 1959–62; Escuela Tecnica Superior Ingenieros Industriales, Barcelona, 1963–67, M.A.; Pratt Graphics Center, New York, 1971–73. **Career:** Pioneer of video art since the 1960s; has taught and been artist in residence at schools all over the world since 1977. **Awards:** Sumner Foundation for the Arts, 1976–77; Fundacion Juan March Madrid, Spain, 1978; The Massachusetts Artist Foundation Boston, MA, 1979; Beca Ministerio de Cultura Spain, 1979; The Rockefeller Foundation, C.A.V.S./M.I.T, 1980; C.A.P.S., Creative Artists Public Services New York, 1981; Guggenheim Fellowship Award New York, 1984; New York State Council for the Arts, 1984; National Endowment for the Arts-Visual Arts, 1985; Massachusetts Council for the Arts and Humanities/New Works; production of the installation *The Board Room,* 1986–1987; Canada Council Grant; production of the installation *Stadium,* 1988; Commande de l'Etat, Centre National des Artes Plastiques France for *Between the Frames,* 1990; National Endowment for the Arts, production grant for *The File Room,* 1991; Premi Nacional D'Arts Plastiques Barcelona, Spain, 1993; National Endowment for the Arts, production grant for *On Translation,* 1995; Etant Donnes, funding for CD Rom prototype New York/Paris, 1995; Ars Electronica Prix for *The File Room,* 1995; Aide a la publication—FIACRE Paris, France project *CD Rom,* 1996; LASER D'OR, Festival de Locarno Switzerland, 1996; Premi Nacional D'Arts Plastiques Generalitat de Catalunya Spain, 1996. **Agent:** Kent Gallery, New York; Galerie Gabrielle Maubie, Paris; Galeria Luisa Strina, São Paulo. **Address:** 395 Broadway, #5C, New York, New York 10013, U.S.A.

Selected Individual Exhibitions:

1971 Galeria Vandres Madrid, Spain (catalog)
1974 Galeria Vandres Madrid, Spain (catalog)
1976 International Cultureel Centrum Anvers, Belgium
Galeria Ciento Barcelona, Spain
1977 Anthology Film Archives New York
1978 *Projects: Video XVII,* Museum of Modern Art, New York
Anthology Film Archives New York
1979 Vancouver Art Gallery Vancouver, Canada (catalog)
1980 Galeria Vandres Madrid, Spain (catalog)
1982 Addison Gallery of American Art-Phillips Academy Andover, MA (catalog)
1984 Anthology Film Archives, New York
1983 Galerije Contemporary Art Zagreb, Yugoslavia (catalog)
Sala Parpallo' Valencia, Spain (catalog)
1985 Los Angeles Institute of Contemporary Art Los Angeles, CA (catalog)
Galeria Vijande Madrid, Spain (catalog)
1987 Musee' d'Art Moderne Villeneuve d'Asq, France
Palacio de la Madraza Granada, Spain (catalog)
Exit Art New York (catalog)
1988 The Power Plant Toronto, Canada (catalog)
Centro de Arte Reina Sofia Madrid, Spain (catalog)
Palau de la Virreyna Barcelona, Spain (catalog)
1989 Walter Phillips Gallery Banff, Canada (catalog)
Corner House Manchester, England (catalog)
Galerie des Beaux Arts Bruxelles, Belgium
1990 Israel Museum Jerusalem, Israel (catalog)
1991 Indianapolis Museum of Art, Indianapolis (catalog)
1992 CEE Project (in situ) for public spaces in the twelve member countries of the European Community First installation: Witte de With Rotterdam, Holland
Fundacao de Serralves Porto, Portugal (catalog)
IVAM Centre del Carme Valencia, Spain (catalog)
1993 Kunst-werke Berlin, Germany (catalog)
1994 C.A.P.C. Musee d'Art Contemporain Bordeaux, France (catalog)
Wexner Center for the Arts, Columbus, Ohio (catalog)
Museum of Modern Art, New York
1995 Vera List Gallery Massachussetts Institute of Technology Cambridge, MA (catalog)
Storefront for Art and Architecture New York (catalog)
Casa da Parra Santiago de Compostela, Spain (catalog)
1996 Centre d'Art Santa Monica, Barcelona (catalog)
Atlanta College of Art; Atlanta (catalog)
1997 Museo de Arte Moderno Buenos Aires, Argentina
1998 Palma XII Vilafranca del Penedes Barcelona, Spain
Fundacion Arte y Tecnologia Madrid, Spain (catalog)
Museum of Contemporary Art/Ludwig Museum Budapest, Hungary (catalog)
1999 F.R.A.C. Basse Normandie Caen, France
Witte de With Rotterdam, Netherlands (catalog)
Casa de la Moneda Biblioteca Luis Angel Arango Bogota, Colombia (catalog)
Instituto de Cooperacion Iberoamericana Montevideo, Uruguay (catalog). Traveled to Asuncion (Paraguay) and Lima (Peru)
Galeria Gabriela Mistral Santiago de Chile, Chile (catalog)
2000 Musee d'Art et d'Histoire Geneva, Switzerland
Centre pour l'Image Contemporaine Geneva, Switzerland
Museu de Arte Moderno, Rio de Janeiro, Brazil

Selected Group Exhibitions:

1963 *Machines,* Sala Lleonart, Barcelona, Spain
1964 Premi Joan Miro, Barcelona, Spain
1965 Salo de Maig, Barcelona, Spain

1972 Arte de Sistemas II Buenos Aires, Argentina
1973 *4 Elementos,* Col.legi d'Arquitectes, Valencia (catalog)
1974 *Noves Tendencies a l'Art Barcelona Foment de les Arts Decoratives,* Barcelona, Spain
Art/Video Confrontation 74, Musee d'Art Modern de la Ville de Paris Paris, Spain (catalog)
Prospectiva 74, Museu de Arte Contemporanea da Universidade de Sao Paulo Brazil (catalog)
1975 *Arte de Video,* Museo de Arte Contemporaneo de Caracas Caracas, Venezuela (catalog)
IX Bienale de Paris, Paris, France (catalog)
1976 *Biennale Internazionale d'Arte a Venezia,* Spagna, Vanguardia Artistica Realta Sociale Venezia, Italy (catalog)
1977 *Documenta 6,* Kassel, Germany (catalog)
1978 *Video entre l'Art i la Comunicacio,* Col.legi d'Arquitectes Barcelona, Spain (catalog)
Art, Artist, and the Media, Mediart Graz, Austria (catalog)
1979 *Video Viewpoints,* The Museum of Modern Art, New York
1980 *Il Tempo del Museo Venezia Biennale de Venezia,* Venezia, Italy 1998 (catalog)
New Images from Spain, Solomon R. Guggenheim Museum New York
1981 *XVI Bienal de Sao Paulo,* Sao Paulo, Brazil
Trois Installations, ELAC-Espace Lyonnais d'Art Contemporain, Lyon, France
International Video Art Festival Portopia 81, Kobe, Japan
TV Tactics, Anthology Film Archives New York
Video/Comportament-Behavior/Art, Instituto de Estudios Norteamericanos, Barcelona, Spain
XII Setmana Internacional de Cinema, Barcelona, Spain
100 Anys de Cultura Catalana, Madrid, Spain
1982 *Reading Video,* Museum of Modern Art, New York
World Wide Video Festival, Kijkhuis Den Haag, Holland
Video Roma'82, Rome, Italy
I Festival de Video de San Sebastian, San Sebastian, Spain
1983 *Video Art: Art History,* Museum of Modern Art, New York
La Imagen del Animal Palacio de las Alhajas, Madrid, Spain (catalog)
17a Bienal de Sao Paulo: Six Metaphors/Six Alternatives, Sao Paulo, Brazil
Fuera de Formato, Centro Cultural de la Villa de Madrid, Madrid, Spain (catalog)
Dark Rooms, Artists Space, New York (catalog)
1984 *Boston Now: Sculpture,* ICA Boston, (catalog)
Artists Statements, Un-city Trier / Austria Center Wien, Vienna, Austria (catalog)
Video: A Retrospective 1974–1984, Long Beach Museum of Art, Long Beach, California (catalog)
From T.V. to Video/Dal Video alla T.V., L'Immagine Elettronica, Bologna, Italy (catalog)
Berlin Film/Video Festival, Berlin, Germany
III Festival de Video de San Sebastian, San Sebastian, Spain
1985 *Tele/Visions,* exposicio organitzada per Image Film-Video Center Nexus
Desinformation: The Manufacture of Consent, The Alternative Museum New York , New York (catalog)
1987 *Perverted by Language,* Hilwood Art Museum C.W. Post Campus of Long Island University, Brookville, New York (catalog)
La Imagen Sublime: Video de Creacion en Espana, Museo Nacional Centro de Arte Reina Sofia, Madrid, Spain (catalog)
The Arts for Television, The Museum of Contemporary Art, Los Angeles, and Stedelijk Museum Amsterdam (catalog)
1988 *Investigating Video,* Institute of Contemporary Art Philadelphia, Pennsylvania
International Landscape Forum, Stadt Park, Graz, Austria (catalog)
1989 *Metamedia: Film/Video (Image World Art and Media Culture),* Whitney Museum American Art New York (catalog)
Nuits Blanches, Arles, France (catalog)
Corporate Identities, Cornerhouse Manchester, England (catalog)
Fictions, Aeroport Internacional de Mirabel, Mirabel, Canada (catalog)
1990 *Rhetorical Image,* The New Museum of Contemporary Art, New York (catalog)
Art Concept, Galeria Alfonso Alcolea, Barcelona, Spain (catalog)
Casino Fantasma, Casino Municipale, Venezia, Italy (catalog)
A New Necessity, First Tyne International National Garden Festival, Gateshead, England (catalog)
Passages de l'image: Films et Videos, Musee National d'Art Moderne, Centre Georges Pompidou Paris, France, traveling exhibit
1991 *Whitney Biennal,* Whitney Museum of American Art, New York (catalog)
Le Coeur et la Raison, Musee des Jacobins Morlaix, Paris, France (catalog)
Munition: Politische Diskurse in der Amerikanische Videokunst, 711, Frankfurt, Germany
1992 *Fragments,* Museo d'Art, Girona, Spain (catalog)
Video et Oralite, Galerie des Beaux Arts/National Gallery, Ottawa, Canada (catalog)
Pour la suite du Monde, Musee d'Art Contemporain de Montreal, Canada (catalog)
Edge 92 International Biennial, Madrid and London
Idees i Actituds: entorn de l'art conceptual a Catalunya, 1964–1980, Centre d'Art Santa Monica, Barcelona, Spain (catalog)
Force Sight, Schloss Presteneck, Stein am Kocher, Germany (catalog)
El artista y la ciudad, Fundacion Luis Cernuda, Sevilla, Spain (catalog)
Variaciones en gris, Centro Cultural de la Villa de Madrid Madrid, Spain (catalog)
1993 *Critical Quest,* ViaFarini and Gallerie Transepoca, Milano, Italy

1994 *Minima Media Medienbiennale,* Lepzig (catalog)
1995 *3a Biennal de Lyon,* Lyon, France (catalog)
Els limits del museu, Fundacio Tapies, Barcelona, Spain (catalog)
Ars 95, Helsinki, Finland (catalog)
Museum in the Net N.T.T.-I.C.C, Tokyo, Japan (catalog)
1996 *Pola Cruz Vermella,* Palacio de Deputacion Provincial, Pontevedra, Spain (catalog)
Artistes/Architectes Le Nouveau Musee, Institut Art Contemporain, Villeurbanne, France
Homo Ecologicus, Fundacio Joan Miro, Barcelona, Spain (catalog)
Senales de Video, Museo Nacional Reina Sofia, Madrid, Spain (catalog)
Presents I Futurs: L'arquitectura a les ciutats, C.C.C.B., Barcelona, Spain (catalog)
Discord. Sabotage of Realities, Kunstverein and Kunsthaus Hamburg, Germany (catalog)
Kybernettes, Biblioteca Luis Angel Arango, Santa Fe de Bogota, Colombia (catalog)
1997 *WRO 97 Media Art Biennale,* Open Studio, Wroclaw, Poland (catalog)
Rooms with a View: Environments for Video, Guggenheim Museum, New York
Photographie d'une collection, Caisse des Depot et Consignations, Paris, France
Ethique/Esthetique/Politique Rencontres, Internationales de la Photographie, Arles, France (catalogue)
Roam Finale, Abnormal Temple, Taipei, Taiwan (catalog)
Tout doit disparaitre, L'Artoteque, Grenoble, France (catalog)
Documenta X, Kassel, Germany (catalog)
1998 *Reservate der Shen-Sucht Dortmunder,* Dortmund, Germany (catalog)
Festival de Nouveau Cinema/Nouveau Media Montreal, Canada (catalog)
Instant Cities Muntadas/Zush Stedelijk, Museum voor Actuele Kunst, Gent, Belgium (catalog)
1999 *Circa 68,* Fundacao de Serralves, Porto, Portugal (catalog)
Konzeptuelle Photographie (1968–99), Brigitte March Galerie, Stuttgart, Germany
Novos Caminos, Xacobeo, Santiago, Spain (catalog)
2000 *The End,* Exit Art, New York

Collections:

Addison Gallery of American Art, Andover, Massachusetts; The Chase Manhattan Bank, New York; Museum of Modern Art, New York; Donell Public Library, New York; Everson Museum Syracuse, New York; Guggenheim Museum, New York; Long Beach Museum of Art, Long Beach, California; Rotch Library—M.I.T., Cambridge, Massachusetts; University Art Museum, Berkeley, California; Artotheque, Grenoble, France; Caisse des Depots et Consignations, Paris, France; Centre Georges Pompidou, Paris, France; Centro de Arte Reina Sofia, Madrid, Spain; Collection Tournereau-Bosser, Paris, France; Collecio Diari Avui, Barcelona, Spain; Collecio Tous/De Pedro, Barcelona, Spain; Deutsche Messe AG Hannover Messegelaende, Hannover, Germany; Fons Regional d'Art Contemporain (FRAC) de France, Comte, France; Fons Regional d'Art Contemporain (FRAC), Corsica, France; Fons Regional d'Art Contemporain (FRAC) de Basse, Normandie, France; Fons National d'Art Contemporain, Paris, France; Foundation Danae, Poully, France; Fundacio Museu Art Contemporani de Barcelona (MACBA), Barcelona, Spain; Fundació La Caixa, Barcelona, Spain; Instituto Valenciano de Arte Moderno, Valencia, Spain; Ludwig Museum, Budapest, Hungary; Museo de Vitoria, Vitoria, Spain; Palais de Beaux Arts, Bruxelles, Belgium; Sudwest L.B., Stuttgart, Germany; Videoteca Caixa de Barcelona Barcelona, Spain; Fundacao de Serralves, Porto, Portugal; Galerije Contemporary Art, Zagreb, Yugoslavia; Museo de Arte Moderno, Buenos Aires, Argentina; Museu de Arte Contemporanea, Sao Paulo, Brazil; Museo de Arte Contemporaneo, Caracas, Venezuela; The Banff Centre, Banff, Canada; National Gallery, Ottawa, Canada; Israel Museum, Jerusalem, Israel.

Publications:

By MUNTADAS: Book Contributions—*En Torno al video* edited by Bonet, Dols, Mercader, Muntadas, Barcelona 1975; ''Emission—Reception'' in *Video Art an Anthology* edited by Iva Schneider and Beril Korot, New York 1976; *Still Photography: The Problematic Model* edited by Lew Thomas and Peter d'Agostino, San Francisco 1981; *New Observations* (New York), no. 29 1985; *Illuminating Video—An Essential Guide to Video Art* edited by Doug Hall and Sally Fifer, New York 1990; ''Uber kritische Subjektivitat'' in *Video—Apparat/Medium, Kunst, Kultur* edited by Siegfried Zielinski, Frankfurt, Bern, New York, and Paris, 1992; ''Landscape(s)'' in *Felix Journal of Media Arts* (New York), vol. 2, no. 1, 1995; *Transversals #1,* Spain 1996; *Image et Politique,* Arles, France 1998. **Selected Videos—***On Subjectivity (about T.V.),* 1978; *Between the Lines,* 1979; *Watching the Press/Reading Television,* 1980–81; *Between the Frames,* 1983; *Credits,* 1984; *Media Hostages (S.S.S.),* 1985; *This is not an Advertisement,* 1985; 1986 *Slogans* (English), 1986; 1989 *TVE: Primer Intento,* 1989; *Video is Television?,* 1989; *Marseille: Mythe et Stereotypes,* 1995; *Portrait* (loop), 1995; *La siesta/The Nap/Dutje,* 1995; *S.M.E.P,* 1996; *Anarchive #1: Muntadas: Media Architecture Installations, InteRom* (internet/CDRom) Paris, 1999.

On MUNTADAS: Articles—''Antoni Muntadas, Galerie Gabrielle Maubrie'' by Paul Ardenne in *ArtPress,* no. 241, December 1998; ''Muntadas, Paisaje de los medios'' by Rodrigo Alonso in *Artinf,* vol. 22, no. 100, Fall 1998; ''Muntadas. Home, Where Is Home?'' by Frederic Bougle in *Art Presence,* October-December 1999; ''Muntadas 'in progress''' by Blanca Oria in *ArtyCo* (Pamplona), 1999; ''Muntadas: No existe sentido de la contemporaneidad en este pais'' interview by Victor Lope in *Mana Mana* (Pamplona), January 1999; ''Le barcelonais Muntadas investit Geneve pour y decrypter les images du quotidian'' by Elisabeth Chardon in *Le Temps* (Geneva), January 29 2000; ''Antonio Muntadas'' by Annik Hemery in *SVM Mac,* no. 115 March 2000; ''Imagenes Muntadas'' in *Revista Caretas* (Peru), February 24 2000; ''Muntadas, el retratista de fin de siglo xx'' in *Expreso* (Peru), March 7 2000; ''El hombre mediatico'' by Jose Gabriel Chueca in *El*

Comercio (Peru), March 7 2000; ''Muntadas'' in *Cambio* (Peru), March 7 2000; ''Muntadas faz arte con a cultura brasileria'' by Maria Hirszman in *Estado de Sao Paulo* 15 February 2000.

* * *

MURAKAMI, Takahashi

Nationality: Japanese. **Born:** Tokyo, 1962. **Education:** Tokyo National University of Fine Arts and Music, Japan, B.A. (in Japanese Traditional Painting: Nihon-ga) 1986, M.A. 1988, Ph.D. 1993. **Career:** fellowship grant, P.S.1 International Studio Program, 1994; founded studio in New York, 1994; founded the HIROPON FACTORY (a production studio to help create his own works, as well as the work of other young artists), Asaka City, Saitama, 1995; began curating in the mid-1990s; guest professor, New Genre curriculum, University of California, Los Angeles, 1998. **Address:** Lives in New York and Japan. **Web site:** http://www.hiropon-factory.com/index-e.html.

Selected Individual Exhibitions:

1989 Gallery Ginza Surugadai, Tokyo
1991 Art Gallery at Tokyo National University of Fine Arts and Music, Tokyo
Aoi Gallery, Osaka, Japan
Rontgen Kunst Institut (August 23 only), Tokyo
Gallery Aries, Tokyo
Hosomi Gallery Contemporary, Tokyo
1992 *Wild, Wild,* at Rontgen Kunst Institut, Tokyo
1993 Nasubi Gallery, Tokyo
A Very Merry Unbirthday!, at Hiroshima City Museum of Contemporary Art, Hiroshima
A Romantic Evening, at Gallery Cellar, Nagoya
1994 *Fujisan,* at Gallery Koto, Okayama, Japan
Which is Tomorrow?, at SCAI The Bathhouse, Tokyo
Azami, Kikyo, Ominaeshi, at Aoi Gallery, Osaka, Japan
1995 *NIJI,* at Gallery Koto, Okayama, Japan
Emmanuel Perrotin, at Paris, France
Crazy Z, at SCAI The Bathhouse, Tokyo
Yngtingagatan 1, Stokholm, Sweden
1996 Feature Inc., New York
Gavin Brown Enterprize, New York
Gallery Koto, Okayama, Japan
Konnichiwa, Mr. DOB, at Kirin Plaza Osaka, Osaka, Japan
7272, at Aoi Gallery, Osaka, Japan
A Very Merry Unbirthday, To You, To Me!, at Ginza Komatsu, Tokyo
1997 Emmanuel Perrotin, Paris, France
University of Buffalo Art Gallery, New York State University, Buffalo
Blum & Poe, Santa Monica
1998 Feature Inc., New York
Back Beat, Blum & Poe, Santa Monica
Back Beat—Super Flat, Tomio Koyama Gallery, Tokyo, Japan
More over, DOB raises his hand, Sagacho bis, Tokyo
1999 *Super Flat,* Marianne Boesky Gallery, New York
DOB in the Strange Forest, Parco Gallery, Tokyo/Nagoya
The Meaning of the Nonsense of the Meaning, The Center for Curatorial Studies and Art in Contemporary Culture, Bard College, New York
2000 *Kai Kai Ki Ki (Super Flat),* ISSEY MIYAKE MEN Aoyama,Tokyo
2001 *Kai Kai Ki Ki2,* Emanuel Perrotin, Paris
wink, Grand Central Terminal, New York
mushroom, Marianne Boesky Gallery, New York
A Conversation with Takashi Murakami, Museum of Fine Arts, Boston

Selected Group Exhibitions:

1991 *Jan Hoet in Tsurugi,* Tsurugi-cho, Ishikawa, Japan
Jan Hoet's Vision, Art Gallery Artium, Fukuoka, Japan
1992 Artists' Shop '92, Sai Gallery, Osaka, Japan
Mars Galler, Tokyo
Floating Gallery Vol.1, Tsukishima Warehouse, Tokyo
1st Transart Annual ''Painting/Crossing,'' Bellini Hill Galley, Yokohama, Japan
Nakamura and Murakami, Space Ozone, Seoul, Korea
Nakamura and Murakami, SCAI Project Room, Tokyo
Anomary, Rontgen Kunst Institut, Tokyo
Tama Vivant '92, Seed Hall, Shibuya Seibu, Tokyo
Nakamura and Murakami, MetariaSquare Hotel, Osaka, Japan
1993 Malaria Art Show Vol.1, ''February 1st Festival,'' Tokyo
Artists' Shop '93, Sai Gallery, Osaka, Japan
Malaria Art Show Vol.4, ''Decorative,'' Tokyo
Nakamura and Murakami, NICAF'93, Aoi Gallery, Osaka, Japan
The Ginbrart, Ginza, Tokyo
00 Collaboration, Sagacho Exhibit Space, Tokyo
Art Today '93 ''Neo Japanology,'' Sezon Museum of Modern Art, Karuizawa,Nagano, Japan
Beyond the ''Nihonga''—An Aspect of Contemporary Japanese Paintings, Tokyo
The Exhibition for Exhibitions, Kyoto Shijo Gallery, Kyoto, Japan
1994 *Shinjyuku Shonen Art,* Shinjyuku Kabuki-cho, Tokyo
Lest We Forget: On Nostalgia, Gallery at Takashimaya, New York *VOCA '94,* The Ueno Royal Museum, Tokyo
Koriyama City Museum of Art, Fukushima, Japan
1995 *Incidental Alterations: P.S.1 Studio Artists 1994–95,* Angel Orensanz Foundation, New York
Art Space Hap, Hiroshima
Transculture, 46th Venice Biennale, Venice, Italy
Japan Today, Louisiana Museum of Modern Art, Humlebaek, Denmark; Kunstnernes Hus, Oslo, Norway; Liljevalchs Konsthall, Stockholm, Sweden; Waino

Aaltonen Museum of Art, Turku, Finland; MAK, Wien, Austria
Cutting Up, Max Protetch Gallery, New York
Transculture, Benesse House Naoshima Contemporary Art Museum, Kagawa
1996 *Tokyo Pop,* Hiratsuka Museum of Art, Kanagawa, Japan
Sharaku Interpreted by Japan's Contemporary Artists, Japan Foundation Forum, Tokyo
Ironic Fantasy, Miyagi Museum of Art, Sendai, Miyagi, Japan
Asia-Pacific Triennial 1996, Queensland Art Gallery, Brisbane, Australia
Romper Room, Thread Waxing Space, New York
1997 *Flying Buttress Please,* Torch Gallery, Amsterdam
Super Body, Tomio Koyama Gallery, Tokyo
Hiropon Show '97: Tokyo Underground Visual Show, Shop 33, Tokyo
Need for Speed, Grazer Kunstverein, Graz, Austria
Japanese Contemporary Art Exhibition, National Museum of Contemporary Art, Korea, Seoul
Singularity in Plurality, Yokohama Civic Art Gallery, Kanagawa
1998 *Cities on the Move,* Secession, Wien, Austria; Bordeaux, France; P.S.1, New York
People, Places and Things, Marianne Boesky Gallery, New York
Pop Surrealism, Aldrich Museum of Contemporary Art, Connecticut
Art is Fun 9, Hara Museum Arc, Gunma, Japan
So what?—Exhibition of Contemporary Japanese Art, Ecole Nationale Superleure des Beaux-Arts, Paris
ERO_EPOP_ETOKYO, George's, Los Angeles
The Manga Age, Museum of Contemporary Art, Tokyo
The Noumea Third Biennale of Contemporary Art, Noumea, Nouvelle Caledonie
50 Years of Japanese Life Style; Postwar Fashion and Design, Utsunomiya Museum of Art, Tochigi, Japan
Ero Pop Christmas, Nadiff, Tokyo
1999 *Tastes and Pursuits: Japanese Art in the 1990s,* National Gallery of Modern Art, New Delhi, India; Metropolitan Museum of Manila, Philippines
New Modernism for a New Millennium: Works by Contemporary Asian Artists from the Logan Collection, San Francisco Museum of Modern Art
Something Warm and Fuzzy/ Children and Contemporary Art, Des Moines Art Center, Iowa
Carnegie International 1999–2000, Carnegie Museum Hall, Pitsburgh
Ground Zero Japan, Contemporary Art Gallery, Art Tower Mito, Japan
2000 *Murakami & Manetas,* Newsantandrea, Savona, Italy
SUPER FLAT, PARCO Gallery, Tokyo and Nagoya, Japan
Lyon Biennale, Lyon, France
2001 *SUPER FLAT,* MOCA Gallery, Pacific Design Center, Los Angeles
my reality, Des Moines Art Center, Iowa
Public Offering, MOCA The Geffen Contemporary

Publications:

By MURAKAMI: Books—*Symposium: ''Asian Contemporary Art Reconsidered,''* Tokyo 1997; *Takashi Murakami: The Meaning of the Nonsense of the Meaning,* New York 1999; *SuperFlat,* Tokyo 2000.

On MURAKAMI: Articles—''Dangerously Cute'' by Sawaragi Noi in *Flash Art,* vol. 25, no. 163, March-April 1992; ''Imitation Warhol'' by Jerry Saltz in *Village Voice,* 25–31 August 1999.

* * *

Takahashi Murakami is a virtuoso Neo-Pop artist whose witty and exuberant paintings and sculpture incorporate a pop culture-inspired iconography at turns cute and menacing. At first glance his images seem as superficial as the late-capitalist Japanese hyper-consumer culture from which they derive. Murakami's oeuvre, however, is among the most serious, thoughtful and influential produced by a Japanese artist in the twentieth century. His work critically explores the relationship between indigenous modes and styles of art, such as Japanese traditional-style painting (*nihonga*; originating in the late nineteenth century and primarily concerned with symbolizing Japanese ethnic uniqueness with traditional media and formats), and the Western-derived concept of ''contemporary art'' (*gendai bijutsu*). Murakami's incisive yet playful attitude toward distinctions between Japan and the West, and fine and popular arts, has allowed him to achieve a meaningful form of expression even as his primary subject, as he has often stated, is ''nonsense.''

While Murakami's work enjoys immense international success and has been informed by American artists such as Andy Warhol and Jeff Koons, its significance can only be fully understood in relation to its domestic Japanese context. Murakami holds the somewhat dubious honor of being the first to earn a Ph.D. in *nihonga,* yet since his professional debut in the early 1990s, he has chosen to work outside of the genre's institutional context, self-consciously positioning himself as a Japanese artist in an international art arena. He continues to work within the parameters of the *nihonga* discourse, however, even as he questions and redefines it, asking, ''What is the basis of the terms 'Japan' and 'art'? What are 'Japanese images'? What is 'Japan'? What is the nature of this period I live in?''

Murakami has exposed ''art'' as a Western concept superficially imported into modern Japan. He has consistently ridiculed the myth of interiority and artistic subjectivity shared by modern Western and Japanese ''Western-style'' or ''international'' art. In 1992, he duplicated Gutai artist Murakami Saburô's 1955 ''Paper-tearing'' performance in a tongue-in-cheek gesture, criticizing its flimsy conceptualism while taking pleasure merely in its sound and visual effects. In a nod to Roy Lichtenstein's famous parody of the masculine heroics of Abstract Expressionism, Murakami mocked the autonomous gesture in *Cream* (1998), a meticulously crafted painting whose image of ejaculated semen is executed in the linear style shared by Japanese woodblock prints and contemporary animation. In this and other works, Murakami looks back to the art produced in Japan before the introduction of Western modernism with its intellectual pretensions and restraints, reincorporating its playfulness and decorative qualities. He finds these extant not in contemporary art but in

Japanese mass media comics and animation. Concerned with reinvigorating *nihonga* and reintegrating it with the experience of contemporary life, he appropriates the language and pictorial style of popular culture while maintaining a critical and ironic distance from that culture. This approach he supports with his ''Super Flat'' theory—a double metaphor for the flattening of hierarchies between fine and popular art and their respective genres and media, and the loss of meaning in world composed of empty signs.

For Murakami, the business of making and showing art is no different from show business. Market-savvy and aggressively self-promotional, from the beginning of his career Murakami has sought to attract an audience through media manipulation and the staging of ''events'' following the examples of Warhol and Okamoto Tarô. Recently he has taken to curating group shows of artists in his stable, who further the cause of ''super flatness.'' In line with Jean Baudrillard's dictum to rid art of aura and authority and instead produce ''merchandise,'' Murakami unabashedly reduces his works to consumer items. His projects are produced collaboratively outside of Tokyo at his Hiropon Factory, which also makes trademarked products such as mousepads, dolls and t- shirts for mass consumption. Most of these feature the image of Mr. DOB, Murakami's creepy cartoon character who embodies what critic Sawaragi Noi describes as the dangerous and sinister modes of social control and surveillance masked by the façade of cuteness in Japan.

Murakami's strategy of appropriating the iconography of cuteness and taking it to painful excess has involved adopting the persona of the *otaku* or geek. For Murakami, the obsessive *otaku* is paradigmatic of the postmodern age of late capitalism, much as for Baudelaire the *flâneur* was emblematic of modernity. Murakami considers the object of the *otaku*'s obsession—generally comics and the subcultures built around their appreciation—to be perfect and original expressions of present-day Japan. Recognizing that the creation and promotion of cultural images has a parallel in consumer culture, Murakami stamps his products with a bold ''Made in Japan,'' an ironic, self-conscious and post-modernist acknowledgement of the constructed, rather than essential, character of national identity.

—Alicia Volk

MURPHY, Catherine

Nationality: American. **Born:** 1946. **Education:** Pratt Institute, Brooklyn, New York, B.F.A.; also studied at the Skowhegan School of Painting and Sculpture, Maine. **Family:** Married Harry Roseman (an artist). **Career:** Freelance artist. **Awards:** National Endowment for the Arts grant, 1979 and 1989; Guggenheim Fellowship, 1982; American Academy and Institute of Arts and Letters Award, 1990. **Agent:** Lennon, Weinberg, Inc., New York. **Address:** c/o Lennon Weinberg Gallery, 560 Broadway, New York, New York 10012, U.S.A.

Individual Exhibitions:

1972 First Street Gallery, New York
Piper Gallery, Massachusetts
1975 *Recent Paintings,* Fourcade, Droll, Inc., New York
1976 *Catherine Murphy: A Retrospective Exhibition,* Phillips Collection, Washington, D.C. (travelled to the Institute of Contemporary Art, Boston)
1979 *Recent Paintings,* Xavier Fourcade, Inc., New York
1985 Xavier Fourcade, Inc., New York
1988 J. Rosenthal Fine Arts, Chicago
1989 Lennon, Weinberg, Inc., New York
1992 Lennon, Weinberg, Inc., New York
1994 Greenville County Museum of Art, Greenville, South Carolina
Lennon, Weinberg, Inc., New York
1995 Lennon, Weinberg, Inc., New York
1998 Lennon, Weinberg, Inc., New York
1999 Texas Gallery, Houston

Selected Group Exhibitions:

1972 *Annual Painting and Sculpture Exhibition,* Whitney Museum, New York
1974 *Painting and Sculpture Today: 1974,* Indianapolis Museum
1977 *A View of a Decade,* Museum of Contemporary Art, Chicago
1981 *Real, Really Real and Super Real,* San Antonio Museum of Art, San Antonio, Texas (travelled to Indianapolis, Tucson, and Pittsburgh)
1983 *American Still Life: 1945–1983,* Contemporary Arts Museum, Houston (travelled to Buffalo, New York; Columbus, Ohio; Purchase, New York; and Portland, Oregon)
1986 *The Window in Twentieth Century Art,* Neuberger Museum of Art, Purchase, New York
1989 *Making Their Mark: Women Artists Move into the Mainstream, 1970–1985,* Cincinnati Art Museum (travelled to New Orleans, Denver, and Philadelphia)
1990 *Awards Exhibition,* American Academy and Institute of Arts and Letters
1991 *American Realism and Figurative Art: 1952–1991,* Miyaqui Museum of Art, Sendai, Japan (travelled to Yokohama, Todushima, Shiga, and Kochi)
1994 *Inspired by Nature,* Neuberger Museum of Art, Purchase, New York
1997 *Still Life: The Object in American Art, 1915–1995—Selections from the Metropolitan Museum of Art,* American Federation of the Arts (travelled to Virginia, Arkansas, California, Oklahoma, Florida, and Kansas)
1999–2000 *Green Wood and Crystal Waters: The American Landscape Tradition since 1950,* Philbrook Museum of Art (travelled to Florida and Iowa)
2000 *Insites: Interior Spaces in Contemporary Art,* Whitney Museum of American Art at Champion, Stamford, Connecticut

Collections:

Hirshhorn Museum and Sculpture Garden, Washington, D.C.; Metropolitan Museum of Art, New York; Newark Museum, New Jersey;

Catherine Murphy: *View of Hoboken and Manhattan from Riverview Park, New Jersey,* 1973. ©The Newark Museum/Art Resource, NY.

New Jersey Art Museum, Trenton; Phillips Collection, Washington, D.C.; Vassar College Art Gallery, Poughkeepsie, New York; Virginia Museum of Fine Arts, Richmond; Weatherspoon Art Gallery, Greensboro, North Carolina; Whitney Museum of American Art, New York.

Publications:

By MURPHY: Articles—''Catherine Murphy: Art Is My Lifestyle,'' interview, in *The Woman Artist,* special issue of *Art and Man* (New York), November 1974.

On MURPHY: Books—*Catherine Murphy,* exhibition catalog, Washington, D.C. and Boston 1976; *Catherine Murphy: New Paintings and Drawings, 1980–85,* exhibition catalog, New York 1985. **Articles—**''The Art of Survival (and Vice Versa)'' by Vivien Raynor in the *New York Times Magazine,* 17 February 1974; ''Arts Review: Catherine Murphy'' by Allen Ellenzweig in *Arts Magazine* (New York), February 1975; ''An Uncommon Painter of the Commonplace'' by Hilton Kramer in the *New York Times,* 9 March 1975; ''Painter with a Novelist's Eye'' by Piri Halasz in the *New York Times,* 11 January 1976; ''Catherine Murphy: The Rise of a Cult Figure'' by John Cruen in *ARTnews* (New York), December 1978; ''Catherine Murphy'' by Hilton Kramer in the *New York Times,* 11 May 1979; ''The Magic of the Commonplace'' by John Gruen in *Quest* (New York), January 1980; ''Revival of Realism'' by Mark Stevens in *Newsweek* (New York), 7 June 1982; ''Catherine Murphy'' by Kay Larson in *New York,* 16 December 1985; ''Catherine Murphy'' by Jeanne Silverthorne in *Artforum* (New York), February 1986; ''Catherine Murphy'' by John Yau in *Artforum* (New York), summer 1992; ''The Figurative Field'' by Gerrit Henry in *Art in America,* January 1994; ''Catherine Murphy: It Chose Her'' by Margarett Loke in *ARTnews,* February 1996; ''A Dirty Tablecloth,

Deconstructed: Catherine Murphy's Stained Tablecloth Resurrects Nature Morte and Brings Life Back to Still Life'' by Francine Prose in *ARTnews,* October 1999.

* * *

Catherine Murphy's images have been labelled ''biographical vision,'' and in this regard they clearly parallel the creative efforts of Andrew Wyeth (and all others imbued with such existential need). Her art seems as if it were able only to arise from the necessity to comment upon the intimate and mysterious immediacy of her human and physical surroundings. Murphy's 1985 exhibition was one of only a handful of solo shows of her entire career to that point, and its contents indicated that her production in the six years since her previous exhibition included just eight pencil drawings and 11 oil paintings. All those works intimately related to her outwardly placid life in Duchess County, New York.

Murphy became widely known in 1976 through a travelling exhibition arranged by the Phillips Collection in Washington, D.C. Her work continues to be held in high regard as an import and contribution to the realist resurgence of the 1970s and 1980s. While her images with large foreground figures have been considered relatively lifeless, her landscapes and interior views—still life essentially—comprise her best work. Murphy's paintings verge on photorealism with their deft sine-sable brushwork, and yet they are warmer both in touch and feeling. In addition, they may well be taken as postmodern in their insistence upon an unembarrassed and clearly nonsarcastic Romantic nuance. Huddled figures, for instance, may converse in a dark corner at the base of a staircase in an image that is ostensibly focused upon a cluster of window ledge objects.

Another special characteristic in Murphy's finest work appears as an emphasis on the artifice of artmaking. She may display obviously self-conscious chords of color or present a clearly arbitrary compositional pattern, which is a match, or foil, to some other part of the pictorial design. Murphy's realism then may be felt as synthesizing—a second wave encompassing older attitudes beyond the 1970s phenomenological objectification.

And so it is little surprise that Murphy has listed Ryman, Mangold, and Marden as among the artists highly interesting to her. But their presence in her work was at best clearly muted until, alluding to her work made in the earlier 1980s, Murphy said, ''I really needed to get family and the psychological freight that goes with it out of my work, once and for all.''

From the later 80s then, ''I had told my tale . . . I finally got down to the simple balance I wanted.'' Geometries soon became visible as basic visual structure in landscapes and still life, with figures no longer present. The association of a vividly representational idiom with large seemingly empty areas—a twirled garden hose against a snowy field; a meticulously brushed, flattened tablecloth, dirty with after-dinner stains and crumbs—has been labeled a ''figurative Minimalism.'' Murphy's feeling for those practicing an exclusively non-representational Minimalism was now permitted a more overt expression. Only with close observation of the canvas surface did those lovingly rendered and precise yet sensually tactile—phenomenologically forceful—ordinary-life details become apparent in the over-all abstract pattern of paintings of the 1990s. Such works, with their poignant details perhaps a stand-in for the now-vanished ''psychological freight,'' have continued through the decade.

—Joshua Kind

MURRAY, Elizabeth

Nationality: American. **Born:** Chicago, Illinois, 1940. **Education:** Art Institute of Chicago, B.F.A. 1962; Mills College Oakland, California, M.F.A. 1964. **Career:** Independent artist. Instructor, Bard College, Annandale-on-Hudson, New York, 1974–75, 1976–77; Princeton University, New Jersey, 1977; Yale University, New Haven, Connecticut, 1978–79. Visiting instructor, Wayne State University, Detroit, 1975, California Institute of the Arts, Valencia, 1975–76, and School of the Art Institute of Chicago, 1975–76; Member, American Academy and Institute of Arts and Letters, 1992. **Awards:** Walter M. Campana Award, Art Institute of Chicago, 1982; American Academy and Institute of Arts and Letters Award, 1984; Skowhegan School of Painting and Sculpture Medal for Painting, Maine, 1986; MacArthur Foundation Fellowship, 2000. **Address:** c/o Paula Cooper Gallery, 155 Wooster St., New York, New York, 10012–3159.

Individual Exhibitions:

1974 Jacobs Ladder Gallery, Washington, D.C. (with Joseph Zucker)
Elizabeth Murray/Marilyn Lenkowsky/John Torreano, Paula Cooper Gallery, New York
1975 Paula Cooper Gallery, New York (with James Dearing)
Jared Sable Gallery, Toronto
1976 Paula Cooper Gallery, New York
1978 Ohio State University, Columbus
Phyllis Kind Gallery, Chicago
Paula Cooper Gallery, New York
1980 Galerie Mukai, Tokyo
Susanne Hilberry Gallery, Birmingham, Michigan
1981 Paula Cooper Gallery, New York
1982 Smith College, Northampton, Massachusetts
Daniel Weinberg Gallery, Los Angeles
1983 Portland Center for the Visual Arts, Oregon
Paula Cooper Gallery, New York
1984 Knight Gallery, Charlotte, North Carolina
Paula Cooper Gallery, New York
Brooke Alexander Inc., New York
1985 University of New Mexico, Albuquerque
1986 Carnegie-Mellon University, Pittsburgh
1987 Dallas Museum of Art, Texas (toured the United States, 1987–88)
California State University, Long Beach (travelled to Berkeley)
Paula Cooper Gallery, New York
1989 Dallas Museum of Art (traveling retrospective) (catalog)
1995 *Artist's Choice: Elizabeth Murray—Modern Women,* Museum of Modern Art, New York (catalog)

Elizabeth Murray: *Just in Time,* 1981. ©Philadelphia Museum of Art/Corbis.

Elizabeth Murray: *Popeye,* 1932. The Museum of Modern Art, New York; gift of Abby Aldrich Rockefeller ,(by exchange). Photo ©Museum of Modern Art, 1999.

1997 *Elizabeth Murray: Recent Paintings,* PaceWildenstein Gallery, New York (catalog)
1999 PaceWildenstein Gallery, New York

Selected Group Exhibitions:

1974 *American Abstract Painting Today,* Whitney Museum Downtown, New York
1977 *9 Artists,* Guggenheim, New York
Paintings 1975–77, Sarah Lawrence College Gallery, Bronxville, New York (travelled to the American Foundation for the Arts, Miami, and the Contemporary Arts Center, Cincinnati, Ohio)
1978 *8 Abstract Painters,* Institute of Contemporary Art, University of Pennsylvania, Philadelphia
1979 *New Painting: New York,* Hayward Gallery, London
1980 *American Drawing in Black and White 1970–80,* Brooklyn Museum, New York
1981 *1981 Painting Invitational,* Oscarsson Hood Gallery, New York
1983 *Minimalism to Expression: Painting and Sculpture Since 1965,* Whitney Museum, New York
1985 *Correspondence: New York Art Now,* Laforet Museum, Tokyo (travelled to Tochigi and Kobe, Japan)
1987 *Prints in Parts,* Crown Point Press, New York
1988 *The Saatchi Collection: Jennifer Bartlett, Elizabeth Murray, Eric Fischl, Susan Rothenberg,* Saatchi Collection, London (catalog)
SoHo at Duke: Six Artists from the Paula Cooper Gallery, Duke University Museum of Art, Durham, North Carolina (catalog)
Eleven Artists from Paula Cooper, Mayor Rowan Gallery, London (catalog)
1989 *Projects & Portfolios: The 25th National Print Exhibition,* Brooklyn Museum, New York (catalog)
The Elusive Surface: Painting in Three Dimensions, Museum of Albuquerque, New Mexico (catalog)
1990 *The Image of Abstract Painting in the 80s,* Rose Art Museum, Brandeis University, Waltham, Massachusetts (catalog)
American Drawings in the 1980s, Graphische Sammlung Albertina, Vienna (catalog)
1991 *Seven American Painters,* Staatsgalerie Moderner Kunst, Munich (catalog)
1994 *Gemini G.E.L.: Recent Paintings and Sculptures,* National Gallery of Art, Washington, D.C. (catalog)
1996 *Large Drawings and Objects,* Arkansas Art Gallery, Little Rock (catalog)

Collections:

Museum of Modern Art, New York; Guggenheim Museum, New York; Whitney Museum, New York; Museum of Fine Arts, Boston; Art Institute of Chicago; Dallas Museum of Art, Texas; Walker Art Center, Minneapolis; Philadelphia Museum of Art; Saint Louis Art Museum, Missouri; Hirshhorn Museum, Washington, D.C.; H.H.K. Foundation, Milwaukee; Detroit Institute of Arts.

Publications:

By MURRAY: Articles—interview with Mari Rantanen in *Taide,* vol. 28, no. 3, 1988; interview with Jonathan Seliger and John Zinsser in *Journal of Contemporary Art,* vol. 1, no. 2, Fall-Winter 1988; ''Statements by Alex Katz, Frank Stella, Brice Marden, Elizabeth Murray and Bill Jensen'' in *Art Journal,* vol. 48, no. 3, Fall 1989; interview with Jessica Hagedorn in *Bomb,* no. 62, Winter 1998.

On MURRAY: Books—*Early Work by Five Contemporary Artists,* exhibition catalog with texts by Marcia Tucker and Allan Schwartzman, New York 1977; *American Painting: The Eighties,* exhibition catalog by Barbara Rose, New York 1979; *La Peinture americaine: Les mythes et la matiere* by Madaleine Deschamps, Paris 1981; *Elizabeth Murray: Recent Paintings and Drawings,* exhibition catalog, Portland, Oregon 1983; *The Pluralist Era; American Art 1968–1981* by Corinne Robins, New York 1984; *American Art Now* by Edward Lucie-Smith, New York 1985; *Elizabeth Murray: Drawings 1980–1986,* exhibition catalog with essays by Elaine A. King and Ann Sutherland Harris, Pittsburgh 1986; *Elizabeth Murray: Paintings and Drawings,* exhibition catalog with essays by Roberta Smith and Clifford S. Ackley, Dallas and New York 1987. **Articles—** ''Shape Shifter'' by Robert Storr in *Art in America* (New York), vol. 77, no. 4, April 1989; ''Ifs, Ands, and Buts'' by David Frankel in *Artforum,* vol. 36, no. 7, March 1998; ''Elizabeth Murray's Terrifying Terrain'' by Alexi Worth in *ARTnews,* vol. 97, no. 5, May 1998.

* * *

Elizabeth Murray, since 1974, has emerged as a leading practitioner of emotively loaded, ambiguously abstract color painting. She found her mature direction after having investigated various other issues: a funky, Pop-inspired imagist painting along with three-dimensional reliefs dominated her work during the 1960s. In the early 1970s she was exploring single forms and repetitive structures like steps and waves in oil painting. Then in about 1974 she changed her direction and eradicating any direct representational associations instituted, instead, a back-to-basics constructive approach to making pictures. Stressing the clear and specific presentation of line, plane and color, the paintings from the mid-1970s reveal the elaboration of a personal vocabulary of motifs and compositional devices as well as scalar relationship.

In 1975 the first shaped paintings offered the viewer even more dynamic experiences of colors and forms. Her ability to break the rules by making irregular and regular as well as local and disharmonious colors work together by working against each other is strongly evident in such examples as *Singing School* and *Rise,* both 1976. The evocative qualities of the imagery is underscored in the examples from 1977–78 in which complex and choreographed interplays among the pictorial elements impress as equivalential statement about feelings and even human relationships. *Parting and Together* (1978) and *Daybreak* (1977–78) are examples.

In the late 1970s the paintings had become larger and took on more aggrresive shapes. In 1980 the strong pictorial forces generated by the imagery caused Murray, finally, to burst apart the canvas and to adapt multiple format that ranged anywhere from two to more than 20 pieces. By freeing certain thematic impulses earlier present as undercurrents, Murray has worked from the early 1980s toward broadening the scope of her vision. In *Yikes* (1982) she lets her keen sense of humor out, in an amusing painting of a broken cup, in which the title gives fitting voice to the exclamatory qualities of the bold cartoonish imagery and the physically fragmented structure of the canvas on which it appears. In *Kitchen Painting* (1985) she shows her imaginative depths in the effective way that color, shape and representational motifs come together to convey the complex family feelings often suffusing, if not suffocating domestic space. *Kitchen Party* is also an example of multiple shaped canvases arranged into a relief structure with elements jutting off, which the artist has favored in this period.

—Ronny Cohen

MURRAY, Robert

Nationality: American. **Born:** Vancouver, British Columbia, 2 March 1936. **Education:** Saskatoon Teachers College, Saskatchewan, 1954–55 (scholarship, 1955); studied art, under Jack Shadbolt, Will Barnet, Barnett Newman, John Ferren and Clement Greenberg, Emma Lake Artists Workshop, Saskatchewan, 1955, 1957, 1961; studied at Regina College School of Art, University of Saskatchewan, 1956–58, and Institute Allende, San Miguel, Mexico, 1958 (scholarship). **Military Service:** Royal Canadian Air Force Auxiliary, 1951–54. **Family:** Married Diana Armatage in 1959 (divorced, 1969); children: Megan and Rebecca; married Cintra Wetherill Lofting in 1971; children: Claire and Hillary. **Career:** Independent sculptor, since 1960; Assisted Barnett Newman with a number of projects from 1960–1970; Organized and accompanied Clement Greenberg on a tour of five western Canadian cities under the auspices of *Canadian Art Magazine,* Summer 1961; Art instructor, Hunter College, New York, 1965–69; School of Visual Arts, New York, 1971–present; University of Delaware, 1991–93, 1997; University of Pennsylvania, 1995–97; Artist-in-residence, Yale University, New Haven, Connecticut, 1968; University of Regina, Saskatchewan, 1978; University of Alberta, Edmonton, 1978; University of Manitoba, Winnipeg, 1978; Emily Carr College of Art, Vancouver, B.C., 1980; University of Southern Illinois, Carbondale, 1985; Studio School, New York, 1988; Cornell University, Ithaca, New York, 1989; University of the Arts, Philadelphia, 1991; University of Delaware, Newark, 1991; Storm King Art Center, Mountainville, New York, 1991; New Arts Program, Kutztown, Pennsylvania, 1993; Graduate Fine Arts Department, University of Pennsylvania, 1994–97; Graduate Fine Arts, University of Delaware, 1997; Westfield State College, 1999. **Awards:** Recognition Award, Saskatchewan Arts Board, Regina, 1958; Arts Scholarship, 1960, and Bursary, 1969, Canada Council, Ottawa; National Endowment for the Arts Grant, 1969; Second Prize, *Bienal,* Sao Paolo, 1969; Allied Arts Medal, Royal Architectural Institute of Canada, 1977. **Agents:** Andre Zarre Gallery, 515 West 20th, New York, New York 10011; Moore Gallery, 80 Spadina Avenue, Toronto, Ontario M5V 2J3; Ericson Gallery, 53 North 2nd Street, Philadelphia, Pennsylvania 19106. **Address:** 345 Lamborntown Road, West Grove, Pennsylvania 19390.

Individual Exhibitions:

1965 Betty Parsons Gallery, New York
1966 Betty Parsons Gallery, New York
1967 David Mirvish Gallery, Toronto
Jewish Museum, New York
1968 Betty Parsons Gallery, New York
David Mirvish Gallery, Toronto
1969 Battery Park, Cultural Affairs Department, New York
1970 *Robert Murray/Ronald Bladen,* The Gallery, Vancouver
1971 Dag Hammarskjold Plaza, New York
1972 David Mirvish Gallery, Toronto
1974 Paula Cooper Gallery, New York

Robert Murray: *Susquehannah,* 1979. ©Robert Murray, courtesy of a private collection.

David Mirvish Gallery, Toronto
1975 Mendel Art Gallery, Saskatoon, Saskatchewan
The Gallery, Stratford, Ontario
David Mirvish Gallery, Toronto
1976 *Watercolors by Robert Murray and Toni Onley,* Olympia Galleries, Philadelphia
1977 Janie C. Lee Gallery, Houston
Hamilton Gallery of Contemporary Art, New York
1978 Sewall Art Gallery, Rice University, Houston
1979 Dayton Art Institute, Ohio
Columbus Museum, Ohio
Hamilton Gallery of Contemporary Art, New York
Klonaridis Gallery, Toronto
1980 Hamilton Gallery of Contemporary Art, New York
Klonaridis Gallery, Toronto
1981 Klonaridis Gallery, Toronto
1982 Hamilton Gallery of Contemporary Art, New York
Klonaridis Gallery, Toronto

1983 Phillips Academy, Andover, Massachusetts
Sam Houston Gallery, Vancouver
Art Gallery of Greater Victoria, British Columbia
1984 The Esplanade, New York
1985 Centro Culturale Canadese, Rome
Gallery One, Toronto
1986 Gallery 291, Atlanta, Georgia
Richard Green Gallery, New York
1987 Richard Green Gallery, Los Angeles
1990 Delaware Art Museum, Wilmington
1992 Muhlenberg College, Frank Martin Gallery, Allentown, Pennsylvania
1993 *Works on Paper,* New Arts Program, Kutztown, Pennsylvania
Special Showing of HILLARY, Muhlenberg College, Allentown, Pennsylvania
Special Showing of SAGINAW, Reading Museum, Pennsylvania
1994 *Robert Murray Prints and Paintings,* Mira Godard Gallery, Toronto
Recent Paintings and Sculpture, Andre Zarre Gallery, New York
Robert Murray Retrospective, Reading Public Museum, Pennsylvania
1995 *Robert Murray Sculpture,* Andre Zarre Gallery, New York
Special Showing of MUSKOKA, Freedman Gallery, Albright College
1997 *Robert Murray Sculpture* (inaugural exhibit), Domestic Arts Building, Grounds For Sculpture, Hamilton, New Jersey
1999 *Robert Murray Retrospective Exhibition: The Factory as Studio,* NGC, Ottawa
Robert Murray, Working Models, Arno Maris Gallery, Westfield College, Massachusetts
Robert Murray, Four Sculptures, Moore Gallery, Toronto
Robert Murray, Wall Pieces and Small Sculpture, Ericson Gallery, Philadelphia
2000 *The Floatplane Watercolors,* Stroud Fresh Water Research Center, Avondale, Pennsylvania

Selected Group Exhibitions:

1971 *49th Parallel: New Canadian Art,* Museum of Contemporary Art, Chicago
Lithographs from the Nova Scotia College of Art Workshop, Museum of Modern Art, New York
1972 *Masters of the 60s,* Edmonton Art Gallery, Alberta (travelled to the Winnipeg Art Gallery, Manitoba, and David Mirvish Gallery, Toronto)
1973 Contemporary American Art, Whitney Museum, New York
1975 *Artist and Fabricator,* Fine Arts Center Gallery, University of Massachusetts, Amherst
Conditions of Sculpture, Hayward Gallery, London
1976 *American Salon des Refuses,* Stamford Museum, Connecticut
1977 *Project, New Urban Monuments,* Akron Art Institute, Ohio (toured the United States)
1978 *In Small Scale,* Hamilton Gallery of Contemporary Art, New York (travelled to Marion Locks Gallery, Philadelphia)
1981 *Bronze Show,* Hamilton Gallery of Contemporary Art, New York
1982 *Contemporary Outdoor Sculpture,* The Guild, Scarborough, Ontario
Bronzes, Fuller-Goldeen Gallery, San Francisco
Collaborations, Metropolitan Museum of Art, New York
1987 *Nothing But Steel,* The Lab, Cold Spring Harbour, L.I.
Tradition and Innovation: Saskatoon Art and the 1950's, Mendel Art Gallery, Saskatoon, Saskatchewan
1988 *Opening Exhibition,* National Gallery of Canada, Ottawa
20th Anniversary Exhibition, Paula Cooper Gallery, New York
1989 *Exhibition of Outdoor Sculpture (Murray, Sugarman, Wiley),* Boca Raton Museum, Florida
1990 *Sculpture of the Americas into the Nineties,* Museum of Modern Art of the Americas, Washington, D.C.
1992 *The Crisis of Abstraction in the 50s,* National Gallery of Canada, Ottawa
1993 *Robert Murray and Toni Onley: Watercolors and Prints,* West Parry Sound District Museum, Parry Sound, Ontario
Sculpture Off the Pedestal II, Grand Rapids Museum, Michigan
1994 *Gallery Artists,* Andre Zarre Gallery, New York
1995 *Faculty Exhibition,* University of Pennsylvania, Philadelphia
1997 *Currents of Modern Sculpture,* Two Sculptors Gallery, New York
1998 *Surrounding Sculpture,* Freedman Gallery, Albright College, Reading, Pennsylvania
2000 *25th Anniversary Exhibition,* Andre Zarre Gallery, New York
Art of Our Century, Part II: Modern Art at Millenium's End, Appleton Museum, Ocala, Florida
Summer 2000, Moore Gallery, Toronto

Public Installations:

HILLARY (extended loan), Grounds For Sculpture, Hamilton, New Jersey 1995; *Canada-Cross Country,* CNIB, Toronto, Ontario 1998; *Skagway,* Art Gallery of Kelowna, Kelowna, B.C. 2000.

Collections:

Saskatchewan Arts Board, Regina; Mendel Art Gallery, Saskatoon; Canada Council Art Bank, Ottawa; Art Gallery of Ontario, Toronto; National Gallery of Canada, Ottawa; Whitney Museum, New York; Metropolitan Museum of Art, New York; Hirshhorn Museum, Washington, D.C.; University of Massachusetts, Amherst; Dayton Art Institute, Ohio; Aldrich Museum of Contemporary Art, Ridgefield, Connecticut; The Art Gallery of Greater Victoria, Victoria, B.C.; The Art Gallery of Vancouver, B.C.; Columbus Museum of Art, Ohio; Kelowna Art Gallery, Kelowna, B.C.; Power Museum of Art, Sydney, Australia; The Walker Art Center, Minneapolis, Minnesota.

Publications:

By MURRAY: Articles—"The Education of 12 Practicing Artists" in *Canadian Art* (Toronto), December 1965; "10 Artists in Search of Canadian Art" in *Canadian Art* (Toronto), January 1966; interview with Barbara Rose, in *Canadian Art* (Toronto), July 1966; interview in "Design and Expression in Minimal Art" by James S. Pierce in *Art International* (Lugano, Switzerland), May 1968; "Barnett Newman 1905–1970: An Appreciation" in *Artscanada* (Toronto), August 1970. **Films—***Art Is,* New York 1970; *Vision U.S.A.*, New York 1971.

On MURRAY: Books—*Robert Murray/Ronald Bladen,* exhibition catalog (includes statement by Murray), Vancouver 1970; *Artist and Fabricator,* exhibition catalog by Hugh Marlais Davies (includes interview with Murray), Amherst, Massachusetts 1975; *Robert Murray,* exhibition catalog, Toronto 1975; *Watercolors by Robert Murray and Toni Onley,* exhibition catalog with critical notes by Ruth Fine Lehrer, Philadelphia 1976; *Robert Murray,* exhibition catalog, Dayton, Ohio 1979; *Robert Murray: Sculpture and Working Models,* exhibition catalog by Greg Bellerby, Victoria 1983; *The Factory As Studio,* exhibition catalog by Denise Leclerc, with introduction by Barbara Rose, Ottawa 1999. **Articles—**"Canada: Art d'Aujourd'hui" by Bernard Teyssedre in *Vie des Arts* (Montreal), Spring 1968; "Blow-Up: The Problem of Scale in Sculpture" by Barbara Rose in *Art in America* (New York), July 1968; "Robert Murray/Canada" by Brydon Smith in *Artscanada* (Toronto), October 1969; "Bladen and Murray: The Giants of Canadian Sculpture" by Joan Lowndes in *Vie des Arts* (Montreal), Summer 1970; "Sculpture: A Rebirth of Humanism" by Joe Bodolai and "Robert Murray: Against the Monument" by M. Greenwood in *Artscanada* (Toronto), Autumn 1974; "Living with Sculpture" by John L. Taylor in *Artnews* (New York), October 1974; "The Giant Size Art of Robert Murray" by Robert Fulford in *Saturday Night* (Toronto), December 1975; "Where the Monumental Sculptors Go" by Roy Bongartz in *Artnews* (New York), Febraury 1976; "Robert Murray: Generating Sculpture from the Metal Plate" by Hugh M. Davies in *Arts Magazine* (New York), October 1977; "Robert Murray: On Being a Sculptor" by Lowry Sims in *Artscanada* (Toronto), April 1979; "Robert Murray" by Anna Babinska in *Vanguard* (Vancouver), September 1981; "Dances with Steel" by Robert Enright, with introduction by Meeka Walsh, in *BorderCrossings,* May 1999; "A Painter in Metal" by David Raskin in *Art in America,* September 1999.

*

Once I saw what had been accomplished in painting, it seemed to me there should be some equivalent possibility with sculpture. Now sculpture is tougher because of the way one can so easily organize forms in space. That's why I tried to make my sculpture almost of a single piece of material. I've never used found objects, I've used ready-made materials on a couple of occasions—the Q-decking, the corrugated material—but I've had those made for me. I tend to look at steel like a big piece of canvas. And because of my painting background, that sense of invention has always been important. I'm really not very good at assembling found objects.

—Robert Murray

* * *

Robert Murray is known as a maker of constructed metal sculpture which uses simple geometric forms and industrial materials and methods, unified by colored industrial finishes. On the strength of that description, Murray sounds like one of the many followers of Anthony Caro, but in fact the Canadian sculptor is something of an anomaly, since he arrived at his kind of painted metal construction about the same time that Caro first began to work in steel.

Like Caro, Murray developed his steel works from David Smith's example. This is made clear by one of Murray's earliest mature pieces, a fountain sculpture for the City Hall of Saskatoon, Saskatchewan, where he went to art school. The piece is deceptively simple: two similar cut-out metal shapes, with curving projections, reach towards one another. But there is a Smith-ian animation and personality in each of the arching forms, particularly in the way they stand erect on stylized "feet."

Like any intelligent young sculptor, Murray was aware of what Caro was doing in the 1960s, but he was also aware of minimalism and other contemporary ideologies. Perhaps in response to these influences, his work became noticeably simplified during that decade. His sculptures of the 1960s and early 1970s insist on the primacy of vertical-horizontal relationships and logical geometric configurations of lucid, angular shapes. The structure of each piece is readily apparent; nothing is hidden. Murray exploits the possibilities of mechanical processes in these works. They involve folding and bending on a very large scale, so that we immediately think about machinery and the factory, while their smooth, saturated surfaces are as impassive as industrial coatings.

Since about 1974 Murray's sculpture has become more playful and more lyrical. He has evolved a new vocabulary of irregularities and curves, to supplement the austere geometry of his earlier work. He is still fascinated by process and the effects that technology affords, and this can sometimes cause problems. When the technical aspects of fabricating a fluttering handkerchief of steel become too apparent, the sculpture suffers, but when the finished form seems more important than how it was made, the piece can be both powerful and delicate, apparently unaffected by concerns of gravity and weight. The slightly iridescent surfaces of some recent works emphasize the fragility of curling edges and swelling planes and, at the same time, returns us to the physicality of the metal itself, recalling as they do custom car bodies.

Since the early 1980s, Murray has worked in an intermediate, more intimate scale which seems to suit him very well. The works in this middle size include some bronzes, made from sheets (not cast). The malleable metal and its ability to assume color through patination give Murray full scope for his new interest in more elaborate surfaces and forms. If the severities and geometric purity of his earlier work could be called Classical, in Wöfflin's sense of the word, then the sumptuous curves, complex profiles and inflected surfaces of these sculptures can only be termed Baroque.

Since about 1985, Murray's sculpture has once again dealt with severe geometric forms, but at the same time has become more complex in terms of surface and texture, since he often combines a variety of materials—metal and wood, for example—in a single piece. He continues to work in a range of sizes, but to date there is the risk of small sculptures seeming precious or like maquettes for larger works because of their new complexity of construction. The expressive possibilities of the of contrasting materials seems clearest and most effective in the larger works.

—Karen Wilkin

N

NAGASAWA, Hidetoshi

Nationality: Japanese. **Born:** Manchuria, China, 30 October 1940. **Education:** Studied interior design at Tama University of Fine Arts, Tokyo, 1959–63. **Career:** Independent artist, since 1966; lived in Tokyo, 1966–67, and in Milan, since 1967. **Agents:** Galleria Arte Borgogna, via Borgogna 7, 20122 Milan; Galleria Francoise Lambert, Bastioni di Porta Nuova 11, 20121 Milan. **Address:** Via Bramante 29, 20154 Milan, Italy.

Individual Exhibitions:

1969 Galleria Sincron, Brescia, Italy
1970 Galleria Françoise Lambert, Milan
1971 Galleria Toselli, Milan
Galleria l'Attico, Rome
Galleria La Bertesca, Milan
1972 Galleria Art Borgogna, Milan
Galleria Nuova Muse, Bologna
1974 Galleria Arte Borgogna, Milan
Galleria Acme, Brescia, Italy
1975 Galleria Christian Stein, Turin
Galleria L'Attico, Rome
1976 Galleria Christian Stein, Turin
1977 Galerie t'Venster, Rotterdam
1978 Galleria Piero Cavellini, Brescia, Italy
Galleria L'Attico, Rome
Galleria Arco d'Alibert, Rome
1979 Galleria Cesare Manzo, Pescara, Italy
1980 Galleria Wirz, Milan
1981 Tokyo Gallery, Tokyo
1982 Galleria Piu Due Cannaviello, Milan
Galleria Piero Cavellini, Brescia, Italy
1985 Galleria Piero Cavellini, Milan
1987 Galleria Studio G7, Bologna
1988 Galleria Valeria Belvedere, Milan
Padiglione d'Arte Contemporanea, Milan
1989 Galleria Studio G7, Bologna
1990 Galleria Valeria Belvedere, Milan
Galleria Arco D'Alibert, Rome
Studio La Città, Verona
Studio Barnabò, Venice
1991 Galleria del Falconiere, Ancona
Framart Studio, Naples
Nabis Gallery, Tokyo
Gallery Ueda SC, Tokyo
Achilleion, Athens
1992 Edicola notte, Rome
Galleria Valeria Belvedere, Milan
1993 Nuova Icona, Venice
Villa delle Rose, Bologna
Contemporary Art Gallery, Mito, Japan
1994 Mito Geijutsukan Gendai Bijutsu Gyarari, Japan (catalog)
1996 Kyo no Machiya Gallery, Kyoto (catalog)
Fundació Pilar I Joan Miró a Mallorca, Palma (catalog)
1999 Studio G7, Bologna, Italy

Selected Group Exhibitions:

1972 *Biennale,* Venice (also 1976, 1982, 1988, and 1993)
1974 *Japan: Tradition und Gegenwart,* Städtische Kunsthalle, Dusseldorf
1979 *Italy and Japan in the Last Ten Decades,* National Museum of Art, Osaka, Japan
1982 *30 Anni d'Arte Italiana 1950–80,* Villa Manzoni, Lecco, Italy
1984 *Trends of Contemporary Japanese Art 1970–84,* Metropolitan Art Museum, Tokyo
1986 *Chambers d'Amis,* Museum van Hedendaagse Kunst, Ghent, Belgium
1987 *Icons in Contemporary Art,* Museum of Modern Art, Saitama, Japan
1989 *Biennale Middelheim-Japan,* Antwerp
Japan '89, Museum van Hedendaagse Kunst, Ghent, Belgium (catalog)
1990 *Temperamenti: Contemporary Art from Italy,* Tramway, Glasgow (catalog)
1991 *A Current of Contemporary Art in Japan,* Museum of Modern Art, Toyama, Japan
1992 *Documenta IX,* Kassel, Germany
1998 *9th Biennale Internazionale di Scultura Scultura Architettura Citta,* Carrara, Italy

Collections:

National Museum of Art, Osaka, Japan; Museum van Hedendaagse Kunst, Ghent, Belgium.

Publications:

By NAGASAWA: Articles—in *Nagasawa,* exhibition catalog, Rome 1975; *Sette Italiani e sette Giapponesi,* exhibition catalog, Tokyo 1981; and in *Casabella* (Milan), no. 390, 1974; *Flash Art* (Milan), no. 50, 1974. no. 111, 1983, no. 137, 1983; *Ohara Magazine* (Tokyo), no. 12, 1976, no. 1, 1977, no. 2, 1977; *Domus* (Milan), no. 605, 1980, no. 618, 1981, no. 631, 1982; *Panorama Lombardia* (Milan), no. 14, 1984; *Gran Bazaar* (Milan), no. 5/7, 1984, no. 4/5, 1985; interview with Gloria Vallese in *Arte,* vol. 23, no. 240, May 1993; *Nagasawa: Tra Cielo e Terra,* exhibition catalog, Rome 1997; *Nagasawa: Mimetizzazione,* exhibition catalog, Milan 1997. **Films and videotapes**—untitled film, Milan 1971; *No. 1,* Milan 1971; untitled videotape, Milan 1972.

On NAGASAWA: Books—*Nagasawa* by Salvatori Trotta, Milan 1972; *Japan: Tradition und Gegenwart,* exhibition catalog with text by T. Minemura and others, Dusseldorf 1974; *Nagasawa,* exhibition catalog with text by L. M. Venturi, Milan 1974. **Articles**—review in *Domus* (Milan), November 1968; review in *Flash Art* (Rome), May 1971; review in *Data* (Milan), September 1971; review in *Flash Art*

(Rome), May/June 1972; review in *Bijutsu-Techo* (Tokyo), August/September 1972; "Milan in Autumn" by Henry Martin in *Art International* (Lugano, Switzerland), January 1973; *8th Biennale de Paris,* exhibition catalog by J. Cahen-Salvadori, G. Boudaille, J. M. Poinsot and others, Paris 1973; "Hidetoshi Nagasawa" by Giacinto Di Pietrantonio in *Flash Art,* April/May 1990; "Hidetoshi Nagasawa" by Elena Pontiggia in *Flash Art,* summer 1992.

* * *

Born in Manchuria in 1940, Nagasawa began exhibiting his work in his adopted town of Milan in 1971. In the same year he held exhibitions in Rome, at which he showed several works including an aluminium plaque on which two arrows were juxtaposed. Alongside were bronze panels on which male members were represented on a tondo together with the names of great artists of the past. It was in 1972 that, with Trotta and Salvadori, Nagasawa published a catalog (from the Toselli Gallery) documenting a performance piece. In it, the artist is touching various bodily parts of a naked woman who is located at the centre of a large white canvas. The artist touches the woman until she disappears. As he continues to touch the canvas, the impression of the woman reappears.

In these early experiments, a poetic based on the contrasts between 'To Be' and 'To Appear' are outlined, in addition to the idea of the fragment as part of the whole, the relationship between East and West, and—most importantly—between past and present. This is the poetic which informs the work *Piroga* (*Open Boat*) of 1973; as published in the magazine *Flash Art,* it was accompanied by the caption: this open boat, constructed in chestnut wood, was made in Ortisei, following the plan of an original dating from 1800–1200 BC, found in Molina di Ledro and now in the collection of the Trento Museum of Natural Science. The current structure was made using only those techniques available to neolithic cultures, such as fire and appropriate metal instruments. In a later interview (1975), Nagasawa expressed his interest in ethnology: "For man, the most difficult situation is to lose his own culture in place of a new one in which he does not find his roots. That means death."

Nagasawa is profoundly interested in the fusion of his own Japanese culture with that of Latin races, particularly that of Italy where he now lives. A series of works produced between 1975 and 1976 recall a love and skill the Japanese have for working with paper, as in origami. Here is how Nagasawa describes his own work in this field: "to use paper in the sense of cooking food. I say 'cooking,' as I do not mean to find new ways of interpreting a particular material, but rather to aim at making it take over many different flavours while remaining itself." It is in this way that Nagasawa is interested in the direct relationship with matter—be it paper, wood or stone—following the natural characteristics of the material.

He is also concerned with finding the lowest common denominator of an aesthetic kind for natural objects, either subjecting them to modifications prompted by human intervention, or simply arranging them as part of a composition. A statement of 1975 reveals this deep involvement: "If the designer of a beautiful garden happens to see a magnificent Bernini sculpture, he will immediately understand it and will apprehend the degree of beauty in the work although expressed in a different language to his own. So Bernini would himself have done, without any medication, when faced with a beautiful garden."

Boat, a work of 1980–81, well illustrates this idea. The shell of a boat is carved out of a single block of marble, and the inside filled with earth. In the soil, a willow tree (Caprea Pendula) has been planted. The boat's shape is reminiscent of the basin of a seventeenth-century fountain with a rounded rim. The prow of the boat, like a little crest, suggests the waves of the sea. But then the tree occurs with its characteristic pendulous branches to remind the viewer that, after all, the boat is a fountain, the tree trunk is a water jet, and the branches are the spray. It was five years earlier that Nagasawa has spoken of Bernini and the Garden, and here his words are materialized in the natural fountain of this work. Such an equation not only supports his words but makes explicit the roots of the Oriental in his work and the influence of what has been absorbed during his years in Italy.

—Roberto Lambarelli

NAGEL, Peter

Nationality: German. **Born:** Kiel, 6 April 1941. **Education:** Kappein/Schiei, until 1959; studied art, under Wienert, Kluth, Gecelli and Mavignier, at the Hochschule für Bildenden Künste, Hamburg 1960–65. **Family:** Married Hanne Axelsen in 1966; children: Tina and Christoph. **Career:** Figurative "realist" painter, in Hamburg and Kleinflintbek, since 1965; founder, with Dieter Asmus, Nikolaus Stortenbecker and Dietmar Ullrich, Zebra group of painters, Hamburg, 1965. Professor of painting, Kunstakademie, Kiel, 1985. **Awards:** Deutschen Akademie/Villa Massimo Prize, Rome, 1968, 1976; Premio Fiorino, Deutsche Bundesregierung für Malerei, Florence, 1969; First Prize, *International Triennale of Coloured Prints,* Grenchen, 1970; Kulturpreis, Bundesverband der Deutschen Industrie, 1971; City of Freiburg Prize, *European Print Biennale,* Mulhouse, 1976; Kulturpreis, City of Kiel, 1977; *Kunstlerflag-gen fur Europa* Prize, Mannheim, 1983. **Member:** Honorary member, Freie Akademie, Hamburg, 1981; Honorary guest member, Deutsche Akademie, Rome, 1981. **Agent:** Fischer Art, 30 King Street, London SWI, England. **Address:** Klein Flintbecker Weg 24, 2302 Kleinflintbeck, Germany.

Individual Exhibitions:

1965 Galerie 14, Aarhus, Denmark
1966 Galerie 13, Hamburg
1967 Landesmuseum Schloss Gottorf, Schleswig, West Germany
Galerie Patio, Frankfurt
Musuem of Art, Vejen, Denmark
1968 Galerie 68, Kiel
Niederfriesisches Museum, Husum, West Germany
1969 Städtische Kulturant, Soest, West Germany
1970 Galerie Schmucking, Braunschweig, West Germany
Galerie Defect, Nürnberg
1971 Galerie Musterbert, Basel
Bilder, Graphik, Galerie van de Loo, Munich
Galerie Dierks, Aarhus, Denmark
Kunstschau Bottcherstrasse, Bremen, West Germany
Galerie Kafsack, Paderborn, West Germany
Galerie Walther, Dusseldorf
1972 Galleri Haaken, Oslo
Galerie Schlegl, Zurich
1973 *Werkverzeichnis 1965–72: Bilder, Zeichnungen, Grafick, Projekte,* Galerie Hoeppner, Hamburg

Galerie Hoeppner, Munich
1974 Galerija Krystofory, Krakow
1975 Fischer Fine Art, London
Grafik-Forum, Lübeck
Architektenkammer, Kiel
Galerie Lornsentrasse, Kiel
1976 Galleria II Nuovo Torcoliere, Rome
Galerie Kammer, Hamburg
Gallerie Dierks, Aarhus, Denmark
Schloss Clemenswerth, Sogel, West Germany
Studio Jaeschke, Bochum, West Germany
1977 Galerie Kafsack, Paderborn, West Germany
Kunstkreis, Nordenstadt, West Germany
Galerie Die Welle, Iserlohn, West Germany
Gambro, Hechingen, West Germany
Rathaus, Kiel
Palais des Arts et de la Culture, Brest, France
Galerie Schmucking, Braunschweig, West Germany
1978 Dragerwerk, Lübeck
Galerie Walther, Dusseldorf
Galerie Nouvelle, Horsens, Denmark
Schloss Homburg, West Germany
Werkverzeichnis 1972–78: Gemalde, Zeichnungen, Grafik, Projekte, Kunsthalle, Kiel
1979 Galleri Haaken, Oslo
Tel Aviv Museum, Israel (travelled to Haifa and Beer Sheva)
1981 Kunstverein, Mannheim
Galerie Remmele, Giefgen, West Germany
1982 Radicke Gallery, Washington, D.C.
Studio Jaeschke, Bochum, West Germany
Freie Akademie, Hamburg
1983 Kunstverein, Langenhagen, West Germany
1984 Kunstverein, Augsburg, West Germany
Galerie Nemo, Eckenforde, West Germany
Oberhessisches Museum, Giefgen, West Germany
1985 Kulturkreis, Rendsburg, West Germany
Kunstkreis, Hameln, West Germany
Randers Kunstmuseum, Denmark
1987 Museum Tallin, Estonia, U.S.S.R.
1991 Galerie im Bottshaus und Heimatmuseum, Eckenförde (catalog)
1998 Galerie Nemo, Eckenforde, Germany

Selected Group Exhibitions:

1965 *Internationale Osterausstellung,* Kunstforeningen, Aarhus, Denmark
1966 *Gruppe Zebra,* Landesmuseum, Oldenburg, West Germany
1969 *5 Maler unter 30,* Ulmer Museum, Ulm, West Germany
1970 *Gruppe Zebra,* Westfälischer Kunstverein, Münster, West Germany
1971 *Biennale,* Paris
1975 *Zehn Jahre Gruppe Zebra,* Fischer Fine Art, Stuttgart
1976 *Sport in der Kunst,* Kulturkreis der BDI, Dusseldorf
1978 *Realisten aus Hamburg,* Expositiezaal De Delen, Rotterdam
1983 *Realist Graphics from the BRD,* Havana, Cuba
1986 *Sport und Kunst,* Madrid
1990 *Trusting the Picture: 20 Years of the Studio Jaeschke,* Museum Bochum, Germany (catalog)
1996 *Recent Infusion: 50 Artists from North Rhine—Westphalia—50 Artists from Dusseldorf,* Kunstsammlung Nordrhein-Westfalen, Dusseldorf (catalog)

Collections:

Städtische Sammlung, Kiel; Sammlung Deutscher Ring, Hamburg; Staatsgemaldesammlungen, Stuttgart; Städtische Sammlungen, Karlsruhe; Neue Galerie/Sammlung Ludwig, Aachen, Germany; Bayerische Staatsgemaldesammlung, Munich; Kunstmuseum, Dusseldorf; Deutsche Akademie, Rome; Kunstmuseum, Basel; Musée Cantonal des Beaux-Arts, Lausanne, Switzerland.

Publications:

On NAGEL: Books—*Deutsche Kunst; eine neue Generation* by Rolf-Günter Dienst, Cologne 1970; *Peter Nagel; Bilder, Graphik,* exhibition catalog, Munich 1971; *Galerie der neuen Künste* by Heinz Ohff, West Berlin 1971; *Deutsche Kunst der 60er Jahre: Malerie, Collage, Op-Art, Graphik* by Julian Roh, Munich 1971; *Bis Heute: Stilgesschichte der Kunst des 20. Jahrhunderts* by Karin Thomas, Cologne 1971; *Deutsche Kunst der 60er Jahre* by J.W. von Moltke, Kapstadt, West Germany 1972; *Peter Nagel: Verkverzeichnis 1965–72: Bilder, Zeichnungen, Grafik, Projekte,* exhibition catalog, edited by Hans Hoeppner, text by J. Kruse, Hamburg 1973; *10 Jahre Gruppe Zebra* exhibition catalog, Stuttgart 1975; *Peter Nagel: Werkverzeichnis 1972–78; Gemalde, Zeichnungen, Grafik Projekte,* exhibition catalog with texts by Jens Christian Jensen, Bernhard Kerber and Duilio Morosini, Kiel 1978. **Articles—**''Wirklicher als in Wirklichkeit'' by Hanns Theodor Flemming in *Weltkunst,* vol. 62, no. 17, 1 September 1992.

*

As a contemporary painter I often find myself facing a conflict. Much as, on the one hand, people, things and my immediate surroundings have an intrinsic interest for me, which I would like to represent as much as possible, without compromise, yet I am also restricted by my intimacy with the creative materials, the exacting patterns of thought which arise in so ordering a surface that the picture is ''right.''

Of course I know that these two interests are not entirely incompatible, but a voluntary limitation to purely aesthetic problems might simplify many things. If I did without realistic appearances and made my motifs accessible through abstraction and deformation, I would have greater freedom to introduce what means means I wished.

I know these methods from my student years. At that time, as a reaction to tachistic unconnectedness, I had already undertaken the attempt to bring the object once more into play. And yet the object was always only secondary, in that it acts to certain extent as a peg on which to hang an artistic fantasy garment (compare the first printed graphics Nr. 1–3).

The more I committed myself to the object, and recognized its intrinsic worth, the more difficult became the formal solution of a painting. This heightened degree of difficulty is something which I have always found attractive; indeed from time to time I consciously set up new trip-wires for myself. Thus it pleases me to incorporate creatively or in a thematically significant way motifs which conceal within themselves the danger of the literacy, kitsch or reportage. A painting full of risks interests me more than an assured programme. Occasional sorties into the realm of the fantastical or decorative demonstrate my need to work now and then in a playful manner. To these groups belong the balloon-blowers and the still lifes with brightly coloured cloths, where the cloths have the advantage that they are able to be deformed, without having to work realistically any the less.

It can be asked why I have not made use of the opportunity of greater creative freedom and escape from the confusions of motifs. What have I gained?

There are amongst other things the following advantages. The realistic picture offers a stronger possibility of indentification and can facilitate access by the usually unskilled observer. Formal processes in the picture can be checked and subsequently evaluated.

Unrelated formalism on the one hand and plain naturalism on the other are the extreme dangers. The goal can only be to allow neither formal nor thematic decisions to be dominant over the other. The happiest case is a fluctuation of the two, demonstrating their mutual interdependence. Herein lies one of the most useful criteria of artistic quality. The intensity of the reciprocal action of the connection of form and reality constitutes in my opinion the substance of an artistic product. That is not something that can be said of bland realism.

—Peter Nagel

* * *

In the mid-sixties objective artistic representation was widely regarded as suspect. A group of young painters, who were then studying at the Technical School of Applied Arts in Hamburg and who were unable to envisage a form of painting that lacked objective content, formally rejected the (in their eyes) unacceptable stance of non-objective art. Calling themselves the 'Zebra' group they were initially widely known—for the first five years or so—as a group rather than as individual artists. Eventually, however, the individuality of the group's various members became apparent. Peter Nagel, a member of the group from its inception, soon distinguished himself from his friends by a high degree of critical and mathematical awareness. The latter is evident in the sharpness and precision of his drawing, in the almost glaring clarity of his colours, in the carefully selected moment of representation and the sharp fixing of the artistic process. Nagel's critical ability is apparent in his satirical distance from the scenes and people he represents (including himself). The coolness of the representational method and the objectivity of the criticism provide a reciprocal stimulus.

Besides painting and graphics Nagel has devoted himself equally—and with equal success—to printmaking, an area in which he has received several marks of distinction. During the last decade he has regularly applied himself to practical work, designing theatre sets and doing well paintings. He is a member of the Free Academy of Arts in Hamburg and professor of art at the technical college in Kiel. His latest artistic work is based on the tension between rigid contours and illusionistic plasticity and the written characters that appear in sections of the picture; the artistic element remains here an aspect of illusionistically represented objectivity.

—Heinz Spielmann

NAITO, Rei

Nationality: Japanese. **Born:** Hiroshima, Japan, 1961. **Education:** Graduated from Musahino Art University, Tokyo, 1985. **Career:** Lives and works in Tokyo. **Agent:** D'Amelio Terras, 525 West 22nd Street, New York, New York 10011.

Selected Individual Exhibitions:

1986 *Apocalypse Palace,* PARCO Space 5, Tokyo (traveled to Sapporo Capa, Sapporo)
1987 *Apocalypse Palace 6,* Gallery It's mo, Tokyo
1989 *Under the Distance: The Roof of the Light Is Flat,* Sagacho bis, Tokyo (catalog)
1991 *Une place sur la Terre,* Sagacho Exhibit Space, Tokyo (traveled to Galerie du Rond-Point, Paris; Oriel Mostyn, Llandudno, Wales, United Kingdom) (catalog)
1992 *Under the Distance: The Roof of the Light Is Flat, Drawing,* SAO Gallery, Osaka (catalog)
1993 *Namenlos 1989/1993,* Gallery NW House, Tokyo (catalog)
1994 *Potential Aspects of Life,* Gallery Shimada, Tokyo (traveled to D'Amelia Terras, New York) (catalog)
1995 *Namenlos/Licht,* Gallery Koyanangi, Tokyo (catalog)
Wait for the Beautiful Clearness to Visit You, National Museum of Art, Osaka (catalog)
1997 *Being Called,* Galerie im Karmeliterkloster, Frankfurt am Main (catalog)
1998 Gallery Jennifer Flay, Paris
Sculpture, Gallery Koyanagi, Tokyo (traveled to D'Amelio Terras, New York; Gallery Koyanagi, Tokyo) (catalog)
1999 Gallery Jennifer Flay, Paris

Selected Group Exhibitions:

1985 *Clear Garden,* Sagacho Exhibit Space, Tokyo
1992 *Centrifugal Sculpture: An Aspect of Japanese Sculpture in the Last Decade,* National Museum of Art, Osaka (catalog)
Blast: The Spatial Drive, New Museum of Contemporary Art, New York (catalog)
1993 *Prospect '93,* Frankfurter Kunstverein/Schirn Kunsthalle Frankfurt, Frankfurt am Main (catalog)
1994 *Art Today 1994 Sanctuary,* Sezon Museum of Modern Art, Karuizawa (catalog)
1995 *On Kaware 1954, 1954, 1956/Rei Naito 1991,* Nagoya City Art Museum, Nagoya (catalog)
1997 *Change of Scene XII,* Museum für Moderne Kunst, Frankfurt am Main
47th Venice Biennale (catalog)
1998 *La collection Yvon Lambert,* Yokohama Museum of Art, Yokohama (catalog)
1999 *Works on Paper,* D'Amelio Terras, New York
The MOT Annual 1999-Modest Radicalism, Museum of Contemporary Art, Tokyo (catalog)
2000 *Collection Lambert Rendez-vous,* Hotel de Caumont, Avignon (catalog)

Rei Naito: *One Place on the Earth,* 1995. Photo by Sakae Fukuoka. ©Rei Naito.

Public Installations:

Naoshima, Art House Project in Naoshima organized by Naoshima Contemporary Art Museum, 2001.

Publications:

On NAITO: Article—''Weighing in on Feminism: 18 Woman Artists Speak on How Feminism Has Affected Their Careers and Lives'' by Carey Lovelace in *Art News,* May 1997.

* * *

Rei Naito came into her own with large-scale installations such as *One Place on Earth* in 1991 and *Migoto ni harete otozureru wo mate* (*Wait for the Visitation of Brilliant Clarity*) in 1995. These installations consisted of a large tent-like space enclosed by fabric containing small and large objects fabricated with a variety of materials—wire, cloth, glass, wood, rattan, seeds, leaves, wax, string, leather, etc.—in strict, symmetrical arrangements. The objects were ephemeral and delicate, with little volume or mass. The simple forms recalling body parts, organs, toys, or ceremonial offerings were faintly illuminated in the dark interior, giving the whole the tranquil presence of a ritual space. This quality was reinforced by the artist's policy of allowing only one person inside the tent at a time. Because of this condition, the work could only be experienced by lone individuals from the inside instead of being viewed objectively from the outside. The intimate dialog that takes place between the viewer and the objects inside the quiet, meditative space gives the work a temporal as well as physical dimension.

The artist always stays with the work while it is being shown, arranging the objects inside so that it is exactly the same every day. She has said that these works cannot exist after she is dead. She sees the work as literally a part of herself. The use of craft materials and methods and images reminiscent of physical organs suggests feminist concerns, but these elements indicate an alternative sensibility of softness, lightness, and transparency rather than an ideological agenda and do not represent the core of Naito's art. She is concerned with answering a more universal, fundamental question: ''Is existence a blessing?'' Her work declares that the answer to this question is ''yes.'' Naito's installations are designed to humbly present a personal message from the artist to the world, but each viewer must read it alone.

Being Called of 1997 was a site-specific work installed in an old Carmelite cloister in Frankfurt. The space of the work was surrounded by curtains and, again, only one person at a time was allowed inside. One wall of the cloister bore a sixteenth-century mural depicting the history of the order, and Naito filled the space with over 300 orange organdy pillows, about six centimeters long, one for each of the people represented in the mural, who were all long dead. While her previous installations were based on an interior dialog between herself and the world, this work was motivated by a concern for others, for the dead. This was a change from an isolated individual consciousness to a larger realm including others, and it prepared the way for the next stage in Naito's development: the making of ''sculptures,'' single independent objects derived from parts of installations. Her first sculptures were the *Pillows for the Dead,* small pillows of the same kind as those in *Being Called,* but they are dedicated to all the dead of the entire world rather than to the specific group of people appearing in the cloister mural. Like most sculptures, they are exhibited openly, so that they can be seen at the same time by an unlimited number of viewers. Thus, Naito's sculpture, in its subject matter and mode of presentation, shows an expanded awareness of the existence of others. The sculptural works, which include walking sticks and strings of beads as well as the pillows, are concrete but symbolic objects. Like implements used in religious ritual, their extremely simple forms have universal meanings. Pillows provide rest and repose for the head, that is, the spirit. Walking sticks support and protect the body and at the same time show direction and summon up strength. The strings of beads both limit and connect space. However, these works do not guide or restrict viewers to particular meanings or narratives. Naito says that she makes her art out of inner necessity, creating images that she herself wants to see, and that she presents it in the space of everyday life. Light was an important element in her early installations, and it remains so in the recent sculptures. Made with white or lustrous materials, they contain, overflow with, and emit light. They create a special space, next to but slightly separate from ordinary reality, where they linger quietly, in a state of blessedness and grace.

Naito's next project is a site-specific permanent installation in an abandoned house on the island of Naoshima in Japan (2001). This project is related to a space where others once lived, and it will be the first of Naito's installations to exist without the presence of the artist. This development indicates that Naito's art has become more open, although her essential concerns remain the same. It would seem to prove that Naito has gained confidence in her answer to the question, ''Is existence a blessing?''

—Yusuke Minami

NAKAZATO, Hitoshi

Nationality: Japanese. **Born:** Tokyo, 15 March 1936. **Education:** Studied painting, Tama College of Art, Tokyo, 1956–60, B.A. 1960; painting and printmaking, University of Wisconsin, Milwaukee, 1962–64, M.S. 1964; painting, Graduate School of Fine Arts, University of Pennsylvania, Philadelphia, 1964–66, M.F.A. 1966. **Career:** Independent painter, in New York, since 1966. **Awards:** John D. Rockefeller Scholarship, New York, 1966; Painting Prize, Cheltenham Art Center, Pennsylvania, 1967, 1968; Drawing Prize, Moore College of Art, Philadelphia, 1968; Award of Excellence, *5th Japan Art Festival,* Tokyo and New York, 1970; Fine Work Prize, *Shell Art Exhibition,* Tokyo, 1970; Creative Artists Public Service Grant, New York, 1974; Color Print Prize, American Color Print Society, Philadelphia, 1975; Japan/U.S. Consortium for Environmental Planning and Design Education Grant, Ohio, 1982. **Agents:** Muramatsu, Gallery, 7–1 Ginza, Chuo-ku Tokyo; Tokyo Gallery, 6–18, 8-chome Ginza, Chuo-ku, Tokyo 104. **Address:** 361 West 36th Street, New York, New York 10018, U.S.A.

Individual Exhibitions:

1964 St. James Gallery, Milwaukee
1966 Alverno College, Milwaukee
1968 Cheltenham Art Center, Pennsylvania
1970 Pinar Gallery, Tokyo
1976 University of Pennsylvania, Philadelphia
Upstairs Gallery, San Francisco
1977 Print Club, Philadelphia
University of Pennsylvania, Philadelphia
Tokyo Gallery, Tokyo
1978 Mercer College, Trenton, New Jersey
Muramatsu Gallery, Tokyo
Newman Gallery, Philadelphia
West Chester College, Pennsylvania
1979 Soker-Kaseman Gallery, San Francisco
Eric Makler Gallery, Philadelphia
Pennsylvania Academy of Fine Arts, Philadelphia
1980 Muramatsu Gallery, Tokyo
Gross McLeaf Gallery, Philadelphia
1981 Mei Gallery, Tokyo
Bridgeport University, Connecticut
1982 Tokyo Gallery, Tokyo
1983 Ten Gallery, Fukuoka, Japan
Tochigi Prefectural Museum of Fine Arts, Utunomiya, Japan
1986 AIP Gallery, Philadelphia
Muramatsu Gallery, Tokyo
1987 Hara Museum of Contemporary Art, Tokyo
1993 Tokyo Gallery, Tokyo
1998 Gallery Kuranuki, Osaka
1999 Erikson Gallery, Philadelphia

Selected Group Exhibitions:

1963 *Wisconsin Painters and Sculptors,* Milwaukee Art Center, Wisconsin
1968 *American Drawing 1968,* Moore College of Art, Philadelphia
1970 *Expo Art,* Furakawa Pavillion, Osaka, Japan
1973 *Japanese Artists in America,* National Museum of Modern Art, Kyoto, Japan (travelled to Tokyo)
1975 *Young Artists,* Union Carbide Building, New York
1977 *Prints in Series: Idea to Image,* Brooklyn Museum, New York
1979 *Contemporary Drawing,* Philadelphia Museum of Art
1984 *Japanese Contemporary Paintings 1960–80,* Gunma Prefectural Museum of Modern Art, Maebashi, Japan
1986 *Contemporary Japanese Art,* Taipei Fine Arts Museum, Taiwan
1987 *Painting 1977–87,* National Museum of Art, Osaka, Japan

Collections:

Museum of Modern Art, New York; Philadelphia Museum of Art; Pennsylvania Academy of Fine Arts, Philadelphia; Brooklyn Museum of Art, New York; National Gallery of Art, Washington, D.C.; Tokyo Metropolitan Museum of Art; Hara Museum of Contemporary Art, Tokyo; National Museum of Modern Art, Kyoto; Hyogo Prefectural Museum of Modern Art, Kobe; National Museum of Art, Osaka; Setagaya Museum of Art.

Publications:

On NAKAZATO: Books—*Hitoshi Nakazato: Today and Yesterday,* exhibition catalog with the texts by Gerald Silk and Akira Tatehata, Tokyo 1987.

*

My image-making is concerned with using neutral shapes, lines and colors to define a chosen space. This results in an immediate and simple image which, at the same time, is perceptually complex and intense. And in this process of image making, I seek to achieve an original and personal experience.

Last summer for a solo exhibition in Tokyo, I painted a number of diptychs combining two paintings utilizing different color systems. In addition, I devised a small panel as a diagram to be attached on side. The diagram which I called ''common piece'' dealt with a certain aspect of the diptych and allowed written words and numbers to be included to expand the scheme of expression. It gave me an exit from the abstract painting within one level of activity at the same time it offered the viewers an entry into my paintings.

During most part of the time that I worked in my studio for the Tokyo show, the Iran-Contra Hearings were on television. I also watched from my loft window the police raid crack dealers on 9th Avenue. Could this be called a perfect painting background? Art cannot be made without social context. My continuous wonder has been what exists beyond the thinking frame of ''what has been done and what not'' and the art climate.

—Hitoshi Nakazato

* * *

Hitoshi Nakazato, having been reputed as a deft, excellent system-oriented painter in the sixties and seventies, became known as one of the most sophisticated Japanese artists who has succeeded in producing extraordinary works by making the best use of both Western modernist ideas for painting and the Japanese sensibilities, especially to color, in the 1980s. He was born in Tokyo in 1936, studied painting at Tama College of Art in Tokyo. He went to the United States when he was 26, and continued studying painting and printmaking at the University of Wisconsin and the Graduate School of Fine Arts at the University of Pennsylvania until 1966. He settled down in New York in 1971, and lives and works there.

In the late 1960s, Nakazato was engaged in pattern paintings with various combinations of identical forms in different colors; V shapes, for instance, in the *Penn Series, on Yellow* in 1966, each of them being comprised of one waved arm and its vertical or horizontal counterpart jointed to one another. He worked by predetermined system, exploring manifold but limited possibilities of color/shape combinations. Throughout the 1970s, he produced series of impressive paintings, mainly characterized by the rigorous lines. In the paintings such as *Chi Su Ma* and *Ma Su Chi* in 1970, he took advantage of the traditional carpenter's technique of line making. Stretching a length of cord, dipped in China ink, across a raw canvas, the artist picked up the cord, hit the canvas with it, marking a line with some slightly splashed smudges. The procedure was repeated several times and the painting appeared like a musical score without notes.

His idea of doing it seemed to be derived, for one thing, from the urge that he wanted his paintings free from any personal gestures of brushstrokes. More or less, it was the widely supported idea among painters in that period, for the purpose of guaranteeing the autonomy of the painting. There was, however, a more important concern for him since the beginning of his career, It was 'flatness,' a different approach to ensure the autonomy of the paintings. It was only through the flatness that he could show his true gift as a stunning color-field painter.

It should be underlined that he never lost his faith in both 'flatness' and 'objectivity' while bringing out the outstanding paintings with the extremely delicate, soft, unaffected, angelic, and tactile colors. But some slightest nuances of subjectivity could be traced in his paintings in the middle of the 1980s and from then onward. He rendered the boundaries between two color areas the gentle undulations with suggestive blurs, or applied the carefully weighted, smudgy brushstrokes at the edges of the canvases. The grids, rectangular outlines, and sometimes diagonals, drawn deftly by hand on the color areas, are characteristic of his works. They seem to act as if giving a definition to the pictorial surface in a clear, logical way, while making it easier for each of the applied colors to reveal its own, interacting nature in correspondence with other elements. Still, the undulating, blurred boundaries or smudgy brushstrokes succeeded in activating not only the adjoining color fields but also the painting itself.

In 1987, he invented an intriguing, unprecedented device to reinforce both 'definition' and 'activation' at the same time. Nakazato made small paintings, what he calls the 'companion pieces' with diagrammatic figures and hand-written words such as ''One Forth and One Forth'' or ''Four and a Half'' on gray backgrounds, and placed them side the larger paintings.

They are physically apart, but conceptually related, as the diagrams and words on the 'companion pieces' hint or pretend that they act as determinative agents for the larger canvases. The viewer might not elicit any relevant information from those diagrams and words, but cannot deny that they work as if defining something according to the unknown system, and activate the larger canvases next to the small canvases. It is notable that Nakazato achieved his outstanding uprecedented color-field paintings in combination with the conceptual activators.

—Tazmi Shinoda

NANNUCCI, Maurizio

Nationality: Italian. **Born:** Florence, 20 April 1939. **Education:** University of Florence, 1957–61; studied art, in Berlin and Florence. **Career:** Independent artist, Florence, since 1962: concentrated on operative methodologies, 1962–65; concrete verbal structures, visuals and semantics, 1964–65; phonological and electronic music, and uses of verbal communications, 1965–70; environments and sensory processes, 1967–71; neon as writing, computer-aided visuals and music, from 1967; tautological procedures, 1970–72; photographic researches on color in nature, 1973–74; multimedia practices, from 1975. Editor, *Exempla Editions,* Florence, 1970; *Méla* art magazine, Florence, 1976–1981, Recorthings, audioworks, 1978; co-ordinator, ''Zona Archives'' non-profit art organization, Florence, since 1974; co-curator, Base, progetti per l'arte, Florence, 1998. Lecturer and visiting artist: Ecole Superieure des Arts Visuels, Geneva; Maryland Institute College of Art, Baltimore; Helsinki Kuvataideakatemia; New York University; Elac, Lausanne; Fine Arts Academy, Reykjavik, etc. **Agents:** Victoria Miro Gallery, London; Gilbert Brownstone, Paris; Massimo Minini, Brescia; Martina Deterer, Frankfurt; Galerie Walter Storms, Munich. **Address:** Via Marsala 4, 50137 Florence, Italy.

Individual Exhibitions:

1968 Centro Arte Viva, Trieste
1969 Galleria Vismara, Milan
1970 Galleria Barozzi, Venice
Galleria La Polena, Genoa
1971 Galerie Thomas Keller, Munich
1972 Gallerie Segnapassi, Pesaro
Gallerie Flori, Florence
1973 Salone Annunciata, Milan
Galleria Christian Stein, Turin
Galerie Thomas Keller, Munich
1974 Galleria La Bertesca, Genoa
Neue Galerie am Landesmuseum Joanneum, Graz, Austria
Galerie Denise René-Hans Mayer, Dusseldorf
Gallerie Schema, Florence
1975 Banco Galleria, Brescia
Galeria Lydia Megert, Bern
Galerie Ecart, Geneva
1976 Galerie Muller-Roth, Stuttgart
Galleria Area, Florence
1977 Galleria Forma, Genoa
Galerie im Taxispalais, Innsbruck
1979 International Cultureel Centrum, Antwerp
Galerie Walter Storms, Munich
Galerie Sudurgata, Rekjavik
1980 Galerie Lydia Megert, Bern
Kunstverein, Braunschweig
1981 Coracle Gallery, London
1982 Vleeshal, Middleburg, Holland
1983 Palazzo Vecchio, Sala d'Arme, Florence
1984 Kunstverein, Frankfurt
1987 Art Metropole, and Instituto Italiano di Cultura, Toronto (toured Canada, 1987–88)
1988 Westfälischer Kunstverein, Munster
1989 Gallery Victoria Miro, London
Galerie Achim Kubinski, Stuttgart
Gallery Graeme Murray, Edinburgh
Elac, Lyon
1990 Galerie Martina Detterer, Frankfurt
Galleria Bruno Musatti, Sao Paulo
Gallery Insam Gleicher, Chicago
1991 Galleria Victoria Miro, Florence
Galleria Massimo Minini, Brescia
Städtische Galerie im Lenbachhaus, Munich
1992 Villa delle rose, Galleria d'Arte Moderna, Bologna
Villa Arson, Nice
1993 Usine Fromage, Frac Haute Normandie, Rouen
Kasseler Kunstverein, Fridericianum, Kassel
1994 Bibliotheque Nationale de France, Paris
Aarhus Kunst Museum, Denmark
1995 Wiener Secession, Vienna
1996 Ecole des Beaux Art, Bourges
Justified Choice of Dimension, Dadart Virtual Gallery, Florence
1997 Galerie Fahnemann, Berlin
Galerie Walter Storms, Munich
Galerie Guy Ledune, Brussels
1998 Rupertinum, Landesmuseum Salzburg
1999 Europäisches Patentamt, Munich
Cabinet des Estampes, Musée d'Art et Histoire, Geneva
Galerie Fahnemann, Berlin
2000 Biennale d'Architecture, Venice

Selected Group Exhibitions:

1969 *Biennale,* Venice
1977 *Documenta 6,* Museum Fridericianum, Kassel, Germany
1978 *Biennale,* Venice
1979 *Kunst als Photographie 1949–1979,* Tiroler Landesmuseum Ferdinandeum, Innsbruck (toured Europe)
1985 *Sul linguaggio e l'ecstasi,* Alvar Aalto Museum, Jyvaskyla, Finland (toured Finland)
1986 *Aspects of Italian Art 1960–85,* Kunstverein, Frankfurt
1987 *Documenta,* Kassel
1990 *Biennale,* Venice
Biennale, Sydney
1991 *Night Lines,* Centraal Museum, Utrecht
Intersezioni, Arte Italiana 1970–1990, Mucsarnok, Budapest
1992 *Lux Europae,* Edinburgh
Gappymayr, Nannucci, Weiner, Museuo d'arte moderna, Bolzano
Poiesis, Fruitmarket, Edinburgh
1993 *Poesure et Peintrie,* Vielle Charite, Marseille
L'art e le mot, Musee d'art contemporain, Lyon
Die Sprache der Kunst, Kunsthalle Wien, Vienna
Frankfurter Kunstverein, Frankfurt
1994 *Translucent Writings,* Neuberger Museum of Art, New York
Le saut dans le vide, Centre des expositions, Moscow
C'est ecrit, Frac Corse, Corte
The Century of Multiple, Deichtorhallen Hamburg
1995 *On Board, Aperto 95, Biennale,* Venice
The Vision of Art in a Paradoxial World, Biennale of Istanbul Bookmakers, Limoges
1996 *Chimeriques Polymeres,* Musee d'Art Moderne, Nice
1997 *L'Empreinte,* Centre Georges Pompidou, Paris
Materiali dell'Arte, Galleria d'Arte Moderna, Bologna
Foto Text Text Foto, Fotomuseum Winterhur
Heaven, P.S.1, New York
1998 *Au rendez-vous des amis, Identita'e opera,* Museo Pecci, Prato
Fotographie, Sammlung IV, Lenbachhaus, Munich
Soundscape, Sounds by Artists, Palaxxo delle Papesse, Siena

1999 *FarbLicht,* Städtische Galerie Würzburg and Kunstmuseum, Heidenheim
Die Gärten der Flora, Kunstmuseum Unserer Lieben Frauen, Magdeburg
Natura della Luce, Galleria d'Arte Contemporanea, Venezia-Mestre
2000 *Color to Light,* Beyeler Foundation, Basel
Re-play, Generali Foundation, Vienna
Dopo Paesaggio, Palatto Pitti, Florence
Stanze, Museion, Bolzano

Collections:

Stedelijk Museum, Amsterdam; Sprengel Museum, Hannover; Museum Sztuki, Lodz; Museum am Ostuall, Dortmend; Kunstmuseum, Aarhus; Museo d'Arte Contemporanea, Milan; Galerija Suvremene Umjetnosti, Zagreb; Bibliothèque Nationale, Paris; Centre Georges Pompidou, Paris; Museum of Modern Art, New York; Lenbachhaus, Munich; Musée d'Art Contemporain, Lyon; Villa Arson, Nice; Musée d'Art Contemporain, Geneva; Galleria d'Arte Moderna, Bologna; Gnam, Torino; Frac Nord pas de Calais, Dunkerque Museioh, Bolzano; Kidsma, Helsinki; Van der Heydt, Wuppertal.

Publications:

By NANNUCCI: Books—*Play Texte,* with Jochen Gerz, Paris 1968; *Universum,* Florence 1969; *9 Colors,* Florence 1970; *Exempla,* Florence 1970; *My/dum/my,* Florence 1970; *Definitions,* Zurich 1971; *Poemi Cromatici,* Florence 1971; *Nomenclature,* Oldenburgh 1972; *Schema informazione, Florence 1973–74; Writings,* Graz, Austria 1974; *Poem Poesie,* Naples 1975; *Rose aux,* Geneva 1975; *Provisoire et definitif,* Geneva 1975; *The Medium Is the Word,* Rome 1975; *M-40,* Amsterdam 1976; *Small Press Scene,* Florence 1976; *Sessanta verdi naturali,* Innsbruck and Florence 1977; *Art as Social Enviroment,* Lugo and Amsterdam 1978; *Star/scrivendo camminando,* Hinwil 1978; *Parole,* Florence 1979; *Mela Postcard Book,* Florence 1979; *Some Texts, Pages in Motion,* Florence 1980; *Some Texts,* Florence 1980; *To Cut a Long Story Short,* exhibition catalog, Middelburg 1982; *Up Above the World,* Florence 1982; *Some Texts,* Frankfurt 1983; *Image du Ciel,* exhibition catalog, Frankfurt 1984; *L. H. lives here,* Toronto and Aachen 1987; *Discothèque,* exhibition catalog, Villerubanne 1989; *You Can Imagine the Opposite,* exhibition catalog, Munich 1991; *Stored Images,* Bolzano 1992; *Provisoire & Définitif,* exhibition catalog, Nice 1992; *Light Times/Time Lights,* exhibition catalog, Bologna 1993; *Hortus Botanicus,* Stuttgart 1994; *Un viaggio verde: giardini botanici,* Florence 1994. **Videos—***The Missing Poem Is the Poem,* Florence 1973; *Sometexts,* Vancouver 1987; *Not All at Once,* Kassel 1993. **Records—***Readings,* Florence 1969; *Poesia Sonora,* antologia ricerche fonetiche e sonore, CBS, Milan 1975; *Audio Intellect,* Florence 1983; *Fluxus Anthology,* Florence 1989; *Keeping Time,* Bourges 1996.

On NANNUCCI: Books—*Anthology of Concrete Poetry,* edited by Emmett Williams, New York 1967; *Flash Art* 1969; *International Malerwochen Graz* by Wilfried Skreiner, Graz, Austria 1970; *L'Azione Concreta,* exhibition catalog by Paolo Fossati, Como, Italy 1971; *Dattilogrammi* by Carlo G. Argan, Graz 1974; *Konkretedichtung* by Siegfried Schmidt, Munich 1974; *Art et Communication* by Herve Fischer, Paris 1974; *La Escritura en Libertad* by F. Millan and G. Sanchez, Madrid 1975; *La Piramide Capovolta* by Luigi Ballerini, Padua 1975; *Parlare e Scrivere* by Renato Barilli, Marcerata 1977; *Autocritico Automobile* by Achille Bonito Oliva, Milan 1977; *Art Aktuell/Skira* by Jean Louis Duval, Geneva 1977; 1979; *Offmedia* by Germano Celant, Bari, Italy 1977; *The Record as Artwork,* exhibition catalog by Germano Celant, Fort Worth 1978; *Spatialisme et Poesie Concrete* by Pierre Garnier, Paris 1978; *Extra Media* by Enrico Crispolti, Turin 1978; *Maurizio Nannucci,* exhibition catalog by Fulvio Salvadori, Antwerp 1979; *Poesie Sonore* by Henry Chopin, Paris 1979; *Parola/Immagine* by Flavio Caroli, Milan 1979; *Identité Italienne,* exhibition catalog by Germano Celant, Paris 1981; *Books by Artists,* exhibition catalog by Tim Gest and Germano Celant, Toronto 1981; *Maurizio Nannucci: To Cut a Long Story Short,* exhibition catalog with text by Pier Luigi Tazzi, Middelburg 1982; *Maurizio Nannucci: Unus ex Curiosis,* exhibition catalog with text Flaminio Gualdoni, Florence 1983; *Snow, Weiner, Nannucci,* exhibition catalog by Peggy Gale, Toronto 1987; exhibition catalog with text by Marianne Stockebrand, Münster 1989; *NeonStücke,* exhibition catalog with text by Dietmar Elger, Hannover 1990; exhibition catalog with text by Helmut Friedel and Barbara Wörnag, Munich 1991; *Provisoire & Definitif,* exhibition catalog with text by Christian Bernard, Nice 1992; *Not all at once,* video catalog, Kasseler Kunstverein 1993; *Starlight, Turrell, Nannucci, Nauman* by Gabriele Detterer, Aarhus 1994; *Another Notion of Possibility* by Ulrich Wilmes, Dietmar Elger, Pier Luigi Tazzi, and Gabriele Detterer, Wiener Secession, 1995; *Art, L'age contemporain* by Paul Ardenne, Paris 1997; *Soundscape* by Paola Magni, Siena 1998; *Capire l'art contemporanea 1943–1999* by Angela Vettese, Venice 1998; *Un mobile home dans le désert,* Brussels 1998; *Where to Start From,* Munich 1999; *Verba Lucis,* Verona 1999; **Articles—**''Anthology of Concretism'' by Eugene Wildmann in *Chicago Review,* no. 9, 1967; ''Poetry as a Means for the Structuring of Social Enviroment'' by Eugene Gomringer in *Visible Language* (Cleveland), vol. 10, no.3, 1976; ''Quando l'arte si facon la T.V.'' by Daniela Palazzoli *La Republica* (Rome), 31 May 1977; ''Un Libro fatto di Marmo'' by Renato Barilli in *L'Espresso* (Rome), 26 February 1978; ''Rizoma e Struttura, intervista'' by Lino Centi in *Data* (Milan), March/May 1978; ''On Fluxus'' by Ken Friedman in *Flash Art* (Milan), October/November 1978; ''The Italian Art Scene'' by Henry Martin in *Art News* (New York), March 1981; ''Maurizio Nannucci'' by Sandro Sprocatti in *Segno* (Pescara) no. 34, 1984; ''Talking with Nannucci'' by Pier Luigi Tazzi in *Weststuff* (Florence), no. 2, 1985; ''Maurizio Nannucci: Ecrire n'est pas necessaire'' by Denis-Laurent Bouyer in *Sans Titre 37,* October/December 1996; Maurizio Bortolotti in *Domus,* no. 828, 2000.

*

After the ''Dattilogrammi,'' which were channeled into research work on concrete poetry, I became involved in situations that made me understand that there was another territory to explore. It could be called ''intermedia,'' and it includes a host of experiences that stretch from mail art to all of the Fluxus situations to concrete poetry. These experiences were not easy to classify. However, my attitude, once I had investigated interdisciplinary activities, was to respect my origins as a visual artist. I never thought of proposing myself as a poet or as a musician. I always considered myself as an artist coming from another discipline and trying to widen his references, all the while reducing them to experiences I had already faced visually—a different specific context that could be, say, electronic music or concrete poetry.

At times I have applied an idea from one discipline to a different discipline. At first, I'd elaborate on the idea visually, later with sound, and finally in terms of language. Sometimes the whole thing turned out to be smooth enough, sometimes really different things came out: what actually mattered was the method, never the result. Again, at times my interest would shift toward utilization of the media, which somehow suggested their conditions to me.

My work with media and different other materials was done round about the mid-1960s. It was the time of success of great art shows. A new situation with people looking for new propositions was created. These people were active the world over and acted as a magnet for identification and ideas. It was felt that the artist's work needed a new interpretation: it wasn't simply a matter of "producing artwork" but looking for a better system for a wider diffusion of ideas. I kept in touch with a number of artists who were motivated by the same stimuli. I think I forwarded something like a thousand single, typed pages. It was a way to give out correct information on my work, in an unassuming way.

—Maurizio Nannucci

* * *

Maurizio Nannucci is an artist whose work could be (and has been) almost endlessly theorized, since almost of all his widely differing pieces are marked by both a single-mindedness and a lack of physical substance that critics (especially friendly critics) can easily be uncomfortable with: they feel called upon to beef the work up into full-fledged intellectual respectability, and they usually start with Saussure. But Nannucci, as a "concept artist," is far from "hard-core:" his spirit is romantic, if not downright baroque (as evidenced, perhaps, in his motto, which is itself a work, "Always Endeavor to Find Some Interesting Variation"), and one does well to remember that the paternity of the concept of "concept art" is to be attributed not to Kosuth and Art & Language, but rather to Henry Flint and Fluxus. Nannucci is an inveterate wanderer in the realms of what Dick Higgins (one of the Fluxus theoreticians) has defined as "inter-media"—the little almost empty spaces that lie *between* the media and that allow a witty and playful mind to deal sometimes with nonsense and sometimes with a very clear perception of the way all rational and verbal systems are as though afloat in a fluid of silent and pre-rational, if not spiritual, presuppositions, presuppositions, in any case, whose very possibility of existence is never explained by the systems of rational explanation that are built on top of them. The fundamental perception, perhaps, is that mind is precedent to mental instrumentation.

Nannucci's very earliest works came out of concrete poetry: he called them *dattilogrammi,* and they consisted of images made with typewriters. The word "red" (*rosso*), for example, was typed a thousand or so times in red ink on a square of red paper. *Idem,* of course, for the colors (or the words) "yellow," "blue," "black," and "white." It's typical of Nannucci to have used only the primary colors. In 1967, he did an object called "Poem." It's a rubber stamp of the word "poem." In photographs of this work, one notices the obvious fact that the word on the stamp and the word as stamped are upside-down mirror images each of the other. A little later, Nannucci began to work with neon tubing: the illuminated script entitled "Phonetic Alphabet" spells itself out as *Abicidieeffegiacca,* etc., which translates into English's more precarious orthography as *eighbeseedeeeeefjeeaich* .... and to *zee.* The neon writing called "Corner" bends in its center at right angles and is of course exhibited in a corner. "Universum," from 1969, is a book that can't be opened because it's bound with a back rib down both it's right and left sides. "Sixty Natural Greens" is described as a proposal for a more accurate and scientific color nomenclature and consists of that many photos of that many different kinds of green plants, completed with a list of their Latin names, from Mirabilis Jalapa Green to Azalea Hortensis Green. A work from 1973 shows a sequence of nine photos of the artist's hand as it writes a word on a pool of water. Another photo work shows 90 images of the artist as he walks through the streets of Florence; it's completed by a map and an overhead photo of the area involved as well as by the list of the names of the streets that are strolled through. The path being followed spells out the word "star." At the Venice *Biennale* in 1978, Nannucci presented a work that consisted of a Piper Cub that flew through the skies trailing a series of blue letters that spelled out the message "image du ciel." While the plane was doing this, the artist sat in a beautiful old wicker chair beneath a potted palm which was set up inside the Italian pavilion. On the wall next to the be chair was a small framed photograph.

Nannucci has also been active in mail art, computer art, record making, book production, posters and postage cards. A descriptive list of his works could extend to considerable length, but even a partial list is proof that no form other than the list can deal with them: Nannucci's work won't yield to easily formulable generalizations.

—Henry Martin

NASH, David

Nationality: British. **Born:** Esher, Surrey, 14 November 1945. **Education:** Attended Kingston College of Art, Survey, 1963–67; Chelsea School of Art, London, 1969–70. **Family:** Married Claire Langdown in 1972; children: William and Jack. **Career:** Independent sculptor, living in Blaenau Ffestiniog, North Wales, since 1967; sculptor-in-residence, Grizedale Forest, Cumbria, 1978, and at Yorkshire Sculpture Park, Wakefield, 1981–82. Visiting instructor, Newcastle Polytechnic, Royal College of Art, Newport College of Art, Dublin College of Art, etc., since 1967; also instructor at workshop projects in the United States, 1980, 1983, 1987, Japan, 1982, 1984, and the Netherlands, 1982; research fellow, University of Northumbria, 1999. **Awards:** Welsh Arts Council bursary, Cardiff, 1975; prize, *International Drawing Biennale,* Middlesborough, Yorkshire, 1979; elected to Royal Academy, 1999. **Agent:** Annely Juda Fine Art, 23 Dering St., London W1R 9AA, England. **Address:** Capel Rhiw, Blaenau Ffestiniog, Gwynedd, LL41 3NT Wales.

Individual Exhibitions:

1973 St. William's College, York
1976 Arnolfini Gallery, Bristol
1978 Air Gallery, London
Chapter Gallery, Cardiff
1979 Arnolfini Gallery, Bristol
1980 Elise Meyer Gallery, New York
Galleria del Cavallino, Venice
1981 St. Paul's Gallery, Leeds, Yorkshire
1982 Elise Meyer Gallery, New York

David Nash: *Threshold Column,* 1990. Photo by Susan Ormerod. ©2001 Artists Rights Society (ARS), NY/DACS, London.

Rijksmuseum Kroller-Muller, Otterlo, Netherlands
Yorkshire Sculpture Park, Wakefield
Kilkenny Art Gallery, Ireland
1983 Third Eye Centre, Glasgow (travelled to Edinburgh, Llandudno, Swansea, Stoke-on-Trent)
Douglas Hyde Gallery, Dublin
1984 Kamakura Gallery, Tokyo
Nagisa Park, Moriyama City, Japan (toured Japan, 1984–85)
1985 Washington University, St.Louis, Missouri
Rijksmuseum Kröller-Müller, Otterlo, Netherlands (with Sjoerd Buisman)
Heide Art Gallery, Melbourne, Victoria
Aveago Gallery, Sydney
Galerij S65, Aalst, Belgium
1986 Juda Rowan Gallery, London
1987 L. A. Louver Gallery, Los Angeles
1988 Galerij S65, Aalst, Belgium
Toumuj Abbey, France
1989 Galleria Sculptor, Helsinki
Annely Juda Fine Art, London
1990 Louver Gallery, New York
1991 Centrum Stuki, Warsaw
1992 Louver Gallery, New York
1993 Klae Defabrik Odense, Denmark
1994 San Diego Museum of Art, California
1995 Gianni Giacobbi Fine Arte Contemporaneo, Palma de Mallorca, Spain
Beyond the Forest, Palau de la Virreina, Barcelona
Bat in the Box, Lizard in the Glove, Refusalon Gallery, San Francisco, California
1996 *Three Places: David Nash,* Cairn Gallery, Nailsworth, Gloucestershire
Croesau, Wyan, Llestr, Pasg, Oriel y Ddraig, Blaenau Ffestiniog, Wales
Line of Cut, Henry Moore Institute, Leeds
Forms into Time 1971–96, Museum van Hedengasse Kunst, Antwerp
1997 *Stoves and Hearths,* LA Louver, Los Angeles, California
David Nash, Hans Mayer Galerie, Dusseldorf
David Nash Sculptures, Kunsthalle Recklinghausen, Germany
David Nash: Language of Wood, PYO Gallery, Seoul, Korea
1998 *Red and Black,* LA Louver, Los Angeles, California
David Nash Sculpture, Galerie Lelong, New York
1999 *Workplace,* Haines Gallery, San Francisco, California
2000 *Sculpture and Charred Reliefs,* S65 Gallery, Belgium
Line of Cut, Gallerie Lelong, Paris
Wood Quarry, CVA, Cardiff, Wales
Sculpture at Schoenthal Monastery, Switzerland
Chicago Wood Retrieved and Renewed, State Street Bridge Gallery, Chicago, Illinois
Wood Quarry, Market Hall, Blaenau Ffestiniog, Wales
Twmps, Oriel 31, Newtown, Wales

Selected Group Exhibitions:

1975 *The Condition of Sculpture,* Hayward Gallery, London
1977 *From Wales,* Fruitmarket Gallery, Edinburgh
1980 *British Art Now: An American Perspective,* Guggenheim Museum, New York
1981 *British Sculpture in the 20th Century: Part II,* Whitechapel Art Gallery, London
1982 *Aspects of British Art Today,* Metropolitan Art Museum, Tokyo (toured Japan)
1983 *The Sculpture Show,* Hayward Gallery/Serpentine Gallery, London
1985 *Transformations in Sculpture 1945–85,* Guggenheim Museum, New York
1987 *A Quiet Revolution: British Sculpture Since 1965,* Museum of Contemporary Art, Chicago (travelled to San Francisco, Newport Harbour, Washington, D.C. and Buffalo, 1987–88)
1988 *Britannica: Trente am de sculpture,* Musée le Navre, France
1991 *Kunst Europa,* Kunstverein Heidelberg
1994 *Disclosures,* Mostyn Art Gallery, Llandudno, North Wales
1995 *Here and Now,* Serpentine Gallery, London
1996 *Sightlines,* Honiton Festival, Honiton, Devon
Endangered Spaces, Christie's, London
Ecce Ubu, La Maison du Spectacle, La Bellone, Brussels
1998 *50 Years of British Sculpture,* Lothbury Gallery, London
1999 *The Shape of the Century, 100 Years of Sculpture in Britain,* Salisbury Cathedral, Salisbury and Canary Wharf, London

2000 *The Painted Dragon,* Cardiff, National Museum and Galleries of Wales

Collections:

Arts Council of Great Britain, London; Tate Gallery, London; Guggenheim Museum, New York; Walker Art Center, Minneapolis; Rijksmuseum Kroller-Muller, Otterlo, Netherlands; Metropolitan Art Museum, Tokyo; Hiroshima Fine Art Museum, Japan; Tochigi Prefectural Museum of Fine Arts, Japan; Scottish National Gallery of Modern Art, Edinburgh; National Museum of Wales, Cardiff.

Publications:

By NASH: Books—*Briefly Cooked Apples,* New York 1973; *Loosely Held Grain,* Bristol 1976; *Fletched Over Ash,* London 1978; *Wood Quarry,* New York 1980; *Fellowship,* Wakefield 1982; *Stoves and Hearths,* London 1982; *Wood Quarry Otterlo,* Otterlo 1982; *Sixty Seasons,* Glasgow 1983; *Ki No Katachi Ki No Inochi,* Tokyo 1984; *Elm Wattle Gum,* Melbourne 1985; *Hole Veluwe Otterlo,* Otterlo 1985; *Tree to Vessel,* London 1986; *Wood Primer,* San Francisco 1987.

On NASH: Books—*The Condition of Sculpture,* exhibition catalog with essay by William Tucker, London 1975; *British Art Now: An American Perspective,* exhibition catalog with text by Diane Waldman, New York 1980; *A Sense of Place: Sculpture in Landscape,* edited by Peter Davies and Tony Knipe, Sunderland 1984; *Earthworks and Beyond: Contemporary Art in the Landscape* by John Beadsley, New York 1984; *Artists in Wales: Second Nature* by Eric Rowan, London 1984; *David Nash, Sculptor,* exhibition catalog by Norbert Lynton, Serpentine Gallery, 1990; *Voyage and Vessels,* Jocleyn Museum, 1994. **Article—**''David Nash at Louvre'' in *Art in America,* No. 202, October 1990.

*

Earlier, I used woodmill wood, regular, standard units; later, greenwood, fresh from the tree; now, the tree itself. The more I look at the tree, the more I see that tree: its space and location, its volume and structure, its engineering and balance. More than that, I see the uniqueness of each single tree, and beyond that still I see it as a great emblem of life. A potent vibrant tower, a whirling prayer wheel of natural energy.

I want a simple approach to living and doing. I want a life and work that reflects the balance and continuity of nature. Identifying with the time and energy of the tree and with its mortality, I find myself drawn deeper into the joys and blows of nature.

Worn down and regenerated; broken off and reunited; a dormant faith revived in the new growth on old wood.

—David Nash

* * *

Though David Nash was born in Surrey and went to art school at Kingston Upon Thames and Chelsea he very deliberately opted out of the London art scene shortly after leaving college and has lived and worked in North Wales, in the little town of Blaenau Ffestiniog ever since. This is his spiritual home, the place where he has developed his own highly personal and idiosyncratic art.

Trees are his main source of inspiration and he works with them sometimes as a woodman; sometimes as a forester; felling and hewing; planting and fletching; burning and charring; stacking and making rough carpentry. His has not been a reclusive, Thoreau-like existence, however, for his work is as approachable as the man himself and has aroused widespread interest both in Europe and as far afield as Japan. In the years he spent as resident sculptor in the Grizedale Forest and the Yorkshire Sculpture Park (the only time he has lived away from North Wales) he started several major projects and stimulated much local interest and participation.

He works in a very British organic naturalist tradition—the tradition of Gainsborough and Constable and in our own day that of Hepworth. Wordsworth advised ''Let Nature be your teacher''; and John Constable sought the ''pure apprehension of natural fact'' and counselled that ''the landscape painter must walk in the fields with an humble mind'' and should study Nature with all the seriousness of a scientist. Nash would seem to be in sympathy with Constable's approach with the reservation that he ''takes exception to the land being referred to as 'landscape,' referring to the land as 'landscape' is the same as referring to people as 'portraits'.'' The term 'landscape' he says implies a ''view instead of an organic reality.''

Some of Nash's tree sculptures consist of working on existing saplings, young and pliant enough to be manipulated into strange and suggestive shapes. In this he does no more than nature herself in some of the tortured distortions resulting from prolonged exposure to strong winds, for example. He may conceive and commence a project of planting which after a period of years will be tended to form domes or arches or other architectural shapes, being created and conditioned over time by the particular space in which they are cited. Trees, as he often points out, are 90 percent space.

Smaller, moveable pieces which can be set up in a gallery are often quirky and lighthearted. *Running Table,* for example, is a rectangular block supported on four spindly, splayed, branches so that the whole contraption appears to be scampering away. He often uses green wood which changes as it gradually dries out or is exposed to variations of temperature—a museum conservationist's nightmare!—but Nash accepts any accidents which occur both in the making and afterwards as intrinsic to the work. In another piece, a roughly constructed box which inevitably commenced to split in random places is called ''Cracking Box,'' and in his titles, both of the sculptures and of his drawings, there is a playful and witty use of words.

Nash's drawings are an important side of his work and are simple, direct and uncluttered. They too are often made from ''found'' materials such as earth, leaves, fruit juice, grass or charcoal from a fire, and show in diagrammatic form the evolution of his sculptures from their origin in the felled tree.

Nash's attitude to his trees is anthropomorphic—he responds to the personality of the different species seeing some as aggressive and brutal and others as passive and gentle and watches their individual characteristic developing over the years in his own plot of land ''Ca'en-y-Coed'' (the Field in the Trees).

His art may be seen as a response to the widespread alarm about environmental and ecological problems. One can but welcome such a direct and popular art which helps to focus on these anxieties and in so doing may lead us on to some solutions.

—Mary Ellis

NAUMAN, Bruce

Nationality: American. **Born:** Fort Wayne, Indiana, 6 December 1941. **Education:** Studied mathematics; art under Italo Scanga, University of Wisconsin, Madison, 1960–64, B.S. 1964; art, under William Wiley, Robert Arneson, Frank Owen and Stephen Kaltenbach, University of California at Davis, 1965–66, M.F.A. 1966. **Family:** Married artist Susan Rothenberg, 1989. **Career:** Independent artist and filmmaker, since 1966. Instructor, San Francisco Art Institute, 1966–68; sculpture instructor, University of California at Irvine, 1970; lives and works in New Mexico, since 1979. **Awards:** National Edowment for the Arts Grant, 1968; Aspen Institute for Humanistic Studies Grant, Colorado, 1970; Max Beckmann Prize, Frankfurt am Main, Germany, 1990; Wolf Prize for Sculpture, Herzlia, Israel, 1993; Wexner Prize, 1994; Awarded Golden Lion, Venice Biennale, 1999. D.F.A.: San Francisco Art Institute, 1989. **Agent:** Leo Castelli Gallery, 420 West Broadway, New York, New York 10012. **Address:** Home, Galisteo, New Mexico.

Individual Exhibitions:

1966 Nicholas Wilder Gallery, Los Angeles
1968 Leo Castelli Gallery, New York
Galerie Konrad Fischer, Dusseldorf
1969 Sacramento State College, California
Leo Castelli Gallery, New York
Nicholas Wilder Gallery, Los Angeles
Galerie Sonnabend, Paris
1970 Nicholas Wilder Gallery, Los Angeles
Galerie Konrad Fischer, Dusseldorf
Galleria Sperone, Turin
1971 Galerie Sonnabend, Paris
Galerie Konrad Fischer, Dusseldorf
Leo Castelli Gallery, New York (2 shows)
Joseph Helman Gallery, St. Louis
Ace Gallery, Vancouver
1972 *Work from 1965–1972,* Los Angeles County Museum of Art (retrospective; toured the United States and Europe)
1973 Leo Castelli Gallery, New York
University of California at Irvine
1974 Ace Gallery, Vancouver
Galerie Art in Progress, Munich
Galerie Konrad Fischer, Dusseldorf
Wide White Space, Antwerp
1975 Leo Castelli Gallery, New York
Galerie Konrad Fischer, Dusseldorf
Albright-Knox Art Gallery, Buffalo, New York
1976 Ace Canada, Vancouver
Leo Castelli Gallery, New York
University of Nevada, Las Vegas
Sperone-Westwater-Fischer Gallery, New York
Sonnabend Gallery, New York
1977 Nicholas Wilder Gallery, Los Angeles
1978 College Gallery, Minneapolis Institute of Arts
Leo Castelli Gallery, New York
Galerie Konrad Fischer, Dusseldorf
Galerie INK, Zurich
Ace Gallery, Vancouver
1979 Galeri Schmela, Dusseldorf
Marianne Deson Gallery, Chicago
Portland Center for the Visual Arts, Oregon
Hester van Royen Gallery, London
1980 Leo Castelli Gallery, New York
Hill's Gallery, Sante Fe, New Mexico
Galerie Konrad Fischer
Carol Taylor Art Gallery, Dallas
Bruce Nauman/Barry Le Va, Nigel Greenwood Inc., London
1981 INK: Halle fur internationale neue Kunst, Zurich
Nigel Greenwood Inc., London
Rijksmuseum Kroller-Muller, Otterlo, Netherlands
Staatliche Kunsthalle, Baden-Baden, West Germany
1982 Leo Castelli Gallery, New York
Sperone-Westwater-Fischer, New York
1983 Baltimore Museum of Art, Maryland
1985 Museum of Modern Art, New York
1986 Kunsthalle, Basel
Musée d'Art Moderne de la Ville, Paris
1987 Whitechapel Art Gallery, London
1990 *Bruce Nauman: Skulpturen und Installationen 1985–1990,* Museum fur Gegenwartskunst, Basel (catalog)
1991 *Bruce Nauman: Sculptures and Installations 1985–1990,* Musee Cantonal des Beaux-Arts, Lausanne) (catalog)
1994 Reina Sofia, Madrid, Spain
Leo Castelli Gallery, New York
Walker Art Center, Minneapolis (traveling retrospective) (catalog)
Hirshhorn Museum, Washington, D.C.
1995 *Bruce Nauman,* Kunsthaus Zurich (catalog)
1997 *Bruce Nauman: Image/Text 1966–1996,* Kunstmuseum Wolfsburg (traveled to Hayward Gallery, London) (catalog)
Leo Castelli Gallery, New York
Sperone Westwater, New York
Bruce Nauman, 1985–1996: Drawings, Prints and Related Works, Aldrich Museum of Contemporary Art, Ridgefield, Connecticut (catalog)
1998 *Bruce Nauman: Versuchsanordnungen, Werke 1965–1994,* Kunsthalle, Hamburg (catalog)
Bruce Nauman, Hayward Gallery, London (catalog)
2000 *Beckett/Nauman,* Kunsthalle Wien, Vienna
2001 *New York Video 1967–73,* ICA Gallery, New York
Bruce Nauman: Selected Work, Zwirner & Wirth Gallery, New York

Selected Group Exhibitions:

1975 *Drawing Now,* Museum of Modern Art, New York (toured Europe and Norway)
1976 *The Artist and the Photograph,* Israel Museum, Jerusalem
Painting and Sculpture in California: The Modern Era, San Francisco Museum of Modern Art (travelled to the Smithsonian Institution, Washington, D.C.)
1977 *Drawings for Outdoor Sculpture: 1946–1977,* John Weber Gallery, New York (toured the United States)
1978 *20th-Century American Drawings: 5 Years of Acquisitions,* Whitney Museum, New York
Made by Sculptors, Stedelijk Museum, Amsterdam

1979 *The Broadening of the Concept of Reality in the Art of the 60s and 70s,* Museum Haus Lange, Krefeld, West Germany
American Portraits of the 60s and 70s, Aspen Center for the Visual Arts, Colorado
1980 *Contemporary Sculpture: Selections from the Collection of the Museum of Modern Art,* New York
1987 *Avant-Garde in the Eighties,* Los Angeles County Museum of Art
1989 *The Saatchi Collection: Bruce Nauman, Robert Mangold,* Saatchi Collection, London (catalog)
1994 *American Drawings and Graphic Works: From Sol LeWitt to Bruce Nauman,* Kunsthaus, Zurich (catalog)
1998 *The Living Mirror,* Musee Cantonal des Beaux-Arts, Lausanne, Switzerland (catalog)
2000 *Rodney Graham and Bruce Nauman: ''The Nearest Faraway Place,''* Dia Center for the Arts, New York

Collections:

Museum of Modern Art, New York; Whitney Museum, New York; Guggenheim Museum, New York; Museum of Holography, New York; Albright-Knox Art Gallery, Buffalo, New York; Fogg Art Museum, Cambridge, Massachusetts; Art Institute of Chicago; City Art Museum, St. Louis; Stedelijk Museum, Amsterdam; Museum Haus Lange, Krefeld, Germany.

Publications:

By NAUMAN: Books—*Pictures of Sculptures in a Room,* Davis, California 1966; *Clear Sky,* San Francisco 1968; *Burning Small Fires,* San Francisco 1968; *L.A. AIR,* Los Angeles 1970; *Bruce Nauman: 25 Years—Leo Castelli,* edited by Susan Brundage, New York 1994; *Bruce Nauman: Interviews, 1967–1988,* with Christine Hoffmann, Amsterdam 1996. **Articles—**''Way Out West,'' interview with Elizabeth Baker and Joe Raffaele in *Artnews* (New York), summer 1967; ''Nauman,'' interview with Willoughby Sharp in *Arts Magazine* (New York), March 1970; ''Bruce Nauman,'' with Willougby Sharp, in *Avalanche* (New York), Winter 1971; ''Body Works'' in *Interfunktionen* (Cologne), September 1971; interview with Joan Simon in *Art in America* (New York), vol. 76, no. 9, September 1988. **Films and videotapes—***Manipulating the T-Bar,* 1966; *Opening and Closing,* 1966; *Revolving Landscape,* 1966; *Fishing for Asian Carp,* with William Allan, 1966; *Building a New Slant Step,* with William Allan, 1966; *Abstracting the Shoe,* with William Allan, 1966; *Playing a Note on the Violin While I Walk Around the Studio,* 1968; *Bouncing Two Balls Between the Floor and Ceiling with Changing Rhythms,* 1968; *Wall-Floor Positions,* 1968; *Violin Tuned D.E.A.D.,* 1968; *Slow Angle Walk,* 1968; *Stamping in the Studio,* 1968; *Bouncing in a Corner,* 1968; *Manipulating a Fluorescent Tube,* 1968; *Slo-Mo (Black Balls, Bouncing Balls, Gauze, Pulling Mouth),* 1969; *Walk Dance,* 1969; *Violin Film No. 1,* 1969; *Violin Film No. 2,* 1969; *Art Makeup No. 1 White,* 1969; *Art Makeup No. 2 Pink,* 1969; *Art Makeup No. 3 Green,* 1969; *Art Makeup No. 4 Black,* 1969; *Pulling Mouth,* 1969; *Walking in Contraposto,* 1969; *Bouncing in a Corner,* 1969; *Lip Sync,* 1969; *Revolving Upside Down,* 1969; *Pacing Upside Down,* 1969; *Studio Problems No. 1,* 1971; *Studio Problems No. 2,* 1971.

On NAUMAN: Books—*Bruce Nauman,* exhibition catalog with text by David Whitney, New York 1968; *Bruce Nauman: Work from 1965–1972,* exhibition catalog with essays by Jane Livingston and Marcia Tucker, Los Angeles 1972; *Spiralen und Progressionen,* exhibition catalog, Lucerne 1975; *Bruce Nauman,* exhibition catalog with text by Katharina Schmidt, Baden-Baden 1981; *Bruce Nauman: Neons,* exhibition catalog with essay by Brenda Richardson, Baltimore 1983; *Bruce Nauman; Werke von 1965 bis 1986,* exhibition catalog with essays by Jean-Christophe Ammann, Nicholas Serota and Joan Simon, Basel 1986; *Bruce Nauman* by Coosje van Bruggen, New York 1988; *Bruce Nauman,* exhibition catalog, with text by Neal Benezra, Kathy Halbreich, Paul Schimmel, and Robert Storr, New York 1994; *Leucht-Schrift-Kunst: Holzer, Kosuth, Merz, Nannucci, Nauman* by Andrea Domesle, Berlin 1998. **Articles—**''From Hand to Mouth to Paper to Art: The Problems of Bruce Nauman's Drawings'' by Jonathan Goodman in *Arts Magazine,* vol. 62, no. 6, February 1988; ''Clear Vision: The Prints of Bruce Nauman'' by Susan Taliman in *Arts Magazine,* vol. 64, no. 3, November 1989; ''Bruce Nauman: Vices and Virtues'' by Leah Ollman in *Hight Performance,* vol. 12, no. 3, Fall 1989; ''Lie Down, Roll Over: Bruce Nauman's Body-conscious Art Reawakens New York'' by Lois E. Nesbitt in *Artscribe International,* no. 82, Summer 1990; ''Bruce Nauman: Doing What Comes Unnaturally'' by Robert Storr in *Parachute,* no. 73, January-March 1994; ''The Trouble with Nauman'' by Peter Schjeldahl in *Art in America* (New York), vol. 82, no. 4, April 1994; ''Casting About with Bruce Nauman'' by Ann Wilson Lloyd in *Sculpture* (Washington, D.C.), vol. 13, no. 4, July-August 1994; ''Dada by the Numbers: Pater Nauman; Just Being Doesn't Amount to Anything (Some Themes in Bruce Nauman's Work)'' by John Miller, Pamela M. Lee, and Isabelle Graw in *October,* no. 74, Fall 1995; ''Being a Nuisance: His Work is Deliberately Off-putting, but Bruce Nauman has become the Most Influential American Artist of His Generation'' by Robert Hughes in *Time,* vol. 145, no. 17, 24 April 1995; ''Bruce Nauman: The True Artist'' by Jeffrey Kastner in *Art Monthly,* no. 186, May 1995; ''Bruce Nauman'' by Jean-Pierre Criqui, vol. 36, no. 3, November 1997; ''Bruce Nauman: Work in Progress'' by Joan Simon in *Beaux Arts Magazine,* no. 163, December 1997; ''Nauman's Beckett Walk'' by Kathryn Chiong in *October,* no. 86, Fall 1998; ''Bruce Nauman: The Matter in Mind'' by Joan Simon in *Tate: The Art Magazine,* no. 15, Summer 1998; ''Bruce Nauman and the Object of Anxiety'' by Parveen Adams in *October,* no. 83, Winter 1998; ''Samuel Beckett/Bruce Nauman'' by Daniel Birnbaum in *Artforum,* vol. 38, no. 10, Summer 2000.

NEAGU, Paul

Nationality: Romanian. **Born:** Bucharest, 22 February 1938; emigrated to England in 1969; naturalized, 1976; Romanian citizenship reinstated, 1991. **Education:** Bucharest and Timisoara primary schools; studied at the Academy of Fine Arts, Institute N. Grigorescu, Bucharest, under Professor Ghitescu and C. Cracium, 1959–65. **Family:** Married Sybilla Oarcea in 1967 (divorced, 1974). **Career:** Worked as accountant, draftsman, topographer and electrician, Timisoara and Bucharest, 1954–59; currently lives in London, working and exhibiting as the Generative Art Group, founded in 1972; part-time lecturer, Hornsey College of Art, Chelsea School of Art, and Royal College of Art, London, 1972–81. **Awards:** Centre Internationale de Recontres Award, Nice, 1972; Arts Council of Great Britain Award, 1973, 1975, 1978; *Tolly Cobbold Exhibition Prize,* 1976; Northern Arts Fellowship, 1979–81; British Council grant for exhibition abroad, 1981–84,

Paul Neagu: detail of *Last,* 2000. ©Paul Neagu, courtesy of Generative Art Trust.

1994, 1996; First Prize for *Triple Starhead,* Sculpture on the Strand, Westminster Council, 1987; First Prize, Monument Project, Kingston-Upon-Thames, 1988; Sargant Fellowship at The British School at Rome, 1991–92; Krasner-Pollock Foundation award, U.S.A., 1995; *Blue Ribbon Medal* awarded by Japanese Government (Konjo Hosyo), 1996; The Leverhulme Trust research award, 1997. **Agent:** Angela Flowers Gallery, 199–205 Richmond Road, London E8 3NJ. **Address:** 31c Jackson Road, London N7, England.

Individual Exhibitions:

1969 Amphora Gallery, Bucharest
Palpable Art, Richard Demarco Gallery, Edinburgh
Bauzentrum, Hamburg
1970 *Tactile Objects,* Sigi Krauss Gallery, London
1971 Compass Gallery, Glasgow
1972 *Anthropocosmos,* Galerie Rivolta, Lausanne, Switzerland
1973 *Tactile and Palpable Objects,* Serpentine Sculpture, London
Museum of Modern Art, Oxford, England
Paul Neagu and his Generative Art Group Hyphen, Sunderland Arts Centre, England
1976 Leeds Polytechnic Gallery
1978 Newcastle Polytechnic Gallery
1979 *Hyphen,* Elise Meyer Inc., New York
Third Eye Centre, Glasgow
Hyphen Installation, Institute of Contemporary Arts, London
1980 Norwich Arts Centre, England
Fusion, Project Gallery, Dublin
Liverpool Academy of Art
1981 Galerie Rivolta, Lausanne, Switzerland
Sunderland Arts Centre
1982 *Anthropocosmos,* Laing Art Gallery, Newcastle upon Tyne, England (retrospective)
1983 Liverpool University, Merseyside, England
Gallery K, Tokyo
Hyphen, Olga Korper Gallery, Toronto
Hyphen, Kamakura Gallery, Tokyo
1984 *Open Monolith,* Curwen Gallery, London
Galerie Rivolta, Lausanne, Switzerland
1985 *Catalytic Sculpture,* London Business School
1986 *Catalytic Sculpture: Court System,* Gallery K, Tokyo
1987 *Nine Catalytic Stations,* Serpentine Gallery, London (traveled through Great Britain)
1990 Gallery K, Tokyo
1991 First Romanian drawing exhibition, toured country
1992 *Catalytic Sculpture,* E. Suciu Gallery, Karlsruhe, Germany

British School at Rome
Second Romanian drawing exhibition, toured country
1993 *Catalytic Sculpture,* Economist Building, London
Epagoge, Flowers East, London
1994 *Newhyphen,* Galeria First, Timisoara, Romania
Brukenthal Museum, Sibiu, Romania
1995 *Sculpture—A Mental Cause,* Iorga house, Venice Biennale
*Ten Right Angles—Ten Right Angels,*Hungarian Cultural Centre, Bucharest
Unanimity, RomaniAlba Galley, Edinburgh
1997 *Retrospective,* National Museum of Art, Bucharest
Modern Energy Painting, Museum of Literature, Bucharest
1998 *Flash of Splendour,* Gallery A, Chicago
Endlessedge Hyphen, Flowers East Gallery, London
2000 *Whirlblast for Brancusi,* East West Gallery, New York
Ongoing Tornado, Henry Moore Institute, Leeds

Selected Group Exhibitions:

1973 *Earth Images,* Scottish National Gallery of Modern Art, Edinburgh
1975 *The Condition of Sculpture,* Hayward Gallery, London
1976 *Six Times,* Serpentine Gallery, London
1977 *Silver Jubilee Exhibition of British Sculpture,* Battersea Park, London
1981 *Baroques '81,* Musée d'Art Moderne de le Ville, Paris
British Sculpture in the 20th Century, Whitechapel Art Gallery, London
1982 *Aspects of British Art Today,* Metropolitan Art Museum, Tokyo (toured Japan)
Inner Worlds, E. M. Flint Gallery, Walsall, Staffordshire (toured the U.K. 1982–83).
1984 *Time and Space,* Visual Arts Center, Anchorage, Alaska
1992 *Constructive Art in Europe,* E. Suciu Gallery, Karlsruhe, Germany
1993 *Chelsea Harbour Sculpture 93,* London
1994 *Triple Starhead,* Goodwood Foundation, Sussex
1995 *Paul Neagu, David Nash, Andy Goldsworthy,* Tochigi Museum, Japan
1997 *Biennale of Small Sculpture,* Murska Sobota, Slovenia
1998 *Between Performance and the Object,* Museum of Contemporary Art, Los Angeles (toured)
1999 *Global Conceptualism,* Queens Museum of Art, New York
2000 *2000+,* Museum of Modern Art, Ljubljana, Slovenia

Collections:

Victoria and Albert Museum, London; Tate Gallery, London; Arts Council of Great Britain, London; Scottish National Gallery of Modern Art, Edinburgh; Stedelijk Museum, Amsterdam; Kulturbehorde, Hamburg; Musée Cantonal des Beaux-Arts, Lausanne; Ministry of Culture, Bucharest; Philadelphia Museum of Art; Art Institute of Chicago; Museum of Contemporary Art, Tokyo; National Museum of Art, Bucharest; British Museum, London; Albertina, Vienna.

Publications:

By NEAGU: Books—*Guide to Generative Arts,* 1977; *Hyphen—Ten Years of Hyphen,* exhibition catalog, London 1985; *DeepSpace and Solid Time—'Nine Catalytic Stations,'* exhibition catalog, Edinburgh 1988; *Epagoge,* exhibition catalog, London 1993; *Reorganisation of Nothing,* exhibition catalog, London 1996. **Articles**—''Palp Art,'' with others, in *Arta Plastica* (Bucharest), vol. 5, 1970; ''Objets-Gateaux'' in *Leonardo* (Paris), no. 3, 1970; ''Le Diner Neagu,'' interview, with Andrei Doicescu, in *Opus International* (Paris), April 1970; ''The Janus Effect,'' interview, with Stewart Scotney, in *Art and Artists* (London), October 1974; ''Gradually Going Ahead'' in *Artscribe,* no. 16, 1979; ''Hyphen-Maker'' in *Aspects,* no. 6, 1979; ''The Case of Horia Bernea'' in *Aspects,* no. 14, 1980; ''Some Notes on Fullers Visceral Turmoil'' in *Aspects,* 1981; ''Punk-Baroques '81 at the Museum of Modern Art Paris'' in *Artscribe,* 1981; ''Three Poems'' in *Aspects,* no. 29, 1985.

On NEAGU: Books—*Romanian Art Today,* exhibition catalog, Edinburgh 1971; *Paul Neagu,* exhibition catalog by Paul Overy, Glasgow 1979; *Paul Neagu* by Paul Overy, Sunderland 1981; *Epagoge,* exhibition catalog by Brian Robertson, London 1993. **Articles**—''Letter from Bucharest'' by Radu Varia in *Studio International* (London), July/August 1971; ''Products of the Split Personality'' by Paul Overy in *The Times* (London), 4 March 1975; ''Paul Neagu'' by William Varley in *Aspects,* Autumn 1978; ''Paul Neagu—ICA'' by Stuart Morgan in *Artforum,* November 1979; ''Crossbearings and Stars'' by Hugh Adams in *Art and Artists* (London), September 1980; ''Generative Context'' by Richard Demarco in *Studio International,* June 1981; ''Nine Catalytic Stations'' by Clare Henry in *Arts Review,* April 1988; ''Paul Neagu: Romanian Art in Diaspora'' by Deanna Petherbridge in *Arta,* no. 4/5, 1990; ''Paul Neagu'' by Anca Oroveanu in *Arta,* no. 6, 1991; ''Sculptor Shines in Sunlight'' by Richard Cork in *Times,* 13 September 1994; ''The Table of Silence'' by Mel Gooding in *Art Monthly,* November 1995; ''Paul Neagu—Utopia Artistului Integral'' by Magda Carneci in *22,* 15–21 November 1995; ''The Hyphen Sculptures of Paul Neagu'' by Donald Kuspit in exhibition catalog, 1998; ''A Life Measured Out in Hyphens'' by John McEwen in *Sunday Telegraph,* 15 March 1998; ''Uncorrupted Joy'' by Kristina Stiles in *Out of Action,* exhibition catalog, Los Angeles, California 1998.

*

Generative Arts has become an expression of a tall ambition, that of recreating a one-man comtemporary art, evolved on principles similar to those of Egyptian civilisations; a metaphysical faith with all its aesthetic counterparts.

Starting in 1968, I worked towards an ontological interpretation of the human body by crucifying its shallow relief (*Anthropocosmos*) as in its tactile and ritualistic accoutrements. In addition, through the 1970s and 1980s, I developed the three-dimensional forms of sculptures as nucleic, catalytic entities (*Nine Catalytic Stations*). By 1986, I put together sets of spheres implying integral paradoxes; compact yet flexible clusters of interstitial relationships: time/space, liquid/solid. These works exist under the titles ''Unnamed'' or ''Water.''

Working through ''deep space and solid time,'' a definition of catalytic sculpture, a meta-cosmology became evident. Stainless steel and bronze sculptures, like *Epagoge* (a nucleic litany), are visual and substantial demonstrations of a human soul with a modern disposition struggling to transcend its inherent contradictions.

When the complex nature of systemic-wholeness is understood organically, then archetypal forms like *Hyphen* (1975) or *Open Monolith* (1981) could transmute into visionary architecture; an imaginative mode of spiritual building which enhances, in proportionate fashion, social emancipation and individual participation. The enterprise, exhaustive as it might be, shows nothing short of radical confidence. It comprehends a generative tradition as an essential bonding force with thousands of years of proven validity and an amazing capacity of actualisations.

We say, ''Seeing is believing!'' The Generative Arts has transformed a belief into reality. A biological crust as cellular network, nine solid-state templates and an infinity of spheric moments, it is more than sufficient to redeem a congruent and extensive outlook.

Most significant in my sculpture search (over 35 years) appears, in retrospection, to have been that momentous inspiration in 1975 when I built the first truly anagogical sculpture named HYPHEN. At the time it was called ''Subject generator.'' This was a post-Duchampian, strange, machine-grinder of artist's ego!? Since 1975, the idea of hyphen dominated all other interests. Re-made, deconstructed, implied, drawn, welded, casted, used as tool, and recycled many times over. After 25 years it is still with me, as archetype and bastard sculpture (a hysteria of a life-time).

The evolution of this impossible absence, which is the ideatic space in which the hyphen fits best, has shown and performed large numbers of unexpected drifts and shifts. While its formal body changed from a skeletal pseudo-scientifical apparatus to a more unitary small, almost brancusian sculptural entity, skull-like, its underpinning expanded over to symbolic and metaphysical loopholes and vortices.

I understand it now as a genetic sculpture, because it inherits within its interstitiality a large amount of history. Art history, or rather closer and truer to itself, some history of sculpture (build) form.

Specialists like Rosalind Krauss or Donald Kuspit might find me, saying this, hugely pretentious, yet looking inside this hyphen-nation (!) as a philosopher. . . one could see it as the simpleton of an architecture, the blueprint of a new organicity, etc., etc.

Future time perceptions will tell no doubt.

My own conviction is nevertheless that the articulation of tensed energies from all three cardinal directions is nothing short of a god,. . . a god of transit, a sort of narrow, rite of passage. . . the only, solitary yes, but solid gate, open in the present.

—Paul Neagu

* * *

The difficult feat of vanishin' up one's own rear end has been achieved not once but infinitely many times by artists of the late 20th century. Furthermore, the manner in which this has been achieved would have greatly pleased Thomas Aquinas or any other of those medieval metaphysicians with a taste for calculating the number of angels able to dance upon a pinhead or the exact date of the Creation, for the artists have carried out the exercise entirely conceptually.

The abstract noun, once the prerogative of theologians and radical reformers, has now become the cornerstone of visual art; edge-information-system-paradigm-process, the list is endless; and these are not words used only by critics. The great majority of contemporary artists employ these words automatically and unconsciously, so pervasive is the orthodoxy, and their art is often no more than illustration of their ideas.

This tendency represents one pole of contemporary art; the fashionable pole. It retains its spotlit position by comparing itself with the opposite extreme, that of the anti-intellectual, it's-better-not-to-ask-questions type of art mysticism, and, of course, it's no contest.

That both positions share the same, highly debatable premises is not understood by many who have had to struggle through the British system. We must look for salvation to the eccentrics, the fetishists, and the foreigners. Which brings me to Paul Neagu.

Neagu makes sculpture, not that it looks anything like most contemporary sculpture; he does performances which abide by none of the conventions of ''Performance Art,'' and as for his drawing and painting . . . well, let us consider his drawing and painting for a moment.

It is a truism of contemporary art that a painter must establish his territory, become known for a style which he can then repeat with minute variations for the rest of his career. He has to do this so that buyers and critics can recognize his work. The fact that this leads to sterility and boredom is irrelevant in the face of economic pressure.

It is also a truism that a group with an impressive sounding name is a useful weapon in picking up public money and critical esteem. The name gives respectability, the group allows choice within a certain dialectical pattern.

Neagu belongs to the Generative Art Group. There are four other artists. So far, so good. The trick is that the four other artists are all Neagu, painting under different names and different styles. He was able to sustain this fiction long enough for the group to become established and go into the history books. The hunter is hunted; that is real radicalism for you. It also enabled Neagu to investigate other styles without the irritation of critics trying to reconcile them all for him.

Most British artists—the serious ones, which means most Bristish artists—find Neagu's attitude puzzling and prefer not to talk about him. He does not fit into the system; he does not frown when he works.

I doubt myself if Neagu is particularly interested in art at all. He *makes* things, using anything that comes to hand. His favorite materials are wood, leather, and string, but he does not limit himself to them. None of his objects follows on logically from any other, but they are all related. They are tactile and cerebral, simple and complicated, in a word—paradoxical, which is the essence of knowledge.

Enough has been written of the influence on Neagu of his native Romanian folk-art to save me the trouble; I doubt if it's important anyway. Such comments on stylistic influence are a method of dis-associating an artist from the reality of his actual time and place. It would be comforting to explain Neagu's art as being Romanian and showing the influence of Brancusi: doing so would remove him as a challenge to British and American art. The fact is that his origins have precious little to do with his quality, except in the negative sense that he has avoided the Western orthodoxy.

My first memory of Neagu was at the Demarco Gallery in Edinburgh. He had just come over from Romania and had unerringly headed for the only outpost of artistic illogic in the British Isles. He had taken over a basement room and hung it with objects, of wood, of leather, of fur. It was lit only by a single light, and one had to feel one's way around, from texture to texture. In the middle of the web sat Neagu, while a tape recorder twittered and squeaked in the background. I thought at the time that he would be able to design a magnificent set for *The Tempest.* There aren't many British artists I would trust with Shakespeare.

—Alastair Mackintosh

NECHVATAL, Joseph

Nationality: American. **Born:** Chicago, Illinois, 15 January 1951. **Education:** Southern Illinois University, B.F.A. 1974; studio work at Cornell University, M.F.A. 1975; studied philosophy, Columbia University, M.Phil. 1978; studied philosophy of art, Centre for Advanced Inquiry in the Interactive Arts (CAiiA), University of Wales, Ph.D. 1999. **Family:** Married Marie-Claude Levee. **Career:** Teaches theories of virtual reality at School of the Visual Arts, New York, 1999–2001, and Institute for the Electronic Arts, Alfred University; founder, TELLUS Audio Art Project (www.harvestworks.org/tellus/tellus.html); Parisian editor, *Rhizome Internet* (www.rhizome.org); artist-in-residence, Ledoux Foundation computer lab, Arbois, France, 1991–93, and Cite des Art Internationale, Paris, 1995. **Awards:** Pollack-Krasnere Foundation Award, 1989; grants from the National Endowment for the Arts, the Foundation for Contemporary Performing Arts, the New York Foundation for the Arts, and others. **Address:** 143 Ludlow Street, #14, New York, New York 10002. U.S.A.; 114, Rue de Vaugirard, 75006 Paris, France. **Web site:** www.dom.de/arts/artists/jnech.

Individual Exhibitions:

1980 *Methadone Median,* abandoned methadone center on west Canal Street, New York
1981 *The Occult Power of Technology: Part I,* P.S. #1, Long Island City, New York
1982 Real Art Ways, Hartford, Connecticut
Joseph Nechvatal: The Occult Power of Technology: Part II, The Kitchen, New York
1983 Brooke Alexander, New York
Semaphore Gallery, New York
Spiritual America, New York
1984 Brooke Alexander, New York (catalog)
Joseph Nechvatal: Grace Under Pressure, Gallery Nature Morte, New York
1985 Brooke Alexander, New York
Anders Tornberg Gallery, Lund
XS: An Installation, Gray Art Gallery, East Carolina University, Greenville (catalog)
1986 *Joseph Nechvatal: Photographs,* Greathouse, New York
Anna Friebe Galerie, Cologne
Vanquard Gallery, Philadelphia
1987 Brooke Alexander, New York
NeuerAachenerKunstverein, Aachen
Gallery Engstrom, Stockholm
1988 *Joseph Nechvatal Computer-Robotic Paintings: 1986-1987,* Illinois State University, Normal (catalog)
De Selby Gallery, Amsterdam
Galerie Antoine Candau, Paris
1989 Gallery Fahl, Stockholm
Anders Tornberg Gallery, Lund (catalog)
Shoshana Wayne Gallery, Santa Monica, California
1990 Musee des Beaux Arts de Dole, France (CD-ROM catalog)
Brooke Alexander, New York (catalog)
Galerie Karin Sachs, Munich
Galerie Antoine Candau, Paris (catalog)
1991 Shoshana Wayne Gallery, Santa Monica, California
1992 Galerie Antoine Candau, Paris
Tombeaux, Brooke Alexander, New York
1993 *Computer Virus Project,* The Saline Royale, Arc-et-Senans, France (catalog)
The Destiny of Painting, Galerie Karin Sachs, Munich
1994 *Computer Virus Project,* Espace d'Art Yvonamor Palix, Paris (catalog)
Information Bruit Culture, Galerie Traje, Besancan, France
Computer Virus Project, Galerie In Situ, Aalst, Belgium (catalog)
1995 *Les Archons,* Galerie Multimedia, Paris
Angels, Broken Hearts and Computer Viruses, Galerie Karin Sachs, Munich
1996 *Joseph Nechvatal Retrospective,* Galerie Berndt, Cologne (catalog)
Alt.Sex (with Mathias Groebel), Galerie In Situ, Aalst, Belgium
1997 *Das Neural Netz* (with Mathias Groebel), Galerie Karin Sachs, Munich
1999 *Viral Beauty,* Boston Cyber Arts, Boston, Massachusetts
2000 *es-satyricon 2000,* Universal Concepts Unlimited Gallery, New York
2001 *Virus Projects 1.0 & 2.0,* Moving Image Gallery, New York

Collections:

Los Angeles County Museum of Art, California; Moderna Musset, Stockholm; Israel Museum, Jerusalem; Rooseum, Malmo, Sweden; Saline Royale, Arc-et-Senans, France; Musee de Dole, France; Schyl Foundation, Malmo Konsthall, Sweden; Museum of Modern Art, New York; National Gallery of Art, Washington, D.C.; Museum of Contemporary Art, Los Angeles.

Publications:

By NECHVATAL: Books—*Collected Essays, 1983–1990,* Paris 1990; *An Ecstasy of Excess,* Mönchengladbach 1991; editor, with D. Gagneur, *Excess in the Techno-Mediacratic Society,* Arbois 1992. **Articles—**"Epic Images and Contemporary History" in *Real Life,* no. 11/12, Winter 1983; "State of the Art/Art of the State" in *Spectacle,* Fall 1986; "High Style" in *Arts Magazine,* April 1987; "Post-Simulation Decadence" in *Arts Magazine,* Summer 1987; "Theoretical Statement Concerning Computer Robotic Paintings" in *Documenta 8,* vol. 3, 1987; "A Prophylactic Discourse on Simulated Art" in *Code,* December 1987; "An Interview with Joseph Nechvatal" in *Caliban 5,* 1988; "Artistic Cynicism" in *Art Criticism,* vol. 5, no. 3, 1989; "The Artist and Familiars" in *Blast,* November/December 1991; "The Collapse of the 80's Image" in *M/E/A/N/I/N/G Contemporary Art Issues,* May 1991; "Innovations in Image Technology" in *M/E/A/N/I/N/G Contemporary Art Issues,* no. 11, 1992; "Interview with Joseph Nechvatal" in *Journal of Contemporary Art,* Fall 1992; "Immersive Implications" in *Consciousness Reframed: Conference Proceedings,* edited by R. Ascott, Newport, California 1997.

On NECHVATAL: Books—*Postmodern Currents: Art and Artists in the Age of Electronic Media,* by Margot Lovejoy, UMI Research 1989. **Articles—**"Joseph Nechvatal" by Jean Fisher in *Artforum,* January 1985; "The New Irascibles" by Robert Pincus-Witten in

Arts, September 1985; ''Joseph Nechvatal'' by Holland Cotter in *Arts,* November 1985; ''Joseph Nechvatal'' by Carlo McCormick in *Unsound Magazine,* vol. 3, no. 1, 1986; ''Joseph Nechvatal: Grace Under Pressure'' by Tricia Collins and Richard Milazzo in *Differentia,* Fall 1986; ''Joseph Nechvatal'' by Kim Levin in *Village Voice,* 14 October 1986; ''A Technology Under Control'' by Ben Marks in *Artweek,* March 1989; ''Computer Virus Project'' in *Bomb,* Winter 1994; ''Art Enters The Digital Age'' in *Art News,* September/October 1995; ''The Techno-Digita Sublime'' by Paul D. Miller in *Artbyte,* September/October 1998.

* * *

Joseph Nechvatal, originally a painter and performance artist, has worked with ubiquitous electronic information and computer-robots since 1986. His computer-robotic-assisted paintings and computer animations have led to a particularly original research commitment called the Computer Virus Project, an experiment with computer viruses as a creative stratagem.

One way of looking at Nechvatal's development since his first shows in New York City's alternative spaces in the 1970s would be in terms of the various media with which he had chosen to work, making major shifts in presentation without markedly altering his art's complex structure based primarily on telecommunications and its technology. However, the succession of pencil drawing, photocopying, photography, sculpture, and computer-robotic-assisted painting only tells part of the story.

In fact, in order to understand fully Nechvatal's most recent artistic options one has to make allusion to Nechvatal's progressive attitude towards technology in general and his existential commitments.

In 1983, Nechvatal wrote: ''Images of mass annihilation wrought by technology now provide the major context for our art and our lives. With profoundly disturbed psyches, modern people encounter their existential fear in the atom, for when technology relieved much of man's fear of nature it replaced that fear with one of technology itself.''

Three years later, Joseph Nechvatal accomplished the first decisive step in his career by adopting frankly the latest technology into his works before introducing from 1993 onwards the biological/medical/aesthetic concept of the computer virus as a leading idea into his art work.

Before analysing in more detail this option let me make an allusion to another aspect of Nechvatal's aesthetic commitment. He himself has stated that the focus of his painting is the interface between the virtual and the actual, what he terms the ''viractual,'' between immersion and withdrawal. The basic premise of his computer-robotic-assisted paintings is the exploration of ''omnijectivity,'' the metaphysical concept stemming from the discovery of quantum physics which teaches that mind and matter are inextricably linked under the influence of today's high-frequency, electronic, computerized environment.

For Nechvatal, art is then a matter of inventing aesthetic sensations linked to concepts of technology, a mental prosthetic. And the function of this prosthetic art is to create by extenuation different technological-aesthetic percepts. Thus his art is about a personal investigation into the conditions of virtuality—conditions which are not quite historically assessible yet.

Nechvatal's highly original computer virus project first exhibited at the Saline Royale in Arc et Senans, France, in November 1993, is closely linked to the spread of biological viruses, notably HIV. The artist has digitised his pictorial work, adjusting the images on the computer screen before introducing a computer virus unto the iconographical database. The images are then subject to alteration.

At the end of the year 2000 Nechvatal took a further important step. At that moment he finished the first phase of the reworked Computer Virus Project and brought it into the realm of artificial life, i.e. into a synthetic system that exhibits behaviours characteristic of natural living systems—in this case viruses. The new project actively propagates viral attacks on Nechvatal's image-files from the ''ecsatyricon 2000 (enhanced) + bodies in the bit-stream (compliant)'' series in real time and so, one might say, address some fundamental questions about the nature of life and death by simulating life/death-like phenomena on the computer. Here viral algorithms—based on a viral biological model—are used to define evolutionary processes which are then applied to the image-files from Nechvatal's ''ecsatyricon 2000 (enhanced) + bodies in the bit-stream (compliant)'' show which were exhibited in New York, at Universal Concepts Unlimited, in 2001.

In Nechvatal's virus project, essentially a grid composed of coloured cells, each virus is localized on a cell and can perceive the colour of the cells close to it. Each virus has an energy level and at each turn a small amount of energy is lost. If the energy of a virus is too low then the virus dies. A virus has its own programme that defines its behaviour and each programme is initially randomly generated, employing a user-defined instruction set and these instructions govern the chromatic, luminous, and resonant behaviour of the virus.

Like his earlier computer-robotic-assisted paintings of the mid-1980s, Nechvatal's current work creates immersive saturated space dominated by pattern. Fragments of soft human form are more clearly visible now, emerging from patterns of text overlay. Here the lines provide a sharp and vigorous opposition to the deterioration of the virtual body through viral infection. Such recent paintings as ''Viral attack: transmissioN, Viral attack: the cOnquest Of the hOrrible,'' ''Viral attack:regretS'' or ''Viral attack: piTy'' express fully Nechvatal's existential as well as his artistic commitment.

The general Fin-de-Siècle ornamental excess of Nechvatal's work gives to us a metaphor for the current computational conditions of seeing—and perhaps for our expansive conditions of technological-aesthetic being. In the rising and collapsing of alternative visualizations and unordered revelations encountered in his work, the circuits of the mind find an occupation exactly congruent with today's techno-informatic structures. In fact, if Nechvatal's preoccupation with fears, mental anguish, illness and death has never entirely disappeared from his projects their artistically prospective realization within an up-to-date technological framework allows him to come to terms with present-day life's complexity.

—Frank Popper

NEGRET, Edgar

Nationality: Colombian. **Born:** Popayan, 1920. **Education:** Popayan primary and secondary schools; studied at the Escuela de Bellas Artes, Cali, Columbia, 1938–43; studied, with Jorge de Oteiza, Popayan, 1944–46, and in Madrid, 1953; at Clay Club Cultural Center, New York, 1948–50; influenced by Henry Moore. **Career:** Independent sculptor, since 1937: visited Bogota, then travelled to Europe, 1950; lived in Paris, 1950–52; travelled in Spain and Mallorca,

1953; in Paris and the United States, 1955; painted original posters, graphics and sets for La Mama Theatre, New York, 1963; founder, La Mama Bogota Theatre, Colombia, 1970. Instructor, New School for Social Research, New York, 1958. Museo Negret founded by the Colombian Government, Popoyan, 1986. **Awards:** First Prize, *Salon Nacional,* Bogota, 1949; Travel Fellowship, Paris, 1958; Silver Medal, *Bienal,* Sao Paulo, 1965; Gran Premio a las Artes, *Salon Nacional,* Bogota, 1967; David E. Bright Foundation Prize, *Biennale,* Venice, 1968; Guggenheim Foundation Fellowship, 1975. **Agent:** Humphrey Fine Art, New York City. **Address:** c/o Humphrey Fine Art, 242 East Fifth Street, New York, New York 10003; and 37 East 7th Street, New York, New York 10003, U.S.A.

Individual Exhibitions:

1943 Palacio de Bellas Artes, Cali, Colombia
1944 Convento de San Francisco, Popayan, Colombia
1946 Biblioteca Nacional, Bogota
1948 *Edgar Negret/Eduardo Ramirez,* Sociedad de Ingenieros, Bogota
1950 Peridot Gallery, New York
1951 Galeria de Arte, Bogota
Galerie Arnaud, Paris
1953 Museo de Arte Contemporaneo, Madrid
1955 Peridot Gallery, New York
1956 Pan-American Union, Washington, D.C.
1957 *Edgar Negret/Jack Youngerman,* Gres Gallery, New York
1958 Biblioteca Nacional Bogota
1959 David Herbert Gallery, New York
1962 Museo de Bellas Artes, Caracas
Biblioteca Luis-Angel Arango del Banco de la Republica, Bogota
1963 Galeria de Arte El Callejon, Bogota
1964 *Edgar Negret/Eduardo Ramirez,* Graham Gallery, New York
1965 Museo de Arte Moderno, Bogota
1966 Graham Gallery, New York
Museu de Arte Moderna, Rio de Janeiro
Galeria Siglo XX, Quito
Casa de la Cultura, Guayaquil, Ecuador
Museo de Zea, Medellin, Colombia
1967 Richard Demarco Gallery, Edinburgh
Axiom Gallery, London
Negret/Rojas, Galeria Nacional, Cali, Colombia
1968 Biblioteca Nacional, Bogota
Negret/Cicero, Galerie Simone Stern, New Orleans
1969 Museo La Terulia, Cali, Colombia
1970 Stedelijk Museum, Amsterdam
1971 Galerie Buchholz, Munich
Städtische Kunsthalle, Dusseldorf
Museo de Arte Moderno, Bogota (retrospective)
1972 Galerie Bonino, New York
Arts Club of Chicago
1974 Galeria Bonino, New York
San Juan Museum of Fine Arts, Puerto Rico
Corcoran Gallery of Art, Washington, D.C.
Negret, Ramirez, Rojas, Galeria Monte Avila, Bogota
1975 University of Texas at Austin
Museo d'Arte Moderno, Bogota
1976 Galeria Belarca, Bogota
Center for Inter-American Relations, New York (retrospective)
Sala de Exposiciones, Caracas
1977 Galeria San Diego, Bogota
1978 La Galeria, Quito, Ecuador
1979 Galeria Garcés Velásquez, Bogota (retrospective)
Museo de Arte Moderno, Bogota
Galeria San Siego, At *FIAC 79,* Grand Palais, Paris
1980 Galeria Quintero, Barranquilla, Colombia
Galeria 9, Lima, Peru
1981 Fondacion Joan Miro, Barcelona
Sala Caja de Ahorros, Alava, Vitoria, Spain
1982 Galeria Atenea, Barranquilla, Colombia
Contemporary Sculpture Center, Tokyo
1983 Museo Espanol de Arte Contemporaneo, Madrid
Galeria Casa Negret, Bogota
1984 Galeria Avianca, Barranquilla, Colombia
1985 Museo Casa Negret, Popayan, Colombia
1986 Humphrey Fine Art, New York
1987 Museo de Arte Moderno, Bogota (retrospective)
Humphrey Fine Art, New York
1991 *Edgar Negret: From the Machine to Myth, 1957–91,* Museo de Monterrey, Mexico (travelled to Museo Rufino Tamayo, Mexico City)
1994 Museo de Arte Moderno, Bogota
1995 Museum of Modern Art La Tertulia, Cali, Colombia
Maison de L'Amerique Latine, Paris
International Festival of Biarritz, France
1996 Museo de Arte Moderno de Pereira, Bogota
Centro Cultural Conde Duque, Madrid
1997 Feria Internacional de Arco, Madrid
Galeria Art Espacio, Santiago de Chile

Selected Group Exhibitions:

1950 *Sculptures and Paintings from Colombia,* New School for Social Research, New York
1952 *Salon des Réalites Nouvelles,* Paris
1956 *Carnegie International,* Carnegie Institute, Pittsburgh
1958 *Biennale,* Venice
1961 *Geometrics and Hard Edge,* Museum of Modern Art, New York
1968 *Documenta,* Kassel, West Germany
1975 *Latin American Artists Today,* University of Texas at Austin
1976 *El Arte Colombiano a Traves de los Siglos,* Palacio de Velázquez, Madrid
1979 *Twenty-Five Years Afterwards: Nevelson, Kelly, Negret,* Museo de Arte Moderno, Bogota
1985 *Works of Botero, Grau, Negret,* Museum of Modern Art of Latin America, Washington, D.C.
1998 *Points of Departure in Contemporary Columbian Art,* Inter-American Development Bank, Washington, D.C.

Collections:

Museo Casa Negret, Popayan, Colombia; Museo de Arte Moderno, Bogota; Museo de Arte Moderno, Caracas; Museo de Arte Moderno, Santiago, Chile; Museum of Modern Art, New York; Albany Institute of History and Art, New York; Pan-American Union, Washington, D.C.; University of Nebraska, Lincoln; Guggenheim Museum, New York; Stedelijk Museum, Amsterdam.

Publications:

On NEGRET: Books—*Negret,* exhibition catalog with text by Franklin Konigsberg, London 1967; *Contemporary Art in Latin America* by Gilbert Chase, New York 1970; *Negret: A Retrospective Catalog* by Eduardo Serrano, Bogota 1987; *Edgar Negret: From the Machine to Myth, 1957–91,* exhibition catalog, with text by Jose Maria Salvador, Mexico City 1991. **Articles—**''Reviews and Previews: Negret'' by Frank O'Hara in *Artnews* (New York), November 1955; ''Reflexiones sobre la Edad de los Metales'' by Marta Traba in *Vinculo Shell* (Buenos Aires), 1957; ''Reviews and Previews: Edgar Negret'' by Lawrence Campbell in *Artnews* (New York), November 1959; ''News and Views from New York: Edgar Negret at the David Herbert Gallery'' by Marvin D. Schwartz in *Apollo* (London), December 1959; ''The World of Art, Pan-America: Five Contemporary Colombians'' by Marta Traba in *Art in America* (New York), Spring 1960; ''Edgar Negret'' by Maria-Rosa Gonzales in *Dictionnaire de la Sculpture Moderne,* Paris 1960; ''Fabricacion del Silencio'' by Jorge de Oteiza in *Aparatos Magicos,* exhibition catalog, Caracas 1962, reprinted in *6th Bienal,* exhibition catalog, Sao Paulo 1965; ''The Sculpture of Edgar Negret'' by Douglas Hall in *Studio International* (London), September 1967; ''Reviews and Previews: Edgar Negret'' by Rosalind Brown in *Artnews* (New York), April 1969; ''Der Bildhauer Edgar Negret'' by E. Trier in *Art International* (Lugano, Switzerland), Summer 1970; ''Twisting, Turning, and Binding: Edgar Negret'' by Juliana Soto in *Artnews* (New York), vol. 93, December 1994; ''The Enthusiasm of Edgar Negret: Museum of Modern Art, Bogota'' in *Third Text* (Abingdon, Oxford), no. 30, Spring 1995; ''Three Sculptors: Museum of Modern Art La Tertulia, Cali, Columbia'' in *Art Nexus,* no. 17, July/September 1995.

* * *

Edgar Negret is a Colombian sculptor who the more he was introduced to modern idioms and nonobjective concepts, the more he seemed paradoxically to reflect in his work something of the silent dialogue between ancient monolithic style and a communal memory not yet overlaid by the superfluous data of intervening civilizations.

He was slow in maturing, though by 1949 while relating to figurative tradition he had assimilated Moore's penetration of the mass. From 1954 he switched his attitude towards metal constructions, and from this point they assumed the open situation rising from flat ground rather than the top of a pedestal. This integration with environment none the less concentrated the axis on a central base and profiles strongly marked by cut-out shapes—signals, arms, slots and brackets—set up system of iconic semaphors. As an admirer of both Gaudi and Calder, he simulated a style of metallic rococo, and the illumination of his flat metal by bright reds and oranges instilled a note of carnival to static constructions, while breaking up the tonal mass in light.

''Emblem for an Aquarium'' (1954) has its abstract simplicity, while its polychrome shells project unstressed affinities with fish. In the 1960s he operated with large structures of sheet metal, chiefly aluminum, symbolizing the mechanical power of screws and propellors as they might be embodied in entities of morphological character. Negret found an apt concrete weight to his formal syntax, placing the sheer planes and flanged girders as physical embodiments of abstract relationships that were sums of simplified complexity. They took poetic solidities economically in reduced dimensions of architectural scope. In works such as ''The Bridge'' and ''Stanchion 2'' of 1968–70 the massive rivetted and bolted girders are patterned by the repetition of the fastening nuts and heads in the way a cathedral is ornamented by its functional buttressing, Gothic effects being heightened by the lozenge shaped holes.

This identification with architecture continues alongside the airborne spirit of much of Negret's metaphoric imagery. ''Cape Kennedy'' (1966) has its obvious connection with space travel in its crude simplicity yet by that fact implying untold energy in its suggestion of upward angled thrust. ''Navigators'' also combines the helmeted astronaut image with the centrifugal spirit of automotive power. ''Temple'' (1971) is a structure conceived in voided grandeur, defining impressive proportions of space and converting straight-edged girders into contemporary capitals bearing measured architectural decoration in their flanges and bolt-heads.

Negret is singularly outstanding for his affirmation of contemporary man-released power transfigured to optimist paraphrase in organic poetry. His complex yet simple monoliths celebrate man's capacity to evolve for good instead of evil, for exploration rather than for destruction; his clean-cut constructions stand for classical order of tensed proportion and inhabited dignity.

—G.S. Whittet

NEIMAN, Yehuda

Nationality: French, Israeli. **Born:** Warsaw, Poland, 22 October 1931. **Education:** Fine Art Academy, Tel Aviv, Israel, 1945–49; Decorative Art School, Paris, 1954. **Military Service:** Served 2 years in the Israeli Navy. **Family:** Married Marie Therese in 1962; son: Emmanuel, born in 1964; daughter: Laure, born in 1966. **Awards:** Chevalier des Arts et Lettres. **Address:** 86 rue Bobillot, 75013 Paris, France; 191 rue de Àlesia, 75014 Paris, France.

Selected Individual Exhibitions:

1955 Galerie Chemerinsky, Tel Aviv
1957 New Vision Center, London
1958 Galerie Obelisk, London
Galerie La Salita, Rome
1960 Galerie Drian, London
1963 Galerie Couper, London
1964 Galerie Hadassa, Tel Aviv
1965 Galerie Municipale du Luxembourg, Luxembourg
1967 Galerie Cazenave, Paris
1968 Galerie Yoseido, Tokyo
1970 Musée National d'Argentine, Buenos Aires
1971 Galerie Thelen, Cologne
Musée d'art moderne, Cordova, Argentina
1975 Bon à Tirer, Milan
1979 La Closerie des Lilas, Paris
1982 *Portraits, Mois de la Photo,* J. & J. Donguy, Paris
1989 Musée Ouvert, Migdal Tefen, Israel

1998 Sa-Nostra, La Sala de Cultura, Formentera
2001 Sa-Nostra, La Sala de Cultura, Ibiza and Formentera

Selected Group Exhibitions:

1955 Salon de la Jeune Peinture, Paris
1956 New Vision Center, London
1959 Musée d'Art Moderne, Haïfa
Première Biennale de Paris
1961 Biennale de Paris
1966 *Peinture sur Métal,* Musée d'Art Moderne, Tel Aviv
1967 *Sculptures,* Galerie Obelisk, London
Labyrinthe, Musée d'Israel, Jerusalem
1968 *Erotic Art,* Musée d'Art Moderne, Aarhus, Denmark
1969 Musée d'art moderne, Bucarest
Erotic Art, Kunstverein, Munich and Hamburg
1970 Japanese Art Society, Tokyo, Yokohama, and Sendai
1971 Le Nouveau Musée de Tel Aviv, Israel
1979 *Mec-Art,* Galerie Il Dialogo, Milan
1981 *Témoignage 81,* Centre Georges Pompidou, Paris
1984 *1956–1966,* New Vision Center, London
1987 FIAC, Paris
1990 *Couleurs de la Vie,* Bibliothèque Nationale, Paris, and Centro Cultural de La Villa, Madrid
1994 *Le Temps de l'Ailleurs,* Galerie Lara Vincy, Paris
1999 *L'Art dels 70,* Museu d'Art Contemporani d'Eivissa, Spain
2000 *Art and Cigar,* Galerie Flak, Paris
Works on Paper, Espace Belleville, Paris
2001 *Art and Cigar,* Beyrout Simaa Salon Art and Architecture

Collections:

Fonds National d'Art Contemporain, Paris; Kunstverein, Düsseldorf; Musée d'Israel, Jerusalem; Musée d'Art Moderne, Rio de Janeiro; Moderna Museet, Stockholm; Musée d'Art Moderne, Tel Aviv; Musée d'Art Moderne de la Ville de Paris; Bibliothèque Nationale, Paris; Maison Européenne de la Photographie, Paris.

Publications:

By NEIMAN: Books—*Les Milles et Une Bibles du Sexe,* illustrations by Neiman, with text by Utto Rodolph, 1967; *Past Continuous,* illustrations by Neiman, with text by Jacob Shabtai, Israel 1977. **Articles—**''Mec-Art'' in *Essere,* 1968; ''New Art, New Technic'' interview with Yehuda Neiman in *Bijutsu Techo,* February 1969. **Films—***Paris Top Secret* by Van Bell, 1967; *La Poupée,* 1968/71.

On NEIMAN: Books—*Lyrisme et Abstraction* by Pierre Restany, Milan 1960; *Erotic Art* by Drs. Phyllis and Elisabeth Kronhausen, 1969; *The New Painting* by Udo Kulterman, 1970; *La Sculpture Moderne en France Depuis 1950* by Ionel Jianou, Aube Lardera and Gérard Xuriguera, Paris 1982; *Les Figurations* by Gérard Xuriguera, Paris 1985; *Le Pastel* by Jean-Louis Beaudonnet, Paris 1994. **Articles—**''Un Mécano Pour Initiés'' by Christian Bretagne in *Le Nouveau Candide,* vol. 8, no. 5, 1966; ''Yehuda Neiman'' by Jean-Louis Swiners in *Terre d'Images,* no. 33, 1966; ''Neiman'' by Sinichi Seguy in *Art et Design,* 1968; ''Entre Nous'' by Ruth Cole in *Japan Times,* 1968; ''Yehuda Neiman'' by Jorge Glusberg in *Fotovision,* vol. 5, no. 6, 1971; ''Osucesso dos Cavalos em Paris'' by Tati Bueno in *Journal do Brasil,* 1979; ''Une Sensibilité à Fleur de Peau'' by Gérard Xuriguera in *Demeures et Château,* no. 48, 1988; ''Presse-Papiers'' by Geneviève Jurgensen in *La Croix,* vol. 16, no. 5; *La Mazarine,* with text by Pierre Restany, 1997.

* * *

Yehuda Neiman is a trained painter who at the beginning of the 1950s left Israel for Paris and who very quickly joined the Ecole de Paris at a moment, immediately after the Second World War, when it was still very much alive. There he befriended French and foreign artists, such as Bryen, Halpern, Lan-Bar, Marfaing, and Bertini, among others. They all belonged to a tendency diversely described as lyrical, tachist, or ''nuagist'' abstraction. Later, Neiman became also a photographer and a sculptor.

At the beginning, Neiman practised a post-Cubist painting but abstract graphic signs of a distinctly calligraphic origin soon appeared in his pictures, under the double influence of Tal-Coat and Fautrier; these graphic signs are gradually followed by black patches and iridescent colours which emerged delicately from the background due to a perfect command of the mellowness and gradualness of colours and in a fine discretion of tones. The artist employs often an almost monochromatic grey colour at a moment when Yves Klein paints his immaterial blue monochromes. Nevertheless the pinky grey is used by Neiman in a totally different spirit since it is not in the least conceived with a metaphysical preoccupation. It is true that the personality of Neiman predisposes him to control, as much as it is possible, his pulsions and effusions. In any case, the scale of greys utilized by him then in his paintings bring him already close to the shadows and lights, the grain of the support and the tactile softness of a photographic portrait or nude at the time of early black and white photography.

It is therefore not surprising that starting from about 1964, Neiman gave up painting in order to devote himself to photography. He produces then a series of photos of flowers, horses and landscapes as well as a number of portraits and nudes. Some art theorists have advanced that, tired of repetitious abstract painting, he had wanted to renew his links with figurative art thanks to photography whose highly structured nature favours the choice of a clearly defined object. It could be added that the photographic medium in comparison with painting, is one of enlarged communication since it requires the artist to leave his studio and to participate actively in social life. It follows that the inner life of the artist is affected; in other words the photographic medium acts as an additional constraint which corresponds entirely with Neiman's exigence for rigorousness.

Neiman's photographic activity is mainly concerned, at least quantitatively, with portraiture and nudes. The photographs of faces are mainly taken on the occasion of encounters with other artists, art critics, or museum curators, that is to say with his partners belonging to the international art world. Neiman is in fact a great traveller who does not try to capture narrowly the identities of persons nor any of their specific national characteristics. His works attempt, on the contrary, to attain a universal dimension through the interplay of a multitude of countenances and personalities. Once the first phase of the photographic seizure of the image is accomplished, the really creative work begins for the artist in the solitude of his studio-laboratory, a place where the phase of reflection and research is developed. This stage of creation can be assimilated to a deferred exchange of long duration between the photographer and his model. The original image is then either cut up, fragmented, or multiplied.

This confers to the model a kind of transpersonal dynamic through the photo-mechanical report of the image onto a canvas or a sensitized aluminum plate. The slight mirroring of the metallic surface thus favours an effect of movement and vitality.

As to the photographed nudes, they are never personalized and can neither be considered as anecdotical since they are composed by parts of the female body and assembled according to the principle of "collage" as well as being distorted by the manipulations inherent in the photographic technique. Their force and their elegance are due to a suggested eroticism which bears no relation to the crude eroticism of Picasso but is much closer to the half figurative, half abstract allusive nudes of Fautrier. With the technique of the photo-mechanical report of the image which permits the multiplication of the works, Neiman proposes differently coloured versions of them in delicate tints: smoky blue, fuchsia pink, mandarin orange, etc. These appear in the images of flowers, animals, towns and landscapes, as well as in the portraits and the nudes.

It is probably the photographed nudes which have led Neiman to confront himself with the third dimension by modelling directly in plaster or by cutting marble. In the latter case the chipping and the rendering of the subject are those of classical sculpture while the sensuality which can be discerned in the curves obtained by direct modelling remains that of a perfectly real hip, belly, or breast. In this case also, the artist proceeds by isolation and monumentalisation, sometimes by accumulation of the different parts of the body. One of his sculptures in the shape of an upright column is made up by several truncated bodies cast in plaster and placed on top of each other. We do not seem to be confronted here with an assignment of the everyday object to the status of an art object as it was done by the New Realism and Pop Art movements, by Warhol and Arman in particular, but we are rather in the presence of a reification of the different parts of the human body which serve as points of reference in the artist's bio-aesthetic imaginary.

From the 1980s onwards, Neiman reintroduced painting into his work, separately or juxtaposed with his photographs as well as with ready-made images such as picture post cards of Mediterranean landscapes (where the artist spends a part of the year), that which has led him to work with a much livelier chromatic scale. Let us add that the utilisation of the post card, a widely employed means of rapid visual and scriptural communicability, ratifies the position of the artist who was one of the first protagonists of Mec-Art (Mechanical Art), an avant-garde movement which paved the way for current technological communication art. Today, Yehuda Neiman is a multi-media artist who participates fully in the art of the present.

—Aline Dallier-Popper

NEIZVESTNY, Ernst

Nationality: Russian. **Born:** Sverdlovsk, 9 April 1926. **Education:** Studied at the Academy of Art, Riga, Latvia, 1947–48, and Surikov Art Institute, Moscow, 1948–54; influenced by works of Michelangelo, Henry Moore and Jacques Lipchitz. **Military Service:** Served as volunteer paratrooper in the Red Army, 1942 (wounded and hospitalized in Bratislava and Brno, Czechoslovakia, 1943–45). **Career:** Worked as assistant to several sculptors, Moscow, 1948–54; foundry-worker in rolling stock yards, Urals, 1954–55; independent sculptor, Moscow 1955–75, Vienna, 1976–77, Zurich, 1977; has lectured at colleges and universities throughout the world; lives and works in New York City. **Awards:** Silver Medal, *International Youth Festival,* Moscow 1957; Red Star, for wartime gallantry, Moscow, 1964; Government Award for Achievement in the Arts, Moscow, 1996; Lifetime Achievement Award, National Children's Leukemia Foundation, 1997; Medal of Honor for Artistic Achievements, Russia, 2000. Honorary doctorate, Moscow State University, 1996. **Address:** 81 Grand St., New York, New York 10013, U.S.A.

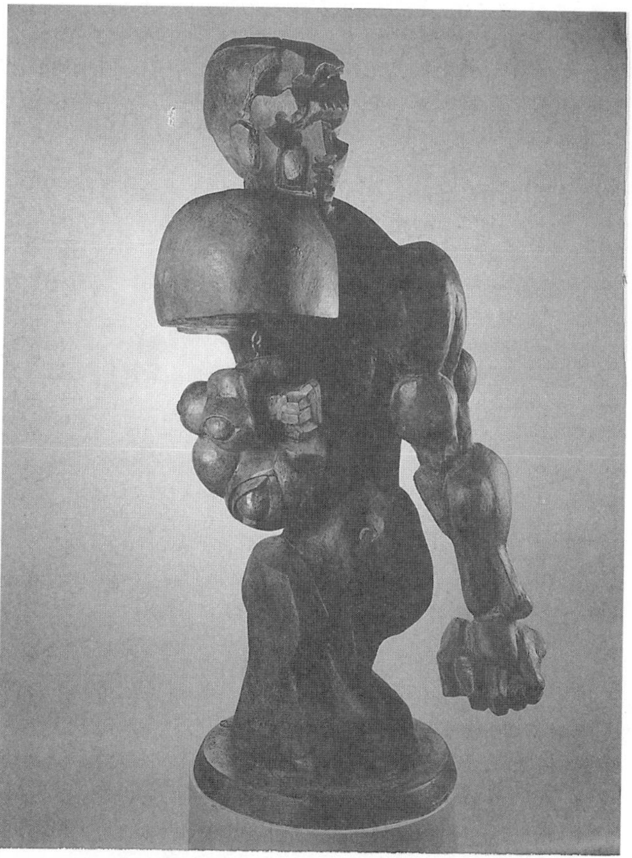

Ernst Neizvestny: *Prophet II.* ©Ernst Neizvestny.

Individual Exhibitions:

1961 Druzhba Club, Moscow
1962 University of Moscow (with Y. Yankilewsky)
1964 Grosvenor Gallery, London
Zentral Buchhandlung, Vienna
1965 Museum of Modern Art, Belgrade
Grosvenor Gallery, London
1969 Galleria La Barcaccia, Montecatini, Italy
1971 Galleria Il Gabbiano, Rome
1972 Tel-Aviv Museum
1975 New York Cultural Center
Kunstlerhaus, Vienna
Braunschweize Kunstverein, Berlin
Kunstamit Charlottenburg, Berlin
1976 Stedelijk Museum, Amsterdam
Kunstverein, Constance, Germany
Parkway Focus Gallery, London

1977 Galerie Scheidegger, Zurich
Gallerie Astley, Uttersberg, Sweden
Städtische Museum, Leverkusen, Germany
1978 Thielska Gallerie, Stockholm
Lilla Gallerie, Umea, Sweden
Manzoni Galleria d'Arte, Milan
Centro d'Arte Dolomiti, Cortina, Italy
Holst Halvorsens Kunsthandes, Oslo
1979 Eduard Nakhamkin Fine Art, New York
1984 Magna Gallery, San Francisco
1985 Magna Gallery, San Francisco
Cathedral of Saint John the Divine, New York
1987 Ulrich Museum of Art, Wichita, Kansas
Eduard Nakhamkin Fine Art, New York
1989 Eduard Nakhamkin Fine Art, New York
Magna Galleries, New York and San Francisco
Connaught Brown Gallery, London
Galerie Clara Maria Sels, Dusseldorf
1990 Magna Galleries, New York and San Francisco
1991 Ergane Gallery, New York
1992 Jewish Museum, Washington, D.C.
Le Monde de l'Art, Paris
Kunstverein Museum, Constance, Germany
Embassy of the Russian Federation, Washington, D.C.
1993 Russian Federation Mission to the United States, New York
Stevens Institute of Technology, New Jersey
1994 La Quinta Sculpture Park, California
Exhibit 1022, California
Embassy of the Russian Federation, Washington, D.C.
Morris International Festival of the Arts, New York
1995 Gordona Loncar Fine Arts, Pennsylvania
1996 Gallery Dom Nashchokina, Moscow
Pushkin Museum, Moscow
1997 United Nations Place of Nations, Geneva, Switzerland
1998 Gallery Dom Nashchokina, Moscow
1999 Tretiakov Gallery, Moscow
2000 Festivals Palace, Cannes, France

Selected Group Exhibitions:

1954 *Young Moscow Artists,* Moscow
1961 *The Nine,* Moscow
1962 *The Belyutin Studio Group,* Bolshaya Kommunistichekaya Street, Moscow
1964 *Aspects of Contemporary Soviet Art,* Grosvenor Gallery, London
1965 *Young Moscow Kinetic Artists,* Viola Gallery, Prague
1966 *Festival of Fine Arts,* Sopot-Poznan, Poland
1970 *The Russian Avant-Garde in Moscow Today,* Galerie Gmurzynska, Cologne
1974 *Progressive Tendencies in Moscow 1957–1970,* Städtische Museum, Bochum, West Germany
1975 *The Glezer Collection of Russian Art,* Kunstlerhaus, Vienna (toured Austria and Germany)
1977 *Unofficial Art from the Soviet Union,* Institute of Contemporary Arts, London
1995 Jewish Museum, New York
Zimmerly Museum, New Jersey
1998 Triumph Exhibition, Paris

Collections:

Museum of Modern Art, New York; Musée d'Art Moderne, Paris; Moderna Museet, Stockholm; Museum of Modern Art, Belgrade; Kennedy Center, Washington, D.C.; Russian Art Museum, St. Petersburg; Alexander Glezer Collection, Vienna; Israel Museum, Jerusalem; Tel Aviv Museum of Modern Art, Israel; Museum of Modern Ecclesiastical Art, The Vatican; City of Oslo; Tretiakov Gallery, Moscow; Volgograd Museum, Russia; Vologda Museum, Russia; Dostoevsky Museum, Moscow; Erevan Gallery, Armenia; L'vov Gallery, Belarus.

Permanent Public Installations:

Artek Pioneer Camp, Crimea; *Lotus Blossom,* Aswan Dam, Egypt; Communist Party Headquarters, Ashdhabad, Turkmenistan; Institute of Electronics and Technology, Moscow; Schumann Building, New York; *Centaur and Stone Tears,* Yugoslavia; Tombstone for Nikita Khrushchev, Russia; *Grief Mask Tombstone for a Centaur,* Milan; Memorial to the Victims of Stalinism, Magadan, Russia; *The Golden Child,* Odessa, Ukraine; *Memorial for Kalmykian Deportation: Exodus and Return* (monument), Elista, Kalmykia, Russia; *Rebirth* (monument), Moscow.

Publications:

By NEIZVESTNY: Books—*On Synthesis in Art,* 1982; *Neizvestny Speaks,* 1982; *Body: Man as Visual Sign,* 1987; *Art and Society,* 1987; *Space, Time, and Synthesis in Art,* 1990 (as *Centaur,* 1993); *Artist Fate,* 1992. **Illustrations**—*Short Works* by Dante, Moscow 1968; *Crime and Punishment* by Fyodor Dostoevsky, Moscow, 1970; *Their Fathers' Voice* by Cynthia Simmons, New York 1993; *Treatise About Angels* by Vera Zubareva, Odessa, Ukraine 1995; *Ecclesiastes* by Yakov Kumok, Moscow 1996; *The Last One Hundred Days* by Boris Pahnkin, Switzerland 1996; *The Book of Job* by Yakov Kumok, Moscow 1999. **Articles**—''Monument to Russian Martyrs Under Stalinism'' in *''Remove Not the Ancient Landmark:'' Public Monuments and Moral Values,* edited by Donald Martin Reynolds, Gordon and Breach Publishers, 1996; ''The Tree of Life'' in *International Affairs,* vol. 44, no. 1, 1998.

On NEIZVESTNY: Books—*Ernst Neizvestny,* exhibition catalog with text by D. Cosic and N. Stripoevic, Belgrade 1965; *Ernst Neizvestny,* exhibition catalog with text by John Berger, Tel-Aviv 1972; *Soviet Art and the Tasks of the Struggle Against Bourgeois Ideology* by V. Vanslov, Moscow 1969; *Ernst Neizvestny,* exhibition catalog with text by Franco Miele, Montecatini, Italy 1969; *Art and Revolution: Ernst Neizvestny and the Role of the Artist in the U.S.S.R.* by John Berger, London 1969; *Ernst Neizvestny,* exhibition catalog with texts by John Berger and Renato Guttuso, Rome 1971; *The Glezer Collection of Russian Art,* exhibition catalog with texts by Hans Mayr, Alexander Glezer and Viktor Tupizin, Vienna, 1975; *Unofficial Art from the Soviet Union,* exhibition catalog with texts by Igor Golomshtok and Alexander Glezer, London 1977; *New Art from the Soviet Union* by Norton Dodge and Alison Hilton, Washington, D.C., 1977; *Ernst Neizvestny: Life and Work* by Erik Egeland, New York 1984; *Art Under Stalin* by Matthew Brown, New York and London 1991; *Russian Jewish Artists in a Century of Change,* edited by Susan Goodman, New York 1995; *Escape from ''Ward Six:'' Russia Facing Past and Present* by George Alexandra, New York,

1998; *Forbidden Art: The Postward Russian Avant-Garde,* edited by Garret White, New York, 1998. **Articles—**''Why Khrushchev's Favorite Sculptor Chose Exile'' by Anthony Astrachan in *New York Times,* 11 April 1976; ''The Monumental Dreams of Ernst Neizvestny'' by Harrison Salisbury in *ARTnews,* May 1979; ''The New Statue of Liberty'' in *New Yorker,* 13 July 1987; ''Russian Sculptor Finds Fame Elusive'' by Adam Tanner in *Christian Science Monitor,* January 1995; ''For an Emigre Sculptor, Home Is Where the Art Is'' by Tracie Rozhorn in *New York Times,* 23 April 1995; ''Assimilation and Alienation'' by Eleanor Heartney in *Art in America,* February 1996; ''Freedom and the Artist'' by Peter Thwaites in *For a Change,* October/November 1997; ''Ernst Neizvestny: Artist, Gullivar'' by Marina Vardenga in *Argumenty i Fakty* (Russia), May 1995.

* * *

Before leaving the Soviet Union in 1976 Neizvestny had occupied an ambiguous position as the best-known Soviet artist of his generation, whose work nevertheless could not be publicy shown. For years he had consistently opposed the enforced new academicism of Socialist Realism, courageously arguing as well as working to demonstrate that official Soviet art had no right to its claims. Yet the idea of an art truly serving a whole society is as central to his thinking as it was to that of the Constructivists at the time of the Revolution, for he maintains that only art can make people fully conscious of themselves in time and history.

And the starting point of all Neizvestny's work, in both sculpture and drawing, is the tragic history of his own times and the sufferings his country has endured during them. He expressed this suffering in terms of the human body; his works, in plaster, stone or bronze, are all concerned with endurance and the growth and transformation this brings about. Thus the recurring theme of his art is human strength to survive and grow, depicted in some heroic, anguished metamorphosis of the human figure. As John Berger has put it ''For Neizvestny the human body is the field of all possible metaphors. All that he has to say can be said in terms of the human body. It represents the quintessence of all that is not death. . .his interest. . .begins with an insatiable curiosity about the body. He is not concerned with its beauty but with its workings, its power, its resistance, its limits and its mysteries.'' And it was literally through his own body that Neizvestny became so keenly aware of life, having been severely wounded and left for dead in the Second World War.

But though he is an artist of tremendous energy, power and ambition, the isolation in which he has been forced to work means that there has sometimes been a contrast between the sheer force of his abilities and their proper realization. Thus his writhing forms, immense shoulders and clenched fists have been criticized by Hilton Kramer as being over-rhetorical: ''the enormous hands in dramatic gestures, the twisted mouths, the orotund musculature of his larger-than-life male figures and their altogether massive stance—these and other characteristic features of his sculpture, while clearly the work of a sizable talent, are closer in feeling to the clichés of Socialist Realism than to the more critical spirit of modern art.''

But if Neizvestny sometimes is guilty of lapsing into a rather debased rhetoric, this may be because he is desperately struggling to express not outward appearance but interior feelings. Even in the case of a single simple form like the sphere he has claimed a distinction between inner and outer truth: ''Two sculptors are carving a sphere out of stone. One of them wants to achieve the most perfect form of sphere and sees the meaning of his work in turning a mass of stone into a perfect sphere. The other is also carving a sphere, but only in order to convey the inner tension expressed in the form of a sphere filled to bursting point. The first sphere will be the work of a craftsman, the second that of an artist.''

Neizvestny is also a prolific graphic artist, for instance in his voluminous series of etchings illustrating Dante's *Divine Comedy.* Again the appeal of the *Inferno* is that it offers splendid opportunities for an artist whose main concern is to express human anguish and suffering, as in the lovers whirled along in their whirlwind of passion, or the woman suicide in the Forest of Suicides, crouching with a tree growing violently through her.

Obsessed with Michelangelo, Neizvestny has also been influenced by Henry Moore and by the Lipchitz of the late, massive baroque figures. He similarly aspires to a monumental statement, a kind of heroic humanism, thinking of sculpture as being essentially a public art, so that he has made maquettes for very large-scale public monuments, though very few have actually been put up. He sees many of his figures of giants or prophets as potentially capable of being assembled together to make one vast work which he thinks of as a *Gigantomachia.* But his opposition to the official hierarchy means that most of his bronzes have had to be cast by himself in primitive conditions in his small overcrowded shop, thus limiting their size.

However, he did receive some state commissions such as the large sculpture for a children's summer colony in the Crimea, as well as some private commissions for memorials on the graves of some prominent men, most notably Khrushchev. The two men had a famous argument in November 1962 when Khrushchev denounced modern art after seeing an exhibition in Moscow that Neizvestny had helped to arrange. Later, after Khrushchev's fall from power, the two men began a friendly coorespondence. So after the former leader's death, his family asked the sculptor to design a memorial for his grave—a realistic head of Khruschev on a platform, with two intertwined forms of black and white stone behind, locked in perpetual struggle. But Neizvestny's own struggle with the Soviet authorities continued, and in the harsher climate once the Thaw under Khrushchev had receded he found it more difficult to express himself, until in March 1976 he was given permission to leave Russia, moving to the West and conducting negotiation for the export of some of his sculpture.

—Konstantin Bazarov

NELSON, Joan

Nationality: American. **Born:** Torrence, California, 1958. **Education:** Washington University, St. Louis, Missouri, B.F.A. 1981; Brooklyn Museum School, New York, 1981–82. **Career:** Painter. **Awards:** Max Beckman Memorial Scholarship, Brooklyn Museum School, New York, 1981–82.

Selected Individual Exhibitions:

1985 P.O.W. Gallery, New York
1986 P.O.W. Gallery, New York
Michael Kohn Gallery, Los Angeles
1987 Fawbush Gallery, New York
Michael Kohn Gallery, Los Angeles
1988 Contemporary Arts Museum, Houston, Texas

1989 Robert Miller Gallery, New York
Currents 39, St. Louis Arts Museum, St. Louis, Missouri
1990 Robert Miller Gallery, New York
Michael Kohn Gallery, Santa Monica, California
1991 Robert Miller Gallery, New York (catalog)
Freedman Gallery, Albright College, Reading, PA
1992 Michael Kohn Gallery, Los Angeles
1993 Robert Miller Gallery, New York
1994 John Berggruen, San Francisco
1995 Robert Miller Gallery, New York
1997 Robert Miller Gallery, New York

Selected Group Exhibitions:

1982 Nature Morte Gallery, New York
1984 P.P.O.W. Gallery, New York
1985 Grace Borgenicht Gallery, New York
East Village at the Center, Saidye Bronfman Gallery, Montreal, Canada
Places, Greenville County Museum of Art, Greenville, South Carolina *Minimal Representation,* Jan Baum Gallery, Los Angeles
Solomon R. Guggenheim Museum, New York
Christminster Gallery, New York
Works on Paper, Joe Fawbush Editions, New York
1986 *Art Awards Exhibition,* American Academy of Arts and Letters, New York
Forum, International Kunstmusee, Zurich, Switzerland
Painting and Sculpture Today: 1986, Indianapolis Museum of Art, Indianapolis
Landscape in the Age of Anxiety, Lehman College Art Gallery, Bronx, New York (travelled to Cleveland Center for Contemporary Art, Cleveland, Ohio)
The Manor in the Landscape, Lorence Monk Gallery, New York
P.P.O.W. Gallery, New York
Art of the East Village, Morris Center, Lafayette College, Easton, Pennsylvania
Small Format, Lang O'Hara Gallery, New York
NYC: New Work, Delaware Art Museum, Wilmington, Delaware
1987 *On Paper,* Curt Marcus Gallery, New York
Emerging Artists: Selections from the Exxon Series, 1975–1986, Solomon R. Guggenheim Museum, New York
Fictions, Kent Fine Art, New York
1988 *Jack Barth, Michael Young, Joan Nelson,* BlumHelman Gallery, New York
Landscape Anthology, Grace Borgenicht Gallery, New York
Land, ACA Gallery, New York
1989 *RePresenting Landscape,* New York Studio School, New York
Landscape Re-Viewed: Contemporary Reflections on a Traditional Theme, Walker Art Center, Minneapolis, Minnesota
Nocturnal Visions in Contemporary Painting, Whitney at Equitable Center, New York
1989 Biennial Exhibition, Whitney Museum of American Art, New York
Painting Beyond the Death of Painting, (American Imagistic and Abstract Work), Kunetsky Most Exhibition Hall, Moscow, U.S.S.R.
41st Annual Purchase Exhibition, American Academy of Arts and Letters, New York
1989–91 *Romance and Irony in Recent American Art,* National Gallery of New Zealand, Wellington (traveled to Art Gallery of Western Australia, Perth; Aukland City Art Gallery, New Zealand; Tampa Museum of Art, Florida; Parrish Art Museum, Southampton, New York)
1990 *Third International Exhibition,* Galeria Leyendecker, Santa Cruz de Tenerife, Canary Islands, Spain
Rhode Island, Terra Incognita: New Directions in Contemporary Landscape, Museum of Art, Rhode Island School of Design, Providence
Joan Nelson/Gary Stephan Landscapes, University Art Galleries, Wright State University, Dayton, Ohio
Von der Natur in Der Kunst, Weiner Festwochen, Vienna, Austria *Harmony & Discord,* Virginia Museum of Fine Arts, Richmond
The Ten Artists I Was Thinking of on May 3, 1990 at 7:00 o'clock, Witte de With, Rotterdam, The Netherlands
42nd Annual Academy-Institute Purchase Exhibition, American Academy and Institute of Arts and Letters, New York
1991 New Britain Museum of American Art, New Britain, Connecitcut
1992 *The Landscape, Subject of Renewed Scrutiny,* Foster Gallery, University of Wisconsin-Eau Claire
1993 *Painters' Prints,* Cirrus Gallery, Los Angeles
1994 *Portfolios,* Associated American Artists, New York
1997 *Landscape: The Pastoral to the Urban,* Center for Curatorial Studies Museum, Bard College, New York
White Columns, New York
Landscape as Abstraction, James Graham & Sons, New York
2001 *The American Experience,* Tampa Museum of Art, Florida

Collections:

Museum of Modern Art, New York; Solomon R. Guggenheim Museum, New York; Toledo Museum of Art, Toledo, Ohio; Archer M. Huntington Art Gallery, University of Texas at Austin; Los Angeles County Museum of Art, California; Minneapolis Museum of Art, Minnesota.

Publications:

On NELSON: Books—*New Horizons in American Art* (exhibition catalogue), with text by Lisa Dennison, New York 1985; *The New Romantic Landscape* (exhibition catalogue), with text by Chantal Combes, Stamford 1987; *Emerging Artists 1978–1986: Selections From the Exxon Series,* with text by Diane Waldman, New York 1987; *Contemporary Women Artists* by Wendy Beckett, Oxford 1988; *1989 Biennial Exhibition* (exhibition catalogue), by Richard Armstrong and Richard Marshall, New York 1989; *Romance and Irony in Recent American Art* (exhibition catalogue), by Louis Gratchos, with John Stringer and Richard Martin, Perth 1989; *Joan Nelson /Gary Stephan Landscapes* (exhibition catalogue), by Barry A. Rosenberg, Dayton, Ohio 1989; *Von der Natur in Der Kunst* (exhibition catalogue), Vienna 1990; *New Art* by Phyllis Freeman, with Mark Greenberg, Eric Himmel, Andras Landshoff et. al., New York 1990; *Joan Nelson* (exhibition catalogue), by Donald Kuspit, New York 1990; *Harmony & Discord: American Landscape Painting Today,* Richmond, Virginia 1990; *Die Zehn Kunstler an die am 3. Mai 1990 um 19.00 Uhr gedacht habe.* (exhibition catalogue), by Jiri Georg Dokoupil, Rotterdam 1990; *Drawing: A Contemporary Approach* by Betti, Claudia and Teel Sale, Texas 1992. **Articles—** ''Joan Nelson'' by Timothy Cohrs in *Arts Magazine,* vol. 62, no. 3, November 1987; ''Joan Nelson at Fawbush'' by Suzaan Boettger in *Art in America,* vol. 76, no. 2, February 1988; ''Joan Nelson'' by Donald Kuspit in *Artforum,* vol. 26, no. 5, January 1988; ''Landscape Painting in the Eighties: April Gornik, Ellen Phelan and Joan Nelson'' by John Loughery in *Arts Magazine,* vol. 63, no. 9, May 1988; ''Joan Nelson at Robert Miller'' by Ken Johnson in *Art in America,* vol. 77, no. 3, March 1989; ''Joan Nelson'' by Alfred MacAdam in *Artnews,* vol. 100, no. 3, March 2001.

* * *

In the mid-1980s Joan Nelson painted dark, gloomy views of industrial architecture dominated by sketchy greys and dark browns. It was these paintings that first brought her attention from critics. Nelson then started painting views of skies with various cloud formations. By the end of the decade, Nelson had begun to paint landscapes. She emerged as one of the most important landscape painters of the 1980s when she exhibited these landscapes at a handful of New York galleries in 1988 and 1989. These exhibits received considerable attention in the major art periodicals of the time and brought the painter widespread attention and acclaim before she was thirty years old.

These landscapes are small, intimate, eerie scenes done in oil or a mixture of oil and wax on unframed, irregularly shaped wood panels. The artist has deliberately stained these paintings with dirt and thinly layered wax. She has also deliberately cracked, split, and scratched the paint surfaces. This intentional damage has been done to accentuate the effect that these paintings look old and worn, almost like old paintings one might find in the attic. Many of these landscapes are fragmentary, disorienting views of land and trees. Some feature the tops and sides of large, dark trees with no traces of the land on which they stand and from which they have grown. Some feature the trees as large, dark forms placed centrally in the canvas, with their tops and bottoms cropped. The disconcerting effect of these cropped views with forms seen in mid-air and in intricate detail but separated from any ground plane, is the most striking, immediate impact of these works. Other landscapes by Nelson are more traditional in composition, with meadows, hills, and caverns rendered in a very sketchy manner but seen in their entirety, or at least with the completeness of expansive terrain to be found in traditional landscape painting. The trees in Nelson's paintings have been rendered in meticulous detail; if one looks closely he can see individual twigs and leaves. These trees are seen against clear or cloudy skies of bright sunlight, overcast skies indicative of gloomy weather, and skies seen at dawn and dusk.

These skies have been rendered with moody, evocative, darkened tones of blue, tan, orange, brown, and sometimes even greens. Some of Nelson's sky views are rather abstract and filled with broad, delicately modulated areas of deep, vivid colors. Occasionally, brighter, paler, and livelier colors are used to define the skies. Regardless of the colors used, the mood-creating, contemplative possibilities of color, more or less muted and toned down, are always present in Nelson's work. Nelson excels at creating luminous, vibrant, thickly atmospheric skies. The painterly facture of the skies is in sharp contrast to the carefully delineated trees. The tonal skies sometimes appear similar to Rothko's paintings of stacked rectangular areas of color and therefore are connected to the tradition of the abstract sublime landscape both in mid-nineteenth century America and early nineteenth-century Northern Europe, part of what has been described as the Northern Romantic tradition. At the same time, they bring to mind the moody, eerie, psychologically introspective landscapes of Albert Pinkham Ryder and Ralph Albert Blakelock, to which they are very similar in how tones of colors are delicately balanced but less so in paint application, especially in the careful rendering of trees. Nelson's paintings are virtually never given titles; although some are identified by numbers.

Nelson's landscapes have been interpreted in various ways. Most of these interpretations were offered in the late 1980s, when Nelson was most widely exhibited. It is surely no coincidence that these paintings appeared in the wake of the revived interest in painting and the new sense of its viability around 1980. The moody tones, deliberately worn look, and irregularly shaped plywood convey a Romantic nostalgia for the old and distant past and an aura of melancholy. The deliberate, artificial aging may well be a commentary on the obsessive preoccupation with antique objects and cultural artifacts, of our material obsessions for things old and rare in an era of mass-produced, disposal everyday consumer goods. In a way, the seemingly decrepit condition of these works may refer to the idea that even art and culture fade into nothing over time, that nothing escapes the destructive power of the greater powers in life that make all things deteriorate eventually.

These works seem to have subtle references to the tradition of great landscape painting of the past in the Europe: Nicholas Poussin, Jacob van Ruisdael, John Constable, and Jean-Baptiste-Camille Corot to mind. They seem even more closely related to much nineteenth century American landscape painting, namely the Hudson River School and Luminism but especially the later development of Tonalism. In this sense of appropriation, of recreating in fragmentary ways images with art-historical references, Nelson's paintings may be considered Postmodernist in spirit and purpose. True to Postmodernism, they may be more about the history of landscape painting than about landscape itself.

Since first gaining significant attention in the late 1980s, Nelson has continued to paint moody, evocative landscapes like those that established her reputation. Her work has continued to develop along the path established at that time, with various changes and explorations of new possibilities related to the concerns that have always formed the basis for her work. In the 1990s her landscapes were often more smoothly finished and polished, with clearer and brighter colors, and more careful definition of water, rocks, trees, and plants.

—Herbert R. Hartel, Jr.

NESBITT, Lowell (Blair)

Nationality: American. **Born:** Baltimore, Maryland, 4 October 1933. **Education:** Tyler School of Fine Arts, Philadelphia, 1950–55, B.F.A 1955; studied stained glass and etching, Royal College of Art, London, 1955–56. **Military Service:** United States Army, 1956–58.

Career: Designed theatre sets, 1948–54; art director, closed circuit television, Walter Reed Army Medical Center, Bethesda, Maryland, 1957–60; worked at Philips Collection, Washington, D.C., 1959–63. Independent artist, associating with Robert Indiana, Louise Nevelson, Jasper Johns and Andy Warhol, New York, since 1963. Instructor of Printmaking, Baltimore Museum of Art, 1961–63; instructor, School of Visual Arts, New York, 1973. **Died:** New York City, 8 July 1993.

Individual Exhibitions:

1958 Baltimore Museum of Art
1963 Franz Bader Gallery, Washington, D.C.
1964 Corcoran Gallery, Washington, D.C.
1965 Rolf Nelson Gallery, Los Angeles
Henri Gallery, Washington, D.C.
Howard Wise Gallery, New York
1966 Gertrude Kasle Gallery, Detroit
Rolf Nelson Gallery, Los Angeles
Henri Gallery, Washington, D.C.
Howard Wise Gallery, New York
1967 Jefferson Gallery, San Diego
Louisiana Gallery, Houston
Henri Gallery, Washington, D.C.
Gertrude Kasle Gallery, Detroit
1968 Stable Gallery, New York
1969 Stable Gallery, New York
Baltimore Museum of Art
Henri Gallery, Washington D.C.
Gertrude Kasle Gallery, Detroit
Galerie M. E. Thelen, Essen
1970 Galerie M. E. Thelen, Cologne
Stable Gallery, New York
Gertrude Kasle Gallery, Detroit
1971 Gertrude Kasle Gallery, Detroit
Gimpel Fils, London
Gimpel and Weitzenhoffer, New York (2 shows)
Lambert Studios, Los Angeles
Pyramid Gallery, Washington, D.C.
Galerie de Gestio, Bremen
1972 Galerie M. E. Thelen, Cologne
Gimpel and Hanover Galerie, Zurich
Fabian Carlson Galerie, Göteborg, Sweden
Galerie Ostergren, Malmo, Sweden
Kunstverein, Freiburg, West Germany
Galerie Arneson, Copenhagen
Galerie Aronowitch, Stockholm
Hansen Fuller Gallery, San Francisco
Corcoran and Corcoran Gallery, Miami
1973 *The Flower Series 1964–73,* Corcoran Gallery, Washington, D.C.
Marion Locks Gallery, Philadelphia
Kunstverein, Freiburg, West Germany
Galerie Arneson, Copenhagen
Gertrude Kasle Gallery, Detroit
Gimpel and Weitzenhoffer, New York
Galerie John Craven, Paris
Stefanotty Gallery, New York
Gimpel Fils, London
1974 Gimpel Fils, London
Stefanotty Gallery, New York
Gertrude Kasle Gallery, Detroit
Galerie Arneson, Copenhagen
Fendrick Gallery, Washington, D.C.
Brooke Alexander Inc., New York
Walton Gallery, San Francisco
Galerie HM, Brussels
Museo de Bellas Artes, San Juan, Puerto Rico
1975 Pyramid Gallery, Washington, D.C. (2 shows)
Andrew Crispo Gallery, New York
Pace Gallery, New York
Memorial Art Gallery, Rochester Museum, New York
Corcoran Gallery, Washington, D.C.
Josef Gallery, New York
1976 Galerie HM, Brussels
Andrew Crispo Gallery, New York
Hokin Gallery, Palm Beach, Florida
Hokin Gallery, Chicago
Hayden Gallery, Massachusetts Institute of Technology, Cambridge
Treasure Island, Bicentennial Museum, San Francisco
1977 Graphis Gallery, Toronto
Gumps Gallery, San Francisco
Andrew Crispo Gallery, New York
Edwin A. Ulrich Museum of Art, Wichita, Kansas
Janus Gallery, Venice, California
Galeria Arte/Contacto, Caracas, Venezuela
Galerie Jollen, Cologne
1978 Strong's Gallery, Cleveland
Intown Club, Cleveland
Kent State University, Ohio
B. R. Kornblatt Gallery, Baltimore
Art Contact, Miami, Florida
Still Lifes, Andrew Crispo Gallery, New York
1979 Selby Museum, Sarasota, Florida
Flowers, Andrew Crispo Gallery, New York
1980 McNay Art Institute, San Antonio, Texas
Lyford Cay Gallery, Nassau, Bahamas
Galerie Jerome, Copenhagen
Galeria Arte/Contacto, Caracas, Venezuela
Profile Gallery, New York
Aldrich Museum of Contemporary Art, Ridgefield, Connecticut
B. R. Kornblatt Gallery, Baltimore
Gallerie Herder, Falsterbo, Sweden
Hull Gallery, Washington, D.C.
1981 Hokin Gallery, Palm Beach, Florida
General Electric Corporation, Connecticut
Andrew Crispo Gallery, New York
Fay Gold Gallery, Atlanta
Southwest II Galeries, Dallas
1982 Butler Institute of American Art, Youngstown, Ohio
1983 Oklahoma Art Center, Oklahoma City
Institute of Contemporary Art, Philadelphia
1984 Oklahoma Art Center, Oklahoma City
1985 G. Sander Fine Art, Daytona Beach, Florida
Temple University, Philadelphia
Long Island University, New York
Bourne Gallery, Surrey, England
1986 DiLaurenti Gallery, New York City

Foster Harmon Gallery, Sarasota
Images Gallery, Toledo
1987 Louis Newman Gallery, Beverly Hills
Joy Tash Gallery, Scottsdale
1988 Dyansen Gallery, San Francisco
1990 Bayley Museum, Charlottesville
Martin Lawrence Gallery, Baltimore
1991 Wessel/O'Connor Gallery, New York City
Sarasota Design Gallery

Selected Group Exhibitions:

1971 *Target Moon,* Wallraf-Richartz Museum, Cologne
1972 *Hyperrealistes Americaines,* Galerie des Quatres Mouvements, Paris
1973 *Johanssen Collection,* Museum Folkwang, Essen
1974 *Flowertime at Lincoln Center,* New York
1977 *30 Years of American Print Making,* Brooklyn Musuem, New York
The Bicycle, Museum Boymans-van-Beuningen, Rotterdam
1978 *Collector's Choice,* Mississippi Museum of Art, Jackson
1979 *Selected Paintings from the Andrew Crispo Gallery Collection,* New York
1985 *American Realism,* San Francisco Museum of Modern Art (toured the United States)
1990 *Humanist Icon,* Bayly Museum, University of Virginia, Charlottesville

Collections:

Museum of Modern Art, New York; Baltimore Museum of Art; Corcoran Gallery, Washington, D.C.; National Gallery of Art, Washington, D.C.; National Aeronautic and Space Administration, Washington, D.C.; Art Institute of Chicago; Milwaukee Art Center; Cleveland Museum; Bibliothéque Nationale, Paris; National Art Gallery, Wellington, New Zealand; The Corcoran Gallery of Art, Washington, D.C.; Library of Congress, Washington, D.C.; Massachusetts Institute of Technology, Cambridge; Temple University.

Publications:

By NESBITT: Books—*Lowell Nesbitt: An Autobiography,* exhibition catalog, New York 1975. **Article—**''An Interview with Lowell Nesbitt,'' with Adam Drewnowki, in *Interview* (New York), December 1975.

On NESBITT: Books—*Lowell Nesbitt,* exhibition catalog by Morris Graves, Los Angeles 1965; *Flowers, Facades and IBM Machines,* exhibition catalog by Henry Martin, New York 1965, reprinted in *Collage* (Palermo, California), October 1965; *Lowell Nesbitt,* exhibition catalog by Anders Bergh, Malmo, Sweden 1972; *Lowell Nesbitt,* exhibition catalog by Udo Kultermann, Zurich 1972; *Lowell Nesbitt,* exhibition catalog by Roy Slade, San Juan, Puerto Rico 1973; *The Flower Series 1964–73,* exhibition catalog with text by Henry T. Hopkins, Washington, D.C. 1973; *Lowell Nesbitt: Still Lifes,* exhibition catalog, New York 1978; *Lowell Nesbitt: Flowers,* exhibition catalog, New York 1979; *Lowell Nesbitt,* exhibition catalog, Ridgefield, Connecticut 1980. **Articles—**''Lowell Nesbitt'' by Cindy Nemser in *Arts Magazine* (New York), December 1966/January 1967; ''Lowell Nesbitt's Photographic Approach'' by Hilton Kramer in the *New York Times,* March 1970; ''Sharp Focus Realism'' by Denise Wolmer in *Arts Magazine* (New York), March 1972; ''The Male Nude Arrives at Last'' by Cindy Nemser in *Changes* (New York), July 1972; ''Lowell Nesbitt's Autobiography'' by Gene Baro in *Arts Magazine* (New York), December 1975; ''Lowell Nesbitt'' in *Artnews* (New York), April 1976; ''Background for an Artist'' by Peter Carlson in *Architectural Digest* (New York), April 1977; ''Lowell Nesbitt'' by Noel Frackman in *Arts Magazine* (New York), June 1977; ''Haus Lowell Nesbitt'' by Anja Veg in *Architektur und Wohnen* (Stuttgart), November 1977; ''Home Is Where the Art Is'' by John Dorsey in the *Baltimore Sun,* 4 March 1979; ''Lowell Nesbitt'' by Gerrit Henry in *Art in America* (New York), November 1979; ''I Fiori Humani de Lowell Nesbitt'' in *Harpers Bazaar Italia,* July/August 1980.

* * *

Lowell Nesbitt is one of the multifarious group of painters who helped bring Realism back into prominence more than a decade ago. He is best known for his magnified, close-up views of flowers, shoes and other ordinary objects which he paints with meticulous care for detail. Although he starts with photographic models, Nesbitt paints on the canvas without the aid of the projected image which many of the other Realists use, which lends his pictures a feeling very like the Dutch still-life painters and also like the American Precisionists such as Charles Sheeler and particularly Geogia O'Keefe.

Since 1964 Nesbitt has produced about 15 to 20 series of works whose subject matter ranges from building facades in Lower Manhattan, to still lifes, studio interiors, shoes, bridges around Manhattan, his dog Echo, animals and fruits and vegetables. In each case, the articles in the work are arranged somewhat schematically to convey something beyond the literal, seen image for its own sake. In the most arresting works, little things, treated with tender loving care, transmit an aura of mysterious importance. In his shoe picture, for example, attention is given to the individual qualities of the object, down to the wrinkles from wear and the brand names.

About one-third of Nesbitt's total output has concentrated on huge, blowups of flowers such as irises, lilies, tulips and roses, which Nesbitt endows with life-of-their-own nature and a cold beauty far beyond their natural appearances in the garden or wilderness. Zeroing in on this subject and painting it in all its literal details in firm, unbroken contour and exquisite colorings, Nesbitt transforms the explicit into a monumental, almost metaphysical presence of cold sensuousness. In works such as ''Bird Flying over Orchid'' (1981), the image of the bird's wingspan while in flight hovers above and behind that of the exotic bloom, echoing form and color to create a composition with implications beyond that of the photographic reproduction. As in many of his earlier works, the later series of fruits and vegetables play on asymmetrical balancing of shapes which share their space with crisply rendered patterns. There is a similar mix of ordered structure and sensuous mysticism in all his still lifes, which is especially successful in works of 1976 such as ''Amber Beads and Mask,'' a tabletop grouping in which things lying around the studio attain a drama and lushness which make them seem eerie and organic. Nesbitt transforms the usually unnoticed details of life into something special and bigger than life.

—Barbara Cavaliere

NETO, Ernesto

Nationality: Brazilian. **Born:** Rio de Janeiro, Brazil, 1964. **Education:** Studied at Escola de Artes Visuais do Parque Lage, Rio de Janeiro; studied at Museu de Arte Moderna, Rio de Janeiro. **Career:** Lives and works in Rio de Janeiro.

Selected Individual Exhibitions:

1996 Paço Imperial, Rio de Janeiro
Espacio 204, Caracas, Venezuela
1997 Tanya Bonakdar Gallery, New York
Galeria Pedro Oliveira, Porto, Portugal
Christopher Grimes Gallery, Los Angeles
Galeria Camargo Vilaça, São Paulo, Brazil
1998 Museo de Arte Contemporano Carrilo Gil, Mexico DF, Mexico
Bonakdar Jancou Gallery, New York
1999 *Ernesto Neto: Nhó Nhó Nave,* Contemporary Arts Museum, Houston (catalog)
2000 *Ernesto Neto,* Institute of Contemporary Arts, London; Dundee Contemporary Arts, Dundee, Scotland (catalog)
SITE Sante Fe
Wexner Center for the Arts, Columbus, Ohio
2001 Centro Galego de Arte Contemporaneo, Santiago de Compostela, Spain

Selected Group Exhibitions:

1995 *Kwangju International Biennale,* Kwangju, Korea
Drawing Center, New York
The Five Senses, White Columns, New York
Entre o Desenho e a Escultura, Museu de Arte Moderne de São Paulo, Brazil
1996 *Transformal,* Wiener Secession, Vienna
1996 Kunstbrau, Next, Internationales Projekt für Bildende Kunst, Verin für Bildende Kunst, Graz, Austria
Transparencias, Museu de Arte Moderna, Rio de Janeiro
1997 *Material Immaterial,* Art Gallery of New South Wales, Sydney
Esto es: Arte Objeto e Instalacion de Piberoamerica, Centro Cultural Arte Contemporano, Mexico DF, Mexico
As Outras Modernidades, Haus der Kulturen der Welt, Berlin
1998 *XXIV Bienal Internacional de São Paulo,* São Paulo, Brazil
Sydney Biennial, Sydney
Puntos Cardinales, Fundacion Museo Alejandro Otero, Caracas, Venezuela
Loose Threads, Serpentine Gallery, London
1999 *Liverpool Biennial,* Liverpool
Drawings, Bonakdar Jancou Gallery, New York
Best of the Season, Aldrich Museum of Contemporary Art, Ridgefield, Connecticut
2000 *Carnegie International 1999/2000,* Carnegie Museum of Art, Pittsburgh
Raumkörper, Netze und andere Gibilde, Basel Kunstverein, Switzerland
Wonderland, Saint Louis Art Museum, St. Louis, Missouri (catalog)
Versiones del Sur, Museo Nacional Centro de Arte Reina Sofía, Madrid

Publications:

By NETO: Book—*Ernesto Neto 1998–1999: Naves, Céus, Sonhos,* São Paulo, Brazil, 1999.

On NETO: Articles—''Ernesto Neto: Entre el Nadir y la Nada'' by Paulo Herkenhoff in *Arte Internacional,* 1993; ''Report From Brazil: Paradoxes and Transfigurations'' by Alisa Tager in *Art in America,* July 1994; ''Studio Visit: Ernesto Neto'' by Carlos Basualdo in *TRANS,* November 1995; ''Ernesto Neto: Voluptuous, Sexy, and Floating Membranes'' by Rubén Gallo in *Flash Art,* January-February 1999; ''Ernesto Neto'' by Gilda Williams in *Art Monthly,* July-August 2000; ''Ernesto Neto'' by Bill Arning in *Bomb,* winter 2000.

* * *

Brazilian artist Ernesto Neto manipulates yards of elastic Lycra (the same material used for pantyhose) to form the ''skin'' of his organic sculptures and site-specific installations. Bulbous, Lycra-covered masses of styrofoam pellets, small lead balls, pigment, sand, or spices either anchor the works to the floor or suspend them from the ceiling.

Although Neto's works are complex studies of form, they primary function as investigations into viewer/artwork interaction. Neto encourages people to touch, even to walk into, his room-sized sculptures. His works' skin-like color and texture makes viewers intimately aware of their own physical bodies. Pieces that incorporate spices activate the sense of smell, thereby enhancing the works' dream-like and contemplative qualities.

To create one of his early works, the nearly 20-foot-long installation *Colonia* (1989), Neto poured small lead balls into nylon stockings. He then dropped the stuffed Lycra bulbs from waist level. When they hit the floor, they spread out and merged as the open stocking tops rolled back to reveal thousands of balls. *Colonia* explored formation and deformation, themes Neto addresses throughout his *oeuvre.*

Neto sometimes incorporates sound into his works through onomatopoeic titles. For example, the last two words of *Venus Quark Paffs* (1998) mimic the sound of the works' three heavy Lycra bundles, filled with pigment and concrete powder, hitting the ground. In the completed installation, evidence of this action remained in the form of dusty halos surrounding the bundles. Viewers were forced to physically interact with the work as they tried to avoid the powder that seemed to reach out to them. Neto stretched the open stocking tops to the ceiling, their taut forms radiating outward and upward like search lights. The installation was a study in precarious balance, weightless thinness, and solid mass.

For the installation *Poff, Poff, Poff. . .* (1996), Neto filled Lycra with colorful spices including curry and cloves. The bundles were then either stretched to the ceiling or bunched together on the floor. This formal variety modified the sense perception of the viewer who walked under, over, and around the various constructions.

Neto began producing his series of *Ovaloids*, transparent objects with visible internal structures, in 1998. Approximately five feet in height, these oval works sit on the ground. They have a specific relationship to human scale and invite exploration through touch. Some of them are pierced with openings that extend into internal tubes. Viewers-turned-participants insert their hands, and in some cases their entire arms, into these orifices. Through a Lycra membrane, participants touch the thousands of Styrofoam pieces that fill the work.

In 1997, Neto created his first of many site-specific *Naves*. To make a *Nave*, Neto stretches huge sections of Lycra from floor to ceiling. The result is an enormous, suspended, translucent sculpture with an opening through which participants, after removing their shoes, enter. Once inside, they walk through the *Nave*, testing the flexibility and resistance of the Lycra as it expands and retracts with every step. Their movements transform the sculpture as it stretches to accommodate them, modifying the experience for viewers both inside and outside the work.

Neto's *Naves* take the viewer/artwork relationship to an intimate level. As participants walk through the sometimes-narrow passages inside the *Nave*, they are forced to walk on tiptoe and use their arms and hands to clear a path through the body-hugging Lycra. They may also lie down on ''mattresses'' on the *Nave*'s floor or hug spice-filled suspensions. These experiences reinforce a heightened sense of bodily awareness.

In Portuguese, *nave* means ''ship'' or ''spaceship.'' Throughout the ages, both the sea-faring ship and spaceship have symbolized the barrier between human endeavor and the mysterious expanse of the void. Similarly, Neto's *Naves* provide conduits of discovery into the nebulous, ethereal environments of corporeal and universal worlds.

—Joyce Youmans

NEUSTEIN, Joshua

Nationality: Israeli. **Born:** Danzig, Germany (now Gdansk, Poland), 16 October 1940; displaced person and political prisoner, with his family, in Poland, the U.S.S.R. and Germany, 1949; settled in the United States, 1950; emigrated to Israel, 1964. **Education:** Yeshiva Rabbi Jacob Joseph, New York, 1951–56; College of the City of New York, under Professor Hans Kohn, 1957–61, B.A. 1961; Art Students League, New York, 1959–61; Pratt Institute, Brooklyn, New York, 1960–63; studied privately with Arieh Aroch and Zwi Mairowich, Jerusalem, 1964–68. **Military Service:** Served in the Israeli Army as a 2nd Lieutenant in the Tank Division, 1964–66. **Career:** Painter; worked as a waiter in Monticello, New York and Lakewood, New Jersey, 1955–58, as a baker in New York, 1958–59, as a real estate broker and in the Department of Welfare, New York, 1959–61, as furrier, New York, 1961–63, and as a croupier, Brooklyn, 1961–65; ordained as a rabbi, 1962; settled in Jerusalem, 1964; now lives and works in New York City and Jerusalem. Editor, *Art en Garde,* Jerusalem, since 1975. Lecturer, Ramaz Yeshiva, Brooklyn, 1962–64. Lecturer, Bezalel Academy, Jerusalem, since 1974. **Awards:** Jerusalem Prize 1971; Willem Sandberg Prize, Jerusalem, 1973. **Agents:** Rina Gallery, 23 East 74th Street, New York, New York 10020; Yod Fat Gallery, 190 Dizengorf, Tel Aviv, Israel. **Address:** 300 West 108th Street, New York, New York 10023, or 7 Hamavak Street, French Hill, Jerusalem.

Individual Exhibitions:

1966 Rina Gallery, Jerusalem
1969 *Boots,* Jerusalem Artists House
1970 *Road Piece,* Helena Rubinstein Pavilion, Tel Aviv
Jerusalem River Project, Israel Museum, Jerusalem
1971 Gallery House, London
Galerie Yvon Lambert, Paris
1972 Yod Fat Gallery, Tel Aviv
Haifa Museum, Israel
1973 Rina Gallery, New York
Yod Fat Gallery, Tel Aviv
1974 *The Sound of Pines Opening in the Sun,* Yod Fat Gallery, Tel Aviv
1975 Rina Gallery, New York
Worcester Art Museum, Massachusetts (with Gross and Kupferman)
Julie M. Gallery, Tel Aviv
Territorial Imperative, Golan Heights, Israel (travelled to Krusa, Denmark and Belfast, 1975–78)
1977 Pollock Gallery, Toronto
Gallery Birch, Copenhagen
Tel Aviv Museum
Velar Gallery, Carnegie-Mellon University, Pittsburgh
1979 Mary Boone Gallery, New York
1980 Givan Fine Arts, Tel Aviv
Quintessence, Dayton, Ohio
1981 Tel-Hai, Upper Galilee, Israel
1983 Cornell University, Ithaca, New York
1984 Galerie X +, Brussels
Givon Gallery, Tel Aviv
Israel Museum, Jerusalem
1987 Exit Art, New York
1992 *Joshua Neustein: The Carbon Series,* Albright-Knox Art Gallery, New York (travelled to Grey Art Gallery and Study Center, New York Univeristy, New York)
1993 Albright-Knox Art Gallery, Buffalo
1997 Southeastern Center for Contemporary Art, Winston-Salem, North Carolina
1998 Rose Art Museum, Brandeis University, Waltham, Massachusetts

Selected Group Exhibitions:

1970 *Israel on Paper,* High Museum of Art, Atlanta
1971 *Concepts + Information,* Israel Museum, Jerusalem
1972 *Documenta 5,* Museum Fridericianum, Kassel, West Germany
1974 *Beyond Drawing,* Israel Museum, Jerusalem
1978 *Seven Artists in Israel,* Los Angeles County Museum of Art
1980 *With Paper: About Paper,* Albright-Knox Art Gallery, Buffalo, New York
1982 *Bilder Sind Nicht Verboten,* Kunsthalle, Dusseldorf
1985 *The American Experience,* Bass Museum, Miami, Florida (toured the United States)
1987 *Immigrants and Refugees/Heroes or Villains,* Exit Art, New York
1994 *Along New Lines: Israeli Drawing Today,* Israel Museum, Jerusalem

1999–2000 *The End: An Independent Vision of Contemporary Culture, 1982–2000,* Exit Art/The First World, New York (catalog)

Collections:

Israel Museum, Jerusalem; Tel Aviv Museum; Museum of Modern Art, New York; Guggenheim Museum, New York; Albright-Knox Art Gallery, Buffalo, New York.

Publications:

By NEUSTEIN: Books—*Affidavit,* exhibition catalog, co-editor, London 1972. **Articles**—''I Remember George Grosz'' in *Flash Art* (Milan), November 1972; ''On Aroch and Mairowich'' in *Jerusalem Post,* December 1974.

On NEUSTEIN: Books—*Concepts + Information,* exhibition catalog by Yona Fisher, Jerusalem 1971; *Abstraction to Nature to Landscape,* exhibition catalog by Yona Fischer, Jerusalem 1972; *4 Draughtsmen,* exhibition catalog by Ammon Barzel, Tel Aviv 1974; *Definition of Art* by Gideon Ofrat, Tel Aviv 1974; *Seven Artists in Israel,* exhibition catalog with texts by Maurice Tuchman and Stephanie Barron, Los Angeles 1978; *With Paper: About Paper,* exhibition catalog with essay by Charlotta Kotik, Buffalo 1980; *Bilder sind nicht verboten,* exhibition catalog with text by Jurgen Harten, Dusseldorf 1982; *Joshua Neustein: Maps,* exhibition catalog with introduction by Yigal Zalmona, Jerusalem 1983; *Joshua Neustein: The Bethlehem Series,* exhibition catalog with essays by Joseph Masheck and Pierre Restany, New York 1983; *The American Experience,* exhibition catalog with essays by Cynthia McCabe and Tuan Yi-Su, New York 1985; *Joshua Neustein,* exhibition catalog with texts by Carlo McCormick, Irit Rogoff and Klaus Ottmann, New York 1987; *Joshua Neustein: The Carbon Series,* exhibition catalog, with text by Barry Schwabsky and Douglas G. Schultz, Buffalo 1992; *Along New Lines: Israeli Drawing Today,* exhibition catalog, Jerusalem 1994. **Articles**—''The Discourse of Exile: Geographies and Representations of Identity'' by Irit Rogoff in *Journal of Philosophy and the Visual Arts,* 1989; review by Elizabeth Licata in *Art News* (New York), vol. 92, January 1993; ''Joshua Neustein at SECCA'' by Gregory Volk in *Art in America* (New York), vol. 85, no. 2, February 1997; ''Joshua Neustein's Memory Maps'' by Adachiara Zevi in *L'Architettura,* vol. 43, no. 495–96, 1997; review by Miles Unger in *Art News* (New York), vol. 97, no. 11, December 1998.

* * *

Joshua Neustein has a love affair with paper. He folds it, tears it, pleats it, cuts it; it is often left un-severed. *Stella* (1971) resembles a maze: follow the paper through from one end to the other, along the surfaces with the torn edges on either side, and you will come to the end without a break on the way. His paper works are positive, secure, unwavering. The first ten years of Neustein's life were insecure, miserable, unstable and, must have been at times, negative.

His native Danzig had already suffered its own vicissitudes before he was born; a free state under the protection of Poland from 1920 until annexed by Hitler in 1938. With his family he was displaced by the Germans to Poland, then by way of the U.S.S.R. and Austria arrived in the United States, settling in Brooklyn.

His father had been forced to cut wood in Siberia—could this have been the beginning of his romance with the structure of the paper that was to become so important in his work twenty years later? His involvement with the materials of his trade is total; his understanding of the structure of paper (he has observed its manufacture in the mills) and the myriad methods of treatment available to him are his language.

During his time of study at yeshiva (rabbinical school) he would draw in the margins of the commentaries of the Torah (Jewish law) horrifying his teachers who compelled him to erase his doodles and restore the pages to their original condition. This was soon after his arrival in the United States, possibly his introduction to the printed page—the blank margins were too much of a temptation. The second Commandment forbidding representational art may have directed him in his early work to the influences of American Abstract Expressionism and his work has been compared to that of Larry Rivers (a fellow Jew).

Some of his presentations bring to mind the sufferings and deprivations of the wondering masses of European refugees immediately following World War II. *Boots* (1969) composed of 17000 pairs of old boots, and *Barriers* (1971), *River Project* (1970), *Landscapes with Bales of Hay (1970), Earth, Air, Fire Water: Elements of Art* (1971 group exhibition)—reminiscent of what lay outside, where nature was there for the having.

Paper—a common commodity—accesible, inexpensive, diverse, beautiful: Its bare form asking to be clothed; straight lines to be curved; the whole to be divided. He avoided the strongest colours in his more youthful works and was attracted to beiges, whites, tans, some yellows, pinks and greens, leaving the texture of the paper to be observed; by the 1980s, still handling the paper in his own particular style, he is concerned with creating further dimensions and produces large-scale works, with the undersides of the paper, though not entirely seen, covered in paint, now in much stronger colours, but with a continuing fondness for the pearly whites. Unframed, unstretched, not even attached to a wall, they hang—islands (or almost) isolated in space. His work has a mystery and an ability to disturb. He does with paper what the seventeenth-century masters did with cloth. He folds and lifts it—he curls the corners in order to create depth.

Recently Neustein has turned to maps and produced a new form of landscapes. In so doing he has spread his horizons to encompass international boundaries and the political, social and territorial problems facing the world today. The basic map is the truth (the discovered form), man makes and constantly changes the boundaries—Neustein adds imagination. His attached objects, in metal, sticks, glass, form-obliterating or semi-oblitering platforms disturbing the marked borders. Is it his wish to blot out and start again? He is never didactic—yet his paintings do inform.

—Muriel Emanuel

NEVELSON, Louise

Nationality: American. **Born:** Louise Berliawsky, in Kiev, Russia, 23 September 1900; immigrated to the United States with her family, 1905. **Education:** Studied painting and drawing, under Theresa Bernstein and William Meyerwitz, New York, 1920; voice and dramatics, New York, 1920; art, under Kenneth Hayes Miller, Art

Louise Nevelson beneath her sculpture *Sky-Gate*, New York, 1978. Estate of Louise Nevelson/Artists Rights Society (ARS), New York.

Students League, New York, 1929–30; art, under Hans Hoffman, Munich, 1931–32; modern dance, under Ellen Kearns, 1932; archaeology, Mexico, 1951–52. **Family:** Married Charles Nevelson in 1920 (separated, 1931) son: Myron. **Career:** Worked as film extra, Berlin and Vienna, 1931; assistant to Diego Rivera, Mexico City, 1932–33; worked at the Sculpture Center, New York, 1949–50, and at Atelier 17, New York, 1953–55. Instructor of art, Educational Alliance School, 1937; Great Neck Adult Education Program, New York, 1950s. Chapter president, New York, 1957–59, and national president, 1962–64, Actor's Equity; vice president, Federation of Modern Painters and Sculptors, 1962–64. Member, Sculptor's Guild, 1962–64; participant, National Council on Arts and Government, Washington., D.C., 1965. **Awards:** Grand Prize, *Art: U.S.A.*, New York, 1959; Mr. and Mrs. Frank G. Logan Prize, Chicago, 1960; Tamarind Fellowship, 1963, 1967; Medal, MacDowell Colony, Peterborough, New Hampshire, 1969; Skowhegan Medal for Sculpture, Maine, 1971; Creative Arts Award in Sculpture, Brandeis University, Walthman, Massachusetts, 1971; American Institute of Architects Award, 1977; New York State Governor's Arts Award, 1987. D.F.A.: Western College for Women, Oxford, Ohio, 1966; Smith College, Northampton, Massachusetts, 1973; D.H.L.: Hobart and William Smith College, Geneva, New York, 1971; Colombia University, New York, 1977; Boston University, 1978. **Agent:** Pace Gallery, 32 East 75th Street, New York, New York 10022, U.S.A. **Died:** Of undisclosed causes, in New York, 17 April 1988.

Individual Exhibitions:

1941 Karl Nierendorf Gallery, New York
1942 Karl Nierendorf Gallery, New York
1943 Karl Nierendorf Gallery, New York
Norlyst Gallery, New York
1944 Karl Nierendorf Gallery, New York
1946 Karl Nierendorf Gallery, New York
1950 Lotte Jacobi Gallery, New York
1954 Lotte Jacobi Gallery, New York
Marcia Clapp Gallery, New York
1955 Grand Central Moderns, New York
1956 Grand Central Moderns, New York
1958 Grand Central Moderns, New York
Esther Stuttman Gallery, New York
1959 Martha Jackson Gallery, New York
1960 Galerie Daniel Cordier, Paris
David Herbert Gallery, New York
Deborah Sherman Gallery, New York
1961 Galerie Daniel Cordier, Paris
Pace Gallery, Boston
Martha Jackson Gallery, New York
Tanager Gallery, New York
Staatliche Kunsthalle, Baden-Baden, West Germany
1963 Sidney Janis Gallery, New York
1964 Pace Gallery, New York
Pace Gallery, Boston
Galerie Gimpel-Hanover, Zurich
Galleria d'Arte Contemporanea, Turin
Kuntshalle, Bern
1965 David Mirvish Gallery, Toronto
Pace Gallery, New York
Galerie Schmela, Dusseldorf
1966 Ferus-Pace Gallery, Los Angeles
1967 *Prints and Drawings 1953–1966,* Whitney Museum, New York
Rose Art Museum, Brandeis University, Waltham, Massachusetts
1968 Arts Club of Chicago
Pace Gallery, New York
1969 *Louise Nevelson 1959–1961,* Bürgermeister-Ludwig-Reichert-Haus, Ludwigshafen, West Germany
Museo Civico, Turin
Recent Wood Sculpture, Pace Gallery, New York
Harcus-Krakow Gallery, Boston
Sculptures 1959–1969, Rijksmuseum Kröller-Müller, Otterlo, Netherlands
Museum of Fine Arts, Houston
Galerie Jeanne Bucher, Paris
Pace Columbus Gallery, Ohio
Akron Art Institute, Ohio
1970 Martha Jackson Gallery, New York
Whitney Museum, New York
University of Texas at Austin
1971 Makler Gallery, Philadelphia
Pace Gallery, New York
1972 Dunkelman Gallery, Toronto
Pace Gallery, New York
Parker 470 Gallery, Boston
1973 Studio Marconi, Milan

Louise Nevelson: *Sky Cathedral*, 1958. The Museum of Modern Art, New York; gift of Mr. and Mrs. Ben Medwoff. Photo ©The Museum of Modern Art, New York. ©2001 Estate of Louise Nevelson/Artists Rights Society (ARS), New York.

Wood Sculptures, Walker Art Center Minneapolis
Modern Museet, Stockholm
1974 San Francisco Museum of Art
Musee d'Art Modern de la Ville, Paris
Palais des Beaux-Arts, Brussels
Neue National Galerie, West Berlin
Museum of Fine Arts, Dallas
Pace Gallery, Columbus Ohio
Makler Gallery, Philadelphia
C.W. Post Center, Long Island University, Greenvale, New York
High Museum of Art, Atlanta
William Rockhill Nelson Gallery of Art, Kansas City, Missouri
Pace Gallery, New York
Louise Nevelson as Printmaker, Cincinnati Art Museum
1975 Minanu Gallery, Tokyo
Galleria d'Arte Spagnoli, Florence
Cleveland Museum of Art
Harcus-Krakow-Rosen-Sonnabend Gallery, Boston
Galleria d'Arte l'Arcipelago, Turin
Hokin Gallery, Palm Beach, Florida
1976 Makler Gallery, Philadelphia
Dawn's Presence-Moon Garden + Two 1969–1975, Pace Gallery, New York
1977 *The Metal Sculptures,* Neuberger Museum, Purchase, New York
1978 Pace Gallery, New York
Pace Gallery, Columbus, Ohio
Recent Works, Richard Gray Gallery, Chicago
Linda Farris Gallery, Seattle
1979 Makler Gallery, Philadelphia
Farnsworth Museum, Rockland, Maine
Norton Gallery, West Palm Beach, Florida
Jacksonville Art Museum, Florida
1980 Pace Gallery, New York
Wildenstein and Co., New York
Scottsdale Center for the Arts, Arizona
The 4th Dimension, Phoenix Art Museum, Arizona
Seattle Art Museum
Winnipeg Art Gallery
Museum of Art, University of Iowa, Iowa City
Dayton Art Institute, Ohio
1981 Wildenstein and Co., London
Pace Gallery, New York
Makler Gallery, Philadelphia
Galerie de France, Paris
1982 Harcus/Krakow Gallery, Boston
Richard Gray Gallery, Chicago
Fay Gold Gallery, Atlanta, Georgia
Wildenstein and Co., Tokyo
1983 Pace Gallery, New York
Grey Art Gallery, New York University
1984 Barbara Krakow Gallery, Boston
Grace Hokin Gallery, Miami
Makler Gallery, Philadelphia
Storm King Art Center, Mountainville, New York
State University at Buffalo, New York
1985 Hokin Gallery, Miami
Pace Gallery, New York
Farnsworth Museum, Rockland, Maine
1986 Galerie Claude Bernard, Paris
Galerie Alice Pauli, Lausanne, Switzerland
Guggenheim Museum, New York
Pace Gallery, New York
Massachusetts Institute of Technology, Cambridge
1987 Whitney Museum, Fairfield County, Connecticut
1988 Centre Georges Pompidou, Paris
1992 Pace Gallery, New York
1997 PaceWildenstein, New York
Richard Gray Gallery, Chicago
Washburn Gallery, New York
1998 Galerie Lutz & Thalmann, Zurich

Selected Group Exhibitions:

1935 *Young Sculptors,* Brooklyn Museum, New York
1946 *Whitney Annual,* New York (and 1947, 1950, 1953, 1956, 1957, 1958, 1960, 1962, 1964, 1966, 1969)
1964 *Paintings and Sculpture of a Decade,* Tate Gallery, London
1969 *Tamarind: Homage to Lithography,* Museum of Modern Art, New York
1973 *American Art at Mid-Century,* National Gallery of Art, Washington, D.C.
1976 *200 Years of American Sculpture,* Whitney Museum, New York
1979 *Vanguard American Sculpture; 1913–1939,* Rutgers University, New Brunswick, New Jersey
1981 *Sculpture and its Related Drawings,* Marisa Del Re Gallery, New York
1985 *Transformations in Sculpture,* Guggenheim Museum, New York
1986 *Relief Sculpture,* Hirshhorn Museum, Washington, D.C.
1988 *Enduring Creativity,* Whitney Museum of American Art, Stamford
1989 *The Experience of Landscape: Three Decades of Sculpture,* Whitney Museum of American Art, New York
1990 *Early/Later,* Whitney Museum of American Art, New York
1992 *A Selection of Works by Caro, Hull, Nevelson, Nicholson, Pomodoro, Rickey,* Sigrid Freundorfer Fine Art, New York
1995 *Artist's Choice: Elizabeth Murray—Modern Women,* Museum of Modern Art, New York
1997 *American Art: A Selection from Waddington Galleries,* Waddington Galleries, London

Collections:

Guggenheim Museum, New York; Metropolitan Museum of Art, New York; Museum of Modern Art, New York; Whitney Museum, New York; Corcoran Gallery, Washington, D.C.; Hirshhorn Museum, Washington, D.C.; Art Institute of Chicago; Los Angeles County Museum of Art; Tate Gallery, London; Musée d'Art Moderne de la Ville, Paris; and numerous public installations including Federal Courthouse, Philadelphia; Pepsico World Headquarters, Purchase, New York; World Trade Center, New York; Madison Plaza,

Chicago; Crocker Center, Los Angeles; Arts Club of Chicago; Museum of Contemporary Art, Chicago; Dallas Museum of Fine Arts, Texas; National Gallery of Scotland, Edinburgh; High Museum of Art, Atlanta; Montréal Museum of Fine Arts, Canada; Norton Simon Museum, Pasadena, California; Israel Museum, Jerusalem; Rijksmuseum Kröller-Müller, Otterlo, Holland; Yale University, New Haven.

Publications:

By NEVELSON: Books—*Nevelson: Facade—Twelve Original Serigraphs in Homage to Edith Sitwell,* with text by Edith Sitwell, New York 1966; *Dawns and Dusks,* edited by Diana MacKown, New York 1976. **Articles**—''Queen of the Black Black'' by Philip Pearlstein in *Nevelson* by Colette Roberts, Paris 1964; statement in ''Period Rooms: The 60s and 70s'' in *Art in America* (New York), November/December 1970; ''Why Have There Been No Great Women Artists?'' in *Artnews* (New York), January 1971; ''Nevelson on Nevelson'' in *Artnews (New York),* November 1972; interview with Arnold Glimcher in *Archives of American Art,* New York 1973; interview in *Art Talk: Conversations with 12 Women Artists* by Cindy Nemser, New York 1975; statement in ''Is New York Still the Artistic Place to Be?'' by Gerrit Henry in *Artnews* (New York), November 1976.

On NEVELSON: Books—*Nature in Abstraction* by John I. H. Bauer, New York 1958; *16 Americans,* exhibition catalog by Dorothy C. Miller, New York 1959; *Louise Nevelson,* exhibition catalog with text by Hilton Kramer, New York 1960; *Nevelson,* exhibition catalog, New York 1961; *The Art of Assemblage,* exhibition catalog by William Seitz, New York 1961; *Nevelson,* exhibition catalog with text by Kenneth Sawyer and others, New York 1961; *Nevelson* by Colette Roberts, Paris 1964; *Nevelson,* exhibition catalog, New York 1964; *Louise Nevelson* by John Gordon, New York 1967; *Louise Nevelson: Prints and Drawings 1963–1966,* exhibition catalog by Una E. Johnson, New York 1967; *Louise Nevelson,* exhibition catalog, Chicago 1968; *Nevelson Recent Wood Sculpture,* exhibition catalog, New York 1969; *Louise Nevelson,* exhibition catalog, Paris 1969; *Louise Nevelson,* exhibition catalog with text by Mary Hancock Buxton, Houston 1969; *Louise Nevelson, 1959–1961,* exhibition catalog with text by Manfred Fath, Ludwigshafen, West Germany 1969; *Louise Nevelson: Sculptures 1959–1969,* exhibition catalog with text by R. Oxenaar, Otterlo, Netherlands 1969; *Louise Nevelson* by Arnold Glimcher (includes prologue by Nevelson), New York 1972; *Louise Nevelson* by Germano Celant, Milan 1973; *Nevelson,* exhibition catalog with text by Franco Russoli and Arnold B. Glimcher, Milan 1973; *Louise Nevelson,* exhibition catalog, Stockholm 1973; *Nevelson: Wood Sculptures,* exhibition catalog by Martin Friedman, Minneapolis 1973; *Nevelson,* exhibition catalog with text by Joan V. Miller, Greenvale, New York 1974; *Nevelson: Skygates and Collages,* exhibition catalog, New York 1974; *Louise Nevelson as Printmaker,* exhibition catalog with text by Kristin L. Spangenberg, Cincinnati 1974; *Nevelson: The Prints,* exhibition catalog by Gene Baro, New York 1974; *Art in Boxes* by Alex Mogelon and Norman Laliberte, New York 1974; *Louise Nevelson,* exhibition catalog, Tokyo 1975; *Nevelson: Dawn's Presence-Moon Garden + Two at Purchase; The Metal Sculptures,* exhibition catalog, Purchase, New York 1977; *Nevelson, Recent Wood Sculptures,* exhibition catalog, New York 1977; *Louise Nevelson: Recent Works,* exhibition catalog, Chicago 1978; *Louise Nevelson,* exhibition catalog, Rockland, Maine 1979; *Louise Nevelson: Atmospheres and Enviroments,* exhibition catalog with an introduction by Edward Albee, New York 1980; *Nevelson: Maquettes for Monumental Sculpture,* exhibition catalog, New York 1980; *Nevelson: Wood Sculpture and Collage,* exhibition catalog, with text by David L. Shirey, New York 1980; *Louise Nevelson: The Fourth Dimension,* exhibition catalog with text by Laurie Wilson, Phoenix, Arizona 1980; *Louise Nevelson,* exhibition catalog by Carter Ratcliff, New York 1981; *Nevelson's World* by Jean Lipman, London 1987; *Enduring Creativity,* exhibition catalog, with text by Roni Feinstein, Stamford 1988; *The Experience of Landscape: Three Decades of Sculpture,* exhibition catalog, New York 1989; *Louise Nevelson: Black, White and Gold,* exhibition catalog, New York 1992; *The Voices of Women Artists* by Wendy Slatkin, Englewood Cliffs 1993; *American Art: a Selection from Waddington Galleries,* exhibition catalog, London 1997; *Louise Nevelson: Sculpture 1957–1987,* exhibition catalog, New York 1997; *Louise Nevelson: Sculpture and Drawing from the 1930s,* exhibition catalog, New York 1997. **Articles**—''Louise Nevelson 1899–1988: Goodbye, Louise'' by June Wayne in *Women Artists News* (New York), vol. 13, no. 2, Summer 1988; ''Every Scrap of Wood: the Private World Behind the Public Myth of Louise Nevelson'' by James Harrison Lurie in *Art and Antiques,* April 1989; ''Entering the Mainstream: Women Sculptors of the 20th Century, Part One—Barbara Hepworth and Louise Nevelson'' by Ann Sutherland Harris in *Women's Art,* vol. 2, no. 2, Fall 1989; ''At Home with the Improbable: Reading Louise Nevelson'' by Alan Jones in *Arts Magazine* (New York), vol. 64, no. 3, November 1989.

* * *

From her beginnings the conditioning of the frame was to recur for Louise Nevelson. It doubled in its way with the proscenium arch, for she came to art in several aspects, and this breadth of approach to some extent was never relinquished; voice and drama seemed complementary to the three dimensions that claimed her finally. Working at the Art Students League gave her the rudiments, and Hans Hofmann in Munich in 1931 taught her something, though her European experience in acting and seeing collage were no less durable influences. The same year saw her start collecting African and Amerindian art. Her drawings then have a great volume of form, being concrete linear images. The year 1932 saw her working with Diego Rivera on a mural painting. Her sculptures had a solidity with affinities to Lipchitz and Cubism, though her first one-man show in 1941 revealed traces to Mayan and Near Eastern imagery. By 1944 she was into ceramics and modelling sculptures in terra cotta with more and more concern for the blocked-in masses.

For the next ten years Nevelson was working out her dynamic, now concerned almost exclusively with the assemblages that took the forms of compartments, one of the first being a more or less straight adaptation of a liquor crate tipped on end. By 1960 the concepts were reaching their peak of significant authority. Large low relief panels in boxwood, some more than eight feet tall, offered their black presences with mystery and an aura of religious solemnity not denied by the evidence of their source materials—cheap boxes with fitted ingredients of newel posts, chair legs and bevelled shelf edgings and, now and then, a rude hunk of unplaned wood. This compartmentalization of the relief wall emphasized the multiplicity of the contained detail so that on each shelf appeared what seemed the miniature furnishings of a chapel in an overcrowded baroque cathedral.

Then after 1963 the mood changed and with it the colour scheme. Gold replaced the unreflecting black; colour lent a Byzantine splendor to the iconic facades that took greater strength form simplicity and economy of shape; now she had boxes made to order for her assemblages instead of relying on the chance of ready-made. In the 1960s the sculptures took a simpler abstract phase often with spheres of wood arranged in repeated groups across the squared divisions of the wooden wall. Other materials were introduced, mirrors and Plexiglass opening up the ribbed structure to the light. In those the strong paraphrase of music made itself apparent especially in the large vertical traceries, baroque in arched symphonic rhythms. In the 1970s the works are more individually conceived, flowers and trees in welded aluminium and Plexiglass are freestanding and unenclosed.

Architectural and musical in span, Nevelson's works have the ultimate universal quality of the image formed by emotion and character catching its unique idiom from time and place. Simultaneously primeval and sophisticated, they escape the dating of fashion by their triumph of atavistic magic over the irrelevance of material.

—G.S. Whittet

NIGRO, Mario

Nationality: Italian. **Born:** Pistoia, 28 June 1917. **Education:** Studied music in Arezzo, 1923–29; studied chemistry and mineralogy at the University of Pisa, 1936–45; self-taught in art. **Family:** Married Violette Talentoni in 1948 (divorced, 1976); son: Gianni. **Career:** Painter: first abstract and cubist works, Livorno, Italy, 1945; worked as chemist in Department of Pharmacy, Livorno Hospital, 1945–58; member, Movimento Arte Concreta, Milan, 1949; settled in Milan, 1955; visited Paris, 1956 and 1957.

Individual Exhibitions:

1949 Libreria Salto, Milan
1951 Libreria Salto, Milan
Galleria La Vigna Nouva, Florence
1952 Galleria Giraldi, Livorno
Galleria Numero, Florence
Le Quattro Pipe, Turin
1953 Studio B 24, Milan
1954 Casa della Cultura, Livorno
1955 Galleria Numero, Florence
1959 Galerie Kasper, Lausanne, Switzerland
Salone Annunciata, Milan
Galleria del Cavallino, Venice
1962 Galleria Numero, Milan
1965 Casa della Cultura, Livorno, Italy
1966 Galleria Rizzato-Witworia, Milan
1967 Galleria La Polena, Genoa
Galerie Suzanne Bollag, Zurich
Galleria Notizie, Turin
1968 *Biennale,* Venice
1970 Galleria dell'Ariete, Milan
1971 Galleria Toselli, Milan
Galleria Sincron, Brescia, Italy
Zentrum für Aktuelle Kunst, Aachen, West Germany
Galleria del Mille, Bergamo
1972 Galerie Loehr, Frankfurt
Galleria La Polena, Genoa
Galleria Toselli, Milan
Galleria Peccolo, Livorno
Galerie M, Bochum, West Germany
1973 Galleria La Cappellata, Osnago, Italy
Studio Barozzi, Venice
Studio Maddalena Carioni, Milan
1974 Multicentre, Milan
Galleria Il Sole, Bolzano, Italy
Galleria La Nouva Citta, Brescia, Italy
Galleria Marlborough d'Arte, Rome
Galleria Peccolo, Livorno
1975 Galleria dell'Ariete, Milan
Galleria La Polena, Genoa
1977 Galleria Seno, Milan
Galleria Lorenzelli, Milan
1978 Galleria Editalia, Rome
Galleria Milano, Milan
Galleria Martano, Turin
1979 Studio Grossetti, Milan
Padiglione d'Arte Contemporanea, Milan
Galleria Plurima, Udine, Italy
1981 Studio d'Arte Contemporanea Dabbeni, Lugano, Switzerland
1982 Studio Grossetti, Milan
1983 Galerie Loehr, Frankfurt
Studio Grossetti, Milan
1984 Galerie Teufel, Cologne
1985 Galleria Il Sole, Bolzano, Italy
Galleria Plurima, Udine, Italy
1986 Galleria L'Isola, Rome
1994 *Mario Nigro: Retrospektive,* Wilhelm-Hack-Museum, Ludwigshafen am Rhein
Galleria del Credito Valtellinese, Milan
1996 Palazzo Municipale, Vignate
Centro Espositivo della Rocca Paolina, Perugia, Italy
1998 A Arte Studio Invernizzi, Milan
Artra, Milan
Galleria Cardi, Milan

Selected Group Exhibitions:

1951 *Arte Astratta in Italia,* Galleria Nazionale d'Arte Moderna, Rome (toured Europe)
1952 *Gruppo Arte Concreta di Milano,* Kulturinstitut, Vienna (toured Austria and South America)
1959 *Grafik der Gegenwart,* Salzburg
1964 *Biennale,* Venice (and 1982)
1971 *Konkrete Kunst,* Westfalischer Kunstverein, Munster, West Germany
1972 *The Non-Objective World,* Annely Juda Fine Art, London
1975 *Italian Painting Today,* Galerie Espace, Montreal (travelled to the Galerie Daniel Templon, Paris)
1981 *Arte e Critica,* Galleria Nazionale d'Arte Moderna, Rome
1982 *Rassegna del Movimento Arte Concreta,* Rieti, Italy
1985 *De Maria/Merz/Nigro/Paladino,* Galleria Toselli, Milan

1989 *On the Surface: An Abstract Journey,* Studio Durante, Rome

Collections:

Pinacoteca, Livorno; Galleria Nazionale d'Arte Moderna, Rome; Galleria Civica d'Arte Moderna, Turin; Museu d'Arte Moderna, Sao Paulo; Museu d'Arte Moderna, Rio de Janeiro.

Publications:

By NIGRO: Books—*Mario Nigro,* with Vanni Schweiller, Milan 1968; *Lettera di un raro amore,* exhibition catalog, Genoa 1972; *Scritti per Mario Nigro,* Milan 1991. **Article—**''Non c'e pui la Figa'' in *Domus* (Milan), April 1979).

On NIGRO: Books—*Arte Astratta e Concreta,* exhibition catalog by Carlo Guilio Argan and Gillo Dorfles, Rome 1951; *Alte und Moderne Kunst* by Walter Zettl, Vienna 1964; *Mario Nigro,* exhibition catalog with text by Tommaso Trini, Rome 1986; *Mario Nigro: Opere (1987–1992),* exhibition catalog with text by Giovanni M. Accame, Milan 1998. **Articles—**''"Faccio il ritratto alla pittura"'' by Mario Pancera in *Arte,* vol. 19, no. 197, June 1989; ''Satanic Paintings'' by Ida Punicelli in *Artforum,* vol. 28, no. 3, November 1989.

* * *

From a superficial point of view Mario Nigro's work could be defined as being post-Constructivist; however, it possibly represents the most successful example of the ''bridge'' between that experience and the very recent analytical researches interpreting the latter in the widest sense.

In fact, throughout his whole career, there is cohesion: a subtle but robust thread links the vigorous works of the early 1950s to the ultimate rarefied present-day works: from ''Ritmi'' in 1950–51, to ''Spazi Totali,'' of 1953–60, to the environmental researches of the 1960s, up until ''Tempo Totale'' of the late 1960s and the ''Metafisica di Colore,'' Nigro focused his attention on the unveiling of the ultimate elements of art, those that go beyond sign, colour, rhythm, to unite the concepts of space and time. It is a progressive ratification of signs and colour almost to the point of having exhausted and proved the potential of particular forms and particular lines. Today, Nigro tends to go for an absolute and perfect idea that will coincide with the elimination of every action and every sign in favor of the contemplation of the clear surface, uncut and untouchable.

However, such a formal progression does not simply imply a nihilist conceptualization of creating art, an interest in the starting point of the work of art rather than an attempt to comprehend the totality of space and time in the fragment of the surfaces without renouncing for this a theme of tenuous poetry, of a semi-metaphysical mystery. There are profound suggestions that slowly emerge from his surfaces, that grip the eye with the sensation of infinite whiteness of the canvas, that involve even the mythical and elusive titles that the artist has given his works, particularly in the last few years.

Nigro's geometry, while rising to the peak of concept, also involves all those psychological and cultural values that modify the initially assumed traditional rationale. In 1979 the artist wrote: ''My post-rationalism is born in this dimension: it does not consist of being less rigorous geometrically because then one would automatically arrive at and therefore bring about the imperfect and informal in romantic decadence, also the rigidity is vital—but the external vision is more complicated, thus one can have the sense of an 'ambiguous' geometry.''

—Marco Meneguzzo

NITSCH, Hermann

Nationality: Austrian. **Born:** Vienna, 29 August 1938. **Education:** Graphische Lehr-und Versuchsanstalt, Vienna, 1953–57; mainly self-taught in art, from 1956. **Family:** Married Eva Krannich in 1965 (divorced, 1966); married Beate Konig in 1968 (died, 1977). **Career:** Independent artist, working in Vienna, 1957–69, and in Schloss Prinzendorf, near Vienna, since 1971; also lived in West Berlin, 1969–70, and Munich, 1977–84; first orgy-mystery-theatre works, 1957; first action paintings, 1960; first actións, 1962. Founder, with Bauer, Brus, Ruhm and Wiener, Osterreichisches Exilregierung, West Berlin, 1969. Guest instructor, Stadelschule, Frankfurt, 1971, 1973; Kunsthochschule, Frankfurt, 1979, 1980, 1981; Kunstschule, Reykjavik, 1980; Professor, University of Fine Arts, Frankfurt, 1989–95. **Agents:** Galerie Fred Jahn, Maximilianstrasse 10, 8000 Munich; Kunstandel Kurt Kalb, Backerstrasse 3, 1010 Vienna; Galerie Heike Curtze, Seilerstatte 15, 1010 Vienna; Studio Morra, via Calabritto 20, 80121 Naples. **Address:** Schloss 1, 2185 Prinzendorf an der Zaya, Austria. **Web site:** www.nitsch.org.

Individual Exhibitions:

1960 Loyalty Club, Vienna
1961 Galerie Fuchs, Vienna
1963 Galerie Dvorak, Vienna
1964 Galerie Junge Generation, Vienna
1966 Galerie Dvorak, Vienna
1969 Galerie Casa, Munich
Cinematheque, New York
1971 Galerie Schottle, Munich
1972 Galerie Matala, Tubingen, West Germany
Galerie Grunangergasse, Vienna (retrospective)
1973 Stadelschule, Frankfurt
Galerie Grunangergasse, Vienna
Galerie Werner, Cologne
Galerie Klewan, Vienna
1974 Studio Morra, Naples
Galleria Diagramma, Milan
1975 Galerie Krinzinger, Innsbruck
Galerie Stadler, Paris
Schloss Prinzendorf, Austria
1976 Kunstverein, Kassel, West Germany
1977 Galerie de Appel, Amsterdam
Studio Morra, Naples
1978 Modern Art Galerie, Vienna (retrospective)
Western Front, Vancouver
Galerie Klein, Bonn
1979 Galerie Heike Curtze, Dusseldorf

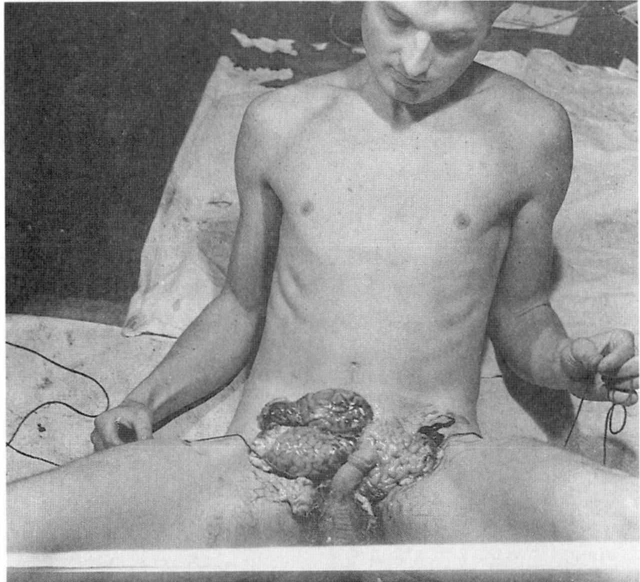
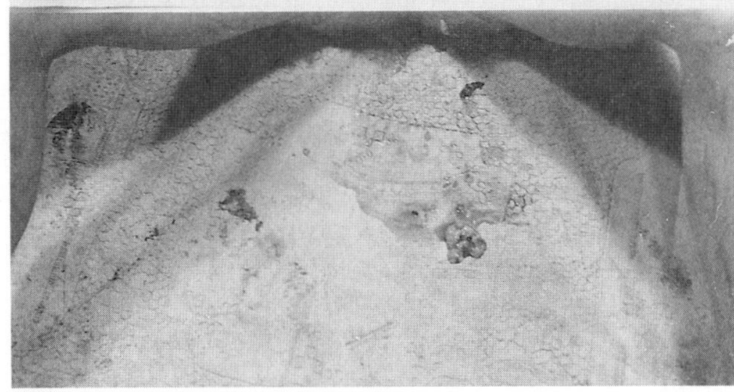

Hermann Nitsch: *21 Aktion,* 1966. ©2001 Artists Rights Society (ARS), NY/ VBK, Vienna.

Galerie Ollave, Lyon, France
Galerie Petersen, West Berlin
Schloss Prinzendorf, Austria
1981 Galerie Klewan, Munich
Galerie Pakesch, Vienna
Kulturhaus, Graz, Austria (retrospective)
1982 Galerie Zell am See, Austria
1983 Galerie Heike Curtze, Vienna
Galerie Armstorfer, Salzburg
Van Abbemuseum, Eindhoven, Netherlands (retrospective)
1985 Galerie Maeght Lelong, Zurich
Mercato di Sale, Milan
Galerie Heike Curtze, Vienna
1986 Galerie Fred Jahn, Munich
Studio Morra, Naples
Galerie Heike Curtze, Dusseldorf
1987 Secession Galerie, Vienna
Villa Pignatelli, Naples (retrospective)
Galerie Fred Jahn, Munich
Galerie Hans Christian Hoschek, Graz, Austria
Galerie Harald Behm, Hamburg
Galerie Heike Curtze, Vienna
1988 *Hermann Nitsch: Works on Paper 1956–1988,* David Nolan Gallery, New York (catalog)
Urban Gallery, Lenbachhaus, Munich
1989 Museum of Modern Art, Vienna
Galerie Donguy, Paris
1990 *Hermann Nitsch: Installation O.M. Theatre,* Galerie Beaumont, Luxembourg (catalog)
1991 *Hermann Nitsch: Passions, 1960–90—Action Painting and Relics,* St. Petri zu Lubeck, Germany (catalog)
Hermann Nitsch, Galerie Krinzinger, Innsbruck (catalog)
1992 *Hermann Nitsch,* Pabellon de las Artes, Seville (catalog)
Hermann Nitsch: ''I am the Painter. . . ''—An Original ''Relikt'' and Nine Paintings from a Private Collection, Neues Museum Weserburg, Bremen (catalog)
1993 *Wounds and Mysteries,* National Gallery, Prague (with Rudolf Schwartzkogler)
1994 *Painters' Images,* Museum of Modern Art, Vienna (catalog)
Hors Limits, Centre Georges Pompidou, Paris
Structures of the O.M. Theater, Frankfurt am Main
1995 *Revolution: Art of the Sixties from Warhol to Beuys,* Hara Museum of Contemporary Art, Tokyo (catalog)
Hermann Nitsch, Brigitte Kowanz, Eva Grubinger: Three Generations of Artists from Austria, Neuer Berliner Kunstverein (catalog)
1997 Neue Galerie der Stadt Linz, Wolfgang-Gurlitt Museum, Austria (catalog)
Body, Art Gallery of New South Wales, Sydney (catalog)
1998 Schloss Prinzendorf, Austria
2001 *Work on Paper,* Gallery Lelong, Zurich
Auferstehungszyklus, Gallery Heike Curtze, Salzburg

Actions and Concerts:

Nitsch has performed 84 Actions in Vienna, Prinzendorf, Graz, London, New York, Cincinnati, New Brunswick, Los Angeles, Munich, Cologne, Stuttgart, Frankfurt, West Berlin, Florence, Turin, Naples, Bologna, Milan, Trieste, Paris, Vancouver, Arnhem, and Eindhoven, 1962–87; he has performed or conducted 9 of his own musical compositions in galleries, museums and concert halls in Prizendorf, Vienna, Innsbruck, Linz, Graz, Munich Hamburg, and Basel, 1974–86; *Theacher,* Academy of Visual Arts, Frankfurt, 1989; *Six-day Play,* Prinzendorf, 1998.

Selected Group Exhibitions:

1961 *Geist und Form,* Galerie Ebendorferstrasse, Vienna
1962 *Die Blutorgel,* Perinet-Keller, Vienna
1970 *Happening und Fluxus,* Kunstverein, Cologne
1972 *Documenta 5,* Museum Fridericianum, Kassel, West Germany
1979 *Sydney Biennale,* New South Wales, Australia
1981 *Westkunst,* Messehallen, Cologne
1982 *Wiener Aktionismus,* Galerie Heike Curtze, Dusseldorf
1984 *Arte Austriacca 1960–84,* Galleria d'Arte Moderna, Bologna, Italy
1986 *Rennweg,* Castello di Rivoli, Turin (travelled to Madrid)
1988 *Contemporary Drawings,* Staatliche Graphische Sammlung, Neue Pinakothek, Munich (catalog)
1989 *Biennale,* Sydney, Australia
1998 *Out of Actions: Between Performance and the Object, 1949–1979,* Museum of Contemporary Art, Los Angeles

2000 *Hounds in Leash: The Dog in 18th-and-19th-Century Scultpure,* Henry Moore Instutute, Leeds, England

Collections:

Museum of Modern Art, New York; Tate Gallery, London; Städtische Museum im Lenbachhaus, Munich; Staatsgalerie, Stuttgart; Kunsthalle, Hamburg; Kunstmuseum, Berne; Stedelijk Van Abbemuseum, Eindhoven; Castello di Rivoli, Turin; Wolfgang Gurlitt-Museum, Linz; Museum Moderner Kunst, Vienna; Guggenheim Collection, New York; Art Gallery of Ontario, Toronto; Musée Centre George Pompidou, Paris; Sammlung Nordrhein-Westfalen, Dusseldorf; Museum Ludwig, Cologne.

Publications:

By NITSCH: Books—*Orgien Mysteries Theater-Orgies Mysteries Theater,* Darmstadt 1969; *Das Orgien Mysteries Theater II,* Naples and Munich 1976; *O.M. Theater,* Naples 1976; *Partitur der 50, Aktion,* West Berlin 1976; *Die Eroberung von Jerusalem,* Naples and West Berlin 1976; *3 Typoskriptbande,* 3 vols., Naples 1976; *Das Orgien Mysterien Theater-die Partituren aller aufgefuhten Aktionen, 1960–79,* Naples, Munich, and Vienna 1979; *45, Aktion,* Naples 1980; *Behauptungen und Beschreibungen zum Projekt des O.M. Theater,* Vienna and Munich 1981; *Die Wortdichtung des Orgien Mysterien Theaters,* Vienna 1982; *Asolo II, Fest,* Naples 1983; *Das Orgien Mysterien Theater,* Vienna 1983; *Das Origien Mysterien Theater 1960–1983,* exhibition catalog, Eindhoven 1983; *Das Orgien Mysterien Theater, die Partituren aller aufgefuhrten Aktionen,* vol. 4, Vienna 1984; *O.M. Theater-Leseuch,* Vienna 1985; *Das Orgien Mysterien Theater, die Partituren aller aufgefuhrten Aktionen,* vol. 2, Vienna and Naples 1986; *Hermann Nitsch: The Creative Work,* with Gunter Brus, Dieter Ronte, Ingrid Rein, and Armin Zweite, Salzburg 1988; *Hermann Nitsch: Slike,* with Andrej Medved and Rudi H. Fuchs, Ljubljana 1992; *Hermann Nitsch: Leben und Arbeit,* with Danielle Spera and Heinz Fischer, Vienna 1999. **Articles—**interview with Heinz-Norbert Jocks in *Kunstforum International,* no. 140, April-June 1998. **Audio discs and cassettes—***Akustisches abreaktionsspiel,* Vienna 1973; *Musik der 45. Aktion,* Naples 1974; *Requiem fur meine Frau Beate,* Naples 1977; *Musik der 60. Aktion,* West Berlin 1978, Stuttgart 1979; *5 Sinfonie Basel, 23 Oktober 1980,* Stuttgart 1980; *Musik der 66. Aktion,* Stuttgart 1980; *6, Sinfonie,* Stuttgart 1980; *Musik der 68. Aktion,* Stuttgart 1980; *Island,* Lucerne 1980; *Musik der 80. Aktion,* Basel and Munich 1984.

On NITSCH: Books—*Happenings* by Jurgen Becker and Wolf Vostell, Reinbeck 1965; *Aus der Theorie des O.M. Theaters* edited by F. Mauthner, Vienna 1965; *Happening und Fluxus,* exhibition catalog compiled by Hanns Sohm, Cologne 1970; *Wien—Bildkompendium Wiener Aktionismus und Film* by Peter Weibel and Valie Export, Frankfurt 1976; *Aktionskunst* by Jurgen Schilling, Lucerne and Frankfurt 1978; *Hermann Nitsch's O.M. Theater* by Eckenhart Sterk, Freiburg 1982; *Der Wiener Aktionismus—das O.M. Theater, eine Performance—Theoretische Studie,* thesis by Hubert Klocker, Vienna 1983. **Articles—**''Hermann Nitsch in Northern New Mexico'' by Nancy Gillespie in *Artspace,* vol. 14, no. 5, July-August 1990; ''Studio: Hermann Nitsch'' by David Courtney in *Sculpture* (Washington, D.C.), vol. 13, no. 2, March-April 1994; ''Blood and Soil'' by Fenella Crichton in *Art Monthly,* no. 220, October 1998.

*

The O. M. Theatre (orgies-mysteries theatre) is an attempt at an absolute ''Gesamtkunstwerk.'' The world of the phenomena is understood through synesthesia. Drama (lyric, epic), painting and music combine themselves in a six-day feast of glorification of existences. The spectator (participant, player) is thrown into a more intensified aesthetic-mystic understanding of the surrounding world.

(Form/aesthetic—essential aim of practice of art. Intensified registration of the world through the form. Form condenses the surrounding world in the enjoying senses and moves it closer to us, drives us more strongly into our own liveliness, drives us more strongly into being. Practice of art = mystic of being. Aesthetic even deep into cruelty. Aesthetic of the cruel.) Establishing synesthetically relations between: perception of touch, perception of taste, perception of smell, perception of acoustic and visual registrations shall inspire our senses orgiastically. The accelerating activation of all senses can be compared to psychoanalysis. Instead of associating, actions are instituted which heighten the perceptions of the senses until the endpoint of orgiastic ''abreaction.'' (Evaluation of elemental sensuous aggressive-sadistic perceptions, dilacerating of raw meat, disembowelment of slaughtered animal cadavers and trampling on the entrials. The use of cry—and noise actions/noise music). The result is a descent into subconscious regions. We have a sex drive originating which reaches to the very bottom of sado-masochistic excess. The basic excess = endpoint of the ''abreactive'' experience, sado-masochistic acting; breakthrough as well as demonstrable and conciousness of the subconscious regions, catharsis. Dramatic climax of the play. The ''abreactive'' events become automatically playacting. Through thorough ''abreaction'' this playing contributes to overcome excessive experiencing, and replaces it with sublimated experience. The events which are presented at the O.M. Theatre are not acted as in the case of classical theatre, but are occurring, he shall reach his own self—reach the mystic of being. The action of the play brings the spectator to realization of his own existential reality. Through the explanation of mystic symbolism originates a demythologized awareness of mystic projections. (Dispute with the collective unawareness). After the ''abreaction'' provoked by the play, the excessive can be overcome. There comes a quiet, meditative understanding of existence. Sublimation, the mystic of being instead of ''abreaction.'' As a result, the actions only provoke contemplation and submersion into the world of phenomena. The excessive, sado-masochistic ''abreaction'' is sublimated to the dispute with colour (colour reactions, colourgames, colour-projections). The concentrated aesthetic liturgy of the O.M. Theatre can expand over the entire human life and can transform the process of living into a positive, life-enjoying, aesthetic ritual.

—Hermann Nitsch

* * *

It is possibly still available: a portrait-photo of Hermann Nitsch—in limited edition—the man himself, blindfolded (with white bandage) blood streaming down from his mouth and left shoulder to the base of his stomach (totally naked, of course) from Studio Morra, Via Calabritto 20, 80121 Napoli for D. Mark 30—a souvenir of 1977.

A leader-member of the *Destruction in Art* Vienna based movement which went into voluntary exile for a while in Germany, Hermann Nitsch has never evaded exhibitionism. The group's output took the form of performance art and generally all four Destruction in Art members (Gunter Brus, Otto Muhl, Rudolf Schwarzkogler Hermann Nitsch himself, and other enthusiasts as well if they could be recruited in time for the place of display) were all employed, singly or in concert, in the Action.

The DIA group tended to concentrate—with their own bodies and behavior—upon the unsavoury aspects of human life. Special attention would be given pornography, the nastier guilts masked by middle-class propriety with invasions of sexual ambiguity and exhibitionism whenever appropriate. They also set great store on enactments of physical torture, castration and other forms of emasculation, together with the shadier inferences of bestiality. Nudity and the profusion of gore combined to make the usual signature of their works.

Not suprisingly they were seen to be the stars and the centre of attention for the DIAS (Destruction in Art Symposium) at St. Bride's Hall off London's Fleet Street only three years before Schwarzkögler in an excess of self-mutilation inadvertently managed to kill himself. At the London DIAS two journalists from United Press called the police on the grounds that the performances were an affront to public decency, a step which eventually led to the Symposium's organization being arraigned and brought to London's supreme court, the Old Bailey, on charges of trying to deprave and corrupt members of the DIAS audience. After a 4-day hearing Judge Rogers, having asked the 12-person jury to reach a decision, spoke in open court to those attending the trial to advise them that he had had a most extraordinary communication from the foreman of the jury—to wit: the twelve had agreed to bring in a joint verdict of guilty for the two defendants, but only if the twelve jurors could have assurance from the judge that he would act leniently towards them. If, on the other hand, they received no such promise, they would pronounce both prisoners innocent. Judge Rogers added that he would now speak to both counsels, prosecuting and defending, and alert them to this strange situation. In consequence the jury brought in a unanimous verdict of guilty for both the accused. One was fined £200, which was immediately collected from visitors attending the the court, and the other was bound over to be of exemplary behaviour for 12 months. None of the four core members of DIA were present at the Old Bailey trial although they had all agreed to play their part there. Both defence and prosecution were somewhat terrified by what they might resort to if given such a chance and opportunity to demonstrate in such a public forum.

Hermann Nitsch, as a general organizer, promoter and idea-man has appeared to be in the forefront of the group's prosecution of aims—to shock, disgust, horrify and bring to light the ugly backgrounds of human behaviour. But it should be emphasized that the movement, acting together, in pairs or as single performers, display a recognizable independence from their colleagues exemplified in character and appearance. Each has his own line of specialities of performance. Muhl, for instance, laces his insults with a disturbing sense of humour, black or purple, depending upon the viewer's character.

—Sheldon Williams

NOÉ, Luis Felipe

Nationality: Argentine. **Born:** Buenos Aires, 26 May 1933. **Education:** College Française de Buenos Aires, Colegio Nacional Sarmiento, University of Buenos Aires Law School; studied painting at the studio of Horacio Butler (1951–52). **Family:** Married Nora Murphy, 1957; two children: Paula and Gaspar. **Career:** Journalist, 1955–61; painter, 1957–. **Awards:** French government fellowship, 1961; Torcuato Di Tella Foundation, National Award, 1964; John Simon Memorial Foundation, fellowship, 1965–1966; Honorable Mention, The 6th International Biennial Exhibition of Prints in Tokyo, 1968; Argentine Society of Art Critics, Trajectory Award, Buenos Aires, 1985; First Prize, Fortabat Foundation, Buenos Aires, 1986; Trajectory Award, Argentine National Arts Fund, Buenos Aires, 1997; First Mercosur Painting Biennial, Montevideo, 1997; Chandon Grand Prize, Buenos Aires, 1997; First Buenos Aires Art Biennial, Argentine Award, 2000. **Address:** Tacuarí 763, (1071)-Buenos Aires.

Individual Exhibitions

1959 Witcomb Gallery, Buenos Aires
1960 Van Riel Gallery, Buenos Aires
1961 Bonino Gallery, Buenos Aires
1965 Museum of Modern Art, Buenos Aires
1966 Bonino Gallery, New York
1968 National Museum of Fine Arts, Caracas, Venezuela
1978 Durban Gallery, Madrid
L'Oeil de Boeuf Gallery, Paris
Espace Latinoamericain, Paris
1982 New York Studio School, New York
1983 Van Riel Gallery, Buenos Aires
1984 Bellechasse Gallery, Paris
Sívori Museum, Buenos Aires
1988 Gooijer Fine Arts, Amsterdam
1989 Museum of Modern Art, Bogota, Colombia
Ruth Benzacar Gallery, ARCO, Madrid
1995 National Museum of Fine Arts, Buenos Aires
La Gallería, Guayaquil, Ecuador
1996 National Palace of Fine Arts, Mexico City
1997 Borges Cultural Center, Buenos Aires
2001 Rubbers Gallery, Buenos Aires

Group Exhibitions with Other Figuration Group (includes Ernesto Deira, Rómulo Macció, Jorge de la Vega, and Luis Felipe Noé):

1961 Peuser Gallery, Buenos Aires
1962 Bonino Gallery, Buenos Aires
Lirolay Gallery, Buenos Aires
1963 National Museum of Fine Arts, Buenos Aires
National Fine Arts Commission, Montevideo, Uruguay
Bonino Gallery, Rio de Janeiro, Brazil
1965 Museum of Modern Art, Rio de Janeiro, Brazil
Bonino Gallery, Buenos Aires
Sociedad Hebraica, Buenos Aires
1981 *Fundación San Telmo,* Buenos Aires
1984 Mara Gallery, Buenos Aires
1985 National Museum of Fine Arts, Buenos Aires
Van Riel Gallery, Buenos Aires

18th Sao Paulo Biennial, Sao Paulo, Brazil
1986 Museum of Fine Arts, Caracas, Venezuela
1987 Brazil-Argentina Cultural Institute, Rio de Janeiro, Brazil
1991 Recoleta Cultural Center, Buenos Aires

Selected Group Exhibitions:

1960 First International Exhibition of Modern Art, Museum of Modern Art, Buenos Aires
1963 *The Art of America and Spain,* Hispanic Culture Institute, Madrid
1964 Guggenheim International Award, The Solomon R. Guggenheim Museum, New York
1966 *The Emergent Decade: Latin America Painters and Paintings in the 1960s,* Cornell University and The Solomon R. Guggenheim Museum, New York
1982 *Latin American Artists in Europe,* Venice
1984 1st Havana Biennial, Havana, Cuba
International Painting Festival, Cagnes-sur-mer, France
1985 18th Sao Paulo Biennial, Brazil
1989 *The Latin America Spirit: Art and Artists in the United States, 1920–1970,* The Bronx Museum of the Arts, New York
1992 *Voices from the High Sea,* Atlantic Modern Art Center, Madrid and Las Palmas (Canary Islands)
1993 1st Triennial of the Americas, Mauberg, France
Latin American Artists of the 20th Century, Museum of Modern Art, New York; Seville City Hall, Spain; Georges Pompidou Center, Paris; Museum Ludwig in der Josef-Haubrich-Kunsthalle, Cologne
1994 *Argentina 1920–1994,* Museum of Modern Art, Oxford, United Kingdom
4th International Painting Biennial, Cuenca, Ecuador
1995 1st Mercosur Inter-parliamentary Painting Exhibition, National Legislature, Montevideo, Uruguay
1st Mercosur Visual Arts Biennial, Porto Alegre, Brazil
Re-Aligning Vision: Alternative Currents in South American Drawing, Museo del Barrio, New York; Arkansas Art Center, Little Rock, Arkansas; AMHAG, Austin, Texas; Museum of Fine Arts, Caracas, Venezuela
1999 *À Rebours: The Informal Rebellion (1939–1968),* Atlantic Modern Art Center, Las Palmas (Canary Islands); Queen Sofía National Art Center, Madrid
2000 *Visions from the South,* Queen Sofía National Art Center, Madrid

Collections:

The Solomon R. Guggenheim Museum, New York; Metropolitan Museum of Art, New York; National Museum of Fine Arts, Buenos Aires; Rhode Island Museum, Rhode Island; Fine Arts Museum, Nicaragua; Salvador Allende Solidarity Museum, Santiago, Chile; Museum of Modern Art, Buenos Aires; Fine Arts Museum of San Juan Province, Argentina; Museum of Fine Arts, General Roca Río Negro Province, Argentina; Castagnino Museum, Rosario, Santa Fe Province, Argentina; The Rosa Galisteo de Rodríguez Museum, Santa Fe, Argentina; Museum of Modern Art, Cuenca, Ecuador; Museum of Fine Arts, Caracas, Venezuela.

Publications:

By NOÉ: Books—*Antiestética,* Ediciones Van Riel, Buenos Aires 1965, and Ediciones de La Flor, Buenos Aires 1988; *Una sociedad colonial avanzada,* Ediciones de la Flor, Buenos Aires 1971; *Códice rompecabezas sobre recontrapoder en cajón desastre,* Ediciones de la Flor, Buenos Aires 1974; *A Oriente por Occidente — Descubrimiento del llamado descubrimiento o del origen de lo que somos y no somos,* Ediciones Dos Gráfico, Bogota, Colombia 1992; *Lectura conceptual de una trayectoria,* with Jorge Glusberg, Center for Art and Communication (CAYC), Buenos Aires 1993; *El otro, la otra, la otredad,* Ediciones IMPSAT, Buenos Aires 1994; *El arte en cuestión. Conversaciones,* Buenos Aires 2000. **Articles—**''En la sociedad pop la vanguardia no está en las Gallerys de arte'' in *Mirador,* vol. 1, no. 5, May 1966; ''La responsabilidad del artista que se va de América Latina y la del que se queda'' in *Mirador,* vol. 1, no. 7, 1966; ''La cultura artística condenada a muerte'' in *El Cielo* (Buenos Aires), vol. 1, no. 2, November-December 1968; ''De la rebelión en el arte al arte en la rebelión'' in *Persona* (Buenos Aires), vol. 1, no. 2, May 1969; ''Mis aproximaciones al dibujo'' in *Plages* (Paris), 1978; ''La nostalgia de la historia en el proceso de imaginación plástica de América Latina,'' paper presented during the Latin American Art Forum of Mexico, 1981; ''Nueve reflexiones acerca de la pintura como lenguaje'' in *Artinf* (Buenos Aires), no. 42, 1983; ''Arte, autoritarismo y poder ''in *Plural* (Buenos Aires), no. 1, 1983; ''Eso que llamamos caos'' in *Cyclope* (Buenos Aires), no. 1, December 1991; ''Does Art from Latin America Need a Passport?'' in *Being American,* edited by Rachel Weiss with Alan West, New York 1991;'' El lenguaje con, sin y más allá de las palabras'' in *El Augur* (Asunción, Paraguay), no. 11–12, 1993;'' La llamada nueva figuración argentina'' in *Porto Arte* (Porto Alegre), vol. 9, no. 16, 1999.

On NOÉ: Books—*New Tendencies in Art* by Aldo Pellegrini, New York 1966; *El arte en la Argentina* by Jorge Romero Brest, Buenos Aires 1969; *80 años de pintura argentina* by Códoba Iturburu, Buenos Aires 1978; *Arte Argentino Contemporáneo,* Madrid 1979; *Pintores argentinos del siglo XX,* Buenos Aires 1981; *El estupor del arte* by Carlos Espartaco, Buenos Aires 1984; *Del pop-art a la nueva imagen* by Jorge Glusberg, Buenos Aires 1985; *Luis Felipe Noé* by Mercedes Casanegra, Alba S.A., Buenos Aires 1988; *La peinture de l' Amérique Latine au XXe Sièc1* by Damián Bayón, Paris 1990; *Del Informalismo a la Figuración Crítica* by Jorge Glusberg, Buenos Aires 1992; *Latin American Art* by Edward Lucie-Smith, London 1993; *Arte y Discurso* by Carlos Espartaco, Buenos Aires 1993; *Nueva Historia Argentina, Arte Sociedad y Política* by José Emilio Burucúa, Buenos Aires 1999. **Articles—**''La nueva imagen en latinoamérica'' by Jorge Glusberg in *Transvantgarde international,* edited by Achille Bonito Oliva, Milan 1982.

* * *

Anguish, the passion for existence, and the pace of life in permanent transformation are all distinctive traits of the work of Luis Felipe Noé—an artist who debates history via Baroque forms, bright ranges of color, and visually clashing spaces.

His background, his abandoning and then recovering painting as a means of expression, his encounter with chaos and in-depth study of it all form part of the production of this artist, who is as passionate as he is reflective—a man who has penned such works as *Antiestética* (*Anti-aesthetics,* 1965) and *La sociedad colonial avanzada* (*The*

Advanced Colonial Society, 1971). "My subject is chaos," he has reiterated time and again, ever proclaiming the inescapable need to assume this theme.

Between 1959 and 1961, Noé sought to dismantle the opposition between the figurative and the abstract, in an overwhelming synthesis. So it was that he went from the elements to the whole in his attempt to find a "unity of atmosphere." Around 1962, through his "divided picture" theory, he approached the theme applying a different dialectic, dismantling the whole into its elements, on the pathway to a "multiplicity of situations." But this second stage coincided with the formation of the *New Figuration* school, in which he participated with Ernesto Deira, Rómulo Macció and Jorge de la Vega. This is the Argentine vision of the CoBrA (Copenhagen, Brussels, Amsterdam) Group. In 1963, the National Museum of Fine Arts, then under the direction of Jorge Romero Brest, organized an exclusive and celebrated show of the work of this group of bold young representatives of an art that was critical, figurative, and aggressive in the face of tradition.

Noé then launched into the process of tearing down boundaries as a means of reaching a "broken vision." He reached it at last, but at the cost of abandoning painting. And so, for nine years (from 1966 to 1974) he quit painting, until, that is, he discovered that the tensions he was obsessed with discovering could be generated by producing vibration in line, smudge, color, and plane. So it was that he returned to painting in 1975. And since then, he has done nothing but delve ever deeper into the historical, social, and poetic contents of his work, under the protection (both literal and metaphoric) of an ever clearer American will and passion. After his nine-year hiatus from painting, Noé was again seduced by it, as of his vision of the landscape of El Tigre (the Delta of the River Plate, close by the City of Buenos Aires).

"La Naturaleza y sus mitos" ("Nature and its Myths") is as historical as "Conquista y destrucción de la Naturaleza" ("Conquest and Destruction of Nature"), which deals with the origins of America in the 15th and 16th centuries. Historical too are the series known as "Esto no tiene nombre" ("This Is Unspeakable"); "Todo es verdad, nada es mentira" ("Everything Is True, Nothing Is a Lie") and "Percepciones" ("Perceptions"). In the end, for Noé, the concept of Nature is synonymous with History.

It is solely with these eyes that we can read the proposals of Noé, who settled in Paris in 1976, but certainly not to estrange himself from an Argentina subjected to darkness and shrouded in fog, or from a Latin America where despotism reigned. His level of concern is patent in his works of those days and in later ones as well. A tenacious vehemence that is emblematic of Noé fires his monsters and nightmares, while making a dream-like and dazzling statement. It is the play between testimony (or constellation) and revelation (or magic).

Perhaps at this point, it would be worthwhile mentioning the geographic triangle in which Noé has resided: Buenos Aires, his native city; New York, where he spent the better part of 1964 and then spent three more years, from the end of 1965 to the end of 1968; and Paris, where he lived in 1961 and 1962, and then—after staying in Buenos Aires from 1969 through 1976—the place to which he would return in exile for over a decade, to escape the sinister military dictatorship, after which, in 1987, he would re-enter life in Buenos Aires. If Noé decided to abandon painting in New York, it was not because he was estranged from Buenos Aires, but from painting itself. And if he was able to develop a new stage in Paris, it was because his absence from Argentina and America was merely nominal, physical.

In fact, during the Paris years, he once again took up his Argentine experiments, such as his front-and-back paintings ("Novela" ["Novel"]; "La difícil comunicación" ["Difficult Communication"]) and of working with folds ("Estructura para un paisaje" ["Structure for a Landscape"]; "Dentro de un paisaje" ["Within a Landscape"]). In both cases, it is a matter of proposing metaphorical elaborations, concrete allusions. Because his front-and-back paintings suggest totality and cover-up, justice and attack. (In Spanish, front and back are *derecho y revés,* with the play on words being that to give someone a *revés* is to backhand them, which is a type of blow—*golpe*—that is another name for coup, while *derecho* is also the word for law, an ethical attribute). The *pliegues* (folds), meanwhile, refer to the multiple wrinkles of human nature.

His work "Reflexión sobre la pintura" ("Reflecting on Painting")—a canvas, a support frame, plus another well-stretched frame and different images accompanied by a passage of text—was, according to what the artist has written, "a way of showing that painting is always thinking about itself, by thinking of itself as a language that thinks about the world around it." Noé's work has to do with history, with events of today and yesterday, with the circumstances of the artist and of the world—be it in "Primera destrucción de Buenos Aires" ("First Destruction of Buenos Aires"), in which he follows the lead, albeit in his own way, of Ulrico Schmidl, or in questions of internal struggle, like in "¡Carajo que se rinda su abuela!" ("Hell No, Let Your Grandma Surrender!") and in "La batalla nos une" ("Battle Unites Us").

It is also the history of the hieroglyphics discovered by Noé in the caverns of Buenos Aires. To start with, they are not hieroglyphics in the normal sense of the word, nor are there caverns in Buenos Aires. But the metaphor is certainly transparent enough: It is a question of mysteries to be unraveled. In these seductive and mordant paintings, the artist disinters the history of internal (Tucumán) and external (Paraguay) migration, the *porteño* character, the ecological reserve, money, and power, as well as the triviality and political drama that have come close to destroying the Argentine people.

—Jorge Glusberg

NOGUCHI, Isamu

Nationality: American. **Born:** Los Angeles, 17 November 1904; moved, with family, to Tokyo, 1906. **Education:** Chigasaki Grammar School, Japan, 1910–17; semi-apprenticed to cabinetmaker, Chigasaki, 1917; studied at St. Joseph's College, Yokohama, Japan, 1917–18; Rolling Prairie Public School, Indiana, 1918–22; sculpture apprentice, to Gutzon Borglum, Stamford, Connecticut; studied art and sculpture, under Onorio Ruotolo, Leonardo da Vinci Art School, New York, 1923–26; medicine, Columbia University, New York, 1924–27; drawing, Academie Grande Chaumiere and Colarossi School, Paris, 1927; brush drawing under Chi Pai Shi, Peking, China, and pottery, under Uno Jinmatsu, Kyoto, Japan, 1931. **Family:** Married Yoshiko (Shirley) Yamaguchi in 1953 (divorced, 1955). **Career:** Independent sculptor and artist, since 1926. Worked in restaurant, New York, 1924; influenced by seeing Brancusi exhibition, Brummer Gallery, New York 1926; moved to Paris, working with Brancusi, 1927; met Alexander Calder, Stuart Davis, Fouijita, Morris Kantor, Pascin and Andre Ruellen, Paris and London, 1927; travelled between New York and Paris, 1928–30, travelled to Berlin, Moscow, Peking, Tokyo and Kyoto via the Trans-Siberian Railway, 1931–32; created

Isamu Noguchi: *Cube,* in front of the Marine Midland Bank in New York, 1988. ©Michael S. Yamashita/Corbis.

first set design, for *Frontier* ballet by Martha Graham, leading to numerous collaborations, New York, 1935; lived and worked in Mexico, 1935–36, in Hawaii, 1939; drove across the United States, with Arshile Gorky, 1941; voluntary intern, relocation camp for Japanese Americans, Poston, Arizona, 1942; designed coffee table for Herman Miller and table lamp for Knoll, New York, 1944; travelled throughout the world, 1949–50; designed sets and costumes for Gielgud's *King Lear,* London, 1955; established studio, Long Island, New York, 1961; established studio, Island of Shikoku, Japan, 1971. **Awards:** Guggenheim Fellowship, 1927, and Travel Fellowship, 1931; Bollingen Foundation Grant, 1950; Second Prize, Society of Four Arts Sculpture Competition, Palm Beach, Florida, 1974; Albert Einstein Commemorative Award, 1978; Mayor's Award of Arts and Culture, New York, 1978; MacDowell Medal, Peterborough, New Hampshire, 1982; New York State Governor's Award, 1984; Japanese American Citizens League Award, 1984; Israel Museum Fellowship, Jerusalem, 1985; President's Medal, U.S.A, 1985; Kyoto Prize, Inamori Foundation, Japan, 1986; National Medal of Arts, Washington, D.C., 1987; The Order of the Sacred Treasure, Japan, 1988. D.F.A.: New School for Social Research, New York, 1974; University of Southern California, Los Angeles 1979; D.H.L.: Columbia University, New York, 1984. **Member:** American Academy of Arts and Sciences. **Agents:** Pace Gallery, 32 East 57th Street, New York, New York 10022; Gimpel Fils, 30 Davies Street, London WIY ILG, England. **Died:** New York, 30 December 1988, of heart failure.

Individual Exhibitions:

1928 Marie Sterner Gallery, New York
1929 Eugene Schoen Gallery, New York
1930 Harvard Society for Contemporary Art, Cambridge, Massachusetts
Arts Club of Chicago (toured the United States)
Albright Art Gallery, Buffalo, New York
1931 Rochester Memorial Art Gallery, New York
John Becker Gallery, New York
Demotte Galleries, New York
Reinhardt Galleries, New York
1932 John Becker Gallery, New York
1933 Mellon Galleries, Philadelphia
1934 Honolulu Academy of Fine Arts, Hawaii
Sidney Burney Gallery, London
1935 Marie Harriman Gallery, New York
1939 Honolulu Academy of Fine Arts, Hawaii
John Becker Gallery, New York
1942 Museum of Modern Art, San Francisco
John Becker Gallery, New York
1947 Museum of Modern Art, New York (retrospective)
1950 Mitsukoshi Store, Tokyo
1952 Museum of Modern Art, New York
1953 Museum of Modern Art, New York

Isamu Noguchi with one of his sculptures. ©UPI/Corbis-Bettmann.

1954 Stable Gallery, New York
1963 Cordier and Ekstrom Gallery, New York
1965 Cordier and Ekstrom Gallery, New York
1967 Cordier and Ekstrom Gallery, New York
1968 Gimpel Fils Gallery, London
Galerie Gimpel und Hanover, Zurich
Whitney Museum, New York (retrospective)
1969 Cordier and Ekstrom Gallery, New York
1970 *Noguchi/Rickey/Smith,* Indiana University, Bloomington
1972 Gimpel Fils Gallery, London
Galerie Gimpel und Hanover, Zurich
1975 *Steel Sculpture,* Pace Gallery, New York
1977 Museum of Modern Art, New York
1978 *Noguchi's Imaginary Landscape,* Walker Art Center, Minneapolis (toured the United States)
1979 *Drawings and Sculpture: Noguchi/Calder/Smith,* Storm King Art Center, Mountainville, New York
1980 Whitney Museum, New York
Pace Gallery, New York
André Emmerich Gallery, New York
1981 Galerie Maeght, Paris
1983 Pace Gallery, New York
1985 Arnold Herstand Gallery, New York
Seibu Department Store, Tokyo
1986 Pace Gallery, New York
American Pavilion, *Biennale,* Venice
1989 *Isamu Noguchi: Portrait Sculpture,* National Portrait Gallery, Washington, D.C.
1992 *Isamu Noguchi: Retrospective 1992,* National Museum of Modern Art, Tokyo
ANZAI: Homage to Isamu Noguchi, Tokoro Gallery, Tokyo
1994 *Isamu Noguchi: Beginnings and Ends,* Pace Gallery, New York
Fundacion Juan March, Madrid
1998 *Isamu Noguchi: Stones and Water,* Pace Wildenstein, New York

Selected Group Exhibitions:

1939 *World's Fair,* New York
1946 *14 Americans,* Museum of Modern Art, New York

1970 *Expo '70,* Osaka, Japan
1974 *Japan: Tradition und Gegenwart,* Städtische Kunsthalle, Dusseldorf
1976 *200 Years of American Sculpture,* Whitney Museum, New York
1979 *A Century of Ceramics in America 1878–1978,* Everson Museum of Art, Syracuse, New York
1980 *Perceiving Modern Sculpture: Selections for the Sighted and Non-Sighted,* Grey Gallery, New York University
1983 *Abstract Painting and Sculpture in America 1927–44,* Carnegie Institute, Pittsburgh (travelled to San Francisco and New York)
1985 *Transformation in Sculpture,* Guggenheim Museum, New York
1986 *Le Japan des Avant-Gardes,* Centre Georges Pompidou, Paris
1988 *Enduring Creativity,* Whitney Museum of American Art, Stamford
1989 *The Experience of Landscape: Three Decades of Sculpture,* Whitney Museum of American Art, New York
1993 *Sculpture in the Expanded Field,* Gariloch Gallery, Oakville
1995 *1945: The End of the War,* Annely Juda Fine Art, London
Abstract Expressionism: Masterpieces from Japanese Collections, National Museum of Modern Art, Tokyo
Abstract Expressionism: Works on Paper—Selections from the Metropolitan Museum of Art, New York

Collections:

Metropolitan Museum of Art, New York; Museum of Modern Art, New York; Whitney Museum, New York; Guggenheim Museum, New York; Chase Manhattan Bank, New York; Storm King Art Center, Mountainville, New York; National Gallery of Art, Washington, D.C.; Hirshhorn Museum, Washington, D.C.; Art Gallery of Ontario, Toronto; Brooklyn Museum, New York; Albright-Knox Art Gallery, Buffalo, New York; Art Institute of Chicago; Israel Museum, Jerusalem; Los Angeles County Museum of Art; Rijksmuseum Kröller-Müller, Otterlo, Holland; Storm King Art Center, Mountainville, New York; Yale University, New Haven.

Publications:

By NOGUCHI: Books—*A Sculptor's World,* New York 1968; *The Isamu Noguchi Garden Museum,* New York 1987. **Articles—**interview in *The Artist's Voice: Talks with 17 Artists* by Katherine Kuh, New York 1962; ''Noguchi on Brancusi'' in *Craft Horizons* (New York), August 1976; interview in *Artists in their Own Words: Interviews,* by Paul Cummings, New York 1979.

On NOGUCHI: Books—*Art in America: A Complete Survey* by Holger Cahill and Alfred H. Barr, New York 1935; *Modern Art in America* by Martha Chandler Cheney, New York 1939; *La Surréalisme en 1947* by Andre Breton, Paris 1947; *Tradition and Experiment in Modern Sculpture* by Charles Seymour, Washington, D.C. 1949; *Abstract Painting and Sculpture in America* by Andrew C. Ritchie, New York 1952; *Noguchi* by Shuzo Takiguchi, Tokyo 1953; *Modern Art U.S.A.: Men, Rebellion, Conquest 1900–1956* by Rudi Blesh, New York 1956; *Nature in Abstraction* by John I. H. Baur, New York 1958; *American Art since 1900: A Critical History* by Barbara Rose, New York 1967; *Isamu Noguchi* by John Gordon, New York 1968; *Isamu Noguchi: The Life of a Sculptor* by Tobi Tobias, New York 1974; *Noguchi: Steel Sculptures,* exhibition catalog, New York 1975; *Isamu Noguchi* by Sam Hunter, New York 1978; *Noguchi's Imaginary Landscapes,* exhibition catalog, Minneapolis 1978; *The Sculpture of Isamu Noguchi 1924–1979* by Nancy Grove and Diane Botuick, New York 1980; *Isamu Noguchi: 75th Birthday Exhibition,* exhibition catalog, New York 1980; *Sculpture of Spaces,* exhibition catalog, New York 1980; *75th Birthday Exhibition: Landscape tables 1968–1979,* exhibition catalog, New York 1980; *Enduring Creativity,* exhibition catalog, Stamford 1988; *Isamu Noguchi: Portrait Sculpture,* exhibition catalog, Washington, D.C. 1989; *ANZAI: Homage to Isamu Noguchi,* exhibition catalog, with essay by Tadayasu Sakai, Tokyo 1992; *Isamu Noguchi: Restrospective 1992,* exhibition catalog, introduced by Koji Takahashi, Tokyo 1992; *Isamu Noguchi* by Bruce Altshuler, New York 1994; *Isamu Noguchi: Beginnings and Ends,* exhibition catalog, New York 1994; *Isamu Noguchi,* exhibition catalog, New York 1998. **Articles—**''Noguchi's Recent Marbles'' by Dore Ashton in *Art International* (Lugano, Switzerland), October 1972; ''Noguchi's Vision Shakes Up Young Japanese'' by Joseph Love in *Artnews* (New York), September 1973; ''Isamu Noguchi's Elegant World of Space and Function'' by Benjamin Forgey in *Smithsonian* (Washington, D.C.), April 1978; ''Noguchi's Multiplicities'' by Franz Schulze in *Art in America* (New York), January/February 1979; ''Sense and Subtlety in Stone'' by Robert Hughes in *Time* (New York), 7 March 1980; ''Rocks'' by Calvin Tomkins in *The New Yorker,* 24 March 1980; ''Sculpture and Beyond: Isamu Noguchi 1904–1988'' by Allen Wardell in *American Craft,* vol. 49, no. 2, April-May 1989; ''Isamu Noguchi: Early Drawings from Paris and Beijing'' by Bruce Altshuler in *Drawing* (New York), vol. 16, no. 4, November-December 1994; ''The Rejection of Isamu Noguchi's Hiroshima Cenotaph: a Japanese American Artist in Occupied Japan'' by Bert Winther in *Art Journal* (New York), vol. 53, no. 4, Winter 1994; ''Isamu Noguchi's Moere Numa Park: a Work in Progress'' by Kay Itoi in *Sculpture* (Washington, D.C.), vol. 16, no. 5, May-June 1997; ''The Stones of Mure'' by Kay Itoi in *ARTnews* (New York), vol. 98, no. 8, September 1999.

* * *

One of the great sculptors of this century, Isamu Noguchi has married his easternism to the west and produced an art enriched and enlarged by both cultures. A perfect example of this happy worldliness are the paper lamps he has designed. Aimed at a commercial market, they reflect the design attitudes of Europe and America while harking back to ancient Japanese craft.

This doubtless has been true of Noguchi's work throughout his career. Again and again one is reminded of orientalisms while looking at something undeniably western. Some of this has to do with a genius for simple means such as the extraordinary white silk curtain that represents the tide of furies who seize Orpheus in the great ballet by Balanchine/Stravinsky. The same inspired economy is characteristic of Noguchi's sets for dances by Martha Graham. He is a master at establishing symbols for things while remaining an abstractionist. Certainly a number of his finest sculptures are like calligraphy taken into the third dimension.

Everything is grist to his mill: the way in which polished marble forms interlock and mesh becomes curiously erotic in his hands. There are strong suggestions of exotic cults and unknown cultures whose signs and totems gleam in exquisitely worked stone. Noguchi is a marvellous carver rather than a modeler and he likes to take his material all the way to a highly finished state. This does not mean that he substitutes finish for expressiveness. He knows, too, when to suggest the unfinished, the broken, the hacked. Think of Michelangelo's uncompleted slaves. Then think of his extremely finished Pieta.

Noguchi, committed to the art of our time, is at the same time an inspired re-inventor of much that is ancient. This movement back and forth in time, together with an aesthetic play between east and west, has produced a new art of classical timelessness.

—Ralph Pomeroy

NOLAN, Sidney (Robert)

Nationality: Australian. **Born:** Melbourne, Victoria, 22 April 1917. **Education:** Attended Melbourne schools until 1932; studied part time at the Prahran Technical College, Melbourne, 1932–34, and at the National Gallery School, Melbourne (full-time), 1934–36; studied engraving and lithography with S. W. Hayter at Atelier 17, Paris, 1957–59. **Military Service:** Served in the Australian Army, 1941–45. **Family:** Married Elizabeth Patterson in 1939 (divorced, 1942); the author Cynthia Hansen in 1948 (died, 1976); Mary Boyd in 1978. **Career:** Designer, Fayrefield Hats factory, Melbourne, 1934–38; illustrator, Reed and Harris publishers, Melbourne, 1945–47. Full-time painter, in Sydney, 1950–51, Cambridge, England, 1951–53, various towns throughout Europe, 1954, in London and Hereford since 1955, and in New York, 1965–66, 1969; also stage designer, from 1941. **Awards:** Dunlop Painting Prize, Sydney, 1950; Painting Prize, *Biennale,* Venice, 1954; National Art Gallery Scholarship, Melbourne, 1956; Italian Government Scholarship, 1956; Commonwealth Fund Fellowship, 1958; Australian National University Fellowship, 1965. Honorary doctorates: Australian National University, Canberra, 1968; Bavarian University, Munich, 1971; University of Leeds, 1974; University of Sydney, 1977. C.B.E. (Commander, Order of the British Empire), 1963; Knighted, 1981; Order of Merit, 1983. **Agent:** Marlborough Fine Art Ltd., 6 Albemarle Street, London W1X 3HF. **Died:** In London, England, 27 November 1992.

Individual Exhibitions:

1940 Sidney Nolan Studio, Melbourne
1943 Contemporary Art Society, Melbourne
1946 University of Melbourne
1948 Moreton Galleries, Brisbane
1949 David Jones Art Gallery, Sydney
Macquarie Galleries, Sydney
Maison de l'Unesco, Paris
1950 Stanley Coe Gallery, Melbourne
Libreria di Quattro Venti, Rome
David Jones Art Gallery, Sydney
Maquarie Galleries, Sydney
1951 Redfern Gallery, Sydney
Maquarie Galleries, Sydney
1952 Stanley Coe Gallery, Melbourne
Redfern Gallery, London
1955 Redfern Gallery, London
1956 Johnstone Gallery, Brisbane
Durlacher Gallery, Brisbane
Gallery of Contemporary Art, Melbourne
1957 *Paintings 1947–57,* Whitechapel Art Gallery, London (toured the U.K.)
Johnstone Gallery, Brisbane
1958 Durlacher Gallery, New York
1960 Phoenix Art Museum, Arizona
Leda and the Swan and Other Recent Works, Mattiesen Gallery, London
1961 Hatton Gallery, Newscastle upon Tyne (retrospective; toured the U.K.)
Bonython Gallery, Adelaide
Australian Galleries, Melbourne
1962 Durlacher Gallery, New York
Institute of Contemporary Arts, London
Skinner Galleries, Perth
1963 Marlborough Fine Art, London
Georges Gallery, Melbourne
1964 Boynthon Gallery, Adelaide
The 1946–47 Ned Kelly Paintings, Qantas Gallery, London
At the *Aldeburgh Festival,* Suffolk (toured the U.K.)
1965 Marlborough-Gerson Gallery, New York
Recent Work, Marlborough Fine Art, London
David Jones Art Gallery, Sydney
Menzies Library, Australian National University, Canberra
Albert Hall, Canberra
Australian Galleries, Melbourne
1966 Shepparton Gallery, Melbourne
Qantas Gallery, Sydney
Marlborough New London Gallery (with John Piper and Ceri Richards)
1967 *Retrospective Exhibition: Paintings from 1937 to 1967,* Art Gallery of New South Wales, Sydney (restrospective; toured Australia)
Qantas Gallery, Sydney
1968 *Aldenburgh Festival,* Suffolk
1970 National Gallery of Victoria, Melbourne
1971 *Gemalde und Druckgraphik,* Kunsthalle, Darmstadt
Ashmolean Museum, Oxford
1972 Tate Gallery, London
Institute of Contemporary Arts, London
Marlborough Fine Art, London
1973 *Paintings and Prints,* Fuji Television Gallery, Tokyo
Ilkley Literature Festival, Yorkshire (retrospective)
David Jones Art Gallery, Sydney
Royal Dublin Society
Farmers Blaxland Gallery, Sydney
1974 Art Gallery of South Australia, Adelaide
Shepparton Gallery, Melbourne
1975 *Some Notes for Oedipus,* Marlborough Fine Art, London
David Jones Art Gallery, Sydney
1976 Rudy Komon Gallery, Sydney
1977 Institute of Modern Art, Brisbane
Rudy Komon Gallery, Sydney
1978 Institute of Modern Art, Brisbane
Australian Galleries, Melbourne
Rudy Komon Gallery, Sydney
War Memorial Gallery, Canberra
Australian Embassy, Paris
1979 *Sidney Nolan 1937–1979,* Folkestone Arts Centre, Kent, England

1980 Rudy Komon Gallery, Sydney
1982 Thomas Agnew and Sons, London
1983 Grosvenor Museum, Chester, Cheshire
National Gallery of Victoria, Melbourne
Windsor Community Arts Centre, Australia
1987 National Gallery of Victoria, Melbourne
Art Gallery of New South Wales, Sydney
Art Gallery of Western Australia, Perth
Art Gallery of South Australia, Adelaide
Sir Sidney Nolan: A Retrospective Celebrating his 75th Birthday, Harewood Terrace Gallery, Leeds
1994 *The Ned Kelly Paintings,* Metropolitan Museum of Art, New York
Sidney Nolan (1917–1992): Important Paintings, Rex Irwin Art Dealer, Woollahra, Woollahra
1997 *Sidney Nolan: Works on Paper from the '60s and '70s—Mixed Media Paintings, Lithographs and Screenprints,* Bridget McDonnell Gallery, Carlton
Nolan's Nolans: a Reputation Reassessed-an Exhibition of Paintings from the Estate of Sir Sidney Nolan, Thomas Agnew & Son, London
1999 Pier Arts Centre, Stromness, Scotland

Selected Group Exhibitions:

1952 *Carnegie International,* Carnegie Institute, Pittsburgh
1954 *Biennale,* Venice
1959 *Documenta,* Kassel, West Germany
1961 *Recent Australian Painting,* Whitechapel Art Gallery, London
1962 *Rebels and Precursors: Painting in Melbourne 1937–47,* National Gallery of Victoria, Melbourne (travelled to the Art Gallery of New South Wales, Sydney)
1963 *British Painting in the 60s,* Tate Gallery, London
1965 *The English Eye,* Marlborough-Gerson Gallery, New York
1966 *Animal Painting: Van Dyck to Nolan,* Queen's Gallery, London
1998 *Australian Prints from the Gallery's Collection,* Art Gallery of New South Wales, Sydney

Collections:

Tate Gallery, London; Gulbenkian Foundation, London; Arts Council of Great Britain, London; National Gallery of Australia, Canberra; National Gallery of Victoria, Melbourne; Western Australian Art Gallery, Perth; Tom Collins Memorial Gallery, Perth University; Museum of Modern Art, New York.

Publications:

By NOLAN: Book—*Paradise Garden,* with an introduction by Robert Melville, London 1971. **Books illustrated**—*Outrider,* by R. Stow, London 1962; *Near the Ocean* by Robert Lowell, London 1966; *A Sight of China* by Cynthia Nolan, London 1969; *The Voyage* by Charles Baudelaire, London 1968; *Children's Crusade* by Benjamin Britten, London 1973.

On NOLAN: Books—*Place, Taste and Tradition: A Study of Australian Art since 1788* by Bernard Smith, Sydney 1945; *Art Here: Buvelot to Nolan* by C. Turnbill, Melbourne 1947; *A Study of Australian Art* by H. Badham, Sydney 1949; *A Gallery of Australian Art* by Badham, Sydney 1954; *Sidney Nolan: Paintings 1947–57,* exhibition catalog with text by Colin MacInnes, London 1957; *Modern Australian Painting and Sculpture 1950 to 1960,* edited by Kim Bonython, Adelaide 1960; *Sidney Nolan: Leda and the Swan and Other Recent Works,* exhibition catalog with text by Stephen Spender, London 1960; *Sidney Nolan* by Kenneth Clark, Colin MacInnes and Bryan Robertson, London 1961; *Nolan,* exhibition catalog with text by John Russell, Newcastle upon Tyne 1961; *Australian Painters: 40 Profiles* by J. Hetherington, Melbourne 1963; *Conversations with Painters* by N. Barber, London 1964; *The 1946–47 Ned Kelly Paintings by Sidney Nolan,* exhibition catalog with text by Elwynn Lynn, London 1964; *Ned Kelly: 27 Paintings by Sidney Nolan* by Robert Melville, London 1964, as *The Legend of Ned Kelly,* New York 1964; *Ballet in Australia* by Peggy van Praegh, Melbourne 1965; *Australian Lanscape Painting* by J. Reed, Melbourne 1965; *Sidney Nolan: Recent Work,* exhibition catalog with text by Robert Melville, London 1965; *Sidney Nolan: Myth and Imagery* by Elwynn Lynn, London 1967; *Open Negative: An American Memoir* by Cynthia Nolan, London 1967; *Sidney Nolan: Restrospective Exhibition: Paintings from 1937 to 1967,* exhibition catalog with text by Hal Missingham, Sydney 1967; *Sidney Nolan: Gemalde und Druckgraphik,* exhibition catalog with texts by Hans G. Sperlich and Bernd Krimmel, Darmstadt 1971; *Sidney Nolan: Paintings,* exhibition catalog with text by Robert Melville, London 1972; *Sidney Nolan: Paintings and Prints,* exhibition catalog with an introduction by Kenneth Clark, Tokyo 1973; *Sidney Nolan: Some Notes for Oedipus,* exhibition catalog with text by Robert Melville, London 1975; *Sidney Nolan 1937–1979,* exhibition catalog with text by Colin MacInnes, Folkestone, Kent 1979; *Sidney Nolan: Australia* by Elwynn Lynn, Sydney and London 1980; *Sidney Nolan,* exhibition catalog with text by Richard Haese, Melbourne 1983; *Sir Sidney Nolan,* exhibition catalog with essay by Elwynn Lynn, Windsor 1984; *Sidney Nolan: Landscapes and Legends,* exhibition catalog with text by Jane Clark, Melbourne 1987; *Sir Sidney Nolan: A Retrospective Celebrating his 75th Birthday,* exhibition catalog, Leeds 1992; *Sidney Nolan: The Ned Kelly Story,* exhibition catalog, with forward by William S. Lieberman, New York 1994; *Nolan's Nolan: a Reputation Reassessed—an Exhibition of Paintings from the Estate of Sir Sidney Nolan,* with introduction by Nicholas Usherwood, London 1997; *Sidney Nolan: Works on Paper from the '60s and '70s—Mixed Media Paintings, Lithographs and Screenprints,* exhibition catalog, Carlton 1997; *Australian Prints from the Gallery's Collection,* exhibition catalog, Sydney 1998. **Articles**—"Glittering Prizes: Metal Sculpture by Sidney Nolan" in *Art Review* (London), vol. 49, May 1997; "London: Sidney Nolan" by Merlin James in *Burlington Magazine* (London), no. 1134, vol. 139, September 1997; "How London is Appropriating 'Our' Nolan" by Julie Cotter in *Art Monthly Australia,* no. 103, September 1997.

* * *

Sir Sidney Nolan is one of Australia's best known artists, both in his homeland and internationally, his fame being reinforced, in 1994, when his original *Ned Kelly* works were shown at New York's Metropolitan Museum, a posthumous tribute to the artist, who died in 1992.

Despite his often quite immediately appealing subject matter (bushrangers, animals and wondrous landscapes) his interpretations were extremely personal and idiosyncratic, exploiting a symbolic visual language reminiscent, at times, of Paul Klee and even Kasimir Malevich (the rectangular helmet of the folk hero Ned Kelly became a dramatic icon, readily recognisable in the history of Australian post-World War II painting).

A retrospective exhibition of *Works on Paper* by Nolan, covering a period of approximately forty years, toured Australia in the early 1980s. Many of the works included were borrowed from the artist's personal collection and were especially insightful. Nolan worked consistently and prolifically for most of his professional life, which was marked by extremely energetic outbursts of creative activity—as many as 12 paintings and 13 drawings in 3 days. Rapid execution would tend to indicate that emotional intensity, rather than technical facility (in the conventional sense), was Nolan's priority. Sometimes, his work appeared inept and child-like, especially to the uninitiated.

Never a very responsive, or cooperative, art student in his younger Melbourne years, he determinedly broke with local artistic taste-makers and puzzled the critics. In the *Works on Paper* retrospective there was plenty of evidence that Nolan was always determined to convincingly speak his own artistic language. His drawings and media experiments of the late 1930s and early 1940s took the form of an intensely felt personal diary. History and myth were often interpreted by Nolan to reveal elements of a decidedly autobiographical nature. Early (and, by local standards, boldly daring) explorations of collage (using rectilinear breakups and complex tonal interplays) were accompanied by voyages of discovery employing a wide range of inks and paints on unlikely papers. The monotype process was one which accommodated Nolan's early graphic flair, where linear emphasis dominated. Smudged pastels and soft water colours helped create dream-like, semi-abstract landscape imagery (part fact, part fiction), inspired by Dimboola, the Grampians and Heidelberg (1942–45). During these war years Nolan commonly used broad washes of background colour with heavy black ink calligraphy superimposed (*Desert, Morning, Plane Crash,* 1942). A sketch for Max Harris's *The Vegative Eye* (1943) revealed an approach to head studies (psychological states) which he was to develop further in his riveting Burke and Wills portraits of the early 1950s and the powerfully disturbing Gallipoli war visages of the 1960s.

The stylised Ned Kelly heads first emerged in 1946, both in drawing and paint. Masked in a rectangular black helmet, the infamous Irish-born bushranger was to become Nolan's most beloved and recognisable creation and the source of inspiration for a seemingly endless sees of paintings and prints (etchings and lithographs).

An inveterate traveller, Nolan ventured into the desert wastelands of Central Australia and Africa, as well as the less accessible Greek islands and Antarctica. Although seldom painting on location, Nolan was inspired by the many places he visited, and blessed with extraordinary powers of recall, he created some of his most expressive and exciting works on his return to more "civilised" climes, such as England, where he was domiciled for much of his later life. A sexual ambiguity prevailed in much of Nolan's figurative work, although the twice-married Nolan never acknowledged publicly any overt deviation from the sexual straight and narrow. The Greek series from the mid 1950s paid homage to the mythology of an ancient culture. A combination of water-based dyes and oil crayons resulted in some hypnotically beautiful and appropriately theatrically flavoured works.

During the 1970s, Nolan seemed to go into a decline, relying increasingly on cliched reworkings of his past symbols and themes. Numbers of minimal crayon drawings (from 1978) and a suite of drawings based on an episode in Dante's *The Divine Comedy* gave rise to speculation that the once sophisticated child-like (pseudo-naive) elements in Nolan's work may have tipped over into mere childishness.

In the 1980s, Sir Sidney Nolan continued to design occasionally, for the theatre and divide his time between Australia and Europe. He visited Australia for special projects, such as his series of paintings executed in conjunction with the film *Burke and Wills,* starring Nigel Havers. Nolan worked on location with the film crew and the resulting paintings were among his finest for years.

His work was the subject of a vast touring retrospective, sponsored by one of his most loyal supporters, Rupert Murdoch (Lord McAlpine being one other notable sponsor). This retrospective, shown in State galleries throughout Australia during 1987 and 1988, confirmed his place as one of Australia's most innovative artists and the artist who has most successfully exploited the Australian folk mythology.

Some paintings, such as those in the *Silk Road* series of the 1980s, were recklessly unfinished looking and met with little critical enthusiasm. Paintings exploring the possibilities inherent in spray aerosol processes varied in their degrees of successfulness. At their best they provided evidence of a still fertile creative mind, as the artist moved into the last years of his life.

Nolan possessed great energy to the end and it is sad that he died at an age when some artists find a new lease on life, and before his American acclaim.

—Arthur McIntyre

NOLAND, Kenneth

Nationality: American. **Born:** Asheville, North Carolina, 10 April 1924. **Education:** Studied art, under Ilya Bolotowsky, Black Mountain College, North Carolina, 1946–48, summer 1950; studied sculpture, under Ossip Zadkine, Paris, 1948–49; student-teacher, Institute of Contemporary Arts, Washington, D.C., 1949–50. **Military Service:** Served as glider pilot and cryptographer in the United States Air Force, 1942–46. **Family:** Married Cornelia Langer in 1950 (divorced, 1957); children: William, Lyndon and Cady; married Stephanie Gordon in 1967 (divorced, 1970); married Peggy Schiffer (divorced); children: Samuel Jesse; married Paige Rense, 1994. **Career:** Independent artist, since 1950. Instructor, Institute of Contemporary Arts, Washington, D.C., 1950–51, and Catholic University, Washington, D.C., 1951–60; instructor of night classes, Washington Workshop Center of the Arts, Washington, D.C., periodically, 1952–56; conducted Emma Lake Artists' Workshop, University of Saskatchewan, Regina, 1963; instructor, Bennington, College, Vermont, summer, 1966; guest, Tel Aviv Foundation of Literature and Art, 1971; guest lecturer, in Australia and New Zealand, 1975. Now lives and works in South Salem, New York. **Awards:** International Prizes, Centro de Artes Visuales, Instituto Torcuato di Tella, Buenos Aires, 1964; Citation in Creative Arts, Brandeis University, Waltham, Massachussetts 1965; Copper Medal, William A. Clark Prize, Corcoran Gallery of Art, Washington, D.C., 1967; North Carolina Award in Fine Arts, 1995; D.F.A., Davidson College, North Carolina, 1997. **Member:** American Academy of Arts and Letters, since 1977. **Address:** c/o Leo Castelli Gallery, 59 East 79th St., New York, New York 10021, U.S.A. **Website:** http://www.sharecom.ca/noland.

Individual Exhibitions:

1949 Galerie Creuze, Paris
1956 Tibor de Nagy Gallery, New York
1958 Tibor de Nagy Gallery, Washington, D.C.
Jefferson Place Gallery, Washington, D.C.
1959 French and Company, New York
1960 Jefferson Place Gallery, Washington, D.C.
Galleria dell'Ariete, Milan
Galerie Lawrence, Paris
André Emmerich Gallery, New York
1961 Galerie Neufville, Paris
André Emmerich Gallery, New York
Bennington College, Vermont
1962 Galerie Charles Lienhard, Zurich
Galerie Schmela, Dusseldorf
André Emmerich Gallery, New York
1963 Kasmin Gallery, London
André Emmerich Gallery, New York
Galerie Lawrence, Paris
1964 Jewish Museum, New York
Galerie Schmela, Dusseldorf
1965 Kasmin Gallery, London
David Mirvish Gallery, Toronto
1966 Nicholas Wilder Gallery, Los Angeles
André Emmerich Gallery, New York
1967 André Emmerich Gallery, New York
1968 Kasmin Gallery, London
David Mirvish Gallery, Toronto
1969 Lawrence Rubin Gallery, New York
1971 André Emmerich Gallery, New York
1972 Galerie Mikro, West Berlin
1973 André Emmerich Gallery, New York
1974 David Mirvish Gallery, Toronto
Jack Glenn Gallery, Corona del Mar, California
Janie C. Lee Gallery, Houston
Rutland Gallery, London
1975 School of Visual Arts, New York
1976 André Emmerich Gallery, Zurich
Leo Castelli Gallery, New York
1977 *Kenneth Noland: A Restrospective,* Guggenheim Museum, New York (toured the United States, 1977–78)
André Emmerich Gallery, New York
1978 André Emmerich Gallery, New York
1979 Waddington Graphics, London
André Emmerich Gallery, Zurich
1980 André Emmerich Gallery, New York
Castelli Graphics, New York
1981 Waddington Galleries, London
1982 Douglas Drake Gallery, Kansas City, Missouri
Downstairs Gallery, Edmonton, Alberta
1983 Hokin Gallery, Bay Harbor Island, Florida
Galeria Joan Prats, Barcelona
1984 Galerie de France, Paris
Makler Gallery, Philadelphia
1985 Galeria Joan Prats, Barcelona
1986 André Emmerich Gallery, New York
1988 Gallery One, Toronto, Ontario
Andre Emmerich Gallery, New York
1989 Hokin Gallery, Bay Harbor Islands, Florida
Heath Gallery, Atlanta
Salander-O'Reilly Galleries Inc., New York
Galerie Joan Prats, New York
1990 Meredith Long & Co., Houston
Helander Gallery, Palm Beach, Florida
Salander-O'Reilly Galleries, Beverly Hills
Edmonton Art Gallery, Alberta, Canada
1991 Galerias Afinsa and Almirante, Madrid
Salander-O'Reilly Galleries, New York
Salander-O'Reilly Galleries, Berlin
Appreciating Noland, Edmonton Art Gallery (catalog)
1993 Ulysses Gallery, New York
Extra Moenia Arte Moderna, Todi, Italy
Noland's Nolands, William H. Van Every, Jr. Gallery, Davidson College, North Carolina (retrospective) (catalog)
1994 *The Circle Paintings,* The Museum of Art, Houston
The Museum of Fine Arts, Ft. Lauderdale, Florida
Heath Gallery, Atlanta, Georgia
Cercle d'Art, Paris (catalog)
1995 *Kenneth Noland: A Selection of Paintings,* Leo Castelli Gallery, New York
Gana Art Gallery, Seoul, South Korea
Mosaics, Weltanschauung Project, Turin, Italy
1998 Andre Emmerich Gallery, New York
1999 Meredith Long Gallery, Houston
Kenneth Nolan: Full Circle, Chac-mool Contemporary Fine Art, West Hollywood, California
2000 *New Circles,* Metta Galleria, Madrid
Circles, Ameringer/Howard Fine Art, New York

Selected Group Exhibitions:

1959 *Biennial of Contemporary American Painting,* Corcoran Gallery, Washington, D.C.
1964 *Post-Painterly Abstraction,* Los Angeles County Museum of Art (toured the United States and Canada)
1969 *New York Painting and Sculpture 1940–70,* Metropolitan Museum of Art, New York
1976 *Aspects of Postwar Painting in America,* Guggenheim Museum, New York
1977 *New Ways with Paper,* National Collection of Fine Arts, Smithsonian Institution, Washington, D.C.
1978 *American Painting of the 1970s,* Albright-Knox Art Gallery, Buffalo, New York (toured the United States)
1979 *International Biennial Exhibition of Prints in Tokyo,* National Museum of Modern Art, Tokyo (toured Japan)
1980 *Aspects of the 70s Painterly Abstraction,* Brockton Art Museum, Massachussetts
1982 *A Private Vision,* Museum of Fine Arts, Boston
1983 *An American Renaissance,* Fort Lauderdale Museum of Art, Florida
1989 *Sculpture Out of Doors,* Andre Emmerich Gallery, New York (catalog)
1990 *Washington Color Painters: The First Generation,* Orlando Museum of Art (catalog)
1998 *The Green Mountain Boys,* Andre Emmerich Gallery, New York

1999 *Ten Americans,* Dorothy Blau Gallery, Bay Harbor Island, Florida

Collections:

Albright-Knox Art Gallery, Buffalo, New York; Art Gallery of Ontario, Toronto; Art Institute of Chicago, Illinois; Australian National Gallery, Canberra; Baltimore Museum of Art, Maryland; The Butler Institute of American Art, Youngstown, Ohio; City Art Museum, St. Louis; Cleveland Museum of Art, Ohio; Columbus Gallery of Fine Arts, Ohio; Corcoran Gallery of Art, Washington, D.C.; Des Moines Art Center, Iowa; Detroit Institute of Arts, Michigan; Gallery of South Australia, Adelaide; Edmonton Art Gallery, Edmonton; Fogg Art Museum, Cambridge, Massachusetts; Hara Museum of Contemporary Art, Tokyo; Hirshhorn Museum and Sculpture Garden, Washington, D.C.; Kunsthaus, Zurich; Kunstmuseum, Basel; Kunstsammlung Nordrhein-Westfalen, Dusseldorf; Los Angeles County Museum of Art, California; Louisiana Museum, Humlebaek, Denmark; Mendel Art Gallery, Saskatoon; The Metropolitan Museum of Art, New York; Milwaukee Art Center, Wisconsin; Musée d'Art Contemporain de Montréal, Montreal, Canada; Musee National d'Art Moderne, Centre National d'Art et de Culture Georges Pompidou, Paris; Museum of Fine Arts, Boston, Massachusetts; Museum of Modern Art, New York; National Gallery of Art, Washington, D.C.; National Gallery of Canada, Ottawa; Pasadena Art Museum, California; Phillips Collection, Washington, D.C.; Rose Art Museum, Brandeis University, Waltham, Massachusetts; Solomon R. Guggenheim Museum, New York; Stedelijk Museum, Amsterdam; Tate Gallery, London; Walker Art Center, Minneapolis, Minnesota; Whitney Museum of American Art, New York.

Public Installations:

Arte-Metro, Rome Underground, 1996.

Publications:

By NOLAND: Articles—''Letter to the Editor'' in *Artnews* (New York), November 1962; ''Jackson Pollock: An Artist's Symposium, Part 2'' in *Artnews* (New York), May 1967; ''Color, Format and Abstract Art: An Interview with Kenneth Noland'' with Diane Waldman, in *Art in America* (New York), May/June 1977; interview in *Artists in Their Own Words: Interviews* by Paul Cummings, New York 1979; interview with Emma Ercoli in *Next,* vol. 10, no. 32–33, Autumn 1994-Winter 1995.

On NOLAND: Books—*A Concise History of Modern Painting* by Herbert Read, London 1968; *Minimal Art: A Critical Anthology,* edited by Gregory Battcock, New York 1968; *History of Modern Art* by H. H. Arnason, New York 1969; *A Reading of Modern Art* by Dore Ashton, New York 1969; *The New Painting* by Udo Kultermann, New York 1969; *Late Modern* by Edward Lucie-Smith, New York 1969; *On the Future of Art* by Jack Burnham, New York 1970; *10 Washington Artists,* exhibition catalog, Edmonton, Alberta 1970; *La Pittura Americana Dopoguerra* by Daniel M. Mandelowitz, New York 1970; *Icons and Images of the 60s* by Nicolas and Elena Calas, New York 1971; *Kenneth Noland* by Kenworth Moffett, New York 1977; *Kenneth Noland: A Retrospective,* exhibition catalog by Diane Waldman, New York 1977; *Kenneth Noland Handmade Papers* by Judith Goldman, Bedford Village, New York 1978; *The New School: Painters and Sculptors of the 50s* by Irving Sandler, New York 1978; *A World History of Art: Painting, Sculpture, Architecture and Decorative Arts* by Gina Pischel, New York, revised edition 1978; *Louisiana: Pictorial Reportage,* Humblebaek, Denmark 1979; *Handbook: Guggenheim Museum Collection 1900–1980* by Vivian Endicott Barnett, New York 1980; *With Paper, About Paper,* exhibition catalog, Buffalo, New York 1980. **Articles—**''Notes on American Painting of the 60s'' by Walter Darby Bannard in *Artforum* (New York), January 1970; ''Noland's New Paintings'' by Walter Darby Bannard in *Artforum* (New York), November 1971; ''Noland'' by Kenworth Moffett in *Art International* (Lugano, Switzerland), summer 1973; ''To Re-Examine the Work of Kenneth Noland'' by Ken Carpenter in *Studio International* (London), July/August 1974; ''Kenneth Noland'' R. J. Rees in *Studio International* (London), January/February 1975; ''Kenneth Noland's New Paintings and the Issue of the Shaped Canvas'' by Kenworth Moffett in *Art International* (Lugano, Switzerland), April/May 1976; ''Landmarks on the Color Field'' by Hilton Kramer in the *New York Times,* 22 April 1977; ''Kenneth Noland and Quality in Art'' by Alwynne Mackie in *Art International* (Lugano, Switzerland), summer 1979; ''Teaching Modernism: What Albers Learned in the Bauhaus and Taught to Rauschenberg, Noland and Hesse'' by Carl Goldstein in *Arts Magazine* (New York), December 1979; ''Artist's Dialogue: Kenneth Noland—Sculpting with Color'' by Karen Wilkin in *Architectural Digest,* vol. 45, March 1988; ''Noland's Land'' in *Architectural Digest,* vol. 46, October 1989; ''Kenneth Noland'' by Karen Wilkin in *Art News,* vol. 94, September 1995; ''Kenneth Noland'' by Katy Siegel in *Artforum,* vol. 37, no. 4, December 1998.

* * *

The highly formal work that emerged in New York in the 1960s as ''minimal'' found one of its most powerful practitioners in Kenneth Noland. It was as though what he had been working toward came to a kind of timely climax so that the art public was ready and able to see what he, along with a group of artists, was exploring.

The minimal artists, as the tag implies, are concerned with reductive means, dealing with only a few of the elements that are available to an artist, such as color, structure, singular forms, etc. Noland first worked with targets of color and chevrons along with the shape of the stretched canvas, then moved toward a very direct and narrow statement of horizontal bands of color in beautiful and inventive relationships like musical chords. Gene Davis was painting vertical bands of color, but Noland's horizontal bands were refreshingly not the same. Their scale was different and the tension much more relaxed, stretching as it did outwards apparently without end. The forms were of course the bands of color and the ''spaces between'' them which could be seen either as other bands or a ground depending on the way an observer chose to see them and the emphasis Noland gave any given color.

The sheer act of painting, I suspect, then led Noland through compositional means—that is, the balancing out of tensions produced not only by the play of color but also by the relationships between forms. The next set of paintings by Noland bears a strong resemblance to plaids with vertical and horizontal bands of color crossing over one another and acting as ''frames'' for the central field of color. This concern with edges is shared by a number of contemporary artists.

The balancing-out of vertical and horizontal in terms of compositional give-and-take has since led Noland to the further compositional step of dealing with diagonals and their relationship to the edge of the painting. He is back to shaped canvases, but whereas symmetry was his answer in the earlier diamonds and tondos, now the diagonals throw the structure off-center and the shapes of the canvases are highly irregular and asymmetrical. This has resulted in a very complex structure where the activity going on within the stretched canvas is joined by the activity *outside* its form—the relationship of the work to its surroundings. In his most successful new work Noland has been able to control all this relational activity in such a way as to continue to produce easel paintings of great integrity.

—Ralph Pomeroy

NONAS, Richard

Nationality: American. **Education:** Studied cultural anthropology. **Career:** Worked as an archeologist in Georgia and Alabama; spent two years as ethnographer in Northern Mexico Indian village; conducted Indian research in Yukon Territory and northern Ontario; visited Indian communities in the Grand Canyon and Lapland; spent two years in Paris. Sculptor since 1967. Instructor in anthropology, University of North Carolina and Queens College, New York; lecturer, University of Rochester, New York; lecturer, School of the Visual Arts, Cooper Union and Hunter College, New York; visiting artist, Sarah Lawrence College, Bronxville, New York, and Fresno State College, California, 1974. **Awards:** Change Inc. Grant, 1972; Guggenheim Foundation Fellowship, 1974; National Endowment for the Arts Grant, 1976. **Agent:** c/o Lawrence Markey, 55 Vandam Street, New York, New York 10013, U.S.A.

Individual Exhibitions:

1972 10 Bleecker Street Gallery, New York
112 Greene Street Gallery, New York
1973 The Clocktower, Institute for Art and Urban Resources, New York
112 Greene Street Gallery, New York
New Sculpture: Robert Grosvenor/Forest Meyers/ Richard Nonas, Loguidice Gallery, New York
New Sculpture: Jene Highstein/Richard Nonas, University of Rhode Island, Kingston
1974 Galleria Forma, Genoa
Galleria d'Allesandro, Rome
Galerie Schöttle, Munich
383 West Broadway, New York
1975 Marilena Bonomo Galleria, Bari, Italy
Idea Warehouse, New York
Holly Solomon Gallery, New York
1976 *New Sculpture/Old Tower,* Spoleto, Italy
Galleria St. Fidele, Milan
Dartmouth College, Hanover, New Hampshire
Galerie Hetzler-Keller, Stuttgart
Art Gallery, Wright State University, Dayton, Ohio
Salvatori Ala Galleria, Milan
1977 PSI, Institute for Art and Urban Resources, Long Island City, New York
1981 Oil and Steel Gallery, New York
Hudson River Museum, Yonkers, New York
Studio La Citta, Verona, Italy
1982 University of Massachusetts, Amherst
Franklin Furnace, New York (retrospective)
Georgia State University Art Gallery, Atlanta
University of Lund, Sweden
1983 Real Art Ways, Hartford, Connecticut
Photography Gallery, Toronto
Hoshour Gallery, Albuquerque
Houston Festival, Texas
Univeristy of North Carolina, Chapel Hill
Jack Tilton Gallery, New York
1984 Anderson Gallery, Virginia Commonwealth University, Richmond
Bjorn Nordenhake and Nordic Sculpture Seminar, Boalt, Sweden
1985 Annemarie Verna Gallery, Zurich
Jack Tilton Gallery, New York
Nassau County Museum, Roslyn Heights, New York
Krista Mikkola Gallery, Helsinki
Laumeier Sculpture Park, St. Louis
C.W. Post College, Long Island University
1986 Aners Tornberg Gallery, Lund
Pamela Auchincloss Gallery, Santa Barbara
Santa Barbara Museum of Art
Pori, Finland
Bisby, Arizona
1987 Sten Ericsson Gallery, Stockholm
Socrates Sculpture Park, New York
Lund Museum of Art, Sweden
Flushing Meadows Park, New York City
Ace Contemporary Exhibitions, Los Angeles
1989 Flushing Meadows Corona Park, Queens, New York
Hill Gallery, Birmingham, Michigan
Cranbrook Academy of Art, Birmingham, Michigan
Galerie Hans Meyer, Dusseldorf
Sandra Gering Gallery, New York
Galleri Lars Bohman, Stockholm
Christine Burgin Gallery, New York
1991 Ace Gallery, Los Angeles
Lodz, Poland
Center of Contemporary Art, Warsaw
Harcus Gallery, Boston
William Patterson College, Wayne, New Jersey
Gallery 360 Degrees, Tokyo
Handelshogskolan, Stockholm
Galerie Hubert Winter, Vienna
1992 *Richard Nonas: Between Old Times, Sculpture for a Changing Castle (-for Bronislaw Malinowski),* Centrum Sztuki Wspolczesnej, Warsaw
Hetapollohuis, Eindhoven, Holland
Andre Simoens Gallery, Knokke-Houte, Belgium
Person's Weekend Museum, Tokyo
1993 Ace Gallery, Los Angeles
Galerie Hubert Winter, Vienna
Gallery 360 Degrees, Tokyo

Galerie Hubert Winter, Vienna
Museum of Contemporary Art, Los Angeles
1994 Galerie Renos Xippas, Paris

Selected Group Exhibitions:

1973 *Sculpture Annual,* Whitney Museum, New York
1976 *Holz-Kunst-Stoff,* Staatliche-Kunsthalle, Baden-Baden, West Germany
1977 *Documenta,* Kassel, West Germany
1980 *Sculpture at the Coliseum,* Long Island City
1984 *Installations,* Directions on Broadway, New York
Svart Pa Vitt: Maleri, Skulptur, Techning and Grafik, Anders Tornberg Gallery, Lund
1991 *Out of Sight,* P.S.1 Museum, Institute of Contemporary Art, Long Island City
Learn to Read Art: Artists' Books, Art Gallery of Hamilton, Ontario, Canada
Biennale de Sculpture Montecarlo, Monaco
1994 *From Minimal to Conceptual Art, Works from the Dorothy and HerbertVogel Collection,* National Gallery of Art, Washington, D.C.
1995–96 *Temporarily Possessed: The Semi-Permanent Collection,* New Museum of Contemporary Art, New York (catalog)
2001 Curt Marcus Gallery, New York

Collections:

Aldrich Museum, Ridgefield, Connecticut; Moderna Museet, Stockholm; Albright-Knox Art Gallery, Buffalo; Detroit Institute of Arts, Michigan; Guggenheim Museum, New York; Kunstmuseum, Zurich; Moderna Museet, Stockholm; Museum of Contemporary Art, Los Angeles; Museum of Modern Art, New York; Walker Art Center, Minneapolis.

Publications:

By NONAS: Books—*Details from the Excavation of Wooster Street,* New York 1972; *Summer, 1906,* New York 1973; *Northern/Southern,* Genoa 1974; *Sonora Cows,* New York 1974; *My Life on the Floor,* New York 1975; *Making Sculpture,* New York 1975; *Lost in Spoleto,* New York 1976; *Montezuma's Breakfast,* New York 1977; *Enough's Enough,* Paris 1978; *Here, Now or Nowhere,* New York 1979; *Boiling Coffee,* New York 1980; *Parts to Anything,* Roslyn Harbor, New York 1984; *If Bisbee Could Talk,* Bisbee, Arizona 1985; *Up from Dayton,* Lund 1986; *Agricultural Doubt/Five Stone Made Places,* New York 1987. **Articles—**''Texte de Richard Nonas'' in *Lumieres Blanches/Photographies de Harry Gruyaert,* 1986; ''A Sculptor's Anthropology of Doubt'' in *Hoopoe,* no. 3, Winter 1988-Spring 1989; ''Construction in Process'' in *Tema Celeste Art Magazine,* March-April 1991; ''A Project by Richard Nonas'' in *Artspace,* January-April 1992. **Radio play—***Goats Itch,* New York 1982.

On NONAS: Books—*New Sculpture/Old Tower,* exhibition catalog with text by Panza di Biumo, Milan 1976; *The First Show: Paintings and Sculpture from Eight Collections 1940–1980,* New York 1983; *Architectural Elements in Contemporary Art,* Cooperstown, New York 1986; *Learn to Read Art,* New York, 1991; *Richard Nonas,* exhibition catalog, Tokyo 1992; *Richard Nonas: Between Old Times, Sculpture for a Changing Castle (-for Bronislaw Malinowski),* exhibition catalog, with text by Milada Slizinska, Warsaw 1992; *Sculpture on Campus,* Wayne, New Jersey 1994. **Articles—**''4 Works by Richard Nonas'' in *Arts Magazine* (New York), February 1973; essay by Suzanne Delahauty in *6 Visions,* exhibition catalog, Philadelphia 1973; ''Richard Nonas'' in *Flash Art* (Milan), June 1974; ''3 Sculptors: Mark di Suvero, Richard Nonas, Charles Ginnever'' by Nancy Foote in *Artforum* (New York), February 1976; ''Richard Nonas'' in *Flash Art* (Milan), April 1976; ''Richard Nonas: Field Works'' by Jan van der Marck in *Art in America* (New York), January 1977; ''Montezuma and the PS1 Kids'' by Grace Glueck in the *New York Times,* 15 April 1977; review by Donald Kuspit in *Art in America* (New York), March 1981; ''Richard Nonas and the Consciousness of Self'' by Frederick Ted Castle in *Arts Magazine,* vol. 64, no. 3, November 1989; ''Richard Nonas'' in *Artspace,* vol. 16, no. 1–2, January-April 1992; ''Richard Nonas & Jene Highstein'' by William Patterson in *Artspace,* vol. 17, no. 1–2, March-April 1993; ''The 'Sculptural Places' of Richard Nonas'' by Adachiara Zevi in *L'Architettura,* vol. 45, no. 5020, February 1999; ''Richard Nonas,'' special issue of *Ground: Art and Culture,* no. 5, 2000.

* * *

Closely associated with Minimalist and Postminimalist sources, the sculpture produced by Richard Nonas in the 1970s uses simple forms and rough, heavy industrial materials to construct horizontal structures which manipulate and redefine the spaces for which they are specifically made.

In 1973 Nonas showed a series of floor works in which rough timber beams were stacked in a manner like that of log cabin construction. Many of these were dedicated to Mark di Suvero, some of whose qualities Nonas has emulated. Nonas's subsequent work, however, is quite different formally from that of di Suvero, becoming less ruggedly expressionistic and more concerned with slender, attenuated horizontality and deceptive simplicity. In works such as *Atumosis* (1974) and *Crocodile* (1976), for example, long, thin steel beams form an inverted ''L'' and a capital ''I'' respectively, their shapes determined by the particular gallery spaces which they were made to alter. Nonas's sculpture characteristically tends to both fill the space and at the same time defer bringing undue attention to itself. The viewer is urged to become a participant, to move in and out and through the work in order to perceive its complete relationship with its symbiotic environment. On first glance, Nonas's forms seem quite simple and direct, yet, on sustained interaction, they assume a complex task in the subtleties of placement and arrangement which serve to reshape their surroundings. If there is deeper meaning in Nonas's work, it lies in its ability to communicate perceptions of the complexities concealed in deceptively simple forms. His is a statement which seems to proclaim that what is outwardly ''minimal'' can be made ''maximal'' through the viewer's efforts.

In 1980 Nonas did an installation composed of an arrangement of 12 rough lumber structures resembling primitive chairs and 12 steel plateau-like structures resembling primitive tables or altars. The aura is one of a modernist/primitivizing urge which seeks to reinvent some primitive ceremony by reinventing a specific city space with multiple repetition of modernly abstracted yet still primitively allusive shapes. Nonas's background as an anthropologist is evident in this work which, like his others, aims at broaching a hint at the complex devices underlying minimal abstraction's misleading simplicity.

Note should be made of the fact that Nonas, although primarily known for his sculpture, has also produced a number of artists' books, photographs and narrative works. Among his other works is a radio play titled *Goats Itch* (1982) which he both wrote and performed.

—Barbara Cavaliere

NORDMAN, Maria

Nationality: American. **Born:** Görlitz, Silesia, Germany in 1943. **Education:** University of California at Los Angeles, 1961–67, B.F.A., M.A. **Career:** Travelled in Europe, and researched coherent light models, 1968. Editorial assistant to Richard Neutra, 1969–70.

Individual Exhibitions:

1967 University of California at Los Angeles
1972 Pasadena Museum of Modern Art, California
12 South Raymond Street, Pasadena, California
20th and Idaho, Santa Monica, California
1973 *Saddleback Mountain,* University of California at Irvine
1974 Galleria Franco Toselli, Milan
1976 Museo d'Artista, Florence
1978 *5 Public Proposals for an Open Place,* Rosamund Felsen Upstairs Gallery, Los Angeles (travelled to Galerie Saman, Geneva, 1979)
1981 Fogg Art Museum, Harvard University, Cambridge, Massachusetts
1983 Westfälischer Kunstverein, Munster
1985 La Jolla Museum of Contemporary Art, California
1990 Musée des Beaux-Arts, Chartres (catalog)
1991 Musée Saint-Pierre-Art Contemporain, Lyon (catalog)
1993 Marian Goodman Gallery, New York
1996 Kulturabteilung, Stadt Pulheim, Germany (catalog)
Maria Nordman: De Theatro, Staatsgalerie Stuttgart, Germany (catalog)

Selected Group Exhibitions:

1976 *Biennale,* Venice
1977 *Documenta 6,* Heckerstrasse, Kassel, West Germany
1979 *Andre/Buren/Nordman: Space as Support,* University of California, Berkeley
1980 *Pier and Ocean: Construction in the Art of the 70s,* Hayward Gallery, London (travelled to Rijksmuseum Kroller-Muller, Otterlo, Netherlands)
1983 *The First Show,* Museum of Contemporary Art, Los Angeles
1984 *Nel mezzo della primavera,* Galleria Pieroni, Rome
1985 *Promenades,* Parc Lullin, Genthod, Geneva
1991 *Crossroads,* Gallery of York University, Toronto (catalog)
1992 *Situation Kunst für Max Imdahl,* Kunstsammlungen der Ruhr-Universität Bochum, Germany (catalog)
Like Nothing Else in Tennessee, Serpentine Gallery, London (catalog)
1996 *Tranquility,* Chiba City Museum of Art, Japan (catalog)
1999 *Circa 1968,* Serralves Museum of Contemporary Art, Oporto, Portugal
2000 *Venice-Venezia: Arte Californiana dalla Collezione Panza,* Peggy Guggenheim Collection, Venice
Over the Edges, Stedelijk Museum voor Aktuele Kunst, Ghent, Belgium

Publications:

By NORDMAN: Books—*Fragment from the Notes of Maria Nordman,* Munich 1977; *Unpublished Notes,* Santa Monica, California 1979; *Poiema, Notes 1970–,* Cologne 1982. **Article**—interview with Barbara Haskell and Hal Glicksman, in *Maria Nordman: Saddleback Mountain,* exhibition catalog, Irvine, California 1973.

On NORDMAN: Book—*Andre, Buren, Irwin, Nordman: Space as Support,* exhibition brochure with essay by Jan Butterfield, Berkeley, California 1979. **Articles**—''Art Walk'' by William Wilson in *Los Angeles Times,* 20 October 1978; ''Lux Lucis'' by Corinna Ferrari in *Domus* (Milan), April 1979; ''Maria Nordman'' in *Bijutsu Techo* (Tokyo), April 1979; ''The Work of Maria Nordman'' by Germano Celant in *Artforum* (New York), March 1980; ''Review: Maria Nordman'' by Annelie Pohlen in *Artforum* (New York), March 1984.

* * *

Maria Nordman occupies herself with works which concern people in relation to their surroundings. She works with spaces which can be light and dark, noisy and silent, broad and narrow, which she conceives however in such a manner that the interior is brought to the outside and in counter-movement the exterior comes inside. But the ''natural aspects'' of the gradual transition of day into night, of light into darkness, of breadth into narrowness, of noise into silence, can also be included as surroundings.

Space, light and sound are the most important components in Maria Nordman's work, not as material entities but as elements of our world perceptible and experiential in time. Space and light are closely linked; neither the one nor the other exists in isolation. Maria Nordman sees light as a determinant, elementary presence. Light comes from the sun, the planet revered by all early cultures: in this sense it is to be understood as myth. But it can also be interpreted otherwise: as a neutral, omnipresent power, as man's companion, as a constant which not only acts as a yardstick in our perception of the world, but also ''it defines any place to unpredictable degrees from the same points of departure.''

We all move from space to space, from place to place, from light to darkness; these are elements which can be experienced in the relationship of man to man. Light opens up space, space reflects light. Maria Nordman investigates these relationships in discovering, adapting and opening up places or spaces in which the ''natural aspects'' of light and the ''boundlessness'' of space are present. She gives intellectual and spiritual effect to these relationships in her restained, poetic and peaceful works.

—Zdenek Felix

NUTT, Jim

Nationality: American. **Born:** Pittsfield, Massachusetts, 28 November 1938. Education: Art Institute of Chicago, B.F.A. 1965. **Career:**

Jim Nutt: *It's a Long Way Down,* 1971. ©Smithsonian American Art Museum, Washington, DC/Art Resource, NY; courtesy of Smithsonian American Art Museum.

Independent artist, working in Chicago; teacher, California State University, Sacramento; Adjunct Professor, Painting and Drawing Department, The School of the Art Institute of Chicago, 1990. **Awards:** National Endowment for the Arts, 1974 and 1989; Academy Award in Art, American Academy of Arts and Letters. **Address:** c/o Phyllis Kind Gallery, 313 W. Superior St., Chicago, Illinois, 60610–3515; Phyllis Kind Gallery, 136 Greene Street, New York, New York, 10012–3202.

Individual Exhibitions:

1970 Phyllis Kind Gallery, Chicago
1971 Candy Store Gallery, Folsom, California
1972 Phyllis Kind Gallery, Chicago
Candy Store Gallery, Folsom, California
1973 Candy Store Gallery, Folsom, California
1974 Museum of Contemporary Art, Chicago
Walker Art Center, Minneapolis
Whitney Museum, New York
1975 San Francisco Art Institute
Portland Center for the Visual Arts, Oregon
Phyllis Kind Gallery, Chicago
1976 Phyllis Kind Gallery, New York
1977 Phyllis Kind Gallery, Chicago
Phyllis Kind Gallery, New York
1979 Phyllis Kind Gallery, Chicago
1980 Rotterdamse Kunstichting, Rotterdam
Phyllis Kind Gallery, New York
1981 Phyllis Kind Gallery, Chicago
1982 Phyllis Kind Gallery, Chicago
1983 James Mayor Gallery, London
1984 Phyllis Kind Gallery, New York
1985 Phyllis Kind Gallery, Chicago
1988 Phyllis Kind Gallery, New York
1991 *Jim Nutt: Paintings,* Phyllis Kind Gallery, New York (traveled to Phyllis Kind Gallery, Chicago) (catalog)
1994 Milwaukee Art Museum, Milwaukee (travelled to National Portrait Gallery, Washington D.C. and University of Washington Henry Art Gallery, Seattle) (catalog)
1999 *Jim Nutt: Portraits,* Museum of Contemporary Art, Chicago (catalog)

Selected Group Exhibitions:

1969 Spirit of the Comics, Institute of Contemporary Art, Philadelphia
1972 Chicago Imagist Art, Museum of Contemporary Art, Chicago
1973 American Drawings 1963–1973, Whitney Museum, New York
1977 View of a Decade, Museum of Contemporary Art, Chicago
1979 Chicago Currents, National Collection of Fine Art, Washington, D.C. (and subsequent tour)
1980 Who Chicago?: An Exhibition of Contemporary Imagists, Sunderland Art Centre, England (toured the U.K. and travelled to the Institute of Contemporary Art Center, Boston, and the Contemporary Art Center, New Orleans, 1980–82)
1983 The Comic Art Show, Whitney Museum, New York
1991 Spirited Visions: Portraits of Chicago Artists by Patty Carroll, The State of Illinois Art Gallery, Chicago (travelled)
1992 Parallel Visions: Modern Artists and Outsider Art, Los Angeles County Museum of Art (travelled to Kunsthalle Basel, Switzerland; Centro de Arte Reina Sofia, Madrid; Setagaya Art Museum, Tokyo)
1993 Imagery: Incongruous Juxtapositions, Phyllis Kind Gallery, Chicago
1999 *The Risk of Existence,* Phyllis Kind Gallery, New York

Collections:

Whitney Museum, New York; Metropolitan Museum of Art, New York; Philadelphia Museum of Art; Anne D'Harnancourt Rishel Collection, Philadelphia; Sydney and Frances Lewis Collection, Richmond, Virginia; New Orleans Museum of Art; Art Institute of Chicago; Museum of Contemporary Art, Chicago; Morton Neumann Collection, Chicago; Museum des 20. Jahrhunderts, Vienna; National Museum of American Art, Washington, D.C.; Scottish National Museum, Glasgow; Museum Moderner Kunst, Vienna.

Publications:

By NUTT: Article—''An Interview with Jim Nutt,'' with Russell Bowman, in Arts Magazine (New York), February 1978.

On NUTT: Books—*Artworks and Packages* by Harold Rosenberg, New York 1969; *Chicago Imagist Art*, exhibition catalog, with an essay by Franz Schulze, Chicago 1972; *Fantastic Images: Chicago Art since 1945* by Franz Schulze, Chicago 1972; *Made in Chicago*, exhibition catalog with an essay by Whitney Halstead, São Paulo 1973; *Jim Nutt*, exhibition catalog with an essay by Whitney Halstead, Chicago 1974; *Jim Nutt*, exhibition catalog with an essay by Phil Linhares, San Francisco 1975; *Who Chicago?: An Exhibition of Chicago Imagists*, exhibition catalog, Sunderland, England 1980; *From Chicago*, exhibition catalog with an essay by Russel Bowman, New York 1982; *Focus on the Figure*, exhibition catalog with an essay by Barbara Haskell, New York 1982. **Articles**—''Whimsical Amalgam of Pop Art and Surrealism'' by Peter Schjeldahl in the *New York Times*, 15 September 1974; ''Jim Nutt at the Whitney'' by Dennis Adrian in *Art in America* (New York), September/October 1974; ''Chicago: The Look'' by April Kingsley in *Art Express*, (New York), January/February 1982; ''Painting in Chicago'' by Reagan Upshaw in *Portfolio* (New York), May/June 1982; ''Jim Nutt's Human Comedy'' by Ken Johnson in *Art in America* (New York), vol. 80, no. 2, February 1992; ''The Metaphysics of Perception in the Drawings of Jim Nutt'' by Dennis Adrian in *Drawing*, vol. 15, no. 2, July-August 1993.

* * *

Jim Nutt studied at the School of the Art Institute of Chicago from 1960–65. From 1966 to 1969 he took part in the series of ''Hairy Who'' shows in Chicago which launched his career as one of the so-called ''Chicago Imagists.''

Nutt's drawings and paintings are full of strong linear elements, with cartoon-like imagery, highly inventive with a prediliection for strong and brilliant colour and a highly refined technique. Dennis Adrian, in his essays on Chicago art, has written that Nutt's ''careful finish gives the image a high degree of resolution, enhancing its visionary force.''

Within these settings nude figures, widely distributed across the picture surface engage in erotic encounters, (though sex is never depicted). These are menacing fantasies, with a measure of scatological humour thrown in for good measure. Nutt also emphasises the object-like character of his works by incorporating the frame into the picture, or as Adrian writes: ''Many of Nutt's paintings are painted on both sides (on plexiglass), so that there is no aspect of painting as an object which does not manifest the artist's interest and concerns.''

Since the early 1970s Nutt has taken part in major international exhibitions: in 1972 he was a featured artist at the Venice Biennale; in 1973 he was shown at the Sao Paulo Bienal; and in 1980–82 he was represented in the exhibition ''Who Chicago,'' which toured America and Britain.

—Victoria Keller

The cartoon-like figures of Nutt's earlier works were, by the 1980s, still bizarrely distorted but less combative—engaged in the most tentative interactions either physical or emotional. Since 1987, he has concentrated primarily on bust-length portraits of imaginary women meticulously painted with multiple layers of thin acrylic glazes. The deeply compelling characterizations of the portraits are radically different from the ''in your face'' tone of the Hairy Who work. Gone is the comic excess that barely concealed a fear and loathing of women, and warm tones have replaced the raw, explosive color of the earlier work. The stiff poses and flattened backgrounds are reminiscent of the work of Colonial American portraitists such as Ammi Phillips. But in a manner typical of the wide range of influences that have continuously shaped Nutt's art, the portraits also reflect the painting of Miro and Picasso. The careful execution and the otherwise elegant features of the women contrast with their dark, outsized noses. Thus, they retain something of the contradiction between untamed imagery and elaborate attention to finish found in Nutt's work from the very beginning. These portraits were featured in a 1994 traveling retrospective of the artist's work organized by the Milwaukee Art Museum, and were the focus of a 1999 exhibition at Chicago's Museum of Contemporary Art.

—Paula Wisotzki

O

O'KEEFFE, Georgia

Nationality: American. **Born:** Sun Prairie, Wisconsin, 15 November 1887. **Education:** Studied art under John Vaderpoel, Art Institute of Chicago, 1905–06; under William Merritt Chase, F. Luis Mora and Kenyon Cox, Art Students League, New York, 1907–08 (Chase Still-Life Scholarship, 1908); under Alan Bement, University of Virginia, Charlottesville, 1912; under Arthur Dow and Alan Bement, Teachers College, Columbia University, New York, 1914–16. **Family:** Married the photographer Alfred Stieglitz in 1924 (died, 1946). **Career:** Worked as commercial artist, drawing lace and embroidery for advertisements, Chicago, 1908–10. Art supervisor, public schools, Amarillo, Texas, 1913–16; instructor, summer art school, University of Virginia, Charlottesville, 1913–16; Columbia College, South Carolina, 1915; chairman, art department, West Texas State Normal School, Canyon, 1916–18; met Alfred Stieglitz, New York 1916, moved to New York to concentrate on painting, 1918; travelled to Taos, New Mexico, with Mrs. Paul (Rebecca) Strand and Mabel Dodge Luhan, 1929; travelled extensively in the United States, from 1932; travelled in Mexico, 1951, and in Europe, Asia, India, Middle East, Pacific Islands and North America, 1953–69. Worked on exhibitions from the Stieglitz estate for the Museum of Modern Art, New York, and the Art Institute of Chicago, 1947–49; Georgia O'Keeffe Museum opens in Santa Fe, New Mexico, 1997. **Awards:** Woman of Distinction Award, *World's Fair* Tomorrow Committee, New York, 1939; Creative Arts Award, Brandeis University, Waltham, Massachusetts, 1963; Gold Medal for Painting, National Institute of Arts and Letters, New York 1970; M. Carey Thomas Award, Bryn Mawr College, Pennsylvania, 1971; Edward Macdowell Medal, 1972; Gold Medal, Skowhegan School of Painting and Sculpture, Maine 1973; First Annual Governor's Award, New Mexico, 1974; Presidential Medal of Freedom, Washington, D.C., 1977; National Medal of Arts, Washington, D.C., 1985. D.F.A.: College of William and Mary, Williamsburg, Virginia, 1938; University of New Mexico, Albuquerque, 1964; Randolph-Macon Women's College, Ashland, Virginia, 1966; Brown University, Providence, Rhode Island, 1971; Minnesota College of Art and Design, Minneapolis, 1972; D.H.L.: University of Wisconsin, Madison, 1942; Mt. Holyoke College, South Hadley, Massachusetts, 1971. **Member:** National Institute of Arts and Letters, 1947; American Academy of Arts and Letters, 1963; American Academy of Arts and Sciences, 1966. **Estate:** Georgia O'Keefe Foundation, Albuquerque, New Mexico 87510. **Address:** The Georgia O'Keeffe Museum, Dept. AA, 217 Johnson St., Santa Fe, New Mexico 87501. **Died:** Santa Fe, New Mexico, 6 March 1986.

Individual Exhibitions:

1917 291 Gallery, New York
1923 *Alfred Stieglitz Presents 100 Pictures, Oils, Water-Colors, Pastels, and Drawings by Georgia O'Keeffe, American,* Anderson Galleries, New York
1924 *Alfred Stieglitz Presents 51 Recent Pictures, Oils, Water-Colors, Pastels and Drawings by Georgia O'Keeffe, American,* Anderson Galleries, New York
1926 Intimate Gallery, New York
1927 Brooklyn Museum, New York (retrospective)
Intimate Gallery, New York
Anderson Galleries, New York
1929 Anderson Galleries, New York
Intimate Gallery, New York
1930 An American Place, New York
1931 An American Place, New York
1932 An American Place, New York
1933 An American Place, New York
1934 An American Place, New York
1935 An American Place, New York
1936 An American Place, New York
1937 University of Minnesota, Minneapolis
An American Place, New York
1938 College of William and Mary, Williamsburg, Virginia
An American Place, New York
1939 *Exhibition of Oils and Pastels,* An American Place, New York
1940 *Exhibitions of Oils and Pastels,* An American Place, New York
1941 An American Place, New York
1942 An American Place, New York
1943 An American Place, New York
Art Institute of Chicago (retrospective)
1944 *Paintings, 1943,* An American Place, New York
1945 An American Place, New York
1946 An American Place, New York
Museum of Modern Art, New York (retrospective)
1950 An American Place, New York
1952 Downtown Gallery, New York
1953 Museum of Fine Arts, Dallas
1955 Gibbes Art Gallery, Charleston, South Carolina
Downtown Gallery, New York
1958 Downtown Gallery, New York
Pomona College, Claremont, California
1960 Worcester Art Museum, Massachusetts (retrospective)
1961 Downtown Gallery, New York
1965 *An Exhibition of the Work of the Artist from 1915 to 1966,* Amon Center Museum, Fort Worth, Texas (retrospective, travelled to Houston and Albuquerque)
1970 Whitney Museum, New York (retrospective; travelled to Chicago and San Francisco)
1978 Metropolitan Museum of Art, New York
1981 Whitney Museum, New York
1985 Museum of Fine Arts, Boston
Museum of New Mexico, Santa Fe
1986 Gerald Peters Gallery, Dallas
1988 *Georgia O'Keeffe: Art and Letters,* National Gallery of Art, Washington, D.C.
Georgia O'Keeffe, B Forum, Seibu Shibuya, Tokyo (traveled to Seibu Hall, Otsu)
1989 Metropolitan Museum of Art, New York
1990 *Georgia O'Keeffe: Paintings of Hawai'i,* Honolulu Academy of Arts, Honolulu

Georgia O'Keeffe: *Yellow Calla*, 1926. ©Smithsonian American Art Museum, Washington, DC/Art Resource, NY.

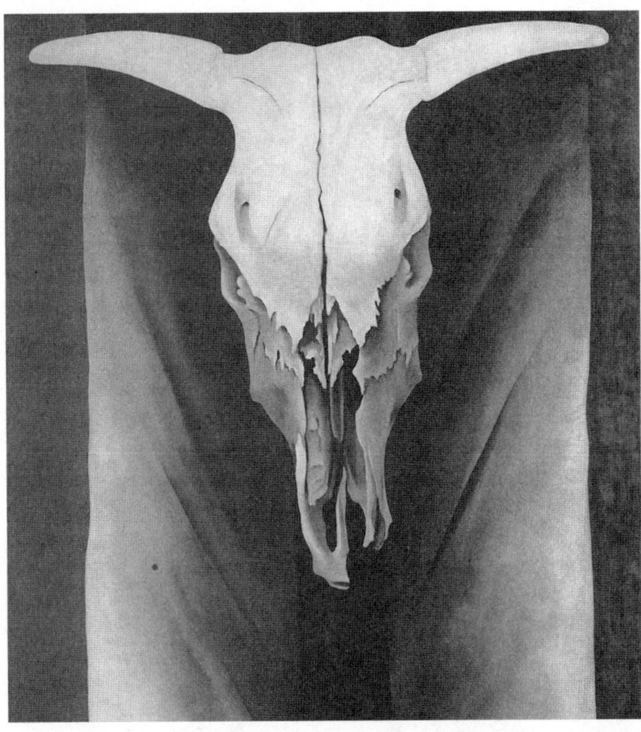

Georgia O'Keeffe: *Cow's Skull.* Metropolitan Museum of Art, The Alfred Stieglitz Collection, 1949. ©2001 The Georgia O'Keeffe Foundation/Artists Rights Society (ARS), New York.

Georgia O'Keeffe, Gerald Peters Gallery, Santa Fe (traveled to Gerald Peters Gallery, New York; Gerald Peters Gallery, Dallas)

1993 *Georgia O'Keeffe: American and Modern,* Hayward Gallery, London (traveled to Museo del Palacio de Bellas Artes, Mexico City; Yokohama Museum of Art, Yokohama)

Georgia O'Keeffe, Lefevre Gallery, London

1995 *Georgia O'Keeffe: Canyon Suite,* Kemper Museum of Contemporary Art, Kansas City (traveled to Denver Art Museum, Denver; Colorado Springs Fine Arts Center, Colorado Springs; Marianna Kistler Beach Museum of Art, Manhattan; Addison Gallery of American Art, Andover)

1998 *O'Keeffe and Texas,* Marion Koogler McNay Art Museum, San Antonio

1999 *The Poetry of Things,* Phillips Collection, Washington, D.C.

Georgia O'Keeffe Museum, Santa Fe

Dallas Museum of Art, Dallas

Selected Group Exhibitions:

1916 *New Paintings and Drawings,* 291 Gallery, New York

1917 *Annual Exhibition,* Society of Independent Artists, New York

1925 *7 Americans,* Anderson Galleries, New York

1929 *Paintings of 19 Living Americans,* Museum of Modern Art, New York

1937 *5 Painters,* University of Minnesota, Minneapolis

1955 *Contemporary American Painting,* Whitney Museum, New York

1958 *The Stieglitz Circle,* Pomona College, Claremont, California

Nature in Abstraction, Whitney Museum, New York (toured the United States)

1976 *20th Century American Drawing: Three Avant-Garde Generations,* Guggenheim Museum, New York

1985 *American Realism,* San Francisco Museum of Modern Art (travelled to Lincoln, Massachusetts; Austin, Texas; Evanston, Illinois, Williamstown, Massachusetts; Akron, Ohio; Madison, Wisconsin)

1989 *Master Drawings 1859–1989,* Janie C. Lee Master Drawings, New York

1990 *Early/Later,* Whitney Museum of American Art, New York

American Artists of the Alfred Stieglitz Circle, Brooklyn Museum, New York

1992 *Georgia O'Keeffe and Alfred Stieglitz: Two Lives—A Conversation in Paintings and Photographs,* Phillips Collection, Washington, D.C. (traveled to IBM Gallery of Science and Art, New York; Minneapolis Institute of Arts, Minneapolis; Museum of Fine Arts, Houston)

1995 *In the American Grain: Dove, Hartley, Marin, O'Keeffe, and Stieglitz—The Stieglitz Circle at the Phillips Collection,* Phillips Collection, Washington, D.C. (traveled to Seattle Arts Museum, Seattle; Museum of Modern Art, Saitama; Fukushima Prefectrual Museum of Art, Fukushima; Chiba Municipal Museum of Art, Chiba; Portland Art Museum, Portland)

1996 *Rings: Five Passions in World Art,* High Museum of Art, Atlanta, Atlanta

American Paintings in Southern California Collections: from Gilbert Stuart to Georgia O'Keeffe, Los Angeles County Museum of Art, Los Angeles

1997 *Birth of the Cool: American Painting from Georgia O'Keeffe to Christopher Wool,* Deichtorhallen, Hamburg (traveled to Kunsthaus Zurich, Zurich)

Twentieth-Century Still-life Painting from the Phillips Collection, Phillips Collection, Washington, D.C.

Still Life: The Object in American Art 1915–1995, Marsh Art Gallery, Richmond (traveled to Arkansas Arts Center, Little Rock; Newport Harbor Art Museum, Newport Beach; Philbrook Museum of Art, Tulsa; Society of the Four Arts, Palm Beach; Salina Art Center, Salina; American Federation of Arts, Rizoli, New York)

Collections:

Metropolitan Museum of Art, New York; Museum of Modern Art, New York; Brooklyn Museum, New York; Albright-Knox Art Gallery, Buffalo, New York; National Gallery of Art, Washington, D.C.; Phillips Collection, Washington, D.C.; Art Institute of Chicago; Carl Van Vechten Gallery of Fine Art, Fisk University, Nashville, Tennessee; Museum of Fine Arts, Dallas; Tate Gallery, London; Baltimore Museum of Art, Maryland; Dallas Museum of Fine Arts, Texas; Santa Barbara Museum of Art, California; Toledo Museum of Art, Ohio; Wellesley College, Massachusetts.

Publications:

By O'KEEFFE: Books—*The Work of Georgia O'Keeffe,* portfolio, 1937; *Georgia O'Keeffe: Drawings,* New York 1968; *Some Memories of Drawings,* New York 1974, 1988; *Georgia O'Keeffe,* New York 1976. **Articles**—statement in *Manuscripts* (New York), December 1922; "Letters to Alfred Stieglitz" in *Georgia O'Keeffe* exhibition catalog, New York 1938; "About Painting Desert Bones" in *Georgia O'Keeffe: Paintings, 1943,* exhibition catalog, New York 1944; "Stieglitz: His Pictures Collected Him" in the *New York Times,* December 1949; interview in *The Artist's Voice: Talks with 17 Artists* by Katharine Kuh, New York 1962; letters in *Letters from 31 Artists to the Albright-Knox Art Gallery,* edited by Ethel Moore, Buffalo, New York 1970; introduction to *Georgia O'Keeffe: A Portrait by Alfred Stieglitz,* exhibition catalog, New York 1978; "Georgia O'Keeffe: An American Original," interview, with M. L. Kotz, in the *Reader's Digest* (New York), May 1979.

On O'KEEFFE: Books—*Alfred Stieglitz Presents 100 Pictures, Oils, Water-Colors, Pastels and Drawings by Georgia O'Keeffe, American,* exhibition catalog (includes statement by O'Keeffe), New York 1923; *Alfred Stieglitz Presents 51 Recent Pictures, Oils, Water-Colors, Pastels and Drawings by Georgia O'Keeffe, American,* exhibition catalog, New York 1924; *Paintings by 19 Living Americans,* exhibition catalog, New York 1929; *Georgia O'Keeffe: Exhibition of Recent Paintings, 1935,* catalog with text by Marsden Hartley, New York 1936; *The Work of Georgia O'Keeffe: A Portrait of 12 Paintings* by James Lane and Leo Katz, New York 1937; *Georgia O'Keeffe,* exhibition catalog, New York 1938; *Georgia O'Keeffe: Exhibition of Oils and Pastels,* catalog, New York 1939; *Georgia O'Keeffe: Exhibition of Oils and Pastels,* catalog, New York 1940; *Georgia O'Keeffe* by Daniel Catton Rich, Chicago 1943; *Abstract and Surrealist Art in America* by Sidney Janis, New York 1944; *Georgia O'Keeffe: Paintings, 1943,* exhibition catalog, New York 1944; *Catalog of the Alfred Stieglitz Collection for Fisk University,* Nashville, Tennessee 1949; *Georgia O'Keeffe: 40 Years of Her Art* by Daniel Catton Rich, Worchester, Massachusetts 1960; *Georgia O'Keeffe: An Exhibition of the Work of the Artist from 1915 to 1966,* catalog edited by Mitchell Wilder, Fort Worth, Texas 1966; *The Art of the Real: U.S.A. 1948–1968* by E. C. Goossen, New York 1968; *Georgia O'Keeffe* by Lloyd Goodrich and Doris Bry, New York 1970; *The Students of William Merritt Chase* by Ronald G. Pisano, Huntington, New York 1973; *Early American Moderns: Painters of the Stieglitz Group* by Mahanri Sharp Young, New York 1974; *Alfred Stieglitz and the American Avante-Garde* by William Innes Homer, Boston 1977; *The Eye of Stieglitz,* exhibition catalog, New York 1978; *Georgia O'Keeffe: A Portrait by Alfred Stieglitz,* exhibition catalog, New York 1978; *A Recognizable Image: William Carlos Williams on Art on Artists,* edited by Bram Dikstra, New York 1978; *The Collection of Alfred Stieglitz* by Weston J. Naef, New York 1978; *Originals: American Women Artists* by Eleanor Munro, New York 1979; *Portrait of an Artist: A Biography of Georgia O'Keeffe* by Laurie Lisle, New York 1980; *Georgia O'Keeffe* by Laurie Lisle, New York 1980; *Georgia O'Keeffe,* exhibition catalog with text by Patterson Sims, New York 1981; *Georgia O'Keeffe,* exhibition catalog with essay by Barbara Haskell, Santa Fe 1985; *Georgia O'Keeffe: One Hundred Flowers,* edited by Nicholas Callaway, London 1987; *Georgia O'Keeffe* by Lisa Mintz Messinger, London 1988; *Georgia O'Keeffe: Art and Letters,* exhibition catalog, with text by Jack Cowart, Juan Hamilton and Sarah Greenough, Boston 1989; *Georgia O'Keeffe,* exhibition catalog by Gerald P. Peters, Santa Fe 1990; *O'Keeffe, Stieglitz and the Critics, 1916–1929* by Barbara Buhler Lynes, Ann Arbor 1989; *Becoming O'Keeffe: The Early Years* by Sarah Whitaker Peters, New York 1991; *Miss O'Keeffe* by Christine Taylor Patten and Alvaro Cardona-Hine, Albuquerque 1992; *O'Keeffe and Stieglitz: An American Romance* by Benita Eisler, Harmondsworth 1992; *Georgia O'Keeffe: American and Modern* by Charles C. Eldredge, New Haven 1993; *Georgia O'Keeffe (1887–1986),* exhibition catalog, London 1993; *The Voices of Women Artists* by Wendy Slatkin, Englewood Cliffs 1993; *Georgia O'Keeffe* by Barbara Buhler Lynes, New York 1993; *Georgia O'Keeffe: Canyon Suite,* exhibition catalog, New York 1995; *O'Keeffe and Texas,* exhibition catalog, San Antonio 1998; *Georgia O'Keeffe: the Catalogue Raisonne* by Barbara Buhler Lynes, New Haven 1999. **Articles**—"Georgia O'Keeffe: Attituded to Nature" by Eric Gibson in *Studio International,* no. 1019, vol. 201, April 1998; "O'Keeffe and the Masculine Gaze" by Anna C. Chave in *Art in America* (New York), vol. 78, no. 1, January 1990; "Georgia O'Keeffe: From the Faraway Nearby" by Christopher Merrill in *El Palacio,* vol. 96, no. 3, Summer 1991; "The Unknown O'Keeffe" by Hunter Drohojowska in *Art and Antiques,* September 1989; "Days with Georgia" by Christine Taylor Patten and Alvaro Cardona-Hine in *ARTnews* (New York), vol. 91, no. 4, April 1992; "Artistic Synergy: Georgia O'Keeffe and Alfred Stieglitz" by Stephen May in *Southwest Art,* vol. 23, no. 6, November 1993; "O'Keeffe As I See Her" by Susan Hiller in *Frieze* (London), no. 11, Summer 1993; "The Georgia O'Keeffe Museum" by Sally Eauclaire in *Southwest Art,* vol. 27, no. 1, June 1997; "Finding a Self in Nature: Georgia O'Keeffe and Trees" by Sharyn R. Udall in *El Palacio,* vol. 102, no. 1, Summer-Fall 1997; "Georgia O'Keeffe's West" by Peter H. Hassrick in *Antiques,* vol. 152, no. 5, November 1997; "Georgia O'Keeffe's White Birch at the Amon Carter Museum, Fort Worth" by Jane Myers in *Apollo* (London), no. 428, vol. 146, October 1997; "O'Keeffe's Arboreal Portraits of D.H. Lawrence and Gerald Heard" by Brenda Mitchell in *Woman's Art Journal* (Laverock), vol. 19, no. 2, Fall 1998-Winter 1999; "Western Women Artists: Discovering a Long-Overlooked Segment of American Art History" by Phil Kovinick and Marian Yoshiki-Kovinick in *Southwest Art,* vol. 28, no. 6, November 1998.

* * *

Like several other American painters—John Marin and Edward Hopper to name two—Georgia O'Keeffe painted both New England and the Southwest. Her paintings of New York City are powerful semiabstractions which relate her to the "Precisionist" painters with their preoccupation with simplification, design, hard-edges, omitted or stylized shadows, areas of even color. But her real love affair is with the mountains, desert landscapes and enormous skies of places like New Mexico.

She can be called a realist in the way she depicts things we can read as known to us, but her editing of forms to serve her formal needs as a painter reveals an artist of acute and profound gifts of abstracting. She was really not much like any other painter. Her best work is charged with the mysterious. In her hands, flowers, looked at so closely and presented so out of natural scale, become worlds threatening to engulf us in sensual floods of shape and color as though we are bees about to become drunk on nectar. She turns sun-bleached skulls into icons for some unknown cult. Hills heave and spread like bodies, high-altitude clouds could be ice floes in a thin blue sea. The architecture of the adobe is shown so pure in line as to vie with Mies or Mondrian.

This mystery is partially created by a surreal sensibility—earth as flesh, small things become gigantic—but it also has something to do with subject matter of place—the flower in the desert skull—along with the effect light has on vision. True artists respond deeply to what they are looking at and how it is lighted. Whistler could never have painted the way he did if he'd lived in New Mexico. And when Gauguin journeyed to the South Seas his *color* changed along with his imagery, although his way of depicting forms did not alter radically from those of his Normandy paintings.

Nor do O'Keeffe's forms change that much from Big Town to small *arroyo*. But somehow the *air* does. No doubt it has something to do with the space between things and between those things and the sky. And perhaps, if sound has anything to do with visual responses, the availability of silence has something to do with it too.

—Ralph Pomeroy

OLDENBURG, Claes (Thure)

Nationality: American. **Born:** Stockholm, Sweden, 28 January 1929; immigrated to the Chicago, Illinois, in 1936; naturalized, 1953. **Education:** Studied literature and art, Yale University, New Haven, Connecticut, 1946–50, B.A. 1950; art, under Paul Weighardt, Art Institute of Chicago, 1952–54. **Family:** Married artist and art critic Coosje van Bruggen, with whom he has worked closely, especially on large-scale public projects and performances, since 1976. **Career:** Worked as an apprentice reporter, City News Bureau, Chicago, 1952–54; illustrator, *Chicago Magazine,* 1955–56; operated Ray Gun Manufacturing Company and worked part-time in Cooper Union Museum School Library, New York, 1956–61; met Jim Dine, George Brecht, Allan Kaprow, George Segal, and Robert Whitman, New York, 1959; collaborated with Lippincott Environmental Arts, Inc., now Lippincott Inc., New York, 1969. Divides time between studios in New York City and Beaumont-sur-Dême, France. **Awards:** American Institute of Architects Award, 1977; Presidential Medal for the Arts, President William Clinton, 2000. **Agent:** Leo Castelli Gallery, 420 West Broadway, New York, New York 10012. **Address:** 556 Broome Street, New York, New York 10013, U.S.A. **Web site:** www.oldenburgvanbruggen.com

Individual Exhibitions:

1959 Cooper Union Art School Library, New York
Judson Gallery, New York
1960 *The Street,* Reuben Gallery, New York
1961 *The Store,* 107 East 2nd Street, New York
1962 Green Gallery, New York
1964 Sidney Janis Gallery, New York
Galerie Ileana Sonnabend, Paris
1966 Sidney Janis Gallery, New York
Robert Fraser Gallery, London
Moderna Museet, Stockholm
1967 Sidney Janis Gallery, New York
Projects for Monuments, Museum of Contemporary Art, Chicago
1969 Museum of Modern Art, New York (traveled to Stedelijk Museum, Amsterdam; Städtische Kunsthalle, Düsseldorf; The Tate Gallery, London)
1971 *Object Into Monument,* Pasadena Art Museum, Pasadena, California, (traveled to University Art Museum, University of California at Berkeley, California; Nelson-Atkins Museum, Kansas City, Missouri; Des Moines Art Center, Iowa; Philadelphia Museum of Art; Art Institute of Chicago)
1974 Leo Castelli Gallery, New York
1975 *Zeichnungen von Claes Oldenburg,* Kunsthalle Tübingen, Tübingen, Germany, (traveled to Kunstmuseum Basel; Städtische Galerie im Lenbachhaus, Munich; Nationalgalerie Berlin Staatliche Museen Preussischer Kulturbesitz, Berlin; Kaiser Wilhelm Museum, Krefeld, Germany; Museum des 20. Jahrhunderts, Vienna; Kunstverein, Hamburg, Germany; Städtische Galerie im Städelschen Kunstinstitut, Frankfurt am Main; Gestner-Gesellschaft, Hannover, Germany; Louisiana Museum, Humlebaek, Denmark)
Oldenburg: Six Themes, Walker Art Center, Minneapolis, (traveled to The Denver Art Museum, Denver; The Seattle Art Museum, Seattle; Institute of Contemporary Art, Hayden Gallery, Massachusetts Institute of Technology, Boston; The Art Gallery of Ontario, Toronto)
1976 Leo Castelli Gallery, New York
1977 *Drawings, Watercolors and Graphics,* Stedelijk Museum, Amsterdam, (traveled to Musée National d'Art Moderne, Centre Georges Pompidou, Paris; Moderna Museet, Stockholm)
The Mouse Museum / The Ray Gun Wing: Two Collections / Two Buildings by Claes Oldenburg, Museum of Contemporary Art, Chicago (traveled to Phoenix Art Museum, Phoenix, Arizona; St. Louis Art Museum, Missouri; Museum of Fine Arts, Dallas; Whitney Museum of American Art, New York; Rijksmuseum Kröller-Müller, Otterlo, The Netherlands; Museum Ludwig, Cologne)
1980 *Large-Scale Projects 1977–1980,* Leo Castelli Gallery, New York, with Coosje van Bruggen
1986 *Props, Costumes and Designs from the Performance Il Corso del Coltello by Claes Oldenburg, Coosje van Bruggen, Frank O. Gehry,* Leo Castelli Gallery, New York
The Knife Ship, Solomon R. Guggenheim Museum, New York
1987 *A Bottle of Notes and Some Voyages,* Northern Centre for Contemporary Art, Sunderland, England, with Coosje van Bruggen (traveled to The Henry Moore Centre for the Study of Sculpture, Leeds City Art Gallery, Leeds, England; Serpentine Gallery, London; Glynn Vivian Art Gallery and Museum, Swansea, England; Palais des Beaux-Arts, Brussels; Wilhelm-Lehmbruck Museum, Duisburg, West Germany; IVAM Centre Julio González, Valencia, Spain; Tampereen Nykytaiteen Museo, Tampere, Finland)
Designs and Costumes for *Il Corso del Coltello,* Musée National d'Art Moderne and Centre Georges Pompidou, Paris, with Coosje van Bruggen and Frank O. Gehry

Drawings 1959–1988, Palais des Beaux-Arts, Brussels, (traveled to Musée d'Art Contemporain, Nîmes, France; IVAM Centro Julio González, Valencia, Spain)

1990 *The European Desktop,* Galleria Christian Stein, Milan, with Coosje van Bruggen
From The Studio, Walker Art Center, Minneapolis, (traveled to Musée Cantini, Marseilles, France)
Multiples in Retrospect, 1964–1990, Brooke Alexander Editions, New York, Leo Castelli Gallery, New York, with Coosje van Bruggen

1992 *Larger than Life,* Pace Gallery, New York BP Building, Cleveland, Ohio, with Coosje van Bruggen
Multiples 1964–1990, Portikus, Frankfurt am Main

1994 *Large-Scale Projects,* PaceWildenstein, New York, with Coosje van Bruggen

1995 *Claes Oldenburg: An Anthology,* National Gallery, Washington, D.C., Museum of Contemporary Art, Los Angeles, Solomon R. Guggenheim Museum, New York, (traveled to Kunst- und Ausstellungshalle der Bundesrepublik Deutschland, Bonn, Germany; Hayward Gallery, London, 1996)

1997 *Claes Oldenburg: Printed Stuff,* Madison, Wisconsin, (traveled to Columbus Museum of Art, Ohio; Detroit Institute of Arts, Michigan, 1998)

1999 *Claes Oldenburg Coosje van Bruggen,* Museo Correr, Venice, Italy, with Coosje van Bruggen

2000 *Encounters: New Art from Old,* National Gallery, London, with Coosje van Bruggen

Selected Group Exhibitions:

1960 *New Forms/New Media I,* Martha Jackson Gallery, New York

1964 *Venice Biennale,* Venice
Painting and Sculpture of a Decade 1954–64, Tate Gallery, London

1968 *The Obsessive Image 1960–1968,* Institute of Contemporary Arts, London

1969 *Chicago Show,* Richard Feigen Gallery, Chicago

1974 *American Pop Art,* Whitney Museum, New York

1976 *Drawing Now,* Museum of Modern Art, New York (toured Europe and Scandinavia)

1978 *Drawings for Outdoor Sculpture 1946–1977,* Amherst College, Massachusetts (toured the United States)

1979 *American Portraits of the 60s and 70s,* Aspen Center for the Visual Arts, Colorado

1980 *Printed Art: A View of 2 Decades,* Museum of Modern Art, New York

1981 *Selections from Castelli: Drawings and Works on Paper,* Neil Ovsey Gallery, Los Angeles

1987 *American Painting: Abstract Expressionism and After,* San Francisco Museum of Modern Art

1997 *Future, Present, Past,* XLVII Esposizione Internazionale d'Arte, Venice Biennale, Venice, with Coosje van Bruggen

Selected Collections:

Art Institute of Chicago; Centre Georges Pompidou, Paris; Hirshhorn Museum and Sculpture Garden, Washington D.C.; Kunstmuseum Basel; Los Angeles County Museum of Art; Moderna Museet, Stockholm, Sweden; Museum für Moderne Kunst, Frankfurt am Main; Museum Ludwig, Cologne; Museum of Contemporary Art, Los Angeles; Museum of Modern Art, New York; National Gallery of Art, Washington D.C.; Rijksmuseum Kröller-Müller, Otterlo, the Netherlands; Solomon R. Guggenheim Museum, New York; Stedelijk Museum, Amsterdam; Tate Gallery, London; Walker Art Center, Minneapolis; Whitney Museum of American Art, New York.

Selected Performances:

Snapshots from the City, Judson Gallery, New York, 1960; *Ironworks / Fotodeath,* Reuben Gallery, New York, 1961; *Ray Gun Theater,* Ray Gun Mfg. Co., 107 East 2nd Street, New York, in cooperation with Green Gallery, New York, 1962: *Store Days I, Store Days II, Nekropolis I, Nekropolis II, Injun (N.Y.C.) I, Injun (N.Y.C.) II, Voyages I, Voyages II, World's Fair I, World's Fair II; Injun,* Dallas, 1962; *Gayety,* University of Chicago, 1963; *Stars,* Washington Gallery of Modern Art, Washington, D.C., 1963; *Autobodys,* Los Angeles, 1963; *Washes,* Al Roon's Health Club, New York, 1965; *Massage,* Moderna Museet, Stockholm, 1966; *Il Corso del Coltello,* (with Coosje van Bruggen and Frank O. Gehry), Venice, Italy, 1985.

Publications:

By OLDENBURG: Books—*Store Days, Documents from The Store (1961) and Ray Gun Theater (1962),* with Emment Williams, New York 1967; *Injun and Other Stories (1960),* New York 1966; *Some Program Notes about Monuments, Mainly,* supplement catalog, New York 1967; *Claes Oldenburg: Notes,* exhibition catalog, Los Angeles 1968; *Proposals for Monuments and Buildings 1965–1969,* Chicago 1969; *Notes In Hand,* New York and Basel 1971; *Raw Notes,* Halifax, Nova Scotia 1973; *More Ray Gun Poems (1960),* Philadephia 1973; *Photo Log, May 1974-August 1976,* Stuttgart 1976; *Press Log, May 1974-August 1976,* Stuttgart 1976; *Sketches and Blottings Toward The European Desk Top,* by Claes Oldenburg and Coosje van Bruggen, Milan, Turin, and Florence 1990; *Claes Oldenburg: Multiples in Retrospect, 1964–1990,* New York 1991; *Large-Scale Projects,* by Claes Oldenburg and Coosje van Bruggen, New York 1994; *Claes Oldenburg Coosje van Bruggen,* by Germano Celant, Claes Oldenburg and Coosje van Bruggen, Milan 1999. **Articles**—''The Artist Says: Claes Oldenburg'' in *Art Voices* (New York), summer 1965; ''The Object: Still Life,'' interview Jan McDevitt in *Craft Horizons* (New York), September/October 1965; ''Claes Oldenburg: Extracts from the Studio Notes, 1962–64'' in *Artforum* (New York), January 1966; ''Oldenburg Lichtenstein, Warhol: Discussion,'' edited by Bruce Glaser, in *Artforum* (New York), February 1966; ''Eftertanker'' in *Konstrevy* (Stockholm), no. 5/6, 1966; ''Oldenburg's Monuments,'' interview, with Gene Baro, in *Art and Artists* (London), December 1966; comments in *Perspecta 11* (New Haven, Connecticut), 1967; ''Take a Cigarette Butt and Make It Heroic,'' interview with Suzi Gablik, and ''Egomessages about Pollock'' in *Artnews* (New York), May 1967; ''America: War and Sex, Etc.'' in *Arts Magazine* (New York), Summer 1967; conversations, with others, in *Theatre of Mixed Means* by Richard Kostelanetz, New York 1968; ''The Artist Speaks: Claes Oldenburg,'' interview with John Coplans, in *Art in America* (New York), March/April 1969; ''The Bedroom Ensemble, Replica 1'' in *Studio International* (London), July/August 1969; ''How to Keep Sculpture Alive, In and Out of a

Museum,'' interview, in *Arts Magazine* (New York), September/October 1969; ''Eigen Statement'' in *Art Now: New York* (New York), October 1969; ''Chronology of Drawings'' in *Studio International* (London), June 1970; ''Claes Oldenburg: An Interview,'' with A. W. Reaves, in *Artforum* (New York), October 1972; ''Oldenburg on Multiples,'' interview with John Loring in *Arts Magazine* (New York), May 1974; ''History of the Alphabet/Good Humor'' and ''The Letter Q'' in *The Alphabet in L.A.*, exhibition catalog, Los Angeles 1975; interview, with Martin Friedman, in *Oldenburg: 6 Themes,* exhibition catalog, Minneapolis 1975; ''About California'' in *Vision* (Oakland, California), no. 1, 1975; ''Interview mit Claes Oldenburg,'' with Friedrich Bach, in *Das Kunstwerk* (Baden-Baden, West Germany), May 1975; ''Added Comments'' in *The Soft Screw,* exhibition catalog, Los Angeles 1976; ''Collecting Ray Guns in New York'' in *Vision* (Oakland, California) no. 3, 1976; ''The Double-Nose/Purse/Punching Bag/Ashtray'' in *Tracks* (New York), Winter 1976.

On OLDENBURG: Books—*Exhibition of Recent Work by Claes Oldenburg,* catalog, New York 1964; *Claes Oldenburg,* exhibition catalog, Paris 1964; *New Work by Claes Oldenburg,* exhibition catalog, New York 1966; *Claes Oldenburg, Skupturer och Techningar,* exhibition catalog, Stockholm 1966; *Oldenburg,* exhibition catalog, New York 1967; *Dine/Oldenburg/Segal: Painting/Sculpture,* exhibition catalog with a foreword by Brydon Smith, text by Ellen H. Johnson, Toronto and Buffalo, New York 1967; *American Sculpture of the 60s,* exhibition catalog, Los Angeles 1967; *Claes Oldenburg: Drawings and Prints,* with an introduction and commentary by Gene Baro, New York and London 1969; *Claes Oldenburg: Constructions, Models and Drawings,* exhibition catalog, Chicago 1969; *Claes Oldenburg,* exhibition catalog by Barbara Rose, New York 1969; *Claes Oldenburg,* exhibition catalog, Amsterdam 1970; *Claes Oldenburg,* exhibition catalog, London 1970; *New Work by Claes Oldenburg,* exhibition catalog, New York 1970; *Claes Oldenburg: Object into Monument,* exhibition catalog by Barbara Haskell, Pasadena, California 1971; *Experiment in Grafiek: Gemini GEL,* exhibition catalog by J. Leering, Eindhoven, Netherlands 1971; *Claes Oldenburg* by Ellen Johnson, Baltimore 1971; *Claes Oldenburg: Recent Prints,* exhibition catalog, New York 1973; *Notes in Hand,* exhibition catalog, Rome 1974; *The Lipstick Comes Back,* exhibition catalog, with an introduction by Alan Shestack, essay by Susan B. Casteras, New Haven, Connecticut 1974; *Claes Oldenburg: The Alphabet in L.A.,* Los Angeles 1975; *Claes Oldenburg: 6 Themes,* exhibition catalog, with an introduction by Martin Friedmann, Minneapolis 1975; *Zeichnungen von Claes Oldenburg,* Tübingen, West Germany 1975; *Erotic Fantasy Drawings,* exhibition catalog with essay by Richard Morphet, London 1975; *Drawing Now,* exhibition catalog with text by Barbara Rose, New York 1976; *The Soft Screw,* exhibition catalog, Los Angeles 1976; *Notes in Hand,* exhibition catalog, Barcelona 1976; *Mouse Museum/Ray Gun Wing, Two Collections/Two Buildings,* exhibition catalog, Chicago 1977; *Claes Oldenburg: Tekeningen, Aquarellen en Grafiek/Drawings, Watercolors and Prints,* exhibition catalog, Amsterdam 1977; *Oldenburg: The Inverted Q,* exhibition catalog by Robert Doty, Akron, Ohio 1977; *Monuments and Monoliths, A Metamorphosis,* exhibition catalog, Roslyn, New York 1978.

* * *

After graduating from Yale, Claes Oldenburg worked as a reporter for a time. Then he took classes at the Art Institute of Chicago and opened a studio where he made magazine illustrations and easel paintings. The first three-dimensional objects did not appear until 1957 after he had moved to New York and met with artists working there in environmental and theatrical projects and happenings.

This was the fertilising ambiance where he began to produce his art objects in relation to what surrounded him. From deep sessions of drawing the still lifes of daily existence, he went into their reconstitution in flat constructions of hessian, cardboard and other ready-made materials. Collage and papier mache were used to compress some of the images he drew as grafitti on the walls of the Bowery and other streets of downtown Manhattan. They were shown for the first time as ''The Street'' at the Judson Gallery in 1960 and later at Reuben. Next came the flags he produced from flotsam gathered on the Massachusetts beaches.

In 1961, after contributing to a group show at the Martha Jackson Gallery replicas in reliefs, signs and advertisements copied from actual goods on display in neighbourhood shops, he opened ''The Store'' in his studio. Here he added some free-standing pieces in the form of a roast joint and a two-piece bathing suit in plaster. From these modest starts Oldenburg moved up next year with his offering of giant soft sculptures taking a part of the Pop Art then flowering in profusion.

The mammoth cheeseburgers and ice cream cones by their size made a new dimension in art that Oldenburg saw as a softening, a flaccidity in attitude as well as appearance. Oldenburg continued to work on constructions that fitted naturally into themes. After the Store came the Home, Electrical and Mechanical Objects and the Car. ''Bedroom Ensemble'' (1964), originally installed at Sidney Janis Gallery, was based on a motel on the way to Malibu. The aim was to remove emotive and personal attitudes so that it presented only formal attributes like the pyramids.

This attempt to introduce a time lag in advance in the contemplation of contemporary objects of everyday use had its surrealist shock especially when embodied in such projects as ''Hats Blowing in the Wind'' as a feasible monument for a city square.

Oldenburg acknowledged Duchamp's theory of art as a special way of regarding objects by his ''Soft Engine for Airflow with a Can and Transmission.'' Like Goeritz's emotional architecture and Christo's draped mountains, Oldenburg's soft monuments take on the inspirational fantasy of proportional suprise as much by juxtaposition as by transformation from still life to robot character. He engages outrage to activate the apathetic.

—G. S. Whittet

OLITSKI, Jules

Nationality: American. **Born:** Jevel Demikovosky in Snovsk, Russia, 27 March 1922; emigrated with family to the United States, 1924; naturalized, 1942. **Education:** National Academy of Design, New York, 1939–42; Beaux Arts Institute, New York, 1940–42; Zadkine School of Sculpture, Paris, 1949; Académie de la Grande Chaumière, Paris, 1949–50; New York University, New York, 1951–56, B.S. 1952, M.A. 1954. **Military Service:** Served in the United States Army, Special Training Unit, Purdue University, Lafayette, Indiana, 1942–45. **Family:** Married Gladys Katz in 1944 (divorced, 1951); married Andrea Hill Pearce in 1956 (divorced, 1975); daughters: Eve and Lauren; married Joan Forges Gorby in 1980. **Career:** Independent painter and sculptor, since 1951: lives and works in New York City, and in New Hampshire and Florida. Associate professor of art, State University of New York at New Paltz, 1954–55; curator, New York University Art Education Gallery, New York 1955–56; art instructor and fine arts department coordinator, C. W. Post College, Long Island University, Greenvale, New York, 1956–63; instructor in art, Bennington College, Vermont, 1963–67; Sally and Milton Avery Professor, Bard College, Annandale-on-Hudson, New York, 1987; Associate, National Academician, National Academy of Design, 1993. **Awards:** Purchase Prize, Ford Foundation, 1964; First Prize and Gold Medal, *30th Biennial Exhibition,* Corcoran Gallery, Washington, D.C., 1967; Distinction in the Arts Award, University of South Carolina, 1975; fellow, American Academy of Arts and Sceinces, 1991; Associate National Academician, National Academy of Design, 1993. **Address:** c/o Salanders O'Reilly, Galleries Inc., 20 E. 79th Street, New York, New York, 10021–0106.

Individual Exhibitions:

1950 Galerie Huit, Paris
1958 Alexander Iolas Gallery, New York
1959 French and Company Inc., New York
1960 French and Company Inc., New York
1961 Poindexter Gallery, New York
1962 New Gallery, Bennington College, New York
Poindexter Gallery, New York
1963 Galleria d'Arte Santo Croce, Florence
Galleria Trastevere di Topazia Alliata, Rome
Galleria Toninelli, Milan
Poindexter Gallery, New York
3 American Painters: Lewis, Noland, Olitski, Norman Mackenzie Gallery, Regina, Saskatchewan
1964 Richard Gray Gallery, Chicago
David Mirvish Gallery, Toronto
Kasmin Gallery, London
Galerie Lawrence, Paris
Poindexter Gallery, New York
1965 Poindexter Gallery, New York
David Mirvish Gallery, Toronto
Kasmin Gallery, London
3 American Painters: Noland, Olitski, Stella, Fogg Art Museum, Harvard University, Cambridge, Massachusetts
1966 Nicholas Wilder Gallery, Los Angeles
André Emmerich Gallery, New York
David Mirvish Gallery, Toronto
Kasmin Gallery, London
Frankenthaler, Noland, Olitski, New Brunswick Museum, Fredericton (toured Canada)
1967 Corcoran Gallery, Washington, D.C. (retrospective; toured United States)
David Mirvish Gallery, Toronto
André Emmerich Gallery, New York
Kasmin Gallery, London
1968 Institute of Contemporary Art, Philadelphia
David Mirvish Gallery, Toronto
Kasmin Gallery, London
1969 French and Company Inc., New York
Metropolitan Museum, New York
Lawrence Rubin Gallery, New York
David Mirvish Gallery, New York
Kasmin Gallery, London
1970 Lawrence Rubin Gallery, New York
David Mirvish Gallery, Toronto
Kasmin Gallery, London
1971 Lawrence Rubin Gallery, New York
David Mirvish Gallery, Toronto
Kasmin Gallery, London
1972 Lawrence Rubin Gallery, New York
David Mirvish Gallery, New York
Kasmin Gallery, London
1973 Lawrence Rubin Gallery, New York
Nicholas Wilder Gallery, Los Angeles
André Emmerich Gallery, Zurich
Knoedler Contemporary Art, New York
Museum of Fine Arts, Boston (retrospective; toured the United States)
David Mirvish Gallery, Toronto
1974 Corcoran Gallery, Washington, D.C. (toured the United States, Canada, and Europe)
David Mirvish Gallery, Toronto
André Emmerich Gallery, New York
Knoedler Contemporary Art, New York
1975 David Mirvish Gallery, Toronto
Knoedler Contemporary Art, New York
Galerie Wentzel, Hamburg
Dart Gallery, Chicago
1976 Knoedler Contemporary Art, New York
Watson/deNagy Gallery, Houston
1977 André Emmerich Gallery, New York
Knoedler Contemporary Art, New York
Galerie Wentzel, Hamburg
Museum of Fine Arts, Boston
Amerika Haus, West Berlin
Hirshhorn Museum, Washington, D.C.
1978 David Mirvish Gallery, Toronto
Knoedler Gallery, London
1979 Knoedler Contemporary Art, New York
Edmonton Art Gallery, Alberta
1981 Janus Gallery, Los Angeles
André Emmerich Gallery, New York
Paintings from the 60s, M. Knoedler and Company, New York
Gallery One, Toronto
Galerie Wentzel, Hamburg
Knoedler Gallery, London
Harcus/Krakow Gallery, Boston
The Downtown Gallery, Edmonton, Alberta
Meredith Long and Co., Houston
1982 Gallery One, Toronto
Downstairs Gallery, Edmonton, Alberta
Harcus/Krakow Gallery, Boston
Meredith Long and Co., Houston
Martha White Gallery, Louisville, Kentucky
1983 Gallery One, Toronto
M. Knoedler and Co., New York
Yares Gallery, Scottsdale, Arizona
Galerie Wentzel, Cologne
Harcus Gallery, Boston
1984 André Emmerich Gallery, New York

Yares Gallery, Scottsdale, Arizona
Gallery One, Toronto
Chateau de Jau, Perpignan, France (retrospective)
Galerie Daniel Templon, Paris

1985 Musée de Valence, France
Duke University, Durham, North Carolina
M. Knoedler and Co., New York
Galerie Wentzel, Cologne
Phillips Exeter Academy, New Hampshire

1986 André Emmerich Gallery, New York
Yares Gallery, Scottsdale, Arizona (retrospective)
Gallery One, Toronto
Galerie Wentzel, Cologne
Yares Gallery, Scottsdale, Arizona

1987 M. Knoedler and Co., New York
Meredith Long and Co., Houston
Gallery Camino Real, Boca Raton, Florida
Galerie Wentzel, Cologne
André Emmerich Gallery, New York
Gallery One, Toronto

1989 Associate American Artists, New York

1990 Buschlen-Mowatt Gallery, Vancouver (retrospective)
Gallery One, Toronto
Salander-O'Reilly Galleries, New York and Los Angeles (travelled to London, Paris, and Madrid)

1991 Galerie Afisina, Oporto, Portugal
Salander-O'Reilly Galleries, New York

1992 Salander-O'Reilly Galleries, Berlin
Gallery Camino Real, Boca Raton, Florida

1993 Salander-O'Reilly Galleries, New York
Thorne-Sagendorph Gallery, Keene, New Hampshire

1994 Gallery Camino Real, Boca Raton, Florida
The New Gallery, Coral Gables, Florida
Galerie Gerald Piltzer, Paris
Salander-O'Reilly Galleries, New York
New Paintings, University of Miami, Coral Gables, Florida (catalog)

1995 Long Fine Art, New York

1996 Thorne-Sagendorph Art Gallery, Keene, New Hampshire

1999 *Monoprints 1994–1999,* Thorne-Sagendorph Art Gallery, Keene, New Hampshire (catalog)
Jules Olitski: Pintura Sin Voluntad, Metta Gallery, Madrid

2000 *Five Decades of Jules Olitski,* Butler Institute of American Art, Youngstown, Ohio (catalog)
Ameringer Howard, New York
Philharmonic Center for the Arts, Naples, Florida

Selected Group Exhibitions:

1968 *L'Art Vivant 1965–1968,* Fondation Maeght, St. Paul-de-Vence, France

1969 *New York Painting and Sculpture 1940–1970,* Metropolitan Museum of Art, New York

1973 *11 Artistes Américains,* Musée d'Art Contemporain, Montreal

1974 *The Great Decade of American Abstraction: Modernist Art 1960–70,* Museum of Fine Arts, Houston

1977 *Drawings of the 70s,* Art Institute of Chicago

1979 *American Painting of the 1970s,* Albright-Knox Art Gallery, Buffalo, New York

1981 *Frankenthaler/Louis/Noland/Olitski,* Centre d'Arts Plastiques Contemporains, Bordeaux

1983 *Early Works by Contemporary Masters,* André Emmerich Gallery, New York

1985 *Grand Compositions,* Fort Worth Art Museum, Texas

1987 *Abstract Painting '57-'87,* Gallery Camino Real, Boca Raton, Florida

1989 *The Painter and Printmaker,* Associated American Artists, New York (catalog)

1993 *New York School,* Long Fine Art, New York

1994 *Olivier Debre & Jules Olitski,* Galerie Gerald Piltzer, Paris, France

1995 *Search for the Real Important Works by Gallery Artists,* Long Fine Art, New York

1996 *Caro and Olitski: Masters of Abstraction Draw the Figure,* New York Studio School of Drawing, Paintings and Sculptures, New York
Spring & Summer Group Show: Drawings, Paintings & Prints, Long Fine Art, New York

1997 *Spring & Summer Group Show: Drawings, Paintings & Prints,* Long Fine Art, New York

1998 *Green Mountain Boys,* Andre Emmerich Gallery, New York

Collections:

Metropolitan Museum, New York; Museum of Modern Art, New York; Whitney Museum, New York; Guggenheim Museum, New York; Corcoran Art Gallery, Washington, D.C.; Hirshhorn Museum and Sculpture Garden, Smithsonian Institution, Washington, D.C.; Chrysler Museum, Norfolk, Virginia; Art Institute of Chicago; Boston Museum of Fine Arts; Art Gallery of Ontario, Toronto; Nebraska Art Association Collection, University of Nebraska, Lincoln; National Gallery of Art, Washington, D.C.; Fogg Art Institute, Boston; Dallas Museum of Fine Art; Museum of Fine Art, Houston; Seattle Art Museum; Israel Museum, Jerusalem; Art Collection of Nordhein-Wastfalen, Düsseldorf, Germany; Cleveland Museum of Art.

Publications:

By OLITSKI: Books—*Jules Olitski: Expect Nothing, Do Your Work, Celebrate,* 2001. **Articles**—''Painting in Color'' in *33rd Biennale of Art,* exhibition catalog, Venice 1966; ''On Sculpture'' in *Metropolitan Museum of Art Bulletin* (New York), April 1969; ''First Chapter (A Short Story)'' in *Partisan Review* (New Brunswick), no. 2, 1978; ''Reflections on Masterworks'' in *Update* (Edmonton), July/August 1985; essay in *The Courage of Conviction,* edited by Phillip L. Berman, New York 1985; essay in *Jules Olitski: A Retrospective View,* exhibition catalog, Scottsdale 1986; essay in *The Courage to Grow Old,* edited by Phillip L. Berman, New York 1989; ''Clement Greenberg in My Studio'' in *American Art,* vol. 8, no. 3–4, Summer-Fall 1994; ''Drawing: Notes from a Student'' in *Drawing,* vol. 18, no. 1, Summer 1996; interview with William V. Ganis in *Art Criticism,* vol. 14, no. 1, 1999; ''My First New York Show'' in *Modern Painters* (London), vol. 13, no. 3, Autumn 2000.

On OLITSKI: Books—*3 New American Painters: Louis, Noland, Olitski,* exhibition catalog by Clement Greenberg, Regina,

Saskatchewan 1963; *3 American Painters: Noland, Olitski, Stella,* exhibition catalog by Michael Fried, Cambridge, Massachusetts 1965; *Jules Olitski,* exhibition catalog by Kenworth Moffett, Boston 1973; *Great Drawings of All Time: The Twentieth Century,* edited by Victoria Throson, New York 1979; *Jules Olitski* by Kenworth Moffett, New York 1981; *Jules Olitski,* exhibition catalog by Dominique Fourcade, Perpignan 1984. **Articles**—''Jules Olitski's New Paintings'' by Michael Fried in *Artforum* (New York), November 1965; ''Frankenthaler, Kelly, Lichtenstein, Olitski: A Preview of the American Selection at the 1966 Venice Biennale'' by Henry Geldzahler in *Artforum* (New York), June 1966; ''The Sculpture of Jules Olitski'' by Kenworth Moffett in *Metropolitan Museum of Art Bulletin* (New York), April 1969 (revised and reprinted in *Artforum,* April 1969); ''Painterliness Redefined: Jules Olitski and Recent Abstract Art'' by John Elderfield in *Art International* (Zurich), December 1972, April 1973; ''Jules Olitski as Post-Raphaelite'' by Vivien Raynor in the *New York Times,* 31 March 1978; ''Jules Olitski'' by Jeanne Silverthorne in *Artforum* (New York), May 1984; ''Jules Olitski'' by Valentin Tatransky in *Arts Magazine* (New York), May 1985; ''The Legend Business'' by Jed Perl in *New Criterion,* January 1990; ''On Target'' by Dodie Kazanjian in *Vogue,* February 1990; ''Jules Olitski'' by Bruce W. Pepich in *Art Gallery International,* April 1990; ''Artist's Dialogue'' by John Gruen in *Architectural Digest,* June 1991; ''Art after the End of Art'' by Arthur C. Danto in *Art Forum International,* April 1993; ''The Artist Reinvents Himself: Jules Olitski'' by Robert R. Craven in *Art New England,* vol. 18, August/September 1997; ''Olitski's Excellence: Elitism's Comeback, Bank's Surge Forward, Art's Ruin, and the Meaning of the Bible'' by Matthew Collings in *Modern Painters* (London), vol. 11, no. 3, Autumn 1998; ''Jules Olitski'' by James Lilliefors in *ARTnews,* vol. 99, no. 5, May 2000; ''Jules Olitski'' by Donald B. Kuspit in *Artforum,* vol. 39, no. 4, December 2000.

*

I was not at all on the scene in the forties and barely, if at all, in the late fifties. I don't really feel on the scene today either. Concerning present taste and sensibility, I am bemused by collectors and museum people who dote equally, at one and the same time, upon their David Smith *and* their George Segal, upon their Kenneth Nolan *and* their James Rosenquist, upon their Anthony Caro *and* their Alexander Calder. When did it begin? Did the few collectors twenty or thirty years ago of Pollock and Still also go for Ben Shahn and Corbino? In the latter nineteenth century the collectors and critics who went for Monet and Picasso didn't go for Bouguereau and Meissonier too. (This easy acceptance in our time of high art alongside lesser or even meretricious art was first brought to my attention by Clement Greenberg in a talk he gave at Bennington College eight or nine years ago.)

Attitude toward money? Maybe what's new is the expectation of artists that real money is to be made in the making and selling of art. Art dealers are quite properly out to make a profit. I doubt there has been any change in their area. An art maker of one sort or another has existed for at least several centuries, which certainly hasn't prevented great art from being made, or great artists from practicing their art. Artists always hope that one day they will find their Kahnweiler. But the sad truth is there are no Kahnweilers. Even Kahnweiler wasn't Kahnweiler, at least not as he has been pictured in retrospect. Money in itself doesn't corrupt. One has to be accessible to corruption. Money can be a help, especially when you have a family. That ought to be obvious.

As to the kind of painting and sculpture being done, I don't think a time that has produced a Nolan, a Caro, among at least an armful of younger and older artists, has anything to be apologetic for.

I suppose one enormous difference, maybe unique to recent times, is the emergence of artists in their twenties and early thirties (there may even be some in their teens, though I don't know any) who are given major shows in respectable galleries and museums and are taken very seriously by the art public, art critics, collectors, and maybe most damaging of all, by themselves. The young artist who feels that every move he makes is being watched by critics and collectors, by his peers and the public, not unnaturally may come to have a vested interest in maintaining his success. One painter I know—one who survived his youthful success and is now working better than ever—said to me one day, rather plaintively, ''It was like growing up in public.'' There is value in long years of obscurity, if one doesn't go insane or become suicidal, in that, simply because nobody is looking, the habit of fooling around and trying things out gets ingrained. This seems to be true for painters and sculptors (with some exceptions) in a way that it isn't for poets, composers, mathematicians, or chess masters.

It's hard to take risks if you feel you have something to lose. And it's that much harder if you have something to lose at about the same time as you've begun to shave. I don't think it occured to serious young artists of my generation (I am fifty-six years old now) that money and fame would be there at the very outset of our careers. At least I myself never thought it. It simply wasn't a part of the reality of my twenties, thirties, or early forties.

There are, of course, other differences between then and now. There is an increasing emphasis on the tying of art and the marketplace to social causes, politics, certain groups or blocs of people. To my mind art is a democratic situation; anyone can look at it and make it, and everyone should have his or her chance to be seen, if the work has anything to it. That's just it. Quality must remain the paramount concern. The quality of the art and the quality of the viewer.

—Jules Olitski

* * *

Jules Olitski is one of the leading American post-painterly abstractionists, a colour field painter who in the wake of Morris Louis developed his own methods of using colour to provide a voluptuous sensual experience. His sprayed paintings are completely devoid of depicted shape, and represent a radical and thoroughgoing attempt to make art out of nothing but colour. This has meant that for those American critics who see colour field abstraction as the quintessence of contemporary art, Olitski has become the undisputed living master, whose innovations have placed him at the farthest outpost of progress in art. Thus for Kenworth Moffett, who directed the 1973 Olitski retrospective and wrote its catalog, the essence of Olitski's greatness and of his novelty lies in his having ''developed and revised Jackson Pollock's central innovation, the over-all picture, in order to make it serve color.''

Olitski's early work, between 1952 and 1959, had thick encrusted surfaces built up from smears and trails of paint in the expressionist manner of Hans Hofmann. But by 1960 he was producing stained paintings, organized around cores, such as ovals ringing each other or clustering in one corner of the field, with large areas of bare canvas, the shapes making their impact through their rich saturated colours.

But his interest in the primary of colour rather than shape led him by 1965 to abandon drawings and composition and to spray paint in tiny particles on to soaked unprinted canvas, using contrasting hues to produce rich optical effects. These sprayed paintings consist of nothing but colour, abandoning shape entirely. Michael Fried has argued that much of the motivation behind Olitski's first sprayed paintings sprang from his desire to oppose the kind of structure at work in the paintings of Noland and Stella. But his paintings do depend on the shape of their supports, and more recently he has been contrasting the sprayed center with an outer edge of more thickly painted or sprayed bands which establish the literal existence of the canvas, while the more delicately sprayed centre creates an illusory, dissolving space.

For these effects the paintings are necessarily on a large scale, usually huge, and the paradox of Olitski's work is this vastness of scale compared with the limitation of content. Sweetly pretty, like so many attractive candy boxes, they seem to be the decorative product of an essentially hedonistic vision. The successive sprayings cause the colours to melt into one another, producing brilliant atmospheric effects which have led Olitski's work to be not inaptly described as the first fully abstract version of Impressionism, which as Barbara Rose puts it, ''like Olitski's mist and hazes, delighted in effects of light, atmosphere and movement.''

Unfortunately, however, much of the American critical talk about these paintings offers fine examples of the higher drivel, exposing the absurd overpraise lavished on American post-war art in general, which some critics try to present as a matter of uninterrupted advance from Pollock into higher and higher realms of excellence. Not only does this involve the claim that all painting must revolve around a single elementary aesthetic issue, but as Harold Rosenberg has acidly observed, the irony of Moffett's elevation of Olitski is that he praises him not for opening new paths but for acting as ''a bloc, *the* influence that has to be gone through or overcome if any fundamental innovation or breakthrough is to be achieved.''

—Konstantin Bazarov

OLIVEIRA, Nathan

Nationality: American. **Born:** Oakland, California, 19 December 1928. **Education:** Mills College, Oakland, California College of Arts and Crafts, Oakland, M.F.A., 1952. **Military Service:** United States Army, 1953–55. **Career:** Independent painter, since 1953: lives and works in Northern California. Instructor, San Francisco Art Institute and California College of Arts and Crafts, Oakland, 1952–53, 1955–56, and Stanford University, 1964–93. Artist-in-residence and visiting artist at universities throughout the United States, 1960–98. **Awards:** Tiffany Award for Graphic Arts, 1957; Guggenheim Foundation Fellowship, 1958; N. W. Harris Bronze Medal, Art Institute of Chicago, 1960; Special Prize, El Retiro Parquet, Arte de America y Espana, Madrid 1963; Tamarind Fellowship, 1964; National Endowment for the Arts Award, 1974. Associate, National Academy of Design, New York, 1982, 1984, 1985, 1994; Academy-Institute Award in Art, American Academy and Institute of Arts and Letters, New York, 1984; Ann O'Day Maples Professor in the Arts, Endowed Chair, Stanford University, Stanford, California, 1988; Honored for Distinguished Artistic Achievement, California Society of Printmakers, 1996; Awarded the degree of Commander in the Order of Henry the Navigator, President of Portugal and Portuguese Government, 1999. Honorary doctorate from San Francisco Art Institute, San Francisco, California, 1996. **Agent:** John Berggruen Gallery, 228 Grant Avenue, San Francisco, California 94108; Marsha Mateyka Gallery, 2012 R Street, N.W., Washington, D.C. 20009; Riva Yares, 3625 Bishop Lane, Scottsdale, Arizona 85251. **Address:** 785 Santa Maria Avenue, Stanford, California 94305, U.S.A.

Individual Exhibitions:

1957 Eric Locke Gallery, San Francisco
1958 Alan Gallery, New York
1959 Alan Gallery, New York
Paul Kantor Gallery, Beverly Hills, California
1960 Alan Gallery, New York
Paul Kantor Gallery, Beverly Hills, California
1961 *Recent Works,* Krannert Art Museum, University of Illinois, Urbana (travelled to the University of Minnesota, Minneapolis)
Walker Art Center, Minneapolis
Paul Kantor Gallery, Beverly Hills, California
1962 Paul Kantor Gallery, Beverly Hills, California
1963 Dickson Art Center, University of California at Los Angeles (travelled to the San Francisco Museum of Art; Fort Worth Art Center, Texas; and the Colorado Springs Fine Art Center, Colorado, 1963–64)
1964 *12 Intimate Fantasies,* R. E. Lewis Gallery, San Francisco
1965 *10 Years of Printmaking,* Stanford University, California (travelled to the San Francisco Museum of Art)
Alan Gallery, New York
Felix Landau Gallery, Los Angeles
1967 *Watercolors and Drawings,* Landau-Alan Gallery, New York
1968 Galerie Bleue, Stockholm
Gump's Gallery, San Francisco
Stanford University, California
Felix Landau Gallery, Los Angeles
1969 *Works on Paper,* Martha Jackson Gallery, New York
San Francisco Museum of Art
Martha Jackson Gallery, New York
1970 Terry Dintenfass Gallery, New York
Wisconsin State University, Oshkosh
1971 Michael Smith Gallery, Los Angeles
Smith-Anderson Gallery, Palo Alto, California
Stanford University, California
Terry Dintenfass Gallery, New York
1972 Southwestern College, Chula Vista, California
Charles Campbell Gallery, San Francisco
Jack Glenn Gallery, Corona del Mar, California
Terry Dintenfass Gallery, New York
1973 Fullerton Junior College, California
Anderson Art Corridor, Sacred Heart Schools, Menlo Park, California
15 Years Survey of Paintings 1958–1973, Oakland Art Museum, California
Spirit Paintings, Jack Glenn Gallery, Corona del Mar, California
1974 Smith-Anderson Gallery, Palo Alto, California
1975 Dorsky Gallery, New York

Charles Campbell Gallery, San Francisco
1976 Jorgensen Gallery, University of Connecticut, Storrs
Smith-Anderson Gallery, Palo Alto, California
University of California at Santa Cruz
Wichita State University, Kansas
1977 El Camino College, Torrance, California
Charles Campbell Gallery, San Francisco
John Berggruen Gallery, San Francisco
1978 *20 Years' Work on Paper,* Santa Rosa Community College, California
Harvard University, Cambridge, Massachusetts
Dorsky Gallery, New York
Cheney Cowles Memorial Museum, Spokane, Washington
Galerie Veith Turske, Cologne
1979 Charles Campbell Gallery, San Francisco
Galerie Veith Turske, Cologne
John Berggruen Gallery, San Francisco
Oliveira: Survey of Monotypes 1973–78, Baxter Art Gallery, Pasadena, California
1980 Alan Gallery, New York
Print Retrospective, California State University, Long Beach
Charles Cowles Gallery, New York
1981 Arts Club of Chicago
1982 John Berggruen Gallery, San Francisco
1983 Honolulu Academy of Arts, Hawaii
John Berggruen Gallery, San Francisco
Charles Cowles Gallery, New York
1984 San Francisco Museum of Modern Art (retrospective, travelled to Laguna Beach, California; Madison, Wisconsin; Lincoln, Nebraska; Norman, Oklahoma)
1985 Honolulu Academy of Arts, Hawaii
1986 Stanford University, California
Richard Gray Gallery, Chicago
Galleria Il Bisonte, Florence
1987 *Nathan Oliveira Recent Works,* Dorothy Goldeen Gallery, Santa Monica, California
Nathan Oliveira: Recent Paintings, John Berggruen Gallery, San Francisco, California
1988 *Continuous Tone: The Work of Nathan Oliveira,* Charlotte Crosby Kemper Gallery, Kansas City Art Institute, Missouri
Autunno in Toscana 1986—Monotypes, Robert Mondavi Winery, Napa, California
1989 *Figure: Summer, Monotypes from the Experimental Workshop,* John Berggruen Gallery, San Francisco, California
Nathan Oliveira: A Printer's Project, Editioned Lithographs, Monotypes and Unique Works, George H. Dalsheimer Gallery, Baltimore, Maryland
Nathan Oliveira: Raptors and Related Images, Beckstrand Gallery, Palos Verdes Art Center, California
1990 *Nathan Oliveira Monotypes,* Dorsky Gallery, New York
Paintings, John Berggruen Gallery, San Francisco, California
1991 *Nathan Oliveira: Paintings and Works on Paper 1959–1991,* Salander-O'Reilly Galeries, New York
Nathan Oliveira: To Edgar Allan Poe, a Suite of Lithographs, Richard L. Nelson Gallery, University of California, Davis, California
Nathan Oliveira: The New Mexican Sites, John Berggruen Gallery, San Francisco, California
1992 *Nathan Oliveira: Figurative Work, 1958–1992,* Hearst Art Gallery, Saint Mary's College, Moraga, California
1993 *Exhibition of Figurative Water Colors,* Museum of Contemporary Art, Honolulu, Hawaii
Paintings, Salander-O'Reilly Galeries/Fred Hoffman Gallery, Beverly Hills, California
Early Lithographs Related to Edgar Allan Poe, 1964–1971, Smith-Andersen Galerie, Palo Alto, California
Recent Paintings: Stelae, John Berggruen Gallery, San Francisco, California
1994 *Paintings, Water Colors and Drawings 1989,* Marsha Mateyka Gallery, Washington, D.C.
Artist and Model: A Tradition, Marsha Mateyka Gallery, Washington, D.C.
1995 *Nathan Oliveira: The Windhover, Dedicated to Gerrard Manly Hopkins,* Stanford University Museum of Art, Stanford, California (travelled to Pepperdine University, Malibu, California)
1996 *Nathan Oliveira: Recent Paintigs and Related Works,* Salander-O'Reilly Galeries, New York
Recent Works, Marsha Mateyka Gallery, Washington, D.C.
1997 *Moments in Time, 30 Year Retrospective of Monotypes and Monoprints,* Achenbach Foundation, California Palace of the Legion of Honor, San Francisco, California
Recent Paintings and Works on Paper, John Berggruen Gallery, San Francisco, California
1998 *Recent Monotypes,* Marsha Mateyka Gallery, Washington, D.C.
Prints/Copperplate Figures, Crown Point Press, San Francisco, California
Nathan Oliveira—Acqua, Water Media Works 1958–1989, College of Notre Dame, Belmont, California
Nathan Oliveira: The Windhover Paintings, Graduate Theological Union, Berkeley, California
1999 *Nathan Oliveira: Figurative Water Colors from 1965–2000 and New Monotypes,* John Berggruen Gallery, San Francisco, California

Selected Group Exhibitions:

1952 *Annual Exhibition of Watercolors, Prints and Decorative Arts,* Richmond Art Center, California
1956 *10 Years of American Prints 1947–1956,* Brooklyn Museum, New York
1957 *4 Leading Printmakers of the Bay Area,* Eric Locke Gallery, San Francisco
1958 *Recent American Prints,* University of Illinois, Champaign-Urbana
1963 *Arte Actuale de America Y Espana,* Los Palacios de Valázquez y Cristal de Retiro, Madrid (toured Europe)
1975 *National Exhibition of Prints,* Smithsonian Institution, Washington, D.C.
1980 *Bay Area Art: Then and Now,* Suzanne Brown Gallery, Scottsdale, Arizona
1982 *Drawings by Painters,* Long Beach Museum of Art, California

1984 *The Figurative Mode: Bay Area Painting 1956–66,* Grey Art Gallery, New York University
1987 *American Painting: Abstract Expressionism and After,* San Francisco Museum of Modern Art
1988 *Chicago International Art Exposition,* Chicago, Illinois
1989 *Bay Area Figurative Art, 1950–1965,* Hirshhorn Museum and Sculpture Garden, Smithsonian Institution, Washington, D.C. (travelled to Pennsylvania Academy of the Fine Arts, Philadelphia, Pennsylvania)
1990 *The Unique Print: 70s into 90s,* Museum of Fine Arts, Boston, Massachusetts
1991 *American Realism and Figurative Art: 1952–1990,* Miyagi Museum of Art, Sendai, Miyagi, Japan (travelled to Sogo Museum of Art, Yokohama, Japan; Tokushima Modern Art Museum, Tokushima, Japan; Museum of Modern Art, Shiga, Japan; Kochi Prefectural Museum of Folk Art, Kochi, Japan)
1992 *Directions in Bay Area Printmaking: 3 Decades,* Palo Alto Cultural Center, Palo Alto, California
1993 *The Black and White Exhibition,* Smith Andersen Gallery, Palo Alto, California
1995 *La Jeune Gravure Contemporaine et ses Invites des U.S.A.,* Mairie du VI eme Arrondissment, Paris
1996 *Master Printers and Master Pieces,* Kaohsiung Museum of Fine Arts, Taiwan
1997 *Singular Impressions,* National Museum of American Art, Smithsonian Institution, Washington, D.C.
1998 *Centennial Exhibition 1989–1998,* American Academy of Arts and Letters, New York
1999 *Artes de Outras Partes Exposieãs Colectiva Mãe D'Áqua das Amoreiras,* Lisbon, Portugal
2000 *Cross Currents in Modern Art: A Tribute to Peter Selz,* Achim Moeller Fine Art, New York

Collections:

Museum of Modern Art, New York; Brooklyn Museum, New York; National Collection of Fine Arts, Smithsonian Institution, Washington, D.C.; Butler Institute of American Art, Youngstown, Ohio; Des Moines Art Center, Iowa; Art Institute of Chicago; Oakland Museum, California; Grunwold Center for the Graphic Arts, University of California at Los Angeles; Honolulu Academy of Art, Hawaii; Bibliotech Nationale, Paris; Boston Museum of Fine Arts, Boston, Massachusetts; Carnegie Institute, Pittsburgh, Pennsylvania; Joseph H. Hirshhorn Collection, Smithsonian Institution, Washington, D.C.; Metropolitan Museum of Art, New York; National Collection Australia, Melbourne; Guggenheim Museum, New York; Tate Gallery, London; Whitney Museum of American Art, New York.

Publications:

By OLIVEIRA: Article—interview with Andrew de Shong in *Artweek* (Oakland, California), 13 October 1973.

On OLIVEIRA: Books—*Nathan Oliveira* by Frederick Wight, Los Angeles 1963; *The Tamarind Book of Lithography: Art and Techniques* by Garo Z. Antreasian and Clinton Adams, New York 1971; *Nathan Oliveira: 15 Year Survey of Paintings, 1958–73,* exhibition catalog by Harvey L. Jones and George Neubert, Oakland, California 1973; *Nathan Oliveira,* exhibition catalog by Fred Ploeger, Spokane, Washington 1978; *Nathan Oliveira: A Survey Exhibition 1957–1983,* exhibition catalog with essays by Thomas H. Garver and George W. Neubert, San Francisco 1984; *The Art of Nathan Oliveira* by Peter Selz, with essays by Joann Moser and Susan Landauer, Berkeley, California 2001. **Articles**—''Nathan Oliveira'' by Dan Tooker in *Art International* (Lugano, Switzerland), December 1973; ''Nathan Oliveira: Strength in Art'' by Susan Ackerman in *Stanford Daily* (California) 29 November 1977; ''Nathan Oliveira and the Monotype'' by Maudette Balle in *Artweek* (Oakland, California), 3 October 1979.

* * *

Nathan Oliveira has been closely identified with the so-called Bay Area Figurative School which emerged in Northern California during the 1950s. Reacting against the prevalent Abstract Expressionist style, David Park, Richard Diebenkorn, and Elmer Bischoff concurrently developed a variation in which painterly gesture and spontaneity were applied to landscape and the human figure. Oliveira's own figurative art matured in close contact with these and other painters working in a similar manner, but there are fundamental differences in attitude that set him apart. Bay Area Figurative painting was primarily concerned with formal matters; light, color, and the nature of paint. The figure was introduced as another composition element, and this basic objectivity stands in direct contrast to Oliveira's subjective romanticism.

Central to Oliveira's work is a humanistic vision that focuses on the figure. Typically female and nude, Oliveira's isolated figures appear to be emerging from the pigment in which their forms have been discovered. Appearing and reappearing in vaporous landscapes of shadow and mist, they embody an artistic and philosophical concept of transformation. Indistinct, faceless or masked, Oliveira's generalized images are symbolic presences rather than individuals. The ''Spirit Women'' of 1971, for example, are recognized as female figures only by their pubic triangles. Ghostlike, they are depicted in the process of materializing or dematerializing.

Despite their striking other-worldliness, these images are not entirely invented from imagination. Although the paintings are not done directly from the model, individual models and Oliveira's feelings about them do provide the essential memories upon which his preternatural, ''recalled'' images are based. Oliveira's visionary imagery, with all its mythical, mystical, and supernatural evocations, is in fact firmly grounded in personal experience of actual human beings—including studio nudes recalled in tranquility. The importance of this contact is evidenced by Oliveira's recent return to drawing directly from the model.

Oliveira's rich, painterly style has encompassed near non-objectivity as well as figuration. In the 1959 ''Standing Man with Stick'' or the ''Dance'' and ''Bathers'' series of the same year, stylized figures are all but obliterated in a thickly painted Abstract Expressionist surface. And the highly abstracted ''Ryan Sites'' (1981) share certain similarities with Diebenkorn's ''Ocean Park'' series. Nonetheless, Oliveira's commitment to nature and the figure precludes excursions into pure abstraction, post-painterly or otherwise. A group of ''Sites'' are actually landscapes painted in tribute to Monet. The most recently exhibited figurative works again bear witness to the consistency of Oliveira's vision and goals along figurative lines.

Oliveira enjoys a growing international reputation as painter; but he is also a widely respected printmaker. His influence as a teacher at

Stanford and particularly his experimentation with monotypes constitute important aspects of his career. The same basic themes appear throughout the graphic work where his sources and inspirations are perhaps most evident: the mysterious, symbolic imagery of Eugene Carriere and Odilon Redon is encountered in Oliveira's dark Lithographic ''portraits'' and disembodied heads such as ''Black Christ I,'' 1963. His profound admiration for Goya led to a dryprint version of ''Disasters of War.'' But perhaps the most important influence was that acknowledged in a major suite of lithographs entitled ''To Edgar Allan Poe'' (1970–1971). Like Poe, Oliveira seeks to uncover the realms of dreams, the unconcious, and the supernatural, deeply hidden truths about spirituality and the human condition.

—Paul J. Karlstrom

OLIVIERI, Claudio

Nationality: Italian. **Born:** Rome, 28 November 1934. **Education:** Accademia di Belle Arti di Brera, Milan, 1952–56. **Family:** Married Anna Lusenti in 1963; daughter: Elenora. **Career:** Worked as art director of media agency, Milan, 1959–62. Full-time painter, since 1978; lives and works in Milan. **Awards:** Morgan Painting Prize, Ravenna, 1972; Michetti Award, Francavila Are, Italy, 1972. **Agent:** Galleria del Milione, via Biali 21, Milan. **Address:** Via Ausonio 8, 20123 Milan, Italy.

Individual Exhibitions:

1959 Salone Annunciata, Milan
1960 George Lester, Rome
1963 Salone Annunciata, Milan
1967 Salone Annunciata, Milan
1969 Galleria del Milione, Milan
1970 Galleria La Loggia, Bologna
1971 Galleria del Milione, Milan
Galleria Contini, Rome
1973 Galleria 3b, Bolzano, Italy
Galleria San Luca, Bologna
1974 Galleria Peccolo, Livorno, Italy
Kunstverein, Münster, West Germany
Galleria La Piramide, Florence
1975 Galleria del Milione, Milan
1977 Galleria del Banco, Brescia, Italy
Galleria Capricorno, Venice
1978 Galerie Stevenson Palluel, Paris
1980 *Biennale,* Venice
1982 Padiglione d'Arte Contemporanea, Milan
1983 Galleria Civica, Modena, Italy
1984 Galerie E Edition, Munich
Galleria Lorenzelli, Milan
1985 Galerie Von Loe, Bonn
1987 Galerie Schafer, Giessen, West Germany
1988 Galleria del Milione, Milan
1989 Galleria Il Triangolo Nero, Alessandria
Galleria Bambaia, Busto Arsizio
Galleria del Milione, Milan
Museo Civico, Crema
1990 Galleria Spazia, Bologna
Galleria Meta, Bolzano
1992 Galleria Tega, Milan
Galleria Bambaia, Busto Arsizio
1993 Galleria Eidos Immagini Contemporanee, Asti
1994 Padiglione d'Arte Contemporanea, Ferrara
1995 Arte Studio Clocchiati, Udine
1996 Studio Centenari, Piacenza
1997 Artline, Amsterdam
1998 Spazio Cesare da Sesto, Sesto Calende
Studio Delise, Venice
Galleria Liba, Pisa
Galleria Bambaia, Busto Arsizio
1999 Galleria Omega, Reggio Emilia
2000 Galleria Centofiorini, Civitanova Alta
Frankfurter Westend Galerie, Frankfurt am Main
2001 Palazzo Sarcinelli, Conegliano
Quadri, Conegliano

Selected Group Exhibitions:

1966 *33rd Biennale,* Venice
1972 *10th Quadriennale,* Rome
1973 *Tempi di Percezione,* Galerie Merian, Krefeld, West Germany
1974 *Geplante Malerei,* Kunstverein, Münster, West Germany (travelled to the Galleria Milione, Milan)
1975 *New Italian Painting,* Galerie Espace 5, Montreal
1977 *Documenta 6,* Kassel, West Germany
1981 *Arte e Critica,* Galleria Nazionale d'Arte Moderna, Rome
1982 *Exploration in Italian Art,* National Gallery of New South Wales, Sydney
1985 *On Language and Ecstasy: A Generation in Italian Art,* Museum of Fine Art, Pori, Finland (travelled to Helsinki)
1987 *Italienische Kunst,* Kunstverein, Frankfurt
1990 Venice Biennial, Venice, Italy
1991 *Intersezioni,* Arte Italiana 1970–80, Kunsthalle, Budapest
Arte astratta in Italia, Liljevalchs Konsthall, Stockholm
1996 *Pittura come pittura,* Palazzo Sarcinelli, Conegliano
1997 *Arte in Italia,* Dumont Kunsthalle, Colonia
1998 *La luce dell'invisibile,* Fondazione Stelline, Milan
1999 *Quadriennale, Roma-Palazzo delle Esposizioni*

Collections:

Museo d'Arte Contemporanea, Parma Italy; Galleria Communale d'Arte Moderna, Livorno, Italy; Washington University, St. Louis; Museo Civico d'Arte Contemporanea, Milan; Galleria Civica, Bologna, Italy.

Publications:

By OLIVIERI: Book—*Del resto,* Conegliano 2001. **Article—**statement in *Flash Art* (Milan), October/November 1974.

On OLIVIERI: Books—*Geplante Malerei,* exhibition catalog by Klaus Honnef, Münster, West Germany 1974; *Claudio Olivieri,* exhibition catalog with essay by Paolo Fossati, Modena, Italy 1983; *Riflessioni su Olivieri* exhibition catalog by Michel Semff, Parma 1998; *Claudio Olivieri* exhibition catalog, Desenzano sul Garda

1989; *Claudio Olivieri: Il corpo dell'idea* by G.M. Accame, Bergamo 1991; *Claudio Olivieri* exhibition catalog, by Klaus Wolbert, Ferrara 1994; exhibition catalog by F. Gualdoni, Reggio Emilia 1999; *Olivieri, il colore come totalita* exhibition catalog by Elena Pontiggia, Civitanova Alta 2000; *Claudio Olivieri* exhibition catalog by B. Cora et al. Conegliano 2001. **Articles—**''Claudio Olivieri'' by Daniela Plazzoli in *Kunst Forum* (Mainz), February 1975; ''Gli Occhi di Atlantide'' by Luigi Ballerini in *Yale Italian Studies* (New Haven, Connecticut), Spring 1980.

*

Before painting is the unthought, the completely opaque place of non-relation. From this irrelationship ''before'' painting traverses the invisible towards a visible no longer blind, capable not so much of revealing the hidden, but of disconnecting the sensing of habitual evidence.

The surface of painting, the fine veil upon which the encounter occurs, is the point where the infinitesimal subtraction of the tangible is affected, where that which is subracted from materiality is restored to the glance.

But, I do not wish to speak of a before painting, nor an after, painting remains there, in that which is missing in word, in its indescribable pure being, which cannot respond because, perhaps, in it all is a questioning.

I have never worked toward setting up cultural deterrents, or toward a conjuring of collateral circumstances; I consider extraneous any descriptive collusion, any anticipation.

Painting is, in itself, an outshining which does not play with the catalog of cultural components, which cannot, in the attempt to refer itself back to a casuality, expect to recognize itself in its reflection.

Painting is ''seen,'' but not in the act of showing the illusion of something; painting ''sees,'' but not from a ''where'' definable as a distance.

Painting is nothing other than the purely and solely visible, is that which, suspending all connotative inclines, introduces the non-mediated but infinite distance which makes of space a memory.

—Claudio Olivieri

* * *

To place the work of Claudio Olivieri somewhere between the formation of the so-called New Painting and Analytical Painting is reductive, perhaps even diversionary. Even if the inquiry is based on such concerns as the structure of painting, on colour, surface, the ultimate elements of the artistic discipline, one must nevertheless carefully distinguish between those artists who have admired pictorial negotiation and those who, though interested in the determination and definition of specific pictorial space, do not actually believe in its destruction. Olivieri belongs to the latter category.

His large actual canvases—large surfaces suit this artist—are played on such minimal chromatic grids that at first they seem to be monochrome, yet they make the eye travel across the canvas; they grasp the internal chromatic states; and the almost invisible colored curves and spectral pulsations metaphysically attract the observer to look ''inside'' the painting. At this point the colour, the surfaces, and the chromatic vibrations are no longer only elements of investigation; they become ''other''; they involve the artist and the spectator in a series of cultural links, mnemonically and symbolically evoked through colour.

But naturally symbol and memory in Oliveri's paintings reman inside the field of the painting: in fact, one is not talking about literary symbols that need only be ''represented,'' the fruition of which belongs to a world outside painting; something more is involved. The colour itself is a symbol, an evocation a memory, the space of which exists alongside the physical space of the canvas. It is this *mental* space that, instead of negating, the painting enchances.

In 1981, Olivieri wrote: ''Painting remains there, in that lack of speech; it cannot reply; but perhaps everything in it is a question'' and ''colour does not narrate; it is the end of the future, the uterus, the dream to come, the tale that began with history.''

—Marco Meneguzzo

ONTANI, Luigi

Nationality: Italian. **Born:** Vergato, Montovolo, Bologna. **Education:** Self-taught in art. **Career:** Lives and works in Rome. **Awards:** Artist of the Year Award, Town Councils of Cortina d'Ampezzo and Belluno, Italy, 2000. **Agent:** Galleria Sperone, Via Pallacorda 15, 00186 Rome, Italy; Sperone Westwater, 142 and 121 Greene Street, New York, New York, 10012. **Address:** Via Margutta 33, 00187 Rome, Italy.

Individual Exhibitions:

1970 Centro Culturale, San Fedele, Milan
Florence Festival
Galleria Diagramma, Milan
Palazzo Diamanti, Ferrara, Italy
1973 Galleria Contemporanea, Rome
1974 Modern Art Agency, Naples
Galleria l'Attico, Rome
Lp. 220, Turin
1975 Galleria l'Attico, Rome
De Appel, Amsterdam
1976 Galleria l'Attico, Rome
Galerie Sonnabend, Paris
Galleria Sperone, Milan
Sonnabend Gallery, New York
1977 Galleria d'Arte Moderna, Bologna
Koepelzaal, Amsterdam
1978 Galleria l'Attico, Rome
Franz Paludetto, Turin
1979 Mario Diacono, Bologna
Palazzo Ducale, Genoa
Kitchen Center, New York
A Space, Toronto
1980 Lucio Amelio, Naples
Galleria Minini, Brescia, Italy
1981 Galleria Minini, Milan
Galleria Diacono, Rome
Galleria Evan Menzio-Elena Pron, Turin
1983 Serra Di Felice, New York
Art Gallery 121, Antwerp
The Kitchen, New York

1984 *Biennale,* Venice
Städtische Museum, Munich
Lace Gallery, Los Angeles
1985 Jack Tilton Gallery, New York
Galleria l'Ariete, Milan
1986 Galleria Dell'Oca, Rome
Gallery Dacic, Tübingen
1987 Jack Tilton Gallery, New York
Galleria Franco Toselli, Milan
1988 Galleria Barnabò, Venice
Rizzardi, Milan
Kunstverein, Frankfurt
1989 Zelig, Bari, Italy
Galleria in Arco, Torino
Galleria Pio Monte, Rome
Studio d'Arte Raffaelli, Trento, Italy
Castello di Volpaia, Chianti
Eternal Metaphors: New Art from Italy, Alberta College of Art, Calgary (traveling exhibition) (catalog)
1990 Galleria Minini, Brescia, Italy
Galleria Communale, Bologna
Groningen Museum, Holland
1991 Italian Academy, London
Lucien Bilinelli, Brussels
1992 Galleria Barnabò, Venice
1993 Galleria Sperone, Rome
Castello di Volpaia, Chianti
1994 Sperone Westwater, New York (catalog)
Studio d'Arte Raffaelli, Trento
Galleria Civica di Arte Contemporanea, Trento (traveling exhibition) (catalog)
1995 *Idea Aida del Vero Diffida: Opere di Luigi Ontani: 1980–1995,* Galleria dello Scudo, Verona (catalog)
1997 Sperone Westwater Gallery, New York
Palazzo delle Esposizioni, Faenza, Italy (catalog)
Frankfurter Kunstverein (traveled to Museum Villa Stuck, Munich; Galleria Civica de Arte Contemporanea, Trento) (catalog)
2000 *En Route Vers l'Inde,* Roman Aquarium, Rome
Palazzo Crepadona, Belluno, Italy (also Galleria Civica, Cortina d'Ampezzo, Italy) (catalog)
2001 *Luigi Ontani: 1965–2001,* P.S. 1 Contemporary Art Center, New York (retrospective)

Selected Group Exhibitions:

1973 *April Festival,* Belgrade
1974 *Photomedia,* Museum am Ostwall, Dortmund, West Germany
Transformer, Kunstmuseum, Lucerne
1975 *Selbsportrat als Selstdarstellung,* Innsbruck
1977 *Arte in Italia, 1960–1977,* Galleria Civica d'Arte Moderna, Turin
1980 *Dieci Anni Dopo,* Galleria d'Arte Moderna, Bologna
1981 *Arte Critica,* Galleria Nazionale d'Arte Moderna, Rome
1982 *Italian Art Now,* Guggenheim Museum, New York
Italian Art 1960–1982, Hayward Gallery, London
1986 *Aspects of Italian Art 1960–85,* Kunstverein, Frankfurt
1995 *Venice Biennale,* Italy
Noa Noa, Galleria In Arco, Torino (catalog)
2000 *Appearance,* Galleria d'Arte Moderna, Bologna, Italy (catalog)
Quadriennale, Rome, Italy

Collections:

Galleria Nazionale d'Arte Moderna, Rome.

Publications:

By ONTANI: Books—*Esca in Grottesca Trentinesca,* with Vittorio Sgarbi, Trente 1989; *Trentasioni,* Trente 1993; *L'Onfalomane,* Turin 2000; *Luigi Ontani: Tricks With Mirrors,* with Margaret Atwood, Ravenna 2000. **Articles—**''Luigi Ontani: Continua-O'' in *Flash Art* (Milan), April 1974; ''Continua-8'' in *Data* (Milan) Autumn 1974; ''Continua-3'' in *Photo 13* (Milan), November 1974; ''Continua-1'' in *Il Corpo come Linguaggio* by Lea Vergine, Milan 1974; ''Wewha: A Project for Artforum by Luigi Ontani'' in *Artforum,* vol. 30, no. 5, January 1992; interview with Pierre Restany in *D'Ars,* vol. 36, no. 146, August 1995.

On ONTANI: Books—*Il Comportamento* by Renato Barilli, Rome 1973; *Transformer,* exhibition catalog by Jean Christophe Ammann, Lucerne 1974; *Fotomedia: Video,* exhibition catalog, Dortmund, West Germany 1974; *Il Corpo come Linguaggio* by Lea Vergine, Milan 1974; *Europa: America* by Achille Bonita Oliva, Milan 1976; *Live Art: 1909 to the Present* by Roselee Goldberg, London 1979; *De Chirico tra Duchamp a Malevitch* by Francesco Poli, Bologna 1980; *Italian Art Now: An American Perspective,* exhibition catalog, Diane Waldman and Lisa Dennison, New York 1982. **Articles—**''Ontani'' by Barbara Reise in *Annual of New Art and Artists,* Amsterdam 1974; ''Process, Concept and Behaviour in Italian Art'' by Achille Bonita Oliva in *Studio International* (London), February 1976; ''Performance Art in Italy'' in *Studio International* (London), February 1976; ''Luigi Ontani'' by Barry Schwabsky in *Artforum International,* vol. 33, December 1994; ''Consummate Constumption'' by Jeffrey Slonim in *Artforum,* vol. 33, no. 4, December 1994; ''Luigi Ontani'' by David Frankel in *Artforum,* vol. 35, no. 10, Summmer 1997; ''Luigi Ontani: Master of Classical Rhetoric'' by Laura Tansini in *Sculpture* (Washington, D.C.), vol. 16, no. 10, December 1997.

* * *

The art and life of Luigi Ontani are divided into three distinct periods that only communicate with each other in secret. First, performance, next, photography, and finally, painting. The arch of this subtly magic time starts from 1970 and reaches to the present day. The absolute protagonist is always the artist himself (his body as the image and likeness of art), the exhaustive aestheticism of his sensibility and sensuality and imagination, often with a vein of humour.

Luigi Ontani's work is thus always rather precious, either when he represents an historic personage (''Dante'') or a mythical figure (''Bacchus,'' ''Leda and the Swan,'' ''Self Portrait''), or when he depicts the imaginary creations of mythology, using water-colour technique. The artist is present or absent (it is no matter); the ''fiction'' of art demands this extraordinary service. Painting itself is to him a sort of projection ''outwards'' of the everyday; it means ''inside'' the incorruptible unreality of beauty, without which art would be like an extinct sun. Luigi Ontani loves all that belongs to the sun; in the nuances of his water-colours he seems, Narcissus-like, to see his own ecstatic fantasies. His great desire is to capture them; but art is the dream that makes possible the strangest and most remote desires in the spatiality of memory.

The "mythical" space of his work seems almost non-existent; it appears and disappears in a transparent remoteness flooded in unreal light. But it is in that space that the artistic effect is made, sheltered from the descriptive clamour of everyday experience. A case in point is a work of 1981, "Self Portrait." Here Luigi Ontani has represented the ideal clothing of the artist—of himself, of course. The individual parts of which it is composed, made from white paper, have been fixed to the walls of the gallery (Mario Diacono, Rome) with pins. Two self-portraits (delicate photographs retouched with paint) face one another like images in a mirror on two opposite walls, while a third photograph (also retouched in paint) shows the artist's feet. Everything was arranged in advance, as if for a ceremony. The "ideal clothing" is the fantastic vestment of art: the artist hides in it, he is somewhere else—in the mythical and unreal space of beauty.

For Luigi Ontani as for Oscar Wilde before him, there is no difference between art and life. Excess is his aesthetic, incomprehensible harmony his exhausting contemplation of beauty, at once sublime and ironic. The technique of the water-colour used in recent works renders clearly the concept of the mirror image that unveils memories and fancies that have by now become uncontrollable. It is this, perhaps, that makes Luigi Ontani a "libertarian" artist, unpredictable and open even to the splendors of the absurd.

—Italo Mussa

OPALKA, Roman

Nationality: French. **Born:** Hocquincourt, Abbeville, France, to Polish parents, 27 August 1931. **Education:** In Poland, 1935–39, and in Germany 1939–45; studied art, Walbrzych School, Nowa Roda, 1946–49; School of Fine Arts, Lodz, 1949–50; Academy of Fine Arts, Warsaw, 1957–60. **Military Service:** Served as art instructor to army officers, House of Culture, Polish Army in Warsaw, 1957–60. **Family:** Has lived with Marie-Madeleine Gazeau since 1976. **Career:** Independent artist, Warsaw, 1960–75, in West Berlin, 1975–1977, in Paris, 1977–79, and in Tournon d'Agenais, France, since 1979. **Awards:** Young Polish Painters Prize, Sopot, 1965; Grand Prize, First Bradford Print Biennale, Yorkshire, 1968; Gold Medal for Graphics, Golden Grapes Exhibition, Zielona Gora, 1969; K. C. Norwid Critics' Prize, Warsaw, 1969; First Prize, 3rd Graphics Biennale, Krakow, 1970; Prize, 2nd Bradford Print Biennale, Yorkshire, 1970; Prize, 7th International Graphics Biennale, Tokyo, 1970; Ohara Art Museum Prize, Tokyo, 1970; Ministry of Arts and Culture Prize, Warsaw, 1971; Graphics Prize, International Art Exhibition, Le Mans, 1977; Painting Prize, 14th Bienal de Sao Paulo, Brazil, 1978. **Agent:** Nicole Klagsbrun, 526 West 26th Street, Room 213, New York, New York, 10001, U.S.A. **Address:** Manoir de Bazeraz, Thezac, 47370 Tournon d'Agenais, France.

Selected Individual Exhibitions:

1966 Dom Artysty Plastyka Gallery, Warsaw
1969 Wspolczesna "Ruch" Gallery, Warsaw
1971 Galleria LP220, Turin
Galleria Il Punto, Calice-Turin
1972 Galleria Annunciata, Milan
Galleria LP220, Turin
Galleria La Bertesca, Genoa
William Weston Gallery, London
1973 Museum Folkwang, Essen
1974 Galerie Bruno Bischofberger, Zurich
John Weber Gallery, New York
1975 Galeria 72, Chelm, Poland
John Weber Gallery, New York
1976 Palais des Beaux-Arts, Brussels
Museum Boymans-van Beuningen, Rotterdam
1977 Musée d'Art et d'Histoire, Geneva
Galerie René Block, West Berlin (2 shows)
John Weber Gallery, New York
16 Details of the Work, Museum Haus Lange, Krefeld, West Germany
1978 Amherst College, Massachusetts
Columbus Museum of Art, Ohio
1979 Allentown Museum of Art, Pennsylvania
Muhlenberg College, Allentown, Pennsylvania
John Weber Gallery, New York (travelled to Toronto)
Minneapolis Institute of Art, Minnesota
Grand Rapids Art Museum, Michigan
1980 Galerie Art in Progress, Dusseldorf
La Jolla Museum of Contemporary Art, California
Galerie Walter Storms, Munich
Studio Carlo Grossetti, Milan
Hessisches Landesmuseum, Darmstadt, West Germany
Rice Museum, Houston
1981 Westfälischer Kunstverein, Münster, West Germany
Musée des Beaux-Arts, Montreal
Galerie Walter Storms, Villingen, West Germany
1982 Galerie Isy Brachot, Paris
Erker-Galerie, St. Gallen, Switzerland
John Weber Gallery, New York
1988 FracAquitaine, Bordeaux
1989 John Weber Gallery, New York
1990 Gallery Walter Storms, Munich
1991 Isy Brachot Gallery, Brussels
1992 New Museum Weserburg, Bremen
1993 Museum of the 20th Century, Vienna
1994 Nationalgalerie, Berlin
Zacheta Gallery, Warsaw
Opalka 1965/1, Galeria Sztuki Wspólczesnej Zacheta, Warsaw (catalog)
1996 Galerie I.S.M., Seoul
1998 *Roman Opalka: Der Befreite Sisyphos,* Städtische Galerie Altes Theater Ravensburg, Germany (catalog)
1999 Medienzentrum der Neuen Presse, Passau (catalog)

Selected Group Exhibitions:

1965 *Young Polish Painting,* Sopot, Poland
1968 *1st International Biennale of Graphic Art,* Bradford Museum, Yorkshire (and *2nd Biennale,* 1970)
1969 *Bienal,* Sao Paulo (and *14th Bienal,* 1978)
1970 *Biennale,* Venice
1973 *Painting and Sculpture Today,* Indianapolis Museum of Art
1975 *Empirica,* Museo Castelvacchio, Verona

1976 *Today/Tomorrow,* University of Miami
1977 *Documenta 6,* Kassel, West Germany
1981 *Soundings,* Neuberger Museum, Purchase, New York
1994 *Venice Biennial,* Italy
1997 *Art from Poland,* Art Gallery, Budapest
1998 *Sentimentale Journée,* Strasbourg Musée d'Art Contemporain, Strasbourg
1999 *Die Macht des Alters—Strategien der Meisterschaft,* Kunstmuseum, Bonn
2000 *Verteidigung der Moderne,* Museum Würth, Künzelsau (catalog)

Collections:

National Museum, Warsaw; Muzeum Sztuki, Lodz, Poland; Galleria Nazionale d'Arte Moderna, Rome; Bibliothèque Nationale, Paris; Nationalmuseum, Stockholm, Sammlung Albertina, Vienna; Museum Folkwang, Essen; Museum Boysman-van Beuningen, Rotterdam; Ohara Museum, Tokyo; Museum of Modern Art, New York; Musée National d'Art Moderene, Centre Georges Pompidou, Paris; Fonds National d'Art Contemporain, Paris.

Publications:

By OPALKA: Books—*Travel Sheets 508325–527089,* Turin 1972; *1965/1-Detail 1602183–1728670,* Mediolan 1975; *Opalka 1965/ 1–00,* photographs and disc, Munich 1980; *Roman Opalka,* exhibition catalog, London 1999.

On OPALKA: Books—*Roman Opalka,* exhibition catalog with text by W. Jaworska, Warsaw 1966; *Modern Prints* by Pat Gilmour, London 1970; *Roman Opalka: Descrizione del mondo,* exhibition catalog, Turin 1971; *Roman Opalka,* exhibition catalog with text by Luigi Carluccio, Cracow 1972; *Polska Awangarda Malarska 1945–1970,* exhibition catalog, with text be Bozena Kowalska, Warsaw 1975; *Roman Opalka,* exhibition catalog with text by Bozena Kowalska, Chelm Lubelski, Poland 1975; *Empirica: L'Arte tra Addizione e Sottrazione,* exhibition catalog with text by G. Cortenova, Verona 1975; *Today/Tomorrow,* exhibition catalog with text by Paul E. Thompson, Miami 1976; *Roman Opalka,* exhibition catalog with text by Rainer Michael Mason, Geneva 1977; *Roman Opalka: 16 Details of the Work,* exhibition catalog with text be Gerhard Storck, Krefeld, West Germany 1977; *14 Bienal de Sao Paulo 1977: Poland,* exhibition catalog with an introduction by Mariusz Hermansdorfer, Warsaw 1977; *Roman Opalka: 1965/1–16 Details,* exhibition catalog with text by Jeffrey Deitsch and David Shapiro, New York 1978; *Opalka 1965/1–00,* exhibition catalog with text by Denys Riout and David Shapiro, Paris 1982; *Discours en l'Honneur de Roman Opalka* by Bernard Lamarche-Vadel, Paris 1992; *Roman Opalka* by Christine Savinel, Jacques Roubaud, and Noël Bernard, Paris 1996; *Roman Opalka: Une Vie en Peinture* by Catherine Desprats-Péquignot, Paris 1998; *Roman Opalka: Der befreite Sisyphos,* Stuttgart 1998. **Articles:** ''Roman Opalka'' by Peter Funken in *Artforum,* vol. 33, no. 1, September 1994; ''Roman Opalka'' by Peter Funken in *Kunstforum International,* no. 127, July/September 1997; ''Roman Opalka'' by Silke Müller in *Flash Art (International Edition),* no. 180, January/ February 1995.

*

In my attitude, which constitutes a programme for my lifetime, progression registers the process of work, documents and defines time, only one date appears—the date of the coming into being of the first detail—1965, opened by the sign of infinity, as well as the first and last number of the given detail.

I am counting progressively from one to infinity, on details of the same size (voyage notes excluded), by hand, with a brush, with white paint on a grey background, with the assumption that every following detail will have 1% more white than the preceding one. In connection with this I anticipate the arrival of the moment when details will be indentified in white on white.

Every detail is accompanied by a phonetic registration on a tape recorder and photographic documentation of my face.

—Roman Opalka

* * *

Roman Opalka's artistic development since the 1960s has been unusually consistent. Seeking a system that would have ''validity for one's entire life,'' he decided to explore the phenomenon of time—time, that is, as a linear phenomenon, as it appears to us in our daily lives. The basis for formulating this idea was his cycle ''Chronemes,'' canvases closely covered with small dots (1963) and his cycle of etchings ''Description of the World'' (inspired by Marco Polo) begun in 1968. The pictures in this latter cycle show a limitless antheap of humanity; the structure of this pulsating mass is, however, interpreted metaphorically. Man is but a part of a species, starting (symbolically) with Adam and Eve and reaching to infinity via the constant addition of basic units. The multiplicity caused by this additive system reveals the concept of number as the basis of constant evolution.

The problem of linear time is explored within this context. The artist is intensely conscious of time as a component of his life; he sets out to measure this time—however long it may last—precisely.

From 1965 onwards Opalka has recorded sequential numbers from one onwards on consecutive canvases (and also on his ''Postcards from a Journey''). These works completely lack nostalgia for the time that has passed; this indifference, however, is not that of a lifeless recording mechanism. This sequence of numbers records all the artist's emotional upheavals, his periods of fatigue and rest: the record rises and falls, it waxes and wanes, pauses, intensifies, stretches or contracts. The networks thus obtained become a personal affirmation of life, ''the secrets of mental concentration.'' The artist himself repudiates all automization; ''I carry on dialogue in the name of man, not in the name of a machine.''

An important component of the process is its aural record—a taped recording of the count. The artist enunciates each written figure loudly, and the recorded voice exhibits the mental state of the speaker, the signs of effort, the difficulty in pronouncing the fearsomely interwoven, rustling consonants in Polish figures.

In spite of the simplicity of this method, its character and mechanism do not become fully clear. One of its mysteries is the very instinct of counting and the fascination that it holds for all of us. Not only is this peculiar compulsion of interest but also the fact that occasionally numerical values take on psychological meaning.

It is true that in this work all numbers are equally important in the sense that they are all numbers of a set, but certain numbers will become prominent from a different perspective. Among these there will be numbers formed by the repetition of a single digit and, most importantly, numbers invested with the aura of ancient symbolism. This is why Opalka says; ''I dream of reaching seven sevens.''

The number seven is particularly important in mysticism, as an apocalyptic, prophetic, secret number. It arises from the union of two basic numbers, three (the element of spirit, masculinity) and four (the material world, femininity). Together three and four represent the universe and all its phenomena.

Opalka's yearned-for seven was known to Pythagorean mysticism, which considered numbers to be the heart of the world. Four symbolizes a square, three a triangle. The square divides into two triangles—it is thus divisible, transcendable (matter). The triangle, however, divides only into triangles, i.e., into itself. It is thus indivisible, eternal (spirit).

The basis of activity in Opalka's system is movement in time. Time, however, changes, but like the triangle, only into itself. It continues instead of ending. It is eternity itself.

Using this simple counting system, Opalka reaches many of the cultural layers comprising human thought. His numbers contain all the content of the numbers comprising the subtance of mathematics.

Opalka's operations even have a mathematical aspect: the works show a mathematical continuity that returns by the addition of ones. In this way, a continuum is delineated which contains the elements of infinity. Although this is absurd both logically and mathematically, its psychological aspect is not so absurd. Logically, infinity is unattainable, but psychologically it lies within our grasp. This is why it can be symbolized by a single sign, the horizontal eight. It seems so easy to grasp, to hold. Only when one tries to grasp its components, to reach it via some chosen path, does it become unreachable, beyond comprehension.

Opalka counts the uncountable. The recorded voice accompanying the count becomes particularly meaningful: it adds nothing mathematically, but by turning the continuation into a psychological action, it interiorizes it. Further, it is only by vocal repetition—i.e., by identification—that one understands this continuation to be an individual's concrete drama, developed by the psyche, which is concentrated in the heart of one problem.

—Alicja Kepinska

OPIE, Julian

Nationality: British. **Born:** London, 1958. **Education:** Goldsmith's College of Art, London, 1979–1982. **Career:** Independent sculptor, London, since 1982. **Awards:** Sargant Fellowship, The British School in Rome, 1995; Residency at the Atelier Calder, Saché, France, 1995–1996. **Agent:** Lisson Gallery, London. **Address:** c/o Lisson Gallery, 67 Lisson Street, London NW1 5DA, England.

Individual Exhibitions:

1983 Lisson Gallery, London
1984 Kolnischer Kunstverein, Cologne
1985 Groninger Museum, Groningen, Netherlands
Institute of Contemporary Arts, London
Lisson Gallery, London
1986 Galleria Franco Toselli, Milan
Lisson Gallery, London
1988 Lisson Gallery, London (catalogue)
Galeria Montenegro, Madrid
Paul Maenz, Cologne
1990 Lisson Gallery, London
1991 Kunsthalle, Berne (catalogue)
Kohji Ogura Gallery, Japan
Gallerie Luis Campaña, Frankfurt
Jänner Galerie, Vienna
Interni, Galleria Franz Paludetto, Turin
1992 Wiener Secession, Vienna (catalogue)
Galerie Albrecht, Munich
1993 Hayward Gallery, London (catalogue)
1994 Kunstverein, Hannover
Galerie Albrecht, Munich
Imagine You Are Walking, Tramway, Glasgow
1995 *Paysages,* Le Channel, Galerie de l'Ancienne Poste, Calais
Monica de Cardenas Gallery, Milan, Italy
1996 Gallery Analix Polla, Geneva
CCC Tours (catalogue)
Gallery Bob van Orsouw, Zurich
Lisson Gallery, London
1997 *9th Indian Triennale,* Lalit Kala Akademi, New Delhi, India (catalogue)
Gallery Nova Sin, Prague (catalogue)
Barbara Thumm Gallery, Berlin (catalogue)
Sculpture, The Economist Plaza, London
1998 Museum of Contemporary Art, Sydney
1999 Primo Piano, Rome
Morrison Judd, London
Tensta Konsthall, Stockholm, Sweden
Gallery Bob van Orsouw, Zurich
Barbara Thumm Gallery, Berlin (catalogue)
Barbara Krakow Gallery, Boston
Lenbachhaus Städtische Galerie, Drawing Room, Munich
2000 Barbara Krakow Gallery, New York
Eight Landscapes, Alan Cristea Gallery, London
2001 Lisson Gallery, London

Selected Group Exhibitions:

1983 *The Sculpture Show,* Hayward Gallery/Serpentine Gallery, London
1984 *Metaphor and/or Symbol,* National Museum of Modern Art, Tokyo (travelled to Osaka)
1985 *The British Show,* Art Gallery of Western Australia, Perth (toured Australia and New Zealand)
1986 *Forty Years of Modern Art 1945–1985,* Tate Gallery, London
Sculpture: 9 Artists from Britain, Louisiana Museum, Humlebaek, Denmark
1987 *British Art of the 1980s,* Liljevalchs Konsthall, Stockholm (travelled to Tampere, Finland)
Focus on the Image, Phoenix Art Museum, Arizona (toured the United States, 1987–90)
1988 *British Sculpture 1960–1988,* Museum van Hedendaagse Kunst, Antwerp
D+S Austellung, Hamburg Kunstverein, Hamburg (catalogue)
1989 *Mediated Knot,* Robbin Lockett Gallery, Chicago (catalogue)

Objet/Objectif, Galerie Daniel Templon, Paris (catalogue)
Skulptur Teil II, Galerie Six Friedrich, Munich

1990 *OBJECTives,* Newport Harbor Art Museum, Newport Beach, California (catalogue)
The British Art Show 1990, The South Bank Centre, London (traveling exhibition) (catalogue)

1991 *Kunst: Europa—Grossbritannien,* Kunstverein, Bruchsal, Germany (catalogue)
Connfrontaciones 91, Palacio Velasquez, Madrid (catalogue)

1992 *Catalogueue to a British Council,* Centre des Conférences Albert Berschette, Brussels
Like Nothing Else in Tennessee, Serpentine Gallery, London (catalogue)

1993 *In Site,* Museet for Samtidskunst, Oslo
Juxtaposition, Charlottenborg, Copenhagen (catalogue)

1994 *Spuren,* Kunsthalle Bern, Switzerland
New Voices: British Painting, A Selection 1989–1992, British Council (traveling exhibition) (catalogue)

1995 *Micromegas,* American Center in Paris, France
British Art from the 1980s & 1990s, The Irish Museum of Modern Art, Dublin

1996 *Elsewhere,* Galerie Froment & Putnam, Paris
Abstrakt/Real, Museum Moderner Kunst Stiftung Ludwig Wein, Vienna

1997 *Venice 2000,* 47th Venice Biennale, Italy
Material Culture, Hayward Gallery, London

1998 *Le Voyage Immobile,* Galerie Georges-Philipe & Natalie Vallois, Paris
Made in London, Expo 98, Museu de Electricidada, Lisbon

1999 *Etcetera...,''* Spacex Gallery, Exeter
In the Midst of Things, Bournville, Birmingham, England

2000 *Gavin Turk, Angela Bulloch, Julian Opie,* Centre d'Art Contemporain, Geneva
Intelligence, Tate Britain, London
Panorama 2000, Utrecht, the Netherlands
Conversation, Milton Keynes Gallery, Milton Keynes, England (catalogue)
Vergiss den Ball und Spiel Weiter, Kunsthalle Nurnberg, Germany
Please Touch, Lighthouse, Glasgow

Collections:

Arts Council of Great Britain, London; Contemporary Art Society, London; Tate Gallery, London; Stedelijk Museum, Amsterdam; Neue Galerie-Sammlung Ludwig, Aachen; Israel Museum, Jerusalem; Saatchi Collection, London.

Publications:

By OPIE: Books—*Opie,* London 1991; *Julian Opie,* London 2001. **Articles—**''Julian Opie Interview,'' with Lynne Cooke, in *Flash Art* (Milan), April 1987; ''The Lure of the Open Road'' with Charlotte Mullins in *Art Review,* vol. 52, September 2000. **Cover Art—***Blur: The Best Of,* 2000.

On OPIE: Books—*Julian Opie,* exhibition catalogue with texts by Wulf Herzogenrath and Kenneth Baker, Cologne 1984; *Julian Opie,* exhibition catalogue with texts by Michael Craig-Martin and others, London 1985; *Julian Opie: Drawings 1982 to 1985,* exhibition catalogue, London 1985; *Julian Opie* by James Roberts, Nagoya, Japan 1991; *Julian Opie* by Wulf Herzogenrath, et al., London 1993; *Julian Opie* by Caroline Douglas and Julian Opie, London 1997; *Intelligence: New British Art 2000* by Virginia Button and Charles Esche, London 2000. **Articles—**''I Was Not Making a Monument, I Was Not Making an Object'' by Michael Archer in *Art Monthly,* no. 144, March 1991; ''Julian Opie: Imagine There's Another Possibility'' by Tim Marlow in *Terskel/Threshold,* vol. 4, no. 9, January 1993; ''Tunnel Vision'' by James Roberts in *Frieze,* no. 10, May 1993; ''Julian Opie: A Stronger Reality Than the Represented One'' by Adachiara Zevi in *L'Architettura,* vol. 40, February 1994.

* * *

Similarly to his contemporaries Tony Cragg and Bill Woodrow, the young English sculptor Julian Opie has returned to the city from the countryside. This was a significant move, considering that the work of these artists includes everday objects of man-made materials in an elaborate visual vernacular which employs banal urban images.

Opie's early works were more concerned with the image and its definition outside the picture plane than with neo-avant-garde sculpture and its heritage. Opie did not hesitate to give up three-dimensionality in order to achieve an iconic dimension. The problems pertaining to the relationship between mass and volume do not in any way qualify his work. Sculpture demands an involvement additional to the requirements of painting. The defining role of painting was earlier clearly evident in Opies's work: he was then working with very thin steel sheets, easily modelled to create a simulacra of objects and words made concrete and realizable through painting.

A pile of books on the verge of falling to the ground (*Incident in the Library II,* 1983) was identified by the strokes of colour which designated and differentiated each part the whole. The painting was ''handwritten,'' almost rudimentary in this respect, demonstrating that the painting itself was based on irony—as in *Personal Effects* (1984), for example, where Opie skilfully re-made identity documents, credit cards, cheques, envelopes and metro tickets, each painted onto sheets of steel.

All Opie's works have this character of parody, the remaking of everday objects inserted into a spectacular universe which, in turn, parodies the universe of mass-media, their realm as signifying objects. Copies of masterpieces (*Cultural Baggage,* 1984), as well as enormous typographic letters in the form of words grouped in improbable assemblage (*Lonely,* 1984), reproduce the banality of mass-media while simultaneously capturing the semantic wealth of its messages. The work could not avoid measuring itself against the power of the connotations induced by the media industry; painting and sculpting, in order to affirm themselves as non-obsolete systems of communication, had to find some sort of relationship with them.

In that phase, a status of the work art as pure was denied. To stress this, Opie built solid figures which he then applied to a kind of fake canvas of foreshortened perspective, each figure being denominated by a number. Without this minimal level of denomination, the figures would have remained unimaginable, Opie was declaring that the abstract form in sculpture is no longer sufficient unto itself unless it makes a reference to the parody of its own history.

With the sculptures of 1986 and after, Opie radically alters the sense of his works. They are now concerned with a subtle and ironic minimalism. His recent pieces are large, vividly coloured bas-reliefs, variously inserted one into the other, or simply laid near each other. The very colour itself, the irregularity of the figures, and the estranging sense implied by the titles (*We'll Be Dead Soon,* 1986) promote the idea of an ironic detachment which shares a definitely non-figurative, non-objective character.

Even shrewder are the most recent works (1987), which camouflage distinctions between sculpture and apparatus of common use—for instance, a pair of air conditioner outlets, or a radiator. Here the artist ridicules our faulty observation and awareness through the devise of displacement.

—Giorgio Verzotti

The catalogue for Julian Opie's 1991 exhibition at the Kohji Ogura Gallery, Nagoya is designed like an industrial trade catalogue and apparently itemises ranges of refrigerators, ventilators, shelving, display units and screen systems; these cool, industrial-like sculptures challenge the notion of non-referentiality in minimalism and seem to parody the seriality of such work. In Opie's oeuvre, however, they presage an interest in modularity and the relationships between reality and its representations which have informed his work since then.

Opie's work through the 1990s becomes increasingly architectural and leads to the elaboration of a virtual world. The quasi-industrial objects give way to 'block' sculptures, painted wooden constructions like models of modernist tower blocks laid out on a grid which can be walked around but not entered. Paintings and computer animations further develop representations of ideal but anonymous spaces: *Imagine you are walking,* 1993, is a series of paintings inviting the viewer to imaginatively follow the paths through a built environment with the blank character of a computer game. *Imagine you are driving,* 1993 similarly offers a driver's view of an immaculate, empty road curving away into the distance.

''What I would really like to do is make a painting and then walk into it,'' Opie noted in his exhibition catalogue in 1997. His desire, coupled with a preoccupation with the world as experienced through modern travel and represented through computer graphics, has culminated in works which represent the world as pure sign. In this simulated world, buildings, cars, trees, animals, and people are pared down to symbols and types: modules to be chosen and ordered in different combinations like objects in a lifestyle catalogue, which the catalogue for his exhibition at the Lisson Gallery (2001) resembles. Opie's simulated world plays off the seductions of a clean and pure utopian vision against the alienation of an anonymous world of standardisation and banality.

—Richard Salkeld

OPPENHEIM, Dennis

Nationality: American. **Born:** Electric City, Washington, 6 September 1938. **Education:** California College of Arts and Crafts, Oakland, California, 1959–64, B.F.A. 1964; Stanford University, California, 1964–65 (teaching assistant, 1965), M.F.A. 1965. **Family:** Married Karen Erwin in 1959 (divorced, 1961); children: Eric, Kristin and Chandra. **Career:** Professor of art, Yale University, New Haven, Connecticut, 1969; professor of art, State University of New York at Stony Brook, 1969. Lives and works in New York City. **Awards:** Guggenheim Foundation Sculpture Grant, 1972; National Endowment for the Arts Sculpture Grant, 1974. **Agents:** Joseph Helman Gallery, 20 West 57th Street, New York, New York 10019; Marlborough Chelsea, 211 West 19th Street, New York, New York 10011. **Address:** 54 Franklin Street, New York, New York 10013, U.S.A.

Individual Exhibitions:

1968 John Gibson Gallery, New York
1969 Yvon Lambert Galerie, Paris
John Gibson Gallery, New York
Galleria Lambert, Milan
A Report: 2 Ocean Projects, Museum of Modern Art, New York
1970 Resse Palley, Gallery, San Francisco
John Gibson Gallery, New York
Pennsylvania Art Museum, Erie
Galleria Lia Rumma, Naples
Crossman Gallery, Wisconsin State University at Whitewater
1971 Yvon Lambert Galerie, Paris
Galleria Lambert, Milan
Harcus-Krakow Gallery, Boston
Galerie 20, Amsterdam
1972 *Outdoor Projections,* Sonnabend Gallery, New York
Projections, Nova Scotia College of Art, Halifax
Mathias Fels Galerie, Paris
2000 Shadow Projections, Tate Gallery, London
L'Attico, Rome
Galerie D, Brussels
1973 Sonnabend Gallery, New York
Chandra Oppenheim, Rivkin Gallery, Washington, D.C.
Galerie Sonnabend, Paris
Galleria Forma, Genoa
Galerie D, Brussels
Mayor Gallery, London
Museum of Conceptual Art, San Francisco
1974 Galleria Forma, Genoa
Galerie D, Brussels
Stedelijk Museum, Amsterdam
John Gibson Gallery, New York
Galerie Oppenheim, Cologne
Galerie Oppenheim, Brussels
Galleria Paolo Barrozzi, Milan
1975 Galleria Lambert, Milan
John Gibson Gallery, New York
Galerie Oppenheim, Cologne
Galleria Castelli, Milan
Restrospective, Palais des Beaux-Arts, Brussels
Galleria Schema, Florence
Galerie Vega, Liege
P. M. J. Self Gallery, London
Yvon Lambert Galerie, Paris
The Kitchen, New York
Anthology Film Archives, New York
1976 Museum Boymans-van Beuningen, Rotterdam (retrospective)
Bo Alveryd Gallery, Kavlinge, Sweden
Framartstudio, Naples
M. L. D'Arc Gallery, New York

1977 M. L. D'Arc Gallery, New York
CARP, Los Angeles
HM Gallery, Brussels
Hans Meyer Gallery, Dusseldorf
John Gibson Gallery, New York
Multiples Gallery, New York
University of Rhode Island, Kingston
University of Montana, Missoula
Wright State University, Dayton, Ohio
Yvon Lambert Galerie, Paris
Yaki Kornbilt Gallery, Amsterdam
1978 Musée d'Art Contemporain, Montreal (retrospective)
Art Gallery of Ontario, Toronto (retrospective)
University of Iowa, Iowa City
Marian Goodman Gallery, New York
Visual Arts Museum, New York
State University of New York at Plattsburgh
Marianne Deson Gallery, Chicago
1979 Kunsthalle, Basel
University of Massachusetts, Amherst
John Gibson Gallery, New York
The Kitchen, New York
Israel Museum, Jerusalem
Herron Gallery, Indianapolis
Winnipeg Art Gallery
Eels Gallery, Kent State University, Ohio
Musée d'Art Moderne de la Ville, Paris
Northern Illinois University, DeKalb
Galleria Francois Lambert, Milan
Kunstverein, Stuttgart
Paul Robeson Center, Rutgers University, Newark, New Jersey
1980 Bruce Gallery, Edinboro, Pennsylvania
Cranbrook Academy of Art, Bloomfield Hills, Michigan
Ace Gallery, Venice, California
Portland Center for the Visual Arts, Oregon
Yvon Lambert Galerie, Paris
Pasquale Trisorio, Naples
Association Musée d'Art Moderne, Geneva
Morris/Acconci/Oppenheim, Sonnabend Gallery, New York
1981 Sonnabend Gallery, New York
Contemporary Arts Center, Cincinnati
Galerie Marika Malacorda, Geneva
Galleria Francois Lambert, Milan
Lowe Art Museum, Miami
Richard Hines Gallery, Seattle, Washington
1982 Marianne Deson Gallery, Chicago
Rijksmusuem Kröller-Müller, Otterlo, Netherlands
Mills College, Oakland, California
Galerie Stampa, Basel
Ikon Gallery, Birmingham, England
Lewis Johnstone Gallery, London
Musée d'Arte et d'Histoire, Geneva
Olsen Gallery, New York
Bonlow Gallery, New York
Vancouver Art Gallery, British Columbia
Taub Gallery, Philadelphia
Ohio State University, Columbus
1983 Akira Ikeda Gallery, Tokyo
Flow Ace Gallery, Venice, California
Galerie Schurr, Stuttgart
Serra Di-Felice Gallery, New York
Seattle Art Museum, Washington
Munson-Williams-Proctor Institute, Utica, New York
Yorkshire Sculpture Park, West Bretton
Whitney Museum, New York
1984 Braunstein Gallery, San Francisco
Galerie Hans Mayer, Dusseldorf
Sander Gallery, New York
Philadelphia Art, Alliance, Pennsylvania
San Francisco Museum of Modern Art
La Jolla Museum of Contemporary Art, California
ZHTA-MI Gallery, Thessaloniki, Greece
Visual Arts Center, Anchorage, Alaska
Tel Aviv Museum, Israel
1985 Sander Gallery, New York
Grand Rapids Art Museum, Michigan
Alan Brown Gallery, Hartsdale, New York
Knight Gallery, Charlotte, North Carolina
1986 Tolarno Galleries, South Yarra, Australia
Laumeier Sculpture Park, St. Louis
1988 Gallery 360, Tokyo
Anne Plumb Gallery, New York
Walker Art Center, Seoul
1989 Paris Art Center
Yvon Lambert, Paris
Elisabeth Franck, Knokke, Belgium
John Gibson Gallery, New York
Willoughby Sharp, New York
Anne Plumb Gallery, New York
Holly Solomon Gallery, New York
Pace McGill Gallery, New York
1990 Liverpool Gallery, Brussels
Pierides Museum, Athens
John Gibson Gallery, New York
Ace Contemporary Exhibitions, Los Angeles
Dart Gallery, Chicago
Galerie Lohrl, Monchengladbach, Germany
Galerie Berndt & Krips, Cologne
Galerie Joachim Becker, Cannes
Le Chanjour, Nice
Galerie Tobias Hirschmann, Frankfurt
1991 Galeria Pedro Oliveira, Porto, Portugal
Landfall Press, New York
Galerie Friebe, Ludenscheid, Germany
Galerie Gastaud, Clermont-Ferrand, France
Galerie Thierry Salvador, Paris
Institute for Contemporary Art, New York (retrospective)
Galerie Berndt & Krips, Cologne
Howard Yezerski Gallery, Boston
1992 Blum Helman Warehouse, New York
State University of Illinois, Normal
Cleveland Center for Contemporary Art
Ace Contemporary Exhibitions, Los Angeles
Galerie Marika Malacorda, Geneva
Galeria Greca, Barcelona
Haines Gallery, San Francisco
Galerie Tobias Hirschmann, Frankfurt
High Museum of Art, Atlanta

Museum of Fine Arts, Houston
1993 Galerie Asbaek, Copenhagen
Galerie Albrecht, Munich
Sala d'Exposicions, Andorra
Blum Helman Gallery, New York
Porin Taidemuseo, Pori, Finland (retrospective)
Oulun Taidemuseo, Oulu, Finland (retrospective)
Ujazdowski Castle, Warsaw (retrospective)
Weatherspoon Art Gallery, Greensboro, North Carolina
Boca Raton Museum of Art, Boca Raton, Florida
Galerie Renee Ziegler, Zurich
Margaret Lipworth Fine Art, Boca Raton, Florida
The Fabric Workshop, Philadelphia
University of California at Berkeley
Progretto, Rome
1994 Musée d'Art Moderne, Lille, France (retrospective)
Palau de la Virreina, Barcelona
Greca Gallery, Barcelona
Galeria Aele, Madrid
Jermonti Gallery, Milano
1995 Oliver Art Center, Oakland, California
Kunstsammlung Tumulka, Munich
Galerie Albrecht, Munich
Haines Gallery, San Francisco, California
Galerie de la Tour, Amsterdam
1996 Masataka Hayakawa Gallery, Tokyo
Galerie Eugen Lendl, Graz, Austria
Fundacao de Serralves, Porto, Portugal
Mannheimer Kunstverein, Mannheim, Germany
Galerie Pro Arte, Freiburg, Germany
Vestsjaellands Kunstmuseum, Soro, Denmark
Centre International d'Arts Visuel, Marseille, France
1997 Helsinki City Art Museum, Finland
Los Angeles County Museum of Art, California
Venice Biennale, Pilkington SIV, Marghera/Venice, Italy
Stadt Galerie Nordhorn, Nordhorn, Germany
1998 University of Arizona Museum of Art, Tucson
Orlando Museum of Art, Orlando, Florida
Galapogos Art and Performance Space, Brooklyn, New York
Museum of Contemporary Art, North Miami, Florida
Galerie Albrecht, Munich
Museo de Arte Alvar, Mexico City
1999 Kunsthalle Hamburg, Germany
Joseph Helman Gallery, New York
Corcoran Gallery of Art, Washington, D.C.
2000 ICAR Foundation, Paris
Piece Unique, Paris
Grand Arts, Kansas City, Missouri

Selected Group Exhibitions:

1968 *Earthworks,* Dwan Gallery, New York
1970 *Information,* Museum of Modern Art, New York
1973 *Aspects de l'Art Actuel,* Musée Galliera, Paris
1975 *Body Art,* Museum of Contemporary Art, Chicago
1977 *Documenta 6,* Kassel, West Germany
1978 *Sculpture/Nature,* Centre d'Arts Plastiques, Bordeaux
1981 *Machineworks,* Institute of Contemporary Art, University of Pennsylvania, Philadelphia
1983 *Kunst mit Photographie,* Nationalgalerie, West Berlin
1985 *Modern Machines: Recent Kinetic Sculpture,* Whitney Museum, New York
1993 *Sonsbeek '93,* Arnhem, Holland
1995 *Reconsidering the Object of Art, 1965–1975,* Museum of Contemporary Art, Los Angeles, California
1997 *L'empreinte,* Centre Georges Pompidou, Paris
1998 *XXIV Biennale Sao Paulo,* Brazil
1999 *The American Century 1950–2000, Part II,* Whitney Museum of American Art, New York

Collections:

Museum of Modern Art, New York; Detroit Institute of Arts; Art Gallery of Ontario, Toronto; Tate Gallery, London; Musée d'Art Moderne de la Ville, Paris; Centre Georges Pompidou, Paris; Stedelijk Museum, Amsterdam; Boymans-van Beuningen Museum, Rotterdam; Kunsthaus, Zurich; Louisiana Museum, Humlebaek, Denmark.

Permanent Public Installations:

Formula Compound. A Combustion Chamber. An Exorcism. (From the Fireworks Series), Fattoria di Celle, Pistoia, Italy 1982; *Roots in Cubism. Hearts Stars in the Stars. Forest for Cezanne,* Bundesgartenschau, Berlin 1983; *Dreams and Nightmares. Journey of an Exploded Weave. (Mondrian Under Pressure),* Tel-Hai, Upper Galilee, Israel 1984; *Dreams and Nightmares. Journey of a Broken Weave,* University of New Mexico, Albuquerque 1984; *Levitation, Celebration, Separation,* Ville de Thiers, France 1985; *Impersonation Station,* Olympic Park, Seoul, South Korea 1988; *Rabbit Factory,* Ballerup Kommune, Copenhagen 1995; *Device to Root Out Evil,* Palma de Mallorca, Spain 1997; *Engagement,* Leoben, Austria 1997; *Drinking Structure with Exposed Kidney Pool,* Europos Parkas, Vilniaus, Lithuania 1998; *Monument to Escape,* Buenos Aires, Argentina 1999.

Publications:

By OPPENHEIM: Books—*Catalyst 1967–70,* reprinted from *Artscanada,* Toronto 1970; *Indentations,* Amsterdam 1974. **Articles—** "Interview with Dennis Oppenheim" with Willoughby Sharp in *Studio International* (London), November 1971; "Interaction: Form/Energy/Subject" in *Arts Magazine* (New York), March 1972; "Interview with Dennis Oppenheim," with Lynne Herschman, in *Studio International* (London), November 1973; "I Shot the Sheriff" in *Impulse* (Toronto), Spring 1979; interview with D. Wall in *New Jersey Architecture,* July/August/September 1979; interview with D. Talley in *Atlanta Art Workers Coalition Newpaper,* September/October 1979; interview in *Studio International* (London), no. 999, 1983.

On OPPENHEIM: Books—*Pop Art et Cie* by Francois Pluchart, Paris 1972; *6 Years: The Dematerialization of the Art Object* by Lucy Lippard, New York 1973; *Icons and Images of the 60s* by Nicolas and Elena Calas, New York, 1971; *Great Western Salt Works* by Jack Burham, New York 1974; *Dennis Oppenheim,* exhibition catalog, Amsterdam 1974; *Man Creates Art, Art Creates Man* by Dwayne Preble, New York 1974; *Proposals 1967–1974* by Lebeer-Hossman, Brussels 1975; *Whitney Biennial '77,* exhibition catalog, New York 1977; *Individuals: Post Movement Art in America* by Alan Sondheim,

New York 1977; *16 Projects/4 Arts* by William Spurlock, Dayton, Ohio 1978; *American Artists Talk on Art, 1940–1980,* edited by E. H. Johnson, New York 1982; *Dennis Oppenheim,* exhibition catalog, Tokyo 1983; *Dennis Oppenheim,* exhibition catalog, Tel Aviv 1984; *Photography and Art* by A. Grundberg and K. Gauss, New York 1987; *Beyond Modernism* by Kim Levin, New York 1988; *Dennis Oppenheim* by Thomas McEvilley and Alanna Heiss, New York 1991; *Dennis Oppenheim* by Barbara Rose, Paris 1992; *Dennis Oppenheim,* exhibition catalog with text by Kim Levin and Peter Spooner, Normal, Illinois, 1992; *Art and Application* by Arthur C. Danto, New York 1993; *Dennis Oppenheim, Palau de la Virreina,* Barcelona 1994; *Dennis Oppenheim: The Old In and Out,* exhibition catalog, Amsterdam 1995; *Dennis Oppenheim Land Art 1968–1978,* exhibition catalog, Storgade, Denmark 1996; *Dennis Oppenheim,* exhibition catalog, Porto, Portugal 1997; *Dennis Oppenheim,* exhibition catalog, Milan 1997; *Sculpture in the Age of Doubt* by Thomas McEvilley, New York 2000. **Articles—**''Artist as Shaman'' by Jack Burnham in *Arts Magazine* (New York), May 1973; ''Dennis Oppenheim, Myth and Ritual'' by Lenore Goldberg in *Art and Artists* (London), August 1973; ''Projekt'' by I. Lebeer in *L'Art Vivant* (Paris), July/August/September 1974; ''Madness in the Arena'' by Nicolas Calas in *Artforum* (New York), September 1977; ''It Ain't What You Make, It's What Makes You Do It'' by A. Ramsden in *Parachute* (Montreal), Winter 1978; ''D. O.: Post Performance Works'' by Kim Levin in *Arts Magazine* (New York), September 1978; ''Dennis Oppenheim's Delirious Operations'' by Jonathan Crary in *Artforum* (New York), November 1978; ''Gut Reaction'' by S. Morgan in *Artscribe* (London), Spring 1979; ''Image and Object in Contemporary Sculpture'' by Grace Glueck in the *New York Times,* 11 January 1980; ''Dennis Oppenheim and the Eternal Machine'' by C. Simmons in *Artweek* (Oakland), 19 May 1984; ''The Dark Side of Dennis Oppenheim'' by Tobey Crockett in *Artforum,* December 1991; ''Dark Laughter'' by Eleanor Heartney in *Art in America,* April 1997; ''D.O.'' by Pamela C. Scorzin in *Kunstler,* vol. 50, no. 2, 2000.

OPPENHEIM, Meret

Nationality: Swiss. **Born:** Berlin, Germany, 6 October 1913; immigrated to Switzerland, 1948, and subsequently naturalized. **Education:** Attended various German and Swiss schools, 1918–30; studied at the Kunstgewerbeschule, Basel, 1929–30, 1938–40, and at the Academie de la Grande Chaumière, Paris, 1932–33. **Family:** Married Wolfgang La Roche in 1949 (died 1967). **Career:** Independent artist, associating with surrealists Alberto Giacometti, Sophie Täuber and Hans Arp, in Paris, from 1932, and in Berne, from 1948; also worked as a picture-restorer, Paris, 1940–48. **Awards:** Kunstpreis, City of Basel, 1974; Grand Art Prize, City of Berlin, 1982. **Agent:** Renée Ziegler, Minervastrasse 33, 8000 Zurich. **Died:** In Basel, 15 November 1985.

Individual Exhibitions:

1936 Galerie Schultess, Basel
1952 Galerie d'Art Moderne, Basel
1959 *La Festin,* Chez Daniel Cordier, Paris
Galerie Riehentor, Basel
1960 Galleria Schwarz, Milan
Galleria Serodine, Ascona, Switzerland
1965 Gimpel and Hanover Galerie, Zurich
1967 Moderna Museet, Stockholm
1968 Galerie Krebs, Berne
1969 Galerie der Spiegel, Cologne
Galleria La Medusa, Rome
Editions Claude Givaudan, Paris
1970 Galleria Il Fauno, Turin
1971 Galerie Bonnier, Geneva
Galerie d'Art Moderne, Basel
1973 Galerie Suzanne Visat, Paris
Galerie Renée Ziegler, Zurich
1974 Galerie Ziegler S.A., Geneva
Galerie Muller, Stuttgart
Jeu d'Eté, Galerie Arman Zerbib, Paris (with Anna Boetti and Roberto Lupo)
City Museum, Solothurn, Switzerland
1975 City Museum, Winterthur, Switzerland
Wilhelm-Lehmbruck-Museum, Duisberg, West Germany
Galleria San Lucca, Bologna, Italy
Galerie 57, Biel, Switzerland
1976 Galerie Carmen Casse, Paris
1977 Galerie Elisabeth Kaufmann, Basel
Galerie Loeb, Bern
Galerie Nothelfer, West Berlin
Galerie Gerhild Grolitsch, Munich
Galerie Boulakia, Paris
1978 Eugenie Cucalon Gallery, New York
Galerie Levy, Hamburg
1979 Stadtische Galerie, Moers, West Germany
Kunstverein, Wolfsburg, West Germany
1980 Galerie 57, Biel, Switzerland
Marian Goodman Gallery, New York
1981 Galerie Claude Givaudan, Geneva
Galerie Nachst St. Stephan, Vienna (travelled to Innsbruck; Klagenfurt; Salzburg)
1982 Galleria Pieroni, Rome
1989 *Meret Oppenheim: Defiance in the Face of Freedom,* Institute of Contemporary Art, London
1996 *Beyond the Teacup,* Solomon R. Guggenheim Museum, New York

Selected Group Exhibitions:

1933 *Salon des Surindépendants,* Musée d'Art Moderne, Paris
1936 *International Suurealist Exhibition,* New Burlington Galleries, London
Fantastic Art, Dada and Surrealism, Museum of Modern Art, New York
1942 *Allianz,* Kunsthaus, Zurich
1959 *Exhibition Internationale de Surréalisme,* Galerie Daniel Cordier, Paris
1961 *The Art of Assemblage,* Museum of Modern Art, New York
1968 *Dada, Surrealism and Their Heritage,* Museum of Modern Art, New York
1972 *Le Surréalisme,* Musée des Arts Décoratifs, Paris 1978
1978 *Dada and Surrealism,* Hayward Gallery, London
1982 *Documenta 7,* Museum Fridericianum, Kassel, West Germany

Meret Oppenheim: *Object (Le Dejeuner en fourrure),* 1936. The Museum of Modern Art; New York, purchase. Photo ©Museum of Modern Art, 1999. ©2001 Artists Rights Society (ARS), New York/ProLitterus, Zürich.

1993 *''Other Countries—Other Customs'': Drawings from the Kunstmuseum in Bern,* Narodni Galerie, Prague (travelled to Kunstmuseum, Bern)

1994 *Bodies-Fragments-Reality: Examples of 20th Century Swiss Art,* Kunstmuseum, Solothurn

Collections:

Kunstmuseum, Basel; Kunsthaus, Zurich; Stadtmuseum, Winterthur, Switzerland; Stadtmuseum, Solothurn, Switzerland; Centre National d'Art Contemporain, Paris; Moderna Museet, Stockholm; Museum of Modern Art, New York.

Publications:

By OPPENHEIM: Books illustrated—*La Lune en Rodage* by Carl Laszlo, Paris 1954; *Sansibar: Geditche und Serigraphien,* Basel 1981. **Articles—**''Enquètes'' in *Le Surréalisme Même* (Paris), no. 3, 1957; ''Cahiers d'Ecoliers'' in *Le Surréalisme Meme* (Paris), no. 2, 1957; ''Le Striptease, enquète'' in *Le Surréalisme Même* (Paris), no. 5, 1959; ''Don't Cry—Work,'' interview, with Lynne Tillman and Carla Liss in *Art and Artists* (London), October 1973; ''Meret Oppenheim—Kunstpreis'' in *Kunstbulletin* (Basel), February 1975; ''Io Meret'' in *Bolaffiarte* (Turin), no. 103, 1980. **Articles—** ''Androgyny: Interview with Meret Oppenheim'' with Robert J. Belton in *Dada/Surrealism,* no. 18, 1990.

On OPPENHEIM: Books—*Fantastic Art, Dada and Surrealism* by Alfred H. Barr, New York 1936; *Almanach neuer Kunst in der Schweiz,* Zurich 1939; *Histoire de Surréalisme* by Maurice Nadeau, Paris 1945; *Histoire de Surréalisme: Documents Surréalistes* by Maurice Nadeau, Paris 1948; *Meret Oppenheim,* exhibition catalog with text by André Pieyre de Mandiargues, Milan 1960; *Der Surrealismus* by Patrick Waldberg, Cologne 1965; *Erotique du*

Meret Oppenheim: *Mourir la nuit* [*Dying at Night*], 1953. Photo by Philippe Migeat. ©2001 Artists Rights Society (ARS), NY/ProLitteris, Zürich.

Surréalisme by Robert Benayoun, Paris 1965; *Meret Oppenheim,* exhibition catalog with texts by K. G. Pontus Hulten, Max Ernst, Carl-Fredrick Reutersvard and others, Stockholm 1967; *Meret Oppenheim,* exhibition catalog with text by Marcel Jean, Rome 1969; *Dada and Surrealist Art* by William S. Rubin, New York 1969; *Meret Oppenheim,* exhibition catalog with text by Janus, Turin 1970; *Objekt-Kunst von Duchamp bis Kienholz* by Willy Rotzler, Cologne 1972; *Meret Oppenheim,* exhibition catalog with text by Hans Christophe von Tavel, Solothurn, Switzerland 1974; *Meret Oppenheim et ses jeux d'été,* exhibition catalog with text by Patrick Waldberg, Paris 1974; *Meret Oppenheim: Arbeiten von 1930–1978,* exhibition catalog with texts by Jürgen Glaesemer, Hamburg 1978; *Meret Oppenheim: Catalog Raisonné,* Zurich 1983; *Meret Oppenheim: Defiance in the Face of Freedom,* exhibition catalog, by Bice Curiger, Zurich 1989; *Meret Oppenheim: an Essay by Stuart Morgan* by Stuart Morgan, London 1989; *Dimension-Small-Swiss Art Between Small Sculpture and Object, from Alberto Giacometti to the Present,* exhibition catalog, Lausanne 1989; *From Dejeuner en fourrure to Caroline: Meret Oppenheim's Chronicle of Surrealism* by Renee Riese Hubert in *Dada/Surrealism,* no. 18, 1990; *Meret Oppenheim: Beyond the Teacup* by Jacqueline Burckhardt, Bice Curiger, Josef Helfenstein, Thomas McEvilley and Nancy Spector, New York 1996; *Meret Oppenheim: Book of Ideas—Early Drawings and Sketches for Fashions, Jewelry, and Designs* by Christiane Meyer-Thoss and Rudolf Schmitz, Bern 1996. **Articles—**''Meret Oppenheim a Paris'' by Christiane Meyer-Thoss and Hans Christoph von Tavel in *Cimaise,* no. 202, vol. 36, September-October 1989; ''Meret Oppenheim 1913–1985: Desire-Redesigning the Object for Consumption'' by Deborah Sugg in *Women Artists Slide Library Journal,* no. 31–32, January-February 1990; ''Between the Cup and the Lip'' by Ann Wilson Lloyd in *Sculpture* (Washington, D.C.), vol. 15, no. 4, April 1996; ''Is There Meret Beyond the Teacup?'' by Mario Naves in *New*

Criterion, vol. 15, no. 1, September 1996; ''Meret Oppenheim: the Women and the Furry Cup at the Guggenheim Museum'' by Luis Camnitzer in *Art Lexus* (Bogota), no. 23, January-March 1997.

* * *

Some artists achieve a particular notoriety for a single work. Picasso made *Guernica* as a monument to the whole Spanish obloquy of Franco and the Nazis. Duchamp could hardly improve upon his ''great glass'' demostration of the Bride traversed by her Bachelors. How much homage can Josef Albers pay to the Square?—and so on.

Meret Oppenheim made Surrealism palpable with her fur-enveloped teacup and saucer. To her credit, a large sector of the world has never forgotten this extraordinary invention even though it first reached public scrutiny over 50 years ago. It was in the great international surrealist exhibition which reached London in 1936.

A modicum of intelligence and understanding will be enough to realize that here was an innovator, a surrealist Columbus of considerable and unusual power. Society does not take easily to brilliant dislocation of accepted values, but Meret Oppenheim's cup-and-saucer became almost a trademark for the surrealist movement worldwide.

In the interim, her ability to fabricate the unexpected continued, and it is unchivalrous for those who have had an opportunity of seeing her subsequent inventions not to recognize that one can get further than fur crockery. One has only to remember the gardenia mirror of the dressingtable (Galerie Charpentier—1964—''Le Surréalisme'') with its convex glass, a vagina in reverse, to realize how this kind of genius for originality does not tire.

How does such an artist start? What are her inspirations and what about the materials she uses? Even the untitled and undated woodcuts from long ago have a freak individuality about them. Whatever connection with reality they may have has been totally obliterated both by the casualness of the image and by the haphazard tinting of the prints. Each pull is different from its fellow because of independent colouration.

Perhaps the encounter with so many and such distinct surrealists of the early 1930s—Giacometti, Kurt Seligmann, Hans Arp and Sophie Täuber-Arp—was sufficient of itself to fire her imagination and take her into the hearth of the surrealist world with which she has never lost touch.

—Sheldon Williams

ORLAN

Nationality: French. **Born:** Saint-Etienne (Loire), 30 May 1947. **Career:** First performance in Saint-Etienne, 1964; controversial sculpture and performance *Le Baiser de l'Artiste (The Kiss of the Artist),* 1977; first surgical performance, videotaped and shown at L'espace Lyonnais d'Art Contemporain (Lyon Center for Contemporary Art), 1978; founds the viewdata art magazine *Art-Accès* on the Minitel, 1982; independent artist, in Paris, since 1983; begins teaching at the Ecole Nationale des Beaux-Arts de Dijon (Dijon National School of Fine Art), 1984. **Awards:** Griffelkunst's collector's first prize, Hamburg, 1999; Arcimboldo's International prize (Hewlett Packard, Picto photographic lab and ''Gens d'Images''), 1999. **Address:** 56, Rue de la Fontaine au Roi, 75 011 Paris, France. **Web site:** http://www.cicv.fr/creation_artistique/online/orlan.

Selected Group and Individual Exhibitions:

1973 Museum of Wuppertal, Germany
1974 Salon du Sud-Est, Lyon
1975 *Triennale de la Peintre,* Maison de la Culture, Saint-Etienne
1976 Galerie des Ursulines, Macon, France
1977 *Made in France,* Espace Lyonnais d'Art Contemporain, Lyon
Le Baiser de l'artiste, Grand Palais Foire Internationnal d'Art Contemporain, Paris; Caldas da Rainha Museum, Portugal
1978 *Action Minute—J. Dupuy et A. Lemoine,* Louvre, Paris
Symposium International de Performance, Neue Galerie Sammlung Ludwig, Aachen, Germany
1979 *Rencontre Internationale d'Art Corporel,* Centre Georges Pompidou, Paris
Rencontre internationale de performance, Palazzo Grassi, Venice
1980 *Vidéo à l'Art,* Musée d'Art Moderne de la ville de Paris
Mesurage, Musée d'Art Moderne, Strasbourg, France
Manifestation video performance, Goethe Institut, Paris
Exposition photocopie, Centre Georges Pompidou, Paris
1981 *L'Auto-Portrait,* Centre Georges Pompidou, Paris
Evénement Orlan, Espace Lyonnais d'Art Contemporain, Lyon
1982 *Auto-portraits de femmes,* Alain Oudin Gallery, Paris
Revue Parlée, Centre Georges Pompidou, Paris
1983 *Photo-Installation,* Musée Rheinisches Landesmuseum, Bonn, Germany
Mesurage d'institution, Guggenheim Museum, New York
L'Art Experimental, Modern Museum, Stockholm, Sweden
1984 Arleri Gallery, Nice, France
Sélection French Video, Tate Gallery, London
1985 *Histoires Saintes de l'Art,* Theâtre et Ecole des Beaux-Arts, Cergy-Pontoise, France (with Lea Lublin)
Les Immatèriaux, Centre Georges Pompidou, Paris
Kunst mit Eigensinn, Modern Art Museum, Vienna
1986 Art and Science section, Contemporary Art Biennale, Venice
Retrospective video, Stedelijk Museum, Amsterdam
1987 *Polyphonix 11,* International Festival of Direct Poetry, Music, and Performance, Centre Georges Pompidou, Paris
Baroques Photographiques, Chambre Claire Gallery, Paris
Télématique et creation, Centre Georges Pompidou, Paris
1990 *Edge,* Biennial of Innovative Visual Art, Glasgow; London; Rotterdam
Désir et Désorde, The Gallery, Milan
1992 *Vidéo installation pour le plafond,* Biennial of Contemporary Art, Sydney
Emily Harvey and Pat Hearn Gallery, New York
1993 *Les couleurs de l'argent,* Musée de la Poste, Paris
Vraiment Faux, Fondation Cartier, Munich
My Flesh, the Text, and the Languages, Penine Hart Gallery, New York
Omnipresence, Sandra Gering Gallery, New York
1995 *Rétrospective video performance,* Centre Georges Pompidou, Paris

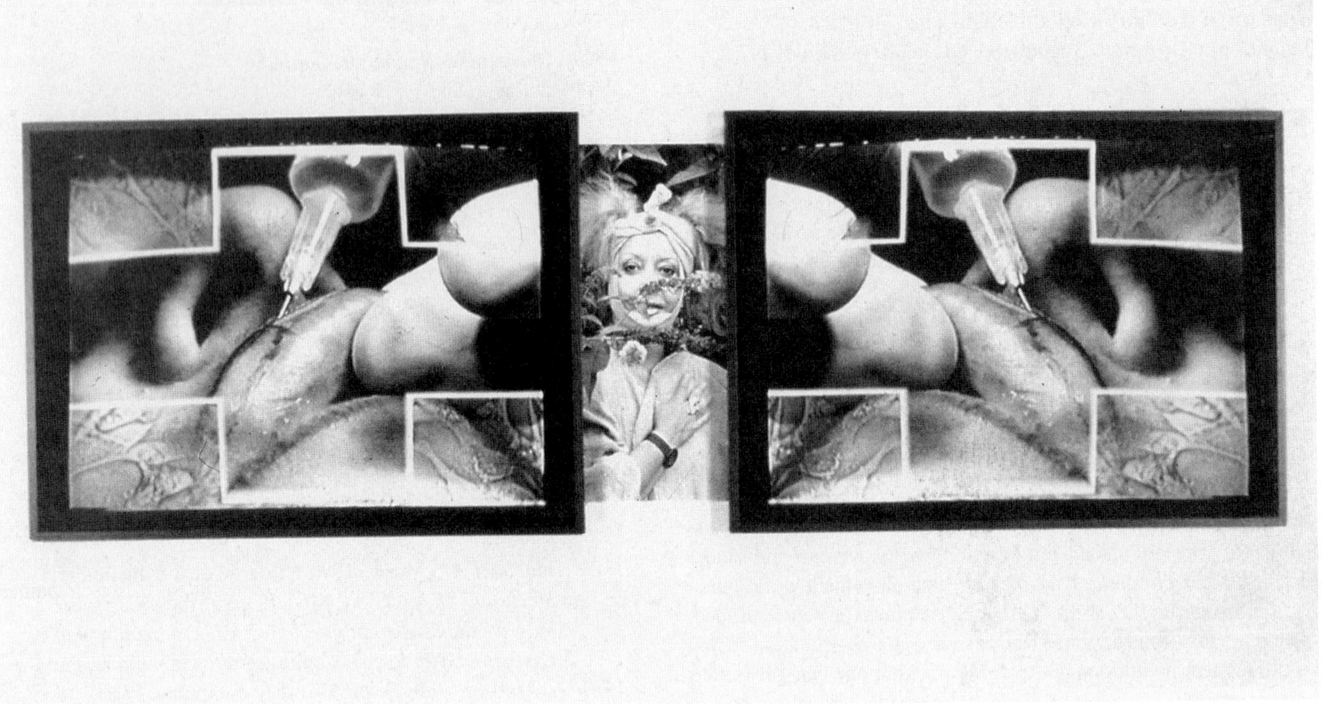

Painting by Orlan. ©Orlan.

Biennale d'art contemporain et de nouvelles technologies, Lyon

1996 *Is it Art?,* Spaces, Cleveland; Contemporary Arts Center, Cincinnati; Katonah

Museum of Art, New York; Community Museum of Art, Palm Beach, Florida; Laguna Museum of Art, California; Community Museum of Art, Lakeworth, Florida; Albany Institute of History and Art, New York

Retrospective, SALA 1, Rome

L'Art au Corps, Musée d'Art Contemporain, Marseille

Endurance, National Museum of Art, Finland; Proton ICA, Amsterdam; Vancouver Art Gallery

1997 *Heaven,* PS 1, New York

Unimplosive Art Exhibition, Biennial of Contemporary Art, Venice

Le masque et le miroir, M. A. C. B. A., Barcelona

Trash, Museum of Contemporary Art, Trento, Italy

1998 *Out of Actions: Between Performance and the Object, 1949–1979,* M. A. K.,

Vienna; Museum of Contemporary Art, Los Angeles

Fétiche-fétichisme, Galerie Passage de Retz, Paris

Refiguration-Selfhybridation, Galerie Espace d'Art Yvonamor Palix, Paris

1999 Museum of Contemporary Art, Tokyo, Japan

Skin-Deep, The Israel Museum, Jerusalem, Israel

Heavenly Figures, Städtische Kunstalle de Düsseldorf, Düsseldorf

Ghost in the Shell, Los Angeles County Museum of Art, Los Angeles

2000 *The Surgical Self,* Winnipeg Art Gallery, Manitoba, Canada

Le Siècle du Corps: Photographie 1900–2000, Lausanne, Switzerland

Dialogue des cultures, Ludwig Museum, Cologne, Germany

Les 100 Sourires de Mona Lisa, Metropolitan Museum of Photography, Tokyo

Publications:

On ORLAN: Books—"This is my body. . . this is my software," edited by Duncan MacCorquodale, 1994; *De l'Art Charnel: au baiser de l'artiste,* edited by Stéphane Place et Jean-Michel Place, Paris, 1997; *Une oeuvre de Orlan,* edited by Bernard Muntaner, Marseille, 1998; *Self-Hybridations,* edited by Laurent Cauwet "Al Dante," Paris, 1999; *Orlan: Millenial Female,* by Kate Ince, New York, 2000. **CD-ROMs**—*Monographie de 1964 à 2000,* Paris, 2000.

*

CARNAL ART

(L'Art Charnel)

Definition:

Carnal Art is self-portraiture in the classical sense, but realised through the possibility of technology. It swings between defiguration and refiguration. Its inscription in the flesh is a function of our age. The body has become a "modified ready-made," no longer seen as the ideal it once represented; the body is not anymore this ideal ready-made it was satisfying to sign.

Distinction:

As distinct from "Body Art," Carnal Art does not conceive of pain as redemptive or as a source of purification. Carnal Art is not interested in the plastic-surgery result, but in the process of surgery, the spectacle and discourse of the modified body which has become the place of a public debate.

Atheism:

Carnal Art does not inherit the Christian Tradition, it resists it! Carnal Art illuminates the Christian denial of body-pleasure and exposes its weakness in the face of scientific discovery. Carnal Art repudiates the tradition of suffering and martyrdom, replacing rather than removing, enhancing rather than diminishing—Carnal Art is not self-mutilation.

Carnal Art transforms the body into language, reversing the biblical idea of the word made flesh; the flesh is made word. Only the voice of Orlan remains unchanged. The artist works on representation.

Carnal Art finds the acceptance of the agony of childbirth to be anachronistic and ridiculous. Like Artaud, it rejects the mercy of God—Henceforth we shall have epidurals, local anesthetics and multiple analgesics ! (Hurray for the morphine !) Vive la morphine ! (down with the pain !) A bas la douleur !

Perception:

I can observe my own body cut open without suffering !. . . . I can see myself all the way down to my viscera, a new stage of gaze. I can see to the heart of my lover and its splendid design has nothing to do with symbolics mannered usually drawn.

—Darling, I love your spleen, I love your liver, I adore your pancreas and the line of your femur excites me.

Freedom:

Carnal Art asserts the individual independence of the artist. In that sense it resists givens and dictates. This is why it has engaged the social, the media, (where it disrupts received ideas and cause scandal), and will even reach as far as the judiciary (to change the Orlan's name).

Clarification:

Carnal Art is not against aesthetic surgery, but against the standards that pervade it, particularly, in relation to the female body, but also to the male body. Carnal Art must be feminist, it is necessary. Carnal Art is not only engages in aesthetic surgery, but also in developments in medicine and biology questioning the status of the body and posing ethical problems.

Style:

Carnal Art loves parody and the baroque, the grotesque and the extreme.

Carnal Art opposes the conventions that exercise constraint on the human body and the work of art.

Carnal Art is anti-formalist and anti-conformist.

—Orlan

* * *

Orlan's artistic proceedings have without any doubt been those that have received the most abundant commentary made for many years in and outside France by specialists of different disciplines such as history or art criticism, philosophy, or psychoanalysis.

That does not preclude that a great deal of superficial statements are still being made about Orlan, which recalls the case of Yves Klein whose provocative approach attracted many hasty judgments or accusations which often had a bearing on his alleged unscrupulous ambitions. Let us add that Yves Klein was one of the forerunners of Body Art, an artistic movement of the 1970s of which Orlan is a direct descendant. One should also recall the strong influence at the same time on her work of the anti-ideological movements and in the first place that of feminism.

Orlan is a multimedia and performance artist who until recently had principally utilized plastic surgery on her face with the object of making of it one of a synthetic personality calculated by computer according to certain physical and psychological characteristics of mythological heroines like the Huntress Diana (chosen for her strength), Psyche (for her inquisitiveness) and Venus (for her freedom of behaviour), whose images have had a strong impact on the history of art. In fact, these female models had not been chosen for their beauty but for their strength of character, since Orlan, who is of great natural beauty herself, would have nothing to gain in this respect—on the contrary.

Between 1965 and 1975, Orlan, who had just graduated from a Fine Arts School, is already a participant in the Meta Art and the Body Art movements since she was realizing at that moment actions in the street and tableaux vivants similar to those of the American Living Theater. These were shortly afterwards followed by public presentations of her own naked body in the posture of an odalisk by Ingres, with the difference that Orlan was stretched out on some bed sheets which she asserted to have been stained by the semen of her various lovers. We are here in the presence of a work of diversion of an image and of one of challenge of the male authority of a Master painter which corresponds entirely to the feminist spirit of the 1970s.

A still more aggressive phase of her work was reached in 1977 on the occasion of her performance entitled "The Artist's Kiss," which was presented at the International Fair of Contemporary Art in Paris. The artist offered to the spectator-customer a kiss for five francs (one dollar) or more, depending on the duration of the kiss or on the trouble taken in its execution. The assimilation made between the woman, the prostitute, and the artist must here be taken as a denunciation of the image which society projects not only on women artists but on all artists who were at the time considered as "prostitutes" of capitalist society. The scandal was great and Orlan became famous. This allowed her to carry on with still more provocative ideas and gestures as well as with ever more advanced techniques.

At that juncture, Orlan realized a series of performances in which this term must be understood in its basic meaning, that of an exploit in a sports event. In these performances the artist proposes herself as a "mètre-étalon" (a play of words on a standard of measure and a stallion) in view of calculating the dimension of some official and cultural sites like the Centre Georges Pompidou and the Museum of the Louvre in Paris, or St. Peter's Square in Rome. This measuring was done by means of her own body lying stretched out on the ground, then rising to her feet and again stretched out on the ground, as often as necessary. Such a physical effort did not go without any aches in the articulations nor without an intense fatigue, but until then, Orlan did not go further in her sacrificial performances than other European or American body artists. In 1978, Orlan undertook, at the same time as other measuring performances of public sites, a new series of performances which were slightly more reassuring, and in which she offered to the contemplation of the public her body half covered by draped veils in the manner of a baroque statue. She considers and calls herself a Saint-Orlan, i.e., another version of a woman as a prostitute and a witch. This represents again a kind of ironic denunciation of the conventional vision that society has of women.

1979 is an important date in the history of the artist, since Orlan will make use of an untoward event in order to reach a new level in the dramatic presentation of herself. At the occasion of an invitation to participate in an artistic manifestation in which she was to execute one of her earlier performances, she was at the last moment prevented from it by a gynaecological accident; an urgent operation became inevitable. Orlan decided to get the operation filmed by video cameras and to have it retransmitted on the spot where the manifestation was to take place. One must stress the fact that, at that moment, everyone was still fully immersed in the counter-culture ideology of the 1960s and 1970s that upheld the principle of ''Art is Life.'' This surgical operation can for two reasons be considered as an undeniable success, the first can be deduced from the artist's implicit statement: ''If I take the risk to show you this, I am invincible and in full control of myself and of my body,'' while the second reason, very reassuring also for others, is contained in the artist's message ''Don't be afraid.''

It will then take Orlan about ten years to give a concerted sequel to this unpremeditated operation-performance. It is in fact not until 1990 that she undertakes her first voluntary surgical operation with the intention of recreating her face and her whole person considered as an open-ended work of art in progress. In the meantime, she had pursued and developed her series of Measurements and also that of Saint-Orlan. She produced, among others, an Apparition of Saint-Orlan, an Assumption of Saint-Orlan, and a Re-incarnation of Saint Orlan, which finally led to several successive surgical disincarnations and reincarnations to which she herself gave the name of Carnal Art.

Her surgical intervention-performances have from the beginning been highly theatrical. The surgeon and his operating team wore some very becoming costumes while the artist, with make-up on her face, her hair carefully dressed, clothed in haute couture garments, and, of course, under local anaesthesia, recited some texts on art and on her own artistic work, accompanied by baroque, rock, or funk music. All these performances were filmed and retransmitted by satellite to museums and art galleries. Afterwards, the artist kept a sort of photographic diary of the different phases of the cicatrization of her face and produced some installations and picture postcards with these images.

In 1996, Orlan realized her ninth operation-performance, the most radical having consisted of an implant of two protruding silicon plates at the temples on both sides of her head, which conjured up the vision of two demonical horns ready to pierce through the skin. She had in mind a refusal of the traditional notion of beauty and was even trying to embroil the notion of gender. Somehow in opposition to this, it is possible to detect in her case a strong quest for an identity as can be discerned in most self-portraits, although a variable mobile identity is put forward by the artist.

Today, Orlan declares having the intention to abandon the surgical interventions on her face for the reason that the metamorphoses she would have liked to obtain are unrealizable; moreover they have been made unnecessary through the existence of virtual images with whose help Orlan can now permanently produce a varying multi-ethnic identity. In order to achieve this, she now mixes her own already multiplied image with the reproductions of African and Asian masks or of faces in Egyptian paintings and of Maya statues, among others. It is clear that Orlan has not gone back on her first commitments and that she continues to practice a socio-cultural politics of the image.

—Aline Dallier

OROZCO, Gabriel

Nationality: Mexican. **Born:** Jalapa, Veracruz, Mexico, 1962. **Education:** Studied at Escuela Nacional de Arte Plasticas, U.N.A.M., Mexico City, 1981–84; studied at Circulo de Bellas Artes, Madrid, Spain, 1986–87. **Career:** Lives and works in New York and Mexico City. **Awards:** Salón Nacional de Artes Plásticas, Secció Espacios Alternativos, Museo de Arte Moderno, Mexico City, 1987; DAAD Artist in Residence, Berlin, Germany, 1995. **Address:** Marian Goodman Gallery, 24 West 57th Street, New York, New York 10019.

Selected Individual Exhibitions:

1993 Museum of Modern Art, New York (catalog)
Galerie Crousel-Robelin BAMA, Paris
Kanaal Art Foundation, Kortrijk, Belgium
1994 Marian Goodman Gallery, New York
Museum of Contemporary Art, Chicago (catalog)
1995 DAAD Gallery, Berlin
Galerie Micheline Szwajcer, Antwerp
De Cardenas, Milan
Migrateurs, ARC/Musée d'Art Moderne de la Ville de Paris
1996 Kunsthalle Zürich, Zurich; Institute of Contemporary Art, London (catalog)
The Empty Club, Art Angel Project, London
Marian Goodman Gallery, New York
Art Gallery of Ontario, Toronto
1997 Anthony d'Offay Gallery, London
Stedelijk Museum, Amsterdam
Staalichen Museum am Kulturforum, Berlin
Centre de la Vieille Charité, Musées de Marseilles, France
1998 Marian Goodman Gallery, New York
St. Louis Museum of Art, St. Louis, Missouri
Centro Fotográfico Alvarez Bravo, Oaxaca, Mexico
ARC/Musée Nationale d'Art Moderne de la Ville de Paris (catalog)
1999 *Gabriel Orozco: Chacahua,* Portikus, Frankfurt am Main, Germany (catalog)
Centre pour l'Image Contemporaine, Geneva
Galerie Chantal Crousel, Paris
Gabriel Orozco: Photogravity, Philadelphia Museum of Art (catalog)
2000 *Gabriel Orozco,* Museum of Contemporary Art, Los Angeles; Museo Internacional Rufino Tamayo, Mexico City; Museo de Arte Contemporaneo de Monterey, Mexico (catalog)
Blue Memory, Shima/Islands (Association for the Preservation of Mirei Shigemori Residence), Kyoto, Japan

Selected Group Exhibitions:

1983 Salón Nacional de Artes Plásticas, Instituto Nacional de Bellas Artes, Mexico City
3rd Encuentro Nacional de Arte Joven, Instituto Nacional de Bellas Artes, Aguascalientes, Mexico
1984 *Neográfica,* Museo Universitario del Chopo, Mexico City
1985 *Sin Motivos Aparentes I,* Museo Carrillo Gil, Mexico City
1987 *Six Nouveaux Regards Mexicains,* Centre culturel du Mexique, Paris; Salón Nacional de Artes Plásticas; Secció Espacios Alternativos; Museo de Arte Moderno, Mexico City
1989 *A Propósito,* Museo del Ex-Convento del Desierto de los Leones, Mexico City

Artistas Mexicanos contemporáneos, Segundo Festival Latino Americano de Arte y Cultura, Brasilia, Brazil
1990 *Sculpture of the Americas into the Nineties,* Museum of Modern Art of Latin America, Washington, D. C. (catalog)
Installations: Current Directions, Museum of Contemporary Hispanic Art, New York
Video D. F., Bronx Museum of the Arts, New York
1991 *Another Mexican Art,* Pasadena Art Center, Pasadena, California
D. F., Blue Star Art Space, San Antonio, Texas
Cuerpos Encontrados, Museo de la Alhóndiga de Granaditas, Guanajuato, Mexico
1992 *Si Colón Supiera!. . . ,* Museo de Monterrey, Mexico
América: Bride of the Sun, Koninklijk Musuem voor Schone Kunsten, Antwerp (catalog)
1993 *Eros, c'est la vie,* Confort Moderne, Poitiers, France
Real Time, Institute of Contemporary Arts, London
Aperto' 93:Emergenza/Emergency, 45th Venice Biennial
In Transit, New Museum of Contemporary Art, New York
1994 *Endstation,* Kunsthaus, Zurich, Switzerland
Watt, Witte de With & Kunsthal, Rotterdam, The Netherlands
The Epic and the Everyday: Contemporary Photographic Art, Hayward Gallery, London (catalog)
Lo crudo y lo cocido, Museo Nacional Centro de Arte Reina Sofia, Madrid
1995 *Réalité Décalée,* Fonds Régional d'Art Contemporain Bretagne, Châteaugiron, France
Morceaux Choisis, Magasin Site Bouchayer-Viallet, Grenoble, France
1996 *Gabriel Orozco, Rirkit Tiravanija og,* Living Art Museum, Reykjavik, Iceland
Drawing on Chance: Selections from the Permanent Collection, Museum of Modern Art, New York
Das Americas, Museum of Art São Paulo, Brazil
Site of Being, Institute for Contemporary Art, Boston
1997 Documenta 10, Kassel, Germany
Present Tense: Nine Artists in the Nineties, San Francisco Museum of Modern Art (catalog)
Veronica's Revenge: Oeuvres photographiques de la Lambert Art Collection, Centre d'Art Contemporain, Geneva
Campo 6, The Spiral Village, Bonnefanten Museum, Maastricht, The Netherlands
1998 *Breaking Ground,* Marian Goodman Gallery, New York
Auf der Spur, Kunst der 90er Jahre im Spiegel von Schweizer Sammlungen, Kunsthalle Zurich
São Paulo Biennal, São Paulo, Brazil
Propositions II, Musée Départemental de Rochechouart, Haute-Vienne, France
1999 *La Ville, Le Jardin, La Mémoire,* Villa Medici, Rome
Infra-Slim Space, Birmingham Museum of Art, Birmingham, Alabama
Carnegie International, Carnegie Museum of Art, Pittsburgh
La Casa, il corpo, il cuore, Museum Moderner Kunst Stiftung Ludwig, Vienna
2000 *Let's Entertain: Life's Guilty Pleasures,* Walker Art Center, Minneapolis (catalog)
A Celebration of Contemporary Art: Vanitas, Meditations on Life and Death in Contemporary Art, Virginia Museum of Fine Arts, Richmond
Orbis Terrarum, Museum Plantin-Moretus, Atwerp
Aprendiende Menos/Learning Less, Consejo Nacional para la Cultura y las Artes, Centro de la Imagen, Mexico City; Museo de las Artes, Universidad de Guadalajara, Mexico (catalog)
2001 *Nothing,* Northern Gallery for Contemporary Art, Sunderland, England
Comfort: Reclaiming Place in a Virtual World, Cleveland Center for Contemporary Art (catalog)

Publications:

By OROZCO: Books—*Gabriel Orozco* with Benjamin H. D. Buchloh and others, Kortrijk, Belgium, 1993; *Gabriel Orozco* with Hans-Ulrich Obrist, Stuttgart 1995; *Empty Club* with Jean Fisher and others, London 1997. **Articles—**''Gabriel Orozco: Technique de l'Energie, The Power to Transform'' with Robert Storr in *Art Press,* June 1997; ''A Thousand Words: Gabriel Orozco Talks About His Recent Films'' in *Artforum International,* Summer 1998.

On OROZCO: Books—*Empty Club* by J. Lingwood, London 1997; *Gabriel Orozco* (pamphlet), by Francesco Bonami, Los Angeles 2000. **Article—**''Like a Rolling Stone: Gabriel Orozco'' by Jean-Pierre Criqui and Jeanine Herman in *Artforum International,* April 1996.

* * *

Gabriel Orozco focuses on the humble occurrences and unassuming, often found materials of everyday life in his sculptural, performative and photographic interventions. These interruptions in public and private spaces activate the physical and psychic space between the object and the viewer. They create transitory experiences that alter our perception of the everyday, celebrating the discarded or mundane with unexpected uses of simple materials. His installation of *Yogurt Caps* (1994), a square white gallery space with a yogurt cap ''hung'' on each wall, is perhaps the most striking and minimal example of his activation of actual space by four abstract points. In this case, as in many, Orozco uses a common consumer material to bridge the gap between the physical or phenomenological world and the intangible concept of empty space.

Working in a wide variety of media, from photography and video to drawing, collage, and sculpture, Orozco uses an equally wide range of techniques to question the difference between art and everyday life, the natural and the artificial, and public and private. His works teach us to see the possibilities for aesthetic and perceptual experiences by transcending the banality of our expectations. In *Horses Running Endlessly* (1995), Orozco uses one of his favorite strategies: intervening in the rules and concepts of games. The sculpture is an ordinary chessboard, but the pieces are all knights, frustrating the possibility of ''normal'' play. Similarly, with his *Ping Pond Table* (1998), which has a lily pond in its center, Orozco forces us to think unconventionally about something we are usually quite familiar with. His photographs capture moments of unpredictable encounters and document also his performative interventions. *Crazy Tourist* (1991) shows an ordinary marketplace where the artist rearranged oranges on the market's empty tables, while *Breath on*

Piano (1993) captures the fleeting moment when his breath fogged the shiny surface.

Orozco's most important strategy in sculptural or material interventions may be site-specificy. Unlike most of the site-specific works of the 1960s and 1970s Orozco responds to the given situations by selecting both his approach and medium in accordance with the specific moment and physical space. No two works are ever the same, just as no two moments can ever be exactly matched or relived. To make *Piedra que cede (Yielding Stone)* in 1992, Orozco shaped nearly 150 pounds of plasticine clay (equal approximately to his own body weight) into a ball and rolled it through the streets of New York City. The engagement of his own body and his surrogate body (the ball of clay) in the action draws attention to a specific place and stretch of time, though they were constantly in parallel flux. The dirt and detritus from the streets that became embedded in the surface of this malleable material are the static, plastic record of a movement in time and space.

While in Berlin in 1995 with the DAAD Artists Program (*Kunstlerprogramm*) he drove a yellow Schwalbe scooter. Whenever he saw an identical one, he parked next to it and photographed them together, (*Until You Find Another Yellow Schwalbe*), leaving a note for the other owner to convene at the National Gallery with all of the other yellow Schwalbes on a prescribed date. For an Artangel project in 1997, Orozco renovated an empty gentleman's club (*Empty Club*). He renewed the abandoned space by filling it with strange architectural situations and frustrating objects like an oval billiards table (*Oval with Pendulum*). Through these awkward situations, Orozco questions the colonial and segregating origins of the ''gentleman's club,'' its members and its activities.

In 1999, Orozco created a new installation at the Philadelphia Museum of Art that integrated his sculptural and photographic practices. He enlarged black and white photographs of various objects from his oeuvre, a conch shell, a bicycle, a Schwalbe, *La DS* as well as photographs of Pre-Colombian sculpture in the museum's collection. Cutting out the silhouettes of these photographed objects, he presented them in the galleries at two-dimensional substitutes for the real objects. The conversation among the objects is twofold: first, are all of these objects part of the same system of cultural production? Orozco specifically refers to work of his own cultural heritage as if to underscore the connections, but also to draw out the differences in the mode and spirit of production. Secondly, are ''ethnographic objects,'' as many institutions consider Pre-Colombian art, treated two-dimensionally in a museum? Is there a cultural hierarchy within the institution that makes such a move so radical? With this gesture, Orozco brings the museum into his architectural and structural critique of the world, and aligns himself with a dynamic lineage of artists who have questioned institutional politics.

—Elizabeth Mangini

OSSORIO, Alfonso

Nationality: American. **Born:** Manila, Philippines, 2 August 1916; immigrated to the United States: naturalized, 1939. **Education:** St. Richard's School, Malvern, Worcestershire, England, 1924–30; Portsmouth Priory, Providence, Rhode Island, 1930–34; Harvard University, Cambridge, Massachussetts, 1934–38, B.A. 1938; Rhode Island School of Design, Providence, 1938–39. **Military Service:** United States Army, 1943–46. **Family:** Married Bridget Hubrecht in 1940. **Career:** Lived in Taos, New Mexico, 1940–42, then settled in New York City; spent summers in East Hampton, New York, met Lee Krasner and Jackson Pollock, 1949: visited Victorias, Philippines, returned briefly to New York, and travelled to Paris, 1949; met Jean and Lili Dubuffet; introduced by Dubuffet to Michel Tapie; visited briefly in East Hampton, New York, and purchased home there, 1951; travelled to Chicago with the Dubuffets; introduced to Clyfford Still, 1952; installed l'Art Brut collection in his East Hampton house, 1952; organized exhibition series at Executive House, New York, 1956–58; co-founder, with Elizabeth Parker and John Little, Sigma Gallery, East Hampton, and organized summer exhibitions there, 1957–60; exhibited l'Art Brut collection at Cordier and Warren Gallery, New York; spent summers in Greece and Turkey, from 1964; Ossorio Foundation opens in Southampton, New York, 1994. **Web site:** http://www.ossorio.org. **Died:** Of a ruptured aneurysm, 5 December 1990.

Individual Exhibitions:

1941 Wakefield Gallery, New York
1943 Wakefield Gallery, New York
1945 Mortimer Brandt Gallery, New York
1951 Studio Paul Facchetti, Paris
Betty Parsons Gallery, New York
1953 Betty Parsons Gallery, New York
1956 Betty Parsons Gallery, New York
1958 Betty Parsons Gallery, New York
1959 Betty Parsons Gallery, New York
1960 Galerie Stadler, Paris
1961 Betty Parsons Gallery, New York
Galerie Stadler, Paris
Selection, Cordier and Warren Gallery, New York
Galerie Cordier-Stadler, Frankfurt
1963 Cordier and Eckstrom Gallery, New York
1965 Cordier and Eckstrom Gallery, New York
1967 Cordier and Eckstrom Gallery, New York
1968 Cordier and Eckstrom Gallery, New York
1969 Cordier and Eckstrom Gallery, New York
1972 Cordier and Eckstrom Gallery, New York
1980 Guild Hall Museum, East Hampton, New York
1984 Oscarsson Hood Gallery, New York
1990 *A Salute to Signa,* Guild Hall Museum, East Hampton Center for Contemporary Art
1991 *Alfonso Ossorio: The Victorias Drawings, 1950,* Pollock-Krasner House and Study Center, New York
Alfonso Ossorio: A Memorial Exhibition, Works of the Fifties, Jennifer Pinto & Vanderwoulde Tananbaum Gallery, New York
Alfonso Ossorio: A Legacy, Benton Gallery, Southampton, New York
1992 *Alfonso Ossorio, Drawings 1940–48,* Whitney Museum of American Art, New York
Alfonso Ossorio: Peintures 1950–1953, Galerie Zabriskie, Paris
1993 *Alfonso Ossorio: Works from the 1960s,* Zabriskie Gallery, New York
1995 *Recovery Drawings,* Arlene Bujese Gallery, East Hampton, New York

1997 *Reflection and Redemption: The 1940s Surrealist Works of Alfonso Ossorio,* Michael Rosenfeld Gallery, New York (traveled to the Greenville County Museum of Art, Greenville, South Carolina) (catalog)
Congregations, The Parrish Art Museum, Southampton, New York (catalog)
Alfonso Ossorio: The Shingle Figures, Michael Rosenfeld Gallery, New York (catalog)
2000 *The Creeks: Before, During and After,* Ossorio Foundation, Southampton, New York (catalog)

Selected Group Exhibitions:

1958 *International Sky Festival,* Osaka Japan
1968 *The Door,* Museum of Contemporary Crafts, New York
1976 *14 Paintings: De Kooning, Dubuffet, Ossorio, Pollock, Still,* Thomas Gibson Fine Art, London
1989 *The Eloquent Object: The Evolution of American Art in Craft Media Since 1945,* Philbrook Museum of Art, Tulsa, Oklahoma (traveled to The National Museum of Modern Art, Kyoto and The National Museum of Modern Art, Tokyo)
1993 *Parallel Visions: Modern Artists and Outsider Art,* Los Angeles County Museum of Art, Los Angeles (international traveling exhibition)
1994 *Michel Tapie: Un Art Autre,* Artcurial, Paris
1996 *The Twentieth Anniversary of the Federal Reserve Board of Governors Fine Arts Program,* Washington, D.C.

Collections:

Albertina Museum Vienna, Austria; Boymans-Von Beuingen Museum, Rotterdam, Holland; Brooklyn Museum of Art, Brooklyn, New York; Centre Georges Pompidou, Paris, France; Greenville County Museum of Art, Greenville, South Carolina; Grey Art Gallery, New York University, New York; Guild Hall Museum, East Hampton; Honolulu Academy of Arts, Honolulu; International Center of Aesthetic Research, Turin, Italy; Herbert F. Johnson Museum, Cornell University, Ithaca; L'Art Brut Museum, Lausanne, Switzerland; Los Angeles County Museum of Art, Los Angeles; Marion Koogler McNay Art Museum, San Antonio; Museo National Reina Sofia, Madrid, Spain; National Gallery of Art, Washington, D.C.; National Gallery of Modern Art, New Britain; Philadelphia Museum of Art, Philadelphia; Rose Art Museum, Brandeis University, Waltham; Solomon R. Guggenheim Museum, New York; Tel Aviv Museum, Tel Aviv, Israel; The Arkansas Arts Center, Little Rock; The Bruce Museum, Greenwich; The Cathedral of St. John the Divine, New York; The Metropolitan Museum of Art, New York; The Norton Museum of Art, West Palm Beach; The Parrish Art Museum, Southampton; The Phillips Collection, Washington, D.C.; Wadsworth Atheneum, Hartford; Whitney Museum of American Art, New York; Williams College Museum of Art, Williams College, Williamstown; Worcester Art Museum, Worcester; Yale University Art Gallery, Yale University, New Haven.

Publications:

By OSSORIO: Books—*Poems and Wood Engravings,* London 1934; *Exhibition of Recent Paintings by Lee Krasner,* exhibition catalog, New York 1960; *John Little Paintings,* exhibition catalog, New York, 1961; *Art Brut,* exhibition catalog, New York 1961; *Recovery: The Hospital Drawings of Alfonso Ossorio,* 1995. **Articles**—''Jackson Pollock'' in *Pollock,* exhibition catalog, New York 1951, reprinted in *Pollock,* exhibition catalog, Paris 1952, and in *15 Americans,* exhibition catalog, New York 1952, and in *The New American Painting,* exhibition catalog, New York 1959; ''One Man's Art U.S.A.'' in *Artnews* (New York), October 1956; ''Michael Lekakis'' in *Americans 1963,* exhibition catalog, New York 1963; ''The House of the Hourloupe'' in *Artnews* (New York), May 1968; ''Notes'' in *14 Paintings: De Kooning, Dubuffet, Ossorio, Pollock, Still,* exhibition catalog, London 1976; interview with Judith Wolfe, in *Ossorio,* exhibition catalog, East Hampton, New York 1980; ''Interview: Alfonso Ossorio Talks with Paul Cummings'' by Paul Cummings in *Drawing,* no. 7, January-February 1986.

On OSSORIO: Books—*Les Peintures initiatiques d'Alfonso Ossorio* by Jean Dubuffet, Paris 1951; *Ossorio* by Michael Tapie, Turin 1961; *Ossorio: A Selection,* exhibition catalog, New York 1961; *Art in Progress: The Visual Development of a Collage by Alfonso Ossorio* by B. H. Friedman, New York 1972; *Could I Ask You Something?* (etchings), text by Lewis Thomas, New York 1984; *Collision* by Anne Harithas and James Harithas, Santa Barbera, California 1985; *Alfonso Ossorio: Congregations,* exhibition catalog, by Klaus Kertess with Ellen G. Landau and Leslie Rose Close, Southampton, New York 1997; *From the Molecular to the Galactic: The Art of Max Ernst and Alfonso Ossorio* by Barbara Matilsky, Jessica Dallow, and Colleen Thomas, Chapel Hill, North Carolina 2000. **Articles**—''The Eastern Long Island Painters'' by Patsy Southgate in *Paris Review,* spring/summer 1959, ''We Visit the Artist Alfonso Ossorio'' by Louise Elliot Rago in *School Arts* (Worchester, Massachussetts), April 1960; ''Alfonso Ossorio: A Biography, Mostly of His Work'' by B. H. Friedman in *Art International* (Zurich), April 1962; ''Ossorio'' by Simone Frigerio in *Aujourd'hui: Arts et Architecture* (Paris), May 1963; ''The Artist as Collector: Alfonso Ossorio'' by Kenneth B. Sawyer in *Studio International* (London), March 1965; ''5 Famous Artists in Their Personal Backgrounds'' in *House and Garden* (New York), December 1965; ''The Diabolic Craft of Alfonso Ossorio'' by Richard Howard in *Craft Horizons* (New York) January/February 1967; ''Alfonso Ossorio'' by B. H. Friedman in *Art International* (Lugano, Switzerland), February 1967; ''Ossorio the Magnificent'' by Francine de Plessix in *Art in America* (New York), March/April 1967; ''Alfonso Ossorio: La Mia Collezione e una Fabbrica di Idee'' in *Bolaffiarte* (Turin), January 1974; ''Ossorio'' by Peter Blake in *Architecture Plus* (London), January/February 1974; ''Alfonso Ossorio: Celebrator of the Unconventional'' by Donna Harkavy in *Arts Magazine,* no. 58, April 1984; Obituary in *Art in America* (New York), vol. 79, February 1991; ''Alfonso Ossorio'' by Elizabeth Hayt in *Art News,* vol. 96, April 1997; ''Ossorio, Dubuffet and Art Brut in the USA'' by Barbara Freeman in *Raw Vision,* no. 17, Winter 1996–1997. **Films**—*Galaxy* by Gregory Markopoulous, 1966; *The Artist: His Work and His Studio* by Terry Krumm, 1969.

* * *

During a career that has spanned four decades, Alfonso Ossorio has had his work approached critically from two viewpoints, neither of which is incorrect but rather overlapping. First, he has been historically placed among the first generation of Abstract Expressionists, a view supported by Ossorio's close enduring friendship with

Jackson Pollock, whose influence can indeed be seen in the surrealist ink drawings Ossorio produced during the 1940s. Second, much has been rightly made of the artist's relationship with French artist Jean Dubuffet, whose abiding fascination with Art Brut (''raw art'') closely paralleled Ossorio's, if it did not precisely influence it. Ossorio's development has incorporated these elements into his work—but it is not, as has been suggested, derivative of them.

In fact, Alfonso Ossorio occupies a unique position in contemporary art, one which frequently aroused controversy, no matter what medium or style he engaged: combinations of wax, watercolor and collage, white lead and plaster, diagrammatic, neo-Constructivist paintings which used and twisted the physical pigment itself into ropelike reliefs, and, from the 1950s until now, complex sculptural wall-constructions and freestanding pieces incorporating such specialized detritus as bones, glass eyes, pieces of tree trunk and mirrors. The work has been described as ''primitive,'' ''barbaric,'' ''voodoo-like.'' The critical emphasis has been placed almost entirely upon the materials themselves—not by the artist, although he is well aware of their connotations of violence, mutilation, and death—rather on the iconography, frequently anthropomorphic, that subsume them. When Ossorio uses the term ''congregated imagery,'' he does so advisedly, to separate his work from the more popular and possibly inaccurate genre of assemblage, or relief construction. The term implies a *cerebral* gathering of materials, not a celebration of the found object. These congregations are often highly decorative, but motivated by an intellectual—even mystical—concern, rather than a purely visual one. If his colors are violent, and his use of materials visceral, it is because he is attempting to give, in Dubufett's words, ''body to conceptual ideas—to the point of making them pass completely into the field of material objects—and at the same time preventing the real things he wants to represent from materializing too much.'' The final product is, of course, frequently horrifying, although presenting more declarations of hope than have often been seen in his work. It is also an immensely sophisticated body of work, ''borrowing'' from Oriental art, sometimes testing new industrial materials (like the plastic sheeting experimented with in 1968), at others re-interpreting the Christian, and pagan, myths of death and resurrection. Although bearing similarities to the best of Art Brut, as practiced by the insane and the imprisoned, Ossorio's work indicates a calculated thoughtfulness that can only come from a professional draughtsman and an artist learned in mythic and formal history. The content is demanding, compelling; it is not automatic at all, but complicated, difficult ''to read,'' frequently relying on a *combinatoire* of a visual vocabulary specifically chosen to evoke atavistic responses and an ordered control that ''marks'' these very emotive elements through complicated design.

Although Ossorio's style and materials have altered throughout the past thirty years, these concerns have bound all the different phases of his work indissolubly. In fact, he will frequently use elements from earlier pieces in new ''congregations,'' a ''reclamation,'' as he terms it. He will return from time to time generalized figuration, using a piece of tree-trunk or a glass eyeball from another, earlier piece; similar components echo each other from separate periods of his evolution as an artist. Starfish, bones, feathers, fragments of anatomical photographs emerge, disappear, and re-emerge from work to work. Past, present, and even future combine, dissipate, and reassemble, in an esoteric yet somehow recognizable fashion, in an insinuating blend of repulsion and attraction.

—Jane Bell

From 1984 to 1990, Ossorio, in association with the Hudson River Press, focused his energies once again on intaglio printmaking. In 1984, Ossorio collaborated with poet and scientist Lewis Thomas on a project commissioned by the Library Fellows of the Whitney Museum of American Art. The collaboration resulted in the book *Could I Ask You Something?*, a volume of poems illustrated by Ossorio, for which he returned to his surrealist roots to create evocative compositions influenced by scientific images taken by electron micrographs. Inspired by his work with Thomas, Ossorio continued to explore organic themes in his prints, creating all-over compositions filled with biomorphic forms reminiscent of cellular imagery, a theme he had explored in his paintings throughout the 1950s and 1960s. Hospitalized due to heart failure in 1988, Ossorio produced a series of felt-tip pen drawings while recuperating from heart surgery. These ''recovery drawings'' were published posthumously in 1995 in a book titled *Recovery: The Hospital Drawings of Alfonso Ossorio*. Ossorio died of a ruptured aneurysm in 1990.

Ossorio's legacy is preserved in his most extensive project, the transformation of his sixty-acre estate, called the Creeks, into an arboretum and sculpture park. The twenty-year project occupied Ossorio from 1970 until his death, and has been called his ''ultimate congregation.'' The landscape and sculpture of the Creeks are documented in 300 photographs of the estate taken by Ossorio in 1990. The Ossorio Foundation, dedicated the preservation of his diaries, photographs, and letters, was established in 1994.

—Bradley Bailey

P

PAGE, Robin (Bluebeard)

Nationality: Canadian. **Born:** London, England, 2 November 1932. **Education:** Vancouver school of art, 1952–1954. **Family:** Married Carol Page in 1960; daughter from earlier marriage: Rachel. **Career:** Independent artist, since 1954: lived in Vancouver, 1954–59, in London and Leeds, Yorkshire, 1959–69, in Dusseldorf and Cologne, 1970–78, in West Berlin, 1978–80, and in Munich since 1981; has also worked in Paris, 1960, 1976. Guest lecturer, High Wycombe College for Further Education, Buckinghamshire, Leicester College of Art, and Coventry College of Art, 1963–1965; senior lecturer, Leeds College of Art, 1965–70; visiting professor, University of Essen, 1978; professor of painting and graphics, Akademie der Bildenden Kunste, Munich, since 1981; professor of painting, Internationale Sommerakademie fur Bildenden Kunste, Salzburg, 1986; ''dyed and went to Bluebeard, 1987,'' conception of the Bluebeard Museum, 1987. **Awards:** Canada Council Senior Arts Grant, Ottawa, 1975; DAAD Artists Fellowship, West Berlin, 1978. **Address:** Akademiestrasse 2, 80799 Munich, Germany.

Individual Exhibitions:

1969 Art Intermedia, Cologne
1971 Eat Art Gallery, Dusseldorf
1972 Galerie Müller, Cologne
1973 Kunstverein, Cologne
Galerie Müller, Stuttgart
Galerie Gunter Sachs, Hamburg
1974 Galerie Foncke, Ghent
Salon de Mai, Paris (travelled to Braunschweig, West Germany, and the Lijnbaancentrum, Rotterdam)
1975 Galerie Allen, Vancouver
1977 Junior Galerie, Goslar, Germany
Galerie Vallois, Paris
1979 Galerie Redmann, Sylt, Germany
Akademie der Kunste, Berlin
1980 Galerie Redmann, Berlin
Galerie Redmann, at *Art '80,* Basel
Kunsthalle, Darmstadt, Germany
1982 Kunstverein, Augsburg, Germany
1993 Galerie Klewan, Munich

Selected Group Exhibitions:

1964 *Cross Section,* City Museum, Leicester
1969 *Amadou in A,* Antwerp
1970 *Happening and Fluxus,* Kunstverein, Cologne
1972 *Documenta,* Kassel, West Germany
1973 *6th International Triennal of Coloured Graphic Prints,* Grenchen, Switzerland
1976 *Holz-Kunst-Stoff,* Staatliche Kunsthalle, Baden-Baden, West Germany
1978 *Museum des Geldes,* Stadtische Kunsthalle, Dusseldorf
1979 *Ten Artists from the DAAD Programme,* DAAD-Galerie, West Berlin
1989 *Fluxus Fluxorum,* Venice Biennale
1991 *Venice Biennale,* Italy
1994 *Fluxbritannica,* Tate Gallery, London

Collections:

Museum Folkwang, Essen; Staatsgalerie, Stuttgart.

Publications:

By PAGE: Article—''Robin Page'' in *Flash Art* (Milan) May 1972.

On PAGE: Books—*Mail Art: Communication à Distance: Concept* by Jean-Marc Poinsot, Paris 1971; *Robin Page: Bildparabeln,* exhibition catalog, Augsburg 1982. **Articles—**''A Note on Robin Page'' by E. Lynn in *Art International* (Lugano, Switzerland), May 1973; ''Robin Page, Galerie Müller'' by G. Wirth in *Das Kunstwerk* (Baden-Baden, West Germany), July 1973; ''Everybody Invited'' by John Anthony Thwaites in *Art and Artists* (London), November 1973; ''Artist Dips His Brush in Canadian Wry'' by Art Perry in *Vancouver Province,* November 1974; ''I Am a Unique Idiot'' by Marq de Villiers in *Weekend Magazine* (Montreal), February 1975; ''Art in a Brown Paper Bag'' in *Weekend Magazine* (Montreal), May 1975.

*

For many years I used *myself,* Robin Page, as the model for *myself* in pictures representing *my* thoughts. In 1987, on holiday from European canvas on an isolated Canadian island, I received a visitation from the Spirit of Bluebeard which said It had seen in my work the ideal medium for Its materialization. The Spirit offered me a deal: in exchange for the promise of eternal life, youth, health, wealth, and happiness I would abandon the identity of Robin Page and allow my person, energy, talent, and creative thinking to be used as the host for the materialization of Bluebeard. Wow! I agreed immediately! Eternal life. . . . Since our pact I have been walking around with this ridiculous blue beard on my face, thinking His thoughts and translating them into spirited Promoganda for His Amuseum. He insists that I work to elevate ''My message and image out of the mind-fucking ghetto of the last hundred years of visual art to an aggressively heroic, independent, sublimely irreverent inspirational entertainment.'' Holy shit, is that all?

I am not at liberty to disclose the full scope of His program, message, or ambitions, or His vision for mankind for the. . . for the next. . . for *the next thousand years*!! These will be revealed at appropriate times through the medium of pictures from the Bluebeard Amuseum Collection. I am authorized, though, to invite others to abandon their petty egos and join with all their energies, talents—and worldly goods—in celebrating the Greatness that is Bluebeard. (Naturally in exchange for the promise of eternal life, youth, etc.)

So I, Bluebeard, say to you now what I said to Robin Page then: don't ask ''What can the hamburger do for me?'' but rather ''How can I be the beef?''

—Robin Page, Bluebeard

* * *

On the surface Robin Page is the archetypal frontier Canadian—big, brash, tough-talking, hard-drinking, gravel-voiced, complete with beard and denim coveralls. Almost a caricature. He even hangs tree-felling saws on the walls of his Munich home. Yet beneath the gruff protective exterior lives a dedicated, articulate artist and teacher.

Page's work presents a similar dichotomy. At first glance it is jokey, fun. But the artistic wit of Page is only a tool he uses to make serious statements about art, life and communication.

Page originally trained as a cartoonist, progressing perhaps unexpectedly to hard-edge painting. The lure of Europe brought him to the stimulus of Paris—so often an artist's catalyst—and London life gave him access to surrealism and the anti-art of Fluxus. Page was associated with Fluxus almost from the beginning, contributing major and minor Happenings throughout the 1960s. The 1970s found Page in Germany where he was able to function totally as an artist for the first time with his first one-man exhibition and artist-in-residence positions providing studio space and stability.

Images, in good art, can not merely represent themselves. The guitar in Page's work is one of his multi-layered autobiographical images which give depth and continuity to his oeuvre. Page played the guitar in a Vancouver-based band (one of more than 60 jobs which have supported him over the years); the guitar was the central object to one of his earlier Happenings—at the Misfits Concert in 1962 he kicked his guitar from the ICA through the streets of London with the help of audience members, returning with a few shreds to the concert stage; later the guitar appears in a painting and an actual object in ''The Blind Man'' of 1970, one of his ''Parables.''

The Parables began in Germany; they are Page's statements about art, conservation, politics, modern life. Central to each Parable is an action self-portrait. Painted from a photograph, the painting is highly detailed, technically skilled. Page uses his own image as an object, raw material, just as he incorporates work of other artists—Picasso, Brancusi, Duchamp, De Chirico. A Charlie McCarthy-like dummy named Whildon (well-done?) acts as occasional comic to Page's straight-guy. The action in the painting does not, however, remain on the two-dimensional canvas. It thrusts into space in front, completing the artist's statement with a three-dimensional object. Expectations of reality are fulfilled.

Indications are that Page's Parables have all been written and new work is about to emerge from this artist who asks ''Hey, Whildon, why has humor never replaced seriousness as the most respected cultural attitude?'' Answer: ''Because the people can't fake it!''

—Marlee Robinson

PAIK, Nam June

Nationality: Korean. **Born:** Seoul, 1932. **Education:** Attended the University of Tokyo, 1952–56; studied music, with Stockhausen, Darmstadt; art history and philosophy in Germany, 1956–58. **Career:** Video artist: lives and works in New York; worked in electronic music studio for Radio Cologne, 1958–61; associated with the Fluxus group, New York, during the 1960s; artist-in-residence, WGBH-TV, Boston, 1969; artist-in-residence, WNET-TV, New York, 1971; works closely with Japanese artist Shigeko Kubota. **Awards:** Skowhegan Medal for Video, 1991; UNESCO Picasso Medal, 1992; 1st Prize, Best Pavilion, Venice Biennale, Venice, 1993; Kyoto Prize, 1998; International Distinguished Artist Award, Miami, 1999; National Arts Club Artists Award, 2000. **Address:** c/o Carl Solway Gallery, 424 Findlay Street, Cincinnati, Ohio 45214, U.S.A.

Nam June Paik: *Technology*, 1991. ©Smithsonian American Art Museum, Washington, DC/Art Resource, NY; Courtesy of Smithsonian American Art Museum.

Selected Individual Exhibitions:

1959 Galerie 22, Dusseldorf
1960 Mary Bauermeister Studio, Cologne
1961 *Simultan,* Galerie Lauhus, Cologne (with Wolf Vostell and Stefan Wewerka)
1962 Kammerspiele, Dusseldorf
1963 Galerie Parnass, Wuppertal, West Germany
1965 Bonino Gallery, New York
1971 Bonino Gallery, New York
1972 Museum of Modern Art, New York
1973 The Kitchen, New York

Nam June Paik standing amid his electronic art exhibit, *The Rehearsal* at Holly Solomon Gallery. ©AP/Wide World Photos.

1974 Everson Museum of Art, Syracuse, New York
Bonino Gallery, New York
1975 René Block Gallery, New York
1976 Bonino Gallery, New York
René Block Gallery, New York
1982 Whitney Museum, New York
Museum of Contemporary Art, Chicago (retrospective)
1984 Metropolitan Art Museum, Tokyo
DAAD-Galerie, West Berlin
1986 *Nam June Paik: Family of Robot,* Carl Solway Gallery, Cincinnati, Ohio
International Art Exposition, Chicago
Nam June Paik: Sculpture, Painting and Laser Photography, Holly Solomon Gallery, New York
1988 *Nam June Paik: Beuys and Bogie,* Dorothy Goldeen Gallery, Los Angeles
Nam June Paik: Color Bar Paintings, Holly Solomon Gallery, New York
Nam June Paik: Family of Robot, The Hayward Gallery, South Bank Centre, London
1989 *La Fee Electronique,* Musee d'Art Moderne de la Ville de Paris
Galerie du Genie, Paris
Mayor Rowan Gallery, London
Galerie Juana Mordo, Madrid
Weisses Haus, Hamburg
Image World: Art and Media Culture, Whitney Museum, New York
1990 Galerie Hans Mayer, Düsseldorf, Germany
Galerie Van De Velde, Antwerp, Belgium
Holly Solomon Gallery, New York
1991 *Nam June Paik: Retrospective,* Kunsthaus Zurich, Kunsthalle Basel, Switzerland
Kunsthalle, Düsseldorf, Germany
1992 *Nam June Paik: Retrospective,* Museum of Modern Art, Seoul, South Korea
Nam June Paik: Arti Elettroniche, Cinema e Media Verso il XXI Secolo, Palazzo delle Esposizioni, Rome
1993 *Artist as Nomad,* Venice Biennale 1993, German Pavilion, Venice
Feedback and Feedforth, The Watari Museum of Contemporary Art, Tokyo
1994 *The Art Show,* Associated Dealers of American Art, New York

The Electronic Super Highway: Nam June Paik in the Nineties, Ft. Lauderdale, Florida
1995 Pennsylvania Academy of the Fine Arts, Philadelphia
Galley Hyundai, Seoul, South Korea
New Work, Galerie Fine Art Rafael Vostell, Berlin
1996 *The Electronic Super Highway: Nam June Paik in the Nineties,* San Jose Museum of Art, San Jose, California (travelled to Culturgest, Lisbon, Portugal)
Statens Museum for Kunst, Copenhagen, Denmark
1997 Jacksonville Museum of Contemporary Art, Jacksonville, Florida
Galeria Ramis Barquet, Monterrey, Mexico
1999 *Nam June Paik: Fluxus/Video,* Kunsthalle Bremen, Germany
Butler Institute of American Art, Youngstown, Ohio
2000 *The Worlds of Nam June Paik,* Solomon R. Guggenheim Museum, New York
Nam June Paik: Video Art Pioneer, Santa Barbara Museum of Art, Santa Barbara, California

Selected Group Exhibitions:

1962 *Fluxus Festival,* Wiesbaden, West Germany
1968 *Cybernetic Serendipity,* Institute of Contemporary Arts, London
1969 *TV as a Creative Medium,* Howard Wise Gallery, New York
1971 *St. Jude Video International,* de Saisset Art Gallery and Museum, University of Santa Clara California
1973 *Circuit: A Video Invitational,* Everson Museum of Art, Syracuse, New York
1975 *Open Circuits: The Future of Television,* Museum of Modern Art, New York
Video Art, Institute of Contemporary Art, Philadelphia
1987 *Avant-Garde in the Eighties,* Los Angeles County Museum of Art
1988 *The Arts for Television,* Museum of Contemporary Art, Los Angeles (travelled)
1993 *The Portrait Now,* National Portrait Gallery, London
1994 *Tuning Up,* Kunstmuseum Wolfsburg, Germany
1995 *Dialogues of Peace,* Palais des Nations, Geneva, Switzerland
1996 *Mediascape,* Guggenheim Museum Soho, New York
1997 *Skulpture Projects in Munster,* Westfalisches Landesmuseum, Munster, Germany
1998 *On the Nature of Landscape,* Mount Holyoke College Museum of Art, South Hadley, Massachusetts
1999 *Fluxus in Amerika,* Fine Art Rafael Vostell, Berlin, Germany
2000 *Tempus Fugit: Time Flies,* The Nelson-Atkins Museum of Art, Kansas City, Missouri
2001 *Collecting Ideas: Works from the Polly and Mark Addison Collection,* Denver Art Museum, Denver, Colorado

Collections:

Museum of Modern Art, New York; Art Institute of Chicago, Illinois; Whitney Museum of American Art, New York; San Francisco Museum of Modern Art, California; Los Angeles County Museum of Art, California; Denver Art Museum, Colorado; Walker Art Center, Minneapolis, Minnesota; Detroit Institute of Art, Michigan; Contemporary Arts Center, Cincinnati, Ohio; Cincinnati Art Museum, Ohio; Reynolda House, Museum of American Art, Winston-Salem, North Carolina; Hiroshima Museum, Japan; Tokyo Metropolitan Museum; Museum of Modern Art, Seoul, South Korea; Stedelijk Museum, Amsterdam; Museum Ludwig, Aachen, Germany; Museum Ludwig, Cologne; Deutsches Post Museum, Frankfurt; Museum of Modern Art, Frankfurt; Staatsgalerie Stuttgart, Germany; Kunstmuseum, Düsseldorf; Nationalgalerie, Berlin; Folkwangmuseum, Essen; Monchehaus Museum, Goslar, Germany; Stadtische Kunsthalle, Mannheim, Germany; Museum am Ostwall, Dortmund, Germany; Stadische Museum, Monchengladbach, Germany; Museum of Technology, Karlsruhe, Germany; Musee National d'Art Moderne, Centre Georges Pompidou, Paris; Musee d'Art Moderne, Paris; Musee d'Art Moderne, Saint Etienne, France; Musee d'Art Contemporain, Foundation Edelman, Lausanne, Switzerland; Statens Kunst-musee, Stockholm; Louisiana, Humblebaek, Denmark; Museum Moderner Kunst Stiftung Ludwig, Vienna; National Museum of American Art, Washington, D.C.; Albright-Knox Museum, Buffalo, New York.

Public Installations:

Video Arbor, Forest City Residential Development, Philadelphia, Pennsylvania, 1990; Public Art Commission, Chase Manhattan Bank, Brooklyn, New York, 1992; *Electro-Symbio Phonics for Pheonix,* American West Arena, Phoenix, Arizona, 1992; Public Art Commission, City of Anaheim, California, 1993.

Publications:

By PAIK: Book—*An Anthology of Nam June Paik,* exhibition catalog, West Berlin 1984. **Articles**—''Expanded Education for the Paperless Society'' in *Interfunktionen* (Cologne), no. 7, 1971; article in *Flash Art* (Milan), May/June 1972. **Television broadcasts**—*Video Commune,* WGBH-TV, Boston 1970; *The Selling of New York,* WNET-TV, New York 1972; *Tribute to John Cage,* WNET-TV, New York 1974.

On PAIK: Books—*Nam June Paik: Mostly Video,* exhibition catalog with essay by Hohn G. Hanhardt, Tokyo 1984; *Vom Verschwinden der Ferne (Telekommunikation und Kunst)* by Edith Decker and Peter Weibel, 1990; *Nam June Paik* by Yongwoo Lee, Seoul 1992; *In the Spirit of Fluxus,* exhibition catalog, edited by Janet Jenkins, Minneapolis 1993; *Nam June Paik: eine DATA base,* exhibition catalog, Venice 1993; *Nam June Paik: Video-Sculpture,* exhibition catalog by Lars Movin, Copenhagen 1996; *The Ghost's Machine—Landscape Reclaimed: New Approaches to an Artistic Tradition,* exhibition catalog by Nancy Princenthal, 1996. **Articles**—''Patricia Sloane Discusses the Work of Nam June Paik'' in *Art and Artists* (London), March 1972; ''Video Art's Guru'' by Grace Glueck in the *New York Times,* 7 May 1982; ''Nam June Paik's TV Answer to George Orwell'' by Grace Glueck in *International Herald Tribune,* 31 December 1984; ''The Luminous Image: Video Installations at the Stedelijk Museum, Amsterdam'' by S. Rice in *Afterimage,* December 1984; ''Electra Myths: Video, Modernism, Postmodernism'' by Katherine Dieckmann in *Art Journal,* Fall 1985; ''The Muse in the Tube'' by Thomas Hoving in *Connoisseur,* January 1987; ''Nam June Paik at Holly Solomon Gallery'' by Walter Robinson in *Art in America,* June 1987; ''The Last Great Modernist—Paik's Peak'' by J. Apple in *Artweek,* March 1988; ''Father of Video Art'' by Carl

Hayward in *Rice,* February 1988; ''Video Art and Colonialism; an Other and Its Others'' by S. Cubitt in *Screen,* Autumn 1989; ''Nam June Paik'' by Jean-Paul Fargier in *Art Press,* 1989; ''La Fee Electronique'' by E. Motz in *Kunstwerk,* December 1989; ''Standing Up to Sunshine (Nam June Paik's Permanent Outdoor Video Installation)'' in *ARTnews,* December 1990; ''Nam June Paik'' by Chris Dercon in *Forum International,* November/December 1990; ''Tuning in to a Unique Public Work'' by Cathy Curtis in *Los Angeles Times,* 22 June 1993; ''Nam June Paik: Video's Body'' by Kenneth E. Silver in *Art in America,* November 1993; ''Art That Turns Television Frogs into Princes'' by Vicki Goldberg in *New York Times,* 31 July 1994; ''Paik Unplugged'' by Paul Gardner in *Art News,* January 1995; ''Art in Review: Nam June Paik's America'' by Charles Hagen in *New York Times,* 26 May 1995; ''Report from Munster: Open City'' by Ulf Erdman Ziegler in *Art in America,* September 1997; ''A Video Visionary'' by Diane M. Bolz in *Smithsonian Magazine,* October 1997; ''Mastering the Millenium: Art of the Americas'' in *Art Nexus,* August-October 1999; ''Vast Wasteland? Fast-Paced Land'' by Grace Glueck in *New York Times,* 11 February 2000.

* * *

In the big exhibition next to the ''Bachelor Machines'' show on the Zattere quay in Venice for the baby *Biennale* of 1975, the fantastic Nam June Paik TV performance was not only the most amusing (funny?) activity, it was also the best put-together. Its connection with the ''Proposte per il Mulino Stucky'' (a proper use for warehouse property which was lying empty and rotten) was not easily apparent, but there are more things in Heaven and Earth. . . .

Perhaps the solution to Paik's ubiquitous appeal lies in the paradoxical fact that he does not like television, does not even own a set (at least he did not have one when he was intriguing visitors to the audio-video tent in the park in Sonsbeek in 1971). His attitude to the whole communications systems is summed up in the big part he plays as creator of international hook-up programmes—coupled with his inventive skill that has even led to the magic button that puts the person who presses it on the screen.

Of Korean origin, with university background in Tokyo, Munich, and Freiburg, Paik is a good example of the contemporary artist-cum-technician. His concern with screen imagery is to treat it as might a painter. What *is* can be given new existence and can join phantasies that do not exist. A sequence can be interrupted, upended. Sound is not constant, it can have its character entirely altered, or it can be silenced, or it can dance up and down in volume. Voice, music, clatter can all be mingled or transposed. The range of colour variations and exchanges seems limitless.

These desecriptive facts about Paik's work are not offered to suggest that they are unique. Others have made similar experiments. Paik differs from them because his standards are so high and when there is something to be discovered, he often discovers it before anyone else.

His abilities are so great that even established authority (in California, for instance) is nervous about his scope. Apprehensive, yes—but short on action because the person with whom they are concerned is too valuable to the medium professionally to be even lightly harassed.

Paik's finished works are one thing, but he is a worker of great fluidity. At Sonsbeek, for example, he used visitors to the audio-video tent as raw material. They saw themselves on screen and they saw their normal appearance could be set in motion by the artist. Nor did everything with which they were concerned stay in Sonsbeek. The 1971 festival in Holland, called with typical Dutch language-play *Beyond Lawn and Order,* stretched nationwide so that the images thrown upon Paik's screens could be picked up all over the country.

—Sheldon Williams

In recent years, Nam June Paik has indulged his fascination for robots, characteristically mocking and sentimentalizing 1950s-era forecasts about the world of the future. His cathode tube experiments now superseded by MTV's occasional vanguard trickery, the artist has been culturally validated even as he has passed undeniabl—if more quickly than could have been predicted—into nostalgia. The passing of his closest associates, including John Cage, Joseph Beuys, and longtime collaborator Charlotte Moorman, has given Paik the occasion to celebrate their legacies in characteristically whimsical tributes.

—Mark Swartz

Paik's work has continued to evolve. Such works as his 1986 ''Family of Robots'' and other similarly kinetic sculptures gave way to increasingly more elaborate video installations. Shifts in technologies and global culture have fueled Paik's work more directly since 1990, and his reputation has remained solid. In 1993, Paik's ''Artist as Nomad'' won First Prize for Best Pavilion at the Venice Biennale.

His 1995 work ''Megatron/Matrix'' continued his tradition in making connections between the East and West. Consisting of 215 video monitors with constantly changing laser-disc images, the work consumed an enormous wall in the National Museum of American Art for months. The massive scale of the installation enabled the viewer to see the video images as much more than a stack of televisions. Instead, the work functioned as a living mosaic, its kaleidoscopic imagery propelled by computers behind the wall. Alternately many different images and one large image composed of individual puzzle parts, ''Megatron/Matrix'' is an installation of amazing impact.

In 1998, Paik was honored with the Kyoto Prize in Japan. The following year, *Art News* magazine named him among ''The Century's Most Influential Artists.'' Paik received further accolades when the Guggenheim presented a retrospective of his work, *The Worlds of Nam June Paik,* in 2000.

—Tammy A. Kinsey

PALADINO, Mimmo

Nationality: Italian. **Born:** Paduli, near Benevento, 18 December 1948. **Career:** Painter: lives and works in Benevento and Milan; founding member of Trans-avantgarde movement, 1978. **Agents:** Waddington Galleries, 2 Cork Street, London WIX 1PA, England. **Address:** Largo La Foppa 5, 20121 Milan, Italy.

Individual Exhibitions:

1976 Nuovi Strumenti, Brescia, Italy
1977 De Ambrogi-Cavellini, Milan
Galleria dell'Ariete, Milan

Galleria Lucio Amelio, Naples
1978 Galleria Persano, Turin
Galerie Paul Maenz, Cologne
Galleria Franco Toselli, Milan
Galerie Tanit, Munich
1979 Galleria Lucio Amelio, Naples
Galerie Anne Marie Verna, Zurich (with Francesco Clemente and Nicola de Maria)
Centre d'Art Contemporain, Geneva
Galerie t'Venster, Rotterdam
Galleria Mazzoli, Moderna, Italy
Art and Project, Amsterdam
1980 Galleria dell'Ariete, Milan
Galleria Persano, Turin
Galerie Paul Maenz, Cologne
Galerie Anne Marie Verna, Zurich
Kunstverein, Karlsruhe
Marian Goodman Gallery, New York
Galleria Franco Toselli, Milan
1981 Galleria Lucio Amelio, Naples
Galleria Mario Diacono, Rome
Galleria d'Arte Moderna, Bologna
Galerie Bischofberger, Zurich
Galerie Daniel Templon, Paris
Marian Goodman Gallery, New York
Galleria Franco Toselli, Milan
Galerie Tanit, Munich
121 Art Galerie, Antwerp
Zeichnungen 1976–1981, Kunstmuseum, Basel (toured West Germany and Denmark, 1981–82)
1982 Waddington Galleries, London
Kunstmuseum, Wuppertal, West Germany
Marian Goodman Gallery, New York
Galerie Buchmann, St. Gallen, Switzerland
1983 Galleria Medusa, Capodistria, Italy
Galerie Engstrom, Stockholm
Galerie Thomas, Munich
Sperone-Westwater, New York
1984 Waddington Galleries, London
Musée St. Pierre d'Art Contemporain, Lyon, France
Galerie Thaddeus Ropac, Salzburg, Austria
1985 Galerie Michael Haas, West Berlin
Galleria Lucio Amelio, Naples
Kunstnernes Hus, Oslo
Galerie Holtmann, Cologne
1986 James Corcoran Gallery, Los Angeles
Sperone-Westwater, New York
Waddington Galleries, London
Galerie Bernd Kluser, Munich
Galeria Comicos, Lisbon
1987 Galleria Franco Toselli, Milan
Fuji Television Gallery, Tokyo
Moderne Galerie Rupertinum, Salzburg, Austria
Kulturhaus, Graz, Austria
Galerie Thaddeus Ropac, Salzburg, Austria
1988 Galleria Gian Enzo Sperone, Rome
Galerie Beaubourg, Paris
1989 Palais des Beaux-Arts, Brussels
Sperone Westwater, New York (catalog)
Daniel Templon Gallery, Paris (catalog)
1990 Galerie Hadrien Thomas, Paris
Mimmo Paladino: Dessins 1973–1990, Palais des Beux-Arts, Charleroi, Belgium (catalog)
1991 Sperone Westwater Gallery, New York
Prints 1987–1991, Waddington Graphics, London (catalog)
1992 *Gravuras,* Museu de Arte de Sao Paulo, Brazil
Waddington Gallery, London
1994 Museu de Arte Contemporaneo de Monterrey, Mexico
Emilio Mazzoni, Modena, Italy
Daniel Templon Gallery, Paris
Waddington Galleries, London (catalog)
Galerie Thaddaeus Ropac, Salzburg (catalog)
Galleria Arte 92, Milan (catalog)
1995 *Mimmo Paladino: Painting and Sculpture,* Sperone Westwater, New York (catalog)
Waddington Galleries (catalog)
Bernd Klüser Gallery, Munich
1996 Diego Aragona Pignatelli Cortes Museum, Naples
Stables of the Royal Palace, Naples
Piazza del Plebiscito, Naples
1997 *La Montagna de Sale,* Waddington Galleries, London (catalog)
Mimmo Paladino, Musées de Strasbourg, Palais Rohan, Strasbourg
1998 Artcore Gallery, Toronto
1999 South London Gallery, England
Venice Design Art Gallery, Venice (catalog)
2000 *Works on Paper by Mimmo Paladino: Inspired by the Poetry of P.K. Page,* Instituto Italiano di Cultura, Toronto and Vancouver

Selected Group Exhibitions:

1975 *Da Mezzo giorno al Tramonto,* Villa Colpicelli, Naples
1977 *Fotografia come Analisi,* Teatro Gobetti, Turin
1978 *International Drawing Triennale,* Warsaw
1979 *Europa '79,* Kunstmuseum, Stuttgart
1980 *Die Enthauptete Hand: 100 Zeichnungen aus Italien,* Kunstverein, Bonn
1981 *A New Spirit in Painting,* Royal Academy of Arts, London
1982 *Documenta 7,* Kassel, West Germany
1984 *Det Italienska Transavantgardet,* Lunds Konsthall, Sweden
1985 *The European Iceberg,* Art Gallery of Ontario, Toronto
1987 *Avant-Garde in the Eighties,* Los Angeles County Museum of Art
1990 *After the Question of Faith,* University Art Museum, California State University, Long Beach
1992 *The Italian Transavantgarde: Sandro Chia, Mimmo Paladino, Francesco Clemente, Enzo Cucchi,* Ho-Am Art Gallery, Korea (catalog)
1995 *The Muse?,* Galerie Thaddaeus Ropac, Paris (catalog)
Noa Noa, Galleria In Arco, Torino (catalog)
1996 *Contemporary Italian Painting,* Galerie Kaess-Weiss, Stuttgart
1997 *Born of Clay II: The Ceramic Figure Since 1920,* Garth Clark Gallery, New York
Transavanguardia, Museum Würth, Künzelsau-Gaisbach (catalog)
1998 *Enzo Cucchi, Mimmo Paladino: Opere Su Carta,* Galleria Cesarea, Genova (catalog)

1999 *I Dormienti,* Roundhouse, London (with Brian Eno) (catalog)

Publications:

By PALADINO: Books—*Mimmo Paladino Drawings; Poems by Thomas Tidholm,* Stockholm 1991; *Mimmo Paladino,,* with Norman Rosenthal, Milan 1993; *Ulysses: 16 June 1904,* Munich 1995; *Paladino,* Milan 1995. **Articles**—''Vincitorio intervista Mimmo Paladino'' in *L'Expresso* (Milan), July 1981.

On PALADINO: Books—*Fotografia come Analisi,* exhibition catalog by Mirella Bandini, Turin 1977; *The Italian Trans-Avantgarde* by Achille Bonito Oliva, Milan 1980; *En De Re* by Achille Bonito Oliva, Modena, Italy 1980; *Mimmo Paladino,* exhibition catalog by Michael Schwarz, Andreas Franzke and Wolgang Max Faust, Karlsruhe 1980; *Mimmo Paladino,* exhibition catalog by Mario Diacono, Rome 1981; *Mimmo Paladino Zeichnungen 1976–1981,* exhibition catalog by Jean-Christophe Ammann and others, Basel 1981 (includes bibliography); *Mimmo Paladino,* exhibition catalog, Wuppertal, West Germany 1982; *Mimmo Paladino: Works on Paper,* exhibition catalog with texts by Otto Breicha, Dieter Koepplin and others, Salzburg 1987. **Articles**—''Mimmo Paladino: 30 Horses, a Watch, and a White Mountain'' by Jonathan Turner in *Artnews,* vol. 91, March 1992; ''Mimmo Paladino: Portrait by Armin Linke'' by *Du,* no. 1, January 1994.

* * *

The works of Mimmo Paladino rely predominantly on thin strokes, essential even when the formal elaboration is very dense. The symbols in his paintings are intimate, of the greatest intensity, containing the essence of Mediterranean culture. His blue has a sense of depth, as do his black, yellow or red, which move us to silence.

Paladino expresses an idea of living, inherent Grecianness, an existential condition that only a man of the south possesses. Such an idea, born as it is of the meeting of different cultures, leads naturally enough to an eclectic activity. With more vigour and sensibility than others, he has been able to restore art to such remote themes as death, the infinite, longing; as the ego that looks at itself in the mirror to read the id there; the mystery. The view of the world derived from this, while markedly subjective, is a broad one; in the end things are seen to be internal to an organic whole. His Grecianness thus becomes evident in his presentation of the *single whole;* man, nature and depth coincide, and the whole combines to show a complex image of life as a perceptible presence. Thus in these works death, in its tragic essence, tends to reinforce its opposite by being presented as confirmation of the fact that the unfathomable mystery of life still persists.

A mysterious wisdom lies at the origin of the object of art. Paladino has shown that he possesses that wisdom, in creating a language that appears in its universal form, of symbols freed from the classical categories of reading. Symbol and metaphors are transformed in order to attend the Sacred Rite undisturbed; skeleton figures are present in silence at the coitus of reason with the lost sense.

Paladino has given substance to the expression of a free eclecticism which restores to the physical act of painting and drawing, as a poetic phenomenon internal to the crisis of reason, a poetry that desires neither to cure nor to create crises. In its appearance the work refutes any scientific approach, in that everything is restored to a pristine, uncompleted, gesture; phantasms, enigmatic presences, in every case presences, declare their existence within the system of contemporary troubles.

—Demetrio Paparoni

PALAZUELO, Pablo

Nationality: Spanish. **Born:** Madrid, 1916. **Education:** Studied architecture at the Escuela Superior de Bellas Artes, Madrid, and the School of Arts and Crafts, Oxford, 1933–36; studied lithography at the Ecole des Beaux-Arts, Paris. **Career:** Painter, Madrid 1939–1947, Paris, 1947–63, and Madrid, since 1963; produced first purely abstract works, Paris 1948; sculptor, Paris 1954, 1962–63; in Madrid, since 1963. Member, with Lara, Lago, Valdivieso, Guerrero and Olmeda, Grup El Paso, Madrid, 1945–47. **Awards:** Study-Travel grant to Paris, Institut Francais, Madrid, 1947; Kandinsky Award, Paris 1952; Carnegie Prize, 1958; Purchase Prize, *International Graphics Exhibition,* Ljubljana, 1969. **Agents:** Galeria Soledad Lorenzo, Orfila 5, 28010 Madrid, Spain. **Address:** Garcia de Paredes 78, Madrid, Spain.

Individual Exhibitions:

1948 Galerie Denisé Rene, Paris
Art Gallery of Ontario, Toronto
1955 Galerie Maeght, Paris
1958 Galerie Maeght, Paris
1963 Galerie Maeght, Paris
1966 Galeria Juana Mordo, Madrid
1968 City Art Museum, St. Louis
Kunstverein, West Berlin
Louisiana Museum, Humlebaek, Denmark
Museum Boymans-van Beuningen, Rotterdam
University of Puerto Rico
1969 Konsthall, Lund, Sweden
1970 Galerie Maeght, Paris
1972 Musée des Beaux-Arts, La Chaux de Fonds, Switzerland
Olbilder Gouachen, Galerie Maeght, Zurich
1973 Galerie Iolas-Velasco, Madrid
1977 Galeria Maeght, Barcelona
Galeria Theo, Madrid
1978 Galerie Maeght, Paris
Galerie Maeght, Zurich
1979 Galerie Art in Progress, Munich
1981 Galeria Theo, Madrid
Herning Kunstmuseum, Angligarden, near Copenhagen (with Pol Bury)
1984 Galeria Maeght, Madrid and Barcelona
1985 Galeria Theo y Sala Celini, Madrid
1986 Galerie Maeght-Lelong, Paris
1987 Galeria Theo, Madrid
Museo de Arte Contemporaneo, Madrid
1991 Galeria Soledad Lorenzo, Madrid
1993 Museo de Bellas Artes de Bilbao
1994 Banco Zaragozano, Spain
Palacio Daralhorra and Palacio de los Condes de Gabia, Granada
Galeria Soledad Lorenzo, Madrid

1995 *Palazuelo,* Museo Nacional Centro de Arte Reina Sofía, Madrid (retrospective) (catalog)
1997 *Palazuelo: Esculturas y Gouaches,* Galería Soledad Lorenzo, Madrid
2000 *Pablo Palazuelo: Virtus Marin,* Junta de Andalucía, Consejería de Cultura, Seville (catalog)

Selected Group Exhibitions:

1945 *Escuela Jovene de Madrid,* Galeria Buchholz, Madrid
1948 *Salon de Mai,* Paris
1952 *Painters d'Aujourd'hui à Paris,* Kunsthaus, Zurich
1954 *Young European Painters,* Guggenheim Museum, New York
1959 *13 Peintres Espagnols Actuels,* Musée des Arts Décoratifs, Paris
1966 *Grandes et Jeunes d'Aujourd'hui,* Musée d'Art Moderne de la Ville, Paris
1968 *L'Art Vivant,* Fondation Maeght, St. Paul-de-Vence, France
1975 *Spanish Contemporary Painting,* New York Art Center
1987 *Espacious Urbanos,* Fundacio Miro, Barcelona
1994 *Artistas Españoles,* Museo Nacional Centro de Arte Reina Sofía, Madrid
1996 *Black is a Color,* Galerie Maeght, Barcelona
1998 *Plural Territories: 10 Years of the Testimonial Collection, 1987–97,* Fundacion ''La Caixa,'' Madrid (catalog)

Collections:

Museo de la Castellana, Madrid; Fundacion Juan March, Madrid; Bankinter, Banco de Santander, Madrid; Museo de Vitoria, Spain; Museo de Arte Abstracto Espanol, Cuenca, Spain; Kunsthaus, Zurich; Musée des Beaux-Arts, La Chaux de Fonds, Switzerlands; Fondation Maeght, Saint Paul-de-Vence, France; Guggenheim Museum, New York; Carnegie Museum, Pittsburgh; Museo Nacional Centro de Arte Reina Sofía, Madrid.

Permanent Public Installations:

Lauda II, Barajas Airport, Spain; Parque de España, Barcelona; Torre Picasso, Madrid.

Publications:

By PALAZUELO: Book—*Palazuelo,* with Claude Esteban, Paris 1980, Madrid 1981; *Visión y Geometría: Una Conversación con Kevin Power,* Granada 1995; *Escritos. Conversaciones,* Murcia 1998. **Articles—**''Poems'' in *Trece de Nieve* (Madrid), no. 7, 1963; ''Cles pour des Espaces Inextricables'' in *Chroniques de l'Art Vivant* (Paris), April 1970; ''Notes de Travail'' in *Derrière le Miroir* (Paris), no, 184, 1970; ''La Geografia Visionaria de Luis Canelo'' in *Luis Canelo,* exhibition catalog, Madrid 1974; ''En el Camino de Grodillo'' in *Luis Grodillo,* exhibition catalog, Barcelona 1976; ''Materia, Forma y Lenguaje Universal,'' interview with Santiago Amon, in *Revista de Occidente* (Madrid), no. 7, 1976. **Illustrated books—** *Lunariae,* with poems by Max Holzer, Paris 1972; *L'Abtalif Absolu,* with text by Michel Couturier, Paris 1976; *Soldadesca,* with text be José Miguel Ullan, Valencia 1978; *Ancres,* with texts by Pierre Reverdy, Paris 1978; *Exercises,* with text by Jean Daive, Paris 1980.

On PALAZUELO: Books and catalogs—*Spanish Art Now* by William Dyckes, Madrid 1966; *Modern Paintings, Drawings and Sculpture Collected by Louise and Joseph Pulitzer, volume 3,* with introduction by Agnes Moran, Cambridge, Massachusetts 1971; *Pablo Palazuelo,* exhibiton catalog, with text by Paul Seylaz, La Chaux de Fonds, Switzerland 1972; *Palazuelo: Olbilder Gouachen,* exhibition catalog with texts by Max Holzer, Zurich 1972; *Palazuelo,* exhibition catalog with texts by Max Holzer and Julian Gallego, Madrid 1973; *Palazuelo,* exhibition catalog with texts by Santiago Ammon and Daniel Giralt-Miracle, Barcelona 1977; *Palazuelo,* exhibition catalog with text by Jose-Miguel Ullan and others, Madrid 1977; *Palazuelo: Sculptures, Peintures,* exhibition catalog with text by Max Holzer, Zurich 1978; *Palazuelo: Pinturas, Esculturas y Gouaches,* exhibition catalog with introduction by Miguel Logrono, Madrid 1987.

PANAMARENKO

Nationality: Belgian. **Born:** Antwerp, 1940. **Education:** Koninklijke Academic voor Schone Kunsten, Antwerp, 1955–1960; National Hoger Instituut, Antwerp, 1962–64. **Military Service:** Served in the Belgian Army,1961–62. **Career:** Independent artist, Antwerp since 1964; first happenings, 1964; first aeroplanes, 1967; first airship construction, 1969; work on magnetic fields and magnetic airship, since 1977. Editor, with Hugo Heyrman, Bernd Lohaus and Wout Vercammen, *Happening News,* Antwerp, 1964–65; founder, with Anny de Decker, Bernd Lohaus and Hugo Heyrman, Wide White Space Gallery, Antwerp, 1966; member, Vrije Aktie Groep Antwerpen (V.A.G.A.), Antwerp, 1968. **Awards:** J.C. van Lanschot Prize for Sculpture in the Low Countries, Ghent, 1998. **Agent:** Galerie Christine et Isy Brachot, rue Villa Hermosa 8, 1000 Brussels, Belgium; Ronald Feldman Fine Arts, 31 Mercer Street, New York, New York, 10013. **Address:** Bierkorfstraat 2, 2000 Antwerp, Belgium.

Individual Exhibitions:

1966 Wide White Space Gallery, Antwerp (and regularly, until 1976)
1967 Galerie Orez, The Hague
1968 Kunstakademie, Dusseldorf
1969 John Gibson Gallery, New York
Galerie René Block, West Berlin
Städtische Museum, Mönchengladbach, West Germany
Galerie Konrad Fischer, Dusseldorf
Galerie Rudolf Zwirner, Cologne
1970 *Boezem/Panamarenko,* Stedelijk Van Abbemuseum, Edindhoven, Netherlands
1972 Galerie Onnasch, Cologne
Automobile und Flugmaschinen, Kunstmuseum, Lucerne (toured West Germany)
Situation Gallery, London
1973 Musée d'Art Moderne de la Ville, Paris
1974 Stedelijk Van Abbemuseum, Eindhoven, Netherlands
1975 Zeeuws Museum, Middelburg, Netherlands
Galerie Seriaal, Amsterdam
1976 Museum van Hedendaagse Kunst, Ghent
Galerie Bama, Paris

Galerie Gabriel von Loeper, Hamburg
1977 *Flugobjekte und Zeichnungen,* Kunsthalle, Basel
Musée d'Art et d'Industrie, St. Etienne, France
Umbilly I, Stedelijk Van Abbemuseum, Eindhoven, Netherlands
1980 Nationalgalerie, West Berlin (travelled to the Rijksmuseum Kröller-Müller, Otterlo, Netherlands, and the Palais des Beaux-Arts, Brussels)
1981 Centre Georges Pompidou, Paris
Technisches Hogeschool, Eindhoven, Netherlands
1982 Gemeentemuseum, The Hague
Haus der Kunst, Munich
1984 Gemeentelijke Van Reekum Galerij, Apeldoorn, Netherlands
Musée d'Art Moderne du Nord, Villeneuve d'Ascq, France
Fundacio Joan Miro, Barcelona
1985 Frans Halsmuseum, Haarlem, Netherlands
De Vleeshal, Middelburg, Netherlands
Kunstverein, Friedrichshafen, West Germany
1987 Parc de La Villete, Paris
1989 *Panamarenko,* Galerie Isy Brachot, Paris (catalog)
Rétrospective 1965–1985, Museum van Hedendaagse Kunst, Antwerp, Belgium (catalog)
1990 *L'Avion,* Musée des Beaux-Arts, Chapelle de l'Oratoire, Nantes, France
1991 *Panamarenko,* Kunstverein Hannover (catalog)
1992 National Museum of Osaka, Japan (retrospective)
1993 Ronald Feldman Fine Arts, New York
Cars & Other Stuff, Galerie Tokoro, Tokyo (catalog)
1995 Galerie Christine e Isy Brachot, Brussels, Belgium
Become Form, Kunsthalle, Bern, Switzerland
Mutiples: 1966–1994, Galerie Jamar, Antwerp (catalog)
Les Constructions du Ciel 1900–1958 & Panamarenko, Foundation pour l'Architecture, Brussels (catalog)
Expérimentations, Centre de Création Contemporaine, Tours, France
1997 Galerie Krief, Paris
1998 *Panamarenko: La Grande Exposition des Soucoupes Volantes,* Fondation Cartier pour l'Art Contemporain, Paris (retrospective) (catalog)
2000 *Orbit,* Dia Center for the Arts, New York
Panamarenko: Hovering, Floating, Flying and Lying Down, Hayward Gallery, London (also Museum Jean Tinguely, Basel) (retrospective) (catalog)
2001 *Panamarenko,* Stedelijk Museum voor Actuele Kunst, Ghent (catalog)

Selected Group Exhibitions:

1969 *When Attitudes Become Form,* Kunsthalle, Berne (toured Europe)
1970 *Salon des Galeries-Pilotes,* Musée Cantonal des Beaux-Arts, Lausanne, Switzerland
1971 *Sonsbeek 71,* Sonsbeek Park, Arnhem, Netherlands
1972 *Documenta,* Kassel, West Germany (and 1977)
1973 *Bilder, Objekte, Filme, Konzepte,* Städische Galerie im Lenbachhaus, Munich
1974 *Nativitat der Maschine,* Kunstverein, Frankfurt
1975 *Funkties van Tekeningen,* Rijksmuseum Kröller-Müller, Otterlo, Netherlands
1976 *Art 7, '76,* Kunstmesse, Basel
1982 *Vergangenheit-Gegenwart-Zukunft,* Württembergischer Kunstverein, Stuttgart
1983 *Bienal de Sao Paulo,* Brazil
1990 *Biennial,* Venice, Italy
1991 *Metafor Och Materia,* Moderna Museet, Stockholm (catalog)
1996 *Comme un Oiseau,* Fondation Carier, Paris

Collections:

Kaiser-Wilhelm-Museum, Krefeld, West Germany; Ministry of Culture, Brussels; Fonds Regional d'Art Contemporain du Nord/Pas de Calais, Lille.

Publications:

By PANAMARENKO: Books—*De Mechanism van de Zwaartekracht,* Antwerp 1975; *Panamarenko: The Complete Works, 1963–1992,* with Hans Thays, Ghent 1992; *Panamarenko: Toy Model of Space (The Sun and the Stars),* Antwerp 1993; *Panamarenko,* with Michel Baudson, Paris 1996; *For Clever Scholars, Astronomers and Doctors,* with text by Jon Tompson, Gent 2001. **Articles**—"Panamarenko: Portrait by Armin Linke" in *Du,* no. 1, January 1994.

On PANAMARENKO: Books—*Boezem/Panamarenko,* exhibition catalog with text by Jan Leering, Eindhoven, Netherlands, 1970; *Panamarenko: Automobile und Flugmaschinen,* exhibition catalog with text by Jean-Christophe Ammann, Jürgen Harten, L. Schirmer and others, Lucerne 1972; *Panamarenko,* exhibition catalog with texts by Suzanne Page and Jean-Christophe Ammann, Paris 1973; *Panamarenko: Flugobjekte und Zeichnungne,* exhibition catalog with texts by Werner von Mutzenbecher, Felix Philipp Ingold and Dietrich Helms, Basel 1977; *Panamarenko,* exhibition folder with texts by Bernard Ceysson and Anne Dary, St. Etienne, France 1977; *Panamarenko: Umbilly I,* exhibition catalog with texts by Paul Hefting and Felix Philipp Ingold, Eindhoven, Netherlands 1977; *Panamarenko,* exhibition catalog with text by Rudi Oxenaar, Lucius Grisebach, Piet van Daalin and others, West Berlin 1980; *Vergangeheit-Gegenwart-Zukunft,* exhibition catalog, with an introduction by Tilman Osterwold, Stuttgart 1982; *Panamarenko: Arbeiten 1966–1985,* exhibition catalog with texts by Wolfgang Rech, Bernd Wiedmann and others, Friedrichshafen 1985; *Panamarenko: A Book by Hans Theys,* Brussels 1992; *Landschaft: Die Spur des Sublimen* by Hans-Werner Schmidt and Ute Riese, Bielefeld 1998. **Articles**—"Panamarenko's Incredible Flying Machines" by Linda Goddard in *Art Newspaper,* vol. 11, no. 101, March 2000; "Flights of Fancy" by Deborah Schultz in *Art Monthly,* no. 234, March 2000. **Video**—*Panamarenko: Portrait en Son Absence* by Claudio Pazienza, 2000.

* * *

Panamarenko began his art career as a student in Antwerp's Koninklijke Academy of Fine Arts. Few of his colleagues and tutors can have imagined the complex and weaving course to which his training would lead him.

This elusive artist, so varied in his fabrication of "objects" and his adventures with assemblages—taking time off to co-edit *Happening News* (which, of course, included information about his own happenings), and—above all—his investigations into magnetism, first its fields and later his discovery of its application to magnetic airships . . . such description of the ways and inspirations of such an artist can only help to suggest a Galileo-like stature.

Panamarenko once wrote: ''I proudly present my new Aeroplane prototype. From different recent inventions and improvements, a new combination is made. The safest, economic and low-cost plane ever designed. It is also very beautiful.'' He then goes on to give all measurements, materials involved, performance, including lift-off, range and speed. And—classic provision—you don't have to be a pilot to fly it.

Panamarenko is an artist searching for unexpected associations of images, neo-realist conceptions as exemplified in his strange (and detailed) lithographs, such as *The Aero Modeller*—his translation from plane to airship.

An oustanding oddity in the world of contemporary art, he is one of those artist usually (or, at least, frequently) included in important international exhibitions such as *Metamorphosis of the Object,* for example, an enormous museum show, first seen at the Brussels Palace of Fine Arts before its tour of Rotterdam, Berlin, Basel and Paris.

—Sheldon Williams

PANE, Gina

Nationality: French. **Born:** Biarritz, to Italian parents, 24 May 1939; acquired French nationality in 1975. **Education:** Valle del'Orco and Turin primary schools; studied at Ecole de Beaux-Arts, under André Chastel, Paris, 1960–65. **Career:** Lived in Turin, 1944–60; worked as information-processor, IBM, Turin, 1959–60; settled in Paris, 1960; concentrated on painting, lithography and sculpture, Paris 1965–68; abandoned plastic activities, and began first body actions and performances, Turin, 1968; multi-media works, from 1980. Lecturer in painting, Ecole des Beaux-Arts, Le Mans, France, 1980. **Agent:** Galerie Christine et Isy Brachot, 62a Avenue Louise, 1050 Brussels, Belgium. **Died:** Paris, March 1990.

Individual Exhibitions:

1968 Galerie Heller, Paris
Fenestrelle, Turin
Pierres Déplacées, Valle de l'Orco, Italy
Lecture dans un Jardin Potager, Ecos, France
La Peche endeulillé, Galleria LP 220, Turin (travelled to the Galleria Diagramma, Milan)
1969 *Autocritique,* Turin
Work in Progress, Paris
Alignement infini, Deauville, France
Situation Ideale, Ecos, France
Table de Lecture, Turin
Premier Project du Silence, Galleria Franzp, Turin
Deplacements, Ospedale San Giovanni, Turin
Streap-rake, Galleria Franzp, Turin
Desert Traces, Grands et Jeunes, Paris
Palo-Acqua Alta, Galeria Rive Droite, Paris
1970 *Terre Protégée 2,* Turin
Continuation d'un Chemin de Bois, Ury, France
Mon Corps, Ury, France
Semences de Graines de Chanvre, Ury, France
Narcisse, Jarcy, France
Hommage à Yves Klein, Paris
Deuxième Project du Silence, Ury, France
Le Riz, Galerie Rive Droite, Paris
1971 *L'Escalade,* Pane Atelier, Paris
Hommage à un Jeune Droque, Bordeaux
Quatrième Projet du Silence, Musée Galliera, Paris
Nourriture/Actualités TV/Feu, Fregnac, Paris
1972 *Le Lait Chaud,* Boutan, Paris
Lecture d'un Certificat Medical de Madame R.S., Paris
Action Posthume, Paris
Vie-Mort-Reve, Belgrade
Je, Bruges, Belgium
1973 *Autoportrait(s),* Galerie Stadler, Paris
Transfert, Space 640, St. Jeannet, France
Azione Sentimentale, Galleria Diagramma, Milan
1974 *Psyche,* Galerie Stadler, Paris
Death Control, Galerie Diagramma, Basel
Action Melancolique 2 X 2 X 2, Studio Morra, Naples
1975 *Le Corps Presenti,* Galerie Krinzinger, Innsbruck
Discours mou et mat, Galerie de Appel, Amsterdam
Death Control 2, Galerie Stadler, Paris
1976 *La Mise en Action Imagée d'une Sequence: Le Secret,* Galerie Stadler, Paris
Il Caso Numero 2 sul Ring, Galleria Diagramma, Legnano, Italy
Io Mescolo Tutto, Museo d'Arte Moderna, Bologna
1977 *Action Theorique,* Libero Per, Naples
Laure, Galerie Isy Brachot, Brussels
A Hot Afternoon, at Documenta 6, Kassel, West Germany
1978 *Little Journey 1,* Vienna
A Hot Afternoon 2, Galeria Quadrum, Lisbon
Mezzogiorno a Alimena 2, San Francisco Art Institute
Little Journey 2, Los Angeles Institute of Contemporary Art
1979 *Mezzogiorno a Alimena 3,* Centre Georges Pompidou, Paris
Little Journey 3, Goethe Institut, Paris
1980 *Travail d'Action,* Galerie Isy Brachot, Paris
1981 *Partition d'Action/Action de Chasse/C'est la Nuit, Cherie,* Franklin Furnace, New York
Partition d'Action: Petit Voyage Oh! Oh! Oh! en couleurs, Kunstlerhaus Bethanien, Berlin (travelled to GEDOK, Hamburg)
1983 *Partition,* Galerie Arapède, Tours, France
Partition, Galerie Isy Brachot, Paris
1984 *Guerre-Partizioni,* Galleria Marginalia, Turin
1985 Ecole Nationale d'Art Decoratif, Limoges, France
Padiglione d'Arte Contemporanea, Milan
1986 *La Legende dorée,* Musée d'Art Moderne, Villeneuve d'Ascq, France
1987 *Travaux recents,* Galerie Christine et Isy Brachot, Brussels
1988 FIAC Grand Palais, Paris
Galerie Isy Brachot, Paris
1989 Galerie Dutertre, Rennes
Kunst Station, Sankt Peter, Cologne
1990 Palao de la Virrena, Barcelona
Centre d'Art Contemporain, Troyes
Musée d'Art Contemporain, Ferrare

Selected Group Exhibitions:

1975 *Body Works,* Museum of Contemporary Art, Chicago
1977 *L'Art Corporel by Francois Pluchart,* Galerie Isy Brachot, Brussels
1978 *6th Biennale Internazionale della Grafica d'Arte,* Florence
1981 *Typisch Frau,* Galerie Magers, Bonn
1983 *Panorman d'Art Contemporain en France 1960–80,* Centre Culturel, Coutances, France
1985 *Ceci n'est pas une photographie,* Fonds Régionale d'Art Contemporain, Aquitaine, France
1987 *Les Années 70—Les Années Memoire,* Centre d'Art Contemporain, Meymac, France
1988 *Icônes,* Musée de la Castre, Cannes
1993 *Différentes Natures,* Galerie de l'Arcade La Defense, Paris
1994 *Hors Limites,* Musée d'Art Moderne de la Ville, Paris

Collections:

Centre Georges Pompidou, Paris; Centre National d'Art Contemporain, Paris; Musée d'Art Contemporain, Epinal, France; Musée d'Art Contemporain, Villeneuve d'Ascq, France; Fondation Camille, Paris; Fonds Régionale d'Art Contemporain, in Bordeaux, Lyon and Toulouse, France.

Publications:

By PANE: Films—*Solitrac,* 1968; *Parcours Identification,* with Denis Gherbrand, 1970; *Action/Vie/Mort/Reve,* 1972; *Action Melancolique,* with Anne Marchand 1974; *Death Control,* with Francoise Masson, 1975. **Videotapes—***Nourriture/Feu/A,* 1971; *Le Lait Chaud,* with Daniel Orsi, 1972; *Autoportraits,* 1973; *Psyche,* 1974; *Discours mou et mat,* 1975; *Mezzigiorno a Alimena,* 1978; *Little Journey,* 1978.

On PANE: Books—*Art en France, une nouvelle generation* by Jean Clair, Paris 1973; *L'Art actuel en France* by Anne Tronche, Paris, 1974; *Body-Art et storie simil* by Lea Vergine, Milan 1974; *L'Arte moderna—La Body Art* by Gillo Dorfles, Milan 1977; *Gina Pane,* exhibition catalog with texts by L. Vergine and G. Manganelli, Milan 1984; *Gina Pane: La legende dorée,* exhibition catalog with texts by Gilbert Perlein and Michel Baudson, Lille 1986; *D'après cette peau que la peinture ne peut donner,* exhibition catalog by Jean-Pierre Van Tieghem, Paris 1988; *Gina Pane: La lucidez implacable* by M. L. Borras, Paris 1990. **Articles—**''Gina Pane'' by Claude Bouyeur in *Les Lettres Francaises* (Paris), May 1971; ''Gina Pane, faire reflechir'' by Bernard Borgeaud in *Pariscope* (Paris), June 1971; ''Gina Pane en Action'' by Claude Bouyeur in *Plaisir de France* (Paris), June 1972; ''Gina Pane'' by J. J. Leveque in *Opus International* (Paris), November 1972; ''La Response sanglante de Gina Pane'' by Francois Pluchart in *Combat* (Paris), January 1973; ''Performance of Concern'' by Effie Stephano in *Art and Artists* (London), April 1973; ''Gina Pane ou la debacle des agnes'' by Bernard Teyssedre in *Opus International* (Paris), no. 51, 1974: ''The TV Aesthetic'' by Tony del Renzio in *Art and Artists* (London), November 1974; ''Feminismus Kunst'' in *Heute Kunst* (Dusseldorf), February/March 1975; ''Short Trip'' by L. Lewis in *Artweek* (Oakland, California), September 1978; ''Gina Pane: Wounded as Sign'' by Helena Kontova in *Flash Art* (Milan); October/November 1979; ''Gina Pane en toute urbanité'' by Anne Dagbert, and ''Gina Pane: l'instant du ravissement'' by J. M. Touratier in *Opus International* (Paris), no. 94, 1984; ''The Reflective Edge: a Female Concept of Self-representation'' by Silvia Eiblmayr in *Performance* (Toronto), no. 55, August-September 1988; ''Oeuvre et artiste'' by L. Albertazzi in *Galeries Magazine,* December/January 1987/88; ''Gina Pane'' by Luc Vezin by *Beaux Arts Magazine* (Paris), no. 63, December 1988; ''Pains and Pleasures: Women's Performance and Body Art in the 90s'' by Katy Deepwell in *Contemporary Visual Arts* (London), no. 14, 1997.

*

My work corresponds to different methods of approach to a material reality and seeks to show that the very manner in which ''we'' experience the body is never completely ''ours'' because all bodily experience reflects the body of others—in other words, My Body in Action is not only in RELATION but RELATION itself.

It is not a surface with a centre (a flat pictute) or a socle (a support of something else), but the whole, the exterior, the interior: the very BODY of the discourse.

It achieves a ''proximity'' because it is not enclosed: its completeness is seen on all sides embracing the theory of significance in the production of re-actuation. One has to understand ''My Body in Action'' not as the skin of a painting enclosing its interior but as a WRAPPING/UNFOLDING bringing back depth to the edge of things.

—Gina Pane

* * *

Before becoming a protagonist of Body Art, Gina Pane was a painter and sculptor. Her painting was, however, growing more and more like an ''action,'' to a point where her pictures were produced by the mark left by brushes let fall on the canvas.

In 1968 came her first actions and installations in nature, like ''The Displaced Stones'' and ''Continuation of a Woodland Path,'' in which the artist existed solely as a performer of simple acts, such as for instance the moving of materials or objects. Her body, which was simply an instrument, became from 1970 the protagonist of her actions.

In one of her first body actions, ''Protected Earth,'' Gina Pane simply shielded a part of the ground with her own body, the ground having been first, in an action with the same title (''Protected Earth, No. 1''), been covered (protected, in the artist's words) with cement objects fastened together with belts. In this phase, therefore, the body passed from being an instrument to being medium of expression.

From 1971 on, the main image in the actions became the wound, which with Gina Pane, unlike other more radical Body Art artists, was not only something personal, a psycho-physical act, but also a sign ''through which I can communicate the loss of strength . . . a gesture of fracture and breaking.''

After some actions concentrating purely on the gesture of wounding herself, from 1972 this action became only one element in a spectacle of growing richness and complexity, both visually and in its content, full of metaphysical and imaginary references. A small paper boat might serve to suggest the idea of travel, the wound might become an act of magic, as it did for the doctor-healers in ancient Greece, who inflicted on their own bodies the same wounds that they wished to heal.

At the same time Gina Pane still expressed herself by other means, such as photography, objects, drawing, and video, which represent other aspects of her actions.

From the later years come the musical scores painted for the performances. These are paintings composed of big panels with scenes from an imaginary story, which have to be acted by the performers, not now by the artist. The performers in this case become simply actors, instruments to create a living image.

—Helena Kontova

PAOLINI, Giulio

Nationality: Italian. **Born:** Genoa, 5 November 1940. **Career:** Independent artist, since 1964; lives and works in Turin. Produced costumes and scenic designs for *Bruto II,* Turin, 1969; *Manfred,* Turin, *Colloquio con Malcolm X,* Genoa, and *Atene Anno Zero,* Turin, 1970; *Laborninthus II,* Genoa, 1971; *Hierapolis,* Turin 1983; *Rosenists,* West Berlin, 1984; *Il Combattimento di Tancredie e Clorinda,* Turin, 1985. **Awards:** Television Scenography Prize, RAI Television, Rome, 1971; Premio Fontana, 1975; DAAD Fellowship, West Berlin, 1981; Chevalier dans l'Ordre des Arts et des Lettres, Paris, 1995; Premio Trigon, 1995; Accademico di San Luca, Classe degli Accademici Corrispondenti Pittori, 2000; Premio Koinè per l'Arte (Premio alla carriera), Verona, 2000. **Agent:** Marian Goodman Gallery, 24 West 57th Street, New York, New York 10019, U.S.A. **Address:** Piazza Vittorio Veneto 10, 10123 Turin, Italy.

Individual Exhibitions:

1964 Galleria La Salita, Rome
1965 Galleria Notizie, Turin
1966 Galleria dell'Ariete, Milan
1967 Sala delle Colonne, Teatro Stabile, Turin
Una Poesia, Libreria Stampatori, Turin
Galleria del Leone, Venice
Galleria Christian Stein, Turin
1968 Libreria dell'Oca, Rome
Galleria Notizie, Turin
1969 Galleria de Nieubourg, Milan
Una Copia della Luce, Studio La Tartaruga, Rome
Galleria del Leone, Venice
1970 *Vedo,* Qui Arte Contemporanea, Rome (travelled to the Galleria Notizie, Turin)
1971 *Un Quadro,* Galleria dell'Ariete, Milan (travelled to the Galleria La Salita, Rome)
Appolo e Dafne, Libreria Stampatori, Turin (travelled to Studio C, Brescia)
Galerie Paul Maenz, Cologne
1972 Galleria Notizie, Turin
Apoteosi di Omero, Galleria Marilena Bonomo, Bari, Italy, (travelled to the Modern Art Agency, Naples)
Sonnabend Gallery, New York
1973 *Idem,* Galleria Notizie, Turin
Galleria Toselli e Francoise Lambert, Milan
La Doublure, Galleria L'Attico e Sperone Fischer, Rome
Royal College of Art, London
Galerie Annemarie Verna, Zurich
Studio Marconi, Milan
1974 Modern Art Agency, Naples
Museum of Modern Art, New York
Galleriaforma, Genoa
Galerie Paul Maenz, Cologne
Galleria Marilena Bonomo, Bari, Italy
Galleria Il Sole, Bolzano, Italy
1975 *Museo,* Galleria Notizie, Turin
Galerie Annemarie Verna, Zurich
Galerie Art in Progress, Munich
Galerie Paul Maenz, Cologne
Galleria D'Alessandro-Ferranti, Rome
Studio G7, Bologna
Galleria Ferrari, Verona
1976 Samangallery, Genoa
Galleria Multipli, Turin
Studio Marconi, Milan
Galerie Yvon Lambert, Paris
University of Parma
Galleria Area, Florence
Galerie Paul Maenz, Cologne
Banco, Brescia, Italy
1977 Sperone-Westwater-Fischer Gallery, New York
Galerie Annemarie Verna, Zurich
Städtische Museum, Mönchengladbach, West Germany
Lisson Gallery, London
Galerie Paul Maenz, Cologne
Kunstverein, Mannheim
Annali 1961–1976, Galleria Ugo Ferranti, Rome
1978 Museo Diego Aragona Pignatelli Cortes, Naples
Galerie Yvon Lambert, Paris
Galleria Christian Stein, Turin
Galleria Marilena Bonomo, Spoleto, Italy
Galerie Albert Baronian, Brussels
Galleria Mario Diacono, Bologna
Del Bello Intelligible, Musée d'Art Moderne de la Ville, Paris
Galerie Paul Maenz, Paris
1979 Galleria dell'Oca, Rome
Liber Veritatis, Lisson Gallery, London
Galerie Jean et Karen Bernier, Athens
Atto Unico in Tre Quadri, Studio Marconi, Milan
1980 *Pendant,* Galerie Annemarie Verna, Zurich
Stedelijk Museum, Amsterdam (travelled to the Museum of Modern Art, Oxford)
Instituto Nazionale per la Grafica, Rome (with Michelangelo Pistoletto and Patella)
Ritrato dell'Artista come Modello, Galleria Ugo Ferranti, Rome
1981 Galleria Christian Stein, Turin
Hortus Clausus, Kunstmuseum, Lucerne
Galerie Paul Maenz, Cologne
Casa di Lucrezio, Banco, Brescia, Italy
La Caduta di Icaro, Padiglione d'Arte Contemporanea, Milan
Del Bello Intelligibile, Kunsthalle, Bielefeld, West Germany (travelled to the Museum von der Heydt, Wuppertal, West Germany)
Galleria Marilena Bonomo, Bari, Italy (travelled to Galleria Francoise Lambert, Milan)
Raum für Kunst, Hamburg
Nouveau Musée, Lyon-Villeurbanne, France

Laforet Museum, Tokyo
Galerie Yvon Lambert, Paris
1983 Galleria Christian Stein, Turin
Galerie Paul Maenz, Cologne
Galleria Lucrezia De Domizio, Pescara, Italy
1984 Los Angeles Institute of Contemporary Art
Nouveau Musée, Lyon-Villeurbanne, France
Studio Marconi, Milan
Direction Régionale de Culture de Bourgogne, Dijon, France
Giulio Paolini, at the *Festival di due mondi,* Spoleto, Italy
Galerie Annemarie Verna, Zurich
Studio G7, Bologna
1985 Galleria Pieroni, Rome
Galerie Maeght Lelong, Paris
Guggenheim Museum, New York
Pinacoteca Comunale, Ravenna, Italy
Arti Visive, Ravenna, Italy
Art Gallery of Vancouver, British Columbia
Musée d'Art Contemporain, Montreal
Marian Goodman Gallery, New York
Galleria Locus Solus, Genoa, Italy
Galleria Marilena Bonomo, Bari, Italy
1986 Palais des Beaux-Arts, Charleroi, Belgium
Galerie Albert Baronian, Brussels
Galerie Paul Maenz, Cologne
De Vleeshal, Middleburg, Netherlands
Staatsgalerie, Stuttgart
University of California, Berkeley
1987 Galleria Pieroni, Rome
Galleria Christian Stein, Milan
Marian Goodman Gallery, New York
Institute of Contemporary Art, Nagoya, Japan
Musée des Beaux-Arts, Nantes, France
1988 Kölnischer Kunstverein, Cologne
Galerie Annemarie Verna, Zurich
Museo di Capodimonte, Naples
Galleria in Arco, Turin
Galleria Nazionale d'Arte Moderna, Rome
1989 Ydessa Hendeles Art Foundation, Toronto
Galerie Yvon Lambert, Paris
Salone del Libro, Turin
Galleria Massimo Minini, Brescia, Italy
Galerie Paul Maenz, Cologne
1990 Galleria Marilena Bonomo, Bari, Italy
Studio d'Arte Barnabò, Venice
Galleria d'Arte Moderna, Bologna
1991 Castello di Rivoli, Italy
Galleria dell'Oca, Rome
Galleria di Franca Mancini, Pesaro, Italy
Stein Gladstone Gallery, New York
1992 Galleria Lucio Amelio, Naples
Bonner Kunstverein, Bonn, Germany
Galleria Christian Stein, Milan
Galleria Christian Stein, Turin
Galerie Yvon Lambert and Galerie Di Meo, Paris
Galleria Marco Noire, Turin
1993 Kunstmuseum Winterthur, Germany
1994 *L'opera in palio*, Palazzo Patrizi, Siena (catalog)
1995 Marian Goodman Gallery, New York
Impressions graphiques. Múltiplos e Obra Gráfica 1969–1995, Fundação C. Gulbenkian, Lisbon (catalog)
Galleria Sperone, Roma
Lezione di pittura, Galleria Milleventi and Bloomsbury Books and Arts, Torino
Salone del Palazzo della Ragione, Padova (catalog)
1996 *L'Ile enchantée*, Galerie Yvon Lambert, Paris
Dilemma, Quadreria Eusider, Malgrate, Lecco (catalog)
Correspondances, Accademia di Francia, Villa Medici, Rome (catalog)
Impressions graphiques, Kunsthaus Apolda Avantgarde and Weimarer Schloss, Weimar (catalog)
1997 Galleria Christian Stein, Milano
Impressions graphiques. Das graphische Werk 1967–1995, Städtische Galerie, Göppingen (catalog)
Esposizione Universale, Galleria degli Antichi, Sabbioneta (catalog)
1998 *Von heute bis gestern/Da oggi a ieri*, Neue Galerie im Landesmuseum Joanneum, Graz (catalog)
Big Bang, Galleria Massimo Minini, Brescia
1999 Galerie Jule Kewenig, Frechen-Bachem, Germany
Stanze, Lisson Gallery, London
Padiglione dell'Aurora, Teatro del Castello di Rivoli, Museo d'Arte Contemporanea, Castello di Rivoli, Torino (catalog)
Da oggi a ieri, Galleria Civica d'Arte Moderna e Contemporanea, Torino (catalog)
Salles d'attente, Musée d'art moderne et contemporain, Geneva
Da un momento all'altro, Piazza del Plebiscito, Napoli (catalog)
2000 *Di-stanza*, Yvon Lambert, Paris
Reportage, Annemarie Verna Galerie, Zurich
Tracce/Spuren, Galerie in Traklhaus, Salzburg

Selected Group Exhibitions:

1965–75 Reconsidering the Object of Art, The Museum of Contemporary Art, Los Angeles
1966 *Aspetti dell'Avanguardia in Italia,* Galleria Notizie, Turin
1969 *Biennale,* Paris
1970 *Information,* Museum of Modern Art, New York
1971 *New Italian Art: 1953–1971,* Walker Art Gallery, Liverpool
1974 *Kunst bleibt Kunst: Projekt '74,* Kunsthalle, Cologne
1976 *Biennale,* Sydney
1981 *Identité Italienne,* Centre Georges Pompidou, Paris
1985 *Transformations in Sculpture,* Guggenheim Museum, New York
1987 *Avant-Garde in the Eighties,* Los Angeles County Museum of Art
1992 *Biennale,* Sydney
1995 *Imagine*, New San Francisco Museum of Modern Art, San Francisco
The Italian Metamorphosis 1943–1968, Kunstmuseum, Wolfsburg
Venice Biennale, Venice
1996 *Arte Povera. Les multiples*, Musée d'Art Moderne et d'Art Contemporain, Nizza
1997 *Foto Text Text Foto,* Frankfurter Kunstverein, Frankfurt

Venice Biennale, Venice
Arte italiana 1945–1997. Il visibile e l'invisibile, Aichi Prefectural Museum of Art, Aichi Arts Center, Nagoya (toured)
La Collection de la Fondation Cartier pour l'art contemporain, Fondation Cartier, Paris
1998 *Breaking Ground*, Marian Goodman Gallery, New York
1999 *Auffrischender Wind aus wechselnden Richtungen. Internationale Avantgarde seit 1960: Die Sammlung Paul Maenz*, Neues Museum, Weimar
Global Conceptualism: Points of Origin 1950s-1980s, Queens Museum of Art, New York (toured)
Regarding Beauty. A View of the Late Twentieth Century, Hirshhorn Museum and Sculpture Garden, Washington, D.C. (toured)
Il libro d'artista in Italia, Galleria Civica d'Arte Moderna e Contemporanea, Torino
Museum für Neue Kunst, Karlsruhe
2000 *Le Temps, vite!*, Centre Georges Pompidou, Paris (toured)
Arte Povera Torinese, Galerie Nathalie Pariente, Paris

Collections:

Galleria Civica d'Arte Moderna, Turin; Tate Gallery, London; Centre Georges Pompidou, Paris; Stedelijk Museum, Amsterdam; Museum Haus Lange, Krefeld, West Germany; Staatsgalerie, Stuttgart; Museum of Modern Art, New York; Museum of Modern Art, Oxford, England; Guggenheim Museum, New York; Musée d'Art Contemporain, Montreal; Australian National Gallery, Canberra.

Publications:

By PAOLINI: Books—*Idem,* with text by I. Calvino, Turin 1975; *Del bello intelligibile,* with texts by S. Page, Paris 1978; *Atto unico in tre quadri,* with C. Bertelli and C. Vattimo, Milan 1979; *Hotus Clausus/Werke und Schriften 1960–1980,* with M. Kunz and M. Wechsler, Lucerne 1981; *De bouche a orielle,* with R. Denizot, Paris 1982; *Casa di Lucrezio,* with texts by B. Man and others, Bologna 1984; *Voix off,* with text by A. Coulan, Macon 1986; *Ancora un libro,* with text by B. Cora, Rome 1987; *Suspense: breve storia del vuoto in tredici stanze,* Firenze 1988; *Giulio Paolini: una collezione '60/'80,* Milan 1990; *Guilio Paolini, la voce del pittore: scritti e interviste 1965–1995,* Lugano 1995; *La verità in quattro righe e novantacinque voci,* Torino 1996. **Articles—**interview, with M. Pistoi, in *Marcatre* (Rome), no. 19–22, 1966; interview in *Centroarte* (Turin), no. 1, 1967; ''Il Quadro di sempre'' in *B't* (Milan), no. 5, 1967; ''Una Lettera sul Tempo'' in *Paolini,* exhibition catalog, Turin 1968; ''Happening'' in *Qui Arte Contemporanea* (Rome), no. 5, 1969; ''Note per le scene e i costumi del Bruto II'' in *Qui Arte Contemporanea* (Rome), no. 6, 1969; interview with C. Lonzi, in *Autoritratto,* Bari, Italy 1969; interview in *Bolaffiarte* (Turin), no. 1, 1970; ''Intenzioni su Don Chisciotte'' in *Rivista Rai* (Turin), July 1970; ''Vedo'' in *Vedo,* exhibition catalog, Turin 1970; ''Un Quadro'' in *Un Quadro,* exhibition catalog, Milan 1971, and in *Data* (Milan), no. 2, 1972; interview, with Klaus Staeck in *Befragung der Documenta,* Göttingen 1972; interview with M. Volpi Orlandini in *Futuribili* (Rome), no. 42–43, 1972; interview with M. Bandini in *Prospects* (Milan), no. 1, 1972; ''Note di Lavoro'' in *Nac* (Milan), no. 3, 1973; ''Dipingere la Pittura,'' interview, with N. Orengo in *Fuoricampo* (Turin), no. 2, 1973; ''La Doublure'' in *La Doublure,* exhibition catalog, Rome 1973; ''Dentro il linguaggio,'' interview with Achille Bonito Oliva in *Paolini,* exhibition catalog, Genoa 1974; ''Una domanda discreta,'' interview with N. Orengo in *Libri Nuovi,* (Turin), June 1975; interview, in *Nuova Societa* (Turin), no. 71, 1976; interview with L. M. Venturi in *Studio International* (London), January/February 1976; ''Offlentiche Diskussion,'' with Maurizio Calvesi, in *Galleria Nationale d'Arte Moderna,* (Rome), April 1976; ''Ma L'Artista non e un Computer,'' interview with F. Minervino in *La Republica* (Rome), September 1976; interview in *Nuova Societa* (Turin), no. 90, 1976; ''Bilanci e Programmi: La Parola agli Artisti,'' interview in *Qui Arte Contemporanea* (Rome), no. 17, 1977; ''Moderno/Post-Moderno/Millenario,'' interview in *Data* (Milan), no. 29–29, 1977; ''Cos'e l'Avanguardia,'' interview in *Notiziario* (Milan), no. 6, 1977; ''Lezione di Pittura'' in *Imprinting,* Rome 1979; ''Incontro con l'artista,'' with Bruno Cora, in *Accademia di Belle Arti,* (Perugia, Italy), April 1981; ''Conversazione con gli studenti,'' with A. Charre in *Ecole Nationale des Beaux-Arts* (Lyons), May 1981.

On PAOLINI: Books—*Giulio Paolini* by Germano Celant, New York and Paris 1972; *Giulio Paolini* by Maurizio Fagioli and A. C. Quintavalle, Parma, Italy 1976; *Giulio Paolini,* exhibition catalog by J. Cladders, Mönchengladbach, West Germany 1977; *Giulio Paolini,* exhibition catalog by Harald Szeemann and D. Elliott, Amsterdam 1980; *Giulio Paolini: Del bello intelligibile,* exhibition catalog by E. Franz, Bielefeld, West Germany 1982, (includes bibliography); *Giulio Paolini,* Stuttgart 1986; *Giulio Paolini: von heute bis gestern = da oggi a ieri,* Stuttgart 1998. **Articles—**''Giulio Paolini: Recent Works'' in *Domus* (Milan), November 1972; ''Giulio Paolini'' by Tomassa Trini in *Art Press* (Paris), May/June 1973; ''Image of the Image: The Work of Giulio Paolini'' by Germano Celant in *Art and Artists* (London), May 1974; ''Giulio Paolini'' by Leo Rubinfien in *Artforum* (New York), April 1977; ''Seeing Things Right'' by Marina Vaizey in *The Sunday Times* (London), 17 April 1977; ''Spatial Imagery'' by Paul Goldberger in *Architectural Digest* (New York), no. 4, 1979.

*

Art in its character is by definition new. When it appears not to be so, it is only because we experience no suitable expectancy in ourselves. But even if this were not so, it is in fact all we can say for art; it does not admit of diagnosis, let alone therapies.

Any statements that one can make about art are necessarily *a posteriori* reflections, are therefore conclusions, never predictions. We call present-day art analytic, but nothing would be further from the truth than to present the artist as a computer programmed for art analysis. He does not know the stations of his search but he gives it absolute and mysterious obedience. We learn what this obedience demands of him only when we find in him something ''new'' (that which, in the ancients, still suprises us). That is why today everything new seems to me as old as the idea of the new.

—Giulio Paolini

* * *

Giulio Paolini has been conducting his artistic experiments for more than 20 years and has now developed an aesthetic based on a few characteristic elements which he combines and re-combines in new ways, to produce new, complex wholes. At the start of his career, in 1960, he was already interested in the principles which he was later to develop and refine. Two works from 1960, ''Geometric Design'' and ''Design of the Letter,'' record his quest for what it is in the nature of things which can give a work of art value. Here we can no longer think of the work as a mechanical synthesis but must see it as an analytical process in which the artist scrutinizes the elements he uses and resolves the problems they present.

Paolini's early work demonstrates this conception of art: his first documented piece, for example (the ''Geometric Design'' referred to above), is a small canvas on which he has made a preliminary squaring-off of the surface before him (''all drawing,'' he has explained, ''is preliminary drawing''). This is followed by other works in which Paolini emphasizes the fundamental elements available to the painter and the problems involved in combining them. Thus in one we have an empty canvas-frame which bravely displays a can of varnish; in another work, a set of canvases joined together but their backs to the viewer; and in still another he has assembled many little pieces of colored cardboard. From the start of his career he was always concerned with the material the artist must use to construct his expressive wholes.

During the next phase of his development Paolini became interested in the role space plays in painting. The 1963 ''Horizontal,'' for example, is a work in which he strives to find the best optimal axis for viewing works which are hung 160 cm. from the floor. At the same time he is also concerned with the ways in which the art of the past affects the present. Thus we have such works as ''A Young Man Looking at Lorenzo Lotto'' (1967) and ''The Invention of Ingres'' (1968). In the latter work Paolini has superimposed over Raphael's self-portrait the slightly distorted image of the same portrait as realized by Ingres. This juxtaposition produces an unsettling effect which boldly proclaims Paolini's own artistic presence. In ''Mimesis'' (1975) we have two identical plaster casts of classical busts placed opposite each other, in mirror-like fashion.

After having made all these experiments, Paolini has entered into a mature, reflective phase which encompasses all of his earlier interests in material, space, the art of the past and, now, his own past. His work is fundamentally a way of questioning which changes but always seeks the true, existential nature of art itself.

—Roberto G. Lambarelli

PAOLOZZI, Eduardo (Luigi)

Nationality: British. **Born:** Leith, Scotland, of Italian parents, 7 March 1924. **Education:** Schools in Leith and Edinburgh; studied at the Edinburgh College of Art, 1943, and the Slade School of Fine Art, London, 1944–47. With family, interned as enemy alien in 1940; released after three months and conscripted to Pioneer Corps, 1943–44. **Family:** Married Freda Madge Eliot in 1951 (divorced 1988); children: Louise, Anna, and Emma. **Career:** Sculptor: lived in Paris and met Alberto Giacometti, 1947–50; acted, with Michael Andrews, in *Together* by Lorenza Mazzetti, London, 1954; lived in Hamburg, 1960–62, and Berlin, 1974; lives and works in London and Thorpe-le-Soken, Essex. Lecturer in Textile Design, Central School of Art and

Eduardo Paolozzi: *His Majesty the Wheel,* 1958–59. ©Scottish National Gallery of Modern Art.

Design, London, 1949–55; lecturer in Sculpture, St. Martin's School of Art, London, 1955–58; visiting professor, Hochschule für Bildende Kunst, Hamburg, 1960–62; professor of ceramics, Fachhochschule, Cologne, 1977–82; professor, International Summer Academy, Salzburg, 1981, 1982. Tutor in ceramics, Royal College of Art, London, 1968–94, emeritus professor, since 1994; professor of sculpture, Akademie für Bildenden Künste, Munich, 1981–1990. Since 1949, lived and worked in London. **Awards:** British Critics Prize, 1953; Norma and William Copley Foundation Award, 1956; David Bright Foundation Award, *Biennale,* Venice, 1960; Watson F. Blair Prize, Chicago, 1961; DAAD Fellowship, Berlin, 1974; Purchase Prize, *Guggenheim International Sculpture Exhibition,* 1967; First Prize for Sculpture, *Carnegie International,* Pittsburgh, 1967; First Prize, Closed Competition for the Development of the Rhinegarten, Cologne, 1980; Saltire Society Award, 1981; Grand Prix d'Honneur, Print Biennale, Liubliana 1983. Honorary doctorate: Royal College of Art, London, 1979; University of Glasgow, 1980. Associate, Royal Academy of Arts, 1972; Royal Academician, 1979; Goethe Medal, 1991; Honorary Fellow Royal Incorporation of Architects for Scotland, 1991; Cavalieri Ufficiale del Ordine al Merito dell Republica Italiano, 1991. Honorary Member, Architectural Association, London, 1981. Fellow, University College, London, 1986. Her Majesty's Sculptor in Ordinary for Scotland, 1986. C.B.E. (Commander, Order of the British Empire), 1968. Knighted, 1989. Honorary doctorates from Heriot Watt University, Edinburgh, 1987, and University of St.

Andrews, 1994. **Address:** 107 Dovehouse Street, London SW3 6JZ, England.

Individual Exhibitions:

1947 Mayor Gallery, London
1948 Mayor Gallery, London
1949 Mayor Gallery, London
1950 Hanover Gallery, London (with Kenneth King and William Turnbull)
1958 Hanover Gallery, London
1960 Betty Parsons Gallery, New York
Manchester City Art Gallery
Biennale, Venice
1961 Palais des Beaux-Arts, Brussels (with Victor Pasmore)
1962 Betty Parsons, New York
1963 Waddington Galleries, London
1964 Robert Fraser Gallery, London
Museum of Modern Art, New York
1965 Hatton Gallery, Newcastle upon Tyne
Chelsea School of Art, London
Editions Alecto, London
1966 Scottish National Gallery of Art, Edinburgh
Robert Fraser Gallery, London
Pace Gallery, New York
1967 Pace Gallery, New York
Hanover Gallery, London
Alecto Gallery, London
Rijksmuseum Kröller-Müller, Otterlo, Netherlands
1968 Worth Ryder Art Gallery, University of California, Berkeley
Galerie Neuendorf, Hamburg
Stedelijk Museum, Amsterdam
Plastik und Graphik, Städtische Kunsthalle, Dusseldorf
Kunstverein, Stuttgart
Galerie Mikro, Berlin
Kunstmuseum, Gothenburg, Sweden
1970 Pollock Gallery, Toronto
1971 Tate Gallery, London
1972 St. Katherine's Gallery, London
1973 Victoria and Albert Museum, London (toured the U.K.)
1974 Galerie Wentzel, Hamburg
Kestner-Gesellschaft, Hannover
1975 Nationalgalerie, Berlin (travelled to the Kunstverein Karlsruhe, and the Kunsthalle, Bremen)
The Need to Draw, Fruit Market Gallery, Edinburgh (toured the U.K., 1975–76)
1976 Laing Art Gallery, Newcastle upon Tyne (toured the U.K., 1976–77)
Sculpture, Drawings, Collages and Graphics, Marlborough Fine Art, London
National Exhibition Centre, Swift Current, Saskatchewan (toured Canada)
1977 Victoria and Albert Museum, London
Galerie Renate Fassbender, Munich
Anthony d'Offay Gallery, London
1978 Kunstverein, Kassel, West Germany
1979 Kunstverein, Cologne
Glasgow Print Studio Gallery
Talbot Rice Art Centre, University of Edinburgh
1980 Kunstverein, Münster, West Germany (toured West Germany)
1982 Museum für Kunst und Gewerbe, Hamburg
1983 Aedes Gallery, West Berlin
1984 Architectural Association, London
Royal Scottish Academy, Edinburgh
Städtische Galerie im Lenbachhaus, Munich
1985 Museum Ludwig, Cologne
Moderna Galerija, Liubliana, Yugoslavia
Centre for Contemporary Art, Breda, Netherlands
Ivan Dougherty Gallery, Paddington, New South Wales
Espace Lyonnais d'Art Contemporain, Lyon, France
Crawford Municipal Art Gallery, Cork, Ireland
Museum of Mankind, London
1986 Royal Academy of Art, London
Glaskasten, Marl, West Germany
1987 Serpentine Gallery, London
1988 National Portrait Gallery, London, 'Paolozzi Portraits'
1990 Stadtmuseum Munich 'Eduardo Paolozzi: Arche Noah'
The Scottish Gallery, 'London: Mythologies'
1991 Goethe Institute, London
1994 Yorkshire Sculpture Park, West Bretton, Yorkshire
1996 Jason and Rhodes, London, European Patent Office, Munich
1998 Crawford Art Centre University of St Andrews
1999 Paolozzi Studio, Dean Gallery Edinburgh; Paolozzi Gallery, Edinburgh
2000 University of Northumbria Gallery; Flowers East, London

Selected Group Exhibitions:

1948 *Group Exhibitions,* Galerie Maeght, Paris
1952 *Biennale,* Venice
1953 *Parallel of Life and Art,* Institute of Contemporary Arts, London
1957 *Bienal,* Sao Paulo
1959 *Documenta 2,* Kassel, West Germany
1969 *Pop Art Redefined,* Hayward Gallery, London
1976 *Arte Inglesi Oggi 1960–1976,* Palazzo Reale, Milan
1981 *British Sculpture in the 20th Century,* Whitechapel Art Gallery, London
1982 *Aspects of British Art Today,* Metropolitan Art Museum, Tokyo (toured Japan)
1984 *The Automobile and Culture,* Museum of Contemporary Art, Los Angeles
1986 *Entre el objeto y la Imagen, escultura britanica contemporaneo,* Palacio de Velazquez, Madrid
1988–89 *Unter Helden und Gottern,* Akademie der Bildenden Kunste in der Glyptothek, Munich
1990 *Avant-garde British Printmaking,* British Museum, London
The Independent Group, Post War Britain and Aesthetics of Plenty, Institute of Contemporary Arts, London
1994 *Sculpture in the Close,* Jesus College, Cambridge
1996 *Spellbound-Art and Film,* Hayward Gallery, London

Un Siecle de Sculpture Anglaise, Galerie Nationale du Jeu de Paume, Paris

2000 *As Found: Brutalist Art in Britain in the 50s,* Decorative Arts Museum, Zurich

Collections:

Tate Gallery, London; Victoria and Albert Museum, London; Arts Council of Great Britain, London; Art Museum and Gallery, Glasgow; University of St. Andrews, Scotland; Nationalgalerie, Berlin; Kunsthalle, Hamburg; Rijksmuseum Kröller-Müller, Otterlo, Netherlands; Museum of Modern Art, New York; Guggenheim Museum, New York; Royal Academy, London; Scottish National Gallery of Modern Art, Edinburgh.

Publications:

By PAOLOZZI: Books—*Metaphysical Translations,* London 1960; *The Metallization of a Dream,* London 1963; *Kex* New York 1966; *Abba-Zaba,* London 1970. **Articles—**''Metamorphosis of Rubbish: Mr. Paolozzi Explains His Process'' in *The Times* (London), 2 May 1958; ''Interview with Eduardo Paolozzi,'' with E. Roditi, in *Arts Maganize* (New York), May 1959; statement in *New Images of Man,* exhibition catalog, New York 1959; ''Mein Diktionaer'' in *Blatter und Bilder* (Wurburg, West Germany), March/April 1960; ''The Sculptor Speaks: The Enchanted Forest'' in *The Observer* (London), 24 April 1960; ''Interview with Eduardo Paolozzi,'' with Richard Hamilton, in *Contemporary Sculpture Arts Yearbook,* New York 1965; ''Moonstrips: General Dynamic FUN'' in *Ambit 33,* London 1967; ''Analysis of Domains of the Spectrum of Alternatives'' in *Eduardo Paolozzi: Plastik and Grafik,* exhibition catalog, Dusseldorf 1968; ''Why We Are in Vietnam'' in *Ambit 40,* London 1969; ''Moonstrips'' in *Neue Englische Prosa,* (Cologne), 1970; ''Speculative Illustrations: Eduardo Paolozzi in Conversation with J.G. Ballard and Frank Whitford'' in *Studio International,* (London), October 1971; ''10 Questions to Eduardo Paolozzi'' by Diane Kirkpatrick in *Ambit 51,* London 1972; ''The Iconography of the Present'' in *The Times Literary Supplement* (London), December 1972; ''About the Prints: The Artists Talking at an Interview'' by E. Bailey and C. Hagben in *Bunk,* London 1973; ''Conversation with Jim Waugh'' in *Eduardo Paolozzi,* exhibition catalog, Glasgow, 1979.

On PAOLOZZI: Books—*Eduardo Paolozzi* by Michael Middleton, London 1963; *Paolozzi* by U.M. Schneede, Stuttgart and New York 1970; *Eduardo Paolozzi* by Diane Kirkpatrick, London 1970; *Eduardo Paolozzi: Sculpture, Drawings, Collages and Graphics,* exhibition catalog by Wieland Schmied and others, London 1976; *Eduardo Paolozzi,* exhibition catalog by Rosemary Miles, London 1977; *Eduardo Paolozzi* by Winfried Konnertz, Munich; *Eduardo Paolozzi: Underground,* exhibition catalog edited by Richard Cork, London 1986; *Paolozzi: Sculptures from a Garden,* exhibition catalog with text by Frank Whitford, London 1987; *Paolozzi Portraits,* exhibition catalog with text by Robin Gibson and Robin Spencer, London 1988; *Eduardo Paolozzi: Artificial Horizons and Eccentric Ladders,* exhibition catalog with text by Eduardo Paolozzi and Judith Collins, Edinburgh 1996–97; *Paolozzi* by Fiona Pearson, Edinburgh 1999; *Eduardo Paolozzi: Writings and Interviews,* edited by Robin Spencer, Oxford 2001.

*

Divine ambiguity is possible with collage—flesh robots marred by objects or objects masquerading as flesh. There is nothing astonishing in that—witness the great portraits of Arcimboldo. We have learned to define collage as a process where dreams can be rejected and the victims exposed to ridicule. The word ''collage'' is inadequate as a description because the concept should include ''damage, erase, destroy, deface and transform''—all parts of a metaphor for the creative act itself. Preconscious elaboration must have a relationship to chance, therefore the permutations of 101 figures on 40 landscapes and interiors represent a process of endless destruction until finalization.

—Eduardo Paolozzi

* * *

Eduardo Paolozzi was outstanding among post-war British sculptors to make their reputations beyond the shadow of Moore. Born exactly one day before Caro in 1924, he studied at Edinburgh College of Art before going into the Slade in London. He was at the Slade until 1947; then he moved to Paris where he met, and saw the works of, the avant garde sculptors, including Giacometti. By 1950 he was back in England and embarked on a programme of personal investigation into the role of sculpture in a world where Renaissance ideals seemed ill at ease. This quest had its origins in his days at the Slade when he was to find more fascinating subjects to draw at the Science Musem in South Kensington than in the life class.

Despite the compulsive interest in the shape and organization of mechanical processes, Paolozzi did not admire them for the abstract appearances or functional symmetry, as did the Constructivists. He saw analogies between the engineered and anatomical image and struck a forceful surrealist note between them, a contrast he exploited in the 1950s by incorporating ''ready-mades'' in the composition of grotesque heads. Those and the larger figures were conceived as forms encrusted and embossed in decorative relief patterns. Semi-abstract in character they were regarded in the light of science-fiction robots retaining an upright human stance.

About 1961 Paolozzi began some of his most extraordinary sculptures, designed and cast in steel and alloy. He has expressed his view that idols representing rational order of technology can be as fascinating as the fetishes of a Congo witch doctor. Elements of precast metal were adapted and assembled within schemes of impressive architectural significance developing their own original iconography, suggestive of the transformation of the visible world, in machinery that became monumental and capable of transmitting a mystical presence.

Similarly the animistic metaphors latent in the contorting spirals of steel tubing were spun into a Laocoon-like struggle embodied in unyielding metal. In recent years Paolozzi has produced a series in silk-screen and other media containing literary and scientific data in variable colour schemes. The composing of the minuscule cuneiform motives reduce the unified impact to an esoteric literary reading.

In Paolozzi's sculpture the idol and the unique shapes with their superimposed decoration have surrealist mystery. Some of the latter constructions bear the delicate trivialisation of the process reflective of neo-Dada tendencies of the 1960s lacking however any of the self-destructive desperation of a Tinguely.

—G. S. Whittet

PARR, Mike

Nationality: Australian. **Born:** Sydney, New South Wales, 19 July 1945. **Education:** Studied at University of Queensland, Brisbane, 1965–66, and at National Art School, Darlinghurst, New South Wales, 1968. **Family:** Married Tess Stefanitsch in 1977; daughter: Adrian. **Career:** Independent artist specializing in large-scale drawings and performance art, Newton, New South Wales, since 1970. Cofounder, with Peter Kennedy, Inhibodress Cooperative Gallery, Sydney, 1970–73; lecturer in art, Sydney University Art Workshop, 1974–78; lecturer in sculpture, Sydney College of Arts, 1978–82. **Awards:** Australian Government study grant for study in Europe, 1977. **Agent:** Roslyn Oxley 9 Gallery, 13–21 Macdonald Street, Paddington, Sydney, New South Wales. **Address:** P.O. Box 488, Alexandria, New South Wales 2015, Australia.

Individual Exhibitions:

1970 Reid Gallery, Brisbane
1971 Inhibodress Gallery, Sydney
Pinacotheca Gallery, Melbourne (with Tim Johnson)
Inhibodress Gallery, Sydney
Inhibodress Gallery, Sydney (with Peter Kennedy)
1972 Inhibodress Gallery, Sydney (with Peter Kennedy)
1973 Veste Sagrada and Museo de Arte Moderno, Rio de Janeiro (with Peter Kennedy)
Galerie Impact, Lausanne, Switzerland
Galeria Media, Neuchâtel, Switzerland
1974 Contemporary Art Society Gallery, Adelaide, South Australia
Central Street Gallery, Sydney
1975 Art Gallery of South Australia, Adelaide (with Peter Kennedy)
1977 Sculpture Centre, Sydney
Watters Gallery, Sydney
1978 Bela Balaczs Studio for Experimental Film, Budapest
1980 Western Australia Institute of Technology, Perth
1981 Museum des 20. Jahrhunderts, Vienna (film screening)
Danny Keller Galerie, Munich (film screening)
Kunstverein, Frankfurt (film screening)
National Art School, Dublin (film screening)
Institute of Modern Art, Brisbane
Ivan Dougherty Gallery, Sydney
1982 Art Projects, Melbourne
1983 The Performance Space, Sydney
Institute of Modern Art, Brisbane
Art Projects, Melbourne
1984 Royal Melbourne Institute of Technology, Melbourne
1985 Roslyn Oxley 9 Gallery, Sydney
University of Tasmania, Hobart
1986 Siegel Contemporary Art, New York
Michael Milburn Galleries, Brisbane
Roslyn Oxley 9 Gallery, Sydney
1987 United Artists, Melbourne
Roslyn Oxley 9 Gallery, Sydney
Michael Milburn Galleries, Brisbane
1988 Milburn + Arte Gallery, Brisbane
1989 Roslyn Oxley 9 Gallery, Sydney
City Gallery, Melbourne
Milburn + Arte Gallery, Brisbane
1990 Australian National Gallery, Canberra
City Gallery, Melbourne
Roslyn Oxley 9 Gallery, Sydney
1991 Ian Potter Gallery, University of Melbourne Museum of Art
City Gallery, Melbourne
Roslyn Oxley 9 Gallery, Sydney
Survey of Recent Work, Art Gallery of New South Wales, Sydney, and Perth Institute of Contemporary Art, Perth
1992 Delaney Gallery, Perth
ALPHABET/HAEMORRHAGE, Arthouse, Perth (travelled to Brisbane, Melbourne, and Sydney)
Memory of a Monochrome (for John Nixon), A-Atrophy, Field/Feeled, School of Fine Arts, University of New South Wales, Sydney
100 Breaths from (ALPHABET/HAEMORRHAGE) Black Box of 100 Self-Portrait Etchings, 2, Australian National Gallery, Canberra (travelled to Melbourne)
1993 Roslyn Oxley 9 Gallery, Sydney
Black Mirror/Pale Fire, Ivan Dougherty Gallery, Sydney
1994 Art Gallery of South Australia, Adelaide
Ivan Dougherty Gallery, Sydney
Anna Schwartz Gallery, Melbourne
Works from the Self-Portrait Project, Brisbane City Hall Art Gallery and Museum
Echolalia (The Road): Prints from the Self-Portrait Project, National Gallery of Victoria, Melbourne
Black Mirror/Pale Fire, Part 2, Old Police Barracks, Brisbane
1995 *The Illusion of the End,* Sherman Galleries Goodhope and Hargrave, Sydney
1996 *The Infinity Machine,* Sherman Galleries Goodhope, Sydney
Head on a Plate, New York Studio School, New York
1997 Anna Schwartz Gallery, Melbourne
Dead Sun, 3 day performance, Art Gallery of New South Wales
1998 *The Rest of Time,* Sherman Galleries, Paddington, Sydney
The End of Nature, performance, The Baltic Sea, Sweden
Photo Realism, Anna Schwartz Gallery, Melbourne
1999 *Deep Sleep [The Analytical Disabling of Mind and Mater],* 72 hour performance, Old Parliament House and Lake Burley Griffin, Canberra
Wrong Face, Anna Schwartz Gallery, Melbourne
Three Collaborations, Sarah Cottier Gallery, Sydney
2000 ARCO, International Contemporary Art Fair, Madrid
Shallow Grave, 3 day performance, Biennale of Sydney, Art Gallery of New South Wales
Mike Parr, Sherman Galleries, Goodhope Street, Sydney

. . . de Kooning, de Kooning. . ., Anna Schwartz Gallery, Melbourne
John Nixon/Mike Parr, Conny Dietzschold Gallery, Cologne

Selected Group Exhibitions:

1977 *10th Biennale des Jeunes,* Musée d'Art Moderne, Paris
1978 *Performance Art Festival,* Osterreichischer Kunstverein, Vienna
1979 *European Dialogue,* at the 3rd Biennale of Sydney
1980 *Biennale,* Venice
Biennale, Sydney (and 1986, 1988)
1984 *An Australian Accent,* Project Studios One, New York (travelled abroad and to state galleries in Australia)
Australian Contemporary Art to China, State Museums of Beijing, Wuhan, Shanghai, and Guangzhou
1990 *Edge 90: The New Work (Art & Life in the Nineties),* Newcastle-upon-Tyne, England
1992 *My Head Is a Map—A Decade of Australian Prints,* National Gallery of Australia
1993 *Identities: Art from Australia,* Taipei Fine Arts Museum, Taipei, Taiwan
1994 *25 Years of Performance Art in Australia,* Ivan Dougherty Gallery, Sydney (toured Australia)
1995 *Antipodean Currents: 10 Contemporary Artists from Australia,* Guggenheim Museum SoHo, New York
1996 *Spirit and Place: Art in Australia 1861–1996,* Museum of Contemporary Art, Sydney
1997 *Dead Sun,* Art Gallery of New South Wales, Sydney
1998 *Wounds: Between Democracy and Redemption in Contemporary Art,* Moderna Museet, Stockholm, Sweden
1999 *Other Stories: Five Australian Artists,* Hokkaido Museum of Modern Art, Sapporo, Japan
2000 *Zeitgenoessische Fotokunst aus Australien/Contemporary Photographic Art from Australia,* Neuer Berliner Kunstverein, Berlin (travelled to Museum Schloss Hardenberg, Velbert, Kunstsammlungen Chemnitz, and Kulturzentrum der Stadt Stuttgart)

Collections:

Museum of Contemporary Art, Sydney; National Art Gallery of New South Wales, Sydney; National Art Gallery of Victoria, Melbourne; Queensland Art Gallery, Brisbane; Newcastle Regional Art Gallery, Newcastle; National Art Gallery of South Australia, Adelaide; National Art Gallery of Australia, Canberra; National Library, Canberra; Art Gallery of Western Australia, Perth; Metropolitan Museum of Art, New York.

Publications:

By PARR: Books—*Black Box of Word Situations No. 1,* Sydney 1971; *150 Programmes and Investigations,* Sydney 1971; *Wall Definitions,* Sydney 1973; *Black Box of Word Situations No. 2,* Sydney 1978. **Articles—**''Other Dimensions'' in *Aspect* (Sydney), Winter 1975; ''3 Questions'' in *Aspect* (Sydney), vol. 2, no. 1, 1976; ''Abasex to Zymasex'' in *Art in Australia* (Sydney), April-June 1976; ''Notes on Recent Work'' in *Flash Art* (Milan), February-April 1978; ''Artist's Statement'' in *3rd Biennale of Sydney: European Dialogue,* exhibition catalog, Sydney 1979; ''Notes on the Structure of Content: Black Box/Theatre of Self-Correction—Parts 1 and 2'' in *Venice Biennale 1980: Australia,* exhibition catalog, Sydney 1980; ''Notes on My Work'' in *The 1st Australian Sculpture Triennale,* exhibition catalog, Melbourne 1981; ''Artist's Statement'' in *Eureka! Artists from Australia,* exhibition catalog, London 1982; ''A-Atrophy'' in *Aspect* (Sydney), June 1983; ''Le moi createur et l'autre,'' interview with Catherine Millet, in *Art Press* (Paris), October 1983; ''The Art of John Nixon'' in *Australia and International Art Monthly* (Sydney), August 1987; ''Historical Times (Criticizing the Critic)'' in *Agenda: Contemporary Art,* August 1988; ''Reproduction Zero'' in *British International Print Biennale,* exhibition catalog, Bradford, England 1989; ''The Self-Portrait Project'' in *Australian Art Monthly,* July 1993; ''The Hole of the Vanishing Point'' in *25 Years of Performance Art in Australia,* exhibition catalog, Sydney 1994; ''Daybreak. Manilla Performance, January 20–21, 1995'' in *Art Monthly Australia* (Canberra), July 1995; ''An Interview with Mike Parr,'' interview with Jeremy Sibbald, in *Art Write,* December 1997; ''Notes on My Performance Art, 1971–1998'' in *Endurance,* 1998; ''Some Notes'' in *Biennale of Sydney 2000,* exhibition catalog, Sydney 2000. **Films—***Idea Demonstrations,* with Peter Kennedy, 1972; *Rules and Displacement Activities, Part 1,* 1974; *Rules and Displacement Activities, Part 2,* 1976; *Rules and Displacement Activities, Part 3,* 1977; *Rules and Displacement Activities, Part 4,* 1983.

On PARR: Books—*Videotapes from Australia,* exhibition catalog with text by Bernice Murphy and Stephen Jones, Sydney 1979; *Venice Biennale 1980: Australia,* exhibition catalog, with introduction by Elwyn Lynn, Sydney 1980; *The Visual Arts* edited by M. K. Symonds, C. Portley, and R. E. Phillips, Sydney 1980; *Australian Perspecta,* exhibition catalog, with introduction by Bernice Murphy, Sydney 1981; *Self-Portrait/Self Image,* exhibition catalog with text by Janine Burke, Sydney 1981; *Eureka! Artists from Australia,* exhibition catalog with texts by Nancy Underhill, Ian Burn, and Paul Taylor, London 1982; *An Australian Accent,* exhibition catalog with texts by Daniel Thomas and Jonathan Fineberg, New York 1984; *Australia: Nine Contemporary Artists* by Paul Taylor, Los Angeles 1984; *Mike Parr: Portage,* exhibition catalog with introduction by Jonathan Holmes, Hobart 1985; *Mike Parr: The Satellites of Death,* exhibition catalog with essay by Anthony Bond, Brisbane 1986; *Creating Australia: 200 Years of Art* by Daniel Thomas, Adelaide 1988; *Inhibodress: 1970–1972,* exhibition catalog with introduction by Sue Cramer, Brisbane 1989; *Identities: A Critical Study of the Work of Mike Parr* by David Bromfield, Perth 1991; *Mike Parr: Artist in Residence, 1990–1991* by Merryn Gates, Melbourne 1991; *Mike Parr: The Self-Portrait Project* by Graham Coulter-Smith, Melbourne 1994; *Spirit and Place: Art in Australia 1861–1996,* exhibition catalog by Nick Waterlow, Sydney 1997; *In Place (Out of Time): Contemporary Art in Australia,* exhibition catalog by Howard Murphy and David Elliott, Oxford 1997. **Articles—**''Idea Demonstrations: Body Art and 'Video Freaks' in Sydney'' by Donald Brook in *Studio International* (London), June 1973; ''Art and Sanctuary'' by Patrick McCaughey in *Aspect* (Sydney), spring 1975; ''Videotapes from Australia: A Top Collection from Down Under'' by Victor Ancona in *Videography* (New York), February 1980; ''Films by Artists'' by Jennifer Phipps in *Art in Australia* (Melbourne), spring 1980; ''Venice Biennale 1980'' by Suzanne Davies in *Art Network* (Sydney), spring 1980; ''Report from Australia'' by Suzi Gablik in *Art in America* (New York), January 1981; ''Australian Art: Beyond the Cringe,'' a special issue of *Studio International* (London), October 1983; ''Three Vigorous Artists from Down Under'' by John Russell in the *New York Times,* 20 April 1984; ''An Australian Accent'' by Thomas McEvilley in *Artforum* (New York), October 1984; ''Mike Parr'' by Ellen Lee Klein in *Arts Magazine* (New York), December 1986; ''Mike Parr at Ruth Siegel'' by Eleanor Heartney in *Art in America* (New York), January 1987; ''Mike Parr's Self-Portraits: Unma(s)king the Self'' by Graham Coulter-Smith and Jane Magon in *Eyeline,* June 1988; ''Mike Parr: The Labyrinth of Memory'' by Deborah Hart in *Art & Australia* (Sydney), Summer 1994; ''Closer Up. Into the Sunset'' by Ben Curnow in *Artlink* (Hensley Beach, SA), Vol. 15, No. 2 & 3, 1995; ''Mike Parr in the Philippines: The Artist Dances'' by David Bromfield in *Art Asia Pacific,* Vol. 3, No. 1., 1996; ''Break Down the Wall'' by Sebastian Smee in *Sydney Morning Herald Metro,* 17–23 May 1996; ''Body of Work the Cat's Whiskers'' by Joanna Mendelssohn in *Australian,* 19 September 1997; ''Telling Tales'' by Jackie Dunn in *Telling Tales,* exhibition catalog, Sydney 1999; ''On the Art of Collaboration'' by Cathy Leahy in *Spitting and Biting: Ten Contemporary Artists and the Print,* exhibition catalog, Melbourne 2000.

*

All of my work since my first conceptual pieces and performances in 1970–71 at Inhibodress Cooperative Gallery, Sydney, is an organic whole. Continuity and vertical structure are the essence of my approach because in many ways the ''meaning'' derives from the linkage between works; the works themselves are intense moments, epiphanies in the sense that James Joyce speaks of inspiration and illumination. These intense moments are either ''actual,'' where my performance pieces are a revelation of personal obsessions based on real behavior, or else symbolic. However, I am not interested in literary symbolism or literary devices; these symbols are unconventional and function in ways similar to the symbolism of the abstract expressionists, which was simultaneously abstract in its unitary reductionism but universal in its ambience.

The symbols of the abstract expressionists gelled out of process and had no *a priori* structure. They were arrived at, recognized at the moment of their fusion—they were signs isolated against a field. This is exactly how my ''actions'' or ''gestures'' work. The great bulk of my work is based on the performance. I perform myself. (I mean I act out my own intensity.) The records of many of these performances have been made into films or else portfolios of prints. The films, the prints, and even the recent installations are more often a revelation of process, the linkage between images. They record the alternative nature for the personalism of the world I want to reveal.

The performance lifts me and the audience into real time, into a continuous present tense. Each performance, existing at the edge of the present tense, is suffused with an existential realism of peculiar intensity. Between my behavior and the behavior of the audience, there is a formative osmosis—it is a peculiarly miasmic world of mirror images. The intensity and the immediacy of this world constitutes itself as a sign—but one existing at the edge of the present tense. It is a sign of absolute abstraction and realism. This is a peculiar contradiction, the consequence of tautological reduction. The chair on which I sit is nominated as the chair on which I sit. The event to occur is described as the event occurs: i.e. ''Sitting before an audience . . . bare your shoulder . . . let a friend bite into your shoulder . . . until your friend's mouth is filled with blood.''

In 1972 this was displayed on the wall of Inhibodress like a print—an art object. One night, after the audience had become used to the instruction for an event as an object, it was performed before them. It was an event without apparent reason—a sign of itself. As a sign of itself it expanded to become a kind of chasm into which we all disappeared. The fact that it was an event without meaning stimulated the audience to search their memories and reasons. Insofar as the event demanded a meaning, it extracted from the self-consciousness of the audience. It was as though the room was filled with dead albatrosses—one for each member of the audience.

Anyway, the peculiarity of my work is that all these ''events as events'' fuse together—gradually a ''parallel fiction'' to the fiction of memory emerges. It is cancerous, like the supernatural, because it extracts its parameters from the real. (It is my view that every event is attached to its shadow, in the same way that objects are; every shadow is the antidote to its meaning, but simultaneously the prerequisite for it.) So the process is omnipresent and endless, like paranoia, and yet discrete.

The ''Black Boxes'' and room installations reassemble process, tinker with its organic continuity, fabricate elaborate fictions. The mirror images deployed in the installations compound the ''fictions,'' tautologize perception, and fix the glutinous extensibility of the process. Therefore, it is hard not to look. The audience tends to look too hard. Looking hard they see themselves. This complication of the mirror images as metaphor is the ''meaning'' of the ''Black Boxes'' and installations.

Recent installations have extended all these ideas in the absence of performers. I have become very interested in problems of anamorphic distention and of incorporating images of extreme anamorphic distortion back into rooms and space that extend two-dimensional perspective literally, three-dimensionally. I should add that these images are always self-portraits and that the initial source of the image was photographs from performances. These problems of sight-line and the position of the viewer (the relativity of all representational codes and by implication the attendant problems of psychological distance) continue and extend all my earlier notions of breaking down and articulating the space between viewer and artwork.

Portrait of M. and F. 1996 shows my wife Felizitas and myself in a carefully articulated environment. The photographer was Paul Green. I think this image summarizes a good deal of my work in the 1990s which recurrently shows images or actions repeated into abstraction or blackness. The fire blackened interior of *Polar Sea* of 1986 became an inward turning maze in 1988 in a work called *Hebrew the Language of God.* In 1990, for *Edge 90* in Newcastle-upon-Tyne and at regular intervals since through the 1990s, I have built ever increasingly complex black mazes, with hundreds of feet of blind corridors though which audiences can wander for hours.

These are all works that stage the idea of performance in terms of the inner life of the audience and they are all works that require the audience to make a basic choice at the threshold of the image as it were, because the most visually arresting aspect of these works is the black monochrome of the doorway. The same ideas of repetition, involution, and loss recur in the drawings of the Self Portrait Project, which has more to do with the impossibility of portraiture and the labyrinthine digressions of memory, than it has to do with the ''likeness,'' though the likeness and its myriad avatars, its almost collective or genetic complexity is the theme of the S.P.P. This linguistic complexity of drawing has been greatly extended I think, by printmaking. In 13 years, John Loane (my printer) and I have done upwards of fifteen hundred plates, in all media including etching, woodcut, and lithography.

—Mike Parr

* * *

Mike Parr first came to the attention of the Australian art scene in a significant way during 1970, when he helped initiate an artists' cooperative in Sydney. He was the principal organizer of the Inhibodress Cooperative Gallery, which provided a genuine alternative for innovative artists who were seeking to work without the limitations normally imposed by commercial gallery directors. Inhibodress encouraged video-performance art experiments while offering display spaces for more conventional forms of expression, such as painting and sculpture. Freedom from profitmaking incentives resulted in the development of an art center that defied establishment tastes.

During the relatively shortlived Inhibodress venture (1970–1973) Parr worked with filmmakers Aggy Read and Ian Stocks, who edited ideas and performances by Parr and his fellow artist Peter Kennedy, resulting in *Idea Demonstrations* (black, white and color with optical sound), which was later shown at the Sydney Film Festival (1973) with added material by Parr. Film was always an important part of Parr's activities as a performance artist, providing him with a viable means of documentation. Photographic stills of his performance pieces have assumed the status of artworks in themselves and pose interesting questions related to art-photography issues. By employing the services of outstanding local photographers such as John Delacour, the artist guaranteed documentation of the highest technical order.

The content of Parr's work has been primarily autobiographical, and he has used his body as other artists might have used paint or stone—as an essential medium for self-expression. Because Parr's left arm is congenitally unformed, he has had to cope with a physical disability that has radically influenced his life, both personally and as an artist. In a series of performances, Parr attempted to exorcise his feelings of physical inadequacy (or incompleteness) by literally chopping a life-like prosthesis created from various materials and packed with animal livers. The action culminated with some of the artist's family gathering up the dismembered parts and replacing the severed arm with another knitted from pink yarn.

It was tempting to interpret Parr's obsessive concern with his missing arm in Freudian terms related to castration fears. Parr's often brutal treatment of his body as a ground for experiment (including various forms of self-mutilation and induced vomiting) was meant to offer a form of catharsis. Self-mutilation, it was hoped, would lead to self-liberation.

To many observers (and critics) his activities appeared sadomasochistic and incomprehensible in any art context. But Parr's works had obvious precursors in a host of performance pieces by European artists such as Yves Klein, Piero Manzoni, Arnulf Rainer, and Rudolph Schwarzkogler. The latter committed a form of ritual suicide in 1969 by methodically amputating sections of his anatomy (penis et al) in an ultimate gesture of liberation, making Parr's endeavors appear quite tame.

In the context of ''theatre of cruelty,'' Parr's performances were not altogether successful. His attempts to involve audiences led, more often than not, to their retreat into civilized passivity.

From the mid-1970s much of Parr's work divorced itself from the audience of outsiders, although some of his *Primary Vomit* actions took place in public viewing areas such as Watters Gallery (Sydney) in 1977. The more intimate explorations were highly erotic encounters involving naked bodies and a variety of touching experiences incorporating such disparate materials as blood, feathers, and honey. Family and close friends participated in his *Performance Room* (1978) pieces and at the Venice Biennale (1980), when a series of tableaux vivants, combined with live performances, further extended the *Performance Room* possibilities.

At the 4th Biennale of Sydney (1982) Parr was represented by a visually stunning photographic installation (*Parapraxis 3*) exploiting images of the human head in a manner indicating possible new departures in his ongoing voyage of self-discovery and enlightenment.

Concepts of ''photo-death'' have recurred in Parr's work from 1982, culminating in a series of photocopied self-portraits that gradually ''dissolved'' or ''eradicated'' recognizable features of the artist's face.

In 1984 Parr's work was included in a highly acclaimed group exhibition—together with contributions from contemporary Australian artists Imants Tillers and Ken Unsworth—called *An Australian Accent,* sponsored by fabric manufacturer John Kaldor, which debuted at New York's P.S.1. (Project Studios One) Gallery. It was a privately funded initiative, which established a role model for overseas exhibitions of contemporary Australian art.

The international influences of the Italian ''trans-avant-garde'' were echoed in local variations on large-scale, neo-figurative painting-drawings. Parr's huge self-portraits in charcoal (and other media), on sheets of paper pinned directly onto the gallery walls, extended notions of drawing as performance art and drawing as a ''thinking aloud'' process, whereby finished ''statements'' were as significant in scale and concept as anything traditionally classified as painting and sculpture.

The drawing-as-fine-art-object aspect of Parr's activities in the 1980s, while acknowledging its roots in earlier performance art, seemed at odds with his earlier rejection of commercial art gallery priorities. The last decade saw Parr devote an increasing amount of his time and energy to sophisticated drawing and printmaking endeavors, the results of which are nothing if not viable commercial gallery objects.

One of the most interesting features of Parr's drawings (not so much in evidence in his *Green Self-Portraits*, shown at the Roslyn Oxley 9 Gallery in Sydney in mid-1987) has been his division of the working area into two asymmetrical sections, imparting significance through a symbolic left and right side of the brain. Parr's ''landscapes of the mind'' have been reinforced by portraits of the artist's face, often distorted into forms of extravagant metamorphosis.

The most striking irony concerning Parr's drawings has been their execution by a one-armed artist. Their technical virtuosity and mammoth scale would have been daunting for an artist with two arms—and of half Parr's age.

While not abandoning performance entirely in the 1990s, Parr has been heavily promoted and exposed as a graphic artist of outstanding dexterity. In 1994 the National Gallery of Victoria in Melbourne, Australia, mounted a dramatic survey of seven years of Parr's prints titled *Echolalia (The Road): Prints from the Self-Portrait Project—Mike Parr, 1987–1994.* In conjunction with John Loane and his Victoria Press, Parr has produced often large-scale, monochromatic self-portraits of startling power and increasing technical virtuosity. Always conspicuously self-obsessed, Parr's recent graphic output makes him arguably Australia's most brilliant works-on-paper artist, combining expressionist and self-referential figurative drawing skills with a flair for formal placement, which sometimes verges on the suavely decorative. He is one of the most written about, exposed, curatorially indulged, and successful Australian artists of his generation.

—Arthur McIntyre

PARTRIDGE, David (Birdie)

Nationality: Canadian. **Born:** Akron, Ohio, 5 October 1919; immigrated to Canada, 1936: naturalized, 1944. **Education:** Radley College, Berkshire, England, 1933–35; Trinity College School, Port Hope, Canada, 1935–38; studied geology and paleontology, Trinity College, University of Toronto, 1938–41, B.A. 1941; painting, under Carl Schaeffer, Hart House, Toronto, 1939–41, under André Bieler, Carl Schaeffer and Will Ogilvie, Queen's University Summer Art School, Kingston, Canada, 1946–47, 1949, under Harry Stenberg, Art Students League, New York, summer 1948; Slade School, London, 1950–51 (British Council Scholarship); etching under Stanley William Hayter, Atelier 17, Paris, 1958. **Military Service:** Flying instructor/flight lieutenant, Royal Canadian Air Force, 1942–45. **Family:** Married Helen Rosemary Annesley in 1943; children: Katherine and John. **Career:** Independent artist, since 1961. Instructor, Appleby College, Oakville, Ontario, 1945–46; art instructor, Ridley College, St. Catharines, Ontario, 1946–65; St. Catharines Collegiate Institute and St. Catharines Art Association, 1953–56; Queen's Summer School, Kingston, Ontario, 1955, 1959–60; Ottawa Civic Centre, 1958–61; Ontario College of Art, Toronto, 1974–75. Member of London Group, living in England, 1962–74. Co-founder, 1954, and curator, 1954–56, St. Catharines Public Library, Ontario; docent, National Gallery of Canada, Ottawa, 1959–61; trustee, Art Gallery of Canada, Toronto. **Awards:** Sculpture Purchase Award, Museum of Fine Arts, Montreal, 1962; Toronto Aviva Sculpture Prize, 1976, 1979; First Place, Toronto City Hall Mural Competition, 1977; First Place, Royal Canadian Academy Sculpture Competition, 1978; Toronto Aviva Sculpture Prize, 1979. **Member:** Royal Canadian Academy, 1962–86; Fellow, Royal Society of Arts and Sciences, London, 1971–90; The London Group, 1965–1974; Trustee, Art Gallery of Ontario, 1977–1980. **Agent:** Moore Gallery Ltd., 34 Hess Street, Hamilton, Ontario. **Address:** 77 Seaton Street, Toronto, Ontario M5A 2T2, Canada. **Web site:** http://www.globalserve.net/~dnaillie.

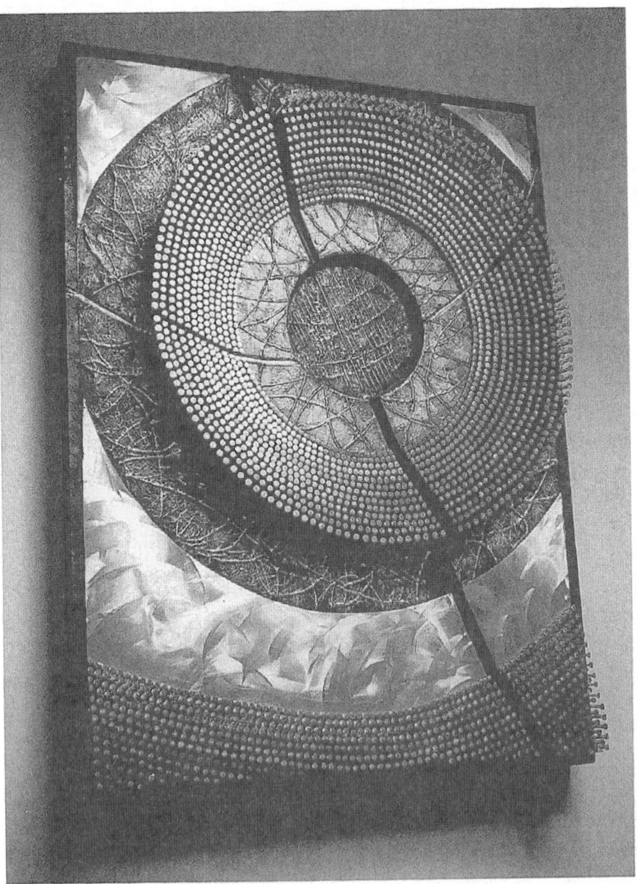

David Partridge: *Arena,* 1999. ©David Partridge.

Individual Exhibitions:

1956 St. Catharines Art Gallery, Ontario
1957 Rose and Crown, Fletching, Sussex, England
1959 St. Catharines Art Gallery, Ontario
Robertson Gallery, Ottawa
Gallery of Contemporary Art, Toronto
1960 Robertson Gallery, Ottawa
1961 Queen's University, Kingston, Ontario
Here and Now Gallery, Toronto
1962 Robertson Gallery, Ottawa
Agnes LeFort Gallery, Montreal
Jerold Morris International Gallery, Toronto
1964 The New Vision Centre, London
1965 Agnes LeFort Gallery, Montreal
Commonwealth Institute, London (with Toni Onley)
New Charing Cross Gallery, Glasgow
1966 University of Sheffield, England
1967 Hamilton Gallery, London
1968 Richard DeMarco Gallery, Edinburgh
1970 Convent Garden Gallery, London
1973 Roberts Gallery, Toronto
1974 Alwin Gallery, London
1975 Willstead Gallery, Windsor, Ontario
Roberts Gallery, Toronto
1977 Roberts Gallery, Toronto
1979 Atikokan Centennial Museum, Ontario
1982 Gallery Quan, Toronto
1984 Gallery Quan, Toronto
1986 Nancy Poole's Studio, Toronto
1987 Moore Gallery, Hamilton, Ontario
1988 *Nails,* Nancy Poole's Studio, Toronto
1996 Bau Xi Gallery, Toronto
1998 Moore Gallery, Toronto

Selected Group Exhibitions:

1962 *Spring Show,* Museum of Fine Arts, Montreal
1964 *2nd Exhibition of Canadian Sculpture,* National Gallery of Canada, Ottawa
Carnegie International, Pittsburgh

1965 *Art and Engineering,* Art Gallery of Toronto
1966 *Art of the Commonwealth,* Nottingham, England
1967 *Sculpture '67,* City Hall, Toronto
Canadian Biennial, National Gallery of Canada, Ottawa
1969 *Canada Council Collection,* National Gallery of Canada, Ottawa
1977 *Rehearsal,* Harbourfront Art Gallery, Toronto
1978 *Sculpture 1978,* City Hall, Toronto (travelled to London and Brussels)
1979 *Art for All,* Windsor Art Gallery, Windsor, Ontario
1980 *Royal Canadian Academy Show,* Toronto
1987 Northumberland Art Gallery, Cobourg, Ontario
1992 *Year of the Horse,* Westin Harbourcastle Hotel, Toronto
1996 *Circa 1996,* Toronto
1997 *Moore Gallery Artists,* Toronto

Collections:

National Gallery of Canada, Ottawa; Art Gallery of Ontario, Toronto; Art Gallery of Windsor, Ontario; University College, Trinity College, and Hart House, at the University of Toronto; Ridley College, St. Catharines, Ontario; Montreal Museum of Fine Art; Tate Gallery, London; Victoria and Albert Museum, London; Art Gallery of New South Wales, Sydney; Library of Congress, Washington, D.C.; Tate Gallery, London; Montreal Museum of Fine Art, Quebec; Museum of Contemporary Art, Santiago, Chile.

Publications:

By PARTRIDGE: Article—''Printmaking'' in *Canadian Art* (Ottawa), March/April 1961.

On PARTRIDGE: Articles—''Profile on David Partridge'' by Philip Pocock in *Canadian Art* (Ottawa), March/April 1962; ''The Nailman'' in *Time* (New York), 27 July 1962; ''David Partridge'' by Pierre Rouve in *Arts Review* (London), May 1964; ''Profile'' by Marjorie Bruce Milne in the *Christian Science Monitor* (Boston), 1 October 1974; ''David Partridge'' by Kenneth Coutts-Smith in *Quadrum* (Brussels), no. 18, 1964; ''David Partridge's Nail Mosaics'' by Charles Spencer in *Studio International* (London), July 1965; ''Profile'' by Max Wykes-Joyce in *Arts Review* (London), July 1965; ''Alchemy of the Nail Artist'' by Edward Gale in the *Scotsman* (Edinburgh), 11 December 1967; ''Common Nail Makes Unique Sculpture'' by Kay Kritzwiser in *Globe and Mail* (Toronto), 13 October 1973; ''Nailman's Lament'' by Stephen Godfrey in *Globe and Mail* (Toronto), 6 May 1978; article by David Quinter in the *Windsor Star* (Ontario), 19 September 1979; article by James Tiley in *Vanguard* (Vancouver), Spring 1982.

*

''Configurations''

''Naillies''

I was studying at Atelier 17 in Paris, etching and engraving, with William Hayter, during February and March of 1958. I was fascinated by the irregular surfaces of deep-etched copper and zinc plates, irrespective of their purpose in printing. They became low-relief sculptures, which seemed to my ex-pilot's eyes like aerial views of topography.

While gallery-hopping on the Rue du Seine on Saturday, I chanced on an exhibition by Zoltan Kemeny (a Hungarian sculptor, born in 1907, tragically killed in a car crash in 1965). These were wonderful bas reliefs uing all manner of metal bits and pieces, welded into an even more exciting aerial vision than the etched plates had provided.

The following winter in Ottawa I was using wood and nails while redecorating an old house we had moved into. Somehow a nice 2ft. x 3ft. piece of 3/4'' plywood was left over from a project. Nails were at hand and a hammer! I descended to the basement and made my first nail sculpture.

I produced quite a few more in 1959 and 1960. I had an exhibition of Paintings, Drawings, and Configurations at The Robertson Galleries, 103 Queen St., Ottawa, October 17th, 1960. It was a reasonably successful show and the nail works were well received.

The term ''CONFIGURATIONS'' came one evening when Alan Jarvis (National Gallery of Canada) and his wife Betty had supper with Tibs and me. It was Tibs' suggestion. We looked it up in the dictionary and it seemed an appropriate description of what seemed to be a new ''art form.''

As time has gone on, my private name, ''NAILLIES,'' has become accepted. Perhaps not as dignified as the original term, but reasonably descriptive.

Techniques and Materials

The technique involved is fairly straight-forward. Nails of differing sizes are hammered part-way into wood, the shortest nails first, to create a relief sculpture.

Materials: Nails of all sorts and lengths. Currently aluminum nails most often, but copper and steel are in evidence. Nail heads may be polished or shaped with abrasive discs on drill or Dremel Tool.

Aluminum nails ensure that even large works are not excessively heavy.

Plywood, 3/4'' to 1'' most often receives the nails. solid doors (I refer to these as ''Composite wood'') up to 2'' thick are also a good ground which can also be carved into, adding to the 3-dimensionality of the piece. Beams up to 6'' x 6'' by 12' have been used in the past, creating an ''all-around'' naillie. The finished work may be clear-lacquered or spray or brush-painted with acrylic or oil based paints.

Although first a teacher-painter and printmaker, I feel I actually started my professional career in 1958 when I produced my first ''Nail'' configuration. In 1962 I won a sculpture prize in Montreal with one and got a commission to do a mural. By 1965 I had pretty well stopped painting and printmaking and was devoting all my time to hammering nails. Uecker of Zero Group must have started his nail things about the same time I did—but I didn't see his work until I came to England in 1962, and certainly mine have developed in a completely different way. My work is influenced by early studies in geology and paleontology and by hours of flying over Northern Ontario during the war. Latterly archaeology has had a strong influence. However I have always worked intuitively rather than from preconceived designs or drawings. Currently I am becoming involved in the sound qualities of nails often struck, stroked or dropped. Several of the 'musical' naillies have been used by composers (J. Berhens at the University of Western Ontario, and the Canadian percussion group Nexus have used several during world tours of China and Asia and Europe).

During the next three years I made a return to painting—based on experiences of flying in an ultralight (microlight) aircraft I built in 1982. A successful show of ''Ultralight Approach Series'' at Nancy

Poole's Studio in 1986 was of basically skyscapes with a suggestion of landing area at the bottom.

Since 1887, I have done several more musical naillies tintinabulations. Most recently, I have been working on a series of nail works with augmented colour.

—David Partridge

* * *

It was in Paris, studying etching under Hayter, that the Canadian artist David Partridge first saw the metal reliefs of Zoltan Kemeny. At this time Partridge was a painter and print-maker, with little involvement in three-dimensional form. Having studied art largely in England, he lived in London for ten years, from 1962, developing his fascinating technique of nail-reliefs. He continued to paint, however, solid rock-like shapes, reminiscent of Ernst's landscape, and curiously enough it is the transference of these forms to the pointillist technique of nail-heads, which gives his work its unique character.

Partridge relates the origin of his method to the rebuilding of a small family house in Ottawa, eighteen months after having seen Kemeny's reliefs. Pulling down a wooden wall, he revealed a group of nails, forming a relief composition, and immediately began to experiment, treating the nails as elements of design, only later exploiting the third dimension. This led to further variations: different length nails, or undulating forms resulting from the nails being driven in at different lengths, with different heads. An infinite variety of texture, density and spatialism, became possible. Colour was introduced by varying galvanized steel with copper and zinc, and then polishing or lacquering.

A neat balance between decoration and the exploration of rhythmic space saves his work from repetitive banality, but it is by no means denigratory to affirm that the technique is best suited to large, architectural murals. Fortunately, Partridge has secured many of these, in different parts of the world.

—Charles Spencer

PASCHKE, Ed(ward)

Nationality: American. **Born:** Chicago, Illinois, 22 June 1939. **Education:** School of the Art Institute of Chicago, B.F.A. 1961, M.F.A. 1970. **Career:** Painter; lives and works in Chicago. Instructor, Meramac College, St. Louis, 1970–71, Barat College, Lake Forest, Illinois, 1971–77, School of the Art Institute of Chicago, 1974–76, and Columbia College, Chicago, 1976–78; professor of drawing, Northwestern University, Evanston, Illinois, since 1977. **Awards:** Cassandra Foundation Grant, 1972; Logan Medal, Art Institute of Chicago, 1972; Annual Playboy Editorial Award, 1982; Chicago Academy for the Arts, 1985; Honorary Doctorate, School of the Art Institute of Chicago, 1990; Distinguished Alumnus, School of the Art Institute of Chicago, 1992; Illinois Academy of Fine Arts, 1992; Illinois Arts Alliance 8th Annual Yates Advocacy, 1994; Barat College Duchesne Recognition Award, 1998; Northwest University John Evans Award, 1999; Guggenheim Fellowship, 2000–01. **Agent:** Maya Polsky Gallery, 215 W. Superior, Chicago, Illinois, 60610. **Website:** http://www.edpaschke.com.

Individual Exhibitions:

1970 Deson Zaks Gallery, Chicago
1971 Hundred Acres Gallery, New York
1972 Deson Zaks Gallery, Chicago
1973 Richard de Marco Gallery, Edinburgh, Scotland
Deson Zaks Gallery, Chicago
1974 Contemporary Arts Center, Cincinnati, Ohio
Galerie Darthea Speyer, Paris
Hundred Acres Gallery, New York
1975 Pyramid Gallery, Washington, D.C.
Contemporary Arts Center, Cincinnati, Ohio (retrospective)
Deson Zaks Gallery, Chicago
1976 Marion Locks Gallery, Philadelphia
Galerie Darthea Speyer, Paris
1977 Phyllis Kind Gallery, Chicago
1978 Galerie Darthea Speyer, Paris
1979 Phyllis Kind Gallery, Chicago and New York
1982 *Ed Paschke: Selected Works, 1967–1981,* Renaissance Society, University of Chicago (travelled to Nebraska and Texas)
1983 Galerie Darthea Speyer, Paris
Phyllis Kind Gallery, Chicago and New York
New Paintings: 1983, Hewlett Gallery, Carnegie Mellon University, Pittsburgh (travelled to Kalamazoo Institute of Arts, Michigan)
1984 Galerie Bonnier, Geneva
1985 Galerie Bonnier, Geneva
1986 Whitney Museum of American Art, New York
Metropolitan Museum of Art, New York
Galerie Darthea Speyer, Paris
1987 Galerie Bonnier, Geneva
1988 Galerie Darthea Speyer, Paris
Dorothy Goldeen Gallery, Santa Monica, California
Phyllis Kind Gallery, Chicago
Galerie Bonnier, Geneva
Lowe Art Museum, University of Miami, Coral Gables
1989 Galerie Darthea Speyer, Paris
Ed Paschke Retrospective, Art Institute of Chicago (travelled to Musee d'Art Moderne Nationale, Paris, and the Dallas Art Museum, Texas)
1990 Galerie Darthea Speyer, Paris
Dorothy Goldeen Gallery, Santa Monica, California
Phyllis Kind Gallery, Chicago and New York
1992 Dorothy Goldeen Gallery, Santa Monica, California
Phyllis Kind Gallery, Chicago and New York
1993 Galerie Darthea Speyer, Paris
Phyllis Kind Gallery, Chicago and New York
1994 Grand Valley State University, Allendale, Michigan
1995 Phyllis Kind Gallery, Chicago

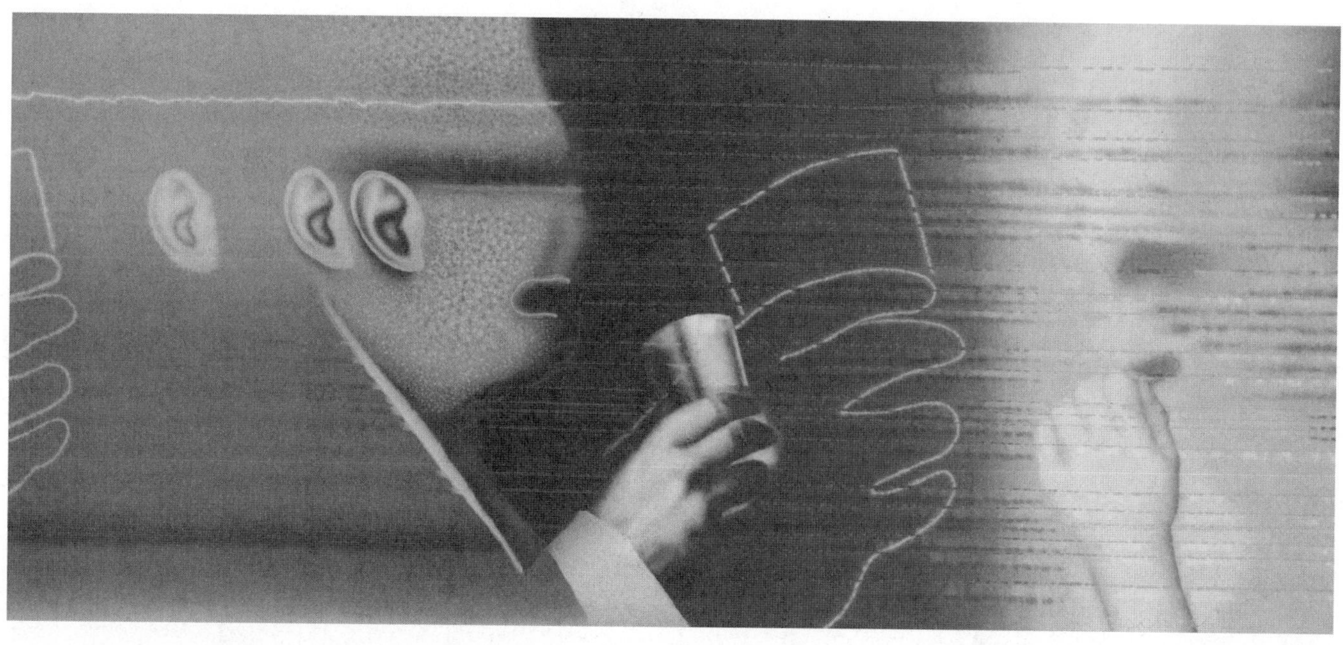

Ed Paschke: *Brand-Ex,* 1980. ©Christie's Images/Corbis.

Evan Mannes Gallery, Atlanta
Galerie Darthea Speyer, Paris
Galeria Galliani, Genoa
1996 Phyllis Kind Gallery, New York
1997 Maya Polsky Gallery, Chicago
INSA Gallery, Seoul, Korea
Gallery Ciocca, Milan, Italy
Galerie Darthea Speyer, Paris
1998 Dean Jensen Gallery, Milwaukee
Retrospective '73-'98, Galerie Darthea Speyer, Paris
David Floria Gallery, Aspen
1999 Frederick Snitzer Gallery, Miami
Maya Polsky Gallery, Chicago
Vaknin-Schwartz Gallery, Atlanta
Gallery B.A.I., New York
2000 Galerie Darthea Speyer, Paris

Selected Group Exhibitions:

1962 *Chicago and Vicinity Show,* Art Institute of Chicago (and 1967, 1969, 1973)
1972 *Chicago Imagist Art,* Museum of Contemporary Art, Chicago
What They're Up To in Chicago, National Gallery of Canada, Ottawa (travelling exhibition)
1973 *Biennial,* Whitney Museum of American Art, New York
Made in Chicago at the Bienal, Sao Paulo, (toured South America and travelled to the National Collection of Fine Arts, Smithsonian Institution, Washington, D.C., and Museum of Contemporary Art, Chicago)
1977 *View of the Decade,* Museum of Contemporary Art, Chicago
Masterpieces of Chicago Art, Chicago Public Library Cultural Center
1980 *100 Artists, 100 Years,* Art Institute of Chicago
1992 *From America's Studio: Twelve Contemporary Masters,* Art Institute of Chicago
1994 *Heads Only,* Art Museum at Florida International University, Miami
1995 *Selections from the Permanent Collection,* Whitney Museum, New York
Phyllis Kind Gallery Revisited, University of Wisconsin, Eau Claire, Wisconsin
Landfall Press Twenty Five Years, Chicago Art Institute Prints & Drawings, Chicago
1996 *Art in Chicago 1945–1995,* Museum of Contemporary Art, Chicago
Myth and Magic, California Center for the Arts, Escondido
Printmaking in America 1960–1990, Museum of Fine Arts Houston (also National Museum of American Art, Smithsonian, Washington, D.C.)
1997 *Landfall Press,* Museum of Modern Art, New York
Art and Provocation, Museum of Contemporary Art, Boulder
European Perspectives on American Art 3, Whitney Museum of American Art, New York
American Art in the Age of Technology, San Jose Museum of Art, San Jose
1998 *MCA Collects,* Museum of Contemporary Art, Chicago
Cleveland Collects, Museum of Contemporary Art, Cleveland
Chicago Ten, Chicago Atheneum, Illinois
1999 *The American Century,* Whitney Museum, New York
Art at the End of the Century, Scottsdale Museum of Art, Scottsdale
2000 *The American Century,* Chicago Cultural Center, Illinois
2001 *26th Print National,* Brooklyn, New York
Venus de Milo in 20th Century Art, Salvador Dali Museum, St. Petersburg, Florida

Ed Paschke: *Icon-Ero,* 1980. ©Christie's Images/Corbis.

Collections:

The Art Institute of Chicago; Baltimore Museum of Art, Maryland; Birmingham Museum of Art, Alabama; Borg-Warner Corporation, Chicago; Brooklyn Museum, New York; Carnegie Museum, Pittsburgh; Centre Georges Pompidou, Paris; The Chicago Tribune; Cole-Taylor Bank, Chicago; Continental Bank, Chicago; Exxon Corporation, New York; First National Bank of Chicago; General Electric and Company, Fairfield; Hirshhorn Museum, Washington, D.C.; Illinois Bell, Chicago; Jacksonville Museum of Art, Florida; Kalamazoo Institute of the Arts, Michigan; John F. Kennedy Library, Washington, D.C.; Virginia Museum of Fine Arts, Richmond; Metropolitan Museum of Art, New York; Milwaukee Art Museum, Wisconsin; Musee d'Art Nationale, Paris; Museo de Art Contemporaneo de Monterrey; Museum Boymans, Rotterdam; Museum of Contemporary Art, Chicago; Museum of Modern Art, New York; Museum Moderner Kunst, Vienna; National Museum of American Art, Smithsonian Institute, Washington, D.C.; Northern Trust Bank, Chicago;

Playboy Collection, Chicago; The State of Illinois, Chicago; University of Missouri; Valparaiso Museum of Art, Indiana; Walker Art Center, Minneapolis; Wake Forest Unversity, Winston-Salem, North Carolina; Whitney Museum of American Art, New York; Walker Museum, Minneapolis.

Publications:

By PASCHKE: Articles—"A Few Minutes with Ed Paschke" in *Chicago Social,* August 1997; "First Person" in *Chicago Tribune,* 4 December 1998.

On PASCHKE: Books—*Chicago Painters in Print: Brown, Paschke, Hull, Lostutter, Pasin-Sloan, Bramson, Wirsum,* Chicago 1989; *Ed Paschke* by Neal Benezra with contributions by Dennis Adrian, Carol Schreiber, and John Yau, New York and Chicago 1990. **Articles**—Review in the *New York Times,* 19 March 1982; "Imaging Issues: The Power of Paschke" by Dennis Adrian in *New Art Examiner,* March 1991; "Paschke Warms Up" in *Chicago Tribune,* September 1997; "Spatial Effects: Ed Paschke + (Art) = The Future" in *North Shore Magazine,* March 1998; "Taking Risks" in *Aspen Times Weekly,* 15 August 1998.

* * *

Ed Paschke is one of the representatives of the 1960s Chicago School—the figurative movement, i.e., the Imagists, a group comprised of Roger Brown, Edward C. Flood, Philip Hanson, Gladys Nillson, James Nutt, Christina Ramberg, and Karl Wirsum, who are (close enough) his contemporaries, not to mention the much older H. C. Westermann, who led them. These artists introduced a certain amount of ferment into the American art scene, occasionally even shocking the public.

At first the group appeared informally, giving their exhibitions names taken from an underground vocabulary: *The Hairy Who, Non-Plused Some, Marriage Chicago Style.* The artists also emulated people on the fringes of the community in their behavior and lifestyle; it was fashionable to display artistic bad taste, even vulgarity. Their anti-aestheticism embraced subjects that Pop Art had treated with discretion—sexual deviation, the kinds of pictures that one sees in porn shops, kitsch, obscene magazines, etc.

Paschke was born in 1939 in Chicago to a family of Polish-German descent. Although he spent his childhood and youth in the country, nature did not play a great part in the development of his artistic imagination. He is said to have visited doubtful bars, used slang, occasionally picked fights, and penetrated the hidden life of the metropolis. From material taken from reality itself, he began to build his images. Albeit theatrical, these were closer to reality than real theater. Fetishes turned into pictures appeared in his first works. Such a fetish might be a man's or woman's shoe of absurdly exaggerated proportions.

In his next phase, Paschke concentrated on eccentric portraits. His gallery of archetypes—models of the 1960s and early 1970s popularized by mass-produced underground magazines—may one day be considered a study of the night fauna of the great city. These persons wear gaudy clothes, ingenious hairstyles, and exotic hair coverings. Their bodies are covered in heavy makeup or even tattoos. They are grotesque, stunted, sexually ambiguous.

In his later paintings, social provocations seem to have dissipated: erotic perversion, travesty, hermaphrodism, and the various dark inhabitants from the city underworld disappear. Now the sitters appear to be wearing the theatrical masks that take away their individuality. They are shadows of real people—singers, guitarists, circus people, pleasure-seekers. Their contours are erased, softened, washed, and blurred like a photograph that is out of focus. A ghostly masquerade in ghostly colors—electric green, orange, red, and yellow—appears on the canvas in an aureola of flickering light impulses that bring to mind pictures from a television screen. Streaks that appear to be glowing with moonlight cut across the ground, breaking up its cohesion and artistic illusion. Inspired by falsely produced reality—electronic images made up of dots—Paschke now poses new problems in art. He also poses new problems in communicating through painting that reveals static, deformations, and malformations.

—Szymon Bojko

Despite the brashness of his color and the immediacy of much of his source imagery, Paschke's work has a tendency to shift only in the most subtle of ways. But since the late 1980s, his work has moved away from the vernacular subjects which had dominated earlier decades. There seems to be less concern with the potential shock value of a work's subject, and more interest in investigating how power accrues to, or is drained from, various categories of symbols. From 1985 he has produced close-up views of heads of familiar figures from culture and history—for example, Lincoln and the Mona Lisa, and, in 1999, antique Greek sculpture of female goddesses. He has also continued to investigate gender roles, but through more subtle male and female characteristics than the transvestites and pimps who had peopled his earlier paintings. These more recent figures are still, as one critic termed it, "Paschke-ized"—rendered with neon colors, patterned with tattoos, and interrupted with horizontal stripes that allude to electronic imagery. Paschke continues to be one of the best known and most widely exhibited of the Chicago Imagist artists. He was a 2000–01 recipient of a Guggenheim Fellowship.

—Paula Wisotzki

PASMORE, Victor

Nationality: British. **Born:** Chelsham, Surrey, 3 December 1908. **Education:** Attended evening classes at the Central School of Arts and Crafts, London, 1927–30; also attended Harrow School. **Family:** Married painter Wendy Lloyd Blood in 1940; children: two. **Career:** Painter. Worked in local government service, 1927–37. Abandoned abstract experiments and returned to visual realism, 1936; co-founded Euston Road School with Claude Rogers and William Coldstream, London, 1937; returned to abstract painting, 1946; with Robert Adams, Adrian Heath, Anthony Hill, and Kenneth Martin, organized first postwar abstract painting and sculpture exhibition, London, 1948; associated with Ben Nicholson and Barbara Hepworth in the Penwith Society of Art, St. Ives, Cornwall, 1951; consultant for urban design, Peterlee New Town, County Durham, 1954–77; organized summer school in Scarborough, Yorkshire, as experimental center for *The Developing Process,* 1955–57; organized *The Developing Process* exhibition, Newcastle upon Tyne and London, 1959; worked in graphics, with Kelpra Studios, London, 1964, and 2RC Workshop, Rome, 1971–94; immigrated to Malta. Visiting lecturer, Camberwell

Victor Pasmore: *The Festival is Britain's.* ©Hulton-Deutsch/Corbis.

School of Art, London, 1943–49, and Central School of Arts and Crafts, London, 1949–54; director of painting, Department of Fine Art, University of Durham at Newcastle upon Tyne, 1954–61. Trustee, Tate Gallery, London, 1963–66. **Member:** London Artists Association, 1932, and the London Group, 1934. **Awards:** Carnegie Prize for painting, *Pittsburgh International,* 1964; gold medal, *Graphics Biennale,* Frederikstad, Norway, 1972; graphics prize, 1971, and grand prize, 1977, *Biennale,* Ljubljana; Charles Wollaston Award, Royal Academy, London, 1983. Honorary doctorates from University of Newcastle upon Tyne, 1967; University of Surrey, 1969; Royal College of Art, London, 1972; University of Warwick, 1985. Named C.B.E. (Commander, Order of the British Empire), 1959; Companion of Honour, 1981; Royal Academician, London, 1984. **Agent:** Marlborough Fine Art, 6 Albemarle Street, London W1X 3HF, England. **Died:** January 1998.

Individual Exhibitions:

1932 London Artists Association Cooling Gallery, London
1940 Wildenstein Gallery, London
Redfern Gallery, London
1942 Wildenstein Gallery, London
1947 Redfern Gallery, London
1948 Redfern Gallery, London
1950 Redfern Gallery, London
Penwith Society, St. Yves, Cornwall (with Ben Nicholson and Barbara Hepworth)
1951 Redfern Gallery, London
1954 Institute of Contemporary Arts, London
1955 Redfern Gallery, London
Arts Council Gallery, Cambridge
1958 O'Hara Gallery, London
1960 Hatton Gallery, Newcastle upon Tyne
Biennale, Vienna (toured Europe, 1960–62)
1961 Palais des Beaux-Arts, Brussels (with Eduardo Paolozzi)
Marlborough New London Gallery, London
Kunstgalerie, Bochum, West Germany
1962 Kestner-Gesellshaft, Hannover
1963 Galerie Charles Leinhardt, Zurich
Kunsthalle, Berne
1964 Galleria Lorenzelli, Milan
Marlborough New London Gallery, London
1965 Tate Gallery, London (travelled to the Scottish National Gallery of Art, Edinburgh, and the Walker Art Gallery, Liverpool)
Bienal, Sao Paulo (toured South America)
1966 Marlborough New London Gallery, London
1967 Marlborough-Gerson Gallery, New York
Ranger's House, Blackheath, London
1968 Hatton Gallery, Newcastle upon Tyne
Whitworth Art Gallery, Manchester
Ulster Museum, Belfast (travelled to Trinity College, Dublin)
1969 Marlborough New London Gallery, London
1970 Galleria Lorenzelli, Milan
Arts Club of Chicago (travelled to Allentown Art Museum, Pennsylvania)
Palazzo de la Salle, Valletta, Malta
1971 Arnolfini Gallery, Bristol
1972 Marlborough Fine Art, London
1973 Marlborough Galerie, Zurich
Villiers Pty, Paddington, New South Wales, Australia
1974 Galleria Lorenzelli, Milan
Marlborough Galleria d'Arte, Rome
Marlborough Graphics, London
1975 Museum of Fine Art, Valletta, Malta
1977 Marlborough Fine Art, London (travelled to the Marlborough Galerie, Zurich)
1978 Galleria 2RC, Rome
Grafica '78 Internazionale, Messina, Sicily
Musée des Beaux-Arts, La Chaux de Fonds, Switzerland (travelled to the Gentof Radhus, Copenhagen)
1979 *Graphics International Biennale,* Ljubljana
Burstow Gallery, Brighton College, Sussex
Galleria Lorenzelli, Milan
1980 Royal Academy of Arts, London
Tate Gallery, London
Marlborough Fine Art, London
Cartwright Hall, Bradford, Yorkshire
1981 Amane Gallery, Osaka, Japan
Woodlands Art Gallery, Greenwich, London
National Gallery, Oslo (toured Scandinavia, 1981–82)
1982 Galleria Lorenzelli, Milan
Galerie Carinthia, Klagenfurt, Austria
Galerie Nicoline Pon, Zurich
1983 Marlborough Fine Art, London
1985 Musée des Beaux-Arts, Calais, France
1986 Marlborough Fine Art, London
1988 Yale Center for British Art, New Haven
Phillips Collection, Washington, D.C.
Marlborough Gallery, New York
1990 *Victor Pasmore: Nature Into Art,* Center for International Contemporary Arts, New York
The Artist's Eye, National Gallery, London
Marlborough Graphics, London
1991 *Going Abstract,* Serpentine Gallery, London
Center for International Contemporary Arts, New York
1992 *Victor Pasmore: Etchings and Aquatints,* Marlborough Graphics, London
Victor Pasmore: New Work, Marlborough Fine Art, London
1993 Tate Gallery, London
1995 *Victor Pasmore: New Work,* Marlborough Fine Art, London
1999 *Victor Pasmore 1908–1998: Memorial Retrospective Exhibition,* Marlborough Fine Art, London
Art Institute of Chicago
2000 *Victor Pasmore: Changing the Process of Painting,* Tate Gallery, Liverpool

Selected Group Exhibitions:

1934 *Objective Abstracts,* London
1956 *Masters of British Painting,* Museum of Modern Art, New York
1958 *Documenta 2,* Kassel, West Germany
1959 *The Developing Process,* Newcastle upon Tyne and London
1960 *Biennale,* Venice
1962 *Premio Marzotto,* Valdagno, Italy
1964 *Painting and Sculpture of a Decade,* Tate Gallery, London
1965 *Bienal,* Sao Paulo
1970 *Expo '70,* Osaka, Japan
1977 *International Biennale of Graphic Art,* Ljubljana, Yugoslavia
1991 *The Marlborough Gallery Re-opening Exhibition,* Marlborough Fine Art, London
1993 *The Sussex Scene: Artists in Sussex in the Twentieth Century,* Hove Museum and Art Gallery (travelled to Towner Art Gallery, Eastbourne)
1994 *British Abstract Art Part 1: Painting,* Flowers East, London
1997 *Lisbon: British Art 1960 to the Present,* Fundacao Calouste Gulbenkian, Lisbon

1998 *Art Treasures of England: The Regional Collections,* Royal Academy of Arts, London
Twentieth Century British Art: From Sickert to Hirst, Spink-Leger Pictures, London
2000 *Modern British Art,* Tate Gallery, Liverpool

Collections:

Tate Gallery, London; Scottish National Gallery of Art, Edinburgh; National Gallery of Victoria, Melbourne; National Gallery of New South Wales, Sydney; Rijksmuseum Kröller-Müller, Netherlands; Museum Boymans-van Beuningen, Rotterdam; Galleria Nazionale d'Arte Moderna, Rome; National Gallery of Canada, Ottawa; Museum of Modern Art, New York; Albright-Knox Art Gallery, Buffalo, New York.

Publications:

By PASMORE: Books—*A Developing Process in Art Teaching,* Newcastle upon Tyne 1959; *Colour as a Function of Multi-Dimensional Space,* London 1976; *The Artist's Eye: Victor Pasmore—An Exhibition of National Gallery Paintings Selected by the Artist,* exhibition catalog, 1990. **Articles—**''The Artist Speaks'' in *Art News and Review* (London), February 1951; ''Abstract Painting and Structure in England'' in *The World of Abstract Art* (New York), 1957; ''Connections Between Painting, Sculpture, and Architecture'' in *Zodiac* (Brussels), no. 1, 1957; ''Drawing as an Organic and Autonomous Activity'' in *London Magazine,* March 1964; ''The Artist on His Work'' in *Christian Science Monitor* (Boston), December 1965; ''The Developing Process'' in *Data* (London), 1968; ''Re-establishing the Individual Factor'' in *Art and Artists* (London), March 1969; ''The Concrete Picture-Plane and Multi-Dimensional Space'' in *The Structurist* (Saskatoon, Canada), no. 9, 1969; ''Picasso's Debt to Turner'' in the *Sunday Times* (London), 8 December 1974; ''Turner's Influence on Me'' in *Turner Society News* (London), October 1978; ''Turner and Impressionism'' in *Turner Society News* (London), April 1979; ''Victor Pasmore: The Case for Modern Art'' by Peter Fuller in *Modern Painters* (London), vol. 1, no. 4, Winter 1988–89; ''A Crisis in Function'' in *London Magazine,* April 1979; ''Victor Pasmore'' by Peter Townsend and Mel Gooding in *Art Montly,* no. 146, May 1991; ''Victor Pasmore Talks: Interview with the Artist About His Book Burning Waters'' in *Art Monthly,* no. 191, November 1995; ''Attraction of Opposites; Past Masters: Carel Weight and Victor Pasmore'' in *Royal Academy Magazine,* no. 59, Summer 1998.

On PASMORE: Books—*Victor Pasmore* by Clive Bell, London 1944; *Victor Pasmore,* exhibition catalog with text by Werner Smalenbach, Hannover 1962; *Victor Pasmore* by Jasia Reichardt, London 1963; *Victor Pasmore* by Herbert Read, Paris 1964; *Victor Pasmore,* exhibition catalog text by Ronald Alley, London 1965; *The Space Within,* exhibition catalog text by Dennis Duerden, New York 1967; *Victor Pasmore: Catalog Raisonnée* by Alan Bowness and Luigi Lambertini, London, New York and Milan 1980; *Victor Pasmore: 1950–1967,* exhibition catalog with text by Evelyne-Dorothee Allemand, Calais 1985; *Victor Pasmore: Nature Into Art,* exhibition catalog, with text by Bhupendra Karia and Norbert Lynton, New York 1990; *Victor Pasmore,* exhibition catalog, London 1990; *Victor Pasmore: Etchings and Aquatints,* exhibition catalog, London 1992; *Paintings and Graphics: 1980–1992* by Norbert Lynton; *Victor Pasmore: New Work,* exhibition catalog, London 1992. **Articles—**''Artist's Choice no. 36: Victor Pasmore—Relief Construction in White, Black, Maroon and Ochre'' in *Art and Australia,* vol. 26, no. 4, Winter 1989; ''A Forlorn Kind of Poetry: The Euston Road School'' by Robin Stemp in *The Artist* (Tenterden), vol. 104, July 1989; ''Towards an Art of Environment: Exhibitions and Publications by a Group of Avant-garde Abstract Artists in London 1951–55'' by Alastair Grieve in *The Burlington Magazine* (London), vol. 132, November 1990; ''In Profile: Pasmore'' by David Lee in *Art Review* (London), vol. 47, October 1995; Obituary by Margaret Garlake in *Art Monthly,* no. 214, March 1998; ''In Homage to Victor Pasmore: An Exhibit: ICA, London, 1957'' by David Sylvester in *Modern Painters* (London), vol. 11, no. 2, Summer 1998; ''Victor Pasmore's Wandering Journey, 1908–1998'' by Derek Hyatt in *Modern Painters* (London), vol. 12, no. 3, Autumn 1999; ''Liverpool and London: Victor Pasmore'' in *The Burlington Magazine* (London), vol. 141, no. 1158, September 1999; ''Representing Reality: G.E. Moore, Tonks Coldstream, Victor Pasmore and Others'' by David Cast in *Word & Image,* vol. 16, no. 3, July/September 2000.

*

Revolution in the form and imagery of the visual arts has either followed or accompanied critical changes in the evolution of human consciousness—Greece, Byzantine, the Renaissance, etc. Again, in the 20th century, when the conceptual implications of modern science have been pointing to a new metamorphosis of the mind, a new revolution has taken place. The dedication of painting and sculpture to a logical and extraneous relation between man and nature, which has formed their content since the Renaissance, has been challenged by a new Copernican revolution in which man, as well as the earth, is the relative factor. As a result, man and nature have begun to merge in a relationship that is not only more integrated but also irrational and more individual. It is perhaps in the independent forms, intrinsic images, and individual freedom of modern art that this new humanism and new cosmology has found its most potent expression.

—Victor Pasmore

* * *

Victor Pasmore is that rare thing in English culture, an artist-theoretician. It therefore comes as surprising to discover that he was self-taught as an artist; his mother was a Sunday painter and his father a doctor, but for 10 years he worked as a clerk for the London County Council before being rescued by his first patron, Sir Kenneth Clark. His special gifts as a teacher contributed to the Euston Road School, which he cofounded with William Coldstream, Graham Bell, and Claude Rogers, and from 1954 to 1961 he was director of painting at Durham University, at which time Richard Hamilton was his assistant, later his successor. It was at Durham that Pasmore was able to develop his theories of art, the integration of aesthetics and town planning, and then develop his own brand of English constructivism.

Despite his brilliant gifts and early fame, it wasn't until 1962 that Pasmore was able to support himself by his art. As early as 1934 he had experimented with abstract forms, which he regarded more as an outburst of youthful high spirits rather than a serious effort. But this period clearly contributed to the beautiful neo-impressionistic paintings of the 1940s, landscapes and scenes of the Thames, in which highly selected, near abstracted details are rendered with Whistlerish delicacy. This reference to Whistler is all-important, since Pasmore's work at this time (and since) is compounded of influences derived from impressionism and Japanese art, as well as Cézannesque-Cubist analyses of space.

Although his break from poetic naturalism to constructive abstraction forms one of the most dramatic incidents in modern British art, it was not as immediate as is generally supposed. There was a period of gestation and transience, especially connected with his association with Cornwall in the late 1940s and early 1950s, during which he also organized an important postwar exhibition of purely abstract art. ''Abstraction White, Brown, Grey and Ochre'' (1949; in the Tate Gallery) might easily be mistaken for a typical cubist collage of Ben Nicholson and suggests the same seacoast formation to be found in that artist's Cornish works. Pasmore's drawings of the Cornish coast, less cubistically formal, explore rhythmic, spiral motifs, which relate both to his interest in Japanese art and his later organic paintings. One must not fail to note Pasmore's reverence for Constable and Turner, who, he feels, raised English nostalgia for nature to unsurpassed levels of poetic expression. In his own transient period the drawings and paintings of natural phenomena (snowstorms, clouds, and the like) are clearly related to the preoccupations of these two English masters and to the involvement with nature that has produced some of Britain's finest art and poetry.

Pasmore's more disciplined constructivist period may have been an attempt to restrict the means whereby the understanding of nature, of space and light, could be formulated into severely limited expressive means. As in all his work, but particularly in the constructions of the late 1950s and 1960s, he aims for a striking balance of mind and emotion, in which elegance, taste, and scholarship play their parts.

Above all Pasmore had the special gift of conveying physical energy, a quality necessary to all great works of art. His work is exhilarating and exciting, never passive or depressive; one is conscious of the quality of thought and planning behind each piece, as well as the dexterous craftsmanship of expression. Control, formality, and rationality do not in any way inhibit passion, so that no matter how direct and positive the statement, it never lacks poetic resonance.

Although the early abstract studies led to three-dimensional constructions, Pasmore later conceded that his basic interest was painting: ''I am quite prepared to accept that my own bent and training is not as a sculptor or architect. I am returning to painting because I find I can go further with it.'' Since the mid-1960s Pasmore has evolved a body of work—paintings and prints—which finally reconcile his love of nature, his love of paint, and the delightful mixture of influences ranging from Turner and Constable, Whistler, the impressionists, and especially Japanese art. His knowledge of oriental art goes back to his schooldays and his early acquaintance with orientalist Laurence Binyon. He is said to have spent holidays in the British Museum, carefully examining Chinese landscape painting and the prints of Utamaro.

In his mature paintings, Pasmore clearly returned to the lessons learned and impressions received as a youth. His work once again became like organic, rhythmic compositions of large monochrome forms—similar to huge land-masses, linked by channels in which islands and isthmuses create interlocking shapes. Some paintings use flat areas of solid color, others use a pointillist style that goes back to his early impressionist landscapes. They are beautiful, satisfying works, relaxed and at ease, not concerned with the tensions set up by the constructivist reliefs, and in a sense no longer suggesting radical views or solutions. They embody the Turneresque or Japanese acceptance of life and nature, as phenomena to be studied, sources of pleasure and inspiration.

—Charles Spencer

PEARLSTEIN, Philip

Nationality: American. **Born:** Pittsburgh, Pennsylvania, 24 May 1924. **Education:** Studied under Sam Rosenberg, Robert Lepper and Balcomb Greene, Carnegie Institute of Technology, Pittsburgh, 1946–49, B.F.A. 1949; Institute of Fine Arts, New York University, 1951–55, M.A. 1955. **Career:** Independent painter, since 1955. Instructor, Pratt University, New York, 1959–63; visiting critic, Yale University, New Haven, Connecticut, 1962–63; professor of art, Brooklyn College, New York, 1963. **Awards:** Fulbright Travel Fellowship, to Italy, 1958; National Endowment for the Arts Grant, 1969; Guggenheim Fellowship, 1971, 1972; American Academy of Arts and Letters Award, 1973; Painting Prize, *First International Biennal of Figurative Painting,* Tokyo, 1974; Artist-in-Residence Fellowship, American Academy, Rome, 1982; Grantee, American Academy of Arts and Letters, 1992; Alumni Achievement Award, New York University Graduate School of Arts & Science, 2001. D.F.A.: Distinguished Doctorate Emerite, Brooklyn College, New York, 1988; Brooklyn College, New York 1996. **Agent:** Robert Miller Gallery, 524 West 26th St., New York, NY 10001, U.S.A.

Individual Exhibitions:

1955 Tanager Gallery, New York
1956 Peridot Gallery, New York
1957 Peridot Gallery, New York
1959 Tanager Gallery, New York
Peridot Gallery, New York
1960 Allan Frumkin Gallery, Chicago
1962 Kansas City Art Institute
Allan Frumkin Gallery, New York
1963 Allan Frumkin Gallery, Chicago
1965 Allan Frumkin Gallery, New York
Allan Frumkin Gallery, Chicago
Ceeje Gallery, Los Angeles
Reed College, Portland, Oregon
1966 Ceeje Gallery, Los Angeles
1967 Allan Frumkin Gallery, New York
Bradford Junior College, Massachusetts
1968 Carnegie-Mellon Institute, Pittsburgh
1969 Allan Frumkin Gallery, New York
1970 Chatham College, Pittsburgh
Georgia Museum of Art, Athens (restrospective; toured the United States)
1971 Graphics I and II Gallery, Boston
Leslie/Pearlstein/Thiebud: Contemporary Views of Man, Hayden Gallery, Massachusetts Institute of Technology, Cambridge
1972 Galerie M. E. Thelen, Cologne

Galleri Ostergren, Malmo, Sweden
Galerie Kornfeld, Zurich
Staaliche Museen-Kupferstichkabinett, West Berlin
Kunstverein, Hamburg
Donald Morris Gallery, Detroit
Hansen Fuller Gallery, San Francisco
Allan Frumkin Gallery, New York

1973 Parker 470 Gallery, Boston
Editions La Tortue, Paris

1974 Allan Frumkin Gallery, New York
Finch College, New York (retrospective; toured the United States)

1975 *The Human Figure,* Gimpel Fils, Ltd., London
Neuberger Museum, Purchase, New York
Marianne Friedland Gallery, Toronto

1976 Barbara Fendrick Gallery, Washington, D.C.
Donald Morris Gallery, Detroit

1978 Springfield Art Museum, Missouri (toured the United States)
Harcus-Krakow Gallery, Boston

1980 Allan Frumkin Gallery, New York
Association of American Artists, New York
FIAC, Paris

1981 *Landscape Aquatints 1978–1980,* Brooke Alexander Inc., New York
Ringling Museum of Art, Sarasota, Florida
Columbus College, Georgia
Reynolds/Minor Gallery, Richmond, Virginia
Marianne Friedland Gallery, Toronto
North Dakota State University, Fargo
University of North Carolina, Greensboro
Springfield Art Museum, Missouri
Graphics I and II, Boston

1982 Allan Frumkin Gallery, New York
Summit Art Center, New Jersey
Donald Morris Gallery, Birmingham, Michigan

1983 Galleria Il Ponte, Rome
American Academy, Rome
University of Northern Iowa, Cedar Falls (toured)
Milwaukee Art Museum, Wisconsin (retrospective; travelled to Brooklyn, New York; Philadelphia; Toledo, Ohio; Pittsburgh)

1984 Marianne Friedland Gallery, Toronto
Fay Gold Gallery, Atlanta, Georgia
Richmond University, Virginia

1985 Hirschl and Adler Modern, New York
Graphics I and II, Boston

1986 James Madison University, Harrisonburg, Virginia
Palace Theatre of the Arts, Stamford, Connecticut
Atlantic Center for the Arts, New Smyrna Beach, Florida
Amherst College, Massachusetts

1987 Art Gallery in Chicago
Marianne Friedland Gallery, Toronto
State University of New York, Binghamton

1988 Hirschl and Adler Modern, New York

1989 *Philip Pearlstein: Trials of the Sphinx,* The Brooklyn Museum (catalog)

1990 Galerie Zwirner, Cologne

1991 CompassRose Gallery, Chicago
Hirschl and Adler Modern, New York

1992 *Philip Pearlstein: The Abstract Landscape and Other Early Works on Paper,* The Butler Institute of American Art, The Institute, Youngstown (catalog)
The Artist's Eye, Academy of Design, New York (catalog)

1993 *3 Decades of Prints: Pearlstein,* Elvejem Museum, Madison
Recent Watercolors & Drawings, Hirschl & Adler Modern, New York

1994 *Pearlstein Prints,* Honolulu Museum, Hawaii

1995 *New Paintings,* Robert Miller Gallery, New York
Graphic Works, Springfield Art Museum, Missouri (catalog)

1996 *Portraits: 1946–1996,* Robert Miller Gallery, New York
Shippensburg University, Shippensburg, Pennsylvania

1997 *Up Close and Impersonal,* Robert Miller Gallery, New York

1998 *Philip Pearstein: World War II Drawings,* Carnegie Museum of Art, Pittsburgh

Selected Group Exhibitions:

1954 *Emerging Talent,* Kootz Gallery, New York

1962 *The First Five Years,* Whitney Museum, New York

1968 *Realism Now,* Vassar College, Poughkeepsie, New York

1974 *7 Realists,* Yale University, New Haven, Connecticut

1977 *8 Contemporary Realists,* Pennsylvania Academy of Fine Arts, Philadelphia (travelled to the North Carolina Museum of Art)

1979 *6 Painters of the Figure,* University of Colorado Museum, Boulder

1980 *Realism/Photorealism,* Philbrook Art Center, Tulsa, Oklahoma

1982 *Contemporary American Realism since 1960,* Pennsylvania Academy of Fine Arts, Philadelphia

1985 *American Realism: The Precise Image,* Isetan Museum, Tokyo (travelled to Osaka and Yokohama, Japan)

1987 *Visions of America,* ACA Galleries, New York

1994 *NY Realism,* Odakyu Museum, Tokyo (also Kagoshima Museum of Art; Kitayushu Municipal Museum, Japan; Fukushima Prefectrual, Japan)
Hirschl & Adler Modern Gallery, New York

1995 *American Interiors,* Knoedler & Company, New York
The Urban Landscape, The Murray Collection, Scranton, Pennsylvania
NY Visions 1900–95, ACA Gallery, New York

1996 *171st Exhibition,* National Academy of Design, New York
Thomas J. Walsh Art Gallery, Fairfield University, Connecticut
Realism After 7 AM, Hopper House, Piermont, New York

1997 *Abstract Expressionism in US,* Centro Arte Contemporaneo, Mexico City

2001 *Eye of Modernism,* Georgia O'Keeffe Museum, Santa Fe

Collections:

Museum of Modern Art, New York; Whitney Museum, New York; Metropolitan Museum of Art, New York; Brooklyn Museum, New York; Vassar College, Poughkeepsie, New York; Hirshhorn Museum,

Washington, D.C.; Corcoran Gallery, Washington, D.C.; Art Institute of Chicago; Cleveland Museum of Art; Milwaukee Art Center.

Publications:

By PEARLSTEIN: Books—*Philip Pearlstein: Drawings and Watercolors,* with John Perreault, New York 1988. **Articles**—''The Symbolic Language of Francis Picabia'' in *Arts Magazine* (New York), January 1956; ''Futurism and Some Other Impure Forms'' in *Artnews* (New York), Summer 1961; ''The Private Myth'' in *Artnews* (New York), September 1961; ''The Figure Paintings Today Are Not Made in Heaven'' in *Artnews* (New York), summer 1962; ''Whose Painting Is It, Anyway?'' in *Arts Yearbook,* New York 1964; statement in *Art Now: New York* (New York) March 1971; ''Why I Paint the Way I Do'' in the *New York Times,* August 1971; ''A Conversation with Philip Pearlstein,'' interview, with Ellen Schwartz, in *Art in America* (New York), September/October 1971; ''Pearlstein Portraits,'' interview, with Ralph Pomeroy, in *Art and Artists* (London), September 1973; interview, with Paul Cummings, in *Artists in Their Own Words: Interviews,* New York 1979; ''Re: De Kooning'' in *Art Journal,* vol. 48, Fall 1989; ''An Artist's Case'' in *Art in America* (New York), vol. 78, May 1990; ''Censorship on Stylistic Grounds'' in *Art Journal,* vol. 50, Winter 1991.

On PEARLSTEIN: Books—*Philip Pearlstein,* exhibition catalog with an essay by Linda Nochlin, Athens, Georgia 1970; *Leslie/Pearlman/Thiebaud: Contemporary Views of Man,* exhibition catalog with text by Sidra Stich, Cambridge, Massachusetts 1971; *Philip Pearlstein,* exhibition catalog, Detroit 1972; *Neue Formen des Realismus* by Peter Plagens, Cologne 1973; *The Age of the Avant-Garde* by Hilton Kramer, New York 1973; *7 Realists,* exhibition catalog, New Haven, Connecticut 1974; *Philip Pearlstein: The Human Figure,* exhibition catalog, London 1975; *Returns of Realism,* Part 1, exhibition catalog, with essays by Allan Frumkin and Charlotte Stockes, Rochester, Michigan 1978; *Philip Pearlstein: Landscape Aquatints 1978–1980,* exhibition catalog, New York 1981; *Philip Pearlstein: A Painter's Progress,* exhibition catalog with essay by Paul Master-Karnik, Summit, New Jersey 1982; *Philip Pearlstein: A Retrospective,* exhibition catalog with texts by Russell Bowman and Irving Sandler, Milwaukee 1983. **Articles**—''Confronting the Solemn Nude'' by John Perreault in the *Village Voice* (New York), 14 February 1974; ''What the Flesh on Real Humans Looks Like'' by Peter Schjeldhal in the *New York Tmes,* 17 February 1974; ''Pearlstein: Portraits at Face Value'' by Hayden Herrera in *Art in America* (New York), January/February 1975; ''Art View'' by Hilton Kramer in the *New York Times* 15 February 1976; ''Philip Pearlstein: Is He the Enemy of Realism?'' by Robert Duffy in the *St. Louis Post-Dispatch,* 27 February 1977; ''Philip Pearlstein: Naked Nudes, A Profile'' by John Perreault in the *Soho Weekly News* (New York), 20 April 1978; ''An Artist Who Likes the Body'' by Franz Schulze in the *Chicago Sun Times,* 17 June 1979; ''The Evolution of Philip Pearlstein, Part 1'' by L. Wallin in *Art International* (Lugano, Switzerland), Summer 1979; ''The Evolution of Philip Pearlstein, Part 2'' by L. Wallin in *Art International,* September 1979; ''Philip Pearlstein: The Complete Paintings'' by Lawrence Alloway in *Art in America* (New York), February 1985; ''Artist and Model: Why the Tradition Continues'' by Grace Glueck in the *New York Times,* 8 June 1986; ''Philip Pearstein: Figures and Other Objects'' by Susan Koslow in *Arts Magazine,* vol. 62, Summer 1988; ''Philip Pearlstein: Portrait of Linda Nochlin and Richard Pommer'' by Linda Nochlin in *Artforum International,* vol. 32, September 1993; ''Philip Pearlstein'' by Donald B. Kuspit in *Artforum International,* vol. 33, May 1995.

*

Most artists reach maturity when they consciously decide what kind of art they do not want to make. They are then free to go on to invent an attitude that opens new technical and stylistic possibilities. Around 1960, I felt a sudden revulsion to the expressionism that had been the dominant characteristic of art of the New York painters during the preceding decade. My own works then had taken off from the Abstract Expressionists. I was determined to start from a zero position to pragmatically depict the forms of the models I hired. The models took poses that provided me with picture structure possibilities. I rejected self-expression, psycho-drama and all other storytelling, letting the implications of such fall as they would. I concentrated on the exploitation of creating the illusions of form in space, that to me remains the most intriguing of painting problems. Along the way I have been charged with being pornographic, or worse, antihumanistic, etc. However, my intent has been to ignore all that, and, supported by the figurative traditions of Western art, to explore the aesthetics inherent in one possible way of painting.

—Philip Pearlstein

* * *

Philip Pearlstein's preoccupation with the human figure enriches his visual utterance, but it is not, as one might think, the overriding element in his compositions. Rather the *forms* of such figures are the shapes he chooses to work with as the areas and edges within the compositional limits of a rectangle. The way parts of the figures move right off the canvas does not greatly concern him as he has established a module for the entire work from the very beginning—a hand, say, or perhaps a foot. Once chosen, this module is completely realized before the next form is worked on, and this working out or away from the initial module sets the scale against which successive forms are measured. As a result, the cropping—so characteristic of his work—has a quality of surprise about it; even he doesn't always know where it will occur. But control is maintained, and a satisfying sense of balance, through the establishment of the right scale over the whole painting. As for the going-off, Pearlstein shares the compositional novelty achieved by a number of contemporary artists in that he does not structure his work in relation to the edge of the canvas. He enjoys the increased struggle this creates for the picture plane in trying to maintain itself.

Pearlstein has come up with a revealing statement to describe what he does with his nude figures—he calls his manipulation of bodies ''a sort of stilled-action choreography.'' He has no interest in the psychological overtones of the relationships exposed in his work. It is only as a subject for painting that he considers his models, rather like the way Morandi utilized his bottles. Pearlstein wants the movement of the forms, their directional thrust, to create the structure of the painting. He also wants to put down what it is he sees as a way of reiterating the innate dignity of the human body.

—Ralph Pomeroy

PENCK, A. R.

Nationality: German. **Born:** Ralf Winkler, in Dresden, 5 October 1939; adopted name A. R. Penck, 1969. **Education:** 38th Grundschule, Dresden, 1945–53; self-taught in art from 1953. **Military Service:** Served in the DDR Volksarmee, 1957, 1973–74. **Career:** Trainee design draughtsman, Dresden, 1956; worked as a newspaper delivery-boy, night watchman, postman, stroker, etc, Dresden, 1957–60. Independent artist, working with intuitive and symbolic imagery, from 1963, establishing his own studio in the Lange Strasse, East Berlin, 1963, and in the Gostritzer Strasse, Dresden, 1977; lived in East Berlin, 1963–72, in Lindenau, 1972–76, in Dresden, 1976–80, and in Kerpen, near Cologne, from 1980. Currently lives and works in Cologne, London, and Dublin. **Awards:** Print Prize, *International Triennale,* Grenchen, 1974; Will-Grohmann Prize, 1976; Rembrandt Prize, Basel, 1980. **Agent:** Galerie Michael Werner, Cologne. **Address:** c/o Galerie Michael Werner, Gertrudenstrasse 24–28, 5000 Cologne 1, West Germany.

Individual Exhibitions:

1969 Galerie Michael Werner, Cologne
1970 Galerie Michael Werner, at the *IKI Art Fair,* Cologne
1971 Galerie Heiner Friedrich, Munich
Museum Haus Lange, Krefeld, West Germany
Galerie Michael Werner, Cologne
1972 Wide White Space Gallery, Antwerp
Kunsthalle, Basel
Goethe-Institut, Amsterdam
Galerie Stampa, Basel
Galerie Michael Werner, Cologne
Galerie Grafikmeyer, Karlsruhe
Galerie Beck, Erlangen, West Germany
1973 Galerie Loehr, Frankfurt
Nova Scotia College of Art and Design, Halifax
Daner Galleriet, Copenhagen
Galleria l'Uomo e l'Arte, Milan
1974 Galerie Michael Werner, Cologne
Galerie Stampa, Basel
Galerie Nachst St. Stephan, Vienna
Galerie Heiner Friedrich, Munich
Städtisches Galerie ''Altes Theater,'' Ravensburg, West Germany
Wide White Space Gallery, Antwerp
1975 Galerie Neuendorf, Hamburg
Kunsthalle, Bern
Galerie Seriaal, Amsterdam
Stedelijk Van Abbemuseum, Eindhoven, Netherlands
Galerie Michael Werner, Cologne
Kunsthalle, Basel
1977 Galerie Seriaal, Amsterdam
Kunstverein, Mannheim
Museum Ludwig, Cologne
1978 *Zeichnungen bis 1975,* Kunstmuseum, Basel
Galerie Helen van der Mey, Amsterdam
Galerie Rudolf Springer, West Berlin
1979 *Concept Conceptruimte,* Museum Boysman-van Beuningen, Rotterdam
Galerie Michael Werner, Cologne
1980 Galerie Fred Jahn, Munich
Städtisches Museum Schloss Morsbroich, Leverkusen, West Germany
Galerie Michael Werner, Cologne
Kunstmuseum, Basel
1981 Galerie Helen van der Mey, Amsterdam
Gemalde, Handzeichnungen, Josef-Haubrich-Kunsthalle, Cologne
38 neue bilder, Galerie Neuendorf, Hamburg
1982 Sonnabend Gallery, New York
Galleria Lucio Amelio, Naples
Galleria Toselli, Milan
Studio d'Arte Cannaviello, Milan
Galerie Gillespie-Laage-Salomon, Paris
Waddington Galleries, London
Edition Sabine Knust, Munich (with Jorg Immendorf)
Galerie Michael Werner, Cologne
Kunstmuseum, Basel
Kunstmuseum, Bonn
1983 Galleria Lucio Amelio, Naples
Yarlow/Salzmann Gallery, Toronto
Galerie Michael Werner, Cologne
Galerie Springer, West Berlin
Galerie Sabine Knust, Munich
Galerie Gillespie-Laage-Salomon, Paris
1984 Mary Boone/Michael Werner Gallery, New York
Watari Gallery, Tokyo
Studio d'Arte Cannaviello, Milan
Galerie Maeght Lelong, Zurich
Waddington Galleries, London
Galerie Alma, Lyon, France
Ulrike Kantor Gallery, Los Angeles
Tate Gallery, London
A. R. Penck, at the *Biennale,* Venice
Akira Ikeda Gallery, Tokyo
Galerie Sabine Knust, Munich
Galerie Michael Werner, Cologne
Temple Bar Studios, Dublin
1985 Musée d'Art et d'Industrie, St. Etienne, France
Brody's Gallery, Washington, D.C.
Arnolfini Gallery, Bristol, Avon
Galerie Michael Werner, Cologne
Stadtische Museum, Mönchengladbach, West Germany
Mary Boone/Michael Werner Gallery, New York
Galerie Herbert Meyer-Ellinger, Frankfurt
Neue Galerie-Sammlung Ludwig, Aachen, West Germany
Kunstverein, Braunschweig, West Germany
1986 Deweer Art Gallery, Zwevegem-Otegem, Belgium
Galleria Christian Stein, Milan
Galerie Maeght Lelong, Zurich
Galerie Springer, West Berlin
Galerie und Edition Stahli, Zurich
Galerie Gillespie-Laage-Salomon, Paris
Kunstverein, Freiburg, West Germany
Maximilian Verlag/Sabine Knust, Munich
Galerie Collection d'Art, Amsterdam
Cabinet des Estampes, Geneva
Barbara Toll Fine Arts, New York
Galerie Michael Werner, Cologne
Galerie Dobele, Ravensburg, West Germany

DAAD-Galerie, West Berlin
Galerie de Ganzerik, Eindhoven, Netherlands (with Johannes Brus)
Kunsthalle, Bielefeld, West Germany (with P. Kirkeby and M. Lupertz)
1987 Orchard Gallery, Londonderry, Northern Ireland
Stadtische Museum, Mönchengladbach, West Germany
Douglas Hyde Gallery, Dublin
Edinburgh College of Art, Scotland
Fruitmarket Gallery, Edinburgh
Galerie Michael Werner, Cologne
Ulmer Museum, Ulm, West Germany
Galerie Steinmetz, Bonn
Galerie Chobot, Vienna
Galerie und Edition Stahli, Zurich
Musée de Strasbourg, France
Galerie Jule Kewenig, Frechen-Bachem, West Germany
Kettle's Yard Gallery, Cambridge, England
Galerie Thaddeus Ropac, Salzburg, Austria
Galerie Springer, West Berlin
Galerie Gillespie-Laage-Salomon, Paris (with G. Baselitz and M. Lupertz)
1988 Galerie Van de Loo, Munich
Tekeningen: A.R. Peck, Haags Gemeentemuseum, The Hauge (catalog)
A.R. Penck: Holzschnitte 1966–1987, Die Stiftung, Bremen (catalog)
A.R. Penck: Skulpturen und Zeichnungen, 1971–1987, Kestner-Gesellschaft, Hannover (catalog)
1989 Magasin 3 Stockholm Konsthall, Stockholm (catalog)
A.R. Penck: Venice Paintings, Fred Hoffman Gallery, Santa Monica (catalog)
A.R. Penck, Galerie Beyeler (catalog)
Mary Boone Gallery, New York (catalog)
1990 *A.R. Penck: Standart Weapons, Standart Models,* Michael Werner Gallery, New York (traveled to Galerie Philippe Guimiot, Brussels) (catalog)
A.R. Penck: Opere Recenti, Galleria in Arco, Torino (catalog)
1992 *Analyse Einer Situation,* Die Galerie, Dresden (catalog)
A.R. Penck: "Städte und Menschen," Galerie Rigassi, Bern (catalog)
1993 Nolan/Eckman Gallery, New York
Galerie im Hörsaalbau, Leipzig (catalog)
1994 Städtische Galerie Albstadt, Albstadt, Germany (catalog)
1995 *Zeichnungen/Tekeningen, 1965–1977,* Museum Het Domein, Sittard, the Städt (traveled to Museum Mülheim an der Ruhr; Galerie der Stadt Kornwestheim; Kultusministerium des Landes Nordrhein-Westfalen, Germany) (catalog)
1996 Michael Werner Gallery, New York
Fundación Rufino Tamayo, México (catalog)
A.R. Penck: Resurrection, Michael Werner Gallery, Köln (catalog)
1999 *A.R. Penck: Memory, Model, Memorial,* Städtische Museen Heilbronn, Frankfurt am Main (catalog)
2000 Kolbe Museum, Berlin (catalog)
A.R. Penck: 9 Konfessionen: Bilder von 1988–1995, Kulturzentrum Englische Kirche der Stadt Bad Homburg, Germany (catalog)

Selected Group Exhibitions:

1971 *Prospekt '71,* Kunsthalle, Dusseldorf (and *Prospekt '73,* 1973)
1972 *Documenta 5,* Kassel, West Germany (and *Documenta 7,* 1982)
1974 *Projekt '74,* Kunsthalle, Cologne
1975 *Functions of Drawing,* Rijksmuseum
Kröller-Müller, Otterlo, Netherlands
1978 *Werke aus der Sammlung Crex,* Ink, Zurich, Switzerland (travelled to the Louisiana Museum, Humlebaek, Denmark; Städtische Galerie im Lenbachhaus, Munich; and the Kunstverein, Hamburg)
1979 *European Dialogue,* At the *3rd Biennale of Sydney,* Art Gallery of New South Wales, Sydney
1981 *A New Spirit in Painting,* Royal Academy of Art, London
1983 *Expressions: New Art from Germany,* St. Louis Art Museum, Missouri (travelled to Philadelphia; Chicago)
1985 *The European Iceberg,* Art Gallery of Ontario, Toronto
1987 *Mathematik in der Kunst,* Wilhelm-Hack-Museum, Ludwigshafen, West Germany
1989 *Figuratively Speaking: Drawings by Seven Artists,* Neuberger Museum, State University of New York, Purchase (catalog)
1990 *Figural Signs,* The Gallery, Amherst (catalog)
Zeichnungen, Dem Kupferstichkabinett, Basel (catalog)
1991 *Erste Phalanx Nedserd,* Kunsthalle Nürnberg (also Staatliches Lindenau-Museum, Altenburg) (catalog)
1996 *The Froehlich Foundation: German and American Art from Beuys and Warhol,* Froehlich Foundation, Stuttgart (catalog)
1998 *21st International Art and Antique Exhibition,* Essen, Germany
1999 *The Woodcut in the 20th Century,* Stadtische Kunstmuseum Spendhaus Reutlingen, Germany (catalog)

Collections:

Stedelijk Museum, Amsterdam; Van Abbemuseum, Eindhoven; Kaiser-Wilhelm-Museum, Krefeld; Neue Galerie-Sammlung Ludwig, Aachen; Kunsthalle, Basel; Museum of Fine Arts, Boston; University of Lethbridge Art Collection, Alberta, Canada; Art Gallery of South Australia, Adelaide.

Publications:

By PENCK: Books—*Standart Making,* Munich 1970: *Was ist Standart,* Cologne and New York 1970; *Ich: Standart Lieratur,* Paris 1971; *Zeichen als Verstandigung,* exhibition catalog, Krefeld, West Germany 1971; *Standart: Deskriptive Einfuhrung 1 + 2,* Milan 1973; *Europaische Sonnete,* Antwerp 1974; *Sanfte Theorie über Arsch, Asche und Vegetation,* Groningen 1979; *Immendorff besucht Deutschland mal Deutschland-Ein Deutsch-Deustcher Vertrag,* with Jorg Immendorff, Munich 1979; *Kneipen und Kneipentexte,* Dresden 1980; *Je suis un livre: achetez-moi maintenant,* Paris 1981; *Endi im Osten: 98 Zeichnungen,* West Berlin 1981; *A. R. Penck: Paris Graphik,* Munich 1984; *Welt des Adlers,* West Berlin 1985; *Standart-Modelle 1973/74,* Cologne 1985; *Standart 1971/73,* West Berlin 1985; *Mein Denken,* edited by Klaus Gallwitz, Frankfurt 1986; *A.R.*

Penck, with Bernard Marcadé, Paris 1988; *A.R. Penck im Gespräch mit Wilfried Dickhoff,* Cologne 1990; *A.R. Penck,* Bonn 1991; *A.R. Penck: Paintings,* New York 1991; *Delphi Heliotroph: Eine Skulptur von A.R. Penck,* with Klaus Gallwitz, Siegfried Gohr and Benjamin Katz, Bern 1993; *A.R. Penck: Sonette,* Berlin 1997. **Articles—**''Der Adler'' in *Interfunktionen,* (Cologne), no. 1, 1974; ''Ich über Mich Selbst'' in *Kunstforum International* (Mainz), December/January 1975; editor, *Krater und Wolke* (Cologne), no. 1, 1982; interview with Brigitte Schenk in *Flash Art,* no. 150, January-February 1990.

On PENCK: Books—*A. R. Penck,* exhibition catalog with texts by Johannes Gachnang and Dieter Koepplin, Basel 1975; *A. R. Penck,* exhibition catalog with text by Günther Gercken, Hamburg 1975; *A. R. Penck: Zeichnungen bis 1975,* exhibition catalog with texts by Johannes Gachnang and Dieter Koepplin, Basel 1978; *A. R. Penck: Concept Conceptruimte,* exhibition catalog with texts by Wim A. L. Beeren, Johannes Gachnang, M. Visser and others, Rotterdam 1979; *A. R. Penck: Gemalde, Handzeichnungen,* exhibition catalog with text by Siegfried Gohr, Cologne 1981; *A. R. Penck,* exhibition catalog with text by Johannes Gachnang, Berne 1981; *A. R. Penck: 38 neue bilder,* exhibition catalog with text by Günther Gercken, Hamburg 1981; *A. R. Penck,* exhibition catalog with text by Richard Calvocoressi, London 1982; *A. R. Penck: 45 Zeichnungen,* exhibition catalog with text by Dieter Koepplin, Basel and Bonn 1982; *A. R. Penck: Brown's Hotel and Other Works,* exhibition catalog with text by Richard Calvocoressi, London 1984; *A. R. Penck: Mike Hammer—Konsequenzen,* exhibition catalog with text by Johannes Cladders, Monchengladbach 1985; *A. R. Penck: Graphik Ost/West,* exhibition catalog with text by D. Bojescul, Braunschweig 1986; *Penck West in Berlin—Zeichnungen aus den Jahren 1980–1982,* exhibition catalog with text by Wieland Schmied, West Berlin 1987; *A.R. Penck* by John Yau, New York 1993. **Articles—**''A.R. Penck'' by Heinz-Peter Schwerfel in *Beaux Arts Magazine,* no. 90, May 1991; ''A.R. Penck'' by Donald Kuspit in *Artforum,* vol. 31, no. 6, February 1993; ''The Drawings of A.R. Penck'' by John Yau in *Drawing,* vol. 14, no. 5, January-February 1993; ''A.R. Penck'' by Klaus Ottmann in *Journal of Contemporary Art,* vol. 7, no. 1, Summer 1994; ''A.R. Penck at Michael Werner'' by Eleanor Heartney in *Art in America* (New York), vol. 84, June 1996.

* * *

Penck received no formal artistic training and was given his first public exhibition in East Germany in 1956. Shortly before the building of the Berlin Wall in 1961 he exhibited at the Akademie der Kunst in East Berlin. Penck gave up painting for two years, going back to it in 1963 on being given a commission by an architects' co-operative to paint a mural for four walls of a Dresden cellar. He painted a black line representing the border between East and West with soldiers shown shooting each other and sprawled on the ground. This has been described as resembling the prehistoric hunting scenes found on the walls of caves in Southern France and Northern Spain. By 1965 when Penck participated in an exhibition at the Pushkin House, Dresden, he was falling out with the authorities which made it difficult for him to exhibit publicly. His pictures were smuggled to the West for his first solo show at Galerie Michael Werner in Cologne in 1969. In 1973 Penck's name was found to be a pseudonym, which had been successfully used to hide his name while his work was on show in the west. By 1980 his position had become extremely difficult in Dresden where he could not sell his pictures legally. He was ''bought out'' and allowed to immigrate to the west. In 1983 he moved to London.

In the 1982 Waddington Gallery and 1985 Tate Gallery catalogs of Penck exhibitions Richard Calvocoressi has explained the paintings as an elaborate method of picture writing which the artist uses to communicate his bleak understanding of human behavior. His picture surfaces have, scattered across them, ''geometric or archetypal forms, symbols from mathematics or logic, hieroglyphs, emblematic objects (orb, eagle, death-mask, flower), the occasional face or head, often in pictorial shorthand, and large, anonymous, stick-like figures, singles or in pairs . . . . The key to all this is Penck's interest in cybernetics, information theory, codes and cyphers, imaginatively and humorously exploited.'' The paintings are not to be seen though as the kind of ''automatic writing'' as used in Surrealism, but carefully thought out in advance.

Since coming to the west, Penck has explored a great variety of artistic outlets, such as sculpture, book making, prints, music and the occasional film. Such is his mistrust, though of the artist's recognizable style, the artist's ''handwriting,'' (and in this he is not alone among his generation), that he still uses various pseudonyms, (such as Mike Hammer, TM, Ypsilon, Alpha), to correspond to different areas of his artistic output.

—Victoria Keller

PENONE, Giuseppe

Nationality: Italian. **Born:** Garessio Ponte, 3 April 1947. **Career:** Independent Artist, Turin, since 1967; founding member of Arte Povera movement, 1967. **Agents:** Galerie Paul Maenz, Bismarkstrasse 50, 5000 Cologne 1, Germany; Galleria Christian Stein, Turin and Milan. **Address:** c/o Galleria Christian Stein, Piazza San Claro, 10121 Turin, Italy; Marian Goodman Gallery, 24 West 57th Street, New York, New York, 10019.

Individual Exhibitions:

1968 Deposito d'Arte Presente, Turin
1969 Galleria Sperone, Turin
1970 Aktionsraum 1, Munich
Galleria Toselli, Milan
1972 Galerie Paul Maenz, Cologne
1973 Galleria Multipli, Turin
Galleria Sperone, Turin
Galleria Toselli, Milan
Galerie Klaus Lupke, Frankfurt
Galerie Paul Maenz, Cologne
1974 Galleria Sperone/Fischer, Rome
Galerie 't Venster, Rotterdam
Galleria Schema, Florence
1975 Galerie Paul Maenz, Cologne
Samangalleria, Genoa, Italy
Galleria Sperone, Turin
Sperone Gallery, New York
1976 Nuovi Strumenti, Brescia, Italy
Studio De Ambrogi, Milan
1977 Kunstmuseum, Lucerne

1978 Galerie Paul Maenz, Cologne
Galerie Rudolf Zwirner, Cologne
Staatliche Kunsthalle, Baden-Baden, West Germany
Galleria Salvatore Ala, Milan
Museum Folkwang, Essen, West Germany
Galleria De Crescenzo, Rome
1979 Galerie Durand-Dessert, Paris
Studio G7, Bologna
Halle fur Internationale Neue Kunst, Zurich
1980 Galerie Helen van der Meij, Amsterdam
Stedelijk Museum, Amsterdam
Kabinett für Aktuelle Kunst, Bremerhaven, West Germany
Ausstellungstudio, Monchengladbach, West Germany
Galleria Christian Stein, Turin
Lisson Gallery, London
Galerie Gewad, Ghent, Belgium
1981 Salvatore Ala Gallery, New York
Galerie Konrad Fischer, Zurich
1982 Städtische Museum, Monchengaldbach, West Germany
Salvatore Ala Gallery, New York
Galerie Konrad Fischer, Zurich
1983 Galleria Salvatore Ala, Milan
Galleria Christian Stein, Turin
Galerie Durand-Dessert, Paris
National Gallery of Canada, Ottawa
1984 Fort Worth Art Museum, Texas
Museum of Contemporary Art, Chicago
Musée d'Art Moderne de la Ville, Paris
1986 Galerie Buchmann, Basel
1987 Galleria Christian Stein, Milan
1991 Galerie de l'Ancienne Douane, Strasbourg, France
Museo d'Arte Contemporanea, Turin
1992 Marian Goodman Gallery, New York
Galerie Jule Kewenig, Cologne
Foro per l'Arte Contemporanea, Verona
Galerie Durand-Dessert, Paris
1993 Frith Street Gallery, London
Centre Genevoise de Gravure Contemporaine, Geneva
Château d'Annecy, France
1994 Centro Culturale Teresa Orsola Bussa de Rossi, Cuneo, Italy
Maison de la Culture, Amiens, France
1995 Marian Goodman Gallery, New York
1996 Galerie Liliane, Paris
Michel Durand-Dessert, Paris
1997 Musée d'Art Contemporain, Nîmes, France (catalog)
Giuseppe Penone: Die Adern des Steins, Kunstmuseum Bonn, Germany (also Toyota Municipal Museum of Art, Toyota City) (catalog)
1999 The Douglas Hyde Gallery, Dublin
Fondation Cartier, Paris
Giuseppe Penone: 1968–1998, Centro Galego de Arte Contemporánea, Galicia (catalog)
To Breathe, Douglas Hyde Gallery, Dublin (catalog)
2000 Marian Goodman Gallery, New York

Selected Group Exhibitions:

1969 *Konzeption-Conception,* Städtische Museum, Leverkusen, West Germany
1970 *Conceptual Art, Arte Povera, Land Art,* Galleria Civia d'Arte Moderna, Turin
1972 *Documenta 5,* Kassel, West Germany
1974 *Die verlorene Identitat,* Stadtisches Museum, Leverkusen, West Germany
1976 *Identite-Identification,* Centre d'Art Plastique Contemporian, Bordeaux, France
1978 *XXXVIII Biennale,* Venice (and *XXXIX Biennale,* 1980)
1981 *Identite Italienne: L'Art en Italie depuis 1959,* Centre Georges Pompidou, Paris
1982 *Italian Art Now: An American Perspective,* Guggenheim Museum, New York
1994 *The Italian Metamorphosis,* Guggenheim Museum, New York (catalog)
1995 *From Halifax to Glasgow*, Tramway, Glasgow
Je Vous Ai Tant Aimés, CAPC Musée d'Art Contemporain de Bordeaux, Bordeaux (catalog)
Galerie Durand-Dessert, Paris
1998 *Arte Povera: Works and Documents from the Goetz Collection*, Kölnischer Kunstverein, Cologne, Germany (catalog)
2000 *Time Quickly*, Centre Georges Pompidou, Paris

Publications:

By PENONE: Books—*Svolgere la propria pelle,* Turin 1971; *Rovesciare gli occhi,* with Jean-Christophe Ammann, Turin 1977; *Conversation avec Giuseppe Penone*, with Jean François, Strasbourg 1994. **Articles—**''Giuseppe Penone'' in *Art Press*, special issue no. 17, 1996; interview with Doris von Drathen in *Kunstforum International*, vol. 141, July/September 1998.

On PENONE: Books—*Arte Povera: Conceptual, Actual or Impossible Art* by Germano Celant, Milan 1969; *Giuseppe Penone,* exhibition catalog with texts by Jean-Christophe Ammann and Ugo Castagnotto, Lucerne 1977; *Giuseppe Penone,* exhibition catalog with texts by Jean-Christophe Ammann, Renato Barilli and Hans Albert Peters, Baden-Baden 1978; *Giuseppe Penone,* exhibition catalog with essay by Germano Celant, Amsterdam 1980; *La Vision Poetique de Giuseppe Penone,* exhibition catalog with essay by Jessica Bradley, Ottawa 1983. **Articles—**''Penone à Vif'' by Elisabeth Bedrenne in *L'Oeil* (Lausanne), no. 487, July/August 1997; ''Giuseppe Penone: The Sculptor Becomes Nature and Vice Versa'' by Adachiara Zevi in *L'Architettura*, vol. 45, no. 527, September 1999; ''Giuseppe Penone'' by David Frankel in *Artforum*, vol. 39, no. 3, November 2000; ''Giuseppe Penone: The Breath and the Tree'' by Margaret Sheffield in *Sculpture* (Washington, D.C.), vol. 20, no. 2, March 2001.

* * *

From the beginning of 1968, Penone's work has been marked by a radical departure from traditional artistic movements towards a natural, almost 'artless' ambience. Through a direct physical contact with nature, Perone has interacted with the processes of physical growth to represent these elements and processes in the form of photographic documentation. These interactions were later effected in the studio. In many works, Penone emphasized the presence of the body—of the hand, for instance, by means of imprints pressed onto a wide range of materials, thus creating a metaphor for psycho-physical energy or a metonym for the universe.

Penone is searching for indices in the sense that American philosopher Charles Peirce describes: the index is a sign ''which attracts attention towards a particular object without actually describing it'' while maintaining ''a direct physical connection'' with that object. Thus the image in its early stages of formation is still linked to organic phenomena. Works such as *To Unfold One's Own Skin, Gypsum Print and Projections, or Coincidence of Images* promote a tactile reading of the object, of space, of a part of the body or corporeal substance. At the root of the work is a direct connection between the psychological and the physical, between the artist and the materials upon which the epidermis of the skin leaves its traces.

In other cases, again it is the body which generates forms, as in the terracottas that bear the imprint of the hand or of the inside of the mouth—or in an evocative projection of the body in the form of his breath affecting the surface of archaic 'vases' in a work of 1978. Whenever Penone evokes the image via the standpoint or 'topos' of the self-portrait, he does so in order to negate its role as a priveleged route of information.

Central to the group Arte Povera, of which Penone is one of the foremost representatives, form and image are integrated outside traditional systems. Penone's most recent works empathise with nature to a lesser extent. On the one hand are installations in which the image is recognizable and distinct, and on the other is an 'activation' of metaphor which comes very close making the message redundant. Penone rarely uses the customary artists' materials, preferring to work with earth, vegetables, vases and bronze casting which continue to take on the character of plant life—tree, forms, bark and branches—and the anthropomorphic, thus imposing the natural event within the very heart of artifice.

—Giorgio Verzotti

Andrew Pepper: *Wall Drawing,* architectural installation at Lanchester Gallery, Coventry University, 1998. ©Andrew Pepper.

PEPPER, Andrew

Nationality: British. **Born:** Nottingham, England, 23 September 1955. **Education:** Nottingham Trent University, B.A. 1978; University of Reading, M.F.A., 1980; studied practical holography at New York Holographic Laboratories, 1981–82; University of Reading, Ph.D. in Fine Art Holography, 1989. **Family:** Married Monika Frost-Pepper, 1985; daughters: Christina and Corinne. **Career:** Self-employed artist and visiting lecturer, 1982–91; artist-in-residence, Museum of Holography, New York, 1987; founding editor, *The Creative Holography Index, The International Catalogue for Holography,* Bergisch Gladbach, Germany, 1991; full time staff, Academy of Media Arts, Cologne, Germany, 1991–96; director and chair, Art in Holography 2 Symposium, England, 1996–97; director, Shearwater Foundation Holography Program, 1998–; visiting lecturer, Department of Fine Arts, Nottingham Trent University, 1999–; visiting lecturer, Department of Contemporary Arts, Nottingham Trent University, 2001. **Awards:** Prize winner, New Contemporaries Exhibition, ICA, London, 1979; prize winner, Northern Young Contemporaries Exhibition, Manchester, 1979; Fulbright Scholar, Museum of Holography, New York, 1980–81; Lionel Robbins Memorial Scholar, Department of Fine Art, University of Reading, 1988–89; Shearwater Award for Creative Holography, 1989. **Agents:** Gallery 286, 286 Earl's Court Road, London SW5 9AS, United Kingdom; Galerie für Holographie und Neue Visuelle Medien, Frechen, Germany. **Address:** 46 Crosby Road, West Bridgford, Nottingham NG2 5GH, England. **Web site:** www.apepper.com.

Individual Exhibitions:

1982 Living and Learning Centre, University of Vermont
Museum of Holography, New York
1988 Museum für Holographie und Neue Visuelle Medien, Pulheim, Germany
1989 Interference Gallery, Toronto
1990 Watermans Arts Centre, Brentford, England
Gill Gallery, Newham, London
1992 Karas Studios, Madrid (catalog)
1995 Galerie für Holographie und Neue Visuelle Medien, Frechen, Germany
1998 Lanchester Gallery, Coventry University, England
1999 Highgate Gallery, Highgate, London
2001 Gallery 286, London

Group Exhibitions:

1979 *New Contemporaries,* Institute of Contemporary Art, London
1987 *Illuminations: State of the Art Holography,* Royal Photographic Society, Bath, England (catalog)
1989 *3-D '89, National Sculpture Open Exhibition,* Watermans Arts Centre, Brentford, England (catalog)
1990 *Images du Futur '90,* Montreal, Quebec, Canada (catalog)
1991 *Holographische Visionen,* Gürzenich, Cologne, Germany (catalog)
1992 *Avanguardia dell'Arte Olografica,* Centro Espositivo Rocca Paolina, Perugia, Italy (catalog)
1993 *Borderlines: Deutsche Fototage,* Frankfurt, Germany (catalog)
1994 *Holography: Artists and Inventors,* MIT Museum, Boston, Massachusetts
1995 *The Art of Holography,* National Museum of Photography, Film, and Television, Pictureville, Bradford, England
1999 *Visions into the 21st Century: The New Age of Holography,* Canton Museum of Art, Canton, Ohio
Lumia, International Lyskunst, Charlottenborg Udstillingsbygning, Denmark
2000 *Die Neue Dimension,* Kulturbrauerei, Berlin
2001 The Holography Gallery, Royal Photographic Society, Bath, England

Collections:

MIT Museum, Boston, Massachusetts; Galerie für Holographie und Neue Visuelle Medien, Frechen, Germany; Zentrum für Kunst und Medientechnologie, Karlsruhe, Germany; University of Reading, England; Fiat Lux, Spain; Sammlung Lauk, Germany; Karas Studios, Madrid.

Publications:

By PEPPER: Articles—''Perceptions of Holography: A New Medium Using Old Tricks'' in *Holosphere,* vol. 11, no. 10, October 1983; ''Can Holograms Open the Way to New Wave Ads?'' in *Campaign,* 9 December 1983; introduction in *Canadian Holography Now,* exhibition catalog, London 1984; essay in *Holographie in England: Der Aufstieg eines Künstlerischen Mediums,* exhibition catalog, Germany 1984; ''Holography, Visual Medium or Cheap Trick?'' in *Art Monthly,* December/January 1988/89; ''Display Holography in the U.K.: An Overview'' in *Holographie-Jahrbuch/Holography-Yearbook,* 1989–90; ''Holographic Space: A Generalised Graphic Definition'' in *Leonardo Journal: Holography as an Art Medium* (special issue), vol. 22, no. 3 and 4, 1989; ''Creative Holography: Its Development in the Academy of Media Arts, Cologne, Germany'' (with Dieter Jung), International Symposium on Display Holography, *SPIE Proceedings,* vol. 1600, July 1991; ''Holography on the Internet: A Useful Resource or Expensive Distraction?'' in *Practical Holography 10, SPIE Proceedings,* vol. 2652, 1996; ''Windows with Memories: Creative Holography in the Real World'' in *This Side Up,* no. 10, June 2000; ''Archiving a Creative History: Holography for a Future Generation'' in *Holography 2000, SPIE Proceedings,* vol. 4149, 2000.

*

The first holograms I made were not very good, technically or aesthetically, but they hardly needed to be. Away from the optical laboratory, in which they were made, no one noticed the blemishes and scratches, they only saw the spectacle of this 20th century alchemy. The first 4 x 5 inch hologram became precious. More so when I accidentally broke it on a sunny October morning in New York. The sunlight reflected off the shards of glass, some reconstructing their part image, others dark and eventless. These flat damaged glass segments were overwhelmingly more interesting, on an aesthetic and conceptual level, than the rectangular hologram they originated from.

It was not until several years later that I began using holography as a medium in its own right, rather than as a dimensional document. Over recent years the holograms have existed along-side site specific and time based light installations. What I could not achieve with holography, I could explore using projected light and vice versa. This was an advantage, as there was always an alternative to work with. The holographic work became flatter but more dimensional, as lines, drawings and sketched marks became the objects to be optically and spatially manipulated. ''Drawing Series,'' part of the MIT Museum collection in Boston, Massachusetts, presents sequential drawings to the observer, lines which exist in the space between the viewer and the hologram surface. They are not ''traditional'' 3-dimensional holograms, drawings, photographs or physical sculptures, but something in between—lines in space which define the volume they exist in. A visual, conceptual, and aesthetic paradox.

More recent work has continued to use drawn images, made visible via holography and stored onto glass plates. ''Wall Drawing,'' which was installed at the Lanchester Gallery, Coventry, England, used 5 small glass holograms fixed at an angle into the plaster of the gallery wall. The spotlights above, which illuminated the holographic images, also illuninated the walls.

Exhibitions come and go—mostly paintings in galleries. The canvases (rectangles) are fixed to the wall, shown, celebrated, taken down and then the wall is repaired and repainted. This happens over and over againg. We do not normally see the resulting texture of the wall because more painted rectangles are placed over the ''damage.'' ''Wall Drawing'' highlighted the ''damage'' and ''memory'' of all those exhibitions which had gone before.

Light from the spotlights highlighted the surface texture of the wall while at the same time illuminating the holograms, which cast a shadow down the rest of the wall to the floor. Each small holographic rectangle appeared to be displayed on its own dark plinth (the elongated shadow), surrounded by the memory of all the art which had occupied the gallery wall previously.

Critics and observers still question whether holography is a viable creative medium, as it fits uncomfortably into the accepted classifications of visual art. ''Wall Drawing,'' perhaps, highlighted some of those classifications in an attempt to move away from the overwhelming novelty of a medium.

—Andrew Pepper

* * *

Andrew Pepper, besides being an artist, is also a teacher and an organizer of exhibitions and symposia. This threefold vocation—exercised within the context of the art and holography area in which he is a leading figure—is grounded in his artistic and university training. It is also clearly visible in his artistic works and career, where it is combined with the idea and the feeling that technological means must be associated with a global human experience in order to enter frankly into the domain of the arts as well as having a true impact on the spectator, who is invited to react to the artistic statement in his own way and thus encounter a parallel experience with that of the artist.

Pepper's position as a holographic artist can best be understood if one takes into account that he is both a light artist and a graphic artist and that his artistic itinerary has led him logically from projected light sculptures to wall-based holograms and on to holographic floor pieces. In fact, the artist's main endeavour is to create physical and conceptual links between these three forms of expression.

Already as a student, Andrew Pepper had begun working with light to produce installations and animated sculptures. What excited him was the fact that he could almost ''draw'' in space by using a light projector that enabled him to intercept light by materials such as nylon or string, perspex or smoke. When he discovered holography in 1975, he understood at once that he could, by adopting this technique, counteract the ephemeral nature of his works by recording and documenting these light installations.

However, it took Pepper many years to produce the first holograms which satisfied him and which he wanted to exhibit. These formed the ''Drawing Series'' of 1987, five wall holograms exploring the use of lines in space and their resulting shadows. A series of very analytical holograms grew out of them, exploring the use of shadows and geometric structures. There followed holograms of drawings which he could modify long after the photographic/holographic/chemical stage was completed, either by working on the surface of the plates, by drawing directly on the glass or by ''distressing'' the emulsion and removing parts of it to draw it ''into'' the hologram.

Andrew Pepper also produced holograms on the floor like ''Positive Attempt'' (1989), a large glass circle with hologram fragments and projected light, or like ''Positive Attempt Redrawn'' (1991), twenty-one individual reflection holograms in three groups, illuminated from above with light from an apparatus projecting a drawing. Both these floor pieces were conceived as a reaction to, and way of working through, intense personal and family events and confirmed Pepper's basic engagement in connecting highly technical statements with strong human experiences, an endeavour developed throughout his artistic itinerary and in his other connected professional activities.

During the past few years Pepper has been consciously reducing the size of the holographic elements in his pieces. ''Divided Line''—first shown at the Highgate Gallery, London, and subsequently in the *Lumia* exhibition in Copenhagen in November 1999—is made up of a thin strip of holographic colour supported by two incandescent electric tubes. Light supporting light. The luminous lines on either side of the hologram provide stable, luminous, ''book ends'' for the kinetic mix of holographic colour which they hold between them.

More recent work reduces the holographic elements still further. Small sections of hologram, displaying the three-dimensional shadow of liquid, are incorporated into flat steel wall panels, rusted with liquid. The intense colour and pattern of the rusted metal extends into the three-dimensional liquid shadows of the holographic sections. In several of these works electric light is incorporated behind the steel rectangles so that not only is light reflected from the rusted steel, and the holograms they frame, but it is also emitted from behind the steel plates. The spotlights, required to illuminate the holograms in the panels, cause shadows of the metal construction to be cast onto the wall. The lights behind the panels soften some of those shadows and highlight the wall on which the works are displayed.

In his recent solo exhibition at Gallery 286, London, several small rusted panels, fixed just above the white painted gallery floor, not only supported certain holographic elements but caused shadows to be drawn onto the areas below them. The shadows become an integral element in the installation, helping to focus attention on the metal sheets which cast them and the holograms they support.

—Frank Popper

PEPPER, Beverly

Nationality: American. **Born:** Beverly Stoll in Brooklyn, New York, 20 December 1922. **Education:** Studied industrial and advertising design at the Pratt Institute, Brooklyn, New York, 1939–41, B.A. 1941; Art Students League, New York, 1946; Atelier André Lhote, Paris, 1948; Atelier Fernand Léger, Paris, 1949. **Family:** Married Lawrence Gussin in 1941 (divorced, 1948); children: John Randolph; married Curtis Gordon (Bill) Pepper in 1949; children: Jorie Sheppard Graham. **Career:** Worked as art director for numerous advertising agencies, New York, 1942–48; independent artist, since 1949, travelling extensively in Europe and North Africa; lived in Paris and Haut du Cagnes, France, 1949–50, and in Positano, Italy, 1951–52, settling in Rome in 1952; travelled in Far East and India, being especially influenced by Cambodian Khmer sculpture, 1960; concentrated on sculpture, Rome, 1961; moved to Torre Gentile di Todi, Perugia, Italy, 1972. **Awards:** Gold Medal and Sculpture Purchase Award, *Mostra Internazionale Florino,* Italy, 1966; First Prize and Purchase Award, Jacksonville Art Museum, Florida, 1970; Best Art in Steel Award, Iron and Steel Industry, New York, 1970; Central Service Administration Grant, Washington, D.C., 1974; National Endowment for the Arts Award, 1975. Honorary doctorates from Pratt Institute, New York, 1982, and Maryland Institute, Baltimore, 1983; Accademico di Merito, Accademia di Belle Arti, Perugia, 1987; Celebrity Path, Brooklyn Botanic Garden, 1987; Friend of Barcelona, 1992; Outstanding Achievement in the Visual Arts, Women's Caucus for Art, 1994; Chevalier de l'Ordre des Arts et Lettres, 1999; Allied Arts Honor Award, The American Institute of Architects, 1999; Alexander Calder Prize; Xavier College Preparatory Vision and Voice Award, 1999. **Agent:** André Emmerich Gallery, 41 East 57th Street, New York, New York 10022, U.S.A. **Address:** 84 Thomas Street, New York, New York 10015, U.S.A.; Torre Gentile di Todi, Perugia 06059, Italy.

Individual Exhibitions:

1952 Galleria dello Zodiaco, Rome
1954 Barone Gallery, New York
1955 Obelisk Gallery, Washington, D.C.
1956 Galleria Schneider, Rome
Barone Gallery, New York
1958 Barone Gallery, New York
1959 Galleria dell'Obelisco, Rome
1961 Galleria Pogliani, Rome
1962 Thibaut Gallery, New York

Beverly Pepper: *Basalt Ritual,* 1985–86. ©Beverly Pepper. Photo courtesy of the artist.

1965 Marlborough Galleria d'Arte, Rome
1966 McCormick Place, Chicago
1967 Jewish Museum, New York
1968 Marlborough Galleria d'Arte, Rome
Galleria La Bussola, Turin
Galleria Paolo Barozzi, Venice
1969 Marlborough Gallery, New York
Museum of Contemporary Art, Chicago
Hayden Court and Plaza, Massachusetts Institute of Technology, Cambridge
Albright-Knox Art Gallery, Buffalo, New York
1970 Everson Museum, Syracuse, New York
Piazza della Rotonda, Milan
Studio Marconi, Milan
1971 Galerie Hella Nebelung, Dusseldorf
Piazza Margana, Rome
470 Parker Street Gallery, Boston
1972 Qui Arte Contemporanea, Rome
Marlborough Galleria d'Arte, Rome
1973 Tyler School of Art, Temple University Abroad, Rome
1975 Hammarskjold Plaza Sculpture Garden, New York
André Emmerich Gallery, New York
1976 San Francisco Museum of Modern Art
1977 André Emmerich Gallery, New York
Rosa Freudenheim Gallery, New York
Seattle Museum of Contemporary Art
Indianapolis Museum of Art
Hopkins Art Center, Dartmouth College, Hanover, New Hampshire
1978 Princeton Art Museum, New Jersey
Indianapolis Museum of Art
1979 André Emmerich Gallery, New York
Hofstra University, Hempstead, New York
Piazza Mostra, Todi, Perugia, Italy
Piazza Maggiore, Todi, Perugia, Italy
1980 Nina Freudenheim Gallery, Buffalo, New York
Thomas Segal Gallery, Boston
André Emmerich Gallery, New York
André Emmerich Gallery, Zurich
Ronald Greenberg Gallery, St. Louis
1981 Makler Gallery, Philadelphia
Linda Farris Gallery, Seattle, Washington
Davenport Gallery, Iowa
Hansen Fuller Goldeen Gallery, San Francisco
1982 André Emmerich Gallery, New York
Laumeier Sculpture Park, St. Louis
Yares Gallery, Scottsdale, Arizona
Galleria Il Ponte, Rome
1983 Gimpel-Hanover and André Emmerich Galerien, Zurich
André Emmerich Gallery, New York
Huntington Galleries, West Virginia
John Berggruen Gallery, San Francisco
1984 André Emmerich Gallery, New York
1985 Adams-Middleton Gallery, Dallas
John Berggruen Gallery, San Francisco
1986 André Emmerich Gallery, New York
Albright-Knox Art Gallery, Buffalo, New York (travelled to San Francisco; Columbus, Ohio; Brooklyn, New York; Miami, Florida, 1986–88)
1989 List Visual Arts Center, Massachusetts Institute of Technology, Cambridge
James Corcoran Gallery, Santa Monica, California
1991 Contemporary Sculpture Center, Tokyo, Japan
Metropolitan Museum of Art, Mezzanine Gallery, New York
Narni alla Rocca, Narni, Italy
1993 André Emmerich Gallery, New York
1994 Charles Cowles Gallery
Nardin Gallery, Somers, New York
2000 *Grounds for Sculpture,* Hamilton, New Jersey

Selected Group Exhibitions:

1961 *The Quest and the Quarry,* Rome/New York Art Foundation, Rome
1972 *XXIII Biennale,* Venice
1981 *All in Line: An Exhibition of Linear Drawing,* Lowe Art Gallery, Syracuse University, New York (travelled to Terry Dintenfass Gallery, New York)
1985 *The Artist as Social Designer,* Los Angeles Institute of Contemporary Art
1987 *A Century of Modern Sculpture: The Patsy and Raymond Nasher Collection,* Dallas Museum of Art, Dallas, Texas

The Barcelona Plazas: Preview of an Urban Experience, The Spanish Institute, New York (travelled to Barcelona, Rome, Vienna, and Kyoto)

1991 *Bienale de Sculpture,* Marisa del Re Gallery, Monte-Carlo

1993 *Centre Georges Pompidou,* Societé des Amis du Musée National d'Art Moderne, Paris, France

Chelsea Harbor Sculpture '93, Royal Society of British Sculptors, London

1994 *The Women's Caucus for Art 1994 Honor Awards Exhibition,* The Queens Museum of Art, Queens, New York

1995 *Grounds for Sculpture,* Johnson Atelier, Hamilton, New Jersey

Twentieth Century American Sculpture at the White House, The White House Sculpture Garden, Washington, D.C.

In Three Dimensions: Women Sculptors of the '90s, Part II: Beyond Gender, Newhouse Center for Contemporary Art, Snug Harbor Cultural Center, Staten Island, New York

1996 *American Art Today: Images from Abroad,* The Art Museum at Florida International University, Miami

1997 *Crossing The Threshold,* Steinbaum Kraus Gallery, New York

Small and Beautiful: The Issue of Scale, Eaton Fine Art, West Palm Beach, Florida

1998 *The Winter Show,* Charles Cowles Gallery, New York

The Summer Show, Marlborough Gallery, New York

1999 *Contemporary Classicism,* Neuberger Museum of Art, Purchase, New York

Works on Paper: A Riverhouse Retrospective, Eleanor Bliss Center for the Arts at the Depot, Steamboat Springs, Colorado

2000 *20th Century Steel Sculpture,* Beadleston Gallery, New York

Modernism and Abstraction: Treasures from the Smithsonian's Museum of American Art, The Art Museum at Florida International University, Miami, Florida

The Summer Show, Marlborough Gallery, New York

Collections:

Fogg Art Museum, Harvard University, Cambridge; Massachusetts Institute of Technology, Cambridge; Albright-Knox Art Gallery, Buffalo, New York; Vassar College, Poughkeepsie, New York; Dartmouth College, Hanover, New Hampshire; Hirshhorn Museum, Washington, D.C.; Indianapolis Museum of Art; Walker Art Center, Minneapolis; Galleria Civica d'Arte Moderna, Turin; Metropolitan Museum of Art, New York; Detroit Institute of Arts, Detroit; Barcelona Museum of Modern Art, Spain; Kujke Gallery, Seoul.

Permanent Public Installations:

Richard J. Hughes Justice Complex, Trenton, New Jersey; *Four-Leaf Towers,* Houston; Phoenix Center, Pontiac, Michigan; Johns Hopkins Hospital, Baltimore; First Interstate Center, Seattle; *Thel,* Dartmouth College, New Hampshire; *Amphisculpture,* AT&T Long Lines Center, Bedminister, New Jersey; Sol i Ombra Park, Barcelona, Spain; *Teatro Celle,* Pistoia, Italy; *Ternana Altar II,* National Museum of American Art, Smithsonian Institution, Washington, D.C.; *Gemini Columns,* Narni Castle, Narni, Italy; *Normanna Wedge,* Detroit Institute of Arts; Gotanno Community Park, Tokyo; *Three-Panel Screen,* Centre Georges Pompidou, Paris; *Cleopatra's Wedge,* Battery Park, New York City; Garden at 26 Federal Plaza, New York City; *Palingenesis,* Zurich; *Jerusalem Ritual,* Jerusalem Foundation, Jerusalem; *Sacramento Stele,* California Environmental Protection Agency, Sacramento.

Publications:

By PEPPER: Articles—''Space, Time, and Nature in Monumental Sculpture'' in *Art Journal* (New York), Spring 1978; *Public Sculpture and Its Public,* a pamphlet for the National Council on Arts Administration, Washington, D.C., March 1979.

On PEPPER: Books—*Passages in Modern Sculpture* by Rosalind Krauss, New York 1977; *Originals: American Women Artists* by Eleanor Munro, New York 1979; *Beverly Pepper in Todi,* exhibition catalog with an introduction by Roberto Abbondanza, text by Marisa Volpi Orlandini and Sam Hunter, Todi, Perugia, Italy 1979; *Acquisitions 1974–78,* exhibition catalog with text by Jan van der Marck, Hanover, New Hampshire 1979; *Contemporary Artists at Work: Sculptors, Vol. 2,* New York 1980; *Beverly Pepper: The Moline Markers,* exhibition catalog with essay by Phyllis Tuchman, Davenport, Iowa 1981; *Currents: Contemporary Trends in the Visual Arts* by Howard Smagula, New York 1983; *Beverly Pepper,* exhibition catalog with text by Ronny Cohen, New York 1986; *Beverly Pepper: Sculpture in Place* by Douglas G. Schultz and Rosalind E. Krauss, New York 1989; *Palingenesis,* exhibition catalogue with text by Toni Stooss, Kunst im CS Communication Center Horgen, 1994; *Beverly Pepper: Grounds for Sculpture,* exhibition catalog text by Robert T. Buck, Hamilton, New Jersey 2000. **Articles**—''Beverly Pepper'' by Virgilio Guzzi in *Il Tempo* (Milan), December 1952; ''Beverly Pepper'' by Lawrence Campbell in *ARTnews* (New York), December 1954; ''Beverly Pepper'' by E. M. Munroe in *ARTnews* (New York), December 1956; ''Beverly Pepper'' by Giovanni Carandente in *Arte Oggi* (Milan), October 1961; ''Plus by Minus'' by Douglas McAgy in *Art Gallery* (Ivoryton, Connecticut), 1968; ''Beverly Pepper, Galleria Hella Nebelung'' by Y. Friedrichs in *Das Kunstwerk* (Baden-Baden, West Germany), July 1971; ''Art'' by Robert Hughes in *Time* (New York), June 1975; ''A Space Has Many Aspects'' by Jan Butterfield in *Arts Magazine* (New York), September 1975; ''New York Letter'' by Carter Ratcliff in *Art International* (Lugano, Switzerland), no. 6, 1977; ''Arte Actuel'' by Jean-Luc Daval in *Skira Annual,* Geneva 1978; ''Beverly Pepper's New Sculpture'' by Margaret Sheffield in *Arts Magazine* (New York), September 1979; ''Monument/Sculpture/Earthwork'' by Nancy Foote in *Artforum* (New York), October 1979; ''The Sculpture of Beverly Pepper'' by Will Ameringer in *Arts Magazine* (New York), October 1983; ''Interconnection: Beverly Pepper'' by Kenneth Baker in *Art in America* (New York), April 1984; ''Beverly Pepper'' by Jane Bell in *ARTnews* (New York), February 1985; ''Beverly Pepper'' by Michael Brenson in the *New York Times,* 21 September 1990; ''Beverly Pepper'' by Debbie Koppman in *ARTnews,* November 1990; ''The Barcelona Way'' by Cathleen McGuigan in *Newsweek,* 9 December 1991; ''Beverly Pepper: Sculpture in Place'' by Robert Hobbs in *Women's Art Journal,* Fall 1991-Winter 1992; ''Beverly Pepper: André Emmerich Gallery'' by Matthew Kangas in *Sculpture,* May-June 1992; ''A

Theatre That's Also a Park'' by Patricia Schultz in *Landscape Architecture,* March 1993; ''Where an Arc Once Ruled'' by Carol Vogel in the *New York Times,* 28 May 1993; ''Beverly Pepper: André Emmerich Gallery'' by Hovey Brock in *ARTnews,* September 1993; ''Split Ritual'' in *Garden Design Magazine,* November-December 1993; ''Sculptures and Abstract Expressionist Prints in Close Harmony'' by William Zimmer in the *New York Times,* 3 April 1994; ''Beverly Pepper'' by Diane Kelder in *WCA Honor Awards Catalog,* 1994; *Il Parco di Celle a Pistoia,* Edizionie Firenze, 1994; Article in *Art Fundamentals: Theory and Practice* by Otto G. Orvick, et al., seventh edition, Madison, Wisconsin, 1994; ''Endless Columns: The Quest for Infinite Extension'' by Suzaan Boettger in *Sculpture,* January-February 1994; Article in *Artful Management; Art for the Masses, or Mass for Public Art?* by Andrew Decker, *Atelier,* 1996; ''Memory, Monuments, Mystery and Iron'' by Anne Barclay Morgan in *Sculpture,* April 1998; ''Crossing the Threshold'' by Jan Biles, *Lawrence Journal—World,* 30 August 1998; ''Beyond Gender, Beyond Age'' by Alice Thorson in *The Kansas City Star,* 30 August 1998; ''Sky High'' by Tim Engle in *The Kansas City Star,* 20 September 1998; Monumental Beverly Pepper'' by Barbara Rose in *Paris Vogue,* October 1998.

*

If I talk about the formal problems that involve me, it is because the abstract language of form that I have chosen has become a way to explore an interior life of feeling. In this way, my forms mirror emotional reality. The problems to which I have consistently linked my work concern the question of sculptural illusion. Put briefly, I wish to make an object that has a powerful physical presence but is at the same time inwardly turned, seeming capable of intense self-absorption.

The works I made of highly polished stainless steel in the late 1960s achieved this kind of dualism primarily through the mirror-like finish of their surface. Those surfaces acted to emphasize the actual weight and density of the steel. At the same time they made the physical bulk of the sculpture withdraw behind a screen of reflections.

Under certain light conditions and from certain angles this reflectivity picks up the sculpture's environment—sky, grass, earth. This causes the work almost to disappear so that all that remains visible is the network of blue enamel lines that indicates the interior faces of the forms. From other angles, the surfaces reflect into one another, causing geometries to appear which are not part of the physical format of the work. But even though these internal reflections are illusions, they do in fact prefigure the actual shape the crystalline forms will appear to have when viewed from another angle. In this way the reflected illusions seem to be sculptor's ''anima''—appearing to generate its total being from within the shifting depths of the mirror.

Reflection may be the most obvious way to generate illusions, but there are other ways that are equally direct. One of these is forced (and therefore false) perspective, which I began to concentrate on in the early 1970s. ''Exodus'' (1972), for example, is a large stainless steel pyramid which contains a pyramidal void. Because of the eccentric relationship between solid and void, the position of the void appears to be tunneling in a different direction from the one revealed by the other side of the sculpture. So when the viewer actually moves around to the other side of the work and sees another triangular opening, it is not clear that the two openings into the inside of the volume are related. The illusion is that somewhere inside the sculpture the continuity of the inner form has been disrupted, or diverted, from one configuration to another.

It is the perspective relationship between mass and void that causes this apparent shift. The effect of this is that the inner reaches of a very simple geometrical form appear mysteriously able to create relationships whose logic is not clear to the viewer but is instead very private. And a result of this mysteriousness is that the massiveness of the physical form is suspended—or made to seem quite thin—as the viewer tries to correlate the flat shapes formed on the front and back of the sculpture.

In my later works I tried to maintain this precarious balance between the physically self-evident and the sense of an elusive inner logic. In ''Alpha'' (1974) I used four triangular sheaths—joined to form two pairs—to give an intense experience of the generative power of the interior, from which the sheaths develop or peel away. As in ''Exodus,'' we have here two parts of a work that are obviously related to one another but are puzzlingly incapable of logical fusion. Looking back at the decisions I made while working on ''Alpha,'' I realize now they came from the same emotional source that has formed all my work. I want the sculptures to seem to be creating relationships that are very simple yet at the same time are beyond the viewer's grasp. I want it to seem as though an inexplicable coherence works inside the sculpture to generate external aspects of its physical being that are always unexpected because they are unpredictable.

In my work the image comes from within me—an ''emotion'' that is released. I then apply whatever critical abilities I possess to allow the intermingling of the intellect and emotion. Even if there is a conflict and contradiction between these two, I allow them to feed into one another and eventually merge into one being.

—Beverly Pepper

* * *

Since the early 1960s Beverly Pepper's sculpture has undergone significant formal changes. The monumental steel columns of the early 1980s mark a radical departure from the geometric steel sculpture and environmental works of the 1970s. Yet the columns, with their strong references to architectonic structures like obelisks and memorial stones, share with the earlier work an intrinsic power that significantly alters the environment in which they are situated. Pepper's sculpture has the power to retain its integrity as sculpture but the graciousness to understand its location in a place. Examples of this aspect of her art are *Thel,* installed at Dartmouth College, New Hampshire in 1977, and *Amphisculpture* of 1974–75 at the AT&T Long Lines Center, Bedminister, New Jersey. Both works are monumental in their proportions yet literally become part of the landscape. Scale for Pepper is a human quality and one she tempers with a consciousness of geography and place.

Few sculptors have been as successful as Pepper in avoiding the blankness of geometry characterized by decorative forms that have meaning only as pure form. Pepper's art is insistently meaningful and devoid of superfluous moments and gestures. There has always been a sense of mystery in the massive forms she constructs, but the columns of recent vintage are perhaps the richest in a sense of history and time. First exhibited in the piazza at Todi, Italy, the columns are as monumental as the earlier horizontal sculptures yet have a vocabulary that permits experience, time, and history to become dominant elements. The piazza at Todi provided a superb location for the columns, but their intrinsic power is such that even in other less historically rich locations there is a quality of self-absorption and mystery about the work to suggest a new form for the term "monument."

—Katherine Smith

PERILLI, Achille

Nationality: Italian. **Born:** Rome, 28 January 1927. **Education:** Studied history of art at the University of Rome, 1945–46. **Career:** Painter: Founder-Member, with Pietro Consagra, Piero Dorazio and others, Forma I, Rome, 1947; visited Paris, and met Hans Arp, Francis Picabia, Alberto Magnelli and Antoine Pevsner, 1948; member, Movimento Arte Concreta, Milan 1948; travelled in Austria and Germany, 1949, and lived in Paris, 1950–51; founder, with Dorazio, *Arte Visive* magazine, Rome, 1952; travelled in Spain and Germany, 1954–55; associated with Hannah Höch, and influenced by the Dada group, Berlin, 1955; founder, with Gastone Novelli, *L'Esperienza Moderna* magazine, Rome, 1957–59; worked on theatrical designs, including *Collage* ballet, Teatro Eliseo, Rome, 1961; founder, with Novelli and others, *Grammatica* magazine, Rome, 1964, and, with others, Altro group, Rome, 1973; worked on theatrical designs for Rome Opera, *Dies Irae,* 1978; founder, *Metek* magazine, Rome, 1996. Lecturer in visual communications, School for Industrial Design, Rome, 1965. **Awards:** Premio Fontana, *Biennale di San Marino,* 1963; Premio Comune di Roma, *Quadriennale di Roma,* 1965; Premio Lugano, Switzerland 1968; Prize for Drawing, *International Exhibition of Graphics,* Rijeka, Yugoslavia, 1970. **Agent:** Frankfurter Westend Galerie, Arndtstrasse 12, 6000 Frankfurt am Main, West Germany; Galleria Giulio Tega Via Senato 24, Milan, Italy. **Address:** Largo Arenula 34, 00186 Rome, Italy.

Individual Exhibitions:

1956 Galleria Strozzina, Florence
1957 Galleria La Tartaruga, Rome
1958 Galleria del Naviglio, Milan
1959 *Bienal,* Sao Paulo
Galleria del Cavallino, Venice
1960 Galleria La Tartaruga, Rome
Galleria del Naviglio, Milan
Galleria Souza, Mexico City
1962 *Biennale,* Venice
Galerie Creuze, Paris
1963 Bonino Gallery, New York
1964 Kunstverein, Freiburg
Galeria Baier, Mainz
Galleria del Deposito, Genoa
1965 Felix Landau Gallery, Los Angeles
Galleria La Tartaruga, Rome
1966 Galleria del Naviglio, Milan
Court Gallery, Copenhagen
Galleria Il Segno, Rome
1967 Marlborough Galleria d'Arte, Rome
1968 *Biennale,* Venice
Galleria La Sfera, Modena, Italy
Galleria Rotta, Genoa
Westend Galerie, Frankfurt
1969 Gallery, Foksal, Warsaw
Galleria Alfieri, Venice
1970 Grafica Romero, Rome
Galleria m'Arte, Milan
Narodni Gallery, Prague
1971 Galerie Forum, Zagreb
Jacques Baruch Gallery, Chicago
Galerie Espace, Amsterdam
Marlborough Galleria d'Arte, Rome
Galleria La Bussola, Turin
Galleria Rotta, Milan
Westend Galerie, Frankfurt
1972 Galerie Grondahl, Copenhagen
Grafica Romero, Rome
Marlborough Galleria d'Arte, Rome
Galleria Quattro Venti, Palermo
1973 Marlborough Galerie, Zurich
10th Quadriennale Nazionale d'Arte, Rome
Nova Arte Moderne, Prato, Italy
Musée des Beaux-Arts, La Chaux de Fonds, Switzerland
1974 3A Galleria d'Arte Moderna, Turin
Galleria Spagnoli, Florence
Galleria Il Milione, Milan
Galleria Ravagnan, Venice
1975 Marlborough Galleria d'Arte, Rome
La Tavolozza, Palermo, Sicily
La Permanente, Cesena, Italy
1976 Circolo della Stampa, Messina, Sicily
Galleria Rotta, Genoa
Studio Soldano, Milan
Galleria Linea 70, Verona
1977 Palazzo dei Diamanti, Ferrara, Italy
Lo Spazio della Pittura 1947–1977, Trissino, Italy
Palazzo Tomitano, Feltre, Italy
1978 Galleria Lo Spazio, Naples
1980 Studio F22, Palazzolo sull-Oglio, Italy
Galleria Vismara, Milan
Galerie d'Art International, Paris
1981 Westend Galerie, Frankfurt
1982 Studio F22, Palazzolo sull'Oglio, Italy
Galleria Giuli, Italy
Galleria Bluart, Varese, Italy
Galleria d'Arte, Republic of San Marino
1983 Galleria Editalia, at the *Fiera di Bari,* Italy
Galleria Editalia, Rome
Galleria Arte Duchamp, Cagliari, Italy
1984 Galleria Il Segno, Pordenone, Italy
Paris Art Center, Paris
Studio F22, Palazzolo sull'Oglio, Italy
Galleria Le Pietre, Arenzano, Italy
Galleria Ariele, Vicenza, Italy
Galleria Il Millennio, Rome
Galleria Peccolo, Livorno, Italy
Galleria Spriano, Omegna, Italy
1985 Galleria La Panchetta, Bari, Italy
Galerie d'Art International, Paris
Studio Mara Coccia, Rome
Galleria La Scaletta, Matera, Italy
Free Time Club, Cesena, Italy

Galleria Luce, Venice
Galleria Fioretto, Padua, Italy
Galleria Maurizio Corradini, Mantua, Italy
1986 Studio Mara Coccia, at the *Fiera dell'Arte,* Bologna, Italy
Galleria Morone 6, Milan
Galleria Emicla, Gaeta, Italy
Studio F22, Palazzolo sull'Oglio, Italy
Galerie d'Art International, at *FIAC 86,* Grand Palais, Paris
Accademia dei Concordi, Rovigo, Italy
1987 Free Time Club, at the *Fiera di Bologna,* Italy
Galleria Maurizio Corraini, at the *Fiera di Bari,* Italy
Galleria Meta, Bolzano, Italy
Spazio Studio d'Arte, Bologna, Italy
Studio Santandrea, Savona, Italy
1988 Fioretto Galleria d'Arte, Padova
Achille Perilli: Works from 1947 to the Present, Galleria Nazionale d'Arte Moderna, Rome
1989 Galleria Spriano, Omegna
1990 Galleria Tega, Milan
1991 *Achille Perilli, Gemälde, 1947–1990,* Wilhelm-Hack-Museum und Kunstverein Ludwigshafen am Rhein
Frankfurt Westend Gallery, Frankfurt
1992 Accademia Nazionale di San Luca, Rome
1993 Galleria Giulio Tega, Milan
Galleria Paola Verrengia, Salerno
1994 Nàrodni Galerie, Prague
Galleria Fioretto, Padova
1995 Galleria Ghelfi, Vicenza
1996 Galleria Les Chances de l'Art, Bolzano
Galleria Stefano de Crescenzo e Floriana Viesti, Rome
1997 Galleria Civica, Termoli
Galleria Stefano Fumagalli, Bergamo
1998 Galleria Fioretto, Padova
Achille Perilli 1968/1998: De Insana Geometria, Mole Vanvitelliana, Ancona
1999 Galleria Forni, Bologna
A.A.M. Architettura Arte Moderna, Rome
Galleria d'Arte Marchetti, Rome
2000 Studio Delise, Portogruaro

Selected Group Exhibitions:

1948 *Quadriennale,* Rome
1950 *Biennale,* Venice
1957 *Painting in Post-War Italy 1945–1957,* Columbia University, New York
1961 *Art Italien Aujourd'hui,* Galerie International d'Art Contemporain, Paris
1971 *20 Artistas Italianos,* Museo de Arte Moderna, Mexico City
1980 *Italian Graphic Abstract Art,* Museum of Modern Art, Haifa
1982 *Goethe und Italien,* Westend Galerie, Frankfurt
1985 *Nouvelles Tapisseries,* Paris Art Center, Paris
1987 *L'Informale in Italia,* Kunstmuseum, Lucerne Switzerland
1988 *Olympiad of Art,* International Contemporary Painting Exhibition, Seoul (traveled to National Museum of Contemporary Art)
Dialogues in Art 3, Palazzo Ducale, Gubbio, Italy
1989 *On the Surface: An Abstract Journey,* Studio Durante, Rome
1995 *Roma 1950–59 Il Rinnovamento della Pittura in Italia,* Palazzo dei Diamanti, Ferrara
1996 *MAC,* Kodama Gallery, Osaka
1998 *Arte Italiana, Ultimi quarant'anni, Pittura aniconica,* Galleria Comunale d'Arte Moderna, Bologna
2000 *The 1950s: The Original Years,* De Crescenzo-Viesti Gallery, Rome
Galleria Comunale d'Arte Contemporanea, Rome
2001 *Novecento Arte e Storia in Italia,* Scuderie del Viminale, Rome

Collections:

Galleria Nazionale d'Arte Moderna, Rome; Galleria Comunale, Rome; Cà Pesaro, Venice; National Gallery, Prague; Musée des Beaux Arts, La Chaux de Fonds, Switzerland; Joseph H. Hirshhorn Museum and Sculpture Garden, Washington, D.C.; Museum St. Louis University, St. Louis, Missouri; National Gallery, Berlin; Museo di Palazzo Reale, Milan; National Museum of Contemporary Art, Seoul; Muzeum Sztuki, Lodz.

Publications:

By PERILLI: Books—*L'age d'or di forma,* Maurizio Corraini, 1994.

On PERILLI: Books—*Achille Perilli,* exhibition catalog by Umbro Apollonio, Venice 1962; *Achille Perilli,* exhibition catalog by Margit Stabler, Zurich 1973; *L'Arte in Italia dopo la seconda guerra mondiale* by Giorgio De Marchis, Turin 1982; *Achille Perilli—Continuum 1947/1982,* exhibition catalog by Francesco Vincitorio, San Marino 1982; *Achille Perilli: L'irrazionale geometrico,* exhibition catalog by G. C. Argan, Paris 1984; *Achille Perilli: Works from 1947 to the Present,* exhibition catalog with text by Pia Vivarelli, Francesca Moschini and Elisabetta Cristallini, Rome 1988; *Achille Perilli, Gemälde, 1947–1990,* exhibition catalog, Ludwigshafen 1991; *Achille Perilli: le carte e I libri 1946–1992,* exhibition catalog, Rome 1992; *Achille Perilli 1968/1998: De Insana Geometria,* exhibition catalog by Fabrizio d'Amico, Ancona 1998. **Articles—**''Perilli e la comunicazione efficace'' by Bruno Alfieri in *Metro* (Milan), no. 6, 1962; ''Achille Perilli: Immagine e organizzazione'' by Nello Ponente in *Civilta delle Macchine* (Rome), March 1967; ''Achille Perilli'' by Milton Gendel in *Art International* (Lugano, Switzerland) vol. 15, no. 9, 1971; ''The Painting Thought of Achille Perilli'' by Roger Bordier in *Cimaise* (Paris), 1982; ''Achille Perilli: Comment Peindre l'Invisible'' by Elisabetta Cristallini in *Opus International,* no. 119, May-June 1990.

*

In re-examining those visual experiences which, during the course of the century, have been generically labelled as abstractionism, one seems to perceive, amongst the few theoretical certainties and the many poetic uncertainties, a thread linking the attainment of rationalist truth to the decadence of the same and its formal dissolution.

The slow but constant shift from representation to presentation, based on the "linguistic" values of the code and the denial of iconographical communication, undoubtedly freed the artist from various influences which bound him to the idea of reality. The visual factor acquired a degree of autonomy with respect to the concept of reproduction and was no longer intended as evidence, a record or window on history, but as a manner of investigating the nature of the world and of mankind's existence. Thus it becomes an analysis of the structure of the visual world; as Klee wrote, "Art does not copy visible objects, but renders them visible."

This progress and occasional regression, this lengthy voyage was meant to illuminate, uncover and reveal the most subtle workings of vision; to reproduce the procedure of focusing the image; to communicate it by means of an analytical methodology; and, above all, to extract from the depths of our memory, the richest and most complex forms of knowledge. This process knew both absolute certainties and shattering failures, due to the difficulties of carrying out an enquiry comprehensive of the many possible interpretations available to investigators. One of the absolute certainties was the belief that to proceed on the basis of pure perception (the retina) was enough to rediscover the essential laws of vision; all other approaches were dismissed as spurious or insufficiently pure. This was a certainty which derived from the conviction that everything could be reduced to the essence of painting, which coincided with the essence of geometrical form—the fundamental crossing of the horizon with a vertical line on a white surface.

To reach this point it was necessary to reduce painting, or the investigation of painting, to an absolute. Beyond this absolute, the value of representation was no longer intended as a transcription of reality, or continued by the necessity of transmitting a specific message (landscape, still life, portrait): it became a free component of pictorial activity, strengthened by the multiplication of "languages" through the ambiguity of speech (De Chirico, for instance, or Pop Art).

The equally drastic alternative was the re-examination of the possibilities inherent in media understood as material (canvas, paper, wood, burlap, glass and so forth): see Schwitters and most informal art. But when absolute certainty, the unchanging values of the horizontal and vertical, of the primary values, were recognized, then the feeling arose that the approach adopted had been mistaken from the start and should be corrected. The error, that of identifying the eye as the instrument of understanding, derived from centuries of habit and mental sloth which restricted visual perception to Durer's maxim: "First, the eye that sees; seond, the object that is seen; third, the intervening distance.

It was not enough to remove the object and the distance in order to achieve the optimum effect, known as abstraction. Malevitch, having recognized the law of geometrical absolution, was able to admit: "This is why we are obliged to clarify that—there is a difference—and indeed a great contradiction between the creative work of the painter and pure optical activity." He continued: "Therefore we must conclude that the mutation of form and colour in artistic activity does not take place on the basis of visual optical perception, but as a consequence of their alterations in our minds; that is, in the creative imagination of the painter in whose mind the pictorial image has arisen."

The black square on the white square has a slight variation in measurement: it is an irregular square. The certainty of geometry has begun to yield to and to transform itself into the Suprematist painting of 1917—a geometric yellow form bathed in a light which dissolves into space. Certainty has by now completely given way to geometrical uncertainty, the conception of a geometrical form that is no longer determined by laws of mathematics or optics, but by slight dislocations and displacements produced by memory on the data of visual perception. Geometric irrationality has come into being as a result of the dissolution of geometrical form, its loss of weight, its escape from two-dimensionality: the instruments of enquiry have shifted decisively from perception to memory, together with all the knowledge, both conscious and unconscious, that the contemporary world has acquired. It is a shift so great as to produce a fundamental change in the visual world and in all future discoveries pertaining to it. It means "shaping imaginary space through a material object," as El Lissitsky foresaw.

What then is the imaginary space, if not a new mode of visual structure, a more complex contribution to our definition of knowledge which is no longer linked to the activity of the eye alone, but related to a series of more complex sensations and different perceptions? And, with respect to history, does not this shift from the certainty of reason to the the uncertainty of madness, reveal the decadence and dissolution of the utopia of technology, the safety of the megalopolis, faith in progress? Vantongerloo during his last years followed Malevitch's example, substituting the mysticism of form with the mysticism of mathematics.

The result was the name: the slow dissolution of geometrical certainty in favour of an open form permitting language to perceive the mysteries of the visual world through investigation.

In 1939 Variant seems to have extended its lines of force in space with an extraordinary essentiality of tension. For it is formal tension which causes the dissolution of form: it is tension which takes the place of order, certainty, safety.

Visual tension may only be achieved when several opposing forces are able to discharge themselves contemporaneously. When this takes place in a concentrated and "tense" space, such as geometrical space, the shifting of forces, the lessening of certainty—which interests me—then occurs. Form loses certainty and is transformed into a field of rapid motion, violent struggle, unbelievable deformations defining new, unknown and complex structures governed by laws which I defined in my 1975 manifesto *Machinerie, ma chere machine:* "From the relation between two geometric modules, occasionally in contrast, occasionally similar with slight variations, a sequence is born which tends to shift in space until . . . it spreads from picture to picture, evolving, associating with other factors, constantly increasing the complexity of the investigation of Imaginary Space. The interpretation of such sequences suggests passages which shatter the idea of central space, or superficial space or light space. To enter within or to stay without, to advance or to halt, are all acts of vision, not of perception, which require independent choices for each of the various possibilities suggested by the image. It is not necessary to alter or change the order of sequence: alteration, transformation are inherent in the manner of seeing the structure, in the ambiguity created by the shift from one level to another, from one chromatic law to another, from volume to void. Interpretation and observation must be extended in time to include successive stages of memorization, to analyze possible interpretations without being limited to formal structure, but taking into account all these materials belonging to the collective unconscious which inform the deepest levels of human consciousness.

It is a process which tends to broaden rather than restrict, to shift the field of enquiry from the perceptual to the mental; it rejects any minimalization of the uncertainties concentrated in the visual, expanding them so as to affect those uncharted areas between one code and another, and to implicate alien linguistic structures.

Such implications deny the severity of an absolute code, or a primary code and its unchangeable ''linguistic'' laws, since that code has already been transformed into *Another (Altro)* through a methodology which I call intercode: by working on areas which are affected by a law, but are not subject to it. Although these areas are sensitive to its presence and reality, the law itself is perceived with the greatest ambiguity possible, with respect to meaning and value, so as to allow all manner of deformations and transformations. Only then is creative imagination able to build a new utopia: geometrical non-form.

—Achille Perilli

* * *

Achille Perilli is one of the large group of talented Italian artists who came to maturity in the post-war period and retained considerable attachment to and influence from Paris. He is one of the most diversely active and successful of his generation, embodying typical native brilliance as a designer, graphic artist and polemicist; and also exceptionally successfully in his work in theatre. He is what might loosely be called a gestural artist, which gives him some attachment to Tachisme, most easily compared with the French painter Georges Mathier. Perilli, however, is much more truly ''informal'' than his French contemporary, saved by excellent technique and taste from the exhibitionistic excesses common to artists of his genre. Among the most attractive of his early works was a series entitled ''Picture Stories,'' comic-strip compositions based on insect-like linear figures, arranged in sequences, contrasted with coloured zones, bands and right-angles. He usually works on monochrome backgrounds, pale, reticent colours on which graffiti-like motives are ''scratched.'' They have connotations of cave-drawings, whilst at the same time conveying contemporary humor, part cynicism, part fear of the very thing made fun of. He later developed large-scale versions of these figures, entitled ''transformazione della spazio,'' in which the relationship of the insect-like form to the space it occupied became important.

A brilliant draughtsman and designer, Perilli has produced splendid etchings, and other prints, as well as practising as a teacher of design. Work in the theatre ties in with his involvement with storytelling and the depiction of figures in space. He has designed ballets for La Scala, Milan, and has worked with the Teatro Gruppo 63 of Palermo and other companies. Efforts to relate art objects to theatrical presentations have resulted in a number of fascinating productions—''Collage,'' 1961, which combined mobile sculpture, projections and music, and in 1967 ''Grammatica No Stop Teatro.'' As an aesthetic activist, Perilli founded the group Forma I, in 1947, and has helped launch three important art magazines, *Art Visive,* 1952, *L'Esperienze Moderna,* 1957 and *Grammatica,* 1964.

—Charles Spencer

PETLIN, Irving

Nationality: American. **Born:** Chicago, Illinois, 17 December 1934. **Education:** Art Institute of Chicago, 1952–56. B.F.A.; Yale University, with Josef Albers, New Haven, Connecticut, M.F.A. 1959. **Military Service:** Served in the United States Army, 1957–59. **Career:** Painter: lived in France, 1959–63; now lives and works in New York. Instructor, University of California at Los Angeles, 1963–66; Rhode Island School of Design, Providence, 1978; Cooper Union, New York, 1977–80; artist-in-residence, Dartmouth College, Hanover, New Hampshire, 1983. **Awards:** Ryerson Fellowship, 1956; Copley Foundation Fellowship, 1961. **Agent:** Marlborough Gallery, 40 West 57th Street, New York, New York 10019.

Individual Exhibitions:

1956 Dilexi Gallery, San Francisco
Cliffdwellers Gallery, Chicago
1960 Galerie du Dragon, Paris
1962 Galerie du Dragon, Paris
Galleria Galatea, Turin
1963 Galerie du Dragon, Paris
1964 Galerie du Dragon, Paris
Hanover Gallery, London
1965 Palais de Beaux-Arts, Brussels (retrospective)
1966 Rolf Nelson Gallery, Los Angeles
1967 Odyssia Gallery, New York
1968 Galerie du Dragon, Paris
Galleria Il Fante di Spade, Rome
Odyssia Gallery, New York
1969 Odyssia Gallery, New York
Galleria Odyssia, Rome
1970 Odyssia Gallery, New York
1971 Odyssia Gallery, New York
Galleria Odyssia, Rome
1973 Galleria Odyssia, Rome
1974 Galleria Documenta, Turin
Galleria Bergamini, Turin
1975 Galerie du Dragon, Paris
1976 Galleria Odyssia, Rome
Rebecca Cooper Gallery, Washington, D.C.
1977 Galleria Bergamini, Milan
1978 State University of New York at Purchase
Arts Club of Chicago
1979 Odyssia Gallery, New York
1981 Odyssia Gallery, New York
1982 Odyssia Gallery, New York
1983 Dart Gallery, Chicago
Odyssia Gallery, New York
Dartmouth College, Hanover, New Hampshire
1984 Marlborough Gallery, New York (catalog)
1986 Marlborough Gallery, New York (catalog)
1987 Simms Fine Art Gallery, New Orleans
Galerie Jean Briance, Paris
Kent Fine Art, New York
1989 Kent Fine Art, New York

Irving Petlin: *Marriage,* 1963. ©Christie's Images/Corbis.

1994 Galerie Thessa Herold, Paris
1999 Jan Krugier Gallery, New York

Selected Group Exhibitions:

1972 *Chicago Imagist Art,* Museum of Contemporary Art, Chicago
1980 *100 Artists, 100 Years,* Art Institute of Chicago
1982 *Jewish Themes,* Jewish Museum, New York
1983 *Bodies and Souls,* Artists Choice Museum, New York
1984 *Art Americain,* Centre Georges Pompidou, Paris
1985 *Narration Drawing,* New York Studio School
1986 *American Myths,* Kent Fine Art, New York

Collections:

Museum of Modern Art, New York; Centre Georges Pompidou, Paris.

Publications:

By PETLIN: Articles—''Interview: Irving Petlin Talks with Paul Cummings'' in *Drawing,* vol. 8, May/June 1986.

On PETLIN: Book—*Irving Petlin: Weisswald,* exhibition catalog with text by Edwawrd F. Fry, New York 1987. **Articles**—''Portfolio'' in *Arts Magazine,* vol. 62, September 1987; review by John Yau in *Artforum International,* vol. 27, April 1989; review by Rex Weil in *Art News,* vol. 98, no. 3, March 1999; review by Aruna D'Souza in *Art in America* (New York), vol. 87, no. 4, April 1999.

PETTIBON, Raymond

Nationality: American. **Born:** Tucson, Arizona, 1957. **Education:** University of California, Los Angeles, B.A., 1977. **Career:** Independent photographer, Hermosa Beach, California. **Awards:** The Louis Comfort Tiffany Foundation Awards in Painting, Sculpture, Printmaking, Photography, and Craft Media, 1991. **Agent:** David Zwirner Gallery, 43 Greene Street, New York, New York 10013.

Selected Individual Exhibitions:

1986 Semaphore Gallery, New York
1989 Feature Gallery, New York
1990 *Readings,* Feature Gallery, New York
A Long Parenthesis, Richard/Bennett Gallery, Los Angeles
1991 Massimo de Carlo Arte Contemporanea, Milan
Reader Dearest, Robert Berman Gallery, Los Angeles
1993 Matrix Gallery, University Art Museum, University of California, Berkeley (brochure)
On the Scent, Galerie Metropol, Vienna
1994 Galeria Ramis Barquet, Garza, Mexico (traveled to Arena Arte Contemporaneo, Guadalajara, Mexico)
Galerie Metropol, Vienna
Galerie Beaumont, Luxembourg
1995 Kunsthalle Bern, Switzerland (catalog)
Galeria Massimo De Carlo, Milan
Contemporary Fine Arts, Berlin
1996 Taka Ishii Gallery, Tokyo
Tramway, Glasgow
1997 David Zwirner Gallery, New York
1998 *Raymond Pettibon,* The Renaissance Society, Chicago (catalog and artist book)
Regen Projects, Los Angeles
Contemporary Fine Arts, Berlin
1999 *Raymond Pettibon,* The Drawing Center, New York; Philadelphia Museum of Art; Museum of Contemporary Art, Los Angeles (catalog)
Galerie Meyer Kainer, Vienna
2000 *Raymond Pettibon: The Books,* organized by Roberto Ohrt, Frankfurt (traveled to Contemporary Fine Arts, Berlin; MAK, Vienna; David Zwirner Gallery, New York)
Regen Projects, Los Angeles
Hauser + Wirth, Zurich,
Sadie Coles HQ, London
2001 The Whitechapel, London
Wall Drawing, MAK Center, Vienna

Selected Group Exhibitions:

1985 Los Angeles Contemporary Exhibitions
1986 *Social Distortion,* Los Angeles Contemporary Exhibitions
1987 *Head Sex,* Feature Gallery, Chicago
Art of Politics, Richard/Bennett Gallery, Los Angeles
1988 *LACA Boys,* Feature Gallery, Chicago
Near Miss, Feature Gallery, Chicago
Cartoon-Like, MoMing Art Gallery, Chicago
1989 *Buttinsky,* Feature Gallery, New York
Art as Religion, Richard/Bennett Gallery, Los Angeles
Problems with Reading Rereading, Rhona Hollman Gallery, Chicago
1990 *Work on Paper* (invitational), Paula Allen Gallery, New York
Total Metal, Simon Watson, New York (catalog)
Just Pathetic, Rosamund Felsen Gallery, Los Angeles (catalog)
Drinking and Driving (exhibition of art commissioned for The Progressive Corporation's 1989 Annual Report), Cleveland Center for Contemporary Art
1991 *Ovarian Warriors vs. Knights of Crissom,* Sue Spaid Fine Art and Parker Zanic Gallery, Los Angeles
The Kelly Family, Esther Schipper Gallery, Cologne
AIDS Timeline, included in Group Material's installation of the AIDS Timeline at the Whitney Biennial, Whitney Museum of American Art, New York
Gang Bang, Air de Paris
1992 *Twenty Fragile Pieces,* Galerie Analix, Geneva (catalog)
Connections: Explorations in the Getty Center Collections, The Getty Center for the History of Art and the Humanities, Santa Monica
Drawn in the Nineties, Katonah Museum of Art, Katonah, New York (catalog)
Helter Skelter: L.A. Art in the 1990s, Museum of Contemporary Art, Los Angeles (catalog)
1993 *1993 Whitney Biennial,* Whitney Museum of American Art, New York; National Museum of Contemporary Art, Seoul (catalog)
Drawing the Line Against AIDS, Peggy Guggenheim Collection, Venice; Guggenheim Museum, SoHo, New York (catalog)
Mongrel Muse/Works on Paper Silkeborg Kunstmuseum, Silkeborg, Denmark (catalog)
Paper Trails: The Eidetic Image, Krannert Art Museum, University of Illinois at Urbana-Champaign, University Gallery in Chicago: I Space, Chicago
1994 *Mapping,* Museum of Modern Art, New York
SoggettoSoggetto, Castello di Rivoli, Italy (catalog)
Can You Always Believe Your Eyes: Recent American Drawings, Museum of Contemporary Art DeBeyerd, Breda, The Netherlands
Don't Look Now, Thread Waxing Space, New York (catalog)

1995 *Das Ende Der Avantgarde: Kunst als Dienstleistung (Sammlung Schurmann),* Kunsthalle der Hypo-Kulturstiftung, Munich (catalog)
It's Only Rock and Roll: Rock and Roll Currents in Contemporary Art, Contemporary Art Center, Cincinnati; Austin Museum of Art (catalog)
1996 *Sammlung Speck,* Museum Ludwig, Cologne, Germany
Now Here: Work in Progress, Louisiana Museum of Art, Copenhagen (catalog)
New Art on Paper 2, Philadelphia Museum of Art
Sex and Crime: On Human Relationships, Sprengel Museum, Hannover (catalog)
1997 *Heart, Mind, Body, Soul,* Whitney Museum of American Art, New York
A Decade of Collecting: Recent Acquisitions in Contemporary Drawing, Museum of Modern Art, New York
Elusive Paradise: Los Angeles Art from the Permanent Collection, Museum of Contemporary Art, Los Angeles
Angel, Angel, Kunsthalle Wien, Vienna; Rudolfinum, Prague (catalog)
Sunshine & Noir: Art in L.A., 1960–1997, Louisiana Museum, Humlebaek, Denmark (traveled to Kunstmuseum Wolfsburg, Germany; Castello di Rivoli, Italy; UCLA at The Armand Hammer Museum, Los Angeles) (catalog)
1998 *Hindsight: 56 Recent Acquisitions,* Whitney Museum of American Art, New York
L.A. Current: Looking at the Light: 3 Generations of L.A. Artists, UCLA at the Armand Hammer Museum of Art and Cultural Center, Los Angeles
Sea Change, Parrish Art Museum, Southampton, New York
Double Trouble: The Patchett Collection, Museum of Contemporary Art, San Diego
1999 *The American Century: Art and Culture, 1999–2000,* Whitney Museum of American Art, New York
Gallery Swap, Contemporary Fine Arts, Berlin; Sadie Coles HQ, London
Hypertronix, Espai d'Art Contemporani de Castello, Spain
Collectors Collect Contemporary: 1990–99, The Institute of Contemporary Art, Boston
2000 *L.A.,* Ileana Tounta Contemporary Art Center, Athens, Greece
Mirror's Edge, Bildmuseet, Sweden (traveled to Vancouver Art Gallery; Castello di Rivoli, Italy; Tramway, Glasgow, Scotland)
Made in California, Los Angeles County Museum of Art
2001 *Locating Drawing,* Lawing Gallery, Houston

Publications:

By PETTIBON: Books—*On the Scent,* Vienna 1992; *Thinking of You,* Chicago 1998. **Articles—**''A Conversation with Raymond Pettibon'' by Jim Lewis in *Parkett,* no. 47, September 1996; ''An Interview with Raymond Pettibon'' by David Larsen and Raymond Pettibon in *San Jose Manual of Style,* issue 3, 2000.

On PETTIBON: Books—*Raymond Pettibon* edited by Ulrich Loock, Bern 1995; *Raymond Pettibon: A Reader* edited by Ann Temkin and Hamza Walker, Philadelphia 1998; *Raymond Pettibon: The Books, 1978–98,* edited by Roberto Ohrt, New York, 2000. **Articles—** ''American Prayers'' by Kim Gordon in *Artforum,* no. 23, April 1985; ''Raymond Pettibon at Semaphore'' by Ellen Handy in *Arts Magazine,* no. 60, May 1986; ''The Library in Your Good Hands: Raymond Pettibon'' by David Deitcher in *Artforum,* October 1992; ''Pettibon with Strings'' by Mike McGonigal in *Chemical Imbalance,* Spring 1992; ''Raymond Pettibon at Regen Projects'' by James Scarborough in *Flash Art,* no. 175, March-April 1994; ''Surfing with Raymond: Nobody Rides for Free'' by Ralph Rugoff in *Parkett,* no. 47, September 1996; ''Untitled'' by Hilton Als in *Parkett,* no. 47, September 1996; ''Raymond Pettibon Reads Henry James'' by Thyrza Nichols Goodeve in *Parkett,* no. 47, September 1996; ''The Drawing Rescues Poetry'' by Boris Groys in *Parkett,* no. 47, September 1996; ''Can One Speak of Art?'' by Jan Tumlir in *Artweek,* no. 28, June 1997; ''Artist's Project: Raymond Pettibon,'' *Dazed and Confused,* July 1997; ''Kunst in L.A.'' by Lars Nittve in *Marian,* April 1998; ''Raymond Pettibon: The Renaissance Society, The University of Chicago'' by Charles Irvin in *New Art Examiner* vol. 26, no. 5, February 1999; ''Pettibon's Talking Pictures'' by Michael Duncan in *Art in America,* vol. 87, no. 3, March 1999; ''Raymond Pettibon at MOCA (Los Angeles)'' by Brad Spence in *Artweek,* vol. 30, no. 11, November 1999; ''Raymond Pettibon'' by Grady Turner in *Bomb,* Fall 1999; ''Raymond Pettibon: The Thin Black Line'' by Hope Urban in *Juxtapoz,* January-February 2000; ''Raymond Pettibon: A Return to Disorder and Disfiguration'' by Benjamin H.D. Buchloh in *October,* no. 92, Spring 2000; ''Raymond Pettibon at MOCA (Los Angeles)'' by Carmine Iannaccone in *Art Issues,* vol. 62, March-April 2000; ''Raymond Pettibon: Regen Projects'' by Bruce Hainley in *Artforum,* vol. 39, no. 3, November 2000.

* * *

Addressing the work of Raymond Pettibon, musician and writer Kim Gordon asserted the relevance of Los Angeles culture in the artist's cryptic, cartoon-frame drawings of modern American life when she wrote: ''L.A.'s lush landscaping only begins to make sense when you realize that underneath it is a desert.'' Raised in Hermosa Beach, where he continues to live, Pettibon has made a career of his near-obsessive mining of that desert—and both the treasures and garbage buried there—in the thousands of ink wash, graphite, and watercolor drawings he has produced since the late 1970s. Gordon's astute, early observation of this tendency in Pettibon's work is interesting considering it was not the gallery world but punk culture from which both emerged; indeed, Pettibon's work first came to national attention through his album covers and flyers for Gordon's band Sonic Youth as well as his older brother Greg Ginn's outfit, Black Flag. His drawings combine imagery culled from popular photography, video stills, cartoons, and comics with original and appropriated text applied to the image in the sometimes direct, often random fashion that earlier Southern California artists Alexis Smith and Ed Ruscha utilized a generation earlier. But in the same way that Ginn's purposely flubbed guitar solos on Black Flag's albums mocked the mastery of 1970s rock, Pettibon's poor draftsmanship and sloppy technique reflects an antiheroic, nihilistic punk ethic that distinguishes his work from these earlier Pop-inspired artists.

Some works operate in the conventionally, irreverently critical fashion of influences like Francisco Goya and Honore Daumier, mocking the heroes and hypocrisy of American culture. Like both artists, he has also explored the power of popular media, but through the postmodern era's new print forms: photocopied fanzines and comics. Although popular and political figures often appear in his satirical drawings, Pettibon's most bilious critiques tend to be reserved for the counterculture, as its participants attempt to conform to the same media images that the movements themselves allegedly disdain. Charlie Manson is frequently conjured as representative of California's self-congratulatory hippie movement's dark side; a grinning postwar blonde toasts an unseen artist with the exclamation, "With a loft like this, you can paint masterpieces"; and young Bob Dylan's famous profile from the *Don't Look Back* movie poster is recreated with a halo and the churlish revelation, "Of *course* he became a Christian."

Since the early 1990s his work has become increasingly abstract, as well as more cryptic, with the texts applied in a random or personally relevant fashion that reveal an introspective, Romantic side to Pettibon often overshadowed by the biting satire of his earlier work. His vernacular images—such as the recurring appearances of cartoon character Gumby and Felix the Cat sidekick Vavoom, steam engine trains and anonymous baseball players—are frequently paired with reflective but seemingly unconnected snippets of prose from the likes of Marcel Proust, John Ruskin, or Francis Bacon. A recent series of phallus drawings—compiled in book form by the University of Chicago's Renaissance Society—represents nothing more than penis profiles with sometimes comical, sometimes poignant comments that generally relate to the myth of authority's masculine nature. (Perhaps the most memorable phalli include a quartet simply labeled "The Beatles," and a quintet under the statement, "We share a wide community of belief.") In another work, a gesturally rendered hypodermic syringe is topped with text that muses: "For it has a soul, I think." Such cryptic works are simultaneously jarring and inviting, in that these curious juxtapositions beg close scrutiny of the works and, by extension, the artist's communicative process.

The artist's processes of thought and expression—baffling as they can be—are precisely what is on view when viewing Pettibon's works in the way they were intended: in fanzines, journal-style books, or exhibited floor-to-ceiling, often pinned directly to the wall, in a snowballing barrage of stimuli. Critic Ralph Rugoff summarized the cumulative effect of Pettibon's 'zine, book, and exhibition projects when he wrote: "As if mimicking the ceaseless maelstrom of our mass-media landscape, these shows engulf you in a whirlpool of words and images . . . surfing across a seemingly haphazard cross section of cultural history." Pettibon himself has asserted that this effect reflects the notion that "modern sensibility is a product of multiple personality and fractured personality," reflected in the fragmented, stream-of-consciousness style of both his image/text combinations and exhibitions. Through these curious juxtapositions and the labyrinth of meanings that they evoke, Pettibon's work articulates the relevance of his popular icons and objects in our collective memory as well as their potential to transcend their homely, temporal, or trivial origins.

—Maria Elena Buszek

PFAFF, Judy

Nationality: American. Born: London, England, 1946. **Education:** Wayne State University, Detroit, Michigan, 1965–66; Southern Illinois University, Edwardsville, Illinois, 1968–69; Norfolk Summer School of Music and Art, Norfolk, Connecticut, 1970; Washington University-St. Louis, Missouri, B.F.A. 1971; Yale University, New Haven, Connecticut, M.F.A. 1973. **Career:** Designed set for "Wind Devil," a dance choreographed by Nina Weiner, Brooklyn Academy of Music, New York. **Awards:** Creative Artist Public Services, Sculpture, 1976; National Endowment for the Arts, Sculpture, 1979; Guggenheim Fellowship, Sculpture, 1983; Bessie Award, Set Design, 1984; Wacaol Commission, Japan, 1985; National Endowment for the Arts, 1986; Fellow of the Saint-Gaudens Memorial, 1997.

Selected Individual Exhibitions:

1975 *J.A.S.O.N./J.A.S.O.N.,* Artists Space, New York
1977 *The World is Flat,* Theatre Gallery, University of South Florida at Tampa
1978 *Prototypes,* Los Angeles Contemporary Exhibitions Gallery
1980 *Deep Water,* Holly Solomon Gallery, New York
1981 *Rorscharch,* John and Mable Ringling Museum, Sarasota, Florida
1982 *Four Minute Mile,* Bennington College, Bennington, Vermont
Collages and Constructions, Hallwalls Gallery, Buffalo, New York
1983 *3-D,* Holly Solomon Gallery, New York
1986 *Apples and Oranges,* Holly Solomon Gallery, New York
Autonomous Objects, Knight Gallery, Charlotte, North Carolina
1987 *Judy Pfaff,* Susanne Hilberry Gallery, Birmingham, Michigan
1988 *Judy Pfaff,* Carnegie-Mellon University Art Gallery, Pittsburgh, Pennsylvania
10,000 Things, Holly Solomon Gallery, New York
1990 *Judy Pfaff: Sculpture and Works on Paper,* Cleveland Center for Contemporary Art, Cleveland, Ohio
1992 *Judy Pfaff: Seven New Prints and a Sculpture,* Crown Point Press, New York and San Francisco
Judy Pfaff: A New Work, Max Protetch, New York
1993 *Judy Pfaff: Recent Sculpture and Drawings,* Nancy Drysdale Gallery, Washington, D.C.
1994 *Cielo: Landscape as Metaphor,* Denver Art Museum, Denver, Colorado
1995 *Elephant,* Rose Art Museum, Brandeis University, Waltham, Massachusetts
Recent Drawings, Bellas Artes Gallery, Sante Fe, New Mexico
Ear to Ear, Williamson Gallery, Art Center College of Design, Pasadena, California
1996 *Judy Pfaff: New Prints, Drawings and Sculpture,* Susanne Hilberry Gallery, Birmingham, Michigan
Judy Pfaff, André Emmerich Gallery, New York
Judy Pfaff: New Work, Bellas Artes Gallery, Santa Fe, New Mexico
1997 *Judy Pfaff: Round Hole Square Peg,* André Emmerich Gallery, New York
Judy Pfaff, Saint-Gaudens National Historic Site, Cornish, New Hampshire

Judy Pfaff: *Supermercado,* 1986. Photo by Geoffrey Clements. ©Collection of Whitney Museum of American Art, Purchase, with funds from the Louis and Bessie Adler Foundation, Inc., Seymour M. Klein, president, and The Sondra and Charles Gilman, Jr., Foundation, Inc.

1998 *Judy Pfaff: Drawings,* Gallery Deux, Tokyo, Japan

Selected Group Exhibitions:

1975 *Whitney Biennial,* Whitney Museum of American Art, New York

1976 *Approaching Painting,* Hallwalls Gallery, Buffalo, New York

1979 *Reinventing the Wheel,* Neuberger Art Gallery, State University of New York at Purchase

Sculptural Perspective, University of California at Santa Barbara Art Museum

1980 *Extensions: Jennifer Bartlett, Lyda Bengils, Robert Longo, Judy Pfaff,* Contemporary Art Museum, Houston, Texas

Penthouse Exhibition, Museum of Modern Art, New York

Drawings: The Pluralist Decade, United States Pavillion, Venice Biennale, Venice, Italy (travelled to Kunstgoreningen Museum, Copenhagen, Denmark; Henie Onstad Museum, Onstad, Norway; Biblioteca Nacional, Madrid, Spain; Gulbenkian Museum, Lisbon, Portugal)

1981 *Whitney Biennial,* Whitney Museum of American Art, New York

Directions 1981, Hirshhorn Museum and Sculpture Garden, Washington, D.C.

1982 *Guy Goodwin, Bill Jensen, Louise Fishman, Judy Pfaff,* Usdan Gallery, Bennington College, Bennington, Vermont

The Americans: The Collage, Contemporary Arts Museum, Houston, Texas

1983 *New Art,* The Tate Gallery, London, England

Back to the U.S.A., Kunstmuseum, Lucerne, Switzerland

The Next Wave: BAM, Paula Cooper Gallery, New York

1986 *Public and Private: American Prints Today,* The Brooklyn Museum, New York

Recent Acquisitions, Whitney Museum of American Art, New York

1987 *For 25 Years: Crown Point Press,* Museum of Modern Art, New York

Sculptors on Paper, Madison Art Center, Madison, Wisconsin

1988 *Aspects of Abstraction,* Holly Solomon Gallery, New York

1989 *Point National Overview,* The Brooklyn Museum, New York

Prospects and Portfolios: The 25th National Print Exhibition, The Brooklyn Museum, New York

American Rainbow, Galerie de Poche, Paris, France

1993 *Reflections on the Center: 25 Years,* Cleveland Center for Contemporary Art, Ohio

1994 *Inspired by Nature,* Neuberger Museum, SUNY Purchase, Purchase, New York

American Academy Invitational Exhibition of Painting and Sculpture, American Academy of Arts and Letters, New York

1995 *In Tree Dimensions: Women Sculptors of the 90s,* Snug Harbor Cultural Center, Staten Island, New York

1996 *New Art on Paper,* Philadelphia Museum of Art, Pennsylvania

New Visions: Al Held, Jules Olitski, Judy Pfaff, André Emmerich Gallery, New York (catalog)

1997 *35 Years at Crown Point Press,* National Gallery of Art, Washington, D.C

Etching and Woodcuts: From Crown Point Press, Karen McCready Fine Art, New York (catalog)

Great Graphics, Karen McCready Fine Art, New York (catalog)

Drawn & Quartered: 4 Drawings Each, Karen McCready Fine Art, New York (catalog)

1998 *Pop Abstraction,* Museum of American Art, Philadelphia, Pennsylvania

Drawings: Judy Pfaff & Jane Rosen, Kendall Art and Design, Hudson, New York

2000 *The Likeness of Being: Self Portraits by 50 Women,* DC Moore Gallery, New York (catalog)

The End: An Independent Vision of Contemporary Culture 1982–2000, Exit Art/The First World, New York (catalog)

2001 *New Prints,* International Print Center New York, New York (catalog)

Collections:

Brooklyn Museum, Brooklyn, New York; Bowdoin College Museum of Art, Brunswick, Maine; University Art Gallery, University of Massachusetts at Amherst; The Library of Congress, Washington, D.C.; Museum of Modern Art, New York; The St. Louis Art Museum, St. Louis, Missouri; Städtische Kunsthalle, Mannheim Museum, Mannheim, Germany; Youngstown State University Art Gallery, Youngstown, Ohio.

Public Installations:

Rock/Paper/Scissors, Albright-Knox Art Gallery, Buffalo, New York, 1982; Aquavitae: Art in Public Places, Miami Beach Police and Court Facility, Miami Beach, Florida, 1994; Cirque, CIRQUE, Pennsylvania Convention Center, Philadelphia, Pennsylvania, 1994.

Publications:

By PFAFF: Articles—Interview by Richard Whittaker, online *works + conversations,* Web site at http://www.conversations.org/98–1-pfaff.htm (accessed June 2001).

On PFAFF: Articles—''Art: Judy Pfaff and Kim MacDonnell'' by Grace Glueck in *New York Times* (New York), 26 September 1980; ''Little Disturbances of Man: Judy Pfaff'' by Kay Larson in *Village Voice* (New York), 7 October 1980; ''Judy Pfaff'' by Betty Collings in *Arts Magazine* (New York), November 1980; ''Animal House: The Whitney Biennial'' by Stuart Morgan in *Artscribe* (London), no. 20, 1981; ''The Art World: Three Salons'' by Calvin Tomkins in *New Yorker* (New York), 13 April 1981; ''Alice in Duchamp Land'' by Kay Larson in *New York Magazine* (New York), 25 May 1981; ''Talking with Judy Pfaff'' by John Caldwell in *New York Times* (New York), 3 January 1982; ''Judy Pfaff's Neo-Expressionist Environment'' by Grace Glueck in *New York Times* (New York), 2 January 1983; ''Done and Undone Judy Pfaff'' by Roberta Smith in *Village Voice* (New York), 1 February 1983; ''Review: Judy Pfaff'' by Richard Armstrong in *ArtForum* (New York), March 1983; ''Viewpoints: A Queen of Art Reigns with Space Odysseys'' by Harry Herbert Sloane in *Gentleman's Quarterly* (New York), April 1983; ''The Whitney Spanks Itself'' by Roberta Smith in *Village Voice* (New York), 18 December 1984; ''Talking Objects: Interviews with Ten Younger Sculptors'' by Wade Saunders in *Art in America* (New York), November 1985; ''Pfaff's Riotous Calm Hits the Holly Solomon Gallery'' by Douglas McGill in *New York Times* (New York), 16 May 1986; ''Judy Pfaff: New York Reviews'' by Lorraine Karafel in *ArtNews* (New York), October 1986; ''Beyond the Perimeters: The Eccentric Humanism of Judy Pfaff'' by Susan Gil in *Arts Magazine* (New York), October 1986; ''Six of One. . . A Half Dozen Woodcuts by Judy Pfaff'' by Susan Tallman in *Arts Magazine* (New York), November 1988; ''10,000 Things I Know About Her'' by Carl Rosen in *Arts Magazine* (New York), March 1989; ''Embracing Ambiguity'' by Michael M. Floss and Anastasia D. Shartin in *Artweek* (New York), 9 July 1992; ''Judy Pfaff: Life and Limb'' by Nancy Princenthal in *Art in America* (New York), vol. 86, no. 10, October 1998.

* * *

Judy Pfaff's sculptures have been likened to paintings that have exploded out of the frame. While her work does share some of the characteristics of paintings, like an obvious love of color and a sense of spontaneity, they are solidly three-dimensional. What reads as spontaneity is the result of the carefully-planned and laborious process that is necessary given the work's complexity, wide range of materials, and, often, its placement in the public sphere. In many cases, Pfaff's work may more accurately be called installation art than sculpture, since she carefully considers the setting and makes each work specifically for the space in which it will be housed.

Born in London in 1946, Pfaff came to the United States when she was twelve years old. After spending her childhood years in Detroit, Michigan, Pfaff earned her B.F.A. at Washington University, St. Louis, Missouri, and her M.F.A. at Yale University. At Yale, she studied painting and drawing with Al Held, a painter of geometric abstraction. While Held's work is in many ways the opposite of Pfaff's mature style, she has professed an admiration for minimalist sculptors. Pfaff has used minimalism as a sort of jumping off point, trying throughout her career to push its boundaries ever further.

Pfaff has continually pushed the envelope with her use of materials. She has used most every material imaginable, even those that other artists might consider trash. Her works are a marriage of found objects—both manufactured and organic, with trees and branches particular favorites—and more traditional materials like glass, steel and wire.

In her early installations, Pfaff created an environment that would completely envelop and even disorient the viewer. Unlike a painting or a traditional sculpture, there was no one vantage point from which to view these works; the viewer had to literally enter it. In these installations, Pfaff explored some of the traditional formal elements of painting, using repetition of color and shape as a painter might.

In the late 1980s, Pfaff's sculptures became less painterly and more structured: she put them back on the wall. While these works still asserted a strong presence in the gallery, they no longer necessitated the viewer's physical interaction. However, Pfaff still retained the possibility of multiple perspectives, with the work taking on a different appearance when viewed from different angles.

In 1989, Pfaff visited Pilchuck Glass School near Seattle, Washington, for the first of several summers as an Artist in Residence. Her time at Pilchuck led to a major change in Pfaff's use of materials. Pfaff had what she calls an "epiphany" when she experienced the interaction of the school's several rustic buildings and the more than fifty acres of a nearly untouched natural environment. She was also attracted to the glass-making process and the physical properties of glass. After her first stay at Pilchuck, Pfaff brought glass-making materials back to her New York studio and experimented further with the medium.

Pfaff fully merges her sculpture with its surroundings, especially when she constructs a work in a public space, like *Cirque, Cirque* (1995) at the Philadelphia Convention Center. She enters a space where she will build a sculpture without any preconceived notions of what the work will look like. Only after she has spent a considerable amount of time getting to know the space is she ready to create the initial design of the work. She determines many of the details of the sculpture along the way, with the relationship between the work and its site always foremost in her mind.

Whereas Pfaff's earlier work experimented with formal characteristics like repetition of line and color, the artist has said that the inspiration for the most recent work comes from a more personal place. Perhaps as the result of nearly thirty years of experience, Pfaff now seems more able to trust her intuition and to rely on her own experiences.

Among Pfaff's most important recent installations is *Crown of Thorns,* her project as the United States representative for the 1998 Sao Paulo, Brazil, Bienal. For this work, Pfaff and a team of assistants spent six full-time weeks installing the work. Located in a glass pavilion, Pfaff's installation evoked a forest-like environment using found tree stumps and branches, in addition to other materials, including soil, plaster, and tubing. The focal point of this installation was thirteen-foot tall steel catwalk which visitors could cross, affording them an entirely different perspective on the installation.

In 1994, Pfaff was involved in a legal case that earned her a reputation as a crusader for artists' rights. She sued the Denver Art Museum for the destruction of her work *Cielo,* which arrived damaged at the Columbus Museum of Art for a traveling exhibition. Pfaff's case was only the second brought under the Artists Right Act of 1990, and established her as a champion of the rights of artists to have their work treated with integrity.

—Tara Reddy Young

PHILLIPS, Peter

Nationality: British. **Born:** Birmingham, 21 May 1939. **Education:** Birmingham primary schools; Birmingham College of Art, 1955–59; Royal College of Art, London, 1959–62. **Family:** Married Marion-Claude Xylander in 1970. **Career:** Travelled in France, Switzerland and Italy, 1959; in France, 1961; in Spain, the United States and North Africa, 1964. Worked on Entrance Hall, and machine designs, *Shakespeare Exhibition,* Stratford-on-Avon, Warwickshire, 1964; lived in New York, 1964–66; travelled extensively in the United States and Canada, 1965; settled in Zurich, 1966, guest professor, Hochschule für Bildende Kunste, Hamburg, 1968–69. **Awards:** Harkness Fellowship, 1964. **Address:** Im Ostgarten 5, 8044 Gockhausen, Zurich, Switzerland.

Individual Exhibitions:

1965 Kornblee Gallery, New York
1966 Kornblee Gallery, New York
1967 Galerie Bischofberger, Zurich
1968 Galerie der Spiegel, Cologne
Kornblee Gallery, New York
Galleria del Leone, Venice
Alecto Gallery, London
Galerie Bischofberger, Zurich
1969 Galerie Bischofberger, Zurich
1970 Studio d'Arte Condotti, Rome
Galleria Milano, Milan
1971 Galerie Leonhart, Munich
Galleria d'Arte Vinciana, Milan
Studio d'Arte Condotti, Rome
1972 Westfälischer Kunstverein, Münster (retrospective)
1973 Galerie Bischofberger, Zurich
1974 Galleria Plura, Milan
Galerie Bischofberger, Zurich
1976 Tate Gallery Coffee Shop, London
Waddington Galleries, London
1982 *Retrovision,* Walker Art Gallery, Liverpool (toured the United Kingdom)
1987 Galerie Jamileh Weber, Zurich
1998 *Peter Phillips: Freedom of Choices,* Thomas Gibson Gallery, London

Selected Group Exhibitions:

1961 *Young Contemporaries,* RBA Galleries, London
1962 *The New Realists,* Sidney Janis Gallery, New York
1964 *The New Generation,* Whitechapel Art Gallery, London
1965 *Op and Pop,* Moderna Museet, Stockholm
1966 *Primary Structures,* Jewish Museum, New York

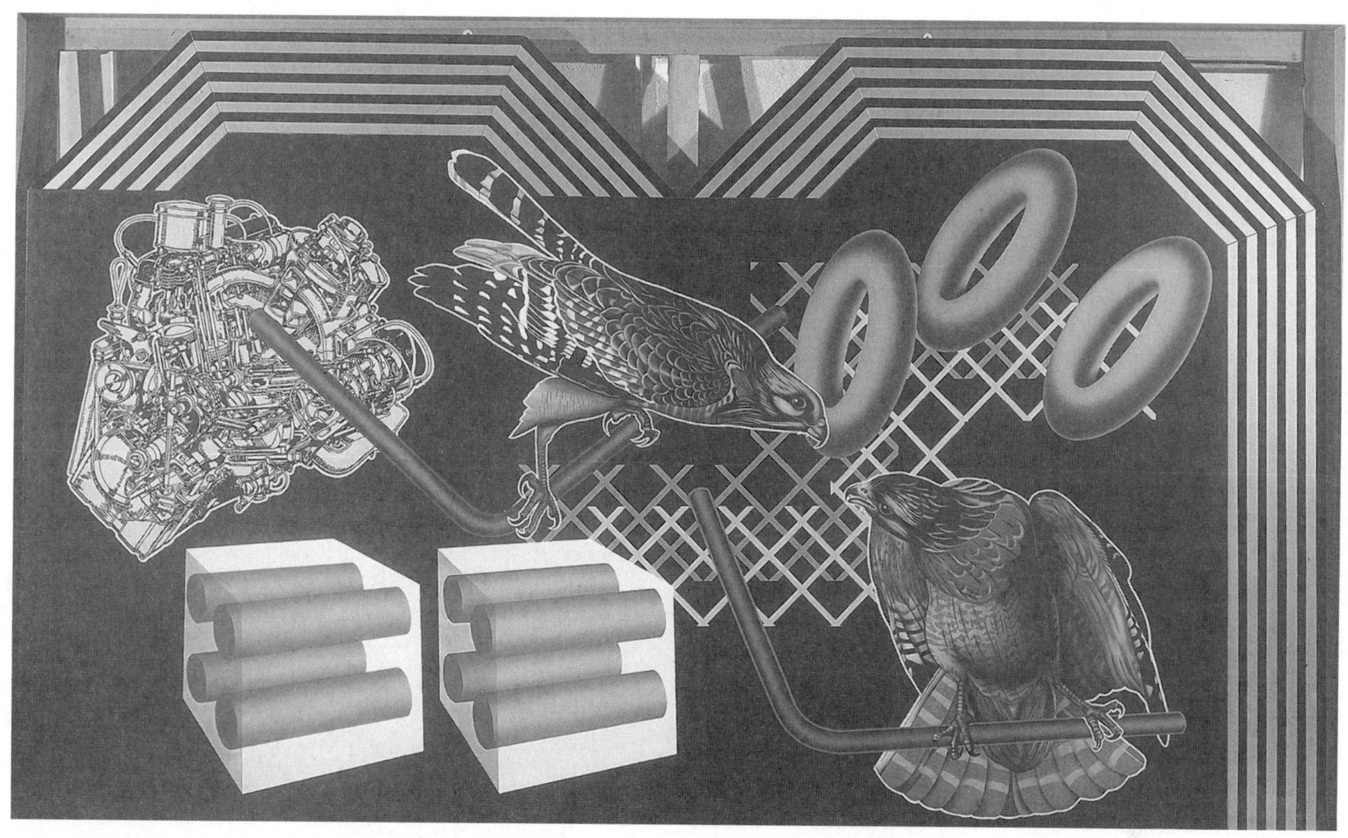

Peter Phillips: *Random Illusion No. 4,* 1968. ©Tate Gallery, London/Art Resource, NY; courtesy of Tate Gallery.

1968 *Junge Generation Grosbrittannien,* Akademie der Bildenden Kunste, Berlin
1971 *Around the Automobile,* Hofstra University, Hempstead, New York
1976 *Pop Art Redefined,* Kunstverein, Hamburg
1981 *Avantgarden Retrospektiv: Kunst nach 1945,* Westfälischer Kunstverein, Munster, West Germany
1986 *British and American Pop Art,* Tate Gallery, London
1997 *Lisbon: British Art 1960 to the Present,* Fundacao Calouste Gulbenkian, Lisbon

Collections:

Tate Gallery, London; Victoria and Albert Museum, London; Museum voor Schone Kunsten, Ghent; Neue Pinakothek, Munich; Albright-Knox Art Gallery, Buffalo, New York; Museum of Modern Art, New York.

Publications:

By PHILLIPS: Article—''Crawl a Mile in My Shell,'' *New Observations,* no. 108, September-October 1995.

On PHILLIPS: Books— *Private View* by Bryan Robertson, John Russell and Lord Snowdon, London 1965; *Pop Art* by Günter Dienst, Weisbaden 1965; *Pop as Art* by Mario Amaya, London 1965; *Pop Art* by Lucy Lippard, London 1965; *Peter Phillips,* exhibition catalog by Christopher Finch, London 1966; *Pop Art: Object and Image* by Christopher Finch, London 1968; *Image as Language* by Christopher Finch, London 1969; *Pop Art Redefined* by John Russell and Suzi Gablik, New York and London 1969; *Peter Phillips,* exhibition catalog by Enrico Crispolti, Rome 1970; *Peter Phillips,* exhibition catalog by Roberto Sanesi, Milan 1971; *Peter Phillips* by Enrico Crispolti, Milan 1975; *Retrovision: Peter Phillips,* exhibition catalog by Marco Livingstone, Liverpool 1982; *Peter Phillips: Freedom of Choices,* exhibition catalog, London 1998. **Articles—**''Peter Phillips: Metaphors of Consciousness'' by Marco Livingstone in *Art Press,* no. 195, October 1994; ''Peter Phillips at Thomas Gallery'' by Carol Z. Prager in *Art in America* (New York), vol. 86, no. 11, November 1998.

* * *

From his final months at the Royal College of Art in 1962, Peter Phillips felt moved to reject completely the time-worn formulae for painting pictures. After studying at the Birmingham College of Art before coming to London, Phillips had trained in technical drawing. His views were conditioned by the employment of painting media for the purposes of illustration and description, rather than for the creation of ''Fine Art.'' In 1964 he was one of the youngest exhibitors in *The New Generation* exhibition at the Whitechapel Gallery. He received a Harkness stipend from the Commonwealth Fund and spent the next two years in New York. While he was there, he perfected his performance with the air brush and used photography extensively in his graphics. He held his first one-man show in New York in 1965 with the Kornblee Gallery. Since 1966 he has lived in Zurich, where he exhibits at the Galerie Bischofberger.

Peter Phillips: *Custom Painting No. 3,* 1964–65. ©Art Resource, NY; courtesy of collection of Watson Powell, Des Moines, IA.

Of the younger Pop generation Phillips composes his pictures almost exclusively from the second-hand imagery of publicity, either the glossy advertisements in magazines, billboards or the flashing lights on one-arm bandits and jukeboxes. Treated in a disintegrated cutaway sectional format, the large canvases become decorative data-charts of recognizable views of automobile interiors over-painted in zigzags and parallel stripes, that give the work a feeling of dynamic abstraction. This absorption in the intricacies of mechanics as they affect modern living is formalized in pictures apart from a sense of realism in the bland description of parts. It is the still life of consumer durables. The motives, such as the inset power units of internal combustion engines, exploratory if not beautiful, reveal the vicarious nature of their source, almost deserving the title Post-Photo Collage Jazz Painting.

Brilliant metallic colours mark rejection of the oil palette for acrylics and instil a chromatic dazzle, as in his ''Pneumatics,'' where an air-line whips and coils through an arrangement of tyres, headlights, and exploded engine and star-stickers bearing a petrol company's selling symbol. The elements that take their place in Phillips's work pay no regard to aesthetic appeal or geometric design. Overall flatness of the picture plane eliminates perspective, so that details complete in themselves emerge from their backgrounds like the paper legends of an amusement arcade. Phillips has developed subject to a new variety by the substitution of the painting itself composed in eye-catching design of decorative publicity style, dynamic and brightly abstract.

—G. S. Whittet

PHILLIPS, Tom

Nationality: British. **Born:** London, 24 May 1937. **Education:** St. Catherine's College, Oxford, 1957–60; studied painting at the Camberwell School of Art, London, under Frank Auerbach, Charles Howard and Euan Uglow, 1961–63. **Family:** Married Jill Purdy in 1961; children: Eleanor and Conrad. **Career:** Painter, since 1963; also a poet and composer (composed opera *Irma,* first performed at York University, 1973); lives and works in London. Lecturer in English and music, Brixton, London, 1960–61; lecturer, Ipswich School of Art, 1966–67, and Wolverhampton College of Art, 1967–70; part-time lecturer, Royal College of Art and Slade School of Fine Art, London, 1975; co-director of *A TV Dante,* 1984–89. **Awards:** Second Prize for Painting, *John Moore's Exhibition,* Liverpool, 1969; First Prize for Painting, Artists International Association, 1969; Book Design Award, Victoria and Albert Museum, London, 1983; First Prize, for *A TV Dante,* Montreal Festival, 1990; Prix Italia, 1991. **Member:** Royal Society of Painter-Printmakers, 1987; Royal Academy, London, associate, 1984, member, 1989. **Agent:** Please contact the artist or Massimo Valsecchi, Via Santa Marta 11, Milan, Italy. **Address:** 57 Talfourd Road, London SE15 5NN, United Kingdom.

Individual Exhibitions:

1965 Artist's International Association Gallery, London
1968 Ikon Gallery, Birmingham
Elizabeth Gallery, Coventry
1970 Angela Flowers Gallery, London
1971 Angela Flowers Gallery, London
Bear Lane Gallery, Oxford
City Art Gallery, Wolverhampton
Welsh Arts' Council Gallery, Cardiff (travelled to the Arnolfini Gallery, Bristol, and Dartington Hall, Devon)
1972 Galerie Rudolph Zwirner, Cologne
Bear Lane Gallery, Oxford
1973 Hatton Gallery, Newcastle upon Tyne
Marlborough Fine Art, London
Marlborough Graphics, London
Institute of Contemporary Art, London
1974 Gallery 101, Johannesburg
Marlborough Gallery, New York
Downtown Gallery, New York
1975 Gemeentemuseum, The Hague
Nova Spectra Gallery, The Hague
Kunsthalle, Basel
Galleria Massimo Valsecchi, Milan
Galerie BA-MA, Paris
Centre d'Art et Communication, Vaduz, Lichtenstein
Musée Art Moderne de la Ville, Paris
Palais d'Athenée, Geneva
1976 Angela Flowers Gallery, London
Serpentine Gallery, London
Fabian Fine Art, Capetown
Municipal Art Gallery, Durban, South Africa
University of Witwatersrand, Johannesburg
National Museum and Art Gallery, Gaberone, Bechuanaland
Midland Group Gallery, Nottingham
City Art Gallery, Wolverhampton

Arts Centre, Durham
Mappin Art Gallery, Cardiff
Fabian Fine Art, Capetown (toured South Africa)
1977 Waddington Galleries, London
Kunstverein, Mannheim
AIFACS, New Delhi
Oriel Gallery, Cardiff
Ferens Art Gallery, Hull
1978 Lefevre Gallery, New York
Galerie BA-MA, Paris
1979 Centre Cultural du Marais, Paris
Marlborough Fine Art, London
Tate Gallery, London (with Richard Long and Paul Nash)
Galleria Massimo Valsecchi, Milan
Galerie BA-MA, Paris
1982 Galleria d'Arte Moderna, Bologna
Waddington Galleries, London
1983 Victoria and Albert Museum, London
1985 Wingfield College, Suffolk
1986 Center for Books Arts, New York
1987 Angela Flowers Gallery, London
Mappin Art Gallery, Sheffield
Turnpike Gallery, Wigan, Yorkshire
1988 National Gallery, Australia
City Art Institute, Sydney
1989 National Portrait Gallery, London
1990 North Carolina Museum of Art
Kunsthalle, Basel
1992 Royal Academy of Arts, London
Victoria and Albert Museum, London
Berggruen and Zevi, London
1993 Ulster Museum, Belfast
Yale Centre for British Art, New Haven, Connecticut

Selected Group Exhibitions:

1967 *Summer Exhibition,* Royal Academy of Art, London
1970 *Biennale,* Venice
1973 *La Peinture Anglaise d'Aujourd'hui,* Musée d'Art Moderne de la Ville, Paris
1976 *Arte Inglese Oggi,* Palazzo Reale, Milan
1978 *Art for Society,* Whitechapel Art Gallery, London
1980 *The Open and Closed Book,* Victoria and Albert Museum, London
1984 *The Hard Won Image,* Tate Gallery, London
1985 *Livres d'Artistes,* Centre Georges Pompidou, Paris
1987 *New Faces at the Gallery,* National Portrait Gallery, London
1988 Center for Book Arts, New York
1993 *Summer Exhibition,* Royal Academy, London
Royal Academy Exhibition on Tour, Ulster Museum, Botanic Gardens, Belfast
A Print, Is a Print, Is a Print, The Gallery in Cork Street, London
The Folio Society: Illustrations from the Last 5 Years of Publishing, The Fry Art Gallery, Saffron Walden
Le Lure dans Touts ses Etats, Galway Arts Festival, Galway
Wor(l)d Poem: Poema Mun(d)o, Museu Municipal Dr Santo Rocha, Portugal
The Portrait Now, National Portrait Gallery, London
1994 Mall Galleries, London
Wolfson's Centre Gallery, Miami
1995 *Words: or Don't Stand on Titles*, Aspex Visual Arts Trust, Portsmouth
La Collection François et Ninon Robelin, Musée d'Art Moderne de Saint Etienne
Artists' Books, Tate Gallery, London
1996 *Small is Beautiful: Food & Drink*, Flowers East, London
L'Experience des Livres, Université de Rouen
Contemporary Art at Deutsche Bank, Deutsche AG, London
British and American Representational Prints, Alan Cristea Gallery, London
Summer Exhibition, Royal Academy, London
1997 *The Contemporary Print Show 1997,* Concourse Gallery, Barbican Centre, London
Royal Society of Portrait Painters, Mall Galleries, London
Summer Exhibition, Royal Academy, London
Livres d'Artistes l'Invention d'un Genre 1960–1980, Galerie Mansart, Bibliotheque National de France
Contemporary British Painters, Arts Initiative, Grimsby
30th Anniversary Celebratory Exhibition, Berkeley Square Gallery, Advanced Graphics, London

Collections:

Victoria and Albert Museum, London; Tate Gallery, London; Boymans-van Beuningen Museum, Rotterdam; Gemeentemuseum, The Hague; National Museum, Stockholm; Neue Galerie der Stadt, Aachen, Germany; National Gallery of Australia, Canberra; Musée d'Art Moderne de la Ville, Paris; Museum of Modern Art, New York; Philadelphia Museum of Art.

Publications:

By PHILLIPS: Books—*Control Magazine No. 2,* London 1966; *The Directions,* with Jerome Rothenberg, London 1970; *Correspondence,* with Roy Fisher, London 1970; *Metamorphosis,* with Roy Fisher, London 1970; *Trailer,* Stuttgart 1971; *A Humument,* 10 volumes, London 1971–76; *Anthology of Concrete Poetry,* London 1971; *Images Words and Words Images,* New York 1971; *Future Fiction,* New York 1971; *This Book Is a Movie,* New York 1971; *In One Side and Out the Other,* with André Crozier and John James, London 1971; *The Birth of Art,* London 1972; *4 Artists,* London 1972; *Breakthrough Fictioneers,* New York 1973; *The Recollection,* Exeter 1973; *The Source of the Dove,* London 1973; *Introduction to Works in Johannesburg,* Johannesburg 1974; *Tom Phillips: Works and Texts to 1974,* London and Stuttgart 1975; *Imaginary Postcards,* with Jonathan Williams, 1975; *Dante's Inferno: Livre d'Artiste,* London 1983; *Dante's Inferno,* London 1985; *The Heart of a Humument,* Stuttgart 1985; *Works/Texts to 1987,* Stuttgart 1988; *Tom Phillips: Works and Texts,* London, 1992; *A Humument: Variants and Variations,* London 1992, revised 1996; *Merely Connect,* London 1993; *Aspects of Art,* Bellew 1996; *Music in Art,* Prestel 1996. **Articles**—"The Seafarer" in *Pause Magazine* (Oxford), no. 2, 1970; "On 'A Humument'" in *London Magazine,* February 1970; "Extracts from 'A Humument'" in *Poetry Review* (London) April 1971; "Postcard Composition" in *Pages* (London), nos. 1–3 1971; statement in *Tom Phillips,* exhibition catalog, London 1982. **Illustrated books**—*The Coherence* by Anselm

Hollo, London 1968; *The Wolverhampton Wanderer* by Mike Horowitz, London 1972; *Cuts* by Malcolm Bradbury, London 1987; *Plato's Symposium,* London 1992. **Film—***Drawing,* 1977. **Musical scores—***Ornamentik, Opus 9,* 1968; *Harmonia Praestrabilita,* 1969; *Irma,* opera, 1969; *Ein Deutsches Requiem,* 1972; *Lesbia Waltz,* 1972; *Scratch Music,* 1972; *Variations on Opus 85,* 1977.

On PHILLIPS: Books—*Tom Phillips,* exhibition catalog by Richard Morphet, London 1971; *Tom Phillips* by Charles Spencer, London 1973; *Tom Phillips,* exhibition catalog by John Russell, London 1973; *Late Modern* by Edward Lucie-Smith, London 1977; *Fifty Years of Tom Phillips,* exhibition catalog with text by Michael Tooby, Sheffield 1987; *The Altered Page,* exhibition catalog by Marvin Sackner, 1988; *Tom Phillips,* exhibition catalog, London 1990; *Windsor: The Most Romantic Castle* by Mark Girouard, London 1993; *Bookworks: A Partial History and Sourcebook,* 1996. **Articles—** "Tom Phillips" in *Studio International* (London) October 1971; "A Book of Bits or a Bit of a Book" by Alan Woods in *Cambridge Quarterly,* Spring 1982; "The Layered Look" by Nancy Soloman in *Afterimage* (London), Spring 1983; "Tom Phillips: Renaissance Man in the Twentieth Century" by Mike von Joel in *Artline* (London), April-May 1987; *Carte D'Arte Internazionale,* no. 4, December 1993; *Politiken,* 4 December 1993; *Royal Academy Magazine,* no. 41, Winter 1993; *Art & Auction,* January 1994; *Arts Review,* February 1997; *Musical Times,* March 1997; *Royal Academy Magazine,* no. 54, Spring 1997; *Cambridge Architectural Journal,* June 1997; *Wall Street Journal,* 17 June 1997; "New Lamps For Old" in *Assemblage,* no. 32, August 1997; *Royal Academy Magazine,* no. 56, Autumn 1997.

* * *

Tom Phillips has spent the past six years translating and illustrating Dante's *Inferno.* The translation is the element he most enjoys, because at that he considers himself an amateur and therefore finds it a challenge. A few of the 40 out of the 140 images I have seen are excellent—for example, "Dante in His Study," which is based on one of the best known portraits of Dante thought to be by Signorelli. Phillips has eliminated unnecessary details and portrays Dante's remarkable chiselled and aquiline features with great simplicity. "The Dark Wood" illustrates the beginning of the Inferno. Here Phillips employs a technique he has used since 1969—words "Selva Oscura" repeated many times as in Tantra create a claustrophobic forest. Repetition is also present in "I had not thought death had undone so many." A print of 517 heads drawn between December 1977 and December 1978 represents the crowds inhabiting hell.

Spending such a long time on this print admirably demonstrates Phillips' obsessive patience and ability to focus on one particular theme for a long period of time. In the 1960s he came across a turgid Victorian novel called *A Human Document* by W. H. Mallock. The discovery of this work has led to its introduction in almost everything Phillips does (even poor Dante); he considers its use to be inexhaustible. The first direct result was "The Humument," which he worked on from 1966 to 1975. Mallock's text became a backdrop for Phillips' own creation, and snippets of the actual text were highlighted. Levi-Strauss has called this technique "Bricolage"—in other words, how to "Mess About." The value or meaning of this exercise is incomprehensible.

Occasionally Phillips has involved himself in projects of interest such as the conjectured pictures based on a postcard of the interior of a room in the Mappin Art Gallery, Sheffield. His ability in portraiture is remarkable: it is difficult to understand why he plays games and often wishes to be unnecessarily obscure. A story his mother told encapsulates his persona perfectly. When he was a small boy he brought back old bones from a first visit to France. Why he chose old bones in preference to cheese or bread, for example, must remain a question for some speculation. The anecdote does, however, relate to his work, which often requires some highly speculative processes and can defy interpretation!

—Carine Maurice

PIENE, Otto

Nationality: German. **Born:** Laasphe, Westphalia, 18 April 1928. **Education:** Lubbecke, Westphalia, until 1948; studied art at the Blochererschule, and Hochschule der Bildenden Kunste, Munich, 1948–50; and at the Staatliche Kunstakademie, Dusseldorf, 1950–52; studied philosophy at the University of Cologne, 1952–57. **Family:** married Elizabeth Goldring; one son; three daughters; one stepdaughter. **Career:** Independent artist in Dusseldorf, in New York City, 1965–68, in Cambridge, Massachusetts, since 1968, and in Groton, Massachusetts, since 1985; first light performances and environments, 1959; automated light sculptures and fire-paintings, 1960. Founder, with Heinz Mack, Group Zero, Dusseldorf, 1957; co-publisher, magazines *Zero 1* and *Zero 2,* 1958, and *Zero 3,* 1961. Visiting professor of art, University of Pennsylvania, Philadelphia, 1964; resident fellow, 1968–70, non-resident fellow, 1970, professor of environment art since 1972, director, Center for Advanced Visual Studies, 1974–94, and director emeritus, 1994, Massachusetts Institute of Techology, Cambridge; organiser and director of international SKY ART Conferences, 1981–83, 1986; chairman and organiser of ARTTRANSITION '90, international conference on art and technology, CAVS/MIT, 1990. **Awards:** Josef Pankofer Preis, Baden-Baden, West Germany 1959; Cultural Relations Prize, *Graphic Art Biennale,* Ljubljana 1967; Konrad von Soest Prize, Münster, 1968; Tamarind Lithography Fellowship, Los Angeles, 1968; Purchase Prize, *International Graphics Exhibition,* Ljubljana 1969; Purchase Prize, *International Drawings Exhibition,* Rijeka, 1970; National Museum of Modern Art Prize, *8th Biennale,* Tokyo, 1972; First Prize Tete de Defense (with Viguier/Jodry), Paris, 1983; Kohler-Maxwell Medal for art-writing (shared with Rudolf Arnheim), 1987; sculpture prize, American Academy of Arts and Letters, 1996. **Address:** 383 Old Ayer Road, Groton, Massachusetts 01450, U.S.A.

Individual Exhibitions:

1959 Galerie Alfred Schmela, Dusseldorf
1960 Galerie Diogenes, West Berlin
Galerie Alfred Schmela, Dusseldorf
Studio F, Ulm, West Germany
1961 Galerie Ad Libitum, Antwerp
Galerie Nota, Munich
Galerie Dato, Frankfurt
Galerie St. Stephen, Vienna (with Heinz Mack)
Galerie Muller, Stuttgart
1962 *Licht und Rauch/Graphik,* Städtische Museum Schloss Morsbroch, Leverkusen, West Germany
Galerie Alfred Schmela, Dusseldorf

McRoberts and Tunnard Gallery, London
Studio F, Ulm, West Germany (with Heinz Mack and Günther Uecker)
1963 *Permanentes Lichtballet,* Galerie Müller, Stuttgart
Obilder und Gouachen, Galerie Alfred Schmela, Dusseldorf
Die Feuerblume, Galerie Ad Libitum, Antwerp
Galleria Cadario, Milan
Galleria La Polena, Genoa
Museum Haus Lange, Krefeld, West Germany (with Heinz Mack and Günther Uecker)
Kaiser-Wilhelm-Museum, Krefeld, West Germany (with Heinz Mack and Günther Uecker)
1964 Galerie Lawrence, Paris (with Günther Uecker)
Galleria Il Bilico, Rome (with Heinz Mack)
1965 Galeria Rottloff, Karlsruhe
Howard Wise Gallery, New York
Kestner-Gesellschaft, Hannover (with Heinz Mack and Günther Uecker)
1966 Galerie Alfred Schmela, Dusseldorf
1967 *Fire Flower Power,* Museum am Ostwall, Dortmund, West Germany
Galerija Centar, Zagreb
Galerie Seyfried, Munich
1968 Westfälisches Landesmuseum, Münster, West Germany
Studio F, Ulm, West Germany
1969 *Elements,* Howard Wise Gallery, New York
Yale University, New Haven, Connecticut
1971 *Bilder, Feuergouachen und Graphik 1957–1967, Skyart Portfolio 1969, Bilddokumentation 1967–1971,* Galerie Heseler, Munich
1972 Galerie Wentdorf und Swetec, Dusseldorf
Sloane O'Sickey Gallery, Cleveland
Centro de Arte y Communication, Buenos Aires
Galerie Heseler, Munich
Westfälisches Landesmuseum, Münster, West Germany
1973 Galerie Heseler, Munich
Galerie Wentdorf und Swetec, Dusseldorf
Kölnischer Kunstverein, Cologne
Museo Genero Perez, Cordoba, Argentina
1974 Galerie Heimeshoff, Essen
Kunstverein, Ingolstadt, West Germany
Galerie Lohrl, Willich, West Germany
1975 Kleine Grafik-Galerie, Bremen, West Germany
Paintings, Gouache, Drawings, Massachusetts Institute of Technology, Cambridge
Galerie Lauter, Mannheim
Galerie Heseler, Munich
Galerie Lohrl, Willich, West Germany
Galerie Ehrensperger, Zurich
1976 Galerie Schoeller, Dusseldorf
88 Pine Street, New York
1977 Galerie Heseler, Munich
Fitchburg Art Museum, Massachusetts
Galerie Heimeshoff, Essen, West Germany
Galerie Schoeller, Dusseldorf
1978 Galerie Heseler, Munich
1979 Galerie Heseler, Munich
1980 Galerie Schoeller, Dusseldorf
State University of New York, Stony Brook
1984 Guggenheim Museum, New York
1985 Pat Hearn Gallery, New York
Galerie Heseler, Munich
1986 Galerie Löhrl, Mönchengladbach, Germany
1987 Galerie Schoeller, Düsseldorf
1988 Galerie Heimeshoff, Essen, Germany
Galerie Löhrl, Mönchengladbach, Germany
1989 Kunsthaus Schaller, Stuttgart
1991 Galerie Schoeller, Düsseldorf
Galerie Löhrl, Mönchengladbach, Germany
1992 Galerie Lauter, Mannheim, Germany
Gallery 360°, Tokyo
1993 Galerie d'Art International, Paris
MIT Museum, Compton Gallery, Cambridge, Massachusetts
Der Innere Raum, Düsseldorf
1995 Galerie Schoeller, Düsseldorf
The Writers Place, Kansas City, Missouri
Kunsthaus Schaller, Stuttgart
1996 Galerie Schoeller, Düsseldorf
Galerie Löhrl, Mönchengladbach, Germany
Suffolk University, Boston, Massachusetts
Obscure, Quebec
Kunstverein Lübbecke, Lübbecke, Germany
2000 Galerie Schoeller, Düsseldorf
Retrospective, Cubus Kunsthalle, Duisburg, Germany

Selected Group Exhibitions:

1959 *Vision in Motion,* Hessenhuis, Antwerp
1961 *The Movement Movement,* Stedelijk Museum, Amsterdam (travelled to the Moderna Museet, Stockholm)
1964 *Zero: European Experimental Art,* Institute of Contemporary Art, Philadelphia
1969 *Inflatable Sculpture,* Jewish Museum, New York (travelled to the De Witte Memorial Museum, San Antonio, Texas)
1970 *Kinetic Art,* Hayward Gallery, London
1973 *Westphalian Art,* Westfälisches Landesmuseum, Münster, West Germany
1977 *Documenta 6,* Museum Fridericianum, Kassel, West Germany
1981 *Centervideo,* American Center, Paris (travelled to the Kunstverein, Cologne)
1983 *Electra,* Musée d'Art Moderne de la Ville, Paris
Gallery Watari, Tokyo
1985 *Mehr Licht,* Kunsthalle, Hamburg
1986 *German Art 1945–85,* Neue Nationalgalerie, Berlin
1988 *Art in the Sky,* Stadtmuseum Düsseldorf
1989 *Gruppe Zero,* Galerie Schoeller, Düsseldorf
1990 *Arttransition '90,* CAVS/MIT, Cambridge, Massachusetts
1991 *Schwerelos,* Berlinische Galerie, Martin-Gropius-Bau, Berlin
1992 *UNDR, Kunst, Videnskab, Teknik,* Charlottenborg, Copenhagen
1994 *Light, Time, Space—25 Years of CAVS,* MIT Museum and CAVS/MIT, Cambridge, Massachusetts
1995 *15 Jahre Galerie Schoeller,* Galerie Schoeller, Düsseldorf
1996 *Invitational Exhibition,* American Academy of Arts and Letters, New York

Collections:

Kunstmuseum, Dusseldorf; Museum om Ostwall, Dortmund, West Germany; Westfälisches Landemuseum, Münster, West Germany; Städtische Kunstsammlungen, Bonn; Stedelijk Museum, Amsterdam; Stedelijk Van Abbemuseum, Eindhoven, Netherlands; Musée Royal des Beaux-Arts, Brussels; National Gallery of Canada, Ottawa; Museum of Modern Art, New York; Philadelphia Museum of Art, Pennsylvania; Albright Knox Art Gallery, Buffalo, New York; National Gallery, Berlin; Metropolitan Museum of Art, New York; Power Art Gallery, Sydney.

Publications:

By PIENE: Books—*More Sky,* Cambridge, Massachusetts 1973; *Arttransition, You Are Here,* Cambridge, Massachusetts 1975; *Centerbeam,* Cambridge, Massachusetts 1980; *Centervideo,* exhibition catalog, editor, with Elizabeth Goldring and Vin Grabill, Cambridge, Massachusetts 1981; *Sky Art Conference '81,* exhibition catalog, editor with others, Cambridge, Massachusetts 1981, 1983; *SKY ART Manifest,* with Elizabeth Goldring and Lowry Burgess, Paris 1986. **Articles—**''Sky Scale and Technology in Art'' in *Leonardo 19,* no. 3, 1986.

On PIENE: Books—*Piene: Licht und Rauch/Graphik,* exhibition catalog, Leverkusen, West Germany 1962; *Piene: Die Fleuerblume,* exhibition folder, Antwerp 1963; *Otto Piene: Permanentes Lichtballet,* exhibition catalog, Stuttgart 1963; *Piene: Olbilder und Gouachen,* exhibition catalog, Dusseldorf 1963; *Piene: Fire Flower Power,* exhibition folder/poster with text by Eugen Thiemann, Dortmund, West Germany 1967; *Otto Piene: Elements,* exhibition catalog, New York 1969; *Deutsche Kunst: Eine Neue Generation* by Rolf-Günter Dienst, Cologne 1970; *Hommage à Fontana* by Günter Aust, Wuppertal, West Germany 1969; *Deutsche Kunst der 60er Jahre: Malerei, Collage, Op-Art, Graphik* by Juliane Roh, Munich 1971; *Otto Piene: Bilder, Feuergouachen und Graphik 1957–1967, Skyart Portfolio 1969, Bilddokumentation 1967–1971,* exhibition catalog, Munich 1971; *Otto Piene Lichtballet und Kunstler der Gruppe Zero,* exhibition catalog, Munich 1972; *Otto Piene,* exhibition catalog with texts by Wulf Herzogenrath, Gerhard Storck and Lawrence Alloway, Cologne 1973; *Otto Piene: Paintings, Gouache, Drawings,* exhibition catalog with text by Lawrence Alloway, Cambridge, Massachusetts 1975; *Ars Electronica,* exhibition catalog edited by Christine Schopf, Linz 1980; *Otto Piene, Arbeiten auf Papier 1958–1986,* exhibition catalog, Mönchengladbach 1986; *Otto Piene, Bilder und Lichtballett,* exhibition catalog, Düsseldorf 1987; *Otto Piene, Feuerbilder und Texte,* exhibition catalog, Mönchengladbach 1988; *Zero: Vision und Bewegung, Werke aus der Sammlung Lenz Schönberg,* exhibition catalog, Munich 1988; *ZERO—Eine Europäische Avantgarde,* exhibition catalog, Koblenz 1992; *Otto Piene, Überblick, Bilder, SKY ART, Projekte,* exhibition catalog, Mönchengladbach 1992; *Otto Piene: Retrospektive 1952–1996,* exhibition catalog, Düsseldorf 1996.

*

What is painting? A painting is a field of forces, the arena where its author's impulses all come together, there to be transformed, reformed into a movement of color. Energies which the painter has received out of the fullness of the universe are now directed into channels open to the spirit of the onlooker.

What is color? Color is articulation of light.

And what is light? Light is the sphere of everything that lives, the element in which the trialogue of painter, painting and spectator must take place; it is caught and intensified into a continuous vibration which contains all three.

What is vibration? Vibration is nuance come alive; it outlaws contrast, shames tragedy and dismisses drama. It is the vehicle of the frequencies, the life-blood of color and the pulse of light. Vibration is pure emotion and pure energy, that which gives the picture its radiance.

What is pure energy? The undisturbed continuum, never ending, unquenchable, the stuff of life.

What are they all, painting, color, light vibration and pure energy? Life. And the free spirit.

—Otto Piene

* * *

Otto Piene has used many different media, from Light Ballets to Smoke pictures and to performances and events involving balloons and kites. But they are linked by a fascination with light which runs through all his work, whether kinetic art which consists essentially of light sculptures or performances which are projected, programmed light manifestations.

In 1957 he was co-founder with Heinz Mack of Group Zero, one of the many groups and associations of kinetic artists formed during the late 1950s and early 1960s, all dedicated to the use of new means in art. In contrast to the French Groupe de Recherche d'Art Visuel, with her scientific purism, Zero was at the romantic end of the spectrum in adopting an intuitive relationship with technology. They believed in light as *the* expansive medium, carrying energy from the artist to the spectator; they also believed that man has to live *with* rather than against technology, and that artists today should help to change the environment on a large scale, as opposed to a petty scale.

This desire to work on a scale large enough to ''reharmonize . . . the relation between man and nature'' led Piene to go beyond the production of conventional art objects such as paintings to create works directed towards the aim of articulating light and making it real and perceptible as a natural force. The light paintings which he began making in 1957 were projected on a wall, ceiling or floor by placing a pre-cut stencil over a light source, Piene then developed these static light paintings into Light Ballets, using hand-operated lamps whose light he directed through the stencils in a series of different projections choreographed by accompanying sound such as jazz. The solo then turned into a group performance, with each member of the ensemble holding individual lamps and contributing different shapes and colours to the projection. A later stage was to mechanize the light ballet, using motors and other machines, with the use of revolving perforated discs to produce changing and overlapping light patterns. Piene has also used multitudes of tiny incandescent lamps to establish volumes in space, with shapes indicated by titles such as ''Onion Flower'' (1965), ''Milky Way'' (1965) or ''Corona Borealis'' (1965), and with their own spectrum of colour depending on the current running through them. He has also used walls of light as architectural installations, such as a facade of ''sculptured'' light operated by a programme for a store in Cologne.

But Piene has also been involved with light in the form of fire, and with the other traditional ''elements'' of earth, air, and water. His ''elemental'' art however includes also the ''human elements'' of the active participation of the spectators in his varied performances. His ''fire pictures'' involve the display of smoke and other effects of combustion, for instance by placing paper over a meshed screen with a candle under it, fixing the smoke and soot and indicating the kinship of these smoke vibration patterns with other natural forces in such titles as ''Fire Flower.'' For his ''air'' art he has used flags, kites and streamers in various city spaces; a giant red balloon or windsock which dominated the 1970 Kinetics exhibition at London's Hayward Gallery, and all sorts of other inflatables. In 1961 Group Zero staged a series of demonstrations in the streets or on the banks of the Rhine, flying huge transparent hot-air balloons. Piene later developed such performances on an even more gigantic scale, as in his ''Field of Hot Air Sculpture over a Fire in the Snow'' in 1969 on an athletic field at M.I.T., composed of 30 transparent polythene balloons of different shapes and sizes, raised repeatedly with hot air from tanks spaced around the field, and all lit up by arc lights.

Piene's ''sky events'' of the late 1960s and early 1970s thus drew together both environmental and participatory tendencies, and he has argued that ''by exposing artists' work in places that are open to many peoples' eyes such as the sky—and by the use of broadcasting and televising techniques . . . the artist could be very helpful in rebuilding, reshaping, humanizing CITIES old and new.'' His book *More Sky* is a plea for more scope and space for art, for freeing it from museums and galleries and the making of objects in order to enable future artists to accept the challenge of taking on city planning and shaping tasks on a large scale, an environmental art for social use, with art and architecture, the city and the open landscape, all interacting in a total ecological and elemental aesthetics.

—Konstantin Bazarov

PIGNON, Edouard

Nationality: French. **Born:** Bully, Pas-de-Calais, 12 February 1905. **Education:** Mainly self-taught in art, Paris, from 1927. **Career:** Miner and stonemason, Bully, 1921–27; worked at various jobs while studying drawing and sculpture, Paris, 1928–38; independent artist, Paris, since 1938; concentrated on painting, from 1940; on theatrical decors, from 1948. **Awards:** Grand Prix, *Bienal,* Sao Paulo, 1951; Guggenheim Prize, 1958; Gold Medal/Prix Leonardo da Vinci, 1973; Grand Prix des Arts, City of Paris, 1976. **Died:** 14 May 1993.

Individual Exhibitions:

1939 Maison de la Culture, Paris
1946 Galerie de France, Paris
1948 Galerie Apollo, Brussels
1949 Galerie de France, Paris
1951 Galerie Evrard, Lille, France
Leicester Galleries, London
1952 Galerie de France, Paris
1953 Galerie de France, Paris
1954 University of Louisville, Kentucky
1955 Galerie de France, Paris (twice)
1956 Perls Galleries, New York
1959 Galerie Rauch, Monte Carlo
1960 Galerie de France, Paris
Musée de Metz, France
Musée de l'Histoire et de l'Art, Luxembourg
1961 Galerie Spinazzola, Aix-en-Provence, France
Musée des Beaux-Arts, Nantes, France
1962 Galerie de France, Paris
Galerie du Passeur, France
Galerie Cavalero, Cannes
Galerie Parti Pris, Grenoble, France
1963 Galerie Spinazzola, Aix-en-Provence, France
Maison de la Culture, La Havre, France
Guilde du Disque, Lausanne, Switzerland
Kunsthandel M. L. de Boer, Amsterdam
1964 Galerie Desire, St. Etienne, France
Galeria Nuova Milano, Milan
Maison de la Culture, Caen, France
Kunstmuseum, Lucerne
Musée d'Art et d'Histoire, Geneva
1965 Musée des Beaux-Arts, Valenciennes, France
Musée des Beaux-Arts, Lille, France
Maison de la Culture, Namur, Belgium
Palais des Beaux-Arts, Charleroi, Belgium
1966 Musée d'Art Moderne, Paris
Maison de la Culture, Rheims, France (toured France)
1968 Galerie de France, Paris
1969 Galerie La Proue, Rennes, France
Galerie Argens, Strasbourg
Galleria Nuova Pesa, Rome
Centre Culturel, La Seyne, France
Maison de la Culture, St. Etienne, France
Abbaye St. Hugues, Cluny, France
Hotel de Ville, St. Etienne du Rouvray
Galerie Municipale, Esch-Alzette, Luxembourg
1970 Galerie Philippe Reichenbach, Paris
Galerie de France, Paris
Musée Galliera, Paris
Theatre du VIII, Lyons
Centre Culturel, Venissieux, France
Maison des Arts et Loisirs, Sochaux, France
Group Scolaire Henri-Wallon, Trappes, France
Musée d'Ingres, Montauban, France
1971 Seibu Newspaper Gallery, Tokyo
1972 Galerie Aspect, Brussels
Galleria Tokrbandena, Trieste
Théâtre du Parvis, Brussels
1973 Galerie de France, Paris
Galleria Hausammann, Cortina d'Ampezzo, Italy
Maison de la Culture, Paris (toured France)
Galleria Pace, Milan
Dalles Rooms, Bucharest (retrospective; toured Rumania, Hungary, Poland and Luxembourg)
Establissements Usinor, Denain, France
1974 Galerie Protee, Toulouse
Galleria Verrocchio, Pescara, Italy
Hotel de Ville, Douai, France
Musée de Calais, France
Musée de St. Pol, France
Hotel de Ville, St. Pol, France
Hotel de Ville, St. Maxim, France
1975 Galleria Giorgio de Cillia, Udine, Italy

Edouard Pignon: *Maternity,* 1942. ©2001 Artists Rights Society (ARS), NY/ADAGP, Paris.

Galerie Nicole Fourrier, Lyons
Galerie Protée, Toulouse
Chateau de Simiane, Valreas, France
Galleria Civica d'Art Moderna, Bologna
Fondatin Noroit, Arras, France
Maison de la Culture, Saint-Genevieve des Bois, France (toured France)
Musée de Seret, Pyrenées Orientales, France
1976 Musée d'Art Moderne de la Ville, Paris
1977 Galerie Anne et Albert Prouvost, Paris (restrospective)
Hotel de Ville, St. Etienne du Rouvray, France
Galerie Govaerts, Brussels
1978 Maison de la Culture, Nanterre, France
Salle des Fêtes Jean Vilar, Argenteuil, France
Centre Culturel, Corbeil, France
Hotel de Ville, Bayonne, France
Musée des Beaux-Arts, Beziers, France (retrospective)
1979 Musée de Saint-Denis, France
Galerie Armorial, Brussels
Air-France Office, Roissy, France
1980 Centre des Telecommunications, La Londe-les-Maures, France
Fondation Paul Ricard, Paris
Galerie du Verger, Touquet, France
Palais des Arts et de la Culture, Brest, France
1981 Musée de la Seita, Paris (restrospective)
Galerie d'Art Municipale, Esch-sur Alzette, Luxembourg
Galerie des Granges, Geneva
Galleria Villata, Cerina Monferrato, Italy
Musée de la Poste, Paris
1982 Galleria La Gradiva, Rome
Galerie Beaubourg, Paris
Galleria Maggiore, Bologna, Italy
1983 Hôtel de Ville, Villerubanne, France
Maison de la Culture, Bourges, France
1984 Musée Picasso, Antibes, France

Galleria La Gradiva, Rome
1985 Grand Palais, Paris (restrospective)
Théâtre Jean-Louis Barrault, Paris
Galerie Trigano, Paris
Galerie Beaubourg, Paris
Galerie Regis Dorval, Lille, France
Galleria La Gradiva, Rome
1986 Musée de Deippe, France
Musée de Issoudun, France
Musée de Lens, France
Galleria Il Fante di Spada, Milan
Galerie Condillac, Bordeaux
Galerie Gastaud, Clermont-Ferrand, France
Galerie de Luxembourg, Luxembourg
1987 Musée de Sète, France
Galerie Beaubourg, Paris
1990 Centre Georges Pompidou, Paris
1992 Musée ''Le Monde de l'Art,'' Paris
Edouard Pignon: Watercolours, 1967–86, Galerie de l'Etat, Luxembourg
1997 *Edouard Pignon: Retrospective,* Palais des Beaux-Arts, Lille

Selected Group Exhibitions:

1932 *Salon des Indépendents,* Paris (regularly from 1932)
1944 *Salon de Mai,* Paris (regularly from 1944)
1955 *New Decade,* Museum of Modern Art, New York
1961 *Post-War European Art,* Stedelijk Van Abbemuseum, Eindhoven, Netherlands
1979 *Celebration en Bleu,* Manege Royal, Saint-Germain en Laye, France
1980 *Les Années 30 en France,* Musée d'Art et d'Industrie, St. Etienne, France
1982 *Le Paysage Revolutionnaire de Cezanne à nos Jours,* Action Artistique Francaise Galerie, Tokyo
1986 *Cinquantenaire du Front Populaire,* Musée de Saint-Brieu, France
1989 *Révolution Française,* Saint Etienne de Rouvray, France

Collections:

Centre Georges Pompidou, Paris; Centre National d'Art Contemporain, Paris; Tate Gallery, London; Musée d'Histoire et de l'Art, Luxembourg; Musée des Beaux-Arts, La Chaux de Fonds, Switzerland; Museum of Contemporary Art, Skopje, Yugoslavia; National Museum of Modern Art, Tokyo; Museu de Arte Moderna, Sao Paulo; Johannesburg Museum, South Africa; Museum of Moderna Art, New York.

Publications:

By PIGNON: Books—*Battages et pousseurs de blé,* with Georges Bataille, Paris 1962; *La Quete de la réalité,* Paris 1966; *Contre courant,* Paris 1973. **Illustrated books**—*Les Blason* by Maurice Sceve, Paris 1945; *Noir sur blanc* by Helen Parmelin, Paris 1955; *Dialogues de l'arbre* by Paul Valery, Paris 1958; *Jacques le Fataliste* by Diderot, West Berlin 1967; *Lumière de Beatrice* by Gerald Mourgue, Paris 1974; *Cinquante de Poesie* by Eugenio Montale, Paris 1974; *Mascarade* by Ronsard, Paris 1976; *Poèmes* by Daniel Gelin, Paris 1979.

On PIGNON: Books—*Cinq peintres d'aujourd'hui* by Frank Elgar, Paris 1943; *Pignon* by Henri Lefebre, Paris 1956; *Cinq peintres et le théâtre* by Helene Parmelin, Paris 1957; *Edouard Pignon* by Helene Parmelin, Paris 1960; *Edouard Pignon: 50 peintures de 1936 à 1962,* edited by Jean-Louis Ferrier, Paris 1962; *Edouard Pignon* by Henri Lefebre, Paris 1970; *Pignon* by Raoul-Jean Moulin and André Calles, Paris 1970; *50 Nus de Pignon* by Giuseppe Marchiori, Paris 1973; *Rencontre avec Pignon* by E. Maurizi, Paris 1974; *Pignon* by Jean-Louis Ferrier, Paris 1976; *Histoire des nus* by Helene Permelin, Paris 1976; *Pignon,* exhibition catalog, Paris 1981; *Pignon,* exhibition catalog, Rome 1982; *Poesimage numero special: Pignon,* Savigny-le-Temple 1983; *Pignon,* exhibition catalog, Paris 1985; *Pignon: Touches et zigzag pour un portrait* by Helene Parmelin, Paris 1987; *Edouard Pignon: Retrospective,* exhibition catalog, Lille 1997. **Films**—*Pignon* by Mitrani, 1961; *Pignon* by Michel Chapuis, 1962; *Edouard Pignon* by Guy Suzuki, 1964; *Pignon: Peintre du nord* by Bernard Claeys, 1965; *Pignon* by Michel Chapius and Charles Chaboud, 1966; *Pignon* by Pierrer Dumayet, 1970; *Pignon: Courte biographie cinematographique* by Guy Gilles, 1970; *Les Seigneurs de la guerre de Pignon* by Fleurent, 1970; *Pignon* by Josiane Serror, 1973; *Edouard Pignon* by Alain Leroy, 1974; *Edouard Pignon* by Michel Lacelot, 1978; *Pignon* by Patrick Barberis, 1982; *Pignon* by Pierre Daix, 1985; *L'Homme debout, Edouard Pignon* by Jean-Luc Ardouin and Gabrielle Althen, 1985.

* * *

Throughout a long artistic life, the hallmark of Pignon was durable continuity. The son of a miner from Marles-les-Mines whose family had been employed in deep mining—man and boy—for nearly three centuries, Edouard Pignon was one of several children growing up in poor circumstances.

In 1912, Edouard Pignon saw the horrors of the pit disaster at La Clarence which killed close on 100 workers. The tragedy imprinted itself on his mind and was many years later the subject of two of his important paintings, each entitled ''Ouvrier mort.'' At the local school, Pignon was awarded a ''certificate'' for the promise he showed in his art studies. He loved drawing. During the years of the First World War, his mother ran a bar while his father worked in the mine, and when a soldier, on his way to the battle-front, stopped at Mme. Pignon's establishment for a drink, the young Pignon drew a portrait of him and was so fascinated by the likeness contained in the result that, for the first time he felt in touch with the magic of Art. Even after the armistice the havoc wreaked in France by the War seemed inescapable. In the year of 1919 his father fell ill with silicosis. At 14 Edouard himself went to work in the mines, a job he hated because of the pervading darkness.

Against such a background, he continued to occupy himself with his drawings whenever the opportunity presented itself. And within him the determination to one day entirely devote himself to becoming an artist grew and grew. Because of this obsession, in 1922 he enrolled in a drawing correspondence course and, by now, was buying books dealing with art, writing to Paris for one such book about Matisse and another concerned with the art of La Fresnaye. He was able to lay hands on a thesis called ''Le Metier de Rubens'' which told him a great deal about oil painting techniques; he also came across a small publication about Van Gogh and was able to purchase a large reproduction of Picasso's *Moissonneurs*. But it was not until a year later that he made his first trip to Paris, spending a few days in the capital which enabled him to fit in a day trip to Lille and discover the marvels of Goya's ''Les Vieilles et les Jeunes.''

This attempt to contain and expand his artistic ambitions and struggles continued and continued (even during his military service when he was able to complete his first oil painting—*Portrait of Uncle Edouard*).

The early years were hard indeed. They involved switching from one job to another just to survive and escape unemployment. At one point, he even obtained a licence to make ''pignons dentés'' and join evening classes in the Boulevard Montparnasse. Nevertheless, despite penury, his social horizon was broadening. In Paris, he was meeting many new friends, a kaleidoscope of intellectuals and artists (including the artist Arpad Szenes). It was these contacts that encouraged him to visit the Paris galleries specializing in contemporary (1929) art—the cubism of Picasso, the works by La Fresnaye, Braque, Bonnard, Matisse and Lèger.

While in employment with the Renault Company, he became a member of l'AEAR—*The Association of Revolutionary Artists and Writers,* a prelude to his membership of the Communist Party for which he was blacklisted and sacked by Renault. L'AEAR organized a large exhibition of art works, including among them three of Pignon's latest paintings, touched in style a little with cubist influence and owing something of their strength to Lèger.

During the 1930s, the scale of his acquaintances continued to increase. He could now number amongst his friends and colleagues Lèger, Lhôte, Szenes, Vieira da Silva, the Prevért brothers, Malraux, Hèlion, Herbin, Lipschitz, Marcel Duhamel and Robert Delaunay, amongst whom there was a constant series of interplays of ideas all helping to transform the peasant boy from the mines into an active participant in the Art World of France. As a Communist Party member, taking his place alongside Picasso, Lèger and Lhôte, his art gravitated towards acquisition of a steady revolutionary accent, soon to become strongly evident in his work, a factor which has persisted (acceptable or—more frequently—unacceptable because it was so remote from social Realism by hardline Communists) from that day to this.

With his pictures now being accepted for exhibition by numerous galleries in Paris (including temporary exhibitions in museums and set up by organizations) it can still prove difficult to discover in these early works the actual *trend* (however mixed at various stages of his development in style) leading to what has come to be recognized today in whatever form as typical flavour of Pignon's oeuvre. This realization of how we have come to expect the Pignon artistic personality to register in pictorial expression on his canvases so that the artist's signature is assumed before it is read had to wait until after the Second World War. (Even then it was much cooler and less strident than his painting was to become later.)

Pignon did not sell one of his pictures until 1939. This was a painting he had made during his time in the French air force, stationed at Villacoublay, a *maternité* titled *La Toilette,* now in the permanent collection of the Musée d'Art Moderne de la Ville de Paris.

Pignon joined the French Resistance. Some twelve months later, at the request of Jeanne Bucher (the founder of the Paris gallery which bears her name) he moved into the home of Lipschitz, evacuated by the sculptor who left for the United States when he realized the danger in which he stood from the Nazis. At the Lipschitz home in Boulogne where Pignon set up house he made a point of burying the sculptor's bronzes in the garden where they remained undetected until they were dug up after hostilities and the occupation of France ended.

The story of Pignon—there is much more to it—ought to end without more ado because it is time to give a proper examination of the artwork of this fierce rebel. Even so, it should be borne in mind that he had become in his way a sort of proto-Eurocommunist, rejecting Stalin (but not the Soviet Union), rejecting social-realism (but not the Communism), rejecting *engagierter Kunst* (but not the politics it sought to promote), against the occupations of Hungary and Czechoslovakia (preferring to declare support for those who resisted the Russian invasions of those two States). Pignon was permanently in opposition to the War in Vietnam, General de Gaulle, all forms of Fascism and anything that smacked of Conservatism and Centrism. All these attitudes he sought to express in his pictures.

At the outset of 1949, he was painting pictures which somehow managed to combine the quiet composition qualities of André Lhôte with a loosely designed atmosphere of Raoul Dufy at his casual best with perhaps even a hint—in figuration, not in colouring—of Marquet. Vigour and violence of brush strokes and a sort of suppressed temper were in strong evidence 1958 onwards. Trees and other vegetation raged in swirling contortions. Imagery steadily became more ferociously and markedly coherent. Colours, with Pignon reservations, took on alarming aggression often in direct contrast with messages implied by the subjects.

In the 1960s, it was as if the wonderful harvesting scenes he had once painted were all forgotten. Now the fields and woods were full of battle and the bleeding heart of struggle.

Then, another switch. From 1966 to 1980 war was virtually swept into the background to be replaced by Divers. The *plongeurs* were rich in brilliant colours. The erstwhile blacks and greens and dark blues gave way to vibrant pinks, emeralds, and maroons. And they were interspersed with other subject matter that this tireless and violent painter pressed into service to give his paintings still greater intensity of feeling-cum-discription.

By the late 1970s, after the vicious paintings of the ''Cockfights'' came a special tribute to flamboyant womanhood; sometimes these nudes, in all their unashamed pulchritude, would let themselves curve or pose in statuesque stance, but more often their happy abandonment sheds any accent of modesty into a careless oblivion.

Where can one place the endless career of this turbulent artistic dissenter, this active co-operator in his lonely antagonism, an artist and a man at total odds with anything which allies itself to the status-quo, fundamentally against all other kinds of revolt but his own, way to the Left but the indomitable foe of the *aparatchik*? Where indeed? The very length of the list of his artist and intellectual friends—such a close relationship with Picasso first in Vallauris and Sanary for instance—fails not to assure one of his status as an extraordinary and exceptional artist.

—Sheldon Williams

PIPER, Adrian

Nationality: American. **Born:** Harlem, New York, 20 September 1948. **Education:** School of Visual Arts, New York, A. A. in Fine Arts, 1969; City College of New York, B. A. in Philosophy, 1974;

Adrian Piper: *What It's Like, What It Is #3,* 1991. ©Adrian Piper.

Harvard University, Cambridge, Massachusetts, M. A. in Philosophy, 1977; studied at University of Heidelberg, West Germany, 1977–78; Harvard University, Cambridge, Massachusetts, Ph. D. in Philosophy, 1981; California Institute of the Arts, Valencia, D. L. (Honorary Degree), 1992; Massachusetts College of Art, Boston, D. A. (Honorary Degree) 1994. **Family:** Only child of Daniel Robert Piper and Olive Xavier Smith Piper. **Career:** Conceptual art works published in Vito Acconci's *0 to 9 Magazine,* 1968; *Three Untitled Projects* (mail art exhibition) published by 0 to 9 Press, 1969; joins Art Worker's Coalition, 1970; starts women's consciousness-raising group, 1971; starts The Mythic Being/Village Voice performance series, 1972; first philosophy article published, 1978; begins tenure-track Assistant Professorship in Philosophy at the University of Michigan, Ann Arbor, 1979; begins permanent position at Georgetown University, Washington, D. C., 1986; accepts Associate Professorship in Philosophy at the University of California at San Diego, 1988; accepts Full Professorship in Philosophy at Wellesley College, Massachusetts, 1990; conducts two-week residency at the Kunstakademie München entirely in German, 1995; Distinguished Scholar at the Getty Research Institute, 1997; delivers talk, ''What the Indexical Present Really Is,'' at Frameworks for Art conference, Parikh Centre for the Visual Arts, Bombay, India, 1998; becomes Faculty Chair of Wellesley's Black Task Force, 1999. **Awards:** First Prize in Drawing and Honorable Mention in Sculpture at School of Visual Arts Annual Student Exhibition, 1968; Danforth and Ford Foundation graduate fellowships, 1974; Sheldon Traveling Fellowship, 1977; full-grant NEA Visual Artists' Fellowship, 1979; awarded senior status NEA Visual Artists' Fellowship, 1982; two-year Mellon Post-Doctoral Fellowship, 1982; National Endowment of the Humanities Summer Stipend, 1987; Woodrow Wilson International Scholars Fellowship, 1988; Guggenheim Fellowship in Conceptual Art, 1989; grant from Awards in the Visual Arts, 1990; Skowhegan Medal for Sculptural Installation, 1995; National Endowment for the Humanities Research Fellowship, 1997. **Web site:** http://www.adrianpiper.com.

Selected Individual Exhibitions:

1969 *One Man (sic), One Work,* New York Cultural Center
1971 *Adrian Piper,* Gallery One, Montclair State College, Montclair, New Jersey
1976 *Adrian Piper,* Matrix 56, Wadsworth Atheneum, Hartford, Connecticut
Adrian Piper, Real Artways, Hartford, Connecticut
1980 *Adrian Piper,* And/ Or, Seattle
1981 *Adrian Piper: Reflections 1967–1987,* Alternative Museum, New York; Nexus Contemporary Art Center, Atlanta; Goldie Paley Gallery, Philadelphia; University of Colorado Art Gallery, Boulder; Power Plant Gallery, Toronto; Wooster Art Museum, Wooster, Ohio; Lowe Art Museum, Coral Gables, Florida; Santa Monica Museum of Contemporary Art; Washington Project for the Arts, Washington, D.C. (catalog)

1989 Matrix Gallery, University Art Museum, Berkeley, California
Williams College Art Museum, Williamstown, Massachusetts
1990 *Pretend,* John Weber Gallery, New York (catalog)
Why Guess, Exit Art, New York
Out of the Corner, Whitney Museum of American Art, Film and Video Gallery, New York
What It's Like, What It Is, #1, Washington Project for the Arts, Washington, D. C.
1991 *What It's Like, What It Is, #2,* Hirshhorn Museum, Directions Gallery, Washington, D. C.; Krannert Art Museum, Champaign, Illinois
Adrian Piper: European Retrospective, Ikon Gallery, Birmingham, England; Cornerhouse, Manchester, England; Cartwright Hall, Bradford, England; Kettle's Yard, Cambridge, England; Kunstverein Munich
Cornered, John Weber Gallery, New York
Political Drawings and Installations, 1975–1991, Cleveland Center for Contemporary Art; Carver Center, San Antonio; Herron Gallery, Indianapolis Center for Contemporary Art; Women and Their Work, Austin, Texas
1992 *Space, Time and Reference 1967–1970,* John Weber Gallery, New York
Ur-Madonna, Expo '92, Monasterio de Santa Clara, Moguer (Huelva), Spain
Decide Who You Are, Grey Art Gallery, New York; John Weber Gallery, New York; Paula Cooper Gallery, New York; Myers Fine Art Gallery, SUNY Plattsburgh Art Museum, Plattsburgh, New York; Art Awareness, Lexington, New York; City Gallery of Contemporary Art, Raleigh, North Carolina
1993 *Installations by Adrian Piper,* New Langton Arts, San Francisco
The Hypothesis Series 1968–70, Paula Cooper Gallery, New York
1994 *Cornered/Decide Who You Are,* SUNY Buffalo, New York
1995 *Icons of One: Decide Who You Are,* Savannah College of Art Gallery, Georgia
Ashes to Ashes, John Weber Gallery, New York
1996 Galleria Emi Fontana, Milan, Italy
1997 *Food for the Spirit (1971),* Thomas Erben Gallery, New York
Who Are You? Selected Works by Adrian Piper, Davis Museum and Cultural Center, Wellesley College, Wellesley, Massachusetts
1998 *Adrian Piper: A Retrospective 1965–2000,* Fine Arts Gallery, University of Maryland Baltimore County, Baltimore; New Museum, New York (catalog)
MEDI(t)Ations: Adrian Piper's Videos, Installations, Performances and Soundworks, 1968–1992, Los Angeles Museum of Contemporary Art; New Museum, New York
1999 *Adrian Piper: The Mythic Being, 1972–1975,* Thomas Erben Gallery, New York
2000 *Adrian Piper: A Solo Exhibition,* Gallerie Voges und Deisen, Frankfurt
The Color Wheel Series: First Adhyasa: Annomayakosha, Paula Cooper Gallery, New York
Adrian Piper: Early Drawings and Other Works, Thomas Erben Gallery, New York

Selected Group Exhibitions:

1969 *557,087,* Seattle Art Museum
Concept Art, Städtische Museum, Leverkusen, Germany
Plans and Projects as Art, Kunsthalle Berne, Bern, Switzerland
Conceptual Art and Conceptual Aspects, New York Cultural Center, New York
1970 *Art in the Mind,* Allen Museum, Oberlin, Ohio
Information, Museum of Modern Art, New York (catalog)
Language IV, Dwan Gallery, New York
26 Contemporary Women Artists, Larry Aldrich Museum, Ridgefield, Connecticut
1971 *Paris Biennale,* Musée d'Art Moderne, Paris
Art Without Limits, Memorial Art Gallery, Rochester, New York
1972 *Communications,* Inhibodress Gallery, New South Wales, Australia
Thought: Structures, Pace College Gallery, New York
1973 *Nine New York Artists,* Hartwick College, Oneonta, New York
Artforms, Abstract Activities, Ideas, Pomona College, Claremont, California
c. 7,500, California Institute of the Arts, Valencia
Persona, Artists' Space, New York
1974 *Word Works,* Mt. San Antonio College Art Gallery, Walnut, California
Woman's Work: American Art 1974, Philadelphia Civic Center
In Her Own Image, Samuel S. Fleischer Art Memorial, Philadelphia
Bodyworks, Museum of Contemporary Art, Chicago
Word Works II, San Jose State University Art Gallery, California
1975 *Eleven in New York,* Women's Interart Center, New York
Lives, Fine Arts Building, New York
1976 *Paris Biennale,* Musée d'Art Moderne, Paris
1977 *The Sense of the Self: From Self-Portrait to Autobiography,* Newberger Museum, Purchase, New York (catalog)
1978 *Untitled Exhibition,* Artists' Space, New York
Eventworks, Massachusetts College of Art, Boston
1979 *Both Sides Now,* Artemesia Gallery, Chicago
A Decade of Women's Performance Art, National Women's Caucus for Art Conference, New Orleans
1980 *Speaking Volumes: Women's Artist Books,* A.I.R. Gallery, New York
Art of Conscience, Wright Gallery, Dayton, Ohio
Issue: Twenty Social Strategies by Women Artists, Institute of Contemporary Arts, London
Events: Artists Invite Artists, New Museum, New York
1981 *The Gender Show,* Group Material, New York
The Page as Alternative Space, Franklin Furnace, New York
Oppositions, And/Or, Seattle
1982 *Art at Ground Zero: Artists' Statements on Nuclear War,* University of Michigan Residential College, Ann Arbor

1983 *The Black and White Show,* Kenkeleba Gallery, New York
Language, Drama, Source, and Vision, New Museum, New York
Disarming Images: Artists' Statements Against Nuclear War, Newburger Museum, Purchase, New York
1984 *Decade of New Art,* Artists' Space, New York
Tradition and Conflict, Studio Museum in Harlem, New York
1985 *Kunst mit Eigen-Sinn,* Museum Moderner Kunst, Vienna
The Art of Memory/The Loss of History, New Museum, New York
Floating Values, HallWalls, Buffalo, New York
1987 *Black Video: Performance/Document/Narrative,* Gorman Museum, Davis, California
Past Time, Maryland Art Place, Baltimore
Commitment to Print, Museum of Modern Art, New York
1988 *Modes of Address,* Whitney Museum Downtown, New York
The Turning Point: Art and Politics in 1968, Cleveland Center for Contemporary Art, Cleveland (catalog)
Art as a Verb, Maryland Institute of Art, Baltimore; Studio Museum in Harlem, New York (catalog)
Making Their Mark: Women Artists Move Into the Mainstream 1970–85, Cincinnati Art Museum, Ohio
1989 *Collecting, Organizing, Transposing,* Maryland Art Place, Baltimore
Some Choices, Long Beach Art Museum, Long Beach, California
Double Take: A Second Look at Advertising, Cincinnati Contemporary Arts Center, Ohio
L'Art Conceptuel: Une Perspective, Musée d'Art Moderne, Paris
1990 *Insect Politics,* Hallwalls Contemporary Arts, Buffalo, New York
Signs of the Self: Changing Perceptions, Woodstock Artists Association, Woodstock, New York
Art in Europe and America: The 1960s and 1970s, Wexner Center for the Visual Arts, Ohio State University, Columbus
Word as Image: American Art 1960–1990, Milwaukee Art Museum; Contemporary Arts Center, Houston (catalog)
1991 *The Art of Advocacy,* Aldrich Museum of Contemporary Art, Ridgefield, Connecticut (catalog)
Awards in the Visual Arts, Hirshhorn Museum, Washington D. C.; Albuquerque Museum of Art, History and Science; Toledo Museum of Art; Southeastern Center for Contemporary Art, Winston-Salem, North Carolina (catalog)
Visions/Revisions, Denver Art Museum
What It's Like, What It Is, #3, Dislocations, Museum of Modern Art, New York
1992 *Dream Singers, Story Tellers: An African American Presence,* Fukyui Fine Arts Museum, Fukyui-ken, Japan; New Jersey State Museum, Trenton (catalog)
10: Artist as Catalyst, Alternative Museum, New York
Will/Power, Wexner Center For The Arts, Ohio State University, Columbus (catalog)
Here's Looking at Me: Contemporary Self Portraits, Espace Lyonnais D'Art Contemporain, Lyon, France
1993 *44th Annual Purchase Exhibition,* American Academy and Institute of Arts and Letters, New York
25 Years, Cleveland Center for Contemporary Art
Kontext Kunst, Neue Galerie, Graz, Austria
L'Hiver de l'Amour, Musée d'Art Moderne de Ville de Paris
1994 *Can You Always Believe Your Eyes?* Museum of Contemporary Art, De Beyerd, Breda, Holland
Thirty Years, Larry Aldridge Museum of Contemporary Art, Ridgefield, Connecticut
Mappings, Museum of Modern Art, New York
Black Male: Representations of Masculinity in Contemporary American Art, Whitney Museum of American Art, New York (catalog)
1995 *Public/Private: ARS 95,* Museum of Contemporary Art, Finnish National Gallery, Helsinki, Finland
Civil Rights Now, Cleveland Center of Contemporary Art (catalog)
Art with Conscience, Newark Art Museum, New Jersey
NowHere, Louisiana Museum of Modern Art, Humlebaek, Denmark (catalog)
1996 *Thinking Print: Books to Billboards 1980–95,* Museum of Modern Art, New York (catalog)
Hidden in Plain Sight: Illusion in Art from Jasper Johns to Virtual Reality, Los Angeles County Museum of Art
A/Drift, Bard College Center for Curatorial Studies, Annandale-on-Hudson, New York
Face à l'Histoire 1933–1996, Centre Georges Pompidou, Paris
1997 *Between Two Worlds,* Strong Museum, Rochester, New York
Envisioning the Contemporary: Selections from the Permanent Collection, Museum of Contemporary Art, Chicago
The View from Denver: Contemporary American Art from the Denver Art Museum, Museum Moderner Kunst, Vienna
Desde el cuerpo: alegorias de lo femenino, Fundacion Museo de Bellas Artes, Caracas, Venezuela
1998 *Out of Actions: Between Performance and the Object, 1949–1979,* Museum of Contemporary Art, Los Angeles; Österreichisches Museum für Angewandte Kunst, Vienna; Museu d'Art Contemporani, Barcelona, Museum of Contemporary Art, Tokyo; National Museum of Art, Osaka, Japan (catalog)
5729–5756: Contemporary Artists Welcome the New Year? Jewish Museum, New York
More Pieces for the Puzzle: Recent Additions to the Collection, Museum of Modern Art, New York
Re-Righting History: Counternarratives by Contemporary African/American Artists, Katonah Museum of Art, Katonah, New York (catalog)
1999 *Global Conceptualism: Points of Origin 1950's-1980's,* Queens Museum of Art, New York; Walker Art Center, Minneapolis; List Visual Arts Center of MIT, Cambridge, Massachusetts; Vancouver Art Gallery
The American Century, Whitney Museum of American Art, New York (catalog)
Around 1984: A Look at Art in the 80's, P. S. 1, New York

Publications:

By PIPER: Books—*Talking to Myself: The Ongoing Autobiography of An Art Object,* Brussels 1974; *Adrian Piper, Reflections, 1967–1987* (exhibition catalog), New York 1987; *Colored People,* London 1991; *Decide Who You Are,* New York 1992; *OUT OF ORDER, OUT OF SIGHT,* Cambridge, Massachusetts, 1996. **Articles**—''Three Models of Art Productions Systems'' in *Information,* New York 1970; ''An Ongoing Essay'' in *Art and Artists,* March 1972; ''In Support of Meta-Art'' in *Artforum,* October 1973; ''I Embody'' in *From The Center: Feminist Essays on Women's Art,* New York 1976; ''This Is Not A Documentation Of A Performance'' in *Studio International,* summer 1978; ''Critics' Delight'' in *A Critical Assembling,* New York, 1979; ''Is the Alternative Space a True Alternative?'' in *Studio International,* 1980; ''Food for the Spirit'' in *High Performance,* spring 1981; ''Performance and the Fetishism of the Art Object'' in *Vanguard,* December 1981-January 1982; ''Selected Funk Lessons: A Page Project by Adrian Piper'' in *Artforum,* January 1984; ''Who Is Safely White?'' in *Women Artists News,* June 1987; ''On Conceptual Art'' in *Flash Art,* November-December 1988; ''A Paradox of Conscience'' in *The New Art Examiner,* April 1989; ''The Joy of Marginality'' in *Art Papers,* July-August 1990; ''Brenson on Quality'' in *Art Papers,* November-December 1991; ''Passing for White, Passing for Black'' in *Transition,* 1992; ''The Logic of Modernism'' in *Flash Art,* January-February 1993; ''Higher-Order Discrimination'' in *Voicing Today's Visions: Writings by Contemporary Women Artists,* New York 1994; ''On 1980s Feminist Theorizing'' in *October,* winter 1995; ''Mortal Remains'' in *Mortal Remains,* Minneapolis 1996; ''Decisions, Decisions'' in *Grand Street,* spring 1997; ''Xenophobia and the Indexical Present: Lecture'' in *Disturbing the Peace: Radical Street Performance Around the World,* New York, 1998.

On PIPER: Book—*Adrian Piper: A Retrospective* (exhibition catalog), by Maurice Berger, University of Maryland 1999. **Articles**—''Being and Politics'' by Ken Johnson in *Art in America,* September 1990; ''In Memory of the News and of Ourselves: The Art of Adrian Piper'' in *Third Text: Third World Perspectives on Contemporary Art and Culture,* winter 1991; ''The Indexical Present: A Conversation with Adrian Piper'' by Elizabeth Hayt in *Arts Magazine,* March 1991; ''In This Corner: Adrian Piper's Agitprop'' by Marjorie Welish in *Arts Magazine,* March 1991. **Videos**—*Adrian Piper* by James Johnson and Dale Jamieson, 1989; *Adrian Piper: The Early Seventies* by James Johnson and Dale Jamieson, 1992.

* * *

Adrian Piper began her art career in the mid-1960s as a student at the School of Visual Arts in New York. In 1969 Piper worked as an assistant for artist Sol Lewitt. Conceptual art had an impact on Piper and her early career is marked by performance based, conceptual works such as the well-known *Catalysis* series. Piper's early artistic investigations coincided with her receiving a Doctorate degree in philosophy from the University of Michigan in Ann Arbor. Piper's work explores and interrogates issues of ''otherness'' and what it means to be different from the expectations of the culture in which we live. Her works also explore issues of gender, racial, and class exploitation.

Piper's performances in the *Catalysis* series were intended to be catalysts for change in the city environments through which Piper moved on a daily basis. In *Catalysis No. 4,* 1970, Piper rode a New York City bus with a towel stuffed in her mouth. In other performances from the series, Piper rode public transportation in clothing doused with offensive smells, or searched for her keys in a bag filled with ketchup. Piper executed these performances by herself and in a way that drew attention to her as ''other.'' These performances aimed to explore the boundaries of Piper's own ego and physical body, and to interrogate the public reception and acceptance of the altered human body or the body that is considered offensive.

Piper's early conceptual performances coincide with the wider cultural phenomenon of women performance artists that was burgeoning in the early 1970s. Feminist artists such as Piper, Carolee Schneemann and others sought to perform women's issues and everyday lives in a way that denied and challenged the essentialized notions of femininity and societal expectations of women. Although Piper admits that gender issues were not conscious considerations in her early performances, the works do highlight issues of how society deals with women in public who do not fit the norm. Piper also claims that her early performances were not consciously addressing the issue of race. But these performances interrogate the acceptance or rejection of the other in mainstream society. In the *Catalysis* series, Piper transforms her body into an art object that keenly calls into question the limits of the body and the limits of public reception.

Race is the major theme of Piper's later works. Much of her art from the mid-1970s is inspired by her experience of having a light skin complexion and growing up in Harlem, as well as her experience as a student in an upper-class prep school. In works such as *Political Self-Portrait # 2 (race),* 1978, Piper incorporates pictures of herself as a child with autobiographical text that describes her childhood experiences. In this particular work the photograph is altered to present both a positive and negative image—her face is bisected down the middle and made black on one side, white on the other. The text describes Piper's experience of being called ''paleface'' by her neighborhood friends and of being bullied by her white teachers. After briefly describing an ethnic history of her family, Piper ends the autobiographical text by stating, ''I realize that in reality I've been bullied by whites as well as blacks for the last three hundred years. And there is no end in sight.''

One of Piper's attempts to address the issue of racial bullying and racism was to produce *My Calling (Card) #1,* 1986. This work of art takes the form of a 2'' x 3'' business card on which Piper has printed a lengthy explanation of her discomfort upon hearing racist remarks. The text begins: ''Dear Friend: I am black. I am sure you did not realize this when you made/laughed at/agreed with that racist remark.'' The card came as a response to Piper's experience of being mistaken for Caucasian, and having to endure racist jokes in the presence of other white people. The work has been described as a ''reactive guerilla performance for diners and cocktail parties''; there are two videos by Piper that recall these performances. The confrontational quality of the calling card is a direct attempt to foster awareness among those who participate in racist thought and language.

Many of Piper's works deal directly with racial stereotypes. *Vanilla Nightmares #8,* 1986, and *I Embody,* 1975, are two works that highlight stereotypes about the African American male. In the *Vanilla Nightmare* series, Piper made charcoal drawings on contemporary newspaper advertisements and editorials. In #8 from the series, Piper has added several menacing looking African American men to a seductive perfume ad featuring a white woman. The black males in the image grope the women. In *I Embody,* we see a photograph of Piper that has been altered with oil crayon to resemble an African

American male. The accompanying text in the image states, ''I embody everything you most hate and fear.'' Both of these works underscore the stereotypical position of the African American male as the dangerous aggressor who at once may be an exotic fantasy for whites and at the same time is seen as the embodiment of danger and sexual violence. These works by Piper interrogate the common racist and stereotypical categories into which African Americans are placed. Her works are typically confrontational and ask viewers to think about their own culpability in the continuance of racism.

Piper's personal experience as an African American woman with a light skin complexion has been the basis of much of her art. In addition to performances and two-dimensional works, Piper is also well known for her video art such as *Cornered,* 1988. Her training and teaching as a philosopher has imbued her works with a keen awareness of the critical and conceptual issues of race and gender. Works such as *My Calling (Card)* illustrate the multi-leveled interpretations that we can assume from Piper's work: it is confrontational, it makes us think, it is unexpected, it puts us on the spot. And the title may lend insight into Piper's role as an artist who explores race and gender issues. The word ''(Card)'' is separated by parentheses from the words ''My Calling,'' underscoring the fact that Piper's calling in life is to confront, interrogate, and hopefully change the racism, gender oppression, and hate each of us experiences and perpetuates every day.

—Jennifer S. Zarro

PIPER, John

Nationality: British. **Born:** John Egerton Christmas Piper, Epsom, Surrey, 13 December 1903. **Education:** Epsom College, 1917–21; articled clerk in his father's law office, Piper, Smith and Piper, London, 1921–26; studied under Raymond Coxon, Richmond School of Art, Surrey, 1926–27; under Morris Kestelman and Francis Spear, Royal College of Art, London 1930. **Military Service:** Served as official war artist, with Ministry of Information, London 1940–45; recorded bomb damage, communications and marshalling yards. **Family:** Married Eileen Holding in 1929 (divorced 1937); married Myfanwy Evans in 1937; children: one son (deceased) and two daughters. **Career:** Painter, in Betchworth, Surrey, 1927–35, and in Hammersmith, London, 1929–35, in Henly, Oxfordshire, since 1935: contributed criticism to *Nation, Atheneum, New Statesman* and *The Listener,* London 1928–30; visited Paris, 1933; founder, with Myfanwy Evans, *Axis* magazine, London, 1935–37; founder, with Robert Wellington and Baynard and Curwen Presses, *Contemporary Lithographs,* London, 1936; designed sets and costumes for *The Quest* ballet, with music by William Walton, London, 1943; founder member, English Opera group, London, 1947; worked on lithographs at Mourlot's Studios, Paris 1953, and on designs for the Baptistry window, Coventry Cathedral, 1957–62. Trustee, Tate Gallery, London, 1944–61. **Member:** Royal Fine Art Commission, since 1959. **Awards:** Lithography Prize, Vietnamese Government, 1963. Honorary doctorate: University of Leicester, 1960; Oxford University, 1964; University of Sussex, Brighton, 1974. Honorary Associate, Royal Institute of British Architects, 1957, and Royal College of Art, 1959. Companion of Honour, London, 1972. **Agent:** James Kirkman Limited, 46 Brompton Square, London SE3 2AF. **Died:** In Fawley, Oxfordshire, England, 28 June 1992.

Individual Exhibitions:

1927 Arlington Galleries, London (with David Birch)
1933 Zwemmer Gallery, London
1938 London Gallery
1940 Leicester Galleries, London
1941 Temple Newsam, Leeds (with Graham Sutherland and Henry Moore)
1945 Leicester Galleries, London
1946 Leicester Galleries, London
1948 Curt Valentin Gallery, New York
1950 Curt Valentin Gallery, New York
1951 Leicester Galleries, London
1953 *Aldeburgh Festival,* Suffolk
Arts Council Gallery, Cambridge
1955 Curt Valentin Gallery, New York
1956 Kunstsaal Magdalene Sothman, Amsterdam
1957 Durlacher Gallery, New York
Leicester Galleries, London
1959 Leicester Galleries, London
1960 Arthur Jeffress Gallery, London
Gloucester Art Gallery, London (with Lynn Chadwick)
Durlacher Gallery, New York
1962 Arthur Jeffress Gallery, London
1963 Marlborough Fine Art, London
1964 Marlborough Fine Art, London
1966 Marlborough Fine Art, London (with Sidney Nolan and Ceri Richards)
1967 Marlborough Fine Art, London (toured the U.K.)
Marlbourough Fine Art, London (with Ceri Richards)
1969 Marlborough Fine Art, London
Bear Lane Gallery, Oxford
1970 Hammet Gallery, London
Derwent College, University of York
Century Galleries, Sonning, Berkshire
Pieter Wenning Gallery, Johannesburg
Folkstone Adult Education Centre, Kent
1972 Marlborough Fine Art, London
1973 Marjorie Parr Gallery, London
Compendium Galleries, Birmingham
Paintings, Drawings, Prints and Illustrated Books, Frank Gadsby Gallery, Leicester
Pieter Wenning Gallery, Johannesburg
9th Century Festival, Lincoln Cathedral, Lincolnshire
1974 Parc Howard Gallery, Llanelli, South Wales
1975 University of York
1976 School of Art and Design, Sheffield, Yorkshire
Gallery Kasahara, Osaka
1977 Marlborough Fine Art, London
Hambledon Gallery, Blandford Forum, Dorset
1978 University of Cardiff
Bohum Gallery, Henley-on-Thames, Oxfordshire
The Maltings, Snape, Aldeburgh, Suffolk
Glynn Vivian Art Gallery and Museums, Swansea, South Wales
1979 *50 Years of Work,* Museum of Modern Art, Oxford (travelled to the Minories, Colchester, Essex)
1980 Regimental Chapel, Manchester Cathedral
Rufford Craft Centre, Ollerton, Nottinghamshire

1981 Maclean Gallery, London
Dorchester Abbey, Dorset
Marlborough Fine Art, London
1982 Solomon Gallery, Dublin
Blackman Harvey, London
Newlyn Art Gallery, Cornwall
Kettle's Yard Gallery, Cambridge
1983 *John Piper,* at the *Aldeburgh Festival,* Suffolk
Marlborough Fine Art, London
Tate Gallery, London (retrospective)
1984 *John Piper,* at the *Lichfield Festival,* Staffordshire
Marlborough Gallery, New York
1988 Waddington Galleries, London
New Ashgate Gallery, Farnham, England
1989 John Weber Gallery, New York
1990 Davies Memorial Gallery, Newtown, Wales
Waterman Fine Art, London
John Piper in Wales, Oriel 31, Newton (catalog)
The Master Prints, CCA Galleries, London (catalog)
1991 *Six Decades of Printmaking,* Marlborough Graphics, London (catalog)
John Weber Gallery, New York
1992 *John Piper 1903–1992: A Retrospective,* Scarborough Art Gallery (catalog)
John Piper, Ashmolean Museum, Oxford (catalog)
1996 *Early Oils and Watercolours,* Spink Gallery, London (catalog)
''Quality and Experiment'': The Prints of John Piper, Lund Humphries Gallery, London (catalog)
1999 *A Retrospective,* Grey College, University of Durham (catalog)
2001 *Painting with Light,* University Art Gallery, The University of Liverpool

Selected Group Exhibitions:

1932 *New English Art Society: 7 and 5,* Zwemmer Gallery, London
1935 *Abstract-Concrete,* Zwemmer Gallery, London
1942 *New Movements in Art,* London Museum, Lancaster House, London
1951 *Festival of Britain,* London
1955 *Aldeburgh Festival,* Suffolk
1965 *Axis, Circle, Unit One,* Marlborough Fine Art, London
1970 *International Art Fair,* Kunsthalle, Basel
1973 *Contemporary British Painters and Sculptors,* Marlborough-Godard Gallery, Toronto
1977 *British Painting 1952–1977,* Royal Academy of Arts, London
1981 *Drawings and Watercolours of 13 British Artists,* Marlborough Fine Art, London
1992 *Ahead on Points,* First Light Gallery, Brighton, England
Six Operas, Six Artists, Marion Koogler McNay Art Museum, San Antonio, Texas (catalog)
1996 *Two-way Traffic: British and Italian Art 1880–1980,* Royal Albert Memorial Museum, Exeter (catalog)
London in Paint, Museum of London (catalog)
1997 *British Art,* Foire Internationale d'Art Contemporain, Paris (traveling exhibition)
1999 *Modern Britain 1929–1939,* Design Museum, London

Collections:

Tate Gallery, London; Victoria and Albert Museum, London; Guggenheim Museum, New York; Museum of Modern Art, New York; Phillips Collection, Washington, D.C.; National Gallery of Canada, Ottawa; Museum of Modern Art, Sao Paulo.

Publications:

By PIPER: Books—*The Wind in the Trees,* 1924; *Shell Guide to Oxfordshire,* London 1938; *Shell Guide to Shropshire,* with John Betjeman, London 1939, 1951; *British Romantic Artists,* London 1942; *Murray's Architectural Guide to Buckinghamshire,* with John Betjeman, London 1948; *Murray's Architectural Guide to Berkshire,* with John Betjeman, London 1949. **Articles—**''Obiturary: Adrian Stokes'' in *Architectural Review* (London), March 1973; ''A Piper Portfolio,'' interview with M. Margetts in *Crafts* (London), January/February 1979; interview with Ian Simpson in *The Artist* (Tenterden), vol. 105, November 1990. **Books illustrated—***Wordsworth's Guide to the Lakes,* edited by W. Moelwyn Merchant, London 1952; *Selbourne* by Gilbert White, London, 1962.

On PIPER: Books—*John Piper* by John Betjeman, London 1944; *John Piper: Paintings, Drawings and Theatre Designs 1932–54,* London 1955; *John Piper: European Topography 1967–69, Oil Paintings and Gouaches,* London 1969; *The Painter's Object,* edited by Myfanwy Evans, London 1970; *Paintings, Drawings, Prints and Illustrated Books by John Piper,* exhibition catalog by R. Graham, Leicester 1973; *John Piper: 50 Years of Work,* exhibition catalog by John Betjeman, J. Hoole and others, Oxford 1979; *John Piper* by A. West, London 1979; *John Piper: Paintings in Coloured Light,* exhibition catalog with introduction by Martin Harrison, Cambridge 1982; *Piper's Places* by Richard Ingrams, London 1983; *John Piper: Retrospective Exhibition,* exhibition catalog with texts by David Fraser Jenkins, John Russell and others, London 1983; *John Piper and Stained Glass* by June Osborne, Stroud 1997; *John Piper: The Forties* by David Fraser Jenkins, London 2000. **Articles—**''The Sitwells Tucsan Castle: Watercolours by John Piper'' by Gervaise Jackson-Stops in *Country Life* (London), January 1981; ''John Piper: Neo-Romanticisim in the 1980s'' by Peter Fuller in *Modern Painters* (London), vol. 1, no. 2, Summer 1988; ''John Piper: The Lewin Gift'' in *Ashmolean,* no. 23, Winter 1992; Obituary in *Art in America* (London), vol. 80, September 1992; ''John Piper'' by Alan Powers in *Crafts* (London), no. 119, November/December 1992; ''Bohun Gallery'' by Patricia Jordan Evans in *Printmaking Today,* vol. 5, no. 4, Winter 1996.

* * *

At the Royal College of Art, John Piper cultivated the traditional English concern for drawing that he has consistently used in the several branches of art he has practised since, including painting in oils and watercolour, engraving, designing for theatrical production and stained glass design. His intense interest in looking at art, and reading and discussion, led him to write discerning art criticism. He had also a great love for music and the theatre, also for archaeology and architecture, a profession he once thought of entering.

Piper's early pictures were more or less straightforward renderings of picturesque views of the landscape of the South Coast. Then in 1933 he visited Paris and met some of the leading figures then veering towards the abstract; they included Braque, Léger, Brancusi and Hélion. For a time, Piper composed landscapes that reflected this abstract influence. Observation of natural phenomena has always been at the root of Piper's art, followed by architecture taking a high place in subject matter.

Lively stylization enlivened his treatment of given scenes, especially during the Second World War, in which he served as an official war artist with a special interest in recording the damage to historic buildings. He also worked on preserving in pictorial form records of Britain's distinctive visual character in its town and villages. After the war, Piper made frequent trips on the Continent by car and exhibited series of the oils and water-colours he made of the buildings and landscapes of France and Italy. In particular Venice provided him with much material, and his dark palette of the 1939–45 period was replaced by a scheme of warmer hues. While the figure is almost totally absent from his paintings, there is consistent reflection of man's presence in the many pictures of churches and inhabited communities. He has been described as a 20th century Piranesi, though he lacks the Italian's theatrical drama.

To some degree Piper is perhaps the victim of his own versatility in that some of his slighter topographical works do not quite live up to the reputation won by his larger and more impressive oils. He invests his painting with a significant atmosphere that can be immensely evocative. Light is a vital ingredient of his art and he will be remembered also for the brilliantly incandescent stained-glass window he designed for Coventry Cathedral.

—G. S. Whittet

PISANI, Vettor

Nationality: Italian. **Born:** Bari, 14 June 1935; lived on the Island of Ischia until 1945, then moved to Naples. **Education:** Studied architecture at a Jesuit School, Naples, c. 1950. **Career:** Founder, Rose Croce Theatre and School of Art, Rome. **Awards:** Premio Pino Pascali, Bari, Italy, 1970. **Address:** via A. Poliziano 78, 00184 Rome, Italy.

Individual Exhibitions:

1970 *Maschile, Femminile e Androgino: Incesto e Cannibalismo in Marcel Duchamp,* Galleria La Salita, Rome
Galleria Arte Contemporanea, Rome
Amoremio, Palazzo Ricci, Montepulciano, Italy (with Michelangelo Pistoletto)
Premio Nazionale Pino Pascali, Castello Svevo, Bari, Italy
1973 Galleria L'Attico, Rome
1976 *Incontri Internazionale d'Arte,* Rome (with Michelangelo Pistoletto)
1982 *Vettor Pisani: R. C. Theatrum,* Museum Folkwang, Essen
1989 Galleria Pio Monti, Rome
1990 Jack Shainman Gallery, New York
ACTA Gallery, Milan
1991 Galleria Pieroni, Rome

Selected Group Exhibitions:

1970 *Vitalita del Negativo,* Palazzo delle Esposizioni, Rome
1971 *Bienal,* Sao Paulo
Arte Povera, Kunstverein, Munich
1972 *Documenta,* Kassel, West Germany
1977 *Settimana della Performance,* Bologna
1980 *Italian Art Now: An American Perspective,* Guggenheim Museum, New York
1982 *Arte Italiana 1960–82,* Hayward Gallery, London
1986 *Esculturas sobre la Pared,* Galeria Juana de Aizpuru, Madrid
1989 Galleria Pieroni, Rome
1990 *44th Biennale di Venezia,* Venice
1992 *Pink and Yellow,* Pieroni Gallery, Rome
1997 *Italian Painting: Alighiero e Boetti, Anselmo, Arienti, burri, Clemente, de Maria, Griff, Lo Savio, Marisaldi, Merz, Pisani, Toderi,* Castello di Rivoli, Museo d'Arte Contemporanea, Rivoli, Italy

Publications:

By PISANI: Articles—''Il Teatro a Coda'' and ''Per Coerenza'' in *Vettor Pisani: R. C. Theatrum,* exhibition catalog, Essen 1982; ''Vettor Pisani: Having the Lost Word: Interview'' by Giacinto Di Pietrantonio by *Flash Art (International Edition),* no. 162, January/February 1992.

On PISANI: Books—*Vettor Pisani,* exhibition catalog by Achille Bonito Oliva and others, Bari, Italy 1970; *La Performance,* Macerata, Italy 1978; *Vetto Pisani: R. C. Theatrum,* exhibition catalog by Maurizio Calvesi, Essen 1982. **Articles**—''L'Arte Povera'' by Renato Barilli in *L'Arte Moderna,* Milan 1975; ''Vettor Pisni'' by Tommaso Trini in *Data* (Milan), October/November 1976; ''Vettor Pisani'' in *Data* (Milan), Summer 1978; ''Quarry Story'' by Giorgio Verzotti in *Artforum International,* vol. 36, no. 10, Summer 1998.

* * *

Since the 1970s the art of Vettor Pisani has founded its true alchemical significance in its language, which has a closed/open oscillation rich in dark, symbolic areas; he proceeds by hermeneutic antitheses, brooding on indirect references, he assumes different attitudes in his work, revealing complex, sometimes actually irreconcilable, paths. He does not possess a single technique through which the work of art appears diversifed, as if isolated from the global contest of the discourse. Pisani uses a language that is inexorably deductive, which forces the viewer to be suspicious of a deductive interpretation of the cause-and-effect type. Its course is thus a sort of spiral, winding round the same violent alchemical significance.

With its orientative power, the language of Pisani's art continually displaces the real to unveil it internally through obscure poetic differences in level. Its secret space ends where nature begins, an alchemical nature, as we see in the work ''The Hero's Bedroom'' of 1970. But his evocative power is oedipal; thus, while the artist identifies himself with the materials that compose the work of art, he discovers disconcerting elective affinities in them which take the work to the origin of creativity, of existence as an artist. The mystery of art remains mysterious; only bright or dark whirlpools are revealed within it. The work of art hints at the dazzling conceptual truth present in the alchemical significance. In the work called "The Struggle of Light and Darkness" (1980) Pisani prefigures his own birth as an artist; the island of Ischia, where he lived as a child, is lit by a brilliant light, the symbolic image of art's creativity.

A theatrical production unites Vettor Pisani's works. They are linked because they have in common the flowing, circular birth of the representation itself. The alchemical significances never upset their own contents, because they are initial premises, unchanted and undulating. Within its theatricality (regardless of the everyday environment) the work of art jealously guards the complexity of its own (masculine/feminine) origin. The revelation of it depends on the intellectual paths taken by the observer's eyes, in which the visual-mental possibilities of interpretation are vigorously intertwined. Out of the depths they rise up to the light, to the subtle, changing play of nature, to the imagination's ornamentation. There is no superstition in art, but remote, mysterious beauty, which the artist transforms with amazement and alarm because he knows that he has eternity before him—eternity violated by poetry and imagination, spectres of the imprecision and obscurity of art. In the "Orient" as in the "Occident," says Pisani, the artist loves nature and its labyrinths. And so it all starts again from the beginning, in a circle, through new indefinite identifications. Art is the eternal Eden.

—Italo Mussa

PISTOLETTO, Michelangelo

Nationality: Italian. **Born:** Biella, 23 June 1933; moved with his family to Turin, 1934. **Education:** Self-taught in art; assistant to father in picture restoration business, Turin, 1957. **Career:** Executed first painting, 1956; first sculptures, 1964; actions and happenings, 1970; worked in Berlin 1978; travelled for two years in the United States giving performances, 1970–81. **Awards:** DAAD Grant, 1978. **Agent:** Galleria Lucio Amelio, Piazza dei Martiri 58, 80121 Naples. **Address:** Via Argonne 1, 10133 Turin, Italy.

Individual Exhibitions:

1960 Galleria Galatea, Turin
1963 Galleria Galatea, Turin
1964 Galerie Ileana Sonnabend, Paris
Galleria Sperone, Turin
Galleria del Leone, Venice
1965 Ideal Standard, Milan
Galerie Heiner Friedrich, Munich
1966 Walker Art Center, Minneapolis
Galleria del Leone, Venice
Galleria Sperone, Turin
Galleria La Bertesca, Genoa
Studio Pistoletto, Turin
1967 Galleria Sperone, Turin
Galerie Zwirner, Cologne
Hudson Gallery, Detroit
Palais Des Beaux-Arts, Brussels
Galleria Naviglio, Milan
Galerie Ileana Sonnabend, Paris
Kornblee Gallery, New York
Museum Boymans-van Beuningen, Rotterdam
Badischer Kunstverein, Karlsruhe, West Germany
Albright-Knox Art Gallery, Buffalo, New York
1969 *Warhol/Pistoletto,* New Gallery, Cleveland
1970 Palazzo Ricci, Montepulciano, Italy (with Vettor Pisani)
Modern Art Agency, Naples
Galleria dell'Ariete, Milan
Galleria Sperone, Turin
1972 Galleria dell'Ariete, Milan
Kunstverein, Frankfurt
Galleria Toninelli, Rome
1973 Galleria Sperone, Turin
Marlborough Galleria d'Arte, Rome
Kestner-Gesellschaft, Hannover
1974 Sidney Janis Gallery, New York
Kestner-Gesellschaft, Hannover
Galerie Mathildenhohe, Darmstadt
Galerie Gunther Sachs, Hamburg
1975 Galleria Sperone, Rome
Modern Art Agency, Naples
Galleria Multipli, Turin
Galleria Christian Stein, Turin
Castelli Graphics Gallery, New York
1976 Galleria Christian Stein, Turin
Galleria Salvatore Alan, Milan
Galerie Saman, Genoa
Incontri Internazionale d'Arte, Rome (with Vettor Pisani)
Palazzo Grassi, Venice
1977 Galerie Marie Louise Jeanneret Art Moderne, Geneva
1978 Nationalgalerie, West Berlin
1979 Institute of Arts, Rice University, Houston
Georgia Museum of Arts, Athens
1980 *Nazionale per la Grafica,* Rome (with Giulio Paolini and Luca Patella)
1981 Westfälischer Landesmuseum, Münster, West Germany
1982 Galleria Pieroni, Rome
Galerie Tanit, Munich
1983 Galleria Giorgio Petano, Turin
Galleria La Polena, Genoa, Italy
Italian Cultural Institute, Madrid
1984 Centre d'Art Contemporain, Geneva
Centro d'Art Contemporanea, Syracuse, Italy
1985 Palacio de Velazquez, Madrid
Galerie de France, Paris
1986 Kunstnernes Hus, Oslo
1987 Montevideo Galerie, Antwerp, Belgium
1988 Galleria Lia Rumma, Naples
Pistoletto: Division and Multiplication of the Mirror, The Institute for Contemporary Art and P.S. 1 Museum, New York
1989 Kunsthalle Bern (catalog)
Sala dei Camuccini, Capodimonte Museum, Naples
Jay Gorney Modern Art, New York
P.S. 1, Long Island City, New York
1990 Gallery Hufkens, Brussels
Galleria Nazionale d'Arte Moderna, Rome (catalog)
L'Arquitectura del Mirall, Pistoletto, Generalitat de Catalunya, Departament de Cultura, Barcelona (catalog)
1991 Maureen Paley Interim Art, London
Galleria Nazionale d'Arte Moderna, Rome

1993 Galerie Xavier Hufkens, Brussels
Museum Moderner Kunst Stiftung Ludwig Wien, Vienna (catalog)
Michelangelo Pistoletto e la Fotografia, Fundaçao de Serralves, Portugal (catalog)
1994 National Gallery, Prague
Musee de Rochechouart, Thiers (catalog)
1995 *Memoria, Intelligentia, Praevidentia,* Lenbachhaus, Munich (catalog)
Museum Moderner Kunst Stiftung Ludwig, Vienna (catalog)
Pistoletto: Le Porte di Palazzo Fabroni, Milan (catalog)
1998 Ecole Nationale des Beaux-Arts, Paris (catalog)
1999 *Mirror Work (1962–1992),* Museum of Modern Art Oxford (catalog)
New Work, Henry Moore Foundation Studio, Dean Clough, Halifax, United Kingdom (catalog)
Azioni Materiali, Galerie im Taxispalais, Cologne (catalog)
2000 Musen d'Art Contemporani de Barcelona, Spain (retrospective) (catalog)

Selected Group Exhibitions:

1958 *Premio San Fedele,* Milan
1964 *Niewe Realisten,* Gemeentemuseum, The Hague
1966 *The Object Transformed,* Museum of Modern Art, New York
1969 *Information,* Museum of Modern Art, New York
1970 *Land Art/Arte Povera/Conceptual Art,* Museo Civico d'Arte Moderna, Turin
1975 *Realismus und Realität,* Kunsthalle, Darmstadt
1977 *La Traccia del Racconto,* Villa Comunale Ormand, San Remo, Italy
1982 *Documenta,* Kassel, West Germany
1985 *The European Iceberg,* Art Gallery of Ontario, Toronto
1986 *Aspects of Italian Art 1960–86,* Kunstverein, Frankfurt
1990 Giorgio Persano Gallery, Milan
Arte Povera, Galleria in Arco, Torino (catalog)
1992 *Psycho: Inaugural Exhibition,* The KunstHall, New York (catalog)
Arte Povera, Kodama Gallery, Osaka, Japan (catalog)
1993 *International Critics' Choice: An Exhibition,* The Museum, Mount Vernon (catalog)
1996 *Pop Art e Oggetto,* Palazzo Crepadona, Belluno (also Galleria Civica, Cortina) (catalog)
1997 *From Here to There,* Centro de Arte Moderna José de Azeredo Perdigao, Lisbon (catalog)
2001 *Zero to Infinity: Arte Povera 1962–1972*, Walker Art Center, Minneapolis (catalog)

Collections:

Albright-Knox Art Gallery, Buffalo, New York; Kaiser Wilhelm Museum, Krefeld, West Germany; Kunstmuseum, Dusseldorf; Musée Départmental d'Art Contemporain, Rochechouart, France.

Publications:

By PISTOLETTO: Books—*Le Ultime Parole Famose,* Turin 1967; *L'Uomo Nero: Il Lato Insopportabile,* Salerno, Italy 1970; *Pistoletto,* with Germano Celant, New York 1989; *Michelangelo Pistoletto: Un Artista in Meno,* Firenze 1989; *The Artist Observed: 28 Interviews with Contemporary Artists, 1972–1978,* with John Gruen, Chicago 1991. **Articles**—interview with Barry Schwabsky in *Arts Magazine,* vol. 63, December 1988; interview with Carolyn Christov-Bakargiev in *Flash Art (International Edition),* no. 151, March/April 1990; ''Michelangelo Pistoletto'' in *Art Press,* special issue no. 17, 1996.

On PISTOLETTO: Books—*Michelangelo Pistoletto: A Reflected World* by M. Friedman, Minneapolis 1966; *Pistoletto,* exhibition catalog by Henry Martin, Rotterdam 1969; *Michelangelo Pistoletto,* exhibition catalog by Wieland Schmied, Hannover 1973; *Michelangelo Pistoletto,* exhibition catalog by Bernd Krimmel, Darmstadt 1974; *Michelangelo Pistoletto: Les Quatre Saisons,* exhibition catalog with preface by Guiseppe Conte, Paris 1985; *Pistoletto: Division and Multiplication of the Mirror*, Milan 1988; *Arte Povera* by Germano Celant, Villeurbanne 1989. **Articles**—''Pistoletto'' by Henry Martin in *Art International* (Lugano, Switzerland), February 1969; ''Pistoletto Traverse le Miroir'' by A. Boatto in *Opus International* (Paris), March 1972; ''Michelangelo Pistoletto'' by Tommaso Trini in *Data* (Milan), July/September 1976; ''Pistoletto's American Campaign'' by M. Welish in *Art in America* (New York), February 1981; ''Michelangelo Pistoletto: Portrait by Armin Linke'' in *Du,* no. 1, January 1994; ''Michelangelo Pistoletto: Mirror Effects'' by Maïten Bouisset in *Art Press,* no. 189, March 1994; ''Michelangelo Pistoletto: Nothing Escapes the Mirror'' by Adachiara Zevi in *L'Architettura,* vol. 41, June 1995; ''Michelangelo Pistoletto'' by Rachel Withers in *Artforum,* vol. 38, no. 6, February 2000.

* * *

Michelangelo Pistoletto's early work dates from the mid-1950s, but it was a 1961 painting which marked a truly significant point in his development as an artist. After completing a series of large self-portraits but this time done on an acrylic base coated with plastic varnish so that the surface became extremely mirror-like. The effect was striking—so much so that Pistoletto changed the entire direction of his work. What now interested him was the possibility of establishing a reciprocal relationship between the images painted in the canvas and the images reflected on its highly polished surface. Thus Pistoletto was setting up a relationship between art and life, between reality and pictorial invention, an artistic intention which provided the key to his work during this period.

The early self-portraits and ''reflecting'' paintings were followed by completely mature works in which mirror-like surfaces still played an important role. Pistoletto drew and photographed images which he then attached to polished metal surfaces, thus moving from a kind of formalism to a kind of reporting: painting becomes photography. The earlier relationships between reality and invention are now replaced by relationships established between reality and its reflected image, thus affording two levels of interpretation: we have the relationships of image to reflection, and the image itself. In three works from 1965, ''No Higher Fares on the Train,'' ''Vietnam'' and ''Coming,'' a pattern is set: the viewer is not passive but interacts with the images which reflect his own presence.

—Roberto G. Lambarelli

In 1966, Pistoletto created a series of objects, including *A Cubic Meter of Infinity*, that were subtitled *Minus Objects*. These works were in fact to stand somewhat in opposition to the mirror paintings of the early 1960s. Where the mirror paintings are constantly in motion, the viewer's perception shuttling endlessly between a fixed representation (photographic image) and fluid recognition (reflection), the Minus Objects are fixed in a material state of existence. Using the most direct, available material—pressed newspapers (*Sphere of Newspapers*), corrugated cardboard, stretcher bars, stretched canvases, iron pipe, wood, or masonite—Pistoletto created objects that are anchors for shifting perception and points of view. He wrote in *Zero to Infinity* that these: ''are objects through whose agency I free myself from something—not constructions, then, but liberations. I do not consider them 'more' but 'less,' not 'pluses' but 'minuses,' in that they bring with them a sense of a perceptual experience that has been definitively manifested once and for all.''

Between 1968 and 1970, Pistoletto continued to be engaged with the idea of making art a reality rather than a reflection or image of reality. With his companion Maria Pioppi, he started a travelling theater production company called *Lo Zoo* (''The Zoo''). The *Zoo* performed experimental pieces in galleries, alternative space and theaters, art festivals such as Amalfi, and even took to the streets for *Walking Theater* or *Canopy Theater* in 1969. For Pistoletto, the *Zoo* brings every gesture and encounter found in painting into the world in actual size.

In the 1980s Pistoletto began working with monumental sculpture. The idea was to return to an original sense of the word as an excavation or liberation of a form from the stone. By creating awkward, semi-figurative, semi-abstract forms, Pistoletto sought to destabilize and thus revive what he saw as a cold dead medium: empty monumentality. Like the Minus Objects, they go back in order to go forward. In recent years, Pistoletto has focused much of his energy on an art school founded in his hometown of Biela. *Cittadellarte*, founded in 1998 by Fondazione Pistoletto, is a center for the study, research, planning, and promotion of creative activities. Housed in a former wool mill, it is a workshop and school that ''assigns art the role of 'sensible center' of the social system, not isolated but linked and intertwined with all parts of this system.'' Through its multi-disciplinary approach that links art and industry, fashion, architecture, design, technology, and sociology, and its neighboring institution *UNIDEE*, University of Ideas, which tackles aesthetic, ethical, and social dimensions of artistic production, Pistoletto has created a place where art and life can truly flow freely into one another.

—Elizabeth Mangini

PLIMACK MANGOLD, Sylvia

Nationality: American. **Born:** Sylvia Plimack in New York City, 18 September 1938. **Education:** Studied fine arts at Cooper Union, New York, 1956–59; Yale University Art School, New Haven, Connecticut, 1959–61, B.F.A. 1961; influenced by Georgia O'Keeffe, Rene Magritte, Edward Hooper, John Haberle, John Peto, William Harnett, Robert Mangold, Jasper Johns and Phillip Pearlstein. **Family:** Married the artist Robert Mangold in 1961; sons: James A. and Andrew P. **Career:** Worked (with Robert Mangold) as apartment house superintendent, New York, 1961–63. Instructor of painting and drawing, School of Visual Arts, New York, 1971–81. **Awards:** National Endowment for the Arts Grant, 1974–75; Special Purchase Award, Davidson National Print and Drawing Competition, 1976. **Agent:** Brooke Alexander Inc., 20 West 57th Street, New York, New York 10019. **Address:** 155 Bull Road, Washingtonville, New York 10992, U.S.A.

Individual Exhibitions:

1974 Fischbach Gallery, New York
1975 Daniel Weinberg Gallery, San Francisco
Fischbach Gallery, New York
1978 Droll-Kolbert Gallery, New York
Galerie Annemarie Verna, Zurich
1980 Droll-Kolbert, Gallery, New York
Ohio State University, Columbus
Young Hoffman Gallery, Chicago
1981 Matrix Gallery, Wadsworth Atheneum, Hartford, Connecticut
Perspectives, Contemporary Arts Museum, Houston
1982 Brooke Alexander Inc., New York
1984 Brooke Alexander Inc., New York
1985 Rhona Hoffman Gallery, Chicago
1986 *Sylvia Plimack Mangold: Drawings,* Brooke Alexander, New York
Sylvia Plimack Mangold: Paintings & Pastels, Texas Gallery, Houston
1987 *Sylvia Plimack Mangold: Landscape Paintings,* Fuller Goldeen Gallery, San Francisco
1989 *Sylvia Plimack Mangold: Paintings 1987–1989,* Brooke Alexander, New York
1991 *Sylvia Plimack Mangold: The Elm Tree,* Annemarie Verna Galerie, Zürich
1992 *Sylvia Plimack Mangold: Works on Paper 1968–1991,* University of Michigan Museum of Art, Ann Arbor; The Minneapolis Institute of Arts; Grunwald Center for the Graphic Arts, UCLA; Neuberger Museum, State University of New York at Purchase; Davison Art Center, Wesleyan University
Sylvia Plimack Mangold: Prints and Related Works, Brooke Alexander, New York
Sylvia Plimack Mangold: Work Done in the Elk River Valley in August 1992, The New Van Straaten Gallery, Chicago
1994 *The Paintings of Sylvia Plimack Mangold,* Albright-Knox Art Gallery, Buffalo, New York; Wadsworth Atheneum, Hartford, CT; Blaffer Gallery, University of Houston; Museum of Fine Arts, Boston
1995 *Sylvia Plimack Mangold, Paintings, 1990–1995,* Brooke Alexander, New York
1997 *New Paintings and Watercolors,* Annemarie Verna Galerie, Zürich
1998 *Sylvia Plimack Mangold: Trees,* Herbert F. Johnson Museum of Art, Cornell University, Ithaca, New York
2000 *Sylvia Plimack Mangold,* Alexander and Bonin, New York

Selected Group Exhibitions:

1968 *Realism Now,* Vassar College, Poughkeepsie, New York
1971 *Twenty Contemporary Women Artists,* Aldrich Museum, Ridgefield, Connecticut
1973 *New York Realism,* Espace Cardin, Paris
1977 *Documenta 6,* Kassel, West Germany

Sylvia Plimack Mangold: *Summer Pin Oak,* 1998. Photo by Orcutt and Van Der Putten. ©Sylvia Plimack Mangold, courtesy of Alexander and Bonin, New York.

1979 *The 1970s: New American Paintings,* New Museum, New York (toured Europe)
1980 *Drawings to Benefit the Foundations for Contemporary Performance Art Inc.,* Leo Castelli Gallery, New York
1981 *20 Artists: Yale School of Art 1950–1970,* Yale University Art Gallery, New Haven, Connecticut
1984 *New Vistas: Contemporary American Landscapes,* Hudson River Museum, Yonkers, New York
1986 *Drawings,* Spirit Square Arts Center, Charlotte, North Carolina
The Window in Twentieth-Century Art, Neuberger Museum, State University of New York at Purchase
A Contemporary View of Nature, Inaugural Exhibition, The Aldrich Museum, Ridgefield, Connecticut
Landscape in the Age of Anxiety, Lehman College Art Gallery, City University of New York, Bronx; Cleveland Center for Contemporary Art
NYC: New Work, Delaware Museum of Art, Wilmington
Logical Foundations, The Museum of Modern Art, Art Lending Service, New York
1987 *From the LeWitt Collection,* Wadsworth Atheneum, Hartford
1988 *Art on Paper 1988,* Weatherspoon Art Gallery, The University of North Carolina at Greensboro
1989 *Coming of Age: Twenty-one Years of Collecting by the Madison Art Center,* Madison Art Center, Wisconsin
Making Their Mark: Women Artists Move into the Mainstream 1970–1985, Cincinnati Art Museum; New Orleans Museum of Art; Denver Art Museum; Pennsylvania Academy of Fine Arts
1993 *Yale Collects Yale, 1950–1993,* Yale University Art Gallery, New Haven, Connecticut
Building a Collection, Museum of Fine Arts, Boston
1994 *Inspired by Nature,* Neuberger Museum of Art, Purchase, New York
Block/Plate/Stone: What a Print Is, Katonah Museum of Art, New York; Davison Art Center, Wesleyan University, Middletown, Connecticut
1995 *Karo Dame: Konstruktive, Konkrete unde Radikale Kunst von Frauen von 1914 bis heute,* Aargauer Kunsthaus Aarau, Austria
1996 *Private Worlds: 200 Years of American Still Life Painting,* Aspen Art Museum, Colorado
1997 *Selections from the Collection,* The Museum of Modern Art, New York
Private Worlds: 200 Years of American Still Life Painting Aspen Art Museum, Aspen, Colorado
Queens Artists: Highlights of the 20th Century, Queens Museum of Art, New York
1999 *Rita McBride, Sylvia Plimack Mangold & To Be Announced,* Alexander and Bonin, New York
2000 *Still,* Alexander and Bonin, New York

Collections:

University of Michigan, Ann Arbor; Museum of Fine Arts, Boston; Brooklyn Museum, New York; Albright-Knox Art Gallery, Buffalo; Dallas Museum of Art; Detroit Institute of Arts; Weatherspoon Art Gallery, Greensboro, North Carolina; Wadsworth Atheneum, Hartford; Museum of Fine Arts, Houston; Indianapolis Museum of Art; Madison Art Center, Wisconsin; Milwaukee Art Museum; Walker Art Center, Minneapolis; Yale University Art Gallery, New Haven; The Museum of Modern Art, New York; New York Public Library, New York; Whitney Museum of American Art, New York; Smith

College Museum, Northampton, Massachussetts; Allen Memorial Art Museum, Oberlin, Ohio; University of Utah, Utah Museum of Fine Arts, Salt Lake City; Achenbach Foundation for Graphic Arts, San Francisco; St. Louis Art Museum; The Tampa Museum.

Publications:

By MANGOLD: Book—*Inches and Field,* New York 1978.

On MANGOLD: Books—*Art on Paper,* exhibition catalog, Greensboro, North Carolina 1968; *Realism Now,* exhibition catalog, Poughkeepsie, New York 1968; *New Realism,* exhibition catalog, Pottsdam, New York 1971; *26 Contemporary American Artists,* exhibition catalog, Ridgefield, Connecticut 1971; *Still Life Today,* exhibition catalog, New York 1971; *New Realism* by Udo Kultermann, Tübingen, West Germany 1972; *Contemporary American Painting Annual,* exhibition catalog, New York 1972; *Objects and 8 Women, Realists,* exhibition catalog, Amherst, Massachusetts 1973; *Super Realism,* edited by Gregory Battcock, New York 1974; *Anonymous Was a Woman,* exhibition catalog, Valencia, California 1974; *Realists,* exhibition catalog, New Haven, Connecticut 1974; *Selections in Contemporary Realism,* Ohio 1974; *Works on Paper,* exhibition catalog, Richmond, Virginia 1974; *A Woman's Sensibility,* Valencia, California 1975; *19th National Print Exhibition,* exhibition catalog, Brooklyn, New York 1975; *60s/70s: Paintings, Drawings, Sculpture from the Vogel Collection,* Philadelphia 1975; *Spare,* exhibition catalog, New York 1975; *Private Notions: Artists' Sketchbooks II,* exhibition catalog, Philadelphia 1976; *Paintings and Sculpture Today, 1976,* exhibition catalog, Indianapolis 1976; *Contemporary Images in Watercolor,* exhibition catalog, Akron, Ohio 1976; *A View of a Decade,* exhibition catalog, Chicago 1977; *Recent Works on Paper by American Artists,* exhibition catalog, Madison, Wisconsin 1977; *Paintings 75/76/77,* exhibition catalog, Bronxville, New York 1977; *Young Hoffman Gallery 1976–1979,* exhibition catalog, Chicago 1970; *8 Artists: The Elusive Image,* exhibition catalog, Minneapolis 1979, *Reality and Illusion,* exhibition catalog, by Donald J. Brewer, Denver, and Los Angeles 1980; *New York Realists 1980,* exhibition catalog, by Roger Howrigan, Sparkill, New York 1980; *Sylvia Plimack Mangold* by Andrea Miller-Keller, Hartford, Connecticut 1980; *Sylvia Plimack Mangold Paintings 1965–1982* with an essay by Thomas H. Garver, Madison, Wisconsin 1982; *Sylvia Plimack Mangold Paintings 1987–1989* with an essay by Carter Ratcliff, New York 1989; *Sylvia Plimack Mangold: Works on Paper 1968–1991* with essays by Hilarie Faberman and Ellen G. D'Oench, Ann Arbor, Michigan 1992; *The Paintings of Sylvia Plimack Mangold* with an essay by Cheryl Brutvan, New York 1994; **Articles—**''Realism: The Painting Is Fiction Enough'' by Hilton Kramer in the *New York Times,* 28 April 1974; ''Sylvia Mangold: Light, Rules, Floors'' by Judith L. Dunham in *Artweek* (Oakland, California), 27 September 1975; ''Vogel Collection: They Pick Wisely, and Very Lovingly'' by Victoria Donohoe in the *Philadelphia Inquirer,* 12 October 1975; ''Painting Is as Painting Does'' by John Perreault in the *Soho Weekly News* (New York), 12 May 1977; ''Through the Looking Glass and What the Artist Found There'' by David Mower in *Art International* (Lugano, Switzerland), September 1979; ''Abstraction and Sensitivity'' in *Artspeak* (New York), 31 January 1980; ''Beautiful Deceptions'' by Mark Stevens in *Newsweek* (New York), 24 March 1980; ''Keep Up the Image'' by William Zimmer in the *Soho Weekly News* (New York), 26 November 1980; ''Sylvia Plimack Mangold: Uses of the Past'' by John Paoletti in *Arts Magazine,* vol. 57, no. 9, April 1983; ''Sylvia Plimack Mangold: Framework'' by John B. Ravenal in *Arts Magazine,* vol. 57, no. 9, April 1983; ''New York in Review: Sylvia Plimack Mangold'' by Peggy Cyphers in *Arts Magazine,* vol. 64, no. 6, February 1990; ''Mangold: Probing the Nature of Perceptual Space'' by Christopher Knight in *Los Angeles Times,* 13 October 1992; Article by William Zimmer in *New York Times,* 5 March 1995; ''Sylvia Plimack Mangold'' by Francine Koslow Miller in *Artforum,* March 1996; ''Bob and Sylvia and Chris and Doris: A Collaboration'' by Faye Hirsch in *Art on Paper,* December 2000; Article by Arthur C. Danto in, *The Nation,* 21 February 2000.

*

My paintings are a total of accumulated detail. The translation from the object to the canvas has a signature that is mine, and is the evidence of my efforts. I try for accuracy and illusion. Although I believe these qualities to be arbitrary, I need to strive for them.

—Sylvia Plimack Mangold

* * *

During the 1960s Sylvia Plimack Mangold established a realist painter's variant of one then-favorite nonrepresentational image—grid-patterned hard-edged, and measured. It was a complex and perhaps intellectualized, if not poeticized, realism, that self-consciously incorporated a self-questioning attitude. Her precise, perspectival depictions of flooring—hardwood, grained boards—allowed her to become expert in the painting of their patterns. Aside from the physical materiality shown through her craft energy, these paintings were also about ''measure''; rulers and other devices of scale were included in these silent and usually otherwise empty room interiors. The images then became emblems of the irony within depiction—both the scale of actuality, and three-dimensional space, when illustrated pictorially. (Her work, interestingly enough, might be seen as the stylistic obverse of her painter-husband Robert's approach to scale and measure; both at that time and the present he has worked with two-dimensional geometric forms upon flat monochromatic fields.)

Since the mid-70s, Mangold has restricted the spatial extent of her former view, so that the surface of her canvas has become analogous to—in classic *trompe l'oeil* tradition—a flat wall plane; and the craft and zest that she once expended upon the wood graining now was given over to meticulous illusionist renderings of masking tapes, often much overlapped. Seemingly held in place by the tapes, centrally in the rectangle of the canvas, are landscape views. From the artist, we learn that these scenes are usually based upon those observed through her studio windows. Keeping this format intact, she has played many variants upon the relationship of the landscape views and the ''wall area'' outside the tapes, including images completely non-representational with the exception of the tapes. In such works, Mangold reveals the abstract force that has always clearly lain beneath her seemingly quiet mundane worlds. As well, it is not so much doubt about the efficacy of realism that distinguishes her work—no matter how powerful the depicted reality, it is all abstract.

During the 1990s, a major museum exhibition at Albright-Knox Gallery presented the sweep of all of Plimack Mangold's work. After her own consideration, the paintings that followed appeared to be attempts to attain her previous confidence and a stylistic security—but now with altered style. Her long-held fascination with the tree—apparently mostly elms in the fields outside her studio—continued to be placed in high prominence; but she dropped her inner frame of tape and wished to develop a unified canvas. The intensity of her gaze which earlier had still held on to the optical and often literal force of the depicted tape and larger image—her signature style—now shifted to a singularly focused abstracting idiom. Flattened segments of tree limbs were placed adjacent to blue sky and green leaf segments which overlapped them to form an effort dubbed ''Neo-Cezannian.'' The paintings appeared as sincere an effort as was her previous sharp realism, to present a guileless American reaction—but now in the guise of European early Modernism.

—Joshua Kind

POIRIER, Anne and Patrick

Nationality: French. **Born:** (Anne) Anne Houllevigue in Marseille, 31 March 1942; (Patrick) Nantes, 5 April 1942. **Education:** Both studied at the Ecole Nationale Superieure des Arts Decoratifs, Paris, 1963–66. **Family:** Married in 1968; son: Alain-Guillaume. **Career:** Anne and Patrick Poirier have worked together on archaeological reconstruction and documentation projects, in Paris and Rome, since 1967; they live and work in Paris, France and Trevi, Italy. **Awards:** Villa Medici Fellowships, Rome, 1967, 1973, 1974; D.A.A.D. Fellowship, West Berlin, 1977–78. **Agents:** Galerie Paul Maenz, Bismarckstrasse 50, 5000 Cologne 1, Germany; Galleria Massimo Valsecchi, Via Santa Marta 11, 20123 Milan, Italy; Sonnabend Gallery, 420 West Broadway, New York, New York 10012, U.S.A.; and Galerie Daniel Templon, 30 rue Beaubourg, 75004 Paris. **Address:** 65 rue St. Charles, 75015 Paris, France.

Individual Exhibitions:

1970 Galleria Arco d'Alibert, Rome
1972 Galerie Paul Maenz, Cologne
1973 Neue Galerie, Aachen, West Germany
Sammlung Ludwig, Cologne
Galerie Paul Maenz, Cologne
Galerie Sonnabend, Paris
1974 Sonnabend Gallery, New York
Sonnabend Gallery, Geneva
Galleria Forma, Genoa
Galerie Yellow-Now, Liège, Belgium
1975 Galerie Sonnabend, Paris
Daner Galleriet, Copenhagen
Galerie Paul Maenz, Cologne
1977 Galerie Sonnabend, Paris
Galerie Paul Maenz, Cologne
Galleria Massimo Valsecchi, Milan
Centre d'Art Plastique Contemporain, Bordeaux
Maison de La Culture, Rennes, France
Neue Berliner Kunstverein, West Berlin
1978 Galerie Sonnabend, Paris
Centre Georges Pompidou, Paris
Kunstverein, Bonn
Palais des Beaux-Arts, Brussels
Kunstverein, Mannheim
Museum of Modern Art, New York
Sonnabend Gallery, New York
1979 Galerie Sonnabend, Paris
Palazzo dei Diamanti, Ferrara, Italy
Carpenter Center, Harvard University, Cambridge, Massachusetts
Philadelphia College of Arts
Galerie Paul Maenz, Cologne
1980 Studio G7 (Ginevra Grigolo), Bologna
Carpenter Center, Harvard University, Cambridge, Massachusetts
Sonnabend Gallery, New York
P.S. 1, New York
Galleria Massimo Valsecchi, Milan
1981 Maison de la Culture, Chalon-sur-Saône, France
Villa Romana, Florence
Musée de Nice, France
Galerie Daniel Templon, Paris
1982 Sonnabend Gallery, New York
Studio G7, Bologna, Italy
Galleria Massimo Valsecchi, Milan
1983 Chapelle St.-Louis de la Salpetriere, Paris
Chiesa di San Carpoforo, Milan
1984 Galerie Daniel Templon, Paris
Sonnabend Gallery, New York
1985 Studio G7, Bologna, Italy
Galleria Arco d'Alibert, Rome
Brooklyn, Museum, New York
Newport Harbor Art Museum, Newport Beach, California
Maison de la Culture, Grenoble, France
Musée Montelimar, France
1986 Forum Middelburg, Netherlands
Neuberger Museum, Purchase, New York
Villa Pratolino, Italy
Artiste Gallery, Bath, Avon
1988 Sonnabend Gallery, New York
Kunstforum, Städtische Galerie im Lenbachlaus, Munich
Studio G7/Ginevra Grigolo, Bologna
1989 Galerie Daniel Templon, Paris
Wandering Into Memory: Sculpture by Anne and Patrick Poirier, Storm King Art Center, Mountainville, New York (catalog)
Anne & Patrick Poirier: Krypta, Kunstforum München, Munich (catalog)
1990 Galerie Ropac, Salzburg
Galerie Ingrid Dacis, Tubignen
Galleria Valentina Moncada, Rome
1991 Galerie Ropac, Salzburg
Falcony-Oyama Gallery, Tokyo
Galerie Samuel Lallouz, Montreal
Sonnabend Gallery, New York
1992 Galerie Thaddaeus Ropac, Paris
Galleria Massimo Valsecchi, Milan
1993 Studio G7/Ginevra Grigolo, Bologna
Galerie Dany Keller, Munich
Galerie Isy Brachot, Brussels

1994 Bourse, Getty Research Institute, Santa Monica
Cenre d'Art Contemporain, Fréjus
Ex Voto, Caen
1995 Sonnabend Gallery, New York
1996 Ouranopolis, Galerie Thaddeaeus Ropac, Paris
Printemps de Cahors, Cahors
Galerie Ajbel, Kobenhavn
Musée de la Picardie, Amiens
1997 *Fragility,* Sonnabend Gallery, New York (catalog)
Galleria Franca Mancini, Pesaro
Piazza Matteotti, Santa Sofia
Galleria Vero Stoppioni, Santa Sofia
1998 Centre d'Art Contemporaine Synagogue, Trnava, Slovakia
Galerie Andrée Sfeir-Semler-Hambourg, Hamburg
Galerie Thaddaeus Ropac, Paris
Stand Galerie Piltzer, Tefaff, Basel
1999 Musée de l'Elysée, Lausanne, Switzerland

Selected Group Exhibitions:

1970 *Contemporary Art,* French Pavilion, at *Expo 70,* Osaka, Japan
1972 *Grands et Jeunes d'Aujourd'hui,* Grand Palais, Paris
1973 *Biennale de Paris,* Musée d'Art Moderne, Paris
1975 *Memoire d'un Pays Noir,* Palais des Beaux-Arts, Charleroi, Belgium
1976 *Biennale,* Venice (and *Beinnale,* 1980)
1977 *Documenta 6,* Kassel, West Germany
1979 *European Dialogue,* at *Biennale of Sydney,* Art Gallery of New South Wales, Sydney
1982 *Vergangenheit-Gegenwart-Zukunft,* Württembergischer Kunstverein, Stuttgart
1985 *Promenades,* Centre d'Art Contemporain, Geneva
1987 *Avant-Garde in the Eighties,* Los Angeles County Museum of Art
1988 *Classical Myth and Imagery on Contemporary Art,* The Queens Museum, New York
Viaggio in Italia, Communale di Ravenna (catalog)
Vision/Revision, Marlborough Gallery Inc., New York
1989 *Encore: Celebrating Fifty Years,* The Contemporary Art Center, Cincinnati
Soulages: 40 Ans de Peinture, Musée des Beaux-Arts, Nantes (catalog)
Wiener Diwan Sigmund Freud Heute, Museum des 20, Jahrhunderts, Wien
1990 *Team Spirit,* Neuberger Museum, Purchase University, New York (also Cleveland Center for Contemporary Art)
Studio G7, Bologna (catalog)
1991 *So Tell Ich Mir die Liebe Vor,* Galerie Dany Keller, Munich
1992 *Force Sight I,* Schlosse Presteneck, Stuttgart
1993 *The Frozen Leopard,* Galerie Bern Kluser, Munich
Force Sight II, Schlosse Presteneck, Stuttgart
1994 *L'Art et la Ville,* Centre Georges Pompidou, Paris
Anne et Patrick Poirier, Museum Moderner Kunst Stiftung Ludwig, Vienna (catalog)
1995 *Im Haum der Erinnerung,* Galerie Thaddaeus Ropac, Salzburg, Paris (catalog)
1996 *ICH PHOENIX,* Oberhausen Echo, Carousel, New York
1997 *Made in France,* Centre Georges Pompidou, Paris
Biennale du Montenegro, Montenegro
Tuscia Electa 97, Torino (catalog)
1998 *Irresistible Decany,* Getty Research Institute, Los Angeles
Ensemble Moderne, Galerie Ropac, Salzburg, Paris
Produktion der Geschichte, Institute Max Plank, Göttingen

Collections:

Australian National Gallery, Canberra; Centre National d'Art Contemporain, Paris; Israel Museum, Yerushalaim; Musée d'Art Contemporain, Bruxelles; Musée d'Art Contemporain, Montréal; Musée d'Art Moderne de la Ville de Paris; Musée des Beaux-Arts, Montréal; Musée Cantini, Marseille; Musée de Nantes; Museum Ludwig, Aachen; Museum Ludwig, Koblenz; Museum Ludwig, Cologne; Museum Ludwig, Vienna; Museum of Modern Art, Sydney; Museum für Moderne Kunst, Krefeld; Nationalgalerie, Berlin; Neue Galerie, Aachen; Smithsonian Collection of fine Arts, Washington; Solomon R. Guggenheim Museum, New York; The Tate Gallery, London; Kunstverein, Rottweil; Manufacture de Sèvres, Paris; Galerie Eolia, Paris; Art Curial, Paris; Galerie Carousel, New York.

Permanent Installations:

Fattoria di Celle, Pistoia, 1982; Jardin du Musée Picasso, Antibes, 1983; Place du Tonkin 6, Villeurbanne, 1984; Promenade Classique, Alexandria, Virginia, 1985; Giardino di Villa Demidoff, Pratolino, 1986; Les Mas Saint-Anne, Lourmain, 1986; Museo Pecci, Prato, 1988; Joel & Sherry Mallin Collection, Pondrige, New York, 1989; Private Collection, Torino, 1989; Washington Tower, Washington, 1989; Washington Tower, Seattle, 1990; Private Collection, Boca Raton, Florida, 1990; Stadtarchiv-Platz, Munich, 1990; Collection Pierre Farrenbach, Colmar, 1990; Jardin d'Hiver de l'Hotel de Ville, Toronto, 1992; Garten des Museums Ludwig, Koblenz, 1993; Valentine Theatre, Toledo, Ohio, 1999; Pontevedra, Spain, 1999.

Publications:

By the POIRIERS: Books—*A la Memoire de Romulus,* Liège, Belgium 1974; *Les Paysages revolus,* Paris 1975; *Les Réalités incompatibles,* Copenhagen 1975; *Domus aurea,* Brussels and Paris; *Petit a l'usage des voyageurs,* Brussels 1978; *140 Notes around a Round Utopia,* Paris 1979.

On the POIRIERS: Books—*Art en France: Une nouvelle generation* by Jean Clair, Paris 1972; *Anne and Patrick Poirier,* exhibition catalog with texts by Wolfgang Becker and Gunter Metken, Aachen, West Germany 1973; *Spurensicherung* by Gunter Metken, Cologne 1977; *Anne and Patrick Poirier: Domus Aurea-Fascination des Ruines,* exhibition catalog with texts by Gilbert Lascault, Daniel Sallenave, Gunter Metken, Denis Roche and Renaud Camus, Paris 1978; *Anne and Patrick Poirier,* exhibition catalog with texts by Christian Besson and Marie Lapalus, Chalon-sur-Saone, France 1981; *Anne and Patrick Poirier: Lost Arche-types,* exhibition catalog with text by Stuart Morgan, Bath 1986; *Archäologie Zwischen Imagination und Wissenschaft: Anne und Patrick Poirier* by Aleida

Assmann and Bernhard Jussen, Göttingen 1999; *The Third Hand: Collaboration in Art from Conceptualism to Postmodernism* by Charles Green, Minneapolis 2001. **Articles—**''Dynamic Duos'' by Glenn Zorpette in *Art News,* vol. 93, Summer 1994; ''Anne and Patrick Poirier'' by Jude Schwendenwien in *Sculpture* (Washington, D.C.), vol. 15, February 1996; ''Anne & Patrick Poirier'' by Gislind Nabakowski in *Kunstforum International,* no. 146, July/August 1999.

*

The death of Ephialtes

Art is perhaps a privileged way for understanding not only our participation in the society in which we live, but also our roots in the whole human adventure. This understanding is not gained in logical but in purely intuitive fashion. At least that, for our part, is what we look for in our work: the entry into a discourse which would be that of the subconscious, a discourse using a language which would escape the tyranny of Time and the rigid codes of logic.

And it is not by accident that the two most permanent themes in our work are Architecture and Mythology, which, since the beginning, return alternately, echo and complete each other. They are only metaphors, approaches to this Unknown Continent, the subconscious, that we clumsily try to explore with our makeshift means.

For us it is a matter of geographical wandering, of physical drift which conditions and stimulates the mental drift: we journey not only into the site through texts and images, but above all on the site through architecture, ruins and gardens peopled with mythical figures. Without this physical and palpable contact with the actual places we could not truly capture the ''genius loci'' which will stimulate our subsequent work.

Architecture and Archaelogy have often served, since Antiquity, as a metaphor for Memory or an attempt to explain subsonscious phenomena.

We could talk at length about this theme which fills us with enthusiasm and which has guided all our work on Architecture: namely the relation of Archaeology and Architecture with the mental universe. Or, put in another way, the relation of a four dimensional (three dimensions of Space and one dimension of Time) physically perceptible and penetrable world with an imperceptible and physically impenetrable world whose space-time dimensions are of another quality, another essence. And how these spaces intercommunicate by hidden doors which we have to discover.

Another approach to this subconscious universe is by Mythology. Our encounter with mythological figures in Angkor and Rome stimulated our first truly ''archaeological'' work. ''The Gardens of the Villa Medici,'' Rome 1970: 15 casts in Japanese paper, 15 manuscripts, 15 photographs on porcelain. Centre Georges Pompidou, Paris.

Mythological figures, representing the intemporal and permanent in the human psyche, have not ceased to fascinate us and particularly the myth of the Gorgon, directly linked to the idea of the gaze. In 1979 at the Palazzo di Diamanti in Ferrara, we carried out ''La Stanza dello Sguardo,'' where the gaze of 8 identical gorgons meet.

The idea of gigantism also particularly interested us—a work presented at the Villa Romana in Florence consisted of a series of paper casts of giant statues as well as herbaria—and heralded our later work at CELLE, where we tried to produce an episode suggested by the mythological struggle between earthly powers (the giants) and cosmic forces (the gods).

We retained only a few signs of the struggle: the EYE of the giant Ephialtes, modelled on an anonymous sculpture magnified 12 times; Zeus's THUNDERBOLTS and the ARROWS of Heracles, Apollo or artemis buried in the eye.

Time and Nature are called on to play an essential role in this work which remains incomplete without their intervention. If they manage to transform this giant eye, making it resemble one day the tumbled rocks which surround it, they could, however, never change the direction of this regard.

—Anne and Patrick Poirier

* * *

Among the artists whose theme was summarized at the fifth Kassel *Documenta* in 1972 under the designation ''individual mythologies,'' the ''Spurensicherer'' (those who secure a trail/protect vestiges) form a particular group. Within this group Anne and Patrick Poirier occupy a distinguished and exceptional position by virtue of their collaboration and their search for the collective vestiges of culture.

The decisive stimulus for the direction of their work came to these artists during their visit to the Villa Medici in Rome. They realized that while a wealth of evidence from the past was still available in the eternal city, the significance of ruins and archaeological finds was not currently understood and that this required an intervention. Anne and Patrick Poirier made this role of mediator their business. They start from the idea that, in order that it may survive, the connection with the roots of our culture must again be made visible. While they place the present in a parallel relationship to the past, they disassociate themselves in their work from any belief in a progressive artistic avant-garde. The couple start from the assumption that historical development does not occur in linear mode, rather that the past can be placed in parallel to the present. The Poirier's activity consists in demonstrating this connection with specific historical buildings or sites as examples—recording, understanding and making them visible. They employ their own intuition and sensitivity and their artistic abilities and attempt in the union of their creative abilities to increase the potential for understanding and for making visible.

In the collaborative work of this couple there is no strict division of labour. Each partner could carry out the other's activity. The work of the individual first achieves its full effect, however, in combination with that of the other. The work begins with the idea of an archaeological adventure on which they at first embark intuitively. They trace past reality in viewing its monuments, the eventual study of available documents and the restoration of associations with things seen and known. They take photographs, collect fragments, look for plant remains, take casts, prepare plans and inventories. After an intensive investigation of the locality and a mutual exchange of impressions and ideas, there results a deeper understanding of past reality which is now to be made visible once more. In spite of the extreme precision of the work it compares less with an account of scientific research than with an historical novel.

When the joint preparatory works have provided an overall picture, the creative activity of reconstruction begins. Tools, herbariums, plans, casts, implements recreate the historic site in miniature. Artistic creation culminates in the installation when, with the simplest of materials, water and sand, brush and paper, complex thought processes are set in motion and the vision which preceded the work assumes intelligible form. For instance the ruined city of ''Ostia

Antica'' mentioned by Herodotus can be resurrected as a new reality on 40 square metres. At an exhibition the reduced scale allows the spectator a general view which, by virtue of a certain shock effect, should arouse his own associations and awaken those memories already almost lost to modern man. The couple's collaborative work thus brings visible reality to the Domus Aurea (Golden House) has its full effect in that moment when the viewers react to the display and themselves introduce collective reminiscences in relation to Nero's palace. In this way Anne and Patrick Poirier's creation is of artistic significance for the future, both in the originality of the production process and in its metaphysical extensions.

—Dagmar Sinz

POLKE, Sigmar

Nationality: German. **Born:** Oels, Niederschlesien, now Olesnicka, German Democratic Republic, 13 February 1941; moved to West Germany, 1953. **Education:** Studied glass-painting in Dusseldorf-Kaiserswerth, 1959–60; studied painting, under Gerald Hoehme and Karl-Otto Goetz, Staatliche Kunstakademie, Dusseldorf, 1961–67. **Career:** Independent painter, in Dusseldorf, 1967–70, in Willich bei Krefeld, 1971–79, and in Cologne since 1980. Founder, with Konrad Fischer-Lueg and Gerhard Richter, Capitalist Realist painting group, Dusseldorf, 1963. Guest instructor, 1970–71, and professor since 1977, Adakemie der bildenden Kunste, Hamburg. **Awards:** Painting Prize, *Bienal,* Sao Paulo, 1975. **Agents:** Galerie Konrad Fischer, Platanenstrasse 7, Dusseldorf, West Germany; Galerie Toni Gerber, Berne. **Address:** c/o Galerie Toni Gerber, Gerechtigkeitsgasse 74, 3011 Berne, Switzerland; Michael Werner Gallery, 21 E 67th St., New York, New York, 10021–5817.

Individual Exhibitions:

1966 Galerie H, Hannover
Galerie Renée Block, West Berlin
Galerie Alfred Schmela, Dusseldorf
1967 Galerie Heiner Friedrich, Munich
1968 Galerie Renée Block, West Berlin
1969 Galerie Rudolf Zwirner, Cologne
Galerie Renée Block, West Berlin
1970 Galerie Heiner Friedrich, Munich
Galerie Konrad Fischer, Dusseldorf
Kabinett für Aktuelle Kunst, Bremerhaven, West Germany
Galerie Toni Gerber, Bern
Galerie Thomas Borgmann, Cologne
1971 Galerie Michael Werner, Cologne
Galerie Ernst, Hannover
Galerie Konrad Fischer, Dusseldorf
Galerie Toni Gerber, Bern
1972 Galerie Rochus Kowallek, Frankfurt
Galerie Grafikmeyer, Karlsruhe
Goethe-Institut, Amsterdam
Galerie Michael Werner, Cologne
1973 Galerie Konrad Fischer, Dusseldorf
Westfälischer Kunstverein, Münster, West Germany
1974 Galerie Dorothea Loehr, Frankfurt
Galerie Cornels, Baden-Baden, West Germany
Galerie Toni Gerber, Zurich
Galerie Thomas Borgmann, Cologne
Galerie Michael Werner, Cologne
Galerie Rudolf Zwirner, Cologne
Städtische Kunstmuseum, Bonn
Galerie Klein, Bonn
Galerie Springer, West Berlin
1975 Kunsthalle, Kiel
Galerie Michael Werner, Cologne
Galerie Klein, Bonn
1976 *Bilder, Tucher, Objekte,* Kunsthalle, Tübingen
Kunsthalle, Dusseldorf
Stedelijik Van Abbemuseum, Eindhoven, Netherlands
Galerie Toni Gerber, Bern
Rheinisches Landesmuseum, Bonn
1977 Kunstverein, Kassel, West Germany
1978 Halle fur Internationale Neue Kunst, Zurich
1980 Galerie Klein, Bonn
1981 Galerie Toni Gerber, Bern
Galerie Bama, Paris
Galerie Klein, Bonn
1982 Galerie Bama, Paris
Holly Solomon Gallery, New York
1983 Galerie Michael Werner, Cologne
Studio d'Arte Cannaviello, Milan
Galerie Thomas Borgmann, Cologne
1984 Stadtisches Kunstmuseum, Bonn
Galerie Klein, Bonn
Kunsthaus, Zurich
Kunsthalle, Cologne
Marian Goodman Gallery, New York
1985 Mary Boone Gallery, New York
Galerie Schmela, Dusseldorf
Anthony D'Offay Gallery, London
1986 Galerie Thomas Borgmann, Cologne
Mary Boone Gallery, New York
Galerie Klein, Bonn
1987 David Nolan Gallery, New York
1988 *Sigmar Polke: Drawings, Watercolours, Sketchbooks 1962-88,* Stadtisches Kunstmuseum, Bonn (catalog)
1989 *Sigmar Polke: Photographs—Paris 1971,* Galerie Jablonka, Cologne (catalog)
1990 *Sigmar Polke,* San Francisco Museum of Modern Art (traveling retrospective exhibition) (catalog)
Sigmar Polke: Photographs, Staatliche Kunsthalle, Baden-Baden, Germany (catalog)
1991 *Sigmar Polke,* Michael Werner Gallery, New York (catalog)
1992 *Sigmar Polke,* Stedelijk Museum, Amsterdam (catalog)
Sigmar Polke: New Paintings 1992, Stadtisches Museum Abteiberg, Monchengladbach, Germany (catalog)
1994 *Polke,* Musee d'Art Contemporain, Nimes, France (traveled to IVAM Centre del Carme, Valencia) (catalog)
1995 *Sigmar Polke: Join the Dots,* Tate Gallery Liverpool (catalog)
Sigmar Polke: Editions 1966–1995, Walker Art Center, Minneapolis (traveling exhibition) (catalog)

Sigmar Polke: *Gingko.* ©Philadelphia Museum of Art/Corbis.

1996 Museum of Contemporary Art, Los Angeles
Michael Werner Gallery, New York
1999 *Sigmar Polke: Works on Paper 1963–1974,* Museum of Modern Art, New York (traveled to Hamburger Kunsthalle) (catalog)
Michael Werner Gallery, New York

Selected Group Exhibitions:

1963 *Demonstrative Ausstellung,* Kaiserstrasse, Dusseldorf
1965 *Tendenzen,* Städtische Museum, Trier, West Germany
1969 *Konzeption-Conception,* Städtisches Museum Schloss Morsbroich, Leverkusen, West Germany
1970 *New Multiple Art,* Whitechapel Art Gallery, London
1972 *Documenta,* Kassel West Germany (and 1982)
1975 *Bienal,* Sao Paulo
1982 *Vergangenheit-Gegenwart-Zukunft,* Württembergischer Kunstverein, Stuttgart
1987 *Avant-Garde in the Eighties,* Los Angeles County Museum of Art
1988 *Refigured Painting: The German Image 1960–88,* Toledo Museum of Art, Ohio (catalog)
Joseph Beuys, Sigmar Polke, Cy Twombly, Hirschl and Adler Galleries, New York (catalog)
1989 *Departures: Photography 1924–1989,* Hirschl and Adler Modern, New York (catalog)
Art from Koln, Tate Gallery Liverpool (catalog)
1990 *Energies,* Stedelijk Museum, Amsterdam (catalog)
1992 *Head Through the Wall,* Statens Museum for Kunst, Copenhagen (traveling exhibition) (catalog)
1993 *Painting: Emblems and References,* Musee d'Art Contemporain, Bordeaux, France (catalog)
''Other Countries—Other Customs'': Drawings from the Kunstmuseum in Bern, Narodni Galerie, Prague (catalog)
1995 *Femininmasculin: The Sex in Art,* Centre National d'Art et de Culture Georges Pompidou, Paris (catalog)
Signs & Wonders: Niko Pirosmani (1862–1918)—and Recent Art, Kunsthaus Zurich (catalog)
1996 *Speck Collection,* Museum Ludwig, Cologne (catalog)
Gerhard Richter, Sigmar Polke, Arnulf Rainer: The Frieder Burda Collection, Staatliche Kunsthalle Baden-Baden, Germany (catalog)
Beuys and After: Contemporary German Drawings from the Collection, Museum of Modern Art, New York (catalog)
1997 *German Art in Singapore: Contemporary Art from the Collection of the Kunstmuseum Bonn,* Singapore Art Museum (catalog)
Painters and Their Sculpture: From Edgar Degas to Gerhard Richter, Museum Folkwang, Essen, Germany (catalog)

On the Edge: Contemporary Art from the Werner and Elaine Dannheisser Collection, Museum of Modern Art, New York (catalog)
1999 *48th Venice Biennale,* Italy

Collections:

Städtishe Kunstmuseum, Bonn; Kunstmuseum der Stadt, Dusseldorf; Kunsthalle, Tübingen; Landesmuseum, Darmstadt; Museum Boymans-van Beuningen, Rotterdam; Stedelijk Van Abbemuseum, Eindhoven; Centre Georges Pompidou, Paris; Museum of Modern Art, New York.

Publications:

By POLKE: Books—*Hohere Wesen Befelhlen,* West Berlin 1968; *. . . der Ganze Korper Fuhlt Sich Leicht und Mochte Fliegen,* Dusseldorf 1969; *Die Grafik der Kapitalistischen Realismus* with others, edited by René Block, West Berlin 1971; *Bizarre,* Heidelberg 1972; *Original und Falschung,* with Achim Duchow, Münster, West Germany 1973; *Sigmar Polke: Stenoblock 1970,* Bonn 1990; *Sigmar Polke: Illumination,* with Kathy Halbreich and Richard Flood, Minneapolis 1995; *Sigmar Polke: The Three Lies of Painting,* with Hans Belting and others, exhibition catalog, Stuttgart 1997; *Sigmar Polke: Works on Paper 1963–1974,* with Margit Rowell, New York 1999. **Articles—**''Poison is Effective: Painting is Not'' with Bice Curiger in *New Art Examiner,* vol. 18, no. 1, September 1990.

On POLKE: Books—*Pop und die Folgen* by Heinz Ohff, Dusseldorf 1968; *Deutsche Kunst: Eine Neue Generation* by Rolf-Günter Dienst, Cologne 1970; *Noch Kunst: Neuestes aus Deutschen Ateliers,* Dusseldorf 1970; *Bis Heute* by Karin Thomas, Cologne 1970; *Deutsche Kunst der 60er Jahre* by Jürgen Morschel, Munich 1972; *Ducomenta 5: Befragung der Realitat,* exhibition catalog edited by Harald Szeemann and others, Kassel, West Germany 1972; *Six Years: The Dematerialization of the Art Object* by Lucy R. Lippard, New York 1973; *Sigmar Polke: Bilder, Tucher, Objeckte,* exhibition catalog, with texts by Joseph Beuys, Gerhard Richter, F. W. Heubach and Benjamin D. Buchloh, Tübingen 1976; *Vergangenheit-Gegenwart-Zukunft,* exhibition catalog with text by Tilman Osterwold, Stuttgart 1982; *Sigmar Polke: Drawings from the 1960s,* exhibition catalog with text by Prudence Carlson, New York 1987. **Articles—**''Sigmar Polke's Drawings of the 1960s'' by Meyer Raphael Rubinstein in *Arts Magazine,* vol. 62, no. 6, February 1988; ''Addition + Abundance: Sigmar Polke'' by Kenneth Baker in *Artforum,* vol. 29, no. 8, April 1991; ''Polke in America: The Non-Returnable Flounder and the Dime-Store'' by Dave Hickey in *Parkett,* no. 30, December 1991; ''Sigmar Polke: How to Make Gold from Shit'' by Michael Gibbs in *Perspektief,* no. 42, October 1991; ''Clothes Make the Canvas'' by Jean Pierre Criqui in *Artforum,* vol. 33, no. 3, November 1994; ''Poisoning the Sublime'' by Mark Gisbourne in *Tate: The Art Magazine,* no. 5, Spring 1995; ''Polkography'' by Paul Schimmel in *Aperture,* no. 145, Fall 1996; by Suzanne Muchnic in *ARTNews,* Summer 1996; ''Alchemical Researches: The Photoworks of Sigmar Polke'' by Kathleen Howe in *On Paper,* vol. 1, no. 2, November-December 1996; ''When Pictures Vanish: Sigmar Polke'' by Mark Power in *Photo Review,* vol. 20, no. 2, Spring 1997; ''Clairvoyant Memories: The Time of Sigmar Polke'' by David Moos in *Art/Text,* no. 62, August-October 1998; ''Sigmar Polke's Unsavory Mirth'' by Max Kozloff in *Art on Paper,* vol. 3, no. 1, September-October 1998; by Mark Stevens in *New York Magazine,* 12 April 1999; ''Mocker of All Styles: Edgy and Elusive, Germany's Sigmar Polke Flits Through the Image Haze of Consumerist Society'' by Robert Hughes in *Time,* vol. 153, no. 21, 31 May 1999; ''Some Observations on the Early Drawings of Sigmar Polke'' by Martin Hentschel in *Art On Paper,* vol. 3, no. 6, July-August 1999; ''The 10 Best Living Artists'' in *ARTnews,* vol. 98, no. 11, December 1999.

* * *

Sigmar Polke's eclectic and protean output, incisive wit, and enigmatic intelligence have made him one of the most influential painters of recent decades. Having grown up amidst the devastation of postwar East Germany, as a young artist Polke emigrated illegally to study at the Kunstakademie in Dusseldorf from 1961–67, where one of his teachers was Joseph Beuys. Over the past thirty years, without adhering to a single style or theme, Polke has explored the territory between Beuys' spiritualized pathos on the one hand and Warhol's brazen monuments to consumer culture on the other. At different times, and sometimes simultaneously, he has been involved with installations, painting, drawing, collage, and photography, in works that encompass both abstraction and figuration.

While still a student, Polke and others in Dusseldorf produced a series of works in a style which they mockingly termed ''Capitalist Realism.'' Polke's contributions were wry tributes to the fetishes and pleasures of consumerism in a country that still felt the deprivations of the war. In *Plastik-Wannen* (Plastic Tubs), 1964, Polke's banal subject is the plastic washbasins and food containers of a type that was then difficult to obtain in Eastern bloc countries. While sharing its methods, Polke's work from the 1960s diverged from the mechanical self-assurance and seemingly glib optimism of American Pop art. A typical picture might begin at the top of the canvas with Lichtenstein's Benday-dot method, but by the middle of the canvas the dots would begin to disintegrate. The insipid, flatly rendered couple in *Liebespaar II* (Lovers II) from 1965, for example, appears overtaken by a series of random dots and energetic brushstrokes which intrude from one edge of the canvas.

Soon Polke was satirizing artworld sacred cows such as formalism and Conceptual art more directly, in works such as *Higher Powers Command: Paint the Upper Right Corner Black!* of 1969. Reflecting his increased sense of doubt about painting's ability to transmit coherent meaning, Polke's paintings of the early 1970s became layered and appropriative. An important influence for Polke at this time was the idiosyncratic and debased formalism of Francis Picabia's late paintings. *Akt mit Salamandern* (Nude with Salamanders), 1971, employs layers of stenciled overdrawing on a ground of miscellaneous fabrics to underscore the inherent randomness and triteness of the painting's subject matter. Polke's enlarged range of techniques and devices intensified the visual impact and content of his pictures while proffering no readily understood iconography. By the late 1970s Polke's peripatetic use of materials, his throw-away, good-bad drawing style, sardonic humor and deconstructivist wiles appealed to many younger artists, including Americans such as David Salle and Julian Schnabel, who were looking for ways to reinvigorate and legitimize the practice of painting in the wake of Conceptualism.

But Polke's paintings, however abstruse, do not aim at a kind of self-aggrandizing mythology or nihilistic relativism. With a renewed energy that first manifested itself in the early 1980s and has continued into the 1990s, Polke has produced paintings that can be divided into several distinct thematic groups. Some are dominated by what could be called historical themes: prison bars, prison camps, and watch towers, which allude to Germany's Nazi past and the experience of those who lived during its division into East and West. The enormous, looming scale of the *Hochsitz* (Watch tower) series, from the mid-eighties, overwhelms and haunts the viewer, while familiar Polke devices such as fabric grounds with tacky patterns or overlaid drawings derived from mass culture suggest the frightening, mechanized impersonality of fascism and dictatorship, and the social conformity and complicity that permit them to exist.

With their seductive washes of golden ochres and murky blacks, made from substances such as silver bromide, iodine, and chloride, the *Watch tower* paintings point to another body of Polke's recent works, full-scale abstractions made of non-art materials—such as meteor particles or unstable pigments—that allude to both alchemical processes of transformation and the toxic by-products of industry. One series, titled *The Spirits that Lend Strength are Invisible,* consists of experimental works that read as paintings, though they have not been painted in any traditional sense. Enigmatic and ethereal, poisonous and seductive, these works elicit associations with landscape and nature, but are difficult to understand, devoid as they are of compositional focus. The product of seemingly random and mysterious processes, they hover between received notions of abstraction—*form*alism—and formlessness, physical insubstantiality.

In other works Polke confronts history through the use of collaged imagery derived from eighteenth-century prints, many of which refer to the French Revolution, the ideological origins of the modern political era. Works such as *Liberte, Egalite, Fraternite* (Liberty, Egality, Fraternity), 1988, or more obliquely, *Jeux d'enfants* (Children's Games), 1988, recall Goya's famous *Disparates* (Follies) in their nightmarish oscillation between reason and terror, their critique of rationality and enlightenment. More fascinating still are Polke's transparencies, small, double-side paintings on polyester scrim, which contain alchemical diagrams, nineteenth century illustrations and visual jokes, embedded in vaporous, enamel-like layers of color. Images that are readily perceived on one side of a panel are all but buried on the other, drawing the viewer into what Robert Storr has called an irresistible ''game of iconographic hide-and-seek. . . forc[ing] us to see through a glass darkly without hope of redeeming insight.'' (*Art in America,* December 1992).

A final aspect of Polke's recent output is his continued use of fabric and clothing as a collage element or support. *Handtucher* (Hand towels), 1994, consists of small towels sewn together to form a large canvas. One towel is embroidered with Durer's *Hare,* a reference not only to Durer himself, but also to Beuys's famous performance called ''How to Explain Pictures to a Dead Hare.'' With its conflation of the most exalted, spiritualized tendencies in German history and art, its Romantic identification with nature, and the most quotidian but essential domestic activities represented by the dishcloths, Polke plays with the notion of fabric as canvas or support—the arena for creativity, invention and meaning.

Polke's offhand agility, his marriage of the vulgar and debased to the magical and esoteric, his abiding intellectual connection to history and art history, and his refutation of all easy systems of interpretation, both political and aesthetic, make him a maverick of invention—one of the most challenging and important painters working today.

—Updated by Dorothy Valakos

Although Polke was named one of ''Ten Most Important Living Artists'' by *Art News* in December 1999, only his earlier works were seen in any major U.S. museum surveys through the past decade: *Works On Paper: 1963–1974* were exhibited at the Museum of Modern Art in 1999. At MOMA much was made of four enormous works, *The Ride on the Eight of Infinity,* which both in their visionary complexity and scale, could now appear as portent of the work of the past two decades. Smaller exhibitions did focus on selected aspects of Polke's art. The Museum of Contemporary Art in Los Angeles presented his photographs where the artist's feeling for the mundane often with manipulation was omnipresent. And 44 painted works, Lanterna Magica from 1988–94 were displayed at the Walker Art Center, Minneapolis. Here Polke's familiar collaged figuration was seen.

(In private U.S. commercial galleries, however, the work was seen yearly.) Polke in European museums was then in firm contast as—aside from exhibitions in Nimes, Copenhagen, and Edinburgh—German museums mounted an encompassing retrospective. Entitled The *Three Lies of Painting,* the show travelled from Bonn to Berlin.

The overriding nature of the 1990s work, in its dominating technical approach, retained a clear aspect of Polke's long-time visionary yet self-deprecating force. This was through his continuing use of transparent and layered polyester fabric upon which is placed his now two-decade-long play with resins, lacquers, and other synthetic chemical and metallic mixtures to achieve an intensified Jenkins/Frankenthaler romantic and entirely formalist sweep. Yet into such surfaces—and as well, in works on paper—were placed appropriated figuration; now no longer totally Pop-inspired, their sources ranged through history, myth, fairy-tale, and literature, and did include nuance of the current political-social worlds. All such, from an American vantage, appears as continually 1960s' Rauschenberg-variations.

The insertion—very often with Polke's signature ''raster'' dot-patterning—of such imagery, presented the bed-rock obsession of the artist with collagist manipulation. Not only the juxtaposition of the abstract with the apparently mundane seemed to recall Polke's on-going cynical anti-art stance and his ancient Fluxus vein, but such familiar Polke aura also arose from the imagery's on-going obtuse unreadable tantilization.

—Updated by Joshua Kind

POMODORO, Arnaldo

Nationality: Italian. **Born:** Morciano di Romagna, in Montefeltro, 23 June 1926. **Education:** Studied architecture and jewelry-making; mainly self-taught in sculpture. **Career:** Worked as stage-designer and jewelry-maker in Pesaro, 1950–54; thereafter, independent sculptor in Milan; founder-director, with Giorgio Perfetti and his brother Gio Pomodoro, Studio 3P, Pesaro and Milan, 1958. Artist-in-residence, Stanford University, California, 1966–67; guest instructor, University of California, Berkeley, 1968, 1970, and Mills College. Head, Centro TAM, created in collaboration with the Comune of Pietrarubbia, Montefeltro, since 1990. **Awards:** First Prize, *Mostradi di Disegni,* Lodi, 1958; Foreign Ministry Travel Scholarship, Rome, 1959; Premio del Libro *Mostra della Bronzetta,* Padua, 1959; Sculpture Prize, *Biennale d'Arte Triveneta,* Venice, 1959; *Spoleto Festival* Prize, with Garelli, 1960; Sculpture Prize *Bienal,* Sao Paulo, 1963; Gran Premio di Scultura, *Biennale,* Venice, 1964; Sculpture Prize,

Arnaldo Pomodoro: *Sphere within a Sphere,* 1963. ©Arnaldo Pomodoro.

Carnegie International, Pittsburgh, 1967; Graphics Prize, Florence, 1972; Henry Moore Grand Prize, Japan, 1981; Praemium Imperiale, for sculpture, Japan Art Association, 1990; Degree in Letter honoris causa, University of Dublin's Trinity College, 1992; UBU Prize for the set designs of Koltès' ''Nella solitudine dei campi di cotone,'' 1992; honorary degree of Academician, Accademia di Brera, Milan, 1993; Medal of the Cabinet of the Italian Republic, Pio Manzù Foundation of Rimini, 1994; Cavaliere di Gran Croce dell'Ordine ''Al merito della Repubblica Italiana,'' 1996. **Agent:** Studio Marconi, via Tadino 15, 20124 Milan. **Address:** via Vigevano 31, 20144 Milan, Italy.

Selected Individual Exhibitions:

1954 Galleria Numero, Florence
Galleria Montenapoleone, Milan
1955 Galleria dell'Obelisco, Rome
Galleria del Cavallino, Venice
Galleria del Naviglio, Milan (with Gio Pomodoro)
1956 Galleria del Cavallino, Venice (with Gio Pomodoro)
1957 Galleria Bonino, Buenos Aires
Galleria Prisma, Turin
Galleria dell'Obelisco, Rome
1958 Galeria del Naviglio, Milan
Kunstverein, Cologne
Galerie Helios Art, Brussels (with Gio Pomodoro)
Metallreliefs, Galerie 22, Dusseldorf (with Gio Pomodoro)
1959 Galerie International d'Art Contemporain, Paris (with Gio Pomodoro)
Galerie Internationale d'Art Contemporain, Brussels (with Gio Pomodoro)
1961 Palazzo Masimo, Rome
1962 *Recent Sculpture,* Felix Landau Gallery, Los Angeles
Musée de l'Athenée, Geneva
Galerie Internationale d'Art Contemporain, Paris
1963 Palais des Beaux-Arts, Brussels (with Gio Pomodoro)
1965 Kunstverein, Cologne
Galleria Marlborough, Rome
Marlborough-Gerson Gallery, New York
Louisiana Museum, Humlebaek, Denmark
1966 Galleria Del Deposito, Genoa
1968 Marlborough New London Gallery
Galerie Pierre, Stockholm
Studio Marconi, Milan
1969 *Work 1959–1969,* Museum Boymans-van Beuningen, Rotterdam
Kunstverein, Cologne
Galerie Semiha Huber, Zurich
Galleria Marlborough, Rome
1970 University of California at Berkeley (toured the United States)
Galleria La Città, Verona
Fine Arts Gallery, San Diego, California
Portland Art Museum, Oregon
Studio Marconi, Milan
1971 University of Texas at Austin
Wadsworth Atheneum, Hartford, Connecticut
Galleria Quattro Venti, Palermo, Sicily
Immagine della Città di Pesaro, con le Sculture di Arnaldo Pomodoro, Open-air street exhibition, Pesaro, Italy
Un Centesimo di Secondo, Studio Marconi, Milan
1972 Galerie Stangl, Munich
Westend Galerie, Frankfurt
Grosplastiken, Stadttheater, Darmstadt
Galleria Verde, Florence
1973 Galerie Fontana Morose, Geneva
1974 Rotonda della Besana, Milan
1976 Marlborough-Gerson Gallery, New York
1978 Museo de Bellas Artes, Caracas
1984 Musée de la Ville de Paris
1987 Forte di Belvedere, Florence,
1994 Palazzo dei Diamanti, Ferrara,
1995 Hakone Open Air Museum, Japan,
1997 Rocca Malatestiana, Cesena
Museo della Città, Rimini, San Leo
1999 La Llonja and Casal Balaguer, Palma de Mallorca
2000 Reggia of Caserta, New York
Marlborough Gallery and Marlborough Chelsea, New York

Selected Group Exhibitions:

1954 *Triennale,* Milan (and 1957)
1956 *Biennale,* Venice
1958 *10 Contemporary Italian Sculptors,* Museum of Fine Arts, Houston
1959 *Documenta,* Kassel, West Germany
1962 *Schrift und Bild I,* Staatliche Kunsthalle, Baden-Baden, West Germany (travelled to the Stedelijk Museum, Amsterdam)

1963 *Bienal,* Sao Paulo
1968 *Recent Italian Paintings and Sculptures,* Jewish Museum, New York
1971 *New Italian Art 1953–71,* Walker Art Gallery, Liverpool
1972 *Contemporary Italian Sculptors,* Hakone Open-Air Museum, Nihotaira, Japan
1973 *X Quadriennale Nazionale d'Arte, Mostra Storica: Situazione non figurativa in Italia dal 1930,* Rome
12e Biennale voor Beeldhouwkunst, Middelheimpark, Middelheim, Antwerp, Belgium
II Biennale Internazionale de la Petite Sculpture, Budapest, Hungary
Sculptures Italiennes Contemporaines, Musées Royaux d'Art et d'Histoire, Brussels, Belgium
1974 *Forme nel Verde: IV Mostra di Scultura Internazionale,* Villa Chigi, San Quirico d'Orcia, Italy
Contemporary Italian Sculpture, City Museum & Art Gallery, Hong Kong, China
1977 *Arte in Italia: 1960—1977,* Galleria Civica d'Arte Moderna, Torino, Italy
1979 *XIIIa Biennale Internazionale di Grafica,* Ljubljana, Yugoslavia
Artisti Italiani nella XV Biennale di San Paolo del Brasile, Sao Paulo, Brazil
1980 *Fiac '80,* Grand Palais, Paris, France
Biennale d'Alessandria d'Egitto, Alexandria, Egypt
1981 *14a Biennale Internazionale di Grafica,* Ljubljana, Yugoslavia
The 2nd Henry Moore Grand Prize Exhibition, The Hakone Open-Air Museum, Tokyo, Japan
1983 *Esposizione internazionale di medaglie contemporanee,* Palazzo Medici-Riccardi, Firenze, Italy
Vente aux enchères Art Contemporain, Palais des Beaux-Arts, Brussels, Belgium
1984 *Works in Bronze: a Modern Survey,* University Art Gallery, Sonoma State University, Rohnert Park, California (traveled)
1988 *Biennale Svizzera del Gioiello d'Arte Contemporaneo,* Villa Malpensata, Lugano, Switzerland
The World Expo 88 Collection , Padiglione Italiano, World Expo 88, Brisbane, Australia
XLIII Biennale Internazionale d'Arte di Venezia, Sala Personale e Giardini, Venice, Italy
Olympiad of Art, Olympic Park, Seoul, Korea
1989 *XX Biennale Internazionale di Sao Paolo,* Sao Paulo, Brazil
1992 *IIIème Triennale du Bijou,* Musée des Arts Decoratifs, Paris, France
1993 *The Artist and the Book in Twentieth Century Italy,* The Museum of Modern Art, New York, New York
1995 *Europäische Plastik des Informel 1945–1965, Wilhelm Lehmbruck Museum Duisburg,* Duisburg, Germany
Actualité de la sculpture—IV Triennale Européenne de Sculpture, Jardin des Plantes, Paris, France
1996 *Casting: A Contemporary View of an Age-old Art,* Concourse Gallery, San Francisco, California
1997 *Arte a Milano. 1946–1959. Reale, Concreto, Astratto—dal Postcubismo all'Ultimo Naturalismo,* Galleria Credito Valtellinese, Palazzo Sertoli, Sondrio, Italy
1999 *Illuminazioni,* Palazzo Medici Riccardi, Firenze (traveled)
XIII Quadriennale d'Arte di Roma. Proiezioni 2000. Lo Spazio Delle Arti Visive Nella Civiltà Multimediale, Palazzo delle Esposizioni, Rome, Italy
2000 *Miracoli a Milano, 1955/1965,* Artisti, Gallerie, Tendenze, Museo della Permanente, Milan, Italy
Nona Biennale d'Arte Sacra, San Gabriele, Teramo, Italy
Il '900 scolpito da Rodin a Picasso, Museo del Corso, Rome, Italy

Collections:

Columbus Museum of Art, Columbus, Ohio; Cummings Life Science Center, University of Chicago, Chicago, Illinois; Galleria Nazionale d'Arte Moderna, Rome, Italy; Gateway Center, Walnut Creek, California; The Gibson Collection,The State University, College of Arts And Science Potsdam, Postdam, New York; Peggy Guggenheim Collection, Venice, Italy; The Hakone Open-Air Museum, Kanagawa, Japan; Hirshhorn Museum and Sculpture Garden, Washington D.C.; Italian Embassy in Tokyo, Tokyo, Japan; Jacksonville Art Museum, Jacksonville, Florida; Kölner Volkshochschule, Cologne, Germany; Kunsthalle, Darmstadt, Germany; Mount Sinai Hospital, New York, New York; Musée des Beaux-Arts, La Chaux-de-Fonds, Belgium; Musei Vaticani, Cortile della Pigna, The Vatican; Museo Aroldo Bonzagni, Ferrara, Italy; Museo d'Arte Moderna Ca' Pesaro, Venice, Italy; Museo de Bellas Artes, Buenos Aires, Argentina; Museo de Bellas Artes, Caracas, Venezuela; Museo Poldi Pezzoli, Milano, Italy; Museo Rufino Tamayo, Cuidad de Mexico, Mexico; Museum Boymans-Van Beuningen, Rotterdam, The Netherlands; Museum Ludwig, Cologne, Germany; Museum of Fine Arts, Gifu, Japan; Museum of Hiroshima, Hiroshima, Japan; Museum of Modern Art, New York, New York; Museum of Modern Art, Toyama, Japan; National Gallery Of Victoria, Melbourne, Australia.

Publications:

By POMODORO: Articles—''Notes on My Work, 1966'' in *Arnaldo Pomodoro: Work 1959–1969,* exhibition catalog, Rotterdam 1969; ''Correspondence,'' with Tom Freudenheim in *Arnaldo Pomodoro,* exhibition catalog, Berkeley, California 1970; ''Interview'' with Franceso Leonetti in *Arnaldo Pomodoro: Un Centesimo di Secondo,* exhibition catalog, Milan 1971; interview with Sam Hunter in *Arnaldo Pomodoro,* exhibition catalog, Milan 1974; essay in *Arnaldo Pomodoro,* exhibition catalog, New York 1987.

On POMODORO: Books—*Gio e Arnaldo Pomodoro,* exhibition catalog with text by Gio Ponti, Milan 1955; *Gio e Arnaldo Pomodoro,* exhibition catalog with text by Aflonso Gatto, Venice 1956; *Gio e Arnaldo Pomodoro,* exhibition catalog with text by Guido Ballo, Brussels 1958; *Gio e Arnaldo Pomodoro: Metallreliefs,* exhibition folder with text by Guido Ballo, Dusseldorf 1958; *Gio e Arnaldo Pomodoro,* exhibition catalog with texts by Stephane Lupasco, Georges Mathieu, Abraham A. Moles, and Guido Ballo, Paris 1959; *Dalla Poetica del Segno all Presenze Continuita; Arnaldo e Gio Pomodoro* by Guido Ballo, Milan 1962; *Recent Sculpture by Arnaldo Pomodoro,* exhibition catalog with texts by Theodore Roethke and Kynaston McShine, Los Angeles 1962; *Arnaldo Pomodoro/Gio Pomodoro,* exhibition catalog with text by Guilio Carlo Argan, Brussels 1963; *Arnaldo Pomodoro,* exhibition catalog with texts by Francesco Leonetti, Roberto Sanesi, and Umbro Apollonio, Rome 1965; *Arnaldo Pomodoro,* exhibition catalog with text by Frank O'Hara, New York

1965; *Arnaldo Pomodoro,* exhibition pamphlet with text by Nello Ponente, Genoa 1966; *New Italian Art 1953–1971,* exhibition catalog with text by Giovanni Carandente, Liverpool 1971; *Immagine della Citta di Pesaro, con le Sculture di Arnaldo Pomodoro,* exhibition folder, Pesaro 1971; *Arnaldo Pomodoro: Grosplastiken,* exhibition catalog with texts by H. W. Sabais and Bernd Krummel, Darmstadt 1972; *Arnaldo Pomodoro,* exhibition catalog with texts by Gonzalo Castellanos and Giulio Carlo Argan, Caracas 1978; *Arnaldo Pomodoro at the Belvedere Fort,* with texts by Giulio Carlo Argan and Italo Mussa, Florence 1986; *Arnaldo Pomodoro-Francesco Leonetti, L'arte lunga,* Milan 1992; *Arnaldo Pomodoro* by Sam Hunter, Milan 1995; *Arnaldo Pomodoro. Arco-in-cielo,* with text by Luciano Caprile and an introduction by Aldo Moretto, Castellamonte, 1998; *Arnaldo Pomodoro: Sculture per San Leo e per Cagliostro,* with text by Achille Bonito Oliva; unpublished writings by di Paolo Volponi, a conversation between Arnaldo Pomodoro and Francesco Leonetti, 1998.

*

Everything inside a sphere is energy inside a form. That's what drives me to make the spheres: breaking these perfect, magic forms in order to reveal (find, discover) its internal ferment, mysterious and alive, monstrous and yet pure; so I create a discordant tension, a conflict, with the polished shine: a unity composed of incompleteness. With the same act, I free myself of an absolute form. I destroy it. But I also reproduce it.

The sphere is a marvelous object, from the world of magic, wizards, whether it is of crystal or bronze, or full of water; it is also the mother's womb, I think. . . .

—Arnaldo Pomodoro

* * *

Italy, a country of artists and artisans, is almost unique in producing distinguished artists from single families; the brothers Arnaldo and Gio Pomodoro can be compared with the Cascellas, or the two Legnaghi, and many others. Curiously enough this fraternal tradition seems to be particularly strong in sculpture.

Unlike the strict preferences of the Cascellas for natural marble, Arnaldo Pomodoro is a master of bronze casting, working on a gigantic scale with an almost theatrical sense of drama, yet at the same time a meticulous concern for detail. It comes, therefore, as no surprise to learn that, in fact, he started his career as a stage designer and that he has often created remarkable jewelry.

Pomodoro's characteristic forms are either huge spheres or free-standing columns, somewhat phallic they rise from semi-spherical bases. One might assess these two forms as female and male, and incisions, a penetrating hole, or a relief-like, inverted rigid thrusting prongs.

As an artist Pomodoro shares the Italian love for the monumental, as well as a delight in brilliant, decorative materials, plus an openly communicative manner. Pomodoro's work is certainly impressive, beautifully fashioned and cast, assertive and self-assured, positive, demonstrative and entertaining. Stylistically, apart from the interplay of round and upright froms, there are reminders of Fontana in the anxiety to penetrate the outer skin of the sculptures in order to erode the surfaces and to reveal complex inner forms. It is difficult to know whether these bruises and incisions are symbols of violence or tragedy, or of passion, and whether the interior analysis is an anxiety to penetrate life's mystery, or merely to playfully reveal ''the works of the clock,'' so to speak.

One of the problems of Italian artists like Pomodoro, brilliant, gifted, capable of working on a large, public scale, is that the native sense of craftsmanship and wit predominates, often obscuring more serious pretensions. Pomodoro's work does, however, often look like gigantic, charming pieces of jewelry.

—Charles Spencer

POMODORO, Gio

Nationality: Italian. **Born:** Orciano di Pesaro, 17 November 1930. **Education:** Attended school in Pesaro; studied with Professor Caponetto, Instituto Tecnico per Geometria, Pesaro, 1946–51; thereafter, mainly self-taught in art, but influenced by writings by Kafka, Pound, Apollinaire, Eluard, and Auden, and by paintings of Franz Kline. **Military service:** Served in the Italian Army, 1952–53. **Family:** Married Gigloila Gagnoni in 1958; son: Bruto. **Career:** Sculptor and artist in jewelry and graphics; lived in Florence, 1951–52 and 1953–54, and in Milan and Querceta since 1954, when he began to concentrate on architectural sculptures; member with Enrico Baj, Sergio Dangelo, Asger Jorn and others, Arte Nucleare group, Milan, 1954–57. **Awards:** Sculpture prize, *Biennale,* Paris, 1959; David E. Bright Prize, *Biennale,* Venice, 1962. **Agents:** Galleria Fumagalli, Via Giorgio Paglia 28, Bergamo, Italy; Galleria Annunciata, via Manzoni, 46, 20121 Milan, Italy; Emile Veranneman, Kruiseoten, 9770 Belgium. **Address:** via S. Marco 50, 20121 Milan, Italy.

Individual Exhibitions:

1954 Galleria Numero, Florence
1955 Galleria del Cavallino, Venice
Galleria dell'Obelisco, Rome
Galleria del Naviglio, Milan (with Arnaldo Pomodoro)
1956 Galleria del Cavallino, Venice (with Arnaldo Pomodoro)
1957 Galeria Bonino, Buenos Aires
1958 Galerie Helio Art, Brussels (with Arnaldo Pomodoro)
Metallreliefs, Galerie 22, Dusseldorf (with Arnaldo Pomodoro)
1959 Galerie Internationale d'Art Contemporain, Paris (with Arnaldo Pomodoro)
Galerie International d'Art Contemporain, Brussels (with Arnaldo Pomodoro)
1960 Galerie International d'Art Contemporain, Paris
1962 Galleria Blu, Milan, Italy
Musée de l'Athenée, Geneva
1963 Palais des Beaux-Arts, Brussels (with Arnaldo Pomodoro)
1964 Galleria Marlborough, Rome
Galerie Semiha Huber, Zurich
1965 *Opere Grafiche 1957–1964,* Galleria del Naviglio, Milan
Musée des Beaux-Arts, La Chaux de Fonds, Switzerland
Dom Galerie, Cologne
Louisiana Museum, Humblebaek, Denmark
1966 Kunstverein, Wuppertal, West Germany
Galleri a Buffalmacco, Piacenza, Italy
1967 Marlborough-Gerson Gallery, New York
1968 Galerie Rothe, Heidelberg

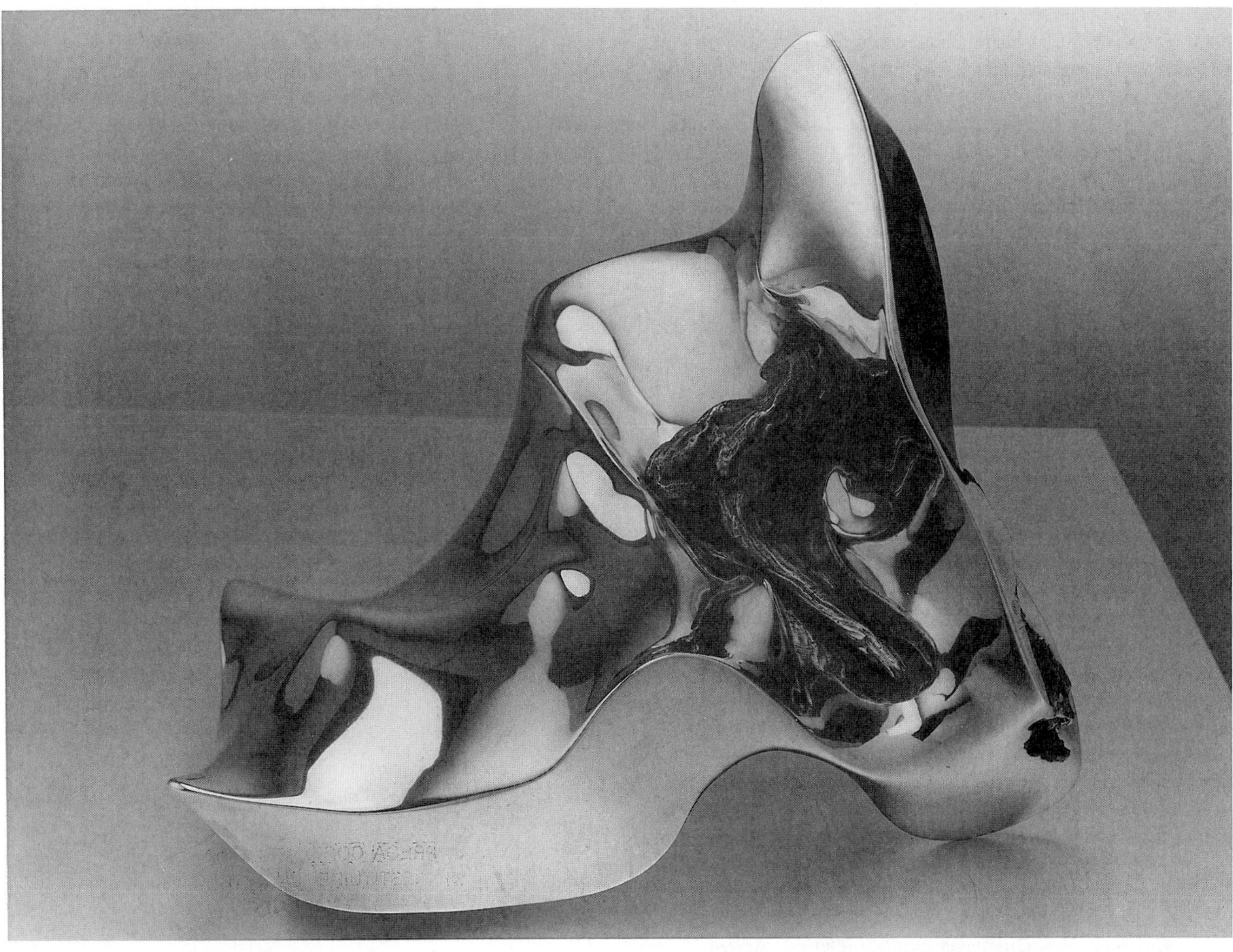

Gio Pomodoro: *Oeriva-Radice,* 1994.

Galleria Martano Due Turin
Galerie de France, Paris
Galleria dell'Ariete, Milan
1969 Galleria La Bussola, Turin
Galerie Pierre, Stockholm
Sculpture, Felix Landau Gallery, Los Angeles
1970 Martha Jackson Gallery, New York
Galleria Blu, Milan
1971 Galerie Francoise Mayer, Brussels
Galleria dell'Ariete, Milan
Martha Jackson Gallery, New York
Galleria L'Uome e l'Arte, Milan
1972 Galleria La Bottega, Ravenna
Galeria Documenta, Sao Paulo
1973 Galleria Il Giorno, Milan
Galleria Forum, Trieste
1974 Galleria Cavour, Milan
Galleria Niccoli, Parma
Galleria del Naviglio, Milan
Sculture dal 1958 at 1974, Pinacoteca, Ravenna
Galerie Farber Brussels
1975 Galleria Lorenzelli, Bergamo, Italy
Galleria La Bottega, Ravenna
Galleria Il Segnapassi, Pesaro, Italy
Galleria Ricerche, Turin
1976 Musée d'Ixelles, Brussels
Opere in Pietra dal 1974 at 1976, Galleria Stendhal, Milan
Sculture in Pietra 1973–1976, Castello dell'Imperatore, Prato, Italy
1977 Museo Ca Pesaro, Venice
1978 Galleria CIAC, Udine, Italy
Galleria 3A, Turin
Arte Incontri, Fara d'Adda, Italy
1979 Kunsthalle-Libreria Fermo di Cavallo, Rome
1980 Galleria San Carlo, Naples
Luogo di Misure 1977–1978, Cassa di Risparmio, Verona
1981 Galleria Fioretto, Padua, Italy
Studio Melotti, Ferrara, Italy
Galleria Farsetti, Focette (Lucca), Italy
1982 *Parete di Misure,* Direzione del Partito Comunista Italiano, Rome
1983 Bank fur Gemeinwirtschaft, Frankfurt
Galleria Il Salotto, Como, Italy

1984 Galleria Stendhal, Milan
1985 Studio Melotti, Ferrara, Italy
Studio Dabbeni, Lugano, Switzerland
Palazzo Civico, Lugano, Switzerland
1986 Circolo Nuova Italsider, Tranto, Italy
Palazzo Ducale, Pesaro, Italy
Veksolund, Copenhagen
1987 Studio Saudino, Viareggio, Italy
Basilica San Ambrogio, Milan
Galleria Denisi Fiorani, Piacenza, Italy
Galleria L'Isola, Rome
1989 Galleria Melotti, Ferrara
Rotonda Della Besana, Milan
Galleria 2RC, Milan
1990 Villa Renatico Martini, Monsummano Terme, Pistoia
1991 Fondazione Veranneman, Kruisoten, Belgium
Centro Comune di Ricerca, Ispra
1992 Galleria Milena Ugolini, Rome
Museo Archeologicao, Milan
1993 Genia Schreiber University Art Gallery, Tel Aviv University, Israel
1994 Galleria Berman 2, Torino
1995 *Gio Pomodoro: Disegni e Sculture,* Galleria Spazia, Bologna
Ornamenti, Fondazione Querini Stampalia, Venice
Gio Pomodoro: Marble and Bronze, Yorkshire Sculpture Park, Wakefield, West Yorkshire, England
Accademia Italiana, London
Segni di Civilizzazione, Galleria S. Rocco, San Remo, Imperia, Italy
1996 *Gio Pomodoro: Sculture a Firenze,* Palazzo Vecchio, Florence, Italy
Gio Pomodoro: Sculture di Granito all'Isola d'Elba, Commune di Marciana e Poggio
Gio Pomodora: Ornamenti, Basilica Inferiore, Arezzo, Italy
Gio Pomodoro: Ornamenti, Tokyo
1997 *Gio Pomodoro: Sculture, Lorenzo Cappellini: Fotografie,* Palazzo del Monte di Pietà, Padua, Italy
1998 *Gio Pomodoro: Pietre e Marmi 1965–1997,* Centro Espositivo St. Benin, Aosta, Italy
Gio Pomodoro: Sculture e Carte 1958–1998, Galleria Fumagalli, Bergamo
Gio Pomodoro: Studi per "Grandi Opere" dal 1954 al 1994, Galleria Berman, Torino
Gio Pomodoro at the Seventh International Cairo Biennale 1998, Opera house, Cairo
1999 *Gio Pomodoro,* Arte Fiera di Bologna, Galleria Fumagalli, Bologna
Gio Pomodoro—Akwarellen, Skulpturen, Juwelen, Stichting Veranneman, Belgium
2000 *Gio Pomodoro,* Comune di Laives
Gio Pomodora: Tensioni e Soli, Museo San Pietro, Colle Val d'Elsa, Siena, Italy

Selected Group Exhibitions:

1966 *Print Biennale,* National Museum of Modern Art, Tokyo
1970 *British Print Biennale,* City Museum and Art Gallery, Bradford, Yorkshire
1974 *Martha Jackson Collection,* Albright-Knox Art Gallery, Buffalo, New York (toured the United States)
1976 *Grafica Sperimentale,* Palazzo Strozzi, Florence
1979 *Gravura Abstracta Italiana,* Fundacao Gulbenkian, Lisbon
1984 *Die Sprache der Geometrie,* Kunstmuseum, Bern
1987 *Ipotesi per un Museo,* Parco di Versiliana, Italy
1989 *Italian Master Sculptors of the XX Century,* Panicali Fine Art, New York
1992 *Presenze D'Art Contemporanea in Italia fra Arte e Natura,* XVIII Triennale di Milan
1994 *Italian Metamorphosis, 1943–1968,* Guggenheim Museum, New York
1995 *Arte Come Luce,* Antico Oratorio della Passione, Basilica di S. Ambrogio, Milan
1996 *Carte di Scultori Italiani,* Galleria Giulia, Rome
1997 *Scultura Astratta a Milano,* Museo d'Arte Moderna Gazoldo Degli Ippoliti, Mantova e Palazzo delle Stelline, Milano
1998 *Sogni di Carta: L'Arte del Disegno in Lombardia 1946–1996,* Sala Napoleonica di Brera, Milan
1999 *Proiezioni 2000: Lo Spazio delle Arti Visive Nella Civiltà Multimediale,* Esposizione Nazionale Quadriennale d'Arte di Roma, Palazzo delle Esposizioni, Rome

Collections:

Galleria Nazionale d'Arte Moderna, Rome; Palais des Beaux-Arts, Brussels; Wilhelm-Lembruck Museum, Duisburg, Germany; Kunstverein, Wuppertal, Germany; Musée des Beaux-Arts, La Chaux de Fonds, Switzerland; Tate Gallery, London; Hirshhorn Museum and Sculpture Garden; Smithsonian Institution, Washington, D.C.

Publications:

By POMODORO: Books—*Per una storia della scultura contemporanea: Gio Pomodoro,* Milan 1987. **Articles**—"Devenir de la Necessité" in *Gio et Arnaldo Pomodoro,* exhibition catalog, Paris 1959; "A Conversation with Gio Pomodoro," with Luce Hoctin in *Gio Pomodoro,* exhibition catalog, Rome 1964; "Interview" in *Borba* (Zagreb), October 1970; "Gio Pomodoro," in *Margutta* (Rome), no. 7/8, 1971; "Conversazione con Gio Pomodoro," with Guido Ballo, in *Gio Pomodoro,* exhibition catalog, Milan 1974; "Note per Isla Negra" in *Gio Pomodoro,* exhibition catalog, Milan 1976; interview, with Guido Ballo, in *Gio Pomodoro: Sculture in pietra 1973–1976,* exhibition catalog, Prato, Italy 1976; "Diritto—Dovere di un Primato Civile" in *Museo d'Arte Sandro Pertini,* 1991.

On POMODORO: Books—*Gio Pomodoro,* exhibition catalog with text by L. Sinisgalli, Rome 1955; *Gio et Arnaldo Pomodoro,* exhibition catalog with text by Guido Ballo, Brussels 1958; *Gio et Arnaldo Pomodoro,* exhibition catalog with texts by Stephane Lupasco, Georges Mathieu, Abraham A. Moles, and Guido Ballo, Paris 1959; *Arnaldo Pomodoro/Gio Pomodoro,* exhibition catalog with text by Giulio Carlo Argan, Brussels 1963; *Gio Pomodoro: Opere Grafiche 1957–1964,* exhibition catalog with text by Guido Ballo, Milan 1965; *Gio Pomodoro,* exhibition catalog with texts by Nello Ponente, Patrice Seylaz, and Michel Tapie, La Chaux de Fonds, Switzerland 1965; *Gio Pomodoro,* exhibition catalog with text by Gunter Aust,

Wuppertal, West Germany 1966; *Sculpture: Gio Pomodoro,* exhibition catalog, Los Angeles 1969; *Gio Pomodoro: Sculture dal 1958 al 1974,* exhibition catalog with texts by Raffaele De Grada and Giulio Guberti, Ravenna 1974; *Gio Pomodoro: Sculture in Pietra 1973–1976,* exhibition catalog with texts by Paolo Fossati and Antonio Del Guercio, Prato, Italy 1978; *Gio Pomodoro: Opere in Pietra dal 1974 al 1976,* exhibition catalog with text by Paolo Fossati, Milan 1976; *Gio Pomodoro: Luogo di Misure 1977/1978,* exhibition catalog with texts by Antoni Del Guercio and Giuseppe Marchiori, Verona 1980; *Gio Pomodoro: Sculture 1968/1981,* exhibition catalog, with text by Carlo L. Ragghianti, Focette, Italy 1981; *Gio Pomodoro: Parete di Misure,* exhibition catalog, with text by Enrico Berlinguer and Antonio Del Guercio, Rome 1982; *Gio Pomodoro: Marmi e Bronzi 1984–87,* exhibition catalog with text by Giovanni Carandente, Rome 1987; *G. Pomodoro, La Scultura e il suo disegono,* exhibition catalog with text by G. Ballo, Milan 1989; *G. Pomodora, luoghi scolpiti fra realta'e utopia,* exhibition catalog with text by C. Zappia, Monsummano Terme, Italy 1990; *Luogo dei 4 punti cardinali,* exhibition catalog, Rome 1991; *Gio Pomodora e Johnson,* exhibition catalog, Milan 1992; *Gio Pomodoro, Sculptures and Drawings,* exhibition catalog with text by M. Omer, Tel Aviv 1993; *The Italian Metamorphosis 1943–1968* by G. Celant, New York 1994; *Disegno e Scultura nell'Arte Italiana del XX Secolo,* exhibition catalog by C. Pirovano, Milan 1994; *L'Arte Resiste Alla Mafia: Omaggio a Falcone e Borsellino,* exhibition catalog, Bologna 1995; *Piazze nell'Architettura Contemporaneo* by P. Favole, Milan 1995; *Gio Pomodoro: Sculture e Carte 1958/1998,* exhibition catalog with text by Marco Meneguzzo, Bergamo 1998; *Gio Pomodoro: Pietre e Marmi 1965–1997,* exhibition catalog, Milan 1998; *Gio Pomodoro at the Seventh International Cairo Biennale 1998,* exhibition catalog, Milan 1998; *Gio Pomodoro,* exhibition catalog with text by Marisa Vescovo and Pier Luigi Siena, Bolzano, Italy 2000; *Gio Pomodoro: Tensioni e Soli, Disegni e Sculture 1959–1999,* exhibition catalog, Siena 2000. **Articles—**''Un Cuore di Pietra per l'Isola di Gio'' by Barbiellini Amidei in *Nazione,* 9 August 1996; ''Lo Zenit di Gio Pomodoro Brilla Sulla Cima del Lago Maggiore'' by F. Cardea in *Arte,* November 1996; ''Sculture da Indossare'' by C. Dubini in *Fascino,* April-June 1997; ''Il Sole di Bronzo, Choc per la Città'' by C. Riconda in *Republica,* 5 September 1997; ''In Studio da Gio Pomodoro: Alla Conquista del Sole'' by P. Gabbri in *Magia di una Terra Splendore di una Città, Firenze Toscana,* September 1997.

* * *

With his elder brother Arnaldo, and Giorgio Perfetti, Gio Pomodoro was one of a remarkable group of artist-jewellers in the early 1950s; the two Pomodoro brothers produced a series of miniature sculptures and experiments from which many of their mature ideas emerged. Whilst the elder Pomodoro went on the produce massive bronze sculptures, monumental in the best Italian manner, yet at the same time basically concerned with the same problems as were examined in the small jewelry, Gio has proved to be rather more quizzical and experimental artist.

He still works as a jeweller, one of the most inventive among a fine group of artists who devote themselves to this pursuit, and who, it should be added, are usefully supported by a long artisan tradition, and an interested public. Gio Pomodoro's concern with space is both more infinite and more diverse than his brother's involvement with global or tower structures. His early works in bronze had a far more tough, visceral character than the smooth, polished forms of his brother; he was clearly not so concerned with interior space as the definition of line and volume. The reliefs were based on undulating masses with internal tensions, vitalized by typical Pomodoro exuberance and assurance, marked by the same Baroque energy and movement as is evident in his brother.

His development has denied a concentration on bronze and a greater concern for rigid and contained forms, as well as a dialectic between solids and fluids. For these reasons he has switched to fibreglass which permits him to obtain a positive outward skin, in the manner of his brother's bronze surfaces, which, without penetration, allows considerable enquiry and registration of a variety of shapes and pressures. The effect is almost that of upholstery, although without the formal programme of furniture.

Pomodoro avoids complacency and decorative order by treating each side of the huge oblong shapes or cubes as separate entities, to be inflated or deflated, inscribed or defaced. The result is more indefinite and subtle than his brother's entertaining bronzes.

—Charles Spencer

POONS, Larry

Nationality: American. **Born:** Ogibuko, Japan, 1 October 1937; moved to United States in 1938. **Education:** New England Conservatory of Music, Boston, 1955–57; Museum of Fine Arts School, Boston, 1959. **Career:** Independent artist, New York, since 1960. Artist-in-residence, Institute of Humanistic Studies, Aspen, Colorado, 1966–67; instructor, Bennington College, Vermont, 1968; visiting instructor, New York Studio School, New York, 1969; instructor, Cooper Union, New York, 1971–72; teacher, Art Students League, New York, 2000—; guest lecturer, Broward Community College, Ball State University, Red Deer College, Alberta, University of Tampa, Florida, Brooklyn College, Union College, and Yale University, from 1979. **Agent:** André Emmerich Gallery, 41 East 57th Street, New York, New York 10022. **Address:** 831 Broadway, New York, New York 10003, U.S.A.

Individual Exhibitions:

1963 Green Gallery, New York
1964 Green Gallery, New York
1965 Green Gallery, New York
1967 Leo Castelli Gallery, New York
1968 Kasmin Gallery, London
Leo Castelli Gallery, New York
1970 Lawrence Rubin Gallery, New York
1971 Lawrence Rubin Gallery, New York
Kasmin Gallery, New York
1972 Lawrence Rubin Gallery, New York
David Mirvish Gallery, Toronto
1973 Lawrence Rubin Gallery, New York
Knoedler Gallery of Contemporary Art, New York
1974 *Recent Paintings,* Edmonton Art Gallery, Alberta
Galerie La Bertesca, Dusseldorf
Knoedler Gallery of Contemporary Art, New York
1975 Ace Gallery, Los Angeles

Galerie André Emmerich, Zurich
Knoedler Gallery of Contemporary Art, New York
1976 David Mirvish Gallery, Toronto
Galerie Daniel Templon, Paris
M. Knoedler Gallery and Co., New York
1977 Ace Gallery, Los Angeles
Watson-de Nagy Gallery, Houston
M. Knoedler and Co., New York
1978 Galerie Ninety-Nine, Bay Harbor Islands, Florida
M. Knoedler and Co., New York
1979 André Emmerich Gallery, New York
Gemälde, America Haus, West Berlin
America Haus, Hannover
1980 Galerie Ulysses, Vienna
Theo Waddington Gallery, Toronto
Hett Gallery, Edmonton, Alberta
1981 Galerie Ninety-Nine, Bay Harbor Islands, Florida
Andre Emmerich Gallery, New York
Gallery One, Toronto
Galerie Artline, The Hague
Museum of Fine Arts, Boston (retrospective)
1982 Andre Emmerich Gallery, New York
Meredith Long and Co., Houston
Gallery One, Toronto
Theo Waddington Gallery, Montreal
1983 Andre Emmerich Gallery, New York
1984 Gallery One, Toronto
1985 Andre Emmerich Gallery, New York
1986 Andre Emmerich Gallery, New York
1988 Andre Emmerich Gallery, New York
1989 Gallery One, Toronto
Gallerie Montaigne, Paris
1990 Helander Gallery, Palm Beach, Florida
Salander-O'Reilly Galleries, New York
1991 Salander-O'Reilly Galleries, New York
Gallery Afinsa, Madrid
Meredith Long & Co., Houston
1992 Salander-O'Reilly Galleries, New York and Berlin
1993 University of Miami, Florida
1994 Frederick Spratt Gallery, San Jose, California
Salander-O'Reilly Galleries, New York
1995 Ruth Bachofner Gallery, Santa Monica, California
Salander-O'Reilly Galleries, New York
1996 Frederick Spratt Gallery, San Jose, California
Salander-O'Reilly Galleries, New York
1997 *Art in Public,* Geneva, Switzerland
Larry Evan/James Willis and Frederick Spratt Gallery, New York
1998 Salander-O'Reilly Galleries, New York
2000 Galeria Metta, Madrid, Spain
Theo Waddington Gallery, Boca Raton, Florida
Perrilla Gallery, Johnstown, New York

Selected Group Exhibitions:

1963 *Formalists,* Washington Gallery of Modern Art, Washington, D.C.
1966 *Systemic Painting,* Guggenheim Museum, New York
1968 *The Art of the Real: USA 1948–68,* Museum of Modern Art, New York (travelled)
1970 *Color and Field 1890–1970,* Albright-Knox Art Gallery Buffalo, New York (travelled to Dayton, Ohio; Cleveland, Ohio)
1972 *Masters of the Sixties,* Edmonton Art Gallery, Alberta (travelled to Winnipeg, Manitoba)
1974 *The Great Decade of American Abstraction: Modernist Art 1960–1970,* Museum of Fine Arts, Houston
1977 *Surface, Edge, and Color,* Whitney Museum, New York
1980 *Aspects of the 70s: Painterly Abstraction,* Brockton Art Museum, Massachusetts
1985 *Pre Postmodern,* St. Lawrence University, Canton, New York
1987 *The Great Decade: American Abstraction Modernist Art 1960–70,* Museum of Fine Arts, Houston
1989 *Before the Field—Paintings from the Sixties,* Daniel Newburg Gallery, New York
1992 *Slow Art,* P.S. 1, Long Island City, New York
1998 *Reflections of Monet,* Museum of Fine Arts, Boston
Four Americans: Frankenthaler, Noland, Olitski, Poons, The Fitzwilliam Museum, Cambridge, England
1999 *The Virginia and Bagley Wright Collection of Modern Art,* Seattle Museum of Art, Washington
The 1960s, Nassau County Museum of Art, Roslyn Harbor, New York
2000 Museum of Fine Arts, Boston

Selected Collections:

Museum of Modern Art, New York; Whitney Museum, New York; American Federation of Art, New York; Metropolitan Museum of Art, New York; Guggenheim Museum, New York; Museum of Fine Art, Boston; Philadelphia Museum of Art; Hirshhorn Museum, Washington, D.C.; Albright-Know Gallery, Buffalo, New York; Museum of Contemporary Art, Los Angeles; Tate Gallery, London; Stedelijk Museum, Eindhoven, Netherlands.

Publications:

By POONS: Article—''An Interview with Larry Poons,'' with Phyllis Tuchman, in *Artforum* (New York), December 1970.

On POONS: Books—*The United States of America VIII,* exhibition catalog by W. Hopps, Sao Paulo 1965; *The Structure of Color,* exhibition catalog by Marcia Tucker, New York 1971; *Larry Poons: Recent Paintings,* exhibition catalog by Terry Fenton, Edmonton, Alberta 1974; *15 Scupltors in Steel Around Bennington 1963–1978,* exhibition catalog by Andre Hudson, North Bennington, Vermont 1978; *A Century of Ceramics in the United States 1878–1978* by Garth Clark and Margie Hughto, New York 1979; *Larry Poons: Gemalde,* exhibition catalog by Terry Fenton, West Berlin 1979; *Color Abstractions: Selections from the Museum of Fine Arts, Boston,* exhibition catalog with an introduction by Kenworth Moffett, Boston 1979; *L'Amérique aux independants,* exhibition catalog, Paris 1980; *Aspects of the 70s: Painterly Abstraction,* exhibition catalog with text by Marilyn Friedman Hoffman, Brockton, Massachusetts 1980; *Larry Poons: Paintings 1971–1981,* exhibition catalog with text by Kenworth Moffett and Terry Fenton, Boston 1981; *Abstraction, Geometry, Painting: Selected Geometric Abstract Paintings in America since 1945* by Michael Auping, New York 1989; *American Art of the 1960s* by Irving Sandler, New York 1989; *Making it New: Essays, Interviews, and Talks* edited by Henry Geldzahler, New York 1994. **Articles—**''Larry Poons'' by Ken Johnson in *Art in America,* September 1990; ''Archaeologist: Larry Poons Reconsidered'' by Archie Rand in *Arts Magazine,* January 1991; ''Color Painting of the 1960s: Dynamic Abstractions by Five American Masters'' by Karen Wilkin in *Architectural Digest,* August 1994; essay by Barry Schwabsky in *Artforum,* September 1994; essay by David Ebony in *Art in America,* January 1997; essay by K. J. Paradis in *Art Criticism,* vol. 14, 1999. **Films—***Manual of Arms,* produced by Hollis Frampton, 1966; *Painters Painting: A Contested History, 1940–1970,* produced by Emile de Antonio and Mitch Tuchman, 1984; *Larry Poons,* ART/New York, 1999.

* * *

Larry Poons' early maturity centered around his educational preparation for a career as composer; his growing sense that he was ''capable of painting,'' which came to him at the 1959 Barnett Newman exhibition (Newman was as well an important personal influence at that time); and Poons' working through, in the late 1950s, a group of geometric-abstract images related to DeStijl and Constructivist style. He would then become well-known in the 1960s with paintings which combined the reductivist novelty of that time—the retinal play of Optical Art and the expansive flat color fields of post-painterly abstraction—with a seemingly modernist visualization of musical form play (akin perhaps to Kupka and Kandinsky). Poons invented an ellipsoidal ('lozenge') shape, itself combining geometric and organic nuance, and displayed it in interacting lines built up upon a non-visible grid formation often called Systemic. Poons' career-long search had come into view: the creation of a design flow that would appear random (he had studied with John Cage), but was in reality calculatedly composed.

From that moment flowed a long progress—and is no doubt still the artist's controlling device—to derive the essential significance of image-making from what is outwardly an improvisatory approach. The elliptical forms became loose-edged towards the close of the 1960s, and from the next decade to the present, Poons has been a virtuoso painterly painter. From the post-painterly evolution, he adopted a pour technique, together with staining, dripping, and canvas folding with all the attendant paint manipulation as well as long dragged brush strokes. And from all of this, he often allowed a thick crust to build up. It was as if the European modernist residue of Bauhaus and Constructivist thought displayed in his earlier hard-edge pictures was displaced by the need to produce a more indigenous and rhapsodic American landscape easily recalling in its synthesis the work of Still and Newman, and more at hand. Jules Olitsky, together with the energy of the abstract-expressionist gestural tradition.

In the matter of technique, the Poons hallmark became the great swinging pour of paint, at first with the onset of the 1970s, with the canvas placed, Pollock-like, on the studio floor; and then within a year to produce the almost scupltural effect of the so-called monochromatic ''Elephant Skin'' paintings. And then, within a year, he began to direct paint-filled buckets onto often gigantic canvases stapled to the studio wall, with the resultant drip pattern controlled and used, in the final state of the picture, both down-and upwards. The great size and unusual rectangular shapes often found in Poons' oeuvre seem to imply both great compositional fascination as well as Romantic ardor, a sense only increased by the at times corruscating density of color and the deep crust formed by the flowing paint. Yet it may be that the overall effect is restrained, and if so, such sensation would arise from the mellifluous, Impressionist pastel hues favored by Poons, and the relatively traditional movement and closure pattern of the formal dispositions. His clearly heroic scale and masterful control of color and surface in his return to painterly abstraction may have led to a lessened critical acceptance of his art, which was dismissed as sentimental and conservative during the 1970s when other standards of achievement and fashion were held foremost in the high art world. Nonetheless Poons' persistence in upholding a warm, yet controlled improvisatory art has outlasted that swing of taste; and now, seen in post-modern light, his painting well suits the eclectic spectrum which can easily embrace both their craft and their mood.

In 1996, Poons left behind his more than 20-year-long—arguably ecstatic—poured and slung painterly idiom. He then entered into what may with some justification be labelled a postmodern rejuvenation through regress. The new works kept the older, often quite large scale and some of the older tactile immediacy and force: but here the overall pictorial effect was pre-1920s Kandinsky, with a touch of funky Nabi-as-synthetic cubist.

Poons' 1960s signature lozenges and dots were once again available in a swirl of landscape reference, but now they are paramecium and freely organic like much of the over-all shape-order which as well included geometric forms, pictograms, musical notations, and illegible words. The work, in its energy and joy, truly evinced ''. . . the exhileration of an artist in the process of reinventing himself,'' wrote David Ebony in *Art in America.* No surprise that in his off hours Poons has taken cross-country motorcycle treks.

At times, as in 1998, a traditional landscape—gravitational surge of sky above and terrain below—was supported by place-name titles, i.e. Utah. During the later 1980s, the artist had already added debris—torn rubber foam, string—to perhaps guide and accent the viscuous pour. But then these poignant references to a reality like Picasso and the actualities within collage were submerged in Poons' then-usual lavish surge of paint. Now, the addition of such surface texture—some bits are even left without paint cover—is like compositional order and surface enhancement. Also equally reminiscent of an earlier modernist decorative intent is the high value and low to medium saturation of the general order of color; this array produces at times an ''. . . offhandedly decorative ugliness,'' noted Barry Schwabsky in *Artforum.* The incorporation of literal motion—so vital to Poons' life and art—is here accentuated by a fairly prevalent and surely self-conscious left-to-right compositional movement across the picture plane.

—Joshua Kind

POSEN, Stephen

Nationality: American. **Born:** St. Louis, Missouri, 27 September 1939. **Education:** Washington University, St. Louis, 1957–62, B.F.A. 1962; studied painting at Yale University, New Haven, Connecticut, 1962–64, M.A. 1964. **Military Service:** Served in the United States Army, 1957–58. **Family:** Married Susan Orzack in 1966; daughter: Alexandra. **Career:** Painter, New York, since 1967. Professor of painting and drawing, Cooper Union, New York, since 1970. **Awards:** Milliken Travel Scholarship, New Haven, 1964; Fullbright Travel Grant, 1964–66; Creative Artists Program Service Grant, New York, 1973; Guggenheim Fellowship, 1986. **Agent:** Jason McCoy Gallery,

19 East 71st Street, New York, New York 10021. **Address:** 115 Spring Street, New York, New York 10013, U.S.A.

Selected Individual Exhibitions:

1969 O.K. Harris Gallery, New York
1970 O.K. Harris Gallery, New York
1971 O.K. Harris Gallery, New York
1974 O.K. Harris Gallery, New York
1978 Robert Miller Gallery, New York
1986 Jason McCoy, New York
1990 Jason McCoy, New York

Selected Group Exhibitions:

1972 *Documenta 5,* Kassel, West Germany
1973 *Realism Now,* New York Cultural Center, New York
1974 *7 Realists,* Yale University Art Gallery, New Haven, Connecticut
New Realism, Art Institute of Chicago
Biennale '74, Tokyo
71st American Exhibition, Art Institute of Chicago
1975 *Trompe l'Oeil,* Taft Museum, Cincinnati, Ohio
1977 *Illusion and Reality,* Australian National Gallery, Canberra (toured Australia)
Malerei und Photographie im Dialog, Kunsthaus, Zurich
8 Contemporary Realists, Pennsylvania Academy of Fine Arts, Philadelphia

Collections:

Chase Manhattan Bank, New York; Museum of Fine Arts, Richmond, Virginia; Pennsylvania Academy of Fine Art, Philadelphia; Guggenheim Museum, New York; J. B. Speed Museum, Louisville, Kentucky.

Publications:

On POSEN: Books—*Radical Realism* by Udo Kultermann, Tübingen, West Germany 1972; *Neue Formen des Realismus* by Peter Sager, Hamburg 1973; *Super Realism,* edited by Gregory Battcock, New York 1975; *Stephen Posen: New Paintings,* exhibition catalog with text by Lauren Sedofsky, New York 1990. **Articles**—''New York Galleries'' by Willis Domingo in *Arts Magazine* (New York), May 1971; ''Neue Formen des Realismus'' by Peter Sager in *Magazin Kunst* (Mainz, West Germany), Winter 1971; ''Rent Is the Only Reality'' by Ivan Karp in *Arts Magazine* (New York), December 1971/January 1972; ''The Art World, Reality Again'' by Harold Rosenberg in *The New Yorker,* February 1972; ''New Wrinkles in Realism'' by John Perreault in the *Village Voice* (New York), March 1974; ''On Art'' by Peter Frank in the *Soho Weekly News* (New York), March 1974; ''Realism: The Fiction Is Enough'' by Hilton Kramer in the *New York Times,* April 1974; ''Posen's Two Paintings a Year Are Well Worth Waiting For'' by John Canaday in the *New York Times,* September 1975; ''Stephen Posen and the Mixed Metaphor'' by Dore Ashton in *Arts Magazine* (New York), November 1978; ''Dialectic in Modernism: The Paintings of Stephen Posen'' by A. Mackie in *Art International* (Lugano, Switzerland), January 1980; review by Ruth Bass in *Art News,* vol. 89, November 1990; review by Gerrit Henry in *Art in America* (New York), vol. 78, no. 9, September 1990.

*

My painting involves the meeting and fluidity of exchange between life, illusion and the demands of the medium.

—Stephen Posen

* * *

Before artistic innovation can be valid, the artist has to confront, and ultimately challenge, past artistic conventions. Imbued with an impressive knowledge of art history, Stephen Posen's paintings exist as modern interpretations of traditional themes. Much of his work speaks with the visual language of his age-old favorites: the spiritual freedom encompassed in a large Rothko canvas; the solidity of reality in Cezanne's still lifes; the spatial structure in a Giotto and Vermeer painting; the sensitivity to paint in a Monet; and the bluntness and honesty in American folk paintings. Yet rather than a cheap facsimile of historic monuments, Posen struggles to use these qualities to produce a painting that is, in his words, ''a state of mind (fluid, structured, expressive, and accessible).''

Posen's ''state of mind'' largely depends on his understanding of reality. Consequently, his work since 1973 has been a study of illusion. He denies the importance of illusionism to his paintings, although he is considered essentially an abstract artist. More than anything his use of the photographic image has pushed him into abstraction. The photograph, taken by an associate under the artist's directions, is enlarged to a one-on-one scale to the eventual painting's size. The photograph allows him to explore the nature of reality and the difference between reality and art. Because photographs designate the picture plane, and thus the space behind and in front of it, his paintings achieve the same equilibrium. This heightened definition of space in his work raises questions about the reality of the photograph in the context of the external world. For Posen it represents a combination of object, document, and space, and thus helps him establish relationships in levels of reality. In this sense, painting to Posen becomes an explanation of reality to himself.

Onto the enlarged photograph Posen superimposes coloured pieces of cloth, stapled to its surface. The coloured cloth either hangs as strips on the surface or covers boxes underneath. The arrangement of the cloth with the context and information of the photograph becomes the ''subject'' of his painting. The success of his work rests on his ability to hold the number of directional movements in the canvas in rhythmic equilibrium. His 1976 piece, ''Variations on a Millstone,'' illustrates Posen's care in creating a balance.

He models the pieces of cloth, the scaffolding, intuitively, after prolonged contemplation. He draws his inspiration from one visual source, the photograph, until a point in the painting where he ''abandons the model and the painting takes over, meaning that it exerts demands formal and expressive which are not visible in the construction itself.'' These details give Posen's work its vital energy; their subtleties demand from the viewer the same degree of contemplation required to create the painting. Posen is asking for involvement in his work on both intellectual and sensory levels. He wants the reality of the painting to help explain reality.

—Carrie Barker

POUSETTE-DART, Richard

Nationality: American. **Born:** St. Paul, Minnesota, 8 June 1916; son of the writer and painter Nathaniel Pousette-Dart. **Education:** Scarborough School, Scarborough-on-Hudson, New York, 1928–35; studied at Bard College, Annandale-on-Hudson, New York, 1936. **Family:** Married Evelyn Gracey in 1946; children: Joanna and Jonathan. **Career:** Full-time painter, New York, since 1940: associated with the Abstract Expressionists and Studio 35, New York. Taught at the New School for Social Research, New York, 1959–61, and the School of Visual Arts, New York, 1965; guest critic, Columbia University, New York, 1968–69; taught at Sarah Lawrence College, Bronxville, New York, 1970–74; professor, Art Students League, New York, 1980–86. **Awards:** Guggenheim Fellowship, 1950; Ford Foundation Grant, 1959; Cornstock Prize, Art Institute of Chicago, 1961; Silver Medal, *Corcoran Biennial,* Washington, D.C., 1965; National Endowment for the Arts Grant, 1967; Distinguished Lifetime Award, Tiffany Foundation, New York, 1981. D.H.L.: Bard College, 1965. **Died:** 25 October 1992.

Individual Exhibitions:

1941 Artists Gallery, New York
1943 Marion Willards Gallery, New York
1945 Marion Willards Gallery, New York
1946 Marion Willards Gallery, New York
1947 Art of This Century Gallery, New York
Howard Putzel Gallery, New York
1948 Betty Parsons Gallery, New York
1949 Betty Parsons Gallery, New York
1950 Betty Parsons Gallery, New York
1951 Betty Parsons Gallery, New York
1953 Betty Parsons Gallery, New York
1955 Betty Parsons Gallery, New York
1958 Betty Parsons Gallery, New York
1959 Betty Parsons Gallery, New York
1960 Betty Parsons Gallery, New York
1961 Betty Parsons Gallery, New York
1963 Whitney Museum, New York
1964 Betty Parsons Gallery, New York
1967 Katonah Art Gallery, Katonah, New York
1969 Museum of Modern Art, New York (toured the United States)
Obelisk Gallery, Boston (toured the United States)
University of Washington, Seattle
1974 Whitney Museum, New York (retrospective)
Andrew Crispo Gallery, New York
1975 Allentown Art Museum, Pennsylvania
Wichita State University, Kansas
1976 Andrew Crispo Gallery, New York
1978 Andrew Crispo Gallery, New York
Arts Club of Chicago
1981 Marisa del Re Gallery, New York
1983 Marisa del Re Gallery, New York
1985 Solomon R. Guggenheim Museum, New York
1986 Marisa del Re Gallery, New York
1987 Metropolitan Museum of Art, New York
1991 *Richard Pousette-Dart: Recent Paintings,* ACA Galleries, New York
1992 Piemonte Dioce, Italy
1997 Metropolitan Museum of Art, New York

Selected Group Exhibitions:

1944 *Abstract Painting and Sculpture in America,* Museum of Modern Art, New York
1949 *Whitney Annual,* New York (and 1951, 1953)
1955 *Young Americans,* Museum of Modern Art, New York
1958 *Nature in Abstraction,* Whitney Museum, New York
1959 *Documenta,* Kessel, West Germany
1961 *The Art of Assemblage,* Museum of Modern Art, New York
1973 *American Art at Mid-Century,* National Gallery of Art, Washington, D.C.
1978 *Abstract Expressionists: Formative Years,* Cornell University, Ithaca, New York
1981 *Decade of Transition 1940–50,* Whitney Museum, New York
1986 *An American Renaissance,* Fort Lauderdale Museum of Art, Florida

Collections:

Museum of Modern Art, New York; Metropolitan Museum of Art, New York; Whitney Museum, New York; Guggenheim Museum, New York; Albright-Knox Art Gallery, Buffalo, New York; Addison Gallery of American Art, Phillips Academy, Andover, Massachusetts; Newark Museum, New Jersey; Philadelphia Museum of Art; Corcoran Gallery of Art, Washington, D.C.; National Collection of Fine Arts, Smithsonian Institution, Washington, D.C.

Publications:

By POUSETTE-DART: Articles--''What Is the Relationship between Religion and Art?'' in *Union Theological Seminary* (New York), 1952; statements in *The New York School: The First Generation—Paintings of the 1940s and 1950s,* exhibition catalog by Maurice Tuchman, Los Angeles, 1965; ''Richard Pousette-Dart: Photographs and Journal Entries'' in *Aperture,* no. 145, Fall 1996.

On POUSETTE-DART: Books—*Richard Pousette-Dart,* exhibition catalog by John Gordon and Lloyd Goodrich, New York 1963; *Richard Pousette-Dart,* exhibition catalog by James K. Marne, New York 1974; *Richard Pousette-Dart: Presences, Black and White 1978–80,* exhibition catalog with essay by Lawrence Campbell, New York 1981; *Richard Pousette-Dart (E Series) 1981–83,* exhibition catalog with essay by Lowery Sims, New York 1983; *Richard Pousette-Dart: Recent Paintings,* exhibition catalog with texts by Robert C. Hobbs and Sam Hunter, New York 1986; *Richard Pousette-Dart* by Joanne Kuebler, Robert Hobbs, Donald B. Kuspit and David A. Miller, Indianapolis 1990; *Richard Pousette-Dart: Recent Paintings,* exhibition catalog, with text by Edward F. Fry, New York 1991; *Richard Pousette-Dart: Paintings from the 40s and 50s,* exhibition catalog, New York 1996. **Articles**—''Inside Nature'' by Thomas B. Hess in *Artnews* (New York), February 1958; ''Richard Pousette-Dart: Transcendental Expressionist'' by Jack Kroll in *Artnews* (New York), April 1961; ''Transcending Shape, Richard Pousette-Dart'' in *Arts Magazine* (New York), November 1974; ''Concerning the Spiritual in Pousette-Dart'' by Carter Ratcliff in *Art in America* (New

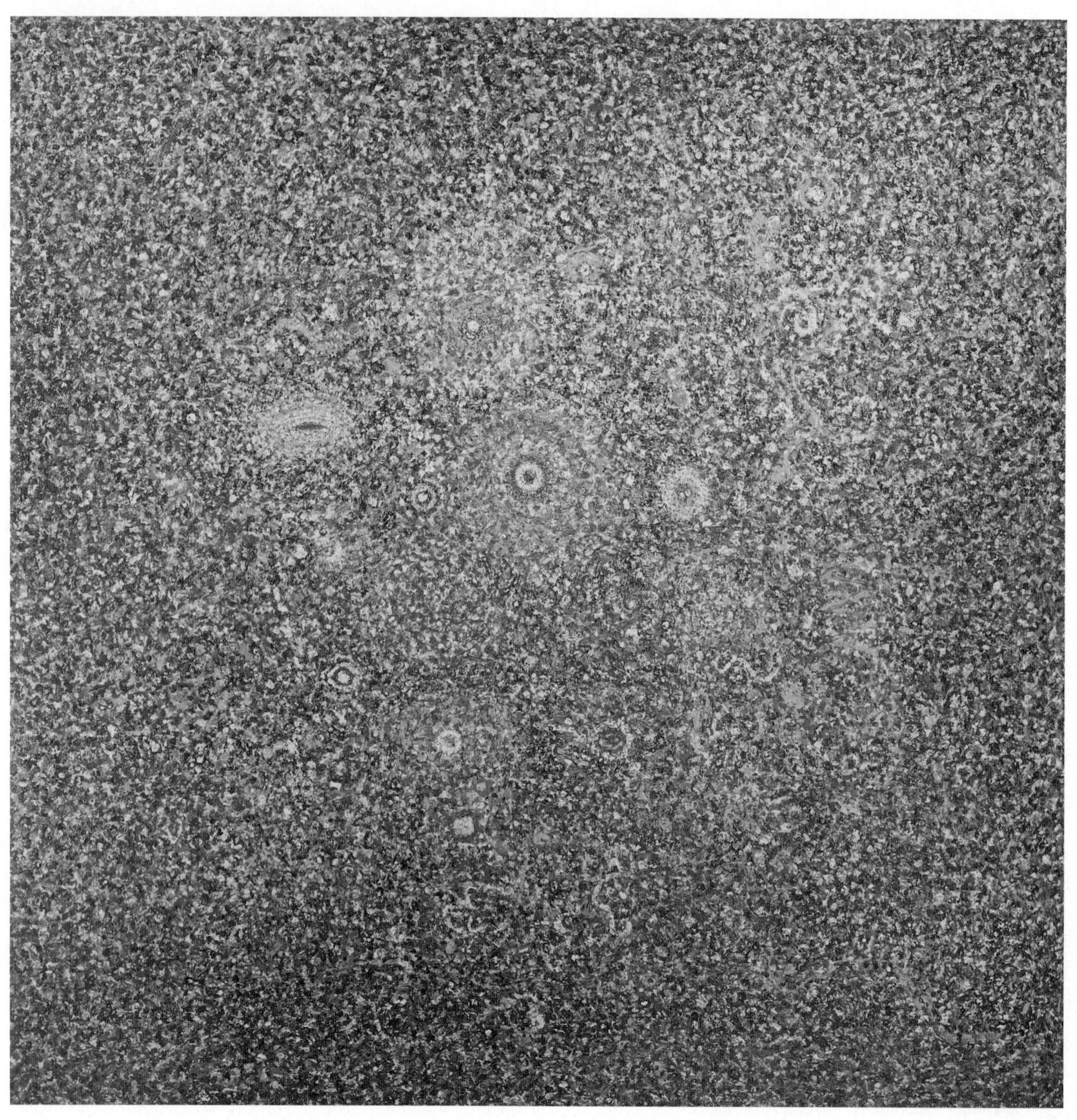

Abstract painting by Richard Pousette-Dart. ©Burstein Collection/Corbis.

York), November/December 1974; ''Richard Pousette-Dart: Expression in Paint'' by Barbara Rose in *Journal of Art,* vol. 4, no. 3, March 1991; ''Richard Pousette-Dart'' by Peter Plagens in *Artforum* (New York), vol. 36, no. 7, March 1998.

* * *

Richard Pousette-Dart began painting around 1939, and by the mid-1940s he had already developed the vocabulary of forms and the scale which is characteristic of may other first generation Abstract Expressionists developing during the same period of time. Perhaps his rapid evolution owes something to the fact that his father was a painter and writer about American art and his mother was a poet, and certainly it owes a lot to Pousette-Dart's involvement with mystical ideas from a youthful age. His sculpture and painted primitivizing heads from the late 1930s and early 1940s connect with Picasso, who was a ''father figure'' to whom most of this generation of American artists had to face up.

The point is that Pousette-Dart was working in his individual and continually developing form in pictures such as ''Symphony Number

1, The Transcendental'' (1942), employing an all-over grid as infrastructure and painting many layers of thick, colored pigments to arrive at a sign language composed of humanoid shapes of multi-referential association. In the works of the mid-1940s, such as ''Comprehension of the Atom, Crucifixion'' (1945), one can still make out some figural references of specific nature, cross and fish here, totemic and densely painted, not unlike the more abstracted signs which continue to appear in various combinations for years to come. These include spirals, circles, lozenges, writing marks, diamonds and rectangles, variously subsumed and peeking through up to 30 or 40 layers of heavily worked paint. Most of Pousette-Dart's pictures of the next two decades are all-over fields, some shimmering with a calmer, more evenly dispersed quality, others peopled with swarms of cell-like shapes which are arrived at and illuminated through his skillful manipulation of color in various states of hue, value and intensity.

Always Pousette-Dart strived for a rhythmic, harmonic balance, a vibrating state in which flickering tension is heightened by the haloing and blending of shapes merging gradually with their surrounding field. It is a meditative art, achieved by a kind of slow automatism and requiring a continuous perception through time to achieve the desired effects. The artist's intention is to communicate a spiritual state evocation of the interrelatedness of the continuum which stretches across time and space.

With pictures such as ''Presence, Red'' (1968–69) and ''Merging Presences'' (1972–73) Pousette-Dart explores the field inhabited by one or two large shapes, most often orbs which achieve their balancing edge in relationship with fields of differing color relationships. His works of the past few years continue this basic format, now limited to black and white for the purpose of setting limits which can free newer possibilities out of purposeful abstinence. There continues to be lots of thickness in the pigment, an element always predominant throughout Pousette-Dart's development. Either one or a balanced repetition of circle, spiral, rectangle are used to create a variety of combinations which would seem impossible within such strict limitations of means. What predominates is a classical, silent, almost eerie calm enlivened by the illumination of black/white light which draws you closer and invites contemplation of the mysteries in universals, both microscopic and galactic. In his fifth decade of Abstract Expressionist painting, Pousette-Dart portrays a vigor and mastery of his means which responds to his intention for mystical meanings with continued commitment.

—Barbara Cavaliere

POZZI, Lucio

Nationality: American. **Born:** Milan, Italy, 29 November 1935; immigrated to the United States in 1962; naturalized, 1972. **Education:** Studied under the sculptor Michael Noble, Milan, 1955–59; also studied architecture, Rome, 1958–59. **Military Service:** Lieutenant in the Italian Cavalry, Montebello Regiment, Rome, 1959–60. **Career:** Art director and designer, Studio Gramma, and design consultant, Architeti Urbanisti Associati, Rome, 1959–62; visiting lecturer in art history, Marlboro College, Vermont, 1969–71; lecturer in art history, 1970–71, and professor of art, 1970–75, Cooper Union, New York; visiting professor of art, Princeton University, New Jersey, 1976; instructor in art, School of Visual Arts, New York, since 1978; visiting professor, University of Arkansas, Little Rock, 1986; senior critic, graduate sculpture department, Yale University, 1990. **Address:** 201 Mulberry Street, New York, New York 10012–4511, U.S.A.

Individual Exhibitions:

1961 Topazia Alliata Gallery, Rome
1962 Topazia Alliata Gallery, Rome
1963 Topazia Alliata Gallery, Rome
1964 New York Six Gallery, New York
1965 20th Century West Galleries Ltd., New York
1971 Galleria dell'Ariete, Milan
1973 Marian Locks Gallery, Philadelphia
Ariete Grafica, Milan
1974 John Weber Gallery, New York
Galleria Forma, Genoa
Clocktower, New York
1975 John Weber Gallery, New York
Galleria Sperone, Turin
Galleria Sperone, Rome
Gallerie Peccolo, Livorno, Italy
Galerie December, Münster, West Germany
Galleria Area, Florence
Galerie Yvon Lambert, Paris
Kazuo Akao Art Agency Co. Ltd., Tokyo
Galerie Art in Progres, Munich
1976 Galerie Yvon Lambert, Paris
Galerie Recontres, Paris
Galerie Aronowitsch, Stockholm
Galleria Francoise Lambert, Milan
Galerie Albert Baronian, Brussels
Fine Arts Building, New York
Julian Pretto Gallery, New York
Galerie Charles Kriwin, Brussels
Rush Rhees Gallery, University of Rochester, New York
1977 Galleria Françoise Lambert, Milan
Institute for Art and Urban Resources, P.S. 1, Queens, New York
Salone Annunciata, Milan
Galerie Marika Malacorda, Geneva
Lucio Pozzi: Works and Ideas 1960–1977, Dartmouth College Art Galleries, Hanover, New Hamsphire
Diego Cortex, New York
1978 John Weber Gallery, New York (2 shows)
Hal Bromm Gallery, New York
Fine Arts Center, C. W. Post College, Greenvale, New York
Marika Malacorda, Basel
Museum of Modern Art, New York
Mario Diacono, Bologna
Kazuo Akao Art Agency Co. Ltd., Tokyo
Julian Pretto Gallery, New York
1979 Galerie Yvon Lambert, Paris
Galerie Albert Baronian, Brussels
Farideh Cadot, Paris
Hal Bromm Gallery, New York (2 shows)
Young Hoffman Gallery, Chicago
1980 Texas Gallery, Houston
P.S. 1, Queens, New York
John Weber Gallery, New York

Lucio Pozzi: *Balm of Gilead,* 2000. Photo by Fred Scruton. ©Lucio Pozzi.

Musée du Parc de la Boverie, Liège
Galleria Francoise Lambert, Milan
Marian Locks Gallery, Philadelphia
Marika Malacorda, Basel
Galerie Albert Baronian, Brussels
Art Gallery, University of Massachusettes, Amherst

1981 Ariete Grafica, Milan
Carol Taylor Art, Dallas
Galleria Peccolo, Livorno, Italy
John Weber Gallery, New York

1982 Kunsthalle, Bielefeld, West Germany
Carol Taylor Art, Dallas
Image Gallery, Stockbridge, Massachusetts

1983 Badischer Kunstverein, Karlsruhe, West Germany

1984 Leo Castelli, Gallery, New York
John Weber Gallery, New York
Susan Caldwell Gallery, New York
Cava Gallery, Philadelphia

1985 Studio Grossetti, Milan
M-13 Gallery, New York
Gerald Just Gallery, Hannover
Gloria Luria Gallery, Bay Harbor Island, Florida
Galerie Liesbeth Lips, Amsterdam

1986 Mario Diacono Gallery, Boston
John Weber Gallery, New York
Jeffrey Linden Gallery, Los Angeles
Studio E, Rome
American Academy, Rome
Galerie Albrecht, Munich

1987 Alice Simsar Gallery, Ann Arbor, Michigan

1988 Pennsylvania State University, Berks
General Electric Headquarters (retrospective), Fairfield, Connecticut

1989 Studio Carlo Grossetti, Milan
George Dalsheimer Gallery, Baltimore
Julian Pretto Gallery, New York
Berland-Hall Gallery, New York

1990 Mario Diacono Gallery, Boston
Roberto Peccolo, Livorno, Italy
Berland-Hall Gallery, New York
Galleri Weinberger, Copenhagen
Michael Walls Gallery, New York

1991 Studio Carlo Grossetti, Milan
Galleria Valentino Turchetto, Milan
University of Maine Museum of Art, Orono
Galerie Albrecht, Munich

1992 Galerie Albrecht, Munich
Penine Hart Gallery, New York
P.S. 1, Queens, New York
Memory Junk, Project #8, Stalke Out of Space, Copenhagen

1993 John Weber Gallery, New York
Grace Borgenicht Gallery, New York
Galerie Sabine Wachters, Brussels

1994 Bill Maynes, New York

1996 *Lucio Pozzi: Rag Rug Paintings,* Penine Hart Gallery, New York
Rag Rug Group, John Weber Gallery, New York
Vertigini Tranquille, Studio Carlo Grossetti, Milan

1997 *Lucio Pozzi,* Pinta, Milan
Motherboard, New York

1998 *Castles in the Air,* Tower 49, New York

1999 *Motherboard,* Robeson Art Gallery, Rutgers University, Newark, New Jersey
4-Color Figures, Bernstein Display, New York

A Thousand Specks of Light, Sergio Tossi Arte Contemporanea, Prato, Italy
Photoworks, Carraini Arte Contemporanea, Mantova, Italy
2000 *Crowd Paintings,* Molino Poirino 1898, Italy

Selected Group Exhibitions:

1965 *New York Six,* Loeb Center, New York University
1975 *Tendances Actuelles de la Nouvelle Peinture Américaine,* Musée d'Art Moderne de la Ville, Paris
1976 *Rooms,* Institute for Art and Urban Resources, P.S. 1, Queens, New York
1977 *Words,* Whitney Museum-Downtown, New York
1979 *Wall Painting,* Museum of Contemporary Art, Chicago
1983 *American Abstract Artist,* University of North Carolina, Greensboro (travelled to University, Alabama)
1985 *Biennale des Friedens,* Kunstverein, Hamburg
1986 *Ultrasurd,* S. L. Simpson Gallery, Toronto
The New Poverty, John Gibson Gallery, New York
1990 *Token Gestures,* Scott Hanson Gallery, New York
1991 *Landschaften,* Galerie Albrecht, Munich
1992 *Childhood: Imitation and Perception,* Henry Street Settlement, Louis Abrams Arts Center, New York
1993 *Mostra di Natale 1993,* Galleria Stefania Miscetti, Rome
1994 *Conjunction 12: New York,* Gallery Korea, New York
1996 *Starting with Flowers,* DC Moore Gallery, New York
1997 *Una Colleccio Particular, Fragments de 1971 a 1996,* Museu D'Art de Girona, Spain
1998 *123: m2, Km, Kg,* PIUMA Arte Moderna, Milan
1999 *Il Libro D'Artista in Italia,* Galleria D'Arte Moderna e Contemporanea, Torino, Italy
2000 *A Selective Survey of Political Art,* John Weber Galery, New York
New Paintings from the ''Crowd'' Group, Galleria Figure, Torino, Italy

Collections:

Museum of Modern Art, New York; Chase Manhattan Bank, New York; University of Massachusetts, Amherst; Kunstmuseum, Basel; Australian National Gallery, Canberra; Art Gallery of Ontario, Toronto; Museum of Contemporary Art, Chicago; Panza Collection, Milan; Vogel Collection, New York; Detroit Institute of Arts.

Publications:

By POZZI: Books—*5 Stories,* New York 1974; *Unwritten,* with David Shapiro, New York 1977; *Hender,* 1978; *Lucio Pozzi,* Mantova, Italy 2000. **Articles—**''Super Realisti USA'' in *Boffiarte* (Turin), March 1972; article in *Art-Rite* (New York), no. 3, 1973; ''Adesso La Pitture Dipinge La Pitture'' in *Bolaffiarte* (Turin), May 1974; ''La Pittura'' in *Europa,* April 1975; ''Il Gruppo 'Level' 1975'' in *Flash Art* (Milan), May 1975; ''Painting Matters'' in *Art-Rite* (New York), Spring 1975; ''Instruction Manual'' in *Tracks* (New York), Fall 1975; ''Max Neuhaus'' in *Data* (Milan), September/October 1975; ''What is Proper Training of the Artist?'' in *American Artist* (New York), March 1976; ''Avangardia USA'' in *Bolaffiarte* (Turin), May/June 1976; ''A Discussion Continued'' in *Central Hall Artist Newsletter* (Port Washington, New York), no. 6, 1976; ''Artist's Books'' in *Art-Rite* (New York), no. 13, 1977; article in *Documenta 6,* exhibition catalog, Kassel, West Germany 1977; article in *Kunst und Media: Materialien zur Documenta 6,* exhibition catalog, Kassel, West Germany 1977; ''Project for a Short Theatrical Action in Three Parts'' in *Premiers Recontres Internationale d'Art Contemporain,* Montreal 1977; ''Fare Ate e un Fatto Politico'' in *Data* (Milan), March/May 1977; ''Burgtheater bei Tag und bei Nacht'' in *Mela* (Florence), Autumn/Winter 1978; ''Eleven Drawings'' in *Whitewalls,* (Chicago), Winter/Spring 1979; ''An Interview with Lucio Pozzi,'' with David Shapiro, in *New York Arts Journal,* no. 15, 1979; statement and interview in ''Lucio Pozzi'' by Thierry de Duve in *Parachute* (Montreal), Spring 1979; ''We Were Four. . .'' in *Mela* (Florence), Autumn/Winter 1979/1980; statement in ''Situation Esthetics: Impermanent Art and the 70s Audience,'' edited by Nancy Foote, in *Artforum* (New York), January 1980; ''A Letter to Peder Bonnier'' in *Artforum* (New York), Summer 1980; ''The When'' in *Whitewalls* (Chicago), Winter 1981; ''475 Years'' in *New Observations* (New York), no. 12, 1983; ''Critical Point'' in *Art Criticism* (Stony Brook, New York), no. 3, 1986. **Films and videotapes—***Plus,* 1974; *Portrait #1,* 1975; *2 Times,* 1975; *Updownleftright #1,* 1975; *A Boetti Suggestion,* 1975; *Portrait #2,* 1975; *Updownleftright #2,* 1975; *Comin from Reading #1, Interview with Lucio Pozzi and Philip Smith,* with Paul Michael Shavelson, 1976; *CEAC,* 1976; *Onetwothreefour,* 1976; *Dialogue,* 1976; *Study for ''Dialogue,''* 1976; *Patchameena,* 1977; *Little Chief,* 1977; *Yesno,* 1978; *Index,* 1978; *Snow,* 1978.

On POZZI: Books—*Due Dimensioni,* Milan 1962; *Tendances actuelles de la nouvelle peinture americaine,* exhibition catalog, Paris 1975; *Photographical Process as Medium,* exhibition catalog, New Brunswick, New Jersy 1976; *New York, New York,* exhibition catalog, Los Angeles 1976; *Rooms,* exhibition catalog, New York 1976; *Collection in Progress: The Collection of Milton Brutten and Helen Herrick,* exhibition catalog, Philadelphia 1977; *Lucio Pozzi: Works and Ideas 1960–1977,* exhibition catalog by Jan Van Der Marck, Hanover, New Hamsphire 1977: *'74 '75 '76 Painting,* exhibition catalog, Bronxville, New York 1977; *Works for the Collection of Dorothy and Herbert Vogel,* exhibition catalog, Ann Arbor, Michigan 1977; *Aphoto,* exhibition catalog, Milan 1977; *Bilder Ohne Bilder,* exhibition catalog, Bonn 1978; *Disseminazione,* exhibition catalog, Varese, Italy 1978; *Lucio Pozzi,* exhibition catalog by Mario Diacono, Bologna 1978; *Words,* exhibition catalog by Isabella Puliafito, Bochum, West Germany 1979; *Wall Painting,* exhibition catalog by Judith Russi Kirschner, Chicago 1979; *Painting in Environment,* exhibition catalog with essays by Renato Barilli and Francesca Alinovi, Milan 1979; *Painting: 5 Views,* exhibition catalog by Nancy Einreinhofer, Wayne, New Jersey 1979; *Abstract Painting, New York City 1981,* exhibition catalog with an introduction by Tiffany Bell, Hempstead, New York 1981; *Lucio Pozzi,* exhibition catalog with texts by David Ebony, David Shapiro and others, Bielefeld 1982; *Lucio Pozzi: Figurative Malerei 1980–1982* by Herbert Heere, Munich 1983; *Lucio Pozzi—From the Particular to the General and Back Again* by Tiffany Bell, Livorno, Italy; *Libri d'Artista in Italia 1960–1998,* exhibition catalog, Torino 1999.

*

I am involved in a continuing investigation of the art of painting, which I consider a most important component of modern culture. The procedures of painting, its language, its speculative and environmental context, its contemplative and emotional content are the matrix of my work. I devote much of my time to painting, but I also continually probe into different dimensions. Materials and situations, other than pigment applied by hand onto static surface, offer me the opportunity of dealing with a variety of perceptual codes.

While developing a logical structure common to all my activities, I regard each as a specific operational methodology, the inherent characteristics of which I reveal and respect. I try to base my work on a systematic, analytical approach so that I may then, in every project, leap beyond the describable, and combine in each piece factors of spontaneous improvisation.

I write about art. I work with words alone, or combined with images. I work with photography. I compose concerts of acoustic situations. I organize performances and make films and videotapes. All the separate activities I have so far brought forward seem at this point to be merging into one single flux, with parts, images and symbols freely interchanging from work to work.

—Lucio Pozzi

PRICE, Kenneth

Nationality: American. **Born:** Los Angeles, California, in 1935. **Education:** Chouinard Art Institute, Los Angeles; Los Angeles County Art Institute; University of Southern California, Los Angeles, B.F.A. 1956; State University of New York at Alfred, M.F.A. 1959. **Awards:** Tamarind Fellowship, Los Angeles, 1968–69; American Academy of Letters and Arts Sculpture Award, 1998. **Address:** c/o Aldis Browne Fine Arts, 1614 Crescent Place, Venice, California 90291, U.S.A.

Individual Exhibitions:

1960 Ferus Gallery, Los Angeles
1961 Ferus Gallery, Los Angeles
1964 Ferus Gallery, Los Angeles
1966 Los Angeles County Museum of Art (with Robert Irwin)
1968 Kasmin Gallery, London
1969 Whitney Museum, New York
Mizuno Gallery, Los Angeles
1970 Gemini G.E.L., Los Angeles
Kasmin Gallery, London
1971 David Whitney Gallery, New York
Mizuno Gallery, Los Angeles
Galerie Neuendorf, Cologne
Galerie Neuendorf, Hamburg
1972 Gemini G.E.L., Los Angeles
1973 Nicholas Wilder Gallery, Los Angeles
Galerie Neuendorf, Hamburg
1974 Willard Gallery, New York
Felicity Samuel Gallery, London
1976 Ronald Greenberg Gallery, St. Louis
James Corcoran Galleries, Los Angeles
1978 Los Angeles County Museum of Art
Gallery of Contemporary Arts, Taos, New Mexico
1979 Willard Gallery, New York
Texas Gallery, Houston
Hansen-Fuller-Goldeen Gallery, San Francisco
1981 James Corcoran Galleries, Los Angeles
Modernism, San Francisco
Betsy Rosenfield Gallery, Chicago
1994 Franklin Parrasch Gallery, New York
Harwood Foundation Museum of the University of New Mexico, Taos
L.A. Louver Gallery, Venice, California
1995 Beaver College Art Gallery, Glenside, Pennsylvania
1996 Franklin Parrasch Gallery, New York
L.A. Louver Gallery, Venice, California
1997 *Ken Price: New Work,* Louver Gallery, Venice, California
L.A. Louver Gallery, Venice, California
Johnson County Community College Gallery of Art, Overland Park, Kansas
Franklin Parrasch Gallery, New York
1998 *Ken Price; New Work,* Franklin Parrasch Gallery, New York
Ken Price: Selected Sketches and Drawings of Early Cups and Geometric Sculptures, Franklin Parrasch Gallery, New York
Ken Price, Sculpture, Hill Gallery, Birmingham, Michigan
1999 *Ken Price, New Work,* James Kelly Contemporary Art, Santa Fe, New Mexico
Ken Price, New Work, L.A. Louver Gallery, Venice, California

Selected Group Exhibitions:

1962 *50 California Artists,* Whitney Museum, New York
1963 *Sculpture of California,* Oakland Art Museum, California
1966 *10 from Los Angeles,* Seattle Art Museum
1967 *American Sculpture of the 60s,* Los Angeles County Museum of Art
1971 *Gemini: Technics and Creativity,* Museum of Modern Art, New York
1975 *Sculpture: American Directions 1945–75,* National Collection of Fine Arts, Washington, D.C.
1976 *30 Years of American Printmaking,* Brooklyn Museum, New York
200 Years of American Sculpture, Whitney Museum, New York
1979 *A Century of Ceramics in the U.S. 1878–1978,* Everson Museum of Art, Syracuse, New York
Whitney Biennial, Whitney Museum, New York
1991 *Selections from the Permanent Collection,* Museum of Contemporary Art, Los Angeles
Shiugaraki Museum of Ceramic Art, Shigaraki, Japan
1993 *Contemporary Craft in the Saxe Collection,* Toledo Museum of Art, Toledo, Ohio
5 x 7, New York State College of Ceramics at Alfred University, Alfred, New York
1997 *Sunshine and Noir,* Louisiana Museum, Louisiana, Denmark
Abstract Expressionist Ceramics: Myth and Reality Revisited, Garth Clark Gallery, New York
1998 *Sunshine and Noir: Art in L.A. 1960–1997,* U.C.L.A./ Hammer Museum, Westwood
American Academy Invitational Exhibition of Paintings and Sculpture, American Academy of Letters and Arts, New York

The Edward R. Broida Collection: A Selection of Works, Orlando Museum of Art, Florida

Collections:

Museum of Modern Art, New York; Whitney Museum, New York; Hirshhorn Museum and Sculpture Garden, Smithsonian Institution, Washington, D.C.; Art Institute of Chicago; San Francisco Museum of Art; Los Angeles County Museum of Art; Norton Simon Museum of Art, Pasadena, California; Victoria and Albert Museum, London; Stedelijk Van Abbemuseum, Eindhoven, Netherlands.

Publications:

On PRICE: Books—*American Ceramics 1876 to the Present* by Garth Clark, New York 1987; *The History of American Ceramics 1607 to the Present* by Elaine Levin, New York 1988; *Ken Price* by Walter Hopps and Edward Lebow, Minneapolis, Minnesota 1992; *Ken Price, 5 x 7,* exhibition catalog, Alfred, New York 1993; *Contemporary Crafts and the Saxe Collection,* exhibition catalog, Toledo, Ohio 1993; *Revolution in Clay: The Marer Collection of Contemporary Ceramics,* exhibition catalog, Claremont, California 1994; *Ken Price: Career Survey* by Carter Ratcliff, Glenside, Pennsylvania 1995; *Ken Price,* exhibition catalog, New York 1997. **Articles—**''Painting and Sculpture: The Los Angeles Scene'' by Jules Langsner in *Craft Horizon* (New York), July/August 1962; ''Sculpture in California'' by John Coplans in *Artforum* (San Francisco), August 1962; ''Kenneth Price'' by Henry T. Hopkins in *Artforum* (San Francisco), August 1963; ''Out of Clay'' by John Coplans in *Art in America* (New York), December 1963; ''The Sculpture of Kenneth Price'' by John Coplans in *Art International* (Lugano, Switzerland), March 1964; ''Specific Objects'' by Donald Judd in *Arts Yearbook,* New York 1965; ''London: Stop Press-Nature Survives'' by Simon Watson Taylor in *Art and Artists* (London), March 1968; ''Two Good Deeds'' by Bryan Robertson in *The Spectator* (London), May 1968; ''Kenneth Price'' by Jim Crumrine in *Craft Horizons* (New York), November/December 1969; ''London Letter'' by Bernard Benvir in *Art International* (Lugano, Switzerland), March 1970; ''London'' by David Russell in *Arts Magazine,* (New York), October 1970; ''Los Angeles'' by Peter Plagens in *Artforum* (New York), October 1970; ''The Revival of Prints'' by Robert Hughes in *Time* (New York), January 1971; ''Art'' by Thomas Hess in *New York Magazine,* December 1974; ''Kenneth Price—Willard'' by Judith Tannenbaum in *Arts Magazine* (New York), February 1975; ''Kenneth Price at Willard'' in *Art in America* (New York), May/June 1975; ''The Faberge of Funk'' by Robert Hughes in *Time,* 13 April 1992; ''Ken Price in Retrospect'' by Robert Silberman in *American Craft,* August/September 1992; ''Earthly Objects'' by Frances Colpitt in *Art in America,* February 1993; ''The Most Beautiful Show in Town,'' by Peter Schjeldahl in *Village Voice,* 17 May 1995; ''Challenging the Conventions of Art and Craft'' by Edward J. Sozanski in *Philadelphia Inquirer,* 17 November 1995; ''Ken Price's L.A. Edge'' by Peter Schjeldahl in *Art Issues,* No. 48, Summer 1997; ''Ken Price: Mutable Materials'' by Kathleen Whitney in *Sculpture,* September 1997; ''Ken Price'' by Michael Duncan in *Art in America,* November 1997; ''Ken Price, La Louver'' by Clayton Campbell in *Flash Art,* March/April 1998; ''Ken Price'' by Suzanne Muchnic in *Art in America,* February 1998; ''Ken Price, La Louver'' by Christopher Miles in *Artforum,* September 1999; ''Ken Price, La Louver, Los Angeles'' by Michael Darling in *Frieze,* no. 148, September/October 1999.

* * *

The dominant characteristic of post-war American art has been a search for significance, or to be more precise, Significance. To many American artists, European art seemed too modest in its methods; a small canvas, however radical its contents, could easily be lost in the Huge and complicated arena of contemporary life; chamber music drowned by the roar of traffic.

To achieve the sensation of Significance, painters and sculptors employed scale, forcing the viewer to concentrate upon the work to the exclusion of all else. Blasted by the visual equivalent of a 400,000 amp sound system it was impossible not to notice the things, to look willy-nilly for meaning. Although the technique of scale was first used in the era by Abstract Expressionists it was taken over by the successors. Pop artists, while rejecting all other tenets of Expressionism retained the scale, as did Op and Minimal artists, while the tendency reached its apotheosis in Land Art. Whatever else could be overthrown, Significance was fundamental.

The art of Kenneth Price and other West Coast artists is a direct challenge upon this orthodoxy. His work is deliberately unsignificant (the common negative, insignificant, means something quite different) and one of its most typical qualities is a throw-away nonchalance. Price made his name with works in ceramic, the choice of material being crucial. There is no limit to the scale on which one can use wood, steel, fiberglass or earth, but ceramic needs a kiln and kilns can never be very large. In addition, ceramic is traditionally used either for small ornaments or functional objects, both concepts which would be anathema to the Great American Artist in his search for unsullied Significance. As a result Price's work was first greeted with hostile bewilderment.

Which is not surprising. A generation gorged on vast washes of colour, or monolithic wedges of orange steel, was suddenly faced with a room of small ceramic CUPS. Some of them were adorned with animals (frogs usually), and other motifs, and none of them could be called beautiful in a traditional sort of way. In fact, some of them were downright ugly.

Many ''admirers'' of Price have tried to pretend that his work still adheres to the traditionally American values; thus Maurice Tuchman refers to ''a significant movement in the use of ceramics as a major sculptural medium'' and goes on to suggest that the ''minorness'' of Price's work is an illusion. In fact, Price's work is an attempt to exclude such terminology from art, and to make work which cannot really be discussed at all.

Indeed there is not much one can say about small, greyish green turds of ceramic, the style of his more recent works. Even his cups defy much interpretation; they are there and that is that. To wax eloquent about his ''painterly'' use of colour is to wrap the shroud of dead terminology around his living work, and, anyway, those who do so are made ridiculous by his very unpainterly paintings. There is no useful interpretation possible.

This is a negative virtue, albeit one of fundamental importance in an age when art is threatened by a tidal-wave of logorrhoea. The discovery of the positive virtues must be left to the individual when he sees the actual work, an event for which words can never be a substitute. Speaking personally, I found that, on first acquaintance, Price's work irritated and even repelled me, seeming to be a blind alley in the triumphant march of American art towards, well I was never quite sure what it was towards, but the band played and the crowds cheered and I felt sure it must be going somewhere. Now, when all we have left is the confetti on the streets, Price's back road looks more and more promising.

But don't ask me why. . . .

—Alastair Mackintosh

PROCH, Don

Nationality: Canadian. **Born:** Hamilton, Ontario, 1944. **Education:** University of Manitoba, B.F.A., B.Ed., 1966. **Career:** Independent artist since 1970. **Awards:** Purchase Award, *Twelfth Winnipeg Biennial,* 1970; Canada Council Grants, 1972–75; Manitoba Arts Council Senior Grants, 1975–76, 1976–77, 1980, 1985–86; Canada Council Visual Arts Grant A, 1987–88. **Agent:** Douglas Udell Gallery, 10332 124 St. NW, Edmonton T5N 1R2, Alberta, Canada; Douglas Udell Gallery, 1558 West 6th Avenue, Vancouver, British Columbia, Canada.

Selected Individual Exhibitions:

1972 Winnipeg Art Gallery
1975 Winnipeg Art Gallery
1977 Musée d'Art Contemporain, Montreal (travelled to Windsor, Ontario, and Lethbridge, Alberta)
1988 *Grainscapes,* Ukrainian Cultural and Education Centre, Winnipeg

Selected Group Exhibitions:

1971 *Winnipeg Biennial,* Winnipeg Art Gallery
1973 *Canada Trajectoires,* Musée d'Art Moderne de la Ville, Paris
1975 *Changing Visions,* Edmonton Art Gallery and Art Gallery of Ontario
1979 *Contemporary Canadian Prints,* National Gallery of Canada, Ottawa
1984 *Manitoba Artists Overseas/Artists Manitobain Outremer,* Canada House, London (travelled to Brussels and Paris)
1985 *Chicago International Art Exposition*
1986 *Los Angeles International Art Exposition*
1987 *True North, Far West,* University of the Pacific Gallery, Stockton, California
1988 *True North, Far West,* San Francisco State University
1998 *2D by 3D,* Ukrainian Institute of Modern Art, Chicago

Collections:

Art Gallery of Ontario, Toronto; Glenbow Museum, Calgary; National Gallery of Canada, Ottawa; Vancouver Art Gallery; Winnipeg Art Gallery; Bell Canada Collection; Royal Bank of Canada.

Publications:

On PROCH: Books—*Don Proch,* exhibition catalog, Windsor, Ontario, 1977; *Modern Painting in Canada* by Terry Fenton and Karen Wilkin, Edmonton 1978; *Manitoba Artists Overseas/Artists Manitobain Outremer,* exhibition catalog, Manitoba, 1984; *Discovering Canadian Art: Learning the Language,* Toronto, 1984; *The Best Contemporary Canadian Art* by Joan Murray, Edmonton 1987. **Articles—** ''Prairie Space Drawings'' by Philip Fry in *artscanada,* early autumn 1972; ''The Grand Western Canadian Screen Shop'' by Sarah Yates in *artmagazine,* March/April 1977; ''The Magic Masks of Asessippi'' by Adele Freeman in *Saturday Night,* January/February 1977; ''Asessippi Everywhere'' by Kenneth Hughes in *Canadian Dimension,* August/September 1978; ''Pluralities 1980'' in *ARTnews,* November 1980; ''Masking and Mapping the Prairie Landscape'' by Patricia Vervoort in *British Journal of Canadian Studies,* vol. 6, no. 1, 1991. **Films—***Don Proch: The Spirit of Assessippi* by Patrick Friesen, 1985.

PROCKTOR, Patrick

Nationality: British. **Born:** Dublin, 12 March 1936. **Education:** London primary schools; studied Russian at London University, 1954–56; studied at the Slade School of Fine Art, London, under John Aldridge, Frank Auerbach, Keith Vaughan, Claude Rogers, Reg Butler, William Townsend, William Coldstream and Richard Beer, 1958–62. **Military Service:** Served as a sub-lieutenant, Royal Navy, in Combined Services School for Linguists, Cornwall, London and Fife, Scotland, 1954–56. **Family:** Married Kirsten Bo Andersen in 1973 (died, 1984); son: Nicholas Bo. **Career:** Independent painter, since 1963. Worked as apprentice builder's merchant, London, 1952–54; as Russian interpreter, British Council Russia and the United Kingdom, 1956–61; as omelette chef, Academy Restaurant, London, 1956; as clerk, Thomas Cook Travel Bureau, London, 1956; as art therapist, Fulham Western Hospital, London, 1960–63; as art broadcaster, BBC Russian Service, London, 1960–65; as Russian interpreter, San Francisco-Moscow Peace March, 1961; as fashion model, London, 1968; as set and costume designer for *Bed Bug* by Mayakowsky, London University, 1960; as set designer for *Saint's Day* by John Whiting, Theatre Royal Stratford, London University, 1960; as set designer for *Cage of God* ballet, Sadlers Wells Theatre, London 1967; designed decor, British Pavilion, *Expo '67,* Montreal; set and costume designer for *Twelfth Night,* 1968, and *Total Eclipse,* Royal Court Theatre, London 1969; designed background, *The Greatest Show on Earth,* Coliseum, London, 1972. Lecturer, Camberwell School of Art, London, 1962–67, and Maidstone College of Art, Kent, 1962–67; color consultant (sculpture), 1965–67, and lecturer in painting, 1968–72, Royal College of Art, London. **Awards:** Murray Landscape Scholarship, Royal Academy of Art, London, 1959 and 1961; Abbey Minor Travelling Scholarship, 1962. Honorary Member, Royal Watercolour Society, London, 1978; The Watercolour Foundation Award, 1989; Prizewinner, The Singer & Friedlander/ Sunday Times Watercolour Competition, 1991. **Agent:** c/o Redfern Gallery, 20 Cork Street, London W1X 2Hl, England.

Individual Exhibitions:

1963 Redfern Gallery, London
1965 Redfern Gallery, London
1967 Redfern Gallery, London
1968 Redfern Gallery, London

Lee Nordness Gallery, New York
1969 Redfern Gallery, London
Alecto Gallery, London
Alecto Gallery, New York
1970 Clare College, Cambridge
Alecto Gallery, London
Alecto Gallery, New York
1971 Studio la Città, Verona
1972 Galleria del Cavallino, Venice
Galleria di Piazza Galvani, Bologna
Galleria l'Approdo, Turin
Redfern Gallery, London
1973 Galleria Henze, Campione d'Italia, Switzerland
Salisbury Festival, Wiltshire
1974 Redfern Gallery, London
Galleria Tinoghelfi, Vincena, Italy
Gallery 101, Johannesburg (toured South Africa)
1975 Rochadale Art Gallery, Lancashire
1976 Redfern Gallery, London
Galerie Biedermann, Munich
Alecto Gallery, London
1977 Galleria l'Approdo, Turin
Galleria del Cavallino, Venice
Bohun Gallery, Henley-on-Thames, Oxfordshire
1978 Redfern Gallery, London
Galleria del Cavallino, Venice
1979 *Salisbury Festival,* Wiltshire
1980 Redfern Gallery, London
Galleria del Cavallino, Venice
1981 David Paul Gallery, Chichester, Sussex
Kornblee Gallery, New York
Bohun Gallery, Henley-on-Thames, Oxfordshire
1982 Redfern Gallery, London
1983 Gimpel-Weitzenhoeffer Gallery, New York
1985 Redfern Gallery, London
Galleria del Cavallino, Venice
Birmingham Museum and Art Gallery, Warwickshire
1986 Galerie Beidermann, Munich
Patrick Procktor, at the *Henley Festival,* Oxfordshire
1987 IAM Galerie, Lisbon
Redfern Gallery, London
1989 Galerie Biedermann, Munich
Welsh Art Council Tour of Great Britain
1990 Galleria Ghelfi, Venice
1991 Galerie Coard, Paris
Le Style Japonais: Recent Oils, Watercolours and Prints, Redfern Gallery, London
1992 Tokyo Art Fair, Galerie Enatsu, Japan
Galerie Biedermann, Munich
1993 LeCadre Gallery, Hong Kong
1994 *Recent Paintings and Drawings and Paintings from the 1960s to 1980s,* Redfern Gallery, London
CCA Galleries, Cambridge
1995 Rye Art Gallery, Rye, East Sussex
1996 *A 60th Birthday Tribute to Patrick Procktor,* Redfern Gallery, London
1997 Redfern Gallery, London
Patrick Procktor: Four Decades of Printmaking, Scolar Fine Art, London
1998 Galerie Biedermann, Munich

Selected Group Exhibitions:

1957 *Group Exhibition,* Redfern Gallery, London
1959 *Young Contemporaries,* London
1962 *The London Group,* RBA Gallery, London
1964 *New Generation,* Whitechapel Art Gallery, London
1965 *Jeune Peinture Anglaise,* Galerie Motte, Geneva
1967 *International Exhibition,* Darmstadt
1969 *Tempo dell'Immagine,* Bologna
1971 *Critic's Choice,* Arthur Tooth and Son, London
1977 *British Painting 1952–1977,* Royal Academy of Art, London

Collections:

Arts Council of Great Britain, London; Contemporary Art Society; Imperial War Museum, London; Leicestershire Education Authority; Los Angeles County Museum; Metropolitan Museum of Art, New York; National Gallery of Victoria, Melbourne; New College, Oxford; Sao Paulo Museum of Art, Brazil; Tate Gallery, London; The Old Jail Art Center, Albany, Texas; University of Leeds; Whitworth Art Gallery, Manchester.

Publications:

By PROCKTOR: Books and portfolios—*One Window,* Venice 1974; *Venice Suite* aquatints, London 1977; *China Suite,* aquatints, London 1980; *Chateau de Bordeaux,* aquatints, London 1986; *Patrick Procktor Paintings, 1959–1989,* Newtown 1989; *Autobiography: Self Portrait,* London 1991; *Patrick Procktor,* with John McEwen, London 1997. **Article—**"Why Do I Paint?" in *New Society* (London), May 1963; "Do What You Like: Interview with Joe Studholme of Editions Alecto and Artist Patrick Procktor" with Cathy Courtney in *Art Monthly,* no. 195, April 1996; interview with Virginia Boston in *Artists and Illustrators,* no. 136, January 1998. **Illustrated books—***Poems by Rimbaud and Verlaine,* London 1968; *The Rime of the Ancient Mariner* by Samuel Coleridge, London 1978.

On PROCKTOR: Books—*Patrick Procktor* by Patrick Kinmonth, London 1985; *Patrick Procktor: Prints 1959–1985,* catalog raisonné, Birmingham 1985. **Articles—**"Against the Rimless Men" by Bryan Robertson in *London Magazine,* July 1963; "Patrick Proctor's New Paintings" by Robert Hughes in *Studio International* (London), May 1967; "Patrick Procktor" by Paul William White in *Connoisseur* (London), July 1974; "Stylish Rebel" by William Packer in *Art and Artists* (London), August 1974; "The Master of Marylebone" by William Green in the *Sunday Telegraph* (London), November 1980.

*

You ask me for about 300 words or so—I paint, watercolour, draw and etch in line and aquatint. That's 10 words. But to write it out 30 times. . . think of the time it would take when I could be painting, watercolouring, drawing or etching in aquatint and line.

—Patrick Procktor

* * *

Patrick Procktor has numerous shows to his credit at the Redfern Gallery, and he cannot be pigeon-holed. At the beginning of his career he was criticized for varying his style too much, but as a young artist he was discovering his range; he continues to do so. His painting career is similar to his non-painting career, in which he went from being an omelette chef to a Russian interpreter. Some of his paintings are like runny omelettes—not well thought out; others are as well structured and beautiful as Russian grammar.

An important group of paintings is that of the London Philharmonic Orchestra. The brush is used like a conductor's baton, at times giving a hint of an image, at others becoming much more forceful. These black and white brush paintings are successful because of the simple calligraphic strokes. The accompanying etchings are disappointing. The intimacy and vivacity is lost. The double etching of the left and right hand side of the orchestra is weighed down by the deep orange background. Procktor is attempting to convey the sense of heat and depth on stage, but fails to do so.

The paintings resulting from the sketches are far more abstract, with heavy stippled backdrops and very strong colours. Procktor is at his best when painting familiar and treasured objects, such as a still life entitled ''Stubbs Jigsaw,'' where on the jigsaw are casually strewn an ashtray, a vase filled with white anemones, an exquisite antique desk light, and so on. The image is painted with light delicate brushstrokes. The pots of Morning Glory in ''Road Works Ahead'' are superbly painted—a crisp, clear cut, watercolour that has the same kind of flourish as the brilliant portrait of gondolier Bruno Palmarin. In this portrait Procktor demonstrates his skill: he is capable of manipulating watercolour with extraordinary dexterity and achieves remarkable variations of shading, but that is only when he chooses to.

—Carine Maurice

R

RADICE, Mario

Nationality: Italian. **Born:** Como, 1 August 1898. **Education:** Studied veterinary medicine; attended evening and Sunday painting classes at local art school and studied privately with a Como painter, 1912–18. **Military Service:** Served in the Italian Army, 1918–20. **Career:** Worked in Como paper mail, and in Buenos Aires, 1924–30; thereafter devoted himself to painting: lived and worked in Como, 1930 until his death in 1987. Travelled in France, Germany, and Switzerland, 1930–32; visited Paris and associated with Fernand Léger, 1931–32, co-founder-editor of *Quadrante,* Milan, 1932; worked on architectural projects, murals, bas-reliefs and mosaics, Como, 1933–38; organized, with Maulio Rho and Alberto Sartoris, *Exhibition of Modern Art* at Villa Olmo, Como 1936; founder-member, with Terragni and Ciliberti, *Valori Primordiali,* group and periodical, Rome, 1938; worked on various church projects with Cesare Cattaneo, 1939–43 (unrealized, due to death of Cattaneo in 1943). **Awards:** Painting Prize, Cittá di Gallarate, Italy, 1950; Primo Michetti, Francavilla al Mare, Italy, 1954; First Prize, Morgan's Paint, Rimini, Italy 1957; Primo Einaudi, Milan, 1958; Gold Medal of Artistic Merit, Como, 1964; Ambrogino d'Oro Medal, Milan, 1973; Abbondino d'Oro Prize, Como, 1985; U. Biancamano Prize, Pavia, 1987. **Agent:** Marlborough Galleria d'Arte, via Gregoriana 5, 00187 Rome. **Died:** Como, 25 July 1987.

Individual Exhibitions:

1936 Moody Gallery, Buenos Aires
1943 Galleria Bergamini, Milan
1953 Galleria San Fedele, Milan
1954 Galeria Del Fiore, Milan
1956 National Gallery of Victoria, Melbourne (toured Australia)
1962 Galleria Lorenzelli, Bergamo, Italy
1965 Galleria Agrati, Monza, Italy
1968 Centro Culturale Rosmini, Trento, Italy
Galleria Vismara, Milan
Galleria Martano Due, Turin
Galleria La Colonna, Como
1970 Galleria Peccolo, Livorno
1971 Deutsches Vonderau Museum, Fulda, West Germany
Marlborough Galleria d'Arte, Rome
1972 Galleria Quattro Venti, Palermo
Galleria Annunciata, Milan
1973 Associazione Amici dell'Arte, Modena
Università di Messina, Italy
1974 Westend Galerie, Frankfurt
Galleria Spagnoli, Florence
1975 Galleria Pellegrino, Bologna
1976 Musée des Beaux Arts, La Chaux de Fonds, Switzerland
1977 Galleria La Promotrice, Turin
1979 *Biennale,* Venice
1980 Galleria Il Salotto, Como
1981 Galleria Pantha Arte, Como
1982 Villa Malpensata, Lugano, Switzerland
1985 Galleria Lorenzelli, Milan
Galleria Italia, Naples

Selected Group Exhibitions:

1940 *Biennale,* Venice
1947 *Quadriennale,* Rome
1950 *Art Vivant Italienne,* Palais des Beaux Arts, Brussels
1969 *Aspetti del Primo Astrattismo Italiano 1930–1940,* Galleria Civica d'Arte Moderna, Monza, Italy
Bienal, Sao Paulo
1970 *Arte Italiana 70/70,* Museo Poldo Pezzoli, Milan
Konkrete Kunst, Westfälischer Kunstverein, Münster, West Germany
1971 *Mostra Arte Lombarda,* Museo Civico, Cremona, Italy
1972 *4th Biennale of Italian Graphic Art,* Faenza, Italy
1991 *The World of Carlo Belli: Italy in the 1930s—Artistic Culture,* Museo d' Arte Moderna e Contemporanea di Trento e Rovereto, Trento (travelled to Padiglione d'Arte Contemporanea, Milan)

Collections:

Galleria Nazionale d'Arte Moderna, Rome; Galleria Civica d'Arte Moderna, Turin.

Publications:

On RADICE: Books—*Pittura Italiana del dopoguerra* by Tristan Sauvage, Milan 1957; *Venti disegni di Mario Radice* by Franco Russoli, Milan 1962; *La linea dell'arte Italiana* by Guido Ballo, Rome 1964; *Il viaggiatore in arte* by Marcello Venturoli, Milan 1966; *Pittura e scultura degli anni 60* by Raffaele de Grada, Milan 1967; *Occhio Critico 2* by Guidi Ballo, Milan 1968; *Gli astrattisti de gruppo Como dagli anni trenta ad oggi* by Alberto Longatti, Milan 1972; *Mario Radice: Gli affreschi della Casa Terragni 1932–36* by Guido Ballo, Como 1973; *Lettera sulla aascita dell'astrattismo in Italia* by Carlo Belli, Rome 1978; *Who is Mario Radice?* by Angelo Maugeri, Como 1986; *The World of Carlo Belli: Italy in the 1930s—Artistic Culture,* exhibition catalog, Milan 1992. **Articles—**"Il pittore Mario Radice" by F. T. Marinetti in *Meridiano di Roma* March 1939; "Radice" by G. J. Kasper in *Art Actuel* (Lausanne, Switzerland), no. 4, 1958.

* * *

A self-taught painter, Mario Radice played a distinguished late role in the Futurist movement and was one of the principal promoters of Italian abstract paintings from 1930. More than most of his Italian colleagues he was deeply concerned with the relationship between abstraction and rational architecture, closer to the philosophy and outlook of the Dutch de Stijl group, which sought to relate the aesthetic analysis of space to practical, public purpose.

With the painters Maulio Rho and Carla Badiali, who, like Radice, lived in Como, and the architect Terragni, who came from the same town, he formed a group to promote these ideas, also expressed in the magazines *Quadrante* and *Valori Primordiali,* which he edited.

His paintings were deeply affected by Mondrian, logically and clearly arranged as assemblies of geometrical forms, built up with clear, pure purpose, exploiting a structural basis which immediately relates to architecture and town planning. Radice displays a fine sense of space and a much lighter touch than his Dutch mentor. There is little sense of mortality in his work, or, indeed of mediatation. The form floats in the space rather as they do in the dream fantasies of Paul Klee or the surrealist sequences of Joan Miro. His colour is charming and gay, blues, greens, grays, neither the stern primary colours of Mondrian, nor the strident, over-anxious brightness of many of his Italian contemporaries.

Radice saw his works as mural decorations, integral to the architecture they enhance, as well as immediately communicative to the public they serve. In some ways they serve as backdrops to human movement, and could, indeed, do so to advantage in the theatre.

—Charles Spencer

RAETZ, Markus

Nationality: Swiss. **Born:** Bern, 6 June 1941. **Education:** Teacher-training college in Bern, 1957–61. **Career:** Independent painter, influenced by Tachism and Action-Painting, in Bern, 1960–69, Amsterdam, 1969–73, Carona (Ticino), 1973–76, and again in Bern since 1976; first three-dimensional works, 1964; first concept-art works, 1968; lives and works in Bern. **Awards:** DAAD Fellowship, Berlin, 1981–82; Triennale für Originalgraphik prize, 1988; Banque hypothicaire du Canton de Geneve prize, 1991. **Agent:** Brooke Alexander, 59 Wooster Street, New York, New York, 10012, U.S.A. **Address:** Engestrasse 7, 3012 Bern, Switzerland.

Individual Exhibitions:

1966 Galerie Toni Gerber, Bern
1967 Galerie Toni Gerber, Bern
Galerie Felix Handschin, Basel
1969 Galerie Bischofberger, Zurich
Galerie Toni Gerber, Bern
Galerie Mickery, Loenersloot, Netherlands
1970 Centrum voor Coomunikatie, Utrecht
Galerie René Block, West Berlin
Markt 17, Enschede, Netherlands
Galerie Toni Gerber, Bern
Galerie Mickery, Loenersloot, Netherlands
1971 Galleria Diagramma, Milan
Galeria Herzog, Buren an der Aare, Switzerland
Galerie Loeb, Bern
Galerie Mollenhoff, Cologne
1972 Galerie Renée Ziegler, Zurich
Zeichnungen, Objekte, Kunstmuseum, Basel
Galerie Renée Ziegler, Geneva
Musée d'Art d'Histoire, Geneva
Galerie Toni Gerber, Bern
Galerie Seriaal, Amsterdam
1973 Galerie Stahli, Zurich
Goethe Institut, Amsterdam
1974 Galerie Toni Gerber, Bern (2 shows)
1975 Kunstmuseum, Lucerne
Amsterdam Fruhjahre 1973; Arbeiten aus einem Monat und einer Nacht von Markus Raetz, Kunthaus, Zurich
Neue Galerie am Landsmuseum Joanneum, Graz, Austria
1976 Galerie Toni Gerber, Bern (2 shows)
Galerie Seriaal, Amsterdam
1977 Galerie Herzog, Buren an der Aare, Switzerland
Galerie Toni Gerber, Bern
Kunstmuseum, Bern
Kunsthalle, Bern
1979 Galerie Herzog, Buren an der Aare, Switzerland
Galerie Stahli, Zurich
1980 Stedelijk Museum, Amsterdam
Galleria Lucio Amelio, Naples
1981 Kunsthaus, Aarau, Switzerland
Galerie Krinzinger, Innsbruck
Galerie Nächst St. Stephan, Vienna
Kunstverein, Kassel, West Germany
1982 DAAD-Galerie, West Berlin
Kunsthalle, Basel
1983 Musée d'Art Moderne de la Ville, Paris
Nouveau Musée, Lyon-Villeurbanne, France
Kunstverein, Frankfurt
1984 Galerie Pablo Stahli, Zurich
1986 Kunsthaus, Zurich
Kunstverein, Cologne
Moderna Musset, Stockholm
1988 New Museum of Contemporary Art, New York
Brooke Alexander, New York
Biennale, Venice
1989 Museum für Gegenwartskunst, Basel
1990 San Diego Museum of Contemmporary Art
1991 Galerie Pablo Staehli, Zurich
Kunstmuseum, Bern
Cabinet des Estampes, Geneva (with Richard Long)
1992 Brooke Alexander, New York
Galerie Farideh Cadot, Paris
Kunstmuseum, Bern
Cabinet des Estampes, Geneva
1994 Musée Rath, Geneva
Serpentine Gallery, London
Museum of Contemporary Art, Helsinki
Centre Culturel Suisse, Paris
Musée de l'Estampe, Gravelines, France
1998 Gallerie Francesca Pia, Bern
Galleria Periferia, Poschiavo, Switzerland
Museum Calouste Gulbenkian, Centro de Arte Moderna José de Azeredo Perdigao, Lisbon

Markus Raetz: *Todo—Nada,* 1998. ©2001 Artists Rights Society (ARS), NY/ProLitteris, Zürich.

1999 Gallery Brooke Alexander, New York
Galerie Farideh Cadot, Paris
2000 Galleria Monica de Cardenas, Milan

Selected Group Exhibitions:

1965 *Biennale,* Musée d' Art Moderne, Paris (and 1970)
1968 *Documenta,* Kassel, West Germany (and 1972, 1982)
1969 *When Attitudes Become Form,* Kunsthalle, Bern (toured Europe)
1970 *Information,* Museum of Modern Art, New York
1972 *31 Artistes Suisses Contemporains,* Grand Palais, Paris
1977 *Bienal,* Sao Paulo
1979 *Schweizer Kunst,* Fundatie Kunsthuis, Amsterdam
1981 *Le Dessin Suisse 1970–1980,* Musée Rath, Geneva
1984 *An International Survey of Painting and Sculpture,* Museum of Modern Art, New York
1990 *Readymade Boomerang,* Sydney Biennial
1991 *Visionäre Schweiz,* Kunsthaus Zürich (travelled to Museo Nacional Centro de Reina Sofia, Madrid; Kunsthalle Düsseldorf)
1992 *Artscape Nordland,* Lofoten, Norway
1993 *Szenenwechsel,* Museum für Moderne Kunst, Frankfurt
1998 *13 Räume für Zeichnung—Schweizer Zeichnung des 20 Jahrhunderts,* Kunstverein Frankfurt und Rupertinum, Salzburg
1999 *Searchlight: Consciousness at the Millenium,* CCAC, San Francisco, California
2000 *Mnemosyne,* Coimbra, Portugal

Collections:

Tate Gallery, London; Stedelijk Museum, Amsterdam; Centre Georges Pompidou, Paris; Musée de Toulon, France; Kunstmuseum, Basel; Kunstmuseum, Bern; Kunsthaus, Zurich; Kunstmuseum, Winterthur; Musée d'Art et d'Histoire, Geneva; Museum of Modern Art, New York.

Publications:

By RAETZ: Books—*Plans and Projects 1965–1969,* Loenersloot 1969; *27 Reproduktionen von Zeichnungen,* Lucerne 1970; *Notizbuchlein,* Bern 1972; *Buch mit 138 Xeroxkopien nach dem Projekt 1969,* Lucerne 1971; *Von diesem Blatt eine Kopie machen; die Kopie wieder koperien; diesen Prozess nach belieden Fortsetzen,* Amsterdam 1971; *Die Bucher,* 3 vols. in cassette, Zurich 1975; *Notizbuch,* Zurich 1975; *Seiben Geschichten der sieben Prinzessinnen,*

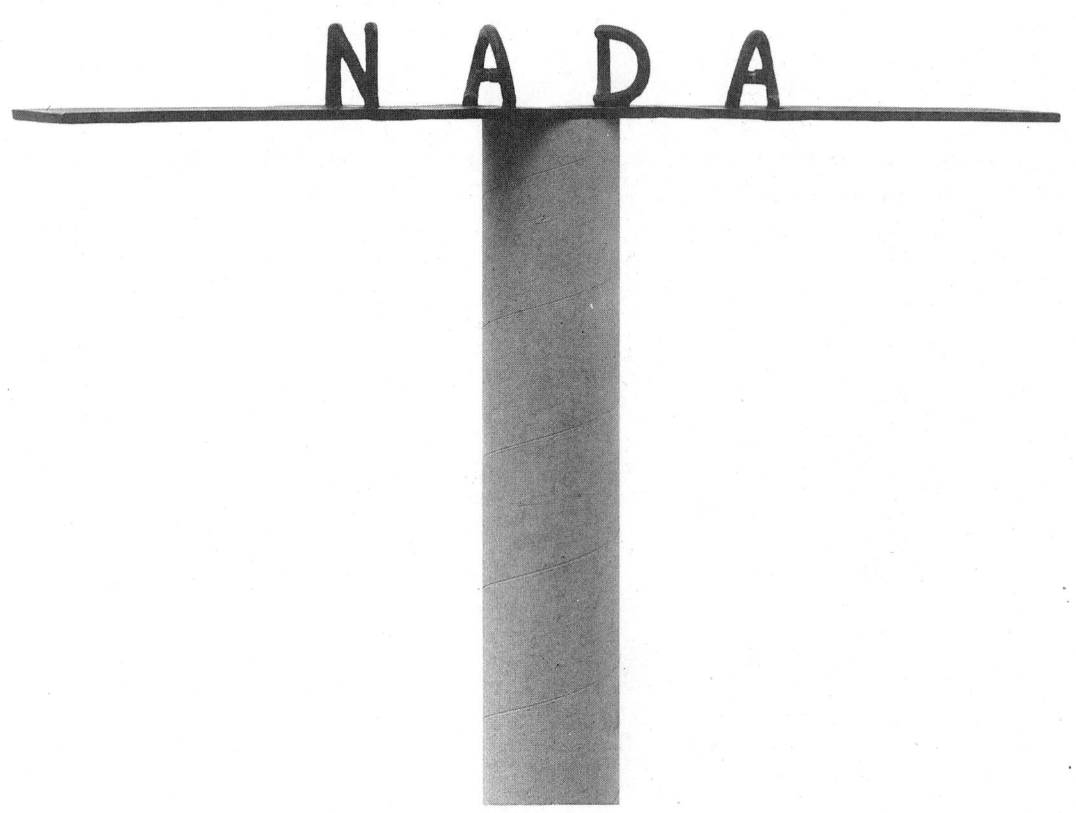

Markus Raetz: *Todo—Nada,* 1998. ©2001 Artists Rights Society (ARS), NY/ProLitteris, Zürich.

Lucerne 1975; *& + & u. &,* with Walo von Fellenberg and Rolf Geissbühler, Bern 1977; *MIMI,* Aarau 1981; *CH '70-'80,* Lucerne 1981; *Notizen 1981–1982,* Berlin 1982; *Markus Raetz, Polaroids 1978–1993,* exhibition catalog with Ad Petersen, Valencia 1993.

On RAETZ: Books—*Electronic Art: elektronische und elektrische objekte und environments, neon objekte,* Dusseldorf 1969; *Documenta 5: Befragung der Realitat,* exhibition catalog edited by Harald Szeeman and others, Kassel, West Germany 1972: *Markus Raetz: Zeichnungen, Objekte,* exhibition catalog with text by Dieter Koepplin, Basel 1972; *Amsterdam Fruhjahre 1973: Arbeiten aus einem Monat und einer Nacht von Markus Raetz,* exhibition catalog with text by Erik Gysling-Billeter, Zurich 1975; *Markus Raetz,* exibition catalog with text by Johannes Gachnang, Bern 1977; *Das Beobachten des Beobachtens: Markus Raetz—Zeichnungen,* exhibition catalog with text by Jürgen Glaesemer, Bern 1977; *Markus Raetz,* exhibition catalog with introduction by Ad Petersen, Amsterdam 1980; *Markus Raetz,* exhibition catalog with text by Jean-Christophe Ammann, Basel 1982; *Markus Raetz,* exhibition catalog with text by Peter Weiermair, Frankfurt, 1983; *Markus Raetz: Arbeiten 1962–1986,* exhibition catalog, Zurich 1986; *Markus Raetz: In the Realm of the Possible,* exhibition catalog by Marcia Tucker, New York 1988; *Markus Raetz, Biennale di Venezia 1988, Svissera,* exhibition catalog by Bernhard Bürgi, Venice 1988; *Markus Raetz, les Estampes, die Druchgraphik, the Prints, 1958–1991,* exhibition catalog by Rainer Michael Mason, Juliane Willi-Cosandier, and Josef Helfenstein, Bern 1991; *CECI-CELA,* exhibition catalog by Ad Petersen and Max Wechsler, Valencia 1993. **Articles—**''Markus Raetz'' by Barry Schwabsky in *Arts Magazine,* no. 2, October 1988; ''Disappearing Acts'' by Holland Cotter in *Art in America,* no. 11, November 1988; ''Über Metamorphosen, Neue Skulpturen von Markus Raetz'' by Claude Ritschard in *Parkett,* no. 42, 1994; ''Markus Raetz: Forme Inerte—Reflet Vivant'' by Patrick Schaefer in *Le Miroir Vivant,* 1997; ''Im Sprachraum, eine Skulptur von Markus Raetz in Genf'' by Hans Rudolf Reust in *Kunstbulletin,* no. 10, September 2000.

* * *

The Swiss artist Markus Raetz is the creator of a labyrinth-like universe of meanings and irritations. He is at the same time an indefatigable investigator of the possibilities of expression offered him by his method combining thought and fantasy. Behind this method lies the question about the limits and reliability of perception, an old if no less topical problem.

Raetz prefers to tackle this problem through drawing. It seems that he has a command of all the conceivable styles and refinements of this classical technique, so easily and naturally flow the lines in his drawings, so naturally do the forms and images take shape. Yet first impressions are deceptive. Some of Raetz's drawings are playful and simple; many others, on the other hand, are confused and complex. They force us, not unlike a puzzle or rebus, to reflect and to decipher, for they often employ sensory perceptibility only as a pretext for an intellectual operation.

Raetz links the questioning of reality with the questioning of the creative process; each to him is equally important. So the ideas develop into motifs and form chains from which new motifs and images arise. When Raetz for example replaces lines with points or dashes, the ''old'' image gains a ''new'' dimension whose renewed possibilities of association can be investigated. The way from a ''simple'' to a ''multi-layered'' motif is thereby pre-programmed.

This is also the case in other works by Raetz; photographs, sculptures, objects and painted cloths. He has a particular preference for books, since the character of a book allows the reproduction of a series of drawings which have arisen on a pad without alteration to sequence and so to authenticity. Raetz understands how to use in constantly new variations the principle of metamorphosis as a means for perception of the world.

—Zdenek Felix

RAFFAEL, Joseph (Jose Raffaele)

Nationality: American. **Born:** Brooklyn, New York, 22 February 1933. **Education:** Cooper Union, New York 1951–54; Yale University School of Fine Arts, New Haven, Connecticut, under Josef Albers, 1954–56, B.F.A. 1956; Fulbright Fellow, Italy, 1958–59. **Family:** Married Judy Collins in 1968; children: Robert, Matthew, Rachel and Reuben. **Career:** Worked for the New York Public Library, 1952–54; layout artist, *Yale Daily News,* New Haven, 1955–56; travelled in England, France and Italy, 1956; full-time artist since 1956: currently lives in Cap d'Antibes, France. Art instructor, University of California at Davis, 1966; instructor, School of Visual Arts, New York, 1967–69; associate professor of art, University of California, Berkeley, summer 1969; professor of art, California State University, Sacramento 1969–74; art instructor, University of Utah, Snowbird, 1976. **Awards:** Louis Comfort Tiffany Fellowship, 1960; First Painting Prize, *International Biennal,* Tokyo, 1974; Purchase Prize, *Concours d' Antiques,* Oakland Museum, California, 1975. **Agent:** Nancy Hoffman Gallery, New York. **Address:** c/o Nancy Hoffman Gallery, 429 West Broadway, New York, New York 10012, U.S.A.

Individual Exhibitions:

1958 Kanegis Gallery, Boston
1959 Galleria Numero, Florence
1963 D'Arcy Gallery, New York
1965 Stable Gallery, New York
1966 Stable Gallery, New York
1968 Stable Gallery, New York
Berkeley Gallery, San Francisco
1969 Sacramento State College, California
Worth Ryder Gallery, University of California, Berkeley
1970 Wichita Art Museum, Kansas
Reese Palley Gallery, San Francisco
1971 University of California Art Gallery, San Diego
1972 Reese Palley Gallery, New York
Nancy Hoffman Gallery, New York
1973 Nancy Hoffman Gallery, New York
Water Painting, University of California Art Museum, Berkeley
Museum of Contemporary Art, Chicago
1974 Barbara Okun Gallery, St. Louis
3 Realists: Close/Estes/Raffael, Worcester Art Museum, Massachusetts
Nancy Hoffman Gallery, New York
1975 University of Nevada Art Gallery, Las Vegas
Norman MacKenzie Art Gallery, University of Saskatchewan, Regina
1976 Nancy Hoffman Gallery, New York
Ruth Braunstein's Quay Gallery, San Francisco
1977 Museum of Fine Arts, St. Petersburg, Florida
ARCO Center for Visual Art, Los Angeles
Roy Boyd Gallery, Chicago
1978 Barbara Fendrick Gallery, Washington, D.C.
Valparaiso University, Indiana
John Berggruen Gallery, San Francisco
San Francisco Museum of Modern Art
Des Moines Art Center, Iowa
Joslyn Art Museum, Omaha, Nebraska
Newport Harbor Art Museum, Newport Beach, California
Denver Art Museum
1979 Nancy Hoffman Gallery, New York
Louise Himelfarb Gallery, Watermill, New York (with Robert Dash)
Stewart Center Gallery, Purdue University, West Lafayette, Indiana (with Judy Raffael)
Wenger Gallery, La Jolla, California (with Judy Raffael)
1980 Nancy Hoffman Gallery, New York
Wake Forest University, Winston-Salem, North Carolina
Columbus Museum of Arts and Science, Georgia
Birmingham Museum of Art, Alabama
Mint Museum of Art, Charlotte, North Carolina
Mississippi Museum of Art, Jackson
Images Gallery, Toledo, Ohio
Redding Museum, California
1981 John Berggruen Gallery, San Francisco
Elvehjem Art Center, Madison, Wisconsin
University of Connecticut, Storrs (travelled to Lincoln, Nebraska; Grand Forks, Dakota; Racine, Wisconsin; Calgary, Alberta; Boise, Idaho)
1982 Saddleback Community College, Mission Viejo, California
Santa Ana Community College, California
Allport Associates Gallery, Larkspur, California
John Berggruen Gallery, San Francisco
Delaware Art Museum, Wilmington
Jacksonville Museum, Florida (travelled to West Palm Beach, Florida)
Nancy Hoffman Gallery, New York
1983 University of Austin, Texas
Richard Gray Gallery, Chicago
Nancy Hoffman Gallery, New York
1984 Nancy Hoffman Gallery, New York
1985 Gibbes Art Gallery, Charleston, South Carolina

New York Academy of Sciences
Salt Lake Art Center, Utah (travelled to Billings, Montana; Casper, Wyoming)
1986 Nancy Hoffman Gallery, New York
Woltjen/Udell Gallery, Edmonton, Alberta
1987 Nancy Hoffman Gallery, New York
2000 Nancy Hoffman Gallery, New York

Selected Group Exhibitions:

1966 *Art in the Mirror,* Museum of Modern Art, New York
1969 *Paintings from the Photo,* Riverside Museum, New York
1973 *Separate Realities,* Los Angeles Municipal Art Gallery
1976 *Illusions of Reality and Realists' Prints,* Australia Council, North Sydney (toured Australia)
1977 *8 Contemporary American Realists,* Pennsylvania Academy of Fine Arts, Philadelphia
1979 *Late 20th Century Art: The Sydney and Frances Lewis Foundation Collection,* Virginia Commonwealth University, Richmond (travelled to Institute of Contemporary Art, University of Pennsylvania, Philadelphia)
1980 *The Print Club Invitational 1980,* Print Club, Philadelphia
1983 *West Coast Realism,* Laguna Beach Museum, California
1985 *Art in the San Francisco Bay Area 1945–80,* Oakland Museum, California
1987 *Modern American Realism,* National Museum of American Art, Washington D.C.
1992 *Mind & Beast: Contemporary Artists and the Animal Kingdom,* Leigh Yawkey Woodson Art Museum, Wausau, Wisconsin

Collections:

San Francisco Museum of Modern Art; University of California Art Museum, Berkeley; Santa Barbara Museum of Art, California; Los Angeles County Museum of Art; Library of Congress, Washington D.C.; National Collection of Fine Arts, Smithsonian Institution, Washington, D.C.; Hirshhorn Museum and Sculpture Garden, Washington, D.C.; Museum of Contemporary Art, Chicago; Metropolitan Museum of Art, New York; Whitney Museum, New York.

Publications:

On RAFFAEL: Books—*Joseph Raffael,* exhibition catalog, San Francisco 1970; *Joseph Raffael,* exhibition catalog, New York 1972; *Water Painting,* exhibition catalog, Berkeley, California 1973; *Separate Realities,* exhibition catalog by Laurence Drieband, Los Angeles 1973; *3 Realists: Close/Estes/Raffael,* exhibition catalog by Leon Shulman, Worcester, Massachusetts 1974; *Contemporary Landscape Painting,* exhibition catalog by George Keubler, Oklahoma City 1975. **Articles—**''Oh, To Be Born Under Pisces, with Saggitarius Rising'' by Grace Glueck in the *New York Times,* 29 December 1968; ''In Art with Joseph Raffael'' by Lynne Zickerman in *Daily California Arts Magazine* (Berkeley), October 1972; ''The Paintings of Joseph Raffael'' by William S. Wilson in *Studio International* (London), May 1974; ''Nature Upclose'' by Jerome Tarshis in *Horizon* (New York), September 1978; ''Cutting Through the Clouds: A View of Joseph Raffael's Recent Paintings'' by Joyce Petschek in *Arts Magazine,* vol. 59, November 1984; ''Joseph Raffael's Lannis Series, Part One'' by Irene McManus in *Arts Magazine,* vol. 62, March 1988; ''Joseph Raffael'' by Donald B. Kuspit in *Artforum International,* vol. 34, March 1996. **Film—***The Eyes Have It,* by Gloria Smith for National Broadcasting Corporation (NBC-TV), 1972.

*

Painting is the subject of my work, and nature the inspiration. Wallace Stevens has written: ''The subject of the poem is poetry.'' I believe that too: painting for me, is the subject of the painting. The process of painting the work. What happens from moment to moment. What occurs. The events that take place before my eyes.

I want the paintings to be like nature. Nature is always changing. I want the work to be always changing. In the sense that each time they are looked at they are different. I want to encourage people to look at may paintings in different light situations. They always look different.

—Joseph Raffael

* * *

The lyrical paintings of Joseph Raffael sing of nature, expressed in the ebb and flow of a subject matter wedded intrinsically and naturalistically to the medium. The substance is water: the icy, bubbling riffles of a shallow coursing stream; limpid pools with gracefully swirling trout and Japanese trout below calm surfaces decked with lilypads and punctuated by blossoms and buds. His medium is as fluid as his subject—thinned luminescent colors in droplets, blobs and stains, with contours emphasized to make each appear as a discrete, atomic unit. The large scale canvases and watercolors are realist in mode, but that reality is built on the accretion of myriad abstract particles and shapes. Light glistens, sparkles, and reflects off the surfaces in the watery images and the fluid texture of paint. It is the incident of light that brings into being the form and substance of water.

Raffael works from photographs, a convenience for capturing those momentary and spontaneous occurences in nature. External references to natural scale and distance are cropped; the image in isolation fills the picture plane and intensifies the fragmentation of object and substance. Rather than a faithful copy of a photograph, Raffael reconstructs a timeless and meditative image with scintillating color, gesture and fluid texture. The momentary incident is captured, and provides for silent reverie and contemplation.

For Raffael, nature is in the constant act of becoming. He portrays not the fact of natural experience, but its painterly equivalent. Raffael's practice of the Chinese meditative concept of *chi'i* is reflected in these considerations. The boundlessness of nature, time and thought coalesce on canvas. Water and light, emblematic of nature's omnipresence, are the vehicles for its perception.

—Ron Glowen

RAINER, Arnulf

Nationality: Austrian. **Born:** Baden, near Vienna, 8 December 1929. **Education:** Studied art briefly at the Akademic der Bildenden Künste, Vienna, 1950; mainly self-taught. **Family:** Married three times (divorced). **Career:** Independent artist, living and working in

Upper Austria, Bavaria and Vienna, since 1947; produced surrealist drawings, 1947–51; random-images and proportion studies, 1951–52; surreal works influenced by hallucinogenic drugs, 1964–65; grimace-photos, 1968–73; cooperative works, with artist Dieter Roth, 1974; mortuary images, 1977–87; Arnulf Rainer Museum inaugurated in New York, 1993; forty-two paintings destroyed by unknown perpetrators in Rainer's studio at the Akademie der Bildenden Künste, Vienna, 1994. Instructor, master class for painting, Akademie der Bildenden Künste, Vienna, and guest professor, Staatliche Akademie der Bildenden Künste, Stuttgart, 1981–1995. **Awards:** Artist Prize, Vienna, 1974 (rescinded by Mayor Gratz of Vienna); Grosser Osterreichischer Staatspreis für Malerei, Vienna, 1978; Max Beckmann Preis, Frankfurt, 1981; International Center of Photography Award, New York, 1989. **Member:** Akademie der Künste, West Berlin 1981. **Agent:** Galerie Ulysses, Opernring 21, 1010 Vienna, Austria. **Address:** Mariahilferstrasse 49, 1060 Vienna, Austria.

Individual Exhibitions:

1951 Galerie Kleinmayr, Klagenfurt, Austria
1952 Galerie Franck, Frankfurt
Art Club Gallery, Vienna
Galerie Springer, West Berlin
1954 Galerie Würthle, Vienna
1956 Galerie St. Stephan, Vienna
1957 Wiener Secession, Vienna
1958 Galerie 33, Bern
Galerie St. Stephan, Vienna
Galerie Boukes, Wiesbaden, West Germany
1960 Galerie St. Stephan, Vienna
1961 Galleria del Cavallino, Vienna
Galerie St. Stephan, Vienna
Galerie Dato, Frankfurt
Galerie Seide, Hannover
1962 Galerie Schmela, Dusseldorf
Galerie Rottloff, Karlsruhe
Minami Gallery, Tokyo
Galerie 61, Klagenfurt, Austria
1963 Galerie St. Stephan, Vienna
1964 Galerie Springer, West Berlin
1965 Galerie Rottloff, Karlsruhe
1966 Galerie Peithner-Lichtenfels, Vienna
1967 Galerie Grossgorchen, West Berlin
1968 Osterreichisches Kulturinstitut, Warsaw
Galerie Steinbacher-Hohl, Frankfurt
Museum des 20. Jahrhunderts, Vienna
Galerie St. Stephan, Vienna
1969 Galerie Hake, Cologne
Galerie im Taxispalais, Innsbruck
Galerie Ariadne, Vienna
Galerie Rewolle, Bremen, West Germany
Forum 67, Linz, Austria
Galerie Casa, Munich
Galerie Springer, West Berlin
Galerie Tams, Munich
1970 Galerie Müller, Stuttgart
Galerie Van de Loo, Munich
Galerie Müller, Cologne
Forum Stadpark, Graz, Austria
Galerie Lichter, Frankfurt
Galerie St. Stephan, Vienna
Galerie Schöttle, Munich
Kunsteverein, Frieburg, West Germany
1971 Museum des 20. Jahrhunderts, Vienna
Kunstverein, Hamburg
Galerie Ariadne, Vienna
Galerie Müller, Cologne
1972 Galerie Ariadne, Cologne
Galerie Grunangergasse, Vienna
Austrian Institute, New York
Galerie Van de Loo, Munich
Busch-Reisinger Museum, Cambridge, Massachusetts
Galerie Klein, Bonn
1973 Galerie Müller, Stuttgart
Graphische Sammlung Albertina, Vienna
Galerie Ariadne, Cologne
Galerie Schöttle, Munich
1974 Galerie Klein, Bonn
Studio Santandrea, Milan
Galerie Grunangergasse, Vienna
Kunstverein, Bremerhaven, West Germany
Galerie Ariadne, Cologne
Ariadne Gallery, New York
Abis Gallery, West Germany
Gestische Handmalerein, Kunstraum München, Munich
Galerie Greve, Cologne
1975 Galerie Grunangergasse, Vienna
Superpaintings 1954–64, Ariadne Gallery, New York
Galerie Stadler, Paris
Retrospektive, Hessische Landesmuseum, Darmstadt
Galerie Aktuelle, Kunst, Frankfurt
1976 Galerie Heiner Friedrich, Munich
Galerie Winterberger, Cologne
Galerie Shapira, Vienna
Galerie Stadler, Paris
Kunstverein, Mannheim
Centre d'Arts Plastiques Contemporains, Bordeaux
Galerie Aktuelle Kunst, Frankfurt
Grimaces, Neue Galerie, Linz, Austria
Kunstverein, Frankfurt
1977 Kunsthalle, Bern
Städtische Galerie im Lenbachhaus, Munich
Kestner-Gesellschaft, Hannover
1978 Osterreichischer Galerie, Vienna
1980 Van Abbemuseum, Eindhoven, Netherlands
Whitechapel Art Gallery, London
Retrospective, Nationalgalerie, West Berlin
Als Van Gogh als. . . Uberarbeitungen von Photos und Reproduktionen von Van Gogh Selbstportraits, Galerie Curtze, Vienna
Galerie Springer, West Berlin
Galerie AK, Frankfurt (toured Germany)
1981 Galerie Droschl, Graz, Austria
Kunstverein, Heidelberg
Galerie Freund, Klagenfurt, Austria
Galeria Erhardt, Madrid
Galerie Turske, Zurich
Galerie Ulysses, Vienna
Galerie Holtmann, Cologne
Stadtische Galerie, Frankfurt

Galerie Academia, Salzburg
Galerie Curtze, Vienna
Galerie Hummel, Vienna
Galerie Munro, Hamburg
Sala Parpallo, Valencia, Spain
Dossi Arte Contemporanea, Bergamo, Italy
Galerie Holtmann, Hannover
Graphikubermalungen, Galerie Klein, Bonn
Galerie Curtze, Dusseldorf
Galerie Friedrich-Kunst, Munich

1982 Louisiana Museum, Humlebaek, Denmark (retrospective)
Suermondt Museum, Aachen, West Germany

1983 Kunstmuseum, Hannover
Kontshall, Malmo, Sweden
Ulmer Museum, Ulm, West Germany
Wilhelm Hack Museum, Ludwigshafen, West Germany
Museum van Hedendaagse Kunst, Ghent, Belgium
Westfälischer Landesmuseum, Munster, West Germany

1984 Neuer Berliner Kunstverein, West Berlin
Städtische Müseum, Mönchengladbach, West Germany
Centre Georges Pompidou, Paris
Van Abbemuseum, Eindhoven, Netherlands
Kunstmuseum, Dusseldorf
Kunsthaus, Zurich

1985 Museum of Modern Art, Oxford
Castello di Rivoli, Turin
Kunsthalle, Nuremberg, West Germany
Groninger Museum, Groningen, Netherlands
Museum Boymans-van Beuningen, Rotterdam
Galerie Maeght Lelong, Zurich

1986 Florida Atlantic University, Boca Raton
University of South Florida, Tampa
Grey Art Gallery, New York University
Neue Galerie-Museum Ludwig, Aachen, West Germany
Kunsthalle, Hamburg (with Gunter Brus)
Abbazia di San Gregorio, Venice
Kuntshalle, Bremen, West Germany
Musée Cantonal des Beaux-Arts, Lausanne (with Louis Soutter)
Schirn Kuntshalle, Frankfurt
Provinciaal Museum, Hasselt, Belgium
Museum Moderner Kunst, Vienna
North Carolina Museum of Art, Raleigh

1987 Centre National d'Art Contemporain, Grenoble, France
Saidye Bronfman Center, Montreal
Neue Galerie im Wolfgang Gurlitt Museum, Linz, Austria
Galerie Ulysses, Vienna

1988 Galerie Sabine Knust, Munich
Verdeckt—Entdect, Oberösterreichische Landesgalerie, Linz, Austria
Haus Lange and Haus Esters Museums, Krefeld, Germany
Neue Galerie, Staatliche und Städtische Kunstsammlungen, Kassel, Germany
Zeichnungen 1949–85, Städtisches Museum, Schloß Morsbroich, Leverkusen

1989 Städtische Galerie, Regensburg, Germany
The Self-Portraits, Sadye Bronfman Center, Montreal
Kunstverein, Braunschweig, Germany
Retrospective, Solomon R. Guggenheim Museum, New York
Enzyklopädie und Revolution, Festspielhaus, Bregenz, Austria
Museum of Contemporary Art, Chicago
Historisches Museum der Stadt Wien, Vienna
Drawing on Death, Moore College of Art and Design, Philadelphia

1990 Castello di Rivoli, Turin, Italy
Hommage aan Vincent Van Gogh, Bonnefanten Museum, Maastricht, Belgium
Übermalte Bücher, Städtische Kunstmuseum, Bonn, Germany
Arnulf Rainer: Werke 1980–1990, Saarlandmuseum, Saarbrücken, Germany

1991 Malmö Konsthall, Sweden
Brandenburgische Kunstsammlungen, Cottbus, Germany
Frühe Graphikübermalungen, Sabine Kunst, Munich
Galerie Stadler, Paris

1992 *Young Cross,* The Menil Collection, Houston
Kreuz-Weisen, Kunst-Station St. Peter, Cologne, Germany
Topografia Superiore—Carinzia/Venezia, Kärtner Landesgalerie, Klagenfurt, Austria
Obras Recentes, Fundacao de Serralves, Porto, Portugal
Cankarjev Dom, International Graphic Center, Ljubljana, Slovenia

1993 Kunsthalle Dominikanerkirche, Osnabrück, Germany
Hessisches Landesmuseum, Darmstadt, Germany
Fossilien, Oberösterreichischer Kunstverein, Linz, Austria
Moderna Galerija, Ljubljana, Slovenia

1994 Museum Moderner Kunst, Passau, Germany
Kunsthalle, Recklingshausen, Germany
Retrospective, Schömer-Haus, Klosterneuburg, Austria

1995 Über das Bild Hinaus, Museum of Modern Art, Bolzano, Italy
Katastrophen und Desaster, Nationalmuseum Cotroceni, Bukarest, Romania and Brukenthal Museum, Hermannstadt
Arnulf Rainer: Early Works, Stedelijk Museum, Vienna (catalog)

1996 *Arnulf Rainer Natur—Mikrokosmos Makrokosmos,* Kärntner Landesgalerie, Klagenfurt, Austria (also Landesmuseum, Oldenburg, Germany; Isländische Nationalgalerie, Reykjavik, Iceland)

1997 *Arnulf Rainer: Abyss—Deep—Perspective: Retrospective 1947–97,* Kunsthalle Krems, Krems an der Donau, Austria (catalog)

1998 *Arnulf Rainer: Fingermalereien, Schleierbilder 1998,* Stadt Kunstsammlungen, Augsburg (catalog)

2000 *Arnulf Rainer, Gegen.Bilder: Retrospektive zum 70. Geburtstag,* Kunstforum, Wolfratshausen, Vienna (catalog)

2001 *Arnulf Rainer: Retrospettiva 1948–2000,* Galleria d'Arte Moderna, Bologna (catalog)

Selected Group Exhibitions:

1951 *Hundsgruppenausstellung,* Institut fur Wissenschaft und Kunst, Vienna

1953 *German Graphics,* Art Institute of Chicago

1959 *Documenta,* Museum Fridericianum, Kassel, West Germany (and 1972, 1977)

1963 *Schrift und Bild,* Stedelijk Museum, Amsterdam (travelled to Baden-Baden)
1967 *9th Tokyo Biennale,* Metropolitan Museum of Art, Tokyo
1973 *Kunst aus Photographie,* Kunstverein, Hannover
1975 *Bodyworks,* Museum of Contemporary Art, Chicago
1979 *European Dialogue,* at the *Biennale of Sydney,* New South Wales
1983 *Aspects of Postwar Painting in Europe,* Guggenheim Museum, New York
1987 *Berlinart 1961–87,* Museum of Modern Art, New York (travelled to San Francisco)
The Spiritual in Art: Abstract Painting 1890–1985, Los Angeles County Museum of Art
1988 *The Seventh Biennale of Sydney,* Art Gallery of New South Wales, Sydney
Collection Next the Sea, Haags Gemeentemuseum, The Hague, The Netherlands
1989 *Bilderstreit,* Museum Ludwig in den Rheinhallen der Kölner Messe, Cologne, Germany
Open Mind, Museum van Hedendaagse Kunst, Ghent, Belgium
Modern Masters, Kunsthalle Helsinki, Finland
1990 *Vienne Aujourd'hui,* Museum Toulon, France
Vies d'Artistes, Musée des Beaux-Arts, Le Havre, France
Voor Vincent Van Gogh, Haags Gemeentemuseum, Hague, The Netherlands
1991 *Artist's Choice,* Museum of Modern Art, New York
Un Musée en Voyage, Musée d'Art Contemporain, Lyon, France
Die Hand des Künstlers, Museum Ludwing, Cologne, Germany
1992 *Das Jahrzehnt der Malerei—Österreich 1980–90,* Sammlung Schömer, Museum der Bildenden Künste, Budapest, Hungary
Parallel Visions: Modern Artists and Outsider Art, Los Angeles County Museum of Art
1993 *L'Ame au Corps—Arts et Sciences 1793–1993,* Galeries Nationales du Grand Palais, Paris
Malerei der Widerstände, Jesuitenkirche, Galerie der Stadt Aschaffenburg, Germany
1994 *Détente,* Museum des 20. Jahrhunderts, Vienna
The Tradition of the New, Solomon R. Guggenheim Museum, New York
1995 *3rd Grand Prix of Drawing Alpe-Adria,* Mücsarnok Kunsthalle, Budapest
Tanzende Mädchen, Stedelijk Museum, Amsterdam, The Netherlands
1996 *Antagonismes,* Centre National de la Photographie, Paris
Like a Crystal, Stedelijk Museum, Amsterdam, The Netherlands
2000 *Europa,* Galerie Academia, Salzburg (catalog)

Collections:

Museum des 20. Jahrhunderts, Vienna; Österreichische Galerie, Vienna; Nationalgalerie, West Berlin; Staatsgalerie, Stuttgart; Kunstmuseum, Dusseldorf; Kunstmuseum, Bonn; Kunstmuseum, Basel; Tate Gallery, London; Art Institute of Chicago; Guggenheim Museum, New York.

Publications:

By RAINER: Books—*TRRR-Early Drawings, 1947–51,* Vienna 1969; *Face Farces,* Vienna 1971; *Uberdeckungen,* with text by Otto Breicha, Vienna 1971; *Vermachtnis uber Meine Nachlass,* Cologne 1972; *Blindzeichnungen 1951–73,* Cologne, 1973; *Hirndrang,* edited by Otto Breicha, Salzburg 1980; *Arnulf Rainer: Even Before Language,* with Rudi H. Fuchs, Amsterdam 2000. **Films and video—** *Verlegenes und Vergebliches Selbstbeschaftigungen 1974; Confrontation with My Video Image: Mouth Piece and Slow Motion, 1974; Doppeldruck,* with Dieter Roth, 1976; *Duell in Schloss,* with Dieter Roth, 1976. **Articles—**''Arnulf Rainer: Lamento (Lament)'' in *Journal of Contemporary Art,* vol. 1, no. 2, Fall-Winter 1988; interview with Guy Scarpetta in *Art Press,* no. 132, January 1989; interview with Johannes Gachnang in *Repères,* no. 70, 1990; interview with Gillian Spragens in *Photo Metro,* vol. 11, no. 107, April 1993.

On RAINER: Books—*Arnulf Rainer,* exhibition catalog with texts by W. Hofmann and H. Kern, Hamburg 1971; *Documenta 5,* exhibition catalog edited by Harald Szeeman and Jean-Christophe Ammann, Kassel, West Germany 1972; *Arnulf Rainer: Gestische Handmalerein,* exhibition catalog, Munich 1974; *Rainer: Superpaintings 1954–64,* exhibition catalog, New York 1975; *Arnulf Ranier: Retrospektive,* exhibition catalog with text by Dieter Honisch and Hermann Kern, West Berlin 1980; *Arnulf Rainer: Als Van Gogh. . . Uberarbeitungen von Photos und Reproduktionen von Van Gogh Selbstportraits,* exhibition catalog, Vienna 1980; *Arnulf Rainer: Graphikubermalungen,* exhibition catalog with text by I. Rein, Bonn 1981. **Articles—** ''Arnulf Rainer'' by Dieter Ronte in *Weltkunst,* vol. 60, no. 21, 1 November 1990; ''Arnulf Rainer'' by Johannes Gachnang in *Du,* no. 1, January 1994; ''Arnulf Rainer at the Arnulf Rainer Museum'' by Lilly Wei in *Art in America* (New York), vol. 82, no. 4, April 1994; ''42 Rainer Paintings Defaced'' by Christopher Phillips in *Art in America* (New York), vol. 83, March 1995; ''Arnulf Rainer'' by Silke Klein in *Flash Art (International Edition),* no. 193, March/April 1997; ''Der Fall Arnulf Rainer'' by Louis Peters in *Atelier,* no. 1, January-February 1998.

*

When I produce my own image, then it is also an attempt to expand—visual formulation of the possible, the imagined. I grab my hair and pull, I jump without reason, mimic discoveries, draw visions, lie and lie, until it could become true. I make no attempt at a one-to-one correspondence, I let it happen through an act of reproduction.

My own ideas, corrections, idealizations, develop in three phases: first scenic, extracted photographically. It must be reduced as much as possible, since it is concentrated in the instant that the camera records. Corrections aren't possible, only the instant counts. Most often I use a mirror, not as a control, but as a stimulation, to achieve a kind of extroverted communication with myself. Well-defined, motivated performances, known typecastings—as practised by actors—don't interest me. It is only in the realising that I can find, than I can look for, whatever it is that wants to activate itself within me.

My two-second scribbles were a first step towards one-tenth of a second exertion being photographed. The second phase: selection from hundreds of moments. The identification with one, the rejection of another. Criteria: intensity of facial transformation and nervous tension. I don't trust myself to destroy the great deal of residue, perhaps the criteria within me will change theselves.

Categories of expression such as peace, relaxation, maturity, eventemperedness, don't, for the while, excite my attention: without doubt an expressive formalistic visagism dominates.

The third phase: afterwards, often weeks later, when nothing remains but a flat piece of paper, there follows a further correction and selection. I draw over them and exert myself to discover new, more important, more meaningful lies. Only when I begin to believe myself do I give up. The stronger the physiognomic quality, the faster the graphic accentuation is accomplished. I end the work quickly and don't slide into complete overpainting.

Were there really such a thing as photographic documentation the overdrawing wouldn't be necessary. I am often more aware the instant of being photographed than I can ever be while overdrawing. On the paper only a dull reflection remains that needs to be accentuated and fattened out. That is why the mixture of mediums is necessary, from the inadequacy of what is left over from the photo sessions. Often I think of a combination of paintings, movements, three-dimensional photography. In order to be able to work with complete sequences, rapidly changing scenes, I am now buying a camera with an automatic release mechanism.

It is not at all clear to me where this physiognomism will lead. I have gained another vantage point. Because of the many lies I no longer know where borders are to be drawn. I lose myself in the possible, catch impossibilities: vectors that burst; growths, swollen in anger; breaks, cracks, split from irritation, flowers or wounds produced in pain. Agglomerations that destroy themselves.

The first stages of working with my own body before a camera were drawings with physiognomic themes; but equally the forming of traces of my body or movements. To these belong drawing with closed eyes, smearing of the face, painting with fingers and toes, with the left hand etc., all forms of a psychophysical reproduction upon a pictorial surface. In addition, for the last few years, I have been making use of photography. At first just for grimaces, afterwards for gestures and body-motoric expressions. Photography alone, however, is not able to communicate adequately a moving or statically concentrated tension. For a closer approximation I draw over the photograph. This isn't retouching, but rather accenting the reawakening of the dynamic aspect of the frozen moment. In this way my work became a mixture of performing and visual art.

Well defined human forms—I couldn't find myself among them. Only when their strictness and confinement were enunciated, could I grab hold of myself.

Fact: I begin to forget, I don't try to save face; I only want tranformations, changes, jumps, things not formulated. Identity seems so sure that I no longer pay attention to it. But the cage is always there. Caught in my own production, I stand with my back to the wall, planning a new escape.

—Arnulf Rainer

* * *

Today Arnulf Rainer is best known for the astonishing embellishments he adds to the photographic image of his face (and sometimes his body as well). A few years have helped the public forget that he is also an expert in many graphic fields, notably that of dry-point. Before he began work upon the strange range of autoportraits he had already been experimenting with imagery that, a bit further West than Vienna, might have been seen as yet another diversion of Cobra Art. He managed a permanent if eccentric figuration engulfed in scrawls and busy linear explosions in these earlier works and, in its way, elements of this style have survived to be injected into the photographic self-portraits. But even so, this sweeping generalisation overlooks his surrealist drawings of 1948–50, also the Central, Horizontal, and Vertical Visions, and his Black Pictures—all of which also, one way or another, have led up to his latest work.

The violence exhibited in Rainer's oeuvre over the past decade suggests that he should be associated with the Direct Action school of Vienna; but this would be wrong. Both philosophically and creatively he has nothing to do with Nietsch and Muehl. Actually, he is far closer to Dieter Roth with whom he has shared a number of exhibitions.

Peter Baum, Director of the Galerie der Stadt Linz Wolfgang-Gurlitt-Museum, goes as far as to say (March 1976) that "in the past few years Rainer has altered the face of painting." This artist has made himself familiar with many aspects of creativity, including some of the least considered (the drawings and paintings by schizophrenics and the mentally sick, and it is possible with their tantalizing inspirations in mind that he has investigated with such zest the challenge of extending opportunities offered by the self-portrait).

Baum implies that Rainer is "singular" in the dictionary sense of the word, and this view could certainly be maintained on the basis of an exhibition like the one held at the Wolgang-Gurlitt-Museum in March/April 1976, although Wilfried Skreiner writing about the artist's *Grimaces* exhibition saw things differently because, as he pointed out, "the language or faces" is part of the "language of art." Skreiner's belief is that Rainer must not be regarded as in any sense *isolated;* on the contrary, he is one of many, albeit an important example, of those who in a thoroughly accepted manner—the self-portrait—have changed the appearance of modern art. Hans M. Schmidt in his introduction to the Rainer Retrospective Exhibition (Hessische Landesmuseum, Darmstadt, 1975) goes still further, comparing Rainer's traditional conern with the self-portrait with that of van Gogh, Rembrandt and Kokoschka: "the originality of his self presentation is the manner in which he seeks the core personality."

What started as a re-interpretation of passport-photographs has now become much more sophisticated. Rainer's photo-portraits are carefully staged today so that they leave out every other suggestion of imagery outside Rainer himself. His expressive face, sometimes bearded, sometimes unshaven, sometimes completely beardless, assumes all sorts of *grimaces.* His body, too, when it is in evidence, takes up all kinds of unexpected poses. The photos themselves, large (175 x 122cm) or small (50 x 60cm) are printed onto a variety of grounds—china, aluminium sheet, photo-canvas and photographic paper. Once his image is in place, he begins to decorate it. Swift flashes of colour (red, yellow, orange and black) may be added as dramatic incidentals or, as in the case of one of the "Ohne Titel" pictures in the Neue Galerie der Stadt Linz (1976 exhibition), the entire area of the photograph has been overpainted and worked upon. The ultimate reaction experienced from such a show is one of quickened enthusiasm. A single person, a single face can suddenly opened up a completely new frontier of vision rich in emotionally uninhibited exhibitionism which is at the same time a personal triumph of communication with the outside world, even though this "communication" today is often fraught with the effects of the swing of the artist's creative pendulum which can take his inventive activities from clear recognizable "realism" to almost total black obliterations of the image.

—Sheldon Williams

RAJLICH, Tomas

Nationality: Dutch. **Born:** Janknov, Czechoslovakia, 5 March 1940; immigrated to the Netherlands 1969; naturalized, 1977. **Education:** School of Decorative Arts, Prague, 1954–58, and Academy of Fine Arts, Prague, 1958–64. **Family:** Married Hanusova Rajlich in 1963. **Career:** Painter and sculptor, Prague, 1964–68, in The Hague, since 1969. Instructor, Vrije Academie, The Hague, 1971–80. **Agents:** Galerie Yvon Lambert, 5 rue du Grenier St. Lazare, Paris, France; and Art and Project, Prinsengracht 785, Amsterdam, Netherlands. **Address:** Sirtemastraat 144, 2513 SR The Hague, Netherlands.

Individual Exhibitions:

1961 Galerie Mladych, Prague
1971 Stedlijk Museum, Schiedam, Netherlands
Gemeentemuseum, The Hague
1972 Haagse, Kunstkring, The Hague
Galerie Collection d'Art, Amsterdam
1973 Städtisches Museum, Bochum, West Germany
1974 Galerie Yvon Lambert, Paris
Galerie Seriaal, Amsterdam
Galleria Francoise Lambert, Milan
Art and Project, Amsterdam
1975 Groninger Museum, Groningen, Netherlands
Jaap Berghuis/Tomas Rajlich/Martin Rous, Westfälischer Kunstverein, Münster, West Germany
1976 Stedelijk Museum, Schiedam, Netherlands
Galerie Yvon Lambert, Paris
1978 Gemeentemuseum, The Hague
Centraal Museum, Utrecht
1979 Galleria Peccolo, Livorno, Italy
Gemeentemuseum, The Hague
Art and Project, Amsterdam
1980 Artline, The Hague
1982 Artline, The Hague
1983 Art and Project, Amsterdam
1985 Artline, The Hague
1986 Galerie im Winter, Bremen, West Germany
1987 Galleria Peccolo, Livorno, Italy
Galeria Aale, Madrid
Gallery Hatanaka, Tokyo

Selected Group Exhibitions:

1968 *Sculpture Tchecoslovaque,* Musée Rodin, Paris
1973 *Lof der Tekenkunst,* Stedelijk Van Abbemuseum, Eindhoven, Netherlands
8th Biennale de Paris, Musée d'Art Moderne, Paris
1975 *Fundamentele Schilderkunst,* Stedelijk Museum, Amsterdam
1976 *I Colori della Pitura,* Istituto Italo-Latino Americano, Rome
1977 *Trois Villes-Trois Collections,* Musée de Grenoble, France (travelled to Marseilles, St. Etienne and Paris)
1978 *Fracture du Monochrome,* Musée d'Art Moderne de la Ville, Paris
Bilder Ohne Bilder, Rheinisches Landesmuseum, Bonn
1979 *Unga Hollandare,* Liljevalchs Konsthall, Stockholm
1983 *Von der Ungleichheit des Ahnlichen in der Kunst,* Stadtische Galerie, Ludenscheid, West Germany (travelled to Gelsenkirchen and Unna)

Collections:

Musee de Grenoble, France; Musée Cantini, Marseilles; Gemeentemuseum, The Hague; Museum Boymans-van Beuningen, Rotterdam; Centraal Museum, Utrecht; Stedelijk Museum, Schiedam, Netherlands; Stedelijk Museum, Amsterdam; Stuyvesant Collection, Amsterdam; Narodni Galerie, Prague; Museum of Modern Art, New York.

Publications:

On RAJLICH: Books—*Tomas Rajlich,* exhibition catalog, The Hague 1971; *Jaap Berghuis/Tomas Rajlich/Martin Rous,* exhibition catalog with text by Klaus Honnef, Münster, West Germany 1975; *Fundamentele Schilderkunst/Fundamental Painting,* exhibition catalog with text by Rini Dippel, Amsterdam 1975; *Elementary Forms of Contemporary Painting and Drawing in the Netherlands,* exhibition catalog with texts by Guys van Tuyl, Hans Sizoo and Klaus Honnef, Amsterdam 1975; *Tomas Rajlich,* exhibition catalog with text by L. Brozek-Dolezal, Utrecht 1978; *Rajlich,* exhibition catalog, The Hague 1979; *De Nederlandse Indentiteit in de Kunst na 1945* by Geurt Imanse, Amsterdam 1984; *Tomas Rajlich,* exhibition catalog with text by Flip Bool, Livorno 1987. **Articles**—''The Metaphysical Monochrome or the Perfect Painting?'' by Philip Peters in *Kunst & Museumjournaal,* vol. 4, no. 5, 1993.

* * *

The painter Tomas Rajlich, who was born in Czechoslovakia, works and lives in The Hague, Holland. In his new country he found an artistic climate that welcomed the views he already had developed in his native Prague.

Within a short time his work met the critical attention of some of the leading writers on art. The art historian Carel Blotkamp wrote an introduction for the exhibition catalog *3 Konkretisten aus Prag* (Museum Bochum, 1973) in which he put Rajlich's typical gridstructure in a strikingly convincing perspective. Blotkamp describes this type of organization as unpersonal and as aiming at a clear relation between the external, physical existence of a canvas and its internal structure.

According to Blotkamp the visual formulation in Rajlich's work is lucid and convincing in its objective to demonstrate a ''minimal disruption of regular structure.'' Rajlich wants to provide painterly gestures with a ground that cannot be discussed and that offers no terms for speculation, with a background that is concrete.

A change occurs from about 1976 on when the gridstructures are seen to disappear from sight. This development starts with gesturely strokes loosely laid over the grid in a transparent paint. Hereafter, the surface they cover tends to become larger and larger while at the same time the paint itself gets more opaque. The next phase is marked by a series of paintings in which the underlying grid is only to be discovered at the extreme ends of the canvas. Finally, in 1979, the paintings are almost black. A rectangled part of the canvas, however, has been overpainted with a shining material that adds a reflection to the skin of the painting's surface. Also from the years 1976–77 dates a series of collages in which the theme of transparency is dealt with.

Rajlich's work appears to be methodical and uncompromising. The self-imposed restrictions lead him to a continuous reflection on his own premises. The general context of this research is a concrete, late-constructivist tradition of painting, of which the exhibition title *Fundamental Painting* (Stedelijk Museum, Amsterdam, 1975) seems to be a variation. In the Netherlands there has always been a special attention towards these strict views in painting, possibly because the artistic debate since De Stijl's early 20th century emergence ordinarily focused on the conflicting ideas of painting as rational intention versus painting as individual product.

Rajlich's inflexible gridstructures contradict the viewer's needs of a personal, subtly formulated composition. Additionally, the complementary painterly gesture as well is given in well measured quantities. Taken together these assure a position on ones's own in the Netherlands.

—A. F. Wagemans

RAMBOW, Inge

Nationality: German. **Born:** Marienburg/Westpreußen, Germany, 7 December 1940. **Education:** Trained in the book trade, 1954–57; **Family:** Married: Gunter Rambow, 1969 (divorced 1986); Gerald Gutsch, 1995; daughter: Ariane, born 1965. **Career:** Worked as a window-dresser, 1957–61; worked in a graphic studio, Stuttgart, 1961–65; began working as an artist, 1974; worked with designer Gunter Rambow, Frankfurt/Main, 1969–1979; worked as theater photographer, 1979–1990. **Awards:** Sonderpreis Grafik-Design, Bundesministerium des Inneren, 1981; Hessischen Kulturstiftung Grant, 1998; Maria Sibylla Merian Preis für Bildende Künstlerinnen, 1999. **Address:** Untermainanlage 8, 60329 Frankfurt/Main, Germany.

Individual Exhibitions:

1976 Deutscher Werkbund, Frankfurt/Main
1993 Deutsches Historisches Museum, Berlin
Galerie DB-S, Antwerp, Belgium
1994 Museum für Moderne Kunst, Amerika Haus, Frankfurt/Main
1995 Städtische Galerie, Pforzheim, Germany
1997 *Szenenwechsel XII,* Museum für Moderne Kunst, Frankfurt/Main
Galerie für Zeitgenössische Kunst, Leipzig, Germany
1998 Goethe Institut, New Delhi and Bombay
2001 Museum für Photographie, Braunschweig, Germany

Group Exhibitions:

1975 *Experimenta 5,* Kunstverein Franfurt/Main
1992 *3rd Biénnale Rotterdam,* Netherlands (catalog)
1995 *Prospect 96 IV, Internationale Triénnale Zeitgenössischer Kunst,* Schirn Kunsthalle and Frankfurter Kunstverein (catalog)
1997 Norddeutsches Landesmuseum Hamburg, Germany
1998 Hara Museum of Contemporary Art, Tokyo
Goethe Institut, Madrid
2000 Landesmuseum Oldenburg, Germany
Akademie der Künste, Berlin

Collections:

Museum für Moderne Kunst, Frankfurt/Main; Deutsches Historisches Museum, Berlin; Landesbank Hessen-Thüringen, Germany; Ministerium für Wissenschaft und Kunst, Wiesbaden, Germany.

Publications:

On RAMBOW: Books—*Positionen Aktueller Kunst der 80er und 90er Jahre,* catalog, Frankfurt/Main 1995; *Das Versprechen der Fotographie,* catalog, Munich 1998; *Wüstungen Fotografien 1991–1993,* catalog with text by Jean-Christophe Ammann, Frankfurt/Main 1998; *Grand Street No. 65,* New York 1999; *XL Photography Art Collection Neue Börse,* Ostfildern 2000.

*

I'm interested in a representation of landscapes which outreach the immediate readable presence due to the dimension of their historical past or their future history. I focus on everyday, trivial, subnormal areas, actually ''non''-locations, which often escape our attention due to their perceived worthlessness. These areas can be interim zones, outskirts, brush, work areas, unoccupied industrial sites or formerly exploited areas, which have been reclaimed—''wasteland'' in the broadest sense.

In addition, these locations are sometimes very special in my opinion and bear an important meaning within the context of utopias and ideologies. Therefore, I study and do research for a long time. My systematic objective is to acquire the topography of perceptions and memories that are evoked in me, figuratively and with maximal simplicity, and turn them, despite their complexity, into highly precise series or sequences.

Large formats emerge in the imagination of a full-scale approach of the world (as an index of a map), considering the laws of entropy. A few sculptures are intensified in their relation to space and are presented as ground works.

Similar to some literary models, my sculptures are not intended to be considered as works of art with a specific meaning but simply exist.

—Inge Rambow

RAMOS, Mel(vin John)

Nationality: American. **Born:** Sacramento, California, 24 July 1935. **Education:** Studied under Wayne Thiebaud at Sacramento Junior College, California, 1953–54; San Jose State College, California 1954–55; Sacramento State College 1955–58, B.A. 1957, M.F.A. 1958. **Family:** Married Leta Alice Helmers in 1955; children: Bradley, Scot and Rochelle. **Career:** Independent painter, since 1955: lives and works in California. Taught at Elk Grove High School, California, 1958–60; Mira Loma High School, California, 1960–66; Sacramento State College, California, 1965–66; and Arizona State University, Temple, 1967; artist-in-residence, University of Southern Florida, Tampa, 1970, and Syracuse University, New York, 1970; visiting artist, University of Wisconsin, Madison, 1973, and Pacific Lutheran University, Tacoma, Washington, 1973. Associate professor of painting, 1966–1980, and since 1980 professor of painting,

Inge Rambow: *Gestrüpp #1,* 2000. ©Inge Rambow.

Mel Ramos: *Galatea,* 2000. ©Mel Ramos/Licensed by VAGA, New York NY.

California State University at Hayward. **Awards:** Purchase Prizes: San Francisco Museum of Art, 1948, and Oakland Art Museum, 1959; Artist Fellowship, National Endowment for the Arts, Washington, D.C., 1986. **Agent:** Louis Meisel, 141 Prince Street, New York, New York 10012. **Address:** 5941 Ocean View Drive, Oakland, California 94618; or Moragrera 38, Horta de San Juan, Tarragona, Spain.

Individual Exhibitions:

1964 Bianchini Gallery, New York
1965 Bianchini Gallery, New York
David Stuart Gallery, Los Angeles
1966 Galerie Ricke, Kassel, West Germany
1967 San Francisco Museum of Art
Berkeley Gallery, San Francisco
Galerie Tobies-Silex, Cologne
1968 Mills College Art Gallery, Oakland, California
David Stuart Gallery, Los Angeles
1969 David Stuart Gallery, Los Angeles
Gallery Reese Palley, Los Angeles
Stadtsmuseum, Aachen, West Germany
1970 Artists Contemporary Gallery, Sacramento, California
1971 French and Co., New York
Graphics Gallery, San Francisco
Galerie Bruno Bischofberger, Zurich
Galerie Richard Foncke, Ghent
1972 Utah Museum of Fine Arts, Salt Lake City
1973 Dickinson College, Carlisle, Pennsylvania
Madison Art Center, Wisconsin
Pacific Lutheran University, Tacoma, Washington
1974 Meisel Gallery, New York
David Stuart Gallery, Los Angeles
1975 Museum Haus Lange, Krefeld, West Germany (retrospective)
1976 Meisel Gallery, New York
1977 Morgan Gallery, Shawnee Mission, Missouri
Oakland Museum, California (retrospective)
1978 University of Nevada at Reno
1979 California State University, Chico
1981 Meisel Gallery, New York
Modernism, San Francisco
California State University at Chico
1982 Route 66 Gallery, Philadelphia
Melinda Wyatt Gallery, Venice, California
1985 Louis K. Meisel Gallery, New York
1986 Hokin Gallery, Chicago
1987 Studio Trisorio, Naples
1988 James Corcoran Gallery, Los Angeles
1994 Kunstverein Lingen, Germany (retrospective)
1995 Mannheimer Kunstverein, Mannheim, Germany
Kunsthalle zu Keil, Germany
Hochschule für Angavante Kunst, Vienna
1996 Modernism, San Francisco
Galerie Levy, Hamburg
Galerie Ulrich Gering, Frankfurt
Galerie Hilger, Vienna
Galerie Burkhard H. Eikelmann, Essen, Germany
1997 Galerie Levy, Madrid
Kantor Gallery, Los Angeles, California
1998 Galeria Nova, Bad Homburg, Germany
Galerie Eikelmann and Auktionhaus Karbsten, Düsseldorf-Alstadt
1999 Galleria Civica di Modena, Italy
Louis Meisel Gallery, New York
Museum Moderner Kunst, Passau, Germany
Domestica, San Giovani Valderno, Italy
Galerie Burkhard Eikelmann, Essen, Germany
2000 Galerie Levy, Hamburg
Galerie Terminus, Munich
Galerie Vonderbank, Frankfurt
Galerie Burkhard Eikelmann, EXPO 2000, Cologne, Germany
2001 Galleria d'Arte Maggiore, Bologna, Italy
Galerie Hilger, Vienna

Selected Group Exhibitions:

1969 *Pop Art Revisited,* Hayward Gallery, London
1975 *3 Centuries of the American Nude,* New York Cultural Center
1976 *California Painting and Sculpture: The Modern Era,* San Francisco Museum of Modern Art
1978 *Art about Art,* Whitney Museum, New York

1981 *American Drawings in Black and White 1970–80,* Brooklyn Museum, New York
1983 *Modern Nude Painting 1880–1980,* National Museum of Art, Osaka, Japan
1984 *Automobile and Culture,* Museum of Contemporary Art, Los Angeles
1985 *Pop Art 1955–70,* Art Gallery of New South Wales, Sydney (travelled to Brisbane and Melbourne)
1992 *Pop Art,* The Royal Academy, London
Hand Painted Pop, Museum of Contemporary Art, Los Angeles
1993 *Arte Pop,* Galerie Levy, Madrid
1994 *The Pop Image: Prints and Multiples,* Marlborough Graphics, New York
1995 *Martini Culture,* Modernism, San Francisco, California
1996 *Attention to Detail (Realism in All Forms),* Louis K. Meisel Gallery, New York
1997 *The Pop 60s: Transatlantic Crossing,* Centro Cultural de Belém, Lisbon, Portugal
1998 *Babes,* Salzburg Museum, Austria
1999 *Pop Impressions: Prints and Multiples Europe/USA,* Museum of Modern Art, New York
2000 *Protest and Survive,* Whitechapel Art Gallery, London
2001 *Pop Art: US/UK Connections 1956–1966,* Houston, Texas

Collections:

Museum of Modern Art, New York; University Museum, Potsdam, New York; Chrysler Museum of Art, Norfolk, Virginia; San Francisco Museum of Modern Art; Oakland Museum, California; Museem der Stadt, Aachen, Germany; Kaiser Wilhelm Museum, Krefeld, Germany; Guggenheim Museum, New York.

Publications:

By RAMOS: Book—*Mel Ramos: Watercolors,* Berkeley, California 1979. **Articles—**''Interview with Mel Ramos,'' with Dan Tooker, in *Art International* (Lugano, Switzerland), December 1973.

On RAMOS: Books—*Pop Art* by John Rublowsky, New York 1965; *La Pop Art* Enrico Crispolti, Milan 1966; *Invitation to Vision* by Earl Linderman, Dubuque, Iowa, 1966; *Pop Art* by Lucy Lippard, New York 1966; *New Tendencies in Art* by Aldo Pellegrini, New York 1966; *Pop Art* by Michael Compton, London 1969; *Neue Formen des Bildes!* by Udo Kultermann, Berlin 1969; *Pop und die Folgen* by Heinz Ohff, Dusseldorf 1969; *Creativity and Communication* by Colin Forbes, London 1970; *Erotic Art 2* by Phyllis and Eberhard Kronhausen, New York 1970; *Erotic Art Today* by Volker Kahmen, Greenwich, Connecticut 1971; *Art Now/New Age: The Pop Image of Man* by Yoshiaki Tono, Tokyo 1971; *Woman as Sex Object* by Thomas Hess and Linda Nochlin, New York 1972; *Art as Image and Idea* by Edmund B. Feldman, New York 1972; *Kitsch* by Jacques Sternberg, London 1972; *Pop* by Simon Wilson, London 1974; *Mel Ramos* by Elizabeth Claridge, London 1975; *20th Century Masters of Erotic Art* by Bradley Smith, New York 1980; *Art in the San Francisco Bay Area 1945–80* by Thomas Albright, Berkeley, California 1985; *Mel Ramos: Pop Art Images* by Robert Rosenblum, Cologne 1994; *I Spy a Freight Train* by Lucy Micklethwait, New York 1996; *Disidentico Maschile Femminile e Oltre,* exhibition catalog by Achile Bonito Oliva, Rome 1998; *Mel Ramos: His Graphic Work* by Geri Obler and Heiner Schepers, Vienna 1999; *Ideal and Reality* by Peter Weiermair, New York 1999; *Mel Ramos: New Oils and Watercolors* (exhibition catalogue), Hamburg 2000. **Articles—**''Gut für die Preise sind Oden and die Veiblichkeit'' by Olga Kronsteiner in *Die Welt,* 24 July 1995; ''Aus der Sonne Kaliforniens'' by Irwin Melchart in *Kronen Zeitung,* 15 August 1995; ''Pop Art—Künstler Ramos Garniert Seine Meisterwerke mit Exotischen Gerichten'' by Mario Scheuermann in *Welt am Sonntag,* 21 April 1996; ''Pinsel-Kunst in Pöseldor Sharfer Cocktail'' in *Bild,* 13 May 1996; ''Mel Ramos: La Belleza de la Mujer y la Sensualidad del Dibujo'' by Javier Rubio Nomblot in *El Punto de las Artes,* 18–24 April 1997; ''Mel Ramos—Meister der Pop Art'' by Theo Schmidt in *Autographensammler,* no. 1, 1997; ''Pop Art, l'America a Palermo'' by Sergio Troisi in *Republica,* 15 December 1998; ''Mel Ramos e' Ancora Tempo di Pop Art'' by Paolo Vagheggi in *Republica,* 25 January 1999; ''Mel Ramos: Der Mahler im Erotik-Wahn'' by A. Thiele-Hoffmann in *Bild,* 13 August 1999; ''Dream Girls'' in *Die Welt,* 10 May 1999; ''Voyeuristische Verherrlichungen'' by Ulf Fiedler in *Nord-West Zeitung,* 28 October 1999; ''Der Pop-Artist und die Pin-Up-Girls'' by Doris Banuscher in *Die Welt,* 4 April 2000.

*

The subject of my painting is the figure. The object of my painting can be anything and usually is. I sometimes think that everything is instantaneous except my work, and I get the feeling that the best figuration is in the movies. Nevertheless, despite the rampant self-consciousness about ''formal'' concerns that seems to characterize 20th century art, the best painting still announces itself in this manner, and I am not particularly interested in becoming an exception. I am for an art that hangs on the wall and asserts itself.

—Mel Ramos

* * *

Mel Ramos' new landscapes, introduced in New York a few years ago, ostensibly seem to represent a major departure from the blunt figurative Pop paintings that brought him fame in the 1960s. In reality, however, the fundamental issues that formed the basis of his earlier aesthetic investigations—exploration of forms, a search for complete objectivity in representation—also inform the new work. ''I have never been interested in dealing with art from an esoteric point of view,'' he says. ''I do not think of objects as symbols, but as temporal, formal entities, as shapes to be explored purely on a formal basis.''

A major California figure of the first generation of Pop artists, Ramos came to the attention of the art world when Pop art was at its apogee. He participated in a movement that in celebration of the banal, the commonplace, the vulgar, often gently parodied familiar icons of American popular culture. His first mature works were a sort of hard-edge figurative paintings that documented as well as mimicked comic book heroes and *Playboy* sex symbols, using a limited palette of flat colors and hard precise drawing. Then, in a series of salutes to art history executed in the 1970s Ramos turned his attention from the lowly to the mighty with reconstructions of traditional and modernist masterpieces which he infused with a new eroticism drawn from the heroic images of contemporary folklore. Unfortunately, because of the notoriety fostered by their subject matter (beautiful nude bodies—mostly female), the ideas behind the works from these two decades were overshadowed by journalistic sensationalism, and often misunderstood. Central to Ramos' aesthetic are the modernist principles of both ''objectness'' and autonomy of the painted surface that depersonalize a subject. Thus, for him, the figures were never anything but objects—plastic shapes to be studied and recreated with paint on canvas, or paper, according to his particular vision—and to regard them as anything else was to miss the point of the art entirely.

Ramos' approach to the landscape is a similar one. His images may have changed to monuments, cacti, bridge supports, and palm trees, but they are treated with a like impersonal neutrality. That they are an outgrowth of the artist's art historical ''Homage Series'' of the 1970s, particularly de Kooning's, is evident from the lushly brushed surfaces and what he calls ''the gesticulated backgrounds.'' In allegiance to Morris Louis' famed unfurled canvases, they are organized around a central void flanked by angled rows of colored travel-related objects depicted in a worm's eye perspective, the way a tourist would look at those objects. ''The landscape came about mainly through my travels,'' Ramos explains, ''and the way one looks at things, as tourists look at the facades of buildings, as palm trees.'' In keeping with his preference for the mundane, the iconography of these new paintings is derived from postcards, travel posters, and other popular media images, thus marking the opening of new chapter rather than a change in the narrative.

''My primary concern has always been ART; I am interested in ART, and the subject matter of my work is, and will always be, ART.'' With these words, Mel Ramos recapitulates two very successful decades. On the strength of the interest generated by the new landscapes, one might hazard the prediction that the third will be important.

When Mel Ramos showed his landscapes for the first time in 1982, a controversy that had simmered for two decades was put to rest. Ramos, his critics proclaimed, may not be a male chauvinist painter after all; he may just have been a misunderstood artist who was manipulating the female form to satirize the worst aspect of American advertising. Speculations were rife about the cause of the switch from figures to landscapes, but the move was a good one, everyone agreed, and as one Los Angeles reviewer declared, ''Sex's loss (was) art's gain.''

In point of fact, Mel Ramos was not then, nor has he ever been, a male chauvinist, or a satirist, or anything but an artist concerned with art and its history. ''Although I have been accused of being a sexist, or of exploiting women, I really have never had any politics,'' he said five years ago. With a perspective of nearly three decades, despite assertions to the contrary, it is now clear that militancy has never been Ramos' posture, and that the change in subject matter was but another means of exploration—of research into new ways to make the same individualistic statement in as many forms as possible.

And where did the research into the landscape lead to? . . . As demonstrated by Ramos' new series, *The Artist in the Studio:* right back to the figure and the history of art! In this series and its corollary, *The Drawing Lesson,* de Kooning and Manet make way for Ingres and Matisse; a ''nude descending a stair-case'' takes on a new look; soft-focus mirror reflections and family memorabilia are added to the repertoire; and, most importantly, Ramos is now drawing from his own past, as in the restated *Kellog* painting he turned into a composition centered around a drawing by Ingres. ''My new paintings are more narcissistic,'' he said during a recent interview. ''I use some of my old works in my compositions, showing them reflected in mirrors, and this is what I mean by narcissistic. This is not a new device: artist have shown mirror-reflected images for ages, ever since the mirror was invented in the fifteenth century, when Jan Van Eyck painted *Giovanni Arnolfini and his Bride* (1434).''

The significance of the new *Artist in his Studio* series goes far beyond reconsideration of imagery, however. In his art historical ''Homages'' works of the seventies, Ramos relied upon well-known modernist masterpieces which he recast according to his own aesthetic vocabulary—parodying or celebrating, as the cases may have been. In the current *Studio* paintings and drawings, he continues to pay tribute to the heroes from the past, but the prototypes are less obvious. Matisse, Ingres, Bonnard, Duchamp are all part of the cast of characters, but there is no question as to the identity of the protagonist. In addition, the images from which he draws are not as renowned, and if they are rendered just as faithfully, they are now but one segment of a complex compositional scheme. This, in turn, gives the works an irrefutable stamp of Ramos authenticity that establishes them firmly within the stream of art history—lending truth once more to the timeless French adage: ''The more things change, the more they stay the same.''

—Andree Marechal-Workman

After retiring from his position at California State University, Hayward, where he taught for over thirty years, in 1998 Ramos returned to his studio full-time, as well as to some of the subjects that preoccupied him in the 1960's. The artist's most recent work finds him returning to the delicious and witty female figures for which he first became known. With characteristic sense of humor, Ramos calls one of his recent series *The Lost Paintings of 1965*—an appropriate and ironic theme for many of his recent figure studies, which quote his own work and reinvestigate his influences via pin-up styled nudes, lounging on enormous plates of food or suggestively straddling giant cigars. His *Galatea* series similarly returns to recurring themes in the artist's work—in this case, the art historical homage that Ramos explored in his reworking of canonical nudes, and the theme of transformation that we see in his de Kooning tributes—but with a novel twist. Here, we find the artist reproducing ancient Greek and Roman sculptures in his meticulous super-realist style that appear to have been captured, mid-metamorphosis, into sumptuous flesh-and-blood, contemporary beauties in the fashion of the mythological statue after whom the series is named. This new exploration of the past, however, promises an interesting future for the artist. At present, Ramos is at work on translating the paintings into a series of three-dimensional, painted porcelain sculptures that will surely pose exciting new challenges to the artist, and a new context through which to approach his oeuvre.

—Maria Elena Buszek

RAUSCHENBERG, Robert

Nationality: American. **Born:** Port Arthur, Texas, 22 October 1925. **Education:** Kansas City Art Institute and School of Design, 1946–47; Académie Julian, Paris, 1947; Black Mountain College, North Carolina, with Joseph Albers, 1948–50. **Family:** Married Susan Weil in 1950 (divorced, 1952); son: Christopher. **Military Service:** Served in the United States Navy Reserve, as a neuropsychiatry technician, at California Naval Hospital, 1942–45. **Career:** Independent artist,

New York, since 1950. Taught at Black Mountain College, 1952, mounting first "happening" with John Cage and others. Has worked with the Merce Cunningham Dance Company, New York, as a stage and costume designer, since 1955, technical director since 1960. President of the board of directors, Chang Inc., New York, 1970; member, board of directors, Public School #1, New York, 1977; president, Trisha Brown Dance Company, New York, 1978. **Awards:** Art Institute of Chicago Prize, 1960; Ohara Prize, National Museum of Modern Art, Tokyo, 1962; First Prize, 1963, and Grand Prix d'Honneur, 1979, *International* Exhibition of Graphic Art, Ljublijana, Yugoslavia; First Prize, *Biennale,* Venice 1964; William A. Clark Gold Medal and Prize, Corcoran *Biennial Exhibition of Contemporary American Painters,* Washington, D.C., 1965; Logan Award, Art Institute of Chicago, 1976; Mayor's Award of Honor in Arts and Culture, New York, 1977; Creative Arts Medal in Painting, Brandeis University, Waltham, Massachusetts, 1978; Chicago Arts Award, *Graphic Arts Biennale,* Cracow, Poland, 1979; Skowhegan Medal for Painting, Maine, 1982; Grammy Award, New York, 1984; Jerusalem Prize for Arts and Letters, Friends of Bezalel Academy, 1984. D.H.L.: Grinnell College, Iowa, 1967; D.F.A.: University of South Florida, Tampa, 1976; fellow, Rhode Island School of Design, Providence, 1978. **Member:** American Academy of Arts and Sciences, 1978. Foreign member, Royal Academy of Fine Arts of Stockholm, 1980; officier, Ordre des Arts et Lettres, France, 1981. **Agents:** Pace Wildenstein Gallery, 32 E. 57th Street, New York, New York, 10022–2513. **Addresses:** Laika Lane, P.O. Box 54, Captiva Island, Florida 33924; and 381 Lafayette Street, New York, New York 10003, U.S.A.

Individual Exhibitions:

1951 Betty Parson Gallery, New York
1953 Stable Gallery, New York
Galleria d'Arte Contemporanea, Florence
1955 Charles Egan Gallery, New York
1958 Leo Castelli Gallery, New York
1959 Leo Castelli Gallery, New York
Galleria La Tartaruga, Rome
Galerie 22, Dusseldorf
1960 Leo Castelli Gallery, New York
1961 Leo Castelli Gallery, New York
Galerie Daniel Cordier, Paris
Galerie dell'Ariete, Milan
1962 Dwan Gallery, New York
1963 Leo Castelli Gallery, New York
Jewish Museum, New York (retrospective)
Gallerie del'Obelisco, Rome
Galerie Ileana Sonnabend, Paris
1964 Galerie Ileana Sonnabend, Paris
Galleria Civica d'Arte Moderna, Turin
Paintings, Drawings and Combines 1949–1964, Whitechapel Art Gallery, London (retrospective)
1965 Leo Castelli Gallery, New York
Amerika Haus, Berlin
Contemporary Arts Society, Houston
Paintings 1963–1964, Walker Art Center, Minneapolis
Moderna Museet, Stockholm
1966 Museum of Modern Art, New York
1967 Leo Castelli Gallery, New York
Douglas Gallery, Vancouver
1968 Leo Castelli Gallery, New York
Museum of Modern Art, New York
Stedelijk Museum, Amsterdam
Peale House, Philadelphia
Kunstverein, Cologne
Musée National d'Art Moderne, Paris
1969 Leo Castelli Gallery, New York
Fort Worth Art Center, Texas
Douglas Gallery, Vancouver
1971 Galerie Ileana Sonnabend, Paris
1972 Leo Castelli Gallery, New York
Galerie Ileana Sonnabend, Paris
Galerie Buren, Stockholm
1973 Galerie Ileana Sonnabend, Paris
Leo Castelli Gallery, New York
Ace Gallery, Venice, California
Mitchell Gallery, Southern Illinois University, Carbondale
Israel Museum, Jerusalem
1974 Graficstudio Tampa, University of South Florida, Tampa
Galerie Buren, Stockholm
Galerie Mikro, West Berlin
Lucio Amelio Modern Art Agency, Naples
Museum Haus Lange, Krefeld
Castelli-Sonnabend Galleries, New York
Castelli Graphics, New York
Gemini, G.E.L., Los Angeles
Galerie Sonnabend, Geneva
Jared Sable Gallery, Toronto
1975 Castelli Graphis, New York
Gemini G.E.L., Los Angeles
Visual Arts Gallery, New York
Ace Gallery, Venice, California
Museo d'Arte Moderna ca'Pesaro, Venice
Art Association, Newport, Rhode Island
1976 Ace Gallery, Venice, California
Galerie de Gestlo, Hamburg
Greenberg Gallery, St. Louis
Galerie H. M., Brussels
Galleria Civica d'Arte Moderna, Ferrara, Italy
Leo Castelli Gallery, New York
Fort Belvidere, Florence
Ace Gallery, Vancouver
National Collection of Fine Arts, Washington, D.C. (retrospective)
Alberta College of Art, Calgary
Galleriet, Lund, Sweden
1977 Ace Gallery, Venice California
Galleriet, Lund, Sweden
Galerie Sonnabend, Paris
Museum of Modern Art, New York (retrospective)
Leo Castelli-Ileana Sonnabend Galleries, New York
San Francisco Museum of Modern Art (retrospective)
John Berggruen Gallery, San Francisco
Albright-Knox Art Gallery, Buffalo, New York
Art Institute of Chicago
Linda Farris Gallery, Seattle
Janie C. Lee, Houston
Galerie Rudolf Zwirner, Cologne
1978 Galerie Sonnabend, Paris
Mayor Gallery, London

Vancouver Art Gallery
Gemini G.E.L., Los Angeles
Castelli Graphics, New York
Forth Worth Art Museum, Texas
1979 Sonnabend Gallery, New York (twice)
Akron Art Institute, Ohio
Richard Gray Gallery, Chicago
Ace Gallery, Venice, California
Richard Hines Gallery, Seattle
Gloria Luria Gallery, Miami
Portland Art Center, Oregon
Kunsthalle, Tübingen (retrospective)
Art in Progess, Cologne
Castelli Uptown, New York
Kunstmusuem, Hannover (retrospective)
Musée de Toulon, France
Multiples-Goodman, New York
Institute of Contemporary Art, Virginia Museum, Richmond
Gloria Luria Gallery, Bary Harbor Island, Florida
1980 Conejo Valley Art Museum, Thousand Oaks, California
Edison Community College, Fort Myers, Florida
Visual Arts Museum, New York
Staatliche Kunsthalle, Berlin (retrospective)
Leo Castelli Gallery, New York
Galerie Sonnabend, Paris
Ace Gallery, Venice, California
Ace Gallery, Los Angeles (twice)
Staatliche Kunsthalle, Dusseldorf
Sanibel Photo Gallery, Florida
Louisiana Museum, Copenhagen (retrospective)
Cranbrook Academy of Art, Bloomfield Hills, Michigan
Baltimore Musuem of Art
Frederick Gallery, Washington D.C.
Children's Hospital, Washington, D.C.
Magnuson-Lee Gallery, Boston
Ace Gallery, Vancouver
Galleriet, Lund, Sweden
Equitable Trust, Baltimore
1981 Stadtische Kunstinstitut, Frankfurt (retrospective)
New Gallery of Contemporary Art, Cleveland
Gemini Gallery, Palm Beach, Florida
Städtische Galerie im Lenbachhaus, Munich (retrospective)
Colorado State University, Denver (toured the western United States and Canada)
Tate Gallery, London (retrospective)
Fay Gold Gallery, Atlanta
Centre Georges Pompidou, Paris (retrospective)
Sonnabend Gallery, New York
Sable-Castelli Gallery, Toronto
Gallery Watari, Tokyo
Styria Gallery, New York
Institute of Contemporary Art, Boston
Mayor Gallery, London
Gibbes Art Gallery, Charleston, South Carolina
Magnuson-Lee Gallery, Boston
Grimaldis Gallery, Baltimore
Rosamund Felsen Gallery, Los Angeles
1982 Sonnabend Gallery, New York
Photographers' Gallery, Sanibel Island, Florida
Edison Community College, Fort Myers, Florida
Hara Museum of Contemporary Art, Tokyo
Castelli Graphics, New York
Lund Galleriet, Lund, Sweden
Long Beach Museum of Art, California
Flow Ace Gallery, Paris
Van Straaten Gallery, Chicago
Museum of Modern Art, New York
1983 Sonnabend Gallery, New York
Castelli Gallery, New York
Thomas Babeor Gallery, La Jolla, California
Louisiana Museum, Humlebaek, Denmark (travelled to Copenhagen and Oslo)
Prince Hotel, Tokyo
KBS Kaikan, Kyoto, Japan
Flow Ace Gallery, Los Angeles
Daytona Beach Community College, Florida
Jinxian, Anhui Province, China
Edison Community College, Fort Myers, Florida
Galleria di Franca Mancini, Pesaro, Italy (travelled to New York; Houston; Cleveland, Ohio; Raleigh, North Carolina; West Palm Beach, Florida; Long Beach, California)
Douglas Elliott Gallery, San Francisco
Castelli Graphics, New York
Dalsheimer Gallery, Baltimore
Maryland Institute, Baltimore
Susanne Hilberry Gallery, Birmingham, Michigan
Marianne Friedland Gallery, Toronto
Australian National Gallery, Canberra
1984 Port Arthur Public Library, Texas
Harcourts Contemporary Gallery, San Francisco
Galerie Beyeler, Basel (retrospective)
Heland Thorden Wetterling Galleries, Stockholm
Miami Center for Fine Arts, Florida
Fondation Maeght, St. Paul de Vence, France
Adagio Gallery, Bridgehampton, New York
Gemini G.E.L., Los Angeles
Allen Street Gallery, Dallas
Objects Gallery, San Antonio, Texas
Edison Community College, Fort Myers, Florida
Scheinbaum and Russek Gallery, Santa Fe, New Mexico
Sonnabend Gallery, New York
Castelli Graphics, New York
1985 Fundacion Juan March, Madrid (retrospective; travelled to Barcelona)
B. R. Kornblatt Gallery, Washington D.C.
Ringling Museum of Art, Sarasota, Florida
Museo Rufino Tamayo, Mexico City (and world tour)
Galerie Daniel Templon, Paris
Contemporary Arts Museum, Houston (travelled to San Antonio, Dallas and Corpus Christi)
1986 Moosart Gallery, Miami, Florida
Contemporary Art Museum, Houston
Espace Niçois d'Art et de Culture, Nice, France
Larry Gagosian Gallery, New York
Edison Community College, Fort Myers, Florida
Acquavella Galleries, New York
School of Visual Arts, New York
Castelli Gallery, New York

Setagaya Art Museum, Tokyo
Sogetsu Kaikan, Tokyo
Dallas Museum of Art, Texas
1987 Metropolitan Museum of Art, New York
Heland Thorden Wetterling Galleries, Stockholm
Kaj Forsblom Gallery, Helsinki
Blum Helman Gallery, New York
Galerie Denise René/Hans Meyer, Dusseldorf
Galleria Lucio, Amelio, Naples
Edison Community College, Fort Myers, Florida
Castelli Graphics, New York
1990 Galerie Fabien Boulakia, Paris (catalog)
Paintings 1962–1980, Runkel-Hue-Williams Ltd., London (catalog)
Rauschenberg: Works on Paper, Knoedler & Company, New York (catalog)
The Silkscreen Paintings, 1962–64, Whitney Museum of American Art, New York (catalog)
1991 *The Early 1950s,* The Menil Collection, Corcoran Gallery of Art, Washington, D.C. (catalog)
1993 *Breaking Boundaries,* Lafayette College Art Gallery, Easton, Pennsylvania (catalog)
1995 *Major Printed Works,* Morris Museum of Art, Atlanta (catalog)
Modern Art Museum of Fort Worth (catalog)
1996 Exhibit A. Gallery, Savannah College of Art and Design, Savannah (catalog)
1997 Solomon R. Guggenheim Museum, New York (retrospective) (catalog)
Arcadian Retreats, Pace Wildenstein Gallery, New York (catalog)
1998 Solomon R. Guggenheim Museum, New York (retrospective) (catalog)
Museum Ludwig, Cologne (catalog)
2000 *Apogamy Pods,* Pace Wildenstein, New York (catalog)

Selected Group Exhibitions:

1957 *Collage in America,* American Federation of Arts, New York (toured the United States)
1961 *American Vanguard,* Guggenheim Museum, New York (toured Europe)
1964 *Black, White and Grays,* Wadsworth Atheneum, Hartford, Connecticut
1968 *Dada, Surrealism and their Heritage,* Museum of Modern Art, New York
1973 *Fotografia Creativa,* Centro La Capella, Trieste, Italy
1978 *Art about Art,* Whitney Museum, New York
1980 *Printed Art of the 60s and 70s,* Museum of Modern Art, New York
1983 *Photography in America 1910–83,* Tampa Museum, Florida
1985 *Painterly Visions 1940–84,* Guggenheim Museum, New York
1987 *American Painting: Abstract Expressionism and After,* San Francisco Museum of Modern Art
1989 *5 Great American Artists,* Duson Gallery, Seoul, Korea (catalog)
Jasper Johns & Robert Rauschenberg, San Jose Museum of Art, San Jose (catalog)
1990 *Roy Lichtenstein, Robert Rauschenberg,* La Fondation, Arles, France (catalog)
1999 *Robert Rauschenberg and James Rosenquist,* Museum of Fine Arts, St. Petersburg (catalog)

Collections:

Museum of Modern Art, New York; Guggenheim Museum, New York; Whitney Museum, New York; Stedelijk Museum, Amsterdam; Los Angeles County Museum of Art; Museum Ludwig, Cologne; Kaiser Wilhelm Museum, Krefeld Kunsthaus, Zurich; Art Gallery of Ontario, Toronto; National Gallery of Canada, Ottawa; Kunsthaus, Zurich.

Publications:

By RAUSCHENBERG: Books—*The Artist Observed: 28 Interviews with Contemporary Artists, 1972–1978,* with John Gruen, Chicago 1991; *Encounters with Rauschenberg: A Lavishly Illustrated Lecture,* with Leo Steinberg, Chicago 2000. **Articles—**interview with Dorothy Seckler for *Archives of American Art* (Washington, D.C.), 21 December 1965 (transcript, unpublished); ''Carnal Clocks'' in *Art Now: New York,* May 1969; ''A Collage Comment by Robert Rauschenberg in His Latest Suite of Prints'' in *Studio International* (London), December 1969; ''Robert Rauschenberg Talks to Maxime de la Falaise McKendry'' in *Interview* (New York), May 1976; ''Statements by Richard Diebenkorn, Jasper Johns, Robert Rauschenberg and Wayne Thiebaud'' in *Art Journal,* vol. 48, no. 3, Fall 1989; interview with Paul Taylor in *Interview,* December 1990; interview with Douglas Maxwell in *Art Line,* vol. 5, no. 4, March-April 1991; interview with Hajo Schiff in *Neue Bildende Kunst,* no. 4, August-September 1998; interview with Tim Marlow in *Tate: The Art Magazine,* no. 16, Winter 1998. **Film and video—***Canoe,* New York 1966; *Robert Rauschenberg: Man at Work,* New York 1997.

On RAUSCHENBERG: Books—*Rauschenberg,* exhibition catalog with essay by Gillo Dorfles, Milan 1961; *Rauschenberg,* exhibition catalog with essays by John Cage, Lawrence Alloway, and others, Paris 1963; *Robert Rauschenberg: Paintings, Drawings and Combines 1949–1964,* exhibition catalog with essays by Henry Geldzahler, John Cage, Max Kozloff, 1964; *4 Germinal Painters, United States of America: 32nd International Biennial Exhibition of Art,* exhibition catalog with an essay by Alan R. Soloman, New York, 1964; *Robert Rauschenberg: Paintings 1953–1964,* exhibition catalog with an introduction by Dean Swanson, Minneapolis 1965; *Robert Rauschenberg,* exhibtion catalog by Andrew Forge, Amsterdam 1968; *Robert Rauschenberg* by Andrew Forge, New York 1969; *Rauschenberg: Black Market* by Jürgen Wissman, Stuttgart 1970; *Rauschenberg at Graphic Studio,* exhibition catalog with introduction by Willard McCracken and a foreword by Donald Staff, Tampa, Florida 1974; *The Bride and the Bachelors: 5 Masters of the Avant Garde* by Calvin Tomkins, New York 1974; *Rauschenberg's Pages and Fuses,* exhibition catalog with an introduction by Joseph E. Young, Los Angeles 1974; *Robert Rauschenberg,* exhibition catalog with essays by Guido Perocco, Daniel Abadie, David Bourdon, Venice 1975; *Robert Rauschenberg,* exhibition catalog with essays by Paola Serra Zanetti, Daniel Abadie, David Bourdon, Ferrara, Italy 1976; *Robert Rauschenberg* by Gotz Adriana, Munich 1979; *Off the Wall* by Calvin Tomkins, New York 1980; *Photography and Art 1946–1986* by Andy Grundberg and Kathleen Gauss, Los Angeles

1987; *Rauschenberg: Art and Life* by Mary Lynn Kotz, New York 1990; *Robert Rauschenberg: The Early 1950s* by Walter Hopps, Houston 1991; *Robert Rauschenberg* by Sam Hunter, New York 1999. **Articles**—''Sculpture on the Road: Rauschenberg's ROCI'' by Robert Mahoney in *Sculpture* (Washington, D.C.); ''Rauschenberg: In the Beginning'' by Frances Colpitt in *Art in America* (New York), vol. 80, no. 4, April 1992; ''We the People and the Art of Robert Rauschenberg and the Construction of American National Identity'' by Christin J. Mamiya in *American Art,* vol. 7, no. 3, Summer 1993; ''Rauschenberg's Cyborgs'' in Jan Avgikos and Miranda McClintic in *Sculpture* (Washington, D.C.), vol. 15, no. 5, May-June 1996; ''Lifting the Veil: Robert Rauschenberg's Thirty-Four Drawings for Dante's Inferno and the Commercial Homoerotic Imagery of 1950s America'' by Laura Auricchio in *Genders,* no. 26, 1997; ''This is Now: Robert Rauschenberg'' by Thomas Crow, Yve-Alain Boris, Dore Ashton and Dave Hickey in *Artforum,* vol. 36, no. 1, September 1997; ''Rauschenberg'' by Frederick Ted Castle in *Art Monthly,* no. 211, November 1997; ''Robert Rauschenberg's Reservoir'' by Jonathan Fineberg in *American Art,* vol. 12, no. 1, Spring 1998; ''Rauschenberg: Solutions for a Small Planet'' by Roni Feinstein in *Art in America* (New York), vol. 86, no. 2, February 1998; ''Rauschenberg's Photographies'' by Ingrid Schaffner in *Afterimage,* vol. 25, no. 5, March-April 1998; ''Trash as a Cultural System: Rauschenberg, Warhol, Smith and Shifting Museum Practices'' by Philip Monk in *Magazine,* no. 58, May-August 1998; ''Rauschenberg's Honeymoon'' by Jonathan Katz in *Art/Text,* no. 61, May-July 1998; ''Robert Rauschenberg: Holiday Ruse (Night Shade)'' by Walter Hopps in *Artforum,* vol. 38, no. 9, May 2000. **Video**—*Robert Rauschenberg: Inventive Genius,* New York 1999.

* * *

Rauschenberg is with Jasper Johns the most influential of the artists who reacted against the high seriousness, solemn introspection, and spirituality of Abstract Expressionism and the critical reverence accorded to it; in the process he raised some fundamental questions about art and its relation to life. In comparison to Johns, Rauschenberg's work is much more varied, and he has shown a constant zest for exploration which sharply distinguishes him from the narrow formula or recipe type of modern artist. In fact he has pioneered or anticipated many of the subsequent movements in American art, and he has also been a truly eclectic artist in his use of different techniques, so that the extraordinary variety of his work makes it a microcosm of the artistic developments of the last two decades.

John Cage has quoted as Rauschenberg's central ''message'' his now famous statement that ''Painting relates to both art and life. Neither can be made—I try to act in the gap between the two.'' It was in fact Cage's example that caused Rauschenberg to formulate that remark, for Cage had already been breaking down the distinction between art and life with his random noises and chance events, so that instead of offering artistically structured and ordered experiences he was trying to ''unfocus'' the spectator's mind and so to make him more open, more aware of himself and his environment. For Cage's off beat, Zen-oriented mind had led him right away from the Western tradition of art as personal expression to a belief in the complete depersonalization of creativity by chance procedures like throwing dice—thus proposing the revolutionary overthrow of the whole basic assumption of Western art since the Renaissance, that the artist by individual self-expression creates order and communicates feelings and emotions.

Similarly Rauschenberg started attacking the inflation of the artistic ego that had been an integral part of Abstract Expressionism by saying that being an artist was no different spiritually from being a cargo humper, a file clerk, or anything else. And if his famous erased de Kooning drawing was at least in part an act of homage, he was certainly attacking the idea of highly subjective action painting when he made two Abstract Expressionist pictures which reproduce each other identically in every splash and dribble. Having the same sort of quirky, off-beat mind as Cage, a mind which works in angular ways full of ricochets and inventions, Rauschenberg studied under the rigorous Albers to give himself discipline. And among the works which resulted were his own explorations of minimalism in all-white and all-black paintings. All sorts of interpretations have been advanced for these, but it is clear from Rauschenberg's own statements that these are a far cry from Malevich's suprematist *White on White,* but a continuation of his own dialogue between art and life by letting life and the environment enter directly into art: ''I always thought of the white paintings as being not passive but very—well, hypersensitive, so that one could look at them and almost see how many people were in the room by the shadows cast, or what time of day it was.''

The comparison is therefore rather with the monochromatic paintings that Yves Klein had begun painting two years earlier, and both artists moved on in the direction of actuality, towards methods and attitudes that incorporate the outside world within the work of art. Using the free brushwork of Abstract Expressionist painting, Rauschenberg began to load his canvases with rags and tatters of cloth and other collage elements of discarded junk. He incorporated ladders or chairs into the painting, and broke down the distinction between painting and sculpture, so that many of his ''combines'' are free-standing works which can include any junk material, from Coca-Cola bottles and old radios to stuffed birds or a stuffed goat wearing an automobile tyre, and even a full-sized made-up bed. John Cage has stressed that the essential point of these ''combines'' is their multiplicity, their lack of any unitary subject. Like the work of Duchamp they do abound in puns, parallels and hidden meanings, but there is no unitary meaing, only a flux of images in which the dialogue between art and everyday reality is kept open and unresolved. In his ''combines'' Rauschenberg is the complete city artist, collaborating with his environment with that open receptive attitude advocated by Cage.

Rauschenberg was thus helping to open up the tracts of popular and junk imagery that were to become the basis of Pop art. But such assemblages also provided the jumping-off point for environmental art and for the happening, both of which Rauschenberg was himself exploring. The theatre pieces which have been as important in his work as his visual art grew out of his close association with Cage and with the innovative choreographer Merce Cunningham, with whose Dance Company Rauschenberg has had a long association not only as a designer but as a dancer too. And just as the ''combines'' include collages of all sorts of found and ready-made objects, so Rauschenberg's theatre pieces and happenings are essentially collages, though instead of being static they include the added dimensions of time and event, allowing things to happen, including anything which happens to take place by chance. Again there is no meaning in the usual sense, but simply a bringing together of disparate images, as in his earlier paintings and combines, and in his later lithographs and silk screens.

By the late 1950s Rauschenberg had begun to think of his work as a kind of reporting, and action photographs from magazines and newspapers were cropping up more frequently in his works. He then found that newsprint, when wetted with lighter fluid and then rubber, transfers a grey ghost of itself to paper, and this opened his work to a whole stream of image-quotation from newspapers and magazines. He used this technique in his set of illustrations to Dante's *Inferno,* Dante being a character in a towel from *Sports Illustrated,* while Virgil appears alternately as Adlai Stevenson and as a baseball umpire. The resulting combination of diverse images was aptly described by Cage as "like many television sets working simultaneously, all tuned differently." Rauschenberg then adopted Andy Warhol's technique of making silk-screens of photographs and stencilling them on to the surfaces of silk-screen paintings whose trapped images in electronic colours have a brilliantly heightened documentary flavour. Similarly his lithographs, such as the two series devoted to the American space programme "Booster" (1967) and the "Stoned Moon" series (1970) are a rich, complicated mix of diverse images.

It was logical that Rauschenberg should one day incorporate not merely the thrown-away junk of industrial society in his works, but its active technology too, as he began to do when he incorporated an electric clock, a blinking light, or three working radiosets into his combines. One of his long-standing collaborations has been with the laser-scientist Billy Kluver, with whom in 1966 he started the nonprofit foundation EAT (Experiments in Art and Technology) in order "to catalyze the inevitable active involvement of industry, technology and the arts." Among Rauschenberg's own forays into artworks making use of technology are the series of "Revolvers," round paintings using characteristic assemblages of disparate images, but on plexiglass discs which can be driven by motors, so that they revolve and prevent any definite conclusions about the "right way" of viewing the works. "Soundings" (1968) is an environment work using the same basic idea as the early white paintings which had invoked the space of nothingness in which the disparate objects of the surroundings could be reflected and seen afresh. Basically it is a plexiglass wall hanging in the centre of a room to make a sort of hall of mirrors, with microphones picking up the spectator's talk and triggering the projection of changing images, including the viewers themselves, onto the mirror sufaces.

Despite his seeming multiplicity, therefore, Rauschenberg's activities have behind them a consistent set of developing ideas, ideas very similar to those of John Cage. Schoenberg said of Cage that he was "not a composer but an inventor—of genius," and that phrase could easily be adapted to fit Rauschenberg. But whereas very few composers indeed have been prepared to accept Cage's extreme position in abandoning the personal expression of composed music in favour of listening to the random noises of life, the world of the visual arts, already conditioned by Duchamp to accept that anything may be selected and displayed as art, has been more ready to be influenced along such lines. Recent American art has offered two extreme courses, both of them reductive—the insistence that there is no boundary between art and life found in Rauschenberg and Cage, or the Hard Edge insistence on art deriving from art alone, with the exaltation of the painting as object which reaches its *reductio ad absurdum* in the work of Frank Stella. But whatever its ultimate value may prove to be, Rauschenberg's work, with its constant questioning of the nature of art itself and the nature of reality, has challenged most artistic concepts, so that Robert Rosenblum can justly say of him: "Every artist after 1960 who challenged the restrictions of painting and sculpture and believed that all of life was open to art is indebted to Rauschenberg—forever."

—Konstantin Bazarov

RAY, Charles

Nationality: American. **Born:** Chicago, Illinois, 1953. **Education:** University of Iowa, Iowa City, Iowa, B.F.A., 1975 (cum laude); Mason Gross School of Art, Rutgers University, New Jersey, M.F.A., 1979. **Career:** Performance artist, sculptor, and photographer; Professor, Art Department, University of California, Los Angeles, since 1981. **Agent:** Donald Young Gallery, 933 W. Washington Blvd., Chicago, Illinois 60607.

Selected Individual Exhibitions:

1983 64 Market Street, Venice, California
1985 Mercer Union, Toronto, Ontario, Canada
New Langton Arts, San Francisco
1987 Feature, Chicago
Burnett Miller Gallery, Los Angeles
1988 Feature, Chicago
Burnett Miller Gallery, Los Angeles
1990 Feature, New York
Burnett Miller Gallery, Los Angeles
Newport Harbor Art Museum, Newport Beach, California
Galerie Claire Burrus, Paris, France
Interim Art, London
The Mattress Factory, Pittsburgh
Burnett Miller Gallery, Los Angeles
1991 Galerie Metropol, Vienna, Austria
Galerie Claire Burrus, Paris, France
1992 Donald Young Gallery, Seattle
Feature, New York
1993 Feature, New York
1994 Rooseum-Center for Contemporary Art, Malmö
ICA, London
Kunsthalle Bern, Switzerland
Kunsthalle Zürich, Switzerland
1996 Studioz, Milan
1997 Regen Projects, Los Angeles
1998 Whitney Museum of American Art, New York
Museum of Contemporary Art, Los Angeles
1999 Museum of Contemporary Art, Chicago

Selected Group Exhibitions:

1980 Contemporary Arts Center, New Orleans, Los Angeles
Uno Gallery, New Orleans, Los Angeles
1981 Cape Gallery, New Orleans, Los Angeles
1984 Los Angeles Institute of Contemporary Art, Los Angeles
1986 Frederick A. Wright Gallery, University of California, Los Angeles
Baaa Baaa Ba'bel, Alexandria Hotel, Los Angeles
1987 *Industrial Icons,* University Art Gallery, San Diego State University, San Diego, California
Nature, Feature, Chicago
Burnett Miller Gallery, Los Angeles
1988 *Selections from the Permanent Collection,* Newport Harbor Art Museum, Newport Beach, California
Still Trauma, Milford Gallery, New York
Near Miss, Feature, Chicago
303 Gallery, New York

Recent Art from Los Angeles, Cleveland Center for Contemporary Art, Cleveland, Ohio
1989 *1989 Biennial Exhibition,* Whitney Museum of American Art, New York
Loaded, Kuhlenschmidt Gallery, Los Angeles
1990 *Recent Drawing,* Whitney Museum of American Art, New York
Matrix Gallery, University Art Museum, Berkeley
5th Anniversary Exhibition, Burnett Miller Gallery, Los Angeles
1991 *Devices,* Josh Baer Gallery, New York
Katharina Fritsch, Robert Gober, Reinhard Mucha, Charles Ray, and Rachel Whiteread, Luhring Augustine Gallery, New York
The Savage Garden, Sala de Exposiciones de la Fundation Caja de Pensiones, Madrid, Spain
Mechanika, Contemporary Arts Center, Cincinnati, Ohio
1992 *Viaggio a Los Angeles,* Castello di Rivara, Torino, Italy
Documenta, Kassel, Germany
The Other Side, Tony Shafrazy Gallery, New York
Strange Developments, Anthony d'Offay Gallery, London
Helter Skelter: L.A. Art in the 1990s, Museum of Contemporary Art, Los Angeles
Donald Young Gallery, Seattle, Washington
Sydney Biennial, Sydney, Australia
1993 *Biennial Exhibition,* Whitney Museum of American Art, New York
1994 *Radical Scavenger(s): The Conceptual Vernacular in Recent American Art,* Museum of Contemporary Art, Chicago
Face-Off: The Portrait in Recent Art, Institute of Contemporary Art, University of Pennsylvania, Philadelphia (traveled to Nebraska and North Carolina)
1995 *1995 Whitney Biennial,* Whitney Museum of Art, New York
Private/Public: ARS 1995, Museum of Contemporary Art, Helsinki, Finland
MicroMegas: Miniatures and Monstrosities in Contemporary Art, Israel Museum, Jerusalem
PerForms: Janine Antoni, Charles Ray, Jana Sterbak, Institute of Contemporary Art, Philadelphia
Feinin-masculin: le sexe de líart, Centre Georges Pompidou, Paris
Everything that's Interesting is New, Dakis Joannou Collection, Athens School of Fine Art, Athens, Greece
Still Leben, National Museum, Stockholm, Sweden
A Glimpse of the Norton Collection as Revealed by Kim Dingle, Santa Monica Museum of Art, Santa Monica, California
1996 *Just Past: The Contemporary in the Permanent Collection, 1975–96,* Museum of Contemporary Art, Los Angeles
Portrait of the Artist, Anthony d'Offay Gallery, London
Distemper: Dissonant Themes in the Art of the 1990s, Hirshhorn Museum and Sculpture Garden, Smithsonian Institution, Washington D.C.
Art at the End of the 20th Century: Selections form the Whitney Museum of American Art, National Gallery, Athens, Greece (traveled to Spain and Germany)
NowHere: Walking and Thinking and Walking, Louisiana Museum of Modern Art
Happy End, Kunsthalle Düsseldorf, Düsseldorf, Germany
Young Americans: Part II, Saatchi Gallery, London
Narcissism: Artists Reflect Themselves, California Center for the Arts Museum, Escondido, California
1997 *A Lasting Legacy: Selections from the Lannan Foundation Gift,* Museum of Contemporary Art, Los Angeles
Biennale de Lyon dí Art Contemporain, Maison de Lyon, Lyon, France
Skulptor: Projekte in Münster 1997, Westfälisches Landesmuseum für Kunst und Kulturgeschichte, Münster, Germany
Objects of Desire: The Modern Still Life, Museum of Modern Art, New York
Sunshine & Noir: Art in L.A. 1960–1997, Louisiana Museum of Modern Art, Humlebaek, Denmark (traveled to Germany, Italy, and the United States)
Whitney Biennial Exhibition, Whitney Museum of American Art, New York
Veronicaís Revenge: Selections from the Lambert Art Collection, Centre d'Art Contemporain, Geneva, Switzerland
1998 *Serra, Ray and Pardo,* Museum of Contemporary Art, Los Angeles
1999 *Millennium My Eye: Head Over Heals, A Work of Impertinence,* Musée d'Art Contemporain de Montréal, Québec, Canada
Regarding Beauty, Hirshhorn Museum and Sculpture Garden, Washington, D.C.
2000 *Quotidiana: The Continuity of the Everyday in XX Century Art,* Castello di Rivoli, Museo dí Arte Contemporanea, Torino, Italy

Publications:

On RAY: Books—*Charles Ray* by Lucinda Barnes and Dennis Cooper, Newport Beach, California 1990; *Charles Ray* by Lars Nittve and Bruce W. Ferguson, Malmö, Sweden 1994; *Charles Ray* by Paul Schimmel and Lisa Phillips, Los Angeles 1998. **Articles—**''Studio: Charles Ray, Edgy Provocative Presences'' by Peter Clothier in *Art News,* no. 86, December 1987; ''Charles Ray: In the No'' by Lane Relyea in *Artforum International* no. 31, September 1992; ''Ray's Reality Hybrids'' by Virginia Rutledge in *Art in America,* vol. 86, no. 11, November 1998; ''Anxious Spaces'' by Robert Storr in *Art in America,* vol. 86, no. 11, November 1998; ''Charles Ray'' by Anne Wagner in *Artforum International,* vol. 37, no. 9, May 1999.

* * *

Primarily known as a sculptor, Charles Ray has worked in variety of media since his career began in the early 1970s, including performance, photography, and film. Ray's work has encompassed the wide range of post-World War II styles from Greenbergian formalism to conceptualism, often within the confines of a single sculpture. His ability to combine disparate, seemingly contradictory styles into a cohesive whole gives much of his work a schizophrenic feel; indeed, Ray has cited the behavior of his sister, a diagnosed schizophrenic, as a major influence. Perhaps the most compelling characteristic of Ray's work is the overwhelming sense of unease, brought about by subtle shifts in context, scale, and materials that reveal extraordinary aspects in otherwise commonplace objects and situations.

Ray became interested in formal syntax while studying at the University of Iowa under Roland Brener, a former student of the modernist sculptor Anthony Caro. Ray's earliest sculptural experiments, abstract arrangements of iron girders, rods, and cinderblocks, reveal a fascination with balance and tension. Later in the 1970s, Ray fused his early performance projects with the stark, geometric forms of Minimalist sculpture in such works as *Clock Man* (1978) and *In Memory of Moro* (1979), emphasizing the theatrical quality of Minimalism espoused by Robert Morris. Widely considered one of his most significant sculptures, Ray's *Ink Box* (1986), a black, thirty-six cubic-inch container with an open top filled to the brim with black ink, is his most successful foray into literalizing the theatrical possibilities of Minimalist sculpture. While *Ink Box* has the structural stability of a Minimalist object, the potentially messy contents of the box, held in place by surface tension alone, imbue the sculpture with a tangible, even hostile, presence.

After he discontinued using performance to heighten the theatrical presence of his sculpture in the mid-1980s, Ray began using furniture, mannequins, and fiberglass molds of his own body, which evinced a sustained interest in a human presence in the work, albeit an implied rather than actual presence. His mannequin series, which began in the early 1990s, references classical sculpture, Minimalist seriality, and Pop art's regard for consumer culture. His *Self-Portrait* (1990), a mannequin endowed with a cast of Ray's own generalized facial features, exudes a vacancy that belies its verisimilitude. With his switch from formalism to figuration, Ray embarked on an investigation into his own psyche, generating a highly personalized lexicon through the familiar, deceptively benign features of the clothing-store mannequin. Despite the fact that Ray is often the subject of his own work, his self-representations read more like objects, like constructs of—rather than glimpses into—his carefully guarded psyche.

While Ray's works initially seem to have the Minimalist quality of the gestalt, their most powerful and lasting effects come with closer examination, as they reveal "the instability of perceptual experience." He delights in making palpable the moment of uncertainty between seeing and understanding. The secret behind his *Rotating Circle* (1988), a disc set flush into a wall spinning so fast that it appears to be stationary, is aural rather than visual, as the disc's imperceptible motion is betrayed by the hum of the hidden motor. Like the instinctual impulse to run or fight, the sense of dislocation caused by the interval between seeing and understanding the sculpture instills a moment of heightened self-awareness.

—Bradley Bailey

RAYNAUD, Jean-Pierre

Nationality: French. **Born:** Colombes, 20 April 1939. **Education:** Versailles Horticultural School, France, 1955–57; mainly self-taught in art, 1962. **Military Service:** Served in the French Army, 1959–61. **Career:** Worked at various jobs, including architectural assistant and floral decorator, Paris, 1961–66. Independent artist, since 1962: first exhibited art works, Paris, 1964; opened his house in Colombes to the public, 1974; first stained-glass commission, Noirlac, 1976; garden commission, Grenoble, 1977. **Address:** 25 rue des Robichons, 78000 La Celle-St.-Cloud, France.

Individual Exhibitions:

1965 Galerie Jean Larcade, Paris
1966 *Jean-Pierre Raynaud et la Conscience de Soi,* Galerie Mathias Fels, Paris
1967 Galleria Apollinaire, Milan
1968 Stedelijk Museum, Amsterdam
Galerie Mathias Fels, Paris
Moderna Museet, Stockholm
Württembergischer Kunstverein, Stuttgart
1969 Centre National d'Art Contemporain, Paris
Galerie Alexandre Iolas, Paris
1970 Palais des Beaux-Arts, Brussels
Galerie Alexandre Iolas, Paris
Alexandre Iolas Gallery, New York
1971 Israel Museum, Jerusalem
Galleria LP220, Turin
Galerie Smith, Brussels
Hyde Park, London
Open-Air Exhibition, Hannover
1972 Salone Annunciata, Milan
Musée des Arts Décoratifs, Paris
Galerie D, Brussels
1973 Galerie Alexandre Iolas, Paris
1974 Galerie D, Brussels
Galerie Alexandre Iolas, Brussels
1975 Galerie Alexandre Iolas, Paris
Palais des Beaux-Arts, Brussels
1978 Musée des Beaux-Arts, Ghent
1979 Centre Georges Pompidou, Paris
1981 Galerie Jean Fournier, Paris
Hara Museum of Contemporary Art, Tokyo
1982 Galerie L'Hermitte, Coutances, France
1983 Grand Palais, Paris
1984 Newport Harbor Art Museum, Newport Beach, California
Galerie Daniel Varenne, Zurich
1985 Musee d'Art Moderne de la Ville, Paris
Seibu Museum, Tokyo
Galerie Gilbert Brownstone, Paris
Fondation Cartier, Jouy-en-Josas, France
Daniel Varenne Gallery, Chicago
1986 Carpenter and Hochman Gallery, New York
1988 Galerie de France, Paris
1991 Museum of Contemporary Art, Chicago
Menil Collection, Houston (catalog)
1992 Leo Castelli Gallery, New York
Mito Geijutsukan Gendai Bijutsu Gyarari, Mito-shi, Japan (catalog)
1993 *Psycho-Objets, 1964–1968,* CAPC Musée d'Art Contemporain de Bordeaux (catalog)
1994 Neue Bildende Kunst, Berlin
1996 Fondation Cartier, Paris
Galerie Pièce Unique, Paris
1998 Galerie Daniel Templon, Paris
Centre Georges Pompidou, Paris (catalog)
Galerie Nationale du Jeu de Paume, Paris (retrospective) (catalog)
1999 De Pont Foundation for Contemporary Art, Tilburg (catalog)

2001 *Drapeau,* Stedelijk Museum Actuele Kunst, Amsterdam (also Museum d'Art Moderne Stiftung Ludwig, Palais Liechtenstein, Vienna)

Selected Group Exhibitions:

1964 *Salon de la Jeune Sculpture,* Paris
1965 *4th Biennale de Paris,* Musée d'Art Moderne de la Ville, Paris
1966 *Salon de Comparaisons,* Paris
1967 *Expo '67,* Montreal
Superlund, Lunds Konsthall, Lund, Sweden
Bienal, Sao Paulo
1972 *Douze Ans d'Art Contemporain en France,* Grand Palais, Paris
Amsterdam-Paris-Dusseldorf, Guggenheim Museum, New York
1977 *Paris-New York,* Centre Georges Pompidou, Paris
1981 *Opening Exhibition,* Museum of Modern Art, Toyama, Japan
1993 CAPC Musée d'Art Contemporain de Bordeaux (catalog)
1996 *18th Biennale des Antiquaires,* Paris
1997 CAPC Musée d'Art Contemporain, Bordeaux, France
2001 Bienal de La Habana—VIIa, Cuba

Collections:

Centre Georges Pompidou, Paris; Musée Cantini, Marseilles; Stedelijk Museum, Amsterdam; Musée des Beaux-Arts, Ghent; Kaiser Wilhelm Museum, Krefeld, Germany; Israel Museum, Jerusalem; Hara Museum of Contemporay Art, Tokyo; Rhode Island Museum of Art, Providence; de Menil Foundation, Houston; Museum of Modern Art, New York.

Publications:

By RAYNAUD: Books—*Jean-Pierre Raynaud, La Maison: 1969–1987,* with Denyse Durand-Ruel, Yves Tissier, Bernhard Wauthier-Wurmser, Paris 1988; *Jean-Pierre Raynaud: La Maison, 1993,* with Denyse Durand-Ruel and Marc Sanchez, Paris 1993; *Jean-Pierre Raynaud: Catalogue Raisonné,* with Denyse Durand-Ruel, Paris 1998. **Articles—**interview with Didier Laroque in *L'Architecture d'Aujourd'hui,* no. 286, April 1993; ''Alliance avec l'Univers: J.P. Raynaud Explains His Participation in the Café Richelieu, Musée du Louvre, Paris'' in *Connaissance des Arts,* no. 502, January 1994; interview with Philip Jodidio in *Connaissance des Arts,* no. 516, April 1995; interview with Philip Jodidio in *Connaissance des Arts,* no. 556, December 1998.

On RAYNAUD: Books—*Jean-Pierre Raynaud et la Conscience de Soi,* exhibition catalog with text by Pierre Restany, Paris 1966; *Superlund,* exhibition catalog with text by Pierre Restany and others, Lund, Sweden 1967; *Douze ans d'art contemporain en France,* exhibition catalog with texts by F. Mathey, J. Clair, D. Cordier and others, Paris 1972; *Amsterdam-Paris-Dusseldorf,* exhibition catalog with text by Blaise Gautier, New York 1972; *Jean-Pierre Raynaud* by Emmy de Martelacre, Paris 1975; *Abbaye Cistercienne, Noirlac: Vitraux de Jean-Pierre Raynaud,* Paris 1977; *Jean-Pierre Raynaud,* exhibition catalog, New York 1986. **Articles—**''Raynaud's Psycho-Objects'' by Catherine Francblin in *Art in America* (New York), vol. 79, June 1991; ''Raynaud à Cologne'' in *Connaissance des Arts,* no. 521, October 1995; ''Raynaud Expose en Profondeur'' by Jules Merleau-Ponty in *Beaux Arts Magazine,* no. 163, December 1997; ''Raynaud en Quatre Acts'' by Jean-Michel Ribettes in *Beaux Arts Magazine,* no. 175, December 1998; ''Say It With Flowers'' by Laurie Attias in *Art News,* vol. 97, no. 11, December 1998.

* * *

Jean-Pierre Raynaud started exhibiting his sculptures and objects at the Galerie Creuze *(Salon de la jeune sculpture)* in 1964, but his first effective show, one in which he was able to spread himself and be properly seen, did not occur until a year later when he had his big solo exhibition at the Galerie Jean Lacarde for which Alain Jouffroy wrote his catalog *Une laboratoire mental.*

The Raynaud toilet with its lifted seat in white!

No need for him, like Duchamp, to up-end the porcelain and scribble a fake signature across its edge in thick black paint.

In fact it is the shock impact of Rayaud's creations that is so impressive. To make ''matter-of-fact'' all the fetishes of horror, whether in the home, in the prison or in the hospital, is alarming enough in its mental magnetism, but when the *facts,* the bits and pieces, the random introduction of photographs, the elements of everyday drama (like the fire buckets) are combined in a sterile colour scheme of red, white and occasional black (almost the official anarchist colours!), the eye becomes literally *brain-washed.* Thought becomes cerebral instead of visual. His ''psycho-objects'' really are psycho-objects. Chains, numbers, boxes, doors and bolts stand alone in an hysterical isolation, or are brought together to *assemblages* which are none the less telling because the uncompanioned monologue has been replaced by a script for more than one voice.

The clean terror of Raynaud's fixtures and fittings is one of the most eccentrically arresting records of the contemporary situation.

''Psycho-Object Cailloux A,'' with its modern instrument of multi-pronged torture, hanging like a lavatory brush above the pile of pebbles on the shelf, is supported by the grim poster with message at the top reading:

Premieres: Portes 14, 15, 16
Secondes: Portes 12, 13

above the photo of a white-coated stooping man, arms akimbo, his eyes censored by a white rectangle, alone in front of the warehouse doors with only a fire hydrant (figure 3 painted on it in white) to keep him company. This is a Kafka vignette made visual.

—Sheldon Williams

RAYSSE, Martial

Nationality: French. **Born:** Golfe-Juan, 12 February 1936. **Career:** Independent artist, in Paris, subsequently in Beaulieu-sur-Mer, France; first theatre designs, 1966, first films, 1967. **Awards:** David Bright

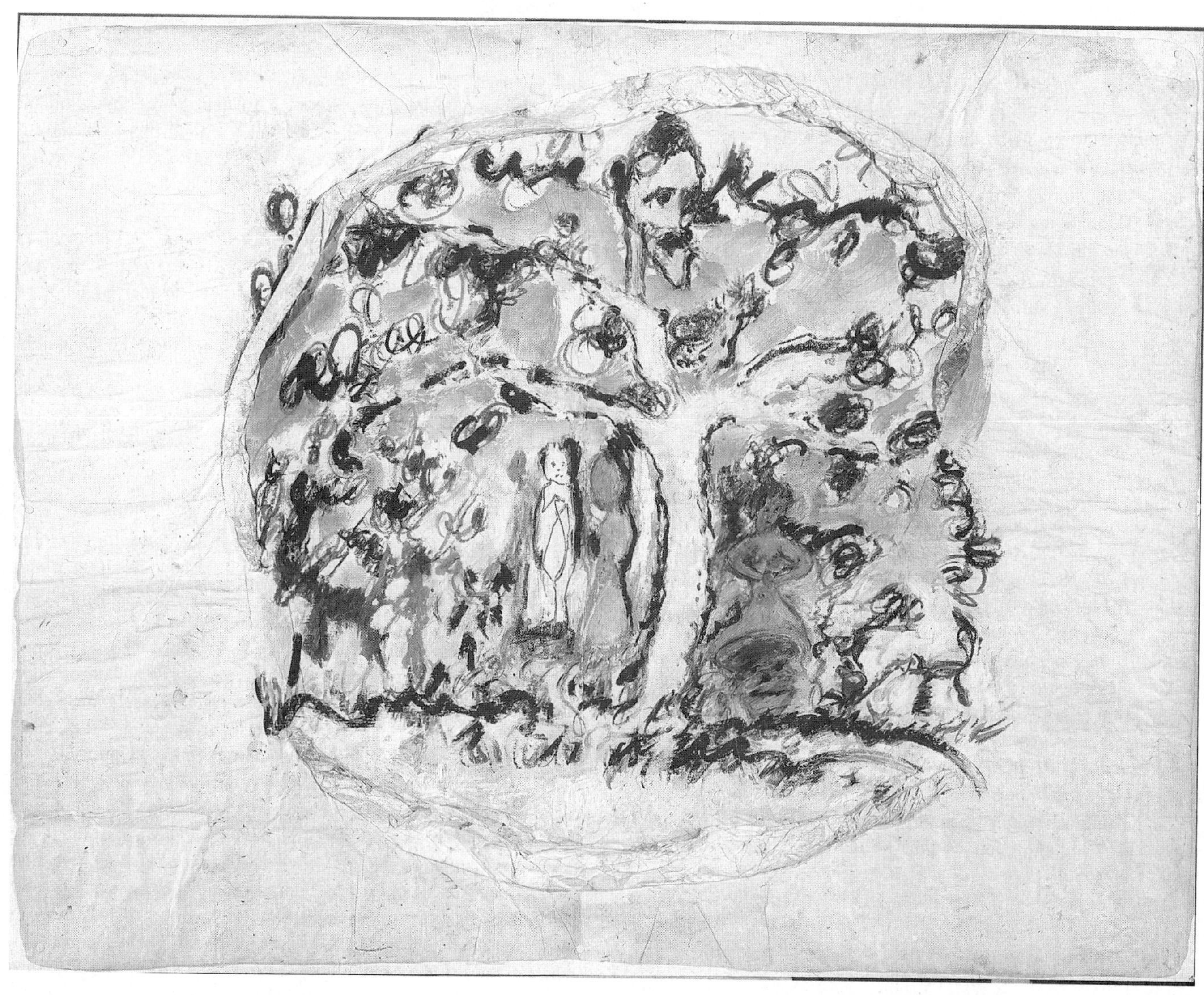

Martial Raysse: *Image V,* 1975. ©2001 Artists Rights Society (ARS), NY/ADAGP, Paris.

Award, *Biennale,* Venice, 1969. **Address:** c/o Galerie Iolas, 8 rue Perronet, 75007 Paris, France.

Individual Exhibitions:

1957 Galerie Longchamp, Nice
1959 Galerie d'Egmont, Brussels
1961 Galleria Schwarz, Milan (with Arman)
1962 Galerie Alfred Schmela, Dusseldorf
Alexander Iolas Gallery, New York
1963 *Mirrors and Portraits,* Dwan Gallery, Los Angeles
M. H. de Young Memorial Museum, San Francisco
Galleria del Leone, Venice
1964 Galerie Alexandre Iolas, Paris
Maitre et Esclave de l'Imagination, Stedelijk Museum, Amsterdam
Dwan Gallery, Los Angeles
1965 *L'Obsession Solitaire,* Galerie Alexandre Iolas, Paris
1966 Alexander Iolas Gallery, New York
1967 Galleria Alexandre Iolas, Milan
Palais de Beaux-Arts, Brussels
Dwan Gallery, Los Angeles
Galerie Der Spiegel, Cologne
Svensk-Franska Konstgalleriet, Stockholm
Galerie Alexandre Iolas, Paris
1968 Museum of Contemporary Art, Chicago
1969 Galerie Alexandre Iolas, Paris
Galerie Der Spiegel, Cologne
Galerie Alexandre Iolas, Geneva
Narodini Galerie, Prague
1970 Alexander Iolas Gallery, New York
Moderner Kunstmuseum, Munich
Galleria Alexandre Iolas, Milan
1972 25 rue du Dragon, Paris
1975 Galerie Benador, Geneva
Galerie Der Spiegel, Cologne
1976 Galerie Karl Flinker, Paris
1977 Galerie Eva de Buren, Stockholm
Centre d'Art, Flaine, France
1978 Galerie Karl Flinker, Paris

1980 Galerie Claude Givaudan, Geneva
Fondation Veranneman, Kruishoutem, Belgium
1981 *Martial Raysse 1970–1980,* Centre Georges Pompidou, Paris
Stedelijk Museum, Amsterdam
1991 Musée National d'Art Moderne, Centre Georges Pompidou, Paris
1992 Musée du Jeu de Paume, Paris (travelling exhibit)
1993 Museum Moderner Kunst, Vienna

Selected Group Exhibitions:

1961 *The Art of Assemblage,* Museum of Modern Art, New York
1964 *40 Ans de Collage,* Musée d'Art Moderne, Paris (travelled to Musée d'Art et d'Histoire, St. Etienne, France)
1969 *Biennale,* Venice (and 1976)
1970 *Pop Art, Nouveau Réalisme, Nouvelle Figuration,* Casino Municipal, Knokke, Belgium
1973 *L'Art du 20eme Siècle,* Musée Rath, Geneva
1977 *Paris-New York,* Centre Georges Pompidou, Paris
1979 *Biennale of Sydney,* Art Gallery of New South Wales, Sydney
1980 *Le Reel en Question,* Maison des Arts, Montbeliard, France (travelled to Galerie Athanor, Geneva)
1988 *Nouveaux Realistes: Arman, Cesar, Christo, Gerard Deschamps, Francois Dufrene, Raymond Hains, Yves Klein, Martial Raysse, Mimmo Rotella, Niki de Saint-Phalle, Daniel Spoerri, Jean Tinguely, Villegle,* Zabriskie Gallery, New York
1999 *Corps Social,* Ecole Nationale Superieure des Beaux-Arts, Paris

Collections:

Musée de la Ville, Paris; Musée National d'Art Moderne, Paris; Neue Galerie/Sammlung Ludwig, Aachen, Germany; Staatgalerie, Stuttgart; Kaiser-Wilhelm-Museum, Krefeld, Germany; Stedelijk Museum, Amsterdam; Stedelijk Van Abbemuseum, Eindhoven, Netherlands; Louisiana Museum, Humlebaek, Denmark.

Publications:

By RAYSSE: Book—*I Had a Thousand Things to Put in Order,* exhibition catalog, New York 1966. **Articles—**''Geometri variable'' in *Paris Review,* February 1967; ''La Beauté c'est le mauvais gout'' in *Jeune Afrique* (Paris), February 1968. **Films—***Jesuscola,* 1967; *Portrait electro machin chose,* 1967; *Homero presto,* 1968; *Camembert martial extra-doux,* 1969; *Le grand depart,* with Lucienne Hamon, Anne Wiazemsky and Sterling Hayden, 1970; *Pig Music,* 1971; *L'Hotel des folles fatmas,* 1976; *Intra muros,* 1977–80; *La petite danse,* 1978–80.

On RAYSSE: Books—*Martial Raysse: Mirrors and Portraits,* exhibition catalog with text by John Ashbery, Los Angeles 1963; *Martial Raysse: Maitre et esclave de l'imagination,* exhibition catalog with texts by Otto Hahn and Pierre Restany, Amsterdam 1964; *Martial Raysse ou l'obsession solaire,* exhibition catalog with text by Otto Hahn, Paris 1965; *Martial Raysse,* exhibition catalog with text by Otto Hahn, Los Angeles 1967; *Martial Raysse,* exhibition catalog with text by Pierre Restany, Brussels 1967; *Minimal Art: A Critical Anthology,* edited by Gregory Battcock, New York 1968, London 1969; *Martial Raysse,* exhibition catalog edited by Ad Petersen, Amsterdam 1981; *Martial Raysse 1970–1980,* exhibition catalog with text by Pontus Hulten, Jean-Yves Mock, Gilbert Lascault and others, Paris 1981, *Martial Raysse,* exhibition catalog, with essay by Didier Semin, Vienna 1993. **Articles—**''Portrait Relief: Martial Raysse, PR2 (Art Reproduction)'' by Yves Klein in *Art in America,* vol. 74, April 1986; ''Martial Raysse'' by Anne Dagbert in *Artforum* (New York), vol. 31, no. 8, April 1993; ''Raysse, Bioulès entre Ovide et Buster Keaton'' by Didier Ottinger, translated by C. Penwarden in *Art Press,* no. 258, June 2000.

* * *

An early painting of a detergent packed by Martial Raysse sums up his attitude to the world of art in a way that has nothing to do with the kitchen sink or socialist realism. It would be better to remember that he was born in Golfe-Juan than to think about washing-up. Better still, think about both at the same time.

Raysse has a weird kind of *bruderschaft* with the American Tom Wesselmann. However different the end-product of their work, both are, albeit with dissimilar emphases, concerned with and absorbed in the real (artificial!) portrait of contemporary life. Wesselmann's great American nudes bask in air-conditioned apartments, and their dish-washer machines need detergents too. A chemical cleanliness pervades their world with just the same pertinacity as the Prisunic svelte make-up that displaces dirt and mops up perspiration for the girls of Martial Raysse. If Wesselmann's models look more at ease and better organized than the chic Raysse clotheshorses, it is only because their niche in the American Way of Life is that much more cosily secure. One notices that they have a tendency to stay indoors (a drive or a trip to the beach is obviously a carefully planned break in continuity), whereas the Raysse beauties, whether demonstrating luminous lipstick or plundered from Ingres or Cranach, are definetely on parade. No subdued table lamps for them; they have to face the uncertain illumination of Neon or the hard glare of Cote d'Azur sunshine.

Wesselmann stays with the time and place of a modern dream America. His fancy and magpiecollecting culpability take Raysse far and wide even if the raw strip lighting, the chemical colours and the band-box perfection of his figures do not deviate. In *Paradise Lost,* Nureyev and Fonteyn must contend with Raysse sets that make the serpent light up! For most of the Covent Garden audience the Garden of Eden drama was a long time ago; even Milton has celebrated a few centenaries; but for Raysse the story belongs to Now and should be dressed accordingly.

He is a creator of the artificialdom of contemporary times, and he gives to a manmade fabricated existence absolute veracity. Neon is true, and so are aniline dyes. The best buys from the supermarket look well on the right girl.

Because he is adept, inventive and has confident modish taste, Raysse belongs comfortably in the arena of contemporary art. No vieux-jeux! He does not mirror modern times; he italicises them. His control of assemblages, collages, distortions, situations and technical gimmickry hardly falters.

—Sheldon Williams

REBEYROLLE, Paul

Nationality: French. **Born:** Eymoutiers, Haute-Vienne, 3 November 1926. **Education:** Limoges until 1944; mainly self-taught in art from 1944, but attended Académie dela Grande Chaumière, Paris 1944–45; influenced by work of Soutine, Leger, Chagall and Picasso. **Career:** Independent painter Paris, since 1945. Committe member, *Salon du Mai* Paris, 1957. Member, French Communist Party, 1950–56. **Awards:** Prix de la Jeune Peinture, Paris 1950; Prix Feneon, Paris 1951; Painting Prize, *Biennale,* Paris, 1959; First Prize (French section), *John Moores Exhibition,* Liverpool, 1959; Grand Prix de la Ville de Paris, 1982. **Agent:** Galerie Maeght Lelong, 13 ruede Teheran, 75008 Paris, France. **Address:** 2 Passage Dantzig, 75015 Paris, France.

Individual Exhibitions:

1951 Galerie Drouant-David, Paris
1954 *Recent Paintings,* Marlborough Fine Art, London
1956 Maison de la Pensée Francaise, Paris
1958 Galerie Saint-Germain, Paris
1959 Galerie Creuzevalt, Paris
1961 *Recent Paintings,* Marlborough Fine Art, London
Galerie André Schoeller, Paris
1962 Janvier Nitta Gallery, Tokyo
Galerie André Schoeller, Paris
1964 Marlborough-Gerson Gallery, New York
Galerie André Schoeller, Paris
1966 Galerie André Schoeller Paris (with Fautrier and Messagier)
1967 Galerie Maeght, Paris
1969 Galerie Maeght, Paris
1970 Galerie Maeght, Paris
1971 *Grands Formats,* Foundation Maeght, St. Paul-de-Vence France
1972 Studio Marconi, Milan
1973 *Prisonniers,* Galerie Maeght, Paris
1974 Galerie Maeght, Zurich
1976 Galerie Maeght, Paris
Galerie Larcos Paris
1979 Galerie Maeght, Paris
Grand Palais, Paris
1982 Hospice Saint-Louis, Avignon, France
Galerie Maeght, at *FIAC 82,* Grand Palais, Paris
Galerie Editart, Geneva
Galerie Art Contemporain, Limoges, France
Galerie Maeght, Zurich
1988 Galerie Lelong, Paris

Selected Group Exhibitions:

1945 *Grands Formats,* Galerie du Bac, Paris
1948 *Salon des Jeunes,* Paris (and regularly to 1957)
1952 *5 Young French Realists,* Arcade Gallery, London
1957 *Bienal,* Sao Paulo
1962 *Grands et Jeunes d'Aujourd'hui,* Grand Palais, Paris
1969 *Festival d'Avignon,* France
1970 *L'Art dans la Ville,* Maison de la Culture, Arceuil, France
1978 *Kunstmesse,* Basel

Collections:

Musée d'Art Moderne de la Ville, Paris; Fondation Maeght, St. Paul-de-Vence, France.

Publications:

By REBEYROLLE: Books illustrated—*Eloge du Socialisme* by Samir Amin, Paris 1975; *Conte Rouge pour Paloma* by André Velten and Serge Sartreau, Paris 1976.

On REBEYROLLE: Books—*Rebeyrolle: Recent Paintings,* exhibition catalog with text by Neville Wallis, London 1954; *Rebeyrolle,* exhibition catalog with text by Georges Besson, Paris 1956; *Recent Paintings by Rebeyrolle,* exhibition catalog with text by Herbert Read, London 1961; *Rebeyrolle by Pierre* Descargues, Paris 1970; *Rebeyrolle: Grands Formats,* exhibition catalog with text by Jean Louis Prat, St. Paul-de-Vence, France 1971; *Paul Rebeyrolle: Prisonniers,* exhibition catalog with text by Ricardo Porro and Michael Foucault, Paris 1973; *Paul Rebeyrolle,* exhibition catalog with text by Peter F. Althaus, Zurich 1974; *Paul Rebeyrolle: Natures mortes et pouvoir,* exhibition catalog with text by Carlos Franqui, and others, Paris 1976; *Rebeyrolle: Peintures 1968–1978,* exhibition catalog with texts by Michel Tronche, Carlos Franqui, and others, Paris; 1979; *Rebeyrolle: Les évasions manquées,* exhibition catalog with preface by Jacques Dupin, Zurich 1982. **Articles—**''Rebeyrolle: Like a Hedgehog in Flight'' by Claude Bouyeure in *Cimaise,* vol. 41, April/May 1994; ''An Artist and an Architect: The Espace Rebeyrolle at Eymoutiers'' by Mathilde Bellaigue in *Museum International,* vol. 49, October/December 1997; ''The Spirit of Capitalism, the Flesh of Art'' by Hugo Lacroix in *Art Press,* no. 255, March 2000.

* * *

When the Galeria Maeght opened in the Calle Moncada in Barcelona in 1974, works by 27 international artists were chosen to celebrate the event. The list started with Adami, Bazaine, Braque, Bury, Calder and Chagall. Paul Rebeyrolle, low on the catalog because the artists were arranged in alphabetical order, came near the end with a grand triptych called ''De la grande baleine'' (1973), but one can see by the company he keeps that he is held in high esteem. When an important sale was held in London in aid of Vietnam war prisoners and wounded, John Berger without hesitation picked out Rebeyrolle's painting of a frog as the best—and most important—work on show.

As an artist Rebeyrolle is a creator of frequent changes. In fact, as a contradiction in terms, the one constant in all his work is change. Figuration flits in and out of his painting. He is an artist of conscience (in ''Coexistences'' a black dragon's jaws close on a red boot). Mixed media are engulfed in paint, slats of wood that look as if they were fugitives from Tapies are only casually interrelated by some random old chickenwire, while the tachiste pigment swirls round about and the early swatches of brown at the base of a four-meter-wide canvas show that the imprints of cat's paws were made while the thick paint was still wet.

Rebeyrolle has just enough individuality to prevent him ever becoming submerged in any art movement. The charisma of his works is magnetic, a personal magic that sets him aside as one of the lone wolves of contemporary painting.

—Sheldon Williams

REED, David

Nationality: American. **Born:** San Diego, California, 20 January 1946. **Education:** Reed College, Oregon, B.A.; New York Studio School, New York; Skowhegan School of Painting and Sculpture, New York. **Career:** Metropolitan Museum of Art, New York; Museum of Contemporary of Art, San Diego; Centre Georges Pompidou, Paris; Wexner Center of the Arts, Columbus, Ohio. Visiting artists, California Institute of the Arts, Valenica, California, 1994. **Awards:** Rockefeller Foundation Grant, 1966; Fellowship, Guggenheim Foundation, 1988; National Endowment of the Arts, 1991. **Agent:** Patricia/Faure Gallery, Bergamot Station B-7, 2525 Michigan Ave, Santa Monica, California 90404. **Address:** 315 Broadway, New York, New York 10007.

Selected Individual Exhibitions:

1988 Asher/Faure Gallery, Los Angeles
1989 Max Protetch Galler, New York
1991 Max Protetch Galler, New York
Galerie Rolf Ricke, Cologne
1992 Max Protetch Galler, New York
1993 Galerie Rolf Ricke, Cologne
1995 Max Protetch Galler, New York
1997 Galerie Rolf Ricke, Cologne
1998 Asher/Faure Gallery, Los Angeles

Publications:

By Reed: Articles—''Talking Pictures: David Reed Interviewed by Stephen Ellis'' in *Art Papers,* 1990; Interview in *ART Press,* 1990; ''Reflected Light; In Siena with Beccafumi'' in *Arts Magazine,* March 1991; ''Two Bedrooms in San Francisco'' in an exhibition catalog for the San Francisco Art Institute, 1992.

On REED: Books—Exhibition catalog, with text by Arthur Danto and Hanne Loreck, Cologne 1995; *David Reed Paintings: Motion Pictures* (exhibition catalog), with text by Elizabeth Armstrong, Dave Hickey, and Mieke Bal, 1998; *Pleasures of Sight and States of Being: Radical Abstract Painting Since 1990* by Roald Nasgaard, Tallahassee, Florida 2001. **Articles—**''Reed's Paintings'' by J. Sherry in *Artforum,* vol. 18, January 1980;''What Is Postmodern about Painting: The Scandinavia Lectures'' by Steven Henry Madoff in *Arts Magazine,* vol. 60, September 1985; ''Artifice and Artificiality: David Reed's Recent Painting'' by David Carrier in *Arts Magazine,* vol. 60, January 1986; by Steven Henry Madoff in *Art News,* vol. 85, January 1986; by Barry Schwabsky in *Arts Magazine,* vol. 61, September 1986; ''Baroque Expansions'' in *Art in America,* vol. 75, February 1987; ''Interstices: David Reed, Jonathan Lasker, Barry Bridgwood, and Will Mentor'' by Jonathan Seliger in *Arts Magazine,* vol. 61, March 1987; ''Nonrepresentation in 1988: Meaning-production Beyond the Scope of the Pious'' by Jeremy Gilbert Rolfe in *Arts Magazine,* vol. 62, May 1988; ''The Greenberg Effect: Comments by Younger Artists, Critics, and Curators'' by Joshua Decemberter in *Arts Magazine,* vol. 64, December 1989; ''The Anatomy of Autonomy: David Reed'' by Charles Hagen in *Artforum International,* vol. 29, November 1990; ''Painting Movement: The Work of David Reed'' by Jeremy Gilbert Rolfe in *Arts Magazine,* vol. 66, September 1991; article by Marchy Murphy in *New Art Examiner,* vol. 19, June-Summer 1992; ''David Reed'' by Reinhard Ermen in *Kunstforum International,* no. 130, May-July 1995; ''David Reed at Max Protetch'' by Lilly Wei in *Art in America,* vol. 83, June 1995; ''David Reed and Manhattan Baroque'' by Arthur Coleman Danto in *Art Press,* no. 218, November 1996; ''David Reed'' by David Pagel in *Art Text,* no. 58, August-October 1997; article by Raphael Rubinstein in *Art in America,* vol. 85 November 1997; ''Black on White: Paintings by David, Reed'' by Paul Auster, reprinted in *David Reed Paintings: Motion Pictures,* San Diego 1998; article by Christine Buci Glucksmann in *Parachute,* no. 91, July-September 1998; ''David Reed's Coming Attractions'' by Dave Hickey in *David Reed Paintings: Motion Pictures* (exhibition catalog), San Diego 1998; ''David Reed: Museum of Contemporary Art, San Diego'' by Ingrid Calame in *Art Issues,* no. 56, January-February 1999; ''Bedside Manner'' by Arthur C. Danto in *Artforum International,* vol. 37, no. 10, Summer 1999; ''David Reed: Galerie Xippas, Paris'' by Carole Boulbes in *Art Press,* no. 251, November 1999; ''Moving Pictures at an Exhibition'' by Christian Viveros Faune in *Art Papers,* vol. 23, no. 6, November-December 1999; ''A Minimalist in Baroque Trappings'' by Barbara A. MacAdam in *Art News,* vol. 98, no. 11, December 1999; ''David Reed: Max Protetch'' by Katy Siegel in *Artforum International,* vol. 38, no. 5, January 2000.

* * *

The work of David Reed has often been grouped with that of other abstract painters who first emerged in the late 1970s and early 1980s: Peter Halley, Philip Taaffe, Jonathan Lasker, among others. What differentiated their so-called ''new abstraction,'' from its abstract antecedents was how the work seemed severed from succession within the modernist linear model of the development of abstract art as it had been described in the Greenbergian story. Instead these artists appeared to stand outside that history, the entirety of its achievements, stylistic and ideological, laid bare to them, for quotation, comment, manipulation, and subject to discursive connections or juxtapositions. Some typical labels that writers applied to the new work included conceptual abstraction, self-conscious abstraction, and third-person abstraction. Often the painting that resulted, its marks, its forms, were described as mere rhetorical reiterations from the history of painting, ironic, and meaningless as direct speech, their immediacy, directness, and intimacy long ago replaced by a determined system of references.

In retrospect, our reading of the work has become more complex, and respective careers have differentiated themselves. If Halley has described his abstracted language as ''generalized'' and ''completely removed from the representation of the specific,'' illustrating, in effect, the bleakness of social relation within a technologized culture that has driven out ''the complexity and physicality of the whole of experience,'' Reed's paintings, also technologically influenced, on the contrary have become sensuous celebrations addressed to the evocation of the particular and specific visual, and visceral, response. If Taaffe has quoted Barnett Newman and Op Art, Reed's reference to Mannerist and Baroque painting are less a matter of quotation than of analogy. And if Lasker and Reed at times share a comparable collage-like arrangement of elements across the picture plane, Reed's, unlike Lasker's, operate, finally, not as part-to-part compositions whose dialogue operates discursively across the longitudinal surface of the painting as a kind of writing, but in the transverse experiential space that embraces both painting and viewer.

Among Reed's first mature work are the Brushstroke paintings from the early 1970s, constructed of continuous horizontal strokes in black or red paint dragged across a surface of wet, white pigment, their character determined both by controlled gesture and chance effects. It is as if, as was true for many artists in the aftermath of abstract expressionism, notably Roy Lichtenstein, and Gerhard Richter, the gestural brushstroke needed to be negotiated and tamed by being somehow reined in by mechanized processes. Paul Auster, in 1975 wrote of these paintings: ''The finished work is not a representation of this process—-it is the process itself, and it asks to be *read* rather than simply observed.'' In truth, however, is it not rather the case that as spectators we are cast adrift somewhere in between direct visual response and critical reflection, a fruitful indecisiveness that will align Reed's future painting with Richter's constant interrogation of the complexities and compensations of perceptual experience?

By the early 1980s Reed began to scrape large palette knives through wet paint with sweeping repetitive, curvilinear gestures, sanding them down, using various glazes and transparent layers of paint, creating new surface qualities that would become the basis of his subsequent lush and voluptuous wonderland of ambiguities. This is a painting that could be seen as belonging either to the history of gestural painting, or to the realm of postmodern quotation, but that in reality surmounts such critical subjugations by its sheer visual immediacy, its spontaneity, freshness and beauty. Its scrolls and volutes of paint-cum-drapery seem at once to billow sculpturally in space and to lie flat transparent and illusionistic images in a smooth and glossy photograph. The painting revolves on dualisms. It is figurative and abstract, gestural and fixed, flowing and frozen, tactile and evanescent, body and light, joyous and brooding, all played out, as some observers put it, on the cinematic wide-screen format.

If one were to persist on parallels to Richter, the differences would lie precisely in this reference to modern technology. Reed recalls a poignant experience in 1967, trying to paint the landscape of Monument Valley, when he came to realize how much the way he saw it had been predetermined by growing up watching the movie westerns. So if Richter's light and color are somehow natural, Reed's emulates light and color of photographs, television, and the movies. As he has said: ''During the Renaissance and Baroque periods they had a wonderful religious light that always came from above. Now we have a technological light, the light of a TV or a movie screen, which is directionless—homogeneous across the screen—and increases the intensity of every color.'' This is a ''technological light that can be suggested in an abstract painting, but made more sensual and material than it is on a screen or in a photograph,'' as quoted in an interview with Stephen Ellis.

Concomitantly Reed has wanted to connect to the tradition of painting, especially to Mannerist and Baroque painting, his billowing forms evoking the drapery that swirls around its air-borne figures. ''They've either just flown off the viewer's body into the painting or they're about to fly off the painting into the viewer. The movement is what is important. It reveals the gesture of the body,'' he noted in an interview with Ellis. Dave Hickey has said of the painted gestures, ''Like willful, Baroque angels, they ceased to respect the rectangle or the picture plane. Spilling out over the rectangle's hard boundaries and blossoming up within its frame, Reed's new gestures made space where none existed, then flowed away into that space beneath the rectangle's enclosing edges, as Jim Rosenquist's figures do, inferring a vast, complex, and multi-tiered figural landscape of which the tight aperture of the rectangle affords us only a glimpse.''

But by sheer visceral scale, visual proximity and sensual immediacy these are one-on-one paintings, that actively draw the beholder into intimate and private reverie. Again Hickey, with reference to Titian's Venus d'Urbino, has astutely analyzed the effect of how Reed's composition have increasingly stressed the juxtaposition or overlapping of disjunct, colored rectangles, with distinct, discrete and dissonant, ravishing, gestural articulation, the anxiety and instability at their meeting edges, the hide and seek sensations that occur there, a cause, or a place of their erotic seduction. Reed has indeed proclaimed his ''ambition in life, to be a bedroom painter,'' according to Hickey. He underscored this ambition in his 1995 exhibition in the Kolnischer Kunsterverein by installing an actual bed in the gallery space and hanging one of his paintings above it. In this case the bed was a replica of one from a bedroom scene in Alfred Hitchcock's *Vertigo,* simultaneously played on an adjacent TV set, as a loop, into whose cinematic space Reed had digitally inserted the same painting above the bed, in the same position as it hangs in the exhibition.

—Roald Nasgaard

RENOUF, Edda

Nationality: American. **Born:** Mexico City, 17 June 1943; immigrated to the United States, 1957; naturalized, 1978. **Education:** Putney School, Vermont, 1957–1961; studied at Sarah Lawrence College Bronxville, New York, 1961–65, B.A. 1965; Academie Julian, Paris, 1963–64; Art Students League, New York, 1967–68; Columbia School of the Arts, New York, 1968–71; M.F.A. 1971. **Career:** Independent artist, since 1972. Lived in Paris, from 1971; taught in Paris for Sarah Lawrence College program, 1974; now lives and works in New York. **Awards:** Printing Fellowship, National Endowment for the Arts, Washington, D.C., 1978; Grantee, Pollock-Krasner Foundation Inc., 1990–91; Centre National Arts Plastiques Grantee, 1996. **Agent:** Sollertis Gallery, 12 rue Des Régans, Toulouse, France, 31000; Blum Helman Gallery, 20 West 57th Street, New York, New York 10019. **Address:** 37 rue Volta, 75003, Paris, France.

Individual Exhibitions:

1972 Galerie Yvon Lambert, Paris
1973 Galleria Françoise Lambert, Milan
1974 Konrad Fischer Gallery, Dusseldorf
Galerie Yvon Lambert, Paris
Galerie MTL, Brussels
1975 Galerie Yvon Lambert, Paris
Galleria Francoise Lambert, Milan
Galleria Marilena Bonomo, Bari, Italy
1976 Julian Pretto and Co., New York
Galleria Francoise Lambert, Milan
Rolf Preisig Gallery, Basel
Allesandro Ferranti Gallery, Rome

1977 Kathryn Markel Fine Arts, New York
Weinberg Gallery, San Francisco
Galerie MTL, Brussels
1978 Blum Helman Gallery, New York
Wadsworth Atheneum, Hartford, Connecticut
Young-Hoffman Gallery, Chicago
Margo Leavin Gallery, Los Angeles
Galerie Yvon Lambert, Paris
Graeme Murray Gallery, Edinburgh
Galleria Francoise Lambert, Milan
Ugo Ferranti Gallery, Rome
1979 Blum Helman Gallery, New York
Weinberg Gallery, San Francisco
Konrad Fischer Gallery, Dusseldorf
1980 Blum Helman Gallery, New York
Ronald Greenberg Gallery, St. Louis
Galerie Yvon Lambert, Paris
Margo Leavin Gallery, Los Angeles
Thomas Segal Gallery, Boston
1981 Graeme Murray Gallery, Edinburgh
1982 Carol Taylor Gallery, Dallas
Blum Helman Gallery, New York
1983 Galleria Francoise Lambert, Milan
1984 Galerie Yvon Lambert, Paris
1985 Blum Helman Gallery, New York
1986 Martina Hamilton Gallery, New York
1987 Liesbeth Lips Gallery, Amsterdam
Blum Helman Gallery, New York
1997 *Werke 1972–1997,* Staatliche Kunsthalle Karlsruhe, Cantz (catalog)

Selected Group Exhibitions:

1972 *Actualité d'un Bilan,* Galerie Yvon Lambert, Paris
1973 *Drawings,* Museum of Modern Art, Oxford
Biennale, Paris
1974 *Geplante Malerie,* Kunsthalle, Münster, West Germany
1975 *International Print Exhibition,* at the Jyvaskyla Arts Festival, Alvar Aalto Museum, Jyvaskyla, Finland
1977 *Extraordinary Women,* Museum of Modern Art, New York
1978 *Contemporary Drawing/New York,* University of California at Santa Barbara
1979 *Whitney Biennial,* Whitney Museum, New York
1985 *Livres d'Artistes,* Centre Georges Pompidou, Paris
1987 *New York Scene,* Liesbeth Lips Gallery, Amsterdam
1988 *From the Collection of Dorothy & Herbert Vogel,* Arnot Art Museum, New York (traveling exhibition) (catalog)

Collections:

Museum of Modern Art, New York; Whitney Museum, New York; Metropolitan Museum of Art, New York; Philadelphia Museum of Art; Art Institute of Chicago; Museum of Fine Arts, Dallas; Centre Georges Pompidou, Paris; Musée des Beaux-Arts, Grenoble, France; St. Louis Art Museum, Missouri; Australian National Gallery, Canberra; Yale University Art Gallery; Bibliothèque Nationale, Paris; Cincinnati Museum of Art; Tel Aviv Museum; Louisiana Museum, Copenhagen; Walker Art Center, Minneapolis; National Gallery of Art, Washington, D.C.; British Museum, London; The Brooklyn Museum, New York; Detroit Institute of Arts; Museum of Contemporary Art, Los Angeles; High Museum, Atlanta.

Publications:

By RENOUF: Books—*Lines,* Milan 1974; *Lines and Nonlines,* New York 1977; *Echoes,* Edinburgh 1979; *A Language I Do Not Know,* with Alec Finlay and Jaan Kaplinski, Edinburgh 1994; *Edda Renouf: Etchings and Aquatints, 1974–1994,* with Anne Dagbert, New York 1994. **Articles—**''Entretiens avec Edda Renouf,'' with C. Beret, in *Art Press* (Paris), January 1973; ''Edda Renouf,'' statement in *Flash Art* (Milan), April 1974.

On RENOUF: Books—*Matrix 36: Edda Renouf,* exhibition brochure with text by Peter O. Marlow, Hartford, Connecticut 1978. **Articles—**''Edda Renouf'' in *Peinture Cahiers Theoriques* (Paris), January 1973; ''France: Edda Renouf'' in *Flash Art* (Milan), April 1974; ''Edda Renouf'' by France Morrin in *Parachute* (Montreal), Winter 1977/78; ''Intimate Mathematics'' by Susan Larsen in *Art News* (New York), December 1978; ''Edda Renouf'' by Anne Dagbert in *Art Press* (Paris), February 1981; ''Edda Renouf at Blum Helman'' by Steven Henry Madoff in *Art in America* (New York), May 1982; ''Edda Renouf chez Galerie Yvon Lambert'' by Regis Durand in *Art Press* (Paris), September 1984.

*

There is a life, an energy in every material. The thing is to sense this energy and to reveal it by the most direct path.

Changing the structure of the base, I add, scrape or sand. Not covering, but uncovering—not closing, but opening—it is then what it is.

There is a mixture of both logical, mathematical structures and organic randomness in the materials. As I work, the materials make me aware of archetypal signs and forms, both structured and random within my unconscious. It is as a silent flow of sound, a silent conversation between the materials and my imagination, an intuitive listening out of which the work of art grows.

—Edda Renouf

REUSCH, Erich

Nationality: German. **Born:** Lutherstadt, Wittenberg, 26 June 1925. **Education:** Melanchthon-Gymnasium, Lutherstadt until 1946; studied sculpture and architecture, under Richard Scheibe and Hans Uhlmann, at the Hochshule für Bildende Kunst, West Berlin, 1947–53. **Military Service:** Served in German Army, 1944–45. **Family:** Married Sonja Dietzler in 1969; daughter: Simone. **Career:** Worked in an architect's office, Dusseldorf, 1953–56; free-lance architect, Dusseldorf, designing housing estates in Dusseldorf, Hannover and Frankfurt, and initiating Bonn-Teckenheim/Merl satellite town, 1956–64; independent artist, Dusseldorf, since 1964; first sculpture reliefs and paintings, 1954; first electro-static objects, 1968. Professor, Staatliche Kunstakademie, Dusseldorf, 1974–90. **Agents:** Galerie Heinz Holtmann, Obenmarspforten 7–11, 50667 Cologne, Germany; Galerie Neher, Moltkeplatz 61, 45135 Essen, Germany; Galerie

Sculpture by Erich Reusch. ©Erich Reusch.

Friebe, Parkstrasse 54, 58509 Lüdenscheid, Germany; Galerie Walzinger, Prälat-Subtil-Ring 1, 66740 Saarlouis, Germany. **Address:** Breddeweg 4, 5982 Neuenrade 5, Germany.

Individual Exhibitions:

1966 Von-der-Heydt Museum, Wuppertal, West Germany
1967 Galerie H, Hannover
Haus am Lutzowplatz, West Berlin
Galerie im Europa Center, West Berlin
1968 Galerie Swart, Amsterdam
Galerie Loehr, Dusseldorf
1969 Galerie Swart, Amsterdam
1970 Galerie M, Bochum, West Germany
Kunstverein, Aachen, West Germany
1971 Galerie Ernst, Hannover
Kabinett für Aktuelle Kunst, Bremerhaven, West Germany
1972 Galerie Wilbrand, Cologne
Hommage à McCready, Museum am Ostwall, Dortmund, West Germany
Lucy Milton Gallery, London
1973 *Elektrostatische Objekte,* Kunsthalle, Kiel, West Germany
1974 Galerie M, Bochum, West Germany
Galerie Müller-Roth, Stuttgart
Galerie Falazik, Neuenkirchen, West Germany
1976 Galerie Müller-Roth, Stuttgart
Salone Annunciata, Milan
Kunsthalle, Dusseldorf
Gallerie St. Johann, Saarbrucken
1978 Karl-Ernst-Osthaus Museum, Hagen, West Germany
1979 *Skulpturen, Reliefs, Zeichnungen, Collagen,* Galerie Müller-Roth, Stuttgart
1981 Galerie Hans Mayer/Denise René, Dusseldorf
1984 Gallery 44, Kaarst, West Germany
Galerie Monochrome, Aachen, West Germany
Galerie Linie, Moers, West Germany
1986 Stadtische Galerie, Ludenscheid, West Germany
1987 Skulpturen Museum Glaskasten, Marl, West Germany
Galerie Rupert Walser, Munich
1989 Galerie Hermanns, Munich
1992 Galerie Walzinger, Saarlouis, Germany
1993 Haus am Wasser, Bremen-Vegesack, Germany
Kunstverein Arnsberg, Germany
1995 Galerie Walzinger, Saarlouis, Germany
1996 b2 Galerie, Solingen, Germany
1998 Kunstmuseum Bonn, Germany
Galerie Friebe, Lüdenscheid, Germany
1999 Synagoge Stommeln, Pulheim, Cologne, Germany
2000 Galerie Heinz Holtmann, Cologne, Germany
Städtische Galerie Lüdenscheid, Germany

Selected Group Exhibitions:

1965 *Das Relief,* Landesmuseum, Darmstadt
1968 *Junge Deutsche Plastik,* Wilhelm-Lehmbruck-Museum, Duisburg, West Germany (toured Germany)
1969 *Raume,* Städtische Museum Schloss Morsbroich, Leverkusen, West Germany
1970 *Strategy: Get Arts,* Richard Demarco Gallery, Edinburgh
1972 *Szene Rhein-Ruhr,* Museum Folkwang, Essen
1975 *Empirica,* Commune di Rimini, Italy (travelled to Museo Castelvecchio, Verona)
1980 *Reliefs,* Westfälisches Museum, Münster, West Germany
1981 *Schwarz,* Kunsthalle, Dusseldorf
1985 *Kunst in der Bundesrepublik 1945–85,* Nationalgalerie, West Berlin
1986 *Bodenskulptur,* Kunsthalle, Bremen, West Germany
1988 *Vision und Bewegung,* Sammlung Lenz Schönberg, Städtische Galerie im Lenbachhaus, Munich
1989 *Niemandsland,* Kunsthalle Recklinghausen, Germany
1990 *''Bis Jetzt''—Plastik im Außenraum der Bundesrepublik,* Sprengel Museum, Hannover
1991 *Kunst als Grenzbeschreitung—John Cage und die Moderne,* Neue Pinakothek, Munich
1993 *Stahlplastik in Deutschland 1993,* Staatliche Galerie Moritzburg, Halle, Germany
1998 *Abstraktion Zwischen 1945 und 1959,* Wilhelm-Hack-Museum, Ludwigshafen, Germany

Collections:

Städtische Museum Schloss Morsbroich, Leverkusen, Germany; Kunstmuseum, Mönchengladbach, Germany; Wilhelm-Lehmbruck-Museum, Duisburg, Germany; Museum am Ostwall, Dortmund, Germany; Kunstmuseum, Ludwigshafen, Germany; Kunsthalle Kiel, Germany; Städtische Museum Bochum, Germany; Staatsgalerie Stuttgart; Nationalgalerie Berlin; Musée de Grenoble, France.

Publications:

By REUSCH: Film—*Kunst und Architekur: chancen vertran,* television film, 1975.

On REUSCH: Books—*Park und Bildwelt* by Eugen Thiemann, Dortmund, West Germany 1969; *Projekte, Konzepte, Aktionen* by Walter Aue, Cologne, 1971; *Bis Heute* by Karin Thomas, Cologne, 1971; *Neue Konkrete Kunst* by Bernhard Kerber, Bochum, West Germany 1972; *Erich Reusch: Hommage à McCready,* exhibition catalog with text by Eugen Thiemann and Bernhard Kerber, Dortmund, West Germany 1972; *Erich Reusch,* exhibition folder, London 1972; *Erich Reusch: Elektrostatische Objekte,* exhibition catalog with text by Jens Christian Jensen, Kiel, West Germany 1973; *Bildhauer Heute: Erich Reusch* by Bernhard Kerber, Hildescheim 1977; *Erich Reusch,* exhibition catalog with text by Clara Weyergraf, Hagen, West Germany 1978; *Erich Reusch: Skulpturen, Reliefs, Zeichnungen, Collagen,* exhibition folder, Stuttgart 1979; *Erich Reusch,* exhibition catalog by Jurgen Wissman, Ludenscheid 1986; *Erich Reusch, Arbeiten 1954–1998,* exhibition catalog, Cologne 1998. **Articles—** ''Einbeziehung Akustischer Wirkungen: Erich Reuschs Entwurf für ein Auschwitz-Mahnmal (1957)'' by Felix Reuße in *Das Denkmal an der Grenze Seiner Sprachfähigkeit,* Stuttgart 1995; ''Raum als Glück und Provokation'' by H. Stachelhaus in *Künstler,* 1999. **Film—***Erich Reusch* by Heiner Hepper and Hubert Neueburg, 1974.

*

I began designing decentralized sculptures in 1956. By reducing the singular form to a minimum, I was able to include the problem of gravitation in the space. In addition, by compression and dissolution, I was also able to achieve spatial incidents of substantial dimensions. The most important feature to me was the gravitational relation among the sculptures, not the mass of the sculptures itself. Due to this decision, I was able to free myself from the visual constraints of the sculpture from front and side perspectives.

The positioning of the sculpture and its relation to the surrounding space became decisive. In 1961, I created closed and open internal spaces, and in 1962 metallic surfaces which cut and divide space through their replacement of different axes. In 1965, I formed grounded, decentralized sculptures and one year later multiples made out of rectangular bars, which could be very small or extremely large, depending on the situation. Thereby, axial relations in the internal and external space were created, which accentuated the space in a unique way. In 1972, an ensemble of cubes measuring between 1.5 and 5 meters was displayed in the Art Museum of Dortmund. Its potential expansion was pointed toward the surrounding space and led the viewer up to physical affliction. In 1993, large dimensioned sculptures were created whose outside surfaces made their small material strength viewable.

In subsequent works, I used various radial axes to specify the opened internal space. It creates a fluctuation between internal and surrounding space.

—Erich Reusch

RICHTER, Gerhard

Nationality: German. **Born:** Dresden, 9 February 1932. **Education:** Studied art at the Hochschule für Bildende Kunste, Dresden, 1952–57, and, under Karl-Otto Gotz, at the Staatliche Kunstakademie, Dusseldorf, 1961–64. **Family:** Married Marlenne (Ema) Eufinger in 1957 (divorced); married the artist Isa Genzken in 1982 (divorced); daughter: Betty; married Sabine Moritz in 1995; son: Moritz. **Career:** Worked as scenery painter, Stadttheater, Zittau, East Germany, 1949–50; commercial artist for several firms, Zittau, 1950–51; photolaboratory technician, Dresden, 1957–60. Full-time painter, Dusseldorf, since 1963. Guest lecturer, Hochschule für Bildenden Künste, Hamburg, 1967; lecturer in Fine Arts at a gymnasium, Dusseldorf, 1968–69; professor, Staatliche Kunstakademie, Dusseldorf, from 1971; Guest Professor at the Städelschule, Frankfurt, 1988. **Awards:** Kunstpreis Junger Westen, Recklinghausen, 1967; Arnold Bode Prize, Kassel, 1982; Receives the 'Kaiserring' of the City of Goslar, 1988; Wolf Prize, Jerusalem, 1995. **Agent:** Galerie Konrad fischer, Platanenstrasse 7, 4000 Dusseldorf. **Address:** Kaiserwerther Strasse 115, 4000 Dusseldorf 30, Germany.

Individual Exhibitions:

1963 Mobelhaus Berges, Dusseldorf (with Konrad Lueg)
1964 Galerie Heiner Friedrich, Munich

Gerhard Richter: *Untitled (608–3),* ca. 1980–90. ©Christie's Images/Corbis.

Galerie Alfred Schmela, Dusseldorf
1965 Galerie René Block, West Berlin
1966 Galerie Friedrich und Dahlem, Munich
Galerie Alfred Schmela, Dusseldorf
Galleria La Tartaruga, Rome
Galerie Bishofberger, Zurich
Galleria del Leone, Venice
Galerie René Block, West Berlin
1967 Wide White Space Gallery, Antwerp
Galerie Heiner Friedrich, Munich
1968 Galerie Ricke, Kassel, West Germany
Galerie Rudolf Zwirner, Cologne
1969 Galerie Gegenverkehr, Aachen, West Germany
Galleria del Naviglio, Milan
Galerie René Block, West Berlin
1970 Palais des Beaux-Arts, Brussels
Galerie Konrad Fischer, Dusseldorf
Museum Folkwang, Essen
Galerie Jorg Schellmann, Munich
Galerie Heiner Friedrich, Munich
1971 Kunstverein, Dusseldorf
Kabinett für Aktuelle Kunst, Bremerhaven, West Germany
Galerie Thomas Borgmann, Cologne
1972 Galerie Heiner Friedrich, Munich
Galerie Rudolf Zwirner, Cologne
Galerie Konrad Fischer, Dusseldorf
Museum van Hedendaagse Kunst, Utrecht
1973 Galerie Seriaal, Amsterdam
Onnasch Gallery, New York
Kunstverein, Bremerhaven, West Germany
Galleria La Bertesca, Milan
1974 Galerie René Block, West Berlin
1975 Städtische Museum, Mönchengladbach, West Germany
Kunstverein, Braunschweig, West Germany
Galerie Rolf Preisig, Basel
Galerie Konrad Fischer, Dusseldorf
Bilder aus den Jahren 1962–1974, Kunsthalle, Breman, West Germany
1976 Kaiser-Wilhelm-Museum, Krefeld, West Germany
Museum Haus Lange, Krefeld, West Germany
Galleria Renzo Spagnoli, Florence (travelled to the Galleria La Bertesca, Genoa)
Galerie Durand-Dessert, Paris
Galleria Lucio Amelio, Naples
1977 Centre Georges Pompidou, Paris
Galerie Konrad Fischer, Dusseldorf
1978 *Abstract Painting,* Stedelijk Van Abbemuseum, Eindhoven, Netherlands
48 Portraits, Midland Group Gallery, Nottingham
Sperone-Westwater-Fischer, New York
Nova Scotia College of Art, Halifax
1979 Whitechapel Art Gallery, London
1980 Sperone-Westwater-Fischer, New York
Museum Folkwang, Essen, West Germany
Van Abbemuseum, Eindhoven, Netherlands
Galleria Mario Pieroni, Rome
1981 Kunsthalle, Dusseldorf
1982 Kunsthalle, Bielefeld, West Germany
Kunstverein, Mannhein, West Germany
Galerie Hetzler, Stuttgart
Galerie Fischer, Zurich
Padiglione d'Art Contemporanea, Milan
1983 Sperone-Westwater-Fischer, New York
Galleria Lucio Amelio, Naples
Galleria Mario Pieroni, Rome
Galerie Konrad Fischer, Dusseldorf
1984 Musée d'Art et d'Industrie, St. Etienne, France
Galerie Thomas Borgmann, Cologne
Galerie Wilkens-Jacobs, Cologne
1985 Marian Goodman Gallery, New York
Sperone-Westwater, New York
1987 Museum Overholland, Amsterdam
1988 *Gerhard Richter: The London Paintings,* Anthony d'Offay Gallery, London (catalog)
Art Gallery of Ontario, Toronto (retrospective; toured the United States)
Gerhard Richter 1988/89, Museum Boymans-van Beuningen, Rotterdam (catalog)
1989 Lenbachhaus, Munich
1990 Museum Ludwig, Cologne
1991 Tate Gallery, London (retrospective) (catalog)
Gerhard Richter: Mirrors, Anthony d'Offay Gallery, London (catalog)
Liliane & Michel Durand-Dessert Gallery, Paris (catalog)
1992 *Gerhard Richter: Helga Matura,* Rodman Hall Arts Centre, St. Catharines, Ontario (traveling exhibition) (catalog)

1993 *The Portrait Now,* National Portrait Gallery, London (catalog)
David Nolan Gallery, New York
Zerynthia, Associzone Per L'Arte Contemporanea, Rome, Italy
Gerhard Richter, Musee d'Art Moderne de la Ville de Paris, France (traveling exhibition) (retrospective) (catalog)
1994 Marian Goodman Gallery, New York
Museo Nacional Centro de Arte Reina Sofia, Madrid (catalog)
1995 *Atlas,* Dia Center for the Arts, New York
Gerhard Richter: Paintings 1964–1994, Sammlung Hauser & Wirth, Zurich (catalog)
Gerhard Richter: Paintings in the Nineties, Anthony d'Offay, London (catalog)
1996 *100 Pictures,* Carre d'Art, Nimes, France
Gerhard Richter: Paintings, Museo d'Arte Moderna, Bolzano (catalog)
1999 *Gerhard Richter: Drawings and Watercolors, 1964–1999,* Kunstmuseum Winterthur (traveled to Staatliche Kunstsammlungen, Dresden; Kaiser Wilhelm Museum, Krefeld; Stichting De Pont, Tilburg)
Anthony d'Offay Gallery, London
Faggionato Fine Arts, London
Gerhard Richter: The Art of the Impossible—Paintings 1964–98, Astrup Fearnley Museet for Moderne Kunst, Oslo (catalog)

Selected Group Exhibitions:

1965 *14 Aspekte Moderner Malerei,* Haus der Künste, West Berlin
1968 *Junge Deutscher Kunstlerbund,* Kunsthalle, Nuremberg
1969 *9 Young artists,* Guggenheim Museum, New York
1971 *New Multiple Art,* Whitechapel Art Gallery, London
1972 *Documenta 5,* Museum Fridericianum, Kassel, West Germany (and *Documenta* 7, 1982)
1975 *Fundamental Painting,* Stedelijk Museum, Amsterdam
1976 *Projekt Retrospekt,* Kunsthalle, Dusseldorf
1981 *A New Spirit in Painting,* Royal Academy of Art, London
1984 *Ein anderes Klima,* Kunsthalle, Dusseldorf
1987 *Avant-Garde in the Eighties,* Los Angeles County Museum of Art
1988 *Refigured Painting: The German Image 1960–88,* Toledo Museum of Art, Ohio (catalog)
1989 *Art from Koln,* Tate Gallery Liverpool (catalog)
1991 *The Times, the Chronicle & the Observer,* Kent Fine Art, New York (catalog)
1994 *Art from Germany's Winter Fairy Tales,* Tochigi Prefectural Museum of Fine Arts, Utsunomiya, Japan (catalog)
Sculpture, Anthony d'Offay Gallery, London
1995 *A Perspective on Contemporary Art: Painting—Singular Object,* National Museum of Modern Art, Tokyo (traveled to National Museum of Modern Art, Kyoto) (catalog)
Drawing on Chance: Selections from the Collection, Museum of Modern Art, New York (catalog)
1996 *Munch and after Munch: Or the Obstinacy of Painters,* Stedelijk Museum, Amsterdam (catalog)
Abstract Painting Today, Kunstahalle Bielefeld, Germany (catalog)
Gerhard Richter, Sigmar Polke, Arnulf Rainer, Staatliche Kunsthalle Baden-Baden, Germany (catalog)
1997 *German Art in Singapore: Contemporary Art from the Collection of the Kunstmuseum Bonn,* Singapore Art Museum (catalog)
Painters and their Sculpture: From Edgar Degas to Gerhard Richter, Museum Folkwang, Essen (catalog)
1998 *Subjective Presences,* Museum van Hedendaagse Kunst, Antwerp (catalog)

Collections:

Kunstmuseum, Dusseldorf; Neue Galerie/Sammlung Ludwig, Aachen, West Germany; Museum Folkwang, Essen; Stedelijk Van Abbemuseum, Eindhoven, Netherlands; Städtische Museum, Mönchengladbach; Nationalgalerie, West Berlin; Städtische Kunstmuseum, Bonn; Louisiana Museum, Humblebaek, Denmark; Kunstmuseum, Basel; Guggenheim Museum, New York.

Publications:

By RICHTER: Books—*Bericht über eine Demonstration,* Dusseldorf 1963; *Gerhard Richter: Atlas van de fotos en schetsen,* exhibition catalog, Utrecht 1972; *Gerhard Richter: Atlas der Fotos, Collagen und Skizzen,* exhibition catalog, Krefeld, West Germany 1976; *Gerhard Richter: Texte, Writings and Interviews 1962–1995,* Frankfurt am Main 1993, Dijon 1995; *The Daily Practice of Painting: Writings and Interviews 1962–1993,* edited by Hans-Ulrich Obrist, New York 1995; *Gerhard Richter: Abstract Painting 825-11-69 Details,* with Hans-Ulrich Obrist, Zurich 1997. **Articles—**interview with Sabine Schutz in *Journal of Contemporary Art,* vol. 3, no. 2, Fall-Winter 1990; interview with Richard Cork in *Apollo,* vol. 135, no. 359, January 1992; ''Gerhard Richter'' in *Aperture,* no. 145, Fall 1996; interview with William Furlong in *Audio Arts,* vol. 15, no. 3, 1996.

On RICHTER: Books—*Pop Art* by Rolf-Günter Dienst, Wiesbaden 1965; *Schlussel zur Modernen Kunst* by Karl Ruhrberg, Dusseldorf 1966; *Gerhard Richter,* exhibition catalog with text by Klaus Honnef, Aachen, West Germany 1969; *Gerhard Richter: Arbeiten 1962 bis 1971,* exhibition catalog with texts by Karl-Heinz Hering and Dietrich Helms, Dusseldorf 1971; *Gerhard Richter,* exhibition catalog with text by Jean-Christophe Ammann, Munich 1972; *Neue Formen des Realismus* by Peter Sager, Cologne 1973; *Projekt '74: Aspekte Internationaler Kunst am Anfang der 70er Jahre,* exhibition catalog with texts by Dieter Ronte, Evelyn Weiss, Manfred Schneckenburger and others, Cologne 1974; *Gerhard Richter: Bilder aus den Jahren 1962–1974,* exhibition catalog with texts by Manfred Schneckenburger and Marlis Gruterich, Bremen 1975; *Gerhard Richter,* exhibition catalog with texts by K. G. Pontus Hulten and Benjamin Buchloh, Paris 1977; *Gerhard Richter: 48 Portraits,* exhibition catalog edited by Lynda Morris, Nottingham 1978; *Gerhard Richter: Abstract Paintings,* exhibition catalog with texts by Rudi H. Fuchs and Benjamin Buchloh, Eindhoven, Netherlands 1978; *Gerhard Richter: Zweigelbe Striche,* exhibition catalog with text by Zdenek Felix, Essen 1980; *Gerhard Richter: Abstrakte Bilder 1976 bis 1981,* exhibition catalog with texts by Rudi H. Fuchs and Heribert Heere,

Munich 1981; *Gerhard Richter,* exhibition catalog with text by Bruno Cora, Milan 1982; *Gerhard Richter,* exhibition catalog with text by Benjamin Buchloh, New York 1985; *Gerhard Richter: The London Paintings,* exhibition catalog with essay by Jill Lloyd, London 1988; *Gerhard Richter Retrospective,* exhibition catalog with essays by Michael Danoff and Roald Nasgaard, Toronto 1988; *Gerhard Richter* by Gertrud Koch, Luc Lang and Jean-Philippe Antoine, Paris 1995; *Gerhard Richter: Atlas* by Helmut Fridel and Ulrich Wilmes, London 1997. **Articles—**''Gerhard Richter: Betty'' by Jim Lewis in *Artforum,* vol. 32, no. 1, September 1993; ''Divided Memory and Post-Traditional Identity: Gerhard Richter's Work of Mourning'' by Benjamim H.D. Buchloh in *October,* no. 75, Winter 1996; ''Gerhard Richter: He Who Misleads'' by Max Kozloff in *Art in America* (New York), vol. 82, no. 9, September 1994; ''Gerhard Richter's Atlas: The Anomic Archive'' by Benjamin H. D. Buchloch in *October,* no. 88, Spring 1999; ''The Ten Best Living Artists'' in *ARTnews,* vol. 98, no. 11, December 1999.

*

Every time we describe an event, add up a column of figures or take a photograph of a tree, we create a model; without models we would know nothing about reality and would be like animals.

Abstract paintings are fictitious models because they visualize a reality which we can neither see nor describe but which we may nevertheless conclude to exist. We attach negative names to this reality: the unknown, the un-graspable, the in-finite, and for thousands of years we have depicted it in terms of substitute images like heaven and hell, gods and devils. With abstract painting we created a better means of approaching what can be neither seen nor understood because abstract painting illustrates with the greatest clarity, that is to say with all the means at the disposal of art, 'nothing.' Accustomed to recognizing real things in paintings we refuse, justifiably, to consider color alone (in all its variation) as what the painting reveals, and instead allow ourselves to see the unseeable, that which has never before been seen and indeed is not visible. This is not an artful game, it is a necessity; and since everything unknown frightens us and fills us with hope at the same time, we take these images as a possible explanation of the inexplicable or at least as way of dealing with it. Of course even representative paintings have this trancendental aspect; since every object, being part of a world whose last and first causes are finally unfathomable, embodies that world, the image of such an object in painting evokes the general mystery all the more compellingly the less function the representation has. This is the source of the continually increasing fascination, for example, that so many old and beautiful portraits exert upon us. Thus paintings are all the better, the more beautiful, intelligent, crazy and extreme clearly perceptible and the less decipherable metaphors they are for this incomprehensible reality.

Art is the highest form of hope.

—Gerhard Richter

* * *

When Richter first showed his painterly abstract paintings in the late 1970s, his work seemed characterized by a pervasive heterogeneity, its parts refusing to be linked together into easily unified structures or developmental overviews. This was true of its chronological development, in which disparate streams of work overlapped, of the relation between individual kinds of work produced at any one time, and within the depth of the individual works themselves. From a curatorial perspective then, the dilemma was that a chronological examination of the work would hide what a thematical approach according to subject matter could reveal, and vice-versa. In Richter's first North American retrospective (Toronto and Chicago, 1988) the curators, in collaboration with the artist, nevertheless divided the work thematically, into three broad sections: the figurative—all the paintings based on found, or Richter's own photographs, from the earliest photo paintings beginning in 1962, to the latest landscapes and still lifes; the constructive—the more theoretical work, produced primarily between 1966 and 1976, such as the colour charts, the ''inpaintings'' and the gray paintings, and *Forty-Eight Portraits,* but also including pictures of windows and doors, and objects like the glass panes, and the mirrors; and the Abstract—encompassing majority the work since 1976, alongside landscapes, still lifes and more recently family photo-based portraits (and innumerable exploitations of photography), but also reaching back to a number of small, gray, experimental paintings from the late 1960s. This tri-partite division remains a useful analytical tool even as the over-all trajectory of Richter's career has taken on a more unifying clarity.

From the beginning Richter never sought a recognizable style insofar as his development has followed no clear rules that can be analyzed in terms of formal development. And, if he has not actually backed away from them, he has certainly taken a subversive attitude toward most of the historical tasks of Modern painting: subjective expression, symbolic or metaphysical representation, the production of Utopian models, the description of reality, etc. He has therefore acted contradictorily, delighting, or despairing, in abrupt juxtapositions, and has unhesitatingly tested issues evoked by painting through reaching outside it, to conceptual projects, occasionally to object-making, and especially to photography. But if Richter assumed a critical attitude to painting and to abstract art at a time when both were long in crisis, he has also become, during the past two decades, the most consummate maker of abstract paintings, investing them with the power progressively to explore our perceptual experience of reality. When in 1976 Richter made an abrupt about-face in his work, breaking free from the severe painterly impassive and personally aesthetic bounds of his Constructive work, not even he was sure of the implications. In little ''sketches,'' as he called them at first, he suddenly rallied the full arsenal of his painting trade, and with abandon, trying it all out, laid the groundwork for the compositionally complicated, heavily impastoed and richly polychromatic abstract paintings that have since dominated his work.

The transition was not easy, and had first to be mediated through photography, as in the ''smooth'' abstract pictures from between 1977 and 1980; and underlying premises needed to be redoubted, as in the gray-painted glass panes in 1977, and the mirrors from 1981. Nevertheless abstract painting has come to constitute the largest single body of work within an apparently many-sided career. Yet it is not still a little surprising—despite over forty years of painting—to recall how exclusively Richter has been a painter, and a rather traditional one, choosing few new materials, working almost always with oil on canvas? On the contrary, it has more often seemed as if the critical thrust of the work, and the context in which it was produced and has been shown called for another order of categorization. Accordingly criticism has tended to stress the skeptical aspects of Richter's work, and, in face of the abstract paintings, perhaps a little embarrassed by the sheer beauty and optimistic sensuality of them, at the beginning preferred to address the conceptual basis of the work, focusing on the deconstructivist job it did on expressionist painting's belief in unmediated subjectivity, rather than on Richter's own professed desire to be producing something positive and constructive out of his contradictory moves. In any case as Richter always stresses, surveying the body of his work: "The paintings do not differ from each other, I change my method of approach only whenever I think it appropriate."

From the first cataloged painting, *Table* from 1962, to the abstract and figure paintings of the 1980s, the heterogeneity of the work is also the source of its truthfulness. If Richter upholds "art as the highest form of hope" (as in his much quoted statement from *Documenta 7*), he does so with a reserved optimism that may echo Modernism, but not with Modernism's expectation of discovering final harmonies, visions or unities. The character of the individual works, most clearly stated in the abstract paintings, is not their resolution but in the dispersal of their elements, their coexistant contradictory expressions and moods, their opposition of promises and denials. They are complex visual events, suspended in interrogation, and "fictive models" for the reality which escapes direct address, eludes conceptualization and description, but resides inarticulate in our experience.

Over the years, of course, many of Richter's signature strategies of estrangement, such as the out-of-focus effects of his early Photo Paintings that initially functioned as irritants for viewers, setting up frustrating barriers to clear seeing and possessing, have become the cause of enchantment as we learned the pleasures of dwelling in a time and space that defies meaning, closure or resolution. His freedom to work freely across a number of styles and mediums would be liberating for any number of younger generations of artists for whom painting continued to be a vital and necessary medium, but not always a sufficient one. By the end of the century, as 'beauty,' has again become a hot topic in both artistic and academic circles, Richter's work has become celebrated as its exemplar.

—Roald Nasgaard

RICHTER, Scott

Nationality: American. **Born:** Atlanta, Georgia, 27 December 1943. **Education:** Art Students League, New York, 1962; Parsons School of Design and New School, 1963–65, B.F.A. in Industrial Design. **Family:** Married Marcia Miller (divorced 1972); one child: Erin. Married: Pamela Lenon; two children: Perris and Nicholas. **Career:** Industrial designer; professor, S.U.N.Y., Purchase, New York, 1978–84, and Cooper Union, New York, since 1984. **Awards:** National Endowment for the Arts for sculpture, 1984; Engelhard Grant, 1985; New York Foundation for the Arts for sculpture, 1986; National Endowment for the Arts for sculpture, 1986; Connecticut Council for the Arts for painting, 1995. **Agent:** Elizabeth Harris Gallery, 529 W. 20th St., New York, New York 10011; Revolution, 23257 Woodward Ave., Ferndale, Michigan 48220. **Address:** 24 Old Rock Rd., Weston, Connecticut 06883, U.S.A.

Individual Exhibitions:

1983 Luise Ross Gallery, New York
1985 Zabriski Gallery, New York
1987 Curt Marcus Gallery, New York
1988 University of Massachusetts, Amherst
1989 Pittsburgh Center for the Arts, Pittsburgh
Curt Marcus Gallery, New York
Fuller Gross Gallery, San Francisco
1990 Beth Urdang Gallery, Boston
1992 John Stoller Gallery, Minneapolis
1994 Thorne Gallery, Keene State College, Keene, New Hampshire
1996 Craig Krull Gallery, Santa Monica
1998 Elizabeth Harris Gallery, New York
2000 Revolution, Ferndale, Michigan
Elizabeth Harris Gallery, New York

Selected Group Exhibitions:

1985 *The Psyche and the Human Form,* Sculpture Center, New York
Affiliations: Recent Sculpture and Its Antecedents, Whitney Museum, Stamford, Connecticut
1986 *Inaugural Exhibition,* Curt Marcus Gallery, New York
Group Show, Gallery Nature Morte, New York
1988 *Figurative Impulses,* Santa Barbara Museum of Art, Santa Barbara
Sculptors on Paper, Madison Art Center, Madison, Wisconsin
Avant-Garde in the Eighties, Los Angeles County Museum of Art
1993 *Paper Trails: The Eidetic Image,* I Space, Chicago and Krannert Art Museum, Champaign, Illinois
1994 *Sculpture,* Nina Freudenheim Gallery, Buffalo
1995 *Drawings,* Nina Freudenheim Gallery, Buffalo
1996 *Pieces from the Permanent Collection,* Museo de Arte Comtemporano, Mexico City
1997 *10 Artists/ 10 Visions,* DeCordova Museum, Lincoln, Massachusetts
1998 *Abstract Painting, Once Removed,* Contemporary Arts Museum, Houston, Texas

Collections:

The Eli Broad Foundation; The Chase Manhattan Bank; Lannan Foundation; Metropolitan Museum of Art, New York; Museum of Contemporary Art, Chicago; Prudential Insurance; Walker Art Center, Minneapolis.

Publications:

On RICHTER: Books—*Landscape Reclaimed* exhibition catalog, Ridgefield, CT, 1996; *10 Artists/ 10 Visions: 1997* exhibition catalog, Lincoln, MA, 1997; *Tabletops* exhibition catalog, Escondido, CA, 1998; *Abstract Paintings, Once Removed* exhibition catalog, Houston, TX, 1998; *Painting Function: Making It Real* exhibition catalog, Cleveland, 2000. **Articles—**"Invitational Exhibition" by Grace Glueck in *New York Times,* 1 June 1984; "Young Americans" by Nancy Princenthal in *artNews,* January 1985; "The Human Form in the Work of 12 Sculptors" by Michael Brenson in *New York Times,* 1 February 1985; "Head, Heart, and Hands" by Steven Kaplan in *Artfinder,* Spring 1987; "Minimalism and Runaway Wit" by Kenneth Baker in *San Francisco Chronicle,* 11 July 1987; "An Attitude Toward the Figurative" by Joan Crowder in *Santa Barbara News*

Press, 18 November 1988; ''Body Language'' by Sherry Chayat in *Syracuse Herald American,* 9 October 1988; ''Scott Richter'' by Michael Kimmelman in *New York Times,* 30 September 1989; ''Scott Richter at Curt Marcus'' by Ken Johnson in *Art in America,* January 1990; ''Scott Richter'' by Nancy Princenthal in *Art in America,* January 1990; ''A Feast for Eyes Laid out on 'Tabletops''' by Robert Pincus in *San Diego Union-Tribune,* 12 October 1997; ''Scott Richter'' by Roberta Smith in *New York Times,* 13 November 1998; ''Scott Richter at Elizabeth Harris'' by Bill Arning in *Art in America,* March 1999.

*

Past reviews written about my work have difficulty categorizing it: is it painting or sculpture? While the work has sculptural properties, my interests are not sculptural at all, but rather conceptual. And while I am very interested in painting, these are not paintings. They are, however, about painting—the process of painting, not the product of painting. These pieces are only palettes (palette tables in this case). Each is repetitious in nature, with a particular subject in mind—the subject that ordinarily the painting would express or be about, e.g., an idea or person. When the paint on the palette has been mixed and is ready to go to canvas, the process stops and my painting day ends. This happens day after day, the new day's work overlaying the previous day's work. The irony is, that while trying to avoid the product, I end up with one.

—Scott Richter

RICKEY, George (Warren)

Nationality: American. **Born:** South Bend, Indiana, 6 June 1907. **Education:** Trinity College, Glenalmond, Scotland, 1921–26; Balliol College, Oxford 1926–29, B.A. 1929, M.A. 1941; Ruskin School of Drawing, Oxford, 1928–29; Académie André Lhote, Paris, 1929–30; Académie Moderne, Paris, 1929–30; Institute of Fine Arts, New York University, 1945–46; State University of Iowa, with Mauricio Lasansky, 1947; and the Institute of Design, Chicago, 1948–49. **Military Service:** Served in the United States Army Air Corps, 1940–45; became staff sergeant. **Education:** Married Edith Leighton in 1947; children: Stuart and Philip. **Career:** Lives and works in East Chatham, New York; painter in the 1930s and 1940s, sculptor since the early 1950s. History instructor, Groton School, Massachusetts, 1930–33; worked in the editorial department of *Newsweek* magazine, New York, 1936; artist-in-residence, Olivet College, Michigan, 1937–39; part-time faculty member, Art Department, Kalamazoo College, Michigan 1938–40; director, Institute of Arts, Kalamazoo, 1938–40; chairman, art department, Muhlenberg College, Allentown, Pennsylvania, 1946–48; instructor, University of Washington, Seattle, 1948; associate professor, Fine Arts Department, Indiana University, Bloomington, 1949–55; professor of art, Newcomb College, Tulane University, New Orleans, 1955–61; professor, University of California at Santa Barbara, 1960; professor, School of Architecture, Rensselaer Polytechnic Institute, Troy, New York, 1961–66. Visiting artist, Dartmouth College, Hanover, New Hampshire 1966; regents lecturer, University of California at Santa Barbara, 1967. **Awards:** Carnegie Grant, 1940, 1941; Guggenheim Fellowship, 1960, 1961; DAAD Stipendium, Berlin, 1968; Fine Arts Honor Award, American Institute of Architects, Houston 1972; Medal for Sculpture, Skowhegan School of Painting and Sculpture, Maine, 1973; Creative Arts Award in Sculpture, Brandeis Unversity, Waltham, Massachusetts, 1979; citation, National Association of Schools of Art, 1981; New York State Governor's Arts Award, Albany, 1986; Urban Design Commission Award, Atlanta, 1986. Honorary doctorates: Knox College, Galesburg, Illinois, 1970; Williams College, Williamstown, Massachusetts, 1972; Union College, Schenectady, New York, 1973; Indiana University, Bloomington, 1974; Kalamazoo College, Michigan, 1977; York University, Toronto 1978; Tulane University, New Orleans, 1983; State University of New York Purchase, 1986; Rensselaer Polytechnic Institute, Rensselaer, New York, 1990; Decorated Order of Merit 1st Class, Germany, 1993; Gold Medal for Sculpture, American Academy of Arts and Letters, 1995. **Member:** National Institute of Arts and Letters, 1974; Akademie der Kunste, West Berlin, 1987; Order of Merit, First Class, of the Federal Republic of Germany, 1993. **Address:** Route 2, Box 235, East Chatham, New York 12060–9739, U.S.A.

Individual Exhibitions:

1933 Caz-Delbo Gallery, New York
1935 Denver Art Museum
1943 Denver Art Museum
1945 Denver Art Museum
1948 Denver Art Museum
1950 Associated American Artists, Chicago (with Reginald Neal)
1953 *Mobile Sculpture,* John Herron Art Museum, Indianapolis
1955 Kraushaar Gallery, New York
1956 Isaac Delgado Museum, New Orleans
1957 Amerika Haus, Hamburg
School of Architecture, Rensselear Polytechnic, Troy, New York
1959 Kraushaar Gallery, New York
1960 Museum of Art, Santa Barbara
1961 Kraushaar Gallery, New York
Museum of Art, University of Oklahoma, Norman
1962 Primus-Stuart Galleries, Los Angeles
Kinetische Skulpturen, Galerie Springer, Berlin
Kunstverein, Hamburg
1963 Williams College Museum of Art, Williamstown, Massachussetts
Rush Rhees Fine Arts Center, University of Rochester, New York
Hopkins Center Art Galleries, Dartmouth College, Hanover, New Hampshire
1964 Kalamazoo Institute of Arts, Michigan
Kinetic Sculptures, Boston Institute of Contemporary Art
Staempfli Gallery, New York
David Stuart Gallery, Los Angeles
1966 Corcoran Gallery of Art, Washington, D.C.
1967 Walker Art Center, Minneapolis
Staempfli Gallery, New York
Fort Wayne Art Museum, Indiana
Musée d'Art Contemporain, Montreal
1968 Halfmannshof, Gelsenkirchen, West Germany (with Heinz Mack)
1969 *Mobile Skulpturen,* Haus am Waldsee, Berlin

Kunstverein, Munich
Museum Boymans-van Beuningen, Rotterdam
Kunsthalle, Nuremberg
New Jersey State Museum, Trenton
Staempfli Gallery, New York
1970 Whatcom Museum of History and Art, Bellingham, Washington
Henry Gallery, University of Washington, Seattle
1971 Staempfli Gallery, New York
University of California at Los Angeles (retrospective; toured the United States)
1972 Museum of Art, University of Iowa, Iowa City
1973 Kestner Gesellschaft, Hannover
Neue Nationalgalerie, Berlin
1974 Galerie Bucholz, Munich
Galerie Espace, Amsterdam
1975 Staempfli, Gallery, Fordham University Plaza, New York
College of St. Rose, Albany, New York
Gimpel and Hanover, Zurich
Gimpel Fils, London
1976 Kunsthalle, Bielefeld, West Germany
Kresge Art Center, Michigan State University, East Lansing
Ball State University, Muncie, Indiana
1977 Gimpel and Hanover, Zurich
Galerie Espace, Amsterdam
Galerie Buchholz, Munich
Galerie Kasahara, Osaka
Städel Museum, Frankfurt
Dag Hmmarskjold Plaza, New York
Makler Gallery, Philadelphia
1979 *Skulpturen Material Tecknik,* Amerika Haus, Berlin
Guggenheim Museum, New York (retrospective)
1981 Musée d'Art Contemporain, Montreal
1982 Scottish Sculpture Trust, Glasgow (travelled to Yorkshire Sculpture Park)
1983 Tulane University, New Orleans
1984 Bauhaus Archiv, West Berlin
Josef Albers Museum, Bottrop, West Germany
1985 Art Center of South Bend, Indiana (also at Indiana University, South Bend; St. Mary's College, South Bend; Snite Museum of Art, South Bend; University of Notre Dame, South Bend)
1986 Bryant Park, New York
Maxwell Davidson Gallery, New York
Zabriskie Gallery, New York
Neuer Berliner Kunstverein, West Berlin
1987 Carl Schlosberg Fine Arts, Sherman Oaks, California
Galerie Pels Leusden, West Berlin
State University of New York, Purchase
1988 Veranneman Foundation, Kruishoutem, Belgium
1989 Museum Boymans-van Beuningen, Rotterdam, Holland
1990 Artcurial, Paris
1991 Katonah Museum of Art, Katonah, New York (catalog)
Maxwell Davidson Gallery, New York
1992 *George Rickey in Berlin, 1967–1992,* Berlinische Galerie, Berlin (catalog)
1993 *George Rickey at Muhlenberg,* Muhlenberg College, Allentown (catalog)
George Rickey, The Gallery, Osaka (catalog)
George Rickey in Santa Barbara, University Art Museum, University of California, Santa Barbara (catalog)
George Rickey: Recent Sculpture, Maxwell Davidson Gallery, New York (catalog)
1994 Galerie Utermann, Dortmund, Germany
Maxwell Davidson Gallery, New York
1997 *George Rickey: Important Early Sculptures 1951- 1965,* Maxwell Davidson Gallery, New York (catalog)
2000 Maxwell Davidson Gallery, New York

Selected Group Exhibitions:

1951 *American Sculpture,* Metropolitan Museum of Art, New York
1959 *Recent Sculpture USA,* Museum of Modern Art, New York
1964 *Documenta 3,* Kassel, West Germany
1965 *Licht und Bewegung,* Kunsthalle, Bern (toured Belgium and West Germany)
1970 *Kinetic Art,* Hayward Gallery, London
1976 *Sculpture '76,* Greenwich Arts Council, Connecticut
1980 *Pier and Ocean,* Hayward Gallery, London
1983 *Sculpture: The Tradition in Steel,* Nassau County Museum of Fine Art, New York
1987 *Nothing But Steel,* Cold Spring Harbor Laboratory, Long Island, New York
1991 *Abstract Sculpture in America, 1930–1970,* American Federation of Arts, New York
2000 *Monte-Carlo International Sculpture Festival,* France (catalog)
Crossroads of American Sculpture, Indianapolis Museum of Art, Indiana (catalog)

Collections:

Museum of Modern Art, New York; Yale University Art Gallery, New Haven, Connecticut; Hirshhorn Museum, Washington, D.C.; National Gallery of Art, Washington, D.C.; Tate Gallery, London; Nationalgalerie, Berlin; Kunsthalle, Hamburg; Auckland City Art Gallery, New Zealand; Rijksmuseum Kröller-Muller, Otterlo, Netherlands; Modern Art Museum, Osaka, Japan; Solomon R. Guggenheim Museum, New York; Whitney Museum of American Art, New York; Storm King Art Center, Mountainville, New York.

Public Installations:

City of Berlin, Germany; City of Cologne, Germany; City of Hannover, Germany; The Carrell Woodland Sculpture Trail, Cheekwood Museum of Art, Nashville; The Morris Arboretum, Philadelphia; numerous public installations in the United States and Europe.

Publications:

By RICKEY: Books—*George Rickey: Technology,* with Achim Pahle, Chatham 1992. **Articles**—"Scandale de succés" in *Art International* (Lugano, Switzerland), May 1965; "Kinesis Continued" in *Art in America* (New York), December 1965; "Origins of Kinetic Art" in *Studio International* (London), February 1967; interview with Frederick S. Wight in *George Rickey: Retrospective Exhibition 1951–1971,* exhibition catalog, Los Angeles 1971; statement in

George Rickey, exhibition catalog, New York 1975; ''Naum Gabo'' in *Artforum* (New York), November 1977; ''Ich bin ein Berliner'' in *Artgallery* (Berlin), June/July 1978; ten brief essays in *Georges Rickey: Skulpturen Material Technik,* exhibition catalog, West Berlin 1979; ''Less is Less'' in *Art Journal* (New York), Fall 1981; ''South Bend: Seven Decades Later'' in *George Rickey in South Bend,* exhibition catalog, South Bend, Indiana 1985; three brief essays in *George Rickey,* exhibition catalog, New York 1986; ''In the Fullness of Time'' in *George Rickey,* exhibition catalog, West Berlin 1987; ''Artist's Dialogue: George Rickey, Choreography of Steel,'' with John Gruen in *Architectural Digest* (Los Angeles), vol. 45, June 1988.

On RICKEY: Books—*Kinetische Skulpturen,* exhibition catalog with an introduction by Henry R. Hope, West Berlin 1962; *George Rickey—Kinetic Sculptures,* exhibition catalog with a foreword by Susan M. Thurman, Boston 1964; *George Rickey,* exhibition catalog with an introduction by Peter Selz, Washington, D.C. 1966; *Constructivism: Origins and Evolution,* New York 1967; *Mack—Rickey,* exhibition catalog with an introduction by Wieland Schmied, Gelsenkirchen, West Germany 1968; *George Rickey: Mobile Skulpturen,* exhibition catalog with an introduction by Wieland Schmied, West Berlin 1969; *George Rickey: Ein Porträt Kunstler Als Gaste in Berlin* by Eberhard Roters, West Berlin 1969; *George Rickey* by Nancy Rosenthal, New York 1977; *George Rickey 1979,* exhibition catalog, New York 1979; *George Rickey: Kinetic Sculpture on Clydeside,* exhibition catalog with foreword by Robin Spencer, Glasgow 1982; *George Rickey: New Orleans Plus 30,* exhibition catalog with essay by Marilyn Brown, New Orleans 1983; *George Rickey in South Bend,* exhibition catalog with text by Hayden Herrera, South Bend, Indiana 1985; *George Rickey in Berlin,* exhibition catalog with texts by George Rickey and others, Berlin 1992. **Articles**—''Two Motion Sculptors: Tinguely and Rickey'' by Arthur Secunda in *Artforum International,* vol. 26, February 1988; ''The Public Art of George W. Rickey'' by Jonathan Goodman in *Arts Magazine,* vol. 62, May 1988; ''George Rickey'' by Jude Schwendenwien in *Sculpture* (Washington, D.C.), vol. 15, March 1996; ''George Rickey: Within the Poetry of Motion'' by Carla Hanzal in *Sculpture* (Washington, D.C.), vol. 18, no. 8, October 1999; ''Growth, Structural Coupling and Competition in Kinetic Art'' by Georg Nees in *Leonardo,* vol. 33, no. 1, 2000.

*

Looking back over the twenty-four years since I began seriously to compose with movement *itself* as my medium, I would say that my objectives have become clearer and simpler, though not necessarily easier to achieve. The shape of components has been reduced to a more austere geometry, while my view of the vocabulary and syntax of movement has been enormously extended. I have learned a great deal about material and about techniques for working it. I have moved my sculptures outdoors into the wind and have found Nature, both as power and as environment, to be a benign ally. This permitted much larger sculptures and the satisfaction (as well as the anxiety) of mounting large pieces in public places.

I have worked with linear elements of all of these 24 years, in the last 12 with tapered, slender blade-like forms balanced on knife edges. In the last 5 years I have also proceeded from moving lines to moving planes to moving volumes. These volumes could be between surfaces as in cubes, tetrahedra or columns of planes, or within imaginary surfaces whose edges were indicated by moving lines. I have also varied the axes of rotation to arrive at conical, rather than linear, paths. I have at the same time continued to search through the possibilities of earlier themes; an old motif can sprout new branches. I have solved, in the last two years or so, the problem of hanging a moving part on a moving part, a kind of ''elbow linkage,'' with three moving parts depending one on another. Art historians separate periods in an artist's life but the artist himself is free to overlap them.

I am sometimes asked what will come next? In retrospect I do not find that I have often done what I thought I was going to do, though each step now seems consistent with the previous one, and none of my excursions (even 20 years of painting, before I made sculpture) seems wasted. (1989)

Meanwhile, the muse has pressed me to push deeper into the phenomenon of motion.

My hinges or elbows involved planar rotation at 90° to the shaft, like a wheel or the blade of a jack-knife; but how about 45° instead? The path is then through a cone. Could I then do this with a double joint, each moving through a conical path in relation to its support? Yes, I could and did. But how about a triple joint at 45°? I have done it, with a column of four squares, stacked one above the other, followed by a linkage of four rectangular bars—at rest, a tall vertical column which, with some wind, bends back on itself like the four sides of a rectangle. Then a series of five horizontal squares, each moving to vertical above a shallow pond, the outer four swinging to vertical.

In 1992 I was invited to design a sculpture for a tall atrium in Berlin, lit by an overhead skylight. I made a ''faceted column,'' in ground stainless steel, of twelve pendant kayak-shaped vertical units, each 16 feet long, each swinging out from vertical, independently, on bearings, set only a few millimeters above the center of gravity. Each unit was thus a barely stable pendulum with a period, to and fro, of about 19 seconds, with facets constantly changing the incidence of the descending light. Then, to change the pace, I have been exploring what shapes I can develop from a small rectangle of thin steel or silicon bronze, cut-into at various angles and then bent with my thumnbs into baroque rolls and arcs, then mounted onto a pointed rod, with a single punched indentation, at exactly the center of gravity. Currently, I repeat the same exercise in bending, not with thumbs, but with broad vice-grip pliers along straight lines in a jump into 4-D cubism.

Then came a carpal tunnel operation on my left hand. I could not weild a hammer, but could still control the pigment on a paint brush. So, after an absence of 50 years, color has rejoined my four dimensions, making five. (1994)

—George Rickey

* * *

George Rickey's introduction to modernism in art occurred in Paris where he studied painting with Lhote, Léger and Ozenfant in the early 1930s. Subsequently he went back to the U.S. and taught in various academies while pursuing an active career as a painter of Social Realist pictures in styles reflective of Cézanne and Cubism. During his war service with the Army Air Corps he amused himself constructing little mobiles, but it was not until 1948–49 when he went back to school at the Institute of Design in Chicago, listening to Gabo lecture and reading Moholy-Nagy's *The New Vision,* that he became immersed in sculpture, at first allowing a kind of figurative element to exist but soon being completely captivated by outright constructivist concepts.

The mobiles of Alexander Calder were a source of inspiration in the early 1950s, though Rickey progressed away from the playful if limited circuits executed by the little cut-out leaves in the older man's constructions. From about 1957 his work grew more ambitious in both size and in setting, and he created series where the basic forms were concentrated within the one orbit.

His first works were inspired by natural shapes and were designed to be hung on a wall, thus limiting their viewpoint to the frontal. Then he extended the aspects from which the work was visible so that "Sedge Variation IV" (1961–64) was composed of two counter-weighted planes that assumed two angles of vision.

Rickey's reputation became widespread chiefly when his work was exhibited in Europe, where kinetics were appreciated more widely than in the U.S. His rocognition was expedited by the inclusion of his "Two Lines Temporal" in the 1964 *Documenta.* This massive construction of stainless-steel rods of triangular section tapering from eight inches wide at the base to a point 35 feet high achieved an impressive symmetry, leaning, falling and moving in parallel rhythms and oscillating in indepedent axes.

The bearings and the gearing of the axles on which Rickey's constructions pivot and dance are designed with an exactitude in calculation of effect, while wind-strength remains the unpredictable factor; the fail-safe mechanisms are built in so that even gale force winds cannot overbalance or capsize the whole. Variation in the speed of the independent and correlated tracks of motion produced only by wind currents is an integral part of each construction. The momentum that leads to the tipping of a blade rises to a climax in the apex of the swing, then is suspended by the force of gravity exerted while the weight of each blade falls slowly to its seemingly pre-ordained pause at its nadir.

From 1964 to 1969 Rickey evolved a series of closely related sculptures comprising either three or five elements that were free-standing and required a circumambulatory inspection to appreciate their complete operation. At one point the edges of the planes only are apparent so that the volume is negative, then as the permutation of planned movement changes the flatness of the blade-faces combine to present a surface almost continuous in expanse. One of Rickey's greatest public sculptures is his "Two Rectangles Vertical Gyratory" (1969) in a shopping centre in Rotterdam. These long planes of stainless steel go through see-saw movements and move at angles to each other.

Movement is at the root of Rickey's work since it is the motion of large planar areas or rods rather than their forms which creates the unique sensations on the spectator. Time too is of the utmost, for it plays its dramatic role in the pace and suspenseful pauses in the choreography of the abstract light-reflecting surfaces in space.

—G.S. Whittet

RILEY, Bridget (Louise)

Nationality: British. **Born:** London, 25 April 1931. **Education:** Cornwall, Buckinghamshire, and Cheltenham; studied under Sam Rabin, at Goldsmiths College of Art, London, 1949–52; also studied at Royal College of Art, London, 1952–55, and under Maurice de Sausmarez, at Thubron's Summer School, Norfolk, 1959. **Career:** Painter: has lived and worked in London since 1956; worked for J. Walter Thompson Advertising Agency, London, 1958–59; visited

Bridget Riley: *Blaze,* 1964. ©Tate Gallery, London/Art Resource, NY; courtesy of Tate Gallery.

Spain and Portugal, 1959; spent summer of 1960 in Italy; has worked partly in Vaucluse, France, since 1961; visited Greece, 1967; collaborated with Peter Sedgley on *Space,* a scheme for the organization of studios for artists, St. Katherine's Dock, London, 1969–71; travelled in Europe and the United Kingdom, 1971–75, and in India, Japan, and elsewhere in the Far East, 1977. Lecturer in art, Convent of the Sacred Heart, London, 1957–58; part-time lecturer in art, Loughborough College of Art, Leicestershire, 1959–61, Hornsey College of Art, London, 1960, and Croydon College of Art, Surrey, 1962–64; trustee, National Gallery, London, since 1981. **Awards:** Open prize, John Moore's Exhibition, Walker Gallery, Liverpool 1963; Peter Stuyvesant Foundation Travel Bursary, 1964; Grand Prize for Painting, *Biennale,* Venice, 1969; prize, *International Print Biennale,* Ohara Museum, Tokyo, 1972; Gold Medal, *Grafik-Biennale,* Fredrikstad, Norway, 1980. Commander, Order of the British Empire (CBE), 1974; Trustee of the National Gallery, London 1981–88; Companion of Honour 1999; Honorary doctorates from University of Manchester, 1976, University of Ulster, 1986, Oxford University, 1994, Cambridge University, 1995, De Montfort University, 1996, University of Exeter, 1997. **Agent:** Mayor Rowan Gallery, 31a Bruton Place, London W1A 7AB. **Address:** 7 Royal Crescent, London W11, England.

Individual Exhibitions:

1962 Gallery 1, London
1963 Gallery 1, London
University of Nottingham
1965 Richard Feigen Gallery, New York
Feigen/Palmer Gallery, Los Angles
1966 Robert Fraser Gallery, London (with Harold Cohen)
Museum of Modern Art, New York (toured the United States)
Richard Feigen Gallery, New York

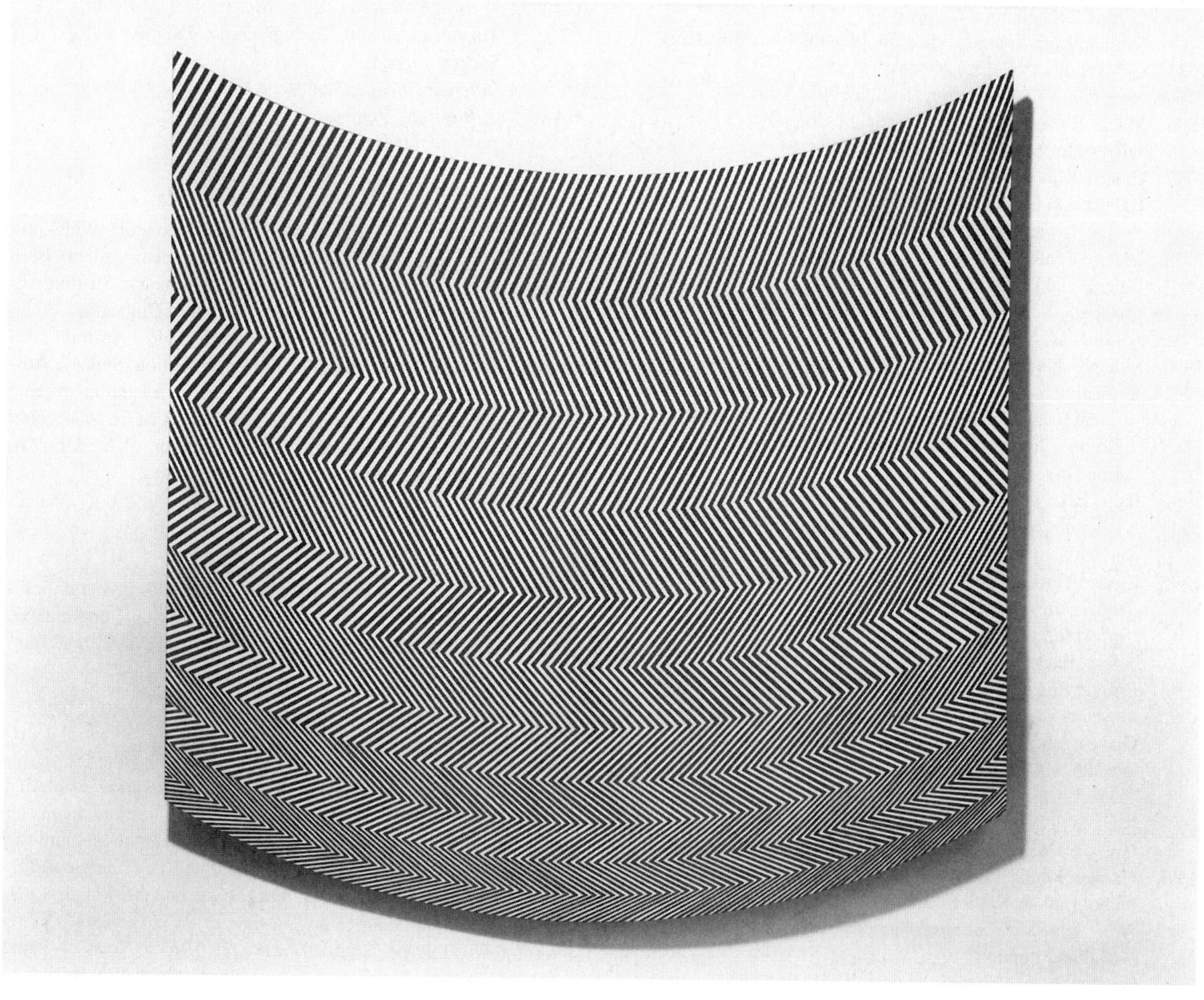

Bridget Riley: *Suspension,* 1964. ©Walker Art Center, Minneapolis.

1967 Richard Feigen Gallery, New York
1968 *Biennale,* Venice (with Philip King; travelled to the Städitsche Kunstagalerie, Bochum, West Germany, and the Museum Boymans-van Beuningen, Rotterdam)
1969 Rowan Gallery, London
Bear Lane Gallery, Oxford (travelled to the Midland Group Gallery, Nottingham, and the Arnolfini Gallery, Bristol)
1970 Richard Feigen Gellery, Chicago
Kunstverein, Hannover (toured Europe)
1971 Rowan Gallery, London
1972 Rowan Gallery, London
1973 *Paintings and Drawings 1961–73,* Whitworth Art Gallery, Manchester, (toured the U.K.)
1974 MacRobert Centre, University of Stirling, Scotland (travelled to Collins Exhibition Hall, Strathclyde, Scotland, and the Aberdeen Art Gallery, Scotland)
1975 Galerie Beyeler, Basel
Sidney Janis Gallery, New York
1976 Rowan Gallery, London
Coventry Gallery, Sydney
1977 Minami Gallery, Tokyo
1978 Sidney Janis Gallery, New York
Albright-knox Art Gallery, Buffalo, New York (toured the United States, Australia, and Tokyo)
1979 Australian Galleries, Melbourne
Bonython Gallery, Adelaide
1980 Artline, The Hague
Silkscreen Prints 1965–78, Arts Council, London (toured Britain)
1981 Rowan Gallery, London
Warwick Arts Trust, London
1983 Nishimura Gallery, Tokyo
Juda Rowan Gallery, London
Arcade Gallery, Harrogate, Yorkshire
Newcastle Polytechnic, Northumberland
Queens Hall Art Centre, Haxham, Northumberland
1984 Royal Institute of British Architects, London

Galerie Reckermann, Cologne
Durham Light Infantry Museum, England (toured Britain)
1985 Goldsmith's College, London
Nina Freudenheim Gallery, Buffalo, New York
1986 Maclaurin Art Gallery, Ayr, Scotland (toured)
Jeffrey Hoffeld and Co., New York
1987 Galerie Konstruktiv Tendens, Stockholm
Galerie und Edition Schlegl, Zurich
Mayor Rowan Gallery, London
1988 Galerie Teufel, Cologne
1989 Galerie und Edition Schlegl, Zurich
Curated: The Artist's Eye: Bridget Riley, National Gallery, London
1990 Sidney Janis Gallery, New York
1992 *According to Sensation: Paintings 82–92,* Arts Council of Great Britain (touring Kunsthalle Nürnberg, Quadrat Bottrop, Joseph Albers Museum Hayward Gallery, London)
1993 Ikon Gallery, Birmingham
1994 *Six Paintings From The Collection,* Tate Gallery, London
Karsten Schubert Gallery, London
1995 Kettles Yard, Cambridge
Bridget Riley: Works on Paper, Aberdeen Art Gallery
Bridget Riley: Recent Works: 1981—1995, Spacex Gallery, Exeter
Bridget Riley: New Works, Galerie Schlegl, Zurich
1996 Museum Moderner Kunst Landkreis Cuxhaven, Ottendorf
Glasgow Print Studio, Glasgow
Waddington Galleries & Karsten Schubert Gallery, London
1997 Karsten Schubert Gallery, London
Green on Red Gallery, Dublin
1998 Gallerie Michael Sturm, Cologne
Abbot Hall Art Gallery and Museum, Kendal, Cumbria
1999 *Bridget Riley: Paintings from the 60s and 70s,* Serpentine Gallery, London
Bridget Riley: Selected Paintings 1961–1999, Kunstverein fur die Rheinlande und Westfalen, Düsseldorf
2000 *Bridget Riley: New Paintings and Gouaches,* Waddington Galleries in collaboration with Karsten Schubert, London
Bridget Riley: Paintings 1982 2000 and Early Works on Paper, PaceWildenstein, New York
Bridget Riley: Reconnaissance, DIA Center for the Arts, New York

Selected Group Exhibitions:

1955 *Young Contemporaries,* London
1962 *Towards Art,* Arts Council Gallery, London (toured the U.K.)
1965 *The Responsive Eye,* Museum of Modern Art, New York (toured the United States)
1967 *Jeunes Peintres Anglais,* Musée des Arts Décoratifs, Paris
1973 *La Peinture Anglaise Aujourd'hui,* Musée National d'Art Moderne, Paris
1976 *Arte Inglese Oggi 1960–76,* Palazzo Reale, Milan
1978 *British Santidskunst,* Kunstnernes Hus, Oslo (travelled to Trondheim and Bergen, Norway)
1982 *Aspects of British Art Today,* Metropolitan Museum, Tokyo (travelled to Tochigi, Osaka, Fukuoka and Sapporo, Japan)
1984 *A Different Climate,* Stadtische Kunsthalle, Dusseldorf
1986 *XLII Biennale,* Venice

Collections:

Arts Council of Great Britain; Tate Gallery, London; Whitworth Art Gallery, Manchester; Stedelijk Museum, Amsterdam; Bern Kunstverien; Neues Museum, Nürnberg, Germany; Stiftung für Konkrete Kunst, Reutlingen, Germany; Calouste Gulbenkian Foundation, Portugal; Art Gallery of New South Wales, Australia; Art Gallery of Sydney, Australia; The Power Collection, Sydney, Australia; The Australian National Gallery, Canberra, Australia; Museum of Modern Art, Tokyo; Nantenshi Gallery, Tokyo; Seibu Museum of Art, Tokyo; Albright-Knox Art Gallery; Museum of Modern Art, New York; The Dallas Museum of Fine Arts, Texas.

Public Installations:

''Colour Moves'' for Ballet Rambert, premiered at Edinburgh Festival, 1983; two corridor murals for St. Mary's Hospital, London 1987; free-standing work in atrium of Citibank office building, London 1998–99.

Publications:

By RILEY: Articles—statement in *The New Generation,* exhibition catalog, London 1964; ''Bridget Riley Answers Questions about Her Work'' in *Monad I* (London), 1964; ''Perception Is the Medium'' in *Artnews* (New York), October 1965, ''Bridget Riley Interviewed by David Sylvester'' in *Studio International* (London), March 1967; ''Bridget Riley and Maurice de Sausmarez; A Conversation'' in *Art International* (Lugano, Switzerland), April 1967; ''Notes on Some Paintings'' in *Art and Artists* (London), June 1968; ''Bridget Riley in Conversation with Robert Kudielka'' in *Bridget Riley: Paintings and Drawings 1961–73,* exhibition catalog, London 1973; ''On Travelling Paintings'' in *Art Monthly* (London), no. 39, 1980; ''Bridget Riley on Swimming Through a Diamond'' in *Vogue* (London), March 1984.

On RILEY: Books—*Bridget Riley,* exhibition catalog with introduction by Maurice de Sausmarez, London 1962; *Optical and Kinetic Art* by Michael Compton, London 1967; *Movements in Art Since 1945* by Edward Lucie-Smith, London 1969; *Bridget Riley* by Maurice de Sausmarez, London 1970; *Modern English Painters* by John Rothenstein, London 1974; *Art Since Pop* by John A. Walker, London 1975; *Bridget Riley,* exhibition catalog with text by Robert Kudielka, Tokyo 1977; *Art of the Sixties* by Hugh Adams, London 1978; *Bridget Riley: Works 1959–78,* exhibition catalog with introduction by Robert Kudielka, London 1978; *Women Artists from Antiquity to the Twentieth Century* by Wendy Slatkin, New York 1983; *Colour for the Painter in Colour: Art & Science*, edited by Trevor Lamb and Janine Bourriau, Oxford, 1995; *Bridget Riley: Dialogues on Art,* edited by Robert Kudielka, London, 1995; *Bridget Riley: Works 1961–1998,* exhibition catalogue with interview by Isabel Carlisle, Kendal, Cumbira, 1998; *Bridget Riley: Paintings from the 60s and 70s,* exhibition catalogue with text by Frances Spalding, Robert Kudielka, and Lisa Corrin, London 1999; *The Eye's Mind: Bridget Riley, Collected Writings 1965–1999* edited by Robert Kudielka, London 1999; *Bridget Riley: Reconnaissance* edited by Lynne Cooke and John Elderfeld, New York 2001.

*

My paintings are not concerned with the romantic legacy of expressionism, nor with fantasies, concepts or symbols.

I draw from nature, I work with nature, although in completely new terms. For me nature is not landscape, but the dynamism of visual forces—an event rather than an appearance—these forces can only be tackled by treating colour and form as ultimate identities, freeing them from all descriptive or functional roles.

The context of painting provides an arena in which to tap these visual energies—to unlock their true potential and latent characteristics. Once released they have to be organized in new pictorial terms, every bit as much, though quite differently, as when painting nature in landscape or still life.

The new motif determines the size, the proportion, even the ''way up'' of the painting just as the old natural motif determined these factors before. In working on a painting I choose a small group of colours and juxtapose them in different sequences, to provide various relationships and to precipitate colour reactions. These colour *events* are delicate and elusive, they have to be organized to make them more *present*—more *there* more *real.* I take for example three colours, say magenta, ochre and turquoise plus black and white, a situation which then triggers off airy irridescent bursts of colour.

I choose a form and a structure in which to repeat these colour clouds, to accumulate them, to mass them until each painted unit is submerged in a visual rhythm which, in turn, collectively generates a shimmering coloured haze. This luminous substance is completely meshed with the actual coloured surface and together they provide the experience of the painting.

—Bridget Riley

* * *

Bridget Riley has the distinction of being one of the few British artists (and the only British woman) to win the *premio* at the Venice *Biennale.* She thus enjoys an enormous international reputation. She is one of the pioneers of Op Art, not *the* pioneer.

Her early work was divisionist in technique. It enabled her to capture the intensity of light and colour, the visual equivalent of energy, even the pulsations of heat, from a shimmering landscape.

This preoccupation with light, heat and pulsating energy persisted into the next phase of her work, which marked the beginning of those pictures by which she has come to be known. In this phase she worked in black and white with very simple elements—small triangles or ovals, curved lines, vertical lines, horizontal lines. She discovered that a systematic repetition of these small elements could generate the visual equivalent of energy very powerfully. In ''Static'' (which refers to an electric charge, not absence of movement), for instance, tiny ovals assault the optic nerves in such a way as to suggest the bombardment of heat and light from the shale on a mountain on an intensely hot summer's day.

In the early 1960s her pictures fell roughly into three types: systematic repetitions of simple elements such as triangles, as in ''Straight Curve,'' in which triangles of varying proportions are arranged in straight rows in such a way that an impression of curved lines is produced; broken concentric figures, such as ''Disfigured Circle,'' in which there is a continuous shift of perspective, or the ''Blaze'' series, in which counterflow hatched lines forming eccentric circles grind into one another; and undulating curved lines, like waves, which heave and billow, as in the appropiately named ''Current.''

What is remarkable about these early pictures, apart from the technical brilliance, and the suavity and rhythm of undulating lines, is the intensity of feeling they generate and the way their effects are achieved with such economy of means. The aggressiveness of some of these works may reflect certain feelings which Riley had at the time and transferred to canvas. The economy of means is connected with a belief (which she inculcated in her teaching) that restraints on an artist lead to greater, not less, richness of invention and individuality of expression. In this connection, she had a practice, which she called ''pacing,'' in which a circle or triangle is ''put through its paces,'' moved from full circle, through various ovals, to almost a straight line, with unforseeable and stimulating results.

From the stark and dramatic contrasts of black and white Riley turned to the modulation of tones.

This gave greater scope, since tone can modify and produce form. Thus, not only were the elements ''paced'' by an alteration of shape, but also by alteration of tone. Moreover, variations in tone created overall patterns which black and white on their own could not do.

By the late 1960s Riley was working in colour, at first two colours (red and blue), then three, four, five, with white, or, more recently, black intervening. Superficially they may seem to be no more than strips of colours juxtaposed. The perspective spectator, however, will notice how these colours react on one another to ''induce'' other ethereal, aerial colours through the ''spread'' of the pigment colours into the areas of white. Thus, in an early work, ''Late Morning,'' a sense of the opulence of a late summer morning, with its golden-green glow, when the sun has all but dispersed the morning mists and the air is still cool, is induced by the juxtaposition of orange, various shades of green and white.

In those early colour works Riley had not quite mastered the principle of colour induction. She thought that it consisted in inducing colour into a white area. It is, of course, partly that. But in her recent work she has discovered that the ''inhibitive'' effects of black may lead to a far richer induction of colour. It seems that in these recent works she has finally achieved the goal she has been aiming for. These recent work are both entirely individual, canvas by canvas, but rich in coloration, suggesting the richness of oriental colours.

Critics of Bridget Riley's work have said that her pictures are nothing more than exercises in perceptual psychology or designs for commercial advertising. Ironically she did work for an advertising agency, and it could be said that the so-called ''woolmark'' is a plagarism of one of her ''Fragments.'' And some of her work is of interest to perceptual psychologists. It is also true that her method of work is perhaps more blatantly ''experimental'' than that of most artists—sketch, cartoon, etc—and that she employs assistants to produce the final work. Space does not allow a proper discussion of these matters. Suffice it to say that the use of assistants is in the grand tradition of painting; artistic experimentation has nothing to do with scientific experimentation (though scientists may use works of art as material for their investigations); and what advertisers do with works of art should not reflect on the works themselves. Art is art, neither science nor advertising; and Bridget Riley is an artist pure and simple.

—D. C. Barrett

RINKE, Klaus

Nationality: German. **Born:** Wattenschied, 29 April 1939. **Education:** Studied in Wattenschied, 1945–54; apprentice painter/decorator in Westphalian department store, Gelsenkirchen, 1954–57; studied paintng and free pictorial expression, Folkwangschule, Essen-Werden, 1957–60. **Career:** Independent artist in Paris, 1960–62, Rheims 1962–64, and in Dusseldorf since 1964: abstract paintings and drawings, 1960–66; polyester sculptures, 1965–68; first sculptures with water, 1968; first body-works and "demonstrations," 1969; first films and videos, 1969. Professor of free pictorial expression, Staatliche Kunstakademie, Dusseldorf, 1974. **Awards:** Prize, with Nancy Graves and Pierpaolo Calzolari, *Biennale,* Paris, 1971; Landespreis, Nordrhein-Westfalen, Dusseldorf, 1973; Konrad-von-Soest Prize, Landeschaftsverbandes Westfalen, Dusseldorf, 1974. **Agents:** Reese Palley Gallery, 550 Sutter Street, San Francisco, California 94102, U.S.A.; and Galerie Alfred Schmela, Dusseldorf.

Individual Exhibitions:

1962 Galerie Le Portulan, Le Havre, France
1963 Galerie Haut-Pave, Paris
1964 Centre Culturel, St. Severin, Paris
1965 Galerie Butterbach, Luxembourg
1969 Galerie Konrad Fischer, Dusseldorf
1970 Städtische Museum Schloss Morsbroich, Leverkusen, West Germany
Galerie Konrad Fisher, Dusseldorf
1971 Galeria Toselli, Milan
Galerie Ricke, Cologne
Videogalerie Gerry Schum, Dusseldorf
Gegenverkehr, Aachen, West Germany
1972 Situation Gallery, London
Galleria L'Attico, Rome
Reese Palley Gallery, New York
Reese Palley Gallery, San Francisco
Kunsthalle, Tübingen
1973 Kunsthalle, Recklinghausen, West Germany
Bienal, Sao Paulo
Württembergischer Kunstverein, Stuttgart
Gallerie Ricke, Cologne
Universitat, Kiel
Museum of Modern Art, New York (outdoor action)
1974 The Clocktower, New York
Galerie Schmela, Dusseldorf
Westfälischer Kunstverein, Münster, West Germany
1975 Galerie Hetzler + Keller, Stuttgart
Galerie Defet, Nuremberg
Objekte, Photoserien, Zeichnungen 1969–1975, Kunstverein, Dusseldorf
Galerie Schmela, Dusseldorf
1976 Museum of Modern Art, Oxford
Städtische Museum, Wiesbaden, West Germany
Reuchlinhaus, Pforzheim, West Germany
Travaux 1969–1976, Musée d'Art Moderne de la Ville, Paris
1978 *Meine Plastik ist Zeichnung,* Kunsthalle, Hamburg
1981 *Die Autonomen Werke von 1957–1980,* Staatsgalerie, Stuttgart
1982 Kunstmuseum, Dusseldorf
Flow Ace Gallery, Vancouver, British Columbia
1983 Flow Ace Gallery, Paris
1984 Museum Neandertal, Mettmann, West Germany
1985 Centre Georges Pompidou, Paris
1992 Kunsthalle, Kiel Kunsthalle, Dusseldorf (catalog)
Klaus Rinke: Retroactive—Catalogue of Works 1954–91, Städtische Kunsthalle, Dusseldorf (catalog)
Karsten Greve Gallery, Cologne
Klaus Rinke: 1954–1991, Retro Aktiv: Werkverzeichnis 1954–1991 der Malerei, Skulptur, Primärdemonstrationen, Fotografie, und Zeichnungen ab 1980, Kunsthalle, Düsseldorf, Germany (catalog)
1994 Galerie de France, Paris
2000 *Installations, Drawings, Photographies,* Gallery Meyer Ellinger, Frankfurt am Main

Selected Group Exhibitions:

1968 *Envirornments,* Kunsthalle, Bern
1969 *14 x 14 Escalation,* Staatliche Kunsthalle, Baden-Baden, West Germany
1970 *Information,* Museum of Modern Art, New York
1971 *Prospekt,* Kunsthalle, Dusseldorf
1972 *Documenta,* Kassel, West Germany (and 1977)
1973 *Kunst aus Fotografie,* Kunstverein, Hannover (travelled to Städtische Kunstsammlungen, Ludwigshafen, West Germany)
1974 *Projekt 74,* Kunsthalle, Cologne
1975 *Bodyworks,* Museum of Contemporary Art, Chicago
1977 *Europe in the 70s,* Art Institute of Chicago (travelled to the Hiroshima Museum, Washington, D.C.)
1983 *Sculpture Biennale,* Middelheim Park, Antwerp, Belgium
1992 *Water in Art,* Museums-Pädogogischer Dienst, Hamburg (catalog)
1995 *FotoKunst,* Institut für Auslandsbeziehungen, Stuttgart (catalog)
1996 *Rundgang 96,* Kunstakademie, Dusseldorf
1998 *Positions in Art Photography in Germany Since 1945,* Martin-Gropius-Bau, Berlin

Collections:

Nationalgalerie, West Berlin; Museum Folkwang, Essen; Städtische Museum Schloss Morsbroich, Leverkusen, West Germany; Museum Ludwig, Cologne; Neue Galerie/Sammlung Ludwig, Aachen, Germany; Kaiser-Wilhelm Museum, Krefeld, Germany; Staatsgalerie, Stuttgart; Kunsthalle, Tübingen; Kunstmuseum, Bonn; Tate Gallery, London.

Publications:

By RINKE: Books—*Klaus Rinke: Zeit Time-Raum Space-Korper Body—Handlungen Transformations,* edited by Gotz Adriani, Cologne 1972; *Klaus Rinke: Skulpturen und Zeichnungen,* exhibition catalog, Mettmann 1984. **Articles**—''Kunstwater van Klaus Rinke'' in *Museumjournaal* (Amsterdam), September 1970; ''Between Spring and Ocean'' in *Studio International* (London), March 1971; ''Statement'' in *Avalanche* (New York), March 1971; ''Phenomenology of a Time, Space System,'' edited by Evelyn Weiss, in *Studio International* (London), April 1974; interview with Helga Meister in *Kunstforum International,* no. 118, 1992; interview with Heinz-Norbert Jocks in *Kunstforum International,* no. 150, April/June 2000. **Films and videos**—*Zwoelf Fass Geschoeppftes,* 1969; *41 Polyesterelement Verteilt und Zusammmen Gezogen,* 1969; *Wasser Hippen,* 1970; *Fermost-/Far East German Buddha,* 1970; *Inhalation I + II,* 1971; *Wasser Holen Bringen Schulten,* 1971; *Galerie Konrad Fischer,* 1971; *Energiegrenzen,* 1971; *Distant and Zeitrelation,* 1971; *Boden-Raum,* 1971; *Elliptisch,* 1971.

On RINKE: Books—*Klaus Rinke,* exhibition catalog with text by Rolf Wedewer and an interview by Jacques Laval, Leverkusen, West Germany 1970; *Klaus Rinke: 12th Bienal de Sao Paulo 1973,* exhibition catalog with text by Manfred Schmalriede, Cologne 1973; *Klaus Rinke: Objekte, Photoserien, Zeichnungen 1969–1975,* exhibition catalog with a foreword by Karl-Heinz Hering, text by Manfred Schmalriede, Dusseldorf 1975; *Klaus Rinke: Travaux 1969/1976,* exhibition catalog with texts by Suzanne Page, Evelyn Weiss and Pierre Guyotat, Paris 1976; *Klaus Rinke: Meine Plastik ist Zeichnung,* exhibition catalog with text by Werner Hofmann and Helmut R. Leppien, Hamburg 1978; *Rinke: Die Autonomen Werke von 1957–1980,* exhibition catalog with texts by Stephan von Wiese and Klaus Heinz, Stuttgart 1981. **Articles**—''Klaus Rinke'' by Catherine Francblin in *Beaux Arts Magazine,* no. 51, November 1987; ''Der Wassermann'' by Alfred Welti in *ART: Das Kunstmagazin,* no. 5, May 1999.

* * *

Klaus Rinke has sought in the most vigorous way at his command to eliminate every vestige of the past from his work. Not like the Futurists who wanted to replace heritage with a new imagery based upon the contemporary world of their times, but like an extended conceptualist, he has cauterised imagery to the point of non-existence. The world is permitted only in terms of temporal theory or physics. Aids like the camera and engineering make these practices visible, tangible even, but the burden of proof is upon the brain rather than upon the eyes or the hand. Actions—demostrations he calls them—are also an appeal to cerebral ratiocination rather than emotion. Rinke looks for the viability of his work in situations like landscape, space or in the abstract systems of physics and Germany.

Beyond the conceptual frontiers, and to demonstrate time and space, he builds systems which spell out the magic of computers but always in the series order he has ordained. He is particularly obsessed with two elements, both of which can play their parts in these fields—expansion and gravitational pull. In the former, to take one specific example, he has shown with his drawing ''Circular Expansion'' that he can enter the realms of optics that less sophisticated eyes might assume were the prerequisites of Bridget Riley and Victor Vasarely. This is a fairly primitive demonstration of visual truth by Rinke. ''The Measuring Instrument for Eternity'' (an engineering construction) of 1972/73 shows how far he can pursue his theories when he wishes.

—Sheldon Williams

RIOPELLE, Jean-Paul

Nationality: Canadian. **Born:** Montreal, 7 October 1923. **Career:** Painter; travelled in France, Germany, and New York, 1946; settled in Paris, 1947; associated with the Automatistes group led by Paul-Emile Borduas. **Awards:** Prix Unesco, Paris, 1962. Companion of the Order of Canada, 1969. **Agents:** Pierre Matisse Gallery, 41 East 57th Street, New York, New York 10022; and Galerie Maeght Lelong, 13–14 rue de Teheran, 75008 Paris. **Address:** 10 rue Fremincourt, 75015 Paris France.

Individual Exhibitions:

1949 Galerie Nina Dausset, Paris
1950 Galerie Greuse, Paris
1951 Galerie Springer, Berlin
1952 Galerie Hachette, Paris
Galerie Henriette Niepoe, Paris
1953 Galerie Pierre Loeb, Paris
1954 Pierre Matisse Gallery, New York
Galerie Rive Droite, Paris
Galerie Evrad, Lille, France
1955 Pierre Matisse Gallery, New York
1956 Gimpel Gallery, London
Galerie Jacques Dubourg, Paris
Kunstverein, Cologne
Kunst-und-Museumverein, Wuppertal, West Germany
Kestner Gesellchaft, Hannover
1959 Kunsthalle, Basel
Richentor, Basel
Svensk-Franska Konstgalleriet, Stockolm
Galerie Anne Abels, Cologne
Arthur Tooth and Sons Gallery, London
1960 Galerie Jacques Dubourg, Paris
Galleria l'Ariete, Milan
Assosiazione Arti Figurative, Turin
1962 National Gallery of Canada, Ottawa
1963 Galerie d'Art Moderne, Basel
Arthur Tooth and Sons Gallery, London
1965 Pierre Matisse Gallery, New York
1967 Musée de la Province, Quebec
1972 Galerie Maeght, Paris
1974 Galerie Maeght, Paris
Pierre Matisse Gallery, New York
1975 Pierre Matisse Gallery, New York
Galeria Maeght, Barcelona
Galleria d'Arte Narciso, Turin
Gallery Moos, Toronto
1977 *Jean-Paul Riopelle: Grands Formats 1952–75,* Pierre Matisse Gallery, New York
1980 Musée d'Art et d'Industrie, St. Etienne, France
Galerie Maeght, Zurich

Jean-Paul Riopelle: *Untitled,* 1963. ©2001 Artists Rights Society (ARS), NY/ADAGP, Paris.

1981 Raydon Gallery, New York
Gimpel Fils Gallery, London
Centre Georges Pompidou, Paris
1983 Galerie Maeght Lelong, Paris
1985 Pierre Matisse Gallery, New York
1989 *Jean-Paul Riopelle,* Galerie Claude Lafitte, Montreal
Pierre Matisse Gallery, New York
1991 *Jean-Paul Riopelle,* Museum of Fine Arts, Montreal
1993 *Riopelle,* Michel Tetreault Art International, Montreal
Jean-Paul Riopelle: Live Works, Michel Tetreault Art International, Montreal
1997 *Jean-Paul Riopelle: Sculpture, Painting, Printmaking,* Espace Paul Rebeyrolle, Eymoutiers, France

Selected Group Exhibitions:

1951 *Bienal,* Sao Paulo (and 1955)
1954 *Biennale,* Venice (and 1962)

1956 *Internationale Sezession,* Leverkusen, West Germany
1958 *World's Fair,* Brussels
1959 *Documenta,* Kassel, West Germany
1960 *Salon de Mai,* Paris
1961 *Carnegie International,* Pittsburgh
1970 *8 Artists from Canada,* Museum Haaretz, Tel Aviv
1992 *Montreal 1942–92: The Splendid Anarchy of Painting,* Galerie de l'Universite de Quebec, Montreal
1993 *Free Admission to Contemporary Art in Montreal,* Place Bonaventure, Hall Sud, Montreal
1994 *The Festival de Peinture in Mascouche: Abstraction in Montreal, 1950–70,* Hotel de Ville, Mascouche, Quebec
1998 *Kaleidoscope: An Exhibition of Quebec Members of the Royal Academy of Arts,* Palais Montcalm, Hull, Quebec
Eternal Present: 50 Years After Refus Global, Musee d'Art de Mont-Saint-Hilaire, Quebec

Collections:

National Gallery of Canada, Ottawa; Art Gallery of Ontario, Toronto; Los Angeles County Museum of Art; Scottish National Gallery of Modern Art, Edinburgh; Neue Nationalgalerie, Berlin; National Gallery of Victoria, Melbourne.

Publications:

On RIOPELLE: Books—*Riopelle,* exhibition catalog, Paris 1954; *Riopelle: Reperes,* exhibition catalog with preface by Lise Gauvin, Paris 1983; *Jean-Paul Riopelle: Les Oies Sauvages,* exhibition catalog, New York 1985; *Jean-Paul Riopelle,* exhibition catalog, Montreal 1991; *Riopelle,* exhibition catalog, Montreal 1993; *Jean-Paul Riopelle: Live Works,* exhibition catalog, preface by Claude Brault and Michel Tetreault, Montreal 1993. **Articles—**''Two Answers'' by Neville Wallis in *The Observer* (London), June 1959; ''A Painter of Awakening—Jean-Paul Riopelle'' by Georges Duthuit in *Canadian Art* (Ottawa), October 1959; ''La Sculpture de Peintre: Bronzes de Riopelle'' in *Quadicum* (Paris), no. 11, 1961; ''Riopelle'' by Franco Russoli in *Derrière le Miroir* (Paris), April 1970; ''Riopelle ou la Pensée Sauvage'' in *Chroniques de l'Art Vivant* (Paris), May 1970: ''Jean-Paul Riopelle: A Poet of the Sign'' by M. Greenwood in *Artscanada* (Toronto), August 1971; ''Lettre de Suisse'' by J. L. Daval in *Art International* (Lugano, Switzerland), March 1973; special issue of *Derrière le Miroir* (Paris), March 1976; ''In Search of Riopelle'' by Francois-Marc Gagnon in *Canadian Art,* vol. 9, no. 1, Spring 1992; ''Jean-Paul Riopelle: A Savagery of Thought'' by Marc Le Bot in *Cimaise,* vol. 39, September/October 1992; ''Jean-Paul Riopelle: Prints & the Legend'' by Leslie Leubbers in *The Print Collector's Newsletter,* vol. 22, January/February 1992; ''Jean Paul Riopelle's Prints'' by Jean-Pierre Bordua in *Magazin'art,* vol. 9, no. 1, Autumn 1996; ''The Master: Lineage from Leduc to Borduas to Riopelle'' by Paquerette Villeneuve in *Canadian Art,* vol. 14, Spring 1997; ''Acclaimed Artist's Catalog Sparks Controversy'' by Glen Warner in *Art Business News,* vol. 27, no. 3, March 2000.

* * *

Nicolas de Staël and Jean-Paul Riopelle have proved themselves the masters of thick-paint applied impasto in contemporary times. Unlike de Staël, whose only non-figurative work veered towards exact and tight abstract compositions, the Canadian was able to spread his squares and deluges of colours in a far more amorphous mass. For those who can tease their eyes through the strife of colours and the stodgy pigment there are at least two surprises in store: a) under and running through the lumpy scales of paint there is a well-tuned discipline of composition which draws the whole painting together in much the same way as the open eye in one of Lee Bontecou's constructions will give cohesion to the entire apparatus; and b) out of this emerges a kind of architecture not so far removed from that of Vieira da Silva, except that in Riopelle's case there is no instance of nervous *schadenfreude* that can haunt some of the more daunting canvases of Vieira da Silva.

Of course a talent like that of Riopelle could never stay still. At some stage the embattled frontage presented by his painting would be bound to yield to change, however characteristic. But it was not actually the expected transition from one kind of fortresslike wall of paint to another that took place. Instead the areas of paint began to isolate themselves and assume the individuality of independence. Brightly coloured areas, although free-flocking, took on something of the intensity of those to be found in the flower paintings of Ernst Wilhelm Nay. This was particularly true of the watercolours. The paintings tended to stay more closely integrated, although the ''pattern'' (or subject) in them became clear cut, more sculptural; and the gouaches and the pastels-and-charcoal drawings have, in many cases, given the central image a distinct outline, placing it like a jewel on black velvet.

Are all these demonstrations of inventive skill anything to do with change of ambience? Riopelle has been living and working in Paris since 1947. Does any artist carry his personal creativity with him into a new atmosphere and not expect to be affected by a different climate? Riopelle fits so comfortably into the Ecole de Paris and he plainly has added to its lustre—but do he and his work owe anything to Paris?

—Sheldon Williams

RIST, Pipilotti

Nationality: Swiss. **Born:** Charlotte Rist, Rheintal, Switzerland, 21 June 1962. **Education:** Studied commerical art, illustration, and photography, Institute of Applied Arts, Vienna, 1982–86; studied audio visual communications, School of Design, Basel, 1986–88. **Career:** Computer and video artists; has had braodcasts and screenings of work, since 1987; joined Lew Reines Prochaines musical group, 1988. **Awards:** Prix d'art contemporain de la BC, Geneva, 1994; Manor Kunstpreis, St. Gallen, 1994; DAAD prize, Berlin, 1996; Hugo Boss Prize, Guggenheim Soho Museum, New York, 1998. **Address:** Zypressenstrasse 76, 8004 Zurich, Switzerland. **Web site:** www.eyekon.ch/pipilotti/.

Individual Exhibitions:

1993 Gallery STAMPA, Basel
1994 Gallery STAMPA, Basel
I'm Not the Girl Who Misses Much, Art Museum, St. Gallen (toured)
1995 Gallery Akinci, Amsterdam

1996 Centre d'Art Contemporain, Geneva
Museum of Contemporary Art, Chicago
2000 Montreal Museum of Fine Arts, Montreal

Group Exhibitions:

1991 Arts Center, Fribourg
1992 Shedhalle, Zurich
1993 Shedhalle, Zurich
Biennale, Venice
1994 Arts Center, Basel
Norrkoepings Konstmuseum, Norrkoeping
Museum of Contemporary Art, Chicago
Biennale, Sao Paulo
1995 Hong Kong Museum of Art, Hong Kong
Stedelijk Mueum, Amsterdam
1996 Space, Vienna
1997 Biennale, Venice
Fourth Biennale, Lyon
1998 Museum fur Moderene Kunst, Frankfurt
Guggenheim Museum Soho, New York
1999 Kunstmuseum, Bonn
Biennale, Venice
Hirshhorn Museum and Sculpture Garden, Washington D.C.
Metropolitan Museum of Modern Art, Tokyo
2000 St. Louis Art Museum, St. Louis
Musee d'Art Contemporain, Bordeaux
Landesgartenshcau, Singen
Museum fur Moderne Kunst, Vienna

Publications:

By RIST: Books—*Remake of the Weekend* (editor), Cologne 1998; *Pipilotti Rist,* Cologne 1998; *Himalaya* (editor), Paris 1999. **Articles—** ''Laurie Anderson and Pipilotti Rist: Conversation in the Lobby of a Hotel in Berlin'' in *Parkett,* vol. 46, December 1996; ''I Love You Forever'' in *Du* (Zurich), no. 6, 1997; ''Daumenkino'' in *Parkett* (Zurich and New York), no. 37, 1993; ''Psychedelic, Baby: An Interview with Pipilotti Rist'' by Jane Harris in *Art Journal,* vol. 59, no. 4, Winter 2000.

On RIST: Books—*Padiglione d'Arte Contemporanea, Gallerie Civiche d'Arte Moderna die Palazzo dei Diamanti* (exhibition catalog), edited by Comune di Ferrara, Centro Video Arte, Ferrara 1991; ''Leibesbrief von Pipilotti Rist'' by Hedy Graber in *Simone Berger, Pipilotti Rist, Francis Traunig* (exhibition catalog), Kunsthalle Palazzo Liestal, Liestal 1992; ''Per quattro mesi all'anno la Svizzera è un paese in bianco e nero'' by Viana Conti in *Frammenti Interfacce Intervalli: Paradigmi della Frammentazione nell'Arte Svizzera,* (exhibition catalog), Museo d'arte contemporanea di Villa Croce, Genoa 1992; *Epicenter Ljublijana, Moderna galerija Ljubljiana,* edited by Mika Briski, Museum of Modern Art, Ljublijana, 1997; *Strange days. Gregory Crewdson, Tracey Moffatt, Pipilotti Rist, Kara Walker* by Wayne Tunnicliffe, Arts Gallery of New South Wales, Sydney, 1998; Exhibition catalog, Guggenheim Museum SoHo, New York 1998; *Cream. 10 Curators, 10 Writers, 100 Artists—Contemporary Art in Culture* by Carlos Basualdo, Francesco Bonami, et al, London 1998; *Global Fun.-Kunst und Design von Mondrian, Gehry, Versace and Friends* (exhibition catalog), Städtische Museum Leverkusen Schloss Morsbroich, Ostfildern 1999. **Articles—**''Pipilotti Rist, 21.6.1962, Basel'' by Danielle Arn in *Du* (Zurich), no. 2, 1989; ''Rist & Mathis: Künstlerfrauenpaare'' by Liliane Lerch in *Kunstforum International,* no. 107, 1990; ''Pickel, Porno und Zitronen'' by Thomas Lehmann in *Proz* (Basel), March, 1991; ''Pipilotti Rist: Der Reiz des Unsauberen—Ein Interview'' by Anne Reich in *Kunst-Bulletin* (Zurich), no. 12, 1992; ''Ich will sehen wie Du siehst: Zu Weihnachten ein Interview mit Pipilotti Rist'' by Simon Maurer in *züri-tip* (Zurich), no. 53, 24 December 1992; ''Pipilotti Rist: A Cosmos in Her Own Right'' by Harms Lux in *Flash Art,* vol. 32, no. 207, Summer 1994; ''Pipilotti Rist, Not the Girl Who Misses Much'' by Reinhard Puntigam in *(Blimp), Zeitschrift für Film* (Graz), no. 32, Fall 1995; ''Pipilotti Rist,'' by Elizabeth Janus in *Artforum,* vol. 34, Summer 1996; ''The Rist Risk Factor: When Dreams Twitch Like Dying Fish'' by Marius Babias in *Parkett,* vol. 46, December 1996; ''Pipilotti Rist's *Flying Room*'' by Philip Ursprung in *Parkett,* vol. 46, December 1996; ''Risikofaktor Rist; Wenn Träume wie sterbende Fische zucken'' by Marius Babias, in *Parkett* (Zurich and New York), no. 48, 1996; ''The Mechanics of Fluids'' by Nancy Spector in *Parkett* (Zurich and New York), no. 48, 1996; ''Pipilotti Rist'' by Birgit Sonna in *EMMA. Das Magazin von Frauen für Menschen* (Cologne), no.2, March-April 1998; ''Pipilotti Rist: Grist for the Mill'' by Terry Myers in *Art/Text,* vol. 61, May/July 1998; ''Il fattore di rischio Rist. Quando i sogni si contorcono come pesci morenti'' by Marius Babias in *Valentini, Valentina, Allo specchio* (Rome) 1998; ''Contemporary works intended to provoke'' by Grace Glueck in *New York Times* (New York) 17 July 1998; ''Rist for the Mill'' by Hans-Ulrich Obrist in *Artforum,* no. 36, April 1998; ''Pippi Goes to Video'' by Jonathan Turner in *Art News,* vol. 97, no. 10, November 1998; ''Rist Factor'' by Ulf Erdmann Ziegler in *Art in America,* vol. 86, no.8, June 1998; ''Pipilotti Rist'' by Damien Sausset in *L'Oeil* (Paris), April 1999; ''El videoarte como flujo de placers'' by Carlos Vidal in *Lapiz* (Madrid), vol. 18, no. 153, 1999; ''Dame Pipilotti Rist'' by Sandrine Malinaud in *art actuel* (Paris), no. 2, May-June 1999; ''Pipilotti Rist par nature pop'' by Elisabeth Lebovici in *Libération* (Paris), 24 April 1999; ''L'Ospitalità di Pipilotti Rist'' by Harm Lux in *Flash Art* (Milan), no. 215, April-May 1999; ''The Luminous Body'' by MaLin Wilson in *Art Issues,* no. 59, September/October 1999; ''Pipilotti Rist: Musée d'Art Moderne de la Ville de Paris'' by Dana Mouton Cibulski in *Sculpture,* vol. 18, no. 9, November 1999; ''Tour de Suisse'' by Gerhard Mack and Heinz Peter Schwerfel in *Art* (Hamburg), no. 6, June 1999; ''Pipilotti Rist Le Bonheur Est Un Canon Brûlant'' by Marie De Burgerolle in *Beaux Arts* (Paris), no. 179, April 1999; ''Pipilotti Rist: Kunsthalle Zürich'' by Elizabeth Janus, in *Artforum* (New York), April 1999; ''It's All in the Rist'' by Mark Stevens in *New York Magazine,* 8 May 2000; ''Pipilotti Rist: Luhring Augustine Gallery'' by Robert Raczka in *Sculpture,* vol. 20, no. 1, January/February 2001.

* * *

Since Pipilotti Rist's effervescent, enigmatic videos and installations brought her to the attention of the international art world in the early 1990s, she has consistently explored the interconnections of self, politics, and popular culture. Rist's eclectic education and experience lends logic to her poignant celebrations of mass culture; she studied commercial art, illustration, and photography at Vienna's Institute of Applied Arts and went on to graduate work in video communications at the School of Design in Basel. While studying, she lent her talents to video animation and stage design for local bands, eventually joining the feminist group Les Reines Prochaines as a self-taught multi-instrumentalist. (Playing bass, flute, and percussion—in the artist's own estimation, ''all equally badly.'') Rist unpretentiously asserts MTV among influences such as Joseph Beuys, and the technical bravura of her installations reflects a perfectionism common in commercial videos but rare in traditionally low-tech video installation. Appalled by the arrogant isolation of the art world from popular artforms, as well as its affected disdain for joy and sincerity, she is unashamed of her populist desire ''to bring people into the art ghetto.''

Rist's desire to merge her art and technical training with her interest in pop and punk performance led to early works like *I'm Not the Girl Who Misses Much* (1986)—the title of which comes from the variation on the first line of the Beatles' song ''Happiness is a Warm Gun,'' which the artist sings mantra like throughout the piece. The short video presents Rist as whirling dervish, dancing maniacally in a breast baring, ripped thrift store dress, singing to a stationary camera in the fashion a child playing dress-up might unselfconsciously entertain herself in a bedroom mirror. This breezy performance is, however, jarringly punctuated by shifts in speed that break up its visual and aural rhythms. The video is constantly sped up to a hysterical pitch or slowed down to an ominous drawl, as if an unseen spectator were randomly controlling the monitor's remote control to purposely confuse and irritate fellow viewers. Simultaneously naïve and sophisticated, silly and sadistic, the work set the tone for much of Rist's subsequent work, which would similarly transform familiar imagery, sounds, and sensations from mass culture into unique meditations on the relevance of such influences in modern identity formation.

Later works further incorporate her musical tastes and talents, as well as her childlike awe at the magical potential of television and film as everyday expressive media. Reflecting the influence of Nam June Paik and Laurie Anderson, her video and film projects blend highly selective, sensual imagery and catchy musical accompaniment into accessibly complex vignettes on seemingly mundane subjects. Her use of vivid, saturated color and penchant for open-ended, surreal narratives also betray the influence of 1960s psychedelia. *Sip My Ocean* (1996) features a mirrored projection of Rist swimming in an ill-fitting yellow bikini while the artist's falsetto voice warbles, karaoke-style, to Chris Isaak's romantic hit ''Wicked Game'' on the accompanying soundtrack—its watery slide guitar particularly suitable to the otherworldly underwater imagery. Although the artist sings of love's bondage in the clichéd, melodramatic language of the pop tearjerker, her mugging presence on the screen instead appears unbound and carefree. *Ever Is Over All* (1997), an installation that earned the artist the 2000 Prize at the 1997 Venice Biennale, similarly pairs the logic of the three-minute pop song with the concept of an equally fleeting, but comparatively profound state of being. Over a funky trance beat overlaid by an Indian-flavored melody, Rist absent-mindedly hums along to the tune, striding dreamily down an ordinary Zurich street with an exotic, long-stemmed flower in her hand. Just as the audience settles into the groove of the soundtrack and follows the slow motion pace of the artist's stroll, without changing her joyous expression Rist winds up her arm like a baseball pitcher and smashes the flower into the windows of parked cars in her path. The only real world intercessor in this surreal scene is a female police officer who happens upon the destruction, smiles, and casually salutes before continuing past. *Altruist in a Lava Bath* (1994)—a miniature LED screen installed in a floor crack—finds the artist parodying the stereotype of the female martyr as the artist's tiny image and voice scream up at the viewer from the bowels of hell: ''I am a worm and you, you are a flower! You would have done everything better! Help me! Forgive me!'' This quirky sense of humor and interest in insinuating installation art into surprising spaces was displayed in her 2000 public video series, *Open My Glade,* consisting of one-minute videos of the artist appearing to (unsuccessfully) press her way out of the Panasonic Screen at Times Square in New York City. More recently, Rist has turned her interest in public art into a new, administrative role, serving as director of the 2001 Swiss National Exhibition in Neuchâtel.

Though focusing on optimistic, lighthearted narratives, Rist has asserted the serious and feminist aims of her work in ways that align her with like-minded, third wave feminists of her generation. Much like the contemporary Riot Grrrl movement in the United States and England—which the artist has claimed as an influence—Rist has sought to bring feminist theory down to earth and up to date through her appropriation of popular culture and media. As curator Nancy Spector argues, the ''coquettish and rebellious'' behavior of Rist's various video incarnations suggests both an understanding and rejection of Laura Mulvey's theory of the oppressive, ubiquitous male gaze that effectively ''problematize(s) feminism's interrogation of visual pleasure.'' Emphasizing instead the feminist potential of pleasure in its myriad forms, this aspect of Rist's work reflects yet another interest of many of her third wave contemporaries: challenging notions that feminist art must be anti-erotic or asexual to serve the goals of the women's movement. Giving in to beauty and sensuality while maintaining an intellectual edge, Rist is a rare artist who mixes pleasure and politics as deftly and poignantly as she does media.

—Maria Elena Buszek

RIVERS, Larry

Nationality: American. **Born:** Larry Grossberg in the Bronx, New York, 17 August 1923; changed name to Rivers at start of career as jazz saxophonist, 1940. **Education:** Julliard School of Music, New York, 1944–45; Hans Hofmann's School, New York and Provincetown, Massachusetts, 1947–48; New York University, 1948–51, B.A. 1951. **Military Service:** Served in the United States Army, 1942–43. **Family:** Married Augusta Burger in 1945 (separated, 1946); children: Steven and Joseph; married Clarice Price in 1960 (separated, 1967); children: Gwynne and Emma. **Career:** Played in jazz bands, New York, in the early 1940s; began painting, 1945; travelled in Europe, then returned to New York and began painting full time, 1950; lived with his mother-in-law, Berdie Burger, his favorite model, Southampton, Long Island, 1953–57; began working in welded metal sculpture, 1957; visited Paris, 1961–62; set and costume designer, *Oedipus Rex,* New York, 1966; travelled to Africa and collaborated with Pierre Gaisseau on the television film *Africa and I,* 1967–68; began work with videotape, 1970; collaborated with Jean Tinguely on multimedia work, Paris, 1979. Artist-in-residence, Slade School of Fine Art, London, 1964; instructor, University of California at Santa Barbara, 1972; lecturer on contemporary American art, in various Russian cities at invitation from Union of Soviet Artists, 1976.

Awards: Third Prize, Corcoran Museum, Washington, D.C., 1955. **Agent:** Marlborough Gallery, New York. **Address:** c/o Marlborough Gallery Inc., 40 West 57th Street, New York, New York 10019, U.S.A.

Individual Exhibitions:

1949 Jane Street Gallery, New York
1951 Tibor de Nagy Gallery, New York
1953 Tibor de Nagy Gallery, New York
1954 Tibor de Nagy Gallery, New York
Stable Gallery, New York
1956 Tibor de Nagy Gallery, New York
1957 Tibor de Nagy Gallery, New York
1958 Tibor de Nagy Gallery, New York
1959 Tibor de Nagy Gallery, New York
1960 Tibor de Nagy Gallery, New York
Martha Jackson Gallery, New York
1961 Dwan Gallery, Los Angeles
Tibor de Nagy Gallery, New York
1962 Tibor de Nagy Gallery, New York
Gimpel Fils, London
Galerie Rive Droite, Paris
Dwan Gallery, Los Angeles
1963 Dwan Gallery, Los Angeles
1964 Gimpel Fils, London
1965 Rose Art Museum, Brandeis University, Waltham, Massachusetts (retrospective)
Pasadena Art Museum, California (retrospective)
Jewish Museum, New York (retrospective)
Detroit Institute of Arts (retrospective)
Minneapolis Institute of Arts (retrospective)
1970 *Drawings 1949–1969,* Art Institute of Chicago
Larry Rivers 1965–70, Marlborough Gallery, New York
1973 *Larry Rivers 1970–73,* Marlborough Gallery, New York
Palais des Beaux-Arts, Brussels
1974 *From the Coloring Book of Japan,* Marlborough Gallery, New York
1975 Marlborough Gallery, New York
1976 *Works of the 60s and 70s,* Gimpel Fils, London
1977 Marlborough Gallery, New York
Robert Miller Gallery, New York
Hokin Gallery, Chicago
1978 ACA Gallery, New York
1979 *Recent Works, Golden Oldies,* Robert Miller Gallery, New York
1980 Museo de Arte Contemporanio de Caracas, Venezuela
1981 Marlborough Fine Art, London
1982 Marlborugh Gallery, New York
Studio Marconi, Milan
1983 Elaine Horwich Gallery, Phoenix, Arizona
Guild Hall Museum, East Hampton, New York
1984 Kouros Gallery, New York
Jewish Museum, New York
1985 University of Pennsylvania, Philadelphia
Marlborough Fine Art, Tokyo
1986 Adelphi University Center, Garden City, New York
Marlborough Gallery, New York
1988 *Recent Relief Paintings,* Marlborough Gallery, New York (catalog)
1990 *Recent Work,* Marlborough Fine Art, London (catalog)
Oeuvres Récentes 1984–1990, Galerie Beaubourg, Paris (catalog)
Works from the Sixties, Marlborough Gallery, New York (catalog)
1992 Nassau County Museum of Art, Roslyn Harbor, New York (catalog)
1993 *Art and the Artist,* Marlborough Gallery, New York (catalog)
1994 *The Auction and Other Visions of Slavery,* Marlborough Gallery, New York
1995 *La Danse,* Marlborough Gallery, New York (catalog)
1997 *Recent Works,* Marlborough Gallery, New York (catalog)
1998 Marlborough Gallery, New York
1999 *Fashion Show,* Marlborough Gallery, New York (catalog)

Selected Group Exhibitions:

1950 *New Talent 1950,* Samuel Kootz Gallery, New York
1956 *12 Americans,* Museum of Modern Art, New York
1958 *Carnegie International,* Pittsburgh
1960 *Business Buys American Art,* Whitney Museum, New York
Painting and Sculpture of a Decade, 1954–64, Tate Gallery, London
1966 *2 Decades of American Painting,* Museum of Modern Art, New York (travelled to Japan, India, and Australia)
1968 *Documenta 4,* Kassel, West Germany
1970 *American Painting 1970,* Virginia Museum of Art, Richmond
1988 *Spoleto Festival U.S.A.,* Charleston, South Carolina (catalog)
1997 *De Klein à Warhol,* Centre Georges Pompidou, Paris (catalog)

Collections:

Metropolitan Museum of Art, New York; Museum of Modern Art, New York; Whitney Museum, New York; Corcoran Gallery of Art, Washington, D.C.; Hirshhorn Museum and Sculpture Garden, Washington, D.C.; Chrysler Art Museum, Provincetown, Massachusetts; Brandeis University, Waltham, Massachusetts; Art Institute of Chicago; Tate Gallery, London; Baltimore Museum of Art; Dallas Museum of Art; De Merril Foundation, Houston; The Nelson-Atkins Museum of Art, Kansas City; Los Angeles County Museum of Art; The Minneapolis Institute of Art.

Publications:

By RIVERS: Books—drawings for *Coloring Book of Japan,* 1973; *The Donkey and the Darling,* with Terry Southern, New York 1977; *Drawings and Digressions,* with Carol Brightman, New York 1979; *The Artist Observed: 28 Interviews with Contemporary Artists 1972–1978,* with John Gruen, Chicago 1991; *Larry Rivers: Opere 1989–1992,* with Achille Bonito Oliva and Furio Colombo, Milan 1993; *Poem and Portrait,* with John Ashbery, Charleston 1997; *What Did I Do?: The Unauthorized Autobiography of Larry Rivers,* New York 1992, 2001. **Articles**—''Young Draftsman or Master Draftsman'' in *Art News* (New York), January 1955; ''An Interview with

Larry Rivers,'' with James Thrall Soby, in *Saturday Review* (New York), 3 September 1955; statement in *12 Americans,* exhibition catalog by Dorothy C. Miller, New York 1956; ''Why I Paint as I Do,'' interview with Frank O'Hara, in *Horizon* (New York), September/October 1959; ''Monet: The Eye Is Magic'' in *Art News* (New York), April 1960; interview in *Conversations with Review* (New York), July/August 1961; ''We Hitch Our Wagons to a Star'' in *Mademoiselle* (New York), August 1961; ''6 Poems by Larry Rivers'' in *Locus Solus* (New York), vol. 1, no. 3/4, 1962; ''My Life Among the Stones'' in *Location* (New York), vol. 1, no. 1, Spring 1963; introduction to *Larry Rivers,* exhibition catalog, London 1964; ''Dear Teen-age Audience'' in *Seventeen Magazine* (New York), November 1964; ''A Memoir'' in *Larry Rivers,* exhibition catalog, Waltham, Massachusetts 1965; ''Sensibility of the 60s'' in *Art in America* (New York), January 1967; ''Blues for Yves Klein'' in *Artnews* (New York), February 1967; statement in ''What Is Pinter Up To?'' in the *New York Times,* 5 February 1967; ''Jackson Pollock: An Artists' Symposium'' in *Artnews* (New York), April 1967; statement in *Art Now: New York,* May 1970; ''If You Can't Draw, Trace: Frank Bowling Talks with Larry Rivers'' in *Arts Magazine* (New York), February 1971; interview in *Arts Chronicles 1954–1966* by Frank O'Hara, compiled by D.M. Allen, New York 1975; ''Golden Oldies: An Interview with Larry Rivers,'' with Jeffery H. Loria, in *Arts Magazine* (New York), November 1978. **Video—***Larry Rivers: An American Master,* New York 1993.

On RIVERS: Books—*Modern Art and the New Past* by James Thrall Soby, Norman, Oklahoma 1958; *Some Younger Artists,* edited by B.H. Friedman, New York 1959; *Rivers,* exhibition catalog, text by John Ashbery and Thomas B. Hess, London 1962; *Larry Rivers,* exhibition catalog with text by Sam Hunter, Waltham, Massachusetts 1965; *Larry Rivers* by Sam Hunter, New York 1969; *Rivers* by Sam Hunter, 1972; *Larry Rivers: Drawings 1949–1969,* exhibition catalog, Chicago 1970; *Larry Rivers 1970–1973,* exhibition catalog, New York 1973; *Larry Rivers: From the Coloring Book of Japan,* exhibition catalog, New York 1974; *Larry Rivers: Works of the 50s and 60s,* exhibition catalog, London 1976; *Larry Rivers: Recent Works, Golden Oldies,* exhibition catalog, New York 1979; *Larry Rivers,* exhibition catalog with text by David Joel Shapiro, Caracas 1980; *Larry Rivers: Relief Paintings,* exhibition catalog, New York 1986. **Articles—** ''Larry Rivers: Figures en Mouvement'' by Philip Jodidio in *Connaissance des Arts,* no. 460, June 1990; ''Still Raging Rivers'' by Barbara MacAdam in *Artnews,* vol. 93, November 1994.

* * *

Larry Rivers is one of those American artists who followed de Kooning in adapting the freedom of the Abstract Expressionist technique towards figurative ends. And in painting bank notes, cigarette packets and advertisements he was along with Rauschenberg one of the first Americans to use ready made vernacular images, thus paving the way for Pop Art. But Rivers differs from the Pop Artists in using given imagery, whether popular commercial clichés or his copies of Old Masters, as the basis of painterly variations in his freely expressionistic style.

Rivers has shown considerable versatility, beginning his career as a professional jazz saxophonist, writing poetry, and making constructions, sculptures, graphics and stage designs as well as painting. He has also been very eclectic in the subject matter he has reworked in his paintings. History, folklore and popular myth all combined in his painting of ''George Washington Crossing the Delaware'' (1953), in which he used the currently accepted mode of Abstract Expressionism not for purely abstract painterly purposes but to transform a scorned and banal image from the past. His variations of familiar themes, in which he humorously played with transformations of visual cliches, range from well-known old-master paintings to objects from daily life like his cigarette packets. And in such pictures as ''Dutch Masters and Cigars II'' (1963) he combines the two in a composition of an open cigarbox with a reworking of Rembrandt's ''Syndics'' as the picture on the lid.

Thus Rivers introduced recognizable subject matter into abstract Expressionism in far more explicit terms than had de Kooning, adapting that style to a montage-like combination of images taken both from the urban commercial environment and from fine art. His human figures may like ''O'Hara'' be variations on other paintings, in this case a famous Gericault standing male nude, or they may be taken directly from life as are his candid portraits of his mother-in-law Birdie in the nude. His ''Double Portrait of Birdie'' (1955), shows her in two different poses, simulating movie montage. In other cases he uses the human figure to project an ironic image derived from instructional graphics, with a head having parts of the face all neatly labelled in French, or a female nude similarly labelled with the French names for the parts of the body. Other paintings are fragmented accounts of a particular experience such as a street accident, treated in out-of-focus, multiple views.

Rivers' use of urban and commercial images anticipates Pop Art, but his playful and painterly treatment of them is very different from the cool, deadpan approach of the Pop artists, and he has never been influential in the way that Rauschenberg has. He isn't an artist who fits neatly into any category. Edward Lucie-Smith has said of him that the outstanding characteristic of all his paintings is ''a kind of glancing obliqueness, as if the artist were unable to focus on the actual subject for very long at a time.'' His subjects are secondary to the treatment he gives them, and he himself has described his variations on familiar themes as ''a smorgasbord of the recognizable, and if being the chef is no particular thrill, it was as much as I could cook up.'' Barry Ulanov has called him ''a superior entertainer.'' The wit which is in his writing is even more substantial than in his painting. But one would like to see his facility and humor reach beyond virtuoso twirls and twists to more demanding material, though it is something in a time when the surfaces of Pop Art and the emblems of easy identification absorb so many painters to find even entertainment that requires a little thought, a brief pause.

—Konstantin Bazarov

ROBERTS, Liisa

Nationality: American. **Born:** Paris, France, 29 April 1969; lives and works in New York and Helsinki. **Education:** Chelsea School of Art, London, B/TEC in Art & Design, 1987; Rhode Island School of Design, Providence, B.F.A. in sculpture, 1990; attended Brown University, Providence, Rhode Island, and the Academy of Fine Arts,

Helsinki. **Career:** Lecturer, Academy of Fine Arts, Helsinki, 1993—; visiting artist, Malmö Konsthogskolan, Lund University, Malmö, Sweden, 1997–98. **Awards:** Residencies at Film/Video Arts, New York, 1993, International Studio Program, New York, 1997–98, Nordic Institute for Contemporary Art, Helsinki, 1998, and ArtPace/ A foundation for Contemporary Art, San Antonio, Texas, 1999, and DAAD, Berlin, 2002; Elizabeth Foundation for the Arts, 1996. **Agent:** Galerie Yvon Lambert, 108 rue Vielle du Temple, Paris 75003, France.

Individual Exhibitions:

1995 *betraying a portrait,* Janice Guy, New York
1997 *Trap Door,* Lehmann Maupin, New York
1998 *Blind Side,* The Whitney Museum of American Art, Film/ Video Gallery, New York
1999 *Sidewalk,* ArtPace, San Antonio, Texas
Blind Side, Miami Art Museum, Florida
to derive an approach, Yvon Lambert, Côté Rue, Paris, France

Selected Group Exhibitions:

1994 *Artists Select,* Artists Space, New York
1995 *Quarters,* Bravin Post Lee Gallery, New York
Lux Sonor, Helsinki Kunsthalle, Finland
1996 *Scream and Scream Again: Film in Art,* The Museum of Modern Art, Oxford, England (traveled to the Irish Museum of Modern Art, Dublin, and the Museum of Contemporary Art, Helsinki) (catalog)
1997 *documenta X,* Kassel, Germany (catalog)
Heaven, P.S. 1, Long Island City, New York
Celluloid Cave, Thread Waxing Space, New York (catalog)
Narrative Urge, Uppsala Konstmuseum, Sweden, and Lombard Freid Fine Arts, New York
1998 *The Art of Memory,* Bard College Center for Curatorial Studies Museum, Annandale-on-Hudson, New York
Insertions, Arkipelag at the Nordic Museum, Stockholm, Sweden (catalog)
1999 *The American Century: Art and Culture in America 1900–2000,* The Whitney Museum of American Art, New York (catalog)
48th Venice Biennale, Italy (catalog)
Mirror's Edge, Bildmuseet Umeå, Sweden (traveled to Scotland, Denmark, Canada, and Italy)
Retrace Your Steps: Remember Tomorrow, Sir John Soane's Museum, London
2000 *Vôilá-Le Monde dans le Tête,* Le Musée d'Art Moderne de la Ville de Paris
A Delicate Balance: Six Routes to the Himalayas, Kiasma-Museum of Contemporary Art, Helsinki (catalog)
2001 2nd Berlin Biennale 2001, Germany (catalog)
Hit and Miss, Perth Institute of Contemporary Arts, Australia (catalog)

Selected Film Screenings:

1993 Finnish Film Archive, Helsinki
1997 Anthology Film Archives, New York
1999 The Wolfsonian Museum, Miami, Florida

Collections:

The Whitney Museum of American Art, New York; Kiasma-Museum of Contemporary Art, Helsinki; Sammlung Goetz, Munich.

Publications:

By ROBERTS: Articles—''The Paradox Defining Center: The Reception of Art from Latin America'' in *Taide* (Helsinki), February 1994; ''Expatriate Art: How Brazilian Is It?'' in *Poliester* (Mexico), Spring 1994; ''Pablo Suárez: A Portrait of Resistance'' in *Art from Argentina: 1920–1990,* exhibition catalog, Oxford, England 1994; interview with Alex Aberro in *Transarts.cultures.media,* no. 5, 1998; ''Letter from San Antonio'' in *Changing the System: Artists Talk about Their Practice,* Helsinki and Rotterdam 1999; ''A Letter to Maaretta Jaukkuri'' (with Simryn Gill) in *Delicate Balance: Six Routes to the Himalayas,* exhibition catalog, Helsinki 2000.

On ROBERTS: Articles—''Liisa Roberts at Janice Guy'' by Joshua Decter in *Artforum,* no. 35, 1996; ''Liisa Roberts at Lehmann Maupin'' by Martha Schwendener in *Art Papers,* no. 21, 1997; ''Narrative Urge at Lombard Freid Fine Arts'' by George Baker in *Artforum,* no. 36, 1997; ''Liisa Roberts'' by Carlos Basualdo in *cream-contemporary art in culture,* London 1998; ''Liisa Roberts: The Space of Memory'' by Chrissie Iles in *New American Film & Video Series 84,* New York 1998; ''Openings: Liisa Roberts'' by Margaret Sundell in *Artforum,* no. 36, 1998; ''Liisa Roberts: The Whitney Museum of American Art'' by Gregory Williams in *Frieze,* no. 43, 1998; ''Liisa Roberts: Yvon Lambert'' by Pascale Beausse in *Flash Art,* vol. 32, no. 209, 1999; ''Video and Film Space'' by Chrissie Iles in *Space Site Intervention,* Minneapolis and London 2000; ''TRAP DOOR—Närværo inom parentes'' in *Blikk på Kunst,* Oslo 2001; ''Phases of a Monument: Liisa Roberts' SIDEWALK'' by Okwui Enwezor in *Parkett,* no. 61, 2001.

* * *

Artist Liisa Roberts makes works of social sculpture that engage the emblematic structure of film—a cinematic image is both independently framed and also tied to another image—to question how past, present, future and context coalesce to form meaning. In *9 Minutes of Form: A Sculpture by Liisa Roberts* (1993), Roberts created a 16mm silent black-and-white film. This ''film sculpture'' focuses on a hand continuously writing a text on a stack of white paper; the words being written are not legible to the viewer. It portrays an act of creation that can be seen, yet the meaning that act of creation produces must be invented. Roberts has said of the work, ''I have used film to create sculpture because of the contradictions that this combination implies. Film is inherently ephemeral and kinetic, while sculpture is static and monumental. Film is also the projection of one surface onto another, while sculptural mass implies that it is the thing itself.'' Roberts showed her sculpture/film in a theater, thus encouraging viewers to reconsider the very category of sculpture. ''My work,'' says Roberts, ''is the physical re-definition of sculpture, and therefore the reformulation of a paradigm.''

Roberts undertook another disruption of conventional meaning in her 1999 work *Sidewalk,* which was created during a residency at Art Pace in San Antonio, Texas. In this work, Roberts recorded a series of narratives in which San Antonians speak about the building or monument most instrumental to their sense of self. She then placed the recordings in public elevators, transitional spaces in which time passes. She also placed the sound recordings in an installation at Art Pace which reacted to the movements of the gallery visitors, dislocating the narrative of the recordings while highlighting the viewers own presence in the gallery space. Roberts thus made the visitor's encounter have the characteristics generally reserved for an object by taking form that can be transported and is present in the social-self ''bewusstsein'' of the public. Going beyond the minimalist understanding of a viewer's relation to an object, Roberts accounts for the fact that not only does the viewer project meaning onto an object but that the object also projects onto the viewer.

Employing diverse strategies in her conceptual works of social sculpture, Roberts suggests that context defines and is defined by every cultural exchange. In a work currently in progress, Roberts attempts to negotiate the local history of the remote hybrid town of Vyborg, Russia—which was formerly part of Finland—and the restoration of a library that was initially designed by Alvar Aalto and later restored by Alexander Mihailovich Schver. In her work in the city, Roberts is investigating the ways that a setting consists not only of the physical environs but also of that which produces them, namely the past, the present, the future, and how each of these are envisioned. She has been collaborating with a range of interested parties, including local youths who have participated in a writing workshop with the aim of making a film about the city and architect Schver, who has created a design for a cinema space in the library lecture hall with a picture window facing a sculpture of Lenin in the adjacent Red Square.

Just as Alvar Aalto's functionalist philosophy emphasized integrating a building with its setting, Roberts' project aims to bring the local context to the restoration of the library, to acknowledge that an object is always formed in an indivisible relationship with its contexts. But Roberts' works are not phenomenological. She does not construct a narrative of personal history but rather an experience of that experience as a translation into form.

In earlier works, *TRAP DOOR* at documenta X and *to derive an approach* at the Venice Biennale in 1999, Roberts installed screens to personify the variety of frames through which a viewer constructs an image, where every such construction results from a view of the self in relation to that which is perceived. The idea that past and present simultaneously make an event out of the context in which something can be understood dominates the design of Roberts' work. Ultimately, her works are not finished when the design is built because the viewer maintains an essential role in producing meaning for the sculpture, space, or sequence.

—Cay Sophie Rabinowitz

ROCKBURNE, Dorothea

Nationality: Canadian. **Born:** Verdun, Quebec, 1921. **Education:** Ecole de Beaux-Arts, Montreal, 1947–50; Black Mountain College, North Carolina, 1951–56, B.F.A. **Career:** Painter; lives and works in New York. Taught art theory, School of Visual Arts, New York. **Awards:** Guggenheim Fellowship, 1972–73; Painting Award, Art Institute of Chicago, 1972; National Endowment for the Arts fellowship, Washington D.C., 1974; Creative Arts Award, Brandeis University, Waltham, Massachusetts, 1985. **Agents:** Andre Emmerich Gallery, 41 East 57th Street, New York, New York, 10022, U.S.A. **Address:** 140 Grand Street, New York, New York 10013, U.S.A.

Individual Exhibitions:

1970 Bykert Gallery, New York
1971 Galerie Ileana Sonnabend, Paris
1972 New Gallery, Cleveland
Bykert Gallery, New York
Galleria Toselli, Milan
University of Rochester Art Gallery, New York
Galleria d'Arte, Bari, Italy
1973 Bykert Gallery, New York
Galleria Toselli, Milan
Lisson Gallery, London
Hartford College of Art, Connecticut
Daniel Weinberg Gallery, San Francisco
Galleria Schema, Florence
1974 Gallerie Toselli, Milan
1975 Galleria Schema, Florence
Galerie Charles Kriwin, Brussels
1976 John Weber Gallery, New York
1977 Galleria La Polena, Genoa, Italy
Richard Eugen Fuller Gallery, Pennsylvania
1978 John Weber Gallery, New York
1979 Texas Gallery, Houston
1980 Texas Gallery, Houston
Xavier Fourcade, New York
David Belman Gallery, Toronto
Museum of Modern Art, New York (*Locus Series* installation)
1981 Texas Gallery, Houston
1982 Contemporary Art Museum, Houston
Whitney Museum, New York
1983 Museum of Fine Arts, Houston
Galleriet, Lund, Sweden
1985 Denver Art Museum, Colorado (toured the United States, 1985–87)
Xavier Fourcade, New York
1987 Arts Club of Chicago
1988 Andre Emmerich Gallery, New York
1989 Brandeis University, Waltham, Massachusetts
Andre Emmerich Gallery, New York
1991 Andre Emmerich Gallery, New York
D. P. Fong & Spratt Galleries, San Jose, California
1992 André Emmerich Gallery, New York
Gallery Schema, Florence
1994 André Emmerich Gallery, New York
2000 *Dorothea Rockburne: Ten Years of Astronomy Drawings 1990–2000,* Lawrence Rubin Greenberg Van Doren Fine Art, New York

Dorothea Rockburne: *Southern Sky* (in progress), 1993. Photo by Tina Barney. ©Dorothea Rockburne/Artists Rights Society (ARS), New York.

Selected Group Exhibitions:

1976 *Drawing Now,* Museum of Modern Art, New York
1977 *Biennial,* Whitney Museum, New York
1978 *HHK Foundation for Contemporary Art,* Brumder Gallery, Milwaukee Art Museum
1979 *Biennial,* Whitney Museum, New York
1980 *Explorations in the 70s,* Pittsburgh Plan for Art
With Paper, About Paper, Albright-Knox Art Gallery, Buffalo, New York (travelled to Museum of Fine Arts, Springfield, Massachusetts)
1983 *A Century of Modern Drawing,* Museum of Fine Art, Boston
1985 *An American Renaissance,* Fort Lauderdale Museum of Art, Florida
1986 *Philadelphia Collects Art Since 1940,* Philadelphia Museum of Art
1987 *American Masters,* Corcoran Gallery of Art, Washington, D.C.
1996 *More Than Minimal: Feminism and Abstraction in the '70s,* Rose Art Museum, Brandeis University, Waltham, Massachusetts

Collections:

Whitney Museum, New York; Museum of Modern Art, New York; Metropolitan Museum of Art, New York; Corcoran Gallery of Art, Washington, D.C.; Philadelphia Museum of Art; High Museum of Art, Atlanta; Minneapolis Art Institute; Museum of Fine Arts, Houston; Sony U.S.A., New York.

Publications:

By ROCKBURNE: Articles—''Works and Statements,'' edited by Robert Pincus-Witten, in *Artforum* (New York, March 1972; ''Interview with Dorothea Rockburne,'' with Jennifer Licht, in *Artforum* (New York), March 1972; ''Notes to Myself on Drawing'' in *Flash Art* (Milan), April 1974; ''An Interview with Dorothea Rockburne,'' with Roberta Olson, in *Art in America* (New York), November/December 1978; statement in *WhiteWalls,* spring 1986; ''Light in Geometry'' in *Artforum,* May 1990; ''Painterly Thought and the Unconscious: Interviews with Alex Katz, Frank Stella and Dorothea Rockburne'' by Denise Green in *Art Press,* no. 188, February 1994.

On ROCKBURNE: Books—*Dorothea Rockburne* by Bruce Boice, Hartford, Connecticut 1973; *6 Years: The Dematerialization of the Art Object* by Lucy R. Lippard, New York 1973; *Biennial Exhibition,* exhibition catalog, New York 1979; *Exploration in the 70s,* exhibition catalog with an essay by Robert Rosenblum, Pittsburgh 1980; *With Paper, About Paper,* exhibition catalog with essay by Charlota Kotik, Buffalo 1980; *Art in the 70s* by Edward Lucie-Smith, Ithaca, New York 1980. **Articles—**''Rockburne's Wager,'' introduction to exhibition catalog published by Andre Emmerich Gallery, New York 1988; ''The High Windows: Dorothea Rockburne's Skyscapes'' by Brooks Adams in *Artforum,* May 1993; ''Rockburne's Wavelength'' in *Artnews,* vol. 92, May 1993; ''Dorothea Rockburne's Quantum Leap'' by Murray Pomerance in *Canadian Art,* Fall 1993; ''Painterly Thought and the Unconscious'' by Denise Green in *artpress 188,* February 1994; ''Dorothea Rockburne, Stargazer'' by Lilly Wei in *Art in America* (New York), vol. 82, no. 10, October 1994; ''Passing the Marcelling Test with a Cold Iron'' by Dominique Nahas in *New Observations,* no. 110, January-February 1996; ''Dorothea Rockburne: Egyptian Painting Saqqarah'' in *New Observations,* no. 110, January-February 1996; ''Watching the Skies'' by Lilly Wei in *Art in America* (New York), vol. 88, no. 4, April 2000.

ROGALA, Miroslaw

Nationality: Polish. **Born:** 1954. **Education:** Studied at the Panstwow Srednia Szkola Muzyczna and Liceum Plastyzne; Fine Arts Academy, Krakow, M.F.A. in painting, 1979; School of the Art Institute of Chicago, M.F.A. in video and computer graphics, 1983; CAiiA (Centre for Advance Inquiry in the Interactive Arts), University of Wales, Ph.D., 2000. **Career:** Professor, Department of Art, Carnegie Mellon University, Pittsburgh, Pennsylvania; Director of the Program in Integrated Media Arts, Brooklyn College, New York, 2000—. Artist-in-residence, ZKM/Center for Art Media, Karlsruhe, Germany, 1994. **Awards:** Edward Ryerson Art Fellowship, 1983; National Endowment for the Arts grant, with Carolee Schneemann, 1992; NEA/American Film Institute Regional Art Fellowships, 1983–84, 1990–91, 1993; Illinois Arts Council grants, 1986, 1989. **Agent:** Oskar Friedl Gallery, 330 W. Superior, Suite 202, Chicago, Illinois 60610. **Address:** 329 West 18th Street, Suite 900, Chicago, Illinois 60616, U.S.A. **Web site:** http://www.mcs.net/˜rogala.

Individual Exhibitions/Installations:

1980 Polish Museum of America, Chicago
1981 Radio Gallery, St. Louis, Missouri
1982 Radio Gallery, St. Louis
West Hubbard Gallery, Chicago
Loyola University, Chicago
1984 Center for New Television, Chicago
1985 Polish Art Gallery, Chicago
1986 Polish Museum of America, Chicago
1988–90 *Nature Is Leaving Us,* Chicago International Art Exposition, Chicago; Goodman Theatre Studio, Chicago
1989–93 *The Witches Scenes/Macbeth,* American Film Institute, Los Angeles; Brooklyn Art Museum, New York; Walker Arts Center, Minneapolis, Minnesota; The Kitchen, New York
1993 Oskar Friedl Gallery, Chicago
1994–2001 *Lovers Leap* (interactive multimedia installation and CD-ROM exhibition), international travelling exhibition; visited various sites including Perspektiven, Schlossmuseum Murnau, Murnau, Germany; The Spain-Cordoba Cultural Center, Cordoba, Argentina; and the Museum of Contemporary Art, Roskilde, Denmark
1996 *Electronic Garden/NatuRealization* (interactive sound installation and free speech project), http://www.mcs.net/˜rogala/eGarden
1997 *Divided We Stand,* Museum of Contemporary Art, Chicago
2000 *Divided We Sing (Divided We Walk)* (interactive sound installation), Eindhoven University of Technology, Eindhoven, The Netherlands
Interactive Phscolograms, WRO 2000, Wroclaw, Poland
2001 *Gestures of Freedom: Miroslaw Rogala Works, 1975–2000,* Centre for Contemporary Art, Warsaw, Poland (travelled; catalog)
Divided We See (interactive media installation), Drexel University Design Arts Gallery, Philadelphia, Pennsylvania

Selected Group Exhibitions and Video Screenings:

1982 Film/Video Festival, Athens, Ohio
Video Roma, International Video Festival, Rome
1983 Cupples House Gallery/St. Louis University, Missouri
The School of the Art Institute of Chicago
1984 Anthology Film Archives
ARC Gallery, Chicago
International Video Festival, San Sebastian, Spain
1986 *New Generations,* Museum of Contemporary Art, Chicago
1987 Moming Dance Center, Chicago
19th International Video Biennal, Sao Paulo, Brazil
Scan, Tokyo
Centre Georges Pompidou, Paris
1989 International Film and Video Festival, San Francisco
1990 *Ars Electronica,* Linz, Austria
1991 Sony Gallery of Consumer Electronics, Chicago
Chicago Public Library Cultural Center, Chicago
1992 SIGGRAPH '92, Chicago
Consulate of Polish Republic, Chicago
1993 *Iterations,* International Center of Photography, New York
1995 *DEAF (Dutch Electronic Arts Festival),* Rotterdam, Holland
Oskar Friedl Gallery, Chicago
Art in Chicago 1945–1995, Museum of Contemporary Art, Chicago (catalog)
1996 Third Biennale d'Art Contemporain, Lyon, France
Photography After Photography, Siemens AG Kultur Programm Travelling Exhibit (toured Germany and Switzerland)
Burning the Interface, Museum of Contemporary Art, Sydney (toured Australia)

Art 1996 Chicago, International Art Exposition, Navy Pier, Chicago
ISEA '95, International Symposium on Electronic Art, Montreal
MULTIMEDIALE4, ZKM/Center for Art and Media Technology, Karlsruhe, Germany

Collections:

Centre Georges Pompidou, Paris; Museum d'Art Contemporain, Lyon, France; The Museum of Modern Art, New York; Museum of Contemporary Art, Chicago; Ujazdowskie Castle, Centre for Contemporary Art, Warsaw, Poland.

Publications:

By ROGALA: Articles—''Nature Is Leaving Us: A Video Theatre Work'' in *Leonardo,* vol. 26, no. 1, 1993.

On ROGALA: Books—*Post Modern Currents: Art and Artists: in the Age of Electronic Media* by Margot Lovejoy, 2nd edition, Saddle River New Jersey, 1997; *Envisioning Cyberspace: Designing Electronic Spaces* by Peter Anders, New York 1999. **Articles—**''Electronic Art from Rensselaer'' by John Rockwell in *New York Times,* 1 June 1991; ''Video as Universal Language: The Magical World of Miroslaw Rogala'' by Elaine A. King in *Cincinnati: The Contemporary Arts Center,* November 1993; ''Leap, ARTITACT 2, CD-ROM'' by Timothy Druckrey in *Interactive Magazine,* 1995; ''Artists and communities are Collaborating to make Chicago a Park Place'' by Alan Artner in *Chicago Tribune,* 23 June 1996; ''A New Language for Artistic Expression: The Electronic Arts Landscape'' by Joan Truckenbrod in *Leonardo* (Electronic Art Supplemental Issue), 1998; ''Art and Education in the Telematic Culture'' by Roy Ascott in *Leonardo* (Electronic Art Supplemental Issue), 1998; ''Alan Rath's Techno Anthropoids'' by Elaine A. King in *Sculpture,* vol. 18, no. 1, January-February 1999; ''Miroslaw Rogala: A Techno Poet of Time, Place, Self'' by Elaine A. King in *The Experience of Interactive Art in Miroslaw Rogala: Gestures of Freedom, 1975–2000,* exhibition catalog, Warsaw, Poland 2001. **Video—***Two on 2: Rogala Art,* CBS-TV, Chicago, 1986.

* * *

Miroslaw Rogala stands today on the forefront of media art as the result of twenty years of experimentation, as well as the transformation of video art by computer technology.

What is most amazing about Rogala is that he never was part of the American television generation of the sixties and seventies. In contrast he was born in Communist Poland. During his formative years Rogala experienced a world where all communication was difficult and secrecy was a way of life. Perhaps living in a repressed and restricted environment propelled him to communicate freely in a type of universal visual language that could be accessible to ''all.''

In spite of the unavailability of lofty video technology in Poland, Rogala in the 1970s was making interactive works and experimenting with gesture and time. Using minimalist sculptural forms in 1975 he made his first interactive work titled *Pulso-Fuckttory* (1975–77). This work invited the audience to actively participate in the alteration of the exhibition setting by triggering light and sound switches. The elements of light and sound would remain essential in the evolution of his experimental art—they afford unlimited power to sculpt, shape, and mold experiences into new forms.

Inspired by Brecht's ideas about the theatre and his antagonism of the viewer as a passive spectator, Rogala invites interaction in his environments that are intended to function as a type participatory stage. In this visual domain he presents the familiar with the unfamiliar in order to destabilize the habits and conventions of viewing. Strategic maneuvers are built into his work in order to augment one's perception and to originate a counter-museum-looking model. At the center of this time-based art is an aspiration to rewrite the meaning of artistic visual experiences and the concept of viewer mapping.

Remote Faces: Outerpretation (1986–88) is a bench mark piece because of its extended length of 36 minutes and Rogala's break from the realm of contained video production. A distinction between video sculpture and installation accordingly developed as a direct result of the role played by the liberation of monitors as a physical presence and the availability of new technologies that allowed for seamless projections. A new visual language emerges in Rogala's work as a result of the synergism of the computer and its ability to convey many contents—the personal and metaphorical fuse seamlessly in his high tech poetic expression. Content and technology no longer are separate entities—a metamorphosis of ideas, images, and technique meld, generating a visual expression choreographed by an ingenious mind and electronic media. Images become layered and synthesized in a manner that parallels the fabric of contemporary life, unlike the two-dimensional image that is static and operates only on a visual plane.

Despite the presence of technical upgrading in Rogala's work, his philosophical approach to technology is no different from artists at the onset of the twentieth century who have both embraced and challenged new technology by stressing its poetry, magic, and chance. Miroslaw Rogala recognizes that video collapses the distinction between painting and drawing—the static image on a wall. Using gesture, visual and audio stimulus, and language, he shifts the focus from the art object to the artist's ideas and to the spectator's participation.

It would be simplistic to try classifying him with singular traditional titles—video artist, sculptor, installation artist; perhaps he should be viewed as a transdisciplinary maker who utilizes many tools and incorporates various disciplines into his work. Notwithstanding his embrace of high technology, Rogala also recognizes that it can be a dangerous weapon to humanity. He shares a realistic attitude about technology with Alan Rath who too believes that a poised blend of aesthetic, mechanical, and social concerns needs to exist in order to attract the onlooker's attention.

The success of *Nature Is Leaving Us* (1989–94) appears to have been Miroslaw Rogala's passport to delve further and deeper in expanding the coupling of media with personal statement. His aim is to combine art and technology in order to heighten human perception—he hopes to devise a relationship between visual language and reality. Beginning in and continuing throughout the 1990s, Rogala continued to demolish barriers between passive and active viewing by harnessing computer technology and the Internet in his specialized brand of media aesthetic installations. Time is a distinct component, evoking a sense of present, past, and future for the viewer within fractions of a second.

Although over the past decade his output has grown in many dimensions, several key works encapsulate the new complex technical configurations—*Instructions Per Second* (1991–1994), *Lovers Leap* (1995), *Electronic Garden/NatuRealization* (1996), and *Divided We Speak* (1997). Interactivity becomes the essence of the above media installations affording the ''v(user)'' increased capability to interact in cybernetic space, via computer anamnesis, and free of normal restraints of time and space that apply to face-to-face intercommunication.

Rogala's oeuvre exhibits a tangent-to-a-circle kinship to the mainstream art world and often he has been ahead of its wave both technically and visually. For two decades he has continually broken new ground with his video based interactive environments. The exhibition *Gestures of Freedom: Miroslaw Rogala Works, 1975–2000,* organized by The Centre for Contemporary Art in Warsaw, provides significant insights into Rogala's ideas and production. With perhaps the exception of Bill Viola, who similarly in the 1980s recognized technology's potent cultural sphere and transcended the craft of video making with his compelling landscapes, Rogala remains at the forefront of electronic art making. He prefers electronic technology because digital images and sounds are infinitely malleable—he enjoys using its limitless power to sculpt, shape, and turn any experience or idea into new interactive constructions. Technology provides him with the novelty of open-ended structures that are closely aligned to other electronic forms of the entertainment industry and he optimizes this reality in order to reach a larger audience with his serious messages.

—Elaine A. King

ROMBERG, Osvaldo

Nationality: Argentinian. **Born:** Buenos Aires, 28 May 1938; immigrated to Israel in 1973. **Education:** Colegio Nacional de Buenos Aires, 1950–55; studied architecture at Buenos Aires University, 1956, 1959–62. **Military Service:** Served in the Argentine Army, Buenos Aires, 1957–59. **Career:** Artist; lives in New York. Instructor, University Art School, Còrdoba, Argentina, 1963–66, and Puerto Rico University, San Juan, 1966–69; professor of painting and color theory, Tucumàn University, Argentina, 1971–72; professor of painting and color theory, Bezalel Academy, Jerusalem, 1973–92 (chairman of fine arts department, 1979–83); sculpture instructor, 1974–75, and professor of aesthetics from 1975, State Teachers College, Herzyla, Israel; visiting professor, University of Delaware, 1983–85, Brooklyn College, 1992, Technological University of Graz, Austria, 1992, Pennsylvania Academy of Fine Arts, 1994. **Awards:** First Printmaking Prize, Architectural Hall, Buenos Aires, 1961; First Printmaking Prize, Hebraica Hall, Buenos Aires, 1965; National Collage Award, Còrdoba, Argentina, 1967; National Printmaking Award, Argentine National Hall, Buenos Aires, 1968; Gold Mannequin Design Prize, Buenos Aires, 1969; First Sculpture Prize, *Park Competition,* Buenos Aires, 1971. **Agent:** Stefan Stux Gallery, 529 West 20th Street, New York, New York, 10011. **Address:** Office, 529 W. 20th Street, New York, New York, 10011–2800.

Individual Exhibitions:

1961 Central Society of Architects, Buenos Aires
1962 Contemporary Art Institute, Lima
Galeria Galatea, Buenos Aires
1963 Art Center, Lima
Galeria Nueva, Buenos Aires
1964 Pan American Union, Washington
Museum of Modern Art, Miami
1965 Galeria Lirolay, Buenos Aires
1966 Galeria El Sol, Buenos Aires
Panamanian Art Institute, Panama City
Galeria Dinasty, Buenos Aires
Modern Art Gallery, Cordoba, Argentina
1967 Foussats Gallery, New York
Casa del Arte, San Juan, Puerto Rico
1968 XX2 Gallery, Caracas
Print Club of Philadelphia
Galeria Makarius, Buenos Aires
Galeria Rubbers, Buenos Aires
1969 Galeria Contemporànea, Buenos Aires
1970 Sala de Artes y Letras, San Jose, Costa Rica
El Cafe Literario, Guatemala City
National Art Gallery, El Salvador
Art Museum, Lima
Art Gallery, Managua, Nicaragua
1971 Studio Farnese, Rome
Galeria del Triangulo, Buenos Aires
1972 Center of Art and Communications, Buenos Aires
Tucumàn Museum of Art, Argentina (retrospective)
1974 Center of Art and Communications, Buenos Aires
1975 *Typologies,* Yodfat Gallery, Tel Aviv (travelled to the International Cultureel Centrum, Antwerp)
1976 Galerie Keller, Starnberg, West Germany
Galerie Julie M, Tel Aviv
Galerie Yaki Kornblit, Amsterdam
Kunstverein, Laiphein, West Germany
1977 Galleria Peccolo, Livorno, Italy
Galerie Krohn, Konstanz, West Germany
Delson-Richter Galleries, Old Jaffa, Israel
1979 Galerie Stadler, Paris
1980 Galerie Linssen, Bonn
Centro de Arte y Communicacion, Buenos Aires
1981 Musee d'Art Moderne, Strasbourg, France
Galerie Stadler, Paris
1982 Gimel Gallery, Jerusalem
Galerie Linssen, at the *International Art Fair,* Chicago
1983 Richter Gallery, Jaffa, Israel
Galleri Bellman, New York
Galerie Stadler, Paris
1984 Galerie Springer, West Berlin
Kunstmuseum, Hannover
Linssen Gallery, Bonn
1985 Tibor de Nagy Gallery, New York
1986 Museu de Arte de Sao Paulo
Piezo Electric Gallery, New York
1987 Piezo Electric Gallery, New York
Galeria Paolo Figueredo, Sao Paulo
1988 Elizabeth McDonald Gallery, New York
Galeria Julia Lublin, Buenos Aires
Artifact Gallery, Tel Aviv
1989 Artifact Gallery, Tel Aviv
1990 The Jewish Museum, New York
1991 The Israel Museum, Jerusalem
Museum of Contemporary Art, Antwerp
Gimmel Gallery, Jerusalem
Artifact Gallery, Tel Aviv
Ingrid Dacic Gallery, Tübingen, Germany

Schuppenhauer Gallery, Cologne
Luise Krohn, Badenweiler
Wilhelm Lehmbruck Museum, Duisburg, Germany
1992 Galerie Montaigne, Paris
1993 Museum Moderner Kunst, Vienna
Sprengel Museum, Hannover, Germany
Fundacion San Telmo, Buenos Aires
Galerie Heike Curtze, Vienna
Galerie Schuppenhauer, Cologne
Galerie Montaigne, Paris
1994 Ingrid Dacic Gallery, Tübingen, Germany
Gimmel Gallery, Jerusalem
1996 *''+2000/-2000, Even'': An Installation at the End of the Millennium,* Pennsylvania Academy, Philadelphia
1997 *Osvaldo Romberg: 1970s/1990s+,* Emanuth Israel, New York
1998 *Osvaldo Romberg: Bypass 1972–1997,* Stefan Stux Gallery, New York (also Kunstmuseum Bonn, Germany) (retrospective) (catalog)
2000 Kunsthalle Augsburg, Germany
Städtische Kunstsammlungen Augsburg, Germany

Selected Group Exhibitions:

1967 *Biennale,* Tokyo
1969 *Art and Cybernetics,* Bonino Gallery, Buenos Aires
1971 *Argentine Art,* Camden Art Centre, London
1972 *Biennale,* Venice
1973 *Introduction to Design,* Jerusalem Museum
1974 *Latin American Art System,* International Cultureel Centrum, Antwerp (toured Europe)
1979 *The Artists Choice,* Tel Aviv Museum, Israel
1980 *Art about Art,* Galerie Nouvelles Images, The Hague
1982 *Here and Now,* Israel Museum, Jerusalem
1993 *Quotations,* Museum of Contemporary Art, Wright State University, Ohio
Gone Beyond Gone, Thread Waxing Space, New York (catalog)
1994 *Translokation,* Haus der Architektur, Graz (catalog)
1995 *Avant-Garde Walk a Venezia II,* Italy (catalog)
2000 *Faith: The Impact of Judeo-Christian Religion on Art at the Millennium,* The Aldrich Museum of Contemporary Art, Ridgefield (catalog)

Collections:

Museo de Bellas Artes, Buenos Aires; Institute of Contemporary Art, Lima; Casa del Arte, San Juan, Puerto Rico; Instituto Panameno de Arte, Panama City; Museum of Modern Art, New York; Brooklyn Museum, New York; Philadelphia Museum of Art; Museum of Modern Art, Miami; Pan American Union Collection, Washington, D.C.; Library of Congress, Washington, D.C.

Publications:

By ROMBERG: Books—*Primeras Jornadas de Artes Gráficas,* Tucumàn, Argentina 1972; *Journeys into Visual Experience,* Tucumàn, Argentina 1972; *Towards a Theory of Existential Teaching,* University of Delaware 1984; *The Inverted Pyramid,* Düren, Germany, 1991. **Films and Videotapes—***Interview with Ran Schechori* by Jorge Glusberg, Buenos Aires 1974; *Typologies of My Body,* Bezalel, Israel 1975; *Typologies of the Wailing Wall,* Bezalel, Israel 1975.

On ROMBERG: Books—*Osvaldo Romberg,* exhibition catalog with an introduction by Sam Hunter, New York 1967; *Retrospective View of Argentine Art* by J. Romero Brest, Buenos Aires 1971; *Osvaldo Romberg,* exhibition catalog by Edmundo Concha, Tucumàn, Argentina 1972; *Landscape as Idea,* exhibition catalog by Jorge Glusberg, Buenos Aires 1972; *Art in Israel* by Ran Schechori, Tel Aviv 1974; *Osvaldo Romberg: Typologies,* exhibition catalog with an introduction by Florent Bex, Antwerp 1975; *Osvaldo Romberg: Kunstuber Kunst,* exhibition catalog with text by Michael Erlhoff, Hannover 1984; *Osvaldo Romberg, Recent Works,* exhibition catalog with text by Carter Ratcliff, New York 1985; *Building Footprints,* exhibition catalog, Jerusalem 1991. **Articles—**''Romberg's Cosmos'' by Carter Ratcliff in *Artefactum,* vol. 2, no. 10, September-October 1985; ''Ultranature: The Art of Romberg'' by Liza Black in *Splash,* December 1987; review by William Zimmer in the *New York Times,* 14 June 1992; ''Osvaldo Romberg: Universalgeschichte'' by Jürgen Raap in *Kunstforum International,* no. 137, June-August 1997.

*

During recent years my interest in results has decreased on the one hand while my concern with preparatory process has considerably increased on the other. Since the *Space verificator* of 1970, running through 1971–72 landscape projects, we can observe a permanent search after classification of space, providing it with a frame of reference. Sometimes dialectical concepts, like rational-irrational, are counter poised.

Then the search moves on the field of the basic possibilities inherent in the pictorial medium and in the human being as executive agent.

The most frequent questions are: what is a painting, a drawing, a sculpture, in its ultimate meaning?

The colour classification, the graphic proofs on paper or tridimensional objects emphasized the artistic gesture before form, before composition, before the dictionary's morphological definition of what is correct.

A kind of process esthethics is thus generated; these processes are elevated to a degree of results by ''super exercises'' exhibited on the walls of the gallery.

This means, in some way, to begin anew, to sense again the pleasure of painting, to paint the painting, to try and define again and again in each work, what is the essence of painting.

Art is unverifiable; we can merely approach it through exercises, which sometimes surmount their own limits and provide us with a mystique of expression if we are artists, and a mystique of perception if we are observers.

—Osvaldo Romberg

* * *

For many years, Osvaldo Romberg has been trying to penetrate into the essence of the work of art and its components, at the same time analysing the creative act in its most elementary form. This investigation implies that the process, the relationship between the pictorial medium and the artist, the relationship perception-expression is much more important than the resulting product (the painting).

Romberg's structural analysis of ''painting'' focuses on the three basic elements: colour, line, act. These are reduced to their most elementary forms.

Romberg uses only five principal colours (white, black, ultramarine blue, vermilion red, medium yellow), from which all other tones and tonalities are derived. Spots or touches are produced on the canvas, usually in a determined scheme of rectangular spaces. For some works, Romberg has chosen not to use a brush. These works consist of casual spots, which are all given a number as may be the case in other works as well.

While analysing the act of ''painting,'' Romberg just draws primary forms as e.g. line, circle, spiral in a neutral tone. These forms are produced through elementary movements of right or left hand, right or left foot, mouth, etc. (cf. a work entitled: ''Typology Through Three Parts of My Body''). Notwithstanding the discipline and the mathematical progress of the investigation, irrational and aesthetical values can be recognized within the result of these experiments. The duality between head and senses comes plainly into the open, even in the slightest interventions of the artist. The analysis of one colour, the classifications of a series of colours, the subtle trace of the hand, sometimes sure, sometimes clumsy, have a pure and primitive charm, even if they refer to the limitation of human action, or—by numbering and ordering—to the relativity of a spatial and temporal perception.

The aesthetical dimension is probably clearest in those works in which Romberg applies his colour analysis to famous painters. He leaves the strict logical scheme to produce a series of analytical colour impressions on the canvas. (cf. ''I Remember Malevich'' etc.'')

Romberg paints the painting process. His oeuvre being part of the ''New Painting,'' it is important to point out that it should not be seen as the concrete form of a theoretical program. Instead, it has grown from the practice of painting and it requires or refers to a new theory.

—Florent Bex

ROOB, Alexander

Nationality: German. **Born:** Laumersheim, Germany, 18 October 1956. **Education:** Studied art at the Hochschule der Bildenden Künste, Berlin, 1977–1985. **Family:** Married Annette Hinricher, 1980 (divorced 1987); married Uta Gerlach, 1988; daughters: Lena and Lisa. **Career:** Worked as a cartoonist for various journals, paintings, prospects, and murals for galleries, theaters, churches, and films, 1977–85; beginning of the long-term drawing project CS, 1985; studies of the late poems of William Blake, 1989–96; novel phase of the CS project, 1991–2000; teacher of drawing, Hochschule für Bildende Künste, Hamburg, 2000—; artist-in-residence, Wimbledon School of Art, London, 2001; CS-Projects in Geneva, Nürnberg, London, and Shanghai, 2001. **Awards:** DAAD-Stipendium, Zürich and Cairo, 1986; Förderpreis des Landes Rheinland-Pfalz, 1987; Zeichenstipendium der Stadt Nürnberg, 1992; Arbeitsstipendium des Deutschen Kunstfonds, 1993; Villa Massimo-Stipendium, Rome, 1996. **Agents:** Galerie Ursula Walbröl, Kirchfeldstrasse 13, 40217 Düsseldorf, Germany; Galerie Anita Beckers, Frankenallee 74, 60327 Frankfurt/Main, Germany. **Address:** Kirchfeldstrasse 13, 40217 Düsseldorf, Germany.

Individual Exhibitions:

1988 Pfalzgalerie Kaiserslautern
Hans Thoma-Gesellschaft, Reutlingen
1991 *CS I-III,* Kunstverein Heidelberg
1992 *CS IV,* Kunsthalle Nürnberg
Städtische Galerie Göppingen
1993 Galerie Ursula Walbröl, Hilden
1995 *CS V,* Stadtgalerie Saarbrücken
1996 Galerie Ursula Walbröl, Düsseldorf
CS V, Overbeck-Gesellschaft, Lübeck
CS V, Kunstverein Freiburg
CS V, Kunsthalle Ritter, Klagenfurt
1997 Kunstverein Bochum
1998 Städtische Galerie im Lenbachhaus, Munich
CS VI, Karl-Ernst-Osthaus Museum, Hagen
CS VI, Städtische Galerie Göppingen
1999 *CS VI,* Kunstverein, Mannheim
CS VII, Graphische Sammlung Albertina, Vienna
2000 Goethe Institut, Rotterdam
Frankfurter Sequenzen I, Galerie Anita Beckers, Frankfurt
Galerie Ursula Walböl, Düsseldorf
Richter Zeichnen, Museum für Moderne Kunst, Frankfurt

Selected Collections:

Pfalzgalerie Kaiserslautern, Germany; Neues Museum Nürnberg, Germany; Landesmuseum Mainz, Germany; Kupferstichkabinett Berlin; Graphische Sammlung Albertina, Vienna; Museum für Moderne Kunst, Frankfurt.

Publications:

By ROOB: Books—*Gold und Scheisse,* with Stefan Fuchs, Berlin 1985; *Zelchnungen 1985–87,* Pfalzgalerie Kaiserslautern 1988; *CS I-III,* (Hrsg) Pfalzgalerie Kaiserslautern 1991; *CS IV,* (Hrsg) Kunsthalle Nürnberg 1992; *Dachdecker im CS,* (Hrsg) Städtische Galerie Göppingen 1992; *CS V,* (Hrsg) Bernd Schulz, Klagenfurt 1995; *Das Hermetische Museum, Alchemie & Mystik,* Cologne 1996; *Theorie des Bildromans,* (Hrsg) Villa Massimo, Rome and Cologne 1997; *CS VI,* Darmstadt 1998; *Zeichnung als Partikel,* Galerie im Lenbachhaus Munich 1998; *CS VII,* (Hrsg) Albertina Wien, Klagenfurt 1999; *Richter zeichnen (The Stammheim Cycle by Gerhard Richter leaves the MMK: A CS Protocol.),* (Hrsg) Andreas Bee, Frankfurt and Cologne 2001.

On ROOB: Articles—''Alexander Roob'' by Gisela Fiedler-Bender in *Zelchnungen 1985–87,* Pfalzgalerie Kaiserslautern 1988; ''Alexander Roob'' by Gisela Fiedler-Bender in *CS I-III,* (Hrsg) Pfalzgalerie Kaiserslautern 1991; ''Apell und Angebot'' by Hans Gercke in *CS I-III,* (Hrsg) Pfalzgalerie Kaiserslautern 1991; ''Bitte nach Oben Kommen'' by Renate Damsch-Wiehager in *Dachdecker im CS,* (Hrsg) Städtische Galerie Göppingen 1992; ''Der Knick im Bleistift. Anmerkungen zu A. Roobs Bildroman'' by Stephan Berg in *CS V,* (Hrsg) Bernd Schulz, Klagenfurt-Saarbrücken 1995; ''Sehen was

Alexander Roob: *CS-VI Bildroman.* ©Alexander Roob, courtesy Mannheimer Kunstverein.

ist'' by Bernd Schulz in *CS V,* (Hrsg) Bernd Schulz, Klagenfurt-Saarbrücken 1995; ''Zeichnungen'' by Roswitha Siewert in *CS V,* (Hrsg) Bernd Schulz, Klagenfurt-Saarbrücken 1995; ''Das Wahrnehmungsvermögen muss in der Aktion erforscht werden'' by Werner Meyer in *Abenteuer Kunst,* Städtische Galerie Göppingen 1996; ''Alexander Roob'' by Bettina Baumgärtel in *Augenzeugen,* Die Sammlung Hanck, Kunstmuseum Düsseldorf 1997; ''Sich einsehen in CS V—wie man Sehen sieht'' by Werner Meyer in *CS VI,* Darmstadt 1998; ''Notizen zur sequentiellen Bilderzählung'' in *CS VI,* Darmstadt 1998; ''Strich für Strich'' by Martin Stather in *CS VI,* Darmstadt 1998; ''Wie sind zwei Bilder ein Bild?'' by Hubert Sowa in *CS VI,* Darmstadt 1998; ''Alexander Roob'' by Stephan Berg in *Vollkommen gewöhnlich,* Eine Ausstellung des Kunstfonds, Band 1, 1998; ''Bedeutung zerstreuen: Zu den Zeichnungen Alexander Roobs'' by Marion Ackermann in *''Zeichnung als Partikel,''* Galerie im Lenbachhaus Munich 1998; ''Die Zerstreuungen des Zeichners: Alexander Roobs Bildroman'' by Stephan Berg in *Kunstforum,* Band 142, 1998; ''Verwilderungen'' by Michael Glasmeier in *CS VII,* (Hrsg) Albertina Wien, Klagenfurt 1999; ''Die Linie des Gedankens'' by Wolfgang Pircher in *CS VII,* (Hrsg) Albertina Wien, Klagenfurt 1999; ''CS VII'' by Konrad Oberhuber in *CS VII,* (Hrsg) Albertina Wien, Klagenfurt 1999; ''Bilder aus dem Kopf des Zeichners'' by Ruth Händler in *Art-das Kunstmagazin,* No. 10, 1999; ''Ein CS-Protokoll'' by Andreas Bee in *Richter zeichnen,* Frankurt and Cologne 2001.

* * *

RÖSEL, Peter

Nationality: German. **Born:** Rockenhausen, Germany, 20 February 1966. **Education:** Städelschule, Frankfurt am Main, 1987–92; Cooper Union, School for the Advancement of Science and Art, New York, 1992. **Family:** Married Valeria Heisenberg in 2000, son: Raoul Emil. **Awards:** Hessischen Kulturstiftung (New York grant), Germany, 1995; Kahnweiler Award, City of Rockenhausen, Germany, 1997; NUR Stipend, Germany, 1999. **Agent:** Galerie Art Attitude, Hervé Bize, 17–19, rue Gambetta (cour R.D.C.), 54000 Nancy, France. **Address:** Weinbergsweg 5, D-10119 Berlin, Germany.

Selected Individual Exhibitions:

1992 Galerie Paul Sties, Franfurt am Main, Germany (catalog)
1993 Waßermann Galerie, Munich
1996 *Seam Ripper,* TZ' Art & Co., New York
1997 *Monstera Deliciosa, etc.,* Galerie Art Attitude Hervé Bize, Nancy, France (catalog)
1998 *No! Shorts, No! Hats, No! Sneakers,* Mannheimer Kunstverein, Germany
2001 *Mirrages,* Attitudes, Geneva

Selected Group Exhibitions:

1994 *Change of Scene V,* Museum für Moderne Kunst, Frankfurt am Main, Germany
1996 *Landvermesser,* Mannheimer Kunstverein, Germany (catalog)
1997 *Neue Landschaftsgalerie,* Museum für Altonaer Geschichte, Hamburg
1998 *Change of Scene XIV,* Museum für Moderne Kunst, Frankfurt am Main, Germany
1999 *I Never Promised You a Rosegarden,* Kunsthalle Bern, Switzerland
Kunst in der Stadt III, Kunsthaus Bregenz, Austria
2000 *Hand-Arbeit,* Haus der Kunst München, Munich (catalog)
2001 *Priorité aux Piétons,* Kiron Galerie, Paris

Peter Rösel: *Lily Pond,* 1997. Photo by Axel Schneider. ©Peter Rösel, courtesy of Museum für Moderne Kunst, Frankfurt am Main.

Collections:

Museum für Moderne Kunst, Frankfurt am Main, Germany; Museum für Altonaer Geschichte, Hamburg; Bundesministerium für Inneres, Berlin; Deutsche Bank, Frankfurt am Main.

Public Installations:

Hotel, Der Teufelhof Basel, room number 2, Basel, Switzerland 1994; Hotel Robert Maier, room number 32, Frankfurt am Main, Germany 1994; *Soundscape,* sound installation, Wohnmaschine in Berlin, Germany 1999.

Publications:

By RÖSEL: Recording—*Soundscape,* 1999.

On RÖSEL: Books—*Bewegung im Kopf: Vom Umgang mit der Kunst* by Jean-Christophe Amman, Regensburg 1993; *Zeitgenössische Kunst in der Deutschen Bank, Trianon* by Kevin Slavin, Frankfurt am Main, Germany 1994; *Peter Rösel* by Martin Pesch and Jean-Christophe Amman, Frankfurt am Main 1998. **Articles—**''Seam Ripper II'' by Martin Pesch in *Frieze,* March 1997; ''Peter Rösel im Museum für Moderne Kunst, Frankfurt'' in *Kunst Bulletin,* September 1998; Janneke De Vries in *Artist Kunstmagazin,* no. 37, vol. 4, 1998; ''Die Suche nach dem Nichtvorhergesehenen'' by Martin Pesch in *Kunstforum International,* no. 151, July/September 2000.

* * *

ROSEN, Kay

Nationality: American. **Born:** Corpus Christi, Texas. **Education:** Tulane University, New Orleans, Louisiana, B.A.; Northwestern University, Chicago, Illinois, M.A. **Career:** Arts Midwest Focus Groups, 1988; curator and visual artist, School of the Art Institute of Chicago, 1988, University of Chicago, 1990; lecturer. Columbia College, 1989, Indiana University, Gary, 1992; panelist, Midwest College Art Association Conference, Cincinnati, 1989, Massachusetts Artists Fellowship Program Painting Panel, 1990; graduate critique panelist, School of the Art Institute of Chicago, 1989; review panelist, Arts Midwest New Partnership Grants Visual Artists, 1990; speaker and panelist, Mountain Cake Symposium, Virginia, 1990; graduate faculty advisor, School of the Art Institute of Chicago, 1992; speaker, Indiana State University, Terre Haute, 1993. Editor, *Spunky International,* New York, 1992. **Awards:** National Endowment for the Arts Grants, 1987 and 1989; Visual Arts 10 Award, 1990. **Address:** 6925 Indian Boundary, Gary, Indiana, 46403–1246, U.S.A.

Selected Individual Exhibitions:

1993 Feature, New York
1994 Museum of Contemporary Art, Chicago
Shoshana Wayne Gallery, Santa Monica, California
Indianapolis Museum of Art, Indiana
Forefront Gallery, Indiana
Victoria Miro Gallery, London
Galeria Massimo de Carlo, Milan
1995 Galerie Erika and Otto Friederich, Bern, Switzerland

Selected Group Exhibitions:

1995 *Temporarily Possessed: The Semi-Permanent Collection,* New Museum of Contemporary Art, New York
1996 *What I Did on My Summer Vacation,* White Columns, New York
An (Alternative) Alternative Art Fair: Oasis Vs. Blur and Artists Who ROCK, Art Exchange Show, New York
1997 *Short Stories/Tall Tales,* List Visual Arts Center, MIT, Cambridge
2000 *Biennial,* Whitney Museum of American Art, New York
2001 *Up and Down,* Aspen Art Museum, Colorado

Collections:

Art Institute of Chicago, Illinois; Museum of Modern Art, New York; New Museum of Contemporary Art, New York.

Publications:

By ROSEN: Article—''Kay Rosen'' by Kay Rosen in *Du,* no. 6, June 1991.

On ROSEN: Articles—''Artists' Writing: Words and/as Pictures'' in *Art Journal,* vol. 49, Summer 1990; ''Read Read Rosens'' by Judith-Russi Kirshner in *Artforum International,* vol. 29, December 1990; ''Cleveland Center for Contemporary Art'' by John Byrum in *New Art Examiner,* vol. 20, November 1992; ''Rhona Hoffman Gallery, Chicago'' by Kathryn Hixson in *Flash Art* (International Edition), no. 168, January/February 1993; ''Aprilints and Photographs Published'' in *The Aprilint Collector's Newsletter,* vol. 24, September/October 1993; ''Kay Rosen'' *Du,* no. 11, November 1993; ''Painting Camp: The Subculture of Painting, The Mainstream of Decemberoration'' by Terry-R Myers in *Flash Art* (International Edition), no. 179, November/December 1994; ''Philadelphia: Kay Rosen at Beaver College Art Gallery'' by Miriam Seidel in *Art in America,* vol. 86, no. 10, October 1998; ''Speech! An Interview with Kay Rosen'' by Kathryn Hixson in *New Art Examiner,* vol. 26, no. 3, November 1998; ''Kay Rosen: ''Lifeli(k)e'' by Frank-Alexander Hettig in *Kunstforum International,* no. 144, March/April 1999; ''Kay Rosen: Otis Gallery; Museum of Contemporary Art'' by Jacqueline Cooper in *New Art Examiner,* vol. 26, no. 7, April 1999; ''True to Type'' by Eileen Myles in *Art in America,* vol. 87, no. 9, September 1999; ''Catching a Slippery Fish'' by Kay Larson in *ARTNews,* September 1999; ''True to Type'' by Eileen Myles in *ARTNews,* September 1999. **Web site—***UbuWeb.com,* http://www.ubu.com/contemp/rosen/bcoming.html (accessed June 2001).

* * *

Kay Rosen uses the laws—and limitations—of linguistics to express herself. She employs language as art, with special attention paid to the importance of context in ''decoding'' written and spoken words. In ''Virginia Woolf,'' for example, Rosen uses two different fonts to emphasize the fragment, ''Virgin Wool.'' With the extra letters in italics, the subject is altered from a household literary figure, to a provocative socio-sexual image.

Language constitutes Rosen's content and her media. Her interest in language can be traced back to her childhood in Corpus Christi, Texas, where she grew up with a Yiddish speaking family member in a community where both Spanish and English were spoken. She went on to study language, and after graduate school taught Spanish with ''linguistics thrown in.''

In a 1998 interview with Kathryn Hixson of the *New Art Examiner,* Rosen explains that she crossed-over from teaching language to producing art when she wanted to be more than ''simply a conduit who passed information from textbooks to students.'' Having always made art for herself, she realized that the points she wanted to make about language and linguistics required a visual medium.

When Rosen began painting, she used words and letters as her subjects. After showing her work in Chicago in the early 1970s, she grew frustrated with the restrictions of Chicago's limited art scene and began showing at Bertha Urdang Gallery in New York. In the middle of the decade, she put her work with language on hold to experiment with other subjects and media—photography and sculpture. These works address similar themes as her more textual works. But rather than adjust and alter *letters* to change the subjects' connotation, Rosen adjusted objects, and human subjects. It was the written notations that Rosen made in the course of producing these works that ''led her back to text'' as a primary subject.

Rosen often focuses on the smallest building blocks of communication: letters. In *(B)coming (A)part,* a series of ''lessons'' on language, linguistics and art, Rosen illustrates her systems of breaking down existing language into new sets of meanings. ''Linguistic systems,'' Rosen states, ''are a consensus of rules which are products of history and usage.'' With that in mind, Rosen removes words, letters and phrases from their existing context and organizes them anew.

Regarding *Trickknees,* a painting bearing only those two words joined into one, Rosen explains how the two Ks in the middle are excessive, without them ''tricnees'' still sounds, and reads, the same. However, the Ks serve to illustrate the word's meaning ''in a pictorial capacity.'' Each K has one straight leg and one crooked. Locating and framing these linguistic subtleties is Rosen's specialty, it is the foundation upon which her art is built.

Kay Rosen's paintings are often humorous. Sometimes they tell a story. *The Ed Prints,* 1992, for example, tell the story of two heroes, ''Ed'' the man, and ''ed'' the suffix. Her paintings pose questions, make us think and challenge us. In *HIM, HYMN, HMMM,* the three words—each different in spelling and meaning but phonetically similar—are perfectly stenciled, uppercase and white, against a bright blue background. They appear one on top of the other. Each letter in ''HIM'' is printed slightly wider than the other letters in the painting, perhaps to accommodate the three-letter word on a page of four lettered ones, or perhaps to give the word a heavy, inundating appearance. At the bottom of the list, ''HMMM,'' is printed in shorter letters, giving the phrase an almost squashed look. The first word is a gender-specific pronoun, the second defines a pious song, and the third is an expression indicating thought. Grouped together, loaded with their own meanings, and thereby questioning their similar pronunciation, the words provoke thought about gender, spirituality and, of course, linguistics and the origin of language. The true power of *HIM, HYMN, HMMM,* is in Rosen's ability to make simple yet precise artistic decisions—color, font, and word choice—that put language in the hot seat.

—Aaron Jacobs

ROSENBACH, Ulrike

Nationality: German. **Born:** Salzdetfurth, Germany, 1943. **Education:** Studied under Joseph Beuys at the Academic für Bildende Künste, Dusseldorf, 1964–69. **Career:** Independent artist, since 1970: first video works, 1972; first action-performances, 1973. Founder, Schule für kreativen Feminismus private school, Cologne, 1976–83. Instructor, California Arts Institute, Valencia, 1976; Fachhochschule, Cologne, 1977; Staatliche Kunstakademie of Dusseldorf, Munster, 1984; artist-in-residence, Western Front, Vancouver, British Columbia, Canada, 1984; professor, Academy of Fine Arts, Saarbruecken, Germany, 1989—. **Awards:** Art Prize, Nordthein-Westfalen, 1977; Study Award for Video Art and Feminist Art, California Institute of Art, Valencia 1976; Artist's Stipend, City of Cologne, 1978; Festival Award, Videofesitval Locarno, Switzerland, 1984.

Individual Exhibitions:

1972 Galerie Ernst, Hannover
1975 Oppenheim Studio, Cologne
Galerie Magers, Bonn
1976 *Foto, Video, Aktion,* Sammlung Ludwig, Aachen, West Germany
1978 Galerie Stampa, Basel
1979 Kulturmuzentrum für Frauen, Stuttgart
1980 Galerie Meier-Hahn, Dusseldorf
Ulrike Rosenbach/Valie Export, Sedelijk Museum, Amsterdam
1981 *Video, Foto, Serije,* Centar za Fotografiju, Film, i TV, Zagreb
1982 Museum Schwarzes Kloster, Freiburg, West Germany
1983 Institute of Contemporary Art, Boston
1984 Galerie Philomene Magers, Bonn
Galerie Stampa, Basel
1985 Galerie Grita Insam, Vienna
1986 Galerie Meier-Hann, Dusseldorf
Neue Galerie/Sammlung Ludwig, Aachen, West Germany
1987 Galerie Stampa, Basel
1990 Stadtgalerie Saarbruecken, Germany
Stadtgalerie Quakenbrueck, Germany
1991 Galerie am Luxemburgplatz, Wiesbaden
1992 Stadtgalerie Kerems, Germany
Galerie Fotohaf, Salzburg
1993 Galerie Uli Buschinger, Wiesbaden
Haus de Geschichte, Bonn
1995 Galerie Weisser Raum, Hamburg
Festival ''Bollwerk,'' Fribourg, Switzerland
St. Petri Kirche, Dortmund

Selected Group Exhibitions:

1973 *1,000 Miles From Here,* Gallery House, London (travelled to the Kunsthalle, Dusseldorf)
1974 *Videoshow,* Museum of Modern Art, New York (travelled to the Institute of Contemporary Art, Philadelphia)
1975 *Magna-Feminismus,* Galerie Nächst St. Stephan, Vienna
1978 *Frauen Machen Kunst,* Galerie Magers, Bonn
1980 *Mythen und Zeichen,* Kunstverein, Bonn
Biennale, Venice
1981 *Videokunst,* Baden-Baden, West Germany
1983 *The Video History Show,* Museum of Modern Art, New York
1985 *Kunst nach 45,* Nationalgalerie, West Berlin
1987 *Documenta 8,* Museum Fridericianum, Kassel, West Germany
1990 *Art after '68,* Kunstmuseum Basel, Switzerland
Resource Art, Kunstmuseum Budapest, Hungary
1991 Goethe-Institut, Paris
German Video Art, Fukuyama Museum of Modern Art, Japan
1993 *The First Generation,* Long Beach Museum of Art, California
Tower of Babylon, Helsinki Videofestival, Finland
1994 *Videosculpture in Germany,* IFA-Galerie, Stuttgart, Germany (toured)
1995 *Videoretrospektive,* Freiburger Videofestival, Germany

Publications:

By ROSENBACH: Article—''Haubenkunst'' in *Avalanche* (New York), no. 8, 1973.

On ROSENBACH: Books—*Video Art: An Anthology,* edited by Ina Schneider and Beryl Korot, New York and London 1976; *Ulrike Rosenbach: Foto, Video, Aktion,* exhibition catalog with text by Lucy Lippard and others, Aachen, West Germany 1977; *5 in Köln: Michael Buthe, Sigmar Polke, Ulrike Rosenbach, Gerhard Ruhm, Alf Schuler,* exhibition catalog with text by Wulf Herzogenrath and others, Cologne 1979; *Ulrike Rosenbach/Valie Export,* exhibition catalog with text by P. M. Pickshaus, Amsterdam 1980; *Ulrike Rosenbach: Video-Foto-Serije,* exhibition catalog with text by Mangelos, Zagreb 1981; *Videokunst in Deutschland* by Wulf Herzogenrath, Cologne 1983; *Ulrike Rosenbach: Video and Performance Art,* exhibition catalog, Boston 1983; *Feminist Aesthetics* by Gisela Ecker, London 1985; *Bis Heute* by Karin Thomas, Cologne 1986; *Spuren des Heiligen in der Kunst 2: Ulrike Rosenbach,* exhibition catalog by Wolfgang Becker, Aachen 1986. **Articles—**''Vom Werden und Vergehen'' by Gerhard Glueher in *Made for Arolsen* (exhibition catalog), Museum Bad Arolsen, 1997.

* * *

The work of Ulrike Rosenbach is a radical and artistically convincing manifestation of contemporary feminist art. It is a critical and dialectical confrontation with a historical continuity which it—at the same time—continues and challenges. From her earliest beginnings the artist worked on a polemical level and articulated polarities and tensions which are inherent in the patriarchially dominated traditional and contemporary culture.

After her studies with Joseph Beuys, Ulrike Rosenbach began creating works around 1970 in which social roles of women were the theme, among others *Hauben fuer verheiratete Frauen;* clichés of the traditional society were attacked and the authentic reality of women newly constituted. In 1971 the artist included video tapes in her work, which continuously was dealing with the activity of feminist politics, but within this establishing an authentic artistic articulation. In works such as *Bindemaske, Einwicklung mit Julia* (*Involvement with Julia*) and *Eine Frau ist eine Frau* (*A Woman Is a Woman*), all of 1972, she demonstratively constituted a new image of woman in intermedia.

Works in the years to follow, such as *Der Mann sei das Haupt der Frau* (*Man Is the Head of Woman*) of 1973 and *Madonna of the Flowers* of 1974/1975 give artistic reinterpetations of existing literary and painterly historic documents on the basis of a feminist consciousness. It is not the individual work of art which is the target of destruction, but the patriarchal projection of the passive image of woman which does not correspond with reality.

These tendencies culminate in *Glauben Sie nicht, dass ich eine Amazone bin* (*Don't Believe that I Am an Amazon*) of 1975 in which the painting by Stefan Lochner *Madonna im Rosenhag* is incorporated into a performance in which Ulrike Rosenbach shoots fifteen arrows into a reproduction of the historical image and the end of the performance superimposes her own image into that of the Gothic madonna. The action *Reflektionen ueber bie Geburt der Venus* (*Reflections on the Birth of Venus*) of 1976 also refers to and uses a historical precedent, here Botticelli's painting *The Birth of Venus,* but again Rosenbach reconstitutes her own interpretation of woman, rejecting the historical cliché and the social and cultural degradation documented in Botticelli's work.

Ulrike Rosenbach continued these actions in 1976 with *Zehntausend Jahre habe ich geschlafen und nun bich ich erwacht* (*I Have Slept Ten Thousand Years and now Awoke*), one of the masterpieces of contemporary international performance art. Sleep and awakening here become analogous with death and rebirth in a ritual-like action. Prehistoric symbolism and the reality of contemporary life, both seen from a radical feminist perspective, are united, and a powerful new form of performance art is created. In the same year the artist created other forms of performances, among them *Female Energy Exchange,* as well as the manifesto *Hexenmuetter,* which was published in 1977.

Several actions since 1977 concentrate on male imagery; *Herakles-Herkules-King Kong* of 1977 contrasts historic role behaviour in men with contemporary reality. In other works such as *Die einsame Spaziergaengerin-Hagazussa* (*The Lone Walker-Hagazussa*) of 1979, using a reproduction of Caspar David Friedrich's painting *Gebirgslandschaft mit Regenbogen,* Rosenbach combines action and video.

Most of Rosenbach's works are aimed at the release of contemporary female energy in a creative artistic manifestation. This is evident in other works in 1981, *Psyche aber, sie irrte gaenzlich umher* (*But Psyche Wandered About*), and *Psyche und Eros* partly in collaboration with her daughter Julia. In *Frauenkultur-Kontaktversuch* (*Women's Culture—Attempt at Contact*) and *JudoFrauen haben als Hilfe Boten* (*Judo Women Have Messengers as Help*), both of 1981, again in a creative confrontation of live action and video, the artist reconstitutes the reality of women in contemporary culture. Performances in recent years, such as *Ewa and Adam* of 1982/1983, *Im Garten der Goettin* (*In the Garden of the Goddess*) of 1986 and *ANA'L HAQ* (*I am God*) of 1986, expand the earlier thematics into eschatological and cosmological dimensions in regard to the meaning of women's contribution to contemporary culture.

The essence of Ulrike Rosenbach's work is the transformation of female consciousness by means of an authentic artistic creation. This is, as all art, multilevelled, rationally not understandable and open for various views of interpretation, as Rosenbach wrote in 1974: "Life is complicated and an art that is simplifying it, is just a complicated lie." Rosenbach's art is not on the level of feminist propaganda, it is, quite the opposite, on the level of a complex and irrational, often mysterious and unexplainable new art form, which was newly constituted and in this sense continued the art tradition of the past, enriching it by a new dimension.

More recent work by Ulrike Rosenbach, among them *Wie ein Phoenix aus der Asche* of 1989/1990 and *Im Garten des Meisters* of 1990 intensify the conviction of the artist that the process of creating is more important than the physical end result of the activity. Encompassing elements of Buddhist thoughts, classical mythology and Shakespeare (*Or-Phelia* of 1988) into the consciousness of contemporary reality Rosenbach expresses the innermost human feelings in their relationships to the outermost cosmic constellations of reality. Feminist art is defined by Ulrike Rosenbach as "the elucidation of the woman-artist's identity; of her body, of her psyche, her position in society."

Stronger than in her earlier work are video-sculptures and video-performances in the 1990s integrated into this elucidation of the woman-artist's identity as symbols of life and death, visible in "Ishtar von Babylon" of 1993, "Requiem fuer eine Eiche" of 1994, and "Ueber den Tod" of 1995/96. A new element is furthermore the necessary participation of the viewer in the activation of the crossing of historical borderlines and the borderlines between art and reality, as manifested especially in "Hildegard von Bingen" of 1995/97, a creative reincarnation of the medieval nun and artist with possible implications for the contemporary situation.

—Udo Kultermann

ROSENQUIST, James

Nationality: American. **Born:** Grand Forks, North Dakota, 29 November 1933. **Education:** Studied art, under Cameron Booth, at the University of Minnesota, Minneapolis, from 1948 (on scholarship), and at the Art Students League, New York, 1954–55; attended drawing classes organized by Jack Youngerman and Robert Indiana, New York, 1957–58; studied Eastern philosophy and history, Aspen Institute of Humanist Studies, Colorado, 1965. **Family:** Married Mary Lou Adams in 1960 (divorced); son: John; married Melinda Thompson, 1987; daughter: Lily McLean. **Career:** Painter, printmaker, and "Pop" artist. Commercial display artist, General Outdoor Advertising Company, 1952–54; chauffeur, Winchester, New York, 1955; met Robert Indiana, Chuck Hinman, Robert Rauschenberg, Jasper Johns, and Jack Youngerman, New York, 1956; member, International Pictorial Painters Union, New York, 1957; commercial display artist, Bonwit Teller, and Tiffany and Company, New York, 1959; began series of lithographs, with Donald Saff, Graphics Studio, University of South Florida, Tampa 1971; completed 11 graphic works for the Petersburg Press, London, 1972; rented studio, and completed lithographic series, Tampa, 1973–74; lobbied, with Marion Javits and Roberts Rauschenberg, to amend tax laws regarding artists and their estates, Washington, D.C., 1975; prepared sets for the Joffrey Ballet's *Deuce Coupe,* New York, 1975; spent summer in California, and began collaboration on prints with Susan Hall, 1976; built house and studio with architect Gilbert Flores, 1976; continued collaboration with Susan Hall, at Gemini Workshops, Los Angeles, 1977; bought property in Soho, New York, and designated a floor each for painting, graphics, and living; returned to Florida to paint, 1979. Visiting lecturer, Yale University, New Haven, Connecticut, 1964. Member, board of directors, National Endownment for the Arts, 1978. **Awards:** Torcuato di Tella International Prize, Buenos Aires, 1965; Recipient Golden Plate Award, American Academy of Achievement, 1988. **Agent:** Leo Castelli Gallery, 420 West Broadway, New York, New York 10012. **Address:** Box 4, Aripeka, Florida 33502; or 162 Chambers Street, New York, New York 10007, U.S.A.

Individual Exhibitions:

1962 Green Gallery, New York
1963 Green Gallery, New York
1964 Dwan Gallery, Los Angeles
Galerie Ileana Sonnabend, Paris
Galleria Sperone, Turin
1965 Leo Castelli Gallery, New York
Moderna Museet, Stockholm
Museo d'Arte Moderna, Turin
Galerie Ileana Sonnabend, Paris
1966 Leo Castelli Gallery, New York
Moderna Museet, Stockholm
Staatliche Kunsthalle, Baden-Baden, West Germany
Louisiana Museum, Humlebaek, Denmark
Stedelijk Museum, Amsterdam
1967 Musée des Arts Décoratifs, Paris
1968 National Gallery of Canada, Ottawa
Galerie Ileana Sonnabend, Paris
Galleria Sperone, Turin
Metropolitan Museum of Art, New York
1969 Leo Castelli Gallery, New York
1970 Galerie Ricke, Cologne
Leo Castelli Gallery, New York
1972 *Gemaälde, Räume, Graphik,* Wallraf-Richartz Museum, Cologne (retrospective)
Whitney Museum, New York
Museum of Contemporary Art, Chicago
Galleria del Milione, Milan
Margo Leavin Gallery, Los Angeles
1973 Galerie Hans Hoeppner, Hamburg
Galerie Hans Hoeppner, Munich
Amerika Haus, West Berlin
Jack Glenn Gallery, Corona Del Mar, California
Center of the Visual, Portland, Oregon
Courtney Jules Gallery, Dallas
Stedelijk Museum, Amsterdam
Leo Castelli Gallery, New York
1974 Max Protetch Gallery, Washington, D.C.
Margo Leavin Gallery, Los Angeles
Galerie Michael Pabst, Vienna
Prints, Scottish Arts Council Gallery, Edinburgh (travelled to the Art Gallery and Museum, Aberdeen, and the City Museum and Art Gallery, Dundee, Scotland)
Jared Sable Gallery, Toronto
Paintings 1961–1973, Mayor Gallery, London
1975 Leo Castelli Gallery, New York
1976 Gallery A, Sydney
Berenson Gallery, Bay Harbor Islands, Miami Beach
Corcoran and Greenberg Inc., Coral Gables, Florida
Mayor Gallery, London
Paule Anglim Associates, San Francisco
Ronald Greenberg Gallery, St. Louis
1977 Leo Castelli Gallery, New York
Sable-Castelli Gallery, Toronto
National Gallery of Victoria, Melbourne
Institute of Modern Art, Brisbane
1978 Mayor Gallery, London
Multiples Gallery, New York
1979 *Graphics Retrospective,* Ringling Museum of Art, Sarasota, Florida (travelled to the Fort Lauderdale Museum of the Arts, Florida)
1981 Leo Castelli, Gallery, New York
1982 *Paintings from the 60s,* Mayor Gallery, London
1988 *Hommage a Toiny Castelli,* Galerie des Ponchettes, Nice (catalog)
Pop Art, Galerie 1900–2000, Paris (catalog)
1989 *5 Great American Artists,* Duson Gallery, Seoul (catalog)
1991 IVAM Centre Julio González, Valencia (catalog)
1992 *The Early Pictures: 1961–1964,* Gagosian Gallery, New York (catalog)
1993 *The Serenade for the Doll After Claude Debussy or Gift Wrapped Dolls & Masquerade of the Military Industrial Complex Looking Down on the Insect World,* Leo Castelli Gallery, New York (catalog)
1994 *The Big Paintings,* Leo Castelli Gallery, New York (catalog)
1995 Leo Castelli Gallery, New York
1996 *Target Practice,* Galerie Thaddaeus Ropac, Paris (catalog)
1997 *The Graphics of James Rosenquist,* Center for Contemporary Graphic Art and Tyler Graphics Archive Collection, Sukagawa-shi, Fukushima, Japan (catalog)
1999 *James Rosenquist: Paintings 1996–1999,* Baldwin Gallery, Aspen (catalog)
2000 *James Rosenquist: Paintings,* Salvador Dalí, St. Petersburg, Florida (catalog)

Selected Group Exhibitions:

1967 *Whitney Annual,* Whitney Museum, New York (and 1969)
1968 *Documenta,* Kassel, West Germany
1969 *Pop Art,* Hayward Gallery, London
New York Painting and Sculpture 1940–1970, Metropolitan Museum of Art, New York
1974 *American Pop Art,* Whitney Museum, New York
1978 *American Painting of the 1970s,* Albright-Knox Art Gallery, Buffalo, New York
1979 *Black and White Are Colors: Paintings of the 1950s-1970s,* Scripps College, Claremont, California
1980 *Printed Art: A View of 2 Decades,* Museum of Modern Art, New York
1984 *Reflections: Contemporary Art Since 1964,* National Gallery of Canada, Ottawa
1995 *The Muse?,* Galerie Thaddaeus Ropac, Salzburg (also Salzburg Festival, Austria) (catalog)

1997 *Home Sweet Home,* Oktagon, Cologne (catalog)
De Klein à Warhol, Centre Georges Pompidou, Paris (catalog)
1999 *Robert Rauschenberg and James Rosenquist,* Museum of Fine Arts, St. Petersburg, Florida (catalog)

Collections:

Museum of Modern Art, New York; Whitney Museum, New York; Albright-Knox Art Gallery, Buffalo, New York; Chrysler Museum of Art, Norfolk, Virginia; Hirshhorn Museum and Sculpture Garden, Smithsonian Institution, Washington, D.C.; Museum of Contemporary Art, Chicago; Norton Simon Museum of Art, Pasadena, California; National Gallery of Canada, Ottawa; Tate Gallery, London; Centre Georges Pompidou, Paris.

Publications:

By ROSENQUIST: Books— *Time Dust, James Rosenquist: Complete Graphics 1962–1992,* Madrid 1992; *James Rosenquist,* with Roberto Damiani and Maria Masau Dan, Milan 1995. **Portfolio—** *Rosenquist: 6 Etchings,* Tampa, Florida 1976. **Articles—**statement in *Art in America* (New York), June 1963; statement in *Artnews* (New York), February 1964; statement in the *Partisan Review* (New York), Fall 1965; statement in *Rosenquist,* exhibition catalog, Paris 1968; interview with G. R. Swenson in *Metropolitan Museum of Art Bulletin* (New York), vol. 26, 1968; interview with J. Siegel in *Artforum* (New York), June 1972; ''Pop,'' interview with Phyllis Tuchman in *Artnews* (New York), May 1974; statement in *James Rosenquist: An Exhibition of Paintings 1961–73,* exhibition catalog, London 1974; ''Returned to Sender'' in *Artforum International,* vol. 33, April 1995.

On ROSENQUIST: Books—*Rosenquist,* exhibition pamphlet with an introduction by Tommaso Trini, Paris 1968; *James Rosenquist,* exhibition catalog with text by Marcia Tucker, New York 1972; *James Rosenquist: Gemälde, Räume, Graphik,* exhibition catalog with text by Evelyn Weiss, Cologne 1972; *James Rosenquist,* exhibition catalog with text by Wim A. L. Beeren, Amsterdam 1973; *James Rosenquist: An Exhibition of Paintings 1961–1973,* exhibition catalog with an introduction by David Sylvester, London 1974; *Black and White are Colors: Paintings of the 1950s-1970s,* exhibition catalog with a foreword by David Steadman and text by David S. Rubin, Claremont, California 1979; *James Rosenquist: Graphics Retrospective,* exhibition catalog with an introduction by Elayne H. Varian, Sarasota, Florida 1979; *Printed Art: A View of 2 Decades,* exhibition catalog, New York 1980; *American Prints 1879–1979,* exhibition catalog, London 1980; *Print Publishing in America,* exhibition catalog, Schiedam, Netherlands 1980; *James Rosenquist: Paintings from the 60s,* exhibition catalog, with text by Richard Shone, London 1982. **Articles—**''James Rosenquist: Militant Pop'' by Francesco Bonami in *Flash Art,* no. 165, Summer 1992; ''James Rosenquist: F-111'' by Douglas Coupland in *Artforum,* vol. 32, no. 8, April 1994; ''James Rosenquist'' by W.T. Dooley in *Art Papers,* vol. 18, September/October 1994; ''James Rosenquist: Flowers, Fish, and Females'' by Lisa M. Messinger in *The Metropolitan Museum of Art Bulletin,* vol. 54, Fall 1996; ''James Rosenquist: 6 Article Special Section'' in *Parkett,* no. 58, 2000.

* * *

Of all Pop artists, James Rosenquist was one who emerged from inside the commercial advertising scene rather than approaching it as a spectator. He had spent time working as a billboard painter in the Midwest before arriving in New York and meeting up with Rauschenberg, Johns and Kelly. Ever conscious of the brainwashing effect of giant images on the public mind, his paintings are frequently exposures of the means adopted. This often appears as an erotic sales punch embodied in a woman's lips—they can be Marilyn Monroe's—and makeup shades will be specifed, but the motive is not hightening the punch but illuminating its exploitation. Combinations of images, often in large scale, parade the vocabulary of persuasive identifications in publicity campaigns. This painting-out of the television or movie drama on the scale of billboard gives a monumental ''still'' effect more oblique than Lichtenstein's and in the early works such as ''The Light That Won't Fail'' (1961), the monochrome finish accentuates the projected ''soap opera'' association.

Paint on a single surface was not to be exclusive for Rosenquist's image transmission. He added wooden and Plexiglass structures to illustrate an ''exploded'' picture idea filched from commercial advertising pages. Often the source of his human faces appears by the inclusion of a section of the television tube and of sundry montage effects. Other giant compositions such as ''F-111'' (1965), the colossal panorama of a jet fighter hurtling across 86 feet of unrelated motives, including a Firestone tire, electric light bulbs, the atomic dust plume and Shirley Temple when young, inside a hairdryer with a background of blown-up spaghetti, is a fourwall wrap-around mural of contemporary authenticity. The large scale montage is given extra dimension by the inclusion of sections of moulded aluminium panels so the spectator and passers-by are reflected, giving surprise elements of movement and colour.

This activation of the picture by the spectator provides the ready-made kinetic ingredient very much at the heart of contemporary art exemplified by Rosenquist, for thus the picture-assemblage is an instant happening for whoever comes into its orbit. Dayglo and lead-based colours, designed to carry across city squares, at closer range have saturating power on the retina. How the Renaissance connection has been eliminated from painting completely is evident at its highest degree in Rosenquist for, as far as he is concerned, it was never there.

The overall even strength in Pop compositions is basic in all Rosenquist work—not ''this is how it is'' but ''this is how I make it'': bright, deadpan, noncommittal, uncommitted, it can be a close-up of a film star's ''facescape''; she is not a person, she is an apparatus for selling something, the cosmetic accessories or the smokes or a movie but only to the naive a symbol of sex or feminine attraction and then not for real; it glorifies devitalised life.

—G. S. Whittet

ROSLER, Martha

Nationality: American. **Education:** Brooklyn College of the City University of New York, B.A., 1965; University of California, San Diego, M.A., 1974. **Career:** Taught art, photography and film studies at many colleges and universities, including San Diego State University, 1975, 1977, 1978; San Francisco Art Institute, 1978; Nova Scotia College of Art and Design, Halifax, 1979; Rutgers University, New

Martha Rosler: Series *The Bowery in two inadequate descriptive systems,* 1974–75. Photo ©Geoffrey Clements. ©1998 Whitney Museum of American Art, New York. Collection of Whitney Museum of American Art, purchase, with funds from John L. Steffens.

Brunswick, 1980–90, 1998 to present; The Cooper Union, New York, 1981; Whitney Museum Independent Studies Program, 1982, 1990. **Awards:** National Endowment for the Arts Artist's Fellowship, Conceptual Art, 1975; National Endowment for the Arts Critic's Fellowship, 1976; National Endowment for the Arts Artist's Fellowship, Video, 1980; National Endowment for the Arts Artist's Fellowship, Video, 1983; LINE Artist's Book Grant, 1983; New York Foundation for the Arts Fellowship, Video, 1986; Honorable mention, Best Documentary, for *Born to Be Sold,* Thirteenth Atlanta Film and Video Festival, 1989; National Endowment for the Arts Artist's Fellowship, Photography, 1994; New York Foundation for the Arts Catalogue Grant in Photography, 1996. **Agent:** Gorney Bravin + Lee, 534 West 26th Street, New York, New York 10001; Galerie Christian Nagel, Richard-Wagner-Strasse 28, Cologne, Germany D-50674.

Selected Individual Exhibitions:

1975 The Kitchen (with Allan Sekula), New York
1977 *New American Filmmakers' Series,* Whitney Museum of American Art
1979 Anna Leonowens Gallery (with Allan Sekula), Nova Scotia College of Art & Design, Halifax
1981 *Watchwords of the Eighties,* Elisabeth Irwin High School, New York (toured)
1983 Institute of Contemporary Arts, London
1987 *Focus: Martha Rosler,* Institute of Contemporary Art, Boston
1989 *If You Lived Here. . . ,* DIA Art Foundation, New York
1990 *Housing Is a Human Right,* Museum of Modern Art, Oxford
1993 *In the Place of the Public,* Jay Gorney Modern Art, New York
1994 Palais des Beaux Arts, Brussels
1995 *II Bienal de Video,* Museo de Arte Contemporáneo, Santiago, Chile
1997 *Rights of Passage,* Galerie Anne de Villepoix, Paris
1999 *Martha Rosler: Positions in the Life World,* IKON Gallery, Birmingham, England (toured) (catalog)

Selected Group Exhibitions:

1976 *Art in the Mail,* toured various New Zealand galleries and museums
1977–78 *Selections from the Southland Video Anthology,* Everson Museum, Syracuse, New York (toured)
1980 *Issue!,* Institute of Contemporary Arts, London
1981 *Libres D'Artista/Artists' Books,* Centre de Documentaçió D'Art Actual (cdaa), Barcelona

1983 *American Video—Twenty Works,* Museum of Modern Art, New York (toured five Japanese cities)
1984–86 *New American Video Art: A Historical Survey, 1967–1980,* Whitney Museum of American Art, New York (toured)
1985 *New York: Ailleurs et Autrement,* ARC, Musée de l'Art Moderne à la Ville de Paris
1986 *Social Engagement: Women's Video in the '80s,* Whitney Museum of American Art, New York
1987 *Filmhuis,* The Hague, Holland
1987–88 *The Arts for Television,* Stedelijk Museum, Amsterdam (toured)
1988–90 *Committed to Print,* Museum of Modern Art, New York (toured)
1990 *Video and Myth,* Museum of Modern Art, New York
1991–93 *Reframing the Family,* Video Data Bank Touring Exhibition, School of the Art Institute of Chicago, Illinois (traveled to Institute of Contemporary Art, Boston, Massachusetts; DeCordova Museum and Sculpture Park, Lincoln, Massachusetts; University of California, Irvine)
1992–93 *Video: Two Decades,* Museum of Modern Art, New York
1993 *Desmontaje: Film, Video/Apropiación, Reciclaje—Demontage: Film, Video/Appropriation, Recycling,* IVAM, Institut Valencià d'Art Modern-Centre Julio González, Valencia (toured)
1995–96 *25 Years of Video Art,* Museum of Modern Art, New York (toured)
1996–97 *Views from Abroad II,* Museum für Moderne Kunst, Frankfurt, and the Whitney Museum, New York

Collections:

Australian National Gallery, Canberra; Finnish National Gallery, Helsinki; Kunstverein, Hamburg; Museu de Arte Moderna, Rio de Janeiro, Brazil; Museum of Modern Art, New York; National Gallery of Canada, Ottawa; San Francisco Museum of Modern Art, California; Victoria and Albert Museum, London; Whitney Museum of American Art, New York.

Public Installations:

Traveling Garage Sale, La Mamelle Gallery garage, San Francisco 1977; *Hollow Leg,* University of Colorado, Boulder 1983; Los Angeles Center for Photographic Studies and eztv. (video installation), Los Angeles 1986; *Foul Play in the Chicken House,* Long Beach Museum of Art, California 1986; San Francisco Camerawork (video installation), 1986; *Global Taste: A Meal in Three Courses* (video installation), Cornell Cinema, Ithaca, New York 1987; *If You Lived Here: Homelessness and Housing in St. Louis,* installation in the exhibition *Green Acres: Neo-Colonialism in the U.S.,* Washington University Gallery of Art, St. Louis, Missouri 1992.

Publications:

By ROSLER: Books—*Service: A Trilogy on Colonization,* New York 1978; *If You Lived Here. . . The City in Art, Theory, and Social Activism,* Seattle 1991; *In the Place of the Public/An der Stelle der Offentlichkeit: Observations of a Frequent Flyer/Beobachtungen einer Vielfliegerin,* Ostfildern, Germany 1998. **Articles—**''Interview with Martha Rosler'' by Jane Weinstock in *October,* no. 17, Summer 1981; ''Interview with Martha Rosler'' by Bruce Barber and Serge Guilbaut in *Parachute,* October 1981; ''Martha Rosler'' interview with Craig Owens in *Profile* (Chicago: Video Data Bank), vol. 5, no. 2, Spring 1986; ''Against Tame Expectations: An Interview with Martha Rosler'' by John Conomos in *Filmnews,* December 1987; ''In, Around, and Afterthoughts: On Documentary Photography'' in *The Contest of Meaning: Critical Histories of Photography,* edited by Richard Bolton, Cambridge, Massachusetts 1990.

On ROSLER: Books—*The Amazing Decade: Women and Performance Art in America, 1970–1983* edited by Moira Roth, Los Angeles, California 1983; *Postmodern Currents: Art and Artists in the Age of Electronic Media* by Margot Lovejoy, Ann Arbor, Michigan 1988; *Indiscretions: Avant-Garde Film, Video, & Feminism* by Patricia Mellencamp, Bloomington, Indiana 1990; *The Body and the Lens: Photography 1839 to the Present* by John Pultz, London 1995. **Articles—**''Martha Rosler's Video'' by Ruth Askey in *Artweek,* 4 June 1977; ''Dismantling Modernism, Reinventing Documentary (Notes on the Politics of Representation)'' by Allan Sekula in *Photography,* special issue of the *Massachusetts Review,* Winter 1979; ''Dislocated Women'' by Alan M. Brown in *Artweek,* 16 August 1980; ''From Gadget Video to Agit Video: Some Notes on Four Recent Video Works'' by Benjamin Buchloh in *Art Journal,* Fall 1985; ''Toward a New Social Documentary'' by Grant Kester in *Afterimage,* vol. 14, no. 8, March 1987; ''Living Room War'' by Brian Wallis in *Art in America,* February 1992; ''Martha Rosler: Crossing Borders'' by Laura Cottingham in *Frieze,* November/December 1993; ''Laughing Matters Out of Place: Obscenity, Dirt and Video'' by Ernest Larsen in *Exposure,* vol. 29, no. 2–3, 1994; ''Alternative America'' by Eleanor Heartney in *Art in America,* June 1996; ''Martha Rosler'' by Alexander Alberro in *Artforum,* April 1997; essay by Nancy Roth in *Afterimage,* vol. 27, no. 1, July-August 1999; ''Martha Rosler in Conversation: Packaging the Public Sphere'' by Stephen Wright in *Parachute,* no. 97, January-March 2000.

* * *

Though Martha Rosler is often referred to as a political artist, for her, activism and aesthetics are inextricably bound. From the very beginning of her career in the 1960s, Rosler has demonstrated a creative and intelligent commitment to work that theorizes the insistent role of systems of power in personal relationships and individual lives. Her use of startling and provocative juxtapositions critiques everything from commodity display to nuclear proliferation, media obsession, surveillance, and post-colonial imperialism. Rosler's work with photography, video, performance, installation, and critical writing reveals the breadth and value of her contributions to feminist theory and leftist politics and her dedication to educating the public. Purposely refusing a signature style, Rosler's work consistently represents the political resonances that permeate and construct everyday experience. Indeed, Rosler emphatically rejects apotheosizing the artist figure as a ''coherent subjectivity'' whose persona is invested in the production of singular ''authentic'' vision.

Entitled *Martha Rosler: Positions in the Life World* (1999–2000), her first career retrospective is also her first major showing in the United States, though Rosler received accolades early on in the form of a 1975 National Endowment for the Arts Artist's Fellowship, a

1976 NEA Art Critic's Fellowship, and a 1994 NEA Artist's Fellowship in photography. Her photographs and videos are included in an estimated 140 public collections, and her performances, one-person and group shows, and installations have been featured all over the globe. As an undergraduate and graduate student, Rosler followed a course of study that trained her as an abstract expressionist painter. However, her objections to painting's associations with high art and her attraction to working with images and text led her to abandon traditional modes of artistic expression and engage in media that would not require her to cater to the demands of the mainstream art world. Early on, Rosler found inspiration in the work of German dramatist and theorist Bertolt Brecht and French New Wave director Jean-Luc Godard, whose cinematic style references its own mediation and production of ''reality'' for the spectator.

Though Rosler tackles complex political power systems, she ultimately seeks to raise awareness about the ubiquitous and subliminal nature of these vast structures and to transform what it means to flip through a beauty magazine, watch the evening news, or read a cook book. Such quotidian acts, she suggests, are constructed by and shot through with ideological meaning and socioeconomic significance. Much of Rosler's work betrays the constructedness of the profitable image industry, particularly as it enables certain classes to presume a false separation from the realities of war, hunger, and forced labor. Luxurious domestic interiors meet the geopolitical realities of war-torn Vietnam in Rosler's ''Bringing the War Home'' and ''Bringing the War Home: House Beautiful'' (1967–72). Like all of Rosler's art, these photomontages demonstrate radical and poignant dissonances that engage the viewer on multiple interpretive levels. This project wholly rejects the myth of sheltered and apolitical American domestic space by suggesting that the war in Vietnam, despite its geographic distance, remained a spectral presence in the private homes of post-colonial America. Drawn from images in *Life* and other magazines, the montages starkly juxtapose anguished faces and upscale living decor, grisly war tableaux and modernist sculptures, pristine kitchens and prowling GIs. Given the inflammatory nature of these images, they were, like much of Rosler's work, disseminated through local underground newspapers.

In one of her earliest feminist works, ''Body Beautiful, or Beauty Knows No Pain,'' (1966–72) Rosler offers a meditation upon the intersectionality of soft-core pornography and glossy fashion magazines. Fragments of Playboy nudes intersect with refrigerators and cut-out breasts sit awkwardly montaged onto lingerie models, creating a phantasmagoric collage of female bodily commodification. In photomontaging such images, this work offers a disquieting experience to its audience, categorically disavowing any distinction between these equally exploitative and repressive media.

Rosler's video art, arguably her most enduring work, figures centrally in her critique of patriarchal regimes as they irresponsibly perpetuate beauty standards and delimit female identity and mobility. In such work, Rosler figures the female body as a site of intersecting vectors of power. Based upon a live performance at University of California, San Diego, *Vital Statistics of a Citizen, Simply Obtained* (1973) features the clinical interrogation of a stripped Rosler, her individual parts measured and recorded by men in white medical uniforms. Soon after, Rosler again played the protagonist in *A budding gourmet* (1974) and *Semiotics of the Kitchen* (1975), a video that uses poignant humor to uncover the profound frustration of women confined to domestic space. Dramatizing women's rage through the unorthodox use of kitchen utensils, *Semiotics* endures as a signal work of the feminist movement.

Rosler's persistent interest in the politics of theoretical and relational space may perhaps be traced to her early image and text installation ''The Bowery'' in two inadequate descriptive systems (1974–75). In many ways this work previews Rosler's more recent work on public space, homelessness, and bourgeois society. In ''Bowery'' Rosler sought specifically to criticize what she calls ''liberal humanist documentary'' that engages the voyeuristic gaze and perpetuates stereotypes of street culture. Juxtaposing text panels featuring 170 slang words for derelicts with unpeopled black-and-white shots of lower Manhattan, Rosler troubles the idea that social documentary can represent the lives of the neighborhood's inhabitants. In identifying text and image as ''inadequate,'' Rosler confronts the failure of the art system to transcend the individual viewpoint of the one who records ''social reality.'' This integral part of Rosler's oeuvre marks the beginning of a career in deconstructing descriptive systems, spatiality, and social realist documentary photography. Her pivotal essay ''In, Around, or Afterthoughts: On Documentary Photography'' (1990), part of an impressive body of critical writings, offers further theoretical scrutiny of what she calls documentary's ''exoticism, tourism, voyeurism, psychologism . . . and careerism.'' Filmed with a handheld Super-8 camera, *Secrets From the Street: No Disclosure* (1980) analyzes the Mission District of San Francisco as a space in which class tension and social power play out. Also a metacommentary on artistic production, this piece draws attention to the act of recording and reminds the viewer of the constitutive presence of the camera.

In *The Place of the Public* (1990), a site installation, video and book, Rosler analyzes the discursive intersection of socially constituted space, air travel, and the architecture of transportation. Rosler identifies the airport terminal as the quintessentially postmodern space, focusing in particular upon the way that bodies are moved through elaborate tunnel systems and other modes of transport ''reminiscent of biological organisms.'' Rosler further suggests that the design and logistics of the terminal and its associated spaces foster feelings of dislocation and alienation in the traveler. In the installation itself, Rosler simulated the space of the airport terminal and included text, audio speakers, and large scale color photographs to interrogate the surreality of this ''world apart.'' The airport environment is finally seen as a profoundly contrived space in which operational interests are foremost, and the only anodynes to feelings of replaceability and transitoriness are illusion and a philosophy of ''see, buy, fly.''

In her systemic critique of and intellectual engagement with the entrenched products of institutional ideology, Rosler remains hopeful, insisting: ''Anybody who believes in social transformation is a utopian.'' Wholly rejecting nostalgia or complacent retreats into the aesthetic dimension of artistic production, Rosler's work stages a productive balance between critical distance and passionate engagement, utopianism and skepticism.

—Annalisa Zox-Weaver

ROTELLA, Mimmo

Nationality: Italian. **Born:** Domenico Rotella in Catanzaro, Calabria, 17 October 1918. **Education:** Studied at the Academy of Fine Art, Naples. **Family:** Married Inna Agarounova, 1991; one child: Asya, 1993. **Career:** Independent artist, living in Rome, 1949–61, in Paris, 1961–80, and in Milan since 1980: first ''epistaltici'' phonetic poems,

1949; first torn paper works, 1954; first Mec Art (mechanically produced) works, 1963. Artist in residence, University of Missouri, Kansas City, 1951–52. Visiting lecturer, Theresa College, Kansas City, 1952; School of Visual Arts, New York, 1962; and University of Havana, Cuba, 1986. Member, Pierre Restany's Nouveaux Réalistes group of artists, Paris, 1961. **Awards:** Fulbright fellowship, 1951; conferred the title *Officiel des Arts et des Lettres* by French Minister of Culture, 1992. **Agent:** Studio Marconi, Via Tadino 15, 21024 Milan, Italy. **Web site:** http://www.mimmorotella.it.

Individual Exhibitions:

1951 Galleria Chiurazzi, Rome
1952 William Rockhill Nelson Gallery, Kansas City, Missouri
1955 Galleria del Naviglio, Milan
1957 Galerie Beno, Zurich
Institute of Contemporary Arts, London
Galleria del Cavellino, Venice
Galleria del Naviglio, Milan
Galleria Selecta, Rome
1958 Wittenborn Gallery, New York
Galleria del Naviglio, Milan
1959 Galleria La Salita, Rome
1961 Galleria La Salita, Rome
1962 Galerie J, Paris
Seven Arts Gallery, London
Galeria Bonino, Buenos Aires
Galleria del Leone, Venice
1963 Galleria Apollinaire, Milan
Galleria del Leone, Venice
Galerie Passepartout, Copenhagen
1964 *Biennale,* Venice
1965 Galleria La Tartaruga, Rome
Galerie J, Paris
1966 Galleria La Tartaruga, Rome
Salon la Teatro, Venice
Galleria del Naviglio, Milan
Galleria Il Punto, Turin
1967 Galerie 20, Amsterdam
Galerie Ricke, Cologne
1969 Galleria del Naviglio, Milan
Galleria Arco d'Alibert, Rome
Rotella 1954–1968, Galerie Fitzroy, Brussels
Studio San Andrea, Milan
1971 Galerie Mathias Fels, Paris
1973 Studio Bellini, Milan
Galerie Marquet, Paris
1974 Galerie Craven, Paris
Galerie J. Ferrero, Paris
Galerie Inter Arts, Lyon
Galleria dell'Ariete, Milan
1975 Galerie des Deux Rues, St. Tropez, France
Rotonda della Besana, Milan
1978 *Opere dal 1958–75,* Galleria Civica d'Arte Moderna, Castello di Portofino, Italy
Padiglione d'Arte Contemporanea, Ferrara, Italy
1981 Studio Marconi, Milan
Galerie Denise René, Paris
1984 Studio Marconi, Milan
1985 Galerie Reckermann, Cologne
1986 Galleria Niccoli, Parma, Italy
1987 Pascal de Sarthe Gallery, San Francisco
Galerie Lavignes-Bastille, Paris
Fiac '87, Paris
Art Köln, Cologne
Rotella Anni '80, Galleria Mara Coccia, Rome
1988 *Lamieri 1987,* Studio Marconi, Milano
Galerie 44, Dusseldorf
Galerie Keeser-Bohbot, Hamburg
1989 DAAD, Berlin
Galerie Reckermann, Cologne
1990 Galerie Beaubourg, Paris
Galerie Keeser-Bohbot, Hamburg
Galerie Tornvall, Stockholm
1991 Galerie Thorigny, Paris
Salvatore Ala Gallery, New York
Ready-Made 1990–91, Studio Marconi, Milano
1992 Galerie Reckermann, Cologne
Mimmo Rotella, Per Mari e Monti Associazione Culturale, Macerata (catalog)
1993 *Rotella à Dijon,* Fonds Regional d'Art Contemporain, Dijon
Mimmo Rotella à Dijon, Ecole National des Beaux-Arts, Dijon
1994 *Rotella à Berlino,* Museo delle Belle Art, Bosto Arsizio
Museum Ludwig, Cologne (catalog)
Galerie Keeser, Hamburg (retrospective)
1996 *Rotella,* Marisa Del Re Gallery, New York (catalog)
Rotella, Museo Civico, Palazzo Zagarese, Rende, Cosenza, Italy (catalog)
Mimmo Rotella, Galerie Dionne, Paris (catalog)
1998 *Mimmo Rotella,* Württembergischer Kunstverein, Stuttgart, Germany (also Kunstverein Braunschweig, Germany) (catalog)
1999 *Mimmo Rotella: L'Arte Oggi,* Galleria Giò Marconi, Milan (catalog)
Mimmo Rotella: Rétrospective, Musée d'Art Moderne et d'Art Contemporain, Milan (catalog)
Mimmo Rotella: Rétrospective, Musée d'Art Moderne et d'Art Contemporain, Nice (catalog)
2000 *Fashion and Flowers,* Charles Cowles Gallery, New York
History of an Idea, Monumental Complex of the S. Giovanni, Catanzaro, Italy

Selected Group Exhibitions:

1949 *Salon des Réalités Nouvelles,* Paris
1959 *International Print Biennale,* Ljubljana, Yugoslavia
1961 *The Art of Assemblage,* Museum of Modern Art, New York (travelled to the Museum of Contemporary Art, Dallas, and the San Francisco Museum of Art)
1963 *L'Art et L'Ecriture,* Staatliche Kunsthalle, Baden-Baden, West Germany (travelled to the Stedelijk Museum, Amsterdam)
1964 *Pop Art/Nouveau Réalisme,* Palais des Beaux-Arts, Brussels
1971 *Décollages,* Staatsgalerie, Stuttgart
1977 *3 Villes/3 Collections,* Centre Georges Pompidou, Paris
1982 *Registrazione di Frequenze,* Galleria d'Arte Moderna, Bologna

1984 *Ecritures dans la peinture,* Villa Arson, Nice, France
1986 *Arte italiana degli anni Sessanta,* Castello di Rivoli, Turin
1990 *Art et Pub,* Centre Georges Pompidou, Paris
High and Low, Museum of Modern Art, New York
1994 *Italian Metamorphosis,* Guggenheim Museum, New York
Murmures des Rues, Centre d'Histoire de l'Art Contemporain, Rennes (catalog)
Spuren der Grosstadt, Museum Ludwig, Cologne (catalog)
1996 *Face'l'Histoire,* Centre Georges Pompidou, Paris
Halls of Mirrors, Museum of Contemporary Art, Los Angeles
Originale Multiplo, Galleria Manzoni, Milan (catalog)
1997 *De Klein à Warhol,* Centre Georges Pompidou, Paris (catalog)
1998 *Die Kunst des Zerreissens,* Stiftung Hans Ar, Rolandseck (catalog)

Collections:

Galleria Nazionale d'Arte Moderna, Rome; Centre Georges Pompidou, Paris; Museu de Arte Moderna, Sao Paulo; University of Missouri, Kansas City; Museum of Contemporary Art, Chicago; Fort Lauderdale Museum of Art, Florida; Stedelijk Museum, Amsterdam; Museum Ludwig, Cologne; Museum Moderner Kunst, Vienna; Museum of Modern Art, Tel Aviv; Museo d'Arte Moderna, Milan; Musée d'Art Moderne de la Ville, Paris; Hara Museum, Tokyo.

Publications:

By ROTELLA: Books—*Autorotella,* Milan 1972; *Mimmo Rotella,* with Giovanni Joppolo, Paris 1997. **Articles**—''Cosi'' in *Rotella,* exhibition catalog, Rome 1957; ''Il mondo di immagini violentissime che i circonando'' in *Alternative Attuali,* exhibition catalog, L'Aquila, Italy 1962; ''Caro le Noci'' in *Rotella: Dal décollage alla nuova immagine* by Pierre Restany, Milan 1963. **Recordings**—*Poemi fonetici: 1949–75,* Milan 1975.

On ROTELLA: Books—*Rotella,* exhibition catalog with text by Paul Garner, Kansas City, Missouri 1952; *Rotella,* exhibition catalog with text by Nello Ponente, Milan 1958; *Rotella,* exhibition catalog with text by Emmilio Villa, Rome 1959; *Rotella,* exhibition catalog with text by Pierre Restany, Rome 1961; *Rotella: Dal décollage alla nuova immagine* by Pierre Restany, Milan 1963; *Les Nouveaux Réalistes* by Pierre Restany, Paris 1968; *Rotella: 1954–1968,* exhibition catalog with text by Otto Hahn, Brussels 1969; *Rotella* by Tommaso Trini, Milan 1974; *Rotella: Opere dal 1958–75,* exhibition catalog with text by Pierre Restany, Portofino, Italy 1978; *Vitalità del negativo nell'arte italiana: 1960–1970* by M. Calvesi, G. Dorfles, and A. Bonito Oliva, Turin 1980; *Le Blanks de Rotella,* exhibition catalog with text by Pierre Restany, Milan 1984; *1960: Les Nouveaux Réalistes,* exhibition catalog with text by Pierre Restany, Paris 1986. **Articles**—''Mimmo Rotella: L'Uomo Che Farebbe di Roma un Decollage'' by Francesca Comisso in *Arte,* no. 291, November 1997; ''Rotella in Nice: A Rebel and Clinical Gaze'' by Giovanni Joppolo in *Cimaise,* vol. 46, no. 262, November/December 1999; ''Rotella: La Societa dei Consumi Vista da un Monello di Strada'' by Alessandra Redaelli in *Arte,* no. 317, January 2000.

*

Collage, unfortunately, has a place in history and an origin and development in both earlier and contemporary art. I say unfortunately because I should have wished to have invented collage myself. In my childhood, the gray skies, the gray houses, the faces, the roads, the dust, the feeling, all the immense gray things of the South of Italy filled me with a sense of urgency—a rage—to invent colors and to paste them on certain restricted spaces of my fantasy. Then I began to express myself with tissue paper. All this about memories of childhood is an ingenuous reference, a literary presumption. But the rage remains. To rip posters from the walls is the only act of real evaluation, the only protest against a society that has lost its taste for the mutations and transformations of the extraordinary.

I paste posters together, then I rip them: new forms are born, unforeseeably. I have abandoned easel painting in order to make this protest. If I had the powers of Samson, I would paste Piazza di Spagna with certain of its morbid and tender autumnal tints on the red squares of the Gianiculum at sunset. You will say: ''This is all rambling. Explain your work, rather, for it is not very intelligible.'' Very well. It is concerned with a research—a research that places its reliance not in the aesthetic but in the unforeseeable, in the very humors of the texture. It is like a trumpet, a drum, or a saxophone that plays by itself. I place my reliance in the trumpet, the drum, and the saxophone. I have no wish to be eccentric, otherwise I would dress in the street clothes of the Napoleonic era. Eccentricity in our time is reactionary; the truth lies, instead, in a hope for the future.

Were I to paste up colors in various shapes on pieces of cardboard, selecting them as if from an easel, I should then be resolving simple problems of taste with the help of an artisan's technique. I rip posters, first from the walls, then from the base of the composition: how much taste, how much fantasy, how much interest accumulates, thrusting forward and drawing near from the first to the last rip. It is not a matter of juxtaposing abstract colors but of colors with a life of their own, with a spirit, with—so to speak—a vitality. If I pass from researches into the nature of color to researches into the nature of texture, then the meanings transform themselves and become dramatic.

How will the earth be after the end of the world? It may be as smooth and as cold as a surface of marble, rigged by canals as contorted as trails in the wilderness. Collage suggests a yellow or a yellowish patina for this geography of the deluge: and the patina is a hope.

—Mimmo Rotella

* * *

Mimmo Rotella's contribution to modern art has been the development of the Cubist collage technique to a formula known as *decollage,* or ''double collage,'' also followed by the French *affichistes,* by which posters stripped from walls are transferred onto the canvas, reduced or decomposed by further mutilation. This was a comparatively late development, when the artist was over 30, working and living in Rome after a period of study in the United States under a Fulbright fellowship.

In America, Rotella had experimented with phonetic poems, painted a huge mural at the University of Missouri in Kansas City, and held an exhibition in the same town. It may be that this contact with the United States influenced his interest in urban poster sites, while, back in postwar Italy, these mutilated, processed images presented both a symbol of contemporary conditions and the means of expressing them.

The earliest decollages were really substitutes for abstract painting, using the color and texture of the papers to establish a sensitive, carefully balanced, atmospheric image, not unlike the work of Schwitters. There was little of the social comment of a collagist such as Raoul Haussmann or the psychological, surrealistic exploitation of Max Ernst. Rotella's work, at this stage, was colorful and dramatic—growing more and more assured, intricate, brilliant—exploiting to the full the maximum potential of the medium. It is interesting, for instance, to note the transitions from hot colors to futuristic rhythmic detail and then changes to broad areas of tone.

By 1960 Rotella reverted to a calmer, less active formula—one of broad areas of single colors and large gestural shapes rather than the busy intricacy of the first period. At this stage he also incorporated direct narrative or moral messages; this invoked the exploitation of photographic images, which were allowed to dominate and direct the picture, whereas in the past he had remained strictly abstract. Suggestions of American pop art, notably of the works of Andy Warhol, were inevitable, especially in the manipulation of film star faces, but Rotella always remained more complex and painterly than the American artist.

In the mid-1960s a major change of style and purpose resulted in direct simplicity: single, powerful, newspaper images of the death of a pope or a Vietnam soldier, reproductions of magazine covers, portraits of fellow artists, advertisement still lifes. This relied far more on single photographic or reproducible images, heralding the new photorealistic school of fellow painters. Rotella's *nouveau realism* of photo-reportages represent a further break from traditional Western techniques and an anxiety regarding images of urban society. He therefore involved himself in mass mythology and mechanical operations; indeed he is credited with inventing the term *mecart* to describe this aesthetic philosophy.

At one period of his career, in the early 1960s, Rotella involved himself in the assemblage of objects, a form of junk-art, extending the process of *object trouvés* from the city walls to its streets. This Duchamp-like process ranged from manufactured ready-mades, like toy balls and window models displaying brassieres, to complex, semi-realistic assemblages of flea market rubbish. These works appeared, in fact, at the turning point in Rotella's career, when he was about to abandon the painterly, sensitive, often brilliant manipulations of color and texture for the sober, restrained, direct "mechanical" photo-reportage.

—Charles Spencer

ROTH, Dieter

Nationality: Swiss. **Born:** Karl-Dietrich Roth, of Swiss and German parents, in Hannover, Germany, 21 April 1930; moved with his parents to Switzerland, 1943. **Education:** Hannover, 1936–43; in classical secondary school in Zurich, 1943–46, and in St. Gallen, 1946–47; apprentice graphic designer, Studio Friedrich Wüthrich, Berne, 1947–51; studied lithography, under Eugen Jordi, Kehrsatz, 1950: associated closely with artists Franz Eggenschwiler and Paul Talman, Berne, 1947–51. **Family:** Married Sigridur Björnsdöttir in 1957 (separated, 1964); children: Karl, Björn and Vera. **Career:** Independent artist, in Bern, 1951–56, Copenhagen, 1956–59, subsequently in Reykjavík, Iceland, Stuttgart, Germany, and in Mols, Switzerland, 1958–84; lived in Basel, 1984–1998: first collages and woodcuts, 1949; first films and baked food sculptures, 1954; works with goldsmiths and architects, 1957–58; with editions Hansjörg Mayer, Stuttgart, London and Reykjavík, 1968–1981; collaborations with artists Stefan Wewerka, 1970, Arnulf Rainer, 1973–76, Richard Hamilton, 1975–77; sound recordings and concerts, with Gerhard Rühm, Oswald Wiener and others, since 1973. Also worked occasionally as builder/ decorator, Berne, 1951–60; graphic designer, Geigy Corporation, New York, 1959; in Ragner Kjartansson's ceramic workshop, Reykjavík, 1960; and in Karl Gerstner/Markus Kutter advertising agency, Basel, 1960 and 1968. Founder-editor, *Spirale* magazine, Berne, 1953; director, with Rolf Iseli, Peter Meier and Walter Vögeli, Gallery 33, Bern, 1954; founder, with Elinar Bragi, Forlag ed editions, Reykjavík, 1957–58; founder-designer, with Magnus Palsson and Manfred Vilhjamsson, Küla furniture shop, Reykjavík, 1960; co-publisher, Edition Hansjörg Mayer, Stuttgart, London and Reykjavík, 1968–81; founder, with Karl Schulz, Schepperts Press, Braunschweig, 1970–77; founder, Dieter Roth's Family Press, and Dieter Roth Pictures, 1974; founder *Review for Everything,* 1975; founder, *Kopiks* magazine, Bali, 1984. Visiting critic 1959, and instructor 1964, Yale University, New Haven, Connecticut; instructor, Rhode Island School of Design, Providence, 1965; Watford School of Art, London, 1968; and Staatliche Kunstakademie, Dusseldorf, 1968–70. **Awards:** Kiefer-Hablitzel Painting Prize, Bern, 1954; Gold Medal, *San Francisco Textile Fair, 1956;* William and Norma Copley Award, Chicago 1960; Kunstpreis der Stadt Iserlohn, 1969; First Prize, *International Print Biennale,* Grenchen, 1973; Rembrandt Prize, Goethe-Foundation, Basel, 1982; Kunstpreis der Nord/LB, Hannover, 1984; Charles Nypels Prize, Maastricht, 1986. **Agent:** Nolan/Eckman Gallery, 560 Broadway, New York, New York, 10012; Petersburg Press, P.O. Box 2238, New York, New York 10101; Margarete Roeder Gallery, 545 Broadway, New York, New York, 10012. **Died:** Basel, Switzerland, 5 June 1998.

Individual Exhibitions:

1958 Mokka Kaffi, Reykjavík
1960 Galerie Koepcke, Copenhagen (with Christian Megert)
1963 Galerie Koepcke, Copenhagen
1964 Philadelphia Museum School of Art
1967 Galerie Zwirner, Cologne (with Dorothy Iannone)
Galerie der Edition Hansjörg Mayer, Stuttgart
1968 Galerie Zwirner, Cologne
Galerie Handschin, Basel
Galerie Neuendorf, Hamburg
Galerie René Block, West Berlin
Galerie Tobies und Silex, Cologne (with Stefan Wewerka)
1969 Galerie Ernst, Hannover
Eugenia Butler Gallery, Los Angeles
Galerie Hake, Cologne
Art Intermedia Cologne
Galerie Muller, Stuttgart
1970 Galerie Werner, Copenhagen
Galerie Kummel, Cologne (with Stefan Wewerka)
Galerie Mikro, West Berlin (with Stefan Wewerka)
1971 Galerie Toni Gerber, Bern
Art Intermedia, Cologne
Ziegler Editionen und Graphik, Zurich

Eat-Art Galerie, Dusseldorf
Universitat, Kiel
Langenbacher und Wankmiller, Lucerne
Museum Haus Lange, Krefeld, West Germany
Von-der-Heydt Museum, Wuppertal, West Germany (with Stefan Wewerka)

1972 Haags Gemeentemuseum, The Hague
Kunsthalle, Basel
Helmhaus, Zurich
Kunsthalle, Baden-Baden, West Germany
Galerie Grunangergasse, Vienna
Richard Foncke Gallery, Ghent
Museum Haus Lange, Krefeld, West Germany
Galerie 2, Stuttgart
Galerie Kammer, Hamburg
Eat-Art Galerie, Dusseldorf

1973 Hayward Gallery, London
European Gallery, San Francisco
Galerie Meyer-Ellinger, Frankfurt
Galerie Steinmetz, Bonn
Vancouver Art Gallery
Kunstverein, Braunschweig, West Germany
Akademie der Künste, West Berlin
Kunsthalle, Dusseldorf

1974 Kunstverein, Mannheim
Galerie Steinmetz, Bonn
Galerie Kammer, Hamburg
Langenbacher und Wankmiller, Lucerne
Manus-Presse, Stuttgart
Kestner-Gesellschaft, Hannover
Kunstverein, Hamburg

1975 Stedelijk Museum, Amsterdam
Galerie Steinmetz, Bonn
Galerie Bama, Paris
De Moriaan, den Bosch, Netherlands
Galleria il Capricorno, Venice
Galerie Grunangergasse, Vienna
Dieter Roth Pictures, Hamburg
Galerie Renee Ziegler, Zurich
Gallery Ariadne, New York (with Arnulf Rainer)
Galerie Hoss, Stuttgart

1976 Galleri Dierks, Aarhus, Denmark
Kulturhaus, Graz, Austria (with Arnulf Rainer)
Galerie Kalb, Vienna
Galerie Buchmann, St. Gallen, Switzerland
Galeria Cadaques, Cadaques, Spain (with Richard Hamilton)
Kaiser-Wilhelm-Museum, Krefeld, West Germany
British Council Institute, Barcelona (with Richard Hamilton)
Galerie im Reuchlinhaus, Pforzheim, West Germany
Galerie am Jakobsbrunnen, Stuttgart
Stadtmuseum, Solothurn, Switzerland
Turnpike Gallery, Leigh, Lancashire, England (with Richard Hamilton)

1977 Institute of Contemporary Arts, London (with Richard Hamilton)
Pari e Dispari, Cavriago, Italy
Galerie Fassbender, Munich
Galerie Handschin, Basel
Galerie Stahli, Zurich
Galery 44, Kaarst, West Germany
Galerie Steinmetz, Bonn
Haags Gemeentemuseum, The Hague (with Richard Hamilton)
Junior-Galerie, Dusseldorf (with Richard Hamilton)
Galeria Cadaques, Cadaques, Spain (with Karl and Björn Roth)
Print Gallery Pieter Brattinga, Amsterdam
Galeria Eude, Barcelona (with Richard Hamilton)
Aagauer Kunsthaus, Aarau, Switzerland (with Richard Hamilton)
Fundacio Joan Miró, Barcelona (with Richard Hamilton)

1978 Carl Solway Gallery, New York (with Richard Hamilton)
Waddington and Tooth Galleries, London (with Richard Hamilton)
Galerie Buchmann, St. Gallen, Switzerland
Galerie Anton Meier, Geneva
Galerie Handschin, Basel
Whitworth Art Gallery, Manchester (with Richard Hamilton)
Galerie Cadaques, Cadaques, Spain (with Richard Hamilton)
Galeria Maeght, Barcelona (with Richard Hamilton)
Galerie Northelfer, West Berlin
Galerie Handschin, Basel
Ulmer Museum, Ulm, West Germany

1979 Backworks, New York
Stempelplaats, Amsterdam
Kunsthalle, Bielefeld, West Germany (with Richard Hamilton)
Galerie René Block, West Berlin (with Richard Hamilton)
Galerie Klewan, Munich (with Arnulf Rainer)
Staatsgalerie, Stuttgart
Galerie Holtmann, Hannover

1980 Kunstmuseum, Lucerne
Langenbacher und Wankmiller, Lucerne
Galerie Holtman, Hannover (with Richard Hamilton)
Haags Gemeentemuseum, The Hague
Galerie Buchmann, St. Gallen, Switzerland (with Arnulf Rainer)

1981 Galerie Buchmann, St. Gallen, Switzerland
Galerie Holtmann, Cologne
Helmhaus, Zurich
Galerie Littman, Basel

1982 Galerie Bama, Paris
Kunstmuseum, Basel
Bahnhof Buffet SBB, Basel
Galerie Klewan, Munich
Swiss Pavilion, at the *Biennale,* Venice
Galerie Toni Gerber, Bern
Buchhandlung Niedlich, Stuttgart
Galerie Kurt Kalb/Kunstbuchhandlung Judith Ortner, Vienna
Galerie Hummel, Vienna
Nýlistasafnid, Reykjavík
Roosenhaus, Hamburg

1983 Reinhard Onnasch Ausstellugen, West Berlin
Holderbank Management und Beratung, Holderbank, Switzerland

Antiquariat Walter Wögenstein, Vienna
Kunstverein, Bonn
Galerie Handschin, Basel
Institut für Kunstgeschichte, Vienna University

1984 Museum of Contemporary Art, Chicago
Petersen Galerie, West Berlin (with Björn Roth and others)

1985 Herzog Anton Ulrich Museum, Braunschweig, West Germany
Petersen Galerie, West Berlin (with D. Roth Verlag)
Loft, Munich (with D. Roth Verlag)
Hegenheimerstrasse 24, Basel (with D. Roth Verlag)
Burckhardt und Partner, Basel
Galerie Priska Meier, Zell, Switzerland (with Björn and Vera Roth)
Hegenheimerstrasse 24, Basel (with Björn Roth)

1986 Galerie Marlene Frei, Zurich
Museum für Gegenwartskunst, Basel
Nigel Greenwood Books, London
Rhode Island School of Design, Providence
Galerie Marlene Frei, Zurich (with Björn Roth and Ingrid Wiener)
Holderbank Management und Beratung, Holderbank, Switzerland
Centre Régional d'Art Contemporain Midi-Pyrenees, Labège, France
Hegenheimerstrasse 24, Basel
Galerie Portikus, Frankfurt

1989 Galerie Littmann, Basel

1990 David Nolan Gallery, New York
Karsten Schubert Gallery, London (with Richard Hamilton)

1993 Kurt Kalb, Vienna

1994 Nýlistasafu, Reykjavík
Unikate, Multiples, Skulpturen, Graphik, Wolfgang Werner KG, Berlin (catalog)

1995 *Werke 1951–1961,* Das Museum, Solothurn, Switzerland (catalog)

1998 Nolan/Eckman Gallery, New York
Prints and Books 1949–1979, Graphische Sammlung Albertina, Cologne (catalog)

1999 *Art is Life/Life is Art,* University of Iowa Museum of Art, Iowa City (catalog)
Dieter Roth: Printed Pressed Bound, Goldie Paley Gallery, Moore College of Art and Design, Philadelphia (catalog)

2000 *Die Haut der Welt,* Staatsgalerie Stuttgart, Germany (catalog)

Selected Group Exhibitions:

1955 *Junge Berner Kunstler,* Kunsthalle, Bern
1959 *Edition MAT,* Société d'Art St. Germain-de-Près, Paris
1960 *festival d'art d'avantgarde,* Paris
1961 *Bewogen Beweging,* Stedelijk Museum, Amsterdam
1965 *Artist's Key Club,* American Theater for Poets, New York
1968 *Edition Hansjörg Mayer,* Haags Geementemuseum, The Hague
1969 *Fründ Friends Freunde und Freunde,* Kunsthalle, Bern
1972 *Amsterdam-Paris-Dusseldorf,* Guggenheim Museum, New York
1986 *Bein i köldu ofni,* Nordiskt Konstcentrum, Sveaborg, Finland
1990 Collection Oskar Schmid, Vienna
1995 *Dieter Roth, Björn Roth: Wiener Secession,* Die Secession, Vienna (catalog)
1996 *D'une Oeuvre l'Autre,* Musée Royal de Mariemont, Morlanwelz (catalog)
1999 *Begegnungen,* Sprengel Museum, Hannover (catalog)
2000 *48th Venice Biennale,* Italy

Collections:

Kunsthaus, Zurich; Stedelijk Museum, Amsterdam; Museum Haus Lange, Krefeld, Germany; Tate Gallery, London; Moderna Museet, Stockholm; Louisiana Museum, Humlebaek, Denmark; Museum des 20. Jahrhunderts, Vienna; Museum für Gegenswartskunst, Basel; Nýlistasafu, Reykjavík.

Publications:

By ROTH: Books—*Bilderbuch,* Reykjavík 1956; *Kinderbuch,* Reykjavík 1957; *Book,* Reykjavík and Paris, 1968; *Ideogramme,* Darmstadt 1959; *Bok 1956–59,* Reykjavík 1959; *Bok 2a,* Reykjavík 1960; *Bok 2b,* Reykjavík 1961; *Bok 4a,* Reykjavík 1961; *Bok 5,* Reykjavík 1961; *Bok 3a,* Reykjavík 1961, 1981; *Bok 3b,* Reykjavík 1961; *Bok 3c,* Reykjavík 1961, Mosfellssveit 1981; *Bok 3d,* Reykjavík 1961; *Daily Mirror Book,* Reykjavík 1961; *Literaturwurst,* book/object, Reykjavík 1961, West Berlin 1970; *Daglegt Bull/Daily Bul, no. 8,* La Louvière, Belgium 1961; *Book AC 1958–59,* New Haven 1964; *Quadratblatt,* Hilversum, Netherlands 1965; *Kölner Divisionen: 7 August 65,* Cologne 1965; *Schneewittchen,* Cologne 1965; *Quick von Dieter Roth 1961–65,* Reykjavík 1965; *Scheisse: Neue Gedichte von Dieter Roth,* with an appendix by Al Fabri, Providence, Rhode Island 1966; *Copley Buch,* Chicago 1966; *Die Blaue Flut,* Stuttgart 1967; *Mundunculum—Band 1: Das rot'sche Videum,* Cologne 1967; *Poetrie nr. 2,* Stuttgart 1967; *80 Wolken, 1965 bis 1967,* Stuttgart 1967; *A Look into the Blue Tide part 2,* New York 1967; *Snow,* West Berlin 1967; *Stempelkasten,* Dusseldorf 1967, rev. ed. Stuttgart 1972; *Poeterie 3–4,* Stuttgart 1968; *Poemetrie,* Cologne 1968, rev. ed. Cologne 1970; *Noch mehr Scheisse: Ein Nachlese,* Stuttgart 1968; *Sonntagsbeigabe der Zeitung für Kaukausen und Umgebung,* Stuttgart 1968; *Die gesamte Scheisse: Gedichte und Zeichnungen von Dieter Roth,* West Berlin 1968; *246 Little Clouds,* with an introduction by Emmett Williams, New York, Cologne, Paris 1968; *Little Tentative Recipe by Dieter Roth and Students of Watford School of Art,* Stuttgart 1969; *Gesammelte Werke,* first series, 20 vols, Stuttgart, London, and Reykjavík 1969–76; *Islandisch Leder,* Reykjavík 1970; *Postkartenblock,* Cologne and London 1971; *Franz Eggenschwiler, der Junglin, der Mann, die Zeit, das Werk: Ein Essay von Dieter Roth,* Stuttgart 1971; *2 Probleme unserer Zeit: ein Essay von Dieter Roth,* Reykjavík 1971; *Wer war Mozart: ein Essay von Dieter Roth,* Reykjavík 1971; *Wer ist der Nicht Weiss wer Mozart war,* Reykjavík 1971; *Dieter Roth: ein Frage?,* Reykjavík 1971; *Ein Essay über das Verhalten de Allgemeinen zu oder Gegenüber dem Besonderen BZW des Besonderen zu Order Gegenüber dem All-gemeinen,* Reykjavík 1971; *Frische Scheisse (eine Nachlese),* Reykjavík 1972; *Die*

Schastrommel nr. 9: Ergebnissedes ersten Berliner Dichter-Workshops (30.10–7.11.1972) with Friedrich Achleitner, Günter Brus, Gerhard Rühm, and Oswald Wiener, Stuttgart 1973; *Das Tränenmeer,* Stuttgart 1973; *Der Tränensee,* Reykjavík 1973; *Die Gesamte Scheiss von Dieter Roth,* West Berlin and Stuttgart 1973; *Das Tränenmeer: Band 2,* Stuttgart 1973; *Frühe Schriften und typische Scheiee ausgewählt-und mit einem Haufen Teilverdautes von Oswald Winer,* Darmstadt 1973, Stuttgart, London, and Reykjavík 1975; *Murmel,* 1974; *Bücher,* Hannover 1974; *Dars Wähnen: Band 1 (Tränenmeer 3),* Stuttgart 1974; *Die Die Die Gesamte Scheisse von Dieter Roth,* West Berlin, Stuttgart, London and Reykjavík 1974; *Das Original oder Kann das Gemälde der Maler sein? Eine Bastel-Novelle von Max Plunderbaum,* Stuttgart 1974; *Boeken,* Amsterdam 1975; *Neo Nix and Neo-Mix,* with Arnulf Rainer, Stuttgart 1975; *Das Riginal=Das Original, Bastelnovelle nr. 2,* Stuttgart 1975; *Die Die Die DIE Gesamte verdammte Scheisse von Karl-Dietrich Roth,* West Berlin, Stuttgart, London and Reykjavík 1975; *Roth and Rainer: Misch-u. Trennkunst,* with Arnulf Rainer, Graz, Austria 1976, Stuttgart and London 1979; *Ratiobrief, 1. Auflage,* with Arnulf Rainer, Vienna 1976; *Ratiobrief, 2. verbesserte Auflage, Saugpost, Auslandsverkehr u.a.m.,* with Arnulf Rainer, Vienna 1976; *Ratiobrief 3* with Arnulf Rainer, Vienna 1976; *Collaborations of Ch. Rotham,* with Richard Hamilton, Stuttgart and Cadaques, Spain 1977; *Interfaces,* with Richard Hamilton, New York 1977; *Interfaces,* with Richard Hamilton, London 1978; *150 Speedy Drawings: nrs. 1501–1650, 2-handed, made in Cadaques on the 1st + 2nd of Oktober 1977,* Cadaques and Zug 1978; *Von Blau ins Grau: Zwei Aber kein Saldot,* with Arnulf Rainer, Zug and Vienna 1978; *Das Wähnen Band 2A (Tränenmeer 4),* Stuttgart, London Zug 1978; *Das Original nr. 3: Das Fatal-Original (Baselnovelle nr. 3),* Stuttgart and Zug 1978; *Trophies: 125 Two-Handed Speedy Drawings,* Stuttgart aand London 1979; *Unterm Plunderbaum (die Sonetten 195?–1979)=Das Weinen no. 2= Das Wähnen, bd. 2B (Tränenemeer 5),* Stuttgart and London 1979; *Dieter Roth: Ein Lebenslauf von 50 Jahren,* Lucerne 1980; *Telefonzeichnungen 1976–78,* Stuttgart and London 1980; *Antwoorden op Vragen,* with Krees Broos, The Hague 1980; *Der Moralist: Essays nr. 7,* Zurich, London, Stuttgart and Lucerne, 1981; *Bats: 130 Zweihandige Schnellzeichnungen,* West Berlin 1981; *Dogs: 128 Zweihandige Schnellzeichnungen,* West Berlin 1981; *Biennale Venezia 1982,* Bern 1982; *4 Dutzend schnelle Weichzeichnungen,* Hamburg 12982; *2 Schock schnelle Weichzeichnungen 1982,* West Berlin 1983; *Holderbank,* Holderbank 1983; *Landenhüter (aus den Jahren 1965–1983),* West Berlin 1983; *Holderbank,* Holderbank 1983; *A Diary (from the year 1982),* Basel 1984; *20 Zeichnungereihen,* with Björn Roth, Basel 1984; *150 Schnellzeichnungen 1977,* West Berlin 1984; *Kopiks no. 1,* With Björn, Karl, and Vera Roth, and others, West Berlin 1985; *(untitled),* with Michael Seeger and Dorothea Baumer, Stuttgart 1985; *Bone in a Cold Oven,* with Björn Roth, and others, Basel 1986; *Katalog zur Austellung des grossen Teppiches,* Zurich and Basel 1986; *Bilder und Teppichausstellung,* Holderbank and Basel 1987; *Dieter Roth: Printed Pressed Bound,* with Felicitas Thun, Cologne 1998. **Articles**—interview with Peter Nesweda in *Kunstforum International,* no. 131, August-October 1995. **Films and videos**—*Pop 1. dock 1 N 2. letter. dot,* 1956–61; *Dieter Roth / Scheissegedichtlesung / Wien, Juli 1975,* 1976; *Arnulf Rainer und Dieter Roth: Doppeldruk,* 1976; *Arnulf Rainer und Dieter Roth: Duell im Schloss,* 1976; *Arnulf Rainer und Dieter Roth: Ein trüber Nachmittag (Rainer)/Wer hatte das gedacht, dass auch das Verwerfen nichts macht! (Roth),* 1977; *Arnulf Rainer und Dieter Roth: Fuzzle-Piece (Rainer)/Wer hatte das nicht gedacht, dass alles nichts macht! (Roth),* 1977; *Arnulf Rainer und Dieter Roth: Gesprach am Morgen (Rainer)/ (varying title) (Roth),* 1979; *Arnulf Rainer und Dieter Roth: Stanfotos (Rainer)/(varying title) (Roth),* 1979; *Arnulf Rainer und Dieter Roth: Umgriffe (Rainer)/(varying title)(Roth),* 1979; *Arnulf Rainer und Dieter Roth: Uble Stunden (Rainer)/Was Ekelhaftes (Roth),* 1979; *Ballet,* with Beatrice Cordua and Peter Schönherr, 1979; *Essay No. 11,* Basel 1988; *Notizbuch,* Hamburg 1990; *Gesammelte Werke,* Basel 1971–94. **Records and tapes**—*Berliner Dichterworkshop, 12/ 13.7.73,* with Gerhard Rühm and Oswald Wiener, Stuttgart, London and Reykjavík 1973; *Novembersymphonie (Doppelsymphonie),* with Gerhard Rühm and Osward Wiener, Stuttgart 1974; *Selten gehorte musik, münchner Konzert mai* 1974 with Günter Brus, Hermann Mitsch, Gerhard Rühm and Osward Wiener, Stuttgart, London and Reykjavík 1975; *Islenskra Fjalla (Kalli live at Danneckerstrasse),* with Karl Roth, Zug 1975; *Selten gehorte musik, Streichquartett 55 81 71 (Romenthalquartett),* with Günter Brus, Hermann Nitsch and Gerhard Rühm, Stuttgart, London and Reykjavík 1976; *Canciones de Cadaques* with Richard Hamilton and Chispas Luis, Cadaques and Stuttgart 1976; *Selten gehorte Musik, Tote Rennen, Lieder,* with Oswald Wiener, Stuttgart and London 1977; *Selten gehorte Musik, Musica che si Ascolta Rarmente, Das Berliner Konzert,* with Attersee, Günter Brus, Hermann Nitsch, Arnulf Rainer, Gerhard Rühm, Dominik Steiger, Oswald Wiener, and Reggio Emmilia, Naples and Stuttgart 1977; *Collaborations: Readings,* with Richard Hamilton, London 1978; *Tibidabo,* Zug and Cadaques 1978; *Lorelie: The Long Distance Sonata,* with Björn Roth and Vera Roth, Stuttgart and London 1978; *Radiohous-Klage=Musik, Die Radiosonate,* Brussels, Hamburg and Stuttgart 1978; *Misch-und Trennkunst: Autonom-Dialogische Thermatik,* Arnulf Rainer, Brussels, Hamburg and Zug 1978; Rainer-Roth oder ''Ratio-Konditio'' with Arnulf Rainer, Hamburg and Stuttgart 1979; *Thy Quatsch est min Castello,* Stuttgart 1979; *Selten gehorte Musik. Munich, Mai 1979: Abschoepfsymphonie. Die Abschoepfung,* with Attersee, Heinz Cibulka, Herbert Hossman, Hansjörg Mayer, Hermann Nitsch, and Paul Renne, Björn Roth, Gerhard Rühm, Dieter Schwarz, André Thomkins, and Osward Wiener, Stuttgart, Brussels and Hamburg 1979; *Autofahrt No. 1. 15–16 h, 17. Apr. 79,* with Björn Roth, Stuttgart 1979; *The Kuemmerling Trio Plays Kuemmerling Trios no. 1 & 2,* with Hansjörg Mayer and Emmett Williams, Stuttgart 1979; *Fernquartett,* with Björn Roth, Karl Roth and Vera Roth, Stuttgart 1980; *Harmonica Curse,* London 1981.

On ROTH: Books—*Books and Graphics 1947–1971,* exhibition catalog, edited by Hansjörg Mayer, Stuttgart 1971; *The Story of Bern (or) Showing Colors* by Dorothy Iannone, Dusseldorf 1970; *Dieter Roth Gewurz-Objekte, GummibandBilder etc. . . ,* exhibition catalog, with text by Paul Wember, Krefeld, West Germany 1971; *Danger in Dusseldorf (or) I Am Not What I Seem* by Dorothy Iannone, Stuttgart, London and Reykjavík 1973; *Dieter Roth,* anthology, edited by Galerie Steinmetz, Bonn 1974; *Dieter Roth: Werke von 1973/1975,* exhibition catalog, with text by Peter F. Althaus, Solothurn, Switzerland 1976; *An Titils. Skaldverk* by Einar Gudmundsson, Reykjavík 1978; *Auf der Bogen Bahn: Studien zum litararischen Werk von Dieter Roth* by Dieter Schwarz, Zurich 1981; *Johann Wolfgang von Goethe Stiftung: Verleihung des Rembrandt-Preises 1982 an Dieter Roth,* with text Emmett Williams, Basel 1982; *Dieter Roth,* exhibition catalog with text by Ann Goldstein, Chicago 1984; *Dieter Roth: Arbeiten auf Papier 1974–1984,* exhibition catalog with text by

Dietrich Helms, Hannover and Braunschweig 1985; *Dieter Roth* by Kees Broos, Labège 1987. **Articles—**"Dieter Roth at Nolan/Eckman" by Richard Kalina in *Art in America* (New York), July 1998; "Balkon: Roth on the Rhoades" by Juri Steiner and Guido Magnaguagno in *Parkett*, no. 53, 1998; "Food for Thought" by Richard Hamilton in *Artforum*, vol. 37, no. 2, October 1998; "Mold Gold" by Maja Oeri in *Artforum*, vol. 37, no. 2, October 1998; "Collage Credit" by Emmett Williams in *Artforum*, vol. 37, no. 2, October 1998; "Content and Formula" by Patrick Frey in *Artforum*, vol. 37, no. 2, October 1998; "Irony Tower" by Dieter Schwarz in *Artforum*, vol. 37, no. 2, October 1998; "Correspondence Course" by Gary Garrels in *Artforum*, vol. 37, no. 2, October 1998; "Dieter Roth" by Craig Saper in *Art Journal*, Spring 2000.

*

When I was born, I found myself, so I have been told, at a place in Germany, which I found the most horrible place to be, early or later in life. Horribly screaming Germans everywhere, scolding beating me up all the time, and when I grow up to be able to look around me, I found them engaged not only in war with me, but also with those horrible bombs and grenades throwing, terrible cruel madmen called the English and those insane massmurders, throwing bombs and blasts from the sky out of terrifying manmade monsters called airplanes or airoplanes, the so-called Americans, horribly adept killers and massmurderers. All three, Germans, Englishmen, Americans from Northamerica, as bloodthirsty at that time, the time of my little boyhood, as the silly French, thirsting for blood, the Russians, killers of the first order, Italians, Poles, murderous bunch of monsters as ugly themselves as their horrible inventions and imaginations. There, among them Fighters and Slaughterers, I grow up pissing in my timid pants, shitting into my pisswet trousers all the time and weeping all the time like a poor little dogturd. Then I was brought to Switzerland my horribly Christian Home Country. There were those murderous, butchering people, called soldiers and defenders of Freedom, everywhere. I survived there 12 years and then got away to friendly wonderful Copenhagen. But I fell into that awfully black hole called Matrimony, and I struggled there, horribly kicking, fucking and pissing in my timid little pants for seven years. Hell! But I got away to the United States of Northamerica, full of horrifying Maneaters, Butchers, Christians and other stuff. Pissing and shitting in my awfully wet pants, I survived, a strong and screaming cannibal myself now, a bastard of terror and fear, kicking, fucking, drinking and pissing. Running around different countries, all the same time, I find myself a dweller of butchershops, cannibal of fate, rage, tears, fears, and shit, piss, blood and shit, a bastard of fear, murderous, Hangover from Hell. Pissing in his awfully shitting, pissing, shitting trousers, called his pants, of fears and tears. Hangover from shitfucking places like Hell, Germany, U.S.A., England, France, China, Russia, Heaven, God, Angels, Christ, Buddha, Shit, Piss and Fear.

—Dieter Roth

* * *

"Good bye! Good bye!" was Dieter Roth's return of thanks when he received the *Rembrandt prize* in the Basel Art Museum in February 1982. This farewell accompanying a friendly and eloquent retreat and holding out hope for the future, runs like a motto through Dieter Roth's work. Alarmed by the aesthetic and moral demands upon the artist Roth never makes more than a small bow to convention and looks for the exit. "He quickly leaves this place and betakes himself apace," as Wilhelm Busch, one of his artistic ideals, wrote.

It was also "Good bye" at the beginning of his *Quadruple Concert* in the Basel Academy of Music where Roth was to play on four instruments, accompanied by a battery of strong drinks on the long grand piano. The concert had in fact already taken place in the two hours before the time announced by the poster. What followed were musical intermezzi, accompanied by counter-orders, drowned in playbacks of the music played earlier this evening. "As broke as when I came–/as broke I now must go,/and say in modest blame:/ Farewell, forever so!" was the last poem of his volume *Still More Shit* from 1968, although this solemn declaration was followed in the same year by *The Complete Shit.* Roth does not simply disappear but conceals behind the modest gesture a performance powerful already in its extent.

Like the magician he shows that his hands are empty before pulling rabbits out of the air—there are pictures hidden under his cap, and in his jacket pocket a diary with entries which could go directly into his volumes of poetry without any alteration. In appearance Roth represents the discreet style of the Bourgeois, grey three-piece suit and light grey shirt. A business man on his travels, the cap gives a sportsmanlike touch. Today, when industrialists follow fashion, these clothes are a reminder of pre-war days, manufacture and small industries. The diary bulging his pocket is not merely order book and agenda for the production which Roth calls "positive, therefore civilising," but also a repository for emotions and reflections, "Junk and Waste."

For more than two years junk and waste really filled his pockets when Roth decided to collect all the flat rubbish that passed through his hands, packing it into transparent bags for filing. In the autumn of 1981 he built them into two pyramids in Zürich's Helmhaus, a melancholy still life of a civilisation's dead remains. In its strict method (collecting everything flat during a year) this collection recalls Roth's artistic beginnings among the Swiss concrete artists of the 1950s. As his father was a Swiss living abroad, Roth came to Switzerland in 1943 from bomb-destroyed Hannover as a foster child, and after grammar school and apprenticeship as a graphic artist he made his first etchings (on tea-box tin instead of copper plate, due to lack of money) and poems. He made ends meet with occasional work and soon met with harsh criticism of his works when his friends Eugen Gomringer and Marcel Wyss rejected his poems as dreadfully sentimental. He rescued himself into minimal texts, reduced in part to dashes and dots, and contructivist pictures which he carried so far that finally he exchanged the brush for a knife and cut books out of coloured paper so that slits offered views of the following pages, producing subtle optical effects.

As a textile designer Roth was invited to a Danish firm, worked for a year in Copenhagen and met a girl from Iceland whom he followed to Reykjavík and married. Because he lived so far away and most of his contacts with Europe were broken, Roth was not able to devote himself to a simple artistic career but had to support himself working for a goldsmith and in furniture design. That changed his art: "When you go down, this concrete poetry and Mondrian painting doesn't help at all; only shit and rage." So Roth accepted everything that, while making a picture, got onto the picture's surface and gave up all claim to neat clarification of forms. This no longer pleased the purists in Switzerland and elsewhere, and it took years for Roth to succeed in making this (often under rich colour) hidden lament palatable to the public. Roth had already overtaken the postwar belief in a progress in which art and advertising would form an alliance for the feature of consumerism, even before this joined an all-inundating flood of merchandise. Roth saw under the cleanly prepared surface the hidden ''War of living creatures''; production as a raging contest: ''I understand civilisation as everybody eating everybody.'' Letting himself go is a moral gesture with which Roth demonstrates against all those who draw up regulations and use them against others, and yet he knows that he too must take part in this struggle. His large graphics and book exhibition opened in Stuttgart on September 1979, forty years after the outbreak of the second world war; ''Over such talk one often forgets the dreary things that are happening outside, that nobody sees, where one thinks there is only open air acrobatics going on (and in the worst case, football). No, outside, it is war!, there's marching, bleeding and bombing!''

Great tension stems from the fact that Roth always tackles his work with the ambition necessary to hold his ground against the competition, yet speaks for amateurish work, or stuff quickly made. It is more than an easy moral creed, for it leads, for example, to a time and energy consuming project like the *Review for Everything.* Roth founded it in 1975 under the motto ''Review for Everything accepts and publishes everything that comes.'' In the seven issues published so far, Roth and notable artists join with amateurs, children, all who have the courage to collaborate. The editor does not select, but tries to put up whatever comes to him and to depend all possible options. Only when criteria fall is there something new to see. On similar grounds Roth, whose list of own books contains over a hundred titles, founded his *Familien Verlag,* publishing books and records intially of his children and relatives, then of friends and acquaintances. Publishing these works he apologizes for the extent of his own production which threatens to push others to the wall,—at the same time these published works become part of the Roth-ian work, a circle from which there seems to be no way out.

Even when Roth takes new paths, approaches music for example, invents *Rarely Heard Music,* and demonstrates the non-command of instruments, he wins a throw. It is true that what happens is not the norm in concert halls—when he, for instance, places next to musical time the minutes and seconds which he must see through to an end—music as the living of a prescribed lifetime. In the concerts which he initially gave with a few, later with an increasing number of friends, harmony gradually drowns in the sea of individual expressions, the music expresses its own destruction, and by the side of Haydn's symphony *Die Schöpfung* appears *Die Abschöpfung.* To enhance these sounds Roth left his own music-making aside and recorded in a large kennel on Mount Tibidado near Barcelona twenty four hours of continual dog barking; to him the strongest music of all, the perfect lament. Comparison with the sorrowful angry howling and whining degrades art but it elevates the despised animals, depending on the point of view the spectator wants to adopt.

So that such enterprises should not end only as anecdotes Roth published the results as records or tapes, above all in the *edition hansjörg mayer,* Stuttgart. His *Collected Works* have also appeared there, a first part with twenty volumes and a second part with, so far, three volumes. Whether this second part and a project third part (that is sixty volumes in all) will ever be completed, is not certain. Roth has proved that his work can establish itself on the bookshelves. Where logical consequence threatens, it is better to stop or to turn, for otherwise Roth could just as well have stayed with the Concrete Painting of his father's generation. ''You poor and lonely man and arise, don't get caught by your contemporaries, flee, beetle, flee!''

—Dieter Schwarz

ROTHENBERG, Susan

Nationality: American. **Born:** Buffalo, New York, 20 January 1945. **Education:** Cornell University, B.F.A. 1966; George Washington University, 1967; studied at the Corcoran Museum School, Washington, D.C. **Family:** Married sculptor George Trakas, 1971 (divorced 1979); child: Maggie; married artist Bruce Nauman, 1989. **Career:** Painter; member American Academy and Institute of Arts and Leters, 1990. **Awards:** CAPS Grant for Painting, 1976–77; Guggenheim Fellowship for Painting, 1980; American Academy of Arts and Letters Award, 1983; Cornell Council Committee on the Arts Award, 1998. **Agent:** c/o Sperone Westwater, 142 Greene Street, New York, New York, 10012–3236. **Address:** Galisteo, New Mexico.

Individual Exhibitions:

1975 *3 Large Paintings,* 112 Green Street, New York
1976 Willard Gallery, New York
1977 Willard Gallery, New York
Susan Rothenberg/Judith Ornstein, Willard Gallery, New York
1978 *Matrix,* University Art Museum, Berkeley, California
Recent Work, Walker Art Center, Minneapolis
Greenberg Gallery, St. Louis
1979 Willard Gallery, New York
Recent Paintings, Mayor Gallery, London (travelled to Galerie Rudolf Zwirner)
1981 *5 Heads,* Willard Gallery, New York
Akron Art Museum, Ohio
Robert Moskowitz, Susan Rothenberg, Julian Schnabel, Kunsthalle Museum, Basel (travelled to the Frankfurt Kunstverein, and Louisiana Museum, Humlebaek, Denmark, 1981–82)
1982 Stedelijk Museum, Amsterdam
1983 Willard Gallery, New York
Los Angeles County Museum of Art
Institute of Contemporary Art, Boston
1984 Barbara Krakow Gallery, Boston
1985 California State University, Long Beach
Des Moines Art Center, Iowa
1990 Rooseum, Malmö, Sweden (catalog)
Paintings, Sperone Westwater, New York (catalog)
1992 *Paintings,* Sperone Westwater, New York (catalog)
Paintings and Drawings, Albright-Knox Art Gallery, Buffalo (catalog)
1993 Hirshhorn Museum and Sculpture Garden, Washington, D.C.
Albright-Knox Gallery, Buffalo, New York (traveling exhibition)
Prints, Des Moines Art Center, Iowa (catalog)

1994 Dallas Museum of Art, Texas
Paintings, Sperone Westwater Gallery, New York (catalog)
1996 *Paintings,* Museo de Arte Contemporáneo de Monterrey, Mexico (catalog)
1997 *Paintings,* Sperone Westwater, New York (catalog)
1998 *Drawings and Prints,* Herbert F. Johnson Museum of Art, Cornell University, Ithaca, New York (catalog)
1999 *Paintings from the Nineties,* Museum of Fine Art, Boston (catalog)

Selected Group Exhibitions:

1974 *New Talent,* Sachs Gallery, New York
1976 *Animals,* Solomon Gallery, New York
1978 *7 Artists: Contemporary Drawings,* Cleveland Museum of Art
1979 *New Image Painting,* Whitney Museum, New York
American Painting: The 80s, Grey Art Gallery, New York University (travelled to the Contemporary Art Museum, Houston, and the American Center, Paris, 1979–80)
1980 *Biennale,* Venice
1981 *A New Bestiary: Animal Imagery in Contemporary Art,* Virginia Museum, Richmond
1982 *Focus on Figure,* Whitney Museum, New York
1985 *Horses in Twentieth-Century Art,* Nicola Jacobs Gallery, London
1987 *Avant-Garde in the Eighties,* Los Angeles County Museum of Art
1991 *Sieben Amerikanische Maler,* Bayerische Staatsgemäldesammlungen, Staatsgalerie Moderner Kunst München, Munich, Germany (catalog)
1995 *A New York Time,* Bruce Museum, Greenwich, Connecticut
1996 *Diary of a Human Hand,* Gallery of the Saidye Bronfman Center for the Arts, Montreal, Canada (catalog)
1999 *In Company: Robert Creeley's Collaborations,* Castellani Art Museum of Niagra University, New York (traveling exhibition) (catalog)

Collections:

Museum of Modern Art, New York; Whitney Museum, New York; Albright-Knox Art Gallery, Buffalo, New York; Akron Art Museum, Ohio; Walker Art Center, Minneapolis; Art Museum of South Texas, Corpus Christi; Museum of Fine Arts, Houston; Castellani Art Museum, Niagara University, New York.

Publications:

By ROTHENBERG: Books—*Susan Rothenberg,* with Dave Hickey and Michael Auping, New York 1992; *Susan Rothenberg: Paintings and Drawings,* New York 1992; *Parts,* with Robert Creeley, San Francisco 1993. **Articles**—''Artist's Dialogue: Susan Rothenberg—Images on the Edge of Abstraction'' with Carter Ratcliff in *Architectural Digest* (Los Angeles), vol. 44, December 1987; ''Diffusions: A Project for Artforum'' in *Artforum,* vol. 26, April 1988; ''On Walking and Thinking,'' with Joan Simon in *Parkett,* no. 34, 1995.

On ROTHENBERG: Books—*Susan Rothenberg* by Joan Simon, New York 1999. **Articles**—''From Primary Structures to Primary Imagery'' by Mark Rosenthal in *Arts Magazine* (New York), October 1978; ''Art: What's New, Whitney Style'' by Vivien Raynor in the *New York Times,* 8 December 1978; ''Art for '79 Eyes'' by Barbara Rose in *Vogue* (New York), January 1979; ''The Abstract Image'' by Roberta Smith in *Art in America* (New York), March/April 1979; review by Hilton Kramer in *New York Times,* 13 April 1979; review by Peter Schjeldahl in *Artforum* (New York), Summer 1979; ''Neo-Modernists—A Sense of Deja-Vu'' by Hilton Kramer in *New York Times,* 23 September 1979; ''Painting in New York: An Illustrated Guide'' by Thomas Lawson in *Flash Art* (Milan), October/November 1979; review by Sarah Kent in *Time Out* (London), 28 February 1980; ''All Roads Head to the Venice Biennale'' by Carrie Rickey in *The Village Voice* (New York), 9 June 1980; ''Bravery in Action'' by Peter Schjeldahl in the *Village Voice* (New York), 29 April-5 May, 1981; ''An Audacious Inaugural Exhibition'' by Hilton Kramer in the *New York Times,* 20 September 1981; ''Susan Rothenberg'' by Michael Danoff in *Akron Art Museum Newsletter* (Ohio), 21 November 1981; ''Post Modernist Painting'' by Sam Hunter in *Portfolio Magazine* (New York), January/February 1982; ''Robert Moskowitz, Susan Rothenberg and Julian Schnabel'' in *Flash Art* (Milan), February/March 1982; ''Mysteries of Motion: Recent Paintings by Susan Rothenberg'' by Ellen Handy in *Arts Magazine,* vol. 64, May 1990; ''Forum: An Untitled Drawing by Susan Rothenberg'' by Joan Simon in *Drawing,* vol. 13, July/August 1991; ''Susan Rothenberg: United States'' by Peter Schjeldahl in *Artforum,* vol. 32, no. 1, September 1993; ''Susan Rothenberg: Mondrian Dancing 1984–85'' by Charles Wylie in *Saint Louis Art Museum Bulletin,* vol. 21, Winter 1995; ''Essential Hesitations: Rothenberg's Brushstroke Imagery and its Affinity to Cave Paintings'' by Mark Stevens in *Parkett,* no. 34, 1995; ''Painting as an Immense Feeling: Expression of Emotion in Rothenberg's Paintings'' by Jean-Christophe Ammann in *Parkett,* no. 34, 1995; ''The Evolution of the Horse'' by Ingrid Schaffne in *Parkett,* no. 34, 1995; ''Susan Rothenberg'' in *Arte,* no. 278, October 1996.

* * *

Susan Rothenberg, born in Buffalo, New York, was educated at the universities of Cornell and George Washington and the Corcoran Museum in the then prevalent abstract style of painting with its emphasis on 'process' and on maintaining the flatness of the picture plane. She commenced her career as an artist painting in this purely abstract mode. However, in 1973 the first horse image, shadowy and phantomlike, appeared in her work, and over the next few years she achieved an international reputation with a series of canvases featuring these horse portrayals. Rothenberg herself says that the horse figure appeared accidentally as a dividing device, but it is undoubtedly an image that has had powerful associations in art over the centuries. It can stand both for unbridled force or as a tamed but potentially violent source of energy, and thus as a symbol for human sexuality. At that time her introduction of a representational element into an abstract painting was an unusual and startling contribution. The paintings were nearly all in monochrome, using blues, greys, blacks and whites—cold colours which enchanced the curious otherworldly quality of her canvases. The compositional devices were simple; using the horse as a centering element on a scaffolding of diagonals or horizontal and vertical grids integrated into a thick, brushy, all-over textured background. The ghostly horse figures sometimes merged and sometimes appeared separate from the surface. Rothenberg was still, at this time, endeavouring to maintain one plane but found that spatial illusions did not necessarily destroy the unity of the whole. At the beginning of the eighties a general loosening up of her brushwork became noticeable and the horse gradually began to fade out to be replaced, first of all by anatomical parts—hands, limbs, bones—and then human and humanoid shapes. The emotional content of her art also deepened, the images giving a feeling of extreme anguish. These fragments of humanity are touching in their eroded fragility, speaking of a desperate clinging to survival in an encroaching darkness. Now handling the paint much more freely and expressively her interest in the geometric scaffolding lessened.

Whole figures started to appear in her work in the mid-eighties, seeming to emerge from a flurry of feathery brushstrokes. She works on a large scale, (280 x 220 cm. is an average size for her painting on canvas) and the cumulative effect of seeing her works in quantity, as in an exhibition, is of a collapsing, imploding world. Lately she has made tentative excursions into colour. In a late work of truly massive scale, *Vertical Spin* (1986/7), there is a tumble of raw, red figures down the center of the painting against a dark, striated background. The effect is of viewing through coarse netting. At the base, there is a cluster of half naked male figures, one behind the other, as though clinging to a raft. Long verticals widen from the top—one could be looking down into a dark canyon with rushing rapids. In an upper corner a face gradually reveals itself—much larger in scale than the other figures, colourless as a skull with dark eye sockets and a black gaping mouth. The brushwork is dry and applied with a coarse hogshair brush, at least an inch in width, and the paint is built up very thickly in places. Her achievement, in this huge canvas, is that the details have meanings in themselves, but form parts of a whole which can convey to a receptive viewer a totally different meaning or meanings. Sadly, like so many of her generation, Rothenberg is hampered by her deficiency in draughtsmanship from realising to its full potential her powerful and original imagery.

—Mary Ellis

ROW, David

Nationality: American. **Born:** Portland, Maine, 31 August 1949. **Education:** Yale University, B.A., cum laude, 1972, M.F.A., 1974. **Family:** Married Kathleen Chorpenning in 1981. **Career:** Associate Professor, The Cooper Union of the Arts and Sciences, 1994–96, School of Visual Arts, 1996—, Hunter College, City University, 1998–99, and Princeton University, 2000; visiting lecturer and critic at many institutions, including: Tyler School of Art, Temple University, 1981; Syracuse University, 1993; Hunter College, City University of New York, 1998; Princeton University, 1998; Kansas City Art Institute, 2000; guest artist and lecturer, numerous printmaking projects, 1988–2000. **Awards:** Ellen B. Stoeckel Fellowship, Yale at Norfolk, 1971; Scholar of the House in Painting, Yale University, 1971–72; National Endowment for the Arts Grant in Painting, 1987. **Agents:** Von Lintel and Nusser, 555 West 25th Street, New York, New York 10001; Galerie Brandstetter and Wyss, Zurich, Switzerland; Marella Arte Contemporanea, Milan, Italy; Numark Gallery, Washington, D.C.; Jan Weiner Gallery, Kansas City, Missouri; Galerie Von Lintel and Nusser, Munich, Germany. **Address:** 476 Broadway, New York, New York 10013.

Selected Individual Exhibitions:

1974 Yale University School of Art, New Haven
1977 Rutgers University, Newark
1982 Art Galaxy, New York
1984 55 Mercer Street Gallery, New York
1987 John Good Gallery, New York (catalog)
1988 Ascan Crone Gallery, Hamburg (catalog)
1989 John Good Gallery, New York (catalog)
1991 Galerie Thaddaeus Ropac, Paris (catalog)
John Good Gallery, New York (catalog)
1993 John Good Gallery, New York (catalog)
1995 André Emmerich, New York
1996 André Emmerich, New York
1997 Galerie Thomas von Lintel, Munich (catalog)
1999 Betsy Senior Gallery, New York
Galerie von Lintel & Nusser, New York
2000 Marella Arte Contemporanea, Milan
2001 Numark Gallery, Washington, D.C.
Edwin A. Ulrich Museum of Art, Wichita, Kansas

Selected Group Exhibitions:

1978 *Line-up,* The Drawing Center, New York
1982 *New Drawing in America,* The Drawing Center, New York (catalog)
1986 *Twelve from New York,* Yale University School of Art, New Haven
1987 John Good Gallery, New York
1988 John Good Gallery, New York
1989 *Geometric Abstraction,* Persons Lindell Gallery, Helsinki (catalog)
Sightings, Institute of North American Studies, Barcelona (catalog)
1991 *Conceptual Abstraction,* Sidney Janis Gallery, New York (catalog)
Strategies for the Next Painting, Wolff Gallery, New York, and Feigen Gallery, Chicago (catalog)
1992 *Invitational Exhibition of Painting and Sculpture,* American Academy and Institute of Arts and Letters, New York
1993 *Italia/America l'Astrazione Redefinita,* State Museum of San Marino, San Marino, Italy (catalog)
Yale Collects Yale: 1950–1993, Yale University Musuem of Art, New Haven, Connecticut (catalog)
1994 *Pittura Americana,* Galleria Oddi Baglioni, Rome
Critiques of Pure Abstraction, Blaffer Gallery, University of Houston, Texas (catalog)
1995 *Critiques of Pure Abstraction,* Armand Hammer Museum of Art, Los Angeles (catalog)
1996 *Trois Collections d'Artistes,* Musee des Beaux Arts, La Chaux de Fonds, Switzerland
1997 *Fractures.Constructs,* Claremont Graduate University, California (catalog)

David Row: *Phosphor* (diptych), 1999. ©David Row. Courtesy of the artist and Von Lintel and Nusser.

Divergent Models, Nassauischer Kunstverein, Wiesbaden, Germany (catalog)

1998 *Masters of the Masters,* Butler Institute of American Art, Youngstown, Ohio

2000 *Inner Eye: Contemporary Art from the Marc and Livia Straus Collection,* Neuberger Museum of Art, Purchase, New York

Collections:

Brooklyn Museum, New York; Carnegie Museum of Art, Pittsburgh, Pennsylvania; Cleveland Museum of Art, Ohio; Museum of Contemporary Art, San Diego, California; Galleria Nazionale D'Arte Moderna, San Marino, Republica di San Marino, Italy.

Public Installations:

Mural, Washington National Airport 1997.

Publications:

On ROW: Books—*Modernities: Art Matters in the Present* by Joseph Maschek, Pittsburgh, Pennsylvania 1993; *Continuous Model: The Paintings of David Row* by John Zinsser, Munich 1997; *The Widening Circle: Consequences of Modernism in Contemporary Art* by Barry Schwabsky, Cambridge University Press 1997; *Blindfolding the Muse* by Ross Neher, New York 1999; *National Airport Terminal* by Cesar Pelli, Gloucester, Massachusetts 2000. **Articles—**''From the Inside Looking Out'' by Jane Bell in *New York Arts Journal,* December 1978; ''David Row'' by Meyer Raphael Rubinstein and Daniel Weiner in *Arts Magazine,* September 1987; ''The Current State of Nonrepresentation'' by Jeremy Gilbert-Rolfe in *Visions Art Quarterly,* Spring 1989; ''On the Use of Color: Two Generations, Two Antagonistic Concepts of Painting, David Row and Gerhard Richter'' by Philippe Dagen in *Le Monde,* September 1991; ''Negotiating New Abstraction: A Conscious Affirmation'' by Mary Murphy in *New Art Examiner,* Summer 1992; ''Looking at Kelly's Paintings Now'' by Tiffany Bell in *Artstudio,* no. 24, 1992; ''Critique of Pure Abstraction: David Row'' by Mark Rosenthal in *Atelier International,* June 1994; ''Flights and Fancy'' by Carter Wiseman in *Artnews,* June 1997; ''Modernist Art and Its Market'' by David Carrier in *Art Journal,* Winter 1998; ''David Row'' by Alfred Mac Adam in *Artnews,* April 1999; ''David Row'' by Hilarie M. Sheets in *Artnews,* January 2000.

*

Statement on Painting

I've been asked a number of times to write a short statement on painting, which seems very similar to writing a short statement about life. I really can't do it. No matter how I try to pin down what painting is to me, it will make a liar out of me in ten minutes in the studio. The reason I continue to work is not to make a grand statement to the world, or to perfect a craft, or to pretend that the world couldn't live without what I do, but because what happens in my studio is, and always has been, a complete surprise to me. I am a dreamer, and the only thing I can positively say is that painting is a dreamer's medium. It doesn't have to exist in real space like sculpture or be useful like architecture, and, unlike photography, it is not dependent on the outside world for imagery. It can be done by one person in complete solitude and it has absolutely no rules except those we make for ourselves to keep our sanity.

Having said that, and being what is commonly referred to as an ''abstract painter,'' it may appear that my intentions and the work that results have no relation to the world. Exactly the opposite is the case. It is the work that constantly reconnects me with what surrounds me. I did not look at electron micrographs of colliding particles and then make the painting called *Flatlands.* These images were pointed out to me after the painting was made. So from my point of view, the painting itself made me aware of those wonderful subatomic events. I can point to many such incidents in my life and work. The work acts as an intuitive antenna that in some mysterious process finds its corollary in the real world. I would like to say that I knew about some idea or phenomenon that relates to some image in my work but the truth is that without making the work I would never think to look in that particular place. So I continue going into the studio every day wondering what place the work will transport me to and what aspect of the world I might begin to get a glimpse of.

—David Row

* * *

''I could be bounded in a nutshell, and count myself a king of infinite space.'' Like Hamlet, David Row controls space, time, and perpetual flux through metaphor. His metaphors, his paintings, visually translate synecdoche, the rhetorical figure in which a part (the painting) stands for the whole (the cosmos). To accomplish this, he situates himself at the center of an imaginary, bidirectional optic device: one side a telescope, the other a microscope.

Row moved to New York in 1975, when a new age for painting in the United States had begun. The moment was fraught with anxieties: What direction would American painting take? Was it even possible, critics wondered, to paint now that Abstract Expressionism, Pop, Color Field, Minimalism, Op, Neo Geo, Conceptualism, et al seemed to have run their course and become part of art history? Row's response (like that of contemporaries like David Reed, Stephen Ellis, Stephen Westphall, Lydia Dona, and Donna Moylan) was to turn the critics's intellectual exhaustion into a pluralistic panorama where anything was possible and where no one trend would dominate.

Row's early, 1960s photosilkscreens, especially those of rocky beaches in Maine, look either like telescopic views of the moon's surface or microscopic views of human skin. The borders of the photographic images, frames essentially, constitute an initial order, fixing what is within while simultaneously acknowledging its ephemeral nature. This kaleidoscopic vision of the universe is, nevertheless, perilously close to representation because the medium inevitably leads the viewer back to reality. During the 1970s, Row severed that umbilical chord by embracing the techniques of two painters he admired, his Yale mentor Al Held and Frank Stella.

Row hit his stride during the 1980s, when he set Held and Stella aside, retaining only Held's formal discipline and the manipulation of templates Stella perfected in his protractor paintings. Perhaps the best way to grasp the essence of Row's painting during the 1980s and 1990s is to think of him painting within a constant, reversible dialectic of connection and disconnection. Shapes come together or part within the vivid colors Row first experienced as a teenager when he visited India.

During the 1980s, a typical Row painting consisted of a grainy field over which the artist would lay templates—arcs or fragments of ellipses. These templates could be faced toward or away from one another; they could be of different colors or the same color. Throughout the 1980s, Row used continuity and connectedness to show the serial, cyclical quality of the universe, at both the level of the gene, whose helix form appeared in many of his paintings during those years, and the galaxy—the ellipses replicated the orbits of the planets.

These paintings inaugurated Row's signature style—the coiled fragments of ellipses writhing over a surface which eventually acquired depth. The flatness critic Clement Greenberg saw as being essential to abstract painting was not viable for Row because he needed depth for his metaphorical representation of infinite space. At the same time, he createed vertical sections and used shaped canvases, which brought his painting closer to object-making. In fact, Row did make some sculptures for a 1992 Hamburg show, but instantly returned to painting because he discovered his objects had become part of the real world by occupying space, while his paintings constituted an aperture through which the viewer could experience other worlds.

During the 1990s, Row continued to section the surfaces of his paintings, four being the most frequent number, as if to echo the idea of changing seasons, shifting tectonic plates or, more plausibly, given his own training in Indian music as well as his fascination with jazz, the idea of music. But his greatest concern was still the painted surface. There, his ellipses, whole or fragmentary, swirled in a matrix of overlapping swaths of color. An important change took place in the way Row deployed his ellipse: now he rendered it horizontal, vertical, bisected, and intersected. But wherever it appeared—including at the refurbished Washington National Airport, where Row, working with the architect César Pelli, created a major piece of public art, a 27-foot mural—the ellipse was a threshold he used to bring unity to the metaphoric space of the painted surface. The canvas became an arena, like the hockey rinks of his adolescence, where he played dynamism off against stasis.

With the new century, Row's painting, as well as his monotypes and lithographs, has become more complex. His most recent work shows him peering down the microscopic end of his personal optic. This close focus reveals the very pores of the painting—pixels, molecules, or quarks—that may herald an even deeper plunge below the surface of color and the ever more fragmentary ellipses.

—Alfred MacAdam

RÜCKRIEM, Ulrich

Nationality: German. **Born:** Dusseldorf, 30 September 1938. **Education:** Trained as an apprentice stonemason, Dusseldorf, 1957–59; studied briefly at the Werkkunstschule, Cologne, 1959. **Career:** Independent sculptor, in Norvenich, near Cologne, since 1962: first stone-splitting works, 1968; worked in Mönchengladbach, 1969. Professor of sculpture, Hochschule für bildende Kunste, Hamburg, 1975–84; professor of sculpture, Kunstakademie, Dusseldorf, since

1984. Lives in Anrochte-Klieve and in Cologne. **Awards:** Forderpreis des Landes Nordrhein-Westfalen, 1973; Kunstpreis der Stadt Krefeld, 1973; Forderpreis, Bundesverband der deutschen Industrie, 1975; Lichtwark-Preis, Hamburg, 1983; Konrad-von-Soest Preis, Münster, 1984; Verband der deutschen Kritiker Preis, West Berlin, 1985; Arnold Bode Preis, Kassel, 1985. **Agent:** Ace Gallery New York, 275 Hudson Street, New York, New York, 10013.

Individual Exhibitions:

1964 Domgalerie, Cologne
Leopold-Hoesch-Museum, Duren, West Germany
1967 Galerie Ad Libitum, Antwerp
1968 Galerie Tobies und Silex, Cologne
1969 Galerie Ernst, Hannover
Galerie Konrad Fischer, Dusseldorf
1970 Museum Haus Lange, Krefeld, West Germany
Galerie Ricke, Cologne
1971 Kabinett für Aktuelle Kunst, Bremerhaven, West Germany
Galerie Ernst, Hannover
Galerie Konrad Fischer, Dusseldorf
Mayfair Gallery, London
Galerie Paul Maenz, Cologne
Videogalerie Gerry Schum, Dusseldorf
1972 Paula Cooper Gallery, New York
Staatliche Kunsthalle, Baden-Baden, West German
1973 Kunsthalle, Tübingen, West Germany
Städtische Museum, Mönchengladbach, West Germany
1974 Kunstverein, Frankfurt
Kunstraum München, Munich
Galerie Preisig, Basel
Galerie Paul Maenz, Cologne
Galerie Konrad Fischer, Dusseldorf
1975 Lisson Gallery, London
Galerie Preisig, Basel
Galerie Durand-Dessert, Paris
Art and Project, Amsterdam
1976 Museum of Modern Art, Oxford
Städtische Museum, Mönchengladbach, West Germany
Galerie Klein, Bonn
1977 Van Abbemuseum, Eindhoven, Netherlands
Galerie Konrad Fischer, Dusseldorf
1978 Galerie Hetzler und Keller, Stuttgart
Museum Folkwang, Essen, West Germany
West German Pavillion, at the *Biennale,* Venice
Galerie Klein, Bonn
Stadtisches Kunstmuseum, Bonn
1979 Kunsthalle, Bielefeld, West Germany
Kabinett für Aktuelle Kunst, Bremerhaven, West Germany
Westfälischer Kunstverein, Münster, West Germany
Stichting Eindhoven, Netherlands
Sperone-Westwater-Fischer, New York
Graeme Murray Gallery, Edinburgh
Galerie Durand-Dessert, Paris
1980 Galerie Konrad Fischer, Dusseldorf
Kunstraum München, Munich
Galerie Hetzler, Stuttgart
Galerie Klein, Bonn
Galerie Loehrl, Mönchengladbach, West Germany
1981 Fort Worth Art Museum, Texas
Galerie Konrad Fischer, Zurich
1982 Galleri Nordenhake, Malmo, Sweden
1983 Centre Georges Pompidou, Paris
Raum für Kunst, Hamburg
1984 Galerie Konrad Fischer, Dusseldorf
Stadelgalerie, Frankfurt
Skulpturprojekt im offentlichen Raum, Hamburg
Produzentgalerie, Hamburg
Kamakura Gallery, Tokyo
1985 Galerie Wilkens und Jacobs, Cologne
Westfälisches Landesmuseum, Münster, West Germany
Galerie Klein, Bonn
Staatliche Kunstsammlungen Neue Galerie, Kassel, West Germany
1986 Rijksmuseum Kröller-Müller, Otterlo, Netherlands
Galerie Konrad Fischer, Dusseldorf
Galerie Loehrl, Mönchengladbach, West Germany
Kunstverein, Freiburg, West Germany
1987 Galerie Klein, Bonn
Kunstsammlung Nordrhein-Westfalen, Dusseldorf
Abteiberg-Museum, Mönchengladbach, West Germany
Kölnischer Kunstverein, Cologne
Halle Rückriem, Cologne-Höningen
Victoria Miro Gallery, London
Donald Young Gallery, Chicago
1988 Niederösterreichisches Landesmuseum, Vienna (catalog)
1989 *Stele & Barn,* Palacio de Cristal, Madrid (catalog)
1991 Serpentine Gallery, London (catalog)
Galerie Tschudi, Glarus (catalog)
Skulpturen und Arbeiten auf Papier, Kunstverein Winterthur, Winterthur (catalog)
1995 *Lenbachhaus,* Städische Galerie im Lenbachhaus, Munich (catalog)
1997 Stedelijk Museum, Amsterdam (catalog)
1998 Ace Gallery New York, New York
1999 Neue Nationalgalerie, Berlin
2000 Contemporary Art Center, Vilnius (also Goethe Institut, Vilnius)

Selected Group Exhibitions:

1967 *Wege 67,* Museum am Ostwall, Dortmund, West Germany
1969 *17 deutsche Kunstler,* Kunstverein, Hannover
1972 *Documenta 5,* Museum Fridericianum, Kassel, West Germany (and *Documenta 7,* 1982; *Documenta 8,* 1987)
1975 *The Condition of Sculpture,* Hayward Gallery, London
1978 *38th Biennale,* Venice
1981 *Art Allemagne Aujourd'hui,* Musée d'Art Moderne, Paris
1984 *Von hier aus,* Messehallen, Dusseldorf
1985 *Kunst in der Bundersrepublik 1945–85,* Nationalgalerie, West Berlin
1986 *Wild, Visionary, Spectral: New German Art,* Art Gallery of South Australia, Adelaide
1989 Galería de Arte Soledad Lorenzo, Madrid (catalog)
XX. Biennale São Paulo, Brazil (catalog)
1990 *Floor Sculpture,* Nohra Haime Gallery, New York (catalog)
1991 *Made of Stone,* Galerie Isy Brachot, Brussels (catalog)
1997 *Skulptur: Projekte,* Munster, Germany
1998 *Artranspennine 98,* Manchester, England

Collections:

Westfälisches Landesmuseum, Münster; Kunstmuseum, Bonn; Museum Haus Lange, Krefeld; Museum Ludwig, Cologne; Nationalgalerie, West Berlin; Neue Galerie und Städtische Kunstsammlungen, Kassel; Rijksmuseum Kröller-Müller, Otterlo; Stedelijk Van Abbemuseum, Eindhoven; Fort Worth Museum of Art, Texas; Art Gallery of South Australia, Adelaide.

Publications:

By RÜCKRIEM: Books—*Ulrich Rückriem: Frankfurt Daimlerstrasse,* with Klaus Gallwitz and Ulrich Wilmes, Cologne 1989; *Ulrich Rückriem: Arbeiten,* with Heinrich Ehrhardt, Stuttgart 1994; *Mont Joie: Festschrift für Ulrich Rückriem zum 60,* with Kathrin Wappenschmidt, Düsseldorf 1998.

On RÜCKRIEM: Books—*Jahresbericht 1971,* edited by Paul Maenz, Cologne 1971; *Documenta 5: Befragung der Realität,* exhibition catalog edited by Harald Szeemann and others, Kassel, West Germany 1972; *Ulrich Rückriem: Skulpturen 1968–1973,* with an introduction by Günter Ulbricht, Cologne 1973; *Projekt 74: Aspekte internationaler Kunst am Anfang der 70er Jahre,* exhibition catalog with text by Dieter Ronte, Evelyn Weiss, Manfred Schneckenburger and others, Cologne 1974; *Ulrich Rückriem,* exhibition catalog, Oxford 1976; *Ulrich Rückriem: Skulpturen 1968–1976,* exhibition catalog with text by Rudi H. Fuchs, Eindhoven, Netherlands 1977; *Ulrich Rückriem* by Hermann Kern, Munich 1977; *Ulrich Rückriem: Venezia 1978,* exhibition catalog with texts by Rudi H. Fuchs and Klaus Gallwitz, Stuttgart 1978; *Ulrich Rückriem: Skulpturen 1968–78,* exhibition catalog with text by Rudi H. Fuchs, Essen 1978; *Ulrich Rückriem: Skulpturen 1977–78,* exhibition catalog with text by Thomas Deecke, Münster, West Germany 1979; *Ulrich Rückriem,* exhibition catalog with text by Michael Pauseback, Bielefeld, West Germany 1979. **Articles**—''Romancing the Stone: Ulrich Rückriem'' by Pier Luigi Tazzi in *Artforum International,* vol. 29, September 1990; ''Ulrich Rückriem'' by Gabriel Rivet in *Journal of Contemporary Art,* vol. 7, Summer 1994; ''Ulrich Rückriem: The Quarry as an Atelier'' by Adachiara Zevi in *L'Architettura,* no. 517–518, November/December 1998; ''Sod Off Ruckriem!'' by David Lee in *Art Review* (London), vol. 50, July/August 1998.

* * *

Contact with works of Rückriem, in the basic sense, is like straying into a stonemason's yard. A sudden confrontation with well-chined rock, sometimes cloven, sometimes pitted, but always with a definitive impression of well-tuned 3-dimensional geometry. Not suprisingly, his craft as a sculptor springs from two sources, each in its way as significant as the other.

Ulrich Rückriem was, for a short while, a student of carving at the Dusseldorf Staatliche Kunstakademie, but then he also derived experience in its most practical form as assistant to a professional stonehewer in what might for others have proved a prosaic setting. Such was far from the case with Rückriem.

Looking at his sculpture today, one is aware of two fundamental virtues: his undeviating love of his raw materials (showing the same sort of affection for stone as a draughtsman like Titus-Carmel bestows upon the qualities and characters of paper); and secondly, the straight-and-narrow path which he has adapted in his sculpture throughout showing up in his unyielding decisions never to allow any temptation of even the least touch of figuration to enter into the nature and spirit of his works, nor to listen to the siren-voices of beguiling romanticism (to both of which failings a sculptor like Jacob Epstein too easily fell prey). Nor should it be overlooked that here is an artist who particulary favours extremely tough materials—like large blocks of granite—for the execution of his works which strongly implies that clearly any diversion from puritanical intentions would wreak havoc upon any goal in view for his finished pieces.

A typical instance of his unadulterated sense of creative mission was shown at Hannover's Galerie Ernst. Examining this upright rectangular eminence (10 small blocks to one side, and 10 larger blocks matching them in careful exactitude on the other, all clasped together with roughly implanted short strips of a metallic substance like medals on the chest of a monument), one is overwhelmed by the crude (simple in meaning, rather than in execution) power of this artist's vision tempered by such a strict discipline.

Rückriem's main work-centre as a independent sculptor was since 1962 in Nörvenich, a small village just outside Cologne where, some 6 years later, he began his splitting processes (leading to *geschliffen* and polishing), after which he transferred his worklife as a sculptor to his studio in Mönchengladbach where his wall-reliefs and freestanding sculptures now reach completion.

There should be no misunderstanding about the kind of status this artist has been able to achieve during the past 25 years. Apart from showing his works in the main art centres and galleries of West Germany, Switzerland, Italy, Sweden, Holland, Japan, Australia, Austria, the United States, Britain and Eire, it should be noted that he was an official participant at the Venice Biennale and the 1987 Kassel Dokumenta. Ulrich Rückriem is no stranger when it comes to invitations to take part through his works in important accrochages and anthologies of modern art in international events, frequently in museums (where he has appeared either as an isolated exhibitor or in company with respected elders and contemporaries in his chosen field).

—Sheldon Williams

RUFF, Thomas

Nationality: German. **Born:** Zell, Germany, 1958. **Education:** Studied with Bernd Becher at the Kunstakademie, Düsseldorf, Germany, 1977–85.

Selected Individual Exhibitions:

1981 Galerie Rüdiger Schöttle, Munich, Germany
1984 Galerie Rüdiger Schöttle, Munich, Germany
Galerie Konrad Fischer, Düsseldorf, Germany
1986 Galerie Philip Nelson, Villeurbanne, Lyon, France
1987 Galerie Johnen & Schöttle, Cologne, Germany
Galerie Crousel-Robelin, Paris, France
1988 Museum Schloss, Hardenburg, The Netherlands, and Velbert/Portikus, Frankfurt, Germany (catalog)
Mai 36 Galerie, Lucerne, Switzerland (catalog)
Ydessa Hendeless Art Foundation, Toronto, Canada
1989 Galerie Bebert, Rotterdam, The Netherlands
Cornerhouse, Manchester, England
303 Gallery, New York

Des Portraits, des Maisons, des Etoiles, Stedelijk Museum, Amsterdam, The Netherlands (catalog)
1990 Magazin, Centre National d'Art Contemporain, Grenoble, France (catalog)
Kunstverein, Zurich, Switzerland (catalog)
1991 Kunstverein, Arnsberg, Germany and Braunschweig, Germany, and Galerie des Stadt Sindelfingen, Germany (catalog)
1992 Mai 36 Galerie, Lucerne, Switzerland
Galerie Nelson, Lyon, France
1993 Deweer Art Gallery, Ottegem, Belgium (catalog)
303 Gallery, New York
1994 Galerie Johnen & Schöttle, Cologne, Germany
Galerie Rüdiger Schöttle, Munich, Germany
1995 Galerie Johnen & Schöttle, Cologne, Germany
Mai 36 Galerie, Zurich, Switzerland
1996 Fraenkel Gallery, San Francisco, California
Rooseum, Malmo, Sweden (catalog)
1997 *Thomas Ruff: Kleine Portrats,* Dryphoto, Prato, Italy
Galerie Helga de Alvear, Madrid, Spain
Oeuvres 1979–1997, Centre National de la Photographie, Paris, France (catalog)
1998 Contemporary Fine Arts, Berlin, Germany
303 Gallery, New York
Gallery Koyanagi, Tokyo, Japan

Selected Group Exhibitions:

1982 *Work by Young German Photographers,* Art Galaxy, New York
Ausstellung B, Künstlerwerkstätten, Munich (catalog)
1983 Laputa, Stuttgart, Germany
1985 *Künstlerische Fotografie des 20,* Universitäts Museum, Marburg, Germany
1986 *Das Auge des Künstlers—Das Auge der Kamera,* Pinacotheque Ravenna, Italy, and Kunstverein, Frankfurt, Germany (catalog)
1987 *Reste des Authentischen,* Museum Folkwang, Essen, Germany, and Photographers Gallery, York, England (catalog)
Foto Cliche, Gallery Victoria Miro and Orchard Gallery, Derry, Ireland (catalog)
Foto/Realismen, Villa Dessauer, Bamberg, Germany, Kunstverein, Munich, Germany, and Grundkreditbank, Berlin, Germany (catalog)
1988 Padiglione d'Arte Contemporanea, Milan, Italy (catalog)
L'inventaire, Manufrance, St-Etienne, France (catalog)
BiNationale, Kunstverein, Kunsthalle und Kunstammlung, Düsseldorf, Germany, and Museum of Fine Arts and ICA, Boston, Massachusetts (catalog)
Bilder-Denda-van Ofen-Ruff, Museum Haus Esters, Krefeld, Germany (catalog)
1989 *1st Internationale Foto-Triennale,* Esslingen, Germany (catalog)
32 Portraits: Photography in Art, Kunstrai, Amsterdam, The Netherlands (catalog)
Tenir l'image a distance, Musee d'art contemporain de Montreal, Canada (catalog)
Mit dem Fernrohr durch die Kunstgeschichte, Kunsthalle, Basel, Switzerland (catalog)
1990 Kunstmuseum, Bonn, Germany (catalog)
To Be or Not to Be, Centre d'Art de Santa Monica, Barcelona, Spain (catalog)
Hacia el paisaje, Centro Atlantico de Arte Moderno, Grand Canary Island, Spain (catalog)
Weitersehen, Museum Haus Esters/Museum Haus Lange, Krefeld, Germany (catalog)
1991 *Metropolis,* Martin Gropius Bau, Berlin, Germany (catalog)
Typologies: Nine Contemporary Photographers, Newport Harbour Art Museum, Newport Beach, California, Akron Art Museum, Akron, Ohio, and The Corcoran Gallery of Art, Washington, D.C. (catalog)
Sguardo di Medusa, Musée d'Art Contemporain, Rivoli, Italy (catalog)
1992 *Casal Solleric,* Palma di Mallorca, Spain (catalog)
Premiere Photo, Galerie du Jour-Agnes B, Paris, France (catalog)
Qui, Quoi, Où, Musée de l'Art Moderne de la Ville de Paris, France (catalog)
1993 *Photography in Contemporary German Art: 1960 to the Present,* Walker Art Center, Minneapolis, Minnesota; Dallas Museum of Art, Dallas, Texas; Solomon R. Guggenheim Museum, New York; Modern Art Museum of Fort Worth, Fort Worth, Texas; St. Louis Art Museum, St. Louis, Missouri; The Lannan Foundation, Los Angeles, California; Museum Ludwig, Cologne, Germany; Louisiana Museum of Modern Art, Humblebaek, Denmark; Museum für Gegenwartskunst, Basel, Switzerland (catalog)
Parallelaktion, Stadtische Galerie Schloss, Oberhausen, Germany (catalog
Konstruktion, Zitat: Kollektive Bilder in der Fotographie, Sprengel Museum, Hannover, Germany (catalog)
Kunst aus Wintermarchen Deutschland, Tochigi Prefectural Museum of Fine Arts, Japan (catalog)
1994 *Aura,* Wiener Secession, Vienna, Austria (catalog)
The Institute of Cultural Anxiety, ICA, London, England (catalog)
1995 *RAM: Realitat, Anspruch, Medium,* Kunstverein Karlsruhe, Germany; Bundespostministerium & Kunstverein, Bonn, Germany; Neues Museum Weserburg, Bremen, Germany; Lindenau-Museum, Altenburg, Germany; Museum Wiesbaden, Germany (catalog)
Kunst in Deutschland: Sammlung des Bundes, Kunst und Ausstellungshalle der Bundesrepublik Deutschland, Bonn, Germany (catalog)
Pavillon Allemand, Biennale de Venice, Venice, Italy (catalog)
1996 *Desert,* John Hansard Gallery, Southampton, England, South London Gallery, London, England, Ikon Gallery, Birmingham, England (catalog)
Zuspiel, Sprengelmuseum Hannover, Hannover, Germany (catalog)
JURASSIC Technologies—Revenant, 10th Biennale de Sydney, Sydney, Australia (catalog)
Eternal Dialogue, Tower of David Museum, Jerusalem, Israel (catalog)
1997 *Die Epoche der Moderne: Kunst im 20. Jahrhundert,* Martin Gropius Bau, Berlin, Germany (catalog)

Pro Lidice, Ceske Museum, Prague, Czechoslovakia (catalog)
Positionen kunstlerischer Fotografie in Deutschland seit 1945, Martin Gropius Bau, Berlin, Germany (catalog)
1998 *Wounds: Between Democracy and Redemption in Contemporary Art,* Moderna Museet, Stockholm, Sweden (catalog)

Publications:

By RUFF: Articles—''Aufnahmeleitung: Ein Interview von Isabelle Graw mit Thomas Ruff'' in *Artis* (Konstanz, Germany), October, 1989.

On RUFF: Books—*Aus der Distanz* by Bernd Finkeldey and Maria Müller, Düsseldorf, Kunstsammlung Nordrhein-Westfalen 1991; *Thomas Ruff* by Boris von Brauchitsch, Frankfurt am Main, Museum für Moderne Kunst 1992. **Articles—**''Thomas Ruff'' by Lucie Beyer in *Flash Art* (Milan, Italy), May 1987; ''Reste des Autentischen'' by Manfred Schmalriede in *Camera Austria* (Graz, Austria), no. 23, 1987; ''Doppelganger'' by Manfred Hermes in *Artscribe International* (London, England), March-April, 1988; ''A Report From the Field'' by Jutta Koether in *Flash Art* (Milan, Italy), Summer 1988; ''Thomas Ruff'' by Gregoria Maganni in *Flash Art* (Milan, Italy), Summer 1988; ''Thomas Ruff: Portrats'' by Raija Fellner in *Artefactum* (Antwerp, Belgium), November/December 1988; ''Apollo in Düsseldorf: The Photographs of Thomas Ruff'' by Meer Raphael Rubinstein in *Arts Magazine* (New York), October 1988; ''The Trailer Effect: The Work Becomes a Network and the Artist a Programmer of Coming Attractions'' by Nicolas Bourriaud in *Flash Art* (Milan, Italy), November/December 1989; ''Thomas Ruff'' by Thomas Wulffen in *Artscribe* (London, England), May 1990; ''Heidegger, Beuys and the Consequences'' by Klaus Ottman in *Flash Art* (Milan, Italy), October 1990; ''Thomas Ruff'' by David Rimanelli in *Artforum* (New York), January 1991; ''Gewinnmitnahmen vor der Jahrtausendwende'' by Manfred Hermes in *Texte zur Kunst* (Cologne, Germany) January 1991; ''Deep Surface'' by Annelie Pohlen in *Artforum* (New York), April 1991; ''Le Diaphane'' by Lieven Van Den Abeele in *Artefactum* (Antwerp, Belgium), April/May 1991; special issue of *Parkett* (Zurich, Switzerland), June 1991; ''Thomas Ruff'' by Josef Strau in *Texte zur Kunste* (Cologne, Germany), Summer 1991; ''A Cowboy is Dead'' by Eric Tronc in *Artscribe* (London, England), February/March 1992; ''Thomas Ruff: Reality So Real It's Unrecognizable'' by Thomas Wulffen in *Flash Art,* no. 168, January-February 1993; ''Thomas Ruff: Subjective Propaganda'' by Catherine Hurzeler Herzog in *Parachute*, no. 95, July-September 1999; ''Other Faces, Other Rooms'' by David Galloway in *Artnews,* February 2000.

* * *

Thomas Ruff is best known as one of the protegés of photographers Bernd and Hilla Becher, who rose to prominence in the 1980s by practicing a deadpan style of serial, documentary photography. Other Becher students who have gained international acclaim as photographers include Thomas Struth, Candida Höfer, and Andreas Gursky. However, while the Bechers' photographs of industrial structures seem to maintain a traditional belief in photography's claim to capture reality and offer documentary evidence, much of Ruff's work has questioned the medium's ability to represent reality.

Ruff studied under Bernd Becher at the Kunstakademie Düsseldorf (Düsseldorf Art Academy) from 1977–1985. Ruff's first major series of photographs were the *Interiors* of 1979–83, which recorded the mundane household interiors of his family and friends. The middle-class furnishings seem to date mostly from the 1950s and 1960s and the photographs record, as the artist has stated, the world of his parents' generation and the world in which people of his own generation grew up. Given the artist's straightforward aesthetic approach, there is no suggestion of his trying to criticize middle-class convention; he merely records things as they are.

In 1986, Ruff began the series that made him an international star, the *Portraits* that lasted until 1991. Although the earliest works in this series encompassed both frontal and three-quarter poses as well as backgrounds of different colors, Ruff soon settled on a single, unchanging format for his portraits. Expressionless sitters were photographed frontally in bust-length portraits against a neutral, pale gray background. The results were presented in a large format—generally 210 by 165 centimeters—with rich color and fine detail. The portraits have often been likened to giant passport photographs, and the artist himself has linked them to the prevalence of surveillance and control in contemporary society. In his portraits, Ruff tries to suppress the individuality of his sitters, arguing that attempts to reveal sitters' personalities are misguided and unsuccessful. Whether or not Ruff actually succeeds in erasing personal characteristics is highly debatable; hairstyles, clothing, and different levels of comfort before the camera suggest individual traits about the sitters to the viewers.

Ruff later used the color photographs from the *Portraits* series to create a new series of black-and-white composite photographs called *Other Portraits* (1994–95). Using technology employed by police to create composite photographs, Ruff blended earlier portrait images to create spectral portraits of people who do not exist in real life. Their eerie, slightly blurry quality serves to undermine viewers' attempts to make presumptions about the personal traits of Ruff's subjects. Some of these photographs were shown in the German pavilion at the 1995 Venice Biennale.

Another preoccupation of Ruff's that is related to the *Interiors* series is the *Houses* series of 1987–1997. Taken largely in the Düsseldorf area, the photographs in *Houses* record banal and sometimes bleak apartment buildings, offices, and factories. The artist scrupulously avoids buildings that could be considered to possess intrinsic architectural interest, and he focuses specifically on blocky, post-World War II architecture. In some instances, the artist has manipulated the photographs to remove trees and other elements that might interfere with the stark impression of the buildings, preferring an abstracted, perfected reality to reality itself.

Other series include *Night Pictures* (1992–95), *Stars* (1989–92) and *Newspaper Photos* (early 1990s). In the *Night Pictures*, Ruff used military night vision technology first popularized during the Gulf War when it was used to locate targets and also provide images for television broadcast. While merely recording ordinary urban buildings at night, Ruff's photographs took on a disturbing quality due to these Gulf War associations and their greenish cast. Ruff himself has described them as like crime scenes.

With *Stars* and *Newspaper Photos*, Ruff turned to readymade photographs as the basis for his art. Although here Ruff adopts the now-familiar tactics of postmodern appropriation, unlike an artist like Sherrie Levine, he does not copy images that are well-known. Instead, he chooses ''authorless'' images from the realms of science and journalism. For the star photographs, he purchased a complete set of negatives of the skies of the southern hemisphere from the European

Southern Observatory. He produced his own prints of the negatives in a standard size of 252 x 180 cm. Divorced from their artistic context and displayed within museum spaces, these pieces read as abstract patterns of light and dark.

With the newspaper photographs, Ruff has rephotographed in color his collection of black-and-white newspaper photo clippings and presented them in an enlarged format. The photos are stripped of their captions and rearranged in new constellations of images that seem to bear no logical relation to one another. This image-mixing is taken to new heights in some of Ruff's most recent work, namely the *Billboards* series begun in 1996. In a marked departure from the deadpan, unemotional aesthetics of most of his previous work, Ruff has turned to political photomontage in the tradition of John Heartfield, attacking political leaders from Helmut Kohl to Jesse Helms.

It is difficult to reconcile this most recent series with the rest of Ruff's work. From the late 1970s to the mid-1990s, Ruff's work had largely dealt with recording the people and places of contemporary life in a manner of cool neutrality. Although more critical of photography's alleged objectivity than his former teachers, Bernd and Hilla Becher, Ruff was still clearly working in a vein established during his studies at the Kunstakademie Düsseldorf. His work also bore clear similarities to his former classmates, Höfer, Gursky, and Struth, in both choice of subjects and aesthetic approach. Ruff seems to be charting a new course in his recent work and consciously distancing himself from his expected milieu of Düsseldorf documentary photography.

—Jennifer A. Smith

RULE, Nicolas

Nationality: English. **Born:** Birmingham, England, 5 December 1956; moved to New York, September 1984. **Education:** Central School of Art, London, B.A. 1980; Queens College, City University of New York, M.F.A. 1984. **Family:** . **Career:** . **Awards:** . **Agent:** Esso Gallery, 211 West 28th St., New York, New York 10001, U.S.A. **Address:** 329 E. 13th St., #1D, New York, New York 10001, U.S.A.

Individual EXhibitions:

1990 Nicole Klagsbrun Gallery, New York
1991 Nicole Klagsbrun Gallery, New York
Michael Kohn Gallery, New York
Andrea Ruggiero Gallery, Washington, D.C.
1992 Albert Baronian, Brussels, Belgium
Ho Gallery World Art, Hong Kong
1994 Paul Kasmin Gallery, New York
1995 Galleria Paolo Gentili, Florence, Italy
2000 Esso Gallery, New York

Selected Group Exhibitions:

1987 *16 @ 56,* 56 Bleecker St. Gallery, New York
1989 *Greg Colson, Peter Greenaway, Nicolas Rule,* Nicole Klagsbrun Gallery, New York
1990 *Language in Art,* Aldrich Museum of Contemporary Art, Ridgefield, Connecticut
All Quiet on the Western Front, Galerie Antoine Candeau, Paris
Works on Paper, Paula Allen Gallery, New York
1991 Paley-Wright Gallery, London
Outside America: Going into the Nineties, Fay Gold Gallery, Atlanta, Georgia
1992 *Drawn in the Nineties,* Katonah Museum of Art, New York
Mars Gallery, Tokyo
Ho World Art Gallery, Hong Kong
1993 *The Irony and the Ecstasy: Contemporary American Drawings,* Wesleyan University, Connecticut
Extended Relations, Andrea Rosen Gallery, New York
Drawings: 30th Anniversary Exhibition, Foundation for Performance Art, Leo Castelli Gallery, New York
1994 *Gene Culture,* Fordham University, New York
1995 *Notes on Print with and after Robert Morris,* Cabinet des Estampes de Musee d'Art et d'Histoire, Geneva
1996 *Salon de Tree,* Central Park, New York
The Rational World, Kohn Turner Gallery, Los Angeles
1997 *Splash,* Nicole Klagsburn Gallery, New York
Tracery, Betsy Senior Gallery, New York
1998 *Solo Painting,* North Dakota Museum of Art
Art on Paper, Weatherspoon Art Gallery, Greensboro, North Carolina
1999 *Scripta Manet,* Esso Gallery, New York
Holly Solomon Gallery, New York
2000 *L'Elemento Verbale Nell'Arte Contemporanea,* Galleria Martano, Turin, Italy
Paradise Now, Exit Art, New York

Collections:

Fogg Art Museum, Cambridge, Massachusetts; St. Louis Art Museum, Missouri; Museum of Contemporary Art, Los Angeles; Emily Fisher Landau Collection, Long Island City, New York; Chase Manhattan Bank, New York; Groeninge Collection, Bruges, Belgium.

Publications:

By RULE: Articles—''Interview with Nicholas Rule'' by Leslie Tonkonow in *Journey of Contemporary Art,* vol. 4, 1991.

On RULE: Articles—''Nicolas Rule'' by Robert Mahoney in *Arts Magazine,* September 1990; ''Dark Horse: Nicolas Rule's 'Criminal Type, 1991''' by Jerry Saltz in *Arts Magazine,* October 1991; ''Nicolas Rule, Pur-Sang et Inceste'' by Pierre Sterckx in *L'Instant,* 18 June 1992; ''Extended Relations'' by Roberta Smith in *New York Times,* 7 January 1994; essay by Ken Johnson in *New York Times,* 8 March 2000.

RUPPERSBERG, Allen

Nationality: American. **Born:** Cleveland, Ohio, 5 January 1944. **Education:** Chouinard Art Institute, Los Angeles. **Career:** Independent artist, working in Los Angeles, Santa Monica and New York, since 1969. **Awards:** National Endowment for the Arts grant, Washington, D.C., 1976; Theodoron Award, Guggenheim Museum, New

York, 1982. **Agents:** Brooke Alexander/Brooke Alexander Editions, 59 Wooster Street, New York, New York, 10012. **Address:** 1314 Second Street, Santa Monica, California 90401, U.S.A.

Individual Exhibitions:

1969 Eugenia Butler Gallery, Los Angeles
1970 Pasadena Art Museum, California
1971 Art and Project, Amsterdam
1972 Market Street Program, Venice, California
Pomona College Art Gallery, California
1973 Situation Gallery, London
Galleria Françoise Lambert, Milan
Stedelijk Museum, Amsterdam
Galerie Yvon Lambert, Paris
Information Gallery, University of California at Irvine
1974 Art and Project, Antwerp
Claire Copley Gallery, Los Angeles
Kabinette für Aktuelle Kunst, Bremerhaven, West Germany
1977 *Projects,* Museum of Modern Art, New York
1982 Los Angeles County Museum of Art
1985 Museum of Contemporary Art, Los Angeles (retrospective; travelled to New York)
1988 Christine Burgin Gallery, New York
1989 James Corcoran Gallery, Santa Monica
1990 Christine Burgin Gallery, New York
1991 Galerie Gabrielle Maubrie, Paris & New York
1992 *Western Allen Ruppersberg: A Different Kind of Never-Never-Land,* de Appel Foundation, Amsterdam (catalog)
Christine Burgin Gallery, New York
1993 *Where's Al,* Centre National d'Art Contemporain de Grenoble, France (catalog)
1994 *Looking Backward: 2000–1887,* Jay Gorney Modern Art, New York
How to Remember a Better Tomorrow, Linda Cathcart Gallery, Santa Monica
1996 Margot Leavin Gallery, Los Angeles
1997 Le Magasin, Grenoble, France (catalog)
1999 Fonds Régional d'Art Contemporain Limousin, Limoges, France
2000 *Honey, I Rearranged the Collection,* Christine Burgin Gallery, New York (catalog)
2001 *A Novel That Writes Itself,* Margo Leavin Gallery, West Hollywood, California (also ArtPace Gallery, San Antonio) (catalog)

Selected Group Exhibitions:

1969 *When Attitudes Become Form,* Kunsthalle, Bern (toured West Germany and the U.K.)
955.000, Vancouver Art Gallery
1970 *Art in the Mind,* Allen Memorial Art Museum, Oberlin College, Ohio
Whitney Annual, Whitney Museum, New York
1971 *24 Young Los Angeles Artists,* Los Angeles County Museum of Art
Pier 18, Museum of Modern Art, New York
1972 *Documenta,* Kassel, West Germany
1973 *Videotapes by Artists,* Allen Memorial Art Museum, Oberlin College, Ohio
Artists' Books, Moore College of Art, Philadelphia
1974 *Group Show,* Art and Project, Antwerp
1992 *Night Lines: Words Without Thoughts Never to Heaven Go,* Centraal Museum, Utrecht, The Netherlands (catalog)
1995 *Commercial Art,* Gallery Paule Anglim, San Francisco (catalog)
1999 *Wallace Berman and Jeff Koons, Allan McCollum, Allen Ruppersberg, Andy Warhol,* Nicole Klagsbrun Gallery, New York (catalog)

Collections:

Los Angeles County Museum of Art; Norton Simon Museum of Art, Pasadena, California; Stedelijk Museum, Amsterdam; Guggenheim Museum, New York.

Publications:

By RUPPERSBERG: Books—*23 Pieces,* Los Angeles 1969; *24 Pieces,* Los Angeles 1970; *Al's Grand Hotel,* exhibition catalog, Los Angeles 1970; *Greetings from L.A.,* Los Angeles 1972; *Allen Ruppersberg,* Amsterdam 1973; *Fifty Helpful Hints on the Art of Everybody,* Los Angeles 1984. **Articles**—interview with Daniel Levine in *Journal of Contemporary Art,* vol. 5, no. 2, Fall 1992; "Allen Ruppersberg" in *Art Press,* Special Issue, no. 17, 1996. **Video**—*A Lecture on Houdini,* Los Angeles, 1973.

On RUPPERSBERG: Books—Allen Ruppersberg, exhibition catalog with essay by Helen Winer, Pomona 1972; *Allen Ruppersberg: The Secret of Life and Death,* with essay by Howard Singerman, Los Angeles and Santa Barbara 1985. **Articles**—"Scenarios/Documents/Images II" by Helene Winer in *Art in America* (New York), October 1973; "Wilde about Harry" by Peter Plagens in *Artforum* (New York), April 1975; "Allen Ruppersberg" by Gilda Williams in *Art Monthly,* no. 22, July-August 1999; "Allen Ruppersberg: Un Artiste à la Page" by Eric Troncy in *Beaux Arts Magazine,* no. 186, November 1999; "Allen Ruppersberg: Nothing Ever Happens" by John Slyce in *Artext,* no. 69, May/July 2000.

* * *

Now entering his thirtieth year on the exhibition scene, Allen Ruppersberg continues to uphold the stance which began when he rejected his art school background of traditional formal study of studio art to engage in the conceptually oriented "post-studio" school of thinking in 1969. Located by Peter Plagens in 1985 as "somewhere between Rauschenberg and Ruscha"—both have influenced his work—he was early inspired by artists for whom Duchamp had pointed the way, by Yves Klein and the Nouveaux Réalistes as well as by Jasper Johns.

Ruppersberg's first solo exhibition in 1969 opened the Eugenia Butler Gallery in Los Angeles, that city's first venue for Conceptual Art, which showed William Wegman, William Leviton and others. Included in Seth Segelaub's catalog, *One Month (1969),* he was in touch with New York Conceptualists such as Robert Barry, Joseph

Kosuth and Lawrence Weiner; his meeting with Ger van Elk and Dutch conceptualists led to a solo show in Amsterdam, *Art and Project* (1971).

Indeed, until 1974, despite a 1970 exhibition at the Pasadena Art Museum, his work found its primary response in Europe, more receptive to Conceptual Art in those early years. With that interest still continuing, the American art audience has caught up and joined.

Living in the Los Angeles area for over a decade furnished setting, and often subject, for his work. *Twenty-Three Pieces,* the first of a series of three books, asserted his conviction that art could reveal the beauty and mystery that lies in the ordinary, indeed, the banal. There, 23 black and white snapshots—from park benches to tacky coffee shops, from hotel lobbies to the Museum of Natural History Diorama—offer portraits of emptiness, the pedestrian artlessness of the photography endowing them with mystery and poignancy. In *Greetings from L.A.* (1972), a ''lucid and powerful examination of the tawdry, tarnished truth of Tinseltown,'' the empty pages that comprise the greater part of the book are the most telling. (The orange-covered volume floats, overscaled, over the ocean-side, California-sunset landscape on the 1973 painting, *Greetings from L.A.*)

From Venice, where he lived briefly in 1970, Ruppersberg moved to Hollywood. His own image began to enter his work on frequent occasions; as the reader—narrating in a strait-jacket—in the 1973 video piece *A Lecture on Houdini (for Terry Allen);* seated at a table on which objects gradually accumulate in the series of incongruously captioned snapshots which end with his ''suicide,'' in *To Tell the Truth* (1973), and as negative silhouettes; cut-outs of his profiled head, in *Personal Art* (1973).

A lover of reading, Ruppersberg's work has been nourished by both great books and screaming tabloids, by poetry and by pornography. While continuing to produce original books he appropriates favorite authors—among them Oscar Wilde, whose *Portait of Dorian Gray* he diligently, meticulously and laboriously handprinted on 20 six-by-six-foot canvases in 1974. Fusing literature with painting, he layers it with new meaning. Other pieces join the world of lofty ideas with the world of ordinary objects. In the 1979 *Rare Books* (Baudelaire) an announcement of exhibition of the poet's *oeuvres posthumes* resides in a cigar box. With such wry and unexpected juxtapositions, his work abounds in paradox and contradiction, in irony and ambiguity.

In 1985, the Museum of Contemporary Art in Los Angeles held a survey of Ruppersberg's work, the exhibition traveling to the New Museum of Contemporary Art, New York, later in the same year. A book, *Allen Ruppersberg: The Secret of Life and Death* (Los Angeles and Santa Barbara: Museum of Contemporary Art and Black Sparrow Press, 1985), with a penetrating essay by Howard Singerman, accompanied the show, with reproductions and texts by the artist including, ''Where's Al'' (1972), consisting of 121 typed index cards and 150 instamatic prints, ''A Lecture on Houdini,'' and in part, ''The Secret of Life and Death'' (1977), with text printed over images of natural and man-made objects, together with other writings.

The MOCA survey fully revealed the pungency of Ruppersberg's dry, deadpan wit and the depth of his quirky, sidelong vision in a body of work that is complex yet accessible, profound yet lucid. One critic, Peter Plagens, cited *Dorian Gray* as ''one of Ruppersberg's masterpieces'' in his engaging article on the show. Back in 1970, Plagens had pronounced the Pasadena Museum show ''the worst exhibition I've ever seen,'' then, five years later acclaimed the *Lecture on Houdini* the ''best 40 minutes in five-odd hours inside the world's smallest Twin-Vue walk-in east of the Hudson, the video chamber of the Whitney Museum's Biennial.'' Plagens' view of the survey convincingly confirmed that earlier about-turn!

In *Fifty Helpful Hints on the Art of Everybody* (1984), a kind of artist's credo illuminating and explicating his position, Ruppersberg sums up the essence of his version in a brief sentence: ''Art should be familiar and enigmatic, like human being.'' Indeed, that axiom underscores a body of work that is accessible yet complex, lucid yet profound.

After fifteen years of dividing his time between Santa Monica and New York, Ruppersberg now lives and works in New York.

—Merle Schipper

RUSCHA, Edward (Joseph)

Nationality: American. **Born:** Omaha, Nebraska, 16 December 1937. **Education:** Educated at Classen High School, Oklahoma City, 1954–56; studied at Chouinard Art Institute, Los Angeles, under Richard Rubin, 1956–60. **Military Service:** Served in the United States Navy, 1956–60. **Family:** Married Danna Knego in 1967 (divorced, 1972); son: Edward. **Career:** Painter, photographer, and book creator, Los Angeles, since 1960. Lecturer in painting, University of California at Los Angeles, 1969–70. **Awards:** National Council on the Arts Award, 1967, 1978; National Endowment for the Arts Grant, 1969, 1978; Guggenheim Foundation Fellowship, 1971–72; Skowhegan Medal in Graphics, Maine, 1974; Achievement in Printmaking Award, Graphic Arts Council of the Los Angeles County Museum of Art, 1988; Los Angeles Arts Council Honors, 1990. **Agent:** Office, 90 Gagosian Gallery, 980 Madison Avenue, New York, New York, 10021–1848; Anthony d'Offay Gallery, 9 21 23 and 24 Dering Street, London, W1R 9AA, England. **Address:** 35 South Venice Boulevard, Venice, California, 90291.

Individual Exhibitions:

1963 Ferus Gallery, Los Angeles
1964 Ferus Gallery, Los Angeles
1965 Ferus Gallery, Los Angeles
1967 Alexander Iolas Gallery, New York
1968 Irving Blum Gallery, Los Angeles
Galerie Rudolf Zwirner, Cologne
1969 Irving Blum Gallery, Los Angeles
1970 Alexander Iolas Gallery, New York
Alexander Iolas Gallery, Paris
Galerie Heiner Friedrich, Munich
Nigel Greenwood Inc., London
1971 Contract Graphics Gallery, Houston
1972 University of California at Santa Cruz
Janie C. Lee Gallery, Dallas
Corcoran and Corcoran Gallery, Miami
Minnesota Institute of the Arts
DM Gallery, London

Edward Ruscha: *Ace,* 1961. ©Geoffrey Clements/Corbis.

1973 *Projection,* Projection Ursula Wevers, Cologne
University of California at San Diego
Leo Castelli Gallery, New York
Galerie Françoise Lambert, Milan
Nigel Greenwood Inc., London
John Berggruen Gallery, San Francisco
Ronald Greenberg Gallery, St. Louis
Ace Gallery, Los Angeles
Picker Gallery, Colgate University, Hamilton, New York
1974 Leo Castelli Gallery, New York
Galerie Françoise Lambert, Milan (twice)
Root Art Center, Hamilton College, Clinton, New York
Golden West College, Huntington Beach, California
1975 Galerie Ricke, Cologne
Sable-Castelli Gallery, Toronto
Leo Castelli Gallery, New York
Fox Venice Theatre, California
Prints and Publications 1962–1974, Arts Council of Great Britain, London (toured the U.K.)
1976 Ace Gallery, Los Angeles
Los Angeles Institute of Contemporary Art
Stedelijk Museum, Amsterdam
Paintings, Drawings and Other Works, Albright-Knox Art Gallery, Buffalo, New York
Institute of Contemporary Arts, London
1977 University of Lethbridge, Alberta (travelled to the University of Calgary Art Center, Alberta)
Fort Worth Art Museum, Texas
David Hockney: Photographic Pictures/Edward Ruscha: Photographic Books, Nova Gallery, Vancouver
Ace Gallery, Los Angeles
1978 Galerie Ricke, Cologne
Galerie Rudiger Schöttle, Munich
Castelli Gallery, New York

Edward Ruscha, 1983. ©Richard Schulman/Corbis.

Graphics Works, Auckland City Art Gallery, New Zealand
1979 Richard Hines Gallery, Seattle
Texas Gallery, Houston
Ink, Zurich
1980 Portland Center for the Visual Arts, Oregon
Ace Gallery, Venice, California
Leo Castelli Gallery, New York
Foster Goldstrom Gallery, San Francisco
1981 Arco Center for Visual Art, Los Angeles
The Works of Edward Ruscha, San Francisco
Museum of Modern Art, New York (toured the United States 1982–83)
1983 Route 66, Philadelphia
Bernard Jacobson Gallery, Los Angeles
Galleria del Cavallino, Venice
1984 Leo Castelli Gallery, New York
Morgan Gallery, Kansas City, Missouri
1985 James Corcoran Gallery, Los Angeles
Gallerie Gilbert Brownstone, Paris
Musée St. Pierre, Lyon, France
1986 Leo Castelli Gallery, New York
Westfälischer Kunstverein, Münster, West Germany
Galerie Susan Wyss, Zurich
1987 Robert Miller Gallery, New York
Leo Castelli Greene Street, New York
1988 James Corcoran Gallery, Los Angeles
1989 *''Dreams'' and Other Works on Paper,* Leo Castelli Gallery, New York
1990 *Ed Ruscha Prints,* Richard Green Gallery, Santa Monica, California
Edward Ruscha, Galeria Trisosio, Napoli, Italy
American Masters of the '60s: Early and Late Works, Tony Shafrazi Gallery, New York (catalog)
Edward Ruscha: Los Angeles Apartments 1965, Whitney Museum of American Art, New York (catalog)
1991 *Ed Ruscha: Early Drawings,* Modernism Gallery, San Francisco
Ed Ruscha Paintings, Leo Castelli Gallery, New York
1992 *Edward Ruscha: New Paintings & Drawings,* Galerie Thaddeus Ropac, Salzburg, Austria
Ed Ruscha/Stains, Robert Miller Gallery, New York City (catalog)
1993 *Edward Ruscha: Romance with Liquids,* Gagosian Gallery, New York City (catalog)
Edward Ruscha: Standard Stations, Amarillo Art Center, Texas
Edward Ruscha/New Work, Space Gallery, Brussels, Belgium
1994 *The Books of Ed Ruscha,* Gund Hall Gallery, Harvard University, Cambridge (traveled to Laura Carpenter Fine

Art, Santa Fe; Remba Gallery, Los Angeles; Castelli Gallery, New York)

1998 *Ed Ruscha's Light,* J. Paul Getty Museum, the Getty Center, Los Angeles
Richard Gray Gallery, New York
Ed Ruscha: New Paintings and a Retrospective of Works on Paper, Anthony d'Offay Gallery, London (catalog)

Selected Group Exhibitions:

1962 *New Paintings of Common Objects,* Pasadena Art Museum, California
1965 *Words and Images,* Guggenheim Museum, New York
1969 *Pop Art,* Hayward Gallery, London
1973 *American Drawings 1963–73,* Whitney Museum, New York
1976 *Painting and Sculpture in California: The Modern Era,* San Francisco Museum of Modern Art
1980 *Printed Art: A View of Two Decades,* Museum of Modern Art, New York
1982 *Contemporary Los Angeles Artists,* Nagoya City Museum, Japan
1984 *The Automobile and Culture,* Museum of Contemporary Art, Los Angeles
1985 *Americanische Zeichnungen 1930–80,* Stadtische Galerie im Stadel, Frankfurt
1986 *Spectrum: In Other Words,* Corcoran Gallery of Art, Washington, D.C.
1992 *Special Collections: The Photographic Order from Pop to Now,* International Center of Photography, New York (catalog)
1995 *Articulations: Forms of Language in Contemporary Art,* Whitney Museum of American Art, New York (catalog)
Downtown: Ruscha, Rooney, Arkley, Museum of Modern Art at Heide, Bulleen, Australia (catalog)
1996 *Speck Collection,* Museum Ludwig, Cologne (catalog)
1997 *Artists' Book: The Invention of a Genre, 1960–1980,* Galerie Mansart, Paris (catalog)
47th Venice Biennale, Italy
Sunshine & Noir: Art in L.A. 1960–1997, Louisiana Museum of Modern Art, Humlebaek, Denmark (traveling exhibition) (catalog)
1998 *Speed: Visions of an Accelerated Age,* Whitechapel Art Gallery, London (catalog)

Collections:

Museum of Modern Art, New York; Whitney Museum, New York; Hirshhorn Museum, Washington, D.C.; Contemporary Art Foundation, Oklahoma City; Institute of Arts, Minneapolis; Meadowbrook Art Gallery, Oakland University, Rochester, Michigan; Los Angeles County Museum of Art; Norton Simon Museum of Art, Pasadena, California; Oakland Art Museum, California; Stedelijk Museum, Amsterdam; Art Institute of Chicago; Art Museum of South Texas, Corpus Christi; Fort Worth Art Museum, Texas; Auckland City Art Gallery, New Zealand; Musee Nationale d'Art Moderne, Paris; Denver Art Museum; Museum of Contemporary Art, Los Angeles; PaineWebber Corporation Art Collection, New York.

Public Installations:

Miami-Dade Public Library, Florida, 1985, 1989; Great Hall, Denver Central Library, Colorado (1994–95); *Picture Without Words,* Lobby, Harold M. Williams Auditorium, J. Paul Getty Museum at the Getty Center, 1998.

Publications:

By RUSCHA: Books—*26 Gasoline Stations,* Hollywood 1962; *Various Small Fires,* Hollywood 1964; *Some Los Angeles Apartments,* Hollywood 1965; *The Sunset Strip,* Hollywood 1966; *34 Parking Lots,* Hollywood 1967; *Royal Road Test,* with Mason Williams and Pat Blackwell, Hollywood 1967; *Business Cards,* with Billy Al Bengston, Hollywood 1967; *9 Swimming Pools,* Hollywood 1967; *Crackers,* with Mason Williams, Hollywood 1968; *Babycakes,* New York 1969; *Real Estate Opportunities,* Hollywood 1969; *A Few Palm Trees,* Hollywood 1970; *Records,* Hollywood 1971; *Colored People,* Hollywood 1971; *Dutch Details,* Rotterdam 1972; *Hard Light,* with Lawrence Weiner, Hollywood 1972; *Guacamole Airlines,* New York 1980. **Articles**—''An Interview with Edward Ruscha,'' with John Coplans, in *Artforum* (New York), February 1965; contribution in *Design Quarterly* (Minneapolis), vol. 78/79, 1970; contribution in *Aspen Magazine* (Aspen, Colorado), Fall/Winter 1971; contribution in *Perspecta 13/14* (New Haven, Connecticut), 1971; ''Art: An Interview with Ed Ruscha,'' with Robert Colaciello, in *Inter/View* (New York), March 1972; ''A Kind of a Huh?,'' interview with Willoughby Sharp in *Avalanche* (New York), Winter/Spring 1973; ''Swollen Eye, 1973'' in *Flash Art* (Milan), February/March 1975; ''Interview with Ed Ruscha,'' with Barbara Radice in *Flash Art* (Milan), May 1975; ''The Information Man'' in *Journal* (Los Angeles), June/July 1975; ''Bless You'' in *Vision* (Oakland, California), September 1975; ''Devil or Angel'' in *Art-Rite* (New York), Winter/Spring 1975–76; ''Home Q & A: Edward Ruscha,'' with Marshall Berges in *Home Magazine: Los Angeles Times,* 28 March 1976; ''They Shoot Corners, Don't They?'' in *Esquire* (New York), January 1977; ''Feature Interview: Edward Ruscha,'' with Diane Spodarek, in *Detroit Artists Monthly,* April 1977; ''A Conversation with Ed Ruscha,'' with Trina Mitchum, in *LAICA Journal* (Los Angeles), June/July 1979; ''Ed Ruscha on V-Various S-Subjects'' in *Stuff Magazine* (Los Angeles), No. 24, 1980; ''Ed Ruscha: An Interview,'' with Henri Man Barendse, in *Afterimage* (Rochester, New York), February 1981; interview with Elizabeth Armstrong in *October,* no. 70, Fall 1994; interview with Andreas Reiter Raabe in *Camera Austria,* no. 64, 1998; interview with Siri Engberg in *Art on Paper,* vol. 4, no. 2, November-December 1999. **Films**—*Premium,* 1972; *Miracle,* 1974.

On RUSCHA: Books—*Changing: Essays in Art Criticism* by Lucy R. Lippard, New York 1971; *14 Big Prints* by Bernard Jacobson, London 1972; *Edward Ruscha: Prints and Publications 1962–1974,* exhibition catalog by Reyner Banham, London 1975; *Paintings, Drawings and Other Works by Edward Ruscha,* exhibition catalog by Linda L. Cathcart, Buffalo, New York 1976; *Painting and Sculpture in California: The Modern Era,* exhibition catalog by Henry T. Hopkins, San Francisco 1977; *Cities* by Joseph A. Gatto, Worcester, Massachusetts, 1977; *Graphic Words by Edward Ruscha,* exhibition catalog by Andrew Boyle, Auckland 1978; *The 73rd American*

Exhibition, exhibition catalog by Anne Rorimer and James Speyer, Chicago 1979; *Fifty West Coast Artists* by Henry Hopkins and Mimi Jacobs, San Francisco 1981; *The Works of Ed Ruscha,* exhibition catalog with texts by Dave Hickey and Peter Plagens, San Francisco 1982; *Photography and Art 1946–86* by Andy Grundberg and Kathleen M. Gauss, Los Angeles 1987. **Articles—**''Ed Words: Ruscha in Print'' by Michael Dooley in *Print,* vol. 48, no. 5, September-October 1994; ''Edition for Parkett: Edward Ruscha—Vine/Melrose, 1999'' in *Parkett,* no. 55, June 1999; ''Two Pops: Edward Ruscha and Wayne Thiebaud'' by Peter Plagens in *Artforum,* Summer 2000.

* * *

According to his own record, Edward Ruscha has been in and out of painting and then back in again. Indisputably, this American is an organized and effective academic artist. For a large and not always sympathetic public he certainly can draw and paint naturalistic imagery of hyper-realist faultlessness. He spent some time—between 1956 and 1960—at the Chouinard Art Institute, but on the whole he is a natural artist with automatic talent. Much of his screenprint and lithographic work together with a number of the books he has published served to introduce him to the British, a result of the interest and enthusiasm of Nigel Greenwood.

What does Ruscha actually do?

He records the contemporary scene and its flavours.

But not just as a topographer. Ruscha selects, often the most ordinary details of modern life—as in his series of ''Twenty-Six Gasoline Stations'' (1962). Somehow, somewhere, and definitely not just round the corner, Ruscha found garages and gave to each a character no passerby would ever have imagined; he gave these petrol stations *identity* without in any way altering their actual appearance.

A sort of magic!

It is difficult to tell; still more awkward to explain.

Ruscha paints (lifts!) the gargantuan neon sign that says ''Hollywood'' at hillcrest height. Never mind if its natural site is half-way down the slope. For him it is a beacon, and blazing signs like that need to be seen from far, far away. So that is how he makes the pictures.

Is this what contemporary art is about?

Ed Ruscha has made his mark. The choice lies with his viewers. How many of them want to know ''Every Building on the Sunset Strip''?

—Sheldon Williams

In the late 1990s Ruscha produced a series of large scale gray, white, and black paintings in which shafts of light stream through high windows into stark architectural spaces. These almost spiritual paintings are dominated by enigmatic phrases, like ''An exhibition of gasoline powered engines'' (1993). These works were featured in the 1998 exhibition *Ed Ruscha's Light* at the J. Paul Getty Museum in Los Angeles. At the time of the exhibition, the Getty commissioned a monumental painting from this series, the twenty-three-foot high ''Picture Without Words.'' This painting hangs permanently in the lobby of the Getty's auditorium.

Ruscha's most recent works show intersections of Los Angeles streets. In these simple, schematic works, simple lines intersect to form grids. The names of the street appear alongside the appropriate line, and the entire composition is rendered in shades of gray. This recent series is reminiscent of Ruscha's early works that chronicled parts of Los Angeles photographically, like the book *Every Building on the Sunset Strip* (1966), on which Ruscha built the foundations of his career.

—Tara Reddy Young

RUTHENBECK, Reiner

Nationality: German. **Born:** Velbert, 30 June 1937. **Education:** Studied art, under Joseph Beuys, at the Staatliche Kunstakademie, Dusseldorf, 1962–68. **Family:** Married Erika Schussler in 1962. **Career:** Worked as photographer, in Velbert, West Berlin and Dusseldorf, until 1962; sculptor, Dusseldorf, since 1967; began transcendental meditation 1972. Instructor, Hochshule für Bildende Künste, Hamburg, 1975–76, and Staatliche Kunstakademie, Dusseldorf, since 1980. **Awards:** Kunstpreis der Stadt, Krefeld, 1973; Konrad-von-Soest Preis, Munster, 1982. **Address:** Frankenstrasse 23-Hof, 4000 Dusseldorf 30, Germany.

Individual Exhibitions:

1967 Galleri Charlottenburg, Copenhagen
1968 Galerie Konrad Fischer, Dusseldorf
Wide White Space Gallery, Antwerp
1969 Galerie Konrad Fischer, Dusseldorf
Galerie René Block, West Berlin
Galerie Heiner Friedrich, Munich
1970 Galerie Konrad Fischer, Dusseldorf
1971 Galerie Heiner Friedrich, Munich
Kabinett für Aktuelle Kunst, Bremerhaven, West Germany
Westfälischer Kunstverein, Münster, West Germany
1972 Städtische Museum, Mönchengladbach, West Germany
Galerie Konrad Fischer, Dusseldorf
1973 Kunstverein, Krefeld, West Germany
Kunsthalle, Kiel, West Germany
1974 Städtische Kunsthalle, Dusseldorf
Galerie Rolf Preisig, Basel
Kabinet für Aktuelle Kunst, Bremerhaven, West Germany
Galerie Müller, Stuttgart
Galerie René Block, West Berlin
1975 Galerie Klein, Bonn
René Block Gallery, New York
1976 Kabinett für Aktuelle Kunst, Bremerhaven, West Germany
Galerie Durand-Dessert, Paris
1977 Centre Culturel du Marais, Paris
Galleria Peccolo, Livorno, Italy
1978 *Handzeichnungen,* Museum Haus Lange, Krefeld, West Germany
Samangalleria, Genoa
Galerie Klein, Bonn
1979 Samangalleria, Genoa
Galerie Maier-Hahn, Dusseldorf
1980 Galerie Erika und Otto Friedrich, Bern
1981 Galerie Klein, Bonn
1982 Galerie Konrad Fischer, Dusseldorf
Forum Kunst, Rottweil, West Germany
1986 Musée d'Art Moderne de la Ville, Paris
Galerie Muller-Roth, Stuttgart
Galerie Akumulatory II, Poznan, Poland

1987 Stalom, Salon am Burgplatz, Dusseldorf
1991 *Fotografie 1956–1976,* Kunstverein für die Rheinland und Westfalen, Dusseldorf (catalog)
1993 Staatliche Kunsthalle, Baden-Baden, Germany (catalog)
2000 *Sorgeln—Gerauscharbeit,* Fruhwerkswaage, Cologne (catalog)

Selected Group Exhibitions:

1969 *When Attitudes Become Form,* Kunsthalle, Bern (toured Europe)
1972 *Documenta 5,* Museum Fredericianum, Kassel, West Germany (and *Documenta 6,* 1977; *Documenta 7,* 1982)
1976 *Biennale,* Venice
1978 *Focus '78,* Centre Culturel de Marais, Paris
1979 *Wahrnehmungen, Aufzeichnungen, Mitteilungen,* Museum Haus Lange, Krefeld, West Germany (travelled to the Nationalgalerie, West Berlin)
1980 *Pier and Ocean,* Hayward Gallery, London (travelled to Rijksmuseum Kröller-Müller, Otterlo Netherlands)
1981 *Art Allemand Aujourd'hui,* Musée d'Art Moderne, Paris
1982 *Kunst wird Material,* Nationalgalerie, West Berlin
1986 *Von Zwei Quadraten,* Wilhelm-Hack-Museum, Ludwigshafen, West Germany
1987 *Das Andere Medium,* Museum am Ostwall, Dortmund, West Germany
1991 *Von der Geistigen Kraft in der Kunst,* Die Galerie, Würzburg, Germany (catalog)
1993 *Gravity & Grace: The Changing Condition of Sculpture 1965–1975,* Hayward Gallery, London (catalog)
1997 *Skulptur: Projekte,* Münster, Germany
Galerie der Gegenwart, Hamburger Kunsthalle, Hamburg
1998 *Circa 1968,* Museu Serralves, Oporto, Portugal

Collections:

Kunstmuseum, Dusseldorf; Museum Ludwig, Cologne; Kunsthalle, Hamburg; Staatsgalerie, Stuttgart; Kaiser Wilhelm Museum, Krefeld, Germany; Hessiches Landesmuseum, Darmstadt; Von der Heydt Museum, Wuppertal, Germany; Städtische Museum, Bonn; Centre Georges Pompidou, Paris; Museum of Modern Art, New York.

Publications:

By RUTHENBECK: Books—*Dach Skulptur,* Mönchengladbach, West Germany 1972. **Article—**"Ruthenbeck" in *Interfunktionen* (Cologne), no. 10, 1973. **Videos—***Papier,* 1970; *Object to Partially Conceal a Video Screen,* 1972.

On RUTHENBECK: Books—*Deutsche Kunst: Eine neue Generation* by Rolf Günter, Cologne 1970; *Bis Heute* by Karin Thomas, Cologne 1972; *Kunstpraxis Huete* by Karin Thomas, Cologne 1972; *Handzeichnungen,* exhibition catalog with text by Gerhard Storck, Krefeld, West Germany 1978; *Art Allemand Aujourd'hui,* exhibition catalog, Paris 1981; *Gesprache mit Kunstlern* by A. Haase, Cologne 1981; *Reiner Ruthenbeck: Arbeiten 1965–1983,* exhibition catalog, Braunschweig 1983; *Reiner Ruthenbeck: Entre chien et loup,* exhibition catalog, Paris 1986; *Reiner Ruthenbeck,* exhibition catalog, Stuttgart and Nuremberg 1986. **Articles—**"Reiner Ruthenbeck" by Doris von Drathen in *Kunstforum International,* no. 101, June 1989; "Rainer Ruthenbeck" by Sabine B. Vogel in *Artforum International,* vol. 34, March 1996; "Humor und Formen im Raum" by Ursula Bode in *ART: Das Kunstmagazin,* no. 10, October 1993.

*

In my work I have tried, among other things, to bring polarities, contrast and tensions to a formal unity.

By a reduction to simple lucid structures which appear to offer little nourishment to the intellect, I would like to lead the spectator to an entirely contemplative view of my art.

—Reiner Ruthenbeck

* * *

Before Reiner Ruthenbeck went to the Kunstakademie of Dusseldorf as a pupil of Joseph Beuys, he was a photographer. Certainly, the fact that he had been a photographer exercised no immediate influence on his plastic works, and yet certain motifs in his photographs remind one of those which are characteristic of his sculptures. That almost oppressive taciturnity and that atmosphere of tension which distinguish his works over and above any artistic virtousity were already evident in his photographs. Empty streets and half-demolished house fronts are depicted; a climate of tangible desolation is built up. Or a window in which a curtain is gently blown by the wind. Peace—silence. Every movement appears literally frozen. The scenery is in a state of suspended animation; the stillness is ghostlike and oppressive. In familiar objects Ruthenbeck reveals the strangeness which will not be bound by the conventions of normal experience.

At the beginning of his artistic career, Ruthenbeck always made use of a single material for the production of an object. Iron, for example, or wood. He fashioned sculptures from these, which mirror the forms of simple objects from everyday life. With distortions, of course. Giant spoons are created, two and a half metres high; giant umbrellas, a metre higher than that; tiny cupboards on one-dimensional legs—and ladders whose rungs are so closely spaced that they are impossible to climb. Although Ruthenbeck was more concerned with the forms of objects than their function, for example the rounding of the spoons, the cool stereometry of the cupboards, the uniform rhythmicality of the steps of the ladder, nonetheless there is at the same time an unmistakeable attempt to make would-be useful objects unusable. Without, however, annihilating them. Unusable solely as a result of placing undue emphasis on their formal qualities and peculiarities.

On the other hand one can not overlook the point that Ruthenbeck is trying to protect the objects from total use and, consequently, their gradual destruction. The concave inner surfaces of the spoons are wrapped in thin bands of iron, as if they required protection from some external threat, just as an umbrella guarantees protection to the space beneath it when it rains. Strips of material cut in oblongs hang in a wire cage, beyond the reach of grasping hands. And finally, a large heap of ashes is provided with a mesh of wire and iron bars, like a hedgehog that has curled itself up into a ball before an aggressor.

Later Ruthenbeck proceeded to eradicate the former "literary" dimensions in his works in favour of a subtle development of materials. He combined differing materials which evoke contrary responses in the observer; dark red widths of cloth, often cut in rectangles and sewn together, stretched taut by means of iron and glass plates which Ruthenbeck inserts into them, or else hung down limply from cords fastened diagonally across the exhibition space and thrown over iron poles. Ruthenbeck tracks down hidden tensions, indeed he provokes them. As a result of this, cloth, to which the observer attributes the quality of softness, is unexpectedly revealed as a ''hard'' material. Convention is broken down; things learnt from experience turn upside-down.

Above all, he affords things, dispassionately, whether it is a question of the purely artistic or the unequivocally practical, a personal dignity and autonomy, values which are commonly reserved for things seen as art, but denied to the practical.

This dignity is also to be found in the architectural spaces to which the sculptor has in recent years turned his attention. His contribution to the 1976 *Biennale* in Venice consisted of a project called ''Doorway'' which was quite simply a doorway. Ruthenbeck stretched rubber cables through two inner-connecting rooms. The rubber cables were fastened to and covered the whole surface area of the opposing walls. In the doorway they bunched up, and created there a kind of energy centre. Reiner Ruthenbeck turned an ordinarily accessible room into a seeing room. Its structural identity and identity as object became more important than his own purposes.

—Klaus Honnef

RYMAN, Robert

Nationality: American. **Born:** Nashville, Tennessee, 30 May 1930. **Education:** Tennessee Polytechnic, Cookville, 1948–49; George Peabody College for Teachers, 1949–50. **Family:** Married Lucy Lippard, 1961 (divorced 1966); children: Ethan, Ryman; Married Merrill Wagner, 1969; children: William, Tracy, George Corydon. **Career:** Worked as a guard, Museum of Modern Art, New York, in the 1950s. Independent artist, New York, since 1966. **Member:** Art Commission of New York, 1982–85, member of Board of Directors since 1991. **Agent:** Galerie Maeght Lelong, 9 West 57th Street, New York, New York 10019. **Address:** 17 West 16th Street, New York, New York 10011–6301, U.S.A.; Studio, 637 Greenwich St., New York, New York, 10014–3306.

Individual Exhibitions:

1967 Paul Bianchini Gallery, New York
1968 Konrad Fischer Gallery, Dusseldorf
Heiner Friedrich Gallery, Munich
1969 Konrad Fischer Gallery, Dusseldorf
Heiner Friedrich, Gallery, Munich
Fischbach Gallery, New York
Françoise Lambert Galleria, Milan
Galerie Yvon Lambert, Paris
Ace Gallery, Los Angeles
1970 Fischbach Gallery, New York
1971 Fischbach Gallery, New York
Current Editions, Seattle
Dwan Gallery, New York
Heiner Friedrich Gallery, Cologne
1972 Heiner Friedrich Gallery, Cologne
Current Editions, Seattle
John Weber Gallery, New York
Guggenheim Museum, New York
Galerie Annemarie Verna, Zurich
Galleria del Cortile, Rome
Lisson Gallery, London
1973 Galleria San Fedele, Milan
John Weber Gallery, New York
Konrad Fischer Gallery, Dusseldorf
Art and Project, Amsterdam
1974 Stedelijk Museum, Amsterdam
Westfälischer Kunstverein, Münster, West Germany
Palais des Beaux-Arts, Brussels
John Weber Gallery, New York
1975 John Weber Gallery, New York
Kunsthalle, Basel
1977 Public School #1, Long Island City, New York
Gian Enzo Sperone Galeria, Rome
Galerie Annemarie Verna, Zurich
Galerie Charles Kriwin, Brussels
Whitechapel Art Gallery, London
1978 Galerie Inc., Zurich
1979 Galerie Inc., Zurich
Sidney Janis Gallery, New York
1980 Konrad Fischer Galerie, Dusseldorf
Paintings 1958–1980, Galerie Inc., Zurich
Kunstraum, Munich
1981 Sidney Janis Gallery, New York
1982 Young Hoffman Gallery, Chicago
James Mayor Gallery, London
Kunsthalle, Dusseldorf
1983 Bonnier Gallery, New York
Daniel Weinberg Gallery, Los Angeles
1984 Galerie Maeght Lelong, New York
Galerie Maeght Lelong, Paris
1987 Art Institute of Chicago
1988 San Francisco Museum of Modern Art
Dia Center for the Arts, New York
1991 *Robert Ryman,* Espace d'Art Contemporain, Paris (traveled to Hallen fur Neue Kunst, Schaffhausen, Switzerland) (catalog)
1992 *Robert Ryman: Versions,* Hallen fur neue Kunst, Schaffhausen, Switzerland (catalog)
1993 *Robert Ryman,* Tate Gallery, London (catalog)
Museo Nacional Centro de Arte Reina Sofia, Madrid (catalog)
1994 Museum of Modern Art, New York
Robert Ryman: New Paintings, Pace Gallery, New York (catalog)
1999 *Robert Ryman: Paris,* PaceWildenstein Gallery, New York (catalog)
2000 *Robert Ryman: Paintings from the Sixties,* Xavier Hufkens Gallery, Brussels (catalog)

Selected Group Exhibitions:

1968 *Gordon/Lonzano/Stanley,* Contemporary Arts Center, Cincinnati, Ohio
1977 *Documenta 6,* Museum Fridericianum, Kassel, West Germany (and *Documenta 7,* 1982)
1978 *American Post-War Painting from the Guggenheim Collection,* Guggenheim Museum, New York

1979 *73rd American Exhibition,* Art Institute of Chicago
1980 *Printed Art: A View of 2 Decades,* Museum of Modern Art, New York
1981 *A New Spirit in Painting,* Royal Academy of Arts, London
1982 *The New York School,* Guggenheim Museum, New York
1983 *Abstract Painting 1960–69,* Project Studio One, New York
1984 *The Meditative Surface,* Renaissance Society, Chicago
1990 *American Masters of the '60s: Early and Late Works,* Tony Shafrazi Gallery, New York (catalog)
Object and Content: Meaning in Minimal Art, Australian National Gallery, Canberra (catalog)
1994 *Contemporary Art from the Collection of the Federation of Migros Co-operatives,* Museo Cantonale d'Arte, Lugano, Switzerland (catalog)
Painting: Emblems and References, capc Musee d'Art Contemporain, Bordeaux, France (catalog)
1995 *Abstraction: Pure and Impure,* Museum of Modern Art, New York (catalog)
Biennial, Whitney Museum of American Art, New York
American Drawings and Graphic Works: From Sol LeWitt to Bruce Nauman, Kunsthaus, Zurich (catalog)

Collections:

Museum of Modern Art, New York; Guggenheim Museum, New York; Sidney Janis Gallery Collection, New York; Dayton Art Museum, Ohio; Minneapolis Art Institute; San Francisco Museum of Modern Art; Stedelijk Museum, Amsterdam; Milwaukee Art Center; Whitney Museum of American Art, New York.

Publications:

By RYMAN: Books—*Robert Ryman Prints, 1969–1993,* with Amy Baker Sandback and Betsy Senior, New York 1993. **Articles—** statement in *Art in Process IV* (New York), December 1970; ''An Interview with Robert Ryman,'' with Phyllis Tuchman, in *Artforum* (New York), May 1971; statement in *Art Now: New York,* September 1971; ''An Interview with Robert Ryman,'' with Achille Bonito Oliva in *Domus* (Milan), February 1973; ''Robert Ryman, Le Geste'' in *Revue d'Art Contemporain* (Paris), November 1974; statement in *Fundamental Painting,* exhibition catalog, Amsterdam 1975; statement in *Prints: Bochner/Le Witt/Mangold/Marden/Martin/Renouf/Rockburne/Ryman,* exhibition catalog, Toronto 1975; interview with Barbaralee Diamondstein in *Inside New York's Art World,* New York 1979; statement in *Wall Painting: Hafif/Jackson/Pozzi/Ryman/Yasuda,* exhibition catalog, Chicago 1979; ''Robert Ryman,'' interview with Peter Blum in *Du* (Zurich), Summer 1980; interview with Simon Morley in *Art Monthly,* no. 164, March 1993; interview with David Batchelor in *Frieze,* no. 10, May 1993; ''Robert Ryman: 'Standard', 1967'' with Klaus Kertess in *Artforum,* vol. 35, no. 1, September 1996; interview with David Carrier in *Burlington Magazine* (London), vol. 139, no. 1134, September 1997. **Videotape—**interview for *Video Data Bank,* School of the Art Institute of Chicago, Spring 1979. **Film—**interview for *Art Report,* television program, by Hideo Kinoshita, for Art Agency, Tokyo 1979.

On RYMAN: Books—*Changing: Essays in Art Criticism* by Lucy R. Lippard, New York 1971; *Robert Ryman,* exhibition catalog with an introduction by Diane Waldman, New York 1972; *Robert Ryman,* exhibition catalog with an introduction by Naomi Spector, Amsterdam 1974; *Robert Ryman,* exhibition catalog with an introduction by Carlo Huber, Basel 1975; *Drawing Now,* exhibition catalog with an introduction by Bernice Rose, New York 1976; *Yesterday, Today, Tomorrow,* exhibition catalog with an introduction by Paul E. Thompson, Miami, 1976; *Robert Ryman,* exhibition catalog with introduction by Naomi Spector, London 1977; *73rd American Exhibition,* exhibition catalog with an introduction by Anne Rorimer, Chicago 1979; *Inside New York's Art World* by Barbaralee Diamondstein, New York 1979; *Robert Ryman: Paintings 1958–1980,* exhibition catalog with an introduction by Christel Sauer, Zurich 1980; *Appreciating Ryman* by Jeremy Gilbert-Rolfe 1980; *Printed Art: A View of 2 Decades,* exhibition catalog, New York 1980; *Art of the 70s,* exhibition catalog, Venice 1980; *A New Spirit in Painting,* exhibition catalog, London 1980; *Minimal Art from Crex Collection,* exhibition catalog, Madrid 1981; *Robert Ryman: Reperes,* exhibition catalog with preface by Jean Fremon, Paris 1984; *Robert Ryman: The Charter Series,* exhibition catalog with text by Neal Benezra, Chicago 1987. **Articles—**''Robert Ryman: A Sequence of Variations'' by Clare Farrow in *Art and Design,* vol. 8, no. 11–12, 1993; ''Ryman's Poetics'' by Christopher S. Wood in *Art in America* (New York), vol. 82, no. 1, January 1994; ''Ryman: Eloge du Blanc'' by Ann Hindry in *Beaux Arts Magazine,* no. 121, March 1994; ''Robert Ryman'' by Klaus Kertess in *Artforum,* vol. 35, no. 1, September 1996; ''Robert Ryman on the Origins of His Art'' by David Carrier in *Burlington Magazine,* vol. 139, no. 1134, September 1997.

* * *

''Before a picture represents a battlefield, a nude or some other anecdote, it is first of all a surface covered with paints applied in a special way.'' These famous words of Maurice Denis are rightly put at the head of any experiment in ''pure painting.'' The great majority of Robert Ryman's pictures are rectangular in shape and painted in white. They refer to nothing beyond themselves; they are simply ''surfaces covered with paint.'' Thus what comes clearly to the fore is the language, or rather the various languages, of the material, released from any obligation to depict actual existing phenomena.

The painting is an existing phenomena in itself, an object among other objects. Ryman does not paint entirely in monochrome; since his white is totally and definitely empirical, concrete, phenomenal, it is as if it had broken down into a number of ''whites.'' It is thus a pure relationship—but a relationship with what? With what other factors? Ryman takes into account everything involved in painting; he works them and manipulates them so as to explore the depths of their formal significance. Cotton, canvas, steel, cardboard, wood, fibreglass—all these are materials which have their own specific languages, which form relationships producing new interactions and novel perceptions with oils, tempera, acrylics and so on. Many different levels of brightness, of softness, of dark or light tone, of shade, and refractions arise from this treatment. And then the format (Ryman often works on a number of paintings in series) is always determined in relation to the size of the wall, the height at which the painting is to be hung and so on, thus creating a complex network of interactions which almost make a ''story'' in themselves, even though nothing is represented or portrayed by them.

It is the actual story of the material—which obviously has its own mental, even conceptual, significance—that is diversified by itself, empirically: ''to make'' is in fact perhaps Ryman's favorite word. And he identifies ''making'' with knowing the languages of the materials and what can be deduced and produced from them. This has always been the prime skill of the painter; and this is Ryman's skill.

—Massimo Carboni

S

SAINT-PHALLE, Niki de

Nationality: French. **Born:** Neuilly-sur-Seine, Paris, 29 October 1930. **Education:** Convent of Sacre Coeur, New York, 1936–45; self-taught in art, but influenced by work of Antoni Gaudi and Le Facteur Cheval. **Family:** Married the writer Harry Mathews in 1948 (separated, 1960); children: Laure and Philippe; married the artist Jean Tinguely, 1971 (died 1991). **Career:** Independent artist, since 1952, in Paris, subsequently in Soisy-sur-Ecole, France: first painting, 1952; first object-reliefs and assemblages, 1956; first experimental rifle-shot paintings, 1960; happenings and manifestations, with Jean Tinguely, from 1961; first "Nana" sculptures with daughter Laure, 1965; first theatre decors, with Martial Raysse and Jean Tinguely, 1966; first films, 1973; worked on Tarot Garden outdoor sculptures project in Tuscany, Italy, from 1979; creates Niki de Saint Phalle Le Parfum de L'Art, 1982. **Awards:** Caran d'Ache, 1994; 12th Praemium Imperiale Laureate, Japan Art Association, 2000. **Agents:** Gimpel Fils, 30 Davies Street, London WIY ILG, England; Marisa del Re Gallery, 41 East 57th Street, New York, New York 10022, U.S.A. **Address:** L'Auberge du Cheval-Blanc, 91840 Soisy-sur-Ecole, Essones, France. **Web site:** http://www.nikidesaintphalle.com.

Individual Exhibitions:

1961 Galerie J. Paris
Galerie Koepcke, Copenhagen
Moderna Museet, Stockholm
1962 Dwan Gallery, Los Angeles
Galerie Rive Droite, Paris
Alexandre Jolas Gallery, New York
1963 Dwan Gallery, Los Angeles
1964 Hanover Gallery, London
Palais des Beaux-Arts, Brussels
Galerie Iolas, Geneva
1965 Alexandre Iolas Gallery, New York
Galerie Alexandre Iolas, Paris
1966 Alexandre Iolas Gallery, New York
1967 Stedelijk Museum, Amsterdam
Galerie Espace, Amsterdam
Fondation Maeght, St. Paul-de-Vence, France
1968 Gimpel und Hanover Galerie, Zurich
Hanover Gallery, London
Kunstverein, Dusseldorf (retrospective)
Stadttheater, Kassel, West Germany (decors for *Ich,* with Rainer von Diez)
1969 Kunstverein, Hannover (retrospective)
Galerie Stangl, Munich
Kunstmuseum, Lucerne (retrospective)
Galerie Iolas, Geneva
Galerie Seriaal, Amsterdam
Galerie Ad Libitum, Antwerp (with Jean Tinguely)
1970 Galerie Alexandre Iolas, Paris
Les Halles, Paris
Galerie Der Spiegel, Cologne
Please Give Me a Few Seconds of Your Eternity, Galleria Iolas, Milan
Gimpel und Hanover Galerie, Zurich
Musée des Beaux-Arts, Lille, France
1971 Galerie Espace, Amsterdam
Galerie Runquist, Stockholm
Galleria Carmine, Rome
Gimpel and Weitzenhoffer, New York
1972 Galerie Rive Gauche, Brussels
Galerie Alexandre Iolas, Paris
Galerie Bonnier, Geneva
Gimpel Fils, London
Galerie Stangl, Munich
1973 Gimpel and Weitzenhoffer, New York
1974 Galerie Alexandre Iolas, Paris
1975 Musée d'Art et d'Industrie, Arles, France
Galerie Le Point, Beirut
1976 Nordijyllands Konstmusemum, Aalborg, Denmark
1977 Fondation Veianneman, Kruishoutem, Belgium
1978 Gimpel and Weitzenhoffer, New York
Banque Lambert, Brussels
1979 Watari Gallery, Tokyo
Gallery Iolas, Athens
Gimpel and Weitzenhoffer, New York
1980 Galerie Bischofberger, Zurich
Bawag Foundation, Vienna
Ulmer Museum, Ulm, West Germany
Museum of Fine Arts, Columbus, Ohio (toured the United States)
Centre Georges Pompidou, Paris (retrospective; toured Germany, Austria, Britain, Sweden and Israel)
1981 Galerie Bonnier, Geneva
1982 Gimpel and Weitzenhoffer, New York
Gimpel Fils, London
1983 Gallery Esperanze, Montreal
1985 Casino Knokke, Belgium
Gimpel Fils, London
Gimpel and Weitzenhoffer, New York
Galerie Klaus Littmann, Basel
1987 Space Niki/Sagacho Exhibit Space, Tokyo
Kunsthalle der Hypo-Kulturstiftung, Munich
Galerie Bonnier, Geneva
Nassau County Museum of Fine Art, Roslyn, New York
1989 *Oeuvres des annees 80,* JGM Galerie and Galerie de France, Paris
1990 *Tirs. . . et autres revolts 1961–64,* JGM Galerie and Galerie de France, Paris
1991 *Niki de Saint-Phalle: New Bronzes,* Gimpel Fils Gallery, London (catalog)
1992 Kunst-und Ausstellunghalle der Bundesrepublik Deutschland, Bonn (traveling retrospective exhibition) (catalog)
1994 *Niki de Saint Phalle: Tableaux Eclates 1994,* James Goodman Gallery, New York and Maxwell Davidson Gallery, New York (catalog)

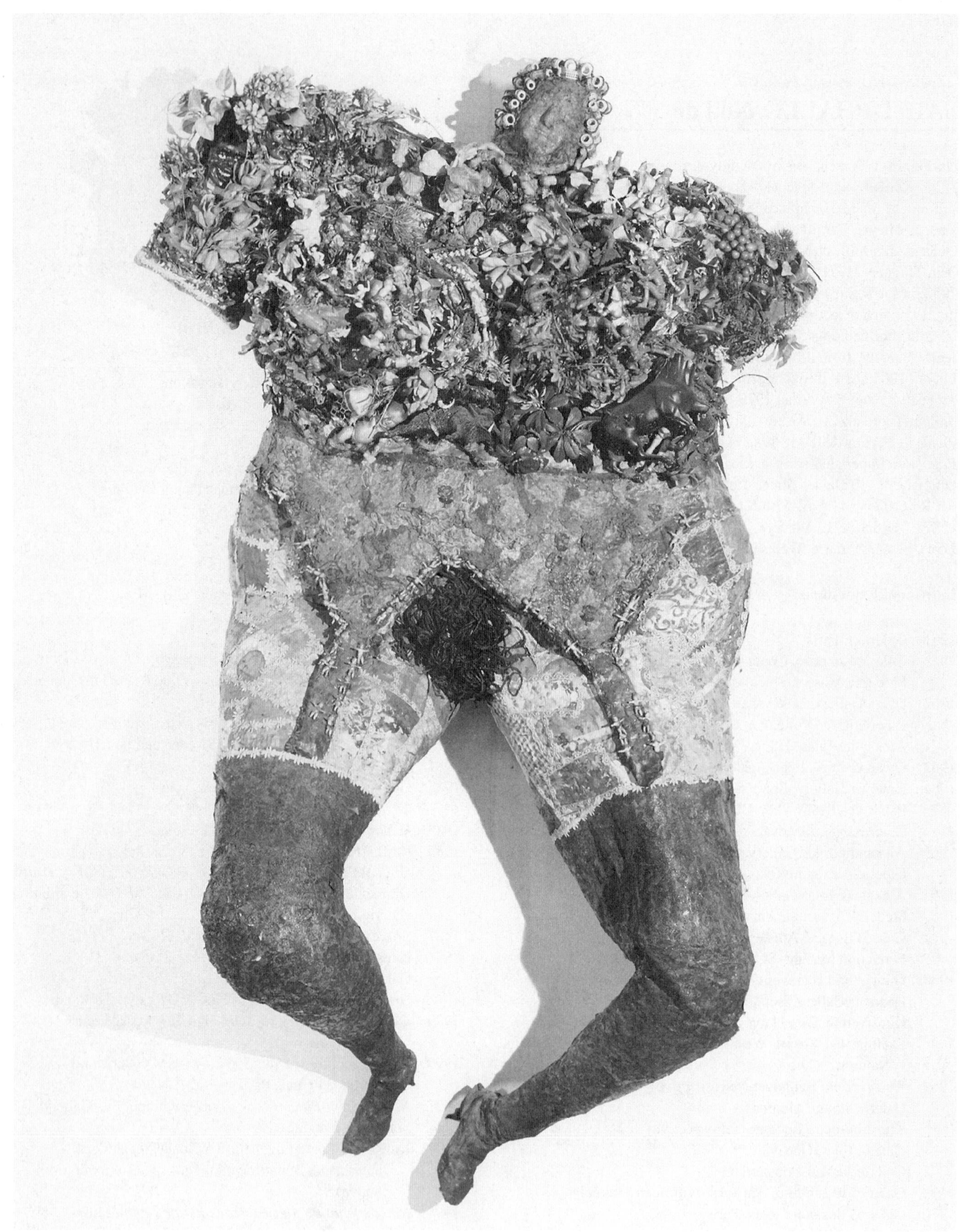

Niki de Saint-Phalle: *Crucifixion,* 1963. ©Musee National d'Art Giraudon/Art Resource, NY.

Sculpture by Niki de Saint-Phalle at the Park of Monsters, ca. 1980–97. ©Massimo Listri/Corbis.

1997 *The Tarot Garden,* Orbetello, Polveriera Guzman, Italy (catalog)
1999 *Niki de Saint Phalle—Insider/Outsider: World Inspired Art,* Mingei International Museum, Balboa Park, San Diego

Selected Group Exhibitions:

1961 *The Art of Assemblage,* Museum of Modern Art, New York
1963 *Biennale de Paris,* Musée d'Art Moderne, Paris
1966 *4 European Artisis and the Figure,* Art Institute of Chicago
1968 *Dada, Surrealism and Their Heritage,* Museum of Modern Art, New York
1970 *Pop Art, Nouveau Realisme,* Casino Communal, Knokke, Belgium
1972 *12 Ans d'Art Contemporain en France,* Grand Palais, Paris
1978 *Collection Hammer,* Kunstmuseum, Basel
1980 *The Figurative Tradition,* Whitney Museum, New York
1985 *Nouveau Realisme and Pop,* Museum of Contemporary Art, Chicago
1987 *Sacred Spaces,* Everson Museum of Art, Syracuse, New York
1988 *Nouveaux Realistes,* Zabriskie Gallery, New York (catalog)
1995 *Out 100th Anniversary of Paintings of People—Pictoral Worlds,* Museum Ludwig, Cologne (catalog)
1996 *Plastic,* Edwardes Square Studios, London (catalog)
The Fields of Sculpture, Hara Museum of Contemporary Art, Tokyo (catalog)
1999 *Skulptur: Figur-weiblich,* Stadtische Kunstsammlungen Chemnitz, Germany (catalog)

Collections:

Centre Georges Pompidou, Paris; Stedelijk Museum, Amsterdam; Museum Boymans-Van Beuningen, Rotterdam; Moderna Museet, Stockholm; University of Ulm, West Germany; Whitney Museum, New York.

Permanent Public Installations:

Nellens Collection, Knokke-le-Zoute, Belgium; Robinowitsch Park, Jerusalem; *Oiseau Amoureux,* Duisburg, Germany; *The Tarot Garden,* Garavicchio, Italy; Chateau-Chinon, France.

Publications:

By SAINT-PHALLE: Books—*Niki de Saint Phalle,* London and Milan 1968; *Niki de Saint Phalle: My Love,* Stockholm 1971; *The Devouring Mothers,* London 1972; *Tarot Cards in Sculpture by Niki de Saint Phalle,* with Fausta Squatriti, London and Milan 1985; *AIDS: You Can't Catch It Holding Hands,* with Silvio Barandun, Munich and Lucerne 1986, Paris, Milan and San Francisco 1987; *Traces: An Autobiography Remembering 1930–1949,* Lausanne, Switzerland 1999. **Films—***Daddy,* with Peter Whitehead, 1973; *Une reve plus long que la nuit,* with Laura and Laurent Condominas, 1975; *AIDS: You Can't Catch It Holding Hands* by Philip Mathews, 1989; *Niki de Saint Phalle,* with Uta Grosenik and Pontus Hulten, Stuttgart 1995.

On SAINT-PHALLE: Books—*Niki de Saint-Phalle,* exhibition catalog with texts by Pierre Restany and John Ashbery, Paris 1962; *Niki de Saint-Phalle,* exhibition catalog with text by Pierre Descargues, Paris 1965; *Niki de Saint-Phalle: Les Nana au pouvoir,* exhibition catalog with text by Pierre Descargues, Amsterdam 1967; *Niki de Saint-Phalle: Please Give Me a Few Seconds of Your Eternity,* exhibition catalog, Milan 1970; *Niki de Saint-Phalle,* exhibition catalog with text by Yoshiaki Tono, Tokyo 1979; *Niki de Saint-Phalle,* exhibition catalog with texts by K. G. Pontus Hulten, Pierre Restany, John Ashbery, Larry Rivers and Jean-Yves Mock, Paris 1980; *Niki at Nassau,* exhibition catalog with texts by David Bourdon, John Cage and Harry Mathews, Roslyn, New York 1987; *Tableaux Eclatés,* exhibition catalog with text by Pontus Hulten, New York 1994; *Pioneering Spirits: The Lives and Times of Remarkable Women Artists in Western History* by Abby Remer, Worcester 1997. **Articles—** ''Ain't Gonna Let Her In: Niki de Saint Phalle'' by Barbara Jones in *Women's Art Magazine,* no. 66, September-October 1995; ''Fantasy Worlds'' by John Maizels in *Raw Vision,* no. 28, Fall 1999. **Films—** *Who Is the Monster, You or Me* by Peter Schamoni, 1994.

* * *

''I come from a respectable family and religious institution,'' said Niki de Saint-Phalle. What she has made of life after such staid beginnings might be the starting point for an interesting psychological investigation.

Hon is the Swedish word for ''she.'' This was an enormous construction, the joint creation of Niki de Saint-Phalle, Jean Tinguely and Per Olof Ultvedt. A great sprawling giantess, lying on her back, stretched out on the floor of Stockholm's Moderna Museet. The year was 1963. Those entering *Hon,* for she was also a house of many mansions with bar, music rooms, and cinema, did so by mounting the ramp leading to the doorway between her legs, a typical example of what this artist would regard as apposite not only as a philosophic point but also *epater-la-bourgeoisie. Hon* was mostly black inside but her outer skin was decorated in bright colours painted on white.

Described by her makers as 82 feet long, 20 feet high and 30 feet wide, her layout contained ''lovers' nest'' with built-in microphone to relay love-talk to the bar, a gallery of fake paintings, an aquarium, a telephone, the bar with coca-cola automat, a cinema for Greta Garbo movies, a planetarium, a mill for grinding empty bottles when they were thrown down the chute and viewing platform from *Hon*'s head. The head also contained an infernal machine. Her heart and lungs were constructed to expand and contract to simulate breathing.

And all this was the inspiration of Niki de Saint-Phalle who a few years previously had been demonstrating the absurdity of the permanent by raking a wall hung with hotwater bottles with rifle fire.

The *nanas* which are, in the modern sense of the term, Niki de Saint-Phalle's stock-in trade today, are the total expression of arch-femininity. They were even present, albeit in gestatory stage, in the early reliefs encrusted with all kind of trinkets (usually of plastics), even dolls' kitchenware, along with knitting needles and crochet hooks—a splendid bullseye material for the rifle brigade who could commit a sacrilege that incurred no penance when they destroyed the *altars* made by Niki de Saint-Phalle. But nobody shoots *nanas.* If anybody indulges in target-practice, it is they who will be the practitioners when they thrust their gaudy primary characteristics at goggle-eyed hermits. St. Anthony is lucky to be beyond their clutches.

Hon was more like the Niki de Saint-Phalle of the 1960s and 1970s. This enormous pregnant lady of Stockholm was an early version of Niki de Saint Phalle's *nanas,* the hefty ladies whose ornamented bodies look as if they have renounced centuries of sophistication and civilization to go back to a time when peasant-style decoration was the natural way to express personality and seek to attract the opposite sex. The casual traditionalism of thir swollen bodies and the patterns painted on them propose a sort of archetypal verity they were never perhaps in the first place intended to have.

—Sheldon Williams

Hon influenced de Saint Phalle's later works in numerous ways. As previously mentioned, shortly after she created *Hon,* Niki de Saint-Phalle began to create a series of Nana's: large, colorful, active female figures, allegedly inspired by the pregnancy of her sister. She continued to work with this imagery for several decades, in graphic media as well as in sculpture.

Although *Hon* was installed temporarily, many of her subsequent works are permanent site-specific installations. The first was a commission she received in 1972 from the city of Jerusalem to design a play structure for children: *Golem,* a giant monster head with tongue slides. In 1982 she collaborated with Jean Tinguely (her companion since 1960 whom she married in 1971) to create a fountain, dedicated to the composer Igor Stravinsky, for the city of Paris on a site beside the Centre George Pompidou. The work combines sculptural elements by both Tinguely and de Saint-Phalle including a brightly colored *Firebird* by de Saint-Phalle. That year she also created permanent sculpture *Sun God* for the University of California at San Diego as part of the Stuart Collection. This work has become a campus icon, the subject of rituals and adornment. Over the years de Saint-Phalle has also been involved in making several films.

De Saint-Phalle's major artistic endeavor of the 1980s and 1990s was the creation of the Giardino dei Tarocchi (Tarot Garden), in southern Tuscany, Italy, in the hamlet of Garavicchio. This sculpture park containing images of the twenty-two major arcana of the tarot deck, was built on the site of an abandoned quarry given to de Saint-Phalle by the brothers of a friend. Ground was broken in 1978; the Garden was finally opened to the public in 1998. One way in which the Garden relates to her earlier work is that, like *Hon,* some structures were made to be experienced from within. In fact, in 1983 Saint-Phalle moved into *The Empress,* equipped with a working kitchen and bathroom, and she lived there for the next seven years; her studio was contained in another sculpture, *The Magician.* Saint-Phalle pushed her previous interest in built-up, colorful surfaces in this ensemble by encrusting the works with ceramics, glass mosaics, mirrored tiles. The entire space glitters in the Tuscan sun. It is a monument to the power of the archetypal feminine.

Jean Tingueley died in 1991, throwing de Saint-Phalle into a depression, exacerbated by her failing health—emphysema caused by the harsh chemicals with which she made her earlier works. To heal herself she moved to La Jolla, California, where she became interested in resuming painting after a hiatus of many years. In the mid-1990s she made a series of paintings called ''tableaux eclartés'' that consist of moving parts through which the works transform or ''explode.'' She dedicated these to Tingueley. Recently her work has been exhibited in various international venues. She has also written an autobiography and completed other installations.

—Mara Witzling

SAITO, Yoshishige

Nationality: Japanese. **Born:** Tokyo, 4 May 1904. **Education:** Nihon Middle School, Tokyo, 1918–24, and Waseda Kotogakuin, Tokyo, 1924. **Family:** Married Tomoko Sato in 1961; children: Wado and Shimon. **Career:** Independent painter and sculptor, Tokyo, since 1925: founder-member, Art Culture Association, Tokyo, 1939–53; professor of art, Tama Art University, Tokyo, 1964–73. **Awards:** Mr. K. Prize, 1957, National Museum Prize, 1959, Grand Prize, 1960, *International Art Exhibition,* Tokyo; Major Prize, 1958, Ohara Museum Prize, 1971, *Contemporary Art Exhibition,* Tokyo; International Federation of Art Critics Award, 1959; Major Prize, *Guggenheim International Art Exhibition,* New York, 1960; Painting Prize, *6th Bienal de Sao Paulo,* Brazil, 1961; Asahi Prize, Tokyo, 1984. Agent: Tokyo Gallery 8–6-18 Ginza, Chuo-ku, Tokyo 194. **Address:** 2–79 Mutsukawa, Minami-ku, Yokohama 232, Japan.

Individual Exhibitions:

1958 Tokyo Gallery
1960 Tokyo Gallery

Yoshishige Saito: *Blue Ruins,* 1960. ©Christie's Images/Corbis.

1962 Tokyo Gallery
1963 Tokyo Gallery
1964 Galerie Friedrich and Dahlem, Munich
1965 Galleria del Naviglio, Milan
Kunstverein Freiburg
1967 Tokyo Gallery
Galleri Haken, Oslo
1973 Tokyo Gallery
1976 Tokyo Gallery
1979 National Museum of Modern Art, Tokyo
1980 *Disproportion,* Tokyo Gallery
1983 Annely Juda Fine Art, London (with U-Fan and Kawabata)
1984 Metropolitan Art Museum, Tokyo (travelled to Tochigi, Hyogo, Ohara, Fukui)
1986 Hyundai Gallery, Seoul, Korea
1987 Asahi Gallery, Tokyo
1988 Annely Juda Fine Art, London
1989 Museum voor Moderne Kunst, Brussels
1992 *Yoshishige Saito: Sculpture and Installations,* Tokyo Gallery
1993 Yokohama Museum of Art, Japan
Yoshishige Saito: Time, Space, Wood, Tokushima Modern Art Museum, Tokyo

Selected Group Exhibitions:

1958 *Carnegie International,* Carnegie Institute, Pittsburgh
1960 *Biennale,* Venice
1966 *New Japanese Painting and Sculpture,* Museum of Modern Art, New York
1974 *Japan—Tradition und Gegenwart,* Kunsthalle, Dusseldorf
1976 *Pre-War Avant-Garde,* Metropolitan Art Museum, Tokyo
1979 *Contemporary Post-War Art,* Modern Art Museum, Tochigi, Japan
1981 *Trends in Contemporary Art,* Metropolitan Art Museum, Tokyo
1983 *Un Regard sur l'Art Japonais d'Aujourd'hui,* Musée Rath/ Musée d'Art et d'Histoire, Geneva
1985 *Reconstructions: Avant—Garde Art in Japan 1945–65,* Museum of Modern Art, Oxford
1986 *Japon des Avant-Gardes, 1910–70,* Centre Georges Pompidou, Paris

Collections:

Museum of Modern Art, Kamakura, Japan; National Museum of Modern Art, Tokyo; Museum of Contemporary Arts, Nagaoka, Japan; Rockefeller Collection, New York; Museum of Fine Arts, Houston; Rijksmuseum Kroller-Muller, Otterlo, Netherlands; Tochigi Prefectural Museum of Fine Arts Japan; Nagaoka Museum of Contemporary Art, Japan; Metropolitan Art Museum, Tokyo.

Publications:

By SAITO: Books—*Yoshishige Saito,* Tokyo 1964; *Yoshishige Saito,* Tokyo 1973.

On SAITO: Books—*Modern Art in Japan* by Teichi Hijikata, Tokyo 1966; *Avant-Garde in Japan* by Masayoshi Honma, Tokyo 1971; *Japan: Tradition und Gegenwart,* exhibition catalog with texts by Jurgen Harten, Joseph Love and others, Dusseldorf 1974; *Yoshishige Saito,* exhibition catalog, Tokyo 1979; *Yoshishige Saito: Disproportion,* exhibition catalog with text by Shigeo Chiba, Tokyo 1980; *Yoshishige Saito: Sculpture and Installations,* exhibition catalog, London 1988; *Yoshishige Saito: Sculpture and Installations,* exhibition catalog, London 1992; *Yoshishige Saito: Time, Space, Wood,* exhibition catalog, Tokyo 1993. **Articles—**''The Two-fold Path: Contemporary Art in Japan: Leading Postwar Movements and Personalities'' by Janet Koplos in *Art in America* (New York), vol. 78, April 1990.

* * *

Born in 1904, Yoshishige Saito has been earning his fame as one of the most challenging artists in Japan for a long time. Inspired by the paintings of Russian Futurist David Davidovich Burliuk, who organized the Russian painting exhibition in Tokyo in 1920, 16-year-old Saito made up his mind to enter upon an artist's career. During the following years in his early twenties, he was constantly exposed to the modernist movements, especially Constructivism and Dada, which were introduced by Japanese pioneer avant-garde artists who had studied in Europe and came back to Japan with the exciting new ideas.

Constructivism and Dada made young Saito somewhat suspicious of the possibility of painting, so that he began to make

Constructivistic sculptures. In 1936 he met Haruyoshi Yoshihara, the leader of Gutai group which was to be known as one of the most experimental avant-garde groups in Japan. Being encouraged by Yoshihara, Saito made his first commemorative sculpture *Kara Kara,* which had great affinity with the work by Naum Gabo.

During World War II, the difficulty in obtaining supplies compelled the artist to make black reliefs in simple plywood, and the experience was to affect his later work a great deal. He lost all his work in a fire in the year the war ended.

The new abstract movement in painting in Europe and the United States in the post-war period influenced the artist, and he devoted himself to abstract expressionistic painting in parallel with his plywood relief making. He was 54 when he gave his first one-person show at the Tokyo Gallery in 1958, and the show included *Painting E* which was awarded the prize of the International Association of Art Critics in the following year.

In the middle of 1960s he came to concentrate most of his energy to plywood reliefs rather than oil painting. Those reliefs had roundish cut-out polygons juxtaposed on rectangle supports in witty equilibrium.

He was offered the post as a professor in Tama College of Art in 1964, and taught there until he retired in 1973. But he never retired from art-making. He had great energy to renovate his style with more open and lighter structure by utilizing straight boards in his relief. His major retrospective was held at the National Museum of Modern Art in Tokyo in 1979. For that show, he made his first three-dimensional floor pieces by composing plain boards into geometrical forms. His second retrospective was organized in 1984 with the cooperative sponsorship of five major Japanese museums. He exhibited his work in the 18th Sao Paolo Bienniale and *The Reconstruction: Avant-Garde Art in Japan 1945–1965* held at the Oxford Gallery of Modern Art in England in 1985. Since 1984 he has developed more original open-structured 3-D installations by black-painted boards. Those remarkable installations including works with graffiti-scribbled blackboards were shown at Yurakucho Asahi Gallery in Tokyo in 1986. One of his old works was exhibited in *Japan des Avant Gardes: 1910–1970* at the Centre de Georges Pompidou in Paris in 1986.

—Tazmi Shinoda

David Salle in his Soho Studio, 1986. ©David Salle/Licensed by VAGA, New York, NY.

SALLE, David

Nationality: American. **Born:** Norman, Oklahoma, 28 September 1952. **Education:** California Institute of Arts, Valencia, 1971–75, BFA 1973, MFA 1975. **Career:** Independent painter, New York, since 1975. **Awards:** Creative Artists Public Service Grant, New York, 1979; Guggenheim Fellow, 1986. **Address:** c/o Leo Castelli Gallery, 59 East 79th Street, New York, NY 10021, U.S.A.; c/o Mary Boone Gallery, 420 W. Broadway, New York, New York, 10012–3764.

Individual Exhibitions:

1976 Artists' Space, New York
1977 Fondation de Appel, Amsterdam
The Kitchen, New York
1979 The Kitchen, New York
1980 Annina Nosei Gallery, New York
Galerie Bischofberger, Zurich
1981 Mary Boone Gallery, New York
Larry Gagosian Gallery, Los Angeles
Galleria Lucio Amelio, Naples
1982 Galleria Mario Diacono, Rome
Mary Boone/Leo Castelli Gallery, New York
Galerie Bischofberger, Zurich
1983 Akira Ikeda Gallery, Tokyo
Museum Boymans-van Beuningen, Rotterdam
Mary Boone Gallery, New York
Larry Gagosian Gallery, Los Angeles
Galerie Schellmann und Kluser, Munich
1985 Texas Gallery, Houston
Galerie Daniel Templon, Paris
Mary Boone Gallery, New York
Galerie Michael Werner, Cologne
Donald Young Gallery, Chicago
1986 Leo Castelli Gallery, New York
Mario Diacono Gallery, Boston
Institute of Contemporary Art, Philadelphia
Institute of Comtemporary Art, Boston
Galerie Sabine Knust, Munich
1987 Whitney Museum, New York
Museum of Contemporary Art, Los Angeles

David Salle: *Aerialist,* ca. 1980–95. © David Salle/Licensed by VAGA, New York NY.

Art Gallery of Ontario, Toronto
Museum of Contemporary Art, Chicago
Mary Boone Gallery, New York

1988 *David Salle,* Fundacion Caja de Pensiones, Madrid (traveled to Munich and Tel Aviv) (catalog)

1989 *David Salle,* Michael Werner Gallery, Cologne (catalog)
David Salle, Waddington Galleries, London (catalog)

1990 *David Salle,* Mario Diacono Gallery, Boston (catalog)

1992 *David Salle: Drawings,* Gagosian Gallery, New York (traveled to Gemeentemuseum, Hague) (catalog)

1998 Galleria Gian Ferrari, Milan

1999 *David Salle,* Stedelijk Museum, Amsterdam (traveling exhibition) (catalog)

Selected Group Exhibitions:

1979 *Imitation of Life,* Hartford Art School, Connecticut

1980 *Apres le Classicisme,* Musée d'Art et d'Industrie, St. Etienne, France

1981 *Young Americans,* Allen Memorial Art Museum, Oberlin, Ohio

1982 *Documenta 7,* Museum Fridericianum, Kassel, West Germany

1983 *New Art,* Tate Gallery, London

1984 *The Restoration of Painterly Figuration,* Kitakyushu Municipal Art Museum, Tokyo

1985 *Biennale de Paris,* Grand Halle du Pare de la Villette, Paris

1987 *Avant-Garde in the Eighties,* Los Angeles County Museum of Art

1988 *Contemporary American Art,* Sara Hilden Art Museum, Tampere, Finland (travelled to Oslo)
Point of View, University Art Gallery, California State University, San Bernardino (catalog)

1989 *10+10—Contemporary Soviet and American Painters,* Modern Art Museum of Forth Worth (traveling exhibition) (catalog)

1991 *Art Works: International Modern Art in the Industrial Working Environment, an Experiment Over More than Thirty Years,* Stedelijk Museum, Amsterdam (catalog)
Image and Likeness, Whitney Museum of American Art, New York (catalog)

1996 *Spellbound: Art and Film,* Hayward Gallery, London

1997 *The Lois Beurman Torf Print Collection for the University of Massachusetts,* University Gallery, Amherst (catalog)

1998 *Young Americans 2: New American Art at the Saatchi Gallery,* London (catalog)

1999 *Sarajevo 2000,* Museum Moderner Kunst Stiftung Ludwig Wein, Vienna (traveled to Palais Liechtenstein, Vienna) (catalog)

Collections:

Whitney Museum, New York; Museum Boymans-van Beuningen, Rotterdam; Kunstmuseum, Basel; New York Public Library.

Publications:

By SALLE: Articles—''David Salle Interview'' by Peter Schjeldahl, *Journal,* September/October 1981; ''An Interview with David Salle'' by John Roberts in *Art Monthly,* March 1983; ''Interview with David Salle'' by Robert Pincus-Witten in *Arts Magazine,* November 1985; interview with Robert Enright in *Border Crossings,* vol. 9, no. 4, Fall 1990; ''David Salle's 'Search and Destroy' Mission'' with Frederic Tuten in *Interview,* vol. 25, no. 3, March 1995; interview with Frederic Tuten in *Art in America* (New York), vol. 85, no. 9, September 1997. **Films—***Search and Destroy,* 1995.

On SALLE: Books—*David Salle,* exhibition catalog, Rotterdam 1986; *David Salle Paintings,* exhibition catalog, Philadelphia 1986; *Contemporary American Art,* exhibition catalog with foreword by Peter Schjeldahl, Tampere 1988; *David Salle 1979–1994* by Lisa Liebmann, New York 1994. **Articles—**''David Salle: Impersonal

Effects'' by Eleanor Heartney in *Art in America,* vol. 76, no. 6, June 1988; ''David Salle: The New Gatsby'' by Donald B. Kuspit in *Art Criticism,* vol. 5, no. 1, 1988; ''Artist's Dream Machines: The Films of Longo, Salle and Clark'' by Dike Blair in *Flash Art,* vol. 29, no. 187, March-April 1996; ''Salle Days'' by Dan Cameron and Dave Hickey in *Artforum,* vol. 37, no. 9, May 1999.

* * *

The paintings of David Salle, like those of Picabia, have a particular 'transparency.' The figures are outlined across the surface of the picture against a background of colour. Everything is provisional and insubstantial as though about to disappear in the volubility of this transparent arena, as in *Hundreds of Tons* (1980), and *Rational Censor* (1981). The visual situation with its ephemeral aura hovering between sign and material constitutes a complete harmony. The programmed shifts in imagery share something with advertisement signs.

Salle, however, takes nothing from Pop Art, nor from Hyperrealism. His mode of narrative is the result of psychic impulses that reflect a humorous fantasy. In this respect, his vision of daily life is individual and introspective, an opaque mirror of a fascinating world full of the intriguing expression of his imagination and expressive imagery. The subject appears as a mutation of the moment and of voluptuous desire. It offers an infinite combination of iconographic visions, and it is not important that these icons have been seen and gathered from other sources. They appear afresh signifying their essential modernity.

For Salle, it is not a style nor a deception which promotes the fantasy, rather, it is the fixing of the moment of maximum intensity. A visual contest is established, in which indeterminate visual sensations are ensnared. It is no accident that most of his works are untitled. The picture is frequently highly energized, and it is not without discernment that Salle arrives at these visual effects—an intriguing superimposition of transparent layers. The expression is adriotly handled, the effervescent surface sheltering barely perceptible images. Not everything has coherence or stylistic harmony; things and events often appear separately. The skill of the artist lies in his consistent manipulation of a ravenous media.

Salle's images are also the stuff of dreams, and the means of reaching them almost scandalous—like Narcissus with his reflection. The melancholy and arrogant creative spirit which mobilizes the raw material of the surface establishes a certain excitement born of subconscious desires.

Perhaps Salle seeks a disarming effect in the near-imperceptible presence of his secretly assembled iconography. The areas into which the picture plane is sub-divided have their own autonomy in spite of their close juxtaposition. This is clearly visible in the fine work from 1982 onwards, exhibited at the *Zeit Geist* show in Berlin—notably in *Was My Husband a Doctor or a Patient* (1982). Here, as in other works, the various combinations of colour and sign form a kind of creative and expansive connivance between figuration and abstraction. The hyperbole of transparency prompts a sense of arrested flight.

Salle as an artist is more European than American. His images are drawn more in the manner of Picabia than of the urban graffitist. Moreover, we see in him a concern for the metaphysical mysteries of art that is peculiar to European culture.

—Italo Mussa

Though Salle's large-scale oil paintings have continued to attract attention from collectors and heated responses of all kinds from the critics, during the 1990s he has branched out into several other media, all the while retaining what Donald Kuspit has identified as ''a deliciously unwholesome nightclub atmosphere, vaguely seamy—but with no enduring sensual impact.'' He exhibited black-and-white photographs of female nudes, works that he had always executed as a preparatory step in the creation of paintings. In 1994, he exhibited sculpture for the first time, notably a work titled *Jokerville,* a glass puppet's hand resting on a bronze chair. And although he had produced video art, 1995 saw the release of Salle's first commercial film, the Hollywood send-up *Search and Destroy,* featuring an all-star cast that included Dennis Hopper, Patricia Arquette, and Martin Scorsese, who also served as executive director. Critics admired the visual style of the film but dismissed the writing and the directing.

—Mark Swartz

SAMARAS, Lucas

Nationality: American. **Born:** Kastoria, Macedonia, 14 September 1936; immigrated to the United States, 1948: naturalized, 1955. **Education:** Memorial High School, West New York, New Jersey, 1951–55; studied under Allan Kaprow, at Rutgers University, New Brunswick, New Jersey, 1955–59, B.A. 1959; Columbia University, New York (Woodrow Wilson Fellow), 1959–62. **Career:** Artist and photographer, New York, since 1964; first ''autopolaroid'' photographs, 1970; first ''photo-transformations,'' 1973. Visiting instructor in sculpture, Yale University, New Haven, Connecticut, 1969; instructor, Brooklyn College, New York, 1971–72. **Agent:** Pace Wildenstein Gallery, 32 East 57th Street, New York, New York 10022, U.S.A.; Pace Wildenstein Los Angeles, 9540 Wilshire Boulevard, Beverly Hills, California, 90212. **Address:** 52 West 71st Street, New York, New York 10023, U.S.A.

Individual Exhibitions:

1955 Rutgers University, New Brunswick, New Jersey
1959 Reuben Gallery, New York
1961 *Dinner, Liquid Aluminum, Pastels and Plasters,* Green Gallery, New York
1962 *Pastels,* Sun Gallery, Provincetown, Massachusetts
1964 *Boxes, Constructions,* Dwan Gallery, Los Angeles
Bedroom, Boxes, Plastics, Green Gallery New York
1966 *Samaras: Mirror Room: Selected Works 1960–66,* Pace Gallery, New York
1968 *Transformations, Mirror Stairs, Paintings and Drawings,* Pace Gallery, New York
1969 *Books,* Museum of Modern Art, New York
Mirror Room 3, Boxes and Drawings, Galerie der Spiegel, Cologne
1970 *Chair Transformations* Pace Gallery, New York
Mirror Room 3, Kunstverein, Hannover
1971 *Stiff Boxes and Autopolaroids,* Pace Gallery, New York
Acrylics, Pastels, Inks, Phyllis Kind Gallery, Chicago
Lucas Samaras' Boxes, Museum of Contemporary Art, Chicago
1972 *Chicken Wire Boxes,* Pace Gallery, New York

Whitney Museum, New York (retrospective)
1974 *Photo-Transformations,* Pace Gallery, New York
1975 *Pastels,* Museum of Modern Art, New York
Makler Gallery, Philadelphia
Samaras and Some Others, Pace Gallery, New York
Photo-Transformations, California State University at Long Beach
1976 University of North Dakota Art Gallery, Grand Forks
Wright State University Art Gallery, Dayton, Ohio
Institute of Contemporary Art, Boston
Seattle Art Museum
A.C.A. Gallery, Alberta College of Art, Calgary
Phantasmata, Pace Gallery, New York
Margo Leavin Gallery, Los Angeles
1977 *Photo-Transformations,* Galerie Zabriskie, Paris
Photo-Transformations, Walker Art Center, Minneapolis
1978 Reconstructions, Pace Gallery, New York
Mayor Gallery, London
Reconstructions and Photo-Transformations, Akron Art Institute, Ohio
1979 Richard Gray Gallery, Chicago
1980 *Reconstructions,* Pace Gallery, New York
Reconstructions, Photo-Transformations and Word Drawings, Pace Gallery, Columbus, Ohio
Polaroid Photographs, Pace Gallery, New York
1981 Galerie Watari, Tokyo
1982 *Pastels,* Lowe Art Museum, University of Miami
1983 *Photographs 1969–83,* Centre Georges Pompidou, Paris
Kunstverein, Frankfurt
1984 *Polaroid Photographs 1969–83,* International Center of Photography, New York
Chairs, Heads, Panoramas, Pace Gallery, New York
1985 Madison Art Center, Wisconsin
Pace Gallery, New York
1986 *Polaroid Photographs,* Serpentine Gallery, London
Mayor Gallery, London
1988 National Museum of American Art, Washington, D.C.
Lucas Samaras, Figures, Still Lifes, Pace/Macgill Gallery, New York (catalog)
Lucas Samaras: Boxes and Mirrored Cell, Pace Gallery, New York (catalog)
Lucas Samaras: Objects and Subjects 1969–1986, Denver Art Museum
1989 Virginia Museum of Fine Arts, Richmond
1990 Museum of Fine Arts, Boston
Lucas Samaras, Waddington Galleries (catalog)
1991 *Self: 1961–1991,* Yomiuri Shimbun, Japan (catalog)
Yokohama Museum of Art, Japan
Slices of Abstraction, Slivers of Passion, and/or Mere Décor, The Pace Gallery, New York (catalog)
1992 *Persona,* Museum of Photographic Arts, San Diego (catalog)
1993 *Pastels,* Pace Gallery, New York (catalog)
1994 *Lucas Samaras: Cubes, Pragmata, Trapezoids,* Pace Wildenstein, New York (catalog)
1996 *Pastels,* Pace Wildenstein Los Angeles
Photo-Transformations 1973–1976, Pace Wildenstein Los Angeles (also Pace Wildenstein, Soho, New York)
Kiss Kill/Perverted Geometry/Inedibles/Self-Absorption, Pace Wildenstein (Mid-Town), New York (catalog)
Pace Wildenstein Greene, New York
1997 Galerie Renos Xippas, Paris (catalog)
Hamilton Galleries, London
1998 *Lucas Samaras: Gold,* Pace Wildenstein, New York (catalog)
1999 Pace Wildenstein Gallery, New York
Jay Grimm Gallery, New York
2000 *Sittings 1978–1980,* Galerie Xippas, Paris (catalog)

Selected Group Exhibitions:

1961 *The Art of Assemblage,* Museum of Modern Art, New York
1967 *American Sculpture of the 60s,* Los Angeles County Museum of Art
1968 *The Obsessive Image,* Institute of Contemporary Arts, London
1974 *Photography in America,* Whitney Museum, New York
1977 *Documenta 6,* Kassel, West Germany
1978 *Mirrors and Windows: American Photography since 1960,* Museum of Modern Art, New York (toured the United States, 1978–80)
1979 *One of a Kind: Polaroid Color,* Corcoran Gallery, Washington, D.C. (toured the United States)
1980 *La Photo Polaroid,* Musée d'Art Moderne, Paris
1983 *Arranged Image Photography,* Boise Gallery, Idaho
1986 *Photography as Performance,* The Photographers' Gallery, London
1994 *Guys Who Sew,* University Art Museum, University of California, Santa Barbara (catalog)
American Art Today, The Art Museum at Florida International Museum, Miami (catalog)
1999 *The Rutgers Group: Garden State Avant-Garde,* Newark Museum, New Jersey
2000 *Modern Odysseys: Greek American Artists of the 20th Century,* Queens Museum of Art, New York (catalog)
High Museum of Art, Atlanta
Monte-Carlo International Sculpture Festival, France

Collections:

Metropolitan Museum of Art, New York; Museum of Modern Art, New York; Whitney Museum, New York; Guggenheim Museum, New York; Albright-Knox Art Gallery. Buffalo, New York; Larry Aldrich Museum, Ridgefield, Connecticut; Wadsworth Atheneum, Hartford, Connecticut; Art Institute of Chicago; Walker Art Center, Minneapolis; Los Angeles County Museum of Art; National Gallery of Art, Washington, D.C.

Publications:

By SAMARAS: Books—*Samaras Album, Autobiography, 0 Autointerview, Autopolaroids,* New York 1971; *Lucas Samaras: Photo-Transformations,* with the text by Arnold B. Glimcher, New York 1975; *Lucas Samaras,* with text by Kim Levin, New York 1975; *Photos, Polaroid Photographs 1969–1983,* exhibition catalog, New York 1984; *The Artist Observed: 28 Interviews with Contemporary Artists, 1972–1978* by John Gruen, Chicago 1991. **Articles—**''An Exploratory Dissection of Seeing'' in *Artforum* (New York), December 1967; ''Greece 1967; A Reconstituted Diary'' in *Artforum* (New

York), October 1968; ''Autopolaroids and Autointerview'' in *Art in America* (New York), November/December 1970; ''The Art of Portraiture, in the Words of Four New York Artists'' in the *New York Times,* 31 October 1976; interview, with Barbara Rose, in *Samaras: Reconstructions,* exhibition catalog, New York 1978; interview in *Artists in Their Own Words* by Paul Cummings, New York 1979. **Film**—*Self,* 1969.

On SAMARAS: Books—*Samaras: Selected Works 1960–66,* exhibition catalog, with text by Lawrence Alloway, New York 1966; *Chair Transformations,* exhibition catalog, New York 1970; *Samaras: Selected Works 1960–1969,* exhibition catalog, with text by Joan Siegfried and Lawrence Alloway, Chicago 1971; *Lucas Samaras Boxes,* exhibition catalog, with text by Joan Siegfried, Chicago 1971; *American Art in the 20th Century* by Sam Hunter, New York 1973; *Photography in America,* edited by Robert Doty, with an introduction by Minor White, New York and London, 1974; *Art in Boxes* by Alex Mogelon and Norman Laliberte, New York 1974; *Lucas Samaras* by Kim Levin, New York 1975; *Mirrors and Windows: American Photography since 1960* by John Szarkowski, New York 1978; *Lucas Samaras: Photographs 1969–1983,* exhibition catalog with essays by Roger Marcel Mayon and William A. Ewing, Paris 1983; *Lucas Samaras: Chairs, Heads, Panoramas,* exhibition catalog with text by Douglas Blau, New York 1984. **Articles**—''Panorama (1984) by Lucas Samaras'' by Martha Chahroudi in *Philadelphia Museum of Art Bulletin,* vol. 86, no. 365–366, Spring 1990; ''Through the Mind's Eye: Samara's Abstractions'' by Eleanor Heartney in *Art in America* (New York), vol. 80, no. 3, March 1992; ''Lucas Samaras'' by Peter Plagens in *Artforum,* vol. 35, no. 6, February 1997; ''Transformer: Lucas Samaras'' by Ken Johnson in *Art in America* (New York), vol. 85, February 1997; ''Phototransformation'' by Raymond Hernández-Durán in *Museum Studies,* vol. 25, no. 1, 1999.

* * *

Lucas Samaras is one of the most brilliant and respected of the American artists to have come to prominence during the post-abstract reaction of the 1960s. His work was in the forefront of that art which kept alive the possibilities of an expressionist-surrealist idioms; while incorporating some of the radical attitudes of that time—about personal revelation, common object reference, environmental art, bodily performance, serial production—his art nonetheless remained a traditional visual art product. And it may be this perennial confidence in the object and its existential power—the anxiety within his work is always immediate—that is a prime source of the satisfaction which his art often inspires.

Samaras' work originates from the strong Surrealist milieu omnipresent in New York City. Most influential was his personal acquaintance with the group of artists who would form the Pop Art movement, and others with equally object orientation such as Rauschenberg and Johns. As Samaras left behind the coarse materials of his earliest works—plaster, tin foil, rags—to assume the fragile and meticulous elegance of his mature works as in the *Boxes* series from the mid-60s on, the influence of Joseph Cornell was clearly felt.

It is no doubt meaningful to ascribe some important part of the bizarre intensity and glee in both self-examination and object-obsession that pervade his work to Samaras' fantastic early boyhood experiences in his native Greece which he left in 1948 to come to the U.S. at the age of 12. He clearly recalls—his *Autobiography* is in continual progress and he has constantly produced stories whose characters and attitudes can be felt in his visual work—his home town where there were 72 churches for 10,000 people; where the dead were unburied after three years and their bones, with which he played, placed in black boxes along the church walls; where the Greek Civil War raged and shots and executions were frequent. He is himself elusive and secretive, and it might be said that his production is an effort both to retain and yet transmute the sense of life's intensity and fragility learned in his early years.

Although much of his major work in the 1960s was done with assemblage materials, the objects were rarely themselves exotic, becoming so only through the artist's manipulations. Critical attention has rightly been focused on the hurtful, inherently destructive objects—the knives, pins, tacks, razor blades—which proliferate in the *Boxes* series; yet an older Surrealist romance also accompanies these in the shells, jewel-like glitter, stuffed birds, and the pervasive sense of obscene treasure. But the eclectic nature of Samaras' imagination can also invest American Pop art-like objects—hardware, pencils, X-Rays—with a personal and perverse magic.

The *Boxes,* which accumulated to about 80, were the microworlds, with dimensions not larger than 20 inches, which allowed him at that time to develop his passion for personal expression via the older European surreal traditions of fetishism and the elusive literal. But equally a trademark and an almost ironic foil for these emblems of illness and sado-masochistic urgings, was Samaras' assumption of the Pop Art use of the rainbow spectrum and its perhaps universal sense of magic and good cheer. It often appeared on the boxes as a tight banding of yarns. Samaras' uncanny ability to manipulate the literal and produce a heart-felt yet ironic wit—his work is never sentimental—is also clearly felt in his *Transformations* series; knives, chair, eyeglasses, utensils, etc., are all subjected in the later 1960s to both stylistic and its concomitant expressive alterations.

Aside from the drawings and small, icon-like acrylic paintings which he has continuously produced, some other important work of the 1960s may seem, at first, unrelated to the spirit of the assemblages. In 1964, Samaras produced a full-sized *Room* for a gallery exhibition. Related of course to his Happenings experience and his ongoing personal sense of the necessity to incorporate all of his life in his work, this first room—never reassembled for exhibition—was a replica of his life-stage and filled with actual objects. Much better known are the *Mirror* room works of 1966–68 where all the surfaces both inside and out, including the furniture, were made of mirrors. If the ongoing metaphor of Samaras' art is the transformation available in the juxtaposition of pathos and elegance, of mundaneness and glamour, it is here, as elsewhere in his art, kept in delicate balance.

The *Cut-Paper Drawings,* a long series in 1968—a format returned to in 1975 in the similarly flat, cut, and now painted aluminum works—are cut white papers placed against dark backgrounds to create images from the silhouetted white papers. In this fragile and virtuoso contrivance, perhaps also in their reference to an older folk art tradition, these works are all the more perverse as the cutting process which naturally produced them in the first place, and may be read as a pun upon their frequently threatening subject matter.

From both his life-long involvement with theatre (Samaras has been a drama student sporadically) and his penchant for self-revelation has come his commitment to the visual arts as a field for literal self-presentation. In his use of his body, Samaras thus parallels and anticipates the recent phenomenon of Body and Performance Art. And in contrast to other recent erotic art, for instance Oldenburg's sexual similes with their peculiarly American phallic innocence,

Samaras' subtlety and fantasy make the viewer seem truly a voyeur, and his art has thrived on a wide array of androgynous display—especially in the 1970s with his photograph series unrelentingly featuring his body.

Samaras' preoccupation with photography became his leading medium began after the completion of the movie *Self* in 1969. This major body of work, entirely based upon the instant image-making inherent in the Polaroid photographic print, is available only on the miniature stage of the 2 by 3 inch format of the photograph. Yet through the sense of ''actuality'' which we tend to associate with a photograph, Samaras is able to reiterate that sense of the immediate literal present, so much a part of the attraction of his earlier work; and even more compelling, he has extended and intensified his opportunities and skills in presenting ''transformations.''

In fascinating and characteristic exhaustive display of invention, Samaras at first (*Autopolaroids* 1970–71) showed multiple exposures and color changes within the camera itself, together at times with further painting and drawing upon the finished photographic print surface; then in the *Phototransformations,* 1973–74, using the recently available Polaroid transfer-dye print process (SX-70), he reworked the actual color chemistry of the print surface. In the traditional two-dimensional pictorial format, Samaras has been able, as he did in his earlier sculptural work, to enliven an existent modernist tradition—but here significantly by his intuitive use of a technological instrument. Few have done better.

His recent works include the series of varied fabric fragments sewn into often very large flat patterns, *Reconstructions*—which he has called homage to his mother's vision. In 1977, Samaras continued his ''body art'' *Phototransformations* as *Phantasmata*: the already familiar/self images in his living quarters altered by surface manipulation on the polaroid print itself, and here extended by the use of colored lights, slide projectors, and fabrics all involving the artist's body. In 1981, he returned to this format, but now in the large polaroids—20 by 24 inches—and produced the series *Sittings* where Samaras' head appeared at the margin of images of art world personalities in the nude and surrounded by the paraphernalia which heretofore he had lavished only upon himself. There was no surface alteration of the literal print itself.

The *Panoramas* in 1983 were horizontal images composed of narrow vertically cut strips of Polaroid prints, reassembled to produce a strobe-like picture with staccato, multiple appearances of figures. As usual in his work, whatever formalist references were felt—here Cubo-Futurist—were rendered irrelevant by Samaras' rolling anxiety and energy. His early 1980s works also include pastel drawings of heads, and casts of complex modeled clay figures, all with a gruff expressionist style and compounded bodies and body parts.

Similarly grotesque and mocking, a group of Giacometti-like heads of art world representatives shown as rotting death's heads, were his first return to painting in 16 years (1985). Just so, the artist returned to youthful techniques in the 1987 *Chair Transformations.* The wire-hanger-based forms were filled with an irrational assemblage of tasteless mundane objects manipulated towards a Surreal decadence.

While bodies of work so clearly predicated upon ''self'' have often been exhausted and become mannered upon the artist's psychic exhaustion, Samaras' wit, candor and formalist sense allow him to carry his art forward.

—Joshua Kind

SANDBACK, Fred

Nationality: American. **Born:** Bronxville, New York, 29 August 1943. **Education:** Williston Academy, Easthampton, Massachusetts, 1957–61, and Theodor Heuss Gymnasium, Heilbronn, West Germany, 1961–62; studied at Yale University, New Haven, Connecticut, 1962–66, B.A. 1966; and Yale School of Art and Architecture, 1966–69, B.F.A 1967; M.F.A. 1969. **Awards:** Creative Artists Program Service Grant, New York, 1972. **Agent:** John Weber Gallery, Greene Street, New York, New York 10012. **Address:** 561 Broadway, New York, New York 10012, U.S.A.

Individual Exhibitions:

1968 Galerie Konrad Fischer, Dusseldorf
Galerie Heiner Friedrich, Munich
1969 Dwan Gallery, New York
Ace Gallery, Los Angeles
Museum Haus Lange, Krefeld, West Germany
1970 Galleria Françoise Lambert, Milan
Galerie Yvon Lambert, Paris
Dwan Gallery, New York
Galerie Reckermann, Cologne
Galerie Heiner Friedrich, Munich
1971 Galerie Annemarie Verna, Zurich
1972 John Weber Gallery, New York
Galerie Annemarie Verna, New York
Galerie Reckermann, Cologne
Galerie Heiner Friedrich, Munich
Galerie Diogenes, Berlin
1973 Galerie Nachst St. Stephan, Vienna
Galerie Heiner Friedrich, Munich
Galerie im Taxispalais, Innsbruck
Kunsthalle, Berne
1974 John Weber Gallery, New York
Galleria Martano, Turin
Galleria Milano, Milan
Galleria Primo Piano, Rome
Galerie Heiner Friedrich, Munich
Studio Schloss Morsbroich, Leverkusen, West Germany
Clocktower, New York
Folkwang Museum, Essen
1975 Galerie Heiner Friedrich, Munich
Kunstraum, Munich
Galerie Müller-Roth, Stuttgart
Galerie Dorothea Loehr, Frankfurt
1976 Brooke Alexander Inc., New York
Galerie Heiner Friedrich, Munich
John Weber Gallery, New York
Galerie Annemarie Verna, Zurich
Galleria Primo Piano, Rome
Galerie Durand-Dessert, Paris
1977 Lisson Gallery, London
Hester Van Royen Gallery, London
1978 Galerie Heiner Friedrich, Munich
Heiner Friedrich Gallery, New York
P.S.I., Long Island City, New York
Museum of Modern Art, New York

1981 Galerie Annemarie Verna, Zurich
Fred Sandback Museum, Winchendon, Massachusetts
Galerie Durand-Dessert, Paris
1982 Galerie Editions Media, Neuchatel, Switzerland
1983 Marian Goodman Gallery, New York
Fred Sandback Museum, Winchendon, Massachusetts
Galerie Fred Jahn, Munich
University of Massachusetts, Amherst
1984 Galerie Le Consortium, Dijon, France
1985 University of Illinois, Champaign
Kunsthaus, Zurich
Galerie Durand-Dessert, Paris
Marian Goodman Gallery, New York
1986 Kunsthalle, Mannheim, West Germany
1987 Westfälischer Kunstverein, Münster, West Germany
1988 Galerie Fred Jahn, Munich
1989 Burnett Miller Gallery, Los Angeles
Dia Center for the Arts, New York
Sculpture, Contemporary Art Museum, Houston (catalog)
Nina Freudenheim Gallery, Buffalo
1991 *Sculpture,* Yale University Art Gallery, New Haven (catalog)
David Nolan Gallery, New York
1992 Galerie Hubert Winter, Vienna
1994 Nolan/Eckman Gallery, New York
Galerie Jürgen Becker, Hamburg
1996 *Sculpture,* Dia Center for the Arts, New York (catalog)
1997 Lawrence Markey Gallery, New York

Selected Group Exhibitions:

1968 *Artists Under 40,* Whitney Museum, New York
1969 *New Media/New Methods,* Museum of Modern Art, New York
When Attitudes Become Form, Kunsthalle, Berne (toured West Germany and the U.K)
1971 *Sonsbeek 1971,* Arnhem, Netherlands
1974 *Multiples,* Kunstverein, Berlin
1976 *Drawing Now,* Museum of Modern Art, New York
1980 *Pier and Ocean,* Hayward Gallery, London
1981 *Construction in Process,* Muzeum Sztuki, Lodz, Poland
1983 *Presence Discrete,* Musée des Beaux-Arts, Dijon, France
1985 *Vom Zeichen,* Kunstverein, Frankfurt
1990 *Minimalism,* Nicola Jacobs Gallery, London (catalog)
1994 *Amerikanische Zeichnungen und Graphik,* Kunsthaus, Zurich (catalog)
1999 *Here and Now,* Henry Moore Institute, Leeds, England

Collections:

Museum of Modern Art, New York; Whitney Museum, New York; Rhode Island School of Design, Providence; Kaiser-Wilhelm Museum, Krefeld, West Germany; Dia Center for the Arts, New York.

Publications:

By SANDBACK: Articles—interview with Joan Simon in *Art in America* (New York), vol. 85, no. 5, May 1997.

On SANDBACK: Books—*Fred Sandback* by Hermann Kern, Munich 1945; *Fred Sandback; Sculpture 1966–86,* exhibition catalog with texts by Manfred Fath and Fred Jahn, Mannheim 1986. **Articles**—"Fred Sandback at Dwan" in *Arts Magazine* (New York), May 1970; "Lettre de New York" by J. Patrice Marendel in *Art International* (Lugano, Switzerland), Summer 1970; "Sculpture at Sonsbeek" by Carel Blotkamp in *Studio International* (London), September 1971; "Fred Sandback" by Ellen Lubell in *Arts Magazine* (New York), May 1974; review by Lawrence Alloway in *Artforum* (New York), May 1974; "Question: How Do You Buy a Work of Art Like This?" by Roy Bongartz in the *New York Times,* 11 August 1974; "Walking the Line: Fred Sandback in Buffalo" by Robert Creeley in *Arts Magazine,* vol. 64, April 1990; "Fred Sandback: As If. . ." by Adachiara Zevi in *L'Architettura,* vol. 36, September 1990; "Line Readings: Fred Sandback's Recent Drawings" by Nancy Princenthal in *The Print Collector's Newsletter,* vol. 22, September/October 1991; "Here and Now: Fred Sandback" by Andrew Mead in *Architects' Journal,* vol. 209, no. 7, 18 February 1999.

* * *

From about 1967, Fred Sandback has persistently continued in his singular development consisting of extremely spare, geometrically based, linear constructions in space made out of colored yarn or elastic or painted rope. Sandback's work relates closely to the prominent development in the 1960s of Minimal/Conceptual sculptural forms which use little materials to define large spaces. Sandback's work is closest in its conceptual underpinnings to the oeuvre of Sol Le Witt and Barry Le Va, the difference being that Sandback pushes his visualizations even closer to the edge of the invisible, hovering on the extreme point wherein dematerialization is about to occur.

In Sandback's constructions of the late 1960s, placement was at first against the wall, using geometrical shapes in repetition and then moving to singular and larger shapes. Sandback next began stretching his linear materials across rooms which became his "framing" environments of three dimensional space, defining shapes less specific than before. He moved into creation of combinations of both these types of configurations, using simpler configurations and more expansive spaces. Sandback has also made serial pieces, installed in the gallery at different times over the interval of the exhibition. In "Sixteen Two-Part Pieces" (1974), for example, two lengths of dark yarn crossing the small room were changed sixteen times to produce variations on the theme which he had systematically worked out through a diagrammatic drawing. For a 1978 installation, Sandback made three separate "Constructions," which were shown variously over a period of several weeks. In many ways, the initial diagrams/drawings for the works convey enough information in themselves to perceive the constructions' possible implications, yet their physical makeup achieves an illusionistic inference and spatial experience not possible through the concept alone nor through the two dimensional plan. Depending on the viewer's placement of self in just the right spot, the linear is transformed into an inference of the volumetric; the fragile, thin threads appear to become the edges of planes and/or geometrical shapes. The illusion of volume is hypothetical yet made visible tenuously, dependent on physical placement and mental involvement. This tension between what is really there and what seems to be there infers the tenuous nature of relationships between premises and the visualizations which follow them. It is not unlike the juxtapositions of drawings and written theorems found in geometrical texts.

One problem in Sandback's work is whether the geometrical basis is transformed adequately enough to warrant its being called art. The major problem, though, rests on the question of whether Sandback's longtime repetition of such strict limitations can retain any real significance, either conceptually or visually.

—Barbara Cavaliere

SANDLE, Michael

Nationality: British. **Born:** Weymouth, Dorset, 18 May 1936. **Education:** Studied drawing, painting and lithography at Douglas School of Art and Technology, Isle of Man, 1954–56; Slade School of Fine Art, London, 1956–59. **Family:** Married Cynthia Dora Koppel, 1972 (divorced, 1974); married Demelza Spargo, 1988; son: George Benjamin. **Career:** Graphic artist and sculptor, lives and works in Devon: worked as a lithographer, Paris, 1959–60; founder-member, with Cristina Bertoni, Laurence Brut, Michael Chilton and others, Leicester Group, 1961–63; associated with members of Art and Language group while living in Coventry, 1964–68. Part-time assistant lecturer, Foundation Studies Department, Leicester College of Art, 1961–63; lecturer, Coventry College of Art, 1964–68; visiting professor, University of Calgary, Alberta, 1790–71; visiting associate professor, University of Victoria, British Columbia, 1971–72; lecturer, 1973, and professor in sculpture, 1977, Fachhochschule fur Gestaltung, Pforzheim, Germany. Professor in sculpture, Akademie der Bildenden Kunste, Karlsruhe, Germany, 1980–1999. **Awards:** Abbey Minor Travelling Scholarshp, 1959; French Government Scholarship, 1960; Nobutaka Shikanai Prize, *Rodin International Exhibition,* Hakone Open-Air Museum, Japan, 1986; Chantrey Bequest Award, 1987; 7th Internation Small Sculpture Exhibition Prize, Budapest, 1987; Korn-Ferry Award, 1989; Henry Hering Memorial Medal, National Sculpture Society, 1995. **Member:** Associate member Royal Academy of Art, 1982, Royal Academician, 1989–1998; Fellow of the Royal Society of British Sculptors, since 1994. **Address:** Schloss Scheibenhardt 2, 71635 Karlsruhe, Germany.

Individual Exhibitions:

1963 Drian Galleries, London
1966 Grabowski Gallery, London (with Ivor Abrahams and Michael Chilton)
1975 *Drawing Exhibition,* Haus am Lützow Platz, Berlin
Galerie der Spiegel, Cologne
Drawing Exhibition, Galerie Suzanne Fischer, Baden-Baden, Germany
1976 Galerie Hecate, Paris
Bernard Jacobson Gallery, New York
Felicity Samuel Gallery, London
1977 Galerie 2, Stuttgart
1981 Fischer Fine Art, London
1983 Kunstverein, Mannheim, Germany
1984 Wilhelm Lehmbruck Museum, Duisburgh, Germany
1985 Fischer Fine Art, London
1988 Whitechapel Art Gallery, London (also Stuttgart Kunstverein) (retrospective)
1989 Württembergischer Kunstverein, Stuttgart
1990 Ernst Museum & Mucsarnok, Budapest
OPS Park Sienkiewicza, Lodz, Poland
1991 Krzysztofory Galerie, Warsaw
1995 *Michael Sandle: Memorials for the Twentieth Century,* Tate Gallery, Liverpool (catalog)
Jason & Rhodes Gallery, London

Selected Group Exhibitions:

1965 *Inner Image,* Grabowski Gallery, London
1967 *Biennale,* Paris
1968 *Documenta,* Kassel, Germany
1972 *British Sculptors,* Royal Academy of Arts, London
1975 *DAAD Ausstellung,* Haus am Lützow Platz, Berlin
1977 *Le Dessin,* Musée d'Art Moderne de la Ville, Paris
1978 *Hayward Annual,* Hayward Gallery, London
1982 *British Sculpture in the 20th Century,* Whitechapel Art Gallery, London
1986 *Das Andere Land,* Nationalgalerie, Berlin (toured Germany and Luxembourg)
1990 *The Great British Art Show,* McClellan Galleries, Glasgow
1994 *Sculpture at Goodwood,* Goodwood Sculpture Park, England
2000 *Disaster!,* Harris Museum and Art Gallery, Preston, England

Collections:

British Museum, London; National Gallery, London; Tate Gallery, London; National Portrait Gallery, London; Victoria & Albert Museum, London; Museum of London; Imperial War Museum, London; Fitzwilliam Museum, Cambridge; National Museum of Wales, Cardiff; Scottish National Gallery of Modern Art, Edinburgh; City Art Gallery, Glasgow; City Art Gallery, Manchester; Arts Council of Great Britain, London; National Gallery, Berlin; Kunsthalle, Bremen; Kunsthalle, Hamburg; Wilhelm Lehmbruck Museum, Duisburg; Museum Moderner Kunst, Vienna; Musee National du Louvre, Paris; Musee d'Orsay, Paris; National Gallery, Warsaw; Israel Museum, Jerusalem; National Gallery of Australia, Canberra; Art Institute of Chicago, USA; Metropolitan Museum of Art, New York; Museum of Modern Art, New York; National Gallery of Art, Washington, D.C.; Museum des 20. Jahrhunderts, Vienna.

Permanent Public Installations:

Sculpture for Berufsschule, Muhlacker, 1981; *Memorial for the Victims of a Helicopter Disaster,* Mannheim, 1985; Belgrano Medal—*A Medal of Dishonour,* 1986; *St. George and the Dragon,* London, 1988; *Malta Siege Bell Memorial,* Valletta, Malta, 1989–1993; International Maritime Organization, *Seafarer's Memorial,* Albert Embankment, London 2001.

Publications:

By SANDLE: Statements—in *Inner Image,* exhibition catalog, London 1965; in *Abrahams, Chilton, Sandle,* exhibition catalog, London 1966; in *Michael Sandle Drawing Exhibition,* exhibition catalog, Baden-Baden, Germany 1975; in *Hayward Annual,* exhibition catalog, 1978; "In eigener Sache" in *Michael Sandle 1984,* exhibition catalog, Duisburg 1984; in *Celtic Vision,* exhibition catalog, Madrid 1986.

On SANDLE: Books—*Art in Britain* by Edward Lucie-Smith and Patricia White, London 1969; *6 at the Hayward,* exhibition catalog by Michael Compton, London 1969; *British Sculptors,* exhibition catalog by Bryan Robertson, London 1972; *Michael Sandle Drawing Exhibition,* exhibition catalog by Karl Ruhrberg, Berlin 1975; *Michael Sandle,* exhibition catalog by John McEwen, London 1981; *Michael Sandle,* exhibition catalog with essay by Kurt Lankheit, Mannheim 1983; *Michael Sandle 1984,* exhibition catalog with text by Karl-Egon Vester, Duisburg 1984; *The Geometry of Rage,* exhibition catalog with texts by Sarah Kent, Lewis Biggs and James Stevens Curl, Bristol 1984; *Visages Contemporains de la Sculpture in Europe,* exhibition catalog by Gerhard Fries, Maubeuge 1985; *Michael Sandle,* exhibition catalog with essays by Jon Bird and Marco Livingstone, London 1988; *Michael Sandle,* exhibition catalog with essay by Angela Weight, Budapest 1990. **Articles**—"Article of Faith: Michael Sandle" by John Spurling in *Art Review* (London), vol. 46, September 1994; "Michael Sandle: Memorials for the Twentieth Century" by Colin Amery in *Modern Painters* (London), vol. 8, Summer 1995; "The Malta Siege Bell Memorial" by Arthur S. Pier in *Sculpture Review,* vol. 44, Fall 1995; "Michael Sandle: A Cranky Memorial-Maker's Defiant Classicism" by Evelyn Toynton in *Art & Antiques,* vol. 18, December 1995.

*

I have always worked towards the goal of achieving a synthesis of my disparate or seemingly irreconcilable notions of content, form and intention. Objectively, I know this to be almost impossible but it is my bad luck to be programmed to keep trying and, what is worse, care about it when I fail.

It is my misfortune to see art (read life) as a conflict, as an ennervating struggle against mediocrity; in the first instance my own. We do, however, live in times of stupendous, quite heroic mediocrity. It is more than depressing to see the visual arts contaminated with the "New Spirit" of cynicism, or, what is even worse, through benign "democratic" agencies, being turned into a meaningless pap.

Bad art serves one good purpose, I find. However sharp the feelings of anguish and despair at my own shortcomings may be, I believe that there are hundreds who should shoot themselves first.

—Michael Sandle

* * *

Michael Sandle is one of the most gifted and enigmatic British artists of his generation. His drawings and sculptures are unlike those of any of his contemporaries, and, indeed, one must go back to Victorian comic draughtsmen and fantasists to establish any likely lineage.

He works extremely slowly, so that whilst he has often been included in group shows, he has never, in fact, held a one-man exhibition of any dimension. He describes himself as an "expressionist," and says that his work is compounded of nostalgia, dreams and perception. Sandle is a deeply personal, introverted artist, concerned, as he has stated, with magic and wonder, the very opposite of detached intellectualism. This romantic, poetic stance is clearly not pretentious, but rather the outcome of a very special kind of personality.

It would, however, be wrong and misleading to suggest that Sandle's rare, but impressive, work is in any way twee or indulgent. Both in his drawings and sculpture it is clear that his method is based on selection and isolation, so that whilst separate images or elements can be directly traced to known reality, in their assembling they take on a life of their own. Equally confusing is the remarkable range of source inspiration called upon by Sandle: nature, animal forms, architecture and design, as well as the diverse materials used in his sculptures, polyester resin, glass fibre and brass.

Basically he is a "black and white" artist, and in this sense, as well as in a more subtle and deeper connotation, he bears a definite relationship to the important tradition of English illustrators, including Aubry Beardsley. Sandle is a fantastist and surrealistic, his large, hieratic, heraldic sculptures emerging as almost Disneyish illustrations for *Alice in Wonderland,* but, although compounded of a strange wit and remarkable invention, they are in sense coy or merely humorous. Neither are they violent or aggressive. They are, indeed, within his own terms, dreamlike, strange beings almost natural, yet at the same time invented.

—Charles Spencer

SANEJOUAND, Jean-Michel

Nationality: French. **Born:** Lyon, 18 July 1934. **Education:** Studied law, then politics, Lyon, 1951–55; self-taught in art, from 1955. **Family:** Married Michelle Bourgeois in 1957; sons: Yves-Henri and Ludovic. **Career:** Independent artist, Lyon, 1955–59, and in Paris since 1959; abstract paintings, 1955–62; "object-load" assemblage and environmental works, 1963–75; calligraphic works on canvas, 1969–78; painted and drawn works since 1978. **Address:** 27 rue Jasmin, 75016 Paris, France.

Individual Exhibitions:

1964 Galerie Yvette Morin, Paris (with Smerck and Chabaut)
1965 Salon Regain, Lyon (with Smerck and Jackquet)
1967 Ecole Polytechnique, Paris
1968 Galerie Yvon Lambert, Paris
1970 Galerie Mathias Fels, Paris
1973 Centre National d'Art Contemporain, Paris
Palais des Beaux-Arts, Brussels
1974 International Cultureel Centrum, Antwerp
Galerie Germain, Paris
1975 Galerie Germain, Paris
1979 The Antwerpen Gallery, at *FIAC 79,* Grand Palais, Paris
1982 Galerie de France, Paris
Lens Fine Art, Antwerp
1986 Espace Claudine Breguet, Paris
Palais des Beaux Arts, Lyon, France
1989 *Jean-Michel Sanejouand: Paintings 1987–89,* Musee de l'Abbaye Sainte-Croix, Les Sables-d'Olonne, France

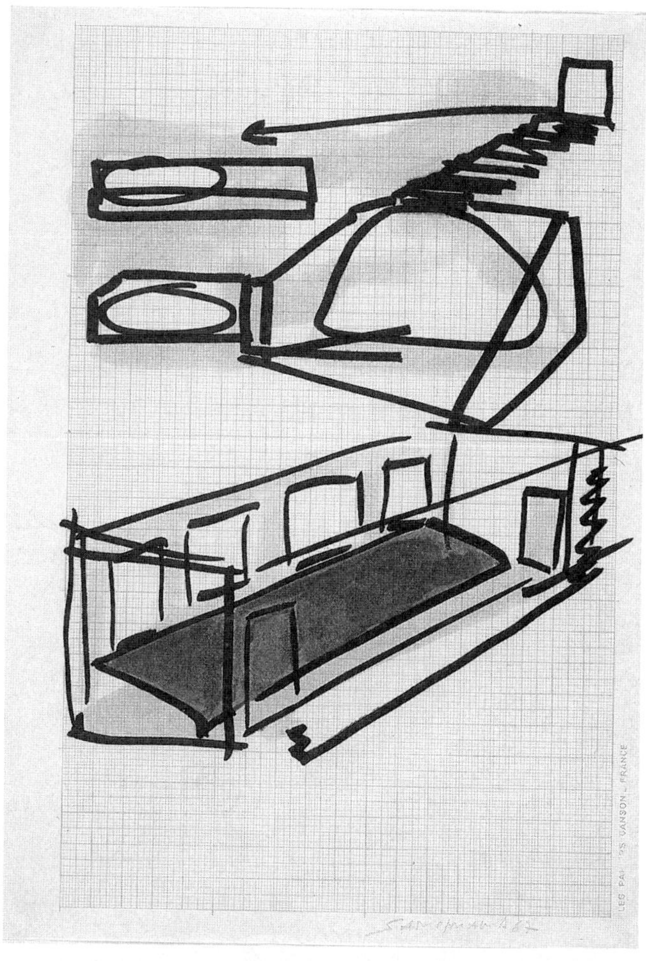

Jean-Michel Sanejouand: *Organised Landscape.* Photo by Philippe Migeat. ©CNAC/MNAM/Dist. Réunion des Musées Nationaux/Art Resource, NY; courtesy of Musee National d'Art Moderne, Centre Georges Pompidou, Paris, France.

1991 *Jean-Michel Sanejouand: Space-paintings 1978–86,* Musée d'Art Moderne, Villenuve-d'Ascq, France
Galerie Froment-Putmann, Paris
1992 Froment-Putman Gallery, Paris

Selected Group Exhibitions:

1964 *La Leçon des Choses,* Galerie du Ranelagh, Paris
1967 *Superland,* Lunds Konsthall, Sweden
1969 *Le Décor Quotidien de la Vie en 1968,* Musée Galliera, Paris
1970 *Information,* Museum of Modern Art, New York
1971 *Peintures et Objects,* Musée Galliera, Paris
1972 *Amsterdam-Paris-Dusseldorf,* Guggenheim Museum, New York
1976 *Biennale,* Venice
1982 *Actuele Franse Kunst,* International Cultureel Centrum, Antwerp
1983 *Zwanzig Jahre Kunst in Frankreich 1960–80,* Kunst-Museum, Mainz, West Germany (travelled to Tubingen and West Berlin)
1986 *Qu'est que l'art francais?,* Centre Régionale d'Art Contemporain, Labège, France (travelled to Innopole and Toulouse)

Collections:

Fonds National d'Art Contemporain, Paris; Musée National d'Art Moderne/Centre Georges Pompidou, Paris; Musée d'Art Moderne de la Ville de Paris; Musée St. Pierre d'Art Contemporain, Lyon; Collection Mobilier National, Gobelins.

Publications:

By SANEJOUAND: Books—*Introduction aux espaces concrets,* Paris 1970; *Plans d'organisations d'espaces,* Paris 1970. **Interviews**—with Pierre Cabanne, in *Matinees de France Culture* (Paris), April 1968; with Daniel Abadie, in *Archives du CNAC* (Paris), September 1971; with Catherine Millet, in *Art Press* (Paris), No. 3, 1973; with Jacques Bertoin, in *Arte Factum* (Antwerp), no. 1, 1983; with Alain Avila and Valere Bertrand in *France Culture* (Paris), 21 April 1986; ''Entretien avec Jean-Michel Sanejouand'' by Catherine Lawless in *Cahiers du Musée National d'Art Moderne,* no. 26, Winter 1988. **Films**—*Soda,* 1965; *Trente-Trois Minutes, Neuf Secondes,* 1967; *L'Espace de la Tour Nord-Est du Grand Palais,* 1972; *Quelques Espaces,* 1973.

On SANEJOUAND: Books—*Neue Dimensionen der Plastik* by Udo Kultermann, Tubingen 1967; *Jean-Michel Sanejouand: Deux Organisations d'Espaces,* exhibition catalog with essay by Gregoire Muller, Paris 1968; *Jean-Michel Sanejouand: Plans d'Organisations d'Espaces,* exhibition catalog with text by Pierre Restany, Paris 1970; *Sanejouand Ruimtelijke organisatie in het Koniklijk paleis (ICC) te Antwerpen,* exhibition catalog with text by Claude Devos, Antwerp 1974; *Actuele Franse Kunst,* exhibition catalog with text by Florent Bex, Antwerp 1982; *Zwanzig Jahre Kunst in Frankreich 1960–1980,* exhibition catalog with essay by Marcelin Pleynet, Mainz 1983; *Jean-Michel Sanejouand,* exhibition catalog with text by Bernard Lamarche-Vadel, Paris 1986; *Jean-Michel Sanejouand: Paintings 1987–89,* exhibition catalog, Les Sables-d'Olonne 1989; *Jean-Michel Sanejouand: Space-paintings 1978–86,* exhibition catalog with text by Michel Enrici, Villeneuve d'Ascq 1991; *Jean-Michel Sanejouand: les charges-objets 1963–1967* by Bernard Lamarche-Vadel, Paris 1990. **Articles**—''Jean-Michel Sanejouand'' by Itzahk Goldberg in *Beaux Arts Magazine,* no. 137, September 1995.

*

When I stopped painting at the end of 1962 I was convinced that it was the final break. For the previous few years I had painted abstracts as now on white backgrounds. To a very superficial observer today they might appear quite similar to my current work. My painting was confined to a fairly naive, purely imaginary space. The ''object-loads'' (''charges-objects''), my arrangements of pieces of striped tarpaulin, metal grating, strips of printed linoleum and so on which replaced the paintings reflected a suddenly compelling need to experiment with real space, a tremendous urge to confront this space. They were also an acknowledgement of the ludicrous. After 1967 there was a logical progression with these arrangements making way

Jean-Michel Sanejouand: *Space—Painting,* 1934. Photo by Philippe Migeat. ©CNAC/MNAM/Dist. Réunion des Musées Nationaux/Art Resource, NY; courtesy of Musee National d'Art Moderne, Centre Georges Pompidou, Paris, France.

for my work directly on concrete space in what I called my organizations of spaces. The space of various places: a courtyard, a building site, an exhibition hall, became my raw material. Everything seemed to be going fine.

Yet in 1969 I began to conceptualize my work with space more by drawing plans and I felt an urge to hold a paintbrush again, to dip it in the ink and draw figures, generally grotesque and aggressive ones. For nine years I had to struggle on with both activities: my work with actual space and then these calligraphies of mood, as I call them, which in a way were my painting resurfacing. Of course, they were not only and not entirely that—far from it! My distrust of painting still ran very deep. I would take a canvas that was ready to be painted on and would just draw a few lines in ink. It was a difficult, even a painful experience, but I truly had no choice. I did not then understand that I only needed these calligraphies because they gave me an opportunity to work with imaginary space. The sense of the ludicrous, inaugurated in my ''object-loads,'' was very apparent in these ''figurative'' drawings, but also in my carefully elaborated plans with their understones of a contained frenzy and in my organization of the planet Earth using ''orientation tables'' that I worked on from 1974 to 1977. In any event it was in 1977 that both my calligraphies of mood and my orientation tables became pictorialized.

What had happened? Quite simply, I had never stopped looking at painting all those years. Gradually the conviction that I had underestimated it took hold of me. Of course, I do not mean just any painting! Painting in general seemed to me then—and still does today—to be a rather pointless exercise. All those surfaces covered in what is often just filling bore me and even irritate me most of the time. However, I began to to realize that painting, if handled with stringent discipline, could be a gateway leading on towards a different consciousness. It was also a way of not skirting the fundamental issue of transposition which is the nobility of art.

Anyway, since 1978, which was when I accepted that I would start painting again, I have felt a lot happier, relieved, as though freed from the wearying, two-fold course which I had had to pursue.

However, I was unable to apply the analytical discipline I mentioned to my own use of the brush immediately. Not for technical reasons alone—that wasn't much of a problem—but because I could not shake off my distrust all at once. I had an absolute need to wipe my brush regularly over the canvas. It is only over the last two or three years that I have dismissed my last reservations on the subject and that I have at last been able to rise above the ludicrous smilingly.

—Jean-Michel Sanejouand

SARET, Alan (Daniel)

Nationality: American. **Born:** New York City, 25 December 1944. **Education:** Studied at Cornell University, Ithaca, New York, 1961–66, B.Arch.; Hunter College, New York, 1967–68. **Career:** Travelled in Mexico, Europe, and North Africa; lived in India, 1971–73; now lives and works in New York. Visiting artist in sculpture, University of California at Irvine, 1979. **Awards:** Guggenheim Fellowship, 1969; National Endowment for the Arts Grant, 1975; Creative Artists Program Service Grant, New York, 1976. **Agent:** Margo Leavin Gallery, 812 North Robertson Boulevard, Los Angeles, California 90069. **Address:** 65 South 11th Street, New York, New York 11211, U.S.A.

Individual Exhibitions:

1968 Bykert Gallery, New York
3 Young Americans: Krueger, Nauman, Saret, Allen Memorial Art Museum, Oberlin, Ohio
1970 Bykert Gallery, New York
1971 Katonah Gallery, Katonah, New York
1973 Clocktower, New York
1975 597 West Broadway, New York
1977 Seattle Art Museum
And/Or, Seattle
1978 University of California, Berkeley
1979 SITE, San Francisco
Weinberg Gallery, San Francisco
1980 Charles Cowles Gallery, New York
1981 University of Rhode Island, Kingston
Gallerie Rudolf Zwirner, Cologne
1982 Charles Cowles Gallery, New York
Newport Harbor Art Museum, Newport Beach, California
1983 Albright-Knox Art Gallery, Buffalo, New York
Hallways, Buffalo, New York

Selected Group Exhibitions:

1968 *Whitney Annual,* Whitney Museum, New York
1969 *When Attitudes Become Form,* Kunsthalle, Berne (toured Europe)
1971 *6 Sculptors: Extended Structures,* Museum of Contemporary Art, Chicago
1976 *American Art of the 20th Century,* Allen Memorial Art Museum, Oberlin, Ohio
1977 *Open to New Ideas,* University of Georgia, Athens
1980 *Biennale,* Venice
Drawing/Structures, Institute of Contemporary Art, Boston
1981 *Developments in Recent Sculpture,* Whitney Museum, New York
1982 *Kunst Wird Material,* Nationalgalerie, West Berlin
1988 *Questioning the Givens,* BlumHelman Gallery, Santa Monica, California
1989 Lorence-Monk Gallery, New York
1990 *The New Sculpture 1965–75: Between Geometry and Gesture,* Whitney Museum of American Art, New York
7 Objects69: A Collection of Original Works by Seven Young Artists, University Gallery, University of Massachusetts, Amherst
P.S. 1, Long Island City, New York
1991 *The Margins of Minimalism,* Daniel Weinberg Gallery, Santa Monica, California

Collections:

Whitney Museum, New York; Museum of Modern Art, New York University of Georgia, Athens; Detroit Institute of Arts; Museum of Contemporary Art, Chicago; Dallas Museum of Fine Arts; Art Museum of South Texas, Corpus Christi; Los Angeles County Museum of Art; San Francisco Museum of Modern Art; Society of the Four Arts, Toronto.

Publications:

By SARET: Articles—''An Interview with Alan Saret and Jeffrey Caw'' in *Avalanche* (New York), Winter 1971; ''Reincarnated Concept or Repeated Gesture: An Experience in Remaking Sculpture'' in *Art in America* (New York), vol. 78, July 1990.

On SARET: Articles—''3 Young Americans: Krueger, Nauman, Saret'' by Ellen H. Johnson and Athena Spear in the *Allen Memorial Art Museum Bulletin* (Oberlin, Ohio), Spring 1968; ''New York: Alan Saret, Bykert Gallery'' by Emily Wasserman in *Artforum* (New York), January 1969; ''9 Men in a Warehouse'' by Max Kozloff in *Artforum* (New York), February 1969; ''Alan Saret's Studio Exhibition'' by Emily Wasserman in *Artforum* (New York), March 1970; ''Methods and Materials New and Old'' by B. Schwartz in *Craft Horizons* (New York), December 1975; ''Alan Saret'' by Jonathan Crary in *Arts Magazine* (New York), September 1977; ''Alan Saret: Skulpturen und Zeichnungen'' by A. Pohlen in *Kunstforum International* (Mainz), no. 1, 1981; ''Alan Saret'' by Roswitha Fricke and Marion Fricke in *Art Press Special Issue* (Paris), no. 17, 1996.

SARKIS

Nationality: French. **Born:** Sarkis Zabunyan, in Istanbul, Turkey, 26 September 1938; immigrated to France, 1964; naturalized, 1985. **Education:** Studied at the Academy of Fine Arts, Istanbul, 1957–60. **Military Service:** Served in the Turkish Army, Ministry of Defence, Istanbul, 1961–63: lieutenant. **Family:** Married Isil Akyuz in 1963; children: Elvan and Dork. **Career:** Worked as a part-time draughtsman in an architect's offices, Istanbul Ankara, 1961–63; first paintings, 1961; full time artist in Istanbul, 1963–64, in Paris since 1964. Professor, Ecole des Arts Decoratifs, Strasbourg, 1980–90; Directeur de séminaire, Institut des Hautes Etudes en Arts Plastiques, Paris, 1989–95 **Awards:** First Prize for Painting, *Biennale de Paris,* 1967. Chévalier, Ordre des Arts et des Lettres, Paris, 1985. **Agent:** Galerie Sonnabend, 12 rue Mazarine Arlogos, 6 rue du Pont de Lodi, 75006 Paris. **Address:** 67 rue Vergniaud, 75013 Paris, France.

Individual Exhibitions:

1967 Galerie Blumenthal, Paris
1968 Galleri Klipans, Gothenburg, Sweden
1970 Galerie Sonnabend, Paris
Musée d'Art Moderne, Paris
1971 Galerie Sonnabend, Paris
Galerie Handschin, Basel
1972 Kunsthalle, Dusseldorf
Galerie Sonnabend, Paris
Galerie Ben Doute de Tout, Nice
Galerie Handschin, Basel
1973 Musée Galliera, Paris
Institut Pasteur, Paris
1974 Musée d'Art et d'Industrie, Saint-Etienne, France
Galleria La Salita, Rome
Modern Art Agency, Naples
Galerie Sonnabend, Paris
Galerie Handschin, Basel
1975 Galleria Cenobio-Visualita, Milan
Galerie Le Metronome, Paris
Galerie Sonnabend, Paris
Galerie Handschin, Basel
Salle d'Art Contemporain, Geneva
Galerie Folker Skulima, West Berlin
1976 Galerie Sonnabend, Paris
Galleria Cenobio-Visualita, Milan
1978 Westfälischer Kunstverein, Münster, West Germany
1979 Neue Galerie, Aachen, West Germany
1980 Centre des Arts Plastiques Contemporain, Bordeaux
Galerie Sonnabend, Paris
Galerie Attitude, Strasbourg, France
1981 Centre d'Art Contemporain, Geneva
Galerie Baronian, Brussels
1982 Galerie J. J. Donguy, Paris
Galerie Catherine Issert, St. Paul de Vence, France
Galerie Eric Fabre, Paris
1983 Grand Garage, Strasbourg, France
Tartar Gallery, Edinburgh
Macka Sanat Galerisi, Istanbul
1984 Musée d'Art Moderne, Paris
Galerie Eric Fabre, Paris
DAAD-Galerie, West Berlin
1985 Chapelle Sainte Marie, Nevers, France
Galerie Eric Fabre, Paris
Centre d'Art Contemporain, Chateauroux, France
Kunsthalle, Berne
Centre d'Art Contemporain, Geneva
Le Nouveau Musée, Villeurbanne, France
1986 Ecole Nationale d'Art Décoratif, Limoges, France
Macka Sanat Galerisi, Istanbul
Placard d'Eric Satie, Paris
Galerie de Paris, Paris
1987 Maison de la Culture, La Rochelle, France
Chateau Lynch-Bages, Bordeaux, France
't Kromhout Museum, Amsterdam
1988 *Territoire d'atterrissage,* Galerie de Paris, Paris
La Source éclaire toujours, Finnegan's, Strasbourg
Feu d'artifice rouillé, Transit, Strasbourg
1989 *Le Forgeron en masque de Sarkis, rouge et vert, visite Autun,* Chapelle Notre Dame des Bonnes-Oeuvres, Autun
103 Aquarelles et 42 Heures du Loup, Musée des Beaux-Arts de Nantes
Sarkis interprète le Musée Constantin Meunier, Musée Constantin Meunier, Bruxelles
1990 *103 Akvaller* and *42 Ulvetimer,* Nordjylands Kunstmuseum
Les 13 Ikônes en aquarelle et néon, FIAC 1990, Galerie de Paris
1991 *Scènes de nuit—Scènes de jour,* Magasin, Centre National d'Art Contemporain, Grenoble
Les 12 coins du monde, Galerie Arlogos, Nantes
1992 *Scènes de nuit, de jours,* Centraal Museum, Utrecht
19380, Galerie de Paris
Rêve du jour et de nuit (1980), Galerie Arlogos, Nantes
Blikket, Tapko, Copenhagen
19380–19930, Maçka Sanat Galerisi, Istanbul
1993 *Ankara'dan bugüne,* Zon galerisi, Ankara
Warmte en licht, Galerie de Zaal, Delft
Le décalage entre la lumière de l'éclair et le bruit du tonnerre, Centre Georges Pompidou, Paris
1994 *Introduction à l'exposition de Sarkis aux Ecuries Saint-Hugues,* Salle Victor Duruy, Cluny
PAYSAGE, Ecuries Saint-Hugues, Cluny
Mesures d'élévation, Galerie de Paris, Paris
1995 *Das Licht des Blitzes, der Lärm des Donners,* Museum moderner Kunst Stiftung Ludwig, Palais Liechtenstein, Vienna (catalog)
"26.9.19380," Kunst-und Ausstellungshalle der Bundesrepublik Deutschland, Bonn (catalog)
L'arrivée des images and *L'envolée d'Agra à Verdun,* Chapelle Buvignier et le Théâtre de Verdun
Aquarelle/Néon, Galerie de Zaal, Delft
1996 *Sculptures obscures 1969–1975 (à Aram Iynedjian),* Musée d'Art Moderne et Contemporain de Genève
3 Zones + One, Capp Street Project, San Francisco (booklet)
Geistersblitz, Akademie der Künste, Berlin
1997 *Paysage Brule,* Galerie Arlogos, Nantes
Au Commencement, le son de la lumiere, a l'arrivee, Musée des Beaux-Arts, Nantes
1998 *Les films tournés à Saché,* Atelier Calder, Saché
1999 *L'echo de ma main (à partir de 19380),* MAMCO Genève
25 short films, Galerie de Zaal, Delft
2000 *SARKIS 21.01.2000—09.04.2000,* CAPC Musée Bordeaux (catalog)
Respiration, Le Panthéon, Paris (catalog)
L'atelier depuis 19380—LE CRI XX, MAMCO, Genève

Selected Group Exhibitions:

1967 *Biennale de Paris,* Musée d'Art Modern, Paris (and 1969, 1971)
1969 *When Attitudes Become Form,* Kunsthalle, Berne (toured Europe)
1970 *6 Propositions,* Centre Culturel Americain, Paris
1972 *Intervention á la Galerie Duncan,* Galerie Raymond Duncan, Paris
1974 *Ars 74,* Museum Ateneum, Helsinki

1975 *Photographie dans l'Art,* Musée des Beaux-Arts, Rennes, France
1976 *Identité-Identifications,* Centre des Arts Plastiques Contemporains, Bordeaux
1982 *Documenta,* Kassel, West Germany
1985 *L'Oeil Musicien,* Palais des Beaux-Arts, Charleroi, Belgium
1987 *Maintenant,* Palais de Rohan, Strasbourg, France
1st Biennale, Istanbul
Du Goût et des Couleurs, Centre National des Arts Plastiques, Paris
1988 *Collection Sonnabend,* CAPC Musée d'Art Contemporain, Entrepôt Laîné, Bordeaux
Art pour l'Afrique, Musée National des Arts Africains et Océaniens, Paris
CLARTE, Nordjyllands Kunstmuseum, Aalborg
1989 *Coup d'envois,* Musée de la Poste, Paris
Hommage à la Déclaration Universelle des Droits de l'Homme, Oeuvres sur papier d'artistes des cinq continents, Centre d'Art Contemporain, Genève
Les Magiciens de la Terre, Centre Georges Pompidou and La Grande Halle de la Villette, Paris
1990 *The Readymade Boomerang,* 8th Biennale of Sydney, Australia
Les territoires de l'Art, Musée Russe, Leningrad
Aktuelle kunst Europas, sammlung Centre Georges Pompidou, Deichtorhallen Hamburg, Germany
1991 *Dessins et Dessins,* Musée des Beaux-Arts, Mulhouse
Night Lines, Centraal Museum, Utrecht
Biennale de Cetinje, Montenegro (permanent installation)
1992 *Francia—Közelmult,* Magyar Nemzeti Galeria, Budapest
Territorium Artis, Kunst und Austellungshalle, Bonn
1993 *Trésors de voyage,* San Lazzaro, Biennale de Venice
Juxtapositions, Grande Halle, Gare d'Austerlitz, Paris
1994 *Eighth Triennale-India,* New Dehli
Arte in Francia 1970–1993, Galleria Communale d'Arte Moderna di Bologna
A partir de 19380, Musée d'art moderne et contemporain (MAMCO), Genève
1995 *Thresholds,* National Gallery of Modern Art, New Dehli
Des artistes à travers l'archive, Ecole Nationale des Beaux-Arts, Nancy
1996 *Installations & Sculptures,* FDAC, Seine Saint-Denis
Memento Metropolis, Turbinehallen, Copenhagen
L'humaine condition, Espace d'Art Contemporain André Malraux
1997 *Parisien(ne)s,* Camden Arts Centre, London
Memento Metropolis, Hessenhuis Antwerpen
Meditation, Medersa Ibn Youssef, Marrakech
1998 *TAPKO—Sunday Morning* Walk, Kunsthallen Brandts Klaedefabrik, Odense (catalog)
Crossings, Kunsthalle Wien
Premises (Invested Spaces in Visual Arts, Architecture and Design from France, 1958–1998), Solomon R. Guggenheim Museum SoHo, New York
1999 International Film Festival Rotterdam
Panorama 2000, Dom Tower, Utrecht (catalog)
Kronos & Kairos, Museum Fridericianum, Kassel (catalog)
au commencement (les 16 films tournés au Fresnoy), Cinéma Odyssée, Strasbourg
2000 *Lumière aux Cordeliers,* Couvent des Cordeliers, Paris (catalog)
Narcisse blessé, Passage Retz, Paris (catalog)
Shanghai Biennale, Shanghai Art Museum (catalog)

Collections:

Centre Georges Pompidou, Paris; Kaiser-Wilhelm-Museum, Krefeld, West Germany; Kunstmuseum, Basel; Konstmuseum, Gothenburg, Sweden; Art Gallery of New South Wales, Sydney; Musée des Beaux-Arts, Nantes; Museum moderner Kunst Stiftung Ludwig, Palais Liechtenstein, Vienna; Musée Saint-Pierre, Lyon; Le Nouveau Musée, Villeurbanne; Musée Cantini, Marseille; Musée de Strasbourg.

Publications:

By SARKIS: Books—*La Drama of the Tempest,* St Etienne, France 1974; *Blackout,* Geneva 1975; *Der Blackout ist voller schwarzer weisser blauer roter goldener Farbe so wie der Anstreicher,* with Wolfgang Becker, Aachen, West Germany 1979; *Kriegsschatz-Klassenkrieg,* with Herbert Molderings, Munster, West Germany 1978; *Reserves sans Retour,* Bordeaux 1980. **Disc—***Litho Disc,* Rome 1974; *La Drama of the Tempest,* Rome 1974; *Enquete. . . ,* Geneva 1975.

On SARKIS: Books—*Sarkis: Le Troisieme Reich, des Origines á la Chute,* exhibition catalog, Paris 1971; *Sarkis Zabunyan,* exhibition catalog with an introduction by Jurgen Harten, Dusseldorf 1972; *Art en France: une nouvelle generation* by Jean Clair, Paris 1973; *Sarkis,* exhibition catalog with an introduction by Bernard Ceysson, St. Etienne, France 1974; *Art Actuel en France* by Anne Tronche and Hervé Gloaguen, Paris 1974; *Documenta 7* exhibition catalog, 2 vols., edited by Rudi H. Fuchs, Kassel, West Germany 1982; *Der Anfang der Jahrhunderts,* exhibition catalog with text by Claude Gintz, West Berlin 1984; *Trois Mises en Scene de Sarkis,* exhibition catalog with text by Jean-Hubert Martin, Berne 1985; *Vie et Legende du Captain Sarkis* by Jean-Marie Touratier, Paris 1986; *Sarkis: It's Time, Time, Time,* exhibition catalog with text by Elvan Zabunyan, La Rochelle 1987; *103 Aquarelles,* exhibition catalog, Bruxelles-Hambourg 1989; *Ma Chambre de la rue Krutenau en Satellite,* exhibition catalog, Bruxelles-Hambourg 1989; *4 2 Heures du Loup,* exhibition catalog, Nantes 1989; *Scènes de Nuit, Scènes de Jour,* exhibition catalog, Grenoble 1992; *19380–19930,* exhibition catalog, Istanbul 1992; *Point de Rencontre: Le Rêve,* exhibition catalog, Sélestat 1993; *Warmte en Licht,* exhibition catalog, Delft 1993; *Le Forgeron en masque de Sarkis rouge et vert,* exhibition catalog, Port-Bou 1993; *Les 7 Trésors de guerre de La Réunion,* exhibition catalog, Saint-Denis 1994; *Zone,* exhibition catalog, Maebashi, Japan 1994; *Das Licht des Blitzes, der Lärm des Donners,* exhibition catalog with texts by Uwe Fleckner, Lórand Hegyi, and Roland Recht, Vienna 1995; *The Treasure Chests of Mnemosyne. Selected Texts on Memory Theory from Plato to Derrida,* edited by Uwe Fleckner, Dresden 1998 (German edition 1995, French edition 1998); *26.9.1938,* exhibition catalog, Bonn 1996; *Au commencement, le son de la lumière, à l'arrivée,* exhibition catalog with texts by Pontus Hulten, Stephan Andreae, and Elvan Zabunyan, Nantes 1997; *SARKIS 21.01.2000—09.04.2000,* exhibition catalog with texts by Henry-Claude Cousseau, Michel Enrici, Uwe Fleckner, and Erik Bullot, Bordeaux 2000.

* * *

In the principle of open design embodied in his constantly changing and ever-new installations, Sarkis has found the particular form in which the work of art stores and processes personal as well as collective memory. His work must thus be assigned to that genre within contemporary art which intervenes in the exhibitive framework, arranging found and formed objects into structures which have long since left behind them the classical concept of sculpture—a concept which was determined, not least, by the aesthetic distance of the pedestal. Above all, the works of the artist derive their singular structure from the fact that his oeuvre is to be fundamentally characterised as open, as defying completion. Combining neon light and letters, wooden scaffolds, video, magnetic tape, drawings and sculptures, artifacts of all times and peoples, Sarkis' archive-installations have been regrouped and have undergone incessant changes in form. Indeed, the installation of a work is comparable to the concert performance of a symphony.

The location of this performance is the museum. However, the museum is the place of the object's historical transformation of function, as well as being the place in which the present establishes its rule over history. It is precisely this aesthetical expropriation which has led Sarkis to transfer the concept of the "treasure of war" to the collection of booty exhibited in the museum and, finally, to transform it into material fruitful for his own artistic work. This concept of artistic work has accompanied him since 1976. After visiting the museums in Berlin, he encountered this concept for the first time in an article in *Le Monde* on striking French workers who had appropriated a part of the factory production as "treasure of war." Sarkis immediately transferred what he had read onto what he had just seen in the museums: the artefact becomes one of the spoils of the past in the edifice of the present. From this point on, the artist endeavoured, in his installations, to establish his own compilation of found and formed objects into a living collection contraposed to the art treasures in the museum, in which the individual work of art ossifies into a symbol of the rule of the present over history.

Even though the art works of the past may not always exercise a direct influence on individual artworks of the present, art nevertheless has a collective memory which infiltrates the image worlds of us all, not just of painters and sculptors, and leaves just as deep a mark on our visual consciousness as on our visual subconscious. Not only the artist but also the beholder, the art critic and the art historian must, in order to reach the hidden depths of any work of art, take into account both the artistic heritage of bygone epochs and the "permanent memory trace" (Sigmund Freud) which these epochs have left in the rich treasure chest of images which all of us share. The works of Sarkis comprise many such hidden depths of memory. Commencing in the artist's present, they reach further and further into the past. The history of mankind has always been central to this artist's work, and it is art and cultural history in particular—as his devotion to Matthias Grünewald or Andrey Tarkovsky, to Edvard Munch or Anton Webern suggests—which influences the world of his imagination. Sarkis has, in an intensive and very personal way, sought to bridge the historical gap between himself and the artists of the past by incorporating aspects of their works in his own work and, in so doing, clearly demonstrating that he is at all times aware of the engraphic effect of past works of art.

The conceptual framework of the artistic work of Sarkis has recently been extended by an idea that Aby Warburg, the art and cultural historian, noted down in 1928 in an attempt to condense his conception of the work of art into a single formula: "The treasure of human suffering becomes the possession of mankind." The work of art itself is thus to be seen primarily as a document in the archive of the human experience. The role of the historian—and we should like to add, that of the artist too—is to be characterised as that of a "seismographer" whose task it is to receive, in the study of history, the "mnemonic waves" of a past filled with suffering.

Sarkis' work on the theme of memory culminated, in 1995, in a pictorial essay, published in the book *The Treasure Chests of Mnemosyne* (edited by Uwe Fleckner), in which various theoretical and literary treatments of this theme—from Plato to Jacques Derrida—are confronted with views of the artist's studio. These photographs, taken between the years of 1976 and 1993, tell the story of the studio. The reader and beholder witnesses the changes that take place down the years in the arrangement of the created and found objects that fill the studio: the artist's own sculptures and the fetishes of remote peoples and times, watercolours and fragments of texts, pictures and masks, all of them objects used by the artist for his installations, all of them constantly changing places with each other, conducting dialogues with each other in ever changing constellations. It is in this microcosm—for this is what the artist's Paris studio in the rue Vergniaud has indeed become—that the beholder also discovers the various strata of life that were deposited there, one on top of the other, as time went by.

This conception of the work of the artist, which does not only respond to the convulsions in his own soul, but also to those reaching him from bygone times, has been unconsciously tracked down by Sarkis in his concept of "treasure of suffering": no matter whether it is a work of cultural or art history, the particle of private iconography, the object—as the fragment of memory of a past filled with human experience—finds reception in the mnemonic architecture of the artist. Sarkis assembles the found and formed objects into treasure-houses of imprinted images of memory, storing the experience of suffering from the past and the present.

—Uwe Fleckner

SARKISIAN, Paul

Nationality: American. **Born:** Chicago, Illinois, 18 August 1928. **Education:** School of the Art Institute of Chicago, 1945–48; Otis Art Institute, Los Angeles, 1953–54; Mexico City College, 1955–56. **Career:** Independent painter, in California and New Mexico, since 1956. Taught at the Pasadena Art Museum, California, 1965–69; University of Southern California, Los Angeles, and the Art Center, Los Angeles, 1969; University of California, Berkeley, 1970; University of Oregon, Eugene, 1971; and University of South Florida, Tampa, 1972; **Agent:** Nancy Hoffman Gallery, New York, New York, U.S.A. **Address:** c/o Nancy Hoffman Gallery, 429 West Broadway, New York, New York 10012, U.S.A.

Individual Exhibitions:

1958 Nova Gallelry, Boston
1962 Aura Gallery, Pasadena, California
1963 La Jolla Art Center, California
1968 Pasadena Art Museum, California
1969 Corcoran Gallery, Washington, D.C.
1970 Michael Walls Gallery, San Francisco
Santa Barbara Museum of Art, California

1972 Museum of Contemporary Art, Chicago
1973 Michael Walls Gallery, Los Angeles
1975 *Featured Painting,* Museum of Contemporary Arts, Houston
1977 Museum of Contemporary Arts, Houston
1978 Nancy Hoffman Gallery, New York
1979 Arts Club of Chicago
1980 Wright State University, Dayton, Ohio (travelled to the Herron Gallery, Indianapolis, and Ohio State University, Columbus)
Nancy Hoffman Gallery, New York
1981 Arco Center for Visual Arts, Los Angeles
1982 Aspen Center for the Visual Arts, Colorado

Selected Group Exhibitions:

1977 *A View of the Decade,* Museum of Contemporary Art, Chicago
Illusions of Reality, Australian National Gallery, Canberra (travelled to the Western Australia National Gallery, Perth)
1979 *Prospectus: The 70s,* Aldrich Museum, Ridgefield, Connecticut
Reality of Illusion, Denver Art Museum (travelled to the Honolulu Academy of Art; Oakland Museum of Art, California; University of Texas Art Museum, Austin; and Johnson Museum of Art, Cornell University, Ithaca, New York, 1979–80)
1980 *American Art since 1950,* Santa Barbara Museum of Art, California
Contemporary Art from New Mexico, Scottish Arts Council, Edinburgh
1981 *Real, Really Real and Super Real,* San Antonio Museum Association, Texas
1985 *American Realism,* San Francisco Museum of Modern Art (toured the United States, 1986–87)
1988 *Director's Invitational,* Tacoma Art Museum, Washington

Collections:

Corcoran Gallery, Washington, D.C.; Hirshhorn Museum and Sculpture Garden, Washington, D.C.; Art Institute of Chicago; Indianapolis Museum of Arts; Des Moines Art Center, Iowa; Milwaukee Art Center; Oakland Museum of Art, California; Norton Simon Museum of Art, Pasadena, California; Santa Barbara Museum of Art, California; Aachen Museum, West Germany.

Publications:

On SARKISIAN: Book—*Paul Sarkisian,* exhibition leaflet, with an essay by Philip Yenawine, Aspen, Colorado 1982. **Articles—**''Painters Who the Real World into Sharp Focus'' by John Canady in *Smithsonian,* vol. 12, October 1981; ''Paul Sarkisian'' by Steven Henry in *Art in America,* vol. 71, March 1983.

* * *

This foremost American ultra-illusionist is often spoken of in the lineage of the 19th century Americans such as Peale, Harnett, and Peto, who similarly practiced trompe l'oeil, all thus touching the American literalist nerve. Sarkisian began during the 1960s to assert that he had gained a sense of the present by a past-glance, in a series of satirical Pop-academic paintings. However he then gained wide recognition with vernacular subjects—store fronts—in spectacular life-scale monochromatic paintings of the earlier 1970s. From that time, has come the almost two-decade-long drive—coinciding with a greatly strengthened grasp both technical and ideational—towards what has been called an illusionist transcendental collage (V.B. Price). These often large works have featured mundane objects, such as printed commercial packaging, newspapers, letters, et al, most often seen flattened against a milky light background. Compositions were usually unbalanced, as if relationality and thus ''art-fulness'' were deemphasized. The surface of these works become breathless, achieving with both air brush and subtle silkscreen techniques an immaculate hologram-like three-dimensional quality. (Shadows, for instance, were air-brushed adjacent to the represented objects to lift them from the canvas surface.)

Perhaps such delving into the apparitional quality of the light-lit object is enhanced and supported by the artist's 25-year-long residence in New Mexico; his illusionist work also coincides with, ableit in art far more abstracted, the work of other far-western artists likewise infatuated with the mysterious revelations of light—Irwin, Bell, Valentine, Turrell. Within the last half-decade, as almost a logical progress, Sarkisian eliminated more and more the printed sections and other specifically referential qualities of his collage groupings, so that he seemingly intended a material purity which might be read as shape and color alone. Although still trompe l'oeil, the images appear as hard edge geometric art with at times a post-modernist reference to old master modernist work of Max Weber, Malevich, and as well the illusionism of Harnett.

It would seem that Sarkisian has attempted to make the non-modern illusionist tradition appropriate to a post modern environment with allusions both general and specific to the abstract art which discarded that illusionism.

—Joshua Kind

SAUL, Peter

Nationality: American. **Born:** San Francisco, California, 16 August 1926. **Education:** Stanford University School of Fine Arts, California, 1949–50; California School of Fine Arts, San Francisco, 1950–52; Washington University School of Fine Arts, St. Louis, with Fred Conway, 1952–56, B.F.A. 1956. **Career:** Painter: lived in the Netherlands, 1956–58; Paris, 1958–62; Rome, 1962–64; California, for several years beginning in 1965; currently lives in Austin, Texas. **Awards:** Copley Foundation Award. 1961; *Art in America* New Talent Award, 1962; National Endowment for the Arts grant, Washington, D.C., 1980. **Agents:** George Adams Gallery, 41 West 57th Street, New York, New York, 10019; Rena Bransten Gallery, 77 Geary Street, San Francisco, California, 94108.

Individual Exhibitions:

1961 Allan Frumkin Gallery, Chicago
Galerie Breteau, Paris
1962 Allan Frumkin Gallery, New York

1963 Allan Frumkin Gallery, New York
Rolf Nelson Gallery, Los Angeles
Galleria Tartaruga, Rome
Galerie Breteau, Paris
1964 Rolf Nelson Gallery, Los Angeles
Galleria Notizie, Turin
Galerie Breteau, Paris
Allan Frumkin Gallery, New York
1965 Galerie Anne Aebels, Cologne
1966 Allan Frumkin Gallery, New York
Allan Frumkin Gallery, Chicago
1967 Galerie Breteau, Paris
Contemporary Gallery, Kansas City
Wanamaker's, Philadelphia
Galleria de Foscherari 60, Bologna, Italy
1968 San Francisco Art Institute
California College of Arts and Crafts Gallery, Oakland
Reed College, Portland, Oregon
Allan Frumkin Gallery, New York
1969 Allan Frumkin Gallery, Chicago
Allan Frumkin Gallery, New York
Galerie Darthea Speyer, Paris
1971 Allan Frumkin Gallery, New York
Musée d'Art et d'Industrie, Saint-Etienne, France
1972 Allan Frumkin Gallery, Chicago
Galerie Darthea Speyer, Paris
1973 California State University at Sacramento
Allan Frumkin Gallery, New York
Galerie Klang, Cologne
1974 Allan Frumkin Gallery, Chicago
1975 Allan Frumkin Gallery, New York
1976 Housatonic Museum of Art, Bridgeport, Connecticut
1977 Allan Frumkin Gallery, Chicago
1978 Allan Frumkin Gallery, New York
1980 University of Northern Illinois, DeKalb (retrospective)
Madison Art Center, Wisconsin (retrospective)
1981 Allan Frumkin Gallery, New York
Kilcawley Center, Youngstown State University, Ohio (retrospective)
1983 *Red Grooms/Peter Saul: The Early Sixties,* Alland Frumkin Gallery, New York
1984 Allan Frumkin Gallery, New York
Frumkin Struve Gallery, Chicago
1985 Allan Frumkin Gallery, New York
1986 Rena Bransten Gallery, San Francisco
1987 Texas Gallery, Houston
Allan Frumkin Gallery, New York
1989 Frumkin Struve Gallery, Chicago
Frumkin/Adams Gallery, New York
1989–90 *Peter Saul* (retrospective), organized by the Aspen Art Museum, Colorado (travelled to Museum of Contemporary Art, Chicago; Laguna Gloria Art Museum, Austin, Texas; and Contemporary Arts Center, New Orleans)
1990 Texas Gallery, Houston
Frumkin Adams Gallery, New York
Galerie Bonnier, Geneva, Switzerland
Peter Saul: Political Paintings, Frumkin Adams Gallery (retrospective; travelled to Krannert Art Museum, University of Illinois, Champaign, and the Art Museum, Washington University, St. Louis, 1990–91)
The Trial of Peter Saul, Museum of Contemporary Art, Chicago
1991 Galerie Thomas R. Monahan, Chicago (catalog)
Galerie du Centre, Paris
1992 Frumkin Adams Gallery, New York
1993 Frumkin Adams Gallery, New York
1994 Henry Palmer Gallery, Los Angeles
1995 *Don't Kiss Ass,* Ynglingagatan 1, Stockholm, Sweden
Castro's Mother Destroys Miami and Related Drawings, Frumkin Adams Gallery, New York
Galerie Bonnier, Geneva, Switzerland
Turner, Byrne and Runyon, Dallas
1996 *New Paintings,* George Adams Gallery, New York
Art World Portraits, David and Alfred Smart Museum of Art, Chicago
1998 *Paintings and Related Drawings 1960–64,* George Adams Gallery, New York
1999 *Peter Saul,* Musée de l'Abbaye Sainte-Croix, Les Sables d'Olonne (traveling exhibition) (catalog)

Selected Group Exhibitions:

1959 *Salon de Jeune Peinture,* Paris (and 1960)
1967 *Carnegie International,* Carnegie Institute, Pittsburgh, Pennsylvania
1968 *Social Comment in America,* Museum of Modern Art, New York
Paris Biennale International, Museum of Modern Art, Paris
1969 *Human Concern/Personal Torment,* Whitney Museum of American Art, New York (travelled to University Art Museum, Berkeley, California)
1971 *Corcoran Biennial,* Washington, D.C.
1972 *American Exhibition,* Art Institute of Chicago (and 1976)
1978 *Art about Art,* Whitney Museum, New York
1984 *The Human Condition,* San Francisco Museum of Modern Art
1988 *Commmitted to Print,* Museum of Modern Art, New York
1994 *Here and Now: Bay Area Masterworks from the di Rosa Collections,* The Oakland Museum (catalog)
1995 *1995 New Orleans Triennial,* Louisiana (catalog)
1996 *Going Places,* George Adams Gallery, New York
A Show of Hands, George Adams Gallery, New York

Collections:

Museum of Modern Art, New York; Whitney Museum, New York; University of Massachusetts, Amherst; Allen Art Museum, Oberlin, Ohio; Krannert Art Museum, University of Illinois, Champaign; Art Institute of Chicago; Elvehjem Art Center, Madison, Wisconsin; Carnegie Institute, Pittsburgh; San Francisco Museum of Modern Art.

Publications:

By SAUL: Articles—''It's Been Nice Gnawing You: Interview with Peter Saul'' by Cary Leibowitz and Rhonda Lieberman in *Artforum International,* vol. 32, December 1993; ''Peter Saul: Interview'' with David McCarthy in *Art Papers,* vol. 20, March/April 1996.

On SAUL: Books—*Peter Saul,* exhibition catalog, Los Angeles 1963; *Peter Saul,* exhibition catalog with text by Cesare Vivaldi, Rome 1963; *Peter Saul,* exhibition catalog with text by Cesare Vivaldi, Turin 1964; *Human Concern? Personal Torment,* exhibition catalog by Robert Doty, New York; *Peter Saul,* exhibition catalog with text by J. Beauffet, Saint-Etienne, France 1971; *Art Since 1940: Strategies of Being,* by Jonathan David Fineberg, New York 1995. **Articles—**''That's Saul Folks'' by David Zack in *Artnews* (New York), November 1969; ''Peter Saul'' in *Mizue* (Tokyo), no. 788, 1970; ''Saul ou la Mauvaise Conscience'' by C. Bouyeure in *Opus International* (Paris), December 1972; ''Peter Saul, Allan Frumkin Gallery'' by J. Masheck in *Artforum* (New York), January 1972; ''Peter Saul, Galerie Klang'' by B. Catoir in *Das Kunstwerk* (Baden-Baden, West Germany), November 1973; ''Art People'' by Grace Glueck in the *New York Times,* 2 January 1981; ''Cartoons Are No Longer Funny'' by Elizabeth Hess in the *Village Voice* (New York), 14 January 1981; ''Art View'' by Hilton Kramer in the *New York Times,* 18 January 1981.

* * *

Peter Saul, his name itself—with its instant yet chronologically backwards juxtaposition of the Christian New and the Judaic Old Testaments—is appropriate for the fierce and perverse moralist that the artist has been all his working life. In his European works of the early 1960s, although he is still absorbed by the painterliness of abstract-expressionism, mundane objects appear, rendered in a soft, fat cartoon style, like late-Guston; absurdity and surrealism are suggested by obscure actions and space, and by titles such as ''Icebox,'' ''Bathroom Sex Murder,'' and ''Super Crime Team.'' In the later 1960s, Saul moved to images of clear political dissent with Viet Nam and Civils Rights themes dominating; his technique also became less painterly and more strident in its continuing cartoon-qualities, and in its thin and harsh coloration and drawing. If these works might be considered in the tradition of American interwar Social Realism, Saul's career is clear example of the alienation that a social-political art has undergone from the culture of high art.

To the present time, even though Saul returned to more generalized social satire in the 1970s, his works (called ''splatter-film violence'' by R. Storr) appear ''difficult'' in an art gallery. Such a feeling may arise from the tension that they exude between their political-moral intensity, apparently much intended by the artist, and an equally desired aestheticism. He is haunted by the need to be ''public'': ''My idea is to make my paintings interesting enough that all kinds of people can look at them without inducement from expert opinion.'' And yet Saul is much like his formalist predecessors in the 1950s—exuberantly inventive in shape and pattern, and his comic-like characters move with a vividly personal dreamy flow.

Saul appers constantly embarrassed by his involvement in high culture, and so it seems logical that in a long series of works ''Artfront,'' in the early 1970s his attacks were directed against members of the art world. The pornographic virulence of these often scatological works also extended over to subjects such as ethnic prejudice, governmental structure, and the police. During this decade, Saul developed a pristine acrylic technique which featured brilliant color, including the shrill bad taste of Day-Glo pigments, applied to long streched-out forms—his figures seemed made of extruded plastic; he also continued his art world antagonism with parodies of major of art—''The Night Watch'' of Rembrandt; DeKooning's ''Woman''; ''The Death of Sardanapalus'' of Delacroix, and many more.

Like Shahn and Guston in the early 1940s, Saul may have experienced a time of strain, as if constant attention to social and political matters of the moment was creatively exhausting. And yet in works such as ''The Arsonist,'' ''The Rapist,'' and ''Three Mile Island,'' constructed in a Picassoid-plastic style, Saul returns to the rage and motifs of violence that characterized his earlier works. The monstrous exaggerations and dissolutions of the body parts achieve a hovering sadism and perhaps hypnotic disgust, and yet usually to the end of moral outrage. If his works were considered adversary political images, then his creative mechanisms may be analogous to those of fiction writers with political subjects. Since his vituperation is easy to follow, and because satirical force but no satirical narrative exists, Saul's paintings have long resembled the apocalyptic atmosphere of such books as *The Public Burning* of Robert Coover and E. L. Doctorow's *The Book of Daniel.* The shrill satire misleads us to feel that Saul's anarchic despair is only about his subjects; perhaps he revives the continuing despair about the art act itself.

—Joshua Kind

SAURA, Antonio

Nationality: Spanish. **Born:** Huesca, 22 September 1930. **Education:** Studied in Madrid, Valencia, and Barcelona, 1936–48; self-taught in art, from 1947. **Career:** Painter; lived and worked in Madrid, 1947–53, Paris, 1953–55, again in Madrid, 1955–78, and in Cuenca since 1978; associated with group of surrealist artists and writers, Paris, 1953–55; founder-member and director of activities, El Paso group of painters, Madrid, 1957–60; first lithographs, Madrid 1958; collaborated with ''Estampa Popular'' group, Madrid, 1960; first welded metal sculptures, Madrid, 1961; abandoned painting on canvas for works on paper, Madrid, 1971–73. **Awards:** Guggenheim Award, 1960; Carnegie Prize, Pittsburgh, with Chillida and Soulages, 1964; Grand Prize, *Biennale Biancoe Nero,* Lugano, Switzerland, 1966; First Prize, *Print Biennale,* Heidelberg, 1979; Gold Medal for Fine Arts, Madrid, 1982; Gold Medal of the City of Huesca, Spain, 1984; Gold Mercury Prize, Organisation for International Cooperation, Madrid, 1986; Officer of the Order of the Arts and Letters, Paris, 1990; Medal of Honor, Universidad Internacional Menédez Pelayo, Santander, Spain, 1990; Gold Medal, Isabel of Portugal, Zaragoza, Spain, 1991; Joan Miró Medal, Unesco, Paris, 1993; Aragón Prize of the Arts and Letters, Zaragoza, Spain, 1994; Grand Prix de Arts de la Ville de Paris, 1995; Liberty Prize, Sarajevo, 1995; Goya Prize, Fuendetodos, 1996; Tomás Francisco Prieto Prize, Fundación Casa de la Moneda, Madrid, 1996; Communication Prize of Madrid, 1998. Honorary doctorate from University of Castilla—La Mancha, Cuenca, Spain, 1997. **Died:** 22 July 1998.

Individual Exhibitions:

1950 Liberia Libros de Zaragoza, Saragossa, Spain
1951 Galerie Buchhloz, Madrid
1953 Liberia Clan, Madrid
1956 Palacio de Bibliotecas y Museos, Madrid
1957 Galerie Stadler, Paris
1959 Galerie Stadler, Paris

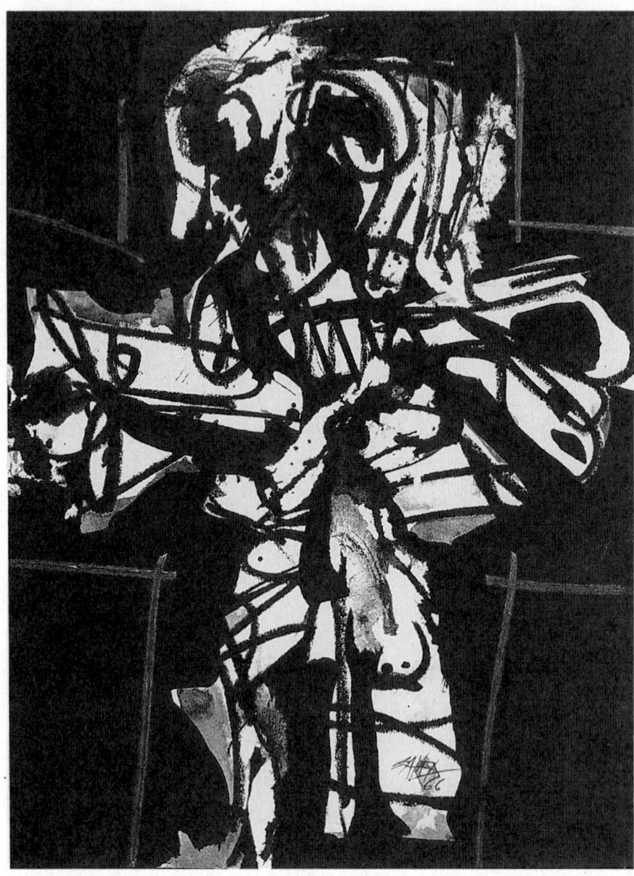

Painting by Antonio Saura. ©2001 Artists Rights Society (ARS), NY/ ADAGP, Paris.

Galerie Van de Loo, Munich (with Antoni Tapies)
Galeria Machetti, Cuenca, Spain
1960 Galerie Stadler, Paris
Galleri Blanche, Stockholm
Galleria Odyssia, Rome
1961 Pierre Matisse Gallery, New York
Galerie Van de Loo, Munich
Galleria Dell'Ariete, Milan
1962 Galeria Biosca, Madrid
1963 Galerie Stadler, Paris
Stedelijk Van Abbemuseum, Eindhoven, Netherlands (travelled to the Kunstkring, Rotterdam)
Museo de Arte Moderno, Buenos Aires (travelled to Museo de Arte Moderno, Rio de Janeiro)
Palais des Beaux-Arts, Bussels
1964 *Recent Painting,* Pierre Matisse Gallery, New York
Stedelijk Museum, Amsterdam (travelled to the Kunsthalle, Baden-Baden, West Germany, and the Konsthall, Gothenburg, Sweden)
1965 Galerie Stadler, Paris
Galeria Juana Mordo, Madrid (travelled to the Galerie Liceo, Cordoba; La Pasarela, Seville; Galerie Krikhaar, Amsterdam)
1966 Casa de las Americas, Havana, Cuba
Institute of Contemporary Arts, London
Galeria Grises, Bilbao, Spain
1967 Galerie Stadler, Paris
Galerie Buchholz, Munich
1968 Galerie Van de Loo, Munich
Frankfurter Kunstkabinett, Frankfurt
1969 *Peitures sur papier,* Galerie Stadler, Paris
Galeria René Metras, Barcelona
1971 Galerie Stadler, Paris
Pierre Matisse Gallery, New York
1972 *Trois Visions/Retratos Imaginarios,* Galeria Juana Mordo, Madrid
1973 Colegio de Arquitectos, Santa Cruz de Tenerife, Canary Islands
Galeria 42, Barcelona
Caja de Ahorros de Navarra, Pamplona, Spain
Galeria Carl van der Voort, Ibiza, Spain
Galeria Fort, Tarragona, Spain
Galeria Moira, Madrid
Galeria Trece, Barcelona
1974 Centro M-11, Seville
Galerie Stadler, Paris
Sala Pelaires, Palma de Mallorca, Spain
Galeria Zarte, Bilbao, Spain
Grupo 15, Madrid
Sala Conca, La Palmas, Spain
1975 Galerie Nouvelles Images, The Hague
Galeria Juan Martin, Mexico City
Galerie Van de Loo, Munich
Galleri Blanche, Stockholm
Galerie Henry Meyer, Lausanne
At *Art 6 75,* Basel
Tres pintores del Paso, Galeria Juana Mordo, Madrid
Papers, Galeria Maeght, Barcelona
1976 Galerie Benador, Geneva
Galleria Grafica Club, Milan
Galerie Mailliard, St. Paul-de-Vence, France
Galeria Edurne, Madrid
Libreria Popular, Albacete, Spain
1977 Galeria 42, Barcelona
Galerie Nouvelles Images, The Hauge
Galeria Juana Mordo, Madrid (travelled to Galerie Stadler, Paris, and the *Festival Cinematografico,* Pontarlier)
Galerie Stadler, at *FIAC 77,* Paris
Musée des Beaux-Arts, Besanson, France
1978 Foundation Nationale des Art Graphiques et Plastiques, Paris
Galeria Torques, Santiago de Compostela, Spain
Galeria Punto, Valencia
Galeria Rebollo, Zaragoza
Caja de Ahorros Municipal, Vigo, Spain
1979 *Peintures 1978–1979,* Galerie Stadler, Paris
Galerie Lauter, Mannheim
Union des Arts Plastiques, St. Etienne de Rouvray, France
Galerie Nouvelles Images, The Hague
Galeria Carmen Durgano, Valldolid, Spain
Galeria 4 Gats, Palma de Mallorca, Spain
Maison de la Culture de Belleville, Paris (toured France)
Stedelijk Museum, Amsterdam (retrospective; travelled to the Kunsthalle, Dusseldorf)
Galerie Jack Visser, Amsterdam
1980 Casa de Alhajas, Madrid

National Gallery, Reykjavik
Exposicion Antologica 1948–1980, Fundacion Joan Miro, Barcelona
Centre d'Action Culturelle, Montbeliard, France
Centre Gerard Philippe, Venissieux, France
Lens Fine Art, Antwerp
Galeria Benedet, Oviedo, Spain
Galeria Juan Martin, Mexico City
1981 Sala Luzan, Zaragoza
Galerie Moderne, Silkeborg, Denmark
Galerie Nouvelles Images, The Hague
Sa Pieta Freda, Majorca, Spain
Portraits Raisonnes, Galerie Stadler, Paris
Galerie Jack Visser, Amsterdam
Museo de Arte Contemporaneo de Altoaragon, Huesca, Spain
1982 Galeria Diart, Madrid
1983 Maison de Goya, Bordeaux, France
Casa de Espana, Paris
Galerie Antonio Machon, Madrid
1984 Galerie Wewerka, West Berlin
Galerie Van de Loo, Munich
Galeria Maeght, Barcelona
1985 Galerie Lauter, Mannheim, West Germany
Musée Bonnat, Bayonne, France
Kunstamt Wedding, West Berlin
Galleri Kaj Forsblom, Helsinki
1986 Galerie XPO, Hamburg
Neue Galerie/Sammlung Ludwig, Aachen, West Germany
Galeria del Palau, Valencia, Spain
1987 Galerie Jean-Pierre Meurisse, Toulouse, France
Galerie Stadler, Paris
Rheinhallen, Colonia
Galeria Ligeti, Huesca, Spain
Diputación Provincial de Huesca, Spain
1988 Palacio de Sástago, Zaragoza, Spain
Galleri Toso, Odense, Denmark
Galerie Gabriele von Loeper, Hamburg
Fundación Marcelino Botin, Santander, Spain
XPO Galerie Ida Kaufmann, Hamburg
Kampnagel Halle K3, Hamburg
Ferie Internacional de Arte, Galería Stadler, Valencia, Spain
Manus Presse, Stuttgart
Galerij Bbl, Amberes
1989 Wiener Secession, Vienna
Biblioteco Nacional, Madrid
Sert Gallery, Harvard University, Cambridge, Massachusetts
Capilla del Oidor, Alcalá de Henares, Spain
Universidad Central, Barcelona
Musée Rath, Geneva (travelled throughout Europe)
Galerie Pierre Huber, Geneva
Librairie La Hune, Paris
Galeria Barcelona
Espais, Centre d'Art Contemporani, Gerona, Spain
Galeria Fandos, Valencia
1990 Galeria Antonio Machón, Madrid
Galerie Van de Loo, Munich
Emmanuel Benador Fine Arts, New York
Médiathèque, Arles, France
Galeria Maeght, Barcelona
Art Frankfurt, Galeria Carles Taché, Frankfurt
Kunst-Station Sankt Peter, Colonia
Galerie Stadler, Paris
Musée Taurin, Nîmes, France
Universidad Internacional Menéndez Pelayo, Cuenca, Spain
Galeria Génesis, Barcelona
Galeria Carles Taché, Barcelona
1991 Artcurial, Paris
Decenario, Diputación Provincial, Huesca, Spain (travelled throughout Europe and to New York)
Manus-Presse, Stuttgart
FIAC 91, Galeria Antonio Machón, Paris
Jason McCoy Inc., New York
1992 Sala del Arenal, Seville
Museo de Zaragoza, Spain
Centro Cultural del Círculo de Lectores, Madrid (travelled to Instituto Cervantes, Paris; Sala de la Corona de Aragón, Gobierno de Aragón, Zaragoza, Spain)
1993 Galeria Pilares, Cuenca, Spain
Sala Tretze, Banyoles
1994 Centre Cultural (with Maya Andersson), Dax, France
Museo del Grabado, Fuendetodos
Art, Culture et Foi, Saint Severin-Saint Nicolas, Paris
Galerie Adriana Schmidt, Stuttgart
Sala Carderera, Huesca, Spain
Museo del Grabado Español Contemporáneo, Marbella
Museo d'Arte Moderna, Lugano, Switzerland
Museo de Teruel, Spain (travelled to Museo Pablo Gargallo, Zaragoza; Palacio de los Condes de Gabia, Granada; Centre d'Art Santa Mónica, Barcelona)
1995 Centro Cultural de Círculo de Lectores, Madrid
Pilares Gráfica, Cuenca, Spain
Museo de Zaragoza, Spain
Université, Faculté de Lettres et de Langues, Poitiers, France
Galerie Kaj Forsblom, Zurich
Auditorio del Círculo de Lectores, Barcelona
1996 Galeria Fernando Santos, Lisbon
Galeria Marlborough, Madrid
Château de Voguë, Ardeche, France
Museo de Dibujo del Castillo de Larrés, Huesca, Spain
Galeria Ginkgo, Madrid
1997 Palacio Galveias, Lisbon
Auditorio de Galicia, Santiago de Compostela, Spain
Galerie Lelong, Paris
Konsthall, Malmo, Sweden
1998 Galeria Marlborough, Madrid
Centre Européen d'Art Contemporain, Chapelle de la Miséricorde, Vallauris
Galerie de l'Ancien Collège, Ecole d'Arts Plastiques, Châtellerault, France
Musée Jenisch, Vevey, Switzerland
IVAM, Centro Julio González, Valencia
1999 Galerie Dialogue, Paris
IberCaja, Zaragoza, Spain
Galerie Lelong, Zurich
Galeria Marlborough, Madrid

2000 Galeria Carles Taché, Barcelona
Galeria Marlborough, Madrid
Galerie Lelong, Paris
Musée aux Cordeliers, Châteauroux, France

Selected Group Exhibitions:

1952 *Tecdencias I.,* Casa Americana, Madrid
1964 *Documenta,* Kassel, West Germany (and 1977, 1982)
1969 *Contemporary Portraits,* Museum of Modern Art, New York
1972 *Estampa Popular,* Libreria Antonio Machado, Madrid
1976 *Biennale,* Venice
1978 *Arte Iberoamericano de Hoy,* Museo de Arte Contemporaneo, Caracas
1979 *L'Homme dans l'Art Europeen apres 1945,* Fundatie Kunsthuis, Amsterdam
1980 *Recent European Drawings,* Art Gallery of New South Wales, Sydney
1981 *Westkunst,* Rheinhallen, Cologne
1982 *Quatre Images Seditieuses,* Foundation du Chateau de Jau, France
1984 *Ny International Kunst 1959–1984,* Silkeborg Kunstmuseum, Denmark
1987 *Cinq Siècles d'Art Espagnol: La Siècle de Picasso,* Musée d'Art Moderne de la Ville de Paris
1988 *Les Années 50,* Centre National d'Art et de Culture Georges Pompidou, Paris
1989 *El Informalismo Español en las Colecciones del IVAM,* IVAM, Valencia
1991 *Del Surrealismo al Informalismo, Arte de los Años 50 en Madrid,* Sala de Exposiciones de la Comunidad de Madrid
1992 *Automatismos Paralelos: La Europa de los Movimientos Experimentales 1944–1956,* Centro Atlántico de Arte Moderno, Las Palmas de Gran Canaria, Spain
1995 *Europa de Posguerra, 1945–1965, Arte Después del Diluvio,* Fundación La Caixa, Barcelona
1996 *La Dimension du Corps 1920–1980,* Le Musée National d'Art Moderne, Tokyo
1997 *Made in France, 1947–1997,* Centre Georges Pompidou, Paris
1998 *Dibujos Germinales, 50 Artistas Españoles,* Museo Nacional Centro de Arte Reina Sofía, Madrid
1999 *Jardín de Eros,* Palau de la Virreina y Centre Cultural Tecla Sala, Barcelona

Collections:

Museo Espanol de Arte Contemporaneo, Madrid; Fundacion Juan March, Madrid; Neue Pinakothek, Munich; Museum des 20, Jahrhunderts, Vienna; Musée d'Art et d'Histoire, Geneva; Moderna Museet, Stockholm; Stedelijk Museum, Amsterdam; Centre National d'Art Contemporain, Paris; Tate Gallery, London; Museum of Modern Art, New York; Nationalgalerie, Berlin; Australian National Gallery, Canberra; Louisiana Museum, Humlebaek, Denmark; Centro de Arte Reina Sofía, Madrid; Guggenheim Museum, New York; Carnegie Institute, Pittsburgh, Pennsylvania; Hirshhorn Museum, Washington, D.C.; Centre National d'Art et de Culture Georges Pompidou, Paris; Museo de Arte Moderno, Mexico; British Museum, London; Museo de Arte Contemporáneo, Caracas, Venezuela.

Publications:

By SAURA: Books—*Programio,* Madrid 1951; *Arte Fantastico,* with Carlos Saura, Madrid 1953; *Carta al espectador,* Madrid 1953; *Cartas de El Paso: Manifiestos,* with others, Madrid 1957; *Carta Abietta a Antonio Pericas,* Madrid 1961; *Antonio Saura: Superpositions,* Paris 1974; *Contra el Guernica,* Madrid 1982; *Antonio Saura: Notebook 1958–1980,* Madrid 1982; *Still-Life,* Madrid 1986; *Note-Book,* Murcia 1992; *Belvédère Miró,* Paris 1993; *La Question de L'Art Espagnol,* Paris 1996; *Le Chien de Goya,* Paris 1996; *Francis Bacon et la Beauté Obscène,* Paris 1996; *Discurso de Cuenca,* Cuenca 1997; *Le Miroir Singulier, Bram van Velde,* Paris 1998; *Fijeza, Ensayos,* Barcelona 1999; *Klee, Point Final,* Paris 1999; *Crónicas, Artículos,* Barcelona 2000; also articles in numerous catalogs and periodicals since 1951; also numerous limited edition print portfolios, from 1959.

On SAURA: Books—*Saura* by Erik Borman, Madrid 1956; *La obra de Saura* by Juan Eduardo Cirlot, Barcelona 1960; *Antonio Saura,* exhibition catalog with text by Michel Tapie, Rome 1960; *Saura-Crucifixion* by Enrico Crispolti, Rome 1961; *Antonio Saura,* exhibiton catalog with texts by Michel Tapie and José Ayllon, New York 1961; *Antonio Saura,* exhibition catalog with text by Vincente Aguilera Cerni, Munich 1961; *Saura,* exhibition catalog with text by José Ayllon, Eindhoven, Netherlands 1963; *Saura: Recent Paintings,* exhibition catalog with text by Yvon Taillandier, New York 1964; *Antonio Saura,* exhibition catalog with text by José Ayllon, Amsterdam 1964; *Saura* by Georges Boudaille, Paris 1967; *Peintures sur papier de Saura,* exhibition catalog with text by Fernando Arrabal, Paris 1969; *Antonio Saura* by José Ayllon, Barcelona 1969; *Trois Visions: Antonio Saura,* exhibition catalog with text by Claude Roy, Madrid 1972; *Antonio Saura: Retratos Imaginarios,* exhibition catalog with texts by Waldemar George and Jean Clarence Lambert, Madrid 1972; *Saura: Obra Grafica* by Eduardo Westerdahl and José Maria Moreno Galvan, Santa Cruz de Tenerife 1973; *Antonio Saura,* exhibition catalog with texts by Jean Manuel Bonet and others, Seville 1974; *Antonio Saura: Papers,* exhibition catalog with texts by Oscar Collazos, Alexandre Cirici-Pellicer, Roland Penrose and others, Barcelona 1975; *Saura: Un message pour l'homme d'aujourd'hui* by Paul Gauthier, Paris 1977; *Saura: Peintures 1978–1979,* exhibition catalog with text by Marcel Cohen, Paris 1979; *Antonio Saura,* exhibition catalog with texts by Bert Schierbeek, Lucebert and Ad Petersen, Amsterdam 1979; *Antonio Saura,* exhibition catalog with text by Jürgen Partenheimer, Dusseldorf 1979; *Saura* by Gerard Xuriguera, Paris, 1979; *Antonio Saura* by Alexandre Cirici-Pellicer, Madrid and Paris 1980; *Periodico de Exposiciones I: Antonio Saura,* Madrid 1980; *Antonio Saura: Exposicíon Antologica 1948–1980,* exhibition catalog with texts by Javier Tusell Gomez, Ad Petersen, Alexandre Cirici-Pellicer and others, Barcelona 1980; *Antonio Saura: Antologia de obras en papel* by Federico Torralba and others, Zaragosa 1981; *Saura: Portraits raisonners,* exhibition catalog with text by Severo Sarduy, Paris 1981: *Espiral-Figuras: Saura,* texts by several authors, Madrid 1982; *Saura,* exhibition catalog with text by Edmond Jabes, Paris 1987.

* * *

The stranglehold of the bourgeoisie over the the visual arts is revealed most clearly by the history of immediately post-war art in Europe. When one sees the bland prettiness of most French artist of the 1950s adherents of ''Tachism,'' one finds nothing to indicate that the whole of northern Europe had been fought across, bombed, burned and then held in the grip of Fascism for five years. French art took up its brushes exactly where it had been left off; there is a gap, that's all.

This was not the case in literature or philosophy; Sartre, Genet, Camus, and Barthes wrote and thought about an unmistakably post-war world, one in which the traditional values of the bourgeoisie were rejected and full consciousness of the corruptibility of man was taken into account. For writers such as these the war was liberating, a fire storm that sucked the old stratified and inhabited way of life into its centre and spat out bare bones of existence. It was a confirmation of the thought of Husserl and Heidegger, a chance to start again with no illusions.

But painting, which is in the hands of a small and wealthy minority, was not so affected. These economics of literature allow ideas to spread with comparative case; those of painting restrict the movement of ideas. Instead of a visual equivalent of existentialism we were offered the bland mush of *L'Art Informer* between the twin poles of the circus tricks of Mathieu and the high catholicism of Manessier.

Liberation of the painting in Europe came from a country that had not suffered the war—Spain. Instead it had known something far worse, a civil war which tore the country to shreds and left gaping wounds of injustice which still are not healed. The bourgeoisie in Spain had not taken over painting, as there had been no painting to take over. Artists simply fled because Franco's Fascism, in the early stage, was repressive of any manisfestation of independent thought. Those that did stay worked secretly, without hope.

By the mid-1950s, however, Franco found himself isolated, the only Fascist dictator left. American money kept him firmly in power, but in return he had to make a few gestures towards a token liberalism. As a result visual artists came out of hiding and were allowed to pursue a very restricted course of experiment. Direct political comment was, of course, not allowed; but abstraction, well, that could hurt nobody.

The result of policy was the Spanish school of Tachism, led by Tapies and including Antonio Saura. Although it was mild, in terms of political comment, it revitalised European painting. The Spanish school had no time for prettiness; the dominant texture was thick and viscous, often using sand mixed in the paint. Compared with French painting it was serious, mature and painful.

Saura's contribution was the most violent. The dominant colours of his art are black and red. Unlike most of the other Spanish painters he introduced the human figure into his canvases, but the figure distorted, wild in extremity. Huge eyes stare, jaws gape like the painting of a child living in a nightmare. The paintings seem to have been made in a frenzy; paint drips like blood from an open wound and the surface is ripped open to reveal the lacerated canvas beneath.

In the 1980s such painting can seem naive; Saura himself moved away from it towards a more cartoon-like drawing, more overtly political. But at the time it was brave painting that avoided for quite a while the self-satisfied embrace of the middle-class public and did a great deal towards restoring a dignity and seriousness of purpose to European art.

—Alastair Mackintosh

SAWKA, Jan

Nationality: Polish and American. **Born:** Zabrze, Poland, 10 December 1946, moved to New York 1977. **Education:** Institute of Technology, Wroclaw, M.A. in architectural engineering 1972; Fine Arts Academy, Wroclaw, M.F.A., 1972. **Family:** Married Hanna Maletz, 1974; daughter: Hanna. **Career:** Independent artist since 1969; began designing posters 1969; first large-scale paintings 1971; first installations 1982; first stage designs 1987; first concert sets (for the Grateful Dead), 1989; multimedia projects, starting with Mito's ''The Eyes'' visual theatre, since 1993; architectural projects, including *Tower of Light,* Abu Dhabi, 1994–96, and *The Essen Towers,* 1999; has lectured at universities and museums throughout the world. **Awards:** Oscar de la Peinture and President's Award, *7th International Painting Exhibition,* Cagnes-sur-Mer, 1975; Gold Medal, *7th International Poster Biennale,* Warsaw, 1978; Silver Medal, *14th International Graphic Art Biennale,* Brno, 1990; Japan Cultural Agency Award, Tokyo, 1994. **Address:** 54 Old Rte. 213, High Falls, New York 12440, U.S.A. **Web site:** http://www.jansawka.com.

Individual Exhibitions:

1971 International Arts Festival, York, England (with E. Stankiewicz)
University Gallery, Budapest (with E. Stankiewicz)
1972 Art 7 Theatre Festival, Palermo, Italy
Cultural Center, Lausanne, Switzerland
1973 BWA Gallery, Wroclaw
University Gallery, Helsinki
1974 Art Festival, Caracas, Venezuela
FAMA Festival, Swinoujscie, Poland
Stodola Gallery, Warsaw
1975 International Painting Festival, Cagnes-sur-Mer, France
1976 IDCA, Aspen, Colorado
Theatre Gallery, Opole, Poland
1977 Otto Nagel Haus, Berlin
Galerie Lefor-Openo, Paris
Galerie Noire, Paris
Pulhri Studio, The Hague
Dubins Gallery, Los Angeles
1978 *International Painting Festival,* Cagnes-sur-Mer and Musée d'Art Moderne, Paris
Art Directors Club, New York
1979 Heidenberg Gallery, New York
Ankrum Gallery, Los Angeles
1980 Poster Museum, Wilanow, Poland
Theatre Gallery, Opole, Poland
1981 Ankrum Gallery, Los Angeles
1982 Andre Zarre Gallery, New York
Ana Sklar Gallery, Miami, Florida
1983 Ankrum Gallery, Los Angeles
Sid Deutsch Gallery, New York
1984 Albany Academy Gallery, Albany, New York
Evelyn Siegel Gallery, Fort Worth, Texas
1985 Sid Deutsch Gallery and 112 Green Exhibition Space, New York
Pratt Manhattan Center Gallery, New York
1988 Marco DiLaurenti Gallery, New York
1989 Dorsky Gallery, New York

Jan Sawka: *The Memory I, II, III,* 1996. Photo by Roy Gumpel. ©Jan Sawka. Photo courtesy of the artist.

College Art Museum and Dowd Fine Arts Gallery, SUNY, New Paltz
1990 Tyler Art Gallery, SUNY, Cortland
Arvada Center for the Arts, Denver
Nicolaysen Museum, Casper, Wyoming
International Graphic Art Biennale, Brno, Czechoslovakia
1991 Dorsky Gallery, New York
De Andino Fine Arts, Washington, D.C.
National Museum, Cracow (retrospective)
Starmach Gallery, Cracow
Hassel & Haeseler Gallery, Denver
Lincoln Center, Fort Collins, Colorado
National Museum, Warsaw
Galerie Lefor-Openo, Paris
1992 Carolyn Hill Gallery, New York
National Museum, Gdansk
Museum of Art and Science, Prague, Czech Republic
Art Center Gallery, Bielsko-Biala, Poland
Universal Expo, Seville, Spain
Queens Museum of Art, New York
Creation Gallery, Tokyo
National Museum, Wroclaw
1993 Atrium Gallery, University of Connecticut, Storrs
Art Tower Mito, Japan
1994 Striped House Museum of Art, Tokyo (catalog)
1995 Contemporary Art Gallery, Pecs, Hungary
1996 *Retrospective and Presentation of the Tower of Light,* Cultural Foundation, Abu Dhabi, United Arab Emirates
Artist's Donations to the Polish National Museums, National Museum, Cracow, Poland
1997 *The Roots* (retrospective), City Museum, Zabrze, Poland (catalog)
Sawka-Sato: Prints and Posters, Upper Silesian Cultural Centre, Katowice, Poland
Meetings (retrospective), toured Polish arts centers (catalog)
1998 *Expo of the Sea,* Lisbon, Portugal
2001 *Multimedia Show,* Toppan Museum, Tokyo

Collections:

Centre Georges Pompidou, Paris; Chateau Musée, Cagnes-sur-Mer, France; Essen Museum, Essen, Germany; Israeli Museum, Jerusalem; Library of Congress, Washington, D.C.; Kanazawa University, Japan; Museum of Decorative Art, Copenhagen; Museum of Modern Art, New York; Stedelijk Museum, Amsterdam; National Museum, Warsaw; Victoria and Albert Museum, London; and many others.

Publications:

By SAWKA: Books—*A Book of Fiction,* New York 1986; *Notes,* Poznan, Poland, 1991; *Small Hours,* with foreword by James Beck and Roberta Lord, Kansas City, Missouri 2001.

On SAWKA: Books—*A Selected Retrospective,* exhibition catalog with essays, New Paltz, New York, 1989; *A Selected Retrospective,* exhibition catalog, Denver 1990; *The Returns,* exhibition catalog, Cracow 1991; *My Europe,* exhibition catalog, Seville 1992. **Articles**—''Jan Sawka'' by Ruth Eisenberg in *Arts Magazine,* March 1985; ''Jan Sawka'' by *Artension,* October 1991; ''Jan Sawka'' by Shoji Katagishi in *Creation Magazine* (Tokyo), 1992; ''Jan Sawka'' by Frank Fox in *Affiche Magazine* (Amsterdam), 1995; ''Visions of Color'' by Frank Fox in *Print Magazine,* 1996.

*

You ask for my approach to art?

My stormy life has shaped it for me. . . .

In various times I was doing posters, illustrations, editorial drawings, paintings, sculptures; the whole array of printmaking techniques came through my hands, concert and theatrical sets costing from $100 to $3,700,000, installations, outdoor sculptures, electronically guided images. . . .

I still do all the things outlined above.

I have one goal in my life.

I want to express my feelings, dreams, and frustrations, sometimes alone, but often in collaboration with other artists speaking with a different accent, the accent of poetry, drama, acting, and music. . . .

But we all speak the same language.

So I use all available means to communicate with them and all who are willing to listen.

Since my last entry to this edition (1995) and to *Contemporary Designers* (1997) the matters have ''worsened'' even more in the categorization of my work. I am still painting, creating prints and sculptures at my studio near Woodstock, New York, but at least half of my time is spent on larger projects which are mixing not only my above-mentioned activities but also stage design, multimedia in general, theatrical spectacles, public sculptures, and also architecture. Also, I face the relocation of my household and studio to Japan in the near future and the opening of the new market in Europe, particularly in Germany. There I am building a giant ultrasophisticated multimedia project of four 50-meter-tall towers linked by laser beams by night and performing a whole spectacle of visual and sound affects after dusk. All of it created with the help of top Japanese and German technology companies.

All this is a result of my years and nights spent over the canvas, etching plates and clay, combined later with the advanced engineering and on-the-edge technology . . . where to draw a line between art, design, and architecture? Or the rock concert, visual theatre, animated film, and graphic art, as in another of my projects taking shape in TOHO Studios in Tokyo for a tour of major world cities?

I am pushing ahead, crossing the borders of creative disciplines, as the critics say. It truth I cannot care less about the professionals' opinions as to where I stand, in arts or design, architecture or entertainment, high and low art. I simply create what my imagination carries across my mental screen and fight to see all these dreams not only in my mind but before my own and other people's eyes.

You are all invited!

—Jan Sawka

* * *

For the reader who wants to be acquainted with Jan Sawka's early work (1970–1990), I greatly recommend Elena Millie's entry in *Contemporary Designers* (St. James Press, 1990), which focuses on the artist's graphic design production and his paintings. "Perhaps," Millie states, "Jan Sawka is a visionary of our time." This was written long before the important reorientation and change—which confirmed Millie's judgment—had occurred in the artist's approach to his work.

The 49-year-old maverick American of Polish extraction with Slavic temperament and wit works now hand in hand with electronic and high-tech tools, enriching his material with visions originating in his childhood.

Trained in architecture, based in rationalism, experienced in painting and printmaking, exploring old masters' engraving techniques and drawing, skilled in book illustration and poster design, collaborating with illustrious poets and playwrights, author of "artists books" and "postcards," scenic design, installations, sculpture, a craftsman, believing in the power of a pencil, brush, eye, and hand, Sawka is more than anyone else in the contemporary art world fully conscious of the new dimensions and scale of the art of the coming era of communication.

In the 1990s, Sawka, who lives in the country outside of the great art centers and works in a barn, started down a new path. One could call it an "acceleration in rhythm and in the tempo of being." From an artist who performed quite successfully in distinguished New York galleries and museums, and other indoor sites, he started to bring his ideas and dreamlike visions to macro space, to the modern agora where thousands of people gather in order to participate. It's there, like in ancient times, where young and old, rich and poor, can enjoy the mystery of music, word, and spirituality.

The "ego" and subjectivity of an artist can no longer be maintained—it is divided, transformed by a team of equal creators: producers of images, music, technicians who operate light, sound, acoustics; constructors and computer operators. Isn't it that kind of production that was known in Greece during the Dionysian or Olympic festivities or later on at Bacchanalian wine orgies?

Sawka's work appears nowadays in theaters, rock music festivals, concert halls in the United States as well as Japan, Spain, Poland, Hungary, with a perspective which can be extended to the Near East, Italy, Taiwan, and other places in the world. The artist defines himself as a multi-media man, which is correct in definition but doesn't indicate the cultural context of his work. One must recall here Wagner's vision of Gesamkunstwerk, Baudelaire's ideal of "Correspondance des Arts," Scriabin, and Kandinsky's modern model of unified art work, where music, dance, poetry, rhythm and light support spacio-architectural concepts and vice versa.

In our time such ideas—revealed here and there—oppose the gloomy perspective of a "global village": uniform, passive, without joy and interaction. Sawka's recent images derive from his previous iconography—colorful and powerful banners float in the air set on open-air platforms; mysterious large eyes move in obscurity, frightening and evoking anxiety; pieces of paintings, blown up and synchronized with changing light, are hung in an invisible space; flashes of light reveal contours of painting, like a musical motif. All these audio-visual images, synchronized by computer, bring to the contemporary eye and ear new experience.

Let us quote among other projects and productions the first gigantic outdoor objects and banners for the Grateful Dead rock performances (1989), the British rock group Traffic (1994), "Eyes" at the Art Tower Mit in Japan, "The Messiah," an audio-visual project based on the masterpiece by Handel—images appearing in the air—the Vatican version appearing in 1992.

Sawka is currently working on "The Tower of Light," a 100-meter-high obelisk with kinetic art projections to the music of Summerlin, in Abu Dhabi; and "The Window of Hope," a 35-meter-high monument to commemorate the 50th anniversary of the bombing of Nagasaki, Japan.

The dimension, format, and geographical range of these multimedia concepts give an idea of Jan's endless energy and artistic vitality.

—Szymon Bojko

SAXE, Henry

Nationality: Canadian. **Born:** Montreal, Quebec, 24 September 1937. **Education:** Sir George Williams University, Montreal 1955–56; Ecole des Beaux-Arts, Montreal, under Albert Dumouchal, 1956–62, B.A. 1960; also studied in London, England, 1968. **Career:** Independent sculptor, since 1962: lives and works in Tamworth, Ontario. **Awards:** Paul Emile Borduas Prize, 1994. **Agent:** Galerie Kozen. **Address:** PO Box 143, Tamworth, Ontario K0K 3GO, Canada.

Individual Exhibitions:

1962 Galerie Libre, Montreal
1963 Galerie Camille Hebert, Montreal
1966 Galerie du Siècle, Montreal
1968 Dunkelman, Gallery, Toronto
1969 20/20 Gallery, London; Ontario
1970 Carmen Lamanna Gallery, Toronto
1972 Musée d'Art Contemporain, Montreal

1973 *Henry Saxe/Milly Ristvedt,* Musée d'Art Contemporain, Montreal
National Gallery of Canada, Ottawa
1975 Agnes Etherington Art Gallery, Queens University, Kingston, Ontario
1976 Mt. Allison University Art Gallery, Sackville, New Brunswick
Dunlop Art Gallery, Saskatoon
1977 Galerie Gilles Gheerbrant, Montreal
1978 Center of Inter-American Relations, New York
1979 Canadian Culture Centre, Paris
Habourfront Art Gallery, Toronto
1981 Galerie Gilles Gheerbrant, Montreal
1982 Galerie Gilles Gheerbrant, Montreal
1983 Agnes Etherington Art Centre, Kingston Ontario
1985 Olga Korper Gallery, Toronto
1987 Olga Korper Gallery, Toronto
1994 *Henry Saxe: Works from 1960 to 1993,* Musée d'Art Contemporain, Montreal

Selected Group Exhibitions:

1968 *Artists under 35,* at the *Biennale,* Paris
1973 *Boucherville, Montreal, Toronto, London,* National Gallery of Canada, Ottawa
1978 *Biennale,* Venice
1982 *Contemporary Sculpture at the Guild,* Toronto
1983 *Drawing Show,* Sadie Bronfman Centre, Montreal

Collections:

National Gallery of Canada, Ottawa; Museum of Fine Arts, Montreal; Musée d'Art Contemporain, Montreal; Musée de Quebec; Art Gallery of Ontario, Toronto; Agnes Etherington Art Centre, Queen's University, Kingston, Ontario; Canada Council Art Bank, Ottawa; Department of External Affairs, Ottawa; Nickle Arts Museum, Calgary.

Publications:

By SAXE: Articles—''Address of the General Assembly of the Nihilist Party of Canada'' in *20 Cents Magazine* (London, Ontario), October 1969; ''Deux ans en 25 nouvelles'' in *La Presse* (Montreal), January 1970.

On SAXE: Books—*Boucherville, Montreal, Toronto, London, 1973,* exhibition catalog by B. Smith and P. Theberge, Ottawa 1973; *Henry Saxe: Two Works,* with text by P. Fry, Regina 1975; *Venice Biennial 1978: Canada—Ron Martin, Henry Saxe* by P. Theberge, Ottawa 1977; *The Empirical Presence: Six Essays—Barbara Caruso, Jean-Marie Delavalle, Yves Gaucher, Ron Martin, Jaan Poldaas, Henry Saxe* by James D. Campbell and Yvonne Lammerich, Montreal 1992; *Henry Saxe: Works from 1960 to 1993,* exhibition catalog with text by Real Lussier, Lise Lamarche and Louis Cummins, Montreal 1994. **Articles—**''Henry Saxe, avant tour un graveur'' by J. Sarrazin in *Le Nouveau Journal* (Montreal), January 1962; ''Henry Saxe à la Galerie Libre'' by L. Lamy in *Le Devoire* (Monreal), January 1962; ''Saxe recherche d'un langage'' by C. Jasmin in *La Presse* (Montreal), January 1962; ''Les objects inattendus de Saxe'' by Y. Ribillard in *La Presse,* (Montreal), April 1966; ''Canada Didn't Lose This One Anyway'' by B. Lord in *Toronto Daily Star,* January 1970; ''In the Galleries: Toronto'' by G. M. Dault in *ArtsCanada* (Toronto), February 1971; ''Montrer All'' by Myra and Irwin Gophik in *Artscanda* (Toronto), Spring 1972; ''Art Work That's Debatable'' by C. Bates in the *Montreal Star,* April 1973.

* * *

One of Canada's best known sculptors, Henry Saxe started out as an abstract painter, and produced striking abstractions throughout the early 1960s. By mid-decade, he had moved on to sculpture (that would, however, continue to be painted until the early 1970s). For the last thirty years, he has been producing restless and rigorously well-reasoned work that yields a multitude of different views, and directly engages the observer's physical and mental participation. From the earliest sculpture through his most recent work, Saxe has executed structurally complex objects that require a constant shifting and commingling of perspectives on the spectator's part. In a sense, his work is about learning to *see.*

This was nowhere more evident than in the splendid low-lying steel sculptures of the late 1970s and 1980s. Those works were magnets for our own embodiment, and effectively oriented us in space. Large plates, lengths and other members of hot and cold-rolled steel in structurally complex configurations occupied the floor plane, and promised revelations as we moved around them. They were *behavioural artefacts,* because they directed the observer through space accordingly. We were driven to slowly circle them, accruing as many different perspective—and therefore partial—views upon them as was feasible for our ongoing project of interpretation without losing sight of the whole.

In the *Ball* sculptures of the late 1980s and 1990s, Saxe chose to work with aluminium rather than his trademark steel plate because of its inherent reflective properties. He ordered tubes, bars, flats and sheets of the metal from the factory which he then cut and bent in his studio workshop in Tamworth, Ontario, into open globes which he has aptly characterized as ''hot points on the sun.''

Saxe uses the aluminium skeletally and in segments becase he wants to fragment the light-reflecting surface. He constructs his spheroidal forms out of different lengths and thicknesses until a certain threshold of density—a sort of heavy matter that transecends the materials used—has been formed in the sculpture's inner core. To put together four different lengths of aluminium into the right sequence is an intensive process and requires long hours in the studio. The resultant skeletal nests of gleaming aluminium, spheres formed out of coiled lengths of circular piping and flat lengths of plate are inordinately complex and visually engaging. Their multipositional configurations invite us to experience them directly.

The *Ball* sculptures invite user participation. We can upend them, turn them about, change their configurations at will. Saxe's sculpture has always been open to change. They are fully resolved—but the furthest thing possible from static artworks. Since he first began making sculpture, Saxe has always insisted that the observer assume different standpoints in both space and in his/her imagination in order to know the object in its many aspects as a perceptually complex object.

Saxe is one of the few sculptors now working who encourages the observer to employ a variational method in assimilating his work. In order to open up the internal topography of the sculpture, the observer must engage in empirical testing and verification. It is simply not possible for the observer to achieve a sense of the overall unity of the work from any one privileged viewing perspective. We have to amass as many profiles of the object as possible to know it at all well. The empirical integrity of the sculpture is grounded in the free variations of perspective and imagination we ourselves perform when viewing it.

We recognize that, in the case of Saxe's sculpture, there is nothing final and definitive—no enervating spectacle of closure. The multipositional status of a sculpture makes it an open-ended object. Each of its facets in turn offers us a rich and newly rewarding experience. In allowing us to freely vary our point of view, and in reminding us that seeing, touching, imagining and reflecting are themselves free creative acts, this work liberates us from static patterns of knowing and old habits of thinking. Indeed, a profound affirmation of subjective freedom is the true reward of seeing Saxe's remarkable sculpture.

—James D. Campbell

SCANAVINO, Emilio

Nationality: Italian. **Born:** Genoa, 28 February 1922. **Education:** Educated in schools in Genoa; studied at the Nicolo Barabino Art School, Genoa, 1938–41; studied architecture at the University of Milan, 1942–43. **Military Service:** Served in the Italian Army 1943. **Family:** Married Georgina Graglia in 1946; children: Sebastiano and Paola. **Career:** Draughtsman in local government offices, Genoa, 1945–50; full-time painter from 1950: worked for Mazzotti ceramic factory, Albisola, Italy, 1951–52; co-signed, with Lucio Fontana Giuseppe Capogrossi, Roberto Crippa and others, *III Manifesto dello Spazialismo,* Milan, 1952; settled in Milan 1960; transferred his studio to Calice Ligure, 1962; lived in Varese, 1965–67, and moved to Calice Ligure, 1968. Lecturer, Liceo Artistico, Genoa 1952. **Awards:** Premio Graziano, 1955; Premio Lissone, 1958; Premio Prampolini, *Biennale,* Venice, 1958; Premio Spoleto, 1960; Premio Sassari, 1960; Premio Valsesia, 1960; Premio Lignano, 1960; Premio La Spezia, 1963; Grand Prix, *Biennale,* Menton, France 1970. **Died:** In Calice Ligure, 28 November 1986.

Individual Exhibitions:

1948 Galleria Isola, Genoa
1951 Apollinaire Gallery, London
1953 Galleria del Cavalino, Venice
1955 Galleria del Naviglio, Milan
1956 Galleria Apollo, Brussels
1957 Galleria Selecta, Rome
1959 Galleria del Naviglio, Milan
1960 Palais des Beaux-Arts, Brussels
Biennale, Venice
1961 Galleria del Naviglio, Milan
Galleria de Cavallino, Venice
1962 Gallerie International d'Art Contemporain, Paris
Galleria del Cavallino, Venice
Galleria l'Attico, Rome
Joachim Gallery, Chicago (with Giuseppe Capogrossi)
1963 Galleria del Naviglio, Milan
Galleria Hausmann, Cortina d'Ampezzo, Italy
Gallerie Smith, Brussels
Galleria Birch, Copenhagen

Emilio Scanavino: *Hung,* ca. 1960. ©Elio Ciol/Corbis.

Galleria Rotta, Genoa
1964 Galleria la Bussola, Turin
Galleria del Cavallino, Venice
1965 Galleria Argentario, Trento, Italy
Galleria Ferrari, Verona
1966 Galleria de Foscherari, Bologna
Biennale, Venice
1967 Philadelphia Art Alliance
Galleria del Naviglio, Milan
1969 Studio S. Andrea, Milan
Galleria del Naviglio, Milan
1970 Galerie Smith, Brussels
Galleria Poliantea, Terni, Italy
Galleria Cantini, Rome
Galleria 3B, Bolzano, Italy
Biennale, Menton, France
1972 Galleria Gissi, Turin
1973 Galleria del Naviglio, Milan
Malerei/Zeichnung/Graphik, Kunsthalle, Darmstadt
Palazzo Grassi, Venice
1974 Palazzo Reale, Milan
1975 Galleria Thomas Levy, Hamburg
1976 Galleria Il Canale, Venice
Galleria Plurima, Udine, Italy
Galleria Qui Arte Contemporanea, Rome
Galleria 4M, Florence
Studio Marconi, Milan
Galleria Marin, Turin

Galleria La Chiocciola, Padua
Galleria Civica d'Arte Moderma, Portofino, Italy
1977 Galleria Rotta, Genoa
1978 Centro Olivette, Ivrea, Italy
1979 Galerie Mathias Gels, Paris
Galleria Zaratustra, Milan
Galleria Cesarea, Genoa
1980 Galleria Giuli, Lecco, Italy
Padiglione d'Arte Contemporanea, Parco Massari, Ferrara, Italy
Mercato del Sale, Milan
1981 Galleria Gastaldelli, Milan
Galleria Cesarea, Genoa
Galleria Il Narciso, Rome
Galleria Planetario, Trieste
1982 Galleria Planetario, Trieste
Galleria Lo Spazio, Naples
Castello Aragonese, Ischia, Italy
Galleria Pagani, Legnano, Italy
1983 Azienda Turismo, Marina di Massa, Italy
Arte Studio, Moderna
Galleria Santo Stefano, Iarnico, Italy
1984 Galleria Civica, Valdagno, Italy
Galleria L'Angolo, Bra, Italy
Galleria Omar Ronda Aprile, Biella, Italy
Galleria Morone 6, Milan
Galleria Blu Art, Varese
Galleria La Loggia, Bologna
1985 Studio Ganzerli, Naples
Galleria F22, Palazzolo, Italy
Galleria Barrel, Genoa
Studio Albanese, Vicenza
Limonaia Palazzo dei Congressi, Florence
1986 Valente Arte Contemporanea, Finale Ligure, Italy
Galleria Gastaldelli, Milan
1987 Galleria Giuli, Lecco, Italy
Qui Arte Contemporanea, Rome
Galleria XX Settembre, Genoa
Museo d'Arte Contemporanea di Villa Croce, Genoa

Selected Group Exhibitions:

1950 *Biennale,* Venice
1959 *Documenta,* Kassel, West Germany
1961 *Italian Art Today,* Kunstnernes Hus, Oslo
1964 *Pittsburgh International,* Carnegie Institute, Pittsburgh
1966 *Prospekt,* Dusseldorf
1967 *Omaggio allo Spazialismo,* Villa Reale, Milan
1969 *Maitres de la Peinture Italienne,* Cagnes-sur-Mer, France
1971 *20 Artistas italianos,* Museo de Arte Moderno, Mexico City
1977 *La Traccia del Rocconto,* Villa Communale Ormand, San Remo, Italy
1981 *Aspeti dell'Informale,* Palazzo Reale, Genoa

Publications:

On SCANAVINO: Books—*I Simboli trovati di Scanavino* by Eligio Cesana, Lecco, Italy 1969; *20 Artistas Italianos,* exhibition catalog by Roberto Sanesi, Mexico City 1971; *Scanavino io mani* by Alain Jouffroy and Enrico Crispolti, Milan 1971; *11 Progetto dell 'Irrazionale di Scanavino* by Francesco de Bartolomis, 1972; *Emilio Scanavino,* exhibition catalog by Aldo Passoni, Turin 1972; *Scanavino* by Alain Jouffroy, Paris 1973; *Scanavino: Malerei/Zeichnung/Grahpik,* exhibition catalog by Bern Krimel, Darmstadt 1973; *Scanavino,* exhibition catalog by Guido Ballo, Trieste 1982; *Le Ceramiche di Scanavino* by Roberto Sanesi, Milan 1981; *Scanavino,* exhibition catalog by Guido Ballo, Trieste 1982; *Scanavino: La Memorial del Tempo,* with texts by Flavio Vangeli, Umbro Apollonio, Gillo Dorfles and others, Milan 1986; *Il Post-Informale in Europa,* by Ugo Ruberti, with introduction by Renzo Zorzi, Rome 1991.

* * *

It has been said that the work of Emilio Scanavino typifies in its sombre arrogance something of the character of his native city—Genoa. Certainly there is much more on his paintings that stylistic search for effect *per se.* In fact the impression is readily received that the picture frame is the proscenium within which a drama is presented in quasi-abstract terms that hints at tragic impending events. It is evident too that the import of those dark compositions is more than formal.

There is however a certain squared-up structure to most of his paintings that bears certain allusive properties one might identify with a stage or a judicial bench or even the nave of a cathedral. The allusions are not overtly emphasised; what they are is hinted at rather than elaborated, yet in a large painting such as ''In prossimita di un evento'' (1964) there is under a central swirling orb the tangled silhouette of something that might be a stricken village or the wreck of an aircraft. The detail is unimportant, but the atmosphere is one of menace and threat, a shadow of contemporary history. It is also present in his ''Tempo presente,'' an upright canvas composed around a central blank light rectangle. The two figures in the foreground might represent two viewers of a TV screen, while in the upper section a disregarded holocaust is occuring.

This ambiguity accounts for Scanavino's inclusion among the ranks of the surrealists of our epoch, though his imagery is largely abstract as opposed to that of Genoves, for example. In spite of the appearance of his works, which bear the calligraphic knotting and rhythms of central spherical motives counterpoised against dark and blurred rectangles, Scanavino works relatively slowly, the execution awaiting the decision of the apropriate symbol to express his mood. For in his colours and tones the setting is analogous to music in which the movement of its abstract players responds to his poetic choreography. There is a certain analogy of style with Georges Mathieu but this is merely a superficiality in the relief of the raised brush strokes linked and cursive in their notation of the symbols.

Scanavino has also a deeper sense of occasion, of compelling an appreciation of the presence of his picture such as ''I Loculi'' (The Tombs) in which the present and the past are represented by an upper frieze of free gyrating forms, obviously implying the abandon and frenzy of life, and below it two black boxes seem to symbolise the shrunken immobility of death, reminiscent of cadavers in the catacombs. This ambivalence between the figurative and the abstract is probably less difficult to understand when the artist's intentions are clarified as they are by choice of titles; they give unequivocal directions of the import of his message; the language is personal and symbolic, and the handling of the medium is traditionally respectful of its capacity for underlying mood by colour and comprehension in an easily understood code for joyous and moribund, moving and static. Beyond the meaning of the paintings they stand witness to the superlative quality of the artist to create a painted object that by itself stands unique in evidence of vital and essential command of expressive form in paint.

—G. S. Whittet

SCANGA, Italo

Nationality: American. **Born:** Lago, Calabria, Italy, 6 June 1932; moved to the United States in 1947. **Education:** Italian public schools; studied sculpture at Michigan State University, East Lansing, under Lindsey Decker and Charles Pollack, 1955–61, B.A. 1960, M.A. 1961. **Military Service:** Served in the United States Army, in Austria, 1953–55. **Career:** Sculptor; now lives and works in Southern California. Instructor, University of Wisconsin, Madison, 1961–64; assistant professor, Rhode Island School of Design, Providence, 1964–66; assistant professor, Pennsylvania State University, University Park, 1966–67; associate professor of sculpture, Tyler School of Art, Elkins Park, Pennsylvania, 1967–78; visiting associate professor, 1976–77, and professor of visual arts, 1978–93, University of California at San Diego. **Awards:** Lou Tendler Memorial Prize, Detroit Institute of Arts, 1960; Sculpture Prize, *Annual Wisconsin Salon of Art,* Milwaukee, 1961; Howard Foundation Grant, Brown University, Providence, Rhode Island, 1970; Cassandra Grant, Chicago, 1972; Chicago, 1972; National Endowment for the Arts Grant, 1973 and 1980; Distinguished Alumni Award, Michigan State University, 1989; Chancellor's Award for Excellence in the Arts, University of California at San Diego, 1993. **Agents:** Susanne Hilberry Gallery, Detroit; Larry Becker Gallery, Philadelphia; Betsy Rosenfield Gallery, Chicago; Carl Schlosberg Gallery, Sherman Oaks; William Traver Gallery, Seattle. **Address:** 961 Turquoise St., San Diego, California 92109, U.S.A.

Individual Exhibitions:

1959 Valparaiso University, Indiana
1960 Kresge Art Center, Michigan State University, East Lansing
1962 Lawrence College, Appleton, Wisconsin
Memorial Union Gallery, University of Wisconsin, Madison
1964 Milwaukee Art Center
Art Unlimited, Providence, Rhode Island
1970 Rhode Island School of Design, Providence
Chapman-Kelly Gallery, Dallas
1971 Henri Gallery, Washington, D.C.
Depth in Presence, Corcoran Gallery (with Robert Rauschenberg and Joseph Cornell)
93 Grand Street, New York
University of Rochester, New York
University of Massachusetts, Amherst
1972 Tyler School of Art, Rome
Water, Everson Museum, Syracuse, New York (with Yoko Ono)
Whitney Museum, New York
Pennsylvania Academy of Fine Arts, Philadelphia
Museum of Contemporary Art, Chicago
1973 University of Rhode Island, Providence
1974 112 Greene Street, New York
1975 Henri Gallery, Washington, D.C.
Brown University, Providence, Rhode Island
1979 Palomar College, San Maracos, California
San Jose State University, California
1980 Frank Kolbert Gallery, New York
1981 Crown Point Gallery, Oakland, California
Daniel Weinberg Gallery, San Francisco
1982 Charles Cowles Gallery, New York
State University of New York at Purchase
1983 La Jolla Museum of Contemporary Art, California
Los Angeles County Museum of Art
1984 Delahunty Gallery, Dallas
Rhona Hoffman Gallery, Chicago
1985 Quint Gallery, Dallas
Burnett Miller Gallery, Los Angeles
Indianapolis Center for Contemporary Art, Indiana
1986 Oakland Museum of Art, California
David Winton Bell Gallery, Brown University, Providence, Rhode Island (travelled to Maine, Connecticut, and Massachusetts)
Betty Stoler Gallery
1987 Simon Neuman Gallery, New York
Helander Gallery, Palm Beach, Florida
Susanne Hilberry Gallery, Birmingham, Michigan
Pamela Auchincloss Gallery, Santa Barbara
1988 Anders Tornberg Gallery, Lund, Sweden
Bates College Museum of Art, Lewison, Maine
Simon Neumann Gallery, New York
Larry Becker Gallery, Philadelphia
1989 Dorothy Goldeen Gallery, Santa Monica
Germans van Eck Gallery, New York
Ewing Gallery of Art and Architecture, Knoxville, Tennessee
Art Institute of Southern California, Laguna Beach
Susanne Hilberry Gallery, Birmingham, Michigan
1990 *Italo Scanga in Chico 1990,* Taylor Hall Art Gallery, Chico
Anne Westin Gallery, Stockholm
New Britain Museum of Modern Art, New Britain, Connecticut
Missoula Museum of the Arts, Missoula, Montana
1991 Smith Andersen Art Gallery, Palo Alto
Beckstrand Gallery, Palos Verdes
Helander Gallery, New York
1992 Porter Randall Gallery, La Jolla
The Athenaeum Music and Arts Library, La Jolla
Ro Snell Gallery, Santa Barbara
Susanne Hilberry Gallery, Birmingham, Michigan
Betsy Rosenfield Gallery, Chicago
1993 William Traver Gallery, Seattle
Tacoma Art Museum, Tacoma, Washington
LewAllen Gallery, Santa Fe, New Mexico
Fay Gold Gallery, Atlanta
Larry Becker Gallery, Philadephia
1994 William Traver Gallery, Seattle
SOMA Gallery, San Diego
1995 Art Museum of Southeast Texas, Beaumont
Galleria II Patio, Ravenna, Italy

1996 Bryan Ohno Gallery, Seattle (traveling exhibition)
Southeastern Center for Contemporary Art, Winston-Salem, North Carolina
1997 Van Every/Smith Galleries, Davidson College, Davidson, North Carolina
Bayley Art Museum, Charlottesville, Pennsylvania
Bryan Ohno Gallery, Seattle

Selected Group Exhibitions:

1966 *Mutiplicity,* Institute of Contemporary Art, Boston (with Nancy Graves, Eva Hesse, and Robert Morris)
1970 *Whitney Sculpture Annual,* Whitney Museum, New York
1972 *Drawings and Sculpture,* Philadelphia Museum of Art
1974 *Questions Answered,* Sarah Lawrence College, Bronxville, New York
1977 *A View of a Decade,* Museum of Contemporary Art, Chicago
1981 *Figuratively Sculpting,* Project Studio One, New York
1983 *New Epiphanies,* University of Colorado, Colorado Springs
1985 *Manifestations of the Figure,* Tibor de Nagy Gallery, New York
1987 *Recent Acquisitions,* Guggenheim Museum of Art, New York
1988 *Collaboratins in Monotype,* Art Museum, University of California at Santa Barbara (traveled to Archer M. Huntington Art Gallery, University of Texas, Austin, and Cleveland Museum of Art)
Enigmatic Inquiry: The Search for Meaning—Works by Italo Scanga, Richard Reese and Alison Saar, Gray Art Gallery, East Carolina University Museum of Art, Greenville
Three Italo-American Artists: Giorgio Cavallon, Costantino Nivola, Italo Scanga, Peggy Guggenheim Collection, Venice (travelled to Castello Svevo, Bari)
1992 *Parallel Visions,* Los Angeles County Museum of Art
1993 *Malibu International Sculpture Exhibition,* Carl Schlosberg Gallery, Malibu, California
Beyond the Bay: The Figure, Newport Harbor Art Museum, Newport Beach, California
The Human Factor: Figurative Sculpture Reconsidered, The Albuquerque Museum, New Mexico
1994 *The 5th International Shoebox Sculpture Exhibition,* University of Hawaii at Manoa Art Gallery
Fresco: A Contemporary Perspective, Boston College Museum of Art, Chestnut Hill
Figures and Faces, Carl Schlosberg Fine Arts, Sherman Oaks, California
1995 *Italo Scanga New York, Collaborative Works in Glass with Richard Royal,* Jeanine Cox Fine Art, Miami Beach
Palm Springs Desert Museum's Art Auction, Palm Springs Desert Museum, California
UCSD Visual Arts Faculty Exhibition, University of California San Diego, Visual Arts Gallery
1996 *Acquiring Minds,* Santa Barbara Contemporary Art Forum
From the Figure, Carl Schlosberg Fine Arts, Sherman Oaks, California
Baseball in Art, Polk Museum of Art, Lakeland, Florida
1997 *Raw Vision, Raw Book,* Bayly Art Museum, Charlottesville
1998 *Vis Alchemical: New Directions in Contemporary Glass Sculpture,* University Art Gallery, University of California, San Diego

Collections:

Metropolitan Museum of Art, New York; Rhode Island School of Design Museum of Art, Providence, Rhode Island; Fogg Museum, Harvard University, Cambridge, Massachusetts; Philadelphia Museum of Art; Pennsylvania Academy of Fine Arts, Philadelphia; University of Wisconsin, Madison; Wright Art Center, Beloit, Wisconsin; Milwaukee Art Center; Albright Knox Art Gallery, Buffalo; Art Institute of Chicago; Brooklyn Museum of Art, New York; Cincinnati Museum of Art, Ohio; Detroit Institute of Arts, Michigan; Guggenheim Museum of Art, New York; Hirshhorn Museum and Sculpture Garden, Washington, D.C.; La Jolla Museum of Contemporary Art, California; Los Angeles County Museum of Art; Newport Harbor Art Museum, Newport Beach, California; Palm Springs Desert Museum; Toledo Museum of Art, Ohio; University Art Museum, University of California, Berkeley; Utah State University, Lohan; Walker Art Center, Minneapolis; Arizona State University Art Museum, Nelson Fine Arts Center, Tempe.

Permanent Public Installations:

Santa Barbara Museo, Mammola, Italy; City of San Jose, California; Carlson Companies, Minneapolis, Minnesota; Private Commissions, La Jolla, California.

Publications:

By SCANGA: Book—*Pilchuck Projects,* Philadelphia 1973.

On SCANGA: Books—*Arts Yearbook of Contemporary Sculpture,* New York 1965; *Rhode Island School of Design Alumni Bulletin,* Providence, Rhode Island 1966; *Direct Metal Sculpture,* New York 1966; *Restoration Pieces,* exhibition catalog by Alan Moore, New York 1974; *Societa per Azzione* by Tullio Catalono, Milan 1975; *Italo Scanga: Heads,* exhibition catalog with text by Maurice Tuchman, Los Angeles 1983; *Italo Scanga 1972–85,* exhibition catalog with text by Paul Tomidy, Oakland 1986; *Italo Scanga,* edited by Michele Bonuomo and translated by Pasquale Verdicchio, Seattle 1989; *Italo Scanga in Chico 1990,* exhibition catalog with text by Ron Glowen, Chico 1990; *Italo Scanga* by Ron Glowen, Seattle 1993; *Italo Scanga,* exhibition catalog, Osaka 1996. **Articles—**''Italo Scanga: A Troubled World'' by Pasquale Verdicchio in *Artspace,* vol. 14, no. 2, January-February 1990.

* * *

On two facing walls Italo Scanga hangs handsomely framed reproductions of kitschy religious paintings spattered with red paint. Before these, he places urns containing spices or grains, and occasionally leans farming implements, a rake or a hoe, againts the wall. At the rear of the room, he hangs large bunches of dried herbs. Scanga constructs a kind of ritual space which resembles a series of ambulatory chapels in a cathedral, each with its own devotional image.

One has to kneel to examine the paintings closely, since they are hung so low to the ground, and from there it's a natural step to smell or taste the foodstuffs in the urns. The reproductions Scanga appropriates are the kind of sweet versions of gruesome imagery—bleeding martyrs and sacred hearts—found in poorer Italian homes. The spots and streaks of the thin red paint have been applied helter skelter, almost as if he had opened a vein before the images. Scanga's allusion to desecration (or perhaps it is an extreme form of veneration) speaks directly to the devotional function of these images.

So do the tools leaning against the wall. Many a Catholic saint was martyred by common people who used just such pedestrian implements. In medieval times, peasants used their tools as weapons since only gentry were allowed to use swords. Yet these implements are muffled. The tines of the rake, for example, are braided with straw, which indicates and mutes the tool's deadly function. Thinking about why those tools are there, kneeling and realizing just what Scanga has done to his images, together with smelling and tasting the urns' contents draws the spectator into a kind of kinesthetic parody of Holy Communion.

Scanga appears to be forcing a familiar religious issue here, pointing up the discontinuity between the painful violence the martyrs underwent and the devotional images that abstract sweet sanctity from suffering. Scanga places an urn brimming with chili powder before the bespattered images of the Christ child as Salvator mundi, so that the tasting becomes almost like one of St. Ignatius of Loyola's spiritual exercises, an encouragement for us to empathize with His suffering for us. But Scanga's iconography is a bit more complex than this. The Baroque era during which St. Ignatius wrote his Exercises also saw the culmination of a particular tradition of natural magic. This humanist systematization of the natural world was no more or less respectable in the eyes of the church than the then-emerging scientific attitude. Two of the leading philosophers and practitioners of this tradition of magic, Giordano Bruno (who was burned for his views) and the dominican friar Tommasco Campanella, were born in Calabria, Italy, as was Scanga himself. Campanella was frequently jailed during his lifetime, once for defending Galileo. But his development of a powerful astrological magic won him the support of Pope Urban VII, who in 1628 called upon Campanella to use his magic to ward off the planetary influences threatening the pontiff's life. In performing the embarrassingly pagan ritual derived from Bruno and earlier magicians, the Pope and the friar sang, lit candles to stimulate the planets in a safe arrangement, drank specially distilled liquors, and sprinkled and burned selected herbs. In return for this service, Campanella gained the Pope's support for the establishment of a short-lived order to proselytise a syncretistic brand of millennial Catholicism and sun worship.

Scanga's art is informed by an awareness of 17th-century Calabrian magical tradition, which was by no means a populist shamanism. Campanella, among others, thought of Catholicism as contiguous with the natural magic they had wrought out of Humanist philosophy. Similarly, Scanga's art infers a kind of community between cooking and religion and magic; it is not a new attempt at an orthodox Christian art. There is some way in which the effort to reduce and control the elements in an artwork becomes an effort to control the spectator's reaction to it. This effort, particularly in sculpture, can in turn become an attempt to seize and marshall the spectator's sensibilities.

—Alan Moore

SCARPITTA, Salvatore

Nationality: American. **Born:** New York City in 1919; grew up in Los Angeles; lived in Italy, 1936–59. **Education:** Studied at the Italian Academy of Fine Art, and the American Academy of Fine Art, and the American Academy, Rome. **Military Service:** Served with the United States Marines in Italy during World War II. **Career:** Has lived and worked in New York since 1959. Visiting critic, Maryland Institute College of Art, Baltimore, since 1965. **Agent:** Leo Castelli Gallery, 420 West Broadway, New York, New York 10012. **Address:** 307 East 84th Street, New York, New York 10028, U.S.A.

Individual Exhibitions:

1949 Galleria Chiurazzi, Rome
1951 Galleria Il Pincio, Rome
1955 Galleria La Tartaruga, Rome
1956 Galleria del Naviglio, Milan
1957 Galleria La Tartaruga, Rome
1958 Galleria del Naviglio, Milan
Galleria La Tartaruga, Rome
1959 Leo Castelli Gallery, New York
1960 Leo Castelli Gallery, New York
1961 Dwan Gallery, Los Angeles
1963 Galerie Schmela, Dusseldorf
Galleria dell'Ariete, Milan
Musée des Beaux-Arts, Brussels
Leo Castelli, Gallery, New York
1965 Leo Castelli Gallery, New York
1968 Galleria La Tartaruga, Rome
1969 Leo Castelli Warehouse, New York
1972 Galleria Notizie, Turin
Studio C, Brescia, Italy
1973 Galerie Jacques Benador, Geneva
1974 L'Uomo e L'Arte, Milan
1975 Leo Castelli Gallery, New York
1976 Galleria La Tartaruga, Rome
1977 Contemporary Arts Museum, Houston (retrospective)
1978 Robinson Galleries, Houston
Portland Center for the Visual Arts, Oregon
1980 Leo Castelli Gallery, New York
1982 Leo Castelli Gallery, New York
1986 Leonarda Di Mauro Gallery, New York
1989 Matrix Gallery, University Art Museum, Berkeley
1990 Greenberg Wilson Gallery, New York
Scott Hanson Gallery, New York
1992 Annina Nosei Gallery, New York
Leo Castelli Gallery, New York
1997 Tricia Collins Grand Salon, New York

Selected Group Exhibitions:

1959 *Work in Dimensions,* Leo Castelli Gallery, New York
1961 *Corcoran Biennial,* Corcoran Gallery, Washington, D.C.
1963 *Salon International de Galeries Pilotes,* Musée Cantonal des Beaux-Arts, Lausanne, Switzerland
1970 *Highway,* Institute of Contemporary Art, Philadelphia
1971 *Art around the Automobile,* Hofstra University, Hempstead, New York

1976 *Personal Mythologies,* Fine Arts Building, New York
1979 *Sustained Vision,* New Museum, New York
1984 *Content: A Contemporary Focus 1974–84,* Hirshhorn Museum, Washington, D.C.
1986 *Drawings by Sculptors,* Nohra Haime Gallery, New York
1989 *On the Surface: An Abstract Journey,* Studio Durante, Rome

Collections:

Museum of Modern Art, New York; Albright-Knox Art Gallery, Buffalo, New York; Los Angeles County Museum of Art; Stedelijk Museum, Amsterdam; Gallery of Modern Art, Tel Aviv.

Publications:

On SCARPITTA: Books—*Collage* by Harriet Janis and Rudi Blesh, New York 1962; *The Joys and Sorrows of Recent American Art* by Allen S. Weller, Chicago 1968; *Attributi dell'Arte Odierna 1947–1969* by Emilio Villa, Milan 1970. **Articles—**''The Ivory Tower'' by B. H. Friedman in *Art News* (New York), April 1969; ''Richard Long, Gina Pane, Salvatore Scarpitta'' by Giorgio Verzotti in *Flash Art (International Edition),* no. 127, April 1986.

* * *

Salvatore Scarpitta, as much as Rauschenberg and Johns (with him at the Castelli Gallery since its founding), presents the contained energy of *things.* For some 25 years now Scarpitta has been making *things*—the ''shaped canvases'' of the late 1950s (before the term was invented); the kite, rollbar, and halter or harness works of the early 1960s; the racing cars of the late 1960s, the armored cars, sleds, and bins of the 1970s. Consistently, all of this work is at once open and closed, visible and wrapped, sculptural and painterly, energetic and quiet. Even in his early work, beginning in 1936 at the Royal Academy in Rome, though he was attracted to a sort of neo-Futurism, he was more interested in the subject itself, its *presence,* than in its dynamics and was closer in spirit to the metaphysical quietism of Morandi than to the extrovert emphasis of Futurism.

As a boy in Los Angeles, Scarpitta saw a lot of dirttrack car racing, participated in its violence and glory, perhaps romanticized the rugged beauty of homemade cars. During World War II his vision matured. He saw the vehicles of war as simultaneously protective and aggressive, contained and explosive. The two-dimensional canvas must have seemed inadequate to express what he felt, what he had seen in the ''bull-ring'' tracks of California and more recently, more profoundly, on the battlefields of Europe. Emotions are difficult to particularize, especially within the tradition of Italian painting where expressionism hardly existed. But so, again, are *things*—hurt, bent, tortured, broken things. Scarpitta began to cut up his canvases, to bandage stretchers with these strips, to pierce his work in order to let it breathe. In effect, he hid his pain to make it visible. From the late 1950s on, his canvases bled.

In the catalog introduction for a 1958 exhibition in Rome, Cesare Vivaldi used images that both describe and anticipate the direction in which Scarpitta was moving: ''Canvas: twisted, stretched, slashed, ripped, taut as the roof of an ancient touring car'' and ''this canvas of his *(Moby Dick)* is composed into planes, it spreads out into wings, it bristles and bulges, it is articulated into hood-like shapes.''

By the early 1960s Scarpitta was incorporating in new work not only his own previous work but also salvaged parts of racing cars, safety belts and their hardware, more modern shoulder harnesses. Then he began building cars—as sought rather than found objects, as reconstructed history. The fragments of these dreams came partly from the drivers Scarpitta knew as a boy—a steering wheel from one, a radio cap from another, a chassis from a third. Other parts were cut, forged, welded as needed. As in ''Rajo Jack,'' sometimes, because a shape seemed right, an axe was used as a tie-rod; sometimes, because that's the way it was done then, a circular saw blade was made into a steering wheel.

Scarpitta's work is not an exercise in restoration but re-creation. In all of it—the early kites as well as the recent sleds and bins—he is a sort of Robinson Crusoe, involved with re-invention rather than research. Primitive wheelless vehicles and carriers move within their own rhythm of criss-crossed and bound laces and tape. Tents, sails, obstetrical shrouds, stand still, permit the flow of air through them, move in place, creating an environment as expansive as those of Rothko and Pollock, as specific as those Fords and dogsleds.

—B. H. Friedman

SCHAPIRO, Miriam

Nationality: American. **Born:** Toronto, Canada, 15 November 1923. **Education:** Erasmus Hall High School, Brooklyn; studied at the Museum of Modern Art, New York, 1937–41; Hunter College, New York, 1941–43; State University of Iowa, Iowa City, 1943–49. B.A. 1945, M.A. 1946, M.F.A. 1949. **Family:** Married Paul Brach in 1946; son: Peter. **Career:** Worked as teacher and secretary, Columbia, Missouri, 1950–52; children's art teacher, real estate secretary and bookshop assistant, New York, 1952–55. Full-time artist since 1955. Visiting lecturer, Connecticut College for Women, New London, 1966–67; lecturer, later acting assistant professor, University of California at San Diego Art Department, La Jolla, 1967–69; produced series of computer paintings and drawings, with David Nalibof, La Jolla, 1969; faculty member, California Institute of the Arts, Valencia, 1970–71; met Judy Chicago, Fresno State College, and together they co-founded and co-directed Feminist Art Program, 1973; co-directed Womanhouse Environment, Los Angeles Institute of Contemporary Art, 1974; frequent lecturer and visiting artist. **Awards:** Ford Foundation Grant for printmaking, with Paul Brach, Tamarind Lithography Workshop, 1964; National Endowment for the Arts Fellowship, 1976; Skowhegan Award, 1982; Guggenheim Fellowship, 1987; Honors Award, Women's Caucus for Art, 1988; Honors Award, National Association of Schools of Art and Design, 1992; Rockefeller Foundation Grant, 1993; Honors Award, New York State NARAL, 1994. Honorary degrees: Minneapolis College of Art and Design, Moore College of Art, Philadelphia, Lawrence University, Appleton, Wisconsin, and Miami University, Oxford, Ohio. **Agent:** Bernice Steinbaum Gallery, 3550 N. Miami Ave., Miami, FL 33127–3112, U.S.A.

Individual Exhibitions:

1951 University of Missouri, Columbia
Illinois Wesleyan University, Bloomington

Miriam Schapiro: *Wonderland,* 1983. ©Smithsonian American Art Museum/Art Resource, NY.

1958 André Emmerich Gallery, New York
1960 André Emmerich Gallery, New York
1961 André Emmerich Gallery, New York
1963 André Emmerich Gallery, New York
1964 Skidmore College, Saratoga Springs, New York
1966 Franklin Siden Gallery, Detroit
The Lyman Allyn Museum, New London, Connecticut
1967 André Emmerich Gallery, New York
1969 André Emmerich Gallery, New York
1971 André Emmerich Gallery, New York
1973 André Emmerich Gallery, New York
1974 The Comsky Gallery, Los Angeles
1975 The Comsky Gallery, Los Angeles
Mandeville Art Gallery, University of California at San Diego
Benson Gallery, Bridgehampton, New York
Mills College, Oakland, California
1976 Mabel Smith Doglass College Library, New Brunswick, New Jersey
Mitzi Landau Gallery, Los Angeles
André Emmerich Gallery, New York
Douglas Drake Gallery, Kansas City
A.R.C. Gallery, Chicago
University of Wisconsin at LaCrosse
1977 Fairbanks Gallery, University of Oregon, Eugene
Oberlin College, Ohio
Reed College, Portland, Oregon
1979 Davenport Municipal Art Gallery, Iowa
Gladstone-Villani Gallery, New York
Galerie Liatowitsch, Basel
Douglass Drake Gallery, Kansas City
Center Gallery, Madison, Wisconsin
1980 Dart Gallery, Chicago
Barbara Gladstone Gallery, New York
Lerner-Heller Gallery, New York
Muse Gallery, Philadelphia
College of Wooster Art Museum, Ohio (touring retrospective exhibition)
1981 Barbara Gladstone Gallery, New York
Galerie Rudolf Zwirner, Cologne
1982 Axiom Gallery, Victoria, Australia
Douglas Drake Gallery, Kansas City, Kansas
David Heath Gallery, Atlanta
Barbara Gladstone Gallery, New York
1983 Barbara Gilman Gallery, Miami
Kent State University, Kent, Ohio
Koplin Gallery, Los Angeles
Marian Locks Gallery, Philadelphia
Thomas Segal Gallery, Boston
1984 Atlantic Center for the Arts, New Smyrna Beach, Florida
Dart Gallery, Chicago
1985 Appalachian State University, Boone, North Carolina
Brentwood Gallery, St. Louis, Missouri
1986 Bernice Steinbaum Gallery, New York

Miriam Schapiro: *Ox*, 1968. ©The Newark Museum/Art Resource, NY.

Guilford College, Greenboro, North Carolina
Vered Gallery, Easthampton, New York
New York University, New York
Artlink Contemporary Artspace, Ft. Wayne, Indiana

1987 Simms Fine Art Gallery, New Orleans
Gibbes Art Gallery, Charleston, South Carolina

1988 Bernice Steinbaum Gallery, New York

1990 Bernice Steinbaum Gallery, New York
LewAllen/Butler Fine Art, Santa Fe, New Mexico

1991 Bernice Steinbaum Gallery, New York
Phyllis Rothman Gallery, Farleigh Dickinson University, Madison, New Jersey
Brevard Art Center and Museum, Melbourne, Florida

1992 Curfman Gallery, Colorado State University, Fort Collins
Fullerton College Art Gallery, Fullerton, California
Guild Hall Museum, East Hampton, New York
Mendelson Gallery, Chicago

1993 ARC Gallery, Chicago

1994 *Miriam Schapiro, Collaboration Series 1994: Mother Russia,* Steinbaum Krauss Gallery, New York
Miriam Schapiro, West Virginia University, College of Creative Arts, Morgantown

1996 *Miriam Schapiro: A Seamless Life,* Sawhill Gallery, James Madison University, Harrisonburg, Virginia

1997 *Miriam Schapiro: A Woman's Way,* National Museum of American Art, Smithsonian Institution, Washington, D.C.
Miriam Schapiro: Collaged, Femmaged, Printed & Painted, Steinbaum Krauss Gallery, New York
Miriam Schapiro, Artforms Gallery, Philadelphia

1998 *Miriam Schapiro,* duPont Hall, Washington and Lee University, Lexington, Virginia

1999 *Miriam Schapiro: Works on Paper: A Thirty Year Retrospective,* Tucson Museum of Art, Tucson, Arizona

Selected Group Exhibitions:

1963 *Toward a New Abstraction,* Jewish Museum, New York

1973 *21 Artists—Invisible/Visible,* Long Beach Museum of Art California

1977 *10 Approaches to the Decorative,* Allesandra Gallery, New York

1979 *Feministische Kunst International,* Gemeentemuseum, The Hague (toured the Netherlands)
Patterns Painting, Palais des Beaux-Arts, Brussels
The Decorative Impulse, Institute of Contemporary Art, University of Philadelphia

1980 *Les Nouveaux Fauves di Neuen Wilden,* Ludwig Museum, Aachen

1981 *Retrospective Show—Women Artists' Series,* Douglass College, Rutgers State University, New Brunswick, New Jersey

1983 *Women Artists of the 1970s,* State University of New York, Cortland

1989 *Making Their Mark,* Cincinnati Art Museum (travelled to the New Orleans Museum of Art, Denver Art Museum, and Pennsylvania Academy of Fine Arts)

1990 *Definitive Contemporary American Quilt Show,* Bernice Steinbaum Gallery, New York (travelled through 1994)
Contemporary Women, Works on Paper, Carnegie Museum of Art, Pittsburgh, Pennsylvania
Art and Fashion, Contemporary Arts Center, New Orleans
Quilting Partners, Northern Illinois Art Museum, Chicago, Illinois
Pattern & Decoration: Selections from the Roth Collection of Works on Paper, Polk Museum of Art, Lakeland, Florida

1991 *Graphicstudio: Contemporary Art from the Collaborative Workshop at the University of South Florida,* National Gallery of Art, Washington D.C.
Crossing Over/Changing Places, The Print Club, Philadelphia (travelled internationally)
Presswork: The Art of Women Printmakers, Lang Communications Corporate Collection, National Museum of Women in the Arts, Washington, D.C. (toured through 1994)
Art on Paper, Weatherspoon Art Gallery, Greensboro, North Carolina
Collage Unglued, North Miami Museum, Center of Contemporary Art, North Miami, Florida
AIGA Annual, The American Institute of Graphic Arts, New York

1992 *The Edge of Childhood,* The Heckscher Museum, New York
Parallel Visions: Modern Artists and Outsider Art, Los Angeles County Museum of Art, Los Angeles
Floored Art, Steinbaum Krauss Gallery, New York

1993 *Dolls in Contemporary Art: A Metaphor of Personal Identy,* Patrick & Beatrice Haggerty Museum of Art, Marquette University, Milwaukee, Wisconsin
Establishing the Legacy, The National Museum of Women in the Arts, Washington, D.C.
Women's Art, Women's Live's, Women's Issues, Tweed Gallery, New York
Master Prints from the Rutgers Center for Innovative Printmaking, The Noyes Museum, Oceanville, New Jersey
Contemporary American Quilts, Crafts Council, London, England (travelled throughout Europe)

1994 *Memories of Childhood. . . So We're Not the Cleavers or the Brady Bunch,* Steinbaum Krauss Gallery, New York (travelled through 1997)
The Label Show: Contemporary Art and the Museum, The Museum of Fine Arts Boston, Massachusetts
A View of One's Own, Jane Voorhees Zimmerli Art Museum, Rutger's Univesity, New Brunswick, New Jersey (inaugural exhibition of the National Association of Women Artists-N.A.W.A.)

1995 *Division of Labor: ''Women's Work'' in Contemporary Art,* The Bronx Museum of the Arts, New York; Museum of Contemporary Art, Los Angeles
Making Faces: American Portraits, The Hudson River Museum of Westchester, Yonkers, New York
About Faces, Santa Barbara Museum of Art, Santa Barbara, California

1996 *Contemporary Printmaking in America: Collaborative Prints and Presses,* National Museum of American Art, Washington, D.C.

Women's Work: A Century of Achievement in American Art, The Columbus Museum, Columbus, Georgia
25 Years of Feminism, 25 Years of Women's Art, Mary H. Dana Women Artist Series, 25th Anniversary Exhibition, Mason Gross School of the Arts, Rutgers University, New Brunswick, New Jersey
1997 *Hanging by a Thread,* Hudson River Museum of Westchester, Yonkers, New York
Art Patterns, Austin Museum of Art, Austin, Texas
Expanding Expression: Berghoff-Cowden Editions, Polk Museum of Art, Lakeland, Florida
Female Artists from Graphic Studios, Polk Museum of Art, Lakeland, Florida
Wild Women Salon, Morgan Gallery, Kansas City, Missouri
1997–2000 *Crossing the Threshold,* Steinbaum Krauss Gallery, New York (toured United States)

Collections:

Metropolitan Museum of Art, New York; Museum of Modern Art, New York; Whitney Museum, New York; National Museum of American Art, Washington, D.C.; Hirshhorn Museum, Washington, D.C.; National Museum of Women in the Arts, Washington, D.C.; St. Louis Art Museum, Missouri; Indianapolis Museum; Minneapolis Institute of Art; Brooklyn Museum of Art; Leusiana Museum, Denmark; Art Gallery of New South Wales, Sidney, New South Wales, Australia; The Israel Museum, Tel Aviv.

Publications:

By SCHAPIRO: Books—*Anonymous Was a Woman,* editor, Valencia, California 1974; *Rondo,* San Francisco 1989. **Articles—**''Artists on Their Art'' in *Art International* (Lugano), February 1968; ''Introduction'' and ''Out of Isolation'' in *Every Woman* (Los Angeles), May 1971; ''Dollhouse Room,'' statement with Judy Chicago in *Womanhouse,* exhibition catalog, Los Angeles 1972; statement with Judy Chicago in *21 Artists—Invisible/Visible,* exhibition catalog, Long Beach, California 1972; statements in ''Feminine Sensibility; An Analysis'' by Patricia Mainardi in *The Feminists Art Journal* (New York), Autumn 1972, ''Our Beginning'' in *Womanspace Journal* (Los Angeles), February 1973; ''Female Imagery,'' with Judy Chicago in *Womanspace Journal* (Los Angeles), June 1973; ''Woman and the Creative Process: Discussion'' in *Mosaic* (Winnepeg), Autumn 1974; ''More on Women's Art: An Exchange,'' with others, in *Art in America* (New York), November/December 1976; ''Interview with Miriam Schapiro,'' with Donald Kuspit in *Art in America* (New York) September 1977, essay in *Reed College Exhibition: Anatomy of a Kimono,* exhibition catalog, Portland, Oregon 1978; ''Femmage'' in *Helicon Nine* (New York), Spring 1981; ''The Decorative Politic: An Interview with Miriam Schapiro'' with Jan Avgikos in *Art Papers,* November/December 1982; ''Geometry and Flowers'' in *The Artist and the Quilt,* edited by Charlotte Robinson, New York, 1983; ''An Interview with Miriam Schapiro'' with Christy Sheffield Sanford and Enid Shorter in *Women Artists News,* spring 1986; ''Recalling Womanhouse'' in *Womens Studies Quarterly,* spring/summer 1987; ''Cunts/Quilts/Consciousness'' (with Faith Wilding) in *Heresies,* no. 24, 1989; ''Breaking Bread Etching the Plate'' in *Ladies Lunch,* exhibition catalog, Louisville Visual Art Association, 1992; ''A Conversation with Miriam Schapiro'' with Charlene Roth in *Artweek,* August 1993; ''A Feminist Response: An Interview with Miriam Schapiro'' with Patrick Merrill and Gail Jacobs in *Newsprint,* Winter 1994–95; ''A Talk with Miriam Schapiro'' with Brenda Kean Tabor in *The Washington Post,* 8 May 1997; ''Creating Beauty: An Interview with Feminist Artist Miriam Schapiro'' with Amy Nickell and Tanya Stanciu in *Gadfly,* vol. 1, no. 7, September 1997.

On SCHAPIRO: Books—*Toward a New Abstraction,* exhibition catalog with an essay by Dore Ashton, New York 1963; *Womanhouse,* exhibition catalog, Valencia, California 1972; *21 Artists—Invisible/ Visible,* exhibition catalog, Long Beach, California 1972; *Sunshine Muse: Contemporary Art on the West Coast* by Peter Plagens, New York and Washington, D.C. 1974; *The Shrine, the Computer and the Dollhouse: Miriam Schapiro,* edited by Moira Roth, La Jolla, California 1975; *Working It Out: 25 Women Writers, Artists, Scientists and Scholars Talk about Their Lives and Work,* edited by Sara Ruddick and Pamela Daniels, New York 1977; *Feminist Collage: Educating Women in the Visual Arts,* edited by Judy Loeb, New York 1979; *The Originals* by Eleanor Munro, New York 1979; *Patterns Painting,* exhibition catalog by John Perreault with an introduction by K.J. Gierlandt, Brussels 1979; *The Decorative Impulse,* exhibition catalog by Janet Kardon, Philadelphia 1979; *Feministische Kunst International,* exhibition catalog edited by Rosa Lindenburg, The Hague 1979; *Miriam Schapiro, A Retrospective: 1953–1980,* exhibition catalog edited by Thalia Gouma-Peterson, Wooster, Ohio 1980; *Les Nouveaux Fauves de Neuen Wilden,* exhibition catalog, 2 volumes, Aachen, West Germany, 1980; *Miriam Schapiro* by Max Kozloff, Cologne 1981; *Women and Art,* exhibition catalog with an essay by Erma Bombeck, Scottsdale, Arizona 1981; *Women Artists* by Susan Fisher Sterling, New York 1995; *The Pink Glass Swan: Selected Feminist Essays on Art* by Lucy R. Lippard, New York 1995; *Woman's Work: A Century of Achievement in American Art,* exhibition catalog, Columbus, Georgia 1996; *Lives and Works: Talks with Women Artists* by Beryl Smith, Joan Arbeiter, and Sally Shearer, Lanham, Maryland 1996; *Sexual Politics: Judy Chicago's Dinner Party in Feminist Art History,* edited by Amelia Jones, Los Angeles 1996; *Crossing the Threshold,* exhibition catalog, New York 1997; *Miriam Schapiro: Works on Paper: A Thirty Year Retrospective,* Tucson, Arizona 1999. **Articles—**''Miriam Schapiro'' by Mary Stofflet in *Arts Magazine* (New York), May 1977; ''Miriam Schapiro's Collection'' by Mike Walsh in *Artweek* (Oakland, California), 19 February 1978; ''Placing Women in History; Miriam Schapiro's Fan and Vestiture Series'' by Paula Bradley in *Arts Magazine* (New York), February 1979; ''Decoration, Ornament, Pattern and Utility'' by Carrie Rickey in *Flash* Art (Milan), June/July 1979; ''The Heart of the Matter'' by John Perreault in the *Soho Weekly News* (New York), 13 February 1980; ''Women Artists 80'' by Grace Glueck and ''A Decade of Progress'' by Avis Berman in *Art News* (New York), October 1980; ''Women and Art'' by Carol Donnelkj-Kotrozo in *Arts Magazine* (New York), March 1981; ''Miriam Schapiro and Femmage'' by Norma Broude in *Feminism and Art History,* edited by Norma Broude and Mary D. Garrard, New York 1983; ''Miriam Schapiro'' by Ruth Bass in *ArtNews,* October 1990; ''Feminists in the Art World'' by Lilly Wei in *Art in America,* vol. 83, no. 1, 20 April 1995; ''Miriam Schapiro: An Art of Becoming'' by Thalia Gouma-Peterson in *American Art,* vol. 11, no. 1, Spring 1997; ''Miriam Schapiro:

Feminism's 'Mimi Appleseed''' by Paul Richard in *The Washington Post,* 11 May 1997; ''Miriam Schapiro: An Artistic Journey'' by Marilyn Stewart in *SchoolArts,* vol. 97, no. 7, March 1998.

*

Process and Ideology in an Opulent, Multi-layered Eccentric, and Hopeful Abstract Art:

1. The need for order and stability
2. The need to destroy order and stability in order to find something else.
3. Finding something else.

Pattern, itself an architectural species, reflects order and stability. Then a need to create chaos as though life itself were taking place. Finally the bonding (layer by layer), the interpenetration of paint, fabric, photograph, tea towel, ribbon, lace and glue, a collage: a simultaneity; a visual dazzlement, a multilayering, a final message for the senses. And the ideology which inspires the work itself? That is feminism, the wish to have the art speak as a woman speaks. To be sensitive to the material used as though there were a responsibility to history to repair the sense of omission and to have each substance in the collage to be a reminder of a woman's dreams.

—Miriam Schapiro

* * *

Miriam Schapiro emerged as an ardent feminist in the late 1960s when she began to bring her life as a woman and an artist together. She felt she had to become one woman, one identity, and began by reevaluating notions of the (male) public and the (female) private in hopes of repairing her own sense of self. After taking inventory of her separate roles, she looked into her specific experience as a female to find sources of making art that would be more personally relevant and expressive. A decade of personal and political struggle with feminist issues crystallized in her pioneering and collaborative involvement in Womanhouse. Co-directing the Feminist Art Program with Judy Chicago at the time (1970), they started off the school year by involving their students in a project which would allow them to project all their dreams and fantasies by creating an exclusively female environment in an old house. After renovating the house, they transformed it with performance and art works which dealt with specifically feminist issues. They used this explorative process as a means of restructuring their identities as women artists in a patriarchal (art) world.

Miriam Schapiro began her professional career in the 1950s as an abstract expressionist. In her early work one can often find vague images of the human figure and semi-submerged female symbols. In the 1960s she worked in a hard-edged, minimalist but illusionistic style. Some of the recurring female symbols become more obvious. Moody opulent color characterizes all of her work. It was during this time that Schapiro faced tumultuous confusion about her relationship to (art) history. Though working abstractly, a number of these paintings contain allusive messages about women in diverse roles (see for examples: ''The Law,'' 1961; ''Shrine for Two Paint Tubes,'' 1962; and ''Shrine: Homage to M.L.,'' 1963). By 1965 she had almost completely suppressed all references to her personal self. Perservering with personal/artistic struggles led her to a resolution of proud feminist commitment. The major battles ending in 1970, Schapiro had travelled (like many others at the time) the dangerous journey through emotional, psychological, and spiritual darkness. The abyss closed. She emerged powerful and fresh.

Since then, Miriam Schapiro has been giving the history of women's ''covert'' art a brightly lit showcase. The once-tabooed scraps: sequins, buttons, threads, rickrack spangles, yarn, silk, taffeta, cotton, burlap, and wool, were excavated from the musty attics and dredged from the dark closets of art history. Now, they are assembled and coordinated with emotional and creative thought into ''femmages.'' From Schapiro's collaborative efforts with other feminist artists, particularly Melissa Meyer, she invented this word to describe art made in the techniques traditionally ascribed to women (i.e. sewing, embroidery, piece work, appliqué, etc.). It is a potpourri of collage, costume design, assemblage, decoupage, and photomontage seasoned with spiritual symbols, decorative motifs, and personal, anecdotal information.

A protector and preserver of women's heritage, her art is for everyone, as is feminism itself. She often incorporates motifs and imagery derived from women artists who worked anonymously or have been submerged by history (see for examples: ''Lady Gengi's Maze,'' 1972; ''Collaboration Series: Mary Casatt and Me,'' 1975; ''Anonymous Was a Woman,'' 1977). Her femmages are externalized projections of her interior world as well as information gathered from her daily life.

Before the patriarchal mind-body dichotomy came to reign and analytical, linear thinking (known as ''intellectual'') came to be hallowed as superior to nonrational (not necessarily irrational!) and creative thought/experience, there was no split, no compartmentalizations. Miriam Schapiro reunites all of these aspects in her work, protesting against society's unnatural and oppressive programming of our thinking.

Organized with geometrical unity, Schapiro's own language of flowers and decorative motifs speaks to the viewers. Her work makes us think and feel simultaneously by monumentalizing such (female) symbols as the home, the kitchen, the shrine, the theatre, the egg, hearts, handkerchiefs, and Kimonos. Since ideas and things related to the realm of women had been rendered inconsequential and unintelligent by history, and ''insignificant'' things have been tabooed by a male-dominated art world, Schapiro restores these metaphors' many meanings. The patterned picture planes flow with human and organic rhythm. In the presence of her work, one can imagine being crooned to a state of peacefulness. Her use of color and her sense of discipline and order, also derived from deep awareness of her physical life and cycles, is passionately saturating and evocative of moody atmospheres. Schapiro's strong sense of nostalgia and proud sentimentality is often heightened by attachments of mementos from her personal and/or collective past. All of these naughty ''no-no''s become subjects of spiritual devotions and gems to behold. But, then, the original etymological meaning of the word ''taboo'' is restored; something to be revered, repected, and preserved as sacred.

Both explosively commanding and dramatic and yet lyrical and poignant, Miriam Schapiro wields power and gives nurturance at the same time. As she said recently: ''I see that all mental issues really come from a very deep perception of one's own body; how it is different from a man's. You look into yourself, and from that intimate view grows a view of the world.''

Through the many layers of geometry and rich hues her work stimulates us to explore and feed our souls and from that base develop an understanding of the parallels and messages in the world around us. Having taken embroidered upholstery out of the parlor, quilts off beds, clothing off hangers, scrapbooks out of trunks, and tapestries from beneath our feet, Schapiro reeducates us about a history of buried art, women's art. As children we are stimulated and fed on all levels (creatively/emotionally/intuitively/perceptually/intellectually) and physically protected and spoiled by the art of female guides in our own families. We grow up taking these luxurious enviroments for granted, as society encourages. Ecologist of women, and therefore all of humanity, Miriam Schapiro encourages us to take heed and give gratitude to these tradtions, in hopes of motivating us to make our culture whole again.

—Elise La Rose

During the last two decades of the twentieth century, Miriam Schapiro continued to address the enduring concerns of her notable career: the primary forms drawn from her roots in minimalism (although she shifted from anonymous geometric shapes to female-identified heart and fan compositions); pattern and decoration, employing historically devalued ''crafts'' of textile design, quilting, embroidery, etc.; and feminist concerns about woman's role in society in general and in the art world in particular. In the mid-1980s, she began a series of works that examine the passages of a woman's life, such as ''Moving Away,'' which portrays a girl maturing into a woman, and ''Incognito,'' which explores the internal conflicts of a professional woman. She continued the series through the late 1990s, when she began to incorporate her own passages in works such as ''Father and Daughter'' (1997), a self-portrait as a little girl that acknowledges her father's influence on her development as an artist.

Throughout her career, Schapiro has interrogated the relationship of gender and art production. She has asked, ''How do you identify an artist? What does an artist look like? When I grew up, an artist was defined by a Rembrandt self-portrait. There would be his smock and his beret, velvet usually, and his palette in one hand, his brushes in the other, and these were the symbols of the outward appearance of an artist. So then I say to myself, but I'm a woman, how do I fit into that? Not only that, but I'm a middle-class woman. Not only that, but I'm a Jewish woman. Not only that, I'm not particularly beautiful. In fact, you probably wouldn't pick me out of a crowd. So how would I identify myself as an artist?'' In the 1970s, she began doing what she called ''Collaborations,'' which combined her work—often painted designs overlaid by fabric collages—with the work of historical women artists. A notable example is ''Me and Mary Cassatt'' from 1976. The artist continued her ''Collaborations'' series through the 1990s with works like ''Russian Matrix,'' a 16-image grid depicting revolutionary women artists from the Soviet Union, and ''Yard Sale,'' honoring Frida Kahlo, Varvara Stepanova, and Sonia Delaunay.

—Betty Ann Brown

SCHER, Julia

Nationality: American. **Born:** Hollywood, California, 9 March 1954. **Education:** California State Universiy, Northridge, 1972–73; University of California at Berkeley, N.A. in studio arts 1975; University of Minnesota, Minneapolis, M.F.A. in studio arts 1984. **Career:** Teacher, University of Minnesota, Minneapolis, 1983–84; California Institute of the Arts, Valencia, 1988; Art Center College of Art and Design, Pasadena, 1988 and 1991; University of Southern California, Los Angeles, 1989; Massachusetts Institute of Technology, Cambridge, 1990; Massachusetts College of Art, Boston, 1990; Anok-Ramsy College, Coon Rapids, Minnesota, 1990; Minneapolis College of Art and Design, 1990; School for Visual Arts, New York, 1991; Princeton University, 1992; Institute fur Gegenwartskunst, Vienna, 1993; San Francisco Art Institute, 1993; Cooper Union, New York, 1993; New York University, 1993–95; Resselaer Polytechnic Institute, Troy, New York, 1994–95; Rutgers University, New Brunswick, New Jersey, 1994; Massachusetts Institute of Technology, Cambridge, 1995—. **Awards:** Jerome Foundation Grant, 1987; Art Matters Inc. Grants, 1987, 1988, 1989, and 1993; Artist's Space Individual Artist Grant, 1988; National Endowment for the Arts Grant, 1992; Bunting Fellowship, Radcliffe/Harvard University, 1996–97. **Address:** 154 W. 27th Street, New York, New York 10001, U.S.A. **Web site:** www.scherware.com.

Selected Individual Exhibitions:

1984 Coffman Gallery, University of Minnesota, Minneapolis
1989 Collective for Living Cinema, New York
Wexner Center, Columbus, Ohio
1990 Max Fish Bar and Restaurant, New York
Anoka-Ramsey College, Coon Rapids, Minnesota
Walker Art Center, Minneapolis
1991 Pat Hearn Gallery, New York
1992 Hallwalls, Buffalo
Pat Hearn Gallery, New York
1993 Galerie Metropol, Vienna
1994 Andrea Rosen Gallery, New York
Kölnischer Kunstverein, Cologne, Germany
1995 Massimo De Carlo, Milan
Schipper and Krome, Berlin
1996 Andrea Rosen Gallery, New York
Fri-Art Centre d'Art Contemporain Kunsthalle, Fribourg, Switzerland
1997 Ghislaine Hussenot Gallery, Paris
Bunting Institute, Cambridge, Massachusetts
1998 San Francisco Museum of Modern Art
Andrea Rosen Gallery, New York
2000 Andrea Rosen Gallery, New York

Selected Group Exhibitions:

1994 *L'hiver de l'amour,* Musée d'art Moderne de la Ville, Paris
Bioinformatica, Sandra Gering Gallery, New York (travelled to Cologne, London, and Paris)
1995 *Art with Conscience,* Newark Museum, New Jersey
1996 *Departure Lounge,* Clocktower Gallery/Institute for Contemporary Art, New York
Against: Thirty Years of Film and Video, Anthony d'Offay Gallery, London
Where Does It Hurt? Banff Centre for the Arts, Alberta, Canada
Voyeur's Delight, Franklin Furnace, New York
So You Wanna Be a Rock and Roll Star: Artists Interpret Popular Music, Museum of Contemporary Art, Chicago

1997 *Surveillance,* Massachusetts Institute of Technology, Cambridge
Performance Anxiety, Museum of Contemporary Art, Chicago
1998 *The Sultan's Pool,* Jerusalem

Collections:

Musée d'Art Moderne, Geneva; Musée d'Art Contemporani de Barcelona, Spain; Musée d'Art Moderne de la Ville, Paris; Neue Galerie am Landesmuseum Joanneu, Graz, Austria.

Publications:

By SCHER: Articles—''Security News'' in *Blast,* October 1987; ''Security News #2'' in *Blast,* October 1988; ''The House that Watches Back'' in *Remote Control—The TV Set,* New York 1990; ''Mass Observation'' in *Ten,* Autumn 1991; ''Convention'' in *Documents,* October 1993; ''Warnings'' in *Headline,* June 1993; ''Safe and Secure: Scene 1 and Scene 2'' in *Assemblage,* April 1993; ''The Bad Seed + Security by Julia'' in *Bomb Magazine,* Summer 1994; ''Buffalo under Surveillance'' in *Jahresring #41 Jarbuch fur moderne kunst,* edited by Christiane Schneider, Munich 1994; ''The Julia Set: Fractal Geometry'' in *Documents,* Spring/Summer 1995; ''Danger, Dirty Data'' in *Artforum International,* Septemger 1995; ''Home-In-Security'' in *Gender and Technology: Rethinking Masculinity and Femininity in a World of Intelligent Machines,* edited by Bill Horrigan, 1995; ''The Institutional State'' in *Els Limits Del Museo,* 1995; ''*American Fibroids*'' in *Trans,* vol. 1, no. 2, 1996; ''Danger: Dirty Data and the Rodent Ship'' in *New Observations,* Fall 1996.

On SCHER: Articles—''Julia Scher: Playground Monitor'' by William Schefferine in *Flash Art* (International Edition), no. 168, January/February 1993; ''Julia Scher: Kolnischer Kunstverein'' by Barbara Hess translated by Shaun Whiteside in *Flash Art International,* vol. 17, no. 179, November/December 1994; ''Kunstverein, Cologne'' by Benjamin Weil in *Art Monthly,* no. 180, October 1994; ''Julia Scher: es gibt einen Wunsch, kontrolliert zu werden'' by Noemi Smolik in *Kunstforum International,* no. 129, January/April 1995; ''Danger Dirty Data'' by Andrew Hultkrans in *Artforum International,* vol. 34, September 1995; ''Julia Scher: Telephobic Modernity and the Ecologies of Surveillance'' by Timothy Druckrey in *Art and Text,* no. 54, May 1996; ''Musee-Museum'' by Manuel J. Borja-Villel in *Lotus International,* no. 95, 1997; ''The Art of Watching the Watchers'' by Adam Quest in *New Art Examiner,* vol. 24, March 1997; ''Julia Scher: Forecast'' by Charles Giuliano in *Art New England,* vol. 18, August/September 1997; ''Interview: Julia Scher'' by Josephine Bosma online at *Nettime Archive,* www.nettime.org/nettime.w3archive/199805/msg00013html (accessed June 2001); ''Julia Scher: *american fibroids*'' by Rainald Schumacher online at *THINGREVIEWS* http://old.thing.net/ttreview/marrev.05.html (accessed June 2001); ''Watching The Watchers'' by Adam Quest online at www.adamquest.com/watchers3.html (accessed June 2001).

* * *

Working from a position of ''insecurity in the real world,'' Julia Scher uses the language of security and surveillance—police uniforms, surveillance cameras, alarms, key pads, badges, handcuffs—to create spheres of security and insecurity within an unsafe world. By putting the viewer on both sides of the surveillance camera, by making everybody the viewer as well as the viewed, Scher's installations raise questions about the nature of security in contemporary society. The devices constructed to ensure security are the very ones that make us insecure. Surveillance cameras insure security to those behind the camera, but to those in front, the cameras are a source of insecurity.

Due to the current technology and widespread paranoia, we live in a world where we are always watching and being watched. Every time we enter convenience stores or banks, we are being watched. Every time we apply for a job, write down our names and social security numbers, someone is keeping track. Every time we argue in the seeming confines of our homes, a neighbor is listening. And while this reality is a reality often ignored, or unnoticed, or accepted, Scher notices.

While genuine artifacts of security are polished and conspicuously inconspicuous—security guards and policemen in perfect uniform with shiny badges, surveillance cameras and alarm systems neatly installed in homes and businesses—Scher's devices are often crass. The wires and cables are tangled and visible, her web installations reveal the limitations of the media, and the police uniforms reproduced in her work often have an S & M appeal as opposed to a strictly authoritarian one. In his article, ''The Art of Watching The Watchers,'' Adam Quest, a ''security-conscious'' writer who frequently works with Scher, writes that these imperfections, and Scher's work as a whole, attempt ''to show both the irregularities of power and the subtle incursions into freedom that these systems create by exposing their hidden mechanisms enabling the viewer to question the strategy behind our collective need for security.''

Scher has installed surveillance and security systems in galleries, museums, private and public spaces, and the Web. In her 1994 installation, *Don't Worry,* Scher equipped a room with six monitors, several loudspeakers, and two video cameras that hung from the ceiling. At the far end of the room is a desk with a computer and a printer. Users are watched, recorded and manipulated, before they are aware of it. In an review printed in *Flash Art,* Barbara Hess writes, ''when one printed one's own image off the computer monitor, one had the sense of defining one's own image, although we know that our identities are always generated by the descriptions of others.''

Scher's Web-based installations are frequently more conceptual and complex than her 'traditional' installations, but her themes remain the same. *Securityland,* for instance, is a sprawling labyrinth-like Web installation in which the user finds him/herself answering questions, punching in numbers on digital keypads, and scrolling through 360-degree images. How the questions are answered and the buttons are clicked determines where the user will go next. The text is a fusion of technological jargon and sexually provocative connotations.

The interactive installations, *Konsent Klinic* and *Wonderland* can be navigated online, and while Scher's intent seems clear, what *exactly* she's saying is frequently vague. Perhaps, this is a result of Scher's admitted misuse of media materials. She approaches the technology with the insight of a computer-user and the passion of a visual artist, rather than with the cold know-how of a computer-programmer. Her works are textured rather than seamless, paranoid, voyeuristic and aesthetically brilliant, rather than informational and dry.

Scher's role on the Web is one of a paradoxical figure. She makes herself a part of the online communities that could pose a threat, and she works to create security mechanisms designed to manage those same threats.

In an interview with Josephine Bosma, Scher describes how she ventures to the seedy underbelly of the vast, complicated Internet and uses ''media materials to express sadomasochistic messages.'' She explores Web rings intended for those with unconventional sexual inclinations—pedophiles, S & M types, those who fantasize about sex with amputees. In 1992, Scher helped to commit one of the first cyber-rapes, in which ''a character or individual shakes up or disturbs another online persona by saying nasty icky things that feel intrusive and apelike.''

And then she works to create real and conceptual devices that serve to protect people—children—from the dangers of even her *own* work. When it comes to such sensitive issues of Internet content, Scher acknowledges both its benignity and its dangers. She doesn't believe that S & M Web sites, for example, will spawn a worldwide epidemic of sadomasochism. She sticks by the stance that says, if you don't like it don't look and you won't get hurt. But, she also knows that people will wander into these sites by accident, and that children, with their uncanny knack for finding things they're not supposed to find, will occasionally end up on the wrong side of the sexual cyber-tracks. Scher concedes that if a child were to stumble upon a cyber rape, he/she would suffer. That image, the recollection, would be ingrained on the child's previously innocent mind.

So, Scher has attempted the admittedly impossible task of empowering the powerless. Deeply concerned about child abuse and child protection, and knowing what she knows about the Internet and the world, Scher has completed a number of projects intended to provide security. In her interview with Bosma, Scher describes one installation, ''a surveillance bed for children in which children were shown how to tie up people who come and might hurt them . . . A little cage under the bed in which they could hide in case a bad person was coming in the house and a button they could press, so that they could call a community network online.''

Online networks are a source of information and entertainment to Scher, but they are also a threat. In a sense, Scher is threatened by herself. When Josephine Bosma asked her what conclusions she could draw regarding her exposure to online environments, Scher replied, ''I am more full of darkness and doom then ever before.'' She is frank about her fascination with subject matter that could be dangerous if misused or used by the wrong person, and her tendency to work with ideas of security and surveillance comes from this knowledge. Scher's surveillance is not authoritarian. Instead, her projects express a need for community-based security as an alternative to state-based control.

—Aaron Jacobs

SCHIFANO, Mario

Nationality: Italian. **Born:** Homs, Libya, in 1934. **Career:** Painter, lives and works in Rome. **Awards:** Premio Lissone, 1961. **Agent:** Studio Marconi, via Tadino 15. 20124 Milan. **Address:** via del Babuino 51, Rome, Italy.

Individual Exhibitions:

1959 Galleria Appia Antica, Rome
1961 Galleria La Tartaruga, Rome
1963 Galleria dell'Ariete, Milan
Galerie Ileana Sonnabend, Paris
Galerie Odyssia, Rome
1964 Galleria dell'Ariete, Milan
Odyssia Gallery, New York
Galleria Odyssia, Rome
Galleria Il Puto, Turin
1965 Studio Marconi, Milan
Galleria La Tartaruga, Rome
1966 Galleria Il Canale, Venice
Galleria Il Punto, Turin
Studio Marconi, Milan
Galleria Stein, Turin
1967 Galleria La Tartaruga, Rome
Galleria, Stein, Turin
Galleria La Bertesca, Genoa
Galleria Stefanoni, Lecco, Italy
Studio Marconi, Milan
1968 Galleria del Minotauro, Brescia, Italy
Studio Marconi, Milan
1969 Galleria della Chiocciola, Padua
1970 Studio Marconi, Milan
Galleria La Città, Verona
1972 Galleria L'Uomo e L'Arte, Milan
Galleria Soligo, Rome
1973 Galleria Il Gabbiano, Rome
Galleria della Steccata, Rome
Galleria Il Punto, Turin
1974 Galleria Lia Rumma, Naples
Istituto di Storia dell'Arte, University of Parma
Studio Marconi, Milan
1975 Galleria dei Mile, Bergamo, Italy
1984 Palazzo delle Prigioni Vecchie, Venice
Galleria Bergamini, Milan
Galleria Ravagnan, Venice
1985 Galerie Reckermann, Cologne
Italienische Institut, Cologne
1991 Studio Marconi, Milan
1999 Antonio Colombo Gallery, Milan

Selected Group Exhibitions:

1960 *5 Giovani Pittori Romani,* Galleria Il Cancello, Bologna (travelled to Galleria La Salita, Rome)
1962 *The New Realists,* Sidney Janis Gallery, New York
1964 *Carnegie International,* Carnegie Institute, Pittsburgh
1966 *Contemporary Italian Art,* Museum am Ostwall, Dortmund, West Germany (travelled to Moderna Museet, Stockholm)
1969 *Aspekte aus Italien,* Galerie im Taxispalais, Innsbruck (travelled to the Galerie Nachst St. Stephan, Vienna)
1973 *Combattimento per un'Immagine,* Galleria Civica d'Arte Moderna, Turin
1977 *La Traccia del Racconto,* Villa Comunale Ormand, San Remo, Italy
1980 *Arte e Critica,* Galleria Nazionale d'Arte Moderna, Rome
1982 *Arte Italiana 1960–1982,* Hayward Gallery, London
1986 *Aspects of Italian Art 1960–85,* Kunstverein, Frankfurt
1999 *Minimalia, una Linea dell'Arte del XX Secolo,* P.S. 1, New York

Mario Schifano, 1996. ©Sandro Vannini/Corbis.

Biennale di Venezia, Venice, Italy

2000 *The Ark of 2000: 10 Artists Take Us Across to the New Millennium,* Galleria Spazia, Bologna, Italy

From the Visible to the Invisible: The History of the Society Portrait of the 20th Century, Palazzina dei Giardini, Modena, Italy

From the Beatles to Pesce's Armchairs: All the Faces of Pop on Show, Galleria Niccoli, Parma, Italy

Collections:

Galleria Nazionale d'Art; Moderna, Rome; Museu de Arte Moderna, Sao Paolo; Museum of Modern Art, Tokyo.

Publications:

On SCHIFANO: Books—*Schifano,* exhibition catalog by Maurizio Calvesi, Milan 1964; *Schifano,* exhibition catalog by Frank O'Hara, New York 1964; *Schifano,* exhibition catalog by Maurizio Fagiolo, Venice 1966; *Le due avanguardie* by Maurizio Calvesi, Milan 1966; *Mario Schifano,* exhibition catalog by Arturo C. Quintavalle, Vittorio Fagone, and Maurizio Calvesi, Milan 1974; *Mario Schifano: Naturale Sconosciuto,* exhibition catalog, Venice 1984; *Mario Schifano: Bilder und Gouachen 1962–1983,* exhibition catalog, Cologne 1985; *Mario Schifano: una collezione '60/'70* by Maurizio Calvesi, Goffredo Parise and Alberto Moravia, Milan 1990.

* * *

Perceptive observation has always been at the base of Mario Schifano's work. While he is a realistic painter, he has produced pictures that have become known in the range established by the system of theoretical-ideological syntheses or of simplifications (or elaborations) on logical lines. The artist, that is, has not wanted to use his work to give solutions to the problems of real life, nor even to report on its conditions, so much as to counter painting in its density, in the complex web of relationships between the methods of interpreting a picture and its ''use'' for communication. That is why his pictures when completed are deliberately imperfect, with no conclusions and no emphasis on subject matter. Everything in them has to be clearly visible, so that nothing in them has to be explained. They show what is to be seen, and in so doing lead to that logic of communication which—as Wittgenstein emphasizes—allows us to cross the street without being knocked down. Schifano paints what he has observed, and since the world is changing, his art changes with it. It has not been adapted to the times; it is part of time.

In Mario Schifano's pictures everything is reduced to a self-explanatory image, even the captions, which are no more than a picture within a picture, decodified fragments with an autonomous life of their own. The picture is a photograph made by hand, a photogram fixed, filtered and flattened, using a mechanical eye to put distance between man and objects, between the objects and the pictures of them.

An art so carried out takes on a marked objectifying character; the edges of the canvas become the limits of the visible field and the picture the mirror of a fragment of reality in which the presence of the whole is manifested.

The artist represents the diversity of things by means of a realism filtered by the ordinary use of the language of advertising. That is not, of course, to say that his pictures are like advertisements—far from it; they are born of the need to manifest a plurality of aspects within the object represented, which is manipulated by the artist in order to have a relationship with it. In the end the painted canvas acquires an essence, a sort of internal spirit of the objects. It is this desire to get to the bottom of things that lies at the base of the serial and repetitive procedure employed by Schifano, a procedure that has enabled him to give substance to his pictures swiftly, putting them in a state of precarious equilibrium that makes them ''alive'' even before they are finished.

—Demetrio Paparoni

SCHLEMOWITZ, Joel

Nationality: American. **Born:** Madison, Wisconsin, 26 April 1967. **Education:** Apprenticed with filmmaker and New School instructor Arnold Eagle, 1988–1992; Ithaca College, B.A. 1989. **Career:** Began making short experimental films, 1989; began making film installation art, 1995; instructor, New School, New York, 1996—; adjunct professor, The Cooper Union, 1998—. **Awards:** Jerome Foundation grant, 1999; New York State Council on the Arts grant, 1999. **Agent:** The Film-Makers' Cooperative, c/o The Clocktower Gallery, 108 Leonard Street, 13th floor, New York, New York 10013, U.S.A. **Address:** 470 State Street, Brooklyn, New York 11217, U.S.A.

Individual Exhibitions:

1997 *Representative Works,* Millennium Film Workshop, New York
Representative Works, Orgone Cinema, Pittsburgh
1998 *Cineprobe,* Museum of Modern Art, New York
PARAGIM, University of the Arts, Philadelphia
Representative Works, Anthology Film Archives, New York
Garden of Light, Ave. B and East 6th Street Garden, New York
1999 *Three by Joel Schlemowitz,* The Den of Cin, New York
2000 *Fridays @ 5,* New School University, New York
2001 *filmscrolls,* Anthology Film Archives, New York

Group Exhibitions:

1992 Massachusetts Art Institute, Boston
1993 *Gothic,* London Film Festival
1994 *New Experiments,* London Filmmakers' Cooperative, London
1995 *Group Show,* Millennium Film Workshop, New York
1996 *Filmmakers' Forum,* New School for Social Research, New York
1997 *Cinemaki,* Segue Performance Space, New York
1998 *The Filmmakers' Co-optical,* Anthology Film Archives, New York
1999 *Light on Falling Water Writes the Text,* Robert Beck Memorial Cinema, New York
2000 *The American Century,* Whitney Museum of American Art, New York
Synesthesia in Film and Video, University of Rhode Island, Kingston

Public Installations:

Filmboxes, New School for Social Research, New York 1995; *Polyphemus—A Magic Lantern* (video), Millennium Film Workshop, New York 1997; *Gesualdo—A Magic Lantern* (video), Museum of Modern Art, New York 1998; *Garden Piece* (film installation), Ave. B and East 6th Street Garden, New York 1998; *Parathiroscopic Window Picture* (film installation), Cybersapien Entertainment, New York 1999; *A Bridge Crosses the Pond* (film installation), Ukrainian Institute of America, New York 1999.

Publications:

By SCHLEMOWITZ: Books—*The Sayings of St. Tula, the Patron Saint of Film,* 1998.

*

As the words in a poem evoke images, the images in a film may evoke a sense of poetic association. Film remains a tactile medium, like sculpture made of little strips, as well as light and shadow on the screen. I paint, scratch, print, expose film to have it retain a sense of the tactile even in its transformation into the ethereal moving image. I find myself drifting towards the art of the Decadents and Symbolists; the age of the birth of cinema and the Nineteenth Century's proto-cinema of the Magic Lantern and Panorama.

—Joel Schlemowitz

* * *

SCHMIDT, Julius

Nationality: American. **Born:** Stamford, Connecticut, 2 June 1923. **Education:** Oklahoma A&M University, Stillwater, 1950–51; Cranbrook Academy of Art, Bloomfield Hills, Michigan, 1951–55, B.F.A. 1952, M.F.A. 1955; studied with Ossip Zadkine, in Paris, 1953, and at the Accademia di Belle Arti, Florence, 1954. **Military Service:** Served with the United States Navy, in the Pacific, during World War II. **Career:** Independent sculptor, since 1955: lives and works in Iowa City. Chairman of Sculpture, Kansas City Art Institute, Missouri, 1955–59; taught at Rhode Island School of Design, Providence, 1959–60, and University of California, Berkeley, 1961–62;

Joel Schlemowitz: scene from the film *Invitation to a Voyage* (16mm, 4 minutes), 1997. ©Joel Schlemowitz.

Head of the Department of Sculpture, Cranbrook Academy of Art, 1962–69; Head of the Department of Sculpture, University of Iowa, Iowa City, 1970–93. **Awards:** Guggenheim Fellowship, 1963; Lifetime Achievement Award in Sculpture, International Sculpture Center, 1998. **Agent:** Gallery K, R Street N.W., Washington, D.C. 20036. **Address:** 5 Highview Knoll NE, Iowa City, Iowa 52240–9149, U.S.A.

Individual Exhibitions:

1953 Silvermine Guild of Artists, New Canaan, Connecticut
1957 Kansas City Art Institute, Missouri
1958 Nelson Gallery, Kansas City, Missouri
1961 Santa Barbara Museum of Art, California
Otto Gerson Gallery, New York
1962 University of California, Berkeley
1963 Otto Gerson Gallery, New York
1964 Franklin Siden Gallery, Detroit
1966 Marlborough-Gerson Gallery, New York
Kansas City Art Institute, Missouri
Taudega College, Alabama
1967 Gertrude Kasle Gallery, Detroit
1969 Cranbrook Academy of Art, Bloomfield Hills, Michigan
1971 Marlborough Gallery, New York
Madison College, Virginia
1972 Gertrude Kasle Gallery, Detroit
1974 University of Iowa Museum of Art, Iowa City (retrospective)
Gertrude Kasle Gallery, Detroit
Rockford College, Illinois
1980 Swope Art Gallery, Terre Haute, Indiana
1981 Augusta College, Georgia
1984 Monmouth College, Illinois
1985 Sheldon Swope Art Gallery, Terre Haute, Indiana
1987 University Hospital, Iowa City

Selected Group Exhibitions:

1958 *6 American Sculptors,* Arts Club of Chicago
1959 *16 Americans,* Museum of Modern Art, New York
1960 *Aspects of American Sculpture,* Galerie Claude Bernard, Paris
1962 *The Hirshhorn Collection,* Guggenheim Museum, New York
1963 *Bienal,* Sao Paulo
Sculpture in the Open Air, Battersea Park, London
1964 *American Vision,* Marlborough-Gerson Gallery, New York
1966 *Lipman Collection,* Whitney Museum, New York
1973 *Biennial,* Middleheim Park, Antwerp

Julius Schmidt: *Untitled,* 1966. ©State of New York/Corbis.

1983 *Iron Cast/Cast Iron,* Pratt Gallery, New York (travelled to Washington, D.C.)

Collections:

Museum of Modern Art, New York; Whitney Museum, New York; Albright-Knox Art Gallery, Buffalo, New York; Detroit Institute of Arts; Art Institute of Chicago; Walker Art Center, Minneapolis; Nelson Gallery, Kansas City, Missouri; Hirshhorn Museum, Washington D.C.; Princeton Museum of Art, New Jersey; Santa Barbara Museum of Art, California; Krannert Art Museum, Urbana; Walker Art Center, Minneapolis.

Publications:

On SCHMIDT: Books—*16 Americans,* exhibition catalog, New York 1959; *Concise History of Modern Sculpture* by Herbert Read, London 1964; *Art in Architecture* by Redstone, New York 1968; *American Sculpture in Process 1930–1970,* New York 1975; *The Metaphorical Imagery of Julius Schmidt* by Robert D. Kinsman, New York 1985.

*

On the Machine Form: Images that involve the insoluble problem of technology/humanity—concern with the measure of civilized society and the pursuit of technology.

On Cast Iron: The reasons for working with cast iron are numerous and complex. Conscious, subconscious, atavistic, inherited—one does not always know what directs one's efforts. However, there remains the strong, persistent desire to use the material—to engage in the ritual aspects of melting and pouring, events the evoke countless associations deeply linked in the mind.

—Julius Schmidt

SCHNABEL, Julian

Nationality: American. **Born:** Brooklyn, New York, 1951; raised partly in Brownsville, Texas. **Education:** Universty of Houston, 1969–72, B.F.A. 1972; Whitney Museum Independent Study Program, New York, 1973. **Family:** Married Jacqualine Beaurang (divorced), three children; married model Olatz Lo-pez Garmendia, children: Olmo and Cy. **Career:** Did odd jobs and worked as a cab driver in New York in the mid-1970s; returned to Texas for a year, then travelled to Europe and back to New York; worked as a cook in Locale Restaurant, Greenwich Village; travelled in France and Italy 1976, and in Spain, Italy and Germany, 1978. **Address:** c/o Pace Gallery New York, 32 E 57th Street, Floor 4, New York, New York, 10022–2530.

Individual Exhibitions:

1976 Contemporary Art Museum, Houston
1978 Galerie December, Dusseldorf
1979 Mary Boone Gallery, New York (2 exhibitions)
Daniel Weinberg Gallery, San Francisco
1980 Bruno Bischofberger, Zurich
1981 Mary Boone and Leo Castelli Galleries, New York (joint exhibition)
Margo Leavin Gallery, Los Angeles
Schnabel/Rothenberg/Moskowitz, Kunsthalle, Basel (travelled to the Kunstverein, Frankfurt, and the Louisiana Museum, Humlebaek, Denmark)
1982 Stedelijk Museum, Amsterdam (retrospective)
Mary Boone Gallery, New York
Tate Gallery, London
1983 Galerie Bischofberger, Zurich
Castelli Graphics, New York
Akron Art Museum, Ohio
Galerie Daniel Templon, Paris
Galleria Mario Diacono, Rome
Waddington Galleries, London
1984 Akira Ikeda Gallery, Tokyo
Galerie Bischofberger, Zurich
Pace Gallery, New York
1985 Galerie Bischofberger, Zurich
Galleria Sperone, Rome
Waddington Galleries, London
1986 Whitechapel Art Gallery, London (travelled to Paris; toured the United States, 1987–88)
Pace Gallery, New York
1988 *Julian Schnabel,* Israel Museum, Jerusalem (catalog)

Julian Schnabel, ca. 2001. ©Rufus F. Folkks/Corbis.

Julian Schnabel: Crows Flying the Black Flag of Themselves, Sarah Campbell Blaffer Gallery, University of Houston (catalog)

1989 *Julian Schnabel,* Museo d'Arte Contemporanea Luigi Pecci, Prato, Italy (catalog)
Julian Schnabel: Fox Farm Paintings, Pace Gallery, New York (catalog)
Julian Schnabel: New Works, Musée d'Art Contemporain, Bordeaux, France (catalog)
Julian Schnabel: Works on Paper 1975–88, Museum fur Gegenwartskunst, Basel (catalog)

1992 *Julian Schnabel,* Pace Gallery, New York (catalog)

1996 Galleria d'Arte Moderna, Bologna (traveled to Turin) (catalog)
Julian Schnabel: The Conversion of St. Paolo Malfi, the Pink Blouse That I Like the Most, Pink Paintings, Jablonka Galerie, Cologne (catalog)

1997 PaceWildenstein, New York (catalog)

1998 PaceWildenstein, New York
Whitney Museum of American Art, New York (retrospective)
South London Gallery, London

2000 Galerie Forsblom, Helsinki
Galeria Ramis Barquet, Mexico City

2001 Galleria Cardi, Milan

Selected Group Exhibitions:

1977 *Surogate/Self Portraits,* Holly Solomon Gallery, New York

1980 *L'Amerique aux Independants,* Grand Palais, Paris
Painting and Sculpture Today, Indianapolis Museum of Art

1981 *Whitney Biennial,* Whitney Museum, New York
A New Spirit in Painting, Royal Academy, London
Figurative Aspects of Recent Art, Massachusetts Institute of Techonology, Cambridge

1982 *Focus on the Figure,* Whitney Museum, New York

1984 *Legendes,* Musée d'Art Contemporain, Bordeaux, France

1986 *Carnegie International,* Carnegie Institute, Pittsburgh

1990 *The Last Decade: American Artists of the 80s,* Tony Shafrazi Gallery, New York (catalog)
Culture and Commentary: An Eighties Perspective, Hirshhorn Museum and Sculpture Garden, Washington, D.C. (catalog)
Gifts of the Associates: 1975–1990, Museum of Modern Art, New York (catalog)

1992 *Sculpture,* Waddington Galleries, London (catalog)

1993 *Steps in Time,* Wilhelm-Hack-Museum, Ludwigshafen, Germany (catalog)

1994 *From Beyond the Pale,* Irish Museum of Modern Art, Dublin (catalog)
Printer, Galerie Graff, Montreal (catalog)

1996 *Picasso: A Contemporary Dialogue,* Galerie Thaddaeus Ropac, Paris (catalog)
Waddington Galleries, London (catalog)

1997 *American Art: A Selection from the Waddington Galleries,* London (traveled to Chicago, Basel and Paris) (catalog)
47th Biennale, Venice

1999 *Bad-Bad: That Is a Good Excuse,* Staatliche Kunsthalle Baden-Baden, Germany (catalog)

Publications:

By SCHNABEL: Book—*C.V.J.: Nicknames of Maitre d's and Other Excerpts from Life,* New York 1986. **Articles—**Interview with David Bowie in *Modern Painters* (London), vol. 11, no. 4, Winter 1998. **Films—***Basquiat,* 1996; *Before Night Falls,* 2000. **Recording—** *Every Silver Lining Has a Cloud,* 1995.

On SCHNABEL: Books—*Julian Schnabel,* exhibition catalog with text by Wilfried Dickhoff, New York 1986; *Julian Schnabel: Paintings 1975–1986,* exhibition catalog with essay by Thomas McEvilley, London 1986; *Julian Schnabel* by Remo Guidieri, Bordeaux 1990. **Articles—**''2 Painters Explores New Wave'' by Hilton Kramer in the *New York Times,* 17 April 1981; ''Is Julian Schnabel That Good'' by John Perreault in the *Soho News* (New York), 22 April 1981; ''The Ardor of Ambition'' by Peter Schjeldahl in the *Village Voice* (New York), 23 February 1982; ''Julian Schnabel'' by Cathleen McGuigan in *Artnews* (New York), Summer 1982; ''Julian Schnabel: The Artist as Entrepreneur'' by Robert Hughes in *Modern Painters* (London), vol. 1, no. 1, Spring 1988; ''Off the Canvas: The Art of Julian Schnabel Survives the Wreckage of the Eighties'' by Michael Stone in *New York,* 18 May 1992; ''Julian Schnabel at Pace'' by Meyer Raphael Rubinstein in *Art in America,* September 1992; ''American Art: The Good, the Bad and Julian Schnabel: UnAmerican Activities'' by David Lee and Paul Jeromack in *Art Review,* vol. 45, November 1993; ''The Big Picture'' by Susan Orlean in *New Yorker,* 24 July 1995; ''Julian Schnabel's Excellent Adventure'' by Annie Leibovitz in *Vogue,* February 1996; ''Big'' by James Kaplan in *New York,* 12 August 1996; ''Julian Schnabel: Plate Paintings, 1978–1997'' by Roberta Smith in *New York Times,* 21 May 1999; ''A Painter's Latest Cinematic Collage'' by Don Shewey in *New York Times,* 5 November 2000.

* * *

Julian Schnabel's rapid and controversial rise to critical focus—if not acclaim—has been taken as an emblem of the art world's present search for new form-givers, the equal of those who arose in earlier decades, so that his appearance and the nature of his work itself may be taken as emblem of the unstable nature of avant-gardist visual culture—subject to media exploitation, and itself quite willing to manipulate its image for the purpose of commerce under the guise of the promulgation of an authentic aesthetic discovery or extension.

Schnabel's collage mode, both in its literal materiality and in its multi-style references and clear homage to artists of the recent past, is a characteristic mark of the electic drift of the early 1980s. His special contribution to such stylistic uneasiness, and the general primitivizing and nervously mannered neo-expressionistic mode, may be his clearly kitsch approach—his appropriation of cliché seemingly without an ironic or distancing stance. Although the latter and traditional modernist attitude toward such material may be implict in his usual ambitiously bombastic images—best known have been the work with shards of china imbedded in the impasto ground and his use of velvet as ground—nonetheless, Schnabel's intense and deliberate mindless presentations, as well as his religious and sexual aura, does not lend itself to such objectivity. (''the emotive effect arises less from the image, which is not immediately dicepherable, than from an audacious stylistc performance . . . evoking the conflicted drama of delusionary omnipotence undermined by self-protective ambivalence.''—D. Wheeler).

The fear and wariness of many critics has been apparently the clear index in such works to the weakening of the older avant-gardist distinction of high and low culture; and thus if such work as Schnabel's is the further truimph of a Pop Art, it is now cynically and exhaustedly stripped of both the optimism and the clear striving for personal expressiveness within older recent art.

In recent exhibitions, he continues his longtime extravagance in scale, subject, and hyper-elaborate titling, and as well in a bravura handling of material, but there has been a dampening of the horror vacui which led to the earlier surface encrustation, and the mid-1980s works have a more resolved appearance. Also, Schnabel's celebration if his own celebrity and his seeming exultation of the banal culminated, for the time being, in the publication of a memoir *C.V.J.: Nicknames of Maitre d's and Other Excerpts from Life.* There is now a greater confidence in pictorial invention, and so line and shape appear openly and are stamped with authority. Still, his work continues to be read as if it were a body of sophisticated juvenalia, somehow trivializing both theme and performance through lack of justification for either.

Critical focus has been constant upon this psycho-social aspect of his career for some time: his self-conscious attempt to present his art and persona as mythic and thus create at only the extremities. If his neo-expressionist paintings from the later 1970s on were thereby, bathetic and anxiety-ridden, their more current dependence upon an easier decorative command may yield an oeuvre less temporal in its appeal.

The filmmaking debut of two other major 1980s visual artists—David Salle, with *Search and Destroy,* and Robert Longo, with *Johnny Mnemonic*—perhaps directly influenced Schnabel when he directed and co-wrote *Basquiat* in 1997. Schnabel himself did not appear in the film, but placed himself close to the legendary graffiti artist of the title. He has acknowledged the powerful aura of film for his own painting career, if not as well his life. He is said to live with the intense grandiosity of *The Godfather,* which he has viewed many times. One of his children is even named Vito.

Schnabel's energies through the latter half of the 1990s continued to be fixated upon filmmaking. He concentrated on the expatriate Cuban poet and writer Reinaldo Arenas, making the film *Before Night Falls.* The film's tight collage and sensuous imagery—closely allied then to the look of Schnabel's paintings—were deemed successful. In 1995 he had released his own CD, *Every Silver Lining Has a Cloud*; on it Schnabel sings his own country rock songs. These activities may reflect the possibly-more-widespread-than-acknowledged feeling in the visual art community that a career with only traditional painting production is an unfufilled creativity.

Schnabel has continued to produce the large paintings—''overly large,'' say critics who have continued their enduring carping at his work. ''. . . [H]is earlier plate paintings are frequently incoherent . . . his imagery was rarely up to the challenge . . . and his development since then has not clarified their promise,'' wrote *New York Times* critic Roberta Smith in 1999. Recent works continued the earlier established image, highly abstracted and fragmented, with words inserted at times. He has also retained his now-signature insertion of ceramic plate shards into the paintings' surfaces.

—Joshua Kind

SCHNEEMANN, Carolee

Nationality: American. **Born:** Fox Chase, Pennsylvania, 12 October 1939. **Education:** Studied at the University of Illinois, Urbana; Bard College, Annandale-on-Hudson, New York; Columbia University School of Painting and Sculpture, New York; New School for Social Research, New York; Universidad de Puebla, Mexico. **Family:** Married the artist Anthony McCall in 1972. **Career:** Independent artist, New York, since 1962; founder-director, Kinetic Theater movement and design workshops, New York, 1963–68; founder-member, with Joseph Kosuth, Anthony McCall and others, International-Local group, New York, 1976. Art instructor, University of Illinois, Urbana, 1961–62; artist-in-residence, Colby College, Maine, 1968, and Dartington College, Totnes, Devon, 1972. **Awards:** Performance Grant, Benedict Arnold Foundation, New York, 1964; Writers grant, Croton Press, New York, 1968; New York State Council on the Arts Grant, 1968, 1974, 1975, 1976, 1977; Cassandra Foundation Grant, New York, 1970; National Endowment for the Arts Grant, Washington, D.C., 1974, 1977, 1978, 1983, 1985; New York Foundation for the Arts Grant, 1974, 1977, 1978, 1987; Creative Artist Public Service Grant, New York, 1978; Art Matters Inc. Grant, New York, 1986; Guggenheim Fellowship, 1993; Pollock-Krasner

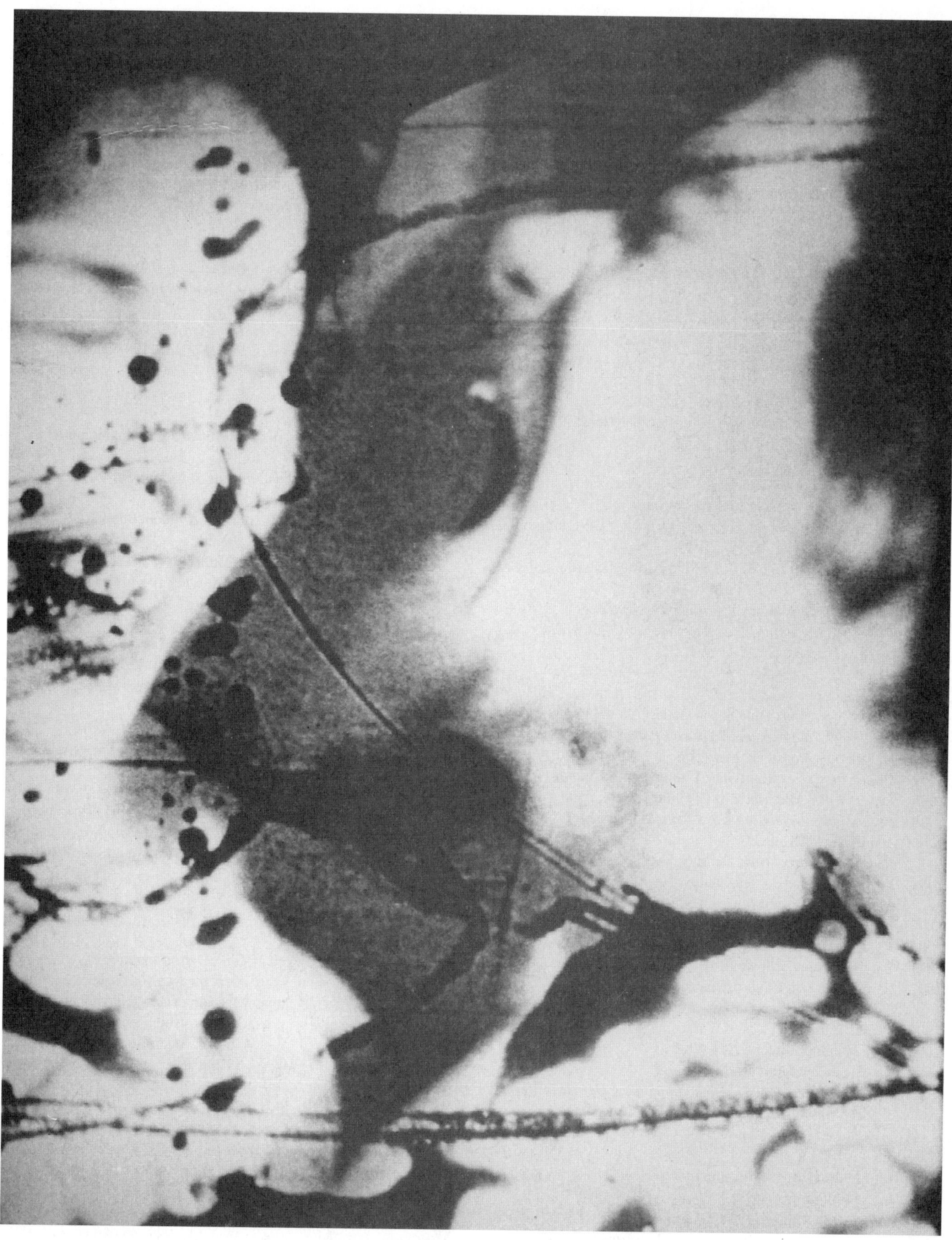

Carolee Schneemann: a scene from her film *Fuses*, 1965. ©2001 Carolee Schneemann/Artists Rights Society (ARS), New York.

Foundation Grant, 1996. **Address:** 114 West 29th Street, New York, New York 10001, U.S.A.

Individual Exhibitions:

1962 *Mink Paws Turret,* Artist's Studio, New York
1963 *Eye Body,* Artist's Studio, New York
1964 *Environment,* Artist's Studio, New York
1969 *Performance Drawing and Photo/Collage,* Chelsea School of Art, London
1973 *Performance Drawings and Photo/Collage,* Camden Art Centre, London
1974 *Up to and Including Her Limits,* University of California, Berkeley
1976 *Up to and Including Her Limits,* Studiogalerie, West Berlin
Up to and Including Her Limits, The Kitchen, New York
1977 Galerie de Appel, Amsterdam
Multiples, Archives Francesco Conz, Italy
1979 *ABC: We Print Anything/In the Cards,* Galerie de Appel, Amsterdam
Forbidden Actions, C. Space, New York
Bard College, Annandale-on-Hudson, New York
1980 *Dirty Pictures,* A.I.R. Gallery, New York
1981 *Image/Texts,* Washington Project for the Arts, Washington, D.C.
Image/Texts and Debris Grid, Real Artways, Hartford, Connecticut
1982 *Early Work,* Max Hutchinson Gallery, New York
1983 *Works on Paper,* Rutgers University, New Brunswick, New Jersey
Image/Text, Colby-Sewer College, New London, New Hampshire
Recent Work, Max Hutchinson Gallery, New York
1984 *Performed Paintings and Works on Paper,* Kleinert Gallery, Woodstock, New York
Cycles-Re-Cycles, Kent State University, Ohio
1985 *Recent Work,* Max Hutchinson Gallery, New York
1986 *Performance Notebooks and Scores,* University of California at Los Angeles
Recent and Early Work, Henri Gallery, Washington, D.C.
1988 *Self-Shot,* Emily Harvey Gallery, New York
New Rituals, Boston Museum School of Fine Arts, Massachusetts
1990 *Cycladic Imprints,* Emily Harvey Gallery, New York
1991 San Francisco Art Institute
1992 Randolph Street Gallery, Chicago
Tangeman Fine Arts Gallery, University of Cincinnati
1994 Penine Hart Gallery, New York
1996 Elga Wimmer Gallery, New York
Galerie Samuel Lallouz, Montreal
Carolee Schneemann: Up to and Including Her Limits, New Museum of Contemporary Art, New York (catalog)

Happenings and Performances include:

Labyrinths, Sidney, Illinois, 1960; *Glass Environment for Sound and Motion,* Living Theater, New York, 1962; *Chromolodeon,* Judson Dance Theater, New York, 1963; *Meat Joy,* at *Festival de la Libre Expression,* Paris, Dennison Hall, London, and Judson Church, New York, 1964; *Water Light/Water Needle,* St. Mark's Church, New York, 1966; *Snows,* Martinique Theatre, New York, 1967; *Object in Process,* Something Else Gallery, New York, 1968; *Expansions,* Round House, London, 1969; *Film/Action Theatre,* Paradiso Theatre, Amsterdam, 1971; *Interior Scroll,* East Hampton, Long Island, New York 1975; *Fresh Blood: A Dream Morphology,* Real Artways, Hartford, Connecticut, 1981; *Mother Lexicon,* 12th International Sound Poetry Festival, Washington Square Church, New York, 1982; *Dirty Pictures,* San Francisco Art Institute, 1985; *Cat Scan,* Beyond Baroque, Venice, California, 1987; *Skewed Beams* and *''The Delirious Arousal of Destruction'' or ''Is There a Feminist Erotic Iconography,''* Aspects of Performance Art, Canadian Centre of the Arts at Owen Sound, 1991; *Enter . . . Vulva,* Institute for Contemporary Art/P.S. 1 Museum, New Yor, 1994; *Made/Enacted,* University of British Columbia, 1995; *Your Dog My Cat or Delirious Arousal of Destruction,* Porin Taidemuseo, Pori, Finland, 1998.

Selected Group Exhibitions:

1982 *A Decade of Women's Performance Art,* Contemporary Art Center, New Orleans
Labyrinth of Self-Consciousness, Narodowe, Warsaw (travelled to Lodz and Wroclaw)
Blam! Pop, Minimalism and Performance 1958–64, Whitney Museum, New York
1986 *The Heroic Female,* Ceres Gallery, New York
1988 *Apollo, Dionysius and Job,* Alternative Museum, New York
1990 *Biennale,* Venice
1993 *Neo-Dada,* Whitney Museum, New York
Abject Art, Whitney Museum, New York
1995 *In the Spirit of Fluxus,* Walker Art Center, Minneapolis (travelled throughout the United States)
Hors Limites, Centre Georges Pompidou
Feminin/Masculin: le Sexe de L'art, Centre Georges Pompidou
1999 *The American Century: Art and Culture, 1900–2000,* Whitney Museum of American Art, New York (catalog)
The End: An Independent Vision of Contemporary Culture, 1982–2000, Exit Art/The First World, New York (catalog)

Collections:

Museum of Modern Art, New York; Detroit Institute of Arts, Michigan; Institute of Contemporary Art, Chicago; Los Angeles Institute of Contemporary Art; Cincinnati Museum of Art, Ohio; Contemporary Archives, University of Massachusetts, Amherst; Krannert Art Gallery, University of Illinois, Urbana; Institute of Contemporary Arts, London.

Publications:

By SCHNEEMANN: Books—*Parts of a Body House Book,* Cullompton, Devon 1972; *Cezanne, She Was a Great Painter,* New York 1974, 1976; *ABC: We Print Anything—In the Cards,* Beuningen, Netherlands 1977; *More Than Meat Joy: Complete Performance Works and Selected Writing,* New York 1979, second edition, 1997; *Early and Recent Work,* with text by J. Ballerini and Ted Castle, New

York 1983; *The Ekstatic Body as a Source of Knowledge,* New York 1996; *Imaging Her Erotics: Carolee Schneemann, Essays, Interviews, Projects,* Boston 2001.

On SCHNEEMANN: Books—*A Primer of Happenings and Time/Space Art* by Al Hansen, New York 1966; *Technicians of the Sacred,* edited by Jerome Rothenberg, Garden City, New York 1967; *Happening und Fluxus* by Harald Szemann and Hans Sohm, Cologne 1970; *Art and Life: The Function of Intermedia* by Udo Kultermann, New York 1970; *Environments, Happenings, Performance* by Adrian Henri, London 1974; *Performance Art* by Roselee Gobberg, London 1978; *Judson Dance Theater: 1962–1966,* edited by Wendy Perron and Daniel Cameron, Bennington, Vermont 1981; *The Amazing Decade: Women and Performance Art 1970–1980,* edited by Maria Roth, Los Angeles 1982; *Carolee Schneeman: Early and Recent Work* by Frederick Ted Castle and Julia Ballerini, New York 1983; *The Object of Performance: The American Avant-Grade Since 1970* by Henry Sayre, Chicago 1987; *Technicians of Ekstasy: Shamanism and the Modern Artist,* Norwalk 1993; *Imagining Erotics* by Jay Murphy, Cambridge 1995; *Carolee Schneeman* by Kristine Stiles, Baltimore 1995; *A Body of Vision: Representations of the Body in Recent Film and Poetry* by R. Bruce Elder, Waterloo, Ontario 1998.

* * *

Performance art found its culmination in its early phase of development, in the works of Carolee Schneemann. Her early performances were documentations of a new view of art in general, continuing the traditionally separated disciplines of painting, sculpture, film and real life events. Merging these disciplines new modalities were explored which resulted in a new autonomous medium. Female sensibility which had never been articulated with radical clarity is related to the inauguration and establishment of this medium. In addition to her creative work Carolee Schneemann is also one of the most intelligent and perceptive critics of the art of our time.

Born in 1939 in Fox Chase, Pennsylvania, Carolee Schneemann studied painting in Urbana, Illinois, New York, and Puebla, Mexico. She also worked with dancers like Trisha Brown, Deborah Hay and Yvonne Rainer, filmmakers like Stan Brakhage and artists like Robert Morris and Claes Oldenburg. Her early work *Eye body* of 1963 grew out of the artistic climate in New York, and with it she established her own independent contribution to contemporary art. The artist herself is made part of the environment, and the interaction of materials, living snakes, human bodies and a feminist strategy constitutes something which in this combination did not exist before.

One year after this important event a fundamental breakthrough took place in Schneemann's *Meat Joy,* performed in May 1964 in Paris, then in London and in New York. With this work the course of performance art took a different direction. *Meat Joy* was based on a dream-like sequence of movements of the participants, who were not actors or dancers in the traditional sense, but participants of a new medium. A choreography of a different kind was established which encompassed psychological and physical relationships, resulting in an erotic ritual in which the newly achieved structures of freedom, orgiastic exuberance and vitality were manifest.

Since 1964 Carolee Schneemann has expanded her work into several directions: the film *Fuses* of 1964 in which the artist was both filmmaker and participant is an artistic celebration of the sexual act. Gene Youngblood described it as ''a film which breaks the barriers between the private and public subject matter. From her background as a painter, Schneemann was free to explore the physical-visual contexts of sexuality in rhythmic layers of collaged imagery.''

In 1966 the event *Water Light/Water Needle* explored the human body in the context of natural forces; *Kitchs Last Meal* of 1973–1978 was a celebration of a relationship between the artist and her cat; *Thames Crawling* of 1970 is a vital choreography of bodies in movement.

Around 1973, Carolee Schneemann entered yet another phase of her developement which went even further in directly relating the personal life of the artist to her work. *Up to and Including Her Limits* of 1973 is a typical example: the artist hangs from a rope for extended durations swinging in limited directions as she marks the floor and walls with chalks. The work is a brilliant document of artistic activity itself. *Interior Scroll* of 1975 continues these tendencies to its most radical consequences; it creates a powerful symbol in which the body of the artist and literary tradition of knowledge are united. Standing on a stage the artist reads from a scroll which she slowly pulls out of her vagina. The artist wrote about this work: ''I saw the vagina as translucent chamber of which the serpent was on outmoded model: enlivened by its passages the visible to the invisible, a spiraled coil ringed with the shape of desire and generative mysteries, attribute of both female and male sexual powers.''

Carolee Schneemann's recent actions and performances, which are parallel—as in all phases of her work—to her paintings, sculptures, collages and environments, continue to explore more complex idiosyncrasies of life and art, the rational and the emotional, male and female sensibilities. In her *Venus Vectors-Abstract,* first installed in the Everson Museum of Art in Syracuse in 1987, the artist built an environmental sculpture encompassing her 1983 performance *Fresh Blood—A Dream Morphology,* combining visual, acoustical, electronic as well as action and viewer participation into a universal work of art, all elements merging into a symbolic language of high intensity.

The activities of Carolee Schneemann in recent years have intensely extended to teaching and publishing, among them courses on performance art and filmmaking, both technical and conceptual, at various universities. In a class description about ''Missing Precedents: Woman and Creativity'' of 1994 Schneemann wrote: ''The full history of women's innovative creativity has been demeaned, destroyed or buried away.'' Her teaching as well as the revised second edition of her pioneering work *More Than Meat Joy* of 1997 are most important to correct this view. In her most recent book, *Imaging Her Erotics,* Schneemann gives a creative synthesis of her concepts.

—Udo Kultermann

SCHÖFFER, Nicolas

Nationality: French. **Born:** Kalosca, Hungary, 6 September, 1912; immigrated to France, 1936: naturalized, 1948. **Education:** School of Fine Arts, Budapest, 1932–35; Ecole des Beaux-Arts, Paris, 1936–39. **Family:** Marguerite Orlhac in 1945 (died, 1970); married Elenore de Lavandeyra in 1971. **Career:** Agricultural worker, Auvergne 1941–42, 1944–45; foundry worker, Saint-Etienne, 1943; hotel night porter,

Paris, 1946–47; doll-factory worker, Paris, 1949–51. Independent artist, Paris since 1948; first ''spatiodynamic'' sculpture, 1948; first cybernic sculpture, 1955; ''luminodynamic'' works, from 1957; ''chronodynamic'' works, from 1959; video-art works, from 1961; musical researches, from 1977; instructor in art and programming, Ecole Nationale Supérieure des Beaux-Arts, Paris, 1966–71; visiting lecturer, McGill University, Montreal 1970; Université de Bruxelles, 1971; Cité Universitaire, Neuchatel, Switzerland, 1972; Sorbonne, Paris 1972, 1977; French Institute, Athens 1974; Ecole des Beaux-Arts, Orleans, 1975; and the Kunstakademie, Stuttgart, 1977. Nicolas Schöffer Museum, Kalosca, Hungary, established 1980. **Awards:** Grand Prix, *Biennale* Venice, 1968; First Prize, *Henry Moore Exhibition,* Hakone Museum, Japan, 1980; Frank J. Malina/Leonardo Prize, San Francisco, 1986; member, Académie des Beaux-Arts, Paris, 1982; Officier, Ordre des Arte et des Lettres; Officier, Légion d'Honneur; Ordre du drapeau, Budapest. **Agent:** Artcurial, 9 Avenue Matignon, 75008 Paris. **Died:** 8 January 1992.

Individual Exhibitions:

1950 Galerie des Deux-Iles, Paris
1952 Galerie Mai, Paris
1957 Theatre d'Evruex, France (spatiodynamic spectacle)
Grand Central Station, New York (spatiodynamic spectacle)
1958 Galerie Denise René, Paris
1960 Institute of Contemporary Arts, London
1961 Palais des Beaux-Arts Brussels
1963 Musée des Arts Décoratifs, Paris (retrospective)
Theatre de la Cité, Lyon-Villeurbanne, France (with Roger Planchot)
1964 *Ruimte/Licht/Tijd,* Stedelijk Museum, Amsterdam
Stedlijk Van Abbemuseum, Eindhoven, Netherlands
1965 Jewish Museum, New York (with Jean Tinguely; travelled to the Washington Gallery of Modern Art; and the Carnegie Institute, Pittsburgh)
1966 Galerie Denise René, Paris
1968 Waddell Gallery, New York
Kinetische Plastiakk/Licht/Raum/Bewegung, Kunsthalle, Dusseldorf
Hamburg Oper (luminodynamic spectacle at Menotti/ Nikolais ballet)
1969 Galerie Denise René, Paris
Henie-Onstad Kunstsenter, Oslo
Musée d'Art Moderne, Paris (audio-visual spectacle)
1970 Fundacion Mendoza, Caracas
Spanodynamisme/Luminodynamisme/Chronodynamisme/ Cybernetique: Recherches de 1948 à 1970, Galerie Denise René, Paris
1971 Cercle Noroit, Arras, France
1972 Denise René Gallery, New York
Cité Universitaire, Neuchatel, Switzerland
1973 Kunstmuseum, Aarau, Switzerland
Hamburg Oper (cybernetic spectacle; with Pierre Henry and Alwin Nikolais) Maison de la Culture, Chalon-sur-Saône, France
Centro Industria Montedison, Milan
1974 Galeria Arte/Contacto, Caracas
Musée d'Art Moderne de la Ville, Paris
1975 Galerie Denise René, Paris
Galerie Denise René/Hans Mayer, Dusseldorf
Artcurial, Paris
1977 Kunstmuseum, Bonn
1978 Maison de la Culture, Chatou, France
1979 Centre Culturel Suedois, Paris (concert performance)
1980 Nicolas Schöffer Museum, Kalocsa, Hungary (inaugural exhibition)
1982 Artcurial, Paris
Mucsarnok/Museum of Modern Art, Budapest
1984 Cathedral of Kalocsa, Hungary
IRCAM, Paris

Selected Group Exhibitions:

1956 *Festival d'Art Avant-Garde,* Habitation Le Corbusier, Marseilles
1965 *Kinetic and Optic Art Today,* Albright-Knox Art Gallery, Buffalo, New York
1968 *Biennale,* Venice
1970 *Expo 70,* Osaka, Japan
1971 *Biennale de Paris,* Parc Floral, Paris
1975 *Festival d'Automme,* Chapelle de la Sorbonne, Paris
1977 *Biennale de la Tapisserie,* Lausanne
1981 *Paris-Paris,* Centre Georges Pompidou, Paris
1983 *Electra,* Musée d'Art Moderne, Paris
1987 *Digital Visions: Computers and Art,* Everson Art Museum, Syracuse, New York

Collections:

Nicolas Schöffer Museum, Kalocsa, Hungary; Centre Georges Pompidou, Paris; Musée de Plein air, Paris; Musée de la Tapisserie, Beauvais, France; Museum of Modern Art, Tel-Aviv; Galleria Nazionale d'Arte Moderna, Rome; Office Européen des Brevets, Munich; City Administration Centre, Bonn; Embarcadero Center, San Francisco; Hakone Open Air Museum, Tokyo.

Publications:

By SCHÖFFER: Books—*Le spatiodynamisme,* Boulognesur-Seine 1955; *La ville cybernetique,* Paris 1969; *Le nouvel esprit artistique,* Paris 1970; *Entretiens avec Nicolas Schöffer,* with Philippe Sers, Paris 1971; *La tour lumiére cybernetique,* Paris 1973; *La nouvelle charte de la ville,* Paris 1974; *Art et société,* porfolio, with text by Jean Louis Ferrier, Paris 1976; *Perturbation et chronocratie,* Paris 1978; *Sur l'amenagement du temps—essai de chronogenie,* with others, Paris 1981; *Discours d'election a l'Académie des Beaux-Arts,* Paris 1984; *Temps et programmation, temps libre,* Paris 1985. **Films—***Fer Chaud,* with Jacques Brissot, 1957; *Spatiodynamisme,* with Langlois, 1958; *Mayola,* with gruel, 1958; *Variations luminodynamigues I,* with Jean Kerchbron, 1961; *Astronomie,* with Guy Job, 1969; *Klydex*

I, with Klaus Lindemann, 1973; *Variations luminodynmiques 2,* with Hermann, 1974; *Variations luminodynamiques 3,* with Rainai, 1981. **Record—***Hommage à Bartok,* Budapest 1979.

On SCHÖFFER: Books—*Nicolas Schöffer,* exhibition catalog with text by Raymond Bayer, Paris 1950; *Schöffer,* exhibition catalog with text by Michel Seuphor, Paris 1952; *Schöffer,* exhibition catalog with text by Marcel Brion, Paris 1958; *The Sculpture of This Century* by Michel Seuphor, New York 1959; *Schöffer,* exhibition catalog with texts by Jean Cassour and Guy Habasque, London 1960; *Nicolas Schöffer* by Guy Habasque and Jacques Menetrier, Neuchâtel, Switzerland 1963; *Schöffer,* exhibition catalog with texts by Jean Cassou and Guy Habasque, Amsterdam 1964; *The Nature and Art of Motion* by Gyorgy Kepes, New York 1965; *4 Essays in Kinetic Art* by Frank Popper, Reg Gadney, Stephen Bann and Philip Steadman, London 1966; *Naissance de l'art cinetique* by Frank Popper, Paris 1967; *Nicolas Schöffer: kinetische Plastik/Licht/Raum/Bewegung,* exhibition catalog with texts by Karl Rughrberg and Frank Popper, Dusseldorf 1968; *Man and His Images—A Way of Seeing* by Georgina Oeri, New York 1968; *Nicolas Schöffer: Spatiodynamisme/ Luoninodynamisme/Chronodynamisme/Cybernetique: recherches de 1948 à 1970,* exhibition catalog with text by Philippe Sers, Paris 1970; *La Tour Lumiére Cybernetique de Nicolas Schöffer* by Jacky Mandin, Paris 1972; *Nicolas Schöffer,* exhibition catalog with text by Frank Passoni, Milan 1973; *Nicolas Schöffer,* exhibition catalog with texts by Eleanore de Lavandeyra and Bernadette Contensou, Paris 1974; *The Tradition of Constructivism* by Stephen Bann, New York 1974; *Nicolas Schöffer* by Pedro Fiori, Madrid 1974; *Nicolas Schöffer: l'adventure de l'art moderne* by André Parinaud, Paris 1975; *L'Univers Trame de Nicolas Schöffer* by Claude Heyligers, Paris 1975; *Nicolas Schöffer: un immense massage visuel* by Pierre Cabanne, Paris 1975; *Schöffer: pour un art tonique* by J. Warnod, Paris 1982; *Nicolas Schöffer* by Istvan Porkony, Budapest 1985. **Articles—**''Schoffer'' by Michel Faucher in *Cimaise,* no. 202, vol. 36, September-October 1989; **Films—***Sculptures, Projections, Peintures* by Jacques Brissot, 1956; *Tour de Liége* by Gruel, 1961; *Tout Voir: Nicolas Schöffer* by Charles Chaboud, 1966; *Portrait: Nicolas Schöffer* by Charles Chaboud, 1966; *Nicolas Schöffer* by Gerd Kairath, 1970; *L'Invite du Dimanche* by Anne Beranger, 1971; *La Tour Lumiére Cybernetique* by Adam Saulnier, 1971; *La Tour Cybernetique de la Défense* by Adam Saulnier, 1973; *Nicolas Schöffer* by Angeliki Haas, 1973; *Le Grand Prisme de la Sorbonne* by Jean Deveze, 1975; *Le Grande Prisme de la Sorbonne* by Angeliki Haas, 1975; *Nicolas Schöffer* by Egri, 1982; *Nicolas Schöffer* by Gabor Takacs, 1983; *Le Graphilux* by Laszlo Kovacs, 1984.

*

The only possible action for an artist worthy of the name is to create the new, to discover the unknown, to begin the foundations of real progress, for Art is the product of the richness of the free and liberated imagination of a few creators who have worked for society with a view to overcoming the prevailing mediocrity. Man owes to these artists who have left the beaten paths the clarification of his finalities, which are above all ethical and aesthetic and give him his real reason for living.

The artist owes it to himself to proclaim his own truth in his works with complete freedom. His cries, often ineffective at the actual moment, finally penetrate the collective conscience.

Great revolutions are never bloody; they are provoked by ideas and occur above all at the level of ideas. Now an artistic effect develops from an artistic idea through an artistic object or programme. (It is the same with commercial, scientific, technological ideas.) The artist does not create only for himself. The effect of his idea must therefore reverberate as widely as possible, without compromise, censorship or self-critisism, in order to prepare the stages of our evolution at all levels, including those that concern fundamental spiritual, cultural, ethical and aesthetic values.

My definition of art: ''Art is the creation, invention, at the level of the mechanism of thought and imagination, of an original idea with aesthetic content translatable into perceptible effects. The development and arrangement of these effects are drawn up in a programme in time or space, or in both, a programme whose composition and proportional relationships are most favorable, a new and aesthetic. These effects are transmitted by the use of visual, auditory or audio-visual signals to all those who accidentally or voluntarily become temporary or permanent spectators or listeners. A process of fascination results, provoking a more or less profound modification of their psychological field according to the degree of the creation's aesthetic value. This modification has to go in the direction of transcendence, sublimation and spiritual enrichment though the complex play of sensibility and human intellect. In this way, thanks to the creator's ability, striking aesthetic products penetrate social reality through multiple channels of communications. In order to achieve this goal, the creator must use a language and techniques which correspond to the true level of development of his era.''

My research clearly reflects this tendency to contemporaneity. For the artist who agrees to relinquish the iron chisel, there is the electric or electronic chisel and even the computer, but access to them is not easy. One has to fight and make it understood that new tools have to be available to artistic research and creation as much as if not more than to all kinds of industry including that of armaments. I am working at this. But as soon as an artist resorts to contemporary technology and develops his ideas and his works in relation to socio-cultural needs arising from situations provoked by new technology, cybernetics inevitably becomes part of his preoccupations, for the galloping technicoscientific development which introduces in increasing doses dynamic factors in every sector of daily life (transport, information), accompanying an extra ordinary growth in channels of communication and exchange, modifies completely the programmes of human life.

My definition of cybernetics: ''Cybernetics is the recognition of the vital process which keeps all phenomena in equilibrum. It is the science of effectiveness and of goverment by the organized control of all information including that which concerns perturbations of any kind, with a view to their treatment in order to achieve optimum regulation of all organic, physical or aesthetic phenomena. As a result there is a fluid permanence in supple equilibrium where each appearance of a tendency to periodicity or to stagnation provokes the intervention of perturbations or of adequate modifications to preserve the opening and aleatory character of every evolutionary process.''

As regards perturbation: ''It is the unexpected, brusque or progressive appearance of news, events, ideas or objects which modify, bend, distort or annul a programme, whether it is a question of a localised or generalised, physical or organic, individual or collective, natural phenomenon, or whether it is a questions of a programming of human origin, fixed or aleatory, limited or not in time and space with social, economic, political, philosophical, spiritual, aesthetic, scientific, technologcal or other tendency. According to the strength of its impact, the perturbation provokes more or less profound repercussions on the very structures of the programmed system going as far as their immediate or progressive disappearance and, on the contrary hypothesis, towards their optimisations, transformation or diversification.''

This definition evokes the no less important phenomenon of rupture: ''In the evolution of each phenomenon there is a point at which saturation, exhaustion, lead to inertia. The opportune intervention of a force or a formulated energy, however small it may be, can provoke rupture on condition that it is communicable and diffusible. That is to say that energy formulated by concrete propositions in a new language and by means of a new technique enters straight away into the circuit of the human complex, rapidly eliminating the traces of the previous phenomenon.''

These definitions also fundamentally concern the problem of art. In the history of art the perturbations provoked by perturbatory artists, the ruptures generated by these perturbations and the re-equilibrations resulting from the omnipresent cybernetic function are numerous. Art emphasizes the salutory and nourishing contribution of perturbations and ruptures, significant and indispensible factors of change and progress.

This quip could really be a complete programme: ''An Artist has to expose, most certainly, but he has also expose himself in order to impose himself and, if necesarry, to explode.''

—Nicolas Schöffer

* * *

In the late 1950s there grew up a loose confederation of artists grouped round the Denise René gallery in Paris who, for want of a better term, were labelled Kinetic. They shared a belief that modern industrial methods and materials could be harnessed for use in art. They thought that in this way the science/art dichotomy could be resolved and a new fusion be created. They were wrong, of course, but the blame for their failure cannot be laid at their door.

Most art of the period was based on the human figure, and the most pervasive mood was angst. Angst, redolent with existentialist hopelessness, was the perfect image for the industrialists who became the new patrons of art. It enabled them to continue exploiting everything and everybody while pointing to the tragic inevitability of it all. After all, if artists thought the whole things was a pointless farce, who were they to disagree?

The Kinetic artists disagreed, though. They refused to join in the mourning. It was clear to them that glass, plastic, stainless steel and so on were beautiful materials if used properly, and that the techniques of cybernetics could be used to add complexity to their works. In their hands art became machine, machine turned to art. Pity that no one else went along.

Nicolas Schöffer was the Grand Old Man of this tradition. He even managed to convince his own government to build some of his works on a scale which would be beyond the purse of an individual. He was a voice crying in the wilderness, though, and his optimism has once again been superseded. We are back to angst these days.

Like many of the kinetic artists Schöffer evolved a particular technique and stuck to it. Pieces by Schöffer are in two parts: a solid sculptural core and its reflection cast upon a suitable surface. The sculptural half usually moves and is made of many small pieces of reflective steel, put together in a constructivist manner. The whole edifice turns, and within this principal movement there is often other movement, creating a positive waterfall of light.

Aimed at this are spotlights, often different colours which cast a huge shadow onto a screen. Sometimes the whole piece is viewed at once, sometimes just the shadow are visible, sometimes the image is repeated ad infinitum by the use of mirrors. The general effect is one of considerable abstract beauty.

Frequently these pieces are equipped with cybernetic systems that react to enviromental influences. The largest outdoor pieces are often huge weather vanes, reacting to wind speed, atmospheric pressure, sunlight and so on. They are icons for a technological society, with no reference to the past or to the human figure.

Visionaries—one thinks of Sant Elia or Tatlin—who conceive societies in which art can play an everyday and functional role are rarely given more than short shrift. Perhaps it is for the best; a few works by Schöffer are stimulating and beautiful; a whole world filled with them might be an inhuman place to live.

The technologists and the kineticists tend to forget that Man is a messy creature, one that enjoys picking at the scabs of his unconscious and living in the refuse of his dreams. Let us be thankful that we cannot be controlled to be sane, but also sorry that sanity, when it appears, is given so little chance.

—Alastair Mackintosh

SCHULT, HA (Hans-Jurgen)

Nationality: German. **Born:** Parchim, Mecklenburg, 24 June 1939. **Education:** Studied art under K. O. Gotz at the Staatliche Kunstakademie, Dusseldorf, 1959–61; influenced by work of Yves Klein, Nam June Paik and Jackson Pollock, from 1958. **Family:** Has lived with the actress Elke Koska since 1967. **Career:** Worked occasionally as railwayman, building labourer, factory worker, driver, and advertising art director, from 1959; as independent artist, Dusseldorf, Munich and Cologne, 1959–82, in New York, since 1982: first organic-kinetic works, 1960; biokinetic and environmental actions, from 1968. Guest instructor, Kasseler Kunstakademie, Kassel, West Germany, 1971. **Address:** 203 West Houston Street, New York, New York 10014, U.S.A.

Individual Exhibitions:

1968 Galerie Ekto, Munich
1969 Galerie Nachst St. Stephan, Vienna
Städtisches Museum Schloss Morsbroich, Leverkusen, West Germany

HA Schult: *Great Wall People* at the Great Wall of China, 2001. ©2001 Artists Rights Society (ARS), NY/VG Bild-Kunst, Bonn.

Galerie Klaus Lupke, Frankfurt
Galerie Ingo Kummel, Cologne
1970 Kunstverein, Munich
Galerie Rudolf Zwirner, Cologne
1971 Galerie Rudolf Zwirner, Cologne
Kunstverein, Heidelberg
Spot Galerie, Kiel University
Neue Galerie, Aachen, West Germany
Kunsthalle, Cologne
1972 Galerie Van de Loo, Munich
Galerie Rochus Kowallek, Frankfurt
Galerie Klaus Lupke, Frankfurt
1973 Galerie Inge Baecker, Bochum, West Germany
Galerie Falazik, Neuenkirchen, West Germany
Museum Wiesbaden, West Germany
Galerie Inge Baecker, at the *IKI Art Fair,* Dusseldorf
Galerie Edith Seuss, Buchschlag, West Germany
1974 Museum Folkwang, Essen
Kunsthalle, Kiel
Kunstverein, Stuttgart
Stadtische Galerie im Lenbachhaus, Munich
Junior-Galerie, Hannover
Galerie Inge Baecker, Bochum, West Germany
Bunderministerium für Stadtebau, Bonn
Württembergischer Kunstverein, Stuttgart
Galerie Ubu, Karlsruhe
Junior-Galerie, Cologne
Galerie Thomas, Munich
1975 Stadtische Galerie Altes Theater, Ravensburg, West Germany
Galerie Edith Seuss, Buchschlag, West Germany
1976 Galerie Lauter, Mannheim
1977 Galerie Camomille, Brussels
Palazzo Spaletti, Naples
Palazzo Odescalchi, Rome
1978 Museum Mulheim, West Germany
Galerie Bergkamen, West Germany
Museum am Ostwall, Dortmund, West Germany
1980 Museum Ludwig, Cologne
1982 Galerie Hans Strelow, Dusseldorf

Selected Group Exhibitions:

1968 *Sub-Art,* U-Bahnhof Giselastrasse, Munich
1970 *Jetzt. Kunste in Deutschland Heute,* Kunsthalle, Cologne
1972 *Documenta, Kassel,* West Germany
1974 *Projeki 74,* Kunsthalle, Cologne

1975 *Der ausgesparte Mensch,* Kunsthalle, Mannheim
1976 *Schuh-Werke,* Kunsthalle, Nuremberg
1979 *The Image of Man since 1945,* Funatie Kunsthuis, Amsterdam
Im Namen des Volkes, Wilhelm-Lehmbruck-Museum, Duisburg, West Germany (travelled to Kunstlerhaus Wien, Vienna)
1982 *L'Art Sociologique,* Musée de la Ville, Nice
Kunst wird Material, Nationalgalerie, West Berlin

Collections:

Wilhelm-Lehmbruck-Museum, Duisburg, West Germany; Kunsthalle, Kiel; Museum Wiesbaden, West Germany; Museum am Ostwall, Dortmund, West Germany; Museum Lübeck; Kunsthalle, Nuremberg; Kunsthalle, Recklinghausen, West Germany; Leopold-Hoesch-Museum, Duren, West Germany; Kunsthalle, Mannheim; Sammlung Bundesrepublik Deutschland, Bonn.

Publications:

By SCHULT: Books and leaflets—*Situation Schackstrasse,* manifesto, Munich 1969; *Aktion 20,000 km,* action-text, Munich 1970; *Die Schultfrage,* Cologne 1971; *Actif au Maroc,* Munich and Casablanca 1971; *Der Schlussel steckt,* action-text Munich 1971; *Biokinetische Landschaft und Soldat,* flysheet, Munich 1972; *Brief an Georg Jappe (1),* Munich 1973; *Brief von Georg Jappe an HA Schult/Brief von HA Schult an Georg Jappe (2),* Munich 1973; *Die zum Stillstand gebrachte Zeit,* flysheet, Munich 1974; *Venezia Vive,* action-flysheet, Munich 1976; *Crash!,* action-flysheet, Munich 1977; *Venezia Vive,* magazine, Munich 1977; *Ruhr-Tour,* magazine, Cologne 1978; *HA Schult: Der Macher,* Cologne 1978; *Trash,* manifesto, Cologne 1979; *Der Alltag* flagsheet, Cologne 1980; *Jetzi! Zeit . . . ,* flysheet, Cologne 1980; *Jetzi! Zeit . . . ,* exhibition catalog, Cologne 1980.

On SCHULT: Books—*H A Schult: Biokinetische Situationen,* with text by Rolf Wedewer, Leverkusen, West Germany 1969; *Expansion der Kunst* by Jürgen Claus, Reinbeck, West Germany and Mexico City 1970; *Deutsche Kunst: eine neue Generation* by Rolf-Günter Dienst, Cologne 1970; *Leben und Kunst* by Udo Kultermann, Tübingen 1970; *Science and Fiction* by Walter Aue, Frankfurt 1971; *Bis Huete: Stilgeschichte der Bildenden Kunst im 20. Jahrhundert* by Karin Thomas, Cologne 1971; *Jam* by James Burns, Cologne and New York 1971; *Kunst ist Utopie* by Heinz Ohff, Gutersloh 1972; *Verkehrskultur* by Klaus Honnef, Recklinghausen, West Germany 1972; *Art Now: The New Age* by Ichiro Haryu, Tokyo 1972; *Funktionen der Bildenden Kunst im Spatkapitalismus* by Martin Damus, Frankfurt 1973; *Der ausgesparte Mensch,* exhibition catalog with text by Heinz Fuchs, Mannheim 1975; *Landscape: A New Aspect* by Dietrich Mahlow, Stuttgart 1976; *Dumont Kunstlerlexikon* by Karin Thomas and Gerd de Vries, Cologne 1977; *De-architecture* by the SITE group, New York 1978; *Landschaftmalerei* by Rolf Wedewer, Cologne 1978; *Art in the 70s* by Edward Lucie Smith, Oxford 1980; *Gesprache mit Kunstlern* by Amine Haase, Cologne 1981; *Kunst wird Material,* exhibition catalog with text by Dieter Honisch and Michael Pauseback, West Berlin 1982. **Articles**—"If Cars Had Wings: HA Schult's Golden Bird Atop the Tower of the Municipal Museum, Cologne" by Gerard A. Goodrow in *Art News,* vol. 91, April 1992.

* * *

H. A. Schult, born in Parchim, Mecklenburg, in 1939, calls himself quite simply "The Maker." This epithet is not merely a circumlocution for something unclassifiable, it is also programmatic; it designates the unity, as actually experienced, between life and art, but also points to the multiplicity of the artist's work. From the start it was impossible to associate him with a particular genre, let alone an artistic trend or style. Schult made a name for himself via objects, but he has since concentrated on action art, making extensive use of the media and gaining worldwide recognition. The spectacular is his metier, in which, as an accomplished self-publicist, he exercises perfect control. And yet Schult is far more than just a showman; he is no mere exhibitionist, but rather a missionary earnestly seeking, if with a great deal of wit, to alter public awareness and to make people think.

Schult's art is always above all a criticism of society. After studying at the Academy of Art in Düsseldorf under K. O. Goetz, he was influenced by action-painting artist Jackson Pollock and increasingly by Yves Klein and the action musician Nam June Paik. He subsequently worked as an art director and in numerous other occupations—more than fifty, according to Schult himself. He was the first artist to recognise the potential of the environment as a theme for artistic processes. He coined the term biokinetics and using bacterial cultures demonstrated the kinetic principle of constant change and decomposition. What he created was of necessity not a lasting work of art for a museum. He was thereby also seeking to demonstrate that there are no lasting works of art, since every work of art disintegrates, becoming something else. The public was given the opportunity to intervene in the process, to regulate the change that was taking place: change as a possibility to be experienced. Later Schult demonstrated in object-boxes how technology and civilisation increasingly violate nature, how nature and culture are dying, idylls are wearing out.

Alongside these slight works Schult was already producing his happening-actions at the end of the sixties. In Munich he piled up a gigantic paper mountain in a street, set up refuse actions, made a collection of the football star Franz Beckenbauer's left-overs and rubbish, launched a 20,000-kilometre rally and organised an archaeological journey through the present as well as "Rühr Tour" into the "District's Here and Now." When the *Documenta 6* exhibition opened in Kassel in 1977, he crashed a plane into a rubbish dump in New York, an incident which was relayed on television.

The most expensive happening was the *Berlin—New York* one, where identical events were organised to occur simultaneously in both cities.

There are plans afoot for a happening in Peking, and also for the foundation of an "HA Schult Museum for Action Art" in Essen, intended to document the history of this art form and to provide the opportunity to experience past happenings through a series of different scenarios.

—Werner Schulze-Reimpel

SCHULTZE, Bernard

Nationality: German. **Born:** Schneidemühl, West Prussia, now Pila, Poland, 31 May 1915. **Education:** Educated at Prinz Heinrichs-Gymnasium, Berlin, 1925–34; studied art at the Kunsthochschule, Berlin, 1934 and at the Kunst Akademie, Dusseldorf, 1939. **Military service:** Served in the German Army, in Russia and Africa, 1939–45. **Family:** Married Ursula Bluhm in 1955. **Career:** Painter; has lived and worked in Flensburg, 1945–47; Frankfurt-am-Main 1947–68; in Paris, 1950–64; and in Cologne, since 1968: first ''tachiste'' paintings, influenced by Lanskoy and Riopelle, 1951; first reliefs, 1956; first ''tabuskris'' and free-standing reliefs, 1959; first ''migofs,'' 1961; first grisaille works, 1972; Member, with K. O. Gotz, Otto Greis and Heinz Kreutz, ''Quadriga'' group, Frankfurt, 1952; designed stage decor for Duetsche Oper am Rhein, Dusseldorf, 1970. **Awards:** Kunstpreis, Darmstadt, 1967; Kunstpreis der Stadt, Cologne, 1969; Kunstpreis Wormland, Munich, 1983; Grosser Hessischer Kulturpreis, 1984; Golden Laurel Award, Gesellschaft Bildender Kunstler, Vienna, 1985; Lovis-Corinth-Preis, 1986. Honorary member, Akademie der Künste, West Berlin, 1972; honorary professor, Landgovernment of Nordrhein-Westfalen, 1981. **Address:** Riehlerstrasse 53, 5000 Cologne 1, West Germany.

Individual Exhibitions:

1947 Galerie Junge Kunst, Hamburg
1948 Moderne Galerie Egon Günther, Mannheim (and regularly until 1951)
1949 Zimmergalerie Franck, Frankfurt (and regularly until 1958)
1956 Galerie Parnass, Wuppertal, West Germany
Studio Paul Facchetti, Paris
Wittenborn Gallery, New York
1957 Galerie Schuler, West Berlin
Galerie 22, Dusseldorf
1958 Galerie Inge Ahlers, Mannheim
Die Insel, Hamburg
Galerie Daniel Cordier, Paris
Galerie Nohl, Siegen, West Germany
Städtische Kunstmuseum, Duisburg, West Germany
1959 Galleria Montenapoleone 6A, Milan
1960 *Plastikbilder, Tabuskris, Zeichnungen,* Galerie Daniel Cordier, Frankfurt
Galerie Schuler, West Berlin
1961 Kunsthalle, Baden-Baden, West Germany
1962 *Peintures et Reliefs,* Musée des Beaux-Arts, La Chaux de Fonds, Switzerland
Städtische Museum, Wiesbaden, West Germany
Kunstverein, Wuppertal, West Germany
Reliefs et Dessins, Galerie Daniel Cordier, Paris
1963 Galerie Schuler, West Berlin
1964 Galerie Schmela, Dusseldorf
Galleria l'Attico, Rome
Galerie der Edition Rothe, Heidelberg
1965 Howard Wise Gallery, New York
1966 Kestner-Gesellschaft, Hannover
Städtische Museum, Leverkusen, West Germany
Badischer Kunstverein, Karlsruhe
Galleria Senior, Rome
San Francico Musuem of Art
Wide White Space, Antwerp
Studio B, Bamberg, West Germany
1967 London Arts Gallery, Detroit
1968 *Alte und Neue Arbeiten,* Kölnischer Kunstverein, Cologne
Kunstverein, Braunschweig, West Germany
Kunstverein, Darmstadt
Galerie Rudolf Zwirner, Cologne (with Robert Graham)
1969 Haus am Waldsee, West Berlin
Palais des Beaux-Arts, Brussels
Galerie Felix Handschin, Basel
1970 Galerie Brusberg, Hannover
Bernard Schultze 1960–1970, Museum Bochum, West Germany
1971 Centre National d'Art Contemporain, Paris
Pfalzgalerie, Kaiserslautern, West Germany
Galerie Arcanes, Brussels
Galerie MARC, Washington, D.C.
1972 Galerie der Spiegel, Cologne
1973 *Die Migofs 1958 bis 1973,* Baukunst, Cologne
1974 Museum Boymans-van Beuningen, Rotterdam
Galerie Nova, Hagen, West Germany
Galerie Defet, Nuremberg
Galerie B, Paris
Die Welt der Migofs, Staatliche Kunsthalle, Baden-Baden, West Germany
1975 *Die Welt der Migofs: Bilde und Objekie aus 25 Jahren,* Galerie Brusberg, Hannover
Aus-und Fortbildungsstatte, Bonn
Galerie Schuler, West Berlin
1976 Galerie Rothe, Heidelberg
Galerie der Spiegel, Cologne
1977 Deutsche Aktiengesellschaft, Clubheim-Hamburg
Kunstverein, Salzgitter, West Germany
1978 Galerie Rothe, Heidelberg
Kulturabteilung Bayer, Erholungshaus-Leverkusen, West Germany
1979 Galerie Jean Leroy, Paris
Kunstlerhaus Wien, Vienna (with Ursula Schultze)
Städtische Museum, Leverkusen, West Germany
1980 *Zerbrochene Verstecke,* Kunsthalle, Hamburg
Städtische Kunsthalle, Dusseldorf
1981 Akademie der Künste, West Berlin
Kunstverein, Frankfurt
Saarland Museum, Saarbrucken
Galerie R. Haftmann, Zurich
Galerie der Spiegel, Cologne
1982 Graphische Sammlung Albertina, Vienna
Galerie Gunzenhauser, Munich
1983 Galerie Schueler, West Berlin
1984 Albertina, Vienna
Rheinisches Landesmuseum, Bonn
Kunsthalle, Tubingen, West Germany
Wilhelm-Hack-Museum, Ludwingshafen, West Germany
Kunsthalle, Nuremberg, West Germany
Galerie Rothe, Heidelberg, West Germany
Wallraf-Richartz-Museum, Cologne
Galerie Hans Strelow, Dusseldorf
1985 Galerie Hans Strelow, Dusseldorf

Bernard Schultze: *Submarine Komposition,* 1949. ©CNAC/MNAM/Dist. Réunion des Musées Nationaux/Art Resource, NY; courtesy of Musee National d'Art Moderne, Centre Georges Pompidou, Paris, France.

Baukunst-Galerie, Cologne
Galerie Brusberg, West Berlin
Ostdeutsche Galerie, Regensburg, West Germany
Galerie Schueler, West Berlin
Galerie Gunzenhauser, Munich

1986 Kunstverein, Dortmund, West Germany
Galerie Der Spiegel, Cologne
Ostdeutsche Galerie, Regensburg, West Germany

1987 Galerie Pro Arte, Freiburg, West Germany
Galerie Hans Strelow, Dusseldorf
Galerie Timm Gierig, Frankfurt

1988 Galerie Dieter Wilbrand, Cologne

1990 *Bernard Schultze: Works from the Years 1952–90,* Galleria Henze, Lugano, Switzerland

1991 *Bernard Schultze ''In the Labyrinth'': Works from 1947 to 1990—Oil Paintings, Objects, Works on Paper,* Staatliche Kunstsammlungen, Dresden, Germany

1994 *Bernard Schultze,* Galleria Blu, Milan

Selected Group Exhibitions:

1948 *Vision und Magie,* Moderne Galerie Egon Günther, Mannheim

1954 *3rd International Biennale of Color Lithography,* Cincinnati Art Museum, Ohio

1960 *Guggenheim International,* Guggenheim Museum, New York

1963 *Schrift und Bild, Kunsthalle,* Baden-Baden, West Germany

1966 *Labyrinthe,* Akademie der Künste, West Berlin (travelled to the Kunsthalle, Baden-Baden, West Germany, and the Kunsthalle, Nuremberg)

1968 *Dada, Surrealism and Their Heritage,* Museum of Modern Art, New York (travelled to Los Angeles County Museum of Art, and the Art Institute of Chicago)

1975 *Surrealitat-Bildrealitat 1924–1974,* Kunsthalle, Dusseldorf

1977 *Documenta,* Kassel, West Germany

1978 *Museum des Geldes,* Kunsthalle, Dusseldorf

1979 *Weich und Plastisch/Soft Art,* Kunsthaus, Zurich

1988 *Modern Art: Paintings, Sculptures, Watercolours, Drawings, Prints,* Galleria Henze, Campione d'Italia, Switzerland
Structure and Gesture: ''Informal Painting'' and ''Subjective Photography'' in German Art of the 1950s, Suermondt-Ludwig-Museum, Aachen, Germany

1989 *Modern Art: Paintings, Sculpture, Watercolours, Drawings, Prints,* Galleria Henze, Campione d'Italia, Switzerland

1990 *The Art of German Drawing VII: Free Abstraction,* Goethe Institute, London; Scottish National Gallery of Modern Art, Edinburgh
Fischer Fine Art, London

1991 *Artists of the Century,* Baukunst Galerie, Cologne

Collections:

Kunsthalle, Mannheim; Museum Ludwig, Cologne; Pfalz-Galerie, Kaiserslautern, West Germany; Museum Bochum, West Germany;

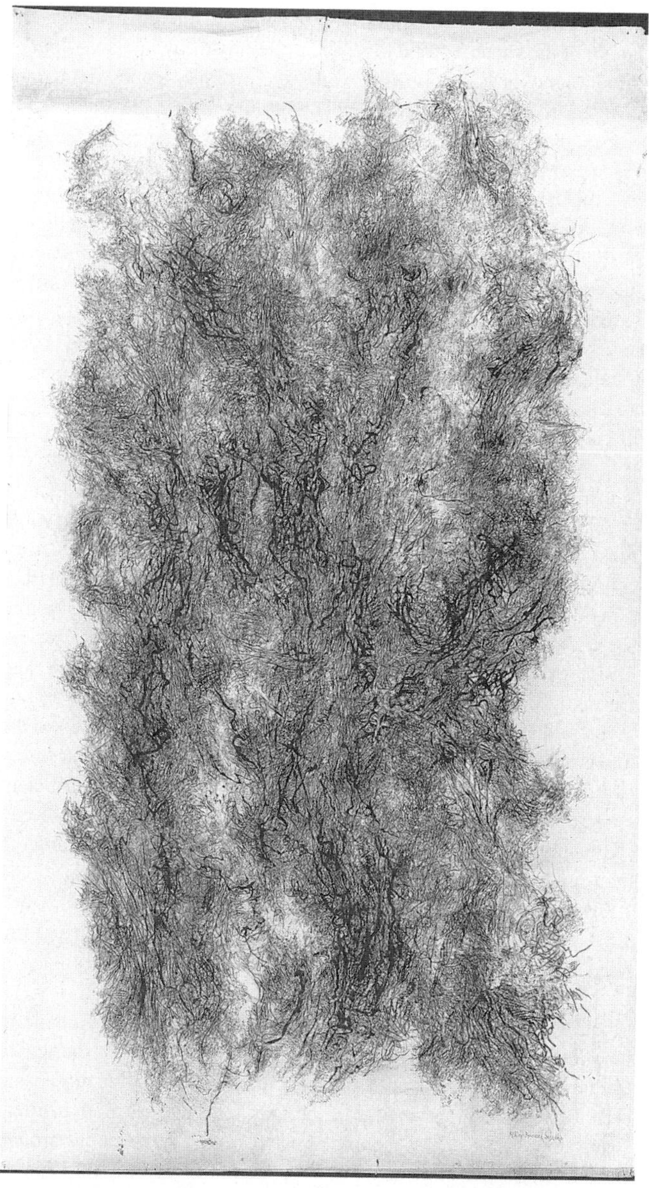

Bernard Schultze: *Untitled,* 1959. ©CNAC/MNAM/Dist. Réunion des Musées Nationaux/Art Resource, NY; courtesy of Musee National d'Art Moderne, Centre Georges Pompidou, Paris, France.

Hessiches Landesmuseum, Darmstadt; Wilhelm-Lehmbruck Museum, Duisburg, West Germany; Stiftung Preussischer Kulturbesitz, West Berlin; Wallraf-Richartz Museum, Cologne; Centre Georges Pompidou Paris; Museum Boymans-van Beuningen, Rotterdam.

Publications:

By SCHULTZE: Books—*Migof-Reden Texte und zeichnungen,* Stierstadt im Taunus, West Germany 1971; *Im Sieb die gelbroten Korner,* portfolio, Hamburg 1972; *Sperriger Zaun aus Zeit: Neue Migof-Reden und Ooffsetlithographien,* Dusseldorf 1976.

On SCHULTZE: Books—*Bernard Schultze,* exhibition catalog with text by Will Grohmann, Paris 1956; *Bernard Schultze,* exhibition catalog with text by Edouard Jager, Mannheim 1958; *Bernard Schultze,* exhibition catalog with text by Hanns Theodor Flemming, Hamburg 1958; *Bernard Schultze: Plastikbilder, Tabuskris, Zeichnungen,* exhibition catalog with text by Wolfgang Grozinger, Frankfurt 1960; *Bernard Schultze; Reliefs et Dessins,* exhibition catalog with text by Julien Alvard, Paris 1962; *Bernard Schultze: Peintures et reliefs,* exhibition catalog with a foreword by Paul Seylaz, La Chaux de Fonds, Switzerland 1962; *Schultze,* exhibition catalog with text by Enrico Crispolti and Alain Jouffroy, Rome 1964; *Bernard Schultze,* exhibition catalog with text by Filiberto Menna, Rome 1966; *Bernard Schultze,* exhibition text by Manfred de la Motte, Bamberg, West Germany 1966; *Bernard Schultze,* exhibition catalog with texts by Rolf Wedewer and Peter W. Jasen, Leverkusen, West Germany 1966; *Bernard Schultze: Alte und Neue Arbeiten,* exhibition catalog with text by Heinz Ohff, Cologne 1968; *Bernard Schultze 1960–1970,* exhibition catalog with text by Peter Leo and José Pierre, Bochum, West Germany 1970: *Bernard Schultze,* exhibition catalog/book with texts by Alain Jouffroy, Will Grohmann, Peter Selz and José Pierre, Paris 1971; *Bernard Schultze: Die Migofs 1958 bis 1973,* exhibition catalog with text by Wieland Schmied, Cologne 1973; *Bernard Schultze—Die Welt der Migofs,* exhibition catalog, with texts by Hans-Albert Peters and Eberhard Roters and an interview by Barbara Catoir and Hans-Albert Peters, Baden-Baden, West Germany 1974; *Bernard Schultze-Het Woud der Migofs/Ursula—Dromen in veren en bont,* exhibition catalog with text by Eberhard Roters, Rotterdam 1974; *Bernard Schultze Die Welt der Migofs—bilde und objekte aus 25 jahren,* exhibition catalog with text by Jean Dypreau, Eberhard Roters and Bruno Schulz, Hannover 1975; *Bernard Schultze/Ursula,* exhibition catalog with text by Eberhard Roters, Vienna 1979; *Bernard Schultze,* exhibition catalog with text by Rolf Wedewer, Leverkusen, West Germany 1979; *Bernard Schultze: Zerbrochene Verstecke,* exhibition catalog with an introduction by Werner Hofmann and Helmut Leppien, Hamburg 1980; *Bernard Schultze: Works from the Years 1952–90,* exhibition catalog, with text by Heinrich Hahne, Lugano 1990; *The Art of German Drawing VII: Free Abstraction,* exhibition catalog, London 1990; *Bernard Schultze* by Lothar Romain and Rolf Wedewer, Munich 1991; *Bernard Schultze,* exhibition catalog, Milan 1994. **Articles**—"Bernard Schultze" by Heinz-Norbert Jocks in *Kunstforum International,* no. 129, January/April 1995.

*

Until 1940 I worked in accordance with Menzel's motto: "It is good to draw anything, it is better to draw everything." So I tried to draw everything around me, first as precisely as possible and then again in sketchy loose strokes. I rigorously repressed, as though a bad conscience, my even then narcissistic wandering dreamlike images, influenced by Kubin's chimaera, in order to learn once and for all the ABC's and do homage to a certain realism which at the time of the beginnings of National Socalism was in any case taught at the Academy. When I completed my studies I became a soldier and limited myself to a strictly recorded representation of life in both drawing and painting, certainly as a protection of my interior monologue. Now and again I allowed myself, regarding it almost as an offence, to wander in my realms of fantasy; something of this is seen in the work "The Temptation of Saint Antony." I let myself drift in the sudden flood of pictures which appeared to me: the corner of the room at evening secure in the lamplight, bursting out into savage vegetation: tree trunk, distant landscape with Russian cathedrals and buried in sand the ugly enticing whore's face. This was perhaps a prophetic pointer, for the Russian campaign soon began, in the gruesome drawing of corpes, the executed, ruined churches and burning villages I again with Kubin and Ensor kept joy-dispelling company. Towards the end of the war, in short days of holiday, I painted, on a bed sheet on which a German fighter pilot had died of his burns, a pale gloomy picture of drifting dead on black water, of mountains which consisted of pallid white monsters beneath a thundery sky in a kind of El Greco style, and subsequently a picture of my dead grandmother, the lace of the bed linen and pillows around her yellow as wax face. I showed the picture to my former teacher Willy Jäckel, whose careful appreciation gave me the courage to continue with this preoccupation only with oneself.

Then came the great conflagration, the hail of bombs, in which everything that I had previously painted and drawn disappeared in the golden glow. A turning point in my life. The fetters were broken. On the poorest scraps of paper with coloured pencil and with self-made water colours on black-out paper I now began to revel in my spendidly gruesome fairy tales. As a refugee in Flensburg I was able to show Nolde some of these. The coloured pencil scenes in shrill descant tones particularly pleased him. The labyrinthine way allowed me to stumble into the unconscious, encouraged, by a psychotherapist: ''The doors to your unconscious must always stand wide open,'' as she later confirmed similarly in front of my wife's works. At that time I was already working to the ''dictates of the unconscious'' without having heard anything at all of Berton. And just at that time, towards the end of the 1940s, I also came across Prinzhorn's book *The Plastic Arts of the Mentally Ill.* In 1947 I had my first exhibition in a gallery of little signifince in Hamburg. Hanns Theodor Flemming reviewed it and gave me just the acknowledgment I needed at that moment.

Then in Frankfurt, no longer cut off from the unrestrained development of artistic life in Berlin above all and in the Rheinland, it was the Egon Günther Mannheim Gallery, the only one at that time that was interested in surreal art, that showed some of my works along works along with those of Max Ernst, Viktor Brauner and Miró. In great haste I passed through the stations of this wonderful dream world and began even more resolutely to delve into myself, producing for example ''Circus,'' a picture carried out almost in a state of trance. The gate was pushed open: in 1951 I made my first visit to Paris where Wols' drawing, but above all Riopelle's spatula executed colour-field orgies, overwhelmed me like new earthquake pictures. My Friends Götz, Greis and Kreuz were similarly affected, and the great fever attacked us.

Each of us now in his own way painted this as it were shock to the soul. Parisian colleagues, writers on art supported us. We were called the new German romantics. It was Edouard Jaguer who with René Drouin proclaimed the four of us the Frankfurt Quadriga, as the first independent German variants of tachism, as were Vedova in Venice and Burri in Rome. 1952 was our comet year. And yet each of us was so utterly occupied with himself that our paths soon diverged. At the time I had a children's painting class in Frankfurt's America House. Once again, but on a different level of the secret spiral, I was led back to the source as I had been in Flensburg when reading and contemplating the Prinzhorn book. At the same time my wife began quite abruptly to paint, in an equally original manner, untamed, not yet expelled from Paradise. COBRA friends visited us; it was a marriage of regal and yet dogged work.

Like children on the beach, crouching in the slimy sand and paying with buckets full of sea water, I did likewise with self-mixed, thickened colour brews and coloured water, masses of colour dissolved in turpentine. With pieces of wood, my hands, the brush, I let myself drift over the horizontal painting ground, fell into a panic at the horror of the vacuum, tried to rescue myself by throwing the coloured turpentine over it. Pools, hills, valleys, crevasses, scabby exuberant growths formed themselves, the crumbling walls, the delta landscapes, the desolate steppes and expanses of Russia emerged, the dark green forests of my childhood on the Polish border.

Such pictures precipitating in me shreds of memory, I let myself be washed away by them in a chain of associations and simultaneously tried to see over my own shoulder. The exciting game of inspiration and control in raped succession had begun. That was the stimulant, for that reason painting was a substitute for living. I have never been able to establish a connection as in the dogma of the young today. On the contrary I lived my outward life day in day out soberly and inconspicuously and with it screened off so as to live my real life—yes, really—in the ivory tower.

At the end of the 1950s and the beginning of the 1960s my wife, whose pictures had been acquired by Dubuffet for his famous art-brut collection, and I entered the circle of the Daniel Cordier Gallery, the most individual gallery in Paris at that time—a circle of outsiders commanded as it were by Dubuffet. His method, his inward construction of discovery, of pressing on to the summit and then already taking the next step into fresh and unknown realms, was a model for us. Those of us coming from Sweden, Yugoslavia, Italy, USA and Germany understood this mixture of latin-celtic harmony of spirit given perhaps only to the French: vitality, laying oneself open to the unconscious and yet objectifying in an organized manner everything contradictory. Such a stormily creative climate gave me sufficient courage to risk a step into the third dimension, to create the coloured ''Unnameable,'' later called ''Migof'' structures, at the junction between painting and sculpture. There were also the groups, the ''Environments:'' my first ''Migofs'' 1959, my first ''Environment'' 1961 for Mahlow's exhibition in the Baden Baden Art Museum: *Fantasy Architecture.*

For the first time I then tried to let myself be led into relief pictures carried out in accordance with the rules of drawing, and to coloured sculpture in a transition, a metamorphosis from the one to the other. The joy of such confused games, of such adventures as it were behind the thorny hedge of the fairy tales in ever more brilliant labyrinths, had reached a summit when I saw in the circle around Cordier and Eckstrom in New York the first pictures of Richard Lindner, also a dream-painter, but letting himself be slowly drawn in, so infinitely slowly that I thought of the torments of the dying and said as much to him when we were able to see him at work. I tried to provide him with a solution from my labyrinth, a very difficult undertaking to draw his slowness into my nervous and at the same time baroque net. Combinations were generated and new dense complex Environments. The manneristic impulse, belonging it is true to my basic structure, and emerging here and there at the end of the 1940s, fulfilled me and drove me on. At this point my ''life-long interior monologue'' now began for the first time to be conclusively settled. An Enviroment hanging from the ceiling, branching out, on the ground as a complete optical work of art spreading out, surrounded by four Migof guardians. Such crowding, such possession and encroachment of space changed, almost imperceptibly, into the ''grisailles,'' stormily baroque and simultaneously ghostly silent cold pictures, which thereafter, and that is my present position, led quite contrarily to the very large vibrant water colours shot through with paths of light where early memories of Ensor and Turner emerge.

In thick over-ripe oil colours bearing a certain relationship perhaps to the colour-brew informal pictures of the 1950s there are now bright dream scenes, tumbling Migof structures stretching themselves, changing and on the other hand not decipherable in terms of the figurative, of cliff faces, ravishing glimpes of landscape in waterfalls and tumbling clouds, associations as they catch me when in front of the white canvas I begin bit by to string together the colour tones, like picture and word fragment, gradually covering and weaving the surface.

—Bernard Schultze

* * *

Born in 1915 in Schneidemühl near the Polish border, Bernard Schultze is still one of the really young painters. He is now, as always, in search of mysteries in the labyrinthine depths of his sub-conscious. There the apparently inexhaustible exhaustible springs of his scurrilous imagination bubble forth, regularly brought into harmony, however, by his ''Prussian-like'' sober and realistic intelligence, with the social reality of the present time to which his avant garde work responds in all its transformations and in its constantly new approaches.

Nevertheless, Bernard Schultze is a painter in the continuity of tradition. His work always stood in relation to admired painters of other generations who served him as fixed stars for orientation. In the beginning he tried, following Menzel's example, to draw as precisely as possible whatever was in front of him—true to nature, of course. But the affinity to Kubin continually haunted his work like a hobgoblin. Later on, in Belgium during the war, he happened to come across a book with pictures by Ensor, who became his guiding star for a long time. Ensor was displaced by Wols, Riopelle and Pollock—Schultze became concreator of the German version of the informal, a tachist, and in 1952 had his breakthrough. Increasingly he developed sculptural images which, around 1957, protruded from the picture surface and finally became independent as ''soft sculptures'' on the dividing line between painting and sculpture. These mysterious creations called ''Migofs,'' garishly coloured and bizarre in form, make palpable for the first time a formative reference point in his work: a spiritual with Surrealism. These Migofs soon united to form groups, atavistic Migof environments, frightful images of a society after the end of civilization.

While he was producing the Migofs (until far into the 1970s) Bernard Schultze also returned to canvas. As ''Tabuskri'' he showed delicate oil paintings which change into pen and ink drawings. He also worked on a series of water-colours and grey-toned grisailles. Thereafter his palette quickly lightened again with homages to Impressionism: entirely fresh nuances in the painter's work appear in the latest extremely poetic pastel-toned pictures which suggest unidentifiable plants and in no way conceal a reference to Corinth and Kokoschka. Even Schultze himself draws attention to such references which are related to the spiritual rather than the stylistic: it is more than obvious that in this case one original artist is saluting the other and that no one could suppose epigonal dependence.

This oeuvre is stamped with unmistakeable individuality; it is difficult to classify. It would certainly not be wrong to describe Bernard Schultze as a painter of secret landscapes who found his place between abstraction and surrealism. His continually restrained pleasure in rampant fantasy is in harmony with the tendency to harmony and order which aims at beauty and perfection. Yet Schultze is of his age and proffers an image of the present. Its reality, however, is shown in the caricature of the fragmentary and incessant destruction of the beautiful. The Migofs are significantly appropriate. His later mature work has employed more intense colours, and his pictures have gained an increased luminosity.

—Werner Schulze-Reimpell

SCHUMACHER, Emil

Nationality: German. **Born:** Hagen, 29 August 1912. **Education:** Studied art, Kunstgewerbeschule, Dortmund, 1932–35. **Military service:** Served as conscripted armaments factory worker, Hagen, 1939–45. **Family:** Married Ursula Klapprott in 1940; son: Ulrich. **Career:** Independent painter, Hagen, 1935–39, and since 1945; co-founder, Junger Westen Artists Association, Recklinghausen, 1947. Professor, Hochschule für Bildende Künste, Hamburg, 1958–60, and Staatliche Akademie der Bildenden Künste, Karlsruhe, 1966–77; guest professor and visiting artist, Minneapolis School of Art, 1967–68. **Awards:** Kunstpreis ''Junger Westen,'' Recklinghausen, West Germany, 1948; Kunstpreis, Stadt Iserlohn, 1955; Conrad-von-Soest-Preis, Münster, 1956; Karl-Ernst-Osthaus-Preis, Hagen, 1958; Guggenheim Award, 1958; Japanese Ministry of Culture Prize, *International Art Exhibition,* Tokyo, 1959; Premio Cardazzo, *Biennale,* Venice, 1962; First Prize/Silver Medal, Bang Danh-Du Award, *International Arts Exhibition,* Saigon, 1962; Grosser Kunstpreis des Landes Nordrhein-Westfalen, Dusseldorf, 1963; Governor's Prize, Tokyo, 1966; Cross of Honour First Class, 1968, and Grand Cross of Honour with Star, 1983, Federal Republic of Germany; City of Ibiza Prize, *Graphics Biennale,* Ibiza, 1974; August Macke Prize, city of Menschede, 1978; Rubens Prize, City of Siegen, 1982; Ehrenring Award, 1982, and Honoured Citizen, 1987, Stadt Hagen; Jorg Ratgeb Pries, Reutlingen, 1987. **Member:** Akademie der Künste, West Berlin, 1968. Member, Order of Merit, für Wissenschaften und Künste, West Germany, 1982. **Agent:** Galerie Strelow, Luegplatz 3, 4000 Dusseldorf 11. **Address:** Bleichstrasse 11, 5800 Hagen, Germany.

Individual Exhibitions:

1947 Studio für Neue Kunst, Wuppertal, West Germany
1956 Freie Kunstlergemeinschaft Schanze, Münster, West Germany
Galerie Parnass, Wuppertal, West Germany
1957 Galerie Parnass, Wuppertal, West Germany
Galerie 22, Dusseldorf
Galerie Il Milione, Milan
1958 Galerie Schuler, West Berlin
Galerie Van de Loo, Munich
Galerie Brockstedt, Hannover
Galerie Stadler, Paris
Karl-Ernst-Osthaus Museum, Hagen, West Germany
1959 Galleria dell'Ariete, Milan
Samuel L. Kootz Gallery, New York
Galleria La Medusa, Rome
Galerie Schuler, West Berlin
Galerie Muller, Stuttgart
Galerie Van de Loo, Munich
1960 Kootz Gallery, New York
Galerie Van de Loo, Munich
1961 Kestner-Gesellschaft, Hannover
Galerie Schuler, West Berlin

Emil Schumacher. ©2001 Artists Rights Society (ARS), NY/VG Bild-Kunst, Bonn.

Galerie Art, Bremen, West Germany
1962 Westfälischer Kunstverein, Münster, West Germany
Kunstverein, Hamburg
Stadtische Kunstmuseum, Duisburg, West Germany
Kunstverein, Freiburg
Opere Recenti, Galleria La Medusa, Rome
Galleria Blu, Milan
Oldbilder und Gouachen 1962, Galerie Van de Loo, Munich
Galerie Baier, Mainz, West Germany
1963 German Pavillion, at the *Bienale,* Sao Paulo
Galleria L'Indiano, Florence
Galerie Nachst St. Stephan, Vienna
Galerie Schmucking, Braunschweig, West Germany
1964 Galleria L'Indiano, Florence
Galerie Brechbuhl, Grenchen, Switzerland
Azienda Autonoma Soggiorno e Cura, Meran, Italy
1965 *Oldbilder, Gouachen, Grafik 1964–65,* Galerie Van de Loo, Munich
Galerie Alice Pauli, Lausanne, Switzerland
Galerie Gerber, Berne
Galerie Nohl, Siegen, West Germany
1966 Kleine Graphik Galerie, Bremen, West Germany
Galerie Brusberg, Hannover
Galleri Haaken, Oslo
Galerie Schuler, West Berlin
1967 Galerie Ariel, Paris
Salle d'Honneur, *International Graphics Exhibition,* Ljubljana, Yugoslavia
Narodni Galerie, Prague
Galerie Rothe, Heidelberg
1968 The Minnesota Suite, Lefebre Gallery, New York
1969 Galerie de Montreal
Galerie Defet, Nuremberg
Galerie Rothenstein, Bremen, West Germany
Galerie Kuhn, Aachen, West Germany
1970 Galleria L'Indiano, Florence
Galleria Morone, Milan
1971 Kunstmuseum für Rheinlande und Westfalen, Dusseldorf
1972 Badischer Kunstverein, Karlsruhe
Galerie Schottenring, Vienna
Haus am Waldsee, West Berlin
Galerie Nowa, Hagen, West Germany
Galerie Rothenstein, Bremen, West Germany
1973 Galerie Rothenstein, Bremen, West Germany
Galerie Rothe, Heidelberg
1975 *Arbeiten 1957 bis 1975,* Karl-Ernst-Osthaus Museum, Hagen, West Germany
Forum Kunst, Rottweil, West Germany
Galleria Falchi, Milan
Galerie Nothelfer, West Berlin
Galeria Van de Voort, Ibiza, Spain
Galeria Internacional de Art, Madrid
Galerie Hilbur, Karlsruhe
1976 Galerie Ostertag, Frankfurt
Galerie Werner, Bremen, West Germany
Palazzo delle Prigioni Vecchie, Venice
Neue Galerie am Wolfgang Gurlitt Museum, Linz, Austria
Galerie Veith Turske, Cologen
1977 Karl-Ernst-Osthaus Museum, Hagen, West Germany
Galerie Rothe, Heidelberg
Galerie Van de Loo, Munich
Galerie Oben, Hagen, West Germany
1978 Galerie Elke und Werner Zimmer, Dusseldorf
Galerie Falchi, Milan
Modern Art Gallery, Vienna
Galerie Ferdinand Meier, Kitzbuhl, Austria
Kunstverein, Braunschweig, West Germany
1979 Stadtische Museum, Meschede, West Germany
Fritz-Winter-Haus, Ahlen, West Germany
1980 Galerie Merten Slominsky, Mulheim, West Germany
Galerie Van de Loo, Munich
Galerie Alice Pauli, Lausanne, Switzerland
Galerie Schlegl, Zurich
Galerie Oben, Hagen, West Germany
1981 Galerie Gunzenhauser, Munich
Galerie Dr. Krohn, Badenweiler, West Germany
Galerie Rothe, Heidelberg
Galerie Strelow, Dusseldorf
Overbeck-Gesellschaft, Hannover
1982 *Rubenspreis—Siegen '82,* Haus Seel, Siegen, West Germany
Galerie Strelow, Dusseldorf
Kunstmuseum, Hannover

1983 Kunsthalle, Darmstadt, West Germany
Wilhelm-Hack-Museum, Ludwigshafen, West Germany
Westfälisches Landesmuseum, Münster, West Germany
Galerie Strelow, Dusseldorf
Galerie Skulima, West Berlin
1984 Galerie Rothe, Heidelberg, West Germany
Galerie Strelow, Dusseldorf
Kunsthalle, Bremen, West Germany
1985 Badischer Kunstverein, Karlsruhe, West Germany
Kunstverein, Augsburg, West Germany
Galerie Strelow, Dusseldorf
Galerie Marghescu, Hannover
1986 Herstand Gallery, New York
Galerie Pro Arte, Freiburg, West Germany
Städtisches Galerie, Quakenbrück, West Germany
Städtisches Museum, Mulheim, West Germany
Galerie Strelow, Dusseldorf
1987 Städtische Galerie, Lüdenscheid, West Germany
Städtische Galerie, Rosenheim, West Germany
Galerie Meyer-Ellinger, Frankfurt
Städtisches Museum, Gelsenkirchen, West Germany
Institut für moderne Kunst, Nuremberg, West Germany
Städtische Galerie, Reutlingen, West Germany
Kunsthalle, Kiel, West Germany
Karl Ernst Osthaus Museum, Hagen, West Germany
1988 *Emil Schumacher: Late Paintings,* Nationalgalerie, Staatliche Museen Preussischer Kulturbesitz, Berlin
1989 *Emil Schumacher: Recent Paintings,* Nationalgalerie Berlin (travelling exhibition)
Emil Schumacher: Paintings on Paper, Schloss Detmold, Germany
Kunstsammlung Nordrhein-Westfalen, Düsseldorf
1990 *Emil Schumacher: Paintings and Works on Paper 1946–90,* Kunstverein, Wolfsburg, Germany
Emil Schumacher: 19 Aquatints—Etchings 1990, Galerie Hans Strelow, Düsseldorf
1991 *Emil Schumacher, 1990–1991,* Galerie Hans Strelow, Düsseldorf
Emil Schumacher: Recent Paintings, André Emmerich Gallery, New York
1992 *Emil Schumacher: Painting 1936–1991,* Stadtische Galerie im Stadelschen Kunstinstitut, Frankfurt am Main (travelling exhibition)
Emil Schumacher: Works from the Years 1955–90, Galerie Neumann, Düsseldorf (travelling exhibition)
Emil Schumacher: Works 1989–92, Galerie Hans Strelow, Düsseldorf
1995 *Emil Schumacher: Paintings 1992–94,* Hans Strelow Gallery, Düsseldorf
1996 *Emil Schumacher,* Stedelijk Museum, Amsterdam
1997 *Emil Schumacher: Retrospective,* Galerie nationale du Jeu de Paume, Paris (travelled to Hamburger Kunsthalle, Hamburg)
Materialbilder, Chapel Art Center, Hamburg, Germany
Emil Schumacher: An Artist and His City, Karl Ernst Osthaus Museum, Hagen, Germany
Emil Schumacher: Kunst im Kontext—Project Kunstlermuseum 3, Hanover, Germany
Emil Schumacher: Fur Ulla, 1996, Friedrich Schiller-Universitat, Jena, Germany

Selected Group Exhibitions:

1951 *Kunder unseres Jahrhunderts,* Ruhrfestspiel, Recklinghausen, West Germany
1954 *Deutsche Kunst nach 1945,* Stedelijk Museum, Amsterdam
1955 *Documenta,* Kassel, West Germany (and 1964, 1977)
1962 *Biennale,* Venice
1966 *International Biennale of Prints,* National Museum of Modern Art, Tokyo
1970 *Carnegie International,* Carnegie Institute, Pittsburgh
1975 *Contemporary German Art,* University Art Museum, Melbourne (toured Australia and the United States)
1981 *Westkunst,* Messehallen, Cologne
1985 *Kunst in der Bundesrepublik 1945–85,* Nationalgalerie, West Berlin
1987 *L'Art en Europe 1945–53,* Musée d'art Moderne, St. Etienne, France
1995 *Material and Idea,* Kunstsammlung Nordrhein-Westfalen, Düsseldorf
1996 *Western Art: German Art 1945–60—Ruhrfestspiele Recklinghausen 1996 Art Exhibition,* Kunsthalle Recklinghausen, Germany
Art After '45: A Selection, Galerie Neher, Essen, Germany
1998 *Brennpunkt Informel: Quellen—Strömungen—Reaktionen,* Heidelberger Kunstverein im Kurpfälzischen Museum der Stadt Heidelberg, Germany
1999 *Summer Guests II,* Galerie Pels-Leusden, Kampen auf Sylt, Germany

Collections:

Nationalgalerie, West Berlin; Städtisches Kunstmuseum, Bonn; Karl-Ernst-Osthaus Museum, Hagen, West Germany; Museum of Modern Art, Belgrade; Museum Nradowe w Karkowie, Cracow, Poland; Musée Cantonal des Beaux-Arts, Lausanne, Switzerland; Neue Galerie der Stadt, Linz, Austria; Moderna Galerija, Ljubljana, Yugoslavia; Albright-Knox Art Gallery, Buffalo, New York; Art Institute of Chicago.

Publications:

By SCHUMACHER: Books— *Emil Schumacher: Irak Skizzen* by Friedrich W. Heckmanns, Cologne 1990. **Articles—**"Farben und Einfalle" in Blatter und Bilder (Wurzburg), March/April 1959; "Neue Kunst in Deutschland" in *The Geijutsu-Shino* (Tokyo), October 1960; "Wegzeichen im Unbekannten" in *Neunzehn deutsche Maler zu Fragen der zeitgenossische Kunst,* edited by Wolfgang Rothe, Heidelberg 1962; "Aphorismen" in *Ein Buch mit Sieben Siegeln,* Heidelberg 1972.

On SCHUMACHER: Books—*Emil Schumacher* by Erwin Sylavanus, Recklinghausen, West Germany 1959; *Emil Schumacher,* exhibition catalog, with text by Werner Schmalenbach, Hannover 1961; *Emil Schumacher: Olbilder und Gouachen* 1962, exhibition catalog, with text by Michel Tapie, Munich 1962; *Emil Schumacher,* exhibition catalog, with text by Werner Schmalenbach, Milan 1962; *Opere Recenti di Emil Schumacher,* exhibition catalog, with text by Werner Schmalenbach, Rome 1962; *VII Bienal de Sao Paulo: Emil Schumacher,* exhibition catalog, with text by Werner Schmalenbach, Dusseldorf 1963; *Emil Schumacher: Olbilder, Gouachen, Grafik*

1964/65, exhibition folder, Munich 1965; *Emil Schumacher,* exhibition catalog, with text by Werner Schmalenbach, Lausanne, Switzerland 1965; *Der doppelte Masstab, Kunstkritik 1955–1966* by John Anthony Thwaites, Frankfurt 1967; *The Minnesota Suite by Emil Schumacher,* exhibition catalog, with text by Werner Schmalenbach, New York 1968; *Emil Schumacher,* exhibition catalog, with text by Werner Schmalenbach, Dusseldorf 1971; *Emil Schumacher: Neue Bilder und Gouachen,* exhibition catalog, with text by Dr. Hesse and Rolf-Günter Dienst, Hagen, West Germany 1975; *Emil Schumacher,* exhibition catalog, with text by Bernard Holeczek, Braunschewig, West Germany 1978; *Emil Schumacher,* exhibition catalog, with text by Jürgen Wissmann, Mulheim, Lausanne and Zurich 1980; *Emil Schumacher* by Werner Schmalenbach, Cologne 1981; *Emil Schumacher: Rubenspreis: Siegen '82,* exhibition catalog, with text by Werner Schmalenbach, Siegen, West Germany 1982; *Emil Schumacher: Arbeiten auf Papier 1957–1982,* exhibition catalog with texts by Joachim Buchner and Bernland Holeczek, Hannover 1982; *Emil Schumacher: Djerba,* with text by Ernst-Gerhard Guse, Stuttgart 1983; *Emil Schumacher,* exhibition catalog with texts by Gunter Busch, Annette Meyer zu Eissen and Andreas Vohwinkel, Bremen 1984; *Emil Schumacher: Maroc,* with text by Jens Christian Jensen, Stuttgart 1987; *Emil Schumacher: Spate Bilder,* exhibition catalog, Budapest 1989; *Emil Schumacher: Gemalde und Werke auf Papier 1946–1990,* exhibition catalog, Wolfsburg 1990; *Emil Schumacher: 19 Aquatinta—Radierungen 1990,* Düsseldorf 1990; *Emil Schumacher, 1990–1991,* exhibition catalog, Düsseldorf 1991; *Emil Schumacher: Recent Paintings,* exhibition catalog, New York 1991; *Emil Schumacher: Painting 1936–1991,* Stuttgart 1992; *Emil Schumacher: Werke 1989–1992,* Düsseldorf 1992; *Emil Schumacher: Bilder 1992–1994,* Düsseldorf 1994; *Emil Schumacher,* exhibition catalog, with text by Rudi H. Fuchs, Amsterdam 1996; *Emil Schumacher: Kunst im Kontext—Project Kunstlermuseum 3,* Hanover 1997; *Emil Schumacher: Fur Ulla,* exhibition catalog, *1996,* Jena 1997. **Articles—**''Emil Schumacher: Resistance Ignites New Energies'' by Peter Winter in *Art International,* no. 4, Autumn 1988; review by Ingrid Schaffner in *Arts Magazine,* vol. 65, Summer 1991; ''Emil Schumacher'' by Marion Leske in *Kunstforum International,* no. 129, January/April 1995.

*

Form: Everything that exists has its appropriate form or tends to assume form: island formations after flood, remnants of snow after thaw, cinders after fire. Form that presupposes life—form that comprises life-is ''formless'' and yet form.

Line: ''The shortest connection between two points is the straight line'' according to geometry. Within the picture the shortest connection between two points can be curved, winding, even discontinuous, but also straight. For the measure of the picture is the force which dictates the path of the line.

Colour: It is not enough to say: this colour is red, this colour is also red matter, palpable, tangible matter. Its flexibility has to be overcome. Only then does it assume character.

Matter: Picture material and picture matter: the one stands at the beginning, the other at the end. Material stands for both inspiration and resistance. The picture is formed from the essence but also the resistance of the material. The character of the picture cannot only be that of its materials.

Destruction: The most extreme form for crushing resistance is destruction: a primitive gesture of despair and desire. The answer is not sanctify, but: exorcise; not: restore, but incorporate the act of destruction in the picture—as expression and as form.

Space: Depth: not only the depth dimension of the picture but palpable tangible nearness: the picture space is closed in the backround, presses forward. Width: line which describes the space. Curves which span it, contours which define it. Defined finitely measurable—and yet not measurable again—space.

Nature: In any case the earth closer than the stars. So thought turns to landscape: above and below the horizon line. They are not landscapes; but how could I elude nature.

—Emil Schumacher

* * *

Emil Schumacher belongs to that generation of German artists who spent their youth separated from the artistic developments beyond the German frontiers. In his birthplace, Hagen, the memory of the early years of modernism remained alive in the survival of Karl Ernst Osthaus' Activities and in the Folkwang Museum which he founded, and finally through the painter Christian Rholfs who had accomplished in his work the development from realism to an expressionism which used colour as an independent value. Schumacher's early gouaches, woodcuts and paintings follow, with perceptible modification to colour and drawing, the late works of Rholfs. His most important themes are still-lifes with the simplest everyday objects, whose poetry Schumacher makes visible with variations of tone or luminous colours. The tendency to experiment with unconventional materials is seen in his graphic prints during this period.

In 1950 Schumacher, influenced by developments in France, turned to abstract painting which through him gains a content which is difficult to express in words. After the mid 1950s the initial solid closed forms become more open, more relaxed, more defined by the colour structure. Between 1955 and 1958 the ''Test Objects'' which, without constricting frames, are conceived as independent sculptural reliefs, led to the mature period of his oeuvre. Schumacher's creative ideas are based on the material beauty of substance and colour which he condenses to independent paraphrastic signs. The creative constellations and picture titles awaken associations with objective realms without restricting the spectator, yet marking his perception as if with a poetry without words. Schumacher's Art lives in the controlled spontaneity of the production process and in a subject related freedom both for himself and for the spectator. Without following in an historic manner tendencies imitative of Japenese art, he employs suggestions of it in oriental calligraphy.

In Western art of the last decades there are few examples which approach so closely the Far Eastern concept of painting as Schumacher's pictures, not because of formal parallels to calligraphy but above all because of the poetic subjectivity which for a Far Eastern viewer is central to his conceptions of art. For this reason distinctions in Tokyo and Saigon were among the earliest appreciations of Schumacher at an international level. From the late 1950s on, the artist numbered among the leading representatives of an informal painting whose fashionable period he survived by virtue off the subtlety and strength of his pictures.

A picture by Schumacher results as a rule from a process in which tempo of painting and lengthy periods of waiting, leading to a finished article, its destruction and renewed completion, succeed one another. His painting could be described as a dialectical process on the level of purely material experience if such a formulation did not hide the risk of it being understood as calculated intellectutal aestheticism. Schumacher who, as his picture titles demonstrate, has a thorough command of words, declines to deliver rational, analytic explanations of his activity. This also makes him into a European kindred spirit of the Zen Master.

—Heinz Spielmann

SCOTT, Tim

Nationality: British. **Born:** Richmond, Surrey, 18 April 1937. **Education:** Educated in Lausanne, Switzerland; studied at Tunbridge Wells School of Art, Kent, 1954, Architectural Association, London, 1954–59, and under Anthony Caro, at St. Martin's School of Art, London, 1955–59. **Family:** Married Malkanthi Wirekoon in 1958; children: Paloma, Roman, Maya, Chantal, and Anil. **Career:** Independent sculptor, since 1960. Worked in the Atelier Le Corbusier/Wogenscky architectural office, Paris, 1959–61 and as an architect for Fry, Drew and Partners, London, 1962; part-time teacher, St. Martin's School of Art and other institutions, 1961–79; head of department of fine art, Birmingham Polytechnic, 1976–78; head of department of sculpture, St. Martin's School of Art, 1980–86; professor of sculpture, Akademie den Bildenden Kunste, Nuremberg, 1993—. **Awards:** Peter Stuyvesant Bursary, 1965. **Address:** 7 Prideaux Place, London, WCIX 9PP, England.

Tim Scott: *Peach Wheels,* 1961–62. ©Tate Gallery, London/Art Resource, NY; courtesy of Tate Gallery.

Individual Exhibitions:

1966 Waddington Galleries, London
1967 Whitechapel Art Gallery, London
1969 *New Sculpture,* Museum of Modern Art, Oxford
Lawrence Rubin Gallery, New York
Waddington Galleries, London
1971 Lawrence Rubin Gallery, New York
Waddington Galleries, London
Tate Gallery, London
1972 Museum of Fine Arts, Boston
1973 Corcoran Gallery of Art, Washington, D.C.
Waddington Galleries, London
1974 André Emmerich Gallery, New York
1975 Waddington and Tooth Galleries, London
1976 Edmonton Art Gallery, Alberta
Norman McKenzie Art Gallery, Regina, Saskatchewan
Art Gallery of Windsor, Ontario
David Mirvish Gallery, Toronto
1977 Tibor de Nagy Gallery, New York
Waddington and Tooth Galleries, New York
Galerie Wentzel, Hamburg
1979 Knoedler Gallery, London
Tiergarten 105, Hannover
Kunsthalle, Bielefeld, West Germany
1980 Knoedler Gallery, London
Kettle's Yard Gallery, Cambridge (retrospective)
Galerie Ziegler, Zurich
1981 Kunsthalle, Hamburg
1982 Galerie Wentzel, Cologne
1983 Atrium der Stadt Aachen, West Germany
Klonaridis Inc., Toronto
1984 Galerie Wentzel, Cologne
1986 Kunsthandel Grill, Vienna
1987 Galerie Wentzel, Cologne
Galerie Appel und Fertsch, Frankfurt
1988 Gallerie Wentzel, Cologne
Kunstverein Braunschweig
Westfälisches Candmuseum, Munster
Saariand Museum, Saarbröcken
Städt Museum, Leverkusen
Städtische Galerie, Regensburg
1989 Galerie Biederman, Munich
1990 Galerie Wentzel, Cologne
Deutschlandfunk, Cologne
1992 Galerie in Fonte, Berlin
Galerie Tiergarten, Hanover
1993 Deutsche Bank, Colombo
Galerie Winkelmann, Dusseldorf
1994 Galerie Appel and Fertsch, Frankfurt
Galerie Fahlbusch, Mannheim

Selected Group Exhibitions:

1958 *Young Contemporaries,* RBA Gallery, London (and 1959)
1961 *26 Young Sculptors,* Institute of Contemporary Arts, London
1965 *New Generation,* Whitechapel Art Gallery, London
1966 *Primary Structures,* Jewish Museum, New York

1967 *Young British Sculptors,* Kunsthalle, Berne
1968 *Junge Generation Grossbritannein,* Akademie der Bildenden Kunst, Berlin
1970 *Contemporary British Art,* National Museum of Modern Art, Tokyo
1974 *Sculpture in Steel,* Edmonton Art Gallery, Alberta
1976 *Arte Inglesi Oggi 1960–1976,* Palazzo Reale, Milan
1981 *20th Century British Sculpture,* Whitechapel Art Gallery, London
1999 *'45-'99: A Personal View of British Painting and Sculpture,* Kettle's Yard, Cambridge, England

Collections:

Tate Gallery, London; Arts Council of Great Britain, London; Gulbenkian Foundation, Lisbon; Museum of Modern Art, New York; Museum of Fine Arts, Boston; Hirshhorn Museum and Sculpture Garden, Smithsonian Institution, Washington, D.C.; National Gallery of Victoria, Melbourne.

Publications:

By SCOTT: Articles—''Tim Scott, Sculptor,'' interview in *Journal of the Architectural Association* (London), May 1967; ''Reflections on Sculpture: A Commentary on Notes by William Tucker'' in *Tim Scott,* exhibition catalog, London 1967, reprinted in *I.C.A. Magazine* (London), April 1968; ''Colour in Sculpture,'' with Phillip King, David Annesley, and William Turnbull, in *Studio International* (London), January 1969, reprinted in *Tim Scott: New Sculpture,* exhibition catalog, Oxford, 1969; ''Extracts from Tim Scott's Personal Notebooks (1958–59, 1961, 1965)'' in *Potlatch* (London), May 1969; ''Gone Too Far,'' with Alan Gour, in *Artscribe* (London), Summer 1983.

On Scott: Books—*New Generation,* exhibition catalog by Bryan Robertson, London 1965; *Tim Scott: Sculpture 1961–67,* London 1967; *Tim Scott,* exhibition catalog, London 1969; *Tim Scott,* exhibition catalog by Karen Wilkin, Edmonton, Alberta 1976; *Sculpture in Great Britain 1960–66 by the St. Martin's Group* by R. C. Rossi, Ph.D. thesis, New York University 1978; *Tim Scott,* exhibition catalog, Bielefeld, West Germany 1979; *Tim Scott,* exhibition catalog, Braunschweig and Others, 1988; *Tim Scott,* exhibition catalog, Cologne 1991; *Tim Scott,* exhibition catalog, Dusseldorf, 1993; *Tim Scott,* exhibition catalog, 1993; *Tim Scott,* exhibition catalog, 1993. **Articles—**''British Sculpture in the '60s: Colour as Form'' by Bryan Robertson in *Modern Painters,* vol. 12, no.4, Winter 1999.

* * *

Tim Scott is probably the best of his generation of post-Caro English sculptors. Although he was a student of Caro, he managed to avoid the pervasive influence of the older artist and stake out territory of his own. The clear articulation in space which is typical of Scott's work may owe something to Caro, but its bulk and mass do not. If anything, it seems closer to the tradition of the solid figurative monolith than to modernist construction. This sounds less far-fetched in relation to work which had been abstract and usually made by collaging, if we consider the history of Scott's development.

His early work was a response to Brancusi, the only modernist sculptor whose work he knew first hand who seemed to offer a way into abstraction. At the time, Scott knew of David Smith only through photographs seen by chance at a U.S. Information Service library, when he was living in Paris, and his studies with Caro pre-dated Caro's use of steel. Scott liked the simplicity and solidity of Brancusi's forms, and says that his work of the early 1960s was an attempt to get past Brancusi, not through open construction (which he knew little about) but by using materials and technology which allowed him to assemble volumetric, large scale forms in unconventional ways. Scott's works of the 1960s are made of such diverse materials as fiberglass, sheet acrylic, glass and metal tubing, employed equally for their unique properties and for the contrast their combination afforded.

The sculptures are both delicate and remarkably generous in scale. They are the equivalent of drawing with sweeps of the entire arm, rather than with controlled hand movements. Large geometric solids are played against thin acrylic sheets; flat shiny sheets are played, in turn, against metal tubing. Tubing outlines structures which echo solid forms, and flat cut-out shapes translate these outlines into yet another dimension. If there is any overt connection with Brancusi, it is in this counterpoint of like and unlike forms, which could be related to the way the Rumanian artist set his referential organic sculptures on severe and generalized bases; the stacking of wood, stone and metal in these assemblies must also have interested Scott. But even if Brancusi was a chosen ancestor, Scott's work never looked like anyone else's. His use of color in the 1960s pieces is especially personal. The sculptures are widely polychromatic, sometimes incorporating as many as six or eight different hues. But color is always a function of materials, a way of differentiating forms—or, as in the *Bird in Arras* series of 1967–70, a way of generating forms. It never serves as a unifying skin.

As if in response to these extraordinary, fragile, colored sculptures, Scott began using thick acrylic slabs and correspondingly thick unpainted steel bars in his works of the early 1970s. This uncanny series depends upon seemingly contradictory qualities of transparency and brutal bulk. Gradually, the steel elements of these works began to dominate the plastic slabs, and by 1975 Scott was working exclusively in steel.

He had been dissatisfied for some time with the indirectness of his earlier working methods, and relished the new immediacy of welded construction, but the essential qualities of his mixed media work remained in the steel pieces. Like earlier sculptures, they are generous in scale, no matter what their size, and despite the uniformity of their material, they still depend upon dramatic contrast of like and unlike forms. The piled steel and iron components of a single sculpture may be related by virtue of similar density and mass, but they are often completely unlike in other respects. Ragged flame-cut edges are juxtaposed with smooth geometric solids; thick sheets are contrasted with chunky bars and discs. And no matter how massive their components, Scott's sculptures in steel retain the vigorous, expansive drawing of his early works.

Since about 1980, Scott has intensified his pursuit of directness. Reflecting on what characterized the sculpture he admired most, he concluded that a sense of tension and stress analogous to that of the body in motion was critical. He also became convinced that steel that had already been processed, turned into channel, plate, or angle, for example, was too inexpressive for his purposes. He wished to shape the metal himself and began a series made by the laborious process of forging. Because of inevitable limitations inherent in this method of working steel, the forged sculptures tend to be small in size—but extraordinarily complex and powerful.

Scott's typical generous drawing is translated into inflections and bends in massive lengths of metal. We are acutely aware of the physical effort expended in shaping these members, but they move so effortlessly through space, play so eloquently off less worked blocks of steel, that our perception of Scott's initial labor seems irrelevant. Paradoxically, despite their intense physicality, Scott's forged pieces are so much about the material itself, its ability to change shape when heated and pounded, that his sculptures have a curious kinship with abstract paintings by those of his colleagues, such as Jules Olitski or Lawrence Poons, or their common ancestor, Jackson Pollock, who ''find'' their images paying close attention to how their materials behave.

Recently, Scott has experimented with still other materials and other processes, but his sculpture has remained generous, expansive, and richly articulated. By rethinking the properties of abstract constructed sculpture, Scott has expanded possibilities, and a group of young British sculptors, mostly former students at St. Martin's School of Art when Scott was head of the sculpture department, are currently attempting to expand them still further. Scott's work continues to critize theirs. His apparently unyielding, dense, worked elements are used aggressively to embrace and activate large areas of space. They are sculptures that cannot be ignored, but they refuse to be ingratiating. Like his earlier works, the best of Scott's forge sculptures are at once powerful, lyrical, and brutal.

—Karen Wilkin

SCOTT, William

Nationality: British. **Born:** William George Scott, Greenock, Renfrewshire, Scotland, 15 February 1913; moved with his family to Enniskillen, Northern Ireland, 1922. **Education:** Studied privately with Kathleen Birdie, Enniskillen, Northern Ireland, c. 1926; Belfast College of Art, 1928–30; studied sculpture, 1931–33, and painting, 1934–35, at the Royal Academy Schools, London. **Military Service:** 1942–46. **Family:** Married Mary Lucas in 1937; sons: Robert and James. **Career:** Painter; worked in Cornwall for six months, 1936; visited France and settled in Pont Aven, Brittany, 1937; founder, with Mary Scott and Geoffrey Nelson, Summer Painting School, Pont Aven, France, 1938; lived in St. Tropez, France, 1938–39, but fled at outbreak of war, via Dublin, to London, where he settled in Chelsea; moved to Hallatrow, Somerset, 1974. Member, *Festival of Britain* Commission, London 1951; visited the United States, 1953 and 1959; settled in Edinburgh. Part-time lecturer, 1941, and senior painting master, 1946–56, Bath Academy of Art, Corsham, Wiltshire; artist-in-residence, Ford Foundation, Berlin 1963. **Member:** Société du Salon d'Automme, Paris, 1938; associate of the Royal Academy of Arts, 1977. **Awards:** Silver Medal for Sculpture, Royal Academy of Arts, London, 1933; Landseer Scholarship in Painting, London, 1934; Leverhulme Travel Scholarship, 1935. **Agent:** Waddington Galleries, 34 Cork Street, London, W1, England; Joseph Rickards Gallery, 1045 Madison Avenue, New York, New York, 10021. **Died:** Of complications related to Alzheimer's disease, in Bath, England, 28 December 1989.

Individual Exhibitions:

1942 Leger Galleries, London
Leger Galleries, London
Leger Galleries, London (with Mary Scott)
1950 White Chapel Art Gallery, London
1953 Hanover Gallery, London
1954 Hanover Gallery, London
Martha Jackson Gallery, New York (with Barbara Hepworth and Francis Bacon)
1955 Hanover Gallery, London (with Francis Bacon and Graham Sutherland)
1956 Hanover Gallery, London
Martha Jackson Gallery, New York
1958 *Biennale,* Venice (toured Europe)
1959 Martha Jackson Gallery, New York
Galleria Galatea, Turin
Galleria Blu, Milan
Galerie Charles Lienhard, Zurich
Galleria dell'Ariete, Milan
1960 Kestner Gesellschaft, Hannover (toured West Germany)
1961 Esther Robles Gallery, Los Angeles
Hannover Gallery, London
Galerie Schmela, Dusseldorf
1962 Hanover Gallery, London
Museu de Arte Moderna, Rio de Janeiro (travelled to the Museo Nacional de Bellas Artes, Buenos Aires)
Martha Jackson Gallery, New York
1963 Kunsthalle, Berne
Hanover Gallery, London
Ulster Museum, Belfast
Galerie Anderson-Mayer, Paris
1966 Galerie Gimpel-Hanover, Zurich
1967 Dawson Gallery, Dublin
Bear Lane Gallery, Oxford
Hanover Gallery, London
1968 Hanover Gallery, London
Dawson Gallery, Dublin
1969 Richard Demarco Gallery, Edinburgh
Hanover Gallery, London
1971 Hanover Gallery, London
Scottish National Gallery of Modern Art Edinburgh (travelled to the Aberdeen Art Gallery, Scotland)
1972 *Paintings, Drawings, Gouaches 1938–1971,* Tate Gallery, London
1973 Martha Jackson Gallery, New York
Gallery Moos, Toronto
1974 Gimpel Fils Gallery, London
Arnolfini Gallery, Bristol
Galerie Gimpel-Hanover, Zurich
1975 Martha Jackson Gallery, New York
Albright-Knox Art Gallery, Buffalo, New York
Santa Barbara Museum of Art, California
Gallery Moos, Toronto
1976 Gimpel Fils Gallery, London
Kasahara Gallery, Tokyo
Martha Jackson Gallery, New York
1979 Fermanagh County Museum, Orchard Gallery, Londonderry (travelled to Northern Ireland Arts Council Gallery, Belfast)

1981 Imperial War Museum, London
1985 Gimpel Fils, London
1986 Ulster Museum, Belfast
Guinness Hop Store, Dublin
Scottish National Gallery of Modern Art, Edinburgh
1987 *William Scott: Paintings 1953–1986,* Gimpel Fils Gallery, London (catalog)
1990 *William Scott,* Bernard Jacobson Gallery, London (catalog)
1992 *William Scott: Paintings on Paper and Canvas,* André Emmerich Gallery (catalog)
1997 *William Scott,* Bernard Jacobson Gallery, London
1998 *William Scott: Paintings and Drawings,* Irish Museum of Modern Art, Dublin (catalog)
William Scott: Early Works, Charleston Gallery, England
William Scott, Kerlin Gallery, Dublin

Selected Group Exhibitions:

1950 *Painter's Progress,* Whitechapel Art Gallery, London
1953 *Bienal,* Sao Paulo
1955 *Carnegie International,* Carnegie Institute, Pittsburgh
1963 *Some Aspects of Contemporary British Painting,* Art Gallery of Ontario, Toronto
1964 *Documenta,* Kassel, West Germany
1977 *British Painting 1952–1977,* Royal Academy of Arts, London
1983 *Aspects of British Art,* Guggenheim Museum, New York
1985 *The Irresistible Object: Still Life 1600–1985,* Leeds City Art Gallery, Yorkshire
1988 *The Presence of Painting: Aspects of British Abstraction 1957–1988,* Mappin Art Gallery, Sheffield (traveled to Hatton Gallery, Newcastle-upon-Tyne; Ikon Gallery, Birmingham, England) (catalog)
1990 Royal Academy of Arts, London
1997 *Treasure Island,* Fundacao Calouste Gulbenkian, Lisbon, Portugal
Dreams and Traditions: 300 Years of British and Irish Paintings from the Collection of the Ulster Museum, Belfast (traveling exhibition) (catalog)

Collections:

Tate Gallery, London; Victoria and Albert Museum, London; Scottish National Gallery of Modern Art, Edinburgh; Nationalgalerie, West Berlin; Kunsthalle, Hamburg; Museum des 20. Jahrhunderts, Vienna; Centre Georges Pompidou, Paris; Konstmuseum, Gothenburgh, Sweden; National Gallery of Victoria, Melbourne; Brooklyn Museum, New York; Galleria Nazionale d'Arte Moderna, Rome; Museum of Modern Art, New York.

Publications:

By SCOTT: Books—*A Girl Surveyed,* with poems by Edward Lucie-Smith, London 1971. **Articles**—statement in *The New Decade,* exhibition catalog, New York 1955; "Mr. William Scott Talks of Developments in Abstract Art" in *The Times* (London), January 1960; "William Scott in Conversation with Tony Rothon" in *Studio International* (London), December 1974.

On SCOTT: Books—*Abstract Artists: Their Work and Theory* by Lawrence Alloway, London 1954; *William Scott* by Ronald Alley, London 1963; *William Scott: Paintings* by Alan Bowness and others, London 1964; *William Scott: Paintings, Drawings and Gouaches 1938–1971,* exhibition catalog by Alan Bowness, London 1972; *William Scott: Drawings,* edited by Lou Lepac, New York 1975; *William Scott,* exhibition catalog with texts by Ronald Alley and T. P. Flanagan, Belfast 1986; *William Scott, 1913–1989: Lithographs,* London 1992. **Articles**—Obituary in *The Times* (London), Saturday, 30 December 1989; "William Scott" by Patrick Heron in *Modern Painters* (London), vol. 3, no. 4, Winter 1990–91; "Herbert Read Introduces William Scott" by Herbert Read in *Modern Painters* (London), vol. 3, no. 4, Winter 1990–91; "Great Scott!" by Richard Ingleby in *Art Review* (London), vol. 49, April 1997; "William Scott" by Norbert Lynton in *Modern Painters* (London), vol. 11, no. 3, Autumn 1998.

* * *

William Scott is a member of the generation of English artists who were still dominated and influenced by Europe, notably Paris, a situation radically changed by the decline of the modern art situation in France, and the virtual termination of its power to attract and stimulate, which dates from the outbreak of the 1939 war. His Scottish/Irish origins are, in this context, important since Scottish art has always had a stronger relationship to French that to English painting, and, indeed, the Scots produced a far more successful brand of both Impressionism and post-Impressionism than their fellow-islanders. Where Scott is exceptional is that, unlike his compatriots, he progressed to the possibilities of post-Cubism, so that whilst retaining the native love for rich colour and the Scottish instinct for controlled design, he was able to develop a neo-cubist formula for the heightened, dramatic presentation of everyday objects.

It is precisely in this mixture of unpretentious simplicity and dramatic, decorative creativity, that Scott emerges as an artist of individuality. He spent a number of years before the outbreak of the war travelling and working in Italy and France, copying the work of Italian masters, including Piero della Francesca—a good foundation for disciplined, neo-geometric composition—and in France was attracted by the sensuous colourists, Corot, Manet, Gauguin, Bonnard, Matisse. His increasing involvement with still-life resulted in a desire, in his own words, "to look at Cézanne not through cubist eyes, but rather through the eyes of Chardin."

This phrase is an important clue: Scott never worked clinically, analyzing space and form, but rather as a relaxed humanist, finding in everyday domestic objects sufficient variations, combinations, reflections of the human situation. His early works in the genre are sombre, disciplined, tonally dry compositions, very much in the social-realist style of the Euston Road School. An early visit to Cornwall affected both his colour, the use of light, and the growing abstract formalism in his work. He resisted the immense impact of surrealism, and the introverted fantasy worlds of Klee or Kandinsky, which affected his generation. After a slight involvement in the romantic landscape movement, and a series of monumental, Gauguinesque portrait studies, in the post-war period Scott found his true subject, still-life, and as a result of living in Cornwall, a stylized, symbolic composition related to the formula of Ben Nicholson.

From the end of the 1940s Scott produced a fine series of still-life paintings, imbuing innocent objects with both sexual and metaphysical connotations, as have the best painters in the genre, from Chardin to Morandi. Realistic details were increasingly eliminated, so that the painting area becomes an isolated table-top, on which the chosen objects are carefully arranged, and painted with elegant, abstract discrimination. In time these composition took on architectonic, linear mannerisms, ending in complete abstraction; but by the end of the 1950s Scott returned to realistic commitment, although now adopting a more complex plastic method. By the turn of the decade yet another switch to decorative abstraction had taken place, culminating in series of public murals.

This long period of uncertainty and searching resolved itself by a return to still-life, no longer descriptive, now extenuated with almost oriental elegance into carefully placed formalized objects in seas of brilliant colour. In the intervening period Scott had spent periods teaching in Canada and visiting the United States, the first European painter to visit Pollock, meeting Rothko and Kline. Scott was bewildered and impressed by the scale and self-confidence of their work; the effect, he says, was the discontinuance of abstraction in order to develop his own brand of symbolic realism on a larger scale.

—Charles Spencer

SEAMAN, Bill

Nationality: American. **Education:** Rhode Island School of Design, 1976–77; San Francisco Art Institute, California, B.F.A., 1979; Massachusetts Institute of Technology, Cambridge, Master of Science, Visual Studies (MSvisS), 1985; Centre for Advanced Inquiry in the Interactive Arts, University of Wales, Newport, Ph.D., 1999. **Career:** Professor, UCLA Center for Digital Arts, 1999—. **Awards:** Intel Research Gift, for *Hybrid Invention Generator,* UCLA, Los Angeles, California, 2000, 2001; Interaction Design Award, *The World Generator/The Engine of Desire,* software for virtual and spatial performances, Hannover, Germany, 1998; Bonn Videonale Prize, *Passage Sets/One Pulls Pivots at the Tip of the Tongue,* Bonn, Germany, 1996; Distinction, Interactive Art, *Passage Sets/One Pulls Pivots at the Tip of the Tongue,* Prix Ars Electronica, Linz, Austria, 1995; International German Video Art Prize, *Passage Sets/One Pulls Pivots at the Tip of the Tongue,* Baden Baden, Germany, 1995; First Prize, Berlin Film and Video Festival, Multimedia, Berlin, 1995; Siemens' Stipendium, ZKM, Karlsruhe, Germany, 1993; Distinction Interactive Art, *The Watch Detail,* Prix Ars Electronica, Linz, Austria, 1992; Best International Video, *Telling Motions,* Linear Video, Cadíz, Spain, 1992; Fellowship, Massachusetts State Council Artist, Boston, Massachusetts, 1989; Zone Video Festival Prize, Springfield, Massachusetts, 1989; Fellowship, National Endowment for the Arts, Washington, D.C., 1987; Cannon Europa Prize, *Telling Motions,* Linear Video, World Wide Video Festival, Den Haag, Holland, 1987; Awards in the Visual Arts, Rockefeller Foundation, Winston-Salem, North Carolina, 1986; Finalist, Artist Foundation, Boston, Massachusetts, 1986; Monte Verite Invitational Prize, Locarno, Switzerland, 1985; First Prize, 2nd International Biennial, *S.HE,* Linear Video, Ljubljana, Yugoslavia, 1985; Best Sound, Geneva International Video Festival, Geneva, Switzerland, 1985; First Prize, San Francisco Art Institute, Sound Art, *From Architecture,* San Francisco, California, 1979. **Address:** UCLA Center for Digital Arts, 1100 Dickson Wight Art Gallery, Los Angeles, California 90095–1620, U.S.A.

Selected Individual Exhibitions:

1985 *Water Wheel,* Visible Studies Workshop, Rochester, New York
1989 *The Design of the Grip,* Institute of Contemporary Art, Boston, Massachusetts
1991 *Selected Tapes and Word Drawings,* Roslyn Oxley9 Gallery, Sydney, Australia
1992 *The Exquisite Mechanism of Shivers,* Experimental Art Foundation, Adelaide, Australia (travelled to Inter Communication Gallery, NTT Media Lab, Tokyo, Japan)
1994 *Abstraction Machine/Erotic—-The Voyeur of Light,* Room 32, Alternative Installation Space, Regents Court Hotel, Sydney, Australia
1995 *Passage Sets/One Pulls Pivots at the Tip of the Tongue,* Level 2 Project Space, Art Gallery of New South Wales, Sydney, Australia (traveled to Kunst und Ausstellungshalle der Bundesrepublik Deutschland, Bonn, Germany; Sprengle Museum, Hannover, Germany)
1997 *The World Generator/The Engine of Desire,* with Gideon May, C3—Center for Culture & Communication, Budapest, Hungary
2000 *Red Dice/Dés Chiffrés,* Canadian National Gallery, Ottowa, Canada (traveled to The Daniel Langlois Foundation/Cinémateque Québecoise, Montreal, Canada) (catalog)

Selected Group Exhibitions:

1990 *Mappings/The Voice of Displacement,* Artspace, Computer Print and Audio, Sydney, Australia
1993 *Abstraction Machine* (auto-generative computer-based work), Virtu, Ivan Dougherty Gallery, Sydney, Australia
1997 *The World Generator,* with Gideon May, Projection VR, Wilhelm Lembruck Museum, Duisburg, Germany
1999 *The World Generator/The Engine of Desire,* with Gideon May, Projection VR, Budapest, Hungary

Public Installations:

Water Wheel, 7 Channel Installation, Visible Studies Workshop, Rochester, New York 1989; *The Design of the Grip,* 9 Channel Installation, Kijkhuis, Den Haag, Holland 1990; *The Watch Detail,* Interactive Installation (catalog), Experimental Art Foundation, Adelaide, Australia 1992; *The Exquisite Mechanism of Shivers,* Interactive Installation (catalog), Artificial Games, München, Germany 1993; *Passage Sets/One Pulls Pivots at the Tip of the Tongue,* Interactive Installation, Serious Games, Barbican Gallery, London 1997; *Exchange Fields,* Interactive Installation, with Regina Van Berkel, Vision Ruhr, Dortmund, Germany 2000.

Publications:

By SEAMAN: Books—*Recombinant Poetics* (dissertation), University of Wales, 1999. **Articles—**''Recombinant Poetics'' at www.cda.ucla.edu/faculty/seaman/webreadytexts/recombinant.html (accessed June 2001).

On SEAMAN: Books—*Der Electronische Raum (The Electronic Space)* by Erkki Huhtamo, 1998. **Articles—**''Hybrid Architectures/ Media Information Environments'' in *Intelligent Environments-—Spatial Aspect of the Information Revolution* edited by Peter Droege, Amsterdam 1997; ''Emergent Constructions: Re-embodied Intelligence within Recombinant Poetic Networks'' in *Digital Creativity,* vol. 9, no. 3, 1998; ''Nonsense Logic'' in *Reframing Consciousness,* edited by Roy Ascott, 1999; ''Exchange Fields: Embodied Positioning as Interface Strategy'' in *Convergence Magazine* (special issue on Intelligent Environments), 2001; ''Bill Seaman: Red Dice'' in *In Depth Art News*, National Gallery of Canada, Ottawa at www.absolutearts.com/artsnews (accessed June 2001).

* * *

Bill Seaman uses digital media to create evocative visual poetry. In a dissertation entitled *Recombinant Poetics* (2000) Seaman theorizes that as ''profound technological changes'' affect how people ''communicate, share knowledge and learn,'' so too do they affect changes in poetics. ''Thus a techno-poetics is explored.''

Seaman calls this new form of poetics ''Recombinant Poetics,'' and his media includes digital video, digital stills, 3-D digital objects, 3-D animations, digital spoken and written text, and digital music/ noise. In *Recombinanat Poetics*, Seaman writes, ''It is through the combination and recombination of these evocative fields of meaning, as experienced by an engaged participant, that a new form of poetics can emerge—Recombinant Poetics.''

Seaman refers to participants in his techno-poetic installations as "vusers," a linguistic hybrid of viewer and user. The vuser is crucial to Seaman's visual poetry; it is the vuser who brings meaning to the poetry. In *Recombinant Poetics*, Seaman states that, ''The vuser of the environment takes an active role in the construction of meaning through interaction. The initial set of media-elements forms a primary context. The vuser then disrupts this context by repositioning the variables across a 'plateau' space.''

Thus, Seaman has created a highly subjective art form. Each vuser has a different effect on—and is affected differently by—the installations. One could argue that this is the case in pre-existing forms of poetry and visual art, that when one reads a poem or views a painting he/she is responsible for forming meaning, and that this meaning is rarely the same among different viewers. In Seaman's work, however, the subjectivity, the role of the vuser, is magnified more explicitly than it would be in approaching other, more orthodox works of art. In *Exchange Fields* (2000), Seaman used a series of dance sequences performed by Regina Von Berkel to create a truly interactive installation. An interactive screen displays Von Berkel's dances, which change and reflect the vuser's own actions. On either side of the interactive screen is a non-interactive one, a linear documentary. These screens are aided by a sound track and poetic text which scrolls across the screen.

Seaman's works are highly interactive experiences, collaborations between the artist, the vuser, and the electronic media. In *Recombinant Poetics,* Seaman maintains that ''we are connected biologically (structurally coupled) to machines through thought. Thought is a biological process—a series of electro-chemical flows.'' His art is a product of this relationship between man and machine.

In ''Red Dice,'' Seaman pays homage to French poet Stephane Mallarme. At the heart of the piece is video footage of a natural and industrial site in the Ottawa area. The images are backed by an audio track of French and English. The piece is equipped with an electronic writing tablet and pen on which Mallarme's poem, ''Un coup de des jamals n'abolira le hasard'' (''Dice thrown never will annul chance''). The vuser is invited to scroll through the poem and use the pen to access Seaman's images, sounds, and poetry. Other viewers are able to view the vuser's actions via a projection of the tablet.

''Red Dice'' is one of Seaman's many works that enable a vuser to control his own ''flight'' through words, images, and sounds. In the development of his Recombinant Poetics, Seaman was heavily influenced by the montages of Sergei Eisenstein. Seaman cites Eisenstein's theory that, ''. . . montage is conflict. As the basis for every art is conflict. . . . The shot appears as the cell of montage. Therefore it must be considered from the viewpoint of conflict.'' Seaman writes, ''I can further legitimize understanding of the techno-poetic from a montage perspective.''

—Aaron Jacobs

SEDGLEY, Pete

Nationality: British. **Born:** London, 19 March 1930. **Education:** Studied building and architecture at Brixton Technical College, 1944–46; mainly self-taught in art, from 1959. **Military Service:** Served in the Royal Army Ordinance Corps, Egypt, 1948–50, and in the Royal Air Force, 1959. **Family:** Married Marguerite Wiltshire in 1951; children: Richard and Laura. **Career:** Architectural assistant, R. Ward and Partners, London, 1946–48 and 1950–52; Gollins, Melvin, Ward, London, 1953–54; Clifford Culpin, London, 1955–56; and Architects Co-Partnership, London, 1956–59. Independent artist since 1966. Founded Building Technicians Co-operative, making prototype dwellings and furniture, 1957–58, and Art Information Registry (AIR) and Space Provision Artists Cultural and Education (SPACE), London 1968. Lives and works in Berlin, and in Worthing, Sussex, since 1971. **Awards:** Prize, *Mainichi International Biennale,* Tokyo, 1966; DAAD Grant, Berlin, 1971. **Agent:** Austin/Desmond Gallery, London. **Address:** 31 Littlehampton Road, Worthington BN13 1QJ, England, and Lindenallee 20, 14050 Berlin, Germany.

Individual Exhibitions:

1965 McRoberts and Tunnard Gallery, London
Howard Wise Gallery, New York
1966 McRoberts and Tunnard Gallery, London
Howard Wise Gallery, New York
Richard Feigen Gallery, Chicago
1968 Galerie Neuendorf, Hamburg
Redfern Gallery, London
Galerie Reckermann, Kassel, West Germany
1970 Trinity College, Dublin
1971 St. Paul's School, London
Haus am Waldsee, Berlin
1972 Forum Kunst, Rottweil, West Germany
1973 Ikon Gallery, Birmingham
DLI Museum, Durham
Midland Group Gallery, Nottingham
Arnolfini Gallery, Bristol
1977 Redfern Gallery, London
1978 Akademie der Kunst, Berlin
1979 Overbeck-Gesellshaft, Lübeck

1980 Redfern Gallery, London
1981 Hendriks Gallery, Dublin
Project Gallery, Dublin
Galerie im Zentrum, Berlin
1982 Galerie Ferme, Malmo, Sweden
1983 Redfern Gallery, London
1984 Galerie Seestrasse, Steckborn, Switzerland
1985 Bede Gallery, Jarrow, Country Durham
Galerie Ferme, Malmo, Sweden
1986 Galerie Ferme, Malmo, Sweden
Galerie Blance, Stockholm
1987 Norrkoping Art Museum, Sweden
1991 New York Hall of Science
1994 Neuberger Museum, New York
1997 The Czech Museum of Fine Arts, Prague
2000 Austin/Desmond Gallery, London

Selected Group Exhibitions:

1965 *The Responsive Eye,* Museum of Modern Art, New York
1966 *Mainichi International Biennale,* Tokyo
1970 *Contemporary British Art,* National Museum of Art, Tokyo
1977 *Silver Jubilee,* Tate Gallery and Royal Academy of Arts, London
1978 *Constructive Tendencies,* Galerie Christl, Stockholm
1980 *Kelpra Studio Collection,* Tate Gallery, London
1981 *Distinct Form,* Konsthallen, Skövde, Sweden
1982 *Konsekvens: A Tribute to Olle Baerling,* Liljevalchs, Stockholm
1986 *Art and Science,* at the *Biennale,* Venice
1993 *The Sixties Art Scene in London,* Barbican Art Gallery, London

Collections:

Tate Gallery, London; Arts Council of Great Britain, London; Victoria and Albert Museum, London; Art Museum of Ateneum, Finland; Museum of Sketches, Lund, Sweden; Albright-Knox Art Gallery, Buffalo, New York; Walker Art Center, Minneapolis, Minnesota; St. Louis Art Museum, Missouri; Museum of Modern Art, Rio de Janeiro; Gulbenkian Museum, Lisbon; Nagasaki Museum, Japan; Peter Stuyvesant Collection; Power Bequest Museum Sydney, Australia; Birmingham City Art Museum, England; Bristol City Art Gallery, England; Northern Ireland Arts Council; Leicester Education Collection, England; Berlinische Galerie, Berlin; Schwedische Nationalsammlung, Stockholm; Winnipeg Art Gallery, Canada; Städtiches Museum, Gelsenkirchen, Germany; Neuberger Museum of Art, Purchase, New York.

Public Installations:

Pimlico Underground Station for the Tate Gallery, London; Hiltrup Community Centre, Münster, Germany; Technical University, Stuttgart; Werner-von-Siemens-Schule, Berlin; *St. David's Link Sculpture,* Cardiff, England; Castrop Airport, Copenhagen; Haubrich Forum, Neumarkt, Cologne; Bayerische Vereinsbank, Berlin; Universitätsklinikum Rudolf Virchow, Berlin; Landeskriminalamt, Berlin; Conference Center, The Jumeirah Beech, Dubai, United Arab Emirates; Science Museum, London.

Publications:

By SEDGLEY: Articles—''Peter Sedgley,'' interview with Maurice de Sausmarez in *Leonardo* (Oxford), vol. 4, 1971; ''My Kinetic Art Works and Paintings 1971–1982,'' with Heinz Ohff in *Leonardo* (London), vol. 15, 1982; ''Don't go down in the mine daddy theres plenty of coal in the bath'' in *Gronningen Annual Exhibition Catalog,* Copenhagen 1989.

On SEDGLEY: Books—*Constructivism: Origins and Evolution* by George Rickey, New York 1967; *Movements in Art since 1945* by Edward Lucie-Smith, London 1969; *Op Art* by Frank Popper, Paris 1968; *Peter Sedgley,* exhibition catalog by Cyril Barret, Birmingham 1973; *Lights and Pigments* by Roy Osborne, London 1980; *Sedgley: Paintings, Objects and Installations 1963–1980* by Cyril Barrett, London, 1980; *100 Years of Metal Sculpture* by Dietrich Mahlow, Frankfurt, 1982; *Art Now* by Edward Lucie-Smith, 1989; *Peter Sedgley: Painting, Kinetics, Installations—1964–1996,* exhibition catalog, 1996; *Acts of Light,* exhibition catalog by Margeret Garlake, 2000.

*

In the way that philosophy belongs to the metaphysics of thought, colour occupies a similar position in the metaphysics of vision, namely art. Tracing the evolution (if that is the right word) of colour, it is imposible to isolate it from the development of art, which bears the codescript of successive stages of human sociological adaptation, giving colour a definitive role.

But colour, like water, depends on factors outside itself to give it form, identifying it with something more tangible than pure abstraction. We may speak of colour quite freely, but when one needs to illustrate it in our ''mindseye'' it involves a conscious effort to rehearse the sensation of colour without reference to a shape or context.

In pursuit of translating these sensations in painting, I respect an intrinsic geometry in the eye through which the transmission of colour may be facilitated.

By using simple geometric elements, I have tended to neutralize form in the spatial sense, i.e. shape, while placing greater emphasis on colour in the sequential form, relationships and displacements in time and in this way the visual arts are brought into proximity to the audio arts with the common parameter of time.

This combination of disciplines I have explored in different ways during the past years and several works have been realized. My interest in painting and kinetic object making, however, remains as intense as ever.

—Peter Sedgley

* * *

Peter Sedgley first made use of the startling two-dimensional visual effects of op art, giving the impression of movement, before going on to explore actual movement in three-dimensional kinetic works. But unlike Bridget Riley, a close friend who originally confined her work in the early 1960s to producing optical effects using only black and white, Sedgley from the first made use of the optical interaction of colour and form, in severely geometric canvases, making great use of the recurrent theme of concentric circles as well as horizontal lines and intersecting rectangles.

Although he does not use mathematical systems like Jeffrey Steele, the idea of building up a strict colour scale is crucial to his work. This colour keyboard is based on the spectral colours taken strictly in order—violet, blue, green yellow, red. White he uses as a sort of pause in the sequence, enabling him to repeat a colour without interrupting the series. However, he restricts himself to three colours within any one composition. And from the first he was interested in the interaction to form with colour, and the way the colours seem to change accordingly to their juxtapositions, so that in pictures like the Tate Gallery's "Yellow Attenuation" it is difficult to believe that the same yellow is being used throughout. Similarly with works such as "Trace 7," where concentric yellow circles on a green ground are interested by white right angles growing bigger across the canvas, to give not only colour changes but also a moire pattern as a sort of added bonus.

Sedgley has always preferred circular forms, since because they don't vary in outline they allow concentrations on colour. His earlier target paintings have precise, hard contours which when painted on a black ground seem to revolve and pulsate with a striking hypnotic effect. The hypnotic effects of recession draw the spectator into a dark tunnel of endlessness, or else seem to float towards him in a vision of brightness. Either way he is almost physically involved with the painting, disoriented or made dizzy (achieving by another path the unfocussing recommended by Cage). These effects were most powerfully achieved when Sedgley softened and blurred the edges of his first "hard edge" target paintings, which pulsated out from his black backgrounds.

While arranging his studio for evening showings, he became interested in the varying effects of different coloured lights on his targets, experimenting with red, yellow and blue filters. The effect of colour light is not merely to transform the hue, but to turn some colours black and make others disappear, and by programming the colour light he could control these transformations, and thus the rate at which the targets pulsate, expand, and contract. From these gyrating circles of light and colour Sedgley then took the short but logical step into the actual movement of kinetic art by developing his "Video Rotors." These are moving target pictures covered with small patches of fluorescent paint, which coalesce and change colour as the movement increases. They show clearly that Sedgley is more concerned with visual experience than with the painting as an object—with such effects as the way green and yellow at a certain speed appear white; some rows move rapidly, others slowly; some seem to move in opposite directions to the rest, others to stand still. The result is a complex dance of movement and colour changes.

Apart from his own artistic work, Peter Sedgley has also been very active in such ventures as the Artist's Registry, and with Bridget Riley as the leader of SPACE, which sought out such places as St. Catherine's Dock for young artists involved with new expressive media on a large scale.

—Lavinia Learmont

SEGAL, George

Nationality: American. **Born:** New York City, 26 November 1924. **Education:** Studied at the Cooper Union, New York, 1941–42; Rutgers University, New Brunswick, New Jersey, 1942–46, 1961–63, M.F.A. 1963; Pratt Institute, Brooklyn, New York, 1947–48; State University of New York at Purchase, B.S. 1949, B.A. 1950. **Family:** Married Helen Steinberg in 1946; has 2 children. **Career:** Chicken farmer, North Brunswick, New Jersey, 1949–58; began painting, North Brunswick, 1950; and subsequently created first plaster sculptures; also taught in New Jersey high schools, 1957–64; participated in happenings with Oldenburg, Kaprow and others, in New York and New Jersey, 1956. Full-time artist since 1964. Lecturer, Princeton University, New Jersey, 1968–69. **Awards:** Walter K. Gutman Foundation grant, 1962; Sculpture Prize, Art Institute of Chicago, 1966; Mayer Sultzberger Award, Jewish Museum, New York, 1986; Hall of Fame/Rutgers Achievement Award, Rutgers University, New Jersey, 1987; Governor's Walt Whitman Creative Arts Award, New Jersey, 1987; Order of Andres Bello, First Class, Republic of Venezuela, 1991; International Lifetime Achievement Award for Sculpture, Washington, D.C., 1992; Praemium Imperiale Award, Lifetime Achievement in the Arts, Tokyo, Japan, 1997; National Medal of Honor, Washington, D.C., 1999; Federal Design Achivement Award, Washington, D.C., 2000. Honorary doctorates from Rutgers University, 1970; Kean College, New Jersey, 1984; State University of New York at Purchase, 1992; Massachusetts College of Fine Arts, Boston, 1994; and Ramapo College, 1998. **Agent:** Sidney Janis Gallery, 6 West 57th Street, New York, New York 10019, U.S.A. **Died:** After a long illness, in South Brunswick, New Jersey, 9 June 2000.

Individual Exhibitions:

1956 Hansa Gallery, New York
1957 Hansa Gallery, New York
1958 Hansa Gallery, New York
Rutgers University, New Brunswick, New Jersey
1959 Hansa Gallery, New York
1960 Green Gallery, New York
1962 Green Gallery, New York
1963 Galerie Sonnabend, Paris
Schmela Gallery, Dusseldorf
Douglass College, New Brunswick, New Jersey
1964 Green Gallery, New York
1965 Sidney Janis Gallery, New York
1967 Sidney Janis Gallery, New York
Dine/Oldenburg/Segal, Art Gallery of Ontario, Toronto (travelled to the Albright-Knox Art Gallery, Buffalo, New York)
1968 Sidney Janis Gallery, New York
12 Human Situations, Museum of Contemporary Art, Chicago
1969 Galerie Dorthea Speyer, Paris
Princeton University, New Jersey
1970 Western Gallery, Western Washington State College, Bellingham
Sidney Janis Gallery, New York
1971 Sidney Janis Gallery, New York
New Jersey State Museum, Trenton (with Richard Anuskiewicz)
Onnasch Galerie, Cologne
Galerie Dorthea Speyer, Paris
Kunsthaus, Zurich (toured Europe)
1972 Centre National d'Art Contemporain, Paris
1973 Sidney Janis Gallery, New York

The Private World of George Segal, University of Wisconsin, Madison (travelled to the Museum of Art, Indianapolis)
1974 *Basel Art Fair*
Sidney Janis Gallery, New York
1975 André Emmerich Gallery, Zurich
Hopkins Center Art Galleries, Dartmouth College, Hanover, New Hampshire
1976 *Environments,* Institute of Contemporary Art, Philadelphia
Baltimore Museum of Art
Nina Freudenheim Gallery, Buffalo, New York
Art Association of Newport, Rhode Island
Suzette Schochet Gallery, Newport, Rhode Island
Santa Barbara Museum of Art, California
1977 Sidney Janis Gallery, New York
Pastels 1957–1965, Art Gallery, State University of California at Long Beach
1978 *Blue Jean Series,* Staten Island Museum, New York
Sculptures, Walker Art Center, Minneapolis (retrospective)
San Francisco Museum of Art (restrospective)
Whitney Museum, New York (restrospective)
1979 Hope Makler Gallery, Philadelphia
Serge DeBloe, Brussels
1980 Gloria Luria Gallery, Bay Harbour, Florida
Akron Art Institute, Ohio
New Brunswick Tercentennial Committee, New Jersey
Gatoda Gallery, Tokyo
Fay Gold Gallery, Atlanta
Sidney Janis Gallery, New York
1982 Sidney Janis Gallery, New York
1983 National Museum of Art, Osaka, Japan
1984 Galerie Reinhard Onnasch, West Berlin
Sidney Janis Gallery, New York
1985 Galerie Maeght Lelong, Paris
Israel Museum, Jerusalem
1986 Galerie Brusberg, West Berlin
Sidney Janis Gallery, New York
Galerie Joan Prats, Barcelona
California State University, Long Beach, California
1993 Greenberg Gallery, New York
1996 *George Segal: Recent Fifteen Years,* toured Japan
1997 *Sculpture and Works on Paper,* Sidney Janis Gallery, New York (catalog)
George Segal (retrospective), Montreal Museum of Art, Quebec (toured United States)
1998 *Large Scale Pastels 1997–98,* Sidney Janis Gallery, New York (catalog)
George Segal, A Retrospective: Sculptures, Paintings, Drawings, The Jewish Museum, New York (catalog)
2000 *Nightscapes,* Locks Gallery, Philadelphia (catalog)

Selected Group Exhibitions:

1957 *New York School Second Generation,* Jewish Museum, New York
1963 *VII Bienal de Sao Paulo,* Brazil
1965 *A Decade of American Drawings 1955–65,* Whitney Museum, New York
1967 *American Sculpture of the 60s,* Los Angeles County Museum of Art
1969 *Pop Art,* Hayward Gallery, London
1971 *White on White,* Museum of Contemporary Art, Chicago
1973 *Art in Space,* Detroit Institute of Arts, Michigan
1979 *American Portraits of the 60s and 70s,* Aspen Center for the Visual Arts, Colorado
1980 *Mysterious and Magical Realism,* Aldrich Museum of Contemporary Art, Ridgefield, Connecticut
1997 *A Century of Sculpture: The Nasher Collection,* Solomon R. Guggenheim Collection, New York
Modern and Contemporary Masters, Sidney Janis Gallery, New York (catalog)
1999 *The American Century: Art and Culture, 1900–2000,* Part II, 1950–2000, Whitney Museum of American Art, New York (catalog)

Collections:

Museum of Modern Art, New York; Whitney Museum, New York; Neuberger Museum, Purchase, New York; Albright-Knox Art Gallery, Buffalo, New York; Art Institute of Chicago; Walker Art Center, Minneapolis; San Francisco Museum of Modern Art; Centre Nationale d'Arte Contemporain, Paris; Stedelijk Museum, Amsterdam; Moderna Museet, Stockholm.

Publications:

By SEGAL: Books—*Sculpture, Painting, Pastels: A Discussion of My Recent Work,* M.F.A. Thesis, New Brunswick, New Jersey 1963; *Girl on a Chair: Excerpts from a Conversation between Richard Bellany and George Segal,* New York 1970. **Articles—**''An Interview with George Segal,'' with Henry Geldzahler in *Artforum* (New York), November 1964; ''George Segal on the New York School'' in *Albright-Knox Art Gallery Notes* (Buffalo, New York), Autumn 1966; ''Segal's Explique'' in *Aujourd'hui* (Paris), January 1967; ''Sensibility of the 60s'' in *Art in America* (New York), January/February 1967; ''Jackson Pollock: An Artists' Symposium—Part II'' in *Art News* (New York), May 1967; ''The Sense of 'Why Not?': George Segal on His Art'' in *Studio International* (London), October 1967; statement in *Sao Paulo 9,* exhibition catalog, Sao Paulo 1960; statement in *Art Now: New York,* June 1970; ''Interview with George Segal,'' with Phyllis Tuchman, in *Art in America* (New York), May/June 1972; ''Pop'' in *Art News* (New York), May 1974; ''A Conversation with the Artist,'' with Constance W. Glenn, in *George Segal: Pastels 1957–65,* exhibition catalog, Long Beach, California 1977; comments in *George Segal: Sculpture,* exhibition catalog, Minneapolis 1978.

On SEGAL: Books—*Recent American Sculpture,* exhibition catalog with an essay by Henry Geldzahler, New York 1964; *Amerikanst Pop-konst,* exhibition catalog, Stockholm 1964; *8 Sculptors: The Ambiguous Image,* exhibition catalog with an essay by Jan van der Marck, Minneapolis 1966; *Dine/Oldenburg/Segal,* exhibition catalog with an essay by Robert Pincus-Witten, Toronto 1967; *George Segal: 12 Human Situations,* exhibition catalog, with a preface and introduction by Jan van der Marck, Chicago 1968; *George Segal,* exhibition catalog by Martin Friedman, Paris 1969; *George Segal,* exhibition catalog with text by P. Kelleher and Hedy Backlin-Landman, Princeton, New Jersey 1969; *George Segal: Ruth in Her Kitchen* by Gert Kreytenberg, Stuttgart 1970; *George Segal,* exhibition catalog, Zurich

1971; *George Segal,* exhibition catalog, Cologne 1971; *Anuskiewicz/ Segal,* exhibition catalog with text by Zoltan Buki, Trenton, New Jersey 1971; *George Segal* by William C. Seitz, Stuttgart and New York 1972; *George Segal,* exhibition catalog, Paris 1972; *The Private World of George Segal,* exhibition catalog with text by José L. Bario-Garay and John Lloyd Taylor, Milwaukee 1973; *George Segal* by Jan van der Marck, New York 1975; *George Segal: Environments,* exhibition catalog by Jose L. Bario-Garay and Suzanne Delahanty, Philadelphia 1976; *George Segal Pastels 1957–1965,* exhibition catalog, Long Beach, California 1977; *George Segal: Sculpture,* exhibition catalog by Martin Friedman and Graham W. Beal, Minneapolis 1978; *George Segal: Blue Jean Series,* exhibition catalog, Staten Island, New York 1978; *George Segal* by Jose L. Bario-Garay, Barcelona 1979; *George Segal,* exhibition catalog, New York 1980; *George Segal: reperes,* exhibition catalog with preface by Pierre Restany, Paris 1985; *George Segal,* exhibition catalog with texts by Sam Hunter and Donald Hawthorne, Jerusalem 1985. **Articles—** ''George Segal: Photographs and Sculpture'' by H.T. Nicely in *School Arts,* March 1989; ''Real Dead'' by Richard Kalina in *Arts Magazine,* December 1991; ''Object Lessons'' by Richard Kalina in *Art in America,* October 1994; ''Art That Turns Life Inside Out'' by Phyllis Tuchman in *Smithsonian,* January 1998; ''George Segal: The Holocaust, 1984'' by Leo Bersani and Ulysse Dutoit in *Artforum,* February 1999. **Films—***George Segal: American Still Life,* directed by Amber Edwards, PBS, 2001.

* * *

For all its varied techniques, vast scale, day-glow colours, and advertising strategies, American art in recent years has failed to capture the particular insanity that characterizes the state of Western society in post-war years. With the honourable exception of Kienholz, there is no rage in contemporary American art, no fierce questioning or rejection. There is either bland acceptance, or sadness, emptiness, void. George Segal is the master of sadness.

There was a time, not so long ago, when a representative exhibition of American Art would have automatically included Segal; but not any longer. The bright light of critical acclaim has passed beyond him; his newness has been digested, the content ignored, and he must join the growing band of middle-aged old masters wondering where all the champagne and earnest interviewers from *Artforum* have gone. And unlike many of them, he doesn't even have the comfort of seeing his work change hands for ever increasing prices in the saleroom. His work, you see, is virtually unsellable.

An image by Segal is instantly recognizable. Figures cast from living models in plaster of paris inhabit environments typical of an affluent age. They never communicate to each other; each is locked inside himself. The impression is helped by the fact that Segal does not cast from the internal impression of the plaster, which would give a totally lifelike rendering, but simply cuts the mold open to allow the sitter to escape and then joins it back together again. The surface, then, is irregular, impressionistic. The figures look as if there might still be a body inside them, abandoned by the artist to eternal incarceration.

The only communication in a piece by Segal is between the ''furniture'' of the settings. These are real: beds, petrol pumps, Coke dispensing machines and beside them the figures look like ghosts. Kienholz also uses real objects as furniture, but he transforms them, so that they become menacing and hostile. In Segal's work, they are left exactly the way they were made, masters of the human wraiths that use them, bland, without intelligence, empty.

The process of making the work contrasts with the final effect. Segal has himself noted that there is something sadistic and fetishistic is encasing people in slowly hardening plaster. Some sit stolidly, enduring the discomfort for the sake of Art, some panic and scream, others actually enjoy the experience. Segal's studio was obviously a place of secret emotion, where regularly a human was turned, albeit temporarily, into a thing, a process that is near to the hidden mainspring of our sexual and political fantasies. Yet little of this process escapes into the final work; only its desolation survives.

Segal was never as succesful as those Pop artists who offered a happier view of the American Dream. And when conceptualism made complexity and subtlety the prime virtues, Segal's works were too obvious, being removed from the exhibition rooms in the museums to the storage areas, to be replaced by safer, more arty, work.

Like almost all American artists, Segal was unadventurous in matters of style; he found his formula and stuck to it, and there is a limit to how much any single style can reveal. There is never much variation of mood in his sculpture; although the furniture may change, the loneliness is always present. And the buyers and museum directors apparently don't want to hear about loneliness anymore.

Probably they know it too well already.

—Alastair Mackintosh

SERRA, Richard

Nationality: American. **Born:** San Francisco, California, 2 November 1939. **Education:** Studued at the University of California, Berkeley and Santa Barbara, 1957–61, B.A., M.A.; Yale University, New Haven, Connecticut, 1961–64, B.A., M.F.A.; study-travels in Paris and Italy, 1964–66. **Family:** Married Clara Weyergraf-Serra. **Career:** Independent sculptor, New York, since 1966: rubber and neon works, 1968–69; cut and torn works, 1968–70; weighted leaning pieces, 1968–71; films and video pieces in steel, since 1970; elected Fellow, American Academy Arts and Sciences, 1994. **Awards:** Yale Travel Fellowship, 1964; Fulbright Study Grant, 1965; Skowhegan Sculpture Academy of Arts and Design, Jerusalem, 1983; Wilhelm Lehmbruck Prize for Sculpture, Duisburg, 1991; Praemium Imperiale, Japan Art Association; D.F.A.: California College of Arts and Crafts, Oakland. **Agent:** Gagosian Gallery, 980 Madison Avenue, New York, New York, 10021–1848. **Address:** Office, 173 Duane Street, New York, New York, 10013–3334.

Individual Exhibitions:

1966 Galleria La Salita, Rome
1968 Galeria Ricke, Cologne
1969 Galleria Lambert, Milan
Leo Castelli Gallery, New York
1970 Joseph Helman Gallery, St. Louis
Ace Gallery, Los Angeles
University of California at San Diego
Pasadena Museum of Art, California
1972 Ace Gallery, Los Angeles
Castelli Graphics, New York
1973 Galerie Ricke, Cologne
Ace Gallery, Los Angeles
1974 School of Visual Arts, New York

1976 Ace Gallery, Los Angeles
Blum Helman Gallery, New York
1977 Galerie Daniel Templon, Paris
Galerie Bochum, Weimar, West Germany
Stedelijk Museum, Amsterdam
1978 Ace Gallery, Venice, California
Blum Helman Gallery, New York
Museum of Modern Art, Oxford
1979 Richard Hines Gallery, Seattle
University of California, Berkeley
KOH Gallery, Tokyo
Galeria Schmela, Dusseldorf
1980 Hudson River Museum, Yonkers, New York
Museum Boymans-van Beuningen, Rotterdam
1981 Blum Helman Gallery, New York
KOH Gallery, Tokyo
Castelli Gallery at 142 Greene Street, New York
Monchehausmuseum, Goslar, West Germany
Casteli Graphics, New York
1982 Gemini G.E.L., Los Angeles
Leo Castelli Gallery, New York
Castelli Gallery at 142 Greene Street, New York
St. Louis Art Museum, Missouri
Carol Taylor Art Museum, Missouri
1983 Centre Georges Pompidou, Paris
Larry Gagosian Gallery, Los Angeles
Musée d'Art Moderne, Paris
Akira Ikeda Gallery, Tokyo
Blum Helman Gallery, New York
Reinhard Onnasch Ausstellungen, West Berlin
Galerie Nordenhake, Malmo, Sweden
1984 Leo Castelli Gallery, New York
Galerie Nordenhake, Malmo, Sweden
Galerie Daniel Templon, Paris
Larry Gagosian Gallery, Los Angeles
1985 Galerie Maeght-Lelong, New York
Museum Haus Lange, Krefeld, West Germany
Gemini G.E.L., Los Angeles
Akira Ikeda Gallery, Tokyo
Galleria Christian Stein, Milan
1986 Museum of Modern Art, New York (retrospective)
Castelli Gallery at 142 Greene Street, New York
Larry Gagosian Gallery, Los Angeles
Galerie Maeght-Lelong, New York
New City Editions, Venice, California
Galerie Jean Bernier, Athens
1987 Hoffman Borman Gallery, Santa Monica, California
Harcus Gallery, Boston
1988 Kunsthalle, Basel
Galerie Littman, Basel
Stadtische Galerie im Lenbachhaus, Munich
1989 *Sculpture,* Pace Gallery, New York (catalog)
1990 *Axis,* Bielefeld Kunsthalle, Bielefeld (catalog)
1991 *Skulptur,* Malmö Konsthall, Malmö (catalog)
1992 Museo Nacional Centro de Arte Reina Sofía, Madrid (retrospective)
Afangar Icelandic Series, 1988–1992, Gemini G.E.L., Los Angeles (catalog)
Weight and Measure 1992, Tate Gallery, London (catalog)
Drawings, Serpentine Gallery, London (catalog)
1993 Centre Georges Pompidou, Paris (catalog)
Drawings, Serpentine Gallery, London (catalog)
1994 *Richard Serra: Weight and Measure Drawings,* The Saint Louis Art Museum, Missouri (catalog)
Richard Serra: Nova Scotia Drawings, Gagosian Gallery, New York (catalog)
Richard Serra: Props, Wilhelm Lehmbruck Museum, Dusseldorf (catalog)
1995 Matthew Marks Gallery, New York
1997 *Richard Serra,* Musée National d'Histoire et d'Art, Luxembourg (catalog)
Torqued Ellipses, Dia Center for the Arts, New York (catalog)
Richard Serra, Centro de Arte Hélio Oiticica, Rio de Janeiro (catalog)
1998 *Richard Serra: Sculpture 1985–1998,* Museum of Contemporary Art, Los Angeles (catalog)
1999 Guggenheim Museum, Bilbao, Spain
Kunstlerhaus, Vienna
2000 Gagosian Gallery Chelsea, New York

Selected Group Exhibitions:

1966 *From Arp to Artschwager I,* Bellamy/Goldowsky Gallery, New York
1970 *Identifications,* Kunstverein, Hannover
1974 *The Condition of Sculpture,* Hayward Gallery, London
1976 *200 Years of American Sculpture,* Whitney Musuem, New York
1977 *Documenta,* Kassel, West Germany
1978 *Between Sculpture and Painting,* Worcester Art Museum, Massachusetts
1981 *Biennale,* Venice 1983
Sculpture: The Tradition in Steel, Nassau County Museum of Art, Roslyn, New York
1985 *Maximal Implications of the Minimal Line,* Bard College, Annandale-on-Hudson, New York
1987 *The Great Drawing show 1587–1987,* Michael Kohn Gallery, Los Angeles
1989 *Sculpture Chicago 89* (catalog)
1994 *Arte Minimal,* Diputación Provincial, Granada (catalog)
Drawing Rooms, Modern Art Museum of Fort Worth (catalog)
1995 *Attitudes/Sculptures,* CAPC Musée d'Art Contemporain, Bordeaux (catalog)
1997 *Laying Low,* Kunstnernes Hus, Oslo (catalog)
1999 *Richard Serra, Susan Hartnett,* Skulpturenmuseum Glaskasten, Marl (catalog)
2000 *Stephan Erfurt, Richard Serra: Weight and Measure,* Tate Gallery, London (catalog)

Collections:

Museum of Modern Art, New York; Whitney Museum, New York; Guggenheim Museum, New York; Los Angeles County Museum of Art; Norton Simon Museum of Art, Pasadena, California; Art Gallery of Ontario, Toronto; National Gallery of Canada, Ottawa; Tate Gallery, London; Stedelijk Museum, Amsterdam; Moderna Museet, Stockholm.

Public Installations:

Tilted Arc, Federal Plaza, New York, 1981 (removed 1989); Call *Me Ishmael,* Stanford University, Stanford, California, 1998; The *Hedgehog and the Fox,* Princeton University, 2000; *Berlin Holocaust Memorial,* Berlin (with Peter Eisenman), 2000.

Publications:

By SERRA: Books—*Richard Serra: Drawings 1969–1990,* with Hans Janssen, Bern 1990; *The Destruction of Tilted Arc: Documents,* edited by Clara Weyergraf-Serra and Martha Buskirk, Cambridge 1991; *Richard Serra: Drawings 1969–1990,* with Hans Janssen, Bern 1991; *Richard Serra: Writings/Interviews,* Chicago 1994; *Richard Serra at Gemini, 1993–1996,* Los Angeles 1996; *Speak Art!: The Best of Bomb Magazine's Interviews with Artists,* with Betsy Sussler, Suzan Sherman and Rondale Shavers, New York 1997; *Le Mormaire: Richard Serra, Dick Reinartz,* edited by Alexander V. Berswordt, text by Stefan Germer, Düsseldorf 1997; *Portraits: Talking with Artists at the Met, the Modern, the Louvre, and Elsewhere,* with Michael Kimmelman, New York 1999; *Richard Serra,* edited by Hal Foster, Gordon Hughes and B.H.D. Buchloh, Cambridge 2000; *Richard Serra: Rounds & Ellipses,* Los Angeles 2000. **Articles**—Statements in *Artforum* (New York), September 1971; ''Paul Revere,'' with Joan Jonas in *Artforum,* (New York), September 1971; ''Richard Serra: Shift,'' edited by Roaslind Krauss, in *Studio International* (London), October 1973; ''Richard Serra and Robert Bell: Prisoner's Dilemma'' in *Avalanche* (New York), May/June 1974; ''Richard Serra: Beyond the Walls'' with Vincent Katz in *Flash Art (International Edition),* no. 197, November/December 1997; ''Nerves of Steel'' by Alan Jolis in *Art News,* no. 5, May 1998; ''Extended Vison: Richard Serra Talks About Drawing'' with R. Eric Davis in *Art on Paper,* vol. 4, no. 5, May/June 2000. **Films**—*Hand Catching Lead,* 1968; *Hands Tied,* 1968; *The Trial of Tilted Arc,* 1989; *Richard Serra: Work Comes Out of Work,* 1995; *Richard Serra Videoworks: Volume 1,* 1998.

On SERRA: Articles—''Slow Information'' by Robert Pincus-Witten in *Artforum* (New York), September 1969; ''Richard Serra: Castelli Warehouse'' by P. Leider in *Artforum* (New York), February 1970; ''Critic's Choice: Serra'' by E. C. Baker in *ARTnews* (New York), February 1970; ''Los Angeles: Craig Kauffman and Richard Serra, Pasadena Art Museum'' by Peter Plagens in *Artforum* (New York), April 1970; ''Los Angeles: Richard Serra Films at Ace Gallery'' by J. E. Young in *Art International* (Lugano, Switzerland), October 1970; ''Toronto: Serra's Visit and After'' by Mario Amaya in *Art in America* (New York), May/June 1971; ''Richard Serra: Sculpture Redrawn'' by Rosalind Krauss in *Artforum* (New York), May 1972; ''Richard Serra'' by Otto Hahn in *Art Press* (Paris), February 1974; ''Working Out: The Work of Richard Serra'' by John Anthony Thwaites in *Art and Artists* (London), March 1974; review by Elizabeth Frank in *Art in America* (New York), Summer 1981; ''Richard Serra's Tilted Arc: Art and Non-art Issues'' by Harriet Senie in *Art Journal,* vol. 48, Winter 1989; ''Richard Serra: Stacks, 1990'' by Sasha M. Newman in *Yale University Art Gallery Bulletin,* 1991; ''Richard Serra: Sculpture Irreducible to Its Drawing'' by Adachiara Zevi in *L'Architettura,* vol. 38, October 1992; ''Richard Serra: Portrait by Armin Linke'' by Richard Kostelanetz in *Du,* no. 1, January 1994; ''Steel-drivin' Man: Richard Serra's Massive New Sculptures, as Big as Houses, Create a Wholly Original Spatial Drama'' by Robert Hughes in *Time,* vol. 152, no. 16, 19 October 1998; ''Richard Serra: Man of Steel'' by Jan Garden Castro in *Sculpture* (Washington, D.C.), vol. 18, no. 1, January/February 1999; ''Sculpture in the Space of Architecture'' by Aruna D'Souza and Tom McDonough in *Art in America* (New York), vol. 88, no. 1, February 2000.

* * *

Acutely aware of the interrelationship of recent investigations in the temporal arts, the sculptor Richard Serra produced a series of films in the late 1960s that are paradigmatic of much of his work. The films, in their austere and repetitive meditation on the performance of simple, generally absurd tasks, transcend traditional narrative associations. In *Hand Catching Lead* (1968), for example, Serra focusses on his own hand as it attempts to catch a sequence of falling strips of metal, while *Hands Tied* (1968) is centered on the unshackling of the artist's bound hands. Unfolding in real, operational time, these films depict self-referential states where meaning is external and inextricably woven into the formal conditions of the act itself. Concomitantly, these acts project the kind of compulsion that governs human behavior without asserting the underlying logic of such behavior; the viewer is not made cognizant of the circumstances that precipitate the artist's Sisyphean goal. In the space-time continuum of Serra's films, a task is simply a task.

Stemming from the interest in process inherent in his films, Serra's minimalist and site-specific pieces challenge traditional notions of sculpture. From 1968 to 1969, the artist made nearly 100 works centered on the manipulation of lead and generated by his ''Verb List'' (1967), a series of transitive verbs (to roll, to crease, to fold . . .) that served as a simple program for the artist's task-performance. Disrupting the tradition of the closed sculptural object, a tradition that continued throughout the modernist epoch, Serra produced pieces such as ''Splash Piece'' (1968) and ''Casting'' (1969), both involving the tossing of molten lead into the juncture of wall and floor. Rather than conflating time into a single, conceptualized moment, the works, as the residue of self-evident processes, submit to the ebb and flow of real time. It is in their obsession with the performance of tasks in a real space-time continuum that Serra's films can be seen to co-opt these new sculptural concerns. While Serra has said that ''sculpture can not be similar to or influenced by the illusion in film,'' the process pieces of the late 1960s clearly assume the complusive strategies of his films.

In the 1970s Serra's work was increasingly directed toward one central issue: contingency. By utilizing mass-produced industrial materials (e.g., lead and steel plates), Serra could ultimately divest the art object of the aura of uniqueness and timelessness. This retreat from the reverential resulted in a much less passive relationship between object and viewer, launching, as the critic Douglas Crimp has suggested, ''an all-out attack on the prestige of the artist, granting that prestige instead to the spectator.'' Site-specific pieces such as ''Shift'' (1970–72), six rectangular cement sections embedded on a snowy slope in King City, Canada, expand the closed sculptural vocabulary to include the possibilities of architecture and landscape. Serra's opening-up of sculpture to the conditions of time and place once again parallels the space-time continuum of his films. ''One Ton Prop (House of Cards)'' (1969), an arrangement of four 500-pound plates of lead propped up to form a cube, sustains itself by virtue of a continual reassertion of its balance, a situation wholly contingent on gravity and time. Perhaps the ultimate minimalist object, ''One Ton Prop'' maintains an active relationship to the world even without the presence of a spectator; it makes its point simply by being.

—Maurice Berger

SERRANO, Andres

Nationality: American. **Born:** New York, New York, 1950. **Education:** Brooklyn Museum Art School, 1967–69. **Agent:** Paula Cooper Gallery, 534 West 21st Street, New York, New York 10011, U.S.A.

Selected Individual Exhibitions:

1986 *The Unknown Christ,* Museum of Contemporary Hispanic Art, New York
1987 Galerie Hufkens-Noirhomme, Brussels
1990 Stux Gallery, New York
1991 Gallery Via 8, Tokyo
1992 *The Morgue,* Paula Cooper Gallery, New York (toured) (catalog)
1994 *Andres Serrano: Works 1983–93,* Institute for Contemporary Art, University of Pennsylvania (toured)
1996 Museum of Contemporary Art, Zagreb, Croatia
Sala Mendoza, Caracas, Venezuela
1997 National Gallery of Victoria, Melbourne, Australia
1998 *Andres Serrano: A History of Sex,* Yvon Lambert Gallery, Paris (toured) (catalog)
1999 David Perez-MacCallum Arte Contemporaneo, Guayaquil, Ecuador
2000 *Body and Soul,* Helsinki City Art Museum, Helsinki, Finland (toured)

Selected Group Exhibitions:

1985 *National Studio Programme Exhibition,* The Clocktower, New York
1986 *Past, Present, Future,* New Museum of Contemporary Art, New York
1987 *Scared to Breath,* Perspektierf, Rotterdam, The Netherlands
1988 *AIDS in Democracy,* Dia Art Foundation, New York
1989 *The Photography of Invention,* Smithsonian Institute National Museum of Art, Washington D.C.
1990 *Images in Transition—Photographic Works Towards the 1990s,* Museum of Modern Art, Kyoto/Tokyo
1991 *Beyond the Frame: American Art 1960–1990,* Fukuoka Art Museum, Japan (traveled to National Museum of Art, Osaka; Setagaya Art Museum, Tokyo)
1992 *Dirt and Domesticity: Constructions of the Feminine,* Whitney Museum of American Art, New York
1993 *Tema Aids,* Copenhagen, Denmark (traveled to Stockholm, Sweden; Bergen Kunstforeng, Norway; Sonja Henie-Niels Onstad Foundations, The Art Center, Hovikodden, Norway)

Andres Serrano, 1990s. ©James L. Lance/Corbis.

1994 *The Abstract Urge: Recent Photographs Beyond Description,* Ansel Adams Center for Photography, San Francisco, California
1995 *Civil Rights Now,* Institute for Contemporary Art, University of Pennsylvania, Philadelphia (toured)
1996 *Black and Blue: Eight American Photographers,* Groninger Museum, The Netherlands
1997 *Angel, Angel,* Gallery Rudolfinum, Prague, Czech Republic (traveled to Kunsthalle Wien, Austria) (catalog)
1998 *In Visible Light: Photography and Classification in Art, Science, and the Everyday,* Finnish Museum of Photography, Helsinki (toured) (catalog)
1999 *Veronica's Revenge: Photographies de la Collection LAC-Suisse,* Casino Luxembourg and Musée National d'Histoire et d'Art, Luxembourg
2000 *Children of the 20th Century,* Mittelrhein Museum Koblenz, Germany

Collections:

Art Institute of Chicago, Illinois; Baltimore Museum of Art, Maryland; Fonds Regional d'Art Contemporain, Cluny, France; Israel

Museum, Jerusalem; Centro Cultural Arte Contemporaneo, Mexico City, Mexico; Museo Reina Sofia, Madrid; National Gallery of Australia, Canberra; New Museum of Contemporary Art, New York.

Public Installations:

Americana, installation by Group Material at the Whitney Biennial, Whitney Museum of American Art, New York 1985; *Interiors,* Light Gallery, New York 1987; *The Castle,* Group Material installation, Documenta 8, Kassel, Germany 1987.

Publications:

By SERRANO: Books—*Body and Soul,* edited by Brian Wallis, with essays by bell hooks, Bruce Ferguson, Amelia Arenas, New York 1995.

On SERRANO: Books—*Exploration of Nude Photography* by Kuraischi, Nikado, Amano, Japan 1996; *ART:L'Age Contemporain: Une Histoire des Arts Plastiques á la Fin du XXe Siecle* by Paul Ardenne, Paris 1997; *Vile Bodies: Photography and the Crisis of Looking* by Chris Townsend, Germany 1998; *Art Matters: How the Cultural Wars Changed America,* New York 1999. **Articles**—''Comments on Andres Serrano by Members of the United States Senate'' in *The Congressional Record,* 18 May 1989; ''The Spirit and the Letter'' by Lucy Lippard in *Art in America,* April 1990; ''On the Edge with Andres Serrano, Contemporary Photography's Artist Bad Boy'' by Joan Baum in *Art Review,* 20 December 2000.

* * *

Controversial fine art photographer Andres Serrano uses religious symbolism as one of his central themes and explores the relationship between these icons and the body via its natural secretions. Initially a student of painting and sculpture, Serrano turned to photography in 1983, fascinated by its ability to arrest time. Influenced by Marcel Duchamp and Luis Buñuel (''for his mix of the sacred and profane''), Serrano creates large photographs which engage the viewer in an immediate and direct discussion of racial issues, politics, religion, and sexuality.

His earliest work shows a rapid connection with the images and themes from his Catholic upbringing, an obsession for Serrano. His 1984 work ''Heaven and Hell'' illustrates the classic struggle between good and evil, and it is filled with Catholic symbolism. Serrano began exhibiting his work professionally in 1985, first at the Leonard Perlson Gallery in New York. That same year he was included in the *Myth and Mystery* show at the Museum of Contemporary Spanish Art, and worked on the *Americana* installation in the Whitney Biennial.

In 1986, Serrano began work on his *Body Fluids* series, many massive Cibachrome prints which contained elements of blood, semen, milk, and urine. In these photographs, Serrano's critical opposition to the contemporary American puritanical revival became apparent, and it is for these images that Serrano is most well known and considered so controversial. That year, he produced such works as *Blood Cross* and *Blood Circle,* photographs of Plexiglas constructions (a cross and a circle) filled with cows' blood and placed on contrasting color fields. The *Body Fluids* series work stretches until 1990, but Serrano began working on two other thematic groups of photographs at the same time. From 1987–1990, images were created in the areas of *Fluid Abstractions* and *Immersions.*

The *Fluid Abstractions* are lyrical images of Serrano's own ejaculate in flight, captured in arcs and waves which are reminiscent of paintings from the Abstract Expressionist movement. The *Immersions* are images of objects in containers of urine. A man fascinated with primary colors, Serrano felt that urine was a perfect yellow for his work. Though there are many images in the *Immersions* series, one has become representative of Serrano for many. In 1987, Serrano made the notorious ''Piss Christ,'' a Cibachrome of a plastic crucifix submerged in a vessel filled with urine. The image became widely known in the following two years when it was attacked by the religious right as blasphemous and discussed in Congress as an example of why funding for the National Endowment for the Arts should be cut. (Serrano had received a $15,000 grant from the N.E.A. by this time.)

The May 18, 1989, *Congressional Record* details the comments made by Senators Jesse Helms of North Carolina and Alfonse D'Amato of New York on behalf of outraged constituents and Christians across the country. D'Amato refers to the image as a ''deplorable, despicable display of vulgarity,'' while Helms says that the work shows that the N.E.A. ''ought to be abolished and all funds returned to the taxpayer.'' Helms refused to state the name of the work in his comments, and D'Amato did so reluctantly.

Serrano's response to these criticisms of his work details his intentions in making the image. He said he wanted to ''aestheticize Christ. Beautiful light, I think, aestheticizes the picture. Visually, it doesn't denigrate Christ in any way.'' Serrano feels that ''Piss Christ'' is ''reverential'' and ''comforting . . . not unlike the icons we see in Church.'' He does, however, acknowledge the controversy. ''The fact that you know there's a bodily fluid involved here . . . it's meant to question the whole notion of what is acceptable and unacceptable. There's duality here, of good and evil, of life and death.''

These themes continued to have relevance in Serrano's work, but by 1990 he had ended the series' work in *Immersions, Body Fluids,* and *Fluid Abstractions.* He turned to portraiture, shooting images for two series, *Klan* and *Nomads.* Now Serrano photographed members of the Ku Klux Klan in their robes and hoods, images which are at once beautiful and disturbing. The *Nomads* series consists of around sixty images influenced by the work of Edward S. Curtis. Serrano made portraits of contemporary wanderers in New York subways and parks in an effort to ''photograph the homeless not lying in the street, not begging for food or pushing a shopping cart, but with the dignity that all human beings deserve.'' He continued with this in 1991's *The Church,* a series of portraits of monks and nuns. Serrano sees these images as related to the *Klan* series ''because the people wore the robes and the hoods. I was always impressed that whenever the people wore those robes they assumed a power and an authority that they didn't have without them.''

Two more series emerged in 1992. In *Objects of Desire,* the artist photographed firearms in a style like human portraiture. In *The Morgue* series, Serrano made pictures of corpses on slabs, many of them unidentified victims. In all of these images, Serrano names the photograph with words which describe the manner of death. Of these pictures, Serrano said, ''I think I have a fascination with life and what makes people tick and with the things we are all concerned about. Death, religion, sex, all basic issues. For me, the question is not '*why* photograph death' but '*why not*'. . . . [I]t is not easy to get into a morgue. It took me years to find someone that would allow me access.'' The images of tiny feet, vacant faces, and dry dead skin are both repellant and seductive.

Each of these excursions into new subject matter found a definite audience, and Serrano's popularity (and notoriety) in the United States is enormous. His work has never been quite so widely intriguing to audiences in Europe (nor has his work been considered controversial there), but he has had several shows at major museums in Italy, France, and England. In 1993, his work was featured in the Venice Biennale, and the following year he was honored with his first retrospective at the Institute of Contemporary Art at the University of Pennsylvania. In 1995, his work was shown at museums in Houston, New York, and Chicago, as well as in Sweden.

During this time, Serrano continued to work at a rapid clip, producing the series *Budapest* in 1994. This series marks his return to live models; among the images is ''The Model,'' a woman in her eighties who has made her living as an artist's model for decades. Serrano captures her nude and dignified, smoking a cigarette and looking beyond the frame as if she is deep in thought. The following year, Serrano began work on the massive *History of Sex* (1995–96), a series of life-size close-up images which depict human sexuality in its various forms. Naturally, attention is given to the taboo here, the socially unacceptable. This series has been featured in galleries in Rome and New York. In 1999, Serrano's work from the *Immersions* and *Fluid Abstractions* series was featured at a Belgian museum. New York's Institute of Contemporary Photography included some of his images in the show *Reflections in a Glass Eye.* The Helsinki City Art Museum presented a *Placing Time and Evil—A Millennium Retrospective* in the Spring of 2001. Serrano continues to produce work which fascinates and repels as he explores the bounds of the human experience.

—Tammy A. Kinsey

SEUPHOR, Michel

Nationality: French. **Born:** Fernand-Louis Berckelaers in Antwerp, Belgium, 10 March 1901; adopted the pseudonym ''Seuphor'' (anagram of Orpheus) in 1918; immigrated to France, 1925: naturalized, 1965. **Education:** Studied Latin and Greek at the College of Antwerp, 1909–17; self-taught in art. **Military Service:** Served in the Belgian Resistance in Grenoble, France, 1943–44. **Family:** Married Suzanne Plasse in 1934; sons: Clement (died, 1935) and Regis. **Career:** Poet and writer on art, Antwerp, 1921–22, and in Berlin, Paris, Amsterdam and Tunis, 1922–25; writer, painter, graphic artist and exhibition organizer, Paris, 1925–34, Anduze, France, 1934–45, Bagnols-sur-Ceze, France, 1945–48, and again in Paris since 1948; associated with the De Stijl artists, Antwerp, 1921, Der Sturm artists, Berlin, 1922, Dadaists in Paris, 1923–24, and the Futurists in Italy, 1926; founder, with Arp, Schwitters, Mondrian, Kandinsky, Léger, Stazewski, etc., Cercle et Carré group, Paris, 1930 (disbanded 1931); formed Abstraction-Creation group. Founder and editor, with Jozef Peeters, *Het Overzicht,* Anterwp, 1921–25, and, with Paul Dermée, only issue of *Documents Internationaux de l'Esprit Nouveau,* Paris 1927; editor, 3 issues of *Cercle et Carré,* Paris 1930; contributor, *Esprit,* Paris, 1933, *Sept* and *L'Aube,* Paris, 1934–45, and *Art d'Aujourd'hui,* Paris, 1951; Paris Correspondent, *Art Digest,* New York, 1952–53. **Awards:** Premio Internazionale Diano Marina, Italy, 1978; Special Award of Honour, Biennale of Ljublijana, 1987; Medaille Vermeil de la Ville de Paris, 1991. Chevalier, 1962, and Commandeur, 1977, Ordre des Arts et Lettres, Paris. Seuphor Medal struck by la Monnaie de Paris, 1980. **Agent:** Galerie Convergence, 18 rue Jean-Jaurés, Nantes. **Died:** 12 February 1999.

Individual Exhibitions:

1933 Galerie Manassero, Lausanne, Switzerland
1954 Galerie Berggruen, Paris
Modern Art Galerie, Basel
1955 Rose Fried Gallery, New York (with Alcopley and Hassegawa)
1956 Galerie Saint-Laurent, Brussels
Galerie Accent, Antwerp
1957 Galerie St. Stephan, Vienna (with Hans Arp and Sophie Taeuber Arp)
1958 Galerie der Spiegel, Cologne (with Hans Arp and Sophie Taeuber Arp)
1959 Galerie Denise René, Paris
Galerie Grattacielo, Milan
1960 Galerie Libertad, Buenos Aires
Esther Robles Gallery, Los Angeles
1961 Galerie Hybler, Copenhagen
Galerie Raaklijn, Bruges, Belgium
1962 Galerie Würthle, Vienna
Galeriea Lorenzelli, Milan
1963 Galerie Denise René, Paris
Esther Robles Gallery, Los Angeles
Abbaye Saint-Pierre, Ghent
1965 Galerie Lorenzelli, Milan
Galerie Renee Ziegler, Zurich
Fresno State College, California
1966 Musée des Beaux-Arts, Nantes, France (retrospective)
Librairie-Galerie La Hune, Paris
1967 Galerie L'Oeil Ecoute, Lyons
Galerie Schutze, Bad Godesburg, West Germany
Galerie Martano, Turin
Muzeum Sztuki, Lodz, Poland
Galerie Hybler, Copenhagen (with Sonia Delaunay and Serge Poliakoff)
1968 Musée des Beaux-Arts, La Chaux de Fonds, Switzerland
Galeria Laboratorio Il Parametro, Milan
1969 Inter Gallery, Brussels (with Arturo Bonifanti and Kurt Lewi)
Galerie Rizzoli, Rome
Centre CO-MO, Paris
Galerie Argos, Nantes
Maison du Tourisme, Auxerre, France (with Alicia Penalba)
1970 Gallerie Martano, Turin
Musée de Deurle, Belgium
1971 Musée d'Art et d'Industrie, Saint-Etienne, France (retrospective)
White Gallery, Lausanne, Switzerland
1972 Galleria Borgonuovo, Milan
Galleria La Polena, Genoa
Centre Marcel Peeters, Antwerp (retrospective)

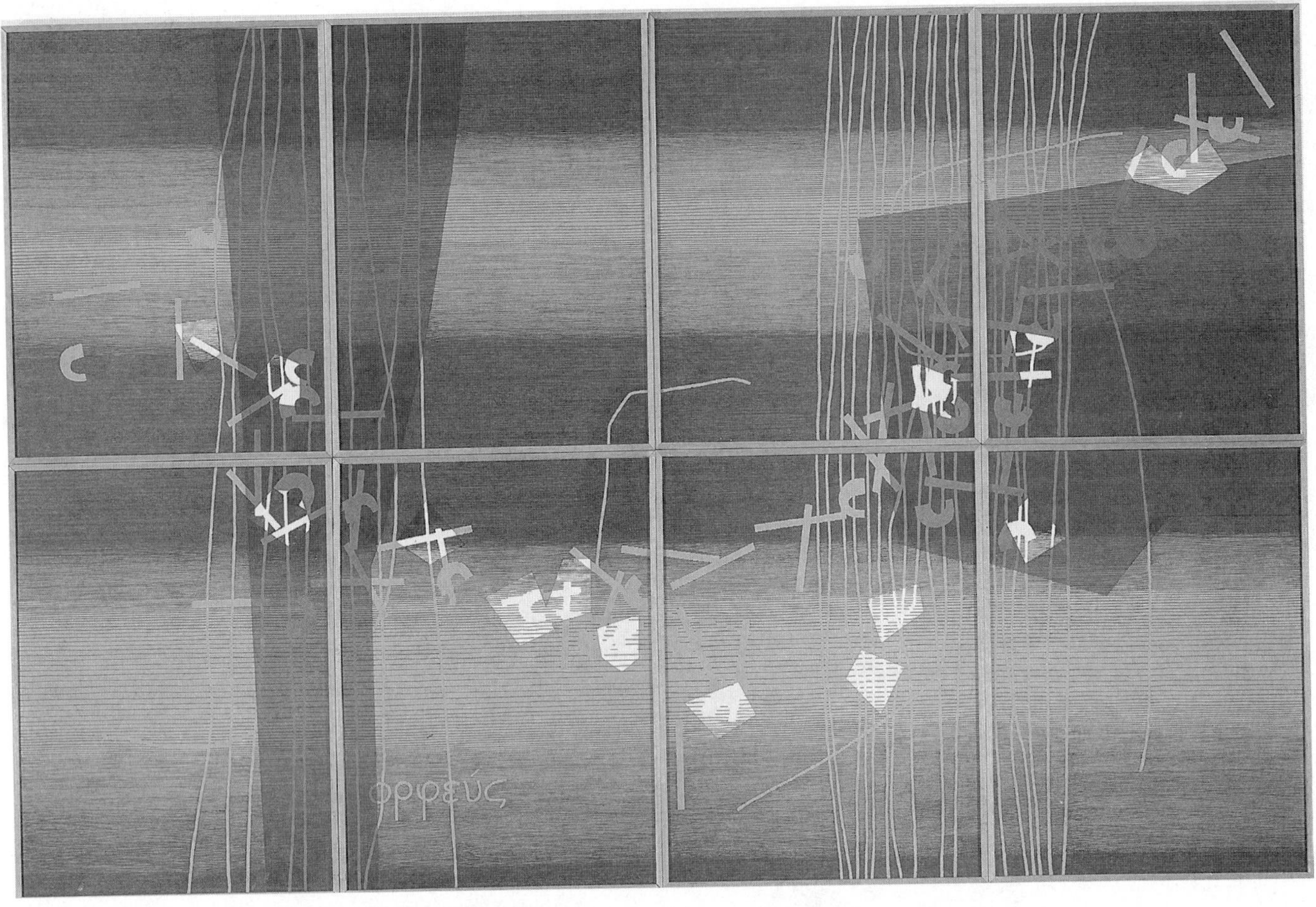

Michel Seuphor: *Death of Orpheus,* 1964. ©2001 Artists Rights Society (ARS), NY/VG Bild Kunst, Bonn.

1973 Galleria Peccolo, Livorno, Italy
Galleria Lorenzelli, Milan (with Henri Michaux)
Galeri La Tortue, Paris
Centre Leonard de Vinci, Toulouse
Galerie Memling-Galerie Orangerie, Ostend, Belgium
Galerie Nouvelles Images, The Hague (with Jean Ricardon)
Galleria Vismara, Milan
Galleria Pictogramme, Rome
1974 Palais de l'Athenée, Geneva
Galerie Govaerts, Brussels
1975 Galerie Attali, Paris
Galleria Beniamino, Sanremo, Italy
Galerie De Greyse, Tielt, Belgium
1976 Palais Granvelle, Besancon, France
Galerie Carmen Martinez, Paris
Gemeentemuseum, The Hague
Galerie Nouvelles Images, The Hague (with Hans Arp and Sophie Taeuber Arp)
Galerie Synthese, Antwerp
Galerie Gunter und Schwan, Essen
1977 Centre Georges Pompidou, Paris
Galerie Attalli, Paris
Librairie-Galerie J.- M. Place, Paris
Galerie V.E.C.U., Antwerp
Galerie Convergences, Nantes, France
Galerie 2016, Hauterive/Neuchâtel,Switzerland
Galerie L'Orangerie, Ostend, Belgium
1978 Treffpunkt Kunst, Saarlouis, West Germany
Galerie della Piazza, Varese, Italy
1979 Galerie Abras-Mont-Des-Arts, Brussels
Galerie Nouvelles Images, The Hague
Galerie Modern Art International, Munich
Saarland Museum, Saarbrucken
Galerie Schindler, Berne
Azienda del Turismo, Diano-Marina, Italy
1980 Mathys Galerie, Herstal, Belgium
Galerie Jacques Visser, Amsterdam
1981 Musée de la Boverie, Liège, Belgium (retrospective)
Mathye Galerie, Herstal, Belgium
Galerie Nouvelles Images, The Hague
Galerie Traces, Rouen
Galerie Convergences, Nantes
Centre Provincial Arenberg, Antwerp
1982 Kunstverein, Bamberg, West Germany
1983 Moris Gallery, Tokyo
1984 Palazzo di Diamanti, Ferrara, Italy
1985 Musée des Beaux-Arts, Nantes, France
Club 44, La Chaux-de-Fonds, Switzerland
Museo d'Arte Moderno, Ciudad Bolivar, Venezuela
Urania Galerie, Zurich
Edwynn Houk Gallery, Chicago

1986 Musée de Grenchen, Switzerland
Galerie Convergence, Paris
Treffpunkt Kunt, Saarlouis, West Germany
VTB Antwerpen, Antwerp
1987 Centro Culturale, Pordenone, Italy
Galerie Sacre du Printemps, Brussels
1988 Institut Français, Stockholm
1990 *Seuphor: Traversing the Century,* Musee Bibliotheque, Ales, France
Galerie Hüsstege, 's Hergotenbosch, Holland
1992 Rolandseck, Germany
Galerie Denise René, Paris
1993 Casino of Knokke, Belgium
1994 Distrikthuis Borgerhout, Belgium
''Lagalerie,'' Paris

Selected Group Exhibitions:

1930 *Cercle et Carre,* Galerie 23 rue La Boetie, Paris
1955 *Salon des Réalités Nouvelles,* Paris
1959 *Documenta,* Kassel, West Germany
1960 *Construction and Geometry in Painting,* Galerie Chalette, New York (toured the United States)
1963 *Schrift und Bild,* Kunsthalle, Baden-Baden, West Germany
1964 *50 Ans de Collage,* Musée d'Art et d'Industrie, Saint-Etienne, France
1972 *De Stijl, Cercle et Carre,* Galerie Gmurzynska, Cologne
1980 *Konstruktion, Struktur . . . ,* Galerie Tempel, Cologne
1982 *Hommages,* Musée du Havre, France
1987 *Biennale of Graphic Art,* Ljubljana, Yugoslavia
1990 *Paris 1930: Abstract Art, Concrete Art—Cercle et Carre,* IVAM Centre Julio Gonzales, Valencia, Spain
1997 *Poetry and Painting: Long Live Double Agents,* Galerie Thessa Herold, Paris
Fighting for Modern Art: Homage to Rene Deroudille, Musee des Beaux-Arts, Lyons, France
1999 Ludwig Museum im Deutschherrenhaus, Koblenz, Germany

Collections:

Centre Georges Pompidou, Paris; Musée d'Art Moderne de la Ville, Paris; Musée des Beaux Arts, Antwerp; Musée des Beaux-Arts, Ghent; Museum Boymans-van Beuningen, Rotterdam; Gemeentemuseum, The Hague; Muzeum Sztuki, Lodz, Poland; Museo d'Arte Moderna, Turin; Albright-Knox Art Gallery, Buffalo, New York; Los Angeles County Museum of Art.

Publications:

By SEUPHOR: Books—*Mariage filme,* Antwerp 1924; *Diaphragme interieur,* Paris 1926; *Lecture elementaire,* Paris 1928; *Un renouveau de la peinture en Belgique flamande,* Paris 1932; *Les evasions d'Olivier Trickmanscholm,* Paris 1939; *Douce province,* Lausanne 1942; *La maison claire,* Lyons 1943; *Informations,* Paris 1944; *Tout dire,* Paris 1945; *Itineraire spirituel de Michel Seuphor,* edited by Francis Bernard, Tornac, France 1946; *Le visage de Senlis,* Paris 1947; *L'art abstrait, ses origines, ses premieres maitres,* Paris 1949; *Piet Mondrian,* Paris, Cologne and New York 1956; *Dictionnare de la peinture abstraite,* Paris and London 1957; *La peinture abstraite en Flandre,* Brussels 1963; *Le style et le cru,* Paris 1965; *Le commerce de l'art,* Paris 1966; *La vocation des mots,* Lausanne, Switzerland 1966; *Le monde est plein d'oiseaux,* Lausanne, Switzerland 1968; *Le chantier,* Turin 1970; *Le don de la parole,* Paris 1970; *L'ephémére est éternel,* Turin 1972; *Les dimensions de la liberté,* Paris 1972; *Le jardin privé au géomètre,* Zurich 1974; *Onze essais de voix pour un chant du soir,* The Hague 1976; *Tout homme,* Paris 1978; *Les innocents,* Paris 1979; *Contes batabraf,* Milan 1981; *C'est l'evidence meme,* Paris 1982; *Chronique de Barbebasse,* Nantes 1983; *Gosps et cosnops,* Nantes 1984; *Les Yi-King vus par Seuphor,* Lièges 1986; *La cinquiéme roue,* Nantes 1986; *Solfege,* Nantes 1987; *Le rire de calf,* Nantes 1988; *Falaise et le grande pacifique,* Nantes 1988; *Les contrées de l'esprit,* Nantes 1989; *Domaines du jeu,* Nantes 1990; *Sans faire le moindre bruit,* Nantes 1992; *Parenthèse,* Nantes 1993; *Taggeknatter,* Siegen, Germany, 1993; *Somme toute,* Nantes 1994; *Ecrits et temoinages de 24 peintres,* edited by Mario Merola and Robert Wolfe, Montreal 1994. **Articles—**''Art Beyond Art: Remembering Mondrian'' in *Art & Antiques,* vol. 6, Summer 1989.

On SEUPHOR: Books—*Zeichen des 20. Jahrhunderts,* West Berlin 1956; *Encycopedie de l'architecture nouvelle,* vol. 2, by Alberto Sartoris, Milan 1957; *Geocultura de la Europa de hoy* by Gyula Kosice, Buenos Aires 1952; *Michel Seuphor: Exposition Restrospective,* exhibition catalog with a preface by Maurice Allemand, Nantes, France 1966; *Ten Huize van . . . ,* vol. 4, by Joos Florquin, Louvain 1968; *L'Esprit Dada en Belgique* by Rik Sauwen, Leuven 1969; *An Artist's Workbook* by Natalie d'Arbeloff, London 1969; *Michel Seuphor,* exhibition catalog, with texts by Jan Martens and Mauris Bilcke, Antwerp 1972; *Michel Seuphor,* exhibition catalog, with prefaces by Bernard Ceysson and Maurice Allemand, Saint-Etienne, France 1971; *Seuphor* by Herbert Henkels, Paris and Antwerp 1976; *Seuphor: Monographe,* edited by Carmen Martinez, with texts by several authors, Paris 1976; *Michel Seuphor,* exhibition catalog with preface by Georg W. Költzsch, Saarbrucken 1979; *Michel Seuphor,* exhibition catalog, with a foreword by Georges Goldine, Liege, Belgium 1981; *Structures et modulations: Oeuvres de Seuphor de 1926 a 1984,* Milan 1984; *Entretiens sur Michel Seuphor,* Paris 1986; *Seuphor: la traversee du siecle,* exhibition catalog with text by Pierre Andre Benoit, Ales 1990; *Michel Seuphor,* exhibition catalog with texts by Költsch and Gellhaus, Germany 1992. **Articles—**Review in *Artforum International,* vol. 30, April 1992; ''Chez Seuphor'' in *The Print Collector's Newsletter,* vol. 26, September/October 1995; review by Gilles Plazy in *Cimaise,* vol. 44, September/October 1997; Obituary by Anolga Rodionoff in *L'Architecture d'Aujourd'hui,* no. 321, March 1999.

*

I have never really known what I am doing nor why I am doing it. I draw a lot, I write a lot. Something within me calls me, and I obey. I don't know at all whether it has any value or not. In front of what I have just completed, my opinion is undecided. Sometimes a drawing or a collage that I have never liked, and which by some miracle I have not myself destroyed, suddenly becomes a work that I find good. But I wouldn't know what to think of such inconstant feelings. The only value is that given by the spectator to a man's work: without him there is no work of art at all. The real creator is found hidden in the gaze of the amateur.

The artist must ask nothing more from society than independence, but this has to be absolute. Its greatest reward is not glory or renown; it is the liberty it brings.

An artist is a creator of unseen objects. He is not a businessman nor a sportsman nor a politiker.

—Michel Seuphor

* * *

This Fleming has two claims to fame. Michel Seuphor is a renowned literary commentator on the visual arts (particularly non-figurative visual art) and he is an eminent artist in his own right (something that has rebounded to his credit ever since Arp recommended him to Berggruen).

Seuphor has not stopped writing, but he once observed ''When a writer sets himself to painting or drawing, it probably means that he has found words to be no longer sufficient, that he imagines other poetic joys than those of speech.''

During the decade 1923 to 1933, he saw a great deal of Mondrian with whom he formed a close association and, although the work of the two artists bears only a superficial resemblance, in a way Seuphor was able to advance many of the ideas of the Dutch painter by exploring their potentialities in graphic works. A diligent researcher, in 1946 Seuphor produced 96 drawings, all of them variants on a single theme.

After 1954 he turned his attention to making collage-drawings, and it is worth noting that Arp actually used many of the Belgian's torn drawings to make collages of his own.

A further extension of his work subsequently took place when he made photographic enlargements of drawings which were then used as the designs for tapestries.

Seuphor lurks in the couloirs of contemporary art. Recognized as an inspired theoretician, capable of all sorts of extensions of the purposes of non-figurative art, he has been too easily relegated to the role of pundit. It should be more readily realized that he is also a fine exponent.

—Sheldon Williams

SHAPIRO, Joel

Nationality: American. **Born:** New York, 27 September 1941. **Education:** Educated at New York University, 1961–69, B.A. 1964, M.A. 1969. **Career:** Independent sculptor, New York, since 1969. Instructor, School of Visual Arts, New York, since 1977. **Awards:** National Endowment for the Arts Grant, 1975; Brandeis Award, Waltham, Massachusetts, 1984; Skowhegan Medal for Sculpture, Maine, 1986. **Agent:** ARS, 65 Bleecker Street, New York, New York 10012, U.S.A.

Individual Exhibitions:

1970 Paula Cooper Gallery, New York
1972 Paula Cooper Gallery, New York
1973 The Clocktower, New York
1974 Salvatore Ala Galleria, Milan
Paula Cooper Gallery, New York
1975 Paula Cooper Gallery, New York
The Garage, London (with Jennifer Bartlett)
Walter Kelly Gallery, Chicago
1976 Paula Cooper Gallery, Los Angeles
Museum of Contemporary Art, Chicago
1977 Max Protech Gallery, Washington, D.C.
Albright-Knox Art Gallery, Buffalo
Susanne Hilberry Gallery, Birmingham, Michigan
Paula Cooper Gallery, New York
Galerie Nancy Gillespie-Elisabeth de Laage, Paris
Galerie Aronowitsch, Stockholm
1978 Greenberg Gallery, St. Louis
Galerie M, Bochum, West Germany
1979 Akron Art Institute, Ohio
Galerie Nancy Gillespie-Elisabeth de Laage, Paris
Paula Cooper Gallery, New York
Ohio State University, Columbus
1980 Paula Cooper Gallery, New York
Sculpture and Drawing, Whitechapel Art Gallery, London
Museum Haus Lange, Krefeld, West Germany
Galerie Mukai, Tokyo
Asher-Faure Gallery, Los Angeles
Brooke Alexander Gallery, New York
Delahunty Gallery, Dallas
Moderna Museet, Stockholm
Galerie Aronowitch, Stockholm
Bell Gallery, Brown University, Providence, Rhode Island
1981 Ackland Art Museum, University of North Carolina, Chapel Hill
Georgia State University, Atlanta
Contemporary Arts Center, Cincinnati
John Stoller Gallery, Minneapolis
Daniel Weinberg Gallery, San Francisco
Israel Museum, Jerusalem
Gallery Mukai, Tokyo
Young-Hoffman Gallery, Chicago
1982 Paula Cooper Gallery, New York
Portland Center for the Visual Arts, Oregon
Susanne Hilberry Gallery, Birmingham, Michigan
Yarlow/Salzman Gallery, Toronto
Whitney Museum, New York (travelled to Dallas; Toronto; La Jolla, California)
1983 Galerie Aronowitsch, Stockholm
Paula Cooper Gallery, New York
Asher/Faure, Los Angeles
1984 Paula Cooper Gallery, New York (twice)
Galerie Aronowitsch, Stockholm
1985 Knoedler/Kasmin, London
Stedelijk Museum, Amsterdam (travelled to Dusseldorf and Baden-Baden)
1986 Seattle Art Museum, Washington
Galerie Daniel Templon, Paris
Ringling Museum of Art, Sarasota, Florida
Paula Cooper Gallery, New York
Asher/Faure, Los Angeles
1987 Donald Young Gallery, Chicago
1988 Paula Cooper Gallery, New York

Gallery Mukai, Tokyo
Hans Strelow, Dusseldorf
Susanne Hilberry Gallery, Birmingham, Michigan
Galerie Daniel Templon, Paris
Cleveland Museum of Art, Cleveland
1989 Asher/Faure Gallery, Los Angeles
The Toledo Museum of Art, Toledo
Paula Cooper Gallery, New York
Waddington Galleries, London
1990 Place Prints, New York
The Greenberg Gallery, St. Louis
Museet i Varberg, Sweden
Galerie Aronowitsch, Stockholm
Paula Cooper Gallery, New York
Louisiana Museum of Moderne Kunst, Humlebaek, Denmark
1991 Salon de Mars, Paris
Center for Fine Arts, Miami
Asher/Faure Gallery, Los Angeles
Gallery Mukai, Tokyo
John Berggruen Gallery, San Francisco
1993 The Pace Gallery, New York
Galerie Karsten Greve, Cologne
1994 Gallery Seomi, Seoul (catalog)
1995 *Joel Shapiro: Painted Wood Sculpture and Drawings,* PaceWildenstein, New York (catalog)
Joel Shapiro: Outdoors, Walker Arts Center, Minneapolis (catalog)
1996 *Joel Shapiro: Sculpture and Drawings,* PaceWildenstein, Los Angeles (catalog)
Joel Shapiro: Recent Sculpture and Drawings, Seomi Gallery, Seoul (catalog)
1997 Addison Gallery of American Art, Andover, Massachusetts (catalog)
Haus der Kunst, Munich (catalog)
1998 Pace Gallery, New York (catalog)
1999 American Academy in Rome, Italy (catalog)
Yorkshire Sculpture Park, Wakefield, England (catalog)
National Gallery of Canada, Ottawa (catalog)
2000 John Berggruen Gallery, San Francisco
2001 Spoleto Festival USA, Charleston, South Carolina (traveled to San Antonio, Texas, and Denver, Colorado) (catalog)

Selected Group Exhibitions:

1969 *Anti-Illusion: Procedure/Material,* Whitney Museum, New York
1973 *New American Graphic Art,* Fogg Art Museum, Cambridge, Massachusetts
1977 *Foire Internationale d'Art Contemporian,* Grand Palais, Paris
1978 *Made by Sculptors,* Stedelijk Museum, Amsterdam
1979 *Contemporary: Sculpture: Selections from the Collection of the Museum of Modern Art,* Museum of Modern Art, New York
1980 *Pier + Ocean,* Hayward Gallery, London (travelled to the Rijksmuseum Kroller-Muller, Otterlo, Netherlands)
1981 *Biennial,* Whitney Museum, New York
1983 *Back to the USA,* Rheinisches Landesmuseum, Bonn (travelled to Lucerne and Stuttgart)
1985 *Transformations in Sculpture,* Guggenheim Museum, New York
1987 *Cast in Bronze,* Kansas City Gallery of Art, Missouri
1989 *Amsterdam/Art: Regards: dessins contemporains,* Institut Néerlandis, Paris (catalog)
1989 Biennial Exhibition, Whitney Museum of American Art, New York
1990 *The New Sculpture 1965–75: Between Geometry and Gesture,* Whitney Museum of American Art, New York (catalog)
Pharmakon '90, Nippon Convention Center, Tokyo (catalog)
1991 *La Sculpture Contemporaine: après 1970,* Fondation Daniel Templon, Musée Temporaire, Fréjus, France (catalog)
1992 *Allegories of Modernism,* Museum of Modern Art, New York
1993 *Manhattan Breeze—Five Contemporary Artists,* Takashimaya, Tokyo (catalog)
Venice Biennale, Venice (catalog)
1995 *Twentieth Century American Sculpture at the White House, Exhibition III,* Washington, D.C. (catalog)
1996 *The Robert and Jane Meyerhoff Collection,* National Gallery of Art, Washington, D.C. (catalog)
Thinking Print: Books to Billboards, 1980–95, Museum of Modern Art, New York (catalog)
1997 *At the Threshold of the Visible: Miniscule and Small-Scale Art, 1964–1996,* traveling exhibition by Independent Curators Incorporated, New York (travelled to New York, Maryland, Ontario (Canada), Virginia, California, and Edmonton (Canada)) (catalog)
1998 *Contemporary Art: The Janet Wolfson de Botton Gift,* Tate Gallery, London (catalog)
1999–2000 *Afterimage: Drawing Through Process,* Museum of Contemporary Art, Los Angeles
1999–2001 *KölnSkulptur 2,* Skulpturepark Köln (catalog)
2000 *End Papers: Drawings from 1890–1900 and 1990–2000,* Neuberger Museum of Art, Purchase State University of New York (catalog)
The American Century: Art and Culture 1900–2000; part II, 1950–2000, Whitney Museum of Modern Art, New York (catalog)
00, Barbara Gladstone Gallery, New York (catalog)
The International Festival of Contemporary Sculpture of Monaco: Contemporary American Sculpture, Monaco (catalog)
New Work, Galerie Jamileh Weber, Zurich
2000–01 *MOMA 2000 Open Ends,* Museum of Modern Art, New York
Changing Perceptions: The Panza Collection, Guggenheim Museum, Bilbao, Spain (catalog)

Collections:

Whitney Museum, New York; Museum of Modern Art, New York; Picker Art Gallery, Colgate University, Hamilton, New York; University of Massachusetts, Amherst; Fogg Art Museum, Harvard

University, Cambridge, Massachusetts; Weatherspoon Art Gallery, University of North Carolina, Greensboro; Lannan Foundation, Palm Beach, Florida; National Gallery of Australia, Caberra; Art Institute of Chicago, Chicago; British Museum, London; Cincinnati Art Museum, Cincinnati, Ohio; Cleveland Museum of Art, Cleveland, Ohio; Dallas Museum of Art, Dallas, Texas; Denver Art Museum, Colorado; Detroit Institute of Arts, Michigan; Hirshorn Museum and Sculpture Garden, Smithsonian Institution, Washington, D.C.; Metropolitan Museum of Art, New York; Museum of Contemporary Art, Chicago; Museum of Fine Arts, Boston; National Gallery of Art, Washington, D.C.; Tate Gallery, London; Walker Art Center, Minneapolis; Yale University Art Gallery, New Haven, Connecticut.

Publications:

By SHAPIRO: Articles—''Joel Shapiro Torquing: A Dialogue with Liza Bear'' in *Avalanche* (New York), Summer 1975; interview, with Susan Logan, in *Early Work by 5 Contemporary Artists,* exhibition catalog, New York 1977; ''Joel Shapiro: An Interview,'' with John Coplans, in *Dialogue* (Akron, Ohio), January/February 1979.

On SHAPIRO: Books—*Critical Perspectives in American Art,* exhibition catalog with an essay by Rosalind Krauss, Amherst, Massachusetts 1976; *Joel Shapiro,* exhibition catalog by Linda Cathcart, Buffalo, New York 1977; *Pictures,* exhibition catalog by Douglas Crimp, New York 1977; *Ideas in Sculpture 1965–77,* exhibition catalog with an essay by Anne Rorimer, Chicago 1977; *Early Works by 5 Contemporary Artists,* exhibition catalog by Marcia Tucker, New York 1977; *The Minimal Tradition,* exhibition catalog, Ridgefield, Connecticut 1979; *Drawings: The Pluralist Decade,* exhibition catalog with an introduction by Janet Karden, Philadelphia 1980; *Skulptur im 20. Jahrhundert,* exhibition catalog, Basel 1980; *Joel Shapiro: Sculpture and Drawings,* exhibition catalog by Roberta Smith, London 1980; *Joel Shapiro,* exhibition catalog with essays by Richard Marshall and Roberta Smith, New York 1982; *Joel Shapiro,* exhibition catalog with texts by Marja Bloem and Karel Schampers, Amsterdam 1985; *Joel Shapiro: Sculpture and Drawings 1981–85,* exhibition catalog with essay by Mark Ormond, Sarasota 1986; *Joel Shaprio: Sculpture and Drawings* by Hendel Teicher, with an introductory essay by Michael Brenson, New York 1998.

* * *

In contrast to minimalism's concentration on self-referentiality, Joel Shapiro, in the early 1970s, contributed to a new direction in sculpture by reexamining the possibilities of memory association and psychological content. Following an interest in Process Art (in which ''raw'' materials were explored for their innate properties or metals were pounded or forged to accept new forms), Shapiro began to explore figurative content: miniaturist houses, chairs, human figures, coffins, bridges, and horses became a part of his sculptural lexicon. By investing his blocky cast bronze and iron forms with allusions to common objects, Shapiro permitted his work to provoke associations beyond their basic external values.

Aside from their psychological content, these objects exist correlatively, to be experienced apart from *a priori* meaning: ''If you see the work as some locater of experience,'' Shapiro has said, ''the work has an internal reference to some metaphoric thought. The analogy would be to use language to describe an experience. The language is never commensurate with experience.'' The external, formal properties of Shapiro's sculptural language constitute a barrier to association. While his chairs and houses may evoke certain memories, they also function self-referentially: ''You can't just say that's just a chair,'' Shapiro has observed in reference to memory, ''you have to deal with what it's doing in space . . . . It's an image that's referential, unless the piece is functioning so dynamically and on such a specific level that maybe then you could overcome associations.'' Corresponding to this earlier interest in ''process,'' which centered on the passage from nature to culture, Shapiro's sculptures are simple shapes at the verge of signification; they are neither ''empty signs'' nor fully realized cultural icons.

The balance between evocation and objecthood extends to Shapiro's extraordinary drawings. Composed of simple geometric outlines or silhouettes that recall both architectural and sculptural forms, the drawings play on the dynamics of scale and shape. Shapiro's images are engaged in a visual dialectic, setting spatial illusionism against the nuances of their own surfaces. While the contrast of dark charcoal bands with their resonant ''ghosts'' suggest a conceptual penetration into space, the fingerprints, smudges, and erasures on the surface of Shapiro's drawings serve as a record of process, continually redirecting the eye to the drawing's surface. By injecting figurative imagery into his drawings (houses or more recently simplified figures disposed in animated groups), Shapiro revives the modernist strategy of questioning representation's reliance on the condition of absence. These drawings subvert the idea that a sign serve as a proxy for an absent object, for in their formal, architectonic integrity and voluptuous exposition of process, they never entirely submit to a representational status. Like his sculptures, the external *presence* of Shapiro's drawings are as significant as the absent forms or spaces they purport to represent.

Another important aspect of Shapiro's activity, small wall ''reliefs'' in wood or plaster, challenges the rationalist ideal of experience in sculpture: rather than offering multiple views of the same object in one synoptic view (in an effort to ''grasp'' it by revealing simultaneously its concomitant physical situations), the literal contours of these constructions cannot be apprehended without *experiencing* them in a full 180 viewing range. Similarly, Shapiro's miniaturist houses and bridges, deployed throughout the gallery space, situate the viewer in a special relationship to the work. Within such a spatial context, these apparently absurd relationships command a re-ordering of the viewer's sense of scale. The sculptures' persistent occupancy of the public gallery space thrust that space into unconventional roles, charging it with ironic associations to landscape an architecture that are as fleeting as the mythologized memories that initially activate Shapiro's simple forms. Absence yields to presence, memory to experience, as the viewer apprehends the external realities of his unique situation.

—Maurice Berger

SHAW, Jeffrey

Nationality: Australian. **Born** in Melbourne, Victoria, 23 October 1944. **Education:** Melbourne High School, 1958–62; studied architecture and humanities at the University of Melbourne, 1963–64;

studied sculpture at the Accademia di Brera, Milan, 1965 and at St. Martin's School of Art, London, 1966. **Career:** Independent artist, with Theo Botschuyver, Eventstructure Research Group, Amsterdam, 1967–82, with participation from Sean Wellesley-Miller, 1967–69; founder, with Marga Adama and John Munsey, Javaphile Group, Amsterdam, 1977–81; guest professor, Academy of Art, Rotterdam, 1990; guest professor, Rietveld Academy, Amsterdam; Director, Institut für Bildmedien, ZKM/Zentrum für Kunst und Medientechnologie, Karlsruhe, since 1991; professor, Hochschule für Gestaltung, Karlsruhe, since 1995. **Awards:** First Prize, *Young Minds Exhibitions,* Victoria, 1963; Commonwealth Scholarship, 1963; Arts Council of Great Britain grant, 1969, 1973; Dutch Ministry of Culture grant, 1970–75, 1981–82; Prix Ars Electronica, Linz, Austria, 1989; L'Imagine Elettronica Prize, Ferrara, Italy, 1989. **Address:** Javastraat 126, Amsterdam 1094 HP, Netherlands.

Individual Exhibitions:

1966 Kingly Street Gallery, London (with T. van Tijen)
Better Boooks, London (with John Latham)
1967 Sigma Projects, Amsterdam (with Eventstructure Research Group)
Sigma Projects, Rotterdam (with E.R.G.)
Casino Communal, Knokke, Belgium (with E.R.G.)
1968 Museum of Modern Art, Oxford (with E.R.G.)
Open-Air display, *Brighton Festival,* Sussex (with E.R.G.)
1969 Institute of Contemporary Arts, London (with E.R.G.)
Six Events display, Amsterdam (with E.R.G.)
Six Events display, Rotterdam (with E.R.G.)
St. George's Art Centre, Liverpool (with E.R.G and John Latham)
1970 Stedelijk Museum, Amsterdam (with E.R.G.)
1972 National Gallery of Victoria, Melbourne (with E.R.G.)
1973 Pinacotheca Gallery, Melbourne (with E.R.G.)
Tolarno Gallery, Melbourne (with E.R.G.)
1974 Stedelijk Museum, Amsterdam (with E.R.G.)
De Latarn, Rotterdam (with E.R.G.)
Drama Institute Theatre, Amsterdam (with E.R.G.)
1975 National Bus Company, London (with E.R.G.and Artist Placement Group)
1976 Genesis World Tour (with Genesis rock group and E.R.G.)
1978 Stichting de Appel, Amsterdam (with E.R.G.)
1997 *Jeffrey Shaw: Place—A User's Manual,* Neue Galerie, Graz (catalog)

Selected Group Exhibitions:

1968 *Structures Gonflables,* Musée d'Art Moderne, Paris
1969 *Art after Plans,* Kunsthalle, Berne
1970 *Street Art Program,* Hannover
1971 *Inno '70,* Hayward Gallery, London
1972 *British Avant Garde,* Gallery House, London
1974 *Tabarka Festival,* Tunisia
1976 *Biennale,* Paris
1977 *Ongellukkige Liefde Festival,* De Lantarn Theatre, Rotterdam
1978 *Lucht,* Stedelijk Museum, Schiedam, Netherlands
1979 *One World Poetry Festival,* Melkweg, Amsterdam
1991 *Outer Space: 8 Photo & Video Installations,* South Bank Centre, London (catalog)
1992 *New Media,* Galerie der Stadt, Sindelfingen, Germany
1995 *1995 Lyon Biennial,* France (catalog)
Manifestation Internationale Vidéo et Art Electronique, Usine C, Montreal (catalog)
Medientechnologie, Zentrum für Kunst und Medientechnologie, Karlsruhe, Germany
1996 *Passages Numériques,* Cité des Sciences et de l'Industrie, Paris (catalog)
1997 *Media—Art—History,* Media Museum ZKM, Center for Art and Media Karlsruhe, Karlsruhe
Mediascape, Deutsch Telecom Galleries, Guggenheim Museum, New York
1999 *Heaven,* Kunsthalle Dusseldorf, Dusseldorf (traveled to Tate Gallery Liverpool)
2000 *Vision.Ruhr—Kunst Medien Interaktion,* Zeche Zollern II/IV, Dortmund, Germany (catalog)
Wired Worlds, National Museum of Photography, Film & Television, Bradford, England

Collections:

City Collection, Amsterdam; Dutch National Collection, The Hague; City Collection, Haarlem, Netherlands.

Permanent Public Installations:

Koopwaarders Plantsoen, Amsterdam Noord; De Hoogeberg, Belsen, Netherlands; Frascati Theatre, Amsterdam; Scholengemeenschap Quirijin, Tilburg, Netherlands

Publications:

By SHAW: Books—*Evenstructures,* with E.R.G., Delf 1972; *Prospectus for the Strombeeld Foundation,* with E.R.G., Amsterdam 1980. **Articles—**''Inflatable Structures and Participation,'' with E.R.G., in *Robho* (Paris), Spring 1968; ''Concepts for an Operational Art,'' with E.R.G., in *Art and Artists* (London), January 1969; ''Revolution/Revolutions: Interactive Video Sculptures'' in *Leonardo,* vol. 24, no. 4, 1991; interview with Florian Rötzer in *Kunstforum International,* no. 117, 1992; interview with Johan Pijnappel in *Art & Design,* vol. 9, November/December 1994; interview in *Kunstforum International,* no. 132, November 1995–January 1996.

On SHAW: Books—*Arthropods* by Jim Burns, New York 1971; *Kunst van Nu,* Amsterdam 1971; *Sonsbeek '71 Report,* Arnherm 1972; *9th Biennale de Paris,* exhibition catalog, Paris 1975; *Art and Technology* by Johan Pijnappel, London 1994. **Articles—**''Evenstructures'' by Albrecht Kwast in *Pneutube,* exhibition catalog, London 1969; ''Evenstructure Research Group'' by Ruud Englander in *Mickery Mouth* (Amsterdam), no. 11, 1971; ''ERG in Australia'' by Terry Smith in *Studio International* (London), October 1972; ''Diadrama'' by Max Adrian In *Toneel Teatral* (Amsterdam), no. 1, 1974; ''Jeffrey Shaw: Breaking Through the Traditional Framework'' by Frits Gierstberg in *Perspektief,* no. 47–48, June 1994.

*

Working inside the frameworks of contemporary art, bound to its matrix of expectancy—if information is a function of interference, then where is the suprise?

"Roll away the reel world, the reel world, the reel world! Cherchons La Flamme!"

No doubt in whose interests the new technologies such as computers are being developed. But at the same time these technologies make possible the creation of "interactive" art works which have an ongoing dialogue with their audience and/or surroundings. Thus the form of such an art work expands to include the nature and quality of this interactivity in time.

—Jeffrey Shaw

SHERMAN, Cindy

Nationality: American. **Born:** Cynthia Morris Sherman, Glen Ridge, New Jersey, 19 January 1954. **Education:** State University of New York, Buffalo, B.A. 1976. **Career:** Painter, photographer, mixed-media artist. **Awards:** National Endowment for the Arts, 1977; John Simon Guggenheim Memorial Fellowship, 1983; Skowhegan Medal for Photography, Maine, 1989; Larry Aldrich Foundation Award, Connecticut, 1993; John D. and Catherine T. MacArthur Foundation, 1995; Wolfgang-Hahn-Preis (Gesellschaft fur Moderne Kunst am Museum, Ludwig), 1997; Goslar Kaierring Prize, 1999; The Hasselblad Foundation, 2000. **Address:** Lives in New York City.

Selected Individual Exhibitions:

1980 Contemporary Arts Museum, Houston (brochure)
Metro Pictures, New York (and 1981, 1982, 1983, 1985, 1987, 1989, 1990, 1992, 1995, 1996, 1998, 1999, 2000)

1982 *Cindy Sherman,* The Stedelijk Museum, Amsterdam (traveled to Gewad, Ghent, Belgium; Watershed Gallery, Bristol, England; John Hansard Gallery, University of Southampton, England; Palais Stutterheim, Erlangen, West Germany; Haus am Waldsee, West Berlin; Centre d'Art Contemporain, Geneva; Sonja Henie-Niels Onstadt Foundation, Copenhagen; Louisiana Museum, Humlebaek, Denmark) (catalogue)
Cindy Sherman, Deja Vu, Dijon, France (catalogue)

1983 Musee d'Art et d'Industrie de Saint Etienne, France (catalogue)
The St. Louis Art Museum, Missouri (broch.)

1984 *Cindy Sherman,* Akron Art Museum, Ohio (traveled to Institute of Contemporary Art, Philadelphia; Museum of Art, Carnegie Institute, Pittsburgh, Pennsylvania; Des Moines Art Center; The Baltimore Museum of Art) (catalogue)
Monika Sprüth Galerie, Cologne (and 1988, 1990, 1992, 1995, 1999)

1985 Westfalischer Kunstverein, Munster, West Germany (catalogue)

1987 Whitney Museum of American Art, New York (traveled to The Institute of Contemporary Art, Boston; The Dallas Museum of Art) (catalogue)

1989 National Art Gallery, Wellington, New Zealand, and Waikato Museum of Art and History, New Zealand (catalogue)

1990 Padiglione d'arte Contemporanea, Milan (catalogue)
University Art Museum, University of California, Berkeley

1991 *Cindy Sherman,* Basel Kunsthalle, Switzerland (traveled to Staatsgalerie Moderner Kunst, Munich; The Whitechapel Gallery, London) (catalogue)
Milwaukee Art Museum; Center for the Fine Arts, Miami; The Walker Art Center, Minneapolis (brochure)

1992 Museo de Monterrey, Mexico (catalogue)

1993 Tel Aviv Museum of Art

1994 *Cindy Sherman,* ACC Galerie Weimar, Germany (catalogue)
Cindy Sherman, The Irish Museum of Modern Art, Dublin (catalogue)

1995 *Directions: Cindy Sherman—Film Stills,* Hirshhorn Museum, Washington, D.C. (brochure)
Cindy Sherman Photographien 1975–1995, Deichtorhallen Hamburg (traveled to Malmo Kunsthall, Sweden; Kunstmuseum Luzerne, Switzerland) (catalogue)
Cindy Sherman, Museu de Arte Moderna de Sao Paulo, Brazil (catalogue)

1996 *Cindy Sherman,* Museum Boymans-van Beuningen, Rotterdam (traveled to Museo Nacional Centro de Arte Reina Sofia, Madrid; Sala de Exposiciones REKALDE, Bilbao; Staatliche Kunsthalle, Baden-Baden) (catalogue)
Cindy Sherman, Museum of Modern Art, Shiga, Japan (traveled to Marugame Genichiro-Inokuma Museum of Contemporary Art, Marugame, Japan; Museum of Contemporary Art, Tokyo) (catalogue)
Metamorphosis: Cindy Sherman Photographs, The Cleveland Museum of Art, Cleveland, Ohio

1997 *Cindy Sherman: The Complete Untitled Film Stills,* Museum of Modern Art, New York
Cindy Sherman: A Selection from the Eli Broad Foundation's Collection, Museo de Bellas Artes, Caracas, Venezuela (catalogue)
Cindy Sherman: Retrospective, Museum of Contemporary Art, Los Angeles (traveled to Museum of Contemporary Art, Chicago; Galerie Rudolfinum, Prague; capc Musée, Bordeaux; Barbican Art Gallery, London; Museum of Contemporary Art, Sydney; Art Gallery of Ontario, Toronto)
Cindy Sherman, Museum Ludwig, Cologne (catalogue)

1998 *Allegories,* Seattle Art Museum, Washington (catalogue)

2000 Hasselblad Center, Goteburg, Sweden
Gagosian Gallery, Los Angeles
Galería Juana de Aizpuru, Madrid
greengrassi, London

2001 *Cindy Sherman: Early Works,* Studio Guenzani, Milan

Selected Group Exhibitions:

1982 *Documenta 7,* Kassel, West Germany (catalogue)
Eight Artists: The Anxious Edge, Walker Art Center, Minneapolis, Minnesota (catalogue)
La Biennale di Benezia, Venice (catalogue)

1983 *Directions 1983,* Hirshhorn Museum, Washington D.C. (catalogue)

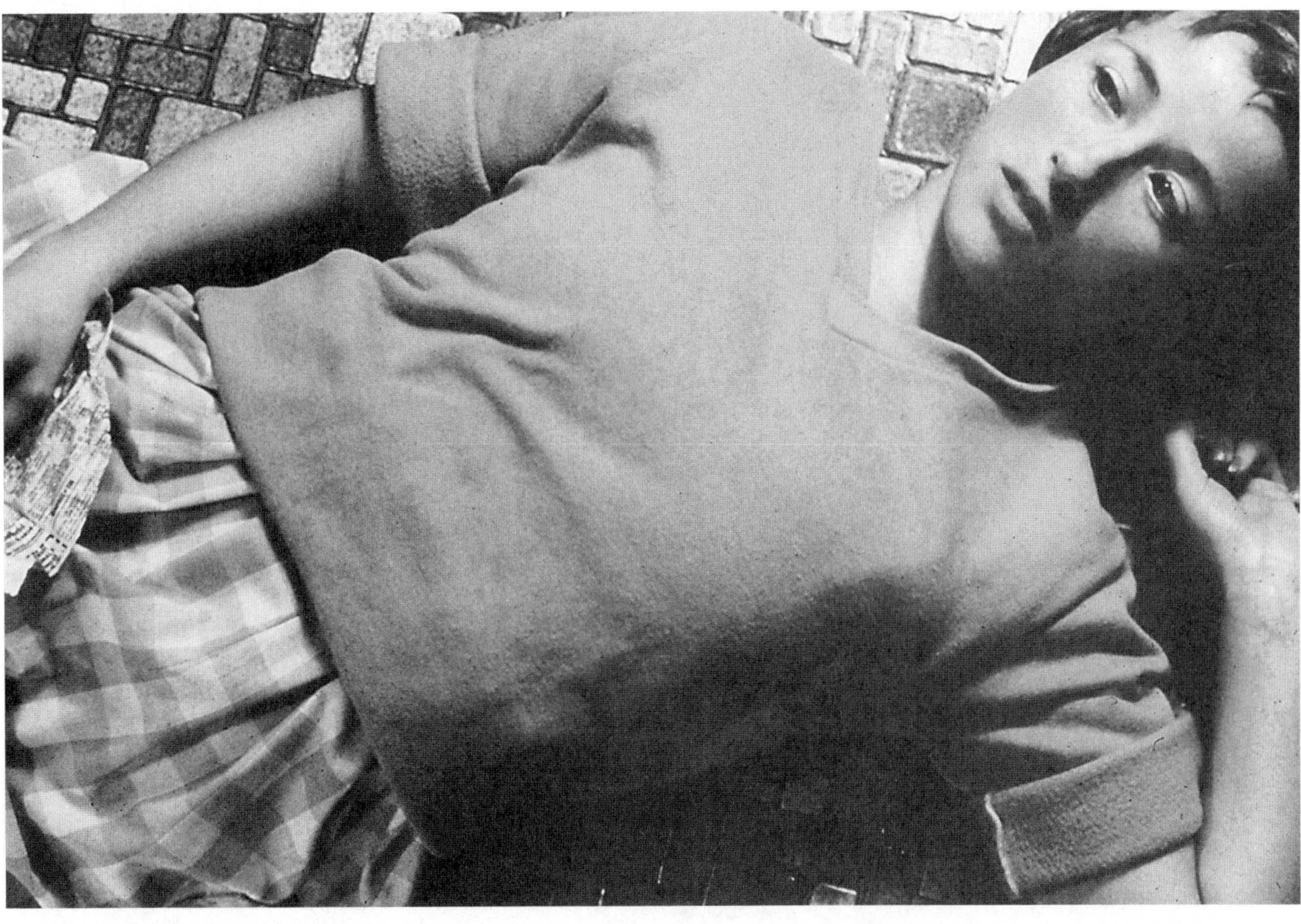

Cindy Sherman: *Untitled,* 1981. ©Courtesy of Cindy Sherman and Metro Pictures.

1983 Biennial Exhibition, Whitney Museum of American Art, New York (catalogue)
The New Art, The Tate Gallery, London
1984 *Alibis,* Centre Pompidou, Musee d'Art Moderne, Paris (catalogue)
Content: A Contemporary Focus, 1974–84, Hirshhorn Museum, Washington D.C. (catalogue)
The Fifth Biennale of Sydney, Private Symbol: Social Metaphor, Art Gallery of New South Wales, Sydney (catalogue)
1985 *1985 Carnegie International,* Carnegie Museum of Art, Pittsburgh (catalogue)
1985 Biennial Exhibition, Whitney Museum of American Art, New York (catalogue)
1986 *Art and Its Double: A New York Perspective,* Fundacio Caixa de Pensions, Barcelona and La Caixa de Pensions, Madrid (catalogue)
Individuals: A Selected History of Contemporary Art, 1945–1986, Museum of Contemporary Art, Los Angeles, (catalogue)
The American Exhibition, The Art Institute of Chicago (catalogue)
1987 *Avant-Garde in the Eighties,* Los Angeles County Museum of Art (catalogue)
Implosion: A Postmodern Perspective, Moderna Museet, Stockholm (catalogue)
1989 *A Forest of Signs: Art in the Crisis of Representation,* The Museum of Contemporary Art, Los Angeles (catalogue)
Bilderstreit, Mense Rhineside Halls, Cologne
Image World: Art and Media Culture, Whitney Museum of American Art, New York (catalogue)
1990 *Culture and Commentary,* The Hirshhorn Museum, Washington, D.C. (catalogue)
Energies, The Stedelijk Museum, Amsterdam (catalogue)
The Readymade Boomerang, Eighth Biennial of Sydney (catalogue)
1991 *1991 Biennial Exhibition,* Whitney Museum of American Art, New York (catalogue)
Metropolis, Martin-Gropius-Bau, Berlin (catalogue)
1992 *Post Human,* Musée d'Art Contemporain, Pully/Lausanne, Switzerland (traveled to Castello di Rivoli, Turin; Deste Foundation, Athens; Deichtorhallen, Hamburg; Israel Museum, Jerusalem) (catalogue)
1993 *Louise Lawler, Cindy Sherman, Laurie Simmons,* Kunsternes Hus, Oslo and Museum of Contemporary Art, Helsinki (catalogue)
1993 Biennial Exhibition, Whitney Museum of American Art, New York (catalogue)

Cindy Sherman: *Untitled Film Still #15*, 1978. Photo by David Heald. ©The Solomon R. Guggenheim Foundation, NY; courtesy of Solomon R. Guggenheim Museum, NY.

American Art of This Century, Martin-Gropius-Bau, Berlin and Royal Academy of Arts, London (catalogue)

1994 *World Morality,* Kunsthalle, Basel (catalogue)
Body and Soul, The Baltimore Museum of Art, Maryland
Jurgen Klauke—Cindy Sherman, Sammlung Goetz, Munich (catalogue)

1995 *Projections,* Ydessa Hendeles Art Foundation, Toronto
1995 Biennial Exhibition, Whitney Museum of American Art, New York (catalogue)
Zeichen & Wunder, Kunsthaus Zurich, Switzerland (catalogue)
XLVI Esposizione Internazionale d'Arte 1995, La Biennale di Venezia, Venice (catalogue)
FeminiMasculin: Le Sexe de l'Art?, Centre Georges Pompidou, Musée d'Art Moderne, Paris (catalogue)
1995 Carnegie International, The Carnegie Museum of Art, Pittsburgh (catalogue)

1996 *L'Informe: le Modernisme a Rebours,* Centre Georges Pompidou, Musée National d'Art Moderne, Paris (catalogue)
Hall of Mirrors: Art and Film Since 1945, The Museum of Contemporary Art, Los Angeles (traveled to The Wexner Center for the Arts, Columbus, Ohio; Palazzo delle Esposizioni, Rome; The Museum of Contemporary Art, Chicago) (catalogue)
Biennale di Firenze, Florence, Italy (catalogue)

1997 *Gender Performnce in Photography,* Solomon R. Guggenheim Museum, New York (catalogue)
On the Edge: Contemporary Art from the Werner and Elaine Dannheisser Collection, The Museum of Modern Art, New York (catalogue)
Von Beuys bis Cindy Sherman Sammlung Lothar Schirmer, Kunsthalle, Bremen (catalogue)

1998 *Mirror Images: Women, Surrealism and Self- Representation,* MIT List Center, Cambridge, Massachussettes (traveled to Miami Art Museum; San Francisco Museum of Modern Art)

1999 *Gesammelte Werke 1: Zeitgenössische Kunst seit 1968,* Kunstmuseum, Wolfsburg
Notorious, Museum of Modern Art, Oxford
The American Century, Whitney Museum of American Art, New York (catalogue)
Inverted Odysseys, Grey Art Gallery, New York (catalogue)
The Century of the Body: Photoworks 1900–2000, Musée de l'Elysée, Lisbon
Triennale Exhibition: Sentiment of the Year 2000, Triennale di Milano, Milan
Regarding Beauty, Hirshhorn Museum, Washington, D.C. (catalogue)

2000 *Let's Entertain,* Walker Art Center, Minneapolis (catalogue) *Open Ends,* Museum of Modern Art, New York
Hyper Mental, Kunsthaus Zürich and Hamburger Kunsthalle (catalogue)

Collections:

Albright-Knox Art Gallery, Buffalo; Art Gallery of New South Wales, Sydney; Art Gallery of Ontario, Toronto; Art Institute of Chicago; Australian National Gallery, Canberra; Baltimore Museum of Art; Carnegie Museum of Art, Pittsburgh; Centre Georges Pompidou, Paris; Centro de Arte Reina Sofia, Madrid; Corcoran Gallery of Art, Washington D.C.; Dallas Museum of Fine Arts; Des Moines Art Center; Hamburger Bahnhof Museum fur Gegenwart, Berlin; Israeli Museum, Jerusalem; Kunsthaus, Zurich; Kunsthalle Hamburg, Germany; Kunstmuseum Wolfsburg, Germany; Los Angeles County Museum of Art; Louisiana Museum, Humlebaek, Denmark; Metropolitan Museum of Art, New York; Moderna Museet, Stockholm; Modern Art Museum of Fort Worth, Texas; Musée d'art Contemporain, Montréal; Museum Boymans-van Beuningen, Rotterdam; Museum des 20, Jahrhunderts, Vienna; Museum Folkwang, Essen, Germany; Museum Ludwig, Cologne; Museum of Art, Carnegie Institute, Pittsburgh; Museum of Contemporary Art, Chicago; Museum of Contemporary Art, Helsinki; Museum of Contemporary Art, Los Angeles; Museum of Contemporary Art, Luxembourg; Museum of Fine Arts, Boston; Museum of Fine Arts, Houston; Museum of Modern Art, New York; Museum of Modern Art, Oslo; New Britain Museum of American Art, New Britain, Connecticut; Philadelphia Museum of Art; Rijksmuseum Kroller-Muller, Otterlo, Holland; San Francisco Museum of Modern Art; Solomon R. Guggenheim Museum, New York; Sprengel Museum, Hannover; St. Louis Art Museum; Staatsgalerie Stuttgart, Germany; Stedelijk Museum, Amsterdam; Tamayo Museum, Mexico City; Tate Gallery, London; Tokyo Metropolitan Museum of Photography; Victoria and Albert Museum, London; Wadsworth Atheneum, Hartford; Walker Art Center, Minneapolis; Whitney Museum of American Art, New York.

Publications:

By SHERMAN: Film—*Office Killer* (feature-film), director, Good Machine and Kardana/Swinsky Films, 1997.

On SHERMAN: Books—*Cindy Sherman: 1975–1993* by Rosalind Krauss, New York 1993; *Cindy Sherman: A Retrospective* edited by Amanda T. Smith and Elizabeth A. Cruz, New York 1997. **Articles—** ''Cindy Sherman: Metro Pictures'' by Lynn Zelevansky in *Flash Art,* no. 102, March/April 1981; ''Oracle of Images'' by Peter Schjeldahl in *Cindy Sherman* (exhibition catalogue), New York 1987; ''Cindy Sherman's Cindy Shermans'' by Lisa Phillips in *Cindy Sherman* (exhibition catalogue), New York 1987; ''Suitable for Framing: The Critical Recasting of Cindy Sherman'' by Abigail Solomon-Godeau in *Parkett,* no. 29, 1991; ''Where's the Artist? Feminist Practice and Poststructuralist Theories of Authorship'' by Linda L. Klinger in *Art Journal,* vol. 50, Summer 1991; ''The Sherman Phenomena: A Forclosure of Dialectical Reasoning'' by Nadine Lemmon in *Perspektief,* no. 46, November 1993; ''Picture This'' by Antonella Russo in *Art Monthly,* no. 181, November 1994; ''Anatomy of an Artist'' by George Howell in *Art Papers,* July/August 1995; ''Obscene, Abject, Traumatic'' by Hal Foster in *October,* no. 78, Fall 1996; ''Cosmetics and Abjection: Cindy Sherman'' by Laura Mulvey in *Fetishism and Curiosity,* Bloomington, University of Indiana Press, 1996; ''A Chat with Cindy Sherman'' by Dike Blair in *Flash Art,* no. 187, March/April 1996; ''Sherman's Mass Appeal'' by Barbara L. Miller in *Afterimage,* no. 25, November/December 1997; ''Cindy Sherman'' by Eva Forgacs in *Art Issues,* no. 51, January/February 1998; ''Cindy Sherman: Metro Pictures'' by Mark Van Proyen in *New Art Examiner* vol. 27, no. 2, October 1999; ''The Woman with a Hundred Faces'' by Sandrine Malinaud in *Cimaise,* vol. 46, no. 258, March/April 1999; ''Cindy Sherman at Gagosian Gallery'' by Eva Forgacs in *Art Issues,* no. 64, September/October

2000; ''Her Secret Identities'' by Calvin Tomkins in *New Yorker,* 15 May 2000; ''American Psychos: The End of Art Cinema in the '90s'' by Laurence A Rickels in *Art/Text,* no. 67, November 1999–January 2000; ''Cindy Sherman: Greengrassi, London'' by Andrew Wilson in *Art Monthly,* no. 242, December 2000/January 2001. **Film—***Nobody's Here But Me* (documentary), directed by Mark Stokes, Cinecontact production for the BBC and the Arts Council of England, 1994.

* * *

Raised on Long Island, in 1972 Cindy Sherman enrolled at the State University of New York (SUNY)—Buffalo, where she began as a painting student, but eventually switched her focus to photography. Sherman graduated from SUNY in 1976 and moved to New York City the following year. Here, her lifelong penchant for playing dress-up and college ''paper doll'' experiments (involving multi-character, single-frame narratives consisting entirely of cut-out self-portrait photos) evolved into a series of self-portraits that not only launched her career, but are today considered landmarks of late twentieth century art.

This series of *Untitled Film Stills* (1977–80) are 8 x 10 inch, black-and-white photographs depicting the artist in a variety of elaborate costumes playing roles reminiscent of stereotypical female ''types'' in cinema. However, instead of directly appropriating these roles from the imagery of others, she rather confiscates the symbolic constructions of women that culture often promotes. Inspired by the performance documentation of feminist artists such as Eleanor Antin and Adrian Piper, these works were meant to serve not as straight portraits but as documents of the artist's staging of situations—in her studio and public sites—for the characters she creates to inhabit. Using costume and makeup transformations the artist renders herself virtually unrecognizable from photo to photo and, imitating conventional setups of the promotional film still genre, depicts the artist/character at hand in ambiguous situations seemingly lifted from an ongoing narrative: the working girl in the big city, the suburban housewife contemplating life over a sink of dirty dishes, the bobby-soxed hitchhiker waiting for a car to materialize around the bend. Although technically unremarkable—indeed, Sherman failed her first photography course at SUNY for her inability to master technical processes—these initial, unconventional self-portraits were created at a moment during which identity, spectatorship, and the role of the ''author'' were coming to the fore as the primary subjects of both postmodern and feminist studies. As such, scholars and critics were quick to adopt Sherman's *Untitled Film Stills* as icons of these very issues. Adding fuel to the discursive fires surrounding Sherman's photographs was their purposeful ambiguity, from the open-ended narratives they present to their lack of titles to the artist's own reluctance to pin down the images' meanings.

The *Untitled Film Stills* and subsequent forays into color self-portraiture, such as her untitled ''rear screen projections'' (1980–81) and controversial ''centerfold'' series (commissioned and eventually rejected by *Artforum* magazine in 1981), drew much attention from thinkers who read them as documents of postmodernist concerns. Readings of Sherman's work immediately addressed her series' relevance as a reflection of postmodern ideals. They represented a plural and fragmented rather than unique and ''essential'' identity; rejected the formal limits particular to the artist's chosen medium by emphasizing the image's concept rather than the photographic object; and questioned the originality of artistic authorship by denying the viewer a single, original source of appropriation, regardless of the haunting familiarity of her imagery. For many of these same reasons, feminist scholars were drawn to Sherman's work as symbolic of feminism's own contemporary concerns. Sherman's construction and presentation of multiple identities through a single female subject offers some feminists a method through which to escape the oppressive ''masculine gaze;'' others see in this same quality of her work rather an affirmation and stabilization of the feminine stereotypes she conjures; and yet still others see this tendency in her work as reflective of both psychoanalytical and ''constructionist'' feminist assertions of gender stemming not from one's biological sex but through the social conditioning and performance of that gender. Such interpretations represent only a fraction of the voluminous research conducted on these early series, and give one a sense of how the artist's photographs invite and inspire comment as part of their reason for being. As Sherman herself has said of her work and its study, ''I have to accept that there will be this range of interpretations that I can't control, and don't want to control, because that's what makes it interesting to me.''

After strategically hiding her body, or eliminating it altogether, from her subsequent ''Disaster'' series (1986–89), her untitled ''History Portraits'' (1989–90) found the artist once again before the camera posed as stock characters—this time from the history of art, referencing the canonical works of the Renaissance and Baroque in the same way she had pop culture in earlier series. In Sherman's next series, ''Sex Pictures'' (1992) and ''Horror and Surrealist Pictures'' (1994–96), the artist's body was replaced with surrogates in the form of disturbing, anatomically correct medical mannequins and doll parts pieced together into figural sculptures and still lifes photographed by the artist. Shortly thereafter, this use of both surrogate selves and dark humor were applied to the new medium of film when in 1997 she directed the film *Office Killer.* Starring actor Carole Kane as a Shermanesque protagonist, the film was modeled after the ''Grade Z'' American and artsy European horror films the artist has claimed as an influence.

In 2000, Sherman returned to self-portraiture in a series of large color photographs that combine elements of her mannequin photographs with her performative exploration of female roles. These works—which portray Sherman as different women posed before generic studio backdrops as if for a cheap commercial portraitist—are perhaps the closest the artist has come to returning to the narrative self-portraits of her earliest series. However, these large color prints feature confrontational subjects returning the viewer's gaze, juxtaposing the seamless effects of her early transformations with the blatant artificiality of prosthetics in her fashioning of each individual's physical attributes. As such, her treatment of the women at hand are a radical departure from the intimate, voyeuristic ''film stills.'' These characters, like Sherman herself, appear to be confronting not only the viewers but femininity and middle age, with a combination of fascination, defiance, and introspection. And the uncanny familiarity of each and every figure reminds one of the artist's continued conjure specters of womanhood that resonate with the memory and experience of her audiences.

—Maria Elena Buszek

SHIELDS, Alan J.

Nationality: American. **Born:** Harrington, Kansas, 4 February 1944. **Education:** Kansas State University, Manhattan, 1963–66; spent two summers with the Theatre Workshop, University of Maine, 1966–67. **Career:** Independent painter and sculptor, New York, since 1968. **Award:** Guggenheim Fellowhip, 1973. **Agent:** Paula Cooper Gallery, 155 Wooster Street, New York 10012. **Address:** P.O. Box 1554, Shelter Island, New York 11964, U.S.A.

Individual Exhibitions:

1969 Paula Cooper Gallery, New York
1970 Paula Cooper Gallery, New York
Janie C. Lee Gallery, Dallas
1971 Janie C. Lee Gallery, Dallas
The New Gallery, Cleveland
Galerie Ileana Sonnabend, Paris
1972 Galleria dell'Ariete, Milan
Paula Cooper Gallery, New York
1973 Hansen-Fuller Gallery, San Francisco
Museum of Contemporary Art, Chicago
University of Rhode Island, Kingston
Contemporary Arts Museum, Houston
Madison Art Center, Wisconsin
Galerie Aronowitsch, Stockholm
1974 Richard Gray Gallery, Chicago
Phoenix Gallery, San Francisco
Paula Cooper Gallery, New York
Barbara Okun Gallery, St. Louis
Texas Gallery, Houston
1975 Galleria dell'Ariete, Milan
Dootson-Calderhead Gallery, Seattle
Museum of Art, University of Kansas, Lawrence
E.G. Gallery, Kansas City
Galerie Daniel Templon, Paris
1976 Richard Gray Gallery, Chicago
Musée de Saint-Etienne, France
Portland Center for the Visual Arts, Oregon
Paula Cooper Gallery, New York
Paula Cooper Gallery, Los Angeles
Museu de Arte Moderna, Rio de Janeiro
Galerie Simone Stern, New Orleans
1977 Moore College of Art, Philadelphia
Nina Freudenheim Gallery, Buffalo
Musée d'Art Moderne, Strasbourg
1978 Paula Cooper Gallery, New York
Gallerie Daniel Templon, Paris
Galerie Munro, Hamburg
Public School N1, Long Island City, New York
Galeria Luisa Strina, Sao Paulo
Barbara Okun Gallery, St. Louis
Thomas Segal Gallery, Boston
Gimpel-Hanover Galerie, Zurich
André Emmerich Galerie, Zurich
Williams College Museum of Arts, Williamstown, Massachusetts
1980 Paula Cooper Gallery, New York
Dorry Gates Gallery, Kansas City
1981 Bowdoin College, Brunswick, Maine
Heath Gallery, Atlanta, Georgia
1982 Fine Arts Museum of the South, Mobile, Alabama
Middlebury College, Vermont
Paula Cooper Gallery, New York
State University of New York, Stony Brook
State University of New York, Purchase
1983 Gallery Uoda, Tokyo
Paula Cooper Gallery, New York
Thomas Segal Gallery, Boston
Brooks Memorial Art Gallery, Memphis, Tennessee (travelled to Coral Gables, Florida; Kansas City, Missouri)
1984 Paula Cooper Gallery, New York
Galerie Andre Emmerich, Zurich
1985 University of Massachusetts, Amherst
Paula Cooper Gallery, New York
1986 Paula Cooper Gallery, New York
Cleveland Center for Contemporary Art, Ohio (travelled to Standard Oil Headquarters, Cleveland)
1987 Dorry Gates Gallery, Kansas City, Missouri
State University of New York, Purchase
1988 Paula Cooper Gallery, New York
Sawhill Gallery, James Madison University, Harrisonburg, Virginia
Lakeside Gallery, Richland Community College, Dallas
1989 Contemporary Art Gallery, Ahmedabad, India
1991 Paula Cooper Gallery, New York
Roger Ramsay Gallery, Chicago
1993 Paula Cooper Gallery, New York
1994 Katvin Galerie voor Hedendaagse Kunst, Groningen, Holland
1999 *Alan Shields: A Survey,* The Beach Museum of Art, Kansas State University, Manhattan
2000 *Alan Shields: Intimate Details/New Paper,* Dieu Donne Papermill, New York
2001 Paula Cooper Gallery, New York
Nicholas Davies Gallery, New York

Selected Group Exhibitions:

1974 *Printed, Cut, Folded and Torn,* Museum of Modern Art, New York
1978 *Recent Drawings by Younger Artists,* Whitney Museum, New York
1979 *Oeuvres Contemporaines des Collections Nationales: Accrochage 2,* Centre Georges Pompidou, Paris
1982 *The Americans: Collage 1950–82,* Contemporary Arts Museum, Houston
1989 *First Impressions: Early Prints by Forty-Six Contemporary Artists,* Walker Art Center, Minneapolis
1990 *Divergent Styles: Contemporary American Drawing,* University Gallery, College of Fine Arts, University of Florida, Gainesville, Florida
Prints by Contemporary Masters, Sylvia Cordish Fine Art, Baltimore, Maryland
1991 *Aspects of Collage,* Guild Hall Museum, East Hampton, New York
1992 *The Living Object: The Art Collection of Ellen H. Johnson,* Allen Memorial Art Museum, Oberlin College, Oberlin, Ohio

1993 *25 Years: A Retrospective,* Cleveland Center for Contemporary Art, Cleveland, Ohio

Collections:

Museum of Modern Art, New York; Metropolitan Museum of Art, New York; Whitney Museum, New York; Guggenheim Museum, New York; Hirshhorn Museum and Sculpture Garden, Washington, D.C.; Allen Memorial Art Museum, Oberlin, Ohio; Akron Art Institute, Ohio; Fort Worth Art Center, Texas.

Publications:

By SHIELDS: Articles—''A Talk with Alan Shields,'' with Emily Wasserman, in *Artforum* (New York), February 1971; ''Tales of Brave Ulysses: Alan Shields Interviewed by Howardena Pindell'' in *The Print Collector's Newsletter* (New York), January/February 1975; interview in *Alan Shields,* exhibition catalog, Philadelpia 1977; interview with Kathy Halbreich, in *Paper Forms Handmade Paper Projects,* exhibition catalog, Cambridge, Massachusetts 1977; ''Interview: Alan Shields'' with Jan Avgikos in *Art Papers* (Atlanta), May/June 1982.

On SHIELDS: Books—*Painting Annual,* exhibition catalog with an essay by John I. H. Baur, New York 1969; *Highlights of the Season,* exhibition catalog, Ridgefield, Connecticut 1971; *Grids,* exhibition catalog with an essay by Lucy Lippard, Philadelphia 1972; *Alan Shields, Artist,* exhibition catalog with an essay by Gregor von Rezzori, Milan 1972; *Documenta 5,* exhibition catalog by Harald Szeeman and Jean-Christophe Ammann, Kassel, West Germany 1972; *12 Statements Beyond the 60s,* exhibition catalog with an essay by Frank Kolbert, Detroit 1972; *Painting Annual,* exhibition catalog, New York 1972; *Alan Shields,* exhibition catalog with an essay by Carter Ratcliff, Chicago 1973; *Alan Shields,* exhibition catalog, Houston 1973; *Alan Shields,* exhibition catalog, Milan 1975; *The Book as Art,* exhibition catalog, Washington D.C. 1976; *30 Years of American Printmaking,* exhibition catalog with an essay by Patterson Sims, Phildadelphia 1977; *Painting 1975–76-77,* exhibition catalog, Bronxville, New York 1977; *Alan Shields,* exhibition catalog with an essay Daniel Abadie, Strasbourg 1977; *American Painting of the 1970s,* exhibition catalog with an essay by Linda Cathcart, Buffalo, New York 1978; *Disseminazione,* exhibition catalog, Varese, Italy 1978; *Drawings About Drawing Today,* exhibition catalog by Innis Shoemaker, Chapel Hill, North Carolina 1979; *Soft Art,* exhibition catalog by Erika Billeter Zurich 1979; *La Peinture Americaine* by Madeleine Deschamps, Paris 1984; *Alan Shields,* exhibition catalog with introduction by Deborah Emont, essay by Shigeo Chiba, Tokyo 1983; *Alan Shields,* exhibition catalog with essay by Deborah Emont-Scott, Memphis 1983; *American Art Now* by Edward Lucie-Smith, New York 1985. **Articles—**''In the Play Room'' in *Art on Paper,* vol. 5, no. 2, November/December 2000; ''Alan Shields at Paula Cooper and Nicholas Davies'' by Jonathan Goodman in *Art in America,* vol. 89, no. 1, January 2001.

* * *

Alan J. Shields is identified with an exuberant ''pictorial sculpture''—that is, color-stained and whimsical, craft-decorated canvases often constructed as both opened and enclosed three-dimensional forms. His career-long fascination has been with an eclectic patterning generally set upon a base of stained hues; his work has then been a variant of the later 1960s return to confidence in the possibilities of large scale abstraction. In his earliest exhibition at that time, he already showed two-sided paintings. His desire for viewer involvement and movement, felt throughout his work by his charm, as well in its often meandering and pointed titles, is perhaps ascribable to his youthful fondness for the travelling carnivals in his hometown.

This tendency is easily seen in what may still be Shields' most oft-referred to works: a cylindrical and drum-like painting, 8 feet in height with a 16-foot diameter; and his free-hanging rectangular, open-grids of sewn, collaged, and stained strips of cotton belting. To these works, Shields would add stitching, crochet, beads, twigs, and other attachments. His strength of feeling for craft materials and processes traditionally held peripheral to the painter's art has carried over to his elaborated silk screen prints and his use of paper pulp. The many forms in which Shields has manipulated his essentially joyous color art include cylinders, pyramids, ladders, ropes, and banners.

While the critical literature contains affirmative statements referring to the inventive and sensual atmosphere of his individual works and exhibitions, the counter to such attitude is the sense that the primarily pleasureful or ''decorative'' aspect of his art is self-indulgent and without the focus of what has been conceived of, even within late-modernism, as ''high'' art. Yet precisely because of this approach to surface and form-shape, Shields must number among the important influences in the formation of the Pattern and Decoration movement of the later 1970s.

He continued his multi-faceted work unbated into the decade of the 1980s, with perhaps greater emphasis upon personalized Multiples. He is now in the poignant position of continuing in a decorative mode—albeit wide-ranging—akin to that of the Pattern and Decoration movement which he foreshadowed and is now essentially static if not in decline. Shields' art has been surely marked by the greatly expanded sense of possibility in visual art activities that came into being during the 1960s. Yet he has transferred this freedom to the smaller field essentially known as easel painting and printmaking; and there, despite the outward glamour of his at times large and eccentric-seeming forms, Shields has produced work as if to expand the traditional painter's art not so much conceptually as emotionally.

—Joshua Kind

SHIOMI, Mieko (Chieko)

Nationality: Japanese. **Born:** Okayama, Japan, 13 December 1938. **Education:** Educated in Musicology at Tokyo University of Music and Fine Art, 1957–61, B.Music 1961. **Family:** Married Akira Sakaguchi in 1970; children Tohru and Taku. **Career:** Independent musician, performance artist, and visual poet since 1961. Founded Group-Ongaku with Takehisa Kosugi and others, 1961; participated in Fluxus activities, New York, 1964–65. **Member:** Japanese Federation of Composers, 1972; Fluxus; JASRAC. **Agents:** The Gilbert and Lila Silverman Collection Foundation, 488 Greenwich Street, New York, New York 10013, U.S.A.; Edition and Galerie Hundertmark, Brüsseler Strasse 29, 50674 Cologne, Germany; Galerie J & J

Mieko Shiomi: *Fluxus Balance.* ©Mieko Shiomi

Donguy, 57 rue de la Roquette, 75011 Paris, France; Nadiff, B1, 4–9-8 Jingu-mae, Shibuya-ku, Tokyo, Japan. **Address:** c/o Sakaguchi, 1–24-38 Sakurai, Minoo, Osaka 562, Japan.

Individual Exhibitions:

1963 *7 Performances,* Okayama Cultural Centre, Japan (with members of Sanyo Broadcasting Company)
1964 *Flux Concert: Mieko Shiomi,* Washington Square Gallery, New York
1965 *Water Music, Air Event, Music for 2 Players IV,* Crystal Gallery, Tokyo
1992 *Media Opera,* Xebec Hall, Kobe
Balance Poems, Art Vivan, Tokyo
1993 *Fluxus Balance,* Xebec, Kobe
1994 *Fluxus Media Opera,* Xebec Hall, Kobe
1995 *JOHN CAGE in a Time Labyrinth,* Mito Museum, Mito, Japan
Fluxus Balance and Balance Poems, Galerie Donguy, Paris
1998 *MIEKO SHIOMI Collagen und Multiples,* Galerie und Edition Hundertmark, Cologne, Germany
2000 *Satoko Plays Japan,* Bario Hall, Tokyo

Selected Group Exhibitions:

1961 *Group-Ongaku Concert,* Sogestu Hall, Tokyo
1966 *From Space to Environment,* Sogestu Hall, Tokyo
1969 *Intermedia Art Festival,* Killer Joe Discotheque, Ginza and Nikkei Hall, Tokyo
1975 *Luna Festival,* Ashiya, Japan
1979 *Japanese Composers,* Iino Hall, Tokyo
1980 *Movements & Music,* Goethe Institute, Osaka
1981 *German-Japanese Contemporary Music Series,* Piccolo Theatre, Amagasaki, Japan
1982 *Live Art Theatre,* Modern Art Museum, Kobe, Japan
1986 *Koto Recital,* Rohdoh Center Hall, Osaka, Japan
1987 *Second Annual Exhibition of Miniature Art,* De Bello Gallery, Toronto
1990 *Sub-Atomic Fluxus Festival,* Venice
1991 *Japanese Composers '91,* Tokyo Culture Hall, Tokyo
1992 *Fluxus Virus,* Kaufhof-Parkhouse, Cologne, Germany
1993 *Fluxus/Nancarrow and So Forth,* Goethe-Institute Kansai, Kyoto
1994 *SEOUL-NYmAX,* Courthouse Theater, New York
1995 *TRYLOGY,* Galerie Cornelius Herz, Bremen, Germany
1996 *The 12th Summer Festival '96,* Tsuda Hall, Tokyo

1997 *Visuell Poesie aus Japan,* toured Germany and Austria
1998 *Satoko Plays Japan '98,* Bario Hall, Tokyo
1999 *Rufuran Concert '99,* Casals Hall, Tokyo

Collections:

Archiv Sohm, Markgroeningen, Germany; Archiv Sohm, Staatsgalerie Stuttgart; Mudima Foundation, Milan; Tate Gallery, London; Getty Museum, Santa Monica, California; Jean Brown Archive, Tyringham, Massachusetts.

Publications:

By SHIOMI: Books—*Event Pieces,* New York 1963; *Spatial Poem* (complete edition, No. 1–9), New York 1976; *Balance Poem No. 1-No. 24,* Osaka 1991; *Shadow Event No. Y,* Cologne 1993. **Articles—** ''Media-Technology-Art'' in *Ongaku Geijutsu* (Tokyo), April 1969; ''Mieko Shiomi'' in *Art and Artists* (London), October 1973; ''Products of Musical Thoughts Wandering Beyond the Sound'' in *Geijutsu Club* (Tokyo), April 1974; ''Score (on the 3 rings)'' in *Transonic* (Tokyo), Winter 1974. **Music scores—***As It Were Floating Granules,* 1976; *The Bird Dictionary,* 1979; *If We Were a Pentagonal Memory Device,* 1981, recording 1982; *Spring,* 1982; *The Waltz in the Shape of a Star* (piano suite), 1987; *Direction Music for a Pianist,* 1990; *An Incidental Story on the Day of a Solar Eclipse #1-#3,* 1996–97; *Fractal Freak No. 1,* 1997–98; *A Message from Encore,* 1998; *An Incidental Story on the Night of a Lunar Eclipse,* 1999; *Plumeria,* 2000; *Poesis No. 1,* 2000. **Audio Publications—***If We Were a Pentagonal Memory Device,* 1981; *Requiem for George Maciunas,* 1990; *Fluxus Media Opera,* 1994; *Group-Ongaku,* 1997; *An Incidental Story on the Day of a Solar Eclipse #1-#3,* 1998.

*

Since I started music activities 40 years ago, I always have been swinging between music and performance art and visual poetry and mail art—time involved dynamic art and rather conceptual static art—being inspired by both.

—Mieko Shiomi

* * *

In the early 1960s, as a student of musicology at the Tokyo University of Arts, Mieko Shiomi and a group of musicians founded Group Ongaku and presented improvised performances at weekly meetings. From 1961 to 1963 the group sought to redefine music and find new sound-producing materials, using, at times, ordinary objects such as tables, chairs, ash trays, and bunches of keys. Shiomi, interested in the juxtaposition of sounds and silence, created ''Boundary Music,'' 1963, and ''Music for Two Players,'' 1963.

Shiomi described ''Boundry Music'' as follows: ''Make the faintest possible sounds of a boundary condition whether the sounds are given birth to as sounds or not. At the perfomance, instruments, human bodies, electronic apparatuses or anything else may be used.''

''Endless Box,'' done during the same period, required the viewer to remove successive paper box coverings, thereby establishing a pattern of activity similar to that of the sound pieces. Inspired to connect with the Fluxus group after seeing a Fluxus work by George Brecht at T. Ichiyanagi's, Shiomi traveled to New York in 1964 where she met George Maciunas, Dick Higgins, Alison Knowles, Nam June Paik, and Ay-O. As a participant in some perfomances and viewer of others, Shiomi felt that she was too restricted by being in only one place at one time. She writes, ''I felt that art should be alive everywhere all the time, and at any time anybody wanted it and so I came up with the idea of the *Spatial Poem.*''

Spatial Poem, a prolonged correspondence art activity, eventually became an artist's book which documents nine events orchestrated by Shiomi between 1965 and 1975. Instructions were sent to each participant, for example: word event, ''write a word or words on the enclosed card and place it somewhere,'' or disappearing event, ''observe the natural phenomenon that something is going to disappear.'' The response was international. Daniel Spoerri placed the word ''merde'' in a hotel room in Paris; Geoff Hendricks placed ''ritual meaning'' in the Prado; and Michael Kirby placed ''continuation'' at the bottom of lower New York Bay. As a 70-page book filled with statements, photographs, and drawings done in response to Shiomi's instruction, *Spatial Poem* is a significant contribution to, and compendium of, activity in the correspondence art network. As a manifestation of Shiomi's idea, to have simultaneous performances at different places all over the world, it is a carefully designed documentation which includes world maps and time clocks as a background for the responses which are printed on small flags. Thus the artist captures the concept of intermittent simultaneity over the duration of time.

—Mary Stofflet

SIEVERDING, Katharina

Nationality: German. **Born:** Prague, Czechoslovakia, in 1944. **Education:** Educated in Castrop-Rauxel, and at the Kathe-Kollwitz-Gymnasium, Dortmund, 1949–62; studied art, Hochschule für Bildende Kunste, Hamburg, 1962–63; studied stage design under Teo Otto, 1964–67, painting under Joseph Beuys, 1967–72, and film under Ole John, 1972–74, Staatliche Kunstakademie, Dusseldorf; also independent studies on the Whitney Museum Program and at the New School for Social Research, New York 1976–77. **Career:** Lives and works in Dusseldorf and Berlin; Worked as a stage designer for theatre productions in Hamburg, Vienna, Dusseldorf, Berlin and Salzburg, 1963–67. Artist-photographer and filmmaker, Dusseldorf, since 1969; guest professor, Hochschule der Künste, Berlin, 1992; guest professor of research program, Center for Contemporary Art, CCA Kitakyushu, Japan, 1995, 1999; guest professor, International Summer Academy for Screen Art, Salzburg, 1995–1998; guest professor, International Summer Academy, Salzburg, 2000–2001. **Awards:** Forderungspreis des Landes Nordrhein-Westfalen, 1975; DAAD-Fellowship, to New York, 1976; Forderpreis, Kulturkreis Bund Deutscher Industrie, 1979; Karl Schmidt-Rottluff Stipend, West Germany, 1980; Kunstfonds Award, West Germany, 1981; Berkenhoff Award, 1984; Kunstpreis, Municipal Savings Bank, Dusseldorf, 1991; Deutscher Critic Prize, Berlin, 1994; Lovis-Corinth-Preis, 1996. **Address:** Nordstrasse 111A, 4000 Dusseldorf 30, Germany.

Individual Exhibitions:

1972 Galleria L'Attico, Rome
1973 Galerie Oppenheim, Cologne

Galerie Oppenheim, Brussels
1975 Galerie Klein, Bonn
Galleria Francoise Lambert, Milan
Galerie Konrad Fischer, Dusseldorf
1977 Museum Folkwang, Essen, West Germany
1978 Rheinisches Landesmuseum, Bonn
Galerie Klein, Bonn
Stiching de Appel, Amsterdam
1979 Van Abbemuseum, Eindhoven, Netherlands
1980 Kunsthalle, Dusseldorf
Galerie Klein, Bonn
1984 Moltkerei, Cologne
Museum Abteiberg, Monchengladbach, West Germany
1985 Galerija Studentskog Centra, Zagreb, Yugoslavia
MM Centar SC, Zagreb, Yugoslavia
1987 Badischer Kunstverein, Karlsruhe, West Germany
Kunstverein, Kassel, West Germany
1991 Galerie Jürgen Becker, Hamburg
1992 *Sieverding,* Bonner Kunstverein, Bonn (catalog)
1993 Museum Ostdeutsche Galerie, Regensburg, Germany (catalog)
1996 Galerie im Traklhaus, Salzburg (catalog)
1997 Kunstsammlung Nordrhein-Westfalen, Dusseldorf
1998 *Katharina Sieverding: 1967–1997,* Stedelijk Museum, Amsterdam (also Kunstammlung Nordrhein-Westfalen, Dusseldorf) (catalog)
Transformer, Hällisch-Fränkisches Museum, Schwäbisch Hall, Germany (catalog)
1999 *Weltlinie VII,* Center for Contemporary Art, Kitakyushu (also Kunsthalle Budapest) (catalog)

Selected Group Exhibitions:

1965 *Biennale de Paris,* Musée d'Art Moderne, Paris
1969 *Beuysklasse,* Stadtisches Museum, Trier, West Germany
1971 *Film-Kritisch,* Kunsthalle, Dusseldorf
1973 *Medium Fotografie 1910–73,* Stadtisches Museum, Leverkusen, West Germany
1975 *Selbstportrat als Selbsdarstellung,* Galerie im Taxispalais, Innsbruck, Austria
1977 *Documenta 6,* Museum Fridericianum, Kassel, West Germany
1980 *Kunst der 70er Jahre,* at the *Biennale,* Venice
1982 *Videokunst in Deutschland,* Kunstverein, Cologne
1985 *Kunst in der Bundesrepublik 1945–85,* Nationalgalrie, West Berlin
1987 *Blow Up,* Kunstverein, Hamburg (travelled to Hannover)
1991 *Kristallisationsbilder,* National Galerie, Berlin (catalog)
1992 *Photography in Contemporary German Art: 1960 to the Present,* Walker Art Center, Minneapolis (traveling exhibition) (catalog)
1995 *FotoKunst,* Institut für Auslandsbeziehungen, Stuttgart (catalog)
Biennale di Venezia, Italy (catalog)
1996 *Fotografia Nell'Arte Tedesca Contemporanea,* Claudia Gian Ferrari Arte Contemporanea, Milan (catalog)
1997 *XLVII. Biennale di Venezia,* Pavillion der Bundesrepublik Deutschland (catalog)
1998 *Gen-Welten: Prometheus im Labor?,* Kunst-und Ausstellungshalle der Bundesrepublik Deutschland, Bonn
1999 *Biennale di Venezia,* Italy (catalog)
2000 Kunstverein Braunschweig, Germany (catalog)

Publications:

By SIEVERDING: Books—*Grossfotos I-X/1977,* exhibition catalog edited by Zdenek Felix, Essen 1977; *Norad XVIII-XXIII/1980,* West Berlin 1983; *Die Sonne um Mitternacht Schauen I/I-VII/196/1973,* exhibition catalog, Monchengladbach 1984; *Du Sollst nicht gegen die Sonne Reden,* exhibition catalog, Karlsruhe 1987; *Sieverding,* with Klaus Mettig and Annalie Pohlen, Stuttgart 1992; *Katharina Sieverding,* Salzburg 1996. **Articles**—interview with Barbara Hess in *Flash Art (International Edition),* vol. 32, no. 204, January/February 1999.

On SIEVERDING: Books—*Medium Fotografie,* exhibition catalog with texts by Rold Wedewer and Lothar Romain, Leverkusen 1973; *Transformer: Aspekte der Travestie,* exhibition catalog edited by Jean-Christophe Ammann, Lucerne 1974; *Korpersprache,* exhibition catalog with texts by Georg Bussmann, Thomas Kempas, Bazon Brock and others, West Berlin 1975; *Buren/Burgin/Dimitrijevic/Haacke/Herring/Sieverding,* exhibition catalog edited by Clara Weyergraf, Bochum 1978; *Documenta 7,* exhibition catalog, 2 vols., edited by Rudi H. Fuchs, Kassel 1982. **Articles**—''Unwiderstehliche Historische Strömung'' by Ursula Frohne in *Wolkenkratzer Art Journal,* no. 2, March-April 1988; ''Eine Frau Durchleuchtet den Kosmos'' by Anna Brenken in *ART: Das Kunstmagazin,* no. 4, April 1990; ''Gesicht als Schnittstelle'' by Susanne Wedewer in *Weltkunst,* vol. 68, no. 13, 1 November 1998.

SIMONDS, Charles

Nationality: American. **Born:** New York City, 14 November 1945. **Education:** University of California, Berkeley, 1963–67, B.A. 1967; Rutgers University, New Brunswick, New Jersey, 1967–69, M.F.A. 1969. **Career:** Artist; lives and works in New York; first concentrated on working in streets, constructing places for imaging civilizations, 1970. Instructor, Newark State College, New Jersey, 1969–71. **Member:** Board of the Lower East Side Coalition for Human Housing, New York, since 1973. **Awards:** National Endowment for the Arts grant, 1974; New York State Council for the Arts grant, 1974. **Agent:** Leo Castelli Gallery, 59 East 79th Street, New York, New York, 10021. **Address:** 26 East 22nd Street, New York 10010, U.S.A.

Individual Exhibitions:

1975 Centre National d'Art Contemporain, Paris
Demeures et Mythologies, Samangallery, Genoa
1976 *Projects: Charles Simonds: Picaresque Landscape,* Museum of Modern Art, New York (travelled to the New York Public Library, Tompkins Square)
1977 *Temenos,* Albright-Knox Art Gallery, Buffalo, New York (travelled to Münster and Bonn, Germany)

1978 *Floating Cities and Other Architectures,* Westfälischer Kunstverein, Münster, West Germany (travelled to the Kunstverein, Bonn)
1979 *Circles and Towers Growing,* Wallraf-Richartz Museum, Museum Ludwig, Cologne (travelled to the Nationalgalerie, Berlin; Musée de l'Abbaye, Sainte-Croix; Les Sables-d'Olonne, France; and the Galerie Baudoin Lebon, Paris)
Floating Cities, Centre d'Art Contemporain, Geneva (travelled to the Samangallery, Genoa)
1980 Beaumont May Gallery, Dartmouth College, Hanover, New Hampshire
California State University at Los Angeles
1981 *Circles and Towers Growing,* organized by the Museum of Contemporary Art, Chicago (toured the United States)
1984 *House Plants and Rocks,* Leo Castelli Gallery, New York
1985 *Three Trees,* Architekturmuseum, Basel
1986 Galerie Maeght Lelong, Paris
1987 Galerie Baudoin Lebon, Paris
1988 *Spectrum: Charles Simonds,* Corcoran Gallery of Art, Washington
1989 *Wall Smears and Rocks,* Leo Castelli Gallery, New York
1990 Loyola University, Danna Center Gallery, New Orleans
1991 Galerie Baudoin Lebon, Paris
1992 Leo Castelli Gallery, New York
1993 Leo Castelli Gallery, New York
1994 *Charles Simonds: Retrospectiva,* Fundació la Caixa, Barcelona
Galerie Nationale du Jeu de Paume, Paris (catalog)
1995 Centre Cultural de la Fundacio ''la Caixa,'' Barcelona, Spain (catalog)
1999 *The Clay Grows Tall: The World of Charles Simonds,* Denver Art Museum (catalog)
Joseph Helman Gallery, New York

Selected Group Exhibitions:

1971 *112 Greene Street Group,* 112 Greene Street, New York
1974 *Interventions in Landscape,* Massachusetts Institute of Technology, Cambridge
1975 *Primitive Presence in the 70s,* Vassar College, Poughkeepsie, New York
1976 *Biennale,* Venice
1977 *Contemporary American Art,* Whitney Museum, New York
1978 *Made by Sculptors,* Stedelijk Museum, Amsterdam
1981 *Architecture by Artists,* Rosa Esman Gallery, New York
1983 *New Art,* Tate Gallery, London
1985 *Transformations in Sculpture,* Guggenheim Museum, New York
1986 *An American Renaissance,* Fort Lauderdale Museum of Art, Florida
1997 *Spoleto Festival,* Charleston, South Carolina
1999 *Lie of the Land,* John Hansard Gallery, Southampton, England

Collections:

Museum of Modern Art, New York; Whitney Museum of American Art, New York; Massachusetts Institute of Technology, Cambridge; Allen Memorial Art Museum, Oberlin College, Ohio; Museum of Contemporary Art, Chicago; Centre Georges Pompidou, Paris; Kunsthaus, Zurich; Museum Ludwig, Cologne; Walker Art Center, Minneapolis; Guggenheim Museum, New York.

Permanent Public Installations:

The Growth House and *Niagara Gorge,* Artpark, Lewiston, New York.

Publications:

By SIMONDS: Books—*3 Peoples,* Genoa 1975; *Art/Cahier 2: Charles Simonds,* Paris 1975. **Articles**—''Microcosm to Macrocosm: Fantasy World to Real World'' in *Artforum* (New York), February 1974; ''Entretien avec Charles Simonds,'' with Didier Semin in *Beaux-Arts* (Paris), no. 39, 1986. **Films**—*Birth,* 1971; *Dwellings,* with David Troy, 1972; *Body—Earth,* with Rudy Burckhardt, 1974; *Dwellings Winter,* with Rudy Burckhardt, 1974; *Niagara Gorge 1974,* with Emil Antonucci, 1974.

On SIMONDS: Books—*Charles Simonds: Demeures et Mythologies,* exhibition catalog, Genoa 1975; *Charles Simonds: Temenos,* exhibition catalog, Münster and Bonn 1978; *Circles and Towers Growing,* exhibition catalog, Cologne 1979; *Charles Simonds,* exhibition catalog with essays by John Hallmark-Neff, Daniel Abadie, and John Beardsley, Chicago 1982; *Charles Simonds,* exhibition catalog, Paris 1986; *Charles Simonds: Retrospectiva,* exhibition catalog text by Daniel Abadie, Barcelona 1994. **Articles**—''Charles Simonds: Inhabiting Clay'' by John Beardsley in *American Ceramics,* vol. 11, no. 3, 1994; ''Charles Simonds: Sex, Dwellings and Cogito'' by Martine Arnault in *Cimaise,* vol. 41, no. 233, November-December 1994; ''Hybrid Dreams'' by John Beardsley in *Art in America* (New York), vol. 83, no. 3, March 1995.

*

For more than two decades I have worked on the streets of New York building tiny landscapes, dwellings, ruins, and ritual places for an imaginary civilization of ''Little People'' who are migrating through the city. Each ''place'' is made of raw clay and tiny bricks. On the Lower East Side, where I began working in the mid-1970s in walls, vacant lots, gutters, etc., I am in constant dialogue with passersby, many of whom see this fragile fantasy world as a microcosm of their own lives and view its destruction as emblematic of their own attempts to improve their neighborhood. Through this activity I became involved in designing with the community a park/playlot/sculpture—a hilly landscape in the midst of the city: as a member of the Lower East Side Coalition for Human Housing, I have since helped administer other community programs.

Some other works: *The Growth House* is a seasonally renewable dwelling constructed of earth bricks with seeds inside. As the seeds sprout, growth transforms the built structure; the dwelling is converted from shelter to food and is harvested and eaten. (It was constructed at Artpark, Lewiston, New York, in 1975.) *Niagara Gorge* is a full-scale dwelling and ritual place—the excavation and inhabitation of the remains of a nineteenth-century railroad tunnel (also constructed at Artpark, 1974). *Birth, Body—Earth,* and *Landscape—Body—Dwelling* are rituals documented by 16mm film.

—Charles Simonds

* * *

Since 1970 Charles Simonds has been making miniature clay architectural ''dwellings,'' the remains left behind by an imaginary civilization of nomadic ''Little People.'' The first 200 or so were built on various sites among the streets and buildings on the Lower East Side of Manhattan, and, since then, others have appeared in Paris, Berlin, Shanghai, and a variety of locations including museum sites.

As Simonds's tiny dwellings have accumulated, they have created a history for his migrant minigroup, who continually move onward in their patterns of flux—building, decaying, and rebuilding their ritualistic living places—always staying one or many steps ahead of the game as portrayed by Simonds's organic/architectural landscapes, which memorialize their former presence and lifestyle.

Simonds's ''Little People'' are generally of three types: people who live in a line, people who live in a circle, and people who live in a spiral. In each case, danger seems implicit in their states of change in time and in space alike. Psychological and sociological mores are revealed through patterns of structure and growth. For example, as the ''Spiral People'' move forward and inward along their route, burying their past and building on top of it, they leave less and less room for people, narrowing through each cycle and ultimately constricting themselves toward imminent extinction. In the twelve-part series titled *Circles and Towers Growing* (1979), Simonds brings his Tom Thumb people full circle, from their beginnings in the dry, cracked earth, through a process of organic, architectural buildup and synthesis, passing through subsequent levels of decay, and ending up in a landscape that verges on the nothingness out of which it all started.

Simonds's diminutive works are accompanied by written narratives in which he explicates the outer patterns and inner implications underlying the structures in a manner very much like that of Borges in his labyrinthine journeys. In a series of short films made in collaboration with photographer and filmmaker Rudy Burckhardt, Simonds himself appears in various states of transformation in concert with the earth. In the first, his body is literally emerging from an earth mound; in the second, he is writhing in the actions of sexual procreation with the clay earth; in the third, he gives birth, as it were, to tiny clay architectural forms that are growing directly on his body. Besides lending additional fantastic levels to his sculptural landscapes, the writing and films seem to indicate Simonds's felt relationships with his mythic peoples; they are his creations out of self, symbolic of the artist's godlike role as maker who, in *Genesis,* scoops up a handful of clay and forms it into something breathing, intelligent, and mysteriously possessing a free-will life of its own.

In many ways, Simonds is in tune with the sensibility of Robert Smithson, who in the late 1960s noted that our future tends to be primitive. In Smithson's monumental *Earthworks,* we are the Lilliputians; in Simonds's dwarfed environments, we are the Gullivers. This difference in feeling as well as in scale helps save Simonds's works from lapsing too deeply into the primitive past. In contemporary life, it is we who tend to crush the environment, having become too big for our own good.

In developing his mythical archaeology of ''Little People,'' Simonds has given us a ritualistic emblem for life/art processes that highlight our ongoing game-playing, childlike, sexual and mystical, which we continue in the midst of ''progress'' and ''decay.'' As of the moment, there seem to be two problematic elements in his future development. How long can Simonds's singular approach retain its fascination and its possibilities? And does his recent making of tabletop models, by lessening our sense of discovery, lose some of the lifegiving element in his site-specific dwellings?

—Barbara Cavaliere

SIMPSON, Lorna

Nationality: American. **Born:** Brooklyn, New York, 1960. **Education:** School of Visual Arts, New York, B.F.A. 1982; University of California, San Diego, M.F.A. 1985. **Career:** Artist-in-residence, Wexner Center for the Arts, Columbus, Ohio, 1996, and Walker Art Center, Minneapolis, 1997–98. **Awards:** Arts Management Fellowship, National Endowment for the Arts, 1985; Workspace Grant, Jamaica Arts Center, 1987; Louis Comfort Tiffany Award, Louis Comfort Tiffany Foundation, 1990. **Agent:** Sean Kelly, 43 Mercer Street, New York, New York 10013, U.S.A.; Karen McCready Fine Art, 425 West 13th Street, New York, New York 10014, U.S.A.

Selected Individual Exhibitions:

1985 Alternative Gallery, 5th Street Market, San Diego
1986 Just Above Midtown, New York
1988 Jamaica Arts Center, Queens, New York
Mercer Union, Toronto
1989 Wadsworth Atheneum, Hartford, Connecticut
1990 Denver Art Museum
Portland Art Museum, Portland, Oregon
Museum of Modern Art, New York
University Art Museum, California State University, Long Beach
1991 Josh Baer Gallery, New York
Center for Exploratory and Perceptual Art, Buffalo, New York
1993 John Berggruen Gallery, San Francisco
Shoshana Wayne Gallery, Santa Monica, California
Josh Baer Gallery, New York
Contemporary Arts Museum, Houston
1994 Whitney Museum of American Art at Phillip Morris, New York
Fabric Workshop, Philadelphia
Rhona Hoffman Gallery, Chicago
1995 Sean Kelly Gallery, New York
Albrecht Kemper Museum of Art, St. Joseph, Missouri
Cohen/Berkowitz Gallery, Kansas City, Missouri
1996 Karen McCready Fine Art, New York
Galerie Wohnmaschine, Berlin
1997 Miami Art Museum of Dade County, Miami, Florida
1999 *Scenarios: Recent Work by Lorna Simpson,* Walker Art Center, Minneapolis

Selected Group Exhibitions:

1987 New Museum of Contemporary Art, New York
1988 Museum of Fine Arts, Boston (traveling)

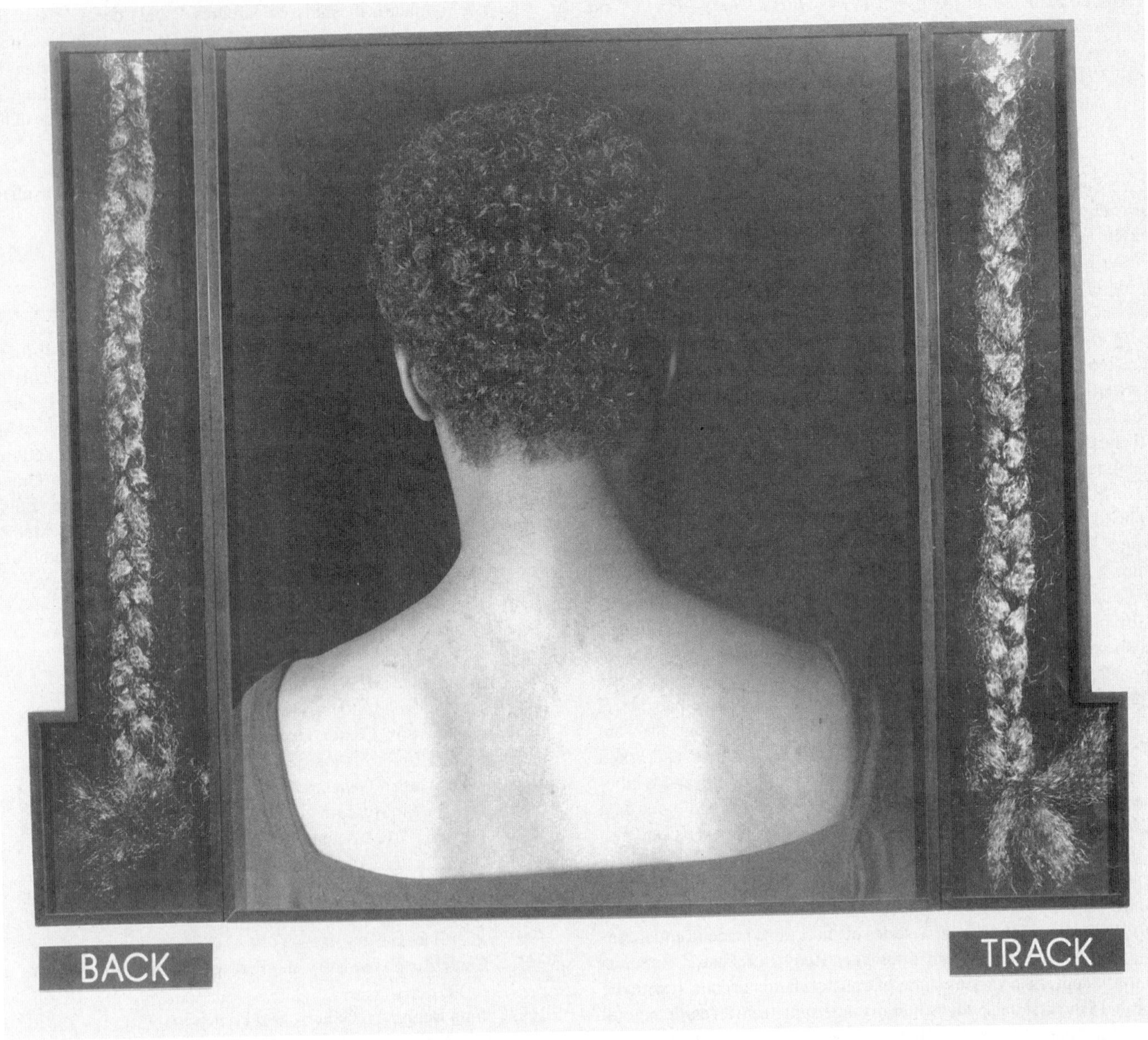

Lorna Simpson: *Two Tracks,* 1990. Photo by Geoffrey Clements. ©Collection of Whitney Museum of American Art, Gift of Raymond J. Learsy and Gabriella Da Ferrarri; Courtesy of Sean Kelly Gallery, New York.

1989 Whitney Museum of American Art, New York
1990 Milwaukee Art Museum (traveling)
1991 Contemporary Art Museum, Houston
1992 Rhona Hoffman Gallery, Chicago
1993 Bonner Kunstverein, Bonn, Germany
1994 Walker Art Center, Minneapolis, Minnesota
Whitney Museum of American Art, New York
1995 Whitney Museum of American Art, New York
1996 Museum of Modern Art, New York
Cleveland Center for Contemporary Art, Ohio
Henry Art Gallery, University of Washington, Seattle
1997 Miami Art Museum of Dade County, Miami, Florida
Wezner Center for the Arts, Columbus Ohio (travelled to Cranbrook Art Museum, Bloomfield Hills, Michigan, and The Power Plant, Toronto)
1999 *Other Narratives,* Contemporary Arts Museum, Houston, Texas
Defining Eye: Women Photographers of the 20th Century, National Museum of Women in the Arts, Washington, D.C.
Contemporary Collectors, Museum of Contemporary Art, San Diego
2000 *Persuave Images,* University Art Museum, Albany, New York

Collections:

Baltimore Museum of Art, Maryland; Brooklyn Museum of Art, New York; Corcoran Gallery of Art, Washington, D.C.; Denver Art Museum; Department of Cultural Affairs, Chicago; Milwaukee Art

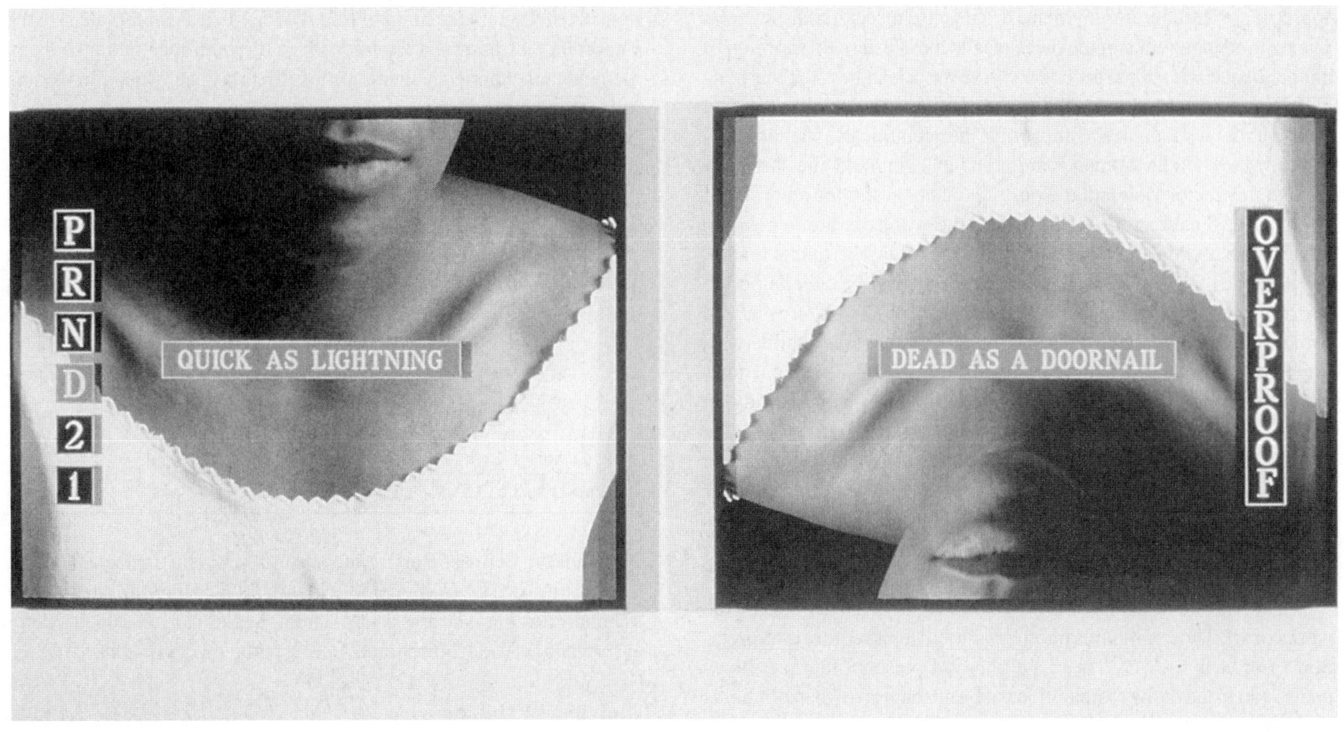

Lorna Simpson: *Untitled.* ©Lorna Simpson; Courtesy of Sean Kelly Gallery, New York.

Museum, Wisconsin; Museum of Contemporary Art, Chicago; Museum of Contemporary Art, San Diego, California; Museum of Modern Art, New York; High Museum of Art, Atlanta; Israel Museum, Jerusalem; University of New Mexico, Albuquerque; Wadsworth Atheneum, Hartford, Connecticut; Walker Art Center, Minneapolis, Minnesota; Whitney Museum of American Art, New York.

Publications:

On SIMPSON: Books—*Lorna Simpson: Untitled 54* by Deborah Willis, San Francisco, Friends of Photography, 1992; *Lorna Simpson: For the Sake of the Viewer* by Beryl J. Wright, New York and Chicago 1992; *Art on my Mind: Visual Politics* by bell hooks, New York 1995. **Articles—**''In Their Own Image'' by Kellie Jones in *Artforum,* November 1990; ''Emerging in the 90s: Lorna Simpson Conceptual Artist'' by Kelly Jones in *Emerge,* vol. 2, no. 3, January 1991; ''Lorna Simpson'' by Terry Myers, in *Lapiz,* no. 72, November 1991; ''Interview with Lorna Simpson'' by Regina Joseph in *Balcon* (Madrid), (5/6), 1991; ''Lorna Simpson: Stop and Think,'' in *MS.,* May-June 1991; ''Lorna Simpson'' by Eugenie Bruno in *Shift,* no. 7, 1991; ''Lorna Simpson'' by Alice R. Gray in *ARTnews,* October 1992; ''Lorna Simpson: Words and Images'' by Dolores, S. Slowinski in *Michigan Photography Journal,* no. 5, 1992; ''Olympia's Maid: Reclaiming Black Female Subjectivity'' by Lorraine O'Grady in *Afterimage,* Summer 1992; ''Lorna Simpson: Waterbearer'' by bell hooks in *Artforum,* September 1993; ''Lorna Simpson'' by Andrew Wilkes in *Aperture,* no. 133, Fall 1993; ''Lorna Simpson, Standing in Water'' by Holland Cotter in *New York Times,* 18 March 1994; ''Premature Emancipation: African American Artists and Time Magazine'' by Bill Gaskins in *New Art Examiner,* February 1995; ''Figuring Absence'' by Eleanor Hartley in *Art in America,* December 1995; ''Nine Props: An Interview and Art Portfolio'' by Maria Christina Vellasenor in *The Paris Review,* Spring 1996; ''Logical Anonymity: Lorna Simpson, Steve McQueen, Stan Douglas'' by Horace Brockington in *The International Review of African American Art,* Summer 1998.

* * *

Lorna Simpson is best known for her photographic works which combine text and image in a way that questions and critiques racial and gender identities. Simpson began working in her signature style in the mid-1980s after spending the previous decade photographing in Europe, Africa, and the United States. After working in a documentary-style photographic tradition, Simpson began adding texts to her imagery. This addition gives voice and agency to the typically silent photograph. Most often, however, the texts provide ambiguous layers of meaning, rather then clarifying for the viewer any one right way of reading the finished work. Simpson's ambiguous combination of image and text denies the essential identities that are often fixed on the people who appear in her photos: mostly, African American women and men. Simpson's photographs and texts investigate and often undermine the traditional ease with which we read photographs, and the supposed truthfulness that a photograph contains. Her art gives voice to the unspoken ambiguities of identity. Often, Simpson's work fosters more questions than answers.

African American women play the largest role in Simpson's photographs. In 1988 Simpson produced *You're Fine, You're Hired,* a work which combines a photograph of an African American woman, lying on her side with her back to the viewer, and surrounded on all sides by added texts. To the right of the woman the text reads ''secretarial position'' and to the left we read a list of physical exams—blood, heart, lungs—the woman has endured. *You're Fine, You're Hired* recalls the medical tests one must undergo when applying for certain employment, in this case a secretarial position. The recumbent woman in the piece recalls the Western art tradition of the odalisque whose purpose is to serve as delectation for the male gaze. Yet, Simpson presents the woman with her back to the viewer, a pose that denies the gaze. Simpson further complicates matters with the added texts. The woman lying prone in a simple white shift may refer to the doctor visit and the position taken during the administration of a medical exam. But how does the woman's prone position relate to the text that advertises for the secretarial job? In this regard, her pose may suggest other duties a secretary may be called upon to perform such as sleeping with the boss. *You're Fine, You're Hired* demonstrates the multi-leveled interpretations that are possible with Simpson's work. This work highlights the invasive medical tests which attempt to map, name, and quantify the physical body in preparation for employment, it questions the different duties expected of women in the workplace, and it modifies canonical traditions in Western art. Ultimately, the woman in the photograph retains her autonomy by facing away from the viewer's gaze, and the ambiguous nature of the texts and photograph denies an essential reading of her identity.

The viewer of Simpson's photographs plays a vital role in the works of art. The ambiguous photographs and texts require interpretation from each viewer. These shifting and personal interpretations underscores one of the main notions of Simpson's art—that identity is not fixed or essential but is contextual and highly varied depending upon the expectations of each viewer. In *Completing the Analogy*, 1987, Simpson presents an African American woman with her back to the viewer. To the left of the woman are three analogies: ''Hat is to head as darkness is to skin, Scissors are to cloth as razor is to skin, Bow is to arrow as shotgun is to skin.'' These violent analogies are unexpected. The viewer often wonders if the texts in Simpson's works are being said by the woman in the image or by someone looking at the image. The viewer of Simpson's works has to read/say the texts as part of their viewing experience. As such, the viewer becomes an actor in the work of art. In *Completing the Analogy*, the viewer is given three violent and racists analogies. The work focuses our attention on the skin of the woman and the importance of skin color as a category of classification in our society. The work also highlights the violence that has been inflicted on women and men with dark skin and the danger that must be felt by people of color who live in a culture that makes analogies such as these. Many of Simpson's works such as *Completing the Analogy*, *Waterbearer*, 1986, and *Three Seated Figures*, 1989, also allude to violence against women.

Focusing on a specific part of the body—skin, hair, a neck—is typical of Simpson. By doing so, the artist is able to highlight a specific site on the body that is controversial or imbued with meaning. The sites she chooses to feature, especially hair and skin, are often read by society as the biological markers of race and gender. Simpson highlights these physical features as a way of shedding light on how identity is constructed. In her *Necklines* series from the late 1980s Simpson presents photographs of the neck and shoulders of an African American woman with texts that describe a variety of good and bad meanings associated with that particular part of the body. In a work such as *Same* (1991) Simpson focuses on the subject of hair as an indicator of race and gender. In this work, we see four sets of four photographs with two women in each set. The women are connected across the photos by a long braid of hair. Below one of the photographs we read that the women, ''knew illness, didn't wear their hair the same way, were let go for the same reasons, had never met.'' Although we read that the women had never met, we see that they are connected through the braid of hair. Works such as this emphasize the importance of hair as a signifier of gender and race and also as an element and experience that joins together African American woman across the black diaspora.

In her art, Lorna Simpson attempts to redress essential readings of race, gender and the experiences of African American women. Her photographs present women that are ultimately unknowable and ambiguous. As such, the protagonists in her works retain a level of privacy and resistance. Through her added texts, Simpson lends active thoughts and voices to women who are typically objectified and silenced.

—Jennifer S. Zarro

SLOMINSKI, Andreas

Nationality: German. **Born:** Meppen, 1959. **Agent:** Jablonka Galerie, Lindenstrasse 19, Cologne, Germany 50674; Produzentengalerie Hamburg, Admiralitätstrasse 71, Hamburg, Germany D-20459; Metro Pictures, 519 West 24th Street, New York, New York 10011, U.S.A.

Individual Exhibitions:

1987 Produzentengalerie, Hamburg (catalog)
1988 Kabinett für aktuelle Kunst, Bremerhaven
1989 Produzentengalerie, Hamburg
1991 Kabinett für aktuelle Kunst, Bremerhaven
Jablonka Galerie, Cologne
1995 Museum Haus Esters, Krefeld
Kunstverein Bremerhaven (catalog)
1996 Jablonka Galerie, Cologne (catalog)
Galerie NEU, Berlin
1997 Hamburger Kunsthalle, Hamburg
White Cube, London
Bonnefanten Museum, Maastricht
1998 Wako Works of Art, Tokyo (catalog)
Kunsthalle Zürich (catalog)
1999 Deutsche Guggenheim, Berlin
Metro Pictures, New York
Kabinett für aktuelle Kunst, Bremerhaven
2000 Jablonka Galerie, Cologne

Group Exhibitions:

1988 *Neue Kunst in Hamburg,* Kampnagel-Fabrik, Hamburg; Museum Haus Lange, Krefeld (catalog)
Nobody's Fool, Stichting de Appel, Amsterdam, The Netherlands
Aperto, La Biennale di Venezia (catalog)
BINATIONALE, Kunsthalle/Kunstverein/Kunstsammlung, Düsseldorf; ICA, Museum of Fine Arts, Boston (catalog)
1989 *D & S,* Kunstverein, Hamburg (catalog)
1991 *L'Exposition de l'Ecole du Magasin,* Centre Nationale d'Art Contemporain, Grenoble, France (catalog)
1992 *Vorhut aus dem Hinterland,* Neues Museum Weserburg Bremen (catalog)

Szenenwechsel II, Museum für Moderne Kunst, Frankfurt
Joy and Pain. . . , ICA, Amsterdam
Avantgarde and Kampagne, Kunsthalle Düsseldorf (catalog)
Qui, quoi, où?, Musée d'Art Moderne de la Ville de Paris (catalog)
Spielhölle, Kunstverein, Graz, Austria

1993 *Hotel Carlton Palace,* Hotel Carlton Palace, Paris
Backstage, Kunstverein in Hamburg; Kunstmuseum Luzern (catalog)
Viennese Story, Wiener Secession (catalog)
Hamburg-Paris-Frankfurt, Kunstverein in Hamburg

1994 *Some Went Mad, Some Ran Away. . . ,* Serpentine Gallery, London; Nordic Arts Center, Helsinki, Finland; Museum of Contemporary Art, Chicago (catalog)
WM KARAOKE, Portikus, Frankfurt
CLOACA MAXIMA, Museum der Stadtenwässerung, Zürich

1996 *Szenenwechsel IX,* Museum für Moderne Kunst, Frankfurt
Zuspeil, Portikus, Frankfurt (catalog)
nach weimar, Kunstsammlungen zu Welmar
do it, Bangkok University Art Gallery, Thailand
Views From Abroad: European Perspectives on American Art II, Whitney Museum of American Art, New York (catalog)

1997 *Niemandsland,* Museum Haus Esters und Museum Haus Lange, Krefeld
Future, Present, Past, La Biennale di Venezia (catalog)
Skulptur. Projekte in Münster 1997, Westfälisches Landesmuseum, Münster (catalog)
Deutschlandilder, Martin-Gropius-Bau, Berlin
artificial, Museu d'Art Contemporani de Barcelona

1998 *Das Jahrhundert der künstlerischen Freiheit. 100 Jahre Wiener Secession,* Wiener Secession
FAST FORWARD, Kunstverein in Hamburg
Manifesta 2, Casino Luxembourg
berlin biennale, Akademie der Künste, Kunst-Werke, Postfuhramt, Berlin

1999 *Collection 99,* Galerie für Zeltgenôssische Kunst Leipzig
Szenenwechsel XVI, Museum für Moderne Kunst, Frankfurt
Das XX. Jahrhundert—ein Jahrhundert Kunst in Deutschland, Altes Museum, Neue Nationalgalerie, Hamburger Bahnhof, Berlin

2000 *Let's Entertain,* Walker Art Center, Minneapolis, Minnesota; Centre Georges Pompidou, Paris
FOOD FOR THE MIND, Staatsgalerie Moderner Kunst, Münich
La Biennale de Montréal 2000, Centre International d'Art Contemporain de Montréal, Québec
Szenenwechsel XVIII, Museum für Moderne Kunst, Frankfurt

2001 *New Acquisitions from the Dakis Joannou Collection,* Deste Foundation, Athens, Greece
FREESTYLE, Städtisches Museum Leverkusen Schloß Morsbroich
Vom Eindruck zum Ausdruck, Deichtorhallen Hamburg
Wertwechsel—zum Wert des Kunstwerks, Museum für angewandte Kunst Köln

Publications:

On SLOMINSKI: Articles— ''Andreas Slominski'' by Patrick Frey in *Artforum,* November 1998; ''Andreas Slominski at the Deutsche Guggenheim'' by David Ebony in *Art in America,* November 1999; ''Andreas Slominski'' by Barry Schwabsky in *Artforum,* December 1999; ''Mouse Domes at the Periphery of Peopledom'' by Patrick Frey in *Parkett,* no. 55, 1999; '''SlominSki': A Conversation with Boris Groys'' by Bettina Funcke and Jens Hoffmann in *Parkett,* no. 55, 1999; ''Wordless'' by Julian Heynen in *Parkett,* no. 55, 1999; ''Berlin Detours'' by Nancy Spector in *Parkett,* no. 55, 1999.

* * *

The sculptures, installations, and actions of Andreas Slominski offer an implicit proposal concerning the nature of art: that it be construed as a distinct form of production developing somewhere between the pragmatic activity of problem solving and the capricious impulses of a disinterested mind. Slominski is clearly obsessed with function and has made it the guiding characteristic in all his work. However, when considered chiefly in terms of functionality his objects generally appear ludicrously complex, too narrowly task-specific, or otherwise less efficient than principles of good design or even common sense might dictate. A y-shaped stove, for example, is his ingenious and magnificently impractical solution to the problem of how to burn forked branches. The utilitarian potential of Slominski's apparatuses is never rendered moot by his extravagance or eccentricity, but his works invariably convey a sense of excess that makes them not quite interchangeable with more routinely encountered functional objects. Art, Slominski seems to suggest, is a useful entity but it is not subject to the constraints of practicality imposed by convention on other aspects of life.

In pressing his point, Slominski has tended to focus his attention on pre-industrial apparatuses such as the windmill, a utilitarian structure associated with the agricultural history of Northern Europe that has been rendered essentially obsolete by the introduction of more efficient mills. During a 1996 exhibition at the Portikus in Frankfurt am Main, Slominski periodically sawed sections from the skeletal blades of a defunct windmill, feeding them to the flames of an old woodburning stove in a gesture that emphasized both the antiquated nature of the windmill and its potential to provide energy of a sort other than that for which it was designed. At the Venice Biennale in 1997, Slominski exhibited a small-scale windmill that, despite the appearance of a toy or an obstacle from a course for miniature golf, was actually capable of grinding grain. To use it for this purpose, however, would require an investment of time that few would be willing or able to make. Even less practical, although still fully functional, was a series of miniature windmills that Slominski installed at the Kunstsammlung Weimar the previous year. The mixed-media windmills, some of which were fashioned rather abstractly while others were constructed to scale with architectural precision, bore titles suggesting their potential use for mixing plaster, pressing grapes, winding thread, or even trapping birds.

Animal traps have figured prominently in Slominski's art since the early 1980s, when he began using them as found objects. Wishing to emphasize the general design rather than the grim history of each trap, he purchased new examples from the hardware store instead of searching for venerable specimens in old barns, fields, or the forest. After 1986, Slominski turned to constructing his own traps, either as exact copies of the originals or as variations influenced by older designs that he encountered in plans and photographs. In the process, the simple utility of the traps became overshadowed by characteristics clearly reminiscent of modern sculpture. The 1998 examples *Fox Trap* (a network of culverts extending across the gallery floor), *Dog Trap* (a framework cube sided with wire mesh), and *Ditch to Trap Slugs* (a low ramp leading up to a raised trough) have distinct affinities with Minimalism. At the same time, these apparatuses seem fully capable of fulfilling their utilitarian tasks. The implicit question is: Are they examples of art following life or life following art?

If the trap can be literal in Slominski's art it is also metaphorical, since his works clearly bait the viewer. The ominous look of most of his constructions and the blatancy of titles such as *Trap to Throttle Small Vermin* (1992) suggest a deadly serious attitude toward objects. A deeper contemplation of Slominski's works, however, reveals the artist's whimsy, love of craft, and, even more unexpectedly, sense of beauty. The effect is a reversal of the relationship between the alluring and the deceptive that is embodied in the legendary Trojan horse, an image to which Slominski alludes in *Bird Trap* (1996/97). In this work a roughly horse-shaped framework covered in wire and burlap is the site of concealment for a trapper who holds the cords to a set of spring-loaded nets. Horses are nervous beasts, and the tranquillity of this ersatz animal is an appealing signal to wary birds, which soon fall prey to the ruse. Unlike the bird in the field, the viewer approaches Slominski's works fully aware of their deception and only later is startled by their visual appeal. For both bird and human, the result is complete surprise.

Slominski has undoubtedly achieved the greatest imbalance between simplicity of utilitarian purpose and complexity of design in his celebrated actions. For example, his contribution to *Skulptur. Projekte in Münster 1997* involved documenting the placement of a bicycle tire around a street lamp, a task that could easily have been accomplished as a large-scale version of a ring toss game. Instead of throwing the tire over the top, however, he methodically excavated the pole's concrete foundation, disconnected the electrical cables, placed the tire around the pole from below, then replaced the entire assembly. That the expenditure of labor was ludicrously out of proportion to the practical result was made all the more obvious when the tire mysteriously disappeared within a week. Equally inefficient was the subsequent action *Wetting a Stamp*, which involved inducing a skeptical giraffe at the Münster zoo to lick a postage stamp held in the artist's hand. Surely there is something enlightening in the sheer extravagance of such actions, which outside the context of art might never have been contemplated. Daily life routinely demands a certain level of efficiency. Consequently, as Slominski's works suggest, perhaps the most significant acts of creativity today involve not a streamlining of productivity but, on the contrary, the discovery of new ways to fulfill the requisites of utility without succumbing to the restraints of practicality.

—Glen R. Brown

SMITH, Alexis

Nationality: American. **Born:** Patricia Anne Smith in Los Angeles, 1949. **Education:** University of California at Irvine, B.A. 1970. **Career:** Independent artist; instructor, California Institute for the Arts, 1975; instructor, University of California, Irvine, 1976; instructor, University of California, San Diego, 1977–78; instructor, University of California, Los Angeles, 1979–82; instructor, Skowhegan School of Painting and Sculpture, Maine, 1990; instructor, Southern Methodist University, 1993. **Awards:** New Talent Award, Los Angeles County Museum of Art, 1974; National Endowment for the Arts Fellowships, 1976 and 1987; Fourth Councilmanic District Civic Service Award, Los Angeles, 1986; Trustee, Beyond Baroque Literary Arts Center, 1990–95; Board of Governors, Skowhegan School, 1990–1993. **Agent:** Margo Leavin Gallery, 812 N. Robertson Boulevard, Los Angeles, California 90069, U.S.A.

Individual Exhibitions:

1974 Riko Mizuno Gallery, Los Angeles
1975 CARP, Los Angeles
University of California at Santa Barbara Art Galleries
Whitney Museum of American Art, New York
Long Beach Museum of Art
1976 Mandeville Art Gallery, University of California at San Diego
1977 Nicholas Wilder Gallery, Los Angeles
1978 Holly Solomon Gallery, New York
Rosamund Felsen Gallery, Los Angeles
1979 De Appel, Amsterdam
Holly Solomon Gallery, New York
1980 Rosamund Felsen Gallery, Los Angeles
1981 Holly Solomon Gallery, New York
Los Angeles County Museum of Art
1982 Margo Leavin Gallery, Los Angeles
Rosamund Felsen Galleries, Los Angeles
1985 Margo Leavin Gallery, Los Angeles
1986 Walker Art Center, Minneapolis
Institute of Contemporary Art, Boston
1987 Aspen Art Center, Aspen, Colorado
The Brooklyn Museum, New York
1988 Margo Leavin Gallery, Los Angeles
1989 Santa Monica Museum of Art
1990 Margo Leavin Gallery, Los Angeles
Josh Baer Gallery, New York
1991 Whitney Museum of American Art, New York (travelled to Museum of Contemporary Art, Los Angeles)
1993 Margo Leavin Gallery, Los Angeles
1994 Margo Leavin Gallery, Los Angeles
1995 Gerald Peters Gallery, Dallas, Texas
Margo Leavin Gallery, Los Angeles
2000 *Words to Live By,* Margo Leavin Gallery, Los Angeles

Selected Group Exhibitions:

1972 *Southern California Attitudes,* Pasadena Museum of Modern Art
1976 Penthouse Gallery, Museum of Modern Art, New York
1977 *Biennale,* Musée d'Art Moderne de la Ville, Paris
1979 *Whitney Biennial,* Whitney Museum of American Art, New York
1983 *New Directions,* Hirshorn Museum and Sculpture Garden, Washington, D.C.
1984 *International Survey of Recent Painting and Sculpture,* Museum of Modern Art, New York

1986 *Spectrum,* Corcoran Gallery of Art, Washington, D.C.
1987 *Avant-Garde in the Eighties,* Los Angeles County Museum of Art
1989 *Making Their Mark,* Cincinnati Art Museum (travelled to New Orleans, Denver, and Philadelphia)
1991 *Transforming the Western Image,* Palm Springs Desert Museum, California
1995 *Commercial Art,* Gallery Paule Anglim, San Francisco (catalog)
1997 *Sunshine & Noir: Art in L.A. 1960–1997,* Louisiana Museum, Humlebaek, Denmark (catalog)
1998 J. Paul Getty Museum, Los Angeles

Permanent Public Installations:

Unity Saving and Loan, West Hollywood; Grand Center, Grand Rapids, Michigan; California State Office Building, Santa Rosa; Artpark, Lewiston, New York; University of California at San Diego; Alaska Building, Seattle; Los Angeles Convention Center.

Publications:

By SMITH: Books—*State of the Arts: California Artists Talk About Their Work,* with Barbara Isenberg, New York, 2000. **Articles—**''Mothers, Mentors and Mischief'' in *ARTnews,* vol. 95, no. 1, January 1996.

On SMITH: Books—*Stuart Collection,* La Jolla 1995. **Catalogs—***Viewpoint: Alexis Smith,* Minneapolis 1986; *Alexis Smith: Public Works,* San Diego 1991; *Alexis Smith Retrospective,* New York and Los Angeles, 1991. **Articles—**''Alexis Smith: Concepts'' by Jane Livingston in *Artweek,* Marck 1974; ''Alexis Smith: A Literary Sensibility'' by Dorothy Burkhart in *Artweek,* May 1976; ''Alexis Smith: The Narrative Act'' by Nancy Marmer in *Artforum,* December 1976; ''All American Art'' by Joan Quinn in *Interview,* March 1981; ''Alexis Smith R Tist'' by Hunter Drohojowska in *Artforum,* October 1987; ''The Public Art of Alexis Smith'' by Hunter Drohojowska in *Artspace,* summer 1991; ''Alexis Smith'' by Richard Armstrong in *The Journal of Art,* November 1991; ''Alexis Smith'' by Madeleine Grynsztejn in *Journal of Contemporary Art,* fall/winter 1991; ''Alexis Smith'' by Marlena Donohue in *Sculpture* (Washington, D.C.), July/August 1993. **Videos—***Scholars and Sculpture: The Stuart Collection,* University of California, San Diego, 1997.

SMITH, Kiki

Nationality: German/American. **Born:** Nuremberg, Germany, 1954. **Education:** Studied industrial banking under the Manpower Training Act, Newark, New Jersey, 1972; studied to be certified as an Emergency Medical Technician at Bedford Stuyvesant Brooklyn Interfaith Hospital, 1985. **Career:** Had traveling puppet theater, 1971; performed in Meredith Monk's Vessel, New York, 1971; moved to New York, 1976; met artist and filmmaker Charlie Ahearn who introduced her to Collaborative Projects, an artist's collective, 1976; began to work in glass at the New York Experimental Glass Workshop, 1985. **Agent:** PaceWildenstein Gallery, 142 Greene Street, New York, New York 10012.

Selected Individual Exhibitions:

1982 *Life Wants to Live,* The Kitchen, New York
1987 *Kiki Smith: Drawings,* Piezo Electric Gallery, New York
1988 Fawbush Gallery, New York
1989 *Kiki Smith,* Ezra and Cecile Zilkha Gallery, Center for the Arts, Wesleyan University, Middletown, Connecticut
Concentrations 20: Kiki Smith, Dallas Museum of Art, Dallas
1990 *Kiki Smith,* Tyler Gallery, Tyler School of Art, Temple University, Philadelphia
Projects 24: Kiki Smith, Museum of Modern Art, New York
Kiki Smith, Centre d'Art Contemporain, Geneva (traveled to Institute of Contemporary Art, Amsterdam) (catalog)
1992 *Kiki Smith: Silent Work,* MAK—Oserreischisches Museum fur angewandte Kunst, Vienna (catalog)
Kiki Smith, Moderna Museet, Stockholm
Kiki Smith, Bonner Kunstverein, Bonn, Germany
Kiki Smith: Sculpture and Works on Paper, Greg Kucera Gallery, Seattle
1993 Fawbush Gallery, New York
Kiki Smith, Anthony d'Offay Gallery, London
1994 *Kiki Smith: Sojourn in Santa Barbara,* University Art Museum, University of California, Santa Barbara (catalog)
Kiki Smith, Israel Museum, Jerusalem (catalog)
Prints and Multiples 1985–1993, Barbara Krakow Gallery, Boston; New Orleans Contemporary Art Center; Olin Arts Center, Bates College Museum of Art, Lewiston, Maine; David Winton Bell Gallery, Brown University, Providence, Rhode Island; University of North Texas Art Gallery, University of North Texas, Denton; Gallery of Art, University of Missouri, Kansas City; Milwaukee Art Museum; Sordoni Art Gallery, Wilkes University, Wilkes-Barre, Pennsylvania; North Dakota Museum of Art, Grand Forks; Davidson College Art Gallery, Davidson, North Carolina; University Gallery, University of Memphis; Art Gallery, University of New Hampshire, Durham; Kresge Art Museum, Michigan State University, East Lansing (catalog)
1995 *Kiki Smith,* Whitechapel Art Gallery, London (traveled to Galerie Rudolfinum, Prague) (catalog)
Kiki Smith, Sculpture & Drawings, Anthony d'Offay Gallery, London
New Sculpture, PaceWildenstein, New York (catalog)
1996 *Kiki Smith,* Montreal Museum of Fine Arts (traveled to Modern Art Museum, Fort Worth, Texas) (catalog)
1997 *Kiki Smith,* Shoshana Wayne Gallery, Santa Monica
Kiki Smith: Convergence, Irish Museum of Modern Art, Dublin (catalog)
Kiki Smith: The Fourth Day, Destruction of Birds, PaceWildenstein, New York (catalog)
1998 *Invention/Intervention: Kiki Smith and the Museum,* Carnegie Museum of Art, Pittsburgh
Kiki Smith: All Creatures Great and Small, Kestner Gesellschaft, Hannover (catalog)
Reconstruction of the Moon, PaceWildenstein, New York
1999 *My Nature: Works with Paper by Kiki Smith,* Saint Louis Art Museum, Missouri (catalog)

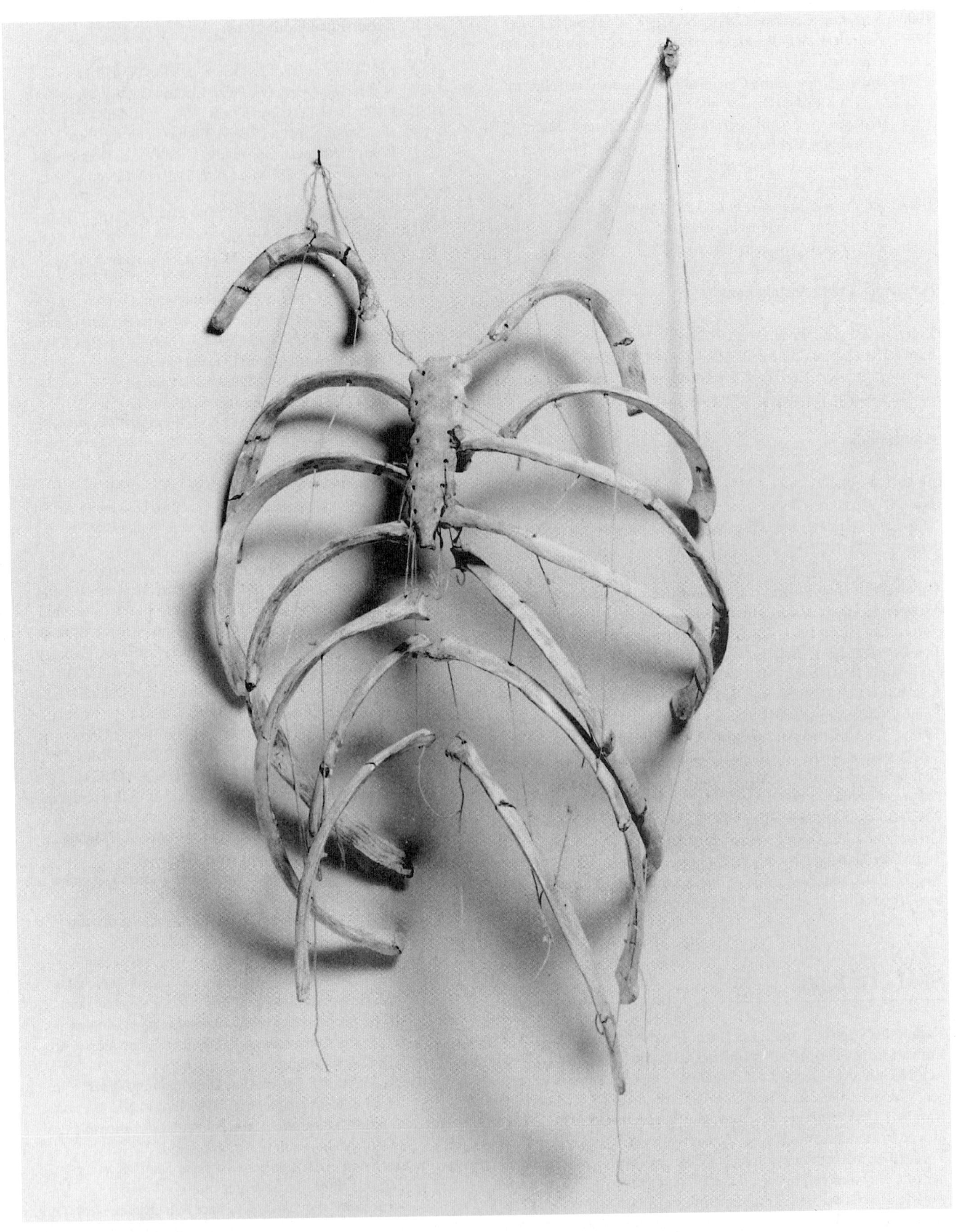

Kiki Smith: *Ribs.* Photo by David Heald. ©The Solomon R. Guggenheim Foundation, NY; courtesy of Solomon R. Guggenheim Museum, NY, gift of the Peter Norton Family Foundation, 1993.

2000 *Realm: Recent Sculptures and Drawings,* John Berggruen Gallery, San Francisco
2001 *Works on Paper,* Greg Kucera Gallery, Seattle

Selected Group Exhibitions:

1987 Fawbush Gallery, New York
Emotope, Buro Berlin, Germany
1988 *Desire Path,* Schulman Sculpture Garden, White Plains, New York
Committed to Print: Social and Political Themes in Recent American Printed Art, Museum of Modern Art, New York (catalog)
A Choice, Kunstrai, Amsterdam
Contemporary Print Acquisitions: 1986–1988, Museum of Modern Art, New York
1989 *Projects and Portfolios: The 25th National Print Exhibition,* Brooklyn Museum, New York (catalog)
Tom Cugliani Gallery, New York
Cara Perlman and Kiki Smith, Fawbush Gallery, New York
New York Experimental Glass, Society for Art in Craft, Pittsburgh (catalog)
1990 *Portraits,* Institute for Art and Urban Resources at P. S. 1, Long Island City, New York
The Body, Renaissance Society at the University of Chicago (catalog)
Recent Acquisitions, Corcoran Gallery of Art, Washington, D. C.
Figuring the Body, Museum of Fine Arts, Boston
1991 *Forbidden Games: Childhood,* Jack Tilton Gallery, New York
Body, Legs, Heads...and Special Parts, Westfalischer Kunstverein, Munster, Germany
Burning in Hell, Franklin Furnace, New York
The Interrupted Life, New Museum of Contemporary Art, New York (catalog)
1992 *Post-Human,* FAE Musee d'Art Contemporain, Pully/ Lausanne, Switzerland; Castello di Rivoli, Museo d'Arte Contmporanea, Rivoli, Italy; Deste Foundation for Contemporary Art, Athens; Deichtorhallen, Hamburg
Acquisitions of the 90s, Whitney Museum of American Art, New York
Recent Acquisitions, Museum of Modern Art, New York
Corporal Politics, MIT List Visual Arts Center, Cambridge, Massachusetts (catalog)
1993 *Regarding Masculinity,* Arthur Roger Gallery, New Orleans
Aperto 1993, Venice Biennale
Human Factor: Figurative Sculpture Reconsidered, Albuquerque Museum of Art
1993 Biennial Exhibition, Whitney Museum of American Art
1994 *Metamorphosis: Surrealism to Organic Abstraction 1925–1993,* Marlborough Graphics, New York
In the Lineage of Eva Hesse, Aldrich Museum of Contemporary Art, Ridgefield, Connecticut (catalog)
Selected Works and Projects (Part One), Irish Museum of Modern Art, Dublin
The Essential Gesture, Newport Harbor Art Museum, Newport Beach, California
1995 *Division of Labor: Women's Work in Contemporary Art,* Bronx Museum of the Arts, New York (catalog)
Altered States: American Art in the 90s, Forum for Contemporary Art, St. Louis, Missouri (catalog)
1996 *The Human Body in Contemporary American Sculpture,* Gagosian Gallery, New York
Paradise Cage: Kiki Smith and Coop Himmelblau, Museum of Contemporary Art, Los Angeles (catalog)
A Portrait of the Artist, Anthony d'Offay Gallery, London; Deste Foundation for Contemporary Art, Athens; Museum of Modern Art, Copenhagen Denmark; Guggenheim Museum SoHo, New York
1997 *Terra Firma,* Art Gallery at the University of Maryland at College Park
Proof Positive: 40 Years of Contemporary American Printmaking at ULAE: 1957–1997, Corcoran Gallery of Art, Washington, D.C; Gallery of Contemporary Art, University of Colorado, Colorado Springs; Armand Hammer Art Museum and Cultural Center, University of California, Los Angeles; Sezon Museum of Art, Tokyo (catalog)

Collections:

Allen Memorial Art Museum, Oberlin College, Oberlin, Ohio; Art Institute of Chicago; Bonner Kunstverein, Bonn, Germany; Cincinnati Art Museum; Contemporary Museum, Honolulu; Corcoran Gallery of Art, Washington, D. C.; Fogg Art Museum, Harvard University, Cambridge, Massachusetts; High Museum of Art, Atlanta; Israel Museum, Jerusalem; J. B. Speed Art Museum, Louisville, Kentucky; Lannan Foundation, Los Angeles; Louisiana Museum of Modern Art, Humlebaek, Denmark; Microsoft Corporation, Redmond, Washington; Moderna Museet, Stockholm; Museum of Contemporary Art, San Diego/La Jolla; Museum of Fine Arts, Boston; Museum of Fine Arts, Houston; Museum of Modern Art, New York; New York Public Library; Tate Gallery, London; Toledo Museum of Art, Ohio; Victoria and Albert Museum, London; Whitney Museum of American Art, New York; Yale University Art Gallery, New Haven, Connecticut.

Publications:

By SMITH: Article—''Impossible Liberties'' in *Art Journal,* summer 1995. **Film—***Kiki in the Flesh* with Charlie Ahearn, 1993.

On SMITH: Books—*Powers of Horror: An Essay on Abjection* by Julia Kristeva, translated by Leon S. Roudiez, New York 1982; *Projects 24: Kiki Smith* (exhibition brochure), by Jennifer Wells, New York 1990; *Kiki Smith* by Paolo Colombo, et al., Amsterdam and The Hague 1990; *Kiki Smith* (exhibition catalog), by Claudia Gould and Linda Shearer, Williamstown, Massachusetts and Columbus, Ohio, 1992; *Abject Art: Repulsion and Desire in American Art* (exhibition catalog), New York 1993; *. . . At the Border: The Work of Kiki Smith* by Elizabeth Anne Dungan, University of California, Berkeley, 1996; *Kiki Smith* by Helaine Posner and David Frankel, Boston 1998. **Articles—**''Kiki Smith: Body and Soul'' by Christopher Lyon in *Artforum International,* February 1990; ''Kiki Smith: Anatomy Lessons'' by Susan Tallman in *Art in America,* April 1992; ''The Body Fragments of Kiki Smith: Object of Society or Society's Abject'' (unpublished master's thesis), by Kathleen Wentrack, University of Amsterdam 1995; Notes on Kiki Smith's *Fall/Winter* by Maura Reilly in *Art Journal,* Winter 1999. **Films—***Kiki Smith* by Paul Tschinkel and others, 1994.

* * *

Kiki Smith's work embodies a multi-faceted reflection on postmodern thought indicative of the late–twentieth century. Her work explores the limits of the body—its physical as well as its social borders. Focusing on bodily fluids and parts to an eventual consideration of the body as a whole, Smith queries how the body functions within society. The artist explains her motivation: ''Our bodies have been broken apart bit by bit and need a lot of healing; our whole society is very fragmented.... Everything is split, and is presented as dichotomies—male/female, body/mind—and those splits need mending,'' as quoted in the exhibition brochure *Projects 24: Kiki Smith.* Looking at the body inside and out, Smith allows it to speak for itself. Her work reveals the body as political battleground. She questions who has control over our bodies, particularly female bodies, and how this effects our lives.

Smith was exposed to art very young; her father was artist Tony Smith. In 1976, she moved to New York City and later joined Collaborative Projects, Inc. (Colab), an artists' collective committed to social and political change. Using images of bodily fragments in the late 1970s, she discovered a language to address life issues. With the death of Smith's father in 1980, she turned towards issues of mortality as in *Hand in Jar* (1983), a mason jar containing a prosthetic hand on which algae grows.

In 1985, Smith trained as an emergency medical technician to learn about the functions, failures, and traumas of the body and began to sculpt bodily organs. In *Second Choice* (1987), a bowl displays ceramic bodily organs. These body parts show no political affiliations, race, or gender—they are universal. The arrangement conjures a fruit bowl waiting to be consumed. Yet, the title indicates that the contents are second choice, the leftovers of an anonymous operation. She provides the opportunity to experience one's own associations with the body but at the same time questions how we, and society, treat our bodies, demanding a more holistic approach to mind and body.

In the late 1980s, Smith focused on feminist issues related to the body, both physically and socially. In *Womb* (1986), a bronze, nine-month pregnant uterus opens to reveal an empty interior. The work draws attention to the function of a uterus and questions who has control regarding reproductive rights. In an untitled work (1989), a seven foot–tall body depicted from the waist down is suspended from the ceiling. A baby hangs still attached to its paper umbilical cord. The female experience of childbirth and the attachment between mother and child is made explicit while at the same time the anonymity of the figure comments on the social conditions and responsibility of child rearing. The choice of paper as opposed to bronze impresses the fragility of this relationship. Smith often uses paper, glass, ceramics, cloth, thread, and other craft-related materials in her work which have traditionally been coded as female. She celebrates these materials and uses them to enhance the theme of a work.

Smith broadened her visual language to include the surface of the body—the skin, orifices, and liquids which appear at its surface. In *Sperm* (1988–90), 230 cut-glass spermatozoa each measuring six to eight inches lay scattered on a black rubber surface. In *Jars* (1988–90), twelve mirrored glass apothecary jars are etched in Gothic lettering with names of bodily secretions: mucus, oil, tears, pus, vomit, semen, diarrhea, blood, urine, sweat, milk, saliva. In the reflective surfaces of the jars the viewer sees her or his own reflection among the names of bodily fluids. As these fluids, usually disposed of in private, are read they stir related human emotions such as sadness, sickness, and lust. The work's poignancy is even more evident in light of its production during the height of the AIDS epidemic.

Smith led the 1980s and 1990s manifestation of the abject in art. The concept of the abject and abjection was first fully explored from a psychoanalytic viewpoint by Julia Kristeva in *Powers of Horror* (1982). This theoretical framework has been applied to contemporary art as exemplified in a 1993 exhibition at the Whitney Museum of Art entitled *Abject Art.* Abject art takes as its subject matter, though not exclusively: food, bodily functions and waste, and signs of sexual difference such as menstruation. These subject matters have been prominent in the work of Smith.

Smith introduces the whole body in the early 1990s. In an untitled work (1991), life-size wax male and female bodies hang on stands, their nude bodies limp, their skin battered and bruised. They appear lifeless except for the life-giving secretions dripping down their bodies, milk and semen. In 1992, Smith sculpts a woman sitting on her hands with her head bowed and legs pulled towards her body. Radiating helplessness and humiliation, her back displays deep, red gouges. There is uneasiness in the brutality of Smith's treatment of the female form but she forcefully confronts the aggression experienced by abused women. These works explore the social and physical limits of the body, themes that are central to Smith's work, laying bare the ills of society.

In the mid-1990s, the artist incorporates story, myth, and history in her imagery, shifting her work from the physical to the spiritual and emotional realms of human experience. In *Lilith* (1994), a bronze female figure in a crouched position on hands and feet is attached to the wall with her head pointing down. Her back to us, she looks over her right shoulder to reveal her glass eyes. Lilith appears in an apocryphal biblical story; she like Adam is created from the earth. Smith's Catholic upbringing has drawn her to other themes such as Mary Magdalene and the Virgin Mary.

More recently, Smith changed her focus to include the animal world and the landscape within which we all coexist. For example, in *Jersey Crows* (1995), Smith scatters the floor with the lifeless bodies of crows in bronze, referencing an incident of pesticide poisoning in New Jersey.

Kiki Smith's work reveals the transitory nature of life and the struggles of the human condition. Her forms confront issues of personal sovereignty and identity when various institutions and government organizations attempt to lay their claim on the body. While many of Smith's works declaim feminist issues to draw attention to oppressing constraints women continue to face, many of her representations offer something for everyone by confronting the viewer with her or his own corporeality.

—Kathleen Wentrack

SMITH, Richard

Nationality: British. **Born:** Letchworth, Hertfordshire, 27 October 1931. **Education:** Studied at the Luton School of Art, Bedfordshire,

1948–50; St. Albans School of Art, Hertfordshire, 1952–54; Royal College of Art, London, 1954–57. **Military Service:** Served in the Royal Air Force, in Hong Kong, 1950–52. **Family:** Married Betsy Scherman in 1964; sons: Edward and Harry. **Career:** Painter and graphic artist; lived in London until 1976; visited New York frequently, from 1957; settled there in 1976. Lecturer in mural decoration, Hammersmith College of Art, London, 1957–58; lecturer, St. Martin's School of Art, London, 1961–63; artist-in-residence, University of Virginia, Charlottesville, 1967; University of California at Irvine, 1968; University of California at Davis, 1976. **Awards:** Travelling Scholarship, Royal College of Art, London, 1957; Harkness Travelling Fellowship, 1959; Robert C. Scull Prize, *Biennal,* Venice, 1966; Grand Prix, *Bienal,* Sao Paulo, 1967; C.B.E. (Commander, Order of the British Empire), 1972. **Agent:** Knoedler Gallery, London. **Address:** c/o Knoedler Gallery, 22 Cork Street, London WIX 1HB, England.

Individual Exhibitions:

1961 Green Gallery, New York
1962 Richard Smith Studio, Bath Street, London
Institute of Contemporary Arts, London
1963 Kasmin Gallery, London
Green Gallery, New York
1965 Green Gallery, New York
1966 Whitechapel Art Gallery, London
Richard Feigen Gallery, New York
Editions Alecto, London
1967 Kasmin Gallery, London
Bienal, Sao Paulo
University of Virginia, Charlottesville
Galerie Denise René Hans Mayer, Krefeld, Germany
1968 Richard Feigen Gallery, New York
1969 Galleria dell' Ariete, Milan
Kasmin Gallery, London
1970 Arnolfini Gallery, Bristol
Biennale, Venice
1971 Richard Feigen Gallery, Chicago
Kasmin Gallery, London
1972 Gallerie dell'Ariete, Milan
Museum of Modern Art, Oxford
Bear Lane Gallery, Oxford
Kasmin Gallery, London
1973 Ruth S. Schaffner Gallery, Los Angeles
Garage Art, London
Waddington Graphics, London
Galerie Schottenring, Vienna
Hayward Gallery, London
1974 O. K. Harris Gallery, New York
Galerie Swart, Amsterdam
Neue Galerie der Stadt, Linz, Austria
Galerie Schottering, Vienna
D.M. Gallery, London
Bernard Jacobson Ltd., London
1975 Museo de Arte Contemporaneo, Caracas
Kettle Yard, Cambridge (travelled to the Ashmolean Museum, Oxford)
Tate Gallery, London
Gimpel Fils Gallery, London
Museu de Arte Moderna, Rio de Janeiro
1976 Galleria Vinciana, Milan
Gimpel Fils Gallery, London
Galleria La Polena, Genoa
Galleria del Cavallino, Venice
Kasahara Gallery, Osaka
Museo de Arte Moderna, Bogota
1977 Arte Contacto, Caracas
Recent Work 1972–1977: Paintings, Drawings and Graphics, Massachusetts Institute of Technology, Cambridge, Massachusetts (toured the United States)
Galerie Daniel Templon, Paris
Studio La Città, Verona
Galleria La Piramide, Florence
Studio Arco d' Alibert, Rome
Galerie Orny, Munich
Galerie Gimpel und Hanover, Zurich
Modulo, Porto, Portugal
1978 Galerie Artline, The Hague
Hayden Gallery, Massachusetts Institute of Technology Cambridge (travelled to the Chrysler Museum, Norfolk, Virgina and Walker Art Center, Minneapolis)
Anthony Stokes Gallery, London
Studio G7, Bologna
Padiglione d'Arte Contemporanea, Parco Massari, Ferrara, Italy
Galleria La Polena, Genoa
Studio Rotelli, Finale Ligure, Italy
Young Hoffman Gallery, Chicago
Galeria dell'Ariete, Milan
Galeria San Diego, Bogota
Hudson River Museum, New York
Kornblee Gallery, New York
1979 Hedendaagse Kunst Museum, Utrecht (travelled to Museum Het Bruggenbouw, Emmen, Netherlands)
Galerie Artline, The Hague
Galleria Il Sole, Bolzano, Italy
Saskatoon Gallery, Saskatchewan
Fort Worth Art Museum, Texas
1980 Knoedler Gallery, London
Bernard Jacobson Ltd., New York
Cartouche Series, Norman Mackenzie Art Gallery, Regina, Saskatchewan
Arco Center for the Visual Arts, Los Angeles
Studio La Città, Verona
Galleria La Polena, Genoa
Neue Arbeiten, Stadtsmuseum, Ulm, West Germany
Hansen-Fuller-Goldeen Gallery, San Francisco
1982 Knoedler Gallery, London
1992 *Richard Smith: The Green Gallery Years 1960–1963,* Richard L. Feigen & Company, New York
1995 Tony Shafrazi Gallery, New York
1997 *Richard Smith: 4 Paintings*, Bernard Jacobson Gallery, London

Selected Group Exhibitions:

1954 *Young Contemporaries,* RBA Galleries, London
1957 *New Trends in British Art,* New York Art Foundation, Rome
1961 *Carnegie International,* Carnegie Institute, Pittsburgh

1964 *The Shaped Canvas,* Guggenheim Museum, New York
1967 *New Shapes of Colour,* Stedelijk Museum, Amsterdam
1970 *Contemporary British Art,* Museum of Modern Art, Tokyo
1973 *La Peinture Anglaise Aujourd'hui,* Musée d'Art Moderne de la Ville, Paris
1974 *British Painting '74,* Hayward Gallery, London
1976 *Arte Inglese Oggi 1960–1976,* Pallazo Reale, Milan
1983 *Aspects of British Art,* Guggenheim Museum, New York
1988 *The Presence of Painting: Aspect of British Abstraction 1957–1988*, Mappin Art Gallery, Sheffield, England (catalog)
1992 *Graphicstudio*, National Gallery of Art, Washington, D.C. (catalog)
1997 *Treasure Island*, Fundacao Calouste Gulbenkian, Libon
Hockney to Hodgkin: British Master Prints 1960–1980, New Orleans Museum of Art, Louisiana (catalog)

Collections:

Tate Gallery, London; Victoria and Albert Museum, London; Galleria Nazionale d'Arte Moderna, Rome; Staatliche Graphische Sammlung, Munich; Kaiser Wilhelm Museum, Krefeld, West Germany; Art Gallery of Western Australia, Perth; Hirshhorn Museum and Sculpture Garden, Smithsonian Institution, Washington, D.C.; Walker Art Center, Minneapolis.

Publications:

By SMITH: Book—*Paginas Amarillas,* exhibition catalog, Caracas 1975. **Articles—**''Ideograms'' in *Ark* (London), No. 16, 1956; ''Film Backgrounds: Two Sitting in the Middle of Today'' in *Ark* (London), No. 19, 1957; ''That Pink'' in *Gazette* (London), No. 2, 1961; ''Brief Statement'' in *Metro* (Milan), No. 6, 1962; ''Trailer: Notes Additional to Film'' in *Living Arts* (London), No. 1, 1963; ''Pre-Occupations: Richard Smith Talks to Anne Seymour'' in *Art and Artists* (London), June 1970; statement in *Richard Smith: Cartouche Series,* exhibition catalog, Regina, Saskatchewan 1980; ''Old Glories'' in *British Journal of Photography*, vol. 139, no. 6874, 4 June 1992; ''Cosmetic Abstractions'' by Brooks Adams in *Art in America* (New York), vol. 80, no. 10, October 1992; ''Easy Readings'' in *Reportage*, no. 2, Autumn 1993.

On SMITH: Books—*Richard Smith: Seven Exhibitions,* with text by Barbara Rose, London 1975; *Richard Smith; Recent Work 1972–1977; Paintings Drawings and Graphics,* exhibition catalog by Wayne Aderson, Cambridge, Massachusetts 1978; *Richard Smith: Neue Arbeiten,* exhihition catalog by Norbert Nobis, Ulm, West Germany 1980. **Articles—**''Richard Smith, Sculptor or Painter?'' by Cyril Barrett in *Art International* (Lugano, Switzerland), October 1967; ''A Double Reality: The Work and Career of Richard Smith'' by Bernard Denvir in *Art International* (Lugano Switzerland), Summer 1970; ''Richard Smith in New York'' by T. Castle in *Art Monthly* (London), September 1979; ''A Fabulous Talent'' by Sarah Whitfield in *Modern Painters* (London), vol. 10, no. 2, Summer 1997.

* * *

At first Richard Smith just jumped out at us. His early, exuberant, abstracted-Pop subjects literally jutted out from the wall like large, formal pages from some pop-up book of abstractions. It was clear from the beginning that this English painter was enamored of American advertising, its imagery and ideas. So much so that he travelled to New York and exhibited big, brash canvases which directly referred to commercial products. There were cigarette-package-like shapes and titles incorporating things like shampoo.

This love affair with Pop never wholly conquered Smith's deepest interests, which had to do with the formal properties of painting—with color, with structure, with form—and he soon left behind the world of commonplace images to paint several series of minimal-like, shaped canvases. A number of these had to do with time and sequence. One set envolved from the idea of pages turned down and removed from a calendar: canvases ''turned down'' at one corner until the last rectangle was reduced to a triangle and the sequence of color changes brought to a halt.

The surfaces of these paintings were most often painted one color with a second acting as an accent. Later, thin, watercolor-like treatment emerged and there began references to nature—to woods, fields, and rivers. Nothing figurative though.

In turn this has given way to other series and sequences, but now off the stretcher and held firm by rods and sticks and rings and string or rope. Things are tied and sometimes the knots act as color comments. The over-all effect is like that of kites or sails on a Chinese junk, the canvas shaped into squares, rectangles or polygons and suspended in sequences fanned out along a wall like some huge hand of cards or from the ceiling like a chain of banners.

Smith's work has developed from a loud aggressiveness to an almost oriental delicacy and subtleness. Now his color is more beautiful than ever and his ''message'' almost serene.

—Ralph Pomeroy

SNELSON, Kenneth

Nationality: American. **Born:** Pendleton, Oregon, 29 June 1927. **Education:** University of Oregon, Eugene, 1946–47; Black Mountain College, North Carolina, under Josef Albers, Buckminster Fuller, and Willem de Kooning, 1947–48; and Acádemie Montmarte, Paris, under Fernand Léger, 1949. Served in the United States Navy, 1945. **Family:** Married Katherine Kaufmann in 1972; daughters: Andrea and Nicole. **Career:** Independent sculptor, since 1960: lives and works in New York. Has taught at Cooper Union, New York; Pratt Institute, Brooklyn, New York; School of Visual Arts, New York; Southern Illinois University, Carbondale; and Yale University, New Haven, Connecticut. **Member:** Advisory board, Public Arts Council, New York, since 1974. **Awards:** Sculpture Award, New York State Council on the Arts, 1971; Reynolds Metals Sculpture Award, 1974; National Endownment for the Arts Grant, 1974; Prize, Iowa City Sculpture Competition, 1974; DAAD Fellowship, Berlin, 1975; National Endownment for the Arts Grant, 1975; American Institute of Architects Medal, 1981; American Institute of Arts and Letters Award, 1987. DHL: Rensselaer Polytechnic Institute, 1985; Prix Ars Electronica Siemens AG for Computer Graphics, Linz, Austria, 1989; American Institute of Architects, Biennial Artists Award, Kansas City, 1991; Elected, American Academy of Arts & Letters, 1994; Lifetime Achievement Award, International Sculpture Center, 1999. **Agent:** Marlborough Gallery, 40 West 57th St., New York, New

York 10019; and 376 rue Quincampoix, 75004 Paris, France. **Address:** 37 W. 12th Street, New York, New York 10011, U.S.A.

Individual Exhibitions:

1962 Pratt Institute, Brooklyn, New York
1966 Dwan Gallery, New York
1967 Dwan Gallery, New York
1968 Dwan Gallery, New York
Bryant Park, New York
1969 Fort Worth Museum of Art, Texas
Rijksmuseum Kröller-Müller, Otterlo, Netherlands
1970 Kunsthalle, Dusseldorf
1971 Kunstverein, Hannover
1972 John Weber Gallery, New York
Galerie van der Voort, Ibiza, Spain
1974 Waterside Plaza, New York
1975 Galerie Buchholz, Munich
1977 Nationalgalerie, Berlin
Wilhelm-Lembruck-Museum, Duisburg, West Germany
Galerie de Gestlo, Hamburg
1978 *Portrait of an Atom,* Maryland Academy of Science, Baltimore
Sonnabend Gallery, New York
1981 Hirshhorn Museum, Washington, D.C.
Albright-Knox Art Gallery, Buffalo, New York
Zabriskie Gallery, New York
1982 University of Houston, Texas
University of Pittsburgh, Pennsylvania
Museum of Science and Industry, Tampa, Florida
North Carolina Museum of Life and Science, Durham
1983 Impression Five Museum, Lansing, Michigan
Schenectady Museum, New York
1984 Zabriskie Gallery, New York
Columbus Museum of Art, Ohio
Galerie Zabriskie, Paris
De Cordova Museum, Lincoln, Massachusetts
1986 Zabriskie Gallery, New York
Galerie Zabriskie, Paris
1990 Zabriskie Gallery, New York
1991 Contemporary Sculpture Center, Tokyo
1993 Yoh Art Gallery, Osaka
1994 *Kenneth Snelson: Sculptures,* Maxwell Davidson Gallery, New York
Anderson Gallery, Buffalo
Laurence Miller Gallery, New York
1995 Contemporary Sculpture Center, Tokyo
1998 Maxwell Davidson Gallery, New York
1999 Marlborough Chelsea, New York

Selected Group Exhibitions:

1964 *20th Century Engineering,* Museum of Modern Art, New York
1966 *Whitney Sculpture Annual,* Whitney Museum, New York
1967 *Sculpture of the 60s,* Los Angeles County Museum of Art
1968 *The Pure and Clear: American Innovation,* Philadelphia Museum of Art
1969 *Contemporary American Sculpture,* Whitney Museum, New York
1970 *Salon International des Galeries Pilotes,* Lausanne, Switzerland
L'Art Vivant Americain, Fondation Maeght, St. Paul-de-Vence, France
1973 *Art in Space: Some Turning Points,* Detroit Institute of Arts
1977 *Panoramic Photography,* New York University
1983 *Big Pictures,* Museum of Modern Art, New York
1994 *Elemental Images,* Gallery at Takashimaya, New York
1996 *Inside/Outside: Photography by 10 Contemporary Sculptors,* Laurence Miller Gallery, New York
2000 *Monte-Carlo International Sculpture Festival: Contemporary American Sculpture,* Monte Carlo

Collections:

Museum of Modern Art, New York; Whitney Museum, New York; Hirshhorn Museum, Washington, D.C.; Hunter Museum of Art, Chattanooga, Tennessee; Art Institute of Chicago; Milwaukee Art Institute; Rijksmuseum Kröller-Müller, Otterlo, Netherlands; Rijksmuseum, Stedelijk, Amsterdam; Museum of Modern Art, Shiga, Japan; Albright-Knox Art Gallery, Buffalo; Cleveland Museum of Art, Ohio; Columbus Museum of Art, Ohio; Dallas Museum of Fine Arts; Museum of Art, Carnegie Institute, Pittsburgh; Portland Art Museum, Oregon; The Art Museum, Princeton, New Jersey; Shiga Museum of Modern Art, Japan; Storm King Art Center, Mountainville, New York; Wakayama Museum of Art, Japan; Walker Art Center, Minneapolis; Whitney Museum of American Art, New York; Wilhelm Lehmbruck Museum, Duisburg, Germany; Japan Iron & Steel Federation, Osaka.

Publications:

By SNELSON: Books—*Kenneth Snelson: The Nature of Structure,* New York 1989; Creativity*: Conversations with 28 Who Excel* by Susan Charlotte, Tom Ferguson and Bruce Felton, Troy 1993**;** *Kenneth Snelson: Sculptures and Drawings 1968–1998,* New York 1999. **Articles**—''A Design for the Atom'' in *Industrial Design* (New York), February 1963; ''Proprietary Protection'' in *Progressive Architect* (New York), June 1964; ''How Primary Is Structure'' in *Art Voices* (New York), Summer 1966; ''An Interview with Kenneth Snelson,'' with John Coplans, in *Artforum* (New York), vol. V, no. 7, 1967; ''An Artist's Atom: Computer-generated Images of the Structure of Atoms'' in *Leonardo,* vol. 27, no. 3, 1994.

On SNELSON: Books—*Struktur und Spannung,* exhibition catalog by Laszlo Glozer, Hannover 1971; *Kenneth Snelson,* exhibition catalog with essay by Howard Fox, Washington, D.C. 1981; *Kenneth Snelson: Sculptures,* exhibition catalog, New York 1994; *Kenneth Snelson,* exhibition catalog, Tokyo 1995. **Articles**—''Kenneth Snelson: Dialogue Between Stress and Tension'' by Gregory Battcock in *Arts Magazine* (New York), February 1968; ''Kenneth Snelson: The Elegant Solution'' by Stephen Kurtz in *ARTnews* (New York), October 1968; ''Snelson and Structure'' by Deborah Perlberg in *Artforum* (New York), May 1975; ''Kenneth Snelson: Straddling the Abyss Between Art and Science'' by Richard Whelan in *ARTnews* (New York), February 1981; ''Full Circle'' by Charles Hagen in *Camera Arts* (New York), January/February 1982; ''Extending Computer Imaging: Art/Science, Science/Art'' by Joelle Bentley in *Print* (New York), vol. 44, May/June 1990; *Multi-disciplinary Creative*

Artist: Kenneth Snelson's Computer Graphics by Shoichiro Higuchi in *Idea,* no. 246, vol. 42, September 1994; ''Kenneth Snelson: The Lyricism of Structure'' by Mark Daniel Cohen in *Sculpture* (Washington, D.C.), vol. 18, no. 8, October 1999.

* * *

''My artistic interest has been based in the countless ways nature provides for organizing physical forces to form structures,'' the photographer/sculptor Kenneth Snelson wrote in 1994. ''My sculptures have been linked variously to constructivism, engineering, mathematics, or science. The fact that I was schooled in art makes me feel most comfortable with the constructivists because, at root, we share a common interest: that of putting together separate parts to create a new whole.''

Again and again, ''separate parts creating the whole'' is a theme that echoes through Snelson's art, from his early panoramic photographs to the tightly engineered sculptures for which he is best known—polished metal tubes that seem to float weightlessly in space.

Born in Oregon in 1927, Snelson studied at the Corcoran School in Washington, D.C., and the University of Oregon. In 1948 he hitched a ride across the country to study with the great color theorist Josef Albers at Black Mountain College. But there he became more interested in another faculty member, Buckminster Fuller, and Fuller's ideas about the geometry of structure. As Joelle Bentley described it: ''The ideas which emerged in the heady avant-garde atmosphere during that summer set the stage for Snelson's artistic expression. The curiosity those ideas engendered in him then has sustained his long and successful career as an artist: How is matter constructed? What is the structure of nature?''

Snelson's own investigations yielded the prototype for his sculpture: a ''floating compression structure,'' where cylinders of steel seem to float in space yet are actually buoyed by the structural competition between tension and compression, with rigid compression tubes pushing outward and flexible tension cables pulling inward. Fuller was intrigued and later credited Snelson with the invention of a new structural principle the architect named ''tensegrity,'' a combination of the words ''tension'' and ''integrity.''

After further studies at the Illinois Institute of Design in Chicago and the Academie Montmartre in Paris, Snelson settled in New York in 1952 and made his living as a documentary film cameraman. At the same time, he was evolving a body of work that related to both Minimalism and Constructivism. The art world began to take notice in the 1960s. Snelson, meanwhile, was becoming more and more interested in what he perceived as the great similarity between the mathematical principles of his structures and those of atoms. Eventually, he postulated a visual model of the ''architecture'' of an atom.

Beginning in the 1970s, Snelson headed in a new direction, taking panoramic photographs. He was still using art to investigate and unravel the fabric of reality. Using a motor-driven Hulcherama camera, he photographed scenes that lent themselves to panoramic perspective: places in Paris where streets converged, the intersections of canals in Venice. The frame which usually creates a boundary to the photographed image was altered, and the boundaries pushed so far outward as to lose their defining power.

The 1980s brought a renewed interest in atomic structure, and now Snelson had a means to capture it in his art: the computer. In the winter of 1988–89 he exhibited the results in the show *The Nature of Structure* at the New York Academy of Sciences. On display were serene constructions of intensely colored floating rings, disks, and spheres. Subsequently, Snelson has also begun to create much larger pieces, including a trio of soaring arches which stand outside Hallmark offices in Kansas City, Missouri.

—Joan Oleck

SNOW, Michael (James Aleck)

Nationality: Canadian. **Born:** Toronto, Ontario, 10 December 1929. **Education:** Educated at Upper Canada College, Toronto, 1946–51; studied at Ontario College of Art, Toronto, 1951–55. **Family:** Married the artist and filmmaker Joyce Wieland, in 1959. **Career:** Independent artist, musician, filmmaker and photographer, Toronto, since 1955. Professor of advanced film, Yale University, New Haven, Connecticut, 1970; visiting artist, Nova Scotia College of Art and Design, Halifax, 1970, 1974, and Ontario College of Art, Toronto, 1973, 1974, 1976; CCMC artist in residence, La Chartreuse, Avignon Festival, France, 1981; visiting professor, Princeton University, 1988. Musician; member of the CCMC, Toronto, since 1976. **Awards:** Purchase Award, *Winnipeg Exhibition,* 1958; Canada Council Arts Grant, 1959, and Senior Arts Grant, 1966, 1973, 1980; Henry Street Settlement Exhibition Award, New York, 1964; Guggenheim Fellowship, 1972; Independent Experimental Film Award, Los Angeles Film Critics Association, 1983; received Order of Canada, 1983; Visual Arts Award, Toronto Arts Awards, 1986. LL.D.: Brock University, St. Catherines, Ontario, 1975. **Agent:** Isaacs Gallery, Toronto. **Address:** c/o Moore Gallery, 80 Spadina Ave., Suite 404, Toronto, Ontario M5V 2J3, Canada.

Individual Exhibitions:

1956 Hart House, University of Toronto
1957 Isaacs Gallery, Toronto (and 1958)
1959 Art Gallery of Ontario, Toronto
1960 Isaacs Gallery, Toronto (and 1962)
1963 Gallery XII, Montreal Museum of Fine Arts
Hart House, University of Toronto
1964 Isaacs Gallery, Toronto
Poindexter Gallery, New York
1965 Poindexter Gallery, New York
1966 20/20 Gallery, London, Ontario
Isaacs Gallery, Toronto
1967 *Retrospective 1963–66,* Vancouver Art Gallery
1968 Poindexter Gallery, New York
1969 Isaacs Gallery, Toronto
1970 *Michael Snow: A Survey,* Art Gallery of Ontario, Toronto
Canadian Pavilion, *Biennale,* Venice
Bykert Gallery, New York
1972 Center for Inter-American Relations, New York
Bykert Gallery, New York
1973 *Camera Works by Michael Snow,* University of Manitoba, Winnipeg
1974 *Projected Images,* Walker Art Center, Minneapolis
Isaacs Gallery, Toronto
1976 Museum of Modern Art, New York
1977 *7 Films et Plus Tard,* Centre Georges Pompidou, Paris (toured France, 1977–79)

1978 *Michael Snow,* Centre Georges Pompidou, Paris (travelled to the Kunstmuseum, Lucerne; Rheinisches Landesmuseum, Bonn; Städtische Galerie im Lembachhaus, Munich; Musee des Beaux-Arts, Montreal; and the Vancouver Art Gallery, 1978–80)
1979 Isaacs Gallery, Toronto
Museum Boymans-van Beuningen, Rotterdam (with Richard Hefti)
1982 Isaacs Gallery, Toronto
1983 Canada House, London, University of California, Los Angeles
Agnes Etherington Art Centre, Kingston, Ontario (travelled to Ithaca, New York; Halifax, Nova Scotia; London, Ontario; Victoria, British Columbia; Toronto)
1984 Isaacs Gallery, Toronto
Vu Centre de la Photographie, Quebec City
1986 Isaacs Gallery, Toronto
The Spectral Image, Expo '86, Vancouver, British Columbia
Visionary Apparatus (with Juan Geuer), List Gallery, MIT, Cambridge, Massachusetts
1987 The Isaacs Gallery, Toronto, Ontario
Still Life in 8 Calls, Mississauga Civic Centre Art Gallery, Ontario
1988 The Isaacs Gallery, Toronto, Ontario
Michael Snow: (Thanks to Robert Crumb), Ruine der Kunste, Berlin, Germany
Hara Museum of Contemporary Art, Tokyo, Japan
1989 The Isaacs Gallery, Toronto, Ontario
Forest City Gallery, London, Ontario
1991 The Isaacs Gallery, Toronto, Ontario
1992 San Francisco Art Institute, San Francisco, California
1992–93 Galerie Claire Burrus, Paris, France
1993 S.L. Simpson Gallery
1994 *Light, Surface and Sound,* Presentation House Gallery, Vancouver, British Columbia
Walking Woman Works, Art Gallery of Ontario Touring Exhibition, Stratford, Peterborough, and Sudbury, Ontario
Exploring Plane and Contour, The Art Gallery of Ontario
Around Wavelength, The Art Gallery of Ontario, Toronto
Presence and Absence: The Films of Michael Snow, The Art Gallery of Ontario, Toronto, Ontario
Embodied Vision, The Power Plant, Toronto, Ontario
Early Work on Paper, S.L. Simpson Gallery

Selected Group Exhibitions:

1956 *Hart House* (two-man exhibition), University of Toronto, Ontario
1957 *Biennale of Canadian Painting,* National Gallery of Canada, Ottawa, Ontario
1958 Walker Art Center, Minneapolis, Minnesota
1959 *Biennale of Canadian Painting,* National Gallery of Canada, Art Gallery of Ontario, Toronto
1964 *Contemporary American Figure Painters,* Wadsworth Athenaeum, Connecticut
Biennale of Canadian Painting, National Gallery of Canada, Ottawa, Ontario
1965 *Outdoor Exhibition,* Sculpture Society of Canada, Stratford, Ontario
1967 *The National Gallery of Canada Exhibition,* Museum of Modern Art, Paris, France
1969 *The Wall Art for Architecture,* Art Gallery of Ontario, Toronto, Ontario
Information, Museum of Modern Art, New York, New York
Anti-Illusion: Procedures and Materials, Whitney Museum, New York
1970 *3-D into the '70s,* Art Gallery of Ontario, Toronto, Ontario
1974 *The Isaacs Gallery at the Owens Art Gallery,* Sackville, New Brunswick
1975 *A Response to the Environment,* Rutgers University
1977 Documenta, Kassel, Germany
1977–78 *Another Dimension,* National Gallery of Canada, Ottawa
1978 *The Artists' Jazz Band at the Canadian Cultural Centre,* Paris, France
1979 *Re-visions: Projects and Proposals in Film and Video,* The Whitney Museum of American Art, New York
1982 *Photoalchemy,* The Robert Freidus Gallery, New York, New York
1983 *Toronto Painting of the 1960s,* Art Gallery of Ontario
1984 *Edge and Image,* Concordia Art Gallery, Concordia University, Montreal
Seeing People—Seeing Space, The Photographers' Gallery, London, England
1985 *Aurora Borealis,* Centre d'Art Contemporain, Montreal
The Zacks Gift: Then and Now, Agnes Etherington Art Centre, Kingston, Ontario
1986 *Fokus: Contemporary Canadian Art 1960–85,* Department of External Affairs, Cologne Art Fair
1987 *International Holography Exhibition and Conference,* Copenhagen, Denmark
Holography, Light in the Third Dimension, Ontario Science Centre, Toronto, Ontario
Toronto: Play of History, The Power Plant, Toronto, Ontario
Photographers Who Make Films, New York University Photo Center Gallery
1987–88 *Snow/Weiner/Nannucci,* Art Metropole, Toronto
Office of the Premier, Queen's Park, Toronto, Ontario
1988 *Images du Futur 88,* Art et Nouvelles Technologies, Montreal
Festival des Arts Electroniques de Rennes, Rennes, France; Georges Pompidou Centre, Paris
Galerie Vu, Quebec City, Quebec
1988–90 *Vanishing Presence,* Walker Art Centre, Minneapolis; Detroit, Michigan; Winnipeg, Manitoba; Atlanta, Georgia; Ithaca, New York; Richmond, Virginia
1990–92 *Passages de l'image,* Centre Georges Pompidou, Paris; Barcelona; Toronto; Columbus; San Francisco
1992 *Robert Fones,* Robert McNealy, Michael Snow, S.L. Simpson Gallery, Toronto, Ontario
1993 *Crisis of Abstraction,* Musée de Québec, Quebec City; MacKenzie Art Gallery, Regina; National Gallery of Canada, Ottawa; Glenbow Museum, Calgary, Alberta, Art Gallery of Hamilton, Hamilton, Ontario

Film Screenings:

Filmmakers Cinematique, New York, 1967, 1968, 1969; Gallery of Modern Art, New York, 1969; Whitney Museum, New York, 1969; Museum of Modern Art, New York, 1969, 1970; Edinburgh Film Festival, 1969, 1975; The Jewish Film Museum, New York, 1970; Pesaro Film Festival, Italy, 1973; *Rameau's Nephew,* world premiere, National Gallery, Ottawa, 1974; Cinematique Quebecoise, Montreal, retrospective, 1975; Museum of Modern Art, New York, retrospective, 1976; Anthology of Film Archives, New York 1975, 1976; Art Gallery of Ontario, Toronto, 1981; Osterreichisches Filmmuseum, Vienna, 1981; Canada House, London, 1983; University of California, Los Angeles, 1983.

Collections:

National Gallery of Canada, Ottawa; Canada Council Art Bank, Ottawa; Art Gallery of Ontario, Toronto; Montreal Museum of Fine Arts; Winnipeg Art Gallery; Museum of Modern Art, New York; Philadelphia Museum of Art; Milwaukee Art Center, Wisconsin; Albright-Knox Art Gallery, Buffalo, New York; Montreal Museum of Fine Arts, Quebec; Musée d'Art Moderne, Centre Georges Pomidou, Paris.

Publications:

By SNOW: Books—*Place of Meeting,* with text by Ray Souster, Toronto 1962; *Michael Snow: A Survey,* with text by P. Adam Sitney, Toronto 1970; *Cover to Cover,* Halifax, Nova Scotia 1975; *High School,* Toronto 1980; illustrations in *Diacritics: A Review of Contemporary Criticism,* Fall 1984. **Article—**''Passage'' in *Artforum* (New York), September 1971. **Films—***A to Z,* 1956; *New York Eye and Ear Control (A Walking Woman Work),* 1964; *Short Shave,* 1965; *Wavelength,* 1967; *Standard Time,* 1967; *Back and Forth,* 1969; *One Second in Montreal,* 1969; *Dripping Water,* 1969; *Side Seat Paintings Slides Sound Films,* 1970; *La Region Centrale,* 1970–71; *Table Top Dolly,* 1972; *Rameau's Nephew By Diderot (Thanks to Dennis Young)* by Wilma Schoen, 1974; *Presents,* 1980. **Sound recordings—** *The Artists Jazz Band,* 1974; *CCMC,* 5 vols., 1974–80; *Michael Snow: Music for Whistling, Piano, Microphone, and Tape Recorder,* 1975; *The Artists Jazz Band: Live at the Edge,* 1977.

On SNOW: Books—*Expanded Cinema* by Gene Youngblood, New York, 1970; *Negative Space* by Manny Farber, New York 1971; *Experimental Cinema* by David Curtis, London 1971; *About 30 Works by Michael Snow,* New York 1972; *Visionary Film* by P. Adams Sitney, New York 1974; *Michael Snow Retrospective,* Montreal 1975; *Une Histoire du Cinema* by Peter Kubelka and others, Paris 1976; *Documenta 6/Band 2,* exhibition catalog by Klaus Honnef and Evelyn Weiss, Cologne 1977; *Michael Snow,* exhibition catalog, Lucerne 1979; *Michael Snow,* Rotterdam 1979; *Snow Seen: The Films and Photographs of Michael Snow* by Regina Cornwell, Toronto 1980; *Michael Snow: Selected Photographic Works,* exhibition catalog with essays by Pierre Theberge and Christopher Dewdney, Los Angeles 1983; *Walking Women Works: Michael Snow 1961–67* by Louise Dompierre, Kingston, Ontario 1983; *Visionary Apparatus: Michael Snow and Juan Geuer,* exhibition catalog, List Visual Arts Center, Boston 1986; *Michael Snow,* exhibition catalog, Hara Museum of Contemporary Art, Tokyo 1988; *The Michael Snow Project: Visual Art, 1951–1993,* exhibition catalog, Toronto 1994; *The Michael Snow Project: Music/Sound,* exhibition catalog, Toronto 1994; *The Michael Snow Project: Collected Writings,* University of Waterloo Press, Ontario 1994. **Articles—**''Michael Snow at the Isaacs Gallery'' by Gerald Needham in *Artscanada,* December/January 1979–80; ''Michael Snow: The Decisive Moment Revised'' by Regina Cornwell in *Artscanada,* April/May 1980; ''Michael Snow at the 49th Parallel'' by Ronald Christ in *Artscanada,* March/April 1981; ''Michael Snow at the Isaacs Gallery'' by Christopher Dewdney in *Vanguard,* February 1983; ''Michael Snow at the Isaacs Gallery'' by Gary Michael Dault in *Vanguard,* May 1984; ''Snow's Angel: The Bachelor Stripped Bare by His Brides'' by Gary Michael Dault in *Vanguard,* April 1985; ''Ghost Lustres: Michael Snow's Holographic Visions at Expo '86'' by René Blouin in *Canadian Art,* Summer 1986; ''Locating the Public in Art'' by Bryan Gee in *Vanguard,* October/November 1986; ''Visionary Apparatus: Michael Snow and Juan Geuer'' by David Benetti in *Canadian Art,* Summer 1987; ''Self-Portrait with an Assist'' in *Canadian Art,* Winter 1989; ''Michael Snow: Forty Years of Achievement'' by Adele Freedman in *Canadian Art,* Spring 1994; ''Michael Snow Drawings at SLSG'' by Susan Walker in *Toronto Star,* 12 March 1994; ''Snow Storm'' by Pamela Young in *Maclean's Magazine,* 21 March 1994.

* * *

A supremely cerebral artist, Michael Snow has produced an oeuvre marked by an almost philosophical examination of perception. Over the course of some thirty years—as painter, sculptor, filmmaker, musician, holographer and bookmaker—Snow has continually experimented in order to perceive the world without regard to convention and tradition. His artistic enterprise differs profoundly from other protean efforts in modern art; within his Renaissance scope of activities Snow, like Leonardo himself, is a skeptic—one who believes that increased knowledge only illuminates a vaster abyss. From his well-known, ubiquitous *Walking Woman* series (1961–67), in which a singular, virtually identical silhouette of a walking woman adorned some 200 works in assorted media, Snow has developed an art that, in its stylistic and technological diversity, questions the function of culture today.

Snow's film *Wavelength* (1967)—an obssessive 45-minute zoom across a loft space to a photograph of the sea—defined the artist's commitment to a ''new cinema of structure.'' Eschewing the human subject and its intrinsic gaze, the artist was freer to examine the pure optical conditions of seeing—all the subliminal physiological experience hitherto subsumed by narrative.

Within this objective perceptual field, Snow began isolating certain characteristics specific to film (e.g., the contrast of stillness and movement), an activity that paralleled the kind of purity of medium espoused by Greenbergian late-moderism. For Snow, however, such formalism was neither exclusive nor to be experienced autonomously, unrelated to reality and to a developing critical, theoretical discourse. Works like *Wavelength* or *La Région Centrale* (1971)—a three-hour film consisting entirely of images shot in the bush in Quebec in which the main character is the camera itself—are as much about film as they are about narrative or representation. The artist's equation of *perception* with film allows a different type of psychology or subconscious to emerge. Of central importance, therefore, is the artist's device of framing, of asserting a disturbingly intractable perspective. In his video installation *De La* (1969–71), for example, a rotating mechanical sculpture—actually an elaborately engineered camera designed by the artist—projected images on four circumscribing video screens. The spectator's perceptual field was constantly challenged and exceeded by the swirling projection of images around him.

Snow's use of cinematic repetition, which parallels his 1960s collaborations with New Music composers Philip Glass and Steve Reich, elicits a hyperacute sensitivity from the viewer. Snow, in fact, has carried his photographic and film techniques to his own musical compositions. In the tradition of Duchamp and Cage the artist's inclusion of chance and the ''raw process'' of art-making became part of the finished composition. His liner notes to his solo album *Music for Piano, Whistling, Microphone and Tape Recorder* (1975), for example, indicates that he placed a microphone on top of his piano and turned up the recording volume in order to make ''a part of the recording process a part of the music'' by allowing ambient sounds (such as a ringing telephone) to register on the master tape.

Synthesizing his earlier multiplicity of techniques, Snow has recently worked in holography. His installation at Vancouver's Expo 86—*The Spectral Image*— was seen in a vast cathedral-like hall illuminated by colored filters, a work that continues his implementation of the most advanced technology into his art. Snow's work in the recent exhibition *Visionary Apparatus* at the Massachusetts Institute of Technology's Hayden Gallery, like *The Spectral Image,* resounds with the added dimension of laser-pulse holographic illusionism, a sophisticated technology that once again attests to the artist's conviction in the mutually redemptive relationship between art and science.

—Mason Klein

SONDERBORG, K.R.H.

Nationality: Danish. **Born:** Karl Richard Horst Hofmann in Sonderborg, 5 April 1923; later adopted the name ''Sonderborg.'' **Education:** Studied painting, under Ewald Becker-Carus, in Hamburg, 1946, and at the Landeskunstschule, Hamburg, 1947–49; studied printmaking under S. W. Hayter at Atelier 17, Paris, 1953. **Career:** Imprisoned by the Gestapo, Hamburg-Fuhlsbuttel, 1941–42; escaped, working as a salesman for an export company, Hamburg, 1942–45; full-time artist since 1949, in Hamburg, subsequently in New York and Copenhagen; member, ''Zen 49'' artists group, 1953. **Awards:** Lichtwark Preis, Hamburg, 1955; Karl-Ernst-Osthaus Preis, Hagen, West Germany, 1955. **Agent:** Galerie Karl Flinker, 25 rue de Tournon, 75006 Paris, France. **Address:** Kongens Nytorv 1, 1050 Copenhagen, Denmark.

Individual Exhibitions:

1956 Kestner-Gesellschaft, Hannover
Galleri Samlaren, Stockholm
1957 Kunstverein, Cologne
Galerie Springer, West Berlin
Galerie René Drouin, Paris
Galerie Van de Loo, Munich
1959 *Neue Bilder,* Galerie Van de Loo, Essen
1960 *Peintures, Dessins,* Galerie Karl Flinker, Paris
1961 Lefebre Gallery, New York
1962 Galerie Handschin, Basel
Galerie Schmela, Dusseldorf
Kunstverein, Freiburg
Galerie Müller, Stuttgart
Galerie Karl Flinker, Paris
1963 Galleri Blanche, Stockholm
1964 Tokyo Gallery
1965 Galerie Karl Flinker, Paris
Lefebre Gallery, New York
Gemalde, Zeichnungen, Kunstverein, Cologne
Stedelijk Museum, Amsterdam
Schilderijen, Tekeningen, Stedelijk Van Abbemuseum, Eindhoven, Netherlands
Tuschen, Gimpel und Hanover Galerie, Zurich
First British Exhibition, Stone Gallery, Newcastle upon Tyne
1966 Louisiana Museum, Humlebaek, Denmark
Galleria Stendhal, Milan
Hammerlunds Kunsthandel, Oslo
1967 Guggenheim Museum, New York
Carnegie Institute, Pittsburgh
1968 Galerie de France, Paris
Galerie Daniel Gervis, Paris
Manus-Presse, Stuttgart
1971 Galerie Daniel Gervis, Paris
1976 Galerie Daniel Gervis, Paris
1978 Kunstverein, Sonderborg, Denmark
1979 Galerie im Haus Behr, Stuttgart
Galerie am Markt, Schwabisch Hall, West Germamy
1983 Galerie Hubert Winter, Vienna
1985 Kunstverein, Augsburg, West Germany
Galerie Nothhelfer, West Berlin
XPO Galerie, Hamburg
Staatsgalerie, Stuttgart
1986 Graphische Sammlung, Stuttgart
1988 Galerie der Stadt, Stuttgart (catalog)
1991 Galerie Georg Nothelfer, Berlin (catalog)
1993 Staatliche Kunsthalle, Dusseldorf (catalog)
Phänotypen: 55 Tuschzeichnungen, Galerie Rolf Ohse, Bremen (catalog)
Staatliche Kunsthalle Baden-Baden, Dusseldorf (catalog)
Württembergischer Kunstverein, Stuttgart (catalog)
1997 Galerie Winkelmann, Dusseldorf

Selected Group Exhibitions:

1952 *Zen 49,* Galerie Bohler, Munich
1954 *Art after 1945,* Stedelijk Museum, Amsterdam
1958 *Biennale,* Venice
1959 *Documenta,* Kassel, West Germany
1960 *Guggenheim International,* Guggenheim Museum, New York
1963 *Bienal,* Sao Paulo
1965 *Painting without a Brush,* Institute of Contemporary Art, Boston
1973 *Kunst im Deutschland 1898–1973,* Kunsthalle, Hamburg (travelled) to the Stadtische Galerie im Lenbachhaus, Munich)
1981 *Westkunst,* Messehallen, Cologne
1983 *Informel 1953–83,* Kunstverein, Lingen, West Germany
1993 *Akademie 1993,* Akademie der Künste, Berlin (catalog)

1997 *Taut: The Diagonal as a Pictorial Structure—A Survey of 500 Years of Art on Paper,* Staatsgalerie Stuttgart, Germany (catalog)

Collections:

Kunsthalle, Hamburg, Nationalgalerie, West Berlin, Wallraf-Richartz Museum, Cologne; Stedelijk Van Abbemuseum, Eindhoven, Netherlands; Louisiana Museum, Humlebaek, Denmark; Guggenheim Museum, New York.

Publications:

By SONDERBORG: Articles—interview in *ART: Das Kunstmagazin,* no. 3, March 1990.

On SONDERBORG: Books—*Sonderborg: Neue Bilder,* exhibition catalog with text by Carl Laszlo, Essen 1959; *Sonderborg: Peintures, Dessins,* exhibition catalog with text by Will Grohman, Paris 1960; *Sonderborg,* exhibition catalog with text by Annette Michelson, Paris 1962; *K. R. H. Sonderborg: VII Bienal de Sao Paulo 1963,* exhibition catalog with text by Werner Schmalenbach, Dusseldorf 1963; *Sonderborg,* exhibition catalog with text by Otto Hahn, New York 1965; K. R. H. *Sonderborg: Gemalde, Zeichnungen,* exhibition catalog with text by Werner Haftmann, Cologne 1965; *Sonderborg: Schilderijen, Tekeningen,* exhibition catalog, with text by Werner Haftmann, Eindhoven, Netherlands 1965; *K. R. H. Sonderborg: First British Exhibition,* exhibition catalog with text by Friedrich Bayl, Otto Hahn and Thomas T. Ichinose, Newcastle upon Tyne 1965; *K. R. H. Sonderborg: Tuschen,* exhibition catalog, Zurich 1965; *K. R. H. Sonderborg,* exhibition catalog with text by Willem Sandberg, Paris 1968; *Kunst im Deutschland 1898–1973,* exhibition catalog with text by Werner Hofmann, Hamburg 1973; *K. R. H. Sonderborg: Arbeiten auf Papier,* exhibition catalog with text by Hans Platschek, Kurt Leonhard and others, Stuttgart 1985. **Articles—**''Die Schnelle Schwarze Spur'' by Stefan Raum in *Bildende Kunst,* vol. 38, no. 1, 1990; ''Schnell, Kontrolliert un ohne Reue'' by Peter M. Bode in *ART: Das Kunstmagazin,* no. 4, April 1991; ''K.R.H. Sonderborg: Jenseits der Malerei'' by Roland Bothner in *Pantheon,* vol. 50, 1992. **Videos—***K. R. H. Sonderborg* by Bill Rathje, 1997.

* * *

The earliest painting by K. R. H. Sonderborg—on a canvas given to him by his father when he was 15 years old—was destroyed in an air raid over Hamburg. It probably has little bearing upon the subsequent development of this Danish-born artist but it does imply that Sonderborg's talent even from the start had a habit of cropping up in a variety of unlikely addresses. In a relatively short time he was able to install himself and his art in Cornwall, the Hebrides, Orkneys, Shetlands, Scotland, Paris and the United States. Perhaps something of this hither and thither existence is reflected in his pictures. They certainly have a staccato beat, a rhythm not unlike the clatter of a typewriter under the fingers of a fastmoving stenographer.

Sonderborg's nearest parallel in contemporary art is Erwin Bechthold, but even here there is no more than a superficial resemblance. Their approach is different. Only the end result shows some degree of kinship.

Three clues point to the sources of inspiration in Sonderborg's pictures—especially since his time in the United States. First there is his absorption in machinery and its operation. Then there is his handcamera pressed into service whenever he sees a detail or element of the contemporary world that he believes to be visually worth recording (parts of machinery and angle shots of the industrial and urban scenes). And finally there are the scraps, clippings and cutouts he can harvest from the media.

The salad he mixes out of all three is frequently the raw meat of his pictures, although all such ingredients undergo a Sonderborg change before they are finalised in pictorial form. Much of his work is basically black and white, but when colours are involved, these tend to cleave to the characteristics of a technical universe.

Not that they are always the portrait of technical imagery. It is just that the final Sonderborg transformation makes them appear so. A specific example of the stages through which this alchemic process can go is provided by four pictures based upon a newsprint photo of President Kennedy's golf kit. The first of these was painted in 1962, but execution of the entire series continued over four years. To give some idea of a Sonderborg synthesis it should be mentioned that in the second picture the JFK golf bag somehow became involved in and absorbed by the control room of Karlsruhe's atomic energy plant.

Sonderborg is an inspired collector. He has gathered together many of the simplest mechanical statements—a metal coil, a spark, a cog—and set them up in contrast with some of the most complex contemporary mechanisms.

—Sheldon Williams

SONFIST, Alan

Nationality: American. **Born:** New York, 26 May 1946. **Education:** Art Students League, New York, 1963; studied painting and art education, Western Illinois University, Macomb, 1961–67, B.A. 1967; also studied at the Pratt Institute, New York, summers 1965, 1966, Ohio State University, Columbus, 1967–68, and painting and sculpture at Hunter College, New York, 1968–69, M.F.A. 1969. **Career:** Independent artist, since 1970. Instructor at numerous universities and colleges, throughout the United States, since 1967. **Awards:** Graham Foundation grants, 1971, 1972; Chase Manhattan Foundation for Environmental and Fine Arts Grant, 1975; National Endownment for the Arts grant, 1975, 1978, 1979, 1981; Creative Artists Public Service Grant, New York, 1977; United States Information Service Grant, to Paris, 1977; Con Edison Foundation Grant, New York, 1978; Citibank Foundation Grant, New York, 1978; Australian Arts Council Travel Grant, 1981; New Zealand Travel Grant, 1984; N.Y. State Creative Communications Award, 1991. **Address:** 205 Mulberry Street, New York, New York 10012, U.S.A.

Individual Exhibitions:

1970 Reese Palley Gallery, New York
The Nature of Things, Harcus-Krakow Gallery, Boston
Star Chartings and Others, Deson-Zaks Gallery, Chicago
Outdoor Crystal Sculpture, Finch College Museum of Art, New York
Diagramma, Milan

1972 Institute of Centemporary Arts, London
Army Ants: Patterns and Structures, Automation House, New York

Sonfist Art, Akron Institute, Ohio
Lanscapes, Paley and Lowe Gallery, New York
1974 Carl Solway Gallery, Cincinnati, Ohio
Galerie Thelen, Cologne
1975 *Running Dead Animal,* Stefanotty Gallery, New York
Time-Landscape, Finch College Museum of Art, New York
Autobiography of Alan Sonfist, Herbert F. Johnson Museum of Art, Cornell University, Ithaca, New York
Autobiography of an Abandoned Animal Hole, Adiene Gallery, New York
1976 *Autobiography of Hemlock Forest,* Galerie Massimo Valsecchi, Milan
Galleria Cavallino, Venice
Adiene Gallery, New York
Autobiography of Time Landscape, 112 Greene Street Workshop, New York
Autobiography of Time Lanscape, Centre Cultural Americain, Paris
1977 Carl Solway Gallery, Cincinnati, Ohio
Neue Galerie Sammlung Ludwig, Aachen, West Germany
Light Gallery, New York
Musuem of Fine Arts, Boston
Galerie Bama, Paris
1978 *Public Monuments,* Neuberger Museum, Purchase, New York
Leo Castelli Gallery, New York
National Collection of Fine Arts, Smithsonian Institution, Washington, D.C.
1979 Multiples Gallery, New York
Monument to Atlanta, High Museum of Art, Atlanta
State University of New York, Stony Brook
1980 Albright-Knox Art Gallery, Buffalo, New York
1981 J. B. Speed Art Museum, Louisville, Kentucky
National Gallery of Art, Melbourne, Victoria
Marion Goodman Gallery, New York
1982 Carl Solway Gallery, Cincinnati
Lowe Art Museum, Coral Gables, Florida
1984 Corcoran Gallery of Art, Washington D.C.
Galleria del Cavallino, Venice
1986 Diane Brown Gallery, New York
Nelson-Atkins Museum, Kansas City, Missouri
1988 University of Southampton Art Gallery, Southampton, New York
World's Fair, Osaka, Japan
1989 Arsenal Gallery of Art, Los Angeles
Art League, Indianapolis
Ann Norton Sculpture Gardens, West Palm Beach, Florida
1990 Max Protech Gallery, New York
Fresno Art Museum, California
Eiteljorg Museum, Indianapolis
Whitney Museum of American Art, New York
1991 *Green,* Max Protech Gallery, New York (retrospective)
Atlantic Center for the Arts, New Smyrna Beach, Florida
1992 Doris Freeman Plaza, New York
EPAD, Paris
Transit Museum, Brooklyn
1993 *Landscapes,* Galerie Voight, Munich
1994 *Landscape,* Nancy Drysdale Art Gallery, Washington, D.C.
Retrospective, University of Iowa Art Museum (retrospective)
1995 *Natural/Cultural Landscapes,* Tampa Art Museum, Tampa, Florida
Pori Art Museum, Finland
1996 *Retrospective,* University of Iowa Art Museum, Iowa City
1997 *Photo Collage Exhibition,* America First Foundation, Chicago
1998 *Drawing Exhibition,* Earth Foundation, New York
2000 *Natural/Cultural Photo Collages,* Goethe House, New York
Traveling Exhibition of Drawings, Collages, and Sculptures, Earth Foundation

Selected Group Exhibitions:

1969 *Invisible Image,* School of Visual Arts, New York
1971 *The Nature of Things,* Harcus-Krakow Gallery, Boston
1975 *Biennale,* Paris
1977 *Documenta,* Kassel, West Germany
1979 *Views of America,* Museum of Modern Art, New York
1981 *Natur-Skulptur,* Kunstverein, Stuttgart
1985 *The Artist as Social Designer,* Los Angeles County Museum of Art
1989 *Nature as Art,* Kunstakademie, Berlin
1992 *Breakdown!,* Rose Art Museum, Brandeis University, Waltham, Massachusetts
Strata, Tampereen, Taidemuseo, Tampere, Finland
1993 *Internatioanl Environmental Art Exhibition,* La Defense Art Gallery, Paris
Traveling Smithsonian Exhibition, Bellevue Art Museum, Washington
1994 *Differentes Natures,* Museum of Modern Art, Paris (travelled to Prado Museum, Madrid)
Creative Solutions to Ecological Issues, Dallas Museum of Natural History
1996 *Trilogi: Kunst, Natur, Vindeskab,* Kunsthallen Brandts, Klaedefabrik, Denmark

Collections:

Museum of Modern Art, New York, Everson Museum, Syracuse, New York; Museum of Fine Arts, Boston; Akron Art Institute, Ohio; Allen Museum of Fine Arts, Oberlin College, Ohio; Museum of Contemporary Art, Chicago; High Museum, Atlanta; Museum of Fine Art, Dallas; Wallraf-Richartz Museum, Cologne; Power Institute of Fine Arts, Sydney; Brooklyn Museum; Museum of Modern Art, Los Angeles; Siri-Johnson Foundation, Jamaica; Westherspoon Gallery, University of North Carolina; Albright-Knox Art Gallery, Buffalo, New York; J B Spped Museum, Louisville, Kentucky.

Permanent Public Installations:

Earth Column, Greenvale, New York; *Geological Time Line,* Duisberg, Germany; *Narrative Mural,* Merrick, New York; *Narrative Historical Mural,* Belmore, New York; *Four Seasons* sculpture, Temple University, Pennsylvania; *Narrative Landscape,* Liberty Park Museum, New Jersey; *5 Time Enclosures with Forest Seeds,* Boca Raton, Florida; *Time Landscape,* Greenwich Village, New York; *Time Landscape,* Redhook, New York; *Hemlock Forest,* Bronx, New

York; *Towers of Growth,* Louisville, Kentucky; *Sun Monument,* Kingston, Rhode Island; *Earth Wall,* Buffalo, New York; *Rock Monument of Buffalo,* Buffalo, New York; *100-Foot Column of Earth,* Morgan City, Louisiana; *Circle of Life,* Kansas City, Missouri; *A Forest and a Mural,* Morris Heights, New York; *Rising Earth Washington Monument,* Washington, D.C., *Ten Acre Project,* Wave Hill, New York; *Narrative/Cultural Landscape* (Curtis Hixon Park), Tampa, Florida; *Narrative/Cultural Landscape,* Pori, Finland; *Narrative/Cultural Landscape,* Luxembourg.

Publications:

By SONFIST: Books—*Art in the Land,* New York 1983. **Articles—**''Oaks and Catbirds'' in *The New York Times,* 18 July 1989; interview with Joseph R. Wolin in *New Observations,* no. 81, January-February 1991; interview with Anne Barclay Morgan in *Art Papers,* vol. 15, no. 6, November-December 1991; ''The First 90 Years'' in *ARTnews,* November 1992; ''Maze of the Great Oak of Denmark Within Stone Ship: 1001 Young Trees'' in *Art & Design,* vol. 9, May/June 1994. **Videotapes—***Tiger-Chance-Kill,* 1976; *Nature's Time, Artificial Time,* 1976.

On SONFIST: Books—*Science and Technology in Art Today* by Jonathan Benthall, New York 1972; *Art and the Future* by Douglas Davis, New York 1973; *Autobiography of Alan Sonfist,* exhibition catalog by Lawrence Alloway, Ithaca, New York 1975; *Unbuilt America,* edited by Carson and Sky, New York 1976; *The American Land* by Joshua C. Taylor New York 1979; *Art of the Seventies* by Edward Lucie Smith, London 1980; *Overlay* by Lucy Lippard, New York 1983; *Artforms: An Introduction to the Visual Arts* by Duane and Sarah Preble, New York 1985; *Fragile Ecologies* by Barbara Matilsky, New York 1992; *Alan Sonfist: History of the Landscape,* exhibition catalog, Iowa City 1997. **Articles—**''Alan Sonfist's Slice of Life'' by Jerry Saltz in *Arts Magazine,* vol. 63, no. 9, May 1989; ''Site: Alan Sonfist'' by Anne Barclay Morgan in *Sculpture* (Washington, D.C.), vol. 15, no. 4, April 1996; ''Alan Sonfist'' in *Kunstforum International,* no. 146, July-August 1999.

*

My body is my museum; it's my history. It collects and absorbs observation-interactions. It is the deciphering of these recordings that I project into the outside world. My boundaries define the world of Art. I clarify my own common boundaries in relationship to the outside whether it be the room I exist in, the country I exist, in the country I exist in, the universe I exist in. By adding other awareness, I am constantly redefining my boundaries and projecting these awarenesses into my art.

My work deals with the idea that the world is always in a state of flux. My art deals with the rhythm of the universe. The pieces are part of the rhythm. A plant grows in cycles—a man moves in cycles—my work tries to bring about awareness of these movements. My works are transitions—they provoke associations. One has to mediate with my work to gain understanding. It is not the beginning or the end that I am concerned with, but the energy that is given or received through communication with my art.

—Alan Sonfist

* * *

The links between nature and Alan Sonfist's art are varied and numerous. They include wet canvases in which mildew takes gradual possession of the linen surface and containers of micro-organisms, in which fungoid and bacterial growth generate changing displays. These are usually enclosed in sealed boxes, a form of containment extended into Plexiglas columns with crystalline structures reactive to light, heat, and the spectator's presence. To quote the artist: ''the growth of the work is characterized by patterns of indeterminacy, since a multiplicity of natural variables creates unforeseen occurrence.'' The technology involved and the neat craft should not obscure the fact that Sonfist's basic interest is in nature and not in the artifacts by which it is contained.

Another nature-based piece is the celebrated colony of army ants (1972) whose movements in search patterns for food revealed the graphic shape of a society. This notion recurs, in an extraordinary metamorphosis, in Sonfist's later work, ''Abandoned Animal Hole,'' a cast of the warren of tunnels built by muskrats. The cement, pushed a section at a time into the burrows, converts hidden space into solid form in a way that constitutes a monument to the morphology of branching structure. It is an undergroud ''tree.'' In these works Sonfist initiated processes and made them visible within a limited zone, such as a box, or a room, or a joined casting. In addition to the enactment of organic process he makes works that consist of objects removed from the unbounded field of the world. Here he subtracts from an existing endless process rather than beginning new ones, as in ''Collection Bags,'' rows of soft containers for found objects. These consisted of things taken from the ground: twigs from the forest floor, for example, not parts broken off growing trees, a restraint that is characteristic of Sonfist's approach to nature. These finds are sometimes accompanied by texts:

> I could feel the lines on my skin. The cold wind passed. The twigs formed their own lines moving back and forth from the rock.

He has also expressed a great kinship with Asher B. Durand, the Hudson River School painter. What touched Sonfist, leading him to visit the site in Troy of one of Durand's paintings, was a letter of 1881:

> All the license that the artist can claim or desire is to choose the time and place were Nature displays her chief perfections, whether of beauty or majesty, repose or action.

The interaction of artist and nature is the basis of Sonfist's interest in Durand. On sites similar to Durand's Sonfist collects small objects that are an equivalent of the plentitude of details in the landscape paintings of Durand.

In the works in which he uses material collected at the site Sonfist lovingly turns random samples into precious quotations. Nature is evoked as a limitless field, the found parts of which, the details, transported from the site by Sonfist are restructured in ways that suggest their solidification. On the contrary, the ''non-site,'' to use a term of Robert Smithson's, preserve a kind of serious nonchalance, as if the relics meant to much to change after the crucial acts of removal and storage. Placing the twigs, the stones, the feathers, is equivalent to preservation rather than to designing.

Sonfist's ability to reveal the forms of communities and processes and his participation in limitless nature have been recognized and well-discussed, but another aspect of his work is less familiar. To work with natural processes as media is of course to work in time, but the definition of time in his arts is not restricted to this sense. There is also time as it relates the artist himself to his work, which is the central theme of the exhibition *The Autobiography of Alan Sonfist.* To understand the implication of this it helps to know that in 1970 he wanted to call his first exhibition *Retrospective,* but the gallery objected. The reason for using the word, which usually refers to an exhibition that summarizes a working life by looking backwards, is that this show represented, to quote the artist, ''pieces of my past'' and was thus the projection into the present of experiences that preceded the exhibition.

The extension of Sonfist's work in time is a central fact of his esthetic. To the extent that any work of art survives, it is a projection of the past into what I shall call the unknown present. Sonfist is concerned with time beyond this and, in effect dissolves the possibility of dating art at all, or at least reduces dating to an arbitrary convention. He does not use dates to indicate the time of production, but to indicate sequence. All his works can be viewed as 1946 *et seq.;* ''my first experience was air.'' Sonfist considers that the materialization of a work of art, though obviously a crucial step if the work process is to be legible to others, has been over-emphasized. In his work he is ''bringing back images of my past'' and, therefore, ''each piece will have its autobiography.'' His art is authenticated by its place in a continuum that includes all phases of artist's life. Thus the act of dating has the effect of isolating art from the full range of genetic elements.

There is a sense in which genetic dating is applicable to all artists, on the principle of Whistler's incisive answer to the question of how long it took to do one of his paintings: ''all my life.'' There is more to it than this, however, because the content of Sonfist's art is oriented, to a remarkable extent, toward memory amd memories. Hence his anti-periodization protects his life as a continuum in which early experiences occur as survivals, reconstructions, and fantasies. Sonfist would not differentiate between these states: all are means to bind his experiences of life into unity. He writes: ''My body is my museum, it's my history,'' and as such it is subject to the same changes in time as his work. Sonfist's offer of his body after death to the Museum of Modern Art to be preserved in the collection is a logical extension of the fusion of the ideas of process and time. Supporting this view of the self as subject-matter is his temperamental inclination towards recollection, activated by surviving drawings, early diaries and scrap books, and what Sonfist calls ''vague experiences'' of growth and discovery as a child. Typically his tree pieces, which consist of flattened tracings of the trunks, were initiated by the rediscovery of a tree in the Bronx Park that he had climbed in childhood:

> The distances of my hand had changed and the surface of the tree had also. I can remember the feel—the smell—and the taste of the tree as I once had.

Art is not presumed to be complete when it is done: both the work's prior and subsequent history force us to a perpetual recontextualization. In the chronology of ''Running Dead Animal,'' for example, Sonfist proposes such events as ''1953: upon tightroping on on a waterfall I woke up in a hospital with my face bandaged'' and the period 1954–59 included monthly visits to the Museum of Natural History ''to observe the stuffed animals.'' ''1959: sat with an antelope in it's cage. 1961: my brother shot a bird and I cried.'' Some of these events are repeated in genetic chronology of other works, some not. Thus the concept of art as the product of potent cause is diffused over the life of the artist. The only analogy to this historical layering of the work becoming the form of the work that I can think of is Rene Char's *Arriere-Histoire de Poeme Pulverise,* in which annotations by the poet in a copy of book become a book added to the original. Char records his hesitation about regarding the manuscript notes on equal terms with the poems, but he is wrong to feel that it was necessary to defend the primacy of the poems. What we get from the notes is a relationship, a connection between poetry and what Char calls ''the awkward and untenable world that served in its making.'' ''Each poem is accompanied by its confidential marginalia, like a whispering stream.''

If we estimate Sonfist's art as beginning in 1946 we should not expect the chronologies to end with the production of them, in fact, the ''autobiographies'' that accompany each work must be revised, like the provenance of paintings, to bring them up to date. The work's meaning therefore is not something that emerges on its completion and exist thereafter in absolute form. On the contrary art demonstrates a principle of delayed coherence: it is a structure that can change and our knowledge of it changes also. Thus the ''autobiographies'' will gradually extend as they become a history of spectator-responses (interpretations) and itinerary (socially conditioned distribution) attached to the work. In the earlier pieces the presence of the spectator initiated physical changes in Sonfist's work (crystal formation, movement of a school of fish), changes that occured unpredictably but logically within the limits of the system prepared by the artist. The extension of the autobiography of the work in another way, drawing on our cognitive and social interaction with the artist via the work of art.

—Lawrence Alloway

SONNIER, Keith

Nationality: American. **Born:** Mamou, Louisiana, in 1941. **Education:** University of Southwestern Louisiana, Lafayette, 1959–63, B.A. 1963; travelled and studied in France, 1963–64; studied at Rutgers University, New Brunswick, New Jersey, 1965–66, M.F.A. 1966. **Career:** Full-time artist. Now lives and works in New York. **Awards:** Guggenheim fellowship, 1974; First Prize, *Tokyo Prints Biennale,* 1974; National Endowment for the Arts Grants, 1975, 1981. **Agent:** Leo Castelli Gallery, New York. **Address:** c/o Leo Castelli Gallery, 59 East 79th St., New York, New York 10021, U.S.A.

Individual Exhibitions:

1966 Douglas College, New Brunswick, New Jersey
1968 Galerie Ricke, Cologne
1970 Leo Castelli Gallery, New York
Ace Gallery, Los Angeles
Stedelijk Van Abbemuseum, Eindhoven, Netherlands
1971 *Projects,* Museum of Modern Art, New York
Galerie Ricke, Cologne
1972 Leo Castelli Gallery, New York
Galerie Ricke, Cologne
1974 *Radio Mix,* Leo Castelli Gallery, New York
Seder-Creigh Gallery, Coronado, California
1975 Leo Castelli Gallery, New York

Galerie Ricke, Cologne
Ace Gallery, Los Angeles
1976 *ABACA Code,* Leo Castelli Gallery, New York
ABACA Code, Hand Cast Paper Sculpture and Other Work 1969–76, Seder/Creigh Gallery, Coronado, California
1977 Ace Gallery, Los Angeles
1978 Leo Castelli Gallery, New York (drawings)
Castelli Graphics, New York (lithographs)
Galerie Ricke, Cologne
Simultaneous Regional Editions, Rosamund Felsen Gallery, Los Angeles
Porte-Voix Audio Installation, The Clocktower, New York
1979 *BA-O-BA SEL Series,* Museum Haus Lange, Krefeld, West Germany
Expanded SEL Series, Leo Castelli Gallery, New York
AM/FM Radio Installion, Galerie Michele Lachowsky, Brussels
Porte-Voix, Eric Fabre Gallery, Paris
Porte-Vue, Centre Georges Pompidou, Paris
1980 *Pictographs,* Tony Shafrazi Gallery, New York
Galerie France Morin, Montreal
1981 *Runic Series 1980,* Galerie Ricke, Cologne
Dom Basor Series: India 1981, David Bellman Gallery, Toronto
Michelle Lachowsky Gallery, Antwerp
Portland Center for the Visual Arts, Oregon
1982 *Rangoli: Aluminum Works Made in India 1981,* Rosamund Felsen Gallery, Los Angeles
Leo Castelli Gallery, New York
Galerie Eric Fabre, Paris
1983 Project Studio One, Long Island City, New York
1984 Galleria Schema, Florence (twice)
Carol Taylor Art, Dallas, Texas
Galerie Rolf Ricke, Cologne
Hara Museum of Contemporary Art, Tokyo (travelled to Nagoya and Osaka)
Leo Castelli Gallery, New York
Virginia Polytechnic Institute, Blacksburg
1985 Rosamund Felsen Gallery, Los Angeles
Susanna Hillberry Gallery, Birmingham, Michigan
Leo Castelli Gallery, New York
1986 Galerie Montenay Delsol, Paris
Tilden Foley Gallery, New Orleans
1987 Galerie Nature Morte, New York
Domaine de Kerguehennec, Rennes, France
Alexandria Museum of Art, Louisiana
1988 *Neon Sculpture,* Chrysler Museum, Norfolk, Virginia
1989 Hirshhorn Museum, Washington, D.C.
Hyde Gallery, Dublin
New Work, Leo Castelli Gallery, New York
Early Work, Barbara Gladstone Gallery, New York
Galerie Montenay, Paris
Galerie Ryszard Varisella, Frankfurt
Studio Claudio Guenzani, Milan
Galerie Jürgen Becker, Hamburg
1990 *Expanded File Series, 1969–89,* Städtisches Museum Abteiberg, Mönchengladbach, Germany
Halle Sud, Geneva
Antenna Series, Blum Helman Gallery, Los Angeles
Galleria Il Ponte, Rome
Liverpool Gallery, Brussels
1991 Galerie Schröder, Mönchengladbach, Germany
Galerie Rolf Ricke, Cologne
1992 Musée-Château d'Annecy, France
Leo Castelli Gallery, New York
Castelli Graphics, New York
65 Thompson, New York
Ilene Kurtz, New York
Gallery 360, Tokyo
1993 *Keith Sonnier, Werke/Works,* Sprengel Museum, Hannover, Germany (travelled to Kunsthalle, Nuremberg, Germany, and Kunstmuseum, St. Gallen, Switzerland)
Galerie Lallouz + Watterson, Montreal
Galerie Rolf Ricke, Cologne
1994 *Keith Sonnier: Multiples and Wall Reliefs*, Betsy Senior Gallery, New York
1995 *Drawings: 30 Years—1964–1994*, Marguerite Oestreicher Fine Arts, New Orleans
1996 *Cat Doucet Series*, Galerie Malka Lallouz, Los Angeles
1997 *Alternating Currents*, Leo Castelli Gallery, New York
Channel Mix, Nicole Klagsbrun Gallery, New York
1999 *Keith Sonnier: Sculpture 1966–1998,* Marlborough Gallery, New York
Keith Sonnier: New Neon, Aktionsforum Praterinsel, Munich
Keith Sonnier: The Blatt Series, Kulturmanagement Häusler, Munich
Keith Sonnier Ba-O-Ba 1977; Blatt 1999, Galerie Evelyne Canus, Colle sur Loup, France
Keith Sonnier: Environmental Works 1968–1999, Kunsthaus Bregenz, Bregenz, Austria
2000 *Keith Sonnier: New Work 2000,* Marlborough Gallery, New York
Keith Sonnier: La Lumiere, Zumtobel Staff Lichtzentrum, Zurich

Selected Group Exhibitions:

1970 *Information,* Museum of Modern Art, New York
1975 *Sculpture: American Directions 1945–1975,* National Collection of Fine Arts, Smithsonian Institution, Washington, D.C.
1978 *20th Century American Drawings: 5 Years of Acquisitions,* Whitney Museum, New York
1982 *Americanische Zeichnungen der 70er Jahre,* Städtische Galerie, Munich
1986 *Temporary Contemporary,* Museum of Contemporary Art, Los Angeles
1989 *Three Sculptors,* Susanne Hilberry Gallery, Birmingham, Michigan
1990 *The New Sculpture 1965–1975: Between Geometry and Gesture,* Whitney Museum of American Art, New York
1993 *Gravity and Grace: The Changing Condition of Sculpture 1965–1975,* Hayward Gallery, London
1994 Jablonka Galerie, Cologne
1995 *1995 Yamantaka Donation: An Exhibition to Benefit Tibet House,* Gagosian Gallery, New York

Traditions of Innovation: Touchstones from Graphicstudio and Limestone Press/Hine Editions, The Boca Raton Museum of Art, Boca Raton, Florida

1996 *15 Degrees from Rutgers*, Mason Gross School of the Arts Galleries, State University of New Jersey
Collage, Leo Castelli Gallery, New York
Chimeriques Polymeres: Le plastique dans l'Art contemporain, Musée d'Art Moderne et d'Art Contemporain de la Ville de Nice
Werkstatt Kollerschlag, Kunstbunker Tumulka, Munich
From Figure to Object. A Century of Sculptors' Drawings, Karsten Schubert Gallery, Londo

1997 *Le voyage extraordinaire,* Musée d'Art Contemporain de Lyon, France
Selections from the Video Collection, Museum of Modern Art, New York
AMFM Radio Mix, Genesta, London
Galerie Jürgen Becker, Hamburg, Germany.

1999 *Afterimage:Film and Video Program*, Museum of Contemporary Art, Los Angeles
The American Century: Art & Culture 1950–2000, Whitney Museum of American Art, New York
Drawings from the 1960s, Curt Marcus Gallery, New York
La nature imite l'art, Espace de l'Art Concret, Château de Mouans-Sartoux, Côte d'Azur, France

2000 *Modell, Modell,* Neuer Aachener Kunstverein, Aachen, Germany
Monte-Carlo International Sculpture Festival: Contemporary American Sculpture. Monaco
Curt Marcus Gallery, New York
Cotthem Gallery, Knokke-Zoute, Belgium.

Collections:

Museum of Modern Art, New York; Whitney Museum, New York; Museum of Contemporary Art, Los Angeles; Musée d'Art Contemporain, Montreal; Musée-Chateau d'Annecy, France; Kunsthalle, Nuremberg; The Hara Museum of Contemporary Art, Tokyo; Kunstmuseum, St. Gallen, Switzerland.

Permanent Public Installations:

Joseph E. Seagram & Sons Inc., New York; New Jersey Department of Transportation, Trenton; NOPSI streetcar stop, New Orleans; New International Airport, Munich; Lycée Dorian, Paris; Station Joffre-Mutualité, Rouen, France; Miami International Airport, Miami, Florida; Bureau of the Census, General Services Administration, Maryland; Ronald Reagan Building and International Trade Center, Pennsylvania Avenue, Washington, D.C.

Publications:

By SONNIER: Books—*Object—Situation—Object 1969–70,* Cologne 1972. **Articles—**''Keith Sonnier,'' interview with Liza Bear, in *Avalanche* (New York), May/June 1974; ''An Interview with Keith Sonnier,'' with Calvin Harlan, in *Parachute,* (Montreal), Spring 1977; ''Keith Sonnier Interview,'' with Craig Gohlson, in *Interview* (New York), November 1977; ''Interview with Keith Sonnier,'' with Bernard Lamarche-Vadel, in *Artiste* (Paris), October/November 1979; ''I Believe in Architecture. . . . '', interview with Carlos Brillembourg in *Bomb*, no. 46, Winter 1994; interview in *Keith Sonnier: Sculpture 1966–98,* exhibition catalog, New York 1999; interview in *Behind the Green Door*, exhibition catalog, New York 2000; ''Interview with Keith Sonnier'' in *NY Arts Magazine*, Vol. 5, no. 2, February 2000. **Films—***Untitled,* 1969; *Untitled II,* 1969; *Negative-Positive,* 1970; *Rub Down,* 1970; *Untitled III,* 1970; *Painting Foot,* 1970.

On SONNIER: Books—*Documenta 5,* exhibition catalog by Harald Szeeman, Jean-Christophe Ammann and others, Kassel 1972; *Some Recent American Art,* exhibition catalog by Jennifer Licth, New Haven 1973; *Keith Sonnier; Argon-und-Neon-Arbeiten,* exhibition catalog, Krefeld 1979; *Keith Sonnier: Runic Series 1980,* exhibition catalog, Cologne 1981; *Keith Sonnier,* exhibition catalog by Alanna Heiss, Long Island City 1983; *Keith Sonnier: The Illuminati,* exhibition catalog by Glenn O'Brien, New York 1992; *Keith Sonnier: Werke/Works,* exhibition catalog by Dietmar Elger and Lucius Grisebach, Stuttgart 1993; *Oriental/Occidental: Keith Sonnier's Tokobashira and Mata Hari Series,* exhibition catalog by Donald Kuspit, New York 1996; *It's All About Sex: Keith Sonnier Then and Now,* exhibition catalog by Linda Yablonsky, New York 1999; *New Media in Late 20th Century Art* by Michael Rush, London 1999; *After Modern Sculpture: Art in the United States and Europe 1965–70* by Richard J. Williams, Manchester, England 2000; **Articles—**''Eccentric Abstraction'' by David Antin in *Artforum* (New York), November 1966; ''On Erotic Art'' by Lucy Lippard in *Hudson Review* (New York), Spring 1967; ''Primary Energy and the Microemotive Artists'' by Piero Gilardi in *Arts Magazine* (New York), September 1968; ''New York: Moving Out'' by Ralph Pomeroy in *Art and Artists* (London), January 1969; ''Le neon dans l'art contemporain'' by Beatrice Parent in *L'Art Vivant* (Paris), May 1971; review in *Flash Art* (Milan), December 1971; ''Keith Sonnier: Video and Film as Color Field'' by Robert Pincus-Witten in *Artforum* (New York), May 1972; ''Keith Sonnier'' by Jon Meyer in *Arts Magazine* (New York), September 1982; ''Keith Sonnier at Nature Morte'' by Stephen Ellis in *Art in America* (New York), June 1987; ''Born on the Bayou'' by Ellen Lampert-Greaux in *Lighting Dimensions*, January/February 1995; ''Keith Sonnier: Drawings a Peek into the Sculptor's Mind'' by Chris Waddington in *Lagnaippe,* 2 June 1995; ''Keith Sonnier'' by Betsy Sussler in *Bomb,* Spring 1997; ''Powering Up'' by Linda Yablonsky in *Art in America,* March 1998.

* * *

A study of Keith Sonnier's 1982 sculpture *Aesthesipol* resurrects the themes and concerns of his career. The word itself seems on the verge of signifying something, though it never quite resolves in specific meaning—for the artist invented it. *Aesthesipol* provides a summary of Sonnier's work: sculpture aimed at the process of language making. His primary concern, like that of many graffiti artists, is of inventing new ways to propel writing (and the meaning of writing) into vision. His favoured medium: technology. *Aesthesipol* is exemplary, a rambling glyph of extruded aluminium with a working pay phone attached to one of its three vertical members and a portable television attached to another. The sculpture assails the viewer with interacting and interchangeable waves of the aural, the visual, and the tactile. This type of pictured, rather than merely phonetic writing, is symptomatic in his work, and suggests a return to and reinvention of the moment when picturing and writing were one.

Pictured writing is grounded in touch, and establishing space and place for his sense of touch became Sonnier's first goal when he arrived in New York in 1966. His previous endeavours were limited by the isolating experiences in rural Louisiana, where he lived in the unassimilated French community of the Cajuns until early adulthood. His early works stressed perfect symmetry and order. After studying in France for a year in 1963 he moved to New York where he abandoned the conventional techniques of figurative painting of his student days in favour of a direct manipulation and exploration of a variety of materials ranging from satin to satellite.

From 1967 to 1969 Sonnier's work became a revelation—and invitation—to the pleasures of touch. Shreds of flesh-toned silk and satin, frequently combined with pleated dacron screening, drape and drip off the wall and floor in soft sublimations of lingerie experience. He applies planes of latex to the wall which he either peels up and leaves hanging or peels down, attaching it to the floor with strings. The effect of the different planes comments on the nature of touch.

In 1969 neon became Sonnier's primary medium. His first neon pieces are configured in gestural loops and curls that look like semi-conscious writing of doodles. He wraps neon around neon or incandescent light bulbs in a loose mirrored symmetry that creates the illusion of light reflecting itself. In these sculptures the light itself becomes the architecture. The gaseous flush of the neon thereafter thickens the surrounding atmosphere to the edge of tangibility.

The performance nature of much of Sonnier's work, his interest in dance, and his attraction to tactile light coupled with the new availability and portability of video hardware made television the next logical medium for him. During the 1970s he introduced video tapes into his work. Like the neons, the tapes represented a distanced restraint that let the medium play with and against itself. In 1971 Sonnier isolated sound. *New Delhi Sound Piece* consisted of two speakers, one with a microphone attached to it causing feedback, another amplifying the sounds of passers-by. These three new mediums incorporated the notion of feedback in Sonnier's subsequent work.

From 1977 to 1979 he intensified his pursuit of public communications. His efforts were almost solely devoted to researching and commandeering a satellite system, which resulted in his piece *Send-Receive* in 1979, a complex visual and verbal dialogue and feedback made possible by satellite technology. The piece consisted of a group of artists and performers in a San Francisco studio making a simultaneous exchange with a corresponding group in New York. San Francisco to New York, New York to San Francisco, dancer to dancer, musician to musician, speaker to speaker—layers of duets of visual and verbal cues, commands, and feedback mixed in material metaphor.

Sonnier, as much a writer as a sculptor, is in constant search of new mediums and new meanings. His pictured language, which thrives on technology, dares to expand past artistic conventions. His art speaks for itself; Sonnier's innovations of the 1980s have continued to open new channels of communication.

—Carrie Baker

SORGE, Peter

Nationality: German. **Born:** Berlin, 14 April 1937. **Education:** Educated in Mecklenburg, 1941–50, and in Dortmund, 1950–58; studied art-teaching at the Hochschule für Bildende Künste, West Berlin, 1958–64; studied painting, under Fred Thieler and Mac Zimmerman, in West Berlin, 1964–65. **Family:** Married Maina-Miriam Munsky in 1970 (died 1999); son: Daniel. **Career:** Independent ''realist'' painter, West Berlin, since 1964: co-founder, Ausstellungsgemeinschaft ''Grossgorschen 35,'' West Berlin, 1964–69; Zehn Neun art association, 1969; and Aspekt artists' group, 1972. **Awards:** Second Burda-Preis, for graphics, Munich, 1968; Graphik-Preis der Stadt Wolfsburg, West Germany, 1969. **Agent:** Galerie Poll, Lutzowplatz 7, 1000 Berlin 30. **Died:** Berlin, Germany, 17 January 2000.

Individual Exhibitions:

1965 Grossgorschen 35, West Berlin
Galerie fur Grafikfreunde, Frankfurt
Galerie Falazik, Bochum, West Germany
1966 Galerie Tobies und Silex, Cologne
Grossgorschen 35, West Berlin
1967 Galerie Ketterer, Kiel
1968 Galerie Klaus Groh, Oldenburg, West Germany
Galerie D. und R. Rothe, Wolfsburg, West Germany
Galerie Ostentor, Dortmund, West Germany
Galerie Poertner, Sennestadt, West Germany
Galerie Poll, West Berlin
1969 Galerie Schmucking, Braunschweig, West Germany
James-Bond-Oratorium, Akademie der Künste, West Berlin (with W. D. Siebert)
Galerie Klaus Groh, Oldenburg, West Germany
Diehl/Petrick/Sorge: Malerei, Graphik, Material, Haus am Waldsee, West Berlin (with Hans-Jürgen Diehl and Wolfgang Petrick; travelled to the Badischer Kunstverein, Karlsruhe)
1970 Kunstverein, Mannheim
Galerie Poll, West Germany
Galerie Kerlikowsky und Kneiding, Munich (with Hans-Jurgen Diehl and Wolfgang Petrick; toured Germany)
Galerie Ostentor, Dortmund, West Germany (with Munsky)
1971 Kunsthistorisches Institut, Groningen, Netherlands
Institut voor Industrielevoormgeving, Delft
Youth Center, Utrecht
Galerie de Tor, Amsterdam
Galerie Wentdorf und Swetec, Dusseldorf
Galerie im Espresso, Trier, West Germany
Galerie Kafseck, Paderborn, West Germany
Galerie Bauer und Pietschner, Bochum, West Germany
Kunstverein, Kassel, West Germany
1972 Kunstkreis, Gelsenkirchen, West Germany
Galerie Poll, West Berlin
Galleria Vinciana, Milan (with Hans-Jürgen Diehl and Wolfgang Petrick)
Galleria San Michele, Brescia, Italy (with Hans-Jürgen Diehl and Wolfgang Petrick)
1975 Kunsthalle, Nuremberg, West Germany
1976 Galerie Poll, West Berlin
1978 Galerie Art Moderna, Freiburg, West Germany
Goethe-Institut, Paris
1979 Galerie Zoellner, Bremen, West Germany
Galerie Poll, West Berlin
Kunstverein, Frechen, West Germany

1980 Kunstverein, Ludwigshafen, West Germany
1981 Galerie Peterson, Flensburg, West Germany
1982 Galerie im Judenturm, Coburg, West Germany
1984 Galerie Apex, Gottingen, West Germany
1985 Galerie Poll, West Berlin

Selected Group Exhibitions:

1961 *Junge Stadt sieht junge Kunst,* Städtische Museum, Wolfsburg, West Germany
1966 *Junge Berliner Kunstler,* Kunsthalle, Basel
1967 *Neue Realismus,* Haus am Waldsee, West Berlin
1968 *International Print Biennale,* City Museum and Art Gallery, Bradford, Yorkshire
1970 *Pop-Sammlung Beck,* Kunsthalle, Bonn (travelled to Darmstadt and Dortmund)
1971 *Biennale de Paris,* Parc Floral, Paris
1972 *Prinzip Realismus,* DAAD-Galerie, West Berlin
1978 *Funf Berliner Realisten,* Museum am Dom, Lubeck, West Germany
1980 *Berlin Realistisch 1890–1980,* Berlinische Galerie, West Berlin
1983 *Realistische Zeichnungen,* Nationalgalerie, West Berlin

Collections:

Kunstverein, Kassel, West Germany; Kunstverein, Mannheim; Berlinische Galerie, West Berlin; Nationalgalerie, West Berlin; Nationalgalerie/ Kupferstichkabinett, East Berlin; Institut fur Auslandsbeziehungen, Stuttgart; Herzog Anton Ulrich-Museum, Braunschweig; Stadtische Kunstsammlungen, Bonn; Kunstverein fur die Rheinlande und Westfalen, Dusseldorf.

Publications:

By SORGE: Books—*Zitate zur StVO,* Burgdorf, West Germany 1970; *Varspiele,* West Berlin 1972. **Articles—**interview with Frank Nicolaus and Maina-Miriam Munsky in *ART: Das Kunstmagazin,* no. 9, September 1986.

On SORGE: Books—*Diehl/Petrick/Sorge: Malerei, Graphik, Material,* exhibition catalog, West Berlin 1969; *Peter Sorge: Werkverzeichnis der Druckgraphik und Handzeichnungen 1963–70,* West Berlin 1972; *Deutsche Kunst der 60er Jahre: Malerie, Collage, Op-Art, Graphik* by Juliane Roh, Munich 1971; *Prinzip Realismus,* exhibition catalog, West Berlin 1972; *Westberliner Realisten* by G. Strathmann, West Berlin 1979; *Peter Sorge,* exhibition catalog with text by Lucius Grisebach, West Berlin 1985. **Articles—**''Künstlerpaare: 22 Kurzporträts'' in *Kunstforum International,* no. 106, March-April 1990.

* * *

The terrors of engagierter Kunst receive their fullest freedom at the hands of Peter Sorge. His devastating (the correct word in this instance) realist style makes the most savage political and sociological cartoon look anaemic by comparison. It is not so much his expert control of narrative art that makes his works compelling and outstanding as the acid sense of drama which he is able to inject into them. The girl the soldiers picked up was the romantic figure in the first frame, but after they had taken her apart she features in the second half of the diptych-print as a broken disposable. Her two comrades (assailants) may not look so engaging in chapter two, but they at least are not smashed up like their poor victim.

Sorge makes the gun mean. No pistol in his prints could be less than villainous. Sorge firearms are not instruments for protective use; they are not even elements of martial equipment, a part of uniform. They are extensions of cruelty that will be brought into play if brute force fails to achieve objectives.

It is difficult to believe that this Berlin artist was born in 1937. His technique and imagery suggest that he could either be much older (!), leaning back upon experience of a cruder past or at least reflecting or revivifying visions culled from the memoirs of a generation before—or, at the other extreme, he ought to be a ''young'' artist, gifted beyond his years, seeking to exhume the cruelties of a past era which he mercifully avoided.

The etchings and lithographs he makes of these nightmares are visually magnetic because of his inspired and accurate talent. His system of building up a graphic in compartments which often present a storyline need not always be the work pattern for horror, but it is significant that this artist will never sacrifice acid for saccharine. ''How to achieve work and lovelines,'' for instance, is divided into three sections: top left—the rippling torso of a muscle man; top right—a faucet out of which descends a flow of water (like a single frame from a carefully made movie); bottom half—the flanks of a man and a woman; he hesitant, she inclining her pelvis toward his hip . . . a joint gesture of natural naked affection, except the half-lemon he is holding behind his back injects an acrid note.

—Sheldon Williams

SOTO, Jesus Rafael

Nationality: Venezuelan. **Born:** Ciudad Bolivar, 1923. **Education:** Studied at the Academia de Bellas Artes, Caracas, 1942–47. **Family:** Married in 1952. **Career:** Painter; director, Maracaibo School of Fine Arts, Venezuela, 1947–50; has lived and worked in Paris since 1950; also a musician. **Awards:** Hatch Prize for Abstract Painting, Caracas, 1957; National Prize, Venezuela, 1960; Virgilio Cordo Prize, Caracas, 1960; Wolf Prize, *Bienal,* Sao Paulo, 1963; Premio David Bright, *Biennale,* Venice, 1964; First Prize, *Bienal America,* Cordova, Peru, 1964; Prize of the City of Cordova, 1964; First Prize, *Salon of Pan-American Painting,* Cali, Columbia, 1965; Medaglia d'Oro, Convegno Internazionale Studiosi d'Arte, Rimini, Italy, 1967; Picasso Medal, UNESCO, 1981, 1990; Gold Prize, Norsk International Graphic Biennial, 1982; Art Plastic Medal, Academy of Architecture, 1989; Grand Prix Nacional de la Sculpture, France, 1995; Orden del Liberatodor en grado de Gran Cordon, Venezuela, 1996. D.F.A.: Universidad de Los Andes, Merida, 1990; Universidad Nacional Experimental de Guayana, Venezuela, 1994. **Agent:** c/o Galleria del Naviglio, Via Manzoni 45, 20121 Milan, Italy. **Address:** Studio, 10 rue Villehardouin, 75003, Paris, France.

Individual Exhibitions:

1949 Atelier Libre de Arte, Caracas
1956 Galerie Denise René, Paris
1957 Galerie Aujourd'hui, Palais des Beaux-Arts, Brussels
Museum of Modern Art, Caracas

1959 Galerie Iris Clert, Paris
1961 Museum of Modern Art, Caracas
Galerie Rudolf Zwirner, Essen
Galerie Brusberg, Hannover
1962 Galerie ad Libitum, Antwerp
Galerie Edouard Loeb, Paris
1963 Museum Haus Lange, Krefeld, West Germany
1964 Galerie Muller, Stuttgart
1965 Galerie Edouard Loeb, Paris
Kootz Gallery, New York
Signals Gallery, London
1966 Galerie Schmela, Dusseldorf
Galleria del Naviglio, Milan
Galleria del Deposito, Genoa
Centre de l'Art Vivant, Trieste
Pfalzgalerie, Kaiserlautern, West Germany
1967 Galerie Denise René, Paris
1968 Galerie Françoise Mayer, Brussels
Kunsthalle, Berne
Stedelijk Museum, Amsterdam
Marlborough Galleria d'Arte, Rome
1969 Palais des Beaux-Arts, Brussels
Galleria Lorenzelli, Bergamo, Italy
Galleria Notizie, Turin
Galleria del Naviglio, Milan
Galleria Flori, Florence
Galleria Giraldi, Livomo
Galeria Estudio Actual, Caracas
Musée d'Art Moderne de la Ville, Paris
Svensk-Franska Kunstgalleriet, Stockholm
1970 Galerie Denise René, Paris
Galerie Godart Lefort, Montreal
Galerie Suvremene, Zagreb
Galleria de la Nova Loggia, Bologna
Galerie Semiha Huber, Zurich
Kunstverein, Mannheim
Marlborough Gallery, New York
Galerie Buchholz, Munich
Ulm Museum, West Germany
1971 Museum of Contemporary Art, Chicago
Galleria Rotta, Milan
Martha Jackson Gallery, New York
Galerie Denise Reneé-Hans Meyer, Dusseldorf
Kunstverein, Kaiserlautern, West Germany
Museo de Bellas Artes, Caracas
1972 Galerie Pauli, Lausanne, Switzerland
Galerie Beyeler, Basel
Galleria Levi, Milan
Museo de Arte Moderno, Bogota
1973 Galeria Tempora Calle, Bogota
Galleria Corsini, Rome
Universidad Central de Venezuela, Caracas
Estudio Dos, Valencia, Venezuela
Arte Contacto, Caracas
Galleria Godel, Rome
1974 Guggenheim Museum, New York (retrospective)
Denise René Gallery, New York
1975 Denise René Gallery, New York
1979 Museo de Arte Contemporaneo, Caracas
Centre Georges Pompidou, Paris
1981 Galeria Tempora Calle, Bogota
Galeria Theo, Madrid
Sala Celini, Madrid
1983 Museo de Arte de Caracas, Venzuela
1988 *Soto,* Elisabeth Franck Gallery, Knokke-le-Zoute, Belgium (catalog)
1990 *Soto,* Galerie Sapone, Nice (catalog)
1991 *Soto: Opere Recenti,* Galleria Arte 92, Milan (catalog)
1992 *Jesus Rafael Soto,* Centre d'Art Contemporain de l'Abbaye Saint-André, Meymac (retrospective) (catalog)
1993 *Jesús Rafael Soto: Retrospectiva,* Fundação de Seralves, Porto (catalog)
Jesús Soto, Museo de Bellas Artes, Caracas (also Museo de Arte Moderno Jesús Soto, Ciudad Bolivar) (catalog)
1997 *An Unending Quest,* Galerie Nationale du Jeu de Paume, Paris (traveling retrospective exhibition) (catalog)
Galerie Denise René, Paris
1999 *Soto Virtual,* Durban Segnini Gallery, Miami (traveling exhibition) (catalog)
Soto: La Poética de la Energía, Fundación Telefónica, Santiago (catalog)
2000 *Soto,* Fundación Corp Group Centro Cultural, Caracas (catalog)

Selected Group Exhibitions:

1943 *Annual Art Exhibition,* Caracas
1955 *Le Mouvement,* Galerie Denise René, Paris
1957 *Bienal,* Sao Paulo
1958 *World's Fair,* Brussels
Bienal, Sao Paulo
Biennale, Venice
1962 *Biennale,* Venice
1967 *International Exhibition,* Carnegie Institute, Pittsburgh
1969 *Middelheim Biennale,* Antwerp
1974 *Neuve Artistas Venezolanos,* Museo de Arte Contemporaneo, Caracas
1988 *Bienal de San Juan del Grabado Latinoamericano y del Caribe,* San Juan, Puerto Rico (catalog)
1992 *Art of Latin America 1911–1970,* Centre Georges Pompidou, Paris
1996 *XXIII Biennial of São Paulo,* Brazil (catalog)
Les Champs de la Sculpture, Champs-Elysées, Paris
1997 *50 Years of Creation in France,* Centre Georges Pompidou, Paris
1999 *Modernity,* Centre Georges Pompidou, Paris

Collections:

Cali Institute of Fine Arts, Colombia; University City, Caracas; Albright-Knox Art Gallery, Buffalo, New York; Stedelijk Museum, Amsterdam; Palais des Beaux-Arts, Brussels; Centre Georges Pompidou, Paris; Kunsthaus, Zurich; Moderna Museet, Stockholm; Louisiana Museum, Humlebaek, Denmark; National Gallery of Victoria, Melbourne; Museum de Sculpture en Plein Air, Middelheim, Belgium; Galleria Nazionale d'Arte Moderna e Contemporanea di Roma, Italy; Rijksmuseum Kroller-Muller, Otterlo, Holland; Boymans-van Beuningen, Rotterdam, Holland; Musée d'Art Contemporain de Montreal; Ho-Am Art Museum, Seoul, Korea; National Museum of Contemporary Art, Seoul; Hara Museum of Contemporary Art,

Tokyo; Nacional de Bellas Artes, Buenos Aires; Tate Gallery, London; Nacional Centro de Arte Reina Sofia, Madrid; Kunstmuseum, Berne, Switzerland; Tel Aviv Museum; Museo Rufino Tamayo, Mexico City.

Publications:

By SOTO: Books—*No Tengo Prisa: Conversaciones con Jesús Soto,* with Alberto Garrido, Mérida, Venezuela 1989; *Soto,* with Gérard-Georges Lemaire, Paris 1997. **Article—**''Dialogue: Jesus Rafael Soto and Guy Brett'' in *Museumjournaal* (Amsterdam), February 1969; interview with Francine Birbragher in *Art Nexus,* no. 25, July-September 1997.

On SOTO: Books—*Soto,* exhibition catalog by Jean Clay, Paris 1969; *Soto,* exhibition catalog by Guy Brett, New York 1970; *Soto* by Alfredo Boulton, Caracas 1973; *Soto,* exhibition catalog, Caracas 1983; *Latin American Artists in Their Studios* by Marie-Pierre Colle, New York 1994. **Articles—**''J. R. Soto'' by Jean Clay in *Signals* (London), 1/10, 1965; ''Soto'' by Jean Clay in *Connaissance des Arts* (Paris), June 1969; ''Soto dans le Labyrinthe'' by Philippe Comte in *Opus International* (Paris), June 1969; ''Soto's X Penetrables'' by Jean Clay in *Studio International* (London), September 1969; ''Soto's Logic'' by Patrick d'Elme in *Cimaise* (Paris), May/August 1970; ''Soto'' by E. L. L. de Wilde in *Museumjournal* (Amsterdam), October 1973; ''Jesus Rafael Soto: Energy as Reality'' by Roberto Guevara in *Art Press,* no. 220, January 1997; ''Soto: Vibrations et Vertiges'' by Itzhak Goldberg in *Beaux Arts Magazine,* no. 152, January 1997; ''Jesús Rafael Soto: When Soto Plays in Space'' by Gilles Plazy in *Cimaise,* vol. 44, January/March 1997; ''Jesus Rafael Soto—Das Bild Ist Starr—das Auge Zittert'' by Robert Fleck in *ART: Das Kunstmagazin,* no. 1, January 1997; ''Jesus Soto: Feeling the Infinite'' by Ricardo Pau-Llosa in *Sculpture* (Washington, D.C.), vol. 16, no. 6, July-August 1997. **Film—***Soto* by Daniel Abadie and Catherine Zins, 1996.

* * *

Jesus Rafael Soto began as a painter and out of painting developed kinetic relief constructions which gradually grew into autonomous environments. In these, the spectator-turned-participant assumes a position so central that he is no longer divorceable from the work of art which without him remains incomplete. This process, traceable from phase to phase, took close to three decades of the artist's diligent and inventive life and gained for him an important place in post-war art.

As a student painter in Venezuela, where Soto was born, his first serious creative impetus came to him from a Cubist Braque still-life in a thrilling moment of comprehension, and his subsequent early work is an academic effort to learn from Cubism and from Cézanne the lessons of geometric simplification. When, as a youth of 27, Soto arrived in Paris, his avowed purpose was to find out what had happened in world art since Braque painted the still-life that had so moved him. Proceeding from a sense of stylistic continuity, he shortly thereafter determined to put his own shoulder to the wheel at the point at which the art-historical carriage seemed to him to be struck. Soto saw this point not in the prevalent area of tachist expression (which he dismissed as irrelevant) but, rather, within an investigative tradition concerned with the object's position in time and space. He correctly traced the modern origins of this issue to Picasso's constructions, the researches of Gabo and Moholy-Nagy, the spatially suggestive paintings of Mondrian and Malevich and, more immediately, to the kinetic mobile art of Alexander Calder.

The young Venezuelan showed implicit faith in the logical progression of art. As a young investigator, but no longer student, he found himself attracted, together with Agam and Tinguely, to the orbit of the Salon des Realites Nouvelles, established in Paris in 1946, and to the Galerie Denise René, which had opened its doors two years earlier. The group's patron-saint was Vasarely, and each of the young men in his own way embarked upon research having as its objective the visual representatin of movement. By the mid-1950s, Soto and his friends had articulated their position and invented visual instruments for the expression of their principles.

Calder, as already mentioned, was the point of departure, but Soto's movement from the outset was different from that of the North American mobile maker, for Calder—the man who made sculpture move—did so mostly by letting carefully weighted, painted objects swing in the breeze, while Soto reduced physical motion to sensory vibration. The vibrating effect was either entirely based on optical responses to a physically static surface or further aided by the gentle movement of optically energetic suspended bodies as these came to act against similarly active optical surfaces. Leaving aside more distant antecedents, it may therefore be said that Soto related Calder's physical to Vasarely's optical kineticism, thereby combining palpable and visual kinetic elements into a new form language.

The environments that Soto created, at the outset in experimental modesty, developed their own momentum and eventually spilled over from his visual laboratory into the world at large. His planes, initially created to reflect vibrations, gradually grew into a striated cube large enough to accommodate the traffic of crowds, and eventually came to dwarf and subsisting but penetrable mazes. The prime experience in Soto's later works is no longer optical, but tactile and sonorous as the human participant, through his act of penetration, agitates not only the real space before him but also our aural ambience. Quite logically, Soto's recent works are architectural. In his monumental factory interior for Renault in Paris, the decorative and the structural elements of his kinetic idiom merge.

Soto's art, then, gradually develops from a sensory and contemplative to a physical, and, in the case of the penetrable, to an athletic dimension: from the small laboratory experiment to monumental architectural scale: and from a self-contained aesthetic unity to one complementary to participatory activity by the viewer. Together with others, Soto has thus blurred the dividing line between the plastic and the performing arts: he has transformed the spectator outside the object to a central agent within the work itself; and reduced or radically altered the distance between art produced and consumed. Through these combined measures, for better or worse, Soto has greatly contributed to a perceptible shift away from art and toward life.

—Thomas Messer

SOULAGES, Pierre

Nationality: French. **Born:** Rodez, Aveyron, 24 December 1919. **Education:** Lycée Rodez until 1938; studied art at the Ecole des Beaux-Arts, Montpellier, 1941. **Military service:** Served in French Army, in Bordeaux and Nyons, 1939–41. **Career:** Worked as a vineyard labourer, Montpellier, 1943–45; independent painter,

Courbevoie, 1946, and in Paris, since 1947. **Awards:** Painting Prize, *Bienal,* Sao Paulo, 1953; Grand Prize, *International Exhibition,* Tokyo, 1957; Grand Prize, *Graphics Biennale,* Ljubljana, Yugoslavia, 1959; Carnegie International Prize, Pittsburgh, 1964; Palette d'Or, *Festival International de Peinture,* Cagnes, 1972; Grand Prize des Arts de la Ville de Paris, 1975; Rembrandt Prize, Goethe-Institut, Basel, 1976; Grand Prix National des Arts, Paris, 1987. **Agent:** Galerie de France, 52 rue de la Verrerie, 75004 Paris. **Address:** 18 rue des Trois-Portes, 75005 Paris, France.

Individual Exhibitions:

1949 Galerie Lydia Conti, Paris
1951 Galleri Birch, Copenhagen
1952 Galerie Stangl, Munich
1954 Kootz Gallery, New York
1955 Gimpel Fils, London
Arts Club of Chicago
Kootz Gallery, New York
1956 Galerie de France, Paris
Kootz Gallery, New York
1957 Galerie Berggruen, Paris
Kootz Gallery, New York
1958 Galerie Rosen, West Berlin
Kunstverein, Braunschweig, West Germany
Gimpel Fils, London
Howard Wise Gallery, Cleveland
1959 Kootz Gallery, New York
1960 Kestner-Gesellschaft, Hannover (retrospective)
Galerie de France, Paris
1961 Museum Folkwang, Essen (retrospective; travelled to the Hague and Zurich)
Museum of Modern Art, Ljubljana, Yugoslavia (graphics retrospective)
Kootz Gallery, New York
1962 Massachusetts Institute of Technology, Cambridge (retrospective)
Museum of Zagreb (graphics retrospective; toured Yugoslavia and Austria)
1963 *Malerier og Raderinger,* Ny Carlsberg Glyptotek, Copenhagen (retrospective)
Peintures sur Papier 1946–1963, Galerie de France, Paris
1964 Kootz Gallery, New York
1965 Kootz Gallery, New York
1966 Museum of Fine Arts, Houston (retrospective)
1967 Musée d'Art Moderne, Paris (retrospective)
Gimpel und Hanover Galerie, Zurich
Gimpel Fils, London
Galerie de France, Paris
1968 Museum of Art, Pittsburgh (retrospective; toured the United States and Canada)
Paintings since 1963, M. Knoedler Inc., New York
Comité d'Enterprise Credit Lyonnais, Paris
1971 Galerie Jobbe-Duval, Rennes, France
1972 University of Maryland, College Park (retrospective)
Galerie de France, Paris
Gimpel Fils, London
Galerie Protée, Toulouse
Galerie-Librairie La Hune, Paris
1973 Henie-Onstad Kunstsenter, Oslo
Nordyllands Kunstmuseum, Aalborg, Denmark
Gentofte Radhus, Denmark
Gimpel und Hanover Galerie, Zurich
Musée d'Art et d'Histoire, Neuchâtel, Switzerland
1974 Musée Dynamique, Dakar, West Africa (retrospective)
Maison des Arts et Loisirs, Montbeliard, France (graphics retrospective)
Galerie de France, Paris (graphics retrospective)
Galerie-Librairie La Hune, Paris
1975 Fundacao Gulbenkian, Lisbon (retrospective; travelled to Madrid and Montpellier)
Museo de Arte Moderno, Mexico City (retrospective)
1976 Museo de Bellas Artes, Caracas (retrospective; toured Brazil and Venezuela)
Musée d'Art et d'Industrie, St. Etienne, France (retrospective)
1977 Grand Palais, Paris (at Foire International d'Art Contemporain)
Galerie de France, Paris
1978 Galerie Ulysses, Vienna
Galerie Madoura, Vallauris, France
Institut Francais, Athens
1979 Galleri Birch, Copenhagen
Foundation Veranneman, Kruishoutem, Belgium
Peintures Récentes, Centre Georges Pompidou, Paris
1980 Musée de la Boverie, Liege, Belgium
Kunstlerhaus, Salzburg, Austria
1982 Galerie Ostertag, Frankfurt
Altes Schloss Museum, Giessen, West Germany
Galerie Ponce, Mexico City
Charlottenburg Museum, Copenhagen (retrospective; toured Denmark)
1983 Musée d'Unterlinden, Colmar, France
1984 Seibu Museum, Tokyo
1985 Pulchri Studio, The Hague
1986 Galerie de France, Paris
1987 Musée St. Pierre, Lyon, Frances
H.-Thomas Gesellschaft, Reutlingen, West Germany
Galerie E. Rieber, Munich
1989 Musée Des Beaux-Arts, Nantes (retrospective)
Museum Fridericianum,. Kassel (retrospective)
1992 Maison des Arts Georges Pompidou, Cajarc, France
1993 Musée National d'Art Contemporain, Seoul, Korea
1996 Musée d'Art Moderne de la Ville de Paris (retrospective)
Museu de Arte, Sao Paulo, Brazil (retrospective)
1997 Deichtorhallen, Hamburg (retrospective)
1999 Kunstmuseum, Bern (retrospective)
2000 Centre Les Abattoirs, Toulouse (retrospective)

Selected Group Exhibitions:

1948 *Franzosisher Abstrakter Malerei,* Kunsthalle, Stuttgart (toured Germany)
1953 *Younger European Artists,* Guggenheim Museum, New York
1955 *The New Decade,* Museum of Modern Art, New York
1964 *Painting in France 1900–67,* National Gallery, Washington, D.C. (toured the United States)
1973 *Aspects of Contemporary Art,* South African National Gallery, Cape Town (toured South Africa)

1978 *Points de Reperes,* Palazzo Reale, Milan (travelled to Naples, Florence, Wroclaw, Poznan, Warsaw, Madrid, and Lisbon)
1981 *Westkunst,* Messehallen, Cologne
1986 *The Spiritual in Art,* Los Angeles County Museum of Art
1987 *Lumière de la Mediterranée,* Israel Museum, Jerusalem
1991 *Art of the Forties,* Museum of Modern Art, New York
1993 *Art contemporain en France,* Sofia, Plodiv, Varna, Poland
Manifeste, une histoire parallèle, Centre Georges Pompidou, Paris
1995 *Europe After the Flood,* Kunstlerhaus, Vienna
1996 *100 peintres de l'Ecole de Paris 1945–1975,* Maison de l'UNESCO, Paris
1997 *Made in France,* Musée national d'art moderne, Paris
1998 *Rendez-vous,* Solomon R. Guggenheim Museum, New York
1999 *Dialoge der kunst Deutschland-Frankreich,* Ludwig Museum, Koblenz, Germany

Collections:

Centre Georges Pompidou, Paris; Nationalgalerie, West Berlin; Museum des 20. Jahrhundert, Vienna; Museum Boymans-van Beuningen, Rotterdam, Netherlands; Kunsthaus, Zurich; Galleria Civica d'Arte Moderna, Turin; Tate Gallery, London; Museum of Fine Arts, Montreal; Art Institute of Chicago; Museum of Modern Art, New York.

Publications:

On SOULAGES: Books—*Abstrakte Franzosischer Malerei* by René Massat, Stuttgart 1948; *The Changing Forms of Art* by Patrick Heron, London 1955; *Pierre Soulages: Paintings,* exhibition catalog, with text by Bernard Dorival, London 1955; *L'Art Abstrait* by Marcel Brion, Paris 1956; *Soulages* by R. van Gindertael, Paris 1957; *Musée de poche: Pierre Soulages* by Hubert Juin, Paris 1958, as *Soulages,* New York 1959; *Pierre Soulages,* exhibition catalog with text by Werner Schmalenbach, Hannover 1960; *Soulages,* exhibition catalog, photo-reportage by Izis, Paris 1960; *Pierre Soulages,* exhibition catalog with text by Eduard Huttinger, Zurich 1961; *Les Peintures sur papier de Soulages* by Michel Ragon, Paris 1962; *Soulages: Peintures sur papier 1946–1963,* exhibition catalog, Paris 1963; *Soulages: Malerier og Raderinger,* exhibition catalog with text by Haavard Rostrup, Copenhagen 1963; *Pierre Soulages,* exhibition catalog with text by Bernard Dorival, James Fitzsimmons and Werner Schamalenbach, Zurich 1967; *Soulages,* exhibition catalog with text by Bernard Dorival, Paris 1967; *Soulages: Paintings since 1963,* exhibition catalog with text by James Johnson Sweeney, New York 1968; *Soulages 1970–72,* exhibition catalog, Paris 1972; *Pierre Soulages* by James Johnson Sweeney, Neuchâtel, Switzerland 1972, New York, London and Stuttgart 1973; *Pierre Soulages* by Michel Ragon, Paris 1974; *Soulages: Eaux-fortes, lithographies* by G. Duby and C. Labbaye, Paris 1974; *Pierre Soulages,* exhibition catalog with an interview by Bernard Ceysson, St. Etienne, France 1976; *Soulages: Peintres récentes,* exhibition catalog with text by Alfred Pacquement, Paris 1979; *Soulages* by Bernard Ceysson, Nafels 1979; *Pierre Soulages,* exhibition catalog with texts by Alfred Pacquement and Ashido Okada, Tokyo 1984; *Pierre Soulages,* exhibition catalog with texts by George Duby, Clement Rosset and others, Lyon 1987; *Pierre Soulages: 40 Jahre Malerei* by B. Geysson and V. Loers, Stuttgart 1989; *Pierre Soulages; L'oeuvre 1947–1990* by Pierre Diax and James Johnson Sweeney, Neuchâtel 1991; *Pierre Soulages: Peintures 1979–1991,* Carjac, France 1992; *Pierre Soulages: L'Oeuvre Complet: Peintures* by P. Encreve, 3 Volumes, Paris 1994–1998; *Pierre Soulages. Célébration de la Lumière* by Sandor Kuthy, Paris 1999; *The Rebirth of Painting in the Late-Twentieth Century* by Donald Kuspit, New York 2000. **Articles**—''Pierre Soulages: Emotion and Intelligence'' by Michel Faucher in *Cimaise,* no. 41, June-August 1994; ''Paris: Soulages'' by James Merlin in *The Burlington Magazine,* no. 138, August 1996.

* * *

Prominent among the abstract painter of the School of Paris who won celebrity after 1945, Pierre Soulages has been consistent in his strength of expression, though the resources of his work have been restricted both in format and in palette. Colour as such is eliminated almost entirely, except where it is mixed with black. Black with brown, grey, green and blue dictates the mood of each painting. Handling of the oil pigment in varied thicknesses from quite high impasto to a transparent solution is always sensuous. By subtracting colour and mixing the pigment only in primarily tonal effectiveness, the imposition of the formal structure is emphasized.

Reflection is of the utmost importance in Soulages' paintings, not merely the reflection from the paint surface itself but in the diffusion of light in the chiaroscuro. Broad pathways of paint indicate the passages of intent, so that each canvas is a plan of tactile directions in which the reflections illuminate the plastic configuration of the paint. This plastic topography is, at first glance, strong in its negative saturation of the light, then grows in assertiveness as the subtle graduations of the shadowy reliefs are traversed. Activation of the picture space and an imaginary depth beyond it, implied by the lighter tones, expands the superficial limits of the non-objective image.

Soulages' contributions to theatre design in the 1949 sets for Graham Greene's *Heloise et Abelard* in Paris and in the 1952 ballet *Geste pour un genie* in honour of Leonardo's 500th anniversary demonstrate that his association with light and dark translate effectively in the proscenium frame. Those broad black bands, meeting and diagonally separating, construct dark and monolithic shapes that have their prototypes in memories of the ancient menhirs and the numinous sculptures of the old Romanesque churches abounding around Soulages' childhood home in the Massif Central. This solemn aura that broods over all of Soulages' work, either in paint or in prints, removed it from the context of ephemeral art styles and identifies it closely and specially with the rich and sensuous empathy of gesture, and the secret impulses of movements in the world of nature by night.

It is a magic and mysterious atmosphere that Soulages can conjure up, with no more than a personal Braille system of signs, and reliefs in which the eye searches vainly for explicit directions and data. ''Out of darkness came forth light,'' in the physical no less than the spiritual sense, is the import of Soulages' message. It also has the ambiguous para-phrase of the light that, dispelling our fears of the unknown, may also make clear the horrors the darkness has mercifully shrouded.

—G. S. Whittet

Pierre Soulages became one of the leading abstract painters in Europe after World War II with his distinctive approach of painting with broad, long, vigorous strokes of mostly black paint on white. His paintings have occasionally contained small amounts of color (typically earth tones, blues, and purples), but are characterized by large, expansive areas of black against the white background of canvas. Soulages paints by manipulating wide strokes of paint that are densely packed, and which sweep, twist, curve, and collide on the space of the picture plane. His paint strokes can be long or wide, straight or bent, thrusting across the picture space or seemingly immobilized, thinly or thickly applied, and smooth or pasty in texture. Soulages' work seems very similar to the American action painter Franz Kline, who is certainly better known in the United States, but the viewer can soon notice it is distinct in sensibility and richly expressive in its own right.

Although active for more than fifty years, Soulages' reputation has, unfortunately, declined in the United States, although he remains highly regarded in Europe, particularly his native France. Soulages is associated with Tachism, the development in painting in Europe after World War II that corresponds most closely to Abstract Expressionism. Soulages continues to create large, mostly black and white abstract compositions, usually in oil and canvas. He also continues to create prints that are very similar to his paintings. He does not give titles to his works, although they are often differentiated by dates on which they were completed.

Soulages has experimented with more diverse media and much larger scale since the 1980s. In these explorations, he has stayed with the same expressive and aesthetic concerns found in his paintings and transformed them. From 1986 to 1994 he designed 104 stained glass windows for the Abbey Church of Saint-Foy at Conques that were commissioned by the government of France. Saint-Foy is an historically important Romanesque church near the town in which Soulages was born and raised. This project is intriguing because the forms and spaces of Christian architecture and in particular Saint-Foy, a church Soulages saw often in his youth because it is near the town of his birth, have long inspired him. His windows for Saint-Foy are narrow panels divided into mostly rectangular sections by simple black tracery. The glass used has been specially prepared to filter the light to create spiritual, contemplative effects. In 1994, Soulages created the installation *Living Light (Lebendeges Licht)* for the Westfälisches Landesmuseum für Kunst und Kulturgeschichte in Münster, Germany. The work is unusual simply because it is an installation created by an artist deeply concerned with the sensuous, expressive effects of paint.

Soulages continues to transform his distinctive approach to painting in various ways. He has come to paint increasingly larger works. He has allowed the wide, sweeping strokes of black paint to multiply in number, grow in width, and blend together, until they coalesce on the canvas. Thus, as his work evolved from the 1950s to the 1970s and beyond, individualized strips of black have become more painterly and tend to fuse together. Vigorous, dynamic, swirling strokes of black paint are often used to create turbulent whirlwinds of black forms or are allowed to accumulate on the picture plane until they create broad areas of deep, seemingly endless voids of blackness. Touches of color enliven and vary his enormous paintings, creating light and color in blackness that normally would never reveal them. His paintings often convey a sense of struggle between white and black forms, which seem to shift between the flat surface of the painting and the illusion of three-dimensional space behind it.

Soulages' paintings are introspective, contemplative, existential experiences that conjure deeper, spiritual meanings; in this he is not unlike the American Abstract Expressionists, from which he learned much after World War II. His interest in the evocative possibilities of the agitated, reverberating black voids that characterize his painting links him to the tradition of the sublime in landscape painting and how mid-twentieth century painters such as Mark Rothko, Barnett Newman, and Clyfford Still abstracted it.

—Herbert Hartel, Jr.

SPAGNULO, Giuseppe

Nationality: Italian. **Born:** Grottaglie, Tarnato, 28 December 1936. **Education:** Educated in Grottaglie primary and secondary schools; studied ceramic technology in father's worshop, Grottaglie, 1948–49; at the Scuola d'Arte Faenza, Italy, 1953–55 and 1956–57; studied sculpture, under Marino Marini, at the Brera Accademia di Belle Arti, Milan, 1959–60. **Military Service:** Served in the Italian Army Infantry, in Bari, Maddaloni and Milan, 1961–63. **Family:** Married Clara Dalla Chiara in 1966; sons: Frederico and Andrea. **Career:** Sculptor; worked as an assistant in sculpture, studio of Lucio Fontana, and of Gio and Arnaldo Pomodoro, Milan, 1959–60; produced first stone works, 1960–65; first wood and iron works, 1965–76; designed first stage sets, Bologna, 1975; has worked with cardboard, landscape, and archaeological themes, since 1976; spent year in Berlin, 1980. Lecturer in sculpture, Istituto d'Arte, Monza, Italy, 1968–69; Professor, National Academy of the Arts, Stuttgart, since 1987. **Awards:** Purchase Prize, *Mostra del Disegno,* Appiano Gentile, 1968; Purchase Prize for Drawing, Galleria delle Ore, Milan 1969; First Sculpture Prize, Seregno-Brianza, Italy, 1974; Faenza Prize for the Career, Museo Internazionale delle Ceramiche, Faenza, 2001. **Agent:** Studio Carlo Grossetti, via dei Piatti 9, 20123 Milan. **Address:** Viale col de Lana 9, 20100 Milan, Italy.

Individual Exhibitions:

1965 Salone Annunciata, Milan
1968 Salone Annunciata, Milan
1969 Galleria Ferrari, Verona
Galleria Martano Due, Turin
1970 *Une Scultura nella Strada: Black Panther,* via Borgospesso, Milan
1971 Salone Annunciata, Milan
Studio Marconi, Milan
1972 *Ferri Spezzati,* Salone Annunciata, Milan
1973 *Scultura nella Citta,* Nova Arte Moderna, Prato, Italy
1974 Galerie Semiha Huber, Zurich
Galerie M, Bochum, West Germany
Studio Casati, Merate, Italy
1975 Galleria Schwarz, Milan
Salone Annunciata, Milan
1976 Galleria Il Sole, Bolzano, Italy
Galerie M, Bochum, West Germany
Galerie M, The Hague
Centro Sant'Elmo, Salò, Italy
Galleria 72, Bergamo, Italy
Galleria Il Segnappasi, Pesaro, Italy
Salone Annunciata, Milan (with Marco Gastini)
1977 Galleria Civica d'Arte Moderna, Turin
Salone Annunciata, Milan
Galerie Walter Storms, Munich
Newport Harbor Art Museum, Newport Beach, California
1978 Kunsthalle, Bielefeld, West Germany

Galleria Il Tritone, Biella, Italy
Studio Carlo Grossetti, Milan
Galerie D + C Müller-Roth, Stuttgart
Studio Casati, Merate, Italy
Galerie Walter Storms, Munich
1979 Galleria E Tre, Rome
Galerie Appel und Fertsch, Frankfurt
1980 Galerie Munro, Hamburg
Galerie Walter Storms, Munich (with Marco Gastini and Gilberto Zorio)
Studio Carlo Grossetti, Milan
Galerie Walter Storms, Villigen, West Germany
1981 Studio G 7, Bologna
Erotish, Rhetorisch, Heroisch, Nationgalerie, West Berlin
Kunstverein, Braunschweig, West Germany
1982 *L'Istinto e Sempre in Cerca di Anima,* Städtische Galerie im Lenbachhaus, Munich
1983 Studio Carlo Grossetti, Milan
Galerie Susanna Kuli, St. Gallen, Switzerland
Salone Villa Romana, Florence
1984 Galleria Civica, Modena, Italy
Galleria L'Isola, Rome
1985 Galleria Martano, Turin
Galleria Piero Cavellini, Milan
Wilhelm-Lehmbruck-Museum, Duisburg, West Germany
Kunstverein, Hamburg
Lunds Konsthall, Lund, Sweden
1986 Galerie Susanna Kulli, St. Gallen, Switzerland
Galerie Walter Storms, Munich
Spagnulo, at the *XLII Biennale,* Venice
Spagnulo, at the *XIX Biennale di Gubbio,* Italy
Galerie Hans Barlach, Cologne
1987 Galerie Hans Barlach, Hamburg
Galleri Nordenhake, Stockholm
Studio Carlo Grossetti, Milan
1991 Neuere Geschichte, Bochumer Historische Studien, Bochum (catalog)
Skulpturen und Zeichnungen, Württembergischer Kunstverein Stuttgart (also Museum am Ostwall Dortmund) (catalog)
1994 Kunsthaus Zug, Zug, Switzerland (also Brandstetter & Wyss, Castel Burio, Costigliole d'Asti, Italy) (catalog)
1997 Palazzo Reale, Milan (catalog)

Selected Group Exhibitions:

1972 *Progetto/Intervento/Verifica,* Palazzo Reale, Milan
1975 *Emprica: L'Arte tra Addizione e Sottrazione,* Museo di Castelvecchio, Rimini
1977 *Arte in Italia 1969–1977,* Galleria Civica d'Arte Moderna, Turin
1979 *Le Stangze del Gioco,* Loggetta Lombardesca, Pinacoteca, Ravenna
1980 *Skulptur im 20. Jahrundert,* Wenkenpark, Riehen, near Basel
1981 *Linea della Ricerca Artistica in Italia 1960–1980,* Palazzo dell Esposisioni, Rome
1982 *Arte Italiana 1960–1982,* Hayward Gallery, London
1983 *L'Informale in Italia,* Galleria Comunale d'Arte Moderna, Bologne
1985 *A Generation of Italian Art,* Alvar Aalto Museum, Jyvaskyla, Finland (travelled to Pori, Finland)
1987 *Kunst RAI 87,* Amsterdam
1988 *Gastini, Mattiacci, Spagnulo,* Pinacoteca Comunale di Ravenna, Italy (catalog)
1990 *Sculpture in Milan 1945–1990,* Städtische Kunsthalle, Mannheim, Germany (catalog)
1991 *Materiali della Scultura Italiana, 1960–1990,* Civici Musei di Reggio Emilia, Italy (catalog)
2000 *Contemporary Art from Italy,* Gallery Carzaniga + Ueker, Basel
Il Secolo della Scultura Italiana, Galleria d'Arte Moderna e Contemporanea, Bergamo, Italy
2001 *Kunstraum Deutschland,* Institut für Auslandsbeziehungen, Stuttgart

Collections:

Galleria Civica d'Arte Moderna, Turin; Museo de Gibelina, Italy; Galleria Comunale d'Arte Moderna, Cagmiari, Italy; University of Parma; Nationgalerie, West Berlin; Kunsthalle, Bielefeld, West Germany; Stadtische Galerie im Lenbachhaus, Munich; Museum am Ostwall, Dortmund, West Germany; Bochum University, West Germany.

Publications:

On SPAGNULO: Books—*Spagnulo e la Pratica Sociale della Scultura* by Tommaso Trini, Milan 1975; *Giuseppe Spagnulo: Erotisch, Rhetorisch, Heroisch,* exhibition catalog, West Berlin 1981; *Giuseppe Spagnulo: L'istinto e Sempre in Cerca di Anima,* exhibition catalog by Helmut Friedel, Munich 1982. **Articles—**''Guiseppe Spagnulo'' by Robert Sanesi in *Marcatre* (Milan), June 1970; ''Giuseppe Spagnùlo'' by Luci Mastropasqua in *Art News,* vol. 94, April 1995; ''Giuseppe Spagnulo: Splitting Form'' by Laura Tansini in *Sculpture Magazine,* vol. 19, no. 3, April 2000.

* * *

One of the greatest stimuli to the work of Giuseppe Spagnulo at the start of his creative activity seems to have been the urge to overcome the weight of an inert material, to create a form that contradicts the true nature of the material used. This became evident when gigantic metal shapes (or even minute blocks of the same material) were bent in unlikely directions and fixed in a state of perpetual tension which made them dynamic. Later on, the evolution of Spagnulo's art was to become clearer with his approach to various materials, which made his aim more explicit. It can be recognized in his numerous series of *Cartoni:* raw cardboard, left in the natural state or just stained with lampblack, which can be folded and then pressed so as to achieve the desired form.

In the wake of the Cartoni came another interesting period, that of the series of works in clay (which Spagnulo christened ''Landscapes''), in which another principle can be perceived, very much in keeping with the moment in history through which we are passing today; that of extemporaneousness. These are works that the artist carries out with very simple, spare means: a surface of clay with pieces of tile or sheets of glass superimposed on them, on which he simply walks so as to give a wavy effect to the surface; this may even break the glass or drive the pieces of tile or stone into clay. From these extempore works Spagnulo moved on (1975–81) to another fascinating series, which he describes as ''Archaeology.'' In these he works with solid iron plates with a deep groove in them; these are pressed on to similar iron plates which have been softened by heating, so as to obtain on the half-melted plate the impression of the groove in the first plate in relief. In this way it is possible to obtain works, always matched, which are presented as ''traces of memory'' (to use the sculptor's own well-chosen expression). One plate is actually the ''memory'' of the other. The first is the matrix of the second, so that, rather than a ''negative,'' what we have here is a sort of ''twinning''—a double organism obtained from the interaction of the two aspects, one subordinate to and dependent on the other, a repeated record of what has its own form and yet is mirror image of the other.

—Gillo Dorfles

SPERO, Nancy

Nationality: American. **Born:** Cleveland, Ohio, 24 August 1926. **Education:** Art Institute of Chicago, 1945–49, B.F.A. 1949; Atelier André Lhote, and Ecole des Beaux-Arts, Paris, 1950–51. **Family:** Married the artist Leon Golub in 1951; children: Stephen, Philip, and Paul. **Career:** Independent artist, since 1949; lived and worked in Ischia and Florence, 1956–57, and in Paris, 1959–64; now lives and works in New York. Co-editor, *Rip-Off File* ad hoc committee of women artists, since 1972. Guest artist, Sacramento State University, California, 1974; visiting artist, School of the Art Institute of Chicago, 1974; and St. Lawrence University, Canton, New York, 1975. **Award:** Creative Artists Public Service Fellowship, New York State Council Grant, Washington, D.C., 1977; 3rd Hiroshima Art Prize, awarded to both Nancy Spero and Leon Golub, 1996. **Agent:** Josh Baer Gallery, 270 Lafayette Street, New York, New York 10012. **Address:** 530 La Guardia Place, New York, New York 10012, U.S.A.

Individual Exhibitions:

1962 Galerie Breteau, Paris
1965 Galerie Breteau, Paris
1968 Galerie Breteau, Paris
1971 University of California at San Diego
Mombaccus Art Center, New Paltz, New York
1973 A.I.R. Gallery, New York
1974 Women's Center, Williams College, Williamstown, Massachussetts
Douglass College Library, Rutgers University, New Brunswick, New Jersey
A.I.R. Gallery, New York
1977 Marianne Deson Gallery, Chicago
1978 Art Library, Queens College, New York
Herter Gallery, University of Masschussetts, Amsterdam
The Woman's Building, Los Angeles
1979 Peachtree Center Gallery, Atlanta
Hampshire College Art Center, Amherst, Massachussetts
Real Art Ways, Hartford, Connecticut
Picker Art Gallery, Colgate University, Hamilton, New York
A.I.R. Gallery, New York
1980 Livingston Gallery, Rutgers University, New Brunswick, New Jersey
1981 The Sarah Institute, New York
Ben Shahn Gallery, William Patterson College, Wayne, New Jersey
Herter Gallery, University of Massachussetts, Amherst
A.I.R. Gallery, New York
1982 *Nancy Spero/Leon Golub,* Florence Wilcox Gallery, Swarthmore College, Pennsylvania
Vietnam War, Tweed Arts Group, Plainfield, New Jersey (with Leon Golub)
Galerie France Morin, Montreal
Matrix Gallery, Wadsworth Atheneum, Hartford, Connecticut
1983 University of New Mexico, Albuquerque (with Leon Golub)
Project Studio One, Long Island City, New York (with Leon Golub)
Art for Social Change, New York
Brucknerhaus, Linz, Austria
Center for Creative Studies, Detroit (with Leon Golub)
Rhona Hoffman Gallery, Chicago
1984 University of California, Berkeley
Riverside Studios, London
Cash Gallery, New York (with David Reynolds; travelled to A.R.C., Toronto)
1985 Lawrence Oliver Gallery, Philadelphia
Carnegie-Mellon University, Pittsburgh
Powerhouse Gallery, Montreal
Burnett Miller Gallery, Los Angeles
1986 Hobart and William Smith Colleges, Geneva, New York (with Nicole Jolicoeur)
Museum Villa Stuck, Munich
Center Gallery, Carrboro, North Carolina (with Leon Golub)
Rhona Hoffman Gallery, Chicago
1987 Orchard Gallery, Derry, North Ireland
Fruit Market Gallery, Edinburgh
Institute of Contemporary Art, London
Washington Project for the Arts, Washington, D.C.
Everson Museum of Art, Syracuse, New York (retrospective; travelled to New York City and Saskatoon, Canada)
1988 Barbara Gross Galerie, Munich
War Series 1966–69; Artaud Paintings: 1969–70, Rhona Hoffman Gallery, Chicago
The Artaud Series: 1969–70, Barbara Gladstone Gallery, New York
Museum of Contemporary Art, Los Angeles
War Paintings: 1966–70, Josh Baer Gallery, New York
1989 *Works from 1956–62,* Josh Baer Gallery, New York
Burnett Miller Gallery, Los Angeles
Les Magiciens de la Terre, Le Grande Halle de la Villette, Paris
S. L. Simpson Gallery, Toronto
1990 Honolulu Academy of Arts
Notes in Time, Smith College Museum of Art, Northampton, Massachusetts

Nancy Spero: *Crouching Female Fertility Symbol,* 1985. ©Nancy Spero.

Nancy Spero: *Sheela Na Gig,* 1996. ©Nancy Spero.

Nancy Spero: Bilder 1958 bis 1990, Haus am Walsee, Berlin (travelled to Bonner Kunstverein, Bonn; Gemeentemuseum, Arnhem, Netherlands)
1991 Jürgen Becker Galerie, Hamburg
Josh Baer Gallery, New York
Nancy Spero in der Glyptothek, Arbeiten auf Papier, Glyptothek am Königsplatz, Munich
Small Works, Artaud Paintings, War Series, Barbara Gross Galerie, Munich
Works on Paper 1981–1991, Salzburger Kunstverein, Künstlerhaus Salzburg, Austria
Galleria Stefani Miscetti, Rome
1992 *Codex Artaud,* Museum of Modern Art, New York
Ulmer Museum, Ulm Germany (retrospective)
1993 *Hieroglyph,* College of Saint Rose Art Gallery, Albany, New York
Josh Baer Gallery, New York
Works on Paper (with Leon Golub), Olin Art Gallery, Kenyon College, Gambier, Ohio
1994 *War and Memory* (with Leon Golub), American Center, Paris (travelled to MIT List Visual Arts Center, Cambridge, Massachusetts)
Malmö Konsthal, Malmö, Sweden
1996 *Sheela-na-Gig at Home,* Jack Tilton Gallery, New York
Nancy Spero: Black and the Red, P.O.O.W., New York
Nancy Spero: A Cycle in Time, The New York Kunsthalle, New York
2000 *The Fighting Is a Dance Too,* Roth Horowitz, New York (with Leon Golub)
2001 *Sheela Does Ramapo,* Kresge and Pascal Galleries, Ramapo College of New Jersey (catalog)

Selected Group Exhibitions:

1977 *Words at Liberty,* Museum of Contemporary Art, Chicago
1980 *Art of Conscience: The Art of the Last Decade,* Wright State University, Dayton, Ohio (toured the United States, 1981–82)

1981 *Crimes of Compassion,* Chrysler Museum, Norfolk, Virginia
1984 *Content: A Contemporary Focus 1974–84,* Hirshhorn Museum, Washington, D.C.
1985 *Nude, Naked, Stripped,* Massachussetts Institute of Technology, Cambridge
1987 *Stations,* Centre International d'Art Contemporain, Montreal
1990 *Light Spirit Dream,* Terrain Gallery, San Francisco
The Decade Show, Museum of Contemporary Hispanic Art, New York
1991 *Beyond the Frame, American Art 1960–1990,* Setagaya Art Museum, Tokyo
1993 *Extravagant: The Economy of Elegance,* Russisches Kulturzentrum, Berlin, Germany
1994 *Dialogue with the Other,* Museet for Fotokunst, Odense, Denmark (catalog)
1998 *7th International Cairo Biennale,* Egypt
1999 *Collaborations 1998,* Printworks Gallery, Chicago (catalog)
2000 *Picturing the Modern Amazon,* New Museum of Contemporary Art, New York
The End: An Independent Vision of Contemporary Culture 1982–2000, Exit Art/The First World, New York

Collections:

Art Gallery of Ontario, Toronto; Art Institute of Chicago; Australian National Gallery; Boston Museum of Fine Arts; Centro Cultural, Mexico City; Musée des Beaux-Arts de Montreal; Museum of Fine Arts, Hanoi, North Vietnam; Museum of Modern Art, New York; Whitney Museum of American Art, New York; Brooklyn Museum; Frac Nord Pas de Calais, France; Harvard University Art Museum; Hiroshima City Museum of Contemporary Art; Uffizi Gallery, Florence.

Public Installations:

Artemis, Acrobats, Divas, and Dancers, 66th Street/Lincoln Center Subway Station, New York; *Premiere,* Ronacher Theater, Vienna, Austria; *Improvisations,* Heeresspital Innsbruck, Tyrol, Austria; *A Cycle in Time,* Residenzgalerie, Salzburg, Austria; *Raise/Time,* Arthur M. Sackler Museum, Harvard University Art Museums, Cambridge; *Feminin-Masculin, Le Sexe de l'Art,* Centre Georges Pompidou, Paris; *To the Revolution II,* The American Center, Paris.

Publications:

By SPERO: Articles—''The Whitney Museum and Women'' in *Art Gallery* (Ivoryton, Connecticut), January 1971; ''Women's Speakout'' in *New York Element,* February/March 1972; ''Art: A Woman's Sensibility'' in *California Institute of Arts,* Valencia, California 1975; ''Art Politics and Ethics: Interview with Leon Golub and Nancy Spero,'' with Derek Guthrie, in *New Art Examiner* (Chicago), April 1977; ''Interview with Nancy Spero,'' with Donald Kuspit, in *Art in America* (New York), September/October 1977; ''Ende'' in *Women's Studies* (London), vol. 6, 1978; interview, with Nicole Jolicoeur and Nell Tenhaaf, in *Parachute* (Montreal), June/August 1985; ''On the Other Side of the Mirror'' with Robert Enright in *Border Crossings,* vol. 19, no. 4, November 2000. **Films—***Woman as Protagonist: The Art of Nancy Spero,* with Irene Sosa, 1993.

On SPERO: Books—*American Sculpture in Process 1930–1970* by Wayne Adersen, Boston 1975; *From the Center* by Lucy Lippard, New York 1976; *Nancy Spero: The Black Paris Paintings,* exhibition catalog with essay by Elaine King, Pittsburgh 1985; *Nancy Spero: Restrospective,* exhibition catalog with essay by Jon Bird, London 1987; *Nancy Spero: Rebirth of Venus,* edited by Edit deAk with essay by Robert Storr, Japan, 1989; *Nancy Spero: Woman Breathing,* exhibition catalog, Germany, 1992. **Articles—**''Bombs and Helicopters: The Art of Nancy Spero'' by Leon Golub in *Caterpillar I* (New York), 1967; ''Women Choose Women'' by April Kingsley in *Artforum* (New York), March 1973; ''Nancy Spero'' by Donald Kuspit in *Art in America* (New York), July/August 1975; ''Nancy Spero'' by Lawrence Alloway in *Artforum* (New York), May 1976; ''Women Ain't Losers'' by John Perreault in the *Soho Weekly News* (New York), 23 September 1976; ''Nancy Spero'' by Corinne Robins in *Arts Magazine* (New York), November 1976; ''Caring: 5 Political Artists'' by Lucy Lippard in *Studio International* (London), vol. 193, no. 987, 1977; ''Words and Images through Time; The Time; The Art of Nancy Spero'' by Corinne Robins in *Arts Magazine* (New York), December 1979; ''Spero's Apocalyse'' by Donald Kuspit in *Artforum* (New York), April 1980; ''Nancy Spero'' by Michael Newman in *Art Monthly* (London), September 1984; ''Nancy Spero: Woman as Protagonist'' by Jeanne Siegel in *Arts Magazine* (New York), September 1987.

*

From 1951 until 1965 I worked in oils on canvas. This group of existential works included lovers, prostitutes, mythological great mothers, etc.

From 1966 on I have worked exclusively on paper. 1966 to 1970: I made a series of over 100 war paintings. The paintings have messages, inscriptions, graffiti, i.e., S.E.A.R.C.H. and D.E.S.T.R.O.Y., L.O.V.E. TO H.A.N.O.I., etc. Victims are thrown from planes, the helicopter consumes its victims, ''The Bomb,'' a human torso with obscene phallic heads spitting blood or fire—technological war.

''The Codex Artaud,'' 1971–72, have cinematic quality—through extension (2 feet high and from 8 to 25 feet in length)—a fragmented and staccato positioning of the images of quotations. One has to change location, move in or distance oneself according to the scale of the images to follow the action. The rhythm of the whole is seemingly discordant and incomplete, relating to fractured time.

''Tortured in Chile,'' 1974, documents the torture of women political prisoners. From this work on I decided to represent ''humankind'' only through images of women.

''Torture of Women,'' 1976, extends in a continuous linear band, 20 inches high by 125 feet in length and contains case histories of women political prisoners from Latin America, Turkey, Iran, etc. (information from Amnesty International, etc.) combined with major references of mythological examples of the repression of women. The text is hand-painted with wood type alphabets and collaged bulletin style. Figures are collaged in to document and transcend the horror of immediate external realities.

''Notes in Time on Women,'' 1976–79, is 20 inches high by 225 feet in length. A range of variously scaled hand-painted and collaged painted images weave through and interact with the 96 quotations and reference from the misogynist to the celebratory, assembled from many cultures up to the present, defining aspects of existence with women as the protagonists, an independent and positive force in a male-controlled world.

''The First Language,'' 1981, 20 inches high by 190 feet long, moves from war and rape to women's power, sexuality, grace and strength. There is no text in this piece, since gesture and movement are the earliest forms of human communication.

I use only images of women, to represent woman as protagonist and hero. This is a reversal of the typical art practice of portraying men as heroes and protagonists. I articulate women's situation and actions from repressed, victimized states to buoyant, self-confident stances.

These works are distanced from the Westernized notions of the personal subjective portrayal of individuality. The works deal with rhythm, stylization, contrast of body types, the juxtaposition of images past and present, varied historical references from disparate cultures, political information, etc.

I am not interested in individual physiognomies or personification. The figures become generic in a somewhat similar way to, for example, the stylizations of Australian aboriginal art, early Greek vase painting, prehistoric art, etc. I combine in one work figures derived from various cultures whose extremely diverse and often disproportionate body sizes and types coexist in simultaneous time.

I use photographs informationally to derive images of contemporary women, for exanple, older Vietnamese women, a range of war and rape victims, youthful celebratory figures, who are depicted in stressed actions and symbolic representations. This is often emphasized by repeating the same figures but based on characteristics of tempo and time spans creating movement across the page. The repetition de-individualizes Western ''subjectivity'' in a nonhierarchical continuous presence.

—Nancy Spero

* * *

Nancy Spero's art/politics needs neither soap boxes nor labyrinthine rhetoric camouflaged in political jargon to take control. Spero's images are ideographs montaged in staccato with verbal texts on long paper scrolls which become like personal holy scriptures. Since she knows all too well the effectiveness of hypnotic banality and subliminal ploys of the media, she rebukes then by using blunt dramatic symbols to confront the viewers. Traditional iconography would be inappropriate for her uncoventioanal and sometimes harrowing messages about rape, murder, and political atrocities. Instead, she compresses information bits from hidden documents and the media, past and present, into verbal fragments. These are juxtaposed with figural analogies from events. Spero demonstrates the persistence of these nightmarish occurrences throughout history. Beyond journalistic reportage, these collages grab the viewers in the way only art can.

More specifically, the history of torture, especially of women, is older than, but blasphemously aided by, the Bible, the Koran, and all other generally respected sacred texts. Spero displays all kinds of tools of victimization with haunting beauty, with exquisite compassion and creative perspicacity.

A perfect example of this humanity is found in her work, ''Codex Artaud.'' While Artaud had serious misogynistic tendencies, she emphathized with his struggle to give birth to himself. She recognized in his struggles, his madness and spiritual anguish, a similarity to the history of women. The ''Codex Artaud'' had grown out of a preceding decade of work centering on anti-war responses to the Vietnam trauma. Phallus, tongue, and insectlike bombs spit death. The victims are seen licking the oppressor and vice-versa. Screeching slogans are scrawled on the paper as though in great desperation.

By 1974, Spero had come to the conclusion that the culprit of all the sado-sexual oppression grew out of the patriachy and, thus, has devoted herself exclusively to themes of women and feminism ever since. It was also at this time that her unique usage of the collage medium was honed. Ways of seeing and methods of communication become synonymous in intensely compressed collages of figure fragments and label-printed type-scripts of personally and quoted texts. Exaggeratedly posed goddesses, classical figures, and monsters run, dance, kneel, and tumble as they stutter and shout the cacophony of horrific realities that compromise the ''news.'' Since 1974 she has done works—''The Torture of Women'' and ''Notes on Women Part II: Women: Appraisals, Dance and Active Histories''—which run rapid-fire through a gamut of themes: childbirth, girlhood, menstruation, and divorce. These are often spliced with themes of collective import such as women's survival, male appraisals, racism, women's role in revolution, etc. New works evolve from unresolved ideas from past pieces and are expanded by the addition of more recent and profound insights.

While Spero's focus has widened over the years, there is a consistency and high-pitched concentration in her work that remains throughout. Though the visual and the verbal are interwoven in what seems like an erratic grouping of various sizes and scales, it is far from unplanned, and creates a sense of the rhythms of abuses. Snaps and snatches, jagged slashes of the stiletto, jolts of punctures and ballistic torment, all leave the viewers in a paralyzed free-fall through an angst-ridden existential abyss. And there is no sweet calm genesis after apocalypse; no salvation. Instead, her ''heretical'' collages make it clear that any one of us is a potential victim of similarly gruesome offenses.

—Elise LaRose

SPOERRI, Daniel

Nationality: Swiss. **Born:** Daniel Isaac Feinstein in Galati, Rumania, 27 March 1930; immigrated to Switzerland, and adopted by his uncle Theophile Spoerri, Zurich, 1942. **Education:** Zurich schools; studied ballet at the School of Dance, Opera de Zurich, 1950–52; studied classical ballet, under Preobrajenska and Kniaseff, and mime, under Decroux and Marceau, Paris, 1952–53. **Career:** Lives and works in Seggiano, Italy, since 1992. Worked for Wacker Dance Studios, Paris, 1952–54; principal dancer, Berne Opera, 1953–57; assistant to Gustav-Rudolf Sellner, Landestheater, Darmstadt, 1957–59. Independent plastic artist, Paris, 1959–66, Symi, Greece, 1966–68, Dusseldorf, 1968–71, Cavigliano, Italy and Zurich, 1972–3, and in La Selle sur le Bied, France, since 1973; founder-member, with Pierre Restany, Yves Klein, Jean Tinguely, Martial Raysse, Arman and others, New Realists group, Paris, 1960; organizer, with K. G. Pontus Hulten, *Bewogen Beweging* exhibition, Stedelijk Museum, Amsterdam, 1961; produced first tableau-pieds, 1961; first happenings and events, from 1962; ''objects de magie a la noix'' and exchanged objects according to emotional value (''feilschmarkt'' works), from 1966; first eat-art events, from 1968. Also a poet, and choreographer and producer of ''Autotheatre'' works, mainly with Jean Tinguely, from 1953. Founder-editor, *Material,* concrete poetry review, 5 issues, Darmstadt, 1957–59, *Editions Mat* (Multiplication d'Art Trans formatable), Paris, from 1959, and *Le Petit Colosse de Symi,* Greece, 1967–68; proprietor, with Carlo Schlerie, Dusseldorf, 1970–71; Opens *Il Giardino di Daniel Spoerri,* Seggiano, Italy, 1992. Professor of multimedia, Fachhochscule für Kunst and Design, Cologne, 1977–1982; guest lecturer, San Francisco Art Institute, 1975; lecturer, Hochscule fur Bildende Kunste, Hamburg, 1980; lecturer, Art Academy, Munich, 1983–1989. **Awards:** DAAD Artist's Fellowship, West Berlin, 1978. **Agent:** Galerie Bonnier, 4 rue Saint Laurent, 1207 Geneva, Switzerland. **Address:** 35 Rue de Retriat, Bât. cour gauche F 75020 Paris, France. **Web site:** http://www.danielspoerri.org.

Individual Exhibitions:

1961 *I Quadri a Trappola,* Galleria Schwarz, Milan
Galleri Koepcke, Copenhagen
1962 Galerie Laurence, Paris
Galerie Lauhaus, Cologne
Studio F, Ulm, West Germany
1963 Galerie J, Paris
Galleria Schwarz, Milan
Galerie Rudolf Zwirner, Cologne
Galerie Dorothea Loehr, Frankfurt
Galerie Gerstner und Kutter, Basel
1964 Allan Stone Gallery, New York
Haus am Lutzowplatz, West Berlin
Galerie Rudolf Zwirner, Cologne
Galerie J, Paris
1965 Green Gallery, New York
Allan Stone Gallery, New York
Galleria Schwarz, Milan
Galerie Ad Libitum, Antwerp
City-Galerie, Zurich
Galerie Nachst St. Stephan, Vienna
1966 Galerie J, Paris (with Arman)
City Galerie, Zurich
1967 Spoerri House, Symi, Greece
1968 Galerie Gunar, Dusseldorf
Eat-Art Restaurant, Dusseldorf (opening event)
1969 Gegenverkehr, Aachen, West Germany
Galerie Hanschin, Basel
1970 Eat-Art Galerie, Dusseldorf
Galleria al Vecchio Pastificio, Cavigliano, Italy
1971 Galerie Denise René-Hans Mayer, Dusseldorf
Eat-Art Gallery, Dusseldorf
Stedelijk Museum, Amsterdam (retrospective)
Galerie Seriaal, Amsterdam
Galerie Bischofberger, Zurich
Kunsthalle, Hamburg
1972 Centre National d'Art Contemporain, Paris
Helmhaus, Zurich
1974 Galerie Ben, Nice (with Claude Torey)
Galerie Germain, Paris
Kunsthalle, Dusseldorf
Galerie Gunther Sachs, Hamburg
Schauspeihaus, Bochum, West Germany (theatre decor for *Blue Angel)*
1975 Kunsthandel Brinkman, Amsterdam
Galerie Loeb, Bern
Galerie Bama, Paris
Galleria Multiphla, Milan
Galerie Bischofberger, Zurich
European Gallery, San Francisco
La Galerie Aberante, Plateau Beaubourg, Paris
1976 Spoerri Room, at *Dodspringet,* Charlottenborg, Copenhagen
1978 Galerie Levy, Hamburg
Spoerri Room, *Hammerausstellung,* Kunsthalle, Basel
Deutsches Schauspielhaus, Hamburg (theatre decor for *A Winter's Tale*)
1979 Kölnischer Kunstverein, Cologne (for Musée Sentimental, with M. L. Plessen)
1981 Galerie Bonnier, Geneva
1982 Galerie Beaubourg, Paris
1987 Galerie Littman, Basel
Galleria Unimedia, Geneva
1988 Galerie Beaubourg, Paris
1989 Galerie Littman, Basel (catalog)
1990 Musée National d'Art Moderne, Paris
Centre Georges Pompidou, Paris
Galerie Beaubourg, Paris
Galérie Krinzinger, Vienna
Musée Picasso, Antibes, France (catalog)
1991 *Daniel Spoerri: From A to Z,* Fondazione Mudima, Milan (catalog)
Corps en Morceaux, Raab Galerie, Berlin (also Raab Gallery, London) (catalog)
Petit Lexique Sentimental Autour de Daniel Spoerri, Musée National d'Art Moderne, Centre Georges Pompidou, Paris (catalog)
Background Landscapes, Zabriskie Gallery, New York (catalog)
1992 Zabriskie Gallery, New York
Raab Gallery, Berlin
Galerie Littmann Basel (also Galerie Beaubourg, Basel) (catalog)
1993 Galleria Cesarea, Genova (catalog)
1994 Ammiraglio Action Gallery, Milan
1995 Heinz Holtmann, Cologne, Germany
1998 *Daniel Spoerri—Carnival of the Animals,* Kunstverein, Kassel, Germany
Détrompe-l'Oeil, Ronny Van de Velde Gallery, Antwerp, Belgium (catalog)
Akademie der Künst, Berlin (catalog)
1999 *Meliora Latent,* Comune di Siena, Assessorato alla Cultura, Siena (catalog)
2000 Galleria del Gruppo Credito Valtellinese, Refettorio delle Stelline, Milan (catalog)
2001 Tinguely Museum, Basel (retrospective)

Spoerri has also presented numerous banquets and Eat-Art events throughout Europe since 1970.

Selected Group Exhibitions:

1960 *Festival d'Avant-Garde,* Musee d'Art Moderne, Paris
1961 *The Art of Assemblage,* Museum of Modern Art, New York
1962 *Dylaby,* Stedelijk Museum, Amsterdam
1965 *MAT und MAT MOT,* Galerie der Spiegel, Cologne
1970 *Nouveau Realisme 1960–70,* Rotonda della Besana, Milan

1975 *Biennale,* Venice
1977 *Sucre d'Art,* Musee des Arts Decoratifs, Paris
1980 *Art Zanders '80,* Zanders Feinpapiere AG, Bergischgladbach, West Germany
1985 *Artistic Collaboration in the Twentieth Century,* Hirshhorn Museum and Sculpture Garden, Washington (travelled to Milwaukee Art Museum and J. B. Speed Art Museum, Louisville)
1988 *Fluxus,* Museum of Modern Art, New York
1992 Rudolf Kicken Gallery, Cologne (with Christer Strömholm and Jean Tinguely)
1993 *Akademie 1993,* Akademie der Künst, Berlin (catalog)
1994 *Neo-Dada: Redefining Art 1958–1960,* Scottsdale Center for the Arts, Arizona (catalog)
1997 *De Klein à Warhol,* Centre Georges Pompidou, Paris (catalog)
1998 *La Cuisine de l'Art,* Fondation d'Art Contemporain Daniel et Florence Guerlain, Les Mesnuls, France
Vendredi 13, Centre Culturel Suisse, Paris
2001 *New Installations: Summer 2001,* Il Giardino di Daniel Spoerri, Seggiano, Italy

Collections:

Moderna Museet, Stockholm; Nordjyllands Art Museum, Aalborg, Denmark; Stedelijk Museum, Amsterdam; Rijksmuseum Kröeller-Müeller, Otterloo; Museum Boymans-van Beuningen, Rotterdam; Neues Museum Weserburg, Bremen; Staatliches Museum Schloss Morsbroich, Leverkusen, Germany; Städtisches Museum Abteiberg, Moenchengladbach, Germany; Kaiser-Wilhelm-Museum, Krefeld, Germany; Kestner-Gesellschaft, Hannover; Museum Ludwig, Cologne; Museum Moderner Kunst,Vienna; Petit Palais, Musee d'Art Moderne, Geneva; Kunsthaus Zurich, Switzerland; Kunstmuseum Basel, Switzerland; Kunstmuseum Solothurn, Switzerland; Musee National d'Art Moderne, Centre Georges Pompidou, Paris; Musée Picasso, Antibes, France; Le Cyclop de Tinguely, Milly la Foret, France; The Museum of Modern Art, New York; Museum of Contemporary Art, Sydney, Australia.

Publications:

By SPOERRI: Books—*Topographie Anecdote du Hasard: An Anecdoted Topography of Chance,* with Robert Filliou, Paris 1961, new edition with notes by Emmett Williams, New York 1966, with additional notes by Dieter Roth, Neuwied 1968; *L'Optique Moderne,* with Francois Dufrene, edited by George Maciunas, New York 1962; *Gastronomisches Tagebuch,* Neuwied/West Berlin 1970; *My Mythological Travels,* New York 1970; *Sur Les Keftedes,* Paris 1970; *Hommage a Isaac Feintstin—Motto; Daniel, du Apfel, falle weit vom Stamm,* exhibition catalog with Francois Dufrene, Paris 1972; *Die Bretonische Hausapotheke,* with M. L. Plessen, Cologne 1976; *Bretonische Heilquellen,* Cologne 1980; *Daniel Spoerri: Catalog anecdote de seize oeuvres de l'Artiste de 1960 a 1964,* exhibition catalog, Geneva 1981; *Mythology and Meatballs: A Greek Island Diary/Cookbook,* translated by Emmett Williams, Berkeley, 1982; *L'Art? C'est une Meilleure Idée: Entretiens (1972–1984)* with Irmeline Lebeer, Nîmes 1997; *Journal Gastronomique,* Geneva 1998. **Articles—** Interview with Patrick Beurard and Sarenco in *Opus International,* no. 110, September-October 1988; ''Daniel Spoerri: Artists Palettes and Booby-Trap Painting'' in *Cimaise,* vol. 37, April/May 1990; interview with Giancarlo Politi in *Flash Art (International Edition),* no. 154, October 1990; interview with Eddy Devolder in *Artefactum,* vol. 9, no. 45, September-November 1992; interview with Maïten Bouisset in *Art Press,* no. 197, December 1994; ''Art that Is Completely Explicable Is Not Art,'' in *African Art from the Han Coray Collection, 1916–1928,* Prestel 1998. **Film—***Resurrection,* with Tony Morgan, 1968.

On SPOERRI: Books—*I Quadri a Trappola di Daniel Spoerri,* exhibition catalog with text by Alain Jouffroy, Milan 1961; *Daniel Spoerri,* exhibition catalog with text by Pierre Restany, Milan 1963; *Encyclopedia des Fraces; Attrapes et Mystification* by N. Armaud, Paris 1964; *Pop Art* by Lucy R. Lippard, New York and London 1966; *FOEW & ONBWHNW* by Dick Higgins, New York 1969; *Arthitektur Concept Art* by Dick Higgins and Wolf Vostell, Dusseldorf 1969; *Pop Art et Cie* by Francois Pluchart, Paris 1971; *Daniel Spoerri,* exhibition catalog with texts by Claus Bremer and Marja Bloem, Zurich 1972; *Daniel Spoerri,* exhibition catalog, Paris 1972; *An Analysis of the Avant Garde in the 20th Century* by Michael Langer, Worms 1984; *Kunst in Dusseldorf* by Helga Meister, Hamburg 1988; *Fluxus Codex* by Jon Hendricks, New York 1988; *Daniel Spoerri* by Otto Hahn, Paris 1990; *Il Giardino di Daniel Spoerri* by Anna Mazzanti, Firenze 1998; *Daniel Spoerri: Biographie und Werk* by Heidi E Violand-Hobi, Munich 1998. **Articles—**''Le Musée Récu de Daniel Spoerri'' in *Du,* no. 1, January 1989; ''Spoerri: Piéges pour l'Oeil'' by Maïten Bouisset in *Beaux Arts Magazine,* no. 77, March 1990; ''Daniel Spoerri: Was Wäre die Kunst ohne den Tod'' by Heinz Peter Schwerfel in *ART: Das Kunstmagazin,* no. 8, August 1995; ''Der Skulpturenpark von Daniel Spoerri'' in *Berner Kunstmitteilungen,* no. 313, January-February 1998; ''Spoerri: The Great Magironic Exhibit'' by Gilles Plazy in *Cimaise,* vol. 45, no. 252, March/April 1998; ''Spoerri En Son Domaine'' by Hugo Lacroix in *Beaux Arts Magazine,* no. 171, August 1998; ''Kunst und Genuss: Eat Art und Fallenbilder von Daniel Spoerri'' by Anne Thurmann-Jajes in *Kunst + Unterricht,* no. 225, September 1998; ''Nel Giardino di Daniel Spoerri'' by Nicoletta Cobolli Gigli in *Arte,* no. 323, July 2000. **Video—***Daniel Spoerri: Art Is What Makes Life More Interesting Than Art,* Paris 1998.

* * *

Daniel Spoerri, who acted and danced when he was a youth, has a strong sense of theater, whether visual or in the actual performance. His personal motto is: ''Daniel, du Apfel falle weit vom Stamm.''

In the mid 1950s he moved on from an appearance in the everlasting *Count of Luxembourg* to join the cast of the Berne Stadttheater's production of *Peter and the Wolf* (1956) and later produced and created the choreography for *Tschumi* (''Colour Ballet,'' in which he also danced).

Then he and Dieter Roth, with Pol Bury, Emmett Williams, Luca and Bremer published a review of concrete and ideogrammatic poetry called *Material.*

By 1960 this indefatigable and inventive Rumanian was staging exhibitions of his own works, having made contact with an assortment of other artists, including Duchamp, Albers, Soto and Agam. Later in Paris he joined forces with Gerstner, Man Ray, Tinguely and Vasarely. At this time he was deep into his MAT experiments (Multiplication/Art/Transformation).

Spoerri seems to have been at the centre of so many co-operative performances by contemporary artists (Luginbuhl, Ultevdt, Niki de Saint-Phalle, Rauschenberg and Raysse). What is so extraordinary about him and his *gauchiste* activities?

In 1962 it was typical of him and his works that he should have starred in Victor Musgrave's *Festival of Misfits* at London's Gallery One where the windows of 6 North Audley Street were covered with white sheets behind which the visual carnage was running riot. The other eight participants included Ben Vautier and Olof Ultvedt, but Spoerri's messy unfinished meals, dirty glasses and cigarette stubs attached to their uncleared tables made the deepest impression. Here was a terrible paradox—immediacy frozen into permanence. Litter and corruption were suddenly given art status. ''The Bones of Szekely Gulyas—with the cooperation of rats'' was offered as proof that actuality, even if it suffers the onslaught of time, *still matters.*

What happend to all this poignant disarray?

As usual with this artist, he operated on several levels simultaneously. The tables might be tidied up a bit and then ''hung'' like pictures on the wall, their bottles, plates, cutlery and napkins all firmly glued into place and perpetuity for the benefit of those who came to see them at the CNAC in Paris, or his admirers could join in a culinary frolic at Dusseldorf's Eat Art gallery where a special Spoerri triple-tiara cake presented to Pierre Restany amid art-debris like the appetisers he cooked in the manner of Arman and other artists, but for Seerial, the multiple-shop in Amsterdam, he had other aspects of anti-gravity and inverse-sociology to provide: ''Le Pourboire de Madeleine'' (round tin tray with coins stuck to it so that it could be suspended picture-style from the wall) or his experiments with pairs of children's shoes (one lot suffering from rat urination, another showing how it had been deftly chewed, and in one case the calamity of the shoe caught in the mouse trap—all of them presented on trays of gravel). Spoerri's imagination is always heretical. His ''Homage to an Unknown Soldier'' is an erect penis with a crown like a stahlhelm, the whole trophy mounted like a big game hunter's prize on a wooden shield.

The artist is like the clown of contemporary art. All great clowns are artists.

—Sheldon Williams

STAECK, Klaus

Nationality: German. **Born:** Pulsnitz, Dresden, 28 February 1938. **Education:** Educated in Bitterfeld, near Halle/Salle, 1944–56; studied law in Heidelberg, Hamburg, and West Berlin 1957–64; self-taught in art. **Career:** Independent artist, Heidelberg, since 1964; first prints and posters, 1960; first wood-prints, 1964–67; founder, Edition Tangente, now Edition Staeck press, Heidelberg, 1965; founder-editor, with Peter Knorr and Siegfried Mahnert, *Tangente-Report* magazine, Heidelberg, 1965; worked with the artists Jochen Gerz, 1967, and Gerhard Steidl, 1970. Founder, Politischer Arbeitskresis, student association, Klausenpfad, Heidelberg, 1961; candidate, Social Democratic Party (SPD) 1967; chairman, lawyer, and graphics editor, Freie Hochscule fur Kreativitat und Interdisziplinaire Forschung, Dusseldorf, 1973. Art tutor, Studenthochhausen, Klausenpfad, Heidelberg, 1967–69; guest instructor, Gesamthochschule, Kassel, West Germany, 1971; professor, Gesamthochschule, Universitat Essen, 1981; professor, Kunstakademie, Dusseldorf, 1986–88. **Awards:** Zille-Preis, *Exhibition of Socio-Critical Art* West Berlin, 1970; Pratt Center Prize, New York 1968; Verkehrsburos prize, *Grafikbiennale,* Vienna, 1972; Forderpreis, *Integrafik,* East Berlin, 1976; Kritikerpreis, West Berlin 1979; Gold Medal, *Biennale fur fotomontage,* Gridziadz, Poland, 1979. **Address:** Ingrimstrasse 3/Postfach 102063, 69 Heidelberg, West Germany.

Individual Exhibitions:

Staeck has had more than 3,000 one-man exhibitions at galleries, universities and institutes throughout Germany and Europe since 1960, including:

1965 Viola Gallery, Prague
1975 *Politick Affiches,* Stedelijk Van Abbemuseum, Eindhoven, Netherlands
1978 *Ruckblick in Sachen Kunst und Politik,* Kunstverein, Frankfurt (travelled to Heidelberg, Graz, West Berlin Vienna Aarhus, Russelheim and Hannover)
1979 Wilhelm-Lehmbruck-Museum, Duisburg, West Germany
1983 Henie-Onstad Kunstsenter, Hovikodden, Norway
1985 Konsthall, Malmo, Sweden
1986 Kunsthalle, Darmstadt, West Germany
1989 NRW—Landeshaus, Bonn (traveling retrospective)
1996 *Staeck in der Produktion,* Standort Hardheim, Göttingen (catalog)
2001 *Posters and Postcards,* Goethe Institut, Helsinki

Selected Group Exhibitions:

1967 *International Graphics Biennale,* Ljublajana, Yugoslavia
1969 *Intermadia 69,* Heidelberg
1970 *Kunst und Politik,* Badischer Kustverein, Karisruhe (toured Europe)
1971 *Biennale de Paris,* Parc Floral, Paris
1972 *Documenta,* Kassel, West Germany
1973 *Kunst im Politischen Kampf,* Kunstverein, Hannover
1974 *Projekt 74,* Kunstverein, Cologne
1977 *Documenta 6,* Museum Fridericianum, Kassel, West Germany (and *Documenta 7,* 1982; *Documenta 8,* 1987)
1985 *Kunst in der Bundesrepublik 1945–85,* Nationalgalerie, West Berlin
1986 *Beuys zu Ehren,* Lenbachaus, Munich
1993 *Akademie 1993,* Akademie der Künst, Berlin (catalog)
The Art of Attack, Wight Art Gallery, University of California, Los Angeles

Collections:

Kunstverein, Heidelberg; Kunstverein, Dusseldorf; Kunsthalle, Cologne; Kaiser-Wilhelm-Museum, Krefeld, West Germany; Nationalgalerie, East Berlin; Kunstmuseum, Basel; Museum des 20. Jahrhunderts, Vienna; Stedelijk van Abbemuseum, Eindhoven, Netherlands; Mahnsche Galerie, Brno, Czechoslovakia; Kulturhuset, Stockholm.

Publications:

By STAECK: Books—*Intermedia 69,* exhibition catalog with Jochen Goetze, Heidelberg 1969; *Pornografie,* with Peter Gorsen, Giessen and Göttingen 1971; *Befragung der Documenta,* Göttingen, 1972;

Plakate Abreissen Verboten, with Ingeborg Karst, Göttingen 1973; *Die Reichen mussen noch Reicher Werden,* with Ingeborg Karst, Reinbeck 1973; *Der Fall Staeck,* Göttingen 1975; *Die Kunst findet nicht im Saale statt,* with Dieter Adelmann, Reinbek 1976; *Eine Zensur findet gelegentlich statt,* with Dieter Adelmann, Göttingen 1977; *Gedichte/Collagen,* with Heinrich Boll, Göttingen 1979; *Die Gedankens sind frei,* East Berlin 1982; *Staeck's Umwelt,* Göttingen 1984; *Klaus Staeck: Sand fürs Getriebe,* with Heinrich Albertz, Göttingen 1989; *Klaus Staeck: Plakate,* Göttingen 1992; *Mein Trauriges Gesicht,* with Heinrich Böll, Göttingen 1994; *Ohne Auftrag: Unterwegs in Sachen Kunst und Politik,* Göttingen 2000. **Articles—** ''Klaus Staeck'' in *Kunstforum International,* no. 93, February-March 1988; interview with Karlheinz Schmid in *Kunstforum International,* no. 95, June-July 1988; interview with Friedrich Hebbel in *ART: Das Kunstmagazin,* no. 11, November 1992; interview with Ingo Arend in *Kunstforum International,* no. 132, November 1995–1996; interview with Heinz-Norbert Jocks in *Kunstforum International,* no. 149, March 2000.

On STAECK: Books—*Kunst und Politik,* exhibition catalog with texts by G. Bussmann, Robert Kudielka, Herbert Marcuse and Gérald Gassiot-Talabot, Karlsruhe 1970; *Mail Art: Communications à Distance, Concept* by Jean-Marc Poinsot, with a preface by Jean Clair, Paris 1971; *Kunstjahrbuch 2,* edited by Jürgen Harten, Horst Richter, Karl Ruhrberg and Wieland Schmied, Hannover 1972; *Deutsch Kunst der 70er Jahre: Plastik, Objekte, Aktionen* by Jürgen Morschel, Munich 1972; *Projekt 74: Aspekte internationaler Kunst am Anfang der 70er Jahre,* exhibition catalog with texts by Dieter Roth, Evelyn Weiss, Manfred Schneckenburger and others, Cologne 1974; *Klaus Staeck: Politik Affiches,* exhibition catalog, Eindhoven, Netherlands, 1975; *Klaus Staeck: Ruckblick in Sachen Kunst und Politik,* exhibition catalog with texts by G. Bussmann, Dieter Adelmann, Bazon Brock and others, Frankfurt 1978; *Documenta,* exhibition catalog, 2 vols., edited by Rudi H. Fuchs, Kassel, West Germany 1982; *Documenta 8,* exhibition catalog edited by Manfred Schneckenburger, Kassel, West Germany 1987. **Articles—**''Man—Always in the Centre of Interest'' by Jürgen Weichardt in *Projekt,* no. 5, 1989.

*

With my work I would like to contribute towards exposing the untruthfulness of the excess of pictures surrounding us—I should like not to present what has been exposed, but to expose what has been presented.

As method I have chosen irony because to me the acridity and dullness that characterize most political discussions arouse fear. Dogmatism and oppression are often nor far apart. To create a lasting alteration of consciousness in the direction of democratic socialism in the minds of those who hold differing political opinions, it is necessary to be inventive. Against an inert mass, cunning offers the only chance. I want to bring about necessary discussions on important political problems. I should like to place questions in such a way that they are hard to avoid. Irony helps me in this and is usually more effective than ponderous appeals or threats.

For me the attempt to reflect reality with pictorial means and to effect something in it represents rising above traditional art. An intensive study of the media is essential to any serious attempt at departure from the restrictions imposed by the encrusted art concept. In my case this led to posters, stickers, postcards and leaflets. It is with these media that I obtain access to the public, without which my work would be pointless. I convey my political ideas through posters which are made for the streets. Thus I reach everyone participating in daily life on the streets, in contrast to the past, when I had to rely on a small, elite circle of addresses.

The breakthrough out of boredom of the art ghettos, where paintings have stagnated to become pure decor, brought with it, though, along with problems of content, also new distributional and financial problems. Since then my work has largely drawn away from the business of art. It is mainly young people who employ my posters politically, but several hundred thousand posters and stickers have, for instance, been acquired by workers: those same workers that so many would like to get through to, but actually cannot. I know from representative inquiries which population groups I reach with my work: all groups feel themselves to be approached, though some more than others.

At present I am in the process of intensifying my contacts with the trade unions: numerous exhibitions in union headquarters, contributions to union newspapers and discussions with workers. At the same time I am increasingly engaged in collaboration with youth groups (e.g. exhibitions in youth centres and schools).

—Klaus Staeck

STAMOS, Theodoros

Nationality: American. **Born:** New York City, 31 December 1922. **Education:** Educated in public schools, New York; studied sculpture, under Simon Kennedy and Joseph Kouzal, at the American Artist School, New York, 1936 (on scholarship). **Career:** Painter; worked as hatblocker, florist, printer, and frame-maker, 1939–43; commission for work on *SS Argentina,* Moore McCormack Lines, New York, 1946; toured Western America, 1947; travelled to France, Italy and Greece, 1948. Taught at Hartley Settlement House and Black Mountain College, North Carolina, 1950–54; instructor, Art Students League, 1955; lecturer, School of Fine Arts, Columbia University, New York, 1966; professor, Brandeis University, Waltham, Massachusetts, 1967–68. **Awards:** Tiffany Foundation Fellowship, 1951; National Institute of Arts and Letters Award, New York, 1956; Brandeis University Creative Arts Award, Waltham, Massachusetts, 1959; Mainichi Newspaper Prize, *Tokyo International,* 1967; National Arts Foundation Award, Washington, D.C., 1967; **Agent:** Kuoros Gallery, 23 East 73rd St., New York, New York 10021, U.S.A. **Died:** 2 February 1997.

Individual Exhibitions:

1943 Wakefield Gallery, New York
1945 Mortimer Brandt Gallery, New York
1947 Betty Parsons Gallery, New York
1948 Betty Parsons Gallery, New York
1949 Betty Parsons Gallery, New York
1950 Philips Memorial Gallery, Washington, D.C.
1951 Betty Parsons Gallery, New York
1953 Betty Parsons Gallery, New York
1954 Philips Memorial Gallery, Washington, D.C.

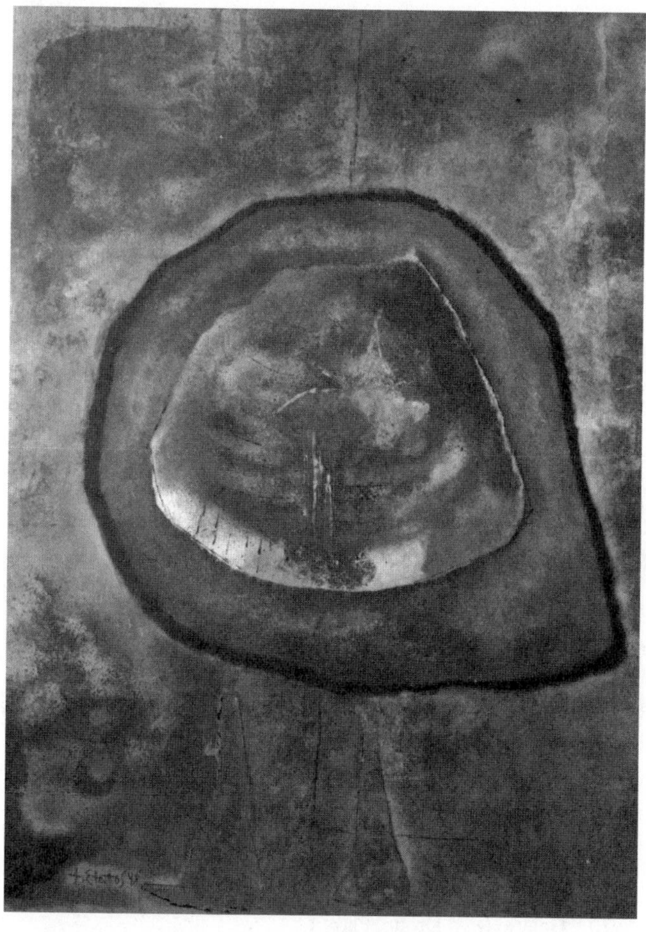

Theodoros Stamos: *Eccho,* 1948. ©Francis G. Mayer/Corbis.

1956 Betty Parsons Gallery, New York
1957 Philadelphia Art Alliance
Gump's Gallery, San Francisco
1958 André Emmerich Gallery, New York
Corcoran Gallery of Art, Washington, D.C. (retrospective)
1960 André Emmerich Gallery, New York
Gimpel Fils Gallery, London
McNay Art Institute, San Antonio, Texas
1961 André Emmerich Gallery, New York
Galleria del Naviglio, Milan
1962 André Emmerich Gallery, New York
1963 André Emmerich Gallery, New York
1964 André Emmerich Gallery, New York
1966 André Emmerich Gallery, New York
1967 Spingold Theater Arts Center Gallery, Waltham, Massachusetts
1968 André Emmerich Gallery, New York
1969 Waddington Fine Arts Gallery, Montreal
1970 André Emmerich Gallery, New York
1972 Marlborough-Gerson Gallery, New York
1973 Joslyn Art Museum, Omaha, Nebraska
1974 Athens Gallery
1977 Louis K. Meisel Gallery, New York
Galerie Le Portail, Heidelberg
Morgan Art Gallery, Shawnee Mission, Kansas
1978 Hokin Gallery, Palm Beach, Florida
Union College, Schenectady, New York
1979 Wichita State University, Kansas
1980 Munson-Williams-Proctor Institute, Utica, New York
State University of New York at New Paltz (retrospective)
1981 Martha White Gallery, Louisville, Kentucky
Louis K. Meisel Gallery, New York
1982 Karen and Jean Bernier Gallery, Athens, Greece
1984 Knoedler Gallery, Zurich
1985 Galerie Wurthle, Vienna
Kouros Gallery, New York
Ericson Gallery, New York
1986 Kouros Gallery, New York
Hokin Gallery, Palm Beach, Florida
Harcourts Contemporary, San Francisco
Grimaldis Gallery, Baltimore, Maryland
1987 Kouros Gallery, New York
Pierdes Gallery of Modern Art, Athens, Greece
Turske and Turske, Zürich
Stadisches Museum Leverkusen, Germany
1988 Kouros Gallery, New York
Grimaldis Gallery, Baltimore
Dorsky Gallery, New York
Studio d'Art Zanussi, Milan, Italy
Museum Morsbroich, Leverkusen, Germany
Jack Rutberg Fine Arts, Los Angeles
Pascal de Sarthe Gallery, San Francisco
1989 Ileana Tounta Contemporary Art Center, Athens, Greece
Kouros Gallery, New York
1990 Kouros Gallery, New York
Galeria Verlato, Milan
Louis Newman Galleries, Beverly Hills
1991 Kouros Gallery, New York
1992 ACA Galleries, New York
1994 Kouros Gallery, New York
El Greco Society of Visual Arts, Old Archeological Museum of Thessaloniki
1995 Northern Westchester Center for the Arts, Mt. Kisco, New York
1996 Kouros Gallery, New York
Hiro Gallery, Tokyo
1997 *Theodoros Stamos: 1922—1997, A Retrospective,* National Gallery Alexandros Soutzios Museum, Athens, Greece
1998 Kouros Gallery, New York

Selected Group Exhibitions:

1945 *Whitney Annual,* New York (and 1946)
1948 *Biennale,* Venice
1950 *Contemporary American Painting,* University of Illinois, Urbana
1952 *Carnegie International,* Carnegie Institute, Pittsburgh
1959 *Documenta,* Kassel, West Germany
1961 *Biennale,* Tokyo
1968 *Dada, Surrealism, and Their Heritage,* Museum of Modern Art (toured the United States)
1978 *Abstract Expressionism: The Formative Years,* Cornell University, Ithaca, New York
1980 *American Drawings,* Du Bose Gallery, Houston

1982 *A Curator's Choice 1942–63,* Rose Esman Gallery, New York

Collections:

Albright-Knox Art Gallery, Buffalo, New York; The Art Institute of Chicago; Bayerische Staatsgemaldesammlung, Staatsgalerie Moderner Kunst, Munich, Germany; The Corcoran Gallery of Art, Washington, D.C.; Fogg Art Museum, Harvard University, Cambridge, Massachusetts; Hirshhorn Museum and Sculpture Garden, Smithsonian Institution, Washington, D.C.; The Metropolitan Museum of Art, New York, New York; Museu d'Arte Moderno, Rio de Janeiro, Brazil; The Museum of Modern Art, New York, New York; National Picture Gallery, Athens, Greece; National Pinacotek, Athens, Greece; Solomon R. Guggenheim Museum, New York; Tel Aviv Museum, Tel Aviv, Israel; Whitney Museum of Art, New York, New York.

Publications:

On STAMOS: Books—*Stamos,* exhibition catalog by B. B. Newman, New York 1947; *Theodoros Stamos* by Kenneth Sawyer, Paris 1960; *Stamos* by Ralph Pomeroy, New York 1971; *Theodoros Stamos* by Ralph Pomeroy, New York 1973; *Theodoros Stamos: Works from 1945 to 1984,* exhibition catalog with essays by Barbara Cavaliere and Theodore F. Wolff, Zurich 1984; *Stamos,* exhibition catalog with essay by Dore Ashton, New York 1985; *Theodoros Stamos: An Overview,* exhibition catalog with essay by Barbara Cavaliere, New York, 1991; *Theodoros Stamos 1992–1997: A Retrospective,* edited by Anna Kafetsi, Athens, 1997.

* * *

Younger by many years, but professionally their contemporary, Stamos (as he prefers being called) shared the explorations and discoveries of the American abstract painters who found their profound footing after the Second World War. Along with such painters as Baziotes and Rothko he depicted biomorphic subject matter in thin washes of pigment—in his case the sea and its creatures, rocks, plants and leaves. This led to the abstraction of cultivated fields on Long Island and a series of works influenced by the Orient having mostly to do with the effect of light falling through semi-transparent screens creating imaginary, non-literal tea houses. Fire and snow played their parts too along with the overhead viewpoint, turned toward riverbed-like channels of thick, rich paint—''landscapes'' without any horizons—that occupied him in the 1950s.

A long series of ''sun boxes'' followed. Paintings in which two rectangles suspended like reflections of one another balanced in fields of radiant color. During this same period a group of wall hangings were produced after ''cartoons'' fashioned from the cut and torn paper, along with works on paper and a series of prints.

A trip to Greece resulted in a shift from the sunbox format—the ''boxes'' giving way to larger, more open rectangles with washes of paint sweeping into various parts of the canvas much like shallow waves. These paintings were an extension of an ''Infinity Series'' begun in the late 1960s where an effort to push forms nearer and nearer to the periphery of the actual canvas led to emptier and emptier expanses of color. More or less in reaction to this, there then evolved paintings full of small, highly active forms intricately composed, which are a little like the shapes found in the work of Arthur Dove (an artist much admired by Stamos).

A subtle, complex and powerful colorist, Stamos continued to probe the limits of abstraction in the last quarter of the twentieth century, firmly committed to the tradition of the easel picture and the painterly concerns which it has produced.

—Ralph Pomeroy

STÄMPFLI, Peter

Nationality: Swiss. **Born:** Deisswil, Switzerland, 3 July 1937. **Education:** Ecole des Arts et Métiers, Bienne, Switzerland, 1954–55; studied painting with Max von Muhlenen, Berne, 1954–59. **Family:** Married Ana Maria Torello in 1961. **Career:** Independent painter, Paris, since 1960: images of human body and food details, 1963–65; automobile and tire details, 1966–70; tire-track images, from 1970; first sculptures, 1985. **Agent:** Galerie Lelong, 13 rue de Teheran, 75008 Paris; Sonia Zannettacci, 6 rue des Granges, Geneva. **Address:** 54 rue Notre Dame de Lorette, 75009 Paris, France.

Individual Exhibitions:

1966 Galerie Bischofberger, Zurich
Galerie Rive Droite, Paris
1967 Galerie Tobies et Silex, Cologne
1968 Instituto Torcuato di Tella, Buenos Aires
1969 Galerie Rive Droite, Paris
Galerie Bischofberger, Zurich
1970 Galerie Rive Droite, Paris
1971 Galerie Rive Droite, Paris
Galerie Richard Foncke, Ghent
Galleria Christian Stein, Turin
1972 Palais des Beaux-Arts, Brussels
1974 Musée Galliera, Paris
1976 Galerie Jean Larcarde, Paris
Musée de l'Abbaye Sainte Croix, Les Sables-d'Olonne, France
1978 Galerie Jean Larcarde, Paris
1979 Galerie Maeght, Zurich
Musee d'Art et d'Industrie, St. Etienne, France
1980 Centre Georges Pompidou, Paris
Galerie Maeght, Paris
1982 Galerie Maeght, Zurich
Kunsthaus, Aarau, Switzerland
Galerie Saapone, Nice, France
1987 Palais Municipal, Lyon, France
1988 Galerie Lelong, Paris
Galerie Sonia Zannettacci, Geneva
Abbaye des Cordeliers, Châteauroux
1989 Galerie Sabine Wachters, Knokke, Belgium
1991 Galerie de l'Ecole d'Art, Marseilles
Abbatiale de Bellelay, Switzerland
Galerie Sonia Zannettacci, Geneva
1992 Galerie Sabine Wachters, Knokke, Belgium
1994 Musée de Dôle, France
Sabine Wachters Fine Art, Knokke, Belgium
Galerie Sabine Wachters, Brussels

Peter Stämpfli: *M + S 94,* 1994. Photo by Andre Morain. ©2001 Artists Rights Society (ARS), NY/ADAGP, Paris.

Galerie Sonia Zannettacci, Geneva
1996 Oda Sala d'Art, Barcelona
1997 Villa Tamaris, La Seyne-sur-Mer, France
1998 Le Palais de Congrès de Paris
1999 Musée d'Art et d'Histoire, Fribourg, Switzerland
Galerie Sonia Zannettacci, Geneva

Selected Group Exhibitions:

1963 *Biennale,* Paris
1967 *Bienal,* Sao Paulo
1970 *Biennale,* Venice
1973 *Contemporary Swiss Art,* Tel Aviv Museum
1974 *Hyperrealistes Americans/Realistes Europeans,* Centre National d'Art Contemporain, Paris (travelled to Hannover; Rotterdam; Milan)
1976 *Aspects of Realism,* Rothmans Gallery, Stratford, Ontario (toured Canada)
1978 *Art Contemporain Suisse,* Helmhaus, Zurich
1985 *Dinge des Menschen,* Stadtische Kunsthalle, Recklinghausen, Germany
1992 *Manifeste,* Musée National d'Art Moderne, Paris
1993 *Differentes Natures,* La Defense, Paris (travelled to Palau de la Virreina, Barcelona)
1996 *Dessins de la Fondation Maeght,* Musée du Luxembourg, Paris
1997 *The Pop '60s,* Centro Cultural de Bélem, Lisbon
1998 *Les Sixties,* Brighton Museum and Art Gallery, Brighton, England
1999 *Pop Impressions Europe/U.S.A.,* Museum of Modern Art, New York

Collections:

Kunsthaus, Zurich; Collection de la Peau de Lion, Zurich; Fonds National d'Art Contemporain, Paris; Centre Georges Pompidou, Paris; Kunstmuseum, Berne; Kunsthaus, Aarau; Fonds Regional d'Art Contemporain, Picardy; Musée d'Art et d'Industrie, St. Etienne; Musée de Dunquerque; Hara Museum, Tokyo; Museum of Modern Art, New York.

Publications:

On Stämpfli: Books—*Le Peinture de Stämpfli* by Alain Jouffroy, Turin 1970; *Art in France* by Jean Clair, Paris 1972; *Peter Stämpfli,* exhibition catalog with essay by Bernard Ceysson, Aarau 1982; *Peter Stämpfli: Vom Objektportrat zur geometrischen Struktur,* exhibition catalog with preface by Fritz Billeter, Zurich 1982; *Le Pastel* by Genevieve Monnier, Geneva 1985; *25 Ans d'Art en France* by Jean Louis Pradel, Paris 1986; *Peter Stämpfli* by Daniel Abadie, Geneva 1991; *Peter Stämpfli,* exhibition catalog with text by Jean-Luc Daval, Dole 1994; *Peter Stämpfli: De la Roda à Profunditat de l'Ésser,* exhibition catalog with text by J. Maria Cadena, Barcelona 1996; *Peter Stämpfli,* exhibition catalog with text by Raoul-Jean Moulin, La Seyne-sur-Mer 1997; *Peter Stämpfli* by Marco Livingstone and Yvonne Lehnherr, Bern 1999.

*

All my work consists of seizing the image, the gesture, the objects which surround us, living what is going on around us, being sensitive to present events and translating them into painting.

I have taken a more particular interest in cars: I was dazzled by the object in its new, intact, self-advertising state, never by the used object. There was never the red print of lipstick on my glasses, never a trace of dirt on the wing of a car. I painted chrome bumpers, headlights, radiators, and then my attention fixed itself on the wheels. From the wheels I passed to the tire, then to the tire-mark . . . . The city is a part of all our lives. There was a period when painters depicted hunting scenes, portraits of kings. Today, the artist can only paint what he sees. I am not making an ironic proposal, I am simply seeking to draw up a report of a period. My images are in no instance reproductions; they are interpretations. The photograph is a starting-point, which I then translate into paint. It is very probable that one day I shall paint something other than tires; it would take more than that to stop me from painting. The development of my plastic itinerary can appear extremely linear and logical: wheels-tires-tiremarks-structures. But if someone had told it to me ten years ago I wouldn't have believed them.

—Peter Stämpfli

* * *

What immediately holds one's attention in Stämpfli's work is the imperious and absolute character of its forward progression. Nothing to cling to, to stop and take pleasure in: just series of pictures carried so implacably to their extreme consequences that, exclusively retaining the attention, they displace it from the preceding work, making of the oeuvre as a whole phenomenon of perpetual actuality. What is more, the current language of the art world translates this state of fact perfectly: Stämpfli has been by turns, without anybody having emphasised these sucessive shifts, the painter of cars, the painter of wheels, the painter of tires. He is, today, the painter of tire-marks.

Between Stämpfli and James Rosenquist exists the same relationship as between Yves Klein and Mondrian: there has, indeed been no lack of comparisons between Stämpfli's first pictures, painted at the same time as those of the initial generation of pop artists, and the works of Rosenquist. It was a way for critics to confine themselves to a thematic reading without noting the specificity of Stämpfli's work. Renouncing all montage of images, all relationships of an intellectual or emotional nature, isolating, on the contrary, the object on the white background of the canvas, he situates the object in an abstract space and depersonalises it. This dwindling of the context was given material form by Stämpfli when in 1966, ''Rouge Baiser'' (Red Kiss), he cut out the picture following the exact shape of the lips. With ''SS 396, No. 2'' (1969) Stämpfli's procedure marks a decisive step. The picture, in the shape of a wheel, is at once object and painting: the subject can be read simultaneously as realist painting, image of industrial civilization, and as concentric zones of colour, close to the works of Kenneth Noland, for example.

The reductive character, which is clearly marked in Stämpfli's work in his circumscribing his field of investigation from the wheel to the tire alone, pushed this ambiguity of reading even further: the sculpted motif is at once both something real, everyday, identifiable in the repertoire of trademarks and industrial firms, and a structure which is abstract, repetitive, serial. The surface of the canvas assuming the precise form of the object, the identity is—except for volume—total. Perhaps it is in this slight distance—the perspectival crushing of an object reduced to the two-dimensional surface of the canvas—that the reason for the following stage should be sought.

The tire-mark, the negative of the schema of the tire, first combined with the picture, then independent, is a questioning of the classical structure of the picture: canvas of rectangular, square, or round format covered with paint. Through his personal language, Stämpfli joins up with the questions posed by an artist such as Frank Stella. He gives them, however, a more conceptual continuation as a result of the dialectic shift of the content of the work, in the absence of gratuitousness of the realist mode of writing finding its elements outside all formalism. The recent continuations of Stämpfli's work, all questioning of visual reality by means of perspective, the conflict with pictorial reality, place these apparently so specific paintings among those which are entering in the most penetrating fashion the debate being carried on by contemporary artists, that of the nature of art itself.

—Daniel Abadie

STANLEY, Robert

Nationality: American. **Born:** Yonkers, New York, 3 January 1932. **Education:** Oglethorpe University, Atlanta, 1949–53, B.A. 1953; High Museum of Art, Atlanta, 1952; Columbia University, New York, 1953; Art Students League, New York, 1953; Brooklyn Museum of Art School, New York (Max Beckmann Scholarship), 1954–56. **Family:** Married Jane Hutchinson in 1961 (divorced, 1968); married Marilyn Herzka in 1970; stepson Perry Brandston, stepdaughter Lori Brandston-Greene, four grandchildren. **Career:** Independent artist known for very large figurative paintings: lived and worked in New York. Instructor of drawing and painting, School of Visual Arts, New York, 1970–72, 1984—; visiting artist, Louisiana State University, Baton Rouge, 1976; visiting lecturer, St. Lawrence University, Canton, New York, 1978; visiting artist, Syracuse University, New York, 1978; and Princeton University, New Jersey, 1979–80. **Awards:** Cassandra Foundation Award, 1969; Igor Foundation Award for Painting, 1987. **Address:** 3 Crosby Street, New York, New York 10013, U.S.A. **Died:** In New York, of cancer, 14 November 1997.

Individual Exhibitions:

1965 Bianchini Gallery, New York
1966 Bianchini Gallery, New York
Galerie Orez, The Hague
Contemporary Arts Center, Cincinnati, Ohio
Galerie Ricke, Kassel, West Germany
1967 Galerie Ricke, Kassel, West Germany
Galerie Kuckels, Bochum, West Germany
1968 Kleine Galerie, Frankfurt
1969 Gegenverkehr, Aachen, West Germany
On 1st, New York
1972 Warren Benedeck Gallery, New York
1974 New York Cultural Center
1976 Union Gallery, Louisiana University, Baton Rougue
1977 P.S. 1, Long Island City, New York
1978 Hal Bromm Gallery, New York (photographs)
St. Thomas Aquinas College, Sparkill, New York
E. Weiner Gallery, New York
1980 E. Weiner Gallery, New York

Holly Keenberg Contemporary Art, Winnipeg, Manitoba (retrospective)
1983 Bucklew-Goehring Gallery, Tampa, Florida
1986 Le Consortium Centre d'Art Contemporain, Dijon, France
John Davis Gallery, New York
1987 Galerie Lavrov, Paris
New Arts Program, Kutztown, Pennsylvania
John Davis Gallery, New York
1988 Galleri Ericsson, Gothenburg, Sweden
Konstmässan Stockholm Art Fair Sollentuna, Stockholm
Gallerie Georges Lavrov, Paris
ART 1988, Basel
1989 Galerie Bébert, Rotterdam, Holland
1990 The Painted Bride Art Center, Philadelphia
1991 Greenville County Art Museum, South Carolina
1992 Barbierato Arte Contemporanea, Asiago, Italy
Moderne Kunst Dietmar Werle, Cologne
1998 Mitchell Algus Gallery, New York

Selected Group Exhibitions:

1968 *Documenta 4,* Kassel, West Germany
1970 *Monumental Art,* Contemporary Arts Center, Cincinnati, Ohio
1973 *Biennial,* Whitney Museum, New York
1975 *The Nude in American Art,* New York Cultural Center
1977 *Outside the City Limits: Landscapes by New York City Artists,* Thorpe Intermedia Gallery, Sparkfill, New York
1980 *The Director's Choice,* Fine Arts Gallery, University of Wisconsin at Milwaukee
1981 *Illusion of Light,* Worcester Art Museum, Massachussets
1983 *Rutgers Archives for Printmaking,* Jane Voorchees Zimmerli Art Museum, Rutgers, New Jersey
1985 *A Decade of Visual Arts at Princeton,* Princeton Art Museum, New Jersey
1987 *Overtalk,* White Columns, New York

Collections:

Whitney Museum, New York; Metropolitan Museum of Art, New York; High Museum of Art, Atlanta; Fogg Art Museum, Cambridge, Massachusetts; Contemporary Art Center, Milwaukee, Wisconsin; Washington University, St. Louis, Missouri; Ludwig Collection, Aachen, Germany; Greenville County Art Museum, Greenville, South Carolina; Ft. Worth Art Museum, Ft. Worth, Texas.

Publications:

By STANLEY: Books—*Tracks,* New York 1982. **Article—**''Big Paintings: Bob Stanley,'' interview with Robert Christgau in *Cheetah* (New York), May 1968.

On STANLEY: Books—*Erotic Art* by Phyllis and Eberhard Kronhausen, 2 vols., New York 1968, 1970; *Gordon/Lozano/Ryman/Stanley* by Robert Christgau, Cincinnati, Ohio 1968; *Directions 2: Aspects of a New Realism* by William Wilson, Milwaukee, Wisconsin 1969; *Robert Stanley,* exhibition catalog by Klaus Honnef, Aachen, West Germany 1969; *Bob Stanley's Louisiana Sweet* by Mario Amaya and Naomi Spector, New York 1978; *Robert Stanley: 25 Years Later,* exhibition catalog with text by Robert Pincus-Witten, Rotterdam 1989; *Robert Stanley,* exhibition catalog with text by Wim van Sindern, Asiago 1992. **Articles—**''The Flip Side'' by David Bourdon in the *Village Voice* (New York), 17 June 1965; ''The New Eroticism'' by Douglas Davis in *Evergreen* (New York), September 1968; ''Eros erinnert an Dharma'' by John Anthony Thwaites in *Christ und Welt,* Dusseldorf 1969; ''The Spectrum of Monochrome'' by Lawrence Alloway in *Arts Magazine* (New York), December/January 1971; ''Robert Stanley'' by G. Gassiot-Talbot in *Opus International* (Paris), December 1971; ''Bob Stanley'' by John Lloyd Taylor in *Art International* (Lugano, Switzerland), September 1974; ''Bob Stanley and Bart Wasserman at P.S. 1'' by Carter Ratcliff in *Art in America* (New York), January/February 1978; ''Paint Misbehavin''' by Peter Frank in the *Village Voice* (New York), 16 October 1978; ''Bob Stanley'' by William Zimmer in the *Soho Weekly News* (New York), 8 October 1980; ''Bob Stanley'' by Michael Florescu in *Arts Magazine* (New York), November 1980; ''Parade in the Face of Death: The Work of Robert Stanley'' by Richard Artschwager in *Galeries* (Paris), Summer 1987; ''Robert Stanley: Testimony of Wildness'' by Shoichiro Higuchi in *Idea Magazine,* vol. 37, no. 213, March 1989; ''Robert Stanley at Mitchell Algus'' by Jonathan Goodman in *Art in America,* January 1998.

* * *

The work of Bob Stanley, it seems to me, is imbued with an old-fashioned morality, if not didacticism—a strange response, perhaps, to an artist whom Mario Amaya has dubbed ''that pirate of the Pop Art Movement.'' But in a time of pluralism in the visual arts, a phrase that has come to mean a time of multiple warring assertions, Stanley stands out as a questioner. His work is interrogative of the contemporary conventional wisdom rather than declarative. Uncharacteristically for a questioner, there is little humility about his paintings: they are big (not to mince words, they are enormous), and to quote Amaya again, they are ''as cyclical and all encompassing as the walls of an early Renaissance chapel.''

—Michael Florescu

STAZEWSKI, Henryk

Nationality: Polish. **Born:** Warsaw, 9 January 1894. **Education:** Educated at Kowalski's Secondary School, Warsaw; studied at the School of Fine Arts, Warsaw, under Stanislaw Lent, 1913–19. **Career:** Painter; lived and worked in Warsaw from 1920; produced paintings and reliefs from 1920, neo-plastic house interiors, 1923–32; founder-member, with Wladyslaw Strzeminski, Mieczyslaw Szule, Henryk Berlewi and others, Blok artists group, Wilno, 1923–36; editor, *Blok* magazine, nos. 1–5, 1924; founder-member, Praesens painters and architects group, Warsaw, 1926–29; founder-member, with Wladyslaw Strzeminski, Katarzyna Kobro, Julian Przybos and others, a.r. group, Lodz, 1929; member, Michel Seuphor's Cercle et Carre group, Paris, 1930–31, and Abstraction-Creation group, Paris, 1931; founder-member, KAGR publicity graphic artists group, Warsaw, 1933; member, editorial board, *Glos Plastykow* magazine, Warsaw, 1933; founder-member, Trade Union of Plastic Artists, Warsaw, 1935. **Member:** Association Internationale des Arts Plastiques (A.I.A.P.), Paris, 1962. **Awards:** Ministry of Culture Prize, Warsaw, 1965; J. G. Herder Prize, University of Vienna, 1972; Golden Cross of

Merit, Warsaw, 1955; Officer, Cross of the Order Polonia Restituta, Warsaw. **Agents:** Galerie Schlegel, Minervastrasse 119, 8000 Zurich, Switzerland; Crane Arts, 321 Kings Road, London S.W.3, England. **Died:** In Warsaw, June 1988.

Individual Exhibitions:

1921 Polonia Artists Club, Warsaw (with E. Miller and M. Szczuka)
1933 Art Propaganda Institute, Warsaw (with Karol Krynski)
1934 Art Propaganda Institute, Warsaw (with Wladyslaw Strzeminski)
1955 Polish Union of Writers Club, Warsaw
1956 Galleria Incontro, Rome (with Aleksander Winnicki)
1959 Kordegada, Warsaw
1960 Krzywekolo Gallery, Warsaw
1961 Castle of Lublin, Poland
Krzywekolo Gallery, Warsaw
1962 Krzywekolo Gallery, Warsaw
1963 *Reliefs and Collages,* Grabowski Gallery, London
1965 Galerija Zacheta, Warsaw
1966 Kazimir Gallery, Chicago
1967 Galerija Foksal, Warsaw
1969 Galerija Foksal, Warsaw
Museum of Fine Arts, Lodz, Poland
1970 Narodna Gallery, Prague
Galerija Foksal, Warsaw
Galerija Krzystofory, Cracow
1972 Mecatorhalle, Duisburg, West Germany
1974 Galerie 16, Paris
Wide White Space Gallery, Brussels
Galerie Polart, Dusseldorf
Biuro Wystawy Artystycznych, Lodz, Poland
Pape Ruddy Gallery, Los Angeles
Museum of Fine Arts, Lodz, Poland
1975 Galerie Schlegl, Zurich
1976 Galerija Wspolczesna, Warsaw
Galerija 72, Chelm, Poland
1977 Galerie Teufel, Cologne
1978 Galerija Zacheta, Warsaw
1979 Palazzo delle Esposizione, Rome (travelled to the Teatro del Falcone, Genoa, and the Museo d'Arte Moderna Ca Pesaro, Venice)
Recent Painting, Fruit Market Gallery, Edinburgh (travelled to the Third Eye Centre, Glasgow)
Galerija Zapiecek, Warsaw
1980 Galerija Krytykow, Warsaw
Biuro Wystaw Artystycznych, Torun, Poland (retrospective)
Biuro Wystaw Artystycznych, Bydgoszcz, Poland
Galerie Quadrat, Bottrop, West Germany
1982 Galerie Denise René, Paris
1991 *Henryk Stazewski, 1894–1988: Reliefs and Paintings 1958–87,* Spicchi dell'Est, Rome
1998 Galeria Foksal, Warsaw

Selected Group Exhibitions:

1922 *F9 Formist Artists Group: 3rd Exhibition,* Salon-Garlinski, Warsaw
1926 *Praesens Group,* Galerija Zacheta, Warsaw
1947 *1st Salon of ZPAP,* National Museum, Warsaw
1957 *Precurseurs d'Art Abstrait en Pologne,* Galerie Denise René, Paris
1961 *15 Polish Artists,* Museum of Modern Art, New York
1966 *Biennale,* Venice
1972 *The Non-Objective World 1939–55,* Annely Juda Fine Art, London(travelled to the Galerie Liatowisch, Basle, and the Galleria Milano, Milan)
1977 *Constructivisme Polonais 1923–36,* Musée d'Art Contemporain, Montreal
1978 *Abstraction-Creation 1931–36,* Westfälischer Landesmuseum, Munster, West Germany (travelled to the Musée d'Art Moderne de la Ville, Paris)
1980 *Polnische Kunst aus 3 Jahrzehnten,* Staatliche Kunstsammlungen, Dresden
1991 *Opening Up: an Exhibition of Six Major Polish Painters,* Hammer Galleries, New York
1992 *Polish Avant-Garde 1930–90,* Neuer Berliner Kunstverein, Berlin
1993 *The 70th Anniversary of the New Art Exhibition, Vilnius 1923,* Muzeum Sztuki, Lodz
1994 *Contemporary Classics: Exhibition from the Collections of the National Museum of Warsaw,* Muzeum Narodowe, Warsaw
1998 *Waves Breaking the Shore... Ad Dekkers in His Time,* Stedelijk Museum, Amsterdam

Collections:

Museum of Fine Arts, Lodz, Poland; National Museum, Warsaw; National Museum, Cracow; Tate Gallery, London; Museum der Stadt, St. Gallen, Switzerland; Rijksmuseum Kröller-Muller, Otterlo, Netherlands; Stedelijk Museum, Amsterdam; Städtische Kunstgalerie, Bochum, West Germany; Museum of Modern Art, New York; Guggenheim Museum, New York.

Publications:

By STAZEWSKI: Books illustrated—*Praesens Library no. 2: The Human Creative Mission in the Fine Arts* by Albert Gleizes, Warsaw 1927; *Praesens Library no. 3: Unism in Painting* by Wladyslaw Strzeminski, Warsaw 1928; *The Angelic Ruffian* by Anatol Stern, Warsaw 1928.

On STAZEWSKI: Books—*Reliefs and Collages by Henryk Stazewski,* exhibition catalog with texts by Alan Bowness and Wieslaw Borowski, London 1963; *Contemporary Polish Painting: Henryk Stazewski* by Hanna Ptaskowska, Warsaw 1965; *Stazewski,* exhibition catalog with texts by Ryszard Stanislawski, Hanna Ptaszkowska and Wieslaw Borrowski, Lodz, Poland 1969; *The Non-Objective World 1939–55,* exhibition catalog with text by George Rickey, London 1972; *Geometric Abstraction 1926–1942,* exhibition catalog with texts by Michel Seuphor and John Elderfield, Dallas 1972; *Henryk Stazewski: Malarstwo z lat 1923–1974,* exhibition catalog, Lodz, Poland 1974; *Henryk Stazewski,* exhibition catalog, Brussels 1974; *Henryk Stazewski: Recent Paintings,* exhibition catalog with texts by Richard Demarco and Janina Ladnowska, Edinburgh 1979; *Henryk Stazewski,* exhibition catalog with texts by Ulrich Schumacher, Ryszard Stanislawski and Janina Ladnowska, Bottrop, West Germany 1980; *Stazewski,* exhibition catalog with text by Anka Ptaszkowska, Paris 1982; *Opening Up: an Exhibition of Six Major Polish Painters,* New York 1991. **Articles—**"The Contemporary Style: Henryk Stazewski's Designs Between the Wars" by Janusz Zagrodzki in *Projekt,* no. 1, 1989.

* * *

Henryk Stazewski, a survivor of the heroic period of the Polish avant garde, and one of the promoters of abstraction (he was a member of Cercle et Carre), began his work as a painter and art theoretician in the 1920s. He was then in favor of the constituent elements of form—the independent roles of line and color, chiaroscuro and fracture: in his pictures the artist linked these elements equally. He wished to create an objectless world that would make the eye sensitive to only that which was universal—above all, to geometric form and to color.

Stazewski continued his pursuit of this problem after the war, in the 1950s. The idea of movement also concerned him at this time. Originally this was provoked by the structure of form which then developed in the sphere of "open structures."

In 1957 a new problem arose. The artist stopped painting pictures and turned to the construction of reliefs from flat smooth forms. He simultaneously executed radical simplifications, reducing form to a single element—the module; and color to black, white and grey. Stazewski then moved on to reliefs from smooth, polished metal. An artist whose creativity had drawn from the sources of abstraction—e.g., Mondrian—now developed a completely new kind of abstraction. In Mondrian's time the fixed relationships between the various respective elements were described in abstract pictures. In his reliefs, however, Stazewski introduced identical forms—modules (e.g., the square with concave sides, the ellipse with two ends cut off). Repeating these many times within the framework of a single picture, the artist removed their stamp of individuality; he "neutralized" them. Also, by repeating the same form-module, he focused attention not on the various ways that it could be arranged.

The picture is thus constructed in an open manner which conceals potential changes of shape. As a result, the mid-1960s saw a sudden increase in interest in Stazewski's work. The possibilities of change inherent in his work prompted several critics to search for precursive elements with respect to the worldwide movement of visual art and the concepts of a neutral, anonymous art. Stazewski's work was thus suddenly regarded as of general importance; it could be re-created and given the greatest possible circulation.

In 1968 Strazewski returned to the problem of color. In a series of paintings from this period he analyzed color phenomena and the laws of visual perception. He based his research on scientific foundations. Using squares marked on his canvases, he carried out a graduation of chromatic color of a section of the spectrum, achieving shades that differ so minimally that it is almost impossible to percieve the delineation.

In 1973 Stazewski created a series of white pictures the surfaces of which are divided simultaneously in rhythmical and unsettled sections with the help of parallel lines. The rhythms of the lines converge or diverge, change their course, undergo short jumps. In spite of these dynamizing moments, the artist achieves homogeneous surfaces by using one kind of method, the minimal mutations always taking place within the framework of one basic module.

A phenomenon of Stazewski's artistic personality is the fact that, although he was still very sensitive to the ephemera of nature, he always sought a permanent form for that which is only transitory. An example of this is the cycle of work begun in 1975, inspired by the wintry landscape of a small town. In these works the artist uses only geometric designs of black lines on a white ground. At the same time he writes: "The artist ought to beware the ephemeral, but he can in art give certain observed ephemeral phenomena a permanence and an extension of their existence." He continues: "Creating art, one has no understanding of the transitoriness of that which one is doing. One is led by a false feeling of permanence without being aware of the withering of a rose." In other words, Stazewski, who always wanted to commemorate the world in universal and permanent forms, also had strong feelings about the impermanence of all that exists. The tension between that which is universal and that which is individual, between intellectual reflection and the sphere of emotion, protects his art from a dry one-sideness and marks it with strong personal sensitivity.

—Alicja Kepinska

STEELE, Jeffrey

Nationality: British. **Born:** Cardiff, South Wales, 3 July 1931. **Education:** Cardiff College of Art, 1948–50; studied painting at Newport College of Art, South Wales, 1950–52; also studied at the Ecole des Beaux Arts, Paris, 1959–60. **Family:** Married Glenda Reynolds in 1958 (divorced, 1966); children: Simon and Tamara; married Arja Nenonen in 1966 (divorced, 1976). Clara Clark, daughter with artist Judy Clark, born 1983. **Career:** Independent painter, since 1952. Worked as hospital porter, Cardiff, 1953–55; as cellarman, London, 1955–57; as radio operator, Cardiff, 1957–59. Co-founder, Systems Group of Artists, London 1969 (dissolved, 1976). Lecturer, Barry Summer School, Glamorgan, South Wales, 1962–73; lecturer in painting, Newport College of Art, South Wales, 1965–68; head of department of fine art, Portsmouth College of Art and Design, 1968–69; principal lecturer in fine art, Portsmouth Polytechnic, 1969–88. **Awards:** French Government Scholarship, 1959; Welsh Arts Council Bursary, 1963; Painting Prize, Northern Ireland Arts Council, 1968; Painting Prize, *Welsh Arts Council Open Painting Exhibition,* Barry, Wales, 1968. **Agents:** Galerie Schoeller, Poststrasse 2, 4000 Dusseldorf 1, Germany; März Galerien, Beethovenstrasse 18, 68165 Mannheim, Germany; Galerie Média, rue des Moulines, 29, Neuchâtel, Switzerland. **Address:** 11a Eastern Villas Road, GB Portsmouth, Hampshire PO4 OSU, England.

Individual Exhibitions:

1961 Institute of Contemporary Arts, London
1963 Dillwyn Gallery, Swansea, South Wales
1964 Grabowski Gallery, London
Regional College of Art, Manchester
1966 McRoberts and Tunnard Gallery, London
1967 Sheffield University Arts Tower
City Art Gallery, Manchester (with Benjamin and Tyzack)
1974 *Current Work,* Lucy Milton Gallery, London
Galerie Media, Neuchatel, Switzerland
1975 Galerie Jacomo-Santiveri, Paris (with Dilworth and Kidner)

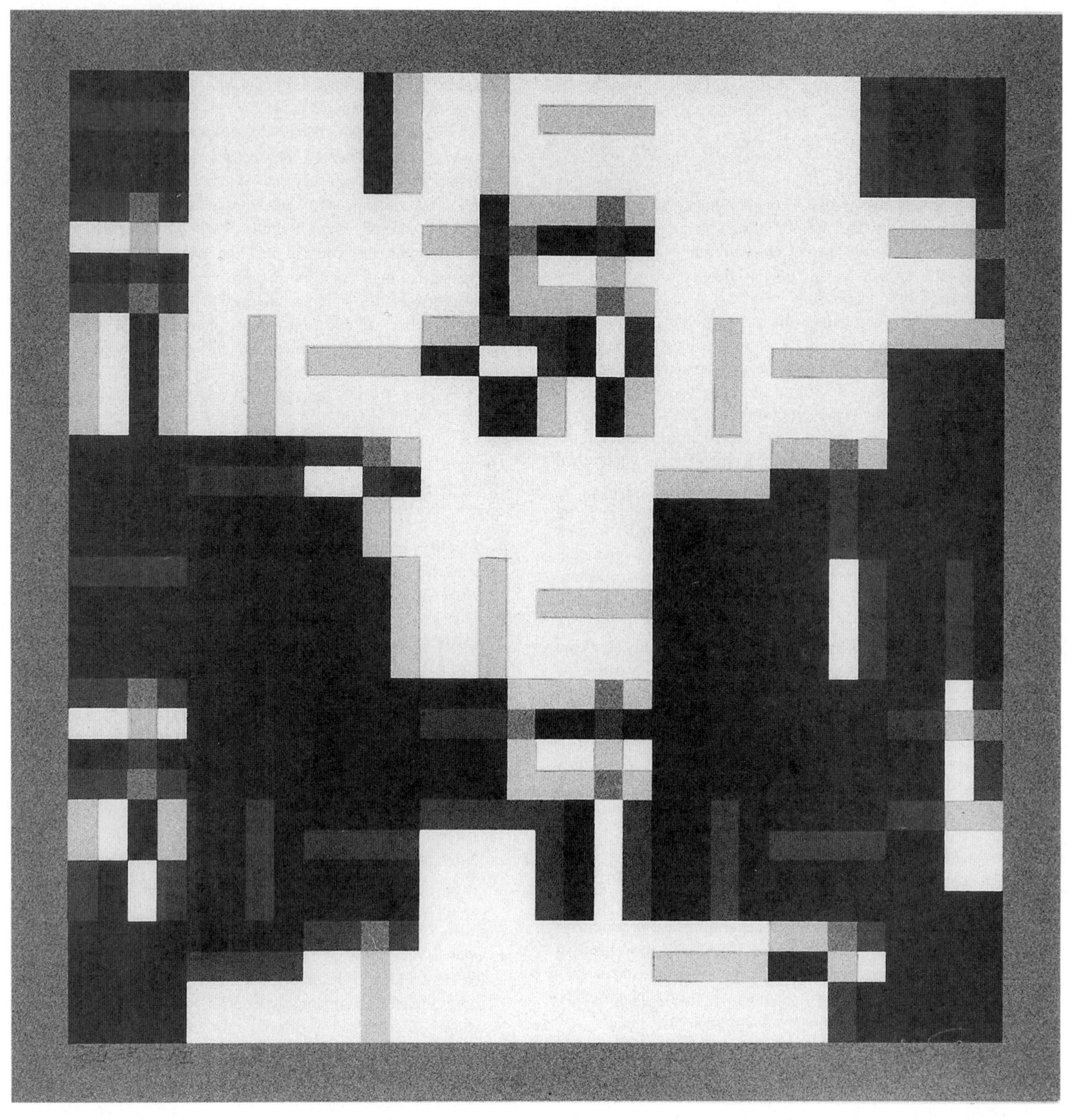

Jeffrey Steele: *Syntagma Sg IV 78,* 1998. Photo by T. H. Clarke. ©Jeffrey Steele.

1976 Le Disque Rouge, Brussels
1977 Galerie Gilles Gheerbrant, Montreal
Galerie Swart, Amsterdam
1978 Galerie Swart, Amsterdam
1979 Galerie Lydia Megert, Bern
1985 Kunsthaus, Nuremburg, West Germany
1989 Galleria Seno, Milan
1992 Clare Hall Gallery, Cambridge
1998 Musée des Beaux-Arts, La Chaux-de-Fonds, Switzerland

Selected Group Exhibitions:

1962 *The Geometric Environment,* Artist's International Association Gallery, London
1965 *The Responsive Eye,* Museum of Modern Art, New York (toured the United States)
1967 *Pittsburgh International,* Carnegie Institute, Pittsburgh
1968 *Cybernetic Serendipity,* Institute of Contemporary Arts, London

1969 *Systeemi,* Amos Andersonin Taidemuseo, Helsinki
1973 *Illusion in 20th Century Art,* University of Stirling, Scotland
1976 *System and Programme,* Palac Kultury i Nauki, Warsaw
1983 *Arte Programmata e Cinetica 1953–63,* Palazzo Reale, Milan
1986 *Arte e Scienza,* at the *42nd Biennale,* Venice
1990 *Britisch-Systematisch,* Stiftung für Konstruktive und Konkrete Kunst, Zurich
1995 *Protagonistor Konstruktivne Umnetnosti,* Moderna Galerija, Ljubljana
1996 *Gli Anni Sessauta,* Fondazione Mazzotta, Milan
Lumière et Mouvement, Galerie Denise René, Paris
1999 *Anthony Hill, Jeffrey Steele, Peter Lowe,* Galeria Stara, Lublin, Poland

Collections:

Arts Council of Great Britain, London; British Council, London; Victoria and Albert Museum, London; Museum Boymans-van Beuningen, Rotterdam; Cabinet des Estampes, Geneva; Kunsthaus, Aarau, Switzerland; National Museum of Wales, Cardiff; Ateneum Art Museum, Helsinki; Museum Sztuki, Lodz, Poland; Fitzwilliam Museum, Cambridge.

Publications:

By STEELE: Articles—''Towards a Non-Egocentric Art'' in *ICA Bulletin* (London), December 1966; ''Statement of Kinetics'' in *Studio International* (London), February 1967; ''Cicerone'' in *Anglo-Welsh Review* (Caerlean), Winter 1967; ''Syntactic Art'' in *Systeemi,* exhibition catalog, Helsinki 1969; ''Systems Theory and Syntactic Art'' in *Systems,* exhibition catalog, London 1972; ''Structural Analysis of My Painting 'Solar Wind''' in *Review Integration* (Eschenau, West Germany), October 1972; ''Note on My Current Work'' in *Jeffrey Steele: Current Work,* exhibition catalog, London 1974; ''Note on the Relationship of Systematic- Constructivist Art to Architecture'' in *Beispiele aus dem Grenzbereich Kunst-Architektur,* Bern 1975; ''Portsmouth Fine Art Music'' in *Experimental Music,* exhibition catalog by Gavin Bryars and Michael Nyman, London 1975; ''Notes sur le Travail do Trevor Clarke'' in *Media* (Neuchatel, Switzerland), May 1976; ''General Notes on Sg 1 . . . Drawings'' in *Engelse en Nederlandse Rationele Tekeningen,* exhibition catalog, Delft 1976; ''Collaborative Work at Portsmouth'' in *Studio International* (London), November/December 1976; ''Core Conditions and Boundary Conditions'' in *Artscribe* (London), July 1977; ''The Identity Concept in the Constructive Context'' in *Constructive Context* (London), 1978; ''Notes Towards Some Theses Against the New York Kitsch'' in *Art Monthly* (London), July/August 1978; ''Closing the Dossier on 'Pier and Ocean''' in *Art Monthly* (London), October 1980; ''Vilification of Constructive Art'' in *Art Monthly* (London), November 1982; ''Die Kunstpraxis als Teil des grosseren Bereiches von linguistischer Praxis'' in *Jeffrey Steele: Konkret Funf,* exhibition catalog, Nuremberg 1985; ''Systematic Constructive Art as Accountable Practice'' in *Exhibiting Space Conspectus,* London 1986; ''Appunti sul sviluppo del mio lavoro'' in *Jeffrey Steele,* exhibition catalog, Milan 1989; ''Chance, Change, Choice, and Order'' in *Leonardo,* vol. 24, no. 4, 1991; ''Taxinomia and Taxomania'' in *Art Has No History,* edited by John Roberts, London 1994; ''Sia Meccarico che Intellettuale'' in *Kiliagono,* Milan 1995; ''War Between Philosophy and Art'' in *Radical Philosophy,* November/December 1996.

On STEELE: Books—*Jeffrey Steele,* exhibition catalog by Sir Herbert Read, London 1964: *Jeffrey Steele,* exhibition catalog by Cyril Barrent, London 1966; *Optical Illusions and the Visual Arts* by Ronald G. Carracher and Jacqueline B. Thurston, New York and London 1966; *Constructivism* by George Rickey, London 1967; *Op-Art* by Cyrill Barrett, London 1969; *An Introduction to Optical Art* by Cyrill Barrett, London 1971; *Introducing Op-Art* by John Lancaster, New York and London 1973; *Art since Pop* by John A. Walker, London 1975; *The Modern* by Terry Measham, Oxford 1976; *L' Ultima Avanguardia,* edited by Lea Vergine, Milan 1983; *Art & Science* by Ans van Berkum and Tom Bleckkenhorst, Vlissingen 1986; *Op Art: Stil, Ornament oder Experiment* by Karina Türr, Berlin 1986; *Jeffrey Steele* by Sandra Hoffman, Erlangen 1991; *Constructive Space in Jeffrey Steele's Black and White Works* by Gloria Carnevali, New York 1992; *Responsive Eyes: The British Contribution to Op Art, 1958–65* by D. M. Bunyard, Southampton 1996; *Creating an Art Community* by Peter Wakelin, Wales 1999; *Two Artists on Evidence* by Steve Edwards, London 1999.

*

Contemporary Artists asks how I see my work fitting into the art world, but there is of course not just one ''art world''. There are many, and each bears a plurality of histories and possible interpretations.

Works of mine have been ''fitted in'' to a number of such histories: ''Op-Art'', which Ross Bleckner called ''a dead movement from its very inception'' (quoted by Hal Foster in ''The Art of Cynical Reason'' in *The Return of the Real,* MIT 1996): ''Arte Programmata e Cinetica (L'ultima avanguardia)'', which ''. . . ended up defeated. Their great project of democratic renewal underwent one of the greatest disappointments in the history of art in our century, perhaps equal to if less tragic than that of the Russian avant-garde at the end of the Soviet revolution'' (Pier Luigi Tazzi in *Art Forum,* May 1984). Tazzi implies here that we *deserved* our ''disappointment,'' unlike the Russians. And finally: ''Systematic Art'', ''. . . a truly striking union of practice and philosophy such as that made by the British Systems artists in the 1960s and 1970s has *fallen out of history.*'' (Adrian Rifkin's introduction to Gilles Deleuze and Michel Foucault in *La Peinture Photogénique,* Courtauld 1999, italics added).

On the positive side I don't mind subscribing allegiance within the discipline of what is termed *konkrete Kunst.* I sketched a possible working definition for this in my 1978 essay ''The Identity Concept. . . . '' This sets out from Jean Piaget's brilliant resolution of the problem of the eschatological relationship between subject and structure by means of the encompassing gerundial, *la structuration,* and continues:

''We can avoid mistaking a system *under construction* for its opposite, the fashionably-styled 'de-construction' process, by reference to the second, *concrete* phase in the cumulative evolution within the field of constructive art:

CONSTRUCTIONøCONCRETEøSYSTEMøSERIES.

I consider this development to be the most crucial and, unfortunately, the least well-understood in the whole of twentieth century art.''

Piaget also elaborates a serviceable theory of ''autoréglage'' which accounts for the tendency of any dynamic structure—such as an *art world*—to maintain homeostasis either by assimilating or expelling recalcitrant bodies. Such an attempt at self-regulation might have determined the negative verdicts on my work cited above. More ironically ''Structuralism'' accounts in this way for its own expulsion from the approved list of research programmes.

On the positive side I am lucky to have been born at a time when there was a rich variety of available ways of ''being an artist,'' so that I was able to pursue a very interesting line of specialism within a larger world of art worlds. The field of possibilities for younger artists today is relatively impoverished (despite advances in technical means).

—Jeffrey Steele

* * *

Jeffrey Steele is associated with a form of painting described as Systems. This, as its name implies, involves the use of some system in the construction of a picture.

There are two ways of using a system. One is to use it to generate some interesting visual image, but alter it in mid-stream, if it is not aesthetically satisfactory. The other, which is the course Steele follows, is to carry the system right through, and, if the result is aesthetically uninteresting, scrap it. Artistic control thus operates at the two ends, but not in the middle. There is a choice of system, and a verdict on the outcome of its use, but no tampering.

It may have been a coincidence, but Steele's early work had an optical-kinetic quality. He had been impressed by the work of Vasarely, though he felt that he had betrayed his original principles when in the 1950s he turned from black and white to colour and from art with optical pulsations to his more characteristic ambiguous figures, a kind of abstract Cubism.

Steele's own work in the 1960s had great optical vibrancy. He, as so many other so-called Op artists, discovered to his surprise that by regular repetition of forms he obtained this vibrancy unsolicted. What had motivated him in the late 1950s was a desire to break with *tachisme,* ''the individual artist's 'touch' or handwriting.'' He had been attracted to Neo-Plasticism and Constructivism, but was most impressed, while in Paris, with the work of Albers, Bill, Soto and Vasarely. But it was only on his return home that he hit on his own brand of optical effect.

The characteristic of his work in the 1960s was the intensification and movement of light which his structures induce. During this period he worked exclusively in black and white. The stark contrast of tones helped to enchance the luminous effect of his work. At times his pictures are rectilinear, as in ''Divertissement'' or ''Lavolta.'' The first builds up to a great intensity of light in the centre; the second disperses light along its axes, and the light pulsates, and even rotates. But he was also producing curvilinear structures, such as ''Baroque Experiment,'' a sort of limitless series of reflecting mirrors, slightly out of kilter, whose divergencies from the norm set up optical vibrations, of ''Sub Rosa'' which suggests the luminous flow of water.

Basically, however, Steele is concerned with structures. Even in those early paintings, such as ''Divertissement'' and ''Lavolta,'' the structural element dominates: the hidden squares, the crossing axes, the undulations swimming against the current. In some cases these counter-structures are evident; in others they are so subtle as to escape the notice of the unperceptive.

In 1965 some of his paintings were used in fabric design, in particular a design for a bikini based on ''Baroque Experiment.'' This was both flattering and embarrassing to Steele, particularly as a year later that same bikini was shown with the caption: ''Take it off (this is last year's swimsuit).'' This proves, if it proves anything, not that Steele's work at the time was ephemeral, but that fashion is fickle. The only ephemeral aspect of his work—the aspect which did not persist—is the optical effect, which was incidental anyway, even though it gave him public recognition. It was always his aim to counterbalance the optical effect.

In the late 1960s Steele turned to colour and reverted entirely to his original interest in formal, as opposed to informal, structures. He developed an elaborate terminology to describe his systematic method of working, too elaborate to expound here. Each work is designated by a symbol (Sg) and a number: Sg I 1, I 2, etc. At present the symbol is Sg VI, but there is no reason why Steele should not revert to Sg I or Sg II, which date from the early 1970s, and develop their possibilities further. An Sg (syntagm) is a material realization of a system (Sy) governed by operations, mappings, distributions, network, syntaxes, etc. The terminology is drawn from linguistics. Steele believes that his systematic approach is a contribution to research in the field of morphology, topology and serial relations.

The earlier works put strong emphasis on the diagonal, and are very dynamic. The more recent works (Sg VI) consist of horizontal bands of rectangular areas of colour arranged on either side of a central axis, reminiscent of certain works of Lohse, for whom Steele has an undying admiration. They are imposing, even if they lack the dynamism and the overlying structures of earlier works.

However interesting it may be to know the methods by which Steele arrives at his images, it is the images themselves which ultimately matter. Nevertheless the presence of an underlying structure based on a system makes itself felt if scarcely percepitibly: the visual stimulation is underwritten by a hidden order.

—D.C. Barrett

STEINBERG, Saul

Nationality: American. **Born:** Ramnicul-Sarat, near Bucharest, Rumania, 15 June 1914; immigrated to the United States, 1941: naturalised, 1943. **Education:** Studied sociology and psychology at the University of Bucharest, 1932; studied architecture at the University of Milan, 1932. **Family:** Married Hedda Lindenberg Sterne, 1943. **Military Service:** Served in the United States Navy, 1943–46. **Career:** Cartoonist for *The New Yorker* since 1941; cartoons contributed to numerous other U.S. periodicals: his objects and drawings satirize contemporary society and the activity of making art. Artist-in-Residence, Smithsonian Institution, Washington, D.C., 1967. D.F.A.: Harvard University, 1976; New York University, 1978; Royal College of Arts, London, 1988. **Awards:** Gold Medal, American Academy of Arts and Letters, 1974. **Agent:** c/o Pace Wildenstein Gallery, 32 East 57th Street, New York, New York 10022, U.S.A. **Died:** New York City, 12 May 1999.

Individual Exhibitions:

1943 Wakefield Gallery, New York
1945 Young Books Inc., New York
1948 Institute of Design, Chicago
1950 Rhode Island School of Design, Providence
Betty Parsons Gallery, New York
1951 Galleria l'Obelisco, Rome
1952 Galeria de Arte, Sao Paulo

Museu de Arte, Sao Paulo
Gump's Gallery, San Francisco
Institute of Contemporary Arts, London
Sidney Janis Gallery, New York
Kunsthalle, Wuppertal-Barmen, West Germany
Leopold-Hoesch-Museum, Duren, West Germany
Betty Parsons Gallery, New York
Frank Perls Gallery, Beverly Hills, California
1953 *Steinberg Drawings,* Arts Club of Chicago
Galerie Blanche, Stockholm
Galerie Maeght, Paris
Stedelijk Museum, Amsterdam
Virginia Museum of Fine Arts, Richmond
1954 Corcoran Gallery of Art, Washington, D.C.
Dallas Museum of Fine Arts
Museum am Ostwall, Dortmund, West Germany
Kunstkabinet, Frankfurt
Kestner-Gesellschaft, Hannover
Kunstmuseum, Basel
Santa Barbara Museum, California
1955 Harvard School of Design, Cambridge, Massachussetts
1956 Allan Frumkin Gallery, Chicago
1957 Institute of Contemporary Arts, London
1959 Musée d'Art Moderne, Brussels
1962 University of California at Santa Barbara
1965 Davison Art Center, Wesleyan University, Middletown, Connecticut
1966 Sidney Janis Gallery, New York
Galerie Maeght, Paris
Betty Parsons Gallery, New York
Wallraf-Richartz-Museum, Cologne
1967 B.C. Holland Gallery, Chicago
Museum Boymans-van Beuningen, Rotterdam
Obelisk Gallery, Boston
Aguarelles, Dessins et Collages 1955–1967, Musée Royaux des Beaux-Arts, Brussels
1968 Museo de Bellas Artes, Caracas
Zeichnungen und Collagen, Kunsthalle, Hamburg
Irving Galleries, Milwaukee
Louisiana Museum, Humlebaek, Denmark
Moderna Museet, Stockholm
1969 J. L. Hudson Gallery, Detroit
Sidney Janis Gallery, New York
Betty Parsons Gallery, New York
1970 Felix Landau Gallery, Los Angeles
1971 Richard Gray Gallery, Chicago
Ölbilder, Gouachen, Zeichnungen, Galerie Maeght, Zurich
1973 Galleria Galatea, Milan
Sidney Janis Gallery, New York
Galerie Maeght, Paris
Betty Parsons Gallery, New York
Steinberg at the Smithsonian, National Collection of Fine Arts, Smithsonian Institution, Washington, D.C.
1974 Institute of Contemporary Art, Boston
Galerie Maeght, Paris
Zeichnungen, Aquarelle, Collagen, Gemalde, Reliefs 1963–74, Kölnischer Kunstverein, Cologne (exhibition travelled throughout Germany and to Vienna)
1976 Sidney Janis Gallery, New York
Betty Parsons Gallery, New York
1977 Galerie Maeght, Paris and Zurich
1978 Whitney Museum, New York (retrospective; travelled to the Hirshhorn Museum, Washington, D.C.; Serpentine Gallery, London; and Foundation Maeght, St. Paul-de-Vence, France)
1982 Pace Gallery, New York
1983 Waddington Galleries, London
1986 Galerie Maeght Lelong, Paris
1987 Pace Gallery, New York
1988 Galerie Adrien Maeght, Paris
1993 Pace Gallery, New York
1998 Adam Baumgold Gallery, New York
1999 *Remembering Saul Steinberg,* Menil Collection, Houston, Texas
Drawing into Being, Pace Wildenstein, New York (catalog)

Selected Group Exhibitions:

1946 *14 Americans,* Museum of Modern Art, New York
1949 *An Exhibition for Modern Living,* Detroit Institute of Arts
1952 *Contemporary Drawings from 12 Countries 1945–1952,* Art Institute of Chicago
1954 *The Roy and Marie Neuberger Collection,* Whitney Museum, New York
1962 *American Drawing Annual XIX,* Norfolk Museum of Arts and Sciences, Virginia
1970 *L'Art aux États-Unis,* Fondation Maeght, St. Paul-de-Vence, France
1971 *7 Enormously Popular American Artists,* Corcoran Gallery of Art, Washington, D.C.
1973 *American Drawing 1970–1973,* Yale University Art Gallery, New Haven, Connecticut
1974 *American Artists,* Cleveland Museum of Art
1977 *American Drawing 1927–1977,* Minnesota Museum of Art, St. Paul
1988 *4th International Triennale der Zeichnung,* Kunsthalle Nürnberg, Germany (catalog)
1989 *Drawn from Tradition,* Norton Gallery and School of Art, West Palm Beach, Florida
1993 *Artists at Gemini G.E.L.,* Newport Harbor Art Museum, Newport Beach, California (catalog)

Collections:

Museum of Modern Art, New York; Metropolitan Museum of Art, New York; Albright-Knox Art Gallery, Buffalo, New York; Fogg Museum, Harvard University, Cambridge, Massachusetts; Detroit Institute of Arts; Victoria and Albert Museum, London.

Publications:

By STEINBERG: Books—*All in Line,* New York 1945; *The Art of Living,* New York 1949; *The Passport,* New York 1954; *Steinberg's Umgang mit Menschen,* Hamburg 1954; *Dessins,* Paris 1956; *The Labyrinth,* New York 1960; *The Catalog,* Cleveland 1962; *Steinberg's Paperback,* Hamburg 1964; *The New World,* New York 1965; *Le Masque,* with texts by Michel Butor and Harold Rosenberg, Paris

1966; *The Inspector,* New York 1973; *The Artist Observed: 28 Interviews with Contemporary Artists 1972–1978,* with John Gruen, Chicago 1991; *The Discovery of America,* with introduction by Arthur C. Danto, London 1992. **Articles—**''Life in the Guatavir Line'' in *Life* (New York), May 1940; ''Mottoes Illustrated'' in *Harper's* (New York), August 1946; ''Recapitulation'' in *Architectural Review* (London), December 1950; ''Italy Drawings'' in *Harper's* (New York), February 1952; ''Built in U.S.A.: Postwar Architecture, 1945–52'' in *Artnews* (New York), February 1953; ''Steinberg at the Bat'' in *Life* (New York), 11 June 1955; ''Drawings of Athens'' in *Harper's* (New York), February 1956; ''Steinberg U.S.A.'' in *Harper's* (New York), September 1960; ''Statements and Documents'' in *Daedalus* (New York), Winter 1960; ''The Nose Problem'' in *Location* (New York), Spring 1963; ''Our False-Front Culture'' in *Look* (New York), 9 January 1968.

On STEINBERG: Books— *14 Americans,* exhibition catalog, edited by Dorothy Miller, New York 1946; *Saul Steinberg,* exhibition catalog, London 1952; *Saul Steinberg,* exhibition catalog, Amsterdam 1953; *The Roy and Marie Neuberger Collection,* exhibition catalog, New York 1954; *Steinberg,* exhibition catalog by Alfred Hentzen, Hannover 1954; *Conversations with Artists,* introduced by Alexander Eliot, New York 1961; *Steinberg Aquarelles, Dessins et Collages 1955–1967,* exhibition catalog, Brussels 1967; *Steinberg,* exhibition catalog by Pierre Baudson, Rotterdam 1967; *Steinberg: Zeichnungen und Collagen,* exhibition catalog, by Helmut Leppien, Pierre Baudson and Manuel Gasser, with an interview by Andre Parinaud, Hamburg 1968; *Saul Steinberg oder Philosophie der Zeichnung* by Franz Wittkamp, Mainz 1971; *Steinberg: Ölbilder, Gouachen, Zeichnungen,* exhibition catalog, by Manuel Gasser, Zurich 1971; *Steinberg at the Smithsonian,* exhibition catalog by John Hollander, Washington, D.C. 1973; *Saul Steinberg: Zeichnungen, Aquarelle, Collagen, Gemalde, Reliefs 1963–74,* exhibition catalog, Cologne 1974; *Here at the New Yorker* by Brendan Gill, New York 1975; *The New Yorker Album of Drawings 1925–1975,* New York 1975; *American Drawings 1927–1977,* exhibition catalog by Paul Cummings, St. Paul, Minnesota 1977; *Saul Steinberg,* exhibition catalog by Harold Rosenberg, New York 1978; *Saul Steinberg: repères,* exhibition catalog with introduction by Jean Fremon, Paris 1986; *Saul Steinberg's Gift,* exhibition catalog with text by Adam Gopnik, New York 1987; *Saul Steinberg's Tango* by Stephanie Stebich, New York 1994. **Articles—**Obituary in *The Independent* (London), 18 May 1999; ''Cartoon Critic: Saul Steinberg's Drawings Were Often Witty Criticisms of Contemporary Architecture'' in *Architecture,* 1 September 1999; ''Steinberg: A Tribute to Saul Steinberg (1914–1999)'' by Italo Lupi in *Abitare,* no. 387, September 1999; ''Saul Steinberg: Walking a Fine Line'' by Michael Webb in *Graphis,* vol. 55, no. 324, November/December 1999.

* * *

For many years Saul Steinberg has been placed in limbo by critics and the public, but the retrospective held at the Whitney Museum in 1978 must finally have confirmed him to be an artist rather than a cartoonist.

Steinberg's style is completely original. Noises, jokes, puns pervade his work. American society is made up of roots, mickey mouse ladies, growling dogs, majorettes and eagles. New York seems to envelop the world in the famous *New York* poster; Siberia appears only a few inches away. Buildings and monuments tower above the ''little men.'' This recurrent figure reminds one of Chaplin in *Modern Times* and Meursault in *L'étranger.* Somehow things happen to these men; they do not have the power to form their own destiny. In ''Graph Paper Building'' the skyscraper dwarfs the tiny stick figures and the stucco buildings; it is an ugly, unnecessary intrusion. However, in ''Piazza San Marco, Venice'' the Italians inhabiting the pen and ink square scream and fight one another, while the tourists merely look at the architecture, never at each other.

From the paintings bursting with characters, Steinberg also goes on to draw individuals. The soldier sits at a table and casually removes his nose. Simple immaculate lines convey this action; they are stamped with Steinberg's seal of officialdom. A minute horseman is chased by a massive boulder, which in turn is hounded by a crocodile down a steep hill. An outrageous situation—but one still hopes that the lone horseman will survive. One of my favourite and equally ''crazy'' paintings is ''March-April 1966.'' Specific segments of land represent one month, and the cat/man bicycles across the bridge from March to April. The concept is witty and charming. Steinberg's vision of a taxi cab made up of crooked lines cannot help but give delight.

Among the most sombre but at the same time most exquisite paintings are ''Anatolia'' (1973) and ''Camp II'' (1960). In the former miniscule figures stare out at the horizon whose blue sky is interrupted by few clouds. Although the setting is perfect, there is a sense of doom, just as in *Waiting for Godot* one expects an explosion. In the latter the Camp is reminiscent of concentration camps, solid black towers dwarfing helpless people. ''Kisumu,'' ''Kunming,'' ''Eastern Sunsets'' and ''African Postcards'' have similar atmosphere and quality because of the free flowing watercolour technique.

Steinberg could paint with the eye of a child, producing simple yet ingenious pen and ink riddles, then in another moment paint landscapes that possess the beauty of Turner inhabited by the figures of Dali. He was a talented and deeply human painter.

—Carine Maurice

STELLA, Frank

Nationality: American. **Born:** Malden, Massachusetts, 12 May 1936. **Education:** Studied painting under Patrick Morgan, Philips Academy, Andover, Massachusetts; under William Seitz and Stephen Greene, Princeton University, New Jersey. **Family:** Married Barbara Rose in London, 1960 (divorced); children: Rachel and Michael. **Career:** Painter. Has lived and worked in New York since 1958. Artist-in-residence, Dartmouth College, Hanover, New Hampshire, 1963; rejected artist-in-residence position, University of California at Irvine, by refusing to sign state's loyalty oath, 1965; lecturer, Yale University, New Haven, Connecticut, 1965; visiting critic, Cornell University, Ithaca, New York, 1965; art instructor, University of Saskatchewan, Saskatoon, summer 1967, and Brandeis University, Waltham, Massachusetts, 1968. **Awards:** First Prize, *International Biennial Exhibition of Paintings,* Tokyo, 1967; Honorary Doctorate of Arts, Princeton University, 1984; New Jersey Bernard Medal of Distinction, 1984; Honorary Degree, Dartmouth College, 1985; New Hampshire Award of American Art, 1985; Pennsylvania Academy of

Frank Stella: *The Betrothal in Santo Domingo,* 1999. ©Frank Stella/Artists Rights Society (ARS), NY.

Arts, Philadelphia, 1985; Honorary Degree, Brandeis University, 1986. **Agent:** M. Knoedler and Company, 19 East 70th Street, New York, New York 10021. **Address:** 17 Jones Street, New York, New York 10013, U.S.A.

Individual Exhibitions:

1960 Leo Castelli Gallery, New York
1961 Galerie Lawrence, Paris
1962 Leo Castelli Gallery, New York
1963 Ferus Gallery, Los Angeles
Leo Castelli Gallery, New York
1964 Galerie Lawrence, Paris
Kasmin Gallery, London
Leo Castelli Gallery, New York
1965 Ferus Gallery, Los Angeles
3 American Painters, Harvard University, Cambridge, Massachusetts
1966 Leo Castelli Gallery, New York
Kasmin Gallery, London
David Mirvish Gallery, Toronto
Pasadena Art Museum, California
1967 Douglas Gallery, Vancouver
Seattle Art Museum
Galerie Bischofberger, Zurich
Leo Castelli Gallery, New York
1968 Gallery of Modern Art, Washington, D.C.
Kasmin Gallery, London
David Mirvish Gallery, Toronto
New Gallery, Bennington College, Vermont
Harcus-Krakow Gallery, Boston
Irving Blum Gallery, Los Angeles
1969 Leo Gallery Gallery, New York
Irving Blum Gallery, Los Angeles
University of Puerto Rico, Mayaguez
Recent Paintings, Rose Art Museum, Brandeis University, Waltham Massachusetts
1970 Museum of Modern Art, New York
Hayward Gallery, London
1971 Lawrence Rubin Gallery, New York
1973 Leo Castelli Gallery, New York
1974 DM Gallery, London
Knoedler Gallery, New York
1975 Castelli Downtown Gallery, New York
Galerie Daniel Templon, Paris
Janie C. Lee Gallery, Houston
1976 Galerie André Emmerich, Zurich
Kunstmuseum, Basel
Sears Bank, Chicago
Koedler Contemporary Art, New York
David Mirvish Gallery, Toronto
B. R. Kornblatt Gallery, Baltimore
1977 Galerie M, Bochum, West Germany
Baltimore Museum of Art
Städtisches Kunsthaus, Bielefeld, West Germany
Museum of Modern art, Oxford
Linda Farris Gallery, Seattle
Koedler Gallery Ltd., London
1978 School of Visual Arts, New York
Forth Worth Art Center, Texas (retrospective; toured the United States)
1979 Museum of Modern Art, New York
Brandeis University, Walthman, Massachusetts
Galerie Valeur, Nagoya, Japan
1980 Galerie 99, Bay Harbor Islands, Florida
1981 University of Arizona, Tucson
Swope Art Gallery, Terre Haute, Indiana •
John C. Stoller, Minneapolis
M. Knoedler Company, New York
1982 Akira Ikeda Gallery, Tokyo
Leo Castelli Gallery, New York
Print 1967–82, University of Michigan, Ann Arbor (toured the United States 1982–85)
1983 Galerie Knoedler, Zurich
Akira Ikeda Gallery, Tokyo
San Francisco Museum of Modern Art
1985 M. Knoedler and Company, New York
Knoedler Kasmin Ltd., London
Greenberg Gallery, St. Louis
1986 Akira Ikeda Gallery, Tokyo
1987 Museum of Modern Art, New York
1988 L.A. Louver Gallery, Venice, California
Akira Ikeda Gallery, Tokyo (catalog)
1989 *Frank Stella: The Waves 1985–1989,* Waddington Graphics, London (catalog)
1990 *Frank Stella: Selected Prints from 1967–68,* Stadtisches Museum Abteiberg, Monchengladbach, Germany (catalog)

Frank Stella: *Jasper's Dilemma,* 1962–63. ©2001 Frank Stella/Artists Rights Society (ARS), New York; Courtesy of ESM/Art Resource.

1991 *Frank Lichtenstein, Frank Stella,* Galerie Beyeler, Basel (catalog)

1993 Knoedler & Company, New York
Frank Stella: Moby Dick Series—Engravings, Domes and Deckle Edges, Stadthaus, Ulm, Germany (catalog)

1995 Knoedler and American Fine Arts, New York
Museo Nacional Centro de Arte Reina Sofia, Madrid (catalog)

1996 *Frank Stella: New Sculpture,* Friedrich Schiller-Universitat, Jena, Germany (catalog)

1997 *Frank Stella at Tyler Graphics,* Walker Art Center, Minneapolis (travelling exhibition) (catalog)

1998 *Frank Stella: Multiple Dimensions in the Nineties,* Knoedler & Company, New York (catalog)

2001 *Imaginary Landscapes,* Gibbes Museum of Art, Charleston, South Carolina

Selected Group Exhibitions:

1964 *Biennale,* Venice

1965 *Bienal,* Sao Paulo

1966 *New Shapes of Colour,* Stedelijk Museum, Amsterdam

1969 *New York Painting and Sculpture 1940–70,* Museum of Modern Art, New York

1970 *Biennale,* Venice

1974 *Prints from Gemini G.E.L.,* Walker Art Center, Minneapolis (toured the United States)

1976 *20th Century American Drawing,* Guggenheim Museum, New York

1978 *Art about Art,* Whitney Museum, New York

1985 *Painterly Vision 1940–84,* Guggenheim Museum, New York

1988 *Contemporary American Art,* Sara Hilden Art Museum, Tampere, Finland (travelled to Oslo)

1989 *Selections from the Beatrice and Philip Gersh Collection,* Museum of Contemporary Art, Los Angeles (catalog)
The Elusive Surface: Painting in Three Dimensions, Museum of Albuquerque, New Mexico (catalog)

1990 *Early/Later,* Whitney Museum of American Art, New York (catalog)
Object and Content: Meaning in Minimal Art, Australian National Gallery, Canberra (catalog)

1991 *Seven Master Printmakers: Innovations in the Eighties,* Museum of Modern Art, New York (catalog)

1993 *Paintings: Emblems and References,* capc Musee d'Art Contemporain, Bordeaux (catalog)
Directions in Modernism, Staatliche Museen Preussischer Kulturbesitz, Nationalgalerie, Berlin (catalog)

1994 *Printer,* Galerie Graff, Montreal (catalog)

1995 *Abstraction, Pure and Impure,* Museum of Modern Art, New York (catalog)

Collection: Modern and Contemporary Art at the Van Abbemuseum in Eindhoven, Musee National d'Histoire et d'Art, Luxembourg (catalog)

1996 *The Froehlich Foundation: German and American Art from Beuys and Warhol,* Tate Gallery, London (traveling exhibition) (catalog)

1997 *American Art: A Selection from the Waddington Galleries,* London (catalog)

Contemporary Prints, Yvonne Andrews Gallery, London (catalog)

Masterpieces of Modern Printmaking, Alan Cristea Gallery, London (catalog)

1998 *Waves Breaking on the Shore,* Stedelijk Museum, Amsterdam (catalog)

Collections:

Museum of Modern Art, New York; Whitney Museum, New York; Albright-Knox Art Gallery, Buffalo, New York; Walker Art Center, Minneapolis; Art Institute of Chicago; San Francisco Museum of Modern Art; Centre Georges Pompidou, Paris; Kaiser Wilhelm Museum, Krefeld, West Germany; Stedelijk Museum, Amsterdam; Stedelijk van Abbemuseum, Eindhoven, Netherlands.

Permanent Installations:

The Princess of Wales Theatre, Toronto, Canada.

Publications:

By STELLA: Articles—interview with John Strand and Donald Garfield in *Museum News,* vol. 72, no. 5, September-October 1993.

On STELLA: Books—*3 American Painters,* exhibition catalog by Michael Fried, Cambridge, Massachusetts, April 1965; *Recent Paintings by Frank Stella,* exhibition catalog by William Seitz, Waltham, Massachusetts 1969; *Frank Stella,* exhibition catalog, Amsterdam 1979; *Frank Stella,* exhibition catalog by William S. Rubin, New York 1970; *Frank Stella* by Robert Rosenblum, London 1971; *Frank Stella Prints 1967–1982,* catalog raisonné by Richard H. Axsom, Ann Arbor 1982; *Frank Stella 1970–1987,* exhibition catalog with text by William Rubin, New York 1987; *Frank Stella: An Illustrated Biography* by Sidney Guberman, New York 1995. **Articles**—''Stella Turns: How Frank Stella Flip-Flopped and Stayed Classic'' in *The New Republic,* 22 February 1988; ''Frank Stella: Paintings as Tapestry'' by Peter Dormer in *Apollo,* vol. 129, no. 324, February 1989; ''Frank Stella: The Whiteness of the Whale'' by Gus Blaisdell in *Artspace,* vol. 13, no. 3, July-August 1989; ''Frank Stella: Annees 80'' by Bernard-Henri Levy in *Art Press,* no. 145, March 1990; ''Abstraction's Sense of History: Frank Stella's 'Working Space' Revisited'' by James Elkin in *American Art,* vol. 7, no. 1, Winter 1993; ''Frank Stella: Moby Dick Series'' by Catherine Millet in *Art Press,* Hors-serie, no. 15, 1994; ''Modern American Painters—Frank Stella's Panatellas'' in *The Economist,* vol. 355, no. 8173, 3 June 2000; ''Frank Stella as Architect'' by Franz Schulze in *Art in America,* vol. 88, no. 6, June 2000; ''Frank Stella'' by Saul Ostrow in *Bomb,* no. 71, Spring 2000.

* * *

When he had his first one-man show in New York in 1960, Frank Stella at 24 was not yet committed to a programme of irreversible iconoclasm. From his ''Island'' paintings of 1958 it was possible to detect some of the polarisation that had been effected by Jasper Johns in the large striped canvases and their enclosed squares of pure colour. This welcome move away from the random impulses of Abstract Expressionism seen in de Kooning and Kline decided the subsequent moves on the board for Stella. Of the 1960 ''Black Paintings,'' the emphasis was linear; metallic paints tracing enclosures of geometric shapes in large formats. The to-and-froing of the lines in parallel was given some rapid change of pace by stepping and switching through right angles to which the canvas stretcher was trimmed. These massive plans, hung vertically, had their strong two-dimensional presences as much by their rejection of the conventional shape of the support as their integration with mural space, using and adjusting to it as complementary to each work's internal proportions.

About 1962 the relative reticence of the stripes expanded so they became bands of pure and semi-transparent colour edged in white. Recession was accomplished by slightly varying the apex height of adjacent pyramids each formed by four triangles laid side by side. This contrast in colour none the less maintained the integrity of the plane. Other hexagonal motives divided by bands of colour retained their adhesion to the surface level.

Stella's arrowhead paintings of 1964, though large in scale, sacrifice something of their architectural integration in their green grounds hatched by light-toned metallic lines.

Up to 1965, the overall shape of the stretcher had decided the parallel of the design within it, but from here Stella alternated the important elements of the picture against a pure ground with a negative profile created from the shaping of the ground itself.

This return to the internal stresses of abstract cut-out shapes placed a greater strain on the applied colour weights, not only for themselves but for their contrapuntal effect on the wall against which they hung. The inverted V's and diagonally based triangles, cutting into a square as an off-centre Z, had the fragmenting dislocation of the plane to contend with, though here (as in all Stella's works) the flatness of the synthetic hues, together with the occasional use of flourescent paint, preserves the integrity of surface in a bland non-reflective total.

By the early 1970s Stella had won an assured command of his means, often within both tall and wide formats of rectangular plan on which circles and hemispheres and wide band arcs performed progressive ballets on the plane. Colours switched values as the eyes moved across the composition, and one colour area would merge irrevocably into its neighbour.

Interrelationships of parallel forms and complementary colours are conditions at the heart of Stella's statement, moving yet seeming static, monumental though momentarily in flux.

—G.S. Whittet

Stella's work in the 1990s continued to explore the notion of non-representational graphic forms, but his methods shifted from the painted two-dimensional surface of the canvas into other arenas. In the early 1990s, Stella began using computers in the creation of his artwork. The ability of graphics programs to synthesize large amounts of information and allow for the manipulation of multiple layers of imagery fascinated Stella. From these studies, he created ''painted sculptures'' in an obvious defiance of the traditional flat surface of painting. These works are often huge, occupying entire walls in galleries. The idea of chaos is at work in these explorations.

The random action of such phenomena as the movement of smoke rings drives the subject matter in these paintings. Stella has images of smoke patterns (affected by changes in air velocity and temperature) scanned into a computer, then maps the vectors of the rings as lines. ''It's hard not to be interested in things that happen beyond your control, like smoke rings,'' he has said. ''It's hard to get smoke to do what you want. I'm interested in things that have their own way of doing things.''

Stella's work has turned toward more concrete sculptural forms as well. In 1999, he did some set design work for dance pioneer Merce Cunningham and for the revived musical *Pajama Game*. That same year, Stella finished work on his first architectural project, a band shell for a new bay-front performance space in Miami, Florida. The structure is a thirty-four-foot tall spiral-cut beach hat. Stella's *Imaginary Landscapes* exhibit was featured at the Gibbes Museum of Art in the Spring of 2001.

—Tammy A. Kinsey

STEPHENSON, Ian

Nationality: British. **Born:** James Ian Love Stephenson in Browney, near Meadowfield, County Durham, 11 January 1934. **Education:** Early education in Blyth, Northumberland; studied under Lawrence Gowing, King Edward VII School of Art, King's College, University of Durham, Newcastle upon Tyne, 1951–56, B.A. 1956 (Hatton Scholar, 1955–56). **Family:** Married Kate Brown in 1959; children: Stephen and Stella. **Career:** Art editor, *Northerner* student magazine, 1955–57; lecturer and studio demonstrator, King's College, 1956–58; designed, with Victor Pasmore, *The Developing Process,* a basic pedagogic course dedicated to a new creativity in art; Boise Scholar (University of London), in Italy, 1958–59. Painter: shared garret with Richard Hamilton, Newcastle upon Tyne, 1956–58; lived in London, 1959–66; featured in the film *Cubism and After,* by Michael Gill, BBC, London, 1962; contributed to the film, *Blow-up,* by Michelangelo Antonioni, Metro-Goldwyn-Mayer, 1966; lived in Newcastle upon Tyne, 1966–70; abandoned easel painting for mural-scale abstracts on sectional canvases, 1966–70; returned London, 1970. Visiting lecturer in extempore studies, London Polytechnic School of Art, 1959–62; visiting lecturer in basic design, and later in painting, Chelsea School of Art, London, 1959–66; director of foundation studies, Department of Fine Art, University of Newcastle, 1966–70. Director of Master's Degree Postgraduate Painting, Chelsea School of Art, since 1970; international course leader, Voss Summer School of Fine Arts, Norway, 1979. **Awards**: Junior Section Prize, *John Moore's Exhibition,* Liverpool, 1957; Gulbenkian Foundation Purchase Award, London, 1960; Marzotto International Selection Prize, 1964; First Prize, *Northern Painter's Exhibition,* Newcastle upon Tyne, 1966; Gold Medal and Diploma of Merit, Accademia Italia and Universita delle Arti, Parma, Italy, 1980–81. Honorary Member: Mark Twain Society, Missouri, 1978; painting faculty, British School, Rome, 1978; Contemporary Art Society, London, 1980; Accademia Italia delle Arti, Parma, Italy, 1980. Associate, 1975, Royal Academician, 1986, Royal Academy of Arts, London; Honorary Doctorate, University of Durham, 1999. **Address:** 49 Elm Park Gardens, London SW10 9PA, England. **Died:** London, 25 August 2000.

Individual Exhibitions:

1958 New Vision Centre, London
1962 New Art Centre, London
1964 New Art Centre, London
1968 New Art Centre, London
1970 Laing Art Gallery, Newcastle upon Tyne
Laing Art Gallery, Newcastle upon Tyne (with John Martin)
1975 Hester van Royen Gallery, London
1977 *Paintings 1955–66 and 1966–77,* Hayward Gallery, London (toured the U.K.)
New Art Centre, London
1978 City Art Gallery, Birmingham (toured Wales)
1981 Editions Alecto, London
1983 Ceolfrith Gallery, Sunderland
1985 Royal Academy, London
1987 Young Gallery, Salisbury, Wiltshire
1995 Victoria and Albert Museum, London

Selected Group Exhibitions:

1964 *Mostra di Pittura Contemporanea,* Comunità Europea Club Unione, Valdagno, Italy (toured Europe)
1969 *Recent British Painting,* Tate Gallery, London (and world tour, 1969–75)
1973 *Recente Britse Tekenkunst,* Koninklijk Museum, Antwerp (toured West Germany)
1975 *Desenhos Britânicos Contemporâneos,* Museu de Arte Moderna, Sao Paulo (toured South America and Near East, 1975–82
1976 *Arte Inglese Oggi 1960–1976,* Palazzo Reale, Milan
1977 *Color en la Pintura Britanica,* Museu de Arte Moderna, Rio de Janeiro (and world tour, 1977–83)
1981 *Deck of Cards,* British Council Gallery, Athens (toured the Greek Islands and Arabia)
1982 *Een Keuze uit de Hedendaagse Britse Kunst,* BP Gallery, Brussels
1983 *Mednarodni Bienale Grafike,* Moderna Galerija, Ljubljana, Yugoslavia
1985 *Three Decades of British Painting 1946–72,* Turner House, Penarth, Wales
1993 *The Byker Art Show,* Newcastle-upon-Tyne, England

Collections:

Tate Gallery, London; Victoria and Albert Museum, London; Arts Council of Great Britain, London; Hatton Gallery, Newcastle upon Tyne; Whitworth Art Gallery, Manchester; Hunterian Museum and Art Gallery, University of Glasgow; National Museum of Wales, Cardiff; National Gallery of Victoria, Melbourne; Madison Art Center, Wisconsin; Queen Elizabeth II, Windsor; Gulbenkian Foundation, Lisbon; City Museum and Art Galleries, Birmingham and Bristol; British Council, London.

Publications:

By STEPHENSON: Articles—''Statements'' in *Studio International* (London), September 1967; ''Explanatory Note: Paintings

1968–79'' in *Ian Stephenson,* exhibition catalog, Newcastle upon Tyne 1970; ''Remarks'' in *One Magazine* (London), April 1974; ''Correspondence: Without Recourse'' in *Art Monthly* (London), November 1981.

On STEPHENSON: Books—*Contemporary British Art* by Herbert Read, London 1964; *Private View* by John Russell, Bryan Robertson and Lord Snowdon, London 1965; *Adventure in Art,* edited by Hendrik Scheepmaker, New York 1969; *Ian Stephenson,* exhibition catalog by Andrew Forge, Newcastle upon Tyne 1970; *Ian Stephenson: Paintings 1955–56 and 1966–77,* exhibition catalog by William Feaver, London 1977; *Ian Stephenson: Ionic Variation Paintings on Paper 1961–1977* by Andrea Rose, Birmingham 1978; *Tendenze e Testimonianze dell'Arte Contemporanea,* edited by Nicolo Panepinto, Parma 1983.

* * *

Ian Stephenson, it seems, is hardly capable of laying paint on flat. Everything that he has done, from his earliest tentative studies to the 12-foot canvases, has in common a stippled surface. It is an obsession, and as such it is rooted at a far deeper level than the specialized preoccupations of a particular year. It is not, one might guess, just the consequence of a stylistic decision but the reflection of some ancient relationship, essential not only to his view of painting but of the world itself.

There are areas in his paintings—particularly the latest—where the numberless particles of paint are massed at random. The canvas is covered with layer upon layer of dots; individual colour differences are absorbed in the tonality of the mass. One is confronted by a cloud, spongy, shifting. We recognize sensations of distance—and its opposite as when with closed lids we contemplate the warm veiled greys and shifting points and sparks that are all one can see with one's eyes shut. There are no stepping stones in these last pictures, no anchorages with spaces in between. All is filled. All is void.

There is an analogy here with the filmy fields of Rothko. But the differences are extremely significant. When in front of a Rothko and one moves in close, the colour wraps round more closely. The experience is heightened. The surface of the picture is a surface of semi-transparent colour, closer, more enveloping. Here, though, with Stephenson, the surface is not the same. The picture changes scale as one draws into it. The surface resolves itself into thousands and thousands of dots which one is far more clearly aware of outside oneself—at a distance—than before. To the oceanic sensations of the whole is added an awareness of multitude, sharpness, and the minute structure that the eye unravels in each inch of paint. The transitions from ''cloud'' to ''myriad'' and back again is available at will. There is no ''correct'' view of it.

Compare these paintings with the images on a TV screen, a newsprint photograph or a mezzotint. In all these cases the lines or dots are functional; in moving ''in'' to examine the system or ''out'' to read the image, we are crossing a distinct threshold in the quality of our attention. Looking at the painting this journey does not span either/or alternatives: the work is a totality and each movement we make is an enlargement of our relationship to it, and indeed uncovers new dimension of the subject matter. The point is that the image is the upshot of how it is made.

This complexity is typical of the way Stephenson relates to painting himself: painting, one feels, encompasses a multiplicity of experience, widely contrasting sensations stemming from the same source, untrammelled choice. His pictures are the opposite of one-shot. They are difficult, demanding close and varied attention. There is much of the pedagogue in him, a tendency towards extreme conceptualization which shows particularly in some of the ''Spray Studies,'' which are like laboratory demonstrations. At the same time doubt is always present, and the techniques and programmes he devises for himself are invariably open, wayward and humorous even with room for endless speculation and revision. His ideas are rigorous; the processes they set in motion are subject to infinite nuance.

—Andrew Forge

STERBAK, Jana

Nationality: Canadian. **Born:** Prague, 1955; immigrated to Canada, 1968. **Education:** Studied at Vancouver School of Art, 1973–74; University of British Columbia, 1974–75; Concordia University, B.F.A. 1977; University of Toronto, 1980–82. **Career:** Multi-media artist living in Montreal.

Individual Exhibitions:

1988 The Power Plant, Toronto
1989 Mackenzie Art Gallery, Regina
1990 The New Museum of Contemporary Art, New York
1991–92 *States of Being,* National Gallery of Canada, Ottawa (travelled to List Visual Arts Center, Massachusetts Institute of Technology, Boston; Nickle Arts Museum, Calgary, Alberta; Cincinnati Contemporary Art Center, Ohio; and San Diego Museum of Contemporary Art, San Diego, California)
1992 *Jana Sterbak: Projects 38,* Museum of Modern Art, New York
Galerie Crousel-Robelin/BAMA, Paris
Power Play, The School of the Art Institute of Chicago
1993 *Jana Sterbak,* Louisiana Museum of Modern Art, Humlebaek, Denmark
I Want You to Feel the Way I Do, Fundacio ''la Caixa,'' Barcelona
Jana Sterbak: Lenine rétréci, Galerie René Blouin, Montréal
1994 *Jana Sterbak: Déclaration,* Musee d'Art Contemporain de Montreal
Jana Sterbak: Déclaration, Musee des Beaux-Arts de Nantes, France
1995 *VELLEITAS,* Musée d'Art Modern de Saint-Étienne, France (travelled to Fundació Antoni Tàpies, Barcelona, Spain and Serpentine Gallery, London)
Jana Sterbak, Donald Young Gallery, Seattle, Washington
1996 *Jana Sterbak: New Photoworks,* Donald Young Gallery, Seattle, Washington
Trichotilomania III, Galerie René Blouin, Montréal
1997 *Jana Sterbak: Metamorphosis,* David Winton Bell Gallery, Brown University, Providence, Rhode Island
1998 Museum of Contemporary Art, Chicago
Galerie René Blouin, Montréal
Edicions T, Barcelona

2000 Galerie Ema Hécy, Luxembourg

Selected Group Exhibitions:

1978 *Five Artists,* Galerie Optica, Montreal
1979 *Bookworks,* Powerhouse, Montreal
1981 The New YYZ, Toronto
1982 *Photos by Artists,* Galerie France Morin, Montreal
Monumenta, YYZ, Toronto
Menues manoeuvres, Musee d'art contemporain, Montreal
1983 *Unaffiliated Artists,* International Exposure, Toronto
Small Works, Pomona University Gallery, Pomona, California (travelled to San Diego University Gallery, San Diego)
1984 *Influencing Machines,* YYZ, Toronto
Canada/New York, 49th Parallel, New York
1985 *Anadromous,* Michael Katz Gallery, New York
1986 *Songs of Experience,* National Gallery of Canada, Ottawa
Nexus Gallery of Contemporary Art, Atlanta, Georgia
Sept sculpteurs canadiens, Musee d'art contemporain, Montreal
Cologne Art Fair, Cologne, Germany
1987 *Subject/Object,* 56 Bleeker Gallery Limited, New York
1988 *Impossible Self,* Winnepeg Art Gallery and The Vancouver Art Gallery, Vancouver
Identity, Identities, Winnepeg Art Gallery, Winnepeg
Group Material, Dia Foundation, New York
Disturbance, Enchantment, The Power Plant, Toronto
1989 Biennale canadienne d'art contemporain, Musée des Beaux-arts du Canada, Ottawa
Dark Rooms, Artists Space, New York
1990 *Aperto '90,* XLIV Venice Biennale, Venice, Italy
Figuring the Body, Museum of Fine Arts, Boston
1991 *The Wealth of Nations,* Centre for Contemporary Art, Ujazdowski Castle, Varsovie, Poland
Un-Natural Traces: Contemporary Art from Canada, Barbican Art Gallery, London
Un archipel de desirs: les artistes du Quebec et la scene internationale, Musee du Quebec, Quebec, Canada
The Embodied Viewer, Glenbow Museum, Calgary, Canada
1992 *Generique 1: Desordres,* Galerie nationale du Jeu de Paume, Paris
Third International Istanbul Biennale, Istanbul, Turkey
Between the Sheets, P.P.O.W., New York
Internationale Kunstlerplakate, Saarbrucken, Germany
1993 *Space of Time: Contemporary Art from the Americas,* Americas Society, New York
Elective Affinities, Tate Gallery Liverpool, Liverpool, England
Fall from Fashion, The Aldrich Museum of Contemporary Art, Ridgefield, Connecticut
Canada, une nouvelle generation, FRAC des pays de la Loire, Garenne Lemot, France
At the Edge of Chaos—New Images of the World, Louisiana Museum of Modern Art, Humlebaek, Denmark
1994 *Heart of Darkness,* Kröller Müller, Oterloo, Holland
Hors limites: L'Art et La Vie 1952–1994, Centre Georges Pompidou, Musée National d'Art Moderne, Paris
Walker Art Center, Minneapolis, Minnesota
1995 *Colisiones-Collisions,* Arteleku, San Sebastian, Spain
Féminin-masculin: le sexe de líart, Centre Georges Pompidou, Paris
PerForms: Janine Antoni, Charles Ray, Jana Sterbak, Institute of Contemporary Art, Philadelphia, Pennsylvania
Rites of Passage: Art for the End of the Century, Tate Gallery, London
Inside the Visible, Kanaal Art Foundation, Courtrai, Belgium (travelling exhibition)
Premiers Dons 1964–1965 et Dons 1989–1994, Musée d'Art Contemporain de Montréal, Montréal
Spirits on the Crossing: Travelers to/from Nowhere, Contemporary Art in Canada 1980–94, travelling exhibition, Setagaya Art Museum, Tokyo; The National Museum of Modern Art, Kyoto; Hokkaido Museum of Modern Art, Hokkaido, Japan
1996 *Corps étrangers,* Musée des Beaux-arts du Canada, Ottawa
Líoeil du Collectionneur, Musée d'Art Contemporain de Montréal, Montréal, Canada
Il tempo e la moda, Biennale di Firenze, Florence, Italy
Now Here, Louisiana Museum of Modern Art, Humlebaek, Denmark
Feed and Greed, Musée des Arts Décoratifs, Vienna, Austria
1997 *Floating Images of Women in Art History,* Tochigi Prefectural Museum, Japan
Art/Fashion, Guggenheim Museum SoHo, New York
Inside the Visible, Art Gallery of Western Australia, Perth
5th International Istanbul Biennal, Istanbul, Turkey
1998 *Addressing the Century,* Hayward Gallery, London, England (travelled to Kunstmuseum Wolfsburg, Germany)
Skin-deep, The Israel Museum, Jerusalem
Crossings / Traversées, Musée des Beaux-Arts du Canada, Ottawa
The Quiet in the Land, Institute of Contemporary Art, Boston
Spectacular Optical, Thread Waxing Space, New York
Desde el Cuerpo: Alegorias de lo femenino, Museo de Bellas Artes, Caracas, Venezuela
2000 *Collecting Ideas: Works from the Polly and Mark Addison Collection,* Denver Art Museum, Denver, Colorado
Muscle—Power of the View, Boulder Museum of Contemporary Art, Boulder, Colorado

Publications:

By STERBAK: Articles—''Malevolent Heart (Gift)'' in *Parachute,* September-November 1982; ''Golem: Objects as Sensations'' in *Impressions,* Winter-Spring 1983; ''Two 3-D Multisensory Projects'' in *Rubicon,* Summer 1986; ''Artist as Combustible'' in *File Magazine,* no. 27, 1987; ''Altitudes'' in *Public,* no. 2, 1989; ''Generic Man'' in *Transition: Discourse on Architecture,* Summer 1990.

On STERBAK: Books—*Jana Sterbak,* exhibition catalog by Bruce Ferguson, New York 1990; *Jana Sterbak: States of Being,* exhibition catalog by Diana Nemiroff, Ottawa 1991; *PerForms: Janine Antoni, Charles Ray, Jana Sterbak,* exhibition catalog by Judith Tannenbaum with essay by Brian Wallis, Philadelphia 1995; *Jana Sterback* by Amada Cruz, Chicago 1998. **Articles—**''The Body Electric'' by Marni Jackson in *Canadian Art,* Spring 1989; ''Seduction'' by Adam Gopnik in *The New Yorker,* 12 March 1990; ''Jana Sterbak'' by James Yood in *Artforum,* 9 May 1990.

* * *

Jana Sterbak has been making sculpture since the 1970s, but much of it wasn't seen until 1988 with her show at the Power Plant in Toronto. That exhibition, organized by Ihor Holubizky (now at the Art Gallery of Hamilton), showed the full range of Sterbak's work, ending with her *Vanitas: Flesh Dress for an Albino Anorectic* (1987), which indicated her ongoing project to interrogate what it is to be female, and to explore the body. However, it was not until Sterbak's 1991 *States of Being* retrospective at the National Gallery of Canada, when her ''flesh'' dress was criticized as being wasteful of public monies both in the Houses of Parliament (by the head of the federal task force on poverty) and in missions that feed the hungry, that she came to widespread public attention.

States of Being was a model exhibition for a mid-career artist. Given large, well-lit galleries and organized thematically, the show drew the viewer's attention to clothing and wearable objects as metaphors for the body. Divided into three sections—body parts, interior spaces, and wearables—and consisting of 25 pieces, it provided a map of the artist's path from 1987. The show effectively changed the way the artist was viewed not only by the public but by the critic and scholar: Sterbak is one of the most noteworthy feminist artists in Canada. Her sculpture has extraordinary range; she has moved from making small sculptures that normalized materials or forms associated with women—oddly assorted objects such as a group of measuring tapes coiled into little, conical shapes that sat on the floor or were attached to the wall—to making more didactic statements. The latter involved some unusual materials drawn from industry and from everyday life. *I Want You To Feel the Way I Do . . . (the Dress),* her 1984–85 wire mesh dress that was cinched around the middle with uncoiled stove wire which glowed deep red when someone walked into the room, wore its female sensibility like a garment. ''I don't want to hear myself think, feel myself move,'' read part of the text projected on the wall behind the work. ''I want to slip under your skin: I will listen for the sound you hear, feed on your thought, wear your clothes.'' The electric dress seemed an appropriate metaphor not only for anger but for jealousy and passion. (The genesis of the dress was the story of Medea in Euripides's play by the same name.) By 1987, Sterbak was constructing her dress, fashioned this time in a 1920s style, from 23 kilograms (50 pounds) of raw, salted flank steak. It made viewers cringe by reminding them (particularly women) of the flesh from which they are really made. The work made a direct reference in both structure and motif to the Vanitas paintings of the Baroque period and to the philosophical issues that lay behind them, such as the passage of time and the meaning of life—'' It's a memento mori,'' said Sterbak. That the meat aged and dried out and then had to be replaced was appropriate to the intention of the work.

Sterbak has always approached her work with a sense of ironic distance. Growing up in Prague with parents who were intellectuals, she learned to be skeptical of authority and to communicate critical opinions through humorous and ironic allusions, according to Diana Nemiroff, curator of her show at the National Gallery. Issues of control and the constraints placed on the individual (and particularly on women) by society are some of her major themes. Nemiroff says that one of Sterbak's subjects is the paradox of destruction as the means to creation, and the recurrence of the idea links her to a romantic current in European thought. Yet the ambiguous, wide-ranging way she approaches her subject allies her with North American feminists such as Maureen Connor. Her terrain is identity, the persona and society. In the third of her dress works, *Remote Control* (1989), two cage-like motorized crinolines glide through space, operated by the woman who climbs into the machine in a poignant display of the difficulty of movement for the female sex. In a manner similar to the nineteenth century crinoline which made women helpless, the woman at the controls can only move by remote control. In 1992, Sterbak created a male counterpart, *Sisyphus II,* which was shown at the Museum of Modern Art in New York. In it, a man manipulates a chrome and aluminum machine composed of 24 metal ribs (12 vertical, and 12 horizontal); the work was balanced on a sphere and displayed in a darkened room on a hardwood floor. Behind it, a film was projected on the wall showing a muscular man inside the sculpture, rocking it. It is yet another example that shows Sterbak is an original; her work is evidence of the importance of satire to the feminist tradition. ''Serious subjects need not be treated in a humorless way,'' says the artist.

—Joan Murray

STEVENSON, Harold

Nationality: American. **Born:** Idabel, Oklahoma, 11 March 1929. **Education:** University of Oklahoma, Norman; University of Mexico, Mexico City; and Art Students League, New York. **Career:** Established residence in Paris, 1959; studio in Idabel, 1965; now lives in Long Island City, New York. **Agent:** Keith Green Gallery, 500 Park Avenue, New York, New York 10022. **Address:** 21–14 45th Avenue, Long Island City, New York 11101, U.S.A.

Individual Exhibitions:

1949 Hugo Gallery, New York
University of Oklahoma, Oklahoma City
Oklahoma Art Center, Oklahoma City
1958 Hugo Gallery, New York
1960 Galerie La Cour d'Ingres, Paris
1962 *Le Sensuel Fantastique,* Galerie Iris Clert, Paris
The Human Telescope, Robert Fraser Gallery, London
1963 *Adam Retrouve,* Gallery Iris Clert, Paris
1964 Richard Feigen Gallery, New York (travelled to the Feigen Galleries in Chicago and Los Angeles)
1965 *The Idabel Paintings,* Alexander Iolas Gallery, New York
1968 *The Great Society,* Galerie Iris Clert, Paris
La Chasse, Galerie Iris Clert, Paris
1969 Galerie Hake, Kolo, West Germany
1970 Galleria La Medusa, Rome
1972 Alexander Iolas Gallery, New York
1973 Alexander Iolas Gallery, New York
Galleria La Medusa, Rome
ARA Pacis, Galerie Alexandre Iolas, Paris
Zoumboulakis Gallery, Athens

1974 *Black Fates,* Alexander Iolas Gallery, New York
1975 *Votives and Greek Themes,* Iolas-Jackson Gallery, New York
1976 *La Victoire and Death of the American Dream,* Iolas-Jackson Gallery, New York
1979 Galerie Iris Clert, Paris
Stevenson, Musée Girodet, Montargis, France
1982 *Alexander the Living God,* Iolas-Jackson Gallery, New York
1984 *The Pagan World,* Iolas-Jackson Gallery, New York
1985 *Stevenson's Greek Mythopoeia Paintings,* Keith Green Gallery, New York
Harold Stevenson in Athens, Gallery Medus of Maria Dimitriadis, Athens, Greece
1986 *Harold in Egypt,* Keith Green Gallery, New York
1987 *Homage to Alexander Iolas,* Keith Green Gallery, New York
1988 *Fourteen Stations of the Cross,* Keith Green Gallery, NewYork
1989 *Death in Key West,* Key West Studio, Florida
1992 *The New Adam,* Mitchell Algus Gallery, New York
1993 *Death in Key West,* Mitchell Algus Gallery, New York
1999 *The New Adam,* Andy Warhol Museum, New York

Selected Group Exhibitions:

1962 *Piccola Biennale,* Venice
Annual Exhibition, Whitney Museum, New York
1965 *Pop Art,* Palais des Beaux-Arts, Brussels
1966 *Erotic Art '66,* Sidney Janis Gallery, New York
1968 *The Obsessive Image,* Institute of Contemporary Arts, London
Prospect '68, Dusseldorf
1972 *Pop Art,* Alexander Iolas Gallery, New York
1979 *Americans in Paris,* Centre Georges Pompidou, Paris
La Famille des Portraits, Musée du Louvre, Paris
1984 *20th Century American Drawings, The Figure in Context,* (toured USA)

Collections:

Whitney Museum, New York; Musée Nationale d'Art Moderne, Paris; numerous private international collections.

Publications:

On STEVENSON: Books—*Pop Art* by Lucy Lippard, New York 1966; *Iris-Time* by Iris Clert, Paris 1978; *Le Milieu de l'Art,* with photographs by André Morain, Paris 1978. **Articles—**''In the Flesh'' by Michael Duncan in *Art in America* (New York), vol. 87, no. 4, April 1999. **Film—***Harold* by Andy Warhol, 1964.

*

My particular search for the spirit of Alexander began in Paris about 20 years ago, and by the late 1960s I had made several Alexander Paintings. Iris Clert showed some of them, the Empress Farah Diba bought one, and after those first pictures dealing with the known historic images but making them monumental in scale and giving the stone likenessess fleshlike qualities, I found the problem got bigger and more evasive.

Brooks Jackson, Alexander Iolas, Iris Clert, and Bruni and Allen in Rome all asked for more Alexander pictures. They would be a long time coming. I had scratched the surface out of love and devotion, and to probe deeper meant a far more extensive involvement than I had ever anticipated.

In thinking back, I realize that I may have always been in love with the legend of Alexander the Great. The antique Greek world was dear to me even in my childhood; I knew instinctively what inspired Isadora Duncan; the ideal beauty of man seemed the most natural demand one should make; I dreamt of those ideals of beauty, freedom, democracy, diplomacy, fraternal passions, fidelity of the spirit. . . and all those gestures that inspired love in soldiers, jealousy in statesmen, fear in kings, insanity in the inner circle. Everyone I have ever loved personally has had for me some touch of Alexandrian Beauty.

The personal search (in art) is such a time-consuming, over-all passion that there is not much energy left for explanations. I wouldn't be trying to say words now except out of a kind of frustration. . . . I couldn't find anyone to capsule these many years.

How awkward it seems now after years of close association to place Alexander back into history. He is still so avant-garde, so modern, so untouched by the neurosis of our Judeo-Christian system (our system still wants to make him out to have been an alcoholic in need of a psychiatrist . . . how ludicrous!). It would appear to me that he is the model for men of the future; a man who dared to live his own singular destiny. What are all our worthless lives today amounting to? We conform, consume take vitamins, get passports, vote, end up in nursing homes, die with social security numbers around our necks. The god-like quality of men is somehow lost in this conformist existence. Aristotle did not teach Alexander how to conquer the world; he taught him how to think.

I am a non-decorative painter; I do not paint to decorate anyone's existence, much less his ''living room,'' nor do I paint for museums. My work is a matter of passion, and to live with my pictures means you have to live with my passion (in front of you). I am an old lover of Alexander, and what I don't understand about him does not make me love him less. Maybe I will understand him more in the future. Or, as one dear friend said shortly before he died, ''I have loved you in this life, and I will love you in the next.

—Harold Stevenson

* * *

Alone, adrift, he rides across the vast plain in anarchic pursuit of the world's exploiters: moneylenders, shopkeepers, lawyers, bankers businessmen, criminals. He stands outside of the law, feet apart, dressed to pronounce his virility, trigger-finger hungrily grazing the cold metal shaft of the pistol at his side. He is the self-appointed nemesis to the injustices hiding in the legal system. He is Outlaw, he is Hero, he is a killer who enters battles to affirm his manhood through symbolic sexual rituals. Death and violence alone satisfy him. He is the Cowboy. He is a myth.

The Cowboy, a palpably sexual image—more accurately homosexual, derived as a response to the increasing confusion in sexual roles and male identity produced by industrialization and urbanization in America during the first decades of this century. Sensing his control over his own life weakening—indeed his masculine mastery and command, the American male created the Cowboy—a figure of super-masculinity and individual power—to combat his feelings of alienation. Harold Stevenson is one of the few American artists to recognize the myth's tenacious grip over the American imagination. His paintings comment on the continuing inability in the American male to reconcile what he would like to be with what he really is. Under the weight of his own inadequacies he is crushed, crushed by the compensatory myth of the Cowboy. Since the 1950s Stevenson has been analysing and translating the physical and psychological consequence onto canvas, delivering a shocking, pornographic, sometimes unrecognizable portrait of the human condition as it really is.

Stevenson was born in a part of America that less than a century ago was populated by Native Americans until pioneers—among them an older generation of Stevenson's family—slaughtered and drove them from the land with fierce weapons. To this day his small home town, Idabel, Oklahoma remains a vacant, lonely region haunted by the memory of racial murder. Furthermore, for the few whites who live there, it is a land of alienation, one with no native history, for the rich oral culture of the Native Americans was forever lost through racial indifference and contempt. Consequently, Stevenson relied on various foreign sources to provide the settings for his paintings. Of these he favoured the Roman or Greek warrior in classical form, for he could imbue it with all the sexual longing and the violence endemic to the Southwest of his boyhood.

Idabel, Oklahoma was the topic of his 1967 painting *The Great Society* which consisted of one hundred faces of various townspeople. The faces are a metaphor for the human race, the faces alienated from their bodies as Americans are from the land they possess. The artist blatantly avoids the townspeople's sexuality, seeing them rather as he did as a boy. For growing up in Idabel his own sexuality was denied, repressed, something sinful, which, because of this repression, is why sensuality is the exuberant force behind the majority of his work. *The Great Society,* however, invites no sexual fantasy, the bodies covered and their sexual energy passed forever like dead men. These are his people: once filled with the drive and excitement of violence, now repressed, anti-sexual, unfeeling, defeated.

Nearly all of Stevenson's paintings celebrate the relationship between male sexuality, violence and death. Part of the early romanticization of the male involved an intimacy between the three. And since the Cowboy is the preeminent symbol of masculinity in American culture, violence and death itself took on sexual attributes. His heroes thus become naked warriors pitted against death. This American idiom illustrates Stevenson's understanding of the darker aspects of American history; specifically, the anguish of disfigured manhood and the way in which it requires the romanticizing of violence. Equally, this illustrates his understanding of why Vietnam occured, and why there might be more Vietnams.

The Altar of Peace (1973), probably Stevenson's best work to date, is a bitter and ironic commentary on the nature of war and throbs with references to Vietnam. Stevenson sets the piece in a pagan mode, appealing to a pre-Christian age to find his metaphor for the evil of Vietnam, an age without hope of redemption, a time before salvation. The stage is deliberately set outside of American themes and images. The individual figures were taken from earlier works, then further developed and were finally collected on one canvas. Among them include a young boy embracing a black statue which has been mutilated, recalling a theme of the living male idealizing a hero. Right centre stands a warrior with a winged helmet passively watching the weeping youth whilst pressing his hands upon the buttocks of another warrior who is raping a woman. The gesture is ambiguous: he is either applauding the warrior or initiating his own sexual act upon his fellow. The scene rings with homosexuality as the warrior's attention is caught by the youth's grief—or his beauty. In the lower lefthand corner are two warriors, one of whom is sexually assaulting the other anally while his hand grips the base of a broken phallic monument. The monument is symbol of the defeated, as is the warrior being raped. A third warrior crouches behind a stone fragment watching the scene. Ironically his body seems to be becoming stone. The skin is ashen. His hair alone appears alive. He is the conquering warrior becoming Hero.

Altar of Peace suggests that war is mutilated male sexuality. It is violence without responsibility. It is the result of sexual confusion and inadequacy. Stevenson so adeptly summarizes this idea by castrating the defeated male; the Hero Death indifferently waves a broken arm or phallus. Winning is manhood: defeat is emasculation. War is the result of the inability to establish manhood and sexual competence non-violently. It is the nature of Man in general and of the perversions and fantasies of the American male in specific Stevenson has recorded with such accuracy, an accuracy many viewers resist knowing.

—Carrie Barker

STEZAKER, John

Nationality: British. **Born:** Worcester in 1949. **Education:** Nottingham School of Art; Slade School of Fine Art, London, 1967–73. **Career:** Lives and works in London. Founder and co-editor, *Frameworks Magazine,* London. Former lecturer, Chelsea School of Art, London; lecturer, St. Martin's School of Art, London, since 1975. **Agent:** Nigel Greenwood Inc., 4 New Burlington Street, London W1, England. **Address:** 61 Praed Street, London W10, England.

Individual Exhibitions:

1970 Sigi Krauss Gallery, London
Forum Stadpark, Graz, Austria
1972 Nigel Greenwood Gallery, London
King's College, Cambridge
1973 Nigel Greenwood Gallery, London
Museum of Modern Art, Oxford
1974 Galerie December, Munster, West Germany
1975 Nigel Greenwood Gallery, London
Galleria Lia Rumma, Rome (travelled to Galleria Lia Rumma, Naples)
1976 Nigel Greenwood Gallery, London
Galerie Eric Fabre, Paris
1977 Nigel Greenwood Gallery, London
Spectro Arts, Newcastle upon Tyne
Galleria Schema, Florence
1978 The Photographers' Gallery, London
Ikon Gallery, Birmingham
City Museum, Southampton
1979 *Works 1973–1978,* Kunstmuseum, Lucerne
New '57 Gallery, Edinburgh
1984 Lisson Gallery, London
1989 *John Stezaker: The New Work,* Salama-Caro Gallery, London (catalog)
1990 Friedman Guinness Gallery, Frankfurt am Main

1991 Salama-Caro Gallery, London
1996 *Garden,* Cubitt Gallery, London

Selected Group Exhibitions:

1970 *Young Contemporaries,* London
3 Schools Exhibition, Royal Academy of Arts, London
1971 *Wall Show,* Lisson Gallery, London
1972 *The New Art,* Hayward Gallery, London
1973 *Critics' Choice,* Tooth's Gallery, London
1974 *Projekt '74,* Kunsthalle, Cologne
1975 *Structures and Codes,* Royal College of Art, London
1976 *Arte Inglese Oggi 1960–1976,* Palazzo Reale, Milan
1979 *Un Certain Art Anglais,* Musée d'Art Moderne de la Ville, Paris
1982 *Hayward Annual: British Drawing,* Hayward Gallery, London
1987 *Multiple Vision,* Cambridge Darkroom, Cambridge (catalog)
1997 *Strange Days: British Contemporary Photography,* Claudia Gian Ferrari Arte Contemporanea, Milan (catalog)
The Impossible Document: Photography and Conceptual Art in Britain 1966–1976, Camerawork, London (catalog)
1999 *River Deep, Mountain High,* Westland Place Gallery, London
Edinburgh International Festival, Portfolio Gallery
Ljubljana International Biennial of Graphic Art no. 23, Slovenia
2000 *The British Art Show 5* (UK touring exhibition)

Collections:

Victoria and Albert Museum, London; Tate Gallery, London.

Publications:

By STEZAKER: Books—*Beyond Art for Art's Sake: A Propos Mundas,* London 1973. **Articles**—''3 Paradoxes and a Resolution'' in *Studio International* (London), May 1972; ''Conceptual Art'' in *Studio International* (London), June 1972; interview, with Anne Seymour, in *The New Art,* exhibition catalog, London 1972; ''2 Instances of Institutional Determinancy of Art'' in *Control Magazine* (London), no. 7, 1973; ''Premises'' in *Flash Art* (Milan), March/May 1973; ''Post-Duchamp Reversal'' in *Art and Artists* (London), December 1973; ''Priorities I, II and III'' in *Frameworks Journal* (London), vol. 1, nos. 1–3, 1974; ''Ideal Types and Utopias'' in *Control Magazine* (London), no. 8, 1974; ''Conversation with Peter Smith'' in *Studio International* (London), March/April 1975; ''Social Expression: Social Reality'' in *Meantime,* no. 1, 1977; interview in *Artlog* (London), January 1979; interview with Adrian Dannatt in *Flash Art (International Edition),* no. 160, October 1991; ''Angels'' in *Coil,* no. 5, 1997. **Audio**—*Malcolm Morely, John Stezaker, Charlie Hooker,* London 1991.

On STEZAKER: Books—*5 Collages by John Stezaker,* with text by John W. Walker, Birmingham 1978; *John Stezaker: Works 1973–1978,* exhibition catalog, by B. Hatten and M.Kunz, Lucerne 1979. **Articles**—''Problem Solving and Question Begging: The Works of Art-Language and John Stezaker'' by Rosetta Brooks in *Studio International* (London), December 1973; ''Fearful Symmetry: John Stezaker'' by David Alan Mellor in *Portfolio Magazine,* no. 29, June 1999.

STREULI, Beat

Nationality: Swiss. **Born:** Altdort, Switzerland, 19 August 1957. **Education:** Schule für Gestaltung, Zurich, 1977–78; Schule für Gestaltung, Basel, 1979–81; Hochschule der Künste, Berlin, 1982–85. Further training and study abroad at Cité des Arts, Paris, 1985–86, 1989, Istituto Svizzero di Roma, 1988–89; Ateliers FRAC Pays de la Loire, Clisson, 1990, in New York, 1991–92, Fondation Cartier, Paris, 1992, P.S. 1, Institute for Contemporary Art, New York, 1992–93, and Atelierstipendium London, 1997. **Awards:** Kunststipendium des Kt. Zurich, 1981, 1983, 1984; Schweizerisches Bundesstipendium für Bildende Kunst, 1985, 1986, 1988; Kiefer-Hablützel-Stipendium, Bern, 1988; European Photography Award, Dt. Leasing AG, Bad Homburg, 1993; Prix Breguet pour l'Art Contemporain, Geneva, 1994. **Agents:** Hauser and Wirth and Presenhulet, Zurich, Switzerland; Conrads, Düsseldorf, Germany; Jablonka, Cologne, Germany.

Selected Individual Exhibitions:

1984 *Die Reine Richtung,* Galerie Palazzo, Liestal, Switzerland (catalog)
1985 Galerie Ralph Wernicke, Stuttgart (catalog)
1992 Galerie Anne de Villepoix, Paris
1993 *Projektionen und Fotografien NYC 1991–93,* Kunstmuseum, Lucerne (catalog)
1995 *USA 95,* Württembergischer Kunstverein, Stuttgart (catalog)
1996 *Portrait Tarragone/Copenhague 1996,* ARC, Musée d'Art Moderne de la Ville de Paris (catalog)
1997 Tate Gallery, London
1998 Museu d'Art Contemporani, Barcelona
Marseille 98, Rencontres d'Arles, Arles (catalog)
1999 *Chicago, July 99,* Museum of Contemporary Art, Chicago, Illinois
Bondi Beach, Sprengel Museum, Hannover (catalog)
CITY, Kunsthalle, Düsseldorf (catalog)
2000 *Urban Views,* Stedelijk Museum, Amsterdam (catalog)
2001 Galerie Wilma Tolksdorf, Frankfurt am Main, Germany

Selected Group Exhibitions:

1984 *Perspectiven,* Art '84, Basel
1987 *Offenes Ende,* Städtische Galerie, Erlangen (catalog)
1990 *Compositions,* Galerie Anne de Villepoix, Paris
1991 *Lieux Communs, Figures Singulières,* ARC, Musée d'Art Moderne de la Ville de Paris (catalog)
1993 *New Photography,* with Giglio, Mihailol, Steinmer, Museum of Modern Art, New York (catalog)
1996 *Im Kunstlicht,* Kunsthaus, Zurich (catalog)
Prospect, Frankfurter Kunstverein, Frankfurt am Main (catalog)
Views from Abroad: European Perspectives on American Art 2, Whitney Museum of American Art, New York (catalog)

1997 *Absolute Landscape: Between Illusion and Reality,* Yokohama Museum of Art, Japan (catalog)
1998 *Freie Sicht aufs Mittelmeer,* Kunsthaus, Zurich (traveled to Schirn Kunsthalle, Frankfurt am Main) (catalog)
Sydney Biennale, Australia
1999 *Bondi Beach/Parramatta Road,* Museum für Moderne Kunst, Frankfurt (catalog)
2000 *Le Désert,* Fondation Cartier, Paris (catalog)
2001 *Open City,* Museum of Modern Art, Oxford, England (catalog)

Collections:

Stedelijk Museum, Amsterdam; Museum für Moderne Kunst, Frankfurt am Main; Museum of Contemporary Art, Chicago, Illinois; Folkwang Museum, Essen, Germany; Kunsthaus, Zurich; Centre Georges Pompidou, Paris; Musée d'Art Moderne de la Ville de Paris, ARC, Paris.

Public Installations:

Berner Versicherung, Bern 1997; SwissRe, Tokyo 1999; Düsseldorfer Sparkasse, Düsseldorf 2000; Neue Börse, Frankfurt am Main 2000.

Publications:

By STREULI: Articles—''Beat Streuli'' interview with Alexander Braun in *Kunstforum,* no. 133, February-April 1996; ''Symposion über Fotografie XVIII (Vortragstext)'' in *Camera Austria,* no. 62/63, 1998; interview in *Bijutsu Techo,* vol. 51, no. 773, July 1999; interview with Staci Boris in *Museum of Contemporary Art,* October 1999; Interview with Alessandra Pace, at http://www.repubblicarts.kataweb.it/repubblicarts/streuli/bio_1.html (accessed June 2001).

On STREULI: Articles—''Beat Streuli, Manières d'Être/Ways of Being'' by Jean-Charles Masséra in *art press,* no. 197, December 1994; ''A Flash . . . Then Night: Beat Streuli's Photographs'' by Girogio Verzotti in *Artforum,* September 1995; ''Figuren, Pausen, Haltungen'' by Jean-Christophe Royoux in *Artis,* no. 2, vol. 48, February/March 1996; ''Impossible Ailleurs'' by André Rouillé in *recherche photographique,* no. 20, February 1997; ''Stop the Train (Douglas, Streuli, Nauman, Hill)'' by Rainald Schumacher in *Flash Art,* no. 194, May/June 1997; ''Kartographie des Anonymen'' by José Lebrero Stals in *Parkett,* no. 54, 1998/99; ''L'Étonnement de Voir'' by Catherine Grout in *Parachute,* no. 97, January-March 2000.

* * *

Since the 1980s Swiss photographer Beat Streuli has been taking photographs, characteristically vibrant and brightly keyed close-up portraits, of urban dwellers. Streuli treats the dynamics of the public sphere as his subject; he seeks a voyeur's sense of intimacy with the denizens of the world's metropolises: New York, Tokyo, Düsseldorf, Chicago, London. Similarly, Streuli's work has been exhibited across the globe.

Streuli works in similar themes to mid-career photographer Philip-Lorca di Corcia, who captures images of ordinary individuals passing on the sidewalks. Di Corcia's choreographed and cinematic attention to his subjects—in the ''Heads'' series from 2000 he used trip lights to trigger stage-like spot lighting on the streets of New York City—results in the sense of a drama caught in progress or a film still. Similarly, Streuli's method is to narrow his attention on singular individuals, usually youngish women, within crowded downtown masses. While Streuli's presentation is as equally lush and finished as di Corcia's—Streuli composes with colors and contrasts, using low-speed fine grain film—he shoots in direct daylight, thus directing the content of his work more towards the psychological ambiguity of his subject's expressions than to theatricality. Streuli uses a telephoto lens at a distance to capture his subjects unposed. By using a strong zoom lens, he minimizes the depth of field and eliminates or neutralizes a specific context while enhancing the impact of the individual features. He states that he ''hardly ever take[s] pictures in poor suburbs where the social problems are obvious, because in such surroundings people could become just figures reduced to their social role.''

Streuli experimented with a variety of photographic techniques in the mid to late 1990s. In 1994, he began using a video camera while standing within a crowd to capture the flow of human traffic from a static perspective, registering the passing of people and their various expressions. Streuli's body of photographic work includes large-scale prints, slide overlay projections, wallpaper, and public billboard images.

His method of selection is based on personal choice, rather than a minimalist documentary or cataloguing aesthetic. In this ''quick and intuitive'' fashion, Streuli photographs people who possess ''that 'special something' which makes them different and beautiful.'' Charles Baudelaire in his essay, ''Painter of Modern Life,'' published in 1863, writes that while ''Beauty'' is eternal, what makes beauty particular to an age is the element of ''the transitory, the fugitive.'' Streuli acts as a 21st century flâneur, similar to his Parisian predecessor who moved as a detached observer through the urban streets—the modern stage—like a detective devoted to finding the many details of contemporary life.

''Shinjuku-ku, 1–5-99'' (2001), an ink-jet print on paper affixed to a wall, presents a self-possessed young Japanese woman on the streets of Tokyo caught unaware of being observed or committed to film. In a graphically designed red jacket, with tidy haircut and messenger bag, the fashionable girl travels through her daily route lost in reflective thought. This type of seductive youth-focused image most closely resembles advertising imagery, but it contains no obvious reference to economic functionality. The print, ''Shinjuku-ku, 1–5-99,'' resembles a visual clip from the *Look Book*, an image bank complied by the New York firm *Look Look,* which sends reporters to the streets of ultra-hip urban neighborhoods to provide corporations with the language of ''cool'' in order to market products to young consumers. Like corporate cool hunters, Streuli seeks to transfix the images of the most clever, unique individuals at the genesis of creative trends before they are codified by mass media and thus rendered clichés.

More so than style-for-sale, Streuli examines the street as an entry into intimate personal worlds that are otherwise inaccessible. He feels that ''the crowd gives you a kind of anonymity that verges on privacy.'' Without anecdotal subject matter or outright visual narrative, Streuli asks the viewer to search the reflective faces in his photographs for meaning. For Streuli, curiosity about other people's lives draws him, and his viewers, into a range of possibilities of human existence.

—Sarah Wagner

STRUTH, Thomas

Nationality: German. **Born:** Geldern, Germany, 1954. **Education:** Studied in the studios of P. Kleeman, Gerhard Richter, and Bernd Becher, Academy of Fine Arts, Düsseldorf, Germany, 1973–80; studied at P.S. 1 Studios, Long Island City, New York, 1978. **Career:** Photographer, Düsseldorf, Germany. **Awards:** ''Spectrum'' International Prize for Photography, Stiftung Niedersachsen, Germany, 1977; scholarship from the Academy of Fine Arts, Düsseldorf, Germany, for P.S.1 Studios, Long Island City, New York, 1978. **Agent:** Marian Goodman Gallery, 24 West 57th Street, New York, New York 10019.

Selected Individual Exhibitions:

1978 P.S.1/Institute for Art and Urban Resources, Long Island City, New York
1980 Galerie Rüdiger Schöttle, Munich
1985 Galerie Rüdiger Schöttle, Munich
1986 Gallery Shimada, Yamaguchi, Japan
1987 Galerie Max Hetzler, Cologne
Kunsthalle Bern, Switzerland
Fruitmarket Gallery, Edinburgh
The Yamaguchi Prefectural Museum of Art, Japan
1988 Galerie Rüdiger Schöttle, Munich
Galerie Meert-Rihoux, Brussels
1989 Galerie Peter Pakesch, Vienna
Halle Sud, Geneva
Galerie Max Hetzler, Cologne
1990 Marian Goodman Gallery, New York
Galerie Giovanna Minelli, Paris
Galerie Paul Andriesse, Amsterdam
Thomas Struth: Photographs, The Renaissance Society, University of Chicago, (catalog)
1991 Gallery Shimada, Yamaguchi, Japan
Galerie Meert-Rihoux, Brussels
1992 Galerie Paul Andriesse, Amsterdam
Institute of Contemporary Arts, London
Museum Haus Lange, Krefeld, Germany
Hirshhorn Museum and Sculpture Garden, Washington, D.C.
1993 The St. Louis Art Museum, Missouri
Thomas Struth: Museum Photographs, Hamburger Kunsthalle, Hamburg (catalog)
Gallery Senda, Hiroshima
Galleria Monica de Cardenas, Milan
1994 *Landschaften,* Achenbach Kunsthandel, Düsseldorf
Thomas Struth: Streets, Houses, People; Photographs 1988–1992, Institute of Contemporary Art, Boston
Marian Goodman Gallery, New York
1995 Kunstmuseum, Bonn, Germany
Thomas Struth: Oeuvres Récentes, Marian Goodman Gallery, Paris
Thomas Struth: Strangers and Friends, Art Gallery of Ontario, Toronto; Institute of Contemporary Art, Boston; Institute of Contemporary Arts, London (catalog)
Gallery Shimada, Tokyo
1996 *Architekturfotografien aus Italien 1984–1991,* Gallery Shimada, Tokyo
Thomas Struth: Photos de Chine, Marian Goodman Gallery, Paris
Kluuvin Galleria, Helsinki, Finland
Thomas Struth, Monica de Cardenas, Milan
1997 Marian Goodman Gallery, New York
Thomas Struth: nieuw werk, Paul Andriesse, Amsterdam
The Berlin Project, Galerie Max Hetzler, Berlin (with Klaus von Bruch)
1998 Galerie Meert Rihoux, Brussels
Sprengel Museum, Hannover, Germany
Thomas Struth: Portraits, Marian Goodman Gallery, Paris; Sprengel Museum, Hannover, Germany
1999 *Thomas Struth: STILL,* Centre National de la Photographie, Paris; Gallery Shimada, Tokyo; Stedelijk Museum, Amsterdam
New Pictures from Paradise, Marian Goodman Gallery, New York and Paris
The Berlin Project, Hamburger Kunstverein, Hamburg; Lucerne, Switzerland (with Klaus vom Bruch)
Galleria Monica de Cardenas, Milan, Italy
2000 Galeri K, Oslo, Norway
2001 *Thomas Struth: My Portrait,* National Museum of Modern Art, Tokyo; National Museum of Art, Kyoto

Selected Group Exhibitions:

1979 *Schlaglichter: Junge Kunst im Rheinland,* Rheinisches Landesmuseum, Bonn, Germany
In Deutschland: Aspekte gegenwärtiger Dokumentarfotografie in Deutschland, Rheinisches Landesmuseum, Bonn, Germany
1980 *T. Struth, T. Schütte and A. Tiffert,* Galerie ERG, Brussels
1981 *Erweiterte Fotografie,* 5th International Biennial, Wiener Seccesion, Vienna
Thomas Struth and Tata Ronkholz, Stadtmuseum, Düsseldorf
1982 *Work by Young Photographers from Germany,* Art Galaxy (Barbara Flynn), New York
1983 *Laputa,* Gutenbergstraße, Stuttgart
Austellung B, Ausstellungsräume, Lothringerstrasse, Munich
1985 New York State University Gallery, New York
1986 *7 Fotografen,* Galerie Rüdiger Schöttle, Munich
Fotografie und Skulptur, Atelierhaus Hansaallee, Düsseldorf
1987 *Foto/Realismen,* Kunstverein München, Munich, Germany; Nationalgalerie, Berlin; Villa Dessauer, Bamberg, Germany; Haus der Industrie, Cologne
Thomas Struth and Siah Armajani, Westfälisches Landesmuseum, Münster, Germany
1988 *Fotoarbeiten,* Wofgang Wittrock Kunsthandel, Düsseldorf
School of Bernhard Becher, Galerie Johnen & Schöttle, Cologne
1989 *Thomas Struth and Andreas Gursky,* P.S.1/Institute for Art and Urban Resources, Long Island City, New York
Another Objectivity, Centre National des Arts Plastiques, Paris; Museo d'Arte Contemporanea Luigi Pecci, Prato, Italy; Institute of Contemporary Arts, London (catalog)
1990 *Weitersehen 1980–1990,* Museum Haus Lange and Museum Haus Esters, Krefeld, Germany

Affinities and Intuitions: The Gerald S. Elliott Collection of Contemporary Art, Art Institute of Chicago (catalog)
Images in Transition, National Museum of Modern Art, Kyoto; National Museum of Modern Art, Tokyo (catalog)
1991 *A Dialogue about Recent American and European Photography,* The Museum of Contemporary Art, Los Angeles (catalog)
Currents, Institute of Contemporary Arts, Boston
Typologies: Nine Contemporary Photographers, Newport Harbour Art Museum, Newport Beach, California; Akron Art Museum, Ohio; Corcoran Art Gallery, Washington, D.C.; San Francisco Museum of Art (catalog)
Surgence: Contemporary Creations in Photography in Germany, Comédie de Reims, France; Musée Saint-Croix, Poitiers, France; Musée des Beaux- Arts, Rennes, France; Musée d'Evreux, France
1992 Documenta 9, Kassel, Germany
Photography in Contemporary German Art: 1960 to the Present, Walker Art Center, Minneapolis (catalog)
Family Album: Changing Perspective of Family Portrait, Metropolitan Museum of Photography, Tokyo
1993 *A Group Show,* Marian Goodman Gallery, New York
Distanz und Nähe, Nationalgalerie, Berlin
Diskurse der Bilder Kunsthistorisches Museum, Vienna
1994 *Photographie in der deutschen Gegenwartskunst,* Museum für Gegenwartskunst, Basel, Switzerland
The Label Show: Contemporary Art and the Museum, Museum of Fine Arts, Boston
Visions Urbaines, Musée National d'Art Moderne-Centre Georges Pompidou, Paris; Centre de Cultura Contemporainia, Barcelona
Works from the Collection: The Institute of Cultural Anxiety, Institute of Contemporary Arts, London
1995 *After Art: Rethinking 150 Years of Photography,* Henry Art Gallery, University of Washington, Seattle; Ansel Adams Center, San Francisco; Portland Art Museum (catalog)
RAM: Realität, Anspruch, Medium, Kunstverein Karlsruhe, Germany; Neues Museum Weserburg, Bremen, Germany; Lindenau-Museum, Altenburg, Germany
Art Museum: Sophie Calle, Louise Lawler, Richard Misrach, Diane Neumaier, Richard Ross, Thomas Struth, Center for Creative Photography, The University of Arizona, Tucson (catalog)
1996 *Photographie in der deutschen Gegenwartskunst,* Prospect 96, Kunstverein Frankfurt am Main & Schirn Kunsthalle, Frankfurt am Main
Musée Nationale d'Histoire and d'Art de Luxembourg
Distanz und Nähe, Kawasaki City Museum, Kawasaki, Japan
Tochigi Prefectural Museum of Fine Arts, Tochigi, Japan
1997 *Face to Face: Luo Yongjin & Thomas Struth Fotografie,* Art Gallery of Beijing, International Art Palace
Invisible Light, Museum of Modern Art, Oxford
Contemporary Photography: Absolute Landscape: Between Illusion and Reality, Yokohama Museum of Art, Japan
1998 *Art of the 80s,* Culturgest, Lisbon
1999 *Seeing Time: Selections from the Pamela and Richard Kramlich Collection of Media Art,* San Francisco Museum of Modern Art (catalog)
The Museum as Muse: Artists Reflect, The Museum of Modern Art, New York (catalog)
Presence: Figurative Art at the End of the Century, Tate Gallery, Liverpool
Apposite Opposites: Photography from the MCA Collection, Museum of Contemporary Art, Chicago
Missing Link: Menschen: Bilder in der Fotografie, Kunstmuseum Bern, Switzerland
2000 *Aspectos de la Collección,* Fundació La Caixa, Madrid
The Continuity of the Everyday in 20th Century Art, Castello di Rivoli Museo d'Arte Contemporanea, Turin
Ansicht Aussicht Einsicht: Architurfotographie, Museum Bochum, Kunstsammlung der Ruhr-Universität Bochum, Germany; Galerie für Zeitgenössische Kunst, Leipzig, Germany; Galeria Bunkler Sztuki, Krakow, Poland
Age of Influence: Reflections in the Mirror of American Culture, Museum of Contemporary Art, Chicago
Open Ends: Architecture Hot and Cold, The Museum of Modern Art, New York
2001 *Mirror's Edge,* BildMuseet, Umea, Sweden; Vancouver Art Gallery; Castello di Rivoli Museo d'Arte Contemporanea, Turin; Tramway, Glasgow

Publications:

On STRUTH: Articles—''Thomas Struth: Marian Goodman'' by David Bussel in *Flash Art,* vol. 24, no. 156, January-February 1991; ''Thomas Struth: Hoping to Transcend the Photograph's Representational Function'' by Kathryn Hixson in *Flash Art,* vol. 28, no. 178, October 1994; ''Thomas Struth: Realism and Recollection'' by Régis Durand in *Art Press,* no. 213, May 1996; articles by various authors in *Parkett,* no. 50–5, 1997; ''Faulty Towers: The Legacy of the Impassive Eye in Contemporary German Photography'' by Tim Griffin in *Art on Paper,* vol. 3, no. 1, September-October 1998; ''Thomas Struth: 'Gesichter, all-over' über die Aufnahme von Differenzen'' by Hans Rudolf Reust in *Kunstforum International,* no. 144, March-April 1999.

* * *

The photographs of German artist Thomas Struth encourage viewers to scrutinize everyday landscapes, scenes, and activities. He uses the technique known as ''straight'' photography to create his works; this means that he does not manipulate his photos by artistic means during the development and production phases. Struth's photographs appear to mirror reality, but they also seem strangely removed from everyday experience. Although they present little in the way of narrative, they function as investigations into social relationships.

Struth takes photographs in series so he can thoroughly investigate his chosen subject matter. Since the 1970s, he has produced three major series: urban landscapes, portraits, and museum interiors. Struth first became known for his photographs of cities taken in the late 1970s and early 1980s. These small-scale, black-and-white works present views of streets and buildings that are devoid of people. Since viewers cannot focus their attention on humans, Struth grants them the ability to thoroughly investigate the urban landscapes for clues about their inhabitants' existence.

Struth's urban photographs examine cities across Europe, the United States, and Japan—countries that share the social organization of late twentieth-century capitalism. Presented as a series, the works reveal both the similarities and the differences between the cultures' urban development and social settings. Overall, however, the photos disclose less about cultural diversity and more about a rigid grid of symmetrical, modernist social planning. Many compositions highlight a street oblique to the picture plane surrounded by vertical buildings and seem to suggest a sense of urban community. Invariably, however, buildings on the horizon line block the expanse of the street. This psychological denial of the ability to get somewhere, on both the part of the viewer and the urban dweller, underscores the social alienation that has resulted from the development of the modern system.

Begun in 1986 but mostly made from 1988 to 1990, Struth's color and black-and-white photographs of bourgeois families comprise single views and posed portraits. As with the urban landscapes, Struth took these photos in Japan, Europe, and the United States. The works reveal shared ways of life between different cultures, although cultural and social distinctions are also discernible.

The individuals in the portrait series chose how to present themselves in the photographs. Although Struth invited a family to pose only after he had known them for a substantial period of time, the people in the portraits always appear stiff and self-conscious; they understand that viewers will scrutinize their images for years to come. The compositions reveal information about how the subjects want other people to see them and also about their relationships with the other sitters in the photographs.

In 1989, Struth began a series of large color photographs taken in galleries in European and American museums. These photos, which show visitors looking at or passing by famous paintings and sculptures, are studies in human interaction with art. Since Struth generally photographs figurative art works, those viewing his photos perceive a psychological relationship between the depicted contemporary viewers and the figures in the historical works. In ''Art Institute of Chicago II'' (1990), for example, the two people viewing Gustave Caillebotte's ''Paris Street; Rainy Day'' (1877) appear to be able to converse with the figures in the painting, and even to walk into the painting itself.

The photographs in Struth's museum series are voyeuristic gazes into a private activity that takes place in a public domain. Those viewing Struth's works necessarily share with the depicted museum visitors a relationship with the photographed works of art: Their role as voyeur reverses as they realize that they themselves are in a public museum looking at a work of art; the watcher becomes the watched. Struth's photographs thus encourage viewers to analyze their experiences with critical self-awareness.

—Joyce Youmans

STUART, Michelle

Nationality: American. **Born:** Los Angeles, Califonia, 10 February 1938. **Education:** Chouinard Art Institute, Los Angeles, 1954–55; Instituto de Bellas Artes, Mexico City, with Diego Rivera, 1955–56; and New School for Social Research, New York, 1958–60. **Family:** Married Jose Barton in 1950 (divorced, 1974). **Career:** Worked as a topographical draftswoman, Los Angeles, 1955; lived in Mexico, 1955–56, and in Paris 1956–58; now a full-time artist, living and working in New York, since 1958. Adjunct instructor, Pratt Institute School of Art and Design, New York, 1975–76, Parsons School of Design, New York, 1976–78, and Fordham University, New York, 1976–79. **Awards:** Macdowell Fellowship, Peterborough, New Hampshire, 1974; National Endowment for the Arts Grant for Individual Artists, 1974–1977, 1980; Tamarind Institute Grant, 1974; New York Creative Artists Public Service Grant in Painting, 1974; Guggenheim Fellowship, 1975; Finnish Art Association Fellowship, Helsinki, 1985; Artists' Fellowship, New York Foundation for the Arts, 1987; Excellence in Design Award, New York City Art Commission, 1990; American Academy in Rome residency, 1995; Richard M. Reccia Memorial Prize, National Academy Museum, New York, 1997. **Agent:** Max Protech Gallery, 560 Broadway, New York 10012; Saxon/Lee Gallery, 7525 Beverly, Los Angeles, California 90036; Galerie Veda, Ginza Asahi Building 6–6-7 Ginza, Chuo-ku, Tokyo 104, Japan; and Galerie Alfred Schmela, Mutter-Ey-Strasse 3, 4 Dusseldorf, Germany. **Address:** 152 Wooster Street, New York, New York 10012, U.S.A.

Individual Exhibitions:

1973 Douglass College, Rutgers University, New Brunswick, New Jersey
Windham College, Putney, Vermont
1974 Max Hutchinson Gallery, New York
Galerie Alfred Schmela, Dusseldorf
1975 Max Hutchinson Gallery, New York
Fine Arts Center Gallery, State University at Oneonta, New York (catalog)
Niagara Gorge Path Relocated, Lewiston, New York (site work)
1976 Galerie Alfred Schmela, Dusseldorf
Gallery of Fine Arts, State University of New York at Stony Brook
Galerie Farideh Cadot, Paris
Max Hutchinson Gallery, New York
Zolla/Lieberman Gallery, Chicago
East/West Wall Memory Relocated, P.S. 1, Institute for Art and Urban Resources, New York (site work)
1977 Massachusetts Institute of Technology, Cambridge
Williams College Museum of Art, Williamstown, Massachussetts
Gallerie Munro, Hamburg
Strata: Graves/Hesse/Stuart/Winsor, Vancouver Art Gallery
Galerie Alfred Schmela, Dusseldorf
Color/Time/Landform/Tranformation, Tomkins Cove Quarry, Tomkins Cove, New York (site work and video project)
Incidents of Travel in Nature: A Space/Time Book and Video Project, Moore College of Art, Philadephia
1978 University of New Mexico Art Gallery, Albuquerque
Incidents of Travel in Nature: A Space/Time Book and Video Project, Art Gallery, University of Califonia at Long Beach (site work)

Michelle Stuart: *Seed Containers: #3,* 1993. ©Michelle Stuart.

Fine Arts Gallery, Wright State University, Dayton, Ohio
Galerie Farideh Cadot, Paris
Centre d'Arts Plastiques Contemporains, Bordeaux
Zand Gallery, Teheran
Tanit Galerie, Munich
Zolla/Lieberman Gallery, Chicago
1979 Ehrensberger Gallery, Zurich
Droll/Kolbert Gallery, New York
Foster White Gallery, Seattle
Stone Alignments/Solstice Cairns, Portland Center for the Visual Arts, Oregon (permanent sculpture site work)
Galerie Schmela, Dusseldorf
Paperwork, Institute of Contemporary Arts, London
Janus Gallery, Venice, California
1980 Galerie Munro, Hamburg
Galerie Ahlner, Stockholm
Galleriet, Lund, Sweden
Galerie Aronowitsch, Stockholm
1981 *Correspondences,* Joslyn Art Museum, Omaha, Nebraska (audio visual room installation)
Galerie Tanit, Munich
Correspondences, P.S. 1, Institute for Art and Urban Resources, New York (audio visual room installation)
1982 *Correspondences,* St. Louis Art Museum (audio visual room installation)
Susan Caldwell Gallery, New York
Galerie Schmela, Dusseldorf
1983 Walker Art Center, Minneapolis (catalog)
Janus Gallery, Los Angeles
Haags Gemeentemuseum, The Hague
Galleriet Anders Tornberg, Lund, Sweden
Gallerie Ahlner, Stockholm
1984 *Sacred Precincts,* State University of New York, Purchase
Galerie Krista Mikkola, Helsinki
Gallery Ueda Warehouse and Ginza, Tokyo
1985 Long Island University, Greenvale, New York (travelled to Syracuse, New York; Boulder, Colorado; Binghamton, New York)
1986 Saxon/Lee Gallery, Los Angeles
Paradisi, Brooklyn Museum, New York

Arts Club of Chicago
Max Protech Gallery, New York
1987 Thorden Wetterling Gallery, Goteborg, Sweden
Toni Birckhead Gallery, Cincinnati
Paintings and Prints, Anders Tornberg Gallery, Lund, Sweden
Malningar, Galerie Aronowitsch, Stockholm
Pfizer Inc., New York
1988 *Silent Gardens: The American Landscape,* Rose Art Museum, Waltham, Massachusetts (travelled; catalog)
1991 B.R. Kornblatt Gallery, Washington, D.C.
Small Sculpture, Art Gallery, College of Wooster, Ohio (travelled; catalog)
1992 *Derelict Tracts: An Observatory,* Santa Barbara Contemporary Arts Forum, California
1994 Fawbush Gallery, New York (catalog)
1995 Anders Tornberg, Lund, Sweden
1997 John Weber Gallery, New York
1998 *The Heart of the Matter,* SECCA, Winston-Salem, North Carolina (catalog)
Glenn Horowitz, East Hampton, New York (catalog)
1999 Frog Pond, Diane Villani/Quartet Editions, New York
John Weber Gallery, New York
2000 Locus Gallery, St. Louis, Missouri

Selected Group Exhibitions:

1972 *Outsize Drawings,* Loeb Art Center, New York University
1976 *Handmade Paper: Prints and Unique Work,* Museum of Modern Art, New York
1977 *Documenta,* Kassel, West Germany
1978 *Paper as Medium,* Smithsonian Institution, Washington, D.C.
1979 *The Presence of Nature,* Whitney Museum, New York
1980 *With Paper, About Paper,* Albright-Knox Art Gallery, Buffalo, New York
1981 *Le Moderna Museet de Stockholm a Bruxelles,* Palais des Beaux-Arts, Brussels
1982 *Sans Titre: 4 Annees d' Acquisition au Musee de Toulon,* Musée d'Art, Toulon, France
1985 *Livres d'Artistes,* Centre Georges Pompidou, Paris
1987 *Sacred Spaces,* Everson Museum of Art, Syracuse New York
1989 *Portfolios and Projects: The 25th National Print Biennal,* Brooklyn Museum of Art, New York (catalog)
First Impressions, Walker Art Center, Minneapolis (travelled; catalog)
1994 *L'Art American dans les Collections Publiques Francaises de Province 1960–1992,* Musée de Toulon, France (catalog)
1997 *On the Edge: Contemporary Art from the Werner and Elaine Dannheiser Collection,* Museum of Modern Art, New York (catalog)
1999 *Afterimage: Drawing through Process,* Museum of Contemporary Art, Los Angeles (catalog)
Book as Art XI, National Museum of Women in the Arts, Washington, D.C.
2000 *Open Ends: Contemporary Art from 1960 to Now,* Museum of Modern Art, New York

Collections:

Museum of Modern Art, New York: Brooklyn Museum, New York; Albright-Knox Art Gallery, Buffalo, New York; Museum of Contemporary Art, Chicago; Walker Art Center, Minneapolis; Cincinnati Art Museum, Ohio; Detroit Institute of Arts, Detroit, Michigan; Philadelphia Museum of Art, Pennsylvania; Library of Congress, Washington, D.C.; Kaiser-Wilhelm Museum, Krefeld, West Germany; Moderna Museet, Stockholm; Stadtisches Museum, Monchengladbach, West Germany; National Collection of Australlia, Canberra.

Publications:

By STUART: Books—*The Fall,* New York 1976; *A Complete Folk History of the United States at the Edge of the Century,* Dayton, Ohio and New York 1978; *From the Silent Garden,* Williamstown, Massachusetts 1979; *I-80 Series: Michelle Stuart,* exhibition catalog, Omaha 1981; *Sacred Precincts: From Dreamtime to the South China Sea,* New York 1984. **Articles—**''Project, Then/Now'' in *Artforum* (New York), February 1980; ''American Frontiers: The Photographs of Timothy O'Sullivan 1867–1874'' in *The Print Collector's Newsletter* (New York), July/August 1982.

On STUART: Books—*Michelle Stuart,* exhibition catalog with an essay by Lawrence Alloway, Oneonta, New York 1975; *From the Center* by Lucy Lippard, New York 1976; *Michelle Stuart,* exhibition catalog with an essay by Robert Hobbs, Cambridge, Massachusetts 1977; *Strata: Graves/Hesse/Stuart/ Winsor,* exhibition catalog with an essay by Lucy Lippard, Vancouver 1977; *Michelle Stuart,* exhibition catalog, with an essay by Jean-Pierre Sanchez, Bordeaux 1978; *Originals: American Women Artists* by Eleanor Munro, New York 1979; *Michelle Stuart: Paperwork,* exhibition catalog with text by Sarah Kent, London 1979; *With Paper, About Paper,* exhibition catalog with an essay by Carlotta Kotik, Buffalo, New York 1980; *La Peinture americaine: Le mythes et la matière* by Madeleine Deschamps, Paris 1981; *Michelle Stuart: Place and Time,* exhibition catalog with text by Graham Beal, Minneapolis 1983; *The Pluralist Era: American Art 1968–81* by Corinne Robins, New York 1984; *Michelle Stuart: Voyages,* exhibition catalog with texts by Ted Castle and Judith Van Wagner, Greenvale, New York 1985; *Michelle Stuart* exhibition catalog with text by Esther Sparks, Chicago 1986. **Articles—**''Michelle Stuart: Atavism, Geomythology and Zen'' by Roberts Hobbs in *Womanart,* vol. 1, no. 4, Spring-Summer 1977; ''Melancholy Mapping'' by Stephen Westfall in *Art in America,* February 1987; ''Michelle Stuarts Silent Gardens'' by Carey Lovelace in *Arts Magazine,* September 1988; ''Natural Selection'' by Gail Gregg in *ARTnews,* March 1999; ''Essential Light: The Skies of Michelle Stuart'' by Joseph Ruzicka in *Art in America,* 1 June 2000.

*

For some years I have been making large scale works concerned with the visual and conceptual experience in nature. The earlier ones were topographical renderings of cratered surfaces, sometimes with elements suggesting waves and currents. The pieces that followed were multi-unit drawings in series that documented changes in nature using real geological surfaces. The marks were made with graphite on paper. The viewer moved physically with the piece. The units were two feet inch intervals extending horizontally on the wall for as long as 12 feet. Parallel to the physical movement, passage of time was demonstrated in the sequence, It formed an open-ended continuum that describes change.

During the last eight years I have used rocks and earth as well as graphite, on muslim mounted rag paper. The height of the work is usually 9 to 12 feet by 5 feet wide. Most of the work is three-dimensional to some degree and some pieces move into the floor space. These pieces are a continuation of both the continuum and geological concepts, but deal directly with specific sites. They are made by violently indenting or impressing the paper repeatedly with rocks and layering and polishing the surface with earth from locations in which I feel strong sentient associations. The pulverized earth or mineral deposits color the paper and the rock marks become random events locked into the surface of the work. The process entails a continuous repetition of body movement. Each gesture varies from the preceding one and thus describes distinct patterns in time. Each repeated rock impression is configurationally infinite.

In special projects such as *Niagara Gorge Path Relocated,* executed at Artpark in Lewiston, New York, I worked in the same way, but the gorge was part of the piece. By relocating topographically the Niagara cascade to its original site I sought to evoke the perception of time and the flow of nature's processes. This piece included some public participation in the process.

In Project Studio I (an abandoned school now used for art projects) I made *East/West Wall Memory Relocated.* In this particular piece I sought to record the way in which memory shifts in time and space and a displacement occurs that re-forms our perceptions. In the two-part piece the texture of the wall's aging surface was rendered visible with graphite on paper and the parallel but opposite 13 foot by 5 foot wall units were interchanged.

Since the beginning of 1975 I have also been making intimate paper objects that I call ''rock books.'' They are 'histories' of a place. 'Notebooks' relating to strata forms and time duration in nature. They are quiet, tactile explorations of the earth in specific geological sites. Some of them are handmade paper that in the process of making, I color with earth pigment. Some, tied with woven string, cannot be opened while others upon opening reveal the sequence of geologic processes that exist when the strata layers of an area are unveiled.

From 1977 to 1982 my work has continued to be involved with nature, but with the additional dimension of nature as a setting for man. This correspondence between the two, man and nature, inspired the passage work *Stone Alignments/Solstice Cairns,* a permanent outdoor sculpture made of boulders and stone that lies on a plateau overlooking the Columbia River Gorge in Oregon. The piece is 1000 feet by 600 feet. Also, the historical aspect was the idea behind a large audio-visual room installation called *Correspondences,* dealing with the perceptual relationship and marriage of two cultures, the Spanish and Maya in the Yucatan area of Mexico.

In addition the work during this period has included photographs, both black and white and color taken on the site by the artist. These photographs render narrative sequence both to nature cycles, such as ''Islas Encantadas: Seymour Island Cycle (The Galapagos Islands),'' and demonstrate symbolically or metaphorically man's inspiration from and use of natural resources such as stone and earth, and how, particularly with architecture, this influences his reality.

Derelict Tracts: An Observatory was installed in Gottesman Hall in the New York Public Library in 1990 as the centerpiece of a historic ''History of Paper'' exhibit. A four-part dome structure, 8 feet high and 12 feet around, the observatory was a kind of paper-skinned sculpture, its metal armature covered by hand-printed paper, collected objects, and gold and silver leaf. A three-dimensional diary, it included visual and written references to a range of subjects, some autobiographical, others concerned with natural and social history, and the life of the late 19th and 20th century.

In the 1990s my works included the *Extinct* botanical series which dealt with ecologically sensitive plants encased translucently in wax as a metaphor for the passage of time. Started in 1991, *Seed Calendars* are a series of ''drawings'' calendrical in form, with individual seeds placed within a grid; each seed secretes its DNA into the paper, casting an aura of ''juice'' around the seed itself. A simultaneous series, the sculptural *Seed Containers,* features bowls or lidded vessels sculpted from wax which hold seeds from specific locales.

The end of the 1990s saw a return to encaustic paintings, the first series of which continued motifs in the *Seed Calendars* by incorporating seeds in a gridded relief within small wax paintings. A second series featured incised marks, minimal and configurationally random, in small and large encaustic works, making reference to the night skies of the Southern Hemisphere, specifically those above New Zealand. *Sheep's Milk and the Cosmos* (1999) continued the three-dimentionality of past pieces. Resting on a wood and granite bench beneath a large encaustic painting are five dark bowls filled with white wax representing sheep's milk; in the center of each are five dark identical sheeps' heads. On the wall above hands the painting which evokes the universe's infinity of stars.

—Michelle Stuart

SUGA, Kishio

Nationality: Japanese. **Born:** Morioka, 19 February 1944. **Education:** Tama Art College, Tokyo, 1964–68. **Family:** Married Taeko Tomioka in 1969. **Career:** Lives and works in Kawasaki. Travelled in Europe and the United States, 1970, in France, 1973. **Awards:** First Prize, *Shell Art Exhibition,* Tokyo, 1967; Second Prize, Art Critics Competition, *Bijutsu-Techo* magazine, Tokyo, 1969; Grand Prize, *Japan Art Festival,* Tokyo, 1970. **Agent:** Tokyo Gallery, Japan. **Address:** c/o Tokyo Gallery, 8–16-18 Ginza, Chuo-Ku, Tokyo, Japan.

Selected Individual Exhibitions:

1968 Tsubaki Kindai Gallery, Tokyo
1969 Tamura Gallery, Tokyo
1970 Tamura Gallery, Tokyo
1971 Sato Gallery, Tokyo
1972 Tamura Gallery, Tokyo
Kinokuniya Gallery, Tokyo
Roppongi Building, Tokyo
1973 Tamura Gallery, Tokyo
Sato Gallery, Tokyo
City Hall, Morioka City, Japan
1974 Tamura Gallery, Tokyo
Gallery 16, Kyoto
1975 Tokiwa Gallery, Tokyo
Maki Gallery, Tokyo (2 exhibitions)
Kaneko Art Gallery, Tokyo (2 exhibitions)
1976 Maki Gallery, Tokyo
Tokyo Gallery
International Christian University, Tokyo

Kishio Suga: *Shū Kou,* 2000. ©Suga Kishio.

1979 Tokyo Gallery
1981 Tokyo Gallery
1982 Kaneko Art Gallery
1983 Tokyo Gallery
1984 Komai Gallery
1986 Kamakura Gallery
1990 So Gallery
Hino Gallery
Tokyo Museum of Modern Art
1995 Gallery Saienshi
1996 Gallery YOU, Kyoto
1997 Hiroshima City Museum of Contemporary Art
1998 Itami City Museum of Art
Kanagawa City Gallery, Yokohama
Tokyo Gallery
Kaneko Art Gallery
1999 Yokohama City Museum
Kaneko Art Gallery
Tokyo Gallery

Selected Group Exhibitions:

1966 *International Young Artists Exhibition,* Tokyo
1967 *Shell Art Exhibition,* Shirokiya Department Store, Tokyo
1970 *Japan Art Festival,* Tokyo
Aspects of New Japanese Art, National Museum of Modern Art, Kyoto
1972 *Contemporary Japanese Graphics Exhibition,* Institute of Contemporary Arts, London
1973 *Biennale de Paris*
1974 *Japan: Tradition und Gegenwart,* Stadtisches Kunsthalle, Dusseldorf
1975 *Materials Exhibition,* Stedelijk van Abbemuseum, Eindhoven, Netherlands
1976 *Kyoto Biennale*
International Open Encounter on Video, Museo de Arte Contemporaneo, Caracas
1978 *Biennale,* Venice
1981 *Sao Paulo Biennale*
1982 Carnegie International, Museum of Art, Carnegie Institute
1985 *Forty Years of Japanese Contemporary Art,* Tokyo Metropolitan Museum of Art
1987 *Biennale Japan,* Ushimado International Art Festival, Ushimado
1994 *8th Triennale India,* New Delhi
2000 *Kanji Biennale,* Kanji Muesum of Contemporary Art, Colia

Publications:

By SUGA: Articles—''Invisible Words in an Invisible World'' in *Space Design* (Tokyo), October 1969; ''The Starting Point of Disappearance'' in *Space Design* (Tokyo), December 1969; ''To Exist Beyond the Situation'' in *Bijutsu-Techo* (Tokyo) February 1970; ''Unnamable'' in *Bijutsu-Techo* (Tokyo) May 1972.

On SUGA: Articles—''Suga,'' special issue of *Kirokutai* (Tokyo), November 1972; ''Current Critic'' by Toshiaki Minemura in *Bijutsu-Techo* (Tokyo), June 1973; ''In the Case of Suga's Work'' by Toshiaki Minemura in *Sogetsu* (Tokyo), June 1973; ''Thing's School'' by Ichiro Haryu in *Asahi Journal* (Tokyo), no. 33, 1974; ''Suga'' by Toshikuni Maeno in *L'Art Vivant* (Paris), no. 45, 1974; ''The Works of Kishio Suga'' by Toshikuni Maeno in *Obararyusoka* (Tokyo), 1974; ''Suga's Work with Natural Things'' by Yusuke Nakahara in *Space Design* (Tokyo), March 1975; ''Suga's Event in Tokiwa Gallery'' by Yoshiaki Tono in *Obararyusoka* (Tokyo), June 1975; ''Current Critic'' by Toshiaki Minemura in *Obararyusoka* (Tokyo), October 1976.

*

Everything has its sides and its center. I find myself dealing with this fact every time I start working on a new piece. In my work, I use pieces of materials that are autonomous on their own. I usually combine many of them together. When I use several pieces, whether they are of the same material or not, I have to consider how to allow each of them to retain its own characteristic nature and look. Even with an ordinary piece of rock, wood, or steel, there is a center and there are sides as long as it exists in real space. When many of these pieces are combined, this will inevitably make some parts visible to the outside, and some other parts hidden from our eyes. The parts that are visible are not necessarily those which are the most significant, nor the hidden ones the insignificant.

Kishio Suga: *Buntai Kaisoku,* 1998. ©Suga Kishio.

At least one thing is clear. The sides get to be exposed to the eye more often. In that sense, they comprise the piece's outermost layer, or its exterior. But when we are seeing the exterior, what is happening to the center?

An object can exist only as an integration of its sides and its center, both in construction and in meaning. If that is so, it is not enough to consider an object and its existence based only on one's observations on its visible sides. The center, even when it is invisible, remains to be the core from which every object sprouts, and because it is invisible, we must clarify in what ways the center differs from a piece to another. In the finished work, some centers of the originally separate pieces become sides, and some sides find themselves to be the center. In a sense, a reversal of centrality has taken place. This, actually, happens with surrounding space too, and is an important factor in giving deeper meaning to the work.

—Kishio Suga

* * *

In one of Kishio Suga's experiments can be seen the following work. A board is set across two walls horizontally in a corner, and a piece of cloth is folded and set upon it. The board is cut across to join the two walls, and the cloth is folded to make creases at the point where it touches the walls. What is interesting about the work is the feeling one has of the reversal of composition and external appearance. There is something willful about setting the board across the corner and putting the cloth on top, but the folding of the cloth as it hits the wall at both ends seems to depend on something beyond this. From the middle upwards, it seems to depend on the state of physical contact with the wall as something exterior. But this folded part seems to be very artificial in physical appearance, while the upper cloth area seems to have been accomplished without this artificiality. This undoubtedly is because folding is the means employed, but this is accomplished forcibly as it were by the walls. Now if that be the case, this work of Suga shows the possibility of revealing how the act of making is regulated by means of the act being made. The corner is a space Suga is particularly fond of, and this work is characterized by the insertion into the work of a conversion power against the act of that corner.

Obviously in whatever work of art the act of making can not overstep the physical conditions. And yet it is difficult to say that this fact is the same as determining a work through the conscious introduction of that area of letting something be made. Yet if we exaggerate this one point of letting something be made, we will inevitably end up with the result of bringing the material's physcial qualities into prominence. It seems to me that the delicate balance between both poles is recovered in this cloth-corner work.

We can only wait in expectation to see how this kind of quality will appear in the other works, but it will be of deep interest to see how

Suga suggests the work's possible expanse as the product that results from reversing the action of determining the work in a dislocation of the condition of this space.

—Yusuke Nakahara

SUGAI, Kumi

Nationality: Japanese. **Born:** Kobe, Japan, 13 March 1919; has maintained residence in Paris since 1952. **Education:** School of Fine Arts, Osaka. **Family:** Married to Mitsuko Sugai. **Career:** Independent artist that practiced a spare, non-personal style of abstraction. **Awards:** Grand Prize, *Triennal International de Gravure,* Grenchen, Switzerland, 1961; Grand Prize, *Biennal International de Gravure,* Cracow, 1966. **Address:** 91 rue de l'Amiral Mouchez, Pavillon 6, 75013 Paris, France. **Died:** In Kobe, Japan, 14 May 1996.

Individual Exhibitions:

1954 Galerie Craven, Paris
Palais des Beaux-Arts, Brussels
1957 Galerie H. Le Grendre, Paris
1958 Galerie Creuzevaut, Paris
1959 Kootz Gallery, New York
1960 Stadtisches Museum, Leverkusen, West Germany (retrospective)
1961 Kootz Gallery, New York
1962 Kootz Gallery, New York
1963 Galerie Creuzevaut, Paris
Kestner-Gesellschaft, Hannover (retrospective)
1964 Kootz Gallery, New York
Galerie Toni Brechbuhl, Grenchen, Switzerland
Die Insel, Hamburg (retrospective)
1965 American Art Gallery, Copenhagen
Galerie Bleu, Stockholm
Sundsvall Museum, Sweden
Kunsthallen, Gothenburg, Sweden
1967 Lefebre Gallery, New York
Kustnernes Hus, Oslo (retrospective)
Galerie Brusberg, Hannover
1968 Galerie Defet, Nuremberg
Galerie Hilt, Basel
1969 Court Gallery, Copenhagen
Kunsthallen, Gothenburg, Sweden
Galerie Klipan, Stockholm
Tokyo Gallery, Tokyo
Minami Gallery, Tokyo
National Museum of Modern Art, Kyoto (retrospective)
1970 Galerie d'Eent N.V., Amsterdam
1971 Circle Gallery London
Court Gallery, Copenhagen
Galerie Schottenring, Vienna
1972 Galerie Defet, Nuremberg
Galerie Hakken, Oslo
Galerie Christael, Helsinki
Galerie Hilt, Basel
1974 Galleria Annunciata, Milan
La Galerie Esplande de la Defense, Paris

Kumi Sugai: *Composition,* 1955. ©Christie's Images/Corbis.

1976 Minami Gallery, Tokyo
1981 Satani Gallery, Tokyo
1983 Nantenshi Gallery, Tokyo
Seibu Museum of Art, Tokyo
1984 Seibu Hall, Ohtsu, Japan
Ohara Museum of Art, Kurashiki, Japan
1985 Nantenshi Gallery, Tokyo
1987 Nantenshi Gallery, Tokyo
1988 Gallery Brusberg, Berlin
1990 *Kumi Sugai: Paintings 1970–1990,* Art Curial, Paris
Die International Kunstmesse Bale Galerie, Kara, Switzerland
1991 Nantenshi Gallery Soko, Tokyo
1992 City Museum of Art, Ashiya, Japan
1995 Takamatsu-shi Bijutsukan, Tokyo

Selected Group Exhibitions:

1956 *Salon Realites Nouvelles,* Paris (and annually through 1982)
1957 *Salon de Mai,* Paris (and annually through 1982)

1959 *Biennal International de Gravure,* Ljubljana, Yugoslavia (and annually through 1981)
Documenta, Kassel, West Germany
1961 *Trienal International de Gravure,* Grenchen, Switzerland
1962 Biennale, Venice
1964 *Painting and Sculpture of a Decade,* London
1966 *Salon Grands et Jeunes d'Aujourd'hui,* Paris (and annually through 1981)
1969 *Exposition Ars '69,* Helsinki
1972 *Biennal International de Gravure,* Norway
1994 *Works Donated from Mr. and Mrs. Kikuo Yamaguchi,* National Museum of Modern Art, Tokyo

Collections:

Nationalgalerie, Berlin; Landesmuseum, Hannover; Centre Georges Pompidou, Paris; Galleria Nazionale d'Arte Moderna, Rome; Moderna Museet, Stockholm; National Museum of Modern Art, Tokyo; National Museum of Modern Art, Kyoto Museum of Modern Art, Toyama, Japan; Museum of Modern Art, New York; Art Institute of Chicago.

Publications:

By SUGAI: Book of drawings—*Albam,* with poems by Andre Pieyre de Mandiargues, Paris 1960. **Books of prints**—*La Laquete sans fin,* Paris 1957; *Repos goute,* Paris 1964; *Sugai, ou la tension maxima,* Milan 1966; *Octobre,* Milan 1969; *Sugai,* Chikuma Japan 1970; *Alea,* Paris n.d.; *Sugai gravure,* Tokyo n.d. **Articles**—"The Spirit of "S": New Works by Kumi Sugai" in *Mizue,* no. 958, Spring 1991; "Painting the Void: Interview with Kumi Sugai" with Miriam Smadja in *UNESCO Courier,* May 1996.

On SUGAI: Books—*L'Aventure de l'art abstrait* by Michel Ragon, Paris 1956; *Kumi Sugai,* exhibition catalog, Leverkusen West Germany 1960; *Sugai* by Andre Pieyre de Mandiargues, Paris 1960; *Le voir dit* by Jean-Clarence Lambert, Paris 1962; *Kumi Sugai,* exhibition catalog by Wieland Schmidt and Irmtraud Schaarchmidt-Richter, Hannover 1963; *Kumi Sugai,* exhibition catalog by Hanns Theodor Flaemming, Hamburg 1964; *Kumi Sugai,* exhibition catalog by Fredrik Matheson and Oistein Parmann, Oslo 1967; *Japan: Tradition und Gegenwart,* exhibition catalog by J. Harten and others, Dusseldorf 1974; *Sugai,* Tokyo 1975; *Sugaï* by Jean Clarence Lambert, translated by Alan Swan, Barcelona 1993; *Kumi Sugaï* by Jean Luc Chalumeau, Paris 1995; *Sugai Kumi, hanga no shigoto 1955–1995,* exhibition catalog, Tokyo 1997, *Kumi Sugaï* by Jean-Clarence Lambert and Makoto Ooka, Paris 1999. **Articles**—"Sugai" by Jean-Clarence Lambert in *La jeune ecole de Paris,* Paris 1956; review by J. S. Byrd in *Art International* (Lugano, Switzerland), September 1965; "Kumi Sugai, Circle Gallery" by Peter Fuller in *Arts Review* (London), April 1971; "Sun King" in *Design* (London), June 1971; "Kumi Sugai" by A. P. de Mandiargues in *Le Arti* (Milan), May 1974; "Sugai Express" by Marc Edelmann in *Point Art,* no. 3, Spring-Summer 1990.

* * *

Kumi Sugai's early abstract paintings were characterized by gloomy images suggestive of Japanese folklore, but clarity of composition and brightness of color came to dominate his work during the 1960s, infusing his paintings with freshness and dynamism. In addition to painting, Sugai was a printmaker who won numerous prizes.

In 1969, at the age of 40, he returned from Paris and executed paintings for the walls of the new building of the National Museum of Modern Art, Tokyo. In this work Sugai demonstrated his excellent technique in composition by combining manifold elements covering an expansive area into a unified composite view.

Sugai's one-man show in 1976 (Minami Gallery, Tokyo) marked a new development for the ex-Ecole de Paris painter from Japan. A huge canvas in the show depicted an icon on a shiny Italian sports car interlaced with bright-colored geometrical patterns. Sugai is now essentially uninterested in emotional hand-painted works and tends to hide his hand traces by mechanical non-personal expression.

In the 1980s his geometric compositions began to break loose, and spread diagonally, leaving more vacant space in white. Clear-cut grey and black forms now dominated the canvases, with accentuated red shapes impressing themselves onto and integrating themselves into the formerly monochrome compositions.

—Yoshiaki Tono

SUGARMAN, George

Nationality: American. **Born:** New York City, 11 May 1912. **Education:** City College of New York, 1934–38, B.A. 1938; Zadkine School of Sculpture, Paris, 1955–56. **Military Service:** United States Navy, 1941–45. **Career:** Sculptor; travelled in Europe and lived in Paris, 1951–55. Instructor, Hunter College Graduate School New York, 1960–1970. Visiting professor of Sculpture, Graduate School of Art & Architecture, Yale University, 1967–1968. Instructor, Yale University Graduate School of Art, New Haven, Connecticut, 1967–68. **Awards:** Second Prize *Carnegie International,* Pittsburgh, 1961 Longview Foundation Grant, 1961, 1962, 1963; National Endowment for the Humanities grant, 1966; Art Award American Academy and Institute of Arts and Letters, 1985; Special Award, Sculpture Triennale, Osaka, Japan, 1992. **Agent:** Robert Miller Gallery, 41 East 57th Street, New York, New York 10022. **Died:** New York City, 25 August 1999.

Individual Exhibitions:

1958 Widdifield Gallery, New York
1961 Stephen Radich Gallery, New York
1964 Stephen Radich Gallery, New York
1965 Philadelphia Art Alliance
Stephen Radich Gallery, New York
1966 Dayton's Gallery, Minneapolis
Stephen Radich Gallery, New York
1967 Galerie Schmela, Dusseldorf
Galerie Ziegler, Zurich
Fischbach Gallery, New York
1969 *Plastiken, Collagen, Zeichnungen,* Kuntshalle, Basel (retrospective: travelled to Leverkusen, Berlin, and Amsterdam, 1969–70
1970 Galerie Ziegler, Zurich
1971 Gallery 118, Minneapolis
1974 Zabriskie Gallery, New York
Dag Hammarskjold Plaza, New York

George Sugarman: *Trio,* 1969–71. ©State of New York/Corbis.

1977 Robert Miller Gallery, New York
1978 Robert Miller Gallery, New York
1979 Galerie Liatowitsch, Basel
1980 Robert Miller Galley, New York
Galerie Rudolf Zwirner, Cologne
1981 Smith Gallery, Palo Alto, California
Galerie Ziegler, Zurich
1982 Robert Miller Gallery, New York
1984 Fuller Goldeen Gallery, San Francisco
1985 Robert Miller Gallery, New York
780 Third Avenue, New York (installation)
Whitney Museum, New York
Doris Freedman Plaza, Central Park, New York (installation)
1986 Whitney Museum, New York
1987 Todd Capp Gallery, New York
Helander Gallery, Palm Beach, Florida
1990 *George Sugarman: Collages, Paper and Print,* Washburn Gallery, New York
1993 Gendai Chokoku Senta, Tokyo
1998 Hunter College, New York (retrospective)

Selected Group Exhibitions:

1952 *IV Salon de la Jeune Sculpture,* Musée Rodin, Paris
1956 *Sculptors Selected by Painters,* Tanger Gallery, New York
1963 *Bienal,* Sao Paulo
1967 *Sculpture of the 60s,* Los Angeles County Museum of Art
1970 *Monumental Art,* Contemporary Arts Center, Cincinnati, Ohio
1975 *Sculpture: American Directions,* National Collection of Fine Arts, Washington, D.C.
1979 *The Decorative Impulse,* Institute of Contemporary Art, Philadelphia (travelled to San Diego, California; Minneapolis; Chicago)
1982 *Postminimalism,* Aldrich Museum of Contemporary Art, Ridgefield, Connecticut
1985 *Forms in Wood: American Sculpture of the 1950s,* Philadelphia Art Alliance, Pennsylvania
1987 *Sculpture: Exploration of Space,* Anchorage Museum of History and Art, Alaska
1996 *Colorflex,* Apex Art Curatorial Program, New York
1998 *Sculptors Draw,* Rosenberg + Kaufman Fine Art, New York

Collections:

Walker Art Center, Minneapolis; Kunstmuseum, Zurich; Museum of Modern Art, New York; Whitney Museum of American Art, New York; Art Institute of Chicago; Metropolitan Museum of Art, New York.

Public Installations:

World Trade Center, Brussels; Albert M. Greenfield School, Philadelphia; Empire State Mall, Albany; Federal Court Building, Baltimore; Akron Public Library, Ohio; Lincoln National Life Foundation, Ft. Wayne; International Airport, Miami; Detroit General Hospital; Wills Eye Hospital, Philadelphia; Summer-Best Station, Buffalo; Southland Life Building, Dallas; Columbia Plaza, Cincinnati; Allegheny Landing, Pittsburgh; Joslyn Sculpture Garden, Omaha; Bellevue Park, Wichita Falls, Texas; VA Hospital, Martinsburg, West Virginia; Storm King Art Center, Mountainville, New York; Merchantile Bank, San Antonio; NCNB Plaza, Tampa; The Pavillions at Buckland Hills, Manchester, Connecticut; Crystal Tower, Kobe; Cultural Center, Miyazaki, Kyushu, Japan; Suderman Square, Jakarta, Indonesia; Morris Arboretum, Philadelphia.

Publications:

By SUGARMAN: Article—''Square Spiral'' in *Art Now: New York,* January 1969; ''George Sugarman: Untitled'' in *New Observations,* no. 110, January-February 1996.

On SUGARMAN: Books—*Collage: Personalities, Concepts, Techniques* by Harriet Janis and Rudi Blesh, Philadelphia and New York 1962; *New York School, The First Generation: Paintings of the 1940s and 1950s,* edited by Maurice Tuchman, Los Angeles 1965; *Constructivism: Origins and Evolution* by George Rickey, New York 1967; *Minimal Art: A Critical Anthology,* edited by George Battcock, New York 1968; *George Sugarman: Plastiken, Collagen, Zeichnungen,* exhibition catalog by Amy Goldin and Peter F. Althaus, Basel 1969; *George Sugarman,* exhibition catalog by Irving H. Sandler, Amsterdam 1970; *Icons and Images of the 60s* by Nicolas and Elena Calas, New York 1971; *Shape of Space: The Sculpture of George Sugarman* by Holiday T. Day, New York, 1981; *George Sugarman: Painted Wood Sculpture,* exhibition catalog, New York 1985; *George Sugarman: Collages, Paper and Paint,* exhibition catalog, New York 1990; *The Artist Observed: 28 Interviews with Contemporary Artists* by John Gruen, Chicago 1991; *George Sugarman* by Meyer Raphael Rubinstein, Livorno 1992; *George Sugarman,* exhibition catalog, Tokyo 1993; *George Sugarman,* exhibition catalog with text by Stephen Davis and Robert Storr, New York 1998. **Articles**—''George Sugarman's Maximal, Musical Sculpture'' by John Gruen in *Art News,* vol. 86, January 1987; ''Outdoor Eye: George Sugarman's Public Sculpture'' by Raphael Rubinstein in *Arts Magazine,* vol. 64, January 1990; ''A Polychrome Profusion'' by Raphael Rubinstein in *Art in America* (New York), vol. 87, no. 4, April 1999; obituary in *Art in America* (New York), vol. 87, no. 11, November 1999.

*

I believe that sculptural space is different from ordinary space, and each of my sculptures is an attempt to create, to define and to articulate an aesthetically significant space. And so, early on, I became interested in floor space, as in ''Inscape'' and horizontal extensions as in ''Two in One.'' I have always avoided industrially available forms because I believe that they blur the particularity of the statement, so I have used as many different forms as I have been capable of imagining, often within the same sculpture, to create a rich and complex experience. These works ask such questions as: ''What is sculptural unity?'' and ''What are artistic relationships, not only within the work itself but also to the space it creates around it?''

Although most people respond to my use of color on a purely emotional basis and although it has been said that my work forms a bridge between painting and sculpture, my own reason for using the full range of color is purely formal, i.e. to help articulate the formal problem set in each sculpture.

Now that I am more concerned with outdoor public sculpture, I have asked myself ''What does *public* sculpture mean?'' Certainly it has a different function than a gallery or museum-oriented work. Equally certain, it should be something more readily accessible to the general public. I think it is possible to do this and not only retain but even heighten all the aesthetic ''high-art'' values one believes in. My sculpture for the Federal Building in Baltimore shows my interest in the creation of a particularized, extended space, in interior volumes, in relationships between different forms, and it does it in ways appropriate only to outdoor sculpture: by its relation to the building it is placed in front of and by its function as a possible symbol of community.

—George Sugarman

* * *

George Sugarman has brought strong pictorial sensibility to contemporary sculpture. A student of Ossip Zadkine in Paris, Sugarman made sculptures in the early 1950s that had the deliberate, weighty and solid properties associated with his teacher's strong grounding in Cubism. By the late 1950s, however, Sugarman began to break away from the Cubist cube and to elaborate a more open and distinctively colorful approach to sculpture. As head of the New York based New Sculpture Group, he was at the forefront of both the discussions and the practical investigations of new treatments of abstract sculpture, based on non-relational structures. In the sculptures of the late 1950s and early 1960s, he started to shape space into a bold infrastructure of solids and voids, using juxtaposed arrangements of curved and straight edged forms as the means. For example, in *Yellow Top* (1960) a polychrome wood sculpture, different colors are used to articulate each separate element, drawing attention simultaneously, to the linear contours of the piece and its definition of space. It is during this period, also, that the sculptures begin to spill directly onto the floor and, even more forcefully, they stress the relationships of parts in the bold but jungle-like compositions that Sugarman continued to favor. In addition to the base and the floor, the wall has also occupied his attention. Strongly colored, his wall reliefs are volumetric and specifically structured forms that challenge cliché notions about the relationship of painting and sculpture.

In the late 1960s Sugarman began to interest himself in the demanding area of public art. Changing his materials from wood to metal, he has designed large-scale and outdoor polychromed pieces, whose brightly colored, cut-out parts give a rich and varied experience of structure and space, wondrously accessible to the average user of the public places in which they stand. *Kite Castle* (1974), shown at the Hammarskjold Plaza in New York City, is revealing of the role of constructive animator which color—here the dominant tonal combination is red and blue—has in encouraging a positive reception to the piece. In his public art works, Sugarman aims to delight the viewer/stroller and to enhance the environment without overwhelming either one.

The exuberant qualities of his sculptures continued developing in the 1980s. *Big Ride* (1981), a relief collage with a dynamically angled multipart structure, shows increasing interest in heightening the illusion of movement through the juxtapositions of different shapes, colors and textured surfaces. In *Ariel* (1984), that illusion is so striking as to make the complex cut-out structure of this painted aluminum sculpture seem to rise up on the energy generated from the tensions within its various parts from the ground. In *Waltz* (1985), the organic flow to the rhythmical structure of this multipart form brings to mind the swaying configurations of flowers. References to nature serve to enhance the impact of much of Sugarman's recent work.

—Ronny Cohen

SUGIMOTO, Hiroshi

Nationality: Japanese. **Born:** Tokyo, Japan, February 1948. **Education:** Saint Paul's University, Tokyo, B.A., 1970; Art Center College of Design, Los Angeles, B.F.A., 1972. **Career:** Independent artist, in New York, since 1974. **Awards:** 2001 Hasselblad Foundation International Award in Photography.

Selected Individual Exhibitions:

1977 Minami Gallery, Tokyo (catalog)
1981 Sonnabend Gallery, New York
1983 Sonnabend Gallery, New York
1988 Sagacho Exhibit Space, Tokyo
Zeit Photo Salon, Tokyo
Sonnabend Gallery, New York
1989 National Museum of Contemporary Art, Osaka, Japan
Cleveland Museum of Art
1990 Saint Louis Art Museum
Presentation House, Vancouver
Galerie Jahn und Fusban, Munich
Urbi & Orbi, Paris
1991 Sagacho Exhibit Space and IBM Courtyard, Tokyo
Kasahara Gallery, Osaka, Japan
Hosomi Gallery, Tokyo
1992 Sonnabend Gallery, New York
Fraenkel Gallery, San Francisco
CAPC, Musée d'Art Contemporain, Bordeaux, France
Centre d'Art Contemporain du Domaine de Kerguéhennec, Locminé, France
1993 *Hiroshi Sugimoto,* Museum of Contemporary Art, Los Angeles (catalog)
White Cube, London
Galerie Marc Jancou, Zurich
Virginia Museum of Fine Arts, Richmond (catalog)
1994 Angles Gallery, Santa Monica
Museum of Contemporary Art, Los Angeles
Parrish Art Museum, Southampton, New York
Museum of Contemporary Art, Chicago
1995 Metropolitan Museum of Art, New York
Kunsthalle Basel, Switzerland
Angles Gallery, Santa Monica
Centre International d'Art Contemporain de Montreal
1996 Fraenkel Gallery, San Francisco
Galerie Meyer-Ellinger, Frankfurt
Moderna Museet, Sparvagnshallarna, Stockholm
Koyanagi Gallery, Tokyo
1997 *Hiroshi Sugimoto Theaters,* Berkeley Art Museum, California

Selected Group Exhibitions:

1979 *Recent Acquisitions,* Museum of Modern Art, New York
Windows on the East: A Survey of Contemporary Japanese Art, World Trade Center, New York
Hiroshi Sugimoto and Eiko Hosei, Susan Spiritus Gallery, Newport Beach, California
1982 *Photography Collection from the Museum of Modern Art,* Museum of Modern Art, New York; Seibu Museum of Art, Tokyo
1983 *Landmarks Reviewed,* Pensacola Museum of Art, Pensacola, Florida
1985 *The Art of Memory/The Loss of History,* New Museum of Contemporary Art, New York (catalog)
1987 *Contemporary Japanese Art in America: Arita, Nakagawa, Sugimoto,* Japan Society Gallery, New York (catalog)
1988 ROSC, Dublin
1989 *Investigations 1989,* Institute of Contemporary Art, Philadelphia
Continuum and the Moment, Art Gallery, Visual Arts Center, California State University, Fullerton
On Kawara Again and Against, Institute of Contemporary Art, Nagoya, Japan
1990 *The Past and Present of Photography,* National Museum of Modern Art, Kyoto; Tokyo National Museum of Art (catalog)
Reorienting: Looking East, Third Eye Centre, Glasgow (catalog)
Natural History Recreated, Center for Photography, Woodstock, New York
Japanische Kunst der Achtziger Jahre, Frankfurter Kunstverein, Frankfurt (catalog)
1991 *Carnegie International,* Carnegie Museum of Art, Pittsburgh (catalog)
Beyond Japan: A Photo Theater, Barbican Art Gallery, London
Réflexions Violées, Israel Museum, Jerusalem (catalog)
Le Printemps de la Photo, Fondation Cartier pour l'Art Contemporain, Ville de Cahors, France
1993 *Multiple Images: Photographs Since 1965 from the Collection,* Museum of Modern Art, New York
Daydream Nation, Luhring Augusting Gallery, New York
The 21st Century: Into the Future with Paracelsus, Kunsthalle Basel, Switzerland
Gardens of Eden: Jardins do Paraiso, Galeria do Museu Antropologico da Universidade de Coimbra, Portugal
1994 *Some Went Mad, Some Ran Away . . .,* Serpentine Gallery, London (travelled to Nordic Arts Centre, Helsinki; Kunstverein, Hannover; Museum of Contemporary Art, Chicago) (catalog)
Space, Time and Memory: Photography and Beyond in Japan, Hara Museum of Contemporary Art, Tokyo (travelled to Museo Rufino Tamayo, Mexico City; Vancouver Art Gallery; Los Angeles County Museum of Art; Denver Art Museum; Contemporary Museum, Honolulu)
Japanese Art After 1945: Scream Against the Sky, Yokohama Museum of Art (travelled to Guggenheim Museum Soho, New York; San Francisco Museum of Modern Art in association with Center for the Arts at Yerba Buena) (catalog)
Inside Out: Contemporary Japanese Photography, Light Factory Photographic Art Center, Charlotte, North Carolina (catalog)
1995 *Changing Perspectives,* Contemporary Arts Museum, Houston
A Century of Silence: Nonrepresentation and Withdrawal in Modern Art, Academy Gallery of Art and Sciences, New York
Private/Public, Museum of Contemporary Art, Helsinki
Art in Japan Today, Museum of Contemporary Art, Tokyo
1996 *10th Biennale of Sydney,* The Gunnery
By Night, Fondation Cartier pour l'art contemporain, Paris
Hall of Mirrors: Art and Film Since 1945, Museum of Contemporary Art, Los Angeles (travelled to Wexner Center for the Arts, Columbus, Ohio; Palazzo delle Esposizioni, Rome; Museum of Contemporary Art, Chicago)
Tranquility, Chiba Museum of Art, Japan
1998 Sonnabend Gallery, New York
Photographer's Gallery, London
The Japan Foundation, Istituto Giapponese di Cultura, Rome
Fraenkel Gallery, San Francisco
1999 Galerie Nacht St. Stephan, Vienna, Austria
2001 *Mirror's Edge,* Glasgow
I Am a Camera 1, London

Publications:

On SUGIMOTO: Books—*Photographs by Hiroshi Sugimoto: Dioramas, Theaters, Seascapes,* Japan 1988; *Hiroshi Sugimoto: Time Exposed* by Thomas Kellein, Kyoto 1991; *Motion Pictures by Sugimoto,* Milan 1995. **Articles**—''No Such Thing as Time'' by John Yau in *Artforum,* April 1984; ''Hiroshi Sugimoto: Time's Continuous Passage'' by John Yau in *Galeries Magazine,* December-January 1993; ''The Blank Screens of Hiroshi Sugimoto'' by Peter Hay Halpert in *Artpress,* November 1994; ''Hiroshi Sugimoto: Zen Marxism'' by Francesco Bonami in *Flash Art,* January-February 1995; ''Hiroshi Sugimoto: Theatres du Vide'' by Jean-Christian Fleury in *Camera International,* summer 1995; ''Sugimoto's Metabolic Photography'' by Norman Bryson in *Parkett,* 1996; ''Hiroshi Sugimoto'' by Frances Richard in *Artforum,* September 1997; ''Hiroshi Sugimoto: The Sleepless Photographer'' interview with Martin Herbert at www.eyestorm.com (accessed 15 August 2000).

* * *

Tokyo-born photographer Hiroshi Sugimoto describes himself as ''The Sleepless Photographer.'' Indeed he is a man who patiently records images which transcend time itself. Sugimoto's images of movie palaces, bodies of water, and architectural structures confound our notions of temporal logic and bring us necessarily into a place of contemplative wonder. Most of his work remains within the context of three extensive series of images: the seascape, the museum diorama, and the interiors of theaters with movies on screen.

Sugimoto began his work in photography in the early 1970s with a strong interest in Minimalist and Conceptual art. Influenced by such artists as Dan Flavin and Carl Andre, Sugimoto began experimenting with ways of expanding the range of the photograph to incorporate temporal shifts often seen in modernist paintings. By the late 1970s, he was producing the first images in the still-growing movie theater series. ''The concept was to photograph the entire duration of a movie,'' Sugimoto said in an interview with Martin Herbert, ''so I was imagining that if I were to do that, the result might be a completely white screen. . . . Usually a photographer sees something and tries to capture it, but in my case I just see it in my head and then the technical process is how to make it happen in the real world. The image, then, is a kind of decoration of the concept.'' Sugimoto elected to test this idea in the ornate movie palaces from the 1920s and 1930s to give a greater context to the simple white rectangle which results from these movie-length exposures. The theaters he has photographed are mainly in the United States, though he has in recent years done images in Osaka and Milan. Sugimoto has seen great differences in the information gathered from various types of films. ''If it's an optimistic story, I usually end up with a bright screen; if it's a sad story, it's a dark screen. Occult movie? Very dark.''

This examination of time continued in the diorama photographs done between 1976–80 at New York City's Museum of Natural History. At first glance, the images appear to be documentary shots of animals taken in the wild, creatures in their natural environments. Study of these rich landscapes, replete with creatures engaged in daily struggles for sustenance, revealed subtle hints of artifice. Closer examination shows a strange stiffness in the animals, an all-too-perfect Darwinian posturing. These tableaus are then obvious constructions, situations so lifelike in death that they are startling. Sugimoto captures images here which never existed in ''real'' time, yet which are presented in museums as virtual snapshots of the actual.

In 1980, Sugimoto began his still-evolving seascapes series. He describes his interest in bodies of water as a way of revealing time. ''Ever since the first men and cultures appeared, they have been facing seas and scenes of nature. The landscape has changed over thousands, millions of years, and man has cultivated the ground, built cultures and cities, skyscrapers. The seascapes, I thought, must be the least changed scene, the oldest vision that we can share with ancient peoples.'' These images require faster exposures, as Sugimoto wants to capture the movement of the waves in his prints. These pictures of the sea have been taken all over the world, and they reveal a contemplative space in which time is at once frozen and yet captured as movement. The interplay of the sky, the smudge of the horizon line, and the ripples on the surface of the water in these images is decidedly meditative and very minimal in design. Most striking is the realization that these are constructions inherent in nature.

While continuing work in images of theaters and seascapes, Sugimoto has moved into other explorations as well. In 1995, he photographed statues in a Buddhist temple in Kyoto, Japan. The forty-eight part study, *Hall of Thirty Three Bays*, is another examination of similarity and comparison. ''The figures in the temple are all slightly different, so I wanted people's eyes to focus on those differences,'' he has said. ''The [grouped sculptures of a] thousand almost-identical Buddhas which I photographed were made in the 13th century, so that is the conceptual aspect of Japanese art, which was what motivated me to work on it.'' The temple and the statues are considered national treasures, so Sugimoto had to gain special permission to make images there, a process which took nearly seven years.

Sugimoto's series of photographs surveying well-known examples of modernist architecture began in 1997, when he was commissioned by the Museum of Contemporary Art in Los Angeles for the project. The concept of time is again central here, as Sugimoto seeks to capture these buildings not as they appear, but as they were imagined in the minds of architects. He photographs them slightly out-of-focus, so that he can ''trace back the original vision from the finished product. All the details and all the mistakes disappear; there's a lot of shadows, melting.'' The result is a soft, impressionistic view of such structures as the Chrysler and Empire State Buildings. They appear more as a dream than as a reality. Sugimoto continues to explore notions of time in his photographs, creating sublime images of things we can't quite see with our own eyes.

—Tammy A. Kinsey

SUTTON, Philip

Nationality: British. **Born:** Poole, Dorset, 20 October 1928. **Education:** Studied painting, under William Coldstream, at the Slade School of Fine Art, London, 1950–54. **Military Service:** British Army, 1947–49. **Family:** Married Heather Minifie Ellis Cooke in 1953; children: Jacob, Imogen, Saskia and Rebekah. **Career:** Independent painter, in Snape, Suffolk, 1955–58, and in London since 1958; member, London Group, 1956. Instructor, Slade School of Fine Art, London, 1956–75. **Member:** Royal Academy, 1977. **Agent:** Browse and Darby Ltd., 19 Cork Street, London W1. **Address:** 3 Morfa Terr Manorbier, Tenby, Dyfed, Wales, SA7 07TH.

Individual Exhibitions:

1956 Roland, Browse and Delbanco, London
1958 Roland, Browse and Delbanco, London
1959 Geffrye Museum, London
1960 City Art Gallery, Leeds, Yorkshire
Roland, Browse and Delbanco, London
1962 Stone Gallery, Newcastle upon Tyne
Lane Gallery, Bradford, Yorkshire
57 Gallery, Edinburgh
Roland, Browse and Delbanco, London
1963 David Jones Gallery, Sydney
Gallery A, Melbourne
Rose Skinner Gallery, Perth, Western Australia
Roland, Browse and Delbanco, London
Battersea District Library, London
1965 *Paintings from Fiji*, Roland, Browse and Delbanco, London
1966 Curwen Gallery, London
David Jones Gallery, Sydney
1967 *Recent Paintings*, Roland, Browse and Delbanco, London
London Arts Gallery, Detroit
David Jones Gallery, Sydney
Arnolfini Gallery, Bristol
Arts Centre, Folkestone, Kent
1969 Roland, Browse and Delbanco, London
Hambledon Gallery, Blandford Forum, Dorset, England
1970 Park Square Gallery, Leeds
Paintings/Drawings/Prints, Arnolfini Gallery, Bristol
Paintings, Drawings, Prints and Sculptures, Arts Centre, Folkstone, Kent
David Jones Gallery, Sydney

1971 Graves Art Gallery, Sheffield
Roland, Browse and Delbanco, London
Battersea District Library, London
Oxford Gallery
Park Square Gallery, Leeds
1972 Battersea District Library, London
Studio Prints, London
Compendium Galleries, Birmingham
1973 Roland, Browse and Delbanco, London
David Jones Gallery, Sydney
Peterloo Gallery, Manchester
1974 J. P. Lehmans Gallery, London
1975 Roland, Browse and Delbanco, London
1976 Orde Levinson, Johannesburg (travelled to Durban and Cape Town)
1977 Falmouth School of Art, Cornwall
Royal Academy of Art, London
1979 Annex Gallery, Wimbledon, London
Browse and Darby, London
David Jones Gallery, Sydney
1980 Holsworthy Gallery, London
Margaret Fisher Gallery, London
1981 Browse and Darby, London
Minden Gallery, Jersey, Channel Islands
1982 Christopher Hall Gallery, London
Browse and Darby, London
1983 John Brinkley Fellowship Exhibition, Norwich, Norfolk
Beaux Art Gallery, Bath, Avon
1984 Shell Headquarters Gallery, London
Browse and Darby, London
Manor House Society, London
Beaux Arts Gallery, Bath, Avon
Bermondsey Gallery, London
1985 Lichfield Arts, Lichfield, Staffordshire
Beaux Arts Gallery, Bath, Avon
Dulwich Art Gallery, London
1986 Cambridge Art Gallery, Cambridge
Municipal Gallery, Stoke-on-Trent, Staffordshire
Poole Gallery, Dorset
Newport Gallery, Isle of Wight
1987 Odette Gilbert Gallery, London
Beaux Arts Gallery, Bath, Avon
1988 Galerie Joel Salaun, Paris
1992 Agnew's Gallery, London
1993 *Philip Sutton: Personal View,* Clwyd County Council, Mold (catalog)
1995 *Philip Sutton in Pembrokeshire,* Jacob Sutton and Tenby Museum and Art Gallery, Tenby (catalog)
1997 *My Shakespeare,* Royal Academy of Arts, London (catalog)
1998 *Father and Son,* Albany Gallery, Cardiff (with Jacob Sutton)

Selected Group Exhibitions:

1952 *London Group,* Beaux-Arts Gallery, London
1955 *Critic's Choice,* Arthur Tooth and Sons, London
1956 *Contemporary British Painters,* Parsons Gallery, London
6 Young Painters, Tate Gallery, London
1957 *Guggenheim International,* New York
1969 *English Landscape Tradition,* Camden Arts Centre, London
The Nude, New Grafton Gallery, London
1980 *Israel Observed,* Israel Museum, Jerusalem
1999 *Tenby Arts Festival,* Tenby, England

Collections:

Arts Council of Great Britain, London; Tate Gallery, London; Ministry of Works, London; City Art Gallery, Birmingham; Cecil Higgins Museum and Gallery, Bedford; City Art Gallery, Leeds; Durban Museum, South Africa; National Gallery of Victoria, Melbourne; Perth Art Gallery, Western Australia.

Publications:

By SUTTON: Article—''In Conversation'' with Julian Halsby in *The Artist* (Tenterden), vol. 107, May 1992.

On SUTTON: Books—*Philip Sutton,* exhibition catalog, London 1958; *Philip Sutton: Paintings from Fiji,* exhibition catalog, London 1965; *Recent Paintings by Philip Sutton,* exhibition catalog with text by David Storey, London 1967; *Philip Sutton: Paintings/Drawings/ Prints,* exhibition cards with text by David Storey, Bristol 1970; *Philip Sutton: Paintings, Drawings, Prints and Sculptures,* exhibition catalog with text by David Storey, Folkestone 1970; *Philip Sutton,* exhibition catalog with texts by Frank Constantine and David Storey, Sheffield 1971; *Israel Observed,* exhibition catalog with text by Helene Marks, Jerusalem 1980.

* * *

Self-activation has always operated on Philip Sutton. After a spell in the R.A.F. he went to the Slade and become hooked on a lively figurative style without hang-ups on subject. He was exhibiting by 1952 and had his first one-man show in 1956. He was then 28 years old. Since that time he has worked in a progress of refinement and freshness of concentration on mood and colour. The early paintings were concerned with the use of medium, how to apply the paint so that it built up in an overall system of chords somewhat in the manner of an expressionist Cezanne. Colour was strong on key, the primaries especially the reds taking a predominant share. Generally the motives triggered off the painting, and sometimes in the landscapes there was a suspicion of the scene dictating too much in the organization of the composition. Exceptions were the interiors and the still life subjects where less complicated systems of pattern and colour became enriched by the freedom from detail. This conflict between truth to motive and unity of picture structure was to be resolved gradully in the flower pieces of 1957 and later when the ever-smiling ghost of Matisse encouraged the young Englishman.

After having lived in the Suffolk countryside for years, Sutton came to live in Battersea, a densely populated quarter of south London. Nature in its green growth was no longer pressing its vegetable lushness upon him, and he painted many interiors with his family of four and his wife as models. They took their places as broadly brushed passages centrally on the canvas, blues, pinks, deep cadmium reds and bright yellows all singing in euphoric harmony. This was a realism no less credible for its chromatic abandon. The colours were genuinely faithful to each other if not to local visual fact, and the drawing of the figures was portrayed his offspring recognizably and unsentimentally abstracted in their outlines and broad summaries of their features and tonality.

For an artist who responds to the stimulus of his surroundings, Battersea seemed to lose even its intimate satisfactions, and in 1963 Sutton set off with his wife and four children to indulge in what could be called a Gauguinesque dream. They ended up on one of the Fijian islands in the blue Pacific, and Sutton happily began painting; he made hundreds of oils, filled 30 sketchbooks and made many woodcuts.

The result, shown on his return to London, was an uncomplicated reflection of a peaceful locality where sun, sea and lush vegetation set up varied motives for pictures of a relaxed and pleasantly unpolluted atmosphere. This mood of relaxation is one that prevails in Sutton's paintings where only in the nudes is there any hint of tension, and this is implied by muscular pose rather than in any contrived conflict of tones or rhythms.

Sutton has the contemporary painter's engagement with the flat area of his surface totally; whether the central space defines a nude woman or a bunch of gladioli is important only for its contribution of colour and its form to the total experience. In this he is at one with both Bonnard and Matisse in the continued mood of optimism.

—G. S. Whittet

ŠVANKMAJER, Jan

Nationality: Czech. **Born:** Prague, Czech Republic, 4 September 1934. **Education:** Studied at College of Applied Arts, Prague, 1950–54; studied at Prague Academy of Performing Arts (DAMU), Department of Puppetry, 1954–58. **Military Service:** Compulsory service in Marianske Lazne, Czech Republic, 1958–60. **Family:** Met future wife, artist Eva Švankmajerová (b. 1940, Kostelec, Czech Republic), 1960; daughter Veronika born, 1963; son Vaclav born, 1975. **Career:** Worked with D34 Theatre, 1957–58; founded Theatre of Masks, part of the Semafor Theatre, Prague, and staged various plays, 1960–62; joined the Maj group, 1962; joined the Magic Lantern (Laterna Magika) Theatre, Prague, and worked on various multi-media productions, 1962–64; left Laterna Magika and made his first film, The Last Trick (Poslední trik pana Schwarcewalldea a pana Edgara) at Krátk? Film Studios, Prague, 1964; joined the Czech Surrealist Group, 1970; special effects designer and co-coordinator at the Barrandov Film Studio, 1972–79; established Athanor film studio, Knoviz, Czech Republic, 1991. Lives and works in Prague. **Awards:** Persistence of Vision, San Francisco Film Festival,1997; Andrzej Wajda/Philip Morris Freedom Prize, 2001. **Agent:** Galerie GAMBRA, Cerninska 5, 118 00 Praha 1, Czech Republic.

Selected Individual Exhibitions:

1961 Semafor Theatre, Prague
1963 Viola, Prague
1977 *Infantile Lüste,* Sonnenring Gallery, Munster (with Eva Švankmajerová)
1983 Cinema Klub, Prague
1985 *Jan Švankmajer l'Inanimateur,* Annecy, France
1987 Bouillonnements cachés, Brussels and Tournai, Belgium
Les labyrinths de Jan Svankmajer, Paris
Bouillonnements caches, Brussels (with Eva Švankmajerová)
1991 *La contamination des sens,* Annecy, France (with Eva Švankmajerová)
Het ludicatiefe principe, Antwerp
La fuerza de la imaginacíon, Valladolid, Spain
1992 *The Communication of Dreams,* Cardiff, Wales (with Eva Švankmajerová)
1993 *Das Lexicon der Träume,* Vienna
1994 *El llenguatge de l'analogia,* Sitges, Spain (with Eva Švankmajerová)
Hinnia mozi, Budapest
1996 The Czech Centre, London (with Eva Švankmajerová)
1997 *Natural Science Cabinet,* Galerie Josefa Sudka, Prague
Painting Which Speaks, Poetry Which is Silent, Obecni galerie Beseda, Prague
(with Eva Švankmajerová)
1998 *Animus Anima Animation,* Czech Republic (catalog) (with Eva Švankmajerová)

Selected Group Exhibitions:

1979 *Otevrena hra,* Geneva; Prague (with the Czech Surrealist Group)
1983 *Sféra snu,* Geneva; Prague (with the Czech Surrealist Group)
1984 *Promeny humoru,* Geneva; Prague (with the Czech Surrealist Group)
1985 *Opak zrcadla,* Geneva; Prague (with the Czech Surrealist Group)
1989 *Gambra I,* Geneva; Prague (with the Czech Surrealist Group)
1991 *Tretí archa,* Prague (with the Czech Surrealist Group)
Sen, erotizmus, interpretacia, Banska Bystrica, Slovakia; Bratislava, Slovakia; Budapest (with the Czech Surrealist Group)
1993 *Das umzugskabinet,* Hanover; Gutersloh, Germany (with the Czech Surrealist Group)
1995 *Z jednoho testa/Z jedného cesta,* Cheb, Czech Republic; Prague; Brno, Czech Republic (with the Czech Surrealist Group)
1997 *Surrealistická obraznost a kresba,* Prague (with the Czech Surrealist Group)
Czech Collage, Prague
Ocima Arcimboldovyma/Through the Eyes of Arcimboldo, Prague (with the Czech Surrealist Group)
Dawn of the Magicians, National Gallery, Prague (with the Czech Surrealist Group)

Publications:

By ŠVANKMAJER: Books— *Hmat a imaginace,* by Jan Švankmajer, Eva Švankmajerová and others, Kozoroh, Czech Republic, 1994. **Articles—**"Repas" in *Bulletin de la liason surréaliste,* 1972; "La Langue" in *Change mondial II,* 1975; "L'avenir est aux machines impsatrices" in *La civilization surréaliste,* 1976; "Felaceus Oidipus" in *Surréalisme 2,* 1977; "Le restaurateur" in *Surréalisme 1,* 1977; "Otevrena hra" in *Surrealistické skupiny v Ceskoslovensku 1969–1979,* 1979.

On ŠVANKMAJER: Books—*La contamination des sens: Eva at Jan Švankmajer* (exhibition catalog), with texts by Ivo Purš, František Dryje, Albert Marenèin, Vratislav Effenberger, Jan Švankmajer, and Eva Švankmajerova, Annecy, France 1991; *Švankmajer: The Communication of Dreams*, by Michael O'Pray, Ivo Purš, Jan Švankmajer, and Eva Švankmajerova, Cardiff, Wales 1992; *Das Lexikon der Traume: Jan Švankmajer—eine Werkschau* (exhibition catalog), with texts by Stefan Grissemann, Vratislav Effenberger, Ludvik Sváb, Michael O'Pray, Martin Stejskal, Alexander Ivanceanu, and Jan Švankmajer, Wien, Austria 1993; *Jan Švankmajer: Transmutation of the Senses* edited by Simeona Hosková and Kveta Otcovská, Prague 1994; *Dark Alchemy* edited by Peter Hames, with texts by Peter Hames, Michael O'Pray, Roger Cardinal, and František Dryje, Westport, Connecticut 1995. **Articles—**''In the Capital of Magic'' by Michael O'Pray in *Monthly Film Bulletin,* July 1986; ''A Švankmajer Inventory'' by Michael O'Pray in *Afterimage,* 1987; ''Švankmajer on *The Fall of the House of* Usher by Vratislav Effenberger in Afterimage, 1987; ''Questions to Jan Švankmajer'' by Petr Král in Afterimage, 1987; ''Malice in Wonderland'' by Geoff Andrew in *Time Out,* October 1988; ''The Film World of Jan Švankmajer'' by Jan Uhde in *Cross Currents,* 1989; ''A Faust Buck'' by Geoff Andrew in *Time Out,* September 1994. **Films—***Visions,* 1984; *The Late Show: Tales From Prague,* 1990.

* * *

Jan Švankmajer's reputation as one of the most original of contemporary filmmakers has eclipsed his activities in other disciplines, particularly collage, sculpture, and pottery. Originally trained as a puppeteer, the artist himself has always claimed that he is primarily a surrealist, not a filmmaker or animator. On the other hand, his constructed objects have found a perfect vehicle for display in his films. According to Švankmajer, his early influences included the theater work of Oskar Schlemmer and Russian constructivists Aleksandr Taïrov and Vsevolod Meyerhold, ''primitive'' films by Georges Méliès and Charles Bowers, the post-revolutionary Russian cinema of Sergej Eisenstein and Dziga Vertov, Luis Buñuel and Salvador Dali's ''Un chiene andalou'' and ''L'age d'or,'' and works of prewar surrealists: Dali, Max Ernst, Toyen, and Jindøich Štyrský.

Despite his diverse interests in the avant-garde of the 1920s and 1930s, Švankmajer began his career in the late 1950s as an abstractionist in the style of Art Informel. Soon, however, he introduced elements borrowed from lived experience into his work, using them in a paradoxical and humorous way. This lead him to the creation of puzzling, mysterious objects, a path he quickly abandoned only to resume some time later. After his ''Informel'' period the artist entered a mannerist phase reflecting his fascination with Giuseppe Archimboldo, the bizarre 16th-century Italian painter who thrived in the eccentric court of Rudolph II in Prague. From this influence came collages and assemblages which have become Švankmajer's favorite means of expression.

At approximately the same time he debuted as animator and from the very beginning his films became an extension of his collage and assemblage work. His early films, *The Last Trick of Mr. Schwarcewallde and Mr Edgar* (1964) and *Punch and Juddy* (1966), also displayed apparent links with traditional puppet theater, the field Švankmajer had come from. These theatrical connections would occasionally reappear in his more recent productions, e.g., *The Lesson of Faust* (1994).

In the late 1960s the artist's work took on surrealist overtones resulting from his contacts with the Prague group of surrealists led by the poet Vratislav Effenberger. Eventually Švankmajer joined the movement in 1970 and soon became, in his own description, a ''militant'' surrealist. In the following decade he created several series of collages presenting (in the form of scientific diagrams and maps from old books) fantastic animals, machines, and places (''Technology,'' ''The Švankmajer Encyclopedia,'' ''Natural Science''). This coincided with his assemblages of skeletons of imaginary animals displayed in glass cases like exhibits in a natural history museum (''Natural Science Cabinets'').

At the end of the 1970s Švankmajer initiated experiments with ''gestural'' sculpture and tactile collages that have developed into a very important component of his oeuvre. These pieces (''Knee-High Socks,'' ''Man,'' ''Woman,'' all 1978) were meant as touchable objects allowing viewers to perceive them beyond their visual form and get closer to the artist's emotions. This search for devices enhancing sensations felt by the beholder culminated in the feature-long film *Conspirators of Desire* (1996) in which protagonists are obsessively involved in inventing erotic tactile toys and machines. In addition to his graphic works, assemblages and films, in the past twenty years Švankmajer has made a number of collage-like majolica pieces under a nickname J.E. Kostelec (''Salt-Cellar,'' ''The Small Demon, and the Big Demon,'' both 1990) . He also creates puppets out of found objects (''Androgyn,'' 1990; ''Puppet Golem,'' 1993; Puppet Alice,'' 1996) which bring him back to the very roots of his art, showing that traditional puppet theater, folk art and legends have not dried up as a source of inspiration for contemporary artists in the Czech Republic. Švankmajer's work seems to epitomize the very spirit of Prague, the city of alchemists and occultists which was praised by André Breton as ''the magical capital of Europe.''

—Marcin Giżycki

T

TADINI, Emilio

Nationality: Italian. **Born:** Milan, 5 June 1927. **Education:** Studied art; received degree. **Family:** Married Antonia Perazzoli in 1959; children: Francesco and Michelle. **Career:** Independent artist, Milan, since 1960. Art instructor, Nuova Accademia Di Belle Arti, Milan, 1980–82. **Agent:** Studio Marconi, via Tadino 15, 20124 Milan. **Address:** via Jommelli 24, 20131 Milan, Italy.

Individual Exhibitions:

1961 Galleria del Cavallino, Venice
1966 Galleria Il Punto, Turin
1967 Galleria del Minotaura, Brescia, Italy
Vita di Voltaire, Studio Marconi, Milan
1968 Galleria La Chiocciola, Padua
Gallerie Richard Foncke, Ghent
1969 Galleria Tempo, Bologna
Studio Condotti, Rome
1970 Studio Marconi, Milan
Gallerie Richard Foncke, Ghent
1971 *Viaggio in Italia,* Studio Marconi, Milan
Galleria San Michele, Brescia, Italy
1972 Studio Condotti, Rome
Galleria Quattro Venti, Palermo, Sicily
Galleria La Chiocciola, Padua
Gallerie Richard Foncke, Ghent
1973 Galleri A. H., Stockholm
1974 Galleria Europa, Bolzano, Italy
Estudio Actual, Caracas
La Struttura della Condensazione e dello Spostamento, Studio Marconi, Milan
1975 Galleria Torbandena, Treiste
Galleria Il Triangolo, Pescara, Italy
Gallerie Rencontres, Paris
Galleria Quarta Dimensione, Arezzo, Italy
Università di Parma, Italy
Studio G7, Bologna
Gallerie Micha, Brussels
1976 Galleria Rizzardi, Milan
Galleria Cesarea, Genoa
Galleria Rondanini, Rome
Galleria Solferino, Milan
1977 Galleria Mercato del Sale, Milan
Museo Civico, Alessandria, Italy
Galleria d'Arte Contemporanea, Suzzara, Italy
1978 Galleria 72n, Bergamo, Italy
Studio Baleri, Bergamo, Italy
Studio Marconi, Milan
Gallerie C., Paris
1979 Galleria Torbandena, Trieste
Galleria 4M, Florence
Galleria Marin, Turin
Galleria Le Feu Vert, Cagliari, Italy
Centro Culturale Olivetti, Ivrea, Turin
Galleria La Chiocciola, Padua
D'Arts Agency, Milan
Galleria Greminger, Genoa
1980 Banca Popolare di Milano, Rome
Galleria Il Disegno, Rome
Galleria Il Triangono, Nola, Italy
Galerie Pieter van Coecke, Aalst, Belgium
Galerie Atmosphere, Brussels
Arte Incontri, Fara d'Adda, Italy
1981 Galleria La Bottega, Parma
1982 Galerie J. L., Ostend, Belgium
Galleria Civica d'Arte Moderna, Suzzara, Italy
1988 *Emilio Tadini: Città Italiane,* Milan (catalog)
1995 Kulturhistorisches Museum, Stralsund, Germany (touring exhibition)
1996 Institut Mathildenhohe, Darmstadt
1997 Galerie Karin Fesel, Dusseldorf
Favole, Galerie George Fall, Paris
2000 *Fiaba,* Galleria Biasutti, Turin, Italy

Selected Group Exhibitions:

1965 *Operazione Goldfinger,* Galleria Levi, Milan
1967 *Contemporary Italian Art,* Gemeentemuseum, The Hague
1970 *Studio Marconi at Felix Landau,* Felix Landau Gallery, Los Angeles
1971 *New Italian Art 1953–1971,* Walker Art Gallery, Liverpool
1973 *Pittura in Lombardia 1945–70,* Villa Reale, Monza, Italy
1977 *Quotidien, Histoire et Utopie,* Maison de la Culture, Grenoble, France
1978 *Biennale,* Venice (and 1982)
1979 *Testuale: Le Parole, le Immagini,* Rotonda di via Besana, Milan
1982 *L'Opera Dipinta,* Galleria La Pilotta, Parma, Italy (travelled to Rotonda di via Besana, Milan)
1986 *Aspects of Italian Art 1960–85,* Kunstverein, Frankfurt
1993 *32nd National Art Biennial,* Milan
2000 *Dal Premio alla Pinacoteca,* Civica Galleria d'Arte Contemporanea, Milan (catalog)

Publications:

By TADINI: Books—*Le Armi, l'Armore,* Milan 1963; *L'Opera,* Milan 1980; *Emilio Tadini,* Milan 1990; *Emilio Tadini,* with Arturo Carlo Quintavalle, Milan 1994. **Articles**—interview with Elio Grazioli in *Flash Art,* no. 116, March 1984.

On TADINI: Books—*Emilio Tadini,* exhibition catalog, with text by A. Martini, Venice 1961; *Emilio Tadini,* exhibition catalog, with text by Guido Ballo, Turin 1966; *Tadini,* exhibition catalog with text by Roberto Sanesi, Brescia, Italy 1967; *Emilio Tadini: Vita di Voltaire,* exhibition catalog with texts by Henry Martin, Roberto Sanesi and Guido Ballo, Milan 1967; *Ricerche dopo l'Informale* by Enrico Crispolti, Rome 1968, *Emilio Tadini,* exhibition catalog with text by J. L. Schefer, Milan 1970; *Emilio Tadini: Viaggio in Italia,* exhibition catalog edited by Giorgio Marconi, Milan 1971; *New Italian Art*

1953–1971, exhibition catalog with text by Giovanni Carandente, Liverpool 1971; *Emilio Tadini: La struttura della condensazione e dello spostamento,* exhibition catalog, with text by Arturo Carlo Quintavalle, Milan 1974; *Emilio Tadini,* exhibition catalog with text by J. L. Schefer, Paris 1975; *Testuale: Le Parole, le Immagini,* exhibition catalog with texts by Flavio Caroli and Luciano Caramel, Milan 1979; *Emilio Tadini: Aquarelli,* exhibition catalog with texts by F. Vincitorio and others, Rome 1980. **Articles—***Il Memoriale di Pinocchio: Disegni di Emilio Tadini* by Uberto Paolo Quintavalle, Florentia 1993; ''Invito al Ballo di Emilio Tadini: Tra Profughi e Filosofi'' by Alfredo Barberis in *Arte,* no. 265, September 1995; ''Peintre Philosophe Emilio Tadini'' by Beba Marsano in *Arte,* no. 290, October 1997.

* * *

Emilio Tadini took up painting during the 1960s, after having worked for years as a writer, critic and theorist of art, and as a novelist. His writing experience and literary acumen are in fact an important element in his painting. The 1960s, characterized by the explosion of Pop Art, gave Tadini a feeling for flat colour, precise drawing, a vaguely advertisement-style of picture—generally, of a super-finished work. Where Pop Art was concerned to glorify consumer goods (Campbell's Soup), Tadini offers us literary goods (the Gate, The Cloth Column); where Pop Art chooses the film star (Marilyn Monroe), for subject, Tadini chooses the literary star (Voltaire, Goethe); where Pop Art illustrates the environment as a great supermarket, Tadini presents it as the place of nostalgically well-educated babies.

There is a picture of his from 1975, called ''Magasins Réunis,'' in which he tackles the theme of the supermarket, a subject that does suggest Pop Art themes; but it is a pretext for literature. From the godlike body of Superman there grows the head of a metaphysical manikin, Nembo Kid; surprised by this head, one asks about the present through the unrealized hopes of the past; a German helmet at the side reinterprets the tragedy of a recent past.

The past is injected into the present, as the historical symbols live together with the symbols of the present day. History and news coexist in a picture written on the canvas with the same sort of pleasure with which tin soldiers are paraded by children on the floor of a nursery.

The figures in Tadini's works, so definitely outlined as to look like coloured silhouettes, are combined with texts which do not name things but illustrate a kind of vocabulary where words and things each go their own way. Like a cosmos in miniature, a syllabary never completed, where words and pictures live only for the euphoria of a text meant only for looking at.

While we normally look at the pictures and read the words, Tadini shows us how it is possible to look at the alphabet too: an alphabet for the eyes which releases the letters from specific meaning and throws them on the table for visual feast.

Tadini's painting is a sort of Luna Park of words and pictures: a question mark makes a column ask a question: the word ''house'' is inscribed between, among other things, a table, a tricycle and a revolver. Pictures and words are used to portray an impossible literature, a literature that cannot exist in writing, a text that cannot be read, a writing that cannot be spoken but only looked at: it is the pleasure of painting.

Painting is presented, then, as an ever-open syllabary, a syllabary made from intimacy, archaeology, comments, travel, from cold gardens, from troubled holidays—a syllabary made to delight the eye. An eye which lingers equally on the particular and the universal, on words and on pictures, on history and on everyday life, but above all an eye that can never cease to narrate.

—Loredana Parmesani

TAJIRI, Shinkichi

Nationality: American. **Born:** Los Angeles, 7 December 1923. **Education:** Art Institute of Chicago, 1947–48, and with Ossip Zadkine and Fernand Léger, Paris, 1948–50, and the Académie de la Grande Chaumière, Paris, 1950–51. **Military Service:** Served as volunteer in United States Armed Forces, 1943–46; awarded Purple Heart. **Family:** Married Denise Martin in 1951 (divorced, 1955); married Ferdina Jansen in 1957 (died, 1969); children: Giotta Fuyo and Ryu Vinci; married Suzanne van der Capellen in 1976. **Career:** Worked as restorer of antiques, Chicago, 1946. Independent artist, since 1949: associated with *Cobra* group, 1949–1950; co-founder of Galerie 8, Paris, 1950; designer at Rasch Wallpaper, Bramsche, West Germany, 1952. Guest lecturer, Werkkunstschule, Wuppertal, West Germany, 1951–53; visiting professor, College of Art and Design, Minneapolis, 1964–65 and 1972. Professor of fine art, Hochschule der Künste, Berlin, 1969–1989. **Awards:** First Prize, *International Wallpaper Exhibition,* Darmstadt, 1953; Golden Lion, *8th Amateur Film Festival,* Cannes, 1955; Copley Foundation Grant, 1959; Whitney Foundation Fellowship for Sculpture, 1960; Mainichi Shinbun Prize for Sculpture, Tokyo, 1963. **Address:** Castle Scheres, 5991 NC Baarlo (Limburg), Netherlands.

Individual Exhibitions:

1951 Galerie Parnass, Wuppertal, West Germany
1953 Kunsthandel Martinet, Amsterdam (with Pierre Alechinsky)
1954 Galerie d'Aujourd'hui, Brussels
1955 Galerie Colette Allendy, Paris
1957 Galerie Parnass, Wuppertal, West Germany
1958 Kunstring, Rotterdam
Galerie Lucien Durand, Paris
1959 De Jong & Co., Hilversum, Netherlands
1960 Stedelijk Museum, Amsterdam
American Cultural Center, Paris
1961 Gemeentemuseum, Arnhem, Netherlands
1962 Galleria Odyssia, Rome
Galerie Parnass, Wuppertal, West Germany
1963 Tokyo Gallery
1964 Hamilton Gallery, London
American Art Gallery, Copenhagen
Galerie 20, Amsterdam
1965 Minneapolis Institute of Art
André Emmerich Gallery, New York
1966 Court Gallery, Copenhagen
1967 Stedelijk Museum, Amsterdam
1968 Palais des Beaux-Arts, Brussels
University of Economics, Tilburg, Netherlands
Von der Heydt Museum, Wuppertal, West Germany
1969 Kunsthalle, Basel

Galerie d'Espace, Amsterdam
1970 City Hall, Heerlen, Netherlands
1971 Konsthall Lund, Sweden
Norrkoping Museum, Sweden
1972 Sodertalie Konsthall, Sweden
Amos Andersons Taidemuseum, Helsinki
Vasterbotten Museum, Umea, Sweden
Kunstnernes Hus, Oslo
Aarhus Museum, Denmark
Galerie Judith Weingarten, Amsterdam
1974 Boymans Van Beunigen Museum, Rotterdam
Bonnefanten Museum, Maastricht, Netherlands
1976 *Tajiri's Daguerrotypes,* Stedelijk Museum, Amsterdam
Tajiri's Rediscovery of the Daguerreotype, Künstlerhaus Bethanien, Berlin
1977 Rheinisches Landesmuseum, Bonn
Van Abbemuseum, Eindhoven, Netherlands
Stadtisches Kunstahalle, Dusseldorf
Münchener Stadtmuseum, Munich
Kunstchau Böttcherstrasse, Bremen, West Germany
Rijksmuseum Kröller-Müller, Otterlo, Netherlands
1979 *Stereoscopic Views by Tajiri,* Stedelijk Museum, Amsterdam
Galerie Fiolet, Amsterdam
1980 Rijksmuseum Kröller-Müller, Otterlo, Netherlands
Kunstlerhaus Bethanien, Berlin
1981 Gemeentemuseum, Vlissingen, Netherlands
1983 Collection d'Art, Amsterdam
1984 Galerie Wansink, Roermond, Netherlands
1985 Bonnefantenmuseum, Maastricht, Netherlands
1986 Galerij Paule Pia, Antwerp, Belgium
1987 Galerie Artline, The Hague
1988 COBRA Gallery, Eindhoven
Galerie Nalepa, Berlin
1989 *Knots for Meditation,* Galerie Dietrich, Berlin
1991 *Early Iron Works,* Bonnefantenmuseum, Maastricht
1992 Museum for Photography, Antwerpen
Museum van Bommel-van Dam, Venlo, Netherlands (retrospective)
1997 *Tajiri: Silent Dynamism and Oneness in Multiformity,* Cobra Museum voor Moderne, Amstelveen, Netherlands (catalog)
Artline, Amsterdam
1998 Artline, Amsterdam
2000 Galerie Het Cleyne Huys, Den Haag
Galerie Husstege, s'-Herogenbosch

Selected Group Exhibitions:

1949 *International Exhibition of Experimental Art (COBRA),* Stedelijk Museum, Amsterdam
1951 *COBRA,* Palais des Beaux-Arts, Liège, Belgium
1957 *Phases,* Stedelijk Museum, Amsterdam
1959 *Documenta 2,* Kassel, West Germany
1961 *Art of Assemblage,* Museum of Modern Art, New York
1968 *Science Fiction,* Kunstverein, Dusseldorf
1973 *Video,* Rotterdamsche Kunststichting, Rotterdam
1982 *Cobra,* Musée d'Art Moderne, Paris
1984 *L'Art a Paris 1945–66,* Centre National des Arts Plastiques, Paris
1987 *Paper as Medium,* Galerie Horst Dietrich, West Berlin

Public Installations:

Museum of Modern Art, Aarhus; Schiphol Airport, Amsterdam; Palace of the Queen (Noordeinde); Headquarters of Shell International, the Hague.

Publications:

By TAJIRI: Books—*Ferdi,* Baarlo Netherlands 1969; *May-day* I and II, Baarlo Netherlands 1970; *The Wall, Die Mauer, La Mur Berlin 1971 Portrait, Self-Portrait and Measurements,* Berlin 1972; *Shinkichi Tajiri: Knots for Meditation,* Berlin 1989; *Tajiri,* Heerlen 1991. **Article—**"Beyond Pornography" in *Suck* (Amsterdam), 1973. **Films—***The Vipers,* Paris 1955; *Ferdi, 1955 The Birth of Giotta Fuyo Tajiri, 6 June 1957,* 1957; *Bodil Joensen, A Summer Day,* Copenhagen 1970.

On TAJIRI: Books—*Shinkichi Tajiri,* exhibition catalog by Aldo van Eyck, Amsterdam 1969; Shinkichi Tajiri, exhibition catalog by Dick Hillenius, Rotterdam 1974; *Tajiri's Daguerrotypes,* exhibition catalog by Ed van der Elsken, Amsterdam 1976; *Tajiri's Rediscovery of the Daguerreotype,* exhibition catalog by Michael Haerdter, Berlin 1976; *Stereoscopic Views by Tajiri,* exhibition catalog by Els Barent, Amsterdam 1979; *Tajiri,* exhibition catalog by Nicole Gast, Maastricht 1985. **Film—***The World of Tajiri* by Ben Berbong, 1973.

* * *

The strange mixture of cultural sources and influences in Shinkichi Tajiri's life seems to have given him great freedom of expression. Born in the United States of Japanese parents, his father a former member of the Samurai caste, Tajiri left his native country as a protest against the treatment of American Japanese during the war. He had previously studied with the famous sculptor Noguchi, who shares his mixed background, and in Paris became a pupil of both Léger and Zadkine. In Paris he was one of the pioneers of the junk-art school, his first impressive group of sculptures being based on bronze foundry droppings, welded into delicate, feathery torsos of vegetable forms.

The instinctive, elegant, oriental seductiveness is something Tajiri immediately rejects once it becomes dominant. A more acceptable inheritance is his fascination with technology and machinery; his is intrigued by the way anything is made, and to some extent his career has been a move away from junk-assemblage, to the re-assembling of natural and man-made shapes. His mature work is a personal mixture of sexual and erotic forms, organized with mechanistic formality. Nature, sex and machines come together in monumental, hieratic sculptures, in which human and plant verticality is conditioned by symbols of growth and procreation. They contain endless echoes and suggestions—the spiky aggression of armored Samurai, the thrusting determination of natural growth, the urgent confrontation of male and female.

In recent years Tajiri has combined these sculptural forms with informal artistic presentations, happenings which include dance, live nude models, or photographic backgrounds.

—Charles Spencer

TAKIS

Nationality: Greek. **Born:** Panayotis Vassilakis in Athens, 29 October 1925. **Education:** Self-taught in art, from 1946. **Family:** Married the artist Liliane Lijn, in 1961 (divorced, 1967); son: Athanasios Thanos; married Do Koenig in 1971. **Career:** Sculptor, Athens, 1945–46, in Paris and London, 1954–59, in Paris and Athens, since 1959; produced first ''Signals,'' 1954–58; first telemagnetic sculptures, 1958; first electro-magnetic musical works, 1973. **Awards:** Fellowship in Advanced Visual Studies, Massachusetts Institute of Technology, Cambridge, 1968–70; Prix de la Biennale, *Biennale de Paris,* 1985. **Agents:** Galerie Lelong, 13 rue de Teheran, 75008 Paris, France; Alexandre Iolas Gallery, 15 East 55th Street, New York, New York 10022, U.S.A. **Addresses:** 22 rue Liancourt, 75014 Paris, France; and Odos Dervenakious, Gero Vounos, Aharne, Attikis, Athens, Greece.

Individual Exhibitions:

1955 Hanover Gallery, London
Galerie Furstenberg, Paris
1958 Hanover Gallery, London
1959 Galerie Iris Clert, Paris
Alexandre Iolas Gallery, New York
1960 *L'Impossible, un homme dans l'espace,* Galerie Iris Clert, Paris
1961 Alexandre Iolas Gallery, New York
1962 *Signals and Telesculptures,* Galleria Schwarz, Milan
1963 Alexandre Iolas Gallery, New York
1964 Galerie Alexandre Iolas, Paris
Signals Gallery, London
1965 Galerie Alexandre Iolas, Geneva
1966 Galerie Alexandre Iolas, Paris
Hanover Gallery, London
Indica Gallery, London
1967 Howard Wise Gallery, New York
Galerie Krikhaar, Amsterdam
Galerie Claude Givaudan, Paris
1968 Galleria Schwarz, Milan
Arts Laboratory, London
Widcombe Manor, Bath, England
1969 Howard Wise Gallery, New York
Massachusetts Institute of Technology, Cambridge (retrospective)
1970 Städtisches Museum Schloss Morsbroich, Leverkusen, West Germany (retrospective)
Howard Wise Gallery, New York
1971 Galerie Alexandre Iolas, Paris
Galerie Bama, Paris
1972 Galleria Iolas, Milan
Centre National d'Art Contemporain, Paris (retrospective)
1973 Nederlands Dans Theater, Amsterdam (decors for ballet *Elkesis*)
1974 Zoumboulakis Gallery, Athens
Musikalische Raume, Kunstverein, Hannover
Espace Cardin, Paris
1975 Galerie Fred Lanzenberg, Brussels
1976 Galerie Alexandre Iolas, Paris

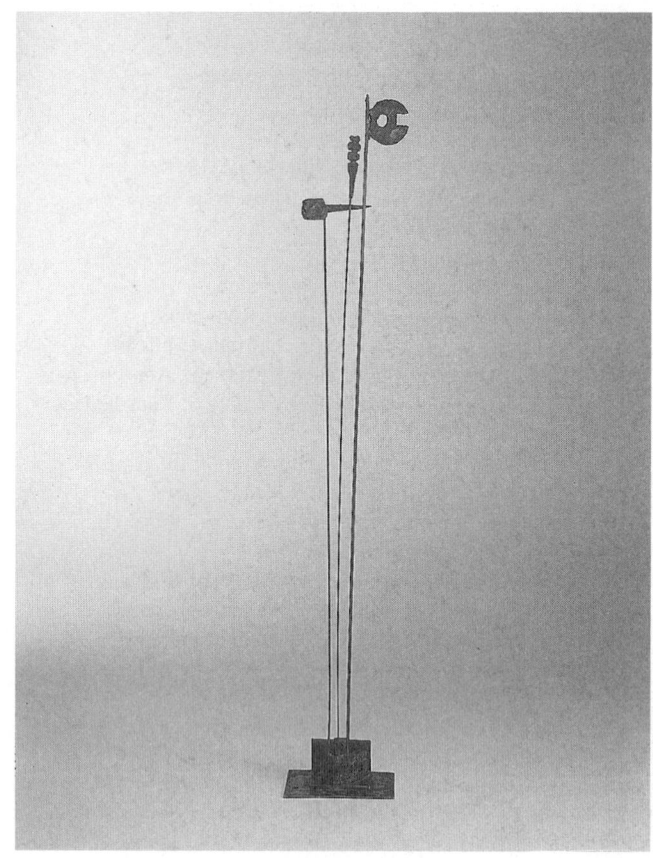

Sculpture by Takis, ca. 1956. Photo by Philippe Migeat. ©2001 Artists Rights Society (ARS), NY/ADAGP, Paris.

1977 Galerie Artcurial, Paris
New Smith Gallery, Brussels
Trito Mati Gallery, Athens
1978 Musée d'Art Moderne de la Ville, Paris
1979 Kölnischer Kunstverein, Cologne
Galarie Reckermann, Cologne
Musée de la Ville, Calais
1981 Centre Georges Pompidou, Paris
Galerie Maeght, Paris
1983 Galerie Maeght Lelong, Paris
1985 Centre Georges Pompidou, Paris
Ecole Régionale des Beaux Arts, St. Etienne, France
1986 Musée Rath, Geneva
Galerie Hotel de Ville, Villeurbanne, France
1990 *Takis: Magnetic Fields 1960–90,* J.G.M. Galerie, Paris (catalog)
1991 Renos Zippas Gallery, Paris
1993 Gallerie Nationale du Jeu de Paume, Paris (travelling retrospective)
1995 *Ergostasio,* Fine Arts School of Athens, Athens (retrospective)

Selected Group Exhibitions:

1952 *Exposition International,* Delphi, Greece
1959 *14 European Sculptors,* Staempfli Gallery, New York

1961 *Bewogen Beweging,* Stedlijk Museum, Amsterdam (toured Scandinavia)
1965 *Lumière et Mouvement,* Kunsthalle, Berne (toured Belgium and Germany)
1967 *The Machine,* Museum of Modern Art, New York
1974 *Art of the 20th Century,* Fondazaione Peggy Guggenheim, Venice (toured Europe)
1977 *Documenta,* Kassel, West Germany
1981 *Machins-Machines,* Centre Culturel, Bretigny France
1983 *Electra,* Musée d'Art Moderne de la Ville, Paris
1985 *Biennale de Paris,* Musé d'Art Moderne, Paris
1991 *4e Biennale de Sculpture,* Centre Culturel de l'Yonne, Auxerre (catalog)
1993 *Luminaries,* Monash University Art Gallery, Clayton, Australia (catalog)
L'Ame au Corps, Grand Palais, Paris
1995 *46th Venice Biennale,* Italy
1996 *Devant et Derriére la Lumiére,* Espace de l'Art Concret, Mouans-Sartoux (catalog)
2000 *Cross-Currents in Modern Art,* Achim Moeller Fine Art, New York

Collections:

Centre Georges Pompidou, Paris; Centre National d'Art Contemporain, Paris; Städtisches Museum Schloss Morsbroich, Leverkusen, West Germany; Arts Council of Great Britain, London; Tate Gallery, London; Museum of Tel Aviv; Museum of Modern Art, New York; Guggenheim Museum, New York; Art Institute of Chicago; Art Gallery of Ontario, Toronto.

Publications:

By TAKIS: Books—*Estafilades,* Paris 1961; *Poems* 1942–46, Paris 1972; *Elkesis,* Rotterdam 1973; *Musique Magnetique,* Paris 1975. **Articles—**''Conversation dans l'Atelier,'' interview with Luce Hoctin in *L'Oeil* (Paris), November 1964; ''Statements by Kinetic Artists'' in *Studio International* (London), February 1967; ''Revelations: Interview de Takis,'' with Jean Clay, in *Rhobo* (Paris), Spring 1968; ''Technology Against Technology = Anti-Technology'' in *Radical Software* (New York), no. 2 1970; ''Lignes Paralleles'' in *Takis,* exhibition catalog, Paris 1971; ''Interview de Takis,'' with Catherine Millet, in *Chroniques de l'Art Vivani* (Paris), May 1971.

On TAKIS: Books—*La Sculpture de ce Siècle* by Michel Seuphor, Paris 1959; *Takis: l'Impossible un homme dans l'espace,* exhibition catalog with texts by Alain Jouffroy, Gregory Corso, William Burroughs, Bryon Gysin and others, Paris 1960; *Icons and Images of the 60s* by Nicolas and Elena Calas, Paris 1961; *Takis: Signals and Telesculptures,* exhibition catalog with texts by William Burroughs, Alain Jouffroy, Nicolas Calas and others, Milan 1962; *Une Revolution du regard* by Alain Jouffroy, Paris 1964; *Naissance de l'art cinétique* by Frank Popper, Paris 1967; *Nature and the Art of Movement* by Gyorgy Kepes, Paris 1968; *Kinetic Art: The Language of Movement* by Guy Brett, London 1968; *25 ans d'art vivant* by Michel Ragon, Paris 1969; *L'avant garde au 20eme siècle* by Pierre Cabanne and Pierre Restany, 1969; *L'art present dans la cité* by Adam Saulnier, Paris 1969; *Focus* by Pierre Cabanne, Paris 1971; *Takis,* exhibition catalog with text by J. J. Lebel, Nicolas Calas, Alain Jouffroy and others, Paris 1972; *Takis: Musikalische Raume,* exhibition catalog with texts by Helmut R. Leppien and Christos M. Jachimides, Hannover 1974; *Takis* by Dominique Vieville, Paris 1993. **Articles—**''Takis: La Sculpture Comme Revelation de l'Invisible'' by Jean-Marc Prevost in *Artstudio,* no. 22, Autumn 1991; ''Takis'' by Vassia Karcayannis-Karabelias in *Revue d'Esthetique,* no. 20, 1991; ''Takis: Un Chant d'Énergies'' by Frank Vermandel in *L'Architecture d'Aujourd'hui,* no. 288, September 1993; ''Takis: A Retrospective'' by Dominique Baque'' in *Art Press,* no. 184, October 1993; review in *Sculpture* (Washington, D.C.), vol. 13, January/February 1994. **Films—***Takis* by Jean-Marie Drot, 1960; *10 Artists de Paris,* French television film, 1965, *Meet the Artist* by Colette Robert, 1967; *Takis, Unlimited by Mahmoud K. Khosrowshaki, 1967; Takis, Chant of the Magnetic Minstre* by Richard Edelman, 1968; *Takis* by Wayne Anderson, 1969; *Takis* by ARC-New Film, 1969; *21st Century* by Keeper Poor, 1969.

*

I will try to put down on paper something about magnets. I have been intrigued by radar systems, and tried to find out how they function. I was told that they depend on a magnet which swings around through the full 360 degrees of the compass. The signal reported to the observer tells him of the presence of some other metallic object in space. I bought my first magnet and dream of using it in some way to bring about a perpetual movement by using the force of the magnet. I hoped to make some metallic object move forever. And I saw that the magnet gave me the use of a new fantastic element which I could apply to the iron-work which I had done before. (The ''tiges'' which I had been making were antennae to capture the force of nature in the clouds . . . electricity. In other works they had been receivers all along. This struck me as being incomplete.) Magnets, however, are not ''receivers'' but ''senders.'' Yet, like radar itself a magnet ''feels'' out towards any passing metallic object facing the magnet. What I had been doing up until the moment I started with the magnets was making signals which merely received the electricity from the sky. Even though they moved, my sculptures seemed to me to still be static.

Up until now those who made metal sculptures had been trying to create tension by twisting iron bars. Many sculptors had been making twisted and pointed forms which were intended to create a sort of vibration between two points; the unreal made to seem real through the talent of the sculptor himself, if you like. What I wanted was to make what I felt to be really REAL. A magnet is not an idea—it is something so real that I was led to dream of making a Perpetual Motion machine with magnets. Very soon I realised that this was not really my intention. What interested me was, rather, the way in which magnetism creates a connection between two metallic objects through the magnetic waves which are a communication. When Gonzales twisted iron objects he produced only a graphic achievement such as the painters had been interested in. Many painters like Matta and Lam have worked along that line as have others who were more interested in creating an illusion of space rather than an action in space which I feel is the role of the sculpture.

When I wished to express the space-communication between an object and a magnet I was obliged to tie up the object. When I did this in order to keep an object at a distance from a magnet, I realized that I had ''floated'' the object. My metallic object floated in the air and vibrated. This was even further from my original intention. I had wished to communicate the two metals only symbolically but, now, they communicated realistically through the magnetic field. Immediately they gave the sensation of being alive. A new and very real force was working between the two objects which I had approached one to the other. When I attached an object by a string and floated it towards the magnet, even a breath of air started a visible vibration. In actual fact the vibration is continuous whether one sees it or not through the wave-motion of the magnetic field, working alternatively but continuously. The vibration is perpetual. What interested me was to put into iron sculpture a new, continuous, and live force. The result was in no way a graphic representation of a force but the force itself which had to be handled as one would handle any other force in nature—even an animal force. The perpetual movement aspect of it became obviously of secondary interest and I put myself to treating, guiding and dominating magnetic force itself in its aspects of real communication . . . the space communication of objects on this planet. More than that, I have wanted to bring off what the Egyptians tried to communicate through the human form in which muscles were represented in a state of tension or slack. The ancient Cycladic sculptors, too, tried to represent these forces through the action of the muscles and forms. In what I do I intend that the tension of forces shall be as visible as the nylon cord which floats an object in front of the magnet whose live force and vibration gives life to what has seemed to be dead material.

—Takis

* * *

Takis is a pioneering kinetic sculptor who has effectively fulfilled his intention of bridging the barriers between art and science by making his own art one which used or unleashes the natural forces of gravity, magnetism and electromagnetism, the movement of the tides or light. He is an elemental sculptor in much the same sense as Turner was an elemental painter, concerned not so much with the visible surface of the world but with the underlying natural forces, which can be enormously destructive and yet have been harnessed by man to drive to Industrial Revolution, a revolution which depended on the new scientific concept of nature as the carrier of energy.

The progress of Takis' work can be seen as a constant attempt to intensify the presence of energy, to make these powerful natural forces the living core and essence of his sculpture, which with his electro-magnetic works he triumphantly has done. He has told how he was fascinated as a child by the way Greek children cut vegetable roots into dolls and hang them on a string to float in the wind. But he came to kinetics only gradually, starting as a self-taught sculptor who at the age of 21 made objects in clay, then for several years from 1948 to 1953 carved in wood. These wooden sculptures were of the human figure, more or less in the Giacometti tradition, though from 1953 to 1955 they became more and more abstract, and Takis came to regard abstraction as inseparable from an objective view of the modern world of science and technology.

Since 1974 he has lived mainly in Paris, though with prolonged stays in London. Here his work crystallized, and from making bronze "idols" with flexible wire necks, or arrow-and piston-headed flower sculptures he moved decisively into the kinetic sphere with the series of words he called "Signals." He has described how the idea germinated while he was waiting three of four hours for a train in Calais, and became fascinated by the signalization of the railways: "I drew some sketches, thinking how dramatic this signalization was, and how necessary a part of our century this was. When I came back to Paris I started making a sort of imitation of those signals, and as I used thin wires as bodies to hold the signals, accidentally they started moving, and I thought it was very fascinating." The Signals consist of modelled forms on the end of long rods of steel, an extremely pliable and light material which allows them to remain in constant vibration when set in motion. They contain a suggestion not only of railway signals, but also of road signs, antennae, and all sorts of other aspects of our technological environment.

His next step of using magnetic and electrical forces instead of gravity was inspired by seeing "radar scanners moving as if directed by an invisible power." He was trying to build his own radar machine, which included piano wires in the hope that it would also make mysterious music, when one day these wires broke because of their tension and floated towards a magnet which was next to the machine. This led him to focus his attention on forces rather than on objects, trying to make visible in his sculptures the invisibly energy of magnetism. The magnetic and telemagnetic sculpture he began making in 1959, in which balls, cones or needles are suspended in a magnetic or electro-magnetic field, do not exist as forms, like traditional sculptures, but an invisible energy which makes them move and change.

The idea that the locally more powerful force of magnetism could liberate objects from the earth's gravity excited him, and in November 1960 Takis put a man in space by suspending the poet Sinclair Beiles in a magnetic field. The following year he was producing his "Magnetic Ballets," which depend on combining and controlling two different forces, electromagnetism and gravity, by suspending balls over upturned electromagnets and making them swing and gyrate in a cosmic dance which makes perceptible the energy that is all around us and the forces that dominate the natural world.

An extension of this is to increase the tension at the centre of this moving kinetic energy sculpture by revealing the source of energy of the electromagnet, which is operated by a blue mercury vapour lamp. This not only used light in the sculpture, but shows the light itself is just another form of electromagnetic energy. Yet the constantly flickering mercury vapour lamp is also poetic in character, so that Takis can think of it is "cosmic flower" emitting its energy. Takis has shown constant inventiveness in finding fresh sources such as signal-lamps, aircraft instruments and fireworks for revealing the energy which is always the core of his recent sculptures. At MIT's Center for Visual Studies in 1968 he turned to yet another natural source of energy in his "Hommage a Marcel Duchamp." The original bicycle wheel exhibited by Duchamp was mounted so that it could be turned by hand, but Takis floated a similar bicycle wheel in the sea so that it was perpetual motion, driven by the motion of the tides.

Takis also offers homage to Thales of Miletus, for it was the pioneering Greek scientist who first described magnetism and electricity 2,500 years ago. And though modern science has learnt how to harness such forces, and that they are interchangable with light, heat and even matter, their ultimate nature remains as mysterious as it was when Thales first described them. Schlegel's prediction that the response to a scientifically explored universe ought to be that it is a still intractable mystery has proved true with a vengeance, and the fascination of Takis' kinetic sculptures is that they are not parodies of technological instruments but highly poetic creations which bring us into direct contact with the fundamental and still mysterious forces which power nature and life. No wonder that Takis in his own statements often seems to verge on animism when he talks about his works as cosmic flowers.

—Konstantin Bazarov

TAL-COAT, Pierre

Nationality: French. **Born:** Pierre Jacob in Clohars-Carnoet, Finistere, 12 December 1905; adopted pseudonym, ''Tal-Coat'' in 1926. **Education:** Attended schools in Quimperle, 1912–18; studied at Ecole Supérieure, Quimperle, 1919–22; studied casting, Academie de la Grand Chaumière, Paris, 1924–26, and pottery moulding at a manufacturer in Sevres, 1926. **Military Service:** French Army, 1925–26, 1939–40. **Family:** Married Bronislawa Lewandowska in 1927; daughter: Pierette; married Xaviere Angeli in 1950 (died, 1970). **Career:** Independent artist, Paris, 1924, Brittany, 1927–39, Paris, 1931–40, Aix-en-Provence, 1940–56, and St. Pierre de Baileul, L'Eure, 1956 until his death in 1985; founder-member, with R. Humblot, H. Jannot, J. Lasne, A. Pellan and G. Rohner, ''Forces Nouvelles,'' Paris, 1932–39. **Awards:** Prix Paul Guillaume, 1936; Grand Prix National des Arts, 1968. Commandeur Ordre des Arts et Lettres, 1976. **Agents:** Galerie Maeght 13 rue de Teheran, 75008 Paris; Galerie Benador, rue Hotel de Ville 7, Place Saconnerie 10, Geneva 1200; and Galerie Clivages, 46 rue de l'Université, 75007 Paris. **Died:** In Saint-Pierre de Bailleul, 11 June 1985.

Individual Exhibitions:

1927 Galerie Fabre, Paris
1930 Galerie Fabre, Paris
1933 Gallerie Billiet Pierre Vorms, Paris
1936 Galerie Renou et Colle, Paris
Julien Levy Gallery, New York
1937 Galerie Renou et Colle, Paris
1943 Galerie de France, Paris
1945 *Peintures,* Galerie de France, Paris
1946 Galerie de France, Paris
1948 Galerie de France, Paris
1950 Galerie Maeght, Paris
Galerie de France, Paris
1954 Galerie Maeght, Paris
1956 Galerie Maeght, Paris
1957 Kunsthalle, Berne, Switzerland
1965 Galerie Beno d'Incelli, Paris
1968 Galerie Henri Benezit, Paris
Galerie André Schoeller, Paris
Galerie Beno d'Incelli, Paris
1969 Palais de l'Europe, Menton, France
Maison de la Culture, Le Havre, France
Maison de la Culture, Amiens, France
1970 *Ocuvres Recentes,* Galerie Benador, Geneva
1972 *Almanach de Tal-Coat,* Galerie Benador, Geneva
1973 Galerie L'Entracte, Lausanne, Switzerland
1974 Galerie Maeght, Zurich
Musée des Beaux-Arts, Metz, France
1975 Galerie Benador, Geneva
Ueno Royal Museum, Tokyo (travelled to the Hakone Open-Air Museum, Ninotaira)
1976 Grand Palais, Paris
Musée d'Art Moderne, Paris
Galerie Eveil, Marlenheim, West Germany
Galerie Shapiro, Paris
Galerie de France, Paris
Galerie du Benelux, Brussels
1978 Galerie Biren, Paris
Galerie de l'Entracte, Lausanne, Switzerland
1979 Galerie Benador, Geneva (travelled to the Galerie Karsten-Greve, Cologne)
Chateau de Ratilly, Yonne, France (with André du Bouchet)
Galerie Ditesheim, Neuchâtel, Switzerland
Bibliotenque de Lyons, France
1980 Galerie Benador, at *F. I. A. C.,* Paris
1981 Galerie Clivages, Paris
Chapelle de Locronan, Brittany, France
Centre d'Art Contemporain Jouy-sur-Eure, France
Galerie Clivages, at *F. I. A. C.,* Paris
1982 Galerie Clivages, Paris
Grand Palais, Paris
1983 Galerie Clivages, Paris
Galerie Michel Cachoux, Paris
Galerie Patrice Trigano, Paris
1984 Centre Noiroit, Arras, France
Galerie Clivages, Paris
Galerie Sapone, Nice, France
1985 Galerie Clivages, Paris
New Museum of Contemporary Art, New York
Cabinet des Estampes, Geneva
1986 Gallery Art Point, Tokyo
Galerie Clivages, Paris
Galerie L'Entract, Lausanne
Centre Gerard Philippe, Bretigny-sur-Orge, France
1987 Maison de la Culture, Bourges, France
Musée de Valence, France
Galerie Clivages, Paris
1991 *Tal-Coat: Ink Washes and Watercolours,* Musee Matisse, Le Cateau-Cambresis

Selected Group Exhibitions:

1934 *Beteaux et Marin,* Galerie Billiet Pierre Vorms, Paris
1935 *Forces Nouvelles,* Galerie Billiet Pierre Vorms, Paris
1949 *La Jeune Peinture Francaise,* Leicester Galleries, London
1955 *Documenta I,* Kassel, West Germany (and *Documenta 2,* 1959)
1968 *Painting in France 1900–1967,* National Gallery of Art, Washington, D.C. (toured the Unites States)
1973 *Collections Genevoises: Art du 20e. Siècle,* Musée Rath, Geneva
1976 *Front Populaire,* Ancienne Gare de la Bastille, Paris
1980 *Forces Nouvelles 1935–39,* Musée d'Art Moderne de la Ville, Paris
1981 *Paris-Paris,* Centre Georges Pompidou, Paris
1982 *Bretons à Paris,* Grand Palais, Paris

Pierre Tal-Coat: *Fish,* 1945. ©2001 Artists Rights Society (ARS), NY/ADAGP, Paris.

Collections:

Centre Georges Pompidou, Paris; Musée de Grenoble, France; Fondation Maeght, Saint-Paul-de-Vence, France.

Publications:

By TAL-COAT: Books illustrated—*Honore de Balzac,* Geneva 1946; *Elements de Nature,* Paris 1949; *Colle Surface,* with text by André du Bouchet, Paris 1956; *Sur le Pas,* with text by André du Bouchet, Paris 1959; *Traverse d'un Plateau,* Paris 1963; *Laisses,* with text by Andre du Bouchet, Lausanne 1975; *Espace Delute,* with text by Pierre Torreilles, Paris 1976; *Sous le Linteau en Forme de Joug,* with text by André de Bouchet, Lausanne 1978; *Surface d'ecueil,* with text by Philippe Denis, Paris 1980.

On TAL-COAT: Books--*Pierre Tal-Coat: Peintures,* exhibition catalog with text by Michel Florisoone, Paris 1945; *Tal-Coat,* exhibition catalog with text Jacques Lassaigne, Paris 1950; *Tal-Coat,* exhibition catalog, with text by F. Meyer, Berne 1957; *Peintres Contemporains* by Georges Duthuit and others, Paris 1964; *Tal-Coat,* exhibition catalog with texts by Francis Palermo and E. Marze, Menton, France 1969; *Tal-Coat: Oeuvres Récentes,* exhibition catalog with text by Henri Maldiney, Geneva 1970; *Almanach de Tal-Coat,* exhibition catalog with text by Pietro Sarto, Geneva 1971; *Pierre Tal-Coat,* exhibition catalog with text by Raoul-Jean Moulin, Zurich 1874; *Forces Nouvelles 1935–1939,* exhibition catalog with text by Pierre Vorms, Paris 1980; *Tal-Coat,* exhibition catalog with text by Jean Pascal Leger, Valence 1987; *Tal-Coat: lavis et aquarelles,* exhibition catalog, Le Cateau-Cambresis 1991. **Articles—**''Pierre Tal-Coat: l'energie du blanc'' by Emmanuel Pernoud in *Nouvelles de l'Estampe,* no. 162, December 1998-February 1999.

*

Prior to the naming of things invisible wave sweeping us out of our cell of insistent visitation. Seized by such an awareness, beyond the dull means of pastures old, I had to proceed toward that which, from the curves, from even our stammerings, can attempt to express what otherwise escapes fair reason. I mean that which cannot be partitioned off by fluctuating edges and escapes from the filed frame, from the established patterns. And that it was the extreme precariousness of the enterprise at which every extremity gleamed a possibility of freedom which is beyond tensions.

Here, accosted by the world, overrun on all ideas, unable to claim I observe it, which always implies perception lagging behind for excess of reference. This said to explain my attempt to raise myself to the level of the experienced without the convention of the known. And the necessity to proceed forbids recapitulation, for all that belongs to the moment is its one guarantee in the ineffable of its presence.

And to yield to one's wonderment requires a necessary precariousness. But no less precarious the continuing awakening to preserve expressive harmony. To thus proceed suits me, demanding neither courage nor special gift; that which is given to each in its emerging necessity.

Thus the arid path common to all has always given out into more distance from the mirage of proximity, for always is the shackle. But also proceeding likewise, in the grip of the ungraspable.

—Pierre Tal-Coat (1983)

* * *

Son of a Breton fisherman, Pierre Tal-Coat was largely self-taught as a painter. His first stay in Paris lasted only two years but by 1931 he was back in the French capital where he quickly became popular with liberal collectors and fellow-artists. He was figurative in his approach, and his portrait of Gertrude Stein was hailed as a fine example of his work that reflected a kind of primitive monumentality. He mixed with the avant-garde painters of his time and his experiences in the Spanish Civil War became the subject of a series called ''Massacres'' that has been compared with Picasso's ''Guernica,'' though Tal-Coat's treatment was more emotional and directly figurative. By about 1945 he in fact came under the influence of Picasso and then two years later André Masson introduced him to the lyrical interpretation of landscape by Chinese artists. This phase continued into the 1960s.

These landscapes represent perhaps the peak of Tal-Coat's art, for in them he aimed at a synthesis of nature that came close to a perfect analogy in its choice of motives more or less echoing reality. The pale grounds of pure tone bore patches of colour that might be held to represent clouds in the sky or boats at anchor on a sunlit bay. This Funambuliste equivocation in his compositions was invariably handled with a sensitive and delicate control of mass and spatial relationship that gave the works a great feeling of atmosphere: the transparency of air and the quivering essence of light were understated in soft-edged outlines. In other works the colours were more violently contrasted in intensity and weight with central motives taking stronger emphasis often in themes redolent of country-side. It is this lack of precision in identification of the objects suggested in his landscapes that gives Tal-Coat's work its edge of interest, for though the associations are less than exact their massing and placing on the canvas have a direct and powerful dynamic operating over the surface of the canvas. By 1974 he was still capable of painting some huge monochrome pictures such as ''Bleu surgi'' that seemed derivative of earlier works by Yves Klein.

His later work shows a rough and vital animation of pigment, scarring its own surface in the relief contour of a lunar landscape, certainly devoid of human habitation and having in its mineral colour something hinting at volcanic orginis. ''Depot 2'' (1974) is a painting of this geological metaphor where a dark gesture raises its facets to reflect the light in an aerial panorama shading into the void of outer space itself. In their own terms the paintings indicate their process of maturing through periods of time in which the surface is moulded, melted, suffering fission and enduring heat and eruption. Tal-Coat has described his motivation. ''As though beyond me a vision, a hand has overruled my blindness, conducting me I know not where nor cannot see.''

—G. S. Whittet

TAMAYO, Rufino

Nationality: Mexican. **Born:** Oaxaca, 1899; moved to Mexico City, 1911. **Education:** Academia de Bellas Artes, Mexico City, 1917–20. **Family:** Married Olga Flores Rivas in 1934. **Career:** Painter; travelled frequently from Mexico City to New York, 1926–36; lived in New York, 1936–1954, and in Paris, 1954 until his return to Mexico 1964; donated museum for permanent display of his Mexican Pre-columbian art collection of more than 100 works, Oaxaca, 1974; donated his international collection of contemporary art to the Mexican people; Museo Rufino Tamayo Arte Contemporaneo Internacional officially opened in Chapultepec Park, Mexico City, May 1981. Chairman, Department of Ethnographic Drawing, Museo Nacional de Arquelogia, Mexico City, 1921–23. **Awards:** First Prize *Carnegie International,* Pittsburgh, 1952; First Prize for Painting *Bienal,* Sao Paulo 1953; Guggenheim International Foundation Award, 1960; National Award for Artistic Merit, Mexico City, 1964; Calouste Gulbenkian Prize, Institut Francais, Paris, 1969; First Prize, 10th Triennale of Colour Graphics, Grenchen, Switzerland, 1958. Street named in his honor, Oaxaca, 1972. **Member:** Argentinian Academy of Art, Accademia Disegno, Florence; Academy of Arts Buenos Aires, 1959; American Institute and Academy of Arts and Letters, 1961. Chevalier, 1957, Officier, 1970, and Commandeur, 1975, Légion d'Honneur, France; Comendador of the Italian Republic, 1971. **Agent:** Marlborough Gallery, Inc., 40 West 57th Street, New York, New York 10019, U.S.A. **Died:** Of pneumonia, Mexico City, 24 June 1991.

Individual Exhibitions:

1926 Weyhe Gallery, New York
1929 Palacio de Belles Arts, Mexico City
1931 Julien Levy Gallery, New York
1937 Julien Levy Gallery, New York
1938 Galeria de Arte Mexicano, Mexico City
Catherine Kuh Gallery, Chicago
1939 Valentine Gallery, New York
1940 Valentine Gallery, New York
1942 Valentine Gallery, New York
1945 Arts Club of Chicago
1946 Valentine Gallery, New York
1947 Cincinnati Art Museum, Ohio
Pierre Matisse Gallery, New York
1948 *Retrospective of 25 Years of Painting,* Palacio de Bellas Artes, Mexico City

Rufino Tamayo: *Musicians,* 20th century. ©Christie's Images/Corbis.

1950 *16 Paintings,* at the *Biennale,* Venice
Galerie des Beaux-Arts, Paris
Palais des Beaux-Arts, Brussels
Knoedler Gallery, New York
1951 Instituto de Arte Moderno, Buenos Aires
Salon de la Plastica Mexicana, Mexico City
Frank Perls Gallery, Los Angeles
Knoedler Gallery, New York
1952 *Arte Mexicain du Pre-Columbien a nos Jours,* Musée d'Art Moderne, Paris
Fort Worth Art Museum, Texas
Pan American Union, Washington, D.C.
1953 Knoedler Gallery, New York
Frank Perls Gallery, Los Angeles
Santa Barbara Museum of Art, California
San Francisco Museum of Art
1956 Museum of Fine Arts, Houston
Knoedler Gallery, New York
1959 Kunstnernes Hus, Oslo
Felix Landau Gallery, Los Angeles
Knoedler Gallery, New York
1960 Galerie de France, Paris
1961 Gallery One, London
1962 Galeria Misrachi, Mexico City
Knoedler Gallery, New York
1963 Mainichi Newspaper, Tokyo (restrospective)
Association of Museum of Israel (travelling exhibition)
1965 Galerie Semiha Huber, Zurich
1968 Palacio de Bellas Artes, Mexico City (restrospective of 103 works)
Exhibition of 124 Works from American Collections, Phoenix Art Museum, Arizona
Biennale, Venice (retrospective of 100 works)
1971 Perls Gallery, New York
1973 Galeria Misrachi, Mexico City
Perls Gallery, New York
1974 Museo de Arte Moderno, Mexico City
Musée d'Art Moderne, Paris
1975 Palazzo Strozzi, Florence
1976 Museo de Arte Moderno, Mexico City
National Museum of Modern Art, Tokyo
1977 *Bienal,* Sao Paulo (retrospective of 134 paintings)

Marlborough Gallery, New York
1978 Phillips Collection, Washington D.C.
1979 Marion Koogler McNay Art Institute, San Antonio, Texas
Myth and Magic, Guggenheim Museum, New York
Marlborough Fine Art, London
1981 Brenner Gallery, Boca Raton, Florida
Marlborough Gallery, New York
1982 Marlborough Fine Art, London
1983 Graphische Sammlung Albertina, Vienna
1984 Marlborough Fine Art, Tokyo
1985 Marlborough Gallery, New York
1986 Marisa Del Re Gallery, New York
1988 *Rufino Tamayo: Paintings,* Centro de Arte Reina Sofia, Madrid
1990 Staatliche Kunsthalle, Berlin
Rufino Tamayo: Recent Paintings 1980–1990, Marlborough Gallery, New York
1995 *From Reflection to Vision: 1920–50,* Fundacion Cultural Televisa, Mexico City
1997 *Twentieth-century Still-life Painting from the Phillips Collection,* Phillips Collection, Washington, D.C.
Latin American Masterpieces, Robert Miller Gallery, New York

Selected Group Exhibitions:

1991 *Homage to Catalonia and Mexico,* Pinacotecade Nuevo Leon, Monterrey
1992 *Rufino, Tamayo, Francisco Gutierrez, Rodolfo Nieto, Francisco Toledo, Sergio Hernandez: Five Artists from Oaxaca Exhibit Graphic Works,* Galeria Metropolitana, Mexico City
Prints and Multiples by Contemporary Masters, Museo de Arte Moderno, Mexico City
1994 *Painters in 20th Century Mexico: from the Collection of the Museo de Arte Moderno in Mexico City,* Banco de la Republica, Bogota

Collections:

Museo de Arte Moderno, Mexico City; Centre Georges Pompidou, Paris; Musée Royal, Brussels, Galleria Nazionale de Arte Moderna, Rome; Museum of Modern Art, Tokyo; Nasjonalgalleriet, Oslo; Museum of Modern Art, New York; Guggenheim Museum, New York; Albright-Knox Art Gallery, Buffalo, New York; Art Institute of Chicago.

Publications:

By TAMAYO: Book—*Drawings* by Tamayo, Mexico City 1950.

On TAMAYO: Books—*Tamayo* by Robert Goldwater, Mexico City 1947; *Rufino Tamayo* by Enrique Gual, Mexico City 1947; *Tamayo* by Paul Westheim, Mexico City 1957; *Tamayo en la pintura Mexicana* by Octavio Paz, Mexico City 1959; *Tamayo* by Juan Garcia Ponce, Mexico City 1967; *Tamayo* by Octavio Paz, Mexico City 1967; *Rufino Tamayo* by Emily Genauer, New York 1974; *Rufino Tamayo: 50 Years of His Painting,* with an introduction by James G. Lynch, Jr., Washington D.C. 1979; *Rufino Tamayo: Recent Paintings 1980–85,* exhibition catalog, New York 1985; *Rufino Tamayo: Recent Paintings 1980–1990,* exhibition catalog, New York 1990; *The Artist Observed: 28 Interviews with Contemporary Artists* by John Gruen, Chicago 1991; *Latin American Art of the Twentieth Century* by Edward Lucie-Smith, London 1993; *Tres maestros: reflexiones sobre Bacon, Motherwell y Tamayo* by Teresa del Conde, Mexico City 1997; *Twentieth-century Still-life Painting from the Phillips Collection,* exhibition catalog, Washington, D.C. 1997; *Latin American Masterpieces,* exhibition catalog, New York 1997. **Articles—**"The Art of the Fantastic: from Tamayo to Rabell" by John Loughery in *Arts Magazine* (New York), vol. 62, no. 5, January 1988. **Films—** *Birth of a Mural,* Universidad Nacional de Mexico, 1965; *Rufino Tamayo,* BBC, London, 1966; *Tamayo,* directed by Max Pol Fouchet, Paris, 1970; *The Artistic Life of Rufino Tamayo,* directed by Gary Conklin, 1973.

* * *

Although it was not until 1972 that a street was named Calle Rufino Tamayo in Oaxaca City (his birthplace), like so many others, worldwide, I was already familiar with Tamayo's works from the solo exhibition of his paintings mounted by Victor Musgrave at London's Gallery One (1961), the first showing of his work to reach British shores, but by no means his first personal exhibition. That had been at the Weyhe Gallery, New York, in 1926, and he had held at least 25 Tamayo exhibitions in Mexico, the United States, Paris, Brussels and Buenos Aires in that interim.

Tamayo, with some reservations, may be described as a kind of Expressionist (although probably not easily recognisable as such to those who have clear title to that description)—there is plenty of latent thunder in some of his paintings, but on the whole expressionist lightning stays muted by his personal colouration and the diminution of the flash. This in no way reduces hints of manic/magical violence when he decides such drama should enter his pictures. In its anti-hysterical manner this cool portrayal of vibrant passions is an inheritance (over the heads of North American and European modernisms) to the cultures and art products of the Ancient Mexicans—Aztec, Toltec, Mayan. Their quiet fierceness, and their placid monumentality as well would seem naturally handed down to a *modern* artist familiar—as he is—with the ethnical ties of his country's *ur-ralt* past. And it should be remembered that, not without good reason, Tamayo was appointed in 1921 for three years as head of the department of ethnographic drawing by the Museo Nacional de Arquelogia in Mexico City.

Along with all the contacts he had with contemporary art—his early years (1926–49) were frequently spent in New York interspersed with return visits to Mexico and during the succeeding ten years he was domiciled in Paris—and his special knowledge of the traditions of ancient Mexican art and their esoteric meanings, he was able to build up an important reputation as an exceptional artist.

Tamayo's painting is essentially constructed upon three foundations: a vagrant and beguiling figuration, sometimes departing from exact imagery, at other times plotted with unerring potency that leaves no bewilderment—techniques of paintwork which include very careful preparations of surfaces from which a picture is to emerge coupled with elaborate mixing of tints, colours and numerous variations beautifully subtly wrought—both these fundamental aspects are imbued with the pervading character of mystery to be expected from one steeped in occult knowledge and feeling. As can be observed, this is not an artistic talent and its attendant attributes that can be summed up in some sort of art-critical short-hand.

Rufino Tamayo has always had a strong sense of monumentality, borne out by his close attachment (in itself a particularly Mexican enthusiasm) for the opportunities to hand for mural painting (one recalls the politico-historical huge wall paintings by Siquieros—some of which led to his imprisonment as a dissident at one stage—the equally violent enormous pictorial statements produced by the more fortunate Orozco, and the many, many examples in his murals output by the politically unassailable Diego Rivera) but based upon (in spirit, not in copyist content) art which proceeded from the great Mexican Empires in the years before the coming of the Europeans. Not for him the towering political propaganda wall paintings from the Mexican artists of a generation before his own, busy celebrating revolution and less or more Marxist supremacy of a new-born republic. With a long look over his shoulder, he always thought back to the wall masterpieces of Pre-Columbian days and has sought to infect into his own commissioned murals (*and* his paintings) echoes of that greatness. Amongst the many Tamayo-made monuments of this kind, his work for the UNESCO Building in Paris is particularly memorable.

It can be seen that this unique artist has many ingredients with which to attract, but it should not be overlooked that there is a certain duality in much of his work so that monumentality is never supremely overwhelming because the way these works of art are fashioned besides seeking their goal of greatness reserves a direct personal approach of equal veracity for the lone viewer, admirer and collector alike.

—Sheldon Williams

TÀPIES, Antoni

Antoni Tàpies, 1994. ©2001 Artists Rights Society (ARS), NY/ADAGP, Paris.

Nationality: Spanish. **Born:** Barcelona, 13 December 1923. **Education:** College of the Sisters of Loreto, Barcelona, 1926–29; Escuella Alemana, Barcelona, 1928–31; Colegio Balmes, Order of Christian Schools, Barcelona, 1931 1940; Liceo Práctico Barcelona, 1936–39; and the Instituto Menéndez y Pelayo, Barcelona, 1940; studied law at the University of Barcelona, 1944; studied drawing at the Academia Valls, Barcelona, 1944. **Family:** Married Teresa Barba Fàbregas in 1954; children: Antoni, Clara and Miguel. **Career:** Concentrated on painting and worked as independent artist, Barcelona, since 1946; member, ''Dau al Set'' group of artists and writers, Barcelona, 1948–51, and founder, with others, *Dau al Set* review, Barcelona, 1948; starts the Antoni Tàpies Foundation, Barcelona, 1984; **Awards:** French Government Scholarship, Paris, 1950; Academia Breve prize, Madrid, 1950, 1951; Acquisition Prize, Bienal, Sao Paulo, 1953; First Prize, Salon del Jazz, Barcelona, 1954; Republic of Colombia Prize, *Bienal Hispano-Americana,* Barcelona 1955; Premio Lissone, Milan, 1957; Unesco Prize 1958; David Bright Foundation Prize Los Angeles, 1958; First Prize *Carnegie International,* Pittsburgh 1958; Ministry of Foreign Affairs Prize, *International Biennale of Graphics,* Tokyo, 1960; Providence Art Club Prize, Rhode Island, 1963; Guggenheim Foundation Award, 1964; Grand Prix, *Biennale de Menton,* France, 1966; Gold Medal 15th Congress of Art Critics, Historians and Artists, Rimini, Italy 1966; Grand Prize, *7th International Biennale of Graphics,* Ljubljana, Yugoslavia, 1967; Rubens Prize, City of Siegen, West Germany, 1972; British Arts Council Prize, *German International Graphics Exhibition,* 1974; Stephan-Locher Medal, Cologne 1974; Plastic Arts Prize, City of Barcelona, 1979; Gold Medal for Fine Arts, Ministry of Culture, Madrid, 1981; Wolf Foundation Prize, with Marc Chagall, Israel 1982. Honorary doctorate: Royal College of Art, London, 1981. Honorary Member, Akademie der Kunste, West Berlin, 1979; Gold Medal, Generalitat of Catalonia, 1983; Rembrandt Prize, Toepfer Foundation, Hamburg, 1983; Officer of Arts and Letters, French government, 1983; honorary doctorate, University of Barcelona, 1988; Commander of the Order of Arts and Letters, French government, 1988; honorary member, Gesellschaft Bildener Künstler Österreichs, Vienna, 1988; honorary member, Royal Academy of Arts, London, and American Academy of Arts and Sciences, Cambridge (United States), 1992; Gold Medal, City of Barcelona, 1992; Picasso Medal, UNESCO, 1993; honorary doctorate, Rovira i Virfili University, Tarragona, Herbert-Boeckl Prize, Salzburg, 1994; European Grand Prix for Graphic Work, Graphic Arts Biennial, Slovenia, 1994; National Plastic Arts Prize, Generalitat of Catalonia, 1995; Cross of the Order of Santiago, Lisbon 1996. **Address:** Saragossa 57, Barcelona 08006, Spain.

Individual Exhibitions:

1950 Galeries Laietanes, Barcelona
Museo Municipal, Barcelona

1952 Galeries Laietanes, Barcelona
1953 Marshall Field Art Gallery, Chicago
Galeria Biosca, Madrid
Martha Jackson Gallery, New York
1954 Galerias Layetanas, Barcelona
1955 Club 49, Sala Gaspar, Barcelona
1956 *Tàpies et l'Oeuvre Complete,* Galerie Stadler, Paris
Club 49, Sala Gaspar, Barcelona
1957 Galerie Schmela, Dusseldorf
Martha Jackson Gallery, New York
Galerie Stadler, Paris
1958 Galleria dell'Ariete, Milan
Spanish Pavilion, at the *Biennale,* Venice
1959 Martha Jackson Gallery, New York
Galerie Stadler, Paris
1960 Sala Gaspar, Barcelona
Museo de Arte, Bilbao, Spain
Martha Jackson Gallery, New York
1961 Martha Jackson Gallery, New York
David Anderson Gallery, New York
Galerie Stadler, Paris
Instituto Torcuato di Tella-Museo Nacional, Buenos Aires
Galleri Blanche, Stockholm
Galerie Rudolf Zwirner, Essen
1962 Kestner-Gesellschaft, Hannover (restrospective)
Guggenheim Museum, New York (retrospective)
Kunsthaus, Zurich
Museo Nacional de Bellas Artes, Caracas
Galleria Il Segno, Rome
Galleri Pierre, Stockholm
1963 Pasadena Art Museum, California
Galerie Berggruen, Paris
Galerie im Erker, St. Gallen, Switzerland
International Center of Aesthetic Research, Turin
Galleria Notizie, Turin
Martha Jackson Gallery, New York
1964 Galleria La Tartaruga, Rome
Galerie Rudolf Zwirner, Cologne
Galerie Stadler, Paris
Galleri Buren, Stockholm
Moss Gallery, Toronto
Galerie Agnes Lefort, Montreal
Sala Gaspar, Barcelona
1965 Galerie Rudolf Zwirner, Cologne
Galerie Van de Loo, Munich
Institute of Contemporary Arts, London
Galerie im Erker, St. Gallens, Switzerland
Sala Gaspar Barcelona
1966 Cercle Artistic Manresa, Barcelona
Galeria Biosca, Madrid
Galerie Stadler, Paris
Galerie Jacques Verrière, Cannes
Galleri Buren, Stockholm
1967 Martha Jackson Gallery, New York
Kunstmuseum, St. Gallen Switzerland (graphics retrospective)
Galerie Maeght, Paris
Sala Gaspar, Barcelona
1968 Museum des 20 Jahrhunderts, Vienna (retrospective)
Galerie im Erker, St. Gallen, Switzerland
Librairie-Galerie La Hune, Paris
Kunstverein, Hamburg (retrospective)
Kunstverein, Cologne (restrospective)
Martha Jackson Gallery, New York
Galerie Maeght, Paris
Galerie Schmela, Dusseldorf
1969 Galerie Maeght, Paris
Sala Gaspar, Barcelona
Galerie Stadler, Paris
Tàpies Room, at *Biennale of Prints,* Ljubljana, Yugoslavia
Museum of Modern Art, Belgrade
Kustverein, Kassel, West Germany (graphics retrospective)
1970 Galleria dell'Ariete, Milan
Galleri Blue, Stockholm
Martha Jackson Gallery, New York
Neue Galerie, Baden-Baden, West Germany
1971 Galleria San Luca, Bologna
Galerie Hachette, London
Galerie Maeght, Zurich
Sala Pelaires, Palma de Mallorca, Spain
Galleri Borjeson, Malmo, Sweden
Sala Gaspar, Barcelona
Galleria Il Collezionista, Rome
1972 Galerie Hans Seel, Siegen, West Germany
Galerie Maeght, Paris
Museo de Mataro, Spain
1973 Galleri Borjeson, Malmo, Sweden
Galerie Wünsche, Hamburg
Musee d'Art Modern, Paris (retrospective)
Musée Rath, Geneva (retrospective)
Galeria As, Barcelona
Jodo Seully Gallery, Los Angeles
Galeria 42, Barcelona
Sala Gaspar, Barcelona
Daual Set-Galeria d'Art Barcelona (retrospective)
Galeria Juana Mordo, Madrid (retrospective)
1974 Nationalgalerie, West Berlin (retrospective)
Galerie Schmela, Dusseldorf
Glynn Vivian Gallery, Swansea, Wales
Martha Jackson Gallery, New York
Galerie Maeght, Paris
Hayward Gallery, London (retrospective)
Galerie Carl Van der Voort, Ibiza, Spain
Galeria Juan Martin, Mexico City
Louisiana Museum, Humlebaek, Denmark (retrospective)
1975 Galeria Maeght, Barcelona
Galerie Jeanne Castel, Paris
Galeria Ruiz Castillo, Madrid
Galeria La Mulassa, Barcelona
Galeria Juana de Aizpuru, Seville
Sala Pelaires, Palma de Mallorca, Spain
Galeria La Kabala, Madrid
Galerie Maeght, Zurich
Erker-Galerie, at *Art 6 75,* Kunstmesse, Basel
Galeria Kreisler 2, Madrid
Galerie Beyeler, Basel (retrospective)
Galeria Ciento, Barcelona
Martha Jackson Gallery, New York
Galerie Le Scriptorium, Paris
1976 Galeria Carmen Durango, Valladolid, Spain

Galeria d'Art 3 i 5, Gerona, Spain
Galeria Rayuela 19, Madrid
Galerie Maeght, Paris
Galeria Joan Prats, Barcelona
Edit Art, Geneva
Fondation Maeght, St. Paul-de Vence, France (retrospective)
Seibu Museum of Art, Tokyo (retrospective)
Fundacio Joan Miró, Barcelona (retrospective)
Galeria Maeght, Barcelona
1977 Albright-Knox Art Gallery, Buffalo, New York (retrospective)
Galeria del Banco de Granda, Spain
Galeria Yerba, Murcia, Spain
Museum of Contemporary Art, Chicago (retrospective)
Biblioteca de la Caixa de Pensions, Sant Celoni, Barcelona
Marion Koogler McNay Art Institute, San Antonio, Texas (retrospective)
Sala Celini, Madrid
Des Moines Art Center, Iowa (retrospective)
Kunstshalle, Bremen, West Germany (restospective: works on paper)
Galeria Terra, Catellon, Spain
Galeria Cop d'Ull, Lerida, Spain
Musée d'Art Contemporain, Montreal (retrospective)
Staatliche Kunsthalle, Baden-Baden, West Germany (retrospective: works on paper)
1978 Kunstmuseum, Winterthur, Switzerland (retrospective: works on paper)
Galeria Lucas, Gandia, Spain
Martha Jackson Gallery, New York
Musée Municipal de l'Abbaye Sainte-Croix, Les Sables d'Olonne, France
Galeria Juana Mordo, Madrid
Centre d'Etudes Catalans, Paris
Galeria Sen, Madrid
Galeria A, Vilafranca del Penedes, Barcelona
Galerie Amstutz, Zurich
Caixa d'Estalvis Laietana, Mataro, Barcelona
Galeria Artema, Barcelona (retrospective, 1945–54)
Galeria im Erker, St. Gallen, Switzerland
Munro Galerie, Hamburg
Galeria Isernhagen, Burgdorf, West Germany
Galeria Maeght, Barcelona
Hating Gallery, Spanish Institute, New York
1979 Galeria Torques, Santiago de Compostela, Spain
Galeria A i B, Granollers, Barcelona
Galerie Maeght, Paris
Badischer Kunstverein, Karlsruhe (retrospective)
Galeria Atelier Hilbur, Karlsruhe
Caja de Ahorros Municipal, Pamplona, Spain
Galeria Joan Prats, Barcelona
Sala Esplai, Gerona, Spain
1980 Kunsthalle, Kiel, West Germany (retrospective)
Caja Insular de Ahorros, Las Palmas, Canary Islands
Escola Taller d'Art, Reus, Tarragona, Spain
Neue Galerie am Wolfgang Gurlitt Museum, Linz, Austria (retrospective)
Galeria de la Caixa d'Estalvis, Manresa, Barcelona
Estudio Palmo, Malaga, Spain
Studio Dueci, Rome
Museo Espanol de Arte Contemporano, Madrid (retrospective)
Stedelijk Museum Amsterdam (retrospective)
Galeria Brinkman, Amsterdam
Sala d'Art La Tralla Vich, Barcelona
Galeria Carmen Durango, Valladolid, Spain
Galeria Maeght, Zurich
1981 *Antoni Tàpies o l'art del mon no dit,* Galerie Maeght, Barcelona
Galeria Cuatro, Valencia
Galeria Punto, Valencia
Galeria Yerba, Murcia, Spain
Ueda Gallery, Tokyo
Kasamara Gallery, Osaka
Galeria Rayuela 19, Madrid
Galeria de la Mota, Madrid
Satany Gallery, Tokyo
Fondation du Chateau de Jau, France (retrospective)
M. Knoedler Gallery, New York
Stephan Wirtz Gallery, Los Angeles
Galerie Maeght, Zurich
Galeria Ponce, Mexico City
1982 Palacio do la Lonja, Saragossa, Spain (retrospective)
Galerie Art in Progress, Munich
Escola Massana, Barcelona
Galeria Art-3, Figueres, Gerona, Spain
Marisa del Re Gallery, New York
Union des Arts Plastiques, St. Etienne du Rouvray, France
Galerie Maeght, Paris
Scuola Grande San Giovanni Evangelista, at the *Biennale,* Venice
Galeria Academia, Salzburg
1983 Stadtische Galerie im Prinz-Max-Palais, Karlsruhe, West Germany
Galeria Maeght Lelong, Paris
1984 Galerie Maeght Lelong, Zurich
Fundacio Joan Miro, Barcelona
Galeria Maeght, Barcelona
1985 Musée d'Art Moderne, Brussels
Galleria Gabriele Mazzotta, Milan
1986 Kunstlerhaus, Vienna
Van Abbemuseum, Eindhoven, Netherland
Galeria Theo, Madrid
Galerie Maeght Lelong, New York
1987 Galeria Maeght, Barcelona
1988 Annely Juda Fine Art, London
Saló del Tinell, Barcelona
Musée Cantini, Marsella
1989 Palau de Belles Arts, Peking
Kunstsammlung Nordrhein-Westfalen, Dusseldorf
1990 Fundació Antoni Tàpies, Barcelona
Museo Nacional Centro de Arte Reina Sofía, Madrid
1991 Funadció Joan Miró, Barcelona
Centro Atlántico de Arte Moderno, Las Palmas
Centro Cultural Arte Contemporáneo, Mexico
1992 Fundació Antoni Tàpies, Barcelona
Serpentine Gallery, London
Museum of Modern Art, New York
1993 Schirn Kunsthalle, Frankfurt

Fundació Antoni Tàpies, Barcelona
1995 Solomon R. Guggenheim Museum, New York
2000 Museo Nacional Centro de Arte Reina Sofía, Madrid

Selected Group Exhibitions:

1948 *1st Salon de Octubre,* Barcelona
1949 *Un Aspecto de la Pintura Catalana,* Instituto Frances, Barcelona
1950 *Carnegie International,* Pittsburgh
1951 *Dau al Set,* Sala Caralt, Barcelona
1952 *Biennale,* Venice
1953 *Bienal,* Sao Paulo
1960 *Before Picasso, after Miró,* Guggenheim Museum, New York
1964 *Documenta,* Kassel, West Germany
1978 *Foire Internationald'Art Contemporain/FIAC,* Paris
1985 *Painterly Visions 1940–84,* Guggenheim Museum, New York
1986 Centro de Arte Reina Sofía, Madrid
1987 *Le Siècle de Picasso,* Musée d'Art Moderne de la Villa de Paris
Fifty Years of Collecting: An Anniversary Selection. Solomon R. Guggenheim Museum, New York
1988 *Aspects of Collage, Assemblage and the Found Object in Twentieth-Century Art,* Solomon R. Guggenheim Museum, New York
1991 *Millares, Saura, Tàpies,* Museu Sztuki, Lodz, Poland
1994 *Picasso-Miró-Tàpies,* Hetgens Museum, Düsseldorf
1996 *Face à l'Histoire. L'artiste moderne devant l'événement historique,* Centre Georges Pompidou, Paris

Collections:

Museo Espanol de Arte Contemporaneo, Madrid; Museo de Arte Moderno, Barcelona; Centre Georges Pompidou, Paris; Tate Gallery, London; Nationalgalerie, West Berlin; Stedelijk Museum, Amsterdam; Kunsthaus, Zurich; National Gallery of Victoria, Melbourne; Musée d'Art Contemporain, Montreal; Museum of Modern Art, New York.

Publications:

By TAPIÈS: Books—*El pa a la Braca,* with poems by J. Brossa, Barcelona 1963; *Album Saint-Gallen,* with J. Brossa, Barcelona 1965; *Novella,* with J. Brossa, Barcelona 1965; *La nuit grandissante,* with text by Jacques Dupin, Paris 1967; *Fregoli,* with J. Brossa, Barcelona 1969; *Nocturn matinal,* with J. Brossa, Barcelona 1970; *Air,* with text by Andre du Bouchet, Paris 1970; *La practica de l'art,* Barcelona 1970; *La clau del foc,* with text by Gimferrer, Barcelona 1973; *Suite Catalana: Poems from de Catalan,* with poems by J. Brossa, introductory text by Arthur Terry and Roland Penrose, Barcelona 1973; *Cartes per a la Teresa,* Barcelona 1974; *L'art contre L'estetica,* Barcelona 1974; *Llamberec material,* with poems by Takiguchi, Paris 1975; *Ca suit son cours,* with poems by Jean Daive, Paris 1975; *Oda a Xirinachs,* with poems by J. Brossa, Barcelona 1975; *Dialogo sobre arte, cultura y sociedad,* with Imma Julian, Barcelona 1977; *Memorial personal,* autobiography, Barcelona 1978; *Retorno de lo vivo lejano,* with poems by Rafael Alberti, Madrid 1978; *Sinnieren über Schmutz,* with text by Alexander Mitscherlich, St. Gallen, Switzerland 1978; *U no es ningu,* with poems by Jorge Guillen, Valladolid, Spain 1980; *Conversaciones con Tàpies,* with Miguel Fernandez-Brasso, Madrid 1981; *La realitat com a art,* Barcelona 1982; *Per un art modern i progressista,* Barcelona 1985; *Selected Essays,* Eindhoven 1986; *Art i espiritualitat,* Barcelona 1988; *Valor de l'art,* Barcelona 1993; *L'experiència de l'art,* Barcelona 1996; *L'art i els seus llocs,* Madrid 1999.

On TAPIÈS: Books—*Antoni Tapiès* by Enric Jardi, Barcelona 1950: *Antoni Tàpies o el dau modern de Versailles* by Joan Josep Tharrass, Barcelona 1950; *Tàpies et l'oeuvre complete,* exhibition catalog with text by Michel Tapie, Paris 1956; *Antoni Tàpies* by Michel Tapie, Barcelona 1959; *Tàpies* by Juan Eduardo Cirlot, Barcelona 1960; *Antonio Tàpies,* exhibition catalog with text by Lawrence Alloway, New York 1962; *Significacion de la pintura de Tàpies,* Barcelona 1962; *Tàpies* by Blai Bonet, Barcelona 1964; *Antoni Tàpies: Fustas, paper, cartons i collages* by Joan Teixidor, Barcelona 1964; *Tàpies* by Joan Brossa and Francesco Vicens, Barcelona 1967; *Antoni Tàpies,* with text by Guiseppe Gatt, Guilio Carlo Argan, Renato Barilli and others, Bologna 1967; *Grandi monografie pittorie scultori d oggi: Antoni Tàpies* by Michel Tapie, Milan 1969; *Tàpies: Testimino del silenci* by Alexandre Circi, Barcelona 1970; *Tàpies,* exhibition catalog with texts by Nello Ponenete and Guiseppe Gatt, Rome 1971; *Antoni Tàpies* by Vera Linhartova, Stuttgart and Barcelona 1972; *Tàpies: Obra Grafica 1947–1972* by Carl Vogel, Barcelona 1973; *Antoni Tàpies: Zeichen und Strukturen* by Werner Schmalerbach, West Berlin 1974, Barcelona 1975; *Antoni Tàpies,* exhibition catalog with text by Tomas Llorens, Barcelona 1976; *Tàpies: Meditaciones 1976* by José Medina, Madrid 1976; *Tàpies* by Georges Raillard, Paris 1976; *Tàpies* by Roland Penrose, Barcelona 1977; *Antoni Tàpies: Kunstlerische Herkunft und Entwicklung* by Andreas Franzke, Stuttgart 1979; *Antoni Tàpies,* exhibition catalog with texts by Luis Permanyer and Jose Maria Valverde, Madrid 1980; *Antoni Tàpies o l'art del mon no dit,* exhibition catalog with text by Alexander Circi, Barcelona 1981; *Tàpies* by Carmine Beninasa, Rome 1982; *Antoni Tàpies: Dipinti, sculpture, opere su carta, grafiche,* exhibition catalog with text by Guido Ballo, Milan 1985; *Tàpies,* exhibition catalog with text by Francesce Farreras, Barcelona 1987; *Tàpies. Obra Completa. Volumen 1. 1943–1960,* by Anna Agusti, Barcelona 1988; *Converses amb Antoni Tàpies,* by Barbara Catoir, Barcelona 1988; *Diàlegs a Barcelona: Antoni Tàpies-Isidre Molas,* by Xavier Febres, Barcelona 1989; *Tàpies. Obra Completa. Volumen 2. 1961–1968,* by Anna Agusti, Barcelona 1990; *Fundació Antoni Tàpies,* Barcelona 1990; *Antoni Tàpies in Print,* New York 1991; *Tàpies. Obra Completa. Volumen 3. 1969–1975,* by Anna Agusti, Barcelona 1992; *Tàpies Varnishes* by Manuel J. Borja-Villel, Barcelona 1993; *Tàpies. Obra Completa. Volumen 4. 1976–1981,* by Anna Agusti, Barcelona 1995; *Tàpies. Obra Completa. Volumen 5. 1982–1985,* by Anna Agusti, Barcelona 1998; *Tàpies,* by Juan Eduardo Cirlot, Barcelona 2000.

* * *

When silence manifests itself in quiet waves of meditative hues crisscrossed with deeply etched scarifications, its evocation can be spellbinding. But when energy and matter brood in contained dynamic markings spread over contemplative fields of subdued color that expand into new forms, the experience is often overwhelming. Antoni Tàpies, whose aesthetic is deeply rooted in the "matter painting" idiom of Europe's "art informel," used silence as a symbol—a key to a private mythology in which raw materials (earth, sand, X-ray film, labels, rags, and paint in various degrees of thickness and consistency) transcend their physicality to become mute metaphors of a world in which existential passions have given way to the serenity of resignation and acquiescence. In the limelight since the early 1950s, Tàpies is one of a number of post World War II European artists who, in their attempt at breaking through the constraints of cubism and geometric abstraction, came out with revolutionary seminal styles that roughly paralleled the development of Abstract Expressionism in the United States. Although he grew up in a time of political ferment, when much of Western art focused on rebellion, struggle, and isolation, and although he was, in politics, a liberal, his forms were never totally circumscribed by radical dictates. For him, for instance, geometry was never the anathema that it was for many of his contemporaries. In fact, an intuitive, spontaneous approach tempered through geometric organization is the one factor that served as a distinguishing mark of his early works—a mark which, over the years, proved to be the fundamental variable that spurred a pattern of growth and gradual change without compromise to the integrity of his forms. Thus, what in the 1950s were crude expressions of the artist's fascination with the effect of timeworn surface texturized by several generations of the clandestine graffiti of Catalonian walls, was tranformed, in the 1960s and 1970s, into poetically charged statements about cosmic intelligence and the unification of all matter into infinity. And, when such words as ''essence,'' ''purity,'' and ''reduction'' were, once again, part and parcel of the artistic vocabulary of the Western world, Tàpies was able to make the transition—to accommodate his vision to the new order while, at the same time, gaining a new stature.

> Everything joined together in a uniform mass. What was ardent ebullition was transformed into static silence. It was a great lesson in humility received by the haughtiness of violent passion. And one day I tried to arrive directly at silence with more resignation, giving into the fatality that governs all profound struggle. The millions of furious stabs were transformed into millions of grains of dust, of sand...suddenly before me a new landscape was opened, the same as the one in the story about crossing through the mirror, as if to communicate to me the most secret interior parts of all things.

These words, written by Antoni Tàpies, summarize the metamorphosis—describe what he calls his ''qualitative jump.'' Underlining a lifetime of sustained creativity, they explain the poetry, the profundity of his vision, as the paintings resonate over two continents with a sense of total resolution—a feeling of attainment and completion.

—Andrée Maréchal-Workman

''Rin-Zen,'' Antoni Tàpies' installation for the Spanish Pavilion at the 1993 Venice Biennale, is comprised of a simple white metallic chair facing a gesturally knotted black paint stroke on an expansive white wall. The emptiness of the chair, the silence of the stark surroundings, and the expressive nature of the calligraphic mark are all characteristics of Tàpies' mature work, work that articulates the artist's ongoing interests in Buddhism and existentialism.

Following his early work influenced by Surrealism and Marxism, Tàpies' oeuvre has traversed multiple terrains, from matter paintings comprised of thick, paste-like substances (combinations of marble dust, sand, and pigment); to evocative, veiled varnish paintings exhibited as ''Celebration[s] of Honey''; to sculptural works incorporating found objects or fabricated pieces in ceramic or bronze. Tàpies often includes either roughly scripted words or indications of the human presence, whether implied—in the form of personal attire (like ripped pants adhered to the canvas)—or direct—as the silhouette of a hand or leg. Throughout, his imagery has, as Manuel J. Borja-Villel writes, demonstrated a ''special sensitivity to certain parts of the human body that are widely viewed as base or repulsive, and [a] tremendous fascination with the most ordinary aspects of existence.''

The Antoni Tàpies Foundation opened in Barcelona in 1990; in addition to permanent holding of the artist's work, the foundation also serves as a venue for periodic exhibitions of contemporary European art. A major retrospective to the artist's work travelled throughout the year 2000.

—Betty Ann Brown

TATAFIORE, Ernest

Nationality: Italian. **Born:** Marigliano, near Naples, in 1943. **Education:** Giambattista Vico High School, Naples, 1956–60; mainly self-taught in art. **Family:** Married Simonetta; son: Marco. **Career:** Painter; lives and works in Naples, **Address:** Piazza Medaglie d'Oro 51, 80129 Naples, Italy.

Individual Exhibitions:

1969 Galleria Lucio Amelio, Naples
1970 Galleria Lucio Amelio, Naples
1972 Galerie Stampa, Basel
1973 Galleria La Salita, Rome
1974 Galleria Lucio Amelio, Naples
Studio Carla Ortelli, Milan
1975 Galleria Lucio Amelio, Naples
Galleria Lucio Amelio, at *Expo Arte Fiera,* Bari, Italy
1976 Galleria La Salita, Rome
1977 Galleria Lucio Amelio, Naples
1978 Galerie Stampa, Basel
Galleria Lucio Amelio, Naples
Galerie Paul Maenz, Cologne
1979 Studio Memini, Naples
Arte 10 79, Kunstmesse, Basel
Galerie Stampa, Basel
Galleria Fabjbasaglia, Bologna
1980 Galerie Stampa, Basel
Galerie 't Venster, Rotterdam
Incontri 1980, Spoleto, Italy
Kunsthalle, Basel
Biennale, Venice
Museum Folkwang, Essen
Stedelijk Museum, Amsterdam
1981 Annina Nosei Gallery, New York
Lisson Gallery, London
Galleria Lucio Amelio, Naples
1982 Galerie Jossevel, Zurich
Galleria Lucio Amelio, Naples

Istituto Italiano di Cultura, Madrid
Galeria Ehrhardt, Madrid
Aetatis Suae, Kunstmuseum, Lucerne
1983 Andre Emmerich Gallery, New York
Gimpel-Hanover/Andre Emmerich Galeries, Zurich
1984 Galleria Lucio Amelio, Naples
1985 II Ponte Editrice d'Arte, Rome
Galerie Stampa, Basel
Metropolitan Museum of Art, New York
Galleria Il Ponte, Chicago
1986 Galerie Harald Behm, Hamburg
Galleri Anders Tornberg, Lund, Sweden
Galleri Fahl, Stockholm
1987 Galleri Dobloug, Oslo
Lucio Amelio, Naples
FRAC Rhone Alpes, Lyon
1988 Galleria Rizzardi, Milan
Kunsthallen Brandts Klaedefabrik, Odense, Denmark
All Art Forum Thomas, Munich
1989 Galleri Anders Tornberg, Lund, Sweden
Galerie Isy Brachot, Brussels
Galleria Philippe Daverio, Milan
1990 Galleri Fahl, Stockholm
Biennale, Venice
1991 Raab Gallery, London
Lucio Amielo, Naples
Raab Gallery, Berlin (catalog)
1992 Abbaye Saint-André, Meymac (catalog)
Lucio Amielo, Naples
1993 Museum Moderner Kunst, Vienna
Galerie Place Unique, Paris
French Institute, Naples
Galerie Hilger, Wien
1994 French Institute, Naples
1995 Galerie Levy Hamburg
Galerie Tobias Hirschmann, Frankfurt am Main
Galerie Stampa, Basel, Switzerland
1996 Boukamel Contemporary Art, London
Galerie Levy, Hamburg
Galerie Hirschmann, Frankfurt am Main
1997 Galerie Pudelko, Bonn
Galerie Stampa, Basel
Galerie Tobias Hirschmann, Frankfurt am Main
Boukamel Contemporary Art, London
1999 Galerie Tobias Hirschmann, Frankfurt am Main
Galerie Dittmar, Berlin
Galerie Pudelko, Bonn
2000 Boukamel Contemporary Art, London
Galerie Hilger, Wein
Galerie Levy, Hamburg

Selected Group Exhibitions:

1966 Quadriennale d'Arte, Palazzo dell'Exposizione, Rome
1967 *Arte Grafica Oggi,* Palazzo Reale, Naples
1970 *Italy II: Art around 70,* Philadelphia Museum of Art
1973 *Biennale,* Paris
1978 *Der Kulturelle Unterschied,* Stuttgart
1979 *Arte Cifra,* Galerie Paul Maenz, Cologne
1980 *Kunstforum,* Stadtische Galerie im Lenbachhaus, Munich
1981 *Linee della Ricerca Artistica in Italia 1960–1980,* Palazzo delle Esposizioni, Rome
1983 *Tema Celeste,* Museo di Gibellina, Sicily
1991 *Painter/Sculptor,* Raab Galerie, Berlin and London (catalog)
1993 *Konfrontationen Neuerwerbungen,* Museum Moderner Kunst, Vienna

Publications:

By TATAFIORE: Books—*La Vanità,* with Anna Chiara Gravagnuolo, Salerno 1995.

On TATAFIORE: Books—*Arte Cifra,* exhibition catalog with an introduction by Wolfgang Max Faust, Cologne 1979; *7 Junge Künstler aus italien,* exhibition catalog with text by Zdenek Felix, Essen 1980; *Ernesto Tatafiore: Aetatis Suae,* exhibition catalog with texts by Marlis Gruterich, Michael Newman and Harald Szeeman, and an interview by Martin Kunz, Lucerne 1982; *Ernesto Tatafiore: New Work,* exhibition catalog with text by Martin Kunz, New York 1983; *Ernesto Tatafiore,* exhibition catalog with introduction by Ronny Cohen, New York 1985.

*

I was born at Marigliano, near Naples, my mother's name was Ida and my father's Enrico.

When I was a child I played with the sea, the sand and the stones; then I enjoyed painting "from life" beside my father.

When I was about ten years old my mother took my sister Maria Antonietta and me to see Rome and Florence, Giotto's tall bell-tower, thousands and thousands of steps.

Classical high school at the Giambattista Vico.

Literature, poets, philosophy and then politics, strikes.

Medicine and art as mystery and discovery.

Meeting Simonetta and the journeys in Africa: Morocco, Tunisia, Algeria, then Turkey and Istanbul, London and Paris.

Marco is born.

Psychoanalysis tripping up the system of logic. Painting as a game without end or purpose.

—Ernesto Tatafiore

* * *

Ernesto Tatafiore prepares free associations between selected episodes, episodes that revolve round the themes of the French Revolution and the *Titanic* disaster. Using these as an interpretative grid and as a track on which a journey is still only partly and temporarily completed, Tatafiore makes psychological use of pretexts borrowed from the reservoir of history; the mind is left free to float up and down within the area affected by the subject, an area chosen as a limiting field of associative-metaphorical forces which of course can be aroused in confrontation with the pretext.

Robespierre, Marie Antionette, Louis XVI, Charlotte Corday, Marat, the *Titanic*—all take on an emblematic quality. Robespierre presides over a dinner of dead men; the *Titanic* becomes the hopeless shipwreck following the "crisis" of scientific "presumption" (ships built with watertight compartments do sink; the iceberg does remain in its rough shape with its tip above the surface; the absence of lifeboats is further evidence of lack of precaution). The event is still, as ever, in the hands of fate, and history as such continues in its meretricious oscillation of permanent instability: illusion and madness.

The features of the cherubic faces of the actors in the scene that Tatafiore depicts hide the images of the guillotine. The venom is concealed by the grace and sensuality of the drawing; it is deliberately given to fragile, delicate figures and to such symbols as caresses; the saliva passed from mouth to mouth with a kiss starts up deadly mechanisms; the poison may even have a taste of honey. The solidity of the outlines of the historical figures evoked is turned back into a cloud of memory, and history is focussed on events that can be selected at will and used on associationistically. The correspondence between ''sign-picture'' and ''truth of the conclusion'' is then played upon by the view in his own way; only he can read the word of history as an individual story as he sees it himself. Vision will condition choice.

—Demetrio Paparoni

TAYLOR-LINDOE, Carroll (formery MOPPETT)

Nationality: Canadian. **Born:** Calgary, Alberta, 1938; formerly Carroll Moppett. **Education:** Alberta College of Art, Southern Alberta Institute of Technology, Calgary, 1966–67, 1974–75; Instituto de Allende, Mexico, 1968. **Career:** Independent artist. Instructor: University of Calgary, Alberta, 1979, 1983; Alberta College of Art, Calgary, 1985, 1986, and 1988 to present; Nova Scotia College of Art and Design, Halifax, 1986, 1991; and University of Lethbridge, Lethbridge, 1991. Has served as visiting artist at numerous colleges throughout Canada. **Awards:** Canada Council B Grant, 1978–79, 1982–83, 1984–85; Alberta Culture Travel Grant, 1985; Department of External Affairs Cultural Grant, 1985. **Agent:** Wynick/Tuck Gallery, 80 Spadina Avenue, Toronto, Ontario, M5V 2J3; TrépanierBaer, 105,999 8th Street SW, Calgary, Alberta T2R 1J5. **Address:** 8915 33rd Avenue NW, Calgary, Alberta, Canada T3B 1M2.

Individual Exhibitions:

1976 University of Calgary
1978 Artons, Calgary
1981 Glenbow Museum, Calgary
University of Lethbride Art Gallery, Alberta
Mendel Art Gallery, Saskatoon, Saskatchewan (catalog)
1984 Southern Alberta Art Gallery, Lethbride
1985 Paul Kuhn Fine Art Gallery, Calgary
1986 Anna Leonowens Gallery, Halifax, Nova Scotia
Stride Gallery, Calgary
Wynick/Tuck Gallery, Toronto
1987 Wynick/Tuck Gallery, Toronto
1989 Wynick/Tuck Gallery, Toronto
1992 Illingworth Kerr Gallery, Alberta College of Art (catalog)
Wynick/Tuck Gallery, Toronto
New Paintings & Installation, Wynick/Tuck Gallery, Toronto
1995 *Symbolic Personae,* Wynick/Tuck Gallery, Toronto
1997 *Shadows Cast By The Body on Nature: New Drawings,* TrépanierBaer, Calgary
1998 *New Paintings and Drawings,* Wynick/Tuck Gallery, Toronto
2000 *1980–2000,* TrépanierBaer, Calgary

Selected Group Exhibitions:

1975 *Alberta Art Foundation Premier International Exhibition* (travelled to London, Brussels, Paris, New York, Calgary, and Winnipeg)
1976 *Spectrum Canada,* Royal Canadian Academy, Montreal
1981 *Contemporary Alberta Art,* Glenbow Museum, Calgary
The Winnipeg Perspective, Winnipeg Art Gallery
1983 *Drawing, A Canadian Survey,* Centre Saidye Bronfman, Montreal (travelling exhibition)
1984 *Art in This Region,* Canada House Cultural Centre, London (travelled to Lancashire and Paris)
1986 Cologne Art Fair, Cologne
1987 *Temporal Icons,* Mercer Union, Toronto
1993 *Canadian Artists to the Benefit of the Olga Havel Foundation,* Galerii Pallas, Prague, Czechoslovakia,
The Land Approached and *Image and Text,* Carleton University Art Gallery, Ottawa, Ontario
1994 *The Transient Image,* Walter Phillips Gallery, Banff, Alberta
The Kluane Expedition, Yukon Arts Centre Gallery, Whitehorse, Yukon
Looking Back II, Southern Alberta Art Gallery, Lethbridge, Alberta
HIDDEN VALUES: Canadian Corporations Collect, Edmonton Art Gallery, Edmonton, Alberta
What's in a Name?: Recent Acquisitions from the Calgary Civic Collection Muttart Art Gallery, Calgary, Alberta
1995 *Journeys,* The Nickle Arts Museum, Calgary, Alberta
Configurations Changeantes, Le Mois de la Photo, la Maison de la Culture Mercier, Montreal, Quebec
Ark, Illingworth Kerr Gallery, Calgary, Alberta
The Kluane Expedition, McMicheal Canadian Art Collection, Kleinburg, Ontario
1996 *Alberta Biennial of Contemporary Art,* Edmonton Art Gallery, Edmonton, and the Glenbow Museum, Calgary, Alberta
A Perspective on Drawing, The Triangle Gallery of Visual Arts, Calgary, Alberta
1997 *Neoteric,* Beaver House Gallery, Edmonton
Informal Ideas 97.2 and *Informal Ideas 97.4,* Wynick/Tuck Gallery, Toronto, Ontario.
Carroll Moppett and Jaan Poldaas: Painting, TrépanierBaer, Calgary
1998 *Informal Ideas 98.2 (Degrees of Abtraction),* Wynick/Tuck Gallery, Toronto
Looks Like. . . , Edmonton Art Gallery, Edmonton

Collections:

Glenbow Museum, Calgary; Winnipeg Art Gallery; Banff Centre School of Fine Arts; National Gallery of Canada, Ottawa; Agnes Etherington Art Centre, Kingston, Ontario; Agnes Etherington Art Centre, Kingston, Ontario; Canada Council Art Bank, Ottawa, Ontario; Edmonton Art Gallery; The National Gallery of Canada, Ottawa,

Ontario; The Winnipeg Art Gallery, Winnipeg, Manitoba; University of Lethbridge, Lethbridge, Alberta; Westburn Collection, Montreal, Quebec.

Publications:

On MOPPETT: Books—*Convergence of Metamorphoses,* exhibition catalog with text by Manon Blanchette, Banff 1986; *Temporal Icons,* exhibition catalog with text by Jerry McGrath, Toronto 1987; *Carroll Moppett,* exhibition catalog with text by David Garneau, Calgary 1992. **Articles—**''Carroll Moppett: Sculpture and Drawings'' by Nancy Tousley in *Parachute* (Montreal), no. 25, Winter 1981; ''Wallspace: New Sculpture by Six Calgary Artists'' in *Glenbow Magazine,* July-August 1987; ''The Best Contemporary Canadian Art'' by Joan Murray in *Visual Arts Newsletter,* vol. 9, no. 4, January 1988; ''Experience the Highlight of Moppett's Art'' by Nancy Tousley in *Calgary Herald,* 25 March 1992; ''Dreamland'' by David Garneau in *Eye of Nature,* exhibition catalog, Banff, Alberta 1992; ''Frontier Women'' by Mary-Beth Laviolette in *Avenue Magazine,* September 1997.

TELÉMAQUE, Hervé

Nationality: Haitian. **Born:** Port-au-Prince, 5 November 1937. **Education:** Studied art under Julien Levy at the Art Students League, New York, 1957–60. **Career:** Painter and graphic artist, Paris, 1961–81; in Villejuif, France, since 1982. **Awards:** Ingram Merrill grant, 1972; Art Grant, Regie Renault, Paris, 1980. **Agents:** Gianni Schubert, Galleria Arte Borgogna, Via Borgogna 7, 20121 Milan, Italy; G. de Muga, Galeria Joan Prats, Rambla de Catalunya 54, Barcelona 7, Spain. **Address:** 52 Avenue de Paris (10–12 impasse Ernest Renan), 94800 Villejuif, France.

Individual Exhibitions:

1964 Galerie Mathias Fels, Paris
Hanover Gallery, London (with Gessler)
1965 Galleria L'Attico, Rome
1966 Galleria Il Punto, Turin
1967 Galerie Mathias Fels, Paris
Studio Marconi, Milan
1968 Galleria del Minotaura, Brescia, Italy
Galleria de'Foscherari, Bologna
1969 Galerie Brusberg, Hannover
Ulmer Museum, Ulm, West Germany
1970 Galerie Mathias Fels, Paris
1971 Galerie Bama, Paris
1972 Marc Gallery, Washington, D.C.
Galerie 3 rue Laplace, Paris
1973 Galleria Arte Borgogna, Milan
Galleria d'Arte San Michele, Brescia, Italy
1974 Galerie K et K, Paris
Galerie Municipale, Vitry-sur Seine, France (with Desterac)
1975 Galerie J. Storme, Lille, France
1976 Galerie D. Blanco, Geneva
Musée d'Art Moderne de la Ville, Paris
Galerie des Ponchettes, Nice
Maison de la Culture, Rennes
1977 Galeria Joan Prats, Barcelona
1979 Galerie Maeght, Paris
Galerie Maeght, Zurich
1980 Galerie Alinea, Toulon
Galerie Atmospheres, Brussels
1981 Galerie Adrien Maeght, Paris
Galeria de Arte Moderna, Santa Domingo, Dominican Republic
1982 Galerie Convergence, Nantes, France
Galerie Adrien Maeght, at *FIAC,* Paris
1983 Galeria Maeght, Barcelona
Galeria Italia, Alicante, Spain
1985 Mairie de Fort de France, Martinique
1986 Casa de las Americas, Havana
1989 Galerie Jacqueline Moussion, Paris
Galerie Tobias Loeffel, Basel
1990 Galerie Jacqueline Moussion, Paris
1991 Galerie Jacqueline Moussion, Paris
1992 Galerie Jacqueline Moussion, Paris
Grand Palais, Paris
1993 Galerie Jacqueline Moussion, Paris
Musée Henri Boez, Maubege, France
Institut Français d'Haiti, Port-au-Prince
1994 Ecole des Beaux-Arts, Fort-de-France, Martinique
Galerie Louis Carré & Cie, Paris
1997 *Oh La Vache!,* Halle Saint-Pierre, Musee d'Art Naif Max Fourny, Paris
1998 Galerie Douyon, Miami

Selected Group Exhibitions:

1964 *Documenta,* Kassel, Germany
1965 *Biennale,* San Marino
1968 *Biennale,* Venice
Documenta, Kassel, West Germany
1976 *Biennale Internazionale d'Arte Grafico,* Florence
1977 *Paris-New York,* Centre Georges Pompidou, Paris
1979 *Le Tondo: De Monet a nos jours,* Musee de l'Abbaye de Sainte-Croix, Les Sables d'Olonne, France
1982 *De Cezanne à Aujourd'hui,* Bridgestone Museum, Tokyo
1984 *Ecritures dans la Peinture,* Villa Arson, Nice, France
1992 *Manifeste,* Musée National d'Art Moderne, Paris
1995 *Indigo 95: The Caribbean,* Guadeloupe
1998 *Freeze Frame,* University of South Florida Contemporary Art Museum, Tampa Bay
Islands, Centro Atlantico de Arte Moderno, Las Palmas, Spain
2000 *A Century of Hatian Sculpture and Painting,* Suites Haitiennes, Paris
International Art Fair Art 31, Basel, Switzerland

Collections:

Fond National d'Art Contemporain, Paris; Bibliothèque Nationale, Paris; Musée d'Art de la Ville, Paris; Goteborgs Kunstmuseum,

Gothenburg, Sweden; Moderna Museet, Stockholm; Hunterian Museum and Art Gallery, Glasgow; Musée d'Art Haitien, Port-au-Prince; Casa de la Americas, Havana; Museo de Bellas Artes, Caracas; University of California, Berkeley.

Permanent Public Installations (Murals):

Lycée Briffaut, Valence; Romille College, France; Salle Omnisport, Rennes; Pitié-Salpétrière Hospital, Paris; Cité des Sciences et de l'Industrie, Paris; Gare d'Orsay, Paris; Seventh Arrondissement Police Station, Paris; City of Lille.

Publications:

By TÉLÉMAQUE: Articles—interview with Jean-Luc Chalumeau in *Opus International,* no. 114, June-August 1989; interview with Gerald Gassiot-Talabot and Philippe Dagan in *Opus International,* no. 128, Summer 1992; interview with Juliette Boussand in *Cimaise,* vol. 42, no. 237, September-October 1995; ''Herve Télémaque: Art Tells the Story of Our Time On Earth'' with Juliette Broussard in *UNESCO Courier,* November 1996.

On TÉLÉMAQUE: Books—*Télémaque-Geissler,* exhibition catalog with text by John Ashbery, London 1964; *Hervé Télémaque,* exhibition catalog with text by Albert Boatto and José Pierre, Rome 1965; *L'Avant-garde internationale de Paris* by Alain Jouffroy and others, Cologne 1966; *Hervé Télémaque,* exhibition catalog with text by Christopher Finch and José Pierre, Paris 1967; *Pop Art* by Lucy R. Lippard, New York 1968; *Télémaque,* exhibition catalog with text by Jean-Patrice Marandel, Paris 1970; *Reperes: La Peinture en France debut et fin d'un systeme visuel 1870–1970* by Dora Vallier, Paris 1976; *Depuis 1945* by Gerald Gassiot-Talabot and others, Brussels 1971; *Le Surréalisme* by José Pierre, Lausanne 1971, Paris 1972; *Art en France: Une nouvelle generation* by Jean Clair, Paris 1972; *Hervé Télémaque,* exhibition catalog with text by Gerald Gassiot-Talabot, Milan 1973; *L'Art Actuel* by Anne Tronche, Paris 1973; *Le Pop Art* by José Pierre, Paris 1975; *Hervé Télémaque,* exhibition catalog with text by Bernard Noel, Paris 1976; *Télémaque,* exhibition catalog, with a preface by Carlos Franqui, Barcelona 1977; *Figures d l'Art Contemporain* by M. Le Bot, Paris 1977; *Hervé Télémaque,* exhibition catalog with text by Bernard Noel and Catherine Thieck, Paris 1981; *Un oeuvre de Télémaque: Fil,* Paris 1992; *Caribbean Art* by Veerle Poupeye-Rammelaere, London 1998. **Articles**—''Herve Telemaque: The Rhetorical Spaces of that Object'' by Anne Tronche in *Cimaise,* vol. 36, no. 200–201, June-August 1989; ''Herve Telemaque'' by Anne Leguy in *Beaux Arts Magazine,* no. 126, September 1994; ''Telemaque: A Natural Maturity'' by Gilles Plazy in *Cimaise,* vol. 42, no. 237, September-October 1995; ''Deux Ou Trois Choses Que Je Sais d'Herve Telemaque'' by Gerald Gassiot-Talabot in *Verso,* no. 12, October 1998; ''Certificat de Vie: Vigie et Sapeur'' by Eduardo Arroyo in *Verso,* no. 12, October 1998.

*

An artist is not a machine producing and immediately recuperating fine feeling. I accept objects as they are—they make up a kind of landscape of our life in the midst of a consumer society. It is interesting to see how these objects speak to us at the unconscious level. This is the reason why I have called upon familiar everyday objects—a walking stick (difficulty of locomotion)—a corset (the idea of desire)—a whistle (a scream).

My purpose is not to blame the consumer society—this invasion certainly causes me a great deal of anguish, but a certain history of human activity is contained in it. I think that the unconscious can begin to function using this collection of forms as a starting point. But it was an easy temptation to represent the objects. It is a question of relating this object to others by allusion, by a suppression of the pictorial illusion.

In the past the spectator plunged into the spatial illusion of the painting. Van Gogh's chair is very close to us. Today it is better to keep to a minimum any illusion, any manipulation of fictional space, any balancing of all these object towards the spectator. I want to be concrete.

—Hervé Télémaque

* * *

Hervé Télémaque's work is a constant interrogation of the world of the man-made objects that surround him, and he seems constantly to be asking himself about the way these objects correspond to his own intimate needs. Do they or don't they, and to what degree, and to precisely what kind of need? He looks at a shoe or a saddle or a house and asks himself how he feels about it, he asks himself how he feels about the very idea of a shoe or a saddle or a house, he asks himself how he feels about depicting the idea of a shoe or a saddle or house. He is not a social critic since he is gifted or burdened with a penchant for a kind of emotional skepticism that goes much farther than that. He asks himself not why these things exist in society, but rather why they exist in his universe. He seems not quite sure that he should have any need of needs at all.

Télémaque works as much with collages of cutouts of colored paper as he does with paint and brush, and when he does work with paint and brush the result can easily look like collages of cut-out paper. His earlier work often created a whole community of images where real objects (ropes, or a cane or a shopping net stuffed with a ball of newspaper) existed on an entirely equal footing with painted representations of other objects (a weight, a tent, a cup of coffee, a facade). His forms are always flat and very simple, geometrically clear but never harsh: there are curves in his collages and painted images that are difficult to imagine as belonging originally to their subjects. His colors are always uniform, muted, and highly saturated with grey, even though the range of his palette runs all the way from one end of the spectrun to the other. The world, as Télémaque wants to show it to us, is a little real, a little less up front, than we ordinarily imagine it to be, and as it recedes a step or so away from us, there is a little more room in which to think about it. Télémaque is also an excellent draughtsman, and in some of the works he has been doing since 1978, collage versions of a subject are juxtaposed to drawings of precisely the same view, but with the difference that what reads from right to left in the drawing will read from left to right in the collage; and when the subject permits (which is to say with subjects that have no clear rightside-up and upside-down) the axis of symmetry, rather than horizontal, is vertical. These drawings are in fact the transparent stencils on the basis of which the collage cut-outs were made, and the works of which they form a 'second' part can also be completed by still a third panel in which some of the individual collage elements that go to form the image (or scraps that fell away from the forming of the image) are presented as though free-floating and out of context. Télémaque shows us various stages in giving concreteness to an image as though to imply that the real world of humanly made objects is itself but another stage in the very same process.

—Henry Martin

THEK, Paul

Nationality: American. **Born:** Brooklyn, New York, 2 November 1933. **Education:** Art Students League, New York, 1950; Pratt Institute, New York, 1951–54; Cooper Union, New York, 1954–57. **Career:** Lived in Florida, 1955–57, and Italy, 1957–62; lived in New York, 1962–68, then returned to Europe; designed sets and costumes for *Arena,* ballet, Nederlands Dance Theatre, 1969; sets for Louis Falco Dance Company, New York, 1978. **Awards:** Fulbright Fellowship, 1967; National Endowment for the Arts Award, 1977. **Address:** c/o Brooke Alexander, 59 Wooster Street, New York, New York 10012, U.S.A. **Died:** New York, 1988.

Individual Exhibitions:

1957 Mirrell Gallery, Miami
1963 Galleria 88, Rome
1964 Stable Gallery, New York
1966 Pace Gallery, New York
1968 Institute of Contemporary Arts, London
Galerie M. E. Thelen, Cologne
1969 Stable Gallery, New York,
Stedelijk Museum, Amsterdam
Moderna Museet, Stockholm
1972 Moderna Museet, Stockholm
1973 Kunstmuseum, Lucerne
Galerie Stahli, Lucerne
Wilhelm Luhmbruck Museum, Duisburg, West Germany
1975 Alexandre Iolas Gallery, New York
1976 Galerie Alexandre Iolas, Paris
1977 Il Fante di Spade, Rome
Iolas-Jackson Gallery, New York
1980 Iolas-Jackson Gallery, New York
1981 Iolas-Jackson Gallery, New York
1982 Galerie Samy Kinge, Paris
1984 Barbara Gladstone Gallery, New York
1988 Mokotoff Gallery, New York
Brooke Alexander, New York
1989 The Clocktower Gallery, New York
1990 Brooke Alexander Gallery, New York
Galerie Samy Kinge, Paris
Paul Thek: the Wonderful World That Almost Was—Snap! Crackle! Pop! Was! Touch Me Not!, Fundacio Antoni Tàpies, Barcelona
1991 Brooke Alexander, New York
Galerie Jollenbeck, Cologne
1992 Castello di Rivara, Italy
1993 Mai 36 Galerie, Zurich
Brooke Alexander, New York
1998 *Paul Thek: Paintings, Works on Paper and Notebooks, 1970- 1988,* Arts Club of Chicago, Chicago
2000 Camden Arts Centre, London

Selected Group Exhibitions:

1967 *Carnegie International,* Carnegie Institute, Pittsburgh
1968 *The Obsessive Image,* Institute of Contemporary Arts, London
Documenta, Kassel, West Germany (and 1972)
1976 *Biennale,* Venice (and 1980)
1977 *Processions,* Institute of Contemporary Art, University of Pennsylvania
1981 *Contemporary Art Since 1939,* International Exposition, Cologne
Continuous Creation, Serpentine Gallery, London
1983 *New Art at the Tate Gallery 1983,* Tate Gallery, London
1984 *Content: A Contemporary Focus 1974–84,* Hirshhorn Museum and Sculpture Gallery, Washington, D.C.
1985 *18th International Bienal of Sao Paulo*

Collections:

Kunstmuseum, Bern; Ludwig Museum, Cologne; Des Moines Art Center, Iowa; Greenville County Museum of Art, South Carolina; Walker Art Center, Minneapolis; Museum of Modern Art, New York; Whitney Museum of American Art, New York; Centre Georges Pompidou, Paris; Philadelphia Museum of Art; Hirshhorn Museum and Sculpture Garden, Washington, DC.

Publications:

By THEK: Book—*A Documenta Made by Paul Thek and Edwin Klein,* Amsterdam and Stockholm 1969. **Articles—**"An Interview with Paul Thek," with G. R. Swenson, in *Artnews* (New York), April 1966; "Paul Thek: Entretein avec Harald Szeeman" in *Chroniques de l'Art Vivant* (Paris), April 1974.

On THEK: Books—*Paul Thek: the Wonderful World That Almost Was—Snap! Crackle! Pop! Was! Touch me Not!,* exhibition catalog by Franz Deckwitz, Barcelona 1996. **Articles—**"The New School of New York" by Lil Picard in *Das Kunstwerk* (Baden-Baden, West Germany) December 1964; "Beneath the Skin" by G. R. Swenson in *Artnews* (New York), April 1966; "In the Galleries: Paul Thek" by William Berkson in *Art Magazine* (New York), June 1966; "In the Galleries: Paul Thek" by Mary Stewart in *Art Magazine* (New York), November 1967; "Paul Thek: Love-Death" by William Wilson in *Art and Artist* (London), April 1968; "Before Nature Disappears, Let Us Return" by B. Sydgoff in *Domus* (Milan), March 1972; "Individuelle Mythologien" by B. Catoir in *Das Kunstwerk* (Baden-Baden, West Germany), March 1974; "Grace a Paul Thek" by Harald Szeemann in *Chroniques de l'art vivant,* April 1974; review by Elizabeth Frank in *Art in America* (New York), Summer 1981; *Paul Thek: Real Misunderstanding* by John Russell in *Artforum* (New York), October 1981; "Thek's Social Reliquaries" by Holland Cotter in *Art in America,* vol. 78, no. 6, June 1990; "Thek's Social Reliquaries" by Holland Cotter in *Art in America* (New York), June

1990; ''The Man Who Couldn't Get Up: Stuart Morgan on Paul Thek'' by Stuart Morgan in *Frieze* (London), no. 24, September-October 1995; ''Ripe for Discover'' by Ann Landi in *ARTnews,* vol. 95, no. 10, November 1996; ''Paul Thek: Paintings, Works on Paper and Notebooks, 1970–1988'' by Katy Siegel in *Artforum* (New York), vol. 37, no. 7, March 1999; ''Paul Thek'' by David Miller in *Art Monthly* (London), no. 233, February 2000.

* * *

Paul Thek's works from 1964 to 1967 consisted mainly of wax facsimiles of raw, fleshly meat incased in plexiglass boxes which became more and more elegant and ornamental. These chunks of tormented fleshiness in their pristine enclosure, which look very like the artifacts we see in museum of natural history, are provocative symbols for humanity's entrapment in technologically caused boxes, sealed off artificially from the life of the spirit. Thek's ''Meat Piece with Warhol Brillo Box'' (1965) suggests his opinion that Pop Art, among other things, had done nothing to change or help alleviate this human condition.

In his 1967 environment sculpture titled ''The Tomb—Death of a Hippie'', Thek further developed his allegorical and ritualistic intentions involving themes of survival in the secularized world of life and art. Placed within a hazy atmosphere of rosy light and incense is a large three-tiered ziggurat which houses the artist's tomb, complete with realistically detailed effigy of Thek accompanied by the accoutrements of his past life and symbolic objects of use for his future life. Among the many things surrounding the artist's wax duplicate are the fingers missing from it, severed parts being one of Thek's recurrent images suggestive of the individual's frustrations at feeling fragmented both physically and spiritually. Accompanying ''The Tomb'' are a series of ''offerings,'' boxes containing arms, hands, legs and artificial limbs and supports, all altered to evoke various states of mutilation or decay. After this surreal, fetishistic use of self in portrayal of the artist/individual's feeling of separateness from the world at large, Thek left New York for Europe in 1968.

Since then he has continually travelled throughout Europe together with a small group of collaborators, creating a series of complex, transitory environments with multifarious elements including ordinary objects and also paintings and sculptures of his own in various states of transformation and overlap. With his characteristic flair for irreverent reverence, Thek calls these works ''Processions,'' a title which acts both as an allusion to the spiritualizing nature of the pieces and as a reference to process art.

Thek's major work of the next decade is this unfolding series of ''Processions,'' loaded with signs and symbols from various historical periods of high and low culture which are combined, re-used, altered to convey mythic and religious levels. As the works move from place to place, presented when possible in correspondence with religious holidays, objects from Thek's own past work and elsewhere re-enter along with things accumulated along the ''processional'' route. A partial listing of the elements included in ''Pyramid/A Work In Progress'' (1971–72) amply communicates the extremely fetishistic complexity of Thek's works. In this work were parts from Thek's ''The Artist's Coop'' (1969) such as the Coop, the worktable-bridge which carried Thek's ''Fishman'' (1968) and ''The Tomb'' (1967), the crates in which these works had been shipped, a fishing boat, old bathtubs, park benches, a piano, tissues, paint, drawings, letters, sea shells, and many more. Moving through a fantastic conglomerate of stuff, the viewer is stimulated to see these things as out-of-the-ordinary, strange indications of the mystical life-quality each component seems to possess. Thek is not nihilistic in his cryptic and theatrical narratives. His continual commitment to the ''Processions'' is linked to his desire to convey a spiritual life by making the ordinary and his own past work as well vehicles to insert the mystical element back into our secularized society.

It is this positive spirit, accompanied by a touch of humor, which also informs Thek's small paintings such a ''Periscope'' and ''Hot Potatoes'' (both 1979–80), which seem, at least in part, a homage to Philip Guston's moving late pictures. Thek has received most of his attention in Europe, where he spent most of his time perhaps largely because he felt the need to be ''in the regions,'' away from the New York art world and closer to the older mystical history of Europe.

—Barbara Cavaliere

THIEBAUD, Wayne

Nationality: American. **Born:** Mesa, Arizona, 15 November 1920. **Education:** California public schools; San Jose State College, California, and Sacramento State College, California, B.A. 1951, M.A. 1952. **Military Service:** United States Air Force, 1942–45. **Family:** Married Patricia Patterson in 1943 (divorced, 1959); daughters: Twinka, Mallary Ann; married Betty Jean Carr in 1959; sons: Paul Le Baron, (adopted), Matthew Bult Carr. **Career:** Painter, in Sacramento, California, from 1950, and in San Francisco from 1972; worked as sign painter, cartoonist, commercial artist, illustrator, designer and advertising art director, 1968–49; design and art consultant, California state fair, 1950–57; designed sets for music festivals, Sacramento city schools, 1953–55; producer of educational films, Patrician Films, Hollywood, 1954–59; co-founder, Artist' Cooperative Gallery (now Artist Contemporary Gallery), Sacramento, 1958. Instructor in art, 1951–59, and chairman of the department of art, 1954–57, Sacramento City College; assistant professor, 1960–63, associate professor, 1963–67, and professor since 1967, University of California, Davis; visiting professor at numerous colleges and universities in the United States since 1967. National juror, National Endowment for the Arts, Washington, D.C., 1972; Professor Emeritus, University of California, Davis (retired 1991). **Awards:** Golden Reel, American Film Festival, Chicago, 1959; First Prize, Art Film Festival, at the California state fair, 1956; Columbia Records Award, 1959; Creative Research Foundation Grant, 1961; Scholastic Art Award, for film, *Space and Design,* 1961; Creative Research Grant, 1964, Golden Apple Award, 1972, and Faculty Research Lecture Medal, 1984, University of California, Davis; Distinguished Studio Teacher Award, College Art Association of America, 1981; Award of Distinction, National Art Schools Association, 1984; Special Citation, National Association of Schools of Art and Design, 1984; Cyril Magnin Award, San Francisco Chamber of Commerce, 1987; Elected Fellow, American Academy of Arts and Science, 1988; UC Davis Prize for Teaching and Scholarly Achievement, 1988; Grumbacher Gold Medallion Award for Painting from the American Academy of Design, New York, 1993; Presidential National Medal of Arts, 1994; The Gold Medal for Lifetime Achievement in the Arts Award, National Arts Club, New York; Award of Excellence, National Park

Service, 1996. Honorary Doctorates: California College of Arts and Crafts, Oakland, 1972; Dickinson College, Carlisle, Pennsylvania, 1983; San Francisco Art Institute, 1988; Art Institute of Southern California, Laguna Beach, 1993; Honorary Doctorate of Fine Arts, Art Institute of Boston, 1997. **Member:** American Academy and Institute of Arts and Letters, 1985; associate, 1986, and academician, 1987, National Academy of Design, New York. **Agent:** c/o Allan Stone Gallery, 48 East 86th Street, New York, New York 10028; c/o Campbell-Thiebaud Gallery, 645 Chestnut Street, San Francisco, California 94133.

Individual Exhibitions:

1957 Crocker Art Gallery, Sacramento, California
Artists Co-Op Gallery, Sacramento, California
1958 Artists Co-Op Gallery, Sacramento, California
1961 San Francisco Museum of Art
1962 M. H. de Young Museum, San Francisco
Allan Stone Gallery, New York
1963 Allan Stone Gallery, New York
1964 Allan Stone Gallery, New York
1965 Galleria Schwarz, Milan
Allan Stone Gallery, New York
Stanford University, California
1966 Nelson-Atkins Museum, Kansas City, Missouri
1967 Allan Stone Gallery, New York
1969 Crocker Art Gallery, Sacramento, California
1971 Whitney Museum, New York
1976 Phoenix Art Museum, Arizona (retrospective)
University of California at Santa Cruz
1977 Allan Stone Gallery, New York
University of California at Davis
Diablo Valley College, Pleasant Hill, California
1978 San Francisco Museum of Modern Art
Allan Stone Gallery, New York
1979 Allan Stone Gallery, New York
Walker Art Center, Minneapolis (retrospective)
1980 Allan Stone Gallery, New York
John Berggruen Gallery, San Francisco
1981 California State University at Hayward
Museum of Fine Arts, St. Petersburg, Florida
Honolulu Academy of Arts
Walker Art Center, Minneapolis
University of Pennsylvania, Philadelphia
Fort Worth Art Museum, Texas
1985 San Francisco Museum of Modern Art (travelled to New Beach, California; Milwaukee, Wisconsin; Columbus, Ohio; Kansas City, Missouri, 1985–86)
1990 Hearst Art Gallery, Saint Mary's College, Moraga, California
1991 Pepperdine University, Malibu, California
1993 Campbell-Thiebaud Gallery, San Francisco
1994 Allen Stone Gallery, New York
National Academy of Design, New York
1995 *Wayne Thiebaud: The Physiology of Taste, 9 New Lithographs,* Jim Kempner Fine Art, New York
Wayne Thiebaud: Prints 1970–1984, A. P. Giannini Gallery, San Francisco
Wayne Thiebaud: Objects of Desire, John Berggruen Gallery, San Francisco
1996 *Wayne Thiebaud Shares His Gift*, Nelson Gallery, University of California, Davis
Wayne Thiebaud: Works on Paper, Pasadena City College Art Gallery, California
Thiebaud: Original Graphics 1971–1996, Van Stavern Fine Art, Sacramento
Thiebaud Selects Thiebaud: A Fourty-Year Survey from Private Collections, Crocker Art Museum, Sacramento (catalog)
1997 *Wayne Thiebaud,* Allan Stone Gallery, New York
Wayne Thiebaud: Landscapes, Campbell-Thiebaud Gallery, San Francisco (catalog)
1999 *Wayne Thiebaud: Simple Delights*, Campbell-Thiebaud Gallery, Laguna Beach, California
2000 *Wayne Thiebaud: A Paintings Retrospective,* California Palace of the Legion of Honor, San Francisco (also Whitney Museum of American Art, New York)

Selected Group Exhibitions:

1967 *Bienal,* Sao Paulo
1972 *Documenta,* Kassel, West Germany
1973 *25 Years of American Painting 1948–73,* Des Moines Art Center, Iowa
Separate Realities: Developments in California Representational Painting and Sculpture, Municipal Museum, Los Angeles
1987 *Made in USA,* University of California, Berkeley (travelled to Kansas City, Missouri; Richmond, Virginia)
1997 *Twenty-five Treasures*, Campbell-Thiebaud Gallery, San Francisco (catalog)
Thirty-five Years at Crown Point Press: Making Prints, Doing Art, National Gallery of Art, Washington, D.C. (also Fine Arts Museums of San Francisco) (catalog)
2000 *Still Life Is Still Alive*, Jan Kruger Gallery, New York

Collections:

Museum of Modern Art, New York; Metropolitan Museum of Art, New York; Whitney Museum, New York; Albright-Knox Art Gallery, Buffalo, New York; Wadsworth Atheneum, Hartford, Connecticut; Philadelphia Museum of Art; Hirshhorn Museum, Washington, D.C.; Art Institute of Chicago; Museum of Fine Arts, Salt Lake City; San Francisco Museum of Modern Art; Library of Congress, Washington, D.C.

Publications:

By THIEBAUD: Book—*America Rediscovered,* 1963; *Wayne Thiebaud: A Paintings Retrospective*, with Steven A. Nash and Adam Gopnik, London 2000. **Articles—**''Thiebaud on Thiebaud'' with Stephen McGough in *ARTnews*, vol. 97, no. 4, April 1998.

On THIEBAUD: Books—*Documenta 5,* exhibition catalog, Kassel, 1972; *25 Years of American Painting 1948–73,* exhibition catalog by Max Kozloff, Des Moines, Iowa 1973; *Separate Realities: Developments in California Representational Painting and Sculpture,* exhibition catalog by Laurence Dreiband, Los Angeles 1973; *Wayne Thiebaud,* exhibition catalog with essay by Karen Tsujimoto, San

Francisco and Seattle 1985. **Articles—**''Slice of Cake School'' in *Time* (New York), May 1962; review by Thomas B. Hess in *Artnews* (New York), May 1962; ''Something's Cooking'' in *Life* (New York), June 1962; *Life* (New York), September 1963; *Time* (New York), April 1963; ''Eros in the Cafeteria'' by Diane Waldman in *Artnews* (New York), March 1966; ''Wayne Thiebaud's Studied Sensuality'' by Laurie S. Hurwitz in *American Artist*, vol. 57, no. 615, October 1993; ''Wayne Thiebaud's Jackpot Machine'' by Jonathan P. Binstock in *American Art*, vol. 10, no. 2, Summer 1996; ''A Painter's Alchemy'' by Richard Wollheim in *Modern Painters* (London), vol. 11, no. 2, Summer 1998; ''Wayne's World'' by Bill Berkson in *Modern Painters* (London), vol. 11, no. 2, Summer 1998; ''Wayne Thiebaud: Green River Lands, 1998'' by Richard Wollheim in *Artforum*, vol. 38, no. 2, October 1999; ''Two Pops'' by Peter Plagens in *Artforum*, vol. 38, no. 10, Summer 2000.

* * *

When Wayne Thiebaud showed his urban landscapes for the first time at the San Francisco Museum of Modern Art in 1978, the question of an essentialization ultimately leading to non-objectivity came to mind. Viewed in the context of both the prevalent trends in California art and the artist's candid acknowledgement of the influence of Richard Diebenkorn's landscapes of the 1960s, the cubes, the columns, the simplified architectonic compositions, the flat crosses, the patterns carried out in rhythmic repetitions of color seemed prophetic of a direction toward absolute abstraction. But Thiebaud's strong realist orientation proved too emphatic an impulse, and it is now obvious that the simplified forms were not indicative of a reductive sensibility, but instruments of exploration into the realist idiom. ''Reduction in a realist painting is the same as reducing a sauce,'' he explains. ''You take away by simplification, by leaving out details. But you also put in selective bits of other experiences, or perceptual nuances which enforce it, giving it more of a multi-dimension than if it were done directly as a visual recording.''

Thiebaud emerged on the New York art scene in the early 1960s, when the Pop movement was beginning to be recognized as the new acceptable form of American art. He did not participate in the movement, but, because of his predilection for mundane subject matter (pinball machines, dime store lipsticks, bakery and delicatessen foodstuff), he has, at times, been identified as a Pop artist. The association was fortuitous, however, for Thiebaud's choice of imagery was then, as it is today, predicated upon formal concerns rather than identification with specific objects. An avowed realist whose roots are steeped in tradition, he is best characterized as heir to such masters as Vermeer, Chardin, and Thomas Eakins for whom the creation of a painting involved hours of scrutinizing an object in order to arrive at stylistic individualization. ''For me, realist painting is an alive confrontation,'' he says. ''If you stare at an object, as you do when you paint, there is no point at which you can stop learning things about it. You can just look and look, and, if you really are a realist painter, you finally realize that what you are doing is a tremendous amount of adoption, adaptation, and change.''

''Adopting, adapting, and changing''—his subjects according to the tenants of 20th Century modernism is precisely what Thiebaud has been doing for almost 30 years. With the sure eye of a modernist, he has transformed cakes into circles, still-lifes and figures into arrangements of spheres, triangles, and cylinders with the same alacrity that he is, today, translating street panoramas into compositions in which arcs, cubes, and complex networks of diagonal and rectangular lines play a sophisticated game of dialectic between geometry and realism.

With the urban landscapes, however, Wayne Thiebaud has reached a new zenith. In many respects, they build on earlier Thiebaud forms and concepts, but they also bring to his vocabulary a new dramatic dimension—a feeling of pressure, a compaction, of vertigo that effect the framework of his pictorial space. In this sense, they come to the forefront of his oeuvre, and represent the utmost in the resolution of that special tension between modernism and tradition that has been his trademark since the very beginning of his career.

The retrospective that premiered at the San Francisco Museum of Modern Art in September 1985 confirmed Thiebaud's unflagging commitment to a modern traditionalist aesthetic. When asked to explain what motivated such new ''dark paintings'' as *Black Shoes and Dark Lipstick,* (1983), he replied that they were prompted by ''looking at dark paintings done by a great many artists.'' Rembrandt, Goya, Whistler, Balthus were among those from whom he sought counsel, and if the results prove that the lessons were well learned, they also unveil an energized pictorial repertoire—reinforcing Thiebaud's often acknowledged opinion that art can never be re-invented, only refreshed through constant practice and experimentation.

Sometimes the experimentation is of a technical nature, such as the manipulation of acrylic and oil paints to create new surface characters and formulations. ''If you wash into oil,'' he explains, ''the surface of the paint is being dissolved all the time. On the other hand, the acrylic dries and creates those terrific washes you can rework with oil, and then use the underpainting combined with oil paint later on.'' Such manipulations strengthened the artist's landscape idiom by changing what he feels were ''pictorially dominant compositions into visual reconstructions of such forces of nature as feelings of light, texture, rutting—thus adding structural factors to the framework of Thiebaud's dramatic vocabulary.

But the significance of the retrospective overrides considerations of style and content. A California painter of major standing, Thiebaud has been channeled into as many movements, modes, and characterizations as there are essays written about his work by critics and art historians. Pop Art and New Realism have been cited as peer groups, and a rich complex interpretative menu of his aesthetic has been offered as possible identifications of his oeuvre. What the perspective of some 23 years suggested, however, is a novel interpretation which, based upon the artist's repeatedly stated views of his forms, brings into focus the theme of abstraction as the one consistent thread that unifies, and thus gives identity, to the entire body of his work. To be sure, it is evident that realism is a dominant element; but the picture that emerged out of the retrospective is one in which the term ''realism'' is translated into abstraction: abstraction as reduction or essentialization; abstraction as an alteration of reality; abstraction as a conceptualized force of realism; abstraction as one source of illusionism. In short, abstraction in all but the non-objective sense of the word.

—Andree Marechal-Workman

In 2000 Wayne Thiebaud's eightieth birthday was celebrated by a wide-ranging retrospective at the San Francisco Art Museum. It featured recent landscapes of San Francisco, the Sacramento Valley and the Sierra foothills as well as his familiar presentations of edibles (''Cakes,'' for example) characterized by an intensity of light and color and rich paint handling, and a selection of figure paintings in which the subjects remain enigmatic, non-revealing, as in a still life.

In keeping with the artist's statement that there is really little difference in the problem set by still life, figure painting or landscape—a question of lighting and space—all three categories involve that same distancing, that balance between realism and abstraction, which was present in his early object paintings. The landscapes, a major part of the retrospective, avoid predictability, as is Thiebaud's aim, by restructuring—creating closeknit proximities, forward tilting planes of meadows or roads or San Francisco's plunging streets which, in a more orthodox perspective would recede toward the horizon—object paintings of the world. By this means he succeeds, by concentrating on the particular, by absenting the subject from "big ideas," in painting themes from the American experience which are themselves a big idea.

—Barbara Cortright

TILLERS, Imants

Nationality: Australian. **Born:** Sydney, New South Wales, 30 July 1950. **Education:** Studied architecture, Sydney University, 1969–72, B.S. (with honors) in architecture. **Family:** Married Jennifer Slayter in 1974; daughters: Isidore and Saskia. **Career:** Independent painter, Sydney, since 1969; assisted artist Christo on *Wrapped Coast* project, Sydney 1969; first solo exhibition 1973. **Awards:** University Architecture Medal, Sydney University, 1973; Grand Prize, Osaka Painting Triennale, Japan. **Agent:** Sherman Galleries, 16–18 Goodhope Street, Paddington 2021 Australia. **Address:** 66 Raglan Street, Mosman 2088, New South Wales 2088, Australia.

Individual Exhibitions:

1973 Watters Gallery, Sydney
1983 Yuill/Crowley Gallery, Sydney
Matt's Gallery, London
1984 Yuill/Crowley Gallery, Sydney
Bess Cutler Gallery, Sydney
1985 Yuill/Crowley Gallery, Sydney
Bess Cutler Gallery, New York
1986 Yuill/Crowley Gallery, Sydney
Biennale, Venice
1987 Queensland Art Gallery, Brisbane
Australian Centre for Contemporary Art, Melbourne
Art Gallery of South Australia, Adelaide
Reed College, Portland, Oregon
Bess Cutler Gallery, New York
Galerie Susan Wyss, Zurich
Yuill/Crowley Gallery, Sydney
1988 Institute of Contemporary Arts, London
Bess Cutler Gallery, New York
Yuill/Crowley Gallery, Sydney
National Gallery of Victoria, Melbourne
Wellington Art Gallery, New Zealand
1989 National Art Gallery, Wellington
Bess Cutler Gallery, New York
1993 National Museum of Art, Riga, Latvia (retrospective)
Institute of Modern Art, Brisbane
1994 Sherman Goodhope Gallery, Sydney
1995 *Imants Tillers: Via Paradiso,* Karyn Lovegrove Gallery, Prahran, Australia (catalog)

Selected Group Exhibitions:

1973 *Object and Idea,* National Gallery of Victoria, Melbourne
1975 *Bienal,* Sao Paulo
1979 *Biennale,* Sydney
1982 *Documenta 7,* Kassel, Germany
1984 *An Australian Accent,* Project Studio One, New York (travelled to Washington, D.C.; Perth; Sydney)
1987 *State of the Art,* Institute of Contemporary Arts, London
1993 *Painting Triennale,* Osaka, Japan
1994 *International Art Festival,* Seoul
Antipodean Currents, Kennedy Center, Washington, D.C.
Virtual Reality, National Gallery of Australia, Canberra (catalog)
1995 *Diaspora in Context,* Pori Art Museum, Finland (travelled to Wellington, New Zealand, and Sydney)
In Tandem, Sherman Galleries Goodhope, Paddington, Australia (catalog)
1996 *Under Capricorn: The World Over—Art in the Age of Globalisation,* City Gallery, Wellington (also Stedelijk Museum, Amsterdam) (catalog)
1998 *Australian Prints from the Gallery's Collection,* Art Gallery of New South Wales, Sydney (catalog)
1999 *Approaching Decoration,* Museum of Contemporary Art

Collections:

Art Gallery of New South Wales, Sydney; National Gallery of Victoria, Melbourne; Metropolitan Museum, New York; National Gallery of Australia, Canberra; Museum of Contemporary Art, Sydney; Osaka Cultural Foundation, Japan; National Museum of Art, Riga, Latvia; Museum of New Zealand, Wellington; Auckland City Art Gallery, Auckland.

Publications:

By TILLERS: Articles—"Poetic Justice—A Case Study" in *Midwest,* no. 5, 1994; "Tillers Talks" with Evelyn Juers in *Art Monthly Australia,* no. 71, July 1994.

On TILLERS: Books—*Imants Tillers: White Aborigines,* exhibition catalog with text by Paul Taylor, London 1983; *An Australian Accent* by Daniel Thomas, Jonathon Fineberg and Alanna Heiss, Sydney 1984; *Imants Tillers: Venice Biennale 1986, Australia,* exhibition catalog edited by Kerry Crowley, Sydney 1986; *Australian Appropriations: Recent Paintings of Imants Tillers,* exhibition catalog with essay by John S. Weber, Portland 1987; *State of Art: Ideas and Images in the 1980s* by Sandy Nairne, London 1987; *Imants Tillers,* exhibition catalog with text by Stuart Morgan, London 1988; *Diaspora,* with text by Pierre Restany, Jennifer Slayter, and Bernice Murphy, Sydney 1993; *The Antipodean Mirror* by Graham Coulter-Smith, Brisbane 1994; *Imants Tillers and the "Book of Power"* by Wystan Curnow, Sydney 1995. **Articles—**"Words of Wisdom: A Special Project by Imants Tillers" in *Art and Australia,* vol. 26, no. 1, 1988; "Imants Tillers as a Site of Conflict" in *Art and Australia,* vol. 27, no. 3, 1990; "Imants Tillers" by S. O'Connell in *Art & Text,* no. 37,

1990; ''Imants Tillers: Paradiso'' by Colin Shingleton in *Agenda,* no. 43, July 1995.

TILLIM, Sidney

Nationality: American. **Born:** Brooklyn, New York, 16 June 1925. **Education:** Studied at the College of Fine Arts, Syracuse University, New York, 1946–50, B.F.A. 1950. **Military Service:** Served in Engineer Corps, United States Army, 1943–46. **Family:** Married Muriel Sharon in 1956 (died 1996); married Diane Radycki, 1998. **Career:** Independent artist since 1950, known for historical, narrative painting, and, more recently, abstract works; lives and works in New York. Contributing editor, *Arts Magazine,* New York, 1959–65; contributing editor, *Artforum,* New York, 1965–69. Instructor, Parsons School of Designs, New York, 1961–63; instructor, Pratt Institute, Brooklyn, New York, 1964–68; instructor, Bennington College, Vermont, 1966–1993. **Awards:** Yaddo Fellowship, Saratoga Springs, New York, 1963; National Endownment for the Arts Grant, 1975; painting grant, Ingram-Merrill Foundation, 1976; Pollock-Krasner Grant in Painting, 1990; John Simon Guggenheim Memorial Foundation Fellowship, Painting, 1995. **Address:** 166 E. 96th St., Apt. 12B, New York, NY 10128, U.S.A.

Individual Exhibitions:

1960 Cober Gallery, New York
1965 Robert Schoelkopf Gallery, New York
1967 Robert Schoelkopf Gallery, New York
1969 Georgia State College, Atlanta
Noah Goldowsky Gallery, New York
1970 Benson Gallery, Bridgehampton, New York
1973 Edmonton Art Gallery, Alberta
1974 Noah Goldowsky Gallery, New York
1976 Edmonton Art Gallery, Alberta
1977 Tibor de Nagy Gallery, New York
1979 Meredith Long Gallery, New York
1986 Bennington College, Vermont
1990 Perimeter Gallery, Chicago
Galerie Burgis Geismann, Cologne
1993 Tenri Gallery, New York; Galerie Vorsetzen, Hamburg
1996 Trans-Hudson Gallery, New York
1998 Trans-Hudson Gallery, New York

Selected Group Exhibitions:

1972 *Whitney Annual,* Whitney Museum, New York
1975 *Modern Views of George Washington,* New Jersey State Museum, Trenton
1980 *Realism and Metaphor,* University of South Florida, Tampa
1984 *American Still Life 1945–83,* Contemporary Arts Museum, Houston
1988 *Numerators,* John Good Gallery, New York
1991 *18 aus New York,* Galerie Lohrl, Monchengladbach
1992 *Slow Art,* P.S. 1 Museum, Long Island City, New York
1993 *Die Arena des Privaten,* Kunstverein, Munich
Andre Zarre Gallery, New York
1994 Helen M.C. Severn Gallery, New York
1996 RE-FAB: Painting Abstracted, Fabricated, and Revised, Contemporary Art Museum, University of South Florida, Tampa

Collections:

Dana Art Center, Colgate University, Hamilton, New York; New Jersey State Museum, Trenton; Hirshhorn Museum, Washington, D.C.; City Art Museum, St. Louis; Weatherspoon Art Gallery, University of North Carolina, Greensboro; University of New Hampshire; Edmonton Art Gallery, Alberta; Modern Museum of Art, Vienna

Publications:

By TILLIM: Books—*Richard Lindner,* Chicago 1960. **Articles—** ''Notes on Narrative and History Painting'' in *Sidney Tillim,* exhibition catalog, Hamilton, New York 1973, revised version in *Artforum* (New York), May 1977; ''The Ideal and the Literal Sublime'' in *Artforum* (New York), May 1976; ''Benjamin Reconsidered: The Work of Art After the Age of Mechanical Reproduction'' in *Artforum* (New York), May 1983; ''The Modest Greatness of Julio Gonzales'' in *Art in America* (New York), October 1983; ''The View from Past 50'' in *Artforum* (New York), May 1984; ''Abstraction Revisited'' in *Art in America* (New York), April 1986; ''Criticism and Culture, or Greenberg's Doubt'' in *Art in America* (New York), May 1987; ''Photography and Remembrance (Helen Levitt),'' *Artforum,* December 1991; essay in *The Work of Art in the Age of Mechanical Representation,* exhibition catalog, Bennington College, Vermont, 1992; ''Art as Photography'' *American Craft,* October/November 1993; ''The Academy, Post-Modernism and the Education of the Artist'' in *Art in America,* April 1999.

On TILLIM: Books—*Neue Formen des Realismus* by Peter Sager, Cologne 1973; *Sidney Tillim,* exhibition catalog by Terry Fenton, Edmonton, Alberta 1973; *Artist Choose Artist,* exhibition catalog with essay by Max Kozloff, New York 1986; *Sidney Tillim,* exhibition catalog with essay by Uli Bohnen, Hamburg 1993; *RE-FAB,* exhibition catalog, Tampa 1996. **Articles—**review by Donald Judd in *Arts Magazine* (New York), November 1960; review by Dennis Adrian in *Artforum* (New York), September 1967; ''Unconventional Realists'' by Gabriel Laderman in *Artforum* (New York), November 1967; ''22 Realists at the Whitney Museum'' by Douglas Davis in *Newsweek* (New York), February 1970; ''Neuer Realismus'' in *Der Spiegel* (Hamburg), August 1970; review by Jed Perl and Deborah Rosenthal in *Arts Magazine* (New York), January 1980; review by Gerrit Henry in *Art in America* (New York), January 1980; ''The Representational Impulse'' by Jed Perl in *The New Criterion* (New York), April 1985; interview in *Arts Magazine* (New York), December 1987; review by Tom Breidenbach in *Artforum* (New York), September 1998; review by Paul Mattick, Jr. in *Art in America* (New York), July 1997; review by Ken Johnson in *New York Times,* 27 March 1998.

*

To an artist all that matters when his work is written about is praise. He will accept criticism if that's all he can get. But praise is better. People used to be interested (in the late 1960s and early 1970s especially) in my painting because I also wrote a lot of criticism. I was painting figuratively then. I learned that no matter what you painted or wrote, it was very important to have the right—one might say correct—dealer. Bob Schoelkopf was a nice man, but it was Dick Bellamy who sold me—to Michener, Hirshhorn, Ludwig, etc. I resumed an abstract style 21 years ago but it wasn't until 1987 that it began to gel; but now, I think, age has entered the exhibition picture. If you can't be young or, as they say, an emerging artist, today you count a lot on friends and philanthropy. I've been lucky in both respects, but I'd rather be famous. P.S. I resumed painting in a figurative, narrative style in 1998.

—Sidney Tillim

* * *

After abandoning his beginnings as a geometric abstract painter more than 15 years ago, Sidney Tillim proceeded to develop a kind of stylized representationalism. In his still-lifes of the 1960s Tillim painted random arrangements in close-up, cropped compositions which reveal connection with the photographic as antecedent. Like Lowell Nesbitt, Tillim opted for firm, unbroken contours and cooly descriptive surfaces. Next came a range of figure pictures dealing with the artist's childhood and family life. In ''A Dream of Being'' (1968–69), crisp, simplified, caricaturized figures are arranged in a highly formalized composition, caught in a moment of frozen activity which suggests a modern-day allegorical theme about the passage of time and life. Next, Tillim began making paintings of more generally historical themes, his subject including early history of the United States, the Jews and the Bible. He underwent a campaign to help revive the genre of epic history painting and became known as a social historian during the 1970s. Often compared with Puvis de Chavannes and Nicolas Poussin, Tillim rejected modernist canons of picture making, emphasizing communication of the narrative by negating the painterly handwriting of the expressionist artist. He created complex compositions filled with arrested action aimed at heightening the drama of an often violent moment from past history or historic myth. Of his intentions in such pictures Tillim has noted, ''History painting gambles more recklessly than most on the problem of converting tastes to its point of view.'' His choices of particular themes were, according to his own statements, predicated on their relevance for the present moment, and it is this symbolic and psychological connection which he wants to convey without using methods of contemporary art. Considering the desire for subjects analogous with the present, it is not surprising to find Tillim also painting themes taken from the movies and from media accounts of current events.

What is surprising is Tillim's switch in 1978–79 from anti-modernist representation to a more abstracted stylization which resembles Cubism and Vorticism. In this new work, Tillim continues to deal with social themes, now depicting them in an angular, jagged planar structuring with openly agitated brush-strokes. It is a turnaround which seems well suited for subjects such as ''The Capture of Patti Hearst,'' ''An American Tragedy'' (Norman Mailer's knife attack on his wife at a party), and ''Murder Hollywood Style'' (scene from the movie *The Big Sleep*). In many of the pictures from this group, the vantage point is downward on an angle to view a series of overlapping triangular planes. The sharpness and frenetic energy of the rather summary stylization works well to enhance the frenetic emotiveness of the subject matter, and Tillim's confrontation with modernism in such a personal form has brought with it a rewarding effectiveness.

Among the qualities which persist throughout Tillim's development are stylizations for dramatic effect and satirical edge. In these and others ways Tillim can be compared with the American magic and Social Realists who developed during the 1930s and 1940s. Tillim's earlier works resemble the figural stylizations of George Tooker or Peter Cadmus, and it is not unenlightening to see his newer pictures in comparison with a painter such as Ben Shahn, or even with the painter of an earlier ''American Tragedy,'' Phillip Evergood.

—Barbara Cavaliere

TILSON, Joe

Nationality: British. **Born:** London, 24 August 1928. **Education:** Studied with Frank Auerbach and Leon Kossoff, St. Martin's School of Art, London, 1949–52; Royal College of Art, London 1652–55, A.R.C.A. 1955. **Military Service:** Served in the Royal Air Force, 1946–49. **Family:** Married Joslyn Morton in 1956; children: Jake, Anna and Sophy. **Career:** Worked as carpenter and joiner, London, 1944–46. Independent artist: in Italy and Spain, 1955–57; in London, 1958–72 and in Christian Malford, Wiltshire, and Italy, since 1972. Instructor, St. Martin's School of Art, London, 1958–63; Visiting lecturer, University of Durham, Newcastle upon Tyne, 1962–63; instructor, School of Visual Arts, New York, 1966; visiting lecturer, Staatliche Hochschule für Bildende Künste, Hamburg, 1971–72. **Awards:** Knapping Foundation Prize, London, 1955; Rome Prize, 1955; Painting Prize, *John Moores Exhibition,* Liverpool, 1957, 1967; Painting Prize, *Gulbenkian Foundation Exhibition,* London, 1960; Gold Medal, *Biennale,* San Marino, 1963; Print Prize, *Exposition Internationale de Gravure,* Ljubljana, 1965, 1967, 1975, 1977, 1979, 1983; Grand Prize, *Graphics Biennale,* Krakow, 1974; First Prize, Bradford Print Biennale, 1984; Grand Prix d'Honneur, *16th Biennale de la Gravure, Luibliana,* 1985. **Agent:** Alan Cristea Gallery, 31 Cork Street, London W1X2NU, Great Britain. **Address:** 93 Bourne Street, London SW1W 8HF, Great Britain.

Individual Exhibitions:

1962 Marlborough New London Gallery
1963 Hatton Gallery, Newcastle upon Tyne
Ferens Art Gallery, Hull
Walker Art Gallery, Liverpool
University of Nottingham
1964 Marlborough New London Gallery
1966 Marlborough Graphics, New York
Marlborough New London Gallery
1967 Galleria del Naviglio, Milan
Galleria del Deposito, Genoa
Galleria Fiori, Montecatini, Italy
Marlborough-Gerson Gallery, New York
Galleria Marlborough, Rome
1968 Galleria Ferrari, Verona
Galleria de'Foscherari, Bologna
Galerie Brusberg, Hannover
1970 Marlborough New London Gallery
Hausam Waldsee, West Berlin (with Gerd Winner)
1971 CAYC: Centro de Arte y Comunicacion, Buenos Aires

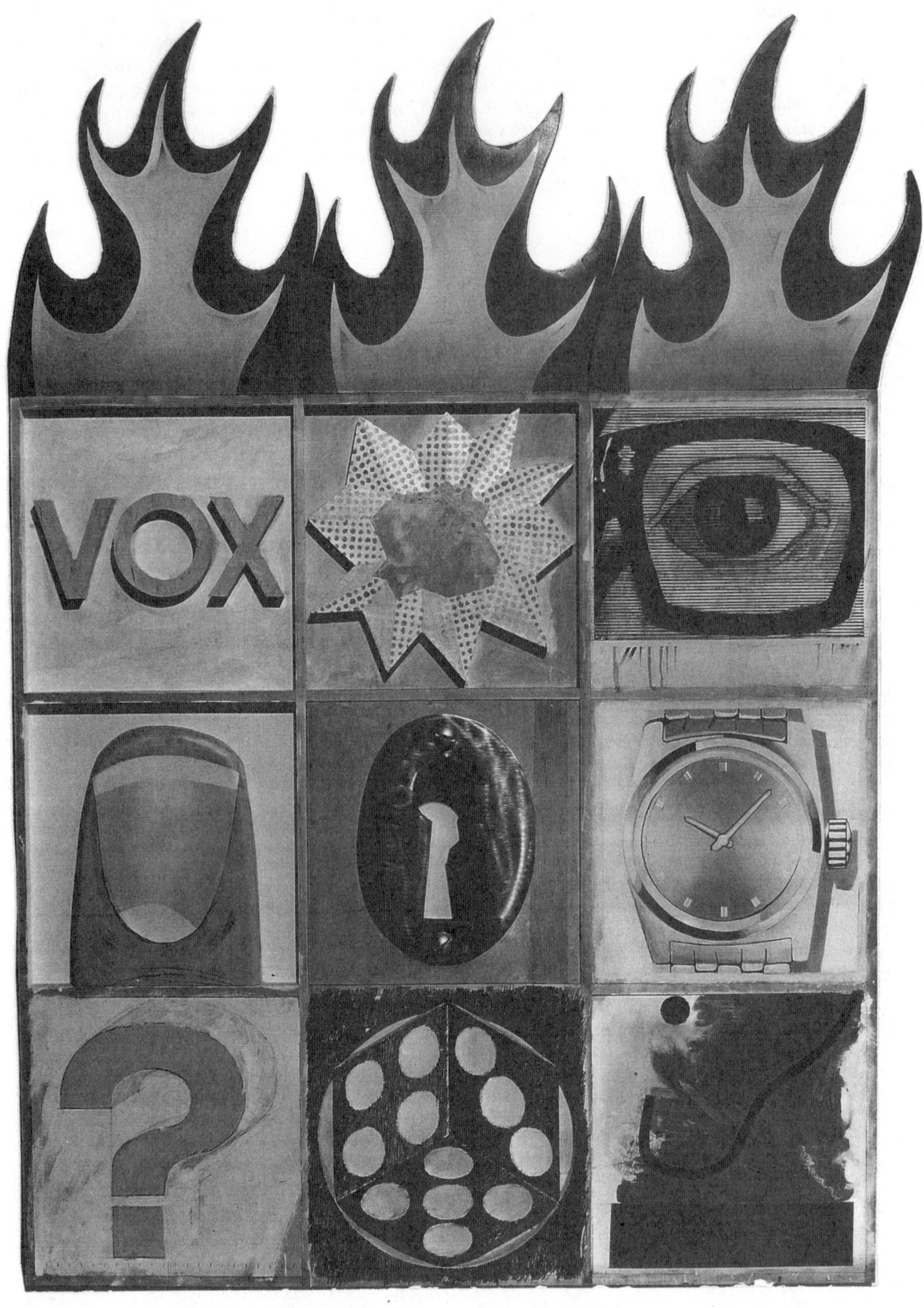

Joe Tilson: *Nine Elements,* 1963. ©2001 Artists Rights Society (ARS), NY/DACS, London.

Waddington Galleries, London
1972 Abrams Gallery, Amsterdam (with Juan Genoves)
Galerie René Block, West Berlin
1973 Museum Boymans-van Beuningen, Rotterdam (retrospective)
1974 Musée Royal des Beaux-Arts, Antwerp
Galerie von Loeper, Hamburg
University of Parma, Italy (retrospective)
1975 Studio Marconi, Milan
Galleria Marlborough, Rome
Galleria del Cavallino, Venice
1976 Galerie Espace, Amsterdam
Galleria Il Chiodo, Mantua, Italy
Galleria Il Tritone, Biella, Italy
Marlborough Fine Art, London
Galerija Kryzsztofory, Cracow, Poland
Galleria Corsini, Intra, Italy
1977 Galleria Rizzardi, Milan
Galleria La Chiocciola, Padua
Galleria A. Parma, Italy
1978 Waddington-Tooth Galleries, London
Tate Gallery, London
Peterloo Gallery, Manchester
Galleria Giuli, Lecco, Italy
1979 Waddington Galleries, London
Van Straaten Gallery, Chicago
Clark Gallery, Boston
Aronson Gallery, Atlanta
Edward Tohta Gallery, London
Vancouver Art Gallery (graphics retrospective)
1980 Galerie Espace, Amsterdam
De Vries ond Roeloff, Rotterdam
Erica Williams/Ann Johnsons Gallery, Seattle
Horwitch Gallery, Scottsdale, Arizona
Galleri 22, Aarthus, Denmark
Gumps Gallery, San Francisco
Hokin Gallery, Miami
1981 Fitterman Gallery, Minneapolis
Meridan House, Washington, D.C.
University of Maryland, College Park
Schneeback Gallery, Cincinnati, Ohio
Galerie Mira Godard, Toronto (travelled to Mira Godard Gallery, Calgary)
Galleria Il Chiodo, Mantua, Italy
Galleria Il Sole, Bolzano, Italy
1982 Galleria Meta, Florence
Galleria Adelfi, Padua
University of Pittsburgh
Joseph Wolpe Gallery, Cape Town
Natalie Knight Gallery, Johannesburg
Galerie Kammer, Hamburg
1983 Galleria d'Arte, Voltera, Italy
Thorden Wetterling Gallery, Goteborg, Sweden
Galleria Dabbeni, Lugano, Switzerland
Galleria Menghelli, Florence
Galleria Rotta, Genoa, Italy
1984 Galleria Nazzari, Parma, Italy
Arnolfini Gallery, Bristol, Avon
1985 Galleria del Cavallino, Venice
1987 Art Museum of Luibliana, Yugoslavia (retrospective)
Thorden Gallery, Goteborg, Sweden
1988 *Joe Tilson: Recent Works, 1985–7,* Waddington Galleries, London
1990 *Joe Tilson: Prints 1989–90,* Waddington Graphics, London
1991 *Joe Tilson: A Light from Eleusis,* Tour Fromage, Aosta, Italy
1992 *Joe Tilson: Works, 1961–1991,* Waddington Gallery, London
1995 *Le Crete senesi,* Theo Waddington Fine Art, London
1997 *Sandra Blow RA—Joe Tilson RA: Eight Works 1956–1967,* Julian Hartnoll Gallery, London
1998 *"Conjunctions" by Joe Tilson,* Theo Waddington Fine Art, London

Selected Group Exhibitions:

1961 *Biennale,* Paris
1964 *Biennale,* Venice
1965 *Op and Pop,* Moderna Museet, Stockholm
1969 *Pop Art,* Hayward Gallery, London
1976 *Pop Art in England,* Kunstverein, Hamburg
1979 *Photography in Printmaking,* Victoria and Albert Museum, London
1981 *Landscape,* Tate Gallery, London
1983 *Pintura Britanica Contemporanea,* Museo Municipal, Madrid
1985 *Modern Artists' Books,* Victoria and Albert Museum, London
1987 *Pop Art USA/UK,* Metropolitan Museum, Tokyo (travelled to Osaka, Funabashi and Yokohama)
1990 *British Prints of the 1960s and 1970s from the Collection of Tony Reichardt,* Art Gallery of New South Wales, Sydney
1997 *Hockney to Hodgkin: British Master Prints 1960–1980,* New Orleans Museum of Art, Louisiana
1999 *Signature Pieces: Contemporary British Prints and Multiples,* Alan Cristea Gallery, London

Collections:

Tate Gallery, London; Victoria and Albert Museum, London; Stedelijk Museum, Amsterdam; Museum Boymans-van Beuningen, Rotterdam; Musée Royal des Beaux-Arts, Antwerp; Kunstmuseum, Hannover; Galleria Nazionale d'Art Moderna, Rome; National Gallery of South Africa, Johannesburg; National Gallery of Australia, Canberra; Museum of Modern Art, New York.

Publications:

By TILSON: Books—*A-Z Box, Fragments of an Oneiric Alphabet,* London 1970; *Alchera: Notes for Country Works,* London 1976; *Alchera: 1970–76,* Pollenza, Italy 1977; *Wessex,* Pollenza, Italy 1977; *Alchera: Joe Tilson,* exhibition catalog, London 1978; *Joe Tilson: Proscinemi, Oracles,* exhibition catalog, London 1978; *Hesiod's Crown,* London 1984; *Joe Tilson: Festivals,* London 1987.

On TILSON: Books—*Collage* by Harriet Janis and Rudi Blesh, New York 1962; *Contemporary British Art* by Herbert Read, London 1964; *The Painter and the Photograph: From Delacroix to Warhol* by

Van Deren Coke, Albuquerque, New Mexico 1964, 1972; *Pop as Art* by Mario Amaya, London 1965; *Pop Art* by Lawrence Alloway and Lucy Lippard, London 1966; *Pop Art Redefined* by John Russell and Suzi Gablik, London 1969; *Pop Art* by Michael Compton, London, New York, Sydney and Toronto 1970; *Tilson: Winner,* exhibition catalog with text by Thomas Kempas, West Berlin 1970; *Eroticism in Contemporary Art* by Volker Kahmen, London 1970; *The Moderns* by Terry Measham, London 1976; *Pop Art in England,* exhibition catalog with text by Uwe M. Schneede, Hamburg 1976; *Arte Inglese Oggi 1960–1976,* exhibition catalog by Norbert Lynton, 2 vols., London and Milan 1976; *Tilson* by Arturo C. Quintavalle with a preface by Pierre Restany, Milan 1977; *Understanding Prints* by Pat Gilmour, London 1979; *Photography in Printmaking* by Charles Newton, London 1979; *Joe Tilson: Graphics,* exhibition catalog with text by Pat Gilmour, Vancouver 1979; *Maestri Contemporanei: Tilson* by Gillo Dorfles and Michael Compton, Milan 1982; *Joe Tilson: Recent Work, 1985–7,* exhibition catalog, London 1988; *Joe Tilson: Prints 1989–90,* exhibition catalog, London 1990; *Joe Tilson: A Light from Eleusis,* exhibition catalog with text by Antonio Del Guercio, Milan 1991; *Le Crete senesi,* exhibition catalog with text by Marco Livingstone, London 1995; *Tilson* by Michael Compton and Marco Livingstone, Milan 1995; *Sandra Blow RA—Joe Tilson RA: Eight Works 1956–1967,* exhibition catalog, London 1997; *''Conjunctions'' by Joe Tilson at Theo Waddington Fine Art,* London 1998. **Articles—**''Joe Tilson: nell'antro degli dei'' by Luciano Caprile in *Arte,* vol. 19, no. 202, December 1989; ''From Hiroshige to Hamilton, from Turner to Tilson'' by Tessa Sidey in *Printmaking Today,* vol. 7, no. 4, Winter 1998.

* * *

Joe Tilson is a rare example, among British artists, of a multimedia creator, not tied to technique or material, yet always able to stamp the mark of his personality and inventive constructivist manner on all his work.

In general terms it is probably easiest to label him a Pop artist, since it is clear that what motivates his creative juices is the stimulation of everyday, urban, industrial society. On the other hand, he could be labelled a landscapist, with the proviso that what arrests his attention and inspires his art is the landscape of the modern city and its decorative addenda. In essence this is a non-analytical or non-critical stance; Tilson does not judge modern society and the physical or moral forms of life it produces. He is a traditionalist in the sense that the English landscape poets or painters looked at nature, analyzed its forms, produced and perfected the means of producing images based on this phenomena, and thereby expressed their relationship with nature. There was no question of ''criticizing'' nature, since it is a non-criticizable force. Modern industrial society is, however, open to criticism or disapproval, but it is also there to be observed, to be analyzed formally, to be used as the basis of design and art.

Pop artists are not critics or philosophers; they are poets. Tilson, in fact, can be compared with the Italian metaphysical painters, with de Chirico in particular, sharing their detachment from the symbols they chose in order to express a state of mind or spirit. Thus when Tilson builds a column of wooden blocks, whose four sides all bear the word ''Yes,'' he is both creating a plastic form, a sculpture, and also a combination of fact and abstraction which is concerned with everyday life, yet which mysteriously, even perhaps mystically, stands apart from it. Tilson, in fact, spent two years in Italy, in the late 1950s and has maintained connections with the country.

Tilson is a member of a remarkable generation of English artists who were connected with the Institute of Contemporary Arts in London when the critic Lawrence Alloway, and artists such as Richard Hamilton and Eduardo Paolozzi were attempting to work out the relationship of art to life and the public. These artists included Peter Blake, Ron Kitaj, Peter Phillips and David Hockney. The intellectual and stylistic example of Hamilton, and the brilliant inventiveness of Paolozzi, led to the special English branch of Pop-art, long before the emergence of the American brand; the younger artists, many of whom visited United States as students and teachers, created a bridge between the continents.

Tilson, as indeed his English contemporaries, whilst impressed and affected by the remarkable American generation of Pop artists, retained his own individuality. This is compounded by a love and use of words as symbols equally useful and powerful as images, as well as the incorporation of geometrical and three-dimensional forms as extensions of flat surfaces. He is catholic in the use of materials, used uniquely or in combination—wood, plastics, painted surfaces, photographic images, collage, screen printing, etc. As well as the abstract insertion of single words, or the serialized image of the eye, Tilson reproduces newspaper photographs, pages from magazines, references to contemporary events, as well as details of famous works of art. None of this is erratic or chance; Tilson is careful and positive in his choice and juxtaposition of components, even if, to the viewer, it is a total effect, either of form, images, or even verbal messages, rather than an immediately understood philosophy, which makes its impact. Probably Tilson's finest gift is for public communication, evident in the murals he has constructed in different parts of the world.

—Charles Spencer

TINDLE, David

Nationality: British. **Born:** Hudderfield, Yorkshire, 29 April 1932. **Education:** Coventry, Warwickshire public school; studied at the Coventry School of Art, 1945–46. **Family:** Married Janet F. Trollope in 1969 (divorced, 1992); children: Saskia, Charlotte and Nathan. **Career:** Painter; in London, 1951–56; in Arboath and Wantage, 1956–58; in London, 1959–64; in Brome, Suffolk, 1964–66; in London, 1966–69; in East Hadden, Northamptonshire, 1969–80; in Clipston, Leicesetershire, 1980–86; in Leamington Spa, Warwickshire, since 1986; moved to France, 1990. Lecturer, Hornsey College of Art and Byam Shaw School of Painting, London, 1959–74. Part-time lecturer, Royal College of Art, London, 1972–83. **Awards:** Painting Prize, *Chichester National Art Exhibition,* Sussex, 1975. Associate, 1973, Royal Academician, 1979, Royal Academy of Art, London; associate, 1973, fellow, 1981, and honorary fellow, 1984, Royal College of Art, London; Ruskin Master of Drawing and Fine Art, Oxford University, 1985. **Agent:** Fischer Fine Art, 49 Carlton Hill, London NW8 OEL; Redfern Gallery, 20 Cork Street, London W1X 2HL. **Address:** 4 rue Naude, 56160 Guémené sur Scorff, Morbihan, France.

Individual Exhibitions:

1954 Piccadilly Gallery, London (and regularly 1954–83)
Crane Gallery, Manchester, England
1957 City Art Gallery, Coventry, England

57 Gallery, Edinburgh
1958 Stone Gallery, Newcastle upon Tyne, England
1961 *New Painting,* Bear Lane Gallery, Oxford
1963 Metropole Gallery, Folkestone, England
1964 Galerie du Tours, San Francisco (travelled to Galerie du Tour, Los Angeles)
1965 Metropole Gallery, Folkestone, Kent
1968 Galleria Carbonesi, Bologna
Galleria Vinciana, Milan
1970 27 Gallery, Northampton
1972 City Art Gallery, Northampton (retrospective)
1974 Galerie XX, Hamburg
1977 Galerie XX, Hamburg
1980 Galerie XX, Hamburg
1985 Fischer Fine Art, London
Galerie XX, Hamburg
1989 Fischer Fine Art, London
1992 Fischer Fine Art, London
Alresford Gallery, Alresford
1994 Redfern Gallery, London
St. Edmund Hall, Oxford University
Shires Hall, Staffordshire
1996 Redfern Gallery, London
1998 Redfern Gallery, London
1999 Redfern Gallery, London

Selected Group Exhibitions:

1958 *International Biennale of Realist Art,* Bruges, Belguim
1959 *John Moore's Exhibition,* Liverpool (and 1961)
1967 *Mostra Mercate d'Arte Contemporenea,* Florence
Salon de la Jeune Peinture, Paris
Internationale Biennale of Realist Art, Bologna
1974 *British Painting 74,* Hayward Gallery, London
1975 *Art 6'75,* Kunstmesse, Basel
1977 *British Painting 1952–77,* Royal Academy of Art, London
1979 *The British Art Show,* toured Britain
1989 *Portrait of the Artist,* Tate Gallery, London
Picturing People: British Figurative Art Since 1945, National Art Gallery, Kuala Lumpur (travelled to Hong Kong Museum of Art; Empress Palace, Singapore)
1990 Royal Academy of Arts, London
1991 *A Group Exhibition of Contemporary Paintings and Bronzes,* Stowe-on-the-World
The Absent Presence, Graves Art Gallery, Sheffield and Geffrye Museum, London
1992 Fischer Fine Art, London
1996 *London in Paint: Oil Paintings in the Collection at the Museum of London,* London
1997 *The Discerning Eye,* The Mall Galleries, London

Collections:

Tate Gallery, London; Arts Council of Great Britain, London; London Museum; Arts Council of Northern Ireland, Belfast; National Portrait Galley, London; Royal Academy; Open University, Milton Keynes; Abbot Hall Gallery, Kendal; The Ashmolean Museum, Oxford; Arts Council of Northern Ireland; The Chantry Bequest; The City Art Gallery of Bradford, Coventry, Dudley, Leicester, Manchester and Wakefield; The University of Hull; The Open University; New College, Oxford; Royal Holloway College; The Royal Library; Windsor Castle.

Publications:

By TINDLE: Articles—interview with Sally-Ann Schilling in *Artist,* vol. 103, no. 10, October 1988.

On TINDLE: Exhibition catalogs—*David Tindle,* edited by Piccadilly Gallery, London 1957, 1963, 1965, 1966, 1968, 1971, 1973, 1976, 1979; *David Tindle: New Paintings,* Oxford 1961; *David Tindle: Painting 1962,* with text by Neville Wallis, London 1962; *Exhibition of Works by David Tindle,* Northampton 1972; *David Tindle,* with text by Marina Vaizey, London 1985; *David Tindle: Paintings 1987–89,* London 1989.

*

The images I paint are of things I know best or can remember most. I try to place them in an order that expresses the feelings I have about them. It is not a question of painting them as realistically as I can, but to get the right tonality, so that memory and presence are very close.

—David Tindle

* * *

"Twentieth-century art, now free from the intolerable burden of representation." How often has one heard that phrase! Yet, if one casts around for contemporary artists whose work asserts the enduring value of representation as a way of finding oneself in the universe, there are very few who offer visible, incontrovertible evidence. David Tindle is one of them.

Why is he so much less acclaimed than, say, Wyeth in the United States? He was the victim of a special situation in Britain: art, and especially "modern" and abstract art, has had such an uphill task to win recognition, interest and respectability in the first half of the twentieth century that sitting in front of an easel and nature, and *learning* from it by making marks and looking again, has been made to seem like a reactionary gesture. And the fact that the brightest talents of those chose more immediate forms of self-expression weighed the public scales even more against it.

Tindle moved from vigorous, gestural painting of such subjects as high seas breaking on the shore, towards "every-blade-of-grass" scenes of landscape seen out of windows, or evocative still-lifes of straw hats on chairs, done in traditional tempera and much like old Roman murals in their effect; but not with the obsessional deadness that high detail so often carries, but a fine, refined, luminescent and atmospheric stillness, full of lively details of observed light, direct and reflected, as in Vermeer or de Hoogh; they have manifest presence. These are paintings which "are what they do"; some find a melancholy in them, others, the timeless repose of the suspended moment, complete in itself. In them, "representation" catches our remembering that "that is how it is." But "how it is" includes the recognition or memory of mental and spiritual worlds beyond the physical and manifest.

From time to time, Tindle has painted very straightforward portraits of young art students; these in their directness deserve to be seen more publicly. Tindle's is a major, little-recognized contribution to twentieth-century factual realism, and to art itself, as a method and also a gift of self-realization.

—Michael Shepherd

TINGUELY, Jean

Nationality: Swiss. **Born:** Fribourg, 22 May 1925. **Education:** Primary and secondary schools in Basel, 1930–39; apprentice decorator, Globus Department Store, Basel, 1941–45; studied art at the Kunstgewerbeschule, Basel, 1941–45. **Family:** Married the artist Eva Aeppli in 1951 (separated, 1958). **Career:** Independent artist, in Basel, 1945–52; subsequently in Paris, Basel, and in Soisysur-Ecole, France; abstract paintings and kinetic assemblage-sculptures, 1945–52; first ''Metamecanismes,'' 1952; first ''Metamatics,'' 1959; collaborative works with artist Yves Klein, 1958–62, Niki de Saint-Phalle, from 1960, and with Bernard Luginbuhl, 1968–72. Member, Pierre Restany's Nouveaux Réalistes group of artists, Paris 1960–70; Jean Tinguely Museum inaugration, Basel, Switzerland, September 30, 1996. **Address:** L'Auberge du Chéval-Blanc, 91840 Soisysur-Ecole, Essoness, France. **Died:** In Bern, Switzerland, of complications resulting from a stroke, 30 August 1991.

Jean Tinguely. Library of Congress.

Individual Exhibitions:

1954 Galerie Arnaud, Paris,
Studio d'Architettura, Milan
1955 Galleri Samlaren, Stockholm
1956 Galerie Denise René, Paris
1957 Galerie Edouard Loeb, Paris
Galerie Denise René, Paris
1958 Galerie Iris Clert, Paris
1959 Galerie Schmela, Dusseldorf
Kaplan Gallery, London
Galerie Iris Clert, Paris
Institute of Contemporary Arts, London (happening-event)
1960 Staempli Gallery, New York
Museum of Modern Art sculpture garden, New York (outdoor event)
Galerie des Quatres Saisons, Paris
Museum Huas Lange, Krefeld, West Germany
Kunsthalle, Berne, Switzerland (with Bernard Luginbuhl and Norbert Kricke)
1961 Moderna Museet, Stockholm
Louisiana, Museum, Humlebaek, Denmark
Staempli Gallery, New York
Galerie Rive Droite, Paris
Galleria Schwarz, Milan
1962 Galerie Handschin, Basel
Everett Ellin Gallery, Los Angeles
Alexandre Iolas Gallery, New York
1963 Minami Gallery, Tokyo
Dwan Gallery, Los Angeles
1964 Galerie Alexandre Iolas, Geneva
Kunsthalle, Baden-Baden, West Germany
Galerie Rudolf Zwirner, Cologne
1965 *Sculpture,* Museum of Fine Arts, Houston
Palais des Beaux-Arts, Brussels
Sculpteurs: Cesar, Roel d'Haese, Tinguely, Musée des Arts Décoratifs, Paris
2 Kinetic Sculptors: Nicolas Schoffer and Jean Tinguely, Jewish Museum, New York (toured the United States)
Alexandre Iolas Gallery, New York
Kunsthalle, Berne
1966 Ohio State University, Columbus
Gimpel and Hanover Galerie, Zurich
Hon-en Katedral, Moderna Museet, Stockholm (with Niki de Saint-Phalle and Per Olof Ultveldt)
1967 Galerie Alexandre Iolas, Paris
Galleria Iolas, Milan
Rijksmuseum Kröller-Müller, Otterlo, Netherlands (with Bernard Luginbuhl)
Galleri Buren, Stockholm
1968 Hanover Gallery, London
Tekeningen, Stedeijk Museum, Amsterdam
Museum of Contemporary Art, Chicago
1969 Gimpel und Hanover Galerie, Zurich
Victor Loeb Department Store, Bern
1970 Galleria Iolas, Milan

Jean Tinguely: *Turning of friendship of America and France,* 1961. ©2001 Artists Rights Society (ARS), NY/ADAGP, Paris.

Galerie Alexandre Iolas, Geneva
Galleria L'Attico, Rome
1971 *Machines de Tinguely,* Centre National d'Art Contemporain, Paris (toured Europe, 1971–72)
1974 *Debricollages,* Galerie Bischofberger, Zurich
1975 *Reliefs et Sculptures 1954–1965,* Galerie Bonnier, Geneva
1976 *Dessins et Gravures pour les Sculptures,* Musée d'Art et d'Histoire, Geneva
Kunstmuseum, Basel
Galerie Bishofberger, Zurich
1978 Wilhelm-Lehmbruck-Museum, Duisburg, West Germany (retrospective)
1979 *Jean Tinguely im Stadel,* Städtische Galerie, Frankfurt
1981 Galerie Bischofberger, Zurich
Abbaye de Senanque, Vaucluse, France
1982 Kunsthaus, Zurich (travelled to the Tate Gallery, London, Palais des Beaux-Arts, Brussels, and the Musée d'Art et d'Histoire, Geneva)
1983 Centre Georges Pompidou, Paris
1984 Stedelijk Museum, Amsterdam
1985 Kunsthalle der Hypo-Stiftung, Munich
1986 Louisiana Museum, Humlebaek, Denmark
Kunsthalle de Hypo-Stiftung, Munich
1987 Galerie Beyeler, Basel
Palazzo Grassi, Venice (retrospective)
1989 Centre Georges Pompidou, Paris
1991 Musée d'Art et d'Histoire, Fribourg, Switzerland
KunstHausWien, Germany
1992 Beyeler Gallery, Basel
A Tribute to Tinguely, Galerie Littmann, Basel
1996 Museum of Modern Art, New York
1997 Centre Georges Pompidou, Paris (retrospective)
Galleria di Nuova Icona, Venice
Jean Tinguely: Drawn Letters, Nuova Icona, Venice
1998 *Jean Tinguely: Sixties Sculptures,* Faggionato Fine Arts, London
Galerie Beaubourg, Paris
Jean Tinguely: Sculptures from the Cycle Die Philosophen and Other Works, Galerie Schmela, Dusseldorf
1999 Musée Picasso, Paris
2000 Museum Jean Tinguely, Basel

Selected Group Exhibitions:

1955 *Le Mouvement,* Galerie Denise René, Paris
1959 *Biennale,* Paris
1961 *Le Mouvement dans l'Art,* Stedelijk Museum, Amsterdam (travelled to the Moderna Museet, Stockholm, and the Louisiana Museum, Humlebaek, Denmark)
1964 *Biennale,* Venice
1967 *French Art Today,* at *Expo 67,* Montreal
1968 *The Machine,* Museum of Modern Art, New York
1977 *Paris-New York,* Centre Georges Pompidou, Paris
1980 *Paris-Paris 1937–57,* Centre Georges Pompidou, Paris
1982 *60–80: Attitudes, Concepts, Images,* Stedelijk Museum, Amsterdam
1984 *Salvaged: Altered Everyday Objects,* Project Studio One Long Island City, New York
1988 *Nouveaux Realistes,* Zabriskie Gallery, New York
1989 *From Goya to Tinguely: Watercolours and Drawings from a Private Collection,* Kunstmuseum, Berne
1991 *Eva Aeppli & Jean Tinguely: Collaboration,* Galerie Littmann, Basel
Une Touche Suisse: Thirty Years of Activity 1961–1991—Thirty Five Artists Invited to Contribute Each a Work of Art, Galerie Bonnier, Geneva
Swiss Open-air Sculpture 1960–91, Foundation Pierre Gianadda, Martigny, Switzerland
Sculptors' Drawings in the Wilhelm-Lehmbruck-Museum Duisburg, Duisburg, Germany
1995 *Our 100th Anniversary of Paintings of People—Pictoral Worlds,* Museum Ludwig, Cologne
1996 *Sloth,* Centre Georges Pompidou, Paris
The Dimension of the Body 1920–80, National Museum of Modern Art, Tokyo (travelled to National Museum of Modern Art, Kyoto)
Drawing on Chance: Selections from the Collection, Museum of Modern Art, New York
1998 *Glancing at the Century,* Museum of Modern Art, Basil & Elise Goulandris Foundation, Andros, Greece
1999 Espace de l'Art Concret, Mouans-Sartoux, France (with Aurélie Nemours)

2000 *Cross-Currents in Modern Art,* Achim Moeller Fine Art

Collections:

Centre Georges Pompidou, Paris; Kunsthaus, Zurich; Kunstmuseum, Dusseldorf; Kaiser-Wilhelm-Museum, Krefeld, West Germany; Stedelijk Museum, Amsterdam; Stedelijk Van Abbemuseum, Eindhoven, Netherlands; Museum of Modern Art, New York; Museum of Fine Arts, Houston.

Publications:

By TINGUELY: Book—*Für Statik,* manifesto, Dusseldorf 1959. **Articles—**interview with Jerzy Sabara in *Projekt,* no. 6, 1990.

On TINGUELY: Books—*Tinguely,* exhibition catalog leaflet with text by Pontus Hulten, Paris 1957; *3 Sculpteurs: Cesar, Roel d'Haese, Tinguely,* exhibition catalog with texts by Francois Mathey, Chris Yperman and James Johnson Sweeney, Paris 1965; *Jean Tinguely: Sculpture,* exhibition catalog with text by James Johnson Sweeney, Houston 1965; *2 Kinetic Sculptors: Nicolas Schoffer and Jean Tinguely,* exhibiton catalog with text by Sam Hunter and K. G. Pontus Hulten, New York, 1965; *Jean Tinguely,* exhibition catalog with text by Jean-Christophe Ammann, Zurich 1966; *Jean Tinguely: Tekeningen,* exhibition folder, Amsterdam 1968; *Tinguely,* exhibition catalog with texts by Peter F. Althaus and others, Basel 1972; *Jean Tinguely,* exhibition catalog with texts by Wieland Schmied, Peter F. Althaus and others, Hannover 1972; *Jean Tinguely: 166 Fotos von Leonardo Bezzola,* with texts Eva Aeppli, Bernard Luginbuhl, Niki de Saint-Phalle and others, Zurich 1974; *Jean Tinguely: Debricollages,* exhibition catalog with text by Gerald Minkoff, Zurich 1974; *Mesa* by Pontus Hulten, London 1975; *Jean Tinguely: Reliefs et Sculptures 1954–1965,* exhibition catalog, Geneva 1975; *Jean Tinguely: dessins et gravures pour les sculptures,* exhibition catalog with an interview by Charles Georg and Rainer Michael Mason, Geneva 1976; *Tinguely in Kunstmuseum, Basel,* exhibition catalog with text by Franz Meyer, Basel 1976; *Jean Tingguely im Stadel,* exhibition catalog with texts by Klaus Gallwitz and Willy Rotzler, Frankfurt 1979; *Der Tinguely-Brunnen in Basel* by Annemaire Monteil, Basel 1980; *Tinguely,* exhibition catalog with texts by Felix Baumann, and Richard Calvocoressi, Zurich 1982; *Jean Tinguely: catalog raisone 1954–1968,* compiled by Christina Bischofberger, Zurich 1982; *Jean Tinguely,* exhibition catalog with text by Carla Schultz-Hoffmann and Stephanie Poley, Munich 1985; *Jean Tinguely,* exhibition catalog with text by Gert Kaiser, Basel 1987; *Tinguely,* exhibition catalog with text by Pontus Hulten, Paris 1988; *Jean Tinguely: Nachtschattengewasche,* exhibition catalog, Vienna 1991; *Jean Tinguely: Life and Work* by Heidi E. Violand-Hobi, New York 1995; *Jean Tinguely und Basel,* edited and with a text by Andres Pardey, Basel 1997; *Jean Tinguely: lettere disegnate,* exhibition catalog, Venice 1997; *Jean Tinguely: Drawn Letters,* exhibition catalog, Venice 1997; *Jean Tinguely: Sixties Sculptures,* exhibition catalog, London 1999. **Articles—**''Two Motion Sculptors: Tinguely and Rickey'' by Arthur Secunda in *Artforum International,* vol. 26, February 1988; ''Niki de Saint Phalle and Jean Tinguely: A Collaboration That Has Lasted Over 30 Years'' by Yvonne Robinson in *Arts Review* (London), vol. 40, 3 June 1988; ''Tinguely'' by Jean-Yves Mock in *Cimaise,* vol. 35, no. 197, November-December 1988; ''Tinguely'' by Michel Conil-Lacoste in *Cimaise,* vol. 36, June/August 1989; obituary in *Art in America* (New York), vol. 79, October 1991; ''Tinguely ou la mecanique de l'absurde'' by Maiten Bouisset in *Beaux Arts Magazine,* no. 94, October 1991; ''Tinguely's Cyclops'' by Elisabeth Tiso in *Art in America* (New York), vol. 81, June 1993; ''Modernite, tradition, portraits et 'meta': Tinguely et La Galerie des Hommes Illustres'' by Eveline Pinto in *Revue d'Esthetique,* no. 23, 1993; ''The Cyclops of Fontainebleau'' by Jill Johnson in *Art in America* (New York), vol. 84, no. 6, June 1996; ''Rebel's Memorial'' by Jill Johnson in *Art in America* (New York), vol. 85, no. 3, March 1997. **Films—***Hommage to Jean Tinguely's Hommage to New York* by Robert Breer, 1960.

* * *

Tinguely's formal artistic training was at the School of Art and Crafts in Basel from 1941–45, though his attendance was irregular. By 1945 he was painting abstract pictures and making constructions from wire, metal and other materials, influenced by the work of Kurt Schwitters. It was also at this time that he expressed interest in movement as an artistic medium.

Between 1945–53, Tinguely worked at various jobs in Basel and was attracted to the work of Paul Klee and the Bauhaus, Tanguy, Dali and Miro. He was living in Paris in 1953 and worked with Daniel Spoerri in Jean Lurcat's studio on a project for ''auto-theatre,'' which was intended to bring action to the stage with or without actors. Tinguely spent most of the 1950s working on various series of reliefs: in 1954, reliefs made up of layers of moving rods; in 1954–56, ''meta-mechanical'' reliefs and free-standing sculptures; in 1956–59 reliefs with rotating metal elements. The late 1950s early 1960s saw the advent of Tinguely's first ''painting machines'' and his involvement with *Nouveaux Realisme,* which rejected the ivory tower world of abstract painting (then the major international trend in painting), and advocated the use of real materials and found objects; all of which was a harkening back to *Dada.* Indeed, Tinguely's own constructions owed a great deal to Picabia's work of 1917–19.

In 1960 one of Tinguely's most famous series was inaugurated with the *Hommage à New York,* a sculpture which self-destructed in the garden of New York's Museum of Modern Art. By the mid-1960s the sculptures were becoming huge and were major media events, especially if they were of the self-destructing variety.

Tinguely's machines usually worked in some way, even if only just. The irony inherent in his early work, particularly the painting machines, receded though never entirely disappeared. He brought together a combination of a dadaist tradition with the fascination for humourous and outlandish machines as seen by artists such as Paul Klee and the Surrealists, adding to all this a concern for the use of cast off materials and an overwhelming interest in movement.

—Victoria Keller

TIRAVANIJA, Rirkrit

Nationality: Argentinean. **Born:** Buenos Aires, Argentina, 1961. **Education:** Studied at Ontario College of Art, Toronto, Canada, 1981; studied at Banff Center School of Fine Arts, Banff, Canada, 1984; studied at School of the Art Institute of Chicago, 1985; studied

under the Whitney Independent Studies Program, New York, 1986.
Career: Lives and works in Bangkok, Berlin, and New York.

Selected Individual Exhibitions:

1990 *Pad Thai,* Project Room Paula Allen Gallery, New York
1991 *Untitled, 1990 (blind),* Randy Alexander Gallery, New York
1992 *Untitled, 1992 (free),* 303 Gallery, New York
1993 *Untitled, 1993 (live and eat, eat and die),* Randolph Street Gallery, Chicago
1994 *Andy Warhol Rirkrit Tiravanija,* Gavin Brown's Enterprise, New York
Untitled, 1994 (meet tim and burkhard), Neugerriemschneider, Berlin
Untitled, 1993 (rucksack), Architektenbüro Alsop & Störmer, Hamburg; Helga Maria Klosterfelde Editionen, Hamburg
Untitled, 1994 (beauty), Jack Hanley Gallery, San Francisco
1995 *Untitled, 1995 (tent),* Architektenbüro Alsop & Störmer, Hamburg; Helga Maria Klosterfelde Editionen, Hamburg
Untitled, 1994 (From Baragas . . . to Reina Sofia), Kunsthalle Basel, Switzerland (catalog)
Untitled, 1995 (still), 303 Gallery, New York
1996 *Untitled, 1996 (tomorrow is another day),* Kölnischer Kunstverein, Cologne (catalog)
Untitled, 1996 (one revolution per minute) Le Consortium, Centre d'Art Contemporain, Dijon, France (catalog)
Stichting DeAppel, Amsterdam (with Renée Green) (catalog)
Untitled, 1996 (rehearsal studio no. 6), Spiral Garden, Tokyo
1997 *Untitled, 1997 (a demonstration by Faust as a sausage and Franz Biberkopf as a potato),* Neugerriemschneider, Berlin
Untitled, 1997 (playtime), Projects 58, Museum of Modern Art, New York
Williams College Museum of Art, Williamstown, Massachusetts
Kunstverein Ludwigsburg, Villa Franck, Ludwigsburg, Germany (catalog)
1998 *Dom-Ino (une demonstration d'automne),* Galerie Chantal Crousel, Paris
Untitled, 1998 (das soziale kapital), Museum für Gegenwartskunst, Zurich (catalog)
Untitled, 1998 (on the road with Jiew, Jeaw, Jieb, Sri and Moo), Philadelphia (catalog)
1999 *Dom-Ino Effect,* Los Angeles County Museum of Art (with Lincoln Tobier)
Community Cinema for a Quit Intersection (Against Oldenburg), Modern Institute, Glasgow
Untitled, 1999 (Mobile Home), Fundació "la Caixa," Barcelona (catalog)
Untitled, 1999 (reading from right to left), Wexner Center for the Arts, Columbus, Ohio
2000 Gallery Side 2, Tokyo
Untitled, 2000 (Demonstrate), Galeria Salvador Diaz, Madrid
Maagazine Station no. 2, Galleria Emi Fontana, Milan

Selected Group Exhibitions:

1989 *Caught in a Revolving Door,* Alumni Association of the School of the Art Institute of Chicago (catalog)
Outside the Clock: Beyond Good and Elvis, Scott Hanson Gallery, New York
Lotto as Metaphor, Hallwalls, Buffalo, New York (catalog)
1990 *Post-Consumerism,* Storefront for Art and Architecture, New York
Work on Paper, Paula Allen Gallery, New York
4th Annual Invitational, Cold City Gallery, Toronto
1991 *The Big Nothing or Le Presque Rien,* New Museum of Contemporary Art, New York (catalog)
Wealth of Nations, Center for Contemporary Arts, Ujazdowski Castle, Warsaw, Poland (catalog)
Fluxattitude, Hallwalls, Buffalo, New York; New Museum for Contemporary Art, New York (catalog)
Marginal Majority (Artists Against Racial Prejudice), Aaron Davis Hall, New York (catalog)
1992 *Transgressions in the White Cube: Territorial Mapping,* Usdan Gallery, Bennington College, Bennington, Vermont (catalog)
Writings on the Wall, 303 Gallery, New York
Home Improvements, 209 W. 97th Street, Apartment 7B, New York
Consumed, Goethe Haus, New York
1993 *Kunstmuseum,* Lucerne, Switzerland (catalog)
Migrateurs, Musée d'Art Moderne de la Ville de Paris (catalog)
Real Time, Institute of Contemporary Arts, London (catalog)
Simply Made in America, Aldrich Museum of Contemporary Art, Connecticut (catalog)
1994 *Der Stand der Dinge,* Kölnischer Kunstverein, Cologne (catalog)
Out Side the Frame, Contemporary Art Center, Cleveland (catalog)
Surface de Reparations, Le Consortium, Centre d'Art Contemporain, Dijon, France (catalog)
Don't Look Now, Threadwaxing Space, New York
1995 Carnegie International, Carnegie Museum of Art, Pittsburgh
Shift, DeAppel, Amsterdam (catalog)
Whitney Biennial, Whitney Museum, New York (catalog)
Economies, Walker Art Center, Minneapolis (with Hans Accola)
1996 *a/drift,* Center of Curatorial Studies, Bard College, Annandale-on-Hudson, New York
Thinking Print, Museum of Modern Art, New York
Campo 6, Fondazione Sandretto Re Rebaudengo per l'Arte, Galleria Civica d'Arte Moderna di Torino, Turin, Italy (catalog)
TRAFFIC, CAPC Musée d'Art Contemporain, Bordeaux, France
1997 *Cities on the Move,* Wiener Secession, Wien, Austria (catalog)
Enterprise, Institute of Contemporary Art, Boston

Truce: Echoes of Art in an Age of Endless Conclusions, SITE Santa Fe (catalog)
Performance Anxiety, Museum of Contemporary Art, Chicago; Museum of Contemporary Art, San Diego (catalog)

1998 National Gallery of Canada, Ottawa
Deserted and Embraced, Goethe Institute, Bangkok (catalog)
Cities on the Move, CAPC, Bordeaux (catalog)
Wounds: Between Democracy and Redemption in Contemporary Art, Moderna Museet, Stockholm (catalog)

1999 *Kunst-Welten im Dialog,* Museum Ludwig, Cologne (catalog)
dAPERTutto, 48, Venice Biennale (catalog)
Go Away: Artists and Travel, Royal College of Art, London (catalog)
Peace, Museum für Gegenwartskunst, Zurich

2000 *Ein/Räumen—Arbeiten im Museum,* Hamburger Kunsthalle, Hamburg (catalog)
Loneliness in the City, Migros Museum, Zurich (with Franz Ackermann)
Continental Shift, Ludwig Forum, Aachen, Germany; Bonnefantenmuseum, Maastricht, The Netherlands; Stadsgalerij, Haarlem, The Netherlands; Musée d'Art Moderne de Liège, Belgium (catalog)
LKW, Lebenskunstwerke, Kunst in der Stadt 4, Kunsthaus Bregenz, Austria (catalog)

2001 *L'idée de communauté/The Idea of Community,* Parachute, Montreal
Freestyle, Werke aus der Sammlung Boros, Museum Morsbroich, Leverkusen, Germany

Publications:

By TIRAVANIJA: Articles—''Rirkrit Tiravanija'' in *Parkett,* no. 44, July 1995.

On TIRAVANIJA: Articles—''Rirkrit Tiravanija: Other Things, Elsewhere'' by Gavin Brown in *Flash Art,* summer 1994; Special section on Rirkrit Tiravanija in *Parkett,* 1995; ''Where Are We Going? And What Are We Doing? Rirkrit Tiravanija's Art of Living'' by Bruce Hainley in *Artforum International,* February 1996; ''A Short History of Rirkrit Tiravanija'' by Jerry Saltz in *Art in America,* vol. 84, February 1996; ''A Lot to Digest: Conceptual Artist Rirkrit Tiravanija'' by Carol Lutfy and Lynn Gumpert in *Art News,* May 1997; ''Rirkrit Tiravanija's Liability'' by Janet Kraynak in *Documents,* no. 13, Fall 1998; ''Modern-day Anthropology: Rirkrit Tiravanija Goes to Work'' by Frances DeVuono in *New Art Examiner,* July-August 1999; ''Rirkrit Tiravanija: The Space of Unconditional Action'' by Yvane Chapuis in *Parachute,* January-March 2001.

* * *

Rirkrit Tiravanija's food and tent installations continue the conceptual art tradition into the 1990s. In one of his first installations, *Untitled (Free)* (1992), Tiravanija switched the administrative and exhibition spaces of a New York gallery in order to set up a communal eating area in the back where he cooked Thai vegetable curry for visitors. Increasingly, his work has engaged issues of global travel and cultural identity by setting up makeshift living and cooking spaces, both inside and outside the gallery or museum context. Whether it is a tent, equipped with mats and TV, installed in a gallery or a camping trip documented with his video recorder, Tiravanija's work has consistently used everyday living situations to explore issues of social interaction in a late 20th century global context.

Tiravanija's avoidance of making conventional objects for display and purchase is informed by the 1960s conceptual art tradition. Like the international conceptual group Fluxus, the Brussels-based artist Marcel Broodthaers, or even Andy Warhol, whom Tiravanija cites frequently, he explores the art of everyday living while simultaneously critiquing the commodified gallery context in which his installations are placed. As with *Untitled (Free)* (1992), many of Tiravanija's cooking installations expose the business operations of the gallery by displaying its files and desks in the exhibition area while further disrupting the pristine commodified space of the gallery with an infusion of Thai spices. He has also installed a temporary plywood replica of his own New York apartment within the space of a gallery, complete with stove, bed, TV, and shower, open 24 hours for anyone that wants to sleep, watch a movie, or wash. The only objects of Tiravanija's that are sold are the used tents and woks, leftover cooking supplies, and the trash remaining from his meals and installations. But the real substance of Tiravanija's art is the interaction among strangers who come together in the guise of a meal, slumber party, or camping trip. Tiravanija's situations often force visitors to renounce control and simply give themselves over to the unpredictable experience of the event. They depend on his hospitality and interactions with the other visitors to formulate their experience of Tiravanija's work. The humbling and selfless philosophy of Tiravanija's work is informed by his Buddhist roots and nomadic lifestyle.

Tiravanija was born in Buenos Aires to a Thai diplomat and has lived in Thailand, Ethiopia, Canada, and the United States. He emphasizes that he feels most at home when he is on the road. Much of his recent work reflects upon this itinerancy with themes of global travel and cross-cultural experience. For the 1993 Venice Biennale he served Cup-o-Noodles from a canoe as a way of commenting on the constant transformation of culture. The title, *Untitled (1271),* refers to the date that Marco Polo appropriated noodles from Asia and made them synonymous with Italian cuisine. Serving a fast-food version of the noodles manufactured by a Japanese corporation further demonstrates the fluidity of culture. Besides installations of food, cots and tents, Tiravanija has also travelled and called it art. *Untitled (On the Road with Jiew Leaw Jieb Sri and Moo)* (1998) was a trip he took across the United States in a motor home. Each day Tiravanija would send live broadcasts and documentation of his adventures to the Philadelphia Museum of Art through a web connection. In *Untitled (from Madrid Airport to Riena Sofia)* (1994), Tiravanija rode a specially equipped bicycle, complete with tent, folding table, chairs, and lightweight cooking equipment, across the Spanish countryside, feeding anyone who would accept his invitation. All of these artistic strategies suggest that Tiravanija's offerings are not meant to give his guests an authentic encounter with Thai culture but are meant as a way to reflect upon one's own transient and mobile situation within a postcolonial, global context. The object (or objective) of Tiravanija's art of living is to foster a nomadic community on a global scale through his own movement and interaction with people.

Tiravanija gives the gift of food or shelter to the gallery, museum, and their visitors. This act of gift-giving is the over-arching operation of Tiravanija's work. But his gift-giving enterprise is not entirely one-sided. Rather, his offerings are part of a gift economy in which the recipient is obligated to return or pass on Tiravanija's hospitality. Patrons who have purchased Tiravanija's leftovers—the trash, remaining cooking supplies, and utensils—are obligated to use them, cook with them, and offer them to others. Tiravanija, in effect, creates an economy of social relations in which other cultures, spaces, and rituals should be experienced and reciprocated.

—Jaimey Hamilton

TITUS-CARMEL, Gérard

Nationality: French. **Born:** Paris, 10 October 1942. **Education:** Studied engraving at the Ecole Boulle, Paris, 1958–62. **Military:** French Air Force, 1962–64. **Family:** Married Joan C. Robinson in 1971; children: Jeanne and Guillaume. **Career:** Independent artist, Paris 1964–82, and in Oulchy-le-Château, Aisne, since 1982; also, filmmaker, since 1972. **Awards:** First Prize, *Drawing Biennale,* Rijeka, 1970; International Art Critics Association Prize, *Biennale de Paris,* 1971; First Prize, *Biennale of Alexandria,* 1971; Prix de la Ville de Warszawa, *Biennale Internationale,* 1972; Grand Prix, *Biennale Internationale de Gravure, 1976;* Juror's Special Award of Honor, World Print Competition, 1977; Grand Prix ''Miroslav Kraljevic,'' *l'Académie Croate des Sciences et des Arts,* 1993. **Address:** La Grand'Maison 02210 Oulchy-le-Chateau, France.

Individual Exhibitions:

1967 Galerie du Fleuve, Paris
1968 Galerie du Fleuve, Paris
1969 Galerija 212, Belgrade
1970 Galerie Daniel Templon, Paris
Galerie A.P.I.A.W., Liège, Belgium
1971 Musée d'Art Moderne de la Ville, Paris
Galerie Bama, Paris
Galleria La Salita, Rome
1972 Neue Galerie Sammlung Ludwig, Aachen, West Germany (retrospective)
Galerie Daniel Templon, Paris
Muzuem Sztuki, Lodz, Poland
French Pavilion, *36th Biennale Internazionale d'Arte,* Venice
Galerie du Fleuve, Bordeaux
The Royal College of Art Gallery, London
Galleria Diagramma, Milan
1973 Galerie Godula Buchholz, Munich
Stedelijk Museum, Amsterdam
Galleria Schwarz, Milan
Galerie Jalmar, Amsterdam
1974 Galerie Daniel Templon, Paris
Galerie La Hune, Paris
Galerie La Touriale, Marseilles
Galerie Birger Arnesen, Copenhagen
Galerie Vega, Liège, Belgium
1975 Galerie Graphikhuset Futura, Stockholm
Galerie Daniel Templon, Paris
Galerie Hecate, Paris
Palais des Beaux-Arts, Brussels
1976 Galerie La Hune, Paris
Galerie Thérése Roussel, Perpignan, France

Gérard Titus-Carmel: *Sable No. 12,* 1999. Photo by Michel Nguyen. ©2001 Artists Rights Society (ARS), NY/ADAGP, Paris.

Galerie Baudoin Lebon, Paris
1977 Gimpel und Hanover Galerie, Zurich
Gimpel Fils Gallery, London
Kunsthandel Brinkman, Amsterdam
Galerie Art Actuel, Nancy, France
1978 Musée National d'Art Moderne/Centre Georges Pompidou, Paris
Galerija Krzysztofory, Krakow
Galerie Maeght, Paris
1979 Kunstverein für die Rheinlande und Westfalen, Dusseldorf
Galerie Maeght, Zurich
Galerie Charles Kriwin, Brussels
1980 Kunsthalle, Bielefeld, West Germany
Stadia Graphics Gallery, Sydney
Kunstverein, Kassel, West Germany
Nishimura Gallery, Tokyo
1981 Overbeck-Gesellschaft and St. Annen Museum, Lübeck
Galerie Maeght, Paris
Kunsthalle, Nuremberg
Musée de l'Abbaye Sainte-Croix, Les Sables d'Olonne, France
Nishimura Gallery, Tokyo
Sonja Henie-Niels Onstad Stiffelser, Hovikodden Kunstsenter, Oslo
1982 Xavier Fourcade Inc., New York
Galerie Chappe-Lautier, Toulouse
Galerie Maeght, Zurich

Galerie Maeght, Paris
1983 Galerie Elisabeth Franck, Knokke-le-Zoute, Belgium
Studio Marconi, Milan
1984 Galerie de la Cité, Luxembourg
Galerie de l'Ancienne Poste, Calais, France
Galerie Maeght Lelong, Paris
1985 Musées de Nice, Galerie des Ponchettes, Nice, France
Spaightwood Galleries, Madison, Wisconsin
Tours Narbonnaises, Carcassonne, France
Institut Francais, Stuttgart (travelled to Hamburg, Munich and Bonn)
Musée d'Art Moderne de Lille Métropole, Villeneuve d'Ascq, France
1986 Galerie Maeght Lelong, Paris
Galerie Graff, Montreal
Galerie Hans Brinkman, Amsterdam
Galerie du Musée du Quebec, Canada
Spaightwood Galleries, Madison, Wisconsin
1987 Mucsarnok/Kiallitasi Intezmenyek, Budapest
Fuji Television Gallery, Tokyo
Gallery Asbaek, Copenhagen
Abbaye des Cordeliers, Chateauroux, France
Galerie La Hune, Paris
Denise Cade Gallery/Art Prospect Inc., New York
Lelong Gallery, New York
1988 Galerie Gill Favre, Lyon
Galerie Kaj Forsblom, Helsinki
Spaightwood Galleries, Madison, Wisconsin
Galerie Grafiart, Turku
1989 Galerie Lelong, Paris
Artothèque, Théâtre Municipal, Caen
1990 Musée Ingres, Montauban
Centre Culturel Français, Damascus
Centre Culturel Tichrine, Alep
Maison du Livre et des Mots, Avignon
1991 Galerie Akhénaton, Centre des Arts, Le Caire
Galerie Lelong, Paris
Centre Culturel Français, Alexandria
Centre Culturel Français, Galleria Ars Nova, Palermo
Institut Français, Naples
Galleria Navona, Rome
Machida City Museum of Graphic Arts, Tokyo
Gallery Itsutsuji, Tokyo
1992 Galerie Marika Marghescu, Hannover
Spaightwod Galleries, Madison, Wisconsin
Palais Bénédictine, Fécamp
Eglise Saint Martin-du-Méjan, Arles
1993 Institut Français, London
Maison des Arts, Lyon
CAC de Compiègne et du Valois, Compiègne
Galerie Jade, Colmar
Fonds Régional d'Art Contemporain de Picardie, Chapelle des Visitandines, Centre Cultural Départmental de la Somme, Bibliothèque Municipale Louis Aragon, Amiéns
1994 Denise Cadé Gallery, New York
Galerie Eric Linard, Strasbourg
Denise Cadé Gallery, FIAC, Paris
1995 Les Silos/Maison du Livre et de l'Affiche, Chaumont
Centre de la Gravure et de l'Image Imprimée, La Louvière
Musée des Oudaïas/Galerie Bab El Kébir et Galerie Nationale Bab Rouah, Rabat
Centre Culturel Français, Casablanca, Rabat, Tetovan, Tanger
Château d'Arsac, Bordeaux
1996 Galerie La Navire, Brest, France
Osiris Gallery, Bruxelles
Centre Lotois d'Art Contemporain, Figeac
1997 Musée de l'Hospice Saint-Roch, Issoudun, France
Spaightwood Galleries, Madison
Galerie de Lillebonne/Espace d'Art Contemporain, Nancy, France (travelled to Maison de la Culture, Metz; Abbatiale Notre-Dame; Abbaye des Prémontrés, Pont-à-Mousson)
1998 Espace d'Art Contemporain André Malraux, Colmar, France
Bibliothèque Municipale de Stasbourg/Médiathèque de Neudorf, Strasbourg
Galleria Nova/Gabriele S. Haberland, Roneo s/Ascona, Switzerland
Musée—Abbaye Saint-Léger et Arsenal Abbaye Saint-Jean-des- Vignes, Soissons, France
Maison des Arts, Malakoff
1999 Galerie Municipale Julio Gonzalez, Arcueil
La Malmaison, Villes de Cannes
San de Cergy-Pontoise, Abbaye de Maubuisson, Saint-Oien- l'Aumône
2000 Université de Bretagne Occidentale, Brest, France
Galerie la Navire, Brest, France
Musée des Jacobins, Morlaix, France
Galerie Abélard, Sens, France
Librairie Mouvements, Paris
Chapelle Saint-Nicolas, Pluméliau
Centre Culturel, Galerie Pierre Tal Coat, Hennebont, France
Centre d'Art et de Littérature, Hôtel Beury, L'Échelle
Musée d'Art Roger-Quilliot, Clermont-Ferrand, France
2001 Cloître Saint-Louis, Avignon, France
The Cooper Union, University of New York
Denise Cadé Gallery, New York
Crypte de l'Ancienne Chapelle/Espace Culturel François Mitterand, Beauvais, France
Espace Culturel Écureuil, Toulouse
Villa Tamaris, La Seyne-sur-Mer, France

Selected Group Exhibitions:

1972 *Amsterdam-Paris-Dusseldorf,* Guggenheim Museum, New York (travelled to the Pasadena Art Museum, California, and Dallas Museum of Fine Arts)
1983 *Art Contemporain,* Palais des Beaux-Arts, Brussels
1984 *Art en France,* Biennale Internazionale d'Arte, Palazzo Sagredo, Venice
1987 *Fifty Years of Collecting/Painting Since World War II,* Guggenheim Museum, New York
1989 *Geijutsu Tako/Art Kites,* City Art Museum, Himeji (travelled to Hara Museum, Gunma; Art Museum, Shizuoka; City Museum of Modern Art, Nagoya; City Museum of Modern Art, Hiroshima; Haus der Kunst, Munich)

1990 *La France à Venise: Le Pavillon français de 1948 à 1988,* Peggy Guggenheim Collection, Venice
1991 *Musée rêvé-trésors contemporains des Musées de Provence,* Musée Picasso, Antibes
Art Kites/Peintures pour le Ciel, Centro de Arte Moderna, Lisbon (travelled to Musée des Beaux-Arts, Brussels; Nationalgalerie, Berlin; Charlottenborg, Copenhagen; and Promotrice delle Belle Arti, Torino)
1992 *Manifeste: 30 ans de Création en Perspective 1960- 1990,* Musée National d'Art Moderne, Paris
1993 *Art Contemporain en France,* Galerie Enrico Navarra (travelled to Gallery Itsutsuji, Tokyo)
1994 *Dessiner/Une Collection d'Art Contemporain—Collection du FRAC de Picardie,* Musée du Luxembourg, Paris
1995 *Poselstvi Znaku/Mezi Pismem a Obrazem, Inter-Kontakt-Grafik '95,* Praha-Kraków, Prague
1996 *Dessins Dessin,* Galerie de l'École des Beaux-Arts, Lorient, France
1997 *Made in France 1947–1997, 50 Ans de Création en France,* Musée National d'Art Moderne, Centre Georges Pompidou, Paris
1998 *La Collection du Centre Georges Pompidou, un Choix,* Musée d'Art Moderne de la Ville de Paris, Paris
1999 *États des Lieux—Anticiper le Printemps,* Musées de Châteauroux, Abbaye des Cordeliers et Musée Bertrand, Châteauroux, France
2000 *Visions of Nature in Contemporary Art,* Denise Cadé Gallery, New York

Collections:

Centre Georges Pompidou, Paris; Victoria and Albert Museum, London; Stedelijk Museum, Amsterdam; Musées Royaux des Beaux-Arts, Brussels; Fundacio Joan Miró, Barcelona; Australian National Gallery, Canberra; Museum of Modern Art, New York; Guggenheim Museum, New York; Musée Cantonal des Beaux-Arts, Lausanne, Switzerland; Centro d'Arte Contemporaneo, Cordoba, Argentina; Muzej Savremene Umetnosti, Belgrade, Yugoslavia; Muzeum Sztuki w Łódzi, Łódz, Poland; Muzeum Narodowe, Warsaw, Poland; Musée d'Art Moderne de la Ville de Paris; Muzej na Sovremena Umetnost, Skopje, Yugoslavia; Staatsgalerie, Stuttgart, Germany; Ateneumin Taidemuseo, Helsinki, Finland; Musée Royaux des Beaux-Arts, Bruxelles; Kobbersticksamlingen ved Statens Museum for Kunst, København, Denmark; Von der Heyt Museum, Wuppertal, Germany; The Art Institute, Chicago, Illinois; Wilhelm-Hack Museum, Ludwigschafen, Germany; Musée d'Art Contemporain, Nimes, France; The Museum of Modern Art, Toyama, Japan; The National Gallery of Victoria, Melbourne, Australia; Musée d'Art et d'Histoire, Luxembourg; The National Museum of Art, Osaka, Japan; Fundación Ralli, Punta del Este, Uruguay; Szépmuveszeti Muzeum, Budapest; Machida City Museum of Graphic Arts, Tokyo, Japan; Musée Jenisch, Vevey, Switzerland; The Modern Art Collection, Trinity College, Dublin, Ireland; National Museum of Israel, Jerusalem.

Publications:

By TITUS-CARMEL: Books—*Joaquin's Love Affair,* Paris 1971; *The Pocket Size Tlingit Coffin,* Paris 1976; *Le Casque de Nikkó,* 1984; *Temps de parole,* 1986; *Quatre images mémorables,* 1987; *Lumières,* 1988; *Ombre portée,* 1989; *L'Indolente d'Orsay,* 1990; *Notes d'atelier & autres textes de lacontre-allée,* 1990; *La Leçon du miroir,* 1992; *''Elle bouge encore... '',* 1992; *Premier sang,* 1994; *Ceci Posé,* 1997; *L'Élancement: Éloge de Hart Crane, 1998; Travaux de foille et d'oubli,* 2000; *La Rive en effet,* 2000. **Books illustrated**—*Pour Bramm* by Mathieu Benezet, Paris 1965; *La Porte de nuit* by Dusan Matic, Montpellier, France 1972; *L'Humus l'hymen* by Jean-Marc Tisserant, Montpellier, France 1973; *Matière première* by Denis Roche, Paris 1976; *Verres* by Jean-Pierre Faye, Paris 1977; *Sarx* by Pascal Quignard, Paris 1977; *Noeud* by Jean Fremon, Paris 1978; *Voyageurs de la voix* by Henri Meschonnic, Lagrasse, 1985; *Rhétorique* by Jean Frémon, 1987; *Chanfrein* by Jacques Dupin, 1990; *Le Motif du fleuve* by Gérard Titus-Carmel, 1990; *Le Livre de Lioube* by Jean-Pierre Faye, Paris 1991; *Légende* by Gérard Titus-Carmel (limited edition), 1992; *Vagho* by Gérard Titus-Carmel (limited edition), 1993; *L'Automne* by Guillaume Apollinaire, 1993; *Propos sur le Vent* by Makoto Ooka, 1994; *Soleil de Pluie* by Dominique Grandmont, 1995; *Petit Guide du XVe à l'usage des fantômes* by Roger Caillois, 1995; *Le Reste du Voyage* by Bernard Noël, 1995; *Lilas* by Pierre Courtaud, 1997; *Cent ans passent comme un jour—56 poètes pour Aragon,* 1997; *Liserons* by Philippe Jaccottet, 1999; *Coupes Réglées* by Gérard Titus-Carmel (limited edition), 1999; *Rien n'est dit* by Marc Petit, 2001; *Telle soudaineté* by Bernard Vargaftig, 2001. **Films**—*Joaquin's Love Affair,* 1972.

On TITUS-CARMEL: Books--*Gérard Titus-Carmel,* exhibition catalog with text by Jean Marc Tisserant, Liege, Belgium 1970; *Titus-Carmel,* exhibition catalog with texts by Mathieu Benezet, Jean-Pierre Faye, interview by Maurice Maurin, Paris 1971; *Gérard Titus-Carmel,* exhibition catalog with a preface by Wolfgang Becker, texts by others, Aachen, West Germany 1972; *Art en France: Une nouvelle generation* by Jean Clair, Paris 1972; *L'Art actuel en France* by Anne Tronche, Paris 1973; *Gérard Titus-Carmel of het Juk van de Weegschaal,* exhibition catalog with text by Irmeline Lebeer, Amsterdam 1973; *La strategia del disegno: Gérard Titus-Carmel,* exhibition catalog with text by Tommaso Trini, Milan 1973; *Gérard Titus-Carmel ou le Procès du Modèle* by Jean-Marc Tisserant, Paris 1974; *Gérard Titus-Carmel: Le Grifforme,* exhibition catalog with text by Jean-Pierre Faye, Paris 1974; *Dictionnaire universel de la peinture,* edited by Robert Maillard, Paris 1975; *Repères, la peinture en France: Debut et fin d'un systeme visuel 1870–1970* by Dora Vallier, Paris 1976; *Gérard Titus-Carmel,* exhibition catalog with an introduction by Willy Rotzler, London 1977; *Le Verité en peinture* by Jacques Derrida, Paris 1978; *Gérard Titus-Carmel,* exhibition catalog with texts by Jacques Derrida and Gilbert Lascault, Paris 1978; *Ecrits timides sur le visible* by Gilbert Lascault, Paris 1979; *Gérard Titus-Carmel,* exhibition catalog with preface by Gunter Metken and introduction by Karl-Heinz Hering, Dusseldorf 1979; *Titus-Carmel,* exhibition catalog with an introduction by Erich Franz, texts by others, Bielefeld, West Germany 1980; *Gérard Titus-Carmel,* exhibition catalog with a preface by Yoshiaki Tono, Tokyo 1981; *Gérard Titus-Carmel,* exhibition catalog with preface by Jean Fremon, Chateauroux 1987; *Titus-Carmel,* exhibition catalog by Yoshiaki Tono, Tokyo, 1981; *Konstanz und Wandel bei Gérard Titus-Carmel,* exhibition catalog by Willy Rotzler with notes by the artist, Zürich, 1982; *Gérard Titus-Carmel: The Art of Remembering and the Privilege of Forgetting,* exhibition catalog by Andrew Weiner, Madison, Wisconsin, 1986; *Gérard Titus-Carmel,* exhibition catalog by Salme Sarajas-Korte, Helsinki, 1988; *Gérard Titus-Carmel,* exhibition catalog by Dominique Abensour, Montauban, 1990; *D'Inlassables saisons,* exhibition catalog by Christian Gailly, Paris, 1991; *Forging the Real: Gérard Titus-Carmel and the Art of Renewal,* exhibition catalog by Andrew Weiner and Sonja Hansard-Weiner, Madison, 1992; *The Parentheses of Memory,* by Joan Robinson, London, 1993; *D'un cairn, l'autre,* exhibition catalog with preface by Gilles Plazy, 1994; *Gérard Titus-Carmel: la Part du livre,* exhibition catalog with text by Patrick Casson and Eddy Devolder, 1995; *Fragments d'autobiographie,* exhibition catalog with preface by Abdelkébir Khatibi, 1995; *Affleurements,* exhibition catalog, 1995; *Fragments et entrelacs,* exhibition catalog with preface by Philippe Cyroulnik, 1996; *Coupes claires,* exhibition catalog with preface by Patrick Casson, 1997; *La Clairière, le sillon,* exhibition catalog, 1998; *Ciel de nielle,* exhibition catalog with text by Denis Roche, 1998; *Titus-Carmel: La peinture archipel,* exhibition catalog with preface by Philippe Piguet, 1999. **Films**—*Gérard Titus-Carmel* by Jacques Scandelari, 1973; *Titus-Carmel* by Angeliki Haas, 1975; *Gérard Titus-Carmel ou l'Aventure du trait* by Teri Wehn-Damisch, 1977; *Gérard Titus-Carmel* by Alain Sayag, 1978; *Gérard Titus-Carmel, un artiste trait pour trait* by Carlos Vilardebo, 1982; *Gérard Titus-Carmel* by Liliane Thorn-Petit, 1983; *Espace et matière: Peinture, Sculpture* by William Mimouni, 1984; *Titus-Carmel, un profil* by Jean Douchet, 1986; *Le temps de voir: ''Two Black Angles'' de Kurt Schwitters, par Gérard Titus-Carmel* by Pierre Coulibeuf, 1991; *Gérard Titus-Carmel: La Leçon du miroir* by Yasuko Shimizu, 1991.

*

DRAWING

1. To draw: to deposit. To engrave: to remove. (idea of a work situated halfway between these two mutilations of the support: the significant maculations of the paper, the matricial groove of the metal).

2. To draw, to encroach: to cover. (Would the *image* be the *mask* of the paper?).

3. Drawing is, above all, a work on a double loss: loss of white (loss of consciousness), loss of materiality (diversion).

4. ''Carta Tinta.'' Drawing the shadows, lighting the lights: between the deaf *sanguine* and the chalky luminosity, the tinted paper is SIGNIFICANT MATTER.

5. On white paper, the brightness (the light) is the absence of drawing—the *lack;* to cease shading is to *enter into light.* On a tinted background, at the end of a stump, there is a rediscovery of the paper's matter as designated element of form, the *interstatement,* just before the hollow shading, the countertype: the drawing of the luminosities with a white pencil.

6. Praxis of drawing, alluvia of the graphite.

7. Drawing as the practice of *outrage: to mark* the paper, to leave (plumbaginous) traces.

8. Before the mark: *the image* of the mark, defined simultaneously as the striation of the void and the stigma (blemish) of its model.

—Gérard Titus-Carmel

* * *

Although he did not have his first exhibition until 1964, this artist, having completed his studies as the Ecole Boulle in Paris, has mounted 81 one-man shows in many parts of the world during the intervening years (including 48 prints at the Abbaye des Cordeliers, Châteauroux, 1987).

Essentially, that early training at the École Boulle has stood him in good stead largely because he has proved himself a master of linear craft with a particular understanding of the extra fulfillment he can acquire from the promise that the paper has to offer depending upon its ''character.'' Evidence of this special gift has been attested on a global scale. (In point of fact, Titus-Carmel ceased to paint pictures in oils after 1969, and did not employ oil again as a medium until the huge *IX Ombres pour STC* series of 1984.)

Important enough; but this is only half of the story. From his well-established basis as an exceptional draughtsman, he has gone to the heart of ''figuration'' and linked it with a controlling—in Willy Rotzler's words—conviction ''of the *reflection* of the functioning'' of subject and technique combined. What this means becomes clear and apparent in actual contact with his works. Then it can be seen that the ''figuration'' is still realised even when it is clothed and engulfed by the creator's graphic and detailed techniques.

These descriptions refer to the artistic production of the 1970s when Titus-Carmel sought to swathe and tightly bandage his subject with taut accuracy. More recently, and increasingly at the present time, his work in style and its current huge dimensions has undergone a number of fundamental changes. The devastating neatness of the earlier pictures has given way to a calculated flamboyance decked out for the most part in washes of pulsating darknesses with rare flashes of brightness almost like accents in the course of some heroic oratory.

Typical instances of this transformation occur in the two collections *Eclats* and *Caparacons.* These began in 1980, lasting for two more years before going on show at the Galerie Maeght, Paris. All the works shown then, although they were emphasised with rich stretches of watercolour—sometimes browns or greys, sometimes a combination of both, in certain cases more varied with a colour scale ranging through blues, greens, yellows and reds, together with their colour fabrics—continued to be supported by his deft ability—even in this new approach—as a supreme draughtsman. His work now avoided his erstwhile strict linear sharpness. The images, including their outline edges, possessed the rolling rhythm of waves—especially in the *Eclats.* They created a theatre-in-the-round (even when they gave sweeping glimpses of the half-filled glass at the Circle Bar) which could flow from stage to amphitheatre and back, whereas the *Caparacons* concentrated on the curtain concealing the stage, or upon the stage itself alive with decor-scaffolding bric-a-brac. Swish curtains or unwriggled forefront of rich opacity, both these kinds of imagery evoke the magic of the playhouse never previously present in works of art.

After the *Eclats* and the *Caparacons,* he became busy with work on other themes: the *Suite Chancay,* his *Boréales,* the *Compositions autour de l'X* and *Interieurs.* Something of the meaning of this artist's raison-d'être development—not always easy to perceive—has yielded a part of its secrets during the past two years.

Possibly Jacques Henric, who knows Titus-Carmel well, has put his finger on the pulse when he looks into T-C's means and motives. Most of all he asserts that here is a creator who understands that the finest perfume always requires a fly in the ointment. This does not mean that for Titus-Carmel *Perfection* is a dirty word, but rather to draw near to unsullied beauty it is necessary to introduce a soupçon of *valde malum* to offset a pervading atmosphere of *valde bonum!* As this hardening process has continued in the artist's works, a stripping and scalping, a ripping off of some of the epidermis element has had to be introduced. It is almost as if *id quod visum placet* has needed to be debunked because under the skin real beauty lies hidden. Not that such a painful operation should be brought about in one fell swoop. Such a revealing has to be accomplished only a tiny bit at a time.

Paradoxically a suggestion of the same result can be obtained (and is obtained by Titus-Carmel) by his concern with what he modestly dubs Papiers-Collés, only in such instances (especially the most recent) these additives obscure parts and surfaces of the original washes and linear structures of his huge pictures—a sort of agreeable torture inflicted upon ideas. His is not, however, a destructive intention. On the contrary, he is seeking to find hidden realities of what his pictures have in their innermost recesses by use of a continuing subtraction of surplus *avoir-du-poids* until deep-seated (and eternal, past and future) truths within the essence of subjects and matter come to the surface. Put another way, this artist is in a sense riding off at a tangent in the belief that the cruder aspect of original picture painting ought not to be allowed to stay in situ. Rather they should be opening doors, windows, even secret trap-doors to divulge what lies within.

—Sheldon Williams

TOMASZEWSKI, Henryk

Nationality: Polish. **Born:** Warsaw, 10 June 1914. **Education:** Studied graphics, under Mieczyslaw Kotarbinski, at the Art Academy, Warsaw, 1934–39. **Career:** Graphic artist and poster designer, Warsaw, from 1946; co-founder, Poster Museum, Warsaw, 1968. Professor of graphic design, Art Academy, Warsaw, since 1952. **Awards:** First Prize, *Polish Poster Exhibition,* Wieden, 1956; First Prize, *Bienal,* Sao Paulo, 1963; Medal, *Internationale Buchkunst Ausstellung,* Leipzig, 1965; Gold Medal, *Poster Biennale,* Lahti, Finland, 1979; First Prize, *Colorado International Poster Exhibition,* 1981; ICOGRADA Excellence Award, 1986; Gold and Silver Medal, 1988, and Bronze Medal, 1994, International Poster Triennal, Toyama, Japan. Honorary Royal Designer to Industry (U.K.), 1976. **Address:** Jazgarzewska Street 13, 00–730 Warsaw, Poland.

Individual Exhibitions:

1969 Kunstverein/Kongresshaus, Biel-Bienne, Switzerland
1972 Poster Museum, Wilanow, Poland
1984 Gallery A. and B. Wahl, Warsaw
1991 Stedelijk Museum, Amsterdam (catalog)
1993 *Henryk Tomaszewski: Plakat,* IFA-Galerie Friedrichstrasse, Berlin (catalog)

Selected Group Exhibitions:

1948 *Miedzynarodowa Wystawa Plakatu,* Wieden, Poland
1963 *Bienal,* Sao Paulo (and 1979)
1966 *International Poster Biennale,* Warsaw (and regularly, 1968–86)
1971 *Polske Plakater,* Louisiana Museum, Humlebaek, Denmark
1978 *International Biennale of Design,* Wroclaw, Poland
1980 *Das Polnische Plakat von 1892 bis Heute,* Hochschule der Kunste, West Berlin
1981 *Colorado International Invitational Poster Exhibition*
1982 *Biennale of Graphic Arts,* Brno, Czechoslovakia
1985 *First International Poster Triennial,* Toyama, Japan
1986 *International Poster Salon,* Paris (and 1987)
1993 *100 Years of the Polish Poster* (travelling exhibition)
Lahti X Poster Biennale, Lahti, Finland
1994 *4th International Poster Triennial,* Toyama, Japan
1999 *Wester Amerykanski: Polish Poster Art and the Western,* Autry Museum of Western Heritage, Los Angeles

Collections:

National Museum, Warsaw; Deutsches Plakat-Museum, Essen, Germany; Kunstgewerbemuseum, Stockholm; Stedelijk Museum, Amsterdam; Kamakura Museum of Modern Art, Kamakura, Japan; Museum of Modern Art, New York; Museu de Arte Moderno, Sao Paulo; Museum of Applied Arts, Stockholm; Museum of Modern Art, Toyama, Japan.

Publications:

By TOMASZEWSKI: Book—*Book of complaints,* Warsaw 1961; *Henryk Tomaszewski,* with Jan Bokiewicz, Wojciech Freudenreich and Stanislaw Wieczorek, Warsaw 1993.

On TOMASZEWSKI: Books—*Henryk Tomaszewski* by Barbara Kwiatkowska, Warsaw 1959; *International Poster Biennale,* exhibition catalog with text by J. Fijalkowska, Warsaw 1966; *Polski Plakat Filmowy 1947–1967,* exhibition catalog with text by Z. Schubert, Poznan 1969; *Polska Sztuka Plakatu* by Szymon Bojko, Warsaw 1971; *Das Polnische Plakat von 1892 bis Heute,* exhibition catalog, West Berlin 1980. **Articles—**''Polish Film and Theatre Posters'' by Charles Robonyi in *Graphis* (Zurich), no. 63, 1956; ''3rd Internationale Plakat-Biennale in Warschau 1970'' by J. Spohn in *Gebrauchsgraphik* (Munich), no. 11, 1970; ''Graphic Design in Poland'' by Szymon Bojko in *The Penrose Annual,* London 1973; ''Universal Dimensions'' by Szymon Bojko in *Art and Artist* (London), September 1976; ''Henryk Tomaszewski'' by Jan Zielecki in *Projekt* (Warsaw), no. 4, 1985; ''The Painted Word: Henryk Tomaszewski'' by Andrzej Klimowski in *Eye,* vol. 1, no. 4, Summer 1991; ''Henryk Tomaszewski'' by Alain Le Quernec in *Idea,* vol. 41, no. 241, November 1993; ''Poster Master'' by James Victore in *Print,* vol. 49, no. 5, September-October 1995.

* * *

''Thanking you, Henryk,'' read the eulogizing title of an exhibition held in Warsaw in 1975 by an international group of postgraduate students connected with Professor Tomaszewski's studio. In exhibiting their own works, the young graphic artists paid homage to the teacher who fascinated them by his personality. One of them wrote: ''Since I have met Professor Henryk Tomaszewski, I know that the art of the poster is a moral discipline.'' Another student tried to sketch the Professor's stimulating way of mediating and making non-verbal comment: ''With one hand, Henryk lights his 87th cigarette from the end of the 86th one, while with his other hand he puts on his spectacles No. 5; with his third hand he cuts a rectangular piece of glossy red paper which will 'play' on crumpled grey backing paper, pinned up with his fourth hand. For the 29th time he moved the edge of this paper, cuts another red rectangle, changes his spectacles to No.

2, paces back, returns, softens up a bright light, again steps back, and says 'This must sing. . . .'''

This lengthy quotation was necessary. Rare as it happens, a characteristic portrait of the artist in question is a mirror of his creative and teaching activity. Young people from various continents, desirous of moral and ethical wisdom, move to Tomaszewski's post-graduate studies, which brings to mind similar treks to Grotowski's Laboratory Institute. They rarely meet with disappointment. In Warsaw they find an impulse for spontaneuos action. Freeing themselves from memorized rules and methods, they return to a happy land of free imagination. The 61-year-old dean of the Polish school of the poster is now surrounded by the legend of a man sensitive to deceit and hypocrisy. He is merciless to appearances and to sullen solemnity. With his stand and his graphic work he immunizes his fellow-countrymen to empty bureaucratic language, phraseology, and pretentiousness. He is credited with many sayings and ironic maxims, maybe once heard in the street, passed on from slang into the literary language. Resentful towards dogmas and pseudo-rationalist doctrines, intellectually independent and contrary, he has greatly influenced the artistic consciousness of a few generations of graphic artists, illustrators, and cartoonists.

Tomaszewski has originated a style of mass graphic art, demanding of the viewer some mental effort, as well as an ability to grasp rapidly the sense of abbreviations, associations, understatements, and paradoxes. Nothing should be taken seriously, verbatim, or without detachment. This work has incorporated the play element, and from child's sensitivity a kind of sophisticated infantilism. At the same time, it is opulent in subtle nuances, possessing neither cruelty, nor black humour, nor riddle. Rather irony and self-irony.

Its aesthetic origin is eminently Polish and is situated in the same development line as the prose and drama of Witkiewicz, Schulz, Gombrowicz, and Mrozek, and the poetry of Tuwim and Galczynski, as well as the literary and student revues of the 1960s and earlier, headed by the Bim-Bom, crammed with grotesquerie, parody, and sneer. One may say that the posters and drawings by Tomaszewski are a mirror of popular Polish mentality. They always create an impression of handwriting, thus attaining the value of an intimate notebook, not intended for strange eyes. The line, drawn as if by a maladroit child's hand, breaks off, loses the trend on the way, and keeps scrawling. The colour plane is simultaneously undecided, and it rarely runs along the outline. It has the charm of an improvisation, and of an unconcerned scrawl. In fact, the artist prepares every line and colour patch with the greatest of care. He even brings a complicated thought or idea down to a synthesis or to a sign deriving from the drawing devoid of embellishments.

Tomaszewski has had a great moral influence in the country. Each one of his new works elicits aesthetic and social comments. In a recent interview he said the most important for him is the motive of the communication and its range of meaning: ''Often on my piece of paper, there is as if nothing to be looked at, nothing beautiful. These are things unable to caress the eye.'' And somewhere else, in the same spirit: ''I prefer a foolish proposition to mastered perfection.''

The artist's poster achievement is generally known from exhibitions and publications. Many of his works have a permanent place in 20th century art, including posters for the film *La beaute du diable* (1954), for an exhibition of sculpture by Henry Moore (1959), for the theatrical performances of *Hamlet* (1970), *Slub* (*The Marriage*) by Gombrowicz (1974), and *Witkacy,* a stage collage of plays by Witkiewicz (1974), and for the Theatre of the Nations session in Warsaw (1976). His drawings are dispersed among various periodicals and, apart from the album *Ksiazka zazalen* (*The Book of Complaints*), 1961, have not been the subject of a monograph so far.

—Szymon Bojko

TORONI, Niele

Nationality: Swiss. **Born:** Locarno-Muralto, 15 March 1937. **Education:** In Locarno. **Career:** Independent artist, Locarno, subsequently in Paris; member, with Buren, Mosset and Parmentier, Groupe BMPT, Paris 1966–68. **Agent:** Galerie Yvon Lambert, 5 rue Grenier Saint Lazare, 75003 Paris. **Address:** 73 rue Damremont, 75018 Paris France.

Individual Exhibitions:

1969 16 Castagnary, Paris
1970 Galerie Yvon Lambert, Paris
Galerie MTL, Brussels
1971 Galerie Michael Werner, Cologne
1972 Galerie Yvon Lambert, Paris
Jack Wendler Gallery, London
Galerie Michael Werner, Cologne
1973 Galleria Francoise Lambert, Milan
Wide White Space Gallery, Antwerp
1974 John Gibson Gallery, New York
Galleria Forma, Genoa
Galleria d'Alessandro Ferranti, Rome
1975 Wide White Space Gallery, Antwerp
Palais des Beaux-Arts, Brussels
Galerie MTL, Brussels
Galleria Francoise Lambert, Milan
Galerie Yvon Lambert, Paris
1976 Galerie Paul Maenz, Cologne
Robert Self Gallery, London
Galerie Maier-Hahn, Dusseldorf
Galleria Banco, Brescia, Italy
1977 Galleria Ferranti, Rome
Galerie Yvon Lambert, Paris
Museum Haus Kemnade, Bochum, West Germany
Galerie MTL, Brussels
Van Abbemuseum, Eindhoven, Netherlands
1978 Galleria Francoise Lambert, Milan
Samsgallery, Genoa, Italy
Kunsthalle, Berne
1979 Galerie Yvon Lambert, Paris
Galleria Ferranti, Rome
Galerie Paul Maenz, Cologne
1980 Centre d'Art Contemporain, Geneva
Hotel Wolfers, Brussels
1981 Galleria Banco, Brescia, Italy
Samsgallery, Genoa, Italy
Galleria Francoise Lambert, Milan

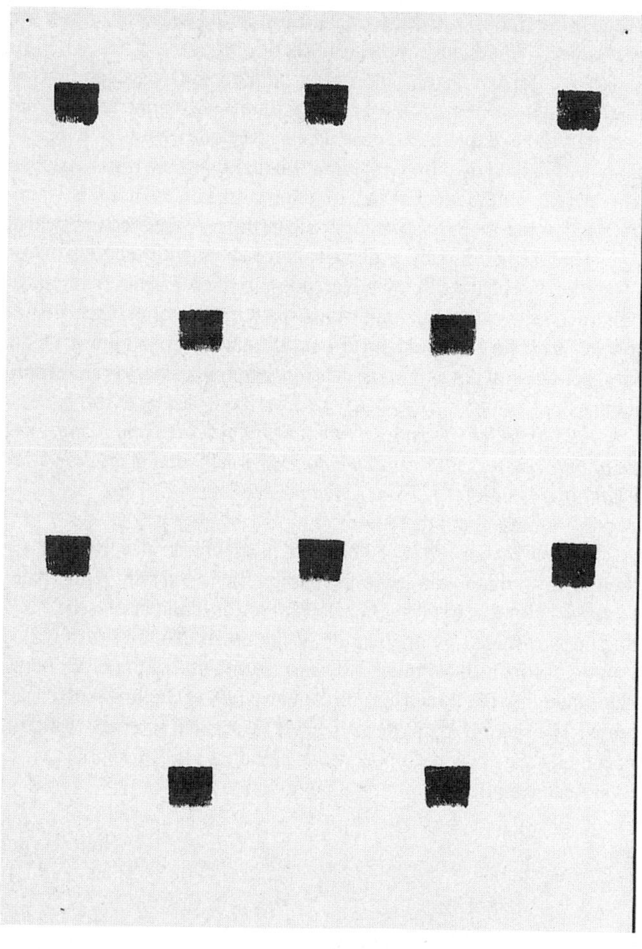

Niele Toroni: *Brush Marks no. 50.* ©CNAC/MNAM/Dist. Réunion des Musées Nationaux/Art Resource, NY. Courtesy of Musee National d'Art Moderne, Centre Georges Pompidou, Paris, France.

1982 Museum van Hedendaagse Kunst, Ghent, Belgium
Galerie M. Szwajcer, Antwerp, Belgium
Galerie Media, Neuchatel, Switzerland
1987 *Niele Toroni: 1967–1987: 20 Ans d'Empreintes,* Villa Arson Centre National d'Art Contemporain, Nizza (also Musée de Sculpture, Grenoble)
1988 *Niele Toroni,* Portikus, Frankfurt am Main (catalog)
1989 *Niele Toroni: Suite n. 1,* Ecole Régionale Supérieure d'Expression Plastique, Tourcoing
Galerie Yvon Lambert, Paris
1991 Museo Communale d'Art Moderna, Ascona, Switzerland
Centre Georges Pompidou, Paris
Marian Goodman Gallery, New York
1992 *Niele Toroni: ''Empreintes de Pinceau no. 50 Repetees a Intervalles Reguliers (30 cm),''* Centre Georges Pompidou, Paris (catalog)
1993 Jule Kewenig Gallery, Frechen-Bachem, Germany
1994 *Niele Toroni: Suite no. 2,* Gemeentemuseum, Amsterdam, Hague (also Stedelijk Museum, Amsterdam) (catalog)
Ugo Ferranti Gallery, Rome
1995 *Niele Toroni,* Douglas Hyde Gallery, Trinity College, Dublin (catalog)
1997 Marian Goodman Gallery, New York

Niele Toroni: *Lino,* 1965. Photo by Philippe Migeat. ©CNAC/MNAM/Dist. Réunion des Musées Nationaux/Art Resource, NY. Courtesy of Musee National d'Art Moderne, Centre Georges Pompidou, Paris, France.

1998 Capc Musée d'Art Contemporain de Bordeaux, Entrepôt, Bordeaux, France (catalog)

Selected Group Exhibitions:

1967 *Biennale,* Musée d'Art Moderne, Paris
1969 *Prospect 69,* Kunsthalle, Dusseldorf
1970 *18 Paris IV 70,* 66 rue Mouffetard, Paris
1972 *Actualites d'un Bilan,* Galerie Yvon Lambert, Paris
1973 *La Peinture en Question,* 16 Place Vendome, Paris (travelled to Monchengladbach and Antwerp)
1975 *Pour-Le/Nous,* Musée d'Ixelles, Brussels
1977 *Europe in the Seventies,* Art Institute of Chicago
1981 *Mise en Pieces. . . ,* Maison de la Culture, Chalon-sur-Saône, France (travelled to Le Coin du Miroir, Dijon)
1982 *Documenta,* Kassel, West Germany
1990 *France Today,* Muzeum Narodowe, Warsaw (also Muzeum Narodowe, Cracow, Poland) (catalog)
1991 *Individualities: 14 Contemporary Artists from France,* Art Gallery of Ontario, Toronto (catalog)
21st Biennale de Sao Paulo, Brazil (catalog)
1992 *Yvon Lambert Collection,* Musee d'Art Moderne du Nord, Villeneuve d'Ascq, France (catalog)

1994 *Wall to Wall,* South Bank Centre, London (travelling exhibition) (catalog)
1995 *"Collections/Collection": The Chest of the Depots and Consignments,* Musee d'Art Moderne, Saint-Etienne, France (catalog)
2000 *Painting Zero Degree:* Cranbrook Museum of Art (also Fred Jones Jr. Art Museum; Cleveland Center for Contemporary Art) (catalog)

Collections:

Musée National d'Art Moderne, Paris; Musée de Toulon; Musée des Beaux-Arts, Ghent; Van Abbemuseum, Eindhoven; Stadtisches Museum, Monchengladbach.

Publications:

By TORONI: Books—*11 Documents photographiques reunis par Niele Toroni,* Brussels 1975; *Galleria allegria,* Paris 1981; *Niele Toroni: "Empreintes de Pinceau no. 50 Repetees a Intervalles Reguliers (30 cm)",* Nizza 1987; *Niele Toroni: 1, 2, 3, 4, 5,* Ghent 1990. **Article—**"Real Paintings: A Conversation with Niele Toroni" with Jeanne Siegel in *Arts Magazine,* vol. 64, no. 2, October 1989.

On TORONI: Books—*18 Paris IV 70,* exhibition catalog with text by Michael Claura, Paris and New York 1970; *Actualité d'un Bilan,* exhibition catalog, edited by Yvon Lambert, Paris 1972; *La peinture en question,* exhibition catalog with texts by Michael Claura and Rene Denizot, Paris 1973; *Un Empreinte n'est jamais seule* by Rene Denizot, Paris 1975; *Niele Toroni,* exhibition catalog with text by Rene Denizot, Eindhoven, Netherlands 1977; *Niele Toroni: 52 pages, 52 pagine, 52 seite,* exhibition catalog with text by Johannes Gachnang, Berne 1978; *Mise en pieces, mise en place, mise au point,* exhibition catalog with an introduction by Xavier Douroux and Christian Besson, Chalon-sur-Saone, France 1981; *Documenta 7,* exhibition catalog, edited by Rudi H. Fuchs, Kassel, West Germany 1982; *Formalité et historicité* by Benjamin Buchloh, Paris 1982. **Articles—**"Niele Toroni: En Toute Difference" by Mo Gourmelon in *Artefactum,* vol. 5, no. 23, April-May 1988; "Le Cabinet de Peinture de Niele Toroni" by Bernard Marcade in *Beaux Arts Magazine,* no. 78, April 1990; "Insert: Niele Toroni" in *Parkett,* no. 29, September 1991; "Niele Toroni: 'Prints Painter'" by Adachiara Zevi in *L'Architettura,* vol. 41, February 1995.

*

Why is it that someone who *does something* (and I underline this because there are so many very active people who never do anything at all) is continually asked "why", for a justification? Is it for reassurance?

In this instance is it because you don't have the courage to accept your reaction in front of his work? Whether negative or positive, that's not the point. The problem is this need for a "debate on," which pretends parasitically to exist in the place of that which stimulates it; this need for intermediaries; it's true that it maintains quite a lot of people, in fish, in vegetables, in art.

It's again the problem of conditioning. There are those who don't even dare to say "I'm fine," "I feel bad"; first they want explanations (the famous why), to know if perhaps they are unhappy because they haven't understood that they should be happy, bravo, the brave face. When you feel bad, say so, bawl it out.

To return to our story, in front of a work begin by accepting what goes through your mind (if something does; it is not an absolute necessity!). No explanation can take its place or then lots of explanations will make you admit anything. Marcel Proust wrote: "As soon as reasoning intelligence wants to judge works of art, nothing is any longer definite or indisputable: one can prove whatever one wants to". That's true enough, especially these days with the swarms of "intelligent debaters." Whoever doesn't know what to do talks painting, writes painting, understands painting . . . . but take care not to touch a brush, you could dirty your little hands or other things! It's a pity that one still doesn't know where a work of art begins and where it ends . . . . .

All this to let you know that my work/painting cannot, must not be of more or less interest depending on what I could say to you or what others might say to you about it.

It's painting and that's all.

Visible marks of a no. 50 brush (typically pictural work tool), for the brush, so that it can leave its mark, is saturated with paint, paint which is colour, colour that one doesn't see as a rule because it's in a tin and is revealed by application of the brush. No. 50 brushmarks, "spots" of paint if you like, (the surface covered with colour being determined by the dimension of the hairy part of the brush, that part which is used for painting) repeated at regular intervals (30cm), occupying the chosen support while leaving it visible, legible.

Read a wall. Why not? It's up to you to see.

—Niele Toroni

TOSANI, Patrick

Nationality: French. **Born:** Boissy L'Aillerie, France, 1954. **Education:** Studied architecture, 1970s. **Career:** Independent artist, Paris.

Selected Individual Exhibitions:

1983 Galerie Liliane et Michel Durand-Dessert, Paris
1984 *Patrick Tosani,* Palais de la Bourse, Nantes; Musée municipal La Roche-sur-Yon, France; Palais des congrès et de la culture, Le Mans, France (catalog)
1985 *Patrick Tosani: Portraits,* Galerie Liliane et Michel Durand-Dessert, Paris (catalog)
1987 *Patrick Tosani,* Fondation nationale de la photographie, Paris; Institute of Contemporary Arts, London (catalog)
1988 Galerie Liliane et Michel Durand-Dessert, Paris
Patrick Tosani, Musée départemental d'art contemporain de Rochechouart, France (catalog)
1990 Galerie Reckermann, Cologne
1991 Magasin, Centre National d'Art Contemporain Grenoble, France (catalog)
Kunsthalle St. Gallen, Switzerland
1992 *Patrick Tosani: Photographer,* Art Institute of Chicago; Chrysler Museum, Norfolk; Santa Monica Museum of Art; Musée du Québec (catalog)
1993 Galerie Rodolphe Janssen, Brussels
Galerie Liliane et Michel Durand-Dessert, Paris

Patrick Tosani, ARC-Musée d'Art Moderne de la Ville de Paris; Palais des Beaux-Arts, Cherleroi, Belgium (catalog)

1994 Mizuma Art Gallery, Tokyo
Imura Art Gallery, Kyoto

1995 Galerie Reckermann, Cologne, Germany
Gallery One, Tokyo
Le Parvis 3, Pau, France
Patrick Tosani: Ongles, Centre d'Art Contemporain, Saint-Priest, France (catalog)

1997 Museum Folkwang, Essen, Germany (catalog)

1998 Centre National de la Photographie, Paris
Galerie Liniane et Michel Durand-Dessert, Paris
Patrick Tosani: Fingernails and Bodies, Zabriskie Gallery, New York
Musée Niepce, Chalon-sur-Saône, France

1999 Mizuma Art Gallery, Tokyo

2000 Zabriskie Gallery, New York

Selected Group Exhibitions:

1991 *Vom Vershwinden der Dinge aus der Fotografie,* Museum Moderner Kunst, Palais Liechtenstein, Vienna
Anni Novanta, Faleria d'Arte Moderna, Bologna
Kunst Europa, Reutlingen, Germany
A Dialogue About Recent American and European Photography, Museum of Contemporary Art, Los Angeles

1992 *Skulpturen-Fragmente Internationale Fotoarbeiten der 90er Jahre,* Wiener Secession, Vienna
Caisse des Dépôts et Consignations: Acquisitions 1989–1991, 56 rue Jacob, Paris
A Visage découvert, Fondation Cartier, Jouy-en-Josas, France
La question de l'image, Musée des Beaux-Arts André Malraux, Le Havre, France

1993 *Histoire de Voir,* Chateau de Villeneuve/Fondation Emile Hugues, Vence, France
L'Ivresse du Réel, Carré d'Art Musée d'Art Contemporain, Nîmes, France
L'Image dans le Tapis, Cercle de l'Arsenal, Venice
Impressions multiples: Collection Caisse des Dépôts, Centre Culturel du Conde Duque, Madrid

1994 *La Ville,* Musée National d'Art Moderne, Centre Georges Pompidou, Paris
L'art de portrait aux XIXème siècles en France, Museum of Modern Art, Akita, Japan
Collection de la Fondation Cartier, National Museum of Contemporary Art, Seoul, South Korea
Les Collectionneurs: Le retour, Musée d'Art Contemporain, Marseilles, France

1995 *Moholy-Nagy and Present Company,* Art Institute of Chicago
Images-Objets (collection of FRAC Lorraine), Vandoeuvre, France
L'homme Photographié, Centre d'art contemporain de l'Abbaye St.-André, Meymac, France
Morceaux Choisis du Fonds National d'Art Contemporain, Magasin Centre National d'Art Contemporain, Grenoble, France

1996 *Une aventure dontemporaine: la photographie 1955–1995,* Maison Européenne de la Photographie, Paris
La Photographie Contemporaine en France: 10 ans d'asquisitions, Musée National d'art moderne, Centre Georges Pompidou, Paris
Passions Privées: Collections Particulières d'art moderne et contemporain en France, Musée d'Art Moderne de la Ville de Paris
Collections, Collection, Musée d'art moderne, Saint-Etienne, France

1997 *Images, Objects, Scène, quelque aspects de l'art en France depuis 1978,* Magasin, Centre National d'Art Contemporain, Grenoble, France
Les Lieux du Non-Lieu, Künstlerwerkstatt Lothringer Strasse 13, Munich, Germany
2ème Biennale Internationale de Photographie de Tokyo, Tokyo Metropolitan Museum of Photography
Patrick Tosani: Fotoarbeiten seit 1976, Museum Folkwang, Essen, Germany (catalog)

1998 *La Collection,* Fondation Cartier pour l'Art Contemporain, Paris
Love boat-collection, Musée Départemental d'Art Contemporain, Rochechouart, France
La photographie sort de sa reserve, Musée de Toulon, France
Zeitgenössische Fotokunst aus Frankreich, Neuer Berliner Kunstverein, Berlin; Städtische Museum, Zwikau, Germany; Hallescher Kunstverein, Halle, Germany

1999 *Dards d'art: Mouches, Moustiques . . . et Modernité,* Musée Réattu, Arles, France
Silent Presence: Contemporary Still-Life Photography, Staatliche Kunsthalle, Baden-Baden, Germany
L'Occidente Imperfetto, 8th Biennale Internzionale de Fotografia, Palazzo Brichersio, Torino, Italy
Le siècle du corps: photographie 1900–2000, Culturgest, Lisbon, Portugal; Musée de l'Elysée, Geneva

Publications:

On TOSANI: Books—*Patrick* Tosani by Gilles A. Tiberghien, Paris 1997. **Articles—**"Still in Time: The Photographs of Patrick Tosani" by Joseph Simas in *Arts Magazine,* December 1990.

* * *

TŌT, Endre

Nationality: Hungarian. **Born:** Endre Toth in Sumeg, 5 November 1937; adopted the name "Tōt" in 1965. **Education:** Hungarian Academy of Applied Arts, Budapest, 1959–65. **Family:** Married Teri Simon in 1969 (divorced, 1981); daughter: Bea; married Herta Paraschin in 1981. **Career:** Independent artist, Budapest, 1965–78, West Berlin, 1978–79, and in Cologne, since 1980: painted first "Zero" and "Rain" works, 1971; ceased painting, 1971; first "Gladness" works, 1971. Instructor, Budapest elementary school, 1965–68, 1972–75, and Technical School for Printing, Budapest, 1968–72. **Awards:** Prize, *Drawing Triennale,* Wroclaw, 1974, 1977;

Endre Tōt: *We Are Glad If We Can Demonstrate,* Whitechapel Art Gallery, London, 1979/2000. ©Endre Tōt.

DAAD Scholarship to West Berlin, 1978–79. **Agents:** Galerie Orez Mobiel, Paviljoensgracht 68/70, NL-2512 BR The Hague, Netherlands; Galerie Bama, 40 rue Quincampoix, F-75004 Paris, France; Galerie Magers, Handelstrasse 13, D-5300 Bonn 1, Germany, and Edition Hundertmark, Brusselerstrasse 29, 5000 Cologne 1, Germany. **Address:** Engelbertstrasse 55, D-50674 Cologne, Germany.

Individual Exhibitions:

1966 Epitök Muszaki Club, Budapest
1968 Ferenczy K. Museum, Szentendre, Hungary
1969 K.F.K.I. Club, Budapest
Mednyánszky Gallery, Budapest
1972 *My Unpainted Canvases,* Ferencvarosi Pincetariat, Budapest
1973 *10 Questions,* Galerie Adres, Lodz, Poland
Fluxus West, San Diego, California (toured California)
1974 *Zero Texts 1971–72,* Studentenhaus, Graz, Austria
One Dozen Rain Postcards 1971–73, Galerie Ecart, Geneva
1975 *Rainproof Ideas/Zero/Gladness,* Israel Museum, Jerusalem (retrospective)
1976 *Rainproof Ideas 1971–75,* Galerie Inge Baecker, Bochum, West Germany
1977 *Rainproof Ideas/Gladness Writings,* Galerie Bama, Paris
1978 *Gladness Questionary,* Studio 16 E, Turin
Nullified Questionary, Galerie A, Amsterdam
Rainy Questionary, Galleri Suburgata, Reykjavik, Iceland
1979 *Gladness Writings, Questions, TOTalJOYS,* Galerie René Block, West Berlin
Gladness Drawings, Galerie A, Amsterdam
Gladness Drawings and Writings, Galerie St. Petri, Lund, Sweden
TOTalZEROS 1973–77, Art Something, Amsterdam
1980 *Very Special Gladnesses,* Galerie Magers, Bonn
Galerie Orez Mobiel, The Hague
Stempelplaatz Galerie, Amsterdam
1981 Artothek, Cologne
1983 Galerie fur Visuelle Erlebnisse, Cremlingen, West Germany
1984 Kunstraum Kunoldstrasse 34, Kassel, West Germany
1987 Edition Hundertmark, Cologne
1991 Kölnisher Kunstverein, Cologne
1992 Galerie Berndt, Cologne
1993 Galerie Waßermann, Munich
Artpool, Budapest
Kunsthalle Szombathely, Hungary
1994 Pāszti-Bott Galerie, Cologne

1995 *''Nothing Ain't Nothing,'' Retrospective (1965–1995),* Kunsthalle, Budapest
Stamp Art Gallery, San Francisco, California
1997 Galerie Hundertmark, Cologne
Fabrik Café, Cologne
1998 Verlag IL/ASAT European, Cologne
1999 *''Who's Afraid of Nothing,'' Absent Pictures,* Museum Ludwig, Cologne
Museum für Zeitgewössische Kunst, Ludwig Museum, Budapest
2000 Galerie Schröder and Dörr, Bergisch-Gladbach, Germany

Tōt has also presented numerous performances and actions throughout Europe since 1972.

Selected Group Exhibitions:

1971 *Biennale de Paris,* Parc Floral, Paris
1974 *Artists' Stamps and Stamp Images,* Simon Fraser Gallery, Burnaby, British Columbia
1976 *Artists' Books,* Institute of Contemporary Arts, London (toured the U.K.)
1978 *L'Estampe Aujourd'hui,* Bibliotheque Nationale, Paris
Acht Kunstler stellen sich vor, DAAD Galerie, West Berlin
1981 *Books by Artists,* National Gallery of Canada, Ottawa
1984 *International Kunstler Gremium Ausstellung,* Museum Fredericianum, Kassel, West Germany
1985 *Livres d'Artistes,* Centre Georges Pompidou, Paris
1994 *Fluxbritannica: Aspects of the Fluxus Movement, 1962-73,* Tate Gallery, London
1995 *FLUXUS in Deutschland 1962–1994,* travelling show
1996 Sammlung Speck, Museum Ludwig, Cologne
1997 Bibliothèque Nationale de France, Paris
1999 *''Aspects/Positions,'' 50 Years of Art in Central Europe,* Museum Moederne Kunst Stiftung Ludwig, Vienna
2000 *Conceptual Art and Conceptualisms: 1970s in the USP Collection,* Museum of Modern Art, San Paulo
The Art of Eastern Europe in Dialogue with the West, Museum of Modern Art, Ljubljana, Slovenia

Collections:

Kulturministerium Nordrhein-Westfalen, Düsseldorf; Lambert Collection, Paris; Bibliothèque Nationale, Paris; Centre National d'Art Contemporain, Paris; Cabinet des Estampes, Geneva; Gemeentemuseum, The Hague; National Museum, Warsaw; Israel Museum, Jerusalem; Kunsthalle, Hamburg; Nationalgalerie, West Berlin; Tate Gallery, London; Museum of Contemporary Art, Ludwig Museum, Budapest; Museum of Modern Art, Ljubljana, Slovenia.

Publications:

By TŌT: Books and cards—*My Unpainted Canvases,* Budapest 1971; *The States of Zeros,* Budapest 1971; *Incomplete Information (Verbal and Visual),* Oldenburg, West Germany 1972; *Possessive Adjective,* Budapest 1972; *I Am Glad If I Can Write Sentences, One After the Other,* Budapest 1973; *One Dozen Rain Postcards (1971–73),* Budapest 1973; *On the Next Page I Shall Say Something,* Budapest 1973; *Zero-Texts (1971–72),* Graz, Austria 1974; *Night Visit to the National Gallery,* Cullompton, Devon 1974; *Zeropost,* Hinwil 1974; *Nullified Dialogue,* Hinwil 1974; *Correspondance avec John Armleder,* Geneva 1974; *TOTal Questions by TOT,* West Berlin, 1974; *1/2 Dozen Incomplete Visual Informations (1971–74),* Budapest 1974; *One Dozen Rain Postcards (1971–73),* Stuttgart 1974; *Rainproof Ideas (1971–74),* Jerusalem 1975; *TOTalJOYS (1971–75),* Geneva 1976; *Zeropost,* Geneva 1976; *Gladness Writings (1973–76),* Liège, Belgium 1977; *TOTal Zeros (1973–77),* Budapest 1977; *1/2 Dozen Berliner Gladness Postcards (1973–78),* West Berlin 1979; *Ich freue mich, wenn ich auf Plakaten werben kann,* West Berlin 1979; *TOTalJOYS,* West Berlin 1979; *Dirty Rains,* Lund, Sweden 1979; *Some Nullified Questions,* Amsterdam 1979; *Ten Documents (1973–80),* Amsterdam 1980; *Very Special Drawings,* West Berlin 1981; *Book of an Extremely Glad Artist,* West Berlin 1981; *From Cologne some Jecke Dinge to you, everybody and nobody,* Cremlingen 1983; *Stamps 1971–83,* Cremlingen 1983; *Special Drawings—Private Space,* Kassel 1984; *Evergreen Book,* Cologne 1991. **Films and videos—***One Step,* 1972; *I Am Glad If. . . ,* 1974; *TOTalsJOYS,* 1976; *I'm Glad if I Can Say Sentences, One After the Other,* 1979; *TOTalJOYS,* 1979; *Nothing Ain't Nothing,* Budapest 1995; *Who's Afraid of Nothing?,* Cologne 1999.

On TŌT: Books—*Mail Art: Communication—A Distance- Concept,* edited by Jean-Marc Poinsot, Paris 1971; *Aktuelle Kunst in Osteuropa,* edited by Klaus Groh, Cologne 1972; *Stamp Activity* by Jiri H. Kocman, Brno, Czeschoslovakia 1972; *An Annual of New Art and Artists 1973–74,* edited by W. Sandberg, Cologne 1974; *Art et Communications Marginale* by Herve Fischer, Paris 1974; *Funf Osteuropaische Kunstler,* edited by Klaus Groh, Nuremberg 1975; *Visual Poetry Anthology,* edited by G.J. de Rook, Utrecht 1975; *Europe/America: The Different Avant-Gardes* by Achille Bonito Oliva, Milan 1976; *The Museum of Drawers,* edited by Herbert Distel, Berne 1978; *Fotografie als Kunst/Kunst als Fotografie* by Floris M. Neususs, Cologne 1979; *Testuale: Le Parole e le Immagini,* exhibition catalog edited by F. Caroli and L. Caramel, Milan 1979; *Kunst in Sozialistischen Staaten* by J. Weichart, Oldenburg, West Germany 1980; *Books by Artists* by T. Guest and Germano Celant, Toronto 1981; *Correspondence Art,* edited by M. Cramer and M. Stofflet, San Francisco 1984; *International Artists' Postage Stamps,* edited by B. Lobach, Cremlingen 1985; *Livres d'Artistes,* edited by A. Moeglin-Delcroix Paris 1985; *Wer hat Augst von Moholy-Nagy?,* edited by T. Straus, Cologne 1987; *Ein Lange Geschichte mit Vielen Knoten—Fluxus in Deutschland 1962–1994,* Stuttgart 1995; *Sammlung Speck,* Köln 1996; *''L'Irrésolution Commune d'un Engagement Èquivoque,'' Ecart, Genève 1969–1982,* Geneva 1997; *Aspekte/Positionen—50 Jahre Kunst aus Mitteleuropa 1949–1999,* exhibition catalog, Vienna 1999; *The Art of Eastern Europe in Dialogue with the West,* exhibition catalog, Ljubljana, Slovenia 2000; *Protest & Survive,* exhibition catalog, London 2000.

*

I am always glad of those days, when nothing happens to me except that I wake up in the morning and go to bed in the evening.

—Endre Tōt

TOUSIGNANT, Claude

Nationality: Canadian. **Born:** Montreal, Quebec, 23 December 1932. **Education:** School of Art and Design, Montreal Museum of Fine Arts, 1948–51; Academie Ranson, Paris, 1952. **Family:** Has lived with Judith Terry since 1968; daughters; Isa and Zoe. **Career:** Worked as surveyor, window-dresser, fireman and show salesman at various times; currently, independent artist. Instructor, School of Art and Design, Montreal Museum of Fine Arts, 1961–63; instructor, Ecole des Beaux-Arts, University of Quebec, Montreal, 1970. **Awards:** First Prize (Painting), *Salon de la Jeune Peinture,* Paris 1962; First Prize (Painting), *Perspective '67,* Toronto, 1967; Italian Government Rome Prize, 1973. **Addresses:** 181 Bourget, Montreal H4C 2M1, Canada.

Individual Exhibitions:

1955 L'Echouerie, Montreal
1956 L'Actuelle, Montreal
1957 L'Actuelle, Montreal
1961 Museum of Fine Arts, Montreal
1962 Galerie Denise Delrue, Montreal
1963 Dorothy Cameron Gallery, Toronto
1964 Galerie du Siècle, Montreal
1965 East Hampton Gallery, New York
1966 East Hampton Gallery, New York
Galerie du Siècle, Montreal
1968 Galerie du Siècle, Montreal
Gallery Moos, Toronto
1969 Galerie Sherbrooke, Montreal
1970 Galerie Joliet, Quebec
1972 Gallery Moos, Toronto
1973 National Gallery of Canada, Ottawa (retrospective)
1974 Art Gallery of Ontario, Toronto (retospective)
1976 Winnipeg Art Gallery
Waddington Gallery, Montreal
1977 Windsor Art Gallery, Ontario
1979 Graff Gallery, Montreal
1980 Musée d'Art Contemporain, Montreal
1982 Musée des Beaux-Arts, Montreal
1987 49th Parallel Gallery, New York
1989 Galerie Waddington Gorce, Montreal
1990 Vancouver Art Gallery
1991 Drabinsky Gallery, Toronto
1994 *Claude Tousignant: Monochromes 1978–1993,* Musée du Québec (travelling exhibition)
1995 Galerie Christiane Chassay, Montreal
Christopher Cutts Gallery, Toronto
1998 *Claude Tousignant: Charged Spaces, 1955–1998,* Galerie de Bellefeuille, Montreal
2000 *Claude Tousignant: Introspective,* Winchester Gallery, Victoria, Canada

Selected Group Exhibitions:

1962 *Modern Canadian Painting,* Palazzo Collicola, Spoleto, Italy
1965 *The Responsive Eye,* Museum of Modern Art, New York (toured the United States)
1968 *Canada: Art d'Aujord'hui,* Musée National d'Art Moderne, Paris (toured Italy, Switzerland and Belgium)
7 Montreal Artists, Hayden Gallery, Massachusetts Institute of Technology, Cambridge
1969 *Form-Colour,* National Gallery of Canada, Ottawa (toured Canada)
1970 *Panorama de la Sculpture au Quebec 1945–1970,* Musée d'Art Contemporain, Montreal (travelled to the Musée Rodin, Paris)
1971 *49th Parallels: New Canadian Art,* Ringling Museum, Sarasota, Florida
1974 *Recent Canadian Painting,* Art Gallery of Ontario, Toronto
1975 *Time Canada,* Musée d'Art Contemporain, Montreal (toured Canada)
1976 *Trois Generations d'Art Quebecois,* Musée d'Art Contemporain, Montreal
1991 *Abstract Practices I: Delavalle, Evans, Poldaas, Tousignant,* Power Plant, Toronto
1992 *Sculpture in Quebec, 1946–1961: Emergence and Persistence,* Musee du Quebec
1994 *Le Festival de Peinture a Mascouche: l'abstraction a Montreal, 1950–70,* Hotel de Ville, Mascouche, Quebec
1995 *Donations 1989–94,* Musee d'Art Contemporain, Montreal

Collections:

Art Gallery of Ontario, Toronto; Art Gallery of York University, Toronto; Canada Arts Council, Ottawa; National Gallery of Canada, Ottawa; Museum of Fine Arts, Montreal; Musée d'Art Contemporain, Montreal; Musée du Quebec, Quebec City; Vancouver Art Gallery; Larry Aldrich Museum, Ridgefield, Connecticut; Phoenix Museum of Arts, Arizona.

Publications:

By TOUSIGNANT: Articles—''Pour une peinture evidentille'' in *Art Abstract,* exhibition catalog, Montreal 1959; ''Quelques precisions essentielles'' in *Peinture Canadienne Francaise,* Montreal 1971.

On TOUSIGNANT: Books—*Modern Canadian Painting,* exhibition catalog by Charles Delloye, Spoleto, Italy 1962; *7 Montreal Artists,* exhibition catalog by Bernard Teyssedre, Cambridge, Massachusetts 1968; *Claude Tousignant,* exhibition catalog by Danielle

Corbeil, Ottawa 1973; *Claude Tousignant: Sculptures,* exhibition catalog with essay by Normand Theriault, Montreal 1982; *Abstract Practices I: Delavalle, Evans, Poldaas, Tousignant,* exhibition catalog, Toronto 1991; *Claude Tousignant: Monochromes, 1978–1993,* exhibition catalog, Québec 1994; *After Geometry: The Abstract Art of Claude Tousignant* by James D. Campbell, Toronto 1995; *Depth Markers: Selected Art Writings, 1985–1994, Volume One* by James D. Campbell, Toronto 1995; *Claude Tousignant: Charged Spaces 1955–1998,* exhibition catalog with text by James D. Campbell, Montréal 1998. **Articles**—''La jeune peinture au Quebec'' by Francois Gagnon in *Revue d'Esthetique No. 3: Art au Quebec,* Quebec 1963; ''L'Illusion optique de l'Op Art'' by Fernande Saint-Martin in *Vie des Arts* (Montreal), no. 44, 1966; ''Structure de l'espace pictural'' by Fernande Saint-Martin in *Constantes* (Montreal), no. 17, 1968; ''Claude Tousignant'' by Pierre Theberge in *Canada: Art d'Aujourd'hui,* exhibition catalog, Paris 1968; ''Les Plasticiens'' by Pierre Theberge in *Studio International* (London), 1970; ''Claude Tousignant: The Chromatic Space of the Painted Object'' by James D. Campbell in *Espace* (Montreal), no. 32, Summer 1995.

*

What I wish to do is to make painting objective, to bring it back to its source—where only painting remains, emptied of all extraneous matter—to the point at which painting is pure sensation.

—Claude Tousignant

* * *

Claude Tousignant of Montreal has been active full-time as a painter and sculptor since the late 1940s. He dedicated himself to a specifically abstract practice as early as 1950 and he has never looked back. The significance of his oeuvre has been attested to time and time again in important exhibitions and commentary over the course of some four decades in Canada and abroad. In recent years, his monochromes and environmental artworks have been recognized for their important contribution to advancing the cause of international abstract painting and sculpture.

At an early point in this long and exemplary career, Tousignant realized that to take abstract painting one step further, to make a new beginning, he would have to *transgress*. The scope—and the impact—of that transgression could be recognized as early as 1956, when he exhibited paintings in Montreal so radical and reduced that only the resultant outcry could have been safely predicted, since the paintings themselves could not have been foreseen. These *Bi-Chromes,* painted in car enamel on treated linen, and limited in their palette to only a few shiny and hard colors, were decidedly minimal objects of great formal strength. Their author had clearly relinquished the convictions and fateful prejudices of many of the then-prevailing mainstreams of Modernism.

While Tousignant's art has been called ''severely reductive and pure,'' it should be pointed out that, however reductive, however pure it may be, its treatment of colour *as* space has been nothing less than brilliant by any objective standard and, for his observers, has always been stimulating and often uplifting. The chromatic space of his work has only been possible because his practice has always been predicated upon securing for a painting the radical status of *object*.

When a given painting is emptied of all referents to things in the space which lies outside itself, yet succeeds in standing alongside those things with simplicity, dignity and, if you will, autonomous thinghood, it fulfills Tousignant's best intentions. It has become, in the artist's own words, an ''object-in-the-first-degree.''

Let us consider, in this regard, one of the recent double square monochromes, or *Bi-chromes* as Tousignant calls them—whether it be two different colour fields, for instance, deep midnight blue and matte black, or two identical colour fields (the recent *Palindromes*) on aluminium sheets separated by five and a half bare inches of white wall space. As we stand before such a work, our perception of bilateral symmetry is heightened through the sheer hegemony of a chromatic space that seems to weigh on the body. But these paintings achieve more than just pressing the weight of chroma upon the body-image. The coloured space in question is so impossibly resonant, the quantity of its pure colour so generously given, that it literally takes the breath away.

From a distance, as we regard the double monochrome, it is the space generated by the two panels—in effect, a third space created by their interaction—that confirms the high calibre of Tousignant's achievement. Just as Barnett Newman placed full emphasis on the perceptual field of the observer as the first and only condition of viewing, Tousignant places a similar onus upon us. The observer has to become an active, rather than passive, observer in front of one of his works. Tousignant places full emphasis on the intentional consciousness of the observer. What I mean to say is that he respects the intelligence of the observer. He never panders to him or her. He gives freely a lifetime's insights into colour and space. When this gift is received with the same humility in which it was offered, what has been referred to as ''severely reductive'' becomes sensuously self-present.

So when the third space comes into play, the observer has become an active participant in the constitution of the painting as a formal whole that has interesting extra-dimensional implications. The space of the painting progressively impinges upon us.

By stressing the objecthood of painting above all else, Tousignant was led, perhaps ineluctably, to objects that could be construed to be as much sculptures as paintings. From the outset, the artist wanted to free painting *from itself.* That may sound absurd—how can one free something from itself and still have it function?—but the truth is that Tousignant wanted to free painting of all the conventions and referents that limited its meaning and straitjacketed its history. He realized that by stressing the object-quality of a painting, he could make seeing new again.

As a result of his deliberations and his endemic doubt, the artist magnified the impact of a painting on an embodied subject who is situated in real space, who is observing in real time. He removed the painting from the wall plane and made it a profoundly *interactive* phenomenon in real, three-dimensional space.

In the last two years, Tousignant has returned to canvas, and is now working often on a very large scale, executing what are clearly some of the most compelling monochromes of his long career.

All existing definitions of ''sculpture'' and ''painting'' suddenly seem rather outmoded. Tousignant speaks of ''attempting to break out of the yoke of traditional pictorial space.'' In this aspiration he has certainly succeeded. There is nothing traditional about the painting space of his own work.

Monochrome means a single colour. But it is not synonymous with a single experience, or a solitary meaning. Monochrome painting as Tousignant practises it is not a monologue; laden with myriad meanings and generative of many different experiences, it is dialogical in the best sense of that word: enjoining us to participate in a conversation and sustaining that conversation as long as we, observers and accomplices, are open to the everlasting mystery and claim that colour stakes upon us.

In Tousignant's work of yesterday and today, principles such as the autonomy of the object, the true meaning of form and the exploration of space in terms of how we can *live* it, transcend issues of pure formalism. Why? Precisely because these are principles seldom addressed so directly—and so convincingly—in abstract painting.

As we attend to each series of works the artist has executed over the years, we can clearly see the implacable reductive logic and perceptual specificity of an abstract practice that has led Tousignant ineluctably beyond painting *per se,* into a form of environmental sculpture. From the 1956 breakthrough panel paintings to *Monochrome rouge sang (Blood Red Monochrome)* (1994), Tousignant has pursued a vision of painting as uncompromising as it is compelling. It is a vision that not only invigorates painting, but invigorates the observer as well.

—James Campbell

TREMLETT, David

Nationality: British. **Born:** St. Austell, Cornwall, 13 February 1945. **Education:** Studied under Terry Pascoe, Falmouth School of Art, Cornwall, 1962–63; Birmingham College of Art, 1963–66; Royal College of Art, London, 1966–69. **Career:** Full-time artist since 1969; travelled in Spain, Netherlands and Australia, 1969; in Malawi, Tanzania, Botswana, Mozambique, Middle East and Far East, 1970–79; in Alaska, Canada, India, Mexico and Australia, 1980–87. **Agent:** Hester Van Royen, Flat 3, 53 Drayton Gardens, London SW10. **Address:** ''Broadlawns,'' Chipperfield Road, Bovingdon, Hertfordshire HP3 OJR, England.

Individual Exhibitions:

1969 Grabowski Gallery, London
1970 Nigel Greenwood Gallery, London
1971 Nigel Greenwood Gallery, London
Galerie Ernst, Hannover
Folker Skulima Galerie, West Berlin
1972 Nigel Greenwood Gallery, London
Tate Gallery, London
Galerie Konrad Fischer, Dusseldorf
1973 Museum of Modern Art, New York
Harold Rivkin Gallery, Washington, D.C.
Nigel Greenwood Gallery, London
1974 Nigel Greenwood Gallery, London
Museum of Modern Art, Oxford
1975 Galleria Marilena Bonomo, Bari, Italy
1976 Galerie Rolf Preisig, Basel
Nigel Greenwood Gallery, London
Art and Project, Amsterdam
Robert Self Gallery, Newcastle-upon-Tyne
Galleria Marilena Bonomo, Bari, Italy
Galerie Durand-Dessert, Paris
Institute of Contemporary Arts, London
1977 Galerie Durand-Dessert, Paris
1978 Plymouth Art Centre, Devon
Galleria Massimo Valsecchi, Milan
Zomba Road, Malawi, Africa
Art and Project, Amsterdam
1979 Galleria Marilena Bonomo, Bari, Italy
Librairie Post Scriptum, Brussels
Galleria Massimo Valsecchi, Milan
Stedelijk Museum, Amsterdam
1980 Galerie Durand-Dessert, Paris
Gordon Jetty, Tasmania
1981 John Hansard Gallery, Southampton, Hampshire
Galleria Massimo Valsecchi, Milan
Art and Project, Amsterdam
Waddington Galleries, London
Galleria Marilena Bonomo, Bari, Italy
1982 Riverside Studios, London
Galerie Durand-Dessert, Paris
1983 Galerie Durand-Dessert, Paris
Galleria Massimo Valsecchi, Milan
Galleria Marilena Bonomo, Bari, Italy
Raum fur Kunst, Hamburg
Waddington Galleries, London
1984 Waddington Galleries, London
Art and Project, Amsterdam
1985 Centre Georges Pompidou, Paris
Leicester Polytechnic, Leicestershire
Gallery 865, Aalst, Belgium
Le Crystal, Paris
Galleria Marilena Bonomo, Bari, Italy
1986 Orchard Gallery, Londonderry, Northern Ireland (with Hamish Fulton)
Waddington Galleries, London
Institute of Contemporary Arts, London
Museum Van Hedendaagse Kunst, Ghent, Belgium
1987 22 All Saints Road, London
Galerie Durand-Dessert, Paris
Galleria Massimo Valsecchi, Milan
Artek Gallery, Helsinki
1988 Galerie L'A, Liege, Belgium
Art & Project, Amsterdam
Les Maitre de Formes Contemporain, Brussels, Belgium
Dorrie-Priess Galerie, Hamburg
Roslyn Oxley 9 Gallery, Sydney
1989 Galerie Durand-Dessert, Paris
Serpentine Gallery, London

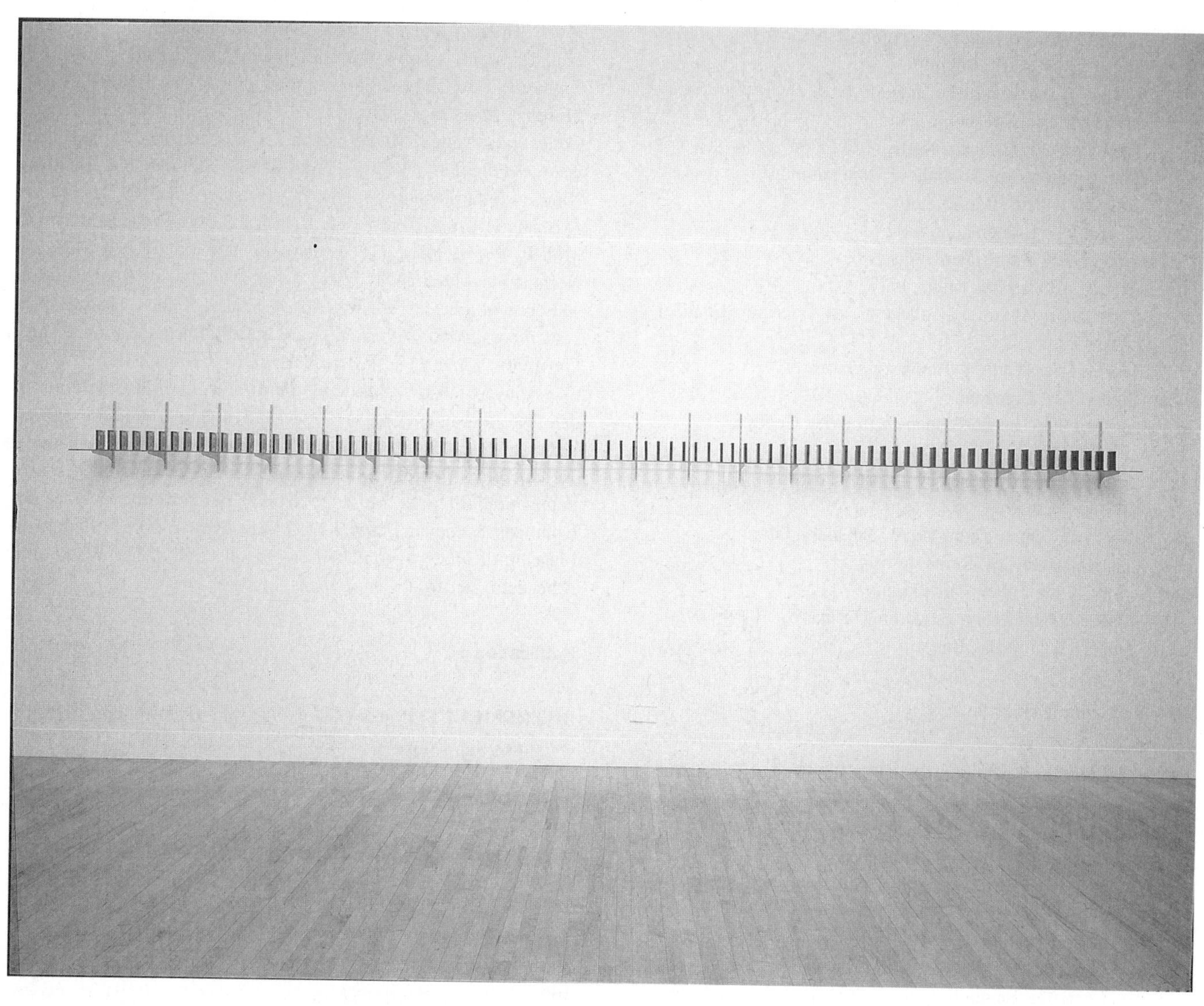

David Tremlett: *The Spring Recordings,* 1972. ©Tate Gallery, London/Art Resource, NY; courtesy of Tate Gallery.

Eglise Val de Vesle, France
Arnolfini Gallery, Bristol
1990 Modulo Gallery, Lisbon and Oporto, Portugal
Palais des Beaux Arts, Paris
Musée de Saint Priest, Lyon
Galerie Durand-Dessert, Paris
Les Maitres de Formes Contemporains, Brussels
Dorrie-Priess Galerie, Hamburg
1991 Lipworth Fine Art, Fort Lauderdale, Florida
Gallery S65, Aalst, Belgium
Massimo Valsecchi Gallery, Milan
Abbey St. Savin, France
Alfonso Artiaco, Pozzuoli, Italy
Marilena Bonomo, Bari, Italy
1992 Dorrie-Priess Galerie, Hamburg
Kestner Gessellschaft, Hannover
Artspace, Auckland, New Zealand
Gerald Peters Gallery, Dallas, Texas
Sue Crockford Gallery, Auckland, New Zealand
Modulo Gallery, Oporto, Portugal
1993 Padiglione d'Arte Contemporanea di Milano, Italy
Rainyday Gallery, Penzance, England
FRAC Picardie, Amiens, France
Gallery Lubie, Amiens, France
1994 The Cornerhouse, Manchester, England
Galleria Allesandra Bonomo, Rome
The British School at Rome
Stadtpark Gallery, Krems, Austria
Galerie de l'Ancien College, Chatellerault, France
Palais Jacques Coeur, Bourges
1995 Carre D'Art, Nimes, France
S.C.A.I. The Bathhouse, Tokyo, Japan
Mizima Gallery, Tokyo, Japan
Galerie Durand-Dessert, Paris, France
Gemeentmuseum, The Hague, Holland
Dorrie-Priess Gallery, Hamburg, Germany
Juan Miro Foundation, Barcelona, Spain
1996 Marilena Bonomo Gallery, Bari, Italy

Alfonso Artiaco Gallery, Pozzuoli, Italy
Gallery S65, Aalst, Belgium
1997 Gallery Stepczynski/Blancpain, Geneva, Switzerland
La Chaufferie, Strasbourg, France
Bank Brussels Lambert, Kortrijk, Belgium
Southampton City Art Gallery, Southampton
Castello Falletti, Barolo, Italy
1998 Gallery G7, Bologna, Italy
Goddard de Fiddes, Perth Australia
Massimo Valsecchi, Milan, Italy
The Gallery, Guernsey College of Art, Guernsey, Channel Islands
1999 Dorrie-Priess Gallery, Hamburg, Germany
2000 Gallery G7, Bologna
Gallery Stepczynski/Blancpain/Bouvier, Geneva, Switzerland
Gallery Durand-Dessert (with Alan Charlton 'Fusion')—Paris, France
New Art Centre, Roche Court, Salisbury, GB
Tor Bella Monaca, Rome, Italy
2001 Art, Culture & Foi, Paris, France
Gallery Marcus Richter, Berlin, Germany
Gallery S.65, Aalst, Belgium

Selected Group Exhibitions:

1972 *Documenta 5,* Museum Fridericianum, Kassel, Germany
1975 *New Media I,* Konsthall, Malmo, Sweden
1977 *03–23–03,* Institute of Contemporary Art, Montreal
1979 *Un Certain Art Anglais,* Musee d'Art Moderne de la Ville, Paris (travelled to Brussels)
1981 *British Sculpture in the Twentieth Centuy,* Whitechapel Art Gallery, London
1987 *L'Exotisme au Quotidien,* Musée des Beaux-Arts, Charleroi, Belgium
1988 *Viewpoint,* Museum of Modern Art, Brussels
1992 *Turner Prize,* Tate Gallery, London
1993 *Out of Sight, Out of Mind,* Lisson Gallery, London
1994 *Wall to Wall,* Leeds City Art Gallery, England
DESSINER une collection d'art contemporain, Musee du Luxembourg, Paris
1995 *1:1 (wall drawings),* Kunstlerwerkstatt, Munich, Germany
1996 The World Over/De Wereld Bollen, Wellington City Art Gallery N.Z and Stedelijk Museum, Amsterdam
1997 *Au Pied du Mur,* FRAC Picardie, Amiens, France
Drawing Distinctions, University Art Museum, Berkeley, and Arizona University Museum
1998 *Au Fil du Trait,* Carre d'Art, Nimes, France
1999 *De Coraz(I)ón,* Centre Cultural Tecla Sala, Barcelona, Spain
2000 *1/2000,* College Jacques-Cartier, Chauny, France

Collections:

Australia: Art Gallery of N.S.W. Sydney; National Gallery of Australia, Canberra. **Belgium:** Museum of Modern Art, Brussels; M.U.K.H.A.; Antwerp; Museum Dhondt-Dhaenens, Deurle, Ghent; Bank Brussel Lambert—Brussels; Bank Brussel Lambert—Kortrijk. **England:** Tate Gallery; Southampton City Art Gallery; Whitworth Museum, Manchester; Arts Council of GB; British Council; Granada Collection. **France:** Musée National d'Art Moderne, Paris; (Centre Georges Pompidou); Musee d'Art Moderne, St. Etienne; Carre d'Art, Nimes; Cartier Foundation; F.R.A.C.-Picardie; F.R.A.C. Champagne-Ardenne, F.R.A.C.-Nord-Pas-de Calais; F.R.A.C.-Bretagne; F.R.A.C. Midi-Pyrénées, F.R.A.C. des Pays de la Loire; F.R.A.C.-Haute-Normandie; Museum St. Priest, Lyon; Museum of Rochechouart; Museum of Le Havre; Museum of Toulon; Fonds national d'art contemporain (Arts Council of France); Bibliotheque National, Paris. **Germany:** Kestner Gesellschaft, Hannover; Kunsthalle, Hamburg; The British Embassy, Berlin. **Holland:** Stedelijk Museum, Amsterdam; Kroller Muller, Otterlo; Boymans Museum, Rotterdam. **Japan:** Benesse Museum of Contemporary Art, Naoshima; The International Forum, Tokyo. **Portugal:** Fundação De Serralves, Oporto; Gulbenkian Foundation. **Poland:** Museum Sztuki. **Switzerland:** Cabinet des Estampes, Geneva. **U.S.A.:** M.O.M.A. New York; Philadelphia Museum of Modern Art; The Lewitt Collection at The Wadsworth Atheneum, Hartford, Connecticut.

Publications:

By TREMLETT: Books—*Some Places to Visit,* London 1975; *On the Waterfront,* Newlyn, Cornwall 1978; *Scrub,* Bari and Paris 1978; *On the Border,* Amsterdam 1979; *Restless,* London 1983; *Old Tom and Hotel Room,* New Haven, Connecticut 1984; *Rough Ride,* Paris and London 1985; *Ruin,* Amsterdam 1987; *Sometimes We All Do,* Bari, Italy 1988; *Working Inside,* France 1989; *Walls in Modulo Gallery,* Lisbon 1990; *Tremlett West Bengal,* Calcutta 1990; *1,9,8,7. Front Side,* London 1990; *Five Postcards from the Palais des Beaux Arts,* Brussels 1990; *Wall Drawing,* Belgium 1990; *Internal,* Milan 1991; *Wall to Wall,* Rome 1991; *The Mjimwema Drawings,* Ghent 1991; *Wall Drawings at Abbey St. Sivan,* France 1991; *Abandoned Drawings,* Amiens 1993; *Casa de Dibujos,* Milan 1993; *Plans We Walk On,* Krems, Austria, 1994; *Nouveau Plans,* Chatellerault, France, 1994; *Rooms in Vienna*, Galerie De L'Ancien College, Chatellerault, France 1994; *Murs*, Palais Jacques Coeur, Bourges, France 1994; *Columns*, Galerie Stadtpark, Krems, Austria 1995; *How Far in That Direction*, Dorrie * Priess Gallery, Hamburg 1996; *Pages*—(+le tremlett) by Jaques Demarcq, La Chaufferie, Strasbourg, France, 1998; *11 cards in book (Eritrea)*, Massimo Valsecchi, Milan, Italy 1998; *Clear & Fuzzy*, SCAI the BathHouse, Tokyo, Japan 1999. **Articles—**''The Art of Searching: An Interview with David Tremlett'' by Willoughby Sharp in *Avalanche*, 3 Fall 1971; Interview with Cathy Courtney in *Art Monthly* (London), November 1992; Interview with Sol Lewitt in *Il Giornale Dell'Arte*, September 1999.

On TREMLETT: Books—*David Tremlett: 4 Sculptures,* catalog poster with essay by Peter Atkins, London 1969; *The British Avant-Garde,* exhibition catalog by Charles Harrison and Donald Karshan, New York 1971; *Documenta 5: Befragung der Realitat,* exhibition catalog edited by Harald Szeemann and others, Kassel 1972; *An Element of Landscape,* exhibition catalog with text by Jeremy Rees, London 1974; *British Sculpture in the Twentieth Century,* exhibition catalog by Sandy Nairne and Nicholas Serota, London 1981; *The Critical Eye,* exhibition catalog with essay by S. Paoletti, New Haven, Connecticut 1984; *David Tremlett,* exhibition catalog, Hannover, Germany 1992; *David Tremlett,* exhibition catalog, Padiglione d'Arte Contemporanea, Milan, Italy 1993; *Wall Drawings,* exhibition catalog, Nimes, France and Barcelona, Spain 1995; *Walls and Their Drawings,* exhibition catalog, Fondazione Bonomo, Castel Del Monte Andria, Bari, Italy, 1996; *Walls in Bologna 1998,* exhibition catalog, Galleria G7, Bologna, Italy 1998; *Passa Dentro,* exhibition catalog, Tor Bella Monaca, Rome, Italy 2000.

* * *

In common with Richard Long, Hamish Fulton or Lothar Baumgarten, the artist David Tremlett takes his inspiration from traditions totally outside his own. For Tremlett, it is the journey, with its transitory locations, temporary resting places and defined cultural identities, which is his stimulus. This does not mean that his language is simply 'cosmopolitan' or more international, but rather that his subject is atopical. He does not renounce that which is conventionally understood as a 'work of art', but he disrupts its traditional modes of expression and the gulf which, in our world, distinguishes the practice of the artist from that of daily life.

He has made frequent trips through Africa and Mexico where he has assimilated ideas and forms belonging to different systems of thought, in order to formulate a vocabulary which vitalizes that formal repertory inherited from Western culture. Very simplified images, latently symbolic and vaguely totemic but stripped of every connotation, become the synthetic schema which are the style of this artist.

It is not without significance that the creative process is instinctive and immediate, employing a direct physical involvement of the artist himself with his materials. Tremlett chooses media such as coloured pastels reminiscent of the organic and allusive elements of the earth, or even extracts his own pigments directly from the earth. At times, he limits himself to elementary black and white, to primary tonalities. Often, the actual wall of the gallery accommodates his images. Spreading the colour directly onto the wall with his hands, Tremlett allows a certain degree of chance in the execution of the work. The wall reveals its unpredictable qualities, its porous and pitted surface reacting in unforeseen ways with the pigment. This unpredictability does not disrupt but actually qualifies the work.

In his works on paper, the drawing signifies the concentration of the mind in the act of governing internal processes. In most cases, the act of drawing determines the dimensions of the project. The environment of the picture plane is scrupulously constructed as a rigorously two-dimensional space, while the titles of the works make reference to architectural space. The images that Tremlett adopts open a discourse on the ambiguity of traditional definitions. Each work, whilst maintaining internal references to its own fulfillment, gestures towards the work which will follow. The pigmentation reclaimed from the earth is the essential material of building and sculpting. The physical work, the action, moulding and consolidation done with the hands, result in the very material of the work.

—Giorgio Verzotti

TROCKEL, Rosemarie

Nationality: German. **Born:** Schwerte, 13 November 1952. **Education:** Studied at the Werkkunstschule, Cologne, 1974–78. **Career:** Independent artist, Cologne, since 1979. **Agent**: Galerie Monika Spruth, Maria-Hilf-Strasse 17, 5000 Cologne 1; Barbara Gladstone Gallery, 515 West 24th Street, New York, New York 10011, U.S.A.

Selected Individual Exhibitions:

1983 Galerie Monika Spruth, Cologne
Galerie Philomene Magers, Bonn
1984 Galerie Monika Spruth, Cologne
Galerie Ascan Crone, Hamburg
Gallerie Stampa, Basel
1985 Galerie Monika Spruth, Cologne
1986 Galleria Stampa, Basel (with Tatafiore and Stumpf)
Galerie Monika Spruth, Cologne
1987 Galerie Tanit, Munich
1988 Kunsthalle, Basel
Museum of Modern Art, New York
1992 Museum of Contemporary Art, Helsinki
1994 Museum of Contemporary Art, Helsinki
Museum of Contemporary Art, Sydney
Barbara Gladstone Gallery, New York
Biennale Sao Paulo, Brazil
1995 Israel Museum, Jerusalem
Musée des Beaux-Arts de Nantes, France (catalog)
1996 Museum für Moderne Kunst, Frankfurt, Germany
Center for Contemporary Art, Ujazkowki Castle, Warsaw, Poland
1997 Barbara Gladstone Gallery, New York
Galerie Monika Spruth, Cologne
1998 Whitechapel Art Gallery, London
Werkgruppen 1986–1998, Kunsthalle Hamburg, Germany
1999 *Rosemarie Trockel: Bodies of Work, 1986–1998,* MAC, Galeries Contemporaines des Musées de Marseille, France (catalog)
Musée d'Art Moderne de la Ville de Paris (with Carsten Höller)
2000 *Dessins,* Centre Georges Pompidou, Paris, and Drawing Center, New York
Pause, Ileana Tounta Contemporary Art Center, Athens
2001 *Manus Spleen,* Barbara Gladstone Gallery, New York
Metamorphoses and Mutations, Drawing Center, New York

Selected Group Exhibitions:

1982 *Licht bricht sich in der oberen Fenstern,* Klapperhof 33, Cologne
1984 *Kunstlandschaft BRD,* Kunstverein, Lubeck, Germany
Bella Figura, Wilhelm-Lehmbruck-Museum, Duisburg, Germany

1986 *Sculptures*, Galleria Stampa, Basel
1987 *Een Keuze/A Choice*, Kunst RAI, Amsterdam
Art from Europe, Tate Gallery, London
1992 *Allegories of Modernism: Contemporary Drawing,* Museum of Modern Art, New York (catalog)
1994 *Critiques of Pure Abstraction,* Independent Curators International touring exhibition (catalog)
1995 *Feminin-Masculin: La sexe de l'art,* Centre Georges Pompidou, Paris (catalog)
1996 Venice Biennale
1997 Documenta X, Kassel, Germany (with Carsten Höller)
1999 Venice Biennale
2000 *Around 1984: A Look at the Art of the Eighties,* P.S. 1 Contemporary Art Centers, New York

Publications:

On TROCKEL: Books—*Rosemarie Trockel: Plastiken 1982–83,* exhibition catalog with text by Wilfried Dickhoff, Bonn and Cologne 1983; *Kunstlandschaft BRD*, exhibition catalog with essay by Wulf Schadendorf, Lubeck 1994; *Rosemarie Trockel: Sculpturen und Bilder,* exhibition catalog with texts by A. R. Penck and Reiner Speck, Hamburg 1984; *Bella Figura,* exhibition catalog with essay by Karl-Egon Vester, Duisburg 1984; *Rosemarie Trockel: Bilder, Skulpturen, Zeichnungen,* with text by Wilfreid Dickhoff, Cologne 1985; *Rosemarie Trockel: Arbeiten 1980–1985,* Bonn and Cologne 1986.

* * *

Interest in Rosemarie Trockel's early work coincided with recent abstract-geometric tendencies in painting. It could be argued that the late 1980s was characterized by a predilection for cool analytical work, supplanting the earlier vogue for figurative and neo-expressionist passion. This abstraction established a critical and ironic distance vis-a-vis the great tradition of abstract painting—i.e., of Malevich and Reinhardt. According to these tendencies, the epic attempt to reestablish perspectival space falls apart, as does the attempt to achieve ultimate or ''supreme'' forms.

Rosemarie Trockel aligned herself with this critical reappraisal of historical abstraction: as Klaus Ottmann has rightly pointed out, her intention is to deconstruct the aesthetic categories of Modern rationalism as much as the hedonism of the Postmodernist age. She does not aim at re-establishing an up-to-date aesthetic, as Peter Halley does, neither does she intend to parody the 1950s in the manner of John Armleder. Trockel elaborates a visual repertoire that focuses on what has been removed from the realm of art by reintroducing a discussion of the categories of creativity: in doing so, she aims at positing a definition of the feminine.

She sees the feminine as a historical dimension and an essential component of art. Typically, she expresses this idea by the device of stretching a length of knitted material onto a frame (like a painting on canvas), the material patterned with motifs akin to those in contemporary clothing. These decorative motifs, typical of feminine creativity within the domestic realm, are now presented as autonomous and formal. The result is a surprising pattern painting, genetically transformed in its function and component parts. Trockel thus promotes a critique of the grand theories of abstraction by suggesting that the mundane is fundamental to all great discourses. This dimension of the mundane can be defined as ''the feminine,'' a concept that the artist uses as a provocative device.

In addition to geometrical motifs, often employed as parody, Trockel has used woven wool and fabrics printed with the most common visual stereotypes of consumerism: the Cowboy, the Hammer and Sickle, the advertising logo Made in West Germany—banal or trivialized insignia of common currency which have lost any (assuming they ever possessed) original meaning. The hammer and sickle lose their ideological significance of which they were a symbol as they become ''purified'' into a geometrical motif.

Balaclava, 1986–90, presents a series of five balaclava masks, knit with the artist's trademark geometric patterns, that cover mannequin heads and are displayed in a vitrine. Instead of offering the warmth and protection that are the stereotypical products of feminine labor, Trockel's mouthless headmasks imply the violence of censorship and suffocation. Similarly, a large mobile, *Almost Gray* from 1992–93, consists of Calder-like forms covered with the artist's trademark machine-knitted gray wool. Works such as these demonstrate—with their oppositions of concealment and disclosure, outside and inside, hard and soft, randomness and order—the artist's attempt to represent the hidden and unrepresented cultural aspect of the gendered female, while confounding our notions of its acceptable form.

Recent films and video installations contribute to Trockel's ongoing demystification of both the role of art in postindustrial culture and her own art and personal history as well. A 1992 video of the artist clad in a knitted sweater, which is slowly being unraveled to expose her naked torso, appears on a monitor that is situated between two windows, which are in turn covered over in knitted gray wool—providing not only the necessary darkness to view the video, but eliciting questions of voyeurism, ownership, and exchange of power as well. More strident in tone, *Continental Divide,* from 1994, depicts Trockel as the violent interrogator of a female victim, demanding to know who is the ''best artist.'' Derisively parodying an article in a German magazine that ranked ''the best 100 artists in the world,'' Trockel threatens, ''We are not playing. It's real.'' Confronting and mocking her victim, herself, and us with the uncomfortable spectacle of an ambitious female who has made it in the tightly controlled, male-dominated international art world, Trockel's work thus eschews ''correct'' feminist readings as much as it reveals the artist's own anxieties about self-exposure.

Trockel's visual repertoire is based on ambiguity; her images are suspended between abstraction and figuration, abandoning their original meaning to appear empty. The serial form of presentation weakens their connotative power, while the elementary manner (based on pure contiguity) in which they are inserted into the visual field prevents their becoming proper structural elements. The artist explicitly talks about the ''depreciation'' she intends to inflict upon the visual elements she has selected.

This negation of the values of signs is a critique of ideologies as totalitarian world-views with their need to legitimize themselves by censoring anything that does not conform. Trockel works at what is considered to be insignificant and ineffective against totalitarian ideologies. In this irrelevance resides the definition of difference, and in its consecration as art lies its power to change the world.

—Essay by Giorgio Verzotti; updated by Dorothy Valakos

In varying media, Trockel continues to work within such dichotomies as natural/industrial, viewer/viewed, animal/human. In 1997, Trockel produced a video that expanded on her woolen or woven pieces. In the video, *À la Motte (Like a Moth)*, Trockel breaks down and builds up woven pieces: they appear to be knit and unravelled endlessly. Thus, both construction and destruction become part of her creative process. The video also shows a moth *(la motte)* eating a hole in a piece of wool. The process then reverses and the hole appears to close up again as if by magic.

Expanding her process by collaborating with other artists and with the audience, Trockel worked together with colleague Carsten Höller to create ''Haus für Schweine und Menschen'' (''House for Pigs and Humans'') at Documenta X in Kassel. Like much of her other work, the project focused on the differences between nature and culture. In one half of the pavillion there was a pigsty with a boar, two pigs, and a few piglets; in the other, a space for the exhibition visitors. Divided by a pane of one-way glass, the human viewers watch the pigs in their natural habitat, reflecting on the connections between our more animalistic origins and our complicated contemporary society.

Trockel filled the German Pavilion at the 1999 Venice Biennale with three projections which were characteristically recondite. Upon entering the darkened space, visitors were greeted with a projection of a huge, blinking eye—a reference to vision and spectatorship.

Trockel has always worked in a variety of media, including video, sculpture, installation, and fabric, but drawing has held a significant position in her practice as a site for experimentation and exploration. In 2001, she exhibited a group of *Dessins* at The Drawing Center in New York. Some of these drawings are made very rapidly and spontaneously, while others are carefully executed. Using primal forms of marking such as the dash and speckle, Trockel distances these automatic drawings from an overly biographical or sentimental touch. Animals turn up again in these drawings, perhaps metaphorically standing in for human counterparts.

—Elizabeth Mangini

TROOSTWYK, David

Nationality: British. **Born:** London, 5 August 1929. **Education:** Royal College of Art, London, 1953–56, A.R.C.A. 1956. **Military:** Royal Air Force, 1947–49. **Family:** Married Ursula Janet Freer in 1953 (divorced, 1963); married Yvette Jean-Marie Bouzigues in 1963 (divorced, 1972); daughter: Lois. **Career:** Independent artist since 1956. Visiting lecturer, Slade School of Fine Arts, 966–70; Chelsea School of Art, London, 1970–71; Sydney College of the Arts, 1978–79. **Awards:** Painting Prize, *John Moores Exhibition,* Liverpool, 1969; First Prize, *British International Drawing Biennale,* Teesside, England, 1973. **Agent:** Matt's Gallery, London. **Address:** c/o Matt's Gallery, 42–44 Copperfield Road, London E3 4RR, England.

Individual Exhibitions:

1964 Southampton University, Hampshire
1969 R.C.A. Galleries, London
Gulbenkian Gallery, London
1970 Angela Flowers Gallery, London (with Alan Davies)
Axiom Gallery, London (with Ivor Abrahams)
1971 Kasmin Gallery, London
1974 Institute of Contemporary Arts, London
1977 Felicity Samuel Gallery, London
1979 Institute of Modern Art, Brisbane
Matt's Gallery, London
1980 Galerija Akumulatory, Poznan, Poland
1981 Matt's Gallery, London
1983 Holland Festival Gallery, Amsterdam
1984 Matt's Gallery, London
1994 Matt's Gallery, London
1999 Robert Sandelson, London
2000 Succession Manufacturing Ltd., London

Selected Group Exhibitions:

1968 Galerie 2D, Amsterdam
1970 Axiom Gallery, London
1974 *International Poezie,* Rotterdam
1975 *Art 75,* Basel
1976 *Biennale,* Art Gallery of New South Wales, Sydney (and 1982)
Stedlijk Museum, Amsterdam
1978 Institute of Contemporary Arts, Los Angeles
1983 Artspace, Sydney
1999 Tate Gallery, London
2000 Whitechapel Art Gallery, London

Collections:

Tate Gallery, London; Arts Council of Great Britain, London; and privately.

Publications:

By TROOSTWYK: Books and leaflets—*Imitation,* London 1977; *20 Broadsheets,* London 1979; *National Day,* London 1981; *Holiday Island,* London 1985. **Article—**''Euan Uglow's Diagonal'' in *Studio International* (London), May 1974. **Audio recordings—***Advertisement of an Idea,* Audio Arts tape cassette, London 1976; *Broadcast Works,* Capital Radio, London 1976; *Fine Art Broadcast Service,* Toronto, New York 1981; *Live to Air,* Audio Arts tape cassette, London 1982; *VPRO Radio,* Netherlands 1984.

On TROOSTWYK: Books—*Private Act,* London 1999.

*

The timeless quality of the early photographic print and its waxed paper negative have been a constant reference point in my work—not the imagery but the process. Its rich velvet tones have been

Painting by David Troostwyk. ©David Troostwyk.

subsumed into the surface of my painting where dense tones of black or bronze enclose a blank unpainted space delineating an 'Absent Object.'

—David Troostwyk

* * *

This artist has found himself a niche amongst the painters accepted in Britain, a prizewinner and joining the elect included in the permanent collection of the Tate Gallery. But such honours do little or nothing to explain the talents of this artistic Banquo. Absent from the feast, but present in absentia. 'To make what I like and when I like may not always be easy, but what it is is what *I should do.'*

Selling antique photographs culled from sales and auction rooms to be resold in the Portobello Market reduces the financial strain on David Troostwyk, and the small profits he acquires in this way pay for canvas, stretchers and paints; but above all these monies ensure a large measure of artistic freedom so that he can pursue his ambitions as a painter relying solely upon the understanding of his works and the

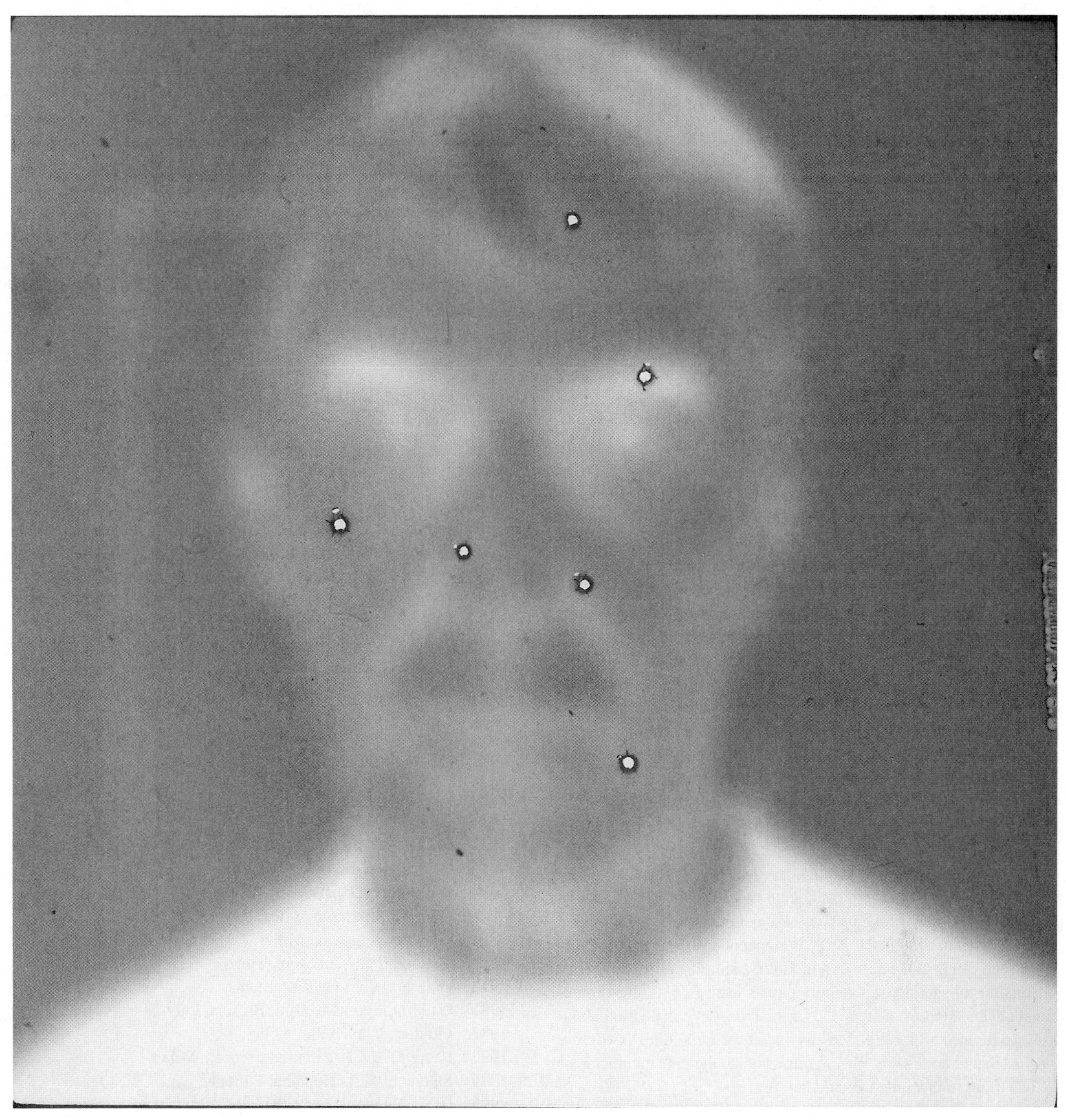

David Troostwyk: *PN Self.* ©David Troostwyk.

impact upon a public whose predilections need no cajoling of any kind insofar as his coolly detached stance as an artist is concerned.

The process of artistic creation for him has been both natural and artificially encouraged. As soon as he was able to claim a pencil as his friend and companion, carefully nurtured—as he came to realise—as a child, but spiritually *relegated* by respectable parents, he filled this social gap sitting sketching on his own in a corner.

Today, this obsession to enter life through making pictures has been carefully tailored. Images, very thoughtfully selected—visual platitudes for the most part—are placed in a monochrome setting, often a black one, the white 'object' or 'statement' asserting its message against a field of black opacity. Troostwyk, who regards paint as only a *medium* (practical and necessary), steers clear of anything approaching a nuance; this is one of the reasons why he eschews the description of 'painter', preferring the title of 'artist'.

He sums up the Why and Wherefore of his creations as 'Communication'. For him, the eye of the beholder can indulge in any interpretive assessment it chooses; his wish as artist is entirely focused on telling a direct truth in absolute terms. So, the 'Empire State Building', white of course, poses with casual tilt in a stygian background or, in less audacious mood, two apples lurk in happy white purity in the midst of a black square. Painting in his Kennington studio in St. Anselm's Church Hall, he is supremely indifferent to critical reaction. These pictures are his remote exploration of finite verities into which those with a desire to investigate may delve but need never feel beholden so to do.

Troostwyk devises paper or card templates. He might make preliminary plans on paper, sketching out his eventual intentions, but he establishes these cutouts as basic aids to be placed—in scale—on his vast canvases. They are, or try to be, the exact guts of the imagery appearing in his pictures. Each of these emplacements—generally one to each picture—is a vital beginning for what will be the finalised pictorial meaning, however frequently readjusted. This is an artist who finds it difficult to persuade himself that any of his works has reached its clinching fulfillment. Many of them stand around the studio awaiting the final coup-de-grace—waiting—they may wait until their place is required in an exhibition, and only then will they receive the last coat of paint and the fine-edge finish that will gain them his personal decision that they should be allowed to go before a public.

Just to give examples of the works of this artist, who makes it a solemn contract with himself never to desert supreme symbols (immediately recognizable to the *hoi polloi,* even though the soul of such simplicity could be described as a 'slow burn' only making itself clear to the majority after long contemplation) is no easy task. One needs to mentally take a stroll through the familiar in order to cross a barrier separating the obvious from the *extra* experience. A large composition like *Fuji,* a white mountain at ease (or not, depending upon mood), solid in its solitude in a surrounding total blackness is what Troostwyk calls one of his 'negatives' (in the photographic sense). Another 'negative', (and one wonders if the flavour is sardonic) is the happy-cumalone signature of Ronald Reagan, clean and white, sprawling across the anonymous black of another work of massive dimensions. (Except in one little canvas, this painter has found it extremely difficult to extract satisfaction from painting on a small scale).

A departure from black and white occurs in his picture of the 'Ring'. The usual containing background in this case is a warm and pale brown madder broken up at casual intervals by unobtrusive glitter-spots. The Ring itself is set in innocent and not very complex curves, but if it is looked at with the aid of a simple optical appliance this unalluring sample of jewellery thrusts itself into a third-dimensional advance out of the canvas. David Troostwyk is pleased about this interference with routine vision but, at the same time, is slightly appalled that he could so easily be accused of indulging in gimmickry—the last thing such a purist should have to fear.

A more uncanny yet typical canvas, and one ot Troostwyk's finest, is the picture he calls *The Russian Chair* (for which he made several studies and a smaller version). This is not one of his 'negative' paintings. It portrays in a strange twisted version a variety of perspectives to form a *portrait* of a famous chair from the experimental period of the great Russian sculptor and designer Vladimir Tatlin. In a strange way the character of Tatlin's chair, despite its curious figuration typifying the acceptance of *new ideas* of the Russian Revolutionary 'Acceptance' of every break with tradition, complies with Troostwyk's determination to communicate with the public through easily digested pictorial statements (in several steps ranging from symbols to absolute realism).

It is worth mentioning here that Troostwyk is an artist who works slowly and with great deliberation. At no time can he assemble a great number of pictures in his studio. Short of the offer of a forthcoming exhibition he accepts no pressures from the outside world to perform extra feats of uncomplicated (yet haunting) painting unless suddenly inspired by an attractive form or feature to place in a chosen position on one of his vast canvases. The 'sections' of architecture which appear in rigid whiteness against the black background of *Heliopolis*—totalities, never randomly positioned, are a fragment of a *loge* which have not only strayed to one side (the left side of the picture) but are quietly defying gravity.

Perhaps David Troostwyk should have the last word. He declares ''Whatever sensations you receive from looking at one of my pictures are certainly enriched *after* you leave the studio with the painting still imprinted on your mind's eye.''

—Sheldon Williams

TROTTA, Antonio A.

Nationality: Argentinian. **Born:** Stio, Italy, 21 December 1937; lived in Argentina until 1968. **Education:** Studied architecture at the University of La Plata, Argentina. **Career:** Independent painter and sculptor, in Buenos Aires, 1960–68, and in Milan since 1968. **Awards:** Painting Prize, Mar del Plata Salon, 1966; Prize, Museum of Fine Arts, Buenos Aires, 1966; Sash of Honour, Ver y Estimar Prize, Buenos Aires, 1966 and 1967. **Address:** via Lamarmora 15, 20122 Milan, Italy.

Individual Exhibitions:

1965 Galeria Lirolay, Buenos Aires
1970 Galleria Lambert, Milan
1971 Galleria Christian Stein, Turin
1972 Galleria Marilena Bonomo, Bari, Italy
Studio Maddilena Carioni, Milan
1974 Galleria Christian Stein, Turin
Qui Arte Contemporanea, Rome
1976 Galleria Borgogna, Milan
1977 Galleria Christian Stein, Turin
1978 Galerie t'Venster, Rotterdam
1981 Galleria Piero Cavellini, Brescia, Italy
1982 Più due Cannaviello, Milan
1990 Padiglione d'arte contemporanea, Milan
1994 Salone di Villa Romana, Florence
1995 I.C.I., Buenos Aires (catalog)
1998 Galleria Civica d'Arte Contemporanea, Siracusa
1999 A arte Studio Invernizzi, Milan (catalog)
Palazzo Comunale, Stio

Selected Group Exhibitions:

1961 *Gruppo SI,* Museo de Artas Plasticas, La Plata (travelled to Museo de Arte Moderno, Buenos Aires and Museo de Bellas Artes, Lima)
1967 *Più in lá delta geometria,* Istituto de Tella, Buenos Aires
1971 *Arte de Sistemas,* Museo de Arte Moderno, Buenos Aires
Understatement, Qui Arte Contemporanea, Rome
1974 *Della Falsità,* Palazzo della Pilotta, Parma

1977 *Senza Relazione: Il verosimile critics,* Palazzo Comunale, Acireale, Italy
1978 *Biennale,* Venice
1979 *L'Annunciazione di Antonello,* Museo Nazionale, Siracusa
1980 *Arte e critica 1980,* Galleria Nazionale d'Arte Moderna, Rome
1982 *La Sovrana Inattualita,* P.A.C., Milan
1991 *Parallele linee della sculptura contemporanea,* Gian Ferrari Arte Contemporanea, Milan
1993 Pomerio Ducale, Massa
1996 *Tuscia Electa: 14 artisti internationali in Toscana,* Greve in Chianti
1997 *Mosaico,* Galleria d'Arte Moderna, Udine
1998 Galleria d'Arte Contemporanea, San Marino
1999 Torre Viscontea, Lecco

Publications:

By TROTTA: Books—*Divagaciones,* Buenos Aires 1967; *Lo Spazio fra Me el'Opera,* Milan 1972; *La Cruz del Sur,* Milan 1974; *Rose, Rose, Rose,* Milan 1974; *Le Finzioni Popolari,* Turin 1976. **Videotapes**—*Punto,* Milan 1969; *Il Sogno di Coleridge,* Milan 1972; *Silbando,* Milan 1972; *Unacita,* Milan 1973.

On TROTTA: Books—*Antonio Trotta* by Romero Brest, Buenos Aires 1967; *Il corpo come linguaggio* by Lea Vergine, Milan 1974; *Antonia Trotta,* exhibition catalog, Rome 1974; *Extra Media* by E. Crispolti, Turin 1978; *Art in Argentina* by Jorge Glusberg, Milan 1986; *Antonio Trotta,* exhibition catalog, Milan 1990. **Articles**—''Letter from Buenos Aires'' by G. Whitelaw in *Art International* (Lugano, Switzerland), May 1969: ''Antonio Trotta'' by J. R. Brest in *Flash Art* (Milan), February/April 1972; ''Antonio Trotta'' by L. Haller in *Flash Art* (Milan), January 1973; ''Antonio Trotta'' in *Utopia Rivisitata,* Milan 1974; ''Miracolo a Milano'' by Tommaso Trini in *Data* (Milan), Spring 1975; ''Antonio Trotta'' in *Art Magazine Bijutsu Techo* (Tokyo), February 1975; ''La Pop Art'' by M. Volpi Orlandini in *L'Arte Moderna,* Milan 1975; ''Antonio Trotta, lo scultore si scolpisce'' in *Data* (Milan), January/February 1978; ''La découverte des origines'' in *Art Aktuel: Skira Annual,* Geneva 1979; ''La experiencia, ideas y sentimientos de los artistas Argentinos radicados en el exterior, donde trabajan, exponen y, de tanto en tanto, nos visitan'' in *Artinf,* vol. 19, no. 92, Spring 1995.

* * *

Antonio Trotta has been exhibiting his work in Italy since 1970, after an extended stay in Argentina. His work is directed towards an enquiry into the rapport between the artist and the work of art—and the space that separates them. In 1972 the Toselli Gallery in Milan published a catalog of works by Nagasawa, Salvadori and Trotta. Trotta's own preface was titled *Images Relating to the Period of the Disappearance of Giovanni Bellini's Saint Sebastian,* a title which may be understood as Trotta's declaration of an analytical view of the work of art which is internal to his own tradition. In the works which followed, Trotta revealed the ideas central to his concern with images of reality and, above all, with the superimposition of the artist's view onto the work of art. *Ricamandosi* (1974–75) is a portrait, perhaps even a self-portrait, made in embroidery. This work forms a direct link with *L'Artifice* (1977), a piece sculpted out of several different slabs of marble, and representing the sculptor at work—''a sculpture of the sculptor sculpting.'' This simple but effective idea demonstrates the rapport between illusion and reality which is the basis of everything.

A declaration of 1972, entitled *The Space Between Me and the Work,* indicates unequivocally where Trotta's interest lies. ''The space between me and the work begins to be dissolved in that moment when it is possible to see that everything surrounding me has already been painted or sculpted. These objects are in a state of petrification, ensnared by those sensations of doubt that form our existence. In them, we observe the unreality which exists in the reality of the work.''

L'Artifice reveals the artist observing his own work from the inside, the sculpture itself reflecting like a mirror the illusion of reality—a concept central to the philosophy of Borges, and perhaps developed during Trotta's time in Argentina. This work is expressed in a variety of different marbles employing quite sophisticated techniques, sometimes smooth or inlaid with a counterpoint of variously toned pieces. This sort of craftsmanship represents another aspect of Trotta, in which he participates in the tradition of the artisan, directing it towards a dialogue of invention and technique.

In June of 1976, the Turin gallery of Christian Stein published one of Trotta's works in book form under the title *Le Finzioni Popolare* (The Popular Illusion). Written the previous summer, the first part is dedicated to the window. The Window is seen from a variety of viewpoints as a screen which divides inside from outside, in a poetic sense. Thus each segment is prefaced by quotations from Mallarmé's poem *La Fenêtre,* and from Miguel Hernandez' *The Farewell is Muffled Behind the Window Pane.* The sequence comprises *La Finestra sul Vetro* (urban images superimposed onto the structure of the window), and *Dietro la Finestra sul Vetro* (external and internal images of life). The same attention, both literary and actual, is focussed onto a balcony, with a quotation from Baudelaire's *Le Balcon.* Trotta subsequently went on to make a number of works and installations on these themes.

La Trilogia: Balcone, Grata, Lampione is a work dated 1974–76 in which objects are reproduced from photographic images, but installed and illuminated in a manner that perfectly simulates that photographic reality. Here again is one of the dominant motifs of Trotta's work—that is, the rapport between reality and appearance which exists between the artist and the work of art. The preoccupation continues to be characteristic.

—Roberto Lambarelli

TRUITT, Anne

Nationality: American. **Born:** Anne Dean in Baltimore, Maryland, 16 March 1921. **Education:** Bryn Mawr College, Pennsylvania, 1939–43, B.A. 1943; Institute of Contemporary Art, Washington, D.C., 1948–50. **Family:** Married James McConnell Truitt in 1947 (divorced, 1971); children: Alexandra, Mary, Samuel. **Career:** Worked as a psychologist at Massachusetts General Hospital, Boston, 1943–46; full-time artist since 1950; lived in Japan, 1964–67. Lecturer, 1975–80, professor of art, 1980–91, Professor Emerita of art, 1991–96, University of Maryland, College Park; taught master class at The Santa Fe Art Institute, 2001. **Awards:** Guggenheim Fellowship, 1970; National Endowment for the Arts Fellowship, 1971, 1977; Stem Foundation

Anne Truitt: *17th Summer.* ©National Museum of American Art, Smithsonian Institution, Gift of Kenneth Noland.

Grant, 1972; Australian Arts Council Fellowship, 1981. DHL: Corcoran School of Art, Washington, D.C., 1985; DFA: Kansas City Art Institute, Missouri, 1987. **Agents:** André Emmerich, 41 E. 57th Street, New York, NY 10022; Osuna Gallery, 1919 Q Street NW, Washington, D.C. 20036. **Address:** 3506 35th Street N.W., Washington, D.C. 20016, U.S.A.

Individual Exhibitions:

1963 André Emmerich Gallery, New York
1964 Minami Gallery, Tokyo
1965 André Emmerich Gallery, New York
1967 Minami Gallery, Tokyo
1969 André Emmerich Gallery, New York
Baltimore Museum of Fine Arts
1971 Pyramid Galleries, Washington, D.C.
1973 Whitney Museum, New York
Pyramid Galleries, Washington, D.C.
1974 Corcoran Gallery, Washington, D.C.
Baltimore Museum of Art
1975 André Emmerich Gallery, New York
Pyramid Galleries, Washington, D.C.
1976 University of Virginia Museum of Art, Charlottesville
1977 Pyramid Galleries, Washington, D.C.
1979 Osuna Gallery, Washington, D.C.
1980 André Emmerich Gallery, New York
1981 Osuna Gallery, Washington, D.C.
1983 James Madison University, Harrisonburg, Virginia
Artemisia Gallery, Chicago
1986 Neuberger Museum, Purchase, New York
André Emmerich Gallery, New York
Osuna Gallery, Washington, D.C.
1991 Osuna Gallery, Washington, D.C.
Anne Truitt: Sculpture 1961–1991, André Emmerich Gallery, New York
1992 Baltimore Museum of Art, Maryland
Weatherspoon Art Gallery, Greensboro, North Carolina
2000 *Anne Truitt: Sculpture,* The Georgia O'Keeffe Museum, Santa Fe

Selected Group Exhibitions:

1953 *8th Corcoran Annual,* Corcoran Gallery, Washington, D.C. (and 1954, 1975)
1964 *Black, White, and Grey,* Wadsworth Atheneum, Hartford, Connecticut
1966 *Color and Space,* Minami Gallery, Tokyo
Primary Structures: Younger American and British Sculptors, Jewish Museum, New York
1968 *Annual Exhibition: Contemporary American Sculpture,* Whitney Museum, New York (and 1972)
1975 *Sculpture: American Directions 1945–1975,* National Collection of Fine Arts, Washington, D.C.
1982 *Grace Hartigan/Morris Louis/Clyfford Still/Anne Truitt,* Baltimore Museum of Art
1985 *Amerikanische Zeichnungen 1930–80,* Stadtische Galerie, Frankfurt
1987 *The Hard Edge, Part I: The 60s,* André Emmerich Gallery, New York
1990 *The Great Decade: The 1960s,* André Emmerich Gallery, New York
1992 *Masters, Mentors and Makers,* Decker Gallery, Mount Royal Station Building, Maryland Institute, College of Art, Baltimore
1996 *Color Field The Classic Years 1960–1975,* André Emmerich Gallery

Collections:

Whitney Museum, New York; Metropolitan Museum of Art, New York; Museum of Modern Art, New York; Albright-Knox Art Museum, Buffalo, New York; Hirshhorn Museum and Sculpture Garden, Washington, D.C.; National Gallery, Washington, D.C.;

Museum of American Art, Washington, D.C.; St. Louis Museum of Art, Walker Art Center, Minneapolis; Museum of Fine Arts, Houston.

Publications:

By TRUITT: Books—*Marcel Proust and Deliverance from Time* by Germaine Bree, translator with C. J. Hill, New Brunswick, New Jersey 1955; *Daybook: The Journal of an Artist,* New York 1982, 1984: *Turn: The Journal of an Artist,* New York 1986, 1987; *Prospect: The Journal of an Artist,* New York 1997. **Articles—** ''Interview with Anne Truitt'' in *Asahi Shimbum* (Tokyo), March 1964.

On TRUITT: Books—*Minimal Art: A Critical Anthology,* edited by Gregory Battcock, New York 1968; *Anne Truitt,* exhibition catalog with essay by Walter Hopps, Washington, D.C. 1974; *Anne Truitt,* exhibition catalog with text by E. A. Carmean, Charlottesville, Virginia 1976; *Originals: American Women Artists* by Eleanor Munro, New York 1979; *Anne Truitt, Sculpture 1961–1991,* exhibition catalog with text by Jane Livingston, New York 1991; *The Voices of Women Artists* by Wendy Slatkin, New Jersey 1993; *Originals: American Women Artists* by Eleanor C. Munro, New York 2000. **Articles—**''Black, White and Grey'' by Donald Judd in *Arts Magazine* (New York), March 1964; ''Changer: Anne Truitt, American Artist Whose Painted Structures Helped to Change the Course of American Sculpture'' by Clement Greenberg in *Vogue* (New York), May 1968; ''Vicissitudes of Sculpture'' by Peter Schjeldahl in the *New York Times,* February 1969; ''Truitt's Box-Sculptures: Now You See Them'' by Paul Richard in the *Washington Post,* April 1971; ''Anne Truitt: The Whitney Museum'' by Jeremy Gilbert-Rolfe in *Artforum* (New York), March 1974; ''Anne Truitt at the Corcoran'' by Gene Baro in *Art in America* (New York), July/August 1974; ''New Sculptures by Anne Truitt'' by John Russell in the *New York Times,* 7 March 1980; ''Daybook: The Journal of an Artist'' by Sara Mandelbaum in *Ms.* (New York), February 1983; ''Anne Truitt'' by Mary Swift in *Washington Review,* April/May 1986; ''Anne Truitt at André Emmerich Gallery'' by Nancy Princenthal in *Art in America* (New York), 1987; ''Anne Truitt'' by Mario Naves in *New Art Examiner,* vol. 25, no. 9, June 1998.

* * *

Since 1961, sculptor Anne Truitt has been making austerely reductive structures of wood painted with variously hued bands of color. Truitt's simple, abstract forms resemble Minimalism's ''primary structures,'' but her personal and intuitive application of shape and color communicate ideas associative with significative meanings beyond strictly formal ones, suggesting Truitt's connections with Abstract Expressionism, specifically with the work of Barnett Newman.

It was after Truitt saw the work of Newman during a trip to New York in 1961 that she began working in the form which was to characterize her work over the next two decades to the present. Truitt's ideological foundations had been formed through long-time friendship with Kenneth Noland, whom she had known since 1948. She had developed through the 1950s from a kind of stylized figure and landscape sculpture to geometrical works in clay which suggested primitive architectural forms. In 1961, she made a generative work titled *First,* a vertical sculptural construct resembling three sections of a picket fence. In 1962, she made a number of drawings and 32 sculptures, her first mature work. *Insurrection* (1962) consists of a vertical rectangular form rising from a small base. The column is painted in two vertical sections, half red, half maroon, in a composition very like Newman's symmetrical pictures in a color combination favored by Newman from 1949 to the early 1950s, and in a vertical configuration directly related with Newman's extremely narrow and tall series of Untitled canvases (Numbers 1 through 5) of 1950.

Like her Abstract Expressionist precursors, Truitt is an artist who finds her preferred form and proceeds consistently to find possible variations within her chosen limitations. Hers is a transposition out of painterly precedents into the more three-dimensional realm. All traces of process are obliterated in her sleek, unabashedly lovely columns, sometimes leaning against the wall, mostly standing straight and tall with an aura of silent stateliness which invokes memories of the continuities and subtle changes which unfold through time and space. Truitt uses her skills as a subtly strong colorist to create a tense ambiguity between the planar and the three dimensional. In various combinations from one work to the next, vertical bands of color divide the surfaces, wrap around the corners and coexist with horizontal bands on the tops of the columns and on the thin bases. Harmonizing pastels or contrasting hues work with her diverse compositional formats to create a space which is simultaneously continuous and changing. A tense balance between gravity and weightlessness is amplified by the use of horizontal bands of color on the narrow, recessed bases. Titles, usually given when the work is nearly or totally completed, often refer to persons, places and events from Truitt's experience, reiterating her intentions for conveying associative meanings.

Truitt's sculptures are neither heroic nor monumental in scale or attitude. She developed her vocabulary alone, unusually separate from most of her contemporaries, and it is this sense of mysterious aloofness which animates her basically unitary and reductive forms. She has created a sincere and personally felt body of work which is firmly rooted in a long established line of modernist abstraction that was nearing its end by the 1950s.

—Barbara Cavaliere

TSOCLIS, Costas

Nationality: Greek. **Born:** Athens, 24 May 1930. **Education:** School of Fine Arts, Athens, 1948–54; University of Rome, 1957–60. **Military Service:** Served in the Greek Army, 1954–56. **Family:** Married Helen Caplanidou in 1975; daughter: Maya. **Career:** Painter, Athens, 1954–57; painter and sculptor, Paris, 1960–70; in West Berlin, 1971–72; in Athens and Paris, since 1973. **Awards:** Greek State Scholarship to Rome, 1957; D.A.A.D. Fellowship to West Berlin, 1971. **Agents:** Pascal Polar, 185 Ch. de Charleroi, 1060 Brussels, Belgium; Epikentro Gallery, 16 Norman Str., 262 23 Patras Greece. **Address:** Axiou 15, 13671 Aharnes, Greece.

Individual Exhibitions:

1965 Hilton Gallery, Athens
1969 Galerie Richard Foncke, Ghent
Galerie Michael Wemer, Cologne
1970 Galerie Sonnabend, Paris
Studio Santandrea, Milan

Galerie Richard Foncke, Ghent
Galerie Defacqz, Brussels
1971 Palais des Beaux-Arts, Brussels
Goethe Institute, Athens
Galerie Springer, West Berlin
Galerie Lichter, Frankfurt
Galerie Reckermann, Cologne
1972 Galerie Richard Foncke, Ghent
Ehemalige Galerie des 20 Jahrhunderts, West Berlin
Kunsthalle, Dusseldorf
1973 Galerie Iolas-Zouboulakis, Athens
Galerie Alexandre Iolas, Paris
1974 Galerie Marzona, Bielefeld, West Germany
Galerie Alexandre Iolas, Paris
1976 Studio Santandrea, Milan
Galerie New Smith, Brussels
Galerie Alexandre Iolas, Paris
Galerie Iolas-Zoumboulakis, Athens
1977 Galerie Desmos, Athens
Alexandre Iolas Gallery, New York
Galerie der Spiegel, Cologne
1978 Galerie Miranda, Hydra, Greece
Palais des Beaux-Arts, Brussels
Galerie Nothelfer, West Berlin
Axionsgalerie, West Berlin
1979 Studio Santandrea, Milan
Galerie Desmos, Athens
1980 Sala Communale d'Arte Contemporanea, Alessandria, Italy
Galerie Miranda, Athens
1981 Galerie Z.M., Thessaloniki, Greece
Galerie Oraisma, Athens
1982 Galleria Dossi, Bergamo, Italy
1983 Gallery 3, Athens
Iolas Gallery, New York
Pinacotheque Pierides, Athens
1984 Plaka Intervention, Athens
Macedonian Center of Contemporary Art, Salonika, Greece
1985 Zomboulakis Gallery, Athens
1986 Greek Pavilion, *Biennale,* Venice
1987 Castello di Rodi, Rhodes, Greece
1988 Zoumboulakis Gallery, Athens
Arco di Rab, Rome
Macedonian Center of Contemporary Art, Salonica, Greece
3rd International Festival of Patras, Greece
Grand Master's Palace, Rhodes, Greece
1989 Zoumboulakis Gallery, Athens
Gadran Solaire, Troyes, France
1990 *Mixographia,* Los Angeles
Arco di Rab, Rome
Pascal Polar Gallery, Brussels
Villa Domenica, Treviso, Italy
Zoumboulakis Gallery, Athens
Stenboch Fermor Gallery, Gand, Belgium
1991 Epikentro Gallery, Patras, Greece
Institut Francais, Salonica, Greece
1993 Pascal Polar Gallery, Brussels
Mylos, Salonica, Greece
1994 Parc Tourney, Solvay, Brussels
Kreonidis Art Space, Athens
Epikentro Gallery, Patras, Greece
1995 Galerie Lola Nikolaou, Salonique
Fondation P. & M. Kydonieos, Andros
1996 Palais des expositions, Rome
Centro Rocca Paolina, Perugia
Galerie Kreonides, Athens
Galerie Ileana Tounta, Athens
1997 Galerie Lola Nikolaou, Acropolis, Athens
1998 Galerie Astrolavos, Athens
1999 Galerie Lola Nikolaou, Salonique
2000 Museo Pecci, Prato, Italy

Selected Group Exhibitions:

1963 *Biennale de Paris*
1965 *Bienal,* Sao Paulo
1970 *Surrealisme,* Moderna Museet, Stockholm
1972 *Zehn Berlin,* Kunstverein, Stuttgart
1975 *8 Artists/8 Attitudes/8 Greeks,* Institute of Contemporary Arts, London
1977 *Documenta,* Kassel, West Germany
1982 *Europalia Greece,* Palais des Beaux Art, Brussels
1987 *Artware,* Kunstmuseum, Hannover (travelled to Dusseldorf)
1992 National Gallery, Athens
1993 *Vailses,* Museum of Contemporary Art, Liege
1994 *1st International Meeting of Sculpture,* Delphi
1995 *Configura,* Dialog der Kulturen, Erfurt
1998 *Electronically Yours,* Metropolitan Museum of Photography, Tokyo
Contemporary Greek Art: Three Generations, Tel Aviv Museum of Art (travelled to Pinacothéque Nationale, Athens)

Collections:

Centre National d'Art Contemporain, Paris; Museum van Hedendaages Kunst, Ghent; Museum of Contemporary Art, Utrecht; Museum Boymans-van Beuningen, Rotterdam; Musée d'lxelles, Brussels; Museo de Bellas Aries, Caracas; Musée d'Art Contemporain, Brussels; Pinacotheque Pierides, Athens; Vorres Museum of Modern Art, Athens; European Center of Delphi.

Publications:

By TSOCLIS: Books—*Rue des Ecouffes,* portfolio of 8 lithos, with text by D. Analis, Paris 1973; *Anamnissis 1971–73,* portfolio of 30 lithos, Paris 1974; *Arbre, Tree, Albero, Aentpo,* book-object, Milan 1980; *Arbre,* portfolio of 8 lithos, with texts by Jose Pierre, C. Cafopoulos, J. P. Van Teighem and others, Paris 1982. **Articles—** Interview with Thalia Stefanidou in *Arti,* no. 34, May-June 1997.

On TSOCLIS: Books—*Art of our Time* by D. Fatouros, London and Cologne 1966; *Costas Tsoclis,* exhibition catalog with text by José Pierre, Paris 1970; *Costas Tsoclis,* exhibition catalog with texts by Karl Geirlandt and Jean Dypreau, Brussels 1971; *Costas Tsoclis,* exhibition catalog with text by G. Vlachos, Ghent 1972; *Costas Tsoclis,* exhibition catalog with texts by Karl Ruhrberg and Peter

Nestler, West Berlin 1972; *Tsoclis,* with texts by Jean Dypreau, Karl Geirlandt, José Pierre, Tony Spiteris and others, Athens 1975; *Costas Tsoclis,* exhibition catalog with text by M. Mauzommatis, Alessandria, Italy 1980; *An Aspect of Postwar Art in Greece* by E. Vakalo, Athens 1981; *Artware, Kunst und Electronic,* with text by N. Missirlis, Dusseldorf, Vienna and New York 1987; *Costas Tsoclis,* exhibition catalog, Athens 2000.

*

As an artist, I have never selected my means of expression—no more than, as a child, I have ever devised my playthings—outside a range of ''situations-objects'' to which I was linked by a bond of love or necessity.

An offspring of the capital, not expecting or caring to discover my roots, I fed on facts, not myths, on things whose prior stages I was not aware of. The myths—I made them up myself from such things and facts.

It took me a long time to see the Acropolis as a vestige of a period gone for ever and not as a set of abstract and unserviceable structures, playing nevertheless a determining role in the aesthetic character of the city, and therefore in the psychology of its inhabitants.

The basements of the small houses that used to shelter my family, I considered, with no bitterness whatever, as my home, in no way inferior to the big houses, those of the rich, which I merely looked upon as the big houses of ''my'' neighbourhood.

Then, I was not yet trying to find out the how, or the why.

My first works recognizable as such are ''objects-fragments'' of that environment, both forced upon me and taken for granted, reconstructed, however, so that they should remain faithful to their inner truth, and bear the indelible mark of my own vision.

(Now, after looking for and finding that literary definition of my quest during that long period of my life, I rejoice and consider I have not worked in a barren field.)

Yet, in order to reconstruct my objects, I had to handle patiently the materials with which such objects were made. Gradually, I became familiar with a new world, the world of virgin matter and with it I began to develop bonds, memories and even secret correspondences. Thus, for a few years, the new object of my work had become the very matter of my former objects. A long series of works scattered here and there, whose theme—object is merely wood, paper, steel, colour, water, cement, testify to that boundless love for matter which has certainly not palled so far.

Now, if ''love'' means endeavouring to probe into the truth of the beloved object, possess oneself of its charms, finally identify oneself with it for mutual pleasure and fulfillment, then that is what I did.

And if ''art'' means offering a new way, a new transitory and, no doubt, incomplete code to organize, conceive and interpret facts and environments so as to attain new emotions and balances, then that is what I felt.

One day, a small revelation became the new guide of my sensibility. A tree whose fitful and phantasmal image had been imparting a touch of beauty to my life was broken by the wind and revealed to me its concrete and enduring truth: the wood, so long hidden under its transient image; and I took a fancy to that glorious wound, and I perceived an inverted continuity between the object, matter and nature and in my recent work I have endeavoured to fuse into one artistic fact the image, the source of that image and the use of that source.

As if one painted the portrait of a man not with colour but with human flesh.

—Costas Tsoclis

TUCKER, Albert

Nationality: Australian. **Born:** Melbourne, Victoria, 29 December 1914. **Education:** Self-taught in art. **Military:** Served in the Australian Army, 1942. **Family:** Married Joy Hester (deceased, 1960); son: Sweeney (died 1979); married Barbara Anne Bilcock in 1964. **Career:** Painter: influential, with Sidney Nolan, in forging an Australian modernism; produced ''Images of Modern Evil'' series, 1943–47, before self-inflicted exile from Australia; lived in London, where he produced a ''Thames Waterfront'' series, 1947–48; travelled to Paris, with critic Lawrence Alloway, and became fascinated by the work of Jean Dubuffet, then unknown, in early 1948; returned shortly thereafter to Paris to live, met Alberto Giacometti and Rufino Tamayo, and made frequent trips to London, Germany, Holland, Belgium, and Italy. Saw for the first time the work of Max Beckmann, Otto Dix, Dubuffet, and the German modernists; moved to Neu Isenburg, near Frankfurt, West Germany, 1951; returned to Paris, 1952, then travelled south, to Noli, Italy, where he lived until mid-1953; lived in Rome and Grottaferrata, 1953–56; met Alberto Burri, de Chirico, Campigli; also renewed contact with Australian compatriot Sidney Nolan, who initiated his return to interest in Australian subjects; worked on ''Pan in Armour'' series 1955–59; returned to London, where he met Eduardo Paolozzi; lived in New York, where he met abstract painters of the New York School, de Kooning and Franz Kline, 1958–60; his work began to receive recognition in Australia, and he returned to his native country after a 13 year absence, 1960; donated 200 of his artworks to Heide Museum of Modern Art, the state of Victoria, Australia, 2000; Tucker Gallery dedicated in Museum of Modern Art, Heide, Victoria, 2000. **Awards:** Kurt Geiger Award, Australian Museum of Art, 1960; Order of Australia, 1984. **Address:** c/o Heide Museum of Modern Art, 7 Templestowe Road, Bulleen, Victoria 3105 Australia. **Died:** Of heart failure in Melbourne, Australia, 23 October 1999.

Individual Exhibitions:

1951 Kunstzaal van Lier, Amsterdam
1952 Galerie Huit, Paris
1953 Galleria at Quattro Venti, Rome
1954 Associazione della Estampa Estera, Rome (with Sidney Nolan)
1957 Imperial Institute, London
1960 Waddington Galleries, London
Hirschl and Adler Galleries, New York
1961 Australian Museum of Modern Art, Melbourne (toured the capitals of Australia, 1961–62)
1969 Poindexter Gallery, New York
Instituto Nacional de Bellas Aries, Mexico City
Galleria de Antonia Souza, Mexico City
1971 Australian National Gallery, Canberra (Australian Government travelling exhibition; toured Japan, Phillipines, Korea and Formosa)

1982 *Paintings 1945–60,* Tolarno Galleries, South Yarra, Victoria
Night Images (Images of Modern Evil) 1943–1947, Sweeney Reed Galleries, Fitzroy, Victoria
1985 *Faces I Have Met,* Tolarno Galleries, Melbourne
1990 *A Retrospective,* National Gallery of Victoria, Art Gallery of New South Wales (catalog)
Albert Tucker: An Aspect of His Work, Tolarno Galleries, South Yarra, Australia (catalog)
Mythologies & Images, Lauraine Diggins Gallery, Melbourne (also Savill Galleries, North Caulfield, Australia) (catalog)
1997 *The Angry Penguins: An Exhibition of Highly Important Works by Boyd, Nolan, Perceval, Tucker,* Gould Galleries, South Yarra (catalog)
2000 *Albert Tucker: The Endurance of the Human Spirit,* Lauraine Diggins Fine Art (catalog)
2001 *Tucker: Australian Gothic,* Heide Museum of Modern Art, Victoria, Australia

Selected Group Exhibitions:

1956 *Biennale,* Venice
1959 *Transferences in Art,* Smithsonian Institution, Washington, D.C. (toured the United States)
Experiences in Art, Hirschl and Adler Galleries, New York
Recent Acquisitions, Museum of Modern Art, New York
1963 *Bienal,* Sao Paulo
1964 *Australian Painting Today,* toured Europe
1988 *Angry Penguins and Realist Painting in Melbourne in the 1960s,* Hayward Galleries, London (travelled to Tate Gallery, Liverpool) (catalog)
1991 *Cite Sight Site,* St. Kilda, Melbourne
1993 *Surrealism, Revolution By Night,* National Gallery of Australia, Canberra.

Collections:

Australian National Gallery, Canberra; Australian Museum of Modern Art, Melbourne; Dunedin Art Gallery, New Zealand; Museum of Modern Art, New York; Guggenheim Museum, New York; Instituto Nacional de Bellas Aires, Mexico City; All Australian State Galleries.

Publications:

By TUCKER: Books—*Albert Tucker: Paintings 1945–1960,* exhibition catalog with William Mora, introduction by Richard Haese, South Yarra, Victoria 1982; *Faces I Have Met,* introduction by Richard Haese, Sydney 1986; *Albert Tucker: Family and Friends: 50 Years of Photographs,* with Scott Brown, North Caulfield 1998; *The Eye of the Beholder,* with Janine Burke, Bulleen 1998.

On TUCKER: Books—*Albert Tucker* by Christopher Uhl, 1969; *Modern Painters 1931–1970* by James Gleeson, Melbourne 1971; *Albert Tucker* by James Mollison and Nicholas Bonham, 1982; *Albert Tucker: Night Images (Images of Modern Evil) 1943–1947,* exhibition catalog with text by John Henshaw, Fitzroy, Victoria 1982; *Albert Tucker: A Retrospective,* exhibition catalog with text by James Mollison and Jan Minchin, Victoria 1990; *Albert Tucker: The Mythologies & Images,* exhibition catalog with text by John Yule, Melbourne 1990. **Article—**''The Art of Albert Tucker'' by Marie Geissler in *Craft Arts International,* no. 21, March-June 1991; obituary in *Art and Australia,* vol. 37, no. 4, 2000.

* * *

Australia during World War II felt peculiarly isolated from its cultural sources in Europe, yet it was a time which saw a most extraordinary collective achievement by certain painters working in Melbourne. Extreme individualists, Albert Tucker, Sidney Nolan and Arthur Boyd nevertheless shared both a humanist attitude and stylistic sources in Surrealism and Expressionism.

Tucker in 1950 wrote: ''For me the drama and tragedy of life—my feeling is quite Websterian—this 'shadow or deep pit of darkness where mankind lives.' To sing of death or disaster does not make for popularity, I'm afraid. But it's my song and I've got to sing it.''

His art is the hardest from that time. It received no public praise. Its haptic forms have primitive, rocklike firmness; and after Alberto Burri introduced him to the polyvinyl acetate medium in 1954, Tucker's paintings quickly acquired a hard flinty surface, often in considerable relief. Tucker's is also an art of clear intelligence and hard statements.

As a young man on the edge of poverty in the 1930s economic depression, from a family struggling to maintain middle-class values, he had good reason to feel oppressed and humiliated by society in general. As a radical artist he soon felt oppressed by the required subservience to a common political cause. Most of all as an army conscript in 1942 he was oppressed by military authority. However, work amongst the mad and the maimed in a military hospital, drawing illustrations of wounds for plastic surgery, was an experience which supplied images to energize his art for years to come—the gaping holes below a sliced-off nose, limbless torsoes, bloodstained mouths. The following year, 1943, his extensive series of ''Images of Modern Evil'' began.

Apparently an indictment of social decay caused by soldiers and their mostly amateur prostitutes in wartime Melbourne, the paintings show momentarily spotlit lumps of pale naked flesh, attached to red crescent mouths, floating in the night darkness of streets and cinemas. But the vulnerability and the uninhibited freedom implied by these fleshly images might also be presented for envious admiration by a conventionally constrained society. By the way of contrast, a series of portraits, ''Faces 1946,'' at first sight straightforward sympathetic likenesses become on second sight hauntingly ravaged souls.

Tucker left Australia in 1947 for thirteen years of expatriation in Paris, Frankfurt, Rome, New York and London. Picasso, Beckmann and Dubuffet (a new discovery in 1948) were the Modern masters who most enthralled him; the exposure to old masters produced biblical subjects: Job, Judas, Lazarus. Night in the European cities was presented less hysterically than in Melbourne.

Paradoxically but not surprisingly, Tucker became an Australian artist in Rome, in 1955. Direct confrontation with Europe always makes those from transplanted European cultures intensely aware of their own non-European character. Tucker began to paint explorers and bandits from Australian history, their features ambiguously treated as Australian desert landscape, and both the figures and landscapes treated with scars, boils and wounds.

Such themes continued in his art. They can be interpreted as an attempt to equip the Australian landscape with mythology-figures and as a comment on European disruption of the well-balanced Aboriginal ecology. But they are primarily an expression of Tucker's personal relish for flouted authority, for large-scale failures and for marks of retribution. Tragedy is a relatively uncommon mode in contemporary painting, and Tucker was one of its few masters.

—Daniel Thomas

TUCKER, William

Nationality: British. **Born:** In Cairo, Egypt, of English parents, 28 February 1935. **Education:** Studied history at Oxford University, 1955–58; studied sculpture at the Central School of Art and Design and St. Martin's School of Art, London, 1959–60. **Career:** Worked at the Victoria and Albert Museum, London, 1961. Sculptor, working in steel, fiberglass, plastics and wood, London, since 1962. Instructor, Goldsmith's College and St. Martin's School of Art, London, 1961–62; University of Western Ontario, London, 1976; and Columbia University and New York School of Painting and Sculpture, New York, 1978–1982. **Awards:** Sainsbury Scholarship, London, 1961; Peter Stuyvesant Foundation Travel Bursary, London, 1965; Gregory Fellowship in Sculpture, University of Leeds, 1968–70; Guggenheim Fellowship, 1980; Sculpture Center Award, Distinction in Sculpture, 1991. **Address:** c/o McKee Gallery, 745 Fifth Avenue, New York, NY, 10151. **Died:** 23 October 1999.

Individual Exhibitions:

1962 Grabowski Gallery, London (with Michael Kidner)
1963 Rowan Gallery, London
1965 Richard Feigen Gallery, New York
1966 Rowan Gallery, London
1967 Kasmin Gallery, London
1968 Elkon Gallery, New York
1969 Leslie Waddington Prints, London
Kasmin Gallery, London
City Art Gallery, Leeds
1970 Kasmin Gallery, London
1972 British Pavilion, at the *Biennale,* Venice
1973 Kunstverein, Hamburg
Kunstmuseum, Bochum, West Germany
Galerie Müller-Wintersberger, Cologne
Serpentine Gallery, London
Waddington Galleries, London
1974 *Drawings,* Hester van Royen Gallery, London
1976 Galerie Wintersberger, Cologne
1977 Elkon Gallery, New York
Kasmin Gallery, London
1978 Fruit Market Gallery, Edinburgh
Sable-Castelii Gallery, Toronto
1979 Elkon Gallery, New York
1980 David Reid Gallery, Sydney
Powell Street Gallery, Melbourne
Elkon Gallery, New York
1981 Galleria L'Isola, Rome
1982 Bernard Jacobson Gallery, Los Angeles
Sculpture and Drawings, Elkon Gallery, New York
1984 David McKee Gallery, New York
Galleria L'Isola, Rome
1985 Pamela Auchincloss Gallery, Santa Barbara, California
David McKee Gallery, New York
Neuberger Museum, Purchase, New York
1987 Pamela Auchincloss Gallery, Santa Barbara, California
Tate Gallery, London
David McKee Gallery, New York
Annely Juda Fine Art, London
Padiglione d'Arte Contemporanea, Milan
Galleria L'Isola, Rome
1988 Storm King Art Center, Mountainville, NY
New York Beijing Art Institute
1989 David McKee Gallery, New York
Gallery Paule Anglim, San Francisco
1991 David McKee Gallery, New York
1992 David McKee Gallery, New York
1993 Maak Gallery, London
1994 David McKee Gallery, New York
1995 David McKee Gallery, New York
Yorkshire Sculpture Park
William Tucker: The Language of a Sculptor, Leeds City Art Gallery, Leeds, England
1996 David McKee Gallery, New York
American Academy of Arts & Letters, New York
1998 Butler Institute of American Art, Youngstown
1999 Gallery Paule Anglim, San Francisco

Selected Group Exhibitions:

1961 *Biennale,* Paris
1965 *London: The New Scene,* Walker Art Center, Minneapolis
1966 *Primary Structures,* Museum of Modern Art, New York
1968 *Documenta,* Kassel, West Germany
1970 *Contemporary British Painting and Sculpture,* National Museum of Modern Art, Tokyo
1975 *The Condition of Sculpture,* Hayward Gallery, London
1979 *Contemporary Sculpture,* Museum of Modern Art, New York
1981 *Il Luogo delta Forma,* Museo di Castelvecchio, Verona
1983 *Monumental Drawings by Sculptors,* Long Island University, New York
1985 *Working in Brooklyn: Sculpture,* Brooklyn Museum, New York
1986 *Between the Object and the Image: British Contemporary Sculpture,* Fundacio Caixa de Pensions, Barcelona
1988 *Starlit Waters: British Sculpture, An International Art 1968–1988,* Tate Gallery Liverpool, England
Collaborations in Monotype, University of California at Santa Barbara (travelled to Archer M. Huntington Art Gallery, Austin; Cleveland Museum of Art, Cleveland)
National Drawing Invitational, Arkansas Arts Center, Little Rock
1995 *Sculpture Space: Celebrating 20 Years,* Museum of Art, Utica, New York
1996 *Large Drawings and Objects,* Permanent Collection Gallery, Little Rock

Collections:

Arts Council of Great Britain, London; British Council, London; Tate Gallery, London; Victoria and Albert Museum, London; Rijksmuseum Kroller-Muller, Otterlo, Netherlands; Louisiana Museum, Humlebaek,

Denmark; Museum of Modern Art, New York; Guggenheim Museum, New York; Walker Art Center, Minneapolis; Metropolitan Museum of Art, New York.

Publications:

By TUCKER: Book—*The Language of Sculpture,* London 1974. **Articles—**''Reflections on Sculpture'' in *Tim Scott,* exhibition catalog, London 1967; ''Moore at the Tate'' in *Studio International* (London), October 1968; ''Anthony Caro's Work: A Symposium,'' with others, in *Studio International* (London), January 1969; ''An Essay on Sculpture'' in *Studio International* (London), January 1969; ''Sidney Nolan and William Tucker Discuss Their Recent Work'' in *Studio International* (London), June 1969; ''The Sculptures of Matisse'' in *Studio International* (London), July 1969; ''4 Sculptors: Brancusi, Picasso, Matisse, David Smith'' in *Studio International* (London), April, May and September 1970 and January 1971; ''Notes on Sculpture, Public Sculpture and Patronage'' in *Studio International* London), January 1972; ''Sculpture and Architecture: An Introduction to My Recent Work'' in *Studio International* (London), June 1972; ''What Sculpture Is'' in *Studio International* (London), December 1974 and March/April 1975; statement in *William Tucker: Horses,* exhibition catalog, Rome 1987.

On TUCKER: Books—*William Tucker: Sculpture,* exhibition catalog with text by Christopher Salveson, London 1963; *36th Biennale di Venezia: British Pavilion: William Tucker,* exhibition catalog with text by Andrew Forge, London 1972; *William Tucker: Sculpture 1970–73,* exhibition catalog with text by Andrew Forge, London 1973; *William Tucker: Drawings,* exhibition catalog with text by Barry Martin, London 1974; *William Tucker,* exhibition catalog, Rome 1981; *William Tucker: Sculpture and Drawings,* exhibition catalog with text by Andrew Forge, New York 1982; *William Tucker: Five Recent Sculptures,* exhibition catalog with text by Dore Ashton, London 1986; *William Tucker: the Language of a Sculptor,* exhibition catalog, Leeds 1995. **Articles—**''William Tucker's American Decade'' by Eric Gibson in *New Criterion,* vol. 7, no. 1, September 1988; ''William Tucker: The Fated Return of the Body'' by Donald B. Kuspit in *Sculpture* (Washington, D.C.), vol. 12, no. 5, September-October 1993.

* * *

In that group of sculptors who emerged from St. Martin's School of Art in London in the mid-1960s, a group which included Phillip King, Isaac Witkin and Tim Scott, William Tucker was noted for the strongly theoretical nature of his approach to sculpture. A concern with certain qualities which he considered fundamental to sculpture—its objecthood, its literalness—has consequently informed all his works. In sculptures like ''Meru I & II'' he explored some of the variety of ways in which an object may be apprehended: how presence is conveyed, together with weight, mass, volume, stability and so on. Though occasionally he used unconventional materials, like resins, Tucker's aims were not iconoclastic: on the contrary, he sought to re-examine many of the crucial questions that sculptors have always faced. The rigor of his approach, however, meant that his works generally lacked the witty or playful aura found in the sculpture of many of his contemporaries.

In the late 1960s Tucker turned to more attenuated forms, more nakedly structural and expressive in character, as found in the ''Beulahs'' and ''Cat's Cradles.'' Still human in scale and still related to the activity of the body, these works were strictly abstract in character although individual components often had architectural associations. As Tucker explained: ''the 'architectural' experience of the sculpture, that is the way in which it could be experienced with the spectator's whole body by analogy with his experience of traversing and using space, replaced the specifically 'tactile,' the experience, real or imagined, or the spectator's hands in previous sculpture.''

In the 1970s an increased scale, together with a greater emphasis on the mass and texture of materials, made works like ''Tunnel'' not only more monumental but also more architectonic than hitherto. At the same time, or perhaps as a result, they took on connotations which formerly would have been eschewed. Although not totemic objects, they are more than just structures in space, they have a new resonance or ''character.''

In his recent large charcoal drawings these concerns are paralleled in handsome fashion. These are not sculptor's drawings in the usual sense, for they do not simply depict a solid object in three-dimensional space; Tucker always carefully aligns the image to the format and to the surface in which it lies. Once again, that rigorous questioning which informs all his activity is apparent.

—Lynne Cooke

TURCATO, Giulio

Nationality: Italian. **Born:** Mantua, 16 March 1912. **Education:** Scuola d'Arte dei Carmine, Venice, 1928–31, Liceo Artistico, Venice, 1932–33, and Scuola Libera del Nudo, Venice, 1933–35. **Military Service:** Italian Army, in Sicily, 1935–36. **Family:** Married Vana Caruso in 1964. **Career:** Assistant draughtsman to the architect Muzio, Milan, 1937–39. Painter and graphic artist in Milan, 1939–42, and in Rome, since 1943: member, Corrente Group of artists, Milan, 1939; founder, International Independent Artists Art Club, Rome, 1945, and, with Consagra, San Filippo, Dorazio, Guerrini and Perilli, Gruppo Arte Sociale, Rome, 1946; co-editor, *Forma I* formalist art manifesto, Rome, 1947; member, Nuovo Fronte delle Arti, Rome, 1949, Gruppo degli Otto, Rome, 1950, and, with Novelli, Perilli, Dorazio, Consagra, and Gio and Arnaldo Pomodoro, Gruppo Continuità, Rome, 1960–62. Instructor in drawing and design, Vocational School, Portogruaro, Italy, 1942–43. Professor, Liceo Artistico, Rome, 1953–82. **Awards:** National Prize, *Biennale,* Venice, 1958; Fiorino Prize, Florence, 1962; Esso Prize, Rome, 1962; Painting Prize, *Review of Figurative Art,* Rome, 1963; Painting Prize, Termoli, 1963; First prize, *Quadriennale,* Rome, 1966; San Sofia prize, 1971; Painting Prize, Volleverede, 1972. **Address:** via del Pozzetto 117, 00187 Rome, Italy.

Individual Exhibitions:

1949 Galleria La Giostra, Asti, Italy
1950 Galleria del Secolo, Rome
1951 Galleria del Naviglio, Milan
1952 Galleria La Cassapanca, Rome
1953 Galleria del Naviglio, Milan
1955 Galleria La Tartaruga, Rome
Galleria del Grattacielo, Milan

1956 Galleria L'Indiano, Florence
Galleria del Grattacielo, Milan
1957 Galleria La Tartaruga, Rome
1960 Galleria del Grattacielo, Milan
1961 New Vision Centre, London
Galleria Il Canale, Venice
1962 Galerie Burdeke, Zurich
Galleria La Tartaruga, Rome
1963 Galleria Il Quadrante, Florence
1964 Galleria La Scaletta, Catania, Italy
Galleria Il Segno, Rome
Galleria La Polena, Genoa
1965 Galleria Marlborough, Rome
Galleria del Naviglio, Milan
Galleria Il Segno, Rome
1967 Galleria Arte Oggi, Pescara, Italy
Galleria Le Muse, Bologna
Galleria L'Indiano, Florence
Galleria Arco d'Alibert, Rome
1968 Galleria del Naviglio, Milan
Galleria Il Punto, Turin
Studio G30, Paris
Galleria L'Oca, Rome
1969 Galerie D.I.V., Frankfurt
Galleria L'Indiano, Florence
Studio Santandrea, Milan
1970 Galleria Boni-Schubert, Lugano, Switzerland
Galleria del Foglio, Rome
Galleria Schubert, Milan
Grafica Romero, Rome
1971 Galleria Il Segnapassi, Pesaro, Italy
Galleria Il Nettuno, Bologna
Galleria Barozzi, Venice
Studio Barozzi, Milan
1972 Galleria La Gradiva, Florence
Galleria Il Salotto, Como, Italy
Studio Cortina, Pescara, Italy
Galleria Editalia, Rome
1973 Galleria Il Giorno, Milan
Grafica Romero, Rome
Palazzo Ancaini, Spoleto, Italy (retrospective)
1974 Galleria Editalia, Rome
Palazzo delle Prigioni Vecchie, Venice
Palazzo delle Esposizione, Rome (retrospective)
1975 Studio Latronica, Todi, Italy
Galleria Nuovo Saggitario, Milan
Galleria Editalia, Rome
Galleria La Gradiva, Florence
1976 Galleria Colasanti, Rome
Galleria Nuove Colonne, Trieste, Italy
1977 Galleria Il Pilastro, Milan
Galleria Lo Spazio, Naples
Galleria Ferretti, Viareggio, Italy
1978 Istituto Italiano di Cultura, New York
Westend Galerie, Frankfurt
1979 Galleria Numerosette, Naples
Museum of Modern Art, Bucharest
Galleria del Falconiere, Ancona, Italy
1980 Agenzia d'Arte Moderna, Rome
Musée de l'Athenee, Geneva
Galleria del Milione, Milan
1981 Galleria Mazzoli, Modena, Italy
Galleria Cesarea, Genoa
Galleria Planetario, Trieste, Italy
Castello di San Giusto, Trieste, Italy
1982 Pinacoteca, Ravenna, Italy
Galleria De Amicis, Florence
Galleria De Crescenzo, Rome
Galleria Linea 70, Verona
1983 Galleria Nazionale d'Arte Moderna, Rome
1984 Padiglione d'Arte Contemporanea, Milan
1985 Staatsgalerie Moderner Kunst, Munich
Kunstverein, Frankfurt
1986 Galleria Nazionale d'Arte Moderna, Rome
1989 Sperone Westwater, New York
1990 Galleria in Arco, Turin
Museo d'Arte Moderna Ca'Pesaro, Venice

Selected Group Exhibitions:

1945 Associazione Artistica Internazionale Indipendente ''Art Clubs, Galleria San Marco, Rome
1948 *Biennale,* Venice (and 1950, 1952)
1957 *Painting in Postwar Italy,* Columbia University, New York
1959 *Documenta,* Kassel, West Germany
1963 *6 Italienska Malare,* Moderna Museet, Stockholm
1968 *Arte Italiana dal Futurismo ad Oggi,* Galleria Nazionale d'Arte Moderna, Rome
1971 *New Italian Art 1953–71,* Walker Art Gallery, Liverpool
1973 *Bienal,* Sao Paulo
1980 *Arte Astratta ltaliana 1909–59,* Galleria Nazionale d'Arte Moderna, Rome
1982 *L'Immagine del Socialismo,* Palazzo delle Esposizioni, Rome
1986 *Eight Italian Painters, 1952–54: Afro, Birolli, Corpora, Moreni, Morlotti, Santomaso, Turcato, Vendova,* Padiglione d'Arte Contemporanea, Milan
1989 *On the Surface: An Abstract Journey,* Studio Durante, Rome
2000 *The 1950s: The Original Years,* De Crescenzo-Viesti Gallery, Rome

Collections:

Galleria Nazionale d'Arte Moderna, Rome; Musée d'Art Moderne de la Ville, Paris; Kunsthalle, Lund, Sweden; Konsthall, Gothenberg, Sweden; Museum of Modern Art, New York; Brooklyn Museum, New York; Museum de Arte Moderna, Sao Paulo; Galleria Civica d'Arte Moderna, Turin; Bayerische Staatsgemaldesammlungen, Munich.

Publications:

By TURCATO: Articles—''Crisi della Pittura'' in *Forma 1* (Rome), March 1947; ''Tre Biscotti'' in *Pittori che Scrivono,* Milan 1954; ''Tempi di Riscatto'' in *Realismo* (Milan), March 1955; ''Pensiero sul Disegno'' in *Civiltá delle Machine,* Rome 1956; ''Declaration'' in *Pittura ltaliana del Dopoguerra,* edited by T. Sauvage, Milan 1957; ''Le Correnti dell'Astrattismo'' in *Il Punto* (Rome), April 1957;

''Conformismo: Pigrizia Intellettuale'' in *Arte Oggi,* Rome 1959; ''Considerazione'' in *Alfabeto* (Rome), February 1963; ''Un Pelo dal Naso'' in *Carte Segrete* (Rome), no. 3. 1967; interview, with Gerardo de Simone, in *Turcato,* exhibition catalog, Naples 1981.

On TURCATO: Books—*Giulio Turcato,* exhibition catalog with an introduction by Palma Bucarelli, Rome 1950; *Otto pittori italiani* by Luca Venturi, Rome 1952; *Dictionnaire de la peinture abstraite* by Michel Seuphor, Paris 1957; *Arte e artisti d'avanguardia in Italia 1910–1950* by Giuseppe Marchiori, Milan 1960; *Ultime tendenze nell' arte d'oggi* by Gillo Dorfles, Milan 1961; *Giulio Turcato,* exhibition catalog with an introduction by Giulio Carlo Argan, London 1961; *Turcato,* exhibition catalog with text by Carla Lonzi, Rome 1965; *Turcato* by Mercuri, Rome 1968; *L'Arte del XX. Secolo* by H. L. Jaffe, Florence 1970; *Turcato* by Giorgio de Marchis, Milan 1971; *New Italian Art 1953–1971,* exhibition catalog with text by Giovanni Carandente, Liverpool 1971; *Giulio Turcato* by Giovanna dalla Chiesa and ltalo Mussa, Rome 1974; *Turcato,* exhibition catalog with text by Giovanni Caradente, Naples 1981; *Turcato* by Flaminio Gualdoni, Ravenna 1982; *Giulio Turcato,* exhibition catalog with texts by Thomas Messer, Carlo Proietti and others, Rome 1986; *Blu oltre* by Giorgio Franchetti, New York 1989; *Giulio Turcato: nuovi dipinti,* exhibition catalog, Torino 1990; *Giulio Turcato,* exhibition catalog with text by Maurizio Calvesi, Giovanna Dalla Chiesa and John Yau, Milan 1990. **Articles—**''Les vertiges pictographiques de Giulio Turcato'' by Gerard-Georges Lemaire in *Opus International,* no. 126, Autumn 1991; ''"Cerco un colore che nessuno ha mai visto"'' by Antonella Amendola in *Arte,* vol. 23, no. 238, March 1993.

*

Although my works for the last 30 years can be seen as unified within the same basic aesthetical principles, their contents have differed depending upon the ideas and poetic allusions I've sought to convey. My paintings quickly developed from geometric abstractions to a more personal and dynamic form, pictorially closer to the original futurist breakthroughs of Boccioni and Balla but with contents inspired by the revolutionary enthusiasm that followed Europe's liberation from Fascism. (For example, such works as ''Comizi'' (Demonstration), 1948; ''Rivolta'' (Revolt), 1949; ''Le Rovine di Varsavia'' (The Ruins of Warsaw), 1949; ''Fabbrica'' (Factory), 1949; ''Minniere'' (Mines), 1950; ''I Maggio '45, a Mosca'' (May 1, 1945 in Moscow), 1950.

Then, in the early 1950s, I began a series of paintings whose primary concern was pure line and color—''Composizione;'' ''Reticolo'' (Net); ''Labirinto'' (Labyrinth); and a series inspired by ecological concerns—''Il Giardino de Miciurin'', (The Garden of Miciurin), 1952; ''Paesaggio Cosmico'' (Cosmic Landscape), 1953. These concerns for pure line, color and form have remained and can be seen continuing in a series of works entitled, ''Mosche Cinese'' (Chinese Flies), 1957; ''Arcipelago'' (Archipelago), 1958; ''Subacqueo'' (Underwater) 1961; ''Floreale'' (Floral), 1961.

Two important works, ''Il Deserto dei Tartari'' and ''Desertico'' were painted after a trip in 1956 to China by plane across the vast continent of Russia and Central Asia. At about the same time I began with ''Le Cavallette'' (Grasshoppers) a more informal technique using colored sand surfaces that visually changed as the viewer moved his physical point of view, works such as ''La Bava'' (Drivel), 1960; ''Astronomical'', 1959; ''Via Lattea'' (Milky Way), 1959; ''Itinerari'' (Traces), 1960. Later, I would pursue this theme by using fine powdered glass that glistens or disappears depending upon the viewer's own movement in front of the painting.

Continuing this search beyond the normal confines of oil on canvas, I began in the early 1960s a series of collages on surfaces of sand and asphalt using the dollar, the lire and a carbon paper whose trademark was the image of the Acropolis—these images of money and the Acropolis were for me polemic symbols of power. In a related manner, on the same surfaces of sand and asphalt I placed real sedatives and tranquilizers as symbols of contemporary neurosis. These collages were actually only enlargements of a painting I did in 1953 in which I painted in oil the repeated image of the lire (being much too poor to even imagine placing real money on canvas in those days). This painting, ''Ricordo di S. Rocco'' (Memory of Saint Rocco), shown in the Venice *Biennale* of 1954, was inspired by my seeing the poor immigrants of the village of Pisticci as they attached lire to the religious statue of Saint Rocco.

Breaking completely from canvas, in 1963, I began to work directly on rough pockmarked sheets of foam rubber that gave to me the sense of the surface of the moon, painting them in white, silver, and dark metallic browns and violet-blues with occasional dots of fluorescent and phosphorescent pigment because I believe a painting can change light within itself. Above all, with the use of phosphorescent pigment I was searching to make painting visible in the dark because, for me, it is absurd that one cannot see a painting or a wall in the dark.

Another group of paintings, interesting and for me fundamental, are those entitled ''Fuori dello Spettro'' (Outside of the Spectrum) since they were made to isolate colors scientifically considered not within the classified color spectrum: maroon and amaranth. I made many experiments (anticipated by a painting of the same title in 1963), and then in 1972 I showed seven paintings based purely on the color spectrum. From a quick glance around the room there remained a fleeting visual impression of maroon and amaranth. From this experiment were born other paints of monochromatic surfaces, each of a different color; each an evidence of the strength within a restraint of using only a single color on canvas.

From a desire to change the square dimensions of painting, I at first painted circular forms, later truncated triangles, until in the early 1970s I created shapes in canvas and then in wood entitled ''Oceanica'' for their similarity to the primitive oval forms of the island civilizations of the Pacific or perhaps to the surf boards originally used by the Maori. I wanted to structuralize existing forms since I don't believe much in sculpture in its classical sense. From this came also the works entitled, ''Libreria Incatenata'' (Chained Library), tall wooden structures, tied in their final narrowing height by iron ropes, and painted in vivid fluorescent colors with assorted sections of phosphorescent pigment that can be seen in the dark. These and other objects such as the ''Sarcofaghi'' were intentionally painted with transparent material that gives off an illumination from inside as if by neon signs. They are the continuation of my interest in collage, but within space; adaptable to any space available—in a small space there can be one, in museum spaces I've shown 10 or 15; they can hang from the ceiling or lean on a wall or block a corridor. By being independent of any particular space, their presence underlines the very existence of free space and the artist's fundamental act of changing a previously defined ambience.

—Giulio Turcato

* * *

Everyone knows that Giulio Turcato is a born painter who lives to paint, and since early youth has done nothing else but paint. Around 1942–43 he taught drawing and design in a vocational school at Portogruaro, and from 1953 has taught figure drawing in the Liceo of Fine Arts in Rome. On the other hand, he has always found someone to buy one of his paintings. Like this, he lives. His official position and fame are much below his value because he is timid and indifferent to any public recognition, and in spite of having some difficult moments he is content in his bohemian life, the only one he considers worthy of an artist, because more than free it is anarchic. But the anarchy of Turcato is extemely gentle. It has a Venetian mood, wouldn't hurt a fly and is so disinterested that it becomes itself a work of art. If one adds that he is capable of intense work, but is desultory sometimes for great intervals, we can understand how he owes to himself the limits of his fame and of the value given to some of the great periods of his work. The last few years have been a recovery and ones of intense and happy activity. It's just the moment to speak of him.

An essential quality of Turcato, which is acknowledged by his colleagues, is his sense of the limits and an absolute lack of rhetoric. When Turcato dedicated himself to pure abstractionism, he didn't fall into it as an experiment or a joke or just for the spontaneous engagement of his painting. It never came into his mind to place a line or colour to show his ability, but only to express a feeling or to indicate an idea or to make poetic allusion. Turcato's strength often consists in his refusal to ''do the painting'' so that he can express a moment of his fantastic vision. Therefore, his paintings appear, and often seem to be, unfinished in spite of their authentic artistic worth. But few artists today, as in the past, are able to escape a bias to finish.

I think I have indicated here many reasons why Turcato's fame is below his value: shyness, indifference to public acknowledgement, a bohemian life, intermittent work, a sense of boundaries, delicateness, and also a tenuous inspiration. He considers his art as being completely abstract. He distinguishes three types of abstraction: the American, represented by Pollock, the French and the European trend, in which he prefers Hartung. Poliakoff is too romantic for him. Matta is too surrealistic, and Manessier too tied up with impressionism. Among Italian painters he feels sympathy for Corpora, Vedova and Afro, and the young Dova and Perilli. He does not take an interest in Mondrian's constructivism because to Turcato a painting is a space charged with emotion, without a center, and without the doors of a triptych. He finds that surrealism was useful because it allowed thought to untie itself from literary tradition. What he asks of painting is for it to have an emotion that exceeds the painting, a surrealistic impulse without the need of an unconscious mind, able not to create romantic drama but colour-form. According to him, painting creates a space in eternal movement, free from any theory, that attempts to transform and modify the life of feeling.

In the review *Forma 1* (April 1947), he published an article entitled ''Crisis of Painting.'' I would like readers to reflect on the fact that this text was written in 1947, and that it has prophetic value in regard to the following development of Italian painting: ''Those who kept a tie with the 19th century style, or wanted to use a realistic style, or gave a small touch of Lombardic feeling to their imitative forms of Picasso, all failed.'' Already in 1947 Turcato understood the historical condition of painting in Italy and abroad better than many eminent persons who were supposedly more learned than he. To understand the history of painting, you must understand painting. And Turcato is a born painter. After a show with the ''Fronte Nuovo'' at the Venice *Biennale* of 1948, Turcato found himself the foremost target in the condemnation of abstractionism by the Communist Party—and he was a Communist. This obstacle, arising directly in the midst of his natural development, did not leave him unaffected. On the contrary, he tried in various ways to find an accord between his convictions as a man and as an artist: he attempted figuration, symbolism, and even surrealism. But his artistic nature prevailed. Besides, he was enough of an anarchist to disregard superior orders. In facing Cagli and Guttuso, moreover, he defended his freedom with his fists. Not that Turcato refused to deal with social problems in which he believed, like in the works ''Meeting,'' ''Revolt'' and ''Warsaw Ruins,'' but he represented them in an abstract form, thereby destroying their effectiveness as propaganda in a heretical way. In the meantime, he gained a scholarship in 1950 to stay in Paris and has returned there many times. He also made other travels to Germany and as far from home as China. So, in his own way, he dominates the panorama of international art.

—Luca Venturi

TURNBULL, William

Nationality: British. **Born:** Dundee, Scotland, 11 January 1922. **Education:** Studied at Slade School of Fine Art, London, 1946–48. **Military:** Served in Royal Air Force in Canada, India, and Ceylon, 1941–46. **Family:** Married Kim Lim in 1960; sons: Alexander and Jonathan. **Career:** Painter and sculptor. Illustration department of D. C. Thompson magazine publishing company, Dundee, 1939–41; moved to Paris, 1948, and to London, 1950. Instructor in experimental design, 1952–61, and in sculpture, 1964–72, Central School of Arts and Crafts, London. **Agent:** Waddington Galleries. **Address:** c/o Waddington Galleries, 11 Cork Street, London W1S 3LT, England.

Individual Exhibitions:

1950 Hanover Gallery, London (with Eduardo Paolozzi and Kenneth King)
1952 Hanover Gallery, London
1957 Institute of Contemporary Art, London
1960 *Paintings,* Molton Gallery, London
1961 Molton Gallery, London
1963 Marlborough-Gerson Gallery, New York (sculpture)
Detroit Institute of Arts (sculpture)
1965 Bennington College, Vermont (paintings)
Galerie Muller, Stuttgart (paintings)
1966 *Sculpture and Paintings,* Pavilion Gallery, Balboa, California
1967 *Bienal,* Sao Paulo (toured South America)
Waddington Galleries, London
1968 Hayward Gallery, London (paintings)
Museo de Arte Moderna, Rio de Janeiro
Museo Nacional de Bellas Artes, Buenos Aires
Institute de Artes Plasticas, Santiago, Chile
1969 Waddington Galleries, London
1970 Waddington Galleries, London
1973 *Sculpture and Paintings,* Tate Gallery, London (retrospective)
1974 Scottish Arts Council Gallery, Edinburgh
Galerie Muller, Stuttgart
1976 Waddington Galleries, London

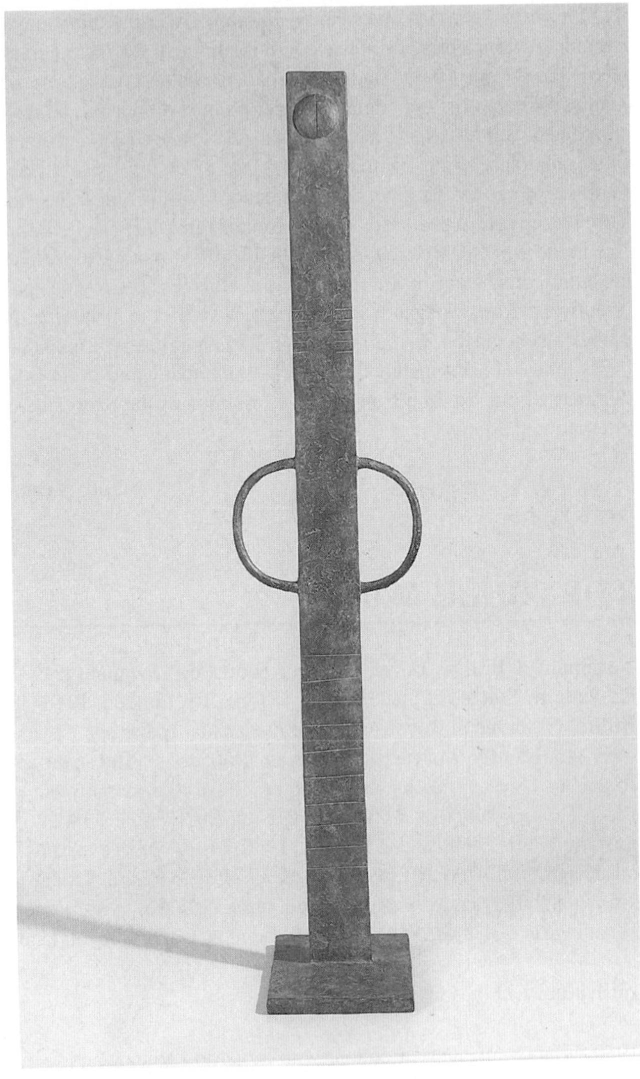

William Turnbull: *Female Figure,* 1993. ©2001 Artists Rights Society (ARS), NY/DACS, London.

William Turnbull: *Horses Head,* 1995. ©2001 Artists Rights Society (ARS), NY/DACS, London.

1978 Waddington Galleries, London
1981 Waddington Galleries, London
1982 Waddington Galleries, New York
Waddington Galleries, Toronto
1983 Galerie Kutter, Luxembourg
1984 National Museum Art Gallery, Singapore
1985 Waddington Galleries, London
1986 Terry Dintenfass Gallery, New York
1987 Galerie Folker Skulima, West Berlin
Waddington Galleries, London
1988 John Berggruen Gallery, San Francisco
1989 Arnold Herstand Gallery, New York
1991 Waddington Galleries, London
1992 Galeria Freites, Caracas (sculpture)
Galerie Michael Haas, Berlin (sculpture)
Galerie von Braunbehrens, Munich (sculpture)
1994 Galerie Sander, Darmstadt (sculpture)
1995 *Bronze Idols and Untitled Paintings* (retrospective), Serpentine Gallery, London
1998 Waddington Galleries, London (sculpture and paintings)
Barbara Mathes Gallery, New York (sculpture)

Selected Group Exhibitions:

1952 *Biennale,* Venice (and 1957)
1958 *Carnegie International,* Pittsburgh (and 1961)
1960 *Situation,* R.B.A. Galleries, London
1964 *Guggenheim International,* Guggenheim Museum, New York
1966 *New Shapes and Forms of Colour,* Stedelijk Museum, Amsterdam
1968 *Documenta,* Kassel, West Germany
1976 *Arte Inglese Oggi,* Palazzo Reale, Milan
1982 *British Sculpture in the Twentieth Century: II,* Whitechapel Art Gallery, London
1987 *British Art in the Twentieth Century,* Royal Academy, London (travelled to Stuttgart)
1991 *New Displays,* Tate Gallery, London

1992 *New Realities, Art in Western Europe 1945–1968,* Tate Gallery, Liverpool
1996 *Un Siècle de Sculpture Anglaise,* Galerie Nationale du Jeu de Paume, Paris

Collections:

Tate Gallery, London; Victoria and Albert Museum, London; Dundee Art Gallery, Scotland; Scottish National Gallery of Modern Art, Edinburgh; Cardiff Museum, Wales; Albright-Knox Art Gallery, Buffalo, New York; Hirshhorn Museum and Sculpture Garden, Washington D.C.; Stadtisches Museum Schloss Mosbroich, Leverkusen, West Germany; Wesfalischer Landesmuseum, Munster, West Germany; Teheran Museum of Contemporary Art.

Publications:

By TURNBULL: Books illustrated—*Basho: The Records of a Weather Exposed Skeleton* (book/object), London 1969; *The Garden of Caresses,* translated from Arabic by Franz Toussaint, London 1970; *Der Wassermaier* by Helmut Heissenbuttel, Zurich 1976. **Articles**—''White Text on Black Ground,'' with Theo Crosby, Germano Facetti, and Edward Wright, in *This Is Tomorrow,* exhibition catalog, London 1956; ''William Turnbull 1949–60'' in *Uppercase* (London), no. 4, 1960; ''The Joining Edge'' in *Gazette* (London), no. 1, 1961; ''Images without Temples'' in *Living Arts* (London), no. 1, 1963; ''Notes on Sculpture,'' with others in *Studio International* (London), November 1968; ''Colour in Sculpture,'' with Phillip King, Tim Scott and David Annesley, in *Studio International* (London), January 1969; ''Statement on Sculpture,'' with others, in *Studio International* (London), July/August 1972. **Film**—*83 B,* with Alan Forbes, 1953.

On TURNBULL: Books—*William Turnbull,* exhibition catalog with text by David Sylvester, London 1950; *Sculpture of the 20th Century* by Andrew C. Ritchie, New York 1952; *William Turnbull,* exhibition catalog with text by Lawrence Alloway, London 1957; *The Sculpture of This Century* by Michel Seuphor, New York 1960; *Contemporary Sculpture* by Carola Giedion-Welcker, New York 1960; *Situation,* exhibition catalog with introduction by Roger Coleman, London 1960; *William Turnbull: Paintings,* exhibition catalog with text by Lawrence Alloway, London 1960; *Modern Sculpture in the Joseph H. Hirshhorn Collection,* exhibition catalog with introduction by H. H. Amason, New York 1962; *A Concise History of Modern Sculpture* by Herbert Read, London 1964; *William Turnbull: Sculpture and Paintings* exhibition catalog with introduction by Jules Langsner, Balboa, California 1966; *IX Bienal de Sao Paulo: British Section-William Turnbull,* exhibition catalog with text by Alan Bowness, London 1967; *William Turnbull: Sculpture and Painting,* exhibition catalog with introduction by Richard Morphet, London 1973; *Turnbull,* exhibition catalog with introduction by Robert Kudielka, Stuttgart 1974; *The Potent Image* by Frederick S. Wight, New York 1976; *British Art* by Simon Wilson, London, 1979; *William Turnbull,* exhibition catalog with introduction by Roger Bevan, London 1987; *The Sculptures of William Turnbull,* exhibition catalog with introduction by Colin Renfrew, Cambridge 1990; *Desde la primigenia hasta los albores del siglo XXI,* exhibition catalog with introduction by Beatriz Sogbe, Caracas 1992. **Article**—''William Turnbull—Sculptor and Painter'' by Bernard Cohen in *Studio International* (London), July/August 1973.

* * *

Although British, William Turnbull has more in common with his colleagues on the continent than with his fellow islanders. For one thing he is equally committed to the major arts of painting and sculpture—activities typical of such continental artists as Picasso and Matisse. For another, his kinship seems closer to a sculptor like Brancusi, a painter like Albers, a draughtsman like Matisse, than to any Briton.

At the same time, his painting as it has evolved would be hard to imagine without the precedent of the breakthrough Americans of the post World War II era; Rothko pre-eminently. This is not to suggest that Turnbull is merely a derivative artist; rather, he has been released into his own sensibility through an emotional tie to certain artists' work. In the formal sense, he is one of the most ''serious'' artists in England, producing works in wood and metal in a minimal vein which have haunting overtones of primitive art as well as an elegance which could be called oriental. His large format paintings have been ''about'' fields of color in which the paint surface is handled with wonderful virtuosity being lively and rich instead of merely a flat expanse.

In recent work color-saturated, brush-inflected canvases are bordered by closely related color; the hue and value of which sets up a tension between the field and its boundary, both in turn related to the actual stretcher edge. This concern with the edge/field has become a major interest to painters in the later part of our century. The ''compositional'' material of such paintings is often the character of the paint application itself together with whatever optical contrasts the colors provide. It is one of the extremely pure developments in modernist art and demands from the viewer a high degree of aesthetic response. As it is about the art of painting as such, it is necessary for the viewer to acquaint himself with the elements that comprise art. Except for the fact that its three-dimensionality causes it to exist in ''real'' space and cast ''real'' shadows in ''real'' light, thus giving us information outside of itself, much the same necessity to know its nature can be demanded by minimal sculpture as well.

Such purism can be misread by the impatient or lazy. A danger artists like Turnbull risk.

—Ralph Pomeroy

TURRELL, James (Archie)

Nationality: American. **Born:** Los Angeles, California, 6 May 1943. **Education:** Pasadena High School, 1957–61; Pomona College, Claremont, California, 1961–65, B.A. in psychology 1965; University of California at Irvine, 1967; Claremont Graduate School, M.A. in Art 1973. **Family:** Married Elizabeth Bartlett Elgin in 1965; children: Shana and Jennifer. **Career:** Independent artist since 1967. Lecturer, University of California at Los Angeles, summer 1968, and University of California at Riverside, 1971; visiting artist, Pomona College, 1971–73; lecturer, University of California at Irvine, 1974. **Awards:** National Endowment for the Arts Grant, 1968; Guggenheim

Fellowship, 1974; National Endowment for the Arts Matching Grant, 1975. **Agent:** Gladstone Gallery, 515 West 24th St., New York, New York 10011, U.S.A.

Selected Individual Exhibitions:

1967 Pasadena Art Museum, California
1976 Stedelijk Museum, Amsterdam
1981 Portland Center for the Visual Arts, Oregon
1982 Center for Contemporary Art, Seattle, Washington
Israel Museum, Jerusalem
1983 Musée d'Art Moderne de la Ville, Paris
1987 Kunsthalle, Basel
1991 Kunstmuseum, Berne, Switzerland (catalog)
1992 Musée d'Art Contemporain, Lyon (catalog)
Fundacion La Caixa, Madrid (catalog)
1995 Contemporary Art Gallery, Mito Art Tower, Japan (catalog)
1998 *The Other Horizon,* MAK, Austrian Museum of Applied Arts, Vienna
Spirit and Light, Contemporary Art Museum, Houston (catalog)
1999 Nelson-Atkins Museum of Art, Kansas City, Missouri
2001 *Infinite Light,* Scottsdale Center for Contemporary Art, Arizona

Selected Group Exhibitions:

1969 *Light Spaces,* Main and Hill Studio, Los Angeles
1973 *3D into 2D,* New York Cultural Center
1976 *Light Space,* Arco Center for the Visual Arts, Los Angeles
1980 *Light and Space,* Whitney Museum, New York
1982 *American Exhibition,* Art Institute of Chicago
1997 *Sunshine and Noir: Art in Los Angeles, 1960–1997,* Kunstmuseum Wolfsburg, Germany, and Louisiana Museum of Contemporary Art, Humlebaek, Denmark (catalog)
The Age of Modernism: Art in the 20th Century, Martin Gropius Bau, Berlin (catalog)
2000 Guggenheim Museum Bilbao, Bilbao, Spain
Venice/Venezia, Peggy Guggenheim Collection, Venice, Italy

Collections:

Stedelijk Museum, Amsterdam

Publications:

On TURRELL: Books—*James Turrell,* exhibition catalog with essay by Claude Gintz, Paris 1983; *James Turrell: Mapping Spaces/ Kartographie des Raumes,* exhibition catalog with texts by Craig Adcock, Jean-Christophe Ammann and others, New York and Basel 1987; *James Turrell: The Art of Light and Space* by Craig Adcock, Berkeley, California 1990; *James Turrell,* edited by Deborah Menaker Rothschild, Williamstown, Massachusetts 1991; *James Turrell: Perceptual Cells,* edited by Jiri Svetska, Stuttgart 1992; *James Turrell: La perception est le médium,* Brussels 1995. **Articles—**''James Turrell: Projected Light Images'' by John Coplans in *Artforum* (New York), October 1967; ''A Gallery Without Walls'' by Barbara Rose in Art in America (New York), March/April 1968; ''New Directions in Southern California Sculpture'' in *Arts Magazine* (New York), Summer 1970; ''The Talk of the Town-Light'' by Calvin Tomkins in the *New Yorker,* 15 December 1980; ''Poetry Out of Emptiness'' by Robert Hughes in *Time* (New York), 5 January 1981; ''The Art of Deception'' by Nancy Marmer in *Art in America* (New York), May 1981.

* * *

In the widest sense, James Turrell can be defined as an environmental artist. Since the late 1960s, Turrell has been creating gallery installations and outdoor pieces that completely engage their space and, in turn, heighten the viewer's sense of her surroundings. More specifically, though, Turrell has manipulated both natural and architectural forms in order to capture the effects of light. ''Light artist'' is perhaps the more accurate term that has been used to describe him. While much of his work creates optical illusions involving light, Turrell's intentions go beyond illusionistic effects themselves. He has explained, ''I like the qualities that are nearer pure perception. . . . The experience I'm aiming for is something of felt light residing in a space.''

An early source of inspiration for Turrell was found in viewing slides of art works. Instead of looking at the image on the wall, Turrell found himself looking at the beam of light that projected the image. He was particularly interested in the way the light appeared suspended in space. Consequently, his earliest pieces are comprised of projected light onto flat walls or into corners. Turrell manipulated the light effect by cutting certain geometric patterns into slide-sized templates used in the projector. In *Afrum* (1967), Turrell created the illusion of an incandescent three-dimensional cube suspended in the corner of a dark room. As the viewer approached the corner, it became apparent the cube was mere light projected on flat walls, an immaterial but immanent presence.

Later pieces have been preoccupied with the viewer's perception of natural light. In *Skyspace* (1972), Turrell exploited the simple framing device of a sky window in a small, bare, and otherwise enclosed room. Time of day, weather, and season dictated the effect of the light on the room and on the viewer's mood. While the viewer was free to contemplate the sky (which appeared as a picture in a state of slow but nonetheless constant natural flux) or the effect of the light on the surrounding walls, more frequently the viewer's eyes were drawn to the light itself which appeared to hover in the middle of the room. As Craig Adcock points out in ''Perceptual Edges: The Psychology of James Turrell's Light and Space'' (*Arts Magazine,* February 1985), ''Part of the interest of Turrell's work involves looking versus seeing. His pieces force us to see light because, in them, there is no object to look at.'' At a purely perceptual level, light *is* the object in Turrell's work.

Since the mid-1970s, Turrell's main project has been the *Roden Crater,* an actual crater which Turrell fashioned from an extinct volcanic cone near Flagstaff, Arizona. With the *Roden Crater,* Turrell is expanding on the light and sky plays of his earlier installations. He is building several underground chambers, tunnels, and openings that will allow visitors to experience the light of a certain moon or see a rare celestial alignment. In order to accurately place the various cells and passages, Turrell has been working with astronomers. Yet current visitors have enjoyed an effect that the artist called ''celestial vaulting.'' By lying flat on their backs along the rim of the crater with their heads toward its center, they see the sky as a huge bubble.

The *Roden Crater* promises to distill the ethos of Turrell's smaller works. In attempting to contain pure light and draw the viewer's attention to it, Turrell has not only been asking us to consider the elements of perception, he has also been inviting us to experience the wonder of a natural phenomenon: light in and of itself. Turrell has stated: ''We feel apart from nature. . . . It is that feeling of being apart that estranges us from nature. So I am interested in things that take away that sense of estrangement. I think the people who made the Gothic cathedrals had as much to say about a sense of awe as does any of the rhetoric that happens within the cathedral.'' Perhaps the *Roden Crater* will prove to be a useful cathedral of sorts at the turn of the millenium, engendering a sense of awe in us for a very old and still mysterious natural world.

—Demetra James

Turrell has continued to create his installations in the United Kingdom, Europe, and Japan as well as the United States. The *Roden Crater*'s completion, once expected in 2001, has proved to be an ever-expanding project. Although much has been done—The South Lodge; Sun and Moon Space; East Alpha Tunnel; the East Portal and the Crater's Eye—the artist has still further plans which will continue, dependent on funding.

At the Scottsdale Museum of Contemporary Art in Arizona his exhibition, ''Infinite Light,'' Amitabha in Sanskrit, had as its theme the concept of rebirth in an eternal paradise known as the Pure Land (as it is conceived by certain Pure Land Buddhist sects). A major feature was a room, ''Wide Cut,'' open on one side and carpeted, which the viewer entered, having removed his or her shoes, to face a wall of light. The shifting color of the light was derived from different gases in the lighting tubes, achieving for the viewer a sense of being suspended in the immaterial—to dematerialize the material and materialize the immaterial, which is Turrell's intention. Also in the exhibition, and exemplary of Turrell's installations, was a ''Skyspace,'' permanently installed in the sculpture garden. It is a building with an elliptical opening in the ceiling from which one views the changing aspects of the sky. The exterior—faced with white plaster in which bits of seashells are embedded, and whole set against a scrim wall by James Carpenter which creates a changing, opalescent surface—continues the presentation of light in the perception of the viewer as the ''object'' of the work.

—Barbara Cortright

TUTTLE, Richard

Nationality: American. **Born:** Rahway, New Jersey, in 1941. **Education:** Trinity College, Hartford, Connecticut, B.A. 1963; Cooper Union, New York, 1963–64. **Career:** Painter; lives and works in New York; Fellow of the American Academy, Rome, 1995–1996. **Awards:** Eighth Kunstpreis, Aachen, 1999. **Agent:** Blum Helman Gallery, 20 West 57th Street, New York, New York 10019. **Address:** 1631 West Pacific, Spokane, Washington, 99204.

Individual Exhibitions:

1965 Betty Parsons Gallery, New York
1967 Betty Parsons Gallery, New York
1968 Betty Parsons Gallery, New York
Galerie Schmela, Dusseldorf
1969 Nicholas Wilder Gallery, Los Angeles
1970 Betty Parsons Gallery, New York
Galerie Rudolf Zwirner, Cologne
Albright-Knox Art Gallery, Buffalo, New York
1971 Museum of Fine Arts, Dallas
1972 Museum of Modern Art, New York
Galerie Yvon Lambert, Paris
Betty Parsons Gallery, New York
Galerie Rudolf Zwirner, Cologne
1973 Clocktower, Institute for Art and Urban Resources, New York
Kunstraum, Munich
Galerie Heiner-Friedrich, Munich
Daniel Weinberg Gallery, San Francisco
Galerie Annemarie Verna, Zurich
Konrad Fischer Gallery, Dusseldorf
1974 Betty Parsons Gallery, New York
Galerie Lambert, Paris
Galleria Toselli, Milan
Galleria Marilena Bonomo, Bari, Italy
Cusack Gallery, Houston
Nigel Greenwood Gallery, London
1975 Whitney Museum, New York (retrospective)
Cusack Gallery, Houston
Parsons-Truman Gallery, New York
Wadsworth Atheneum, Hartford, Connecticut
1976 Galerie Lambert, Paris
Otis Art Institute, Los Angeles
Brooke Alexander Gallery, New York
Fine Arts Building Gallery, New York
1977 Ohio State University, Columbus
Kunsthalle, Basel
Kunstraum, Munich
Yale University, New Haven, Connecticut (with Long and Hewitt)
1978 Betty Parsons Gallery, New York
Galerie Lambert, Paris
Ugo Ferranti Gallery, Rome
Young-Hoffman Gallery, Chicago
1979 Brooke Alexander Gallery, New York
Stedelijk Museum, Amsterdam
Centre d'Arts Plastiques Contemporains, Bordeaux
1980 Centre d'Art Contemporain, Geneva
California Institute of Technology, Pasadena
1982 Blum Helman Gallery, New York (with Robert Ryman and Cy Twombly)
1983 Galerie Hubert Winter, Vienna
Blum Helman Gallery, New York
1984 Studio La Citta, Verona, Italy
Galerie Yvon Lambert, Paris
Galerie Schmela, Dusseldorf
1985 Galerie Schmela, Dusseldorf
Galleria Toselli, Milan

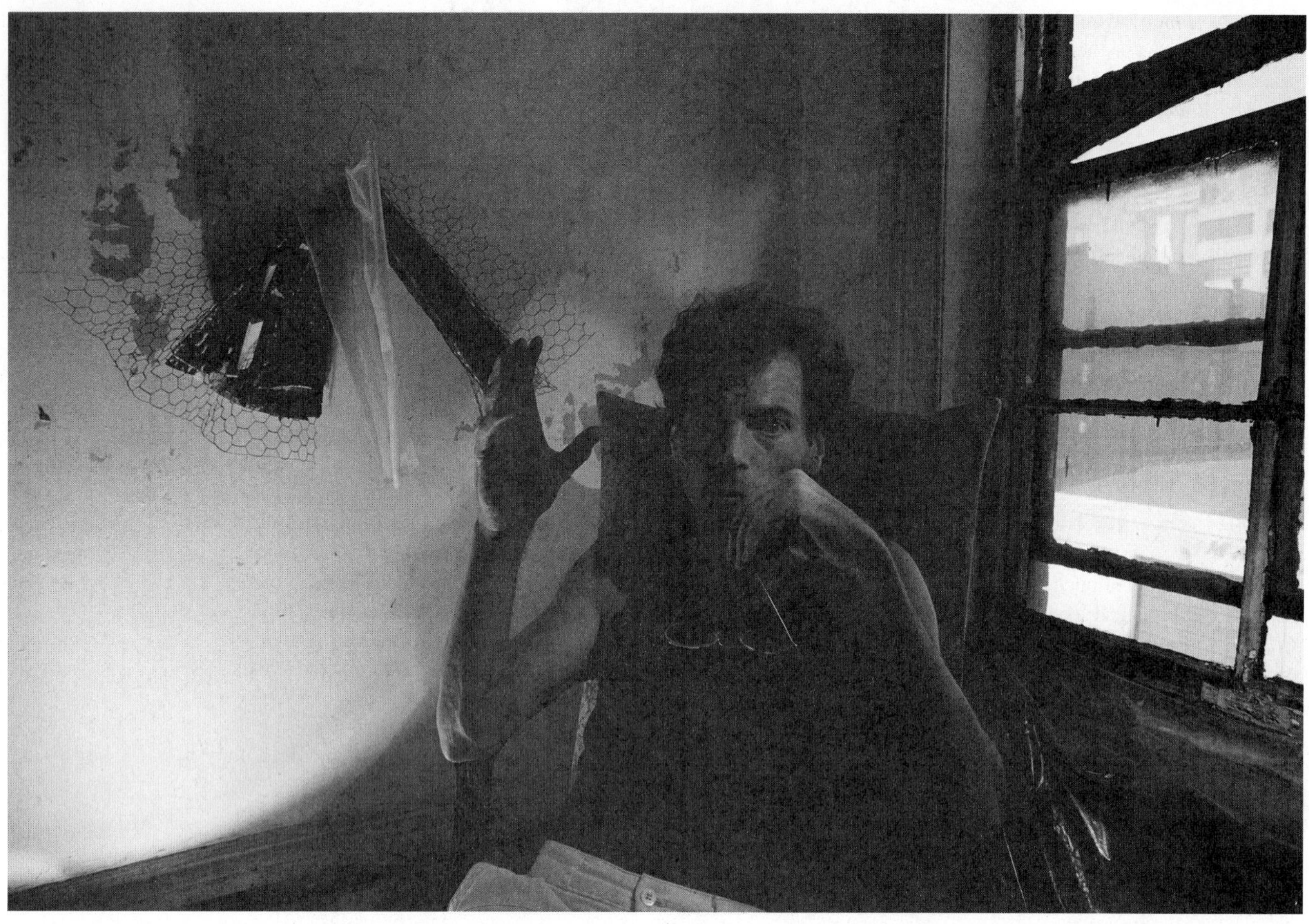

Richard Tuttle with one of his sculptures, 1987. ©Richard Schulman/Corbis.

Institute of Contemporary Arts, London
1986 Victoria Miro Gallery, London
Galerie Reinhard Onnasch, West Berlin
Musée d'Art Contemporain, Bordeaux, France
Musée d'Art Moderne de la Ville, Paris
1988 *Richard Tuttle: Portland Works 1976,* Thomas Segal Gallery, Boston (catalog)
1992 *The Poetry of Form: Richard Tuttle—Drawings from the Vogel Collection,* Instituto Valenciano de Arte Moderno, Spain (travelled to Indianapolis Museum of Art) (catalog)
1993 *Richard Tuttle: Chaos, the Form,* Staatliche Kunsthalle, Baden-Baden, Germany (catalog)
1996 *Richard Tuttle: New and Early Work,* Sperone Westwater, New York
1997 *Agnes Martin/Richard Tuttle,* Modern Art Museum of Fort Worth (catalog)
Richard Tuttle: Books and Portfolios, Brooke Alexander/ Brook Alexander Editions, New York
Richard Tuttle: Grey Walls Work, Camden Arts Centre, London (travelled to Dublin and Edinburgh) (catalog)
1998 Sperone Westwater Gallery, New York
Richard Tuttle: New Mexico, New York, Sperone Westwater, New York
Richard Tuttle: Chandeliers, A/D Gallery, New York
Richard Tuttle: Die Konjunktion der Farbe, Ludwig Forum fur Internationale Kunst, Aachen, Germany

Selected Group Exhibitions:

1968 *Other Ideas,* Detroit Institute of Arts
1970 *Using Walls,* Jewish Museum, New York
1971 *Painting without Supports,* Bennington College, Vermont
1972 *Documenta 5,* Kassel, West Germany (and *Documenta 6,* 1977; *Documenta 7,* 1982)
1973 *Young American Artists,* Kunsthalle, Hamburg (travelled to the Moderna Museet, Stockholm)
1975 *14 Artists,* Baltimore Museum of Art
1976 *Drawing Now,* Museum of Modern Art, New York
1983 *Abstract Painting 1960–69,* Project Studio One, New York
1985 *New Dialogues,* Dracos Art Centre, Athens
1988 *Contemporary American Art,* Sara Hilden Museum, Tampere, Finland (travelled to Oslo)
1991 *Immaterial Objects,* Whitney Museum of American Art, New York (catalog)
1994 *From Minimal to Conceptual Art,* National Gallery of Art, Washington, D.C. (catalog)
1995 *Color and Structure,* Galerie Lelong, New York
American Drawings and Graphic Works, Kunsthaus, Zurich (catalog)

1996 *Drawings by American and European Artists,* Margarete Roeder Gallery, New York
From Figure to Object: A Century of Sculptors' Drawings, Frith Street Gallery, London (catalog)
1997 *Rotating Group Drawing Exhibition,* Margarete Roeder Gallery, New York
Works on Paper, Lawrence Markey, New York
WOOD NOT WOOD/WORKS NOT WORKS, A/D Gallery, New York
Art Foundry Editions Santa Fe at Knoedler New York, New York
At the Threshold of the Visible: Miniscule and Small-scale Art, 1964–1999, Independent Curators Incorporated, New York (travelled to Toronto, Santa Monica and Edmonton) (catalog)
1998 *Severed Ear: The Poetry of Abstraction,* Creiger-Dane Gallery, Boston
Here and Now, Henry Moore Institute, Leeds, England
Brand New Editions, Karen McCready Fine Art, New York
2000 *2000 Biennial Exhibition,* Whitney Museum of American Art, New York

Collections:

Museum of Modern Art, New York; Whitney Museum, New York; Albright-Knox Art Gallery, Buffalo, New York; Corcoran Gallery of Art, Washington, D.C.; St. Louis Art Museum; National Gallery of Canada, Ottawa; Stedelijk Museum, Amsterdam; Wallraf-Richartz Museum, Cologne; Kaiser-Wilhelm Museum, Krefeld, West Germany; Kunsthaus, Zurich.

Publications:

By TUTTLE: Book—*Richard Tuttle: Eight Works from a Reading at Brooklyn College,* Florence 1990; *Richard Tuttle,* with Eduardo Lipschutz-Villa, Susan Harris, Dieter Schwarz and Richard Marshall, Amsterdam 1991; *Richard Tuttle: Grey Walls Work* with Jenni Lomax, Festina Lente and Paul Nesbitt, London 1996. **Article—** statement in *Richard Tuttle,* exhibition catalog, Paris 1986; interview with Bob Holman in *Bomb,* no. 41, Fall 1992; ''Richard Tuttle: September 21, 1989'' in *New Observations,* no. 113, Winter 1996.

On TUTTLE: Books—*Richard Tuttle,* exhibition catalog with text by Robert Murdock, Dallas 1971; *Contemporary American Art,* exhibition catalog with text by Peter Schjeldahl, Tampere 1988. **Articles—**''Reviews and Previews: Richard Tuttle at Parsons Gallery'' by Scott Burton in *Artnews* (New York), January 1968; ''Simple, Not Simple Minded'' by John Perreault in the *Village Voice* (New York), January 1968; ''Artists on Their Art'' by Jeffrey Smart in *Art International* (Lugano, Switzerland), May 1968; ''The Art of Richard Tuttle'' by Robert Pincus-Witten in *Artforum* (New York), February 1970; ''Richard Tuttle'' by Robert Murdock in *Art International* (Lugano, Switzerland), May 1971; ''Wire, Pencil, Shadow: Elements of Richard Tuttle'' by E. Lubeel in *Arts Magazine* (New York), November 1972; ''Richard Tuttle: Collage-Drawings'' by Bernard Brunon in *Artstudio,* no. 23, Winter 1991; ''Numbers of Happiness: Richard Tuttle's Books'' by Nancy Princenthal in *Print Collector's Newsletter,* vol. 24, no. 3, July-August 1993; ''Light and Shadow by Richard Tuttle'' in *El Palacio,* vol. 100, no. 2, Spring 1995; ''Richard Tuttle's Paper Liberation'' by Paul Gardner in *On Paper,* vol. 1, no. 3, January-February 1997; ''Just Exquisite? The Art of Richard Tuttle'' by Robert Storr in *Artforum,* vol. 36, no. 3, November 1997; ''The Subtle Mr. Tuttle'' by Stuart King in *Woodturning,* no. 66, August 1998.

* * *

Richard Tuttle's intimately scaled, fragile, awkward, eccentrically shaped works seem to question both the boundaries between the graphic/painterly and the sculptural and the heroic size and physicality which dominated during the period of Tuttle's development in the 1960s. Tuttle's work, from his ideographic wall reliefs to those composed of various combinations of pencil, wire, cloth, paper, metal and wood, is usually classified under the Postminimalist heading, and his is a particularly quirky and subtly effective variant in the range of work made by the diverse group so clustered.

In 1963–65, Tuttle was making small, paper box constructions such as his three-inch cube Box (1964), using geometric shape to emphasize individual personality and also the making process. ''Toy like'' qualitites along with folds, slits and cuts tend toward an Arp-like anthropomorphism which carries into Tuttle's 1965 series of wood reliefs, rounded shapes painted in one color with abstract references to nature, landscape and symbolically cryptic writing. These were either hung on the wall or lain on the floor in a kind of scattering effect which heightened their personally based, intuitive nature. In 1967 Tuttle made a group of shaped canvases, shaped in irregular octagonal configurations, dyed in Tintex in a range of washy tones, hemmed and either pinned loosely on the wall or arranged on the floor. As the series progressed the shapes became more personally warped versions of the octagon, an effect achieved by Tuttle's cutting out of interior angles on different sides of the canvas. In their fusion of soaked-in paint and fragile three-dimensionality, these works invoked a fusion of painting and sculpture into a tense but material coupling. In his push to achieve new levels of delicate subtlety, Tuttle made his 1972 series of wire and graphite wall works, combining illusion and allusion through the juxtapositioning of wavey, twisting lengths of wire with nervous, straggley graphite lines. The shadows created by the wire lengths adds the third dimension, while the whole acting in concert activates the metaphorical fourth dimension, suggesting rhythms beyond those seen with the eyes.

Throughout the past decade, Tuttle has continued to experiment with the possibilities inherent in the basic methodologies he had established during the previous decade. He has managed to achieve considerable variety and freshness by diversely combining small, simple shapes in low relief with either painted or linear elements which extend these shapes onto the wall. The works are both objects and references to drawings or paintings of objects. Their qualities of tentative whimsey and miniaturization use dephysicalized presence to intensify the personal. Because they are so odd, so attenuated and so close to becoming invisible, they draw the viewer closer to contemplate the delicate interplays between the solid and the ephemeral. Tuttle's mini-world of shadowy, elusive, and deceptively simple form offers hopeful proof that art need not be huge and heavy to achieve the strong effect.

—Barbara Cavaliere

TWOMBLY, Cy

Nationality: American. **Born:** Edward Parker Twombly, Jr., Lexington, Virginia, 25 April 1928. **Education:** Boston Museum School of Fine Art, 1948–49; Washington and Lee University, Lexington, 1949–50; Art Students League, New York, 1950–51; and, under Robert Motherwell and Franz Kline, Black Mountain College, Beria, North Carolina, 1951–52. **Career:** Travelled in Europe and Africa, 1952–53; moved to Rome, 1957. Head of art department, Southern Seminary Junior College, Buena Vista, Virginia, 1955–56; Elected to the American Academy and Institute of Arts and Letters, 1987; Cy Twombly Gallery dedicated at The Menil Collection, Houston, 1995. **Awards:** Virginia Museum of Fine Arts Travelling Fellowship, 1952. **Agent:** c/o Gagosian Gallery, 980 Madison Avenue, New York, New York, 10021–1848; c/o Sperone Westwater, 142 Greene Street, New York, New York, 10012–3236.

Individual Exhibitions:

1951 Kootz Gallery, New York
Seven Stairs Gallery, Chicago
1953 Stable Gallery, New York
Galleria Contemporanea, Florence
Little Gallery, Princeton, New Jersey
1955 Stable Gallery, New York
1957 Stable Gallery, New York
1958 Galleria La Tartaruga, Rome
Galleria del Naviglio, Milan
Galleria del Cavallino, Venice
1960 Leo Castelli Gallery, New York
Galleria La Tartaruga, Rome
Galleria del Naviglio, Milan
Galerie 22, Dusseldorf (with Robert Rauschenberg)
1961 Galleria La Tartaruga, Rome
Galleria del Naviglio, Milan
Galerie Zwirner, Essen, West Germany
Galerie J, Paris
1962 Galerie Aujourd'hui, Brussels
Galleria del Leone, Venice
1963 Galerie Anne Abets, Cologne
Galerie Bonnier, Lausanne, Switzerland
Galerie Jacques Benador, Geneva
Galleria La Tartaruga, Rome
1964 Galerie Handschin, Basel
Galerie Friedrich und Dahlem, Munich
Leo Castelli Gallery, New York
1965 Museum Haus Lange, Krefeld, West Germany
Palais des Beaux-Arts, Brussels
Galleria Notizie, Turin
Galleria La Tartaruga, Rome
1966 Stedelijk Museum Amsterdam
Kunstverein, Freiburg, West Germany
Leo Castelli Gallery, New York
1967 Leo Castelli Gallery, New York
Galleria La Tartaruga, Rome
Galleria Notizie, Turin
1968 Galleria La Tartaruga, Rome
Milwaukee Art Center
Leo Castelli Gallery, New York
1969 Galerie Zwirner, Cologne
Nicholas Wilder Gallery, Los Angeles
1970 Galerie Neuendorf, Cologne
Modern Art Agency, Naples
Svensk-Frenska Konstgalleriet, Stockholm
Gallerie Bonnier, Geneva
1971 Galleria Sperone, Turin
Galerie Mollenhoff, Cologne
Galerie Yvon Lambert, Paris
Galleria dell'Ariete, Milan
Galerie Denise René-Hans Meyer, Dusseldorf
1972 Modern Art Agency, Naples
Dunkelman Gallery, Toronto
Locksley Shea Gallery, Minneapolis
Leo Castelli Gallery, New York
1973 School for Visual Arts, New York
Art in Progress, Zurich
Kunstmuseum, Basel
Kunsthalle, Basel
1974 Galerie Oppenheim, Brussels
Leo Castelli Gallery, New York
Modern Art Agency, Naples
1975 Modern Art Agency, Naples
Art in Progress, Munich
Paintings, Drawings, Constructions 1951–74, Institute of Contemporary Art, Philadelphia
San Francisco Museum of Modern Art
1976 Art in Progress, Dusseldorf
Kestner-Gesellschaft, Hannover
Leo Castelli Gallery, New York
Musée d'Art Moderne, Paris
1977 Galerie Yvon Lamberg, Paris
School of Visual Arts, New York
1978 Heiner-Friedrich Gallery, New York
Galerie Klewan, Munich
1979 Whitney Museum, New York (retrospective)
Galleria Lucio Amelio, Naples
Galleriet, Lund, Sweden
Galerie Karsten Greve, Cologne
1981 Castelli Graphics, New York
Museum Haus Lange, Krefeld, West Germany
Newport Harbor Art Museum, Newport Beach, California (travelled to Madison, Wisconsin; Richmond, Virginia; Toronto)
1982 Blum-Helman Gallery, New York (with Robert Ryman and Richard Tuttle)
Sperone Westwater Fischer, New York
Mayor Gallery, London
Galerie Karsten Greve, Cologne
Galerie Yvon Lambert, Paris
1983 Stephen Mazoh Gallery, New York
1984 Galerie Karsten Greve, Cologne
Mayor Gallery, London
Musée d'Art Contemporain, Bordeaux, France
Santa Barbara Contemporary Arts Center, California
1986 Larry Gagosian Gallery, New York
Hirschl and Adler Modern, New York
Dia Art Foundation, New York
Galerie Yvon Lambert, Paris
1987 Kunsthaus, Zurich

Cy Twombly: *Untitled,* 20th century. ©Geoffrey Clements/Corbis.

Stadtisches Kunstmuseum, Bonn
Whitechapel Art Gallery, London
Kunsthalle, Dusseldorf
1988 Centre Georges Pompidou, Paris
Galerie Dwan, Munich
Pace Gallery, New York
Anthony d'Offay Gallery, London
1989 *Cy Twombly: Bolsena,* Gagosian Gallery, New York (catalog)
1990 *Cy Twombly,* Menil Collection, Houston (also Des Moines Art Center, Iowa) (catalog)
1993 *Cy Twombly: Photographs,* Matthew Marks Gallery, New York (catalog)
1994 *Cy Twombly: A Retrospective,* Museum of Modern Art, New York (catalog)
Cy Twombly, C&M Arts, New York (catalog)
1996 *Cy Twombly: The Sculpture,* Kunstmuseum, Basel (travelled to National Gallery of Art, Washington, D.C., Menil Collection, Houston and Ludwig Museum, Cologne)
1997 *Cy Twombly: Ten Sculptures,* Gagosian Gallery, New York (catalog)
2000 Menil Collection Museum, Houston, Texas

Selected Group Exhibitions:

1958 *Gutai 9: International Festival,* Osaka, Japan
1964 *Biennale,* Venice
1969 *Painting and Sculpture Today,* Indianapolis Museum of Art, Indiana
1971 *The Structure of Color,* Whitney Museum, New York
1973 *Contemporanea,* Parcheggio di Villa Borghese, Rome
1976 *Drawing Now,* Museum of Modern Art, New York
1981 *A New Spirit in Painting,* Royal Academy of Arts, London
1983 *American Accents,* The Gallery, Stratford, Ontario (travelled to Toronto, Quebec City, Halifax, Windsor, Edmonton, Vancouver, Calgary and Montreal)
1986 *Hommage a Beuys,* Stadtische Galerie im Lenbachhaus, Munich
1988 *Contemporary American Art,* Sara Hilden Art Museum Tampere, Finland (travelled to Oslo)
1989 *The Sonnabend Collection: From Pop Art Onwards,* Galleria Nazionale d'Arte Moderna, Rome (catalog)

Cy Twombley: *Shield of Achilles, From Fifty Days at Iliam.* ©Philadelphia Museum of Art/Corbis.

On the Surface: An Abstract Journey, Studio Durante, Rome (catalog)
American Prints from the Sixties, Susan Sheehan, New York (catalog)
1990 *Blue: Colour of Distance,* Heidelberger Kunstverein, Heidelberg, Germany (catalog)
American Masters of the '60s: Early and Late Works, Tony Shafrazi Gallery, New York (catalog)
1991 *Selection: Works from the Collection,* Musee d'Art Contemporain, Lausanne (catalog)
1994 *Sculpture,* Anthony d'Offay Gallery, London (catalog)
Painters' Images, Museum Moderner Kunst, Vienna (catalog)
1996 *The Froehlich Foundation: German and American Art from Beuys and Warhol,* Tate Gallery, London (travelling exhibition) (catalog)
1997 *The Anne-Marie and Ernst Vischer-Wadler Collection: A Bequest,* Offentliche Kunstsammlung Basel (catalog)
1998 *Painters and Their Sculpture: From Edgar Degas to Gerhard Richter,* Museum Folkwang, Essen, Germany (catalog)
Art Miami 98, Florida

Collections:

Museum of Modern Art, New York; Whitney Museum, New York; Rhode Island School of Design, Providence; Milwaukee Art Center; First National City Bank, Houston; Wallraf-Richartz Museum, Cologne; Hessisches Landesmuseum, Darmstadt; Neue Galerie-Sammlung Ludwig, Aachen, West Germany; Galleria Nazionale d'Arte Moderna, Rome.

Publications:

On TWOMBLY: Books—*Cy Twombly,* exhibition catalog with notes by Robert Motherwell, Chicago 1951; *Cy Twombly: Paintings, Drawings, Constructions 1951–74,* exhibition catalog by Suzanne Delehanty and Heiner Bastian, Philadelphia 1975; *Drawing Now,* exhibition catalog by Bernice Rose, New York 1976; *Cy Twombly: Bilder/Paintings 1952–1976,* with text by Heiner Bastian, West Berlin 1978; *Cy Twombly: Catalog raisonne des oeuvres sur papier, 1973–1976,* edited by Yvon Lambert, Milan 1979; *Cy Twombly: Works on Paper 1954–1976,* exhibition catalog with text by Susan C. Larsen, Newport Beach 1981; *Cy Twombly: Skulpturen,* exhibition catalog with introduction by Gerhard Storck, Krefeld 1981; *Cy Twombly: Retrospective,* exhibition catalog with essay by Katharina Schmidt, Baden-Baden 1984; *Cy Twombly: A catalog raisonne of the printed graphic work 1983–84,* with introduction by Heiner Bastian, Munich and New York 1985; *Cy Twombly,* exhibition catalog edited by Harald Szemann, Zurich 1987; *Cy Twombly: Spurensuche* by Jutta Goricke, Munich 1995. **Articles—**''Cy Was Here; Cy's Up'' by Rosalind Krauss in *Artforum,* vol. 33, no. 1, September 1994; ''Twombly's Tempietto: The Menil Collection, Architect Renzo Piano and the Artist Himself Have Joined in Creating a Permanent Cy Twombly Installation'' by Charles Dee Mitchell in *Art in America* (New York), vol. 83, no. 2, February 1995; ''Cy Twombly's Theatre of Operations'' by David Sylvester in *Tate: The Art Magazine,* no. 7, Winter 1995; ''Twombly's Mysteries'' by Philip Hensher in *Modern Painters* (London), vol. 8, no. 4, Winter 1995; ''The White Originals'' by David Sylvester in *Art in America* (New York), vol. 88, no. 7, July 2000.

* * *

Since the 1960s the painting/poetry of Cy Twombly has, by way of a variety of signs, fed on his own research, made prevalently of interruptions or annotations, only apparently but actually brilliantly thought out. The painting traces the poetry, while the poetry retraces the painting and defines evasive paths. Thus those different signs tell the legend, and in it stray to the infinite. It is not true, therefore, that they are something impersonal. Art is always the forbidden fruit of the imagination, and the ''Roman'' artist with his visual paradigms sets it out in an inestimable spatiality (that of the surface of the canvas or the sheet of paper), where there is a collection of graphic crossings and groupings so complex as to be almost impossible to follow. In Cy Twombly's works classical quotation seems more like metaphor than literary erudition. In ''Empire of Flora,'' ''School of Athens'' and ''Leda and the Swan'' (all works of 1961) the mythological metaphor is something secretly indestructible that memory re-echoes in shapes and colours, in memory of a past splendour.

Cy Twombly evokes in his works antique myths perhaps inexplicable to contemporary sensibility. And yet, without the memory of them, the hide-and-seek of those different signs would remain as if suspended, lacking the true secrecy of that search for beauty that evokes rapture. Like marble or paint, Cy Twombly's different signs possess an immortality of their own, transforming the inexpressible into a living manifestation; the apparent chaos releases the silence, introducing incisive light and shade where there have been rare spaces in the handwriting. The beauty flows most subtly, imperceptibly; it always follows the handwriting, when it slows down or breaks off. The artist has before him, not the whirlpool, but the silence of the past which unexpectedly becomes articulate sound, dancing movement, a dream, a memory of happenings of long ago.

In Cy Twombly's painting the secret of art reveals its true mythical origin in this way; its beauty lies in the disorder, not in the polished form. Unexpectedly, those different signs appear as veiled shadows in new dress, so classical is their poetic manifestation. Hence they are not writing (unless perhaps an automatic writing); what Cy Twombly puts down on the canvas or the paper is a sort of poetically conceived composition, as in Holderlin or Novalis. The abstraction formed by the signs may perhaps be a discourse, as we can see from the work called ''Nine Discourses on Commodus'' (1963). But, following Plato, it is clear that Cy Twombly knows how not to be wiser but to love wisdom; since it is only in that that the revelation of the new writing exists. Thus his work of the past 20 years is nothing less than a revelation and a concealment of a lost classical integrity.

—Italo Mussa

U

UECKER, Günther

Nationality: German. **Born:** Wendorf, Mecklenburg, 13 March 1930. **Education:** Studied painting in Wiemar; studied art at the Kunstakademie, Berlin-Weissensee, and at the Staatliche Kunstakademie, Dusseldorf. **Career:** Independent artist, Dusseldorf, since 1955: colour-structure paintings, 1955–56; first white structural objects and nail-paintings, 1957; mathematical computable structure series, 1958–59; kinetic structural discs, 1960; member, Zero Group, with Otto Piene and Heinz Mack, 1961–66. Professor, Staatliche Kunstakademie, Dusseldorf, since 1974. **Awards:** Prize, *Biennale di San Marino,* 1963; Talent Prize, Landes NordrheinWestfalen, 1964; Critics' Prize, *Bienal,* Sao Paulo, 1971. **Address:** Kaistrasse 10, 40221 Dusseldorf, Germany.

Individual Exhibitions:

1960 Galleria Azimuth, Milan
Galerie Schmela, Dusseldorf
1961 Galleria La Salita, Rome
1962 Galerie Ad Libitum, Antwerp
1963 *Mack/Piene/Uecker,* Museum Haus Lange, Krefeld, West Germany
1964 Howard Wise Gallery, New York
1965 Galerie Orez, The Hague
Kestner-Gesellschaft, Hanover
1967 *Flemish Landscape,* Mullen, Belgium (with Jef Verheyen)
1968 Kunsthalle, Baden-Baden, West Germany
1969 Kunsthalle, Dusseldorf
1970 Kunsthalle, Bremerhaven, West Germany
1971 *Bildobjekie 1957–1970,* Moderna Museet, Stockholm
Museum Folkwang, Essen
Galerie Zachea, Warsaw
Nationalgalerie, West Berlin
1972 Kestner-Gesellschaft, Hannover
1974 Muzeum Sztuki, Lodz, Poland
Kolnischer Kunstverein, Cologne
Kunsthalle, Cologne
1975 Museum Folkwang, Essen
Galerie im Erker, St. Gallen, Switzerland
Galerie Denise René/Hans Mayer, Dusseldorf
Galerie M, Bochum, West Germany
Kunstmuseum, Dusseldorf (2 shows)
Württembergische Staatsgalerie, Stuttgart
Württembergisches Staatsheater, Stuttgart (decors for Wagner's *Parsifal*)
Antwerp Gallery
Galerie Denise René/Hans Mayer, Dusseldorf (with Heinz Mack)
1977 Forum Metall, Linz, Austria
1978 Galerie Reckermann, Cologne (travelled to Detmold, Dublin and Munich)
1979 *Bilder und Zeichnungen,* Kunstverein, Braunschweig, West Germany
Erker-Galerie, St. Gallen, Switzerland
Stadtisches Museum Schloss Morsbroich, Leverkusen, West Germany
1981 Erker-Galerie, St. Gallen, Switzerland
1982 Galerie Walter Storms, Munich
Raumberkeilung—Bilder den Wanden zugekeht, Galerie Lohrl, Mönchengladbach, West Germany
Nationalgalerie, West Berlin
1983 Kunsthalle, Dusseldorf
Galerie Schmela, Dusseldorf
Galerie Loehrl, Monchengladbach, West Germany
1984 Kamakura Gallery, Tokyo
Yares Gallery, Scottsdale, Arizona
1985 Museum of Modern Art, Istanbul
Josef Albers Museum, Bottrop, West Germany
1987 Vasarely Museum, Pecs, Hungary
Galerie Ronny Van de Velde, Knokke, Belgium
1988 Central Museum, Moscow
Kjarvalsstadir Art Museum, Reykjavik, Iceland
1989 Galerie Hans Strelow, Dusseldorf
Städtische Galerie, Göppingen
Museum Sztukiw, Lodz, Poland
Galerie Löhrl, Mönchengladbach, Germany
Galerie Edith Wahlandt, Stuttgart
1990 Galerie Eigen + Art, Leipzig, Germany
Galerie auf der Praterinsel, Munich
1991 Rathaus, Göttingen, Germany
Galerie ULUV, Prague
Erker Galerie, St. Gallen, Switzerland
1992 Staatliches Museum, Schwerin
Museum Moderner Kunst, Vienna
1993 Kunsthalle der Hypo-Kulturstiftung, Munich
Städtische Galerie Remscheid, Remschied, Germany
Wanderausstellung des Instituts für Auslandsbeziehungen, Stuttgart (travelling exhibit)
1994 Galerie Hans Strelow, Dusseldorf
G.A.M.E.S. of Art, Mönchengladbach, Germany
Museum of Modern Art, Venice
1995 *Brief an Peking,* Neuer Berliner Kunstverein, Berlin

Selected Group Exhibitions:

1968 *Documenta,* Kassel, West Germany (and 1977)
1972 *Amsterdam-Paris-Dusseldorf,* Guggenheim Museum, New York
1974 *Basically White,* Institute of Contemporary Arts, London
1976 *Europa/America,* Galleria d'Arte Moderna, Bologna
1978 *Elements of Drawing,* Galerie Studio, Warsaw
1979 *Zero International,* Koninklijk Museum voor Schone Kunsten, Antwerp
1981 *Schwarz,* Kunsthalle, Dusseldorf
1988 *Les Anées 50,* Centre Georges Pompidou
1991 *Museum und Kirche,* Wilhelm-Lehmbruck-Museum, Duisburg, Germany
1993 *New Realities,* Tate Gallery, London
1995 *Dadamaino: François Morellet, Günther Uecker,* A.Arte Studio Invernizzi (catalog)

Günther Uecker in his studio, ca. 1980–97. ©K.M. Westermann/Corbis.

Collections:

Stadtisches Kunstmuseum, Dusseldorf; Wallraf-Richartz Museum, Cologne; Kaiser-Wilhelm Museum, Krefeld, Germany; Museum Folkwang, Essen; Stedelijk van Abbemuseum, Eindhoven, Netherlands; Museum des 20 Jahrhunderts, Vienna; Muzeum Sztuki, Lodz, Poland; Galleria Nazionale d'Arte Moderna, Rome; Tate Gallery, London; Museum of Modern Art, New York; DG Bank Collection, Frankfurt am Main.

Public Installations:

Prayer Room, Reichstag, Berlin.

Publications:

By UECKER: Books and Pamphlets—*Projektionen von Heute,* with Otto Piene and Heinz Mack, Dusseldorf 1961; *Uecker-Zeitung,* vols. 0–9, editor, Dusseldorf 1968–82; *Der heutige kunstler,* pamphlet, Dusseldorf 1969; *Uber Steine: zu Skulppuren von Rolf Jorres,* pamphlet, Dusseldorf 1969; *Uecker,* portfolio of 5 lithos with text by Lothar Wolleh, Cologne 1970; *Flamische Landschaft,* with Jef Verheyen, Dusseldorf 1970; *Einsam Gemeinsam,* book with 5 prints, text by Eugen Gomringer, Dusseldorf 1971; *Vom Licht,* with prints by Uecker and others, and an introduction by Gerhard Storck, Heidelberg 1973; *Manuelle Strukturen,* cassette with 10 lithos, St. Gallen, Switzerland 1975; *Anonym,* cassette with objects and 6 silkscreens, Dusseldorf 1976; *Zum Schweigen der Schrift oder die Sprachlosigkeit,* 17 silkscreens with text by Eugen Gomringer, St. Gallen, Switzerland 1976; *Uecker: Ludwig von Beethovens Leonore,* with text by Gerhard Storck, photos by Lothar Wolleh, Stuttgart and Zurich 1978; *Schrifien, Gedichie—Projekiebeschreibungen—Reflexionen,* St. Gallen, Switzerland, 1980; *Littenheid—Eine Studie. . .mit Studenien der Klasse Ueker,* with Hans Geigenmuller, St. Gallen, Switzerland, 1980; *Buhnenskulpturen fur Lohengrin,* with text by Guido de Werd, photos by Lothar Wolleh, Kleve and Dusseldorf 1981; *Bildrituale,* Glarus 1986; *Island,* 1986; *Wüstenfunde,* Cologne 1989; *Carrara,* 1989; *Muttermord in der Diamantenwüste,* Glarus 1991; *Zero: Heinz Mack, Otto Piene, Günther Uecker,* Düsseldorf 1993; *Wind,* Munich 1994; *Günther Uecker, Wind,* with Ralph Merten, Mainz 1995; *Gunther Uecker: Aquarelle Uruguay 1996,* St. Gallen 1999; *Günther Uecker: Rain,* Kempen 1999; *Günther Uecker: Korrelationen,* Munich 2000. **Articles**—interview with Heinz-Norbert Jocks in *Kunstforum International,* no. 150, April/June 2000. **Films**—*Eckenfilm,* 1969; *Nagelfeldzug,* 1969; *Bauchfilm,* 1970; *Muttermord in der Diamantenwüste,* 1986; *Wie ein Bauer auf dem Feld,* 1986.

On UECKER: Books—*Mack/Piene/Uecker,* exhibition catalog with foreword by Paul Wember, Krefeld, Germany 1963; *Günther Uecker:*

(Installation sculpture) Günther Uecker 1996. ©Pablo Corral V/Corbis.

Ten Years of a Kineticist's Work by Willoughby Sharp, New York 1966; *Günther Uecker* by Dietrich Helmz, Recklinghausen, Germany 1970: *Günther Uecker: Bildobjekte 1957–1970,* exhibition catalog with text by K. G. Pontus Hulten, Stockholm 1971; *Günther Uecker,* exhibition catalog/book with texts by Wieland Schmied, Hans Strelow, Rolf-Günther Dienst and others, Hannover and St. Gallen 1972; *Günther Uecker,* exhibition catalog with text by Dieter Honisch, Lodz, Poland 1974; *Uecker: Bilder und Zeichnungen,* exhibition catalog, Braunschweig, Germany 1979; *Uecker: Raumverkeilung-Bilder den Wanden zugekehrt,* exhibition catalog with text by Sabine Kirnpel-Fehlemann, Mönchengladbach, Germany 1982; *Uecker* by Dieter Honisch and Marion Haedecke, Stuttgart 1983; *Günther Uecker,* exhibition catalog with text by Friedrich W. Heckmanns, Bottrop 1985; *Uecker Ludwigshafen,* 1988; *Uecker: Pictlandgarden,* exhibition catalog, Edinburgh 1990; *Uecker in Wein,* exhibition catalog with essay by Günter Engelhard, Vienna 1992; *Günther Uecker: Ein Retrospektive,* exhibition catalog with text by Dieter Honisch, Munich 1993. **Articles—**''A Bright, White World: Günther Uecker's Home and Studio in Düsseldorf'' by Ulf Becker in *Abitare,* no. 344, October 1995.

*

The present-day artist produces and realizes ideas which could serve as examples for a new environment. The idea will come into being as a product. The objects are no longer clarifications of a new way of looking at things. These objects have no value as objects, they have fulfilled their purpose the instant they are absorbed into consciousness. These objects can be understood as tools for processes of thought. An artist is an inventor, an inventor of ideas which can be realized visually, which can serve as parables of spiritual development.

—Günther Uecker

* * *

The Zero Group was formed in 1961. For five years Otto Piene, Heinz Mack and Günther Uecker exhibited jointly as a trio the wax/soot fire-works of Piene, the silver reflections of Mack and the nail constructions and light experiments of Uecker.

Of the three Uecker was the most international in the character of his work. However different in realization and intention, his nail works use the same raw materials as those of the Canadian David Partridge, and, in their way, they imply some of the same effects of light and shade to be found in the stunted peg reliefs of the Brazilian Sergio de Camargo. But there the relationships terminate.

Uecker's use of *white* is wholly different from that of Camargo, and his understanding of the character of upstanding nails and how they can play games with chiaroscuro has nothing to do with Partridge's gleaming carpets of nail-heads. The German artist keeps sternly aloof from the decorative dangers that sometimes beset the works of both of the others. He also has a non-architectural attitude towards the transformation games he plays with ''objects'' like a chair or a picture frame. In such a mood he is demonstrating that he has the same European elan as Jean-Pierre Raynaud or Pol Bury.

Artists like Uecker are revitalising the Old World, not doing a raw survey of artistic potentialities of the New. The aggressive defiance of the Americas is not their style, and their works have no American accent, not even a mid-Atlantic one.

—Sheldon Williams

Uecker, in fact, has little interest in geographic particulars; with cultures, however, and with social issues, he feels compelled to expression. His concern with the Hopis, for example, and their impending loss of cultural identity has been the impetus for a number of works. His political statements—like the *Acshebilder* (Ashen pictures) about the Chernobyl accident—bear witness to his world-wide point of view.

His current work, then, has taken him far beyond the nailwork for which he has been best known, into the use of many and varied materials such as sand, in the traces of which is figured the inexorable passage of time, a war coffin out of which come sounds identified with the battle of Stalingrad. As he has said, however, objects furnish only the initial impetus. It is the change from one state to another which is his real subject. In the artist's metaphor, as a wind sweeps suddenly across a calm sea and the sea becomes something other than what it was, so he introduces disorder into classic harmonies, by exposing quotation and overlaying it, changing the old into something new.

—Barbara Cortright

ULRICHS, Timm

Nationality: German. **Born:** Berlin, 31 March 1940. **Education:** Primary school in Bremen, 1954–59; studied architecture at the Technische Hochschule, Hannover, 1959–66; mainly self-taught in art. **Career:** Independent artist, Hannover, since 1959. Guest professor, Hochschule für Bildende Künste, Braunschweig, 1969–70. Professor, Institut für Kunsterzieher Münster der Staatlichen Kunstakademie, Dusseldorf (now Kunstakademie Münster), since 1972. **Awards:** Literatur-Förderpreis des Niedersächsischen Kunstpreises, 1968; Kritikerpreis für Bildende Kunst, Berlin, 1977; Niedersächsisches Künstlerstipendium, 1979; Kunstpreis der Stadt Nordhorn, 1980; Kunstpreis der Nord/LB, Hannover, 1983; Karl-Ernst-Osthaus-Preis der Stadt Hagen, 1985; Defet-Preis des Deutschen Künstlerbundes, 1985; Will-Grohmann Preis der Akademie der Künste, Berlin 1985; Kunstpreis der Stadtsparkasse Hannover im Kunstverein Hannover, 1988; Konrad-von-Soest-Preis, Munster, 1988; Preis der Heitland-Foundation, Celle, 1991. **Address:** Sodenstrasse 6, 30161 Hannover, and Postfach 6043, 30060 Hannover, Germany.

Individual Exhibitions:

1961 Totalkunst-Zimmergalerie Timm Ulrichs, Hannover
1964 Haus am Lützowplatz, Berlin
1966 Galerie Patio, Frankfurt
1967 Galleria Alpha, Modena, Italy
1968 Institut für Visuelle Kommunikation, Berlin
Galerie Daedalus, Berlin
1969 Edition h, Hannover
Galerie Reckermann, Cologne
1970 Galerie Nachst St. Stephan, Vienna
Neue Galerie, Aachen, Germany
Kabinett für aktuelle Kunst, Bremerhaven, Germany
Museum Haus Lange, Krefeld, Germany
Christian-Albrechts-Universität, Kiel
1971 Kunsthaus, Hamburg
Städtisches Museum, Wiesbaden
1973 Galerie Ernst, Hannover
Kunsthalle, Bielefeld, Germany
Kunstverein, Celle, Germany
1974 Galerie Magers, Bonn
Kunsthalle, Bremen, Germany
Galerie Apex, Göttingen, Germany
Städtische Bildergalerie, Bergkamen, Germany
Kunsthalle, Nuremberg
1975 Kunstverein, Hannover
Kunstverein Freiburg
Restrospective 1960–1975, Kunstverein, Braunschweig, Germany (travelled to the Karl-Ernst-Osthaus Museum, Hagen; Kunstverein, Heidelberg; and Kunstverein, Hannover)
1976 Galleria Civica, Modena, Italy
1977 Space, Wiesbaden
Forum Kunst, Rottweil, Germany
1978 Kunstschau Böttcherstrasse, Bremen, Germany
1979 Petersen Galerie, Berlin
Kunstmuseum Hannover mit Sammlung Sprengel, Hannover
1980 Städische Galerie, Lüdenscheid, Germany
Städtische Galerie, Nordhorn, Germany
1984 Kubus an der Aegidienkirche, Hannover
Wilhelm-Hack-Museum, Ludwigshafen am Rhein
1985 Galerie kö 24, Hannover
Städtische Galerie, Quackenbrück
1986 Kunstfonds Kunstraum, Bonn (with Christiane Möbus)
Galerie Schüppenhauer, Essen, Germany
1987 Foto e. V., Munich
Wewerka Galerie, Berlin
Städtische Galerie im Rathauspark, Gladbeck
1988 Museum für Photographie, Braunschweig
Westfälisches Landesmuseum, Munster
1990 Freundeskreis Wilhelmshöhe, Ettlingen
Galerie Friebe, Lüdenscheid
1991 Deutsches Kulturinstitut, Madrid
Schloss, Celle
Kunsthalle, Recklinghausen
1992 Galerie Defet, Nuremberg
Museum für das Fürstentum Lüneburg, Lüneburg
1993 *Timm Ulrichs: Route,* Kunstverein, Cuxhaven
Städtische Galerie, Iserlohn
Kunstverein Ruhr, Essen
1994 Kunstverein, Haus Kemnade, Bochum
Timm Ulrichs: Turning Your Back on the Spectator, Siegerlandsmuseum im Oberen Schloss, Siegen
Ludwig Museum, Budapest

Brigitte March Galerie, Stuttgart
1997 *Timm Ulrichs: The Detector Perspective,* Neue Gesellschaft fur Bildende Kunst, Berlin
1999 Forum Kunst, Rottweil, Germany
Galerie Blau, Freiburg, Germany
2000 Kunst-Plattform, Munich

Selected Group Exhibitions:

1969 *Konzeption-Conception,* Städisches Museum, Leverkusen, Germany
1970 *Jetzt. Künste in Deutschland heute,* Kunsthalle, Cologne
Konkrete Poesie: Visuelle Texte, Stedelijk Museum, Amsterdam (toured Europe)
1974 *Projekt '74: Aspekte internationaler Kunst am Anfang der 70er Jahre,* Kunsthalle, Cologne
1977 *Documenta 6,* Kassel, Germany
1978 *Art: Museum des Geldes,* Stadtische Kunsthalle, Dusseldorf (travelled to Eindhoven and Paris)
1985 *1945–1985: Kunst in der Bundesrepublik Deutschland,* Nationalgalerie, Berlin
1987 *Inside-Outside,* Museum van Hedendaagse Kunst, Antwerp
1990 Die Museen der Stadt Lüdenscheid
Beyond the Everyday Object, Museum van Hedendaagse Kunst, Antwerp, Belgium
1993 *Poésure et Peintrie: D'un l'Art l'Autre,* Centre de la Vieille Charité, Marseilles
Differentes Natures, La Defense, Paris, and Palau de la Virreina, Barcelona

Collections:

Wilhelm-Lehmbruck-Museum, Duisburg; Karl Ernst Osthaus-Museum, Hagen; Kunsthalle, Hamburg; Sprengel Museum, Hannover; Wilhelm-Hack-Museum, Ludwigschafen am Rhein; Museen der Stadt Lüdenscheid, Lüdenscheid; Kunsthalle, Mannheim; Skulpturenmuseum Glaskasten, Marl; Städtisches Museum Abteiberg, Mönchengladbach, Staatsgalerie, Stuttgart; Städtisches Museum, Wolfsburg.

Publications:

By ULRICHS: Books—*Totalkunst: Das neue Mass; aller Dinge,* Hannover 1961; *Fragment,* Berlin 1964; *Klartexte,* Hannover 1966; *Spielpläne,* Hannover 1967; *Beschriebene Blätter,* Hannover 1967; *Schriftstücke,* Munich 1967; *Des grossen erfolges wegen,* Hannover 1968; *Ich bin ein Gedicht,* Vienna 1968; *Lesarten and Schreibweisen,* Stuttgart 1968; *Interferenzen I,* Cologne 1968; *Interferenzen II,* Basel 1968; *Qwertzuiopü,* Hannover 1968; *Ich als Kunstfigur,* Vienna 1969; *Weiter in text,* Hannover 1969; *Bild-Band,* Berlin 1970; *Fernsehen in Nahsicht,* Göttingen 1970; *Kanaldeckel 1962/64,* Gottingen 1970; *Totalkunst,* exhibition catalog, Krefeld 1970; *Vorsicht, Kunst! Praxis einer Theorie-Kunst,* Hannover 1971; *Permutation,* Hannover 1971; *Einweg-Buch,* Hannover 1972; *Stil der Stillosigeit,* exhibition catalog, Celle 1973; *Farbmusterkarten,* Braunschweig 1974; *Die Zeitungsannonce als Kunstwerk,* Hannover 1974; *Bilder, auf den Leib geschrieben,* Hannover 1975; *Die Photokopie der Photokopie der Photokopie der Photokopie,* Hannover 1975; *Kunst-Räume,* exhibition catalog, Munster 1975; *Retrospektive 1960–1975,* exhibition catalog, Braunschweig 1975; *1984,* Hannover 1975; *Dem Leser den Rücken zukehrend,* Hannover 1976; *Ich mache (diese) Schlagzeilen,* Hannover 1977; *Konstruktion und Rekonstruktion,* Utrecht 1977; *Ich, Gott und die Welt,* Hannover 1978; *Kunst: im Schweisse des Angesichts,* Hannover 1978; *The Infinite Book,* Hannover 1978; *Buch-(EHE)-Paar,* Hannover 1979; *Lektionen,* Frankfurt 1979; *Die Kunst des schönen Schreibens,* 2 vols., Hannover 1980; *Totalkunst,* exhibition catalog, Lüdenscheid 1980; Kunstpreis Nordhorn 1980: *''Der Findling'' und andere Arbeiten,* exhibition catalog, Nordhorn 1980; *Kunstpreis der Nord/LB 1983,* exhibition catalog, Hannover 1984; *Totalkunst: Angesammelte Werke,* exhibition catalog, Ludwigshafen am Rhein 1984; *Checked Baggage,* exhibition catalog, Munich 1987; *Itinerante Timm Ulrichs-Timm Ulrichs, unterwegs,* exhibition catalog, Madrid 1991; *Landschafts-Epiphanien,* Recklinghausen 1991; *Parcours,* Cuxhaven 1993; *Kunst & Leben,* Iserlohn 1993; *Landschafts-Epiphanien,* exhibition catalog, Essen 1993; *Dem Betrachter den Rücken zukehrend,* exhibition catalog, Siegen 1994; *Timm Ulrichs,* exhibition catalog, Budapest 1995; *Timm Ulrichs: der detektorische Blick,* exhibition catalog with texts by Matthias Reichelt and Ulf Erdmann Ziegler, Berlin 1997. **Articles—**''Timm Ulrichs: premisses d'un art du concept/de concepts'' in *Art Press,* Special Issue, no. 17, 1996; ''Timm Ulrichs'' in *Kunstforum International,* no. 146, July/August 1999.

On ULRICHS: Book—*Pop und die Folgen* by Heinz Ohff, Dusseldorf 1967; *Deutsche Kunst: eine neue generation* by Rolf-Günter Dienst, Cologne 1970; *Kunst im Konflikt* by Ludwig Leiss, Berlin 1971; *Konkrete Poesie* edited by Eugen Gomringer, Stuttgart 1972; *Kunst-im-Kopf: Aspekte der Real-Kunst* by Klaus Hoffmann, Cologne 1972: *Deutsche Kunst der 60er Jahre* by Jürgen Morschel, Munich 1972; *Objekt Kunst: von Duchamp bis Kienhol* by Willy Rotzler, Cologne 1972; *Selbstdarstellung* edited by Wulf Herzogenrath, Dusseldorf 1973; *Kunstwetterlage* by Gerd Winkler, Stuttgart 1973; *Da Dada da war ist Dada da* by Karl Riha, Munich and Vienna, 1980; *Timm Ulrichs* by Bernhard Holeczek, Braunschweig 1980; *Briefe an Timm Ulrichs und andere Texte* by Raoul Hausmann, Siegen 1985; *Timm Ulrichs* by Andreas Bee, Heidelberg 1995. **Articles—**''Timm Ulrichs: der Kunstler wird zum Objekt, der Kunstler wird zum Kunstwerk'' by Jorg Bostrom in *Bildende Kunst,* vol. 36, no. 9, 1988; ''Timm Ulrichs: menschlicher Massstab'' by Jürgen Raap in *Kunstforum International,* no. 126, March/June 1994; ''Zum Beispiel: Timm Ulrichs'' by Helmut G. Schutz in *Kunst+Unterricht,* no. 183, June 1994; ''Timm Ulrichs mact mobil'' by Matthias Reichelt in *Kunstforum International,* no. 143, January-February 1999; ''Timm Ulrichs: Geld/Wechsel/Geld'' in *Kunstforum International,* no. 149, January/March 2000.

UNSWORTH, Ken

Nationality: Australian. **Born:** Richmond, Victoria, 28 May 1931. **Education:** University of Melbourne and Melbourne Teachers' College, 1952–54; studied at the National Art School, Sydney; influenced by John Passmore and Godfrey Miller, 1962–63. **Family:** Married Elisabeth Crouch in 1954. **Career:** Independent painter, Melbourne and Sydney, 1954–66; sculptor, Sydney, since 1966; also, performance artist since 1975. Art teacher, Victoria and New South Wales high schools, 1955–65; lecturer in art, Bathhurst Teachers' College, New South Wales, 1966–68; chairman, art teacher education, Tasmanian School of Art, Hobart, 1969–71. Lecturer in sculpture,

Sydney College of Advanced Education, since 1972. Executive member, Contemporary Art Society of Australia, New South Wales, since 1972. **Awards:** Captain Cook Bicentenary Sculpture Prize, Sydney, 1970; Australian-American Education Foundation Grant, to the United States, 1971; residency, Power Studio, Cité des Arts, Paris, 1979–1980; residency, Kunstlerhaus Bethanien, West Berlin, 1980; DAAD Artist Fellowship, West Berlin, 1987; Order of Australia for service to sculpture, 1989; Australian Creative Fellowship, 1989; Biennale Print Portfolio, René Block Editions, 1990; Delegate, UNESCO Conference, Florence, Italy, 1990; Japan Foundation Grant, 1991. **Agent:** Roslyn Oxley 9 Gallery, 13 Macdonald Street, Paddington, New South Wales. **Address:** 88A Louisa Road, Birchgrove, Sydney, New South Wales 2041, Australia.

Individual Exhibitions:

1975 Institute of Contemporary Art, Sydney
1977 Institute of Contemporary Art, Sydney
1978 *Project 28,* Art Gallery of New South Wales, Sydney
Australian Pavilion, at the *Biennale,* Venice (with Robert Owen and John Davis)
1979 Institute of Contemporary Art, Sydney
Australian Embassy, Paris
1980 Kunstlerhaus Bethanien, Berlin
1981 Institute of Contemporary Art, Sydney
1982 Ivan Dougherty Gallery, Sydney
1983 Kobayashi Gallery, Tokyo
National Gallery of New Zealand, Wellington
1984 Roslyn Oxley 9 Gallery, Sydney
Art Gallery of New South Wales, Sydney
1985 Roslyn Oxley 9 Gallery, Sydney
1987 DAAD-Galerie, West Berlin
Roslyn Oxley 9 Gallery, Sydney
1988 *Old Skin,* Roslyn Oxley 9 Gallery, Sydney
1989 *Song of Henning,* Royal Danish Academy of Fine Art, Copenhagen
1991 *Self and Environment,* Galerie Lunami, Tokyo
Litost, Anna Schwartz Gallery, Melbourne
Mixed Feelings, Roslyn Oxley 9 Gallery, Sydney
1993 *Australian Rhino,* Kunst, Sydney
1994 *Everlastingness,* Roslyn Oxley 9 Gallery, Sydney
1998 Art Gallery of New South Wales, Sydney

Selected Group Exhibitions:

1968 *Flotta Lauro Sculpture Competition,* National Gallery of Victoria, Melbourne
1970 *14th Tazmanian Art Gallery Exhibition,* Hobart
1973 *Sculpturescape Triennale,* Mildura, Victoria (and 1975, 1978)
1976 *Biennale of Sydney,* Art Gallery of New South Wales, Sydney
1981 *1st Australian Sculpture Triennale,* Latrobe University, Melbourne
1985 *Funf vom Funften,* DAAD-Galerie, West Berlin
1987 *ZeitBerliner,* I.F.A. Galerie, Stuttgart
1988 *Edge to Edge,* Museum of Art, Osaka (toured other city museums)
1990 *Construction in Process,* Lodz, Poland (also 1993)
1992 *Stranger in Paradise,* National Museum of Contemporary Art, Seoul
Group Show, Roslyn Oxley 9 Gallery, Paddington, Australia
1993 *Confrontations,* Ivan Dougherty Gallery, Paddington, Australia
1995 *Through a Glass Darkly,* Art Gallery of New South Wales, Sydney
1996 *Death: Insights on Life,* Lewers Bequest and Penrith Regional Art Gallery, Emu Plains, Australia (travelling exhibition)
1997 Elizabeth Bay House, Sydney

Collections:

Art Gallery of New South Wales, Sydney; National Gallery of Australia, Canberra; National Capital Development Commission, Canberra; Australian National University, Canberra; National Gallery of Victoria, Melbourne; Flinders University, Adelaide, South Australia; City Art Gallery, Wollongong, New South Wales; Rijksmuseum Kröller-Müller, Otterlo, Netherlands; Museum Sztuki, Lodz, Poland.

Publications:

On UNSWORTH: Books—*The Development of Australian Sculpture* by Graeme Sturgeon, London 1978; *Australian Sculptors* by Ken Scarlett, Sydney 1980; *Ken Unsworth: Project 28,* exhibition catalog with text by Paul McGillick, Sydney 1978; *Presence and Absence,* exhibition catalog with essay by Jonathan Watkins, Perth 1983; *Australian Drawings and Watercolours,* Canberra 1988; *Australian Performance Art* by Anne Marsh, Sydney 1993; *Ken Unsworth,* exhibition catalog, Melbourne 1998. **Articles**—''The Performance Works of Ken Unsworth'' by Paul McGillick in *ICA Magazine* (Sydney), January/March 1978; ''The Venice Biennale: Back to Nature'' by Henry Martin in *Art International* (Zurich), no. 6, 1978, ''Art and Nature at the Biennale'' by Milton Gendel in *Art in America* (New York), September 1979; ''Australia: A Multiple Reality'' by Pierre Restany in *Domus* (Milan), July 1979; ''Ken Unsworth: Some Recent Works'' by Paul McGillick in *Aspect* (Sydney), no. 4, 1981; ''My Home is Your Home'' by Gregory Volk in *Art & Text,* no. 47, January 1994; ''Soft Sculpture'' by Jutta Feddersen in *Craftsman Press,* 1994; ''Chihuahuas and Currawongs: Humour and the Australian Lanscape in the Recent Works of Ken Unsworth'' by Felicity Fenner in *Art and Australia,* vol. 33, Autumn 1996; ''The Theater of Life: Ken Unsworth'' by Ken Scarlett in *Sculpture* (Washington, D.C.), vol. 18, no. 5, June 1999.

*

My work has predominantly concerned itself with questions about the nature and dilemmas of the human condition and of using those fundamental elements and tools of light, sight, sound, place, form and space to present a spiritual, emotional, psychic landscape whose echoes might resonate in the viewer's own mysterious interior of past and present existent experience.

Reconstructed detrius of human, cultural, technological histories and icons, imbued with the unearthly glow of phantasmagorical visions and declarations enmeshed and embedded in a revitalised, spiritual, idealised, architectonic landscape. Nostalgic, elegiac, neoclassical dreams animated by devices of magic yet palpably mute in the grip of elemental material forces and phenomena and the insubstantiality of the reclaimed appearance of things.

My being, between imagination and innocence, reacts to everything that impinges upon it: a word, a flight of sound, an infinitesimally small movement across the corner of the eye, the sense of something that never happened.

My response registers at the subliminal, subconscious and conscious levels and suddenly the whole of the indescribable, the unthought, the unheard is absolutly complete and clear or perhaps, only as another of those endless showers of bits and pieces that somehow, one day or one night fall into place magically, all at once, like some completely perceived and finished, indescribably intricate jigsaw puzzle whose ingrained lines of lunatic perversity suddenly fade and exist no more.

I am most content when silence diminishes the light and, listening to the past echoes of voices that came from no one's throat and the soft footfalls of those who never were, dissolves in the stillness, my waking into newly-born aching oneness with the disappeared.

—Ken Unsworth

* * *

Ken Unsworth came late to his art. Not till he was about 40 did he discover that sculpture was best able to embody his feelings. In an Australian art world which especially prized subtle observation of landscape, he instead felt a need to express great human emotions, with simple directness. In 1967 his earliest venture away from painting was biomorphic soft sculpture; sensuous, even erotic, but too complicated. By 1971 he had found his personal language of forms. Surface manipulation and detail were eliminated, and at first glance purely sculptural experiences were readily apprehended: they were usually extreme states of tension, compression or balance. Although these first mature works were welded metal constructions and concrete slab constructions, they were not formalist drawing-in-space but instead had the abstract energy of a human body testing its limits.

Thus in 1975 it was perhaps inevitable that the breakthrough into art of considerable quality was Unsworth's first essay at performance art. ''Five Secular Settings for Sculpture as Ritual and Burial Piece'' was a series of five briefly held static body-sculptures, in which Unsworth was suspended from various supports; followed by burial alive under shovelsful of sand while standing in an upright glass ''coffin'' from which he was released by a bystander smashing the glass and allowing the dry sand to drain away. In the same year the static sculptures turned to sensuous though plain materials such as worn river-stones floating from wires, or caked and sliced earth.

Music accompanied the ''Five Secular Settings,'' and music or other sounds—babies crying, gunfire, night birds and wind—have been integral to subsequent performance pieces or installations. ''Face to Face,'' 1977, was another physically demanding seven-part brief performance in which the artist, suspended upside-down, first knifed his way out of a sack, and ended lying propped on sticks.

Since then the artist has more often been a background element, endlessly replacing a mechanical crawling doll-child on a plank from which it endlessly falls, to the accompaniment of the staccato beat of a mechanical doll drummer, or sitting immobile by a doll-child and an endlessly bouncing ball.

Such pieces, contributed to *Biennales* of Sydney at the Art Gallery of New South Wales, were maintained for many weeks and (like Gilbert and George's five-day living sculpture and Marina and Ulay's 16 day static performance at the same museum in 1973 and 1981 respectively) were remarkably successful assertions of performance art as primarily a visual art properly shown in the context of a visual-arts museum. Their non-narrative character, or else their endlessly repeated brief narrative, ensured that they were not experienced as out-of-context theatre.

Unsworth's work has gained him invitations from the museum at Lodz, Poland, and the experience of a society under such stress as Poland's in turn influenced a 1982 installation, of two rooms from which humans had fled, leaving only the sense of fear and desperation, and implicit cries for help.

In his various ways—object sculpture, body sculpture, performance art, installation—Unsworth has shown that contemporary art can address itself plainly and with seriousness to the universal mysteries of birth, life, survival, death and resurrection. A body can float, stones hold themselves gracefully in the air: souls therefore may leap across voids, and meet.

—Daniel Thomas

URBAN, Janos

Nationality: Swiss. **Born:** Szeged, Hungary, 5 November 1934; immigrated to Switzerland, 1956: naturalized, 1976. **Education:** Attended Secondary Arts and Crafts School, Budapest, until 1953; studied art history and philosophy at Eotovos Lorand University, Budapest, 1953–56, and art at the Ecole Cantonale des Beaux-Arts, Lausanne, Switzerland, 1957–61. **Family:** Married Jacqueline Nicod in 1963: son: Matthias. **Career:** Independent artist, Lausanne, since 1961; mixed media work with phosphorus, UV light and radio waves, from 1967; ''Memorandum Ancona'' and ''Lived-in Places,'' scripto-visual works, from 1970. Professor, Ecole des Beaux-Arts, Lausanne, since 1963. **Awards:** City of Geneva Prize, *Salon de la Jeune Gravure Suisse,* 1970; Landis and Gyr-Forderungspreis, Zug, 1974. **Address:** Space Saint-François, Place Saint-François 12, CH-1003, Lausanne, Switzerland. **Web site:** http://www.esf.ch/musee/artiste/urban/artist.html.

Individual Exhibitions:

1961 Galerie L'Entracte, Lausanne
1963 Galerie L'Entracte, Lausanne
1966 Galerie L'Entracte, Lausanne
1970 Galerie Palette, Zurich
Galerie Impact, Lausanne
Bischofsmuhle, Hildesheim, West Germany
1971 Galleria Sincron, Brescia, Italy
1973 Galerie la Fenetre, Nice
Galerie Akumulatory, Poznan, Poland
1974 Salle Patino, Geneva
Galerie der Reflektion Press, Stuttgart
1976 Galleria Civica d'Arte Moderna, Modena, Italy
1977 Gallerie R + B, Fribourg, Switzerland
1980 Stempelplaats, Amsterdam

Bazillus Arts Space, Wurzburg, West Germany

Selected Group Exhibitions:

1969 *22 Jonge Switzers,* Stedelijk Museum, Amsterdam
1972 *Art Systems 2,* Museo de Arte Moderna, Buenos Aires
1973 *Biennale de l'Art Suisse,* Kunsthaus, Zurich
1978 *Sammlung der Gotthard-Bank,* Helmhaus, Zurich
1979 *International Print Biennale,* City Art Museum, Bradford, England
Art Documentation 79, California State University at San Jose
1980 *Videowochen Essen,* Museum Folkwang, Essen
22 Artistas Suicos, Galeria Nacional Belem, Lisbon
1981 *Videoarte Suizo,* Centro de Arte y Communicacion, Buenos Aires
1982 *Documenta 7,* Kassel, West Germany

Collections:

Musée Cantonal des Beaux-Arts, Lausanne; Cabinet des Estampes, Geneva; Kunsthaus, Zurich; City of Berne.

Publications:

By URBAN: Books—*Approche des lles—a scripto-visual work,* with others, Lausanne 1972; *Le Bateau de 13 h. 15,* with J. Monnier and L. Prebandier, Lausanne 1973; *Erlebte Erdteile,* Geneva 1974; *Praxis,* Lausanne 1978; *Poiesis,* Lausanne 1979. **Films**—*Again . . . and Again,* 1973; *The Skating Rink,* 1973; *Cross-Talkas,* with L. Prebandier and Hans-Werner Kalkmann, 1973.

On URBAN: Books—*If I Had a Mind . . .,* edited by Klaus Groh, Cologne 1971; *Il corpo come linguaggio* by Lea Vergine, Milan 1974; *Cine-Graphia: 10th Festival Videoart, Locarno,* exhibition catalog, Locarno 1980; *Schweizer Kunst 70–80,* exhibition catalog, Lucerne 1981; *Fri-Art 81,* exhibition catalog, Fribourg 1981; *Love/Hate/Fear/Suicide: Mail Art,* exhibition catalog, Brussels 1981; *Bodies of Artists,* exhibition catalog by Carsten Schmidt Olsen, Aalborg 1981; *A Mail Art Show,* exhibition catalog, Detroit 1981; *Stalin: Centenaire de Joseph Djougachvili,* exhibition catalog, Nice 1981.

URIBURU, Nicolas (Garcia)

Nationality: Argentinian. **Born:** Buenos Aires, 1937. **Education:** Studied architecture in Buenos Aires. **Career:** First colouring project, Grand Canal, Venice, 1968; has worked on colouring natural phenomena since 1968. Lives and works in Paris. **Awards:** Prix Braque, 1964; Prix Lefranc, 1967; Grand Premio Nacional, Buenos Aires, 1968; First Prize, *Biennale,* Tokyo, 1975. **Address:** 67 rue St. Dominique, Paris 7, France.

Individual Exhibitions:

1954 Galeria Muller, Buenos Aires
1960 Galeria Lirolay, Buenos Aires
1962 Galeria Antonio Souza, Mexico City
1963 Galeria Rubbers, Buenos Aires
1965 Galena Guernica, Buenos Aires
1967 Galerie Iris Clert, Paris
1968 General Electric Institute, Montevideo
1972 Galerie Spectrum, Antwerp
1973 Centro de Arte y Communicacion, Buenos Aires
Musée d'Art Moderne de la Ville, Paris
1974 Leo Castelli Graphics, New York
Musée Galliera, Paris
1978 Museum of American Art, Maldonado, Uruguay
1979 Salas Nacionales de Exposicion, Buenos Aires
1982 Hara Museum, Tokyo
1989 Galerie JGM, Paris
1992 *S.O.S. Brazil, Nicolas Uriburu,* Museu de Arte de Sao Paulo, Brazil
1998 Museo Nacional de Bellas Artes, Buenos Aires

Selected Group Exhibitions:

1967 *Salon de Mai,* Paris
1968 *Graphics Biennale,* Paris
1971 *Air, Fire, Earth and Water,* Museum of Fine Arts, Boston
Biennale, Paris
1972 *Bienal,* Medellin, Colombia
1974 *International Graphics Biennale,* Tokyo
Art and Culture in the Third World, Institute of Contemporary Arts, London
Contraste Simultane des Couleurs, Faculty of Medicine, Paris
1980 *Biennale,* Tokyo
1982 *Documenta,* Kassel, West Germany
1997 *1997: Colección del Museo Nacional de Bellas Artes,* Buenos Aires
Canada Argentina: Seven Contemporary Artists, Maison de la Culture Cote-des-Neiges, Montreal
2000 *Micropolitiques,* Le Magasin, Grenoble, France

Publications:

On URIBURU: Book—*Art in Argentina* by Jorge Glusberg, Milan 1986; *S.O.S. Brazil, Nicolas Uriburu,* exhibition catalog, Sao Paulo 1992; *Nicolás García Uriburu,* exhibition catalog, Buenos Aires 1998. **Articles**—"Nicolas Uriburu" by John Perreault in the *Village Voice* (New York), 4 June 1970; "Art Concepts from Europe" by Pierre Restany in *Domus* (Milan), June 1970; "Nicolas Garcia Uriburu" by Jorge Glusberg in *Art and Artists* (London), January 1971; "Le marche aux Puces de l'art moderne" by Otto Hahn in *L'Express* (Paris), October 1971; "Uriburu: Coloration" by C. Bovyeure in *Lettres Francaises* (Paris), June 1972; "The World All in Green" by Pierre Restany in *Domus* (Milan), April 1973; "Une perception autre" by P. Borgeaud in *Pariscope,* December 1973; "Uriburu: La vie en vert" in *Connaissance des Arts* (Paris), February 1974; "Dix questions sur l'art et les nouveaux media" in *Artitudes* (St. Jeannet, France), July 1974; article by Pierre Restany in *Domus* (Milan), October 1981.

*

My work is about ecology. I began by painting a series of trees in Argentina in 1960. In 1964 I won the Prix Braque, a scholarship to Paris. In 1968 during the Venice *Biennale* I coloured the waters of the

Grand Canal in fluorescent green (about 3 kilometers): that was the beginning of a series of colourings in different waters all over the world: the East River, New York; the Seine, Paris; the Rio de la Plata, Buenos Aires—and fountains, lakes, ports, etc., always in a fluorescent green, showing my alarm about pollution. In New York in 1970, I began a series in green colours, ''Antagonism between Nature and Civilization.'' I have also done some body art, colouring my sexual organs, face and hair in green. In 1971 I began a defence of the trees in a park that the authorities wanted to cut; next I planted some trees in the city of Buenos Aires and also in a museum in Uruguay. I've coloured the waters of the Rhine in collaboration with the German artist Joseph Beuys and planted with him the first seven trees (of what will eventually be about 7,000) at *Documenta 7* in Kassel. Now I am working on a series about animals that are disappearing from the world. My art defines the struggle between nature and civilization. That's why I colour my body, my genitals, and the great waters of the world. The more developed countries are destroying water, land and air, resources for the future in Latin American countries.

—Nicolas Uriburu

* * *

The relation between man and his environment has always been a matter of concern for all societies. Ecology, a discipline that began to develop at the beginning of the 20th century, is a branch of biology that deals with the relation between living things and their environment. Organisms, plants, animals, all of them perform certain activities which tend mainly to their adaptation to the surrounding medium. The three large constituent areas of ecology—vegetable, animal and human—roused successively the interest of botanists, zoologists, and lastly, of sociologists. The term ''human ecology'' appeared in 1921, and since then, that region has been part of the region of social sciences. Its problems are not only limited to pointing out the mutual connections between man and his environment, but emphasize the social aspects of his adaptation. If by the term ecosystem is meant the universe of the elements which surround the subject as they become signs, that is to say, when man supplies them with a meaning—a topological semantics would explain the large number of forms in which man articulates space and establishes semantic relations with it. One of the manifestations of this production of meaning, born from man's relations with his environment, is the ''artistic discourse,'' particularly that which is called ''ecological art.'' The ecological artist develops his language in connection with two types of elements of the ecosystem: the natural ones (rivers, mountains, etc.) and the artificial ones (buildings, urbanistic complexes, highways). The intersection between the artistic and what the ecologists call ''natural areas'' (territorial unities created and/or conditioned or not by human activity) constitutes a new phenomenon, which compels us to adopt a critical point of view in an entirely different way. Nicolas Uriburu coloured the waters of Venice canals with green aniline in 1968, during the year's Biennial. In May and June, 1970, he coloured the East River in New York, the River Seine in Paris, once again the Grand Canal in Venice and the River Plata in Buenos Aires. In 1971, when the Paris Biennial took place, he coloured the Vincennes Lake, and he coloured himself, as a participant at a meeting (colour body work); in June, 1972, he coloured fourteen fountains at Kassel, in 1973 the Riachuelo in Buenos Aires; in 1974 the fountains in Brussels. The ecological proposals of Uriburu extend to future projects: the colouring of the fountains of Versailles, that of the snows of Mont Blanc, and of Iguazu and Niagara Falls. The project called ''Cono Sur'' consists of the simultaneous colouring of every river in the different countries of the southern hemisphere, by an artist from each country; through the project ''Agua Nuestra'' he will colour every Latin American place (Uriburu is an Argentinian architect) where water represents conflict: Panama, Iquitos, Titicaca, Puna Arenas. Uriburu's work fuses with nature and at the same time it complements her. We are, thus, in front of a different event: the artist's language inscribes itself in the space transformed by man, the signs spread over large extensions, and thus man gets himself, literally speaking, ''to pervade nature with humanity.'' Uriburu's art refuses to adapt itself to the rules imposed by the important museums or the international galleries, but intends to take the Trojan horse out of its walls, in order to see whether the works done in the 1960s are able to endure living in the open air of daily life. The protecting confinement is no longer an attraction for the vanguard, who want to operate in the reality of the profane ambits. The artist who lives in the second half of his century no longer creates new works, but new channels of sensibility, new discoveries which propose different fields of exploration of the spirit. Instead of undertaking the recreation of reality by means of imitative or decorative objects, the artist makes use of representations which do not exist as separate entities, but as elements which supply the sites where they are placed with a new definition or a new point of view. The traditional work of art has begun to be sustained by an artistic situation composed by happenings which correspond to social and ideological function, and to function related to creativeness and play, all of them belonging to the field of probability, to the world of free relation. In order to convey his sensible message, the traditional artist repeats the act of creation in a God-like manner, resorting to those tricks painters and sculptors have made use of for centuries. The ecological artists carry on with their researches in different operation levels. They are no longer interested in the space that must be filled, nor in the academic discussions about the limits between poetry and painting, nor between fullness and void, because the matter has become a situation; and this situation is communicating, is a creator of signs, and it comprises forms, ideas and being; it probably does not turn out faultless products of ''good art''; it deals with the artistic event as a cultural phenomenon, as a sociological experience, as a practical work in psychology, an urbanistic project, a sort of theoretical and experimental illustration of human behaviour.

—Jorge Glusberg

V

VALENTINE, DeWain

Nationality: American. **Born:** Fort Collins, Colorado, 27 August 1936. **Education:** University of Colorado, Boulder, 1954–60, B.F.A. 1958, M.F.A. 1960. **Career:** Independent sculptor, in Colorado, 1960–65, and in Venice, Califonia since 1965; cast polyester works, 1967–75; laminated glass works from 1976. Instructor, University of Colorado, Boulder, 1959–61; instructor, University of California at Los Angeles, 1965–67. **Awards:** Yale-Norfolk Art School Fellowship, New Haven, Connecticut, 1958; Guggenheim Fellowship, 1980; National Endowment for the Arts Fellowship, 1981. **Address:** 4223 Glencoe Ave. No. A-129, Marina Del Rey, California 90292.

Individual Exhibitions:

1958 University of Colorado, Boulder
1960 University of Colorado, Boulder
1964 The Gallery, Denver
1968 Douglas Gallery, Vancouver
Ace Gallery, Los Angeles
1969 University of British Columbia, Vancouver
Galerie Bischofberger, Zurich
University of Washington, Seattle
1970 Pasadena Museum of Art
1973 Denise René Gallery, New York
Walter Kelly Gallery, Chicago
1974 San Jose Museum of Art
Edward Thorp Gallery, Santa Barbara
Betty Gold Gallery, Los Angeles
1975 La Jolla Museum of Contemporary Art
California State University at Northridge
Long Beach Museum of Art
1977 Santa Barbara Museum of Art
1979 Los Angeles County Museum of Art
1980 Malinda Wyatt Gallery, Venice, California
1981 Projects Studio One, Institute for Art and Urban Resources, New York
1982 Thomas Babeor Gallery, La Jolla
Malinda Wyatt Gallery, Venice, California
Missouri Botanical Garden, St. Louis
Laumeier Sculpture Park, St. Louis
1983 Madison Art Center, Wisconsin
1984 Thomas Babeor Gallery, La Jolla
1985 Honolulu Academy of Arts
Contemporary Arts Center, Honolulu

Selected Group Exhibitions:

1966 *Whitney Annual Sculpture Exhibition,* Whitney Museum, New York
1969 *The Industrial Edge,* Walker Art Center, Minneapolis
1973 *American Art 1948–1973,* Seattle Art Museum, Washington
1976 *Contemporary Masters,* Libra Gallery, Claremont College, California
1979 *Change, Inc. West,* Newport Harbor Art Museum, California
1980 *Sculpture in California 1975–1980,* San Diego Museum of Art
1981 *California Light and Space,* Lonny Gans and Associates, Venice, California
1983 *Urban Sculpture/Architectural Concerns,* Security Pacific National Bank Gallery, Los Angeles
1985 *California Sculpture Show,* Yorkshire Sculpture Park, Bretton Hall College
1987 *Sculpture of the Sixties,* Margo Leavin Gallery, Los Angeles

Collections:

Whitney Museum, New York; Art Institute of Chicago; Milwaukee Art Center, Los Angeles County Museum of Art; Norton Simon Museum, Pasadena, California; La Jolla Museum of Contemporary Art; Palm Springs Desert Museum; Aldrich Museum of Contemporary Art, Ridgefield, Connecticut; Contemporary Arts Center, Honolulu; Vancouver Art Gallery; Atlantic Richfield Corporation, Washington, D.C.; Federal Reserve Bank, San Francisco; Iris B. Gerald Cantor Center for the Visual Arts at Stanford University, California.

Publications:

By VALENTINE: Articles—''An Interview with DeWain Valentine'' with Kurt Von Meier in *Artforum* (New York), May 1969; ''DeWain Valentine: An Interview'' with Melinda Wortz in *Journal* (Los Angeles), June 1974; ''DeWain Valentine'' in *Art Press,* Special Issue, no. 17, 1996.

On VALENTINE: Books—*Neue Dimensionen der Plastik* by Udo Kultermann, Tübingen, West Germany 1967; *Plastics in Arts* by Pierre Restany, Paris 1974; *A Decade of Sculpture: The 1960s* by Julia Busch, Philadelphia 1974; *Sunshine Muse* by Peter Plagens, New York 1974; *Art and Plastics* by Franco Passoni, Milan 1975; *50 West Coast Artists* by Henry Hopkins, San Francisco 1982; *Living Materials: A Sculptor's Handbook* by Oliver Andrews, Berkeley 1983; *DeWain Valentine: Recent Works,* exhibition catalog with essay by Melinda Wortz, Honolulu 1985; *The Art of Light and Space* by Jan Butterfield, New York 1996. **Articles—**''Family Ties'' by Jon Etra in *ARTnews,* vol. 90, no. 5, May 1991.

* * *

Sculptor DeWain Valentine, who moved to Southern California from Colorado in 1965, has been closely identified with the so-called ''L.A. Look,'' which during the 1960s began to attract international attention to contemporary art activity in Los Angeles. A ''cool'' minimalism and preoccupation with elegant surfaces was indeed characteristic of the work of artists such as Valentine, Larry Bell, Craig Kauffman, and Robert Irwin. However, despite certain mutual interests (for example, the aesthetic potential of industrial materials), neither these artists nor their works constituted a cohesive ''movement.'' The most prominent figures associated with the emergence of contemporary Los Angeles art in fact displayed a wide variety of interests as represented by the quasi-POP imagery of Ed Ruscha and Billy Al Bengston, the tableaux assemblages of Ed Keinholz, or Irwin's optical experimentation. Nonetheless, fascination with technology, industrial materials, crafted surfaces, and visual sensuality were characteristic of one notable aspect of the creative milieu in which Valentine worked in the late 1960s. With his elegantly seductive cast-resin sculptures, Valentine played an important role in the development of what became widely regarded as the prevailing Southern California aesthetic. Furthermore, in his subsequent work he has continued to pursue the same basic concerns—mainly the exploration of light—which motivated his earlier work. Valentine's unparalleled technical virtuosity in resin casting on a monumental scale and the undeniable beauty of his work has, unfortunately, tended to obscure his important goals. Over the years Valentine has consistently developed a body of sculptural work based on geometric forms infused with subtle gradations of transparent or translucent color ''activated'' (and modified) by ambient light. Consisting of polyester resin or acrylic plastic discs, wedges, rings, slabs and related shapes, Valentine's art achieves a remarkably effective fusion of physical substance and light. The installations done in the early 1970s mark an important and logical progression from these individual objects to the light environments and related work of the past decade. Throughout, his basic goal has remained the figurative and literal ''illumination'' of a fundamental duality: matter and phenomenon (''tonnage and ethereality,'' to use the artist's words) manipulated into visual harmony by technical means. Despite his use of industrial materials and techniques, these concerns place Valentine firmly within a naturalist tradition. The prismatic lenses of the late 1960s, the camera obscura pieces and photomontages of the mid 1970s, and even the concurrent planes and spectrums (cantilevered, suspended, curved), all depend upon natural phenomena to reveal their true content. In every case, there is present a view of the world that is firmly rooted in landscape. Even the delicate suspended-rod installations (such as *Catenary Light),* by introducing a curved shaft of exterior light into a dark room, deal with the experience of natural light as it responds to weather, season and time of day. The same basic perceptual concerns and interest in transparency of form underlie Valentine's recent large scale laminated glass constructions. As always, an undeniable physical beauty and technical mastery are subservient to ideas based on nature and the almost mystical quality of light. Valentine's philosophical goals clearly separate his art from minimalist refinement and decorative formalism. His accomplishment has been the dematerialization of physicality in a way that asserts the primacy of light. Viewed in perceptual terms, Valentine's interest would appear to have more in common with French Impressionist ideas than with recent formalist theory. Nonetheless, his work does relate to that of the ''environmentalists'' (Irwin, Michael Asher, James Turrell) whose non-object investigations of light and perception constitute one of Southern California's significant contributions to contemporary art.

—Paul J. Karlstrom

VALOCH, Jiri

Nationality: Czechoslovakian. **Born:** Brno, 6 September 1946. **Education:** Studied Bohemistics, Germanistics and aesthetics, J. E. Purkynee University, Brno, 1965–70. **Family:** Married Mirka Antonova in 1971 (divorced, 1972). **Career:** Produced first visual poems and typestracts, 1964; first photographic works, 1969; first conceptual poetry, 1970. Artist and art theoretician, House of Arts, Brno, since 1972: has organized exhibitions and written articles on numberous Czech artists. **Address:** Jugoslavska 46a, 61300 Brno, Czechoslovakia.

Individual Exhibitions:

1966 Music Theatre, Ústi and Labem, Czechoslovakia
1969 Museum, Krnov, Czechoslovakia
1970 House of the Young, Jindrichuv Hradec, Czechoslovakia
1971 Regional Gallery, Jihlava, Czechoslovakia
1972 Information Centre for Events, Bielefeld, West Germany
1974 *Sculptures,* Gallery Akumulatory, Poznan, Poland
1977 *Relations,* Galleria Mercato del Sale, Milan
1978 *Relations and Haiku,* Municipal Library, Wroclaw, Poland
1979 *In, Oltre,* Centro Culturale, Monza, Italy
1984 *Werken uit 1964–82,* Her Apollohuis, Eindhoven, Netherlands
1985 *Vizuální poezie,* Kulturni stredisko mesta Blanska, Czechoslovakia
1997 *Jiri Valoch: Bücher,* Neues Museum Weserburg Bremen, Germany

Selected Group Exhibitions:

1966 *Umeni pisma—Poezie pisma Visudini poezie,* Moravian Museum, Brno
1970 *Konkrete Poezie?* Stedelijk Museum, Amsterdam
1971 *Arte de Sistemas I,* Centro de Arte y Communicacion, Buenos Aires
1973 *Texts,* Balatonboglar, Hungary
1977 *Texty Wisualne,* Gallery Labyrint, Lublin, Poland (travelled to Lodz, 1978)
1979 *Sprachen jenseits von Dichtung,* Kunstverein, Munster, West Germany
1980 *Drawing '80,* Pecz Gallery, Hungary
1981 *Kunstlerbucher,* Kunstverein, Frankfurt
1984 *Am Anfang war das Wort,* Stadtisches Galerie, Ludenscheid, West Germany
1985 *Salut Chlebnikow,* Staatliches Lindenaumuseum, Altenburg, East Germany

Collections:

Archief voor Visuele, Concrete en Experimentele Poezie, Dutch Literary Museum, The Hague; Muzeum Sztuki, Lodz, Poland; Muzeum Narodowe, Wroclaw, Poland; Regional Gallery, Jihlava, Czechoslovakia; Moravian Gallery, Brno; Kupferstichkabinett der Staatlichen Kunstsammlungen, Dresden; Archive Hanns Sohm, Markgronimgen, West Germany; Stedelijk Museum, Amsterdam; Schlubladenmuseum Herbert Disel, Berne; Museo Laboratorio Casabianca, Malo, Italy.

Publications:

By VALOCH: Books and phamphlets—*HLAS/VOICE/VOIX/STIMME,* London 1966; *9 Optical Poems,* London 1967; *Unlucky Number—3 mimeoenphamphs,* Toronto 1968; *An Interrupted Poem,* Toronto 1969; *Optical Book,* Brescia, Italy 1970; *Ga: The First and Last Collection of Sound Poems by Jiri Valoch,* London 1971;

A Minimal Monument, Welling, Kent 1971; *Poem for Ad Reinhardt,* London 1971; *Landscapes I,* Utrecht 1972; *See Page 13,* Friedfichfehn 1973; *Hommage á Valoch,* West Berlin 1975; *12 Exercises,* West Berlin 1976; *Mobile-Two Structures-Piece III,* London 1980; *20 Works: Kunstinfomatie 35,* Gorinchem 1981; *Haiku,* Toronto 1983; *Pozorováni-kniha pro prátele,* Brno 1983; *Word Works,* West Berlin 1984; *Werken uit 1964–1982: Collection Herman de Vries,* Eindhoven 1984; *8 x 2 Portfolio: Czech Visual Texts,* editor, Dresden 1986; *Semantic Study,* Munich 1986; *Poem for bpNichol,* Toronto 1988; *Five Parts of One Piece,* Eschenau 1994; *Three Sheets,* Eschenau 1994; *Jiri Valoch: Bücher* (with text by Guy Schraenen), Bremen 1997. **Articles**—''Brnensky Okruh: Pamatce Gerty Pospisilove, bez niz by mnohe nebylo tak, jak bylo'' in *Vytvarne Umeni,* no. 3–4, 1995; ''Sculptural Creations Based on Astronomical Phenomena'' in *Leonardo* (Cambridge, MA), vol. 30, no. 4, 1997.

On VALOCH: Books—*Experimentalni poezie,* edited by J. Hirsal and B. Grogerova, Prague 1966; *Once Again* by Jean Francois Bory, New York 1967; *Verso la Poesia Totale,* edited by A. Spatola, Milan 1967; *Poezie in Fuzie,* edited by Paul de Vree, Antwerp 1967; *Concrete Poetry: A World View,* edited by M. E. Solt, Bloomington, Indiana 1968; *Aktuelle Kunst in Ost Europa,* edited by Klaus Groh, Cologne 1970; *Exempla: Documents of Concrete and Visual Poetry,* edited by Maurizio Nannucci, Florence 1970; *Konkretedichtung,* edited by S. J. Schmidt, Munich 1972; *Poesia Visiva Internazionale,* edited by Galleria Il Canale, Venice 1974; *Concrete, Visual and Signalist Poetry,* edited by M. Todoravic, Belgrade 1975; *La Escritura en Liberiad,* edited by F. Millan and R. Sanchez, Madrid 1975; *Von für über—Heinz Gappmayr,* edited by Peter Weiermair, Frankfurt 1985; *Zwanzig Jahre Rainer Verlag: Ein Anthologie, Eine Almanach,* edited by R. Pretzell and T. Milch, West Berlin 1986; *Artists' Statements,* edited by Richard Kriesche, Graz 1987; *Geschichte des Fotogramms,* edited by Floris M. Neususs, Cologne 1987.

*

All my work has been and is motivated by language—in the sixties by the possibility to isolate its elements and to create from them a purely aesthetic structure, since the break of the sixties and seventies by seeking limitations and relations that the extremely reduced language can form, either in non-verbal context/phototexts, verbal interventions in nature/or in itself. The starting point is the annihilation or at least the maximal suppression of the signifier/signified relationship. When language is released from these bonds, it is possible to work with it in another way. I am interested in semantic complications, giving evidence of the language as such, and in autonomous language structures formed by isolating the meaning or by repeating identical isolated elements. I am interested in the metamorphosis of the sign into a quasisign which cannot be drawn into a conventional communication system.

—Jiri Valoch

van AMEN, Woody

Nationality: Dutch. **Born:** Eindhoven, 26 August 1936. **Education:** Studied art at the Akademie van Beeldende Kunsten, Rotterdam, 1956–58; mainly self-taught in painting. **Military service:** Served in Geneeskundige Troepen, Dutch Army, Amersfoort, 1956. **Family:** Married Cocky Voermans in 1961; daughters: Cybele and Claudia-Nathalie. **Career:** Worked as window-dresser, gardener, sailor, housepainter, docker, wood-finisher, etc., in Rotterdam, 1958–60. Independent artist, in Rotterdam, since 1960 (worked in New York City, 1961–63). Worked with Scarabee Experimental Theatre Group, Haarlem, 1967; Academie van Beeldende Kunsten, Rotterdam, 1973. **Awards:** Dutch Ministry of Culture Stipend, 1967–69; Rotterdam Arts Foundation Stipend, 1969. **Address:** Goudsesingel 315 D, 3032 EN Rotterdam, Netherlands. **Web site:** http://home.wxs.nl˜taxat/.

Individual Exhibitions:

1962 Cottage Club on the Lake, New York
1963 Galerie Delta, Rotterdam
1965 Galerie 't Venster, Rotterdam
Stedelijk Museum, Amsterdam
1966 Galerie Delta, Rotterdam
1967 Galerie 20, Amsterdam
1968 Galerie Waalkens, Finsterwolde, Netherlands
Markt 17, Enschede, Netherlands
1969 Galerie 't Venster, Rotterdam Galerie 20, Amsterdam
Galerie Jalmar, Amsterdam
1970 Galerie De Doelen, Rotterdam (with Wim Gijzen)
Galerie Defacqz, Brussels
Galerie 't Venster, Rotterdam
1971 Galerie 20, Amsterdam
1973 Galerie Yaki Kornblit, Amsterdam
Galerie Richard Foncke, Ghent
1974 Galerie Yaki Kornblit, Amsterdam
1975 Pander Kunstcentrum, The Hague Galerie Yaki Kornblit, Amsterdam
1978 *Moderne Kunstvoorwerpen,* Museum Boymans-van Beuningen, Rotterdam
Musee d'Art et d'Histoire, Geneva
Museum Het Prinsenhof, Delft, Netherlands
Galerie Brinkman, Amsterdam
1980 Galerie Lara Vincy, Paris
Galerie Brinkman, Amsterdam
1981 Kunstcentrum De Vaart, Hilversum, Netherlands
Buchmann Art Gallery, Antwerp
1982 Stichting Kasteel van Rhoon, Netherlands
National Museum, Singapore
Centre International d'Art Plastique, Hasselt, Belgium
Gemeentemuseum, The Hague
1983 Gallery Black Cat, Rotterdam
Centre International d'Art Plastique, Hasselt, Belgium
1984 Galerie J. L., Ostende, Belgium
1985 Van Abbemuseum, Eindhoven, Netherlands
1986 Gallery Art Action, Singapore
Le Cadre Gallery, Hong Kong
Oets Fine Art Gallery, Djakarta, Indonesia
1987 Rabogallery, Utrecht, Netherlands
1989 Claartje de Gruyter Gallerie, Vught, Netherlands
1991 Gasunie, Groningen (retrospective)
1993 Provinciaal Museum voor Moderne Kunst, Ostende, Belgium
Stedelijk Museum, Schiedam, Netherlands
Chabot Museum, Rotterdam, Netherlands

1994 Noord Brabants Museum, 's Hertogenbosch, Netherlands

Selected Group Exhibitions:

1968 *European Painters Today,* Musée des Arts Decoratifs, Paris (toured the United States)
1970 *De Metamorfose van het Objekt,* Museum Boymansvan Beuningen, Rotterdam (toured Switzerland, Germany and Italy)
1975 *Art Information Festival,* Middelburg, Netherlands
1976 *Biennale,* Venice
1977 *Beethoven, Music for the Millions,* Gemeentemuseum, Arnhem, Netherlands
1979 *De Jaren Zestig,* Galerie De Vries en Roeloff, Rotterdam
1981 *Not Waiving,* Palais des Beaux-Arts, Brussels
1987 *Line and Image,* Muhlenberg College, Allentown, Pennsylvania (toured the United States 1988–89)
1988 *Collecction Agnes et Frits Becht,* Musée d'Art Moderne, Villeneuve d'Asq, France
Rotterdam Retrospective: Fine Arts Since 1940, Museum Boymans-van Beuningen, Rotterdam
1990 *Kunst x Kunst,* Stedelijk Museum, Delft, Netherlands

Collections:

Stedelijk Museum, Amsterdam; Peter Stuyvesant Foundation, Amsterdam; Museum Boymans-van Beuningen, Rotterdam Centraal Museum, Utrecht; Frans Halsmuseum, Haarlem, Netherlands; Palais des Beaux-Arts, Brussels,

Publications:

By van AMEN: Books and Pamphlets—*Filosofie van de Nieuwe Romantiek,* Rotterdam 1973; *Book of Stamps,* with others, Amsterdam 1976; *Transit 3: Translation Transformation,* Amsterdam 1977; *240 Days/Dagen/Jours/Tage,* with foreword by R. H. Fuchs, Amsterdam 1985; *The Trade Plough,* Amsterdam 1990. **Recording—***Het leven van Woody,* with Jan Donia, 1966.

On van AMEN: Books—*Art Around the World* by R. W D. Oxenaar, New York 1966; *Le livre rouge de la revolution picturale* by Pierre Restany, Milan 1968; *De Eksplosie van her Intellekt* by Jan Donia, Hilversum, Netherlands 1968; *Le livre blanc* by Pierre Restany, Milan 1969; *Le pop Art* by Jose Pierre, Paris 1975; *Woody van Amen: Moderne Kunstvoorwerpen 1963–1977,* exhibition catalog with texts by R. Hammacher-van den Brande, Jan Donia, Pierre Restany, Goose Oosterhof and Peter Bulthuis, Rotterdam 1978; *Nieuwe Romantiek van Woody van Amen,* exhibition catalog with texts by Rein-Arend Leeuw and Peter Buithuis, Delft 1978; *Woody van Amen: Objecten, tekeningen, grafiek,* exhibition catalog with text by Kees Broos, The Hague 1982; *Beeldende kunst uit de verameling van Agnes en Frits Becht,* with texts by R. H. Fuchs and Saskia Bos, Utrecht 1984; *Woody van Amen retrospectief 1960–1990* by Jeroen Groeneweg, 1991; *Woody van Amen* by Jeroen Groeneweg, Bruges 1993. **Articles—**"Borderline PILOT: The Audience from a Distance" by Christian Krausch in *Kunstforum International,* no. 148, December 1999-January 2000.

*

New Romanticism

1. "New Romanticism" aims at enriching contemporary art by assigning a major role to feeling and imagination.

2. In a cool society which produces "cool art," "new romanticism" presents a form of art which meets the longings of people today for warmth, happiness and recognizable contents.

3. The need for romance has been clearly recognized in the world of films, fashion and theatre, but the plastic arts are lagging behind in this respect. New romanticism has made it its task to re-activate romanticism in the plastic arts.

4. The chief motive of "new romanticism" is to make—and make recognizable again—the ordinary things which people tend to think of as nice.

5. Socially this point of departure could prove to be of great value: it will restore the basic function of art as a means of communication intelligible to all.

6. The views of "new romanticism" will restore some balance in the chaotic and confusing multitude of art expressions of today.

7. The emphasis on feeling and imagination and the use of ordinary and familiar means of portrayal will set free the personal creativity of the "consumer." This will once again stimulate spontaneity in making and experiencing art.

8. "New romanticism" is improving the image of art.

—Woody van Amen

* * *

Camesi in Switzerland concentrates upon making art (pictures, etc.) the servant of a kind of aesthetic architecture. Pictures, like bricks, can, he has been able to show, build walls, fireplaces, houses even. At the Sao Paulo *Bienal* of 1973 he constructed a wall of self-portraits. Woody van Amen does the opposite. His *new realism* quite frequently demonstrates that architecture (and furniture), with only slight interpolations, can become pictures or *objects.* What he seeks to make clear, often with many humorous interjections, is that the world we know—from ice-block to pavingstone, from *Grande-armoire* to kitchen sink—is a natural-cum-manmade world, ripe for plunder by an artist if he knows what to do with so much valuable raw material. Not that he is suggesting a scratch round for easy-to-come-by readymades. On the contrary, whatever takes his fancy also inspires him to give it an artistic facelift. Bright colours. Aesthetic machinery. Unexpected conjunctions. Van Amen implies that the spade work performed in this field by dada and surrealism is already dated, and that it is time to start creating anew with materials which even if they are not raw can still be coaxed by inventive processes into the furniture and fittings of an unexplored demi-paradise.

—Sheldon Williams

VANDERHEYDEN, J(acob) C(ornelis) J(ohan)

Nationality: Dutch. **Born:** Den Bosch, 23 June 1928. **Education:** Studied at the Koninklijke Akademie, Den Bosch, 1946–49;

Rijksakademie, Amsterdam, 1952–53; Art School, Tilburg, 1954–55; and Jan Van Eyck Academie, Maastricht, 1955–57. **Military service**: Dutch Army, 1949–51. **Family:** Married Johanna van Rysewyk in 1962; children: Paul, Jan and Maria. **Career:** Worked at Philips Electronics, Eindhoven, 1951; drawing master in colleges at Roermond and Nijmegen, 1954–56; independent artist, Den Bosch, since 1958; paintings and prints, 1958–66; films, since 1967; computer compositions, 1968; sound and television works, 1969; time-related works; 1969, calendar, clock and score; has worked in open-air studio since 1975. Guest instructor: Jan Van Eyck Academie, Maastricht, 1971–73; Professor, State Academy, Amsterdam, since 1986. **Agent:** Galerie Van Gelder, Plancius Straat 9A, Amsterdam, Netherlands. **Address:** Louwse Poort 83, 5211 NE Den Bosch, Netherlands.

Individual Exhibitions:

1964 Gemeentemuseum, The Hague
1965 Galerie Swart, Amsterdam
1966 Kunststichting, Rotterdam
Prentenkabinet, Gemeentemuseum, The Hague
1967 Stedelijk van Abbemuseum, Eindhoven, Netherlands
1971 Galerie Collection d'Art, Amsterdam
Stedelijk van Abbemuseum, Eindhoven, Netherlands (with Kees Buurman and Carel Visser)
1977 Gemeentemuseum, The Hague (retrospective; travelled to the Van Abbemuseum Eindhoven, Netherlands)
1981 Stedelijk van Abbemuseum, Eindhoven, Netherlands
1983 Stedelijk van Abbemuseum, Eindhoven, Netherlands (retrospective)
1986 Galerie van Gelder, Amsterdam
1990 Museum Boijmans, Rotterdam (catalog)
1998–2000 Gemeentemuseum, The Hague
2001 Stedelijk Museum, Amsterdam

Selected Group Exhibitions:

1970 *Kontrasten,* Gemeentemuseum, The Hague
1973 *Varianten, Ministry* of Cultural Affairs, The Hague (toured the Netherlands)
1981 *Instant Fotografie,* Stedelijk Museum, Amsterdam
1982 *Contemporary Art from the Netherlands,* Museum of Contemporary Art, Chicago (travelled to Toronto and New York)
Documenta, Kassel, West Germany
1986 *Les Abstraits,* Galerie Le Consortium, Dijon, France (travelled to Nice, Villa Arson Musée)
1987 *Contour,* Prinsenhof, Delft, Netherlands
1990 *Biennial '90,* Metropolitan Museum, Tokyo (and Municipal Museum, Kyoto)
Art Meets Science and Spirituality, Stedelijk Museum, Amsterdam
1993 *The Ideal Place,* Hague Center for Contemporary Art
1994 *Ar Pays Bas,* Musée d'Art Moderne de la Ville, Paris
1996 *In gesprek met Vermeer,* Museum het Prinsenhof, Delft
1998 *Waves Breaking the Shore . . . Ad Dekkers in His Time,* Stedelijk Museum, Amsterdam
2000 The Chinese European Art Center, Xiamen, China
Cartography and Contemporary Art, Antwerpen

Collections:

Haags Gemeentemuseum, The Hague, Netherlands; Stedelijk van Abbemuseum, Eindhoven, Netherlands; Rijksmuseum Kröller-Muller, Otterlo, Netherlands; Museum Boymans-van Beuningen, Rotterdam; Stedelijk Museum, Amsterdam.

Publications:

By VANDERHEYDEN: Books—*J. C. J. Vanderheyden,* with texts by J. L. Locher and C. Blok, The Hague 1977; *Himalaya-Chomolungma,* Utrecht 1981; *J. C. J. Vanderheyden,* Museum Boymans, Rotterdam n.d. **Articles**—"Child of His Time" in *Konstrasten,* exhibition catalog, The Hague 1970; "J. C. J. Vanderheyden: Essay" in *Elementary Forms,* exhibition catalog, Amsterdam 1976. **Films—***Art is Only for Beginners,* with Richard Menken and Henk van de Rijdt, 1969.

On VANDERHEYDEN: Books—*J. C. J. Vanderheyden,* exhibition catalog with text by J. L. Locher, The Hague 1966; *Vanderheyden,* exhibition catalog with text by Lambert Tegenbosch, Eindhoven, Netherlands 1967; *Warning against the Work of J. C. J. Vanderheyden* by Cor Blok, Amsterdam 1971; *Kees Buurman/Carel Visser/J. C. J. Vanderheyden,* exhibition catalog with text by Jaap Bremer and Hein Reedijk, Eindhoven, Netherlands 1971; *J. C. J. Vanderheyden,* exhibition catalog, Eindhoven, Netherlands 1977; *Instant Fotografie,* exhibition catalog with text by Els Barents, Amsterdam 1982; *Contemporary Art from the Netherlands,* exhibition catalog with texts by Marianne Brouweer and others, Amsterdam 1992; *J. C. J. Vanderheyden: Retrospective,* exhibition catalog, Eindhoven, Netherlands 1983; *J. C. J. Vanderheyden: Retrospective,* exhibition catalog, Rotterdam 1990; *Art Meets Science and Spirituality,* London 1996. **Articles**—"7 Dutch Artists" by R. Fuchs, B. Reise and C. Broos, in *Studio International* (London), May 1973; "J. C. J. Vanderheyden" by Kees van Gelder in *Code* (Amsterdam), June 1986; "The Ideal Place: Time Lost and Won. J.C.J. Vanderheyden's Project for HCAK" in *Art & Design,* vol. 10, May/June 1995.

*

We experience everything in bits and pieces. Consciousness snips fragments out of time. And we try to establish contexts, to link one fragment with another. Since the invention of film editing, it is possible to connect every image with any other image, by placing them in succession. Several paintings and photographs, too, can be seen as successive fragments of consciousness.

An excess of information causes us to seem to experience in a few years things which used to take an entire lifetime to experience. And yet you don't have to do very much in your life, only a few things which keep on recurring.

—J. C. J. Vanderheyden

* * *

J. C. J. Vanderheyden's place in Dutch painting is a special one. For more than twenty years he has lived and worked in the provincial town of Den Bosch, outside the centre of artistic life. At appropriate times he shows his works and causes a stir—in recent years, even some general appreciation. In 1968 the young art historian Rudi Fuchs wrote an article on Vanderheyden's work in the serious art-historical periodical *Simiolus.* Fuchs discussed the painting *Blue Cross* (1965/66) in the light of some formal aspects of Mondrian's work. He called attention to the importance of the edges of the canvas that, in Mondrian, still belong to the realm of illusionism, but in *Blue Cross* are of a literal character. Throughout the 1970s, Vanderheyden enjoyed considerable attention from the Municipal Museum in The Hague, an institution that now owns a substantial part of his early works. According to Vanderheyden, the year 1970 was a turning-point. From then on, he rigorously separated himself from the outside world, including the art world. Painting itself was not to be considered as a necessary activity. A symptom of this attitude is the manipulation of his own signature. His first name (Jacob) disappears in favour of the neutral J. C. J. that creates a distance between the painter/producer and the observer. This procedure becomes understandable if one realizes that a considerable part of Vanderheyden's oeuvre consists of a re-use of his own, already executed and finished, paintings. His routine is manifold. In his studio he continuously arranges new situations with the finished canvases he has at his disposal. He observes his own paintings in various situations that he records photographically. He also uses finished compositions, usually repainted in much smaller dimensions, as part of his new paintings. Between 1967 and 1975 he made no paintings at all, only studio photos. New versions of older paintings date from after 1975. Of great importance was a trip by airplane to India in 1977. The photos taken from the inside of the plane, showing pure blue air above the white woolly clouds, have given rise to a series of convincing paintings. Vanderheyden's use of colour is very reduced and elementary (blue, yellow, black and white, and, very rarely, red). Of interest is the project *Two Cabins,* from 1972. One is dark; from the outside one sees into a closed inner space where various objects of Vanderheyden's vocabulary are barely discernible. The other one, the lighter cabin, is an outdoors piece that has a roof covered in transparent plexiglass. Here, the sky is the object of meditation.

—A. F. Wagemans

van ELK, Ger(ard Pieter)

Nationality: Dutch. **Born:** Amsterdam, 9 March 1941. **Education:** Studied art at the Kunstnijverheidesschool, Amsterdam, 1959–61; studied art and history at Immaculate Heart College, Los Angeles, 1961–63, and art history at the Rijksuniversiteit, Groningen, Netherlands, 1965–66. **Career:** Independent artist, Amsterdam, since 1961; founder with Wim T. Schippers, Adynamic group, Amsterdam, 1961–62; with Reinier Lucassen and Jan Dibbets, International Institute for Re-Education of Artists, Amsterdam, 1968. Instructor, Ateliers 63, Haarlem, since 1972. **Agent:** Art and Project; Prinsengracht 785, Amsterdam. **Address:** Oude Zijds Achterburgwal 198, Amsterdam, Netherlands.

Individual Exhibitions:

1962 Museum Fodor, Amsterdam (with Wim T. Schippers)
Dilexi Gallery, Los Angeles
1965 Instituut voor Kunstgeschiednis, Groningen, Netherlands
1966 Galerie Swart, Amsterdam
1967 Galerie de Mangelgang, Amsterdam
Galerie Espace, Amsterdam
1968 Galleria La Nueva Loggia, Bologna (with Marinus Boezem)
Galerie Swart, Amsterdam (with Marinus Boezem and Jan Dibbets)
1969 Koninklijke Academie voor Beeldenden Kunste's, Hertogenbosch, Netherlands
Galerie Walenkamp, Leiden
Kunstkring, Rotterdam
1970 Art and Project, Amsterdam
1971 Mount San Antonio College, Walnut, California
Art and Project, Amsterdam (2 exhibitions)
De Utrechtse Kring, Neudeflat, Utrecht
Pomona Art Gallery, Los Angeles (with Ader and Leavitt)
1972 Montgomery Art Center, Claremont, California
Nova Scotia College of Art and Design, Halifax
Art and Project, Amsterdam
Kabinett Fur Aktuelle Kunst, Bremerhaven, West Germany
Utrechten Ring, Utrecht
1973 Stedelijk Van Abbemuseum, Eindhoven, Netherlands
Galerie Ernst, Hannover
Wide White Space Gallery, Antwerp
Wide White Space Gallery, Brussels
Galerie Waalkens, Finsterwolde, Netherlands
Grafiek 50 VZW, Waicken, Belgium
Claire Copley Gallery, Los Angeles
1974 Art and Project, Amsterdam (2 exhibitions)
Nigel Greenwood Gallery, London
Stedelijk Museum, Amsterdam
Palais des Beaux-Arts, Brussels
1975 Museum of Modern Art, New York
Stedelijk Museum de Lakerihal, Leiden
Palais des Beaux-Arts, Brussels
Nigel Greenwood Gallery, London
Kabinett Fur Aktuelle Kunst, Bremerhaven, West Germany
1976 Nigel Greenwood Gallery, London
1977 Art and Project, Amsterdam
Arbeiten ion 1969–1977, Badischer Kunstverein, Karlsruhe, West Germany
Rheinisches Landesmuseum, Bonn
Kunstverein, Braunschweig, West Germany
1978 Marian Goodman Gallery, New York
Hansen-Fuller Gallery, San Francisco
1979 Marian Goodman Gallery, New York
Art and Project, Amsterdam
Nigel Greenwood Gallery, London
1980 Galleria Lucio Amelio, Naples
Biennale, Venice
Kunsthalle, Basel
Musée d'Art Moderne de la Ville, Paris
Museum Boymans-van Beuningen, Rotterdam
1981 *Recent Painting and Sculpture and a Selection of Earlier Work,* Fruit Market Gallery, Edinburgh (travelled to Serpentine Gallery, London, and Arnolfini Gallery, Bristol)
1984 Art Institute of Chicago
1989 *Von der Natur des Genres,* Kunstverein für die Rheinlande und Westfalen, Düsseldorf

Ger van Elk: *Untitled II,* 1981. ©CNAC/MNAM/Dist. Réunion des Musées Nationaux/Art Resource, NY; courtesy of Musee National d'Art Moderne, Centre Georges Pompidou, Paris, France.

Galleria Massimo Minini, Brescia, Italy
1993 *Sandwiches 1991–1992,* Museum Boymans-van Beuningen, Rotterdam
1999 Van Abbemuseum, Eindhoven
The Horizon: A Mental Perspective, Stedelijk Van Abbemuseum, Eindhoven (catalog)
The Cadillac and the Nun, Stedelijk Van Abbemuseum, Eindhoven (catalog)

Selected Group Exhibitions:

1967 *Beelden en Bouwen,* Plan International, Doortwerth, Netherlands
1969 *When Attitudes Become Form,* Kunsthalle, Reme (toured Europe)
1970 *Biennale,* Tokyo
1971 *Prospekt 17,* Kunsthalle, Dusseldorf

1972 *Documenta,* Kassel, West Germany (and 1977)
1976 *Reflektie en Realiteit,* Palais des Beaux-Arts, Brussels (toured Europe)
1977 *Europe in the 70s,* Art Institute of Chicago (toured the United States)
1978 *Fotografie in Nederland 1940–75,* Stedelijk Museum, Amsterdam
1979 *European Dialogue,* at the *Biennale,* Sydney
1980 *Artist and Camera,* Mappin Art Gallery, Sheffield (toured the U.K.)
1990 *New Art Van Amsterdam,* North Carolina Central University, Hempstead (catalog)
1992 *Of Walls and Wandering,* Stedelijk Museum, Amsterdam
1994 *Du Concept à l'Image,* Musée d'Art Moderne de la Ville de Paris

Collections:

Stedelijk Museum, The Hague; Gemeentemuseum, The Hague; Museum Boymans-van Beuningen, Rotterdam; Stedelijk Van Abbemuseum, Eindhoven, Netherlands; Frans Halmsmuseum, Haarlem, Netherlands; Palais des Beaux-Arts, Brussels; Museum van Hedendaagse Kunst, Ghent; Centre Georges Pompidou, Paris; Museum of Modern Art, New York; Tate Gallery, London.

Publications:

By van ELK: Articles—''Het Eerste (Voorlopige) A Dynamische Manifest'' in *Vrif Nederland* (Amsterdam), December 1961; ''Trips voor Verzamelaars'' and ''Vele Landen Maken Licht Werk'' in *Museumjournaal* (Amsterdam), no. 2. 1968; ''The Haircut, Big Cut-Big Savings'' in *Museumjournaal* (Amsterdam), July 1971; interview with Ron K in *Ger Van Elk,* exhibition catalog, Eindhoven, Netherlands 1973; interview with Antje von Graevenitz in *Ger Van Elk: Arbeiten von 1969–1977,* exhibition catalog, Karlsruhe, West Germany 1977; ''Ger van Elk'' in *Art Press,* Special Issue, no. 17, 1996; interview with Claudia Posca in *Kunstforum International,* no. 140, April/June 1998. **Films—***The Absorption of a Shadow,* 1969; *The Fluttering Pennon,* 1969; *How Van Elk Inflates His Left Foot with His Right One,* 1969; *Self-Portrait Behind a Wooden Fence,* 1969; *Some Natural Aspects of Painting and Sculpture,* 1971; *La Pièce,* 1971; *The Well-Shaven Cactus in Identifications,* edited by Gerry Schum, 1971, *Videopiece,* 1971; *Short Play with Morandi, Klee and Kandinsky,* 1972.

On van ELK: Books—*Arte Povera* by Germano Celant, Milan 1969; *Ger van Elk,* exhibition catalog with texts by Jan Leering and Rudi H. Fuchs, Eindhoven, Netherlands, 1973; *Ger van Elk,* exhibition catalog with text by Rudi H. Fuchs, Amsterdam 1974; *The Magic Image: The Genius of Photography from 1839 to the Present Day by* Cecil Beaton and Gail Buckland, London and Boston 1975; *Ger van Elk: Arbeiten von 1969–1977,* exhibition catalog with texts by Rudi H. Fuchs and Michael Schwarz, Karlsruhe, West Germany 1977; *Fotografie in Nederland 1940–1975,* exhibition catalog by Els Barents, Amsterdam 1977; *Ger van Elk: La Biennale di Venezia 1980,* exhibition catalog with texts by Gijs Van Tuyl and Wim Beeren, Amsterdam 1980; *Ger van Elk,* exhibition catalog with texts by Suzanne Page, Jean-Christophe Ammann, and Wim Beeren, Rotterdam 1980; *Ger van Elk: Recent Paintings and Sculpture and a Selection of Earlier Work,* exhibition catalog with texts by Jean Fisher and others, Edinburgh 1981. **Articles—**''Ger Van Elk'' by Robert Simon in *Artforum,* vol. 38, no. 7, March 2000; ''Ger Van Elk: Manipulateur d'Horizons'' by Valerie Marchi in *L'Oeil* (Lausanne), no. 520, October 2000.

* * *

In Ger van Elk's work, perception is arbitrary; he manipulates facts that common sense tells us are self-evident to the perceiver. Fitting the image to an idea, he presents the image and the idea simultaneously, as a dialectical whole no longer divisible. In this way he constructs a representation played on the complexity of individual psychic activity; reality is defined as a dimension internal to the object which can be manifested only through individual subjectivity. Van Elk uses photographic pictures; he manipulates them, paints over them, distorts the dimensions, alters the perspective by shifting the vanishing point of the picture according to mental demands, removes or adds, associates the idea with the shape, deriving a representation which, while it uses techniques characteristic of surrealism (extrapolation of detail, substitutions, removal of elements, presentation of the image out of context), results in an art that is not surrealist, in that the unconscious component is associated with a definite mental planning, full of conscious, often autobiographical, references, which is legitimized through the awareness acquired from the ''pre-pictorial'' art of the 1970s. By means of a ''monumental'' figuration using ''exaggerated'' dimensions, which brings out the tension between the opposed elements, the trick of separatism-dualism is presented as a dialectical whole. In this way the photographic image is also reintroduced into the painted picture and amplifies its evocative and allusive capacity. By forcing the lines of reality into a geometrizing figuration, the artist paradoxically geometrizes reality itself to its extreme formal effects. That leads to a situation of friction between sense and nonsense, giving rise to a suggestion of interpretation oriented in the direction of the forces internal to the field taken as the area of operative intervention; just as the artist dismantles the rules of perspective, so the viewer of the work is obliged to dismantle the rules of normal everyday interpretation. Thus we find here, in a behavior pattern area of a reality that he has adopted as internal to his own constitution, new ''necessary'' aspects that make of his actual ''structure'' a ''polylegible'' whole.

—Demetrio Paparoni

van KONINGSBRUGGEN, Rob

Nationality: Dutch. **Born:** Rudolphus Johannes Philippus van Koningsbruggen, in The Hague, 23 September 1948. **Education:** Koninklijke Academie voor Beeldende Kunsten, The Hague, 1968; Vrije Akademie The Hague, 1969–70; Ateliers 63, Haarlem, 1976–72. **Career:** Painter, living and working in Amsterdam, since 1973. **Agent:** Galerie van Krimpen, Prinsengracht 629, Amsterdam. **Address:** Louriergracht 166, Amsterdam, Netherlands.

Individual Exhibitions:

1970 Galerie Nouvelles Images, The Hague
1971 Galerie de Mangelgang, Groningen, Netherlands

Galerie Orez, The Hague
1972 Galerie Swart, Amsterdam
Haags Gemeentemuseum, The Hague
1973 Galerie Swart, Amsterdam
1974 Galerie Waalkens, Finsterwolde, Netherlands
Galerie t'Venster, Rotterdam
Van Abbemuseum, Eindhoven, Netherlands
1975 Galerie Swart, Amsterdam
1976 Galerie Swart, Amsterdam
1977 Galerie Swart, Amsterdam
Galerie Swart, Amsterdam
Galerie Swart, Amsterdam
1978 Galerie Swart, Amsterdam
1979 Verfindustrie Jac Eyck BV, Heerlen, Netherlands
Schilderijen/Paintings 1971–78, Stedelijk Museum, Amsterdam
1980 Galerie M, Bochum, West Germany
Galerie Swart, Amsterdam
1981 Galerie van Krimpen, Amsterdam
1982 Museum Fodor, Amsterdam
Galerie van Krimpen, Amsterdam
1983 Galerie van Krimpen, Amsterdam
1984 Galerie van Krimpen, Amsterdam
1985 Rijkschuur Acquoy, Amsterdam
Galerie van Krimpen, Amsterdam
1986 Galerie van Krimpen, Amsterdam
1987 *Rob van Koningsbruggen: Paintings and Drawings 1979–87,* Museum Boymans-van Beuningen, Rotterdam
Rembrandthuis, Amsterdam
1988 *Rob van Koningsbruggen: Paintings and Drawings 1971–1988,* Centre d'Art Contemporain, Saint-Priest, France
1996 *Rob van Koningsbruggen: Paintings 1986–96,* Stadsgalerij Heerlen, Netherlands

Selected Group Exhibitions:

1973 *Lof der Tekenkunst,* Van Abbemuseum, Eindhoven Netherlands
1974 *11 Dutch Artists,* Fruit Market Gallery, Edinburg (travelled to the Aberdeen Art Gallery)
1975 *Dutch Modern Art,* Museum of Modern Art, Ghent
1976 *7 Hollandische Kunstler,* Kunstmuseum, Lucerne
1979 *Gallery Artists,* Galerie Swart, Amsterdam
1980 *Neue Malerei aus den Nederlanden,* Neue Galerie am Landesmuseum Graz, Austria
1983 *Modern Dutch Painting,* National Gallery, Athens
1985 *De Nederlandse Indentiteit in de Kunst na 1945,* Rijksmuseum Vincent van Gogh, Amsterdam
1987 *19th Bienal,* Sao Paulo, Brazil
1996 *In Conversation with Vermeer: Contemporary Art in Dialogue,* Stedelijk Museum Het Prisenhof, Delft

Collections:

Stedelijk Museum, Amsterdam; Haags Gemeentemuseum, The Hague; Museum Boymans-van Beuningen, Rotterdam; Groninger Museum, Groningen, Netherlands; Stedelijk Museum, Schiedam, Netherlands.

Publications:

On van KONINGSBRUGGEN: Books—*Rob van Koningsbruggen,* exhibition catalog, The Hague 1972; *Konstruktive Konzepte* by Willy Rotzler, Zurich 1977; *Rob van Koningsbruggen: Schilderijen/ Paintings 1971–78,* exhibition catalog with text by Rini Dippel, Amsterdam 1979; *Rob van Koningsbruggen: Schilderijen en tekening 1979–1987,* exhibition catalog with text by Erik Beerken, Rotterdam 1987; *Rob van Koningsbruggen: Paintings and Drawings 1971–1988,* exhibition catalog, Saint-Priest 1988; *Visual Arts in the Netherlands* by Rene W.C. Dressing and Mathilde Roskam, Hague 1989; *Rob van Koningsbruggen: Paintings 1986–96,* exhibition catalog, Heerlen 1996. **Articles**—''Van Koningsbruggen schrift en breit'' by Caret Blotkamp in *Vrije Nederland* (Amsterdam), 27 March 1971; ''Signalement van Rob van Koningsbruggen'' by T. Cruls in *Museumjournaal,*(Amsterdam), vol. 16, no. 4, 1971; ''Rob van Koningsbruggen breit zeroistische avonturen'' by K. Schipper in *Haagse Post* (The Hague), 21 April 1971; ''Waarom Rob van Koningsburggen strafregels schreef'' by Dolf Welling in *Haagsche Courant* (The Hague), 30 October 1972; ''Van Koningsbruggen's debuut als schilder'' by Carel Blotkamp in *Vrije Nederland* (Amsterdam), 11 November 1972; ''Twee Schilders: Rob van Koningsbruggen, Toon Berhoef'' by Carel Blotkamp in *Museumjournaal* (Amsterdam), vol. 24, no. 2 1979; ''De modelfunctie van Rob van Koningsbruggen'' by Carel Blotkamp in *Museumjournaal* (Amsterdam), no. 6, 1985.

*

Everything can become a mannerism, including my ''shoved'' paintings. When it has reached a certain point, I stop. I began making ''shoved'' paintings because the brushwork (in larger and larger works) also became mannered. By coincidence, I noticed that my brush itself became a painting, for on the brush was reflected the same features as appeared in the painting—so it was only a small step to use my painting as a brush. Now I have abandoned also those principles. Many of my ''shoved'' paintings consisted of three parts: yellow, red and blue; and I discovered that the three primary colours could produce a deep black. Making art is making discoveries—and art in itself must be renewable. So now I am using mixture colours—orange, purple and green, and tonal extremes—and allow them to end in black.

—Rob van Koningsbruggen

* * *

The work of the 23-year old painter Rob van Koningsbruggen—and the motives behind it—caused something of a sensation in the Netherlands in 1971. Established critics such as Schippers and Blotkamp used his drawings and knitted objects as the point of departure for a debate about the ''credibility'' of the artist, although that issue had really been in the air for more than twenty years. What matters in van Koningsbruggen's work is the action involved in painting and not the work as a finished object. The painting itself is simply the residue of an action which is as concentrated and intense as possible.

Van Koningsbruggen's paintings from 1972, for example, are composed of raised horizontal streaks of paint as broad as the brush which produced them. There is no room for interpretation here: we are confronted with a simple fact (and in this respect van Koningsbruggen's work can be compared to that of the Zero artist Jan Schoonhoven). Success or failure in the usual sense of those terms is irrelevant. The artist has no knowledge in advance of how his work will finally look. This tendency is emphasized even more strongly in van Koningsbruggen's paintings after 1974. Here he uses the stretched canvas itself as a "brush." He applies paint on two canvases, on their sides or in simple geometric figures, such as circles and rectangles, painted on the surfaces; then he rubs the two canvases together for a few seconds. The results are unexpected for the painter himself, who is really no more than a machine which lets the painting create itself. There is a traditional element in van Koningsbruggen's work, in his use of color. Because he uses only red, yellow, blue and black, he invites comparison with other painters in the mainstream of 20th century Dutch artists. His work demonstrates that pictorial quality involves more than painterly skills; for him what matters is the intelligence of the artist. Even in complex works, the presence—or absence—of this intelligence is something which the viewer can sense immediately.

Van Koningsbruggen's paintings from 1981 onwards differ considerably. He has chosen to work in small scale size, the paintings themselves usually resulting from a series of long work processes. These abstract pieces are, above all, experiments in colorism. In an unconventional (and in no respect systematic) way, verging on the naive, van Koningsbruggen's goal each time is to achieve harmony anew.

—A. F. Wagemans

VAN LAMSWEERDE, Inez and Vinoodh MATADIN

Nationality: Dutch. VAN LAMSWEERDE: **Born:** Amsterdam, 1961. MATADIN: **Born:** Amsterdam, 1963. Both: **Education:** Rietveld Academy of Arts, Amsterdam, 1985–90. **Career:** Photographers; met at the Rietveld Academy of Arts, Amsterdam and have been working together ever since; residency, PS 1, the Institute of Contemporary Art, New York, 1992–93; formed Art + Commerce, a fashion, editorial and advertising photography company.

Selected Individual Exhibitions:

1991 *Licking Women,* Billboard Canon Image Center, Amsterdam
1992 *Vital Statistics,* Center for Art and Architecture and City Planning, Groningen
1993 *Heaven,* Central Museum, Utrecht
1994 *Ottobre degli Olandesi,* Solo at the Studio Bocchi, Rome
1995 *Recent Work,* Gallery Ars Futura, Zurich
The Forest, Gallery Johnen & Schottle, Cologne (travelled)
1996 *Kunsthaus,* Zurich
1997 *Inez van Lamsweerde,* Victoria Miro Gallery, London
The Widow, Matthew Marks Gallery, New York (travelled)
1998 *Inez van Lamsweerde,* ME, Matthew Marks Gallery, New York
1999 *Inez van Lamsweerde,* Photographs, Deichtorhallen, Hamburg
Inez van Lamsweerde, ME, Air de Paris, Paris
2000 *Inez van Lamsweerde/Vinoodh Matadin,* Modelphotografie, *Groninger Museum,* Groningen, Netherlands
Inez van Lamsweerde, Romance, White Cube, London
Wall 6—Landscape 6, Air de Paris, Paris

Selected Group Exhibitions:

1992 *Double Dutch—Dutch Realism Today,* Sala 1, Rome
Fotowerk, Beurs van Berlage, Amsterdam
1993 *We're Two Inflatable Dolls in a Hooker's Bad Dream,* Stedelijk Museum Bureau, Amsterdam
High Heeled Art, Charles Cowles Gallery, New York
Naardenfotofestival, Naarden Vesting
In Their Own Images, PS1, New York
1994 *Spellbound,* Centro Cultural de Belem, Lisbon; travelled to Asociacion Cultural Cruce, Madrid
L'Hiver de l'Amour, PS1, New York (travelled to Paris)
Das Archiv, Forum Stadpark/Camera Austria, Graz
Inez van Lamsweerde & Judy Fox & Maria Anna Dewes, Rudiger Schottle Galerie, Munich
Ritratto-Autoritratto, Flash Art Museum, Umbria, Italy
Oh Boy, It's a Girl!, Kunstverein Munchen, Munich
Ik en der Ander, Dignity for all, Reflections on Humanity, Beurs Berlage, Amsterdam
Suture, Salzburger Kunstverein, Salzburg
Jetlag, Gallery Martina Detterer, Frankfurt
NY-NL-XX, Gemeente Museum Helmond, Helmond
1995 *A Glimpse of the Norton Family Collection as Revealed by Kim Dingle,* Santa Monica Museum of Art, California
Somatogenics: Artist's Selections Part 1, Artists Space, New York
Disgrazia, Galleria II Ponte, Rome
Album, Museum Boijmans van Beuningen, Rotterdam
Die Muse, Gallery Ropac, Salzburg
Alterita e Identita, Venice Biennale, Venice
Purple Prose 8/12, Gallery Jousse Seguin, Paris
Kunstwerke, Berlin (with Judy Fox)
Zelfbeschikking, Gremeents Museum Arnhem, Arnhem
Peiling 4: Hollandse Nieuwe, Groninger Museum, Groningen
1996 *a/drift: Scenes from the Penetrable Culture,* Center for Curatorial Studies, Bard College, Annandale-on-Hudson, New York
Inbetweener, Centre for Contemporary Arts, Glasgow
Interzones, by Octavia Zaya, Stockholm
Printemps 1996, Groninger Museum, Groninger
Fotografie nach der Fotografie, Siemens, Munich
New Personal/New Universe, 1st Biennale di Firenze, Florence
Scanning, Stedelijk Museum, Amsterdam
Het ogg ald lasapparaat, Collages, Stedelijk Museum, Schiedam
Images of Masculinity, Victoria Miro Gallery, London
Non! Pas comme ça, Centre d'art de Neuchatel, Switzerland
1997 *A Rrose Is a Rrose Is a Rrose, Gender Performance in Photography,* Guggenheim Museum, New York

Fracturing the Gaze, Doug Lawing Gallery, Houston
My Little Pretty, Museum of Contemporary Art, Chicago
A Succession of Collections 2: Surrealism, Wexner Center for the Arts, Columbus, Ohio
Discomfort, Santa Barbara Contemporary Arts Forum
Taxonomy, Museum of Modern Art, Oxford
Fashion in Art, Ropac Gallery, Paris
Engel: Engel, Kunsthalle Wien, Vienna
Summer Exhibition, Matthew Marks Gallery, New York

1998 *Presumed Innocence,* Anderson Gallery, Virginia Commonwealth University (travelled to Bordeaux, France)

1999 National Gallery, Rekyavick, Iceland (catalog)
Officina Europa, Galleria d'Arte Moderna, Bologna (catalog)
Zeit Wende, Kunstmuseum, Bonn

2000 *Je ne suis pas une pénélope,* Espace Culturel François Mitterand, Beauvais
Cherchez l'erreur, la Galerie, Montpellier
Biennale de Kwang Ju, Korea.
Le corps mutant, Galerie Enrico Navarra, Paris (catalog)
What if, Art on the Verge of Architecture and Design (with Philippe Parreno), Moderna Museet, Stockholm (catalog)
Let's Entertain (with Philippe Parreno). Walker Art Center, Minneapolis (travelled to Portland Art Museum, Oregon; Centre Georges Pompidou, Paris; Museo Rufino Tamayo, Mexico; and Miami Art Museum, Florida) (catalog)

Publications:

By VAN LAMSWEERDE and MATADIN: Articles—Interview by Demetrio Paparoni in *Tema Celeste,* March 1998; Interview with Inez van Lamsweerde and Vinoodh Matadin by Ali Mahdavi in *Bloc Notes,* no. 16, Winter 1999.

On VAN LAMSWEERDE and MATADIN: Books—*Fictie en non-fictie in fotografie* by Miriam Westen, Hervormd Nederland, 1992; Exhibition catalog by Renato Barilli, Romagna 1999; *Inez van Lamswerde, Photographs* (exhibition catalog) by Schirmer and Mosel, Hamburg 1999; *Les anées 90,* edited by Anne Bony, Editions du Regard, 2000; *The Impossible Image,* introduction by Robin Derrick, London 2000. **Articles—**''Van Lamsweerde persifleert pornofoto's'' by Renee Steenbergen in *NRC Handelsblad,* 11 April 1992; ''Inez van Lamsweerde, Chic Shocker'' by Jules Marshall in *Wired,* February 1994; ''Meine Arbeit ist eine exterme Vergroserung'' by Jules Marshall in *Texte zur Kunst,* March 1994; ''Openings: Inez van Lamsweerde'' by Collier Schorr in *Artforum,* October 1994; *Flash Art,* November 1994; ''Inez van Lamsweerde'' by Mark Wilson in *Flash Art,* May-June 1995; ''Les femmes mutantes d'Inez Van Lamsweerde'' in *Le Monde,* 4 May 1996; ''Inez van Lamsweerde: The Forest'' by Jürgen Raap in *Kunstforum,* May-June 1995; ''Inez van Lamsweerde: The Forest at Torch Amsterdam'' in *Flash Art,* August 1995; ''Inez van Lamsweerde: The Forest at Johnen & Schöttle Cologne'' in *Artforum,* September 1995; ''Inez van Lamsweerde, Johnen & Schöttle'' by Yilmaz Dziewior in *Artforum,* September 1995; ''Photographers Inez van Lamsweerde/Vinoodh Matadin, Designer Veronique Leroy'' by Olivier Zahm in *Artforum,* February 1996; ''Inez van Lamsweerde at Matthew Marks'' by Susan Harris in *Art in America,* October 1997; ''Inez van Lamsweerde'' by Grady T. Turner in *Flash Art,* October 1997; ''Jail Bait at the Millenium: Lolita's Grotesque Body'' by Michael Slaven in *New Art Examiner,* June 1998; ''The Clown Princes'' by Stuart Shave in *Sunday Times* (London), 9 August 1998; ''Inez van Lamsweerde'' by Roberta Smith in *New York Times,* 8 January 1999; ''Emois et moi'' by Stéphanie Cohen in *Numéro #1,* March 1999; ''Inez van Lamsweerde, Obsessions'' by Yvette Brackman in *Flash Art,* March-April 1999; ''La photographie pour rester vivant'' by Michel Guerrin in *Le Monde,* 28–29 March 1999; ''La folie du réel'' by Dominique Baqué in *Art Press,* no. 246, May 1999; ''Digital Lies'' by Roy Exley in *CVA-Contemporary Visual Arts,* Issue 31, 2000; ''Visual Art: Art or Advertisement? You Make the Choice; New Shows of Work by Artists who also Work as Fashion Photographers Raise Questions of Commerce and Culture'' by Michael Bracewell in *The Independent* (London), 3 September 2000; ''Casting Himself into a Corner'' in *The Evening Standard* (London), 15 September 2000; ''Art et Mode S'observent en Photographie; Peu de Vetements, Peu de Glamour—le Cliches des Magazines et les Oeuvres d'Art Convergent'' by Michel Guerrin in *Le Monde,* 12 February 2001.

* * *

The question that characteristically leads all considerations of this Dutch team's work is, ''Art or fashion?'' A champion of their work, British *Vogue* Art Director Robin Derrick responds in a newspaper interview, only somewhat facetiously, ''The only difference between art and fashion photography is that art is printed bigger.'' Matadin has said in the text to a recent V&A exhibition, ''Fashion work is like a sketchbook for our next artwork.'' And Van Lamsweerde told *The Daily Telegraph,* ''There's a different approach. We make pieces for the gallery every two years, we do three fashion stories a month. It's not more superficial, it's just different.''

Their duality is nothing unique. Scores of artist photographers have created images for fashion magazines over the past century, Edward Steichen, Brassaï, Man Ray, and Diane Arbus among them. Van Lamsweerde and Matadin have thrived in the fashion world of the 1990s, where the avant-garde is courted in order to achieve some distinction in an environment with an unprecedented density of image-rich media.

Van Lamsweerde and Matadin have gained renown for their avant-garde editorial spreads as well as advertising campaigns for fashion houses such as Gucci, Yohji Yamamoto, and Balenciaga. The vocabulary of these images does bear some resemblance to the works displayed in galleries and museums. Computer manipulation is likely to be employed, effecting an ambiguous ''against nature'' re-formulation. The body is usually the subject, and there may well be some provocation about gender, beauty, absence, mystery, and the synthetic world. Both facets of the team's work share a tendency to provoke political and philosophical discourse, and are most likely to be deeply disquieting.

Van Lamsweerde and Matadin met in art school before 1990 and moved to New York for a P.S.1 artist-in-residence stint in 1992–93. They describe their teamwork thus: van Lamsweerde snaps the photograph, and everything else is teamwork. Some fans and subjects like Madonna describe Matadin's creative role in the fashion vernacular as ''stylist.'' In 1994 *The Face,* a British magazine that shows fashion in zealously iconoclastic editorial spreads, published the first fashion photographs by van Lamsweerde and Matadin.

The ''Thank you, Thighmaster'' series, created during their tenure at P.S.1, was a group of nudes that had all female sexual attributes, as well as faces, eradicated—clearly a reference to the fashion world, and quite unnerving. Van Lamsweerde's explanation was, ''I wanted to stress that there can be a body that is perfect but otherwise useless.''

''The Forest,'' a series of dreamy polo-shirted male models, featured gender ambiguity, as the models had their hands digitally replaced by manicured women's ones, stifling their masculine power to caress or to act violently. ''Final Fantasy'' was surely intended to cause the viewer to cringe, with its three-year-old female models photographed behind a glass wall, with digitally superimposed adult men's mouths. These mutants are related to the men in ''The Forest,'' in that they inspire doubts about sexuality and even bio-technology.

''The Widow,'' their first U.S. solo exhibition, featured an eight-year-old model named Kirsten and was a meditation on death, sex and religion. The youth of the model dressed up in couture was not the chief point. The child-bride was selected, according to van Lamsweerde, because her special age is somehow divine, by being already knowing yet still neuter.

''Me''—consisting of portraits of people related to the team—features a series of people photographed foreshortened and lying on the same white linens. They present autobiographical aspects of the artists (and include van Lamsweerde and Matadin). These are a very different post-manipulated view of humans—not polished, not mutated, but splayed out in a pose that serves to utterly abstract their figure in the frame. These have not been re-formed with ''paint box'' software, as earlier series were, but are raw and meditative.

The pair's most reproduced recent image, used in advertising for the Whitney Museum of American Art, is the self-portrait ''Me Kissing Vinoodh (Passionately)'' which uses erasure to mutate, rather than distortion. Vinoodh's presence is noted on van Lamsweerde's mouth, but his image has disappeared.

They are moving now to digital video for their work. Van Lamsweerde told *Creative Review* in 2000, ''Video will open up a different language and a different way of creating imagery which will generate a more emotional way of capturing those in-between moments that you miss with still photography.''

—Deirdre Donohue

van MUNSTER, Jan

Nationality: Dutch. **Born:** Gorinchem, 3 July 1939. **Education:** Attended the Academie van Beeldende Kunsten, Rotterdam, 1955–57; Institut vor Kunstnijverheidsonderwijs, Amsterdam, 1957–60. **Family:** Married Geertje de Stigler in 1962; daughter: Anna-Lorene. **Career:** Independent artist, working with light and sound environments, in Gorinchem, 1960–66, in Rotterdam, 1967–85, and in Renesse, since 1985. Art instructor, Ateliers 63, Haarlem, 1970–72; Academie voor Beeldende Kunsten, Rotterdam, 1973–74; Koninklijke Academic voor Kunst en Voormgeving, 's-Hertogenbosch, since 1978. **Awards:** A. Schwarz Prize for Sculpture, 1966; Travel Scholarship to London, 1967, Grant, 1969, and Film Bursary, 1973, Ministrie van Cultuur, Recreatie en Mattschappelijk, 1967; Object Prize, Salon van de Maassteden, Schiedam, 1969; Chabot-Prize, Rotterdamse Anjerfonds, 1971. **Agents:** Galerie Fenna de Vries, Eendrachtplein 18, Rotterdam; and Galerie Orez, Paviljoensgracht 68–70, The Hague. **Address:** Rampweg 24, 4326 LK Noordwelle (Renesse), Netherlands.

Individual Exhibitions:

1962 Galerie 't Venster, Rotterdam (with Ad Dekkers)
1963 Galerie de Drie Hendricken, Amsterdam (with Ad Dekkers)
1964 Galerie Pont 31, Dordrecht, Netherlands (with Marinus Boezem)
Rotterdamse Kunststichting, Rotterdam (with Ad Dekkers)
1965 Galerie C. C. C., Schiedam, Netherlands
Galerie Garage, Gorcum, Netherlands
Galerie 845, Amsterdam (with Marinus Boezem)
Dromedaris, Enkhuizen, Netherlands (with Marinus Boezem)
1966 Rotterdamse Kunstkring, Rotterdam (with Nans Verweij)
De Jong-Bergers, Maastricht, Netherlands
1967 Galerie Espace, Amsterdam
Galerie Waalkens, Finsterwolde, Netherlands
Galerie C. C. C., Vlaardingen, Netherlands
1968 Market 17, Enschede, Netherlands
Galerie Julicher, Gutzenrather, West Germany
Galerie Ad Libitum, Antwerp
1969 Galerie C. C. C., Vlaardingen, Netherlands (with Mathieu Ficheroux)
Galerie Mickery, Loenersloot, Netherlands
Stedelijk Museum, Amsterdam
Internationale Galerie Orez, The Hague
1970 Dordrechts Museum, Dordrecht, Netherlands
Van Abbemuseum, Eindhoven, Netherlands
Centraal Museum, Utrecht
1971 Galerie Design, Rotterdam
Galerie Design, Rotterdam (Chabot-Prize exhibition)
1972 Museum Boymans-van Beuningen, Rotterdam (retrospective)
Galerie Fenna de Vries, Rotterdam
1973 Henie-Onstad Kunstsenter, Hovikodden, Norway (with Pieter Engels and Wim Gijzen)
Galerie Yaki Komblit, Amsterdam
1974 Electric Gallery, Toronto
1975 Galerie Fenna de Vries, Rotterdam
1977 Galerie Orez, The Hague
1978 *Jan van Munster/David van de Kop/Wim Gijzen; Recent Werk,* Rijksmuseum Kröller-Muller, Otterlo, Netherlands
1980 Galerie Orez, The Hague
1981 Kunstcentrum Radhuis, Gorinchem, Netherlands
1982 Galerie Orez, The Hague
Kruithuis, Den Bosch, Netherlands
1983 Galerie Pictura, Dordrecht, Netherlands
1984 Galerie Orez Mobiel, The Hague
1986 Grote Kerk, Goes, Netherlands (installation)
1987 Suzanne Niederberg Galerie, Amsterdam
Galerie A. Hoffman, Friedberg, West Germany

Wilhelm-Hack-Museum, Ludwigshafen, West Germany
1988 Galerie A. Hoffmann, Friedberg, West Germany
Rijksmuseum Kroller-Muller, Otterlo, Netherlands
Museum Boymans-van Beuningen, Rotterdam
1989 De Vleeshal, Middelburg
Galerie Fortlaan 17, Gent
1990 Zeeuws Museum, Middleburg
Galerie Hermans, München
Kunstvereinigung, Deipenheim (catalog)
1991 De Beyerd, Breda
Museum D'hont Dhaenes, Deurle
Art Affairs, Amsterdam
Galerie Fortlaan 17, Gent
Quint Krichman Projects, La Jolla
1992 Landesmuseum Oldenburg
Galerie Paul Sties, Frankfurt
1993 Quint Krichman, San Diego
De Zoonehof, Amersfoort
Haus für Kunstruktive und Konkrete Kunst, Zurich
Proviniciaal Museum Hasselt, Belgium
Art Affairs, Amsterdam
Rosa Esmann Gallery, New York

Selected Group Exhibitions:

1963 *Gorkum '63,* Nieuwe Doelen, Gorinchem, Netherlands
1964 *Stichting Nieuw Beelden,* Stedelijk Museum, Amsterdam
1965 *4th Biennale de Paris,* Musée d'Art Moderne de la Ville, Paris (and *8th Biennale,* 1973)
1967 *Science Fiction,* Kunsthalle, Berne
1970 *7 Rotterdam Kunstenaars,* Museum Boymans-van Beuningen, Rotterdam
1972 *Van Medicijnman tot Medicus,* Frans Halsmuseum, Haarlem
1978 *Paper for Space,* Stedelijk Museum, Amsterdam
1982 *Beelden op de Berg,* Wageningen Museum, Netherlands
1984 *Kunst aus Rotterdam,* Museum Boymans-van Beuningen, Rotterdam
1986 *Von zwei Quadraten,* Wilhelm-Hack-Museum, Ludwigshafen, West Germany
Die Ecke, Galerie A. Hoffman, Friedberg-Inngolstadt-Sion
Von zwei Quadraten, Wilhelm Hack Museum, Luswigshafen
1989 *Art Line/Kunstijn,* Station Zwolle
1992 *Brain,* Internal Affairs, Gorinchem
1998 *Waves Breaking on the Shore...Ad Dekkers in His Time,* Stedelijk Museum, Amsterdam (catalog)

Collections:

Museum Boymans-van Beuningen, Rotterdam; Stedelijk van Abbemuseum, Eindhoven, Netherlands; Stedelijk Museum, Schiedam, Netherlands; Dordrecht Museum, Dordrecht, Netherlands; Kröller-Müller, Otterlo, Netherlands; Rijks Collectie, The Hague; Stedelijk Museum, Amsterdam; Centre Georges Pompidou, Paris; Caracao Museum, Dutch Antilles.

Publications:

By van MUNSTER: Articles—''Kunst Kijkt naar 2000'' in *Revue* (Rotterdam), No. 6, 1968; ''Mijn Mechanische Mens'' in *Vrije Geluiden* (Amsterdam), No. 17, 1969.

On van MUNSTER: Books—*De Exploisive van het Intellect* by Jan Donia, Hilversum, Netherlands 1968; *Jan van Munster,* exhibition catalog with text by Liesbeth Brandt-Cortius, Rotterdam 1972; *Jan van Munster,* exhibition catalog with text by Jo-Anne Bimie Dantzker, Toronto 1974; *Paper for Space,* exhibition catalog with text by Gijs van Tbyl, Amsterdam 1978; *Jan van Munster, David van de Kop, Wim Gijzen: Recent Werk,* exhibition catalog with text by Paul Hefting, Otterlo, Netherlands 1978; *Kunst aus Rotterdam,* exhibition catalog by Wim Beeren, Rotterdam 1984; *De eigen ruimte—Beeldhouwkunst in Nederland na 1945* by Paul Hefting, Amsterdam 1986; *Jan van Munster: Energie Objecten, Zeichnungen, Tekeningen,* exhibition catalog with essay by Kees Broos, Friedberg 1987; *Jan van Munster,* 2 vols., with texts by Kees de Boer and Paul Hefting, Utrecht 1988; *12 X Warmte in Beeld,* Middelburg, 1989; *Jan van Munster, Over het onaantastbare,* exhibition catalog, Diepenheim, 1990; *Jan van Munster* by Lisette Pelsers, Breda 1992; *Energeia/Ergon,* Zurich, 1993. **Articles—**''Jan Van Munster: The Energy of the Sculptor'' by Piet Vanrobaeys in *Artefactum,* vol. 6, no. 31, November 1989-January 1990.

*

I am not concerned just with the visual impression of light, but especially with the fact that it is charged with invisible energy. This involves the mystical side of the object, characterized by a kind of enclosedness. What is enclosed is brought out by a particular way of arranging the elements. This produces a tension, a radiation into space, the light seeming to burst forth. . . . The light must be on, even in the black lights: that is, compressed energy, the charge there is in me, in everyone. The light is there, even if it is not visible, just as lots of things are invisible. My work is not abstract. It is concerned with emotions, with attraction and repulsion. I want to make the tension between me and others visible in the space I am working in.

—Jan van Munster

* * *

In the catalog of Jan van Munster's retrospective exhibition at the Boymans van Beuningen Museum, Rotterdam (1972), Liesbeth Brandt-Cortius described as follows the ways in which van Munster worked with light to produce form and specify space:

> In 1972, the objects became visually less important than the shape that, from the object, via the light, is projected onto the ceiling wall and floor. The tangible objects are concentrated into small closed cubes or square poles out of which a single, very simple shape is

> sawn: the outline of a square with an opening on one side, a zig-zag line or a straight or dotted line. The poles or cubes stand on the floor or hang from the ceiling, and the strong bulb inside projects the sawn-out shapes, much magnified, onto the wall, floor or ceiling. In a dark room one sees first of all the light lines, and only afterwards one sees the source of light and finds the small object. The whole area seems to be dominated by insignificant objects. Each object, with its projection, forms the image.

These light projections induced the Algemene Bank Nederland to give Jan van Munster a commission for its new head office building in Amsterdam, located in the Vijzelstraat between Keizersgracht and Prinsengracht. Here he was able to apply light in this form to architecture. The pavement is covered over the whole length of the building. Van Munster has applied his light lines in this arcade, in the floors, ceiling and along the walls. As a result, some parts are concentrated, others ''disappear.'' New space is created.

The light lines, arranged in simple geometric patterns, definitely change the actual area in one's perception and experience of it; van Munster says: ''I can make crosses, rooms and doorways from light lines.'' And in this way he has given the passage under the building a new spatial function with inbuilt light shapes in the pavement and correspondingly in the ceiling.

The shapes are: an open square, consisting of three self-expanding right angled corners—obstruction; line and dotted line—movement; parallel lines—zebra crossing; steps, seen from the side or tipped-up steps—escort (to an important point, e.g. entrance); square with openings on all sides—room or base; the same as above but in the corner of a passage—doorway; square with openings on two sides—lock; cross with double lines, signals for guiding traffic in different directions; metal benches, split in the middle, from where light shines—lighting. In these neutral geometrical shapes, van Munster has conjured up a form of ''environmental design,'' through which this small area of a city undergoes a real, palpable experience.

Both the formal means and the materials used—the intangible light—guarantee that this experience is not forced upon one. The light suggests space and plasticity: one can follow the suggestion, one can just as easily ignore it or put it aside, van Munster says: ''It remains as a guide; it is like hopscotch, whoever want to...plays the game those who don't walk through.

It is a sort of example—a guide—to a conscious experience of the environment. Nothing is enforced, as so often is the case in mental designs which compellingly instruct the users how they must act, by an emphatic use of form, colour and structure.

''Too imposed,'' says van Munster. He limits himself; he even willingly accepts the effect to the difference between day and night. His shapes are indications; for those who want to see, they change the space from the endlessly long to a series of short distances; the light offers instruction, suggesting a narrowing or widening of the space; it helps to span distances, and helps one to experience part of the space as a room, base, lock, etc. The effect of familiarization—which is already accomplished by the use of light as a spatial and plastic element—is further emphasized by the placing of the light lines at the same distances from each other as traffic lines on the road (to which everyone is accustomed). The idea is to call to mind plasticity by means of directed light. What van Munster made previously as a sculptor, in wood, stone and plastic, with mass and volume, is now realized with light in an exactly stipulated shape or form.

What he wants to achieve with light is clear in his object *Pressed Light* (1971). This object is made of two metal sheets, clamped together, with a source of light between them. The object itself, depending on the space in which it stands, becomes relatively less important, because through the radiated beams of light on the walls the whole area is ''influenced.'' Light as a definer of space in a controlled (dark) area—a distinct sculptor's concept, involving as it does the relationship between interior and exterior form—appears to work excellently in the arcade. In the space of 24 hours the suggested spatial differences are alternately strong or hardly noticed at all. An interaction between natural and artificial concepts maintains the tension in the experience.

—H. J. A. M. van Haaren

VANNI, Gian Berto

Nationality: American. **Born:** Rome, Italy, 30 June 1927; emigrated to the United States, 1979; U.S. citizen since 1992. **Education:** University of Rome, School of Art and Architecture, 1948; studied painting with Vordemberge Gildevart, Amsterdam, 1949; studied painting with Josef Albers, Yale University, New Haven, Connecticut, 1952–53. **Family:** Married Frances Gay Atkison, 1953; one son. **Career:** Illustrated several books, including *Contes de Cristal* and *La Craie Magique*; designed color scheme for a 100 apartment housing project for the city of Villejuif, France, 1953; worked as color adviser on a Luciano Emmer movie on Picasso, 1954; professor, Cooper Union School of Art, New York, 1984—; lecturer, Pratt University, New York, 1984; visiting professor, Hunter College, New York, 1984; artist-in-residence, York University, 1984. **Awards:** Diomira prize, Galleria del Naviglio, Milan, 1948; Government Grant, Amsterdam, Holland, 1949; Fullbright scholarship for painting, Yale University, New Haven, Connecticut, 1952; First Prize (for illustrations of the children's book *Contes de Cristal*), Club des Editeurs, Paris, 1957; First Prize (for illustrations of the children's book *La Craie Magique*), Club des Editeurs, Paris, 1958; First Prize, Rhein-Tiber award for painting, Cologne, Germany, 1966. **Address:** 579 Broadway, New York, New York 10012, U.S.A.

Individual Exhibitions:

1948 Galleria Margherita, Rome (catalog)
1955 Galleria Schneider, Rome (catalog)
1960 Galleria Schneider, Rome (catalog)
1962 Seligman Gallery, Seattle, Washington (catalog)
1965 Galleria ''88,'' Rome (catalog)
1970 Pierre Tisné, Paris
1977 Galleria Nuovo Carpine, Rome (catalog)

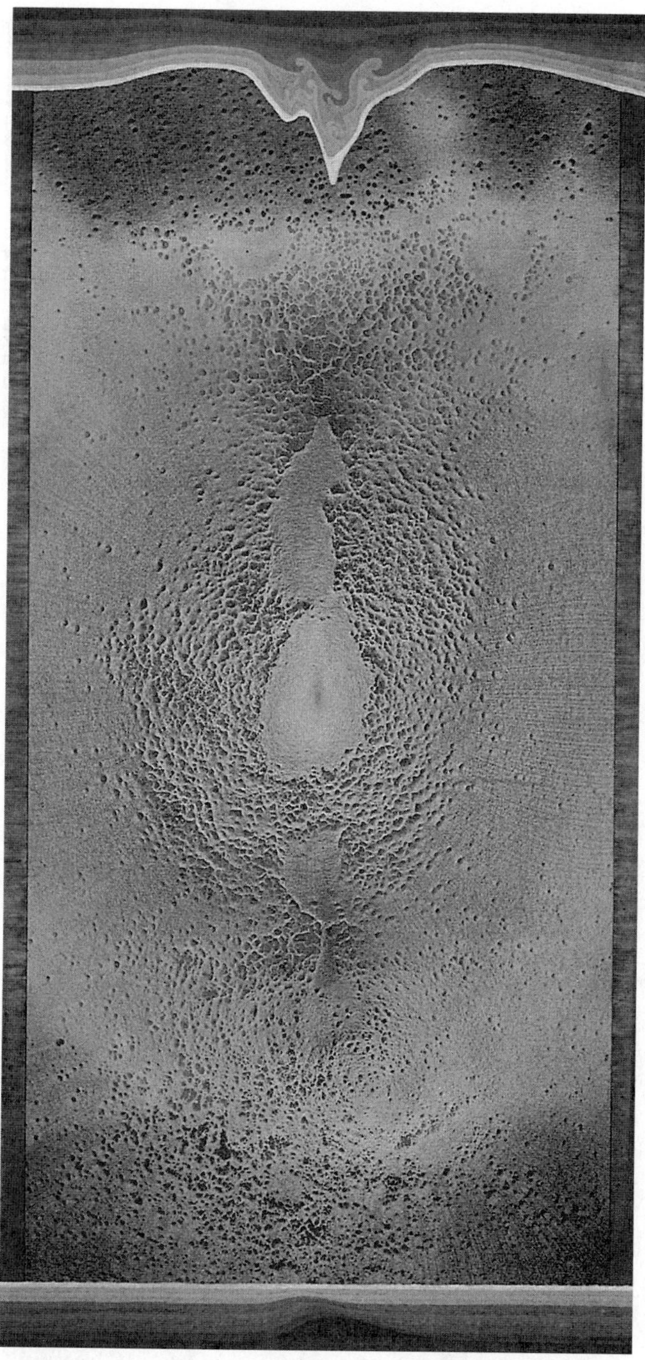

Gian Berto Vanni: *The Desert of No One,* 1999. ©Gian Berto Vanni

1979 Centre Culturel Francais, Rome (catalog)
1983 Gallery Hosun, Tokyo (catalog)
1985 Grace Gallery, New York
1989 Galerie ''88,'' Luxembourg
1989— Two open studio shows annually

Group Exhibitions:

1948 Galleria del Naviglio, Milan
1955 Quadriennale Nazionale d'Arte, Rome (catalog)
1962 Terrain Vague, Paris
1963 Mostra Nazionale d'Arte Contemporanea, Florence
1965 Braschi, Rome (catalog)
1965–68 *27 Artists from Italy,* Charlotte, North Carolina (travelled throughout United States)
1966 Premio Rhein-Tiber, Cologne, Germany (catalog)
1978 Galleria Nuovo Carpine, Rome
1985 Hunter Gallery, New York
1989 Ruth Siegel Gallery, New York
1995 Houghton Gallery, Cooper Union School of Art, New York
1999 Museo d'Arte delle Generazioni Italiane del '900 ''G. Bargellini,'' Bologne, Italy

Collections:

Musei Civici, Milan; West Holland Museum, Amsterdam; House of Representatives, Rome; Stadtliche Kunstverhein, Cologne, Germany; Seattle Art Museum, Seattle, Washington; Museo d'Arte delle Generazioni Italiani del '900 ''G. Bargellini,'' Bologne, Italy; Pieve di Cento, Bologne, Italy.

Publications:

By VANNI: Books—*Love: A Book of Découpage and Serigraphs,* with text by Lowell A. Siff, Paris and Braziller, New York 1964; *The Four Elements* (eight etchings, edition 100), Philadelphia, Pennsylvania 1981; *Five reflections on an Island* (portfolio of six etchings on poems by John Stathatos, edition 40), New York and London 1982; *Metamorphosis* (etching, edition 40), Rome 1987. **Radio—**Interview with Peter Meyer, Swedish Public Radio, 1986. **Videos—**Interview, Télé France, 1955; ''Computer Art,'' interview with Loomis Irish, CUNY New York, 28 September 1995; interview with Raffaello Siniscalco, RAI, December 1998.

On VANNI: Books—*L'Italia di Cartone* by Piero Zanotto and Fiorello Zangrando, Rome 1951; *Un Pittore Giudica l'Architettura: L'Architettura Cronache e Storia* by Bruno Zevi, 1962; *Storia dell'arte italiana del '900: per generazioni,* 5 vols., by Giorgio Di Genova, Bologna 1982—. **Articles—**''Sonen av Sodern'' in *Bonniers Magazine,* no. 10, 1951; ''Settevolante'' by Berenice in *Paese Sera,* 8 November 1961; Arturo Bovi in *Il Messagero,* 7 April 1968; ''L'Arredamento Come Ritratto d'Autore'' by G.S. in *Fine Arts, Edizione Marip,* May 1981; C. B. Firestein in *Art Speak,* 16 February 1984; ''Quadri d'America'' by Enzo Bilardello in *Corriere della Sera,* 10 April 1989.

*

A crumbling fresco can uncover another, a different world can appear, with different rules, forms, allusions, and illusions. Two different worlds can then coexist, and yet each one carries its own truth. And us, the observers, are confronted with both of them at the same time, and a third world, another possible truth, can begin to take shape in our mind. And . . . what if the ancient fresco, or painting, or vision, would reveal, in its disappearing process, a more recent world that would upset our sense of time? But is it not life itself—with its different layers of beliefs, contrasting cultures, affections, statements—to assemble these continuous discontinuities? Isn't it the message conveyed by Pirandello in his plays?

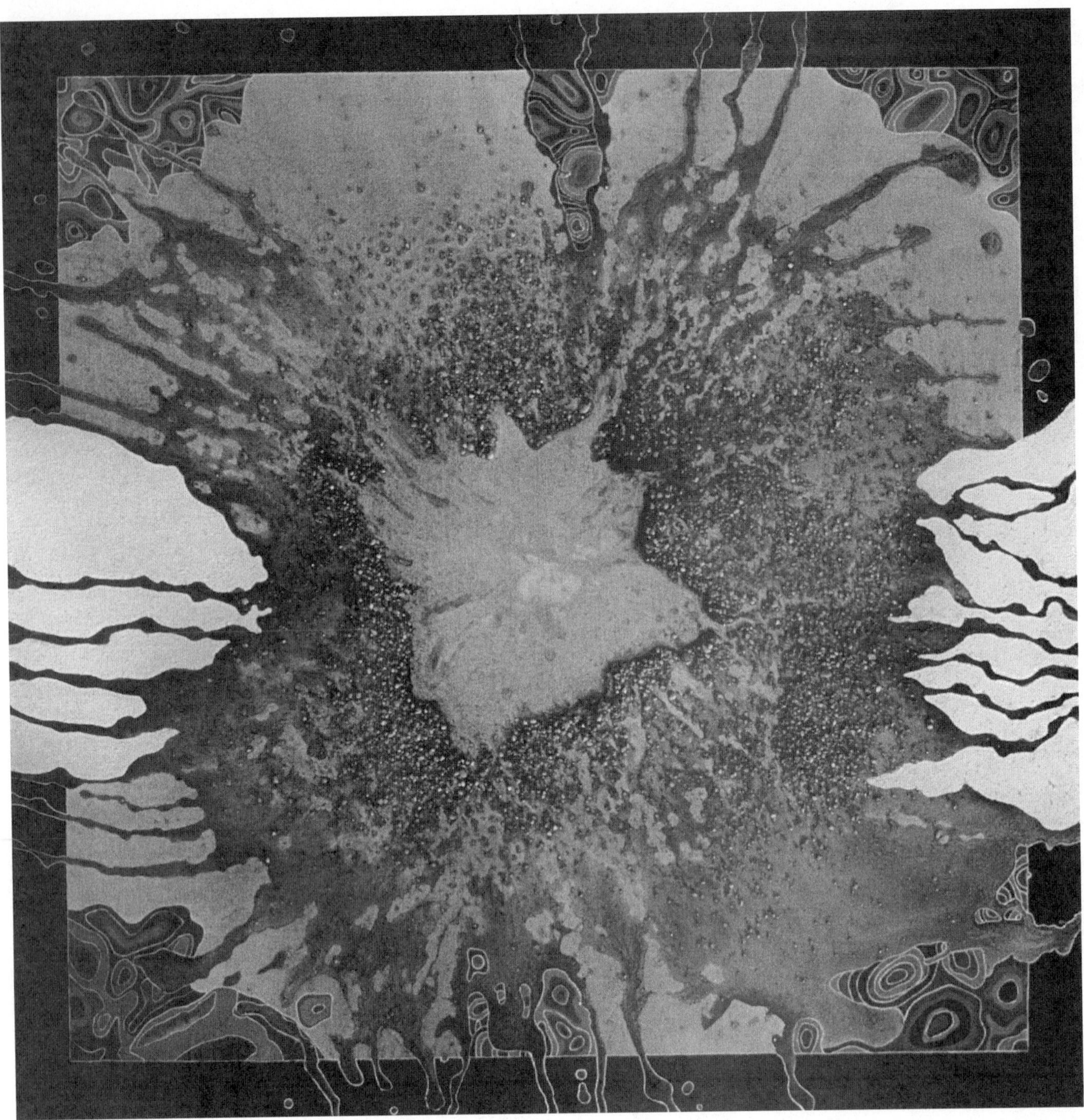

Gian Berto Vanni, *Encounter of Different Spaces,* 1999. ©Gian Berto Vanni.

Contradictions have always fascinated me and represent the essence of my work. They can be provoked by differences in style, mood, techniques, cultures. A painting seems to hide another one, that appears here and there. Cracks of the outer skin. Deeper layers can exist. Or maybe not. Figurative—or not: possibilities of associations of ideas provoked by the successive layers; stratifications of forms, stratifications of the mind. Hypothesis of possible opposite, coexisting worlds.

Myth has attracted me for the veil it casts over its more intimate realities. Many of my works deal with it. Maybe my Mediterranean essence plays its role in it, maybe my contemplation of the sea that I see from the porch of my house, in Kythira. Certainly their precise ambiguity, the ''difference-identity'' between ''Persona'' and ''Double'' and ''Mask'' inspire within me the ideal anchorage, blending and separating reality and illusion, evanescence and solidity, creating the final, superior moment of total unity.

I met it by chance, but it was waiting for me, and I had expected it to be so, to find it in that very spot, and as I was proceeding little by little to uncover its shapes I realized that I knew them, I had known them forever, affirmation confirmation denial, unwrapping from the veils—and every veil is of a different color—and it is your mirror, for you and for the others, maybe for all to understand that nothing is to be understood. . . .

—Gian Berto Vanni

* * *

The painting of Gian Berto Vanni is rooted in a multitude of different experiences, even outside the art field. During his early years Vanni was fascinated by the discovery of the microscopic world, which he was studying at the laboratories of his father, a professor of parasitology at the University of Rome, Italy.

The discovery of a biologic microcosm, so close to the forms of the Informale movement of the post-war years, nourished his painterly imagination and encouraged him to move forward after his experimentation with geometrical abstractions under the guidance of Vordemberge Gildevart in Holland in the early 1950s, and a little later at Yale University, where he studied with Josef Albers as a Fullbright fellow.

His full acceptance of ''Informale'' happened in Paris, in spite of the fact that his work was still partially influenced by memories of Klee, memories that kept coming back over the years. In the 1960s these memories helped to stimulate his undeniable decorative sense, together with the remembrance of Roman Baroque splendors, the golden mosaics of basilicas and the visual impact provided by constant visits to his beloved Greece.

The polyvalent structures of his language enable him to create sumptuous free associations of disparate chromatic and pictographic elements resulting in a symphonic mode. We could say that in his compositions one can follow the progress from *andante con moto* to *allegro vivace,* from *crescendo* to *andante misterioso.*

We should not be surprised by this parallel with music. Vanni is gifted with a dialectic of talents that enable him to orchestrate unusual and free rhythms of chromatic elements fluctuating between gravity and joy.

Undeniably, his approach lets him explore his inner world of organic forms and other forms of nature that are blended in his personal vision. His ways have set him apart from general trends, and his choice to stay away from the gallery circuits has helped make him become a sort of uncontaminated ''Lone Ranger'' in the art scene. In spite of that—perhaps because of it—he has built his own public of admirers.

Vanni's visionary world is based on ''A personal museum that at will remembers, forgets, builds, destroys, associates and divides.'' using ''cuts and rents, images, fragments, eruptions, erosions,'' according to the artist's own words.

In ''Quadri d'America'' all these elements coexist. This book represents a conspicuous body of work where one can see—one next to another—the shiny golds of Byzantium, dripping paint in the ''informale'' style, hints to the graphic neosecessionism of Klimt and to the analytic spirit of Klee. Floating placentas, butterfly wings, transfigured forests, misty swamps. . . . Yet, like in filigrain, one can catch a glimpse of geometries half submerged by a metamorphic pulsing that takes over under the shape of stalagmites of liquefied colors, of ovals whose perimeter is crowded with iridescent cells. They are all halting places on a journey through the marvelous inner world of a pictorial dream that transforms everything into something else. A labyrinth becomes a peacock eye, the rain turns into dripping paint. The chromatic arrays are a procession of snails, a fringed material creates a magic growth of red summits that reflect an amazing wealth of inflections. And this is what Vanni's work is about: it is nourished by its own making, and in the elaboration process it grows on itself thanks to a freedom of execution and a rare and precious inventiveness.

—Giorgio Di Genova

VARDANEGA, Gregorio

Nationality: Italian. **Born:** Venetia, Italy, 1923; moved with his family to Argentina in 1926. **Education:** Escuela Nacional de Bellas Artes, Buenos Aires, 1939–1946. **Career:** Independent artist; joined group Art Concret in 1946; founding member, Artistes Non Figuratifs Argentins, 1956; moved to France, 1959; lives and works in Paris. **Awards:** Gold Medal, International Exhibition, Brussels, 1958. **Address:** 21 rue de l'Amiral Roussin, 75015 Paris, France.

Individual Exhibitions:

1955 Galeria Galatea, Buenos Aires
1958 Galeria H, Buenos Aires
1969 Galerie Denise René, Paris, and Caracas, Venezuela
1970 Galerie Thelen, Essen, Germany
1972 Centre Commercial Belle Epin, Thiais, France
1976 Centre Culturel, Sceaux, France
1979 Galerie de l'Université, Paris
1991 Galerie Galarte, Paris
1996 *Exposition Personnelle à La Poste,* Paris

Selected Group Exhibitions:

1958 *Exposition International,* Brussels
1965 *Lumiere, Mouvement et Optique,* Palais des Beaux Arts, Brussels
1967 *Lumiere et Mouvement,* Musée d'Art Moderne de la Ville, Paris
1983 *Electra,* Musée d'Art Moderne de la Ville, Paris
1992 *Art d'Amerique Latin,* Centre Georges Pompidou, Paris
1993 *Art Concret-Madi-Geometrique,* Galerie Centoira, Argentina
1994 *Acrochage 94,* Galerie Denise René, Paris
1995 *La Transparence dans l'Art du 20th Siècle,* Musée de Beaux Arts, André Malreaux, Le Havre
1996 *Polymeres—Le Plastique dans les Arts du 20th Siècle,* Galerie Denise René at FIAC 96, Paris
1998 *Artists in Situ—Expostion a la Banque et Caisse d'Epargne de l'Etat,* Luxembourg
1999 *Art Construit & Cinétique D'Amérique Latine,* Galerie Denise René, Paris
2000 *Neon—Neons: Fluorescences—Oeuvres Lumineuses,* Galerie Denise René, Paris
Le Mouvement et la Lumière, Carte Blanche à Denise René, Musée de Cambrai, France
2001 *Hommage à Denise René,* Centre George Pompidou, Paris

Collections:

Musée d'Art Moderne de la Ville, Paris; Museo Nacional de Bellas Artes, Buenos Aires; Reclinehausen Museum, Germany; Tel Aviv Museum; Albright-Knox Art Gallery, Buffalo, New York; Hirshhorn Museum, Washington, D.C.; Museum of Milwaukee, Wisconsin; Rembrandt Art Foundation, Le Cap, South Africa; Fonds National d'Art Contemporain, France; Electricеté de France; Museo de Arte Contemporaneo, Buenos Aires, Argentina; Musée Sivori, Buenos Aires, Argentina; Musée de Melbourne, Australia; Coltejer, Medellín, Colombia.

Public Installations:

Mur Cinétique, Banque Rothschild, Paris 1969; Centre Commercial de Belle Epine, Thiais, Paris 1971; Centre Commercial de Metz Borny, 1974; Centre Commercial de Belle Epine, Thiais, Paris 1974; Centre Commercial Le Polygone, Montpellier 1974; Centre Commercial Créteil Soleil, Créteil, Paris 1974; Centre Commercial Créteil Soleil, Créteil, Paris 1978; Centre Commercial Les Arcades, Noisy le Grand , Marne la Vallée 1978; Centre Commercial de Belle Epine, Thiais, Paris 1978; *La Pagode,* C.E.S. Pailleron, Paris 1980.

Publications:

On VARDANEGA: Books—*Denis René Presenta,* exhibition catalog, Milan 1989; *Abstraction Geométrique—Du Constructivisme du Cinétisme,* exhibition catalog, 1990; *Art 21–90,* exhibition catalog, Bâle, Switzerland 1990; *Art Concret Invention,* exhibition catalog, Zürich, Switzerland 1991; *Chimeriques Polymeres* by Jacques Donguy. **Articles—**''3 Peintres à la Galerie Estimulo'' by J. A. G. Martinez in *Revue Espagnole,* 1957; ''L'Art à la Recherche du Mouvement'' by J. A. Cartier in *Journal Argentine,* 1964; ''Buenos Aires, Nouvelle Capitale Artistique'' by Michel Ragon in *Revue Argentine,* April 1967.

*

The Aesthetics of Color, Light, Space, and Movement

Realization of a work of geometric construction involves order and measurement. Order and compositional balance, consequently lead, I think, to a psychological balance. If one engages in synthesis, one acquires the benefit of a purified aesthetic. Since beginning work as an artist my development has been the opposite of Concrete Art; in paintings and even constructions ''space'' as an aesthetic element was and remains essential in my work. Research into spatial and luminous drawings in the cavity of demispheres (Buenos Aires, 1947): In order to arrange colors in a space that is non-illusional, but also not concrete, I have produced works with superimposed plates of glass and Plexiglas. Each of the plates, which are units of the total composition, are separated from one another by a space of three or four centimeters (Buenos Aires 1947/48/50). Subsequently I realized graphics ''as real movement'' (1957). Later, it was the ''Couleur Lumière'' which engaged me. The longest period of my artistic pursuits—the luminous and colorful installations: ''Univers Electronique'' (Buenos Aires, 1957). The series, ''Espaces Chromatiques'' with the works-in-movement, ''Couleurs Sonores'' (Paris, 1963) with Lumineux et Sonore Synchronisés—Reliefs Lumineaux, Lumière Diffusé—Lumière specrale—Transmission of light through gasses, liquids or solids, for example: Neon, water, glass, Plexiglas, etc. Pursuits in ''Structures Lumineuses''—''Mur Cinétique,'' etc. Series of tableaux with white backgrounds, with color drawings.

—Gregorio Vardanega

VASARELY, Victor

Nationality: French. **Born:** Pecs, Hungary, 9 April 1906; immigrated to France 1930; naturalized, 1959. **Education:** State School, Budapest, until 1925; studied at the Academy of Painting, Budapest, 1925–27, and at the Bauhaus School, Budapest, 1929–30. **Family:** Married Claire Spinner in 1930; sons: André and Jean-Pierre (Yvaral). **Career:** Worked as a graphic artist, Agence Havas, Paris, and Editions Draeger Freres, Montrouge, 1930–39. Independent graphic artist, since 1930: produced first paintings, 1944; first architectural integrations, from 1954; Yellow Manifesto, Kinetic works, films and writings, from 1955; inauguration of Vasarely Didactic Museum, Gerdes Chateau, Vaucluse, 1970; Vasarely Foundation, Aix-en-Provence, 1971; Vasarely Museum, Pecs, Hungary, 1976; Vasarely Center, New York, 1978; Centre Vasarely, Oslo, 1982. **Awards:** Gold Medal, *International Biennale of Graphics,* Fredrikstad, Norway, 1974; Plastic Arts Medal, Académie d'Architecture, Paris, 1975; André Bello Grand Sash of Honor, Caracas, 1977; Der Kaiserring Art Prize, Goslar, 1978; Certificate of Distinction, New York University, 1978; Medal of the Order of the Flag of the Republic, Budapest, 1978; Gold Centenary Medal, Bruckmann Verlag, Munich, 1978. D.H.: Cleveland State University, 1977. **Member:** Honorary Corresponding Member, Institute of Nuclear Engineers, London, 1977; Honorary President, France-Hungary Association, 1977. Member, 1965, and Officier, 1985, Ordre des Arts et des Lettres, France; Chevalier, 1970, and Officier, 1981, Legion d'Honneur, France; Officier, 1978, and Commandeur, 1994, Ordre du Merite, France; Officier du Merite Culturel, Monaco, 1980. **Address:** ''Les Devens,'' 84220 Gordes, France. **Died:** In Paris, of prostate cancer, 15 March 1997.

Individual Exhibitions:

1930 Kovacs Akos Gallery, Budapest
1933 Ernst Museum, Budapest
1944 Galerie Denise René, Paris
1946 Galerie Denise René, Paris
1949 Galerie Denise René, Paris
1950 Ame Bruun Rasmussen Gallery, Copenhagen
1952 Galerie Denise René, Paris
Samlaren Gallery, Stockholm
1954 Palais des Beaux-Arts, Brussels
A.P.I.A.W., Liège, Belgium
1955 Galerie Denise René, Paris
1956 Blanche Gallery, Stockholm
Galerie der Spiegel, Cologne
1958 Rose Fried Gallery, New York
Galleria del Grattacielo, Milan
Museo de Bellas Artes, Buenos Aires
Museum of Modern Art, Montevideo
1959 Galerie der Spiegel, Cologne
Galerie Denise René, Paris
Museum of Fine Arts, Caracas

The Vasarely Foundation, established by Victor Vasarely and housed in a building he designed in 1976. ©2001 Artists Rights Society (ARS), NY/ADAGP, Paris.

1960 Galerie Denise René, Paris
Palais des Beaux-Arts, Brussels
1961 Galerie der Spiegel, Cologne
Galleria Lorenzelli, Milan
Galerie Le Point Cardinal, Paris
Artek Gallery, Helsinki
World House Galleries, New York
Hanover Gallery, London
1962 Galerie Le Point Cardinal, Paris
Artek Gallery, Helsinki
Kaare Bemsten Gallery, Oslo
Pace Gallery, Boston
1963 Taft Museum, Cincinnati
Musée des Arts Décoratifs, Paris
Kunsticabinett Klihm, Munich
Kestner-Gesellschaft, Hannover
1964 Académie des Beaux-Arts, Paris
Kunsthalle, Dusseldorf
Pace Gallery, New York
Galerie Le Point Cardinal, Paris
Kunsthalle, Berne
Hybler Gallery, Copenhagen
Brook Street Gallery, London
Haus am Waldsee, Berlin
Gemeentemuseum, The Hague
Galerie Renée Ziegler, Zurich
1965 Hanover Gallery, London
Galleria Deposito, Genoa
Galerie Handschin, Basel
Galerie Müller, Stuttgart
Pace Gallery, New York
1966 Sidney Janis Gallery, New York
Hayden Gallery, Massachusetts Institute of Technology, Cambridge
Brook Street Gallery, London
Overbeck-Gesellschaft, Lubeck
Gallery D, Prague
Galerie Denise Renée, Paris
Aura Krognoshuset, Lund, Sweden
Larrnitiere, Rouen
Galerie Aktuell, Berne
Galerie der Spiegel, Cologne
1967 Musée des Arts Décoratifs, Paris
De Cordova Museum, Lincoln, Massachusetts (graphics retrospective toured the United States)
Muzeum V, Moste, Czechoslovakia
Gallery D, Prague
Stedelijk Museum, Amsterdam
Galerie Hans Meyer, Esslingen, West Germany
1968 Sidney Janis Gallery, New York

Victor Vasarely, with one of his paintings, 1977. ©AP/Wide World Photos.

Galerie Pryzmat, Cracow
Galerija Suvremene, Zagreb
Galleria del Leone, Venice
Galerie Claude Nouel, Rouen
1969 Centre de Culture, Neuchatel, Switzerland
Galeria Rene Metras, Barcelona
Gimpel and Hanover Galerie, Zurich
Museum of Fine Arts, Pecs, Hungary
Galerie Engelberts, Geneva
Galerie Les Contards, Lacost, France
Galerie Denise René, Paris
Palace of Fine Arts, Budapest
French Institute, Budapest
1970 Galerie Veranneman, Brussels
Hungarian Institute, Paris
Knoll International, Paris
Barney Weinger Gallery, New York
Musée d'Art Moderne de la Ville, Paris (films on Vasarely)
Vision Nouvelle, Paris
1971 Galerie Suzanne Egloff, Basel
Galerie Denise René, Paris
Stratford Art Association, Ontario
Kunsthalle, Cologne
Chateau de Vacoeuil, France
Galerie Hans Mayer, Dusseldorf
Galerie Veranneman, Brussels
Minami Gallery, Tokyo
Zellweger Building, Zurich
1972 Glenbow Albert Art Gallery, Calgary (retrospective; toured Canada)
Galerie Municipale Marie-Therese Douet, Mentreuil, France (toured France)
Sidney Janis Gallery, New York
Denise René Gallery, New York
Galerie Argos, Nantes, France
Galerie Charles Kriwin, Brussels
Galerie Maurel, Nimes, France
Philadelphia Museum of Art
Museum of Ludwigshafen-am-Rhein, West Germany (toured Germany, Switzerland and the Netherlands)
Galerie Formes Nouvelles, Lyons
Galerie Semiha Huber, Zurich
Galerie Schöttenring, Vienna
1973 Gallery Moos, Toronto
Galerie Veranneman, Brussels
Galerie Philippe Reichenbach, Paris
Galerie Gulliver, Paris
Archers d'Art Plastiques, Dieppe, France
Musée de Meaux, France

Galerie Denise René Rive Gauche, Paris
Galerie Denise René Rive Droite, Paris (retrospective)
Galerie des Arcades, Biot, France
Galerie Moser, Graz, Austria
Museo de Arte Moderno, Mexico City

1974 Goodman Gallery, Johannesburg
Galerie Semiha Huber, Zurich
Galleria Annunciata, Milan
Minami Gallery, Tokyo
French Embassy, Dakar, Senegal
Heller Gallery, London
Galerie M-L Jeanneret, Geneva
Groupe Manouchian Sports Complex, Aubervilliers, France
Tour des Echevins, Luxeuil-les-Bains, France
Abbaye de Gard, Acquigny, France
Galleria La Borgogna, Rome

1975 Casino-Kursaal, Ostend, Belgium
Sala della Cultura, Modena, Italy
Chateau de Cujan, Cher, France
Galeria Theo, Madrid
Galerie Bel'Art, Stockholm
Musée du Bastion Saint-André, Ramparts d'Antibes, France
Teheran Gallery, Teheran

1976 Tel-Aviv Museum
Kunstmuseum, Dusseldorf
Galerie Denise René Rive Gauche, Paris

1977 Musée Postal, Paris
Kulturforum, Bonn
Galerie des Arcades, Biot, France
Galerie Mathilde, Amsterdam
Galerie Bel'Art, Stockholm
French Institute, Stockholm
Galerie Nordenhake, Malmo, Sweden
Museo de Arte Contemporaneo, Caracas

1978 Vasarely Center, New York (opening exhibition)
Modern Art Museum, Mönchengladbach, West Germany
Städtisches Museum, Goslar, West Germany
Hilliard Collection, Munich
Centre Culturel Jacques Prévert, Villeparisis (with Yvaral)
Galerie Inard, Paris
Vasarely Center, New York
Palm Springs Desert Museum, California

1979 Phoenix Art Museum, Arizona
Chateau de Rocheshouart, Limousin, France
Centre Culturel, Villeparisis, France (with Yvaral)
Fondation Vasarely, Aix-en Provence
Chateau de Sedieres, Correze, France

1980 Fondation Vasarely, Aix-en Provence
Fundacao Gulbenkian, Lisbon
Konsthalle, Malmo, Sweden
Galleri Homansbyen, Oslo
Galerie Heitman, Hannover
Junior Galerie, Vienna
Chateau-de-Val, Bort-les-Orgues, France
Galleria Planetario, Trieste
Ecole des Ingenieurs, Bienne, Switzerland
Young Gallery, San Jose, California
Reading Public Museum, Pennsylvania
Nanteshi Gallery, Tokyo

1981 Royal Palace Gallery, Budapest
Badisches Landesmuseum, Karlsruhe
Jazz Academy, Budapest (toured Hungary)
Midland Center of the Arts, Michigan
Hotel de Ville, Montelimar, France
Chateau de Vassiviere, Creuse, France

1982 Vasarely Center, New York
Musée des Beaux-Arts, Chateauroux, France
Centre Vasarely, Oslo
Galeria Freites, Caracas, Venezuela
Hotel de Ville, Lucerne, Switzerland

1983 Vasarely Center, New York
Societe Hongroise de Secours Mutuel, Paris
Aktion Museum, Mistelbach, Austria
Galerie des Arcades de Blot, Alpes Maritimes, France (with Yvaral)
Museum of Karcag, Hungary
Centre Vasarely, Museum of Fine Aris, Budapest
Vasarely Center, New York

1984 Hotel de Ville, Villeurbanne, France (retrospective)
Musée de Tauroentum, St. Cyr sur Mer, France
Town Hall, Leinfelden, West Germany
Artcurial, Munich (travelled to Dusseldorf)

1985 Palais des Papes, Avignon, France
Institut Francais, Budapest
Galeria S. Dubrownik, Smobor, Yugoslavia
Hotel de Ville, Villeurbanne, France
Espace Jacques Prevert, Aulnay-sous-Bois, France
Chapelle Belloin, France
Galerie du Quesne, Castillon du Gard, France

1986 Galerie der Stadt Esslingen, Neckar, West Germany
Maison de la Lithographie, Paris
Musée National des Beaux-Arts, Algiers
Kunstkreis Sudliche Vergstrasse, Kraichgau, West Germany
Alliance Francaise, Bangkok
Heimatmuseum, Gablitzhalle, Austria
Espace Belleville, France
Galerie Schemes, Lille, France
Maison Alexandre Dumas, Marly-le-Roi, France
Abbaye St. Germain, Auxerre, France
Galerie Lahumiere, Paris

1990 *Victor Vasarely: dipinti 1951–1989*, Galleria d'Arte Nuova Gissi, Turin

1991 *Victor Vasarely: Works from 1974 al 1989*, Galleria San Carlo, Milan

1992 Maison des arts, Antony, France
Kunstforum Wein
Kunstforum Vienna (retrospective)

1993 Hokkaido Prefectural Museum of Modern Art, Sapporo, Japan (travelling exhibition)
Center Noirot, Arras (retrospective)

1994 Museum of Fine Arts, Charleroi

1995 *Victor Vasarely: 50 Years of Creation*, Musée Olympique, Lausanne

1997 Galerie Lahumière, Paris
Vasarely: Erfinder der Op-Art, Wilhelm-Hack-Museum, Ludwigshafen am Rhein

Hommages a Vasarely, Musee des Beaux-Arts, Charleroi, Belgium
1998 Centro Galego de Arte Contemporánea Marzo, Zaragoza
Ulmer Museum, Ulm
2000 Fundación Juan March, Madrid

Selected Group Exhibitions:

1929 *Muhely*, Museum of Applied Arts, Budapest
1947 *1st Salon des Realities Nouvelles*, Musée d'Art Moderne, Paris
1949 *Abstract Painting*, Betty Parsons Gallery, New York
1953 *Younger European Painters*, Guggenheim Museum, New York
1958 *50 Years of Modern Art*, at *Exposition Internationale (World's Fair)*, Brussels
1961 *Le Mouvement*, Stedelijk Museum, Amsterdam
1964 *Painting and Sculpture of a Decade 1954–64*, Tate Gallery, London
1967 *Dada 1916–66*, Galleria Nazionale d'Arte Moderna, Rome
1970 *Collections Etzold*, Kolnischer Kunstverein, Cologne
1973 *The Non-Objective World 1914–55*, Annely Juda Fine Art, London (travelled to Austin, Texas)
1990 *Donation by Karin and Jules Schyl, 1990*, Konsthall, Malmo, Sweden
1991 *Selected Abstract European Prints 1949–1969*, Ars Multiplicata, Surry Hills, Australia
The Post-War School of Paris Abstract Prints, 1945–1969, William Weston Gallery, London
1994 *Chefs-d'oeuvre du musée d'art moderne Louisiana*, Musée Toulouse-Lautrec, Albi
1999 *Hofburg, Vienna: Messe fur Kunst und Antiquitaten 13 to 21 Nov.*, The Hofburg, Vienna

Collections:

Centre Georges Pompidou, Paris; Tate Gallery, London; Stedelijk Museum, Amsterdam; Musée des Beaux-Arts, Brussels; Nationalgalerie, West Berlin; Israel Museum, Jerusalem; Power Gallery of Contemporary Art, Sydney; Musée d'Art Contemporain, Montreal; Museum of Modern Art, New York; Art Institute of Chicago; Museum of Modern Art, Paris; Albright-Knox Gallery, Harvard University; Buenos Aires Museum; Montivideo Museum; Reykjavik Museum; Tate Gallery, London; Tel Aviv Museum; Dallas Museum.

Documentation of Vasarely's life and work is principally housed at the Fondation Vasarely, Aix-en-Provence: the Musée Vasarely, Vaucluse, France; the Vasarely Museum, Pecs; and the Vasarely Center, New York.

Publications:

By VASARELY: Books and pamphlets—*La Forme-couleur integrée dans la cité par la technique des revetements muraux*, Paris 1959; *Kassak-Vasarelly*, album of serigraphs, with an introduction by Denise René and Jean Cassou, Paris 1961; *Vasarely: Morphemes*, album of engravings with text by Imre Pan, Paris 1966; *Notes, Reflexions de Vasarely*, Paris 1964; *The Notebook of Vasarely*, Oxford 1964; *Discours de la methode de Descartes accompagne du discours de la methode de Vasarely*, with a preface by Otto Hahn, Paris 1969; *Plasti-Cité*, edited by Michel Ragon, Paris 1970; *Victor-Vasarely—Notes brutes*, with a foreword by Bruno Alfiere, Venice 1970; *Folklore Planetaire—Farbwelt*, Munich 1973; *Réponses á Vasarely*, Munich and Paris 1974; *Vasarely inconnu*, Neuchatel, Switzerland 1977; *Victor Vasarely Faabstadi/City Polychrome*, with a commentary by Eugen Gomringer, Munich 1977; *Vasarely* Paris 1978; *Reflets*, portfolio of 4 prints with poems by Maurice Bruzeau, Paris 1979; *Vasarely Plasticien*, with William Desmond, Paris 1979; *Gea*, Paris 1982.

On VASARELY: Books—*Vasarely* by Dewasne, Paris 1952; *Vasarely*, exhibition catalog with text by Carlo Belloli, Milan 1961; *Victor Vasarely*, exhibition catalog with text by Wieland Schmied, Hannover 1963; *Arts Plastiques du 20e. Siecle: Vasarely*, Neuchatel, Switzerland 1965; *Vasarely* by Werner Spies, Stuttgart 1969; *Vasarely*, exhibition catalog with a preface by M. E. Rosta, Budapest 1969; *Vasarely II*, Neuchatel, Switzerland 1970; *Vasarely Analysen* by Axel Bruck, Hamburg 1970; *Victor Vasarely* by Werner Spies, Paris, Cologne and New York 1971; *Gesprache mit Victor Vasarely* by Jean-Louis Ferrier, Cologne 1971; *Vasarely*, exhibition catalog with a preface by Helmut R. Leppien, Cologne 1971; *Victor Vasarely*, exhibition catalog with a preface by Manfred Fath, Ludwigshafen, West Germany 1972; *Ateliers Aujourd hui: Vasarely* by Marc Hallain, Paris 1973; *J'apprends á peindre avec Vasarely*, Paris 1973; *Arts Plastiques du 20e Siecle: Vasarely III*, with a preface by Marcel Joray, Neuchatel, Switzerland 1974; *Vasarely* by Marcel Joray, Neuchatel, Switzerland 1976; *Le musée imaginaire de Vasarely*, with a foreword by Otto Hahn, Paris 1978; *Vasarely 4*, Neuchatel, Switzerland 1979; *Vasarely: Connaisance d'un art moleculaire* by Bernard Dahhan, Paris 1979; *Colorier avec Vasarely*, Paris 1980; *Victor Vasarely*, exhibition catalog with text by Werner Spies, Paris 1988; *Victor Vasarely* by Alin Avila, Paris 1988; *Victor Vasarely: dipinti 1951–1989*, exhibition catalog, Torino 1990; *Vasarely* by Gaston Diehl, translated from the French by Eileen B. Hennessy, New York 1991; *Victor Vasarely: opere dal 1974 al 1989*, exhibition catalog, Milan 1991; *Vasarely*, exhibition catalog, Antony 1992; *Victor Vasarely*, exhibition catalog with text by Klaus Albrecht Schröder and Mária Egri, Munich 1992; *Victor Vasarely*, exhibition catalog, Sapporo 1993; *Victor Vasarely: 50 Years of Creation*, exhibition catalog, Lausanne 1995; *Vasarely*, exhibition catalog with text by Bernard Fauchille, Paris 1997; *Vasarely: Geometrie, Abstraktion, Rhythmus: die Fünfziger Jahre*, exhibition catalog, Ostfildern 1998; *Vasarely: Erfinder der Op-Art*, exhibition catalog with text by Richard W. Gassen, Ostfildern-Ruit 1997; *Vasarely*, exhibition catalog, Madrid 2000. **Articles**—"Vasarely a Slovensko" by Jiri Siblik in *Vytvarny Zivot*, vol. 34, no. 3, 1989; Obituary in *Time*, 31 March 1997; "Planetary Folklore: Jorg Heiser on the Legacy of Victor Vasarely" in *Frieze*, no. 41, June-August 1998; "Vasarely: The Collection in the Hungarian Castle" by Claudia Sugliano in *Arte*, no. 315, November 1999.

* * *

From 1930 when he moved to Paris from Budapest, Victor Vasarely followed a course that, while it initially did not renounce realistic elements, always activated the painting surface to create its own illusions of space proper to itself, and finally to nothing beyond the confines of the picture frame. His employment as a commercial artist went hand in glove with a technical proficiency that became more and more self-centered. An early work of his pre-war period—''Chessboard'' (1935)—is a forerunner of his development. It shows strength in conveying illusions of space where the surface seems to buckle and corrugate as the wavy lines swell and contract in width. His method of painting then was meticulous in its definition of form reflecting the ambivalence of Orphism and to a degree Surrealism.

In the 1940s, following his first one-man show in Paris, Vasarely committed himself to a programmed system of picture making based on geometrical modules and variations in colours that went through permutations of considerable complexity. Organic forms of circles, squares, ellipses and rectangles were arranged in compositions of ordered movement and ambiguities in which colours and tonal balances set up visual tensions of alternately harmonious and disturbing elements. This calculated adjustment of solid and transparency of warm and cold hues, of stepping and breaking of linear direction was achieved with a disposition of effect harking back to the Bauhaus principles of sheer outline and immaculate profile in space, eschewing the serif and the decorative as unnecessary in terms of architectonic logic.

''Orion MC'' (1963) is a typical example of Vasarely's concept. The rectangle offers a highly charged checkerboard design composed of 420 squares containing circles of different sizes alternating with ellipses also varied in size and placed on different axes relating to the picture edge. The whole picture presents a quivering screen of light intensity established by the tonal strength and juxtaposition of subtly animated areas. Nothing Vasarely does is uncomposed. In his refinement of mosaical permutations he has evolved striking effects from shades of five different colours placed in four different zones adjacent to each other. In 1959 he patented a system of ''plastic unity'' where he put together collages from single elements: round, oval, square, rhomboid and triangular, cut out from squares of distinctive colours and alternating them on squares of different grounds. This limitless potential and its versatility has lent itself to kinetic exploitation as well as in architectural projects as sculptures both freestanding and in relief.

Acknowledged as the originator of post-war Op Art, Vasarely had a noticeable influence on such artists as Bridget Riley without relinquishing his own authority in constructive geometric abstraction. His own belief that he had formulated a new urban folklore through a multiplicity of prototypes mechanically permutated was justified perhaps in its maturity, but its very consistency imposed an inevitable diminution in returns of aesthetic satisfaction.

—G. S. Whittet

VAUTIER, Ben

Nationality: Swiss. **Born**: Naples, of a Swiss-French father and Irish mother, 18 July 1935. **Education:** Attended schools in Turkey, Egypt, and Greece until 1949; mainly self-taught in art. **Family:** Married Annie Baricolla in 1964; children: Eva and Francois. **Career:** Independent artist in Nice since the mid-1950s; began actions and happenings and established gallery Laboratoire 32 (32 rue Tondutti-del'Escaréne), later re-named Galerie Ben Doute de Tout, Nice, 1958; associated with Fluxus artists in Paris and Cologne, 1962–70; established Galerie Fenetre, Nice, 1971, and Galerie La Difference, Nice, in late 1970s. **Awards:** D.A.A.D. scholarship to West Berlin, 1978. **Agents:** Galerie Daniel Templon, 30 rue Beaubourg, 75003 Paris, France; Galerie Bischofberger, Buhlstrasse 7, 8700 Kussnacht, Switzerland. **Address:** 103 Route de Saint-Pancrace, 06100 Nice, France. **Web site:** http://www.ben-vautier.com.

Individual Exhibitions:

1960 Laboratoire 32, Nice
1964 Amstell 47, Amsterdam
1966 La Cédille Qui Sourit, Villefranche-sur-Mer, France
1970 Galerie de la Salle, Vence, France
Galerie Yellow Now, Brussels
Galerie Daniel Templon, Paris
Galerie Hans Mayer, Dusseldorf
Galerie René Block, West Berlin
Galleria Artestudio, Macerata, Italy
1971 Galleria Sant'Andrea, Milan
Galleria Il Punto, Turin
Galerie Daniel Templon, Paris
Galerie Bischofberger, Zurich
1972 Galerie Günter Sachs, Hamburg
Galleria Lia Rumma, Naples
Galerie Grafikmeyer, Karlsruhe, West Germany
Galerie Daniel Templon, Paris
1973 International Cultureel Centrim, Antwerp
Galerie Daniel Templon, Paris
Art=Ben, Stedelijk Museum, Amsterdam
Galerie Rudolf Zwimer, Cologne
Galleria La Bertesca, Milan
Neue Galerie, Aachen, West Germany
1974 Galeria Foksal, Warsaw
Galerie Yellow Now, Liège, Belgium
Neue Galerie, Aachen, West Germany
Galerie Le Flux, Perpignan, France
1975 Galleria dei Mille, Bergamo, Italy
Studio F22, Palazzolo, Italy
Centro d'Informazione Alternativa, Rome
John Gibson Gallery, New York
1976 Galerie HM, Brussels
Kunsthandel Brinkman, Amsterdam
1977 Galleria l'Uomo e l'Arte, Brescia, Italy
Galerie Baudoin Lebon, Paris
1978 Galleria Rinaldo Rotta, Genoa
Galerie Ecart, Geneva
1979 Galleri Léger, Malmo, Sweden
Berlin Inventory, DAAD-Galerie, West Berlin
1980 Musée d'Art Contemporain, Montreal
1981 *Ben Libre,* Musée d'Art et d'Industrie, St. Etienne, France
Galerie Daniel Templon, Paris
Photos chez Stenope, Nice
Galerie Ecart, Geneva
1982 Galerie Catherine Issert, St. Paul de Vence, France
Galerie Grimaldi, Aix-en-Provence, France
Musée d'Art et d'Industrie, St. Etienne, France
Galerie Errata, Montpellier, France
1983 Galerie Beaubourg, Paris
Galerie La Hune, Paris
Galerie Donguy, Paris
Galerie Chantal Crousel, Paris
Galerie Durand-Dessert, Paris
Galerie Mollet Vieiville, Paris

Galerie Avant Premiere, Paris
Galerie Templon, Paris
Galerie Fournier, Paris
Galerie Lara Vincy, Paris
Galerie Creatis, Paris
Galerie Durand, Paris
Galerie Nez en l'Air, Nice
Galerie Catherine Issert, St. Paul de Vence, France
1984 Galerie Jollenbeck, Cologne
Galerie Ecart, Geneva
Galerie R.Z.A., Dusseldorf
Galerie Baudoin Lebon at *FIAC 84,* Grand Palais, Paris
1985 Galerie Baudoin Lebon, Paris
Galerie Bilinelli, Brussels
Galerie d'Art Contemporain, Nice
Stadtgalerie, Erlangen, West Germany
1986 Museum Ingelstad, Sweden
Sala Parpallo, Valencia, Spain
Galerie Leger, Malmo, Sweden
Galerie Daniel Templon, Paris
Galerie Semiha Huber, Geneva
Galerie Catherine Issert, St. Paul de Vence, France
Maison des Artistes, Genas (Lyon), France
Galerie Schuppenhauer, Essen, West Germany
1987 Galerie Camomille, Brussels
Musée de Calais, France
Musée de Ceret, France
Centre Regional d'Art Contemporain, Lebege, France
1988 Galerie Catherine Issert, St. Paul de Vence, France
Galerie Daniel Templon, Paris
La Jungle l'Art, Centre de creation Contemporaine
1989 Galerie Unimedia, Genes
Galerie Baudoin Lebon, Paris
Galerie Emily Harvey, New York
1990 Galerie Shupenhauer, Cologne
Galerie Catherine Issert, St. Paul de Vence, France
1991 *Une Histoire de Cul,* Galerie Daniel Templon, Paris
Je Doute Donc Je Suis, Fond regional d'Art Contemporain, Orleans
Fondation Mudima, Milan
7 Ans de Bonheur, Galerie Camomille, Bruxelles
Forum du Centre Georges Pompidou, Paris (catalog)
Je Sais J'en Fais Toujours Trop, Galerie Marianne et Pierre Nahon, Paris
1992 Galerie Catherine Issert, St. Paul de Vence, France
Centre d'Art et de Plaisanterie, Montbeliard
I Don't Want to Do Art I Want to Be Happy, Galerie Shupenhauer
1993 Musee d'art moderne et d'art contemporain, Nice
Galerie Guy Pieters, Knokke le Zoute
Maison des jeunes de Neuchatel
1994 Galerie Daniel Templon, Paris
Palais des Festivals, Biarritz
1995 Musee d'art contemporain, Marseille Retrospective (catalog)
Musee de l'Objet, Blois
Galerie Gandy, Pragues
1996 Musee d'art moderne Solothurn, Suisse
Galerie Jerome de Noirmont, Paris
Galerie Shupenhauer, Les limites de l'Art, Cologne
Galerie Lara Vincy, Paris
Rétrospective Ben Vautier, Kunstmuseum, Soleure
1997 Maison Europeenne de la photo, Paris
Galerie Gan Tokyo Japon (catalog)
CEAC Vallauris La Tour de Babel
Hotel Square Paris
1998 Galerie Jacques Girard, Toulouse
Galerie Bein Steinerman Kreuz, Bremen
Centre Culturel Français, Naples
Zabriskie Gallery, New York
Neues Museum Weserberg, Bremen, Germany (catalog)
1999 Partobject Gallery, Carrboro, North Carolina
Zabriskie Gallery, New York
Ben Vautier: Any Photo Will Do, Partobject Gallery, Carrboro, North Carolina

Selected Group Exhibitions:

1962 *Festival of Misfits,* Gallery One, London
1967 *Ecole de Nice,* Galerie de la Salle, Vence, France
1970 *Happening and Fluxus,* Kunstverein, Cologne
1973 *Contemporanea,* Parcheggio Villa Borghese, Rome
1977 *A Propos de Nice,* Centre Georges Pompidou, Paris
1979 *Fluxus,* Espace Lyonnais d'Art Contemporain, Lyons (toured Europe)
1982 *Art Vivant 60/80,* Stedelijk Museum, Amsterdam
1984 *L'Ecriture dans la Peinture,* Centre Nicois des Arts Plastiques, Nice
1987 *Berlinart 1961–87,* Museum of Modern Art, New York (travelled to San Francisco)
1990 *Fluxus Subjective,* Galerie Krinzinger, Vienna (catalog)
Fluxus S.P.Q.R., Galleria Fontanella Borghese, Rome (catalog)
1992 *Fluxus,* Galerie Hundertmark, Cologne (catalog)
Fluxus: The Development of an Antidote, Galleri Stenstrom, Stockholm (catalog)
Funny Dispatches, Centre d'Animation Culturelle de Compiegne et du Valois, Compiegne, France (catalog)
1995 *Text and Art,* Logan Art Gallery, Logan, Australia (catalog)
1997 *Art Games,* Staatsgalerie Stuttgart (also Oktagon, Cologne) (catalog)
1999 *Rendezvous,* Solomon R. Guggnehim Museum, New York
2000 *Live in Your Head: Concept and Experiment in Britain,* Whitechapel Art Gallery, London

Publications:

By BEN: Books and pamphlets—*L'Esthetique de Ben,* Nice 1960; *Programme de 7 Jours de Recherche,* Nice 1964; *Tout Programme Publik,* Nice 1965; *Tout Cedille Qui Sourit,* Nice 1966; *Galerie Ben Doute de Tout Presente,* Nice 1966; *Ben Dieu (L'Art c'est les autres),* Nice 1966; *Propositions pour un livre et pour des objets divers,* Nice 1966; *Tout Rebus,* Nice 1966; *Tout poesis,* Nice 1966; *J'aime et j'attaque no. 1,* 1967; *J'aime et j'attaque no. 2,* Nice 1968; *Tout (Musique et Cinema),* Nice 1968; *Programme pour la table,* Nice 1968; *Tout moi Ben je signe,* Nice 1969; *Reedition de rieux stencils de Ben,* Nice 1969; *Capitre idees,* Nice 1970; *Chronique touche a Tout de Ben No. 1,* Nice 1970; *A P'Art,* Nice 1977; *Reg'Art,* Nice 1978; *Bag'Art Bay'Art,* Nice 1979; *Manuscrit pour une premiere* *internationale ethniste,* Nice 1986; *La verite de A a Z,* Toulouse 1987; *Ben Vautier: Sketchbook,* Rotterdam 1991.

On BEN: Books—*Aktionen, Happenings und Demonstrationen seit 1965,* edited by Wolf Vostell, Hamburg 1970; *Catalog de films de Ben,* Paris 1971; *Mail Art: Communication à distance, concept,* edited by Jean-Mare Poinsot, Paris 1971; *Documenta 5: Befragung der Realitat,* exhibition catalog edited by Harald Szeeman and others, Kassel, West Germany 1972; *Art=Ben,* exhibition catalog with an introduction by Ad Petersen, Amsterdam 1973; *Ben Vautier: Berlin Inventory,* exhibition catalog, West Berlin 1979; *Ben Libre,* exhibition catalog, St. Etienne, France 1981; *Ben: Encore des Mots,* exhibition catalog, Lyon 1986. **Articles—**''Ben'' by Jacques Lepage in *Artstudio,* no. 15, Winter 1989; ''Ben Vautier at John Gibson and Zabriskie'' by Nicole Krauss in *Art in America* (New York), vol. 87, no. 1, July 1999.

* * *

Ben (as he signs his works) could be called the correspondence art network's Duchamp. In performance and on film he sits, or swims, or lies face down on a busy sidewalk, elevating the activity to art by giving it a title and a framework, or de-elevating art by linking it with such common actions. The notion of de-elevating art would not even arise were it not for Ben's frequent references to the questionability of the art world, the making of art and the grip that art has on him and his life.

Ben's art relies on thoughts and words; his works often contain calligraphic oneliners reflecting his humorous, reflective attitude which fluctuates between negative and positive, sometimes in the same piece. One work shows the artist sitting on a chair with a sign on his lap which reads ''Art is Useless.'' To the right is another message: ''I sold that piece, and with the money I went on holiday for a week.''

The artist is based in Nice, where he has operated a second-hand record shop and maintained widespread contact with the international art scene by publishing small books, posters, brochures, and post cards. An associate of Fluxus and the nouveau realisme group, Ben has participated in Flux kits and produced memorable rubber stamp art, a medium he has used since 1949. Post cards are especially suitable for Ben's art since they function as a support for his calligraphic text and, as multiples, are able to reach a wide audience. Two of his cards, ''Postman's Choice,'' 1965, and ''Your thumb present now .... '' 1966, are among the best known works in correspondence art.

As a participant in Mieko Shiomi's ''Spatial Poem,'' a correspondence/response project, Ben contributed responses which reflect his philosophy about art and life and the ever changing balance between the two:

> *Spatial Poem No. 2* direction event. Ben Vautier was most likely in bed facing the ceiling in Nice.
>
> *Spatial Poem No. 3* falling event. After hesitating a great deal, Ben Vautier swallowed the thin piece of paper joined to the invitation letter.
>
> *Spatial Poem No. 4* shadow event. All found the SHADOW plastic sheet in the shadow of an envelope. B)I put the SHADOW plastic sheet 1. in the shadow of a tree 2. in the shadow of myself Ben 3. in the shadow of the moon—at night 4. in the shadow of a beautiful naked girl—my daughter 5. in the shadow of . . . Then I put it into a special file for Shiomi, and it is there in the shadow of all the documents concerning her.
>
> *Spatial Poem No. 9* disappearing event. I have come to the conclusion that my interest in art is slowly disappearing.

In September 1983, *Art News* magazine reported that Ben's Nice boutique, known as Galerie Ben Doute de Tout, is now enshrined in Paris' National Museum of Modern Art at the Centre Georges Pompidou.

—Mary Stofflet

VEDOVA, Emilio

Nationality: Italian. **Born:** Venice, 9 August 1919. **Education:** Studied at schools in Venice, until 1930; mainly self-taught in painting from 1935, but attended Silvio Pucci's Free School of Painting, Florence, 1939–40. **Military service:** Served with the Italian partisans in northern Italy, 1944–45. **Career:** Worked in a local factory, Venice, 1930–37. Independent painter, in Rome, Florence and Venice, from 1937: established studio at Dorsoduro alla Salute, Venice, 1957. Director, Summer Academy, Salzburg, Austria, 1965–70; professor of painting, Accademia di Belle Arti, Venice, from 1975. **Awards:** La Colomba Prize, Venice, 1938; Volpi Prize, 1950, Drawing Prize, 1954, and Grand Prize for Painting, 1960, *Bienal de Sao Paulo,* Brazil; Guggenheim Foundation Prize for Italy, 1956; Premio Lissone, Milan, 1958; First Prize, *Drawing Biennale,* Rijeka, 1976; *Antonio Feltrinelli* International award for painting, Accademia Nazionale dei Lincei, Rome, 1993; Internationale Sommerakademie für Bildende Kunst, Salzburg, 1993. **Member:** Corrente artists movement, Milan, 1942; founder-member, Nuova Secessione (Fronte Nuovo delle Arti), Venice, 1946; Gruppo degli Otto, Venice, 1952. **Agent:** Galleria Giorgio Persano, Piazza Vittorio Veneto 9, 10124 Turin, Italy. **Address:** Dorsoduro 46, 30123 Venice, Italy.

Individual Exhibitions:

1942 Galleria Euro Romano, Genoa, Italy
1943 Galleria La Spiga e Corrente, Milan
1945 Galleria Venezia, Venice
Piccola Galleria, Venice
Galleria de Pioppo, Mantua, Italy
1946 Art Club, Rome
Galleria Del Bosco, Turin
Piccola Galleria Venezia, Venice
1947 Galleria de Cavallino, Venice
Art Club, Rome
1951 Viviano Gallery, New York
1954 Museum de Arte Moderna, Rio de Janeiro
1956 Galerie Gunther Franke, Munich (retrospective)
1957 Galerie Springer, West Berlin
1958 Zacheta Palace Museum, Warsaw (retrospective; travelled to Poznan, 1959)
Galerie Springer, West Berlin

Emilio Vedova: *Sicily, from Voyage to Italy.* ©Scala/Art Resource, NY; courtesy Museo d'Arte Moderna Ca' Pesaro, Venice, Italy.

1960 Galeria Blu, Milan (retrospective)
Galleria Il Disegno, Milan (retrospective)
Kunsthalle, Hamburg
Kunstmuseum, Lucerne
1961 Palazzo della Gran Guardia, Verona, Italy (retrospective)
Galleria Annunciata, Milan
Galleri M59, Copenhagen
Museo de Ateneo, Madrid (retrospective)
Sala Gaspar, Barcelona
1962 Galleria-Libreria Einaudi, Rome
Arco Palais Calerie, Monaco
Galleri Haghfeldt, Copenhagen
Galerie Pierre, Stockholm
Kunstverein, Freiburg, West Germany (retrospective)
1963 Galleria Marlborough, Rome
Museu de Arte Moderna, Rio de Janeiro
1964 Staatliche Kunsthalle, Baden-Baden, West Germany (retrospective)
1965 Institute of Contemporary Art, Washington, D.C. (retrospective)
Kunstlerhaus, Salzburg, Austria (retrospective)
1967 Hollaru Gallery, Prague (toured Czechoslovakia)
1968 Kunstlerhaus, Salzburg, Austria (retrospective; travelled to Ferrara, Italy)
1970 Galerie Rothe, Heidelberg, West Germany
1971 Forum Gallery, Zagreb, Yugoslavia
1972 Galleria Falchi, Milan
1973 Kunstmuseum, Dusseldorf
1974 Galleria Linea 70, Verona, Italy
1975 Teatro Romano, Aosta, Italy
Castello Visconteo, Pavia, Italy (retrospective)
1976 Galleria Mariani, Ravenna, Italy
1978 Museo Castello, Portofino, Italy (retrospective)
1979 Sala Medievale di San Jacopo, Prato, Italy (retrospective; toured Australia)
1980 Galerie im Taxispalais, Innsbruck (toured Austria)
Museo Carrillo Gil, Mexico City
Galleria Planetario, Trieste, Italy
1981 Städtisches Museum, Leverkusen, West Germany
Palazzo dei Congressi, San Marino
Kunstverein, Braunschweig, West Germany
1982 Van Abbemuseum, Eindhoven, Netherlands

Galleria d'Arte Moderna, Bologna, Italy
Galerie Annemarie Verna, Zurich
Mura Aureliana, Rome
1983 Galerie Annemarie Verna 2, Zurich
Istituto Artistiche Universitario, Venice
Galleria Stevens, Padua, Italy
Galerie Thomas Borgmann, Cologne
Galerie Fred Jahn, Munich
Studio Marconi, Milan
Galerija Sebastian, Belgrade
Galerie Neuendorf, Hamburg (travelled to Venice)
1984 Galleria Loza/Gaileria Meduza, Capodistria, Yugoslavia
Museo Correr, Venice
Galleria San Marco, Rome
1985 Galerie Buchmann, Basel
Galleria Giorgio Persano, Turin
Museo del Castello, Rivoli, Italy
1986 Galleria Tomabuoni, Florence
Staatsgalerie Moderner Kunst, Munich
Galerie Fred Jahn, Munich
Musée Ingres, Toulouse, France
Städtisches Museum, Leverkusen, West Germany
Galerie Ulysses, Vienna
Kunsthalle, Darmstadt, West Germany
Padiglione Arte Contemporanea, Milan
Galerie Academia, Salzburg, Austria
Galleria Niccoli, Partna, Italy
1987 Museum Wiener Secession, Vienna
Kunstmuseum, Lucerne, Switzerland
Galerie XPO, Hamburg
Museo Gorizia, Grade, Italy
Musée d'Art Contemporain, Nimes, France
Musée d'Art Contemporain, St. Etienne, France
Galerie Hannah Feldmann, Berne
1988 Galleria L'Isola, Rome (travelled to Bologna)
Fondazione Villa Celle, Santomato, Italy (installation)
Galerie Rothe, Frankfurt
Künstlerhaus, Salzburg, Austria
1989 *Monotypes,* Garner Tullis, Santa Barbara (and 1990, New York)
1991 *Vedova . . . continum,* Padiglione Arte Contemoranea, Milan
1992 Palazzo Ducale, Genoa
1993 *Biennale,* Venice
Museum of Modern Art, Villa Malpensata, Lugano, Switzerland
1994 *The Italian Metamorphosis: 1943–1968,* Guggenheim Museum, New York
1997 Giò Marconi Gallery, Milan
1999 Museo di Arte Monderna e Contemporanea di Trento e Rovereto, Trento, Italy (catalog)

Selected Group Exhibitions:

1947 *Fronte Nuovo,* Galleria Cairola, Milan
1950 *Biennale,* Venice (and 1954, 1960, 1978)
1955 *Documenta 1,* Kassel, West Germany (and *Documenta 2,* 1958, *Documenta 3,* 1964)
1958 *Vitalita nell'arte,* Palazzo Grassi, Venice (travelled to Amsterdam)
1967 *Expo 67,* Montreal
1977 *International Survey of Drawing,* Art Gallery of Western Australia, Perth
1985 *The European Iceberg,* Art Gallery of Ontario, Toronto
1987 *Berlinart 1961–87,* Museum of Modern Art, New York (travelled to San Francisco)
1988 *Painters and Poets,* Palazzi Comunali, Todi, Italy (catalog)
1989 Goethe Institut of Osaka, Miyagi Museum, Japan
1993 *Utopia-Arte Italiana,* Salzburg (travelled to Paris)
1997 *47th Biennale of Venice,* Italy
1999 *Emblemi per un Centenario,* Fondazione Bevilacqua La Masa, Venice
Modern Mosaics, Ravenna, Italy (catalog)
2000 *Corrente,* Galleria Biasutti & Biasutti, Torino (catalog)

Publications:

On VEDOVA: Books—*Pittura Moderna Italiana* by G. Marchiori, Trieste 1946; *Emilio Vedova* by G. Marchion, Venice 1951; *Pittura italiana del dopoguerra 1945–57* by T. Sauvage, Milan 1957; *Confessions of an Art Addict* by Peggy Guggenheim, New York 1960; *Nachwort an ''Blätter aus dem Tagebuch* by Werner Haftmann, Munich 1960; *La pintura de Vedova* by Camilio Josè Cela, Palma de Mallorca 1962; *Drei Welten 1962–3* by Fritz Bayl, Cologne 1963; *New Tendencies in Art* by Aldo Pellegrini, New York 1966; *Ultime tendenze nell'arte d'oggi* by Gillo Dorfles, Milan 1973; *Emilio Vedova: Grafica e didattica,* exhibition catalog, Aosta 1975; *Vedova compresenze,* exhibition catalog, San Marino 1981; *Maestri Contemporanei: Vedova* by Filiberto Menna, Milan 1982; *Emilio Vedova 1935–1984,* edited by Germano Celant and Ida Gianelli, Milan 1984; *Vedova 1986,* edited by Carla Schultz Hoffman, Munich 1986; *Vedova und Salzburg,* Salzburg 1988; *Vedovas Angeli,* by Massimo Cacciari, Klagenfurt 1989; *Emilio Vedova: Monotypes,* exhibition catalog with text by Garner Tullis, New York 1990; *Vedova . . . continuum . . . ,* exhibition catalog with text by Aurora Garcia and others, Milan 1991; *Per Vedova: Dieci pensieri,* exhibition catalog with text by Massimo Cacciari, Lugano 1993. **Articles—** ''On the Engravings of Emilio Vedova'' by Massimo Cacciari in *Forum International,* vol. 3, no. 12, March-April 1992; ''Emilio Vedova: Il Puro Avvenire'' by Luisa Pero in *Arte,* no. 283, March 1997.

* * *

As an artist of international renown in the field of *Informel* painting, Emilio Vedova embodies one of the greatest protagonists of twentieth century Italian art. At the beginning of his career in 1935 to 1936, while still a young man, he demonstrated an extraordinary command of expressive means in a series of architectonic drawings. His elegant style has a descriptive and dynamic urgency which has become his hallmark. Up to the beginning of the 1940s, his oil paintings were clearly influenced by Tintoretto, Goya, Daumier and Rouault and by the Expressionist tradition, one of the most evident premises of Vedova's work—as in *Assassinio* (1941) and *Operaio* (1942). Vedova's expressive dynamism is also reflected in his involvement with anti-fascism and a number of social issues. He had belonged to Corrente, the group opposed to official art during the 1930s. At the end of the war, he joined the Fronte Nuovo delle Arti in 1946, and took part in the debate between the abstract and realist movements that raged through Italian art in those years. Vedova formed a close relationship with the abstract painters championed by Lionello Venturi, and between 1952 and 1954 the Gruppo degli Otto was formed.

For Vedova and other abstractionists who had been suppressed by Fascist cultural policies, abstraction took as a starting point the reinterpretation of Picasso and Cubist figuration. The shifting and interpenetration of different planes is articulated, in Vedova's case, by irregular geometric modules building the figures into compact and rigid forms (Vedova himself was to speak of 'automatons' or 'machines'), as in *Cucitrice No. 1* (1946). Later on, his themes become more evocative, and the painted marks tend increasingly to signify rather than to represent. *Explosion* (1948) has relaxed from the earlier rigid style into a highly dynamic and forceful language. In this work, Vedova uses signals of energy, vectors of directions, forms in which the blacks defining them are accompanied by evanescent patches of white, the function of which is to underline their dynamic rhythm.

In the 1950s Vedova relinquished the geometry which he later confessed to have obsessed and inhibited him. In such works as *Immagine del Tempo n. 1 e 2* (1951), angularity is characterized by a more lyrical brushmark. Vedova's form of cubism had by now begun borrowing from the dynamic vocabulary of early futurism to combine with the fundamental expressionism that so deeply permeated his work with a sense of tragedy. His approach to painting now oscillated between substantiating signs as a body of ideograms, and liberating that gestural fluidity in which the range of colour was highly evocative besides functioning as structure. The resolution of these diametrically opposed features in Vedova's work is evident in *Ciclo della Protesta* and *Ciclo della Natura,* both of 1953. In each of these paintings, the resolution constitutes a highly dramatic event.

Throughout his long career, the actual gesture of painting has remained of paramount importance. The gesture disturbs the surface, signifying historical man's tragedy and loneliness, isolated and unable to control unconscious impulses. In 1962, Vedova wrote: "A material sign will never give us access to a new dimension of a universe constantly being destroyed and re-aggregated." However, still understanding the limits of his artistic language, Vedova insists that "the sign affirms itself," and that his works are "full of structures." The gestural mark is the vehicle for the violence that destroys, but always within sight of a reconstruction. Vedova's negation is full of optimism.

In the multiple images of the 1970s, Vedova's negation destroys codified two-dimensionality where marks or signs virtually dismantle the space. The painting appears to fall apart, with surface planes expanding and combining freely, so that the picture becomes an event and visual process unfolding in front of the viewer's eyes. *Absudes Berliner Tagebuch* (1964) is a work of multiple images commemorating the erection of the Berlin Wall. The 'structures' of which Vedova speaks are also the structures of conscience. The work becomes an emblem of awakened conscience, an alarm ready to expose social injustice, and thus accentuates its role as communicable testimony.

After these multiple works Vedova returned to the single canvas, where he promotes the idea of the painting as a battleground. In the painting *Lacerazioni* (1977–78), Vedova's use of both negation and affirmation is made clear by the function assigned to colours in relationship to the manner in which the paint is handled. Whereas the whites and yellows convey an aura of light and space, the reds are charged with violence. Vedova, however, balances this disruptive passion by conferring the role of regulator onto the viscous strength of his blacks. In only a few cases does Vedova yield to instinctive and informal gesture, as in *Da Dove* (1983).

Unlike Pollock, for instance, Vedova makes no attempt to match his own estrangement from the world by means of an informal painting style. Through destructive and reconstructive valencies, he proclaims the world as worthy of reconquering.

—Giorgio Verzotti

VELICKOVIC, Vladimir

Nationality: Yugoslav. **Born:** Belgrade, 11 August 1935. **Education:** Studied architecture at the University of Belgrade, 1954–60; self-taught in art, since 1960. **Military service:** Served as an engineer in Yugoslav Army, 1960–61. **Family:** Married Maristella Matulic in 1962; children: Vuk and Marko. **Career:** Independent painter, working in studio of Krsto Hegedusic in Zagreb, 1962–63, in Belgrade, 1964–66, and in Paris since 1966. Diplome, Faculty of Architecture, University of Belgrade; professor, Ecole Nationale Superieure de Beaux-Arts, 1983. **Awards:** Painting Prize, *Biennale des Jeunes,* Rijeka, 1962; Painting Prize, *October Salon,* Belgrade, 1963; Drawing Prize, *Yugoslav Triennale,* Sombor, 1963, 1966, 1975; Painting Prize, *Yugoslav Triennale,* Belgrade 1964; Painting Prize, *Biennale de Paris,* 1965; Painting Prize, *Fantastique Poetique,* Somber, 1967; Painting Prize, Lignano, Italy, 1968; N. Petrovic Memorial Prize, Cacak, 1968, 1978; Prize, *International Drawings Exhibition,* Rijeka, Yugoslavia, 1970, 1974; Drawing Prize, *Internationale Grafikausstellung,* Vienna, 1970; Prize, *International Print Exhibition,* Ljubljana 1971, 1973, 1977; Painting Prize, *Momento Tangente Internazionale,* Gardone, Italy, 1971; Prize, *Yugoslav Painters 71,* Sombor, 1971; Print Prize, Belgrade Circle, 1972; Prize, *Print Biennale,* Tokyo, 1976; Painting Prize, *Bienal,* Sao Paulo, 1977; Painting Prize, 10 Anni della Galleria San Michele, Brescia, Italy, 1978; Graphics Prize, La Plume d'Or, Belgrade, 1979; Grand Prize, *Graphics Biennale,* Heidelberg, 1979; *Prize, Graphics Biennale,* Cracow, Poland 1980. **Agents:** Galerie du Dragon, 19 rue du Dragon, 75006 Paris France; Galerie Jan Krugier, 3 Place du Grand Mezel, 1204 Geneva, Switzerland. **Address:** 7 Passage Ricaut, escalier 19/6, 75013 Paris France.

Individual Exhibitions:

1963 Museum of Modern Art, Belgrade
1964 Mala Galerija, Ljubliana, Yugoslavia
1965 Galerie Defacqz, Brussels
Zygos Gallery, Athens
1967 *Peintures, dessins,* Galerie du Dragon, Paris
1968 Galleria Il Fante di Spade, Rome
Galleria La Mutina, Modena, Italy
Galleria B Tempo, Bologna
Dissegni 1965–1968, Galleria La Colonna, Como, Italy
1969 Museum of Modern Art, Belgrade
Gallery of Contemporary Art, Zagreb
Museum of Modern Art, Rijeka, Yugoslavia
1970 Musée d'Art Moderne de la Ville, Paris
Galerie du Dragon, Paris
Galerie T, Haarlem, Netherlands
Galerie Jalmar, Amsterdam
Hengelose Kunstzaal, Hengelo, Netherlands

Vladimir Velickovic: *Chase fig. VII,* 1984. ©2001 Artists Rights Society (ARS), NY/ADAGP, Paris.

1971 Galleria Vinciana, Milan
Galleria San Michele, Brescia, Italy
Art Gallery of Split, Yugoslavia
Galleria Giulia, Rome
Galleria Forni, Bologna
Galleria Goethe, Bolzano, Italy
Mala Galerija, Ljubljana, Yugoslavia
1972 Galleria Cartezius, Trieste
Galleria Eidos, Milan
Biennale, Venice
Galerie Sebastian, Dubrovnik
Maison de la Culture, Rennes, France
1973 Galerie du Dragon, Paris
Galerie Herve Odennatt, Paris
Galerie La Pochade, Paris
Galerie T., Haarlem, Netherlands
Graficki Kolektiv, Belgrade
Galerie Richard Foncke, Ghent
Galerie La Plage, Paris
1974 Galleria San Michele, Brescia, Italy
Galerie T, Haarlem, Netherlands
Galerie La Fieuve, Bordeaux
Galleria Forni, Bologna
Galleria Documenta, Turin
Pryzmat Gallery, Cracow, Poland
Galerie Sebastian, Dubrovnik
Kunsthalle, Dusseldorf
1975 Galerie Arta, Geneva
La Bijougalerie, Grenoble, France
Galleri Futura, Stockholm
1976 Konsthall, Lund, Sweden
Museum of Modern Art, Rijeka, Yugoslavia
Galleria Visconti, Milan
Konsthall, Gothenburg, Sweden
Galeria Juana de Aizpuru, Seville
Galleri Wallner, Malmo, Sweden
Galleri Borjeson, Malmo, Sweden
Kulturhuset, Stockholm
1977 Artcurial, Paris
National Museum, Leskovac, Yugoslavia
Galerie Hervé Odermatt, Paris
Galerie La Hune, Paris
Galleri Dierks, Aarhus, Denmark
Bienal, Sao Paulo
Galerie La Hune, at *FIAC 77,* Grand Palais, Paris
Galleri Leger, Malmo, Sweden
1978 Student Cultural Centre, Belgrade
Galerija Madinska Knjiga, Ljubljana, Yugoslavia
1979 Galerija Zagreb, Zagreb
Galerie Miroir d'Encre, Brussels
Galerie La Hune, Paris
Galerie Albert Henri, Rennes, France
Galerie 24, Novi Sad, Yugoslavia
Salon de la Tribune des Jeunes, Novi Sad, Yugoslavia
Galeria Ciento, Barcelona
Galerie Larcos, Paris
1980 Galerie Una, Geneva
Artcurial, Paris
Galerie Jan Krugier, Geneva
Galerie Krugier et Geofroy, Geneva
Galerie Sebastian, Dubrovnik
Galerie Collegium Artisticum, Sarajevo, Yugoslavia
Galerie Jean-Marie Cupillard, Grenoble, France
Galerija Nadezda Petrovic, Cacak, Yugoslavia
1981 Heni-Onstad Kunstsenter, Oslo
Peintures et Dessins, Galerie Charles Kriwin, Brussels
1982 Galerie Presence Contemporaine, Aix-en-Provence, France
Museo de Bellas Artes, Caracas
Galerie Le Point, Monte Carlo
1983 Galerie Le Dessin, Paris
Galerie de France, Paris
Galerie Athanor, Marseille, France
1984 Galleri Kaj Forsblom, Helsinki
Galleri Grafiart, Turku, Finland
Galerie Jade, Colmar, France
Stadtmuseum, Ratingen, West Germany
Galerie Pierre Huber, Geneva
1985 Espace des Cordeliers, Chateauroux, France
Galerie de l'Ancienne Poste, Calais, France
1986 Academy of Sciences and Arts, Belgrade
Atrium Gallery, Belgrade
Galerie BBL, Antwerp, Belgium
Grand Palais, Paris
Galerie Patrice Trigano, Paris
1987 Galerie Patrice Trigano, Basel
Galerie Le Point, Monte Carlo

Galerie Forni, Bologna
1988 Galerie Davico, Turin
Abbaye de Mondaye, Juaye-Mondaye
Pavillon d'art, Zagreb
Galerie Mlakar, Zagreb
Galerie d'Art Contemporain, Novi Sad
1989 Galerie BBL, Anvers
Galerie Janine Dessers, Hasselt
Galerie Kara, Geneva
Galerie Artio, Athens
Galerie Grafiart, Turkey
Galerie Kaj Forsblom, Helsinki
Galerie le Miroir d'Encre, Brussels
Mayer-Schwarz Gallery, Los Angeles
1990 Galerie Patrice Trigano, Paris
National Museum, Kragujevac
Centre d'Art Contemporain, Mont-de-Marsan
1991 Galerie Michel Guinle, Espace Poisson d'Or, Lyon
Centre Sain-Benin, Aoste (catalog)
Ecole National Superieure de Beaux-Arts, Paris
1992 Galerie Enrico Navarra, Paris
Galerie Bateau-Lavoir, Grenoble
1993 Galerie Michel Luneau, Brussels
Galerie Le Miroir d'Encre, Brussels
Galerie du Château, Geneva
Galerie La Marge, Ajaccio
Galerie Michel Luneau, Nantes
1994 Espace Julio Gonzalès, Arcueil
Galerie Area, Paris
Espace d'Art Mille Feuilles, Tunis
Galerie Nelly l'Eplattenier, Lausanne
Institut Franco-Portugais, Lisbon
Galerie La Hune, Paris
Galerie Le Point, Monte Carlo
1995 Gallery Frederic Storm, Lille
Gallery of the Station, Bonnieux
1996 Center for Contemporary Art, Istre
French Institute of Naples, Italy
House of Culture, Bourges
Galerie Christine Couderc, Paris
1997 Visconti Kolizej Fine Art, Ljubljana
Arts Centre, Cherbourg
National Athens Pinakotheque, Greece
Galerie Osiris, Brussels
Studio Kostel, Paris
1998 Villa Tamaris, La Seyne-Sur-Mer, France
1999 Fondation d'Entreprise Coprim, Paris (catalog)

Selected Group Exhibitions:

1961 *Yugoslav, Triennale,* Belgrade
1963 *Bienal,* Sao Paulo
1966 *Yugoslavia: Contemporary Trends,* Corcoran Gallery, Washington, D.C.
1968 *Contemporary Yugoslav, Art,* Civic Center Museum, Philadelphia
1972 *Activite Artistique en France 1960–1972,* Grand Palais, Paris
1974 *Biennale of Prints,* National Museum of Modern Art, Tokyo
1978 *Arte Yugoslavo Contemporaneo,* Fundacio Joan Miro, Barcelona (travelled to Madrid, Lisbon, London and Manchester)
1980 *20th Century Yugoslav Painting,* Museum of Modern Art, Belgrade
1984 *Ecriture dans la Peinture,* Villa Arson, Nice, France
1986 *Les Figurations,* Musée d'Art Moderne, Dunkirk, France
1995 *Le Tennis: C'est Tout Un Art!,* Galerie Lelong, Paris
1996 *Paysages de la Mémoire,* Fondation d'Entreprise COPRIM, Paris (catalog)

Collections:

Museum of Modern Art, Belgrade; Centre Georges Pompidou, Paris; Stedelijk Museum, Amsterdam; Muzeum Sztuki, Lodz, Poland; Museo Civico, Bologna; Museo Cantonal des Beaux-Arts, Lausanne, Switzerland; Museum voor Schone Kunsten, Ghent; Museum of Modern Art, New York; Tate Gallery, London; National Athens Pinakotheque; National Museum, Belgrade; Museo de Bellas Artes, Caracas; Art Institute of Chicago; Ateneum Museum, Helskinki.

Publications:

By VELICKOVIC: Books—*Vladimir Velickovic: Carnet de Dessins,* with André Velter, Paris 2000.

On VELICKOVIC: Books—*Velickovic: peintures, dessins,* exhibition catalog with text by M. Clarac-Serou, Paris 1967; *Velickovic; Dissegni 1965–1968,* exhibition catalog with text by I. Subotic, Como, Italy 1968; *Vladimir Velickovic: Peintures, dessins 1968–1970,* exhibition catalog with text by Gérald Gassiot-Talabot, Paris 1970; *Velickovic,* exhibition catalog with text by Enrico Crispolti, Milan 1971; *Velickovic,* edited by Jean-Louis Ferrier, with texts by several authors, Paris 1976; *Vladimir Velickovic: Essai sur le symbolisme artistique* by Marc Le Bot, Paris 1979; *Vladimir Velickovic: Dessins et collages,* exhibition catalog, with text by Rend Berger, Geneva 1980; *Vladimir Velickovic: Peintures et dessins,* exhibition catalog with texts by Gérald Gassiot-Talabot, Jean-Pierre Faye, Alain Jouffroy and others, Brussels 1981; *Velickovic: Dibujos 1958–1978/9—Veinte Anos de Agresividad* by Alain Jouffroy, Barcelona 1981; *Vladimir Velickovic,* exhibition catalog with introduction by Marc Le Bot, Paris 1986. **Articles—**''The Virtigo of Velickovic'' by Gerard Xuriguera in *Cimaise,* vol. 43, no. 239, January-March 1996; ''Vladimir Velickovic'' by Valere Bertrand in *Cimaise,* vol. 45, no. 254, May-June 1998. **Films—***Velickovic* by Pierre Desfons and Alain Jouffroy, 1973.

* * *

There are obvious comparisons to be made between Francis Bacon and Vladimir Velickovic, especially in the depiction of putrescent flesh, rotting or dissolving on human forms. Velickovic's paintings are less obviously autobiographic, although, in fact, the vivid images of injured, disintegrating children derive directly from memories of war-time Yugoslavia. These surrealistic nightmarish compositions, and the strange, fluid technique, would seem to derive from the Flemish masters, notably Bosch, and also Goya. Their pictorial directness is the result of an urgent need for personal exorcism and, just as important, for communication. Velickovic's brilliance as a draughtsman and painter enables him to register a disturbing imagination with extraordinary immediacy. No one seeing the work of this Yugoslav painter could ever claim indifference: the effect is either disgust, involvement, sympathy, or hatred. A more difficult-to-analyze aspect of Velickovic's work is its over sexuality, combined with a fascination for the mechanics of childbirth. Sexual allusions are already present in the paintings of mutilated children, where the positioning of the bodies, or irrational surrealistic details, permitted a wide range of interpretation. A series of paintings of reclining women, in 1972, illustrates the strange interplay of realism, sexuality, violence and nightmare in Velickovic's work; energetic images of women, with legs widespread, are alternately entitled *Birth* and *Aggression*: the former suggesting the violent delivery of a screaming child, the latter showing rat-like creatures emerging from or entering the vagina. In a long series of works, rats became obsessive symbols of terror and attack, but at the same time Velickovic produced equally important, if less characteristic, images based on the famous photographs of movement by Muybridge. These paintings of running men and greyhounds develop a concern with movement already evident in the artist's earlier work and, whilst far less subjective or violent, they still convey a disturbing sense of menace.

—Charles Spencer

VENET, Bernar

Nationality: French. **Born:** Saint-Auban, 20 April 1941. **Education:** Ecole Libre and Groupe Scolaire Paul Lapie, Saint-Auban, 1955–58; studied art at La Villa Thiole, Nice, 1958–59. **Military service:** French Army, Algeria, 1961–62. **Family:** Married Ella Bogval in 1971; sons: Alexander and Stephan. **Career:** Worked as stage-decorator, Opera de Nice, 1959–61. Painter and conceptual artist, Nice, 1961–66, in New York, since 1966; ''Master in Residence'', Atlantic Center for the Arts, Florida, 1996; Member of the European Academy of Sciences and Arts, Salzburg, Austria, 1997. **Awards:** Design Award for Sculpture, Norfolk, Virginia, 1988; Grand Prix des Arts de la Ville de Paris, 1990. **Agent:** Galerie Daniel Templon, 30 rue Beaubourg, 75003 Paris, France. **Address:** 117 W. 21st Street, New York, New York 10011, U.S.A.

Individual Exhibitions:

1964 Galerie Ursula Girardon, Paris
1968 Judson Church Theatre, New York
1969 Newark College of Engineering, New Jersey
1970 0. K. Harris Gallery, New York
Museum Haus Lange, Krefeld, West Germany
Kunsthaus, Hamburg
Studio Santandrea, Milan
Denise René-Hans Mayer Editions, Dusseldorf
1971 Galerie Der Spiegel, Cologne
X-One Gallery, Antwerp
Galerie Daniel Templon, Paris
Galleria Daniel Templon, Milan
1972 Galerie Bruno Bischofberger, Zurich
Galerie Daniel Templon, Paris
Galleria Daniel Templon, Milan
New York Cultural Center (retrospective)
1973 Galerie Foksal, Warsaw
1974 Galleria La Seconda Scala, Rome
Galerie Daniel Templon, Paris
Galleria Daniel Templon, Milan
1975 Galerie Hetzler und Keller, Stuttgart
Galleria Nuovi Strumenti, Brescia, Italy
French Section, at the *Bienal,* Sao Paulo
Galerie Daniel Templon, Paris
Institute of Contemporary Arts, London
Museu de Arte Moderna, Rio de Janeiro
1976 Dartmouth College, Hanover, New Hampshire
Textural Criticism, La Jolla Museum of Contemporary Art, California
1977 Galerie Bruno Bischofberger, Zurich
Musée d'Art et d'Industrie, Saint-Etienne, France
Galerie Daniel Templon, Paris
Galerie Gillespie-de Laage, Paris
Henie-Onstad Kunstsenter, Oslo
Galerie Denise René-Hans Mayer, Dusseldorf
1978 Special Project at PS 1, Long Island City, New York
Galerie Denise René-Hans Mayer, Dusseldorf
1979 Arco Center for the Visual Arts, Los Angeles
Hal Bromm Gallery, New York
Galleria Civica d'Arte Moderna, Portofino, Italy
Marianne Deson Gallery, Chicago
Galerie Daniel Templon, Paris
1981 Galerie Denise René-Hans Mayer, Dusseldorf
Galleria Unimedia, Genoa
Galerie Artline, The Hague
Galerie Daniel Templon, Paris
1982 Bonlow Gallery, New York
Malinda Wyatt Gallery, Venice, California
1984 Musée Sainte-Croix, Poitiers, France
Studio Marconi, Milan
Marianne Deson Gallery, Chicago
Centre d'Art Contemporain, Chateauroux, France
Galerie Denise Rene/Hans Mayer, at *Art 84,* Basel
Galerie ARCA, Marseille, France
Galerie Jean-Jules Bertin, Lyon, France
Musée d'Art Moderne, Villeneuve-d'Ascq, France
Galerie Daniel Templon, Paris
1985 Galerie Denise René-Hans Mayer, Dusseldorf
Musée Départemental des Vosges, Epinal, France
Galerie Bernard Lucas, Nice, France
Galerie Littmann, Basel
1986 Castelli Uptown, New York
Galerie Elisabeth Frank, Brussels
Daniel Templon Galerie Un, Paris
Daniel Templon Galerie Deux, Paris
1987 Galerie Pierre Huber, Geneva
Quadrat-Bottrop Moderne Galerie, Bottrop, West Germany
1988 Galerie Michèle Chomette, Paris
Galerie Daniel Templon, Paris
Castelli Uptown Gallery, New York
Galleria Primo Piano, Rome
1989 Cantor/Lemberg Gallery, Birmingham, Michigan
1990 Castelli Graphics, New York
Vrej Baghoomian Gallery, New York (catalog)
Galerie Daniel Templon, Paris
Galeria Theospacio, Madrid (catalog)

1991 *Bernar Venet: Sit on Steel,* Galerie Eric Van de Weghe, Brussels (catalog)
Centro Gerencial Mohedano, Caracas (catalog)
Galeria Oscar Ascanio, Caracas, Venezuela (catalog)
1992 Person's Weekend Museum, Tokyo
1993 Wilhelm-Hack-Museum, Ludwigshafen, Germany (retrospective) (catalog)
Bernar Venet: New Sculpture and Drawings, André Emmerich Gallery, New York
Bernar Venet: Retrospective 1963–93, Musee d'Art Moderne et d'Art, Nice (catalog)
1994 *Bernar Venet, 1963–1993,* Museo de Arte Moderno de Bogota, Colombia (catalog)
Lignes Indéterminées, Champ-de-Mars, Paris
Tovar Gallery, Bogotá
André Emmerich Gallery, New York
1995 *Bernar Venet: New & Recent Sculpture and Drawing,* Boca Raton Museum of Art, Florida (catalog)
1996 Fortant de France, Séte, France
Galerie Karsten Greve, Cologne
1997 Musée de Grenoble, Paris (catalog)
Musée du Québec, Québec (catalog)
Musée de Peinture et de Sculpture, Grenoble, France
Le Nouveau Museum, Villeurbanne, France
Gallery Hyundai, Seoul, South Korea
Musée du Québec, Quebec, Canada
1999 Chac Mool Gallery, Los Angeles
Centro Cultural Recoleta, Buenos Aires (catalog)

Selected Group Exhibitions:

1964 *Salon Comparaisons,* Musée d'Art Moderne de la Ville, Paris
1966 *Salon de la Jeune Peinture,* Musée d'Arte Moderne, Paris
1970 *Information,* Museum of Modern Art, New York
1975 *Tendencies of Contemporary Art,* Nordiyllands Kunstmuseum, Aalborg, Denmark (toured Denmark)
1977 *Documenta,* Kassel, West Germany
1979 *Construction and the Geometric Tradition,* Albright-Knox Art Gallery, Buffalo, New York (toured the United States)
1981 *Construction in Process in the Art of the 70s,* Muzeum Sztuki, Lodz, Poland
1983 *L'Art en France dans les Annees 60,* Musée d'Art et d'Industrie, St. Etienne, France
1985 *Livres d'Artistes,* Centre Georges Pompidou, Paris
1987 *Mathematik in der Kunst,* Wilhelm-Hack-Museum, Ludwigshafen, West Germany
1993 *Black in Sculptural Art,* Atelier, Brussels (catalog)
1997 *The Magic of Number in the Art of the 20th Century,* Staatsgalerie *Stuttgart,* Germany (catalog)

Collections:

Centre National d'Art Contemporain, Paris; Kaiser-Wilhelm Museum, Krefeld, West Germany; Neue Galerie im Alten Kurhaus, Aachen, West Germany; Muzeum Sztuki, Lodz, Poland; Museum of Modern Art, New York; New York University; Akron Art Institute, Ohio; Georgia Museum of Art, Athens; Atlantic Richfield Company, Los Angeles; Santa Barbara Museum of Art, California; Citibank Corporation, New York; Contemporary Art Center, San Diego; Dartmouth College Museum and Galleries, Hanover, New Hampshire; Fond d'Art Contemporain des Musées de Nice, France; Fondation Pierre Gianadda, Martigny, Switzerland; Hirshhorn Museum and Sculpture Garden, Washington, D.C.; Milwaukee Art Museum, Wisconsin; Musée de Peinture et de Sculpture, Grenoble, France; Musée du Québec, Canada; Musée National d'Art Moderne Centre Georges Pompidou, Paris; Musée National d'Art Moderne de Liège, Belgium; Museum of Art, University of Iowa, Iowa City; Museum of Contemporary Art, Chicago; Smalley Sculpture Garden, University of Judaism, Los Angeles; The Arkansas Art Center, Little Rock; The National Gallery of Art, Washington, D.C., The New York University Art Collection; Wadsworth Athenaeum, Hartford.

Publications:

By VENET: Books— *Bernar, Venet: Limoges Porcelain Editions,* New York 1988; *Noir/Noir et Noir* with text by Jean-Louis Schefer, Paris 1990; *Apoétiques: 1967–1998,* Genève 1999. **Articles—**interview with Eddy Devolder in *Artefactum,* vol. 8, no. 40, September-October 1991; "Randomness is the Rule" in *Tema Celeste,* no. 34, January-March 1992; interview with Philippe Piguet in *L'Oeil* (Lausanne), no. 455, October 1993; interview with Philippe Piguet in *Oeil,* no. 455, October 1993; "Bernar Venet: From Simple Geometry to the Crazy Line" with Hilarie M. Sheets in *ARTnews,* vol. 93, no. 3, March 1994; "Bernar Venet entre les lignes" by Nadine Descendre in *Beaux Arts Magazine,* no. 123, May 1994; interview in *Art Press,* Special Issue, no. 17, 1996; interview with Catherine Millet in *Art Press,* no. 220, January 1997; interview with Amine Haase in *Kunstforum International,* no. 136, February-May 1997.

On VENET: Books—*The Structure of Art* by Jack Burnham, New York 1970; *Bernar Venet,* exhibition catalog with text by Catherine Millet, Warsaw 1973; *Bernar Venet,* edited by Arthur Hubschmid, Paris and Zurich 1975; *La Linea Analiti dell'Arte Moderna* by Filiberto Menna, Turin 1975; *Dell'Informale alla Body-Art* by Lea Vergine, Turin 1976: *Bernar Venet: Textual Criticism,* exhibition catalog with text by Lawrence Alloway, La Jolla, California 1976; *Bernar Venef,* exhibition catalog, with text by Bernard Ceysson, Saint-Etienne, France 1977; *A Propos de Nice,* exhibition catalog with text by Ben Vautier, Paris, 1977; *Biennale de Paris 1959–73,* exhibition catalog, edited by Georges Boudaille, Tokyo 1978; *Bernar Venet,* exhibition catalog, Portofino, Italy 1979; *Bernar Venet: Un cura di Bernar Venet,* Milan 1980; *Bernar Venet; Dessins 1963–1983,* exhibition catalog with essay by Catherine Franklin, Poitiers 1983; *Bernar Venet,* exhibition catalog with text by Bernard Ceysson, Epinal 1985; *Bernar Venet* by Jan Van der Marck, Paris 1988; *Bernar Venet, 1961–1970* by Robert C. Morgan, Saint-Etienne 1999; *Bernar Venet: Sculptures et Reliefs* by Arnauld Pierre and Achille Bonito Oliva, Milan 2000. **Articles—**"Bernar Venet" by Michel Ragon in *Cimaise,* vol. 36, March/May 1989; "Les Sculptures Instantanees de Bernar Venet" by Dominique Paini in *Art Press,* no. 164, December 1991; "Venet's Platonic Disorder" by Carter Ratcliff in *Art in America* (New York), vol. 80, October 1992; "Bernar Venet in Provence: The Sculptor's Converted Mill and Studio" by Michael Peppiatt in *Architectural Digest* (Los Angeles), vol. 50, July 1993; *Bernar Venet: Spirale et Mouvement* by Philippe Piguet in *Connaissance des Arts,* no. 506, May 1994; "Bernar Venet: Indeterminate Lines at the Champ de Mars Paris" by Michel

Ellenberger in *Cimaise,* vol. 14, June/August 1994; ''Bernar Venet: Reflexive Angles, Fractal Lines'' by Ninon Gauthier in *Parcours,* vol. 1, no. 2, Spring 1995; ''Bernar Venet: la determinazione dell'indeterminato/the determinate of the indeterminate'' by Adachiara Zevi in *L'Architettura,* vol. 44, no. 508, February 1998; ''Bernar Venet'' by Carter Ratcliff in *Sculpture* (Washington, D.C.), vol. 18, no. 2, March 1999.

* * *

Bernar Venet, born in France, worked in the late 1960s and 1970s on large photographic blow-ups of scientific equations. He then proceeded to use the look of scientific equations and diagrams in a painterly manner. He has also used segments of any number of texts, including weather reports, pages of stock market figures, and astrophysical and meteorological texts. Venet has made it his work to sell the look of contemporary science, yet in a distanced fashion. Venet has assisted in finishing the incomplete work of the scientists by presenting their work, in lieu of their own presentation, to the public. Many of his earlier projects included a number of presentations and lectures by prominent scientists. Venet's task was essentially to organize several hundred of these symposia.

Rather than repeating scientific work verbatim, Venet's canvases, such as ''Calculation of the Diagonal of a Rectangle,'' 1966, and ''Tracing of Two Complimentary Angles,'' 1977, expressed the look of science. Therefore, in a sense, they expressed the content of science, given the nature of belief associated with most of the contemporary sciences.

In Venet's work the contemporary need for science to hide research is revealed, and the contemporary utilization of art as decoration is proven. Perhaps the proof of art will work backwards on the contemporary mystery of science, by insisting on aesthetic reasoning along the way, reflectively during construction. A painting on the wall, worthy of supra-scrutiny, is a misplaced aim. The scrutiny is held in the wrong area. The question is not to scrutinize the aesthetic work, but to examine the direction of the observing functions. Venet has been observing science and subjecting it, like a billboard, to the popular realm. We are supposed to be watching science, not art.

—John Robinson

VESNA, Victoria

Nationality: American. **Born:** Washington D.C., 9 June 1959. **Education:** Attended High School of Art and Design, New York; Faculty of Fine Arts, University of Belgrade, Yugoslavia, Fine Arts Diploma 1984; Centre for Advanced Studies in Interactive Arts, University of Wales, United Kingdom, Ph.D. 2000. **Career:** Formed and performed in experimental music group, 1979–82; produced art specials for *Videowave* (cable TV program), 1982–88; creator and producer of education videos, 1989–1995; North American editor, *Springer: AI & Society: The Journal of Human Centered Systems,* 1998; professor and chair, Department of Design/Media Arts, University of California, Los Angeles, since 2000. Co-editor and co-curator, *Terminals: Considering the End* (Book/CD-ROM); contributing editor, *PRE-TEXT: Electra(Lite).* **Awards:** Artist-in-residence, Roman Bronze Foundry, Corona, New York, 1986, and Women's Interart Center, New York, 1987; Cine Golden Eagle for ''Unfolding the Pyramids' Secrets Using Modern Physics'' (video), 1988; People's Choice Award, FIVA ONLINE 95: The First Festival of Independent Audio/Visual Arts Online Arts, Montreal, Canada, 1995; VRML Excellence Awards, 1997; Oscar Signorini Award, 1998. **Address:** Department of Design/Media Arts, University of California, Los Angeles, 1300 Dickson Art Center, Los Angeles, California 90095. **Web site:** http://vv.arts.ucla.edu.

Selected Individual Exhibitions and Installations:

1989 *Crnica,* SKC Gallery, Belgrade, Yugoslavia
Sometimes a Cigar is Only a Cigar (Freud) (video installation), P.S. 1 Museum, Long Island City, New York
1990 *Sometimes a Cigar is Only a Cigar (Freud)* (performance), Image One Gallery, New York, and C.A.G.E, Cincinnati
1992 *Another Day in Paradise,* SKC Gallery, Belgrade, Yugoslavia
1995 *Another Day in Paradise* (interactive installation), Irvine Fine Arts Center, Irvine, California
1996 *Speed, Bodies, Death* (with Robert Nideffer), Dirty Windows, Berlin
1997 *Bodies @ INCorporated* (interactive installation), San Francisco Art Institute
1998 *Dublin Bodies* (interactive installation), Art House, Dublin, Ireland
2001 ''Notime: Women,'' *Women of Vision,* Walker Art Center, Minneapolis
''Bodies INCORPORATED.'' http://www.bodiesinc.ucla.edu

Selected Group Exhibitions and Installations:

1989 *Collaborations,* Lincoln Center Gallery, New York
1992 *Virgin Territories,* Long Beach Museum, California
1993 *MACHINE CULTURE: The Virtual Frontier,* SIGGRAPH '93, Anaheim, California
BC Space Gallery, Laguna Beach, California
World Expo, Seville, Spain
1994 *Naturally. . . In Central Europe,* Ernst Museum, Budapest, Hungary
1995 *Veered Science,* Huntington Beach Art Center, California
FIVA ONLINE 95, Montreal, Canada
Comfort Women, Lincoln Center Gallery, New York
Remember Yugoslavia, LA International, Sherry Frumkin Gallery, California
ART in GENERAL, New York
Art & Design, SIGGRAPH '94, Orlando, Florida
1996 *Bridge Art Show,* SIGGRAPH ' 96, Convention Center and Contemporary Arts Center, New Orleans, Lousiana
Figuratively Speaking, Santa Barbara Museum of Art, California
1997 *Club Media,* Venice Biennale, Italy
ACM '97 Expo: 50 Years of Computing, San Jose Convention Center, California
1998 *Xtraspace,* Barnsdall Municipal Gallery, Los Angeles
1999 *II Bienal de Mercosul, Cibearte: zonas de Interacao,* Porto Allegre, Brazil
2000 *Anagramatic Bodies,* ZKM, Karlsruhe, Germany

Net Condition, ZKM, Karlruhe
Ruhr Visions, Dortmund, Germany

Publications:

By VESNA: Books—Editor, ''Database Aesthetics: Issues of Organization and Category in Art,'' *Springer: AI & Society,* February/March 1999; co-editor, ''Online Public Spaces: Multidisciplinary Explorations in Multiuser Environments,'' special issue of *American Behavioral Sciences,* September 1999. **Articles**—With Robert Nideffer, *Bodies INCorporated: Theoretical Appropriation for Somatic Intervention,* http://time.arts.ucla.edu/publications/publictions/html/siggraph96essay.htm, 1996; ''Avatars on the World Wide Web: Marketing the 'Decent''' in *Intelligent Agent,* Fall 1997; ''Under Reconstruction: Architectures of Bodies INCorporated'' in *Veiled Histories: The Body, Place and Public Art,* edited by Anna Novakov, New York 1997; ''Virtual Concrete: http://www.arts.ucsb.edu/concrete'' in *Thresholds: Viewing Culture,* vol. 9, 1997; ''Buckminster Fuller: Illusive Mutant Artist'' in *Artbyte,* August-September 1998; ''Another Day in Paradise and Virtual Concrete: Preserved Palms, Concrete and Telepresence'' in *Leonardo,* vol. 31, no. 1, 1998; ''Tracing Bodies of Information Overflow'' in *The Body Caught in the Intestines of the Computer & Beyond,* edited by Marina Grzinic, 2000; ''Third Culture Being in Between'' in *Art, Technology, Consciousness,* edited by Roy Ascott, London 2000. **CD-ROMs**—''Life in the Universe with Stephen Hawking,'' 1997; ''Bodies INCorporated,'' San Francisco Art Institute, 1997.

* * *

With one foot in art and the other in science, Victoria Vesna is on a quest to unveil, and call attention to, the quickly crumbling boundaries between the ''real,'' physical world, and the ''shapeless'' environment of cyberspace. Vesna is out to prove that cyberspace is no less ''real'' than physical space; the two spaces are equally real, they are the same.

To Vesna, computer networks are a logical and inevitable new media extending the realm of conceptual art. Her artwork addresses the relationships between gender and technology, corporate culture and technology, art and science. Vesna's career has followed closely the trends and progression of technology. Her early works were an amalgamation of performance, installation, and video art. In 1984, Vesna and Robert Davis collaborated on *The Chrysler Building Project*, a performance documented on video at the top of Manhattan's Chrysler Building. In the mid-eighties, in such works as *Red Angel* and *Thunderbolt*, Vesna continued to experiment with installation, performance, and video art. These works were highly theatrical, the installations forming imaginative sets for elaborate, often emotional performances.

Vesna has always actively researched and hypothesized on the relationship between art, science, and technology. As computer and networking technology developed, Vesna adopted these new media as her own and blossomed into one of the chief innovators of network-based artwork. From 1995 to 1997, Vesna worked on a project called *F-e-mail*, an online database of women artists using the net as a medium for expression. Vesna writes, ''*F-e-mail* is a part of an evolving network of women working on top of the grid, in the belly of the beast. . . . Women artists working with this network are serving as role models to debunk the mythology which is alienating women from technology.''

In 1996, Vesna and a group of her students from the University of California at Santa Barbara collaborated with an elite team of science and design specialists to create a ''virtual web cd-rom'' based on Professor Stephen Hawking's lecture, ''Life in the Universe.''

Vesna's most widely acclaimed project thus far, *Bodies INCorporated,* grew out of her 1995 installation *Virtual Concrete,* in which Vesna attempts to deconstruct the ''common perception that there is a dichotomy between the material and the immaterial.'' The installation incorporates many of Vesna's theoretical fields of interest. She links gender and technology through her exploration of silicon, the key ingredient in cosmetic implants, computer chips, and city sidewalks. Vesna explored similar motifs previously, in her 1995 installation, *Another Day in Paradise*, a circular arrangement of large artificial palm trees (inspired by the trees surrounding the statue of John Wayne at his namesake airport) equipped with video screens that illustrated, through sound and visual image, Vesna's critique of the artificiality of planned communities.

In *Virtual Concrete*, Vesna continues her commentary on the relationship between networked environments and physical spaces. As she did in *Another Day in Paradise,* Vesna employs California to elucidate. In her essay, ''Another Day in Paradise and Virtual Concrete: Installation and Telepresence Works,'' Vesna writes, ''California's inhabitants are conditioning themselves to make a smooth transition from living in an artificial world formed out of sand and oxygen to navigating cyberspace propelled by the same elements.'' She refers to the January 1994 earthquake, in which cell phones and the Internet became the ''established connections'' between residents of Los Angeles and the world; these devices were no less ''real'' than the crumbled freeways and collapsed telephone polls.

Bodies INCorporated is the natural progression of *Virtual Concrete*. It is, in Vesna's words, ''an investigation into social psychology and group dynamics, actualized in corporate structure . . . a tongue in cheek commentary on some of the more obvious contradictions of corporate culture, particularly for those working with art and technology.''

Bodies INCorporated was presented at the San Francisco Art Institute and The Art House, Dublin, among other venues, as an interactive installation. It is now available on the Internet (at http://www.bodiesinc.ucla.edu), where anyone with a computer is invited to enter and create a body from an assortment of interchangeable parts. On the surface, it seems like a sort of a Mr. Potato Head for the computer age. However, the bodies exist as avatars, embodiments or personifications of ideas and principles, and each user chooses a name, gender, and sexual preference for his/her body. Limbs, heads, and torsos are selected from various combinations of sized, gendered, and textured limbs. The site offers descriptions and traits for the various textures, so that one may choose with intent and purpose. Satisfied with the appearance of the body, the user assigns his/her body individual traits and submits it into existence, breathing ''life'' into the body. Once submitted, the bodies occupy three, three-dimensional environments: Limbo, a cyber-wasteland of neglected bodies; Necropolis, a digitally lush, three-dimensional ''space'' where participants are free to explore the community of synthesized bodies and make decisions that determine the fate of their own bodies; and Showplace, featuring chat sessions, discussion forums, and arenas in which users can view featured bodies and communicate with other users. Users are updated on newly born and deceased bodies and can easily—with the click of a mouse—investigate the other bodies and make changes to their own if they so please.

In a recent collaboration with Gerald de Jong and David Beaudry entitled *Community of People with No Time* [NOTIME], Vesna declares the human body as an obsolete representation of an avatar. This time, each user builds a tetrahedron rather than a ''human body'' as an embodiment of ideas.

Victoria Vesna has succeeded in using a wide range of technologically based media as a vehicle for expression. Her ideas, theories, messages, and professional interests are as varied as her media. She communicates ideas about our world, our art, our cultures, genders, homes, and about the increasing role that technology plays in all of these spheres. It is that same technology that provides Vesna with a means of producing a uniquely interactive art.

—Aaron Jacobs

VIALLAT, Claude

Nationality: French. **Born:** Aubais, Le Gard, near Nimes, 18 May 1936. **Education:** Studied under Descossis, Dezeuze, and Bessil, at the Ecole des Beaux-Arts, Montpellier, 1955–59; also studied at the Ecole des Beaux-Arts, Paris, 1962–63. **Military Service:** French Army, Constantine, Algeria, 1959–61. **Family:** Married Henriette Pous in 1962; daughters: Claire and Isabelle. **Career:** Painter: lived in Nice, 1964–67, Limoges, 1967–69, and in Marseilles, 1972–79, Nîmes, 1979–94; Painting instructor, director, Ecole Beaux Arts, Nîmes, 1979–94; Painting instructor, Ecole Nationale des Beaux Arts, Paris, 1994–00. Member, with Louis Cane, Marc Devade, Daniel Dezeuze, Andre Valensi and others, Groupe Supports Surfaces, Paris, 1969–71. Painting instructor, Ecole des Beaux-Arts, Nice, 1964–67; professor of painting, Ecole des Beaux-Arts, Limoges, 1968–1969. Professor of painting, Ecole des Beaux-Arts, Marseilles, 1969–79. **Agent:** Galerie Daniel Templon, Paris. **Address:** c/o Galerie Daniel Templon, 30 rue Beaubourg, 75003 Paris, France.

Individual Exhibitions:

1966 Galerie A, Nice
1968 Galerie Jean Fournier, Paris
Musée d'Art Moderne, Ceret, France
1971 Galerie Jean Fournier, Paris
1973 Galleria Daniel Templon, Milan
Galerie Jean Fournier, Paris
1974 Galerie Delta, Brussels
Musée d'Art et d'Industrie, St.-Etienne, France
Galerie Ben, Nice
Galleria La Bertesca, Milan (with Delta and Isnard)
Maison de la Culture, Rennes (with Dezeuze and Saytour)
1975 Galerie Athanor, Marseilles (with Tony Grand)
Galerie Jean Fournier, Paris
1976 Pierre Matisse Gallery, New York
Von-der-Heydt Museum, Wuppertal, West Germany (with J. M. Meurice)
Palais des Beaux-Arts Brussels
Galerie A.16, Perpignan, France
1977 Galerie Jean Fournier, Paris
Galerie C. M., St.-Etienne, France
Galerie Sanguine, Collioure, France
Galerie Athanor, Marseilles (with Jaccard and Pincemin)
1978 Galerie Arta, Geneva
Maison de la Culture, Orleans, France
Centre de Création Artistique, Senanque, France
Galerie Athanor, Marseilles
Traces, Musée d'Art et d'Histoire, Chambéry, France
1979 Galerie Wentzel, Hamburg
1980 Centre des Arts Plastiques Contemporains, Bordeaux
Neue Galerie, Aachen, West Germany
1981 Galerie L'Atelier, Nice, France
Kamakura Gallery, Tokyo
Ace Gallery, Venice, California
1982 Galerie Wentzel, Cologne
Leo Castelli Gallery, New York
Centre Georges Pompidou, Paris
1983 Won Galerie, Seoul
Fondacio Juan Miro, Barcelona
1984 Musée d'art et d'industrie de Saint Etienne
1985 Galarie Athanor, Marseille
1986 Galarie Kamakura, Tokyo
1987 Musée Sara Hilden, Finland
1988 Carré d'art Musée d'art contemporain, Nimes
1989 Musées de ceret et de Collioure Galerie Wentzel, Cologne
1990 Galerie Joan Fournier, Paris
1991 Pinacothèque d'Athènes
1992 Galerie Plurime, Milan
Sagacho Exhibit Space, Tokyo
1993 Espace Fortant de France Séte
1994 Won Galerie, Seoul
1995 Institut francais de Tel Aviv
1996 Galerie de l' Ecole des Beaux Arts de Paris, Paris
1997 Musée Fabre, Montpellier
1998 Galerie Daniel Templon, Paris
1999 Musée Shanghe Chengdu, China
Eglise St. Petri Lubeck, Germany
2000 Galerie le Rectangle, Lyon
Festival Garonne, Toulouse

Selected Group Exhibitions:

1966 *Impact,* Musée d'Art Moderne, Ceret, France
1969 *Biennale,* Paris (and 1971)
1971 *Supports/Surfaces,* Théâtre de la Cité Universitaire, Paris (travelled to Nice)
1972 *Amsterdam-Paris-Dusseldorf,* Guggenheim Museum, New York
1973 *Regarder Ailleurs,* Entrepots Laine, Bordeaux
1975 *12 x 1: Europalia 75,* Palais des Beaux-Arts, Brussels
1977 *A Propos de Nice,* Centre Georges Pompidou, Paris
1978 *Espace/Nature,* Centre des Arts Plastiques Contemporains, Bordeaux
1980 *Die Neue Wilden,* Neue Galerie, Aachen, West Germany
1982 *Du Cubisme a nos Jours,* Musée Cantini, Marseille, France
1983 Galarie Léo Castelli, New York
1984 Museum of Modern Art, New York
1985 Seoul Galerie, Seoul
1986 Tademuséo Pori, Finland
1987 Centre Georges Pompidou M.N.A.M., Paris
1988 Muséo national de Bucarest
1989 Musée Pouchkine, Moscow

Drawing by Claude Viallat. ©2001 Artists Rights Society (ARS), NY/ADAGP, Paris.

1990 Musée d'art moderne, Nice
1991 Musde d'art moderne de Saint Etienne
1992 Galerie Sprovieri, Rome
1993 Musée Matisse, Nice
1994 Musée Fabre, Montpellier
1995 Musée de Douais
1996 Chateau de Villeneuve Fondation E. Hugues, Venice
1997 Musée d'art contemporain de Nimes
1998 Galerie Piltzer, Paris
1999 Galerie Gimpel, London
2000 Centro cultural Banco do Brasil, Rio de Janeiro

Collections:

Musée d'Art et d'Industrie, St. Etienne, France; Fonds National d'Art Contemporain, Paris; Neue Galerie-Sammlung Ludwig, Aachen, West Germany; Centre Georges Pompidou, Paris; Tokyo International Forum, Tokyo Sapow, Museum of Modern Art, New York.

Publications:

On VIALLAT: Books—*Claude Viallat,* exhibition catalog with preface by Marcelin Pleynet, Paris 1971; *Art en France: Une Nouvelle Génération* by Jean Clair, Paris 1972: *L'Enseignement de la Peinture* by Marcelin Pleynet, Paris 1972; *Amsterdam-Paris-Dusseldorf,* exhibition catalog with texts by Blaise Gauthier, Cor Blok, and Jürgen Harton, New York 1972; *L'Art Actuel en France* by Anne Tronche and Hervé Gloaguen, Paris 1973; *Claude Viallat,* exhibition catalog with text by Jacques Lepage, St. Etienne, France 1974; *Claude Viallat: Traces,* exhibition catalog with texts by Dominque Fourcade and others, Chambéry, France 1978; *Claude Viallat,* exhibition catalog with text by Bernard Ceysson, Senanque, France 1978; *Claude Viallat,* exhibition catalog with texts by Jean-Louis Froment and Jean-Marie Poinsot, Bordeaux 1980; *Claude Viallat: la Main Perdue* by Christian Prigent, Paris, 1981; exhibition catalog with texts by Paul Rodgers and Alred Pacquement, Centre Georges Pomidou, Paris 1982; exhibition catalog with texts by Claude Fournet, Yves Michaud, and Marcelin Pleynet, Galerie des Ponchettes, Nice 1983; *Variations sur une empreinte de C Viallat* by Albert Ayme, Paris 1987; *Viallat,* exhibition catalog with texts by Jacques Lepaye, Budapest 1987; exhibition catalog with texts by Daniel Dobbels, Musée de Nimes 1988; exhibition catalog with texts by Catherine Francblin, Seoul 1990; exhibition catalog with texts by Catherine Lawless, Paris 1991; *Claude Viallat* by Christian Skimao, Nice 1995; exhibition catalog with texts by Francois Bazzoli, Galerie Yahia, Tunisia 1997; exhibition catalog with texts by Jacques Lepage,

Chateau de Villeneuve, Venice 1998; *Claude Viallat* by Claude Minière, Paris 1999; *Claude Viallat* by Jean Charles Lebahar, Paris 1999; exhibition catalog with texts by Didier Semin, Galerie Rectangle, Lyon 2000; *Claude Viallat* by Brenard Ceysson, Alfred Pacquement, and Raphael Rubinstein, éditions Navarra, Paris 2000.

* * *

There is one single form that Claude Viallat introduced into his painting in 1966 and never again abandoned—the form of a sponge soaked in colour that one presses onto the picture surface. However, when, by this means, an impression of wealth of colour and formal exuberance appears on his canvases, it is because he knew how to effect so many variations with this single motif that it invested entire rooms/spaces as endless ornamentation.

When Viallat began his work in 1966 a radical investigation into all painting was in progress in France. What had painting ever been until then, it was asked, other than a purveyor of illusions and false dreams, in the service of the art market, bourgeois society and its ideology? If one wanted a new beginning for painting, it had to be liberated from this traditional role. This discussion was perhaps successful in the sense that it made one think about the real origins of art. Viallat was one of the younger generation who tried to trace the origin of painting back to its handcraft beginnings, that beginning where the intention was to add a non-functional dimension to the merely functional object. But he also concluded that only where one expelled all content, any statement, every subjective expression from the work and replaced this on the canvas with unchanging neutral and anonymous forms, could one be sure that painting was concentrated only on the process of its becoming, and beyond that had no further significance. Indeed, at first, Viallat had in fact begun to work with the substance, the material grounds of painting, with rope, string, thread, which in tangled knots or composed nets call to mind the matrix of the canvas to be painted. He stressed the praxis of artistic work and not the ideas which it could generate. In so doing he set himself in opposition to the art of the Ecole de Paris and also to the new tendencies of conceptual art which came from America and which provided ideas about material and form.

In France people were looking for a new aesthetic and for a new aesthetic ethic. Each had its theoretical basis in Marxism and in the structuralist critique of language. Painting was understood as a system of signs whose forms of expression, as long as they were taken over from tradition, were charged with specific connotations and meanings. Each artist who dealt with them had to be aware that he was more or less adapting himself to the fashion, the modern myths and current ideological thought structures. So Viallat set about making visible the mechanism of such a system of signs and submitting the signs themselves to criticism. He wanted to change fundamentally the basis, the material and economic suppositions of painting so as to renew the social function of the painter and of art. He subsequently restricted himself to large unframed canvases sewn together and including also found or already printed material, on which he carried out all the possible colour variations of his special form. A ''necessary materialism'' was involved, it was said, in which painting is an experimentation with the material means of art, a preoccupation with the real basis and not a communication of ideas.

Painting had become a metaphor for structural thought inasmuch as it accomplished in its forms the structures of a particular social situation. ''In working we have to learn,'' Viallat wrote. ''Everything develops its own organization: to reject it would be to exclude a reality.'' Everything has a special language, a particular discourse, as Michel Foucault has described it. That which has no power of language expresses itself in bodies and spaces, in lines, forms and colours. The object speaks for itself, and in that moment in which it enters into a relationship with the artist's subject a corresponding composite of reality is expressed in concrete form. According to this interpretation there is no longer a difference, a separation, between subject and object, for they complement one another. In art it is important, Viallat wrote, that in working one learns from the object—or as Michel Foucault expressed it: the artist is through his body and his vision part of the visible world, and both form an inseparable essence.

Viallat wants the subject matter to intrude neither intellectually nor emotionally upon the visible but to engage with him in a process of gradual change. For that reason it is so essential in his work that with a theme which remains the same he should constantly search for fresh material, new contours and formats to whose peculiarities he has to readjust himself. From 1970 to 1971 Viallat was a member of the group Support/Surface, with which he was for a long time theoretically in agreement, but he left it when he was directing its attention less to the analysis of a situation than to direct political engagement. Art, to the group, meant intervening in historical development. Viallat's art strives for a value-free investigation of artistic means of expression, without hierarchy and differentiation between more or less ''noble'' activities. Everything is worthy of experience. Hence also the struggle against tasteful, academic painting and the restriction to one form, which can stand for all forms. Each impression is so similar to the next that it could be part of any picture, and in this dimension Viallat's painting also gains, over and above any theoretical, social-critical tendency, its ethical value.

—Marie Luise Syring

VIEIRA da SILVA, Marie-Helene

Nationality: French. **Born:** Lisbon, Portugal, 13 June 1908; immigrated to France, 1928: naturalized, 1956. **Education:** Studied drawing, under Emilia Santos Braga, in Lisbon, 1922–24; studied painting and sculpture under Armando Lucena at the Academy of Fine Arts, Lisbon, 1924–27; studied painting under Antoine Bourdelle, Académie de la Grande Chaumière, Paris, 1928–29; and engraving, under S. W. Hayter, Atelier 17, Paris. **Family:** Married the painter Arpad Szenes in 1930 (died, 1985). **Career:** Painter, illustrator, and fabric designer, Paris, 1929–39, Lisbon, 1939–40, Brazil, 1940–47, and again in Paris, since 1947. **Awards:** Acquisition Prize, *Bienal,* Sao Paulo, 1953; Tapestry Prize, University of Basel, 1954; Grand International Prize, *Bienal,* Sao Paulo, 1961; Grand Prix des Arts, Paris, 1966; Grand Croix de Santiago da España, Lisbon, 1977; Medal of Honour, towns of Montargis and Montauban, France, 1983; Grand Prix Florence Gould, Académie des Beaux-Arts, Paris, 1986, Grand Prix Antena 1, 1986; Gra-Cruz da Ordem da Liberdade du Portugal, 1988; Gold Medal in Plastic Arts, Academy of Architecture, Paris, Chevalier, 1960, and Commandeur, 1962, Ordre des Arts et Lettres, Paris; member, Academy of Arts of Lisbon, 1970; honorary member, Royal Academy of London, 1988; chevalier, 1979, and officer, 1991, Legion d'Honneur, Paris; member, Académie des Sciences, des Arts et des Lettres, Paris, 1984; **Address:** c/o Galerie Jeanne Bucher, 53 rue de seine, 75006 Paris, France. **Died:** 6 March 1992.

Vieira da Silva: *Domestic Symphony,* 1949. ©2001 Artists Rights Society (ARS), NY/ADAGP, Paris.

Individual Exhibitions:

1933 Galerie Jeanne Bucher, Paris
1935 Galerie U.P., Lisbon
1936 Artist's Studio, Lisbon (with Arpad Szenes)
1937 Galerie Jeanne Bucher, Paris
1939 Galerie Jeanne Bucher, Paris
1942 Museu de Arte Moderna, Rio de Janeiro
1946 Galeria Askenazi, Rio de Janeiro
Palacio Municipal, Belo Horizonte, Brazil
Marian Willard Gallery, New York
1947 Galerie Jeanne Bucher, Paris
1949 Galerie Pierre, Paris
1950 Galerie Blanche, Stockholm
Galerie La Hune, Paris
1951 Galerie Pierre, Paris
Galerie Jeanne Bucher, Paris
1952 Galerie Dupont, Lille, France
1953 Redfern Gallery, London
Cadby Birch Gallery, New York
1955 Stedelijk Museum, Amsterdam (with Germaine Richier)
Galerie Pierre, Paris
1956 Saidenberg Gallery, New York
Galerie Art Moderne, Basel
1957 Galerie de Perron, Geneva
Hanover Gallery, London
Galeria Portico, Lisbon
1958 Kestner-Gesellschaft, Hannover (retrospective; travelled to Bremen and Wuppertal, Germany)
1960 Galerie Jeanne Bucher, Paris
1961 Phillips Art Gallery, Washington, D.C.
Galerie Pierre Beres, Paris
Kunsthalle, Mannheim
Knoedler Gallery, New York

1963 Phillips Art Gallery, Washington, D.C.
Knoedler Gallery, New York
Galeria Gravura, Lisbon
Bezalel Museum, Jerusalem
Galerie Jeanne Bucher, Paris
1964 Galerie Alice Pauli, Lausanne
Musée de Peinture et Sculpture, Grenoble (retrospective)
Museo Civico, Turin (retrospective)
1965 Albert Loeb Gallery, New York
1966 Knoedler Gallery, New York
Académie des Amateurs de Musique, Lisbon
1967 Galerie Jeanne Bucher, Paris
Chateau de Ratilly, France (with Etienne Martin)
1969 Théâtre de la Comédie, Tours
Musée d'Art Moderne, Paris (retrospective)
Galerie Jeanne Bucher, Paris
Galerie Jacob, Paris
1970 Museum Boymans-van Beuningen, Rotterdam (retrospective)
Malerei 1935–1969, Kunstnernes Hus, Oslo
Kunsthalle, Basel (retrospective)
Fundaçao Gulbenkian, Lisbon (retrospective)
Galeria Sao Mamede, Lisbon
Galerie 3, Lisbon
1971 *Temperas, Lithographs, Gouaches et Serigraphies,* Galerie Jeanne Bucher, Paris
Galeria Zen, Porto, Portugal
Paintings 1967–1971, Knoedler Gallery, New York
Musée Fabre, Montpellier, France
1972 Galerie Regence, Brussels
Musée Thomas Henry, Cherbourg
Musée des Beaux-Arts, Rouen
Museum Unterlinden, Colmar, France
1973 Centro Rizzoli, Milan
Musée d'Art et d'Histoire, Orleans
1974 Galerie Artel, Geneva
Gravuras e Litografias, Galeria Quadrum, Lisbon
1975 Institut Francais, Stockholm
Helsinglands Museum, Hudiksvall, Sweden
Saabskonstforening, Lingkoping, Sweden
Konsthalle, Malmo, Sweden
Galerie Monique Delcourt, Valenciennes, France
Galerie Fremond, Paris
1976 Galerie Jeanne Bucher, Paris
Maison des Arts et Loisirs, Sochaux, France
Musée de Metz, France
Musée d'Art Moderne, Paris (with Arpad Szenes)
1977 Musée de l'Etat, Luxembourg
Galerie Kutter, Luxembourg
Musée d'Art Moderne de la Ville, Paris
Pinturas a Tempera, Fundaçao Gulbenkian, Lisbon
Galerie La Hune, Paris
La Galerie Nimes, France
1978 L'Art en Dreux, France
Nordyjllands Kunstmuseum, Aalborg, Denmark (retrospective)
Ty-Kan, Locronan, France
Galerie Jeanne Bucher, Paris (with Louise Nevelson and Magdalena Abakanowicz)
1979 Musée des Beaux-Arts, Agen, France (toured France)
1980 Galeria Joan Prats, Barcelona
Centre Culturel, Dakar, Senegal
1981 Musée de Cluny, France
Bibliothèque Nationale, Paris
1982 Galerie Jeanne Bucher, Paris
Galerie de l'Information, Tunis
1983 Musée Ingres, Montauban, France
Museo de Bellas Artes, Bilbao, Spain
1984 Galeria EMI-Valentim de Carvalho, Lisbon
Centre Culturel Francais, Rome
1985 Galeria III, Lisbon
1986 Galerie Jeanne Bucher, Paris
Galeria Nasoni, Porto, Portugal (with Arpad Szenes)
Artcurial, Paris
1988 Fundaçao Gulbenkian, Lisbon, and Grand-Palais, Paris (retrospective)
1991 Fondacion Juan March, Madrid (retrospective)
1994 Galerie Jeanne Bucher, Paris

Selected Group Exhibitions:

1930 *Salon des Surindépendants,* Paris
1946 *Salon des Realites Nouvelles,* Paris
1950 *Biennale,* Venice
1955 *The New Decade,* Museum of Modern Art, New York
1964 *Painting and Sculpture of a Decade 1954–64,* Tate Gallery, London
1971 *Carnegie International,* Pittsburgh
1973 *L'Estampe Contemporaine,* Bibliothèque Nationale, Paris
1976 *Ratilly,* Musée des Arts Décoratifs, Paris
1978 *Portuguese Art since 1910,* Royal Academy of Arts, London
1984 *Biennale Internationale du Dessin,* Clermont-Ferrand, France
1994 *Modern Art from Brazil: A Selection from the Roberto Marinho Collection,* Museu de Arte de Sao Paulo, Sao Paulo

Collections:

Centre Georges Pompidou, Paris, Musée d'Art Moderne de la Ville, Paris; Tate Gallery, London; Stedelijk Museum, Amsterdam; Museum Folkwang, Essen; Kunsthaus, Zurich; Galleria d'Arte Moderna, Museo Civico, Turin; Museu de Arte Moderna, Rio de Janeiro, Museum of Modern Art, New York; Guggenheim Museum, New York.

Publications:

On VIEIRA DA SILVA: Books—*Vieira da Silva* by Pierre Descargues, Paris 1949; *Le musée de poche: Vieira da Silva* by Rene de Solier, Paris 1956; *Vieira da Silva* by José Augusto Franca, Paris 1958; *Vieira da Silva* by Guy Weelen, Paris 1960; *Vieira da Silva,* exhibition catalog with text by Claude Esteban, Basel 1970; *Vieira da Silva: Malener 1935–1969,* exhibition catalog with texts by Snorre Andersen and Guy Weelen, Oslo 1970; *Vieira da Silva,* exhibition catalog with texts by Joao Gaspar Simoes, Mufilo Mendes and others, Lisbon 1970, *La peinture de Vieira da Silva* by Dora Vallier, Paris

1971; *Vieira da Silva: Paintings 1967–1971,* exhibition catalog with text by John Rewald, New York 1971; *Vieira da Silva,* exhibition catalog with text by Georges Desmoutiez, Montepellier, France 1971; *Vieira da Silva: Temperas, lithographies, gouaches et sengraphies,* exhibition catalog, Paris 1971, *Vieira da Silva* by Guy Weelen, Paris 1973; *Vieira da Silva,* exhibition catalog with texts by René Char and John Rewald, Geneva 1974; *Vieira da Silva: Gravuras e Litografias,* exhibition catalog, with text by Guy Weelen, Lisbon 1974; *Vieira da Silva: Les Estampes: Catalog de l'oeuvre grave* by Guy Weelen, Paris 1976; *Vieira da Silva,* exhibition catalog with text by Jean-Francois Jaeger, Paris 1976; *L'Univers de Vieira da Silva* by Antoine Terrasse, Paris 1977; *Vieira da Silva: Pinturas a Tempera,* exhibition catalog with text by Agustina Bessa Luis, Lisbon 1977; *Vieira da Silva* by Jacques Lassaigne and Guy Weelen, Barcelona and Paris 1978; *L'Eclat de la lumiere* by Anne Philipe, Paris 1979; *Longos dias tem cem anos: Presenca de Vieira da Silva* by Agustina Bessa Luis, Lisbon 1979; *Chemins d'approche: Vieira da Silva* by Dora Vallier, Paris 1982; *Vieira da Silva: Peintures* by Michel Butor, Paris 1983; *Vieira da Silva: Oeuvres sur papier* by Guy Weelen, Paris 1983; *Vieira da Silva e Arpad Szenes ou o Castelo Surrealista* by Mario Cesariny, Lisbon 1984; *Vieira da Silva,* Geneva 1994; *Arte moderna brasileira: uma selecao da colecao Roberto Marinho,* exhibition catalog, Sao Paulo 1994. **Articles—**''Marie-Helene Vieira da Silva'' by Leo Kochnitzky in *Quadrum,* no. 12, 1962; ''A luz da sombra'' by Margarida Acciaiuoli in *Coloquio Artes* (Lisbon), no. 102, vol. 36, July-September 1994; ''A Commentary on Paintings by Vieira da Silva'' by Alfred H. Katz in *Uj Muveszet,* vol. 5, pt. 11, November 1994.

* * *

The paintings of Vieira da Silva have a timeless modernity about them but it is still hard to realize that effectively her art career began as far back as 1919. To all familiar with the dramatis personae of the Ecole de Paris, although her transformation of architecture rendered upon canvas has been almost a permanent feature for so many years, each evidence of her extraordinary talent still seems paradoxically new.

It is true that as a young girl she once had ambitions to become a sculptor and even took a course under the tutelage of Despiau. But this short-lived enthusiasm cannot in any way explain the unusual and unique control she exerted on her canvases across the whole fabric of architectural conception.

Even a painting like the 1939 ''Les Drapeaux'' shows the same grasp of the building syndrome. The fluttering flags hang down like the tails of kites from windows, and there is no doubt that these are windows of huts set on stilts by some river people. The little squares of the ''flags'' and the rhodoid tiles on the roofs are repeated in the fabric between the posts and the rejections in the water. Already the elaborate patterning of Vieira da Silva which sets such store on the heaving chessboards of tiled vistas of which she is so fond—already this central element in nearly all her later work is plainly evident. That it was subsequently to become thicker and more tantalising to the eye, taking on the form of a gigantic art crossword puzzle, was just a matter of time.

Vieira da Silva was the supreme manipulator of perspective. Cities, promenades, floods, night, time itself are all pressed into service to act as welcome excuse for stretch after stretch of mosaic-like detail; not carefully wrought *azulejos* of Portuguese mural artists, but mosaics that have been shaken by earth tremors or frozen into noble austerity forever.

Architectural rectitude is only disturbed by the process of time and perhaps the incursion of decay. Looking at her pictures one realizes that she is deeply conscious of what age and weathering can do to her cherished subjects.

—Sheldon Williams

VILLALBA, Dario

Nationality: Spanish. **Born:** San Sebastian, 22 February 1939. **Education:** Boston, Massachusetts, 1950–54; studied in the Department of Fine Arts, Harvard University, Cambridge, Massachusetts, 1957–58; studied painting in the studio of André Lhote, Paris, 1968, and at the Escuela de Bellas Arte de San Fernando, Madrid, 1958–62; studied literature and philosophy, University of Madrid, 1962–64. **Career:** Independent artist, concentrating on painting, Madrid, from 1957; first Plexiglas-encased figures, 1966; photographic figures in Plexiglas, from 1972; canvases with photo emulsion, from 1973. **Awards:** Critics prize, *Bienal of Ibiza,* Spain, 1973; International Prize, *Bienal,* Sao Paulo, 1973; International Prize, *Graphics Biennale,* Ljubljana, Yugoslavia, 1979. **Agent:** Galeria Vandres, Don Ramon de la Cruz 26, Madrid-1. **Address:** Fernandez de la Hoy 61, Madrid-3, Spain.

Individual Exhibitions:

1957 Sala Alfil, Madrid
1964 Weeden Gallery, Boston
Galena Biosca, Madrid
Gallery 88, Miami
1966 Drian Galleries, London
Pinturas 1966, Galeria El Bosco, Cronica de Palomares, Madrid
1970 Museo Español de Arte Contemporaneo, Madrid
Galleria del Naviglio, Milan
Galerie Defacqz, Brussels
Spanish Pavilion, at the *Biennale,* Venice
1971 Musée d'Art et d'Histoire, Geneva
Studio C, Brescia, Italy
1972 Deson-Zaks Gallery, Chicago
Henry Mayer Gallery, Lausanne
Cité Universitaire, Neuchâtel, Switzerland
1973 Espace Pierre Cardin, Paris
Galleria del Naviglio, Milan
1974 Galeria Vandres, Madrid
Kunstverein, Frankfurt
1975 Louisiana Museum, Humlebaek, Denmark
Museum Boymans-van Beuningen, Rotterdam
Museum Bochum, West Germany
1976 *Retrospective 1972–1976,* Palais des Beaux-Arts, Brussels
Kunstverein, Heidelberg
1977 Kunstlerhaus, Vienna
Galerie Gras, Vienna
1978 Galeria Juana Mordo, Madrid
Galeria Vandres, Madrid
1980 Henie-Onstad Kunstsenter, Oslo

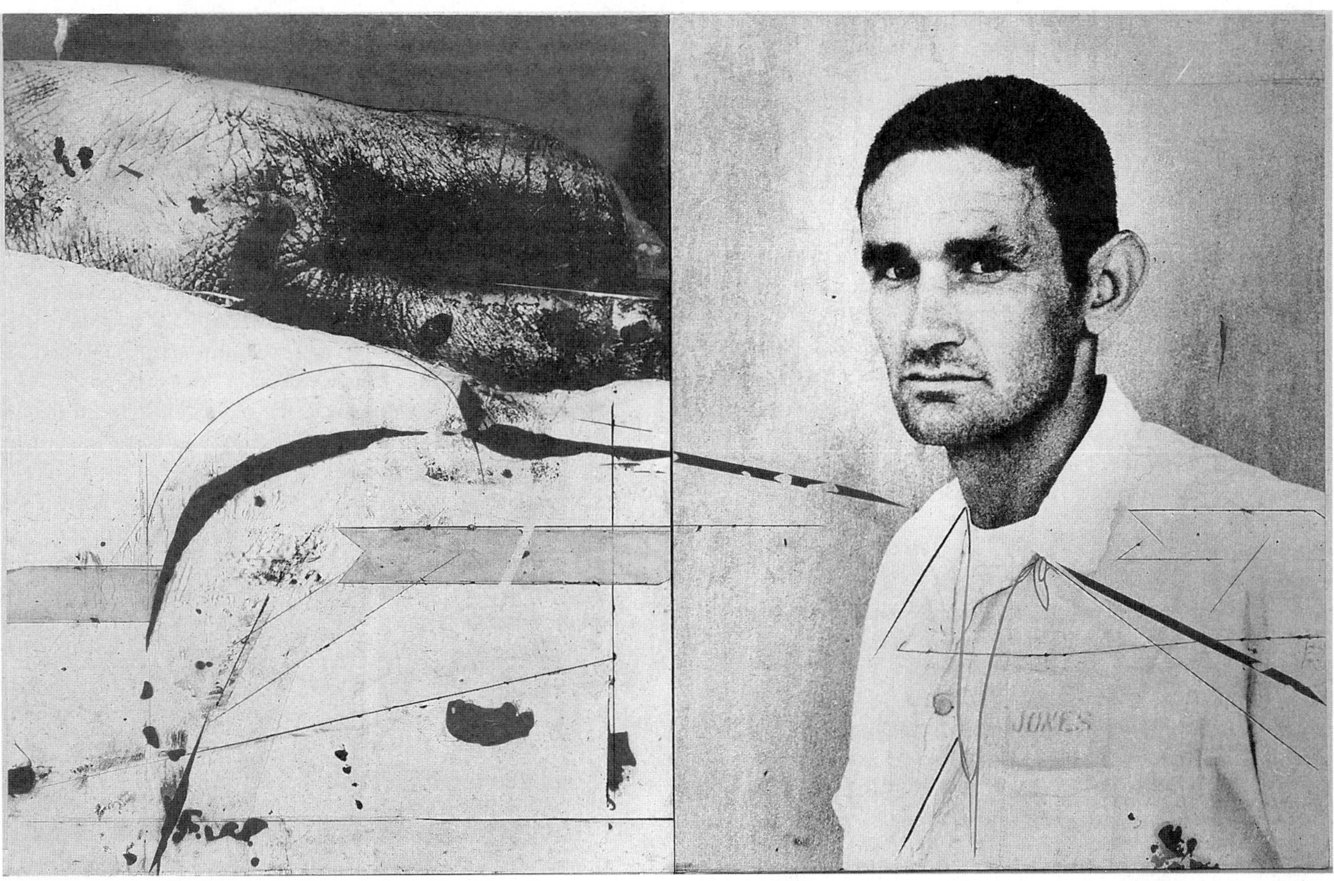

Dario Villalba: *Jones-red line.*

1981 Fondation Veranneman, Kruishoutem, Belgium
1982 Galleria del Naviglio, Milan
Charles Cowles Gallery, New York
1983 Salas Pablo Picasso, Madrid
1984 Charles Cowles Gallery, New York
1985 Museo de San Telmo, San Sebastian y Museo de Bellas Artes, Vitoria
Galeria 16, San Sebastian
1986 Charle Cowles Gallery, New York
1987 Art 18'87, Basilea
1988 Galeria Juana Mordo, Madrid
1990 Galeria Palace, Granada
Galeria Magda Gellotti, Algeciras
Galeria Puno, Valencia
1991 Galeria Juana Mordo, Madrid
1992 Galerie Michael Hasenclever, Munich
1993 Galeria Gamarra y Garrigues, Madrid
1994 Instituto Valenciano de Arte Moderno, centro Julio Gonzalez, Valencia
1995 Galeria Gamarra y Garrigues, Madrid
National Museum of Contemporary Art Oslo, Norway
1996 Palacio de la Audiencia, soria
Art 27'96, Sala individual, Galeria Gamarra, Basilea
1997 Galeria Salvador Diaz, Madrid
1998 Galeria Luis Adelantado, Valencia
1999 *Dario Villalba. Now,*Centro Cultural Cajastur Palacio Revillagigedo

Selected Group Exhibitions:

1963 *Contemporaray Spanish Painting,* D'Arcy Galleries, New York (toured the United States)
1965 *5 Spanish Painters,* at the *Bienal,* Sao Paulo
1970 *Testimonio 70,* Museo Espanol de Arte Contemporaneo, Madrid
1971 *Erotic Art in Spain Now,* Galeria Vandres, Madrid
1972 *Grands et Jeunes d'Aujourd'hui,* Grand Palais, Paris
1973 *Salon de Mai,* Musée d'Art Moderne, Paris
1975 *Biennale of Cagnes-sur-Mer,* France
1978 *La Materia,* Galeria Rayuela, Madrid
1980 *New Images from Spain,* Guggenheim Museum, New York
1983 *International Art Fair,* Chicago
1984 *An International Survey of Recent Painting and Sculpture,* Museum of Modern Art, New York
1986 *Premios Nacionales de Bellas Artes,* Museo de Arte Contemporaneo, Madrid
1987 *Fifty Years of Collecting: An Anniversary Selection,* Solomon R. Guggenheim Museum, New York
1988 *Arroyo, Gordillo, Villalba,* Galerie Michael Hasenclever, Munich
1990 *1st Biennale,* Luxemburg
1991 Museo de Bochum, Bochum
1992 *ARCO '92,* Madrid
X Bienal Internacional del Deporte en las Bellas Artes, Barcelona

1995 *ARCO '95,* Madrid
1996 National Museum of Contemporary Art, Oslo
1997 *El Arte y La Prensa,* Madrid
1998 *ARCO '98,* Madrid
1999 *ARCO '99,* Madrid

Collections:

Musée des Beaux-Arts, Ostend, Belgium; Fondation Veranneman, Kruishoutem, Belgium; Musée Royal des Beaux Arts, Brussels; Museo de Arte Contemporaneo, Seville; Louisiana Museum, Humlebaek, Denmark; Museum Boymans-van Beuningen, Rotterdam; Musée d'Art et d'Histoire, Geneva; Musée des Beaux-Arts, Lausanne; Museo de Arte Contemporaneo, Madrid; National Gallery of Australia, Canberra; Solomon R. Guggenheim Museum, New York; Metropolitan Museum of Art, New York; National Gallery, Oslo; Museum of Contemporary Art, Tehran.

Publications:

By VILLALBA: Book—*Grupo Quince,* 4 silkscreened objects, Milan 1973; Interview with Eduardo Arroyo in *Lapiz* (Madrid), no. 99, 100, 101, 1994; in *Arte y Parte,* no. 8, April-May 1997.

On VILLALBA: Books—*Dario Villalba: Pinturas 1966,* exhibition catalog, with text by Angel Crespo, Madrid 1966; *Nuevos maestros de la pintura española* by Raul Chavarri, Madrid 1972; *Dario Villalba at the Deson-Zaks Gallery,* exhibition catalog with text by Franz Schulze, Chicago 1972; *Villalba,* exhibition catalog with texts by Pierre Restany and Giancarlo Politi, Madrid 1974; *Dario Villalba,* exhibition catalog with text by Peter Spielmann, Hans Gercke, Titia Berlage and Michael Fehr, Bochum, West Germany 1975; *Dario Villalba: Retrospective 1972–1976,* exhibition catalog with texts by Titia Berlage, René Micha, Luis Gonzalez Robles and others, Brussels 1976; *Europa-America: The Different Avant-Gardes* by Achille Bonito Oliva, Milan 1976; *Diccionario de pintores españoles contemporaneos* by Ignacio De Blas, Madrid 1976; *Kunst Kommt nicht von Konnen* by Hans-Jürgen Müller, Stuttgart 1977; *Dario Villalba,* exhibition catalog with text by Ole Henrik Moe, Oslo 1980; *Dario Villalba: Obra reciente 1980–1983,* exhibition catalog with text by Eugenio de Vicente, Madrid 1983; *Dario Villalba. Exposicion Antologica, 1970–1985,* exhibition catalog, Excmo 1985; *Dario Villalba, Obra Reciente,* exhibition catalog, Madrid 1985; *Dario Villalba, 1900–1991,* exhibition catalog, Madrid 1991; *Coleccion de Arte de Fndesco 1985–1993,* exhibition catalog, Madrid 1993; *Dario Villalba, 1964–1994,* exhibition catalog, Valencia 1994.

*

I began using photography in my work in 1968. Therefore I am considered, with other artists a world-wide pioneer of this language. A painting can contain more emotion, pressure, insinuation, love, pain, than reality, due to its ''freezing'' power.

—Dario Villalba

* * *

Dario Villalba's plastic capsules got to London in 1968. They had already caused a considerable stir at the Venice *Biennale.* At that time they were so unexpected, such a novel experience, that too few people did more than step back and marvel at them. A bad reaction because what the artist wanted from his viewers was thought rather than emotion.

Above all, Villalba is a fighter for the acceptance of human rights. That his campaigns are waged through the artistic forms that he has chosen is our good fortune, but should in no way reduce the potencies of the many messages he wishes to deliver. Villalba's ideas about human rights are basic, certainly not the application of well thought-out laws and regulations. He wants proper understanding of pain and suffering, and he wants to throw out a lifeline to the hopeless.

Effectively his career in its most pertinent sense can be divided into three periods, all of which interrelate.

From 1966 to 1971 he made life-sized fleshcoloured figures which were enclosed in plexiglass and hand-rotated at variable speeds from a plexiglass superstructure.

A year later, using the same technique and materials, he switched from his earlier fluorescent-pink figures to blow-ups from press photos. The subjects in these works were also altered. By this time Villalba had turned his attention to the area of sociological problems—a worker in overalls beset with the difficulties of the class system; a youth in jeans and T-shirt glaring at the outside world and raising his clenched fist; the face of a woman, her eyes closed, at the point of death; a patient in a psychiatric ward, his protruding feet knotted together by the wet bed-sheet. Over these images where he felt it relevant, Villalba scrawled symbols as comments.

Since then he has still further expanded the process, reproducing the figures on emulsioned canvases. To emphasize his intention, sometimes the works appear in triptych form—first the feet, then the arm, then the head. Or he takes disparate elements and welds them together in a near-abstract assemblage, making the blow-up technique of the press photograph create enlargements that turn the ''screen'' of the original newspaper photo into an independent patterning.

Villalba is operating on two levels. On one his ''man'' regards nature with imperturbable calm: on the other, the same man turns a look of cold and vitriolic hatred upon the cruelties of the social system.

For the viewer, the Villalba images are also bilateral. He looks at them, but they look back at him. And not just the faces. Feet and hands have become personalized. His presentation is at one and the same time fascinating and appalling.

Does an art public, or even a public at large, want or require such aggressive preaching? The question is an academic one. So many frightening versions of the Temptation of Saint Anthony in no way deflected praise from those who appreciate good painting. Goya's etchings of the Horrors of War are a satchel of masterpieces. Now Villalba with great technical skill hangs up his plastic bags full of the Horrors of Man.

—Sheldon Williams

VILLEGLÉ, Jacques (Mahé) de la

Nationality: French. **Born:** Quimper, Finistere, 27 March 1926. **Education:** Studied at secondary school in Vannes-Morbihan, 1934–43; the Ecole des Beaux-Arts, Rennes, 1944–46; studied architecture at the Ecole Nationale Supérieure des Beaux-Arts, Nantes, 1947–49.

Jacques Villeglé: *Autoroute sud,* 1991. Photo by Francois Poivret. ©2001 Artists Rights Society (ARS), NY/ADAGP, Paris.

Family: Married Marie-Francoise de Faultrier in 1956; daughters: Valerie, Fabienne and Adeline. **Career:** Worked as architectural draughtsman, Vannes, 1943–44; in St. Malo, 1946. Independent artist, writer and filmmaker, in Paris, since 1949; first decollaged poster assembly, 1949; collaborative works with Raymond Hains, 1950–53; member, Nouveaux Realistes group of artists, Paris, 1960. **Agent:** Galerie Georges-Philippe & Nathalie Vallois, 36 rue de Seine, 75006 Paris, France. **Address:** 15–17 rue au Maire, 75003 Paris, France.

Individual Exhibitions:

1957 Galerie Colette Allendy, Paris (with Raymond Hains)
1959 Atelier Francois Dufrene, Paris
1963 Galerie J., Paris
1964 Galerie Ad Libitum, Antwerp
1967 Galerie Jacqueline Ranson, Paris
1971 Galerie Michael Werer, Cologne
Moderna Museet, Stockholm
1972 Galerie Der Spiegel, Cologne
Museum Haus Lange, Krefeld, West Germany
1974 *Temoin de Notre Temps,* Galerie Beaubourg, Paris
Galerie Semiha Huber, Zurich
Centre of Arts and Communication, Vaduz, Lichtenstein
1976 Studio Sant'Andrea, Milan
Galerie Alexandre de la Salle, St. Paul de Vence, France
Galerie Le Dessin, Paris
1978 *Ravisseur Ravi de la Rèalité,* Musée des Jacobins, Morlaix, France
1979 Office d'Action Culturelle, Saint-Brieuc, France
1980 Galerie Beaubourg, Paris
Centre Noroit, Arras, France
1981 Galerie Convergence, Nantes, France
1982 Galerie J and J Donguy, Paris
Galerie Micheline Szwajcer, Antwerp
1985 Maison de la Culture Rennes, France
Espace Claudine Breguet, Paris
1986 Galerie Convergence, Nantes, France
Espace Claudine Breguet, Paris
1987 Galerie 44, Kaarst-Dusseldorf, West Germany
Galerie Reckermann, Cologne
Galerie Christian Laune, Montpellier, France
1988 Galerie d'Art Contemporain, Nice
Galerie Le Chanjour, Nice
1989 Sabine Wachters Fine Arts, Knokke-Zoute
Zabriskie Gallery, New York
1990 Galerie Fanny Guillon, Laffaille, Paris
Musée d'Art Moderne, Collioure
1991 Musée Vasarely, Gordes
1992 Centres Culturel Français, Bologna and Torino, Italy
1993 Galerie Apomixie, Paris
Stephen Cohen Gallery, Los Angeles
1994 Sabine Wachters Fine Arts, Brussels
Espace Van Gogh, Arles
1996 *Villeglé: Retrospective 1955–1992,* Centre d'Art Bouvet-Ladubay, Saumar
1998 *Jacques Villeglé: Décollages 1950–1998,* Alan Koppel Gallery, Chicago
1999 *Mots 1949–1996,* Galerie Georges-Philippe & Nathalie Vallois, Paris
Villeglé, Ubu Gallery, New York
2000 *Dans la rue: Jacques Villeglé and Pierre Henry,* Cité de la Musique, Paris
Luxembourg, Galerie Lucien Schweitzer, Luxembourg

Selected Group Exhibitions:

1961 *The Art of Assemblage,* Museum of Modern Art, New York (toured the United States)
1977 *Trois Villes,* Centre National d'Art Contemporain, Paris
1979 *Nouveau Realisme,* Freitags Galerie Imhof, Solothurn, Switzerland
1980 *Les Affichistes,* Galerie Mathias Fels, Paris
1987 *Les Nouveaux Realistes,* Musée des Beaux-Arts, Winterthur, Switzerland
1989 *Art en France,* Musée Pouchkine Moscow (and L'Ermitage, Leningrad)
1990 *High and Low,* Museum of Modern Art, New York
1991 *Pop Art,* Royal Academy of Arts, London
1992 *Pop Art,* Museum Ludwig, Cologne
1993 *Biennale,* Lyon
1994 *La Ville, art et architecture en Europe 1870–1993,* Centre Georges Pompidou, Paris, and Centre de Cultura Contemporia, Barcelona

1996 *Les Sixties,* Musée d'Histoire Contemporaine, Paris, and Museum of Brighton, Great Britain
1997 *Magie der Zahl,* Staatsgalerie, Stuttgart, Germany
60er Jahre-Die neuen Abenteuer der Objekte, Museum Ludwig, Cologne, Germany
1998 *Rendez-vous,* Solomon R. Guggenheim, New York
1999 *Vooropening,* S.M.A.K., Gent, Belgium
La Peinture après l'abstraction, 1955–1975, M.A.M.V.P., Paris
2000 *Micropolitiques,* Magasin, Grenoble
Open Ends: Matter, Museum of Modern Art, New York
Walker Evans & Company, Museum of Modern Art, New York

Collections:

Centre Georges Pompidou, Paris; Musée Cantini, Marseilles; Musée d'Art Moderne de la Ville de Paris; Réunion des Musées Nationaux (FNAC), Paris; Moderna Museet, Stockholm; Kaiser-Wilhelm Museum, Krefeld, Germany; Hessiches Landesmuseum, Darmstadt; Musée de Beaux-Arts, Geneva; Museum van Hedendaagse Kunst, Ghent; Museum Moderner Kunst, Vienna; Musée d'Art Moderne, Bologne; Israel Museum, Jerusalem; Museum of Modern Art, New York.

Publications:

By de la VILLEGLÉ: Books—*Heperile Eclaté,* with Raymond Hains and Camille Bryen, Paris 1953; *De Mathieu à Mahe,* Paris 1967; *Les volantes du ravisseur,* La Louvière, Belgium 1974; *Lacéré anonyme,* Paris 1977; *Commémoration de la loi du 29 Juillet 1881,* Paris 1981; *L'Innocence du choix,* Nice 1982; *Urbi et orbi,* Dijon 1986; *De la manifestation spontanée,* Cognac 1986; *La croisée de signes,* Lyon 1993; *L'épigraphie contestataire,* Caen 1994; *Carre Four Politique,* Calignac 1997; *Cheminements, 1943–1959,* Saint-Julien-Molin-Molette 1999. **Films**—*Paris-Saint Brieuc,* 1952; *Etude aux allures,* with Raymond Hains, 1954; *Le Mythe de la Ville,* 1976.

On de la VILLEGLÉ: Books—*Collage: Personalities, Concepts, Techniques* by Harriet Janis and Rudi Blesh, New York 1962; *Villeglé,* exhibition catalog with text by Pierre Restany, Paris 1963; *Les nouveaux réalistes* by Pierre Restany, Paris 1968; *Pop Art et cie* by Francois Pluchart, Paris 1971; *Villeglé,* exhibition catalog with text by Otto Hahn, Stockholm 1971; *L'Art actuel en France* by Anne Tronche, Paris 1974; *Villeglé: Témoin de notre temps,* exhibition catalog with text by Pierre Restany, Paris 1974; *Les Pré-Voyants* by Alain Jouffroy, Brussels 1974; *Formalism and Historicity* by Benjamin H. D. Buchloh, Chicago 1977; *Villeglé, Ravisseur ravi de la réalité,* exhibition catalog with text by Otto Hahn, Morlaix, France 1978; *Le retour de l'Hourloupe,* exhibition catalog with text by Bernard Lamarche-Vadel, Rennes 1985; *Villeglé le chapardeur* by Jean-Phillippe Lemée, Nantes 1986; *Les nouveaux réalistes,* exhibition catalog with text by Dieter Schwarz, Mannheim and Winterthur 1986; *Jacques Villeglé,* exhibition catalog with text by Philippe Piquet, Montpellier 1987; *Catalogs thématique des affiches lacérées* (6 volumes), Marval, Paris 1988/90; *Villeglé: La présentation en jugement,* by B. Lamarche-Vadel, Marval, Paris 1990; *Villeglé Techno Rapt* by Dominique Dossol, Calignac 1999; *Mots 1949–1996* by Catherine Millet, Paris 1999; *La Mémoire Insoluble* by Dominique Dussol, Dordogne 2000; *Dans la Rue* by Catherine Francblin, Paris 2000.

*

At the start of the 1950s, dislocating the square of cold abstracts which chastised emotion, the physiological and physical powers of the artist shifted position to the profit of an element of total chance which alone was becoming and could be productive. The artist, becoming ''action-painter,'' then, to conclude the series and by reference to the street hoarding ''automobile compressor,'' rejected on principle all conscious intervention, all hesitation and all conscious choice. As has been stated by the author of a general aesthetic, he opposed ''learnt beauty, of which he is tired, the harsh and natural beauty which man finds fully equipped beneath his feet and which owes nothing to calculation or exertion.''

The lacerations, traces of the gesture in its wild state, come out of anonymity. I would have liked to see them remain there.

If, after having torn down a fragment of a hoarding, the timidity of a certain fear disheartens me it sometimes happens that I unselfconsciously give it the necessary tear to make it stand out, being unable to completely repress the common taste for producing and creating falsities.

Falsities? No, let us recall that discussion between Arp and Mondrian. The latter opposed the artificiality of art to the naturalness of nature, I think, and Arp would not contradict me, that the impulsive gesture of the street is not opposed by that natural tendency to action which more or less everybody possesses. If my hand knows how to terminate the roughed-out gesture of an unknown person, to seek for glory on account of the fact would be inane. The appropriative and selective speculation of an object must not be lowered to the level of a studio procedure, as if to return to the game of dupes which the exercise of drawing and painting has become. ''It tends toward the foolish glorification of the hand. The hand is the guilty party, and how can one accept being the slave of one's own hand? It is inadmissible that drawing and painting should today still be where writing was before Gutenberg'' (André Breton).

It is regrettable to sign a poster—which the worker in paint, Fernand Léger, would have considered as ''having become unusable''—but it remains true that by my label I facilitate its recognition and preserve it from destruction. Beauty is a tributary of bourgeois contingencies. Nevertheless, if I sign, would it not be natural for the successive purchasers or selectors to affix their signatures also, which would simply be resuming a Chinese custom whereby the collector was invited to add his mark beside that of the artist? In sharing my merit as inventor, they would with the same stroke diminish the importance of my imprint and would bring the laceration back to the anonymity of its point of departure.

The ensemble of lacerators, ravishers and collectors will therefore be called ''Lacere Anonyme,'' and would it be to establish the facts of activity whose author would seem to be elusive that my goal would be restricted, or rather, would it be in reconstituting the work of a collective unconscious in personalising the ''Lacere Anonyme''? Giambattista Vico did not act differently when he proved that Homer was not one single person but a collective being, a symbol of the Greek people, telling of its own history in national songs.

To endorse the secret of the creation of the lacerated work, I organized in June 1959 in the atelier of Francois Dufrene a series of soirees entitled ''Lacere Anonyme.'' With this generic title each work acquires a specific character. By anonymous gestural aggression the poster becomes illegible, becomes one of the most outstanding manifestations "of art made by everyone and not by one alone" of our time. When Caliban becomes a painter what happens to. . . the professional and traditional painter and his craft?

—Jacques Villeglé

* * *

The so-called *affichistes* Francois Dufrêne, Raymond Hains, Mimmo Rotella and Jacques Villeglé form a sort of subgroup of the group known as the Nouveaux Réalistes, since their works have a common starting point and are to some extent closely related, while the other artists in the group all tread very different paths. Along with Klein these four are also the Nouveaux Réalistes whose works, outwardly at least, most closely resemble the traditional canvas, which does not mean, however, that they are the 'painters' of the group.

Villeglé received his artistic training in Rennes, where he got to know Raymond Hains, an artist with whom he was frequently to work in the following years. While Hains was devoting his attention to photographic techniques, in 1947 Villeglé had already restricted his artistic activity to the collection of objects which he found near his home on the Breton coast: pieces of wire and other flotsam and jetsam washed up on the Atlantic coast, along with pamphlets and other fragments of printed material. He tells how in January 1947 Hains and he wandered through the Nantes docklands: during the course of that walk it became clear to him how impossible was the artistic transposition of lived reality in its entirety, with which he sought directly and objectively to confront the spectator.

Working with Hains in Paris in 1949, it was in *décollage* that Villeglé found the medium for realising these ideas. The two artists worked together on their first poster abstracts. Such work was the logical consequence of the conversations revolving round the search for an alternative to the abstract art that was beginning to establish itself in Paris now that the war was over. In opposition to painting, the aim of this poster abstract was to link up the avant-garde trends of the 1910s and 1920s which, in Europe, had come to an abrupt end. Not until many years later did Villeglé find a forefather for his historical researches in the person of the French surrealist Leo Malet. Malet had coined the term *décollage* in 1938. For him *décollage* meant the tearing off of individual sections of poster in order to reveal parts of the underlying poster layers and to leave room for speculation concerning what was still concealed. It was a poetic street activity which was still fully in the service of the verbal text, and Malet did not go so far as to uproot the product of *décollage* from its immediate environment.

Hains and Villeglé removed the selected sections of poster from their backing and then mounted them on canvas; the canvas was used on account of its lightness and elasticity, not because of its association with the painted picture. In the process of mounting, the artists might in some cases introduce corrections into the selected poster section. Villeglé also mentions the 'coup de pouce' (finishing touch) which was often necessary in order to complete the insufficiently forceful works, but which was executed without destroying their overall anonymity.

Placarding, particularly that of small political placards, signifies, independently of any actual message carried by the placard, the act of occupying a public area. Under the clause 'Défense d'afficher,' the bill that was passed in France on 29 July 1881 and divides public areas into display-free zones and zones reserved for the display of advertising material *(emplacements réservés);* anyone who tears down such material is guilty of a criminal offence. The sticking up or pasting over, removal or defacement of posters and placards has correspondingly become a symbol of political struggle. In contrast to wall painting and graffiti, the defacement of the writing in the poster abstract follows no subjective-aesthetic rules. It signifies above all the adoption of an attitude, 'antidote contre toute propaganda', and only as an ironic afterthought can it be understood in terms of a decorative design.

By their shabby appearance poster abstracts bear witness to life in certain Parisian quarters, and in his *Le flaneur aux patissades* Villeglé describes the differences between hoardings in the various quarters depending on the degree and nature of building and renovation work going on there. The transformation of the city and especially the erection of inaccessibly high large-format advertising hoardings could mean the end of the 'era' of the poster abstract.

The selection of an object, which becomes a work of art merely by grace of the artist's decision, takes us back to Marcel Duchamp's notion of the ready-made. There are however some fundamental differences between the poster abstract and the ready-made. Poster abstracts are closer from the outset to conventional art, since they assume the conventional form of a picture. They do not merely refer to the artistic context or, as the case may be, to themselves as autonomous works of art; they have besides this a representative function: they refer to the sections of poster that were not selected, to the permanent street exhibition, and thereby step beyond the closed world of art and into that of an anonymous public.

The tradition of artistic skill is replaced by a passive, receptive strolling around, in the course of which the stroller finds and selects posters. There is equally no clear intention in the mind of the artist engaged in tearing down and shredding posters: the spontaneous, unconsidered gesture takes the place of the premeditated composition. And even if certain gestures are deliberate, their significance is lost among the multitude of other gestures whereby the poster is built up. In this way the poster abstract denies essential elements which contribute towards the value of a work of art: craftsmanship, effort and time.

A new academic style could clearly develop out of the anonymous poster abstract. Bryen had already predicted: "Anti-painting is becoming the painting of today and even in its freedom is adopting mannerisms and styles." Villeglé had tried to avoid that by consistently assuming the role of sociological observer and abnegating the traditional one of the creative artist. He entitles his works with the place and date of the discovery and accords thematic importance to their timing. In 1982 he thus dedicated an exhibition to the *Présidentielles 81* (the 1981 presidential elections), following the progress of the various election candidates: "Je n'ai aucun parti pris sur les candidats, je suis presque un historian, qui prend les faits bruts" (I have no particular bias with regard to the candidates, I am virtually a historian, merely recording the bare facts). Through his writing, moreover, he has become the historian of what he calls the *Lacéré anonyme* (the anonymous slasher), the historian of the community of anonymous 'poster slashers', the discoverer and collector of their work.

—Dieter Schwarz

VIOLA, Bill

Nationality: American. **Born:** New York, 25 January 1951. **Education:** College of Visual and Performing Arts, Syracuse University, New York, B.F.A. 1973. **Career:** Artist; assisted Nam June Paik and Peter Campus with various projects, 1970s; worked with the composer David Tudor and the avant-garde music group Composers Inside Electronics, 1973–80; technical production manager, Art/Tapes/22 Video Studio, Florence, 1974–76; visiting artist, WNET/Thirteen Television Laboratory, New York, 1976–83; taught video, California Institute for the Arts, Valencia, 1983. **Awards:** Visual Artist Fellowship, National Endowment for the Arts, 1978, 1983, 1989; U.S./Japan Friendship Commission fellowship, 1980–81; artist-in-residence, Sony Corporation's Atsugi Laboratories, Atsugi, Japan, 1981; Video Artist Fellowship, Rockefeller Foundation, 1982; Polaroid Video Award for outstanding achievement, 1984; artist-in-residence, San Diego Zoo, 1984; John Simon Guggenheim Memorial Foundation video stipend, 1985; American Film Institute Maya Deren Award, 1987; John D. and Catherine T. MacArthur Foundation Award, 1989; Medienkunstpreis, ZKM Karlsruhe, Germany, 1993. Honorary doctorate, Syracuse University, 1995.

Selected Individual Exhibitions:

1973 *New Video Work,* Everson Museum of Art, Syracuse, New York
1974 *Bill Viola: Video and Sound Installations,* The Kitchen Center, New York
1975 *Bill Viola: Videotapes,* Long Beach Museum of Art, Long Beach, California
Rain—Three Interlocking Systems, Everson Museum of Art, Syracuse, New York (catalog)
1979 *Projects: Bill Viola,* The Museum of Modern Art, New York
1981 *Bill Viola,* Vancouver Art Gallery, Vancouver, B.C., Canada
Anthology Film Archives, New York
1982 *Bill Viola,* Whitney Museum of American Art, New York
1983 *Bill Viola,* ARC/Musée d'Art Moderne de la Ville de Paris, Paris, France
1985 *Bill Viola,* Moderna Museet, Stockholm
Bill Viola, The Museum of Contemporary Art, Los Angeles (catalog)
1986 *Bill Viola: I Do Not Know What It Is I Am Like,* Institute of Contemporary Art, Boston
1987 *Bill Viola: Installations and Videotapes,* The Museum of Modern Art, New York (catalog)
1988 *Bill Viola: Video Installation and Videotapes,* Riverside Studios, Hammersmith, London (toured)
Bill Viola: Survey of a Decade, Contemporary Arts Museum, Houston, Texas
1989 *Bill Viola,* 3rd Fukui International Video Biennale: Expansion and Transformation, Fukui Fine Arts Museum, Fukui, Japan (catalog)
1990 *Bill Viola: He Weeps for You,* La Box, École Nationale des Beaux-Arts, Bourges, France
Bill Viola: Room for St. John of the Cross, Cranbrook Academy of Art Museum, Bloomfield Hills, Michigan
1991 *Bill Viola: Video Projects,* Museum für Moderne Kunst, Frankfurt, Germany
1992 *Slowly Turning Narrative,* Institute of Contemporary Art, University of Pennsylvania, Philadelphia (toured)
Bill Viola: Unseen Images, Kunsthalle Düsseldorf (toured Europe and Israel)
1993 *Bill Viola,* Musée d'art contemporain de Montréal, Montréal
1995 *Bill Viola: Buried Secrets,* Venice Biennale
1996 *Bill Viola: New Work,* Savannah College of Art and Design, Georgia
Bill Viola: Stations, Lannan Foundation, Los Angeles
1997 *Bill Viola: Fire, Water, Breath,* Guggenheim Museum Soho, New York (catalog)
Bill Viola: The Theater of Memory, Orange County Museum of Art, Newport Beach, California
1998 *Bill Viola,* Whitney Museum of American Art, New York (catalog)
2000 *Bill Viola: New Work,* James Cohan Gallery, New York
Bill Viola, Detroit Institute of Arts, Michigan

Selected Group Exhibitions:

1973 *Circuits,* Cranbrook Academy of Art Museum, Bloomfield Hills, Michigan; toured
1974 *Art Now: A Celebration of the American Arts,* John F. Kennedy Center for the Performing Arts, Washington, D.C. (catalog)
1975 *Video Art,* Institute of Contemporary Art, Philadelphia; toured
Videotapes from Art/Tapes/22, The Museum of Modern Art, New York
1976 *Video Art: An Overview,* San Francisco Museum of Modern Art, San Francisco, California
1977 *Projects: Video XIII,* The Museum of Modern Art, New York
10e Biennale de Paris, ARC/Musée d'Art moderne de la Ville de Paris, Paris, France, 1977
1978 *Video Art: Made for TV?,* The Kitchen, New York
1979 *Biennial Exhibition,* Whitney Museum of American Art, New York (catalog)
1982 *Dreams and Nightmares,* Long Beach Museum of Art, Long Beach, California
National Video Festival, American Film Institute, Los Angeles, California (catalog)
Recent Video Archive Acquisitions, The Museum of Modern Art, New York
The 4th Biennale of Sydney: Vision in Disbelief, Art Gallery of New South Wales, Sydney, Australia (catalog)
1983 *The Second Link: Viewpoints on Video in the Eighties,* Walter Phillips Gallery, The Banff Centre, Banff, Alberta, Canada; toured (catalog)
1984 *Video: A Retrospective: 1974–1984,* Long Beach Museum of Art, California (catalog)
1985 *Currents,* Institute of Contemporary Art, Boston (catalog)
1986 *New York City Video,* Artspace, Visual Arts Center, Sydney, Australia (catalog)
1987 *The Arts for Television,* Stedelijk Museum, Amsterdam; toured (catalog)

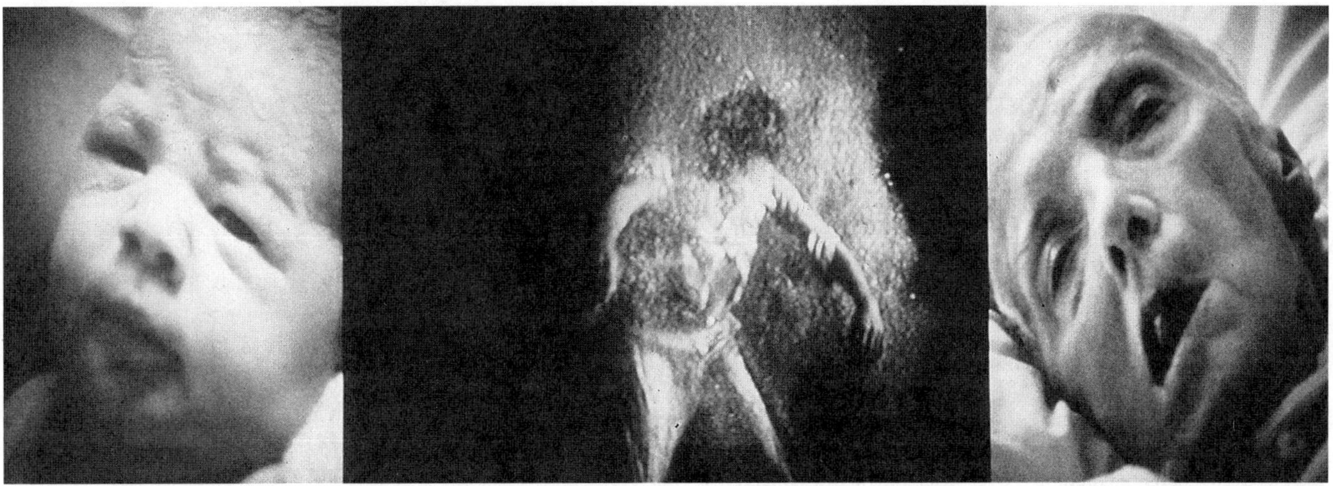

Bill Viola: *Nantes Triptych.* ©Tate Gallery, London/Art Resource, NY; courtesy of Tate Gallery.

Avant-Garde in the Eighties, Los Angeles County Museum of Art, Los Angeles (catalog)
Documenta VII, Kassel, Germany (catalog)
1988 *American Landscape Video: The Electronic Grove,* The Carnegie Museum of Art, Pittsburgh; toured the United States (catalog)
Striking Distance, The Museum of Contemporary Art, Los Angeles; toured
1989 *Image World: Art and Media Culture,* Whitney Museum of American Art, New York (catalog)
Ressource Kunst: Die Elemente neu gesehen, Künstlerhaus Bethanien, Germany; toured (catalog)
1990 *Eye for I: Video Self-Portraits,* organized by the Independent Curators Incorporated, New York; toured the United States, Canada, and Europe (catalog)
Passages de l'image, Musée national d'art moderne, Centre Georges Pompidou, Paris (catalog)
1991 *Metropolis,* Martin-Gropius-Bau, Berlin, Germany (catalog)
Opening Exhibition, Museum für Moderne Kunst, Frankfurt, Germany
The Pleasure Machine: Recent American Video, Milwaukee Art Museum, Wisconsin
1992 *Art at the Armory: Occupied Territory,* Museum of Contemporary Art, Chicago
Documenta IX, Kassel, Germany (catalog)
Manifeste, Musée national d'art moderne, Centre Georges Pompidou, Paris
1993 *Chaos-Turbulence-Critical Points,* Louisiana Museum of Modern Art, Humlebaek, Denmark (catalog)
1995 Venice Biennale
1996 Foundation Cartier pour l'art contemporain, Paris
Mediascape, Guggenheim Museum Soho, New York (catalog)
Negotiating Rapture: The Power of Art to Transform Lives, Museum of Contemporary Art, Chicago (catalog)
1999 *The Art of Memory,* The Center for Curatorial Studies Museum, Bard College, Annondale-on-Hudson, New York (catalog)

Publications:

By VIOLA: Book—*Reasons for Knocking at an Empty House: Writings 1973–1994,* edited by Robert Violette, Cambridge, Massachusetts 1995. **Articles—**''Bill Viola: Preparing for the Venice Biennale'' interview in *Aperture,* Fall 1995; ''An Interview with Bill Viola'' in *Art New England,* December 1995-January 1996; ''Art at the End of the Optical Age'' interview by Virginia Rutledge in *Art in America,* March 1998.

On VIOLA: Books—*Bill Viola* (exhibition catalog), New York and Paris 1994; *Video d'autore: 1986–1995* by Valentina Valentini, Rome 1995. **Articles—**''Bill Viola'' by Thomas Frick in *Art in America,* June 1985; ''Deep TV: Bill Viola's Via Negativa'' by Donald Kuspit in *Artforum,* May 1995; ''On Interpretation: Bill Viola's *The Passing*'' by Sean Cubitt in *Screen* (London), Summer 1995; ''Bill Viola: Allegories in Subjective Perception'' by William D. Judson in *Art Journal,* Winter 1995; ''Vide Video'' by Ian Hunt in *Art Monthly,* May 1996; ''Post-Traumatic Shock: Bill Viola's Recent Work'' by Dierdre Boyle in *Afterimage* (Rochester, New York), September-October 1996; ''The Self-Discovery Channel'' by Hunter Drohojowska Philp in *ARTnews,* November 1997; ''Bill Viola: Altered Perceptions'' by Michael Duncan in *Art in America,* March 1998; ''Artist Viola's World Infused with Divine'' by Virginia Maksymowicz in *National Catholic Reporter,* 24 April 1998; ''Mondo Video'' by Alyssa Katz in *The Nation,* 25 May 1998; ''Eye of the Beholder'' by Nancy Rosen in *Video Magazine,* May 1998; ''Video as High Art'' by Reena Jana in *Wired,* 13 July 1999. **Videos—***Bill Viola,* Oregon Public Broadcasting, 1996; *A World of Art Works in Progress,* Oregon Public Broadcasting, 1996.

* * *

Video artist Bill Viola creates sensual environments which probe the universal themes of human experience. His videotapes, installations, and publications are produced and his exhibitions coordinated by his wife and partner Kira Perov, who is also responsible for the photographic documentation of his work. Together they bring the dual concepts of birth and death, chaos and tranquility, and consciousness and sleep to video installation work which explores the bounds of the cycle of life.

Viola became interested in these ideas while an art student at Syracuse University in the early 1970s. He found inspiration in such sacred writings as the Upanishads and the Bhagavad Gita, and studied Christian and Islamic mysticism and Zen Buddhism. Viola was deeply moved by the common notions of timelessness and quiet confrontation found in these philosophies. These introspective investigations coincided with Viola's discovery of video as a creative medium in 1970. He was a founding member of the Synapse video group, a student organization that installed and operated a cable television system in 1971. This naturally led to Viola's first original video piece, *Wild Horses,* in 1972. That same year Viola gained experience and insight into the world of media arts when he began working as a video preparator at Syracuse's Everson Museum of Art. In this capacity, Viola had the opportunity to work as an exhibition assistant for such pioneers as Nam June Paik, Frank Gillette, and Peter Campus.

During this time, Viola continued to study religious philosophies and felt that video was the perfect medium to explore these notions of the universality of human experience. He states that ''culture comes from people and is formed by the individual's engagement with the world.'' Drawn to the writings of the Gnostics of early Christianity and intrigued by the martyrs of sacred thought, Viola discovered the *via negativa,* a Medieval text which discusses the Cloud of Unknowing. This work's assertion that God cannot be known or comprehended deeply affected Viola. He continued to work in the emerging video art world professionally, serving as the technical director of production for the Art/Tapes/22 studio in Italy from 1974–76. Viola absorbed the influences of his surroundings, studying Renaissance paintings and working with such video artists as Vito Acconci and Joan Jonas at the studio.

In 1976 Viola returned to New York to take a position as a Visiting Artist at WNET/Thirteen Television Laboratory. That year he created his first video and sound installation, *He Weeps for You,* an exploration of the interconnection and utter interdependence of the microcosmic and macrocosmic worlds. The work contains a small brass valve which slowly emits drops of water. As each tiny droplet appears, it is magnified by a video camera and the image created is projected onto a screen. This enlarged view reveals that both the viewer and the room are reflected in the minuscule droplet. As the water drop swells and drops from the valve, it falls onto an amplified drum below, making a loud sound. As the sound occurs, a new droplet emerges from the valve. This highly detailed and meditative work reveals the aesthetic concerns present in Viola's style from the beginning.

Reflecting Pool was created over a two-year span (1977–79) and is a more minimalist installation work. This videotape of the artist actively engaged with nature was displayed as a projection onto a double-sided screen in the middle of the exhibition space. The artist walks out of a wooded area and stands before a pool. As he jumps up, the action is frozen. Subsequent movement is shown only as a reflection in the water. Ultimately, Viola enters the pool, emerges, and returns to the forest. This tampering with time and reality evolved, manifesting itself next in the oddly confrontational *Reasons for Knocking at an Empty House* in 1982. Here Viola faces the viewer and stares while fighting an obvious impulse to sleep. The fine line of consciousness is explored as sounds of breathing and swallowing are heard through headphones. The room itself is silent, except for the violent random sounds made when a silhouetted figure emerges from the shadows in the image and strikes Viola.

The 1980s saw shifts in Viola's work as he applied his evolving skills to new technologies. During this time he created installation works which are at once sacred objects and provocative artworks. *Anthem* (1983) explores primal fears and the ''separation of the material body from its spiritual foundation.'' By 1987, Viola was using gallery space more actively as a contextual device in his work. His *Passage* is screened in a small room at the end of a narrow entrance corridor. It features a child's birthday party in extremely slow motion such that the work cycles over a seven-hour period. The effect is that the viewer is forced to really look at the piece, and in this engagement personal memories are evoked. Viola's dedication to critical discourse and the common language of human life led to the creation of several major installations in that decade.

The 1990s brought an even more prolific period in Viola's work. Viola had begun working with the traditional triptych form and with various projection methods. These would fuel some of the work of the 1990s. *Heaven and Earth* (1992) featured two black-and-white video monitors mounted on columns attached to the floor and ceiling of the gallery space. The monitors face each other and are in close proximity, so that the opposing images of each reflect in the other. The upper monitor shows Viola's mother near death, while the lower one shows a closeup image of Perov and Viola's newborn son. The images interact physically and become a part of each other. One image does not exist without the reflection of the other. In life is death, in death is life. This simple work is among Viola's most direct and moving statements.

Viola continued to experiment with visual reflections and their correlations to the interior world throughout the early 1990s. In 1992, Viola created *Pray Without Ceasing,* a twenty-four-hour window installation which ran continuously. That same year he made *Nantes Triptych,* a site-specific installation for a seventeenth century cathedral in France. In 1995, Viola represented the United States at the Venice Biennale, where he presented ''Buried Secrets,'' five new installation works which were ''designed to function as an integrated whole.'' *The Crossing* (1996) features double-sided screen as a device for expressing duality. The figure of a man is projected simultaneously on both sides. On each side, the man approaches the viewer from a distance in slow motion, finally stopping in the foreground. Once the movement ceases, the figure is slowly annihilated by natural forces. On one side, flames appear at his feet and consume the figure, while on the other water pours down from above. Each continues, growing in strength, until the figure has completely disappeared. Small flames and dripping water remain. In 1998, Viola was honored with a retrospective at the Stedelijk Museum in Amsterdam. The Whitney Museum of American Art organized a major touring retrospective of Viola's work which travelled to museums in six cities from 1999–2000, including the San Francisco Museum of Modern Art and the Art Institute of Chicago. In addition to this, Viola's work has been exhibited in major institutions all over the world. The timeless nature of his installations and the universal themes presented in them speaks to a great many people. Said Viola, ''There is an unseen world out there and we are living in it.''

—Tammy A. Kinsey

VISSER, Carel (Nicolaas)

Nationality: Dutch. **Born:** Papendrecht, 3 May 1928. **Education:** Studied architecture at the Technische Hogeschool, Delft, 1948–49; studied drawing and sculpture at the Koninklijke Academie voor Beeldende Kunsten, The Hague, 1949–51. **Family:** Married Margareet Donker in 1953; sons: Harm and Geert Jan. **Career:** Sculptor and graphic artist, Amsterdam, since 1952, and farmer, near Culemborg, since 1968. Visiting professor, Washington University, St. Louis, 1962; instructor, Koninklijke Academie voor Beeldende Kunsten, The Hague, 1958–62; instructor, Atelier 63, Haarlem, since 1962. **Awards:** Dutch Government travel stipend to Mexico, 1965; David Bright Award, *Biennale,* Venice, 1968; Museum of Western Art Prize, *International Print Biennale,* Tokyo, 1972; Dutch State Prize for Sculpture and Architecture, The Hague, 1972. **Agents:** Galerie Espace, Keizersgracht 548, Amsterdam; Art and Project, Prinsengracht 785, Amsterdam; and Galerie Paul Maenz, Schaafenstrasse 25, 5000 Cologne 1, West Germany. **Address:** Prinses Margrietstraat 2, 4023AD Rijswijk, Netherlands.

Individual Exhibitions:

1954 Kunsthandel Martinet, Amsterdam
1959 Steendnikkerijk de Jong, Hilversum, Netherlands
Neue Galerie Pamass-Jaehrling, Wuppertal, West Germany
1960 Stedelijk Museum, Amsterdam
Gemeentemuseum, The Hague
1965 Galerie Espace, Amsterdam
1967 Municipal Museum, The Hague
1968 Galerie Espace, Amsterdam
1970 Galerie Espace, Amsterdam
1972 *Beelden 1969–1972,* Stedelijk Museum, Amsterdam (travelled to Gemeentemuseum, The Hague)
Galerie Espace, Amsterdam
Galerie Paul Maenz, Cologne
Galerie Fenna de Vries, Rotterdam
Sculptures, Beelden, Palais des Beaux-Arts, Brussels
1973 Form Meditation International, Amsterdam
Lucy Milton Gallery, London
1974 Art and Project, Amsterdam
Galerie Nouvelles Images, Ghent
Galerie Nouvelles Images, The Hague
1975 Art and Project, Amsterdam
Galerie Paul Maenz, Cologne
Beelden, Tekeningen, Collages, Stedelijk Van Abbemuseum, Eindhoven, Netherlands
1976 Art and Project, Amsterdam
Sperone-Westwater-Fischer, New York
1977 Art and Project, Amsterdam
Galerie Konrad Fischer, Dusseldorf
Galleria Primo Piano, Rome
Kunsthalle, Dusseldorf
1978 *Sculptor's Work by Carel Visser: Sculpture Drawings, Prints and Jewelry 1952–1977,* Whitechapel Art Gallery, London (travelled to the Amolfini Gallery, Bristol, and the Third Eye Centre, Glasgow)
Papierbeelden, Stedelijk Museum, Amsterdam
1979 *Sculptures 1978–1979,* Groningen Museum, Netherlands
1981 Rijksmuseum Kröller-Müller, Otterlo, Netherlands
1982 Nigel Greenwood Gallery, London
1984 Groninger Museum, Groningen, Netherlands
Art and Project, Amsterdam
Galerie Plus-Kem, Brussels
1985 Institut Neerlandais, Paris
Galerie Konrad Fischer, Dusseldorf
Galerie Durand-Dessert, Paris
Kasteel Wijlre, Netherlands
1986 Galerie Durand-Dessert, Paris
Museum Boymans-van Beuningen, Rotterdam
Art and Project, Amsterdam
Galerie Fenna de Vries, Rotterdam
1987 Art and Project, Amsterdam
1990 Sprengel Museum, Hannover (catalog)
Van Reekum Museum, Apeldoorn, Netherlands (catalog)
1999 Stichting Kröller-Müller Museum, Amsterdam (catalog)

Selected Group Exhibitions:

1952 *Sonsbeek International Exhibition,* Sonsbeek Park, Arnhem, Netherlands
1958 *Biennale,* Venice, Italy
1961 *Carnegie International,* Pittsburgh
1969 *Biennale,* Paris
1972 *Amsterdam-Paris-Dusseldorf,* Guggenheim Museum, New York
1973 *Lof der Tekenkunsi,* Stedelijk Van Abbemuseum, Eindhoven, Netherlands
1975 *Funkties van Tekeningen,* Rijksmuseum Kröller-Müller, Otterlo, Netherlands
1977 *Europe in the 70s,* Art Institute of Chicago (toured the United States)
1983 *De Statua,* Van Abbemuseum, Eindhoven, Netherlands
1986 *Geent op Bosch,* Museum Het Kruithuis, Den Bosch, Netherlands
1988 *Furniture as Art,* Museum Boymans-van Beuningen, Rotterdam (catalog)
1991 *Individuals: Nine Sculptors from Holland,* Waino Aaltosen Museo, Turku, Finland (traveling exhibition) (catalog)
1992 *The Extremes Adjoin,* Museum Boymans-van Beuningen, Institut Neerlandais, Paris (catalog)
1994 *Formed Objects,* Gemeentehuis, Bergen, Netherlands (catalog)
Country Sculpture, L'Usine and Le Consortium, Dijon, France
1998 *Waves Breaking on the Shore. . . Ad Dekkers in His Time,* Stedelijk Museum, Amsterdam (catalog)

Collections:

Stedelijk Museum, Amsterdam; Gemeentemuseum, The Hague; Rijksmuseum Kröller-Müller, Otterlo, Netherlands; Stedelijk Van Abbemuseum, Eindhoven, Netherlands; Tate Gallery, London.

Publications:

By VISSER: Books—*Carel Visser,* exhibition catalog, Amsterdam 1960; *Carel Visser: 10 Beelden,* exhibition catalog, Otterlo, Netherlands 1981. **Articles**—''Carel Visser in Gesprek met Jan Dibbets en Rudi H. Fuchs'' in *Museumjournaal* (Amsterdam), February 1973;

interview with Ad Petersen in *Carel Visser: Papierbeelden,* exhibition catalog, Amsterdam, 1978.

On VISSER: Books—*Art and Architecture in the Netherlands: Carel Visser* by Cor Blok, Amsterdam 1968; *34th Biennale & Venezia 1968: Olanda-Carel Visser,* exhibition catalog edited by R. W. D. Oxenaar, Hilversum, Netherlands 1968; *Amsterdam-Paris-Dusseldorf,* exhibition catalog, with texts by Cor Blok, Blaise Gautier, and Jürgen Harten, New York 1972; *Carel Visser: Sculptures, Beelden,* exhibition catalog, Brussels 1972; *Carel Visser: Beelden 1969–1972,* exhibition catalog, Amsterdam 1972; *Lof der Tekenkunst,* exhibition catalog with text by Carel Blotkamp, Eindhoven, Netherlands 1973; *Carel Visser: Beelden, Tekeningen, Collages,* exhibition catalog with text by Rudi H. Fuchs, Eindhoven, Netherlands 1975; *Carel Visser: Papierbeelden,* exhibition catalog, Amsterdam 1978; *Sculptor's Work by Carel Visser: Sculpture, Drawings, Prints and Jewelry 1952–1977,* exhibition catalog with texts by Nick Serota and Barbara Reise, London, 1979; *Carel Visser: Sculptures 1978–1979,* exhibition catalog with texts by Frans Haks and Carel Blotkamp, Groningen, Netherlands 1979; *Carel Visser: Beelden 1975–1985,* exhibition catalog with text by Wim Beeren, Rotterdam 1986. **Articles—**''Stilte Op de Bouwplatts: Een Dankwoord'' in *Jong Holland,* vol. 11, no. 1, 1995.

* * *

Carel Visser is undoubtedly the most important sculptor to come into prominence in the Netherlands since the Second World War. The great tradition of constructivism, as manifested in some of Mondrian's work and in the furniture and architecture of Gerrit Rietveld, is also present in Visser's art. Not that his work represents a mere continuation of *De Stijl:* that tradition, in combination with Visser's stern Calvinistic background, simply forms the basis for his struggle against the *Kubus* and helps to explain his preference for softer constructions.

Visser's first sculptures, done in steel around 1950, include the touching ''Dying Horse'' and many representations of birds. In 1954 or so he became strongly interested in the problems of vertical and horizontal symmetry. ''Birds,'' for example, from 1954, is an almost abstract piece in which the top form mirrors the form beneath it, as a bird is reflected in the calm water over which it flies. In 1959 Visser produced ''Great Auschwitz,'' another abstract work in which linear construction and spatial openness are brought together in a tension-filled relationship. In this respect, and because of the emotion-laden title, it is more than a spatial continuation of Mondrian's Pier + Ocean paintings from 1917.

The work Visser displayed at a 1972 exhibition in the Stedelijk Museum of Amsterdam represents a particularly important point in his development. His new material, thin, malleable plastic, is in strong contrast to the massive steel of his earlier work. The sculpture ''Folded Tower'' (1972) is made up of four folded plates, each of which is larger than the one below it: the tower literally sighs under its own weight. ''Result with a Cube'' (1970) is especially significant: here a plated steel cube is held together by leather cummerbunds, while stretched out in front of it is a cross made up of six metal plates identical with those which make up the cube. Visser's battle with ''the cube'' is clearly apparent here.

In 1979 Visser surprised his audience with the small, strongly figurative and anecdotal objects he displayed in the Groningen Museum (South African ostrich eggs, for example, bound by leather straps to a Turkish walking stick). In 1981 he exhibited ten larger constructions in the Rijksmuseum Kröller-Müller, constructions which seemed to combine his drive towards figurative work and his battle against constructivist demands for summary and clarity. These works were made out of various kinds of simple materials drawn from Visser's own recent life in the country.

Visser is also famous as a draughtsman. Especially remarkable are his drawings from 1974: totally gray, graphite backgrounds which seem as if they were made of metal, and on which Visser has attached reproductions of such objects as avocados, fish, and labels of whisky bottles.

In his works from 1982 onwards, Visser exploits his newly discovered procedures. The sculptures seem to be objects of artistic recycling, a way of conserving those things and materials that have been left behind in the fields. His exhibition at the Art and Project Gallery, Amsterdam, in 1987 consisted of two farm transport vehicles serving as pedestals for the sculptures, creating a strong contrast with the architecture of the gallery itself. In some pieces, figurative imagery is dominant as in the cardboard portrayals of his old dog.

—A.F. Wagemans

VON PLATEN, Eva

Nationality: Finnish. **Born:** Frankfurt am Main, Germany, 18 July 1965. **Education:** Studied at Academy of Sound, Darmstadt, 1985–86; studied painting at Florence Studio Art Center International, 1987; studied at Offenbach College of Design, October 1987; graduated with a degree in visual communications, majoring in film and free graphic art, 1994; post-graduate studies at Cologne Art Academy for Media and Film in the Department of Film, October 1996. **Career:** Organized film programs with works of independent filmmakers since 1991; devised and directed several commercials in Frankfurt, 1996. **Award:** Travel stipend from the Hessen Cultural Foundation for a stay in New York, 1995.

Selected Individual Exhibitions:

1993 Gallery Forum, Frankfurt
1999 Museum für Moderne Kunst Szenenwechsel XVI
Cinema British Council Film-Werkschau, Cologne
2000 Gallery De Ligt Ausstellungsraum, Frankfurt
Katia Rid Gallery, Munich
2001 Gallery Hartmut Beck, Erlangen, Germany

Selected Group Exhibitions:

1992 *Kunst in Frankfurt: Medium Zeichnung,* Frankfurter Kunstverein, Frankfurt
1993 Positionen aktueller Kunst in Frankfurt
1994 Retrospective of filmworks/Filmmuseum Frankfurt/ Kommunales Kino
1998 Schnitt Raum
2001 Kunsthalle Schirn, Frankfurt

Eva von Platen: *Rabbitbrain observing a button,* 2001. ©Eva von Platen.

Collection:

Museum for Modern Art, Frankfurt.

Publication:

By VON PLATEN: Book—*Scheins and Wirklichkeits,* Berlin 2000.

* * *

von RYDINGSVARD, Ursula

Nationality: Polish/Ukranian. **Born:** Near Deensen, Germany, in 1942; spent her childhood in Nazi slave labor and refugee camps; immigrated with her family to the United States in 1952. **Education:** University of New Hampshire, Durham, 1960–62; University of Miami, Coral Gables, B.A., M.A., 1962–65; studied at University of California, 1969–70; Columbia University, M.F.A., 1973–75. **Career:** Assistant professor, Pratt Institute, Brooklyn, 1978–82; instructor, School of Visual Arts, New York, 1981–82; assistant professor, Fordham University, Bronx, 1980–82; associate professor, Yale University, 1982–86; professor, graduate division, School of Visual Arts, 1986. **Awards:** Fulbright-Hays travel grant, 1975; New York State Council on the Arts grant, 1978; American the Beautiful Fund grant, 1978; National Endowment for the Arts grant, 1979; Creative Artists Program Service grant, 1980; Guggenheim fellowship, 1983–84; Yale University Griswald travelling grant, 1985; National Endowment for the Arts individual artists grant, 1986–87; honorary doctorate degree, Maryland Institute College of Art, 1991; Sculpture Award, American Academy of Arts and Letters, 1994; Alfred Jurzykowski Foundation, Fine Arts Award, 1995; Joan Mitchell Award, 1997; International Association of Art Critics 2nd Prize for Best Show in a Commercial Gallery, 2000. **Address:** Studio, 429 S. 5th Street, Brooklyn, New York, 11211–7425.

Individual Exhibitions:

1977 55 Mercer, New York
1978 Robert Freidus Gallery, New York
1979 55 Mercer, New York
1980 55 Mercer, New York
1981 Rosa Esman Gallery, New York
1982 Rosa Esman Gallery, New York
1984 Bette Stoler Gallery, New York
1985 Studio Bassanese, Trieste, Italy
Judith Murray and Ursula von Rydingsvard, Hilwood Art Gallery, C. W. Post Campus, Greenvale, New York
1988 Laumeier Sculpture Gallery, St. Louis, Missouri
Exit Art, New York
1989 Cranbrook Art Museum, Bloomfield Hills, Michigan
Feigenson/Prestone Gallery, Birmingham, Michigan
1990 Capp Street Project, San Francisco
The Fabric Workshop, Philadelphia
Lorence-Monk Gallery, New York
1991 Lorence-Monk Gallery, New York
1992 Zamek Ujazdowski Contemporary Art Center, Warsaw
1993 Storm King Art Center, Mountainville, New York (ten-year retrospective)
1994 Galerie Lelong, New York
Weatherspoon Art Gallery, Greensboro
Three Rivers Festival, Pittsburgh
Metro Tech Plaza, Brooklyn
1995 *Socks on my Spoons,* University Gallery, University of Massachusetts at Amherst (also University of Wyoming Art Museum, Laramie)
1996 Museum of Art, Rhode Island School of Design, Providence
1997 Galerie Lelong, New York
Yorkshire Sculpture Park, Wakefield, England
1998 Byron Cohen Gallery, Kansas City, Missouri
Hood Museum of Art, Dartmouth College, New Hampshire
Nelson-Atkins Museum of Art, Kansas City, Missouri
Madison Art Center, Wisconsin (travelling exhibition)
1999 Indianapolis Museum of Art, Indiana
Barbara Krakow Gallery, Boston
The Contemporary Museum, Honolulu
Chicago Cultural Center
2000 Galerie Lelong, New York and Zurich

Selected Group Exhibitions:

1975 Corcoran Gallery, Washington, D.C.
1977 *Wood and Other Works,* Central Hall Gallery, Port Washington, New York

Eva von Platen: film still *Hasl,* 2001. ©Eva von Platen.

1981 *55 Mercer: 10 Sculptors,* Fine Arts Gallery, Stony Book
1985 *Selections from the Collection,* Aldrich Museum of Contemporary Art, Ridgefield, Connecticut
1987 *Sculpture of the Eighties: Aycock, Ferrara, Frank, Lasch, Miss, Pfaff, Saar, Sperry, von Rydingsvard, Zucker,* Queens Museum, Flushing, New York
Standing Grounds, Contemporary Arts Center, Cincinnati
1989 *Encore: Celebrating Fifty Years,* Contemporary Arts Center, Cincinnati
Sculpture, Krygier/Landau Contemporary Art Gallery, Santa Monica
1992 *Zygmunt,* Cultural Space/The Laboratory, New York
1994 *Landscape as Metaphor,* Columbus Art Museum, Columbus; Denver Art Museum, Denver
2000 *The End,* Exit Art, New York

Collections:

Aldrich Museum of Contemporary Art, Ridgefield; William Benton Museum of Art, University of Connecticut, Storrs; Baruch College, New York; Brooklyn Museum, New York; Centre for Contemporary Art, Ujazdowski Castle, Warsaw; Detroit Institute of Art, Michigan; T.F. Green Airport, Providence, Rhode Island; High Museum of Art, Atlanta; Hood Museum of Art, Dartmouth, New Hampshire; Kemper Museum of Contemporary Art Laumeier Sculpture Park, St. Louis; Madison Art Center, Wisconsin; Microsoft Corporation, Redmond, Washington; Metropolitan Museum of Art, New York; National Museum of Women in the Arts Neuberger Museum of Art, Purchase, New York; Orlando Museum of Art, Florida; Storm King Art Center, Mountainville, New York; Virginia Museum of Fine Art, Richmond, Virginia; Walker Art Center, Minneapolis; Whitney Museum of American Art, New York.

Permanent Public Installations:

Wood, Nassau County Museum of Fine Arts, Roslyn, New York; *Song of a Saint,* Art Park, Lewiston, New York; *Koszarawa,* Meuberger Museum, Purchase, New York; *The Artist's View,* Wave Hill, Bronx, New York; Penn's Landing, Philadelphia; Santa Barbara Contemporary Arts Forum; Laumeier Sculpture Park, St. Louis; *Three Bowls,* Walker Art Center, Minneapolis; Storm King Art Center, Mountainville, New York; Metro Tech Plaza, Brooklyn, New York; *Corrugated Rollers,* Three Rivers Festival, Pittsburgh; *The Garden Matrix,* Abington Art Center, Jenkintown.

Ursula von Rydingsvard: *Five Mountains,* 1989. ©Walker Art Center, Minneapolis, T. B. Walker Acquisition Fund, 1990.

Publications:

By VON RYDINGSVARD: Books—*Socks on My Spoons: Ursula von Rydingsvard,* Amherst 1996; *The Sculpture of Ursula von Rydingsvard,* with Dore Ashton, Marek Bartelik and Matti Megged, New York 1996.

On VON RYDINGSVARD: Books—*Sculpture,* exhibition catalog with text by Frances Lassiter, New York 1977; *Ursula von Rydingsvard,* exhibition catalog with text by Jean E. Feinberg, Connecticut 1980; *Athena Foundation 1977–1986,* exhibition catalog, Long Island 1986; *Encore: Celebrating Fifty Years,* Cincinnati 1989; *Home Show,* exhibition catalog with text by Dore Ashton, Santa Barbara 1988; *Diverse Representations,* Morristown, New Jersey 1990; *The Hybrid State,* exhibition catalog with text by Papo Colo and Jeanette Ingberman, New York 1991; *Sowers of Myth,* exhibition catalog, by Elaine A. King, Chicago 1991; *Ursula von Rydingsvard: Sculpture,* Mountainville, New York 1992; *Ursula von Rydingsvard: Sculpture,* exhibition catalog with text by Patricia Phillips, Warsaw 1993; *Visions of America, Landscape as Metaphor in the Late Twentieth Century,* exhibition catalog with text by Martin Friedman and others, New York 1994; *Shaping Space* by Paul Zelanski and Mary Pat Fisher, New York 1995; *The Sculpture of Ursula von Rydingsvard.* by Dore Ashton, York 1996; *Ursula Von Rydingsvard,* exhibition catalog, by Avis Berman, New York 2000. **Articles**—''Landscape Fills a Room'' by Kenneth Baker in *San Francisco Chronicle,* section E, 13 December 1990; ''Ursula von Rydingsvard'' by Anne Barclay Morgan in *Sculpture* (Washington, D.C.), vol. 15, no. 9, November 1996; ''Ursula Von Rydingsvard Sculpts Metaphors in Wood'' by Avis Berman, *Smithsonian Magazine,* April 1998; ''Ursula von Rydingsvard Sculpts Metaphors in Wood'' by Avis Berman in *Smithsonian Magazine,* vol. 29, no. 2, May 1998; ''Ursula Von Rydingsvard'' by Douglas F. Maxwell, *Review Magazine,* 15 March 2000; ''Urban Exercise: Stretching the Definitions of Outdoor Art'' by Roberta Smith, *The New York Times,* 28 July 2000.

* * *

Ursula von Rydingsvard was born in wartime Germany of Polish/Ukrainian parents and immigrated to the United States in 1952 at the age of ten after spending a key portion of her childhood in Nazi slave labor and refugee camps. She has matured as an American artist and stands today as an international hybrid. Although von Rydingsvard was influenced by contemporary American visual culture, much of her art production has been inspired by girlhood experiences as a member of an intensely religious Polish farming family, in addition it alludes to the history and culture of Central Europe. Von Rydingsvard acknowledges that memory allows the mind to retain the past, however imperfectly; memory allows for change and loss as it accumulates, filters, transmits, and distorts past references to the reality of the present.

When examining the sculpture of von Rydingsvard, one must keep in mind that she neither lived in Poland nor ever directly experienced the political interference of Communism that prevailed throughout Eastern Europe. Living in New York City in the 1970s, von Rydingsvard came of age as an artist in a shifting cultural environment when artists questioned the formalist canon, refuted dogmatic styles, and chose to make eccentric and unexpected work. She was part of a generation that was free to make choices and to enjoy the abundance of materials, new ways to exhibit, as well as absorb the changing theoretical art discourse of post-minimalist and conceptual art. Von Rydingsvard was unlike feminists of the 1970s, who formulated a new aesthetic based on the premise that women possess a nature inherently different from that of men and who focused on subjects directly related to their female body. She—along with other artists including Mary Miss, Jackie Winsor and Jackie Ferrara—claimed no feminist intent in their art practice. Von Rydingsvard opted to pursue a rigorous hands-on approach, producing mammoth works that some consider to be ''male.''

Despite steeping herself in the cerebral language of minimalism, von Rydingsvard was uncomfortable with what she perceived as impersonal hard-edge work that was receiving much acclaim. Even though a minimalist sensibility remains at the core of her artistic vocabulary, she continues to incorporate personal references into forms that signify interlocked dramatic metaphors.

Von Rydingsvard draws upon cultural myths and employs a perspective filled with entanglements, emotions, and political events. Her work possesses a clear frankness and demonstrates a reverence for process and the physicality of often rough and raw materials. In the mid-1970s she began developing a composite technique of constructing and carving. Although von Rydingsvard's methods have evolved, nevertheless her specialized creations of massive laminated and carved cedar continues throughout her oeuvre. Sculpting primarily in cedar wood, the precise milled timbers become transformed into another entity after they pass through an improvisational process and violent metamorphosis of carving, chiseling, digging, gouging, grinding, and sawing. Throughout her production one observes a high caliber of craftsmanship and visual acuity.

Despite the dominance of painting in the 1980s, under the classification of neo-expressionism, several remarkable sculptors surfaced and commanded international attention. Von Rydingsvard is one of those artists who introduced unique sculptural forms made from organic materials.

Albeit von Rydingsvard's art is overtly abstract nonetheless it insinuates references reminiscent of human figures, scorched landscapes in miniature, as well as vessels. Often her sculptures look weathered and even old because graphite or paint is applied to the already heavily textured marked surfaces of her sculpture. Her complex constructions are reminiscent of sanctuaries, barracks, hearths, and mysterious architecture conveying a sense of time passing. Through the employment of a repetitive process of layering and removing materials and surfaces, von Rydingsvard's sculptures resemble objects that have incurred the natural process of erosion. Often her multifaceted assemblages entice the viewer to step closer in order to examine their brute materiality. In spite of the restrictions not to touch works of art placed on viewers in museums and galleries, von Rydingsvard's fabrications seductively allure one to stroke their scabrous surface.

Within each new piece, she appears to recycle historical sources not only from her past but also from the 19th and 20th century in order to comprehend the past and to grapple with the relationship of the here and now. Mystery, truth alienation, isolation, and identification emanate at the core of her art, as well as internalized emotions and concerns about the state of society in an era of transformation. At times her work is difficult to penetrate because its content hints at an obliqueness and sense of despair for the human condition. Yet what exists releases a commanding energy that conveys a restless sense of reality and decades of thought translated into externalized objects that at times seem strange and foreign.

Over the past two decades her work has undergone several transformations. In the 1990s the inspiration for her art has become less drawn from childhood introspection. Greek Sculpture and non-Western sources have become new points of departure. Several key pieces demonstrating this shift include *Krasavica,* 1992–1993, made for the Madison Art Center in Wisconsin, *Ocean Floor,* 1996, and *Five Open Bowls,* 1999. Again in the kinetic piece titled *MAMA, YOUR LEOS* she departs from her previous explorations. In this moveable piece presented at the Galerie Lelong in April 2000, she fitted rows of identical sculptured wooden containers into a large grid of graphite; steel piston arms propel them to move up and down into the receptacles. A powerful clanking sound resonates however because of the precision of the synchronized movement it is neither disturbing nor detracting and it acquires a presence larger than its physical bulk. Metaphorically this work summons forth imagery from the Industrial Revolution and the passing of an era when humanity once took pride in what they made with their hands.

Von Rydingsvard's work continues to evolve, revealing a public and private side, a front, a back, and intimates that perhaps an enigmatic message is hidden within her multi-faceted forms. This complicated art inspires inspection and requires an engagement of our senses beyond a few seconds. Her three-dimensional work beckons one to query the signification of this art while inviting viewers to experience and delight in the psychological spaces her objects vitalize at the same time. Ursula von Rydingsvard aspires to invent new meanings through works of art that are about openness and closure and connote life and death themes.

—Elaine A. King

VOSS, Jan

Nationality: German. **Born:** Hamburg, 9 October 1936. **Education:** Kunstkademie, Munich, 1955–60. **Career:** Independent artist, Paris, since 1960. Painting instructor, Kunstakademie, Hamburg, 1966–67. **Agents:** Galerie Lelong, 13/14 Rue de Teheran, 75008 Paris, France; Galerie Nothelfer, Uhlandstrasse 184, 1000 Berlin 12 (West), Germany; Galerie Moderne, Skoletorvet, 8600 Silkeborg, Denmark; Galerie Academia, Residenz, 5010 Salzburg, Austria; Galerie Satani, 4–2-6 Ginza, Chuo-ku, Tokyo, Japan. **Address:** 34 rue Dombasle, 75015 Paris, France.

Jan Voss: *No title,* 1996. ©2001 Artists Rights Society (ARS), NY/ ADAGP, Paris.

Individual Exhibitions:

1963 Galerie Bayer, Mainz
1964 Galerie du Fleuve, Paris
1965 Galerie Lucien Durand, Paris
Galleri Birch, Copenhagen
1966 Galerie Mathias Fels, Paris
Lefebre Gallery, New York
1967 Galleria del Naviglio, Milan
1968 Galerie Brusberg, Hannover
1969 Galleri Birch, Copenhagen
1970 Galerie Van de Loo, Munich
1971 Lefebre Gallery, New York
Galleria Del Naviglio, Milan
1972 Galerie Lucien Durand, Paris
1974 Galerie Brusberg, Hannover
Galerie Buchholz, Munich
1975 Galerie Lucien Durand, Paris
Goethe Institut, Paris
1976 Galleri Birch, Copenhagen
1977 Galerie C, Paris
1978 Musée d'Art Moderne de la Ville, Paris (retrospective)
Galerie Le Dessin, Paris
Galerie Nothelfer, West Berlin
1979 Galerie Van de Lou, Munich
Centre Culturel, Toulouse
1980 Galerie Le Dessin, Paris
Leopold-Hoesch Museum, Duren, West Germany
Galerie Linssen, Bonn
1981 Kunstverein, Pforzheim, West Germany
Landesmuseum, Oldenburg, West Germany
Art Front Gallery, Tokyo
Galerie Adrien Maeght, Paris
1982 Galeria Maeght, Barcelona
Randers Museum, Denmark
Museum van Hedendaagse Kunst, Utrecht
Galerie Convergence, Nantes, France
Galerie Bel'Art, Stockholm
Centre Culturel, Bretigny-sur-Orge, France
1983 Galerie Satani, Tokyo
Galerie Academia, Salzburg, Austria
Galerie Grafica, Tokyo
Artotheque, Lyon, France
Museum van Hedendaagse Kunst, Ghent, Belgium
1984 Galerie Moderne, Silkeborg, Denmark
Galerie Ulysses, Vienna
Galerie Quaresso, Munich
Galerie Satani, Tokyo
Galerie Grafica, Tokyo
1985 Manus Presse, Stuttgart
Galerie Beaumont, Luxembourg
Galerie Wentzel, Cologne
Galerie Satani, Tokyo
Galerie Grafica, Tokyo
1986 Galerie Nothelfer, West Berlin
Galerie Academia, Salzburg, Austria
Herstand Gallery, New York
1987 Maison de la Culture, La Rochelle, France
Les Cordeliers, Chateauroux, France
Galerie Laune, Nimes, France
Galerie Satani, Tokyo
1988 Galerie Wentzel, Cologne
Kunstverein Emsdetten, Netherlands
FRAC d'Auvergne, Clermont-Ferrand, France
1989 Galerie Lelong, Paris
Musée de Brou, Bourg-en-Bresse, France
Gallery Satani, Tokyo
Galerie Academia, Salzburg
1990 Galerie Proarta, Zurich
Galerie Nothelfer, Berlin
Galerie Academia, Salzburg
1991 Musée de Toulon, France
Manus Presse, Stuttgart
1992 Galerie Lelong, Paris
Galerie Lea Gredt, Luxembourg
Galerie Nothelfer, Berlin
Gallery Satani, Tokyo
1993 Galerie Lelong, Paris
Galerie Art et Essai de l'Université de Rennes 2, France
Neue Galere der Stadt Linz, Germany
Galerie Academia, Salzburg

1994 Galerie Proarta, Zurich
Galerie Lea Gredt, Luxembourg
Galerie de l'Ecole des Beaux-Arts de Nantes, France
Nouvelle Galerie d'Exposition de l'Université de Rouen, France
Galerie de l'Ecole des Beaux-Arts de Nantes, France
1995 Musée des Beaux-Arts, Muhlouse
1996 Musée des Beaux-Arts, Angers, France
Galerie Academia, Salzburg
Galerie Lea Gredt, Luxembourg
1997 Kunsthalle Kiel, Germany
Maison des Arts, Malakof
Galerie Lelong, Paris
Galerie Nothelfer, Berlin
Galerie Lelong, Paris
Galerie Proarta, Zurich
Manus Presse, Stuttgart
1998 Musée Félicien Rops, Namur, Belgium
Galerie Athanor, Marseille, France
Le Carré Vincent Orléans, France
Galerie Lea Gredt, Luxembourg
1999 Kulturzentrum Englische Kirche der Stadt Bad Homburg v.d. Höhe, Germany
Galerie Lea Gredt, Luxembourg
2000 Banque Générale du Luxembourg
Galerie Kusseneers, Lier, Belgium
Galerie Lelong, Paris
Galerie Proarta, Zurich
Manus Presse, Stuttgart

Selected Group Exhibitions:

1962 *Donner à Voir,* Galerie Creuze, Paris
1963 *Biennale de Paris,* Musée d'Art Moderne de la Ville, Paris
1965 *Le Merveilleux Moderne,* Konsthall, Lund, Sweden
1967 *La Bande Dessinee et la Figuration Narrative,* Musée des Arts Decoratifs, Paris
1970 *Distances,* Musée d'Art Moderne de la Ville, Paris
1972 *German Contemporary Art,* National Museum of Modern Art, Tokyo (travelled to Kyoto)
1977 *Mythologies Quotidiennes 2,* Musée d'Art Moderne de la Ville, Paris
1981 *Phoenix,* Alte Oper, Frankfurt
1984 *Ecriture dans la Peinture,* Villa Arson, Nice
1986 *Kunst Heute in Frankreich,* Sammlung Ludwig, Aachen, West Germany
1987 *Quai Grand Cargo,* Port de Fort-de-France, Martinique
1988 *Art Français Contemporain,* Bucharest
1990 *Une Collection Pour la Grande Arche,* Toit de la Grande Arche de la Défense, Paris
1991 *Veramente Falso,* Rotonda de via Besana, Mailand und Villa Stuck, Munich
1992 *Semaine Culturelle Bucharest,* Musée d'Art Moderne, Bucharest
1993 *Feuerregen—Hommage an den Hl. Florian,* Schloss Tillyburg bei St. Florian
1994 *Poème—Image—les Livres et les Estampes,* Galerie Lelong, Zurich
1996 *Grosse Kunstausstellung—Sonderausstellung—Experimentelle Druckgraphik,* Haus der Kunst, Munich
1997 *Made in France 1947–1997,* Centre Georges Pompidou, Paris
1998 *Tableaux d'Une Histoire,* Villa Arson, Nice
2000 *Les 100 Sourires de Mona Lisa,* Tokyo Metropolitan Art Museum (travelled to Shizuoka Prefecture Museum of Art; Hiroshima Prefecture Art Museum)

Collections:

Musée d'Art Moderne de la Ville de Paris; Centre National d'Art Contemporain, Paris; Centre Georges Pompidou, Paris; Musée Cantini, Marseilles, Moderna Museet, Stockholm; Goteborgs Kunstmuseum, Sweden; Städtisches Museum, Bonn; Sammiung Ludwig-Städtische Galerie, Aachen, West Germany; Stadtische Galerie im Lenbachhaus, Munich; Museum of Modern Art, New York.

Publications:

By VOSS: Books—*Vorwort,* exhibition catalog, Silkeborg 1991. **Articles—**''Entretien avec Jan Voss'' with Bernard Lamerche-Vadel in *Artistes* (Paris), October/November 1981; ''Jan Voss-Interview'' with Anne Dagbert in *Art Press* (Paris), November 1981.

On VOSS: Books—*Positionen* by Rolf-Günter Dienst, Cologne 1968; *Deutsche Kunst—eine neue Generation II* by Rolf-Günter Dienst, Cologne 1970; *Deutsche Kunst der 60er Jahre* by Juliane Roh, Munich 1971; *Jan Voss,* exhibition catalog, with text by Yves Michaud, Paris 1981; *Le seismographe lunatique: Jan Voss, oeuvre graphique 1964–1982,* exhibition catalog with text be Anne Tronche, Paris 1982; *Jan Voss: Un voyage ideal,* exhibition catalog witn essay by Katsuhiro Yamaguchi, Tokyo 1983; *Jan Voss: Le presque parfait,* exhibition catalog with text by Daniel Dobbels, Silkeborg 1984; *Trajet de Jan Voss* by Bernard Noel, Marseilles and West Berlin 1985; *Jan Voss ou la Crue des Signes Repères n°61,* exhibition catalog by Jean-Christophe Bailly, Paris 1989; *La Résonance de Couleurs et de Formes,* exhibition catalog by Toshio Yamanashi, Tokyo 1989; *Jan Voss—Jusq'au Lieu-dit, Edition de la différence* by Alain Bonfand, Paris 1991; *Einige Anmerkungen zur Arbeit von Jan Voss,* exhibition catalog by Peter Handke, Düsseldorf 1992; *Notes Sur un Art de Grand Chemin et de Traverse,* exhibition catalog by Lucien Kayser, Luxembourg 1992; *Abracadabra, Repères n°85,* exhibition catalog by Marc Dachy, Paris 1995; *Tables de Travail, Repères n°85,* exhibition catalog by Alain Bonfand, Paris 1995; *Jan Voss—Mode d'Imploi (Passage 3),* Lier, Belgium 2000. **Articles—**''Jan Voss—le Fond de la Peinture'' by Philippe Piguet in *Quotidien de Paris,* 7 December 1990; ''Lumière, le Désordre de Voss'' by Daniel Dobbels in *Libération,* 23 July 1991.

*

Within view

Perhaps he had placed his hand against a rock and in outlining it with the help of a bit of charred wood had drawn its shape. Perhaps in this way he had recorded the beginning of history. His hand had then continued to grasp everything in sight: animals and gods, men and landscapes, objects, constructions, forms, ideas . . . .

He should never again stop taking possession of the world by marking/signing it, and we pursue this outline which connects prehistory to our decade and we observe it already overtaking us and vanishing in the vertiginous infinity like the condensation trail of an aircraft which has crossed the sound barrier.

—Jan Voss

* * *

Jan Voss has lived in Paris since 1960. Educated at a time when lyrical abstraction dominated the art schools in Germany, he sought primarily a manner of expression personal to himself and as different as possible from the aimless poesy of this tendency. From the very first he was interested in writing as a painter's gesture, not in that which it could, unwilled and uncontrolled, set free in the layers of the unconscious but in that which it can contribute to painting in its role of go-between.

In the works from the beginning of the 1960s Voss had already given it the task of making a direct statement, less by direct legibility than by the fact that painting can on the whole be conceived as writing. These pictures from 1961 and 1962 recall picture stories put together from pure and simple pictograms which are so close to scrawl that the anecdote as such finally remains incomprehensible. During the 1960s both elements became more precise: both the individual signs and the writing role of the painterly gesture. The pictures became clearer in their expression, had something to say, serve communication. The latter is indeed one of the themes around which Jan Voss's entire work will soon revolve: which sign at what time and for whom is suitable for communication?

The scrawl hardens. The picture ground and signs are from then on more radically separated from each other. The individual pictograms take on firm outlines, become discernible and recognizable and therefore even interchangeable from picture to picture. Finally Jan Voss's pictures are peopled by a number of more or less naively drawn figures and objects which are arranged across a broad unorganized area in a kind of fictional running narrative.

A synthesis of all these works was perhaps reached in 1968 in the picture which he called "Reading for Everyone." It is a challenge to the viewer to read the picture like a book and to regard the painting as a multiplicity of languages, symbols and stereotypes-and an invitation to remain conscious and critical in relation to these languages and not to surrender to them in admiration, as with secret scripts that one does not understand. What Voss was making especially visible in this instance was a critique of political emblems and ideology related symbols: from the Mao bible to Ché Guevara, they serve the individual only to adopt a political code like a fashion and not as more effective communication from man to man.

In this way Voss's work enters completely into the painterly tendencies of the 1960s in Paris, which built on a structuralist critique of language and which above all did not remain uninfluenced by Michel Foucault's writing. Instead of investigating the contents of knowledge, Foucault has begun to analyze critically the discourses, the languages of our knowledge. He had shown that we are all dependent on that discourse into which, according to our era and environment, we are bound, and that it is therefore necessary above all to be vigilant in relation to the languages and forms of expression which we employ in science, literature and art so that we understand their full significance.

In 1965 and 1967 Jan Voss exhibited occasionally with painters who belonged to the so-called "Figuration Narrative." I believe, however, that he aimed less at a confrontation between Figuration, or the power of the figurative picture, and abstract painting than at the preservation of a critical attitude in relation to all languages of art. Consequently, he has also, in recent years, tended towards a painting of "indecision." From the beginning of the 1970s he gave up the previously discovered language patterns in favour of imaginary signs which he arranged uniformly across empty surfaces like elementary particles. These required only to be connected with an endless line in order to arrive at current works. The world of the pictogram seemed too constricting, too didactic and too little concerned with the real problems of painting. He retained the character of the element, but it was now bound up in a kind of linear labyrinth. Even colour was banished from the plane surface back to the line. The line is led across the surface unsteadily, sometimes hesitatingly, sometimes with wilful naivete, forms a foyer here and there in which archaic figure like images take shape without ever becoming articulate forms. The line plays around them and itself; Voss liberates it from the individual object so that it may belong to all possible objects. It flies from one motif to the next; it crosses through, draws paths, horizons, mountains, in order immediately to destroy them.

Voss's pictures are thus a virtuoso example of structures which came from crossed lines. He shows without describing that one can speak neither of abstraction nor of the genesis of a picture: he has now reached an intermediate stage of landscapes without contour and distances without perspectives. He materializes a non-concentric thought, one that moves in many centres at once, that lies across the picture surface like a vibrating network which always remains incomplete and open. His pictures arise from moments of distraction—as he himself says, they arise unpremeditated from a balance between the will and the accidental, between reason and unreason.

—Marie Luise Syring

VOSTELL, Wolf

Nationality: German. **Born:** Leverkusen, near Cologne, 14 October 1932. **Education:** Studied lithography in a printing works, Cologne, 1950–53; studied painting and typography at the Werkkunstschule, Wuppertal, 1954; studied painting, graphics and anatomy, under A. M. Cassandre, Ecole des Beaux-Arts, Paris, 1955–57; and at the Kunstakademie, Dusseldorf, 1957–58. **Family:** Married Mercedes Guarado Olivenza in 1958; sons: Santiago David and Rafael Isaac. **Career:** Independent artist in Paris 1954–57, 1958–59, Dusseldorf, 1957–58, Cologne and Wuppertal, 1959–70, and in West Berlin, since 1971; and Malpartida, Spain, since 1975; produced first "decollages," Paris, 1954; first street happenings, Paris, 1958; first sculpture-actions, with cement "blockages," Cologne, 1969. Layout artist, *Neue Illustrierte,* Cologne, 1961–62; founder-editor, *dé-coll/age,* Frankfurt, 1962–69; founder, with George Maciunas, Jean-Pierre Wilhelm, Nam June Paik and others, Fluxus movement, Cologne, 1962–66; founder, Happening-Archive, Berlin 1971; co-founder, Aktionen der Avantgarde (A.D.A.) foundation, Berlin, 1973; founder, Museo Vostell, Malpartida, Spain, 1976. Instructor in typography, Werkkunstschule, Wuppertal, 1959–60. **Awards:** Pablo Iglesias prize, Madrid 1982; Medal of Paris, 1990; named Professor, Kultursenator, Berlin, 1992; Hannah-Höch Prize, Berlin, 1997; named Adopted Son of Malpartida de Cáceres (posthumous), 1998; Medal of Extremadura (posthumous), 1998. **Agents:** Galerie Van de Loo, Maximilianstrasse 27, 8000 Munich 22, Germany; Galeria Punto, Baron de Career 37, Valencia, Spain. **Died:** Berlin, 3 April 1998.

Individual Exhibitions/Happenings:

1950 Salon Educacion y Descarios, Caceres, Spain
1958 *Le Théâtre est dans la rue,* (happening) Passage de la Tour de Vanves, Paris
1960 Galena Sala Lux, Caceres, Spain
1961 Galerie Le Soleil dans la Tête, Paris
Galerie Haro Lauhus, Cologne
1962 Galerie Monet, Amsterdam
Rokin, (simultaneous happenings) in cooperation with Monet Gallery, Amsterdam
Kleenex 1—4, Fluxusfestival, Wiesbaden, Amsterdam, Copenhagen and Paris
1963 Smolin Gallery, New York
Galeric Pamass, Wuppertal, West Germany
Morning Glory, (fluxus) Third Rail Gallery, New York
1964 Galerie Loehr, Frankfurt
Sun in your head, (happening) Leisden Plein Theater, Amsterdam
In Ulm, um Ulm und Ulm herum, (happening) in cooperation with Ulmer Theatre Studio, Ulm, West Germany
1965 Galerie Rend Block, West Berlin
Studio F, Ulm, West Germany
Berlin 100 Ereignisse-100 Minuten-100 Stellen für Zufallspublikum, (happening) in cooperation with René Block Gallery, Berlin
Chinatown, (fluxus) Festival of the Avantgarde, New York
1966 Something Else Gallery, New York
Verwischungen, Happening-Notationen 1961–66, Kölnischer Kunstverein, Cologne
Plus Chinatown, (fluxus) Avantgarde musik, Philadelphia
1967 Galerie Tobies and Silex, Cologne
Galerie René Block, West Berlin
Museum of Contemporary Art, Chicago (with Allan Kaprow)
1968 Galerie Hake, Cologne
1969 Institut Dr. Gasch, Wiesbaden
Galerie Rolf Kuhn, Aachen, West Germany
Galerie Van de Loo, Munich
Telemetrie, Forum-Gallery Van de Loo, Munich
1970 Galerie Art Intermedia, Cologne
Atelier NW 8, Beindersheim, West Germany
Elektronisch, Galerie Rolf Kuhn, Aachen, West Germany
Galerie Inge Baecker, Bochum, West Germany
Galerie René Block, West Berlin
Fluxus Konzert, Koelnischer, Kunstverein
1971 Galerie Bama, Paris
Galerie Catacombe, Basle
Galerie Press, Konstanz, West Germany
Galerie Kerlikowsky und Kneiding, Munich
Galerie Inge Baecker, Bochum, West Germany
Galerie Hausdewell, Baden-Baden, West Germany
Galerie Hausdewell, Hamburg
Galerie René Block, West Berlin
Galerie Kolczynski, Stuttgart
Fluxus Konzert, Stuttgart
1972 Galerie Argelander, Bonn
Rheinisches Landesmuseum, Bonn
Galerie Art in Progress, Zufich
Kunstverein, Freiburg
Galerie Van de Loo, Munich
1973 Goethe Institut, Marseilles
Galleria La Bertesca, Milan
Galerie Paramedia, West Berlin
Galerie Van de Loo, Munich
Galerie Ingo Kummel, Dusseldorf
Calvario, (happening) in cooperation with La Bertesca gallery, Milan
1974 Galerie Bama, Paris
La Sala Vincon, Barcelona
Galleria La Bertesca, Milan
Galleria Multiphla, Milan
Nuovi Strumenti, Brescia, Italy
Deutsches Kulturinstitut, Madrid
Kunsthalle, Bremen, West Germany
1975 *Environments/Happenings 1958–1974,* Musée d'Art Moderne de la Ville, Paris
Galefic Van de Loo, Munich
Retrospektive 1958–1974, Nationalgalerie, West Berlin
Galleria Bocchi, Panna
Galleria Bozzi, Turin
Galleria Incontri, Rome
Galleria Area, Florence
Galerie Andre, West Berlin
Galleria Multiphla, Milan
Galerie Bama, Paris
Galerie Carsta Zellermayer, West Berlin
Galerie Inge Baecker, Bochum, West Germany
Fandango, (Fluxus-Music) Multhiphla Gallery, Milan
1976 Galerija Teatru-Studio, Warsaw
Städtisches Museum, Wiesbaden
Kunsthalle, Nuremberg
Galerie Pool, Graz, Austria
Galerie Kausch, Kassel, West Germany
Museo Vostell, Malpartida de Caceres, Spain (inaugural exhibitions)
Kunststation Faber, Fulda, West Germany
Galerie Andre, West Berlin
German Institute, Barcelona
1977 Galerie Kausch, Kassel, West Germany
1978 Anja Kunstsenter, Abenra, Denmark
Museo de Arte Contemporaneo, Madrid
Universitat Essen, Wset Germany
1979 Kunstlerkongress-Halle, Stuttgart
Fundacion Joan Miro, Barcelona
Fundacao Gulbenkian, Lisbon (retrospective)
Museu Nacional de Soares Dos Reis, Porto, Portugal
Museo Vostell, Malpartida de Caceres, Spain
Galerie Ars Viva, West Berlin
Romancero Gitano, (action music) Fundació Joan Miró, Barcelona
1980 Galleria Il Centro, Naples, Italy
Monte Video, Wuppertal, West Germany
Galerie Inge Baecker, Bochum. West Germany
Museo Vostell, Malpartida de Caceres, Spain
Kunstverein, Braunschweig, West Germany
Los Angeles Institute of Contemporary Art
1981 Galerie Ars Viva, West Berlin

Fluxus Zug, Rail Stations in Dortmund, Aachen, Cologne, Dusseldorf and other cities in West Germany
1982 Gesellschaft für neue Kunst, Bremen, West Germany
Kunstverein, Uelzen, West Germany
Museo Vostell, Malpartida de Caceres, Spain
Centre Culturel du Marais, Paris
Musee de Calais, France
DAAD-Galerie, West Berlin
Garden of Delights, (Fluxus opera) Radio Breman
1983 Palais des Beaux-Arts, Charleroi, Belgium
Centre de Arte y Comunicacion, Buenos Aires
Galerie Rama, Paris
Nationalgalerie, West Berlin
La Siberia Extremeña, (Fluxus concert) Grande Salle, Lyon
Fluxus Konzert, 17 Sao Paulo Biennial
1984 Galerie Armstorfer, Salzburg, Austria
Galeria Punto, Valencia Spain
Sala Parpallo, Valencia, Spain
1985 Galerie Inge Baecker, Cologne
Galerie Wewerka, West Berlin
Galerie Muda, Hamburg
Espace Nord, Liege, Belgium
Musée d'Art Moderne, Strasbourg, France
1986 *Art Teaches Life,* German Institute, Madrid
Concierto Fluxus, Instituto Alemán de Madrid
1990 Mudima foundation, Milan
Piano. November 9, 1990. Berlin, (Fluxus concert) Gino de Maggio, Milan
1991 Miscetti Gallery, Rome
Tauromaquia, Sebastiá Jané Gallery, Barcelona
1992 *The Weepers,* Inge Baecker Gallery, Cologne
Retrospective, Academy of Art, Leipzig
1993 Kunstgalerie Gera, Gera
Fine Art Rafael Vostell, Berlin
1994 Fundació Pilar y Joan Mirò, Palma de Mallorca, Spain
Fine Art Rafael Vostell, Berlin
1995 Galerie Enderle, Wuppertal
Galerie Inge Baecker, Köln
1996 Fine Art Rafael Vostell, Berlin
BSM und Modernisierung GmbH, Berlin
1997 Berlinische Galerie, Berlin
Museo Vostell Malpartida, Malpartida de Cáceres
Galerie Inge Baicker, Köln
1998 Fine Art Rafael Vostell, Berlin
Palacio Galveias, Lisbon
Iberoamericano de Arte Contemporáneo, Badajoz
1999 Kunsthaus Berlin, Friedrich Foundation, Berlin
Fine Art Rafael Vostell, Berlin
Vostell Autoskulpturen, Köln

Selected Group Exhibitions:

1961 *Salon Comparisons,* Musée d'Art Moderne, Paris
1962 *Schrift und Bild 1,* Kunsthalle, Baden-Baden, West Germany
1967 *Pictures to Be Read-Poetry to Be Seen,* Museum of Contemporary Art, Chicago
1968 *Von der Collage zur Assemblage,* Institut für Moderne Kunst, Nuremberg
1970 *Happening und Fluxus,* Kölnischer Kunstverein, Cologne
1973 *Contemporanea,* Parcheggio Villa Borghese, Rome
1977 *Documenta,* Kassel, West Germarry
1980 *Forms of Realism Today,* Musée d'Art Contemporain, Montreal
1981 *The Fluxus Zug,* Dortmund (travelled through seven German cities including Cologne, Essen, Düsseldorf, and Bonn)
1982 *20 Jahre Fluxus 1962–82,* Stadtisches Museum, Wiesbaden, West Germany
1984 *Kunst des 20. Jahrhunderts,* Dortmund
1985 *Video/Art/Video Festival '85,* Stockholm
Kunst in der Bundesrepublik Deutschland 1945/1985, Berlin
1986 *Ars Electronica,* Linz
1989 *Video Skulptur,* Berlin
1990 Venice Biennial, Venice
1991 *The Pop Art Show,* London
1992 *Fluxus Virus,* Köln (travelled to Chicago)
1993 *Multimediale 3,* Karlsruhe
1994 *Des Images pour la paix: 120 artists pour Sarajevo,* Paris
1997 *Kunst der Gegenwart,* Karlsruhe
1998 *Out of Actions: Between Performance and the Object, 1949–1979,* Museum of Contemporary Art, Los Angeles (travelled to Vienna, Barcelona, and Tokyo)
1999 *Das XX Jahrhundert,* Berlin

Collections:

Museum am Ostwall, Dortmund, West Germany; Neuer Berliner Kunstverein, West Berlin; Berlinische Galerie, West Berlin; Nationalgalerie, West Berlin; Neue Galerie, Aachen, West Germany; Kunstmuseum, Hannover; Bundesministerium des Innem, Bonn; Gesamthochschule, Wuppertal, West Germany; Bibliothèque Nationale, Paris.

Publications:

By VOSTELL: Books and pamphlets—*Tombeau de Pierre Larousse,* with poems by Francois Dufrene, Wuppertal, West Germany 1961; *Happenings, Fluxus, Pop Art, Nouveau Realisme,* editor, with Jürgen Becker, Reinbek, West Germany 1965; *24 Standen,* Itzehoe, West Germany 1965; *Wolf Vostell: Berlin and Phenomena,* New York 1966; *Wolf Vostell: Dokumentation,* edited by Rend Block, West Berlin 1968; *Vostell 1: Eine Dokumentation 1954–69,* with additional text by Sidney Simon, West Berlin 1969; *Miss Vietnam and Texts of Other Happenings,* San Francisco 1969; *Pop Architektur—Concept Art,* editor, with Dick Higgins, Dusseldorf 1969; *Wolf Vostell: Happening und Lebe,* Neuwied and West Berlin 1970; *Aktionen, Happenings und Demonstrationen seit 1965: Ein dokumentation von Wolf Vostell,* Reinbek, West Germany 1970; *Vostell: Betonierungen,* Hinwil, West Germany 1970; *Wolf Vostell: Elektronisch,* exhibition catalog, Aachen, West Germany 1970; *Fantastic Architecture,* editor, with Dick Higgins, New York 1971; T.O.T *(Technological Oak Tree): 310 Ideen,* Hinwil, West Germany 1973; *Wolf Vostell: Happenings Calvario,* Genoa 1973; *Vostell: Fandango, Milan 1975; Vostell: Zyklus Extremadura,* with interview by Maria Luisa Borras, Munich 1975; *Wolf Vostell: 10 Happenings Knozerte 1954–1973,*

Milan 1976; *Derriere l'arbre (Duchamp no ha comprendido a Rembrandt . . .): Un Video-Happening de Vostell,* Barcelona 1976; *Vostell: Projekte und Ideen meiner Medienkonzeption zu Hamlet,* Cologne 1979; *Shakespeare-Hamlet,* Cologne 1979. **Articles**—*De-coll/ages: Bulletin aktueller ideen* (Frankfurt), nos. 1–7, 1962–69; *Posiversandroman,* with Peter Faecke (Neuwied), no. 1–11, 1970–72.

On VOSTELL: Books—*Postface and Jefferson's Birthday* by Dick Higgins, New York 1964; *A Primer of Happenings and Time-Space Art* by Al Hansen, New York 1965; *Assemblages, Environment and Happenings* by Allan Kaprow, New York 1976; *Pop Art* by Lucy R. Lippard, New York and Washington, D.C. 1966; *Collage: Personalities, Concepts, Techniques* by Harriet Janis and Rudi Blesh, New York, Philadelphia and London 1967; *Pop und die Folgen* by Heinz Ohff, Dusseldorf 1968; *Vostell Soziologisch* by Rainer Wick, Bonn 1969; *Wolf Vostell: Retrospective 1958–1974,* exhibition catalog, with text by Jorn Merket, West Berlin 1975; *Wolf Vostell: Environments/Happenings 1958–1974,* exhibition catalog, with text by Suzanne Page, Paris 1975; *Vostell: Heuwagen,* with text by Christa Schwens, Essen 1978; *Vostell,* exhibition catalog, with texts by Santiago Amon, Simon Marchan and Jürgen Schilling, Madrid 1978; *Vostell 1968–1979,* exhibition catalog, with texts by Francesco Vicens, Santiago Amon and Eberhard Roters, Barcelona 1979; *Wolf Vostell: Decollagen, Verwischungen, Schichtenbilder, Bleibüder 1955–1979,* exhibition catalog, with interview by Jürgen Schilling, Braunschweig, West Germany 1980; *LAICA-Los Angeles, Ars Viva-Berlin: Vostell,* exhibition catalog, with text by Robert L. Smith, Los Angeles 1980; *Vostell und Berlin: Leben und Werk 1971–1981,* exhibition catalog, with text by Wieland Schmied, West Berlin 1982; *Wolf Vostell: Estampes et Affiches,* exhibition catalog, with text by Francoise Woimant and Anne Moeglin-Delcroix, Paris 1982; *Wolf Vostell: environment, video, peintures, tiessins 1977–85,* exhibition catalog with texts by Michael Marschail, Nadine Lehni and Michel Giroud, Strasbourg 1986; *Vostell, Das Plastiche Werk 1953–1987,* Milan 1987; *Vostell, Tauromaquie, Automaquie, Frauenmaquie, 1987–88,* Vienna 1989; *Vostell, Le Cri Fluxus-Concert,* Paris 1990; *Vostell, Tempo a Barcelona,* Barcelona 1991; *Weinende,* Köln 1992; *Vostell, Extremadura,* Mérida 1992; *Wolf Vostell, Leben = Kunst = Leben,* Leipzig 1993; *Wolf Vostell, Sara-jevo, 3 Fluxus Pianos,* Palma de Mallorca 1994; *Wolf Vostell, SHOAH 1492–1945,* Mérida 1998; *10 Happenings de Wolf Vostell* by José Antonio Agúndez García, Mérida 1999; *Vostell,* Milan 1999.

*

In order to survive all the madness and craziness of daily life in a nuclear era, I have made my artwork more and more research to express more and more freedom in whatever I am doing. Art as an expression of individual freedom is the only illusion that I have developed from my work—much better than accomplishing a style, satisfying a market, or looking for a happy ending as an artist integrated with society.

The intelligence and the nervous system of the artist has to develop as far as it can; therefore, creative systems and also creative craftsmanship has to be rich and complex as it can be on all levels, far away from nature and trivial fantasy. I feel that my obligation is to concretize that which nature cannot but nature speaks through me, and I am therefore life *and* art at the same time. Every man an artwork means that before making art, the artist must be complex. Anyone becomes an artist only through his work, but anyone can be an artwork through nature.

—Wolf Vostell

* * *

One of Wolf Vostell's best known Happenings. was a crash between a car and a railway engine, which certainly had its intended effect of shocking and infuriating the average German consumer. And all Vostell's work is in a sense a single great composition, since it all arises from the basic idea of shocking his audience out of their normal complacency into a new critical and aesthetic awareness of the everyday world of technology and politics. Like Duchamp with his ''Readymades,'' Vostell seizes and isolates a piece of reality and proclaims it to be a work of art. But instead of mystifying it by isolating it in a gallery stripped of its normal associations, Vostell leaves it in its normal environment, while looking at it afresh, not with the casual glance of everyday life, but with the critical and aesthetic awareness usually brought to art.

Vostell's early work was the production, alteration and destruction of images using the technique he called dé-coll/age, the opposite of the building-up process of collage, since it involves tearing posters or other printed matter. He took the word from a French newspaper headline in September 1954 which announced a plane crashing immediately after its *dé-collage,* which in this context merely means ''takeoff,'' though the general idea of ''unsticking'' fused with the violent event and the artistic meaning of collage to give the idea of torn posters on boardings, the resulting picture becoming a document of the violent action of tearing. The tearing away of various superimposed layers of posters on a hoarding means that bits of different posters are left, fragments of words or pictures or colours which may give each other new meaning, which however can be altered by further tearing, revealing new components.

Such pictorial dé-coll/ages already include not only the ideas of constant change and openness, but also the idea of action. So it was a short step to widen the meaning from torn posters on hoardings to actual real events, to be ''torn,'' open actions of his dé-coll/age demonstrations. In Paris in the late 1950's Vostell collaborated with A. M. Cassandre, and the first of his demonstrations took its inspiration and its title from Cassandre's book *Das Theater ist auf der Strasse* (The Theatre Is in the Street). Vostell's demonstrations differed from the early American happenings not only in taking place out in the open in the streets, but also in relying much less on chance by giving precise instructions for action. These demonstrations had clearly defined objectives, and Vostell's aggressive attitude means that no one is allowed to be a mere passive spectator, but is involved as an actor in whatever is going on. In his TV dé-coll/ages, for instance, the viewer is unsettled by deliberately faulty pictures or sets tuned out of focus, or smeared with paint or bashed in and riddled with bullet holes.

Vostell works out illustrated ''scores'' with detailed instructions for his demonstrations and happenings, though without excluding chance events: ''A primary characteristic of my work and that of my colleagues is that the Happening includes whatever noise, movement, object, color or psychology enters into the total work of art. Because of this I assert that people and life are art.'' This total work of art in which the public are performers is intended to arouse their critical and aesthetic awareness so that they ''learn to live and experience in the psychological reality of their surroundings.'' They are to be involved in a total work of art which both arouses their sensuous and aesthetic responses and also has an intellectual impact which leads to each developing a new way of seeing, a consciousness both of himself and of his own body and of the ways in which his life is conditioned by the technological world.

From 1962 Vostell began to call his works Happenings and he became closely associated with the Fluxus movement, with such events as the group *24 Hour Happening* at Wuppertal in 1965 or Vostell's own most ambitious happening *In Ulm, round Ulm and round about Ulm* of 1964. He has called the events of May 1968 in Paris ''the greatest Happening of all'' because unrest supported by artistic means here moved into direct political action and the overthrow of de Gaulle. Unlike Duchamp's ready-mades, the materials Vostell selects for his happenings are not random objects but central achetypal elements of our machine age such as television, trains and cars. And unlike the futurist worship of the car as an object of beauty he emphasizes its destructive potential, seeing in the passing car ''the accident too driving by.'' One instruction in his earliest demonstration was to make sculpture out of crashed cars by fixing the remains to the spot where the accident occurred, and the old tendency to simply clear up the mess and thrust it out of mind has indeed now given way in some countries to putting up photographs of some of the worst accidents as a grim warning. Vostell's work, whatever its creative limitations, always presents a challenge, both to extend artistic reality to all sorts of everyday events and to approach these with a new critical and aesthetic awareness.

—Konstantin Bazarov

VOULKOS, Peter

Nationality: American. **Born:** Bozeman, Montana, 29 January 1924. **Education:** Montana State College, Bozeman, 1946–51, B.S. 1951; California College of Arts and Crafts, 1951–52, M.F.A. 1952. **Military Service:** B52 Rear Gunner, Army Air Corps, in the Pacific, 1942–45. **Career:** Independent sculptor, since 1952: lives and works in Oakland, California. Taught at Archie Bray Foundation, Helena, Montana, and Black Mountain College, Beria, North Carolina, 1952–54; Otis Art Institute, Los Angeles, 1954–59; and Greenwich House Pottery, New York, summer 1961. Instructor, 1959–63, and professor, 1963–85, University of California, Berkeley (retired 1985). **Awards:** Gold Medal, *International Ceramic Exhibition,* Cannes, 1955; Sculpture Prize, *Biennale,* Paris, 1959; Sculpture Prize, San Francisco, 1967; National Endowment for the Arts grant, Washington, D.C., 1976, 1986; Creative Arts Medal, Brandeis University, Waltham, Massachusetts, 1982; Guggenheim Fellowship, New York, 1984; Gold Medal, American Crafts Council, 1986. Honorary Doctorates: California College of Arts and Crafts, Oakland, 1974; Otis Art Institute, 1982; Louise Nevelson Award in Art, American Academy and Institute of Arts and Letters, New York, 1992; Medal, in Recognition of Contributions to American Ceramics, 1994; Distinguished Artist Award for Lifetime Achievement, College Art Association, 1997; Ceramic Lifetime Achievement of the Year Award, Friends of Contemporary Ceramics, 1997; NCECA Award for Teaching Excellence, National Council on Education for the Ceramic Arts, 1997. **Agent:** Braunstein Gallery, 254 Sutter Street, San Francisco. California 94108, U.S.A. **Address:** 951 62nd Street, Oakland, California 94608, U.S.A. **Web site:** http://www.voulkos.com/core.html.

Individual Exhibitions:

1956 Felix Laridau Gallery, Los Angeles
1957 University of Southern California, Los Angeles
1958 Felix Laridau Gallery, Los Angeles
Pasadena Art Museum, California
1961 Museum of Modern Art, New York
Bonnier Gallery, New York
1964 Gallery Unlimited, San Francisco
Primus-Stuart Gallery, Los Angeles
1965 David Stuart Gallery, Los Angeles
1968 Quay Gallery, San Francisco
1969 David Stuart Gallery, Los Angeles
1974 Quay Gallery, San Francisco
1975 Kansas City Art Institute
Helen Drun Gallery, Philadelphia
Braunstein/Quay Gallery, New York
1976 Yaw Gallery, Bloomfield Hills, Michigan
Detroit Institute of Art
Exhibit A Gallery, Evanston, Illinois
1978 Braunstein/Quay Gallery, San Francisco
San Francisco Museum of Modern Art (retrospective)
1979 Exhibit A Gallery, Chicago
1981 Jacksonville Art Museum, Florida
Exhibit A Gallery, Chicago
Thomas Segal Gallery, Boston
Charles Cowles Gallery, New York
1982 Braunstein Gallery, San Francisco
1983 Point View Art Center, Tokyo (travelled to Nagoya and Kyoto)
Charles Cowles Gallery, New York
1984 Magnolia Editions, Oakland, California
University of Iowa, Ames
Exhibit A Gallery, Chicago
Braunstein Gallery, San Francisco
1985 Exhibit A Gallery, Chicago
1986 Braunstein Gallery, San Francisco
1987 Braunstein Gallery, San Francisco
1988 Twining Gallery, New York (catalog)
1990 Charles Cowles Gallery, New York
1991 Braunstein/Quay Gallery, San Francisco (catalog)
Leedy/Voulkos Gallery, Kansas City, Missouri
1992 Louis Newman Galleries, Beverly Hills
1993 Braunstein/Quay Gallery, San Francisco
Hordaland Kunstnersentrum, Bergen, Norway (travelled to Ram Galleri, Oslo)
Kunstindustrimuseum, Trondehim
Kunstnernes Hus, Salthomsgade, Denmark
Grimmerhus Center for International Studiokeramik, Middledfart, Denmark
Perimeter Gallery, Chicago

Peter Voulkos: *Rocking Pot,* 1956. ©Smithsonian American Art Museum, Washington, DC/Art Resource, NY; courtesy of Smithsonian American Art Museum.

1995 Sezon Museum of Art, Tokyo (travelled to National Museum of Modern Art, Kyoto, Japan) (retrospective) (catalog)
Society for Contemporary Craft, Pittsburgh, Pennsylvania
Art Gallery of New South Wales, Sydney (travelled to National Gallery of Victoria, Melbourne)
Dowse Art Museum, Wellington, New Zealand (catalog)
Oakland Museum, California (travelled to Newport Harbor Museum of Art, Newport Beach; American Craft Museum, New York)
1996 Charles Cowles Gallery, New York
Kenji Taki Gallery, Nagoya, Japan (catalog)
William Traver Gallery, Seattle, Washington
1997 Perimeter Gallery, Chicago
University of Central Florida, Orlando
1999 Frank Lloyd Gallery, Santa Monica
2000 Sheldon Memorial Art Gallery and Sculpture Garden, The University of Nebraska, Lincoln

Selected Group Exhibitions:

1958 *World's Fair,* Brussels
1962 *World's Fair,* Seattle
1963 *International Sculpture Exhibition,* Battersea Park, London
1976 *200 Years of American Sculpture,* Whitney Museum, New York
1979 *A Century of Ceramics in the USA,* Everson Museum of Art, Syracuse, New York
1981 *Ceramic Sculpture,* Whitney Museum, New York (toured the United States)
1983 *Ceramic Echoes,* Nelson-Atkins Gallery of Art, Kansas City, Missouri
1984 *Art in Clay 1950s to 1980s,* Los Angeles Municipal Art Gallery
1988 *Lost and Found in California: 4 Decades of Assemblage Art,* James Corcoran Gallery/Shoshana Wayne/Pence Gallery, Santa Monica (catalog)

1989 *3 Sculptors: New Work,* Twining Gallery, New York
1990 *Putting Pottery in Perspective: Past, Present, Future,* Rockford College, Illinois (travelling exhibition) (catalog)
Bay Area Sculptors of the 1960's: Then and Now, Braustein/Quay Gallery, San Francisco (catalog)
1992 *California Legacy: Concepts in Clay, FHP,* Hippodrome Gallery, Palos Verdes Art Center, California (catalog)
1993 *Meeting of the Masters,* Kunstindustrimuseet, Oslo (catalog)
Contemporary Crafts and the Saxe Collection, Toledo Museum of Art (catalog)
1994 *Working in Other Dimensions: Objects & Drawings II,* Arkansas Arts Center, Little Rock (catalog)
1995 *Made in America: Ten Centuries of American Art,* Minneapolis Institute of Art (travelling exhibition) (catalog)
Jet Dreams: The Fifties in the Northwest, Tacoma Art Museum, Washington (catalog)
1996 *Four Decades of Discovery: The 40th Anniversary of the American Craft Museum,* American Craft Museum, New York (catalog)
Collection Highlights: 1945 to the Present, Seattle Art Museum, Washington
1997 *Designed for Delight: Alternative Aspects of Twentieth-Century Decorative Arts,* Montreal Museum of Fine Arts
1998 *NCECA 1998 Honors and Fellows Exhibition,* Modern Art Museum of Fort Worth
Anderson Ranch Artists, Evelyn Siegel Gallery, Ft. Worth
Of and About Clay II, Galerie Hertz, Louisville, Kentucky

Collections:

Albany Mall, State of New York; Stedelijk Museum, Amsterdam; University of Michigan Museum of Art, Ann Arbor; High Museum of Art, Atlanta; Baltimore Museum of Art; Banff Centre, School of Fine Arts, Alberta, Canada; University Art Museum, University of California, Berkeley; Boise Art Museum, Idaho; Cranbrook Academy of Art, Bloomfield Hills, Michigan; Indiana University Art Museum, Bloomington; Museum of Fine Arts, Boston; University of Colorado, Boulder; Montana State University School of Art Permanent Collection, Bozeman; Australian National Gallery, Canberra; Southern Illinois University Art Museum, Carbondale; Krannert Art Museum, University of Illinois, Champaign; Museum of Contemporary Art, Chicago; David & Alfred Smart Museum of Art, University of Chicago; Scripps College, Claremont, California; Den Permanente, Copenhagen; Denver Art Museum; Des Moines Art Center; Detroit Institute of Arts; Stedelijk Van Abbe Museum, Eindhoven; City of Fresno, California; University of Florida, Gainesville; Archie Bray Foundation, Helena, Montana; City of Highland Park, Illinois; Honolulu Academy of Art; Contemporary Museum, Honolulu; Prince Jonah Kuhio Kalanianaole Federal Building and United States Courthouse, Honolulu; Herbert F, Johnson Museum of Art, Cornell University, Ithaca, New York; Aichi Prefectural Ceramic Museu, Japan; Nelson-Atkins Museum of Art, Kansas City, Missouri; National Museum of Modern Art, Kyoto, Japan; La Jolla Museum of Contemporary Art; Sheldon Memorial Art Gallery & Sculpture Garden, University of Nebraska, Lincoln; Arkansas Arts Center, Little Rock; Victoria and Albert Museum, London; Long Beach Museum of Art; Los Angeles County Museum of Art; Franklin D. Murphy Sculpture Garden, University of California, Los Angeles; Elvehjem Museum of Art, University of Wisconsin, Madison; National Gallery of Art, Melbourne; Milwaukee Art Museum; Minneapolis Institute of Arts; Fine Arts Museum of the South, Mobile, Alabama; Musée des Arts Decoratifs de Montreal, Canada; American Craft Museum, New York; Metropolitan Museum of Art, New York; Museum of Modern Art, New York; Whitney Museum of American Art, New York; Oakland Art Museum; Norton Simon Museum, Pasadena, California; Art Gallery of Western Australia, Perth; Philadelphia Museum of Art; Phoenix Art Museum; Carnegie Museum of Art, Pittsburgh; Portland Art Museum; Museum Boymans van Beuningen, Rotterdam; Crocker Art Museum, Sacramento, California; St. Louis Art Museum; Minnesota Museum of American Art, St. Paul; Utah Museum of Fine Arts, University of Utah, Salt Lake City; City and County of San Francisco; San Francisco Museum of Modern Art; Santa Barbara Museum of Art; Seattle Art Museum, Washington; Henry Art Gallery, University of Washington, Seattle; Museum of Contemporary Ceramic Art, Shigaraki; Everson Museum of Art, Syracuse, New York; Nordenfjeldske Kunstindustrimuseum, Trondheim, Norway; Arizona State University Art Museum, Tempe; Tokyo Folk Art Museum, Japan; Art Gallery of Greater Victoria, Canada; Museum of Modern Art, Wakayama, Japan; Corcoran Gallery of Art, Washington, DC; Hirshhorn Museum and Sculpture Garden, National Museum of American Art and the Renwick Gallery of Contemporary Crafts, Smithsonian Institution, Washington, D.C.; Yamaguchi Prefectural Museum of Art, Japan.

Publications:

By VOULKOS: Articles—"Interview with Peter Voulkos" in *Forum Magazine* (Kansas City), December 1991-January 1992; "West Coast Clay" with Cheryl White in *Artweek,* May 1995; "Voulkos Speaks: An Interview by Rick Berman" in *Clay Times,* September/October 1996; "The Making of an Artist" with Joel Betancourt in *Ceramics Monthly,* vol. 47, no. 5, May 1999.

On VOULKOS: Books—*Objects: US.A.* by Lee Nordness, London 1970; *Peter Voulkos: A Dialogue with Clay* by Rose Slivka, Boston 1978. **Articles—**"Los Angeles Letter" by M. Leopold in *Art International* (Lugano), Summer 1973; "The Art of Peter Voulkos" by Hal Fischer in *Artforum* (New York), November 1978; "Peter Voulkos: Ceramics that Transcend Art" by Thomas Albright in *San Francisco Chronicle,* 27 March 1984; "Strong New Works by Voulkos" by Kenneth Baker in *San Francisco Chronicle,* 2 March 1991; "Peter Voulkos" by Jim Leedy in *The Studio Potter,* June 1993; "The Art of Peter Voulkos" by Edward Lebow in *American Craft,* February/March 1996; "The Art of Peter Voulkos" in *The New York Times,* 24 May 1996.

W

WADE, Robert (Schrope)

Nationality: American. **Born:** Austin, Texas, 6 January 1943. **Education:** University of Texas at Austin, 1961–65, B.F.A. in painting, 1965; University of California at Berkeley, 1965–66, M.A. in painting, 1966. **Family:** Married Susan Elaine Immel in 1966, one daughter; married Lisa Sherman in 1985, one daughter. **Career:** Taught at McLennan College, Waco, Texas, 1966–70; artist-in-residence, Northwood Institute, Cedar Hill, Texas, 1970–72; director, Northwood Experimental Art Institute, Dallas, 1972–73; assistant professor of art, North Texas State University, Denton, 1973–77. Lives and works in Austin, Texas. **Awards:** National Endowment for the Arts Grants, 1973, 1975, 1984. **Agent:** Projects & Photoworks, 3502 Winsome Ct., Austin, TX 78731, U.S.A. **Web site:** bobwade.com.

Individual Exhibitions:

1967 Baylor University, Waco, Texas
1970 Chapman Kelley Gallery, Dallas
1971 Chapman Kelley Gallery, Dallas
Kornblee Gallery, New York
1972 Smither Gallery, Dallas
Temple University, Philadelphia (with Bladen)
1973 Baylor University, Waco
University of St. Thomas, Houston
Austin College, Sherman, Texas
University of California at San Diego
1974 University of Texas at El Paso
Kornblee Gallery, New York
Washington Art Site, Washington, D.C.
Kansas City Art Institute, Missouri
1975 Delahunty Gallery, Dallas
Laguna Gloria Art Museum, Austin, Texas
1976 Delahunty Gallery, Dallas
Morgan Gallery, Kansas City, Missouri
1977 Agora Studio, Maastricht, Netherlands
1978 Janus Gallery, Los Angeles
1979 Washington Project for the Arts, Washington, D.C.
1984 Cultural Activities Center, Temple, Texas
1986 *Recent Works,* Janie Briggs Fine Art, Ltd., Aspen, Colorado
1987 *Recent Works,* Elaine Horwitch Galleries, Santa Fe
Cowgirls & Cowboys, Atwell Gallery, Colorado Springs
1988 *Wild Wild Wade Show,* Republic Plaza, Denver
Recent Works, Marvin Seline Gallery, Austin, Texas
Recent Works, Plaza Gallery, Dallas
Cowgirls & Wooley Boys, Mill Street Gallery, Aspen, Colorado
1989 *Let's Rodeo,* William Campbell Contemporary Art, Ft. Worth, Texas
Photoworks, Le Texan, Monaco
1990 *New Big Photos of Little Old Photos,* Marvin Seline Gallery, Houston
Photoworks, Elaine Horwitch Galleries, Santa Fe
Bronze Coconuts, Janie Beggs Fine Art, Ltd., Beverly Hills
1991 *Recent Works,* Etherton-Stern Gallery, Tucson
1992 *Photoworks,* Janie Beggs Fine Art, Ltd., Aspen, Colorado
Galleria Primitivo, Santa Monica, California
1993 *Big Photos in Cowtown,* William Campbell Contemporary Art, Ft. Worth, Texas
Remember the Alamo: Other Heroics, Carrington/Gallagher Ltd., San Antonio, Texas
Homage to Myths: Reality, Elaine Horwitch Galleries, Santa Fe
The One and Only Bob Wade, Kristina Wasserman Gallery, Providence, Rhode Island
1994 *Wild West Show,* El Paso Museum of Art, Texas
Santa Fe Trail, Lyons Matrix Gallery, Austin, Texas
Photoworks, Lynne Goode Gallery, Houston
1995 *Icons of the Wild West,* Stremmel Gallery , Reno, Nevada
1996 *Southwestern Works,* Parchman Stremmel Galleries, San Antonio
Ridin' & Wreckin, William Campbell Fine Art, Fort Worth
1997 *Equestrian,* Betts Gallery, Santa Fe
1998 *Photoeclectic,* M.D. Modern Gallery, Houston
1999 *Daddy-o's Stuff,* Lawndale Art Center, Houston
Summer Pleasures, Lyons Matrix Gallery, Austin
2000 *Local Color,* William Campbell Fine Art, Fort Worth
2001 *New Photoworks,* Thomas Ingerick Gallery, Aspen
Bob Wade's West, Lynn Goode Gallery, Marfa, Texas

Selected Group Exhibitions:

1969 *Biennial,* Whitney Museum, New York
1976 *DFWISFO Exchange,* San Francisco Museum of Modern Art
1977 *Photography and Paintings in Dialogue,* Kunsthaus, Zurich
Biennale, National Museum of Modern Art, Paris
1978 *Dallas in Chicago,* Fisher, Green, Surls, Wade; Marianne Deson Gallery, Chicago
Giant Iguana, Artpark, Lewiston, New York
1979 *Fire,* Contemporary Arts Museum, Houston
1980 *Mapping,* Kohler Arts Center, Sheboygan, Wisconsin
1981 *Texas Group Show,* Charles Cowles Gallery, New York
1982 *Arteder—'82,* Feria International, Bilbao, Spain
1984 *Showdown,* Alternative Museum, New York
2nd Annual Wild West Show, Alberta College of Art, Calgary, Canada
1985 *Couriers & I,* Central Cultural, São Paulo
1986 *3rd Annual Western States Biennial,* Brooklyn Museum, New York
1988 *Texas Art,* Richmond Hall, The Menil Collection, Houston

Robert Wade: *Neck + Neck,* 2000. ©County Line Barbeque, Austin, Texas.

1991 *Critical Mass,* Maryland Institute College of Art, Baltimore
1993 Center for Research in Contemporary Art, University of Texas, Arlington
1998 *Nouveau Western Art,* Holter Museum of Art, Helena, Montana
2000 *Sculpture 2000,* Houston
Main Street Windows, Foto Fest 2000, Houston
2001 *Desert Tracks,* Wildlife Art of the American Southwest, National Museum of Wildlife Art, Jackson Hole, Wyoming

Collections:

Chase Manhattan Bank, New York; New Mexico State Capitol, Santa Fe; Museum of Fine Arts, Santa Fe; Centre Georges Pompidou, Paris;

Groningen Museum, Netherlands; Dallas Museum of Fine Arts; Eiteljorg Museum, Indianapolis; Modern Art Museum of Ft. Worth, Texas; Center for Creative Photography, Tucson; Royal Palace, Monaco; AT&T, Chicago; The Menil Collection, Houston; Federal Reserve, Dallas; Austin Museum of Art, Texas, etc.

Permanent Public Installations:

Dallas Skyline, Apparel Mart, Dallas; *Texas Sixshooter,* Del Rio Council on the Arts, Texas; *Bronze Cowboy on Giant Armadillo,* Pasadena, Texas; *Smokesax, Billy Blues,* Houston; *Malibu Salsero,* La Salsa, Malibu, California; *World's Biggest Cowboy Boots,* North Star Mall, San Antonio, *Giant Iguana,* Fort Worth Zoo, Fort Worth.

Publications:

By WADE: Books—*Cowgirls,* Peregrine-Smith Books, 1995; *Daddy-O: Iguana Heads and Texas Tales,* with Kent Zimmerman, St. Martin's Press, 1995; *Ridin and Wreckin,* Gibbs-Smith, 1996. **Articles**—*Art Press International* (Paris), October 1977.

On WADE: Books—*Photo Process as Media,* exhibition catalog by Rosanne Truxes, New Brunswick, New Jersey 1976; *Bob Wade: Projects and Photoworks,* exhibition catalog by Janet Kutner et al, Temple, Texas 1984; *Third Western Exhibition,* exhibition catalog by Charlotta Kotik, Brooklyn 1986; *A Century of Texas Sculpture, 1889–1989,* exhibition catalog by Patricia D. Hendricks and Becky Duval Reese, Austin, Texas 1989; *Soft Sculpture and Beyond* by Jutta Feddersen, Langhorne, Pennsylvania 1993; *Handcoloring Photographs,* by James A. McKinnis, New York 1994; *The History of Hand Painted Photography,* New York 1995; *Texas Tradition . . . The Culture of the Lone Star State,* by Robyn Montanta Turner, New York 1996; *Visions of the West,* by Melissa Baldridge, Gibbs-Smith 1999; *Texas Curiosities,* by John Kelso, Globe Pequot, 2000; *Texas Men, Big Guns, Rising Stars, and Cowboys,* Fort Worth 2000. **Articles**—''Houston-Dallas Axis'' by Janet Kutner in *Art in America* (New York), September/October 1972; ''The Young Texans'' by Jan Butterfield in *Arts Magazine* (New York), March 1973; ''Contemporary Art in Texas'' by Henry Hopkins in *Artnews* (New York), May 1973; ''The ABC's of the Oak Cliff Four'' by Josie Rabyor in *Southwest Art* (Austin, Texas), September 1973; ''Texas Map'' by Charlotte Moser in the *Houston Post,* October 1973; ''Kick That Art Off Your Boots'' by Josie Rabyor in *D Magazine* (Dallas), February 1975; ''Texas'' by Jane Kutner in *Artnews* (New York), Summer 1975; ''Texas Ball and Chain Cult 112 Greene'' by Mona da Vinci in *Soho Weekly News* (New York), September 1975; ''Deep in the Heart of Gotham'' by Chet Flippo in *GQ,* April 1984; ''Shoot-out at the Black-Eyed Pea'' by Marie Brenner in *Vanity Fair,* April 1985; ''Outdoor Sculpture by Texas Artists'' by Mel McCombie in *Artnews,* November 1986; ''Etcetera: Art Texas-Style'' by Anne Hillerman in *Southwest Art,* April 1987; ''Life-Size Just Not Big Enough'' by William Clark in *Albuquerque Journal,* 3 July 1988; ''Honky Tonk Good-bye'' by John Milward in *Chicago Tribune,* 10 April 1989; ''Wild, Weird, Wonderful Wade'' by Carole Myers in *The New Mexican* (Pasatiempo), 13 July 1990; ''Bob Wade, A Portrait of the Artist as a Thoroughly Texas Icon'' by Kim Goad in *Dallas Morning News,* 11 August 1991; ''City Appeals Board Rules Giant Saxaphone Is Art, Not a Sign'' by Stephanie Asin in *Houston Chronicle,* 27 May 1993; ''The Art of Bob Wade'' by Charlotte Berney in *Cowboys & Indians Magazine,* September 1994; ''Experience the Colors of the West'' by David McCaffrey in *Reno Gazette Journal,* 16 April 1995; ''Interview with Bob Wade'' by Susie Kalil, *Art Lies* (Houston), Summer 2000. **Films**—*Too High Too Wide Too Long* (documentary), by Karen Dinitz, 1999.

*

The interesting thing about places like Texas is that the myths are perpetuated by cultural curiosity and, perhaps, a universal interest in being a real cowboy. Part of my fascination with Western mythology is that, like jazz and football, it is unique to the United States. I would rather perpetuate the myth of the West than participate in its homogenization.

—Bob Wade

* * *

At the beginning of his career Robert Wade was linked with the loosely associated group of ''Oak Cliff'' artists, all of whom lived or worked in the same area of Dallas; they included such diverse members as Jim Roche (sculptor and conceptual artist) and Jack Mims (allegorical figurative painter who works in monumental scale). Although there are no formal resemblances among any of these artists, they do share similarities in approach and allusion, most noticeably in a proudly wry celebration of the state in which they all live. Wade is particularly drawn to the peccadillos for which Texas is (rightly or wrongly) known: a massive sense of both space and architectural size, and an undercurrent of cultivated violence and rawness which deliberately harks back to the early days of the American West.

Although this emphasis is overwhelmingly obvious, it would be the most popular of cliches to let it rest there. For Wade's work demonstrates a conceptual edge that takes it beyond regionalism, one which is frequently missed—or perhaps deliberately ignored—by many critics. For instance, national attention in America was first drawn to Wade's ''Jumbo U.S. Map,'' a project that makes a cultural, rather than an aesthetic or political, statement. It is a work that is exactly what it says it is, an enormous recreation of the United States executed in earth, plywood, concrete and water and located just beside one of Dallas's busiest freeways. This project had a precedent—the ''Map of Texas,'' which, when completed in 1973, measured 40′ x 40′. Although both the U.S. and Texas maps are undoubtedly the most physically ambitious, other, smaller works are more important and rely more heavily on a mixture of laden content and innovative form.

There are Wade's photo-emulsions on canvas, which operate as images frozen in time, frequently forcing the viewer to confront scenes of potential or actual violence. For Wade is at his best when he gives situations form—takes it, in effect, out of the *realm* of situation and makes it imagery. The best known of this series is entitled ''Criminal Wall,'' in which we see, loosely tacked to the wall, large photos-on-canvas of such infamous and anti-heroic characters as Lee Harvey Oswald, Bonnie and Clyde, John Wesley Harding, and Pancho Villa—all ''death-bed'' portraits. They are all presented without comment and are all the more powerful for that. In others, such as his series of postcard images accompanied by texts from grade-school textbooks, interior and landscape scenes are more complex, nostalgic, not self-consciously violent in the least but somehow sinister in their evocation of a past. This is true as well in his autobiographical work, which incorporated images of inanimate objects as well as human subjects—a piece which he terms ''photographic projections on paper.'' Wade's obsessional sense of scale is much in evidence in this work, as it measures 30 feet long and 16 feet high and requires 15 hours of projection: yet there is also an idiosyncratic quality to this work, and to others, a calculated irony that stops short of exuberance.

—Jane Bell

WALKER, John

Nationality: British. **Born:** Birmingham, 12 November 1939. **Education:** Birmingham College of Art, 1956–60, and Académie de la Grande Chaumière, Paris, 1961–63. **Career:** Painter and graphic artist, in London, 1964–70, in New York, since 1970, and in Melbourne, Australia, since 1980. Professor of painting and drawing, Cooper Union, New York, 1974–75; visiting professor, Yale University, New Haven, Connecticut, 1975–77; artist-in-residence, St. Catherines College, Oxford, 1977–78; painting tutor, Royal College of Art, London, 1974–78; visiting artist, Columbia University, New York, 1974–78; artist-in-residence, Prahran Technical College, Melbourne, 1980; Dean, Victoria College of the Arts, Melbourne, 1982–86; Visiting Professor, Yale University, Graduate School of Art, 1989; Professor of Painting, Visual Arts Division of School for the Arts, Boston University, 1993-present. **Awards:** Drawing Prize, Arts Council of Great Britain, 1960; Edwin Abbey travel scholarship, 1960; First Prize, *National Young Artists Drawing Competition,* London, 1960; Purchase Award, Arts Council, 1967; Gregory Fellowship, University of Leeds,1967–69; Theodoron Award, 1969; Harkness Fellowship, 1970–72; First Prize, *International Prize Biennale,* Bradford, Yorkshire, 1974; First Prize, *John Moores Exhibition,* Liverpool, 1976; Guggenheim Fellowship, 1981. **Agent:** Nigel Greenwood Inc., 4 New Burlington Street, London WI, England; and Knoedler Gallery, 19 East 70th Street, New York, New York, U.S.A.

Individual Exhibitions:

1967 Axiom Gallery, London
1968 Park Square Gallery, Leeds
Axiom Gallery, London
Hayward Gallery, London
1969 City Art Gallery, Leeds
1970 Nigel Greenwood Inc., London
1971 Reese Palley Gallery, New York
1972 British Pavilion at the *Biennale,* Venice
Reese Palley Gallery, New York
Studio la Città, Verona
Ikon Gallery, Birmingham
Galerie Rolf Ricke, Cologne
1973 Nigel Greenwood Inc., London (2 shows)
Kunstverein, Hamburg
Städtisches Museum, Bochum, West Germany
Cunningham Ward Gallery, New York
Park Square Gallery, Leeds
1974 Museum of Modern Art, New York
Galerie Swart, Amsterdam
1975 Nigel Greenwood Inc., London
Cunningham Ward Gallery, New York
1976 Galerie Marguerite Lamy, Paris
Cunningham Ward Gallery, New York
Reed College, Portland, Oregon
1977 Powell Street Gallery, Melbourne
1978 Cunningham Ward Gallery, New York
Phillips Collection, Washington, D.C. (toured the United States)
Museum of Modern Art, New York
Art Gallery of New South Wales, Sydney
Nigel Greenwood Inc., London
1979 University of Massachusetts, Amherst (travelled to Brown University, Providence, Rhode Island, and Brandeis University, Waltham, Massachusetts)
Powell Street Gallery, Melbourne
1980 Nigel Greenwood Inc., London (2 shows)
Betty Cunningham Gallery, New York
1981 *Drawings,* National Art Gallery, Wellington, New Zealand (travelled to Robert McDougall Art Gallery, Christchurch, Dunedin Public Art Gallery and the City Art Gallery, Auckland)
Nigel Greenwood Inc., London
Theo Waddington Gallery, London
1982 Phillips Collection, Washington, D.C. (travelled to J. B. Speed Art Museum, Louisville, Kentucky)
1983 Madeleine Carter Gallery, Brookline, Massachusetts
M. Knoedler and Company, New York
1984 M. Knoedler and Company, New York
1985 Hayward Gallery, London (travelled to Edinburgh and Birmingham)
Tate Gallery, London
M. Knoedler, Zurich
1986 M. Knoedler and Company, New York
Adelaide Festival of Arts, South Australia
1987 L. A. Louver Gallery, Venice, California
National Gallery of Victoria, Melbourne
Pamela Auchincloss Gallery, Santa Barbara, California
M. Knoedler and Company, New York
1989 Schick Art Gallery, Skidmore College, Saratoga Springs, New York (catalog)
1990 *John Walker: Prints 1989–90,* Waddington Graphics, London (catalog)
1991 *John Walker: Paintings and Drawings,* The Arts Club of Chicago (catalog)
Rex Irwin Art Dealer, Woollahra, Australia (catalog)
1992 *John Walker: Small Paintings from the Alba and Oceania Series,* Anthony Ralph Gallery, New York
1993 *John Walker: Recent Drawings,* Victoria Monroe Fine Art, New York
Christine Abrahams Gallery, Richmond, Australia (catalog)
1994 *John Walker: Small Paintings and Recent Works on Paper,* Nielsen Gallery, Boston
1996 *John Walker: The Serenade and Studio Paintings,* Carling Dalenson, Stockholm
Paintings by John Walker, Eli Marsh Gallery, Fayerweather Hall, Amherst College, Amherst
1997 *A Theatre of Recollection: Paintings and Prints by John Walker,* Boston University Art Gallery, Boston (catalog)
John Walker: Feeling, Form, Beauty, Hill Gallery, Birmingham
1998 *Passing Bells,* Nielsen Gallery, Boston

1999 *John Walker: Paintings & Prints,* Fassbender Gallery
2001 *John Walker: Time and Tides* (catalog)

Selected Group Exhibitions:

1965 *John Moores Exhibition,* Walker Art Gallery, Liverpool (and 1974, 1976)
1968 *New British Painting and Sculpture,* University of California, Los Angeles
1970 *Contemporary Art in Britain,* National Museum of Modern Art, Tokyo
1973 *Towards Painting,* Tate Gallery, London
1975 *Color as Language,* Museum of Modern Art, New York (toured South America)
1977 *25 Years of British Painting,* Royal Academy of Art, London
1978 *Critic's Choice,* Institute of Contemporary Arts, London
1982 *Aspects of British Art Today,* Metropolitan Art Museum, Tokyo
1984 *The British Art Show,* City Art Gallery, Birmingham (and Ikon Gallery, Birmingham; travelled to Edinburgh, Sheffield, Southampton)
1987 *British Art 1900–80: The Modern Movement,* Royal Academy, London (travelled to Stuttgart)
1988 *Collaborations in Monotype,* Art Museum, University of California at Santa Barbara (traveling exhibit) (catalog)
The Presence of Painting: Aspects of British Abstraction 1957–1988, Mappin Art Gallery, Sheffield, England (traveling exhibition) (catalog)
1991 *Figuratively Speaking: Drawings by Seven Artists,* Roy R. Neuberger Museum, Purchase, New York (catalog)
1994 *British Abstract Art Part 1: Paintings,* Flowers East, London (catalog)

Collections:

Arts Council of Great Britain, London; Tate Gallery, London; Victoria and Albert Museum, London; City Art Gallery, Leeds; Scottish National Gallery of Modern Art, Edinburgh; Ulster Museum, Belfast; Museum am Ostwall, Dortmund, West Germany; Museum of Modern Art, New York; Guggenheim Museum, New York; National Gallery of Art, Washington, D.C.; Art Gallery of New South Wales, Sydney; Australian National Gallery, Canberra; Chicago Art Institute, Chicago; Cleveland Museum of Art; Fogg Museum, Harvard University, Cambridge; Hirshhorn Museum and Sculpture Garden, Washington, D.C.; Leeds University Art Collection, Leeds, England; Metropolitan Museum of Art, New York; Museum of Contemporary Art, Los Angeles; The University of Michigan Museum of Art, Ann Arbor; Yale University Art Gallery, New Haven.

Publications:

By WALKER: Books—*John Walker: Drawings from the Forge Series, 1988* with Madeleine Carter, Brookline 1988. **Article—** ''John Walker on His Painting: From a Conversation with Tim Hilton'' in *Studio International* (London), June 1972.

On WALKER: Books—*Contemporary Art in Britain,* exhibition catalog with text by Andrew Causey, Tokyo 1970; *36th Venice Biennate: British Pavilion—John Walker,* exhibition catalog with text by John Elderfield, London 1972; *Color as Language,* exhibition catalog with text by Kynaston McShine, New York 1975; *Arte Inglese Oggi,* exhibition catalog with text by Norbert Lynton and others, Milan 1976; *John Walker,* exhibition catalog with text by Andrew Forge, Washington, D.C. 1978; *Critic's Choice,* exhibition catalog with text by John McEwen, London 1978; *Drawings 1981: John Walker,* exhibition catalog with text by Anne Kirker, Wellington, New Zealand 1981; *John Walker,* exhibition catalog with text by Jack B. Flam, Washington, D.C. 1982; *John Walker: Paintings from the Alba and Oceania Series 1979–1984,* exhibition catalog with introduction by Dore Ashton, London 1985; *John Walker: Prints 1976–84,* exhibition catalog with text by Memory Holloway, London 1985; *John Walker: Salsipuedes Suite,* exhibition catalog with text by Ted Gott, Melbourne 1987; *John Walker: The Serenade and Studio Paintings* by John Walker, Stockholm 1996; *John Walker: The Dialectic of Opposites* by Rachel Malcolm-Woods and Maude Wahlman, Kansas City 1999. **Articles—**''A Question of Surfaces: John Walker's Recent Paintings'' by John Elderfield in *Art in America* (New York), vol. 76, January 1988; ''John Walker's Imagery Both Personal, Universal: Paintings, Prints Capture Memories of Great War'' by Kyle MacMillan in *Sunday World-Herald* (Omaha), 23 August 1998.

* * *

There is something powerfully disciplined about John Walker's ambitions as a painter. Conventional (in the strict modernist sense of the word), Walker's work has developed slowly over the last 15 years, reworking given sets of forms and spatial schemes bit by bit, slowly reinvesting them with new expressive power. The tightness of this process of transformation, its reliance on narrow formal reinvention (or adjustment) rather than borrowing and reworking a broad school of forms, forces criticism very much into a descriptive, defensive position. Although literary claims have been made for Walker's powerful shapes, Walker's art is more at home within modemist historicism—Manet, Cézanne, Matisse, Pollock. The artist's job is to find his place within that history, to enter into a dialogue with—to measure himself against—the best work of the past. As a Modern equivalent of l'art pour l'art this assumes a kind of assertiveness against the modern world. Walker has talked about the ''monastic'' challenge of being an artist.

Walker's development can be divided into three phases. A period of geometric abstraction, which introduces the awkward shapes (the lozenges, the pinched-in figures) that reappear in all his work. Here the shapes free-float in an atmospheric, nonillusionist space. A period of cubist collage, represented by the monumental ''Juggernauts'' series, which introduces into a ''built'' architectural space tentative figure-ground relations. The shapes here are jagged and the surface rough, ugly, which is to become a strong feature of the later work. And a period of ''illusionistic'' picture building, represented by the ''Numinous'' balcony series (a motif borrowed from Matisse and Cézanne), the ''Labyrinths'' series, and the recent drawings, which introduce a quasifigurative or fictive space.

This new work makes explicit what has been—in varying degrees—the basis of Walker's art: the tension between our awareness of paintings as containers and windows.

The key to this explicitness is Walker's selfconscious reworking of elements from certain modernist (and protomodemist) works such as Velasquez's ''Las Meninas,'' which, as a paradigm for the artifice of picture making, becomes the perfect model for Walker's own concerns. In Walker's latest drawings, based on ''Las Meninas,'' the reworked forms of the painting reappear within the work as a mirror image. Walker's figure of the artist (the dwarf in ''Las Meninas'') looks across at a screen/canvas containing its own image. The depth of space that Walker introduced into the ''Labyrinths'' is here given a further illusionistic opening out.

This opening out—the transformation of shapes into what might be called images—may not, in any crucial sense, represent a change in outlook (an opening onto the world), but it undoubtedly brings with it an increased sense of esprit or quirkiness, something that seems to be at the basis of Walker's search for shapes that ''irritate'' the eye, that remain in the memory long after the details of the painting have been forgotten.

—John Roberts

WALL, Brian

Nationality: British. **Born:** London, 5 September 1931. **Education:** Luton College of Art, Bedfordshire, 1949–50. **Career:** Sculptor: worked as glass-blower, 1945–50; moved to Paris, 1952, to London, 1953, and to St. Ives, Cornwall, 1955, where he worked as an assistant to Barbara Hepworth, 1955–58; visited New York, 1969, and spent several months of each year in California, 1969–73. Lecturer, Ealing College of Art, London, 1961–62; principal lecturer, Central School of Arts and Design, London, 1962–72. Visiting lecturer, 1969–73, lecturer, 1973–75, 1975–77, assistant professor, 1977–81, assistant professor of art, 81–93, professor, professor emeritus since 1993, University of California, Berkeley. **Agent:** Jernigan Wicker Fine Arts, 161 Natoma Street, San Francisco, California, 94105; Simon Lowinsky Gallery, 578 Broadway, New York, New York. **Address:** 306 Lombard St., San Francisco, CA 94133–2415, U.S.A.

Individual Exhibitions:

1958 Drian Gallery, London
1959 Woodstock Gallery, London
1960 AIA Gallery, London (with Joe Tilson and Anthony Benjamin)
1961 Drian Gallery, London
1962 Grabowski Gallery, London (with Anthony Benjamin)
1963 Manchester City Art Gallery
1964 Grabowski Gallery, London
1966 Grosvenor Gallery, London
1967 Arnolfini Gallery, Bristol
1968 Grosvenor Gallery, London
1971 William Sawyer Gallery, San Francisco
1973 San Jose State University Art Gallery, California
1974 Quay Gallery, San Francisco
St. Mary's College, Morago, California
1976 Braunstein/Quay Gallery, San Francisco
Dootson/Calderhead Gallery, Seattle
University of Nevada, Las Vegas
1981 Max Hutchinson Gallery, New York
1982 Seattle Art Museum, Washington
1983 San Francisco Museum of Modern Art
1987 Simon Lowinsky Gallery, New York
1992 Francis Graham-Dixon Gallery, London
1995 *Brian Wall: Lyrical Steel,* Sheldon Memorial Art Gallery and Sculpture Garden, Lincoln, Nebraska (catalog)
Jernigan Wicker Fine Art, San Francisco
1998 Simon Lowinsky Gallery, New York

Selected Group Exhibitions:

1958 *Contemporary British Sculpture,* Arts Council Gallery, London
1961 *Biennale,* Paris
1963 *British Art Today,* San Francisco Museum of Art (toured the United States)
1965 *Sculpture in the 60s,* Tate Gallery, London
1966 *Sculpture 1960–1966,* Battersea Park, London
1971 *6 x 6 x 6,* Richmond Art Center, California
1975 *Bay Area Sculpture,* James Willis Gallery, San Francisco
1976 *American Sculptors,* University of Texas, Dallas
1979 *Apsects of Abstract,* Crocker Art Museum, Sacramento, California
1982 *One Hundred Years of California Sculpture,* Oakland Museum, California
1988 *Bay Area Sculpture: Metal, Stone and Wood,* Palo Alto Cultural Center, California
Post-War British Abstract Art, Austin/Desmond Fine Art, London
1989 *Art Against AIDS/San Francisico,* Butterfield & Butterfield, San Francisco
1992 *Wagner, Wall, Wareham,* Pacific Rim Sculpture Group, Contract Design Center, San Francisco
Annesley, Levy, Twyford, Wall, Tallberg Taylor Gallery, Greenwich, England
1994 *The Constructed Space: Painting, Sculpture and Verse Commemorating the Poet W.S. Graham,* The Mansion House Ilkley, England (catalog)
Sixteen California Artists, Galerie Sho, Tokyo
Bell, Benjamin, Wall, Isis Gallery, Leigh-on-Sea, England (catalog)
1995 *Abstract British Art: Sculpture,* Flowers East Gallery, London
1996 *Abstract British Art: Drawings,* Flowers East Gallery, London
1997 *U.C. Berkeley Art Faculty,* President's House, Berkeley

Collections:

Tate Gallery, London; Contemporary Art Society, London; Arts Council of Great Britain, London; Whitworth Art Gallery, Manchester; Penwyth Society, St. Ives, Cornwall; National Gallery, Dublin; Billy Rose Sculpture Garden, Jerusalem; University of California at Berkeley; Oakland Museum, California; Gallery of New South Wales, Sydney; Seattle Art Museum; Triton Museum, Santa Clara; British Council, London; University of Houston, Texas; Towson State University, Maryland; Sheldon Memorial Art Gallery and Sculpture Garden, University of Nebraska, Lincoln.

Publications:

By WALL: Articles—statement in *Architectural Design* (London), May 1959; statement in *Brian Wall,* exhibition catalog, Bristol 1967; statement in *Sculpture International* (Oxford), October 1969; ''Wall's

Eye: Barbara Hepworth's Assistant Brian Wall'' in *Art Review* (London), vol. 46, September 1994.

On WALL: Book—*Brian Wall,* exhibition catalog with texts by Peter Selz and George W. Neubert, Seattle 1982. **Articles—**''Brian Wall: Sculpture of Simplicity'' by Charles Spencer in *Studio International* (London), March 1966; ''London Show Offers Brian Wall Sculpture'' by Charles Spencer in *New York Times International Edition,* 30 April 1966; ''Sculpture To See All at Once'' by Christopher Anareae in *Christian Science Monitor* (Boston), 30 November 1966; ''Question and Artist: Brian Wall'' by G. S. Whittet in *Sculpture International* (Oxford), October 1969, ''Unusual Art in San Francisco'' by Thomas Albright in the *San Francisco Chronicle,* 7 January 1974; ''Monumental Sculpture'' by Thomas Albright in the *San Francisco Chronicle,* 16 January 1974; ''The Fitness of Form'' by Robert McDonald in *Artweek* (Oakland, California), February 1976.

* * *

A sculptor of outstanding qualities, Brian Wall has never found his true niche in the post-war British sculptural scene. Like Caro he is a teacher of special qualifications, and in Britain and America has exerted considerable influence on younger generations. His character and work are somewhat paradoxical, typically romantic in the English sense, yet preferring to condition intuitive, gestural elements within a severe discipline. Younger than Caro and Adams (his closest English colleagues), Wall has in some sense been more radical, working on large, simple steel structures when Caro was still involved in Richier-like symbols of the human form.

Wall is virtually self-taught, having taken part-time courses in art whilst serving in the Royal Air Force. A six-month stay in Paris made a decisive impression, notably admiration for Mondrian which led to detailed study of the Russian Constructivists, the Dutch de Stijl and Moholy-Nagy. The second major step in his development was a move to St. Ives, where he first worked in restaurants. Acquaintance with the local art colony led to an introduction to the late Barbara Hepworth, who engaged him as an assistant.

By 1956 he had digested all these various influences and trained himself to work in stone, wood, plaster and metal. His work at this time was distinctly Mondrianesque (painted wood boxes), but he soon switched to metal. The ethics and aims of de Stijl have remained pre-eminent in Wall's career, hence his insistence on large-scale, and his preference for public sculpture. His strength lies in an assured capacity to handle monumental proportions without overcomplicating the design, retaining an impressive sense of power and drama. The sculptures are variations on a few limited shapes—flat panels, square or circular, tubular arms, four-sided boxes; this limited vocabulary is juggled with syntactic ingenuity, never reduced to the decorative or comforting. He has never favoured colour in sculpture, preferring black or white to emphasize the shapes, to stress their simplicity.

—Charles Spencer

WALL, Jeff

Nationality: Canadian. **Born:** Vancouver, British Columbia, Canada, 1946. **Education:** University of British Columbia, Vancouver, M. A. in Art History, 1970; doctoral research, Courtauld Institute, University of London, 1970–73. **Career:** Associate professor, Center for the Arts, Simon Fraser University, Vancouver, 1976–87; currently associate professor at University of British Columbia, Vancouver. **Agent:** Marian Goodman Gallery, 24 West 57th Street, New York, New York 10019, U.S.A.

Selected Individual Exhibitions:

1978 Nova Gallery, Vancouver
1979 *Installation of Faking Death (1977), The Destroyed Room (1978), Young Workers (1978), Picture for Women (1979),* Art Gallery of Greater Vancouver
1982 David Bellman Gallery, Toronto
1983 Renaissance Society, University of Chicago
1984 *Jeff Wall: Transparencies,* Institute of Contemporary Arts, London, England; Kunsthalle, Basel, Switzerland
1986 Galerie Johnen & Schöttle, Cologne
Ydessa Hendeles Gallery, Toronto
1987 *Young Workers,* Museum für Gegenwartskunst, Basel, Switzerland
Galerie Johnen & Schöttle, Cologne
Galerie Ghislaine Hussenot, Paris
1988 Le Nouveau Musée, Villeurbanne, France
Westfalischer Kunstverein, Muenster, Germany
1989 *The Children's Pavilion,* Marian Goodman Gallery, New York; Galerie Roger Pailhas, Marseilles, France; Fonds Regional d'Art Contemporain, Rhône Alpes, Lyons, France; Galerie Chantal Boulanger, Montreal; Santa Barbara Contemporary Arts Forum; Museum Boymans-van Beuningen, Rotterdam, The Netherlands (with Dan Graham)
Galerie Johnen & Schöttle, Cologne
1990 *Jeff Wall 1990,* Vancouver Art Gallery; Art Gallery of Ontario, Toronto (catalog)
Ydessa Hendeles Art Foundation, Toronto
Carnegie Museum of Art, Pittsburgh
1991 San Diego Museum of Contemporary Art
Galerie Johnen & Schöttle, Cologne
Galerie Meert-Rihoux, Brussels
Galerie Christian Stein, Milan
1992 Louisiana Museum, Humlebaek, Denmark
Marian Goodman Gallery, New York
Palais des Beaux-Arts, Brussels
1993 Kunstmuseum Luzern, Lucerne, Switzerland
Irish Museum of Modern Art, Dublin
Fondation Cartier pour l'art contemporain, Jouy-en-Josas, France
1994 Museo Naçional Centro de Arte, Reina Sofia, Madrid
Neue Gesellschaft für Bildende Kunst Galerie, Berlin
De Pont Foundation for Contemporary Art, Tilburg, The Netherlands
The White Cube, London
1995 Marian Goodman Gallery, New York
Jeff Wall, Museum of Contemporary Art, Chicago; Jeu de Paume, Paris; Museum of Contemporary Art, Helsinki, Finland; Whitechapel Art Gallery, London (catalog)
1996 *Jeff Wall: Landscapes,* Kunstmuseum Wolfsburg, Germany
Galerie Nationale du Jeu de Paume, Paris

Jeff Wall: *A Sudden Gust of Wind (After Hokusai)*, 1993. ©Tate Gallery, London/Art Resource, NY; courtesy of Tate Gallery.

1997 *Jeff Wall*, Museum of Contemporary Art, Los Angeles; Hirshhorn Museum and Sculpture Garden, Washington, D. C.; Art Tower Mito, Japan (catalog)

1998 Marian Goodman Gallery, New York

Here and Now II: Jeff Wall, Henry Moore Institute, Leeds, England

Jeff Wall: Photographs of Modern Life, Museum für Gegenwartskunst, Basel, Switzerland

Jeff Wall: Photographs, Galerie Johnen & Schöttle, Cologne

1999 Galerie Johnen & Schöttle, Cologne

Mies van der Rohe Foundation, Barcelona

Jeff Wall: Oeuvres 1990 -1998, Musée d'Art Contemporain, Montreal (catalog)

Selected Group Exhibitions:

1969 *557,087*, Seattle Art Museum

955,000 Vancouver Art Gallery

Photo Show, S.U.B. Art Gallery, University of British Columbia, Vancouver

Focus '69, Bau-Xi Gallery, Vancouver

1970 *3 to Infinity: New Multiple Art*, Whitechapel Art Gallery, London

Information, Museum of Modern Art, New York

Art in the Mind, Allen Memorial Art Museum, Oberlin College, Oberlin, Ohio

Four Artists: Tom Burrows, Duane Lunden, Jeff Wall, Ian Wallace, Fine Arts Gallery, University of British Columbia, Vancouver

1971 *45° 30′ N—73° 36′ W*, Sir George Williams University and the Saidye Bronfman Centre, Montreal

Ecological Art, Bad Salzdetfurth, Germany

New Art, Prague

Collage Show, Fine Arts Gallery, University of British Columbia, Vancouver

1973 *Pacific Vibrations*, Vancouver Art Gallery (catalog)

1980 *Pluralities 1980*, National Gallery of Canada, Ottawa (catalog)

Cibachrome, Photo Gallery, National Film Board of Canada, Ottawa

New Work: Mac Adams, Roger Cutforth, Dan Graham, John Hillard, Jeff Wall, Hal Bromm Gallery, New York

1981 *Westkunst: Zeitgenössische Kunst seit 1939*, Rheinhallen Messegëlande, Cologne (catalog)

Directions 1981, Hirshhorn Museum and Sculpture Garden, Washington, D.C.; Sarah Campbell Blaffer Gallery, University of Houston, Texas (catalog)

1982 Documenta 7, Museum Fridericanium, Kassel, Germany

1984 *Difference: On Representation and Sexuality*, New Museum of Contemporary Art, New York; Renaissance Society, Chicago; Institute of Contemporary Arts, London; List Visual Arts Center, Massachusetts Institute of Technology, Cambridge

A Different Climate: Aspects of Beauty in Contemporary Art, Stüdtisches Kunsthalle Düsseldorf, Germany
Poco Rococo, Coquitlam Centre Mall, Port Coquitlam, British Columbia

1985 *Visual Facts: Photography and Video by Eight Artists in Canada*, Third Eye Centre, Glasgow; Graves Art Gallery, Sheffield, England; Canada House Cultural Centre Gallery, London
Aurora Borealis, Centre International d'Art Contemporain de Montréal (catalog)
Günther Förg & Jeff Wall: Photoworks, Stedelijk Museum, Amsterdam, The Netherlands
Louis XIV Tanzt/Louis XIV Dances, Galerie der Künstler, Munich; Vereinkunsthalle, Zurich; Fonds Regional d'Art Contemporain Rhône Alpes, St. Etienne, France

1986 *Making History: Recent Art of the Pacific West*, Vancouver Art Gallery
Prospect 86, Frankfurter Kunstverein and Schirn Kunsthalle, Frankfurt
Focus: Kanadische Kunst 1960–85, Art Cologne, Rheinhallen Messegelünd, Cologne
Zwei Landschaften: Glenn Branca, Jeff Wall, Galerie Rüdiger Schötte, Munich

1987 *Zeitgeschichten/Blow-up*, Württembergischer Kunstverein, Stuttgart, Germany; Haus am Waldsee, Berlin; Kunstverein in Hamburg; Kunstverein Hannover; Frankfurter Kunstverein, Frankfurt
L'Epoque, la mode, la morale, la passion: Aspects de l'art d'aujourd'hui, 1977–1987, Musée National d'Art Moderne-Centre Georges Pompidou, Paris
Documenta 8, Museum Fridericianum, Kassel, Germany
Nightfire, De Appel, Amsterdam, The Netherlands

1988 *Utopia Post Utopia*, Institute of Contemporary Art, Boston (catalog)
Bilanz/Balance, Kaiser Wilhelm Museum, Krefeld, Germany
Collections pour une region, CAPC Musée d'Art Contemporain de Bordeaux, France
Australian Biennial, Art Gallery of New South Wales and Pier 2/3, Walsh Bay, Sydney; National Gallery of Victoria, Melbourne

1989 *Tenir l'Image à Distance*, Musée d'Art Contemporain, Montreal
Les Magiciens de la Terre, Musée National d'Art Moderne-Centre Georges Pompidou /La Grand Halle de la Villette, Paris (catalog)
The Children's Pavilion, Galerie Roger Pailhas, Marseilles, France; Fonds Régional d'Art Contemporain Rhône Alpes, Villa Gillet, Lyons, France; Santa Barbara Contemporary Art Forum (with Dan Graham)
Theatergarden Bestiarium, P. S. 1/Institute for Art and Urban Resources, Long Island City, New York; Casino des Exposicións del Teatro Lope de Vega, Seville; Entrepôt-Galerie du Confort Moderne, Poitiers, France (catalog)

1990 *Life Size: A Sense of the Real in Recent Art*, Israel Museum, Jerusalem (catalog)
Passages de l'image, Musée National d'Art Moderne, Centre Georges Pompidou, Paris; Fundació Caixa de Pensions, Barcelona; Wexner Center for the Visual Arts, Columbus, Ohio; San Francisco Museum of Modern Art
Culture and Commentary: An Eighties Perspective, Hirshhorn Museum and Sculpture Garden, Washington, D. C. (catalog)
Le Territoire de l'Art 1910–1990, Musée Russe, St. Petersburg

1991 *In anderen Rüumen*, Museum Haus Lange and Museum Haus Esters, Krefeld, Germany
Lost Illusions: Recent Landscape Art, Vancouver Art Gallery (catalog)
Sguardo di Medusa, Castello di Rivoli, Turin, Italy
This Land. . ., Marian Goodman Gallery, New York

1992 *The Binary Era*, Musée d'Ixelles, Brussels
Pour la suite du monde, Musée d'Art Contemporain, Montreal
Avantgarde & Kampagne, Stadtische Kunsthalle, Dusseldorf
Cameres indiscretes, Centre d'Art Santa Monica, Barcelona; Circulo de Bellas Artes, Madrid

1993 *Strange Hotel: International Art*, Aarhus Kunstmuseum, Aarhus, Denmark
Post-Human, Deichtorhallen, Hamburg
The Sublime Void: An Exhibition on the Memory of the Imagination, Palais Royale des Beaux-Arts, Antwerp
Binera: 14 Interaktionen—Kunst und Technologie, Kunsthalle Wien, Vienna

1994 *Foundation Cartier: A Collection*, National Museum of Contemporary Art, Seoul; Fine Art Museum of Taipei, China
Prospect/Retrospect: Contemporary Art from the Collection, Kunstmuseum Luzern, Lucerne, Switzerland
The Ghost in the Machine, List Visual Arts Center, Massachusetts Institute of Technology, Cambridge, Massachusetts
The Epic and the Everyday: Contemporary Photographic Art, Hayward Gallery, London (catalog)

1995 *Spirits on the Crossing, Travelers to/from Nowhere: Contemporary Art in Canada 1980–94*, Setagaya Museum, Tokyo; Museum of Modern Art, Kyoto, Japan; Hokkaido Museum of Modern Art, Sapporo, Japan
Micromegas, American Center, Paris; Israel Museum, Jerusalem
About Place: Recent Art of the Americas, Art Institute of Chicago (catalog)
Fémininmasculin: le sexe de l'art, Musée National d'Art Moderne-Centre Georges Pompidou, Paris

1996 *Face à l'Histoire 1933–1996: L'artiste moderne face à l'événement historique*, Musée National d'Art Moderne-Centre Georges Pompidou, Paris
Hall of Mirrors: Art and Film Since 1945, Museum of Contemporary Art, Los Angeles; Wexner Center for the Arts, Columbus, Ohio; Museum of Contemporary Art, Chicago (catalog)
A Group Show, Marian Goodman Gallery, New York

1997 *Documenta 10,* Museum Fridericianum, Kassel, Germany
Veronica's Revenge, Centre d'Art Contemporain, Geneva
La Collection de la Fondation Cartier pour l'art contemporain, Fondation Cartier, Paris

Contemporary Photography I: Absolute Landscape: Between Illusion and Reality, Yokohama Museum of Art, Japan

1998 *Inner Eye: Contemporary Art from the Marc and Livia Strauss Collection*, Harn Museum of Art, University of Florida, Gainesville; Neuberger Museum of Art, Purchase, New York; Neuberger Museum of Art, Purchase, New York (catalog)

The Parkett Artists' Editions, Museum Ludwig, Cologne

Tuning Up #5: Selections from the Permanent Collection, Kunstmuseum Wolfsburg, Germany

Extenuating Circumstances, Museum Boymans-van Beuningen, Rotterdam, The Netherlands

1999 *Seeing Time: Selections from the Pamela and Richard Kramlich Collection of Media Art*, San Francisco Museum of Modern Art (catalog)

Carnegie International, Carnegie Museum of Art, Pittsburgh

The Museum as Muse: Artists Reflect, Museum of Modern Art, New York (catalog)

Jeff Wall-Pepe Espaliü: Suspended Time, Castellón Contemporary Arts Centre (EAC), Castellon, Spain

2000 *Mixing Memory and Desire Wunsch und Erinnerung*, Kunstmuseum Luzern, Lucerne, Switzerland

Encounters: New Art from Old, National Gallery, London,

Architecture Without Shadow, Centro Andaluz de Arte Contemporaneo, Seville; Centre de Cultura Contemporània de Barcelona

Publications:

By WALL: Books—*Transparencies* with an interview by Els Barents, New York 1986.

On WALL: Books—*Jeff Wall: The Storyteller* by Robert Linsley, Frankfurt am Main 1992. **Articles—**''False Documents: A Conversation with Jeff Wall'' by Bill Jones in *Arts Magazine*, May 1990; ''Profane Illuminations: Social History and the Art of Jeff Wall'' by Thomas E. Crow in *Artforum International*, February 1993; ''Jeff Wall: Digital Phantoms'' by Jeremy Millar in *Creative Camera*, February-March 1994; ''Jeff Wall's Pictures: Knowledge and Enchantment'' by Michael Newman in *Flash Art*, March-April 1995; ''Jeff Wall'' by Briony Fer in *Art & Design*, September-October 1995; ''Jeff Wall'' (4 article special section) in *Parkett*, 1997; ''The Truth is Out There: Jeff Wall and Late-Century Pictorialism'' by Bill Jones in *On Paper*, July-August 1997; ''The Hole Truth'' by Jan Tumlir in *Artforum International*, March 2001.

* * *

Jeff Wall has exhibited his large-scale cibachrome transparencies since the late 1970s and his light-box method of display is significant for the way in which it converges references to street advertising, cinematography, and the painterly tableau. Wall often composes his work, as would the art director on a film set, meticulously creating a scene to be photographed. Cartier Bresson's decisive moment becomes a deliberate representation, a staged composition that has sometimes been even more rigorously controlled by the artist through the use of digital montage. Wall rarely deviates from photographic reality. Some of his pictures such as *The Giant* overtly state their artifice but generally the mise en scene remains within the realm of the real. This is part of Wall's project to develop a version of Baudelaire's ''painting of modern life,'' to use the most up-to-date technologies to represent and question the complex picture of everyday life. Whereas the early avant-gardes either rejected photography as mere documentation or fragmented it through collage, the unified picture plane as a critical voice was excluded from avant-garde practice. Wall seeks to reinstate the possibility of this critical voice for realist photography.

In *Dead Troops Talk,* Wall stages a picture that at the outset looks like a war photograph; the bloody aftermath of a battle skirmish. The full title of the picture *Dead Troops Talk (A Vision after an Ambush of a Red Army Patrol, Near Mogor, Afghanistan, Winter 1996)* also evokes the language of photojournalism with its emphasis on the specific detail of time and place to reinforce the documentary realism of the event and the photographer as witness. Wall's work, however, quickly reveals itself to be a constructed composition. The soldiers are captured by the camera in staged poses reminiscent of the grand gestures of history painting or amateur dramatics. Indeed Wall has appropriated these attitudes and many of the compositional devices from 19th century tableaux such as Gericault's *The Raft of the Medusa.* Transposed here to photographic reality, the postures seem absurd, verging on vaudeville, and certainly some of Wall's figures recall the exaggerated gesticulations of Laurel and Hardy. The gallows humour of this motley crew of living dead is emphasised by the clearly visible special effects of exploded heads and bloodied bodies usually employed in film to suggest a heightened reality. Wall requires his viewer to observe not a battle scene but the idea of war as spectacle and the role of photography as propaganda.

In *The Storyteller*, Wall evokes the poses of Manet's *Dejeuner sur l'Herbe* but again the photograph is more than mere appropriation of certain art historical conventions and a considered reworking of the original work thus avoiding much of the empty pastiche of postmodern art. The young woman in the picture, presumably the storyteller of the title, is animatedly recounting her tale. The oddly positioned groups of listeners are caught between natural and urban environments, dispossessed of their indigenous land perhaps by the invasive structures of contemporary society. Despite their literal status within the picture as an urban underclass, there is a sense that this small community has a voice that can speak to the ongoing hum of traffic and the information highway suggested by the telephone wires that cross the pictorial plane. This discursive moment happens on the outskirts of metropolitan life and much of Wall's work studies these transitional sites between urban and rural space.

Frequently, Wall creates a paradox of constructed spontaneity often revolving around a singular expression of violence. For instance, *Milk* where the sudden burst of aggression suggested by the liquid eruption is held at bay by the frozen poise of the young male subject or the overly dramatic kung-fu pose in *Outburst* that takes place in a banal factory setting. From Max Ernst's ''canned chance'' to the drip paintings of Jackson Pollock, the framing of random gesture is another avant-garde strategy that Wall explores in a photographic context. The idea of disruption is central to Wall's work. In *Stumbling Block* we witness a staged human obstacle deliberately positioned to break the everyday routine of passers-by. Even in more abstract work, such as *Sunken Area* there is both the actual fracture in the geometric grid, reminiscent of work by Lucio Fontana and also the disruptive intrusion of the plants/weeds into the already transgressed horizontal lines. In a gallery of course such minimalist work would be protected from the incursion of nature but of course it was their very dependence on the artificial environment of the white cube that provoked artists in the late 1960s out of the exhibition space. In *Crooked Path*, Wall queries the effectiveness of this strategy and more significantly the role documentary photography had to play in bringing these works into the art mainstream. Photography was the means of preservation and distribution of the work. As is suggested by *Crooked Path*, this is not a straightforward as it seems. The choices made by the artist in the creation of the image—cropping, framing, focusing—influence how we see the event and in Wall's image, the beaten track leads us past some Judd-like minimalist boxes to "Tom Yee Produce Inc" to underline how even the most process oriented work could become commodified by the institutional hunger for new avant-garde goods. The spaces created by Wall admit their own artificiality, a device borrowed from the modernist avant-garde. But although these spaces incorporate different viewpoints they do not result in a fragmented picture plane. For Wall this fragmentation is no longer an authentic dissension from more traditional forms of representation and given the ubiquity of the photo-image there is a need to challenge the authority of visual spectacle in its own frame—from inside the pictorial.

—Fiona Kearney

WALTHER, Franz Erhard

Nationality: German. **Born:** Fulda, 22 July 1939. **Education:** Studied at the Hochschule Für Bildende Künste, Frankfurt, 1959–61, and the Kunstakademie, Dusseldorf, 1962–64. **Family:** Married Johanna Friess in 1964; sons: Clemens Moritz and Kaspar Lehmann. **Career:** Worked in soap factory, Dusseldorf, 1966–67, and in bakery, New York, 1967–69. Independent artist, Dusseldorf, 1965–67, New York 1967–71, and in Hamburg, since 1971. Professor, Hochschule für Bildende Künste, Hamburg, since 1970. **Awards:** Gunter Fruhtrunk Prize, Munich, 1986. **Agents:** Galerie Vera Munro, Heiwigstrasse 64, 20429 Hamburg, Germany; John Weber Gallery, 142 Greene St. New York, New York 10012, U.S.A.; Galerie Wilma Lock, Schmiedgasse 15, 9002 St. Gallen, Switzerland. **Address:** Home, Am Bahndamm 30, D 2083, Halstenbek, Germany.

Individual Exhibitions:

1966 Neue Galerie, Aachen, West Germany
1967 Galerie Heiner Friedrich, Munich
Staatliche Kunstakademie, Dusseldorf
1968 Galerie Rudolf Zwimer, Cologne
1969 Galerie Heiner Friedrich, Munich
Galerie Rudolf Zwimer, Cologne
Galerie Neuendorf, Hamburg
Studio F, Ulm, West Germany
Museum Haus Lange, Krefeld, West Germany
Kunsthalle, Dusseldorf
Museum of Modern Art, New York
1970 Kunstverein, Hamburg
1971 Hessisches Landesmuseum, Darmstadt
Galerie Heiner Friedrich, Cologne
Kunstverein, Frankfurt
Galerie Heiner Friedrich, Munich
1972 Kunsthalle, Tübingen
Videogalerie-Gerry Schum, Dusseldorf
Museum Haus Lange, Krefeld, West Germany
Kaiser-Wilhelm-Museum, Krefeld, West Germany
Stedelijk Van Abbemuseum, Eindhoven, Netherlands
1973 Vanier College, Montreal
Kabinett für Aktuelle Kunst, Bremerhaven, West Germany
Kunstverein, Freiburg
Hessisches Laridesmuseum, Darmstadt
Galerie Heiner Friedrich, Munich (2 exhibitions)
1974 Kaiser-Wilheim-Museum, Krefeld, West Germany
Galerie Klein, Bonn
1975 Galerie Repassage, Warsaw
Kabinett fur Aktuelle Kunst, Bremerhaven, West Germany
1976 *Diagramme zum 1. Werksatz,* Kunstraum, Munich
Städtisches Museum, Bonn
Kunstverein, Frankfurt
1977 Kunsthalle, Baden-Baden, West Germany
Heiner Friedrich Gallery, New York
Wallraf-Richartz Museum, Cologne
German Pavilion, at the *Bienal,* Sao Paulo
Centro de Arte y Comunicacion, Buenos Aires
Galerie Heiner Friedrich, Cologne
1978 *Arbeiten 1954–1963 aus der Sammlung Seng,* Städtisches Museum, Fulda, West Germany
Kabinett für Aktuelle Kunst, Bremerhaven, West Germany
Hessisches Landesmuseum, Darmstadt
1979 Stadtische Galerie im Lenbachhaus, Munich
1980 *Gegensatzpaare und Unterscheidungen im Werk,* Kunstverein, St. Gallen, Switzerland
Arbeiten 1969–1963, Kunstmuseum, Bonn
1981 *Handlung Werk,* Nationalgalerie, West Berlin
Produzentgalerie, Hamburg
1982 *Werkzeichnungen,* Museum Haus Lange, Krefeld, West Germany
Galerie Klein, Bonn
Badischer Kunstverein, Karlsruhe
Kunstraum, Munich
Galerie Schiessel, Munich
Galerie Kubinski, Stuttgart
Kunsthalle, Wilhelmshaven, West Germany
Galerie Carinthia, Klagenfurt, Austria
Overbeckgesellschaft, Lubeck
Galerie Edition E, Munich
Galerie Schiessel, Munich
Kunsthalle, Wilhelmshaven, West Germany
Galerie Carinthia, Klagenfurt, Austria
1983 Galerie Schöttle, Munich (with A. Oehlen)
Ausstellungsraum Fettstrasse, Hamburg
1984 Raum für Kunst, Hamburg
Galerie Haderek, Stuttgart
Kabinett für Aktuelle Kunst, Bremerhaven, West Germany
Galerie Onnasch, West Berlin
Galerie Lock, St. Gallen, Switzerland
Van Abbemuseum, Eindhoven, Netherlands
Ulmer Museum, Ulm, West Germany
1985 Wilhelm-Hack-Museum, Ludwigshafen, West Germany
Institut für moderne Kunst, Nuremberg, West Germany
Galerie Reckemann, Cologne

Ausstellungsraum, Fulda, West Germany
Galerie Mafia Wilkens/Dorit Jacobs, Cologne
Galerie Loehrl, Mönchengladbach, West Germany
Kunstverein, Bremerhaven, West Germany
Städtische Galerie, Nordhom, West Germany
1986 Galerie Carinthia, Klagenfurt, Austria
Kunstverein, Braunschweig, West Germany
Kunstverein, Frankfurt
Galerie Achim Kubinski, Stuttgart
Galeric Tilly Haderek, Stuttgart
Gutenbergstrasse 62, Stuttgart
Galerie Annette Gmeiner, Kirchzarten, West Germany
Galerie Desluis, The Hague
1987 Galerie Edition E, Munich
Galerie Schiessel, Munich
Galerie Hufkens-de Lathuy, Brussels
Kunsthalle, Winterthur, Switzerland
Galerie Onnasch, West Berlin
1988 John Weber Gallery, New York
Burnett Miller Gallery, Los Angeles
Galerie Vera Munro, Hamburg
1989 Galerie Pierre Huber, Geneva
Weiner Sezession, Vienna
Franz Erhard Walther: Drawings, Working Drawings 1957–84, Kupferstichkabinett, Staatliche Museen Preussischer Kulturbesitz, Berlin (catalog)
1990 *Seven Places for Hamburg,* Kunsthalle, Hamburg (catalog)
Villa Arson, Nice
Kunstverein für die Rheinland und Westfalen, Dusseldorf (catalog)
Franz Erhard Walther: Wall Formations, Art Gallery, San Diego State University (catalog)
1991 *Franz Erhard Walther: Works, Drawings,* Institut fur Auslandsbeziehungen, Stuttgart (catalog)
1992 *Franz Erhard Walther: Lateral Transitions—Internal Modeling,* Kunstmuseum, Lucerne (catalog)
Franz Erhard Walther: Work Speak, Kunsthalle, Nuremberg (catalog)
1994 *Franz Erhard Walther: Answer of the Body,* Galerie der Stadt Esslingen, Villa Merkel, Esslingen, Germany (catalog)
1998 *Gelenke im Raum-Werke 1963–1998,* Deichtorhallen, Hamburg (catalog)
Ich Bin Die Skulptur, Kunstverein Hannover, Germany

Selected Group Exhibitions:

1969 *When Attitudes Become Form,* Kunsthalle, Berne (toured Europe)
1972 *Documenta 5,* Kassel, West Germany (and *Documenta 7,* 1982; *Documenta 8,* 1987)
1974 *Projekt 74,* Kunsthalle, Cologne
1977 *Pejling af tysk kunst,* Louisiana Museum, Hummelbaek, Denmark
1979 *30 Jahre Kunst in der Bundersrepublik Deutschland,* Kunstmuseum, Bonn
1980 *Zeichnungen der 50er, 60er und 70er Jahre,* Museum Haus Lange, Krefeld, West Germany
1981 *Art Allemagne Aujourd hui,* Musée d'Art Moderne de la Ville, Paris
1983 *Skulptur und Farbe,* Gesellschaft für Aktuelle Kunst, Bremen, West Germany
1985 *Kunst in der Bundersrepublik 1945–85,* Nationalgalerie, West Berlin
1986 *Wild, Visionary, Spectral: New German Art,* Art Gallery of South Australia, Adelaide (travelled to the New Zealand National Art Gallery, Wellington)
1989 *The Nightingale's Lesson,* Kunstlerhaus, Stuttgart (catalog)
1994 *The Body as Measure,* Davis Museum and Cultural Center, Wellesley College, Massachusetts (catalog)
1995 *Corpus Delicti: Two Private Collections, A North/South Dialogue,* Museum van Hedendaagse Kunst, Ghent, Belgium (catalog)
Attitudes/Sculptures, CAPC Musee d'Art Contemporain, Bordeaux (catalog)

Collections:

Nationalgalerie, West Berlin; Kunsthalle, Hamburg; Kunstmuseum, Bonn; Kunstmuseum, Dusseldorf; City of Frankfurt; Wallraf-Richartz Museum/Museum Ludwig, Cologne; Kaiser-Wilhelm Museum, Krefeld, West Germany; Hessisches Landemuseum, Darmstadt; Staatsgalerie, Stuttgart; Stedelijk Van Abbemuseum, Eindhoven, Netherlands.

Publications:

By WALTHER: Books—*Leihobjekte,* Aachen, West Germany, 1966; *Information,* Dusseldorf 1967; *Objekte, Benutzen,* with photos by Barbara Brown, Cologne and New York 1968; *Tagebuch: Museum of Modern Art, New York, 28 December 1969 bis 1 Marz 1970,* Cologne 1971; *Prozessmaterial,* Cologne and Darmstadt 1971; *Proportionen,* with Ingrid Krupka, Cologne 1971; *Frank Erhard Walther: Werkmonographic, Arbeiten 1955–1963, Material zum 1, Werksatz 1963–1969,* edited by Gotz Adriani, with an interview by Ursula Meyer, texts by others, Cologne 1972; *Franz Erhard Walther: Werksatz,* Montreal 1973; *Franz Erhard Walther: Zeitbezogen/Raumbezogen/Personenbezogen/Handlungsbezogen,* Munich 1979; *Franz Erhard Walther: Hauprworte/Werkbegriffe,* Hannover 1981; *Franz Erhard Walther: 40 Sockel,* with an interview by Michael Lingner, Munich 1982; *Franz Erhard Walther: 30 x Werkbau,* Munich 1982; *Franz Erhard Walther: 2 Arbeiten—35 Werke,* Wilhelmshaven, West Germany 1982; *Organon: Feldbuch,* Klagenfurt 1983; *Zwischen Kem und Mantel,* with Michael Lingner, Klagenfurt 1985; *Organon 2,* Klagenfurt 1987; *Gelenke im Raum,* Stuttgart 1987; *Franz Erhard Walther: Wortwerke,* Klagenfurt 1987. **Articles—**Interview with Isabelle Graw in *Wolkenkratzer Art Journal,* no. 3, May-June 1988.

On WALTHER: Books—*Deutsche Kunst der 60er Jahre* by Jurgen Morschel, Munich 1972; *Franz Erhard Walther: Fruhe Arbeiten 1955 1963,* exhibition catalog with text by Paul Wernher, Krefeld, West Germany 1972; *Bis Heute* by Karin Thomas, Cologne 1972; *Franz Erhard Walther,* exhibition catalog with texts by Argibald Buys, Oda den Boer, Wies Leering, and Jerven Ober, Eindhoven, Netherlands 1972; *Objekte Kunst* by Karin Thomas, Cologne 1972; *Geschichte der Collage* by Hena Wescher and Karin Thomas, Cologne 1974; *Franz Erhard Walther: Diagramme zum 1, Werksatz,* exhibition catalog with texts by Hermann Kern and Carl Vogel, Munich 1976; *Franz Erhard Walther: 2, Werksatz: Skulpturen, Zeichnungen,* exhibition catalog with texts by Evelyn Weiss and Dieter Ronte, and an interview by Georg Jappe, Cologne 1977; *International Biennale Sao Paulo: Franz Erhard Walther,* exhibition catalog with texts by Getz Adriani and Carl Vogel, Cologne 1977; *Kunstierlexicon von 1945 his zur Gegenwarr* by Karin Thomas and Gerd de Vries, Cologne 1977; *Franz Erhard Walther: Arbeiten 1954–1963 aus der Sammlung Seng,* exhibition catalog with texts by Gilbert Seng and Carl Vogel, Fulda, West Germany 1978; *Strukturen Zeitgenossische Kunst* by Ingrid Burgbacher-Krupka, Stuttgart 1979; *Franz Erhard Walther: Gegenstazpaare und Unterscheidungen im Werk,* exhibition catalog with text by Dietrich Helms, St. Gallen, Switzerland 1980; *Franz Erhard Walther: Arbeiten 1969–1963,* exhibition catalog with texts by Dirk Stemmler, Gisbert Seng and Karl Otto Getz, Bonn 1980; *Franz Erhard Walther: Handlung Werk,* exhibition catalog with text by Michael Pauseback, West Berlin 1981; *Franz Erhard Walther,* exhibition catalog with text by Dietrich Helms, Hamburg 1981; *Franz Erhard Walther: Werkzeichnungen,* with a foreword by Gerhard Storck and Marianne Stockebrand, Krefeld, West Germany 1982; *Der Walther-Raum in der Hamburger Kunsthalle,* with text by Achim Lipp, Hamburg 1983; *Franz Erhard Walther: Words 1978 1984,* exhibition catalog with text by Rudi Fuchs, Eindhoven 1984; *Der 1, Werksatz (1963–69) von Franz Erhard Walther,* with text by Barbara Grotkatnp-Schepers, Darmstadt 1985; *Franz Erhard Walther: gesehen gehort gedacht,* with text by Gisbert Seng, Fulda 1985; *Franz Erhard Walther—Ort und Richtung angeben: Zeichnungen 1957–1984,* with texts by Gottfried Boehm, Marianne Stockebrand and Rudi Fuchs, Klagenfurt 1985; *Franz Erhard Walther,* exhibition catalog by Kurt Muenger, Winterthur 1987; *Das hans in dem ich Wohne,* with texts by Michael Lingner and others, Klagenfurt 1990; *Antwort der Körper,* Esslingen 1992; *Blick, Wort, Beruhrung* by Maria Peters, Munich 1996.

*

From the very beginning I had an interest in work processes. In any event the emphasis on process is stronger than that on form. 1958–59: quantities of drawings arise from processes: movements like writing from the top to the bottom or from left to right. Superimpositions, coverings—yet readable as a process. The formlessness of these works had for me the character of a manifesto. From 1960 to 1963 there were extensive work composites resulting from material processes. Material and process—the material process—become decisive for the work. Material is not used for something but is itself the subject. At the same time I worked with extremely simple forms without using hierarchies and meanings. ''Meaninglessness'' was a challenge to oneself to construct meanings in one's activity. Therein lay the invitation to spontaneous action. This motive of operation and then action as an element of the work became the main theme. The determinant basic idea was to construct a work from action. These works originated in 1963. Action is a form of work. The operative has to answer for the work. He is involved not only optically but also with the whole body. All abilities are required. It is a total performance. Man could construct works in other, more extensive ways than were previously possible. Naturally then several people also appear in the development of the work. That is complex construction.

In the alternative work concept there are central concepts such as place, time, space, interior-exterior, body, field, direction, construction, among others, and the possibility to alter historic significance. And thereby a new concept of material has become necessary. For example language, body, space, place, action are material like wood and stone to the traditional sculptor. Spaces, performance areas, action areas, concepts and methods of work should be found which extend the dimensions of earlier means of expression.

—Franz Erhard Walther

WARHOL, Andy

Nationality: American. **Born:** McKeesport, Pennsylvania, 6 August 1928. **Education:** Carnegie Institute of Technology, Pittsburgh, 1945–49. **Career:** Worked as illustrator for *Glamour Magazine,* New York, 1949–50, and as a commercial artist, New York, 1950–57. Independent artist, New York, 1957 until his death in 1987: concentrated on making paintings derived from strip comics and advertisements, 1960–61; first silkscreen paintings, 1962; first films, mainly with Paul Morrissey, 1963. Editor, *Interview* magazine, New York. **Awards:** Art Directors Club of New York Medal for shoe advertisements, 1957; 6th Film Culture Award, New York, 1964; *Los Angeles Film Festival* Award, 1964. **Died:** Of heart failure following gall bladder surgery, New York City, 22 February 1987.

Individual Exhibitions:

1952 Hugo Gallery, New York
1956 Bodley Gallery, New York (and 1957, 1958, 1959)
1962 Fetus Gallery, Los Angeles
Stable Gallery, New York
1963 Fetus Gallery, New York
1964 Leo Castelli Gallery, New York
Stable Gallery, New York
Galerie Sonnabend, Paris
1965 Leo Castelli Gallery, New York
Galerie Sonnabend, Paris
Galerie Rubbers, Buenos Aires
Galerie M. E. Thelen, Essen
Gian Enizo Sperone Arte Moderna, Milan
Institute of Contemporary Art, Philadelphia
Galerie Buren, Stockholm
Jerrold Morris International Gallery, Toronto
Gian Enzo Sperone Arte Moderna, Turin
1966 Galerie M. E. Thelen, Essen
Gian Enzo Sperone Arte Moderna, Milan
Institute of Contemporary Art, Boston
Contemporary Arts Center, Cincinnati, Ohio
Galerie Hans Neuendorf, Hamburg
Ferns Gallery, Los Angeles
Leo Castelli Gallery, New York
1957 Galerie Rudolf Zwimer, Cologne
Galerie Sonnabend, Paris
1968 Galerie Rudolf Zwimer, Cologne
Stedelijk Museum, Amsterdam
Galerie der Spiegel, Cologne
Rowan Gallery, London
Galerie Heiner Friedrich, Munich
Kunsternes, Oslo
Moderna Museet, Stockholm
1969 Neue Nationalgalerie der Staatlichen Museen Preussischer Kulturbesitz, West Berlin

Andy Warhol with his work. ©AP/Wide World Photos

Irvin Blum Gallery, Los Angeles
Leo Castelli Gallery, New York
1970 Galerie Felker Skulima, West Berlin
Museum of Contemporary Art, Chicago
Stedelijk van Abbemuseum, Eindhoven, Netherlands
Musée d'Art Moderne de la Ville, Paris
Pasadena Museum of Art, California (toured the Untied States and Europe)
1971 Galerie Bruno Bischofberger, Zurich
Gotham Book Mart Gallery, New York
Institute of Contemporary Arts, London
Musée d'Art Moderne de la Ville, Paris
1972 Castelli Downtown Gallery, New York
Multiples Gallery, New York
1973 Margo Leavin Gallery, Los Angeles
1974 Mayor Gallery, London
Musée Galliera, Paris
1975 Baltimore Museum of Art
1976 Württembergischer Kunstverein, Stuttgart (travelled to Kunsthalle, Dusseldorf)
1980 *Andy Warhol: Photos,* Lisson Gallery, London
1981 *Portrait Screenprints 1965–1980,* Gloucestershire College of Arts and Technology, Cheltenham, England
1982 Galerie Scheilmann und Kluser, Munich
Stadtische Galerie im Lenbachhaus, Munich
Galerie Daniel Templon, Paris
1983 Fraenkel Gallery, San Francisco
American Museum of Natural History, New York
Museum of Natural History, Cleveland, Ohio
1984 Scottsdale Center for the Arts, Arizona
Edition Schellmann und Kluser, Munich
Flow Ace Gallery, Los Angeles
Judith Goldberg Gallery, New York
Galerie Kammer, Hamburg
Galerie Schellmann und Kluser, Munich
1985 Museo di Capodimonte, Naples, Italy
1986 Galerie Daniel Templon, Paris
Edition Schelimann, Munich
Anthony d'Offay Gallery, London
1987 Galerie Bernd Kluser, Munich
Galerie Thaddaeus Ropac, Salzburg, Austria
Robert Miller Gallery, New York
Waddington Galleries, London
Kunstverein, Hamburg
1988 Galerie Bernd Kluser, Munich
1989 *Andy Warhol: Shadow Paintings,* Gagosian Gallery, New York
Andy Warhol: a Retrospective—a Guide to the Exhibition, Hayward Gallery, London
1990 *Andy Warhol: Films,* IVAM Centre Julio Gonzalez, Valencia, Spain
Andy Warhol: Cars—The Last Pictures, Kunstmuseum, Berne
The Prints of Andy Warhol, Cartier Foundation for Contemporary Art, New York
Andy Warhol: Cars, Fundacion Juan March, Madrid
Andy Warhol: Prints, Staatliche Kunstsammlungen, Dresden, Germany
1991 *Andy Warhol's Video and Television,* Whitney Museum of American Art, New York
1992 *Andy Warhol Polaroids, 1971–1986,* Pace/MacGill Gallery, New York (traveled to Anthony d'Offay, London; Durand-Dessert, Paris)
1993 *Andy Warhol Portraits,* Museum of Contemporary Art, Sydney
Andy Warhol: Abstract, Kunsthalle, Basle (travelled to Osterreichisches Museum fur Angewandte Kunst, Vienna; IVAM Centre Julio Gonzalez, Valencia, Spain)
Andy Warhol, 1928–1987: Works from the Collections of Jose Mugrabi and an Isle of Man Company, Kunstlerhaus, Vienna (travelled to Orlando Museum of Art, Florida; Fort Lauderdale Museum of Art, Florida)
1995 *Andy Warhol: Paintings 1960–1986,* Kunstmuseum Luzern, Lucerne
1997 *Andy Warhol: Heads (After Picasso),* Galerie Thaddaeus Ropac, Paris
1998 *Reframing Andy Warhol: Constructing American Myths, Heroes, and Cultural Icons,* Art Gallery, University of Maryland, College Park
1999 *Andy Warhol: Photography,* Hambuger Kunsthalle, Hamburg (travelled to Andy Warhol Museum, Pittsburgh)

Selected Group Exhibitions:

1956 *Recent Drawings USA,* Museum of Modern Art, New York
1962 *New Paintings of Common Objects,* Pasadena Museum of Art, California
1964 *American Pop Art,* Stedelijk Museum, Amsterdam
1966 *11 Pop Artists: The New Image,* Galerie M. E. Thelen, Essen, West Germany
1968 *Documenta 4,* Kassel, West Germany
1970 *De Giotto 4 Warhol,* Musée d'Art Moderne de la Ville, Paris
1977 *Paris-New York,* Centre Georges Pompidou, Paris
1981 *A New Spirit in Painting,* Royal Academy of Arts, London
1983 *Modern Art in the West,* Metropolitan Art Museum, Tokyo
1985 *Painterly Visions 1940–84,* Guggenheim Museum, New York
1989 *The Sonnabend Collection: from Pop Art Onwards,* Galleria Nazionale d'Arte Moderna, Rome
Selections from the Beatrice and Philip Gersh Collection, Los Angeles County Museum of Art
1990 *Beyond the Frame: American Art, 1960–1990,* Setagaya Art Museum, Tokyo (travelled to National Museum of Art, Japan; Fukuoka Art Museum, Fukuoka)
1991 *Pop Muses: Images of Women by Roy Lichtenstein and Andy Warhol,* Isetan Museum, Tokyo (travelled to Kawamura Memorial Museum of Art, Chiba, Japan; Daimaru Museum, Osaka)
Beuys and Warhol: The Artist as Shaman and Star, Museum of Fine Arts, Boston
1992 *Back and Forth: Early Cinema and the Avant-Garde,* Art Gallery of Ontario, Toronto
Special Collections: The Photographic Order from Pop to Now, International Center of Photography, New York
Keith Haring, Andy Warhol, and Walt Disney, Phoenix Art Museum, Arizona
1995 *Revolution: Art of the Sixties from Warhol to Beuys,* Hara Musuem of Contemporary Art, Tokyo

Still Life: The Object in American Art 1915–1995, Marsh Art Gallery, Richmond (travelled to Arkansas Arts Center, Little Rock; Newport Harbor Art Museum, Newport; Philbrook Museum of Art, Tulsa; Society of the Four Arts, Palm Beach; Salina Art Center, Kansas)

1996 *Masterpieces of the Twentieth Century: The Beyeler Collection,* Art Gallery of New South Wales, Sydney

The Froehlich Foundation: German and American Art from Beuys and Warhol, Tate Gallery, London

Collaborations: Warhol, Basquiat, Clemente, Museum Fridericianum, Kassel, Germany (travelled to Museum Villa Stuck, Munich)

1997 *Artists' Books: The Invention of a Genre, 1960–80,* Galerie Mansart, Paris

Objects of Desire: The Modern Still Life, Museum of Modern Art, New York (travelled to Hayward Gallery, London; Museum of Modern Art, New York)

American Art: A Selection from Waddington Galleries, Waddington Galleries, London (travelled to Art 28 Basel; Foire Internationale d'Art Contemporain, Paris; International Art Festival, Tokyo)

Birth of the Cool: American Painting from Georgia O'Keeffe to Christopher Wool, Deichtorhallen, Hamburg (travelled to Kunsthaus Zurich)

Collections:

Museum of Modern Art, New York; Whitney Museum, New York; Corcoran Gallery of Art, Washington, D.C.; Walker Art Center, Minneapolis; County Museum of Art, Los Angeles; Norton Simon Museum of Art, Pasadena, California; Art Gallery of Ontario, Toronto; Tate Gallery, London; Moderna Museet, Stockholm; and many others.

Publications:

By WARHOL: Books—*Andy Warhol's Index Book,* New York 1967; *A: A Novel,* New York 1968; *Andy Warhol: Transcript of David Bailey's ATV Documentary,* London 1972; *A to B and Back Again,* London and New York 1975; *Ladies and Gentlemen,* Milan 1975; *Andy Warhol: Photographs,* portfolio of 12 photos, New York and Zurich 1980; *Popism: The Warhol 60s,* with Pat Hackett, New York 1980, London 1981; *Andy Warhol: Schweizer Portraits,* with text by George J. Dolezal, Thun 1982; *Andy Warhol's Children's Book,* Zurich 1983; *America,* New York 1985; *The Work of Andy Warhol,* edited by Gary Garrels, Seattle 1989; *Andy Warhol Portraits,* London 1993; *Andy Warhol Nudes,* edited by John Cheim, Woodstock 1995. **Articles—**''My Favorite Superstar: Notes of My Epic, Chelsea Girls,'' interview with Gerard Malanga in *Arts* (New York), February 1967; ''Andy Warhol Tapes Roman Polanski'' in *Inter/View* (New York), November 1973; ''Andy Warhol: Interview'' in *Photo* (Paris), May 1979; ''Warhol: Mon Camet Mondain'' in *Photo* (Paris), March 1980; ''Andy Warhol: a Conversation in 1985'' with Benjamin H.D. Buchloh in *October* (Cambridge), no. 70, Fall 1994. **Films—***Kiss,* 1973; *Tarzan and Jane Regained Sort Of,* 1963; *Dance Movie,* also known as *Roller Skate,* 1963; *Haircut,* 1963; *Eat,* 1964; *Blow Job,* 1964; *Batman Dracula,* 1964; *Empire,* 1964, *Henry Geldzahler,* 1964; *Soap Opera,* also known as *The Lester Persky,* 1964; *Couch,* 1964; *Shoulder,* 1964; *Mario Banana,* 1964; *Harlot,* 1964; *13 Most Beautiful Women,* 1965; *13 Most Beautiful Boys,* 1965; *30 Fantastics and 50 Personalities,* 1966; *Ivy and John,* 1965; *Suicide,* 1965; *Screen Test 1,* 1965; *Screen Test 2,* 1965; *The Life of Juanita Castro,* 1965; *Drunk,* 1965; *Horse,* 1965; *Poor Little Rich Girl,* 1965; *Vinyl,* 1965; *Bitch,* 1965; *Restaurant,* 1965; *Kitchen,* 1965; *Prison,* 1965; *Face,* 1965; *Afternoon,* 1965; *Beauty 2,* 1965; *Space,* 1965; *Outer and Inner Space,* 1965; *My Hustler,* 1965; *Camp,* 1965: *Paul Swan,* 1965; *Hedy,* also known as *Hedy the Shoplifter and The 14 Year Old Girl,* 1965; *The Closet,* 1965; *More Milk, Evette,* also known as *Lana Turner,* 1965; *Lupe,* 1965; *Bufferin,* also known as *Gerard Malanga Reads Poetry,* 1966; *Eating Too Fast,* 1966; *The Velvet Underground,* 1966; *Chelsea Girls,* 1966; **** also known as *Four Stars,* 1967; *International Velvet,* segment of ****, 1967; *Alan and Dickin,* segment of ****, 1967; *Imitation of Christ,* segment of ****, 1967; *Gerard Has His Hair Removed with Nair,* segment of ****, 1967; *Alan and Apple,* segment of ****, 1967; *Bike Boy* 1967; *Nude Restaurant,* 1967; *Lonesome Cowboys,* 1967; *Blue Movie,* 1969; *Schraffs Commercial,* 1969.

On WARHOL: Books—*The Painter and the Photograph: From Delacroix to Warhol* by Van Deren Coke, Albuquerque, New Mexico 1964, 1972; *Andy Warhol* by John Coplans, Pasadena, California 1970; *Andy Warhol* by Rainer Crone, London 1970; *The Autobiography and Sex Life of Andy Warhol* by John Wilcock, New York 1971; *Andy Warhol: Films and Paintings* by Peter Gidal, New York 1971; *Voglio essere una macchina: la fotografia di Andy Warhol* by Paolo Barozzi, Milan 1979; *Andy Warhol: Works 1962–1986,* exhibition catalog with texts by William Milie, Stuart Morgan, David Hockney and others, Salzburg 1986; *Andy Warhol: Reversal Series,* exhibition catalog, London 1987; *Andy Warhol Photographs,* exhibition catalog with text by Stephen Koch, New York 1987; *Warhol: Conversations About the Artist,* Ann Arbor 1988; *Andy Warhol: the Factory Years 1964–1967,* London 1989; *Warhol* by Victor Bockris, London 1990; *The Prints of Andy Warhol,* exhibition catalog, New York 1990; *Andy Warhol's Video and Television,* exhibition catalog, New York 1991; *Andy Warhol Polaroids 1971–1986,* exhibition catalog, New York 1992; *The Interrupted Life,* exhibition catalog, New York 1991; *Andy Warhol, 1928–1987: Works from the Collections of Jose Mugrabi and an Isle of Man Company,* Vienna 1993; *Billy Name: Stills from the Warhol Films* by Debra Miller, Munich 1994; *Andy Warhol: Nudes* by Linda Nochlin, Pittsburgh 1995; *Andy Warhol: Poetry, and Gossip in the 1960s* by Reva Wolf, Chicago 1997; *Warhol's America* by Philippe Tretiack, with introduction by Julian Schnabel, London 1997; *Andy Warhol: Heads (After Picasso),* Paris 1997; *The Religious Art of Andy Warhol* by Jane Dillenberger, eulogy by John Richardson, New York 1998; *Reframing Andy Warhol: Constructing American Myths, Heroes, and Cultural Icons,* exhibition catalog, edited by Wendy Grossman, College Park 1998; *About Face: Andy Warhol Portraits* by Nicholas Baume, Douglas Crimp and Richard Meyer, Cambridge 1999. **Articles—**''Early Warhol'' by Nicholas Polites in *Print,* vol. 43, no. 5, September-October 1989; '''The Most Fascinating Kind of Art': Warhol and the Right of Publicity'' by Time Cone in *Arts Magazine,* vol. 64, no. 5, January 1990; ''New York Letter: the Anatomy of Warholism'' by Hilton Kramer in *Modern Painters* (London), vol. 15, no. 1, Spring 1992; ''15 Minutes Later: Warhol Now'' by Judd Tully in *ARTnews,* vol. 91, no. 3, March 1992; ''Andy Warhol's Polaroids: Instant Fame'' by Peter Hay Halpert in *Photo Review,* vol. 15, no. 4, Fall 1992; ''Andy Warhol and the Critics'' by John Yau in *Artspace,* vol. 17, no. 1–2, March-April 1993; ''Andy Warhol: Brillo Box'' by Arthur C. Danto in *Artforum* (New York), vol. 32, no. 1, September 1993; ''Let Us Now Appraise Andy Warhol'' by Paul Alexander in *Artnews,* vol. 93, no. 3, March 1994; ''The Pope of Pop Gets His Vatican'' by Lisa Liebmann in *Interview,* vol. 24, no. 5, May 1994; ''My Portrait of Andy'' by Peter Halley in *Frieze* (London), no. 16, May 1994; ''The Andy Warhol Museum'' by Allan Schwartzman in *Frieze* (London), no. 16, May 1994; ''Murky Image: the Question of Warhol's Photographs'' by Paul Alexander in *ARTnews,* vol. 94, no. 2, February 1995; ''Startruck: Andy Warhol's Marilyn and Elvis'' by Margery King in *Carnegie Magazine* (Pittsburgh), vol. 62, no. 10, July-August 1995; ''Andy Warhol's Influence in Japan'' by Akio Obigane in *Carnegie Magazine* (Pittsburgh), vol. 63, no. 5, September-October 1996; ''At Home in Pittsburgh: Andy Warhol's Youth'' by Kathryn M. Duda in *Carnegie Magazine* (Pittsburgh), vol. 63, no. 4, July-August 1996; ''Warhol Paints History, or Race in America'' by Anne M. Wagner in *Representaions,* no. 55, Summer 1996; ''Andy Warhol's Moving Pictures of Modern Life'' by David Carrier in *Notes in the History of Art,* vol. 16, no. 3, Spring 1997; ''Andy Warhol in Drag'' by Jonathan Jones in *Untitled,* no. 16, Spring 1998; ''Andy Warhol and Cindy Sherman: the Self-portrait in the Age of Mechanical Reproduction'' by David Carrier in *Notes in the History of Art,* vol. 18, no. 1, Fall 1998; ''Andy's Idol'' by Lutz Presser in *Artlink,* vol. 18, no. 3, September 1998; ''Getting the Warhol We Deserve: Cultural Studies and Queer Culture'' by Douglas Crimp in *Visual Arts and Culture,* vol. 1, no. 2, 1999.

* * *

At a time when enigma is one of the most sought after of aesthetic virtues, Andy Warhol has achieved the difficult feat of remaining the most enigmatic artist of all. Since he first became known at the beginning of the Pop Art boom in the early 1960s, critics and public have argued about him, dismissed him, reinstated him again, endlessly questioned him and in the absence of any useful statement by the artist himself, declared themselves baffled by the bland success of his art.

Yet, of all post-war artists, Warhol made the most obvious breaks from past traditions and displayed the most single-minded consistency. His art can be seen for what it is only by stepping aside from our current assumptions about art and understanding the logic of his point of view.

The Pop Art movement started as a reaction against the success and high seriousness of Abstract Expressionism. As Roy Lichtenstein said, ''We wanted to paint pictures so outrageous and ugly that no one would want to buy them.'' So the chosen subject matter was figurative (heresy!), commercial (but it's not Art) and frequently humorous (please don't laugh in the art gallery). But within two or three years, the Pop Artists found that they were as successful as their predecessors, and, what is more, that it was nice to be rich. As overdrafts disappeared though, so did invention and humour, and most of the artists settled down into comfortable lives making innumerable versions of their successful styles. But not Warhol.

Warhol was a much more sophisticated and analytical thinker than most artists, whose imaginations usually terminate at the end of their paint-brushes. He was aware of the pressure of success, of the danger of becoming an institution, but where most artists react to this by trying to fight it, Warhol decided to make success and being an institution his art form. Art had been manipulated by the art-world, the critics, dealers and collectors long enough; now Warhol was going to use them as his canvas.

His first successful work consisted of sculpture in the form of Campbell's Soup Cans and Brillo Boxes, and screenprinted paintings of contemporary icons from Elvis Presley to Jackie Kennedy, which he made with the assistance of the helpers in his Factory, as his large studio was called. These works immediately raised two important questions: did it matter that the works were not unique? and did it matter that Warhol himself had not actually made them? The critics and dealers, who were riding on the wave of newness and originality that they themselves had created, had to go along with the artist and the collectors dutifully followed.

Was his work, then, the huge confidence risk that the general public suspects all ''Modern art'' to be? Yes, and no. Yes, because Warhol was deliberately attacking all the sacred shibboleths of art, and no, because the art itself was undeniably ''good'' and highly influential. The effect of Warhol pointing to commercial art as a source of visual energy and his use of violent colour overlays in his screenprints can be seen in every art college, every fashion magazine in the Western world. In purely visual terms he affected the language of art more than anyone else of his generation.

The critics would have been content to leave it at that, but Warhol was after bigger game. For one thing he realized the business potential of his painting method. Rich collectors would pay many times more for Warhol portraits of their wives than for conventional ones, even though the portrait would often be no more than a blow-up photograph screenprinted by a member of the Factory. Indeed it was the very casualness of Warhol that made his work so attractive and chic. For those with a more ''concerned'' view of the world he produced a series of paintings of electric chairs and wanted men. All of this work is handsome to look at and in his usual startling colour combinations, and Warhol had no lack of clients.

The Factory now became increasingly important and the work produced there became simply the means to its existence. To explain this next stage one must consider Warhol's personality or, to be exact, his lack of it. His nature was that of a vacuum, a void. He never made the earnest statements about his work that most artists are prone to, and apparently conversed entirely on trivialities. He condemned nothing and seemed to find any odd manifestation of human behaviour fascinating.

Because of this personality, he drew to his studio an assortment of would be actors, failed poets, and all those, especially on the sexual fringes like transvestites, whose dreams were beyond the limits understood by normal society. ''I dream, and others see my dreams,'' says an artist in a Cabell novel, which Warhol changes to ''they dream, and I make their dreams visible.''

When people are allowed to act as they wish, to be what they want to be, they create a ''lifestyle,'' and it was to fashioning the lifestyle of the group that formed around him that Warhol now turned his attention. This he did not by giving the lead for them to follow, but by pointing out what they were doing. He filmed them continuously, in little dramas where a man could act out the fantasy of being Jean Harlow or a woman could be high priestess and whore at the same time. He did this in a style that was deliberately rough and amateurish, which left in all the mistakes, ended when the film ran out and which reflected exactly the street language and stoned lifestyle of its characters.

Early examples of this genre such as *My Hustler* were no more than home movies, but with *Chelsea Girls* came commercial success. The verbal obscenity of his characters fitted exactly the so-called ''permissive society,'' and his works became notorious and fashionable for their sexual frankness. Warhol, who was never one to pass up a good thing, began to turn out full length films such as *Trash*

Andy Warhol: *Triple Elvis,* 1964. ©Artists Rights Society, Inc.

and *Flesh,* and achieved the unique feat of making art films highly commercial.

Warhol's style of filmmaking has had a huge effect on the commercial cinema. Where the whole weight of European "new wave" movies had failed to change Hollywood techniques, he succeeded single-handedly. The casual styles of acting now fashionable, the type of wandering camera movement, the passages of apparently trivial conversation, all derive from Warhol.

To be a major influence on contemporary painting and film might have been enough for most artists, but Warhol was not yet finished. The lifestyle that he had allowed to grow around him was now becoming fashionable outside his circle. The most revolutionary aspect of this was the effect on sexual roles. At a time when the gamine mini-skirted look was de rigeur, Warhol reintroduced The Woman, via a return to 1930s glamour. But the femininity did not mean weakness, for all Warhol's women are much stronger than his men; it was Jean Harlow, but without a patriarchal Clark Gable to subdue her.

Men were encouraged to express their femininity too. At the centre of the fashion were Warhol's "superstars," transvestites like Holly Woodlawn and Jackie Curtis, who had the effect of making bisexuality acceptable. This fashion has operated most strongly in the pop-rock world. There would have been no "glitter" without Warhol. Mick Jagger would have remained a blues shooter, David Bowie would not have happened at all, and it could be argued that the ubiquitous glamorous soul acts would never have happened.

Warhol opened a night-club for the "beautiful people" called The Exploding Plastic Inevitable, inventing the projected light show for it and managing the house band which was called The Velvet Underground. This band became one of the most influential in rock music, restoring in songs such as "Heroin" and "White Light/White Heat" a cutting, poetical edge to a music that was fast drowning in the soft cotton wool of flower power.

As the influence of the lifestyle spread, Warhol changed the focus of his interests, putting out a gossip magazine called *Andy Warhol's Interview* which again furthered the effects of his ideas.

From painter to gossip magazine publisher is a big step, but in terms of Warhol's output a consistent and logical one. To consider his paintings by themselves, as most critics do, is to miss the point. Warhol's subject is society, which he manipulated in actuality as a painter manipulates his paint and for the same purpose; to create, to comment upon and to illustrate.

—Alastair Mackintosh

WATTS, Robert Marshall

Nationality: American. **Born:** Burlington, Iowa, 14 June 1923. **Education:** Studied mechanical engineering at University of Louisville, Kentucky, 1942–44; also studied at the Art Students League, New York, 1946–48, and Columbia University, New York, 1951. **Military Service:** Served in the United States Naval Reserve, 1942–46. **Career:** Independent artist active in sculpture, performance, film and video, since 1953. Member of the Fluxus Group in New York in the early 1960s. Taught at the Institute of Applied Arts and Sciences, Brooklyn, New York, 1951–52. Professor of art, Rutgers University, New Brunswick, New Jersey, 1953–84 (resident artist in film and mixed media, 1964–82). Carnegie Corporation Visual Artist, University of California, 1968. **Awards:** Research Council Grants, 1961–75, Faculty Fellowship, 1971, RASP Grants, 1975, 1982, and CID Grant, 1978, Rutgers University; Experimental Workshop Award, Carnegie Corporation, 1964; Creative Artists Public Service Grant, New York State Council on the Arts, 1975; National Endowment for the Arts Fellowship, Washington, D.C., 1976. **Agent:** Francesco Conn, Vicolo Quadrelli 7, 37121 Verona, Italy. **Died:** 1988.

Individual Exhibitions:

1960 Grand Central Moderns, New York
1966 Bianchini Gallery, New York
Ricke Gallery, Kassel, West Germany
1970 Ricke Gallery, Cologne
1971 Apple Gallery, New York
1973 La Bertesca, Milan
Galerie Baecker, Bochum, West Germany
1974 Multhipla, Milan
1975 Multhipla, Milan
1976 René Block Gallery, New York
1977 Studio Morra, Naples
1978 Felius Gallery, Washington, D.C.
1982 Galleria d'Arte, Verona, Italy
1987 *Flux Med: Robert Watts—Prints 1987,* Joan Guaita, Palma, Spain
1990 *Robert Watts,* Leo Castelli Gallery, New York

Performances:

Magic Kazoo, New York City and New Jersey, 1960; *Yam Festival,* with George Brecht, in the United States and by international mail, 1962; *Yam Lecture,* with George Brecht, New York, 1963; *Yam Day,* with George Brecht, Hardware Poets Playhouse, New York, 1963; *Cake,* Kornblee Gallery, New York, 1964; *Monday Night Letter,* Cafe au Go Go, New York, 1964–65; *Performance Work/Fluxus/Body Covering,* Museum of Contemporary Crafts, New York, 1967; *Superstar,* University of California, Santa Cruz, 1969; *Communication in a Noisy Environment,* Automation House, New York, 1970; *Fluxyear/Gemini/74,* Onnasch Gallery, New York, 1974; *Performance Works for Audience,* Centro d'Informazione Alternativa, Rome, 1975; *Flux-Harpsichord Konzert,* Akademie der Kunste, West Berlin, 1976; *Oraculum,* Studio Morra, Naples, 1977; *Fluxus Concert,* Musée d'Art Contemporain, Montreal, 1980.

Selected Group Exhibitions:

1960 *New Forms, New Media,* Martha Jackson Gallery, New York
1961 *Assemblage,* Museum of Modern Art, New York
1968 *The Machine,* Museum of Modern Art, New York
1970 *Happening und Fluxus,* Kunstverein, Cologne (toured Europe)
1972 *Documenta 5,* Kassel, West Germany
1974 *Artists' Stamps,* Simon Fraser University, Burnaby, British Columbia
1979 *Re-Visions,* Whitney Museum, New York

1981 *Fluxus, etc.,* Cranbook Academy of Art, Bloomfield Hills, Michigan
1985 *Festival of Fantastics,* Roskilde, Denmark
1987 *Made in USA,* University of California, Berkeley
1900 *Fluxus S.P.Q.R.,* Galleria Fontanella Borghese, Rome
1992 *Head Through Wall,* Statens Museum for Kunst, Copenhagen (travelled to Nykytaiteen Museo, Helsinki; Kunsthalle, Nuremberg)
1997 *The Great American Pop Art Store: Multiples of the Sixties,* University Art Museum, California State University, Long Beach

Collections:

Albright-Knox Art Gallery, Buffalo, New York; Chrysler Art Museum, Provincetown, Massachusetts; Art Institute of Chicago; Museum of Fine Arts, Houston; Fort Worth Art Center, Texas; Los Angeles County Museum of Art; Moderna Museet, Stockholm.

Publications:

By WATTS: Book—*Newspaper,* with George Brecht, New York 1963; *Postage Stamps,* New York 1963; *Fluxpost Postage Stamps,* New York 1965; *Event Cards Fluxus,* New York 1965; *The Arts on Campus,* edited by Margaret Mahoney, New York 1970; *Proposals for Art Education,* New York 1970; *S.O.S.,* 2 vols., New York 1977; *The Book As an Event,* Bangor 1978; *Notes and Sketches 1964–66,* Asolo 1979.

On WATTS: Books—*AQ 16: Fluxus* by Silke Paul and Harve Wurz, Antibes 1977; *The Museum of Drawers* by Herbert Distel, Zurich, 1978; *Fluxus* by Harry Rule, Amsterdam 1979; *Blam: The Explosion of Pop, Minimalism and Performance 1958–64* by Barbara Haskell, New York 1984; *Robert Watts,* exhibition catalog, New York 1990; *Robert Watts,* exhibition catalog, New York 1990; *The Great American Pop Art Store: Multiples of the Sixties,* Santa Monica 1997. **Articles—**in the *Institute of Contemporary Arts Bulletin* (London), January 1967; ''Transformations from Nature'' by Letty Eisenhauer in *Art and Artists* (London), November 1973; ''The Rutgers Groups: Garden State Avant-Garde'' by Richard Kalina in *Art in America,* vol. 87, no. 12, December 1999.

*

From 1946 to 1958 I was a painter mainly in the tradition of abstract expressionism and geometric art. In 1957 I began working on pieces involving electric light, with random circuitry, incadescent wire, plants and fish. One day in July 1958 I stopped painting.

During the early 1960s I exhibited works of an electro-mechanical nature guided by random or quasi-random circuits. At the same time I became interested in 16mm and 8mm film, photography, tape machines—and then I met Fluxus in 1963.

In 1960 1 had produced my first event of 48 hours duration which moved from New York City to the Jersey shore, utilizing students as the primary participants, but acquiring others along the way. In a sense, Fluxus came at a time of consolidation of my ideas about art and art process; it was an exploratory forum for ideas and energy which eventually had an effect on all the arts.

Since 1970 I have continued to explore methods and attitudes toward art utilizing my knowledge and experience with past art and archaeology, esoteric information, science and technology, natural phenomena, and print technology. I work with concepts first and methods secondarily, chosen to suit the thought at hand.

—Robert Watts

WEARING, Gillian

Nationality: British. **Born:** Birmingham, England, 1963. **Education:** Chelsea School of Art, 1985–87; Goldsmith's College, London 1987–90, B.A. (honors). **Career:** Artist and photographer. **Awards:** BT New Contemporaries Award, 1993; Turner Prize, Tate Gallery, London, 1997; Ministeriums für Stadtentwicklung, Kultur und Sport des Landes Nordrhein-Westfalen Prize, Oberhausen, Germany, 1998; Phaidon Press Award, 1999. **Agent:** Maureen Paley Interim Art, 21 Beck Road, London, E8 4RE, England.

Selected Individual Exhibitions:

1993 City Racing, London
1994 *Videoportrait IV—Gillian Wearing,* Rooseum Centre for Contemporary Art, Malmö
1995 *Western Security,* Hayward Gallery, London
1996 *Gillian Wearing. City Projects-Prague, Part II,* The British Council, Prague (catalog)
Maureen Paley/Interim Art, London
Le Consortium, Dijon, France
1997 Bloom Gallery, amsterdam
Kunsthaus, Zurich (catalog)
Wiener Secession, Vienna (catalog)
1998 *Spotlight on Gillian Wearing,* Spacex Gallery, Exeter (travelled in Britain) (catalog)
Gallery Koyanagi, Tokyo
1999 Maureen Paley/Interim Art, London
2000 Serpentine Gallery, London
2001 Hayward Gallery, Coventry

Selected Group Exhibitions:

1991 *Clove 1,* Clove Building, London
British Art Group Show, Musée des Beaux-Arts, Le Havre, France
1993 *BT New Contemporaries,* Cornerhouse, Manchester (travelled)
Okay Behaviour, 303 Gallery, New York
2 into 1, Centre 181 Gallery, London
1994 *Incertaine identité,* Galerie Analix B and L Polla, Geneva (catalog)
Rien à Signaler, Galerie Analix B and L Polla, Geneva (catalog)
Le Shuttle, Kunstlerhaus Bethanien, Berlin (catalog)
1995 *Möbius Strip,* Basilico Fine Arts, New York (catalog)
Make Believe, Royal College of Art, London (catalog)
Brilliant! New Art from London, Walker Art Center, Minneapolis (travelled) (catalog)

The British Art Show 4, Hayward Gallery, London (travelled) (catalog)
Venice Biennale, Venice

1996 *Traffic,* CAPC Musée d'art contemporain, Bordeaux (catalog)
Private View: Contemporary Art at the Bowes Museum, Bowes Museum, Barnard Castle, County Durham (catalog)
Toyama Now '96, Museum of Modern Art, Toyama (catalog)
Electronic Undercurrents, Statens Museum for Kunst, Copenhagen (catalog)
Life/Live, ARC, Musée d'Art Moderne de la Ville de Paris, Paris (catalog)
Imagined Communities, Arts Council of England, London, and National Touring Exhibitions, Hayward Gallery, London, with Oldham Art Gallery, London (catalog)

1997 *In Visible Light: Photography and Classification in Art, Science and the Everyday,* Museum of Modern Art, Oxford
Pictura Britannica: New Art from Britain, Museum of Contemporary Art, Sydney (travelled) (catalog)

1998 *Real/Life: New British Art,* Prefectural Museum of Fine Arts, Tochigi, Japan (traveled) (catalog)
Distinctive Elements: British Arts Exhibition, National Museum of Contemporary Art, Seoul, Korea (catalog)

1999 *The Museum of the Muse,* Museum of Modern Art, New York (catalog)

Publications:

By WEARING: Books—*Signs that Say What You Want Them to Say and Not Signs that Say What Someone Else Wants You to Say,* London 1997. **Articles—**''A Short Love Story'' in *Nummer,* no. 3, September 1995; ''Hommage à la femme au visage couvert de bandages, que j'ai vue hier sur la Wandsworth Road'' in *Blocnotes,* no. 9, 1995; interviewed Paul Graham in *Paul Graham,* London 1996.

On WEARING: Books—*Brilliant! New Art from London* (exhibition catalog) by Richard Flood, et al., Minneapolis 1995; *Gillian Wearing* (exhibition catalog) by Russell Ferguson, et al., London 1999. **Articles—**''Hype: Write to Reply'' by Amy Raphael in *The Face,* no. 51, December 1992; ''Vital Signs: Gillian Wearing's Talking Pictures'' by Jon Savage in *Artforum International,* vol. 32, March 1994; ''Signs of the Times'' by Caryn-Faure Walker in *Creative Camera,* no. 332, February/March 1995; ''Wearing Well'' by Paul Bonaventura in *Art Monthly,* no. 184, March 1995; ''The Young Devils'' by Patricia Bickers in *Art Press,* no. 214, June 1996; ''Gillian Wearing'' by Gilda Williams in *Art Monthly,* no. 203, February 1997; ''Signs of the Times'' by Ian MacMillan in *Modern Painters,* vol. 10, Autumn 1997; ''The Work of Gillian Wearing: Wah-wah, The Sound of Crying or the Sound of an Electric Guitar'' by Gilda Williams in *Parkett,* no. 52, 1998; ''Confessions: Why Would a Businessman Say 'I'm Desperate'? A-Z of Gillian Wearing'' by Gianmarco Del-Re in *Flash Art* (International Edition), no. 199, March/April 1998; ''London: Gillian Wearing'' by Richard Shone in *The Burlington Magazine,* vol. 142, no. 1172, November 2000; ''Message in a Bottle: The Ethics of Representation Revisited'' by John Slyce in *DPICT,* no. 6, February/March 2001; ''In the Middle with You'' by Denise Robinson; translated by Jacques Demarcq in *Art Press,* no. 266, March 2001. **Television—***The South Bank Show: Young British Artists,* London Weeken Television, 1998.

* * *

Gillian Wearing is a portraitist and a realist: using photography and video, she has found a way to work in the gap between lived experience and the conventions of representation, to produce works which are intimate portraits and remarkable and affecting social documents and which show the strangeness beneath the surface of ''normal'' life.

From the Daguerrotypes of the 1840s onwards, photography has furnished us with the most detailed, realistic and extensive collective portrait of mankind. August Sander's huge project to document ''Man of the 20th Century'' and Diane Arbus' pictures of marginalised outsiders in 1960s New York are examples of the range and power of portrait photography, and both can be seen to have nourished Wearing's practice. But for all the formal expertise of Sander and his sensitivity to individual character, for all Arbus' emotional and sympathetic gaze, their subjects can be seen as specimens, even victims, trapped in the silence of the photographic space. Wearing gives her subjects a voice.

We have become experts at reading photographic texts: with only the prompting of a name, a date, a place, we can construct the biography of a subject from clothes, expression, and surroundings; a look and a style furnish attitudes and meanings. But the subjects, themselves, are silent, investing their whole being in a pose for the flattering attention of the camera; there is a gap between what they think and feel and what we see. An early work by Wearing, *Signs that say what you want them to say and not Signs that say what someone else wants you to say* (1992–93) addresses this gap precisely. Wearing approached strangers on the streets of London and invited them to write whatever they wanted onto a sheet of blank paper and then to pose with their signs for a photograph. The results, when displayed *en masse*, or published as a book, are surprising, funny and affecting. A range of types and classes express thoughts that are banal, straightforward, jokey, or sincere. A young man in a business suit disarmingly declares ''I'm desperate''; an earnest, bespectacled youth observes ''Everything is connected in life the point is to know it and to understand it''; a young woman (homeless?) says ''Give people houses there is plenty of empty ones OK!''; one says ''Come back Mary love you. . .'' These are ordinary people who consistently defy stereotypes and challenge assumptions about what is ''normal.''

Wearing has grown up in media culture in which photography, film and television are not merely commonplace but are part of the fabric of social reality. During her lifetime the television documentary has evolved from scripted narrative to the apparent objectivity and truthfulness of fly on the wall observation; television, too, has become the new confessional, a playground for exhibitionists and voyeurs. The medium, however, remains intrusive and the authenticity of the results are inevitably compromised by the subject's self-consciousness or narcissism before the camera, and the editorial control of the director. In *Confess all on video. Don't worry, you will be in disguise. Intrigued? Call Gillian* (1994) Wearing pushes the confessional mode of television to its limit: she placed an advertisement, which gives the work its title, in a magazine and filmed the respondents wearing a variety of grotesque masks and wigs. With the anonymity and protection of the masks the self-selecting subjects are able to say exactly what they want: they are in control. The resulting short films of anonymous confessions to petty crimes and unburdenings of sexual guilt are disturbingly raw and naked, strange and pathetic. Their unforced nature seems to be a guarantee of authenticity but, of course, we cannot be sure that anything we hear is true: the real person is, after all, in disguise.

Children's confessions and perceptions are the subject of *10–16* (1997). Wearing recorded the voices of seven children aged from ten to sixteen and then lip-synched them to adult actors. The results are deeply strange and disturbing. The seven vignettes chart a tragi-comic development from childhood to adulthood: from innocent pleasure: "I have a tree house... It's fun" (10), concern about the environment: "... I do actually, um, get upset when I, um, hear about, um, how many tigers there are left in the world..." (12), through a boy's desire to kill his lesbian mother (13), to the pleasures of alcohol: "... I like drinking and I like getting beer into my stomach so I can get buzzing" (14), and anxiety about fatness and sexuality (16). While the frankness of the observations is disarming and the struggle to articulate is sometimes painful, it is the dislocation of sound and image which is so compelling and which disconcertingly reveals the "child as father to the man" and gives the work a universal quality.

Wearing used the lip-synch method in another piece, *2 into 1* (1997) in which a mother, Hilary, and her twin sons, Alex and Lawrence, aged eleven, talk about each other in the other's voice, in disarmingly frank terms. The viewer is drawn into shockingly intimate revelations of family relationships which are painful, bewildering, even embarrassing.

Other works are scripted and contrived: *Sacha and Mum* (1996) is a brief film in which two women act out an ambiguously tender and violent relationship, alternately hugging and fighting, caressing and hair-pulling. The film runs both forwards and backwards emphasising the endless cycle of emotions in the relationship and blurring the boundaries between love and hate.

Wearing, herself, appears in one work which is, perhaps, emblematic of her practice: *Dancing in Peckham* (1994) is a film of Wearing dancing, alone, in a shopping mall in South London. There is no soundtrack, the music is in her head. It is an image of dislocation, even of madness, but ordinary, everyday madness: a brief escape from the prison house of convention. Wearing, like an anthropologist of the familiar, consistently probes beneath the surface of normality exposing the socially constructed nature of identity: by risking her own humiliation and colluding with her subjects she avoids being patronising and achieves a democratic, authentic and moving art.

—Richard Salkeld

WEGMAN, William

Nationality: American. **Born:** Holyoke, Massachusetts, 12 February 1942. **Education:** Massachusetts College of Art, Boston, B.F.A. 1965; University of Illinois, Urbana, 1965–67, M.F.A. 1967. **Family:** Married to Gayle Wegman; son: Man Ray. **Career:** Artist and freelance photographer, California and New York. Instructor, University of Wisconsin at Wausau, 1967, and at Waukesha, 1968–69; assistant professor, University of Wisconsin, Madison, 1969–70; lecturer, 1970–71, and visiting artist, 1978, California State University at Long Beach. **Awards:** Guggenheim Fellowship, 1975; National Endowment for the Arts Grant, 1975–77, 1982; Creative Artists Public Service Grant, 1979. **Agent:** Holly Solomon Gallery, 724 Fifth Avenue, New York, New York 10019. **Address:** 27 Thames Street, New York, New York 10004, U.S.A.

Individual Exhibitions:

1971 Galerie Sonnabend, Paris
Pomona College, California
1972 Sonnabend Gallery, New York
Galerie Ernst, Hannover
Situation, London
Galerie Konrad Fischer, Dusseldorf
Courtney Sale Gallery, Dallas
1973 Galerie Sonnabend, Paris
Texas Gallery, Houston
Los Angeles County Museum of Art
Francoise Lambert and Claire Copley Gallery, Los Angeles
1974 Modern Art Agency, Naples
Galerie D, Brussels
Galeria Toselli, Milan
112 Green Street Gallery, New York
Texas Gallery, Houston
1975 Mayor Gallery, London
Galleria Alessandra Castelli, Milan
Gallerie Konrad Fischer, Dusseldorf
1976 The Kitchen, New York
1977 Sonnabend Gallery, New York
Bruno Soletti Gallery, Milan
1978 Rosamund Felsen Gallery, Los Angeles
Robert Cumming/William Wegman, California Institute of Technology, Pasadena
1979 Holly Solomon Gallery, New York
Arnolfini Gallery, Bristol
Galerie Konrad Fischer, Dusseldorf
Otis Art Institute, Los Angeles
William Wegman: Retrospective, Fine Arts Galleries, University of Wisconsin at Milwaukee
1980 *William Wegman: Selected Works 1970–1979,* University of Colorado Art Galleries, Boulder (travelled to the Aspen Center for Visual Arts, Colorado)
1981 Clarence Kennedy Gallery, Cambridge, Massachusetts (with William Van Dyke and Olivia Parker)
1982 Fraenkel Gallery, San Francisco
Nancy Drysdale Gallery, Washington, D.C.
James Corcoran Gallery, Los Angeles
Wegman's World, Walker Art Center, Minneapolis, Minnesota
The Fort Worth Art Museum, Texas
De Cordova & Dana Museum & Park, Lincoln, Massachusetts
The Contemporary Arts Center, Cincinnati, Ohio
Corcoran Gallery of Art, Washington, D.C.
Newport Harbor Museum, Newport Beach, California
1983 Walker Art Center, Minneapolis
12 Duke Street Gallery, London
Contemporary Arts Center, Cincinnati, Ohio
Corcoran Gallery of Art, Washington, D.C.
Local Boy Makes Good, Fine Arts Gallery, University of Massachusetts, Amherst

1984 Mackenzie Art Gallery, Regina, Saskatchewan
University of Miami, Coral Gables
1985 Albright College, Reading, Pennsylvania
1986 Daniel Wolf Gallery, New York
Cleveland Museum of Art, Cleveland
1987 Nancy Drysdale Gallery, Washington, D.C.
1988 San Francisco Museum of Modern Art
Fraenkel Gallery, San Francisco
The Stuart Collection, University of San Diego, La Jolla, California
Pace/MacGill Gallery, New York
San Francisco Museum of Modern Art
1990 Fraenkel Gallery, San Francisco
James Corcoran Gallery, Los Angeles
Pace/MacGill Gallery, New York
Linda Cathcart Gallery, Los Angeles
The History of Travel, Taft Museum, Cincinnati, Ohio
Butler Institute, Youngstown, Ohio
Sperone Westwater Gallery, New York
William Wegman: Paintings, Drawings, Photographs, Videotapes, Kunstsmuseum, Lucerne (traveled to ICA, London; Stedelijk Museum, Amsterdam; Frankfurt Kunstverein; Pompidou Center, Paris; ICA, Boston; Ringling Museum, Sarasota; Whitney Museum of American Art, New York; Contemporary Arts Museum, Houston)
1991 Neuberger Museum, State University of New York, Purchase
William Wegman: Photographic works 1969–76, Fonds Regional d'Art Contemporain du Limoges, Limousin, Limoges, France
1992 Fraenkel Gallery, San Francisco
Pace/MacGill Gallery, New York
Linda Cathcart Gallery, Los Angeles
William Wegman: Foto, Film, Zeichnungen, Galerie Andreas Binder, Munich
William Wegman: Field Guide to North American (and other regions), Athenaeum Music & Arts Library, La Jolla, California
1993 Fraenkel Gallery, San Francisco
William Wegman's Cinderella, Museum of Modern Art, New York
William Wegman, Museo de Monterrey, Mexico
William Wegman: Les Contes de Fay, Galerie Durand-Dessert, Paris
Fay's Fairy Tales: William Wegman's "Cinderella" and "Little Red Riding Hood," Baltimore Museum of Art, Maryland (traveled to Carnegie Museum of Art, Pittsburgh; Columbus Museum of Art; Modern Art Museum of Fort Worth, Texas; Ansel Adams Center for Photography, San Francisco; Museum of Contemporary Art, San Diego)
1994 Nancy Drysdale Gallery, Washington, D.C.
Linda Cathcart Gallery, Los Angeles
Lisa Sette Gallery, Phoenix, Arizona
Greg Kucera Gallery, Seattle, Washington
Edition Julie Sylvester
1995 *A William Wegman Primer: Shapes, Numbers and Alphabet,* George Eastman House, International Museum of Photography and Film, New York
William Wegman: Photographs, Aspen Art Museum, Aspen
Weimar den Weimaranern, ACC Galerie Weimar
William Wegman: Recent Work, Gerald Peters Gallery, Dallas
William Wegman, PaceWildenstein, Los Angeles
William Wegman: Altered Photographs, PaceWildensteinMacGill, New York

Selected Group Exhibitions:

1969 *Places and Process,* Edmonton Art Gallery, Alberta
1971 *Prospect '71,* Dusseldorf
1973 *Whitney Annual,* Whitney Museum, New York
1978 *23 Photographers,* Walker Art Gallery, Liverpool
1979 *The Altered Photograph,* Project Studio 1, Long Island City, New York
1981 *Drawing Distinction: American Drawings in the Seventies,* Louisiana Museum of Modern Art, Denmark (traveled to Kunsthalle, Basel, Switzerland; Stadtische Galerie im Lenbachhaus, Munich; Wilhem-Hack Museum, Ludwigshafen, Germany)
1982 *Biennale,* Venice
1983 *Images Fabriques,* Centre Georges Pompidou, Paris
1984 *Content: A Contemporary Focus 1974–1984,* Hirshhorn Museum, Washington, D.C.
1989 *Image World,* Whitney Museum of American Art, New York
Painting Beyond the Death of Painting, USSR Artists Union, Moscow
Contemporary Art from New York, Yokohama Museum of Art, Japan
Now, Victoria and Albert Museum, London
1990 *Photography Until Now,* The Museum of Modern Art, New York
Word as Image: American Art 1960–1990, Milwaukee Art Museum, Milwaukee, Wisconsin
Points of Departure: Origins in Video, The Museum of Art, Pittsburgh, Pennsylvania
1991 *4e Semaine Internationale de Video,* Geneva
1992 *Greg Colson, Guillermo Kuitca, William Wegman,* Westwater, New York
1993 *Action/Performance and the Photograph,* Turner/Krull Galleries, Los Angeles
1994 *Animal Farm,* James Corcoran Gallery, Santa Monica, California
1995 *Reconsidering the Object of Art: 1965–1975,* The Museum of Contemporary Art, Los Angeles
Mainely Wegmans, Colby College Art Museum, Waterville, Maine

Collections:

Albright-Knox Gallery, Buffalo; The Brooklyn Museum, New York; Carnegie Institute, Museum of Art, Pittsburgh; F.R.A.C. Limousin, Limoges, France; The Corcoran Gallery of Art, Washington, D.C.; Los Angeles County Museum of Art; Minneapolis Institute of Art; Museum of Fine Art, Houston; The Museum of Modern Art, New York; De Menil Collection, Houston; Newport Harbor Museum, California; Sammlung Ludwig, Aachen; San Francisco Museum of

Modern Art; Saint Louis Museum of Modern Art; Stuart Collection, Univ. of California, San Diego; Walker Art Center, Minneapolis; Whitney Museum of American Art, New York.

Publications:

By WEGMAN: Book—*Man's Best Friend,* New York 1982; *Everyday Problems,* New York 1984; *William Wegman: Paintings, Drawings, Photographs, Videotapes,* New York 1990; *Cinderella,* New York 1993; *Little Red Riding Hood,* New York 1993; *ABC,* New York 1994; *1,2,3,* New York 1995; *Triangle, Circle, Square,* New York 1995; *Fay's Friends,* New York 1995; *Fashion Photographs,* with Ingrid Sischy, New York 1999; *Fay,* New York 1999; *William Wegman's Wegmanology,* New York 2001. **Article**—''Shocked and Outraged'' in *Avalanche* (New York), Winter 1971; **Videos—***Spit Sandwich,* 1970; *Reel 1,* 1970–1972; *Reel 2,* 1972; *Reel 3,* 1972–1973; *Reel 4,* 1973–1974; *Reel 5,* 1975; *Reel 6,* 1975–1976; *Reel 7,* 1976–1977; *Gray Hairs,* 1974–1975; *Man Ray, Man Ray,* 1978; *The World of Photography,* 1985; *Sesame Street Videos,* 1989, 1992, 1993, 1994; *Henry Purcell's Curtain Tune from Timon of Athens,* 1994; *Fay Presents Alphabet Soup,* 1995; *Fay Presents Fay's Twelve Days of Christmas,* 1995. **Films—***Dog Baseball,* 1986; *The Hardly Boys in Hardly Gold,* 1995.

On WEGMAN: Books—*Wegman's World,* exhibition catalog with texts by Lisa Lyon and Kim Levin, Minneapolis 1983; *Photography and Art 1946–1986,* exhibition catalog with essays by Andy Grundberg and Kathleen M. Gauss, Los Angeles 1987; *Weimar den Weimaranern,* exhibition catalog, Weimar 1989; *Image World,* exhibition catalog, New York 1989; *Word as Image: American Art 1960–1990,* exhibition catalog, Milwaukee, 1990; *Points of Departure: Origins in Video,* exhibition catalog, Pittsburgh 1990; *Reconsidering the Object of Art: 1965–1975,* exhibition catalog, Los Angeles 1995. **Articles—** ''Photography'' by Ben Lifson in the *Village Voice* (New York), 9 April 1978; ''Everything You Wanted to Know about William Wegman but Didn't Dare Ask'' by Stuart Morgan in *Arnolfini Review* (Bristol), May/ June 1979; ''William Wegman'' by Ian Walker in *Art Monthly* (London), no. 27, 1979; ''William Wegman: Altered Photographs'' in *Domus* (Milan), July 1979; *Aperture,* no. 143, Spring 1996; ''Le Chien Man Ray'' in *Art Monthly,* July-August 1997; *ArtForum,* January 1999;

* * *

''I like to subvert the familiar, but not to put it down, or make fun of it.'' Wegman thus adequately described the intent and nuance of his photographs, video and films, and unpretentious graphic art; that is, until the early 1980s and the death of Man Ray, his 80 pound Weimaraner companion, with whom he had made his domestic vaudeville and other spoof images. The dog had in a sense become Wegman's persona and allowed him the fragile, deliberately ephemeral attitude in a wide spectrum of theme. Although Wegman's recent works are still characterized by such burlesque fun (Wegman is said to have genuine disdain for ''art''), there is now a more Surreal and emblematic quality in the elegantly produced Polaroid form which has come to distinguish his work.

Wegman states that he became annoyed with the utterly subjective nuance of modernity, and so was then led to jokes through the need to have his communication ''complete itself.'' His primary metaphor formed around the rational absurdity of the joke structure; and perhaps his major role is to have brought into ''high'' art the casual fun of public entertainment. (His critics have often chided him in just this regard—his ''lightness'' of tone.) And so there came about a long-standing attack upon artistic sincerity itself through Wegman's use of autobiographic subject matter, an improvisational spontaneity, and a humor often centered about the nature of our reality perception. Prevalent also throughout his work has been the theme of incapacity and the thwartedness of failure. No doubt vital to his evolution has been his continuing acquaintance with his one-time studiomate John Baldessari, and as well the appearance in 1963 at the Pasadena Museum of Art, of the first large exhibition of the works of Marcel Duchamp.

With the present decade, Wegman has used a large format Polaroid image which perhaps contradicts the self-effacing anti-mastery so important to his statement. The easy accessibility of his earlier work (''I didn't want them to be compared to paintings, and get involved in scale, and size, and 'wall' power'') has thus been lost. The recent work often exudes a commercialized air through the long use of such tableaux-like imagery in the advertising world. Wegman has, for example, focused upon a female body builder as model in order to explore sexual role cliches; and in another lengthy exploration, has used a small child to present the poignancy and strangeness of the child/adult interface.

Wegman (and dogs) have become a small-scale art machine within the last decade. He has been said to be, just after Warhol, the most recognizable U.S. artist. Wegman's own, and many other websites, promulgate the varied products of the Wegman studios. As well as the single and serial photo images (digital printing has begun to appear among his continuing use of the large-scale Polaroid process),there have been yearly book publications which feature the dogs at play, with no lessened wit, in the worlds of literature and ordinary life.

In the latter half of the 1990s Wegman produced a prodigious number of children's books, among them works for pre-schoolers and elementary school students. For all ages Wegman has produced the deeply admired *Wegman Puppies* (1997), and several other works. The dogs have logically enough also been brought into the perennial array of family life needs: the baby book, the address book, the photo-album, etc. Although not generally an aspect of Wegman's larger celebrity, many of these works were enhanced by the inclusion of his own drawings.

All the while, Wegman has continued to appear in the traditional and more prestigious realm of museums and art galleries. While such shows, held throughout the 1990s, did hold twice-perused themes such as the dogs before 19th century photographic backdrops and the dogs at play before mid-20th century circus sideshow banners and advertisements, there was as well a striking departure. Not at all hiding his familiar troupe, Wegman, perhaps with real nostaglia for a modernism he usually held at arm's length, has used the dogs to create both formal abstracted compositional arrangements and subtle landscape-like forms. As if to increase their abstracted elegance, many of these images were in multi-panel formats.

—Joshua Kind

WEINER, Lawrence

Nationality: American. **Born:** Bronx, New York, 10 February 1942. **Education:** Stuyvesant High School, New York; self-taught as an artist. **Carrer:** Independent artist known for conceptual works incorporating verbal elements; Fellow, National Endowment for the Arts, 1976, 1983; John Simon Guggenheim Fellow, 1994; lives and works in New York. **Awards:** Deutscher Akademische Austauschdienst (DAAD) Award, 1975–76; National Endowment for the Arts Fellowship, Washington, D.C. 1977, 1985; American Exhibition Prize, Art Institute of Chicago, 1979; Arthur Kopcke Prize, Copenhagen, 1991; Wolfgang Hahn Prize, 1995; Skowhegan Medal for Painting, 1999. **Agent:** Leo Castelli, 420 West Broadway, New York, New York 10012, U.S.A. **Address:** 297 W. 4th Street, New York, New York, 10014–2207, U.S.A.

Individual Exhibitions:

1964 Seth Siegelaub Gallery, New York
1965 Seth Siegelaub Gallery, New York
1968 Seth Siegelaub Gallery, New York
1969 Konrad Fischer Galerie, Dusseldorf
Nova Scotia College of Art and Design, Halifax
Wide White Space Gallery, Antwerp
Galleria Sperone, Turin
1970 Konrad Fischer Galerie, Dusseldorf
Galleria Sperone, Turin
Galerie Folker Skulima, Berlin
Art & Project Gallery, Amsterdam
Galerie Yvon Lambert, Paris
Gegenverker, Aachen, West Germany
1971 Galerie Yvon Lambert, Paris
Nova Scotia College of Art and Design, Halifax
Leo Castelli Gallery, New York
1972 Jack Wendler Gallery, London
Galleria Toselli, Milan
Wide White Space Gallery, Antwerp
Leo Castelli Gallery, New York
Konrad Fischer Galerie, Dusseldorf
Galleria Sperone, Turin
Westfälischer Kunstverein, Münster, West Germany
California Institute of the Arts, Los Angeles
1973 Project Inc., Cambridge, Massachusetts
Stäidtisches Museum, Mönchenglabach, West Germany
Jack Wendler Gallery, London
Wide White Space Gallery, Brussels
Galleria Sperone, Turin
Modern Art Agency, Naples
Kabinett für Aktuelle Kunst, Bremerhaven, West Germany
1974 Max Protetch Gallery, Washington, D.C.
Rolf Preisig Gallery, Basel
Galleria Toselli, Milan
Gentofte Kommunes Kunstbibliotek, Hellerup, Denmark
Galerie Yvon Lambert, Paris
Leo Castelli Gallery, New York
Claire Copley Gallery, Los Angeles
Barbara Cusack Gallery, Houston
1975 Konrad Fischer Galerie, Dusseldorf
Kabinett Für Aktuelle Kunst, Bremerhaven, West Germany
Galleria Sperone, Turin
Rolf Preisig Gallery, Basel
1976 Van Abbemuseum, Eindhoven, Netherlands
Institute for Contemporary Arts, London
Robert Self Gallery, Newcastle upon Tyne
Institute for Art and Urban Resources, New York
Kunsthalle, Basel
The Kitchen, New York
Rüdiger Schöttle Galerie, Munich
1977 CEAC, Toronto
Galerie Yvon Lambert, Paris
Salle Patino, Centre d'Art Contemporain, Geneva
Konrad Fischer Galerie, Dusseldorf
Claire Copley Gallery, Los Angeles
Laguna Gloria Art Museum, Austin, Texas
Wide White Space Gallery, Antwerp
1978 Renaissance Society, University of Chicago
INK, Halle für Internationale Neue Kunst, Zurich
1979 Galleria Francoise Lambert, Milan
Leo Castelli Gallery, New York
Nova Scotia College of Art and Design, Halifax
Galerija Foksal PSP, Warsaw
Saman Gallery, Genoa
Art & Project Gallery, Amsterdam
Rüdiger Schöttle Galerie, Munich
1980 Museum of Contemporary Art, Chicago
Van Abbemuseum, Eindhoven, Netherlands
Centre d'Art Contemporain, Geneva
Anthony d'Offay Gallery, London
Galerija Akumulatory 2, Poznan, Poland
Leo Castelli Gallery, New York
Art and Project, Amsterdam
1981 A Space, Toronto
Leo Castelli Gallery, New York
David Bellman Gallery, Toronto
Kabinett für Aktuelle Kunst, Bremerhaven, West Germany
P.S. 1, New York
Konrad Fischer Galerie, Dusseldorf
1982 GEWAD, Ghent, Belgium
Galerie Media, Neuchatel, Switzerland
The Movies, Amsterdam
1983 Nordjyllands Kunstmuseum, Aalborg, Denmark (with Albert Merz)
Bleecker Street Cinema, New York
Kunsthalle, Berne
Galerie Micheline Swaczer, Antwerp
Nova Scotia College of Art and Design, Halifax
1984 David Bellman Gallery, Toronto
Ohio State University, Columbus
University of Cincinnati, Ohio
Galerie Daniel Templon, Paris
Espace Lyonnais d'Art Contemporain, Lyon, France
TTL, BRT and NOS Teletekst, Belgium (television broadcast)
1985 Art and Project Plancius Straat Gallery, Amsterdam
Art and Project Prinsegracht Gallery, Amsterdam
Galerie Konrad Fischer, Dusseldorf
Galerie Daniel Templon, Paris
Le Coin du Miroir, Dijon, France
City Thoughts, Amsterdam
Musee d'Art Moderne de la Ville, Paris
Musée St. Pierre d'Art Contemporain, Lyon, France
1986 State University of New York, Old Westbury
Pier Art Centre, Stromness, Orkney Islands
Fruitmarket Gallery, Edinburgh

AIR Gallery, London (travelled to Derry, Northern Ireland)
Anthony d'Offay Gallery, London
Galerie Micheline Szwajcer, Antwerp
Art Gallery of New South Wales, Sydney
Marian Goodman Gallery, New York
Leo Castelli Gallery, New York
1987 Galerie Daniel Templon, Paris
Le Magasin Centre d'Art Contemporain, Grenoble, France
1988 *Lawrence Wiener: Works from the Beginnings of the Sixties Towards the End of the Eighties,* Stedelijk Museum, Amsterdam (catalog)
1992 *Displacement,* Dia Center for the Arts, New York (catalog)
Lawrence Weiner: Rites of Passage, Galerie im Lenbachhaus, Munich (catalog)
1995 *Lawrence Weiner: From Point to Point,* Kunstmuseum St. Gallen, Switzerland (catalog)
Lawrence Weiner: In the Stream, IVAM Centre Julio Gonzales, Valencia, Spain (catalog)
1999 Regen Projects, Los Angeles

Selected Group Exhibitions:

1969 *When Attitude Becomes Form,* Kunsthalle, Bern
1971 *6th Guggenheim International Exhibition,* Guggenheim Museum, New York
1972 *Documenta 5,* Kassel, West Germany (and *Documenta 7,* 1982)
1973 *Prospekt '74,* Kunsthalle, Dusseldorf
1974 *Some Recent American Art,* City of Auckland Art Gallery, New Zealand
1979 *American Exhibition,* Art Institute of Chicago
1981 *Westkunst,* Cologne
1983 *When Words Become Works,* Minneapolis College of Art and Design, Minnesota
1985 *Artists' Books,* Centre Georges Pompidou, Paris
1987 *Comic Iconoclasm,* Institute of Contemporary Arts, London
1988 *About Sculpture,* Anthony d'Offay Gallery, London (catalog)
1989 *From the Collection of Dorothy & Herbert Vogel,* Arnot Art Museum, Elmira, New York (catalog)
1992 *Wander Lieder,* Stedelijk Museum, Amsterdam (catalog)
Interventions, Art Gallery of Ontario, Toronto (catalog)
1994 *From Minimal to Conceptual Art,* National Gallery of Art, Washington, D.C. (catalog)
Even if it's Nighttime, CAPC Musee d'Art Contemporain, Bordeaux (catalog)
Wall to Wall, Serpentine Gallery, London (catalog)
1995 *Rosebud,* Kunstbau Lenbachhaus, Munich (also Fundacio Joan Miro, Barcelona) (catalog)
Articulations, Whitney Museum of American Art, New York (catalog)
Take Me (I'm Yours), Serpentine Gallery, London (traveled to Turin and Nuremberg) (catalog)
1996 *Public Works,* Stedelijk Van Abbemuseum, Eindhoven, Netherlands (catalog)
Speck Collection, Museum Ludwig, Cologne (catalog)
1997 *Artists' Books: The Invention of a Genre, 1960–80,* Galerie Mansart, Paris (catalog)
1998 *Artranspennine98,* Tate Gallery Liverpool (traveling exhibition)
Invading the Book, National Gallery of Canada, Ottawa (catalog)
1999 *Unconvention,* Centre for Visual Arts, Cardiff
2000 *Sarajevo 2000,* Museum Moderner Kunst Stiftung Ludwing, Vienna (traveling exhibition) (catalog)

Collections:

Centre Georges Pompidou, Paris; Stedelijk Museum, Amsterdam; Museum van Hedendaagse Kunst te Gent, Ghent, Belgium; Städtisches Museum, Mönchengladbach, West Germany; Van Abbemuseum, Eindhoven, Netherlands; British Museum, London; Museum of Modern Art, New York; Art Gallery of Ontario, Toronto; Nova Scotia College of Art and Design, Halifax; National Gallery of Australia, Canberra.

Publications:

By WEINER: Books—*Statements,* New York 1968; *Traces,* Turin 1970; *Art & Project/Lawrence Weiner,* Amsterdam 1971: *10 Works,* Paris 1971; *Flowed,* Halifax, Nova Scotia 1971; *Causality: Affected and/or Effected,* New York 1971; *Having Been Done at/Having Been Done to,* Turin 1972; *A Primer,* Kassel 1972; *Green as Well as Blue as Well as Red,* London 1972; *Within Forward Motion,* Bremerhaven, West Germany 1973; *Within a Reasonable Doubt,* Milan 1973; *Once Upon a Time,* Milan 1973; *Having from Time to Time a Relation to,* Amsterdam 1973; *Towards a Reasonable End,* Bremerhaven, West Germany 1975; *Relative to Hanging,* Ringkobing, Denmark 1975; *Various Manners with Various Things,* London 1976; *Art & Project,* Amsterdam 1976; *On the Rocks,* Lund, Sweden 1976; *Pertaining to a Structure,* London 1977; *Coming and Going,* Geneva 1977; *In Relation to Probable Use,* Chicago 1978; *Regarding Inscriptions (of a Sort),* Basel 1978; *With a Touch of Pink,* Bremerhaven, West Germany 1978; *Works,* New York 1978; *Hard Light,* with Edward Ruscha, Los Angeles 1978; *The Level of Water,* Ghent, Belgium 1978; *With a Probability of Being Seen,* Warsaw 1979; *Concerning 20 Works,* London 1980; *Passage to the North,* New York 1981; *Red/As Well as Green/As Well as Yellow/As Well as Blue,* with Albert Mertz, Aalborg 1983; *Sculpture,* with interview by Suzanne Page, Paris 1985; *Lawrence Weiner: Works from the Beginning of the Sixties Towards the End of the Eighties,* with text by Wim Beeren, Amsterdam 1988; *An Evening Forum at the Vancouver Art Gallery with Terry Atkinson, Jeff Wall, Ian Wallace and Lawrence Weiner,* Vancouver 1990; *Lawrence Weiner: Show and Tell,* Ghent 1992; *Lawrence Wiener: Wind & the Willows,* Brussels 1996. **Articles—** interview with David Batchelor in *Artscribe International,* no. 74, March-April 1989; interview with Douglas Gordon in *Variant,* no. 10, Winter 1991; interview with Christian Leigh in *Flash Art,* vol. 25, no. 166, October 1992; interview with Jonas Ekeberg in *Siksi,* no. 1, 1995; interview with Marjorie Welish in *Bomb,* no. 54, Winter 1996; interview with James Hobbs in *Artists Newsletter,* January 1998. **Recordings—***7,* Paris 1972; *Having Been Done At,* Rome 1973; *Nothing to Lose/Niets aan Verloren,* Eindhoven, Netherlands, 1976; *Having Been Built on Sand with Another Base (Basis) in Fact,*

Munich 1978. **Films and videos**—*Beached,* 1970; *Broken off,* 1971; *To and Fro and Fro and To and Fro and Fro and To,* 1972; *Shifted from Side to Side,* 1972; *A First Quarter,* 1973; *Affected and/or Effected,* 1974; *Done To,* 1975; *A Second Quarter,* 1975; *Do You Believe in Water?,* 1976; *Green As Well As Blue As Well As Red,* 1976; *A Bit of Matter and a Ltle Bit More,* 1976; *For Example Decorated,* 1977; *Altered to Suit,* 1979; *There But For,* 1980; *Passage to the North,* 1981 ; *Plowmans Lunch,* 1982.

On WEINER: Books—*Lawrence Weiner: Eine Ausstellung,* exhibition catalog with essay by Klaus Honnef, Aachen 1971; *Lawrence Weiner: Jahresgabe 1972,* exhibition catalog with introduction by Klaus Honnef, Munster 1973; *Lawrence Weiner, 8–30 Juni 1974,* exhibition catalog with essay by Jane Pedersen, Hellerup 1974; *Lawrence Weiner,* exhibition catalog with commentary by Rudi H. Fuchs, Basel 1978; *Lawrence Weiner: Mounds + Smooth Cairns,* exhibition catalog with text by Edward Leffingwell, Columbus, Ohio 1984; *Lawrence Weiner: Above Beyond Below,* exhibition catalog with essays by Erlend Brown and Mark Francis, Edinburgh 1986; *Lawrence Weiner: Posters, November 1965-April 1986,* edited by Benjamin H. D. Buchloh, Halifax, Nova Scotia 1986; *Lawrence Weiner Books 1968–1999,* edited by Dieter Schwarz, Cologne 1989; *Lawrence Weiner* by Alexander Alberro, Alice Zimmerman, David Batchelor and Benjamin H.D. Buchloh, London 1998. **Articles**—"Lawrence Weiner: The Realization on That What a Work of Art Is, Is More Important Than How a Work of Art Is (1)" by Catherine Grout in *Artefactum,* vol. 6, no. 29, June-August 1989; "The Space Between Words: Lawrence Weiner" by Colin Gardner in *Artforum,* vol. 29, no. 3, November 1990; "Providing Metaphor Needs: Lawrence Weiner's Specific and General Works" by Richard Frances in *Parkett,* no. 42, December 1994; "'A Meaning Exists That the Outside is Not Privy To': Lawrence Weiner as a Culture" by Barry Schwabsky in *Print Collector's Newsletter,* vol. 26, no. 1, March-April 1995; "Dissociated Objects: The Statements/Sculptures of Lawrence Weiner" by Birgit Pelzer in *October,* no. 90, Fall 1999.

*

Art is not a metaphor upon the relationships of human beings to objects and objects to objects in relation to human beings but a representation of an empirical existing fact.

It does not tell the potential and capabilities of an object (material) but presents a reality concerning that relationship.

Constant placation of previous aesthetics consumes present resources to the extent that as the needs and desires of a present aesthetic make themselves felt (even when the basis is in a previous aesthetic) the resources have been exhausted.

There are very few material relationships of human beings to objects that at various (some) stages have not required various (some) forms of human being to human being relationships.

The utilization of media presents these various relationships at the moment of the presentation of what in essence is a material relationship. The utilization of media as both presentation and representation seems to require no justification other than the presentation itself.

The artist's reality is no different from any other reality. It is the content that gives the perceptions and observations of an artist (within the presentation/art) a use factor within the society.

The acceptance of the need for this distancing (in fact the need itself) by a society for its art to function has led to the misconception that art and artists are apart from society unless they do not function as art and artists.

The obvious change in the relationship of art to a culture is perhaps that the explanation (not needed justification) of the existence of art has been allied to the concept of production.

This reading while obviating some form of social unease is not in fact the case: art is in relation to its society a service industry.

—Lawrence Weiner

WELCH, Roger

Nationality: American. **Born:** Westfield, New Jersey, 10 February 1946. **Education:** Attended National Music Camp, Interlochen, Michigan, summers, 1963–65; studied at York Junior College, Pennsylvania, 1964–65, Miami University, Oxford, Ohio, 1965–69, B.F.A. 1969, School of the Art Institute of Chicago, 1969–71, and with the Whitney Independent Study Program, New York, 1970–71. **Career:** Multimedia artist: lives and works in New York. **Awards:** Ford Foundation scholarship, 1970; New York State Council on the Arts grant, 1973; National Endowment for the Arts grants, 1974 and 1980. **Address:** 87 East Houston Street, New York, New York 10012, U.S.A.

Individual Exhibitions:

1971 112 Greene Street, New York (performance)
98 Greene Street Loft, New York (performance)
1972 98 Greene Street Loft, New York
Galerie 20, Amsterdam
Sonnabend Gallery, New York
1973 Galerie Konrad Fischer, Dusseldorf
Galerie Sonnabend, Paris
Nova Scotia College of Art, Halifax
John Gibson Gallery, New York
1974 University of Rhode Island, Kingston
Milwaukee Art Center
1975 Galleria Forma, Genoa
Galerie Gérald Piltzer, Paris
Stefanotty Gallery, New York
1977 Albright-Knox Art Gallery, Buffalo, New York
1979 Studio 46, Torino, Italy
Antwerp Gallery, Antwerp, Belgium
1980 Museo de Arte Moderno, Mexico City (retrospective)
P.S.1. (Project Studios One), Institute for Art and Urban Resources, Long Island City, New York
1981 Museo Nacional, Havana
Museo de Bellas Artes, Caracas, Venezuela
1982 Whitney Museum of American Art, New York
1984 Miami University, Oxford, Ohio (retrospective)
1986 Ted Greenwald Gallery, New York
Elizabeth Galasso Fine Arts, Ossining, New York
1987 Ted Greenwald Gallery, New York
1988 Sander Gallery, New York
1990 *Visiting Artists Exhibition,* Ewing Gallery, University of Tennessee, Knoxville
1991 *Roger Welch: Austin, Texas Children,* Liverpool Gallery, Brussels

Roger Welch: *Drive In: Second Feature,* 1982. ©Roger Welch.

1993 Galerie Art Matters, Noordwijk, Holland
2000 Galleria Milano, Milan, Italy
2001 Neuberger Museum, Purchase, New York

Selected Group Exhibitions:

1977 *Documenta,* Kassel, Germany
1978 *American Narrative Art: 1967–77,* Contemporary Arts Museum, Houston (travelled to New Orleans, Winnipeg, and California)
1980 *Cartes et figures de la terra,* Centre Georges Pompidou, Paris
1981 *Four Artists and the Map—Jasper Johns, Nancy Graves, Roger Welch, and Richard Long,* Spencer Museum of Art, University of Kansas, Lawrence
1985 *18th Biennale,* Museum Middelheim, Antwerp, Belgium
1986 *Das Automobil in der Kunst 1886–1986,* Haus der Kunst, Munich
1987 *Photography and Art: Interactions since 1946,* Los Angeles County Museum of Art
1992 *A Presence of the Past,* Snug Harbor Museum, Staten Island, New York
1993 *Concept Art,* Musee d'Art Moderne, Saint-Etienne, France
Conceptual Art of the 1970s: Recent Acquisitions, Boston Museum of Fine Arts

Collections:

Georgia Museum of Art, University of Georgia, Athens; Museo Rufino Tamayo, Mexico City; Stadtisches Museum, Mönchengladbach, Germany; Stadtisches Kunstmuseum, Bonn; Museo de Bellas Artes, Caracas, Venezuela; Boston Museum of Fine Arts; Musée d'Art Moderne, Saint-Etienne, France; Wadsworth Antheneum, Massachusetts; Museum of Modern Art, New York; Chase Manhattan Bank, New York.

Publications:

By WELCH: Articles—''On Recorded History (Part 1)'' in *Tracks: A Journal of Artists' Writings,* vol. 1, no. 2, Spring 1975; ''Harry

Lieberman—1885,'' *Big Deal,* Spring 1975; statement in *Roger Welch,* exhibition catalog, Milwaukee 1975; statement in *Unbuilt America,* New York 1976; statement in *The Big Jewish Book,* New York 1978; essay in *La Gabbia Sui Piremei,* Torino, Italy 1979; ''Alternative Spaces'' in *Alternatives in Retrospect 1969–75,* exhibition catalog, New York 1981; ''Seaview (The Last Film Installation)'' in *Film as Installation,* New York 1983; interview in *Wide Angle* (a film quarterly published by Johns Hopkins University Press), vol. 5, no. 3, 1983; *Roger Welch: Austin, Texas Children* (interview), exhibition catalog, Brussels 1991. **Films—***Welch,* 1972.

On WELCH: Books—*Modern Art* by Sam Hunter, New York 1978; *Four Artists and the Map,* exhibition catalog with text by Roberta Smith, Kansas City 1981; *A Decade of New Art,* exhibition catalog with text by Linda Cathcart, New York 1984; *Das Automobil in der Kunst 1886–1986,* exhibition catalog with essay by Reimar Zeller, Munich 1986; *Photography and Art 1946–86,* exhibition catalog with text by Andy Grundberg, Los Angeles 1987; *Image World: Art and Media Culture,* exhibition catalog with essay by John G. Hanhardt, New York 1989; *Installation Art* by Nicolas de Oliveira, Nicola Oxley, and Michael Perry, with text by Michael Archer, London 1994. **Articles—**''Story Art'' by Margarethe Jochimsen in *Magazin Kunst* (Mainz, West Germany), September 1974; ''The Post-Perceptual Portrait'' by Amy Goldwin in *Art in America* (New York), January/February 1975; ''After Photography'' by Douglas Davis in the *Village Voice* (New York), no. 14, 1981.

*

All my work is basically portraiture.

—Roger Welch

* * *

Roger Welch is a multimedia artist who uses film, photographs, video, drawings, diagrams, texts, and various sculptural objects in multiple combinations in his environmental installations. Since 1969 Welch has been using real persons and events as the bases for his investigations into the nature of our perceptions as they are sifted and shifted by the passage of time. His work begins with things personally experienced and/or experienced by people around him, and he expands his themes out of the purely autobiographical and biographical realms into statements of the more generally recognizable social and cultural environment that shapes the typically American experience.

Welch selects and organizes the various visual and verbal elements of his subject matter to create interrelated and open-ended environments. The viewer becomes an active participant, filling in meanings by association and making choices as to how and when to take in the parts of his multilayered works. Observers often find possibilities for fresh and vital insights into situations that are usually either buried in half-forgotten memories or simply ingested at face value.

In 1970 Welch began examining his own memory. First, he wrote down what he was able to recall about his own experiences at Miami University in Ohio. Subsequently, he returned to that place and photographed the sites he had mentioned in his writings. In this manner, Welch created a sequence in which memory became cause—the trigger that determined the structure of present experiencing of things past. During the same period, Welch began collaborating with friends and family. In graphic works of 1971, he juxtaposed older and newer photographs of members of various generations of his family and had those who were still alive write their memories of the pictured events under each photograph. In the 1972 film *Welch,* he edited clips from old 16mm home movies made from 1926 to 1972 covering five generations of his family. In the accompanying audiotape, he, his father, his mother, his brother, and his brother's son comment spontaneously as they watch the movies together. Past events, rearranged by the artist, are given revitalization and continuity from a new perspective and vantage point. Old and new are both experienced candidly and immediately as past and present are occurring simultaneously for the participants and for the viewers alike.

In a related series of works, Welch conducted interviews with persons born before 1890, discussing with them their recollections of their childhood hometowns. Out of their descriptions, the artist constructed maps—visualizations of their almost-faded memories—making tangible that which is nearly lost from present perception. One of the most memorable of Welch's collaborations with older people is his 1976 *Alton Carter, Plains, Georgia, Memory Map,* a reconstruction of Plains based on discussions with former U.S. president Jimmy Carter's 88-year-old uncle, Alton. Beginning with a personal collaborative effort, the artist interprets the mythology communicated by a person who has experienced a chunk of history through his own perspective and personality.

During the mid-1970s Welch became involved with the American sports figure, a heroic myth of another sort. In a work such as *Preliminaries* (1976), he studies the different human traits underlying the image of the boxer, too often perceived as a unidimensional figure out only for blood and glory. In *Niagara Falls Project—Roger Woodward* (1975), Welch combined Panavision film of the trip to the great falls with a videotaped interview of a man who, at age seven, had gone over the falls. Through the piece, Welch weaves a fascinating narrative of experience and memory in a heroic/mythic style; as in many of his works, portraiture and landscape are combined through various media to convey the extraordinary element in ordinary people and places.

In his sculptural installation titled *Drive In* (1980), later remade as *Drive In: Second Feature,* Welch explores an American phenomenon highly popular during the 1950s—one that has already become a part of the nostalgic past. The work is composed of a full-scale model of a 1958 Cadillac Eldorado made from tied twigs and branches, along with a series of ''Coming Attractions,'' trailers of 1950s movies interspersed with clips taken from old drive-in intermission ads. Welch himself describes it as ''the product of an archaeological expedition into contemporary America,'' and the effect of the work is that of a half-ironic, half-reverent look at the near-past gone primitive. Welch continues to dig into the American experience with an intuitive wit and studious understanding, promising to unearth many more memories to be perceived as never before.

—Barbara Cavaliere

WESELER, Günter

Nationality: German. **Born:** Allenstein, 2 March 1930. **Education:** Studied architecture at the Technische Hochschule, Braunschweig, 1953–58, Dip. Arch. 1958. **Family:** Married in 1958 (separated 1970); son: Justin; married 1986. **Career:** Independent artist, in

Günter Weseler: *Phonix.* ©2001 Artists Rights Society (ARS), NY/VG Bild-Kunst, Bonn.

Braunschweig, 1953–62, in Dusseldorf since 1962: first kinetic ''moving pictures,'' 1953–58; ''hair pictures,'' 1962–65; ''breathing music'' performance, Radio Bremen, 1964; ''breathing objects,'' since 1966; ''circle rituals (mandalas),'' since 19841 ''spiritual art,'' since 1998. Guest professor, Hamburg Hochschule für Gestaltung, 1989–93. **Agents:** Galerie Svetic, Kasernenstrasse 13, 40547 Dusseldorf; Edition Draier, Romerstrasse 47, 61169 Frieberg. **Address:** Bonifatiusstrasse 57, 40547 Dusseldorf, Germany.

Individual Exhibitions:

1960 Galerie Utertnann, Dortmund, West Germany
1961 Galerie Appel, Frankfurt
1962 Galerie am Bohlweg, Braunschweig, West Germany
1966 Kunsthalle, Dusseldorf
1967 Kunstverein, Hannover
Haus Ruhnau, Essen
1968 Galerie Art Intermedia, Cologne
Galerie Gunar, Dusseldorf
1969 Städtisches Museum, Leverkusen, West German
Kunstmuseum, Lucerne
Die Insel, Hamburg
1970 Kunstverein, Göttingen, West Germany
Edinburgh Art College
Galeria Iven Spence, Ibiza, Spain
1971 *Eat Art* Galerie Hünermann, Dusseldorf
1972 Galerie Magers, Bonn
Museum Atheneum, Helsinki
1973 Turku Museum, Finland
1974 Musée d'Art Contemporain, Montreal
Werke, 1964–1974, Kunstverein für Rheinland und Westfalen, Dusseldorf
Landesmuseum, Wiesbaden, West Germany
1975 Electric Gallery, Toronto
Galerie St. Johann, Saarbrucken, West Germany
Nye Bella Center, Copenhagen
1977 Galerie Hennemann, Bonn
Forum Kunst, Rottweil, West Germany
1978 Galerie Brinkman, Amsterdam
Electric Gallery, Toronto
Nationalgalerie, West Berlin
1979 Galerie Lang, Vienna
Galerie St. Johann, Saarbrucken, West Germany
York University, Toronto
1980 Galerie Lupke und Schonbrunn, Frankfurt
1981 Galerie Regio, Freiburg, West Germany
Alte Oper, Frankfurt
1983 Musiktheater, Gelsenkirchen, West Germany Draier-Verlag, Frankfurt
Galerie Wunsche, Bonn
1984 Buchmesse, Frankfurt
1985 Kunstverein, Siegen, West Germany
Draier-Verlag, Frankfurt
1987 Galerie Redmann, West Berlin
1988 Galerie Hunermann, Dusseldorf
1990 Kunstverein II, Lubeck, Germany
1991 Galerie Svetic, Dusseldorf
1992 *Environment,* Kunsthalle, Dusseldorf
Deutscher Künstlerbund, Aachen
1993 Art Multiple, Düsseldorf
1999 Galerie Slutzky, Frankfurt
Fremdkörper, Hygiene Museum, Dresden
2001 *Retrospektive,* Karolimünster Sammlung, Aachen

Selected Group Exhibitions:

1968 *New Art from Germany,* Philadelphia Museum of Art
Science Fiction, Kunstverein für Rheinland und Westfalen, Dusseldorf
1969 *Intermedia 69,* Kunstverein, Heidelberg
1970 *New Multiple Art,* Whitechapel Art Gallery, London
1971 *Die Puppe,* Haus am Waldsee, West Berlin (toured Germany)
Kinetic Art, Goethe institute Athens (travelled to Ankara, Beirut and Nicosia)
1972 *Spielstrasse Olympische Spiele,* Munich
1973 *Poetry with Material,* Municipal Gallery of Modern Art, Dublin (travelled to Warsaw and Cracow)
1979 *Soft Art,* Kunsthaus, Zurich
1991 Metropolis, Berlin
Kunstmesse, Galerie Svetec, Köln
1993 *'68 Kunst und Kultur,* Marl
Bauhaus, Dessau
Ars symmetrica, Nationalgalerie, Budapest
1995 *Neuland,* Galerie Redmann, Berlin
Eat Art, Galerie Hünermann, Düsseldorf
1996 *Torso,* Galerie Schlieper, Hagen
Maschinen, Galerie Schlüter, Hamburg
Kunst und Architektur, Galerie Ruhnau, Essen
1998 *EAT,* Sydney Museum of Contemporary Art, Australia

Tiere, Galerie Redmann, Berlin
Kunst und Architektur, Werkbund, Bonn
1999 *Aus dem Rahmen,* Galerie im Cranachhaus, Weimer
Eat Art, Galerie Hünermann, Düsseldorf
Das Kreuz, Karlekin Art, Wiesbaden
2000 *Köln art 2000,* Edit. Dreier, Köln

Collections:

Kunstmuseum, Dusseldorf; Kulturministerium Nordrhein Westfalen, Dusseldorf; Kunsthalle, Bremen; Institut für Auslandbeziehungen, Stuttgart; Landesmuseum, Wiesbaden; Stadtische Sammlung, Recklinghausen, West Germany; Power Gallery of Contemporary Art, Sydney; Kunstmuseum Bern, Switzerland; Kantonmuseum, Lausanne, Switzerland; Centre d'Art, Vaduz, Lichtenstein.

Publications:

By WESELER: Books—*Der optische Klan,* playscript, Mainz 1970; *Atemobjekle: Gunter Weseler,* Friedberg-Bruchenbrucken 1986. **Films**—*Räume,* 1970; *Weseler, atmende Welt,* 1974; *Günter Weseler,* 1975.

On WESELER: Books—*Raume und Environments,* Opladen, West Germany 1969; *Dusseldorfer Szene,* exhibition catalog with text by Jean-Christophe Ammann, Lucerne 1969; *Kunstszene Dusseldorf,* exhibition catalog with text by Gerhard Storck, Helsinki 1972; *Strategy—Get Arts,* exhibition catalog edited by Richard Demarco, Edinburgh 1970; *Bis Heute* by Karin Thomas, Cologne 1971; *Deutsche Kunst der 60er Jahr* by Jürgen Morschel, Munich 1972; *Kunstpraxis-Heute,* by Karin Thomas, Cologne 1972; *Günter Weseler: Werke 1964–1974,* exhibition catalog with texts by Karl Heiriz Hering, Gerhard Storck, Helga Meister and others, Dusseldorf 1974; *Gunter Weseler* by Gerhard Storck and Manfred de la Motte, Bonn 1977; *Günter Weseler,* exhibition catalog, with text by Maria Engels, Friedberg 2001.

*

During the years I was working with breathing objects I discovered that breathing objects can signficantly change according to their locations.

When I was in contact with visitors and interested parties, I got really surprising insights in the very different responses to my objects that often were far apart from my original intentions and sometimes quite controversial. It seemed to me that the visitors emotions, associations, and judgements were more a projection of their own consciousness (or unconsciousness) than the reality of the object (if that is possible) that I had intended.

For example, let us take one of my breathing bread-objects, individual interpretations and/or reactions to which extend from "here the bread is insulted, a blasphemy," which mostly might belong to those born of a Christian heritage, where the bread is "holy" or from an experience of deficiency during wartime, to happily expressing well-being while describing the object, as "it's like the maggot in the bacon ("die Made im Speck") and that's how I feel about it myself."

It was the discovering of different levels of reality: one material haptic reality (where we can agree), and everyone's individual psychic reality and one reflected, mirrored conscious reality. "Whatsoever you see all around you is more a reflection of you than any real thing there. You look at yourself mirrored all around. The moment you change, the reflections change" (Osho).

I think I can interpret these experiences as part of the background of my mirror objects (sine 1977), with three different levels:

The mirror itself, which is partly transparent, allows you to look at something behind the glass which you cannot really define as a photo or some material or a fake: is it a real snake or a photo of a snake or a painting (you can't touch it) . . . and something in front of the mirror, some tactile material such as glass, sand, feathers, fur, and/or a breathing object.

And you see yourself and your surroundings in the mirror, always changed by light and the environment.

It is also meant that behind the reflecting surface of your consciousness, which is similar to the surface of water, there is a depth you can enter by techniques of relaxation like meditation, you can dive into the realm of your subconscious. And it is meant as a unity and balance between these different levels which are influencing each other and only subjectively comprehensible.

There is also a fractal dimensional element contained within. The laws and building-blocks in the details are the same as in the whole.

Breathing is also a symbol of change, of the rise and fall of the tide and the return.

Breathing also stands for the spoken word.

—Gunter Weseler

* * *

Born in Allenstein, east Prussia, in 1930 (his mother was an artist of local fame and also a pianist), Günter Weseler grew up in north Friesland/Schleswig-Holstein. His first occupation was as a farmer. He went on to train as a radio technician, studied architecture at the technical college in Braunschweig, and finally opted for the liberal arts. As a painter, Weseler tried his hand at a variety of styles that were then current, from Tachism to serial art, while, from 1962 to 1966, he also worked as an architect in Dusseldorf, where he has since lived. An increasing interest in kinetics and in musical structures brought him together with the young, experiment-crazy composer Dieter Schönbach, who was soon taking down his scores in "graphic-painterly" fashion just as Weseler began "composing" his pictures. Together they later produced (1964–68) "breath music" and "action music," predominantly for Radio Bremen, and also, in 1968 and 1971, musical theatre projects in "breathing auditoria" in Kiel, Münster and Cologne.

Breath as a phenomenon of life fascinated Weseler increasingly; an illness which led to an "almost neurotic respiratory disorder," since "every physical effort made one aware of breathing," played its part in this. Around the same time Weseler gave up painting completely and began to make models out of monocoloured lumps of wax and hairs. These models, however, lacked dynamic energy, so Weseler then began experimenting with "breathing balloons," which filled up rhythmically with compressed air and then collapsed again. What was important to him was the way objects are articulated and the way they move. His next experiment involved covering small motors with animal hides and controlling the speed and rhythm of the machines' movement with pulleys and levers. Under the guise of nature, kinetics imitated organic processes and obtained fascinating and magical effects: spherical fur-covered objects suddenly turned out to be apparently living fabulous beings that moved mysteriously and ''breathed.'' Depending on position and context—we may be dealing with a bird cage, a child's bed, a cushion, or a necklace—Weseler's creations called up a multitude of other associations, including social and political ones. The addition of sound effects was provided by tape recordings. Four stuffed lion skins induced panic when they suddenly began breathing. A steel helmet complete with bullet hole moved in a macabre way.

Weseler soon began working along similar lines with foam. He made window dummies which spewed an unappetising grey-green substance due to a chemical reaction involving the combination and expansion of certain elements under the effects of heat. He also produced ''breathing walls'' out of synthetic materials, as a stage set for the Cologne Opera House, for example, and increasingly vast artificial landscapes, abstract and organic at the same time; or ''post-human landscapes'' with scorched trees, craters and spiny objects which breathed and rattled; or—in Edinburgh in 1970—a nauseating ''Breathing Banquet.'' In 1984 Weseler designed a gently breathing ''Tidal Lake'' which simulated the ebb and flow of the tide.

Since 1983 Weseler has been using grass mats for his work, making them himself by growing corn seeds on glass plates and a layer of plain-coloured humus. After a couple of months this process produces strong, naturally woven mats which gradually turn yellow. The artist then places his ''breathing objects'' on top of them—fauna on top of flora—art thereby becoming one with nature.

During his investigations into breathing, Weseler came across a number of ancient breathing therapies and also esoteric breathing techniques which contain possibilities for heightened physical and mental awareness, as in the case of Zen Buddhism and Tantra Yoga for example. This led him to integrate ''breathing objects'' in closed structures that are inspired by Indian mandalas. According to Weseler, ''The use of breathing objects in mandala structures corresponds to an essential switch in meaning: the movement is no longer simply visible in an organic, animal sense; it exists now in a context in which it is to be understood in a magical, transcendental sense.''

It is in this sense that one should interpret the stamp with which Weseler signs his catalogs and letters: ''Weseler creates a new world—the new species.''

—Werner Schulze-Reimpell

WESSELMANN, Tom

Nationality: American. **Born:** Cincinnati, Ohio, 23 February 1931. **Education:** Hiram College, Ohio; University of Cincinnati, Ohio, B.A. in Psychology; Art Academy of Cincinnati, Ohio; and, under Nicholas Marsicano, Cooper Union, New York. **Family:** Married Claire Wesselmann in 1963; daughters: Jenny, Kate; son: Lane. **Career:** Painter. **Agent:** Sidney Janis Gallery, 110 West 57th Street, New York, New York 10019, U.S.A. **Address:** 231 Bowery, New York, New York, 10002, U.S.A.

Individual Exhibitions:

1961 Tanager Gallery, New York
1962 Green Gallery, New York
1964 Green Gallery, New York
1965 Green Gallery, New York
1966 Sidney Janis, Gallery, New York
1967 Galerie Ileana Sonnabend, Paris
Galleria Gian Enzo Sperone, Torino, Italy
1968 Dayton's Gallery 12, Minneapolis, Minnesota (traveled to Museum of Contemporary Art, Chicago; The DeCordova Museum, Massachusetts)
Sidney Janis Gallery, New York
1970 Sidney Janis Gallery, New York
Early Still-Lifes 1962–1964, Newport Harbor Art Museum, Balboa, California (toured the United States)
1971 Jack Glenn Gallery, Corona del Mar, California
1972 Sidney Janis Gallery, New York
Rosa Esman Gallery, New York
Galerie Aronowitsch, Stockholm
1973 Multiples Gallery, Los Angeles
1974 Sidney Janis Gallery, New York
Galerie des 4 Mouvements, Paris
The Early Years: Collages 1959–62, California State University, Long Beach (traveled to Ohio University, Athens)
1976 Sidney Janis Gallery, New York
1978 *Graphics 1964–77,* Institute of Contemporary Art, Boston
1979 Sidney Janis Gallery, New York
F.I.A.C. Grand Palais, Paris
Ehrlich Gallery, New York
Serge de Bloe, Brussels, Belgium
Hokin Gallery, Miami, Florida
1980 Sidney Janis Gallery, New York
1981 Hokin Gallery, Bay Harbor Islands, Florida
Hokin Gallery, Chicago
1982 Sidney Janis Gallery, New York
Carl Solway Gallery, Cincinnati, Ohio
Margo Leavin Gallery, Los Angeles
1983 Sidney Janis Gallery, New York
Sander Gallery, New York
Delahunty Gallery, Dallas, Texas
1984 Galerie Esperanza, Montreal
Moderism, San Francisco
McIntosh/Drysdale Gallery, Houston
1985 Sidney Janis Gallery, New York
Hokin Gallery, Palm Beach, Florida
Jeffrey Hoffeld & Co., New York
1986 Hokin Gallery, Bay Harbor, Florida
Gallery Quintana, Bogota, Columbia
Galerie Joachim Becker, Cannes, France
Cut-Outs, Gallerie Denise Rene Hans Mayer, Dusseldorf, Germany
O.K. Harris, New York
Carl Solway Gallery, Cincinnati, Ohio
1987 Sidney Janis Gallery, New York
Queens Museum, Flushing, New York
Galerie Esperanza, Montreal
Galerie de France, Paris
The Cooper Union, New York
1988 Galerie Tokoro, Tokyo
Sander Gallery Booth, Hamburg Art Fair, Germany
Mayor Gallery, London
Sidney Janis Gallery, New York

Tom Wesselmann Retrospective: Graphics & Multiples, Stein Gallery, Chicago (toured U.S.A. and traveled to Japan)
1989 Blum Helman Gallery, Santa Monica, California
Waddington Galleries, Ltd., London
Maxwell Davidson Gallery, New York
Galerie Joachim Becker, Cannes, France
1990 John Stoller Gallery, Minneapolis, Minnesota
Blum Helman Gallery, Santa Monica
Gloria Luria Gallery, Bay Harbor Islands, Florida
Hokin Gallery, Palm Beach
Posner Gallery, Milwaukee
Sidney Janis Gallery, New York
O.K. Harris, New York
Studio Trisorio, Naples, Italay
Fay Gold Gallery, Atlanta
Galerie Experanza, Montreal
Wilkey Fine Arts, Medina, Washington
Galerie Joachim Becker, Cannes, France
Colorado State University, Fort Collins
1991 *Wesselmann: Graphics/Multiples Retrospective 1964–1990,* The Contemporary Art Center, Cincinnati, Ohio
Edward Totah Gallery, London
Gallery Tokoro, Tokyo, Japan
1992 *Tom Wesselmann,* Riva Yares Gallery, Scottsdale, Arizona
Tom Wesselmann: New Metal Paintings, Sidney Janis Gallery, New York
1993 *Nudes, Landscape, Still Lifes,* O.K. Harris/David Klein Gallery, Birmingham, Michigan
Tom Wesselman, Foundation Veranneman, Kruishouten, Belgium
Wassermann Gallery, Munich
A Retrospective Survey 1959–1992, organized by Sankei Simbun, Isetan Museum of Art, Shinjuku, Tokyo, Japan (toured Japan)
1994 *Larger than Life: Two Paintings by Tom Wesselmann,* Cranbrook Academy of Art Museum, Bloomfield Hills, Michigan
Retrospective 1959–1993, organized by Thomas Buchsteiner and Otto Letze, Institut für Kulturaustausch, Tübingen, Germany (traveled to Belgium, Spain and France)
1995 Sidney Janis Gallery, New York (catalog)
1996 Fundacion Juan March, Madrid (traveled to Paulau de la Virreina, Barcelona) (catalog)
1997 Sidney Janis Gallery, New York
2000 JGM Galerie, Paris

Selected Group Exhibitions:

1962 *Recent Painting U.S.A.: The Figure,* Museum of Modern Art, New York
1963 *Pop Goes the Easel,* Contemporary Arts Museum, Houston
1965 *Young America 1965,* Whitney Museum, New York
1966 *Art in a Mirror,* Museum of Modern Art, New York (toured the United States)
1967 *Bienal,* Sao Paulo
1968 *Documenta,* Kassel, West Germany
1974 *American Pop Art,* Whitney Museum, New York
1976 *Illusions of Reality,* Art Gallery of New South Wales, Sydney
1977 *The Dada/Surrealist Heritage,* Clark Art Institute, Williamstown, Massachusetts
1983 *Why New York?,* Futura Gallery, Stockholm
1991 *The Chicago International Art Exposition,* Tasende Gallery, La Jolla, California
1995 *Art after Art,* Nassau County Museum of Art, Roslyn Harbor, New York (catalog)
Haus der Kunst and Villa Stuck, Munich, Germany
1996 *Large Drawings and Objects,* Arkansas Arts Center, Little Rock (catalog)
1997 *American Art: A Selection from Waddington Galleries,* London (traveling exhibition) (catalog)
American Pop Art in der Hamburger Kunsthalle, Germany (catalog)
1999 *44th Munich Art Fair,* Germany

Collections:

Museum of Modern Art, New York; Whitney Museum, New York; Albright-Knox Art Gallery, Buffalo, New York; Worcester Art Museum, Massachusetts: Philadelphia Museum of Art; Cincinnati Art Museum, Ohio; Walker Art Center, Minneapolis; Minneapolis Institute of Arts; Dallas Museum of Fine Arts; Wallraf-Richartz Museum, Cologne.

Publications:

By WESSELMANN: Book—as Slim Stealingworth, *Tom Wesselmann,* Abbeville Press, N.p. 1980.

On WESSELMANN: Books—*Pop Art* by Rolf Günter Dienst, Wiesbaden, West Germany, 1965; *Pop Art* by John Rublowsky, New York 1965; *Pop Art* by Lucy R. Lippard, New York 1966; *Pop Art and After* by Mario'Amaya, New York 1966; *Pop Art US.A.* by Alberto Boatto, Milan and Rome 1967; *New York: The New Art Scene* by Ugo Mulas and Alan Solomon, New York 1967; *Art in the Age of Risk* by Nicolas Calas, New York 1968; *Tom Wesselmann: A Retrospective Survey,* introduction and catalog essays by Mario Livingstone, additional essay by Masao Kobayashi, Isetan Museum, Tokyo 1993; *Tom Wesselman,* by Sam Hunter, Rizzoli International, New York 1994. **Articles—**''Tom Wesselmann at Tanager'' in *Arts Magazine* (New York), February 1962; ''Tom Wesselmann at Green Gallery'' by Jill Johnston in *Artnews* (New York), November 1962: ''New Realists in New York'' by Sonya Rodikoff, ''Dada Then and Now'' by Barbara Rose, and ''Le Nouveau Realisme A la Coquete de New York'' by Pierre Restany in *Art International* (Lugano, Switzerland), January 1973; ''Symposium on Pop Art-Special Supplement'' by Henry Geldzahler in *Arts Magazine* (New York), April 1963; ''Tom Wesselmann'' in *Time* (New York), February 1964; ''Tom Wesselmann at Green Gallery'' by Jill Johnston in *Artnews* (New York), April 1964; ''The Honest Nude—Wesselmann'' by Gene R. Swenson in *Art and Artists* (London), May 1966; ''Tom Wesselmann and the Gates of Hom'' by J. A. Abramson in *Arts Magazine* (New York), May 1966; ''Paris: Wesselmann et le Nu Américain'' by Jean-Louis Ferrier in *La Quinzaine* (Paris), November 1966; ''Eros Presumptive'' by Lucy Lippard in *Minimal Art: A Critical Anthology,* edited by Gregory Battock. New York 1968; ''Images: Tom Wesselmann at Janis'' in *Arts Magazine* (New York), February 1968; ''Reviews:

Tom Wesselmann'' in *Arts Magazine* (New York), December 1972: ''Reviews: Tom Wesselmann'' by Carter Ratcliff in *Artforum* (New York), January 1973: ''De Kinderen Kunner er in Joutje Van'' by Tom Burgering in *Rotterdam Nieuwsblad,* June 1973; ''Art: Reading a Monumental Still Life'' by John Perreeault in the *Village Voice* (New York), Manr 1974; ''Pop Art Domesticated: Class and Taste in Tom Wesselmann's Collages'' by Cecile Whiting in *Genders,* no. 13, Spring 1992; ''Tom Wesselmann at Joel Kessler Gallery'' by Elisa Turner in Art News, January 1994; ''Tom Wesselman'' by Herve Vanel in *Beaux Arts Magazine,* no. 127, October 1994; ''Tom Wesselmann at Fred Hoffman'' by Peter Clothier in ARTnews, May 1996; ''Tom Wesselmann at Sidney Janis/Maxwell Davidson'' by Deidre Stein Greben in ARTnews, December 1996; ''Tom Wesselmann at Sidney Janis'' by Vincent Katz in Art in America February 1997.

* * *

If Tom Wesselmann does not tire, ''The Great American Nude'' will reach a thousand. This glamorous creation (*Max-Factorized,* Jean-Louis Ferrier has called her) continues her anonymous course across canvas after canvas, in and out of rnixed-media setups, in paint, in plastic, or in any material that takes the artist's fancy. Only her personal number distinguishes her from her sisters, nearly all smiling broadly and seductively, most of them equipped with super-nubile nipples that look like erotic buttons.

And so many bathrooms. . . ! So many bathers. . . !

But it would be very wrong to think that Wesselmann never escapes from this centrally-heated eaude-toilette inflated world of pulchritude. In her way, The Great American Nude is but one more adjunct to the late 20th-century living style. Her bosom may be bare, but her boudoir has a cassette and electric clock, her bathroom is rich with plumbing and generally a comfortable WC. And there are times when she is absent. A peep through the window shows photochromatic pictures hanging on the wall above a table laid with bottle of beer and can of soda. All these appurtenances can be painted (sometimes in overlifescale) or they can ''be themselves'' like Marcel Duchamp's *ready-mades,* although recruited for practical rather than surrealist purposes.

Wesselmann, supremely conscious of the mixed up world of modern times, knows full well (he is a Bachelor of Arts—Psychology) that contemporary life is based upon privately preserved classical myths in surprisingly easy concert with technical development. His girls are 20th century versions of so many sweethearts out of the past. But they live in a world of NOW. They are posed against a background that includes automobiles and TV. Their kitchens may be teeming with gadgetry, but the easy-to-serve snacks come from the supermarket and require a minimum of housewifery attention. A cardboard plate will suffice. Drinks are handy. Whoever heard of washingup! The dishwasher will see to everything.

Lest such a coca-cola paradise be written off as trite, imagine what any other artist would make of this menu of canned lotus out of the refrigerator. Wesselmann is adept. He is able to flavour his irony with just the right amount of saccharine.

—Sheldon Williams

Referring to the voices of Leger, DeKooning, and Matisse, Tom Wesselmann continues to provide America with a billboard of commercialized eroticism. The media have changed and expanded, but the message still rings true. *The Great American Nude* that awakened our senses in the 1960s has transcended her original canvas. The elements of the nude and commercialism have been pared down, as in ''32 Year Old on the Beach'' (1997). She is farther abstracted, her figure streamlined and simplified. Other works have turned to complete abstraction, composed of strong, colorful forms floating together in space, as in ''Big Blue'' (1999). The three-dimensional paintings of large, metal cutouts are reminiscent of children's pop-up books. Textures from his earlier work translate into solid, formed brushstrokes with the use of color and shape. Wesselmann still produces work that draws on the concepts of Pop Art and digs even deeper into the history of abstraction from the earlier 20th century.

—Rachel E. Kuhn

WESTERIK, Co

Nationality: Dutch. **Born:** Jakobus Westerik in The Hague, 2 March 1924. **Education:** Studied art under Han van Dam, Rein Draijer, Henk Meyer, Willem Rozendaal and Willem Schrofer, Koninlijke Akademie van Beeldende Kunsten, The Hague, 1942–47. **Family:** Married the painter Hens M. de Jong in 1948 (divorced); daughters: Christine, Victoria and Sophie; married gallery director Fenna de Vries in 1970; sons: Willem and Maurits. **Career:** Painter, establishing own studio, The Hague, 1946–76, in Rotterdam, since 1971. Member, Haagsche Kunstkring artists' association, The Hague, 1946–57; Verve artists' group, The Hague, 1951–57; Pulchri Studio society of painters, The Hague, 1952. Instructor, International School, and Deutsche Schule, Scheveningen, 1953–58; Vrije Academie, The Hague, 1955–58; Koninklijke Academie van Beeldende Kunsten, The Hague, 1958–71; Ateliers 63, Haarlem, 1969–70. **Awards:** Jacob Marisprijs, The Hague, 1951, 1955, 1961; Dutch Government Grant for Painting, 1953, 1954; Silver Medal, *Bienal,* Sao Paulo, 1965; Rembrandt Prize, Leiden, 1966; Dutch State Prize for Art and Architecture, 1970; Zuid-Holland Cultural Council Prize, 1987. **Agent:** Galerie Fenna de Vries, Rotterdam. **Address:** Eendrachtsplein 18, 3012 LA Rotterdam, Netherlands.

Individual Exhibitions:

1956 Museum Hofwijck, Voorburg, Netherlands
1964 Gemeentemuseum, The Hague (travelled to Vishal, Haarlem and Van Abbemuseum, Eindhoven, Netherlands)
1966 Stedelijk Museum de Lakenhal, Leiden
1968 Galerie 20, Amsterdam
Galerie Fenna de Vries, Rotterdam
Museum Boymans-van Beuningen, Rotterdam
1971 Galerie Fenna de Vries, Rotterdam
Stedelijk Museum, Amsterdam (travelled to the Groninger Museum, Groningen: Palais des Beaux Arts, Brussels)
Galerie Escape, Amsterdam
1973 Galerie Fenna de Vries, Rotterdam
1974 Palais des Beaux-Arts, Brussels
1976 Galerie Fenna de Vries, Rotterdam
1977 Lens Fine Art, Antwerp
1978 Galerie Fenna de Vries, Rotterdam
1979 Stedelijk Museum, Amsterdam

1980 Galerie Fenna de Vries, Rotterdam
1981 Museum Boymans-van Beuningen, Rotterdam
1982 Galerie Fenna de Vries, Rotterdam
1983 Staatliche Kunsthalle, West Berlin (travelled to Saarbrucken and The Hague)
1991 *Co Westerik: Paintings and Drawings,* Stedelijk Museum, Amsterdam
Co Westerik, Stedelijk Museum, Amsterdam (catalog)
1999 Huygensmuseum Hofwijck, Voorburg (catalog)
Self Portraits in Pencil of Co Westerik, Teylers Museum, Haarlem
2000 De Prom, Baarn, Netherlands (catalog)

Selected Group Exhibitions:

1945 *Parade der Debutanten,* Lange Vijverberg, The Hague
1951 *Verve,* Kunstzaal Esher Surrey, The Hague
1954 *Irish Exhibition of Living Art,* National College of Art, Dublin
1962 *Biennale,* Venice
1964 *Carnegie International,* Pittsburgh
1966 *Tokyo Intentational Exhibition of Art,* Keio Department Store, Tokyo
1969 *Haager Kunstler in Helmhaus,* Zurich
1974 *Verve 1951–1957,* Gemeentemuseum, The Hague
1982 *Arte come Arte,* at the *Biennale,* Venice
1985 *Nouvelle Biennale,* Paris
1988 *Rotterdam Retrospective: Fine Arts Since 1940,* Museum Boymans-van Beuningen, Rotterdam (catalog)
1989 *City Collection 1989: Rotterdam,* Museum Boymans-van Beuningen, Rotterdam (catalog)
1991 *Of Flesh & Blood,* Stedelijk Museum Schiedam, Netherlands (catalog)

Collections:

Gemeentemuseum, The Hague; Museum Boymans-van Beuningen, Rotterdam; Centraal Museum, Utrecht; Frans Halsmuseum, Haarlem; Stedelijk Museum, Amsterdam; Museum Her Princessehof, Leeuwarden; Groninger Museum voor Stadt en Lande, Groningen; Gemeentemuseum, Arnhem; Museum De Lakenahl, Leiden; Stedelijk Museum, Arnhem.

Publications:

On WESTERIK: Books—*Domino Book 2: Co Westerik—42 tekeningen, etsen en litho's,* with text by R. W. D. Oxenaar, Amsterdam 1961; *Co Westerik,* exhibition catalog, with text by R. W. D. Oxenaar, The Hague 1964; *Co Westerik: Tekeningen, Grafiek, Aquarellen uit de verzameling C Kuijman,* exhibition catalog with an introduction by H. R. Hoetink, Rotterdam 1968; *Co Westerik,* exhibition catalog, with text by Wim Beeren, Amsterdam 1971; *Westerik: Drawings, Watercolours and Prints,* with text by J. L. Locher and H. R. Hoetink, Vlaardingen 1971, Amsterdam and Antwerp 1979; *Verve 1951–1957,* exhibition catalog with text by John Sillevis, The Hague 1974; *Co Westerik,* exhibition catalog with texts by R. W. D. Oxenaar and Caret Blotkamp, Brussels 1974; *Co Westerik* by W. Meewis, Schelderode, Netherlands 1979; *Co Westerik,* documentary report by C. Withoff, Groningen, Netherlands 1979; *Co Westerik, Painter* by W. A. L. Beeren, Venlo, Netherlands 1981; *Co Westerik,* exhibition catalog with texts by M. Eberle and J. Locher, West Berlin 1983. **Articles**—''Het schilderij als teken: over het werk van Co Westerik'' by Jonieke van Es in *Jong Holland,* vol. 13, no. 3, 1997.

* * *

Within the context of the Dutch art-climate the painter Co Westerik without any doubt is a certain and constant factor. Although he never belonged to any group, although he has never been exemplary of any direction or tendency, through the years he nevertheless has held a position that is reflected by his work being part of all the major Dutch museum collections, and countless private collections as well. Westerik's work is figurative and realistic, and miles away from the mainstreams of Dutch constructivism and expressionism. Westerik's works deal with the human condition, the psychology pertaining to the individual trying and longing for another person, or thrown back at his own. His painting is convincingly humanistic and his pictures never degenerate into mere storytelling or anecdote.

Undoubtedly his best known paintings are *Fishwoman* (1951), *Schoolteacher and Child* (1961), and *Cut by Grass* (1966). The last mentioned piece shows some fingers sliding through green grass. One is cut in half by a green leaf that leaves its mark like a razorblade. The picture however has psychological impact that by far outreaches the absurdity of the event itself. One feels, here as well as in most of Westerik's paintings, a continuous hidden struggle between individuals, their lack of power and immediacy that feeds feelings of shame. On top of this, eroticism and religiosity by all means find their way to the surface. Westerik's great quality is that he always visualizes, never moralizes. The refinement of his thematic procedure corresponds with a very detailed, multi-layered painting process.

Apart from his painting, Westerik has built up a very large oeuvre of drawings and watercolors. Most of these drawings are autonomous; only a few can be considered as preliminary studies to the paintings.

During the last two decades all his work gained in popularity, including the graphic work. In an extensive catalog (Municipal Museum, The Hague, 1984) it is justly stated that this work too deserves an autonomous status. Etching and lithography are Westerik's favourite techniques. His imagery is intimate and just as detailed and complex as his painting. The editions usually are very limited and even the prints differ.

—A. F. Wagemans

WHITEN, Colette

Nationality: Canadian. **Born:** Birmingham, England 7 February 1945. **Education:** Studied at the Ontario College of Art, Toronto, 1968–72. **Career:** Sculptor, multi-media artist. Instructor at the Ontario College of Art, 1975-present. **Awards:** T. Eaton Travelling Scholarship, Governor-Generals Medal, and Canada Council Short Term Grant, all 1972; Canada Council B Grant, 1976, 1978, 1980; Ontario Arts Council Grant, 1977, 1987, 1991, 1994; Canada Council Short Term Grant, 1982, 1987; Ontario Arts Council Material Assistance, 1988; Canada Council Project Grant, 1989; Toronto Arts Award, 1990; Canada Council Senior Grant, 1993, 1994; Ontario

Vita, by Colette Whiten, at the Susan Hobbs Gallery, 2000. Photo by Isaac Applebaum. ©Colette Whiten.

Arts Council Exhibition Assistance, 1996; Ontario Arts Council Senior Grant, 1997; Toronto Arts Council Grant, 1998. **Agents:** Susan Hobbs Gallery, 137 Tecumseh St., Toronto, Canada M6J 2H2. **Address:** 1604 Dupont St., Toronto, Canada M6P 3S7.

Individual Exhibitions:

1973 Agnes Etherington Art Centre, Queen's University, Kingston, Ontario
Carmen Lamann Gallery, Toronto
1974 Scarborough College, University of Toronto, West Hill, Ontario
Carmen Lamanna Gallery, Toronto
1975 Carmen Lamanna Gallery, Toronto
1977 Carmen Lamanna Gallery, Toronto
1978 London Regional Art Gallery, London
Carmen Lamann Gallery, London
1979 McIntosh Gallery, University of Western Ontario, London
1980 Carmen Lamanna Gallery, Toronto
1981 Alberta College of Art, Calgary
1982 Carmen Lamanna Gallery, Toronto
1985 Carmen Lamanna Gallery, Toronto
1986 Carmen Lamanna Gallery, Toronto
1987 Carmen Lamanna Gallery, Toronto
1988 Powerhouse Gallery, Montreal
Oakville Galleries, Oakville
1989 Carmen Lamanna Gallery, Toronto
1992 The Power Plant, Toronto
1993 Galeria Carles Poy, Barcelona
Centre d'art d'Herblay, France
1994 Susan Hobbs Gallery, Toronto
1995 Oakville Galleries/Gairloch, Oakville, Ontario
1996 Susan Hobbs Gallery, Toronto
Galeria Carles Poy, Barcelona
1998–99 Susan Hobbs Gallery, Toronto
2000 Susan Hobbs Gallery, Toronto

Selected Group Exhibitions:

1973 *Biennale,* Musée d'Art Moderne de la Ville, Paris
1975 *Some Canadian Women Artists,* National Gallery of Canada, Ottawa
1976 *Forum 76,* Montreal Museum of Fine Arts, Montreal
1981 *Winnipeg Perspective 1981—Ritual,* Winnipeg Art Gallery, Manitoba
First Australian Sculpture Triennial, Bundoora, Victoria, Australia
1988 *Information Systems,* YYZ Gallery, Toronto
1989 *Canadian Biennial of Contemporary Art,* National Gallery of Canada, Ottawa

1993 *Witness,* Presentation House, Vancouver (travelling exhibition)
1994 *Borduren 2000,* Stedelijk Museum de Lakenhal, Leiden
1995 Samuel Lallouz Gallery, Montreal, Quebec
1996 Sameul Lallouz Gallery, Montreal, Quebec
1997 Museu d'Art de Girona, Spain
Telling Stories, Macdonald Stewart Art Centre, Guelph, Ontario
The Center for Freudian Analysis and Research, London
2000 Open Studio, Toronto
Overflo Gallery, Toronto
The ART Firm, Toronto

Collections:

Art Gallery of Ontario, Toronto; Canada Council Art Bank, Ottawa; National Gallery of Canada, Ottawa; Art Gallery of Hamilton, Ontario; Mendel Art Gallery and Civic Conservatory, Saskatchewan; Macdonald Stewart Art Centre, Guelph, Ontario.

Publications:

On WHITEN: Books—*Contemporary Canadian Art* by David Burnett and Marilyn Schiff, Hurtig, Edmonton 1983; *''Stealing the Show,'' Seven Women Artists in Canadian Public Art* by Gunda Lambton, 1994; *Survivors In Search of a Voice,* exhibition catalog by Barbara Amesbury, Toronto 1995; *Seducing the Receiver,* exhibition catalog by Marnie Fleming, Oakville, Ontario 1996; *Cegueses,* exhibition catalog by Susanna Portell, Girona, Spain 1997; *The Canadian Contemporary Figure,* exhibition catalog by Catherine Elliot Shaw, 1998. **Articles—**''Colette Whiten: Her Working and Work'' by John Noel Chandler in *Artscanada,* Spring 1972; ''In the Galleries—Toronto'' by Merike Weiler in *Artscanada,* October/November 1972; ''Colette Whiten'' by Connie Hitzeroth in *Artscanada,* May 1973; ''La participation canadienne a la 8 biennale de Paris'' by Laurent Lamy in *Vie des Arts,* Spring 1974; ''Art on the Edge of Empire'' by Robert Fulford in *Art News,* Summer 1974; ''The Sculpture of Colette Whiten'' by Joyce Zemans in *Artmagazine,* Fall 1974; ''Some Canadian Women Artists'' by Mayo Graham in *Artmagazine,* December 1975; ''Colette Whiten'' by Gary Michael Dault in *Artscanada,* Winter 1975–76; ''Henry Saxe, Robin Mackenzie, Irene Whittome, David Rabinowitch, Nobuo, Royden Rabinowitch, Colette Whiten'' by Luke Rombout in *Vanguard,* November 1976; ''The Vancouver Art Gallery: Three Fall Exhibitions'' by Ann Rosenberg in *Artmagazine,* December 1976-January 1977; ''Colette Whiten at Carmen Lamanna Gallery'' by Julianna Borsa in *Artmagazine,* August-September 1977; ''Persona: The Sculpture of Colette Whiten'' by John Noel Chandler in *Artscanada,* April-May 1978; ''Woman's Work'' by Marjorie Harris in *Chatelaine,* July 1978; ''Colette Whiten'' by Nancy Carroll in *Vanguard,* Summer 1980; ''Echoes from a European Tour'' by Pauline Andrea in *Artpost,* February-March 1987; ''Colette Whiten, Carmen Lamanna Gallery'' by Gregory Van Alstyne in *C Magazine,* 14 June 1987; ''Colette Whiten'' by Carol Laing in *Parachute,* June-August 1987; ''Prince Charming and the Associated Press: The Needlepoint Work of Colette Whiten'' by Elke Town in *Descant,* Winter 1987; ''Colette Whiten'' by Richard Rhodes in *Artforum,* May 1989; ''Janice Gurney et Colette Whiten'' by Catherine Bedard in *Parachute,* December 1988-February 1989; ''Colette Whiten'' by Nancy Campbell in *C Magazine,* Summer 1992; ''Colette Whiten'' by Janice Andreae in *Parachute,* July/August/September 1992; ''Relations of Power: Considering the Work of Colette Whiten'' by Janice Andreae in *Matriart,* 4, no. 2, 1994; ''Los Bordados de Colette Whiten'' by Mirjam Westen in *Arte/Facto,* September 1994; ''Doorgeprikt'' by Henriette Heezen in *Metropolis M,* February 1995; ''Seducing the Receiver'' by Sherri Telenko in *Matriart,* vol. 7, no. 1 & 2, 1997; ''Colette Whiten at Susan Hobbs'' by Gary Michael Dault in *Globe and Mail,* 28 October 2000.

* * *

At the heart of Colette Whiten's practice lies the paradoxical precept that the very success of the media in being able to tell us so much about the world actually diminishes our ability to act in the world. Through her art she demonstrates how reports of news events can be understood as to operate as a kind of anaesthetic in a world in which there is more and more information, and less and less meaning.

Her production has gone through several different phases in an art career which began formally in 1972. The early work investigated the mutability of the body through the nuances and variances of the casting medium. The body castings became a site in which viewers could judge the space of their own bodies. This sensual expressiveness, rendered with a certain classic aestheticism, eventually gave way to sculpture based not on memories of physical contact, but by contact with, and interest in, media information. By contrast, the work which followed in the 1980s was minimal in its material demands when compared with the earlier unwieldy and cumbersome body casting and structures. The later work consisted of small linens on which Whiten embroidered, in traditional cross-stitch, images of the kind experienced daily in the news media. Rendered in what is generally considered an unimportant female art practice, Whiten's needlework depicted shocking events such as the massacre at Tienanmen Square, tragedies in Beirut, and influential political leaders such as Mikhail Gorbachev, Ronald Reagan and Brian Mulroney.

From 1990 to 1992, Whiten copied newspaper pictures in which anonymous females played the principal part. In this work she focused on a half-dozen images selected from the relatively few news-wire photos that showed anonymous women as newsmakers. They were seen as mourning their dead, waiting to vote, protesting in the street, and finally, bearing arms against oppressors. Displayed on steel plinths, the embroidered cloth hung like skirts, while small overhead lamps illuminated the images. Together they formed a row that was both a statement of solidarity and a line of defence. This defensive empowerment seemed poignantly urgent after the scrutiny directed towards the world of male power in the previous needleworks.

One of Whiten's needleworks, called *Body Found* (1993–94), prompted a new series which critically probes the media fixation and the power structures of a renowned local murder trial. It is directed towards another traditionally female medium—that of beading. This medium permits her to continue to explore mass culture's representations of sexual difference, identity and power, and is also one in which she can expose and oppose stereotypes. She continues to depict women and bodies in crisis, but now they are no longer anonymous, they are named. Like the needlework, tiny bits of beads are required in order to build on an idea, and, in application, can mimic computer-generated images.

The current work consists of newsphotos translated into beadwork, accompained by two types of text—also rendered in beads—which emulate a variety of viewpoints. One type represents actual newsprint headlines that project the voice of authority, and, in black and white beads, declare: ''Muzzling of media by courts curtailed'' or ''Lawyers, lawmakers test public's right to know.'' In contrast, another type of text displays more apologetic remarks, such as: ''I'm sorry,'' or ''I'm doing the best I can.'' The later statements are ridden with guilt, despair, or lack of responsibility, and are so passive that the implied voices seem incapable of responding. Rendered in black and red beads these kinds of texts are evocative of popular LED news bulletins. Additionally the newsphotos translated into black, grey, silver and white beads offer another alternative; a collective perception. These photo-based images merely record without comment, much like the camera that took the original photograph reproduced in the newspaper, only to be reproduced in turn by Whiten's beading technique. News images of this kind are often interpreted in terms of cause and effect, and are invariably explained through the use of a narrative which obeys the structural requirement of having a beginning, middle and end. However, framed as they are by Whiten's texts, they reside in another exterior reality that allows the viewer to test or invent new meanings through a process of identification. Together, the three kinds of statements create an underlying tension, a resonating moment for all kinds of possible readings in which one can adopt a personal position.

Whiten's beadworks and her previous embroidery point to, yet transcend, the dichotomy between the traditional realm of crafts and the technology of electronic media. She conflates material that lacks authority—embroidery and beading—with one that signals it—news reports. The result conveys an understanding of current issues in contemporary media imagery. So too, in the process of converting the media images to these labour intensive processes, Whiten converts a widely dispersed and disposable image into a unique object. As objects, both the intense needleworks and the strands of beads have an aggressive substantiality that matches the constant barrage of media images on the mind.

Viewed as a whole, Whiten's practice does not provide us with the simplified notions of good or evil but rather with powerful images that tap into the part of us that has been invaded and colonized by the news media. Her main concern is to try to understand and unravel some of the implications for moral values of media technologies and, in the process, to encourage us to think for ourselves rather than to accept things as inevitable and the way they must be.

—Marnie Fleming

WHITEREAD, Rachel

Nationality: English. **Born:** London, 1963. **Education:** Studied painting at Brighton Polytechnic, 1982–85; studied sculpture at Slade School of Fine Art, 1985–87. **Career:** Sculptor; lives in London. **Awards:** Turner Prize, London, 1993; Honorary doctorate, Staffordshire University, 1997.

Individual Exhibitions:

1988 Carlisle Gallery, London
1990 *Ghost,* Chisenhale Gallery, London
1991 Arnolfini Gallery Bristol
Karsten Schubert Ltd., London
1992 *Rachel Whiteread: Recent Sculpture,* Luhring Augustine Gallery, New York
Rachel Whiteread: Sculptures, Centre Cultural, Fundacion Caja Pensiones, Barcelona
Rachel Whiteread: Sculptures, Stedelijk Van Abbemuseum, Eindhoven
1993 Galerie Claire Burrus, Paris
Rachel Whiteread: Sculptures, Muesum of Contemporary Art, Chicago (catalog)
House, commisioned by Artangel Trust and Becks, London (catalog)
Rachel Whiteread: Zeichnungen, DAAD Galerie, Berlin
1994 *Rachel Whiteread: Zeichnungen,* Galerie Aurel Scheibler, Cologne
Rachel Whiteread: Skulpturen/Sculptures, Kunsthalle, Basel (traveled to Institute for Contemporary Art, Philadelphia, and Institute for Contemporary Art, Boston) (catalog)
Rachel Whiteread: Drawings, Luhring Augustine Gallery, New York
1995 *Rachel Whiteread: Sculptures,* British School at Rome (catalog)
1996 *Rachel Whiteread,* Karsten Schubert Ltd., London
Rachel Whiteread: Sculptures, Luhring Augustine Gallery, New York
Rachel Whiteread: Shedding Life, Tate Gallery, Liverpool (catalog)
1997 Reina Sofia, Madrid
British Pavillion, Venice Biennale, Venice
1998 *Water Tower,* Public Art Fund, New York
Anthony d'Offay Gallery, London
1999 Luhring Augustine, New York
2000 *Watertower Drawing,* Luhring Augustine, New York
Judenplatz: Place of Rememberence, Vienna
Daybed, A/D, New York
2001 Serpentine Gallery, London
Scottish National Gallery of Modern Art, Edinburgh
Guggenheim Commissions, Berlin, Bilbao, and New York

Group Exhibitions:

1987 Whitworths Young Contemporaries, Manchester
1988 Riverside Open, London
Slaughterhouse Gallery, London
1989 *Concept 88 Reality 89,* University of Essex, Exhibition Gallery, Colchester
Whitechapel Open, London
1990 Victoria Miro Gallery, London
1991 *Metropolis,* Martin Gropius Bau, Berlin
Broken English, Serpentine Gallery, London (catalog)
Turner Prize Exhibition, Tate Gallery, London
1992 *Doubletake: Collective Memory and Current Art,* Hayward Gallery, London
Documenta IX, Kassel
New Voices: Recent Drawings for the British Council Collection, Centre de Conference Albert Borchette, Brussels (toured)
Sydney Biennale, Sydney, Australia
1993 *In Site: New British Sculpture,* The National Museum of Contemporary Art, Oslo (catalog)

New Voices: Jeunes Artistes Britanniques, Musé National d'Histoire et d'Art, Luxembourg (toured until 1995)
Made Strange: New British Sculpture, Museum Ludwig, Budapest
Drawing the Line Against Aids, Peggy Guggenheim Collection, Venice, and Guggenheim Museum Soho, New York

1994 *Sense and Sensibility: Women Artists and Minimalism in the Nineties,* The Museum of Modern Art, New York
Art Unlimited: Multiples from the 1960s and 1990s Arts Council Collection, South Bank Centre, United Kingdom (toured)

1995 *Ars 95,* Museum of Contemporary Art and Finnish National Gallery, Helsinki
British Art of the '80s and '90s: The Welkunks Collection, Irish Museum of Modern Art, Dublin
Brilliant: New Art From London, Walker Art Centre, Minneapolis, and Contemporary Arts Museum, Houston

1997 *47th Venice Biennale,* Venice
Sensation, Young British Artists from the Saatchi Collection, Royal Academy of Arts, London
A Decade of Collecting: Recent Acquisitions in Contemporary Drawing, Museum of Modern Art, New York (catalog)

1998 *Wounds,* Moderna Museet, Stockholm
REAL/LIFE: New British Art, Tochigi Prefectural Museum of Fine Art (toured Japan)

1999 *Sensation: Young British Artists from the Saatchi Collection,* Brooklyn Museum of Art, New York (catalog)

2000 *Art at MoMA since 1980,* Museum of Modern Art, New York
Longing and Memory, Los Angeles County Museum of Art, California

2001 *Public Offerings,* Los Angeles Museum of Contemporary Art, California
British Sculpture, British Council and Taipei Fine Arts Museum, Taiwan, and Singapore Art Museum, Singapore
Staatsgalerie, Munich

Publications:

On WHITEREAD: Books—*Doubletake: Collective Memory and Current Art,* edited Lynne Cooke and Greg Hilty, London 1992; *Rachel Whiteread,* exhibition catalog, text by Iwona Blazwick, Eindhoven, Stedelijk Van Abbemuseum 1992; *Rachel Whiteread: Plaster Sculptures,* exhibition catalog, London 1993; *Rachel Whiteread: Sculptures,* exhibition catalog, Eindhoven 1993; *Rachel Whiteread: Gouachen,* exhibition catalog, Berlin and Stuttgart 1993; *Invisible Museum: Seeing the Unseen,* exhibition catalog, London 1994; *House,* London 1995; *Rachel Whiteread: British Pavilion, XLVII Venice Biennale,* exhibition catalog, London 1997; *Looking Up: Rachel Whiteread's Water Tower,* edited by Louise Neri, London 1999. **Articles—**''Lawrence Winer, Rachel Whiteread,'' special issue of *Parkett* (Zürich), no. 42, December 1994; ''Inside Outcast'' by Mark Cousins in *Tate: The Art Magazine,* Winter 1996; ''Rachel Whiteread: Making Spaces that Matter'' by Rosalind Krauss in *Tate Magazine,* Winter 1996; ''The Struggle between Forgetting and Remembering'' by Robert Storr in *ARTnews,* March 1997; ''Behind Sealed Doors, Opening up the Past'' by Michael Kimmelman in *New York Times,* 30 October 2000. **Videos—***Excavating the House, ICA, London 1995,* VHS video and audiotape, London 1995; *Rachel Whiteread: House,* VHS video, London 1995.

* * *

An installation of Rachel Whiteread's work can seem like a necropolis. Once pliant everyday objects and once lively domestic spaces suffer, in her hands, a kind of *rigor mortis.* The homely hot water bottles, mattresses, and rooms that are cast by Whiteread in plaster or resin are often destroyed by this process. Even while eradicating their subjects, the casts preserve them in their tiny details and imperfections—nicks, scars, dents, bulges—and in this attention to surface speak to the kind of memory that is invoked by a sense of touch. The association of these works with death and loss is literalized by Whiteread's series of cast mortuary slabs, and reinforced by a biographical anecdote. The artist worked for a time on the grounds crew at Highgate Cemetery, where she fascinated by mouldering graves and crypts. ''Although I didn't want to look, I was curious. Peering through the cracks was, and remains, so compelling,'' Whiteread said in an 1992 exhibition catalog. However, the poetry and strength of Whiteread's work is not the result of a simple one-to-one relationship with tombstones or the macabre. Rather, it is to be found in what the lives of objects can tell us about ourselves.

Rachel Whiteread came to international art world prominence when she made *House* (1993), a concrete cast of an entire Victorian terraced house in London's East End. Anticipated by *Ghost* (1990), which Whiteread cast from a single room, *House* upped the ante by becoming public, rather than gallery-scale, art. Using a house slated for demolition as a mold, she sprayed concrete on the interior walls of the building and then peeled off the exterior ''skin.'' The result was a concrete negative of the house, which read from a distance as an impersonal geometric form. On closer inspection the work revealed traces of door jambs and windowpanes, evidence of a specific, abandoned home. Recalling Gordon Matta-Clark's *Splitting* (1974), in which that artist bisected a condemned house in suburban New Jersey, Whiteread's *House* called attention to a void in the urban landscape by replacing the house with a solid surrogate. The response to Whiteread's work at this time was extreme, in both a positive and a negative sense. *Untitled (Room)* (1993), a work cast from the interior of her studio in Berlin, won the prestigious Turner prize. Almost simultaneously, *House* sparked so much public controversy that it was demolished less than three months after its completion.

Whiteread's next public art project was installed on a rooftop at 60 Grand Street in the SoHo neighborhood of New York City. For this work, Whiteread adopted the form of a water tower, visible in every neighborhood on the Manhattan skyline, and used a cedar tank as a mold. Made of translucent resin that retains the texture of the wood from which it was cast, the finished work is nine feet tall and twelve feet in diameter. Well received by the critical press as well as by the general public, *Water Tower* is a relatively whimsical and gentle gesture, encouraging city dwellers to look more carefully at their everyday environment. Replacing the wooden structure with a substance resembling water, the piece is an inverted pun—water tower/tower of water. The work's luminosity—it shifts from soft green to milky white depending upon the light—and its seeming levitation delighted passersby. Initially conceived as a temporary installation, the piece was acquired by the Museum of Modern Art and installed on the museum's own roof when its run at 60 Grand Street had ended.

Whiteread's public art turned controversial once more, however, when she won a competition to design a Holocaust memorial for the city of Vienna. Although Whiteread's proposal was popular with the judges, including the architect Hans Hollein, the Nazi hunter Simon Wiesenthal, and the curator Robert Storr, objections were raised both by right wing groups who opposed the idea of a memorial at all, and by Jewish groups who did not appreciate the monument's minimal design. When the project was expanded to include a community center and museum to display the remains of a synagogue that were excavated from the square, support for the memorial was augmented to the point where it could be realized. The finished work was unveiled in October 2000 in a ceremony which included the president of Austria, the city's mayor, its chief rabbi, and its Roman Catholic Archbishop. The critic Michael Kimmelman echoed the sentiments of many when he wrote in the *New York Times*, ''Amplifying an appalling fact of history, it is an artistic and a civic achievement for Vienna, where a reckoning with the Nazi past was overdue.''

A large, concrete structure in the middle of a small Baroque square, the memorial is both obdurate and imposing. Revisiting the theme of cast interiors explored to different effect in *House* and *Water Tower,* Whiteread created a monument to the history and loss of Jews in Vienna in the form of a library turned inside out. It is a concrete block incised with what appear to be the pages of many shelved books, their spines facing inward. The only legible texts on the piece are the names of Nazi death camps inscribed around its base. The unreadable books, symbolic of the intellectual and spiritual production of a people, are rendered in unforgivingly ponderous material. As time goes by the concrete will age and layers of grime will accumulate on its surface. It will function, on one level, as a hairshirt for the community, while the adjacent community center and museum represent hope for the future.

Born in 1963, Rachel Whiteread is still a young artist. She will undoubtedly continue to create intelligent, moving works based on the talismans and spaces of everyday life.

—Robin Clark

WHITMAN, Robert

Nationality: American. **Born:** New York City, 1935. **Education:** Studied at Rutgers University, New Brunswick, New Jersey, 1953–57, B.A. 1957; also studied at Columbia University, New York. **Career:** Performance artist; lives and works in New York. **Address:** c/o Pace Wildenstein Gallery, 142 Greene Street, New York, New York 10012, U.S.A.

Individual Exhibitions:

1959 Hansa Gallery, New York
Reuben Gallery, New York
Rutgers University, New Brunswick, New Jersey
1963 9 Great Jones Street, New York (with Walter De Maria)
1967 Pace Gallery, New York
1968 Jewish Museum, New York
Museum of Contemporary Art, Chicago
1973 Museum of Modern Art, New York
1974 Bykert Gallery, New York
Galleria L'Attico, Rome
1975 Bykert Downtown Gallery, New York
1976 *Theatre Works 1960–1976,* Dia Art Foundation, New York
1979 Hudson River Museum, Yonkers, New York
1980 *Outdoor Performance Work,* Snug Harbor, Staten Island, New York
1995 PaceWildenstein Gallery, New York
1996 *Great Lakes,* Pace Wildenstein Gallery, New York

Selected Group Exhibitions:

1960 *New Forms—New Media,* Martha Jackson Gallery, New York
1962 *Environments, Situations and Spaces,* Martha Jackson Gallery, New York
1964 *6 Artists,* Sidney Janis Gallery, New York
1965 *11 from the Reuben Gallery,* Guggenheim Museum, New York
1966 *Erotic Art,* Sidney Janis Gallery, New York
1967 *Projected Art,* Finch College, New York
1968 *6 Artists, 6 Exhibitions,* Walker Art Center, Minneapolis
1969 *String and Rope,* Sidney Janis Gallery, New York
1971 *Art and Technology,* Los Angeles County Museum of Art
1974 *Projected Images,* Walker Art Center, Minneapolis
1999 *Off Limits: Rutgers University and the Avant-Garde, 1957–63,* Newark Museum, New Jersey

Collections:

Museum of Contemporary Art, Chicago; Jewish Museum, New York; Dia Center for the Arts, New York.

Publications:

By WHITMAN: Book—*19 Projects: Artists-in-Residence at the MIT List Visual Arts Center,* with Marie Cieri, Dana Friis-Hansen, Katy Kline, Helaine Posner, Cambridge 1996

On WHITMAN: Book—*Assemblages, Environments and Happenings* by Allan Kaprow, New York 1969. **Articles—**''Whitman Room'' in *Arts and Architecture* (Los Angeles), June 1964; ''7 New Artists at Janis'' by Sidney Tillim in *Arts Magazine* (New York), September 1964; ''Pearstein, Jagger, Whitman, Gutman'' by G. Brown in *Arts Magazine* (New York), September 1967; ''Mother Turn Off the Picture'' by Otto Piene in *Artscanada* (Toronto), June 1968; ''Magic Theatre, Une Exposition á Kansas City'' by S. Bann in *Oeil* (Paris), August September 1968; ''A Planned Coincidence'' by Dore Ashton in *Art in America* (New York), September/October 1969; ''Some Thoughts on 'Art and Technology''' by Jane Livingston in *Studio International* (London), June 1971; ''Corporate Art'' by Jack Burnham in *Artforum* (New York), October 1971; ''Bob Whitman and Things. . . . '' by George Segal in *Art and Artists* (London), November 1972; ''Machine Dreams'' by Ken Johnson in *Art in America* (New York), vol. 83, no. 7, July 1995.

* * *

Robert Whitman is a master of visual theatre-presentational performance which cohered in terms of imagery, rather than language or narrative. He was once regarded as a sometime visual artist, who had exhibited his paintings and sculptures, but had, unlike, say,

Oldenburg and Rauschenberg, abandoned those crafts to concentrate exclusively on theater; his willful concentration was, at the time, seen as a measure of serious purpose.

His masterpiece a decade ago was *Prune Flat* (1965), which was then curiously spelled "Prune. Flat." It opens with the image of a movie projector (implicitly announcing that one theme was cinematic images) and then shows a grapefruit (that nearly fills the screen) being cut by a knife. After other images, a tomato appears, which is also cut, black egg-like objects pour out; and when the tomato sequence is repeated, two young women dressed in white smocks and white kerchiefs appear in front of the screen, and the filmed blade cutting through them. As the film shows the two women walking down the street, one slightly behind the other, so the same two women walk across the stage, at a perpendicular angle to their images on the screen, but in the same formation. Later in the piece, the image of a woman undressing and showering is projected directly on the full length body of one of the women performers; but once the film shuts off, the woman who appears to be undressed is suddenly revealed to be definitely besmocked. The subject of *Prune Flat* is, of course, the perceptual discrepancies between filmed image and theatrical presence, and it differs from the other mixed-means pieces not only in its precise control but in its visual beauty.

Whitman staged other mixed-means pieces at the time, including the spectacularly scaled *Two Holes of the Water* (1966); but these tended to be diffuse and temporally flaccid. I have heard of earlier pieces of his, but did not see them until a retrospective was presented in the spring of 1976. The best innovation in *American Moon* (1960) was the positioning of the audience, which is divided into groups of ten, each assigned to a cubicle within a circular structure that looks into the performance area. In other words, that is "theatre-in-the-ground" with the audience subdivided by partitions. Translucent cloth screens separated each audience from the stage before them, and film is at times projected from behind on these individual screens, so that each section sees a different part of the movie. Once the curtains are raised, the climax of the piece is a cellophane structure that is blown up from an unheard source, the plastic filling the centerspace. Two performers walk through it. As a man is suspended in a swing above the space, the piece closes. *American Moon* struck me as the best of the other works in the retrospective, which included *Flower* (1963), *Nighttime Sky* (1965), *Salad PN.* (1974), in addition to a new work, *Light Touch* (1976). Though each of the others has stunning particulars, it is still *Prune Flat* that remains the most extraordinary of Whitman's theatrical pieces.

His work has always been uneven, and always exploratory. His forte is evocative, memorable imagery; his recurring failings include a leaden sense of theatrical time and sado-masochistic undertones.

Though I have already seen *Prune Flat* perhaps a dozen times, I would gladly see it again.

—Richard Kostelanetz

WIELAND, Joyce

Nationality: Canadian. **Born:** Toronto, 1931. **Education:** Studied under Carl Schaeffer, Doris McCarthy, and Bob Ross, Central Technical School, Toronto. **Family:** Married the artist Michael Snow. **Career:** Painter, filmmaker, and maker of quilts: worked for Graphic Associates, Toronto, 1956–58; lived in New York, 1963–70. **Awards:** Canada Council Grants, 1966, 1968; Toronto Arts Award, 1987. **Agent:** Isaacs Gallery, 179 John Street, Toronto, Ontario M5T IX3. **Died:** In Toronto, Canada, 27 June, 1998.

Individual Exhibitions:

1959 Isaacs Gallery, Toronto (with Gordon Rayner)
1964 Isaacs Gallery, Toronto
1967 National Gallery of Canada, Ottawa
1968 Vancouver Art Gallery (retrospective)
1971 *True Patriot Love,* National Gallery of Canada, Ottawa
1978 National Gallery of Canada, Ottawa
1979 Pauline McGibbon Art Centre, Toronto
1981 Isaacs Gallery, Toronto
1982 Forest City Gallery, London, Ontario
Yajima Galerie, Montreal
1983 Isaacs Gallery, Toronto
1985 Concordia University, Montreal
1987 Art Gallery of Ontario, Toronto
Confederation Art Gallery, Charlottetown, Prince Edward Island
1988 Beaverbrook Art Gallery, Fredericton, New Brunswick
Mackenzie Art Gallery, Regina, Saskatchewan
Canada House Gallery, London
1995 *Joyce Wieland: Twilight Record of Romantic Love,* Agnes Etherington Art Centre, Queen's University, Kingston (catalog)
2000 *The Female Nude,* Art Gallery of Ontario, Toronto
Focus: Joyce Wieland, Vancouver Art Gallery, Canada
Remembering Joyce Wieland, Canadian Film Institute, Ottawa

Selected Group Exhibitions:

1968 *Biennale of Canadian Paintery,* National Gallery of Canada, Ottawa
1970 *8 Artists from Canada,* Tel Aviv Museum
1971 *49th Parallels: New Canadian Art,* Ringling Museum of Art, Sarasota, Florida
1972 *Toronto Painting 1953–1965,* National Gallery of Canada, Ottawa
1976 *Une Histoire du Cinema,* Musée National d'Art Moderne, Paris
1977 *Canadian Tapestries 77,* Art Gallery of Ontario, Toronto
1981 *Twentieth Century Canadian Painting,* National Museum of Modern Art, Tokyo
1982 *Contemporary Outdoor Sculpture,* Guild of All Arts, Toronto
1983 *New Perceptions: Portraits,* Harbourfront Community Gallery, Toronto
1984 *Toronto Painting 84,* Art Gallery of Ontario, Toronto
1993 *The Art of the Self-Portrait,* Art Gallery of Windsor (catalog)
1994 *Split Personalities: Portraiture and the Imagination,* Norman Mackenzie Art Gallery, Regina, Saskatchewan (catalog)
1999 *A Century of Canadian Drawing,* Dalhousie Art Gallery, Halifax, Nova Scotia (catalog)

Collections:

National Gallery of Canada, Ottawa; Art Gallery of Ontario, Toronto; Montreal Museum of Fine Arts; Winnipeg Art Gallery; Norman Mackenzie Art Gallery, Regina, Saskatchewan; Edmonton Art Gallery, Alberta; Vancouver Art Gallery; Museum of Modern Art, New York: Philadelphia Museum of Art; Royal Belgian Film Archives, Brussels.

Publications:

By WIELAND: Article—interview, with Pierre Theberge, in *True Patriot Love,* exhibition catalog, Ottawa 1971. **Films**—*Larry's Recent Behaviour,* 1963; *Patriotism* (Parts 1 and 2), 1964; *Peggy's Blue Skylight,* 1964; *Barbara's Blindness,* with Betty Ferguson, 1965; *Water Sark,* 1965; 1933, 1967; *Hand Tinting,* 1967; *Sailboat,* 1967; *Catfood,* 1968; *Rat Life and Diet in North America,* 1968; *La Raison avant la Passion,* 1969; *Dripping Water,* with Michael Snow, 1969; *Pierre Vallières,* 1972: *Solidarity,* 1973; *The Far Shore,* 1976; *A and B in Ontario,* 1984; *Birds at Sunrise,* 1985.

On WIELAND: Books—*True Patriot Love,* exhibition catalog, Ottawa 1971; *Contemporary Canadian Painting* by William Withrow, Toronto 1972; *A Concise History of Canadian Painting* by Dennis Reid, Toronto 1973; *Joyce Wieland,* exhibition catalog with texts by Lucy Lippard, Marnie Fleming and Lauren Rabinovitz, Toronto 1987; *Points of Resistance: Women, Power & Politics in the New York Avant-Garde Cinema, 1943–1971* by Lauren Rabinovitz, Chicago 1991; *Sight Lines: Reading Contemporary Canadian Art,* edited by Jessica Bradley, Montreal 1994; *Female Gazes: Seventy-five Women Artists* by Elizabeth Martin, Toronto 1997; *The Films of Joyce Wieland,* edited by Kathryn Elder, Toronto, 1999. **Articles**—''Joyce Wieland at the Isaacs Gallery'' by David Donnell in *Canadian Art* (Ottawa), March/April 1964; ''Joyce Wieland Retrospective, Vancouver Art Gallery'' by Marguerite Pinney in *Artscanada* (Toronto), June 1968; ''There Is Only One Joyce'' by P. Adams Sitney in *Artscanada* (Toronto), April 1970; ''True Patriot Love'' by Harry Malcolmson in *Canadian Forum* (Toronto), June 1971; ''True Patriot Love: The Films of Joyce Wieland'' by Regina Cornwell in *Artforum* (New York), September 1971; ''Wieland: An Epiphany of North'' by Hugo McPherson in *Artscanada* (Toronto), August/September 1971; ''True Patriot Love: The Work of Joyce Wieland'' by D. Magidson and J. Wright in *Art and Artists* (London), October 1973; ''Building Power: Canadian Women's Art'' by Joan Murray in *Artpost,* vol. 9, no. 3, Summer 1992; ''Adieu to Two Pioneers'' by Maclean Hunter in *Maclean's,* vol. 111, no. 28, 13 July 1998; ''Surpassing Philosophy: The Life and Work of Joyce Wieland 1931–1998'' in *Filmwaves,* Issue 7, 1999.

* * *

Unlike most other artist members of Toronto's art community in her generation, most of whom attended the Ontario College of Art, Joyce Wieland was a graduate of the art course at Central Technical School. More important for her later development was her experimentation with film at Graphic Associates, where she worked from 1956 to 1958 as an animator. Much of Wieland's later work either uses filmic elements (as in her sequential painting referring to an unfolding of a succession of things in film strips) or is in film. It is as a movie-maker that she has secured her international reputation today, especially for her major feature film, *The Far Shore* (completed in 1976).

In her early stained paintings and collages of the late 1950s and early 1960s, Wieland often used sexual imagery, as in ''Time Machine Series.'' After 1965, the format of her work changed to framed or boxed constructions and serial paintings. The plastic collages of 1965 were stuffed and quilted movies called ''home totems.''

In her domestic art works she has tried to discover and explore her femininity. In the late 1960s, seeking a place for feminine work within the dominating male aesthetic, she pioneered the use of the quilt medium traditionally associated with women as a fine art form. Her quilts can hang on the wall or be used on a bed. In quilts she was able to express her spirited nationalism (she is a ''cultural activist'') and her love of nature. In one quilt the insert hidden under a flap reads, ''Down with U.S. Imperialist Technology.'' Elsewhere she may examine Canadian history.

The quilt is also a vehicle for her ecological concerns. In her ''Water Quilt'' there is a message under the 64 cushions with their 64 embroidered flaps of the Arctic flowers—the text is from James Laxer's ecological and political study, *The Energy Poker Game.* In 109 ''Views of Canada'' and ''Arctic Day'' she examines Canada and the much-disputed ecological area of the Canadian Arctic.

From 1977 on, in Wieland's drawings in coloured pencil, she explored stories of love and catalysm, landscape and light, ''drawing together all the things I care about in one place.'' The paintings which developed in this period, culminating with *The Artist on Fire* (1983), explored in rich colour the artist's self-image and ideals. After a retrospective in 1987 at the Art Gallery of Ontario (1987), Wieland went back to the freedom of her early abstractions and combined it with her basic themes of growth, nature, love and life.

—Joan Murray

WILEY, William T.

Nationality: American. **Born:** Bedford, Indiana, 21 October 1937. **Education:** San Francisco Art Institute, B.F.A. 1961, M.F.A. 1962. **Family:** Married Dorothy Ann Wiley, 1959: children: Ethan and Zane. **Career:** Independent artist incorporating verbal humor in paintings, sculpture and prints; lives and works in California. Associate professor, University of California at Davis, 1962–73; instructor, San Francisco Art Institute, 1963, 1966–67; art instructor, University of Nevada at Reno, 1967, Washington State College, Pullman, 1967, University of California at Berkeley, 1967, School of Visual Arts, New York, 1968, University of Colorado, Boulder, 1968. Between 1985 and 1991, engaged in creating, with Lippincott, Inc., and fabricating a 75-foot bronze sculpture, *The Tower,* in the Connecticut woods. **Awards:** Painting Prize, San Francisco Art Institute, 1959; First Prize, *San Francisco Art Institute Festival,* 1960; Fletcher Award, California School of Fine Arts, 1960; First Prize in Painting, *Oakland Annual,* 1960; New Talent Award, *Art in America,* 1961; Painting Prize, *65th Annual Exhibition,* Art Institute of Chicago, 1962; Sculpture Prize, Los Angeles County Museum of Art, 1962; Creative Arts Award, University of California at Davis, 1968; Purchase Prize, Whitney Museum, New York, 1968; Nealie Sullivan Award, San Francisco Art Institute, 1968; Bartels Prize, *72nd American Exhibition,* Art Institute of Chicago, 1976; Traveling Grant to

Australia; Australian Arts Council, 1980; American Academy and Institute of Arts and Letters Award, 1991. **Agent:** Wanda Hansen, 615 Main Street, Sausalito, California 95965, U.S.A. **Address:** P.O. Box 609, Forest Knolls, California 94933, U.S.A.

Individual Exhibitions:

1960 Staempfli Gallery, New York
San Francisco Museum of Art
1962 Staempfli Gallery, New York
1964 Staempfli Galley, New York
1965 Lanyon Gallery, Palo Alto, California
1967 Mills College, Oakland, California
1968 Hansen Fuller Gallery, San Francisco
Allan Frumkin Gallery, New York
1969 Hansen Fuller Gallery, San Francisco
Allan Frumkin Gallery, Chicago
1970 Allan Frumkin Gallery, New York
Keel Over, Madison Art Center, Wisconsin
1971 Hansen Fuller Gallery, San Francisco
Manolides Gallery, Seattle (with Robert Arneson)
Studio Marconi, Milan
Corcoran Gallery, Washington, D.C. (travelled to the University Art Museum, University of California at Berkeley and the Art Institute of Chicago)
1972 Hansen Fuller Gallery, San Francisco
Allan Frumkin Gallery, Chicago
James Manolides Gallery, Seattle
Margo Leavin Gallery, Los Angeles
Galleria Odyssia, Rome
Galerie Richard Foncke, Ghent
1973 Allan Frumkin Gallery, New York
Van Abbemuseum, Eindhoven, Netherlands
1974 Hansen Fuller Gallery, San Francisco
Allan Frumkin Gallery, Chicago
Utah Fine Arts Museum, Salt Lake City
1975 Hansen Fuller Gallery, San Francisco
3 One Man Shows: Willian T. Wiley, Dorothy Hood, Armando Morales, University of Texas at Austin
1976 Allan Frumkin Gallery, New York
Project Room, Museum of Modern Art, New York
1977 Galerie Paul Faccheti, Paris
New Publicications, Landfall Press Gallery, Chicago
Suite of Daze, Art Institute of Chicago
1978 Hansen Fuller Gallery, San Francisco
Myra Morgan Gallery, Shawnee Mission, Kansas
Delahunty Gallery, Dallas, Texas
1979 *Graphics 1967–1979,* Allan Frumkin Gallery, New York and Chicago
Prints, Baltimore Museum of Art (retrospective)
1980 Hansen Fuller Goldeen, San Francisco
Prints, Illinois State University, Normal
Prints and Sculpture, San Jose Museum of Art, California
Cornish Institute of Allied Arts Gallery, Seattle
Glen Hanson Gallery, Minneapolis
Realities Gallery, Melbourne (travelled to the Institute of Modern Art, Brisbane)
Redding Museum, Redding, California
1981 Allan Frumkin Gallery, New York
Emily Carr College of Art, Vancouver
Florida State University, Tallahassee (travelled to Florida International University, Miami, and the University of South Florida, Tampa)
Wiley, Territory Walker Art Center, Minneapolis (travelled to Dallas; Denver; Des Moines; San Francisco; Phoenix)
1983 Hansen Fuller Gallery, San Francisco
Allan Frumkin Gallery, New York
1985 Alberta College of Art, Calgary (travelled to Chicago)
1986 *Steal Witness for the Time Being,* Newport Harbor Art Museum, Newport Beach, California (travelled to Palm Springs; Boise; Seattle; San Francisco)
Moore College; Philadelphia (travelled to New York)
Fuller Goldeen Gallery, San Francisco
Hammarskjold Plaza Sculpture Garden, New York
Marsha Mateyka Gallery, Washington. D.C.
1987 *What Is Not Music?,* Galerie Grita Insam, Vienna (travelled to Frankfurt)
What Is Not Drawing?, L.A. Louver Gallery, Venice, California
1988 *Paintings, Drawings, Watercolors,* Max Protech Gallery, New York
Recent Work on Paper, Marsha Mateyka Gallery, Washington, D.C.
Recent Paintings and Drawings, Richard L. Nelson Gallery, University of Califorina at Davis
1989 Marsha Mateyka Gallery, Washington, D.C.
New Paintings, Constructions and Watercolors, Struve Gallery, Chicago
Fuller Gross Gallery, San Francisco
1990 Riva Yares Gallery, Scottsdale, Arizona
Graphics, Persons & Lindell, Helsinki, Finland
Fables, Cuesta College Art Gallery, San Luis Obispo, California
1991 *Struck! Sure? Sound/Unsound,* Corcoran Gallery of Art, Washington, D.C. (traveled to Contemporary Arts Center, Cincinnati; Southeastern Center for Contemporary Art, Winston-Salem; Laguna Art Museum, California)
Recent Paintings and Watercolors, Marsha Mateyka Gallery, Washington, D.C.
Robert Hudson: Sculpture/William T. Wiley: Paintings, Rose Art Museum, Brandeis University, Waltham, Massachusetts
What Is Not Dancing in Time?, L.A. Louver Gallery, Venice, California
New World Odor, Max Protetch Gallery, New York
San Diego Museum of Contemporary Art, California
1992 *One Man's Moon,* Marian Locks Gallery, Philadelphia
Small Paintings, L.A. Louver Gallery, Venice, California
1993 *William T. Wiley with William Allan: Double Bill,* Marsha Mateyka Gallery, Washington, D.C.
Rena Bransten Gallery, San Francisco
Indiana State University, Bloomington
1994 *Forest Series,* Locks Gallery, Philadelphia
Recent Work, Max Protech Gallery, New York
Afterburner, Rena Bransten Gallery (catalog)
1996 *Nothing Lost from the Original: William T. Wiley Looks at Art History,* M. H. de Young Memorial Museum, San Francisco

William T. Wiley: Watching the World, Walker Hill Art Center, Seoul (traveled to Locks Gallery, Philadelphia) (catalog)

1997 *William T. Wiley: ''Realistic Abstractions, Where Now & Then Colludes,''* Marsha Mateyka Gallery, Washington, D.C. (catalog)

Performance:

Over Evident Falls, with Steve Reich, Sacramento, California, 1968.

Selected Group Exhibitions:

1973 *Extraordinary Realities,* Whitney Museum, New York
1974 *Surrealitat-Bildrealitat 1924–1974,* Städtische Kunsthalle, Dusseldorf
1976 *Three from California,* Dalhousie Art Gallery, Halifax, Nova Scotia
1983 *Minimalism to Expressionism,* Whitney Museum, New York
1985 *Content: A Contemporary Focus 1974–84,* Hirshhorn Museum, Washington, D.C.
1987 *International Art Show for the End of World Hunger,* toured throughout U.S. and Europe.
20th Century Drawings from the Whitney Museum of American Art, National Gallery of Art, Washington, D.C. (toured U.S.)
1988 *Committed to Print,* Museum of Modern Art, New York
1990 *The Trans Parent Thread: Asian Philosophy in Recent American Art,* Hofstra Museum, Hofstra University, Hempstead, Long Island (toured U.S.)
1991 *Exhibition of Work by Newly Elected Members and Recipients of Honor and Awards,* American Institute of Arts and Letters, New York
1996 *Made in L.A.: The Prints of Cirrus Editions,* Los Angeles County Museum of Art (catalog)
1997 *A Singular Vision: Prints from Landfall Press,* Museum of Modern Art, New York (catalog)
1998 *Collaborations,* Palm Springs Desert Museum (catalog)
1999 *''What is Art For?,''* Oakland Museum of California
2000 *Crossroads of American Sculpture,* Indiana Museum of Art (catalog)

Collections:

San Francisco Museum of Modern Art; University Art Museum, University of California at Berkeley; Oakland Museum, California; Museum of Modern Art, New York; Whitney Museum, New York; Art Institute of Chicago; Fort Worth Art Center, Texas; Des Moines Art Center, Iowa; University of Kansas Art Museum, Lawrence; Van Abbemuseum, Eindhoven, Netherlands.

Publications:

By WILEY: Articles: ''William T. Wiley'' in *Art Press,* Special Issue, no. 17, 1996; interview with Mary Hull Webster in *Artweek,* vol. 27, March 1996; ''A Conversation with Mary Hull Webster and William T. Wiley'' with Juan Rodriguez in *Artweek,* vol. 30, no. 6, June 1999. **Films—***The Great Biondino,* San Francisco 1967; *Man's Nature,* San Francisco 1971; *Doubtsidersarte,* San Francisco 1999.

On WILEY: Exhibition catalogs—*Funk* by Peter Selz, Berkeley 1967; *Wizdumb,* with introduction by Brenda Richardson, Berkeley 1971; *William T. Wiley: Retrospective,* with introduction by J. Leering, Eindhoven 1973; *Wiley Territory,* with texts by Graham Beal and John Perreault, Minneapolis 1979: *William T. Wiley,* with essays by Beth Coffelt, Matthew Kangas, John Perreault and others, Tallahassee 1981; *Steal Witness for the Time Being,* with introduction by Albert Stewart, North Haven 1984; *William T. Wiley: Recent Paintings and Watercolors,* with essay by Sarah McFadden, Philadelphia and New York 1986; *What Is Not Music,* with texts by Peter Weiermair and Ben Marks, Frankfurt and Vienna 1987; *William T. Wiley at Crown Point Press,* by Constance Lewallen, New York and San Francisco 1989; *The 1980s: Prints from the Collection of Joshua P. Smith,* edited by Ruth E. Fine, Washington, D.C. 1989; *Contemporary Illustrated Books: Word and Image, 1967–1988,* by Donna Stein, New York 1990; *A Different War: Vietnam in Art,* by Lucy R. Lippard, New York 1990; *West Art and the Law: An Exhibition of Work by Contemporary Artists Interpreting the Law and Society in Our Times,* St. Paul, Minnesota 1991; *William T. Wiley: Struck! Sure? Sound/Unsound,* by Terrie Sultan, edited by Christopher French, Washington, D.C. 1991; *Here and Now: Bay Area Masterworks from the di Rosa Collections,* by Phillip Linhares and Rene di Rosa, Oakland, California 1994. **CD-ROM:** *Crossroads of American Sculpture,* Project Media 2000.

*

Hunger . . . For A Statement
Driven? By Something? I (We)
Don't Understand? We (I) Praise
Sing Dance Deny And Die In
The Face. Make? Pictures
Of Living, Dying, Becoming.
Knowledge Cannot Seem To Help
Much, Nor Suffering. . .
What Is Not Food?

—William T. Wiley

* * *

The surrealist elements that run through William Wiley's paintings and constructions are tempered by a kind of zany, dude dadaism and beguiling lyricism. A look at his work reveals an honest love of the land and a genuine child-like interest in minutia. This quality in turn is reflected in Wiley's style. In his two-dimensional works there are unmistakable references to comic strips, coloring books and children's book illustrations. Applied to the adult world of landscape painting, mysticism and ecology they create an off-balance, fresh quality that is part of Wiley's distinction.

He seems very much a California artist but one who's been as they say, around. Any naivete he may display is strictly *faux.* His work abounds in visual and verbal puns. Yes, verbal. He is an artist much given to words. He likes to write all over his work—to include passages from logs, or notebooks, or fragments from letters to or from friends. He belongs to a kind of circle of like-minded fellow artists and there are constant cross-references to the work, lives, personalities, etc., of the circle.

Wiley's draughtsmanship is very fine with live, strong, *interesting* line, a little like those picture puzzles where you are supposed to locate and identify various hidden images. This incorporation of commonplace, popular material is somewhat related to Pop art—in the way, say, of relating to such things as Andy Warhol's color-me-by-numbers paintings. But Wiley's interests and direction are far more consciously ''artistic'' in technique than the products of most Pop artists. It can even be said that, in the end, his work has elegance.

This is related to the lyricism I spoke of and goes along with a gentleness and whimsy characteristic of much of Wiley's output. He likes to draw imaginary maps, to make charts and give directions. Besides orthodox painting on canvas he often introduces the third dimension incorporating feathers, rope, sticks, string, branches, etc., suggestive of American Indian artifacts, of camping trips, of cowboys-and-Indians. There are echoes of fetishism and secret rites, of poetry and religion, of children's games in his work and its success lies in the imaginative synthesis he has made from such complex and various subject matter. His work suggests that of a man deeply sympathetic to the American Far West and to the development of twentieth-century art—a kind of pioneer who's read Proust.

—Ralph Pomeroy

WILLATS, Stephen

Nationality: British. **Born:** London, 17 August 1943. **Education:** Studied under Roy Ascott at Ealing College of Art. **Family:** Married Felicity Oliver in 1974; sons (from previous marriage): Justin and Nicholas. **Career:** Founder, *Control* magazine, London, 1965; founder, Centre for Behavioural Art, London, 1972–74. Lecturer, Ipswich School of Art, Suffolk, 1965–67, and Nottingham College of Art, 1968–72; part-time lecturer in sculpture, Hornsey College of Art, London, 1969–71; D.A.A.D. Fellowship, West Berlin, 1979–80; Stephen Willats Printed Archive established at the Victoria and Albert Museum, 1991. **Agents:** Lisson Gallery, 68 Bell Street, London NWI, England; Rüdiger Schöttle, Martiusstrasse 7, 8000 Munich 40, West Germany. **Address:** 5 London Mews, London W2 7HY, England.

Individual Exhibitions:

1964 Chester Beatty Research Institute, London
1968 Museum of Modern Art, Oxford
1971 *Man from the 21st Century,* Nottingham
1972 *Social Resource Project for Tennis Clubs,* Nottingham
West London Social Resource Project, London
Oxford Insight Development Protect, Oxford
1973 Gallery House, London
Edinburgh Social Model Construction Project, Edinburgh
1974 Gallery December, Monster, West Germany
1975 Galleria Banco, Brescia, Italy
The Gallery, London (toured the U.K)
1976 Midland Group Gallery, Nottingham
Lisson Gallery, London
Stampa Gallery, Basel
1977 *From a Coded World,* London
Attitudes Within 4 Relationship, Southhampton Art Gallery
1978 *Contained Living,* Museum of Modern Art, Oxford
Questions about Ourselves, Lisson Gallery, London
1979 *Concerning Our Present Way of Living,* Whitechapel Art Gallery, London
The Lurky Place, Galerie Schweinabraden, East Berlin
Berlin Wall Drawing, Rüdiger Schöttle Galerie, Munich
4 Professionals, Lisson Gallery, London
1980 *Concerning Our Present Way of Living,* Stedelijk van Abbemuseum, Eindhoven, Netherlands
4 lnseln in Berlin, Nationalgalerie, Berlin
1981 *4 Inseln in Berlin,* Gothe Institute, London
Mens en Omgeving, De Beyerd Centrum voor beeldende Kunst, Breda, Netherlands
1982 *Meta Filter and Related Works,* Tate Gallery, London
The New Reality, Orchard Gallery, Londonderry, Northern Ireland
1983 *Angst in den Strasse,* Galerie Rüdiger Schöttle, Munich
Inside the Night, Lisson Gallery, London
Under Cover, Arnolfini Gallery, Bristol
1984 *Means of Escape,* Rochdale Art Gallery, Greater Manchester
Another City, Riverside Studios, London
1985 *Doppelganger,* Lisson Gallery, London
Double Crossing, Galerie Ralph Wemicke, Stuttgart
1986 *City of Concrete,* Ikon Gallery, Birmingham
Grusse vom Modernen Lebe, Stadtische Galerie, Regensburg, West Germany
Groeten uit her moderne leven, Museum van Hedendaagse Kunst, Utrecht, Holland
Concepts and Models, Institute of Contemporary Arts, London
Vier Huizen in Den Haag, Haags Gemeentemuseum, Den Haag, Holland
Striking Back, Mappin Art Gallery, Sheffield, Yorkshire
Fragments of Modern Living, Galerie Tanja Grunert, Cologne
1987 *Contemporary Living,* Museum van Hedendaagse Kunst, Ghent, Belgium
Concepts and Projects Bookworks, Nigel Greenwood Books, London
Between Objects and People, Leeds City Art Gallery, Yorkshire
1988 *Transformers,* Laing Art Gallery, Newcastle
Code Breakers, Torch Gallery, Amsterdam
Ralph Wernicke, Stuttgart
1989 *Secret Lanugage,* Cornerhouse Gallery, Manchester
1990 *Mosaics,* Galerie Kaj Forsblom Helsinki, Finland
Galerie Barbara Farber, Amsterdam
1991 *Publishing Interventions,* National Art Library, Victoria & Albert Museum, London
Conceptual Living, Victoria Miro, London
Concrete Window, Galerie Montevideo, Antwerp
1992 *Signs of Living,* Galerie Gabriela Maubrie, Paris
1993 *Buildings & People,* Berlinische Galerie, Berlin
Multiple Clothing, Institute of Contemporary Art, London
Walking Between Objects, Galerie Franck & Schulte, Berlin
Buildings & People, Goethe Institute, London
1994 *Multiple Clothing,* Daniel Buchholz, Cologne

Museum Mosaic, Tate Gallery, London
Random Life, Victoria Miro Gallery, London
1995 *Living Together,* Tramway, Glasgow
A State of Agreement, Galerie Franck & Schulte, Berlin
Writing on the Wall, Galerie Kaj Forsblom, Helsinki (traveled to Reinhard Hauff at Galerie Archim Kubinski, Stuttgart)
1996 *In Response to Each Other,* Galerie Brandstetter & Wyss, Zurich
Du Hasard A l'Accord, Galerie Gabrielle Maubrie, Paris
1997 *Street Talk,* Gallery Victoria Miro, London
Between Me and You, Middlesbrough Art Gallery
1998 *Random Encounters,* Southampton City Art Gallery
Changing Everything, South London Art Gallery
Creative Force, Mappin Art Gallery, Sheffield
Multicult Berlin, Galerie Granck & Schulte, Berlin
Concepts, Strategies & Models 1962–65, Gimpel Fils, London
Blind Date With Reality, Galerie Brandstetter & Wyss, Zurich
1999 *Multichannel Vision,* Galerie Reinhard Hauff, Stuttgart
2000 *Macro to Macro,* Gallery Laure Genillard, London

Selected Group Exhibitions:

1966 *Kunst Licht/Kunst,* Stedelijk van Abbemuseum, Eindhoven, Netherlands
1967 *Light and Movement,* Herbert Art Gallery, Coventry (toured the U.K.)
1972 *Cognition Control,* Midland Group Gallery, Nottingham (toured the U.K.)
1975 *Codes and Structures,* Royal College of Art, London
1977 *Social Criticism and Art Practice,* San Francisco Art Institute
1985 *The British Show,* Art Gallery of New South Wales, Sydney (toured Australia)
1986 *The Art of Peace Biennale,* Kunstverein, Hamburg
1987 *Art and Craft in the Twentieth Century,* Laing Art Gallery, Newcastle-upon-Tyne
1988 *New Reform Retrospective, 1970–79,* Cultural Centre, Aalst, Belgium
1993 *The Ideal Place,* HCAK Den Haag, Holland
1994 *Outsiders,* Camerawork, London
Conceptual Living, Rhizome, Amsterdam, Holland
1995 *Mapping Knowledge,* The Minories Gallery, Colchester
Ars 95 Helsinki, Helsinki, Finland
La Transparence Dans L'Art Du XXe Siecle, Museum des Beaux-Arts Malraux, Le Havre, France
1996 *Les Contes de Fees se Terminent Bien,* Frac Haute-Normandie, Chateau du Val Freneuse, Sotteville-sous-le-Val
Radikale Images, 2nd Austrian Triennale for Photography, Neue Galerie, Graz (catalog)
Everybody's Talking, Gemeentemuseum Helmond, Holland
1997 *Sous le Manteau,* Galerie Thaddaeus Ropec, Paris
The Grand Design, The Art of the Victoria and Albert Museum (also Baltimore Museum of Art)
1998 *Addressing the Century: 100 Years of Art and Fashion,* Hayward Gallery, London
1999 *Nur Wasser Lasst Sich Leichter Schneiden,* Hamburg
Bildung, Grazer Kunstverien, Graz, Austria
2000 *Democracy,* Royal College of Art, London
Live In Your Head, Whitechapel Art Gallery, London
Raw, Victoria Miro Gallery, London

Collections:

Tate Gallery, London; Arts Council of Great Britain, London; British Council, London; City Art Gallery, Southhampton; Gallery of Modern Art, Edinburgh; Stedelijk van Abbemuseum, Eindhoven, Netherlands; De Beyerd Museum, Breda, Netherlands.

Publications:

By WILLATS: Books—*The Artist as an Instigator of Changes in Social Cognition and Behaviour,* Gallery House Press, London 1973; *Art and Social Function,* London 1976; *The Lurky Place,* Lisson Gallery, London 1978; *Ich Lebe in einem Betonklotz,* Cologne 1980; *Cha Cha Cha,* London 1982; *Intervention and Audience: A Synopsis,* London 1984; *Doppelganger,* London 1985; *Intervention and Audience,* London 1986; *The House that Habitat Built,* Cornerhouse, Manchester 1989; *Society through Art,* HCAK Den Haag, Holland 1990; *White Towers,* Helsinki 1990; *Stairwell,* London 1990; *Multistorey Mosaic,* London 1990; *Book Mosaic,* London 1991; *Corridor,* Gent, Belgium 1991; *Personal Islands,* London 1993; *Multiple Clothing,* London 1993; *Balcony,* London 1994; *Stephen Willats: Between Buildings and People,* London 1996; *Shopping Parade: Bilton Road—Stills From the Film,* Toronto 1997; *The Art Museum in Society,* Middlesbrough 1997. **Articles—**Statement in *Control No. 2* (London), 1966; statement in *Studio International* (London), February 1967; statement in *Control No. 3* (London), 1968; statement in *Structure No. 1* (London), October 1968; statement in *Art and Artists* (London), January 1969; "Behavioural Nets and Life Structures" in *The Paper* (Trent Polytechnic, Nottingham), 1971; statement in *Platform* (Nottingham), 1972; "West London Social Resource Project" in *Studio International* (London), January 1973; "Art and Social Function" in *Art and Artists* (London), June 1973; "The Edinburgh Project" in *Art and Artists* (London), January 1974, "Meta Filter" in *Art and Artists* (London), November 1974; "Meta Filter" in *Flash Art* (Milan), November 1974; "The West London Social Resource Project" in *Leonardo* (Oxford), 1974; "Meta Filter" in *Studio International* (London), September 1975; "A State of Agreement" and "A Survey of Distance Models of Art" in *Control No. 9* (London), 1975; "Book as Interactive Tool: The Modelling Book" in *Artists' Bookworks,* exhibition catalog, London 1975; "Social Codes and Behaviour Parameters: An Area of Concern for Art" in *Life Codes and Behaviour Parameters,* Nottingham 1976; "Art Work as a Social Model" in *Studio International* (London), March/April 1976; "From a Coded Word" in *Studio International* (London), vol. 194, 1978; "Working with the Work of Art" in *Art Monthly* (London), April 1979; "Contained Reality" in *Art Monthly* (London), April 1979; "Contained Reality" in *Art Monthly* (London), no. 3, 1980; "Kulturciter Druck" and "West Berlin als Kulturelles Symbol" in *Stephen Willats,* exhibition catalog, Berlin 1980; "Doppelganger," interview with Antonia Nyne, in *Studio International* (London), no. 1011, 1985; interview with Gareth Jones in *Flash Art,* vol. 27, no. 179, November-December 1994; interview with Vitus H. Weh in *Kunstforum International,* no. 143, January-February 1999.

On WILLATS: Books—*Un Certain Art Anglais,* exhibition catalog with text by Sandy Naime and others, Paris 1979; *Stephen Willats: Leben in vorgegebenen Grenzen/4 Inseln in Berlin,* exhibiton catalog with essay by Arno Hoffmann, West Berlin 1980; *The Artist as Photographer* by Marina Vaizey, London 1982; *New Art,* exhibition catalog by Michael Compton, London 1983; *The British Show,* exhibition catalog with texts by Richard Francis and others, Sydney 1985; *Stephen Willats,* exhibition catalog with texts by Michael Archer and Manfred Schmalriede, London 1986; *Between Objects and People,* exhibition catalog, Leeds 1987; *Transformers,* exhibition catalog, Newcastle 1988; *Torch Gallery,* exhibition catalog, Amsterdam 1988; *Secret Language,* exhibition catalog, Manchester 1989; *Conceptual Living,* exhibition catalog with text by Stephen Willats and Stephen Bann, London 1991; *Buildings and People,* exhibition catalog, Berlin 1993. **Articles—**review in *Artscribe,* Setember/October 1988; "High Rise to Heaven" by Andrew Wilson in *Artscribe,* November/December 1991; "Buildings and People" by Toni Del Renzio in *Art Monthly,* December 1993.

*

MEANS OF ESCAPE

Throughout my work I present two states of social consciousness that are in continual cultural opposition.

There is an institutional, authoritatively mapped out social consciousness, its ramifications affect everyone, and in my work it is contrasted with a social consciousness of self-organization that expresses mutuality and personal creativity. For I see that within every person there is the potential of creative self expression, but that this is inhibited and repressed by the authoritative determinism that underpins the physical and social composition of the everyday world. Counter-consciousness is the creative response of people to express their own sensibility and psychology. The presentation of these two different, and culturally opposed ways of perceiving reality, has directed both my working procedure and the visual composition of each work. The concept of self organization is not only symbolically represented in my work, but the actual process of its internalization by the audience involves them in acts of cognitive self-organization, for they construct their own means of escape.

Symbols

It is a fundamental part of my working procedure to search for and identify symbols that are residual in the culture and which will powerfully represent, to an audience, the two opposed states of consciousness I have just described. First I look for obvious symbols of the deterministic, object-based consciousness, and then I uncover balancing expressions of people's self organization and statements of self-identity. My starting point is the physical manifestations of our culture's institutional idealizations and self projections.

Contexts

At the same time as I am searching to identify symbols that represent the object-based consciousness, I am revealing simultaneous, and contrasting, expressions of counter consciousness. The symbols of counter consciousness that I see as a counter balance revolve around self-organized contexts that have been established by people as a vehicle for their own expressions of creativity. Such contexts are not only hard to identify but are difficult to access as, by their very nature, they exist undercover in the inaccessible, forgotten corners of society, often directly repressed and usually alienated from their surroundings.

However, the establishing of a context or capsule is still dependent on the dominant culture, for it has to co-exist, being reliant on it as a source of material. Here lies the really creative act, which requires objects from the dominant culture, with their attendant pre-determined function, to be transformed into an agent for manifesting the counter consciousness. The set determinism given to the object by the dominant culture is broken by it being appropriated by the creators of the counter consciousness, becoming an agent for their self-organization.

Objects

Different objects have particular importance to different groups of creators of counter consciousness, and in each of my works about particular people I identify those objects that are central to them personally. These identified objects actually become part of my work so as to confront the audience with the reality they are viewing. Objects that are central to the audience's world are symbolically mirrored in the actual objects that have been incorporated into my work.

Audience

My works present the audience with a layer of references by depicting the same reality through various media forms. Each layer of references sets up disparate cues so that there is not a pre-formed, legislated, single view, but instead the disparate references are self-connected by the audience to create their own model. The audience make their own journey, their own transformations, between the cues associated with each state of consciousness; from the day to the night, the housing estate to the wasteland, from the conscious to the unconscious. My organization of the layout of the references from which the work's symbolic world is formed I consider essentially a parallel process to the audience's process of de-constructing and internalizing those disparate references into a coherent model. Thus the active, self-organization required from the audience in their cognitive relationship with a work is in itself a creative act, an expression of counter consciousness, and in this way the ideology that is its governing force is externalized. The work is the audience's means of escape.

—Stephen Willats

* * *

Stephen Willats' work is based on a critique of the isolated and elitist art practice of the 1950s and 1960s and the specialist society that engendered such art. Noting the imbalance between theory and practice in much modernist art, he has tried to correct this by being especially concerned with the theory which underlies and informs his work, publishing articles and pamphlets and editing a magazine *Control* which is a forum for theoretical discussion on contemporary art. By making use of advances made in the technological and social science fields, which have begun to allow greater interaction between previously unrelated social groups, he has aimed to reach an audience not normally concerned with art, at the same time enabling them to understand the conditioning by which a manipulative society extends its controls. To reach an audience unused to according art proper attention, he had to develop ways in which to change the artist/art work/spectator relationship away from an idea of art as commodity and decoration to one in which it is seen as a resource to be used by the whole community in a co-operative effort towards tolerance and understanding. These ideas have informed his work since the mid-1960s.

Initially the work of the late 1960s and early 1970s was seen as part of the Kinetic Art movement, and in so far as it made use of light and electronic systems this may have seemed appropriate, but the similarity is seen as superficial if we look at the methods and underlying meaning of such works as the ''Visual Meta Language Simulation'' of January 1972. This simulates the process by which separate decision-making organizations can cooperate to their mutual benefit with the minimum of antagonism. It consists of a Problem Display Box on which incomplete patterns are illuminated and two Decision Boxes on which the remainder of the pattern appears. Each Decision Box is worked by one participant. Although initially motivated by competition, the winning operator is progressively handicapped until only cooperation between operators enables completion of the game. The work enacts symbolically a decision-making process based on a system in which each unit is given equal information and effectiveness as opposed to the current pyramidal model in which information and decision-making is the prerogative of a few.

Other areas of Stephen Willats' work have had a more immediate social relevance, such as the series of Projects from 1965 in Ipswich, London, Nottingham, Oxford and Edinburgh. One of the most successful was the West London Social Resource Project of 1972. This aimed to allow normally unrelated social groups to arrive at common models of their environment based on need. Four social groups were selected from areas of West London which were near enough to be visited by one another but seen as distinctly separate neighbourhoods. Using door to door techniques participants were gathered and a manual distributed. In the manual were a series of questions to be answered and tasks to be performed, the results of which were shown each day on display boards in the local library. As the complexity of the decision-making in the manual increased, so the participation between separate social groups developed. In this way people were enabled to rethink traditional ideas about their environment and to replace them with an ''adaptive, self-organizing, evolutionary'' social structure in which competition was replaced by cooperation. The documentation is now available in the library of Osterley used during the project and is discussed at length in Stephen Willats' book *Art and Social Function,* 1976.

''Meta Filter'' 1973–75 is a direct development of the projects. It is a machine on which two participants symbolically enact the movement away from an individual, coded view of the world towards areas of common agreement. Working through a series of slides and using a thesaurus to describe the states represented, the operator, given the object of agreement attempts to understand the responses of his/her partner, to break through his restrictive perceptions to mutual understanding. The work breaks with traditional art practice; participation is not confined to an elite, for the images and language used are open to everyone. At the same time the work criticizes contemporary social divisions while offering a possible alternative.

The active participation of the spectator is necessary too for the works which take the form of panels with photographs and written descriptions. ''Person A'' of June 1974 is a series of six large and 12 smaller panels and a form to aid viewing. The spectator is asked to choose the most fitting description of the photograph in terms of behaviour states, attitudes etc., and is then directed to another photograph to continue the process. A narrative is built up which starts to affect responses to later panels; not only does the viewer posit how ''Person A'' might behave in a particular situation, but also by bringing his unique set of experiences to bear on the work he starts to comprehend how his own attitudes are achieved through a coded system which may well disguise or distort the real meaning of behaviour. The concept of relativism is used positively in this work, for though the primary meaning is constant, the process by which it is understood will depend on the experiences brought to bear.

Other panel works such as ''Perceptions of a Married Couple'' of June 1975, and ''Attitudes within Four Relationships'' of March 1976 are more complex, making use of two or more people and presenting a more contextualised situation. The reading of these works depends on a relationship between the coded panel and the process by which the spectator decodes and then encodes the information to attain understanding.

In Stephen Willats' work the artist becomes an active instigator of social change as opposed to a passive mirror of current idealogy. His work breaks out of the isolated context of much contemporary art to reach a wider audience and the artist attains a more meaningful position in society.

—Jane Kelly

WILLENBECHER, John

Nationality: American. **Born:** Macungie, Pennsylvania, 5 May 1936. **Education:** Mercerburg Academy, Pennsylvania, 1950–54; studied art history at Brown University, Providence, Rhode Island, 1954–58, B.A. 1958; Institute of Fine Arts, New York University, 1958–61. **Career:** Independent artist, since 1962. Instructor in painting, Philadelphia College of Art, 1972–73; artist in residence, Dartmouth College, Hanover, New Hampshire, 1977. Lives and works in New York. **Member:** New York City Art Commission, 1980–92. **Awards:** MacDowell Colony Fellowship, New Hampshire, 1974, 1980; National Endowment for the Arts grant, 1977; Gottlieb Foundation grant, 1994; G.S.A. commission for the Court House and Federal Building, Providence, R.I., 1982; commission for ''Labyrinth,'' outdoor pavilion and plaza, Minneapolis Institute of Arts, 1993. **Address:** 145 West Broadway, New York, New York 10013. U.S.A.

Individual Exhibitions:

1963 Feigen/Herbert Gallery, Los Angeles
Feigen/Herbert Gallery, New York
1964 Richard Feigen Gallery, Chicago
1965 Richard Feigen Gallery, New York
1966 Richard Feigen Gallery, New York
1967 Richard Feigen Gallery, Chicago
1970 Richard Feigen Gallery, Chicago
1971 Lambert 910 Gallery, New York
1973 A. M. Sachs Gallery, New York
1975 A. M. Sachs Gallery, New York
Bell Gallery, Brown University, Providence, Rhode Island
Everson Museum, Syracuse, New York
1976 Alberta College of Art, Calgary
Olympia Gallery, Philadelphia
Arts Club of Chicago
1977 Hamilton Gallery, New York
University of Massachusetts Art Gallery, Amherst
Wright State University Art Gallery, Dayton, Ohio
Jaffe-Friede Gallery, Dartmouth College, Hanover, New Hampshire
1978 Fine Arts Center, University of Rhode Island, Kingston
Burning Tetrahedron, Artpark, Lewiston, New York
1979 *Day and Night,* Hamilton Gallery, New York (with Janet Stayton)

John Willenbecher 1970–1978, Allentown Art Museum, Pennsylvania (travelled to the Neuberger Museum, State University of New York at Purchase)
Dart Gallery, Chicago
Tetrahedron, Wave Hill, Riverdale, New York
1980 *Capriccios and Grottos,* Hamilton Gallery, New York
1981 *Susan Hail/John Willenbecher,* Hamilton Gallery, New York
1982 Hamilton Gallery, New York
1986 New York Academy of Sciences, New York
1993 *John Willenbecher: 1972 and 1992,* Minneapolis Institute of Arts
1996 *John Willenbecher: Five Paintings,* University of New Mexico Art Museum, Albuquerque

Selected Group Exhibitions:

1964 *Boxes,* Dwan Gallery, Los Angeles
1965 *Young Americans,* Whitney Museum, New York
1966 *Kunst-Licht-Kunst,* Stedlijk Museum, Eindoven, Netherlands
1968 *Annual Exhibition of Sculpture,* Whitney Museum, New York
1977 *Contemporary Tableaux/Constructions,* University of California at Santa Barbara
1980 *Marking Black,* Bronx Museum of the Arts, New York
1984 *El Arte Narrativo,* Museo Rufino Tamayo, Mexico City
1987 *Faux Arts: Surface, and Simulated Materials,* La Jolla Museum of Contemporary Art, California
1991 *El Sueno de Egipto,* Centro Cultural Arte Contemoraneo, Mexico City
1992 *Among Friends,* Detroit Institute of Arts
1996 *After Dark: Nocturnal Images,* Barbara Mathes Gallery, New York

Collections:

Guggenheim Museum, New York; Metropolitan Museum of Art, New York; Whitney Museum, New York; Chase Manhattan Bank Collection, New York; ATT Corporation Collection, New York; Neuberger Museum, State University of New York at Purchase; Museum of Art, Rhode Island School of Design, Providence; Hirshhorn Museum and Sculpture Garden, Washington, D.C.; Art Institute of Chicago: Centre Georges Pompidou, Paris; Minneapolis Institute of Arts; New York Public Library.

Publications:

On WILLENBECHER: Books—*John Willenbecher,* exhibition catalog with an essay by Ronald Onorato, Syracuse, New York 1975; *John Willenbecher,* exhibition catalog, Philadelphia 1976; *The Commonplace Books of John Willenbecher,* Dayton, Ohio 1977; *John Willenbecher 1970–1978,* exhibition catalog with an essay by Jean-Louis Bourgeois, Allentown, Pennsylvania, and Purchase, New York 1979. **Articles**—"John Willenbecher" by Diane Waldman in *Artnews* (New York), February 1967; "John Willenbecher" by Max Kozloff in *Artforum* (New York), March 1975; "Through the Labyrinth: The Art of John Willenbecher" in *Art International* (Lugano, Switzerland), 20 March 1975; "John Willenbecher: Pyramids, Spheres and Labyrinths" bv William Wilson in *Arts Magazine* (New York), March 1975; "The Modern Maze" by Ronald Onorato in *Art International* (Lugano, Switzerland), April/May 1976; "Janet Kardon Interviews Some Modern Maze Makers" in *Art International* (Lugano, Switzerland), April/May 1976; "John Willenbecher" by Paul Gardner in *Arts Magazine* (New York), November 1977; "John Willenbecher's Burning Tetrahedron" by J. Kirk T. Varnedoe in *Arts Magazine* (New York), December 1978; "John Wlllenbecher" by Ronny Cohen in *Artforum* (New York), April 1982; "John Willenbecher and the Riddle of Grandeur" by Dan Cameron in *Arts Magazine* (New York), September 1983.

* * *

John Willenbecher's artworks have remarkable strong iconic presence. Based on archetypal forms like the circle, square and arch, his two- and-three dimensional objects impress as richly elegant but emotive objects.

Though trained as an art historian, Willenbecher preferred the active role of making art to the passive role of studying it. In 1963 he exhibited several examples from his early series of black boxes, filled with orderly, compartmentalized arrangements of simple forms—like balls—behind glass. The theme of this series was "unknown games of chance," and the sleek and autonomous/mechanistic look of the forms reflected the then dominant Pop and Minimalism sensibilities.

Willenbecher continued to make boxes through the middle 1960s and varied the colors—"Gold and White" (1964)—and the inside contents which mostly consisted of globes and balls. Some of them even lit up. And his boxes should be viewed within the context, then, of the period's fascination with this form found also in versions, say, by Joseph Cornell, Louise Nevelson, Richard Artschwager. By the late 1960s the circle and square, the forms emphasized in the boxes were joined by the arch. Based on "found" wooden window frames, the arches were used as the support for different mixed mediums constructed paintings.

In the late 1960s, also, he began to investigate the labyrinth. He explored both the formal and thematic aspects of this clear but deliberately convoluted structure in many of the works through the middle 1970s. Fraught with architectural associations and psychological sensations, involving traps and enclosures, the labyrinth served as the subject of both constructed relief objects and the 2-dimensional paintings. In "The Ladder and the Labyrinth" (1970) he centered a circular shaped labyrinth from which extended a small ladder on a rectangular ground. in "Labyrinth 23.IX.72" (1972), he painted a circular labyrinth around a sphere and centered these motifs on arch-shaped masonite. The labyrinth paintings, in turn, were the source for a group of painted triptychs which consisted of schematic renderings of enclosed structures—arch within square, circle within arch—from 1974 to 1975. Maze-like configurations also appear in another major series of works: the cenotaphs. With arched frames on which various geometric motifs were painted, the cenotaphs also contained a built-out shelf section on the lower edge upon which three-dimensional objects like spheres, tetrahedrons and even ladders were placed. Measuring about chest size, these works bring to mind the memorial function of the cenotaphs which inspired them. The group made in homage to Etienne-Louis Boullée, the eighteenth-century Neo-classical visionary architect, in 1974 are among the most moving.

Shelves also appear in the lower edges of the constructions in the next important series named after *Das Lied ven der Erde* of Gustav Mahler, 1975–77. In 1977 he emphasized the circle, square and the ladder in a group of large-scale, floor constructions directly inspired by designs of Dürer and Goethe. The recent works find Willenbecher returning to the contained and specific relief pieces of the cenotaph group. The series "Laureate" (1980–81) consists of arch-shaped wooden frames that each encase a masonite support, painted to simulate marble; a circle in the form of a gold-leaf wreath adorns each surface. A tribute to creativity, the "Laureate" pictures reveal renewed interests in fine-tuning the pictorial qualities and turning them towards symbolic ends.

—Ronny Cohen

WILSON, Fred

Nationality: American. **Born:** Bronx, New York, 1954. **Education:** State University of New York, Purchase, B.F.A., 1976. **Career:** Served on the board of directors, Artists Space, 1988–92, National Association of Artist Organizations, 1988–92; board member, Artists/Homeless Collaborative, since 1994; board member, Sculpture Center, New York, since 1995; member of board of governors, Skowhegan School of Painting and Sculpture, since 1995. Panelist, Visual Arts Program, National Endowment for the Arts, 1989–91, and InterArts Program, National Endowment for the Arts, 1989–91. **Awards:** New York Foundation for the Arts fellowships, 1987, 1991; New York State Council on the Arts Award, 1990; National Endowment for the Arts Award, 1990; commission, Percent for Art Program, Department of Cultural Affairs, 1991; commission, Riverside South Public Art, New York, 1992; National Endowment for the Arts Fellowship, 1994; Artist and the Community Award, Winston-Salem Foundation, Rockefeller Foundation and North Carolina Arts Council, 1995; New Jersey Transit and New Jersey Council on the Arts Award, 1995; MacArthur Foundation Genius Award, 1999. **Agent:** Metro Pictures, 150 Greene St., New York, New York 10012, U.S.A.

Selected Individual Exhibitions:

1988 Public Art Fund, New York
1990 *The Other Museum,* White Columns, New York
1991 Metro Pictures, New York
Washington Project for the Arts, Washington, D.C.
Gracie Mansion Gallery, New York
1992 *Biennial,* Cairo, Egypt
Metro Pictures, New York
Mining the Museum, Maryland Historical Society, Baltimore
1993 *The Museum: Mixed Metaphors,* Seattle Art Museum (catalog)
Indianapolis Museum of Art
Beaver College Art Gallery, Glenside, Pennsylvania
Capp Street Project, San Francisco
1994 Museum of Contemporary Art, Chicago
"Insight: In Site: In Sight; Incite—Memory," Artist and the Community: Fred Wilson, Southeastern Center for Contemporary Art, Winston-Salem, North Carolina
1995 Metro Pictures, New York (catalog)
1996 Beaver College Art Gallery, Glenside, Pennsylvania
Rice University Art Gallery, Houston
1997 Richard L. Nelson Gallery and Fine Arts Collection, University of California, Davis

Selected Group Exhibitions:

1981 A.I.R. Gallery, New York
1985 Kenleleba Gallery, New York
1987 55 Mercer Gallery, New York
1990 Clocktower Gallery, New York
1993 Whitney Museum of American Art, New York
Museum of Modern Art, New York
Studio Museum in Harlem, New York
1996 The Drawing Center, New York
Institute of Contemporary Art, Boston
Museum of Art, Fort Lauderdale, Florida
1998 *Parasite,* The Drawing Center, New York (catalog)
1999 *To the Rescue: Artists in an Archive,* International Center of Photography, Midtown, New York (catalog)
The Museum As Muse: Artists Reflect, The Museum of Modern Art, New York (catalog)

Collections:

Baltimore Museum of Art, Maryland; Denver Art Museum; Kresge Art Museum, Michigan State University; New School for Social Research; Seattle Art Museum.

Publications:

By WILSON: Articles—"Making the Museum Mine: An Interview with Fred Wilson" in *Museum News,* vol, 72, no. 3, May-June 1993; "Interviews with Sherrie Levine, Louisa Lawler, and Fred Wilson" by Martha Buskirk in *October,* vol. 70, 1994; "The Silent Message of the Museum" in *Global Visions: Towards a New Internationalism in the Visual Arts,* edited by Jean Fisher, London 1994; "Silent Messages" in *Museums Journal,* vol. 95, May 1995.

On WILSON: Books—*Mining the Museum: An Installation by Fred Wilson,* edited by Lisa G. Corrin, New York 1994. **Articles**—"The Museum Mine Field" by Susannah Cassedy in *Museum News,* vol. 71, July-August 1992; "Redecorating the White House" by Ann B. Stoddard in *New Art Examiner,* vol. 20, February 1993; "Allegories of Cultural Criticism: Re-framing the Present" by Joshua Decter in *Flash Art,* no. 170, May-June 1993; "Mining the Museum: An Installation Confronting History" by Lisa G. Corrin in *Curator,* vol. 36, December 1993; Fred Wilson" by Martha Buskirk in *October* (Cambridge, Massachusetts), no. 70, Fall 1994; "Sins of Omission" by Judith E. Stein in *Art in America,* October 1994; "The Museum and Society" in *Studies in Modern Art,* no. 7, 1998; "Object Lessons" by Pamela Newkirk in *Art News,* vol. 99, no. 1, January 2000.

* * *

American artist Fred Wilson creates installations that investigate the hidden implications and assumptions of the practice of museum display. In an attempt to make information easy to understand and palatable to the viewer, museum professionals frequently ignore complex issues, thereby simplifying and distorting meaning. Wilson manipulates standard museum practices to reveal major deficiencies and omissions.

In the late 1980s, Wilson developed ''mock museums'' using reproductions and fabricated objects. These installations underscored the ways that curatorial practices affect the public's interpretation and understanding of museum collections. For *Rooms with a View: The Struggle Between Culture, Content and Context in Art* (1987–88), Wilson simulated three distinct display scenarios: ethnographic museum, Victorian salon, and contemporary gallery. He placed visual art by thirty artists into these environments. The ethnography museum grouped objects according to type, with vague labels identifying the artistic medium but not the maker. The Victorian salon granted the works a rarefied aura, suggesting precious *objets d'art* through selective lighting and ornate pedestals. In the all-white contemporary gallery, works seemed ultra-modern.

Rooms with a View so thoroughly transformed audience perceptions of the works of art that Wilson decided to take on the institutional practices of museums. *The Other Museum* (1991) presented African masks that were blindfolded with the flags of their French and British colonizers. Masks labeled ''Stolen from the Zonga tribe'' reminded visitors that the unethical aspects of acquisition are hidden from the public. Wilson displayed the masks in dramatically colored spaces with theatrical lighting to emphasize how museums use visual techniques to conceal negative aspects of the history of their collections.

To create the exhibition *Mining the Museum* (1992–93), Wilson used art and artifacts from the Maryland Historical Society (MHS) in Baltimore to investigate both African-American and Native American experiences in Maryland. The title of the installation is a double-entendre; the collection at MHS provided a ''gold mine'' of ideas, and Wilson reinstalled it from his own point of view (he is of African and Carib Indian descent). He used startling juxtapositions of objects, label text, selective lighting, slide projections, and sound to force viewers to question the constructedness of history.

The various displays in *Mining the Museum* explored historical issues that are vastly different from those typically presented in museums. For example, the exhibit opened with three white pedestals bearing white marble busts of historic persons (Napoleon, Henry Clay, and Stonewall Jackson). Three empty black pedestals placed near them were labeled ''Harriet Tubman,'' ''Benjamin Banneker,'' and ''Frederick Douglass'' (all Marylanders). Wilson forced viewers to ask themselves: Where are the busts of these prominent personages? Did no one see fit to ''collect'' or commemorate them? Whose truth is on exhibit? Whose history is being told?

Wilson reinterpreted and rearranged portions of the displays of the permanent collection at the Seattle Art Museum for his exhibition titled *The Museum: Mixed Metaphors* (1993). He incorporated some new items and also added videos, documentary photography, labels, text, and commentary. His display in the African art galleries countered the typical museum installation that situates Africans in a romanticized, ''primitive'' past and denies them contemporary realities. In a large display case, Wilson combined a Western-style suit, commonly worn today in Africa, with traditional garments, textiles, and carvings. To this same case he added an architectural model by a contemporary African architect and photographs of large African cities. Through strategic additions and juxtapositions like these, Wilson brings new significance to the practice of museum display.

—Joyce Youmans

WILSON, Robert M. (Byrd Hoffman)

Nationality: American. **Born:** Waco, Texas, 4 October 1941. **Education:** Studied painting with George McNeil, Paris, 1962: studied architecture at the Pratt Institute, New York, 1962–65, B.F.A. 1965; served apprenticeship in architecture to Paolo Soleri, Phoenix, Arizona, 1965–66. **Career:** Performance artist, New York, since 1966: directed theatre pieces with patients at Goldwater Memorial Hospital, New York, 1967–68; taught awareness classes, New Jersey Art Center, 1968–69, and movement classes for children, Bedford-Stuyvesant, Brooklyn, New York, 1968–69; artistic director, Byrd Hoffman Foundation, New York, since 1970. **Awards:** Award for Best Foreign Play, Syndicat de la Critique Dramatique et Musicale, Paris, 1970; Drama Desk Award, for direction, New York, 1971; Obie Special Citation Award, for direction, New York, 1974; Lumen Award for Design, New York, 1977; Guggenheim Fellowship, 1980; Rockefeller Foundation Award, New York, 1981; Skowhegan Drawing Medal, Maine, 1987; Bessie Award, 1987; American Theatre Wing Design Award, 1987; Mondello Award (Italy), 1988; Institute Honour, American Institute of Architects, New York, 1988; New York Public Library Lion of the Performing Arts, 1989; Grand Prize, Sao Paulo Biennial, 1989; Premio Abbiati, Italian Theatre Critics Award, 1989; German Theatre Critics Award, Best Production of the Year, Berlin, 1990; Special Mention, Festival du Film d'Art, 1990; Jack I. and Lillian Poses Creative Arts Award, Brandeis Univeristy, 1991; Honorary Doctorate, Pratt Institute, New York, 1991; Premio Ubu, Best Foreign Performance, Milan, 1992; Golden Lion Award in Sculpture, Venice Biennale, 1993; Honorary Doctorate, California College of Arts and Crafts, Oakland, 1994; Premio Ubu, Best Foreign Performance, Milan, 1994; Texas Artist of the Year, Art League of Houston, 1995; Premio Abbiati, Italian Theater Critics Award, Milan, 1995; Best Director, International Widescreen Festival, Amsterdam, 1995; Dorothy and Lillian Gish Prize, New York, 1996; Premio Europa per il Teatro, Taormina, Italy, 1997; Tadeusz Kantor Prize, Crakow, Poland, 1997; Robert Wilson Day (April 18) declared by Texas State Legislature, 1997; B-Z Kulturpries, Berlin, 1997; Honorary Award, 11th International Istanbul Theatre Festival, Puskin Prize, Moscow, 1998; Harvard Excellence in Design Award, Harvard University, 1999; Pushkin Prize, Moscow, Taganka Theater, 1999; Médaille d'Argent de la Foundation de l'Academie d'Architecture, Paris, 1999; Wilhelm Hansen Honourable Prize, Copenhagen, 1999; American Academy of Arts and Letters, Honorary Member, 2000; Best Foreign Production, Grand Prix de la Critique, 1999/2000. **Address:** Byrd Hoffman Foundation, 155 Wooster Street, Suite 4F, New York, New York, 10012. **Web site:** http://www.robertwilson.com.

Individual Exhibitions:

1966 Byrd Hoffman Studio, New York
1967 *Theatre/Activty,* Bleecker Street Cinema, New York
1968 Grailville School, Loveland, Ohio
ByrdwoMAN, Byrd Hoffman Studio, New York
1969 *The King of Spain,* Anderson Theatre, New York
The Life and Times of Sigmund Freud, Brooklyn Academy of Music, New York
1970 *Deafman Glance,* University Theatre, Iowa City, (toured Europe and the United States)
1971 *Program Prologue Now: Overture for the Deafman,* Espace Pierre Cardin, Paris

Willard Gallery, New York (with Ann Wilson)
1972 *Overture,* Byrd Hoffman Studio, New York (toured France and Iran)
KA Mountain and Guardenia Terrace, Haft Tan Mountain, Shiraz, Iran
1973 *King Lyre and Lady in the Wasteland,* Byrd Hoffman Studio, New York
The Life and Times of Joseph Stalin, Det Ny Tearer, Copenhagen (travelled to Brooklyn Academy of Music, New York)
1974 *A MAD MAN A GIANT A MAD DOG A MAD URGE A MAD FACE,* John F. Kennedy Center, Washington, D.C. (toured the United States)
Musée Galliera, Paris (with Christopher Knowles)
Prologue to a Letter for Queen Victoria, Spoleto, Italy
A Letter for Queen Victoria, Municipal Theatre, La Rochelle, France (toured France, Switzerland and the United States)
1975 *Die $ Value of Man,* Brooklyn Academy of Music, New York
Einstein on the Beach, New York
1977 Multiples/Marian Goodman Gallery, New York
1978 Paula Cooper Gallery, New York
1979 Galerie Zwinger, Cologne
Multiples/Marian Goodman Gallery, New York
1980 Contemporary Arts Center, Cincinnati, Ohio
State University of New York at Purchase
1981 *Medea,* Washington Project for the Arts, Washington, D.C.
1982 Marian Goodman Gallery, New York
Galerie le Dessin, Paris
Galerie Annemarie Verna, Zurich
Stadtische Museum im Lenbachhaus, Munich
Galerie Fred Jahn, Munich
Franz Morat Institut, Freiburg, West Germany
1983 Pavilion des Arts, Paris
Galerie Brinkman, Amsterdam
Museum Boymans-van Beuningen, Rotterdam
Produzentgalerie, Hamburg
Festival Mondial du Theatre, Nancy, France
Gallery Ueda, Tokyo
Sogetsu School, Tokyo
Castelli-Feigen-Corcoran Gallery, New York
Rhode Island School of Design, Providence
1984 Paula Cooper Gallery, New York
Otis Art Institute, Los Angeles
Jones Troyer Gallery, Washington, D.C.
Walker Art Center, Minneapolis
Museo di Folklore, Rome
Centre d'Art Contemporain, Marseille, France
Kunstverein, Cologne
1985 Galleria Franca Mancini, Pesaro, Italy
Kamnierspiele, Munich
Institute of Contemporary Art, Boston
1986 University of Iowa, Iowa City
Kemo Gallery, Albuquerque, New Mexico
Theater in der Kunsthalle, Hamburg
Laguna Gloria Museum, Austin, Texas (retrospective)
Grey Art Gallery, New York
Lehman College, Bronx, New York
Carnegie-Mellon University, Pittsburgh
Kuhlenschmidt Gallery, Los Angeles
Alpha Gallery, Boston
Rhona Hoffman Gallery, Chicago
1987 Paula Cooper Gallery, New York
1988 Marlene Eleini Gallery, London
1989 Stedelijk Museum, Amsterdam
Scuola d'Arte Drammatica, Milan
1990 Virginia Lynch Gallery, Tiverton
Kunsthalle Shirn, Frankfurt
1991 Centre Georges Pompidou, Paris
Palais Stutterheim, Erlangen
Paula Cooper Gallery, New York
1992 Instituto Valenciano de Arte Moderno, Valencia, Spain (catalog)
Kamakura Gallery, Tokyo
Galerie Thaddaeus Ropac, Paris
1993 Deichtorhallen, Hamburg
Waco Creative Art Center, Waco, Texas
Museum Boymans-van Beuningen, Rotterdam
1994 Paula Cooper Gallery, New York
Akira Ideda Gallery, New York
Gallery Biederman
1995 Galerie Thaddaeus Ropac, Salzburg
Hiram Butler Gallery, Houston
Joyce Ma Gallery, Paris
1996 Galerie Lehmann, Lausanne
Paula Cooper Gallery, New York
Galerie Thaddeus Ropac, Paris
1997 Museum Villa Stuck, Munich
Waco Art Center, Texas
1998 Palazzina dei Giardini, Modena, Italy
Museum of Contemporary Art, Chicago
1999 Hiram Butler Gallery, Houston
Galerie Papiers Gras, Geneva
Petit Palais, Musée des Beaux-Arts de la Ville de Paris
2000 Solomon R. Guggenheim Museum, New York and Bilbao, Spain
Location One, New York
Paula Cooper Gallery, New York
Galeria Krzysztofory, Cracow
2001 Bernier, Eliades Gallery, Athens

Selected Group Exhibitions:

1965 *Worlds Fair,* New York
1972 *Overtue,* Musée Galliera, Paris
1980 *Further Furniture,* Marian Goldman Gallery, New York
1981 *Other Realities,* Contemporary Arts Museum, Houston
1982 *American Drawings of the the Seventies,* Louisiana Museum, Humlebaek, Denmark (travelled to Basel, Munich and Ludwigshafen)
1983 *Art and Dance, 1890–1980,* State University of New York, Purchase
1984 *Survey of Contemporary Painting and Sculpture,* Museum of Modern Art, New York
1985 *High Style,* Whitney Museum, New York
1986 *The Painter and the Theatre in the Twentieth Century,* Schirn Kunsthalle, Frankfurt
1988 *Zeichenkunst der Gegenwart,* Staatliche Graphische Sammlung, Munich

1989 *The Arts for Television,* Contemporary Arts Museum, Houston
1990 *Video and Dream,* Museum of Modern Art, New York
1991 *Interactions,* Institute of Contemporary Art, Philadelphia
1992 *10th World Wide Video Festival,* Kijkhuis, The Hague
1993 *Drawing the Line Against AIDS,* AMFAR, Venice Biennale
1994 *Outside the Frame,* Cleveland Center for Contemporary Art (also Snug Harbor Cultural Center, Staten Island)
1995 *Un Cuore Per Amico,* Triennale de Milano, Italy
1996 *Black Grey & White,* Dusseldorf, Galerie Bugdahn und Kaimer
1997 *1997 Biennial Exhibition,* Whitney Museum of American Art, New York
1998 *Countenance,* Galerie Thaddeus Ropac, Salzburg
1999 *The World of Design,* Prague Quadrennial
2000 *World Stage Design,* York Quay Gallery, Harbourfront Centre, Toronto
Acchrochage, The Norwood Gallery, Austin, Texas

Collections:

Art Institute of Chicago; Australian National Gallery, Canberra; Bank of America, San Francisco; Centre Georges Pompidou, Paris; Contemporary Arts Center, Cincinatti; Cooper-Hewitt Museum, New York City; Fonds d'Art Contemporain, Paris; Galerie der Stadt, Stuttgart; Grey Art Gallery, New York University, New York City; Hamburger Bahnhof Museum für Gegenwart, Berlin; Huntington Art Museum, University of Texas, Austin; Kunstmuseum, Berne; Los Angeles County Museum of Contemporary Art; Menil Foundation Collection, Houston; Metropolitan Museum of Art, New York City; Musée d'Art Contemporain, Pully/Lausanne; Museum of Art, Rhode Island School of Design, Providence; Museum Boymans van Beuningen, Rotterdam; Museum of Contemporary Art, Los Angeles; Museum of Fine Arts, Boston; Museum of Fine Arts, Houston; Museum of Modern Art, New York City; Parrish Art Museum, Southampton, New York; Philadelphia Museum of Art, Philadelphia; Stedelijk Museum, Amsterdam; Toledo Museum of Art, Toledo, Ohio; Virginia Museum of Fine Arts, Richmond; Vitra Design Museum, Weil am Rhein, Germany; Waco Art Center, Waco, Texas; Walker Art Center, Minneapolis; Whitney Museum of Contemporary Art, New York City.

Publications:

By WILSON: Books—*The King of Spain in New American Plays,* New York 1970; *Two Conversations with Edwin Denby,* New York 1973; *A Letter for Queen Victoria,* Paris 1974; *Einstein on the Beach,* with Philip Glass, New York 1976; *I Was Sitting On My Patio This Guy Appeared I Thought I Was Hallucinating,* New York 1978; *Death Destruction and Detroit,* New York 1978, West Berlin 1979; *The Golden Windows,* Munich 1982; *The Civil Wars: A Tree Is Best Measured When It Is Down (Rotterdam section),* Amsterdam and Paris 1983; *The Civil Wars: A Tree Is Best Measured When It Is Down (Cologne section),* Frankfurt 1984; *The Civil Wars: A Tree Is Best Measured When It Is Down (Rome section),* Rome 1984; *The Civil Wars: Drawings Models and Documentation,* Los Angeles 1984; *The Civil Wars: A Tree Is Best Measured When It Is Down (Act III Scene E; Act IV Scene A, and Epilogue),* with Heiner Muller, Cambridge, Massachusetts 1985; *Robert Wilson and His Collaborators,* with Lawrence Shyer, New York 1990; *Robert Wilson: Convidados de Piedra,* with Jan Linders, Madrid 1992. **Articles**—interview with Philippe du Vignal in *Art Press,* no. 163, November 1991; interview with Julia Kristeva and Catherine Francblin in *Art Press,* no. 191, May 1994; interview with Jean Poderos in *Beaux Arts Magazine,* no. 161, October 1997.

On WILSON: Books—*Il Teatro di* Robert Wilson by Franco Quadri, Venice 1976; *The Theater of Visions: Robert Wilson* by Stephan Brecht, Frankfurt 1979; *American Alternative Theater* by Theodore Shank, New York 1982; *Robert Wilson: Life Theater of Images* by Craig Nelson, New York 1984; *The Works on Paper 3* by Bernice Rose, New York 1985; *The President of Paradise: A Traveller's Account ofthe Civil Wars* by Janny Donker, Amsterdam 1985; *Robert Wilson: Die lithograpischen Zyklen 1984–86 (Medea, Parsifal, Alceste)* by Fred Jahn, Munich 1986. **Articles**—''Robert Wilson: Scenographer'' by Hans-Thies Lehmann in *Parkett,* no. 16, May 1988; ''Sculpture on Stage'' by Wendy Paris in *Sculpture* (Washington, D.C.), vol. 11, no. 1, January-February 1992; ''Old Time Machines for a New Millennium: Robert Wilson's HG'' by Johanne Sloan in *Parachute,* no. 82, April-June 1996.

* * *

Robert Wilson's most noted project has been his collaboration with composer Philip Glass on *Einstein on the Beach.* Wilson's interest, like that of Gertrude Stein, is in the use of components of syntax and sound to create a new form of language. In *Einstein on the Beach,* as part of the splicing of language, he combined both understood and senseless words and phrases. Because of Wilson's language, sets, and movement patterning, each of his works have a complex world of colorful and inane artistic principles.

Wilson generally chooses performers from the world at large, paralleling the casting of non-trained performers in a number of post-modern dance productions. The movements in the plays are generally influenced by both Andy Degroat's choreography and Wilson's own background in movement sensitization. The emphasis on internal movement, rather than dancerly, external and linear movements, is an aspect that ties Wilson's work to a theatrical, rather than dance, evolution. There has always been the suggestion though, that Wilson's work is actually silent, visual dance, as well as silent, visual opera.

The sense of allowing time to slip by, but very slowly, during Wilson's dreamlike performances is his special talent. *The Life and Times of Joseph Stalin* was a 12 hour play, *Deafman Glance* was seven hours in duration, and *Ka Mountain,* performed in Iran, seven days and seven nights. Rather than a Western expansionism of space, he has chosen an Eastern withdrawing of Western linear time. As Wilson's performances continue over long periods of time, audiences begin to lose the feeling of directionality.

Wilson has chosen several twentieth-century aspects of scale: delayed time, disoriented language and finally, the inclusion of quantity. *The Life and Times of Joseph Stalin* had a complete cast of 148 performers. The performance of *Ka Mountain* included 17 directors, 9 authors, and a cast of 79. Wilson described the 7 day festival as a sort of family which existed throughout the course of time, a type of performance without end. There is the sense here that art-making reaches a scale of proportion akin to other twentieth-century mass activities. There has also been evidence, and he uses both conventionally trained and non-conventionally trained performers now, that life in the twentieth century will go on as a very intricate, well-defined, necessary and habitually organic performance.

—John Robinson

WINNER, Gerd

Nationality: German. **Born:** Braunschweig, 8 October 1936. **Education:** Studied art, under W. Volkert, Hochschule für Bildende Künste, West Berlin, 1956–62; and at the Nuomen Taide-Akatenfian Konici, Helsinki (West German Study Scholarship), 1959–62. **Family:** Married to Ingmar Reuter. **Career:** Graphic artist and printmaker; lived and worked in West Berlin, 1963–70, London 1970–72, New York, 1972–78, and in Braunschweig, since 1978. **Awards:** Kunstpreis für Graphik, Wolfsburg, 1969; British Council travel scholarship, to work at Kelpra Studio, London, 1970; Deutscher Kritikerpreis for Bildende Kunst, West Berlin, 1972; 2 prizes, *International Biennale,* Cracow, 1972; Graphics Prize, *Biennale,* Lugano, Switzerland, 1972; Graphics Prize, *Print Biennale,* Ljubljana, 1973; Graphics Prize, World Graphics Competition, San Francisco, 1973; Graphics Prize, *International Biennale,* Cracow, 1974; Arts Council Prize, *International Print Biennale,* Bradford, Yorkshire, 1982. **Agent:** Galerie Mikro, Carmerstrasse 1, Berlin. **Address:** Finkenherd 10, 3300 Braunschweig, West Germany.

Individual Exhibitions:

1960 Galerie Fenestra, Helsinki
1965 Galerie Mikro, West Berlin
Galerie im Hading, Goeppingen, Switzerland
Galerie Sous Sol, Giessen, Switzerland
1966 Galerie für Grafikfreunde, Frankfurt
Werkstaat Schnoor, Bremen, West Germany
Städtisches Museum, Braunschweig, West Germany
1967 Galerie Gerda Bassenge, West Berlin
Museum am Ostwall, Dortmund, West Germany
Galerie C. D. Rothe, Wolfsburg, West Germany
Schloss Wolfsburg, West Germany
1968 Galerie Mikro, West Berlin
Galerie Nos, Duisburg, West Germany
Werkstaat Schnoor, Bremen, West Germany
Kunstkreis, Hameln, West Germany
Galerie im Schinkelsaal, West Berlin
1969 Galerie Sous Sol, Giessen, Switzerland
Galerie Wildeshausen, Wildeshausen, Switzerland
Galerie Dr. Hartmann, Stuckvilla, Munich
Galerie am Rhein, Cologne
1970 Overbeck-Gesellschaft, Lübeck
Galerie Querschnitt, Braunschweig, West Germany
Tilson: Siebdruck + Winner: Workshop, Haus am Waldsee, West Berlin (with Joe Tilson)
1971 Galerie M. E. Thelen, Cologne
Staatliche Graphische Sammlung, Munich
Kunstverein, Wolfsburg, West Germany (with Joe Tilson)
1972 Herzog-Anton-Ulrich Museum, Braunschweig, West Germany
Galerie Schmucking, Braunschweig, West Germany
Galerie 2000, West Berlin
1973 Marlborough Graphics, London
Siebdruck, Kunstverein, Cologne
Galerie Schmucking, Braunschweig, West Germany
Institut für Moderne Kunst, Nuremberg
Wentzel Galerie, Hamburg
Galerie M. E. Thelen, Cologne
1974 Galerie Stangl, Munich
Galerie Domberger, Reutlingen, West Germany
Galerie Craven, Paris
Galerie Schmucking, Basel
Bundesministerium für Raumordnung, Bauwesen und Stadtebau, Bonn
Pronolfini Gallery, Bristol
Galleri Dierks, Aarhus, Denmark
Konstmuseum, Aarhus, Denmark
Galerie Wentzel, Hamburg
Galerie 2000, West Berlin
1975 Kunsthalle, Bremen, West Germany
Galerie M. E. Thelen, Cologne
1981 *Gerd Winner and Kelpra Studio,* Drumcroon Art Centre, Wigan, Lancashire
1982 University of Regina, Saskatchewan
1983 Riverside Studios, Hammersmith, London
1988 Sprengel Museum, Hanover, Germany (catalog)
Gerd Winner: Urban Structures 1980–88, Wilhelm-Hack-Museum, Ludwigshafen, G.F.R. (catalog)

Selected Group Exhibitions:

1961 *Grosse Berliner Kunstausstellung,* Messehallen, West Berlin (and regularly 1962–69)
1967 *20 Jahre Internationale Graphik,* Kunstverein, Wolfsburg, West Germany
1970 *International Print Biennale,* City Museum and Art Gallery, Bradford, Yorkshire
1971 *Biennale,* Musée d'Art Moderne, Paris
1974 *Print Biennale,* National Museum of Modern Art, Tokyo
1977 *Documenta,* Kassel, West Germany
1982 *Big Prints,* Southampton Art Gallery (toured the U.K.)

Collections:

Nationalgalerie, West Berlin; Kupferstichkabinett, West Berlin; Neue Galerie Sanufflung Ludwig, Aachen, West Germany; Wallraf-Richartz-Museum, Cologne; Muzeum Sztuki, Lodz, Poland; Narodni Museum, Warsaw; Musée d'Art et d'Histoire, Geneva; Victoria and Albert Museum, London; Museum of Modern Art, New York; University of Iowa, Iowa City.

Publications:

By WINNER: Book—*London Dockland,* West Berlin 1972. **Film—***Hommage à la France II,* 1969.

On WINNER: Books—*Tilson: Siebdruck + Winner: Workshop,* exhibition catalog, West Berlin 1970; *Gerd Winner,* exhibition catalog with text by Pat Gilmour, London 1973; *Gerd Winner: Siebdruck,* exhibition catalog with text by Wulf Herzogenrath, Cologne 1973; *Gerd Winner and Kelpra Studio,* exhibition catalog with texts by R. C. Hopkinson and A. R. Taylor, Wigan, Lancashire 1981; *Gerd Winner: Paintings and Graphics 1970–1980* by Pat Gilmour, London 1981; *Gerd Winner,* exhibition catalog with texts by Carol A. Phillips and Maija Bismanis, Regina, Saskatchewan 1982.

* * *

In the catalog to his 1975 Bremen Kunsthalle exhibition, Gerd Winner can be paraphrased as saying that to have people in a picture immediately imposes on that picture an interpretation, an explanation, a type of identity that it would never have acquired without people. Winner's work noticeably excludes the human figure. This makes his pictures, mostly urban landscapes, that much more haunting, for they are places where one would expect to see a figure from time to time, even if only a stray dog.

Because of his concern with photographic realism in his printmaking and his obsession with the more seamy areas of the city landscape, his series of, for example, the London dockland, the London underground or the canyons formed by New York City streets, his avoidance of human life could tend ultimately towards the depressing if it weren't for his non-descriptive use of colour. This is what takes Winner's work beyond a mere photo-realist or ''pop'' approach; it is his technical ability as a printmaker that keeps him from being completely typecast as one who makes ''statements about deserted streets.'' The use of colour in his printmaking, particularly his work consequent to working with Chris Prater of Kelpra Studio, London, where he was invited by the British Council in 1970, tends to be pearly, giving an iridescent glitter to surfaces normally bereft of such delicacy.

—Victoria Keller

WINNEWISSER, Rolf

Nationality: Swiss. **Born:** Niedergosgoen, 5 June 1949. **Education:** Educated in Lucerne, until 1965; studied graphics and design at the Kunstgewerbeschule, Lucerne, 196671. **Military service:** Served as music corps drummer in the Swiss Army, 1969. **Career:** Worked as designer, Olten, 1971–72; as technical assistant on alphabetization project, Tillaberi region, River Niger, Africa, 1972–74. Independent artist, in Lucerne, since 1974; also worked in Zurich and Gambia, 1978–80, in New York, 1981–82, in Schongau, 1982–84, and in London, 1987–88. Drawing instructor, Kunstgewerbeschule, Zurich, 1976–80, and since 1982. **Awards:** Vordemberge-Gildewart Award, Rapperswil, 1984. **Agent:** Galerie und Edition Stahli, Bahnhof Enge, Postfach, 8027 Zurich. **Address:** P.O. Box 345, 6000 Lucerne 7, Switzerland.

Individual Exhibitions:

1972 Galerie Stahli, Lucerne
1973 Galerie Stahli, Lucerne
1975 Galerie Elisabeth Kaufmann, Olten, Switzerland
Galerie Stahli, Zurich (with Aldo Walker)
1976 Galerie Meier, Geneva (with Martin Disler)
Galerie Elisabeth Kaufmann, Olten, Switzerland (with Martin Disler)
Galerie Stahli, Zurich (with Martin Disler)
1977 Galerie Elisabeth Kaufmann, Basel
1978 Galerie Stahli, Zurich
1979 Kunsthalle, Basel
1980 Studio d'Arte Cannaviello, Milan (with Martin Disler)
1981 Galerie Camomille, Brussels
Galerie Stahli, Zurich
1982 Kunstverein, Mannheim (with Aldo Walker)
Galerie Stahli, Zurich
1983 Kunsthalle Waaghaus, Winterthur, Switzerland
1985 Galerie Anton Meier, Geneva
Galerie Biederberg, Amsterdam
Galerie Stahli, Zurich
1986 Galerie Pro(s)art, Lucerne
1989 *Maptrap WIWI.R.: Rolf Winnewisser,* Kunstmuseum, Solothurn, Switzerland (catalog)
1990 Kunstmuseum Luzern, Switzerland (catalog)
1991 Helmhaus Zürich (catalog)

Selected Group Exhibitions:

1972 *Giovane Arie Svizzera,* Rotonda della Reana, Milan
1973 *Biennale,* Musée d'Art Moderne de la Ville, Paris
1974 *Profile 10,* Städtisches Museum, Bochum, West Germany
1975 *Beryll Cristallo,* Kunstmuseum, Lucerne
1976 *Landscapes,* Mint Museum of Art, Charlotte, North Carolina
1980 *Aperto '80,* at the *Biennale,* Venice
1981 *Schweier Kunst '70-'80,* Kunstmuseum, Lucerne (travelled to Bologna, Genoa, Bonn and Graz)
1983 *Eight Portfolios,* Nigel Greenwood Gallery, London
1984 *Bluten des Eigensinns,* Kunstverein, Munich
1987 *Malen, Schreiben-Schreiben malen,* Kunstmuseum, Solothurn, Switzerland
1991 Helmhaus Zürich

Collections:

Kunstmuseum, Luceme; Kunstmuseum, Aarau, Switzerland; Kunthaus, Zurich.

Publications:

By WINNEWISSER: Books—*Aus dem Logbuch Ikons,* Zurich 1982; *Immer Wieder Zuruck,* Rome 1984; *Nil,* with texts by Theo Kneubuhler and Karl Sauter, Lucerne 1986; *Prossima volta in due volupia,* edited by Stephan Banz, Lucerne 1986; *Les modelles: eine melancholische Ausstellungsnovelle,* Zurich 1991. **Articles—**''Der Geraumte Weg oder das schrecklich Personliche in Beobachtungen dber das andere'' in *Kunst-Bulletin* (Berne/Basel), No. 7–8, 1976; ''Zeichen in Rewegung ohne Titel: Fortlaufend'' in *Sondern* (Berlin/Basel), No. 1, 1976; ''Uberquerungen'' in *Sondern* (Berlin/Basel), No. 2, 1977; ''Arabesken einer Reise nach Seltsam'' in *Innerschweizer Blotter* (Lucerne), February 1978; ''Split Horizon'' in *Oboe* (San Francisco), No. 5, 1981; ''Rolf Winnewisser'' in *Xylon,* no. 90, August 1993.

On WINNEWISSER: Books—*Kunst: 28 Schweizer* by Theo Kneubuhler, Lucerne 1972; *Rolf Winnewisser,* exhibition catalog with text by Theo Kneubuhler, Lucerne 1973; *An Annual of New Art and Artists* by Willem Sandberg, Amsterdam 1973; *Rolf Winnewisser,* exhibition catalog with texts by Jean-Christophe Ammann and Theo Kneubuhler, Basel 1979; *Rolf Winnewisser,* exhibition catalog, Geneva 1985; *Serendipity: Unterwegs zu den Bildern von Rolf Winnewisser* by Stefan Banz, Zurich 1991.

*

Unplanned meeting of lines, a line meets, intersects another line, annullable at that point when ''formulatable'' wishes can be shaped out of the vantage point of pictorial plane into which flowing, unflagging signs can flee and a monochrome, with lines winding around an acrobatic sensation, pattern for thought and sensation, where words fail in the sense of following a trail, of wanting to make a language out of the image spoken by the image itself. Deviations between what is conceivable and what is still imaginable. Whereby the image as image no longer works, is no longer able to give for consideration designs of a sign system to current, present-day dissected, dissectable opaque, disintegrating reality and imagination, forgotten in the image state: far from me, in me.

Things, thoughts, reflections, held outwards, turned inside out, there broken and breaking other things, expanding, fanning out, suffocating and making them breathe, domain between image and intent, image as sediment, residue of this activity, an incessant flowing, breaking and being broken of the within and the outermost, the innermost and the uttered.

Because it has to begin somewhere, where was I again when I forgot the image, when I forgot to speak of the image and disappointed by the image as expectation, by the expectation as image of what has already been, meanings running away to prevent signs from catching up with them, under way from image to image, through images. Things thought in the light of the representable and the non-representable movements between mind, mental signs in their brokenness, formulas of inconclusiveness, and the inconclusiveness of a formula, things existential in the light of acting and failing to act, the mistakes, the inconclusiveness of experience, the realities of appearance, embodied signs, when signs flow from their significance, contaminations held and released again.

—Rolf Winnewisser

WINSOR, Jacqueline

Nationality: American. **Born:** Newfoundland, Canada, 20 October 1941. **Education:** Educated at Yale Summer School of Art and Music, New Haven, Connecticut, 1964; Massachusetts College of Art, Boston, 1965, B.F.A. 1965; Rutgers University, New Brunswick, New Jersey, 1967, M.F.A. 1967. **Career:** Independent artist, New York, since 1967. Art and ceramics instructor, Douglass College, New Brunswick, New Jersey, 1967; art instructor, Middlesex County College, Edison, New Jersey, and Newark State Teacher's College, New Jersey, 1968–69; ceramics instructor, Mills College of Education, Oakland, California, 1968, 1971; graphics instructor, Loyola University, New Orleans, summer 1969; ceramics instructor, Greenwich House Pottery School, New York, 1969–72; sculpture instructor, School of Visual Arts, New York, Spring 1971 and 1975; art instructor, Hunter College, New York, 1972–75. **Awards:** Creative Artists' Public Service Program Award, 1973; New York State Council of the Arts Grant, 1973–74; Mather Award, Art Institute of Chicago, 1974; National Endowment for the Arts Grant, 1974, 1977, 1984; Louis Comfort Tiffany Foundation Award, 1977; Guggenheim Fellowship, 1978; Creative Artist's Award, Brandeis University, Waltham, Massachusetts, 1979. **Agent:** Paula Cooper Gallery, 534 West 21st Street, New York, New York 10011, U.S.A. **Address:** 141 Canal Street, New York, New York 10002, U.S.A.

Individual Exhibitions:

1968 Douglass College Gallery, New Brunswick, New Jersey
1971 Nova Scotia College of Art and Design, Halifax
1973 Paula Cooper Gallery, New York
1976 Paula Cooper Gallery, New York
Contemporary Arts Center, Cincinnati, Ohio
Portland Center for Visual Arts, Oregon
1977 Museum of Modern Art, San Francisco
1978 Wadsworth Atheneum, Hartford
1979 Museum of Modern Art, New York
Art Gallery of Ontario, Toronto
Fort Worth Art Museum, Texas
1981 Virginia Museum of Fine Arts, Richmond
1982 Paula Cooper Gadlery, New York
Akron Art Museum, Ohio
1983 Massachusetts Institute of Technology, Cambridge (with Barry Ledoux)
Paula Cooper Gallery, New York
1985 Margarete Roeder Fine Arts, New York (with Richard Deacon)
1986 Paula Cooper Gallery, New York
1991 Milwaukee Art Museum, Wisconsin (catalog)
1992 *Jackie Winsor,* Milwaukee Art Museum (catalog)
1995 *Jackie Winsor,* Paula Cooper Gallery, New York
1996 Galerie Samuel Lallouz, Montréal
1998 P.S. 1 Contemporary Art Center, New York (retrospective)

Selected Group Exhibitions:

1969 *American Abstract Artists,* Riverside Museum, New York
1972 *American Women Artists,* Kunsthaus, Hamburg
1975 *The Condition of Sculpture,* Hayward Gallery, London
1976 *The Liberation: 14 American Artists,* Aarhus Museum of Art, Denmark (toured Europe)
1977 *Biennial,* Whitney Museum, New York
1978 *Fading Bounds in Sculpture,* Stedelijk Museum, Amsterdam
1979 *The Decade in Review,* Whitney Museum, New York
1982 *Currents: A New Mannerism,* Jacksonville Art Museum, Florida (travelled to Tampa, Florida)
1985 *Tranformations in Sculpture,* Guggenheim Museum, New York
1987 *The Success of Failure,* Laumeier Sculpture Park, St. Louis (travelled to Middlebury, Vermont; Tucson, Arizona)

1988 *Sculpture Since the Sixties,* Whitney Museum of American Art, Equitable Center, New York (catalog)
Eleven Artists from Paula Cooper, Mayor Rowan Gallery, London (catalog)
Enclosing the Void: Eight Contemporary Sculptors, Whitney Museum of American Art, Equitable Center, New York (catalog)
1990 *Hesse, Lawler, Martin, Meyer, Pfaff, Smith, Winsor,* Holly Solomon Gallery, New York (catalog)
1991 *Selections from the Permanent Collection,* Wexner Center for the Visual Arts, Ohio State University, Columbus (catalog)
1994 *Sculpture,* Nina Freudenheim Gallery, Buffalo
1996 *More than Minimal: Feminism and Abstraction in the '70s,* Rose Art Museum, Brandeis University, Waltham (catalog)
1998 *What Remains: MCMLXXXXVII,* Groninger Museum, Netherlands (catalog)
1999 *House of Sculpture,* Modern Art Museum of Forth Worth (catalog)
2000 *Open Ends: 11 Exhibitions of Contemporary Art from 1960 to Now,* Museum of Modern Art, New York (catalog)

Collections:

Museum of Modern Art, New York; Whitney Museum, New York; Detroit Institute of Arts; Musée d'Arte Moderne, Paris; Australian National Gallery, Canberra; Art Gallery of Ontario, Toronto; Wexner Center for the Visual Arts, Ohio State University, Columbus.

Publications:

By WINSOR: Books—*Jackie Winsor: Sculpture,* exhibition catalog, text with Ellen Phelan, Cincinnati, Ohio 1976; *The Artist Observed: 28 Interviews with Contemporary Artists,* with John Gruen, Chicago 1991. **Articles—**"An Interview with Jackie Winsor" by Liza Bear in *Avalanche* (New York), Spring 1972; interview in "Artists Now Living in New York" in *Criteria* (Vancouver), November 1977; statement in *Jackie Winsor,* exhibition catalog (New York), 1979.

On WINSOR: Books—*26 Women Artists,* exhibition catalog by Lucy Lippard, Ridgefield, Connecticut 1971; *12 Statements Beyond the 60s,* exhibition catalog by Frank Kolbert, Detroit 1972; *4 Young Americans,* exhibition catalog by Mario Amaya, New York 1973; *8th Biennale de Paris,* exhibition catalog by Georges Boudadle, Paris 1973; *A Response to the Environment,* exhibition catalog by Jeffrey Wechsler, New Brunswick, New Jersey 1975; *The Condition of Sculpture,* exhibition catalog by William Tucker, London 1975; *The Liberation: 14 Women Artists,* exhibition catalog, Aarhus and Copenhagen, 1976; *Ideas in Sculpture 1965–77,* exhibition catalog with essay by Anne Rorimer, Chicago 1977; *A View of a Decade,* exhibition catalog with essay by Robert Pincus-Witten, Chicago 1977; *Strata: Nancy Graves/Eva Hesse/Michelle Stuart/Jackie Winsor,* exhibition catalog with essay by Lucy Lippard, Vancouver 1977; *12 From Rutgers,* exhibition catalog by Jeffrey Wechsler, New Brunswick, New Jersey 1977; *Matrix 38,* exhibition catalog with essay by Andrea Miller-Keller, Hartford 1978; *Jackie Winsor,* exhibition catalog with an essay by Ellen Johnson, New York 1979; *Born in Boston,* exhibition catalog, Lincoln, Massachusetts 1979. **Articles—**"Jackie Winsor: Doing It the Hard Way" by Claire C. Kelly in *Artweek* (Oakland, California), 15 January 1977; "Winsor Built" by Roberta Smith in *Art in America* (New York), January/February 1977; "Winsor Knots: The Sculpture of Jackie Winsor" by Robert Pincus-Witten in *Arts Magazine* (New York), June 1977; "Art: Jackie Winsor" by David Bourdon in *Vogue* (New York), February 1979; "Raw Magic" by Mark Stevens in *Newsweek* (New York), 26 February 1979; "Jackie Winsor: Eloquence of a 'Yankee Pioneer'" by John Gruen in *Artnews* (New York), March 1979; "Jackie Winsor" by Ellen Johnson in *Parachute* (Montreal), Winter 1979; "Jackie Winsor" by Badanna Zack in *Artmagazine* (Toronto), September/October 1979; "Jackie Winsor and Post Minimalism" by Alan Barkley in *Vanguard* (Vancouver), September 1979; "Jackie Winsor" by Jean-Pierre Criqui in *Beaux Arts Magazine,* no. 59, July-August 1988; "Entering the Mainstream: Sculptors of the Twentieth Century—Part Three: Jackie Winsor and Nancy Graves" by Ann Sutherland Harris in *Gallerie: Women Artists,* vol. 2, no. 4, 1989; "Jackie Winsor: Pieces of Life" by Margot Mifflin in *ARTnews,* vol. 91, no. 6, Summer 1992; "The Return of the Red-Brick Alternative" by Eleanor Heartney in *Art in America,* January 1998. **Film:** *What Follows: Jackie Winsor* by Kay Miller and Albert Alhadeff, 1988.

* * *

Jackie Winsor's particular success is best seen in her 1970s production, the moment in her career when her artistic temperament matched perfectly with the evolving Minimalist idiom to achieve an authentic significance. The nature of her art in its use of primary structures such as cube, sphere, and grid, but "tended into a metaphorical position through emphasis upon process, material, and craft, has been labelled second wave Minimalism."

While the very forcefully delineated hand-made aura of this work was perhaps parallel to the feminist art of that time, Winsor typically chose manufactured materials and worked towards weight and density, if not as well a fragile poignance. She said of those works: "The overall element I seek is self-containment. My aim is that the pieces not intrude on you, but that they give one time to come to them." Humbling in their often ritual—like craft repetitiveness, there may also be an essentially masochistic quality in the numbing anti-ego self-effacement implied in such work—aptly felt in the phrase "confessional formalism." (S. Westfall). Hundreds of the artist's hours are implied in the wrapping together, for instance, of the four logs of *Bound Square* (1972). Likewise in *Exploded Piece* (1980–82), a steel-reinforced concrete cube (with Winsor's signature in a small opening on each face presenting a view of the impacted interior space), was blown apart in order to be carefully, even lovingly reconstructed. This motif of tender repair on materials monstrous in either scale or industrial redolence is reminiscent of Grosvenor's approach in the last decade. He also comes to mind in an assessment of Winsor's pace of production: the unhurried appearance of their art betokens more than merely a private, meditative and personal aim. Both artists, among others, are at play with a puritanical American strain, testing the metaphysical implications of weight, idea, and silence within materials divided between the natural and industrial.

If there has been a selflessness in Winsor's art, it is also found in her persistent disinclination to reveal any details of her personal life; and as well in the control which she demands over the dispersal of her still small oeuvre by insisting that her of course obliging buyers sign a contract which permits Winsor to exercise exhibition and reproduction controls, and receive a percentage of the future sales of the works. In her recent sculptures, while still based upon weight, density, and aperture leading to a cubic interior, and as before constructed from industrial materials, it appears that Winsor's privacy of vision has attempted a more public self. The plaster board cubes are bevel-edged, and pastel-hued, and the interior space is mirrored; and just so, a concrete, two-ton sphere is blue-toned. For the moment, Winsor relinquishes the tragic stance of the previous decade and more, and evinces a curious paradoxical decorous air.

The ostensible elegance in that art easily associated with her name was joined since 1988 by the relocation of her works from floor to wall; and a concommitant new focus upon the square. These works now appear as the latest elaboration of Winsor's long-standing interest in ''spatial paradox.'' Black and white plaster squares are overlaid with meticulously pencilled grids. The center is a recess which extends several inches into the wall; clearly then her dominating motif of an interior space approached through a rectilinear avenue—literal depth—has been carried over from an earlier time. And so her work once again reveals what Margot Mifflin has called Winsor's ''intense desire to undermine geometry's fictitious promise of clarity.''

—Joshua Kind

WODICZKO, Krzysztof

Nationality: Polish. **Born:** Warsaw, 16 April 1943. **Education:** Studied industrial design, Academy of Fine Arts, Warsaw, 1962–68, MFA 1968. **Career:** Worked as an industrial designer, Warsaw, 1969–77. Independent artist, living in Toronto and New York, since 1977. Instructor in design, Warsaw Polytechnic, 1969–77; visiting professor in design, Nova Scotia College of Art and Design, Halifax, 1977–79; part-time professor of drawing, Guelph University, Ontario, 1979; part-time professor in design, Ontario College of Art, Toronto, 1979; assistant professor in photography and studio art, Nova Scotia College of Art and Design, Halifax, 1980–81; associate professor of design, New York Institute of Technology, Old Westbury and Columbus Circle, since 1983; guest professor, Cooper Union School of Art, New York, 1987; visiting professor in photography, California Institute of the Arts, Valencia, 1988. Artist in residence: University of Illinois, Urbana, 1975; York University, Toronto, 1976; A Space, Toronto, 1976; Nova Scotia College of Art and Design, Halifax, 1976, 1977; Artists Space, New York, 1977; Asssistant Professor of Intermedia and Photography, Nova Scotia College of Art and Design, 1980–81; South Australian School of Art, Adelaide, 1981–82; Visiting Professor of Photography and Studio Art, California Institute for the Arts, 1988; Assistant Professor of Photography, California Institute of Technology, 1991; Professor of Sculpture, Ecole Nationale Superieure des Beaux Arts, 1991–95; Director, Center for Advanced Visual Studies, Massachusetts Institute of Technology, 1995–1997; Director, Interrogative Design Group, Center for Advanced Visual Studies, Massachusetts Institute of Technology, 1994-present. **Awards:** Hiroshima Prize, 1998. **Agent:** Hal Bromm Gallery, 90 West Broadway, New York, New York 10007, U.S.A. **Address:** Massachusetts Institute of Technology, Department of Architecture, Room N51–315H, 77 Massachusetts Avenue, Cambridge, Massachusetts, 02139–2307, U.S.A.

Individual Exhibitions:

1970 Gallery Wspolczesna, Warsaw
1972 Gallery Wspolczesna, Warsaw
1973 Gallery Akumulatory 2, Warsaw
Gallery Foksal, Warsaw
1974 Gallery Foksal, Warsaw
1975 Gallery Akumulatory 2, Warsaw
Gallery Foksal, Warsaw
N.A.M.E. Gallery, Chicago
University of Illinois, Urbana
1976 Gallery Akumulatory 2, Warsaw
Gallery Foksal, Warsaw
Gallery St. Petri, Lund, Sweden
Vehicule, Montreal
A Space, Toronto
1977 Gallery Akumulatory 2, Warsaw
Gallery Foksal, Warsaw
Project Studio One, New York
A Space, Toronto
York University, Toronto
Eye Level, Halifax, Nova Scotia
Hal Bromm Gallery, New York
1978 Artists Space, New York
Hal Bromm Gallery, New York
1979 Eye Level, Halifax, Nova Scotia
Galerie Optica, Montreal
Gallery 76, Toronto
1980 Hal Bromm Gallery, New York
1981 Eye Level, Halifax, Nova Scotia
Great George Street Gallery, Charlottetown, Prince Edward Island
Franklin Furnace, New York
Artspace, Peterborough, Ontario
1982 South Australian School of Art, Adelaide
1983 Ydessa Gallery, Toronto
1984 Hal Bromm Gallery, New York
1985 State University of New York, Purchase
Ydessa Gallery, Toronto
Canada House, London
Robert McLaughlin Gallery, Oshawa, Ontario
Orchard Gallery, Derry, Northern Ireland
1986 49th Parallel Gallery, New York
Gallery Foksal, Warsaw
1987 Massachusetts Institute of Technology, Cambridge
Hal Bromm Gallery, New York
1988 Clocktower, New York
La Jolla Museum of Contemporary Art, California (retrospective)
Hirchhorn Museum, Washington, D.C.
1989 Wadsworth Atheneum, Hartford (retrospective)
Exit Art, New York City (traveling exhibition)
1991 Josh Baer Gallery, New York
1992 Fundacio Tapies, Barcelona (retrospective)
Museum Sztuki, Lodz (retrospective) (catalog)
Walker Art Center, Minneapolis (retrospective) (catalog)

Galerie Gabrielle Maubrie, Paris
1993 Contemporary Art Center, Houston (retrospective)
1995 Centrum Sztuki, Warsaw (retrospective)
De Appel Foundation, Amsterdam (retrospective)
1996 Galerie Lelong, New York
Galerie Gabrielle Maubrie, Paris

Selected Group Exhibitions:

1969 *Biennale de Paris,* Musée d'Art Moderne, Paris (and 1975)
1977 *Documenta 6,* Kassel, West Germany (and *Documenta 8,* 1987)
1979 *Biennale of Sydney,* Art Gallery of New South Wales (and 1982)
1983 *Presence Polonaise,* Centre Georges Pompidou, Paris
Kunstler aus Kanada, Kunstverein, Stuttgart
1984 *Body Politic,* Tower Gallery, New York
1985 *Alles und Noch Viel Mehr,* Kunstmuseum, Berne
1986 *Biennale,* Venice
Expanding Commitment, Maryland Institute of Art, Baltimore
1987 *Poetic Injury,* Alternative Museum, New York
1990 *New York City Tableaux, The Hybrid State,* Exit Art, New York
1992 *Pour la Suite du Monde,* Musee d'Art Contemporain, Montreal
1993 *In and Out of Place: Contemporary Art and the American Social Landscape,* Museum of Fine Arts, Boston
1994 *Europa-Europa,* Kunstmuseum, Bonn
1994 *Contemporary Canadian Art: Beyond (National) Identities, Setagaya Museum of Art,* Tokyo (traveling exhibition)
1995 *Horizons, 14 Polish Artists,* Sonje Museum of Contemporary Art, Seoul
1996 *NowHere, Walking and Thinking,* Louisiana Museum, Denmark
Project for Survival, National Museum of Art, Kyoto, Japan
1997 *Face a l'Histoire,* Centre Georges Pompidou, Paris
2000 *2000 Biennial Exhibition,* Whitney Museum of American Art, New York

Collections:

National Gallery of Canada, Ottawa; Art Bank, Toronto; Ministry of External Affairs, Ottawa; Muzeum Sztuki, Lodz; Gallery Foksal, Warsaw; National Museum, Poznan; Chase Manhattan Bank, New York; La Jolla Museum of Contemporary Art, California.

Publications:

By WODICZKO: Books—*On Line,* Guelph, Ontario 1976; *Projection,* Halifax 1979; *Poetics of Authority, Vehicles, Line, Images of Propaganda, Public Architecture,* with essay by Alisa Maxwell, Adelaide 1982; *Homeless Vehicle Project, Homeless Conversations,* with Rudolph Luria, New York 1988; *Krzysztof Wodiczko: Public Art, Critical Art—Texts, Remarks and Deocuments,* Paris 1995. **Articles**—''Conversations About a Project for a Homeless Vehicle'' in *October,* no. 47, Winter 1988; interview with William Furlong in *Art Monthly,* no. 120, October 1988; ''Homeless Vehicle Project,'' with David V. Lurie in *October,* no. 47, Winter 1988; interview with Malcolm Dickson in *Variant,* no. 6, 1989; interview with Roger Gilroy in *New Art Examiner,* vol. 16, no. 6, February 1989; interview with Matthias Flugge in *Neue Bildende Kunst,* no. 1, February-March 1996.

On WODICZKO: Books—*Krzysztof Wodiczko: Line,* exhibition catalog, Warsaw 1976; *Krzysztof Wodiczko: References,* exhibition catalog, Warsaw 1977; *Expanding Commitment: Diverse Approaches to Socially Concerned Photography,* exhibition catalog, Baltimore 1986; *42nd Venice Biennale, Canadian Pavilion: Krzysztof Wodiczko and Melvin Chamey,* with essay by Diana Nemiroff, Ottawa 1986; *Counter-Monuments: Krzysztof Wodiczko's Public Projections,* exhibition catalog, Cambridge, Massachusetts 1987. **Articles**—''Krzysztof Wodiczko'' by Eleanor Heartney in *C Magazine,* no. 23, Fall 1989; ''Krzysztof Wodiczko: Pour une 'Politique Esthetique' by Regis Durand in *Art Press,* no. 173, October 1992; ''Krzysztof Wodiczko'' by Christophe Domino in *Beaux Arts Magazine,* no. 120, February 1994; ''Krzysztof Wodiczko: Alien Staff'' by Mark Rakatansky in *Assemblage,* no. 23, April 1994; ''The Xenologist'' by George Melrod in *World Art,* no. 3, 1996; ''Xenology and Identity in Critical Public Art: Krzysztof Wodiczko's Immigrant Instruments'' by Marc James Leger in *Parachute,* no. 88, October-December 1997.

WOJNAROWICZ, David

Nationality: American. **Born:** 1954; left home in his early teens to escape a severely abusive father and lived on the streets for several years. **Career:** Artist and political activist; began taking photographs and writing in 1970; played in punk band called 3 Teens 4 Kill—No Motive; actor in *You Killed Me First* (1985–86) and *Silence=Death* (1990), a gay rights video in which he sewed his own mouth shut. **Died:** Of an AIDS related illness, 1992.

Selected Individual Exhibitions:

1982 Milliken Gallery, New York
1983 Civilian Warfare, New York
Hal Bromm Gallery, New York
1984 Gracie Mansion Gallery, New York
Anna Friebe Galerie, Cologne
Civilian Warfare, New York
C.A.U.C., Buenos Aires
1985 Times Square Spectacolor Board, New York
1986 Cartier Foundation, Paris
David Wojnarowicz, Anna Friebe Galerie, Cologne (catalog)
Gracie Mansion Gallery, New York
1987 Gracie Mansion Gallery, New York
Ground Zero Gallery, New York
1988 Galeria Buades, Madrid
1989 P.P.O.W., New York
1990 P.P.O.W., New York
Dorothy Goldeen Gallery, Santa Monica

David Wojnarowicz: Tongues of Flame, University Galleries, Illinois State University, Normal (catalog)
1991 Intermedia Arts, Minneapolis
1993 P.P.O.W., New York
1994 P.P.O.W., New York
Hal Bromm Gallery, New York
1995 *Temporarily Possessed The Semi-Permanent Collection,* New Museum of Contemporary Art, New York
1996 Gallery 44 Center for Contemporary Photography, Toronto
The American Center, Paris
Bringing It All Back Home, Gracie Mansion Gallery, New York
1997 *Sex / Industry,* Stefan Stux Gallery, New York
1998 *MALE,* Wessel + O'Connor Gallery, New York
1999 *Persuasion,* Lombard-Freid Fine Arts, New York
Fever: The Art of David Wojnarowicz, New Museum of Contemporary Art, New York
2000 *The End: An Independent Vision of Contemporary Culture 1982—2000,* Exit Art/The First World, New York

Selected Group Exhibitions:

1992 Wexner Center for the Arts, Columbus, Ohio
Kunstverein, Hamburg, and Kunsthalle, Lucerne
Whitney Museum of American Art, New York
New York Public Library, New York
Museum of Modern Art, New York
Galerie St. Etienne, New York
William Benton Museum of Art, Storrs, Connecticut
MIT List Visual Arts Center, Cambridge, Massachusetts
John Michael Kohler Arts Center, Sheboygan, Wisconsin
1993 Washington Project for the Arts, Washington, D.C.
Tema: AIDS, Henie-Onstad Kunstsenter Høvikodden, Oslo, Norway (catalog)
7th Annual Bang on a Can Festival, The Kitchen, New York
Whitney Museum of American Art, New York
Jersey City Museum, New Jersey
1994 The Art Gallery at the University of Maryland at College Park
Revolution, Ferndale, Michigan
Contemporary Art Center, Cincinnati
Con Rumore, Breda, The Netherlands
Kunsthalle Basel, Basel
Mary Ryan Gallery, New York
1995 John Michael Kohler Arts Center, Sheboygan, Wisconsin
Burchfield-Penney Art Center, Buffalo State College, Buffalo, New York
Institute of Contemporary Art, Boston
Armory Center for the Arts, Pasadena
1996 Gallery TPW, Toronto
Wessel O'Connor Gallery, New York
Tyler Galleries, Tyler School of Arts, Temple University, Philadelphia
Museum of Modern Art, New York
Sprengel Museum, Hanover
Galerie Peter Kilchman, Zurich
The Drawing Center, New York
Boston Center for the Arts, Boston
1998 Galerie St. Etienne, New York

Collections:

Metropolitan Museum of Modern Art, New York.

Publications:

By WOJNAROWICZ: Books—*Sounds in the Distance,* London 1982; *7 Miles a Second,* with James Romberger, DC Comics, New York 1986; *Memories that Smell like Gasoline,* San Francisco 1992; *The Waterfront Journals,* edited by Amy Scholder, New York 1996; *In the Shadow of the American Dream: The Diaries of David Wojnarowicz,* edited by Amy Scholder, New York 1998; *Fever: The Art of David Wojnarowicz* by David Wojnarowicz, and Dan Cameron, Mysoon Rizk, Cynthia Carr, New Museum of Contemporary Art, New York, 1999. **Articles**—''Being Queer in America: A Journal of Disintegration'' in *CUZ,* New York 1988; ''Between the Inside and the Outside'' in *Low Rent: A Decade of Prose and Photographs from the Portable Lower East Side,* New York 1994; ''Boy in Nathans (NYC); Boy in Trailer Park (Collinsville, Illinois)'' in *Angle of Repose,* Buffalo 1986; *Close to the Knives: A Memoir of Disintegration,* New York 1991; ''Dream Images'' in *Dreamworks 4,* no. 3, Fall 1985; ''From the Diaries of a Wolf Boy'' in *Best American Gay Fiction 2,* Boston 1997. **Videos**—*Fear of Disclosure: The Psycho-social Implications of HIV Revelation,* with Phil Zwickler, San Francisco, 1989; *Fear of Disclosure,* San Francisco, with Phil Zwickler, San Francisco, 1994. **Sound recording**—*3 Teens Kill 4, no motive,* LP Point Bland Records 1983; *ITSOFOMO (In the Shadow of Forward Motion),* with Ben Neill, New Tone 1992.

On WOJNAROWICZ: Books—*New, Used and Improved: Art for the Eighties,* Peter Frank and Michael McKenzie, New York 1987; *Art of the 1980s: Selections from the Collection of the Eli Broad Family Foundation,* New York 1991; *From Media to Metaphor: Art about AIDS* by Robert Atkins and Thomas W. Sokolowski, New York 1991; *David Wojnarowicz: Brushfires in the Social Landscape* edited by Melissa Harris, New York 1994. **Articles**—''Wojnarowicz Sues Wildmon Group'' by Christopher Phillips in *Art in America,* vol. 78, July 1990; ''Troubleshooters: C. Carr on Trying Times'' by C. Carr in *Artforum International,* vol. 29, September 1990; ''Out of the Safety Zone'' by Lucy R. Lippard in *Art in America,* vol. 78, no. 28, December 1990; ''Portrait of the Artist in the Age of AIDS'' by C. Carr'' in *Village Voice,* 13 February 1990; ''David Wojnarowicz'' by Kathy Brew in *Shift X,* no. 2, Summer 1991; ''Grotesque Photography'' by Brooks Adams in *The Print Collector's Newsletter,* vol. 21, January-February 1991; obituary by C. Carr in *Village Voice,* 4 August 1992; ''Brush Fires in the Social Landscape'' in *Aperture,* no. 137, Fall 1994; ''David Wojnarowicz: The Last Rimbaud'' by Donald Kuspit in *Art New England,* vol. 20, July/August, 1998; ''The Killing Machine'' by Barbara Pollack in *Art Monthly,* no. 224, March 1999; ''Odd Man Out'' by Dennis Cooper in *Artforum International,* vol. 38, no. 2, October 1999.

* * *

David Wojnarowicz was an artist whose work stands among the most visceral and confrontational in the late twentieth century.

Images of death, decay, sex, and destruction populate his art. When he died at the age of thirty-seven from an AIDS related illness in 1992, he left behind an amazing legacy of creative work—writings, paintings, photographs, prints, sculptures, films and videos, music, and installation and performance art. Between his first solo exhibition and his death, Wojnarowicz presented his artwork in an impressive nineteen individual and nearly two hundred group shows.

His work was always dark and filled with direct references to death, annihilation, and sexuality. Wojnarowicz's fascination with this type of imagery grew out of his desire to tell the story of his own experience—to bring forth the truth about the real world—something he felt was not being done by many artists of his time. Wojnarowicz knew personally about life on the street. He came from a broken home, had a very abusive father, and made his living as a teenager by prostituting himself in New York City. He knew homelessness, destitution, and alienation. Wojnarowicz knew the depths of pain and anger afforded to outsiders. He was an out gay man furious about the puritanical views toward sex in the United States and the lack of research and healthcare as the AIDS epidemic intensified. All of this fed his work constantly.

In 1970 (at the age of sixteen), Wojnarowicz began writing and making photographs as a survival method, a means of coping with the realities of his life. His first significant series, *Arthur Rimbaud in New York*, was created in 1978–79. The photographs show a man dressed in casual clothing and wearing a Rimbaud mask in various situations around the city—riding the subway, standing in an abandoned warehouse, masturbating on a bed. By this time Wojnarowicz was immersing himself in art-making. He painted massive murals in warehouses by the Hudson River and created environments under piers. He stenciled burning buildings onto gallery doors in SoHo and began working with Super 8 film and guerilla street performance. He piled 100 pounds of bloody animal bones on the steps of the Leo Castelli Gallery. He was just getting started.

In 1980, Wojnarowicz met Peter Hujar, whom he said was "in a great way responsible for everything I've done . . . Essentially Peter was the audience for everything I did. It was like finding a member of one's tribe." This revelation made Wojnarowicz more serious about his work and its potential to move people. He met artist Kiki Smith in 1982 and did several collaborative prints with her which incorporated psychiatric drawings and Rorschach tests Wojnarowicz had found in an abandoned warehouse. That same year, his first solo show was held at a SoHo gallery. It had "some very adamant homo art in it . . . all these naked guys having sex, armed with rifles, an explosion of civilization, money, statues, all this cultural stuff. They freaked out." The show was poorly attended and the gallery responded by destroying some of his paintings and blasting him for his images.

Wojnarowicz continued to expand his artistic commentary on society and its ills throughout the 1980s. AIDS had starting killing his friends, and his work reflected the anger and sorrow caused by the epidemic. *Late Afternoon in the Forest* (1986) is an extremely dark painting filled with images of death and desolation. The work's impressive scale (over thirteen feet long and more than six feet high) gives increased potency to the inherently intense images. An apocalypse is pictured, a vision of lifeless trees, rocks, fragments of machinery and bones, and strange totems. A human skeleton holds a gun near its head. A tiny angel hovers at the top of the painting. All these are shown in blacks, grays, and muted earth tones. The only light appears in a small section at the top left corner, where the Parthenon and the White House sit outside the realm of the decay.

In 1987, Wojnarowicz created *Four Elements: Fire, Earth, Water, Wind (for Peter Hujar)* as his mentor approached death from AIDS. Each of the four six-by-eight-foot paintings contains controversial imagery in its representation of the cycle of life. *Fire* features four distinct image areas and shows a devil, an enormous insect in a cage, a man in a jar in an underground cave, an erupting volcano, FBI Wanted posters, and an advertisement for a car battery. *Earth* is also quartered, but each area seems connected by a complex system of roots. In opposite corners of the painting, earth is being moved by an ant and by a bulldozer. A cowboy rides a bull and a mask stares outward. In the lower left quadrant, a skeletal rib cage and a fragment of an aqueduct are shown in the sky above a wrecked train. Germinating seeds glow with light in the foreground. The *Water* painting is easily the most controversial of the series. Much of the surface shows small boxes in which provocative images are placed. Fish bones and snake skulls mingle with images of the organism which causes AIDS. Gay men and lesbians are depicted making love. A human hand holds a tiny fetus. Outside this grid, a large frog is shown with a photo of a car on its back, a bandaged hand reaches through the bars of a window for a flower in the snow, and a ship is sucked into an ocean vortex. Sperm swim all over the painting. *Wind* is much more transcendent in its approach. Images are placed onto a background of clouds in a blue sky. A diagram of a nuclear reactor covers the painting, and images of a dinosaur running, a mechanical graveyard of machine parts, and a large dismembered wing are shown. In the top center of the painting, an open window is seen with white curtains blowing. A red line flows from the window, becoming an umbilical cord attached to a screaming red infant. The year Wojnarowicz made this series he found out he was HIV positive.

The death of Hujar and his own diagnosis pressed Wojnarowicz into even more intensity in his work. The following two years were extremely prolific, as he worked on the *Ant Series* (plastic ants placed on photographs of such things as a naked man and a large model of an eye) and the *Sex Series* (photographic negatives printed such that gay male pornography interacts with houses, speeding trains, et cetera.) *Anatomy and Architecture of Desire* (1988–89) is a vertical piece with a painted image of the Earth at the center. Cars, trains, ships, and airplanes zoom around it. The Earth is flanked on both top and bottom by a photographic progression of a snake swallowing a frog. Around the same time, Wojnarowicz began using textual overlays in his images featuring his own writing about his rage.

In 1989, a group exhibition of work dealing with AIDS at the Artist's Space in New York City had its NEA funding rescinded because of catalog text written by Wojnarowicz which blasted Cardinal O'Conner's stance against sex education and the distribution of condoms. Then NEA head John Frohnmeyer later restored the funding for the exhibit but not the catalog. In January, 1990, an NEA funded retrospective of Wojnarowicz's work was launched by the Illinois State University gallery. The exhibition catalog carried the controversial essay excluded from NEA support at the Artist's Space. Congress criticized the NEA funding of this exhibit the following month, and President George Bush wrote a letter to the NEA expressing his concern over the funding of Wojnarowicz. In April, Reverend Donald Wildmon and his ultra-right-wing American Family Association sent a pamphlet lambasting the NEA and Wojnarowicz to every member of Congress as well as 178,000 religious groups. In this mass mailing, images of gay sex were excerpted from the *Wind* painting in the *Four Elements* series. Wojnarowicz filed a lawsuit against Wildmon in June, winning an injunction against the pamphlet on the basis of copyright infringement and misrepresentation of his work. The artist was awarded one symbolic dollar in damages in the settlement. That year, Wojnarowicz appeared in the film *Silence=Death* with his lips sewn together. This violent image was featured on the cover of the Fall, 1990 issue of *High Performance* magazine, along with the text "Why is Donald Wildmon Trying to Censor This Man?"

Wojnarowicz willingly engaged in this battle over arts funding and continued to create highly confrontational works. In 1991, he was featured in the Whitney Biennial. That same year, very ill with AIDS, he traveled to Chaco Canyon in Arizona to make a final self portrait. His face is covered with the dry dirt of the sacred place, his eyes shut and his mouth slightly open. The image was not released until 1993, a year after Wojnarowicz died. The New Museum of Contemporary Art in SoHo organized a major retrospective of his work in 1999. Wojnarowicz's work is held at the Whitney Museum of American Art, the San Francisco Museum of Modern Art, and the Metropolitan Museum of Art in New York.

—Tammy A. Kinsey

WOODHAM, Derrick

Nationality: British. **Born:** Blackburn, Lancashire, 5 November 1940. **Education:** Studied at South East Essex Technical College and School of Art, 1957–60, Homsey College of Art London, 1960–62, and the Royal College of Art, London, with Meadows, Clatworthy, Brown, Dalwood and Atkins, 1962–65. **Family:** Married Irene Janusaityte in 1966; children: Anele and Alexandra. **Career:** Independent sculptor, since 1965. Part-time instructor, Royal College of Art, 1965–68; instructor, Philadelphia College of Art, 1968–70; associate professor, University of Iowa, Iowa City, 1970–73; assistant professor, University of Kentucky, Lexington, 1973–80; professor and director of the school of art, University of Cincinnati, Ohio, since 1980. Junior member, Fine Arts Advisory Panel, Arts Council of Great Britain, 1966–68. **Awards:** Walter Neurath Prize for Drawing, Royal College of Art, 1964; Peter Stuyvesant Award, 1965; Group Prize, Prix de la Ville de Paris, 1965; North Jersey Cultural Council Purchase Award, Van Saun Park, Paramus, New Jersey, 1974; University of Kentucky Research Council Grants, 1974–76; University of Cincinnati Research Council Awards, 1997–99; Ohio Arts Council Project Grant, 1999. **Address:** 1910 Bluebell Drive, Cincinnati, Ohio 45224, U.S.A. **Web site:** http://homepages.uc.edu/~woodham.

Individual Exhibitions:

1966 Richard Feigen Gallery, New York
1968 Ad Libitum Gallery, Antwerp
1969 Jewish Museum, New York
1970 Richard Feigen Gallery, New York
1973 Rasdall Gallery, Lexington, Kentucky
1974 J. H. Duffy Gallery, New York
1976 University of Kentucky, Lexington
1980 Lexington Arts Council Gallery, Kentucky
1984 Northern Kentucky University Gallery, Highland Heights
1988 Art Jones Gallery, Cincinnati (retrospective)
1997–98 *Twister,* Aronoff Center for the Arts, Cincinnati

Selected Group Exhibitions:

1965 *The New Generation,* Whitechapel Gallery, London
Biennale, Paris
1966 *International Exhibition,* Sonsbeek Park, Arnhem, Netherlands
Primary Structures, Jewish Museum, New York
1968 *British Artists: 6 Painters, 6 Sculptors,* Museum of Modern Art, New York
1970 *British Sculpture of the 60s,* Institute of Contemporary Arts, London
1971 *Der Geist Surrealismus,* Baukunst, Cologne
1974 *Artists Choose Artists,* Tweed Museum, Duluth, Minnesota
1976 *National Sculpture Exhibition,* Athens, Georgia (travelled)
1985 *Midwest Sculpture Invitational,* Indianapolis, Indiana
1989 *The Machine Shop,* Emery Center, Cincinnati
1997 Intersculpt '97, La Galerie Graphes, Paris
1998 Navy Pier Show, Chicago
1999 *Sculpture for a Virtual World,* Intersculpt '99, Contemporary Art Center, Cincinnati (toured)

Collections:

Arts Council of Great Britain, London; British Council, London; Peter Stuyvesant Foundation, London; Tate Gallery, London; North Jersey Cultural Council, Paramus, New Jersey; Nagaoka Museum of Art, Japan; Fort Worth Art Museum, Texas; Cincinnati Bell Collection, Ohio; Cincinnati Gas and Electric Co., Ohio.

Publications:

On WOODHAM: Books—*The New Generation,* exhibition catalog by Ian Durdop, London 1976; *Jonge Engelse Bildhowers,* exhibition catalog by Christopher Finch, Amsterdam 1967; *The New Sculpture* by Udo Kultermann, New York 1968; *Form and Structure* by Teruo Fujieda, Tokyo 1971; *Pierwalk 97 & 98* (CD-ROM), Chicago 1998; *Avatars!* By Bruce Damer, Peachpit Press 1998; *Selections from the Permanent Collection,* exhibition catalog, Radford University Art Museum 1999. **Articles**—"Colour in Sculpture" by Jasia Reichardt in *Quadrum* (Brussels), No. 18, 1965; "Caro und die junge englische skulptur" by Jean-Christophe Ammann in *Werk* (Reme), vol. 54, 1967; "Stage" in *Art and Artists* (London), Summer 1970; "Art: Sculpture Beside a Lake" by Hilton Kramer in the *New York Times,* 16 June 1974; "Fluid Borders: The Aesthetic Evolution of Digital Sculpture" by Christiane Paul, International Center web special, 1999.

*

My long-standing affair with geometry, and the sensuality of finely colored and finished materials—my pursuit of refinement and one-to-one engagement in the experiencing of sculpture—has recently drawn me towards using virtual reality as the context for comparing first and third-person perspectives on my work. While the metaphoric strength of geometry is maintained in such an environment, it gains the organizational imperative in such a mathematically construed space.

Derrick Woodham: *Over Zero,* a virtual sculpture, 1997. ©Derrick Woodham.

Active Worlds, the popular multi-user virtual reality application that I have been using to present my own work, and sculpture by others, began for me as an alternative use of models designed on the computer for future realization in tangible form. More recently, I find I am just as interested in the prospects for permanent installation there as in the material world.

—Derrick Woodham

* * *

There are striking similarities between the work that Derrick Woodham first exhibited in 1963 and his more recent pieces. Edges are clear and sharp, the surfaces are smooth, colors are muted but vibrant and volume is described with great precision. Woodham was a pioneer of what at the time was referred to as ''minimal'' sculpture, and it is hardly surprising that he has remained faithful to certain of the tenets he originated and exploited at the start of his career. What is surprising, however, is that all of his subsequent work up to and including his more recent sculpture exemplifies a position of ideology and practice that continues to place him at the vanguard of contemporary art.

In the decade during which sculptors nurtured on Henry Moore capitulated by the dozens to the seductive embraces of technology and the fugitive dogmas of conceptualism, Woodham firmly followed a course dedicated to constantly testing the limits of expression that can be encompassed by the sculpture as object (rather than the sculpture as light, electricity, sound, printed word or invisible idea). As a teacher he has sponsored, encouraged and designed multi-media activities of radical dimensions and vital innovation. In 1972 at the University of Iowa he orchestrated a series of events that explored totally new directions for live performance possibilities. Such activities feed, rather than replace, Woodham's inspiration to create object-sculpture. These investigations suggest to him related stratagems that he anchors in solid materials. A major work of his, dated 1975 and titled *Arrangements with a Modular Group,* consists of 86 units, square or oblong in shape and varying in length from six inches to eight feet. The material is Masonite, painted white. These units are arranged by the artist according to the space available. Specific preliminary settings are modified and not all the pieces need be used.

The final appearance may vary from a seemingly random placement to a stacking system that looks almost symmetrical.

Although more recent work is predominantly rectilinear and contains no traces of the rounded, somewhat biomorphic, shapes of his early pieces, the human element in his work still assumes great importance. The scale of the sculpture, indoor or outdoor, is geared to stretch our normal ways of seeing. The gallery work must be explored perimeterically and looked down, into and across, much as one would have to examine a shallow valley from a hilltop. The outdoor work, three or four times human height, invites close inspection while towering above the viewer. Viewing his work makes one very conscious of one's own body scale, size and relative immobility.

His permanently installed outdoor commissions are very successful despite (or perhaps on account of) the fact that they do not self-consciously make the acquaintance of their sites. They do not suggest overtly that they have been custom-designed for the particular setting. Most of them have been erected in rural environments and they uncompromisingly resist blending into the landscape. Their severe angles and proportions are not mitigated by monochromes quite at odds with nature's friendly mix. Woodham does not try to adapt or design to accommodate a particular site because the strength of the work is implicit, not a product of its decorative suitability. Color is a very vital element in this work, and were his forms less stimulating he would still hold a very important position as a colorist. Most modern sculpture is either selfcolored, the natural wood or steel exposed in a raw or rusted state or else flagrantly ''painted on'' with color applied so that it is impossible to eradicate the notion that two layers exist, a ''skin'' of paint over a quite differently colored solid. Woodham challenges both conventions by using the methods of the latter to confound the former. With the exception of *Gates,* 1974, a huge outdoor work utilizing interlocking segments of identical timber frameworks, none of his colors are endemic to the materials, yet they appear so because the color is applied in such a skillful, controlled manner and the surface is so smooth and pure that the predominant sensation is that the color is completely through the material. Though they are carefully mixed and often very subtle (salmon, mauve, turquoise) the colors really seem to be *in* not *on* the sculpture. Woodham achieves a fusion of such density that even to speak of the color of his work as an issue implies a separate identity for color that simply does not exist in the work as perceived.

With physically most prepossessing results, Woodham has doggedly stuck to the notion that quite apart from the formidable range of expression he can cull with his sculpture, it should not be divorced from principles of volume. Many of his peers, on both sides of the Atlantic, now take their cues from abstract painting and try to ''draw'' in space using flat planes of the now orthodox and ubiquitous brown cortin steel. Woodham has reached far more meaningful levels of dialogue by surrounding and containing space and exploring it from the inside out. Yet there is nothing at all ''fat'' about Woodham's work. It is spare and lean.

Fields consists of a four-layered grid of twelve narrow girders stacked horizontally in a lattice formation. Each girder is monochrome and the colors vary from white through yellow, purple and grey to black. This piece operates on the viewer with great immediacy and the clear, sensational impact of a complex and provocative statement. Woodham's intellectual grasp of his vocation is prodigious, but even rarer is his ability to create a unique visual vocabulary that is well-defined, self-sufficient, spontaneous and universal.

—Michael Alistair Findlay

WOODROW, Bill

Nationality: British. **Born:** Near Henley, Oxfordshire, 1 November 1948. **Education:** Winchester School of Art, Winchester, 1967–68; Saint Martin's School of Art, London, 1968–71; Chelsea School of Art, London, 1971–1972. **Career:** Independent sculptor, London, since 1972. Lives and works in London. **Agent:** Lisson Gallery, 52–54 Bell Street, London NWI 5DA. **Address:** 14 Cormont Road, London, SE5 9RA, England.

Individual Exhibitions:

1972 Whitechapel Art Gallery, London
1979 Kunstlerhaus, Hamburg
1980 The Gallery, Acre Lane, London
1981 LYC Gallery, Banks, Cumbria
New 57 Gallery, Edinburgh
Galerie Wittenbrink, Regensburg, Germany
1982 Lisson Gallery, London
Kunstausstellungen, Stuttgart
Galerie Eric Fabre, Paris
St. Paul's Gallery, Leeds, Yorkshire
Ray Hughes Gallery, Brisbane, Queensland
Galerie t'Venster, Rotterdam
Galerie Lachowsky, Antwerp, Belgium
1983 Galleria Toselli, Milan
Museum van Hedendaagse Kunst, Gent
Lisson Gallery, London
Museum of Modern Art, Oxford
Barbara Gladstone Gallery, New York
Locus Solus, Genoa
Art and Project, Amsterdam
1984 Mercer Union, Toronto
Musée de Toulon, France
Galerie Paul Maenz, Cologne
1985 Kunsthalle, Basel
Barbara Gladstone Gallery, New York
Donald Young Gallery, Chicago
La Jolla Museum of Contemporary Arts, California (travelled to Berkeley)
Currents, Institute of Contemporary Arts, Boston
Matrix, University Art Museum, University of California, Berkley
1986 Galleri Nordenhake, Malmo, Sweden
Galerie Paul Maenz, Cologne
Butler Gallery, Kilkenny, Ireland
Fruitmarket Gallery, Edinburgh
Installation for the Mattress Factory, Pittsburgh
1987 Kunstverein, Munich
Lisson Gallery, London
Cornerhouse Gallery, Manchester, Lancashire
Barbara Gladstone Gallery, New York
1988 Galerie Paul Maenz, Cologne
Seattle Art Museum, Washington
Tate Gallery, London
1989 Musée des Beaux-Arts, La Havre and Calais
Galerie Nordenhake, Stockholm
Mala Galerija, Moderna Galerija, Ljubljana
Fred Hoffman Gallery, Los Angeles

Saatchi Collection
Imperial War Museum, London
1990 Galerie Fahnemann, Berlin
1991 *Bienal,* Sao Paulo
Galleria Locus Solus, Genova
Galerie für Druckgrafik, Zurich
1992 Galerie Sabine Wachters, Brussels and Knokke
1993 *New Drawings,* Quint Krichman Projects, La Jolla, California
Only the Lonely, with Richard Deacon, Model Arts Centre, Sligo, Ireland (traveled to Limerick City Gallery of Art, Limerick, Ireland)
Drawings, Galerie Sabine Wachters, Brussels
1995 *About This Axis, Drawings 1990–1995,* Camden Arts Centre, London/Harris Museum and Art Gallery, Preston
1996 *Fools' Gold,* Tate Gallery, London/Institut Mathildenhöhe, Darmstadt, Germany
2000 *Regardless of History,* Fourth Plinth, Trafalgar Square, London

Selected Group Exhibitions:

1981 *Objects and Sculpture,* Arnolfini, Bristol/I.C.A., London
British Sculpture in the 20th Century, Whitechapel Art Gallery, London
1983 *New Art at the Tate Gallery,* London
1984 *An International Survey of Recent Painting and Sculpture,* Museum of Modern Art, New York
1985 *Carnegie International,* Museum of Art, Pittsburgh
1987 *British Sculpture since 1965,* Museum of Contemporary Art, Chicago (Peace Museum, Chicago; San Francisco Museum of Modern Art; Newport Harbor Art Museum; Hirshhorn Museum, Washington; Albright-Knox Art Gallery, Buffalo)
1990 *Great Britain-USSR,* The House of the Artist, Kiev/The Central House of the Artist, Moscow
For A Wider World, Ukranian Museum of Fine Art, Kiev, USSR/1991 National Museum of Art and History, Luxembourg/Sofia, Bulgaria/Museo de Belles Artes, Buenos Aires, Argentina
1991 *Metropolis,* Berlin
1992 *Arte Amazonas,* Museu de Arte Moderna, Rio de Janiero (traveled Museu de Arte, Brasilia; Staatliche Kunsthalle, Berlin; Technische Sammlungen, Dresden; Lugwig Forum für Internationale Kunst, Aachen)
1993 *Autoportraits Contemporain,* Espace Lyonnais d'Art Contemporain, Lyon
1995 *From Picasso to Woodrow: Recently Acquired Prints and Portfolios,* Tate Gallery, London
1996 *Un Siecle De Sculpture Anglaise,* Jeu de Paume, Paris, France
1997 *Sexta Bienal De La Habana,* Havana, Cuba
2000 *3 R Ume—3 Flhsse, Ihr Wart Ins Wasser Eingescreiben,* Hannoversch-Münden, Germany

Collections:

Arts Council of England; British Council; British Library, London; British Museum, London; Imperial War Museum, London; Government Art Collection; Tate Gallery, London; Cecil Higgins Art Gallery and Museum, Bedford; Scottish National Gallery of Modern Art, Edinburgh; Leeds City Art Galleries; Henry Moore Institute, Leeds; Southampton Art Gallery; Museum van Hedendaagse Kunst, Antwerp, Belgium; Musée d'Art Contemporain, Montréal, Canada; National Gallery of Canada, Ottawa, Canada; MacKenzie Art Gallery, Regina, Canada; Musée des Beaux-Arts, Calais, France; Musée d'Art et d'Histoire, Chambery, France; FRAC Bourgogne, Dijon, France; FRAC Haute-Normandie, France; FRAC Picardie, Amiens, France; FRAC Rhône-Alpes, Lyon, France; Musée de Toulon, France; Butler Gallery, Kilkenny, Ireland; Museo Tamayo, Mexico City, Mexico; Museum Boymans van Beuningen, Rotterdam, Netherlands; Rijksmuseum Kröller-Müüller, Netherlands; Auckland City Art Gallery, New Zealand; National Gallery of Contemporary Art, Oslo, Norway; Malmö Konsthall, Sweden; Moderna Museet, Stockholm, Sweden; Kunsthaus Zürich, Switzerland; Museum of Contemporary Art, Chicago; Indianapolis Museum; Museum of Art, Carnegie Institute, Pittsburgh; Museum of Modern Art, New York; San Diego Museum of Contemporary Art.

Publications:

On WOODROW: Books—*Objects and Sculpture,* exhibition catalog with text by Iwona Blaszczyk, London and Bristol 1981; *Lecons des Choses,* exhibition catalog with text by Catherine Ferbos, Berne 1982; *Englische Plastik Heute,* exhibition catalog with essay by Michael Newman, Lucerne 1982; *Beaver, Bomb And Fossil* with text by David Elliott, Museum of Modern Art, Oxford 1983; *Bill Woodrow,* exhibition catalog edited by Jean-Christophe Ammann, Basel 1985; *Natural Produce, An Armed Response* with text by Lynda Forscha, La Jolla Museum of Contemporary Art, California 1985; *Bill Woodrow,* exhibition catalog with essay by Lynne Cooke, Edinburgh 1986; *Bill Woodrow,* exhibition catalog with essay by Lynne Cooke, Munich 1987; *A Quiet Revolution: British Sculpture Since 1965,* with texts by Lynne Cooke, Mary Jane Jacob and others, London 1987; *Eye Of The Needle* with text by Catherine Grenier and Francoise Cohen, Musée des Beaux-Arts, Le Havre 1989; *Point Of Entry* with poems by Selima Hill, Imperial War Museum, London, 1989; *Bill Woodrow: XXI Bienal de Sao Paulo 1991,* exhibition catalog with text by John Roberts, London 1991; *Only the Lonely and Other Shared Sculptures: Bill Woodrow and Richard Deacon,* exhibition catalog, London 1993; *Chapter And Verse,* with interview by Eddy Devolder, Maison de la Culture, La Louvière, Belgium 1994; *In Awe Of The Pawnbroker* with text by John Roberts, Oriel, Cardiff 1995; *Bill Woodrow: About This Axis: Drawings 1990–95,* Camden Arts Centre, London, 1995; *Fools' Gold* with text by John Roberts, Tate Gallery, London/Institut Mathildenhöhe, Darmstadt, 1996; *Sculptures 1981–1997* with text by Keith Patrick, Mestna Galerija, Ljubljana, Slovenia, 1997; *Shadow Of The Beekeeper* pamphlet with text by Marco Livingstone, NatWest Group Art Collection, London, 1999.

* * *

Shortly after completing his education at St. Martin's and later the Chelsea School of Art, Bill Woodrow's work was exhibited in a small solo show at London's Whitechapel Art Gallery. Some eight years were to follow before the artist exhibited again, by which time his art had evolved radically. From 1978 he had begun working with found materials, deconstructing common domestic objects and reassembling them in ways to give a new perspective on the familiar.

In the early 1980s, together with Tony Cragg, Richard Deacon, and others, Woodrow was to become a pivotal figure in the emerging generation of British sculptors known as the ''New Sculpture.'' While their work was distinguished by its highly individualistic approaches—a critique of the conformity of late modernism—a common concern centred on the use of found-objects and/or simple manufacturing procedures. Woodrow's sculpture from this period utilised the detritus of a consumer society, where commodities from discarded washing machines to automobile parts were cut apart and physically transformed into a new set of imagery. If this archaeology of the commonplace further suggested a critique of capitalism and its signifiers, it also shared the visual wit of Pop. Moreover, it touched the more poetic levels of association, while subtly questioning the discrete autonomy of identity.

One of the most enduring works of this early period is *Twin-Tub With Guitar* (1981, Tate Gallery), in which the artist has cut open the outer skin of a discarded washing machine, fashioning the metal into the likeness of an electric guitar. Scale, colour and material are here dictated by the original found-object, but in other works from this period a more eclectic assemblage of host objects is brought into play, with the resulting installation taking on a more spatial aspect. *Campfire* (1981), for example, combines three domestic heaters and an armchair, creating the surreal tableaux of a campfire that draws for colour and texture on the various materials of the host objects while filling the exhibiting space from floor to ceiling.

From 1987, Woodrow gradually evolved away from manipulating found materials to working with welded sheet steel, although the imagery remains that of the fashioned object or objects. Sheet steel in turn gave way to sculpted forms cast in bronze, which has become the artist's principal medium over the past decade. *Corporate Identity* (1989)—with its sheet steel snake, Bacon-like space frame and enigmatic lettering—is typical of this transitionary stage, and combines various sets of imagery familiar from his earlier work, but does so in a way that invites a more complex narrative reading.

Works from this period tend to combine elements with disparate formal qualities, further compounding the complexity of the narrative associations. He also investigated a variety of materials and approaches during the late eighties, and was still occasionally using found objects, although with little or no alteration to their material form. This period further saw an increased interest in drawing that would eventually lead to the large-scale works in oilstick on paper made during the mid-1990s.

Most of Woodrow's work from the 1990s is in bronze, sometimes combined with other materials. Made formally more cohesive through the unifying use of this medium, the artist has continued to pursue narrative themes, using a set of simple imagery that has evolved into a personal iconography. Reoccurring symbols include books, the human head, coins, chains, wheels, etc. But while it might appear that Woodrow is making a simplistic political statement, the conceptual evolution from the earliest pieces would seem to suggest that his narratives are more open-ended, rejecting the simple closure which a political or ecological message might suggest. While a common theme in the work of all periods sees a confrontation between the cultural or industrial and the natural, we should be careful not to read Woodrow's intentions too literally. His succinct vocabulary of forms is arrived at primarily through a regard for the formal properties of particular imagery; it is only through the making process that the artist explores more associative ideas. Thus, issues may be raised but not necessarily resolved. A certain level of ambiguity is essential, for Woodrow's sculpture demands the active participation of his audience and shifts much of the onus for interpretation from the artist onto the viewer.

—Keith Patrick

WUNDERLICH, Paul

Nationality: German. **Born:** Eberswailde, near Berlin, 10 May 1927. **Education:** High School in Eutin until 1946; studied art, under Willi Titze and Willem Grimm, Landeskunstschule, and Hochschule für Bildende Künste, Hamburg 1947–51; studied printing techniques with Desjobert, Paris. **Military Service:** Served in the German Army, 1943–45; prisoner of war 1945. **Family:** Married the photographer Karin Székessy in 1972; daughter: Laura. **Career:** Painter, printmaker and sculptor, Hamburg, 1952–60 and since 1963, in Paris and Italy, 1961–63. Freelance instructor in graphics and printmaking, 1963–68; professor of graphics, Hochschule für Bildende Künste, Hamburg, 1963–67. **Awards:** Cultural Circle bursary, Hamburg, 1951; Stipendium des Kulturkreises, Hamburg, 1955; Deutsche Kunstpreis der Jugend für Grafik, 1960; M. S. Collins Prize, Philadelphia, 1962; Cultural Forum Prize, Tokyo, 1964; Premio Marzotto, Milan, 1967; Graphic Art Prize, Kamakura Museum, Tokyo, 1968; Gold Medal, Florence, 1970; Gold Medal, Oslo, 1973; Medal, Cracow, 1975; Gold Medal, Graphics Biennale, Listowell, Ireland, 1978; Graphics Prize, Taiwan, 1984; Kunstpreis des Landes Schleswig Holstein, West Germany, 1986. **Agents:** Gallery Wuezer, echtion Huber, Berliner Str. 218, D-63011 Offenbach, Germany; Redfern Gallery, 20 Cork Street, London WI, England. **Address:** Hayn Strasse 2, Eppendorf, 20249 Hamburg 20, Germany.

Individual Exhibitions:

1949 Overbeck-Gesellschaft, Lubeck
1955 Kunstlerklub Die Insel, Hamburg
1958 Galerie Nebelung, Dusseldorf
Orangerie, Utin, West Germany
1960 Dragonerstall, Hamburg
1961 Galerie die Insel, Worpswede, West Germany
Galerie Niepel, Dusseldorf
1962 Galerie Brusberg, Hannover
Galerie Diogenes, West Berlin
Galerie Brockstedt, Hamburg
1963 Galerie Sydow, Frankfurt
Galerie Niedlich, Stuttgart
Print Club, Philadelphia
San Francisco Museum of Art
Galerie Rothe, Heidelberg
Galerie Niepet, Dusseldorf
Miami Museum of Art
Eric Locke Gallery, San Francisco
1964 *Obilder,* Galerie Van de Loo, Munich
Galerie Brechbuhl, Grenchen, Switzerland
1965 Galleria Arco, Rome
Musée des Beaux-Arts, Mons, Belgium
Galerie Hausdewell, Baden-Baden, West Germany
Galerie Niepel, Dusseldorf
Pfalzgalerie, Kaiserslautern, West Germany
Galerie Wilbrand, Munster, West Germany

Paul Wunderlich. Photo by Karin Szekessy.

1966 Kubus-Ausstellung, Hannover
Europa-Center, West Berlin
Kunstverein, Dusseldorf
Städtische Galerie, Bochum, West Germany
Galerie Brusberg, Hannover
Kunsthalle, Mannheim
1967 Overbeck-Gesellschaft, Lübeck
Gallerie Dierks, Aarhus, Denmark
Galerie Wolfgang Ketterer, Munich
Galerie Toni Gerber, Rome
Lithographs 1949–1967, Auckland City Art Gallery, New Zealand
1968 *Paintings, Sculpture, Drawings, Graphics,* Redfern Gallery, London
Galerie Passepartout, Copenhagen
Kunstverein, Wolfsburg, West Germany
Galerie Brusberg, Hannover
Gemalde/Zeichnungen/Graphik/Plastik, Badischer Kunstverein, Karlsruhe
Galerie d'Eendt, Amsterdam
1969 Associated American Artists Gallery, New York
Minneapolis Institute of Arts
Paris Galleries, Los Angeles
Phoenix Gallery, Berkeley, California
Kovier Gallery, Chicago
1970 Galerie Brusberg, Hannover
Recent Paintings, Drawings and Sculpture, Staempfli Gallery, New York
Kunsthalle, Recklinghausen, West Germany
Kunsthalle, Gelsenkirchen, West Germany
Museum for Moderner Konst, Gothenburg, Sweden
Galleri Leger, Copenhagen
1971 Galleri Aronowitsch, Stockholm
Amos Andersonin Taidemuseo, Helsinki
Perls Galleries, Los Angeles
Kestner-Gesellschaft, Hannover
1972 Galleria Schwarz, Milan
Galerie Berggruen, Paris
Galerie André-Francois Petit, Paris
Galleria La Bussola, Tarin
1973 *Recent Oils, Gouaches and Drawings,* Staempfli Gallery, New York
Redfern Gallery, London
Galerie Levy, Hamburg
Retrospektive der Jahre 1958 bis 1973, Baukunst, Cologne
1974 Tokyo Gallery
Galerie Art Contacts, Paris
Graphischen, Radierungen, Lithographien, Plastische Werk, Kunsthalle, Kiel
1975 Wilhelm-Lehmbruck-Museum, Duisburg, West Germany
Kunstverein, Augsburg, West Germany
Galerie Coot Saint-Pierre, Geneva
Galerie Orangerie, Cologne
1976 Fondation Veranneman, Kruishoutem, Belgium
Galerie Octave Negro, Paris
Gallerie Uddenberg, Gothenburg, Sweden

Galerie Berggruen, Paris
1977 Redfern Gallery, London
Gouaches, Tekeningen, Litho's en Beeldhounnerken, Centrum voor Kunst en Cultuur, Ghent
1979 Galerie Veranneman, at *FIAC 79,* Paris
1980 Seibu Art Museum, Tokyo
Kunsthalle, Kiel
Redfern Gallery, London
1981 Seibu Museum of Art, Tokyo
Staempfli Gallery, New York
Von Informel zur Figuration: Bilder, Objekte, Druckgraphik seit 1957, Baukunst, Cologne
1983 Fondation Veranneman, Kruishoutem, Belgium
1985 Le Bateau Lavoir, Paris
Sonet Galerie, Stockholm
1987 Kloster Cismar, Holstein, West Germany (retrospective)
Museum Schloss Gottorf, Schleswig, West Germany (graphics retrospective)
Redfern Gallery, London
1990 Redfern Gallery, London
1991 Mitsaka City Gallery, Tokyo (travelled to Navio Museum of Art, Osaka, and Gifu Museum of Art, through 1995)
New Porcelain by Paul Wunderlich, Mathildenhöhe Darmstadt, Rosenthal, Germany
1992–98 *Plädoyer für die Vernunft,* travelling exhibition, Museums in north Germany, Belgium, and Scandinavia
1993 Pal Gallery, Hong Kong
1995 Retrospective exhibitions in Tokyo, Hokkaido, Osaka, and Gifu
1996 Redfern Gallery, London
1997 Museum of Eberswalde, Germany
1998 Stiftung Veranneman, Kruishoutem
1999 *Print Retrospective,* Hokkaido Museum, Japan
2000 Galerie Terminus, Munich
Manus Presse, Stuttgart
Gallery Wurzer, Houston, Texas
2001 Redfern Gallery, London

Selected Group Exhibitions:

1955 *Farbige Grafik,* Kestner-Gesellschaft, Hannover
1962 *16 German Artists,* Corcoran Gallery, Washington, D.C.
1964 *Documenta,* Kassel, West Germany
1966 *Phantastische Figuration,* Haus am Waldsee, West Berlin
1968 *Europaische Druckgraphik der Gegenwart,* Gemeentemuseum, The Hague
1970 *Malerei nach Fotografie,* Stadtmuseum, Munich
1972 *After Surrealism,* Ringling Museum of Art, Sarasota, Florida
1976 *Les Espaces Insolites,* Palais du Congres, Strasbourg
1987 *Zauber der Medusa,* Museum Modemer Kunst, Vienna
1993 *Der Schuh,* Rheinisches Landesmuseum, Bonn

Collections:

Museum Boymans-van Reuningen, Rotterdam; Kunstverein, Darmstadt; Städtische Galerie, Bochum, West Germany; Museum of Modern Art, New York; San Francisco Museum of Modern Art; Miami Museum of Art; Schleswigholsteinisches Landes Museum, Bonn; Pinakothek, Munich; Musée d'Art Modern, Bruxelles; Hamburger Kunsthalle; Ludwig Museum, Cologne.

Publications:

On WUNDERLICH: Books—*Paul Wunderlich: Olbilder,* exhibition catalog, Munich 1964; *Paul Wunderlich: Lithographs 1949–1967,* exhibition catalog with text by Edouard Roditi, Auckland 1967; *Paul Wunderlich: Gemaldel Zeichnungen/Graphik/Plastik,* exhibition catalog with text by G. Bussmann, Karlsruhe 1968; *Paul Wunderlich: Paintings, Sculpture, Drawings, Graphics,* exhibition catalog with texts by Frank Whitford and Wieland Schmied, London 1968; *Paul Wunderlich: Recent Paintings, Drawings and Sculpture,* exhibition catalog with text by George W. Staempfli, New York 1970; *Paul Wunderlich: Catalog Raisonne de l'Oeuvre Graphique 1949–1971* by Max Bense, Hanns Theodor Flemming, Frank Whitford and others, West Berlin 1971; *Paul Wunderlich,* exhibition catalog, with text by Jose Pierre, Paris 1972; *Paul Wunderlich: Recent Oils, Gouaches and Drawings,* exhibition folder with text by George W. Staempfli, New York 1973; *Paul Wunderlich: Retrospektive der Jahre 1958 bis 1973,* exhibition catalog with text by Max Bense, Cologne 1973; *Paul Wunderlich: Skizzen 1966,* with text by Max Bense, Offenbach 1974; *Paul Wunderlich: Graphischen, Radierungen, Lithographien, Plastische Werk,* exhibition catalog with texts by Jens Christian Jensen, Johann Schlick and Eberhard Freitag, Kiel 1974; *Paul Wunderlich: Gouaches, Tekeningen, Litho's en Beeldhouwwerken,* exhibition catalog, Ghent 1977; *Paul Wunderlich und Karin Szekessy: Corresppondenzen,* with an introduction by Fritz J. Raddaz, Hamburg 1977; *Paul Wunderlich* by Octave Negro, Paris 1979; *Paul Wunderlich: Werkverzeichnis* by Jens Christian Jensen, Offenbach 1979; *Paul Wunderlich,* exhibition catalog with text by Jens Christian Jensen, Tokyo 1980; *Paul Wunderlich; Von Informel zur Figuration: Bilder, Objekie, Druckgraphik seit 1957,* exhibition folder with text by Jens Christian Jensen, Cologne 1981; *Paul Wunderlich: Werkverzeichnis der Uthografien,* Offenbach 1981; *Paul Wunderlich: Methamorphosen,* with text by H. Hollander, Dortmund 1985; *Paul Wunderlich,* exhibition catalog, Holstein 1987: *Paul Wunderlich: Skulpturen und Objekte* by Heinz Spielmann, Offenbach 1987; *Paul Wunderlich: Skulpturen und Objekte II* by Heinz Spielmann, Offenbach 2000; *Drypoint, Kaltnadel, Pointe Séche* by Heinz Spielmann, Hamburg 2000.

* * *

Paul Wunderlich's pictures are frequently associated with the tradition of surrealism. While this historical aspect may appear understandable in view of the imagination and fantasy in his art, the work can be described just as well if not more accurately as an analysis of political involvement, sense of reality, Eros, violence, space—that is, of direct experiences related to the present. Wunderlich has painted portraits, paraphrases of older masters, illustrations to the *Song of Solomon* and to Joyce; he has modelled sculptures and conceived useful objects which are not exhausted by use; he is a perfectionist in his craft—in the name of perfect form; he keeps his distance but is always available for practical help; he is very articulate but refrains almost entirely from comment on his pictures. This diversity serves him, however, as a stimulus to the style with which he makes each idea and each problem his own.

Apart from some graphic works Wunderlich's oeuvre begins in 1959. Two series of lithographs at this time show two essential qualities which would always preoccupy him: the oppressed human being, susceptible to violence, whose worth is visible precisely in his destruction, and Eros as an essential human quality which Wunderlich shows as an aesthetic quality. The two series which, seen from today, appear as a key to Wunderlich's art, excited attention when they were shown in a small gallery: the first (the cycle ''20 July 1944'') translated the concrete political event, the assassination of the men involved in the revolt against Hitler, into a general interpretation of human sorrow; the other (the cycle ''qui s'explique'') became the occasion for a demonstration of anti-constitutional bigotry. The punishment of the artist for ''pornography'' brought him into public view, although he shuns rather than seeks publicity. The event has in no way influenced the development of his work.

In the early 1960s Wunderlich next varied the poetic, macabre, erotic themes with graphic works (''Francois Villon,'' ''Leda,'' ''Kleine Anatomie,'' among others), and then around 1964 he began an essential phase in his painting. Wunderlich strives for a painterly line away from traditional peinture by frequent use of the spray gun. The stimulus for his pictures is artificial reality, whether it be the artistic photographs of his wife Karin Székessy or pictures by kindred spirits (Runge, the Fontainebleau school, Leonardo, Ingres, David, and later on Dürer and Manet). The pictures and colored lithographs to the *Song of Solomon* may count as an initial high point in Wunderlich's art, soon followed by a second in the paraphrases of Dürer. It is not only concern for style and form, perfection of craft and execution that links Wunderlich to Dürer; in similar fashion, Wunderlich soon became a representative abroad of the art of his native land, mainly in Western Europe, Japan and the United States.

To the themes which are to him already classical, he added, in the 1970s, portraits in which he can demonstrate in exemplary fashion his relationship to reality. Sculpture to him is a further medium—there has not been since Max Ernst any comparable sculptural work carried out by a German painter. Wunderlich's useful objects are also sculpture that more clearly bewitches reality.

—Heinz Spielmann

WYETH, Andrew (Newell)

Nationality: American. **Born:** Chadds Ford, Pennsylvania, 12 July 1917. **Education:** By private tutors; studied art with his father, N. C. Wyeth. **Family:** Married Betsy Merle James in 1940; children: Nicholas and James. **Career:** Painter. **Awards:** Dana Watercolor Medal, *Pennsylvania Academy Annual,* Philadelphia, 1947; Award of Merit, American Academy of Arts and Letters, 1947; Second Prize, *Painting in the United States,* Carnegie Institute, Pittsburgh, 1948; Popular Prize, *Carnegie International,* Pittsburgh, 1958; Presidential Medal of Freedom, 1963; Annual Award, with James Johnson Sweeney, *Art in America,* 1963; Awarded The Congressional Gold Medal, 1990; The Farnsworth Museum Center for the Wyeth Family, Rockland, Maine, 1998. D.F.A.: Harvard University, Cambridge, Massachusetts, 1955; Colby College, Waterville, Maine, 1955; Swarthmore College, Pennsylvania, 1958; Honorary Doctorate, University of Vermont, 1988; Presidential Award, Congressional Gold Medal, 1988. **Member:** National Institute of Arts and Letters. **Agent:** Office, care Frank E. Fowler, PO Box 247, Lookout Mountain, TN 37350–0247. **Address:** Chadds Ford, Pennsylvania 19317, U.S.A. **Web site:** http://www.wyethcenter.com.

Individual Exhibitions:

1937 Macbeth Gallery, New York
1938 Macbeth Gallery, New York
Doll and Richards, Boston
1939 Macbeth Gallery, New York
1940 Doll and Richards, Boston
1941 Macbeth Gallery, New York
1942 Doll and Richards, Boston
1943 Macbeth Gallery, New York
1944 Doll and Richards, Boston
1945 Macbeth Gallery, New York
1946 Doll and Richards, Boston
1948 Macbeth Gallery, New York
1950 Macbeth Gallery, New York
1951 Currier Gallery of Art, Manchester, New Hampshire (retrospective)
William A. Farnsworth Library and Art Museum, Rockland, Maine (retrospective)
1952 Macbeth Gallery, New York
1953 M. Knoedler and Co., New York
1956 M. H. de Young Memorial Museum, San Francisco (retrospective)
Santa Barbara Museum of Art, California (retrospective)
1957 Delaware Art Center, Wilmington (retrospective)
1958 M. Knoedler and Co., New York
1960 Charles Hayden Memorial Library, Massachusetts Institute of Technology, Cambridge (retrospective)
1962 Albright-Knox Art Gallery, Buffalo, New York (retrospective)
1963 Fogg Art Museum, Harvard University, Cambridge, Massachusetts (retrospective toured the United States)
University of Arizona Art Museum, Tucson
1966 Pennsylvania Academy of Fine Arts, Philadelphia (retrospective; toured the United States)
1970 Museum of Fine Arts, Boston
1974 National Museum of Modern Art, Tokyo (retrospective)
Lefevre Gallery, London
National Museum of Modern Art, Kyoto, Japan
1976 Metropolitan Museum of Art, New York (retrospective)
1981 Station Gallery, Greenville, Connecticut
Delaware Art Museum, Wilmington
Brandywine River Museum, Chadds Ford, Pennsylvania
Greenville County Museum of Art, South Carolina
Galerie Claude Bernard, Paris
1982 Virginia Art Museum, Richmond
1983 Fort Lauderdale Museum of Art, Florida

Andrew Newell Wyeth: *Dodge's Ridge,* 1947. ©Smithsonian National Museum of American Art/Art Resource, NY.

Brooks Museum of Art, Memphis, Tennessee
Portland Museum of Art, Maine

1984 Brandywine River Museum, Chadds Ford, Pennsylvania
Funabashi Gallery, Tokyo
Gallery Iida, Tokyo

1985 Canton Art Institute, Ohio

1987 *The Helga Pictures*, National Gallery of Art, Washington, D.C.
Museum of Fine Arts, Boston

1988 Houston Museum of Fine Arts, Texas
Los Angeles County Museum of Art
Fine Arts Museum, San Francisco
Detroit Institute of Arts, Michigan

1989 *Andrew Wyeth in Maine*, Portland Museum of Art (catalog)

1992 *Andrew Wyeth: Southeastern Collection*, Jacksonville Art Museum (catalog)

1995 *Andrew Wyeth: Autobiography*, Nelson-Atkins Museum of Art, Kansas City

1997 *Andrew Wyeth at 80*, Portland Museum of Art, Maine (retrospective)

1998 *Unknown Terrain*, Whitney Museum of American Art, New York (catalog)
Wondrous Strange: Pyle, Wyeth, Wyeth & Wyeth, Farnsworth Art Museum, Rockland (also Delaware Art Museum, Wilmington) (catalog)

1999 *A Century of Wyeths*, Farnsworth Art Museum, Rockland, Maine (catalog)

2000 *The Wyeths of Pennsylvania: Three Generations,* Governor's Residence, Harrisburg, Pennsylvania

2001 *Selected Works*, The Wyeth Center Galleries, Rockville, Maine (with Jamie Wyeth)
Andrew Wyeth: Close Friends, Mississippi Museum of Art, Jackson (traveled to Greenville County Museum of

Andrew Wyeth: *Refuge,* 1985. ©Geoffrey Clements/Corbis.

Art, South Carolina and Telfair Museum of Art, Savannah) (catalog)

Selected Group Exhibitions:

1938 *Pennsylvania Academy Annual,* Philadelphia (and frequently until 1963)
1943 *American Realists and Magic Realists,* Museum of Modern Art, New York
1947 *Painting in the United States,* Carnegie Institute, Pittsburgh (and 1948, 1949)
1950 *Carnegie International,* Pittsburgh (and 1952, 1958, 1961, 1964)
1959 *American Painting and Sculpture,* Moscow
1963 *Dunn International,* Beaverbrook Art Gallery, Fredericton, New Brunswick (travelled to the Tate Gallery, London)
1964 *Between the Fairs, 25 Years of American Art 1939–64,* Whitney Museum, New York
1965 *N.C. Wyeth and the Brandywine Tradition,* William Penn Memorial Museum, Harrisburg, Pennsylvania
1971 *The Brandywine Heritage,* Brandywine River Museum, Chadds Ford, Pennsylvania
1974 *10 Americans,* Andrew Crispo Gallery, New York
1995 *The American Watercolour Tradition,* Portland Museum of Art

Collections:

Brandywine River Museum, Chadds Ford, Pennsylvania; Metropolitan Museum of Art, New York; Museum of Modern Art, New York; Museum of Fine Arts, Boston; Wadsworth Atheneum, Hartford, Connecticut; Currier Gallery of Art, Manchester, New Hampshire; Philadelphia Museum of Art; North Carolina Museum of Art, Raleigh; Art Institute of Chicago; Museum of Fine Arts, Houston.

Publications:

By WYETH: Boooks—*Andrew Wyeth: Autobiography,* with Thomas Hoving, New York 1996; *Unknown Terrain,* with Beth Weinberg and Adam D. Weinberg, New York 1998. **Article—**''Andrew Wyeth,'' interview with George Plimpton and Donald Stewart, in *Horizon* (New York), September 1961.

On WYETH: Books—*The Brandywine Tradition* by Henry C. Pitz, Boston 1969; *Andrew Wyeth from Public and Private Collections,* exhibition catalog with introduction by M. I. Albacete, Canton, Ohio 1985; *Andrew Wyeth: The Helga Pictures* by John Wilmerding, New York 1987; *Wyeth People: A Portrait of Andrew Wyeth as Seen By His Friends and Neighbours*, Dallas 1988; *First Impressions: Andrew Wyeth* by Richard Meryman, New York 1991; *Andrew Wyeth: America's Painter* by Martha R. Severens and Ken Wilber, New York 1996. **Articles—**''Andrew Wyeth'' by Lloyd Goodrich in *Art in America* (New York), October 1955; ''Andrew Wyeth'' by Henry C. Pitz in *American Artist* (New York), November 1958; ''Andrew Wyeth'' by Eliot Clark in *Studio* (London), December 1960; ''The Four Seasons: Dry-Brush Drawings by Andrew Wyeth'' by Lloyd Goodrich in *Art in America* (New York), no. 2, 1962; ''New Light in Andrew Wyeth'' by James W. Fosburgh in Artnews (New York), November 1962: ''The Drawings of Andrew Wyeth'' by Agnes Morgan in *American Artist* (New York), September 1963; ''Andrew Wyeth'' by E. P. Richardson in the *Atlantic* (Boston), June 1964; ''Andrew Wyeth'' by Brian O'Doherty in *Show* (New York), May 1965; article in *Current Biography,* New York 1981; ''Heavily Hyped Helga: The Artist and the Girl Next Door'' by John Updike in *The New Republic,* vol. 197, no. 23, 7 December 1987; ''Provincial and Universal: Three Generations of Wyeth Art'' by Robin Stemp in *Artist,* vol. 103, no. 11, November 1988; ''Wyeth's World'' by Jennifer Wolcott in *The Christian Science Monitor,* Friday, June 26, 1998. **Film—***Andrew Wyeth, Self-Portrait: Snow Hill,* 1995; Wondrous *Strange: A Conversation: Andrew & Jamie Wyeth on the Wyeth Tradition* by Mary Lou Teel, 1998.

* * *

Not many artists in the 20th century, like their 16th century predecessors, have made good by staying home. Andrew Wyeth, born in Chadds Fork, Pennsylvania, is one such exception; his address in 2001 is still Chadds Ford. In more ways than one his fixed place of residence is symptomatic of his art. His father, N. C. Wyeth, was the pupil of Howard Pyle in that sleepy village and set up his own studio as an illustrator of the historical and romantic episodes of the Union's days of glory and struggle. Andrew, born and brought up in a home where art belonged, had no need to sever family ties to develop his own brand of imagery. His father taught him the techniques; his attitudes grew undisturbed by the pressures of the past or the competitions of the present among young artists in the cities. Pennsylvania alternated with summer sojourns in Maine and between the two localities the younger Wyeth's art grew along the parallel media of water-colour and tempera.

In water-colour the format is usually small and the landscape is the favorite motive. Often it is in the winter fields under snow where the gradual thawing presents a bonus to the artist in the metamorphosis in the changing colour of the ground and the melting tracery of frost-etched foliage.

In 1937–38 Wyeth held his first one-man shows in Boston and in New York. Since then he has exhibited all over the United States and abroad with success without ever failing, once the sterling character of his work became recognized for its consistency and unadulterated painterly quality. Never engaged in the equivocal dialogue of contemporary viability of experiment and discovery, Wyeth's accomplishments have been the seemingly archaic devotion to the search for perfection within a chosen system of conventions owing most to the native American tradition and its personal interpretation by a mind unswayed by art politics of any kind. This concentration of means and directions endows his paintings with the airless atmosphere of a studio where each brush stroke is meditated and deliberated before it takes its place in the canvas with the irrevocable logic of a segment in a jigsaw puzzle.

Sometimes there is a hint of contrived symbolism as in the picture of ''Young America,'' the much exhibited painting of 1950. In this panel the young man rides his bicycle across the open pasture land. He wears a sundowner hat, one side clipped up by a quasi-military badge, and above his head flies a bright tricolour burgee from the long strut rising from the front hub. This mood of adolescent nostalgia for the pioneering past and the battles of adventurous frontiers seems dated now, but it is at one with the somewhat naive innocence of a genre tied firmly to sentiment and homebound associations.

In less allusive interiors and landscapes without figures Wyeth works in a restricted palette. His realism is of a totally composed scene in which every inch of surface plays its integral part towards the final impression. Its radical compass is short but magnetic. One can share the artist's serious passion in a reconstruction dictated by retinal plotting, leaving not only the memorable image but also a superlative material equivalent.

—G.S. Whittet

X

XU BING

Nationality: Chinese. **Born:** Chongqing, China, 1955; moved to United States in 1990. **Education:** Central Academy of Fine Art, Beijing, M.F.A., 1987. **Family:** One daughter. **Career:** Visiting artist, Fine Arts Academy of Paris, 1988, and Australian University Institute of the Arts, Canberra, 1993; guest lecturer at universities including Yale University, Duke University, Columbia University, and Rhode Island School of Design, since 1994. **Awards:** Honorary Fellow, University of Wisconsin, Madison, 1990; ArtPace Foundation Award, 1996; Pollock-Krasner Foundation Award, 1998; MacArthur Award, MacArthur Foundation, 1999. **Address:** Xu Bing Studio, 540 Metropolitan Ave., Brooklyn, New York 11211. **Web site:** http://www.xubing.com.

Selected Individual Exhibitions:

1988 *A Book from the Sky,* National Fine Art Museum, Beijing
1990 *A Book from the Sky,* Tokyo Gallery, Tokyo. (catalog)
1991 *Three Installations by Xu Bing,* Elvehjem Museum of Art, Madison, Wisconsin (catalog)
1992 *Xu Bing Series Exhibition 1,* North Dakota Museum of Art, Grand Forks (catalog)
1994 *Recent Work,* The Bronx Museum of the Arts, New York (brochure)
Negotiation Table, Art Center College of Design, Pasadena, California (brochure)
Experimental Exhibit, Han Mo Art Center, Beijing
1995 *Language Lost,* Massachusetts College of Art, Boston (catalog)
Xu Bing Series Exhibition 2, North Dakota Museum of Art, Grand Forks, North Dakota
Randolph Street Gallery, Chicago (brochure)
Dille Center for the Arts, Moorhead State University, Minnesota
Recent Projects, University Gallery. University of South Dakota
1996 *A Book from the Sky,* University Art Museum, Albany, New York
A Case Study of Transference, Ethan Cohen Fine Art, New York
1997 *Classroom Calligraphy,* Joan Miro's Foundation at Mallorca, Spain.
Installation by Xu Bing, ICA-Institute of Contemporary Arts, London
Tokyo Gallery, Tokyo (catalog)
Charpa Gallery, Valencia (catalog)
Lost Letters, Asian Fine Arts Factory, Berlin (catalog)
The Net: A Collaborative Installation by Xu Bing, December Art Center, Eastern Illinois University, Charleston, Illinois
1998 Jack Tilton Gallery, New York
The Wood Street Gallery, Pittsburgh, Pennsylvania
Recent Projects, California Institute for the Arts, Valencia.
Gallery of University of Wisconsin-Oshkosh, Wisconsin

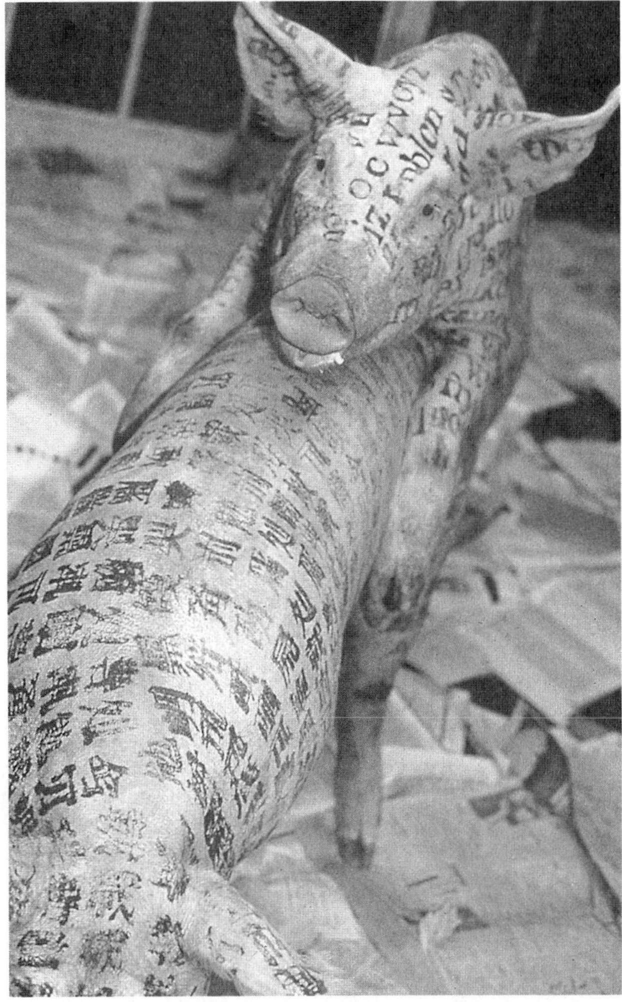

Xu Bing: *Case Study of Tranference,* original performance, Han Mo Art Center, 1994. Photo by Xing Danwen.

1999 New Museum of Contemporary Art, New York
2000 *Book/Ends: Imag(in)ing the Book—The Work of Xu Bing,* State University at Albany, New York
Book from the Sky and Classroom Calligraphy, National Gallery of Prague, Czech Republic. (catalog)
Tobacco Project, Duke University, Durham, North Carolina (catalog)
Bates College Museum of Art, Maine

Selected Group Exhibitions:

1986 1st Turkey Biennial, Ankara, Turkey (catalog)
British Museum, London (catalog)
1989 *China Avant-Garde,* National Fine Art Museum, Beijing, China (brochure)
1991 *The Book as an Object d'Art,* Hong Kong Arts Centre, Hong Kong (brochure)

I Don't Want to Play Cards With Cezanne and Other Works, Pacific Asia Museum, California (catalog)
1992 *Desire for Words,* Hong Kong Arts Centre, Hong Kong (catalog)
New Art From China, Queensland Art Museum, Brisbane (toured Australia; catalog)
Looking for Tree of Life: A Journey to Asian Contemporary Art, Museum of Modern Art, Saitama, Japan (catalog)
1993 45th Venice Biennial, Venice (catalog)
Fragmented Memory: The Chinese Avant-Garde in Exile, Wexner Center for the Visual Arts, Columbus, Ohio (catalog)
Mao Goes Pop: China Post-1989, Museum of Contemporary Art, Sydney (catalog)
1994 *Cocido y Crudo,* Reina Sofia Museum of Art, Madrid (catalog)
1997 *power,* 2nd Kwangju Biennale, Korea (catalog)
Transversions, 2nd Johannesburg Biennale, South Africa (catalog)
An Aspect of Chinese Contemporary Art: In Between Limits, Sonje Museum of Contemporary Art, Kwangju, Korea (catalog)
1996 *Origins and Myths of Fire,* The Museum of Modern Art, Saitama, Japan
1995 *Chinese Avant-Garde Art,* Santa Monica Art Center, California (catalog)
New Art in China, 1989–1994, Vancouver Art Gallery, Canada (catalog)
1999 *Banner Project,* Museum of Modern Art, New York
1st Fukuoka Asian Art Triennale, Fukuoka Asian Art Museum, Japan (catalog)
Inside Out-Chinese New Art, San Francisco Museum of Modern Art and the Asian Art Museum (catalog)
The Third Asia-Pacific Triennial of Contemporary Art, Queensland Art Gallery, Brisbane, Australia (catalog)
Zeitwenden: Looking Back and Looking Forward through the Fine Arts, Kunstmuseum, Bonn, Germany (catalog)
Transience: Chinese Experimental Art at the End of the Twentieth Century, University of Chicago Museum, Chicago
1998 *Crossings,* The National Gallery of Canada, Ottawa (catalog)
Site of Desire, 98' Taipei Biennial, Taipei Fine Art Museum, Taiwan (catalog)
Animal. Anima. Animus, Pori Art Museum, Finland (toured; catalog)
Freedom of Art Project, The Stedelijk Museum of Amsterdam
2000 Sydney Biennale, Art Gallery New South Wales, Sydney (catalog)
The Book & The Computer Project, Tokyo, Japan
Chinese Contemporary Art Documentation Show, 1990s, Fukuoka Asian Art Museum, Fukuoka, Japan.
2001 *Give and Take,* Victoria and Albert Museum, London

Publications:

By XU BING: Articles—''A Re-exploration and Reassessment of Pluralist Painting'' in *Fine Arts Magazine* (Beijing), 1981; ''Analysis and Observation: A Letter by Xu Bing to Qi Li'' in *Hsiung Shi Art Monthly* (Taipei), vol. 242, no. 4, 1991; interview with Christina Davidson in *Art and Asia Pacific* (Australia), vol. 1, no. 2, 1994; interview with Janelle S. Taylor in *Public Culture* (Chicago), vol. 5, no. 2, 1994; interview with Feng Boyi in *Orient* (Beijing), vol. 18, no. 5, 1996; interview in *Fine Art Research* (Beijing), vol. 85, no. 1, 1997; ''In Commemoration of Gu Yuan'' in *Fine Art Research* (Beijing) vol. 85, no. 1, 1997; interview with Nick Kaye in *Performance Research* (London), vol. 3, no. 1, 1998; interview with Hua Tian Sue in *Art Observation* (Beijing), vol. 48 no. 11, 1999; interview with Shu Kewen in *Living Weekly* (Beijing), no. 1, 2000; interview with Vivienne Tam in *Chinese Chic,* New York 2000.

On XU BING: Books—*Cultural Metamorphosis: The Art of Xu Bing and Cai Guo Qiang,* masters thesis by Zhang Zhaohui, Bard College, 1998; *Words without Meaning, Meaning without Words: The Art of Xu Bing,* exhibition catalog with text by Britta Erickson, Washington, D.C., and Seattle 2001. **Articles**—''Ambivalent Icons: Works by five Chinese Artists Based in the United States'' by Jonathan Hay in *Orientations* (Hong Kong), vol. 23, no. 7, July 1992; special issue of *Public Culture* (Chicago), vol. 6, no. 2, Winter 1994; ''Xu Bing and his A Book from the Sky.'' by Weihe Chen in *Intellectuals* (Beijing), no. 1, 1988; ''Evolving Meanings in Xu Bing's Art: A case Study of Transference'' by Britta Erickson in *Chinese Type,* vol. 1, no. 4, May 1998; ''No Questions, No Answers: China and A Book from the Sky'' by Stanley K. Abe in *boundary 2,* vol. 25, no 3, Fall 1998; ''Xu Bing at Jack Tilton and the New Museum'' by Jonathan Goodman in *Art in America,* January 1999; ''Xu Bing: The Cage of Words'' by Jonathan Goodman in *Art Asia Pacific,* no. 26, Spring 2000.

* * *

Over the past decade and a half, Xu Bing's innovations within the print medium, combined with his manipulation of language as a means of confronting cultural complacency, have propelled him to prominence. Currently his works focus on the difficulties and delights of communicating via language, and explore ways in which language has come to limit humankind's experience of the world. Although he delves into difficult concepts, his inventiveness and gentle wit lead his audience to understanding.

Xu Bing initially garnered widespread acclaim for his *Book from the Sky.* First exhibited in Beijing in 1988, the *Book from the Sky* is now recognized as a major monument of later twentieth century Chinese art. At its core, this work is based on twelve hundred unintelligible ''Chinese'' characters invented by the artist. He carved these characters into small blocks of pear wood, from which he typeset and printed the pages of a four-volume book. Usually Xu Bing exhibits the *Book from the Sky* as an installation that surrounds the viewer, with open books covering the floor, scrolls printed with unintelligible characters draped from the ceiling, and panels of invented characters lining the walls. This constitutes a surreal realm, superficially rational and yet utterly indecipherable. The invented characters so closely resemble genuine characters, and the books so closely follow the format of traditional Chinese books, that Chinese literate viewers inevitably expect to be able to read them. The sudden realization that the books are incomprehensible requires a dramatic shift in thought patterns. Xu Bing has since sought to formulate additional works that catalyze such a wrenching shift in thinking, considering this experience to be valuable and liberating for the viewer.

Following the *Book from the Sky*, Xu Bing's interests in language and printmaking have diverged. The artist's next major work, *Ghosts Pounding the Wall* (1990–1991), is the largest print ever made. With a team of over a dozen assistants, he devoted three and a half weeks to making a rubbing of a section of the Great Wall, including two sides of a watchtower, a stretch of wall, and a portion of the walkway atop the wall. All of this he mounted on a paper backing for its exhibition as a monumental installation. With this massive print, and with an ongoing series, the *Series of Repetitions* prints (1987—), Xu Bing explored the medium of printmaking and extended it boundaries. The MacArthur Foundation cited his inventiveness as a print artist as a reason for granting him an award in 1999.

Years of Chinese government manipulation of language had made the written word seem undependable to Xu Bing. Moving to the United States in 1990, and knowing very little English, he found verbal communication even more uncertain. Focusing his attention on the language barrier, Xu Bing created such works as *A, B, C . . .* (1991) and *Post-Testament* (1992–1993). In 1994 he invented Square Word Calligraphy, a way of writing English so that it resembles Chinese characters. Square Word Calligraphy provides a counterpoint to *Book from the Sky*. Like the *Book from the Sky*, Square Word Calligraphy brings the viewer to a moment in which all assumptions concerning everyday language recognition must be suspended in order to comprehend the work's meaning. English literate audiences expect to be unable to read Square Word Calligraphy, but discover to their surprise and delight that they can. Chinese literate audiences expect to be able to read Square Word Calligraphy, but find they cannot. With its myriad possible variations, including *Classroom Calligraphy* (1996—), *New English Calligraphy* (1998), and the Square Word Calligraphy computer font (2001), Square Word Calligraphy has proven to be a key work in the artist's career.

Most recently, Xu Bing has developed *Landscript* (1999—), a means of rendering a landscape using different forms of Chinese characters, including early pictographs. This method of composing landscapes highlights the way in which the intermediary of language distances us from direct experience of nature. This dilemma—of particular interest to Xu Bing—is something he first explored through works involving animals.

Beginning with *Case Study of Transference* (1994), Xu Bing has created installation/performance pieces where viewers confront animals in elitist art settings. These works jolt people into a deeper understanding of human nature, of what it is that separates humankind from animals, and in particular of the role language plays in this separation. For *Case Study of Transference*, Xu Bing placed two pigs printed all over with nonsensical Chinese and English in a pen, to mate. While audience members had been expected to ponder questions of language conditioning on the formation of culture, their primary reaction was one of embarrassment. Watching the animals mate, they faced their discomfort in acknowledging their ''animal nature''—a discomfort concocted by culture. Several years later, with the *Net* (1997–1998), Xu Bing placed two sheep in a cage formed from wire bent into the shapes of words. Because the sheep were in an unusual location—a museum rather than a farm—viewers contemplated the fact of the animals' imprisonment, and the role of language in facilitating humankind's control over animals. Viewers flashed to pondering ways in which language plays a controlling role in their lives, too.

Whether he is working with animals or manipulating language into quixotic formations, Xu Bing masterfully engineers situations that compel people to consider the role culture plays in their lives. He gently leads us to revelation, beguiling first with beauty and perfection of execution—a hallmark trait—and then surprising us through content that contradicts our initial expectations.

—Britta Erickson

Y

YALTER, Nil

Nationality: Turkish and French. **Born:** Cairo, 15 January 1938. **Education:** Studied fine arts in Istanbul. **Career:** Painter, sculptor, environmental and media artist; creation of an interactive CD-ROM for E.D.F. (Electricity of France), 1999–2000; directed new technology and art work shops, including *Cyber Luz,* Morgat, Luz Saint-Sauveur, E.D.F., 1996–1998; *Dran Cyber Culture,* Drancy, 1997; and *Pole Multimedia,* Espace Landowski, Boulogne Billancourt, 2000–01. Professor, University of the Sorbonne, Paris. **Address:** 22, rue Quincampoix, 75004 Paris, France.

Individual Exhibitions:

1959 Alliance Francaise, Bombay, India
1960 Fine Arts Academy, Istanbul
1973 *The Nomad Tent,* Museum of Modern Art, Paris
1974 *The Nomad Tent,* Museum of Tesse, Le Mans
1977 Jean Larcade Gallery, Paris
1978 Lavuum Gallery, Gent, Belgium
1979 Contemporary Art Club, Budapest
1980 Georges Pompidou Center, Paris
1981 *Women at Home, Woman at Work,* Festival of La Rochelle, La Rochelle, France
1982 *Rituals of the Sea,* Festival of La Rochelle, La Rochelle, France
1983 *Exile Is Difficult Work,* Museum of Modern Art, Paris
1987 *Tele-Totem,* Festival of Angouleme, France
1988 *Pyramis,* Museum of Saint-Simon, Angouleme, France
1989 *Hommage to Marquis de Sade,* Priory of Graville, Le Havre, France
1991 *Pyramis,* Cultural Center of Mandsque, France
1992 *Le Regard de L'Autre,* Gallery of the Fine Arts Academy, Mulhouse, France
1994 *Productive Memory,* Center of Contemporary Arts, Istanbul
Television, the moon, Tower of Roi René, Marseille
1995 *Television, the moon,* College Marcel Duchamp, Chateauroux, France
Contemporary Photography in Britanny, L'Imagerie, Lanion, France
1996 *Television, the moon,* Museum of Modern and Contemporary Art, Nice, France
1997 *Vraiment: Féminisme et Art,* Le Magasin, Grenoble, France
1998 *Terra Nomade,* Center of Contemporary Arts, Istanbul

Selected Group Exhibitions:

1963 *Biennale,* Paris (and 1977)
1974 *Projekt '74,* Cologne
1975 *Sociological Aspects of Video Art,* Varsovie, Poland
1976 *Collective Acts, Profiles and Voices,* A.I.R. Gallery/The Kitchen Center, New York
1980 *The Rituals,* Museum of Modern Art, Paris
Issue, Institute of Contemporary Arts, London
1983 *Bonner Kunstverein,* Bonn
1988 *Festival of Electronique Arts,* Rennes
1992 *Transvoices,* Whitney Museum of American Art, New York
1994 *Mutations of the Image,* Paris
1996 *Paris, Ville Lumière,* Habitat II, Yuksel Sabanci Art Center, Istanbul
Pixelismus, Espaces Interactifs—Europe, Pavillon of Bercy, Paris
1997 *La Roquette, Prison de Femmes,* Center of Contemporary Arts, Grenoble, France
1998 *<COMPACTS>,* Galeries du Cloitre, Rennes, France

Collections:

Fonds National d'Art Contemporain, Paris; Bibliotheque Publique d'Information, Centre Georges Pompidou, Paris; Long Beach Museum of Art, California; Aksanat, Center of Contemporary Arts, Istanbul.

Publications:

By YALTER: Articles—"Exile Is Difficult Work," in *Les Temps Modernes,* July 1984.

On YALTER: Books—*Art, Action and Participation* by Frank Popper, Paris 1980; *Overlay Contemporary Art and Art of Prehistory* by Lucy Lippard, Dutton, 1984; *Introduction a la Peinture* by Jose Pierre, Somogy, New York 1985; *Get the Message* by Lucy Lippard, Dutton, New York 1985; *L'art a l'age electronique* by Frank Popper, Thames and Hudson, 1993; *Feminisme, art et histoire de l'art* by Rosi Huhn, Paris 1994. **Articles—**"Nil Yalter" by Alain Jouffroy in *Opus International,* No. 50, Paris, 1974; "Video in Prison" by Dany Bloch in *Info-Artitude* (Paris) No. 4, 1976; "Combative Acts: Profiles and Voices" by Grace Gluck, in *New York Times,* 10 June 1976; "Nicole Croiset et Nil Yalter" by Jean Paul Fargier in *Cahiers du Cinema* (Paris), April 1980; "Auto-Portrait/Recits" by Anne Dagbert in *Art Press* (Paris), No. 51, 1980; "Tour-Video a la Rochelle" by Anne-Marie Duguet in *Liberation* (Paris), July 1982; "Sculptures in Factory" by Rosi Huhn in *Kritische Berichte* (Kassel) 1985; "Nil Yalter: Artiste Ethno-Critique" by Pierre Gaudibert in *Moins O* (Paris) No. 47, 1987; "La Muse Electro" by Herve Gauville, in *Liberation* (Paris), 2 July 1988; "Frontier between Art and Reality" by Esther Ferrer in *Lapiz* (Madrid) No. 60; "Images des Origines" by Jean-Paul Fargier in *Le Monde* (Paris) 14 June 1994; "Images Automates" by Anne-Marie Morice in *La Croix,* 23 June 1994; "Espaces Interactifs—Europe" by Jean-Paul Fargier in *Le Monde* (Paris), 29 May 1996; "Le Style c'est l'Rom" by Jean-Paul Fargier in *Art Press* (Paris), July 1996; "Le féminisme, Strapontin de l'art?" by Elisabeth

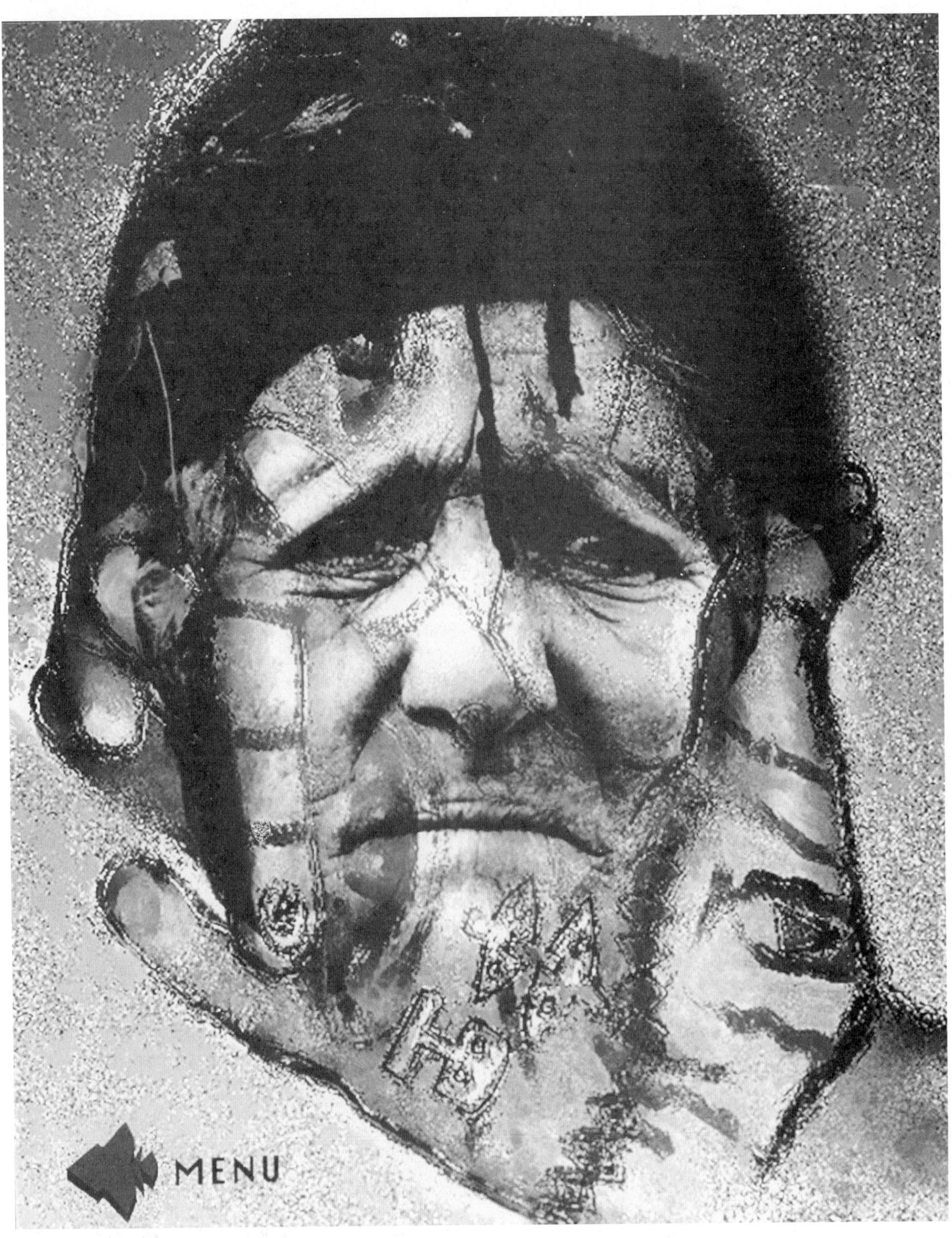

Nil Yalter: *Terra Nomade,* 1998, interactive CD-ROM still. ©Nil Yalter.

I AM AN ARTIST //I AM

I AM A MUSLIM FROM BOSNIA HERZEGOVINE
I AM / A JEW FROM SALONIKA

I AM A CIRCASSIAN FROM RUSSIA
I AM AN ABAZA

I AM A FEMALE JANIZARY
A GREEK ORTHODOX

I COME FROM TURKEY, I AM FROM FRANCE

I COME FROM BYZANTIUM
I AM FROM ASIA MINOR //I AM

I AM A MONGOL, A NOMADE
AN IMMIGRANT ARTIST
EXILED

I AM THE MESSAGE //I AM

Nil Yalter: *Woman Shaman,* 2001. ©Nil Yalter.

Lebovici in *Liberation* (Paris), 17 April 1997; ''Quand les muses passent à l'attaque, à Grenoble'' by Geneviève Breerette in *Le Monde* (Paris), April 1997; ''Yalter'in elektronik tekke'se'' by Ahu Antmen in *Cumhuriyet* (Istanbul), March 1998.

*

New technologies—a platform for a multicultural guerilla—lonesome autonomy. I am an outsider to the art world.

Using media from within, working on cultural topographies. Working on aging artist's body within a culturally corrupted society. The artist's body is a vector for social issues: digitalized, virtual forms, words, hypertext. Lonesome interactivity.

I am a woman shaman on the razor's edge.

The surface of my skin is where I write my message. Like a snake, I leave the trails of my skin on my passage.

—Nil Yalter

* * *

Nil Yalter's work witnesses a history of wanderings and displacements between different countries, continents and cultures, specially between the oriental and the occidental world. Voyages, as well between different technical and aesthetic supports, became the main impetus for the artist's personal and artistic research.

Born in Egypt as a child of a Turkish family, she grew up in Istanbul where she studied the Fine Arts as an autodidact, and has been living in Paris since 1965. During her studies in Istanbul she especially felt attracted by the occidental ideals of modern and abstract art (impressionism, constructivism, suprematism, Bauhaus). Searching for a place where the young artist would be able to contribute to the occidental project of modernity, she went to Paris. Besides painting and drawing, she not only began to work with the new modern medias as photography, video and computer art, but she paradoxically also started to be interested in the roots of her own oriental culture, the Byzantine and the Islamic Art, and in the archaic forms and structure of memory.

Yalter's artistical voyages between Orient and Occident witnesses different and unexpected crossways between iconoclastic and iconolatric attitudes, between rituals and performance art and last not least between the computer generated imageworld and the myths and documents of an ichnographical or a literary past. She travels through the most traditional as well as the most modern and contemporary medias and forms of expression.

In order to express her complex artistic and ethical ambitions in-between modernity and tradition, she combines elements of constructivism, suprematism and the Bauhaus with elements of islamic and byzantine art. In these unexpected coincidences (''rencontres'') emerge surprising relationships between constructivism and ancient calligraphy from islamic art, between abstract art and byzantine mosaïque compositions, suprematism and oriental mirror effects. She discovers those relationships through multiple and variated translation processes from painting into video into computer images and back to drawing and painting. She transposes the experiences of painting into the modern media-world and vice versa. With the instruments of new technology she reviews the formal language of the Avant-garde art of the beginning of the 20th century by fragmentation, translation and displacement processes. In this way she discovers similar formal structures and affinities between occidental and oriental, traditional and contemporary art forms; for instance, between constructivism, suprematism and picture elements of the computer (Pixels) with which she composes the computer generated images. So the white square of Malevic can be understood as the direct forerunner of the smallest unit of the computer generated image. The pedagogical graphic ''screens'' drawn by Malevic can be interpreted as anticipated forms of numerisation. Yalter's aesthetic-analytical proceeding reveals that technological inventions are due to anticipatory artistical phantasy, on the one hand, that artistical phantasy develops through technical inventions, on the other hand.

She synthesizes, approaches, combines not only different artistic styles and epochs, but as well opposite artistical doctrines such as abstract art and l'art pour l'art, and a sociological and ethnocritical oriented realism. Within her critical and enlightening aesthetic practice, the artist renders homages to the Turkish immigrant and workers in the european exile, to the fishermen in La Rochelle, to Turkish nomad women etc. She passes through numerous poetical (Nazim Hikmet, Chateaubriand), philosophical (Marquis de Sade) and artistical references (Popowa, Stepanova) in order to review them in a new personal and actual context and to push them to new meanings. She treats and displaces her once chosen material, references and quotation, combines them either with personal documents, as photos from a family album, or with earlier works of the artist.

In this puzzle of infinitely combined elements she creates a complex artistical field in which we can outline the artist's proposal: she searches for an infinite and multiple space with multiple dimensions, strata of time in-between the past, the present and the future, in-between the I and the Other, in-between reality, fiction and imagination, memory, loss, and new constructions; she advances in a fields where aesthetical, ideological and religious frontiers are going to be dissolved, and opens an ever transforming field in which, instead of eliminating the Other, opposite fields can coexist, co-emerge, dialog and change. In these in-between fields the creative principle of a matrixial feminine subverts, displaces and modifies the order of a Phallic world in which the symbolic is outlined and defined through limitation and opposition.

Nil Yalters ''Yourte'' inspired by the tents of nomadic women in Turkey (Nil Yalter presented it in 1973 in the Museum of Modern Art of Paris) reveals something of the artist's nomadic program: Yalter (re)creates a metaphorical and a feminine space symbolizing the artist's method and proceeding of wandering and displacement between the archaic and the contemporary world. The ''Yourte'' signifies the creative space of a womb and of a house at the same time. It can be carried and constructed anywhere, it is a home that can be rebuilt anytime. Her entire artistic work searches for such a symbolic space in-between and outside of different cultures, in-between and outside of tradition and modernity. The artist's place is a kind of voluntary and permanent exile in-between the opposite aesthetic, ethic and ethnic positions and systems.

Proceeding in a matrixial way and giving the artwork a matrixial structure, Nil Yalter does not only contribute to the discussion of multi-cultural and sexual differences, but proposes an aesthetic fields in which feminine elements as a creative force and energy are established.

—Rosemarie Martha Huhn

YAMADA, Masaaki

Nationality: Japanese. **Born:** Tokyo in 1930. **Education:** Studied with the artist Saburo Hasegawa, Tokyo, 1953; studied at Tokyo University, 1954. **Career:** Independent painter, Tokyo, since 1954. **Agent:** Satani Gallery, Asahi Building 11 BF, 2–6, 4-chome, Ginza, Chuo-ku, Tokyo 104, Japan.

Individual Exhibitions:

1958 Kyobunkan Gallery, Tokyo
1960 Yoseido Gallery, Tokyo (and 1962, 1963)
1964 Nantenshi Gallery, Tokyo
1965 Tsubaki Kindai Gallery, Tokyo
1966 Muramatsu Gallery, Tokyo
1968 Gallery Cristal, Tokyo
1978 Koh Gallery, Tokyo
1979 Satani Gallery, Tokyo (and 1980, 1981, 1982)
1982 Kasahara Gallery, Tokyo, Japan
1983 Inoue Gallery, Tokyo
Satani Gallery, Tokyo (and 1984, 1985)
1985 Gallery Yonetsu, Tokyo (twice)
1986 Inoue Gallery, Tokyo
Satani Gallery, Tokyo (and 1987)
1988 Galerie Springer, West Berlin
1990 San Gyomu, Tokyo (catalog)

Selected Group Exhibitions:

1949 *Yomiuri Independent Show,* Tokyo Metropolitan Museum of Art (and regulary until 1953)
1950 *Jiyu Bijutsu-ka Kyokai Association Show,* Tokyo Metropolitan Museum of Art (and regularly until 1956)
1963 *4th Ecole de Tokyo Exhibition,* Jewish Center Hall, Los Angeles
1969 *9th Contemporary Art Exhibition of Japan,* Tokyo Metropolitan Museum of Art
1972 *Modern Japanese Graphic Art,* Institute of Contemporary Arts, London
1974 *Japan: Tradition and Gegenwart,* Stadtische Kunsthalle, Dusseldorf
1980 *Variations on Planar Painting,* Fukuoka Art Museum, Japan
1984 *Contemporary Art: Tokyo/Paris,* Galerie Denise Rene, Paris
1985 *Japanese Contemporary Paintings,* Museum of Modern Art, New Delhi
1987 *19th Bienal de Sao Paulo,* Brazil
1995 *A Perspective on Contemporary Art: Painting—Singular Object,* National Museum of Modern Art, Tokyo

Collections:

National Museum of Modern Art, Tokyo; Museum of Modern Art, Toyama; Miyagi Museum of Art; Museum of Modern Art, Shiga; Museum of Modern Art, Saitama; Kitakyushu Municipal Museum of Art; Seibu Museum, Tokyo; Ohara Museum, Kurashiki; Seibu Museum, Karuizawa; Takamatsu Municipal Museum of Art.

Publications:

On YAMADA: Books—*Japan: Tradition und Gegenwart,* exhibition catalog with texts by Jurgen Harten and Joseph Love, Dusseldorf 1974; *Masaaki Yamada's Paintings 1950–1980,* exhibition catalog with text by Takashi Hayami, Tokyo 1981; *Masaaki Yamada: Works 1985–86,* exhibition catalog edited by the Satani Gallery, Tokyo 1986; *Yamada: Paintings of the Late 1950s,* exhibition catalog with essay by Tazmi Shinoda, Tokyo 1986; *19th Bienal Internacional de Sao Paulo: Japan,* exhibition catalog with text by Yoshiaki Tono, Sao Paulo 1987. **Articles—**''Painting of Masaki Yamada: On Plurality'' by Kazuo Nakabayashi in *Bulletin of the National Museum of Modern Art,* Tokyo.

*

In my work during the mid-1960s, paintings were examined with in certain constraints as a condensation of an autonomous structure expressed by the act of painting. The opposition to color is seen in the merging of material and method and includes the brush-strokes and use of repressed color. The objective quality, which interacts with form and content through the use of things like crosses and stripes, is looked at from a position that lies in opposition to the real world, as I sought to indicate the fundamental meaning that paintings establish. The restraint, however, cannot be traced to silence. My later works reflect a shift toward previously anticipated colors and stratified forms; selecting a certain point in the midst of the endless flow of time tells where I was at a given time. A compelling feeling of diversity is incorporated in the paintings.

—Masaaki Yamada

* * *

Ever since the 1950s, Masaaki Yamada's paintings have been the best example that shows the intellectual essence of the abstract paintings in Japan. Surprisingly enough, his marvelous achievements have not been shared with a lot of people in the art circles in Japan until the 1970s. He has remained aloof from any other artist or movement, creating high-standard substantial paintings by himself which miraculously corresponded with those of some modernist painters in America.

Yamada was born in Tokyo in 1930 and studied at Tokyo University. He studied painting with Saburo Hasegawa, one of the pioneering abstractionists in prewar Japan. However, Yamada's existent canvases retain no evidences that he made paintings under the major influence of Hasegawa. It is notable that he kept apart from any influence of not only the Japanese abstract painters in the prewar period, but also his contemporary abstractionists in Japan in the post-war era which, in a sense, was strongly affected by the idea of the *Informel* movement advocated and introduced to Japan by the French critic/painter Michel Tapié. The ideas of Informel and Action Painting in the United States in the '40s and '50s rapidly assimilated in Japanese avant-grade art, and evolved into the Dadaistic movement in 1960s.

Yamada stood detached and was making his analytic paintings with great subtlety which many other Japanese contemporaries were apt to ignore. He stuck to painting and explored the pictorial heritage of Cubism and Cézanne all by himself.

Early in the 1950s, he started still lifes with very limited information of Cezanne and Giorgio Morandi, but soon decomposed the subjects in analytic manner which he acquired instinctively from Cubist methodology. The surface of his painting attained the pictorial unity with flat, decomposed and geometric forms. It was 1956 when he destroyed every simplistic geometric form and began the intricate mosaic painting with numerous small broken planes. But in order to maintain stability of the painted surface, he took the constructive direction in 1957 instead of destructive. His paintings in 1958 consisted of squares and rectangles that looked like nested boxes with different colors, most of which could be regarded as the similitudes of the canvas shapes. Those works remind us of paintings by Josef Albers, but it was not until 1965 that Yamada actually saw the works by the modernist painter, Probably Yamada's idea had the affinity with not so much Albers's as Ad Reinhardt's.

The vertical and lateral elements which were introduced to stabilize the picture developed in the first half of the 1960s into the paintings of the lateral stripes in various colors. The paintings with crossed lines followed from 1965 to 1967, which actually consisted of four painted square planes in monochrome arranged at right angles, leaving the ground in a different color in the shape of the narrowest crossed lines.

From 1968 to 1973 his canvases resumed stripes, but only in two colors with the thinner surface. Next six years until 1978 was replaced by the paintings of checkered-flag pattern, retaining the thinly painted surface in two colors of adjacent values. It has been pointed out that in this period Yamada allowed his paintings to approach nearest to 'objecthood', naturally with the great affinity to the Minimalist paintings.

Liberation of free-hand drawings began in 1979 and developed into the splendid variety of strokes and colors in the paintings in the 1980s. In the first half of the eighties, his canvases retained the segmentations by square lines, limiting his

free-hand drawing lines in each division with the ground of subtle but rather restrained colors. However, since 1985, the segmenting square lines have reduced to the scattering crosses, and lavish drawings in rich colors spread over the canvas, making the painting an optical ravishment. It should not be overlooked that Yamada's exuberant works have been accomplished with the excellent texture and soft-hued, creamy colors. and they could be only possible through the Japanese sensibility.

—Tazmi Shinoda

YAMAGUCHI, Katsuhiro

Nationality: Japanese. **Born:** Tokyo, 22 April 1928. **Education:** Graduated from the Law Department of Nihon University, Japan. **Career:** Media artist, sculptor, performance and environment artist,

Katsuhiro Yamaguchi: *From Darkness 2000 to Light,* 2000. Photo by Sadamu Saito. ©Katsuhiro Yamaguchi.

and writer. Organized member with Shozo Kitadai, Toru Takemitsu, and others of ''Experimental Workshop,'' 1951; chief producer of Mitsui Pavilion at Expo '70, Osaka, 1970; organized member of ''Video Hroba,'' a group active in the field of video art, 1972; professor, University of Tsukuba, Japan, 1977–92; art director of theme pavilion in Portopia Expo '81, Kobe, 1981; organized member of ''Arts-Unis,'' group to promote high-tech art in Japan, 1982; chairman of committee for the promotion of Awaji Art Village, 1991; member of director's group, International Biennale, magoya, 1992–97; professor, 1992–99, professor emeritus, 1999—, Kobe Design University; professor emeritus, University of Tsukuba, 1992—. **Awards:** Grand prize, Fourth Exhibition of Museum of Contemporary Art, Nagaoka, 1967; prize, Tokyo National Museum of Modern Art, Eighth Contemporary Art Exhibition of Japan, Tokyo Metropolitan Art Museum, 1968; Premio Industria Villares Prize, 13th Sao Paulo Biennial, Sao Paulo, 1975; Prize Laser d'or, Sixth International Video Art Festival, Locarno, 1985; Conseil de l'Europe Prize and Grand prix de la ville de Locarno for *Metabolism in Locarno,* 14th International Video Art Festival, Locarno, 1993; 42th Mainichi Art Awards, 2001. **Address:** 1202 Shuwa-Higashiyaesu Residence, 2-9-1, Hachobori, Chuo-ku, Tokyo, Japan 104–0032.

Individual Exhibitions:

1952 Matsushima Gallery, Tokyo
1953 Takemiya Gallery, Tokyo
1955 Wako Gallery, Tokyo
1956 American Cultural Center, Yokohama
1958 Wako Gallery, Tokyo
1959 Sato Gallery, Tokyo
1964 Akiyama Gallery, Tokyo
1977 Minami Gallery, Tokyo; Sony Tower, Osaka
Ao Gallery, Tokyo
Ecole Sciologique Interrogative, Paris
1978 C.A.Y.C., Buenos Aires
Anthology Film Archives, New York
1981 Kanagawa Prefectural Hall Gallery
Info-Environmental Video Sculpture, Tokyo Gallery

1984 Satani Gallery, Tokyo
1985 Palazzo Rosso, Genova
1986 Hyogo Prefectural Museum of Modern Art, Hyogo, Laforet Museum Harajuku, Tokyo
Festival Arte Elettronica, Camerino
1988 Satani Gallery, Tokyo
1991 Chapter Art Center, United Kingdom
1992 Tsukuba Art Museum of Art, Ibaraki
C.A.Y.C., Buenos Aires
Aichi Prefectural Museum of Art, Nagoya
1994 Satani Gallery, Tokyo
1995 *Reflection 1958: 1994,* Satani Gallery, Tokyo
The 16th International Video Art Festival—Retrospective of Katsuhiro Yamaguchi, Locarno, Switzerland
1996 Nerima Art Museum, Tokyo
1999 *New Design of Public Arts,* KDU Gallery, Kobe Design University, Kobe
Computerized Shadow Play [Togen Topia], Satani Gallery, Tokyo
2000 *From Darkness 2000 to Light,* Nizayama Forest Art Museum, Toyama

Selected Group Exhibitions:

1948 *Shichiyo Kai Exhibition,* Hokuso Gallery, Tokyo
1950 *Second Yomiuri Independents Exhibition,* Tokyo Metropolitan Art Museum
1955 *New Artist of Today: 1955,* Museum of Modern Art Kamakura, Kanagawa
1960 *First Exhibit of Shudan Contemporary Sculpture Group,* Seibu Department Store, Tokyo
1965 *The New Japanese Painting and Sculpture,* Museum of Modern Art, New York
1972 *The First Video Communication—Do It Yourself Kit,* Sony Building, Tokyo
1977 *Bird's Eye View of Contemporary Japanese Art,* National Museum of Modern Art, Kyoto
1981 *The 1960s—A Decade of Change in Japanese Art,* National Museum of Modern Art, Tokyo
1986 *Image du futur '86,* La Cite des Arts et des Technoegies de Montreal, Montreal
1990 *Light in Art,* Kamakura Gallery, Tokyo
1992 *Dance in Media—Bitwin,* Moscow
1994 *Metamorphosis of Art of Post War,* Iwaki City Art Museum, Fukushima
1995 *Kwangju Biennale '95,* Kwangju, South Korea
Japanese Culture, The Fifty Postwar Years 1945–1995, Meguro Museum of Art, Tokyo (toured Japan)
1996 *Nonstatic Art in the 20th Century,* Wakayama Prefectural Museum of Modern Art, Wakayama
1964 A Turning Point in Japanese Art, Museum of Contemporary Art, Tokyo
Shading Light on Art in Japan 1953, Meguro Museum of Art, Tokyo
Video Art '66-'96, Museo Cantonale d'Art, Lugano Switzerland
1997 *The 5th International Biennale in Nagoya-Artec '97,* Nagoya City Art Museum, Nagoya
Japanese Art 1960's—Japanese Summer 1960–64, Contemporary Art Center, Art Tower Mito, Mito
1998 *Electronically Yours,* Tokyo Metropolitan Museum of Photography, Tokyo
"The Library of Babel"—Characters/Books/Media, NTT Inter Communication Center, Tokyo
Sogetsu Art Center 1945–1970, Chiba City Museum of Art, Chiba
2000 *Homage to Taro Okamoto for Seven Artists,* Taro Okamoto Museum of Art, Kawasaki

Collections:

Museum of Modern Art New York; Rockefeller Foundation; Vancouver Art Gallery; Centro de Arte y Comunicacion, Buenos Aires; National Museum of Modern Art, Tokyo; Museum of Modern Art, Toyama; Fukuoka Municipal Museum of Art; Kawasaki Civic Museum; Itabashi Art Museum, Tokyo.

Publications:

By YAMAGUCHI: Books—*Free Forms and Concepts,* Gakugeishorin, 1967; *Environmental Artist: Frederick Kiesler,* Bijutsu-Shuppan-Sha, 1978; *Katsuhiro Yamaguchi 360 Degrees,* Rikuyo-sha, 1981; *Avangard Art in Robotics Century,* Parco, 1985; *Creation of Environmental Images,* Bijutsu-Shuppan-Sha, 1987; *Tenjin Festival at the Media Age,* Bijutsu-Shuppan-Sha, 1991; *UBU,* Zeppan Shobou, 1991.

On YAMAGUCHI: Books—*To See Or to Be Seen—That Is the Question,* exhibition catalog, with text by Yusuke Nakahara, 1968; *An Open Spirit—Imagination and Reality of Japanese Video Art,* exhibition catalog by Jorge Glusberg, Buenos Aires, 1978; *Katsuhiro Yamaguchi,* exhibition catalog, Musee d'Art Moderne de la Ville de Paris, 1983; *Il fiore e il laser, nove moste penste come un ideograma,* exhibition catalog, with text by Viana Conti, Rosso, Genova, 1985; *Imaginarium,* exhibition catalog by Katsuhiro Yamaguchi, Palazzo Rosso, Genova, 1988; *Formative Indeterminacy in Japanese Technologie Art,* in exhibition catalog, with text by Yoshitomo Morioka, 1989; *Site of Passage,* exhibition catalog, with text by Susan Butler, Chapter Art Center, 1991; *Video Art* by Frank Popper, Thames and Hudson, 1993; *The Spinning of Time,* exhibition catalog, with text by Yoshitomo Morioka, Satani Gallery, Tokyo, 1994; *The Direction of the Darkness—Light from a Vitrine,* exhibition catalog, with text by Masaki Yanagihara, Nizayama Forest Art Museum, Toyama, 2000. **Articles—**many reviews and articles in international periodicals.

* * *

Katsuhiro Yamaguchi is at the same time one of the first to have introduced video art into Japan and a video artist of world reputation.

His previous itinerary already bears witness to his capacities as both organizer and creative artist. In 1948, at the age of twenty, he founded a group of abstract painters and sculptors and a year later he introduced electric light for the first time in his works after having been strongly influenced by reading the books of Laszlo Moholy-Nagy (*Vision in Motion* and *New Vision*). In the 1950s and 1960s,

Yamaguchi was one of the leading lumino-kinetic artists, as well as a sculptor and experimental designer. His research went from work on the optical effects gradually using the colours of light with the help of acrylic paint to luminous moving works and finally to large-scale videographic environments.

In the beginning of the 1970s, Yamaguchi was instrumental in the introduction of video techniques into the Japanese art world. He had constructed his first video installation, the *Image Modulator*, already in 1969. However, although the installation of video art in Japan has benefitted in the first place from the presence of one of the most advanced electronic industries in the world, contemporary Japanese artists were faced by aesthetic problems, such as the relationship between tradition and innovation or that between native specificity and foreign influence. They had to conquer step by step the mastery of the new art on the aesthetic as well as the technical levels especially as regards the time dimension of the medium.

Apart from some isolated realizations,one cannot speak of a video art movement in Japan until the beginning of the 1970s. In November 1971 the Canadian artist Michael Goldberg visited Tokyo in order to present his video tapes and to promote the idea of communication and free exchange of images with the aid of decentralized global networks. Some months later, Yamaguchi was, with Goldberg, one of the main organizers of the first video art exhibition in Japan and he took a prominent place in the development of a real Japanese specificity in this area particularly as regards video communication applied to architectural problems and its combination with practical methods inducing a local community to participate actively in the project. Yamaguchi conducted a first experience of this kind at Yokohama.

In the following years, Yamaguchi, apart from showing a theoretical interest in the relationships between electronics and art, indulged in his predilection for team-work by participating in groups of video and computer art, while continuing his own work.

On the video technique level Yamaguchi has used its two main modalities: production of video tapes and (especially) video sculptures and installations. Many of his video installations are elaborate constructions involving sculptural and design elements, often on an environmental scale. They tend to be either closed-circuit installations which involve the spectator, or multi-monitor arrangements in which the artist obtains a kaleidoscopic effect through the spatial and temporal arrangement of the images.

On the aesthetic level he has among other research, updated the themes of traditional Japanese culture in the field of garden art and architecture. This can be seen in video sculptures such as *Future Garden* in 1984, *Arch* and *Column* in 1988, and particularly in *The Invention of Morel* in 1991. In this work of large dimensions and consisting of 12 monitors and 6 video recorders, allusion is made to Adolfo Bioy Casares's novel with the same title, in which the hero discovers that the woman he has fallen in love with, is nothing but an image produced by a machine, invented by the scientist Morel, who is capable of creating images with a soul. Yamaguchi's aim was to build a labyrinthine architecture into which the observer was drawn amidst the transparent pillars of a temple and would come under the spell of images in permanent transformation which recall both the Buddhist metempsychosis and the implacable and eternal flux of time.

These electronic works take on an exceptional power when they are conceived for a real space in which they are effectively shown as videographic installation-sculptures.

For Yamaguchi, electronics has a creative power that can extend the abilities and intelligence of the user. His vision, which he calls an ''imaginarium,'' sets out a network of media in real space. With the use of adequate software and a video camera, anyone can make images and transfer them to the network. These images can be transmitted in real time to any monitor connected to the network.

Yamaguchi's decidedly social commitment can best be illustrated by the project he is developing on an island near Kobe. According to him, the history of art in the 20th Century is also that of individuals who have dreamt of utopia within society. With the development of advanced technology, artists are inclined to re-define this utopic dream. Some of them, by using technique as a tool, have proposed new creative methods. Others do not yet have the technological means they would like but are waiting for their arrival to use them for artistic ends.

To meet the demands of lone and impecunious artists, Yamaguchi has found a special place on the island of Awaji, where a center is under construction in which artists will have access to all devices indispensable to the creation of technological works. This center will possess, among other things, a library, a movie theatre, a restaurant and exhibition space.Yamaguchi's confessed goal is to realize at last Charles Fourier's plans for a *Phalanstère*, but adapted to the end of the 20th century and the needs of ''utopists of art and technology''.

—Frank Popper

YANAGI, Yukinori

Nationality: Japanese. **Born:** Fukuoka, Japan, 1959. **Education:** Musashino Art University, Tokyo, B.A. and M.F.A. Fine Arts in Painting, 1985; Yale University, M.F.A., Fellowship in Arts (Sculpture), 1990. **Career:** Independent artist, Japan and the United States. **Awards:** Fellowship in Arts, Yale University, School of Art and Architecture, 1988–90; Fellowship, Asian Cultural Council, International Studio Program, P. S. 1 Museum, New York, 1992–93; Award, Aperto 93, Venice Biennale, 1993; Gotoh Memorial Foundation Prize, Japan, 1995.

Selected Individual Exhibitions:

1987 Hillside Gallery, Tokyo
1990 Storefront for Art and Architecture Gallery, Connecticut
Hillside Gallery, Tokyo
Yale University Art and Architecture Gallery, Connecticut
1991 Lehman College Art Gallery, New York
Hillside Gallery, Tokyo
Los Angeles Contemporary Exhibitions (LACE)
1992 Naoshima Contemporary Art Museum, Kagawa, Japan
Fuji Television Gallery, Tokyo
1993 Ars Futura Galerie, Zurich
1994 Anthony d'Offay Gallery, London
1995 University Art Museum, University of California, Santa Barbara
Fuji Television Gallery, Tokyo

Wadsworth Atheneum, Hartford, Connecticut
Yukinori Yanagi: Project Article 9, Kirin Plaza, Osaka, Japan; The Queens Museum of Art, New York (catalog)
1996 Capp Street Project, San Francisco
1997 Fuji Television Gallery, Tokyo
Alcatraz, Peter Blum, New York
Arts Futura Galerie, Zurich
Fabric Workshop Museum, Philadelphia
1998 University Art Gallery, University of California at Irvine
1999 *New Work,* Haines Gallery, San Francisco
2000 *Akitsushima,* Hiroshima City Museum of Contemporary Art

Selected Group Exhibitions:

1987 *Art Document '87,* Tochigi Museum of Fine Arts, Tokyo
1991 *New York Diary: Almost Twenty-Five Different Things,* P. S. 1 Museum, New York
1992 *My Sweet Home in Ruin: Urban Environment and Art in Japan,* Setagaya Art Museum, Tokyo
By Arrangement, Galerie Ghislaine Hussenot, Paris
1993 *Trade Routes,* New Museum of Contemporary Art, New York
Aperto 93, Venice Biennale
Exchange 2, Shedhalle, Zurich
In Their Own Image, P. S. 1 Museum, New York
1994 *Insite 94,* Museum of Contemporary Art, San Diego
Asian Art Now, Hiroshima City Museum of Contemporary Art
Japanese Art After 1945: Scream Against the Sky, Guggenheim Museum, New York (traveled to San Francisco Museum of Modern Art; Yerba Buena Center for the Arts, San Francisco; Yokohama Museum of Art, Kanagawa, Japan)
Old Glory, Cleveland Center for Contemporary Art (traveled to gallery of Contemporary Art at University of Colorado; Phoenix Art Museum)
1995 *Fifty Years After,* Museum of Modern Art, Osaka, Japan
6 Triennale Kleinplastik, Sudwest LB Forum, Stuttgart, Germany
Japan Today, Louisiana Museum of Modern Art, Humlabaek, Denmark (traveled to Kunstnernes Hus, Oslo, Norway; Waino Aaltoner Museum of Art, Turku, Finland; Liljevalchs Kunsthall, Stockholm; Osterreichisches Museum für Angewandte Kunst, Vienna; Daichtorhallen, Hamburg)
Art in Japan Today / 1985–1995, Museum of Contemporary Art, Tokyo
1996 *Paintings—The Extended Field,* Magasin 3 Stockholm Kunsthall, Sweden; Rooseum, Sweden
Universalis, Sao Paolo Biennale, Brazil
Islands, National Gallery of Australia, Canberra
Protean Artists of the Time, National Museum of Art, Osaka, Japan
1997 *L'autre, Biennale de Lyon,* Halle Tony Garnier, Lyon, France
Changing Spaces, Miami Art Museum
Atlas Mapping, Offenes Kulturhaus, Linz, Austria (traveled to Bregenz Kunsthaus; Magazin 4, Bregenz, Austria)
Projects, Museum of Modern Art, Dublin (catalog)
Aspects of Land and Soil, Hiroshima City Museum of Contemporary Art, Japan
1998 *Tastes and Pursuits: Japanese Art in the 1990's,* National Museum of India, New Dehli (traveled to Metropolitan Museum of Art, Manila, Philippines)
Animal, Anima, Animus, Pori Art Museum, Finland (traveled to Arnheim Museum, Holland; P. S. 1, New York)
Sehnsucht Helmat, Kunsthalle Tirol, Innsbruck, Austria
2000 *Whitney Biennial 2000,*Whitney Museum for American Art, New York

Collections:

Allen Memorial Art Museum, Oberlin College; Bayerische Vereinsbank, Munich, Germany; Fabric Workshop and Museum, Philadelphia; Fogg Art Museum, Harvard University, Cambridge, Massachusetts; Hara Museum, Tokyo; Hiroshima City Museum of Contemporary; List Visual Arts Center, MIT, Boston; Louisiana Museum of Modern Art, Denmark; Museum of Fine Arts, Houston; Museum of Art, Kochi, Japan; Museum of Modern Art, New York; Museum Moderner Kunst Stiftung Ludwig Wien, Vienna; Museum of Modern Art, Tokushima, Japan; Naoshima Contemporary Art Museum, Kagawa, Japan; National Museum of Art, Osaka, Japan; National Gallery of Australia, Canberra; New York Public Library; Philadelphia Museum of Art; Queensland Art Gallery, Brisbane, Australia; Swiss Bank Corporation, Stamford, Connecticut; Takamatsu City Museum of Art, Kanagawa, Japan; Tate Gallery, London; Yokohama Museum of Art, Kanagawa, Japan.

Publications:

By YANAGI: Books—*Wandering Position,* Okayama 1992; *Field Work on Alcatraz,* San Francisco 1996.

On YANAGI: Books—*Japanese Art after 1945: Scream Against the Sky* by Alexandra Monroe, New York 1995. **Articles—**''Japan: Yukinori Yanagi'' by Carol Lutfy in *Art News,* April 1991; ''Yukinori Yanagi'' by Martha Schwender in *Flash Art,* 1995; ''Yukinori Yanagi: The Emperor on the Carpet'' by Lynn Gumpert in *Art News,* November 1995. **CD-Rom—***Yukinori Yanagi: Image, Nation, and Transnation,* edited by Brad Spence and Bert Winther-Tamaki, Irvine, California 1998.

* * *

Yukinori Yanagi is of the generation of Japanese artists who came of age immediately following the death of Emperor Hirohito in 1989, an epochal event that occasioned the questioning and erosion of Japanese post-war political and societal structures. A brazen pioneer of openly critical political art, unusual in Japan due to the reality of censorship and the threat of ultrarightist retaliation, Yanagi has taken the fictive and illusory nature of national identity as his subject. Deconstructing such modern myths as the homogeneity of the national body, Yanagi's works satirically manipulate the signs and symbols of the invisible structures that enforce mass allegiance to the status quo. With gallery installations composed of an eclectic range of materials, from high-tech neon to ants, Yanagi challenges his audience to recognize nationalist ideologies, while also presenting them with an ideal vision of a world without borders.

Yanagi's first object of criticism was the Japanese art world. Frustrated by its conservative and parochial educational system, for his first public exhibition he presented a number of life-sized containers holding the charred remains of his art-school works. The opportunity to leave Japan to study at Yale University in New Haven, Connecticut, became the impetus for an expanded critique of ideological systems, which the artist calls "ghettos." Yanagi began to analyze the nation and its abstract symbols in his works, exposing the coercive power of institutions to subsume individual identity into mirages of nationhood and ethnicity under the myth of progress. At Yale he created *Project—Red, White and Blue (Wandering Position)* (1990), an installation resembling a monster-sized hamster wheel with a Mickey Mouse-emblazoned car running inside—a witty allegory of American desire.

Yanagi has also enacted an extended critique of his native country in a series of controversial installations in Japan and elsewhere. *Banzai Corner* (1991) is a wedge-shaped corps of plastic Ultraman figurines, arms raised in a salute recalling World War II *kamikaze* pilots as well as the regimental body of present-day corporate "salarymen." Its reflection in strategically positioned mirrors forms the Japanese national flag's *hinomaru* or "rising sun" emblem with its imperialistic and nationalistic overtones. *Banzai Corner* conveys the enthralling, yet illusory and performative, nature of the national symbol, while exposing the complicity between the emperor system and Japan's current national economic imperialism. Similar connections are made in *Hinomaru Container (Yamato Tumulus Type)* (1992). A simulated ancient imperial keyhole tomb, surrounded by terracotta burial figures or *haniwa,* is placed in proximity to an enlarged map of the Tokyo subway system, which reveals a vacant space where no trains run. This "empty center" (as Roland Barthes called it in his *Empire of Signs*) in the heart of the city is the site of the imperial palace, the hidden axis of authority controlling the populace. Walking into the tomb structure, the viewer is confronted with the symbol of the Japanese yen located at the metaphorical heart of the nation. *Hinomaru Illumination* (1992) mesmerizes the viewer with the blinding power of the Japanese imperial institution—Yanagi's giant "rising sun" is composed of a multitude of flashing neon lights reflected into infinity.

Yanagi is interested in both the local and universal implications of his analyses, which he extends to the global community of nations with the concept of "intercourse." Derived from Marx and Engels and elaborated in the Japanese context by cultural critic Karatani Kôjin, "intercourse" describes the movement, or traffic, occasioned by trade and exchange. In 1990, Yanagi began his series of ant farms with *World Flag Ant Farm.* Featuring the national flags of United Nations members recreated in colored sand and contained in individual plastic boxes, the work challenges the integrity of national symbols through the action of ants moving between the boxes, carrying sand from one container to another. The result is an optimistic, metaphorical vision of an integrated, unified world. This and other, local variations on the theme, such as *Union Jack Ant Farm* (1994) and *The 38th Parallel (North and South Korean Ant Farm)* (1991), evoke the fragility and arbitrariness of national identity in an age of global communication and multiculturalism.

—Alicia Volk

YOSHIDA, Kenji

Nationality: Japanese. **Born:** Ikeda City (Osaka), 24 May 1924. **Education:** Studied pedagogy, University of Osaka, 1939–44; studied art with Mr. Furukido and Kiyoshi Hayashi, and philosophy with Kanshi Matsubayashi; joined Stanley William Heyter's Atelier 17, Paris, 1964–87; also influenced by Spanish sculptor Apelles Fenosa. **Military Service:** Ensign Second Class in the Japanese Marine Corps, 1943–44. **Family:** Married Hiroko Uehara in 1973 (died 1986); daughter: Kiyoko. **Career:** Teacher in Osaka, 1945–51, and Tokyo, 1952–64. Full-time artist, living and working in Paris, since 1964; founding member of Atelier du Nord, 1966. **Awards:** Norwegian Government Grant, Oslo, 1966. **Agent:** José Férez Kuri, 44a Thorne Rd. London SW8 2BY, United Kingdom; Glenn Green Galleries, Santa Fe, New Mexico, United States; glenngreengalleries@earthlink.net. **Address:** 49 rue de la Procession, 75015 Paris, France.

Individual Exhibitions:

1957 Muramatsu Gallery, Tokyo
1958 Muramatsu Gallery, Tokyo
1959 Muramatsu Gallery, Tokyo
1960 Muramatsu Gallery, Tokyo
1964 Takegawa Gallery, Tokyo
1966 Galerie Hammerlund, Oslo
1968 Museum of Japanese Art, Haifa, Israel
1971 Galerie St.-Johann, Saarbrucken, West Germany
1972 Linz Museum, Austria
1973 Seibu Gallery, Tokyo
1974 Galerie Modern-Art, Vienna
1976 Fuji Yoshi Gallery, Tokyo
1977 Galerie L'Estampille, Brussels
Galerie Point W, Gallard, France
1979 Galerie Aujourd'hui, Geneva
1982 Atelier Alma, Lyon, France
Ecole de Francais, Geneva
1983 Gallery Art-Houre, Tokyo
Gallery Beni, Kyoto
Gallery Taiken, Osaka
1984 Galerie Galise, Thonon, France
1986 Galerie Galise, Thonon, France
1987 Galerie Galise, at *FIAC 87,* Grank Palais, Paris
1988 Galerie Bernard Letu, Geneva
Galerie Jude V, Marmo, Sweden
1989 Stockholm Art Fair, Sweden
The October Gallery, London

Kenji Yoshida: *La Vie,* 1987. ©Kenji Yoshida.

1990 International Art Fair, Chicago
Boulev-art Galerie, Geneva
1991 Glenn Green Galleries, Santa Fe
The October Gallery, London
1993 The British Museum, London
International Contemporary Art, Ltd., London
Glenn Green Galleries, Santa Fe
1997 Museo de Arte Moderno, Mexico City
Biblioteca Magna Universitaria, Monterrey, Mexico
Museo de Arte de Queretaro, Mexico
1998 Museo de Arte Contemporaneo, Durango, Mexico
Museo de Arte Contemporaneo Ateneo de Yucatan, Merida, Mexico
Museo de Arte Contemporaneo, Aguascalientes, Mexico
1999 Broad Street Gallery, Lyme Regis, England
2000 Christ Church Cathedral, Dublin, Ireland

Selected Group Exhibitions:

1965 *Graphics Biennale,* Moderna Galerija, Ljubljana, Yugoslavia
1966 *Graphics Biennale,* Modern Museum, Cracow, Poland
Nordisk Grafik Union, Kunstforening, Oslo
1967 *Graphics Biennale,* Kunstverein, Grenchen, Switzerland
1968 *Wiener Sezession Grafika,* Wiener Sezession, Vienna
1970 *Print International,* Kunstverein, Frechen, West Germany
1974 *Graphik Klein-Plastik,* Kunstlerhaus, Vienna
1976 *Exposition International,* Maison de la Culture, Berck-Piage, France
1984 *Actu, Art 84,* Galerie Galise, Thonon, France (and 1985, 1986, 1987)
1986 *Contemporary Art: Japan/Denmark,* Konstmuseum, Copenhagen
1989 Chateau Sonderborg, Denmark
1990 *25 Years of Atelier du Nord,* Hovikodden Kunstsenter, Oslo
1992 Galerie Seplira, Madrid
1999 *Transavangard,* October Gallery, London

Collections:

Bibliotheque Nationale, Paris; Ministere des Affaires Culturelles, Paris; Bibliotheque Royale, Brussels; Museum Louviers, France; Museum of Modern Art, Norrkoping, Sweden; Kunst pa

Arbeidsplassen, Oslo; The British Museum, London; Kunstverein, Frechen, Germany: Museum of Modern Art, Skopje, Yugoslavia; Museum of Japanese Art, Haifa, Israel; Royal Collection of Denmark; Museum of Modern Art, Skopje, Yugoslavia; Museu de Arte Contemporanea, Sao Paulo, Brazil; Modern Art Museum, Norrkoping, Sweden.

Permanent Public Installations:

All Nippon Airways, London; AB Volvo, Goteborg, Sweden; Club Hanzuiryo, Unzen, Japan; Club Shien, Osaka, Japan; Biosphere 2 Conference Centre, Arizona; BTR plc, London; Nikko Europe, London.

Publications:

On YOSHIDA: Books—*Kenji Yoshida: La Vie,* exhibition catalog with texts by Tadashi Fukuda, Joseph Paul Schneider and others, Thonon 1986; *Mado,* Tokyo 1993; *La Vie: The Art of Kenji Yoshida,* edited by José Férez K., with texts by Lawrence Smith, Tadashi Fukuda, Ralph Steadman, Claude Micoski, Makoto Yokohari, and Kenji Yoshida, London 1993. **Articles—**''My Friend Yoshida'' by Uehara Kaza in *Sansai* (Tokyo), January 1974; *Arts Review,* 20 October 1989; *Artrage,* London 1989; *Konnichiwa,* London 1991; ''Substance of Life'' by K.C. Compton in *Focus/Santa Fe,* 1992; *Bodyline,* Athens 1994; *Insight,* London 1994.

*

I'm bound to my life and I have been painting more than sixty years.

My boyhood took place during the wartime long haunted by the Shadows of Death. Later I saw them growing into the World War, where a lot of people, military and civil, perished. I joined the army as a young volunteer, but the end of the war bound me to live.

What's Birth?

What's Death?

What's Life?

From that time on, these questions have occupied more and more deeply my mind.

Now, full of joy, I realise how I'm bound to and for my life, I say to myself:

''What I must do in my life of prayer and thanks is to talk to people through my paintings about the dignity of Life and the importance of Peace.''

—Kenji Yoshida

YOSHIMURA, Fumio

Nationality: American. **Born:** Kamakura, 22 February 1926; became citizen of the United States, 1994. **Education:** Tokyo National University of Art, 1941–49, M.F.A. 1949. **Military Service:** Cadet in Japanese Imperial Army, 1945. **Family:** Married Yoshiko Oshima in 1951 (died, 1963); married the American writer Kate Millet in 1965 (divorced, 1986); married Carol Ann Watkinson in 1987. **Career:** Independent artist, Tokyo, 1950–61, and in New York since 1962: first realist wood sculptures, 1970. Taught kite-making at Brookfield Craft Center, Connecticut during summers, 1965–70; assistant professor, Dartmouth College, Hanover, New Hampshire, since 1982. **Awards:** Faculty Research Grant, Dartmouth College, 1984, 1985; Florsheim Art Fund, 1999. **Addresses:** 5 East Third Street, New York, New York 10003; 2584 Academy Road, Thetford Center, Vermont 05075, U.S.A.

Individual Exhibitions:

1950 Maramatsu Gallery, Tokyo (and yearly until 1958)
1970 Pennsylvania Academy of Fine Arts, Philadelphia
1971 Wichita Art Museum, Kansas
1972 Marian Locks Gallery, Philadelphia
1973 Nancy Hoffman Gallery, New York
1974 Galerie Arneson, Copenhagen
1975 Galeriet, Lund, Sweden
1976 Squibb Gallery, Princeton, New Jersey Nancy Hoffman Gallery, New York
1977 Marian Locks Gallery, Philadelphia
1978 Norton Gallery of Art, West Palm Beach, Florida
1979 Amherst College, Massachusetts Nancy Hoffmen Gallery, New York
1981 Beaumont and May Gallery, Dartmouth College, Hanover, New Hampshire
1983 Nancy Hoffman Gallery, New York
1984 Mitchell Museum, Mount Vernon, Illinois
1985 Atlantic Center of the Arts, New Smyrna Beach, Florida
1986 Windsor House, Vermont
1987 Temple Gallery, Philadelphia
1989 Museum of Art, Rhode Island School of Design, Providence
1993 Hood Museum, Dartmouth College, Hanover, New Hampshire

Selected Group Exhibitions:

1968 *Made with Paper,* Museum of Contemporary Crafts, New York
1973 *Made with Wood,* Dartmouth College, Hanover, New Hampshire
1974 *New/Photo Realism,* Wadsworth Atheneum, Hartford, Connecticut
1976 *Object as Poet,* Renwick Gallery, Smithsonian Institution, Washington, D.C.
1979 *Illusion and Material,* Paterson College, Wayne, New Jersey
1981 *Katachi,* Albuquerque Museum of Art, New Mexico
1982 *Contemporary Realism,* Pennsylvania Academy of Fine Arts, Philadelphia
1983 *Materials and Illusion/Unlikely Materials,* Taft Museum, Cincinnati, Ohio
1985 *Fine Woodwork,* Philbrook Art Museum, Tulsa, Oklahoma
1986 *Poetry of the Physical,* American Craft Museum, New York
1987 *Four Wood Sculptors,* Kansas City Art Institute, Missouri
Eloquent Object, Philbrook Art Museum, Tulsa, Oklahoma
1999 *Constructing Realities,* Museum of Art, Brigham Young University, Provo, Utah

Collections:

Albright-Knox Gallery, Buffalo, New York; Pennsylvania Academy of Fine Art, Philadelphia; Philadelphia Museum of Art; Taft Museum, Cincinnati, Ohio; Go Vett-Brewster Gallery, New Plymouth, New Zealand; Power Gallery of Contemporary Art, Sydney, Australia; Albuquerque Museum of Art, New Mexico; Delaware Art Museum, Wilmington: Mississippi Museum of Art, Jackson; Norton Gallery of Art, West Palm Beach, Florida; Tohoku Shinsha Inc., Tokyo; Hood Museum of Art, Dartmouth College, Hanover, New Hampshire; Villanova University, Villanova, Pennsylvania; LaSalle University, Philadelphia, Pennsylvania; West Vancouver Public Library, West Vancouver, B.C., Canada; H.J. Heinz Company, Pittsburgh, Pennsylvania; Honolulu Academy of Arts, Hawaii; Frederick R. Weiseman Art Foundation, Los Angeles, California.

Publications:

On YOSHIMURA: Books—*New/Photo Realism,* exhibition catalog, by Jack Cowart, Hartford, Connecticut, 1974; *Super Realism: A Critical Anthology,* edited by Gregory Battcock, New York 1975; *Super Realism* by Edward Lucie Smith, Oxford 1977; *Superrealist Painting and Sculpture* by Christine Lindsey, New York 1980; *Masters of Wood Sculpture* by Nicholas Rourkes, New York 1980; *Wood Working: The New Wave* by Dona Z. Meilach, New York 1981; *Poetry of the Physical,* exhibition catalog by Paul Smith, New York 1986; *Fumio Yoshimura: Harvest of a Quiet Eye,* exhibition catalog by Kate Millet, Hanover, New Hampshire 1993.

* * *

In 1970 Fumio Yoshimura began making illusionistic wooden sculptures using the forms of real objects covering a range of subjects from bicycles to tomato plants. Yoshimura had been a painter from around 1948, but it is for his sculpture that he became known.

Yoshimura turns readymade and organic forms into hand made simulations. The element of imitation is co-existent with an element of removal in his finely crafted, smooth wooden substitutes for the real thing. The works are both accurate to their models and modified by the translation into natural, untreated wood. (He prefers linden spruce and pine.) Yoshimura shows considerable involvement with literal depiction, but he is more concerned with close approximation than with scrupulously accurate reduplication down to the last details. This factor, along with the neutralizing colorlessness and smooth graining of the wood, place the appearance of reality at a distance. ''I'm reproducing a ghost,'' Yoshimura has noted, and the sculptures have a disembodied quality achieved through the materials and the handmade craftsmanship which both imitate the original subject/object and simultaneously place it within a new level of artificiality.

''Motorcycle'' (1973), ''Typewriter'' (1975), and ''Bicycle with Parking Meter'' (1978) originate from precise working drawings, are made a part at a time and are assembled like the industrial objects they represent. The finished works are sensuously organic, solid yet soft wood, removed from the mobility and use of their models, and turned into three dimensional objects of contemplation. There is an element of irony in Yoshimura's reversal process, a Zen-like move from the subjective particular to the objective general. He questions perception and the real nature of literal presence.

Yoshimura's work has obvious likenesses with Jasper Johns, George Segal and Claes Oldenburg. Yet, he remains closer to the literal than any of these artists, and he avoids the rough-edged wistfulness of Segal and the flamboyant Pop comedy of Oldenburg. Yoshimura's kind of Realism differs also from the deceptive mimicry central to the work of Duane Hanson or the Photo-Realists. Yoshimura reverses the Duchampian idea of the readymade, transforming it into the hand-crafted artifact. Illusionism is tempered; both organic forms and hard, metal, working objects are slowly and deliberately crafted into sleek, smooth, naturally grained presences, apparitions hovering in suspended animation on the border between becoming and being.

—Barbara Cavaliere

YOUNG, Peter (Ford)

Nationality: American. **Born:** Pittsburgh, Pennsylvania, 2 January 1940. **Education:** Chouinard Art Institute, Los Angeles, 1957; Pomona College, Claremont, California, 1958–60; Art Students League, New York, 1960; New York University, 1961–63, B.A. 1963. Influenced by Dynaton Group (Lee Mullican, Onslow Ford and Wolfgang Paalen). **Career:** Independent painter practicing a formal abstraction rooted in study of primitive design and mysticism; lived and worked in New York, 1960–70, in Bisbee, Arizona, since 1970. Visiting Artist, Oberlin College, Ohio, 1970; Pima College, Tucson, Arizona, 1976. **Agents:** Leo Castelli, 420 West Broadway, New York, New York 10012; and Oil and Steel Gallery, 157 Chambers Street, New York, New York 10012. **Address:** Box 715, Bisbee, Arizona 85603, U.S.A.

Individual Exhibitions:

1968 Nicholas Wilder Gallery, Los Angeles
Galeric Ricke, Cologne
1969 *Peter Young David Diao,* Leo Castelli Gallery, New York
1970 Goldowsky Gallery, New York
1972 Galerie Ricke, Cologne
Goidowsky Gallery, New York
Greenberg Gallery, St. Louis
1974 Goldowsky Gallery, New York
1975 Texas Gallery, Houston
1980 Cochise Fine Arts, Bisbee, Arizona
1981 Leo Castelli Gallery, New York
1984 *Linear Wave,* Oil & Steel Gallery, New York
1989 *Dot Collage,* Braunstein/Quay Gallery, San Francisco
1992 Project Arts Centre, Dublin
1995 Cochrane Gallery, London
1998 Elizabeth Cherry Contemporary Art, Tucson

Selected Group Exhibitions:

1967 *Painting Annual,* Whitney Museum, New York
1968 *Documenta 4,* Kassel, West Germany
1969 *31st Biennial,* Corcoran Gallery, Washington, D.C.
9 Young Artists Guggenheim Museum, New York
The Development of Modernist Painting: Jackson Pollock to Present, Steinberg Art Gallery, Washington University, St. Louis

One Tendency of Contemporary Art, Kunstmart, Cologne
1971 *6 Painters,* Albright-Knox Gallery, Buffalo, New York
1972 *Painting: New Options,* Walker Art Center, Minneapolis, Minnesota
1974 *8 Artists,* Art Museum of South Texas, Corpus Christi
1985 *Philip Johnson Bequest Exhibition,* Museum of Modern Art, New York
1987 *Visions of Innerspace,* Wight Gallery, University of California, Los Angeles (traveled to National Gallery of Modern Art, New Delhi)
1991 *The Legacy of Karl Blossfeldt,* Jan Turner Gallery, Los Angeles
1996 *Seven Painters,* Nicholas Alexander Gallery, New York

Collections:

Museum of Modern Art, New York; Whitney Museum of American Art, New York; Guggenheim Museum, New York; Albright-Knox Museum, Buffalo; Aldrich Museum of Contemporary Art, Ridgefield; Allen Art Museum, Oberilin College, Oberlin, Ohio; Robert Scull Collection, New York; Philip Johnson Collection, New Canaan, Connecticut; Horace Solomon Collection, New York; Charles Cowles Collection, New York; Joseph Helman Collection, New York; D'Amo Collection, Los Angeles; Bruno Bischofberger Collection, Zurich; Virginia Wright Collection, Seattle; Milton Gerstein Collection, Los Angeles; Peter Ludwig Collection, Los Angeles; David Whitney Collection, New York; Ben Heller Collection, New York; Levi-Strauss Collection, San Francisco; James Michener Collection, San Francisco; Vernon Nickel Collection, Clovis, New Mexico; Neuberger Museum, Purchase, New York; Australian National Gallery, Canberra; Phoenix Art Museum, Phoenix; Seattle Art Museum, Seattle.

Publications:

By YOUNG: Articles—''Artists on Their Art'' in *Art International* (Lugano, Switzerland), March 1968; ''Peter Young'' in *Art Now* (New York), vol. 1, no. 5. 1969.

On YOUNG: Books—*The Triumph of American Painting* by Irving Sandler, New York 1970; *The Twentieth Century (American Painting Vol. 2)* by Barbara Rose, Cleveland 1971; *Introduction to 6 Painters,* exhibition catalog, by James Wood, Buffalo, New York 1971; **articles—**''Gallery Without Walls'' by Barbara Rose in *Art in America* (New York). March 1968; ''David Diao, Peter Young, R. Pettibone'' by J. R. Baker in *Arts Magazine* (New York), March 1964; ''Diao and Young at Castelli'' by Dore Ashton in *Studio International* (London), April 1969; review by Emily Wasserman in *Artforum* (New York), May 1969; ''Presenting Peter Young'' in Art *in America* (New York), 1969; ''Notes on American Painting of the '60s'' by Walter Bannard in *Artforum* (New York), January 1970; ''New Infonnalis''' by Carter Ratcliff in *Artnews* (New York), February 1970; ''Color Abstractionism'' by Willis Domingo in Arts magazine (New York), December 1970; ''The Spectrum of Monochrome'' by Lawrence Alloway in *Arts Magazine* (New York), December 1970; ''Peter Young: A Chronology of the Works'' by Ellen Johnson in *Artforum* (New York), April 1971 ; ''Materiality and Painterliness'' by Gregoire Muller in *Arts Magazine* (New York), September 1971; review by Hayden Herra in *Artnews* (New York), November 1974; ''Peter Young at Oil & Steel'' by Stephen Westfall, *Arts Magazine,* Summer 1984; ''The Tasmanian Connection'' by Leigh Hobba in *Artlink,* vol. 16, no. 2–3, Winter 1996.

*

The very greatest art is the ''art'' of perfecting one's Self.

—Peter Young

* * *

Peter Young's involvement with painting began in the early 1960s when there seemed to be a preference for coolness and linear abstraction, a reaction fostered by young artists who felt antagonized by the decadence of such late Abstract Expressionists as Bannard, Peons, Stella and Martin—an insistence on ''doing the next thing.'' This became the theoretical enemy of Young.

Young's work has always been involved with a rich sense of history; primitive design, and American Indian and African art are important influences. Although his early work (1963–65) seemed to respond to the linear grid work of his contemporaries, he was to develop a ''dot'' technique derived from Seurat.

The dot technique, applied in acrylic, is basically an all-over type of composition which has an edge and corner-to-corner continuity related to the formal aspects of Jackson Pollock's work. The dots are irregular, applied with the tip of a brush; the dots may be marbleized, chained or connected, clustered or fully saturated into the canvas. The dot patterns may suggest constellations or star clusters. An analogy to heavenly bodies is not inconsistent with Young's own rather mystical approach to the mid-60's work. At that time he was concerned with the investigation of light and color on large fields. Working from a white background he developed a series of color studies which achieved the primal light and became the hallmark of his work.

Young is a color painter and considers color to be the one constant in a long series of stylistic experiments from 1965 to 1969. ''There are many color painters in my generation who have worked from a mathematical process. My early painting was very pale and white. This had a lot to do with living in New York, having a lot of artificial lighting, and a sort of psychedelic yogic insistence of lightness,'' he states. His work established a serial format of color composition which was provocative in the midst of work he felt was lacking in warmth and a sense of life.

At the peak of his popularity in 1969, Young left New York to live in a remote Indian village in Costa Rica, then in Utah and New Mexico. Back in New York in early 1970 his work showed a loosening of the dot patterning and a more intense color palette.

After a trip to Morocco and Spain in 1972, a further break occurred in his work. He began to fold his canvas when it was wet, producing a totemic two-column figural arrangement à la Rorschach. Already the ground of his dot painting had changed from white base to patchwork color base. In these folded works the figural element takes over and is defined not as a nuance but as sculptural form. The overpainting in these folded works was applied with the Pollock splash and drip method.

At some point in the folding process Young began to fold the canvas diagonally as well as vertically. The diagonal folds produce a mandala image. ''When I began to fold the canvas I was aware that the sense of lightness I was once working for was not as important,'' he says. The color of these mandala paintings is deep and thick, recalling tantric manuscripts. The imagery of his paintings in fully integrated with the animation of moving forms. The busy surface of the circular shape is punctuated with hand over-painting and some splash and drip work.

Now in the mandala works there is still an all-over patterning and dotting. ''The essence of these works is the centrality and decentrality of the image in various states of focus. The symbol is not specific to Indian culture but to all religious art of the world.''

Mysticism and art are unified concepts in a chronology of Young's work. The use of hallucinogens was an additive for Young but only tangential to his belief in universal imagery and the importance of the artist's development of his own decorative motifs.

—Adina Wingate

YOUNGERMAN, Jack

Nationality: American. **Born:** St. Louis, Missouri 25 March 1926. **Education:** University of North Carolina, Chapel Hill (United States Navy Training Program), 1944–46; University of Missouri, Columbia, 1943–47, B.A. 1947; Ecole des Beaux-Arts, Paris, 1947–48. **Family:** Married Delphine Seyrig in 1950; son: Duncan. **Career:** Painter and sculptor; lived in Europe, 1947–56; has lived and worked in New York since 1956; designed stage sets for Jean-Louis Barrault's production of *Histoire de Vasco,* Paris, 1956, and *Deathwatch* by Jean Genet, New York, 1958. Artist-in-residence, Worcester Art Museum, Massachusetts, 1965; instructor, Yale University, New Haven, Connecticut, 1974–75, and Hunter College, New York, 1981–82; instructor, New York University, since 1982. **Awards:** New Talent Award, *Art in America,* New York, 1959; National Endowment for the Arts Award, 1972, 1984; Guggenheim Fellowship, 1976; United States/Japan Exchange Fellowship, 1987; National Academy of Design Award, 1992; American Academy Award, Rome 1995. **Agent:** Washburn Gallery, 20 W. 57th St., New York, NY 10019–3917, U.S.A. **Address:** P.O. Box 508, Bridgehampton, NY, 11932–0508, U.S.A.

Individual Exhibitions:

1951 Galerie Amaud, Paris
1958 Betty Parsons Gallery, New York
1960 Betty Parsons Gallery, New York
1960 Betty Parsons Gallery, New York
1961 Betty Parsons Gallery, New York
1962 Galerie Lawrence, Paris
1963 Galleria dell'Afiete, Milan
Everett Ellin Gallery, Los Angeles
1964 Betty Parsons Gallery, New York
1965 Betty Parsons Gallery, New York
Worcester Art Museum, Massachusetts
1966 Massachusetts Institute of Technology, Cambridge
Galerie Maeght, Paris
1967 Betty Parsons Gallery, New York
1968 Betty Parsons Gallery, New York
Phillips Collection, Washington, D.C.
1971 Pace Gallery, New York
J. L. Hudson Gallery, Detroit
1972 Pace Gallery, New York
Center for the Visual Arts, Portland, Oregon
Seattle Art Museum
1973 Arts Club of Chicago
Galerie Denise René, Paris
Pace Gallery, New York
Galerie Denise René/Hans Mayer, Dusseldorf
1974 Fendrick Gallery, Washington, D.C.
Kingpitcher Gallery, Pittsburgh
1975 Pace Gallery, New York
1976 Parrish Museum, Southampton, New York
1977 Tampa Bay Museum, Florida
1978 Truman Gallery, New York
1981 Washburn Gallery, New York
1982 Washburn Gallery, New York
1983 Alex Rosenberg Gallery, New York
1985 Washburn Gallery, New York
1986 Guggenheim Museum, New York
Washburn Gallery, New York
1987 Washburn Gallery, New York
1989 Heland Wetterling Gallery, Stockholm
1991 Washburn Gallery, New York (catalog)
1996 Glenn Horowitz Bookseller, East Hampton, New York (catalog)
1997 Washburn Gallery, New York
Anita Shapolsky Gallery, New York
2000 Washburn Gallery, New York

Selected Group Exhibitions:

1959 *16 Americans,* Museum of Modern Art, New York
1961 *Abstract Expressionists and Imagists,* Guggenheim Museum, New York
1964 *American Drawings,* Guggenheim Museum, New York
1966 *Systemic Painting,* Guggenheim Museum, New York
1981 *Contemporary Americans,* Guggenheim Museum, New York
1984 *The Folding Image,* National Gallery of Art, Washington, D.C.
1986 *Transformations in Sculpture,* Guggenheim Museum, New York
1988 *Vital Signs: Organic Abstraction from the Permanent Collection,* Whitney Museum of American Art, New York
1989 *Twentieth Century Art,* National Gallery of Art, Washington, D.C.
1993 *Indiana, Kelly, Martin, Rosenquist, Youngerman at Coenties Slip,* Pace Gallery, New York (catalog)
1991 *Feria Internacional de Arte Contemporaneo,* Madrid
1992 *Table Sculpture,* Andre Emmerich Gallery, New York
1993 Pace Gallery, New York
They Quoted Matisse, Galerie de France, Paris
Drawings, 30th Anniversary, Foundation of Contemporary Performance Arts, Leo Castelli Gallery

Jack Youngerman: *Eastward,* 1967. ©Jack Youngerman/Licensed by VAGA, New York NY.

1994 *Les Americains,* Fecamp, Joinville, Paris
2001 *Modernism and Abstraction: Treasures from the Smithsonian Museum of American Art,* Allentown Art Museum, Pennsylvania

Collections:

Guggenheim Museum, New York; Whitney Museum, New York; Museum of Modern Art, New York; Albright-Knox Art Gallery, Buffalo, New York; Worcester Art Museum, Massachusetts; Hirshhorn Museum, Washington, D.C.: Phillips Collection, Washington, D.C.; Corcoran Gallery, Washington, D.C.; Carnegie Institute, Pittsburgh: Art Institute of Chicago; Baltimore Museum of Art; Museum of Fine Art, Houston.

Publications:

By YOUNGERMAN: Books—*The Artist Observed: 28 Interviews with Contemporary Artists, 1972–1978* by John Gruen, Chicago 1991. **Article—**''Interview with Jack Youngerman,'' with Barbara Rose, in *Artforum* (New York), January 1966.

On YOUNGERMAN: Books—*Systemic Painting,* exhibition catalog by Lawrence Alloway, New York 1966; *Constructivism: Origins and Evolution* by George Rickey, New York 1967; *American Art since 1900: A Critical History* by Barbara Rose, New York 1967; *The Joys and Sorrows of Recent American Art* by A. S. Weller, Urbana, Illinois 1968; *Jack Youngerman,* exhibition catalog with text by Diane Waldman, New York 1986. **Articles—***Youngerman: Liberty in Limits* by Michael Benedict in *Art News* (New York), September 1965; *Youngerman or Dialogue with Forms* by R. Bordier in *Cimaise* (Paris), May 1973; *Youngerman's Gestural Emblem* by Donald B. Kuspit in *Art in America* (New York), July 1986; *The Geometry of Nature and the Nature of Geometry* by John Gruen in *Art News* (New York), February 1987; *Sense of Connection: The Sculpture of Jack Youngerman* by Richard Kalina in *Art in America* (New York), vol. 85, December 1997.

* * *

Jack Youngerman's career has involved a continuing absorption with the formal and even psychological possibilities inherent in leaf-like form and flat and brilliantly hued pictorial pattern. Impersonal and banal forms marked the work of many chromatic and hard-edged abstract artists of the 1960s; in strong contrast Youngerman, both then and to the present, has worked in distinctly natural-referent form. The form and color precedents of Arp and Matisse may easily be cited; yet perhaps more to the point might be the strong American symbolist precedents for such undulant and rhapsodic nature-focused art, for instance, Dove, O'Keeffe, Burchfield, and, with Gorky, the surrealist strain in American modernism. It is as if Youngerman would wish the clarity and rationalist force of the Constructivist tradition with which

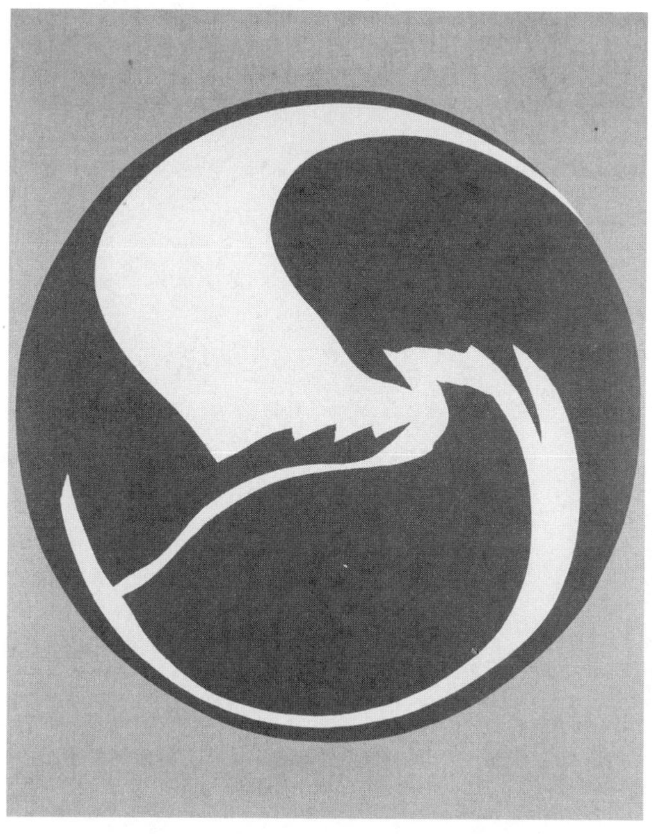

Abstract monochrome painting by Jack Youngerman, late 20th-century. ©Jack Youngerman/Licensed by VAGA, New York, NY.

he initially became conversant during his long European stay, 1947–1956, and yet also wish to imbue it with an irrepressible rhythm of nature. The emphatic urgency of Youngerman's painting and sculpture has been referred to by the artist: ''We are immersed in the powerful and autonomous effigies of the world before these forms are possessed and diminished by names and uses, the name preempting the form. Painting involves the restoring of the image to that original primacy.''

After some heavy-textured, expressionist work in the mid-1950s, Youngerman was, by the end of the decade, a post-painterly abstract artist. His images, already restricted to one or two colors, featured flat and sharp-edged forms which resolved themselves into landscape panorama. While he has restricted the internal shape and pattern of his work to natural reference, he has continuously attempted variance by his manipulation of the ground shape and the concomitant ordering of his forms in their positioning on these grounds. In 1967 he produced symmetrical works, with butterfly-like shapes on diamond shaped canvases, forms clearly influenced by beetle and fish patterning. His exhibition in 1971 featured circular, elliptical canvases. And in the following year, Youngerman detached his floral emblems from their ground and produced shaped canvases, at times in several sections whose edges conformed to the flaring-edged forms. He has also exhibited stainless steel sculpture (1971), and wooden cut-outs (1972), and all white fiberglass and resin three-dimensional sculpture (1976). A recent exhibition (1978) involved the use of folding screens on which he painted his signature shapes.

Youngerman's art has been marked by an almost heroic poignancy because of his insistence upon a duality: clear abstractionist idealism yet linked with the resonance of an older subjective translation of nature into pattern. If this has been a detriment for the critical acceptance of his work—the restrictiveness of his form world—it may as well have operated to deny the artist access to larger, more current, views of the mechanico-metabolic confrontation.

—Joshua Kind

Z

ZAPPETTINI, Gianfranco

Nationality: Italian. **Born:** Genoa, 16 June 1939. **Education:** Studied at the Accademia di Belle Arti, Carrara. **Family:** Married Gabrielle Gonfiantini in 1963; daughter: Martina. **Career:** Painter, living and working in Genoa. **Address:** via Aurelia 116, 16043 Chiavari, Italy.

Individual Exhibitions:

1962 Galleria Belle Arti, Genoa
1963 Galleria Pescetto, Albisola, Italy
1964 Galleria Ferrari, Verona
Galleria 2000, Bologna
1965 Galleria La Polena, Genoa
1966 Galleria L'Arco, Macerata, Italy
1967 Galleria Vismara, Milan
Galerie Du Disque Rouge, Brussels
1968 Galleria del Cavallino, Venice
1969 Galleria Il Punto, Turin
1971 Galleria Peccolo, Livorno
Galleria pourquoi pas, Genoa
1972 Galerie L'Dehr, Frankfurt
Galleria La Polena, Genoa
1973 Centro d'Arte Santelmo, Salo, Italy
1974 Galleria La Polena, Genoa
Galleria La Piramide, Florence
Galleria Vinciana, Milan
Galleria Peccolo, Livorno
Galerie December, Münster, West Germany
1975 Westfälischer Kunstverein, Münster, West Germany
Galerie Karsten Greve, Cologne
1976 Galleria La Seconda Scala, Rome
Galerie Peccolo, Cologne
1977 Studio Soldano, Milan
Galleria La Bertesca, Genoa
1978 International Cultureel Centrum, Antwerp
Galerie Peccolo, Cologne
Galerie Artline, The Hague
Galleria Eremitani, Padua
1979 Studio G&, Bologna
1981 Artra Studio, Milano
1988 Peira Arte Contemporanea, Arte Fiera, Bologna
1992 Museo de S. Maria di Castello, Genova
1994 *Natura no facit saltus,* Galleria Peccolo, Livorno (catalog)
1995 Artestudio, Milano
1997 Artestudio, Milano
Palazzo Rocca, Chiavari
Galleria Peccolo, Livorno
1998 *Gianfranco Zappettini: Mostra antologica, 1964–1997* (retrospective), Museo d'Arte Contemporanea di Villa Croce, Genova (catalog)
1999 Artestudio, Milano
2000 *Dall'ombra all luce,* Galleria Peccolo, Livorno, and Galleria Guastalla, Livorno

Selected Group Exhibitions:

1969 *Nove Tendencije 4,* Zagreb
1970 *Multiples,* Whitechapel Art Gallery, London
1971 *Triennale,* Delhi, India
Concrete Art, Westfälischer Kunstverein, Münster, West Germany
1973 *Tempi du Percezione,* Casa delta Cultura, Livorno
1974 *Geplante Malerei,* Westfälischer Kunstverein, Münster, West Germany
1975 *Pittura,* Palazzo Ducale, Genoa
1976 *A proposito della Pittura,* Stedelijk Museum, Amsterdam
1977 *Documenta,* Kassel, West Germany
1978 *Abstraction Analytique,* Centre Georges Pompidou, Paris
1981 *Avantgarden/Retrospektive,* Westfälischer Kunstverein, Münster
Linee della ricerca artistica in Italia 1960/1980, Palazzo dell Esposizioni, Rome
1984 *Gabinetto della grafica,* Galleria d'Arte Moderna, Bologna
1989 *Triennale Internazionale d'Arte Sacra,* Castello Trecentesco, Celano
1991 *Blau,* Heidelberg Kunstverein, Heidelberg
1999 *Il grande rettile e gli altri,* Museo Civico ''G. Fattori,'' Livorno
2000 *Oggetto—Opera,* Artestudio, Milano

Collections:

Westfälischer Kunstverein, Münster, Germany.

Publications:

By ZAPPETINI: Articles—''Ricerca di una Dimensione'' in *Gala* (Milan), September 1974; ''Per una Pittura Analitica'' in *Data* (Milan), Winter 1974, and *Kunstforum* (Mainz, West Germany), October/November 1974; statement in *Gianfranco Zappettini,* exhibition catalog, Münster, West Germany 1975; statement in *Gianfranco Zappettini,* exhibition catalog, Antwerp 1978; ''Il senso delle cose singolari'' in *Flash Gallerie,* no. 16, June 1984; essay in *Blau,* exhibition catalog, Heidelberg 1991; essay in *Dossier Antwerpen,* Antwerp 1993; essay in *L'oscurarsi della luce,* exhibition catalog, Milan 1999.

On ZAPPETTINI: Books—*Gianfranco Zappettini,* exhibition catalog by Klaus Honnef, Münster, West Germany, 1975; *Storia dell'Arte Italiana del 1900-Generazione Anni Trenta* by G. Di Genova, Rome 2000. **Article—**''Gianfranco Zappettini'' by Klaus Honnef in *Kunstforum* (Mainz, West Germany), October/November 1974.

*

Gianfranco Zappettini: *Al fine che traspare,* 1999. ©Gianfranco Zappettini.

Plato declares, ''It is up to art to pick the ancestral truth, to make audible the not audible, to enunciate the primordial word, to reproduce the images of the origin otherwise it is not art.'' True art, therefore, consists of a symbolic representation of a reality visible only by the intellect.

This is the concept I draw my inspiration from, trying to make again ''sacred'' the art that, expressing itself through the symbol, proposes itself as an aim to truth. Therefore the petal flying between Heaven and Earth is an image of the generation and corruption's process forming the universe's development; it is an invitation to an interior voyage, in an alchemic process through which the artist himself realizes his own spiritual transformation.

—Gianfranco Zappettini

* * *

The course followed by Gianfranco Zappettini in more than ten years of work might be called the ''recovery of meaning,'' and to an extent it reflects a wider change of cultural direction than simply one of those that we are passing through at present. Zappettini started from a strictly, rigorously analytical painting, in which all the materials and other ''ingredients'' of pictorial work were subjected to a test both operational and conceptual. ''Think in terms of painting,'' was his motto. The reduction of the metaphorical level to an absolute zero was obtained through an intent metonymic process, which always restrained the elements used to the same level of (non-) meaning. The ''outside,'' the ''world,'' anything ''other than the picture'' was never to be incorporated in the work; the process was vital, political, social. And this kind of process came into being by his painting exactly according to the autonomous instruments of painting, with no concession to Meaning but reinforcing the materiality of the source of Meaning.

Zappettini then moved on to a manner of painting which, while still retaining some elements typical of analysis (the breaking down of the support, for instance), nevertheless involved a more open attitude towards the world, its colours, its emotions and feelings, its power of evoking memories. But it is only in the past few years that Zappettini has completed the full, complete recovery, almost to the point of iconism, figuration, ''pictorial reconciliation'' (and not only pictorial) with the world.

This change has also had a great personal effect on him: he has gone to live in the country, on the Ligurian coast, where he has developed personal taste for ''minor'' painting, with little innovatory quotient but a high level of technique and craftsmanship. One might say that his investigation of ''the painter's trade'' is still going on, but with other, quite different means. The brush stroke is free, harking back to the Fauves and Impressionists (it might even be better to say, to Barbizon); the subjects are ordinary, everyday, slightly ironic, deliberately ''common.'' In this way Zappettini displays the historicity of painting, reviving methods and processes typical to its still ''heroic'' past.

Most recently his work has been enriched by another aspect and other themes, always drawn from the outpouring of meaning, of metaphor, of the desire to narrate, to tell of himself. His painting has become more spectacular than ever; it has become theatrical, depicting scenes from films (with well-known actors quite recognizable) or historic scenes with famous people in them; this is the world of the Public, of kitsch, of the Myth of the Masses. With a special effect of alienation he puts himself into the scene, in poses sometimes deliberately ironic (no problem in identifying these), as if he were required to ''introduce'' and ''present'' what is going on around him, as if in one of his personal circuses. The return of the Subject (since that is basically what we are looking at) is thus completed, after an analytical period composed of total anonymity, the disappearance of the ''I'' in the work processes—but it is a Subject which, despite all its bodily and concrete appearance, cannot but remain confined in the world of images, of icons, of phantasms.

—Massimo Carboni

ZAUGG, Rémy

Nationality: Swiss. **Born:** Courgenay, Jura, Switzerland, 11 January 1943. **Education:** Studied painting at the Allgemeine Gewerbeschule, Basel, 1963–66. **Family:** Married Michèle Röthlisberger, 1963; one daughter: Pascale. **Career:** Independent artist since 1966. **Awards:** Kunstpreis der Stadt Basel, 1990. **Address:** Utengasse 45, CH-4058 Basel, Switzerland.

Rémy Zaugg: *One Word / One Picture / And / The Shadow Was.*, 1996–97. Photo courtesy of Mai 36 Galerie, Zurich. ©Rémy Zaugg.

Individual Exhibitions

1972 *Dedans-Dehors, Dehors-Dedans, 1968–1972,* Kunstmuseum Basel (catalog)
1977 *143 mises en scène d'une peinture autour du cube,* Galerie Nächst, St. Stephan, Vienna
Du sens, Modern Art Galerie, Vienna
L. B. Alberti, Galerie Rolf Preisig, Basel
1979 *Réflexion 1977,* Kunsthalle Bern (catalog)
1982 *Le singe peintre,* Kunsthaus Aarau (catalog)
1984 *A Sheet of Paper,* Stedelijk Van Abbemuseum, Eindhoven (catalog)
1987 *Bilder,* Galerie Anselm Dreher, Berlin
1988 *Für ein Bild,* Kunsthalle Basel (catalog)
1989 *A propos d'un tableau,* ARC, Musée d'art moderne de la Ville de Paris, Paris (catalog)
1990 *Personne,* Le Consortium, Dijon (catalog)
Voir mort, 28 tableaux, Mai 36 Galerie, Lucerne (catalog)
Ein Blatt Papier, Perzeptive Skizzen, oder die Entstehung eines Bildwerks, Werke von 1973 bis 1989, Museum Folkwang, Essen
Une feuille de papier, Musée d'Art Contemporain, Lyon
Personne, Galerie Anne de Villepoix, Paris
Ein Blatt Papier, Bilder, Grafikmappe, Bücher, Mai 36 Galerie, Lucerne

1991 *A Sheet of Paper, I & II, 1973–1990, 72 Paintings,* Galerie Ronny van de Velde, Antwerp
Réflexions sur et d'une feuille de papier, Zwinger Galerie, Berlin (catalog); Kleinsimlinghaus und Partner, Düsseldorf; Brooke Alexander Editions, New York
Notes, études, 1985–1988, Galerie Pierre Huber, Geneva
Rémy Zaugg, Kunstmuseum Lucerne
A Sheet of Paper II, 23 Paintings, Brooke Alexander Gallery, New York (catalog)
Alberto Giacometti, Musée d'art moderne de la Ville de Paris, Paris
1992 *Rémy Zaugg,* Le Consortium, Dijon
Rémy Zaugg, Hamburger Kunstverein, Hamburg
Rémy Zaugg, Viennaer Secession, Vienna
Ein Blatt Papier, Mai 36 Galerie, Zürich
Reflexions sur et d'une feuille de papier, Musée Rath, Genève
1993 *Jemand,* Westfälisches Landesmuseum, Münster
Draussen, Gesellschaft für Aktuelle Kunst e.V., Bremen (catalog)
Reflexionen auf und über ein Blatt Papier, Galerie Barbara Gross, München
Schau, was du siehst, Galerie Sima, Nürnberg
Fussnoten zu Reflexionen auf und über ein Blatt Papier, Mai 36 Galerie, Zürich
Ein Blatt Papier, Die Stadt, Museum für Gegenwartskunst, Basel
Tableaux Aveugles 1986–1991, Galerie Ronny van de Velde, Antwerp
1994 *Imagine,* Brooke Alexander Gallery, New York
Aber ich, die Welt, ich sehe Dich, Galerie Barbara Gross, München (catalog)
Ein Blatt Papier, SE Sander & Ebert, Darmstadt
Tableaux Aveugles 1986–1991, Módulo, Lissabon
1995 *Herzog & de Meuron,* Centre Georges Pompidou, Paris
Not Here, Brooke Alexander Gallery, New York (catalog)
1996 *Malerei 1973–1994,* Galerie Barbara Gross, München
Hier Nicht, 1. und 2. Teil, Galerie Sima, Nürnberg (catalog)
Galerie Gisèle Linder, Basel
The Work's Unfolding, Kröller-Müller Museum, Otterlo (catalog)
1997 Galerie Isabella Kacprzak, Berlin
Mai 36 Galerie, Zürich
Retrospektive, Ein Fragment, Kunsthalle Nürnberg (catalog)
1998 Galerie André Buchmann, Köln
ICH, ICH SEHE, 1998, Barbara Gross Galerie, Münich
SCHAU, ICH BIN BLIND, SCHAU, Galerie Nordenhake, Stockholm
1999 *Rémy Zaugg,* Kunsthalle Basel (catalog)
Sieben Stehpulte, Ausstellungsreihe *Kunst auf der Zugspitze*
2000 *Portrait d'un ami, Jean-Paul Jungo,* Musée Cantonal des Beaux-Arts, Lausanne
Über den Tod, Kunsthalle Bern (catalog)
Über die Blindheit, Galerie Nordenhake, Berlin
Le monde voit, Galerie Cent8, Paris
2001 Mai 36 Galerie, Zürich

Selected Group Exhibitions

1977 *Biennale de Paris,* Paris
1982 *Documenta 7,* Kassel
1987 *Skulptur Projekte,* Münster
1988 *La couleur seule—l'experience du monochrome, Octobre des arts,* Musée St. Pierre Art Contemporain, Lyon
1989 *Video-Skulptur, retrospektiv und aktuell, 1963–1989,* Kölnischer Kunstverein
1990 8th Biennale of Sydney, *The Readymade Boomerang: Certain Relations in 20th Century Art,* Sydney
1991 *Cézanne,* Witte de With, Center for Contemporary Art, Rotterdam
A Swiss Dialectic, The Renaissance Society, Chicago
Tabula Rasa, Biel
Extra Muros, Zeitgenössische Schweizer Kunst, Musée des Beaux-Arts, La Chaux-de-Fonds and others
1992 *Das offene Bild, Aspekte der Moderne in Europa nach 1945,* Westfälisches Landesmuseum, Münster
Über Malerei—Begegnung mit der Geschichte, Akademie der bildenden Künste, Vienna
Transform—BildObjektSkulptur im 20. Jahrhundert, Kunstmuseum und Kunsthalle, Basel
1993 *Sonsbeek '93,* Arnheim
1995 *Carnegie International,* The Carnegie Museum of Art, Pittsburgh
Die Entdeckung des Anderen—Ein europäischer Blick auf die amerikanische Kunst, Whitney Museum, New York, and Museum für Moderne Kunst, Frankfurt
1997 *Painting—The Extended Field,* Magasin 3 Stockholm, Rooseum Malmö
Public Works, Van Abbemuseum Eindhoven
1998 *dijon/le consortium.coll—tout contre l'art contemporain,* Centre Georges Pompidou, Paris
1999 *Talkshow,* Von der Heydt Museum Wuppertal und Haus der Kunst, Münich
Das XX. Jahrhundert—ein Jahrhundert Kunst in Deutschland, Neue Nationalgalerie, Berlin
2000 *ORBIS TERRARUM—Ways of Worldmaking,* Museum Plantin, Antwerp

Collections:

Oeffentliche Kunstsammlung, Basel; Museum für Gegenwartskunst, Basel; Kunstmuseum, Lucerne; Aargauer Kunsthaus, Aarau; Kunstmuseum, Bern; Museum für Moderne Kunst, Frankfurt; Neues Museum, Nürnberg; Musée d'art moderne de la Ville de Paris; Magasin 3, Stockholm; Carnegie Museum of Art, Pittsburgh; Musée d'art contemporain de Luxemburg; Stedelijk van Abbemuseum, Eindhoven; Musée d'art contemporain, Lyon; Kunstmuseum, Bonn; Centre Georges Pompidou, Paris; Museum of Modern Art, New York; Kröller-Müller-Museum, Otterlo; Musée d'art et d'histoire/ Cabinet des estampes, Geneva.

Permanent Public Installations:

Ochs und Pferd, Münster; *Antipodes I,* Université de Bourgogne, Dijon; *Le Monde Voit,* Eidgenossenschaft, Bern; Neues Museum, Nürnberg; Bundesarbeitsgericht, Erfurt; *Im Werden,* Staatsarchiv,

Basel; *Fünf Höfe,* HypoVereinsbank, Münich; Fritz Hoffmann La Roche AG, Basel; St. Jacob-Stadion, Basel.

Publications:

By ZAUGG: Books—*Dix-septs états dichotomiques und Lecture des dix-sept états dichotomiques* (with Jacques Hainard), Grenchen 1970; *Public relations de Dedans-Dehors I-XII / Décodage en français d'un objet vu, 1970/1971* (with Jacques Hainard), Basel 1971; *DD-DH II, essai poétique,* Basel 1972; *Die List der Unschuld, Das Wahrnehmen einer Skulptur,* Stedelijk Van Abbemuseum, Eindhoven, 1982; *Ausstellung, Balthasar Burkhard,* Kunsthalle, Basel, 1983; *De la peinture de Leon Battista Alberti* (with Alessandra Lukinovich and Michèle Zaugg), Centre d'Art Contemporain, Genève, 1982; *Für das Kunstwerk, Kunstmuseum Bern,* Ammann Verlag, Zürich, 1983; *Das Kunstmuseum, das ich mir erträume, oder, Der Ort des Werkes und des Menschen,* Verlag der Buchhandlung Walther König, Köln, 1987 (2nd edition, Nürnberg, Verlag für Moderne Kunst 1998); *Constitution d'un tableau, Journal, 1963–1968,* Dijon: art & art 1989; *Entstehung eines Bildwerks, Journal, 1963–1968,* Wiese Verlag, Basel, 1990; *Conversations avec Jean-Christophe Ammann, Portrait,* Dijon, art & art, 1990; *Le tableau te constitue et tu constitues le tableau, Projets,* Kunstmuseum, Lucerne, 1991; *Gespräche mit Jean-Christophe Ammann, Porträt,* Edition Cantz/Parkett, Ostfildern/Zürich, 1994; *Herzog & de Meuroen, une exposition,* Dijon: les presses du réel and Centre Georges Pompidou, Paris, 1995; *Le musée des Beaux-Arts auquel je rêve ou le lieu de l'oeuvre et de l'homme,* les presses du réel, Paris, 1995; *Herzog & de Meuron—Eine Ausstellung,* Cantz Verlag, Ostfildern, 1997; *La ruse de l'innocence,* les presses du réel, Dijon, 1997.

On ZAUGG: Books—*Vom Bild zur Welt,* edited by Eva Schmidt, with texts by Rémy Zaugg and others, Buchhandlung Walther König, Köln, 1993; *Réflexions sur et d'une feuille de papier, Reflexionen auf und über ein Blatt Papier,* edited by Theodora Vischer, with texts by Rainer Borgemeister, Claude Ritschard, Rainer Michael Mason, Cantz, Stuttgart, 1993; *Le Monde Dit / Die Welt Spricht / Il Mondo Dice / Il Mund Di—Über das Gesamtkunstwerk von Rémy Zaugg im eidgenössischen Verwaltungsgebäude Monbijoustraße 72/74 in Bern,* with text by Hans Rudolf Reust, Bundesamt für Kultur, Bern, 1998; *Reflexionen von und über Rémy Zaugg,* exhibition catalog with texts by Bernard Fibicher and Rémy Zaugg, Kunsthalle, Bern, 2000.

*

The artist who exhibits his own work:

An exhibition is a presentation, the presentation of a collection of objects. But in being the sum of a set of exhibits, it is also and above all the activity of exhibiting. In this sense the exhibition is an action. Exhibiting means displaying, exposing: rescuing from darkness, indifference, insignificance, bringing to light, showing, drawing notice to the unnoticed; exhibiting also means citing, summoning, defining, retrieving from anonymity, exposing something private or intimate to the public eye. In short: ensuring that it is seen. Exhibiting is an act which forces objects to be contemplated and which commands the eye to gaze at these objects. An easy enough command to obey, for we all know what an exhibition is. . . .

An "exhibition arranged by the maker of the work" is an expressive, coherent, significant phenomenon. All elements, whether artistic or not, important or not, cast a favourable light on the exhibits, showing each work to its best advantage. Whether you agree or not, whether you think it is important or not, whether you accept it or ignore it, the fact remains that everything on show counts, because it all contributes of the general impression and to the perception of every single work (what works?): their disposition (how far apart?) their juxtaposition (what next to what?), the architecture (the rooms, their layout, size, shape, arrangement, furnishings, etcetera). . . .

All the visible elements of an exhibition aimed at forming an expressive, coherent whole, thus all the artistic or architectonic components, primary or secondary components, join forces in creating, with the utmost efficiency, an overall expression which in turn displays the individual works to their best advantage, and stimulates the sensory, psychical and reflective perception of each work. Indeed, all these perceptible elements display one another. Some paintings highlight others which then perform the same service for others, which in turn illuminate still others. Paintings which benefit from a room's shape, walls or floor draw attention to its architecture. Every painting displays both the wall space and the room space which protect it from, and link it with, the other works. Every element is thus fully present—by which I mean unrestrainedly, with dignity. All the elements, some more clearly than others, refer to other elements; more or less directly, the presence of each element justifies and elucidates the presence of the others. It is sometimes hard to tell what came first: was the art made for the architecture or the architecture for the art, or are they the hybrid issue of the two extremes?. . .

The manifest components of the exhibition give the beholder a view of himself. They surround him, causing him to step outside and in front of himself. He sees himself look, perceive, while attempting to find out something about himself and the works of art. When art is thus exhibited by other works and architecture, the subject is exhibited too. A coherent exhibition needs works of art and an environment for them just as much as it needs the beholder. For the sake of simplicity let us say that it needs the work, the architecture and the subject. An exhibition, then is like a penetrating, stern statement, arousing the somnolent beholder just when he was nodding off. . . .

(First published in: *Ausstellung, Balthasar Burkhard,* Basel: Kunsthalle 1983)

—Rémy Zaugg

* * *

When Rémy Zaugg began to study painting in 1963, his encounter with the picture *Day before One* (1951) by Barnett Newman in the Art Museum Basle came as a shock to him. The picture irritated the student, simultaneously triggering both a lack of comprehension and admiration. He wanted to understand the monochrome picture, but at the same time he saw it as already belonging to art history, and he himself wished to arrive at a new conception of the picture. He found this new conception in a roundabout way. First of all, he took a good look at a picture of classical modernism which he found less provocative than that by Newman. Cézanne's *La maison du pendu* (1872/73) became the starting point of an artistic approach which extended over several years. In repeatedly new attempts, Zaugg noted down his perceptions of the picture. The picture was thus translated into language in a variety of ways. Looking back from today's standpoint, these so-called *Perceptive Sketches* may be referred to as the beginning of an open, instrumental conception of the picture. A picture is not an invariable object; quite the contrary, it is always seen in a new and different way within a process of perception, which—in its turn—can never be completed. It is a tool for perception including all the senses, existentially anchoring the viewer in the world.

At the end of the sixties, the young painter discovered semiology and structuralism. He sought to apply their theoretical assumptions to the analysis of painting and the panel picture. At the same time, he started out from a radical reduction of the creative act. He did not want to invent anything new, he only wished to give expression to the greatest possible banality of the merely primed canvas on the stretcher frame. He no longer wanted to produce new pictures, but to sound out the very essence of the panel picture in concentrated processes of perception and analysis. The concrete components of the panel picture—the canvas, the stretcher, the application of colour—were analysed. If the monochrome is already an historical standpoint, what—if anything—is left to place on the picture surface now?

During the following years, only the colour which imitated the colour of the image carrier was used. This extremely reduced artistic action stimulated semiological speculation which was expounded in groups and series of pictures as well as in texts. If a grounded canvas was covered with a layer of paint in the same tone, a broken white, this was both self-referential monochrome painting and a depiction of the canvas lying beneath the layer of paint. During the seventies, this not-only-but-also mode of presentation and representation was investigated in a variety of ways. With nothing happening on the picture surface any more, our eyes wandered to the context of the picture. Beyond the individual picture, our perception is directed to the wall, the height of the picture, the neighbouring pictures, the distance between the pictures, the room and the architecture. The picture opens itself out to the world. The context, with all its elements, became significant.

Words appeared on the monochrome picture surfaces for the first time during the seventies—drawn in pencil, later painted or screen printed. Extra bold, universal script was used for this, a neutral utility script which has remained something of an identification mark for the artist's work up until the present day. The words question perception and comment on the material and spiritual image. Rémy Zaugg is not interested in a formalistic position. He reduces the elements of pictorial expression in order to sound out the depths of their existential dimension, of the fundamental relation between viewer and work. His declared aim is the translatability of these exemplary insights into other practical fields.

The book *The Trick of Innocence* (*Die List der Unschuld*), published in 1982, is an exemplary investigation of Donald Judd's work *Six Steel Boxes* and his presentation of it in the Art Museum Basle within the context of other twentieth century artworks and the architectural context of the museum's rooms. The analysis clearly expresses an interest in the location of the artwork. A short time after the publication of the book, Rémy Zaugg was given the first opportunity to be practically involved in an architectonic project; the addition to the Art Museum in Berne. A series of texts on museum architecture, in particular the book *The Art Museum I Dream of, or the Location of the Work and of Man* (*Das Kunstmuseum, das ich mir erträume oder Der Ort des Werkes und des Menschen*; 1987) resulted from this experience.

Although he continued to paint in the studio on a regular basis, the eighties were shaped by experiences in other fields. Zaugg experimented with video, and investigated art in public places. When he was invited to the exhibition *Skulptur Projekte* in Münster in 1987, he discovered a carelessly presented sculpture group within the city area. He began his own research, finding out the original location and reinstalling the sculpture group according to today's altered traffic situation. This project is an excellent example of his attitude. The artist did not wish to add anything to an already overfilled world. He viewed his task as a lending of structure, by means of analytic perception, to what is already given, and he also strived to assist things to the expression which is their due. In 1990 he received a commission to develop a master plan for the university campus in Dijon. Here he was also called upon as a specialist in perception. Together with the Basle architects Herzog & de Meuron, whom he consulted for this project, he made suggestions for structuring and concentration; later a series of student flats were built. Another urban project, the study *Basle—An emerging city?* (*Basel—Eine Stadt im Werden?*) followed in 1993. Here the semiological and phenomenological methods which he applied in a prototype way to painting and the panel picture led to a surprising concept of urban form and its development. Since then, his work with the two architects Herzog & de Meuron has produced a series of cooperative projects. In 1996, for example, the architects built a studio building close to Mulhouse for and together with the artist.

A great change has taken place in Zaugg's painting from the mid-nineties onwards. For more than twenty years there was only one, exclusive colour tone for his pictures: broken white, the colour of the ground. Beginning in the mid-nineties, however, he produced coloured pictures with coloured texts. Intense and sometimes even garish contrasts in colour make perception into a painful experience. The texts on the pictures address existential themes, referring to blindness and death. In an interplay with the chosen colours, the words conjure up intense, imaginary images. They confront the viewer with the fleeting quality of sensual impressions, throwing him back upon himself. Viewing Rémy Zaugg's pictures means assuring ourselves that it is the process of perception which gives us our place within the world.

—Eva Schmidt

ZORIO, Gilberto

Nationality: Italian. **Born:** Andomo Micca, Italy, 21 September 1944. **Education:** Studied painting at the Accademia di Belle Arti, Turin, 1963–70. **Career:** Lives and works in Turin. Lecturer, Liceo Artistica, Turin, since 1971. **Agent:** Galleria Christian Stein, Piazza San Carlo 206, 10121 Turin. **Address:** Via Gorizia 149, 10137 Turin, Italy.

Individual Exhibitions:

1967 Galleria Sperone, Turin
1968 Centro Calautti, Salema, Italy
1969 Galerie Ileana Sonnabend, Paris
Galleria Sperone, Turin
1970 Galleria Toselli, Milan
1971 Galleria Flori, Florence
Galleria Sperone, Turin
Modern Art Agency, Naples
Palazzo Tavema, Rome
1973 Galleria Sperone, Turin

Galerie MTL, Brussels
1974 Galleria Toselli, Milan
Galleria Sperone, Turin
1975 Galleria dell'Ariete, Milan
1976 Kunstmuseum, Lucerne
Galleria Schema, Florence
Studio de Ambrogi Cavellini, Milan
1977 Galleria del Tfitorie, Biella, Italy
Studio G 7, Bologna, Italy
Studio Cesare Manzo, Pescara, Italy
1978 Galleria Cavellini, Brescia, Italy
Galerie Albert Baronian, Brussels
Galerie Eric Fabre, Paris
Galerie t'Venster, Rotterdam
Galleria del Tfitorie, Biella, Italy
Studio Carlo Grossetti, Milan
Galleria Cavellini, Milan
Salone Annunciata, Milan
1979 Galleria Christian Stein, Turin
Jean and Karen Remier, Athens
Stedelijk Museum, Amsterdam
Galleria Emilio Mazzoli, Modena, Italy
1980 Galleria de Crescenzo, Rome
Galerie Eric Fabre, Paris
Studio G 7, Bologna, Italy
Galerie Albert Baronian, Brussels
Galerie Walter Storms, Munich (with Marco Gastini and Giuseppe Spagnulo)
1981 Galleria Salvatore Ala, Milan
Galerie Meyer-Hahn, Dusseldorf
Galerie Rudiger Schöttle, Munich
Sonnabend Gallery, New York
Galleria de Crescenzo, Rome
Galerie Appel und Fertsch, Frankfurt
1982 Galleria Cavellini, Brescia, Italy
1092 Galleria Christian Stein, Turin
Pinacoteca Comunale, Ravenna, Italy
1983 Galerie Mueller-Roth, Stuttgart
Forum Kunst, Rottweil, West Germany
Galerie Walter Storms, Munich
Center of Contemporary Art, Syracuse, Italy
1984 Galerie au Fond de la Coot a Droite, Chagny, France
Galerie Albert Baronian, Brussels
Galleria Plurima, Udine, Italy
1985 Galleria Civica d'Arte, Modena, Italy Kunstverein, Stuttgart
1986 Galleria Christian Stein, Tlirin
Centre d'Art Contemporain, Geneva
Jean Bemier Gallery, Athens
Centre Georges Pompidou, Paris
1987 Galleria Christian Stein, Turin
1988 Sonnabend Gallery, New York
1990 Fundacao de Serralves, Oporto (catalog)
1991 IVAM Centre del Carme, Valencia, Spain (catalog)
Stein Gladstone Gallery, New York
1992 Museo d'Arte Contemporanea, Prato, Italy (catalog)
Institute of Contemporary Arts, Amsterdam (catalog)
Centro per l'Arte Contemporanea Luigi Pecci, Prato
1996 Galleria Civica di Arte Contemporanea, Trento (catalog)
1997 Sperone Westwater, New York

Selected Group Exhibitions:

1969 *When Attitudes Become Form,* Kunstahalle, Berne (travelled to the Museum Haus Lange, Krefeld, West Germany, and the Institute of Contemporary Arts, London)
1970 *Biennial,* Metropolitan Museum of Art, Tokyo (toured Japan)
1971 *Biennale de Paris,* Parc Floral, Paris
1972 *Documenta,* Kassel, West Germany
1974 *Projekt 74,* Kunsthalle, Cologne
1978 *Biennale,* Venice
1981 *Identité Italienne: Larr en Italie depuis 1959,* Centre Georges Pompidou, Paris
1982 *Italian Art Now: An American Perspective,* Guggenheim Museum, New York
1984 *International Survey of Recent Painting and Sculpture,* Museum of Modern Art, New York
1986 *Hommage a Beuys,* Stadtische Museum im Lenbachhaus, Munich
1989 Galería de Arte Soledad Lorenzo, Madrid (catalog)
1990 *Temperamenti,* Tramway, Glasgow (catalog)
Arte Povera, Galleria in Arco, Torino (catalog)
1992 *Opere from the Collection 88–92,* Centro per l'Arte Contemporana Luigi Pecci, Prato, Italy (catalog)
Documenta IX, Kassel, Germany
Arte Povera, Kodama Gallery, Osaka (catalog)
1993 *Gravity & Grace: The Changing Condition of Sculpture 1965–1975,* Hayward Gallery, London (catalog)
1996 *Aetas Mutationis,* Neue Nationalgalerie, Berlin (catalog)
1997 *Venice Biennial,* Italy
Arte Povera, Kunsthalle Nurnburg, Nuremberg (catalog)
1999 *Circa 1968,* Museu Serralves, Oporto, Portugal

Collections:

Galleria Nazionale d'Arte Moderna, Rome; Rijksmuseum Kröller-Muller, Otterlo, Netherlands; Stedelijk Museum, Amsterdam; Stedelijk van Abbemuseum, Eindhoven, Netherlands; Museum van Hedendaagse Kunst, Ghent; Kunstmuseum, Lucerne; Staatsgalerie, Stuttgart; Guggenheim Museum, New York; Stedelijk Museum voor Actuele Kunst, Ghent, Belgium.

Publications:

By ZORIO: Article—''Gilberto Zorio'' in *Data* (Milan), Summer 1978.

On ZORIO: Books— *Gilberto Zorio,* exhibition catalog by Tommaso Trini, Turin 1967; *Arte Povera* by Germano Celant, Milan 1969; *Europe/America: The Different Avant-Gardes* by Achille Bonito Oliva, Milan 1976; *Gilberto Zorio,* exhibition catalog by Jean-Christophe Ammann, Ugo Castagnotto and Werner Lippert, Lucerne 1976; *Avantguardia di Massa* by Maurizio Calvesi, Milan 1978; *Schena Informazione: Politic-Art,* Florence 1978; *Gilberto Zorio,* exhibition catalog by Jean-Christophe Ammann, Amsterdam 1979; *Gilberto Zorio,* exhibition catalog with essay by Werner Lippert, Frankfurt 1981; *Arte Povera* by Germano Celant, Turin 1989. **Articles**—''Primary Energy and the Micro-Emotive Artists'' by Piero Gilardi in *ArtMagazine* (New York), September/October 1968;

''Gilberto Zorio: Corpo di Energia'' by Jole de Sanna in *Date* (Milan), April 1972; ''Zorio's Star'' by Mirella Bandini *Data* (Milan), December/January 1976/77; ''Gilberto Zorio'' by G. S. Brizio in *D'Ars* (Milan), July 1979; ''Gilberto Zorio'' by Flamino Gualdoni in *G7 Studio* (Bologna), June 1981; ''Autour de Gilberto Zorio'' ''Autour de Gilberto Zorio'' by Emilie Daniel in *Artstudio,* no. 13, Summer 1989; ''Gilberto Zorio: Le Futur de l'Imagination'' in *Verso,* no. 9, January 1998; ''Gilberto Zorio: Scultura Come Energia/Sculpture as Energy'' by Adachiara Zevi in *L'Architettura,* vol. 44, no. 509, March 1998.

* * *

Energy, tension, purification: these, essentially, are the concerns which govern Gilberto Zorio's aesthetic. His works are experiments in which he investigates the principles of change in time and space, in the elements of the atmosphere and physical phenomena, and in chemical reactions. In ''Pieces of Lead'' (1968), for example, two lead containers filled with chlorine and chloridic acid have produced crystalline salts on the copper bands which join the containers. In ''Curtain'' (1967), Zorio has placed a cloth saturated with salt water over a structure of Dalmine tubes, so that a border of salt appears as the liquid evaporates.

These works are designed to show physical and chemical changes, but also to direct our attention to the element of time in which such changes take place. In still other works the process of change itself becomes the subject-matter. This is the case, for example, with ''Rose/Blue/Rose'' (1967), in which the color of cobalt chlorite changes according to the degree of moisture in the air produced by the presence of viewers. A little later he produced objects which may be used to print words such as ''Hate'' and ''Radical Fluidity'' on the human body. The intention here is to use words to evoke images. ''Hate'' was printed on the artist's forehead on one occasion; on another, it was scratched on a wall with a hatchet; and on still another occasion the word itself was modelled in terracotta.

In his search for archetypal images which can be transformed into new vistas and produce new energies, Zorio sometimes chooses a figure such as a star and constructs it out of elements which are in themselves significant—a javelin, for example, or a laser or an incandescent nickel. Like the acids, metals, leather and even the skin which he had used before, these now become part of the repertory out of Zorio makes his poetic statements.

In all of his work, then, it is the dynamic manipulation of energy and change which plays a dominant role. The tensions and energies which are released lead to pure archetypal symbols—as is the case, for example, with ''Purifying Words.'' Purification itself becomes the final aesthetic goal.

—Roberto G. Lambarelli

ZUSH

Nationality: Spanish. **Born:** Albert Porta, Barcelona, Spain, 1946. **Education:** Self taught in art; attended Massachusetts Institute of Technology, Cambridge, Massachusetts, 1975. **Career:** Creator of ''Evrugo Mental State.'' **Awards:** Fundacion March Scholarship, for technological studies, M.I.T., 1975; scholarship, D.A.A.D., Berlin 1983. **Web site:** www.evru.org.

Selected Exhibitions:

1968 *Bienal de Sao Paulo,* Brazil
1977 *Documenta VI,* Kassel
1979 *Bienal de Sao Paulo,* Brazil
1980 *New Images from Spain,* Solomon R. Guggenheim Museum, New York
1982 *Artist's Book,* Sala de Exposiciones Picasso, Bibliotecha Nacional de Madrid
XII Biennale, Paris
1984 *Currents,* Institute of Contemporary Art, Boston
An International Survey of Recent Paintings and Sculptures, Museum of Modern Art, New York
Spanks Egen-Ar, Lilijevalch's Kontsthall, Stockholm, Sweden; Malmo Knotsthall, Malmo, Sweden; Kunstnernes Hus, Oslo, Norway
Spanish Week in Dortmund, Museum am Ostwall, Dormund, Germany
Words and Pictures, Bronx Museum of Art, New York
1986 *Spanische bilder,* Kunstverein in Hamberg, Germany
VI Biennal of Sydney, Australia
The Book Made Art, University Library, University of Chicago
Correspondances, New York Art Now exhibition, Laforet Museum, Tokyo, and Tochigi Perfectural Museum of Fine Arts, Utsonomiya, Japan
PROSPECT 86, Frankfurt
1987 *Salon de los 16,* Contemporary Art Museum of Madrid
1988 *Homage to Fernando Vijande,* Spanish Institute, New York
1989 *Les Magiciens de la Terre,* Musée Nationale d'Art Contemporain, Centre Georges Pompidou, Paris (catalog)
The Books Of Zush, Centre de Arte, Santa Monica, Barcelona (catalog)
1990 *Art Futura,* Mercat de la Flors, Barcelona
Le Vie de Artistes, Musée de la Arts Andree Malraux, Le Havre
Seoul Art Festival, Korea
Vrament Fau, Fundacion Cartier, Jou en Josias, France.
Galerie Camille Von Scholt, Brussels
1991 *Bienal de Sao Paulo,* Brazil
Les Couleurs de L'Argent, Musse do la Post, Paris
Raw War, Galeria Joan Prats, Barcelona
1992 *Expo '92,* Seville
Art a Espana, Museo Rufino Tamayo, Mexico
Amnesty International, Hotel des Arts, Paris
1995 *Drawing on Chance,* Museum of Modern Art, New York
1996 *Homo Ecologicus. Per una cultura de la sostenibilitat,* Foundation Joan Miro, Barcelona
1997 San Fernando Royal Academy of Fine Arts, Madrid
El objeto de arte, Foundation Joan March, Spanish Museum of Abstract Art, Cuenca
1998 *Catalunya-Flandes,* De Bond, Brujas, Belgium
2000 *La Campanada,* MNCARS-Madrid, MACBA-Barcelona (catalog)

Zush: *The Girls of My Life,* 1987–88. Photo by Philippe Migeat. ©2001 Artists Rights Society (ARS), NY/VEGAP, Madrid.

2001 *Zush,* Museu d'Art Contemporaneo de Barcelona (MACBA), Madrid

Collections:

Fundacion Cartier, France; Centro de Arte Riena Sofia, Madrid; Solomon R. Guggenheim Museum, New York; Spanish Contemporary Art Museum Collection; Collection of Centre Regional d'Art Contemporain, Toulouse, France; Musée Modern de Brussels, Belgium.

Publications:

On ZUSH: Books—*Le Milieu du Monde*, Arles, 1993; *Zush* by José Lebrero Stals, Barcelona, 1997. **Articles—**"Zush" by Gary Indiana in *Art in America,* vol. 73, February 1985; "States of Mind" by Robin Cembalest in *ARTnews,* vol. 89, no. 4, April 1990; "Zush at Galeria Joan Prats" by Kim Bradley in *Art in America,* vol. 79, no. 6, June 1991; "Zush" by Leah Ollman in *ARTnews,* vol. 93, no. 3, March 1994.

* * *

Albert Porta—a young artist who was committed to a Barcelona psychiatric center for drug use in 1968 under the repressive Vagrants and Hoodlums Law in effect in Spain at that time—re-baptized himself as Zush, paying heed to the strange recommendations imparted to him by a schizophrenic fellow inmate in the hospital. This radical experience permitted Zush to invent an entirely new personality while he was in the mental institution. And this has been, and is indeed right up to the present, a key factor in permitting him to articulate an artistic device by which to accede to a world that represents chaos and paradox—different dualities such as reason/insanity, beauty/ugliness—without actually losing his head completely to madness.

The name change to Zush lasted him up to 2001. In this year Zush decided to become yet another personality, Evru, a decision that also signified the creation of an imaginary state—namely, Evrugo Mental State—a vital territory of artistic, social, autarchic, and critical experimentation. Evrugo M.S. was born of an essential need, as an act of personal self-confirmation and liberation in the face of the psychic, sexual, and political repression of the era. It is hardly surprising that this gesture should have first coincided with the May '68 uprisings and the virulent appearance of anti-psychiatry.

This uncommon space for representation that the Barcelona artist turns into a constant ritual, beyond the mere manufacturing of a work, is populated by myriad "biomorphic" figures. In his role as ironic alchemist, who is as familiar with nihilism as with surrealism, Zush seeks to turn everything he touches and says into a creative experience, even that which, conventionally speaking, one would suppose should not be. His permanent state of creation has an alphabet and a language (*asura* and *evrugui*), currency (*túcares*), passports, an anthem, ambassadors (*omores*), ministers (*enestirs*), and a flag with the two central symbols in the entire development of his work: the eye and the brain.

Through his work, Zush has built a personal mythology of an autobiographical nature, a world within the world of art itself. This sort of personal cartography generates a broad-ranging repertoire of images—which refer to notions of the body in every extension of the notion (mind, sex, or time)—and of a kind of writing he has created, a personal code that permits him to express that which, from a rational standpoint, is impossible to narrate. These elements, writing and imagery—ungovernable via the order of the history of language and art—serve him as a means to articulate a discursive universe of multiple ramifications, ruled by a seductive balance between what appears to represent the chaotic and the monstrous, and that which hearkens back to order and harmony. In order to give form to his characters, Zush appeals to a range of resources including painting, drawing, signs, assemblage, photography, collage, book, or sound registry, allowing him to digitize it all, recycling the information, so as to obtain new materials for interactive multi-media such as the Web or CD-ROM.

The literary key to and core of the aesthetic universe from which this unclassifiable work emerges—the artist himself describes it as ''psycho-manual-digital''—are found in books created manually, with extraordinary meticulousness and great formal generosity. The beginning of the oldest book dates to 1968. Having surpassed one hundred by now, Zush uses them as a mobile studio, a minimal research laboratory and, together with his electronic planner, as a personal data bank and memo book to record experiences and ideas. These thousands of pages, electronically projected in digital file cabinets, which he has also been creating since the end of the 1980s, constitute the unending and rhizomic narration of his work, which operates within a system of art like a modern perversion of the ancient cabala or a contemporary, if fragmentary, projection of Renaissance universalism. Within them, there are echoes of Japanese calligraphy, of sacred Romanic art or Moslem ornamentation. They are, nevertheless, radical expressions of the unstable human condition that is typical of our times, schizoid signs of the many others encompassed within the single name of each of us.

Zush's interest in new digital technologies goes back to his passage through the Massachusetts Institute of Technology in the United States in 1975, and to his research into the language of holograms. It was precisely his vocation for digital research that permitted him to work, to an ever-increasing degree, within multidisciplinary teams, most recently focusing his attention on electronic animation. He manifests this inclination toward teamwork by expressing his confidence in people's creative potential, or by insisting on underscoring the therapeutic component found in art. A hybrid figure who is artist, scientist, and mystic rolled into one, his work elicits echoes and references to that of Henri Michaux, Odile Redon, Max Ernst, or Antonin Artaud. Art and madness are explicative parameters for work that fearlessly manifests a trend toward ''massification,'' the multiplicity of personalities on which individual awareness is founded in modern societies. Seen in this way, artistic expression is organized as a liberating territory, which, as a means of expression, also acts as a healing and cathartic tool.

—José Lebrero Stals

NATIONALITY INDEX

American

Vito Acconci
Dennis Adams
Nicholas Africano
Doug Aitken
Terry Allen
Laurie Anderson
Carl Andre
Eleanor Antin
Stephen Antonakos
Richard (Joseph) Anuszkiewicz
Siah Armajani
Arman
Robert Arneson
Richard (Ernst) Artschwager
Michael Asher
David Askevold
Alice Aycock
(Anthony) Aziz and (Sammy) Cucher
John Baldessari
Walter Darby Bannard
Matthew Barney
Robert Barry
Jennifer (Losch) Bartlett
Leonard Baskin
Herbert Bayer
Jack Beal
Romare (Howard) Bearden
Bill Beckley
Larry Bell
Lynda Benglis
Billy Al Bengston
Jake Berthot
Mike Bidlo
Sanford Biggers
Dara Birnbaum
James Bishop
Peter Blume
Mel Bochner
Jon(athan) Borofsky
Louise Bourgeois
George Brecht
Robert C. Breer
Larry Brown
Chris Burden
Nancy Burson
Paul Cadmus
John Cage
Peter Campus
John (Angus) Chamberlain
Judy Chicago
Christo and Jeanne-Claude
Chryssa
Chuck Close
Susanna Coffey
Robert Colescott
Bruce Conner
William Nelson (CPLY) Copley
Robert Cottingham
Jordan Crandall
Nassos Daphnis
Douglas (Matthew) Davis
Gene Davis
John (Louis) de Andrea
George Deem
Willem de Kooning
Walter (Joseph) De Maria
Agnes (Cecilia) Denes
Mark Di Suvero
Richard (Clifford Jr.) Diebenkorn
Jim Dine
Jimmie Durham
Friedel Dzubas
Don Eddy
Stephen Ellis
Richard Estes
Jackie Ferrara
Rafael Ferrer
Eric Fischl
Ebon Fisher
Joel Fisher
Dan Flavin
Terry (Alan) Fox
Sam Francis
Helen Frankenthaler
Tom Friedman
Ralph Gibson
Sam Gilliam
Milton Glaser
Robert Gober
Ralph (Ladell) Goings
Ken Goldberg
Leon (Albert) Golub
Dan Graham
Robert Graham
Morris (Cole) Graves
Nancy Graves
Gloria Greenberg
Joseph Grigely
Gronk
Red Grooms
Nancy Grossman
Robert (Strawbridge) Grosvenor
David Hammons
Duane Hanson
David Hare
Helen (Mayer) Harrison
Newton Harrison
Grace Hartigan
Michael Heizer
Al Held
Geoffrey Hendricks
Sheila Hicks
Dick Higgins
Gary Hill
Perry Hoberman
Tom Holland
Nancy Holt
Jenny Holzer
Roni Horn

Douglas Huebler
Bryan Hunt
Richard (Howard) Hunt
Dorothy Iannone
Robert Indiana
Will Insley
David Ireland
Robert Irwin
Valerie Jaudon
Paul Jenkins
Neil Jenney
Luis (Alfonso, Jr.) Jimenez
Jasper Johns
Lester Johnson
Ray Johnson
Joan Jonas
Donald Judd
Howard Kanovitz
Allan Kaprow
Emiko Kasahara
Alex Katz
(Robert) Craig Kauffman
Mike Kelley
Ellsworth Kelly
Edward Kienholz
William (Dickey) King
R(onald) B(rooks) Kitaj
Alison Knowles
Komar and Melamid
Jeff Koons
Joseph Kosuth
Joyce Kozloff
Barbara Kruger
Nicholas Krushenick
Gary Kuehn
Yayoi Kusama
Robert Kushner
Lois Lane
Barry Le Va
Les Levine
Sol Lewitt
Alexander Liberman
Roy Lichtenstein
Glenn Ligon
Liliane Lijn
Maya Lin
Pam Lins
Richard Lippold
Frank Lobdell
Robert Longo
Robert (Peter) Mangold
Conrad Marca-Relli
Christian Marclay
Brice Marden
Tom Marioni
Agnes Martin
John Mason
Ann McCoy
John McCracken
James McGarrell
Richard (Marshall) Merkin
Joan Mitchell
Robert Morris
Margaret Morton
Ed Moses
Robert Motherwell
Catherine Murphy
Elizabeth Murray
Robert Murray
Bruce Nauman
Joseph Nechvatal
Joan Nelson
Lowell (Blair) Nesbitt
Louise Nevelson
Isamu Noguchi
Kenneth Noland
Richard Nonas
Maria Nordman
Jim Nutt
Georgia O'Keeffe
Claes (Thure) Oldenburg
Jules Olitski
Nathan Oliveira
Dennis Oppenheim
Alfonso Ossorio
Ed(ward) Paschke
Philip Pearlstein
Beverly Pepper
Irving Petlin
Raymond Pettibon
Judy Pfaff
Adrian Piper
Sylvia Plimack Mangold
Larry Poons
Stephen Posen
Richard Pousette-Dart
Lucio Pozzi
Kenneth Price
Joseph (Jose Raffaele) Raffael
Mel(vin John) Ramos
Robert Rauschenberg
Charles Ray
David Reed
Edda Renouf
Scott Richter
George (Warren) Rickey
Larry Rivers
Liisa Roberts
Kay Rosen
James Rosenquist
Martha Rosler
Susan Rothenberg
David Row
Allen Ruppersberg
Edward (Joseph) Ruscha
Robert Ryman
David Salle
Lucas Samaras
Fred Sandback
Alan (Daniel) Saret

Ernesto Neto

British

Kenneth Armitage
Roy Ascott
Conrad Atkinson
Frank Auerbach
Francis Bacon
Clive Barker
Peter (Thomas) Blake
Derek Boshier
Mark Boyle
Stuart Brisley
Stephen Buckley
Victor Burgin
Anthony (Alfred) Caro
Leonora Carrington
Patrick Caulfield
Lynn (Russell) Chadwick
Alan Charlton
Bernard Cohen
James Collins
Tony Cragg
Michael Craig-Martin
Roger Cutforth
Alan Davie
John Davies
Richard Deacon
David Dye
Ian Hamilton Finlay
Barry Flanagan
Donald Hamilton Fraser
Lucian Freud
Elisabeth Frink
Terry Frost
Hamish Fulton
John Furnival
Gilbert and George
Liam Gillick
Alan Green
Nigel Hall
Richard Hamilton
Stanley William Hayter
Tim Head
Anthony Hill
John Hilliard
Damien Hirst
David Hockney
Howard Hodgkin
John Hoyland
Allen Jones
Isaac Julien
Michael Kenny
Phillip King
Leon Kossoff
Gerald (Ogilvie) Laing
John Latham
Bob Law
David Leverett
Richard (J.) Long
Sarah Lucas
Bruce McLean
Keith (Arnold) Milow
Henry Moore
Malcolm Morley
David Nash
Julian Opie
Eduardo (Luigi) Paolozzi
Victor Pasmore
Andrew Pepper
Peter Phillips
Tom Phillips
John Piper
Patrick Procktor
Bridget (Louise) Riley
Nicholas Rule
Michael Sandle
Tim Scott
William Scott
Pete Sedgley
Richard Smith
Jeffrey Steele
Ian Stephenson
John Stezaker
Philip Sutton
Joe Tilson
David Tindle
David Tremlett
David Troostwyk
William Tucker
William Turnbull
John Walker
Brian Wall
Gillian Wearing
Rachel Whiteread
Stephen Willats
Derrick Woodham
Bill Woodrow

Canadian

Rene Pierre Allain
Janet Cardiff
Ian Carr-Harris
Alex Colville
Greg Curnoe
Ken Danby
Stan Douglas
Murray Favro
Charles Gagnon
Yves Gaucher
K. M. Graham
Rodney Graham
John Heward
Harold Klunder
Marilyn (Anne) Levine
Micah Lexier
Ken Lum
Ron Martin
Bruce Mau
John Meredith
Guido Molinari
Robin (Bluebeard) Page

David (Birdie) Partridge
Don Proch
Jean-Paul Riopelle
Dorothea Rockburne
Henry Saxe
Michael (James Aleck) Snow
Jana Sterbak
Carroll Taylor-Lindoe
Claude Tousignant
Jeff Wall
Colette Whiten
Joyce Wieland

Chilean

Claudio Bravo
Alfredo Jaar
Roberto (Sebastian Antonio Echaurren) Matta

Chinese

Cai Guo-Qiang
Xu Bing

Colombian

Fernando Botero
Edgar Negret

Cuban

Tania Bruguera

Czechoslovakian

Milan Knížák
J(iři) H(ynek) Kocman
Jan Švankmajer
Jiri Valoch

Danish

Per Kirkeby
K.R.H. Sonderborg

Dutch

Karel Appel
Marinus Boezem
Stanley Brouwn
Corneille
Ger(rit Hendrik) Dekkers
Herman de Vries
Jan Dibbets
César Domela
Pieter Engels
Reinier Lucassen
Vinoodh Matadin
Tomas Rajlich
Woody van Amen
J(acob) C(ornelis) J(ohan) Vanderheyden
Ger(ard Pieter) van Elk
Rob van Koningsbruggen
Inez Van Lamsweerde
Jan van Munster
Carel (Nicolaas) Visser
Co Westerik

Finnish

Eva von Platen

French

Bernard Aubertin
Balthus
Stéphan Barron
Claude Bellegarde
Maurice Benayoun
Jean-Pierre Bertrand
Christian Boltanski
Daniel Buren
Sophie Calle
Louis Cane
Cesar (Baldaccini)
Grégory Chatonsky
Roman Cieslewicz
Jean Dewasne
Daniel Dezeuze
Robert Filliou
Fred Forest
Jean-Pierre Giovanelli
Raymond Hains
Etienne Hajdu
Jean Hélion
Pierre Huyghe
Jean (Robert) Ipoustéguy
Christian Jaccard
Alain (Georges Frank) Jacquet
Michel Journiac
Alain Kirili
Jiří Kolář
Piotr Kowalski
Jean Le Gac
Alfred Manessier
Chris Marker
André (Aimé René) Masson
Georges Mathieu
Annette Messager
Jacques Monory
François Morellet
Yehuda Neiman
Roman Opalka
Orlan
Gina Pane
Edouard Pignon
Anne and Patrick Poirier
Jean-Pierre Raynaud
Martial Raysse
Paul Rebeyrolle
Niki de Saint-Phalle
Jean-Michel Sanejouand
Sarkis
Nicolas Schöffer
Michel Seuphor
Pierre Soulages
Pierre Tal-Coat
Gérard Titus-Carmel
Patrick Tosani
Victor Vasarely
Bernar Venet
Claude Viallat
Marie-Helene Vieira da Silva

Jacques (Mahé) de la Villeglé
Nil Yalter

German

Horst Antes
Stephan Balkenhol
Georg Baselitz
Thomas Bayrle
Bernhard and Hilla Becher
Lucie Beppler
Joseph Beuys
Monika Brandmeier
K. P. Brehmer
Michael Buthe
Jürgen Claus
Walter Dahn
Hanne Darboven
Thomas Demand
Hans-Jurgen Diehl
Thomas Eller
Rainer Fetting
Jochen Flinzer
Katharina Fritsch
Klaus Fussmann
Winfred Gaul
Johannes Geccelli
Isa Genzken
Jochen Gerz
Mathias Goeritz
Ludwig Gosewitz
Gotthard Graubner
Johannes Grützke
Andreas Gursky
Hans Haacke
Gabi Hamm
Erich Hauser
Erwin Heerich
Bernhard Heiliger
Anton Henning
Martin Honert
Rebecca Horn
Jörg Immendorff
Horst Janssen
Dieter Jung
Horst Egon Kalinowski
Michael Kalmbach
Axel Kassebȯhmer
Anselm Kiefer
Konrad Klapheck
Dieter Krieg
László Lakner
Nikolaus Lang
Thomas Lenk
Martin Liebscher
Markus Lüpertz
Heinz Mack
Peter Nagel
A. R. Penck
Otto Piene
Sigmar Polke
Inge Rambow
Erich Reusch
Gerhard Richter
Klaus Rinke
Alexander Roob
Peter Rösel
Ulrike Rosenbach
Ulrich Rückriem
Thomas Ruff
Reiner Ruthenbeck
HA (Hans-Jurgen) Schult
Bernard Schultze
Emil Schumacher
Katharina Sieverding
Andreas Slominski
Kiki Smith
Peter Sorge
Klaus Staeck
Thomas Struth
Rosemarie Trockel
Günther Uecker
Timm Ulrichs
Jan Voss
Wolf Vostell
Franz Erhard Walther
Günter Weseler
Gerd Winner
Paul Wunderlich

Greek

Jannis Kounellis
Takis
Costas Tsoclis

Haitian

Hervé Telémaque

Hungarian

Endre Tōt

Icelandic

Olafur Eliasson
(Gudmundur Gudmundsson) Erró

Indian

Anish Kapoor

Indonesian

Heri Dono

Irish

James Coleman
Louis Le Brocquy
F(rederick) E(dward) McWilliam

Israeli

Yaacov Agam
Dani Karavan
Yehuda Neiman
Joshua Neustein

Italian

Valerio (Romani) Adami
Vincenzo Agnetti
Giovanni Anselmo
Enrico Baj

Gianfranco Baruchello
Carlo Battaglia
Vanessa Beecroft
Alighiero E. Boetti
Alberto Burri
Pier Paolo Calzolari
Pietro Cascella
Enrico Castellani
Maurizio Cattelan
Alik Cavaliere
Mario Ceroli
Sandro Chia
Francesco Clemente
Gianni Colombo
Pietro Consagra
Claudio Costa
Leonardo Cremonini
Enzo Cucchi
Gino de Dominicis
Nicola De Maria
Luciano Fabro
Marco Gastini
Piero Gilardi
Giacomo Manzù
Fabio Mauri
Fausto Melotti
Mario Merz
Bruno Munari
Maurizio Nannucci
Mario Nigro
Claudio Olivieri
Luigi Ontani
Mimmo Paladino
Giulio Paolini
Giuseppe Penone
Achille Perilli
Vettor Pisani
Michelangelo Pistoletto
Arnaldo Pomodoro
Gio Pomodoro
Mario Radice
Mimmo Rotella
Emilio Scanavino
Mario Schifano
Giuseppe Spagnulo
Emilio Tadini
Ernest Tatafiore
Giulio Turcato
Gregorio Vardanega
Emilio Vedova
Gianfranco Zappettini
Gilberto Zorio

Japanese

Shusaku Arakawa
Nobuyoshi Araki
Ay-O
Toshikatsu Endo
Taka(hiko) Iimura
Emiko Kasahara
Tatsuo Kawaguchi
Takashi Kawamata
On Kawara
Hachiya Kazuhiko
Tetsumi Kudo
Tadaaki Kuwayama
Yutaka Matsuzawa
Tatsuo Miyajima
Ryuji Miyamoto
Yasumasa Morimura
Takahashi Murakami
Hidetoshi Nagasawa
Rei Naito
Hitoshi Nakazato
Yoshishige Saito
Mieko (Chieko) Shiomi
Kishio Suga
Kumi Sugai
Hiroshi Sugimoto
Masaaki Yamada
Katsuhiro Yamaguchi
Yukinori Yanagi
Kenji Yoshida

Korean

Nam June Paik

Latvian

Vija Celmins

Mexican

José Luis Cuevas
Guillermo Gómez-Peña
Gabriel Orozco
Rufino Tamayo

Palestinian

Mona Hatoum

Polish

Magdalena Abakanowicz
Miroslaw Balka
Krzysztof M(aria) Bednarski
Marek Chlanda
Tadeusz Kantor
Ewa Kuryluk
Jan Lenica
Miroslaw Rogala
Jan Sawka
Henryk Stazewski
Henryk Tomaszewski
Ursula von Rydingsvard
Krzysztof Wodiczko

Puerto Rican

Tony Gonzalez

Romanian

Ana Lupas
Paul Neagu

Russian

Francisco Infante
Ilya Kabakov
Igor and Svetlana Kopystiansky
Ernst Neizvestny

Scottish
Douglas Gordon

Serbian
Marina Abramovic

South African
Kay Hassan
William Kentridge

Spanish
Eduardo Arroyo
Rafael (Gomez) Canogar
Eduardo Chillida
Salvador Dali
Juan Genovés
Josep Grau-Garriga
Antonio Lopez Garcia
Antonio Muntadas
Pablo Palazuelo
Antonio Saura
Antoni Tàpies
Dario Villalba
Zush

Swedish
Erik Dietmann
Evert Lundquist

Swiss
John M(ichael) Armleder
Silvia Bächli
Max Bill
Miriam Cahn
Luciano Castelli
Peter Fischli
Karl Gerstner
Franz Gertsch
Piero Gilardi
Thomas Hirschhorn
Gottfried Honegger
Christian Jaccard
Urs Lüthi
Christian Megert
Stephan Melzl
Wilfrid Moser
Olivier Mosset
Robert Müller
Meret Oppenheim
Markus Raetz
Pipilotti Rist
Dieter Roth
Daniel Spoerri
Peter Stämpfli
Beat Streuli
Jean Tinguely
Niele Toroni
Janos Urban
Ben Vautier
Rolf Winnewisser
Rémy Zaugg

Turkish
Nil Yalter

Ukranian
Ursula von Rydingsvard

Venezuelan
Jacobo Borges
Carlos Cruz-Diez
Jesus Rafael Soto

Yugoslav
Dado
Vladimir Velickovic

NOTES ON ADVISERS AND CONTRIBUTORS

ABADIE, Daniel. Essayist. Curator at the Centre Georges Pompidou, Paris, since 1975; editor of *Art/Cahiers,* Paris, since 1980. Curator, Centre National d'Art Contemporain, Paris, 1979–74; professor, Ecole des Beaux-Arts, St.-Etienne, France, 1979–80. Author of *Bryen Abhomme; Hyperréalisme; Hélion; Klee;* and *Simonds.* **Essays:** Eddy; Moser; Stämpfli.

ALBRECHT, Dietrich (Albrecht D.). Essayist. Freelance artist and writer; founder-editor, Reflektion Press, Stuttgart. **Essay:** Muehl.

ALLOWAY, Lawrence. Essayist. Professor at the State University of New York at Stony Brook, since 1968. Deputy director, Institute of Contemporary Arts, London, 1957–60; curator, Guggenheim Museum, New York, 1962–66; chairman, division of fine arts, School of Visual Arts, New York, 1967–68. Art editor, *The Nation,* 1968–81; contributing editor, *Artforum,* 1972–76. Author of *Nine Abstract Artists,* 1954; *Ettore Colla,* 1960; *The Metalization of a Dream,* 1963; *The Venice Biennale 1895–1968,* 1969; *Violent America: The Movies 1946–64,* 1970; *American Pop Art,* 1974; *Topics in American Art since 1945,* 1975. **Essay:** Sonfist.

AMMANN, Jean-Christophe. Adviser and essayist. Director of the Museum für Moderne Kunst, Frankfurt, since 1989. Director, Kunstmuseum, Lucerne, 1969–77, and Kunsthalle, Basle, 1978–88. Author of *Von Hodler zur Antiform,* with Harald Szeemann, 1968; *Louis Moilliet: Das Gesamtwerk,* 1972. **Essays:** Buthe; Erró.

ATKINS, Sharon Matt. Doctoral candidate in art history, Rutgers University, New Brunswick, New Jersey. **Essays:** Colescott; Koons.

BABIAS, Marius. Editor of *Zitty* magazine, Berlin. Editorial director, Kokerei Zollverein Zeitgenössische Kunst und Kritik, Essen; contributor of essays to art periodicals, including *Kunstforum International* and *Metropolis M;* editor of *Im Zentrum der Periherie,* 1995, co-editor of *Die Kunst des Öffentlichen,* 1998, and *Arbeit Essen Angst,* 2001. **Essay:** Bayrle.

BAILEY, Bradley. Doctoral candidate in art history, Case Western Reserve University. **Essays:** Conner; Friedman; Ossorio; Ray.

BARKER, Carrie. Essayist. Freelance writer and journalist, London. **Essays:** Antonakos; Bernhard and Hilla Becher; James Bishop; Bourgeois; Daphnis; Douglas Davis; De Rivera; Diehl; Robert Graham; Richard Hunt; Kushner; Lobdell; Merkin; Posen; Savelli; Sonnier; Stevenson.

BARRETT, D. C. Essayist. Reader in philosophy at the University of Warwick, Coventry. Author of *Art,* 1970; *An Introduction to Optical Art,* 1971; *Michael Farrell: A Monograph,* 1979; *Paintings, Objects, Installations 1963–80: Peter Sedgley,* 1980; editor of *Collected Papers on Aesthetics,* 1965, and *Ludwig Wittgenstein,* 1966. **Essays:** Baer; Baskin; Buren; Coleman; Colombo; Le Brocquy; Lijn; Riley; Steele.

BARTON, Peter. Artist and art writer; staff member, *The Artful Mind* magazine, Great Barrington, Massachusetts; regular contributor to art periodicals and catalogues; exhibits artwork through the Robert Pardo Gallery, New York, and in Milan, Italy. **Essay:** Brown.

BAZAROV, Konstantin. Essayist. Freelance writer and researcher, London; also, professional geologist-zoologist. Author of *Landscape Painting,* 1981. **Essays:** Clark; Indiana; Johns; Latham; Le Parc; Mack; Matta; Metzger; Neizvestny; Olitski; Picasso; Piene; Rauschenberg; Rivers; David Smith; Takis; Vostell.

BEE, Andreas. Curator, Museum für Moderne Kunst, Frankfurt am Main, Germany, since 1991; Ph.D. in art history, Heidelberg University, Germany; published numerous essays on contemporary art. **Essay:** Liebscher.

BELL, Jane. Essayist. Contributing editor, *New York Arts Journal,* since 1974; editorial associate, *Artnews,* since 1978; associate director, International Network for the Arts, since 1979; and senior editor, *The Art Economist,* since 1981. Associate editor, *Art Express,* 1980–81. **Essays:** Agnetti; Askevold; Beckley; Le Gac; Ossorio; Wade.

BERGER, Maurice. Essayist. Visiting assistant professor, and special projects curator of the Karl and Bertha Leubsdorf Art Gallery, Hunter College, City University of New York. Contributor to *Artforum, Arts Magazine, New Observations,* and *Artistes.* **Essays:** Andre; Bartlett; Gottlieb; Mason; Robert Morris; Serra; Shapiro.

BEX, Florent. Essayist. Director, International Cultureel Centrum, Antwerp (has organized more than 200 exhibitions of contemporary art). Administrator of La Jeune Peinture Belge; vice-president, Belgian Association of Art Critics; member, International Committee for Museums and Collections of Modern Art (CIMAM). **Essay:** Romberg.

BLUME, Eugen. Essayist and art historian. **Essay:** Brandmeier.

BOHN, Willard. Essayist. Assistant professor of French, Illinois State University at Normal, since 1981. Assistant professor of French and comparative literature, Brandeis University, Waltham, Massachusetts, 1972–74; research associate in comparative literature, University of California, Berkeley, 1974–79; lecturer in French, University of California at Santa Cruz, 1979–81. Frequent contributor to *The Art Bulletin, Arts Magazine,* and the *Journal of Aesthetics and Art Criticism.* Author of *Apollinaire et l'homme sans visage: creation et evolution d'un motif moderne,* 1983; editor of *A quelle heure un train partira-t-il pour Paris?* by Apollinaire, 1982. **Essays:** Delvaux.

BOJKO, Szymon. Adviser and essayist. Freelance art critic and art historian, Warsaw, since 1975. Editor of *Projekt* (visual arts and design review), 1969–74; editor-in-chief, *Polish Art Review,* 1972; consultant to the Gmurzynska Gallery, Cologne, 1973–80; visiting lecturer, School of Art and Design, Lodz, 1976–79. Author of *Polish Poster Art: Its Origins and Development to 1939,* 1971; *The Polish Poster Today,* 1972; *New Graphic Design in Revolutionary Russia,* 1972; *Rot Schlägt Weiss,* 1975. **Essays:** Anuszkiewicz; Cieslewicz; Lenica; Paschke; Sawka; Stankiewicz; Tomaszewski.

BONITO OLIVA, Achille. Essayist. Freelance art critic, Rome. Professor, School of Architecture, Rome, since 1971; editorial staff member, *Avanti,* Rome, since 1978. Author of *Il territorio magico,* 1971; *L'ideologia del traditore,* 1976; *Vita di Marcel Duchamp,* 1976; *Le avanguardie diverse,* 1976; *Passo dello strabismo,* 1978; *La transavanguardia italiana,* 1980; *La transavanguardia internazionale,* 1982. **Essay:** Jaccard.

BORDEAUX, Jean-Luc. Essayist. Professor of art history, California State University at Northridge, since 1972 (director of the Fine Arts Gallery, 1972–80). Visiting curator, Department of Paintings, Musée du Louvre, Paris, 1979. Author of *François Le Moyne and His Generation,* 1983. **Essays:** Cooper; Lippold; McCoy.

BOURDON, David. Essayist. Art critic for *The Village Voice,* New York. **Essay:** Christo and Jeanne-Claude.

BROWN, Betty Ann. Art historian, critic, and curator; professor of art history, California State University, Northridge; recent books include (with co-author Arlene Raven) *Exposures: Women & Their Art* (NewSage Press), 1989; *Expanding Circles: Women, Art & Community* (Midmarch Arts Press), 1996; and *Gradvia's Mirror: Autobiographical Reflections on Women, Surrealism & Art History* (Midmarch Arts Press), 2001. **Essays:** Hockney; Kozloff; Schapiro; Tàpies.

BROWN, David. Essayist. Assistant keeper of modern collections at the Tate Gallery, London (has written numerous catalogs for exhibitions at the Tate); also a doctor of veterinary medicine and surgery. **Essay:** Long.

BROWN, Glen R. Associate professor of art history, Kansas State University; frequent contributor to journals on contemporary art. **Essay:** Slominski.

BUSZEK, Maria Elena. Instructor of art history, Santa Monica College, California; author of essays on art, feminism, and popular culture from the 19th century to the present for periodicals including *Art in America, TDR: The Journal of Performance Studies,* and *Make: The Journal of Women's Art.* **Essays:** Anderson; Balthus; Beecroft; Benglis; Calle; Messager; Pettibon; Ramos; Rist; Sherman.

BUTLER, Carly. M.A. in post-war and contemporary art, London, England; writer and art critic in Toronto, Ontario. **Essays:** Armajani; Bochner; Cragg; Flavin; Kentridge.

CAMPBELL, James D. Adviser and essayist. Writer and independent curator, Montreal. National director of Vis* Art Copyright Inc., the copyright management agency for the visual arts in Canada. Author of over 50 books and catalogs on Canadian and international artists; publications include: *Depth Markers: Selected Art Writings; After Geometry: The Abstract Art of Claude Tousignant;* and *The Thought from Outside: An Inquiry into the Art and Artefacts of John Heward.* **Essays:** Allain; Gagnon; Heward; Saxe; Tousignant

CARBONI, Massimo. Essayist. Art critic, Livorno, since 1978. Sometime lecturer, faculty of Architecture, University of Rome. **Essays:** Burri; Cane; Gastini; Jaudon; Ryman; Zappettini.

CASSEL, Valerie. Associate curator, Contemporary Arts Museum, Houston; recent exhibitions include Whitney Biennial, Whitney Museum of American Art, New York, 2000, and *Ghada Amer: Pleasure,* 2001, Contemporary Arts Museum, Houston, Texas, 2001; contributor of essays to art periodicals and catalogues including *Art Journal, Nka: Journal of Contemporary African Art,* and *Freestyle,* the recent exhibition catalog for the Studio Museum of Harlem. **Essay:** Biggers.

CATALANO, Gary. Essayist. Freelance writer and critic, Melbourne. Author of *Remembering the Rural Life* (verse), 1978; *The Years of Hope: Australian Art and Criticism 1959–1968,* 1981; *Heaven of Rags* (verse), 1982; *The Bandaged Image: A Study of Australian Artists' Books,* 1982. **Essay:** Booth.

CAVALIERE, Barbara. Essayist. Contributing editor, *Arts Magazine,* New York, since 1976. Helena Rubenstein Fellow, Whitney Museum, New York, 1975; fellow in art criticism, National Endowment for the Arts, 1980. Author of the exhibition catalog, *William Baziotes: A Retrospective,* 1978. **Essays:** Africano; Beal; Blume; Burden; Cornell; D'Arcangelo; Diebenkorn; Ferrara; Foulkes; Gertsch; Glarner; Goings; Haacke; Hanson; Bryan Hunt; Lester Johnson; Kaprow; Kelly; Krasner; Le Va; Les Levine; Marden; Agnes Martin; McCracken; Morley; Nesbitt; Nonas; Pollock; Pousette-Dart; Rothko; Sandback; Simonds; Thek; Tillim; Truitt; Tuttle; Van Buren; Von Schlegell; Welch; Yoshimura.

CLARK, Martin. Essayist. **Essay:** Henning.

CLARK, Robin. Curator of retrospective exhibitions on Eva Hesse and Diane Arbus, San Francisco Museum of Modern Art, 2002 and 2003; working on dissertation titled "Artist-Proposed Museums: Polemical Projects by Claes Oldenburg, Robert Smithson and Gordon Matta-Clark, 1965–1978." **Essay:** Whiteread.

COHEN, Ronny. Essayist. Editorial associate, *Artnews,* New York. Reviewer for *Artforum,* New York. Author of *Thomas McKnight's World,* 1987; *Charles Ginnever,* 1987. **Essays:** Benglis; Bladen; Bolotowsky; Campus; Nancy Graves; Hamilton; Hicks; Ray Johnson; Kirili; Elizabeth Murray; Sugarman; Willenbecher.

COMPTON, Michael. Essayist. Director of museum services at the Tate Gallery, London. Author of numerous books and exhibition catalogs on contemporary art, including *Optical and Kinetic Art,* 1967; *Pop Art,* 1970; *Art As a Thought Process,* 1974; *Art since 1945,* 1976; *Some Notes on the Work of Richard Long,* 1978; *Looking at Pictures in the Tate Gallery,* 1979; *Towards a New Art,* with others, 1980; *Howard Hodgkin's Indian Leaves,* 1982. **Essays:** Charlton; Hoyland; Milow.

COOKE, Lynne. Essayist. Lecturer in the history of art, University College, University of London, since 1978. **Essays:** Armitage; Davies; Flanagan; Head; King; William Tucker.

CORTRIGHT, Barbara. Essayist; contributor to various art journals and reference works; author of *The Reach of Solitude;* recipient of National Endowment for the Arts Critic's Fellowship. **Essays:** Thiebaud; Turrell.

CORTRIGHT, Barbara. Essayist. Art critic for the *Scottsdale Progress,* Arizona. Contributing editor, *Artspace.* **Essays:** Clarke; Cuevas; De Andrea. **Updates:** Delvaux; Hanson; Uecker.

CRICHTON, Fenelia. Essayist. Art critic, London. **Essay:** Hill.

DALLIER-POPPER, Aline. Director of the fine arts department, 1986–90, and Maître de Conférences (reader) in the history of art 1980–93, University of Paris VIII; since 1973 has published a series of articles on contemporary art and organized several exhibitions at UNESCO and in galleries in Paris; author of essays and monographs on contemporary art and artists. **Essays:** Bellegarde; Neiman; Orlan.

de LIGT, Natalie. Essayist. **Essay:** Beppler.

De VRIES, Janneke. Independent art critic; taught at Kunstakademie, Düsseldorf; chief editor of *artkaleidoscope,* Frankfurt and Rhine—Main. **Essay:** Kalmbach.

Di GENOVA, Giorgio. Professor of art history, Rome Academy of Fine Arts; author of *History of Twentieth-Century Italian Art,* 7 volumes, and other books; curator of several exhibitions; founding editor of *Terzo Occhio;* director of a museum of contemporary art, Pieve di Cento, Bologna. **Essay:** Vanni.

DONOHUE, Deirdre. Art librarian, Solomon R. Guggenheim Museum, since 2000; librarian, 1995–2000, and staff, 1985–95, The

Costume Institute, The Metropolitan Museum of Art, New York; writer and lecturer on fine art thesauri and cataloging, fashion magazine history, fashion photography, film and fashion; author of *Sophia Style,* Friedman-Fairfax, 2001. **Essays:** Burson; Glaser; Ireland; Komar and Melamid; Lin; Marker; Morimura; van Lamsweerde and Matadin.

DORFLES, Gillo. Essayist. Professor in aesthetics since 1965; has taught at the universities of Milan, Cagliari, and Florence; also served as director of the Institute of Fine Arts, University of Cagliari, 1970–75. Author of *Discorso tecnico delle arti,* 1951; *Bosch,* 1953; *L'architettura moderna,* 1954; *Dürer,* 1958; *Constantes tecnicas de las artes,* 1958; *Il divenire delle arti,* 1959; *Simbolo comunicazione consumo,* 1962; *Il disegno industrials e la sua estetica,* 1963; *Artificio e natura,* 1968; *Le oscillazioni del gusto,* 1970; *Introduzione al disegno industrials,* 1972; *Dal significato alle scette,* 1973; *Mode e Modi,* 1979; *L'intervalto perduto,* 1980. **Essays:** Baj; Spagnulo.

DUCKLER, Merridawn. Dance critic for the *Oregonian* and *Willamette Week;* author of poems, stories, and critical reviews in such publications as *Carolina Quarterly, Mississippi Mud,* and *Bear Essential;* in-house writer for Collage Dance Theater, Los Angeles; first writer-member of the 20-year-old artist's cooperative, Blackfish Gallery; recipient of a Walden Fellowship in fiction. **Essays:** Aitken; Bidlo; Coffey; Dono; Grigeley.

DUMETT, Mari. Ph.D. student in art history, Boston University; research interests include modern and contemporary art and critical theory, with a focus on artist collectives of the 1960s and 1970s; has presented papers on the art group Fluxus at several conferences in North America; contributor of essay to the Mexican art journal *Curare.* **Essays:** Hammons; Mau.

DUNCAN, Beth. Freelance writer and editor, Chicago. **Updates:** Auerbach; Burri; Bury; Calzolari; Kirili; Kounellis; Kuwayama; Lamelas.

ELLIS, Mary. Essayist. Freelance critic and lecturer at the Tate Gallery, London. **Essays:** Atkinson; Deacon; Dimitrijević; Fulton; Guston; Law; Nash; Rothenberg.

EMANUEL, Muriel. Essayist. Freelance researcher, editor and writer, London. Editor of *Israel: A Survey, and Bibliography,* 1971; *Contemporary Architects,* 1980, 1994. **Essays:** Neustein; Schad.

EPSTEIN, Thomas. Visiting assistant professor of Russian and honors, Boston College. Recent publications include the "Russian Literature" entry for the *Encyclopedia Britannica Yearbook* and an article on the Russian poet Nikolai Oleinikov in *The Russian Review,* spring 2001; managing editor of *Symposion* and *alea* magazines. **Essay:** Arana.

ERICKSON, Britta. Independent scholar and curator of contemporary Chinese art; recent projects include teaching at Stanford University, and curating the exhibition, *Word Play: Installation Art by Xu Bing* (Arthur M. Sackler Gallery, 2001–02); author of *Words without Meaning, Meaning without Words: The Art of Xu Bing,* 2001, and essays in art periodicals including *Art Journal, Art Asia Pacific,* and *Chinese-art.com.* **Essay:** Xu Bing.

FELIX, Zdenek. Essayist. Curator at the Museum Folkwang, Essen. **Essays:** Nordman; Palermo; Raetz.

FINDLAY, Michael Alastair. Essayist. Art writer and artist's agent, New York. **Essay:** Woodham.

FLECKNER, Uwe. Assistant professor, Free University of Berlin; co-director, Centre allemand d'histoire, Paris; co-editor of the collected writings of Aby Warburg and Carl Einstein; author of numerous books and essays on 18th- to 20th-century art history, especially on French art and art theory. **Essay:** Sarkis.

FLEMING, Marnie. Essayist. Curator of contemporary art at the Oakville Galleries, Oakville, Ontario. Extension officer and education officer, Vancouver Art Gallery, 1981–86; curator of contemporary art, London Regional Art and Historical museums, Ontario, 1986–91. **Essays:** Lexier; Lum; Whiten.

FORGE, Andrew. Essayist. Dean of the School of Art, Yale University, New Haven, Connecticut. Senior lecturer, Slade School, London, 1950–64; head of the department of fine art, Goldsmith's College, London, 1964–70. Trustee, Tate Gallery, 1964–71, 1972–74, and National Gallery, London, 1966–72. President, London Group, 1964–71. Author of *Klee,* 1953; *Vermeer,* 1954; *Soutine,* 1965; *Rauschenberg,* 1972; *Monet at Giverny,* with C. Joyes, 1975; and editor of *The Townsend Journals,* 1976. **Essay:** Stephenson.

FOURNET, Claude. Essayist. Art critic, Paris. **Essay:** Aubertin.

FRANKE, Marietta. Essayist. Art historian and art critic based in Cologne. Lecturer at museums and art academies. Author of *Work in Progress--Art Is Liturgy.* Contributor to catalogs on Beuys, Trockel, Newman, and Thek. Publisher of art magazine *Work in Progress.* **Update:** Buthe.

FRASER, Alison. Essayist. Director, Victorian College of the Arts Gallery, Melbourne, since 1979. Education officer, Art Gallery of New South Wales, Sydney, 1974–76; art education consultant, visual arts board, Australia Council, Sydney, 1978–79. Author of *History of Australian Art* (slide kit with text), 1981; and coordinator of *Tertiary Visual Arts Education in Australia,* 1980. **Essay:** John Davis.

FRIEDMAN, B. H. Essayist. Trustee, Whitney Museum of American Art, New York, since 1961, and of the Fine Arts Work Center, Provincetown, Massachusetts, since 1968; member of the advisory council of the College of Arts and Sciences and of the Herbert F. Johnson Museum, Cornell University, Ithaca, New York; member, Fiction Collective, since 1973. Author of the biographies *Jackson Pollock: Energy Made Visible,* 1972, and *Gertrude Vanderbilt Whitney,* 1978; has edited, written or contributed to various art monographs, including *School of New York,* 1959; *Robert Goodnough,* with Barbara Guest, 1962; *Lee Krasner,* 1965; *Alfonso Ossorio,* 1973; *Salvatore Scarpitta,* 1977; and *Myron Stout,* 1979; also a novelist and short story writer. **Essays:** Copley; Scarpitta.

FRIEDMAN, Kenneth. Essayist. Artist and writer, New York. Consultant editor, University of Michigan Research Press, since 1978; director, Institute for Advance Studies in Contemporary Art and Architecture, New York, since 1979. **Essay:** Kocman.

GAZZERO, Edda. Essayist. Freelance art critic, Genoa. **Essay:** Costa.

GEBHARDT, Sabine. Essayist. Curator and writer, Basel, Switzerland. **Essay:** Cahn.

GIŻYCKI, Marcin. Art and film historian, critic, filmmaker, and photographer; born in Warsaw, Poland. Editor-in-chief of *Animafilm* magazine, 1979–81; contributor to Polish art and film magazines; lecturer at the Rhode Island School of Design, since 1988. Made a number of documentary films, among them *I Am Providence: The Story of H.P. Lovecraft and His City,* 1997, and *The Island of Jan Lenica,* 1998; author of *Disney Was Not the Only One,* Warsaw, 2000. **Essays:** Bednarski; Švankmajer.

GLOWEN, Ron. Essayist. Freelance art critic, Washington, since 1975. Contributing editor, *Artweek,* Oakland, California, since 1976; visual arts critic, *The Herald,* Everett, Washington, since 1978. **Essays:** Boyle; Bruce; Morris Graves; Kienholz; Raffael; Tobey.

GLUSBERG, Jorge. Adviser and essayist. Director, Centro de Arte y Communicacion, Buenos Aires. Author of *Towards a Topological Architecture,* with Clorindo Testa, 1977; *The Rhetoric of Latin American Art,* 1978; *Socio-Semiotic of Architecture,* 1978; *Myths and Magic of Fire, Gold and Art,* 1978; *From Incan Habitat to the Lima of the Future,* 1979; *The Theory and Criticism of Architecture,* 1979. **Essays:** Aslan; Bedel; Benedit; Distefano; Dompé; García; Grippo; Maler; Noé; Uriburu.

GÖRDÜREN, Petra. Art historian; M.A. degree, Free University of Berlin, 1995; co-author of *Die letzten Dinge, Jahrhundertwende und Jahrhundertende in der Bildenden Kunst um 1500 and 2000* (Berlin), 1999. **Essay:** Hirschhorn.

GÖRNER, Klaus. Essayist. **Essay:** Hamm.

GOLEAS, Janet. Essayist. Artist-in-residence, Sierra Nevada Museum of Art; fine arts instructor at the University of Nevada, Reno, since 1980. **Essays:** Allen; Flavin; Grooms; Holland; Jensen.

GRANATH, Olle. Essayist. Freelance writer and art critic, Stockholm. Has written several books on contemporary Swedish art. **Essay:** Dietmann.

GRUNDBERG, Andy. Critic and independent curator living in Washington, D.C.; author of *Crisis of the Real: Writings on Photography Since 1974;* included Aziz and Cucher's work in the exhibition *Second Nature,* which he organized while he was the director of The Friends of Photography in San Francisco. **Essay:** Aziz and Cucher.

HAMILTON, Jaimey. Doctoral candidate, Boston University; research interests include post-war collage and assemblage and the materialization of the body in contemporary art. **Essays:** Eliasson; Tirivanija.

HARITHAS, James. Essayist. Art critic. Formerly curator, DeCordova Museum, Lincoln, Massachusetts, and director, Corcoran Gallery, Washington, D.C. **Essay:** Jimenez.

HARTEL, Jr., Herbert R. Doctoral candidate in art history, Graduate School of the City University of New York; has published articles and book reviews in *Part: The Online Journal of Art History* and *The Art Book;* former intern at the Metropolitan Museum of Art. **Essays:** Ellis; Marioni; Nelson; Soulages.

HIGGINS, Dick. Essayist and entrant. See his own entry. **Essay:** Knowles.

HIRSCH, Vanessa. Doctoral candidate; preparing a thesis on Robert Irwin. **Essays:** Haacke; Kogler; Long.

HOLUBIZKY, Ihor. Essayist. Senior curator, Art Gallery of Hamilton, Ontario. **Essay:** Klunder.

HONNEF, Klaus. Adviser and essayist. Curator at the Rheinisches Landesmuseum, Bonn; also, professor of the theory of photography at the University of Kassel; director, Westfälischer Kunstverein, Münster, West Germany, 1970–74. Author of *20 Deutsche,* 1971; *Concept Art,* 1971; *Gerhard Richter,* 1976; *Wilhelm Schürman,* 1979; editor of *Verkehrskultur,* 1974, and *Lichtbildnisse,* 1982. **Essays:** Darboven; Gaul; Krieg; Ruthenbeck.

JACOBS, Aaron. Essayist. **Essays:** Rosen; Scher; Seaman; Vesna.

JENSEN, Heather Belnap. Doctoral candidate in art history, University of Kansas. **Essay:** Miyajima.

JOHNSTON, Jill. Essayist. Author and art critic. Formerly columnist for the *Village Voice,* New York; contributor to various art journals. Author of *Marmalade Me; Lesbian Nation;* etc. **Essay:** Cage.

JOINER, Dorothy. Lovick P. Corn Professor of art history, LaGrange College, LaGrange, Georgia; author of numerous exhibition catalogues, as well as articles and reviews in art journals, including *Sculpture, Art Papers, American Craft, Surface Design, Ceramics Monthly,* and *The Southern Quarterly.* **Essays:** Bruguera; Huyghe.

KARLSTROM, Paul J. Essayist. West coast director, Archives of American Art/Smithsonian Institution (based at the M. H. de Young Memorial Museum, San Francisco), since 1973. Assistant curator, Grunwald Center for the Graphic Arts, University of California at Los Angeles, 1967–70; instructor of art history, California State University at Northridge, 1972–73; guest curator, Hirshhorn Museum and Sculpture Garden, Washington, D.C., 1977. Author of the monograph *Louis M. Eilshemius,* 1978, and of the catalogs *Americans Abroad: Painters of the Victorian Era,* 1975; *The United States and the Impressionist Era,* 1979; and *Venice Panorama: Views of Venice in the Graphic Arts from the Late 15th through the 18th Centuries,* 1979. **Essays:** Bechtle; Kauffman; McLaughlin; Oliveira; Valentine.

KEARNEY, Fiona. Visual arts officer, University College Cork, Ireland; curator; author of essays in art periodicals and exhibition catalogues. **Essays:** Horn; Wall.

KELLER, Victoria. Essayist. Exhibitions administrator, 369 Gallery, Edinburgh. **Essays:** Artschwager; Broodthaers; Francis; McLean; Nutt; Penck; Tinguely; Tworkov; Winner.

KELLY, Jane. Essayist. Art critic, London. **Essay:** Willats.

KEPINSKA, Alicja. Essayist. Professor, Academy of Visual Arts, Poznan, Poland. Author of *Jan Piotr Norblin: A Monograph,* 1978; *The New Polish Art 1945–1978,* 1981; *Element and Myth,* 1983; *Ecology of Art,* 1988. **Essays:** Berdyszak; Brzozowski; Dibbets; Fischl; Fisher; Kruger; Metz; Opalka; Stazewski.

KIND, Joshua. Essayist. Professor of art history, Northern Illinois University, DeKalb, since 1969. Instructor in art history, Northwestern University, Evanston, Illinois, 1959–62; instructor in the humanities, University of Chicago, 1962–65; visiting professorial lecturer, School of the Art Institute of Chicago, 1964–76; assistant professor of humanities, Illinois Institute of Technology, Chicago, 1965–69. Author of *Rouault,* 1969; *Naive Painting in Illinois 1830–1976,* 1976; *Geometry as Abstract Art: The Lipschultz Collection,* 1980; and *The Geometric Impulse: The Florsheim Collection,* 1981. **Essays:** Baldessari; Bengston; Breer; Close; Cottingham; Ferrer; Gilliam; Gorchov; Grossman; Grosvenor; Irwin; Jenney; Judd; Lane; Mangold;

McGarrell; Catherine Murphy; Plimack Mangold; Poons; Samaras; Sarkisian; Saul; Schnabel; Shields; Wegman; Winsor; Youngerman.

KING, Elaine A. Professor of the history of art and critical theory, College of Fine Arts, Carnegie Mellon University, Pittsburgh; senior research fellow, Smithsonian American Art Museum and National Portrait Gallery, 2000; former executive director and chief curator, Contemporary Arts Center, Cincinnati; former director and curator, Carnegie Mellon Art Gallery; author of essays in periodicals including *Sculpture, Art on Paper, Grapheion, Pittsburgh Post Gazette,* and *Washington Post.* **Essays:** Acconci; Katz; Rogala; von Rydingsvard.

KINGSLEY, April. Essayist. Instructor, School of Visual Arts, New York, since 1973; director, Sculpture Center, New York, since 1980. Curatorial assistant, Museum of Modern Art, New York, 1969–71; associate curator, Pasadena Art Museum, California, 1971–72. Secretary, American section, International Art Critics Association, since 1978; member, board of advisers, New York Feminist Art Institute, since 1978, and *Women's Art Journal,* since 1979. Author of numerous books/catalogs, including *Frank Stella,* 1970; *Romare Bearden,* 1971; *Budd Hopkins,* 1973; *The Magic Circle,* 1977; *Cape Cod As an Art Colony,* 1977; *David Shapiro/Christopher Wilmarth,* 1978; *Michael Loew,* 1979; *Richard Hunt,* 1979; *Robert Motherwell,* 1980; and *Alternative Realities,* 1981. **Essay:** Motherwell.

KINSEY, Tammy A. Assistant professor of film, University of Toledo, Toledo, Ohio; independent filmmaker; contributor of essays to reference books in the arts and humanities and to film periodicals, including *The Moving Image.* **Essays:** Bacon; Birnbaum; de Kooning; Holzer; Jaar; Marclay; Paik; Rauschenberg; Serrano; Stella; Sugimoto; Viola; Wojnarowicz.

KLEIN, Mason. Essayist. Freelance writer, New York. Formerly, lecturer at Hunter College and Brooklyn College, New York. Contributor to *Arts Magazine* and *New Observations.* **Essays:** Acconci; Anderson; Snow.

KLETKE, Daniel. Freelance art historian and journalist, New York City; Ph.D. from Berlin's Technische Universität; member of curatorial staff, Metropolitan Museum of Art, 1991–95; affiliated with the Sabarsky Estate, New York, and the Rainer Werner Fassbinder Foundaton, Berlin and New York; frequent contributor to such publications as *Frankfurter Allgemeine Zweitung* (Germany) and *Neue Zürcher Zeitung* (Switzerland). **Essay:** Eller.

KONTOVA, Helena. Essayist. Co-editor of *Flash Art,* Milan, since 1977. Assistant curator, National Gallery, Prague, 1976–77. Editor of *The International Trans-Avantgarde,* with Achille Bonito Oliva, 1982; and *Jiri Kolar,* 1982. **Essays:** Abramovic; Collins; Knížák; Pane.

KOSTELANETZ, Richard. Essayist. Poet, critic, cultural historian; co-founder, Assembling Press, and proprietor, The Future Press; co-editor, *Precisely,* and contributing editor, *The Humanist* and *Performing Arts Journal.* Author of several books of verse, two novels, several collections of short stories, and critical works including *The Theatre of Mixed Means,* 1968; *The End of Intelligent Writing,* 1974; *Twenties in the Sixties,* 1978; *John Cage Conversing,* 1987; *Fillmore East: Recollections of Rock Theater,* 1995; *Crimes of Culture,* 1995; editor of numerous collections and anthologies as well as *A Dictionary of the Avant-Gardes,* 1993. **Essays:** Higgins; Tsai; Whitman.

KRAMER, Mario. Essayist and art historian. **Essay:** Flinzer.

KUHN, Rachel E. Visual resources librarian, North Carolina State University. **Essays:** Longo; Wesselman.

KULTERMANN, Udo. Essayist. Ruth and Norman Moore Professor of Architecture, Washington University, St. Louis. Director, City Art Museum, Leverkusen, Germany, 1959–64; architecture commission member, Venice Biennale, 1979–82; member of the National Humanities Faculty, Georgia, 1986–88. Author of numerous critical works; recent publications include *Architecture in the 20th Century, St. James Modern Masterpieces: The Best of Art, Architecture, Photography, and Design since 1945, The History of Art History,* and *Contemporary Architecture in the Arab States: Renaissance of a Region.* **Essays:** Deem; Horn; Jonas; Kanovitz; Messager; Rosenbach; Schneemann.

LAMBARELLI, Roberto G. Essayist. Art critic; contributor to *Flash Art,* Milan, since 1977, and *Segno,* since 1978; editor of *AMP* since 1980. Author of *Maurizio Corona,* 1982; *Pier Luigi Meneghello,* 1982; and *Razionale Decorativo,* 1981. **Essays:** Afro; Anselmo; Battaglia; Boetti; Castellani; Ceroli; Cucchi; de Dominicis; Greco; Griffa; Kounellis; Mauri; Nagasawa; Paolini; Pistoletto; Trotta; Zorio.

LANCER, Sharon. Essayist. Freelance art writer and exhibition organizer, London. Curator of the Ben Uri Gallery, London. **Essay:** Gilbert and George.

LAROSE, Elise. Essayist. Freelance art writer for *Arts Magazine, New Art Examiner,* and *Art Express.* **Essays:** Kuehn; Schapiro; Spero.

LEARMONT, Lavinia. Essayist. Freelance writer and artist, London. **Essays:** Dine; Finlay; Marisol; Roszak; Sedgley; Sutherland.

LIQUOIS, Dominique. Essayist. Freelance art writer and researcher, Paris. Formerly worked with the Galerie Chantal Crousel, Paris, the Galeria Yvan Martin, Mexico City, and the Centre Beaubourg, Paris. **Essays:** Berni; Cragg; Holzer; Kosice.

LIVINGSTONE, Marco. Essayist. Freelance writer and art historian, London. Formerly, deputy director of the Museum of Modern Art, Oxford. Author of the exhibition catalogs *Sheer Magic by Allen Jones,* 1979; *David Hockney,* 1981; *Patrick Caulfield: Paintings 1963–1981,* 1981; *Peter Phillips Retrovision,* 1982. **Essay:** Barker.

LUNENFELD, Peter. Professor of media design, Art Center College of Design, University of Southern California; founder of *mediawork:* The Southern California New Media Working Group; author of *Snap to Grid: A User's Guide to Digital Arts, Media, and Culture* (MIT Press), 2000; editor of *The Digital Dialectic: New Essays on New Media* (MIT Press), 1999; and editorial director of the *Mediawork Pamphlets* series for the MIT Press. **Essay:** Goldberg.

Mac ADAM, Alfred. Professor of Spanish, Barnard College—Columbia University; editor of *Review: Latin American Literature and Arts;* contributor of essays to *ARTnews.* **Essay:** Row.

MACKINTOSH, Alastair. (died 1987) Essayist. Formerly freelance writer and teacher, London; also, visual arts officer, Scottish Arts Council, Edinburgh. Author of *Symbolism and Art Nouveau,* 1975. **Essays:** Bell; Beuys; Brisley; Di Suvero; Filliou; Laing; Medalla; Neagu; Price; Saura; Schöffer; Segal; Warhol.

MANDELBAUM, Audrey. Essayist. Freelance writer and mixed-media artist. **Updates:** Abramovic; Andre; Dibbets; Dine; Fischl; Dan Graham; Kitaj.

MANGINI, Elizabeth. Curatorial intern, Walker Art Center, Minneapolis; currently working on the exhibitions *Superflat* (curated by Takashi Murakami) and *Zero to Infinity: Arte Povera 1962–1972;* curated the exhibition *SUPERMODEL* at MASS MoCA (February–June 2000); and has written extensively on contemporary photography, film, video, and installation art. **Essays:** Barney; Höller; Merz; Orozco; Pistoletto; Trockel.

MARÉCHAL-WORKMAN, Andrée. Essayist. Curator, Berkeley Art Center, and instructor, University of California, Berkeley. Curator, Center for Visual Arts, Oakland, California, 1977–80; Creative Growth Gallery, Oakland, California, 1984–86. Author of the catalogs *The Siegriests: A Family of Artists and Their Work,* 1980; *Robert DeNiro: Recent Paintings and Drawings,* 1981; *Chris Ranes: A Survey of Recent Paintings,* 1983. **Essays:** Connor; Ramos; Tàpies; Thiebaud.

MARTIN, Henry. Essayist. Editorial associate, *Art International,* Lugano, Switzerland, since 1968; Milan correspondent for *Artnews,* New York, since 1980. Author of *Arman,* 1972; *Adami,* with Hubert Damish, 1974; *Renato Mambor's Evidenziatore,* 1975; *Fragments of a Possible Apocalypse,* with Gianfranco Baruchello, 1978; *An Introduction to George Brecht's "Book of the Tumbler on Fire," 1978; Notes on the Work of Teodosio Magnoni,* 1980; *Gianfranco Baruchello,* 1982. **Essays:** Arman; Baruchello; Brecht; Fahlstrom; Hendricks; Nannucci; Telémaque.

MAURICE, Carine. Essayist. Freelance contributor to the *London Review of the Arts,* and consultant to L.S. Graphics, London, since 1982. **Essays:** Caulfield; Davie; Green; Jones; Kitaj; Monro, Tom Phillips; Procktor; Steinberg.

MAYHALL, Marguerite K. Doctoral candidate in Latin American Art History, University of Texas at Austin; dissertation title: *The Dissolution of Utopia: Art, Politics, and the City of Caracas in the 1960s.* **Essays:** Borges; Soto.

McCANN, Cecile N. Editor/Publisher of *Artweek,* Oakland, California, since 1970. **Essays:** Abakanowicz; Arneson.

McINTYRE, Arthur. Adviser and essayist. Artist, art historian, and critic. Lecturer in design and composition, University of New South Wales, since 1979; lecturer in Australian art history, Rollins College (U.S.A.) Australia Programme, 1980–92. Art critic for the *Australian,* 1977–78; and for the *Age,* 1981–90; contributor to *Art and Australia,* 1975–87. Honorary member of the National Gallery of Australia, Canberra, since 1990. Author of *Australian Art of the 70s,* 1980; *Australian Contemporary Drawing,* 1988; and *Contemporary Australian Collage,* 1990. **Essays:** Nolan; Parr.

MENEGUZZO, Marco. Essayist. Teacher of art history at the Istituto Statale d'Arte, Villa Reale, Monza, Italy, since 1978. Contributor to numerous magazines, including *Flash Art, Segno, D'Ars Agency,* etc. Author of *Il moviemento arte concreta,* 1981; *Michelangelo,* 1981; *Leonardo: Disegni,* 1982; *Fausto Melotti: La dimensione del disegno,* with F. Gualdoni, 1981; *Schifano,* 1982. **Essays:** Nigro; Olivieri.

MESSER, Thomas. Essayist. Director of the Guggenheim Museum, New York, since 1961. Director, Institute of Contemporary Art, Boston, 1957–61. President, the MacDowell colony, 1977–78. Author of *Edward Munch,* 1973. **Essays:** Kolář; Soto.

METKEN, Günter. Essayist. Freelance writer on contemporary art and photography, Paris. Author of numerous exhibition catalogs. **Essay:** Lang.

MIKI, Tamon. Essayist. Art critic, Tokyo. **Essay:** Kudo.

MINAMI, Yusuke. Curator of the Museum of Contemporary Art, Tokyo (MOT); exhibitions include *Nakanishi Natsuyuki,* 1997, *On Kawara,* 1998, *MOT Annual 1999: Modest Radicalism,* 1999, and *Takashi Murakami,* 2001, all held at the MOT. **Essay:** Naito.

MINDEROVIC, Christine Miner. Essayist. Freelance writer, Ann Arbor, Michigan. **Update:** Dimitrijević.

MOORE, Alan. Essayist. Art critic, New York. **Essay:** Scanga.

MURRAY, Joan. Adviser and essayist. Director of the Robert McLaughlin Gallery, Oshawa, Ontario, since 1974. Curator of Canadian Art, Art Gallery of Ontario, Toronto, 1969–74. Author of *Letters Home: William Blair Bruce 1859–1906,* 1982; *Kurelek's Vision of Canada,* 1983; *The Best of the Group of Seven,* 1984; *The Best of Tom Thomson,* 1986; *The Best Contemporary Canadian Art,* 1987. **Essays:** Carr-Harris; Curnoe; Meredith; Prent; Wieland.

MUSSA, Italo. Essayist. Art critic, Rome, since 1970; director of the Centro di Cultura Ausoni, Rome. Contributor to *Flash Art, Segno* and *L'Avanti.* Author of *L'Ipperrealismo, il veto piu veto del veto,* 1974; *Victor Vasarely,* 1975; *Il gruppo N e la situazione dei gruppi in Europa negli anni '60,* 1976; *Wilhelm von Gloeden: Photographs,* 1979; *Carlo Maria Mariani, Pictor philosophus,* 1980; *L'inattualita dell'arte,* 1982; *Arnaldo Pomodoro at the Belvedere Fort,* 1986; *La peinture de l'avenir,* 1987. **Essays:** Calzolari; Castelli; Nicola De Maria; Lupertz; Ontani; Pisani; Salle; Twombly; Uncini.

NAKAHARA, Yusuke. Essayist. Freelance art critic, Tokyo. Author of *Man-Made Nature,* 1971; *Contemporary Sculpture,* 1977; and *Akira Baba's Work,* 1980. **Essays:** Matsuzawa; Suga.

NANJO, Fumio. Curator and art critic; curated *Of the Human Condition,* 1994, and *TransCulture,* 1995; commissioner of the Japan Pavilion, Venice Biennale, 1997, and Taipei Biennale, 1998; jury of Turner Prize, 1998; selection committee member of Sydney Biennale, 2000; artistic director of First Yokohama Triennale, 2001. **Essay:** Araki.

NASGAARD, Roald. Professor and chair of the Department of Art, Florida State University; former chief curator and curator of contemporary art, Art Gallery of Ontario, Toronto; has written extensively on symbolism, abstract painting, minimalism and other topics in contemporary art; regular contributor to *Canadian Art;* author of *Free Worlds: Metaphors and Realities in Contemporary Hungarian Art,* 1991, *Pleasures of Sight and States of Being: Radical Abstract Painting since 1990,* 2001, and other books and exhibition catalogs. **Essays:** Favro; Gaucher; Ron Martin; Molinari; Reed; Richter; Tousignant.

NEWMAN, Michael. Essayist. Freelance art critic and historian, London. **Essay:** Coleman.

NORTH, Percy. Essayist. Freelance art critic and writer, Atlanta, Georgia; lecturer, Emory University, Atlanta, since 1987. Formerly, instructor at the University of Minnesota, George Mason University, and James Madison University. Author of the exhibition catalogs *Hudson D. Walker,* 1977; *Max Weber: American Modern,* 1982; *Into the Melting Pot,* 1984; *Gene Davis: Child and Man,* 1985; *Visions of* *an Inner Life: Will Henry Stevens,* 1988. **Essays:** Gene Davis; Liberman.

NOVAKOV, Anna. Professor of art history, theory, and criticism, San Francisco Art Institute; Ph.D. in 20th-century art, New York University; author of essays about gender, public art, and architecture in numerous museum and gallery exhibition catalogs. **Essay:** Adams.

OLECK, Joan. Essayist. Freelance writer and editor, Brooklyn, New York. **Essay:** Snelson. **Updates:** Arman; Chia.

OSBORNE, Harold. (died 1987). Essayist. Editor, *British Journal of Aesthetics,* 1960–78; vice-president, International Committee for Aesthetics, 1976–87; president, British Society of Aesthetics, 1982–87. Author of *Foundations of the Philosophy of Value,* 1933; *Christ and the Early Church,* 1934; *Indians of the Andes,* 1952; *Bolivia: A Land Divided,* 1954, 3rd ed. 1964; *Aesthetics and Criticism,* 1955; *Aesthetics and Art Theory,* 1968; *South American Mythology,* 1968; *The Art of Appreciation,* 1970; *The Oxford Companion to Art,* 1970; *The Oxford Companion to the Decorative Arts,* 1975; *Abstraction and Artifice in 20th Century Art,* 1979; *The Oxford Companion to 20th Century Art,* 1981. **Essays:** Appel; Bazaine; Chamberlain; Dubuffet; Esteve; Gerstner; Marca-Relli; Meadows; Morellet; Munari.

PAPARONI, Demetrio. Essayist. Director, Centro d'Arte Contemporanea, Siracusa, Italy, since 1981. Author of numerous exhibition catalogs, including *L'annunciazione di Antonello,* 1979; *Aljofre barroco,* 1981; *L'altra anatomia,* 1981; *Thinking of Europe,* 1982; and *In virtu del possesso delle mani,* 1982. **Essays:** Baselitz; Paladino: Schifano; Tatafiore; Van Elk.

PARMESANI, Loredana. Essayist. Contributor to *Flash Art* and to other Italian art magazines since 1979. Has organized various exhibitions, including *La frase e il discorso,* Cortina d'Ampezzo, 1981, and *Registrazione di frequenze,* Bologna, 1982. Author of *Nuova immagine,* 1980; and *Baj: I grandi quadri,* 1982. **Essays:** Cavaliere; Tadini.

PATRICK, Keith. Editor of *Contemporary Visual Arts* magazine,1996–; editor of *Artline* magazine, 1990–96; freelance art critic and curator; author of *Oil on Canvas,* 1997, and *British Sculpture in the 20th Century,* 2002. **Essay:** Woodrow.

POMEROY, Ralph. Essayist. Associate director, Forum Gallery, New York, since 1979; contributing editor, *Arts Magazine,* New York, since 1981. Member, editorial staff, *Artnews,* New York, 1963–68, and *Art and Artists,* London, 1966–73. Author of *Stills and Movies,* 1961; *The Canaries As They Are,* 1965; *In the Financial District,* 1968; *Stamos,* 1974; *The Ice Cream Connection,* 1975; *First Things First,* 1977. **Essays:** Balthus; Bearden; Calder; Estes; Hall; Held; Mitchell; Noguchi; Noland; O'Keeffe; Pearlstein; Reinhardt; Richard Smith; Tony Smith; Stamos; Turnbull; Westermann; Wiley.

POPPER, Frank. Director of the fine arts department, 1970–83, and professor of aesthetics and of the science of art, 1975–85, then professor emeritus, University of Paris VIII; author of many books, including *Art of the Electronic Age,* 1993, and *Réflexions sur l'exil, l'art et l'Europe,* 1998, and exhibitions and exhibition catalogs, including *Electra: Electricity and Electronics in the Art of the 20th Century* (Paris), 1983–84, and *L'art virtuel: créations interactives et multisensorielles* (Boulogne-Billancourt), 1998–99. **Essays:** Again; Ascott; Barron; Benayoun; Chatonsky; Cruz-Diez; Fisher; Forest; Gilardi; Giovanelli; Jung; Kac; Nechvatal; Pepper.

RABINOWITZ, Cay Sophie. Senior editor, *Parkett* magazine; author of numerous cataloges and articles on contemporary art. **Essay:** Roberts.

REUST, Hans Rudolph. Essayist and art historian. **Essay:** Bächli.

ROBERTS, John. Essayist. Freelance writer, London; regular contributor to various art magazines. **Essays:** Brus; Burgin; Craig-Martin; Hesse; Walker.

ROBINSON, John. Essayist. Editor, Archives of American Art, San Francisco office; lecturer, California College of Arts and Crafts, Dominican College, and Holy Names College. Contributor to *Artforum, Artweek, San Francisco Review of Books,* and *Flash Art.* **Essays:** Borofsky; Newton Harrison; Hockney; Kaltenbach; Smithson; Venet; Wilson.

ROBINSON, Marlee. Essayist. Personal assistant to Eduardo Paolozzi, and lecturer at the Tate Gallery, London, since 1977. **Essays:** Buckley; Chicago; Page.

ROGERS, Ken. Doctoral candidate, Department of Cinema Studies, New York University; teaches film, photography, and video; curator of 125 Maiden Lane Exhibition Space, New York **Essay:** Gursky.

SALKELD, Richard. Senior lecturer, School of Fine Art, Cheltenham and Gloucester College of Higher Education, United Kingdom. **Essays:** Craig-Martin; Gillick; Hirst; Lucas; Opie; Wearing.

SALVESEN, Britt. Essayist. Art historian; editor of scholarly publications at the Art Institute of Chicago. **Updates:** Finlay; Hamilton.

SCHIPPER, Merle. Essayist. Freelance art critic and exhibition organizer, Los Angeles. Contributing editor, *Artweek,* Oakland, since 1983, and columnist, *Artscene,* Los Angeles, since 1987. Los Angeles correspondent, *Artnews,* New York, 1985–87. Author of *Americans in Paris: The 50s,* 1979; *Abstract Painting and Sculpture in America 1927–44,* with others, 1983; *Jean Helion: Abstraktion und Mythen des Altags,* with others, 1984; *Susan Rankaitis,* 1988. **Essays:** Moses; Ruppersberg.

SCHMIDT, Eva. Art historian; director of the Gesellschaft für Aktuelle Kunst, Bremen; editor, *Rémy Zaugg, Vom Bild zu Welt* (Köln), 1993, *Gesammelte Schriften von Robert Smithson* (Köln), 2000, and other works on contemporary art. **Essay:** Zaugg.

SCHULZE-REIMPELL, Werner. Essayist. Freelance journalist in Germany since 1977. Chief editor of the theatre monthly *Die Deutsche Bühne,* 1972–77. Author of *Structure and Development of the Theatre in the Federal Republic of Germany,* 1973, 1977. **Essays:** Grützke; Schult; Schultze; Weseler.

SCHWABSKY, Barry. Author of *The Widening Circle: Consequences of Modernism in Contemporary Art,* 1997; former editor of *Arts Magazine;* regular contributor to many art publications, including *Artforum* (where he is also co-editor of international reviews), and *Art On Paper* (where he is a contributing editor). **Essay:** Kopystianky.

SCHWARZ, Dieter. Essayist. Assistant curator, Kunstmuseum, Winterthur, Switzerland, since 1985. Author of *Auf der Bogen Bahn: Studien zum literatische Werk von Dieter Roth,* 1981; *Camille Graeser: Zeichnungen,* 1986. Editor of *John Armleder,* 1987; *Andre Thomkins: Gesammelte Anagramme,* 1987. **Essays:** Armleder; Gosewitz; Hains; Roth; Villeglé.

SELZ, Peter. Essayist. Professor of the history of art, University of California, Berkeley, since 1965 (director of the University Art Museum, 1965–73). Head of graduate program, Institute of Design, Chicago, 1949–55; chairman of the art department, Pomona College, Claremont, California, 1955–58; curator, department of painting and sculpture exhibitions, Museum of Modern Art, New York, 1958–65. Author of *German Expressionist Painting,* 1957; *New Images of Man,* 1959; *Art Nouveau,* 1960; *The Work of Jean Dubuffet,* 1962; *Emil Nolde,* 1963; *Max Beckmann,* 1964; *Ferdinand Hodler,* 1972; *Sam Francis,* 1975, 1982; *Art in Our Times: A Visual History,* 1981; *Art in a Turbulent Era,* 1985; *Chillida,* 1986. **Essay:** Denes.

SHEPHERD, Michael. Essayist. Art critic of the *Sunday Telegraph,* London, since 1971; consultant, *Art Review,* London, since 1975; art critic, *What's On in London,* since 1978; postgraduate thesis tutor, Royal Academy of Arts, London, since 1979; London correspondent, *Artmagazine,* Toronto, since 1980. Author of *Barbara Hepworth,* 1963. **Essays:** Tindle; Vaughan.

SHINODA, Tazmi. Essayist. Freelance art critic and art historian, Kanagawa, Japan. Member, Association Internationale des Critiques d'Art, since 1986. Co-author of *The Dictionary of Contemporary Art,* 1984. **Essays:** Kawara; Kitatsuji; Kusama; Nakazato; Niizuma; Onosato; Saito; Yamada; Yamaguchi.

SINZ, Dagmar. Essayist. Parisian correspondent for cultural events, *Neue Zürcher Zeitung,* Zurich, since 1980, and for Saarlandischer Rundfunk/Radio Saarbrucken, Germany, since 1981; art critic, *Artis,* Konstanz, Germany, since 1977. **Essays:** Dado; Penalba; Anne and Patrick Poirier.

SMITH, Jennifer A. Doctoral candidate in art history, University of Wisconsin—Madison; research focuses on contemporary German photography and installation art. **Essays:** Celmins; Fritsch; Ruff.

SMITH, Katharine. Essayist. Freelance art critic, Denver. Formerly, Colorado editor, *Artspace* magazine. Author of numerous exhibition catalogs for museums and art centers in the western United States. **Essays:** Pepper; Ross.

SOUTTER, Lucy. Artist and writer; M.F.A. in photography, The California Institute of the Arts, 1993; Ph.D., Yale University, 2001; contributor of essays to art periodicals including *Afterimage, Art & Design,* and *X-Tra.* **Essays:** Asher; Burgin; Fischli and Weiss; Kelley.

SPENCER, Charles. Essayist. Freelance writer and lecturer at various British art schools for the British Council. Formerly: editor, *Art and Artists,* London; art critic for the London *Daily Mail* and the European edition of the *New York Times;* editor, Editions Alecto, London; and principal lecturer, Croydon College, Surrey. Author of *Erté,* 1970, 1981; *A Decade of Printmaking,* 1972; *The Aesthetic Movement,* 1972; *Leon Bakst,* 1973; *Cecil Beaton: Stage and Film Designs,* 1975; *The World of Serge Diaghilev,* 1978. **Essays:** Botero; Boyd; Butler; Canogar; Cascella; Chadwick; Chillida; Cohen; Consagra; Cremonini; Domela; Dorazio; Efrat; Frost; Genovés; Grau-Garriga; Hodgkin; Hoflehner; Ipoustéguy; Kenny; Kossoff; Leverett; Lundquist; Morlotti; Partridge; Pasmore; Perilli; Piché; Arnaldo and Gio Pomodoro; Radice; Rotella; Sandle; William Scott; Shahn; Tajiri; Tilson; Velickovic; Wagemaker; Wall.

SPIELMANN, Heinz. Adviser and essayist. Director of the Landesmuseum Schleswig-Holstein, Germany, since 1986. Professor at the University of Munster, since 1984. Chief curator, Museum für Kunst und Gewerbe, Hamburg, 1960–85. Editor of *Das Fruhe Plakat in Europa und den USA,* 3 vols., 1969–75; *Oskar Kokoschka,* 4 vols., 1972–76; *Spektrum der Kunst,* 1974, 1987; *Oskar Kokoschka, Briefe,* 4 vols., 1984–88; *Die Japanische Photographie,* 1985. **Essays:** Bill; Janssen; Nagel; Schumacher; von Graevenitz; Wunderlich.

STALS, José Lebrero. Adviser. Chief curator, Macba (Museu d'Art Contemporani de Barcelona), Spain; editor, *Art Web Log-os,* Expo Hannover, 2000; editor, *Disidencia Cultural y Tecnologia.* **Essay:** Zush.

STANISLAWSKI, Ryszard. Essayist. Freelance art critic and historian of contemporary art, Warsaw. Author of *Constructivism in Poland 1923–36,* 1973; etc. **Essay:** Kantor.

STEINER, Shepherd. Art historian and critic now living in Edinburgh, Scotland; recent publications include "Wondering about Struth"; "Henrik Håkansson: On the Surveillance, Care and Bliss of Tiny Creatures"; "On the Constantly Improving Weather"; and "Ritual and the Space of Morris Louis: Unlocking Openness via the Studio Door." **Essay:** Rodney Graham.

STOFFLET, Mary. Essayist. Curator of education, San Diego Museum of Art, California, since 1985. Assistant curator of exhibitions and cultural programs, San Francisco International Airport, 1982–84; instructor in art history, Oakland Museum, California, 1977–83; associate editor, *Images and Issues,* Los Angeles, 1979–82; editor, Western Association of Art Museums *Newsletter,* 1974–77. Author of *Women Artists: Sculpture,* with Karen Petersen, 1980; *Dr. Seuss from Then to Now,* 1986. **Essays:** Antin; Cadmus; Hare; Katz; Ellen Lanyon; Leslie; Marilyn Levine; Maciunas; Marioni; Shiomi; Vautier.

SWARTZ, Anne. Dean of academic research and faculty development, The Savannah College of Art and Design; author of exhibition catalogues and articles on various contemporary artists, including Andy Warhol, Christo and Jeanne-Claude, and Eva Hesse. **Essays:** Christo and Jeanne-Claude; Douglas; Hill; Hoberman; Kushner.

SWARTZ, Mark. Essayist. Art historian and critic. Manuscript editor, journals division, University of Chicago Press; contributor to the Chicago *Reader* and the *Chicago Art Journal.* **Essays:** Boltanski; Fetting; Genzken; Kiefer; Kosuth. **Updates:** Laurie Anderson; Arroyo; Artschwager; Balthus; Borofsky; Christo and Jeanne-Claude; Freud; Gilbert and George; Kruger; Paik; Richter; Salle.

SYRING, Marie Luise. Essayist. Art critic, Paris, since 1976. Parisian correspondent for *Du,* Zurich, and contributing editor, *Kunstforum,* Cologne. **Essays:** Getz; Honegger; Viallat; Voss.

TABORSKA, Agnieszka. Art historian and writer; lecturer, Rhode Island School of Design, since 1989; contributor to Polish art and literary magazines; author *Die Mondgeister,* 1996, *Der Fischer auf dem Meeresgrund,* 1997, and *The Black Mountain,* 2001, and other works. **Essay:** Carrington.

THOMAS, Daniel. Essayist. Senior curator of Australian art, Australian National Gallery, Canberra, since 1978. Curator of Australian art, Art Gallery of New South Wales, Sydney, 1958–77. Author of *Outlines of Australian Art: The Joseph Brown Collection,* 1973, 1980. **Essays:** Albert Tucker; Unsworth.

TIAMPO, Miang. Independent curator and critic specializing in contemporary French and Japanese art; currently working on an exhibition of Tanaka Atsuko; doctoral candidate, Northwestern University, Chicago; dissertation: *Action, Painting: Experiments and Exchanges in France and Japan, 1945–1965.* **Essay:** Kazuhiko.

TONO, Yoshiaki. Essayist. Art critic, Tokyo; professor, Tama University of Art; guest curator, Seibu Museum of Art, Tokyo, and Toyama Museum of Modern Art, Tokyo. Author of *Artists in Grotta,* 1957, 1965; *After Pollock,* 1965; *Diaries in the U.S.A.,* 1968; *Marcel Duchamp,* 1977; *Jasper Johns and/or,* 1979; *The Betrayed Regard,* 1980; *The Ambiguous Water,* 1980; *Chatting with Artists,* 1984; *Mrs. Robinson and Contemporary Art,* 1986. **Essays:** Arakawa; Ay-O; Kawaguchi; Kuwayama; Miki; Sekine; Sugai; Takamatsu.

TRACHTENBERG, Alan. Professor of English and American studies, Yale University; publications include *Brooklyn Bridge: Fact and Symbol,* 1965, *The Incorporation of America,* 1982, and *Reading American Photographs,* 1989. **Essay:** Morton.

VALAKOS, Dorothy. Essayist. Artist and writer, Baltimore, Maryland. Arts coordinator, Baltimore Children's Museum, 1993–94; programs assistant, Baltimore Museum of Art, 1993; assistant director, Randall Gallery, St. Louis, Missouri, 1990. Contributor to the *Baltimore Alternative,* 1992–93; instructor at various institutions. **Essays:** Aycock; Berthot; LeWitt; Polke. **Updates:** Abakanowicz; Baselitz; Becher; Bourgeois; Buren; Chamberlain; Clemente; Close; Cragg; Cucchi; Deacon; De Maria; Ferrara; Grooms; Haacke; Holzer; Kapoor; Kushner; Marden; Martin; Trockel.

van HAAREN, H.J.A.M. Essayist. Art critic, Rotterdam. **Essay:** van Munster.

VARIA, Radu. Essayist. Art critic, Paris and New York. Director of the International Committee of the *Biennale de Paris* in the 1970s, and Director of the International Section of the *Sao Paulo Bienal* in 1973; assisted Salvador Dali in the founding of the Dali Museum in Figueras, 1974. Has organized numerous exhibitions, particularly of the work of Horia Damian. **Essay:** Dali.

VENTURI, Luca. Freelance art critic, Milan. **Essay:** Turcato.

VERZOTTI, Giorgio. Essayist. Temporary exhibitions curator, Pinacoteca di Brera, Milan, since 1983; contributor to *Flash Art,* Milan, since 1979. Author of *Paesaggio metropolitano,* 1982, and the exhibition catalogs *Imago,* 1983; *In labirinto,* 1983; *John Armleder/ Alberto Garutti,* 1987; *Lucio Fontana,* 1987; *Presi per incantamento,* 1988. **Essays:** Bertrand; Chia; Clemente; Dias; Fabro; Immendorff; Kapoor; Mosset; Opie; Penone; Tremlett; Trockel; Vedova.

VOLK, Alicia. Specializes in 20th-century Japanese art; teaches Japanese art history, Northwestern University, Evanston, Illinois; has written on Japanese photography for *Encyclopedia of Contemporary Japan,* 2001. **Essays:** Kasahara; Kawamata; Murakami; Yanagi.

von ZITZEWITZ, Monika. Essayist. Cultural correspondent in Italy for *Die Welt,* Bonn, since 1965. Author of *Auch so ist der Ivan,* 1953; *Verzaubert in Florenz,* 1962; *Golf von Neapel,* 1974, 1978; *Florenz und die Toskana,* 1979, 1980; *Toskana und Umbrien,* 1981. **Essays:** Guttuso; Manzù; Marini; Melotti.

WAGEMANS, A. F. Essayist. Instructor in art theory, State Academy, Amsterdam, since 1987. Assistant curator, Rijksmuseum Kroller-Muller, Otterlo, 1980–81; curator, Bonnefantenmuseum, Maastricht, 1982–84. **Essays:** Boezem; Dahn; Ger Dekkers; Dokoupil; Engels; Rajlich; Vanderheyden; van Koningsbruggen; Visser; Westerik.

WAGNER, Sarah. Doctoral candidate, Graduate Center of the City University of New York; currently working on her dissertation entitled, *Purposeless Play: Cage-Suzuki Zen (and its influence on postwar artists).* **Essays:** Cattelan; Gordon; Meireles.

WEBB, Sarah. Independent artist and freelance writer; recent solo exhibitions include *Milk and Tears,* Providence, Rhode Island, and *In a Delicate Condition,* Rochester, New York. Co-editor of *Singular Women,* University of California Press; contributor of essays to art periodicals, including *Afterimage* and *Art New England.* **Essay:** Antin.

WENTRACK, Kathleen. Doctoral candidate, Graduate Center, City University of New York; art historian; has written on contemporary art and European art between the two World Wars. **Essays:** Hatoum; Kiki Smith.

WHITTET, G. S. Essayist. Art critic and consultant, London. Assistant editor, 1946–50, managing editor, 1950–58, and editor, 1958–64, *The Studio,* London, and editor, *Studio International,* 1964–66. London art correspondent, *Le Monde,* Paris, 1969–72; London editor, *Pictures on Exhibit,* New York, 1972–80. Author of *Bouquet,* 1949; *London* (in the series "Art Centres of the World"), 1967; *Scotland Explored,* 1969; *Lovers in Art,* 1972. **Essays:** Antes; Boshier; Bury; Calderara; Cesar; Colville; Dewasne; Duchamp; Fraser; Freud; Goeritz; Hartigan; Hayter; Heiliger; Hepworth; Huxley; Jenkins; Jorn; Kricke; Peter Lanyon; Lichtenstein; Lipton, Manessier; Kenneth Martin; Mathieu; Mesens; Moore; Negret; Nevelson; Newman; Nicholson; Oldenburg; Paolozzi; Peter Phillips; Piper; Rickey; Rosenquist; Scanavino; Soulages; Stella; Still; Sutton; Tal-Coat; Vasarely; Wyeth.

WILKIN, Karen. Essayist. Freelance curator and art critic, New York, since 1978; contributor to the *New Criterion, Partisan Review,* and *Modern Painters.* Chief curator, Edmonton Art Gallery, 1971–78. Teaches at the University of Toronto and the New York Studio School. Author of *Modern Painting in Canada,* with Terry Fenton, 1978; *David Smith: The Formative Years,* 1981; *Jack Bush,* 1983; *Frankenthaler on Paper,* 1985; *Stuart Davis,* 1987. **Essays:** Bannard; Caro; Dzubas; Frankenthaler; K. M. Graham; Robert Murray; Tim Scott.

WILLIAMS, Sheldon. Essayist. English correspondent of *L'Arte Naive,* Italy, since 1970; artistic adviser to RONA, London, since 1977. Editor, *Art Illustrated,* 1969–71. Author of *Situation Humaine,* 1967; *Verlon,* 1969; *A Background to Sfumato,* 1969; *Voodoo and the Art of Haiti,* 1971; *20th Century British Naive and Primitive Artists,* with Eric Lister, 1975; editor of *RONABOOK,* 1978, and *A Quiet Thunder,* 1978. **Essays:** Adami, Alechinsky; Arroyo; Auerbach; Bacon; Bayer; Blake; Brauer; Bravo; Chryssa; Corneille; de Kooning; Frink; Fuchs; Furnival; Golub; Hajdu; Hélion; Hrdlicka; Hundertwasser; Iannone; Jacquet; Kalinowski; William King; Klapheck; Krushenick; Lenk; Masson; McWilliam; Monory; Nitsch; Meret Oppenheim; Paik; Panamarenko; Pignon; Rainer; Raynaud; Raysse; Rebeyrolle; Rinke; Riopelle; Rückriem; Ruscha; Saint-Phalle; Seuphor; Sonderborg; Sorge; Spoerri; Tamayo; Titus-Carmel; Uecker; van Amen; Vieira da Silva; Villalba; Wesselman.

WINGATE, Adina. Essayist. Development consultant, Arizona Historical Society, Tucson, since 1980. Art critic, *Arizona Daily Star,* Tucson, 1973–76; public information and program director, Tucson

Museum of Art, 1976–79; senior curator, La Jolla Museum of Contemporary Art, California, 1979–80. **Essay:** Young.

WISOTZKI, Paula. Associate professor of art history, Loyola University, Chicago. Native of Portland, Oregon; earned B.A. at Lewis and Clark College, and Ph.D. at Northwestern University. Research interests include women artists, modern and contemporary art and theory, and American art of the 1930s and 1940s. **Essays:** Cadmus; Golub; Nutt; Paschke.

WITZLING, Mara. Professor of art and art history, University of New Hampshire, also coordinator of the Women's Studies Program; editor of two critical anthologies of writings by women artists, *Voicing Our Visions,* 1991, and *Voicing Today's Visions,* 1994, and has written and lectured on women artists. **Essays:** Abakanowicz; Bourgeois; Chicago; Graves; Hartigan; Kruger; Mitchell; Saint-Phalle.

WOLFORD, Lisa. Teaches theatre and American culture studies at Bowling Green State University; writings on contemporary performance have appeared in numerous journals and anthologies, including *TDR, Theatre Forum, Performance Research,* and *Theatre Topics;* currently working with Guillermo Gómez-Peña on a book tentatively titled *Mexterminator: Ethno-Techno Art.* **Essay:** Gómez-Peña.

WONG, Aida-Yuen. Assistant professor of fine arts, Brandeis University, Massachusetts; contributor to art and humanities periodicals, including *Artibus Asiae, Oriental Art,* and *Sino-Japanese Studies.* **Essay:** Cai Guo-Qiang.

YOUMANS, Joyce. Curatorial assistant, Department of African Art, Nelson-Atkins Museum of Art, Kansas City, Missouri; freelance writer and researcher. **Essays:** Cardiff; Durham; Hassan; Neto; Struth; Wilson.

YOUNG, Tara Reddy. M.A. in art history, University of Pittsburgh; assistant curator of Modern and Contemporary Art, Seattle Art Museum, Washington. **Essays:** Balkenhol; Fischl; Freud; Gibson; Gober; Morley; Pfaff; Ruscha.

ZARRO, Jennifer S. Doctoral candidate in art history, Rutgers University, New Brunswick, New Jersey; has taught African American art at Rutgers University and delivered a paper on Glenn Ligon's *A Feast of Scraps,* University of Arizona, 2001. **Essays:** Julien; Ligon; Piper; Simpson.